THE MODERN CATHOLIC ENCYCLOPEDIA

THE MODERN CATHOLIC ENCYCLOPEDIA

Edited by

Michael Glazier and Monika K. Hellwig

A Michael Glazier Book

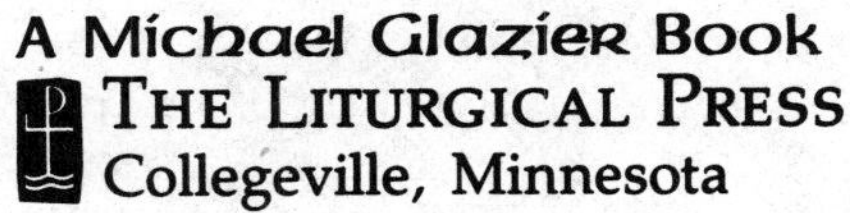

THE LITURGICAL PRESS
Collegeville, Minnesota

A Michael Glazier Book published by The Liturgical Press

Cover design by David Manahan, O.S.B.

Nihil obstat: Robert C. Harren, *Censor deputatus.*
Imprimatur: ✠Jerome Hanus, O.S.B., Bishop of St. Cloud, Minnesota, June 10, 1994.

2 3 4 5 6 7 8

Library of Congress Cataloging-in-Publication Data

The modern Catholic encyclopedia / Michael Glazier, Monika K. Hellwig, editors.
p. cm.
"A Michael Glazier book."
Includes bibliographical references.
ISBN 0-8146-5495-9
1. Catholic Church—Encyclopedias. I. Glazier, Michael.
II. Hellwig, Monika.
BX841.M63 1994
282′.03—dc20 94-21359
CIP

For

John Tracy Ellis
1905–1992

Priest • Gentleman • Scholar

Contents

List of Entries

Preface

A generation has passed since Vatican Council II, and the enthusiasm and euphoria which exhilarated Catholic life in the years that followed the council are misted memories now. The council bequeathed us new hopes, new dreams, new challenges; but, above all, it gifted us with a fresh vision of the Church as a pilgrim people, and this volume is an attempt to give a succinct and contemporary view to the beliefs, practices, and history of this people.

The Church, like a great river, has flowed through two thousand years, changing the landscape of human history. At times, external attempts were made to dam and control its waters; at other times, internal problems hampered and slowed its course and shallowed the great river. But the rains always came, new tributaries rose, and its replenished waters crested and swept obstacles and debris before them.

The seeds which sprouted and became the harvest of Vatican II were mostly sown in the bleak century before it. The names of many of the sowers have slipped from memory, but the vision and work of others flowed, like tributaries, into the life of the Church and they are not forgotten: Migne, Newman, Lagrange, Beauduin, Jungmann, de Lubac, Daniélou, Rahner, Congar. . . . They were men of tradition, deeply aware of the great heritage of two thousand years. The council invited us to a fresh appreciation of the gifts passed to us over the centuries, and we hope that in its limited way *The Modern Catholic Encyclopedia* will help in this task.

It is edited for readers in English-speaking countries, drawn together by a common language and by shared pastoral concerns and challenges. Consequently, men and women from America, Canada, Australia, Ireland, and Britain have written this work for a multinational readership. It is a work of and for our time, and its topics and themes have been chosen to meet the inquiries and religious curiosity of people today. More space and attention are given to contemporary men and women and to modern queries and questions. For instance: Thomas Merton is more attuned to our pressing concerns than are notables from the past such as Thomas à Kempis or Francis de Sales, and for that reason Merton receives greater attention. Dorothy Day, with her gospel of peace and social justice, means more to the young and old of our day than Joan of Arc heading for war and armed to the hilt on horseback. Some questions are breaking like waves on every shore. The role of women in the Church today is one of the most urgent problems confronting the Christian people, and it receives appropriate treatment in two lengthy entries and is also touched on in several shorter ones.

For the first time in history the vital center for scriptural and theological studies has shifted from continental Europe to America and the English-speaking world, and it has moved from the seminary to the college campus. Furthermore, the sacred sciences are no longer exclusive clerical territory; today, many of the most respected scholars in the field are lay men and women. And never before has the study of Scripture become such an accepted and vital part of everyday Catholic life. Consequently, important biblical and theological topics are given preferred treatment. A work like this can perform another useful task by putting its readers more in touch with the valid insights and achievements of modern scholarship. In line with this, entries are devoted to the infancy and passion narratives, and these, in a practical and specific way, illustrate the methods and approach of scholars in their quest to understand and interpret the Scriptures.

A popular reference work of this size has its obvious limitations. Omissions forfeit their space for the welfare of the inclusions. *The Modern Catholic Encyclopedia* is edited for quick and easy consultation; and may it be helpful to many men and women on pilgrimage in our changing world.

MICHAEL GLAZIER
Clearwater, Florida

MONIKA K. HELLWIG
Georgetown University
Washington, D.C.

Acknowledgments

A special note of thanks to Rev. Michael Naughton, O.S.B., the Director of The Liturgical Press, who made the publication of this work possible; and to Brother Aaron Raverty, O.S.B., who, despite many academic duties and commitments, nursed the project from manuscript to book.

Abiding gratitude is due to Professors Helen and Leonard Doohan of Gonzaga University, Spokane, Washington; to Rev. Daniel Harrington, S.J., of Weston School of Theology, Cambridge, Massachusetts; to Professor John F. Craghan of St. Norbert College, De Pere, Wisconsin; to Rev. Thomas Shelley, St. Joseph's Seminary, Yonkers, New York; to Professor Michael Downey, Bellarmine College, Louisville, Kentucky. They all took a personal interest in the progress of the work, and they gave most generously of their time and talents. Their help was truly invaluable.

Deepest thanks to Sister Fay Trombley, S.C.I.C., Newman Theological College, Edmonton, Alberta, whose cheerful help and welcome suggestions made sure that Canadian contributors were well represented in the work; to Rev. Brendan Byrne, S.J., of Melbourne, who graciously helped us to contact and enlist Australian writers for the project; to publisher Michael Gill of Gill & Macmillan, Dublin, and to Rev. Austin Flannery, O.P., of Dominican Publications, Dublin, both of whom helped in so many ways.

Acknowledgment is gratefully given for the occasional use of texts from the New American Bible © 1970 by the Confraternity of Christian Doctrine, Washington, D.C., and from the New Revised Standard Version Bible, Catholic edition © 1989 by the Division of Christian Education of the National Council of Churches of Christ in the U.S.A. All rights reserved.

M.G./M.K.H.

Abbreviations

AA	Vatican II, decree *Apostolicam Actuositatem* (Laity), Abbott, 489–521; Flannery, 766–798
Abbott	Walter M. Abbott, S.J., ed., *The Documents of Vatican II,* New York: The America Press, 1966
AG	Vatican II, decree *Ad Gentes* (Missions), Abbott, 584–630; Flannery, 813–856
CA	John Paul II, apostolic letter *Centesimus Annus* (On the One Hundredth Anniversary of *Rerum Novarum*), Washington: USCC, 1991
CD	Vatican II, decree *Christus Dominus* (Bishops), Abbott, 396–429; Flannery, 564–590
CIC	*Codex Iuris Canonici,* Vatican City: Vatican Polyglot Press, 1983; *Code of Canon Law,* Washington: Canon Law Society of America, 1983
DH	Vatican II, declaration *Dignitatis Humanae* (Religious Freedom), Abbott, 675–696; Flannery, 799–812
DOL	ICEL, *Documents on the Liturgy 1963–1979: Conciliar, Papal, and Curial Texts,* Collegeville, Minn.: The Liturgical Press, 1982
DS	H. Denzinger and A. Schönmetzer, *Enchiridion Symbolorum, Definitionum et Declarationum de Rebus Fidei et Morum,* 35th ed., New York: Herder, 1974
DV	Vatican II, dogmatic constitution *Dei Verbum* (Revelation), Abbott, 111–128; Flannery, 750–765
EM	Instruction *Eucharisticum Mysterium* (On the Worship of the Eucharistic Mystery) from *Sacrosanctum Concilium* (Liturgy), Flannery, 100–105, 1967
EN	Paul VI, apostolic exhortation *Evangelii Nuntiandi,* 8 December 1975; *Evangelization in the Modern World,* Washington: USCC, 1975

Flannery	Austin Flannery, O.P., ed., *Vatican Council II: The Conciliar and Post Conciliar Documents,* Collegeville, Minn.: The Liturgical Press, 1975
GE	Vatican II, declaration *Gravissimum Educationis* (Christian Education), Abbott, 637–651; Flannery, 725–737
GILM	Sacred Congregation for the Sacraments and Divine Worship, *General Introduction to the Lectionary for Mass,* 2nd ed. (1981), Austin Flannery, O.P., ed., *Vatican Council II: More Post Conciliar Documents,* Collegeville, Minn.: The Liturgical Press, 1982, pp. 119–152.
GIRM	Sacred Congregation for Divine Worship, *General Instruction of the Roman Missal,* 4th ed., Vatican City: Vatican Polyglot Press, 1975; ICEL, *Documents on the Liturgy 1963–1979: Conciliar, Papal, and Curial Texts,* Collegeville, Minn.: The Liturgical Press, 1982, 465–533
GS	Vatican II, pastoral constitution *Gaudium et Spes* (Church in Modern World), Abbott, 199–308; Flannery, 903–1001
IM	Vatican II, decree *Inter Mirifica* (The Instruments of Social Communication), Abbott, 319–331; Flannery, 283–292
LE	John Paul II, encyclical *Laborem Exercens, Origins* 11 (24 September 1981) 226–244
LG	Vatican II, dogmatic constitution *Lumen Gentium* (Church), Abbott, 14–96; Flannery, 350–423
MD	Pius XII, encyclical *Mediator Dei,* Washington: National Catholic Welfare Conference, 1947
MM	John XXIII, encyclical *Mater et Magistra* (On a Responsible Approach to Social Progress), New York: Paulist Press, 1962
NA	Vatican II, declaration *Nostra Aetate* (Non-Christians), Abbott, 660–668; Flannery, 738–742
NCWC	National Catholic Welfare Conference
NT	New Testament
OA	Paul VI, apostolic letter *Octogesima Adveniens* (On the Eightieth Anniversary of the Encyclical *Rerum Novarum*), London: Catholic Truth Society, 1971
OpT	Vatican II, decree *Optatam Totius* (Priestly Formation), Abbott, 437–457; Flannery, 707–724
OT	Old Testament
PC	Vatican II, decree *Perfectae Caritatis* (Religious Life), Abbott, 466–482; Flannery, 611–623
PG	J.-P. Migne, ed., *Patrologia Cursus Completus: Series Graeca,* 161 vols., Paris, 1857–1866
PL	J.-P. Migne, ed., *Patrologia Cursus Completus: Series Latina,* 221 vols., Paris, 1844–1855
PO	Vatican II, decree *Presbyterorum Ordinis* (Priesthood), Abbott, 532–576; Flannery, 863–902

PP	Paul VI, encyclical *Populorum Progressio* (On the Development of Peoples), Washington: USCC, 1967
PT	John XXIII, encyclical *Pacem in Terris* (Peace on Earth), Washington: NCWC, 1963
QA	Pius XI, encyclical *Quadragesimo Anno* (On the Fortieth Anniversary of the encyclical *Rerum Novarum*), New York: The American Press, 1947
RCIA	Sacred Congregation for Divine Worship, *Ordo Initiationis Christianae Adultorum,* Vatican City: Vatican Polyglot Press, 1972; ICEL, *Rite of Christian Initiation of Adults,* Collegeville, Minn.: The Liturgical Press, 1988
RN	Leo XIII, encyclical *Rerum Novarum* (Rights and Duties of Capital and Labor), New York: Paulist Press, 1939
SC	Vatican II, constitution *Sacrosanctum Concilium* (Liturgy), Abbott, 137–178; Flannery, 1–36
SRS	John Paul II, encyclical *Sollicitudo Rei Socialis* (On the Twentieth Anniversary of the Encyclical *Populorum Progressio*), Washington: USCC, 1988
ST	Thomas Aquinas, *Summa Theologiae*
UR	Vatican II, decree *Unitatis Redintegratio* (Ecumenism), Abbott, 341–366; Flannery, 452–470
USCC	United States Catholic Conference

ABBESS

"Abbess," the feminine form of "abbot," dates back to the sixth century and refers to the superior of certain communities of nuns. Although in former times, particularly the Middle Ages, certain abbesses exercised considerable ecclesiastical jurisdiction over territories associated with their abbeys, they now have general spiritual and temporal authority over their communities but no sacramental jurisdiction.

PATRICIA DeFERRARI

See also ABBEY; BENEDICTINES.

ABBEY

Refers to the dwelling place and community of men or women religious who are governed by an abbot or abbess they elect. An abbey may be completely independent or may maintain an association with other abbeys of the same order. The physical layout of most abbeys includes the abbey church, refectory, cloister or "dormitory," chapter hall and work area. Depending on its size and its apostolic or contemplative nature, the abbey may also house an infirmary, workshops, schools, guesthouse or retreat center. "Abbey" and "monastery" are generally used interchangeably.

PATRICIA DeFERRARI

See also ABBESS; ABBOT.

ABBOT

An abbot is the head of a religious community of men, such as the Benedictines, Cistercians, and some others. Elected to office, the abbot has ordinary jurisdiction and general authority over his community. "Abbot" derives from the Aramaic and Syriac *abba,* meaning "father."

PATRICIA DeFERRARI

See also ABBEY; BENEDICTINES.

ABELARD, PETER (1079–1142)

Memorable philosopher, theologian, disputant, and lecturer. He earned renown as a teacher in Paris. He tutored and fell in love with Heloise, the niece of Fulbert, a canon of Notre Dame in whose house he lived. When Heloise became pregnant in 1118 after a secret marriage to Abelard, the canon had Abelard mutilated and he retired to the Abbey of St. Denis. Thereafter, he and Heloise carried on a long correspondence, one of the most famous in history. An independent and original thinker, Abelard—who is often regarded as the initiator of Scholasticism—was in constant trouble with more traditional theologians. His teaching on the Trinity was condemned at the Council of Soissons (1121) without giving Abelard a hearing. He dismissed the legends of St. Dionysius as flights of fancy and was forced to leave the Abbey of St. Denis. He then established an oratory near Troyes and called it the Paraclete. In 1125 he was made abbot of St. Gildas; but he relinquished the post ca. 1136 and returned to teach in Paris. He clashed with St. Bernard of Clairvaux who viewed some of his writings as heretical. Consequently, the Council of Sens (1140) condemned several propositions from his writings. Among his many works, *Sic et Non* is particularly significant. In it he assembled

Peter Abelard

apparently conflicting statements in the Scriptures and the Fathers and invited his readers to resolve them. He wrote a commentary on Romans and composed hymns. His ethical writings, especially on the nature of sin, drew censure from his adversaries. Controversy shadowed Abelard all his life; he was a prodigious and challenging author who made his contemporaries think. Abelard died in 1142; and when Heloise died in 1163 she was buried in his tomb.

MICHAEL GLAZIER

See also MIDDLE AGES, THE; PHILOSOPHY AND THEOLOGY; SCHOLASTICISM; THEOLOGY.

ABORTION

In the most general meaning of the term, this refers to the termination of an activity or a process before it reaches its completion or conclusion. When applied to the process of human procreation, it refers to the expulsion or removal from a woman's womb of a fertilized egg, or an embryo, or a fetus, before this new, developing life entity is capable of sustaining life outside the womb.

An abortion may be spontaneous; i.e., it may occur without deliberate intent on the part of the pregnant woman or some other outside agent and without the use of any artificial means. A spontaneous abortion is commonly called a miscarriage. Somewhere between 10 to 15 percent of all pregnancies end in a miscarriage, most of these before the twelfth week of pregnancy, and often without the woman yet being sure she is pregnant. Spontaneous abortions or miscarriages are regarded, from a Christian faith point of view, as sad, even tragic events, often bringing great pain to the prospective parents. But, as spontaneously occurring events, miscarriages are certainly without moral fault.

Despite the Roman Catholic Church's insistence upon conception as the beginning of a new human life, after a miscarriage no effort is made by the Church to baptize the aborted embryo or nonviable fetus, nor is a funeral Mass offered for the deceased life. Respectful disposal of the expelled *conceptus* is called for, but not burial in consecrated ground. With the permission of the parent, the aborted remains may be used for embryonic and fetal research and experimentation.

Most abortions are induced. That is to say, they are brought about intentionally, through the use of various technological or chemical means, by an agent other than the pregnant woman herself. Abortions performed during the first three months of pregnancy are the simplest and safest for the mother if carried out by qualified persons in well-equipped facilities. The most common procedure for such abortions is the vacuum aspiration method, a method that cannot be used after the first twelve weeks of pregnancy. Abortions during the second and third trimesters are correspondingly more painful and less safe for the mother, though the death rate for mothers in the United States from legal abortions is lower than the death rate for mothers in childbirth.

Objections to induced abortions, then, are not leveled against either their monetary cost or their danger to the physical health and safety of women. There is some evidence of psychological trauma in women who abort their pregnancies, but such trauma appears to be highly dependent upon the beliefs and attitudes of the particular woman and her circle of family and friends who support or criticize her choice to abort the pregnancy. There is simply no persuasive evidence that an induced abortion will automatically cause feelings of guilt or shame or depression in all women who choose to abort their pregnancies, however much one might wish it did or think it should.

Some form of induced abortion is now legal in most countries in the world, though few countries have allowed, in law, as unrestricted an access to abortion as has the United States. The 1973 Roe vs. Wade decision of the United States Supreme Court, and that Court's subsequent rulings on legislation in various states aimed at restricting a woman's legal access to abortion, have, in effect, made abortion on demand both legal and accessible to any woman who can afford to pay for it.

The result of these court decisions has been that the number of abortions in the United States now approximates the number of live births with something over 1,500,000 abortions a year being done. For many women abortion has become either a primary means of birth control, as it has been for many years in countries such as Japan and Russia, or it is seen as an essential backup means of birth control to be used when other contraceptive measures have failed.

Moral objections to the practice of abortion are not limited to the Roman Catholic Church, of course, but that Church has long been the most consistent and most articulate critic of abortion, condemning it as a crime against life and as a clear violation of the commandment thou shalt not kill.

The reasons for the Roman Catholic Church's opposition to abortion are clear and straightforward, but its opposition is not nearly as absolute as is sometimes suggested. These reasons also highlight the points at which abortion advocates differ most markedly from the Church.

The first reason for the Church's opposition to unrestricted abortion is that it sees God as the primary author of life and so it regards the conception of new life as a gift from God to be welcomed, respected, and cared for by the entire human community. Conception, pregnancy, and birth are not, in the Church's eyes, private matters, as the Supreme Court would have it, but matters of fundamental concern to God and to the entire human community.

Second, the Church teaches that a new human life is present from the moment of conception so that this new human life possesses the same dignity, the same right to life as any other human person. The Church holds this view on the beginning of human life, not because it has some secret revelation from God on the matter, but for three fundamental reasons. One is the demonstrable, scientific truth that the fertilized egg is both alive and a genetically unique life form. That truth does not yet say the fertilized egg is a human life worthy of the full range of rights to be accorded human persons, but it does say that one is dealing unmistakably with a genetically unique biological life form belonging to the human species, and not simply with an undefined mass of tissue.

A second reason for holding to conception as the beginning of human life is that it is also quite clear that there is and can be no scientific basis on which to determine when this new life should be accorded the moral status of being a human being. All knowledgeable people agree that, if left to develop naturally, the point will come when the newly conceived life can be said to be human. Perhaps that point comes at viability outside the womb, or at the actual point of birth; perhaps earlier with the development of the brain or later with the advent of conscious awareness or self-consciousness.

There is something to be said for all of these positions, but none are beyond question and some degree of arbitrary choice. It seems clear that the determination of when life is to be regarded and treated as human is a matter, not of hard scientific evidence, but of stipulation, not a matter simply of judgment but of decision. The human inability to draw a persuasive line as to when human life starts has persuaded the Church that it is most reasonable and most prudent to accept conception as the beginning of *human* existence.

Third, there is a unity to human life that has its origin and fundamental value in God. It is not our human achievements or the development of our human capacities that is the lasting basis of our human worth and of our claim to rights. It is rather our origin in and final destiny toward God that is the basis of human worth. In such a perspective the human being is of the same worth in his or her mother's womb as after a lifetime of achievements. For he or she is the same person.

Given these three considerations the Church concludes that induced abortion is simply a gross and unwarranted violation of the most basic of human rights, the right to life. To take this life directly and on purpose is simply not a right anyone possesses; hence there can be no legitimate claim of a woman's right to choose to abort a pregnancy. The right to choose is very real and highly respected in Catholic teaching, but that right is located before conception, in the decision to have or not to have sexual intercourse during a woman's fertile period. For this reason cases of pregnancy due to rape—which are rare—or due to other forms of coercion or ignorance pose a distinct and difficult problem for Church teaching, one that has not been fully or adequately addressed.

Despite its teaching on the beginning of human life and its dignity, Church teaching does not absolutely forbid all abortions. It tolerates as regrettable and the lesser of two evils those abortions which are both indirect and necessary to preserve the life of the mother. The principle of double effect has traditionally been employed to determine in particular cases when these two conditions of indirectness and necessity pertain. The reigning moral principle at work affirms that innocent human life may never be directly taken either as an end or as a means to an end, even a good end.

Abortion has been presented to the public as a right to choose, as an essential requirement of the individual freedom so prized in the culture of the

United States. Even abortion advocates admit that it is often a painful choice and always a regrettable one, but a choice they deem essential to every woman's right of self-determination. It seems likely that the Church's teaching about abortion will make little headway in society until that teaching can also address the social, cultural, and economic issues that touch upon the full human dignity and equality of women.

JAMES P. HANIGAN

See also ANTHROPOLOGY, CHRISTIAN; NATURAL LAW; SEXUALITY.

ABSOLUTION

In the 1973 *Rite of Penance* absolution is listed as one of the four "parts" of the sacrament of penance. Sinners who are contrite, confess their sins, and are willing to make satisfaction receive an efficacious sign of God's pardon and peace through the agency of the priest, who extends his hands over the penitent's head and pronounces the formula of absolution, which recalls God's desire to bring reconciliation to the world through the death and resurrection of Jesus (Rom 5:10; 2 Cor 5:19) and the sending of the Holy Spirit for the forgiveness of sins (John 20:22-23). This new rite and the new formula of absolution are the result of a decree of the Second Vatican Council that called for a revision of the sacrament of penance to express more clearly the nature and the effects of the sacrament.

Absolution within the sacrament of penance has taken various shapes in the history of the Church. Initially, baptism into the Church brought about the forgiveness of sins and it was not envisaged, perhaps due to a belief in the imminent second coming of Christ or else to a high expectation of the power of grace, that the faithful would fall again into serious sin. When capital sins such as apostasy, murder, and adultery were publicly known, the sinner was felt to have left the community and the fellowship of the Eucharist. A sinner, however, who genuinely repented and desired to return to the community could not be baptized again, and so public penance was instituted as a "second baptism." After manifesting genuine contrition and having made satisfaction, a penitent would be received back into communion during a liturgical celebration, probably through the laying on of hands by the bishop. This form of absolution, which was in use from the second to the sixth century, was granted only once in a person's lifetime, and so was often postponed until late in life, even the hour of death.

Private and more frequent confession of sins developed from the seventh to the eleventh century and during this time a formula of absolution was developed for use by the priest. By the time of Thomas Aquinas this formula of absolution was firmly established as an essential part of the sacrament.

At the Council of Trent the bishops reacted to the teaching of the Reformers that the proclamation of the Word of God alone brought about the forgiveness of sins. Instead, they stressed the role of the priest as judge, and absolution, therefore, tended to be looked on as a judicial act.

The bishops at the Second Vatican Council wanted to highlight the ecclesial nature of sin: it is an offense against God but also does harm to the Christian community. They also wished to emphasize the ecclesial nature of the reconciliation of the sinner: the Church plays a role through charity, example, and prayer in seeking the conversion of the sinner. Absolution is now set in a more welcoming context of prayer, Scripture reading, and an opportunity for spiritual conversation.

The ecclesial dimension is more dramatically present in the two new rites for *communal* celebration of penance, either with individual confession and absolution, or, in the cases provided for in the law, with general confession and absolution.

WILLIAM C. McFADDEN, S.J.

See also SACRAMENT OF RECONCILIATION.

ABSOLUTION, GENERAL

See GENERAL ABSOLUTION.

ABSTINENCE, PENITENTIAL

Penitential abstinence ordinarily means a temporary refraining from food partially or totally (fasting) or temporary refraining from certain types of food.

Abstinence was a common practice among the Jews of Old Testament times. They observed the Day of Atonement as a strict fast for one day from sundown to sundown each year. Often in times of adversity, the judge, the king, or the prophet would proclaim a fast to show humility before God and to win God's protection. The Jews marked the day of the beginning of the siege of Jerusalem and the day of the burning of the Temple by abstinence. There were certain festival days when leavened bread was forbidden. Abstinence from all "unclean foods" was of strict obligation at all times. The Pharisees of Jesus' time fasted twice a week, Mondays and Thursdays. The purpose of the abstinence was both spiritual and penitential: to avoid unclean foods as an incentive for spiritual cleanness; to be humble before God as befits a sinful people; and to dispose God to look favorably upon them by protecting them from their enemies and granting them prosperity.

In the New Testament, the Synoptic Gospels tell of Jesus passing forty days and forty nights in the desert fasting and praying at the onset of his public ministry. The fasting of Jesus became the model for early Christians. The only specific demand of abstinence imposed upon New Testament Christians was to "abstain from what has been sacrificed to idols and from blood and from what is strangled and from fornication" (Acts 15:29).

The early Christians tended to follow the practices of their Jewish heritage, but, as the links with Judaism became more tenuous, specifically Christian practices developed. In the earliest Christian centuries, Friday, the day of Jesus' death, was observed as a day of abstinence. Also very early, the Friday abstinence was prolonged into Saturday, in some places once a month, in other places every weekend, to commemorate the burial of Jesus and the mourning of the disciples. By the early Middle Ages abstinence was specified as abstinence from flesh meat. Although popes refused to abrogate the general law of Saturday abstinence, so many local indults were granted dispensing from the practice that in effect the law ceased to have any force.

The original Lenten abstinence was as brief as the two days before Easter, Good Friday and Holy Saturday. There were no uniform observances of Lent. The preparation of catechumens for baptism and of penitents for reconciliation, with the accompanying fasting, abstinence, and prayer, became the dominant factor in the development of Lent. In a spirit of solidarity, the faithful joined them to make Lent their own time of retreat and penance. In Rome, Lent was at first three weeks in length, then later six weeks. With the abrogation of abstinence on Sunday, Lent became only thirty-six days until the addition of the four days before the First Sunday of Lent.

In addition to Lent, days of abstinence were Wednesday, Friday, and Saturday of Ember Week, marking each of the four seasons of the year; the four weeks of Advent, the vigils of major feasts, and the Monday, Tuesday, and Wednesday before Ascension Thursday.

Although there were always local modifications, the laws of penitential abstinence remained quite severe until the issuance of *Poenitemini* by Paul VI (17 February 1966). A major thrust of the document was the reassertion of the truth of the constant need for repentance and penitential practices by divine law in light of the gospel and the constant tradition of the Church, but, rather than imposing fasting and abstinence by law, now Christians were to have greater freedom in determining penitential practices deemed most beneficial for them. To preserve the common observance of penance, certain penitential days were to remain: all Fridays throughout the year and the time of Lent. Fridays are to be observed by abstinence from eating meat and Ash Wednesday and Good Friday as days of both abstinence and fasting. Abstinence forbids the eating of meat, but not of eggs, milk or condiments made from animal fat. Fasting allows only one full meal in the course of the day and two smaller meals. All persons who have completed their fourteenth year are bound by the law of abstinence, and those who have become adults (ordinarily, twenty-one years of age) must observe the law of fasting until they are sixty. Conferences of bishops determine more precisely the observance of fast and abstinence. In the United States, the days of required abstinence are Ash Wednesday and the Fridays of Lent, and the days of fasting are Ash Wednesday and Good Friday.

Since *Poenitemini,* penitential abstinence has become largely a matter of self-imposed observance.

CHARLES SKOK

See also FAST/FASTING; SACRAMENT OF RECONCILIATION.

ABSTINENCE, SEXUAL

Sexual abstinence, in its negative sense, is refraining from sexual intercourse or any other use of the sexual faculties; in its positive sense, it can be either a married couple's temporary abstention from sexual relations for spiritual purposes or the permanent abstention from use of the sexual faculties required by the vows of religious or the law of celibacy for priests and bishops of the Western Church.

Jesus himself set the example for sexual abstinence and commended it for his disciples: "There are eunuchs who have made themselves eunuchs for the sake of the kingdom of heaven" (Matt 19:12). The Apostle Paul preferred the life of virginity to that of marriage because "the appointed time has grown short" (1 Cor 2:29) and the unmarried state allows freedom from anxieties and devotion to the service of the Lord (1 Cor 7:32-35). Married couples should refrain from sexual relations only by agreement for a set time to devote themselves to prayer (1 Cor 7:1-7). A current example of sexual abstinence is the practice of natural birth control by the avoidance of sexual relations during the female fertile period (cf. *Humanae Vitae*).

The major issue of sexual abstinence has been the clerical celibacy of the Western Church. There are examples of celibacy in Old Testament times, but usually on a temporary basis regarding soldiers at war and priests and Levites in the course of their Temple service. Early Christians, in a departure from their Jewish heritage, held virginity in high regard, as the lives of so many martyrs attest. The teaching and example of Jesus and of Paul seem to have been the major influence for disciples to espouse themselves to Christ. But there was no universal requirement of celibacy for those serving as deacons, presbyters, or bishops.

The celibacy of the clergy arose more as a custom than as a law. The first attempt to impose celibacy upon deacons, priests, and bishops came in the local Spanish Council of Elvira (ca. 300). In the local Council of Trullo (692) in the East, deacons and priests could not marry after ordination, but they were to live in marriage with the wives they had married previously. Earlier in the West celibacy was stressed as "the more excellent way," but there was no universal attempt to impose it across the board. Gradually there was increased pressure that clerics not marry; if married, that they separate from their wives; and, if they would not separate from their wives, they be deposed. In spite of attempts at reforms by popes and religious leaders who favored a celibate clergy, many priests and bishops openly took wives and had children who often became heirs to their benefices. The centuries-long controversy over the celibacy of priests and bishops was made a matter of universal Church discipline in the First Lateran Council (1123) in which "priests, deacons, subdeacons and monks" were absolutely forbidden "to have concubines or to contract marriages." It recommended that such marriages "be made void." The Second Lateran Council (1139) ordered that those with concubines or in marriages "be separated from their partners, [for] we do not deem there to be a marriage . . ." and that they "do penance commensurate with such outrageous behavior." The Council of Trent (1545–1563) crystallized the earlier discipline: the temporary separation of spouses was allowed; attempted marriages of clerics in holy orders and religious with solemn vows were declared invalid; and lives of virginity and celibacy were superior to the married state.

The issue of clerical celibacy was reexamined in the Second Vatican Council and the position of required celibacy for priests and bishops was again widely discussed in the 1971 Synod of Bishops. Its document, *The Ministerial Priesthood,* reaffirmed the discipline of Trent.

Sexual abstinence, expressed in celibacy, grew out of liturgical law which forbade sexual intercourse the night before communicating at the Eucharist. Its background was primarily cultic, expressing the attitude of something unclean and sinful about sexual intercourse in marriage. The law of celibacy came about to make the law of abstinence effective. The Second Vatican Council made the primary motivation for celibacy "for the sake of the reign of God." The arguments offered in favor of celibacy were its mystical significance, its pastoral effectiveness, and its serious relevance for ascetical and spiritual development. John Paul II has made it clear on several occasions that celibacy expressed in sexual abstinence and observed for the sake of the reign of God will be retained as the discipline and the law for priests of the Western Church.

CHARLES SKOK

See also CELIBACY; HUMANAE VITAE; PRIESTHOOD, THE MINISTERIAL; RELIGIOUS LIFE, ACTIVE; SACRAMENT OF MATRIMONY; SEXUALITY.

ABUSE, FAMILY

Experts agree that religious beliefs play a key role in the behaviors of the violent and the violated. This is particularly true of family violence. Those who commit violence against others (parents against children; spouses against each other; children toward parents and elders) quote the Bible in support of their behavior, and those who are treated violently often believe that the Bible teaches "suffering in silence."

In the prevailing culture of the United States, family violence is called "abuse." Yet some U.S. subcultures consider these behaviors normal and acceptable. Because the concept of abuse is so strongly determined by the cultural context in which a given behavior occurs, the term should be used with great care and sensitivity.

Family Violence in the Bible

Honor and shame, the core cultural values of the Mediterranean world, form the appropriate context for understanding violence in the Bible. These values are the basis for the gender-based division of all of human life in that world. Men preserve and defend honor and must especially guard their wives and daughters. Women, always vulnerable to attack, are associated with shame.

Biblical culture approves physical punishment of male children (Prov 13:24; 22:15; 23:13-14; 29:15, 19) as a normal and acceptable way to raise honorable sons. Such discipline teaches respect for parents and elders and guides the boy into the honorable expression of manliness, which is to suffer in silence (Isa 42:2; 50:6; 53:7; 2 Cor 11:21-30; Mark 15:33-39).

Young girls and women gain honor by being subordinate and submissive to fathers, brothers, and husbands (Sir 22:3; 42:11; 1 Tim 2:11). To behave otherwise is shameful, and such behavior destroys the Middle Eastern family (Sir 9:22; 42:9-10; compare with Eph 5:22).

That boys and girls both rebelled against such treatment can be deduced by mirror-reading various biblical passages. The constant reminder to "honor father and mother" and the repetition of punishments deserved by disrespectful children (Exod 21:15, 17; Lev 20:9; Prov 20:20; 30:11; Sir 3:11, 16) suggests that violence toward elders was no less common than violence toward children.

Women also learned compensating and retaliatory behaviors. Rebecca masterminded the plot in which Jacob deceived his father and defrauded his brother (Gen 27). Bathsheba manipulated David to make Solomon rather than Adonijah his successor (1 Kings 1–2).

Fusing Love with Violence

The Bible indicates that ancient Mediterranean culture consciously fuses love and violence. The sage's observation that: "The Lord reproves the one he loves, as a father the son in whom he delights" (Prov 3:12) is applied to God and Jesus by the author of Hebrews (5:7-10; 12:7-11).

This is no surprise. As the Scholastics taught, all theology is analogy, and ancient Mediterranean thinking about God is rooted in its daily life. Any reading of the Bible indicates that the God revealed therein often behaves like such a Mediterranean father, only more so.

Physical Abuse in the United States

Christians in other cultures who guide their lives by the beliefs and behaviors reflected in the Bible have tended to regard physical violence as normal and acceptable strategy in interpersonal relationships. An early New England diary, *The Memoirs of Abigail Abbot Bailey,* documents Bible-based wife abuse in painful detail.

Since then, however, family violence has been increasingly challenged in this culture and gradually reduced. Violence toward children is illegal everywhere in the U.S., and spouse and elder abuse are also receiving increased attention. Support and advocacy groups continue to form in order to challenge and reduce violence of all kinds among all people.

One thing all Catholics can do to reduce and eradicate family violence from United States' culture is read and reflect upon their Bible and religious beliefs more critically. Only in this way can the culturally inappropriate behaviors inspired by the Bible be properly understood and evaluated.

JOHN J. PILCH

See also CRITICISM, BIBLICAL.

ACADEMIC FREEDOM

This expression evokes the conditions necessary for the faithful and responsible accomplishment of the task a society, be it civil or ecclesial, ascribes to its academics. The basis for such a commission may be seen as threefold: (1) The belief that truth has nothing to fear from truth; (2) The belief that humankind is able, with time and through trial and error, to approach truth; (3) The recognition that society cannot prosper without continuously seeking after truth. Academics, for their part, are expected to pursue truth with courage, determination, objectivity, as well as ecological, societal and moral responsibility since, be it in the domains of the natural or human sciences, they are expected to foster the common good of the whole of the cosmos and of humankind in particular (cf. Pastoral Constitution on the Church in the Modern World [GS 59]; Declaration on Religious Freedom [DH 7]).

In a Christian perspective, belief in the one God, Creator and Savior of the world, firmly grounds the axiom that "truth cannot be contrary to truth" even when it comes to rational truths compared to revealed truths. Vatican I, in its Dogmatic Constitution on Catholic Faith, *Dei Filius,* chs. 1 and 4, had already established this point which Vatican II received and developed in *Gaudium et Spes* 36:2; 59:3; 62:2; the Decree on the Apostolate of the Laity, (AA 7:1-2); and in the Declaration on Christian Education (GE 10:1–2). While recognizing the presence of sin and of serious obstacles in the path of truth, as in the case of all human endeavors, (GS 36:3; 37; AA 7:3), the Church confesses her faith in the recapitulation of all things in Christ (Eph 1:10; cf. GS 38; 45; 58:4) as well as the assistance of the Holy Spirit in humankind's pilgrimage towards the fullness of truth (John 16:13), from which faith comes the impetus for the Christians' commitment to bettering the world in which they live (GS 21:3; 39:2; 43:1).

The service of "teacher"—the theologian realizing but partly this ministry—is found among the gifts the Triune God grants for the building up of the Church, body of Christ (Rom 12:7; 1 Cor 12:28; Eph 4:11; 1 Thess 5:12; Gal 6:6; Matt 23:34), in total subordination to Christ (Matt 23:10)—the source of liberating truth (John 8:32)—and the gospel of the kingdom (Matt 28:20; Gal 1:8-9; 1 Tim 6:3), and threading a fine line between those who run too far ahead (2 John 9) and those who lag too far behind (Gal 2:3-5; 4:8-10; 5:1-4) with an eye to realizing the ideal proposed by Jesus: "... every scribe who becomes a disciple of the kingdom of heaven is like a householder who brings out from his storeroom things both new and old" (Matt 13:32). Discernment as to the orthodoxy of a teaching would seem to come under the purview of a variety of persons: those endowed with a special gift for the task (1 Cor 12:10), colleagues (cf. 1 Cor 14:29), the faithful (1 Thess 5:21; 1 John 4:1-6), the leaders of the community (Acts 15:4, 6, 22-23; Gal 2:2, 6; 1 John 4:6). Such a variety of voices reflects a situation which is altogether healthy and normal in a Church defined as a "communion."

The realm of theology is defined by its fundamental task which is the intelligence of faith, *fides quaerens intellectum.* Thomas Aquinas took this to mean the study of God and all that which pertained to God, through participation in the science of God and of the Blessed made accessible through Scripture and Tradition, thanks to the light of faith (ST I, q. 1, aa. 1–3).

The documents of Vatican II enumerate several tasks expected of theologians. For one, they are strongly encouraged to maintain open dialogue with researchers in the fields of natural and human sciences (GS 44:2; 62:2, 7), as well as in ecumenical circles where it is imperative to recognize and respect a diversity of theological approaches (Decree on Ecumenism, UR 5:1; 6:1; 10:1-2; 11:3; 17:1; GE 11:1). Of course, theologians are invited to make a close and careful study of Scripture, patristics and the liturgy for the benefit of the faithful in general and of the ordained ministers in particular (Dogmatic Constitution on the Church, LG 25, *in fine*; Dogmatic Constitution on Revelation, DV 12:2-3; 23; 24; Constitution on the Sacred Liturgy, SC 16:1). This same task is recalled in LG 67, when treating of Mariology, in which case Vatican II purposely refrains from taking a stand on questions still open to theological debate (LG 54). As for the theological qualifications to be given to the texts of Vatican II in order to ascertain the degree of "authority" involved in "authentic," i.e., "public" and "official," proclamations of the pastoral magisterium (LG 25; DV 10:2; 12:3) the *Addenda* to *Lumen Gentium* refers the inquirer to the norms of theological interpretation. Theology is also called upon to play its part in the inculturation of faith in missionary territories (Decree on the Church's Missionary Activity, AG 22:2).

In order to accomplish their task, theologians are invited to keep in mind two important principles regarding their faith: (1) The very deposit or truths of faith are one thing; other is the manner in which they are formulated just so long as are maintained the same meaning and significance (GS 62:2; UR 6:1); (2) In Catholic teaching, there exists an order or "hierarchy" of truths, since they vary in their relationship to the foundation of the Christian faith (UR 11:3). Equally important is the statement that "In order that such persons (theologians) fulfill their proper function, let it be recognized that all the faithful, clerical and lay, possess a lawful freedom of inquiry and of thought, and the freedom to express their minds humbly and courageously about matters in which they enjoy competence" (GS 62:7; cf. 92:2; LG 37:1, 3; UR 4:7). The last word of this quotation recalls that the "authority" of theologians is based on the degree of their scientific qualifications according to the specific method and rules of theology (GS 62:2). Finally, let us recall that theological research is to be pursued under the light of faith and the guidance of the pastoral magisterium (Decree on Priestly formation, OpT 16:1).

THOMAS R. POTVIN, O.P.

See also THEOLOGY.

ACOLYTE

From the Greek term *akoloutheou,* meaning "follow," acolyte refers to the order of clerics devoted to altar service. They assist the celebrant at Mass, and may distribute Holy Communion as a minister when necessary. The title also refers to any layman who serves at Mass or other liturgical functions. The ministries of acolyte and lector are the two remaining minor orders of the Church.

JOSEPH QUINN

See also LITURGY.

ACTA APOSTOLICAE SEDIS

Translated as "Acts of the Apostolic See," this is the official journal of the Vatican. It is the principal source for the promulgation of canon law, and also includes the authoritative texts of Apostolic Constitutions, encyclical letters, and notable decrees of the Roman Curia. First published in 1909, it is now published monthly by Libreria Editrice Vaticana. The *AAS* is available by subscription, and is commonly found in the libraries of Catholic universities and colleges.

JOSEPH QUINN

See also ACTA SANCTAE SEDIS; PAPACY, THE.

ACTA SANCTAE SEDIS

Translated as "Acts of the Holy See," this was a monthly publication issued in Rome from 1865 through 1908. It contained the principal declarations and decrees of the pope and the Roman congregations, though it was not considered an official publication of the Holy See until 1904 when its contents were pronounced official and authentic. The periodical was superseded in 1909 by the *Acta Apostolicae Sedis.*

JOSEPH QUINN

See also ACTA APOSTOLICAE SEDIS.

ACTA SANCTORUM

See BOLLANDISTS.

ACTIVE ORDERS

See RELIGIOUS LIFE, ACTIVE.

ACTS OF THE MARTYRS

The contemporary accounts of the Church's early martyrdoms. They include the official court records of Christian trials and executions, as well as passions written either by witnesses or later Christian authors who based them on the narrations of witnesses. The most reliable of these accounts are those based on official reports from the trials. The later versions and passions are not considered as credible, particularly those which are decidedly embellished. The writings of St. Augustine indicate that accounts of these martyrdoms have been used in the liturgy of the Western Church since the earliest times.

JOSEPH QUINN

See also MARTYRDOM.

ACTUAL GRACE

See GRACE.

ACTUAL SIN

See SIN.

AD LIMINA APOSTOLORUM

It was a devout custom in the early Church to make a pilgrimage *to the thresholds of the Apostles,* i.e., to the tombs of Peter and Paul in Rome. Canon law currently requires each residential bishop in Europe to visit Rome every five years to pray in the basilicas of St. Peter and of St. Paul, to make a personal report to the pope, and to give a detailed report of the state of his diocese, orally to the pope and in writing to the Consistorial Congregation. Residential bishops outside of Europe need only make the *ad limina* visit every ten years, while continuing to submit a written report every five years.

WILLIAM C. McFADDEN, S.J.

See also BISHOP; CANON LAW.

ADAM, KARL (1878–1966)

Twentieth-century theologian. Born in Bavaria to a family of ten, Adam was educated at the Classical Gymnasium at Amburg and the Philosophical and Theological Seminary at Regensburg, taking his doctorate at the University of Munich in 1904. He was ordained a priest in 1900, became a professor at Munich (1915), held the chair of Moral Theology at Strasbourg (1917) and the chair of Dogmatic Theology, Tübingen (1919). His early works focus on the theologies of the Church Fathers, especially Augustine, but it was his Tübingen lectures on the Church which brought him worldwide fame and a large following among educated laity. His subsequent writings stress the necessity for an understanding of our relationship with Christ in his Mystical Body, especially as related to humanity's search for unity. He was a tireless worker for a union of Christians, a theme in books such as *Christ our Brother, The Son of God, One and Holy,* and *The Spirit of Catholicism.* The latter (1924) has probably been most influential. It was intended to provide a calm, dispassionate, clearly written consideration of the fundamental concepts of the Catholic faith which would explain to all, Catholic and non-Catholic alike, exactly what the Catholic Church is.

Adam opposed the so-called German religion in 1934 with the address on "The Eternal Christ." He was threatened, and his house riddled with bullets, eventually losing his right to lecture.

DAVID BRYAN

See also CHURCH AND STATE; THEOLOGY.

ADOPTION

The relationship arising from adoption affects rights and obligations under canon law. Canon law defers to the appropriate civil law for the determination of whether the relationship has arisen. If a person has been adopted according to the norms of the applicable civil law jurisdiction, that person will be considered as validly adopted for purposes of canon law. Canon 110 provides that children who have been adopted according to the norm of civil law are considered as being the children of the person or persons who have adopted them.

Adoption would bind the adopting parents to the duties of seeing to the baptism of adopted infants and of forming their adopted children in the faith and practice of the Christian life by word and example.

If a person is adopted, notation should be made in the baptismal register, since adoption affects the person's canonical status. The Code of Canon Law provides that generally, upon the baptism of an adopted child, the names of both the adopting parents and the natural parents should be noted in the baptismal register. In many instances, the names of the natural parents would not be known to the adopting parents or the minister of baptism; in such cases, those names are omitted. The local bishop or the conference of bishops may issue special regulations in this regard, which would normally take account of confidentiality and privacy concerns.

Adoption constitutes an impediment to marriage in Church law. A person may not validly contract marriage with those to whom he or she through legal adoption is related in the direct line or in the second degree of the collateral line. The prohibition of marriage in the direct line would include marriage between the adopting parent and adopted child. The collateral line impediment would prohibit marriage between an adopted person and any natural or other adopted children of his or her adopting parents. The local ordinary could dispense this marriage impediment if there were just and reasonable cause in the particular case. The adopted person would still be subject to the impediments arising under canon law by virtue of consanguinity; for purposes of marriage impediments, adoption does not sever ties of blood.

ROBERT C. GIBBONS

See also CANON LAW.

ADORATION, EUCHARISTIC

See EUCHARISTIC DEVOTIONS.

ADVANCE DIRECTIVES FOR MEDICAL CARE

Advance Directives for Medical Care are legal documents enabling people to express the type of medical care they desire if they become incapable of making medical decisions for themselves. There are two kinds of advance directives for health care; the Living Will (LW) and the Durable Power of Attorney for Health Affairs (DPAHA). Both documents were formulated to help avoid unnecessary health care if the person who signed the document becomes incapacitated and can not make medical decisions for himself or herself. The LW which became popular in the mid-seventies, requests the attending physician to remove life support if the person is incapacitated, death is imminent, and life support is merely "prolonging the dying process." The LW is seldom effective because physicians are reluctant to act as legal proxies for their patients and the fact that death is imminent is often difficult to determine. As a result of the ineffectiveness of the LW, the DPAHA was developed in the late 1980s. The agent, or attorney-in-fact of a DPAHA, is a person previously appointed by the one who signs the document. The DPAHA becomes effective when two physicians attest that the patient can no longer make competent health care decisions and it enables the agent to make health care decisions for the incapacitated person even if death is not imminent.

Both the LW and DPAHA have been enacted into law in many states. The moral and legal right to decide the proper medical treatment for incapacitated persons in our care however, does not arise from the state law. Rather, this right and responsibility arises from our relationship as loving human beings and our desire to fulfill our Christian responsibilities. Caring people have been making health care decisions for incapacitated family members and loved ones for centuries. They do not need the civil law to give them permission. However, given the more complex situation in contemporary health care and the tendency in the United States to prolong life beyond benefit for the patient, an advance directive is a useful document. Clearly, attending physicians, especially specialists, often do not know the value system of the patients for whom they care. Moreover, in the United States there is a tendency, especially in acute care facilities, to use all available technology and procedures without asking questions about patient benefit. Both the LW and DPAHA seek to insure patient benefit, but the DPAHA is far more useful than the LW because it names a definite person as proxy or agent, and because it recognizes the patient's value system as expressed by the agent (Chris Hackler and others, eds., *Advance Directives in Medicine,* New York: Praeger, 1989).

Insofar as the teaching of the Catholic Church is concerned, the use of advance directives does not offer any serious moral problems if patient benefit is the focus of the document and its application (Ronald Hamel, "Advance Directives Compatible with Catholic Moral Principles," *Health Progress* 69 [April 1988], no. 3, pp. 36–40). As mentioned, advance directives may be considered a method of facilitating the moral obligation to care for one another. The Pro-Life committee of the U.S. Bishops Conference upon two occasions has taken a rather cautious approach to advance directives (Pro-Life Committee, National Conference of Catholic Bishops, "Guidelines for Legislation on Life Sustaining Treatment," [10 November 1984] *Origins* 14 [24 January 1985], no. 32, pp. 526–528; "The Rights of the Terminally Ill," [2 July 1986] *Origins* 16 [4 September 1986], no. 2, pp. 222–224); however, Catholic conferences in many states have fostered and approved advance directive legislation. Of course, if a person were to request future medical care which is unethical, for example, if one requested to be killed if he contracted Alzheimer's disease, neither the attorney-in-fact nor the health care provider could in conscience fulfill the request. In states which have legislation concerning advance directives, forms for the LW or DPAHA may be obtained from the State Bar Association. An advance directive written from the Christian perspective may be obtained from the Center for Health Care Ethics at Saint Louis University Medical School.

KEVIN O'ROURKE, O.P.

See also DEATH AND DYING; HEALING.

ADVENT

(Lat. *adventus,* an arrival) The four-week liturgical season preceding Christmas in which the Church prepares to celebrate the birth of Christ while also anticipating his second coming. Advent begins on the Sunday nearest to 30 November (the feast of St. Andrew), called the First Sunday of Advent. The Church's liturgical year also begins on this day.

Readings and practices of the Advent season emphasize both penitence and the joyful expectation of the Lord's coming. From the First Sunday of Advent to 16 December, the liturgical focus is on penitence and preparation for the second coming—with readings centered around the messianic prophecies of John the Baptist and Isaiah, and gospel selections which depict Jesus as the fulfillment of those prophecies. Also during this period, violet vestments are worn by the clergy (rose vestments are also acceptable on the Third, or "Gaudete" Sunday), further emphasizing the theme of repentance.

Liturgies of the final week of Advent focus on the approaching birth of Christ, with the role of the Blessed Mother receiving special emphasis. The observation of a preparatory season prior to the celebration of Christmas dates back to the fourth century.

JOSEPH QUINN

See also LITURGY.

AFFIRMATIVE ACTION

Affirmative action is the general name given to various programs meant to redress past discriminatory practices based on sex, race, or other arbitrary standards that prevent people from participating in economic and social institutions.

The existence of such injustice requires positive actions on the part of all aspects of society to redress it. Questions are raised, however, about the nature of these actions.

Some contend that affirmative action means admitting or hiring people who are unqualified. Such, however, is not the case. Affirmative action involves taking minority status into account along with other criteria such as intellectual ability, technical competence, and congruity with organizational values in making admission, employment, and advancement decisions.

Some contend that affirmative action leads to reverse discrimination. Discrimination, however, is more than just not getting a position or promotion. It is a systematic pattern of social marginalization that leaves an individual powerless and unable to participate significantly within society because that person belongs to a particular group. Affirmative action does not have that result.

In order to redress the social consequences of discrimination, it is necessary to focus on more than just admission, employment, and promotion. Attention must be paid as well to the culture of the organization to insure that it is positive for and supportive of minorities. And, steps must be made to provide minorities with the necessary background to apply for positions and with the necessary coaching to work within the formal and informal structures of the organization.

THOMAS SCHINDLER

See also RACISM; SOCIAL TEACHING OF THE CHURCH.

AFRICA, THE CATHOLIC CHURCH IN

Two movements profoundly changed the Catholic Church in Africa from the 1960s onwards: political independence and Vatican II. This article limits itself to sub-Saharan Africa and within these confines to some of the major issues.

Both in Europe and in the colonies the Church had access to the corridors of power. In the French, Belgian, Portuguese and Spanish colonies the Church could be seen as the spiritual counterpart of the country's political and economic presence, a chaplain to the garrison. While in the British colonies the distinct position of the Anglican Church was never successfully challenged, the Catholic Church had established a desirable modus vivendi without the negative connotations of colonial chaplain. This was part of the publicly perceived legacy with which the Church faced the advent of political independence in Africa.

Political Independence

A number of anxieties surfaced quite soon. The majority of the emerging African elite—politician, professional, trade unionist and civil servant—was a product of a Western-style education, frequently received overseas. Among these there was a considerable fascination with a strong centralized government controlling all areas of society, especially education and health. Some were avowedly socialist in outlook while others sought a new creation called African Socialism. Would such a leadership countenance the existence, much less the state subvention, of the Catholic Church's parallel, (and in places superior), system of schools, hospitals, clinics, etc.?

Church leadership in the 1960s was predominantly white. Rome, through Propaganda Fide, stressed the development of an African clergy, especially a diocesan one. Many of the missionary orders, international in character, sought to recruit local membership to their own ranks. This latter was quite legitimate but tragically in some instances African diocesan clergy were pitted against African members of the international orders and societies. There were instances of missionary institutes attempting to hold control of dioceses by having an African member succeed a European bishop member. This territorial outlook did much to slow the development of local diocesan clergy.

Ordination Mass in Ouagadougou, Upper Volta

The end result was that in any high-level discussions with African politicians and civil servants the Church was at a disadvantage in being represented by whites or expatriates. It lacked a seasoned corps of senior African clergy to negotiate with their secular counterparts and fellow citizens. It is true that many of the new secular elite were past pupils of the missions schools, yet one discerns a certain paternalism, the reluctance of the teacher to grant his successful former student adult status.

The Catholic Church is international in its composition and outlook. It presupposes for its activity communication between a nation's hierarchy and Rome, between individual bishops within a national hierarchy. It presumes the freedom of communication (preaching/teaching) of an individual bishop with his people and also the freedom of a national hierarchy to communicate with its own members and to society at large in areas of the public debate. Would independent African governments permit such communication both within the local Church and to the world Church, especially to Rome?

It was difficult to remain optimistic about the outcome of the Church-state relationship as a distinctive pattern of postcolonial politics emerged. The passage from multiparty state to one-party state became increasingly ominous as the public rhetoric identified the nation state with the controlling party and its charismatic leader. To dissent from the party was to absent oneself from the nation, to be unpatriotic. These were some of the challenges facing the Church in the public arena in the immediate aftermath of independence (cf. A. Hastings, *A History of African Christianity, 1950–1975,* London: Cambridge University Press, 1979).

Vatican II

The four sessions of Vatican II, between October 1962 and December 1965, brought hundreds of missionary bishops to Rome. For the greater part they came as pensioners of the Vatican. Practical and grateful men, they had no desire to bite the hand that fed them. Long-suffering in their dependence on Propaganda Fide for annual financial subventions and long-inured to the personal humiliation of begging for funds from the home Churches, they arrived regarding themselves and being regarded as marginal to the debate. The missionary bishops found a voice and departed knowing that the Church of its very nature is missionary. The Macmillan winds of change that had forever changed Africa politically were matched in Rome by the Johannine opening of windows that changed the Church dramatically.

With a few notable exceptions the contribution of the missionary bishops was at the practical level rather than at the theological. Central Europe provided the theological underpinning of the great documents. A wonderful educational process began in Vatican II. The missionary bishops did not remain outside of this; old men began to dream again as the council continued. At a very pragmatic level, they realized that the vote of one missionary bishop from some distant African outpost balanced out the vote of some great European or American metropolitan or Vatican curialist.

The key document of Vatican II is *Lumen Gentium* (The Dogmatic Constitution on the Church), which broke away from the accepted juridic and institutional concept of the Church and emphasized a more biblical and patristic model of the Church as Mystery, Sacrament, and the People of God; a Pilgrim Church for a Pilgrim People. Of particular importance was the theology of the local Church which would be further developed in *Ad Gentes* (The Missionary Activity of the Church). *Gaudium et Spes* (The Pastoral Constitution on the Church in the Modern World) stressed the necessary engagement of the Church with contemporary society and the respective autonomies of the Church and state.

Ad Gentes gave a new theological understanding to the concept of the local Church (diocese) and to the role of the bishop, themes already enunciated in *Lumen Gentium.* The mystery of the Church was to be fully found in the local Church. The bishop was head of that Church, not just the area manager or pope's representative in an outlying satellite of the Catholic Church. The themes of inculturation and human development were also present in *Ad Gentes* and these would be further developed by Paul VI and John Paul II. It would take some time for these theological developments to be studied, apprehended, and put into practical application in the missions, which later were being referred to as the young Churches.

The Young Churches

In the years immediately after the council the indigenization of the episcopate and senior clerical positions received renewed emphasis. Tribal considerations prevented the appointment of African bishops in some instances; a tribe would prefer an expatriate to an African not of their own tribe. Today there are ten residential African cardinals and two curial ones.

Contemporary with the growing indigenization was a heated debate on a missionary moratorium; that missionary congregations should name a future date by which they would withdraw from Africa meanwhile preparing the local clergy for their withdrawal. This did not happen but the composition and number of missionaries changed greatly for a variety of reasons.

In general the missionary societies surrendered their monopoly of a given diocese or territory (the mandate received from Propaganda to staff that mission) to the local diocesan clergy. Missionaries remained on in secondary positions and in new ministries. Many of them began to work in what has become to be known as the Fourth World, the shanty towns growing up in the outskirts of most African cities, now becoming the refuge of the growing number leaving traditional society and the land for an unknown future in the city.

Many international religious orders committed personnel to the young Churches, directing parishes or special ministries but firm in the intention to recruit African members. Where once a particular missionary society managed a diocese, now it was usual for many congregations to work within the same diocese under an African bishop with the diocesan clergy.

A new development of twinning between European African dioceses became quite common. The home Church committed itself to the maintenance of a mission team of priests, religious sisters, and lay personnel to an African diocese. This was building on the earlier tradition of Donum Fidei priests, where individual diocesan priests were seconded for voluntary mission in Africa or South America. Usually a missionary congregation acted as facilitator of these twinning arrangements and provided the preparatory training for the missionary team.

Twenty-five years ago the typical African diocese would have been staffed by a missionary congregation with one of its members as bishop assisted by some missionary congregations of sisters and some local diocesan clergy and sisterhood. Today an African bishop with a growing diocesan clergy and sisterhood is assisted by missionary men and women, priests, religious, and laity, from many nations and communities. Collaborative ministry is the accepted model with the missionaries.

Vocations to the priesthood and religious life are on the increase in Africa, numbers in some areas such as eastern Nigeria being very strong. The Nigerian National Missionary Society of St. Paul now sends priests abroad in reverse mission. Much of the credit for this development goes to Cardinal D. I. Ekanden, the first indigenous bishop in Nigeria. Paradoxically, there has been very little development of the permanent diaconate, though Vatican II envisaged it having a significant role in mission countries.

Probably the greatest vitality of the African Church is among the laity, in education and social activity at the level of the base Christian communities. The Church's ability to organize and educate at this level is highly impressive, so much so that it causes anxiety to governments, more recently, in Kenya and Malawi. The one-party state system feels threatened by such grassroots organizational ability.

One of the outcomes of the liturgical renewal is the use of the vernacular languages for the liturgy. This has ensured that at a time when the new states are seeking to develop a lingua franca, be it English, French, or Swahili, the Church is ensuring the survival of the many hundreds of tribal languages because of their daily use in the liturgy.

A synod of African bishops is slated for 1994. While the agenda has been tightly controlled from Rome, the very fact of the bishops coming together will be a learning experience. Issues deserving serious debate are: (1) The onward march of Islam in northern Nigeria and Somalia, the right wing Islamic fundamentalism that has been waging total war on the Christian population and non-Muslim tribal peoples in the southern Sudan. (2) Inculturation. During his visit to Uganda in 1969, Paul VI challenged the young Churches with the words: "You may and you must, have an African Christianity." This has barely begun. (3) The problem of urbanization: the flight from the land into the cities, creating shanty towns, reminiscent of Sao Paul, "a Fourth World." (4) Social issues such as tribalism, in particular, when one tribe is perceived as receiving more than its fair share as in Kenya, or the monopoly of the one-party state as in Malawi.

All of these issues will be played out to the growing economic divide of North and South at a time when the Church's center of gravity is moving to the South, away from Europe and North America. One can be optimistic about the Church in Africa. National hierarchies have found a voice with a gospel message. An excerpt from the 1992 Pastoral Letter of the Malawi Bishops can stand for the Church in Africa:

"Nobody should ever have to suffer reprisals for honestly expressing and living up to their convictions: intellectual, religious or political.

We can only regret that this is not always the case in our country. We can be grateful that freedom of worship is respected; the same freedom does not exist when it comes to translating faith into daily life. Academic freedom is seriously restricted; exposing injustices can be considered a betrayal; revealing some evils of our society is seen as slandering the country; monopoly of mass media and censorship prevent the expression of dissenting views; some people have paid dearly for their political opinions; access to public places like markets, hospitals, bus depots, etc., is frequently denied to those who cannot produce a party card: forced donations have become a way of life.

It is the Church's mission to preach the gospel which effects the redemption of the human race and its liberation from every oppressive situation, be it hunger, ignorance, blindness, despair, paralysing fear, etc. Like Jesus, the advocate of the poor and the oppressed, the believing community is invited, at times obliged in justice, to show in action a preferential love for the economically disadvantaged, the voiceless who live in situations of hopelessness."

Reaction to the pastoral letter was swift: The expatriate Apostolic Administrator of Mzuzu Diocese (Msgr. John Roche) was expelled to be followed by other missionaries. The bishops held firm and issued another letter in 1993 prior to the national referendum on the one-party or the multiparty state. The bishops of South Africa also took a firm stand with their 1993 pastoral on democracy. The Catholic Church in Africa speaks openly, hopefully, and clearly on the major issues facing the continent.

COLMAN M. COOKE

See also MISSIONS, CATHOLIC, THE MODERN PERIOD; VATICAN COUNCIL II.

AFTERLIFE

See HEAVEN; HELL; LIMBO; PURGATORY.

AGAPE

Agape is one of the Greek words for love, which has come to acquire special meaning for Christians, signifying first of all God's gratuitous love for humanity and all of creation, and humanity's self-giving and other-oriented love in response.

Theologians tend to distinguish *agape* from *eros,* understanding the latter Greek word as possessive and self-centered love, and from *philia,* understood as the human, mutual love of friendship. These words in the New Testament are not so sharply distinguished, though the New Testament almost always uses *agape* and avoids using *eros* when speaking theologically. In the New Testament "God is love (*agape*)" (1 John 4:8). This should not be understood as a contrast, as if the God of the Old Testament were a God of wrath, but as the perfect expression of the Old Testament covenant fidelity of God now in Christ (John 3:16). God's love in Christ is, moreover, pure, unmerited gift, which elicits and enables human love of God and thus the fulfillment of the Old Testament command to love God with one's entire being (Deut 6:5; Matt 22:36-38).

God's generous gift of self also enables fulfillment of the command to love neighbor (Lev 19:18; Matt 22:39; Gal 5:13-14; Jas 2:8). What is "new" about Christ's command to love is that now one is to love in Christ and as Christ loved (John 13:34), and that now neighbor is defined to embrace even the enemy (Matt 5:43-48; Luke 10:30-36).

Agape is the root of all the virtues and is their final completion. Because the early Christians gathered in meals, which included the Eucharist, to express their love for one another, they called these meals their *agape*.

ANTHONY J. TAMBASCO

See also CHARITY; EUCHARIST.

AGE OF REASON

The age at which a person, having acquired the ability to distinguish between right and wrong, incurs moral responsibility for his or her conduct. Traditionally, the Church has held that this normally occurs at about the age of seven, though with a mentally challenged person it may be later.

JOSEPH QUINN

See also THEOLOGY, MORAL.

AGGIORNAMENTO

The term (Italian: "Updating") became common parlance among Catholics because of its use by Pope John XXIII in connection with the need of updating the Church, and because of its acceptance by a majority of the bishops at the Second Vatican Council which he summoned. It is used either in the meaning of an internal spiritual renewal, or an external adaptation of the Church's laws and institutions to the needs of the times.

DAVID BRYAN

See also JOHN XXIII, POPE; VATICAN COUNCIL II.

Vatican Council II

AGNOSTICISM

Agnosticism is a term usually associated with those who are unable to make up their mind about the affirmation or rejection of the existence of God. Agnosticism is a state of uncertainty and ambivalence about the great questions of religion. Sometimes agnosticism is described as a position of neutrality in relation to atheism and theism, or some kind of midpoint between belief and unbelief. Agnosticism more often than not is justified on the claim that there is inadequate empirical evidence for the arguments of religion and so therefore one must suspend judgment. The term "agnosticism" was introduced in the nineteenth century by T. H. Huxley who sought to distinguish his commitment to matters empirical from that of metaphysics which he regarded as "gnostic."

In contrast to this description of agnosticism which could be called philosophical agnosticism there is another form of agnosticism loosely called "theological agnosticism." This latter form of agnosticism recognizes the limitations that attach to all religious knowledge of God. Theological agnosticism expresses itself through a negative theology or what is called apophatic theology.

It must be noted, however, that there is nothing more destructive of good theology than a premature negative theology. Negative theology only succeeds in relation to a prior positive or cataphatic theology. Thus, classical theology in the spirit of Augustine and Aquinas combines both positive and negative moments, giving rise to sophisticated theories of analogy, dialectics, and religious symbolism.

DERMOT A. LANE

See also ATHEISM; PASCAL, BLAISE; THEOLOGY.

AKATHISTOS HYMN

A hymn of praise to the Mother of God. Its author is unknown. For many centuries it has had an honored place in the Eastern Churches, and it is sung standing. Until recently there was no critical edition available, but the Greek and English versions (Fribourg 1958: The University Press) prepared by G. G. Meersseman, O.P., are most critically reliable. The hymn is based on the gospel story of the nativity and consists of a dedication, a preamble and fifty-four stanzas. The deep devotional tone of this great hymn can be gleaned from its opening stanza:

A prince of angels
was sent from heaven
to greet the mother of God
and upon his unbodied word,
seeing thee, O Lord,
    take body,
he stood in ecstasy and
cried to thee this greeting:

Hail! by whom gladness
    will be enkindled;
hail! by whom the curse
    will be quenched.
Hail! righting
    of the fallen Adam;
hail! ransom
    of Eve's tears.
Hail! height unscaled
    by human reasonings;
hail! depth inscrutable
    even to angel's eyes.
Hail! for thou art
    the king's seat;
hail! for thou bearest him,
    who beareth all.
Hail! thou star
    that makes the sun to shine;
hail! thou womb
    of God's incarnation.
Hail! thou by whom
    all creation is renewed;
hail! thou through whom
    the Creator became a babe.
Hail! mother undefiled!

MICHAEL GLAZIER

See also HYMNS; MARY, MOTHER OF GOD.

ALB

(Lat. *albus,* or "white") The full-length white linen robe worn by ministers during liturgical functions. Derived from the Graeco-Roman undertunic, albs are often adorned with colored bands (orphreys) and embroidered with lace extending from the waist to the ankles. This ornamentation, however, should not detract from the simplicity and modesty of the garment, which symbolizes purity of heart.

JOSEPH QUINN

See also VESTMENTS, LITURGICAL.

ALBERT THE GREAT, ST. (ca. 1200–1280)

Albert was born in Lauingen, Germany, of a knightly family around 1200. As a young man, he studied at the University of Padua and while there, became a member of the newly established Dominican Order (1216). He began his long academic career by lecturing in various Dominican houses in Germany. Around 1240, because of his abilities, he was sent to the University of Paris to become a Master in Theology. By 1246 he held one of the two Dominican chairs in theology. It was at that time that he became the teacher and mentor of Thomas Aquinas, and took Thomas with him to Cologne in 1248 to establish a house of studies.

St. Albert the Great

Albert's principal academic contributions were in the fields of natural science and theology. He was also one of the pioneers in the use of Neoplatonic and Aristotelian philosophy as a foundation for Christian theology.

Albert's wisdom and abilities included not only scientific study and theological reflection, but he was also called upon as a leader in the Dominican Order and as a mediator in disputes involving the Church in Germany. Around 1260, he was appointed bishop of Regensburg, but served only long enough to reform the diocese before resigning. His writings are numerous and include remarkably accurate scientific observations and experiments, a *Summa Theologiae,* his *Summa De Creaturis,* as well as commentaries on Sacred Scripture, Aristotle, and on the works of Pseudo-Dionysius. He died in

Cologne in 1280. In 1931, he was canonized and proclaimed as a Doctor of the Church and, in 1941, proclaimed patron saint of those who study natural sciences.

R. B. WILLIAMS, O.P.

See also DOMINICANS; THOMAS AQUINAS, ST.

ALBIGENSES

So called after the town of Albi in southern France, the Albigensians were a branch of the Cathari movement in Europe. A late echo of the Gnostic and Manichaean persuasion, they were dualist, dividing the reality of experience into a world of spirit which is good and a world of matter which is a dark and evil counter-creation. It is conjectured that these ideas might have survived through the centuries in the East and been brought back to western Europe by the Crusaders. We find references to the Cathari or Albigenses mainly in the twelfth and thirteenth centuries.

Because they questioned the goodness of creation, denied that Jesus had a human body, rejected the sacraments, condemned marriage, and were very critical of the institutional structures of the Church, particularly the corruption among hierarchy and clergy, the Church considered them heretics, and persecuted them in various ways. Pope Innocent III in 1208 ordered the first of the "internal crusades" against them, and many thousands were slaughtered. They were also subject individually to the Inquisition. A more reasonable, and spiritual, approach was that of St. Dominic Guzman and his Order of Preachers as he originally planned it (not as they were later engaged by papal authority to conduct the Inquisition). Because the Albigensians usually lived a very austere and disciplined life, the Dominicans were to be begging friars living in the greatest simplicity but deeply schooled in theology so that they might preach effectively to the Albigensians and argue theological points with them.

By the end of the fourteenth century these people no longer existed as a group, though the ideas they propagated recur in subtle forms in subsequent centuries.

MONIKA K. HELLWIG

See also CRUSADES; GNOSTICISM; HERESY/HERETICS; INQUISITION, MEDIEVAL; MANICHAEISM.

ALCOHOLICS ANONYMOUS

The twentieth century has seen the proliferation of self-help groups formed to aid people, of all ages and from all walks of life, who seek relief for a great variety of physical, psychological, and spiritual problems. The best known and the most successful of these is Alcoholics Anonymous (AA) which caters to men and women (and, sometimes, children) who are addicted to alcohol. They are addicts, compulsive drinkers who have become dependent on alcohol.

Alcoholism is a debilitating disease which has plagued humankind over the centuries. All types of treatments have been tried over the years to cope with the problems of the alcoholic. Most have had little or no success, but AA has lifted millions from the havocs of alcoholic addiction. It is a program founded by alcoholics for alcoholics; and it works for those who want to get sober and are willing to make the effort to do so.

Its beginning in Akron, Ohio, in 1935 was fortuitous and almost accidental. Two problem drinkers—Dr. Bob Smith and stockbroker, Bill Wilson—found that by discussing their common problem and by sharing their hopes, failures, and fears they could break the pattern of compulsive drinking and stay sober, a day at a time. They stopped drinking and gained the confidence that they could continue to do so. With some trepidation, they offered their assistance to an inveterate alcoholic in a hospital and set him on the road to recovery. AA was on its way, and in a short time AA groups sprang up in New York and elsewhere. Today such groups meet in countless towns and cities all over the world.

The success of AA is due to many factors; it places a priority on respecting the privacy and anonymity of its members; it is never organized in a business fashion; each group meeting is independent (and any two people with a desire to stop drinking can start a meeting) and it is not affiliated with any political group or Church, but the major asset of AA is its time-tested program which is embodied in its "bible" *Alcoholics Anonymous* (the "Big Book") and is expressed in its famous twelve steps: (1) We admitted that we were powerless over alcohol—that our lives had become unmanageable. (2) Came to believe that a Power greater than ourselves could restore us to sanity. (3) Made a decision to turn our will and our lives over to the care of God *as we understood him.* (4) Made a searching and fearless moral inventory of ourselves. (5) Admitted to God, to ourselves, and to another human being the exact nature of our wrongs. (6) Were entirely ready to have God remove all these defects of character. (7) Humbly asked him to remove our shortcomings. (8) Made a list of all persons we had harmed, and became willing to make amends to them all. (9) Made direct amends to such people wherever possible, except when to do so would injure them or others. (10)

Continued to take personal inventory and when we were wrong promptly admitted it. (11) Sought through prayer and meditation to improve our conscious contact with God as we understood him, praying only for knowledge of his will for us and power to carry that out. (12) Having had a spiritual awakening as the result of these steps, we tried to carry this message to alcoholics, and to practice these principles in all our affairs.

AA offers the suffering alcoholic a program rooted in seasoned experience and sound spiritual principles. It views alcoholism as a disease, not as a moral debility; and it has proved that the disease can be arrested and the recovering alcoholic can live a normal and productive life. Its success has inspired countless other self-help groups to adopt the twelve steps as the basis of their work. AA believes that the active alcoholic adversely affects the lives of family and friends. Hence it established Alanon to enable spouses and adult family members to understand and cope with alcoholism; and the needs of children from an alcoholic home are catered for by another branch known as Alateen.

Alcoholics Anonymous is unique in our time—it shuns publicity; refuses outside financial help; it has opened its arms for decades to men and women of all races and creeds, regardless of social background or financial status or sexual orientation. It offers recovery to those who seek and want it.

EUGENE W. DAVIS

ALEXANDER VI, POPE (1492–1503)

A Spaniard, Rodrigo Borgia (as his name is spelled in Italian) was a blot on the history of the papacy. Created a cardinal by his uncle, Pope Callistus III, Borgia capably administered many high offices, but enriched himself in office, while fathering several children in open immorality. He obtained the papacy by bribery. A gifted administrator, Alexander VI initially pursued justice and order in Rome, while planning the reformation of the Curia and action against the threatening Turks. His pontificate, however, was soon given over to pursuing women, wealth, the arts, and the interests of his family, especially endowing his children with marriages, fiefdoms, and bishoprics. He was conscious of the need to foster the missions and reform monasteries, but such goals were of low priority, in part because he could not reform himself. Alexander is best known for the "Line of Demarkation (1493)" which settled the respective spheres of influence of Spain and Portugal in the voyages of exploration. Incredibly, he also gave the monarchs of Spain and Portugal the right to control the Church in their own colonies.

DAVID BRYAN

See also MISSIONS, CATHOLIC, THE MODERN PERIOD; PAPACY, THE; RENAISSANCE, THE.

ALL SAINTS, FEAST OF

A feast held on 1 November of each year commemorating all Christian saints, known and unknown. It was first celebrated when Pope Boniface IV (608–615) dedicated the Pantheon in Rome to the Blessed Mother and the martyrs (ca. 610). For over a century, the Church in Rome observed the feast on 13 May. In Ireland, however, the date was 1 November, and this eventually became the accepted day for the feast in England and throughout the European continent. Pope Gregory III (731–741) changed the Roman observance to 1 November when he dedicated a chapel in the Vatican Basilica to "All the Saints" on that day (year unknown). The feast of All Saints is a holy day of obligation.

JOSEPH QUINN

See also HOLY DAYS; LITURGY; SAINTS.

ALL SOULS, FEAST OF

A day of solemn remembrance by the Church of all the faithful departed, held each year on 2 November. (If 2 November falls on a Sunday, the feast is observed on 3 November.) The tradition of commemorating the deceased extends back to the seventh century. Odilo of Cluny (d. 1049) is believed to have established 2 November as its date of observance. Pope Benedict XV (1914–1922) in 1915 authorized (for all priests) the offering of three Masses on this day—one for the faithful departed, a second for the pope's intentions, and a third for the intentions of the priest.

JOSEPH QUINN

See also COMMUNION OF SAINTS; PURGATORY.

ALLAIRE, MOTHER VIRGINIE, GREY NUN OF MONTREAL (1882–1969)

Mother Virginie Allaire, S.G.M., was a true pioneer of the Canadian hospital movement, and it is because of her work and unflagging zeal in this field that her name will remain in the pantheon of the Canadian Church. Her life was inextricably bound up with the mission to organize hospitals and to improve the professional training of nurses and hospital administrators. She lived a long life of 86 years, of which 62 were spent in the service of the Grey Nuns of Montreal.

Mother Allaire was of Franco-American heritage (born in 1882 in Grafton, Massachusetts, where many French-Canadians had emigrated), fluently bilingual and an accredited nurse. This background enabled her to appreciate the importance of establishing links between Catholic hospitals throughout North America, while respecting the distinctive characteristics of the Canadian hospital system. It is to this end that she became the president of the first Canadian Conference of Catholic hospitals (the Western Conference, 1921), founded under the auspices of the Catholic Hospital Association of the United States and Canada [CHAUSC]. In 1932, she founded the Quebec Conference of the CHAUSC; subsequently, she was an active participant in the formation in 1939 of a new Canadian body which today is called the Catholic Health Association of Canada.

Determined to upgrade the professional skills of hospital personnel while promoting the significance of spirituality in Catholic hospitals, Mother Allaire accomplished a formidable task throughout Canada. As local superior at the General Hospital in Regina, Saskatchewan (1917–1921), during the First World War, at a time when a great many Canadian soldiers were returning from the front seriously wounded, one of her first priorities was to implement university-level summer courses for nursing-school directors and hospital administrators. She would go on to realize greater challenges as provincial superior of the Grey Nuns of St. Boniface (1921–1925) and as general treasurer of her congregation (1925–1930), in which posts she systematically focused on the development of hospital affairs, both secular administration and care of the sick. But it was truly her election to the rank of second assistant to the superior general and director of the hospitals belonging to the congregation in 1930 which allowed her to carry to term more far-reaching projects. The foundation in 1934 of the Marguerite d'Youville Institute thus remained one of her finest accomplishments. This post-secondary institution which offered a Bachelor of Hospital Science degree became affiliated with the University of Montreal in 1935, and Mother Allaire remained its director until 1946.

Mother Virginie Allaire received numerous honors in recognition of her many years of outstanding contribution to the coordination of hospital work and in recognition of her relentless promotion of excellence in the field of health care. In 1936 she was awarded a doctorate *honoris causa* from the University of Montreal; in 1940, she was awarded the Distinguished Service Certificate of CHAUSC at its Silver Jubilee Convention; in 1947, she was made an Honorary Fellow of The American College of Hospital Administrators and in 1960 an Honorary Fellow of the Canadian Nurses Association; in 1967, she was decorated with the Order of Canada and the centennial medal of the Canadian Confederation. Thus, it is from a number of diverse contexts and sources that these honors were bestowed upon Mother Allaire. But the culmination of these acknowledgments was indisputably the celebration of the Golden and Diamond Jubilees of her religious life. For these ceremonies underlined her devotion to a life in the very tradition of a Church which had seen its role since the Middle Ages as the defender of the poor and the sick.

GÉRALD PELLETIER

See also CANADA, THE CATHOLIC CHURCH IN; HEALING.

ALLEGORICAL MEANING OF SCRIPTURE

Allegorical interpretation searches for abstract or spiritual meanings in biblical texts by identifying their details with major figures or institutions in salvation history. Thus in the parable of the prodigal son (Luke 15:11-32), according to Tertullian, the father is God, the younger son is the Christian, the elder son is the Jew, the patrimony is the birthright of a child of God, the employer is the devil, the feast is the Lord's Supper, and so forth. Allegorical interpretation assumes that the whole story of salvation is present in the details of a particular text. This approach to Scripture is often associated with the Church Fathers of Alexandria, especially Clement and Origen. It is based on methods used by pagan interpreters of Homer's *Iliad* and *Odyssey* as well as by Philo who brought together the Old Testament and Greek philosophy. Some examples of allegorical interpretation appear in the New Testament (see Matt 13:18-23, 36-43; Gal 4:24-27). When insufficient attention is given to the literal meaning, allegorical interpretation runs the risk of reducing every text to the same story and of making arbitrary identifications and connections.

DANIEL J. HARRINGTON, S.J.

See also CRITICISM, BIBLICAL, LITERAL MEANING OF SCRIPTURE.

ALLELUIA

(Hebrew, "praise ye Yah") is a joyful liturgical expression of praise which is found in the Books of Psalms, Tobit, and Revelation. Its liturgical use dates from the early Church and is now used throughout the year except during Lent.

JOAN GLAZIER

See also LITURGY.

ALMSGIVING

All through the Old and New Testaments almsgiving is regarded as an imitation of the gratuitous loving actions of God. In the Old Testament, care for the poor was repeatedly encouraged. Codified forms of almsgiving are found in the Law: e.g., the obligation of leaving part of the crops for gleaning and giving (Lev 19:9; 23:22; Deut 24:20f.; Ruth 2); the triannual tithe for those who had no land such as Levites, foreigners, orphans and widows. The cries of the poor were not ignored and in giving alms the poor were to be treated generously and with dignity (Deut 15:11; Prov 3.27f.; Sir 18:15 ff.). Tobit's plea to his son capitulates the Old Testament attitude toward almsgiving: "Do not turn your face away from the poor man, and God will never turn his face away from you. . . . If you have much give more; if you have little give less—but do not hesitate to give alms. When you give alms do not have any regrets. . . ." (Tob 4:7–11:15f.).

In the New Testament almsgiving received abundant attention. Jesus recommended it, together with fasting and prayer, as the basis of the spiritual life. He asks that our giving be without ostentation (Matt 6:14), without expecting anything in return (Luke 6:35; 14:14). Almsgiving should not be tied by any legal religious code, it should be spontaneous and generous. The New Testament places it in a new and elevated context which is cogently summarized in Matthew 25:40: "I assure you as often as you did it for one of my least brothers, you did it for me." In the Pauline and Johannine epistles, almsgiving is given practical coverage in relation to the needs of the communities for whom they wrote.

Almsgiving is on a different plane from philanthropy; it is not a substitute or a blueprint to solve the perennial problem of poverty; it is concerned giving, transformed by grace, for the kingdom of God.

MICHAEL GLAZIER

See also CHRISTIAN MORALITY; CORPORAL AND SPIRITUAL WORKS OF MERCY; MERCY.

ALPHA AND OMEGA

The first and last letters of the Greek alphabet. In Revelation 1:8 and 22:13, Jesus identifies himself as "the Alpha and the Omega, the beginning and the end, who is, who was, and who is to come." These letters are frequent in the decoration of altars and churches, and are carved into the paschal candle in the annual ceremonies of the Easter Vigil.

DAVID BRYAN

See also BIBLE, NEW TESTAMENT WRITINGS.

ALTAR

In ancient times, a platform on which sacrifices were offered. Throughout the history of the Church, the table on which the Eucharist is celebrated.

The earliest Christian altars would have been the wooden tables in the homes of worshipers. In the ensuing years, Mass was customarily offered at the gravesites of the martyrs, which led to the tradition of placing relics of the saints in or near the altar.

In the fourth century, the growth of Christian communities made the communal meal of the Eucharistic celebration impractical, and the sacrificial aspect of the Mass became more prominent. During this period, churches—with "fixed," or stationary altars made of stone or metal—began to be built over the tombs of martyrs.

Dominican convent chapel, Vence, France

As the Church had emphasized for centuries the singularity of the Eucharistic celebration—one bread for the one body of the Church—tradition dictated that each church have only one altar. In the seventh century, however, the offering of private masses for special intentions became more prevalent, and other altars were added.

From the fifth century until recently, Western churches were often built with their altars facing east—a practice adopted from the Eastern Church. Relics of the saints were exhibited either on or above the altar and, beginning in the tenth century, churches without relics hung paintings of saints behind the altar.

The altar of the modern era is, in many ways, similar to that of the early Church. As a result of liturgical changes implemented by the Second Vatican Council (1962–1965) and the subsequent decrees instituted by the Holy See, altars once again face the congregation, are freestanding, and are situated in such a way that they are the natural focus of attention. Minor altars are now set in separate chapels so as not to detract from the main altar.

JOSEPH QUINN

See also ARCHITECTURE, CHURCH; EUCHARIST.

ALTAR STONE

A consecrated slab of solid stone, measuring about eight by ten inches, upon which the chalice and paten are placed during Mass. Five crosses are inscribed into the stone, one at each corner and the fifth in the center. Below the center cross, at the stone's base, is a hollowed recess containing the relics of two saints. As it is considered the altar proper, the altar stone is "movable"—able to be transferred from one altar table to another according to need. Ministers such as missionaries and military chaplains, who may not have access to a consecrated church, may use an altar stone for the celebration of Mass. They may also use a Greek or Russian *antimensium* (Lat., "that which replaces the table"), a square-shaped cloth, measuring approximately twenty inches, on which the burial scene of Christ is depicted, for this purpose.

JOSEPH QUINN

See also ALTAR; RELICS.

AMBROSE, ST. (ca. 339 [or 337]–397)

Born at Trier, Ambrose was the son of the praetorian prefect of Gaul. Ambrose studied rhetoric, worked as a lawyer ca. 365 in the prefecture of Sirmium (in modern-day Serbia), and became governor ca. 370 of the provinces of Aemilia and Liguria, of which Milan was the capital. When Auxentius, Arian bishop of Milan, died in 374, Ambrose worked to maintain peace between Catholics and Arians who both demanded that he succeed Auxentius as bishop, even though Ambrose had not yet been baptized. After Ambrose accepted the office with some hesitation, he was baptized and a week later ordained a bishop. Ambrose studied Sacred Scripture and theology under his former tutor Simplicianus to prepare himself for new responsibilities. As bishop, Ambrose fought against paganism and Arianism. He successfully opposed the efforts of the pagan Symmachus to restore the Altar of Victory to the Roman Senate House in 382 and 384. He and a great number of the Catholics occupied a basilica in 386 to prevent it from being turned over to the Arians. Ambrose protested the murder of Priscillian and followers in 386 by Maximus and demanded that Theodosius I do public penance for ordering the massacre of 7,000 citizens in Thessalonica in 390. Theodosius complied with Ambrose's order. Ambrose had an important role in the conversion of Augustine and baptized him along with Alypius and Adeodatus at the Easter Vigil in 387.

Many of Ambrose's writings were sermons. Influenced by his reading of Philo and Origen, Ambrose saw a threefold meaning in the scriptural text: literal, moral, allegorical/mystical. Ambrose's exegetical method influenced Augustine's reading and interpretation of the Old Testament. Because of his knowledge of Greek he read the works of Athanasius, Basil, Cyril of Jerusalem, Hippolytus, etc., and was influenced by them in his writings. Ambrose is for that reason an important link between the Eastern and Western Church. Ambrose's most significant ascetical or moral work is the *On the Duties of the Clergy,* a discourse on Christian ethics addressed to the clergy modeled after Cicero's *On Duties.* Ambrose's most significant dogmatic work is the *On the Sacraments,* a series of six addresses given in Easter week to the newly baptized on baptism, confirmation, and the Eucharist. Ambrose's correspondence is of important historical value. Ambrose was also a noted composer of liturgical hymns, including *Aeterne rerum conditor, Deus creator omnium, Iam surgit hora tertia,* and *Intende qui regis Israel.* By his insistence that the emperor must obey the moral law as understood and practiced by the Church, Ambrose has had an effect on Church–state relations that has lasted to this day. Ambrose was named a Doctor of the Church by Boniface VIII in 1295. Feast day, 7 December (4 April in the Book of Common Prayer).

JOHN DILLON

See also CATECHESIS; DOCTORS OF THE CHURCH; FATHERS OF THE CHURCH; HYMNS; SACRAMENTS.

A.M.D.G.

An acronym for the Latin term *Ad Maiorem Dei Gloriam,* meaning "to the greater glory of God." It is a traditional motto of the Jesuits.

JOSEPH QUINN

See also SOCIETY OF JESUS.

AMEN

(*Heb.* "verily") A solemn expression of affirmation first used by the Israelites of the Old Testament to declare their subservience to God's commandments. It was later adopted by the apostolic community, who employed it in both Scripture and the liturgy. The term is used frequently in the Book of Revelation, which refers to Jesus as "the Amen" (Rev 3:14). A key liturgical use of the expression occurs at the end of the Eucharistic Prayer, when it is sung, normally several times, by the congregation.

JOSEPH QUINN

See also LITURGY.

"AMERICA"

America, A Catholic Review of the Week, published by the Jesuits of the United States and Canada, was founded in 1909 by John Wynne, S.J., acting for American Jesuit superiors. After the 1891 failure of a planned Jesuit review, *America* evolved gradually from the Philadelphia-based *Messenger of the Sacred Heart.* Wynne moved the *Messenger* to New York where he converted "a pious magazine into a monthly of general interest." Wynne eliminated articles about Sacred Heart Devotion and included topics "as extensive as are the objects in which Christ Himself is interested." The increased educational level of American Catholics and perennial prejudice against them in American society inspired Wynne to publish articles like those which discussed "Americanism" and opposed American expansionists poised to expel religious orders from the newly annexed Philippines. Other articles appeared on divorce, biblical criticism and papal temporal power.

The Messenger of the Sacred Heart habitually corrected misstatements about Catholicism in the popular press and led to revisions of Catholic articles in *Appleton's Universal Cyclopedia and Atlas.* In 1902 Wynne proposed "a high class and thoroughly Catholic organ" to inform Catholics and discuss current issues. He then split his magazine into the devotional *Messenger of the Sacred Heart* and the more sophisticated *Messenger.* That year Wynne also launched *The Catholic Mind,* a series of inexpensive pamphlets presenting papal documents and articles from European Jesuit journals to American audiences. Despite diffident American Jesuit leaders, by 1907 Franz Xavier Wernz, the Jesuit general, encouraged Wynne—whose model was London's *Tablet*—to transform the *Messenger* into something "more solid and more serious." In 1909, the new *America* sought to help Catholics "distinguish clearly between what is of faith or obligatory in practice and what is only a pious belief or devotion." Wynne urged Catholics to participate in national affairs and public life "instead of forming an element by themselves and standing aloof." He encouraged Catholics, for example, "not to antagonize the public [school] system, but to help to make it as good a working one as possible." Less than a year after *America*'s first edition, Wynne was removed as editor because of his "lordly" autocratic management and his seemingly less than forceful defense of Catholic education.

In its first half-century *America* criticized United States policy in the 1920s toward the anti-Catholic Mexican government. In the 1930s *America* spoke out against "red" Spanish Republicans and in favor of Franco during the Spanish Civil War. While generally supportive of the New Deal, in 1940 *America* advanced isolationist arguments but, by 1945, the magazine judged atomic attacks on Hiroshima and Nagasaki too complex for quick judgments. In the late forties, Editor-in-Chief John LaFarge, S.J., promoted racial equality. *America* became so vehemently opposed to Senator Joseph McCarthy's methods in the 1950s that the Jesuit General uncharacteristically intervened from Rome to order an end to discussion of "merely secular or political matters." In affairs literary, *America*'s contributors included Chesterton, Belloc, Flannery O'Connor, Daniel Berrigan, and Mary Gordon.

America's point of view remains nonpartisan, influenced by official Catholic social teaching and featuring mostly moderate and progressive opinions. Since 1975, *America* has contributed to the ongoing discussion of complex issues like abortion rights, controverted bioethical concerns, the place of theologians in the magisterium, and the role of women in the Church. In recent years *America* has placed renewed emphasis on Catholic and general theological and pastoral issues while continuing to address sociocultural developments, international relations, and political concerns.

JOHN L. CIANI, S.J.

See also SOCIETY OF JESUS.

AMERICAN CATHOLICISM

The Catholic Church in the United States grew in two-centuries' time from virtual insignificance to one of the largest, richest, most influential in universal Catholicism. The first American bishop (John Carroll) was not named until 1789, and until 1908, when its status was changed by Pope Pius X's apostolic constitution *Sapienti Consilio,* the American Church was classified as a mission Church. In 1992 American Catholics comprised 23 percent of the national population, roughly 58 million in a total of 254 million, and their Church has a remarkable reputation for generosity and apostolic commitment. It ranks as a peer Church with the great Churches of Western Christendom, alongside those of France, Germany, Ireland, indeed Italy itself.

American Catholicism—that is, Catholicism in the United States—was fashioned in three distinct, almost mutually exclusive stages.

Christopher Columbus

The faith was planted by priests accompanying the Spanish explorers, who after 1493 arrived with rights conveyed by Pope Alexander VI in the bull *Inter Caetera* to colonize and evangelize along a meridian drawn west of the Azores and Cape Verde islands. (Other lands, mainly to the south, were assigned to the Portuguese.) Spanish explorers pushed along southern routes as far as the Pacific shores, and enjoyed a religious hegemony for ninety-five years. With the defeat of the Spanish Armada in 1588, however, the ascendancy in North America passed to the English. The faith that the Spanish explorers brought catches echoes in old missions and the names of great cities, such as San Antonio, Santa Barbara, San Francisco and Los Angeles. But essentially it is now a relic faith—although one that may be in the process of resuscitation with twentieth-century Hispanic emigration.

American Catholicism's second stage, briefer and more subtle, is identified with the postcolonial era, and the appointment of Father John Carroll in 1784, five years before being named a bishop, to head the American missions. At the time, there were merely twenty-five thousand Catholics in the United States, most of them of British origin, in a population of four million. Centered mainly in Maryland and New York, theirs was a presence not unlike that of Catholic recusants in England—small but consequential. Like their British counterparts, theirs was what historian James O'Toole has termed an "enlightenment Catholicism," with a spirituality based on "the rationality of belief."

The third stage began with the tides of emigration of the 1840s, and introduced a different kind of Catholicism. Emphases suddenly were now on devotional and emotional practices of faith centered about the Mass, Marian devotions, the communion of the saints, novenas and the like. This faith became the norm of the American Church, and dominated until the latter 1960s.

The Church born of emigration encountered hostility from elements of the dominant Protestant and secular societies, but this circumstance seemed to fortify rather than weaken. Barring occasional intramural controversies and ethnic rivalries, as between the German and Irish blocs, American Catholicism internally grew strong and cohesive. Helping was the fact that the immigrants arrived with their own priests. An instant priesthood minimized the problem of defections, and eased the assimilation of faith and people into their new environment. Emigrant Catholicism was strongly responsive to clerical authority and ultramontanist in attitudes toward Rome.

Net results were remarkable in terms both of numbers and institutional infrastructure. By 1900 there was an American Catholic population of twelve million. Vocations were numerous, and an awesome network of schools, hospitals and social services was in the building. Growth was unabated, the high point being reached in 1965, when the American Church boasted a Catholic population of 45,640,619 served by 58,432 priests, 179,954 sisters and nuns, and 14,296 educational institutions. There were 6,095,846 students in Catholic classrooms, and seminaries bulged with 48,992 enrollees. The future appeared insured.

It was not. The total number of Catholics continues to grow, due largely to Hispanic immigration. But in recent years every major institutional division shows serious loss. According to 1992 census figures, priests were down to 52,277 (a misleading number in comparison to 1965, since missionaries and other American priests on duty outside the U.S. are now included in the total, an innovation introduced in 1975). Seminarians had decreased to 6,454; sisters and nuns to 99,337; educational institutions to 9,177; students in diocesan, parochial and private Catholic elementary and high schools to 2,637,480.

Also, after 1965, ideological change began to set in among the rank and file. Today's American Catholics are markedly more independent than their predecessors. A 1992 Gallup Poll indicated that 87 percent of American Catholics believed the Church should end its ban on artificial birth control; 67 percent favored the ordaining of women to the priesthood; 80 percent favored the raising up of women deacons; 70 percent would allow priests to marry; 83 percent approved the use of condoms as a means to prevent the spread of AIDS. These positions are all categorically opposed by the magisterium. With respect to abortion, several polls show opinion among Catholics to be not significantly different from that of Protestants.

The reasons for the transformation from responsiveness to ecclesiastical direction to a kind of internal pluralism have still to sort themselves out completely. Some preliminary conclusions seem reasonable, however.

Certainly the debates of Vatican II are a factor. The openness and intensity of those debates confirmed for many that dissent was not only possible in the Church, but potentially invigorating both to institution and people.

A likely factor too is Vatican II's Declaration on Religious Freedom (*Dignitatis Humanae*). Though narrowly defined in terms of non-Catholics, the document nonetheless spawned exercises of freedom within the Catholic Church itself. This was a development predicted by Jesuit Father John Courtney Murray, principal architect of the declaration. "The ripples will run far," Murray wrote after the council, adding that religious freedom will be asserted "within the church as well as within the world."

Another factor in American Catholicism's new internal pluralism would be Pope Paul VI's 1968 encyclical, *Humanae Vitae,* restating traditional opposition to artificial birth control. That encyclical touched off the most intense dissent in the history of American Catholicism. Studies show, however, that the encyclical did not result in any noticeable disidentification from the Church itself. Another kind of phenomenon occurred. There was a decline in respect for ecclesiastical authority and in aspects of the practice of faith, but dissenters did not leave the Church; they stayed—albeit on their own terms of conscience.

It is at this point that American Catholicism finds itself in the decade of the 1990s. It is a situation that is still evolving, with few indications that ideological distances on dogmatic and moral issues are closing between the magisterium and the faithful.

Complicating matters further are institutional crises born of changed demographics and the dearth of vocations.

American Catholicism, once mainly urban, became largely suburbanized in the years after World War II, a phenomenon resulting in a shifting of focuses and the curtailment of many inner-city apostolates, notably parochial schools, often with no corresponding program developing in the suburbs.

About the same time vocations began their decline. This has forced many dioceses to trim programs and assign duties traditionally associated with priests to religious and laity. A 1988 survey showed that seventy U.S. dioceses had placed parishes or missions under the administration of permanent deacons, religious sisters and brothers, or laypersons, and that parishes or missions in thirty-one of those dioceses were experiencing priestless Sundays. The situation has not improved. A 1991 count showed six hundred American counties to be without any priests whatsoever.

None of this means that American Catholicism is *in extremis.* Despite all the problems, the American Church is vigorous and affluent. (The decline in worshippers has not resulted in a corresponding decline in income.) Still, the American Church is in transition and, with many of the old stabilities gone, unsettled conditions are likely to extend into the indefinite future.

JOHN DEEDY

See also BLACK CATHOLICS; CHURCH, THE.

AMERICANISM

In an 1899 encyclical letter Pope Leo XIII condemned this "ism" as a set of heretical opinions on the need for the Church to adapt to contemporary trends in spirituality and modern culture. There are several ways to perceive the significance of Americanism but in its broadest sense it appears to have been a theology of history based upon the providential conditions of religious liberty and separation of Church and state which have allowed the Church to flourish in the United States, a Church destined to be the model for Catholicity in the modern world. Conscious of the numerical ascendancy of their coreligionists, many of whom were second- and third-generation immigrants of the middle classes, and proud of the proliferation of Catholic schools, hospitals, newspapers and lay societies, the principal prelates and priests associated with Americanism perceived the hand of Providence in the dynamic spirit of the age. The mix of Catholicity and Americanism entailed an understanding of a mutual *transformation* guided by the Holy Spirit's movement in the free climate of American life. Hence, the Church and the age should unite to form a new era in the life of humanity.

The transformationists, or liberals, were led by Archbishop John Ireland of St. Paul, Bishop John J. Keane of Richmond, first rector of The Catholic University of America, Cardinal James Gibbons of Baltimore and Monsignor Denis O'Connell, the bishops' agent in Rome and rector of the North American College. Though Americanism is derived from the spirituality and ecclesiology of Isaac

Hecker, founder of the Paulist Fathers, the "ism" was refined in the heat of controversy with the proponents of strong Catholic identity separate from the culture, one manifested in a strong drive to preserve the Catholic subculture of devotionalism, parish schools, and ethnic particularism, especially among German Americans. Led by Archbishop Michael A. Corrigan of New York, Bishop Bernard McQuaid of Rochester, New York, and Archbishop Frederick Katzer of Milwaukee, these preservationists were not opposed to the gradual Americanization of Catholic institutions to compete with public schools, hospitals, and the press, but they were critical of what they perceived as the inherent anti-Catholic, nativistic, and materialistic core of American culture.

The controversies that shaped the two opposing groups began with the 1886 claim by a Milwaukee priest, Peter Abelen, that since Irish-American bishops were engaged in wholesale discrimination against German-speaking Catholics, the latter should have their own vicars general and their national parishes should be strengthened. While Gibbons was in Rome to be elevated to the cardinate in 1887, Ireland, Keane and O'Connell were on hand for the occasion. Together they responded to the above German American attack. In a letter to Propaganda Fide (responsible for mission areas, including the United States until 1908), Gibbons also defended the Knights of Labor as a legitimate society composed of Catholics eager to promote their interests peacefully, a line of reasoning that influenced the pro-labor elements in *Rerum Novarum* of 1891. The Baltimore prelate also indicated his opposition to the conservatives' position to place on the Index the books of Henry George, social theorist and erstwhile candidate for mayor of New York. This latter move was viewed as a tacit approval of Edward McGlynn, an activist-priest who had been excommunicated by Archbishop Corrigan for refusing to obey his prohibition against participating in the mayoral campaign of Henry George.

The conflict intensified with the public-school issues of 1890 through 1893. John Ireland had devised a plan whereby Catholics sold their schools to the Minnesota towns of Stillwater and Faribault and sent their children there to be taught by sisters, with religion classes held after school hours. Later in an address at a meeting of the American Education Association, John Ireland condoned the propriety of the state's role in education that was viewed as undermining the Third Plenary Council's call for a school in every parish. Ireland's ideas on public education alienated the German community, fearful of the Americanization of the schools, as well as those who viewed public schools as inherently hostile to Catholicity. The conservative-liberal conflict was reflected in disputes among faculty and administration at The Catholic University of America, perceived by the preservationists as a liberal stronghold.

Archbishop Francesco Satolli, the Vatican representative at the Quadricentennial celebration in Chicago (1893), became Pope Leo's apostolic delegate that year. He did not oppose Ireland's school plan, and he later resolved the McGlynn case to the liberals' satisfaction. However, within a year Satolli had shifted his support to the German-conservative alliance because he considered the liberals to be capitulating to the secular forces of modernity.

Throughout this period John Ireland was the most eloquent proponent of Hecker's mission to America. At the Catholic Congresses of 1889 and of 1893 he articulated a vision of an activist Church infused with the spirit of the age. According to Ireland the laity were not baptized and confirmed to merely "save their souls and pay their pew rent" but were to bring Christ to society, so eager for the Catholic principles of good works, social reform and the vitality of the Church as the maker of culture. Satolli's shift of allegiance and the resignations of Denis O'Connell (1895) and John J. Keane (1896) clearly illustrated the conservative ascendancy.

The crisis of Americanism occurred during the 1897 through 1898 period that was initiated by the publication of the French translation of Walter Elliot's biography of Isaac Hecker with a strongly liberal introduction by the French scholar-priest, Felix Klein. It elicited a storm of criticism from the arch-conservative wing of the French Catholic Church led by Charles Maignen. He linked the liberals with the demonic spirit of the age characterized by republicanism, religious liberty, Freemasonry, rationalism, Pelagianism, and an idolatrous capitulation to the secular, godless state. Though Maignen associated John Ireland, John Keane and others with Heckerism and Americanism, the liberals were not deterred and even gained confidence from support of European advocates of reform. Indeed during this time many liberals gathered at the Roman apartment of Denis O'Connell, a place that gained the code name "Liberty Hall." Confident of the imminent victory of Hecker's spiritual vision, Denis O'Connell addressed a Catholic Congress at Fribourg on a "New Idea in the Life of Isaac Hecker" in which he enthusiastically embraced the spirit of the age in political Americanism but criticized its application to ecclesiastical structures. The Hecker biography placed the opposing worldviews in bold relief; the Americanists' historical, developmental model of the Church and the age was inherently incompatible with the reigning ahistorical theological discourse, Neo-Scholasticism.

This dialectic intensified and culminated in Pope Leo's encyclical letter to Cardinal Gibbons, *Testem Benevolentiae* (January, 1899). After establishing that the French edition of the biography of Hecker was "exciting no small controversy on account of opinions introduced concerning the manner of leading a Christian life," Leo stated that the basis of these opinions was the significance of the Church's adapting herself to the spirit of the age by "relaxing her ancient rigor." Though he did not allude to particular Americanists he condemned those "modern popular themes and methods" that were to be "applied not only to accidentals but to the substance of faith" and the claim that the liberty of the age "ought to be introduced into the church."

Some of the new opinions "comprised" under the head of "Americanism" were: the Church should accept the age as experiencing abundant manifestations of the Holy Spirit; the natural virtues are more important than the supernatural; and in religious life contemplation should entirely give way for the age's need for the active apostolate. American conservatives felt vindicated and expressed their gratitude to the pope while the liberals considered Americanism to be a phantom heresy. However they no longer spoke so forcefully on the providential convergence of the Church and the age while the Paulists were demoralized by references to Heckerism.

Americanism and Modernism share a common developmental model of the Church in the modern world. Each group was articulating a fresh apologetic based on historical understandings. The Modernists were very supportive of the Americanists' movement while several Americanists were in accord with the Modernist impulse even though they may not have fully appreciated its methodology and scholarship.

Americanism was, in a sense, vindicated by the ecclesiology and general historical consciousness associated with the Second Vatican Council. However, it remains a protean term. Contemporary heirs of the Americanists represent numerous positions on the liberal-conservative spectrum ranging from the opponents of the expansion of the Vatican's authority over the local Churches to the proponents of a neoconservative rendering of America's providential mission in the world. Those who appropriate the preservationist stance are also a diverse group, such as representatives of the traditionalist critique of the anti-Catholic biases of "secular humanism," and the radical anti-capitalist proponents of Catholic liberationist themes in the social-reform debate. However, the breakdown of the Neo-Scholastic synthesis and the rise of pluralism in theological discourse allow Isaac Hecker's intuitive understandings of a theology of history to be easily appreciated by many contemporary American Catholics.

CHRISTOPHER J. KAUFFMAN

See also AMERICAN CATHOLICISM; GIBBONS, JAMES, CARDINAL; HECKER, ISAAC THOMAS; IRELAND, JOHN.

ANAMNESIS

(Gk., "calling to mind") The liturgical prayer commemorating the passion, resurrection, and ascension of the Lord. Immediately following the consecration in the Mass, it serves as a memorial to Christ's redemption and his salvific presence in the world.

JOSEPH QUINN

See also EUCHARIST.

ANAPHORA

(Gk., "offering") A term adopted from the Oriental Rite. It refers to the Eucharistic Prayer. It includes thanksgiving, invocation of the Holy Spirit, the narrative of the institution by Jesus, the acclamation, the memorial prayer and prayer of intercession.

JOSEPH QUINN

See also EUCHARISTIC PRAYERS.

ANATHEMA

(Gk., "something set aside") A person or object condemned by the Church for apostasy, heresy, or egregious sin. The term was used by St. Paul to repudiate teachings which he considered antagonistic to the true doctrine of the early Church (Gal 1:9), and by the Fathers of the Church to renounce heretics. Later, it was the signal expression used in the condemnatory doctrinal decrees of councils. Anathema signified excommunication in the absolute sense of total separation from the Church.

JOSEPH QUINN

See also EXCOMMUNICATION.

ANAWIM

See POOR, THE.

ANCHORITE

See HERMIT.

ANGELS

The word "angel" is derived from the Greek word *aggelos*. *Aggelos* is in turn a translation of the Hebrew word *mal'akh,* which means messenger. In the Hebrew understanding, one was an angel because of one's function rather than one's being. In the Bible, for example, it is sometimes unclear whether a *mal'akh* is a human or superhuman being; both could deliver messages of God.

Head of an angel, detail, by Duccio di Buoninsegna, Uffizi Gallery, Florence

In English, "angel" has come to signify only supernatural beings, beings who mediate between God and humans. Angels praise God, reveal God's will to mortals, and act on behalf of God. Such beings are present in a variety of religious traditions, including Zoroastrianism and Islam.

Belief in angels has played a significant role in Judaism as well, as is made evident in the Bible. The Book of Genesis speaks of "the angel of the Lord" who stops Abraham from slaying Isaac, and it tells how an angel comes to Hagar in the wilderness. In the Book of Judges, an angel appears to Gideon, and it is an angel who saves Daniel in the lions' den. These are only a few of many places in which angels appear in the Hebrew Scriptures.

In the Christian New Testament, angels testify to the power and divinity of Jesus. They announce his incarnation and birth, and they witness his resurrection. In the Book of Matthew, Jesus describes "twelve legions of angels" who await his command. And angels figure prominently in the Book of Revelations, where they announce the second coming of Christ and the Last Judgment.

As Christianity developed, a tradition emerged of designating several orders or choirs of angels. The number of these orders has varied. However, by the late fifth century, Dionysius the Pseudo-Areopagite had put forth the following hierarchy of angelic beings: Seraphim (described in Isaiah 6:2-3), Cherubim (mentioned in Genesis 3:24, and elsewhere), Thrones, Dominions, Virtues, Powers, Principalities (all described in the epistles of Paul), Archangels, and Angels. The first three, Dionysius said, are dedicated to the contemplation of God. The next three govern the universe; the last three execute orders.

In the Bible, only three angels are mentioned by name: Michael, Gabriel, and Raphael. But Catholic tradition has also maintained a popular belief in guardian angels; it is said that each person has assigned to him or her an angel who acts as guide and protector. Evidence for the existence of guardian angels comes from Matthew 18:10, where Jesus admonishes his followers, "See that you do not despise one of these little ones; for I tell you that in heaven their angels always behold the face of my Father." Though belief in guardian angels has been widespread, the Fathers of the Church (early Christian saints and thinkers) disagreed among themselves concerning the issue. St. Basil, for example, felt that sin drove such angels away, and St. Ambrose contended that the righteous have no guardians, so that their struggle against evil would be more glorious.

Christian tradition also speaks of fallen angels, or angels who disobeyed God. The Second Letter of Peter warns that "God did not spare the angels when they sinned, but cast them into hell." And the Book of Revelation describes a great battle at the end of time between Michael the Archangel and Satan and Satan's angels.

Perhaps the most significant Catholic statement concerning the existence of angels comes from the Fourth Lateran Council, held in the thirteenth century. This council declared that God is the creator of all things, both "the spiritual or angelic world and the corporeal and visible universe." The declaration was echoed in the nineteenth century at the First Vatican Council, and was repeated by Pope Paul VI in 1972.

However, Catholics have differed among themselves concerning exactly what a belief in angels entails. Some have maintained that the doctrine of created, good, personal spiritual beings is a strictly binding truth of faith that has been revealed by God. Others, such as Jesuit theologian Karl Rahner, maintain that the word "revelation" most properly refers only to God: that is, that what is revealed in revelation is always and only God. Since angels are creaturely, says Rahner, their existence "cannot be understood as more than a content of revelation of a secondary and derived character."

Angels have played a significant role in Christian art and iconography throughout the centuries. Early on, angels were depicted simply as young men. Later, they were portrayed as having wings, a device that emphasized their supernatural nature.

THERESA SANDERS

See also APPARITIONS; PROVIDENCE; REVELATION.

ANGELUS

The Angelus is a devotional exercise which enables its users to commemorate the incarnation three times a day. Originally the Angelus was observed only in the evening with the tolling of the "Ave Maria" bell, so named because it called the people to pray three Hail Marys. The dawn and noon bells, each with its three Hail Marys, were added during the thirteenth century. In its present form, each of the three Hail Marys is preceded by a verse and response which tell of the angel's message, Mary's reply, and the resultant incarnation of the Word. The Angelus concludes with a prayer for saving grace accompanied by a peal of the bell.

V. The Angel of the Lord declared unto Mary,
℟. And she conceived of the Holy Spirit. Hail Mary, etc.

V. Behold the handmaid of the Lord,
℟. Be it done unto me according to your word. Hail Mary, etc.

V. And the Word was made flesh,
℟. And dwelt among us. Hail Mary, etc.

Let us pray: Pour forth, we beg you, O Lord, your grace into our hearts: that we, to whom the incarnation of Christ your Son was made known by the message of an angel, may by his passion and Cross be brought to the glory of his resurrection. Through the same Christ our Lord. Amen.

An alternate, using the hymn "Queen of Heaven" in place of the Hail Mary, is often substituted during the Easter season.

DAVID BRYAN

ANGLICAN ORDERS

The question of the validity of Anglican orders has been debated by both Anglicans and Roman Catholics. However, in 1896 Pope Leo XIII issued the encyclical, *Apostolicae Curae,* declaring that the ordinations of deacons, priests, and bishops in the Anglican Church are both null and void because of defect of both form and intention. Much of the controversy revolves around the ordinal of King Edward VI of 1552. Leo saw a defect of intention in the Edwardine ordinal because of its exclusion of the Catholic understanding of the sacrificial nature of priesthood and its replacement with the Protestant view of priesthood devoid of "sacrificing" or "consecrating" elements. Since this ordinal became the norm for ordinations in the Church of England, Leo believed that all these ordinations were invalid because of the use of the "defective" intention formulated by this ordinal.

Some scholars in the Anglican Church answered Leo's objections by stating that their rite of ordination intends to confer the office of priesthood as instituted by Christ with all that it contains, and that the Anglican Church has the same understanding of the Eucharistic sacrifice as found in the Eucharistic Prayer (Canon) of the Mass in the Catholic Church. They also countered his objections by claiming that the words and actions deemed necessary by Leo for a valid ordination are entirely lacking in ordinals dating back to the early Church.

Since 1896 the question of the validity of Anglican ordinations has been a topic of lively debate. Some Orthodox Churches consider Anglican ordinations to be on a par with those of the Catholic Church, and the "Old Catholics" recognize Anglican ordinations and have intercommunion with Anglicans. The Anglican-Roman Catholic International Commission has issued joint statements expressing a common understanding of priesthood and ministry; however as of 1993 the Catholic Church has not changed its official position on Anglican orders as stated by Pope Leo XIII.

ANTHONY D. ANDREASSI

See also ANGLICANISM; ANGLO-CATHOLIC; PRIESTHOOD, THE MINISTERIAL; SACRAMENT OF ORDERS.

ANGLICANISM

The name given to the beliefs and practices of the Church of England and to those Churches which grew from it, such as the Church of South India. Anglicanism began when Henry VIII (1491–1547) led the Church of England out of the Roman communion and put it under his own leadership. What the king wanted was "Catholicism without the Pope," but there were many churchmen in England who wanted far more than that. Although they had to recognize the political nature of the Church, that is, the king's supremacy, they worked to make Anglicanism more than just a tool of the monarchy. Some of these churchmen leaned toward the continental Protestant Reformers, while others hoped to retain as much of Roman Catholic practices and structure as possible. The various factions within Anglicanism reached what they called the *via media,* literally, the middle way, that is, the middle way between the unrestrained biblicism of the Reformed Churches and the supreme power of the Bishops of Rome over Catholic life. Not surprisingly, neither Catholics nor Protestants accepted the notion of the middle way, and in the seventeenth century one group of Protestants, the Puritans, managed to take over the government and "reform" the Church, often by physically destroying what they considered relics of Catholicism. Since that time, Anglicanism has not been threatened by political movements, and, led by several strong archbishops of Canterbury, the Anglicans have worked out their own doctrinal positions. While these are clearly too many and too complex for a brief treatment, it is possible to see the middle way. Anglicans believe, with the Protestants, that the Bible is sufficient in itself for salvation, containing all the necessary truths and guidance. On the other hand, the Anglicans have always had, like Roman Catholics, a strong respect for extrabiblical tradition, especially in the patristic period, and Anglicans accept the authority of the first four ecumenical councils. Anglicanism has a hierarchical form of Church government as well as a sacramental life. It has also given the English-speaking world two unquestioned literary masterpieces, the King James Version of the Bible and the Book of Common Prayer; several leading Anglican divines, such as Richard Hooker (ca. 1554–1600) have been great theologians who have significantly influenced English life both inside and outside the Church. The appeal of Anglicanism to its devotees can perhaps best be seen in the life of John Wesley (1703–1791), the founder of Methodism, who lived and died an Anglican, hoping only to reform his mother Church, not to divide it.

JOSEPH F. KELLY

See also BRITAIN, CHURCH IN; REFORMATION, THE.

ANGLIN, TIMOTHY WARREN (1822–1896)

Journalist, publisher and politician; b. 31 August 1822 in Clonakilty, County Cork, Ireland m. first 1853, at Saint John, New Brunswick, to his cousin Margaret O'Regan (d. childless in 1855) m. secondly, in Saint John in 1862, to Ellen McTavish, by whom he had ten children d. 3 May 1896, Toronto, Ontario.

Born into a well-to-do Catholic family, Timothy Anglin planned to prepare for a legal career but was forced—at the outbreak of the Great Famine in 1845—to take up teaching. On Easter Monday 1849, he left Ireland for Saint John, New Brunswick. In Saint John, Anglin published the *Saint John Weekly Freeman,* emerging as spokesman for the city's burgeoning Irish Catholic population.

In 1861, T. W. Anglin was elected, as an independent, to represent Saint John County and City in the New Brunswick House of Assembly. He was made an executive councilor in the anti-confederate government formed in April 1865, but after imperial authorities proclaimed British North American union desirable for reasons of defense, those who had rejected it were accused of disloyalty. Anglin—whose position on British domination in Ireland was well known—became the focus of the confederates' "loyalty" campaign. During the fall of 1865 the issue of loyalty became even more compelling when the American wing of the Fenian movement, determined to liberate Ireland from Britain, proposed to attack Britain's colonies in North America. Such effective use was made of the loyalty issue that in an election held in May and June of 1866, New Brunswick's "anti" government was toppled.

Now resigned to confederation, in the first general election for the new Canadian House of Commons, Anglin was elected for the Acadian Catholic riding of Gloucester, on New Brunswick's north shore. In Ottawa and in the pages of the *Freeman,* Anglin advanced the cause of New Brunswick's Catholic separate schools. In this bitter, and ultimately unsuccessful, battle he widened the gulf between himself and the province's Protestant politicians under whose pressure he was excluded from the Liberal administration formed in 1873. In reward for his service to the party, Anglin was made Speaker of the House in March of 1874. Following the defeat of the Liberals in 1878 his political career went into decline. Severing his ties with the *Freeman,* in 1883 Anglin moved to Toronto where he took over the *Tribune,* a Catholic weekly. When Liberal support of the paper was withdrawn in 1887 Anglin found himself unemployed. One year before his death, of a blood clot on the brain, Anglin was named chief clerk of the Surrogate Court of Ontario.

In his capacity as journalist and politician, Timothy Warren Anglin encouraged Irish Catholics to transform themselves with God's help. He promoted self-respect by providing "home" news and by supporting the establishment of ethnic-religious organizations. Anglin sympathized with the efforts of labor unions but denounced socialism and communism as threats to the religious underpinnings of Western civilization. He claimed the clergy had a duty to identify and condemn what was unlawful and sinful. But by insisting that the Catholic lay person was as free as anyone to judge political issues for himself he nurtured in New Brunswick's Irish Catholic community an attitude of independence from clerical interference.

PETER DOUGLAS MURPHY

See also CANADA, THE CATHOLIC CHURCH IN.

ANGLO-CATHOLIC

The name given, since 1838, to some High Church Anglicans whose liturgy and doctrines tend to be close to those of the Roman Catholic Church. They put emphasis on the tenets of the Creed and on sacramental life, and claim that they represent the authentic and original beliefs of the Church of England.

JOAN GLAZIER

See also ANGLICANISM.

ANIMALS, A CHRISTIAN APPROACH

Animals, their behavior and appearance, have played an important role in the literature of Christianity from its earliest days. Looking to Genesis, early Christians could understand the right relationship of humans and animals as one of *shalom,* life-giving peace, mirroring the royal rule of the Creator. They could also look to the wisdom literature (e.g., Job 38) to see in animals signs of God's wonderful working. In Isaiah 11 they read of the promised reign of peace, characterized by renewed harmony among animals and humans. Perhaps such thoughts lie behind the phrase in Mark's Gospel (1:13) describing Jesus in the wilderness after baptism: "he was with the wild beasts and angels ministered to him."

In the literature of martyrdom, Christians like Ignatius of Antioch noted that sometimes animals did not attack Christians in the arena where they were condemned to die. Saturus, companion of Perpetua and Felicitas, was not harmed by two beasts, a boar and a bear, according to the rather reliable account of the Passion of those martyrs.

After Constantine's legal recognition of the Christian religion, enthusiastic authors of "epic Passions" embellished earlier, sober accounts of martyrs unharmed by animals. Animals were now pictured as embracing and kissing the martyrs, thus representing the martyrs as having already entered a state of paradisiacal harmony and peace in the reign of Christ.

Lives of early monks have varied and numerous accounts of peaceful relationships among desert solitaries and animals. The tracks of desert animals are described as surrounding the cell of Abba Theona, who provided for their care.

Whether we consider the ravens bringing food to the prophet Elijah in the desert or to St. Benedict in his cave, the message remains similar: animals act as God's messengers and servants to those who obey God.

Such is the explicit message of Sulpicius Severus who exclaims, theologically: "These are your wonders, O Christ! We lose dominion over creatures when we fail to serve the Creator."

"St. Francis' Sermon to the Birds," by Tadeo di Bartolo, 1403

The Lives of Irish saints are especially noteworthy for the prominent place they give to peaceful relationships among holy men and women and the animals. Animals obey those who obey the Creator; the fierce become tame; the proud become meek; the wicked are converted to good or flee the saint's presence.

From early martyrs' Passions to medieval saints' Lives, animals could also be pictured negatively: as harmful instruments of the Evil One, the serpent being most commonly reckoned in this category. Yet even in these cases animals can only harm God's servant if God permits it, which most often means that the "bad" animal retreats after attempting to frighten the saint. A classic example of this type is that of *The Temptation of St. Antony,* depicted in Bosch's famous painting.

Francis of Assisi is often considered the "friend of animals." Accounts in early Lives of this thirteenth-century holy man show him deeply, religiously moved simply by the sight or touch of animals. His "Sermon to the Birds," frescoed by Giotto, remains an appealing icon of this man whose own writings refer to all fellow-creatures as his "brothers" and "sisters."

The medieval Bestiary, heir to the early Christian text *Physiologus,* provided readers and preachers with descriptions of animals and their behavior (both sometimes fantastic) with the purpose of instructing believers in correct Christian belief and behavior.

With the growth of experimental science and an increased emphasis on careful observation of phenomena in the Renaissance and later in the Enlightenment, authors like René Descartes could conceive of animals as soulless machines. The lively "sacramental consciousness" of earlier Christian authors gave way to a view in which animals were relegated to "matter," the stuff of science, and became increasingly objects of research rather than messengers of the Spirit.

Recent, revived interest in the Christian tradition of creation as revelatory of the Creator may well bring renewed understanding of the ways in which the interrelationship of human beings and animals is religiously significant, thus restoring to its proper place a small, but beautiful piece of the Catholic tradition.

WILLIAM J. SHORT, O.F.M.

See also CREATION.

ANNULMENT

The formal declaration by a Church court that a marriage was null and void from the beginning is called an annulment. The word comes from the Latin *ad nullum* (literally, "unto nothing"), and it means a making void, an invalidation. This legal establishment of the nullity of a marriage means that the Church does not recognize the union as valid and sacramental.

An annulment does *not* mean that the marriage had no reality, no significance. The marriage relationship had as much real history, human meaning and moral obligation as the partners invested in it. It may have lasted two months, and have been an ephemeral event in their lives. Or it may have lasted twenty years and produced several children, and been of the greatest importance in their human experience. The Church's annulment does not deny that significance. It simply says that, from the point of view of the Church's canon law, the marriage which appeared to be genuine, was originally defective in some way, and that the Church will not take official cognizance of it as an authentic union.

The annulment of a marriage does *not* declare or imply that the offspring of the marriage are illegitimate. The Church's canons specifically state the opposite, that is, that the children born of the marriage are legitimate (c. 1137).

Sources

There are three canonical sources or causes on which marriage annulments are based: (1) lack of canonical form, (2) a defect of human consent, or (3) an invalidating impediment.

Lack of Canonical Form. The Church requires that the marriages of Catholics take place in the presence of a properly deputed minister (e.g., bishop, priest, or deacon) and two witnesses. This is called the canonical form of marriage (cc. 1108–1117). When a marriage involving at least one baptized Catholic takes place elsewhere, for example, before a Protestant minister or a civil magistrate, then the marriage is invalid for want of form. This is the most common cause of the invalidity of marriages, and the most frequent grounds for annulments.

Defect of Human Consent. Marriage is made by the free consent of the partners. When that consent is gravely defective, a Church court will declare the marriage null. For example, a person might be very immature or under the influence of drugs or severe duress. A person might feel compelled to marry due to some force or fear, or might not intend a permanent or exclusive union. These are considered serious deficiencies in the human consent required for the matrimonial covenant (cc. 1095–1103).

Invalidating Impediment. Church law describes several personal circumstances which prevent persons from marrying. These are called impediments to marriage. Some examples: underage, too close a blood relationship, inability to have sexual intercourse, priestly ordination, or the existing bond of a prior marriage. There are twelve such impediments (cc. 1083–1094). If any one of these conditions can be proven to have existed at the time marriage was entered into, then the marriage can be annulled.

Procedure

The Church's process for declaring the nullity of a marriage is careful and complex. (It is governed by canons 1400–1655, 1671–1691.) It usually begins at the parish level, when one party to a failed marriage comes to the pastor or a member of the pastoral team, and asks for help. The person may be a Catholic or a non-Catholic. A description of the circumstances of the marriage is sent to the diocesan marriage court in the form of a petition. The judge makes an initial decision about the court's jurisdiction and existence of sufficient grounds to go forward with the petition. The court will entertain the petition only after the marriage in question has irretrievably broken down, that is, only after a civil divorce has been granted.

The other partner to the marriage is notified of the petition for an annulment, and is invited to give testimony. Evidence is collected in support of the petition. The evidence can be in the form of documents or the testimony of witnesses, which is then reduced to writing.

The entire marriage case must be examined by a court official whose duty it is to protect the marriage bond; the official must be assured that the evidence presented is sound and serious. Then the whole case is submitted to a panel of three judges who render a decision on whether or not the nullity of the marriage has been established. Their standard of judgment is moral certitude, based on the evidence presented. Their decision is then reviewed in summary form by an appeal court which must confirm it in order for the annulment to be final. At the conclusion of the process, the petitioner is requested to pay a fee to offset the expenses of the court.

After an annulment is granted, both parties to the marriage in question are free to remarry, unless some restriction is placed on one of them because of a particular circumstance which might jeopardize a second union, e.g., a serious psychological disorder.

Annulments have become a widely accepted and frequent means of pastoral reconciliation for those who have experienced the tragedy of divorce.

JAMES A. CORIDEN

See also DIVORCE; SACRAMENT OF MATRIMONY.

ANNUNCIATION

This ancient feast is kept on 25 March and holds the high rank of a solemnity. It commemorates the incarnation of the Son of God. In honor of the incarnation, the old custom of genuflecting during the Creed at the words "he became man" is retained on this day, though suppressed for all other occasions.

Originating in Eastern Christianity, the feast of the Annunciation was introduced in Rome between A.D. 660 and 680. It was celebrated there as a solemnity of the Lord, an emphasis which has been restored in the reforms since the Second Vatican Council. But the Annunciation is also, if secondarily, a festival of Our Lady: It is not to be forgotten that she was, according to Luke (Luke 1:26-38), the first human being to receive the gospel, being evangelized directly by an angelic revelation of God. Luke's Annunciation scene skillfully portrays the humble obedience with which human beings (or the Church, represented by Mary) should receive the Word. There is perhaps a contrast here with the way Eve and Adam disobeyed (Genesis 2 and 3), listening not to an angel of God, but to the prince of the fallen angels. (The identification of the serpent of Genesis with Lucifer, though not made in Genesis, was common by the time of Christ.) Since the Messiah was the expectation of Israel and of all humanity, the scene is further an illustration of the power of hope. We are told that Mary (and, by implication, her prayer) has found favor with God. The Solemnity of the Annunciation, then, also commemorates the power of prayer and meditation. The importance of the Annunciation is underscored by the fact that this is the first mystery of the rosary and is celebrated by the Angelus as well.

"The Anunciation," by Fra Angelico, San Marco, Florence

DAVID BRYAN

See also ANGELUS; INCARNATION; LITURGY; ROSARY.

ANOINTING, SACRAMENT OF

See SACRAMENT OF ANOINTING.

ANSELM, ST. (ca. 1033–1109)

He was born into a family of landowners in Lombardy. After sowing his wild oats, he had a change of heart and entered the monastic school at Bec in Normandy which was run by Lanfranc whom he succeeded as prior in 1063 when Lanfranc moved to Canterbury. He earned respect as a spiritual advisor and as an innovative thinker. He was elected abbot of Bec in 1078 and made several journeys to England. On Lanfranc's death, King William II nominated him to be Archbishop of Canterbury. He immediately fell into a dispute with the crown over Church lands, the right of the Archbishop to hold a council or to go to Rome for advice.

During these years of conflict, Anselm wrote some important works. In 1095 he finished his *De Incarnatione Verbi* and in 1098 he completed his greatest work, *Cur Deus Homo.* He clashed with King William again on the subject of lay investiture and this dispute continued with Henry I, who came to the throne on William's death in 1100. It was eventually resolved by the pope and the king behind his back. As Archbishop, Anselm also became an ardent enforcer of clerical celibacy. He is regarded as the greatest theologian between Augustine and Aquinas, and broke with his predecessors by resorting to reason rather than to arguments based on scriptural texts to defend the faith. He is remembered for his Ontological Argument for the existence of God. He postulated that if we mean God is that than which nothing greater can be conceived, then we cannot conceive this entity except as existing. A staunch intellectual, he held that faith was a precondition to the proper use of Reason (*credo ut intelligam*). His *Cur Deus Homo* was one of the great medieval works on the theology of the atonement. He was declared a Doctor of the Church by Clement XI in 1720.

MICHAEL GLAZIER

See also DOCTORS OF THE CHURCH; EXISTENCE OF GOD; MIDDLE AGES, THE; SOTERIOLOGY.

ANTHONY OF PADUA, ST. (1191–1231)

Born in Lisbon, Portugal, in 1191, and baptized Ferdinand, the young Anthony grew and received his early education at the cathedral school in the city. In 1210 he joined the community of Canons Regular of St. Augustine at the convent of St. Vincent just outside the walls of Lisbon. Two years later he transferred to the monastery of Santa Cruz at Coimbra, where he continued his studies for the priesthood. The canons of Santa Cruz, with both religious and intellectual links to the monastery of St. Victor in Paris, were renowned as scholars, and the monastery of Santa Cruz itself was considered the intellectual center of the kingdom of Portugal.

The Friars Minor had arrived at Coimbra in 1217, establishing themselves there at the chapel of St. Anthony. Ferdinand no doubt encountered the Franciscans as they begged from the canons of Santa Cruz. When the bodies of the five recently martyred friars in Morocco arrived at Coimbra in 1220, he was inspired by their evangelical enthusiasm, in addition to their simple lifestyle, to request a transfer to the Order of Friars Minor. Having received the necessary permissions, Ferdinand joined the friars at the little chapel of St. Anthony, from which he took his new name.

Anthony himself joined a group of friars traveling on mission to Morocco in order to win martyrdom. However, illness forced his return to Portugal. Problems on his return voyage led to his landing at Messina in Sicily rather than Portugal. Joining the local friars at Messina he traveled with them to Assisi where he attended the general chapter of the order at the Portiuncula in 1221, after which he was assigned to the province of Romagna, where he would later serve as provincial minister (1227–1230). Anthony was an effective and popular preacher in both France and northern Italy. Reflecting his fame as a preacher against heretics, in 1223

St. Anthony of Padua, etching

Francis of Assisi wrote a letter to Anthony giving him permission to teach theology to the friars, thus becoming the first lector of theology in the Franciscan Order. His extant writings include two sermon collections, his *Sunday Sermons,* and the *Feastday Sermons,* which were intended to serve as model sermon outlines for preachers. He preached his final lenten sermon cycle at Padua in 1231, retiring to the friary at Campo San Piero because of illness. He died while traveling to Padua on 13 June 1231. He was canonized by Pope Gregory IX on 30 May 1232 within a year of his death, who celebrated Anthony as a great preacher and defender of the faith in service to the Church.

MICHAEL BLASTIC, O.F.M. CONV.

See also FRANCISCANS; MIDDLE AGES, THE.

ANTHROPOLOGY, CHRISTIAN

There are many anthropologies in accord with the many different perspectives available to attempt to understand human existence. Thus we have cultural anthropology, philosophical anthropology, social and political anthropologies, etc. We also have religious anthropologies or ways of understanding human existence that flow from the traditions of the great world religions. Among these religious perspectives there is the Christian understanding of human existence, an understanding that is not in competition with the many secular understandings (as long as they are not reductionist) and an understanding that is in principle in dialogue with other religious understandings.

For Christian anthropology Jesus Christ is the focal paradigm. The Christian is in the most literal sense the *disciple* of Jesus, the one who learns from Jesus how to live authentically. The biblical elaboration of this Christian structure of existence is rich and varied, and it includes both testaments since Jesus was a Jew, and his basic religious formation came from the traditions of Judaism, especially from the Hebrew Scriptures. It was the prophets of Israel who first introduced that structure of existence which we call personhood. Jesus would pioneer a "post-personal" form of existence demanding self-transcendence empowered by the Spirit and actualized in love of neighbor.

Twentieth-century biblical scholarship with its interest in and significant success at the construction of a sound portrait of the historical Jesus has definitely enhanced our knowledge of the salient features of the lifestyle of Jesus of Nazareth. This new knowledge has obvious consequences for a Christian anthropology for which Jesus is *the* illustration of life well lived.

Central to the understanding of the Christian structure of existence is the magnificent portrayal of humanity in the first chapter of the Book of Genesis: humanity is created in the image and likeness of God (1:26). This theme has evoked commentary after commentary down through the centuries as Christian thinkers have attempted to locate precisely what there is about humanity that images God either clearly or faintly. Perhaps we can gain further illumination on this issue by attending to the context of the passage. The God who is to be imaged by humanity is depicted as the creative designer of the world whose freedom shapes the world into a significantly ordered whole. This God, then, would be appropriately imaged by humanity to the extent that creative freedom describes human existence. And since freedom is the hallmark of person, we might say that the Personal God creates human beings to become persons who by so becoming image the divine creative freedom. But humanity did not rise to this task, and the biblical tradition witnesses to human deviation from the beginning. With Christ, the "New Adam," however, God finally formed the true divine image (2 Cor 4:4). Through Christ Christians are empowered to become the image and likeness of God.

The goodness of creation including our creaturely condition with all its finitude and limitations has always been a characteristic theme of Catholic theology. Creation is God's "first gift." Grace or God's self-gift, the "second gift," (not to be understood temporally) has been characteristically understood by the Catholic imagination as the perfection and completion of creation. This traditional Catholic emphasis on the intrinsic connection between creation and salvation must be retrieved today in response to the ecology crisis. Modern theology has been excessively anthropocentric, limiting itself to the understanding of the relationship between God and humanity and this relationship unfolds in the specifically human arena of history. Nature was ceded to the natural scientists whose mechanistic worldview was incompatible with religious portrayals of the world as God's creation. But this modern "division of labor" between nature and history has begun to give way to a new dialogue between scientists and theologians in light of the postmodern critique of the reductionistic rationalism of the modern period. Theologians, for their part, have awakened to the need for a theology of nature critical of the modern ambition to control it for narrowly utilitarian purposes. Without nature there is no home for a history of salvation, and the God who saves is the God who creates.

While it affirms the fundamental goodness of creation, Christian anthropology recognizes the fallen, sinful condition of our world in the doctrine of original sin. At times, however, this doctrine has begotten excessive pessimism among Christians especially when it is expanded into dark theories of predestination. The original purpose of the doctrine of original sin was to profess our universal solidarity of need for the redemptive grace of Christ. To do this Augustine used the biological metaphor of birth (generation, propagation), and his teaching was officially endorsed by the Councils of Carthage, Orange, and, finally, Trent. Contemporary attempts to reformulate this doctrine depart from the biological metaphor in search for an historical one more in accord with our contemporary historical consciousness. Historical consciousness is the recognition that we are intrinsically temporal beings who are antecedently shaped by the past and by the present configuration of our common culture. An example of contemporary approaches to our "inherited sin" would be the notion of social sin which alerts us to the evil consequences of the injustices built into our social, political, and economic structures. These structures, strengthened by the pseudo-legitimations of cultural and religious symbols, deform and distort our consciousness to such an extent that we are not even aware of the evil embedded in them. Thus do they perdure as carriers of the sin of the world.

Other contemporary approaches to original sin translate the "developmental model" of St. Irenaeus (from child to adult) in evolutionary language—original sin would be a "fall" from the original innocence of our prelinguistic ancestors who lived instinctually. Another interesting approach follows the lead of the account in Genesis—original sin is the refusal to accept ourselves as infinitely erotic finite beings. We would be God by dualistically accentuating the "higher" over the "lower"—our infinite élan over our finite capacity, spirit over body, male over female. As Paul sings in the Philippians hymn, Christ saves us by accepting himself in the path of humility which is the truth of our theomorphic nature (Phil 2:5-11). Only in the light of Christ do we really know what sin is.

The core of Christian anthropology is the mystery of grace. Grace is the self-gift of God to us through Jesus Christ. Grace is the Holy Spirit, the divine Power empowering our Christian discipleship. The history of the doctrine of grace provides the depth grammar for understanding Christianity, especially in its Western form. The Greek patristic contribution to this history is summarized in the doctrine of divinization or deification: God became human so that human beings could become divine. This ancient doctrine flows from the Johannine influence on the Greek Fathers—to become divine is to have eternal life now and to be raised up on the last day (John 6:54). For the Western Church, Roman Catholic and Protestant, Augustine's theology of grace is foundational. For Augustine the grace of Christ is at once "operative" and "cooperative." As operative it is "what God does in us without us." This is the good news of Christianity: *God* saves us—God has loved us first. Faith is radical trust in what God has done for us through Jesus Christ. This understanding of grace is the characteristic emphasis of Reformation Protestantism. As cooperative, grace is "what God does in us with us." This is the aspect that is developed by the theology of Thomas Aquinas for whom the word, grace, directly describes not the Holy Spirit but the person justified and sanctified by the Spirit of Christ. For Thomas grace transforms human nature by raising it to parity with God (the "supernatural" level) to such an extent that the deeds done by the graced person are meritorious of life eternal. Employing the Johannine metaphor of friendship with God, Thomas constructed a theology of grace similar to the Greek patristic notion of divinization. This is the typically Catholic emphasis.

Our contemporary historical consciousness alerts us not only to the formative power of the past but also to our creative power for the future. If we are the products of yesterday, we are as well the producers of tomorrow. This insight is extremely important for a contemporary theology of grace. "Where the Spirit of God is, there is freedom" (2 Cor 3:17). Freedom here is not to be identified with the rather pedestrian notion of free will. As the consequence of the presence of the Spirit, freedom is the power to do the good in imitation of Christ. With historical consciousness we can name this good—the good the graced person does is her or his own self. Freedom in the theological sense is one's ability to take one's time and create one's self, and that self will have eternal validity because it is co-created by the Spirit, the presence of eternity in time. With Jesus as paradigm Christians know how to actualize their freedom authentically—here is where love comes in. Love is the *how* of freedom. Love means giving one's self away to others, and one does this as one gives one's time to others, because one *is* one's lifetime. Here the proverb of Jesus that we must lose our lives in order to find them is most apposite (Luke 17:33).

If personhood as freedom in the Spirit is the Christian understanding of human existence, then this ideal cannot be merely an ideal for historically conscious Christians. The Christian vision of freedom in grace must beget a communal *praxis* of liberation for all those whose freedom has been curtailed or negated by the various forms of institutionalized evil—sexism, racism, impoverishment, homophobia, etc. Where the vision of freedom informs the Christian imagination, works of liberation must follow. A holy impatience must create intense dissatisfaction with the *status quo* to the extent that our Christian understanding of existence remains mere theory. Thus have emerged in our contemporary Church the various movements of emancipation of the oppressed. Of these movements the liberation of women is a dramatic illustration.

The anthropocentric cast of modern Western culture masked its androcentric reality. Women, more than half the human species, were, as Christians, free in principle but not in fact. For historically conscious Christians of today this deplorable fact cannot be masked any longer. Our Christian anthropology means nothing until it is put into practice. We can no longer merely *say* with Paul that there is neither male nor female. Women must become equal to men as human beings without any insidious qualification such as equal "but complementary." The status of women cannot be qualified in any way that would make them adjectival to men.

To summarize—Christian existence is personal existence in a community of persons in whom dwells the Spirit of Christ as empowerment for mission to the world. This community—the Church—must create new structures concretely to enable all of its members to live together in the freedom of the Spirit.

MICHAEL J. SCANLON, O.S.A.

See also CREATION; GRACE; ORIGINAL SIN; SALVATION.

ANTICHRIST

In the New Testament, the antichrist is mentioned in the First and Second Letters of John (1 John 2:18, 22; 4:3, and 2 John 7). The First Letter asks, "Who is the liar but he who denies that Jesus is Christ? This is the antichrist, he who denies the Father and the Son." John's second letter adds that there are those "who will not acknowledge the coming of Jesus in the flesh; such a one is the deceiver and the antichrist."

Christian tradition has sometimes connected these statements with the references to beasts found in the Book of Revelation. Understood this way, the antichrist is an evil and blasphemous monster who in the last days will lead many away from Christ. In addition, John's references to an antichrist are often read in conjunction with Paul's warning of a "man of lawlessness" who will proclaim himself to be God (2 Thess 2:3-10).

Throughout Christian history, the antichrist has been identified with various historical persons, including Arians (fourth-century heretics who denied that the Son of God was eternal) and Roman emperors Nero and Caligula. More recently, some Protestant Christian groups have understood the pope to be the antichrist.

Catholic thought has tended in two directions concerning the antichrist. On one hand are those who understand the antichrist to be a historical and personal being. On the other hand are those who interpret the antichrist tradition as referring to any forces that work against the will of God.

THERESA SANDERS

See also ESCHATOLOGY; REVELATION.

ANTIPHON

(Gk., "answering voice") A verse, usually from Scripture, sung or recited before and after (or between the verses of) a psalm or canticle. If the verse is sung, the antiphon establishes its musical phrasing, while also conveying its liturgical or mystical meaning.

JOSEPH QUINN

See also LITURGY OF THE HOURS; MUSIC AND WORSHIP.

ANTIPHONAL

Also called antiphonary, this is the liturgical book containing all sections of the Divine Office (or Liturgy of the Hours) which are to be sung antiphonally, i.e., in the mode of liturgical singing which calls for two groups or voices (such as the cantor and choir, choir and congregation, or two sides of the choir) to sing alternate verses of a psalm or hymn.

JOSEPH QUINN

See also LITURGICAL BOOKS.

ANTIPOPES

An antipope is one who claimed to be the Bishop of Rome without having been chosen in the manner recognized at the time to be valid. Of the thirty-seven usually listed, most were rivals to another claimant now recognized as "authentic." The phenomenon stretches from the third century (St. Hippolytus) to the fifteenth (Felix V), with the twelfth century having no less than twelve. Five were produced by the Great Schism (first half of the fifteenth century).

DAVID BRYAN

See also PAPACY, THE.

ANTI-SEMITISM

Anti-Semitism is a term that is much used, but with little precision. Strictly speaking it could refer to prejudice against either Jews or Arabs. But its origins in the nineteenth century, as well as the history of its usage, have restricted it to hatred and discrimination against Jews. As the French Jewish historian Jules Isaac put it in his volume *The Teaching of Contempt,* "Antisemitism is used nowadays to refer to anti-Jewish prejudice, to feelings of suspicion, contempt, hostility, and hatred toward the Jews, both those who follow the religion of Israel and those who are merely of Jewish parentage."

The term "anti-Semitism" is a nineteenth-century phenomenon. What it represents was already known in the period of the Hebrew Scriptures, and researchers on anti-Semitism such as Fr. Edward Flannery (*The Anguish of the Jews*) have shown that it was a marked feature of pre-Christian Graeco-Roman society.

In the Hebrew Scriptures we read the account of Amalek's vicious attack upon the Jews who were late in leaving Egypt (cf. Deut 25:17-19). Rabbinic commentaries, which are critical in traditional Judaism for biblical interpretation, have always regarded this pericope as prototypical of anti-Judaism. And the Books of Maccabees recall the persistent efforts of Antiochus Epiphanes to suppress the first Jewish rebellion for religious freedom. As we move to the New Testament, we enter an area of some continuing scholarly controversy on the subject of anti-Semitism. While the Hebrew Scriptures record occurrences of anti-Semitic hatred, the question has been raised whether anti-Semitism is actually embedded in the teachings of the epistles and Gospels. No consensus exists today on this critical issue, with many scholars making the argument that the polemics found in the New Testament were in fact Jewish *internal* criticism and therefore cannot be regarded as a form of anti-Semitism. Others have also correctly pointed out that at times we have "globalized" criticisms of Jews and specific Jewish groups of Jesus' day (i.e., the Pharisees) when in fact these denunciations were likely directed only at sections of the Jewish community or particular movements.

On two points, however, there does appear to be emerging agreement among biblical scholars. The first is that many of the biblical texts have surely been interpreted in an anti-Semitic fashion by Church teachers and preachers over the centuries. Thus the tradition of biblical interpretation may in fact be described as "anti-Semitic" even if this does not hold for the texts themselves. Secondly, there are texts, particularly those in the Gospel of John and the Letter to the Hebrews, which must be said to come very close to crossing the anti-Semitic threshhold. Some scholars such as Fr. Raymond Brown have in fact claimed that they are imbued with prejudicial thinking against the Jews to the extent that they should no longer be regarded as authentic catechesis for our time. Brown has in mind such texts as those in John where Jews are equated with the forces of darkness and sinfulness. It does no good in his mind to claim, as some Christians do, that here Jews were simply being used as a prototype of all sinful humanity. For to regard the Jews' principal mission after the Christ Event as exemplifying sinfulness surely provides fertile ground for anti-Semitism.

Whatever the final verdict on New Testament anti-Semitism may turn out to be, there is no doubt that it had taken solid hold in Christian theology and preaching by the time of the Church Fathers. Their era gave rise to the *adversus Judaeos* (i.e., "against the Jews") in which Jewish rituals and interpretations of Scripture were ridiculed and the notion was promoted that God expelled the Jews from their homeland and destroyed their Temple as a punishment for rejecting Christ. They were to persist in this condition until the end of days except for individuals who were willing to undergo conversion. Important Christian thinkers such as Justin, John Chrysostom, and Augustine spoke of the Jews as wanderers over the face of the earth in punishment for their supposed role in the crucifixion. For centuries, this charge of deicide, of Christ-killers, served as the cornerstone of anti-Semitic diatribes.

The Middle Ages continued the polemic against the Jews begun by the Church Fathers. But a moderating trend did appear. The Church of this period did develop legislation which extended a measure of protection to Jews and their religion. While these laws provided some freedom from harassment, they were often breached on the popular level. Efforts at forced conversion were commonplace and these were generally carried out with impunity. In countries such as Spain it was not uncommon for worshippers to leave churches on Good Friday and stone Jews they might meet on the streets. And literature of the period began to depict Jews as "money-grubbing." Such portrayals were frequent in plays and novels.

The period of the Crusades proved especially difficult for Jews. Massacre often replaced mere harassment. False charges abounded (still reflected in village popular piety in some places in Europe) which accused Jews of poisoning wells and slaughtering Christian babies so that their blood could be used in the making of Jewish bread.

In 1215 the Fourth Lateran Council decreed that Jews were obligated to wear distinguishing badges and that they should reside only in certain restricted sections of a city. Though the term was still not in formal use, this legislation in fact laid the foundation for the later Jewish ghetto. In 1492 Jews were expelled from Spain where, for a brief golden age, they had achieved an unprecedented level of dialogue with Christians and Muslims in such cities as Toledo. Portugal followed suit five years later.

The Reformation in the sixteenth century did not usher in any significant improvements for Jews in terms of their social situation. Though Martin Luther initially courted Jewish leaders after his break with Rome, he eventually turned strongly against the Jewish community, authoring several anti-Semitic tracts that came to be admired greatly by the Nazis.

The birth of the modern era saw some improvements for Jews. Having been already accorded some limited civil protection and rights in Poland, they were now allowed a measure of equality in Germany and France. But this was often at the price of secularization and the destruction of communal identity. But new forms of anti-Semitism also emerged. The *Protocols of the Elders of Zion,* a forgery, became extremely popular in many circles. They described a purported Jewish cabal that was intent on controlling the world. And theories of inherent racial impurity began to arise. Jews quickly became prime targets of such theories. Nazism, which resulted in the annihilation of some six million European Jews, represented the most insidious example of such theories. But, while Nazism was qualitatively distinct from more classical forms of anti-Semitism which never advocated total Jewish annihilation, Christians cannot ignore the fact that the Nazis' choice of Jews as their primal targets had everything to do with the centuries of Jewish degradation commonplace in popular Christianity. And certainly classical anti-Semitism provided an indispensable seedbed for public cooperation with Hitler's so-called "Final Solution" to the Jewish question. Hitler himself made the connection explicit when, in responding to two bishops who had come to protest his treatment of the Jews, he said he was only putting into practice what the Church had been teaching for centuries. His great admiration of the Oberammergau passion play is yet another example of an awareness of clear linkage on his part.

While considerable strides have been made in eradicating anti-Semitism in recent decades, this social disease has not totally disappeared. Klan and other radical right groups continue to target Jews as well as African-Americans and Asian Americans. An upsurge of anti-Semitism is evident in parts of Western and Eastern Europe, even in areas where Nazism reduced the Jewish population to a tiny minority. *The Protocols of the Elders of Zion* continue to be distributed in certain circles, including religious ones (both Christian and Islamic).

But, despite the fact that we are still a considerable distance from the time when we can safely declare anti-Semitism as past history, the latter part of the twentieth century has witnessed the most thorough repudiation of its legitimacy from a faith perspective in the history of Christianity. Numerous Protestant denominations have released statements deploring anti-Semitism as unworthy of Christians. For Roman Catholics the major turning point occurred at Vatican Council II which in chapter four of its Declaration on Non-Christian Religions undercut the theological foundations for the classical *adversus Judaeos* tradition and went on to denounce anti-Semitism in explicit terms: ". . . the Church, mindful of the patrimony it shares with the Jews and moved not by political reasons but by the Gospel's spiritual love, decries hatred, persecutions, displays of anti-semitism directed against Jews at any time and by anyone." Subsequent documents from the Vatican such as the 1975 Instruction reaffirmed this condemnation of anti-Semitism: ". . . the spiritual bonds and historical links binding the Church to Judaism condemn (as opposed to the very spirit of Christianity) all forms of antisemitism." Other Church documents, including one from the Polish Episcopal Conference, have declared anti-Semitism a sin. Clearly we are on the road towards reversing the age-old support of anti-Semitism.

JOHN T. PAWLIKOWSKI, O.S.M.

See also HOLOCAUST (NAZI); JUDAISM; OBERAMMERGAU; VATICAN COUNCIL II.

APOCALYPSE

An apocalypse is a literary genre in which a seer is granted a revelation (*apokalypsis* in Greek) of the future and/or the heavenly realm. Since the content of the apocalypses is usually the "last things," it is customary also to use the adjective "apocalyptic" to refer to end-time or eschatological events or figures.

"The Opening of the Seals," Revelation 6, German manuscript, 12th century

The Books of Daniel and Revelation are (at least in part) apocalypses in the canon of Scripture. Within the Synoptic Gospels Jesus' final discourse (Matt 24–25, Mark 13, Luke 21) is sometimes called the "little" or "Synoptic" apocalypse. The most prominent Jewish apocalypses outside the canon are the books of Enoch, 4 Ezra, and 2 Baruch. There are apocalyptic elements in many of the Dead Sea Scrolls and early Christian works (Shepherd of Hermas).

DANIEL J. HARRINGTON, S.J.

See also ESCHATOLOGY.

APOCALYPTIC

See APOCALYPSE.

APOLOGETICS

(Gk. *apologia,* "a defense") In the present context, it refers to a reasoned defense of Christian belief or practice. This facet of theology is as old as the Church, but became an accepted independent, theological discipline only in recent centuries. From the beginning of the Christian era, apologists explained and defended Christian creedal positions. In the second century, there were many articulate apologists, such as Justin Martyr, author of *First Apology, Second Apology,* and *Dialogue with Trypho the Jew.* In the following centuries, we see Clement of Alexandria, Origen, Tertullian, and others playing the apologetical role. In the Middle Ages, the Christian apologists were mostly directed against Islam and Judaism. During the Reformation, apologetics became more polemical and remained so down to the Second Vatican Council. The need to explain and defend Christianity remains as pressing and pertinent as ever, even though the word "apologetics" has gone out of style.

JOSEPH QUINN

See also THEOLOGY, FUNDAMENTAL.

APOLOGIA PRO VITA SUA

See NEWMAN, JOHN HENRY, CARDINAL.

APOPHATIC THEOLOGY

Apophatic theology, also known as "negative" theology, teaches that all language is inadequate when speaking about God. Thus, all positive affirmations of God are only true in a qualified sense, and they need a negative rejoinder rejecting any notion that a certain aspect of God can be fully known or described. This approach is common in the Eastern Church, and it emphasizes wisdom over scientific or intellectual understanding of the nature of God. The reverse of apophatic is kataphatic/cataphatic which means approaching God through what we can know and experience.

ANTHONY D. ANDREASSI

See also KATAPHATIC/CATAPHATIC THEOLOGY; THEOLOGY, SYSTEMATIC.

APOSTASY

(Gk. "desertion") In the Old Testament, the term signifies disobedience to the Lord (Josh 22:22) or desertion from the Jewish faith (1 Macc 2:15). In the apostolic age, it was used to describe a baptized person's abandonment of the Christian faith (Heb 6:1-8), and was applied even against St. Paul when he was accused of rejecting the Mosaic Law (Acts 21:21). In modern Church usage, it refers to the total repudiation of the Christian faith by a baptized (or otherwise received) member of the Church. An apostate is subject to excommunication from the Church.

JOSEPH QUINN

See also EXCOMMUNICATION; FAITH.

APOSTLE

The term *apostle* is derived from the Greek verb *to send* and designates one who is sent out, normally as a commissioned messenger or ambassador. Prior to the NT it was used only occasionally to denote someone or something sent. It occurs only once in the Septuagint. In the NT, where it appears some seventy-nine times, *apostle* is used to refer to messengers in general, to Christ as God's special messenger, and to those sent specifically by the earthly Jesus, the risen Lord, or the Church to continue Jesus' mission on earth.

The term apostle can be used in the general sense of messenger. John's only use of the term is in this category: Jesus says, "Amen, amen, I say to you, no slave is greater than his master nor any messenger [*apostle*] greater than the one who sent him" (John 13:16).

In Hebrews 3:1, Jesus is referred to as "the apostle and high priest of our confession," i.e., God's special messenger.

The most common use of the term, however, is to designate those sent by the earthly Jesus, the risen Lord, or the Church to continue Jesus' mission on earth.

Pauline Letters

In the Pauline letters, where the term appears most frequently in the NT, *apostle* is used to refer to those sent out by local Churches, those falsely representing themselves as legitimate messengers of Christ, and as an important self-designation of Paul. After Paul mentions that Timothy is his partner and coworker he notes, "as for our brothers, they are apostles of the churches, the glory of Christ" (2 Cor 8:23). Paul acknowledges Epaphroditus as having been sent by the Philippians as their apostle to aid him in his imprisonment (Phil 2:25). And in Romans 16:7 Paul appears to refer to Andronicus and Junia as apostles. In 2 Corinthians, Paul refers to his opponents as "false apostles, deceitful workers, who masquerade as apostles of Christ" (2 Cor 11:13).

On numerous occasions, Paul stresses the fact that he is an apostle of Christ and associates his claim with the fact that he has seen the risen Lord, received from him a direct commission to preach the gospel, and functioned successfully as Christ's emissary (Gal 1:11ff.; 1 Cor 9:1-2; 15:3-11; Phil 3:12-16). For Paul, then, apostle meant primarily one who had seen the risen Lord Jesus and who had received from the Lord a commission to preach the Good News.

The Gospels and Acts

John uses the term only in a general sense (see above) and the only Markan use refers to the Twelve whom Jesus had sent out as missionaries (Mark 6:30). Luke uses *apostles* six times in the gospel (6:13; 9:10; 11:49; 17:5; 22:14; 24:10) and some twenty-eight times in Acts. It appears that in Acts 1:21-22 Luke is trying to limit the term both numerically and temporally. The apostles are twelve in number and are made up of those who have been with Jesus from the baptism of John until Jesus' ascension. While the Twelve are apostles (Luke 6:13), Luke did not intend to reserve the title *apostles* exclusively to the Twelve. Unlike Matthew, whose only use of the term refers to the *twelve apostles* (Matt 10:2; Rev 21:14), neither Luke nor Acts uses this phrase. And in Acts, both Paul and Barnabas are unambiguously referred to as apostles (Acts 14:4, 14).

Matthew's reference to the *twelve apostles* (Matt 10:2) reflects the interests of the Church late in the first century, when a desire to legitimate the authentic tradition of the Church against false teachers led to an emphasis on the original guardians of the tradition and their official successors.

Later NT and Early Christian Writings

Revelation 2:2 and the Didache 11.3-6 testify to the immediate ineffectiveness of such attempts at setting numerical and temporal limits. At the very end of the first century one reads about "those who call themselves apostles but are not" (Rev 2:2). And at the beginning of the second century the Didache speaks about the treatment that should be accorded apostles: "Act in line with the gospel precept. Welcome every apostle on arriving, as if he were the Lord. But he must not stay beyond one day. In case of necessity, however, the next day too. If he stays three days he is a false prophet. On departing, an apostle must not accept anything save sufficient food to carry him till his next lodging" (Did 11.3-6).

DENNIS SWEETLAND

See also BIBLE, NEW TESTAMENT WRITINGS; CRITICISM, BIBLICAL; EVANGELIZATION.

APOSTLES' CREED

See CREEDS.

APOSTOLATE OF PRAYER

This organization is heir to the League of the Sacred Heart founded in France in 1844. The group fosters devotion to the Sacred Heart and calls for concerted prayer for a specific monthly intention which is published in its magazine, the *Messenger of the Sacred Heart.*

DAVID BRYAN

See also DEVOTIONS; SACRED HEART OF JESUS.

APOSTOLIC CHURCHES

See APOSTOLIC SUCCESSION; MARKS (OR NOTES) OF THE CHURCH.

APOSTOLIC CONSTITUTION

An apostolic constitution is an ecclesiastical legislative document issued by the pope himself. It treats foundational questions in Church life and practice. The *Sacrae Disciplinae Leges* (25 January 1983), which promulgated the 1983 Code of Canon Law is a prime example of an apostolic constitution. The official texts of apostolic constitutions are published in the *Acta Apostolicae Sedis.*

The apostolic constitutions (plural) is a collection of ecclesiastical law dating from the second half of the fourth century. The full title is *Ordinances of the Holy Apostles through Clement.* The work is a valuable source of information on the religious practices and beliefs of its time.

PATRICIA DeFERRARI

See also ACTA APOSTOLICAE SEDIS; CANON LAW.

APOSTOLIC DELEGATE

The pope's representative having certain supervisory duties over the Church in a particular region or nation. Developing candidates for the episcopacy is a typical concern, but the mandate of each apostolic delegate is unique. In many countries the delegate also has diplomatic status.

DAVID BRYAN

See also PAPACY, THE; PROVINCE.

APOSTOLIC FATHERS, THE

This term was created in 1672 by the scholar J. B. Cotelier to describe five early Christian writers, Barnabas, Clement of Rome, Hermas, Ignatius of Antioch, and Polycarp of Smyrna; later generations of scholars added to this the *Letter to Diognetus,* the *Martyrdom of Polycarp,* and the fragments of Papias' writings; they also distinguished Clement's authentic letter from a homily attributed to him, with the former being labeled 1 Clement and the latter 2 Clement. After its discovery in 1883 the Didache joined the list. The term was intended to cover those writers who lived immediately after the Apostolic Age or who, in some cases, were contemporaneous with it. The term also refers only to orthodox writers and does not include any Gnostic authors. The doctrinal content of these writings is rather thin compared to other Fathers, such as Athanasius or Gregory of Nyssa, but their pastoral content is often high and their historical value is immense. They offer a valuable witness to the life of the earliest Church, especially in Rome and the Eastern Mediterranean.

Clement of Rome

Clement of Rome wrote an epistle to the Church at Corinth ca. 95 in a fraternal attempt to heal a developing schism between older and younger members. Although later papal apologists claimed that this letter proves Rome's early intervention in the affairs of other Churches, Clement did not write in his own name but in that of the Roman community. (Only from references by other ancient writers do scholars know his name.) Clement may have been Jewish; he knows the Septuagint and cites the Old Testament frequently. He alludes to pagan notions, for example, the phoenix as a type of the resurrection, and scholars have found Stoic elements in this thought, an early indication that the Church was opening up to the world.

Clement's epistle is known as the First Epistle of Clement to the Corinthians to distinguish it from a second-century homily known as the *Second Epistle of Clement to the Corinthians,* an erroneous title and attribution, dating from the fourth century and now too well established to be abandoned. The homily is short and simple, urging Christians to virtue and even, if necessary, martyrdom. It also says that the Church preexisted the sun and moon but was called into full being by Jesus Christ. As the earliest extant Christian sermon outside the New Testament, it is a text of great value.

Ignatius of Antioch

Ignatius of Antioch was condemned to the beasts in Rome ca. 112. On his journey there, he wrote seven letters, five to Christian communities in Asia Minor, one to Rome, and a personal one to his fellow-bishop Polycarp of Smyrna. Ignatius described a situation in Antioch in which the community was rent by Judaizers who insisted the Christians follow the Jewish Law and by Docetists, Gentile converts who hoped to protect Christ's divinity by denying that the Son of God ever had a physical body but rather claimed that he had a phantom body. Ignatius was unable to win these groups over, so he decided that the bishop (*episkopos*), whose functions were hitherto uncertain, would be the leader of the community and the source of unity. He compares the bishop to Christ, who appoints the bishop; without the bishop there is no local Church. This organization, apparently unique to Antioch at the time, foreshadowed the monarchical episcopate so familiar from the late second century onward. Ignatius highly praised martyrdom; "to be near the sword is to be near God" (*Smyrneans* 4.2). He also had a strong mystical bent, stressing the possibility of spiritual unity with God, which should be reflected in the spiritual unity of the Church.

Polycarp of Smyrna

Polycarp of Smyrna (d. ca. 156), a city in Asia Minor, wrote an extant epistle to the Philippians, which is actually a cover letter for his collection of Ignatius' letters, but which shows a solid knowledge of the New Testament. Of greater interest is an account of the bishop's martyrdom, called simply the *Martyrdom of Polycarp,* written by one Marcion of Smyrna to the community of Philomelium. It is a vigorous, picturesque narrative with an unforgettable portrait of the aged (eighty-six years old) Polycarp standing firm against the pagans, even to his death at the stake.

Epistle of Barnabas

The *Epistle of Barnabas* dates ca. 130 and deals with the allegorical interpretation of the Bible in opposition to literalist Jewish exegesis; the pseudonymous author (not Paul's companion as Eastern tradition claimed) can thus find references to Christ in the Old Testament which he says is now a Christian book. This work shares the moral teaching of the Didache, that is, there are the Two Ways, one of light and one of darkness. It may be from Alexandria.

Epistle to Diognetus

The *Epistle to Diognetus* dates to the early second century; it is an apology for Christianity, which attacks paganism and Judaism and presents an attractive if idealized view of the faith. Diognetus is unknown, and the name may be symbolic since it means "one who knows God" in Greek; the work is from the eastern Mediterranean.

Didache

The Didache was first published in 1883 by the Greek Metropolitan of Nicomedia, Philotheos Bryennios; he had found it in a Jerusalem parchment. The book's primitive Church order (wandering prophets are a regular feature of the community) caused scholars to date it as early as A.D. 50. Scholarly opinion now dates it to the mid-second century and assumes that it emerged from a Syrian community which had developed little from the first century. Its moral teaching is rather simple and straightforward; given its early date, the liturgical sections are of great value.

Papias of Hierapolis

Papias of Hierapolis in Asia Minor (d. ca. 110) was a millenarian, that is, he believed in an earthly kingdom to be established by Christ. The Church historian Eusebius of Caesarea called him a man of little intelligence, and the few extant fragments of his work do not contradict that view. These fragments do, however, provide a glimpse of early second-century Christianity; for example, Polycarp still prefers oral traditions about Jesus to written ones, proof that the transition from such traditions to the Gospels was not complete at the time.

Shepherd of Hermas

The *Shepherd of Hermas* is the largest work of the Apostolic Fathers; Hermas was a Jewish Christian who wrote in Rome ca. 150. This visionary work tells of apparitions to Hermas by an angel of penance who appears as a shepherd (hence the book's title) and also by the Church, personified as an old woman who gets progressively younger. The book testifies to the continuation of apocalyptic notions in the Church and to the possibility if not the actual practice of a second penance after baptism, a position opposed by rigorists. The many visions in the book had some influence on Christian imagery, most importantly on the view of the Church as a woman.

The Apostolic Fathers have always commanded the attention of patristic scholars, but, as scholars date several New Testament books into the first decades of the second century, the Apostolic Fathers play a continually greater role in biblical studies.

JOSEPH F. KELLY

See also APOSTOLIC SUCCESSION; FATHERS OF THE CHURCH.

APOSTOLIC PENITENTIARY

This tribunal within the Roman Curia has jurisdiction only in the "internal forum," i.e., situations where the privacy of the individual is protected by the strictest "seal" of secrecy. This includes, but is by no means limited to, the sacrament of reconciliation. The tribunal grants absolutions, dispensations, commutations of penances, sanations (validations), and condonations. It also decides questions of conscience. The regulation of indulgences (but not doctrinal questions regarding them) are also within its competency.

DAVID BRYAN

See also CONSCIENCE; CURIA, ROMAN; SACRAMENT OF RECONCILIATION.

APOSTOLIC SIGNATURA

This tribunal within the Roman Curia is a sort of supreme court of the Church. It settles questions of juridical procedure, and the competencies of lower courts, while guarding rights and laws in general; it has supervision of the Roman Rota.

DAVID BRYAN

See also CURIA, ROMAN.

APOSTOLIC SUCCESSION

The doctrine refers to the historical continuity between the present state of the Christian Church and its origins in Jesus and in the college of the apostles. In the Creed, the Church confesses itself to be apostolic. This consciousness of its apostolicity is already affirmed in Ephesians 2:20: "You form a building which rises on the foundation of the apostles and prophets, with Christ Jesus himself as the capstone."

Apostolic Succession in the Ministry of the Apostles

In Roman Catholic teaching, this apostolicity of the Church expresses itself in the formal connection between the episcopate of today and the apostles, that is, in the unbroken ministerial succession of bishops in the Church. *Lumen Gentium* teaches that "the bishops have by divine institution taken the place of the apostles as pastors of the Church" (no. 24). In the early Church, this apostolic succession was used as an argument against heretics and schismatics. Clement of Rome wrote to the Corinthians who had expelled some of their *episcopoi,* urging them to restore these men to their rightful positions on the ground that they had been installed in office according to a pattern of succession in ministry that was apostolic in origin. Against the Gnostics who claimed to possess a secret knowledge, Irenaeus argued that the authentic teaching of the apostles was to be found in the Churches of apostolic origin and in those to whom the apostles had entrusted the care of their Churches. He then proceeded to draw up succession lists of bishops, especially for Rome. Later, Tertullian argued against the heretics that they had no right to prove their teachings from the Scriptures because the Scriptures are the property of the apostolic Churches. In post-Reformation times, the Catholic Church rejected the validity of the orders of the Anglican and Protestant Churches because of their alleged lack of apostolic succession.

Apostolic Succession of the Whole Church in Apostolic Faith and Witness

In recent ecumenical dialogues between Roman Catholics and Christians of other Churches, it has widely been recognized that the notion of apostolic succession as unbroken link between the bishops and the apostles through the imposition of hands, though legitimate, is unduly narrow. Apostolic succession of the episcopal ministry is now seen as an element of the apostolic tradition that the *whole* Church receives from the apostles. As the Lima Document *Baptism, Eucharist and Ministry* puts it, "apostolic tradition in the Church means continuity in the permanent characteristics of the Church of the apostles: witness to the apostolic faith, proclamation and fresh interpretation of the Gospel, celebration of baptism and eucharist, the transmission of ministerial responsibilities, communion in prayer, love, joy and suffering, service to the sick and the needy, unity among the local churches and sharing the gifts which the Lord has given to each" (no. 34). In this perspective, mutual recognition of the ordained ministries may be a possible goal of ecumenical endeavors.

PETER C. PHAN

See also BISHOP; CHURCH, THE.

APOSTOLICITY

See MARKS (OR NOTES) OF THE CHURCH.

APPARITIONS

An apparition is the visible appearance of a supernatural being who is normally inaccessible to human senses. Apparitions of Jesus, Mary, angels, and saints have been reported throughout Christian history.

One of the most famous apparitions took place in Lourdes, France, in 1858. There, the Blessed Virgin Mary appeared several times to a fourteen-year-old girl named Bernadette Soubirous. At the site of the apparitions, a spring welled up, and soon after, the spring was reported to have miraculous healing powers; Lourdes has since become a place of pilgrimage. In 1862 the Church officially recognized the site, and the feast of Our Lady of Lourdes was observed by the universal Church from 1907 to 1969.

There are several other famous instances of apparitions, including appearances of Mary in Guadalupe, Mexico, and at Fatima, in Portugal. Most recently, Mary is said to appear frequently in Medjugorie, a town in the former Yugoslavia.

For the most part, the Church reserves judgment concerning the nature and truth of any particular apparition. In many cases, the Church itself will make no official pronouncement but will allow the local Catholic magisterium, under the leadership of the bishop, to test the truth of and respond most appropriately to reports of apparitions. In all events, however, that an event is supernatural in origin is not to be presumed; rather, it must be proved.

Though significant for piety and devotion, apparitions play a small role in Catholic theology as a whole. They are understood merely as aids to the worship of God, from whom all such supernatural graces are derived. Further, they may never be seen as contradicting or replacing God's revelation in the person and life of Jesus.

THERESA SANDERS

See also FATIMA; GUADALUPE; KNOCK SHRINE; LOURDES.

ARAMAIC

"Aramaic" refers to a cluster of Semitic languages spoken in Palestine in the time of Jesus. It is derived from Aram, the Hebrew name for ancient Syria. Many places in the New Testament reflect the Aramaic background of the writers. In some cases, the Aramaic words themselves are preserved, e.g., Mark 5:41; 7:34; 15:34. Households in Ma'lula and a few other Christian villages of the Anti-Lebanon continue to use a modern form of Aramaic much influenced by the Arabic spoken in the area.

PATRICIA DeFERRARI

ARCHANGEL

See ANGELS.

ARCHBISHOP

A bishop who presides over an archdiocese (the principal see of an ecclesiastical province, constituting one or more dioceses), and is held to be the authoritative teacher of the faith in his region. He has the prerogative to call the bishops of his archdiocese to a provincial council, and also may consider an appeal concerning a decision made by one of his bishops.

JOSEPH QUINN

See also HIERARCHY.

ARCHITECTURE, CHURCH

Public buildings are often referred to by the same name as the particular group of people who use them and/or by the purpose for which they use them. A "church" may be defined as a building designed or adapted for and dedicated to the public worship of the community of believers known as the Church. For the Catholic Church, this is primarily the communal celebration of liturgical rites, most especially the Eucharist and other sacraments, by which they both become and continue as the visible society of the Church. Though each baptized person is a "spiritual temple," the presence of Christ dwelling within is manifested "where two or more are gathered" in his name and it is for this gathering in communion of worship that churches are built. Everything from the location to the size, style, form, and ornamentation of the structure of a church is ultimately designed with this purpose in mind; and the development of these material aspects in church architecture through the centuries reflects something of the theological, ecclesial, and liturgical practice or mind-set of those by whom churches were built. In their construction, the social, political, and economic circumstances of the day have a significant effect as well.

First through Third Centuries

In the first days of its existence, the Christian community was primarily Jewish. They continued to go to the Temple for the "prayers," and then gathered in private homes for the specifically Christian aspects of their communal religious life: baptism, sharing the teaching of the apostles, and "the breaking of the bread." Finding themselves excluded from the Temple, and growing to include increasingly larger numbers of Gentiles, the Church continued to meet in available rooms/homes, adapted for use in their developing liturgy. In these early years, eschatological expectations of Christ's imminent return would make building superfluous, even if it was possible. Though such expectations decreased in intensity, decades of persecutions of varying ferocity kept any architectural development largely limited to a pictorial vocabulary of symbols and images decorating the worship space and expressing the faith of the community. In Rome, similar iconography is found in the catacombs: a labyrinth of underground burial places for martyrs and other holy men and women, whose lives bore witness to the faith and whose memory encouraged the community to persevere to the final victory. Commemorative gatherings in the catacombs mark an early development of the cult of the saints which will be influential in the development of church architecture some centuries later.

Fourth through Eighth Centuries

With the conversion of Constantine, the Church found official acceptance and emerged from the catacombs and domestic churches. The first "churches" appeared, for the most part, in existing public buildings given over to and adapted for worship. Though there were others, the most common form of structure used was the basilica, a large municipal building used by the Romans for legal, commercial, and social gathering. The form was essentially a rectangle, bordered on the long sides with side aisles formed by columns; entered through a narthex (vestibule) on one end and having a large, half-domed semicircular area (apse) on the other end. Roman engineering expertise allowed the use of wide, spacious arches and high cross-vaulted ceilings (the Basilica Nova in Rome rose 114 feet above the floor), which made the larger basilicas very imposing structures. Meanwhile, St. Helena, the mother of Constantine, journeyed to the Holy Land and began the process of erecting shrine churches on those sites associated in the memory of the people with the life of Christ and the early Church.

These two threads, the use of the basilica with its large unified space which was eminently practical for the Eucharistic assembly, and the enclosure of relics or pilgrimage sites with buildings designed for that purpose, laid a foundation for later architectural developments—but the barbarian incursions which led to the collapse of the Roman order by 476 postponed significant growth in church building in the West for several centuries.

In the East, however, the establishment of the new city of Constantinople expressed not only the power and stability of imperial rule there, but a whole new order: a rich, stable, centralized, and spiritualized society, where the secular and ecclesiastical authorities exercised different functions within the same sacred order. With this new order came new building concepts to match, leading to the erection of one of the world's greatest churches. Built in the sixth century under the patronage of the emperor Justinian, in what came to be known as the Byzantine style, the church of Hagia Sophia (Holy Wisdom) is a work of architectural genius whose design remains the basis for Orthodox churches to the present day. The vast, wide-rounded dome seems to convey the transcendent majesty of heaven descending to earth, floating on a circle of light provided by the ring of high windows beneath the dome. With no visible supports, and the structural elements unified by the light and the lavish color of mosaic coverings, the church was designed as an organic whole dedicated to a single theological truth revealed by the light of wisdom: Christ reigns over all, and has established an unchanging divine order in the world. Rather than a decorative element or a mere portrayal of any person or event, the icon (and in a sense, the entire structure was an icon) was a means of access to the divine presence, a means to the experience of God. Neither the celebration of these sacred mysteries in the liturgy, nor the architectural ideal which housed and enhanced it would change for a thousand years. Byzantine influences in the West flowed from the imperial center at Ravenna in Italy, and eventually through the returning Crusaders, lasting even long after the fall of Constantinople in 1453 and the conversion of Hagia Sophia and her sister churches to mosques. With variations in scale and material (the use of wood instead of stone, for instance), the orthodox style spread to and continued in Russia.

Ninth through Eleventh Centuries

In the West, with civil rule in constant flux until Charlemagne and the establishment of the Holy Roman Empire (A.D. 800), religious authority took on much more strength and autonomy than in the East. With the social and economic instability of the Dark Ages, churches were built not by bishops or parishes but by monastic orders. With the liturgical reform of Gregory the Great (A.D. 540–604), there began a "shift in concept of what a 'church' was" (Howard Saalman, *Medieval Architecture,* New York: George Braziller, 1967, p. 17), and with it, architectural modification which became known as the Carolingian renewal. The establishment of the Holy Roman Empire brought about the consolidation of feudalism and the dominance of Benedictine monasticism. The new empire looked back to the order and stability of the Roman Empire, and fostered the adoption of the Benedictine Rule which had been written in the sixth century using the ordered patterns of the Roman family ideal. As in the East, a divinely inspired ordering of society is perceived, though in the West the civil and ecclesiastical authorities function within separate, defined spheres. Architecture too looked back to Rome and to the early Church there. The basic basilica began to develop into what became known as "Romanesque." The old Roman basilica form of a unified building with the single purpose of forward movement and communal unity gradually became a sequence of spatial units delineating a hierarchical (feudal) order. Small side chambers widen into transepts to accommodate crypts and reliquaries as the cult of the saints is revived. The church, now a cruciform structure, rises on massive piers with rounded arches to vaulted ceilings with a three-story elevation of arcade, gallery, and clerestory. In accord with the feudal system, the church becomes more a royal "House of God," a material homage, than a "house for the Church" as a people. By the eleventh century, when the secular clergy (bishops) and their noble patrons can begin to afford to construct cathedrals, the Church itself has become feudal, with Christ portrayed as the overlord, the apostles as vassals, and so on. In liturgy as in society, status, authority and participation are vested in clear sequential units of privilege and obligation—with the laity, as the serfs, having no real role, and the assembly being further and further divided from the mysteries of the sanctuary by the addition of chancel screen, choir, etc. They can, however, participate actively in devotional practices such as the pilgrimage to a shrine; and the growth of such practices leads to architectural additions of ambulatories, side chapels, and crypt chapels. Belfries grew into the towers of various shapes which became characteristic of the Romanesque style, often twin towers with a "wheel window" set between them. Sculpture and arcading displayed decorative genius, with stylized figures and designs proportioned for the available space rather than a realistic human scale. Wonderful regional variations developed, since the Holy Roman Empire was in fact centered in Germany, and the peoples of Western Europe had formed into separate nations by the end of the twelfth century.

Twelfth through Sixteenth Centuries

With the Abbey of St. Denis (1145) and the cathedral of Chartres (1150) seen as proto-Gothic, the Romanesque evolves into Gothic first of all in France, and French influence remained paramount until the beginning of the thirteenth century. Until the Reformation, liturgy remained essentially unchanged and there was therefore no pressing reason to change the basic architectural design of churches. There was however movement toward emphasis on complex ceremonials, on symbolism, mysticism, and the spiritual which was accompanied by growth in technical capabilities (and in wealth) with which to express it. In architecture, a sense of heavenly aspiration and exaltation could be achieved through increasing verticality, accomplished through the mastery of the pointed arch and ribbed vault, the development of flying buttresses which provided external support and allowed piercing of wall with many traceried windows. The windows were soon filled with the vibrant color of stained glass to give an overall effect of soaring beauty. The great Gothic cathedrals were built by experts, in the style of an emergent urban capitalism—a display of the wealth and power of the hierarchy of the Church and the nobility, which was often one and the same. Built in honor of beliefs and aspirations rather than need for worship space, Gothic churches are full of symbolism evoking the transcendent order and majesty of God, the mathematical perfection of creation. For the illiterate masses, they were sermons carved in stone; for the Church, like jeweled caskets to house spiritual treasure. In every aspect, the focus is on "seeing": viewing relics, viewing the Host from a distance (at the elevation of the Mass or in the now centrally placed tabernacle), viewing the extensive carvings and vast windows—even viewing the church itself from a distance as spires and pinnacles rose from the roof and towers. In fact, by the beginning of the fourteenth century, there is so little common participation in worship, that many of the faithful will receive Communion only as viaticum. The Gothic style remained dominant in the building of churches until the sixteenth century when it collided with the Renaissance and the Reformation.

Sixteenth through Nineteenth Centuries

In the sixteenth century, the Council of Trent responded to the Protestant Reformation at least in part by reforming the liturgy, deleting most of the medieval accretions and establishing the restored rites in a rigid body of rubrics. The Counter Reformation emphasis on the triumphal glory of the Church, on clerical discipline and on preaching, came about in Italy within the context of the Renaissance: a "rebirth of ancient Roman culture," when artists, patrons, and scholars were filled with a spirit of admiration and emulation of classical ideals. In Italy, still rich in Roman monuments, and where the Gothic style had never taken firm root, building turned back to classical clarity and order. The hall-like structures better enabled the people to see and hear the preacher; scholarly exploration of classical philosophy and of geometry as a demonstration of absolute truth, led to the use of great symmetry and the "perfect figure" of the circle in the form of the dome. Though classic Roman style was an ideal, a precedent, other elements (new building methods, different modes of living, a different self-view for the Church) made the Renaissance church distinct from either the classic Roman or the Romanesque. Proportions returned to a harmonious human scale and calm serenity, with statues no longer an integral part of the structure, and with fresco replacing stained glass as the source of color. A compound style employing a variety of influences (including the Byzantine), the early Renaissance moved in progressive combinations which quickly evolved into the Baroque. The original church of Constantine, for instance, was torn down by Pope Julius II (amidst some controversy), and a new church begun which, by the time it was finished had already moved from the initially sober classical style to include much of the vivid and intense decorative extravagance of Mannerists such as Michelangelo and Bernini.

Outside of Italy, the Renaissance fascination with antiquity did not really gain popularity until Mannerism had already evolved into the Baroque style in the seventeenth and eighteenth centuries. Retaining the architectural form of classical buildings, the Baroque period moved toward a grand, robust use of all the arts for dramatic effect. Art and illusion transported one into the visionary world of holy mysteries, with the emphasis moving away from the medieval focus on the wages of sin toward portraying the drama of redemption and potential for salvation in eternity. With a proliferation of new feasts established, the cult of the already victorious saints formed the center of Baroque spirituality, making it an overwhelmingly Catholic style contrasting sharply with Protestant austerity. In a subsequent phase called Rococo, the elaborate decorativeness became progressively more refined and subtle.

Church of St. Columba, St. Paul, Minnesota

The eighteenth century brought the usual swing of the pendulum, with an appreciative glance back—once again—to ancient Rome and greater simplicity. However, where the Gothic, Renaissance, and Baroque styles were to some extent expressions of religious experience and particular attitudes toward doctrine, the Neo-classicism of the eighteenth and nineteenth centuries was more a stylistic development: not so much expressing belief or accommodating worship as selecting a style of building from an existing repertoire according to current tastes. Churches and secular buildings all looked the same. The plan for Washington, D.C., included a "national pantheon or church" which was converted into the national patent office and is now a portrait gallery. Secular influences like scientific excavation of ruins made Greek revival particularly popular and its simplicity made it the first really Protestant style. In the late eighteenth and early nineteenth centuries nearly every small town in New England built itself a church with classical portico, two rows of columns, and a steeple. In earlier colonial periods, churches built in the New World varied greatly in style depending on the means, skill, and national origin of the settlers. The nineteenth century saw mostly restorations and revivals, the strongest of which became the Gothic revival. Referring back to nostalgic views of the medieval "age of faith," this in itself was a response of faith to the challenges of intellectual and scientific development, a romantic disenchantment with the materialistic culture of an industrial society. Still, all this was the work of an elite few, with the majority of the faithful involved only in the financing. By the dawn of the twentieth century, however, significant change was on the horizon, in budding liturgical reform and church architecture.

Twentieth Century

The publication of missals for the people, in French by the Abbey of Maredsous (1882) and in German by the Abbey of Beuron (1884), were examples of (and stimulations to) changing attitudes about liturgy and the laity. In the first decade of the twentieth century, Pope Pius X began to stress "active participation in the Sacred Mysteries and in the public and solemn prayer of the Church" (Jovian Lang, O.F.M., *Dictionary of the Liturgy,* New York: Catholic Book Publishing Co., 1989) and urged frequent, even daily, reception of Communion. With this renewed sense of the part of the Christian assembly in worship, the foundations were laid for the liturgical reforms of Vatican II—and for a new cycle of questions and challenges in the design of church buildings and furnishing. It was not a matter of moving focus away from giving glory to God, but of rethinking how God is glorified: is it in the transcendent splendor of the building, or in the communal worship of the people? If the latter, how can the space, the environment in which they gather, contribute to, enhance, the liturgical activity, the sense of prayerful participation? What do we do in church, why and how and in what sort of order? Do we put the focus on bringing every resource of art and imagery to glorify God, or on the Church as assembly with the idea that any building will do, or somewhere in the selective in-between? The questions of how we understand the nature of the Church and her liturgical life, and therefore the purpose of a church building, is intimately connected with the architectural design. The Sacrament reserved in the tabernacle, for instance, (initially done so as to be available for the sick whenever needed) is a special sign of presence encouraging beauty and intimacy in personal piety—but is this the primary purpose of a church building? If it is not, if the primary purpose is active communal worship ("the prayers and the breaking of bread" among a community "of one mind and heart"), then should the design of a church perhaps be more conducive to the sense of sharing a meal, of praying together, with elements assisting private devotion (tabernacle, statues, etc.) placed with reverent care in somewhat less than central positions? This is one of a myriad of similar questions. Since the beginnings of the Modern movement in the 1940s, with its new materials, technical advances and growing liturgical/ecclesial questions, there have been fresh, previously untried solutions of bewildering variety presented. In the postconciliar age of liturgical reform, there continues to be a great deal of vigorous, healthy debate about these and many other related issues, as older churches are renovated and new ones built. Painful as the process can be at times, with different groups wanting to halt or hasten change, the wonder of it is that it is a sign of flourishing life, of the dynamic relationship between the Church and the living God she seeks and meets in worship—and architecture as the art form which perhaps most contributes to her life as a "visible society" of the faithful.

IRENE MOYNIHAN

See also EUCHARIST; LITURGICAL MOVEMENT, THE; LITURGY; SACRAMENTS OF INITIATION.

ARIANISM

See HERESY/HERETICS.

ARISTOTELIANISM

The philosophical system of the Greek philosopher Aristotle (384–322 B.C.) teaches that human knowledge is achieved primarily through sense experience. The highest form of intellectual inquiry is metaphysics where one studies "being" or existence itself. Next comes the study of the changing world of existing things, and this world is composed of both matter and form. Matter is eternal and uncreated, and the forms are the internal principles which determine what a thing is. A form can be likened to the "soul" of an existing thing. The material world undergoes change when matter takes on a new form. Human knowledge comes from sense experience, and Aristotelian epistemology explains the acquisition of knowledge through the mechanics of "active" and "passive" human intellectualization. It holds that the human person has free will. God is understood as thinking or thought itself, although Aristotle himself probably did not think of God as a personal being who created the universe.

Aristotelianism achieved great influence in the Middle Ages in the hands of creative Arabic, Jewish, and Christian thinkers. In the thirteenth century St. Albert the Great and his student, St. Thomas Aquinas, "baptized" and assimilated much of the thought of Aristotle for Christianity, changing parts of it but using much of it to create the Christian philosophical and theological school of thought known as Scholasticism.

ANTHONY D. ANDREASSI

See also PHILOSOPHY AND THEOLOGY; SCHOLASTICISM; THOMAS AQUINAS, ST.; THOMISM.

ARISTOTLE (384/3–322 B.C.)

A Greek philosopher (384/3–322 B.C.). A student of Plato, he did not share his master's idealism and founded a rival school at the Lycaeum where the emphasis was laid on biology rather than mathematics. Whereas Plato held that only the immutable and universal "ideas" or "forms" exist as real, Aristotle asserted that an idea exists only as expressed in the individual object. Only the individual object is real, composed of "form" and "matter." This composition of matter and form led Aristotle to postulate the existence of the "First Cause" who is the "Unmoved Mover" or Pure Act (God). In the early centuries of the Christian era, Aristotle's philosophy was regarded with suspicion largely because it seemed to lead to a materialistic view of the world. However, in the twelfth century, as many of his works were translated into Latin, his thought became better known. The initial hostility to his philosophy began to decrease as theologians such as St. Albert the Great and St. Thomas Aquinas made use of it to elaborate Christian theology. Since then Aristotelianism exercised a profound influence upon Catholic philosophy and theology.

PETER C. PHAN

See also ARISTOTELIANISM; PHILOSOPHY AND THEOLOGY; SCHOLASTICISM.

ARRUPE, PEDRO, S.J. (1907–1991)

Pedro Arrupe was the twenty-eighth superior general (1965–1983) in the 450-year history of the Society of Jesus (Jesuits). The first Basque to lead the Jesuits since their founder, Ignatius of Loyola, Arrupe was born 14 November 1907 in Bilbao, Spain, and entered the Society of Jesus in 1927. When the Spanish government expelled the Jesuits in 1932, Arrupe continued his studies in Belgium, Holland, and the United States. He was ordained a priest in Belgium in 1936.

Pedro Arrupe, S.J.

The next twenty-seven years, from 1938 to 1965, were spent in Japan where he had longed to serve as a missionary. After learning the language he served as a parish priest, director of novices, and then as the first provincial of the Province of Japan. While serving as director of novices near Hiroshima, he experienced the first atomic bomb in 1945, and cared for many sick and dying. It was an experience which marked him for the rest of his life.

His generalate, from 1965 to 1983, coincided with a period of renewal in the Church and in society in general. He led the Jesuit Order through a time of great challenges and opportunities but also of great upheaval when many traditional values, including the basics and future of religious life were questioned and doubted. His guiding principle was the mandate of Vatican II for all religious congregations. This involved a continuous return to the original inspiration of the founder as well as an openness to the signs of the times. For him adaptation and renewal in religious life were to be linked to an effective apostolate in a world of unbelief and injustice. During his entire generalate he worked for adaptation and renewal in the Society of Jesus, beginning in Rome and then taking it on the road to Jesuits all over the world. Arrupe had come face to face with the dehumanizing poverty that afflicts a vast part of the human race and was convinced that religious faith, to be true to itself, had to be vigorous in promoting justice and in opposing injustice, oppression, and social evils such as poverty, hunger, and all forms of racial discrimination. For him, Christ was suffering and dying again in the poor and oppressed.

Arrupe's dream was to unite all the spiritual and apostolic strength of the Jesuits in one mission that would serve the Church and the human family. When the thirty-second General Congregation (its highest legislative body) defined the mission of Jesuits as the service of faith and the promotion of justice in the name of the gospel, Arrupe was delighted.

His influence extended far beyond the Jesuit Order so that he became the spokesman for religious life in the Church. A state of tension developed in 1980 between Arrupe and Pope John Paul II. In August 1981 Arrupe suffered a debilitating stroke and John Paul II named a Jesuit as his personal delegate to direct the Society of Jesus. In September 1983 Father Arrupe's resignation was accepted by the thirty-third General Congregation and his successor, Father Peter-Hans Kolvenbach was elected. For the next ten years Arrupe's days were spent in patient and silent suffering and prayer until his death on 5 February 1991. He was acclaimed as the second Ignatius of Loyola. His three loves were Jesus Christ, the Church, and the Society of Jesus.

VINCENT O'KEEFE, S.J.

See also SOCIETY OF JESUS; VATICAN COUNCIL II.

ART, CHRISTIAN

Sacred art has provided a source of inspiration for the Christian community from early days in its history. The third century "house church" at Dura Europos (in present-day Syria), a neighborhood home renovated for the liturgical needs of the local community, included wall paintings. The baptismal room of this house contains one of the earliest images of Christ, a scene of Christ's *Healing of the Paralytic.* The wall painting at Dura Europos is no mere "illustration" of a biblical text, but rather an image that breaks open for the believer something of the awesome power of baptism. The healing of the paralytic took place at a pool by one of the Jerusalem gates and was a demonstration of the forgiveness of sin. Since in baptism sinners are forgiven, this healing scene is appropriate for a baptistery, visually establishing the link between baptism and healing and forgiveness.

Early Christian art served the assembly of believers by providing insight into the more profound truths of the faith. Narrative illustration was seldom the purpose. There was always a deeper point to be made. For this reason images of Christ were never portraits of what he looked like. Instead they tell us something about who he was, what kind of a person he was. It is perhaps surprising to us that among the many Roman catacomb paintings beginning in the late second century, there are no representations of the crucifixion; in fact none appears until the fifth century, and then they are of the live Christ of the resurrection. Among the most frequent representations was Christ as Good Shepherd, reminding the believer that Christ is the pastor who looks after his flock in all times and places. In times of persecution of the Christian community, it was important to have images that reminded the people of God's fidelity, God's presence. Representations of the moments when God intervened to save the Israelites, such as Moses striking the rock in the desert, Noah and the ark, or the crossing of the Red Sea reminded the Christians of God's fidelity through all the generations of their ancestors, reassuring them that God would continue to be present to them.

Christ the Pantocrator, mosaic, Palatine Chapel, Palermo

The prohibition of "graven images" in the second commandment left a legacy of hesitancy about images, especially statues. Reflection on the fact that God had become visible when Christ took on human nature at his birth gradually broke down the barriers against sacred images. Eastern Christians adopted the practice of the veneration of images in the form of icons with greater enthusiasm than did Western Christians. The veneration of icons led to the bitter Iconoclastic Controversy (A.D. 726–842). At the end of over a century of debate, the acceptance of icons prevailed, to a great extent based on the principle that any devotion to an image in reality passed beyond the image to the saint to whom the image referred. The Eastern Christian Church (the Orthodox Churches) today retains a strong devotion to icons and their veneration is an important part of the liturgy. Examples of important icons include images of the Virgin and of St. Peter from the monastery at Mt. Sinai in the sixth century, the *Virgin of Vladimir* from the twelfth century, and numerous examples from Moscow and Novgorod in the fifteenth century at the height of Russian icon production.

In the Western Roman tradition sacred images took on a variety of forms, including ivory relief carvings, manuscript illuminations, wall paintings, mosaics, architectural relief carvings, free-standing sculpture, panel paintings, and stained glass windows. Among the most splendid of the media in the early centuries were the glass mosaics favored in both the East and the West. These large wall pictures, made of hundreds of thousands of small pieces of colored glass called *tesserae* graced churches in Ravenna and Rome in Italy, and in Constantinople in the fifth through seventh centuries, including the "Golden Age" of the reign of the Emperor Justinian (A.D. 527–565). Memorable Byzantine examples in Ravenna include the funerary image of the deer drinking from the living water (Ps 41/42) in the Tomb of Galla Placidia, the long nave processions toward the altar of female virgins and male martyrs in the Church of S. Apollinare Nuovo, which also includes the earliest *Last Judgment* scene of Christ as shepherd separating the sheep from the goats; the *Transfiguration* composition filling the apse at S. Apollinare in Classe, and the famous images of Emperor Justinian and his wife Theodora at S. Vitale.

Justinian's reign included his rebuilding the church of H. Sophia in Constantinople with its golden dome mosaics. In Rome, in response to the Council of Ephesus (A.D. 431), pronouncing Mary *Theotokos,* (Mother of God), the Church of St. Mary Major was built and luxuriously adorned with mosaics. These still extant fifth-century mosaics depict along the nave scenes from the Hebrew Bible, while the triumphal arch surrounding the apse celebrates the triumph of the church and of Mary in scenes from the infancy of Christ.

Mosaic decoration enjoyed a revival in the Byzantine East in the eleventh and twelfth centuries, exemplified by the Pantocrator (Christ as Judge) images in the domes at the Greek monasteries of Hosios Loukas and Daphni along with the hierarchical arrangement of icons of the Virgin and saints that fill the walls. The Church of St. Mark in Venice, begun in the eleventh century, reflects this "Second Golden Age" revival of mosaics which was continued by the Norman dukes in Sicily who commissioned vast programs of mosaics for their churches in Monreale, Cefalu, and Palermo.

The period of the ninth to eleventh centuries, during the reigns of the Frankish king and Holy Roman Emperor Charlemagne and his successors, followed by the Saxon dynasty of German emperors, the "Ottonians," gave birth to an imperial court art of sumptuous objects commissioned by the emperors and members of their families and courts. The court scriptorium of Charlemagne at Tours produced many sumptuously decorated manuscripts putting together the Hebrew Bible and the New Testament. The Ottonian court, influenced by Byzantine art from Constantinople, introduced into the West images of the dead crucified Christ. Examples such as the Gero Crucifix, presented to the cathedral of Cologne, Germany, by Archbishop Gero (A.D. 969–976) poignantly emphasize the human suffering of Christ in contrast to earlier crucifixions focusing on the divinity of the resurrected Lord.

At the end of the eleventh century in Western Europe a popular religiosity swept art patronage out of the hands of imperial patrons and into the urban churches. The collection and veneration of relics of the saints, propelled by the phenomenon of the religious pilgrimage to Santiago de Compostela in northwestern Spain, produced numerous new churches with chapels displaying reliquaries of intricate goldsmith work for the devotion of pilgrims. In addition elaborate sculptural programs on the entrance portals and the column capitals of both church interiors and cloisters were carved. These sculptural programs, along with the stained glass windows of the following Gothic period have often been popularly described as the "Bible for the illiterate." In a manner of speaking this is true, but the observation often leads to a presumption that the

The Good Shepherd and the Lamb, sculpture, 4th century, Vatican Museum

images illustrated Scripture, following chapter and verse. Instead, images were very carefully selected to help the believers focus on great truths of the faith. Sometimes, as in the case of the "Great Portals" of some major French churches along the pilgrimage routes to Spain, the images were even allied with political agendas, such as at Vezelay where the dedication of the portal representation of the *Mission of the Apostles* at Pentecost coincided with Pope Urban II's preaching of the first crusade. The call to apostleship and going forth to preach the gospel to all the world extended to reclaiming Jerusalem from the Muslims.

A wonderful tension between the opaque tangible reality of the world made holy by the incarnation, and the transcendent splendor of the celestial New Jerusalem provides the vision for Gothic art of the twelfth and thirteenth centuries. Monumental classicizing sculptures play off against immense stained glass rose windows on the facades of great urban cathedrals. The translucency of stained glass, with its jewel-like color filling the open skeletal structures with "divine light," expresses the immateriality, the spirituality of God, lifting the minds of ordinary mortals to contemplation of the order, perfection, beauty, and mystery of God.

A profound religiosity pervades much of the work of the artists of the sixteenth century Italian Renaissance. The Neoplatonic "cult of genius" embraced the artist who now was elevated beyond "craftsman" to divinely inspired genius. Humanist ideals based on a revival of Classicism merged with religious inspiration to produce works like Leonardo's *Last Supper* (A.D. 1495–1498), Michelangelo's *Sistine Ceiling* (A.D. 1508–1512) and *Last Judgment* (A.D. 1534–1541), or Raphael's *Madonna del Granduca* (ca. A.D. 1505). The psychological intensity of the apostles' consternation and Christ's gesture of surrender to the will of the Father in the *Last Supper,* God's "quickening" or enlivening of Adam by sweeping gesture rather than molding him of clay in Michelangelo's *Creation of Adam* on the Sistine Ceiling, or the contemplative tenderness of Raphael's Madonnas continue to stir the hearts and imaginations of viewers.

Tensions erupting with the onset of the Protestant Reformation engendered an artistic response of both deep interior reflection and triumphalism. The work of Domenikos Theotocopoulos (1541–1614), known as El Greco, arrests the viewer with its spiritual intensity. As a devout Catholic working within the environment of fiercely Counter Reformation Spain, El Greco's agitated, flame-like painting style portrays an all-consuming mysticism, an indwelling of the Spirit of God. His paintings of the *Tears of St. Peter* or the *Repentant Magdalen* reflect the contemporary theological debates about grace and repentance. The rebuilding of old St. Peter's in Rome, begun by Bramante and Michelangelo in the sixteenth century, progressed to the grandeur of the work completed by Gianlorenzo Bernini (1598–1680) with his great colonnade embracing the piazza. Bernini's architectural canopy above the altar marking the tomb of St. Peter and his monumental sculpture of the Chair of St. Peter sustained by figures representing the four Fathers of the Church, exuberantly proclaimed the primacy of the Bishop of Rome and the authority and power of the Roman Catholic Church. The heroic drama and transcendency of Bernini's work contrasts with the quiet, contemplative piety of his Calvinist Dutch contemporary, Rembrandt, whose religious paintings and etchings reveal a personal spirituality derived from meditation on Scripture.

By the end of the nineteenth century one can speak of a spirituality in art that is not necessarily linked to religious subject matter. The dignity of simple people in Rembrandt's images is echoed in Van Gogh's paintings of peasant farmers and coal miners. Van Gogh's fiery brushstrokes in a work like *Starry Night* imbue the night sky with the quiver of divine creation. Georges Rouault's *Clown* paintings poignantly and compassionately explore the suffering that is fundamental to the human condition, a suffering awaiting redemption.

Bringing the creative energies of the great artists of our own day to bear on Christians' search for ultimate meaning challenges the Church. A remarkable French Dominican priest, Father M. -A. Couturier, initiated an effort in the early 1950s to engage the Church once again in commissioning significant works of art that provoke encounters with the holy. In a few brief years he involved numerous artists including Léger, Matisse, Rouault, Braque, Chagall, and the architect Le Corbusier at the churches at Assy, Vence, Audincourt, and Ronchamp. Father Couturier's confidence that gifted artists could provide the spiritual art so urgently needed by the Church began a dialogue which awaits continuation. The work of the artists with whom he collaborated, such as Matisse's Stations of the Cross with uncharacteristic violence conveying the disorder of the crucifixion, or the array of works by Lurçat, Rouault, Bonnard, Braque, and Matisse at Assy offer testimony to his conviction that life itself abounds exuberantly in living masters. Their work invites insight into profound truths of the faith, always the role of sacred art.

MARCHITA B. MAUCK

See also ARCHITECTURE, CHURCH.

ARTICLES OF FAITH

Etymologically, article (from the Latin *articulus*) means "joint." Articles of faith are revealed doctrines which are joined together forming the whole of Christian faith and are found in the Church's creeds. Behind this expression lies the affirmation that Christian faith, despite its manifold beliefs, is an organic unity.

An ancient (not literally true) legend has it that to insure uniformity of the faith, the twelve apostles, before going their separate ways, composed a creed, each contributing an article. This creed is known as The Apostles' Creed. Throughout history attempts were made to organize and systematize these articles of faith. Medieval theologians, such as Alexander of Hales, St. Bonaventure and St. Thomas, grouped them into two sets, each composed of seven articles, the first dealing with the Godhead and things eternal, and the second with the humanity of Christ and his work in time.

On the basis of Hebrews 11:6 ("whoever would draw near to God must believe that he exists and that he rewards those who seek him"), St. Thomas argues that all the articles of faith are implicitly contained in two basic beliefs, namely, that God exists and that God exercises providence over human history. Furthermore, he argues that the number of articles of faith may increase with time, though not their substance (see *Summa Theologiae,* II-II, q. 1, aa. 6 and 7).

The Reformation Churches were also concerned with establishing the fundamental articles of faith both to distinguish themselves from the Roman Catholic Church and to promote union among themselves. Thus, the Augsburg Confession (1530), which consists of twenty-one articles summarizing essential Lutheran doctrines and seven articles directed against the abuses in the Roman Church; the Forty-two Articles (1553) and later the Thirty-nine Articles (1563), both of which form the basis of the doctrinal teachings of the Anglican Church.

Vatican II does not use the expression "article of faith," but establishes the principle of the "hierarchy of truths": "In ecumenical dialogue, Catholic theologians . . . when comparing doctrines with one another . . . should remember that there exists an order or 'hierarchy' of truths, since they vary in their relation to the foundation of the Christian faith" (Decree on Ecumenism [*Unitatis Redintegratio*], no. 11). Karl Rahner argues that these foundational articles of the Christian faith include the Trinity, the incarnation, and grace, all three of which can be "reduced" to the one dogma, namely, God as Incomprehensible and Holy Mystery.

PETER C. PHAN

See also CREEDS; DOCTRINE; DOGMA; HIERARCHY OF TRUTHS.

ASCENSION

In the Solemnity of the Ascension, the Church celebrates Jesus' going to his Father at the end of his life. The New Testament references to Jesus' ascension as an event witnessed by his disciples are limited to the writings of Luke (Acts 1:6-11; Luke 24:50-53). In Luke's context, the episode may be taken to indicate (in part) that we should expect no further revelations of Christ as the Risen One: The age of the Spirit, and of the Church, has begun. Accordingly, homilists often stress our need to walk in faith, to be full of expectation and gratitude in respect to the "gifts of the Spirit."

In its original concept, reflected in other New Testament writings, the ascension was more often the equivalent of Jesus' exaltation to the right hand of his Father, by virtue of which he is given the "Name which is above every other Name" (Phil 2:9-11). This exaltation, or glorification, can be seen as the Father's response to Jesus' fidelity. This response, however, did not await the fortieth day after Jesus' death, as Luke's accounts of the ascension might seem to imply: the Father's response is associated with Christ's death and resurrection (Phil 2:8).

The original concept of exaltation to the right hand of the Father also spoke to the early Christians of the return of Jesus. He would be the authentic judge, bringing justice in the name of his Father. Even more, the exaltation and name-bestowing stressed the present and ongoing availability of Jesus as our Mediator (Rom 8:34; 1 John 2:1). He is fully available in prayer, sacrament, and everyday life. We may call on that Name, abide in that Name, baptize in that Name, and do everything in that Name. Thus the Solemnity of the Ascension, correctly understood, highlights the very core of Christian belief.

Until the fourth century, the Church celebrated no separate festival of the ascension, but rather observed Easter through an undifferentiated season of fifty days (see Pentecost). Then, guided by the accounts of Acts 1 and 2, the Church approved the separate celebrations of Ascension Thursday and Pentecost on the fortieth and fiftieth days after Easter. Increasingly, national conferences of bishops are advocating that the ascension be celebrated on the Sunday following the fortieth day, where it could be better known to the faithful.

DAVID BRYAN

ASCENSION OF CHRIST

The Ascension, described as Jesus' being "carried up to heaven" (Luke 24:51) or "lifted up" forty days after his resurrection (Acts 1:9), is an integral part of the mystery of the exaltation of Jesus, and expresses the risen Christ's entry into glory, his session at "the right hand of the Father" where he exercises power over the whole universe, through the Holy Spirit whom he has promised to send upon his disciples. Resurrection, Ascension and Pentecost are therefore intimately linked. Indeed, the Church originally celebrated the mysteries of Ascension and Pentecost together until the end of the fourth century when the feast of Ascension was fixed at forty days after Easter. We shall examine briefly the meaning of Ascension in the Old Testament, then in the New Testament and conclude with a theological interpretation of the Ascension event.

Ascension in the OT

We find prefigurations of ascension, exaltation and session in several psalms of the OT: "Who shall go up to the mountain of Yahweh?" (Ps 24:3); "God goes up to shouts of acclaim" (Ps 47:5); "you have climbed to the heights" (Ps 68:18); "Take your seat at my right hand" (Ps 110:1). The ascension of Enoch who was "taken up" by God (Gen 5:24; Heb 11:5) and Elijah who "went up to heaven in the whirlwind" (2 Kgs 2:1-18) are concrete examples.

Ascension in the NT

While there are only three accounts of the ascension in the NT (Luke 24:50-53; Acts 1:3-11; Mark 16:19-20), there are many allusions to it without specific mention of how it took place. The earliest NT references speak of the "exaltation" of Christ, his being taken up to the glorious presence of the Father: "He was humbler yet, even accepting death, death on a cross. And for this God raised him high" (Phil 2:8-9). References to Jesus' "being lifted on high" in the Gospel of John (3:14; 8:28; 12:32) seem to indicate that his return to the Father was one continuous ascent from crucifixion to exaltation to glory (J. A. Fitzmyer, "The Ascension of Christ and Pentecost," *Theological Studies* 45 [1984] 412). Resurrection, Ascension and Pentecost are also clearly grouped together in Acts 2:33.

NT writers refer to or depict the ascension of Christ in a variety of ways. Only three NT texts actually describe the ascension as an observable event which happened to the risen Christ. Luke 24:50-51 indicates that he was "carried up to heaven" from Bethany, as he was blessing his disciples, on the evening of the resurrection day. Acts 1:1-11 also speaks of Jesus being "taken up to heaven" from the Mount of Olives, but only after several appearances over a period of forty days (also described as "many days" in Acts 13:31), during which he continued to speak to his disciples about the kingdom of God (v. 3). During one of these appearances Jesus, after commissioning his apostles to be his witnesses "to earth's remotest ends" (v. 8), is "lifted up", this time in "a cloud" (v. 9), and two men in white appear, indicating that Jesus "will come back in the same way" as he has gone to heaven (v. 11). These graphic details Fitzmyer (p. 419) describes as "apocalyptic stage props" employed by Luke. In Mark 16:19-20 we find again Jesus' being "taken up to heaven" as happening on the day of his resurrection, with the addition that "there at the right hand of God he took his place."

Theological Interpretation

Luke refers to Jesus as already having entered "his glory" on the day of the resurrection (Luke 24:26), thus indicating that the Emmaus appearance to the two disciples took place from "his glory." The ascension may be understood as a final appearance from "his glory", the last visible leave-taking of the exalted Jesus from the community of his disciples.

Christologically speaking, the ascension means that Jesus, now enthroned at the Father's right hand, has established his universal rule, "far above every principality, ruling force, power or sovereignty." He is also "head of the Church, which is his Body" (Eph 1:21-23). The ascended Christ, far from being absent, fills the whole cosmos in a new way: "The one who went down is none other than the one who went up above all the heavens to fill all things" (Eph 4:10). From now on it is through his Spirit, whom "the Father has promised" (Luke 24:49; Acts 1:4), and whom Jesus now "raised to God's right hand" has poured out (Acts 2:33) or in "the breaking of bread" as in the Emmaus story (Luke 24:35) that Jesus is present in a new way to his followers.

Ecclesially, the ascension implies that the Church now begins to function as the visible embodiment of Jesus. With the ascension the time of the Church begins, marked by the gift of the Spirit and by Christian response to the Spirit in service of the Reign of God. It is through the Spirit of the glorified Christ, "the promise of my Father" (Luke 24:49) that the disciples are empowered to go out and proclaim the Good News.

Finally, the ascension of Christ is the guarantee of human destiny and the fulfillment of Christian hope, as Paul assures the Thessalonians: "We shall be taken up . . . and so we shall be with the Lord for ever" (1 Thess 4:16-17). Indeed, in terms of eschatology, we can affirm that "by his Resurrection and Ascension Jesus did not merely enter into a preexistent heaven; rather his Resurrection created heaven for us . . . Jesus became the pledge and the beginning of the fulfillment of the world, the representative of the new cosmos, the bestower of the Spirit, the head of the Church, the dispenser of the sacraments, and the heavenly mediator of the beatific vision" (P. Phan, *Eternity in Time. A Study of Karl Rahner's Eschatology,* Selinsgrove: Susquehanna University Press, 1988, p. 167).

BRÍD LONG, S.S.L.

See also ASCENSION; JESUS CHRIST.

ASCETICISM

The word "asceticism" is rooted in the Greek term *askesis,* meaning practice or exercise. Early Christians borrowed the term from the world of Greek sports. In early Christian usage asceticism referred to the disciplinary practices by which believers conditioned or trained themselves in preparation for life imperishable (1 Cor 9:24-25). Just as the athlete fixes the mind and the will on a single goal, and directs all effort and energy in its pursuit, so the Christian is to keep the faith while struggling and straining for life's end and purpose (2 Tim 4:7).

The life of Christian discipleship is both gift and task. Asceticism is the activity by which one strives to attain a goal that lies beyond the self: fullness of life in Christ Jesus. This entails rigorous discipline so that one's entire life, and absolutely every dimension of it, is brought into conformity with Christ crucified and risen. Over the course of Christian history there has been a plurality of ascetical practices shaped by various understandings of sin and of sanctity dominant at different periods in the life of the Church.

In early Christian centuries the martyr, who in death is conspicuously conformed to the dying and rising of Christ, was the exemplar of Christian life and holiness. In later generations, when governments were somewhat less hostile to Christianity and when threats of physical violence waned, the martyr's fidelity, courage, and zeal continued to give shape to an enduring profile of Christian asceticism and holiness.

In the mid-third-century Roman Empire, especially in Egypt and parts of North Africa, some Christians fled the urban centers, convinced that the emergent spirit of tolerance toward Christian faith signaled a softening of the radical countercultural call to Christian discipleship. In the desert, far from what they judged as the depravity, debauchery, and decadence of the cities, these Christian ascetics lived alone (*monos*) devoting their lives to harsh penance, silence, prayer, manual labor, and solitude. The roots of Christian asceticism are often thought to rest in this movement away from the world (*fuga mundi*) into the desert. There is evidence, however, of a tradition of autonomous women who embraced virginity as an ascetical discipline much earlier than the mid-third century. By the time of the "Apostolic Church Order" ca. 270, the virgins were recognized as a distinct group alongside widows and deaconesses. Additionally there is a very early current of asceticism found in Syria, that of the *ihidaya,* the "single one" or the one who adopts "singleness." Relatively autonomous celibates, these men and women devoted their lives to ascetical practice, thereby becoming models of the costly discipleship to which all are called by baptism.

It is important to note that while many of these early currents of asceticism developed into communal forms of religious life with vows of poverty, chastity, and obedience, they were originally movements of autonomous lay Christians devoted to a rigorous and disciplined life in Christ.

In the history of Christian spirituality, virginity and celibacy quickly developed as superior forms of life. Celibacy in particular was understood as a form of solitary life that precluded sexuality, marriage, and affective relationships. Virginity and celibacy were regarded as components of the authentic Christian life. Any survey of Christian history will show that the spirituality of the laity, the vast majority of whom marry, was understood as derivative and lesser because of the priority given to virginity and celibacy. Ascesis was often understood quite narrowly, as mortification of the flesh, and rarely was applied to other demanding aspects of the Christian life such as: the rigorous sacrifices entailed in marital and family life, especially caring for one's children; the uncertainties of agrarian life and daily struggles for sustenance; complex decisions about the use and disposition of goods; the chaste exercise of sexuality for non-celibates; responsibility for the earth; the discipline of education and study; care and exercise of the body (nutrition, diet, balance of leisure and work); the tedium of too much work.

Taken as a whole, the history of Christian asceticism may be viewed in terms of two main emphases: the therapeutic and punitive. This history has been at its finest when the focus of asceticism has been on healing and restoration, so that the Christian may be free to focus the mind and heart and soul on the one thing necessary: the love of God which surpasses all understanding. But since asceticism is always associated with sin and its effects, the motifs of punishment for sin, reparation for wrongdoing, *quid pro quo,* and setting straight one's account with God have often gained the upper hand in Church life and practice. Even though an emphasis upon punishment and reparation may have provided opportunity for Christians to identify more closely with Christ in his suffering, passion, and death, Christian asceticism has been skewed when untethered from its therapeutic roots. In some later traditions of asceticism influenced by more positive and humanistic renaissances, e.g., those of Ignatius Loyola or Francis de Sales, there is a notable shift from the exterior to the interior, from the body to the will. In these more positive and humanistic currents, it is primarily the will that needs conditioning, healing, and training. Where there have been excessively rigorous approaches to Christian asceticism, these have been shaped in no small measure by a dualism that scorns materiality, specifically the human body, as if it were a cage within which the "higher" soul or spirit is kept captive.

Exaggerations and wrong-headed ascetical practices throughout Christian history have given rise to a greater measure of prudence regarding ascetical practice in our own day. On the other hand, many contemporary Christians take a negative view, or are altogether indifferent, toward any ascetical practice whatsoever. But spiritual exercise or discipline is an intrinsic dimension of any and all authentic Christian living. Such discipline may be embraced as a permanent factor in a way of life. For example, one may commit oneself to a life of poverty and solidarity with the poor as a member of the Catholic Worker Movement or a l'Arche community. Or one may choose the asceticism of life in a religious community bound by vows of poverty, chastity, and obedience. The disciplines of marital fidelity and nurturing the life of a family are rarely viewed as forms of asceticism, but it is through these that the great majority of Christians are provided ample opportunity to grow in conformity to Christ crucified and risen. In addition to the asceticism which is ineluctably a part of the various life forms within the Christian community, asceticism may also be expressed through periodic disciplines such as almsgiving, fasting, firmer commitment to a regular life of prayer and worship, or renewing one's practice of the corporal and spiritual works of mercy.

Of late there has been increasing attention to the importance of physical exercise, regulated diet, strenuous effort to ward off cardiovascular and other diseases, greater restraint in the consumption of meat, and abstention from alcohol. There seems to be little question about the value of efforts to assure health, fitness, and well-being. But rigors and disciplines undertaken for specifically religious or spiritual motives, especially when they involve conditioning the body through abstinence, fasting, keeping vigil, or embracing a life of material poverty in imitation of Christ, often seem quite incomprehensible to many in the contemporary period.

Current trends that stress the importance of exercise and physical fitness are illustrative of the ever-growing awareness that the person is a unity. He or she is not a combination of separate faculties of intellect and will, nor a mix of body and soul. Intellect and will, body and soul may be recognized as distinct, but they are dialectically inseparable. Each dimension is related to all the others. What affects one of the parts affects the whole. Authentic expressions of asceticism in the life of the Church today tend to be more "holistic," recognizing the interdependence of the different dimensions of the human being. There is less scorn for the body and its sometimes unruly ways. Consequently there seem to be fewer instances of exaggeration and excess in contemporary Christian ascesis. The dualism that underpinned the separation and opposition between mind and body, spirit and matter, has been dealt a fatal blow, at least in principle, by the retrieved and revitalized biblical anthropology which is one of the hallmarks of Christian theology and spirituality in our time.

If the view of the human person grounded in a dualism of body and soul, or matter and spirit, is set aside, then the body in and of itself cannot be seen as the primary target of ascetical practice. Once we begin to see how the various dimensions of the person are all related to one another and affect each other, we can begin to recognize that the human person is above all else a relational being. We are only persons at all because of our relations with other persons. If we could somehow grasp the relational matrix of human personhood, it would altogether alter our understanding of Christian asceticism. Asceticism would then come into view as the ongoing exercise by which the Christian attempts to order his or her relationships rightly: with self, another, others, God, the whole of creation. The focus, then, of ascetical discipline is not upon ever deepening penetration and purification of the self through a solitary journey inward. It is rather more a matter of conforming one's whole person and all of one's relationships, with both human and nonhuman life, to the person of Jesus who in his living, dying, and rising, discloses the mystery of God as a communion of persons in loving relation.

MICHAEL DOWNEY

See also CHRISTIAN SPIRITUALITY; SOUL; SPIRITUAL LIFE; VOWS.

ASH WEDNESDAY

The first day of the Lenten season, so named because of the Church's tradition of marking the foreheads of each member of the faith community with consecrated ashes on this day. Applied to members of the clergy as well as the laity, the ashes serve as a tangible reminder of the Lenten emphasis on penitence.

JOSEPH QUINN

See also LENT.

ASPERGES

(Lat., "you sprinkle") The ceremony in which the celebrant sprinkles holy water over the altar, himself and his assistants, and the congregation during the principal Mass on Sundays. As the sprinkling takes place, verses from Psalm 51 ("purge me with hyssop and I shall be clean. . . .") are sung. The Latin phrasing of this invocation—*Asperges me, Domine*—gives the ceremony its name. In the Easter season, Psalm 51 is replaced with the hymn *Vidi aquam.* The ceremony, which dates back to the ninth century, has in recent years been replaced with the Rite of Sprinkling, during which any appropriate hymn or antiphon may be sung. This rite may be substituted for the Penitential Rite.

JOSEPH QUINN

See also RITUAL; SACRAMENTALS.

ASSUMPTION

The feast of the Assumption (15 August) celebrates Mary's passage to heaven at the end of her life, a divine recognition of her fidelity and her role as mother of the Son of God. The idea that Mary enjoyed an assumption is not affirmed in any direct way by the New Testament, or in the most primitive tradition, but rather developed gradually out of the Church's life of prayer, biblical reflection, and sacrament.

Although praying to Mary is attested from very early times, the first public festival connected with her seems to have begun early in the fifth century in Jerusalem at the site where Mary was thought to have rested on her way from Jerusalem to Bethlehem. This was the feast of the *Theotokos* ("God-bearer," "Mother of God") celebrated on August 15. Later in the century, the feast was transferred to the basilica where Mary's tomb was venerated. Gradually, then, the August feast of the *Theotokos* came to focus on the Dormition ("Falling Asleep") of Mary, and, with this title, was made universal by Emperor Maurice at the end of the sixth century. Rome accepted the feast of the Dormition during the seventh century; in the next century it became known as the Assumption, a name which called attention to the *manner* of Mary's passing. She had been taken up, fully, into heaven.

"The Assumption," detail, by Titian, Basilica dei Frari, Venice

The general concept of "assumption" ("taking up") is biblical. The Old Testament describes the assumption of Elijah (2 Kgs 2), and Jewish tradition supplies assumptions for Moses, Isaiah, and other prophets. The idea seems to be that those who have seen God, or been given revelations of him, have thereby become members of the heavenly court and need to be "taken" there at the end of life. This gave rise to the further idea that assumed prophets were being protected so that they could return as God's witnesses when the prophetic words were fulfilled. Thus Moses and Elijah appear with Jesus in the Transfiguration (Mark 9:2-8), implicitly testifying to him as fulfilling the promises of the Hebrew Scriptures. The idea of protection is also found in Exodus 19:4, where Israel itself is "taken up" on eagles' wings to a place of protection in the wilderness. This theme is repeated in Revelation 12: Lady Israel is again taken on eagles' wings to the desert for protection when evil attacks her son (Jesus) and a persecution rages against her "other children." Insofar as Mary is a figure of the Church, her assumption may be thought to echo that of the lady of Revelation 12. The idea that Mary has been assumed is connected to her having stood in the presence of God (through the angel of the annunciation, through the Holy Spirit's descending to her, and through her life with the Eternal Word). Similarly, in the Catholic experience, Mary is a protected witness to the life of Jesus.

The question of whether Mary has been assumed "body and soul" (not finally defined by the Church until 1950) would not have arisen in Israel, where the human person was always considered to be an indivisible whole. In lands which did divide soul and body, however, the "wholeness" of a personal assumption could not have been preached without reference to the body as well as the soul.

As with the primitive notion of resurrection, an assumed person does not continue to "sleep in the Lord," but is "awake." This idea fits in with Mary's role as intercessor, one who listens to the disciples of Christ. Other aspects of resurrection, however, are not included in Mary's assumption: Mary does not, like Jesus, "reveal the resurrection," nor are there witnesses to her assumption comparable to those who witnessed the resurrection of Jesus.

DAVID BRYAN

ATHANASIUS, ST. (ca. 295–373)

Bishop of Alexandria. Athanasius was born and educated in Alexandria. As deacon and secretary to Bishop Alexander of Alexandria, he accompanied him to the Council of Nicaea (325). He became bishop of Alexandria in 328. Because he refused to yield on Arianism, Athanasius became the enemy of the pro-Arians. His opponents arranged for his removal as bishop of Alexandria and exile to Trier in 336. Athanasius was able to return to Alexandria in 337 after the death of Constantine. In 339 he was again forced to flee, this time to Rome. He remained in exile for seven years. The next ten years in Alexandria (346 to 356) were, relatively speaking, very peaceful and productive. When Emperor Constantius sent soldiers to arrest him, Athanasius escaped into the desert. From his hiding place he directed the Church in Alexandria until the death of Constantius in 361. When Julian the Apostate became emperor in 361, Athanasius was able to return to Alexandria. Julian came to consider Athanasius a disturber of the peace and sent him back into exile. Athanasius returned in 363 after Julian's death. Athanasius was exiled for the fifth and final time in 365 after Valens became the emperor in the East. Owing to the unpopularity of his decision, Valens allowed Athanasius to return early in 366. Athanasius spent the remaining years of his life peacefully trying to repair the harm done to the Church by all the strife and violence. A major theme in Athanasius's many writings was the defense of the Nicene position that the Son was truly God. From 361 onward Athanasius worked to reconcile the semi-Arian party to the Nicene term *homoousios.* In addition Athanasius was concerned to promote the full divinity of the Holy Spirit and the full humanity of Christ against those who opposed these ideas. Athanasius encouraged monasticism in the East through his *Life of St. Antony* which through a Latin translation promoted knowledge of monasticism in the West. Athanasius has been called "the Father of Orthodoxy" by the Greek Church and has been considered one of the four great Fathers of the East by the Roman Catholic Church. He was also named a Doctor of the Catholic Church in 1568. Feast day, 2 May.

JOHN DILLON

See also DOCTRINE, DEVELOPMENT OF; FATHERS OF THE CHURCH; ORTHODOXY; TRINITY.

ATHEISM

Atheism may be described as the formal rejection and denial of the existence of God. There are nearly as many shades of atheism as there are theologies. Broadly speaking one can point to at least three different expressions of atheism: theoretical, practical, and theological.

A great variety of theoretical atheisms exist. One of the most serious forms is reductionist atheism: a view which suggests that religion can be explained away without remainder as a projection of human nature (e.g., L. Feuerbach, K. Marx, S. Freud). Another form of theoretical atheism is the one associated with the birth of the enlightenment which claimed that everything in the world could be accounted for by science, including the God-hypothesis. A third type of theoretical atheism can be found in existentialist atheism which holds that there is an incompatibility between belief in the existence of God and the flourishing of human existence (e.g., A. Camus).

Practical atheism, which seems to be on the increase, is the actual living out of life without reference to or acknowledgement of the possibility of the existence of God. For many, practical atheism arises out of an apathy towards or indifference to the question of God.

Theological atheism, insofar as it is possible to hold these two terms together, denies the existence of God while maintaining the psychological need to affirm the "myth" of God (e.g., D. Cupitt).

Atheism, in whatever form it exists, can have a negative and positive effect on theology. It can be negative when it seeks to destroy faith in others and deny the legitimacy of theological discourse. It can be positive insofar as it continually challenges theology to renew and transform its images of God. Indeed, it has often been remarked that the possibility of atheism provokes the response of religious faith.

The Second Vatican Council in the Pastoral Constitution on the Church in the Modern World (1965) addressed the question of atheism with striking candor, pointing out "that believers can have more than a little to do with the birth of atheism" (no. 19). The council also notes that the dignity of the individual is rooted in God and that therefore this dignity is in danger of being diminished when the existence of God is denied (no. 21). The death of God can give rise to the demise of the dignity of the individual.

Theology in dialogue with atheism will seek to discover the religious dimension of human experience. In doing so theology will want to understand and interpret the vast range of human experiences that people undergo such as experiences of freedom and transcendence (K. Rahner), the experience of an unrestricted desire to know and to love (B. Lonergan), contrast-experiences (E. Schillebeeckx), limit-experiences (D. Tracy). In addition, theology will want to make a distinction between the culturally conditioned expressions of faith in God (what Aquinas called the *modus significandi*) and the infinite reality of God portrayed within these finite expressions (what Aquinas called the *res significata*).

Finally, contemporary theology will have to labor with greater empathy to hear the protests of atheism against religious faith in God: the apathy of believers, the injustices done in the name of God, the presence of superstition and idolatry, the existence of so much evil and suffering in the world. In the end a necessary and constructive tension can and should exist between theology and atheism.

DERMOT A. LANE

See also AGNOSTICISM; FAITH; GOD; THEOLOGY.

ATHOS, MOUNT

The "Holy Mountain" is at the tip of the peninsula of Atke in northern Greece. This semiautonomous republic of Greek Orthodox monks covers an area thirty miles long, five miles wide, and rises 6670 feet above the Aegean Sea. The region was first inhabited by Christian hermits in or around 850. These hermits gradually organized themselves into small communities to promote their spiritual and communal welfare. St. Athanasius the Athonite ("man of Athos") was the first officially to establish a monastic community on the mountain in 963; his community came to be known as the Great Lavra. Several more monasteries were built at Mount Athos in the eleventh century. In 1045 representatives of these communities came together to organize and draft a constitution. One of the foremost provisions of their constitution banned the presence of women and female animals on the mountain, although the monks' success in enforcing the latter provision is uncertain. By 1400 the number of monasteries on the mountain peaked at forty; these received endowments from Russian, Slavic, and Greek Orthodox patrons.

Monastery of Grigoriou, Mount Athos

The Turkish occupation of Thessaloniki, beginning in 1430, and the Greek War of Independence from 1821 to 1829 led to the decline of many of the mountain's communities, including the destruction of libraries and even the deaths of some monks. After Greece won its independence, a period of rebirth and rebuilding occurred. Today Mount Athos hosts twenty monasteries. These houses, along with their great treasures of Byzantine art, medieval manuscripts, and the almost 1500 resident monks, are protected by a provision of the Greek constitution of 1975.

JOSEPH F. KELLY

See also MONASTICISM.

ATTRITION

Sorrow for sin arising from fear of punishment or from a revulsion from the ugly aspects of sins. It is less perfect than contrition which proceeds from the love of God. Luther denied its value, but Thomas Aquinas and most theologians say that attrition is sufficient for the forgiveness of sin in the Sacrament of Reconciliation.

JOAN GLAZIER

See also SACRAMENT OF RECONCILIATION.

AUGSBURG CONFESSION

As the Reformation progressed in its first decade, some figures on both sides hoped that a reconciliation might yet be effected. They were prompted by the horrors of the Peasants' Rebellion, the rise of

Anabaptism, and, on the Protestant side, the progressive dissolution of Reformed unity, symbolized by the failed Colloquy of Marburg (1529) at which Luther and Zwingli divided over the issue of the Real Presence of Christ in the Eucharist. One of Luther's younger lieutenants, the humanist Philip Melanchthon, held onto hopes of reunion longer than most Protestants, and he always tried to keep Luther from a position too radical for reunion. The Catholic Emperor Charles V also hoped for the religious reunion of his German domains, and in 1530 he called a meeting of the Diet (German parliament) at Augsburg. Melanchthon, with Luther's approval, drew up a confession of faith in two parts. The first included central Lutheran teachings, such as basing religious teaching primarily upon the gospel, justification, ecclesiastical orders and rites, the role of civil government, free will, and faith and good works; the second listed abuses to be reformed, including clerical celibacy, episcopal power, confession, and indulgences. The Catholic theologians at the Diet responded to the confession with a "confutation," to which Melanchthon wrote a reply, but the exchange of writings soon degenerated to an exchange of charges. Unity slipped away, but the Augsburg Confession had become an authoritative expression of Luther's teaching. It was published in 1531 for use in the Reformed Churches.

JOSEPH F. KELLY

See also LUTHER, MARTIN; LUTHERANS; REFORMATION, THE.

AUGUSTINE, ST. (354–430)

Born in Tagaste (modern-day Souk-Ahras, Algeria), Augustine was the (eldest?) son of Patricius, a pagan, and Monica, a devout Christian. He studied at Tagaste, Madauros (modern-day Mdaourouch, Algeria) and Carthage. At nineteen Augustine read the now lost *Hortensius* by Cicero which provoked his search for wisdom and the real meaning of life. Dismissing the Christianity which he had learned from his mother, Augustine tried Manichaeism for nine years until Faustus, the Manichaean bishop, was unable to answer Augustine's questions. Augustine had been teaching rhetoric in Carthage for eight years (375 to 383). When he taught in Rome in 384, he no longer openly identified himself as a Manichaean. Augustine received a professorial post in Milan in the fall of 384. He was helped by the sermons of Ambrose who resolved some of Augustine's dilemmas from his time as a Manichaean and who gave Augustine insight on how to read and interpret the Old Testament. Augustine was also helped by reading the Platonists to understand the inner light and the nature of evil. From his study of St. Paul, Augustine came to see that Christ is Redeemer as well as Teacher. Simplicianus, the tutor of Ambrose, related the conversion of the Neoplatonist Marius Victorinus.

Augustine had to face what conversion to Christianity would mean for him. Since he was seventeen he had been living with a mistress to whom he had been faithful and by whom he had a son, Adeodatus, to whom he was intensely devoted. The thought of giving up marriage troubled him deeply, and he was very much moved when Pontitian told him how two civil servants, after having read the *Life of St. Antony,* gave up their careers to become monks. Augustine felt the grace of God when he read Romans 13:13-14. After deciding to give up his teaching career and marriage, Augustine retired to Cassiciacum to prepare for baptism. In March, 387, Augustine returned to Milan to enroll himself in the catechumenate. At the Easter Vigil, 387, Augustine, along with his good friend Alypius and his son Adeodatus, was baptized by Ambrose. In 388 Augustine returned to North Africa and with some friends set up a monastic life at Tagaste.

St. Augustine by Botticelli, fresco painting, 1480, Ognissanti, Florence

In 391, while visiting Hippo Regius (near modern-day Annaba, Algeria), a reluctant Augustine was presented by the people to the elderly bishop Valerius for ordination to the priesthood. After ordaining him, Valerius gave Augustine permission to establish a monastery where Augustine practiced asceticism, studied theology, and began to preach. In 396 Augustine was consecrated as coadjutor bishop to Valerius and from 397 Augustine was bishop of

Hippo. He remained the local bishop until his death and was zealous in his episcopal ministry: regularly preaching to the people, preparing catechumens for baptism, establishing monasteries, caring for the poor and unfortunate, visiting the sick, exercising pastoral care over his priests, administering justice in civil matters, intervening with civil authorities on behalf of the people, and looking after the material needs of the Church. He also was very involved with the affairs of the Church outside of his own diocese which involved frequent travel to African councils and writing against Manichaeans, Donatists, Pelagians, Arians, and pagans.

Many of his writings are involved with these controversies. Of his other writings, two of the most famous are the *Confessions,* the story of his life down to his conversion, written between 397 and 400, and the *City of God,* written between 413 and 426 to refute the charge of pagans that the sack of Rome in 410 by Alaric occurred because the traditional gods and goddesses were no longer worshiped. Augustine's principal dogmatic work is *The Trinity,* published in fifteen books between 399 and 412. Augustine's other writings include his correspondence which numbered over 270 letters covering a period of more than 40 years, more than 500 sermons, philosophical discourses, and the *Retractations,* a review of his literary activity which he published shortly before his death. Augustine's influence in the Western Church cannot be overestimated. He was named a Doctor of the Church in 1295. Feast day, 28 August.

JOHN DILLON

See also DOCTORS OF THE CHURCH; DOCTRINE, DEVELOPMENT OF; FATHERS OF THE CHURCH.

AUGUSTINE, ST., RULE OF

St. Augustine wrote his Rule for his first monastery at Hippo. In eight brief chapters he outlines the purpose and basis of community life. "Before all else, dear brothers, love God and then your neighbor, because these are the chief commandments given to us. The main purpose for your having come together is to live harmoniously in your house, intent upon God in oneness of mind and heart."

Very much a practical Rule of daily life, he sets down specific precepts for all to follow:

> Call nothing your own, but let everything be yours in common. The superior is to distribute food and clothing according to each one's need, as the Acts of the Apostles records "they had all things in common and distribution was made to each one according to each one's need" (4.32,35).
>
> "Be assiduous in prayer" (Col. 4,2) at the hours and times appointed. When you pray to God in psalms and hymns, think in your hearts the words that come from your lips.
>
> Subdue the flesh, so far as your health permits, by fasting and abstinence from food and drink. When you come to table, listen until you leave to what it is the custom to read, without disturbance or strife. Let not your mouths alone take nourishment but let your hearts too hunger for the word of God.
>
> There should be nothing about your clothing to attract attention. Besides, you should not seek to please by your apparel, but by a good life. So when you are together in church and anywhere else where women are present, exercise a mutual care over purity of life. Thus, by mutual vigilance over one another will God, who dwells in you, grant you His protection.
>
> Keep your clothing in one place in charge of one or two. In this way, no one shall perform any task for his own benefit but all your work shall be done for the common good, with greater zeal and more dispatch than if each one of you were to work for yourself alone. For charity, as it is written, "is not self-seeking," meaning that it places the common good before its own. Thus, let the abiding virtue of charity prevail in all things that minister to the fleeting necessities of life.
>
> You should either avoid quarrels altogether or else put an end to them as quickly as possible; otherwise anger may grow into hatred, making a plank out of a splinter, and turn the soul into a murderer. For so you read: "Everyone who hates his brother is a murderer" (1 John 3.15).
>
> The superior should be obeyed as a father. Let him "admonish the unruly, cheer the faint hearted, support the weak, and be patient towards all" (1 Thes. 5.14).
>
> The Lord grant that you observe all these precepts in a spirit of charity as lovers of spiritual beauty, giving forth the good odor of Christ in the holiness of your lives; not as slaves living under the law but as men living in freedom under grace.

ALBERT C. SHANNON, O.S.A.

See also AUGUSTINE, ST.; AUGUSTINIAN ORDER.

AUGUSTINIAN ORDER

The Augustinians, O.S.A., are a mendicant, religious order that traces its lineage to St. Augustine (354–430), bishop of Hippo and Doctor of the Church. In 1256 a number of groups were canonically organized into the Augustinian Order as mendicant friars dedicated not only to community life in prayer, meditation and solitude, but also to the active apostolate in the growing towns. Trained in their study houses at the great medieval universities they responded to the spiritual needs of the faithful throughout Europe and later in Latin and North America. Their missionary apostolate carried them to Africa and the Far East as well. In the seventeenth century 20,000 friars served in over 1000 monasteries. However, the eighteenth and nineteenth centuries brought suppressions by the civil powers, the French Revolution, and subsequent confiscations and secularizations. Eleven provinces were suppressed. Italy alone lost more than 540 monasteries, while in France the order succumbed entirely.

While the Church was recovering from these depredations, the Irish Augustinians sent Fathers John Rossiter in 1794 and Thomas Carr in 1796 to the newly founded American nation. The Augustinians organized their first province in Philadelphia where they erected St. Augustine's Church. As the mendicant orders had done in Europe, the Americans opened their first school, St. Augustine's Academy, in 1811. They soon acquired the Randolph farm outside of Philadelphia from which Villanova College opened its doors in 1843.

Responding to the growing pastoral needs, the Augustinians assumed charge of parishes in nine dioceses and they staffed eleven high schools across the country. In addition to Villanova University, Merrimack College and Biscayne College were organized, and missions were staffed in Peru and Japan. Three provinces were developed in the United States along with three vice-provinces.

In the present age some 3,000 friars serve in 27 provinces in 515 houses with their distinctive black habit consisting of a tunic, a leather cincture and a capuche.

ALBERT C. SHANNON, O.S.A.

See also AUGUSTINE, ST.; AUGUSTINE, ST., RULE OF.

AUSTRALIA, THE CHURCH IN

Aboriginals

Aboriginals came to the Australian continent much earlier than was believed. Cave engravings in South Australia more than forty thousand years old are older than any cave art known elsewhere in the world. Current estimations of the time of the arrival of these first humans range up to sixty thousand years and well beyond.

Following some centuries of occasional contacts, European settlement began after U.S. independence, when Britain chose Botany Bay as an alternative place for the transportation of convicts. The first fleet reached Sydney in 1788 establishing New South Wales.

The impact on the Aboriginals was tragic. Contagious diseases like measles and smallpox killed far more than did the guns of European settlers, and rereadings of early letters and journals suggest that the diseases traveled much faster than did white explorers. Earlier estimations of about 300,000 Aboriginals at first contact are probably well below the true number.

The First Catholics

Almost all the first Catholics were Irish convicts, including three priests, the last of whom left in 1810. Many convicts wrote to their families in Ireland urging them to emigrate to this land of opportunity. The letters included requests for priests, and the pleas reached Rome in 1816. An erratic Irish Cistercian, Fr. Jeremiah O'Flynn, facing charges of insubordination, was offered the task. He volunteered, was pardoned, secularized, and named prefect apostolic of "Bottanibe" (Botany Bay). Refused approval from the London Colonial Office, he impulsively decided to travel without it. He reached Australia in 1817, assuring a skeptical Governor Lachlan Macquarie that the papers would come on a later ship. Eighteen months later Macquarie deported him.

Fr. O'Flynn's inept ministry resulted in the appointment from London of two Catholic chaplains who reached Australia in 1820: Fr. Philip Conolly worked in Van Diemen's Land (Tasmania) and Fr. John Joseph Therry was based in Sydney. People either venerated or detested Therry, and his abrasive character antagonized civil authorities, but he successfully opposed efforts to declare the Church of England the Established Church in 1825.

Distance

Rome placed Australia, still called "New Holland," under the bishop of Mauritius, four thousand miles away, who never saw his new area of jurisdiction. Indeed, distance was the greatest problem faced by the missionaries: Europe was six months away and the new continent entirely lacked roads. But as news spread of vast expanses of grazing lands in the interior, settlers moved their flocks to "squat" on distant tracts regarded as *terra nullius* (unclaimed land). Missionaries rode thousands of miles on circuit visiting them.

No thought was given to Aboriginal rights to the land and when they resisted the invaders, several massacres took place. Dispossessed blacks became beggars on the fringes of white settlement, addicted to alcohol. Christian missionaries, Catholic or Protestant, had little concept of Aboriginal spirituality, and all found conversions difficult.

Catholic Emancipation in England in 1829 brought the appointment of the first Catholics to public office: highly qualified Irishmen Roger Therry and John Hubert Plunkett, who filled senior legal positions in the colony, raising the status of Catholics generally. Plunkett persuaded outstanding Irish pioneer priest Fr. John McEncroe, who had worked in Carolina, to accompany him.

Hierarchy

A young Yorkshire Benedictine, Fr. William Ullathorne, was made vicar general in 1833. He impressed the difficult Fr. Therry, and delighted civil authorities who found that Roman Catholics could be sane, reasonable, and English.

In 1834 the first bishop was appointed, another English Benedictine for a mostly Irish flock: John Bede Polding. He was caring towards the convicts, an effective preacher and catechist, and became an outstanding missionary. His jurisdiction covered the continent, and he traveled thousands of miles, as far as Perth.

In 1836, Governor Sir Richard Bourke enacted the Church Act. Four major Churches, including the Catholic, were accorded equal status as regards payment of ministers and financial assistance for building churches and schools.

Bishop Polding sent Ullathorne to Europe to recruit clergy, and his efforts brought from Ireland eighteen secular priests and seminarians and the Sisters of Charity—all arrived in 1838. He appealed to the English Benedictines for priests without success. But oddly, Polding was then captured by a Benedictine dream of Australia served almost exclusively by monks. On a visit to Rome in 1841 he was made an archbishop, and his request that Sydney be declared an "Abbey-diocese" was granted in 1844.

This Benedictine vision failed and had negative consequences for the Church, with immediate impact on several religious orders which left Polding's archdiocese in the 1840s, members refusing to return while he was alive. Other orders were reluctant to come to Sydney. In the 1840s a remarkable woman, Mrs. Caroline Chisholm, developed an effective Family Migration scheme to care especially for migrant women.

The establishment of new dioceses in Hobart (1842) and Adelaide (1844) began to free large areas from Polding's jurisdiction. Perth, Melbourne, Maitland, Darwin, Brisbane, Goulburn and Bathurst dioceses were created between 1848 and 1865. Most of the new bishops were Irish.

New colonies were established in Tasmania, Victoria, western and southern Australia; the last, Queensland, was separated in 1859. In 1851, gold discoveries in N.S.W. (New South Wales) and Victoria attracted vast numbers of people from overseas. The Church managed to expand enough to care for these immigrants, many of them Catholic.

Education

Self-government was granted to most of the colonies in the 1850s coinciding with a British movement towards separation of Church and state. Payment of ministers of religion was phased out in the 1860s with indications that Church schools would also soon lose funding. Planned government schools would offer "free, compulsory and secular" education to all. The Sisters of Charity, the Mercy Sisters, together with Australian-founded Sisters of the Good Samaritan, and Sisters of St. Joseph (Josephites), developed primary education. Irish Christian Brothers and French Marists educated boys. The Josephites, founded by far-sighted Mother Mary McKillop, were willing to open schools in remote settlements lacking a resident priest.

On Polding's death in 1877, another English Benedictine, Roger Bede Vaughan succeeded him as archbishop and became the spokesman for the Catholic bishops. Following the withdrawal of government funding from Church schools in Victoria in 1872 and then in other states, he wrote a pastoral letter on behalf of the hierarchy in 1878, characterizing public schools as godless and "seedplots of future immorality." Without consulting the laity, the letter deliberately precipitated the withdrawal of state funds from Church schools in N.S.W. in 1880, inflamed Protestants, but galvanized the mostly poorer Catholics into building and supporting their own schools. Many teaching orders came to Australia in the 1870s and 1880s. Church growth is shown by the many new dioceses established between 1871 and 1910: Armidale, Ballarat, Sandhurst, Rockhampton, Lismore, Sale, Wilcannia, Port Augusta (now Port Pirie), Geraldton, and Broome.

Although many bishops believed that government funding for Church schools would soon be restored, eighty years were to pass before this began. Instead, there was a long legacy of ill-feeling between Catholics and Protestants. In the 1890s' depression, Sydney's new Cardinal Patrick Francis Moran encouraged Catholics to work towards the foundation of the Australian Labor Party, which became one of two major political parties when the colonies federated in 1901 as the Commonwealth of Australia. But public funding of Church schools was not restored.

Irish Dr. Daniel Mannix became archbishop of Melbourne in 1913 and was a vigorous critic of government education policies. In 1916 and 1917 he fought referendums intended by Prime Minister William Hughes to impose military conscription. The referendums were defeated, and although it was clear that strongly Protestant states had also opposed them, accusations were made of Catholic disloyalty.

The early 1920s and later the Great Depression saw high unemployment, continuing through the 1930s. Sectarianism sometimes publicly and often secretly excluded Catholics from jobs. Immigration was greatly reduced. But Catholic schools helped raise the social status of their students and many became doctors, lawyers, or entered the civil service. Particularly in Melbourne, Catholics were encouraged to enter academic life. Three new dioceses were created between 1910 and 1950: Wagga Wagga, Toowoomba, and Townsville.

Immigration

After World War II a vigorous immigration policy brought many new Catholics. Australian society and the Church became less isolated in outlook and more cosmopolitan. A postwar increase in vocations to the priesthood and religious life enabled the Church to respond with new parishes, churches, and schools. The Sydney archdiocese was divided in 1951 to establish Wollongong diocese, and again in 1986, forming Parramatta and Broken Bay dioceses.

In 1954, federal opposition leader Dr. Herbert Evatt, trying to strengthen his position, accused the Catholic Social Movement, and its director Mr. B. A. (Bob) Santamaria, of subverting the Labor party. This precipitated a twenty-year split in the party. Bishops divided on the issue, Dr. Mannix and others supporting Mr. Santamaria, while Sydney's Cardinal Norman Gilroy encouraged Catholic loyalty to Labor.

Sectarianism had decreased in the 1960s, and political expediency led both major parties to compete at introducing various forms of assistance to Church schools, until governments funded a substantial part of education costs. Today they maintain such contributions rather than educate the same students more expensively in their own schools. The Catholic Church is by far the largest alternate educator, with an education department in every diocese.

Vatican II

Pope John XXIII and the Vatican Council brought a new enthusiasm to the Australian Church, a keen interest in the debates, and a growing spirit of ecumenism. Hobart's Archbishop Guilford Young was a significant member of the council's Liturgical Commission, and the Mass in English gained speedy acceptance. The birth control issue was followed closely, and there was intense feeling when the encyclical *Humanae Vitae* adopted the minority opinion of the commission of inquiry. Australian bishops responded to the papal call for loyalty, but many Catholics went their own way.

New liturgies, prayer movements, and other changes in the Church brought dismay to a traditionalist minority. Vocations began to dwindle from the mid-1960s with few entering seminaries and novitiates, and many departures. Largely because government funding enabled religious teachers to be replaced with lay, the Catholic school system continues. A positive outcome of having fewer priests has been an increased role for lay men and women. Few dioceses ordain married deacons, but the use of special ministers of the Eucharist is virtually universal.

Australia's bishops are generally conservative, but consult quite widely and the Church has spoken on such issues as Aborigines, poverty, and the care of the divorced. Peer support ministries for those facing a range of problems are increasing. Many parish lay councils exercise genuine authority. Mass attendance has decreased, but parishioners in many places take advantage of educational programs in Scripture and theology. Catholics fill senior positions in the community generally and reach the highest standards of tertiary education; the first two Catholic universities began in the 1990s. Many seminaries have become colleges of theology with mostly lay students—the majority women—taking the degree courses. Religious sisters and brothers serve in ministries once reserved to priests, but women generally are ready for change which has still to occur.

The Catholic Church with 27.3 percent of the national population in 1991, was the largest, followed by the Anglican 23.9 percent and then the Uniting Church. Catholics are quite evenly spread through Australia; N.S.W. has the greatest number: 29.5 percent, Tasmania the least with 18.4 percent. Of Catholics born overseas, one in four is from Italy, about one in eleven from England, followed by Croatia, Malta, Poland, and Ireland.

The Australian Catholic Church faces a new millennium with uncertainties but many strengths, especially a strong laity.

JOHN HOSIE, S.M.

See also MCKILLOP, MARY; MANNIX, DANIEL; MORAN, PATRICK FRANCIS.

AUSTRALIAN CATHOLICS

See McKILLOP, MARY; MANNIX, DANIEL; MORAN, PATRICK FRANCIS.

AUTHORITY IN THE CHURCH

The word "authority" comes from the Latin *auctoritas* which belongs to a family of terms meaning "to cause to grow," "to produce." A person in authority should, accordingly, foster the growth of a society thanks to an invested power to influence or command thought, opinion or behavior. "Authority" is found frequently in the texts of Vatican II, but only once in the Latin translation of the Bible, the Vulgate, which prefers *potestas* = "power." The New Testament Greek uses *dynamis* = "ability," "capacity," "power"; and *exousia* = "the ability to perform an action," "the power which decides."

In the Church of God, "authority," in the basic and fullest sense of the word, belongs to the Triune God, Father, Son and Spirit. This is illustrated by the fact that the ultimate source of "growth" is said to be God alone (1 Cor 3:6-7; 8:6). Furthermore, in the New Testament, "domination" = *kratos* is never attributed to a member of the Church, but only to God and Christ (Luke 1:51; Acts 19:20; Eph 1:19; 6:10; Col 1:11, etc.). The same holds true for "master" = *despotès* (Luke 2:29; Acts 4:19; 2 Pet 2:1; Jude 4); "Lord" = *kyrios* (v.g. Matt 11:25; 1 Cor 8:5-6; Rom 14:9; Phil 2:11)—which explains why Christ can "command" = *kyrieuein* (Rom 14:9; 1 Tim 6:15), but neither Paul (2 Cor 1:24) nor the elders (1 Pet 5:3).

Likewise, only to Christ, but never to his disciples, are attributed the titles: "ruler" = *archôn* (Rev 1:5); "author" = *archègos* (Acts 3:15; 5:31; Heb 2:10; 12:2); "head" = *kephalè* with the meaning of authority, preeminence and superiority (1 Cor 11:3; Col 1:18; 2:10; Eph 1:10, 22; 5:23) and with the meaning of vital principle, source of life (Col 2:19; Eph 4:15). Hebrews 7:24 tells us that Christ's "sacerdotal status" = *hierôsynè* is exclusive *aparabatos*.

The power of the Spirit is manifested by the affirmation that, at his baptism, Jesus was anointed by God with the Holy Spirit and power (Acts 10:38), whereas he was proclaimed the Son of God in power, according to the Spirit of sanctity, through the resurrection from the dead (Rom 1:4; cf. 8:11). The power of the Spirit is also at work in the Church (1 Thess 1:5; Gal 3:5; 1 Cor 2:4; Rom 15:13, 19). It is through the Spirit that the New Covenant is established (2 Cor 3:3, 6, 17-18), that the believer is purified, sanctified and justified (1 Cor 6:11), and becomes a member of the body of Christ (1 Cor 12:13).

This omnipotence of the Triune God is, for the believer, a source of hope since it is the absolute power of a Father of mercy and consolation (2 Cor 1:3-4) whose only-begotten Son has established his dwelling amongst us in order, as truth and life, to lead us to the Father (John 1:14; 14:6) who pours forth his love into our hearts through the Holy Spirit (Rom 5:5) so that we can live in "communion" with them (1 John 1:3; 3:24; 4:13; 2 Cor 13:13). Nor does the Triune God need any "successors" or "replacements" here on earth since they are ever with the believers (Matt 28:20; John 14:16, 23).

When humankind is granted to participate in their power, it is always with the understanding that the source, the model/norm, and the end of such a derived power are none other than the Trinity. This holds true even of civil (Rom 13:1; John 19:11; Wis 6:3) and parental (Matt 23:9; Eph 3:14-15) authority. In turn, "obedience" is due, in the last resort, exclusively to the Triune God no matter how many intermediaries may have been established to lead us to this point. Peter summed up this point very well when, before the Sanhedrin, he stated: "Obedience to God comes before obedience to men" (Acts 5:29; cf. 4:19); as did Paul when he chastised Peter for not acting according to the "truth of the Gospel" (Gal 2:11-14), which gospel of the kingdom of God is the norm not only of the apostles and the angels (Gal 1:6-9; 2 Cor 4:5), but also of all the believers without exception (2 Cor 11:4; 1 John 2:24; Jude 3). In the last analysis, all will have to answer for themselves before the tribunal of God (Rom 14:12).

However, it should be noted that the fundamental empowerment graciously bestowed on believers is that of becoming children of God (John 1:12) through rebirth in water and the Spirit (John 3:5, 8; 7:37-39; 20:22; Rom 8:14-17). Such an empowerment is on the level of "being" and, in fact, of "new being in Christ" (2 Cor 5:17). It is on this basis that Vatican II speaks, in its Dogmatic Constitution on the Church (LG 32), of the fundamental equality among all believers.

Other forms of participation in the power of the kingdom of God are granted the disciples on the level of "action" which has for its purpose fostering the common good (1 Cor 12:7), the building up of the body of Christ (Eph 4:11-16). In such a context, we encounter the power to "bind and loose" (Matt 18:18), "to forgive and retain sins" (Matt 9:8; John 20:23), to judge the world (1 Cor 6:2), the "charisma"/"gifts" (1 Cor 12:1-30; Rom 12:3-8; Eph 4:7, 11-13; 1 Pet 4:9-11; Heb 2:4) along with participation in the regal and sacerdotal functions of Christ (2 Pet 2:5, 9; Rev 1:6; 5:10; 20:6).

Listed among the gifts, we find those of apostle, prophet, teacher, leader (1 Cor 12:28; Rom 12:6-7; 1 Thess 5:12-13; Heb 13:1, 19) as well as shepherd (John 21:15-17; Acts 20:28; Eph 4:11; 1 Pet 5:2-4). The powers of the kingdom of God were granted in a specific and official way to the Twelve (Matt 10:1, par.; 19:28), the Seventy-Two (Luke 10:9, 17-19), Peter (Matt 16:18-19; Luke 22:32; John 21:15-19, 22), the Eleven/Twelve (Matt 28:18-20; Mark 16:15-16; Luke 24:47-49; Acts 1:4, 8), and Paul (Rom 15:19; 2 Cor 10:8; 13:10). During the Last Supper, Jesus instructed the Twelve (Matt 26:20, par.) to "do this in memory of me" (Luke 22:19; 1 Cor 11:24, 25-26; in 1 Cor 11:17-34, Paul does not specify who the presider is). These persons were called upon to render to their brothers and sisters a "service" patterned on that of Christ, who came to serve and not to be served (Mark 10:41-45, par.; John 10:11-17; 13:13-16), for which they remain accountable, primarily, to the Supreme Shepherd (1 Pet 5:4), as well as to the discernment of the community (1 Cor 9:2; 2 Cor 11:6; 12:11-13; Eph 3:4; 1 John 4:1-6), in the light of a common faith (Rom 1:8, 12; 15:14; 1 Cor 15:11; 2 Cor 1:24; 13:5-8; Gal 2:2; 2 Pet 1:12; 1 John 2:24, 27; Jude 5), which is the basis for a common effort, *conspiratio,* between leaders and faithful in the Church of God.

Thus, we see Paul and the other apostles and ministers exercising a delegated authority (2 Cor 3:5-6; 5:18–6:1; Eph 6:20) in and for the building up of the body of Christ, the temple of the Holy Spirit, the Church of God. Chosen to proclaim the gospel of God (Rom 1:1), in which the power of God is at work (Rom 1:16-17), Paul can speak of having engendered, in the gospel, several Churches (1 Cor 4:15; Gal 4:19; 1 Thess 2:7, 11), founding on this fact his right to be obeyed in the domain of disciplinary action (1 Cor 4:21; 5:3-5, 13; 2 Cor 5-11), that of rules and customs (1 Cor 2:16; 4:17; 7:6, 12, 17, 25, 40; 11:16; 14:33-34, 37; 1 Thess 4:1-2; 2 Thess 2:15; 3:6) and to be imitated in so far as he imitates Christ (1 Cor 4:16; 11:1)—in both of these cases the community is invited to play an active role. Moreover, the norm of sound teaching (2 Tim 1:13), the proper interpretation of the gospel (2 Pet 2:20-21; 3:15-17) is to be found with the apostles, the eye witnesses (Luke 24:47-48; Acts 1:8-9; John 20:31; 1 John 1:3; 4:16).

The New Testament testifies to a further delegation of authority within the Church of God, one which often explicitly includes the active participation of the whole community in the form of election and/or prayer. Matthias is chosen to succeed Judas in the apostolic ministry as one of the twelve apostles (Acts 1:15-26). The "Seven" are chosen by the disciples to see to the needs of the Hellenists, and the apostles lay their hands on them (Acts 6:1-7). The prophets and teachers of Antioch, moved by the Spirit in a liturgical setting, send Barnabas and Saul on mission with the laying on of the hands (Acts 13:1-3). Paul and Barnabas, again in a liturgical setting, appoint, in Lystra, Iconium and Antioch in Pisidia, "elders" (Acts 14:23), a group whose existence is equally attested to in the Churches of Jerusalem (Acts 11:30; 15:2, 4, 6; 16:4; 21:18) and Ephesus (Acts 20:17), and whose function seems to be described in Acts 20:28 (cf. 1 Tim 5:17) as a continuation of that of the apostles, namely to "Be on your guard for yourselves and for all the flock of whom the Holy Spirit has made you the overseers, to feed the Church of God which he bought with his own blood." The Pastoral Epistles also speak of these "elders/overseers" whom Titus is commissioned to appoint in each town (Titus 1:5). Yet, we find them already at Paul's side for the laying on of hands on Timothy (1 Tim 4:14) whom we know to be one of Paul's principal collaborators (1 Cor 4:17). Timothy, in turn, will establish elders/overseers who will assume the tasks of teaching and government in the Church of God (1 Tim 3:1-7; 5:22; cf. Titus 1:6-9). In 2 Timothy 2:2, we come very close to the notion of "apostolic succession" in the ministry when Paul exhorts Timothy ". . . those things that you heard from me, through many witnesses, set out for trustworthy men, the kind who will also be competent to teach others." Such a ministry, which is centered on keeping, through the Holy Spirit, the fine deposit (2 Tim 1:14), is no doubt geared to maintaining the "apostolic succession" of the whole Church (Eph 2:20; Rev 21:14) which is to be lived in an atmosphere of fidelity to the teaching of the apostles, fellowship, the breaking of bread and prayer (Acts 2:42).

THOMAS R. POTVIN, O.P.

See also ECCLESIOLOGY; TRADITION.

AUTHORITY OF TRADITION

See TRADITION.

AVE MARIA

See "HAIL MARY."

AVIGNON PAPACY

From 1309 to 1377 the popes, Clement V, John XXII, Benedict XII, Clement VI, Innocent VI, Urban V and Gregory XI, resided at Avignon in France rather than in their traditional See of Rome. Often referred to as the "Babylonian captivity of the Church" it was a scandalous episode in the history of Christianity. At Avignon the popes conducted a very worldly court, using the institutional structures of the Church primarily as a means to raise exorbitant tribute from the local Churches and the ordinary faithful, and selling benefices to the highest bidder.

Clement V moved the papal court to Avignon because Rome was in a condition of anarchy in which one of his predecessors, Boniface VIII, who frequently intervened in international disputes, had been captured and briefly imprisoned by mercenaries of King Philip IV of France. When he died unexpectedly soon after this, Charles II of Naples occupied Rome with troops and influenced the cardinals to elect his protégé, Benedict XI, who also died unexpectedly in less than a year. In a conclave divided along political lines, the pro-French group managed to have the archbishop of Bordeaux elected. Taking the name of Clement V, he decided to seek safety and stability for the papacy by taking up residence in Avignon under the patronage of King Philip. The advantages of this patronage were, of course, countered by disadvantages, including the dwindling respect commanded by the papacy even among the devout.

During the pontificate of John XXII (1316–1334), the scandals of the Avignon papacy, added to a disedifying prior history, prompted four eminent philosophers and theologians of the time, Marsiglio of Padua, John of Jandun, William of Ockham, and Michael Cesena to write anonymous critiques of the way the institutional Church of their time embodied the idea of Church. In particular, they marshalled arguments against any kind of temporal or worldly power in the hands of Church leaders. These arguments were widely influential among scholars and princes. Moreover, the book *Defensor Pacis* of Marsiglio and John went further in the critique of Church authority and proposed that the highest authority in the whole Church should be a general council of laity and clergy which would define orthodoxy in doctrine as well as making practical decisions.

It was not only among scholars and politicians that protests against the scandals of the Avignon papacy were made. St. Birgitta of Sweden, a noblewoman with many influential connections, pleaded unsuccessfully with Urban V to return to Rome. Some years later the indefatigable St. Catherine of Siena, chosen as a mediator between warring Italian city states and Pope Gregory XI, successfully persuaded the latter to return to Rome. Gregory had intended to do this for some time but had faced strong opposition from the French cardinals. He left Avignon in September, 1376, sailed from Marseilles in October, and made a solemn entry into Rome in January, 1377. His return brought new problems because of his harshness to those who opposed him, and in any case by March of 1378 he was dead. Although from this time the popes remained in Rome, the problems of the papacy were not ended because Gregory's death led to the Great Western Schism with its series of rival popes.

MONIKA K. HELLWIG

See also CATHERINE OF SIENA, ST.; GREAT WESTERN SCHISM; PAPACY, THE.

B

BABYLONIAN CAPTIVITY

In 931 B.C. the land inhabited by the chosen people was divided into two kingdoms. The northern kingdom of Israel with its capital in Samaria, fell to the Assyrians in 721 B.C. Nineveh, capital of the Assyrian Empire, itself fell in 612 B.C., giving way to Babylonian supremacy that lasted from 612 to 538 B.C. The Babylonians also defeated the Egyptians at Carchemish in 605, when Nebuchadrezza began an extraordinary forty-three-year reign of power, expansion, and prosperity.

The southern kingdom of Judah remained independent until it fell to Nebuchadrezza, king of Babylon in 587 B.C. The attack was devastating for the kingdom of Judah. The nation was left in ruins, Jerusalem and the Temple destroyed. Large numbers of people were slaughtered, and between ten to fifteen thousand taken off into exile in Babylon. While those deported were a small percentage of the total nation, they included civic and religious leaders, and were the best educated, trained, and most skillful members of the population, and their deportation had an overwhelmingly negative impact on the nation. Judah had been attacked before, but had suffered nothing so great as this. It seemed their national and religious identity was finished.

As was common in those days, once the kingdom of Judah and its capital Jerusalem were conquered the leading inhabitants were taken off into exile. There were several waves of deportations beginning as early as 605 B.C.; three are notable: in 598 to 597 when Jehoiachin was king, in 587 when Zedekia was king, and finally in 582 B.C. During much of this period the great prophet Jeremiah (626–586) warned of the Babylonian threat. The Jews were kept in exile from 587 to 538 until Cyrus conquered the Babylonian Empire (539) and allowed the Jews to return to their homeland in 538.

During their time in exile the Jews suffered much under the harsh treatment of Nebuchadrezza, but after his death they were treated quite well, so that many did not wish to return to Judah when they were offered the opportunity. The prophets of the Exile (Ezekiel and Deutero-Isaiah [chs. 40–55]) consoled and encouraged the people while also challenging them to remain faithful to their religious heritage.

The Babylonian captivity was a time for the Jews to examine their infidelity, against which Isaiah had spoken (Isa 6:11-13), and rethink their commitment to God. In spite of the nation's infidelity, prophets foretold the restoration of an anointed one, and when the first group of exiles were taken to Babylon in 597, the young king, Jehoiachim, was among them.

Babylon destroyed the Promised Land and almost extinguished the faith of the chosen people. Secure in its own power and intoxicated by its own self-aggrandizment, believers saw Babylon as the embodiment of opposition to God's will and to the development of God's people. Prophets denounced its idolatry, pride, cruelty, and immorality (Jer 50:29-32; 51:44-52; Isa 47:7-10). New Testament writers speak of Babylonian opposition to the new Jerusalem of the Church (Rev 21). Peter also refers to imperial Rome under Nero as "this Babylon" (1 Pet 5:13). John, the author of the Book of Revelation, often speaks of the destruction of the great Babylon (Rev 18:1-8).

The initial phase of return from exile, authorized by Cyrus' decree (538 B.C.), was under the leadership of Shesh-bazzar. Response was poor and efforts to restore Jerusalem ineffective. Twenty years later, during the reign of Darius I, Zerubbabel, the provincial governor, and Joshua, the chief priest, began the serious work of restoration, with the encouragement of the prophets Haggai and Zechariah. The Temple was restored by 515 B.C. Sometime later (445–400 B.C.), the leaders Ezra and Nehemiah eventually spearheaded a major renewal of the national religious heritage.

Some Church writers referred to the exile of the popes in Avignon, France, from 1309 to 1377 as the Babylonian captivity of the Church. Seven popes governed the Church from Avignon, until Catherine of Siena (1347–1380) persuaded Pope Gregory XI to return to Rome in 1377.

LEONARD DOOHAN

See also BIBLE, OLD TESTAMENT WRITINGS.

BALTIMORE CATECHISM

The bishops of the Third Plenary Council of Baltimore in 1884, after previous discussion at the First Provincial Council of Baltimore in 1829 and again at the plenary councils of 1852 and 1866, mandated the preparation of a uniform catechism for the United States. The bishops saw the need for a uniform text because many of the catechisms in use at the time were not sufficiently adapted to the understanding of children or were deficient in other respects. Secondly, a single text insured a uniform instructional program no matter where Catholics migrated.

Although a preparatory commission hastily put together a draft of the catechism for the council, it adjourned in December 1884 without an approved manual. The final redaction is the work of John Lancaster Spalding, bishop of Peoria, assisted by Monsignor Gennaro de Concilio, a New Jersey pastor. *A Catechism of Christian Doctrine, Prepared and Enjoined by the Order of the Third Plenary Council of Baltimore* received the imprimatur and was approved by Archbishop Gibbons on 6 April 1885 but was never officially adopted by the body of bishops before publication. The order of the 1885 catechism is Creed, Sacraments, Commandments and Prayer following the order of the *Roman Catechism.* The original version consisted of 421 questions and answers and incorporated the questions in the answers. Very little of the content was original but was taken from other manuals already in use in the United States.

The catechism met with immediate criticism: pedagogically, for its abstract language, monotonous format, and rote learning; theologically, for the equivalence of all doctrines, overemphasis on sin, obligation and fear of punishment, insufficient attention to the significance of the resurrection and to the Holy Spirit. In September 1885, Spalding published an abridged edition that reduced the number of questions-answers to 208 and rearranged the order. This abridged text was never as widely accepted as the original version. Persistent criticism resulted in *A Catechism of Christian Doctrine,* a revised edition of the Baltimore Catechism in 1941 with Francis J. Connell, C.S.S.R., as the chief editor.

Despite the dissatisfaction and negative evaluations, the Baltimore Catechism gained ever increasing circulation. When it was not simply memorized verbatim, it provided a syllabus for Catholic catechetical programs and textbooks until the 1960s. Revised editions continue to be published.

CATHERINE DOOLEY, O.P.

See also AMERICAN CATHOLICISM; BALTIMORE, COUNCILS OF; CATECHESIS; CATECHETICS; CATECHISM.

BALTIMORE, COUNCILS (PLENARY) OF

The First Plenary Council was convoked on 8 May 1852, with Archbishop Francis Kenrick presiding as papal legate. It covered topics and problems of a growing Catholic community including religious teaching, pastoral and parochial life, ritual and liturgy, and the administration of Church finances.

The Second Plenary Council was convoked on 7 October 1866 and, with Archbishop Martin Spalding presiding, it lasted for two weeks. The assembled bishops discussed doctrinal, educational, financial and organizational questions. It issued nine decrees on the care of the 100,000 (of four million) emancipated slaves who were Catholics. The action of the bishops was little more than tokenism as they had played little or no part in the fight against slavery and most regarded segregation a firm norm in American life.

The Third Plenary Council, under the leadership of Archbishop James Gibbons, was a landmark in the history of American Catholicism. It lasted from 9 November to 7 December 1884, and its decrees shaped the course of the Church in America for over a century. It decreed the writing of the series of Baltimore catechisms which had immense and lasting influence. It mandated the establishment of elementary schools in all parishes, and approved the foundation of the Catholic University of America in the nation's capital.

MICHAEL GLAZIER

See also AMERICAN CATHOLICISM; CATECHISM; GIBBONS, JAMES CARDINAL.

BANNS

Banns are public announcements, usually of the intended marriage of two Catholics, but also of someone's candidacy to receive a Sacred Order, with the purpose of uncovering any impediment to the marriage or the ordination.

WILLIAM C. McFADDEN, S.J.

See also CANON LAW; SACRAMENT OF MATRIMONY; SACRAMENT OF ORDERS.

BAPTISM

See SACRAMENTS OF INITIATION.

"BAPTISM IN THE HOLY SPIRIT"

A key experience in the nineteenth-century Holiness Movement and twentieth-century Pentecostalism, baptism in the Holy Spirit is also important in the Catholic Pentecostal renewal. It is described as an awakening to full life in the Spirit, a transformation and an empowerment of faith, which gives rise to joy and praise. McDonnell and Montague give evidence that it was normative in the first eight centuries, and thus argue that it is an authentic charism of Christian initiation; if so, and if the Holy Spirit and the charisms are neglected in the Church, they urge cautious pastoral efforts to help baptized, confirmed Christians to be open to the experience. The RCIA, which asks inquirers to allow their hearts to be "open to the Spirit" (no. 36) and speaks of "following supernatural inspiration" in their deeds (no. 75.2) suggests ways to begin this effort.

MARY BARBARA AGNEW, C.PP.S.

See also FAITH; HOLY SPIRIT; PROPHECY/PROPHET.

BAPTISM OF DESIRE

This term arose out of the medieval discussion trying to reconcile God's universal salvific will (desire to save everyone) with the teaching that baptism is necessary for salvation. It had been recognized since very early Christian times that those who were martyred for the faith while yet unbaptized were deemed to have been baptized in the blood of their martyrdom. It was therefore suggested that even those who died desiring baptism, but were not martyred, could be deemed to be baptized by their desire. But that left the question about people who led good lives in ignorance of the gospel of Jesus Christ, and about people who repented and turned to God as they knew God outside the Christian tradition. Many theologians maintained that these people also had a baptism of desire though this was not an explicit desire of baptism. In a statement of 1949 the Church officially declared that this was correct (DS 3869). In the teaching of the Second Vatican Council it is clear that people of good faith living in other traditions are saved (*Lumen Gentium* 9).

MONIKA K. HELLWIG

BAPTISMAL VOWS

The ancient formula for making baptismal vows is a threefold renunciation of evil and a threefold affirmation of the creed. The latter contains specific acceptance of the Three Persons of the Trinity. In the case of infant baptism the parents and godparents make this renunciation and profession on behalf of the child. In the case of adult baptism the candidate himself or herself does so.

A great pastoral need today is the renewal of baptismal vows, especially by those who were baptized as infants. The most appropriate times for such renewal are the Easter Vigil and Easter Sunday itself. On these occasions the entire congregation is called upon to renew its baptismal commitment after the observance of Lent. However, other occasions are also available. Sundays, with their rite of blessing and sprinkling with holy water, especially during the Easter season, provide a great opportunity for this renewal. The celebration of other sacraments, e.g., confirmation, Eucharist, or penance, is likewise a fitting occasion. Other ways of recalling baptism and its lifelong commitment are the recitation of the Our Father and the Apostles' Creed as well as the making of the sign of the cross, especially in conjunction with the use of holy water.

Ultimately the goal of such renewal is the recollection of one's initial commitment that, in turn, should motivate the believer to participate ever more profoundly in the life and mission of the Church. In this way the obligations assumed in baptism continue to impact one's entire life. Fittingly, funerals celebrate death as that final moment of growth for the encounter with Christ that began at baptism.

JOHN F. CRAGHAN

See also CREEDS; FAITH.

BAPTISTRY

In early Christianity, believers were baptized by immersion in a lake or river. Later, special rooms or buildings were set aside as baptistries (or baptisteries), some recognized as architectural masterpieces,

Baptismal font by Albert Schilling, Basel

like the one in Pisa. Previously located at the entrance to a church to symbolize baptism as the door to membership in the community, recent liturgical reform has recommended that the baptismal font no longer be in a separate location or baptistry, but that it be at the front of the church, close to the altar, thereby manifesting the central importance of baptism and its relationship to the whole Eucharistic community.

LEONARD DOOHAN

See also LITURGY; SACRAMENTS OF INITIATION.

BAPTISTS

At least twenty-seven different Baptist denominations trace their heritage to a religious movement called the Anabaptists who were part of the "radical" or "left-wing" Protestant Reformation of the sixteenth century. This group of Christians did not think Luther and Calvin went far enough in their effort to restore the Church to the purity of the apostolic era. What was missing was "believers' baptism" and separation of the Church from civil authority. These original elements define what a Baptist is to this day.

Since adult baptism was a prerequisite for Church membership, all new followers who were baptized as infants had to be baptized again, hence, the name Anabaptists (rebaptized). An abbreviation of that pejorative label gave the name to one of the largest Protestant bodies.

The Anabaptist tradition developed in two ways. One strand gave rise to a significant group of "peace" Churches—Mennonites, Amish, and Brethren. The other strand helped create the English Puritans and Separatists. Both were countercultural by way of their position on baptism, their peace witness, and their desire to be separate from the government.

The Puritan/Separatist movement produced the pivotal figure of John Smyth (ca. 1570–1612), an Anglican priest who joined the Separatist movement and was instrumental in forming Baptist consciousness.

Roger Williams (ca. 1603–1683) joined the same group and came eventually to the Massachusetts Bay Colony. His views, especially his anti-theocratic convictions, made it necessary for him to move to Providence, Rhode Island, where he founded the First Baptist Church in 1639. The first Baptist Association was formed in Philadelphia in 1707.

By the beginning of the nineteenth century, their evangelical fervor had made them the largest Protestant group in the United States. In time, some of the countercultural edge wore off and there was a serious division over the issue of slavery. In 1845, Baptists became "Southern" and "Northern." The Southern Baptist Convention was and is more conservative, often fundamentalist, and by far the largest branch. The smaller Northern, more progressive and liberal branch, is the American Baptist Church in the U.S.A.

Baptist belief, in general, is near the center of orthodox Christianity; such doctrines as the divinity of Christ with his atonement and resurrection, the authority of the Bible, redemption through Christ, Trinity, Second Coming, heaven and hell are commonly held among Baptists.

Most Baptists stress a personal morality and have a negative view of such individual sins as drinking, gambling, and dancing, just as a strong positive view of a personal, individual relation with Christ is indispensable. No Protestant group is more committed to Sunday schools and none is more enthusiastic about missionary activity.

From the beginning, Baptists have been independent-minded—a "free" Church *par excellence.* Their worship is informal, with no set ritual pattern for all churches; their relation to God is direct and without priestly mediation; they strongly affirm individual interpretation of the Bible; each congregation is a voluntary association of adults who have been reborn; there is no super-church body which has authority to enforce policy for the local congregation; their desire for independence and autonomy has historically made them champions of religious liberty.

There are two Ordinances (i.e., observances ordered by Christ), namely, baptism and the Lord's Supper, neither of which has sacramental power. Baptism occurs after a deeply moving experience of Christ which leads to an adult profession of faith in Jesus as Savior and Lord. Baptism, then, ratifies that experience by full immersion in water; it is a "dying and rising with Christ." Some Baptists hold so strongly to this form of baptism that they believe it is the defining mark of a true Christian.

The Lord's Supper is strictly a memorial meal; Baptists have a meal with Jesus, not Jesus for the meal. Or, as they would say, "Jesus is around the table, not on the table."

Therefore, such "Church" accoutrements as creeds, festival days, orders of clergy, sacraments, banners, hierarchical structures, infant baptism, and clerical vestments are foreign to most Baptists.

Baptists understand themselves to be a gathered Church of believers, a group of regenerated Christian individuals who voluntarily come together for fellowship, preaching, prayer, and to follow Christ as each one's conscience dictates.

It is difficult accurately to know how many Baptists there are. There are many small Baptist groups who do not align themselves with Conventions or Associations. The Baptist World Alliance knows of at least 38 million Baptists in the world. Four of five African-Americans are Baptist; this includes the National Baptist Convention of America (3 million) and the National Baptist Convention of the U.S.A. (6 million). Southern Baptists number about 15 million in the U.S.A. and American Baptists claim about 1.5 million members.

IRA ZEPP

See also PROTESTANTISM; REFORMATION, THE.

BARING, MAURICE (1874–1945)

Born in 1874, Baring was educated at Eton and Trinity College, Cambridge. He wrote articles, biography, poetry, plays, criticism, translations, short stories, and novels. A gifted linguist, he served in the Foreign Office, and later worked as a reporter of the Russo-Japanese War. He discovered Chekhov's work while in Moscow, and helped to introduce it to the West. He was an expert in Russian literature, as seen in his *Landmarks in Russian Literature* (1910), *An Outline of Russian Literature* (1914), and *The Oxford Book of Russian Verse* (1924). Among his novels, '*C*' (1924), *Cat's Cradle* (1925), *Daphne Adeane* (1926), and *The Coat without Seam* (1929) reflect his social world and are still well-regarded for their portrait of the time. Baring's conversion to Catholicism is reflected in two novels of the Tudor era: *Robert Peckham* (1930), and *In my End is my Beginning* (1931). His novella, *The Lonely Lady of Dulwich* (1934), is considered by critics to be his best work, and his anthology *Have You Anything to Declare?* is a classic. He died in 1945.

JOSEPH QUINN

See also BRITAIN, CHURCH IN.

BASIC COMMUNITIES

Basic ecclesial communities (called CEBs both in Spanish and Portuguese) are small groups of Catholics who meet regularly for services of prayer, worship, and communal reflection on both their religious and secular lives. Usually coordinated by lay leaders, CEBs have great interest in the Bible. After reflecting on God's word in light of its historical context and in light of their own lives, experiences, and struggles, these Christians are committed to putting their conclusions into practice both in their personal and their communal lives. CEBs help people to grow in their faith, in a deeper understanding of God's word, and in a greater commitment to justice within the social milieu that surrounds them.

In giving clear and enthusiastic support to CEBs, the episcopal conference at Puebla (1979) saw itself following in the footsteps of Medellín (1968) and the apostolic exhortation of Paul VI, *Evangelii Nuntiandi* (1976), which concludes that CEBs are a source of great hope, a real expression of communion, and a treasure to the whole Church, as long as they live in unity with the local and universal Church.

DENNIS SWEETLAND

See also LIBERATION THEOLOGIES.

BASIL, ST., RULE OF

See BASIL THE GREAT, ST.

BASIL THE GREAT, ST. (ca. 330–379)

Born of a wealthy and distinguished Christian family in Caesarea in Cappadocia (modern-day Kayseri, Turkey), Basil's grandmother Macrina the Elder, his parents Basil the Elder and Emmelia, his elder sister Macrina and two younger brothers Gregory of Nyssa and Peter of Sebaste are all listed among the saints. Basil studied rhetoric at Caesarea, Constantinople, and Athens (where he renewed and deepened his friendship with Gregory of Nazianzus). Basil returned to Caesarea ca. 356 but soon abandoned a career as a rhetorician to dedicate his life entirely to God. After being baptized, Basil visited monastic centers in Egypt, Syria, and Mesopotamia. When Basil returned to Caesarea, he distributed his fortune to the poor and began to live an ascetical life at Annesi. When Gregory of Nazianzus spent some time at this monastic community in 358, they prepared an anthology of Origen's works, the *Philocalia,* and preached to the people. Julian the Apostate, who had studied with Basil, was unable to induce Basil to leave his monastic seclusion to come to court. Basil did leave it, however, ca. 364, when Bishop Eusebius of Caesarea (not to be confused with the first major historian of the Church—Bishop Eusebius of Caesarea in Palestine who had died ca. 339) requested his help against the threat posed by the Emperor Valens, an Arian. Basil became metropolitan of Caesarea when Eusebius died in 370 and held this post until his death. During his nine years as bishop, Basil established a hospital for the sick, a church, and a hospice for travelers which were a lasting tribute to his memory and his love for the poor and unfortunate. It is not surprising then that Basil preached quite strongly to the wealthy on the right use of money and the need to avoid avarice. He was involved in the controversies with the extreme Arian party headed by Eunomius as well as those who denied the divinity of the Holy Spirit. He was unsuccessful in establishing harmony between East and West because of his support of Meletius of Antioch. Basil worked hard to reconcile the Homoiousians to the Nicene position and the success of the Council of Constantinople two years after his death is a testimony to his efforts. Basil's influence in Eastern monasticism was profound: to this day monastic life in the East is based on the ideals he set forth in his monastic Rule. His more significant writings would include his *Letters,* the dogmatic treatises *Against Eunomius* and *On the Holy Spirit.* He also produced homilies on the six days of Creation in Genesis 1:1-26 (*Hexameron*), *Homilies on the Psalms,* and a *Commentary on Isaiah.* Basil was named a Doctor of the Church in 1568. Feast day, 1 January (East), 2 January (West).

JOHN DILLON

See also DOCTORS OF THE CHURCH; FATHERS OF THE CHURCH; HOLY SPIRIT; MONASTICISM; ORTHODOXY.

BASILICA

Originally a characteristic Roman meeting hall, of which several were donated to, or constructed for, the Church by the empire after the period of the persecutions. Many other churches (of various styles) are now given the title "minor basilica" as a way of

Basilica of S. Maria Maggiore, Rome

recognizing their importance locally or historically. Ceremonial privileges are attached to the title.

DAVID BRYAN

See also ARCHITECTURE, CHURCH.

BEA, AUGUSTIN, CARDINAL (1881–1968)

The only son of Karl Bea and Maria Merk entered the Society of Jesus in 1902, after completing two years at the University of Freiburg. During his Jesuit training he became deeply interested in biblical studies. He was ordained in 1912; and from 1917 to 1921 he taught the Old Testament at the German Theologate at Valkenburg, Holland. He was then appointed provincial of Bavaria. After an official visit to Japan, he played a major role in the founding of Sophia University in Tokyo. He went to Rome in 1924 to supervise the studies of Jesuit graduate students, and he taught at the Pontifical Biblical Insti-

Cardinal Augustin Bea

tute and was its rector from 1930 to 1949. He also served on many commissions, including the Pontifical Biblical Commission. He was confessor to Pius XII (1945–1958) and was created cardinal in 1959 and became director of the Secretariate for Promoting Christian Unity. His talent for friendship and understanding together with his expertise in biblical studies enabled him to make significant contributions to ecumenism. He greatly influenced the biblical encyclical *Divino Afflante Spiritu* (1943) and he participated in drafting several Vatican II documents including *Dei Verbum.* Cardinal Bea was a scholar of unusual tolerance and vision and his contribution to the Church, to ecumenism, and to scholarship was immense.

JOAN GLAZIER

See also CRITICISM, BIBLICAL; ECUMENISM.

BEATIFIC VISION

See HEAVEN.

BEATIFICATION

In Roman Catholic usage the process of beatification means a declaration that someone has attained the blessedness of heaven and approval of the title "Blessed" with limited public religious honor. The process is referred to as a cause, which is nothing more than a process that brings about, or helps bring about, the declaration that a particular individual is numbered among the blessed. There are two main stages involved in the process: the first investigates whether the individual has died for the faith or, in the case of non-martyrs, practiced the moral and theological virtues as well as humility in an heroic fashion and, if the Servant of God (as the one being examined is called) is found to have done so, he or she is declared Venerable; the second stage occurs when a miracle is attributed to that person and if the miracle is verified and found to be attributed to the individual, he or she is declared to be blessed.

An investigation into the possibilities of canonization can be begun by the local bishop in whose diocese a person whose renown for holiness extends beyond his or her own neighborhood dies, especially when the reputation for holiness survives after the demise of the individual. The *fama sanctitatis,* renown for holiness, often is not enough as other factors enter into the process. This happened in the case of Fra Angelico, a Dominican Friar who died in 1455 but who was not beatified until 3 October 1982, when Pope John Paul II, directly bypassing the usual process intervened, because the cause had lost popular impetus through the centuries. Many persons outstanding for holiness die and are never even considered for canonization. The reason may well be that there is no one to sponsor the cause. Causes of priests and religious are usually espoused by the dioceses or the religious community to which the deceased was attached but examples of heroic virtue among the laity are only rarely taken up. In many cases this is because of concern about the expense of the process.

In the canonization process a distinction must be drawn between the indispensable and essential expenses as distinct from those of an arbitrary nature. The former are inherent in getting the work done and the latter devotional, promotional, or even beneficial, like holy cards, medals, booklets, etc. The cause of St. John Neumann, the fourth bishop of Philadelphia, was under consideration for over one hundred years and the total expenditures, including both of the items just mentioned, amounted to less than a half million dollars. Certainly the optional items helped spread devotion to the beloved saint but were not essential to the final achievement, the canonization itself. At this time the sum of money expended for the beatification of Mother Katherine Drexel has amounted to approximately $333,250 in ascertainable expenses. The faithful, who are ultimately the promoters of any cause, usually and readily rally to support the cause they want advanced. In the present procedure when the bishop sends the materials to Rome a relator is appointed whose responsibility it is to write a *positio,* which contains everything necessary for the consultors and prelates of the congregation to make their judgments as to the fitness of the candidate for beatification.

In popular parlance much is made of the role of the "Devil's Advocate" which is nomenclature never found in the official process. Officially he was called the Promoter of Faith and his function was to be adversarial, that is, to find what was negative, to be somewhat like a prosecuting attorney. He was to argue against the advocate, who was somewhat like a defense attorney.

If the case deals with a martyr it must be proved that the Servant of God was killed because of hatred of the faith and that the victim made the supreme sacrifice of love for Christ and the Church. In the case of non-martyrs, which is usually the case, it must be shown that the man or woman was so profoundly inspired by Christian love for God and one's sisters and brothers that in daily living he or she practiced all Christian virtues in a truly perfect, exemplary, and heroic manner.

The pope's declaration that a person is declared blessed is not an act of infallibility. The decree declaring the fact usually permits only a specified diocese, region, nation, or religious community to honor with public worship under the title of Blessed a person who had died a martyr for the faith or with a reputation for holiness. Special Masses and particular Offices for the Liturgy of the Hours are provided for the Blessed. Among the more commonly known Blessed in the United States are Kateri Tekakwitha, Katherine Drexel, Andre Bessette, Junipero Serra.

JAMES McGRATH

See also CANONIZATION.

BEATITUDES

A "beatitude" declares someone blessed or happy. In the OT beatitudes appear in the third person ("Happy is the one who/they who . . . ," see Pss 1:1; 32:1-2) and usually in a wisdom context. In the NT the declaration is often eschatological: A person is praised as having a share in God's end-time kingdom or salvation. The four beatitudes in Luke 6:20-23 are cast in the second person plural ("Blessed are you") and promise blessedness to the poor, hungry, weeping, and persecuted. The nine beatitudes in Matthew 5:3-12 are in the third person ("Blessed are they") and exhibit a spiritualizing tendency ("poor in spirit" in 5:3; "hunger and thirst for righteousness" in 5:6). These beatitudes introduce Jesus' Sermon on the Plain (Luke 6:20-49) and Sermon on the Mount (Matthew 5–7), respectively. Seven beatitudes appear at various points in the Book of Revelation (see 1:3; 14:13; 16:15; 19:9; 20:6; 22:7; 22:14).

The Beatitudes in Luke (6:20-23)

"Blessed are you who are poor,
for yours is the kingdom of God.
"Blessed are you who are hungry now,
for you will be filled.
"Blessed are you who weep now,
for you will laugh.
"Blessed are you when people hate you,
and when they exclude you,
revile you, and defame you on
account of the Son of Man. Rejoice
in that day and leap for joy, for
surely your reward is great in
heaven; for that is what their
ancestors did to the prophets.

The Beatitudes in Matthew (5:3-12)

"Blessed are the poor in spirit,
for theirs is the kingdom of heaven.
"Blessed are those who mourn,
for they will be comforted.
"Blessed are the meek, for they
will inherit the earth.
"Blessed are those who hunger
and thirst for righteousness,
for they will be filled.
"Blessed are the merciful, for they
will receive mercy.
"Blessed are the pure in heart,
for they will see God.
"Blessed are the peacemakers,
for they will be called children
of God.
"Blessed are those who are persecuted
for righteousness' sake, for theirs
is the kingdom of heaven.
"Blessed are you when people
revile you and persecute you
and utter all kinds of evil against
you falsely on my account. Rejoice
and be glad, for your reward is
great in heaven, for in the same
way they persecuted the prophets who
were before you.

DANIEL J. HARRINGTON, S.J.

See also BLESSING; EVANGELICAL COUNSELS.

BEAUDUIN, LAMBERT (1873–1960)

A student of Dom Columba Marmion, he was a monk at the Benedictine monastery at Mont-Cesar in Louvain. Many regard him as the key figure in the liturgical movement which he pioneered in Europe. His addresses at the Malines Catholic Conference in 1903 came to be regarded as a blueprint for the liturgical revival. He actively promoted the liturgical education of the faithful and initiated the landmark Liturgical Weeks at Mont-Cesar which aimed to give participants, mostly clergy, a deeper appreciation of texts and rites. He was a friend of Virgil Michel whom he inspired to start the liturgical movement in America. He became professor of liturgy at San Anselmo in Rome where he became editor of *Irenikon.* He inculcated his students with a dedication to liturgical studies and renewal. His articles and books had a select and influential readership; and his *Liturgy, the Life of the Church* (The Liturgical Press, 1926) had a profound impact on readers in the English-speaking world.

MICHAEL GLAZIER

See also LITURGICAL MOVEMENT, THE.

BECKET, ST. THOMAS À (1118–1170)

English archbishop and martyr. A Londoner of Norman descent, he distinguished himself as a lawyer and administrator in the service of Archbishop Theobald of Canterbury but it was his love of hunting, knightly combat, and fine clothes as much as his professional competence which won him the friendship of King Henry II, who appointed him chancellor in 1155. In this capacity he worked hard to undermine the legal and financial exemptions from royal control enjoyed by the Church. The king's influence secured Becket's election to the vacant see of Canterbury in 1162 although he was not a priest: he had to be ordained on the day before his consecration. Being totally committed to any task he undertook, the new archbishop resigned the chancellorship, abandoned his worldly tastes, adopted an ascetic lifestyle, and undertook a vigorous defense of the ecclesiastical privileges which he had previously opposed. Bitter controversy followed between Becket and the king. Despite some mutual concessions made at the urging of Pope Alexander III, the archbishop had to flee to France. An uneasy settlement was arrived at in 1170 and Becket returned to England, where the people acclaimed him as the opponent of tyranny. When he refused to make the conciliatory gestures expected by the king, four knights from the royal household pursued him into his cathedral and murdered him. A local cult sprang up in England, he was canonized in 1173, and King Henry did public penance at his tomb. The shrine of Saint Thomas at Canterbury became the most popular center of pilgrimage in England until the Reformation.

LOUIS McREDMOND

See also BRITAIN, CHURCH IN.

"The Martyrdom of St. Thomas à Becket," Latin Psalter manuscript, 1200

BEDE THE VENERABLE, ST. (ca. 673–735)

Bede's parents entrusted him as a boy of seven to the monks of Wearmouth and soon after to its twin house of Jarrow. Among his teachers were Benedict Biscop and Ceolfrid. Ordained a deacon at the unusually early age of nineteen, he was ordained a priest at thirty. He spent the rest of his life as a monk of Jarrow, probably never traveling outside of northeast England. A productive writer, particularly of biblical works that were famous at the time, Bede is best known today as the author of the *History of the English Church and People* in which he was careful to separate fact from rumor. Bede also composed works for his monastic pupils on proper spelling, versification, and natural phenomena; chronologies (which influenced the custom of dating events from the incarnation); lives of saints; hymns; homilies; prayers in verse; as well as letters. Besides being the author of these works in Latin, Bede is the first-known writer of English prose. Unfortunately his writings in English have not survived. A century after his death Bede was honored with the title Venerable. In 1899 Leo XIII named Bede a Doctor of the Church. Feast day, 25 May.

JOHN DILLON

See also BRITAIN, CHURCH IN; FATHERS OF THE CHURCH; MONASTICISM.

BELLARMINE, ROBERT FRANCIS ROMULUS, ST. (1542–1621)

Doctor of the Church, Jesuit-cardinal, apologist, archbishop of Capua, he was born at Montepulciano in Tuscany on 4 October 1542. Given a Renaissance education, he entered the Society of Jesus despite family opposition. After studying at Florence and Louvain, he was ordained a priest in Ghent in 1570. He became the first Jesuit professor at the University of Louvain, and while studying the Church Fathers, Hebrew and Scripture there, he also used Thomistic thought to refute the writings of Baius. It was there that he began his reputation as a teacher, preacher, and apologist. In 1576 he went to teach at the Roman College where he wrote his famous *Disputations on the Controversies of the Christian Faith,* a systematic defense against the Protestant reformers. During his time in Rome he worked on a catechism, which was widely used for three centuries, and he also helped to prepare a new version of the Vulgate compiled under Pope Clement VIII (1592–1605).

Bellarmine was named rector of the Roman College in 1592, provincial of the Neapolitan province of the Society of Jesus in 1594, personal theologian to Clement VIII in 1597, and a cardinal in 1599. In 1602 he became archbishop of Capua. He poured himself into pastoral work and was committed to the poor. He practiced great personal poverty and prized the ascetical life. After only three years in Capua, he was recalled to Rome by the newly elected Pope Sixtus V to continue his work as defender of the faith. To the displeasure of some more conservative theologians, he would admit only an indirect temporal authority for the pope, and he was sympathetic to some of Galileo's views. He always exercised great moderation in his criticism of his Protestant opponents, avoiding uncharitable remarks and praying for them. Toward the end of his career he withdrew from public life and died at St. Andrew's Novitiate in Rome on 17 September 1621. He was canonized by Pope Pius XI in 1930 and named a Doctor of the Church in 1931. Today his memory is commemorated on 17 September.

ANTHONY D. ANDREASSI

See also APOLOGETICS; CATECHISM; REFORMATION, THE; SOCIETY OF JESUS.

BELLOC, JOSEPH HILAIRE PIERRE (1870–1953)

Author; born in 1870 in St. Cloud, France, he was educated at Cardinal Newman's Oratory School, Edgbaston, and Balliol College, Oxford. In 1896, he married Elodie Hogan of California. He became a naturalized British citizen in 1902, and served in the House of Commons from 1906 to 1910.

Belloc was a prolific writer of diverse talents. With the exception of drama, he made significant contributions to every literary genre. He wrote numerous essays on religious, social, and political topics collected in *On Nothing* (1908), *On Everything,* and *On.* He also wrote a number of historical studies, including *The French Revolution* (1911), *History of England* (four volumes, 1925–1931), and *How the Reformation Happened.* Among his many notable biographies were *Marie Antoinette* (1909), *Cromwell* (1927), Charles II (1940), and *Robespierre* (1901).

Of his novels, *Mr. Clutterbuck's Election* (1908), *The Girondin* (1911), *The Green Overcoat* (1912), and *Belinda* (1928) are considered the best. *The Path to Rome* (1902), which Belloc illustrated himself, is his most highly regarded travel book and *The Servile State* (1912), a satire of Edwardian society, was an important social commentary.

Belloc also wrote several well-regarded volumes of children's poetry—*A Bad Child's Book of Beasts* (1896) and *More Beasts for Worse Children* (1897)—as well as ballads, satires, and epigrams, which can be found in *Collected Poems* (1923).

He taught at Fordham and Notre Dame Universities during his trips to the United States, and was an active journalist throughout his career. (He established the *Eye Witness*—later called the *New Witness*—newspaper.)

Belloc is remembered mostly as a gifted lyric poet and a superb master of the English language. His historical writings, however, are now considered biased and unreliable. He died in 1953.

JOSEPH QUINN

See also BRITAIN, CHURCH IN; CHESTERTON, GILBERT KEITH.

BENEDICT XV, POPE (1914–1922)

Giacomo Della Chiesa, a Doctor of Civil Law and a papal diplomat of much experience, was elected pope in the first weeks of World War I, largely so that the Church could effectively help to bring about a reconciliation of the warring peoples. During the conflict, Benedict constantly raised his voice against the inhuman methods of modern warfare while simultaneously striving to foster peace through diplomatic channels. As his peace initiatives went forward, Benedict mounted a program of universal charity such as the world had never before seen from the papacy. Yet the Pope was attacked from every side, mainly, perhaps, for his refusal to aid the victims of one side only, and his refusal to find fault in only one camp. While the war went on to its bitter end, Benedict did succeed in winning certain concessions on behalf of prisoners, the wounded, and refugees. His proposed seven-point peace plan of August, 1917, was ultimately ignored.

Prohibited from participating in the peace settlement by a secret agreement between Italy and the allies (he was opposed to the total humiliation of Germany), Benedict called for international reconciliation. In the remaining few years of his pontificate he worked for agreements between the Church and the new postwar governments. Relations with France, broken off with the anticlerical acts of 1905, were restored, and Benedict laid the groundwork for reconciliation with Italy which had annexed the Papal States. He promulgated the new code of canon law (largely the work of his predecessor, Pius X), made overtures to the Eastern Orthodox, and encouraged missionary bishops to develop native clergy.

DAVID BRYAN

See also CHURCH AND STATE; PAPACY, THE; PEACE.

BENEDICT OF NURSIA, ST. (ca 480–ca. 547)

On the occasion of the dedication of the rebuilt monastery of Monte Cassino in 1964, Pope Paul VI proclaimed St. Benedict the principal, heavenly patron of the whole of Europe. The title piously exaggerates the place of Benedict but in many respects it is true. St. Benedict did not establish the monastery of Monte Cassino in order to preserve the learning of the ages, but in fact the monasteries that later followed his Rule were places where learning and manuscripts were preserved. For some six centuries or more the Christian culture of medieval Europe was nearly identical with the monastic centers of piety and learning.

St. Benedict was not the founder of Christian monasticism, since he lived two and a half to three centuries after its beginnings in Egypt, Palestine, and Asia Minor. He became a monk as a young man and thereafter learned the tradition by associating with monks and reading the monastic literature. He was caught up in the monastic movement but ended by channeling the stream into new and fruitful ways. This is evident in the Rule which he wrote for monasteries and which was and is still used in many monasteries and convents around the world (see Rule of Benedict).

Tradition teaches that St. Benedict lived from 480 to 547, though we cannot be sure that these dates are historically accurate. His biographer, St. Gregory the Great, pope from 590 to 604, does not record the dates of his birth and death, though he refers to a Rule written by Benedict. Scholars debate the dating of the Rule though they seem to agree that it was written in the second third of the sixth century.

St. Benedict, detail of fresco, Sacro Speco, Subiaco, 1300

St. Gregory wrote about St. Benedict in his Second Book of *Dialogues,* but his account of the life and miracles of Benedict cannot be regarded as a biography in the modern sense of the term. Gregory's purpose in writing Benedict's life was to edify and to inspire, not to seek out the particulars of his daily life. Gregory sought to show that saints of God, particularly St. Benedict, were still operative in the Christian Church in spite of all the political and religious chaos present in the realm. At the same time it would be inaccurate to claim that Gregory presented no facts about Benedict's life and works.

According to Gregory's *Dialogues* Benedict was born in Nursia, a village high in the mountains northeast of Rome. His parents sent him to Rome for classical studies but he found the life of the eternal city too degenerate for his tastes. Consequently he fled to a place southeast of Rome called Subiaco where he lived as a hermit for three years tended by the monk Romanus.

He was then discovered by a group of monks who prevailed upon him to become their spiritual leader. His regime soon became too much for the lukewarm monks so they plotted to poison him. Gregory recounts the tale of Benedict's rescue; when he blessed the pitcher of poisoned wine, it broke into many pieces. Thereafter he left the undisciplined monks.

Benedict left the wayward monks and established twelve monasteries with twelve monks each in the area south of Rome. Later, perhaps in 529, he moved to Monte Cassino, about eighty miles southeast of Rome; there he destroyed the pagan temple dedicated to Apollo and built his premier monastery. It was there too that he wrote the Rule for the monastery of Monte Cassino though he envisioned that it could be used elsewhere.

The thirty-eight short chapters of the Second Book of *Dialogues* contain accounts of Benedict's life and miracles. Some chapters recount his ability to read other persons' minds; other chapters tell of his miraculous works, e.g., making water flow from rocks, sending a disciple to walk on the water, making oil continue to flow from a flask. The miracle stories echo the events of certain prophets of Israel as well as happenings in the life of Jesus. The message is clear: Benedict's holiness mirrors the saints and prophets of old and God has not abandoned his people; he continues to bless them with holy persons.

Benedict is viewed as a monastic leader, not a scholar. Still he probably read Latin rather well, an ability that gave him access to the works of Cassian and other monastic writings, both rules and sayings. The Rule is the sole known example of Benedict's writing, but it manifests his genius to crystalize the best of the monastic tradition and to pass it on to the European West.

Gregory presents Benedict as the model of a saint who flees temptation to pursue a life of attention to God. Through a balanced pattern of living and praying Benedict reached the point where he glimpsed the glory of God. Gregory recounts a vision that Benedict received toward the end of his life: "In the dead of night he suddenly beheld a flood of light shining down from above more brilliant than the sun, and with it every trace of darkness cleared away. According to his own description, the whole world was gathered up before his eyes in what appeared to be a single ray of light" (ch. 34). St. Benedict, the monk par excellence, led a monastic life that reached the vision of God.

ABBOT PRIMATE JEROME THEISEN, O.S.B.

See also BENEDICTINES; MONK; RELIGIOUS ORDERS.

The four types of monks, manuscript detail, Mantova

BENEDICT, ST., RULE OF

The Rule of Benedict (RB) constitutes the basic guide for thousands of Christians who are committed to the monastic movement. Many disciples of Jesus followed the Rule in the past and many still do so today. Written in the sixth century the Rule was followed in thousands of monasteries in Europe, so much so that the Church of the early Middle Ages, beginning especially in the ninth century, was characterized as monastic.

Historians are relatively certain that RB was written by St. Benedict, the founder of the monastery of Monte Cassino, though the historical evidence does not allow a conclusive proof of authorship. St. Benedict's biographer, St. Gregory the Great (pope from 590 to 604), indicates that Benedict "wrote a Rule for monks that is remarkable for its discretion and its clarity of language" (*Dialogues,* Book II, ch. 36). The autograph copy of RB has been lost but scholars believe that we have a faithful copy that is a few centuries and manuscripts away from the original. The best manuscript (Codex San Gallensis 914) stems from the early ninth century and is found today in St. Gall (Switzerland). Another manuscript (Hatton 48 found today in Oxford's Bodleian Library), though earlier by a century, is less faithful because copyists strove to correct the sixth-century Latin.

RB should not be viewed as an exclusively legal code though it includes prescriptions for living in a monastery. The Rule actually contains a treasure of spiritual wisdom concerning the monastic movement in the Church. Its Prologue and seventy-three chapters provide teaching about the basic monastic virtues of humility, silence, and obedience as well as directives for daily living. RB prescribes times for common prayer, meditative reading, and manual work; it legislates for the details of common living such as clothing, sleeping arrangements, food and drink, care of the sick, reception of guests, recruitment of new members, journeys away from the monastery, etc. While the Rule does not shun minute instructions, it allows the abbot to determine in great detail the particulars of common living.

RB, written anywhere between 530 and 560, is not an entirely original document. It depends in great measure on the rules and traditions of Christian monasticism that existed from the fourth century to the time of its writing. Scholars note that rules and writings like those of St. Pachomius (fourth-century Egypt), St. Basil (fourth-century Asia Minor), St. Augustine (fourth- and fifth-century North Africa), Cassian (fifth-century southern Gaul) stand behind RB and at times are clearly evident in the text. The most important source for RB, however, is the Rule of the Master, an anonymous rule written two or three decades before Benedict's Rule. Not infrequently, especially in RB's Prologue and first seven chapters, Benedict copied extensively from the Rule of the Master. Benedict picked up the monastic tradition and even copied from its documents (as was customary at the time); but he also corrected and altered the tradition in significant ways.

Benedict wrote his Rule in the spoken and ordinary Latin of the day. It is not the classical Latin of antiquity nor the scholarly Latin taught in the remaining schools of his time, though occasionally his language is elegant and polished. As the Rule drifts from the classical language it also gives evidence of the breakdown of Latin into more common forms of speech (what later became the Romance languages). Benedict writes with crispness and directness; seldom is he profuse or homiletic.

Compared with the tradition and especially with the Rule of the Master, Benedict legislates for a monastic life that has rhythm, measure, and discretion. His monks are not overdriven by austerities in fasting and night vigils. They do not own anything personally, but they have enough to eat and to drink (even wine when it is available) and to clothe themselves. They work with their hands about six hours a day but they also have leisure for prayerful reading and common prayer. Their sleep is sufficient and they may even take a siesta in summer if needed. The young, the sick, and the elderly are cared for with compassion and attention. The abbot, while he directs all aspects of the common life, must seek counsel from the monks; and the Rule makes provision for his limitations and failings. In short, RB arranges for a monastic life in which the monks may seek God in prayer and reading, in silence and work, in service to guests and to one another.

Benedict's Rule stands tall in the great tradition of Christian monasticism. It is a Christian rule in the sense that its spiritual doctrine picks up on the values of the Bible (e.g., prayer, fasting, service of neighbor) and arranges for a life in which these values can be lived out in community. RB is not written for monastic hermits, though Benedict has high regard for them; it is written for ordinary Christians who wish to immerse themselves in a pattern of living in which the life of Christ can be lived out with understanding and zeal. RB is still used today in many monasteries and convents around the world. The monastics of today do not follow it literally but still find in it much wisdom to live the common life. It still protects the individual and the community from arbitrariness on the part of the abbot or others; it still provides a way of living the Christian life. Monastic communities accept it as their basic inspiration even as they mitigate it, supplement it, or adapt it to the living conditions of today.

ABBOT PRIMATE JEROME THEISEN, O.S.B.

See also BENEDICT OF NURSIA, ST.; BENEDICTINES; MONASTICISM.

BENEDICTINES

Benedictines carry on a monastic tradition that stems from the origins of the Christian monastic movement in the late third century. They regard St. Benedict as their founder and guide even though he did not establish a Benedictine Order as such. He wrote a Rule for his monastery at Monte Cassino in Italy and he foresaw that it could be used elsewhere. Monte Cassino was destroyed by the Lombards about A.D. 577 and was not reestablished until the middle of the eighth century. Meanwhile the Rule found its way to monasteries in England, Gaul, and elsewhere. At first it was one of a number of rules accepted by a particular monastery but later, especially through the promotional efforts of Charlemagne and his son Louis, it became the rule of choice for monasteries of Europe from the ninth century onwards.

The early medieval monasteries of Europe, those for men and women, followed the Rule of Benedict with local adaptations needed in different climes and cultures. They continued, however, the tradition of community life with its common prayer, reading, and work. Some of the monasteries were founded as centers of evangelization of peoples; others carried on a program of education, art and architecture, and the making of manuscripts. Many monasteries were centers of liturgy and learning in the midst of chaotic times and shifting kingdoms.

Benedictine monasteries are often characterized as local institutions with a great deal of autonomy. In the Middle Ages they were often founded by the nobility as centers of prayer, communities that would pray for the people, especially the nobles themselves. The monasteries had little contact with each other though eventually some of them began to relate to each other for the sake of protection from bishops and nobles and for common discipline. The most famous association was that of Cluny, named for the abbey in Burgundy; this monastery was founded in 909/910 and grew to include numerous dependencies. Cluny reformed congregations of black monks, as they were called, in practically all parts of Europe. The abbot of Cluny was in effect the superior of all the dependent monasteries though he administered the multitude of abbeys through appointed priors. Cluny excelled in the splendor and length of its liturgy, so much so that its monks had little time for manual labor or reading.

The Benedictine monasteries waned at the end of the twelfth century, about the time the Church witnessed the rise of the "modern" orders of Franciscans and Dominicans. The Benedictines, though in decline in members and discipline, continued their round of monastic life but at times without their properly constituted head. Not a few monasteries were burdened by a commendatory abbot, a person who was appointed by the pope or a nobleman to oversee and to protect the goods of the monastery.

Often, however, he appropriated the wealth of monastic lands without involvement in the actual life of the community.

In the Middle Ages and up to modern times Benedictine monasteries for men and women often formed various associations or unions in order to promote discipline and mutual assistance. This was in fact mandated by the Council of Trent (1545–1563). Monasteries slowly and with much hesitation followed the directives of Pope Innocent III and the Fourth Lateran Council (1215) to establish visitations of monasteries and regular general chapters for the enactment of legislation.

Many Benedictine monasteries were closed at the time of the Protestant Reformation both because the reformers preached against monastic vows as unevangelical and because secular rulers coveted and seized the abundance of properties owned by the monastics. Congregations of Benedictines continued in the centuries after the Reformation, but most monasteries were closed and expropriated during the Napoleonic era. As a result, their numbers were very few at the beginning of the nineteenth century.

During the course of the 1800s, however, Benedictines experienced a revival. Some congregations, e.g., the Solesmes and Beuronese Congregations, restored a kind of Benedictine monasticism that stressed the enclosed life with its round of liturgical prayer performed with great precision and splendor. Other congregations, e.g., the St. Ottilien Congregation and groupings of American Benedictine women, stressed the missionary endeavors of evangelizing, teaching, and health care. Men and women Benedictines continued to establish new houses in many countries right up to the time of Vatican Council II (1962–1965). Since then the number of Benedictines has declined once again, at least in the First and Second World, but it has increased in other regions, e.g., East Africa and South Korea.

Today Benedictines, both men and women, are still characterized as people who take root in a particular place and who are related to the culture and needs of a specific location. Most are associated together in congregations for purposes of mutual assistance and common discipline. At the same time they vary widely in the type of monastic life they lead. Some pursue an enclosed life with little involvement in the local Church and society; others insist on various degrees of involvement such as education, parochial ministry, evangelization, publication, health care, etc.

In 1887 Pope Leo XIII, who was enamored of the Benedictines, reestablished the College of St. Anselm in Rome. It continues today as an institute for Benedictine students and others who wish to obtain graduate degrees in philosophy, theology, liturgy, and monastic studies. In 1893 the same pope provided the "order" with an abbot primate to oversee the college and to provide spiritual leadership for the Confederation of Benedictine monasteries. The abbot primate does not have direct jurisdiction in the monasteries of the order, though he is still charged with a general concern for the well-being of Benedictines around the world. Thus Benedictines differ from most modern religious orders who have a superior general in Rome.

Benedictines of today continue to group themselves in congregations of monasteries; some, however, especially many communities of nuns, are positioned outside congregations and relate directly to the local bishop and to the abbot primate in Rome. The followers of St. Benedict vary much in the way they carry out the thrust of the sixth-century Rule, but in general they retain essential features of their origins—local gatherings of monastics who endeavor to seek God in a common life of prayer, reading, and service.

ABBOT PRIMATE JEROME THEISEN, O.S.B.

See also BENEDICT OF NURSIA, ST.; MONASTERY; MONK.

BENEDICTION (OF THE BLESSED SACRAMENT)

(Lat., "blessing") An extraliturgical service held as a devotion to the Blessed Sacrament. It begins with the priest placing the consecrated Hosts in a monstrance or ciborium, which he then sets on the altar and enshrouds in incense. Eucharistic hymns—such as *O Salutaris Hostia* and *Tantum Ergo*—are sung (either in Latin or the vernacular) by the congregation, followed by a blessing from the celebrant, in which he forms the sign of the cross with the raised monstrance or ciborium. At the close of the service, the Divine Praises may be sung or recited.

In recent years, particularly since the Second Vatican Council, the Holy See has permitted greater rubrical flexibility; hence the prayers, readings, and hymns may vary. Eucharistic devotion began in the Middle Ages, when, during different periods, members of the Church chose to participate in the Blessed Sacrament by sight.

JOSEPH QUINN

See also DEVOTIONS; EUCHARISTIC DEVOTIONS.

BENEDICTUS

The hymn attributed to Zechariah, the father of John the Baptist, in Luke 1:68-79 is customarily known by the first word in its Latin translation

Benedictus ("Blessed"). Using many biblical phrases and allusions, the hymn celebrates the birth of John as a divine visitation. But the focus is really the birth of Jesus (from the "house of David," see 1:69), who is presented as God's intervention for the salvation of his people in accord with the divine promises in Scripture. John is drawn into the dynamic of God's action in Jesus, but his subordinate role is made clear (see 1:76).

Benedictus (Luke 1:68-79)

"Blessed be the Lord God of Israel,
for he has looked favorably on his
people and redeemed them.
He has raised up a mighty savior
for us in the house of his servant David,
as he spoke through the mouth of his
holy prophets from of old,
that we would be saved from our enemies
and from the hand of all who hate us.
Thus he has shown the mercy promised
to our ancestors, and has remembered
his holy covenant, the oath that he
swore to our ancestor Abraham, to
grant us that we, being rescued
from the hands of our enemies,
might serve him without fear, in
holiness and righteousness before
him all our days.
And you, child, will be called the
prophet of the Most High;
for you will go before the Lord
to prepare his ways, to give
knowledge of salvation to his
people by the forgiveness of
their sins.
By the tender mercy of our God,
the dawn from on high will break
upon us, to give light to those
who sit in darkness and in the
shadow of death, to guide our
feet into the way of peace."

DANIEL J. HARRINGTON, S.J.

See also JOHN THE BAPTIST; INFANCY NARRATIVES, THE.

BENOIT, PIERRE MAURICE (1906–1987)

Maurice Benoit was born in Nancy, Lorraine, France, 3 August 1906. He entered the Dominican Order in 1924, receiving the name Pierre, and was ordained in 1930, after studies at the Saulchoir (Kain, Tournai, Belgium). Shortly thereafter (1933) he was assigned to teach New Testament Greek and exegesis at the Ecole Biblique, the French biblical and archaeological school in Jerusalem. The Ecole in Jerusalem remained his base until his death there on 23 April 1987. His principle teacher was M.-J. Lagrange, the founder of the school. The contributions of Benoit to biblical studies cover a wide range. His was one of the first positive Roman Catholic receptions of form criticism (1946). His many essays on the inspiration of Scripture helped to promote a distinction between inspiration and inerrancy, and this in turn enabled critical work to go on. His essays on hermeneutics also increased theological attention to the Septuagint and to the plurality of senses in the Bible. In his study of the Synoptic Gospels he differed from Lagrange in this: the Gospels do not give us immediate access to the earthly Jesus; they give us access to Jesus only through the mediation of the early Christian community which selectively preserved and shaped the tradition about Jesus.

Benoit is probably best known for his work on the original *Jerusalem Bible* (1956), as NT editor and as commentator on Matthew, Philippians, Philemon, Colossians, and Ephesians. These biblical books were also the object of his teaching at the Ecole, along with a course on the topography of Jerusalem which involved a weekly walk.

His editorial activity also included editing the *Revue Biblique* for many years (1953–1968); he added the archaeological chronicle as a regular feature of the journal. After the death of his colleague De Vaux, he became the general editor of the unpublished fragments from Qumran. This was after the Six Day War (1967) and there was a political impasse over the title of the series. With Milik's help, Benoit worked out a compromise and wrote a preface describing the situation which was accepted by both Israeli and Jordanian authorities. He was succeeded as editor by John Strugnell of Harvard in 1986. He did not have a gift as epigrapher and failed as catalyst and organizer, but brought good sense to oppose sensational views. As interpreter of archaeological data, he succeeded in changing opinion on the location of the Lithostratos, of the trial of Jesus, and on the date of the Ecce Homo arch. He served as director of the Ecole from 1965 to 1972.

In the last two sessions of the Second Vatican Council (1962–1965), he played an important role as theological expert, especially for the documents on divine revelation, the Church, religious freedom, and non-Christian religions. He was a member of the Pontifical Biblical Commission from 1972 until his death. His last major project was a commentary on Colossians. He was an active participant in the Society of New Testament Studies from its beginning, and its president from 1962 to 1963, the first Roman Catholic to hold the post.

BENEDICT T. VIVIANO, O.P.

See also DOMINICANS; ECOLE BIBLIQUE; LAGRANGE, MARIE-JOSEPH, VAUX, ROLAND DE.

BERNARD OF CLAIRVAUX (1090–1153)

Bernard, the founding abbot of Clairvaux Abbey in Burgundy, was one of the most commanding Church leaders in the first half of the twelfth century as well as one of the greatest spiritual masters of all times and the most powerful propagator of the Cistercian reform. He was born in Fontaines-les-Dijon in 1090 and entered the Abbey of Citeaux in 1112, bringing thirty of his relatives with him, including five of his brothers—his youngest brother and his widowed father followed later. After receiving a monastic formation from St. Stephen Harding, he was sent in 1115 to begin a new monastery near Aube: Clairvaux, the Valley of Light. As a young abbot he published a series of sermons on the Annunciation. These marked him not only as a most gifted spiritual writer but also as the "cithara of Mary," especially noted for his development of Mary's mediatorial role. His spiritual writing as well as his extraordinary personal magnetism began to attract many to Clairvaux and the other Cistercian monasteries, leading to many new foundations. He was drawn into the controversy developing between the new monastic movement which he preeminently represented and the established Cluniac order. This led to one of his most controversial and most popular works, his *Apologia.* Bernard's dynamism soon reached far beyond monastic circles. He was sought as an advisor and mediator by the ruling powers of his age. More than any other he helped to bring about the healing of the papal schism which arose in 1130 with the election of the antipope Anacletus II. It cost Bernard eight years of laborious travel and skillful mediation. At the same time he labored for peace and reconciliation between England and France and among many lesser nobles. His influence mounted when his spiritual son was elected pope in 1145. At Eugene III's command he preached the Second Crusade and sent vast armies on the road toward Jerusalem. In his last years he rose from his sickbed and went into the Rhineland to defend the Jews against a savage persecution.

St. Bernard of Clairvaux, detail of manuscript, Abbey of Neuburg

Although he suffered from constant physical debility and had to govern a monastery that soon housed several hundred monks and was sending forth groups regularly to begin new monasteries (he personally saw to the establishment of sixty-five of the three hundred Cistercian monasteries founded during his thirty-eight years as abbot), he yet found time to compose many and varied spiritual works that still speak to us today. He laid out a solid foundation for the spiritual life in his works on grace and free will, humility and love. His gifts as a theologian were called upon to respond to the dangerous teachings of the scintillating Peter Abelard, of Gilbert de la Porree and of Arnold of Brescia. His masterpiece, his Sermons on the Song of Songs, was begun in 1136 and was still in composition at the time of his death. With great simplicity and poetic grace Bernard writes of the deepest experiences of the mystical life in ways that became normative for all succeeding writers. For Pope Eugene he wrote *Five Books on Consideration,* the bedside reading of Pope John XXIII and many other pontiffs through the centuries.

Bernard died at Clairvaux on 20 August 1153. He was canonized by Pope Alexander III on 18 January 1174. Pope Pius VII declared him a Doctor of the Church in 1830.

M. BASIL PENNINGTON, O.C.S.O.

See also ABELARD, PETER; CISTERCIANS; CRUSADES; MYSTICISM.

BERNINI, GIANLORENZO (1598–1680)

Recognized as the greatest sculptor since Michelangelo and a genius in architecture, Bernini was the virtual creator and greatest exponent of the Baroque and of the spirit of the Counter Reformation in art. (Several paintings have also been attributed to him, and he was a playwright and theater designer.)

"The Ecstasy of St. Teresa," detail, by Bernini, S. Maria della Vittoria, Rome

Bernini was born in Naples in 1598 to a devout and talented family, his father, Pietro, being a sculptor in the late Mannerist style. Awarded commissions by Pope Paul V, Pietro moved his family to Rome, the city on which his son's art was to be lavished. The younger Bernini's style in sculpture, developed under his father's tutelage, combined technical virtuosity with great dynamism and emotional insight. Most of his early works were devoted to mythological themes: *The Goat Amalthea* (1615), *Aeneas and Anchises* (1618–1619), *Neptune and Triton* (1620), *The Rape of Persepone* (1621–1622), *Apollo and Daphne* (1622–1624). (The last two as well as his *David* [1623] were done for Cardinal Scipione Borghesi, the Pope's nephew.) Bernini's style drew from many sources (the ancient sculptors, Michelangelo, Carracci, Caravaggio, Reni), but he was the slave of none. Where Michelangelo made the emerging form of a statue adhere closely to the block, Bernini initiated the Baroque style by freeing the work from the limits of the block, allowing it to engage viewers by spilling over into their space. Like Michelangelo, he combined deep piety with a towering temper. He regularly practiced the *Spiritual Exercises* of St. Ignatius, and his personal spirituality became intense in his last years. In an effort to express the various realms of the mystical and the human he used white and variously colored marbles in the same work (e.g., in *The Ecstasy of St. Theresa* in Santa Maria della Vittoria). In architecture, as in sculpture, he became the artist who most fully expressed the upsurge of religious confidence and militant faith that characterizes the Counter Reformation. At St. Peter's, the Piazza, Baldacchino (including its huge statue of St. Longinus), the Chair of Peter (in the apse), and the tombs of Urban VIII and Alexander VII are his. His numerous Roman buildings, fountains, and statuary guarantee that his impress on Rome exceeds that of any other artist on any city. He died in 1680.

DAVID BRYAN

See also ART, CHRISTIAN; REFORMATION, THE; SPIRITUAL EXERCISES OF ST. IGNATIUS OF LOYOLA.

BIBLE, ENGLISH VERSIONS OF THE

Before printing, attempts were made to translate the Bible into English, but the first complete translation from the Vulgate was by John Wycliffe dated 1382 to 1384. With the advent of printing in the sixteenth century and the Reformation, Protestant and Catholic versions began to appear. The first English printed version was by William Tyndale (1525–1531), followed by the complete Coverdale Bible (1535). Other Protestants produced the Great Bible (1539–1541), the Geneva Bible (1560), and Bishop's Bible (1568). In response to the Protestant versions, Catholics produced the Douay-Rheims (1582–1609) from the Vulgate.

The next groups of English versions came from both traditions with the Protestants revising the Bishop's Bible and earlier versions in the Authorized Version (King James 1611). Its language was contemporary and understandable, followed much later by the Revised Version (1881–1885) based on the Greek NT, and the contemporary Revised Standard Version (1946–1952) which was granted a Catholic imprimatur in 1965–1966. The New Revised Standard Version (1986) is widely used.

The Douay-Rheims was revised in the Challoner Revision (1749–1763), the Confraternity Revision of NT (1941), and the Knox Bible (1944–1951). These were all based on the Vulgate. Catholics soon began to use the original biblical languages for their translations in the Westminster Version (1935–1949) and the Kleist-Lilly NT (1950–1954) that used modern English but was considered weak in scholarship. The New American Bible (1952–1970; 1987), with a revision that included Protestant cooperation, is readable, and the Jerusalem Bible (1966; 1985), containing footnotes and comments, has a corrected revision.

Newer translations for the Protestants include Chicago Bible (1931), New English Bible (1961–1970), Good News Bible (1966–1979), the New International Version (1973–1978), and the Living Bible (1962–1971), with the last two reflecting conservative tendencies.

While the variety of versions can be confusing, Catholics should look for reliance on the original texts, readability in contemporary English, and theological interpretations by the various traditions.

HELEN DOOHAN

BIBLE, MANUSCRIPTS OF THE

See MANUSCRIPTS OF THE BIBLE.

BIBLE, NEW TESTAMENT WRITINGS

The writings that comprise the second part of the Christian Scriptures are called the "New Testament." The term is a variant of "New Covenant," which is rooted in the prophecy in Jeremiah 31:31-34, and developed in several NT texts (1 Cor 11:25/Luke 22:20; 2 Cor 3:6; Heb 8:8-13; 9:15; 12:24) to describe God's decisive action in Jesus Christ. On the basis of Paul's reference to the writings of the Mosaic covenant as the "old covenant" (2 Cor 3:14), it was natural that "new covenant" or "new testament" be applied to the Christian texts regarded as sacred and canonical. By the fourth century it was customary to refer to these canonical Christian writings as the New Testament.

The New Testament consists of four Gospels, Acts, thirteen Pauline letters, Hebrews, seven General or Catholic letters, and Revelation. All these books were written in Greek in the Mediterranean basin between A.D. 50 and the early second century. Taken together, these books constitute a library consisting of narratives, letters, sermons, and visions.

The style of Greek in which the NT books were written is usually called Koine ("common") because it is the language of the common people (as opposed to the classical Greek literary language). The influence of the Greek translation of the OT Septuagint is also strong in many books and explains in large part the "Semitic" feel of much NT Greek. Theories about NT books being translations of Hebrew or Aramaic originals are quite dubious.

We do not have the original draft (autograph) of any NT book. Only copies of copies are available. The earliest textual evidence is provided by fragments on papyrus from the second and third centuries. The earliest complete versions of NT books are on vellum manuscripts from the fourth to the ninth centuries. These "uncial" or "majuscule" manuscripts are written entirely in capital letters and without word division or punctuation. The early translations (Latin, Syriac, Coptic, Armenian, etc.) are also sources of textual evidence. All these materials serve as the basis for the critical editions of the Greek NT.

Gospels and Acts

The four Gospels (Matthew, Mark, Luke, and John) tell the story of Jesus' life, death, and resurrection. Mark begins Jesus' story in adulthood in connection with John the Baptist. Matthew and Luke take the story of Jesus back to his birth and infancy, and John goes back to creation ("in the beginning was the Word"). All four Gospels look something like biographies, and in antiquity readers would have assumed they were (though the claims made about Jesus burst the conventions of the biography genre). The first three Gospels offer a "common view" of Jesus and so are called "Synoptic." John presents a different chronology (three Passovers instead of one), different characters (Nicodemus, the Samaritan woman, etc.), and has Jesus speak in long discourses (rather than short sayings).

None of the four Gospels explicitly identifies its author. The traditional ascriptions to Matthew, Mark, Luke, and John were added to the manuscripts later. So one can say that all four Gospels are anonymous. According to second-century traditions Matthew and John were members of the twelve apostles, and Mark was associated with Peter and Luke with Paul. But the composition of the Gospels was more complicated.

Mark appears to have been the earliest Gospel, written around A.D. 70. Writing mainly for Gentile Christians, Mark portrayed Jesus as a healer, a teacher, and the suffering Messiah. He painted a somewhat negative portrait of Jesus' disciples that issues in their abandoning Jesus at the cross. Mark had access to traditions about Jesus that had circulated between Jesus' death (A.D. 30) and his own effort at putting these traditions in narrative form.

Matthew and Luke are second, revised editions of Mark. Both appear to have used Mark's Gospel and a collection of Jesus' sayings (Q). They worked independently and had access to special traditions (M and L). Writing mainly for Jewish Christians, Matthew sought to show how God's promises to Israel have been fulfilled in Jesus of Nazareth and that God's people is now constituted through the abiding presence of Christ. Luke wrote for Gentile Christians and presented Jesus' ministry as a new and decisive period in the history of salvation. Luke's Jesus is prophet, martyr, and example, and the twelve apostles are the principle of continuity between Jesus and the Spirit-led Church. Matthew and Luke composed their Gospels around A.D. 85–90.

John's Gospel was put into final form in the late first century for a largely Jewish-Christian community in the process of being expelled from the synagogue (see 9:22; 12:42; 16:2). It seems to have been the result of a long process of tradition in the

Johannine "school" and to have been based on independent sources: the hymn in 1:1-18, the seven miracles or "signs," the farewell discourses, and the passion account. John's distinctive angle is Jesus the revealer of his heavenly Father. The Cross, rather than being a defeat, is the exaltation of Jesus and his "hour" toward which all his teachings and actions point. Through the exaltation of Jesus eternal life has already begun for believers.

The Acts of the Apostles is the continuation of Luke's Gospel and composed by the same author. It focuses mainly on the exploits of Peter and Paul, and traces the spread of the gospel from Jerusalem to Rome under the Spirit's direction. There is little conflict within the Church, though there is much opposition outside from local Jews and pagans in various places. Throughout, the early Christians do not pose a political threat to the Roman Empire. There is a tendency to idealize life within the Christian community and to present Paul in a different light from the picture that emerges from Paul's own letters.

Pauline Epistles

The thirteen letters attributed to Paul are divided into two groups: those to communities, and those to individuals. In modern editions of the NT they are arranged by length—first to communities (Romans, 1 Corinthians, 2 Corinthians, Galatians, Ephesians, Philippians, Colossians, 1 Thessalonians, 2 Thessalonians), and then to individuals (1 Timothy, 2 Timothy, Titus, Philemon). This arrangement obscures the fact that six of these letters are most likely pseudepigraphic (i.e., written in Paul's name by a later admirer). This conclusion is reached on the basis of language and style, as well as the social setting presupposed by the text and theological content.

Paul's undisputed letters are the oldest documents in the NT. In 1 Thessalonians (A.D. 51–52), Paul renews his friendship with a community he had founded and offers advice on various issues, especially the second coming of Christ. Galatians warns Gentile Christians not to imagine that they have to adopt Jewish observances like circumcision in order to be good Christians. 1 Corinthians presents Paul's advice on divisions in the community, incest, lawsuits, sexual and social status, food offered to idols, the community assembly, and resurrection. 2 Corinthians and Philippians, though written to different communities, take up similar issues: attacks on Paul's ministry, money, life after death, and the threat posed by Jewish-Christian missionaries to Gentile Christians. Philemon is a personal letter in which Paul asks a Christian householder to receive back his runaway slave Onesimus. Paul's last and greatest letter—to the Romans (A.D. 58)—argues that Jews and Gentiles alike needed the revelation of God's righteousness in Christ, that faith is essential to share in this revelation, that Jesus' death and resurrection brought about freedom (from the power of sin, death, and the Law) and made it possible to live in the Spirit, that Israel's rejection of the gospel is not total or final, and that the tensions within the community can be resolved.

The six Deuteropauline letters reflect the efforts of friends and admirers of Paul to keep his spirit alive, and to respond to new situations as they thought Paul himself would have. The practice of pseudepigraphy was fairly common in antiquity and did not bear the stigma that it does today. 2 Thessalonians takes up the issue of the second coming of Christ and urges caution and industry in the present. Colossians addresses a concrete situation, and stresses the importance and sufficiency of the new life available in Christ. Ephesians incorporates much of Colossians and also functions as compendium of Paul's theology with particular attention to how Gentiles have been made members of the people of God through Christ. The Pastorals (1–2 Timothy, Titus) provide advice about Church life and order, and urge Christians to adopt the morals typical of good citizens in the Roman Empire. These letters all reflect conditions in the late first century.

Other Letters

Though vaguely connected with Paul, Hebrews most definitely was written by someone else (only God knows who, said Origen). Its language and theological conceptuality differ greatly from the Pauline and Deuteropauline writings. It appears to address Jewish Christians discouraged in their new faith and tempted to go back to Judaism. The focus is on Christ the high priest and the perfect sufficiency of his sacrificial death on the cross and the new kind of (heavenly) worship that he has inaugurated. Meanwhile, Christians are aliens and exiles on earth but have Christ the pioneer as their leader and guide in pilgrimage.

The General or Catholic epistles are associated with apostles—James, Peter, John (see Gal 2:9), and Jude—but it is doubtful that any of them was directly composed by an apostle. James gives practical advice about how to act in everyday life and criticizes what seems to have been a radical interpretation of Paul's insistence on faith rather than works. 1 Peter takes up the social and spiritual alienation of Gentile Christians in Asia Minor, and urges them to recognize what they have become in Christ: "a chosen people, a royal priesthood, a holy nation, God's own people" (2:9). Jude is a harsh critique of those who pervert God's grace into licentiousness and deny Christ. Most of it is incorporated into 2 Peter, which holds out against scoffers for the second coming in God's own good time and indicates that misinterpretations of Paul may have been at the root of the problem (3:15-16). The three Johannine epistles (1–3 John) continue the story of the Johannine community begun in John's Gospel. There seems to have been a split in the community (1 John 2:19) over the humanity of Jesus (4:2-3).

The Revelation of John (also known as the Apocalypse) is formally a letter (see 1:4; 2–3) but is also an apocalypse and a prophecy (1:1, 3). Its language and thought-world are very different from the Fourth Gospel and the Johannine letters, and there is no real connection to them. It addresses Christians in western Asia Minor in the late first century who seem to have been under pressure to join in civic religious rituals honoring the emperor as a god. Using rich and sometimes bizarre images based on Daniel and Ezekiel, John urged these people to stand firm because the "end" is near. In the end of human history as we know it, their opponents will be defeated and they will be vindicated because God's triumph will be clear to all. Then they will live in perfect happiness with the Lamb of God (Christ) in the perfect city (the new Jerusalem). John's stance toward the Roman Empire differs radically from the cooperative position taken by Paul (Rom 13:1-7), the Pastorals, and 1 Peter. This difference underlines the fact that the New Testament is a library of books, not a single book, and that these books presuppose different historical settings and give different responses. What holds this library together is faith in the person of Jesus Christ.

DANIEL J. HARRINGTON, S.J.

See also BIBLE, OLD TESTAMENT WRITINGS; CRITICISM, BIBLICAL.

BIBLE, OLD TESTAMENT WRITINGS

The term "Bible" comes from the Greek *ta biblia* meaning "the books." It implies, therefore, that the Bible is indeed a collection of books. When the term came into Late Latin, the plural became a singular, i.e., a single book. While the word refers to the Christian Sacred Scriptures, it is also employed to designate the Jewish Sacred Scriptures. From a Christian perspective one speaks of the Old Testament and the New Testament. From a Jewish perspective one speaks of the Bible or the Hebrew Bible since the principal language of those writings is Hebrew.

Canon

The canon is the authentic list of the recognized sacred books of the Jewish and Christian communities. However, the number of books constituting the canon is different. For the Jewish and Protestant communities the canon consists of thirty-nine books. (Although the Jewish canon numbers twenty-four books, this canon accepts the same books as the Protestant community by counting as one book 1 and 2 Samuel, 1 and 2 Kings, 1 and 2 Chronicles, Ezra and Nehemiah, and the Twelve [the minor prophets].) For the Roman Catholic community the canon consists of forty-six books. The seven "extra" books are: Tobit, Judith, 1 and 2 Maccabees, Wisdom, Sirach, and Baruch. There are also additions to Esther and Daniel. Roman Catholics refer to such books and additions as "deuterocanonical" (second canon), i.e., they were recognized as canonical only after a period of hesitation and debate. Jews and Protestants label these books and additions "apocryphal," i.e., hidden or secret writings. While such works deserve to be read, they are not canonical for the Jewish and Protestant communities. It should be noted that the Eastern Orthodox communities also accept these deuterocanonical works and additions with the exception of Baruch.

Division of the Old Testament

There are three sections to the Hebrew Bible: (1) Torah; (2) Prophets; (3) Writings. The Torah consists of the five books of Moses, viz., Genesis, Exodus, Leviticus, Numbers, and Deuteronomy. The Prophets is broken down into the Former and the Latter Prophets. The Former Prophets include Joshua, Judges, 1 and 2 Samuel, and 1 and 2 Kings. The Latter Prophets contain Isaiah, Jeremiah, Ezekiel, and the Twelve (the minor prophets). Finally the Writings embrace Psalms, Job, Proverbs, the Festal Scrolls (Ruth, Song of Songs, Ecclesiastes/Qoheleth, Lamentations, and Esther), Daniel, Ezra-Nehemiah, and 1 and 2 Chronicles.

The ending of the Hebrew Bible is significant. The conclusion of 2 Chronicles (36:22-23) is a repetition of Ezra 1:1-3. This passage, i.e., the decree of Cyrus, king of Persia, announces the end of the Babylonian Exile and the charge to rebuild the Temple in Jerusalem. As a result, the Hebrew Bible ends up on a note of hope, not doom (see 2 Chr 36:15-21).

There are four sections to the Christian Old Testament: (1) Pentateuch; (2) Historical Books; (3) Wisdom Books; (4) Prophetic Books. (These will be discussed in greater detail below.) Similar to the conclusion of the Hebrew Bible, that of the Christian Old Testament is also significant. The last prophetic book, Malachi, ends with the return of Elijah (3:23-

24). Christian tradition saw John the Baptist as fulfilling this role of Elijah (see Matt 11:14; Mark 9:10-13; Luke 1:17). Hence the Christian Old Testament prepares for the coming of Jesus whose way John the Baptist prepared.

Books of the Old Testament

Pentateuch. Derived from Greek meaning "five-volume" (book), the Pentateuch corresponds to the Hebrew Torah, i.e., Genesis through Deuteronomy. Genesis narrates, first, the beginnings of humanity (chs. 1–11) and, then, the stories of the patriarchs (chs. 12–50). These ancestors of Israel (Abraham, Isaac, and Jacob) roamed about the hill country of Canaan (the Promised Land) and received divine promises of a land, offspring, and numerous descendants. Owing to a famine, Jacob's family ultimately migrated to Egypt. Exodus deals with the forced labor of the descendants of Jacob by the king of Egypt and the subsequent exit of the Hebrews from Egypt under the leadership of Moses (ca. 1300 B.C.) that culminates in the making of the covenant between Yahweh and Israel and thus the constitution of Israel as Yahweh's people. Leviticus contains a variety of cultic or ritual legislation that God reveals to Israel at Sinai. Numbers treats the journey of the Israelites from Sinai to the plains of Moab in Transjordan with mention of census figures in chs. 1 and 26 and arithmetical information elsewhere (hence the name "Numbers"). Deuteronomy or "second law" is a recapitulation of Israel's experience up to that point and the final revelation prior to entering the Promised Land. It emphasizes the covenant bond or relationship that is to exist between Yahweh and Israel. The Pentateuch closes with the death and burial of Moses (Deut 34:1-12) within sight of the Promised Land.

The formation of the Pentateuch is an issue hotly debated by scholars. A consensus holds that a number of authors (or schools) employed their traditions to respond to crises from the tenth to the sixth century B.C. This consensus also maintains that oral tradition preceded the written tradition. The end product pulls together both early and late theological views regarding Yahweh and Israel. In the final analysis the Pentateuch is the collection of the foundational events of Israel's relationship with her God.

Historical Books. Joshua, Judges, 1 and 2 Samuel, and 1 and 2 Kings are commonly referred to as the Deuteronomistic History. This history surveys Israel's entrance into the Promised Land under Joshua (ca. 1240 B.C.), the period of the Judges (mainly charismatic military heroes during the period of ca. 1200–1050 B.C.), the beginning of the monarchy under Saul (ca. 1020 B.C.), the rise and ascendancy of King David (ca. 1000–962 B.C.), the reign of King Solomon (961–922 B.C.), the division of the united kingdom of Judah (the south) and Israel (the north) in 922 B.C., the demise of Israel (721 B.C.), and the fall of Judah and Jerusalem (587 B.C.) with subsequent exile in Babylon. The work is theological commentary, developing the doctrine of Deuteronomy, i.e., when Israel was faithful to the covenant, Israel prospered; when Israel was unfaithful to the covenant, Israel was punished. In its final form the Deuteronomistic History offers a message of hope for the future of God's people.

Unlike the Hebrew Bible, the Christian Old Testament sandwiches the Book of Ruth between Judges and 1 Samuel. It is during the time of the Judges that Ruth and her mother-in-law, Naomi, return from Moab to Bethlehem. At the end of the book Ruth marries Boaz and bears a son by the name of Obed and thus becomes the great-grandmother of King David (see Ruth 4:13-22).

1 and 2 Chronicles, Ezra, and Nehemiah are often referred to as the Chronicler's History. Composed as a unified work ca. 400 B.C. (though involving different authors over a period of time), they reflect the problems and concerns of the Persian period (539–333 B.C.). In 1 Chronicles 9:35–29:30 the emphasis lies on an ideal David as founder of the Temple cult while in 2 Chronicles 1:1–9:31 the focus is on Solomon as the builder of the Temple. In 2 Chronicles 10:1–36:23 the work concentrates on the kings of Judah, deliberately omitting those of Israel. The future of the congregation of Israel resides in proper worship in the one Temple in Jerusalem. Ezra and Nehemiah recount the return from Exile, the rebuilding of the Temple, and the resumption of life under the leadership of Ezra and Nehemiah (ca. 450–400 B.C.).

Tobit and Esther deal with life in the Diaspora, i.e., in areas outside the land of Israel. Tobit is a historical novel (ca. 200 B.C.) that describes the trials and joys of two Jewish families. The piety and faith of these families become a model for Jewish existence and religious practice in the midst of adversity. Esther is also a historical novel written in the fourth or fifth century B.C. that tells the story of a universal persecution of Jews in the Persian Empire. Esther, the Jewish Queen of Persia, and Mordecai, her former guardian, are examples of fidelity to the Jewish faith that simultaneously promotes the good of the Persian Empire.

Judith is another historical novel written ca. 150 B.C. that reflects the faith, daring, and resourcefulness of the protagonist. Facing the overwhelming odds of the Assyrian army, she succeeds in winning an enormous victory for her people. Faith in the God of Israel and determination to withstand all odds are hallmarks of this book.

1 and 2 Maccabees deal with the Jewish revolt against Hellenism, i.e., against the impact of Greek culture on the Jews, especially in the person of Antiochus IV Epiphanes who ruled the Seleucid Empire from 175 to 164 B.C. 1 Maccabees written ca. 100 B.C. is a history covering the period from 175 to ca. 104 B.C. that sets out to defend the legitimacy of the Hasmonean dynasty (the Maccabean rulers). 2 Maccabees written ca. 125 B.C. is a rhetorical history covering the period from 180 to 160 B.C. that is intended to instruct and edify the Jewish audience by recounting examples of religious heroism.

Wisdom Books. It has been somewhat traditional to speak of "seven books of wisdom." In addition to wisdom books *per se,* viz., Job, Proverbs, Ecclesiastes/Qoheleth, Sirach, and Wisdom, one included the Psalms and the Song of Songs. While some psalms are wisdom psalms, the Psalms, as a whole, are Israel's prayer book. The Song of Songs is a collection of erotic love poetry and, as such, does not fit under the designation "wisdom books."

As a life style, wisdom sees as its goal the pursuit of the good life. This involves a proper relationship with God that is often expressed as fear of the Lord (see Prov 9:10). As a body of literature, wisdom embraces proverbs, comparisons, hymns, beatitudes, philosophical reflections, instructions, etc. The task of the wisdom teacher was to challenge students by opening their minds to the world around them.

Perhaps written ca. 500 B.C., Job develops a prose folk tale (see 1:1–2:10; 42:7-17) about a totally righteous person (see Ezek 14:14, 20) into a great dialogue about the divine-human relationship, especially as it touches on suffering (chs. 3–41). Unlike the righteous man of antiquity, the Job of the dialogues questions God by lashing out and inquiring about the divine silence. In the end God appears in a storm to Job but disregards his questions because they are wrong. Job must admit his own ignorance and accept mystery as a reality in dealing with this personally concerned God.

The Book of Psalms is a collection of collections. Borrowing from individual collections (cf. Ps 40:12-18 with Psalm 70), the final collection contains 150 psalms and is divided into five books, perhaps in imitation of the Pentateuch. As prayer forms, the psalms reveal Israel's experience with her God both individually and communally. Typical psalm forms include: (1) the lament, i.e., the expression of both individual and communal pain that is brought to God's attention, invoking a response, e.g., Psalm 22; (2) the hymn or psalm of descriptive praise, i.e., praise of God for his ongoing care of the world and people, e.g., Psalm 8; (3) the thanksgiving or psalm of declarative praise, i.e., praise of God for God's help in specific situations, e.g., Psalm 30.

Perhaps completed ca. 500 B.C., Proverbs is a collection of brief, two-line sayings (chs. 10–29). There is a preface of long poetic instructions (chs. 1–9) as well as a conclusion consisting of longer sayings and short poems (chs. 30–31). This biblical book teaches that the pursuit of wisdom is accessible to all. It endeavors to teach the young the right choices they must make in life. In chapters 1–9 wisdom appears as a woman ("Lady Wisdom") who appeals to the young to avoid folly and seek life. To heed her is to gain wisdom.

Ecclesiastes/Qoheleth (the former Greek word translates the latter Hebrew word as some function related to an assembly) is a third-century B.C. work in which the author challenges the accepted wisdom of his day. "Vanity of vanities, all is vanity" captures his iconoclastic thought. Rather than trying to discover the divine purpose in everything, the wise person must accept God's transcendence, the limitations of human knowledge, and the need to deal with both the joys and sorrows of human life.

The Song of Songs (a superlative for "the greatest song") is a collection of love poems that have a certain overall unity. As love poetry, they capture the moods and feelings of the love experiences of humans. The Song also emphasizes mutuality and fidelity between lovers, their sense of devotion, and the sensuousness of their relationship. It is hardly surprising that both Jewish and Christian communities allegorized the Song to reflect, respectively, the bond between Yahweh and Israel and Christ and the Church.

Sirach (also called Ben Sira and Ecclesiasticus—the latter because of Church use) is a work of the early second century B.C. The author, Joshua, son of Eleazar, son of Sira, seeks to deal with the threat of Hellenism by showing that true wisdom is found mainly in Jerusalem, not Athens. Indeed the author insists that wisdom is God's gift of the covenant to Israel (see 24:22).

Wisdom, written perhaps as late as 50 B.C. by a learned Jew in Alexandria, also provides a reaction to Hellenism and its challenge to Jewish faith. As an exhortation, Wisdom reminds the Jewish audience of the impact that learning can have on religious growth. A good Jew should not disparage Greek ways. By the same token a good Jew should not be ashamed of Jewish ways.

Prophetic Books. The names mentioned at the heads of these books substantially identify the words and sayings found there with particular prophets.

However, these words and sayings are the memorabilia of the prophets, not necessarily the literary works of the prophets themselves. Editors have joined together smaller collections of prophetic utterances into a more comprehensive whole.

The prophetic books are traditionally divided into major (Isaiah, Jeremiah, Ezekiel and Daniel—Daniel, however, is not a prophetic book in the Hebrew canon) and minor (Hosea, Joel, etc.) prophets. This designation does not imply the greater importance of the major over the minor prophets. Rather, it expresses the smaller size of the minor prophetic books by comparison with the major prophetic books.

Isaiah consists of three distinct spokespersons: (1) Isaiah of Jerusalem or First Isaiah (chs. 1–39—a time from ca. 740 to 700 B.C.); (2) Second Isaiah (chs. 40–55—a time ca. 540 B.C.); (3) Third Isaiah (chs. 56–66—a time ca. 500 B.C.). Isaiah of Jerusalem preached during the Assyrian crisis of the second half of the eighth century B.C. He emphasizes the holiness of God, the need for faith (see 7:9), and God's choice of the Davidic dynasty as the vehicle for promoting the needs of the people. Second Isaiah preached God's message to the Jewish Exile in Babylon. Sensing the rise of the Persian king, Cyrus, Second Isaiah celebrates that event as God's care for and deliverance of his dejected audience. He teaches the doctrine of monotheism—there is no God besides Yahweh. He also underlines the role of this creator God as redeemer, i.e., Yahweh will bring Israel back from this state of slavery. The form of redemption is a new exodus. Second Isaiah also speaks of the Suffering Servant, probably the symbol of the ideal faithful Jew in exile. Third Isaiah preaches at a time after the return of the exiles to Jerusalem. He deals with deep divisions among the people and reflects his own near despair. But he offers a message of hope in his vision of a new heaven and a new earth (see 65:17).

Jeremiah preached at the most tumultuous time in his country's history, viz., from ca. 626 to ca. 585 B.C. This was the time when the vast Assyrian Empire was tottering and was eventually supplanted by the Babylonians. Apparently supporting the religious and political reform of King Josiah (640–609 B.C.), Jeremiah subsequently became embroiled with the Judean leadership. He denounced idolatry, superficial covenantal conduct, and reliance on Egypt. It was in vain that he urged King Zedekiah (597–587 B.C.) to surrender to Babylon. The outcome was the destruction of Judah, including especially Jerusalem and its Temple. In the subsequent political upheaval Jeremiah was taken to Egypt where he died. Although scholars continue to debate the various sources in the Book of Jeremiah, what does emerge is the portrait of a prophet who courageously struggled with his God, his people, and himself. He remains the model of the persevering spokesperson.

Both Lamentations and Baruch are associated with Jeremiah. Lamentations is an anonymous collection of five poems that catches up the pain and frustration of the Judean population in the aftermath of the destruction of Jerusalem in 587 B.C. While God's people confess their sinfulness in these laments, they also hope for the return of God's mercy. Baruch is an anthology of several different poems as well as the prayer of the exiles and Jeremiah's letter against idolatry. Against the background of the fall of Jerusalem and Exile the editor attributes this work to Baruch, the secretary of Jeremiah, in part because Baruch was well acquainted with Jeremiah's letter to the exiles. However, the book deals not only with the Exile but also with the problems that the exiles experienced in the Diaspora, i.e., those Jews who remained outside the Promised Land.

Somewhat like his contemporary Jeremiah, Ezekiel also preached at the critical time of his people's history. This priest prophet begins his mission to the Judean exiles in 593 B.C. (his last dated prophecy is 571). Hence he preaches both before and after the fall of Jerusalem. Chapters 1–24 warn his audience of the inexorable fall of Jerusalem; chapters 33–48 offer a message of hope for reconstruction in the discouraging period after the fall of the capital city. Ezekiel not only speaks but also acts out or pantomimes his message from God (see chs. 4–5). Significant themes in this prophetic work include: (1) God's transcendent holiness; (2) the need for moral and cultic integrity; (3) personal responsibility; (4) the restoration of Israel as a freely given gift from God.

Daniel is not a prophetic work (see the Hebrew Bible) but a composition consisting of edifying narratives (chs. 1–6; 13–14—the latter are deuterocanonical additions) and apocalyptic (chs. 7–12). As a whole, the book was written around 165 B.C. in response to the attraction of Hellenism and the persecution of Jews who chose to remain faithful to their ancestral religion. The narratives provide edifying tales of faithful Jews, e.g., Daniel in the lions' den. The apocalyptic chapters with their fantastic visions are a form of revelation that assures the Jewish audience that God is still in control of history and that the righteous will ultimately win out (12:2 clearly teaches a resurrection of the dead).

Hosea preached in the northern kingdom of Israel from ca. 755 to 725 B.C., a period of initial calm and subsequent terror (just before the fall of the capital of Samaria). According to chapters 1–3 Hosea follows God's order to marry a woman of loose morals, Gomer, who bears him children with symbolic names. Gomer is unfaithful, leaves her husband, and seemingly falls into slavery. On the basis of this experience Hosea comes to understand God's predicament, viz., Yahweh is married to Israel but Israel has proven unfaithful because of her idolatrous practices. Like Hosea, Yahweh still loves his wife and seeks to renew the marriage bond by returning to Sinai, the place of the honeymoon. Covenantal fidelity and steadfast love are hallmarks of Hosea's preaching.

Scholars date Joel in the Persian period around 400–350 B.C. In chapters 1–2 Joel speaks of a devastating locust plague (it is like an advancing army) and its effect on harvesters, farmers, and cultic personnel. The prophet calls upon the people to repent and then pronounces an oracle, assuring his audience of the end of the plague and the restoration of the land. Employing the imagery of the Day of the Lord, the prophet speaks in chapters 3–4 of the outpouring of the prophetic spirit and God's judgment on the nations. The experience of relief from the plague is the assurance of God's ultimate vindication of Israel.

Amos from the Judean town of Tekoa preached in the northern kingdom of Israel, perhaps ca. 760 B.C. What sets him apart from all other prophets up to that time is that he announces the irrevocable end of Israel. God's covenant with his people notwithstanding, the destruction of the northern kingdom is inexorable. Amos connects this judgment with blatant social injustices of the time—the minority ruling elite have trampled upon and oppressed the majority peasantry. For Amos worship devoid of interhuman justice is a sham because God cannot be honored while the poor are being exploited. Although Israel turns a deaf ear to the prophet, the fall of Samaria in 721 B.C. was in part a catalyst for preserving and updating (see 9:11-15) his words.

Obadiah is the shortest book in the Old Testament. Written probably in the fifth century B.C., the book denounces the country of Edom for its treachery against Judah and Jerusalem in 587 B.C. and thereafter (see Ps 137; Lam 4:21-22). The work calls for vengeance against Edom—specifically the evil the Edomites committed will come back on them. It will suffer what Judah suffered except that Edom will never rise again.

Jonah derives its name from an eighth-century prophet (see 2 Kgs 14:25). It is a short story containing satire. Written ca. 475–450 B.C., the work is a protest against a theology of rigid conformity and a proclamation of God's capacity to be free and hence to give freely. Accordingly the prophet after his adventure in the sea must preach the possibility of repentance to the hated Assyrians, specifically the inhabitants of Nineveh. Contrary to Jonah's expectations and desires the Ninevites repent en masse. In the final chapter the reluctant prophet is hoping that God will relent and punish the city. God's pity surpasses Jonah's all too human calculations.

Micah from the Judean town of Moresheth preached toward the end of the eighth century B.C. At a time of Assyrian domination in the ancient Near East Micah announces that sin is the reason for the forthcoming punishment. He is deeply concerned about social justice and is fearless in attacking the Judean leadership. Later hands kept his message alive, e.g., by applying it to the Babylonian Exile and offering a message of hope to the Jewish exiles (see 4:10).

Nahum, Habakkuk, and Zephaniah are roughly contemporaneous. Zephaniah preached in the early days of King Josiah (640–609 B.C.). He announces the Day of the Lord, i.e., God's judgment against Judah and Jerusalem as well as against foreign nations including the tottering Assyria. However, there is also a dimension of hope or reversal, viz., in the faith of a people small but pleasing to Yahweh. Around 612 B.C. Nahum solemnly pronounced God's vengeance against Nineveh, the capital of the Assyrian Empire. The prophet seems to gloat over Nineveh's destruction. However, this just punishment shows that God has not abandoned Judah—the enemy will not last forever. Sometime during the reign of King Jehoiakim (609–598 B.C.) Habakkuk raised the question of divine justice—after enduring the Assyrians, why must God's people now contend with the Babylonians? What follows is an exchange between Yahweh and Habakkuk. Despite the problem one must continue to maintain an attitude of faith and trust (see 2:4). In the concluding canticle of chapter 3 what is certain is God's absolute power over creation and history, notwithstanding the disturbing political scene.

Both Haggai and Zechariah address the second group of exiles from Babylon who returned to Jerusalem ca. 522 B.C. under the leadership of Zerubbabel, the governor, and Joshua, the high priest. In 520 Haggai urges the restoration of the Temple, arguing that its future glory would surpass that of the old. After denouncing the cultic impurity of the people, he goes to announce blessings, especially the revival of the Davidic dynasty. Beginning in 520 and continuing into the beginning of the next century, Zechariah offers a series of visions and oracles in chapters 1–8 (chs. 9–14 are generally regarded as later works). Like Haggai, Zechariah emphasizes the importance of rebuilding the Temple. Unlike Hag-

Hebrew Bible	**Protestant Bible**	**Roman Catholic Bible**
Torah	*Pentateuch*	*Pentateuch*
Genesis	Genesis	Genesis
Exodus	Exodus	Exodus
Leviticus	Leviticus	Leviticus
Numbers	Numbers	Numbers
Deuteronomy	Deuteronomy	Deuteronomy
Prophets: (a) Former	*Historical Books*	*Historical Books*
Joshua	Joshua	Joshua
Judges	Judges	Judges
	Ruth	Ruth
1 and 2 Samuel	1 and 2 Samuel	1 and 2 Samuel
1 and 2 Kings	1 and 2 Kings	1 and 2 Kings
	1 and 2 Chronicles	1 and 2 Chronicles
Prophets: (b) Latter	Ezra and Nehemiah	Ezra and Nehemiah
		Tobit
Isaiah		
Jeremiah		Judith
Ezekiel	Esther	Esther
Hosea		1 and 2 Maccabees
Joel		
Amos	*Wisdom Books*	*Wisdom Books*
Obadiah	Job	Job
Jonah	Psalms	Psalms
Micah	Proverbs	Proverbs
Nahum	Ecclesiastes	Ecclesiastes
Habakkuk	Song of Songs	Song of Songs
Zephaniah		Book of Wisdom
Haggai		Sirach/Ben Sira/Ecclesiasticus
Zechariah		
Malachi	*Prophetic Books*	*Prophetic Books*
	Isaiah	Isaiah
Writings	Jeremiah	Jeremiah
Psalms	Lamentations	Lamentations
Job		Baruch
Proverbs	Ezekiel	Ezekiel
Ruth	Daniel	Daniel
Song of Songs	Hosea	Hosea
Qoheleth	Joel	Joel
Lamentations	Amos	Amos
Esther	Obadiah	Obadiah
Daniel	Jonah	Jonah
Ezra-Nehemiah	Micah	Micah
1 and 2 Chronicles	Nahum	Nahum
	Habakkuk	Habakkuk
	Zephaniah	Zephaniah
	Haggai	Haggai
	Zechariah	Zechariah
	Malachi	Malachi

gai, he attaches more importance to Joshua than to Zerubbabel. He also underlines the importance of God's activity, not the efforts of the people and the leadership. Also unlike Haggai, Zechariah holds out a hope for a future age that is less imminent.

Around 450 B.C. Malachi addressed a disillusioned Judean audience for whom the new age of Haggai and Zechariah had not come. In this climate he attacks the priests, insists on the people's duty to support the Temple and its personnel, and demonstrates genuine concern for rejected wives. In a later appendix to the book there is the promise of the return of Elijah who will clear the way prior to the Day of the Lord.

JOHN F. CRAGHAN

See also THEOLOGY, BIBLICAL.

BIBLE, READING THE

See READING THE BIBLE.

BIBLICAL ARCHAEOLOGY

The Archaeological Task

Archaeology is the field of studies that attempts to reconstruct the world of antiquity through the recovery and interpretation of its material remains. Literary remains alone do not give an entirely accurate picture of the ancient world since literary works usually represent the perspectives of an elite group. The recovery and interpretation of material remains create a more balanced picture.

There are three significant moments in the archaeological task. The most familiar of the three is excavation which involves the uncovering of material remains through systematic and controlled digging. Excavation has to proceed with accurate recording of the progress and results of digging. The second moment in the archaeological task involves the interpretation of artifacts and other data uncovered during excavation. The goals of this analysis are to reconstruct the chronology of the site and to illuminate its cultural dynamics. The final moment in the archaeological task is publication through which archaeologists share the results of their work. While a project is in progress, preliminary publications will summarize the results of field work and offer tentative and preliminary analysis. When excavation of a site ends, archaeologists publish a final report on the results of their work. The final report describes the excavation project and lists the artifacts recovered. It also offers a synthesis of the vast amount of data uncovered during excavation.

Biblical Archaeology

Biblical archaeology is the discipline that applies the results of archaeological research to the study of the Bible to clarify the cultural and social setting of the Bible. At one time, biblical archaeology was narrowly historical in its orientation. Its focus was on the reconstruction of the political history of the eastern Mediterranean region. The objective of most excavations was to establish the chronology of sites to support the historical value of biblical narratives. Under the influence of New World archaeology, biblical archaeology has broadened its concerns beyond chronology to the society, economy, politics, ecosystems, and population patterns of antiquity to reconstruct the entire culture of ancient Palestine from the prehistoric era down to the end of the Byzantine period A.D. (seventh century).

This broadening of the archaeological task was accompanied by important changes in the presuppositions with which biblical archaeologists approach their work. Data that came from archaeological excavations once were seen as providing an independent and objective support for the historical value of the Bible. Today biblical archaeologists see the complementary relationship that exists between the literary and nonliterary sources of knowledge of the biblical era and its people. They excavate not to prove the historicity of biblical narratives but to explain the meaning of these texts by understanding the people who produced, received, and transmitted them. Interpretation of the material remains which these people left behind helps this process.

Because of the narrower interests of early biblical archaeologists, sites with connections to the Old Testament were once the prime focus of attention. Because of the theological concerns that have characterized New Testament research it was believed that archaeology could have little more than tangential value for understanding the beginnings of the Christian movement. The wealth of literary sources from early Judaism led scholars to consider excavation of Jewish sites an unnecessary luxury.

Archaeology's contribution to biblical studies comes in five general areas. First, recovering the material remains of many ancient Near Eastern peoples makes cross-cultural comparison possible. Second, archaeology can provide a cultural context for events narrated in the Bible in a way that these narratives cannot do themselves. Third, archaeology's recovery of the material remains of ancient cultures provides a supplement to the literary remains already available. Fourth, archaeology sometimes provides a perspective different from the literary texts making possible a more balanced view of events narrated in the Bible. Fifth, archaeology sometimes provides data that can aid the interpretation of an obscure text.

Texts, Documents and Inscriptions

Archaeological excavations in the Middle East have uncovered texts that were unknown before excavation. These texts have provided an understanding of the world in which ancient Israel emerged. During excavations in Syria from 1964 to 1976, an important cultural center from the third millennium came to light: the city of Ebla. The principal find was the city's archives. Archaeologists recovered almost seventeen thousand tablets. Though little more than preliminary work has been done in the interpretation of these tablets, it is obvious that they will have a major impact on our understanding of the history, religion, and culture of the ancient Near East of the Early Bronze Age (3150–2200 B.C.). Though ancient Israel did not emerge in Canaan until more than one thousand years after the fall of Ebla, the Ebla tablets can be an important source for understanding the sometimes obscure vocabulary of biblical Hebrew.

Biblical interpreters are confident about the potential contribution of the Ebla archives to our understanding of biblical Hebrew because of their experience with the tablets found early in this century at Ras Shamra, the site of the ancient city of Ugarit. This city on the Mediterranean coast north of Canaan flourished from 2000 to 1200 B.C. The tablets found there date from the fourteenth century B.C. Ugaritic parallels have illumined obscure passages especially in the psalms and in Job. The Ugaritic texts also preserved the Canaanite myths of the Baal cycle with other Canaanite religious texts. These stories of ancient Canaan have helped interpreters understand the allusions in the Bible to the non-Yahwistic religious traditions of the region. It is now apparent how ancient Israel's beliefs were forged in contact with these religious traditions.

Other finds in the Eastern Mediterranean region have contributed to more nuanced appreciation of the biblical tradition. For example, texts from Mari, an eighteenth-century B.C. site on the Euphrates, have contributed to our understanding of the phenomenon of prophecy in the ancient Near East. Further east along the Tigris River is the site of ancient Nuzi. This site flourished in the sixteenth and fifteenth centuries B.C. Its texts revealed ancient Near Eastern customs and legal practices that biblical traditions reflect.

Excavations in the territory of the second millennium Hittite Empire in Asia Minor uncovered texts that aid in understanding the biblical covenant. The way that the Bible describes ancient Israel's covenant with God resembles the pattern of Hittite treaties.

Finally, archives found at the fourteenth-century site of Amarna in Egypt describe the political, social, and military chaos that reigned in Canaan just before the arrival of the Israelite people. These texts make several references to the *hapiru,* people with no loyalties to established political and social entities. The emergence of the *hapiru* in Canaan may represent a preliminary stage in a process that eventually ended with the Israelite settlement in Canaan.

Unfortunately the territory of the ancient Israelite kingdoms has not yielded the number of inscriptional and documentary finds attested elsewhere in the Near East. Among the few finds that have emerged is the Gezer Calendar. This is a Hebrew text that describes the proper times for various agricultural activities. Another important find is the stele of Mesha, king of Moab. The stele describes the defeat of Israel by Moab in 840 B.C. from the perspective of the Moabites (see 1 Kgs 3:1-27 for the biblical point of view). The text inscribed on the stele shows that the Moabites' conception of their god Chemosh was similar in some ways to the Israelite conception of Yahweh. An inscription found in Jerusalem's Siloam tunnel describes how the tunnel was dug when Judah was preparing for an attack by the Assyrians (see 2 Kgs 20:20). The Lachish ostraca contain correspondence between the defenders of that city and officials in Jerusalem during the final days of the Judahite state.

The textual finds from Palestine would be few and unimportant compared with those from other areas in the ancient Near East were it not for the Dead Sea Scrolls. The discovery of these scrolls in 1947 was the single most important find relating to the Bible. The finds from Qumran help illuminate Palestinian Judaism in the period just before the birth of Jesus.

Another cache of manuscripts found about the same time in Egypt help clarify the first centuries of Church history. The finds come from the town of Nag Hammadi along the Nile in central Egypt. They comprise some 1240 pages of material written in Coptic that reflect the tradition of Christian gnostics of the second and third centuries. One of these works, the Gospel of Thomas, contains sayings of Jesus in a form earlier than those of the canonical Gospels.

Archaeology and the Old Testament

The work of biblical archaeologists is complicated because they turn up few texts or inscriptions from the biblical period. Biblical archaeology is silent for the most part. Interpretation of material remains in-

The synagogue at Capernaum, 2nd century

volves a much more complex and expensive set of procedures than the interpretation of texts. The way archaeologists interpret these material remains depends in part on the interests and theological orientation of archaeologists.

For example, at one point in the development of biblical archaeology the question of history was paramount. Some archaeologists were convinced that archaeology could support the historicity of the biblical narratives about the settlement of the Israelite tribes in Canaan. They used the Bible to interpret their archaeological finds and then used these interpretations to support the historicity of the Bible. The development of modern archaeological methods eliminated such circular reasoning.

Excavations that took place from 1950 to 1972 produced evidence that both supports and contradicts the biblical stories. While the Bible says that the Israelite tribes camped at Kadesh Barnea before entering Canaan (Num 33:16-36; Deut 1:45), archaeology can provide no evidence that people lived at this site before the time of David. The Book of Joshua describes the fall of Jericho and Ai (Josh 2–8), but archaeological evidence shows that there was no major settlement at Jericho and that Ai was unoccupied during the period that witnessed the emergence of Israelites in Canaan. On the other hand, the Bible states that both Lachish (Josh 10:31-32) and Hazor (Josh 11:11) were destroyed violently. Archaeology supports this, but it cannot identify the Israelites as those responsible for the destruction.

The Bible is the product of elite groups in ancient Israel. The focus of the biblical traditions is on public happenings, great political events, and the deeds of prominent figures like leading priests, kings, and prophets. Almost completely lacking in the Bible are the reminiscences and reflections of private people. There is little in the Bible like diaries, biographies, journals, and other literary forms that can give us some hint of what ordinary people thought of their religious traditions and how they lived their lives. Here is where archaeology can be very helpful. Excavation of domestic and industrial buildings, the recovery and analysis of tools, pottery, pollens, and the examination of jewelry and other domestic artifacts can begin to fill the gaps left by the biblical tradition.

For example, Tirzah, the capital of the northern kingdom at one time, produced evidence of two types of domestic buildings. There was unmistakable evidence of larger homes for the rich and the simpler structures for the poor. This not only shows that there was some town planning in the cities of ancient Israel but also that there was social stratification in ancient Israelite society.

Another area where archaeology can be very helpful is in the reconstruction of ancient Israel's worship. Earlier purely literary studies stressed the unique features of ancient Israelite religion. Archaeology has shifted the focus to those features ancient Israel shared with other ancient Near Eastern religions in general and with the Canaanite religion of the Late Bronze Age (1550–1200) in particular.

Archaeology of public and domestic shrines confirms that many ancient Israelites revered other deities, specifically Canaanite fertility gods. Among these were Asherah, the "Mother Goddess." Artifacts discovered at Kuntillet Ajrud suggest that some people thought of Asherah as Yahweh's consort while other Israelites thought of her as the consort of Baal, the Canaanite storm god. Until the Exile, Asherah and Baal were potent rivals of Yahweh for the loyalty of the Israelites.

On a popular level, the claims of Canaanite religion to harness the very life-giving forces of nature for the benefits of worshippers was an attractive alternative to Yahwistic religion with its ethical demands. The prophetic protest against Canaanite religious practice was directed at the genuine threat that non-Yahwistic religion posed to ancient Israel. Archaeology supplies the social, religious, and cultural context for the prophetic protest against Canaanite religion.

Those who ignore the results of archaeological work will continue to minimize the affinity and even continuity of ancient Israelite religion with that of Canaan. Still, archaeology makes it difficult to continue a one-sided emphasis on the uniqueness of ancient Israel. Recent archaeology has shown that in terms of material culture and the behavior it reflects, there was little difference between Canaanite and Israelite religious practices.

Archaeology and the New Testament

Archaeology relating to the New Testament has its own set of problems. First, the theological emphasis in New Testament interpretation has led to ignoring the archaeological record. Second, the material culture of the first Christians was not different from that of other Jews in Palestine.

Excavations in Nazareth and Capernaum has led some archaeologists to describe a phenomenon that they call Jewish Christianity. For example, graffiti and other remains found at Nazareth confirm the use of a synagogue for Christian worship.

Excavations beneath a fifth-century Byzantine church in Capernaum have led some archaeologists to conclude that this church was built over a private home that shows evidence of having been modified for public worship already in the first century. Again graffiti etched on the walls led the excavators to posit this as a shrine in honor of St. Peter.

Excavations of Jerusalem's Church of the Holy Sepulchre and Bethlehem's Church of the Nativity have led to the conclusion that both sites were venerated within less than two hundred years after Christ. Still, archaeology cannot decide whether this veneration represented an historical memory or the localization of pious belief.

Excavations at Sepphoris, the capital of Lower Galilee in Jesus' day, have revealed a cosmopolitan city in which Jew and Gentile were able to live together in peace. Herod Antipas built the city when Jesus was growing up in Nazareth just a few miles away. This had led some to speculate that Joseph may have been a laborer on this building project. Also the discovery of a Roman theater there has led to the suggestion that Jesus' criticism of the scribes and Pharisees as "hypocrites" (see Matt 23) is the use of a metaphor from the theater since one Greek term for actor is "hypocrite" [=mask-wearer since actors wore masks]. Of course, archaeology cannot prove either assertion.

What New Testament archaeology can do for New Testament interpretation is not to prove any historical questions, but to reconstruct the cultural and social setting of first-century Palestine. The preliminary results of the archaeology of this period show that Judaism at this time was a far more diverse religious phenomenon than usually thought. For too long people have understood the Judaism of Jesus' day according to the patterns set by rabbinic Judaism that emerged much later. The results of archaeological work supplemented by renewed study of textual material (the so-called intertestamental literature) shows that early Judaism displayed a remarkable variety of belief and practice determined largely by local variation. The emergence of the Jesus Movement is more understandable against this background.

Conclusion

There are two sources of knowledge about antiquity: literary and material sources. Archaeology concerns itself with the recovery and interpretation of the material remains of antiquity. Together with the literary sources that have survived, archaeology can give people today a glimpse into the people of antiquity. Archaeology helps to reconstruct their world, values, politics, religion, commercial relationships, diet, health, and aesthetic sense. Interest in biblical archaeology will always be keen because it is simply one way we have learned to express our fascination with the Bible, its world and people.

LESLIE J. HOPPE, O.F.M.

See also BIBLE, NEW TESTAMENT WRITINGS; BIBLE, OLD TESTAMENT WRITINGS; CRITICISM, BIBLICAL.

BIBLICAL COMMISSION

The Pontifical Biblical Commission is an organization that is entrusted with overseeing the promotion of biblical scholarship in the Roman Catholic Church. Founded by Leo XIII in 1902 in his Apostolic Letter *Vigilantiae,* the Commission is based in Rome and composed of a number of cardinals, assisted by an international group of biblical scholars who act as consultors.

The Commission was established to promote rather than defend, but its initial work came at a time when Catholic biblical scholarship was struggling with the problems of Modernism. Thus, the Commission's work became more cautious, restrictive, and defensive, as can be seen in its first fourteen statements—negative responses to questions the Commission asked itself. Since the 1950s and Roman Catholicism's acceptance of biblical critical methods in studying Scripture, the Commission has returned to its original purpose of the promotion of biblical scholarship.

Pope Pius X (1903–1914) gave the Commission authority to examine candidates for doctorates in Scripture. Later he declared that the Commission's decrees had the same authority as those of the sacred congregations. However, as time passed, the Commission itself (1955) acknowledged that its earlier decrees were not to be interpreted strictly when they referred to questions of history, geography or authorship, and also admitted that over time its own responses would need further clarification in view of new developments in biblical scholarship. The Commission's respect for biblical scholars and its acceptance of the need for further developments in scholarship were seen in the Commission's silence during the Scripture controversies of 1960 to 1963, and with its instruction in 1964, assuring biblical scholars of their freedom to use form criticism in interpreting the Bible.

LEONARD DOOHAN

See also CRITICISM, BIBLICAL; MODERNISM; THEOLOGY, BIBLICAL.

BIBLICAL CRITICISM

See CRITICISM, BIBLICAL.

BIBLICAL INSPIRATION

See INSPIRATION, BIBLICAL.

BIBLICAL INSTITUTE, PONTIFICAL

See PONTIFICAL BIBLICAL INSTITUTE.

BIBLICAL THEOLOGY

See THEOLOGY, BIBLICAL.

BIDDING PRAYERS

These are intercessory prayers, usually in the form of a litany with response ("Lord, hear our prayer" is typical) which from ancient times have followed the reading of the Gospel or the homily. They are now called "General Intercessions," or, sometimes, the "Prayers of the Faithful."

DAVID BRYAN

See also EUCHARIST; LITURGY.

BIOETHICS

This new field of study, which has immense implications for humankind, can be defined as the examination and study of the moral and social implications of practices and experiments in medicine and the life sciences. It covers such areas as: euthanasia, behavior control, genetic intervention, physician-patient relationship, abortion, fertility control, transplanted and artificial organs, death and dying, and many other areas in genetics and reproductive biology.

Bioethics draws on many disciplines: theological and philosophical ethics, biology, medicine, psychology, sociology, demography, history, economics and law. The awesome advances in medicine and science in the recent decade touch nearly every aspect of human living and dying, and they also raise complex and challenging ethical questions that concern all who work in the expanding field of bioethics.

MICHAEL GLAZIER

See also THEOLOGY, MORAL.

BIRTH CONTROL

See CONTRACEPTION.

BIRTHRIGHT

See SUMMERHILL, LOUISE.

BISHOP

Within Roman Catholicism, the Eastern Churches, and a number of Protestant Churches, a bishop is the leader of Christians united within a specific geographical area, usually referred to as a diocese. The office of bishop is understood as succeeding to the role of the apostles in the early Church and is now structured as the supreme local authority, assisted by priests and deacons as lower ranks within a clerical hierarchy. The principal functions of the bishop are to teach and to maintain authentic Christian doctrine, to govern and to tend to the needs of his diocese, and to preside at worship and encourage growth in holiness in his community. Since the Second Vatican Council the origins of the episcopacy have been seen as more complex, the functions of leadership as more nuanced, and the relationships of bishops to one another and to the pope as enlarged.

Careful examination of the New Testament shows that apostolic succession does not mean simply that the apostles ordained the first bishops who then ordained each succeeding generation. The Churches of the New Testament were variously organized and fixed leadership structures with bishops and a hierarchy evolved only over generations. To begin with, some Churches such as Corinth had a more charismatic and loosely structured leadership (1 Cor 12:27-31). Others such as Jerusalem had a council of elders (Acts 15:2). In Churches such as Philippi leaders are referred to as *episkopoi* and *diakonoi* (Phil 1:1). These are the Greek words for bishops and deacons, but they do not yet imply the structured, hierarchical roles eventually associated with these terms in the later history of the Church. The terms are best understood more generically as "overseers and helpers." "Bishops" are initially referred to in the plural and not in the sense of an individual local authority. Often *episkopoi* is interchanged with *presbyteroi*, "elders" (Acts 20:17, 28), showing again a type of council succeeding to the apostles in the governing of the local Church.

By the last generations of the New Testament period, we have the beginning of a practice whereby one leader seems to emerge from among the *presbyteroi* to have supreme authority in a local community. In the Pastoral Letters, 1 Timothy 3:1-7 and Titus 1:7-11 speak of *episkopos* in the singular, though it is not yet clear that this "bishop" is totally distinct from the *presbyteroi* or that singular bishops are yet ruling in all the local Churches. In any case, by the time of Ignatius of Antioch, writing between the years 108 to 117, a clerical hierarchy is in place. All the official Church ministries in the local community are assumed by a ruling bishop assisted by presbyters (priests) and deacons. In faith, Catholics see this development as the work of the Spirit guiding the Church, so that it can be said that bishops succeed to the apostles. While this is true, one must recognize that the Spirit worked through historical development and that this allows for further historical development in the understanding and function of the episcopacy.

The changing role of bishops is evident over the history of the Church, showing bishops as theologians, feudal lords, builders, spiritual guides, and other types of functionaries. The three traditional functions have persisted over the ages, though in varied manner: to teach, to govern, and to sanctify. The Second Vatican Council reiterated the role of bishops in preaching and in maintaining fidelity to Christian doctrine. Bishops are also commissioned to govern, but this is now encouraged especially as service to the local community to meet their needs on every level, material and social as well as spiritual and personal. Bishops are also designated par excellence to gather the community for worship, especially for Eucharist. In early Christianity the unity of the entire local Church around the bishop was expressed each Sunday by the sending of a particle of consecrated bread from the cathedral Eucharist to every other Church in the diocese to be mingled in the chalice at their own Eucharist. While all these roles of the bishop continue in the Church today, they are in a more nuanced context. While it was recognized from the early Church that the bishop needed help for these functions, the delegation of ministry was kept clerical. Only priests and deacons were given official ministries and these were seen only as sharing in the bishop's. Since the Second Vatican Council, the many ministries assumed over time by the hierarchy are gradually being given back to the Church at large. Clergy/laity distinctions are becoming blurred and one speaks now of diversity of ministries. While the bishop still possesses these ministries, he does not usurp them as officially only his own. Rather he unifies them as the ministries of many in his diocese. Indeed, he sometimes leads and best exercises his ministry by coordinating these roles in capable others.

Recent developments have also stressed the wider role of bishops within the universal Church. Bishops acting in union with one another become the bond of unity whereby local Churches form one, universal or catholic Church. Thus, bishops form a college, so that while each bishop remains the supreme authority in his own diocese, he does not lead in isolation but in communion with the college of bishops. For Catholics, this college, in union with the pope, forms the supreme authority in the Church. The relationship of bishops to pope should not be that of rival powers, but of mutually supporting ministries. Nevertheless, the Second Vatican Council made it clear that bishops are not delegated authority by the pope, but exercise it in their own right. Still, their local authority is to be exercised with consideration of and deference to the Church universal, represented by communion with other bishops and by fidelity to the pope as the source of unity. This wider role of bishops has been enlarged recently by the periodic convocation of synods in Rome, whereby representative bishops from around the world meet with the pope to discuss particular issues. The Second Vatican Council also called for the establishment of national conferences of bishops to make decisions appropriate for the Church beyond single dioceses, yet still oriented to a particular territory.

ANTHONY J. TAMBASCO

See also CONGREGATION FOR BISHOPS; ORDINARY, LOCAL.

BLACK CATHOLICS

Black Catholics in the United States number approximately 2.3 million, one of the fastest growing groups in the Church. A diverse group, they trace their origins in the United States to several sources including: (a) in the east, the colonization of the state of Maryland, the only Roman Catholic colony founded and (b) in the south, the colonization of Louisiana and Florida by Spanish and/or French Catholics. Blacks, who were Catholics and either free or slave, also accompanied the Spanish and French explorers in their exploration of the southwestern part of the United States. Thus, their presence within this country is older than the country itself, dating from 1565. The black or African presence in the Roman Catholic Church is even older, dating back arguably to the baptism of the Ethiopian eunuch in Acts 8:26-40. In its first centuries of existence, the early Church was an African Church with martyrs, bishops, and popes in and from north and east Africa.

The present make-up of black Catholics is equally diverse, consisting of the greater majority who are Catholic from birth, converts, and immigrants from the Caribbean, Central and South America, and Africa itself.

Historically, black Catholics have been a voiceless, invisible minority within the Roman Catholic Church in the United States. Baptized and given only rudimentary instruction during slavery, many left the Church and became Protestant after slavery ended. The Holy See, after the end of the Civil War, had urged establishment of a prefect apostolic or ecclesiastical coordinator for the freed slaves as a means of providing much needed evangelization and spiritual guidance but this was rejected by the American bishops at the Second Plenary Council in Baltimore in 1866 in favor of individual diocesan efforts.

Thus, black Catholics found themselves in a European institution which frowned on the characteristic aspects of black worship which were an important part of their African religious and spiritual heritage, such as singing, shouting, extemporaneous praying, and being moved by the Holy Spirit to testify to their faith in "openly emotional" ways. Most, by the beginning of the twentieth century, found themselves marginalized in predominantly white parishes or segregated parishes. The result was the evolution of a parallel system of parochial schools, parishes, and lay societies such as the Knights and Ladies of Sts. John and Peter Claver which served their needs, both secular and religious.

Black men and women were not initially welcomed into the priestly or religious life. The first black women's religious order, the Oblates of Providence, was founded in 1829 in Baltimore by Mother Mary Elizabeth Lange. A second, the Sisters of the Holy Family, was established in New Orleans in 1852 by Henriette DeLille and Juliette Gaudin. For men no religious orders evolved but, in the nineteenth century, the Society of the Sacred Heart of St. Joseph (The Josephites) and the Society of the Divine Word emerged with vocations in the black community and eventually ordained many black priests. The first, however, Father Augustus Tolton who was ordained in 1886, was a priest of the diocese of Dalton (now Springfield) Illinois. Earlier, the three Healey brothers, children of a black slave mother and an Irish father, became priests in the early 1800s serving as the bishop of Portland, Maine, rector of the Boston Cathedral and president of Georgetown University, respectively. Their blackness was not openly acknowledged, however, until the 1970s.

Required to live on the margins of Catholic society with the authenticity of their Catholic faith often in question, black Catholics persisted in their faith while calling upon Church leaders to denounce the racism manifested by their fellow Catholics and their unequal and marginalized status in the Church. Two avenues initially chosen were the publication of the *American Catholic Tribune,* a weekly newspaper devoted to issues of concern to black Catholics, and the convening of five consecutive national congresses. These congresses stopped in 1892 but were resumed in 1987 with the sixth congress held in Washington, D.C., where the National Black Catholic Pastoral Plan was adopted as a foundation for evangelization and ministry within the black community.

This and the 1992 congress were the result of a reawakening of black Catholics following Vatican II and the struggles for black civil rights. They began to question their passive presence in a Church in which they had been a part for so many centuries, and the presence of God both in their lives and in their Church. Several new organizations emerged as leaders of the call for recognition and inclusion of the black heritage, most importantly the National Black Catholic Clergy Caucus, the National Black Catholic Sisters Conference, the National Black Catholic Seminarians Conference, and the National Black Lay Conference. The Catholic Church was denounced as a racist institution in need of conversion. Calling for greater leadership roles in the Church, they urged the creation of black bishops and the hiring and promotion of blacks in parishes and diocesan offices, and a greater voice for blacks in the Church as a whole.

The result of their efforts has been the establishment, first, of the National Office of Black Catholics, recently replaced by the Secretariat for Black Catholics within the United States Catholic Conference, the appointment of fourteen black bishops, and the establishment of Offices of Black Catholics in dioceses throughout the nation which serve as advocates for the concerns of black Catholics. Segregated parishes were also, for the most part, abolished as were segregated schools and other facilities.

Today, black Catholics are a strong, vocal, and active group within the Church. They participate in many areas at all levels from the NCCB/USCC to local parishes and parochial schools. The National Pastoral Plan has been affirmed by the Church and is being implemented throughout the United States serving as a model for ministry in many dioceses. Though still small in number, there are an increasing number of professional black theologians and other black Catholic scholars who are engaged in the articulation of a black Catholic theology and the inculturation of the Christian message into the heritage and tradition of black Americans.

DIANA L. HAYES

See also BLACK THEOLOGY.

BLACK THEOLOGY

Black theology emerged in the United States in the late 1960s as a direct result of the changes—social, political, economic and religious—taking place in American society because of the demand of black Americans for the civil rights guaranteed by their citizenship but historically denied them.

As a theology whose goal is liberation both from the Eurocentric theological constructs which were heretofore considered universal as well as from the oppression and marginalization of black peoples in the U.S.A., black theology arises from the questions about God's action in their lives which black Christians asked themselves, the black Church and Christianity itself. Although its first systematic articulation did not occur until 1969 with the publication of James Cone's *Black Theology and Black Power,* its first beginnings can be found in the religious understanding the African slaves brought with them from West Africa and maintained despite the distorted Christianity imposed by their slave masters.

This African heritage provided a foundation which enabled the slaves to appreciate and inculturate Christianity into their traditions and worldview, one which did not accept a dualistic separation of the sacred and the secular but saw both as an inseparable whole. This understanding enabled them to rebuild communities of faith from their shattered tribal groupings, opening a way for them to recognize in the Christian God the High God of their own traditions and in the Christian rituals and stories aspects of their own deep faith. As in Christianity, God was creator of all, transcendent yet approachable through prayer and mediators. God was also immanent, acting in the world to help God's creation, alleviating injustice and demanding righteousness from the faithful. It is this understanding of a God who saves, a God who acts in history, a God whose nurturing and sustaining Spirit dwelled amongst them that sustained black Christians through centuries of slavery, segregation, and discrimination. Their religious understanding was revealed in song, story and prayer, as a theology being born.

One of the major sources for black theology, therefore, is the black historical experience in the United States. A second source is Sacred Scripture seen as the source of God's truth and the revelation of God's actions in history on the side of the poor and oppressed. It was a truth that denied the bitterness of their lives and gave them hope for a day of liberation, both spiritual and physical. The Exodus story, especially, was a source for their early theologizing as it spoke of a people whose lives and concerns paralleled their own. A third source for black theology is tradition, the tradition of their particular faith and of their own cultural heritage which were often in tension leading to a Church and religious perspective that was both revolutionary in its call for justice yet also, at times, passive in its hopes for a heavenly resolution.

This tension or dialectic is one that remains a part of black religion, manifesting itself in calls for political action on the part of black Churches and their members on the one hand and a rejection of political engagement for an emphasis on a spiritual liberation in God's time on the other. It came to a head in the growing strain between the nonviolent civil rights movement and the more radical Black Power and Black Nationalist movements of the 1960s. The first, recognizing Jesus Christ as the power over all, called for a conversion of the hearts and minds of Euroamerican Christians while the latter, denying Christianity's legitimacy, called for the attainment of black liberation at any cost.

The civil rights movement, Black Power and Black Nationalism movements are the immediate causes for the emergence of black theology as a systematic articulation of the faith of black Christians in the United States. A new organization, the Society of Negro Churchmen (later Black Churches) issued, in 1967, a Black Power Manifesto which supported the call for Black Power while, also, calling for a reawakening of the dormant black Church to serve as the foundation for a more aggressive effort on behalf of the civil and human rights of black Americans. The authors, all ministers, asserted that religion and politics, the sacred and the secular, were not and could not be separate; how one believes affects how one lives and acts in the world. They saw the need for an expression of Christianity as a source of liberation, physical as well as spiritual, and an articulation of black faith in language that black Americans would recognize and understand.

The two major thrusts of black theology are political and cultural, the first sees theology as a mandate for political activism on the part of the black Church and the empowerment of blacks while the second asserts that, prior to political action, one must first be in touch with the cultural context from which that call arises. James Cone, Major Jones, Albert Cleage, and J. Deotis Roberts are representative of the first group while Gayraud Wilmore and the growing number of black womanist theologians such as Dolores Williams, Jacqueline Grant, Katie Cannon and others are representative of the second. Cone asserts that only a theology expressed in terms of God acting in history on the side of the poor and oppressed is a true Christian theology; it is an active option which overrides all other theological understandings. Black theology is, therefore, a theology of, by, and for black peoples, and God and Jesus Christ are black because the victims with whom they are in solidarity are oppressed simply because of their blackness. This blackness is seen in different ways, ontologically, symbolically, or physically, but the point is that the blackness of God/Christ reveal God/Christ's oneness with black people in their oppression.

The theologians of culture are in basic agreement but note that in order fully to understand and express that theology, one must first look to the roots of the black experience, especially blacks' connections with Africa as well as the experiences which have shaped and formed them into a new people. One must, thus, look at the history, music, literature, art, etc. of black people in order to articulate a true black theology. These theologians appear to be more open to the input of non-Christian as well as nonreligious sources in their understanding of black theology. Despite these distinctions, however, all black theologians see black theology as a theology of praxis which demands action in this world on behalf of marginalized blacks in American society.

Black theology continues to have an impact both in the U.S. and elsewhere. In the U.S., where it evolved as a black male Protestant theology, the input of women and black Catholics is beginning to emerge. Black women theologians define themselves as womanists, feminists of color, who seek in a holistic way to work towards the liberation of all peoples, regardless of race or gender. They critique the failure of black theology to include the perspective of women and of feminist theology to include the voices of women of color, while joining in the critique of Eurocentric theology's claim to speak for all people without recognizing the differences that race and gender bring about in one's God-talk.

At the same time, an emerging group of black Catholic theologians such as Shawn Copeland, Toinette Eugene, Diana Hayes, Bryan Massengale, Jamie Phelps and others are exploring black theology from the context of Roman Catholicism, reclaiming the long history of blacks in the Catholic Church in the U.S. and raising questions which challenge their faith and their Church as well as their fellow black Christians. They are examining Scripture and tradition, exploring the issue of liturgical inculturation and the development of authentic black Catholic liturgies, and developing a new and challenging understanding of the Church, God, Jesus Christ and Mary, calling for an affirmation of religious activism such as Mary first proclaimed in the *Magnificat.*

Black theology can also be found in South Africa where it emerged as the Black Consciousness movement of Steven Biko was first being developed. It has been greatly influenced by the black struggle in the U.S., especially their attack on racism, and serves as a source for reclamation of a Christianity tainted by the heresy of apartheid.

Black theology is a theology which arises from the context of black peoples and seeks to help them understand and defend their faith in a way which is liberating and empowering. It is a recognition of the role that religion has played and continues to play in their lives, one which is lived out in the harsh realities of a world where God continues to act in history to "set the captives free."

DIANA L. HAYES

See also BLACK CATHOLICS.

BLAISE, ST.

Commonly known as St. Blaise, Blasius was a bishop of Sebaste in Armenia during the fourth century who, legend has it, miraculously saved the life of a child who was choking on a fish bone. This led to the faithful seeking his intercessions when sick, and particularly when experiencing a throat ailment. He is one of the fourteen auxiliary saints, and his feast is observed on 3 February. Historical information on St. Blaise is of questionable authenticity.

JOSEPH QUINN

See also SAINTS.

BLASPHEMY

Frivolous or contemptuous thought or expression about God or the sacred, considered seriously sinful because it falsifies the relationship of creatures to the creator and devalues what is most precious and basic in human life—the relationship with God.

MONIKA K. HELLWIG

BLESSING

The Hebrew people of the Old Testament used the term to articulate the experience of divine reconciliation, to account for fertility and prosperity, and as a greeting. Also, the authors of the Book of Psalms employed it frequently to express praise and thanks to the Lord.

Liturgically, the term denotes a ritual in which a priest consecrates a person or object. The Church's liturgical repertoire includes over two hundred of these blessings, and it is now common throughout the Church to conclude all liturgical services with a blessing, usually from the altar.

JOSEPH QUINN

See also RITUAL.

BLESSING, APOSTOLIC

A benediction conferred by the pope at the end either of a liturgical celebration or a papal audience. Traditionally, it carries a plenary, or full, indulgence for those who receive it—either directly or over the radio or television. Bishops may, by vicarious authority, bestow the blessing; similarly, a priest may grant it at his first celebrated Mass, and when he ministers to someone at or near the moment of death.

JOSEPH QUINN

See also INDULGENCES; PAPACY, THE.

BODY AND BLOOD OF CHRIST

See EUCHARIST.

BOETHIUS (ca. 480–524)

Philosopher, theologian, statesman. Like Augustine in the previous century, Boethius was a man of the old Roman world standing at the threshold of the new. Like his father before him, he held the rank of Roman consul, and became a friend and confidant of King Theodoric, the contemporary ruler of Italy.

A poet and philosopher, Boethius had been educated in Athens and Alexandria, and he transmitted to posterity the old Roman idea of the seven liberal arts. More importantly, he began a project to provide Europe with translations and commentaries on some of the principal works of Plato and Aristotle. While most of this project was left incomplete, he was still one of the medieval world's prime sources for the study of logic. In theology he was both perceptive and clear (the latter quality was particularly useful in the turmoil of the Middle Ages). Some of his benchmark definitions are still widely used: *person*: an individual substance of a rational nature; *eternity*: the simultaneous possession, whole and complete, of unending life.

Boethius produced his best known work, *On the Consolation of Philosophy,* after having been accused of treason and sentenced to death by his former patron, King Theodoric. In prose and poetry, his dialogue with Dame Philosophy portrays the pursuit of wisdom as the one lasting consolation among the vicissitudes of life. The book's lack of Christian references caused many modern critics to doubt that Boethius could have been a Christian or have written the theological studies that bear his name. The *Consolation,* however, can be taken as a prisoner's exercise (though not the less profound for being an exercise): He chose to return to material of his school days, to write in a purely philosophical mode, perhaps unaware that this would be his last work. At all events, the authenticity of most of the works which bear his name is now generally accepted, and Boethius remains the great link between the old and the new.

DAVID BRYAN

See also FATHERS OF THE CHURCH; PHILOSOPHY AND THEOLOGY.

BOLLANDISTS

A small group of about six or seven Jesuit scholars who edit the *Acta Sanctorum* (The Lives of the Saints) and other learned hagiographical works. They derive their name from John Bolland who, though not the originator of the idea, began the work of editing critical lives of saints around 1630. With the exception of the era of the French Revolution, the Bollandists have continued their meticulous work through the years and their critical standards render great service to the Church and to scholarship. The *Acta Sanctorum* has had three editions: The Antwerp edition (1634–1795); the Venice edition (1764–1770); and the Paris edition (1863–1869). These differ slightly in arrangement and all extend only to the month of October. The editorial research is necessarily slow; and the work of revision and of completing the year goes on at its unhurried pace.

MICHAEL GLAZIER

See also SAINTS.

BONAVENTURE, ST. (ca. 1221–1274)

Bonaventure was born in Bagnoregio, a small town located about sixty miles north of Rome, Italy. At the time of his birth the Franciscan Order was growing both in numbers and in influence and Bonaventure himself attests to having been cured of a serious illness as a child through the intercession of Francis of Assisi. His commitment to sing the praises of Francis remained an important thread throughout his life. At the age of seventeen, Bonaventure began studies at the University of Paris, where he again encountered the Franciscans, especially the great Alexander of Hales who was his teacher. Bonaventure entered the Franciscans in 1243 and until 1257, when he was elected minister general of the order at the age of forty, studied and taught at the University of Paris. Bonaventure was made a cardinal in 1273, remained head of the order until the chapter of May, 1274, and died in July of that year. He was canonized in 1482 and declared a Doctor of the Church in 1588.

Bonaventure's life encompassed two often opposing roles—that of Scholastic theologian/university professor and that of pastoral leader of a new and growing mendicant order. In fact, this very tension was reflected within the Franciscan Order and was threatening to break it apart. Some members were wary of new developments in the order which seemed to jeopardize the radical ideals of poverty and simplicity espoused by Francis. Others felt that the order needed to adapt and develop with the times, which meant owning books, buildings and property, and holding illustrious positions at the University of Paris. Bonaventure pursued a moderate position, struggling to remain faithful to the ideals of Francis while allowing the order to change and adapt to new circumstances. His *Life of Francis* embodies this tension and Bonaventure's attempts to hold the struggling order together. Because of his intelligence and personal holiness, Bonaventure is called the "Second Founder of the Order."

Bonaventure was a prolific writer. At the beginning of his career, he produced speculative, theological texts and biblical commentaries. After his election as minister general, his thoughts and his writing turn to more pastoral, spiritual concerns. His most well-known mystical work is *The Soul's Journey Into God,* a text that continues to inspire Christians who set out on their own spiritual journeys.

Bonaventure's theology reflects a number of distinctive elements. In true Franciscan fashion, Bonaventure is profoundly aware of the presence of God in creation. In an ascending pattern from inanimate matter to human persons, he sees all of creation as a mirror of God. Second, his theology has been characterized by the phrase "coincidence of opposites." In his life and work, Bonaventure maintained a creative tension between the God who is beyond us and the God who is within us; between intellectual rigor and poetic, mystical expression. Third, his theology is eminently Christocentric. Bonaventure sees united in Christ "the first and the last, the highest and the lowest, the circumference and the center . . . , the Creator and the creature" (*The Soul's Journey Into God*). Finally, Bonaventure's theology builds on the affective theology of Augustine. Bonaventure places love and will (not intellect) at the center of his theology and spirituality. As one moves toward the heights of mystical encounter with God, Bonaventure notes that "affect alone keeps the vigil, and imposes silence on all the other powers" (*The Six Days of Creation*).

St. Bonaventure, detail of altarpiece, Cologne

ELIZABETH DREYER

See also FRANCISCANS; MYSTICISM; SCHOLASTICISM.

BOOK OF COMMON PRAYER

See ANGLICANISM.

"BORN-AGAIN CHRISTIAN"

The popular term for Christians who believe themselves to have undergone a conversion experience, and who consider this experience an important distinction between themselves and other Christians. Claiming this name is their way of witnessing to the reality of the experience and the changed view of life that resulted for them. It is typical of Fundamentalist or Evangelical piety, where conversion represents an enhancement rather than a transformation of previous religious beliefs.

MARY BARBARA AGNEW, C.PP.S.

See also PENTECOSTAL CHURCHES; PROTESTANTISM.

BORRANO, FRANCIS XAVIER (1901–1993)

Born in San Damino d'Asti, a village in northern Italy in 1901, Borrano entered the seminary at Alba, and in the third year of his theological studies abandoned the idea of becoming a diocesan priest. He joined Fr. James Alberione's "Typographical School" which quickly evolved into the Society of St. Paul, a congregation dedicated to the use of modern communications to spread the gospel. He was ordained in 1923, took a degree in philosophy, and for the next seventy years he worked quietly and enthusiastically in various parts of the world.

In 1931 he arrived in New York without a word of English and with little money. He worked among the Italian immigrants, ran a small Italian newspaper, attracted some vocations, and took charge of two rundown parishes in Staten Island, New York. He returned to Rome in 1940 and held various administrative positions. In 1952 he established the Society of St. Paul in Cuba, and moved on to Australia to do the same, where the work of the Paulines is flourishing today. In 1956 the society established its province in America and Francis X. Borrano was elected provincial.

He is best remembered for establishing Alba House in Staten Island where he built one of the most modern publishing plants in the country. He spent the last two decades of his life at Alba Communications in Canfield, Ohio. Francis X. Borrano was a man of great sensitivity with wide cultural interests. He never hesitated to make decisions and never bewailed mistakes or failures. He walked closely with the Lord, and for him Divine Providence was a personal and ever-present reality, not merely a theological term. He died on 16 April 1993.

JOAN GLAZIER

See also AMERICAN CATHOLICISM; AUSTRALIA, CHURCH IN; PAULINES.

BOTTICELLI, SANDRO (ca. 1445–1510)

A Florentine painter of great popularity, Botticelli (b. ca. 1445) was the most individual, if not the most influential, artist in the Florence of his day. In temperament he tended to the neurotic and was much troubled by the religious crisis introduced by the puritanism of Savonarola. Botticelli probably studied under Filippo Lippi; at any rate he utilized the latter's linear style, which he would increasingly infuse with unparalleled grace. About 1470 he came under the influence of Pollaiuoli as he contributed a painting representing *Fortitude* to a series of virtues done by the latter. The *Fortitude* exhibits a vigorous realism, in addition to Botticelli's characteristic grace of line and surety of composition. Although his Sistine Chapel frescoes (1481/1482) do not seem

Sandro Botticelli, self-portrait, detail, Uffizi Gallery, Florence

to have been particularly successful, he began to be greatly in demand from about this time. Between 1480 and 1500 he made his living by setting his shop to producing accessible Madonnas of the gently devout kind. He was perhaps at his best painting on panels for altarpieces. Meanwhile the ethereal tone of his paintings became ever more expressive of emotion. His ideal of feminine beauty was exemplified not only by his Madonnas but by his mythological paintings such as *The Birth of Venus* and the *Primavera.* The 1490s saw his outline illustrations of Dante. By 1500 his style was far different from his original realism: witness the ecstatic *Mystic Nativity.* The years 1500 to 1510 are little known; perhaps to this period belong certain clumsy, almost hysterical works, such as the *Pietàs* in Milan and Munich, and the Zenobius series. Unique in his own time, Botticelli's work fell into obscurity after his death in 1510 until revived in the late nineteenth century.

DAVID BRYAN

See also ART, CHRISTIAN.

BOURGEOYS, MARGUERITE (1620–1700)

A thirty-three-year-old, poised, refined, educated, idealistic French woman named Marguerite Bourgeoys arrived in 1653 along with many soldiers and a few women at the frontier settlement of Ville Marie, Canada (today's Montreal).

Upon arrival in Canada, Marguerite was introduced to Jeanne Mance (also a native of Champagne, France, who had already established a hospital at Ville Marie) by Paul de Maisoneuve saying, "I have brought with me an excellent young woman, a person of good sense and lively intelligence, whose virtue is a treasure which will be a powerful help in Montreal—another product of our Champagne.''

Marguerite had already resisted the temptation to remain with the Ursulines in Quebec, a pitifully poor colony, but luxurious compared to what she saw in Ville Marie.

M. de Maisoneuve and his men began to clear the land and build fortifications. These newcomers were moving into a land occupied by the Iroquois. This gesture alone was bound to generate hostility and fear.

During this time, Marguerite lived in the fort and was relegated to take care of the governor's house. This she did amiably, but, always the prophet, exhorting those around her toward compassion and justice.

A cross had been erected on the top of Mont Royal by M. de Maisoneuve and had been destroyed. Marguerite solicited a couple of expert carpenters and climbed the pathway as far as the promontory and erected a new huge cross—a sign of Christ to the world. (A lighted cross remains there today on this beautiful mountain, on the island of Ville Marie (Montreal), surrounded by the mighty St. Lawrence River.)

A trained teacher, Marguerite desired to teach, but there were no children of school age in Ville Marie. Newborns were few and they found it impossible to survive the harsh climatic conditions of this potentially fertile but very cruel land. There were many needs to which a faithful and intuitive woman could respond. She cared for the sick, comforted the lonely and the troubled, prepared the dead for burial, bleached and mended clothes for the poor; once she even gave away her own blankets and mattress. A worthy testimony is found in the annals of the Hotel Dieu Sisters: "He (Paul de Maisoneuve) could not help but succeed since he had Marguerite Bourgeoys to second him in this undertaking . . . one who has all the characteristics of the valiant women of the scriptures" (Prov 31).

Blessed Marguerite Bourgeoys

Finally, after about four years, the governor gave her the stone stable of the settlement to use as a school and a dwelling for her teachers. Since Jesus' beginnings were allegedly in a stable, Marguerite saw this as a very positive sign. The remnants from the cattle were cleared away, a fireplace built, and the bare necessities were gathered to make a home for the children. The outdoor staircase led to a dovecote, which became the dormitory. Unwilling to leave anything to chance, Marguerite requested and was granted an official act of donation, on 28 January 1658. In the parish registers of Ville Marie, we read that Marguerite Bourgeoys was designated from that day forward as "school mistress." Now she had her school and land adjoining, given in perpetuity to serve for the education/instruction of girls of Montreal. Here she also welcomed native children and adopted some babies. Her first, Marie-des-Neiges (Mary of the Snow), died at ten months.

Marguerite remained always available to the people of the village. She worried about the Christian formation of the few young women and began to bring them together on Sundays and feast days to instruct and encourage them, to hear their concerns and offer counsel. People began spontaneously to call her stable/house, "The Congregation" (gathering place). The colonists, at Marguerite's urging, were asked to gather stones to build a chapel, a place of pilgrimage and a place where she could help them learn to pray. Even then, the wheels of bureaucracy ran slowly and the vicar general, newly arrived in Canada, settled at Quebec, asked her to wait until his visit to Ville Marie. Fifteen years later, she was to begin again.

Six years after her arrival in New France, she retraced her steps to Troyes, France. She went in search of generous young women with solid Christian formation and the ability to pass that education on to others. Marguerite, balancing prudence with audacity, succeeded in having three young women respond to her invitation to come to this "brave new world"; Edmée Chatel, Catherine Crolo, Marie Raisin. Once again Marguerite secured legal contracts; Edmée (her father was the notary) and Catherine committed themselves "to live together and to teach school in Ville Marie." Marie's contract was drawn up in Paris (her father lived there) and Anne Hioux joined the group there. They were aware that they would need to earn their living and Marguerite promised them only bread and soup. On the return trip to Canada, Marguerite was busy caring for the numerous passengers ill with the plague. She knew well from experience the bitter cold of the long Canadian winter, the isolation and the hunger that awaited these courageous women who accompanied her.

Marguerite and her new companions brought new hope to the people of the settlement and the educational and apostolic activities became more diversified. A boarding school was opened, proudly admitting seven young students. A vocational school, aptly named La Providence, was Canada's first school of home economics. The girls were educated in "the principles of humanities" and the science of religion, piety, gentleness, affability, courtesy, and the love of work. These women of the New World needed to learn skills, crafts, cooking and sewing. Marguerite also informally offered courses that today would be known as Family Life Education, Life Skills, Marriage Preparation, Pastoral Care, and Psychology 101. She encouraged her companions to be "*habille dans toutes choses,*" versatile, able to turn a hand to anything.

Among her pedagogical principles was inclusivity. Marguerite believed that boys and especially girls, men, and especially women, rich and poor, Native, French and Canadian, should be afforded the opportunity of education. As Marguerite came to know and understand the native culture, she found it difficult to accept the orientation and emphasis given by France to this Canadian mission of the seventeenth century. Through correspondence, we know that Marguerite desired not to impose a strange civilization on these children of the forest but rather to bring them to Christ in their own milieu. The number of colonists increased and outlying posts were established. In each place a school was established by those trained directly by Marguerite and those who had already become "sisters."

In 1676, Bishop Laval had officially approved the erection of the Congregation de Notre Dame of Mont Royal as a community of secular women; this style of religious life was unheard of at this time.

Another memorable establishment created by the Sulpicians became known as "The Mountain Mission." To the sisters was entrusted the first school for Indian girls in an Indian milieu. Here they moved from their first birch-bark hut to one of the two stone towers which still stand on the grounds of the Grand Seminary in Montreal. The other tower was used as a residence. Two Indian girls who studied at the Mountain Mission, joined the congregation: Marie Thérese Gannensagous and Marie Barb Attontinin. To them was confided the task of teaching at the Mountain Mission. Once again, Marguerite challenged the imposed French pedagogy and the artificial evangelization. Her plea was dismissed by the Court (King of France): "In France, she says, they were convinced that to become Christian meant to become French." Today Marguerite's approach is known as "inculturation."

Among the new recruits that Marguerite brought from France on her third voyage were three of her nieces. Two joined the congregation. A third married and thus it is today that we have lateral descendants of Marguerite in her beloved Canada. Also, by 1685, Marguerite had more than forty sisters of the congregation. The struggle to keep her congregation autonomous, to adhere to her vision of the sisters living *la vie voyageur* was inspired by the biblical story of Mary's journey to care for Elizabeth. Marguerite held fast to her dream and the congregation flourished amid many tragedies and constant setbacks. Fires, wars, autocratic bishops, personal doubt, internal conflict, hunger and poverty were her frequent companions.

Marguerite died in her eightieth year. She is still affectionately referred to as the "Mother of the Colony" or Mother Bourgeoys.

BERNADETTE O'NEILL, C.N.D.

See also CANADA, THE CATHOLIC CHURCH IN.

BRETHREN (AND SISTERS) OF THE COMMON LIFE

See DEVOTIO MODERNA.

BREVIARY

From the Latin meaning a short summary, either the book containing the psalms, prayers, hymns, etc. of the Liturgy of the Hours, or that liturgy itself recited privately.

MONIKA K. HELLWIG

BRIGID, ST. (fl. LATE FIFTH/EARLY SIXTH CENTURIES A.D.)

Abbess, second patron of Ireland (after St. Patrick). According to tradition, born at Faughart, County Louth, and foundress of the great Abbey of Kildare, which incorporated a monastery of monks as well as a nunnery. She endures in the popular memory as helper of the poor and protectress of cattle. Brigid is said to have originated the "St. Brigid's Cross," which used to be the principal religious symbol in the homes of Irish country-people. This is a cross made of straw or rushes with arms of equal length, resembling a swastika except that the arms are not bent. In Eastern as well as Western iconography a similar design was used in pre-Christian art forms as a token of prosperity or good luck. Its association with St. Brigid in Ireland lends some credibility to the theory that this shadowy saint was not a real person but rather the importation into Christian hagiography of the Celtic pagan goddess, Brigit. It is perhaps more likely that some of the attributes of the goddess were transferred in the folk-memory to a pious woman who did good deeds in Ireland shortly after St. Patrick, when a pagan culture would still have been very much alive. A mingling of pagan and Christian themes may also explain why St. Brigid's feast day came to be celebrated on 1 February, the first day of spring, an occasion of annual rejoicing in primitive societies. Some scholars allege that Brigid was not only the abbess but also first bishop of Kildare, which would have implications for the ordination of women to the priesthood if it could be proven—which it has not been.

LOUIS McREDMOND

See also ABBESS; CATHOLICISM, IRISH.

BRITAIN, CHURCH IN

Christianity came early to the island of Britain. Bede's *Ecclesiastical History of the English,* completed in 731, attributes the martyrdom of St. Alban to the persecution of Diocletian (ca. 305), but it is more likely to have occurred under Decius (ca. 254) or even under Severus (ca. 209). Excavations at Silchester, a village southwest of London, have revealed what appears to be the remains of a purpose-built church, possibly the oldest so far discovered in the Roman Empire. Christianity survived the Roman retreat at the beginning of the fifth century, but Anglo-Saxon invaders drove it to the fringes of the island.

The Romano-British form of Christianity never died out. It was revitalized through the evangelization of Northern Britain by Irish missionaries—though the first recorded bishop in Scotland, Ninian, was British by birth. Columba came in 565, establishing a monastery on Iona off the southwest coast of Scotland. Aidan, who traveled to England in 635 to establish a monastery at Lindisfarne off the northeast coast, had been a monk of Iona: it was from Lindisfarne that much of the evangelization of northern England began. In 596, however, the Roman monk Augustine was sent by Pope Gregory to evangelize the Anglo-Saxons. He arrived the following year and established his primatial see at Canterbury—Gregory had intended it to have been London.

There was, therefore, in Britain two distinct religious traditions, a clash most evidently symbolized by adherence to different calendars. At the Synod of Whitby (663/4), presided over by the Abbess Hilda, the Roman party carried the day. Some Celtic monks withdrew to Ireland, but eventually the Church in Britain conformed to the Roman Liturgy, and was indeed remarkable for its loyalty to the papacy: a number of Anglo-Saxon kings chose to spend their final years in Rome. One peculiarity of British (or more particularly English) religious life in the Middle Ages was the dominance of the monastic orders and friars both in the universities and, especially, in the cathedrals. Religious life declined and revived, but recent studies have shown that the devotional life of the people on the eve of the Reformation was flourishing—less so in Scotland, perhaps, than in England and Wales. In both kingdoms, and in the Principality of Wales, the Reformation was an act of state. Priests trained on the continent of Europe attempted to maintain Roman Catholicism despite persecution, and many suffered martyrdom along with lay people who aided them. In 1829 a reluctant government removed most significant legal disabilities endured by Catholics.

By that time changes were already under way which altered the character of British Catholicism. The most important has been Irish immigration. Even after the establishment of the Republic of Ireland there remain no barriers to that country's citizens taking up residence in the United Kingdom, and the Catholic population, especially of the larger cities, was considerably increased by Irish immigrants. In the first quarter of the nineteenth century, for example, the Catholic population of Scotland more than doubled. There was also a number of conversions in the wake of the Oxford Movement, most notably of John Henry (later Cardinal) Newman. These converts were important for the history of Catholicism (one started *The Tablet* in 1840), but did not constitute a significant factor in the spread of the Church.

To cope with expansion, the bishops invited religious orders into Britain from continental Europe, and a number were founded within the country itself. Their chief work, as of the Jesuits and Benedictines who had brought their colleges back to Britain at the end of the eighteenth century, was education. An impressive array of schools was swiftly established, but at enormous financial cost, especially when set alongside the need to construct new churches in town centers. The British government has contributed to the costs of the Catholic education system, more generously in Scotland (since 1918) than in England (since 1944), and the vast majority of Catholic schools are now largely funded by the state while remaining under Catholic ownership and direction. At the end of 1991 there were some 710,000 children in 2,310 Catholic state schools, and just over a further 60,000 in 216 Catholic independent schools. (The total school-going population of the United Kingdom was just over 7.5 million.)

Although until the last quarter of the nineteenth century Catholics were effectively barred from a university education, there was only one attempt, under the guidance of Newman, to open a Catholic university. It was a failure. There have been Catholic colleges for teachers, and those which survive have widened their scope beyond teacher-training. There is now only one seminary in Scotland but four in England and Wales: all have developed links with universities, but are not fully integrated into them. The Jesuit theologate, however, entered the University of London in 1970 as a constituent college, though in so doing it technically ceased to be a Catholic institution. Because there has been no Catholic university, theologians have had to make their way in the state sector.

In penal days England, Wales, and Scotland had been divided administratively into "districts" under vicars apostolic. The hierarchy was restored in England and Wales in 1850 and in Scotland in 1878. There are now four archbishoprics in England, two in Scotland, one in Wales, plus fifteen bishoprics in England, two in Wales and five in Scotland, including the delightfully named Argyll and the Isles, with thirty-five priests and a Catholic population of only eleven thousand. The Archdiocese of Liverpool, in contrast, has an estimated Catholic population of close on half a million. Scotland is a separate episcopal conference, but the Apostolic Pro-Nuncio oversees both. Though not progressive, the bishops of both conferences are relatively liberal in outlook, more so perhaps in England than elsewhere in the United Kingdom. Much of the credit for this is attributed to Cardinal Hume, a former Benedictine abbot appointed archbishop of Westminster in 1976, who is thought to wield considerable authority in Rome.

The total Catholic population of Britain is about 5 million, but of those only ca. 1.5 million regularly attend Sunday Mass. While this still makes Catholicism the largest single worshipping community, there has been a steady decline over the last quarter of this century. Moreover the decrease in numbers of clergy over the same period has been higher for Catholicism than for any other comparable faith. There are now 6,200 priests in England and Wales and just over 1,000 in Scotland.

Throughout the years of persecution priests had to rely for their safety upon lay people. Towards the end of the eighteenth century, as penal laws were relaxed, there was an unsuccessful attempt by some laity to gain a greater say in the administration of the Church in England. Many of the old Catholic families resented the changes brought about in the nineteenth-century British Catholic Church—the introduction of clerical dress, the fostering of Italianate devotional practices, Roman centralization. Without developing an anticlericalism of the continental kind, leading English laity (it is less true of Scotland) kept a discreet distance between themselves and the official Church. The three weekly Catholic newspapers circulating in the British Isles, for example, were all lay initiatives, and although a cardinal presided over the start of the Catholic Institute for International Relations, highly regarded for its justice and development work, much of it now funded by the British government and the European community, CIIR remains staunchly free from clerical control.

Surveys have shown that British Catholics are politically more left-wing than might have been expected from their social class. All positions in British public life except those directly linked to the Crown are now open to Catholics, but none has ever yet held the highest public offices.

MICHAEL J. WALSH

See also BEDE THE VENERABLE, ST.; BECKET, ST. THOMAS À; GILL, ERIC; HOPKINS, GERARD MANLEY; JULIAN OF NORWICH; NEWMAN, JOHN HENRY, CARDINAL; OXFORD MOVEMENT; "THE MONTH"; "THE TABLET"; WALSINGHAM SHRINE.

BROTHERS (RELIGIOUS)

With the parallel term "sisters," "brother" originally referred to any member of the Church, and thus was also used by members of lay religious communities to refer to each other. In the centuries during which such communities were large and numerous, "brother" and "sister" became used almost exclusively of their members. Now this usage is generally further restricted to members of religious societies, whether clerical or lay, who are not in or seeking holy orders. On the other hand, there is a renewed insistence on the fact that *all* members of clerical orders (and not just the unordained among them) are brothers.

DAVID BRYAN

See also RELIGIOUS ORDERS.

BROTHERS OF THE CHRISTIAN SCHOOLS

This religious community of brothers was founded by a French priest, St. John Baptist de La Salle in 1682 in Rheims, France, in order to educate poor boys. De La Salle believed that education of the poor was so difficult that only a religious community could persevere in the endeavor. In addition to the usual vows of poverty, chastity, and obedience he demanded that his brothers take a fourth vow promising that they would seek no personal gain, monetary or otherwise, from their teaching. He offered the brothers a spirituality that encouraged them to form each boy in Christ and his teachings, a noteworthy goal obviously inspired by deeply held gospel values. The community was given papal approval in 1725.

In an effort to reach as many boys as possible, de La Salle involved his brothers in many different forms of education, teaching manual trades in his schools as well as liberal arts, thus taking a broad view of what education means. The community spread quickly throughout France, and by the time of the French Revolution, they numbered almost one thousand brothers. During the Revolution the brothers suffered greatly, and their ranks shrank dramatically. By 1810, however, their numbers were again up to 160, and thereafter they expanded rapidly, spreading to Belgium and even to the island of Reunion in the Indian Ocean, and they numbered almost one thousand by 1822. During the rest of the nineteenth century the community grew rapidly, sending brothers to many nations and attaining an overall strength of ten thousand members. Because of an anticlerical regime in France in the early part of this century, they settled in new places, setting up over two hundred houses in the Americas, Europe, the Near East, Africa and Oceania. By 1960 the total number of professed brothers was over sixteen thousand.

In response to requests from American bishops for brothers to help with the huge numbers of Irish and German Catholic immigrants, they made a brief appearance in Missouri in 1819 and established their first permanent institution in Baltimore in 1845. The brothers flourished through the later nineteenth century, and when secondary education became the norm in the U.S. in the twentieth century, they experienced an even greater institutional expansion. In the post-Vatican II era the Christian Brothers have declined in number like other religious orders in the U.S.

ANTHONY D. ANDREASSI

See also RELIGIOUS ORDERS.

BROWNSON, ORESTES AUGUSTUS (1803–1876)

Author, born in 1803. Brownson was an an accomplished novelist, editor, and author of volumes on

Orestes Augustus Brownson

philosophy and theology. Raised in the strict Puritan tradition, he joined the Presbyterian Church in 1822. In 1824, he became a member of the Universalist sect, of which he would later become a minister. Due to ideological differences, he left the sect and converted to Unitarianism. He was ordained a Unitarian minister, and founded his own Church in 1836. Brownson converted to Roman Catholicism in 1844, and became a controversial figure due to his revolutionary ideas.

As with his religious leanings, Brownson's political beliefs varied throughout his career. He initially embraced socialism, helping to create a Workingmen's Party. Later, he switched allegiance and supported the Democratic Party. Eventually, however, he grew disillusioned with democratic principles—particularly the notion of self-rule by the general populace.

Brownson established the *Boston Quarterly Review* in 1838, which was merged with the *United States Democratic Review* in 1842 and, in 1844, became *Brownson's Quarterly Review.* With the exception of a seven-year period between 1865 and 1872, it remained in publication until 1875. He died in 1876.

Among Brownson's writings are: *New Views of Christianity, Society, and the Church* (1836), *The American Republic* (1865), and *Conversation on Liberalism and the Church* (1870).

JOSEPH QUINN

See also AMERICAN CATHOLICISM.

BUDDHISM

Prince Siddhartha Gautama, founder of Buddhism, was born about 560 B.C. in north India (present-day Nepal) to a Hindu Kshatriya caste of kings. As a child and young man, he was surrounded by privilege and wealth and at the same time was protected by an indulgent father from the misery and pain of life.

In his late twenties, notwithstanding his father's wishes otherwise, Siddhartha chanced upon three "sights" which revealed to him the suffering of every human being—sickness, old age, and death. Soon after these men were spotted, he saw a poor wandering monk who appeared spiritually tranquil and at home in the universe.

Siddhartha was so impressed with the serenity of the monk that he left his family and inheritance and began to search the world for the answer to suffering in this life. This is called "The Night of Great Renunciation." His journey was replete with such self-mortification and asceticism that he was virtually reduced to a skeleton. It eventually dawned on him that his renunciation was just as extreme as the attachment to materialism he had abandoned. There must be another way, which he called the Middle Path (Madhyam Marga). The climax of his spiritual journey was the experience of Enlightenment under a pipal tree, later called the Bodhi Tree, because under that Tree he was Enlightened, saw the Truth of life, and received his Buddhahood. He was now Gautama, the Buddha, the Enlightened One.

The essence of Buddhism centers around Four Noble Truths which is a kind of diagnosis for humanity's ills: (1) All life is suffering; (2) Suffering comes from Desire (Craving); (3) Desire is eliminated by renunciation; (4) One successfully overcomes Desire by following the Noble Eight-Fold Path. The latter consists of (1) Right knowledge, (2) Right thinking, (3) Right speech, (4) Right behavior, (5) Right livelihood, (6) Right effort, (7) Right mindfulness, and (8) Right meditation.

Head of the Buddha, wood, ca. 800, Japan

The end of Enlightenment is Nirvana, an ego-less state which literally means a "burning away." It is a form of "positive" annihilation, a state where boundaries of the self are eradicated to unify the believer with all reality. In Buddhism, there is no God or Supreme Being in the Western sense of a transcendent deity. Nor is there a need for a savior since Buddhism does not see humanity in a state of separation. What is needed are spiritual masters who help us move from darkness (ignorance) to light (knowledge) by guiding us along the Buddha's path.

The Three Refuges, sometimes called Jewels, which are a constant support to the follower are: I take refuge in the Buddha, e.g., the access to guidance and power which Enlightenment provides; I take refuge in the Dharma, e.g., the teachings and path revealed by the Buddha; I take refuge in the Sangha, e.g., the spiritual community of those who truly seek Buddhahood.

There are different strands of Buddhism. Mahayana Buddhism emphasizes prayer and ritual; Hinayana, sometimes called Theravada, stresses meditation and teaching; Vajrayana, found mostly in Tibet, is interested in the psychology of Enlightenment.

Zen, a mystical dimension of Buddhism which came to Japan from China, seeks immediate awareness of reality by way of sitting meditation (Zazen) and by working through Koans, intellectually unsolvable problems, e.g., "What is the sound of one hand clapping?" These Zen schools are respectfully, the Soto and Rinzai schools.

Buddhism as a reform movement in Hinduism deemphasized ritual in the name of compassion, decentralized authority in the name of the personal, and eliminated caste in the name of human equality. It is known as one of the world's most peaceful and ethical religions.

Buddhism is located primarily in Ceylon, Southeast Asia, China, and Tibet. The Buddha died in 480 not far from Benares, India, with his beloved disciple Ananda beside him. His last words were purported to have been: "Whatever is born bears within itself the seeds of death. Work out your salvation with earnestness."

IRA ZEPP

See also ASCETICISM; HINDUISM; MYSTICISM.

BUDKA, NICETAS (1877–1949)

Nicetas Budka, although born in Ukraine in the village of Dobromirka of Zbarazh, Galicia, on 7 June 1877 and having spent most of his life serving the Catholic faithful in Ukraine, is most remembered for his service to the Church as the first bishop of Ukrainian Catholics in Canada.

By the latter half of the nineteenth century most of the four million Ukrainians living in the Austro-Hungarian Empire found themselves at the bottom of the social ladder as peasants. Everyday life meant overpopulation, shortage of land, unemployment, political and social oppression, and starvation. News that a strange land called Canada was welcoming immigrants in order to expand its territory into the prairies left thousands of peasants with the only hope of emigration, a hope which would completely justify the upheaval they would suffer. It would be Bishop Budka's task to help organize their religious, cultural, and national spirituality in their new home, Canada.

Having been appointed as the first bishop of the Ukrainian Catholic Church in Canada on 25 July 1912 by Pope Pius X, and after episcopal ordination on 13 October by Metropolitan Andrey Sheptytsky, Bishop Budka was enthroned at his episcopal see in Winnipeg, Manitoba, on 22 December of the same year, to the great joy of thousands of Ukrainian faithful.

At the time of his installation, Bishop Budka found the 80,000 Ukrainian Catholic faithful being served throughout Canada by twenty priests, five of whom were non-Ukrainians from the Latin Rite; eighty churches and missions; a small number of schools and orphanages under the direction of the Sisters Servants of Mary Immaculate; a minor seminary; and a variety of other religious and national organizations.

The first task of Bishop Budka was to familiarize himself with his extensive nationwide see. Thereby began the countless episcopal visitations conducted under conditions of poverty, loneliness, and harsh wilderness all in the attempt to organize and to bring together the Ukrainian faithful scattered throughout Canada.

In 1914 Bishop Budka convoked in Yorkton, Saskatchewan, the first diocesan assembly so as to examine with his parish priests the living conditions of his faithful in Canada and to adapt to these changed living conditions the rules and regulations of their Church in Ukraine.

Bishop Budka's efforts were rewarded as the number of churches was growing continually as was the number of priests and sisters required to serve them.

At the same time new schools and orphanages were being established to educate the Ukrainian youth and young adults. This helped them to acquire the best religious and academic training and thus preserving their Ukrainian heritage of language, culture, and tradition as well as their Catholic faith.

In 1927 Bishop Budka was forced to resign due to ill health and returned to Lviv, Ukraine. At the time of his departure, Bishop Budka left behind 47 priests, numerous sisters, 299 churches and missions, 200,000 faithful, a number of schools and colleges, an orphanage, a hospital, and a number of other religious and national organizations.

After some time of convalescence in Lviv, Bishop Budka assisted Metropolitan Sheptytsky in spiritual matters until being arrested by the Soviet government in 1946, along with Metropolitan Joseph Slipyj and eight other Ukrainian Catholic Bishops, for their steadfast refusal to renounce their Catholic faith. On 6 October 1949, at the age of seventy-one, Bishop Budka died the death of a martyr and confessor of faith in a Russian labor camp.

The Canadian Catholic Church is indebted to the late Bishop Budka for his great contributions in developing a solid basis for the religious, cultural, and national life of Ukrainian Catholics in Canada.

DAVID MOTIUK

See also CANADA, THE CATHOLIC CHURCH IN.

BULL (PAPAL)

The most solemn kind of papal letter, but most recently restricted mainly to the appointment of bishops.

DAVID BRYAN

See also PAPACY, THE.

BURIAL, CHRISTIAN

See CATACOMBS; CREMATION.

BURKE, JOHN JOSEPH, C.S.P. (1875–1936)

Paulist priest and founder of the National Catholic Welfare Conference. One of nine children, Burke was the son of Irish immigrants Patrick and Mary Regan Burke. Born and raised on New York City's west side, Burke's family was a member of the Irish middle class. Patrick Burke's success as a blacksmith, supplemented with Mary Burke's income from her needlework, provided their family with a comfortable life. Burke's first exposure to the

Paulists came as a child, when his family attended the Paulist parish of St. Paul the Apostle. The influence of the Paulists would result in two vocations from the Burke family, John, and his older brother, Thomas. Burke received his bachelor's degree from St. Francis Xavier College in 1896. Upon graduation, he entered the Paulist novitiate in Washington, D.C., and was ordained a priest in 1899. During his student years in Washington, D.C., Burke received both his S.T.L. and L.S.T. degrees from The Catholic University of America.

Burke's first assignment as a Paulist was to a mission band. For three years he traveled the country with his fellow Paulists conducting one- and two-week missions in Catholic parishes. In 1903 Burke was appointed assistant editor of the Paulist monthly magazine *The Catholic World.* One year later, Burke was named editor, a position he held for the next eighteen years. Under his skillful editorship, Burke returned *The Catholic World* to its scholarly origins, guiding it through the aftermath of Americanism and the shadow of Modernism. As editor, Burke used his position to become an outspoken advocate of social justice, calling for a greater clerical involvement in social action and social reform. His call to "Catholic action" would become the driving force in his life's work. Burke also managed Paulist Press during these years. His commitment to religious publishing led to his role in helping to found the Catholic Press Association, where he served on its executive board for many years.

The U.S. decision to enter World War I would determine Burke's place in the history of the American Catholic Church. In 1917 there were over 15,000 lay and religious organizations in the American Church. The absence of any form of communication and cooperation between these organizations was immediately recognized by Burke to be the greatest barrier to mobilizing the Church's resources to assist in the war effort. Burke soon approached Cardinal James Gibbons with a proposal to form a wartime committee to coordinate the Catholic response to U.S. participation in the war. With his approval, Burke organized the National Catholic War Council (NCWC) in the summer of 1917 in Washington, D.C. That same year he founded the Chaplains' Aid Association to coordinate the Catholic ministry in the military.

In 1918 the NCWC was reorganized and Burke was named chair of the Committee on Special War Activities. He simultaneously served on the Committee of Six, an interfaith committee appointed by the American government to act as an advisory committee to the Secretary of War on religious and moral questions. His service on the committee was recognized in 1919 when the War Department conferred the Distinguished Service medal on him.

After the war, the future of the NCWC was in doubt until the intervention of Pope Benedict XV. Benedict XV appealed to the American hierarchy to maintain the council as a peacetime organization to work in conjunction with the Holy See in its efforts to achieve world peace and social justice. Burke was instrumental in the council's restructuring. Adamant in his conviction that the newly formed National Catholic Welfare Conference be organized on the principles of volunteerism, Burke gave the conference's organization its distinctly American character. He would serve as the conference's general secretary until his death in 1936.

Burke's concerns with the conditions of Catholics, many of whom were immigrants, in postwar America led to his cooperation with the National Catholic Conference of Lay Women in founding the National Catholic School of Social Services (NCSSS) at The Catholic University of America in 1921. Burke's work with the NCSSS further reflects his belief in the need to organize the Catholics of this country in order to best protect and promote their interests.

The Holy See would request Burke's assistance in 1927 to mediate the volatile situation between the Mexican government and the Catholic Church. Burke made two secret trips on behalf of the Holy See in 1927 and 1928. Although he had no official status when he approached the government, his efforts proved instrumental to negotiating a settlement between the Mexican government and the Catholic Church. Burke's continuing interest in the Mexican situation led him to denounce publicly the Mexican government's practices of religious persecution.

Burke's contributions to the Church were recognized in 1927 when the Holy See conferred on him the doctorate of sacred theology, *honoris causa.* His highest honor was to come in September 1936 when the Holy See elevated him to monsignor. John Burke was the first member of a U.S. religious order to receive this honor. Just one month later he died suddenly of a heart attack in Washington, D.C. He is buried in the Paulist mother church in New York.

Devoted to the causes of social justice, education, the press, Catholic organizations, and the needs of immigrants, Burke's concerns for the welfare of the Church in the U.S. and his ardent patriotism forged a vision for the role of the Catholic Church in American society that would influence his life's work and lead to an unparalleled coordination and unity in Catholic action in the U.S. John Burke, Paulist, poet, publisher, administrator, activist, mystic, and visionary, felt deeply, loved faithfully, and lived out his beliefs.

C

CABRINI, FRANCES XAVIER, ST. (1850–1917)

Born into an Italian farming family from Lombardy, Maria Francesca was the youngest of thirteen children. Upon the deaths of her parents in 1870 (she was twenty), she gave up her plans to be a school teacher and decided to be a nun. Her tenacity was already evident when, having been refused by two communities for reasons of health, she went on to accept an offer to take over a mismanaged orphanage (1874) at Codogno. Virulent opposition from the orphanage's foundress forced the bishop of Lodi to close it, but he meanwhile invited Frances to found a society of her own under his patronage. With seven followers, she founded, in an abandoned Franciscan friary at Codogno, the Missionary Sisters of the Sacred Heart of Jesus, devoted to the education of girls. The society was given official status by the bishop in 1880 and by the pope in 1887, while spreading to Grumello, Milan, and Rome. A scant two years later the fame of Frances' work had reached America, and Mother Cabrini, answering an appeal from Archbishop Corrigan, set sail to work with Italian immigrants in New York City. By 1892 she had opened Columbus Hospital in New York, her first in America. Her life's course was now set: During the next twenty-seven years she took her society's works of mercy to all parts of the United States and the Americas (she became an American citizen in 1909), as well as to France, Spain, and England, with further expansion in Italy. At the time of her death the Missionary Sisters, by then 3,000 strong in seventy convents, had founded more than fifty hospitals, schools, and orphanages, and their society had received final approbation from Rome.

St. Frances Xavier Cabrini

Despite the enormous difficulties she faced and overcame, Frances maintained the highest ideals of the gospel. Pope Pius XII canonized her in 1946, the first American citizen to be so honored. Four years later he named her the patron of immigrants everywhere. Feast day, 13 November.

DAVID BRYAN

See also AMERICAN CATHOLICISM; MISSIONS, CATHOLIC, THE MODERN PERIOD.

CALENDAR, LITURGICAL

See LITURGY.

CALVIN, JOHN (1509–1564)

Though a quarter century younger than Luther, John Calvin was the other great "founder" of Protestantism, its first "systematic" theologian through the multiple editions of his unfolding *Institutes of the Christian Religion,* and a determined advocate of Church polity. As spirit and namesake of the developing Calvinistic and Reformed traditions, especially in Europe and the United States, his impact has been felt in religion, politics, economics, literature, and the arts.

Life

Calvin was born Jean Cauvin at Noyon, Picardy, France, in 1509. A gifted, industrious student, he entered the University of Paris in 1523, where he studied theology under Noel Beda, conservative leader of the theology faculty at the Sorbonne, who in 1521 had condemned Luther. By 1528 Calvin was distinguishing himself in the study of law at Orleans, where he studied Greek under Melchior Wolmar, a German scholar, sympathetic to Luther. Following the death of his father in May, 1531, Calvin completed his doctorate in law, then undertook studies of languages and literature, becoming particularly drawn to moral humanism. His first published work, *Commentary on Seneca's Treatise on Clemency,* shows the influence of his classical studies under France's leading humanists. Sometime during this period, impacted by his broadening studies and influenced by close friendship with younger scholars and clerics who had become admirers of rebel thinker Jacques Lefevre, whose ideas anticipated Luther's and who fled Paris for his life at Luther's condemnation, Calvin underwent some undetailed "conversion": "God subdued my heart . . . by a sudden conversion." By 1533 Calvin was among a group of "evangelicals" and Protestants who were forced from Paris. On 4 May 1534, he resigned his benefices at Noyon and repudiated the papacy. Settling first in Basel, Calvin drafted prefaces to Olivetan's French translation of the Bible.

In 1536 the first edition of *Institutes of the Christian Religion* appeared, a work that would be expanded and revised through many editions over the next twenty-five years. Now established as a force in the Reform movement Calvin was persuaded by William Farel to stay in Geneva to further reform and institute order and discipline within religious practice. His *Instruction in Faith* in 1537 sought to establish such discipline. However, Calvin was banished from Geneva in 1538 and spent three years in Strasbourg, studying, writing extensively, and attempting to unite various factions within the Protestant movement.

Geneva during this time became a haven for Protestant refugees from all over Europe. Calvin was drawn back to Geneva in 1541 with the charge to make this city a model Christian community. With the aid of a governing committee, the "Little Council," and its approved *Ecclesiastical Ordinances,* a system of preaching, worship, instruction, and discipline was established to nurture the Christian life. By 1555 all Calvin's opponents had been driven from Geneva, and while he was only a "pastor" in the church, his social and political grip held until his death in 1564.

Thought

The main tenets of Calvin's religious thought are similar in most regards to Luther, though differing significantly on the question of predestination and the nature of Eucharist, as follows.

Humanity is depraved, lost to the knowledge of God, though wanting to know the true God and give him glory. Unable to help themselves or fulfill the stringent requirement of the Law of the majestic and sovereign God, human beings are made righteous solely through faith in Christ as witnessed in Scripture. Works of merit and "drawing" on the "treasure" of merit through a penitential system are of no avail, as the only true, apostolic treasure or deposit for the faithful given to the Church is the "gospel of the glory and grace of God." Thus, knowledge of God is response to the revelation of God in his work as creator and in Scripture, where alone through inspiration of the Holy Spirit God is seen to be Savior of the world in Christ. This revelation is seen only by the elect who are predestined by the will of God to be called to him, part of the unfolding purpose of God from the beginning. The mission of Christ, bound with his suffering and the Cross, were foreseen and foreordained as part of God's eternal purpose. The one, holy, catholic, and apostolic Church is the invisible Church of the whole body of the redeemed through all ages, known only to the sovereign God. The visible Church is the community of believers, glorying in God, professing their faith, and enjoying the sacraments. Baptism is an initiation into the "communion of saints," while the Lord's Supper is the dramatic presence of the real Christ in the individual's communion with God.

Throughout this experience of faithful response one glories in Christ's consummation of the promise given to Adam and humbly realizes one is "elect" by God.

JAMES W. THOMASSON

See also PROTESTANTISM; REFORMATION, THE.

CAMPION, EDMUND, ST. (1540–1581)

English Jesuit and martyr. Born in London, the son of a bookseller. He had a brilliant scholastic career, became a fellow of St. John's College, Oxford, and delivered the formal address of welcome to Queen Elizabeth when she visited the university in 1566. He was ordained deacon in the Church of England in 1569 but had misgivings and soon acquired the reputation of being a cryptopapist. On an extended visit to Ireland he had to go into hiding when it seemed that he might be arrested because of the authorities' suspicions. He made his way in disguise to the English college at Douai in Flanders, where he publicly renounced Protestantism. Continuing to Rome, he joined the Jesuits and was sent for a time to Bohemia. When it was decided in 1579 to send a Jesuit mission into England to fortify the persecuted Catholics, Campion—by now a priest—was chosen to accompany Father Robert Persons and Brother Ralph Emerson. The Jesuits received a warm welcome from the still numerous Catholic gentry in whose houses they preached, celebrated Mass, and administered the sacraments to adherents of the old religion despite the risk of discovery. Campion traveled widely through the midlands and the northern counties of Yorkshire and Lancashire. He also wrote several pamphlets in defense of Catholicism, which he succeeded in having printed and circulated. Government agents eventually tracked him down and brought him to London. Torture followed, a trial in Westminster Hall and execution at Tyburn. He was canonized in 1970.

LOUIS McREDMOND

See also BRITAIN, CHURCH IN; MARTYRDOM; SOCIETY OF JESUS.

CANADA, THE CATHOLIC CHURCH IN

Although Canada's first recorded Catholic Mass was celebrated during Jacques Cartier's expedition in 1534, it was not until the founding of Quebec by Samuel de Champlain, in 1608, that Catholicism was established more permanently. Champlain invited French Recollet priests, and later members of the Society of Jesus, to evangelize the First Nations of New France and to cement the trading partnership between the natives and the French. Catholic missionaries found it difficult to evangelize the Algonkian-speaking peoples of the Laurentian shield: they were nomadic hunter-gatherer peoples who quickly disregarded the "blackrobe's" message once they departed for their winter camps. In 1615, however, the Recollets established a mission among the Ouendat (Huron), a sedentary Iroquoian-speaking people, whose home on the south shore of Georgian Bay had made them important middlemen in the fur trade. When the Recollets failed to Frenchify the Ouendat and left the mission in 1625, the Jesuits assumed their place and employed a greater degree of cultural relativism in their activities, attempting to make Catholicism understandable to the natives through the prism of Ouendat culture. Jesuits created a segregated Christian community among the Bear Clan at Ossossané, a move that split the Ouendat between Christian and traditionalist groups. The tension caused by this division in the ranks, a series of deadly epidemics, and repeated raids by their Iroquois enemies seriously weakened the Ouendat. In 1649, in an unprecedented winter invasion, the Iroquois destroyed the Ouendat homeland, killed six Jesuits, and devastated the Catholic mission.

The setback in Huronia did not deter further evangelization by the Jesuits. French missionaries penetrated the Nipissing district of northern Ontario in 1641, Ojibwa country north of Lake Superior in 1667, Cree settlements on James Bay in 1671, and the Rainy Lake and Lake of the Woods regions of northwestern Ontario in 1731. Although the Jesuit missionaries established their apostolate within the grid established by the French fur trade, they frequently opposed the sale of alcohol to the First Nations and criticized the often "immoral" and unruly behavior of French traders. In an effort to protect First Nations and ensure the success of the missions, Quebec's first bishop, François de Laval (1658–1687) imposed ecclesiastical penalties on brandy traders and petitioned the governor, Louis de Baude, Comte de Frontenac, to prohibit the use of alcohol as a trade good. Merchants, who felt that without alcohol the fur trade might be diverted to the English merchants in New York, won their case despite the pleading of the clergy at the "Brandy Parliament" of 1678. For the victors it was better that native peoples "perish on Catholic brandy than on Protestant rum."

After 1627, only Roman Catholics were permitted to migrate to New France. Influenced by the enthusiasm and renewed piety engendered by the Catholic Reformation in France, members of the secret Company of the Holy Sacrament attempted to establish a Catholic colony at Montreal in 1642. The founders, Paul de Chomedey de Maisonneuve, Jeanne Mance, and Madame de la Peltrie, were inspired by the idea that a New Jerusalem could be created in the Canadian forest. In 1663, Montreal was included in the seigneury granted to the Priests of St. Sulpice, who founded the "Grand Seminaire," which to this day is still one of the primary houses of formation for French Canadian priests. Within this growing Catholic community two new religious orders of women were founded: Marguerite Bourgeois' Sisters of the Congregation (Notre Dame Sisters) in 1653 and Marguerite d'Youville's Sisters of Charity (Grey Nuns) in 1737. Meanwhile, in Quebec City, the capital, the Ursuline Sisters, who arrived in 1639, emerged as the dominant women's teaching order.

While they did not necessarily share the spiritual vision of the founders of Montreal, Catholic farmers and artisans established a line of settlement along the St. Lawrence River, stretching from Montreal Island to Tadoussac. In 1658, the pope named Laval the first vicar apostolic, later bishop (in 1674), of Quebec. The new bishop found his pastoral duties onerous: priests were resistant to episcopal authority, and the peasants, or "habitants," refused to pay their tithes, disrupted religious services by card-playing and horse racing, and appeared negligent in their religious duties. In fact, despite contrary impressions from such historians as Francis Parkman, the bishops and clergy of Quebec were unable to exert much spiritual or social control over the local Catholic population. From 1727 to 1740, three of Laval's successors did not take up permanent residence in New France, thus reinforcing the Church's weakened position in this frontier society. It was also reported that some priests, notably the religious serving at the fortress Louisbourg on Ile Royale (Cape Breton Island) set a very low moral tone among their flock. At the time of "the Conquest" of New France by the British in 1759 to 1760, there were few Canadian-born clergy, no aboriginal clergy, and the bishop, Henri-Marie de Breil de Pontbriand, died before the colony's capitulation.

Although their creed was tolerated "so far as the British Crown would allow," French Canadian Catholics were in a vulnerable position after "the Conquest." There were only 170 priests to serve a population of close to 60,000; there was no bishop for six years; and the male religious of French origin had returned to France. In 1766, Jean-Olivier Briand (1766–1784) was consecrated bishop of Quebec, and recognized by the British as the "Superintendent of the Romish Church." Briand and his successors, most notably Joseph-Octave Plessis (1806–1825), supported the British colonial government in an effort to win concessions for the Church. This alliance was cemented by the official British toleration of the Church in the Quebec Act of 1774, and the Church's support for the British cause during the American War of Independence and during the War of 1812 through 1814. By 1817, the British formally recognized Plessis as "Bishop," raised his salary, and made him an honorary member of the colony's Legislative Council.

Episcopal relations with the laity and lower clergy were more difficult. By 1805, there were only 186 priests for a population of close to 200,000; even the refugee clerics from the French Revolution did not significantly diminish the acute shortage of priests. With so few pastors, tithes remained uncollected, lay churchwardens grew in influence, and criminal and raucous behavior on Sundays and excessive revelry on feast days was not unusual in Quebec. Furthermore, the Church was unable to exert a strong moral influence: prostitution was prominent in Quebec (some 600 prostitutes in a town of 13,000) and the illegitimate birth rate was high. The Catholic religious orders, however, addressed the needs of the colony through their maintenance of orphanages, hospitals, social services, and schools. Through such agencies and academies, women religious kept alive the French language and a sense of the *Canadien* culture.

The British conquest also marked the arrival of other Catholic migrants to British North America's Atlantic colonies. Gaelic-speaking Catholics from the Scottish Highlands concentrated their settlement in eastern Nova Scotia, Cape Breton Island, and the rich agricultural lands of Prince Edward Island. These Scots were joined by the return of French-speaking Acadian Catholics, who had been deported from the area in 1755, and by Irish Catholics, who prior to the Great Famine (1845–1847), were attracted by the Newfoundland fishery, lumbering in New Brunswick, agriculture, and a variety of low-skilled laboring jobs. Formally under the Diocese of Quebec, Catholics in Atlantic Canada did not share the same civil liberties as their French-Canadian coreligionists; it was only in 1789 that Nova Scotia's Catholics could vote, and in 1830 the same rights were given to Catholics in Prince Edward Island. The Maritimes eventually attained episcopal autonomy in 1817, when Edmund Burke (1817–1820) was named vicar apostolic of Nova Scotia, an ecclesiastical territory which also included the colonies of New Brunswick and Prince Edward Island. By 1828, this new ecclesiastical jurisdiction contained 74,000 Catholics, including a significant Micmac Catholic minority. As the Catholic population expanded, more vicariates and dioceses were created so that, by 1847, the region contained five sees. The notable exception was the colony of Newfoundland, whose Irish Catholics had their own vicar apostolic as early as 1795 (prefecture apostolic established in 1784).

The colony of Upper Canada (now Ontario), to the west of Lower Canada (now Quebec), mirrored the Celtic Catholic complexion of the Atlantic colonies, and it also had a small French minority, who were descendants of the eighteenth-century settlers near Fort

Detroit. Between 1786 and 1815, at least 2,500 Scottish Catholics, under the leadership of Loyalist officers defeated in the American Revolution and of priests from Clan Macdonell, settled the agricultural lands of Glengarry, in the eastern portion of Upper Canada. In 1816, Alexander Macdonell became the first vicar apostolic, and later bishop (1826), of Upper Canada. Macdonell's Scots were joined by thousands of Irish-Catholic migrants between 1815 and 1845. Unlike their American cousins, Irish-Catholic immigrants to Canada established their primary settlement grid prior to the Great Famine. They were English-speaking, modestly secure financially, familiar with the system of British governance, showed a preference for rural settlement, and were outnumbered two-to-one by their Protestant countrymen. As a result, the total Catholic population of Upper Canada rarely exceeded 17 percent, until the present day. Until the mid-1840s, Catholic-Protestant relations in Upper Canada were tolerant and amiable. Bishop Macdonell was a member of the ruling elite of the colony, and Irish-Catholic and Protestant laypersons often belonged to the same cultural associations.

In the 1840s the Catholic Church in Canada experienced remarkable change. In Quebec, the failed rebellion of 1837 left a void in French-Canadian leadership that the clergy were only too willing to fill. The episcopacy and clergy of the Province were ardent advocates of Ultramontane piety and polity, and to this they fused a growing sense of French-Canadian nationalism. Religious and cultural identity became inseparable: language and French-Canadian culture were guardians of the faith. In English Canada, the Church became more overwhelmingly Irish. Between 1815 and 1845 the British North American colonies witnessed their largest wave of migrants from Ireland. About 500,000 Irish arrived, of whom about 40 percent were Catholic. While only about one-third of the Irish put down roots in British North America, these Irish established the longstanding Irish settlement grid of such colonies as Upper Canada and New Brunswick. Their numbers were augmented by refugees from the Great Famine who poured into the cities of Saint John, Montreal, Toronto, and Hamilton. In Toronto, for example, sickly, impoverished, and generally unskilled Irish-Catholic migrants increased the proportion of Catholics in the city from 20 percent in 1845 to 26 percent in 1851.

The rising demographic significance of Irish Catholics in major Protestant cities, when added to the assertiveness of French-Canadian politicians, and the increase of Roman triumphalism as the ultramontane spirit spread across Europe and America, contributed to a breakdown in Protestant-Catholic relations in Canada. The establishment of state-funded Catholic separate schools in central Canada and in Nova Scotia prompted an angry response from the Protestant and secular press. Irish nationalist agitation from American Fenians in the 1860s and the anti-Catholic feelings aroused by such itinerant troublemakers as Charles Chiniquy (1809–1899), caused violent clashes between Catholics and Protestants in many Canadian cities. While the Confederation of the principal British Colonies—Quebec, Ontario, New Brunswick, and Nova Scotia—in 1867 brought with it much needed linguistic and religious compromises, sectarian bitterness merely slid into the private affairs of Canadians. Periodically, the Catholic defense of their separate school rights (New Brunswick, 1871; Manitoba, 1890–1897) led to charges of political interference directed at Quebec's Ultramontanes, or prompted public disturbances.

The mid-nineteenth century also witnessed a renewal of the Catholic missionary effort in Canada. The Jesuits reentered Canada in 1842 and established a network of missions among the Anishinabeg peoples (Algonkian), extending from Wikwemikong, on Manitoulin Island in Georgian Bay, to Fort William at the head of Lake Superior. In the same period, French-speaking priests of the Oblates of Mary Immaculate founded missions among the James Bay Cree in the east, at Red River in Manitoba, along the major waterways of the fur trade in the present day provinces of Saskatchewan and Alberta, and on the Pacific Coast in British Columbia and on Vancouver Island. Oblates also set up missions in the far North, in what are now the Yukon and Northwest Territories. Male religious were joined in their endeavor by numerous women's orders, including the Sisters of St. Anne in British Columbia and the Grey Sisters in Manitoba. In the Canadian West, the Oblates ran both the missions and the newly created dioceses and apostolic vicariates. They served as intermediaries between Euro-Canadian and First Nations' communities, attempting to shield the latter from the worst excesses of the former. Oblates and Jesuits also established schools for First Nations' children, recorded their languages in grammars, translated Catholic teaching into usable native texts, and in some residential schools kept a variety of native traditions alive. Recently, however, such schools have been criticized by natives and their Euro-Canadian supporters as having caused the long-term erosion of native culture. This criticism has been so deeply felt that in 1991, the Oblates apologized to First Nations for their role in the European conquest of indigenous peoples.

This struggle between cultures has been a dominant issue in the Canadian Church since 1900. Between 1896 and 1914 close to three million immigrants entered Canada. Catholic migrants from eastern and southern Europe threatened the delicate balance between Canada's English- and French-speaking Catholics. Italian, Maltese, Polish, and Hungarian immigrants brought their own distinctive Catholic traditions with them and formed tightly knit subcultures, which were eventually incorporated into distinctive national parishes, directed by their own priests. Such parishes did not come without struggle, and French- and English-speaking Catholics were frequently slow, reluctant and even hostile to erect separate parochial jurisdictions within their prescribed diocesan grids. Once the Canadian hierarchy became alarmed by Protestant missionary activity among these new Canadians, they were forced to take steps to secure the faith of the Catholic "foreigners." Ukrainian Catholics of the Greek Rite faced particular problems. They were refused their married priests as a result of the Vatican's ban on the migration of such clergy from Europe as of 1894. Led by only a handful of celibate priests, many of whom were French-Canadian or Belgian priests who had transferred from the Latin Rite, Ukrainians were always on guard for potential "latinization" at the hands of their Canadian hosts. In 1912, however, Nicetas Budka (1912–1928), was consecrated apostolic exarch for the Ukrainians of Canada. By the 1920s, Ukrainians and other European Catholics constituted sizeable minorities in the Canadian West, northern Ontario, Toronto, and Montreal.

The immigration question, and the ensuing questions of jurisdiction in the Church, put strains on the relations between French- and English-speaking Catholics. English-speaking Catholics increasingly identified themselves as loyal British subjects who upheld the English language, British law and Parliamentary institutions, and the Imperial connection. They viewed with alarm the growing French-Canadian Catholic migration from Quebec to parts of Ontario and the West, fearing that this demographic shift would jeopardize their own leadership of the Church outside of Quebec. In 1912, English-speaking Catholic bishops of Ontario supported the "Protestant" government's Regulation 17, which prohibited French-language instruction in schools after the second grade. Linguistic relations in the Church soured further during the First World War, 1914 through 1918, when English-speaking Catholics threw themselves into the British war effort, while French-Canadian Catholics resisted the conscription of their sons for a "British" war. French- and English-speaking Catholics also battled for control of the episcopal sees in eastern and northern Ontario, the West, and in the Acadian region of the Maritimes. By the 1930s, many of the western sees were in English hands, as was the predominantly francophone Diocese of Sault Ste. Marie, although the Acadians now had a French-speaking bishop in the Diocese of Chatham (Bathurst), New Brunswick. Although French-Canadian *survivance*—the effort to preserve their language, religion, culture, and autonomy in North America—did not abate during the interwar period, Catholic bishops discovered new unity as they faced Canada's economic and social crisis and the rise of socialism.

The recessions of the 1920s and Great Depression of the 1930s evoked a variety of responses from Canadian Catholics. At St. Francis Xavier University in Antigonish, Nova Scotia, Fathers Moses Coady (1882–1959) and James Tompkins (1870–1953) formed cooperatives among local farmers, fishermen, steel workers, and miners, and reinforced adult education through study groups coordinated by the university's extension department. In Quebec, nationalist politicians in the Action Liberale Nationale, fused the Catholic social teachings found in *Quadragesimo Anno* with an effort to combat political corruption in the province. Although short-lived, the ALN was one of many Catholic Action and Jeunesse groups that was committed to the amelioration of the condition of working people. Elsewhere, Catholic newspaper editors such as Henry Somerville of *The Catholic Register* (Toronto) and Murray Ballantyne *The Beacon* (Montreal) called for social justice and an end to the abuses engendered by the capitalist system. At a more practical level, Catherine de Hueck, a former Russian baroness, founded a network of Friendship Houses in Ottawa, Toronto, and Hamilton, to alleviate the suffering of the urban poor and to combat communist activity among Catholic immigrants from eastern Europe. These charitable and social justice efforts were supported by a few progressive bishops, like Neil McNeil of Toronto (1912–1934), who enthusiastically encouraged the application of papal social teachings in their dioceses. After the Depression and the Second World War, social justice issues were sustained by lay groups like the Young Catholic Workers, religious orders like the Basilian Fathers, and Catholics active in the Co-operative Commonwealth Federation, a social democratic political party, which was released from episcopal censure in 1943.

The Catholic Church in Canada in the postwar period underwent further changes. The arrival of thousands of refugees and immigrants from Europe accentuated the cultural mosaic that was already evident in the Church. By the 1960s Catholics of Italian, Portuguese, Croatian, Polish, and Ukrainian origin were of significant numbers that the model of the bipolar French-English Church was no longer relevant. Moreover, after the loosening of immigration quotas by the Canadian Government in the mid-1960s, Catholic immigrants from Goa, the Philippines, Vietnam, Korea, and Haiti strengthened the cultural variety of the Church in the cities. Postwar immigration also brought an increase in the Catholic population of Oriental Rites, particularly the Maronite and Melkite Christians from the Middle East.

In the 1960s, the Church's dominance as a feature of French-Canadian life was clearly in decline. During Quebec's "Quiet Revolution," which began formally with the victory of the Liberal Party in 1960, the Church lost its place of prominence in the face of Quebec's new political order and its heightened sense of nationalism. The secularization of the education system, hospitals, and social services removed the Church from its omnipresence in Quebec society. The combination of the political revolution, the "aggiornamento" of Vatican II, the secularization of institutions, and the changing social mores of the era, coincided with a turning away from the Church in Quebec. Currently, despite growing interest in such things as charismatic renewal, Church attendance is low in the province, Quebec's birthrate is among the lowest in the Western world, and the voice of the Church is heard less and less in the determination of Quebec's political future.

In "English Canada," the Church's encounter with secular culture has been no less dramatic, although less traumatic in terms of the Church's active adherents. Currently Catholics outside of Quebec maintain one of the highest rates of Church participation among all of Canada's Christian denominations. These Catholics, from a variety of ethnic backgrounds, can now be found in every walk of life, and living in all locales—inner cities, farmsteads, and suburbs. The Vatican recognized the growing importance of the Church outside of Quebec as early as 1946, with the appointment of Toronto's James C. McGuigan (1934–1971) to the College of Cardinals. In the public sphere, Catholics within and outside of Quebec have also become prominent in Canadian political life, so much so that five of the last six Prime Ministers have been members of the Church. Nevertheless, the institutional secularization so marked in Quebec is also taking place elsewhere. In Saskatchewan, New Brunswick, and Ontario, Catholic healthcare facilities are facing increased control by the state, and in some cases complete secularization. Catholic colleges operate in a federated relationship with English Canadian universities, and in the cases of St. Dunstan's (PEI), St. Patrick's College (Ottawa), and the University of Ottawa, these colleges have either shut down or lost their Catholic ethos. Finally, American consumer culture and increasing moral relativism have had a profound effect on Catholic behavior and the ever-widening gap between Church prescription and popular religious practice.

Accounting for 42 percent of Canada's 27.2 million people (1992 estimate), Catholics have been challenged by the social and political changes in the postwar period. Laypersons have become active in their fight against legalized abortion and euthanasia. The Church has recognized the negative effects of its missions to First Nations and has recently defended native rights in such endeavors as Project North, an interfaith effort to stop the MacKenzie Valley Pipeline from destroying native life and the local ecosystems. Bishops and clergy have openly stated their ideals for a renewed Canadian state: the recognition of Quebec as a distinct French-speaking society, fundamental human rights, global development through economic justice, the rights of linguistic minorities, and the preservation of Canada's multicultural fabric. Scholars such as Bernard Lonergan, Marshall McLuhan and Gregory Baum, inspirational writers and caregivers such as Jean Vanier, and clerics such as Paul-Emile Leger have given Canadian Catholics a distinguished international profile.

MARK G. McGOWAN

See also ANGLICANISM; CHURCH, THE; CHURCH AND STATE.

CANDLE, PASCHAL

Blessed on Holy Saturday and lit from the "new fire" at the beginning of the Paschal Vigil, it is a centuries-old symbol of our risen Savior. At the vigil, it is carried through the darkened church by a deacon, who solemnly stops three times before he reaches the altar—each time singing *Lumen Christi* ("Light of Christ"). It is then used by the celebrant when he blesses the baptismal water. During the paschal season, it remains in the sanctuary and is lit during liturgical services. It is also lit during baptisms, and is traditionally placed near the baptismal font. Candles were first used by Christians of the early Church to provide light during predawn services, and in the catacombs. Then as now, they symbolized the divine light of Christ's presence. Five grains of incense—representing Christ's wounds—are encased in the paschal candle.

JOSEPH QUINN

See also LITURGY; PASCHAL MYSTERY.

CANDLEMAS

Held on 2 February, this liturgical celebration is officially known as "The Presentation of Our Lord." It commemorates the presentation of Christ in the

Temple forty days after his birth (Luke 2:22-39). Candles are blessed on this day, and a lighted candle procession is held to symbolize the light of divine revelation that Christ provides.

JOSEPH QUINN

See also LITURGY; SACRAMENTALS.

CANISIUS, PETER, ST. (1521–1597)

Doctor of the Church, Jesuit writer, educator, and preacher, Canisius was born at Nijmegen in the Netherlands on 8 May 1521. He studied at Cologne and at Louvain where he received a degree in canon law. Although his father, a burgomaster, wanted him to be a lawyer and to marry, Peter entered the Society of Jesus in 1543 after hearing a retreat preached by Blessed Peter Faber. He published some works of St. Cyril of Alexandria, St. Jerome and St. Leo the Great. He also attended two sessions of the Council of Trent (1545–1563).

St. Ignatius of Loyola sent Canisius to teach at the Society's first school at Messina in Sicily and later he was assigned to the University of Ingoldstadt in Bavaria to help fight the rising tide of Protestantism. In 1552 he went to Vienna where the Catholic Church had suffered a serious decline and poured himself into pastoral work. By ministering to the sick during a plague, he helped to win back to Catholicism many of the Viennese.

He declined the see of Vienna and instead wrote a famous and important catechism, *Summa Doctrinae Christianae,* which was translated into fifteen languages. He founded an impressive college in Prague and was named a Jesuit provincial. He traveled through much of Germany evangelizing. He also helped to introduce the Society into Poland. From 1559 to 1565 he worked in Augsburg debating with the Protestants and was highly successful in winning people back to Catholicism. In 1580 he was instrumental in the foundation of the University at Fribourg where his preaching helped to keep it Catholic.

Peter Canisius always championed the importance of education and used his own learning in defense of Catholicism. He is called the "Second Apostle to Germany" for his prominent role in the Counter Reformation. He died on 21 December 1597. His feast is commemorated on 21 December.

ANTHONY D. ANDREASSI

See also REFORMATION, THE; SOCIETY OF JESUS.

CANON (SECULAR AND REGULAR)

An individual living under a certain rule (Greek: *kanon,* "measuring stick") of life. In practice the term is used when a large church or cathedral is served by a group of secular clergy called "canons" because they live under mandated duties such as participation in the Liturgy of the Hours. The term may also be used of a group of religious who live under a fixed rule of life and are often connected to a particular church. Among secular clergy, the rank may be mainly honorary.

DAVID BRYAN

See also CATHEDRAL.

CANON LAW

Law in the Church is considered an ordinance of reason formulated and duly promulgated by those officially entrusted with care of the Christian community. It is fundamentally based on Roman law which, unlike some other more familiar legal systems, enunciates general principles, remains legislatively stable over the years, requires equity or a certain malleability in application, and provides for dispensation by competent authorities in particular circumstances. Canon law functions in service to the people of God by respecting the mysteries of theology, by establishing reasonable norms of action for intelligent and free and responsible people, by identifying and helping to balance basic ecclesial values, by articulating certain nondispensable procedures for the protection of rights, and by giving stability to the worldwide visible social and spiritual entity we call the Catholic Church. Basically canon law attempts to fulfill its role by defining certain structures (such as parishes and dioceses), by delineating fundamental internal relations (such as participation in the various sacraments), and by articulating certain rights and obligations which stem from sacramentally based or appointed roles in the Church (such as those of laity, of married persons and of pastors). As a complexus of norms for the ecclesiastical body, canon law provides the principles of order and structure within which particular application is always ultimately at the service of salvation.

The evolution of Church law can generally be divided into three major eras: the *ius antiquum* (old law), the *ius novum* (new law), and the *ius novissimum* (newest law). The first era spans roughly the first eleven centuries; the second, the twelfth to nineteenth centuries; and the third, the late sixteenth century to the present. Scripture was considered the original source of Church law, and there is evidence in the Acts of the Apostles and several epistles of both loose organizational structure as well as certain problem-solving mechanisms. The time of the *ius antiquum* was characterized at first by ad hoc solutions made in local gatherings of clergy and faithful known as synods. Enactments of these synods were called by the Greek name for rule, from whence comes the title "canon" law. For the most part, these synodal decisions were in response to disciplinary transgressions but they also often related to matters of belief, such as the controversies over whether those who had defected during persecutions (the *lapsi*) should be rebaptized when readmitted to the believing community. By the second and third century, several rule books known as Church "orders" indicated how various Christian communities were organized and how they worshipped. The most well-known of these are the Didache, or the *Doctrine of the Twelve Apostles,* and the *Didascalia* or the *Teaching of the Apostles.* Collections of declarations of local synods, sometimes with the addition of papal pronouncements, were evident by the third century. These were usually named for their place of origin (such as the "Hispania" from Spain) or for the person to whom the collection was attributed (such as the "Isidoriana" for Isidore of Seville). Several centuries later, one of these collections was sent by Pope Hadrian I to Charlemagne and was imposed by him as the law of the Carolingian Empire.

In the early fourth century, when Christianity was first recognized as legal and eventually became the official religion of the Roman Empire, the Church began to employ structures and practices similar to those of the civil sector including, for example, the use of territorial divisions called dioceses and provinces, the ceremonial garments of the emperor and his court, and communication by means of decrees and circular letters. When Rome was conquered in 476, many well-established and well-organized existing Church structures fell heir to fulfilling numerous public functions and responsibilities. In the sixth century the writings of Church Fathers (such as Basil and Jerome), as well as the legislation of emperors (such as Justinian), were officially added to the sources of canon law. Because of the somewhat indiscriminate expansion of Christianity and the accompanying decline of belief and observance, various—but mostly unsuccessful—reform measures are evident in Church law during the eighth and ninth centuries.

The period of the *ius novum* dates from the mid-twelfth century when a Camaldolese monk named Gratian compiled the then extant, sometimes conflicting collections of canon law into one large tome which he called the *Concordance of Discordant Canons* (or *Decretum* for short). His work was an attempt to find and make some coherent canonical sense of the numerous ad hoc declarations contained in various synodal and conciliar canons, in writings of Church Fathers, and in papal and imperial decrees. Gratian's monumental *Decretum* was not an official canonical collection, but it became the systematized source studied by and commented on by canonists and canon-lawyer popes, beginning with Alexander III in the late twelfth century. In 1234 Gregory IX commissioned the Dominican friar Raymond of Peñafort to gather the first official collection of canon law. This collection, which contained only the decretal letters of Gregory himself, came to be known as the *Decretals* in contrast to Gratian's *Decretum.* Through the thirteenth and fourteenth centuries, succeeding popes added their own enactments to the *Decretals* of Gregory, and eventually the two immense volumes (the *Decretum* and *Decretals*) became known as the *Corpus Iuris Canonici,* or the "body of canon law." After the Council of Trent (1545–1563), a corrected "Roman" edition of the *Corpus Iuris Canonici* was issued and this, along with the extensive commentaries on the *Decretum* and *Decretals* dating from the late Middle Ages and the Renaissance, were the primary texts for students, scholars, and practitioners of ecclesiastical law until the beginning of the twentieth century.

Trent had ushered in the era of the *ius novissimum,* but eventually Vatican Council I (1869–1870) called for the codification of all canon law. By that time, extensive ad hoc legislation added to the *Corpus Iuris Canonici* and its commentaries had resulted in a mass of canonical material that was difficult to locate, often contradictory, and even more difficult to understand or to reconcile with other conflicting texts. Work on the Code of Canon Law (*Codex Iuris Canonici*) was begun in 1904 under the direction of Cardinal Gasparri and completed in 1917. This provided a great simplification of the morass of previous canonical legislation and was a valuable contribution to the Church in the early twentieth century. However, it also functioned to solidify much of Church structure and practice at a time when most of the world was experiencing major changes. The decades after 1917 resulted in numerous questions, adaptations and interpretations of the Code until, by the time of Vatican Council II (1962–1965), it was obvious that a fresh vision of the Church also required a new look at Church legislation. When John XXIII announced the convocation of Vatican II in 1959, he simultaneously mandated the revision of the 1917 Code. An official commission was formed for this purpose in 1963 but judiciously postponed its work until after the close of the council. In 1967, the first postconciliar Synod of Bishops issued ten principles for revision of the code and, subsequently, specially chosen study groups worked on various sections of the previous code to produce *schemata* that were submitted to bishops, episcopal conferences and ecclesiastical centers of study throughout the world for consultation and comment. In January of 1983, John Paul II officially promulgated the revised Code of Canon Law for the Latin Church. Similarly, in 1990, he promulgated a revised Code of Canons of the Eastern Churches.

The official text of both Codes is Latin, but there are numerous approved translations published by various episcopal conferences throughout the world. The basic unit in the Code of Canon Law is the canon, and there are 1752 canons in the 1983 Code for the Latin Church, in comparison to 2414 canons in the 1917 Code. The canons are grouped into seven Books which treat: I. General Norms; II. The People of God; III. The Teaching Office of The Church; IV. The Sanctifying Office of the Church; V. The Temporal Goods of the Church; VI. Sanctions in the Church; and VII. Procedures. All Church law, however, is not contained in the Code. Ecclesiastical legislation is also found in enactments of ecumenical councils, in apostolic constitutions and documents issued *motu proprio* (on his own initiative) by the pope, in agreements between the Vatican as a sovereign state and other sovereign nations, in liturgical books, in legitimate canonical custom, in the recognized general decrees of episcopal conferences, in laws enacted by diocesan bishops, and in the approved statutes of ecclesiastical organizations such as religious institutes.

Ecclesiastical law is considered universal if it is issued by the supreme legislator (the pope) for the entire Church or for a specific segment of the entire Church, such as clerics. It is considered particular if issued by a lower level legislator (a bishop) for the members of the people of God entrusted to his care within a particular territory. In general, canon law is considered as territorial law in that it usually applies only to those who are within the territory for which the law was enacted, but canon law can also be personal in that it can apply to certain people regardless of where they might be.

ELIZABETH McDONOUGH, O.P.

See also CHURCH, THE; LAW.

CANON OF SCRIPTURE

The word "canon" derives from the Greek *kanōn* (Hebrew *qaneh*), which is a "reed" or "measuring stick." In Christian theology the canon of Scripture is the list of sacred books that serves as the rule or norm of Christian faith and life.

All Christians today accept as the first part of the canon of Scripture the books of the Hebrew Bible. Bibles published under Catholic auspices contain those books as well as seven more books: Tobit, Judith, 1–2 Maccabees, Wisdom, Sirach, and Baruch. These books are sometimes called the Deuterocanonicals or Apocrypha. But for Catholics they are fully canonical. The OT canons of Orthodox Churches contain books over and above what appear in the Catholic canon. All Christians today share the same canon of twenty-seven NT books: four Gospels, Acts, thirteen Pauline Epistles, Hebrews, seven General or Catholic Epistles, and Revelation.

The basic canon of Hebrew Scriptures was probably fixed as early as the second century B.C. And by the late first century A.D. there was a clear distinction between sacred or canonical books and other books, though the status of some books (Song of Songs, Ecclesiastes) remained controversial. The Greek translation (Septuagint) of the Hebrew Scriptures was a Jewish creation and was widely used among Greek-speaking Jews (Philo, Josephus, Paul, etc.). But as Christians adopted the Septuagint as their Bible, Jews either ignored this Greek version or revised it to defend against Christian theological claims. The seven deuterocanonical books were part of the Greek manuscript tradition. The canonical status of these books was debated first by Jerome (against) and Augustine (for), and then by Luther (against) and Catholics (for). The Council of Trent in 1546 followed the tradition of the Latin Vulgate and adopted the wider canon including the seven controverted books. Trent produced a definitive list of OT books, which is followed today in Bibles prepared under Catholic auspices.

By A.D. 200 there was general acceptance in the Churches of the "core" NT books: the four Gospels, Acts, Pauline letters, 1 Peter, and 1 John. By the late fourth century the Greek and Latin Churches had accepted the twenty-seven-book NT canon. The development of the NT canon was facilitated on the one hand by reaction against Marcion in the mid-second century A.D. who rejected the entire OT canon and accepted only ten Pauline letters and Luke's Gospel, and on the other hand by reaction against Gnostic and Montanist attempts to widen the "canon" by including other writings. The operative criteria that entered into the process of NT canonicity appear to have been orthodoxy of content, some association with the "apostles," and use in and acceptance by the Churches. Despite some unclarity about boundaries, it is fair to say that around A.D. 400 the twenty-seven books of our present NT canon were recognized as sacred writings that can serve as the norm or rule of Christian faith and life. In response to Luther's questions about the theological value of some NT books (James, Jude, Hebrews, Revelation), the Council of Trent in 1546 listed the twenty-seven "received" books of the NT. The list was confirmed in various sixteenth- and seventeenth-century Protestant confessions of faith.

Although the content of the canon of Scripture is not a matter of great controversy among Catholics today, there are some interesting questions related to it. How should Christians view the OT and what should they call it? Which Hebrew or Greek text is canonical (since we no longer have the autographs)? Does the presence of the seven additional OT books in the Catholic Bible make any difference? May the Churches add or subtract books from the canon? Are some canonical books more important than others (canon within the canon)? What is the proper relation between canon and Church? How representative is the canon of ancient Israelite or early Church life?

DANIEL J. HARRINGTON, S.J.

See also BIBLE, NEW TESTAMENT WRITINGS; BIBLE, OLD TESTAMENT WRITINGS; MANUSCRIPTS OF THE BIBLE.

CANON OF THE MASS

An approved Eucharistic Prayer is called a canon (from Greek *kanon,* a reed cut as a measuring stick, understood broadly as an established guide, rule, list, or principle). Such a Eucharistic Prayer, or canon, serves as the central spoken prayer of the Eucharistic action itself (Mass). With their roots in earliest Christianity, Eucharistic Prayers in the West were gradually assimilated to, or replaced by, the Roman Canon. Several new canons have been approved since the Second Vatican Council, and some of these use, in part, elements of ancient models.

DAVID BRYAN

See also EUCHARIST.

CANONIZATION

In ecclesiastical usage the term canonization is the process, reserved since the thirteenth century to the pope, by means of which a deceased person is officially sanctioned and approved in the Roman Catholic Church as a saint and is treated as illustrious, preeminent, or sacred. The individual is authoritatively co-opted into the official list of persons accepted and recognized by the Church as a saint, as one who has gone to heaven. These persons, our fellow Christians, who though flawed in heart and mind, have given their all to God, have practiced the virtues heroically, especially faith, hope and charity and, as a consequence, have emerged as individuals who can light the way ahead. These are those declared to have died climbing to get closer to the person of Christ and, in so doing, became God's intimates which qualifies them for the Church's highest honor. There is an immense variety of saints each of which richly embodies what the Christian life is all about and shows the richness of divine gifts.

A saint is one who, by corresponding with grace, has followed the implications of the faith to the fullest degree. The Spirit breathes how and where the Spirit wills, and hence God alone, not the Church, makes saints. The process of canonization, or the declaration of sainthood in earlier times, is simply the discernment and attestation that this or that person is among the elect. Other faiths have their saintly figures but only the Roman Catholic Church has a formal process for singling out those in whom the Christian and Catholic vision has found full growth. Martyrs are those who sacrifice their lives for the sake of principle and they are found also in the secular world where, for example, ceremonies of honor are held at the Tomb of the Unknown Soldier. But only in the theology of the Catholic Church are the "declared heroes" viewed as having intercessory power through which even miracles are expected.

The complicated process with its rigid rules and definite structure for coming to the point of canonization, presently used in Rome by the Congregation for the Causes of Saints, is the natural development of the various means adopted throughout the history of the faith for discovering how God has shaped the lives of these individuals, how he has gifted them for service, loved them faithfully, and made them men and women of influence. The early martyrs were seen as the archetypes of those who, as St. Paul indicated in Philippians, were pressing "on toward the goal for the prize of the upward call of God in Christ Jesus." These martyrs held great attraction for the rest of the faithful because of their ability, both in life and even after death, to manifest supernatural power on behalf of the community of the followers of the "Way." Already in that period these holy persons were viewed as being the center of power and a source of munificence.

This noble army of martyrs who had fallen because of their love for God rose as stars and were proclaimed martyrs, a name which means witnesses, by the voice of the people, and were approved by the local bishops. As time passed and persecutions ceased the Church began to deepen its understanding of the notion of martyrdom to include those who lived lives in pursuit of Christian ideals that dominated their lives. Veneration was then extended to those who, even without dying for the faith, had defended it and suffered for it; these were the confessors of the faith. Shortly after that, outward expression of reverent feelings was extended to those who had been outstanding for their exemplary Christian life, especially by their practices of austerity of life and penance. Some centuries later those who excelled in Catholic doctrine, in apostolic zeal, or in charity and evangelical spirit were considered in the same group as martyrs.

The earliest criterion used to determine which persons were to be put in the category of saints was a unique holiness of life which impressed the faithful, particularly if the individual had a reputation for miracles. With the spread of the faith after the time of Constantine, the list of those who received the cult given to the saints increased greatly and abuses crept in and many unsubstantiated accounts of deeds of valor spread abroad. The Church from its inception guided the thoughts and motions of its members by means of precepts which were backed by the whole force of its authority and here in the matter of canonization there was the intervention of ecclesiastical authority beginning from the sixth century onward. The first papal canonization in which there were positive documents was that of St. Udalricus in 973. With the passage of time various papal norms were issued but it was the future Pope Benedict XIV who (in 1738) wrote the famous treatise *De Servorum Dei beatificatione et Beatorum canonizatione* which was incorporated into the Code of Canon Law published in 1917. That remained the law and practice until the recent appearance of "New Laws for the Causes of the Saints" published in Rome in 1983 which norms still prevail.

How does a Cause begin? The local bishop may begin the investigation after the death of a person who has lived an exemplary Christian life, who has a reputation for holiness, or who has a publicly recognized reputation for martyrdom. There is usually present a conviction that favors are received through intercessory prayer addressed to the individual and in some cases favors granted by God. If, after the investigation carried out in accordance with the norms of the Congregation for the Causes of Saints, the individual is found to have been heroic in the practice of virtues or was a martyr, he or she is declared to be "Venerable" and "private" cult is allowed by praising his or her virtues or praying to him or her.

When it has been established that the Venerable one has worked an authentic miracle invoked in prayer, he or she will be declared Blessed by the Supreme Pontiff. This is not an exercise of infallibility on the part of the pope for he does not declare definitely that the person is in glory but the declaration does give rise to moral certainty. When, after that declaration a second miracle is attributed to the Blessed, the canonization of the Blessed may take place. This is usually done amid the pageantry of St. Peter's with the pope affirming that the Blessed is indeed a saint, worthy of veneration, powerful in intercession and a model of Christian virtue. The cult of the new saint can be extended then to the entire Church and the saint's name is included in the liturgical calendar of the universal Church. This is canonization and the papal declaration is viewed as an exercise of papal infallibility.

JAMES McGRATH

See also HOLINESS; SAINTS; VENERATION OF SAINTS.

CANTICLE

(Lat. *canticulum,* "a little song") A sacred song or chant, other than a psalm, the text of which is taken from Scripture. Three canticles from the New Testament—the *Benedictus* of Zechariah, *Magnificat* of the Blessed Virgin, and the *Nunc Dimittis* of Simeon—are recited daily in the Liturgy of the Hours. The Catholic breviary also includes numerous canticles from the Old Testament.

JOSEPH QUINN

See also LITURGY OF THE HOURS.

CANTOR

(Lat., "singer") Also referred to as precentor, this is the leader of an ecclesiastical choir, who may also select the music for a liturgical service. In the Liturgy of the Hours, the cantor intones the antiphons and leads the singing of the psalms.

JOSEPH QUINN

See also LITURGY OF THE HOURS; MINISTER.

CAPITAL PUNISHMENT

Historically, the argument for capital punishment was rooted in an understanding of commutative justice, which focuses on the obligations and duties members of a society have toward one another, and the responsibility of the state to protect the well-being of its citizens and to insure the common good. As to the first, certain crimes, particularly murder, were seen as so heinous and reprehensible that in justice they demanded a commensurate penalty. Redressing a terrible injustice required an extreme and unique punishment. Some have argued that capital punishment originated in the ancient social desire of blood vengeance for those who murder, suggesting that only by taking the life of a murderer could the debt incurred by his crime be satisfied. In this respect, the justice at work in capital punishment was based in the ancient law of retaliation: "an eye for an eye and a tooth for a tooth" (Deut 19:21). Others have suggested that the severe retribution achieved by capital punishment holds individuals responsible for their actions and demands that they face their consequences.

The second rationale for capital punishment focused on the responsibility of a state or government to protect the well-being of its citizens and safeguard the common good. The execution of criminals was the right and responsibility of those in public authority entrusted with the care of a community. Traditionally, following Romans 13:4 ("It is not without purpose that the ruler carries the sword; he is God's servant, to inflict his avenging wrath upon the wrongdoer."), in executing dangerous criminals the state was seen to be carrying out the will of God. Rulers were divine agents who had received their authority from God; thus, capital punishment was sometimes required by the God-given duty of the state to maintain order and peace.

The medieval Catholic theologian, Thomas Aquinas, argued that every individual in society is a member of that society and must contribute to its welfare; hence, if someone seriously undermines the welfare of society or is a significant danger to it, the common good justifies capital punishment. Using an analogy to a gangrenous limb that must be amputated if it is not to infect the whole body, Aquinas reasoned that sometimes, in order to preserve the overall health of society, a person whose behavior imperils it must be removed (ST, II-II, q. 64, a. 2). Aquinas agreed that "to kill a man who retains his natural dignity is intrinsically evil," but argued that anyone who committed terrible sins against the community deviated so far from rational, human behavior that he forfeited his human dignity, becoming more like a beast than a human being. Following Aristotle, Aquinas believed that "an evil man is worse than a beast, and more harmful" (ST, II-II, q. 64, a. 2). However, Aquinas also maintained that the punishment inflicted must not be done in a vindictive spirit because to delight in the pain and loss suffered by a criminal is a form of hatred, which is the opposite of charity and never justified. Retribution is lawful, Aquinas reasoned, only if the intention is good, namely to insure justice and restore the common good (ST, II-II, q. 108, a. 1).

More recently, a different argument for capital punishment has been advanced which is based on the state's primary function to provide an environment of safety, freedom, justice, and peace for its citizens. On this view, certain crimes, such as murder and terrorism, so severely undermine people's confidence in the state's ability to assure the well-being of its citizens, that capital punishment becomes a symbolic act on the part of the state which works to restore people's trust in its authority and competence. In this respect, the execution of criminals can provide a needed catharsis for anger and outrage when society or individuals have suffered terrible violence.

Whatever reasons can be advanced in support of capital punishment, many theologians and religious people today doubt that it can often be justified. Although the state does have a right to protect its citizens and to punish criminals, this does not mean capital punishment is warranted. There is a strong presumption against capital punishment because taking the life of a person violates the most fundamental ethical norm of respecting life and doing no harm. Traditionally it has been maintained that the evil of capital punishment could be justified when proportionately greater goods, such as justice and the well-being of society, otherwise risked being lost. Today, however, many argue that these goods can be preserved by less severe means.

Although the number of executions in the United States has increased dramatically since 1977, arguments against capital punishment are mounting. First, studies have shown that the threat of execution does not deter criminals. Murder rates vary little between states that have the death penalty and states that do not. Violent crimes such as murder are often the result of emotional arguments among family members, not carefully planned acts whose consequences are calculated. Other times they are acts of impulse or passion, as when someone is frightened or taken by surprise. And when a murder is premeditated, the assailant acts in the confidence of not getting caught.

Secondly, capital punishment can be unevenly and inequitably applied. The majority of those executed are poor, uneducated, and members of racial minorities. These people cannot afford the expert legal advice available to the wealthy and often are discriminated against by juries which reflect the prejudices of a society or can be strongly influenced by public expectations. It is sometimes later demonstrated that those sentenced to death were innocent or were discriminated against in the sentencing process; however, the finality of capital punishment means that a miscarriage of justice cannot be corrected, nor can the executed later benefit from changes in the law or new evidence that could affect their conviction.

Third, one growing argument against capital punishment is that the need for retribution can be satisfied in other ways. Justice demands that criminals not go unpunished, but there are alternatives to capital punishment, such as life imprisonment without parole. One reason in support of this position is that even in cases of extremely violent crime a criminal does not lose all rights. He or she does, for instance, lose the right to freedom, but not the right to life if there is anything short of death that can prevent such violent behavior.

Fourth, capital punishment is a gruesome practice that can harden and desensitize society, thus undermining respect and reverence for life. For people to authorize the state to kill violent offenders of the law can weaken the moral fiber of society by making it casual about death. Executing criminals is inhumane and often contributes to a dangerous vindictive spirit in society. Proponents of capital punishment must demonstrate that respect for life is actually enhanced by violent deaths inflicted by the state. If it is not, then to respond to vicious crimes with capital punishment only perpetuates a cycle of violence. On this view, the overall good of society would be better served by focusing on some of the manifold factors contributing to crime, such as poverty, racism, broken families, and lack of education.

From a Christian perspective, it is difficult to sustain an argument in favor of capital punishment because of the central Christian conviction that human life is sacred and ought to be protected and fostered from conception to death. Although Catholic teaching has allowed the taking of human life in particular circumstances such as self-defense and a just war, the legitimacy of capital punishment has been increasingly questioned. The growing sense of the dignity of the human person as made in God's image and likeness argues strongly against the right to take another's life even where serious injustice has occurred. What Catholic teaching in recent years has come to call "a consistent ethic of life" deeply questions the morality of taking any life, whether that be through abortion, war, euthanasia, or capital punishment.

Additional Christian warrants for proscribing the death penalty are Jesus's command to love our enemies and be reconciled to them. The Gospels provide ample evidence of God's absolute love for every person in Jesus's steadfast ministry to outcasts and sinners. That Christ died that all might live underscores the fundamental Christian belief in moral conversion and regeneration for all people, even the worst sinners. Christians believe in the possibility of new beginnings for everyone, and see that passage from death to life as a reflection of the paschal mystery of Christ. Finally, Christianity is founded on the abundant mercy and gracious forgiveness of God, and those pledged to live in keeping with the character of God are summoned to practice that same merciful forgiveness in their lives. It is for these reasons that most major Christian denominations have denounced capital punishment as inimical with the spirit of Christianity.

PAUL WADELL

See also ANTHROPOLOGY, CHRISTIAN; CHURCH AND STATE; HUMAN RIGHTS; JUST WAR; THEOLOGY, MORAL.

CAPITAL SINS

The capital (Lat. "head" or "chief"), or deadly, sins are usually listed as seven: pride, avarice, envy, anger, lust, gluttony, and sloth or acedia (*Catechism of the Catholic Church,* no. 1866). They are often referred to as vices and are, in fact, a response to basic human powers which can lead us away from growth in love of God, self and others. They may become habits and thus sources or generators of sinful acts. We shall give a brief overview of how the listing of the capital sins developed, then define each one and conclude with a summary of current ways of looking at the capital sins as sources not only of personal but also of corporate sin.

Overview of the Development of the List of Capital Sins

The listing of seven or eight "demons" which beset human life is without scriptural base though all are found in Scripture. Most probably, the origin lies in a post-biblical, monastic context. The number of seven or eight may derive from the spirit which returns with "seven other spirits more wicked than itself" (Luke 11:24-26), and is found as early as the fourth century in the writings of the Egyptian desert monks.

Evagrius of Pontus (d. 399) describes eight *logismoi* (Gk. "evil thoughts") which keep the monk under constant attack. John Cassian (d. ca. 425) who brought the teaching of Evagrius to monastic communities in the West, also listed eight. Gregory the Great (d. 604), to whom is attributed the current list of seven, separated pride from the others, as the root of all sin, and listed seven additional deadly sins also replacing Evagrius' "acedia" with "envy." Gregory's classification influenced the instruction of both monks and laity throughout the Middle Ages. John Climacus (d. 650) and John Damascene (d. ca. 749) carried the tradition forward in the East while the Celtic penitential literature, following Cassian, continued it in the West.

Theologians of the Middle Ages including Hugh of St. Victor, Peter Lombard, Thomas Aquinas and Bonaventure all analyzed the capital sins. John of the Cross (d. 1591) describes how the sins show themselves differently at the different stages of the spiritual life and stresses the need to allow oneself to enter into a process of conversion: "No matter how much the individual does through his own efforts, he cannot actively purify himself enough to be disposed in the least degree for the divine union of the perfection of love. God must take over and purge him in that fire that is dark for him" (*The Dark Night, The Collected Works of St. John of the Cross,* trans. by K. Kavanagh, O.C.D. and Otilio Rogriguez, O.C.D., Washington, D.C.: ICS Publications, 1973, p. 303).

As the Church settled on seven, the major omission from the original lists of eight was *tristitia* ("melancholy"). It was merged with acedia ("apathy") which in English was eventually termed sloth. Vainglory and pride, separate sins in Evagrius' list, merged as pride and Gregory the Great added envy to the list, thus making seven.

Defining the Capital Sins

Pride has been described as the "queen of sins," the "root of all evil," the "beginning of all sin" (Gregory the Great, *Morals on the Book of Job,* Oxford: J.H. Parker, 1845, III, pp. 489–490). It is "to turn one's heart away from one's Maker" (Sir 10:12), from a recognition of God's sovereignty to a false self-aggrandizement and self-centeredness. It is to be distinguished from healthy self-esteem and from a true appreciation of being created "in the image and likeness of God" (Gen 1:27). Linked to pride is vainglory or an undue esteem of self and of one's accomplishments which may reveal itself in great efforts to prove one's excellence or to gain the approval of others.

Avarice, or greed, is an inordinate desire, an insatiable longing for the possession of something. It is often associated with the excessive eagerness to accumulate wealth and to obtain money. It shows itself in a lack of trust in God, in a grasping at material security and in vulnerability especially in the face of an uncertain future. It may lead to the inability to share with others or even to receive from others and the refusal to acknowledge the need for interdependence.

Envy is a tendency to begrudge the good of another because it is perceived as a threat to one's own excellence or glory. Envy expresses both a deep longing for, and a despair of ever receiving, the good things of life. It is related to the scarcity of something that is held dear so that the envious person tries to take from others what he or she longs for. Discrediting or maligning the reputation of others is a common expression of envy. Deep down, envy comes from a radical difficulty in believing that God loves and fashions each one uniquely and personally. It represents a refusal to accept the human condition, particularly one's finiteness as a creature, and a denial of the yearning of the human heart which finds its ultimate completeness only in God.

Anger arises as a defense of self in the face of actual or impending loss of esteem. It often starts with a perceived hurt or injustice, leading to feelings of humiliation and loss of prestige or good name, coupled with the excessive desire to suppress what seems hostile. Fight or flight are common responses to anger. Unbridled anger can lead to vengeful actions that are disproportionate to the injury suffered. When harbored, anger may lead to resentment, hostility, conflict, and an intense urge to retaliate.

Lust is defined as an overmastering appetite or craving for something and is almost always associated with an excessive desire for sexual pleasure. Sexuality is a relational power which bonds one with others in affection, mutual care, intimacy, love and respect. Turned into a disintegrating force, it can lead to the impersonal use or abuse of others for one's own gratification, to relational patterns of domination and submission, and to interpersonal alienation.

Gluttony is usually associated with excessive self-indulgence in eating and drinking but may be linked to insatiable desires for any activity, even exaggerated care for the body through exercise or dieting. Gluttony may stem from an avoidance of facing absolutist expectations of oneself, approval seeking, evasion of intimacy, and a dread of emptiness (M. L. Bringle, *The God of Thinness, Gluttony and Other Weighty Matters,* Nashville, Tenn.: Abingdon Press, 1992, pp. 141–143).

Sloth or acedia, sometimes called the "noonday devil" (Ps 91:6) first referred to monks afflicted by indifference to the obligations to God. It is associated with affectlessness, which gives rise not only to boredom, rancor, apathy, sluggishness, indifference to work but also to restless activity and aggression. Acedia shows itself in a "lack of any feeling for the world, for the people in it, or for the self" (S. Lyman, *The Seven Deadly Sins: A Contemporary View,* London: SCM Press Ltd., 1985, p. 6). Traditionally, acedia is linked to *tristitia* (Lat. "sadness") expressed in melancholy, weariness and general dissatisfaction. Sloth is often fed by poorly used leisure time, overly high expectations, aversion to self-giving love and a lack of creativity in response to one's deepest longings.

Current Views of the Capital Sins

The capital sins, like all sin, have their source in habits of the heart; thus an understanding of the developmental nature of faith leads us to see that the effort to overcome them is part of the lifelong process of conversion. There is today an increased understanding of how corporate and cultural contexts tend to foster sinful attitudes. Contemporary authors are particularly concerned with the society that seems even positively to value the capital sins (S. Lyman and K. Slack). Corporate gluttony and avarice are reflected in world hunger, the energy crisis, misuse and depletion of natural resources, environmental deterioration and world poverty.

Feminist authors, while not denying the traditional list, tend to focus on other personal and social evils which have their source in cruelty (Shklar), and see the traditional list as stemming from the "perverted paradigm" of patriarchal society; in other words, the drives to which men are particularly prone (Daly).

BRÍD LONG, S.S.L.

See also ASCETICISM; CHRISTIAN SPIRITUALITY; SIN; VIRTUE.

CAPITALISM

Capitalism is an economic system which arose in the sixteenth century and flourished in Western Europe, above all in England, as development shifted from commerce to industry. It is still, with modifications, the dominant economic system of the world, even as its industrial base adapts and includes the advances of modern technology in the production of wealth.

Primitive economic systems, if they can be called "systems," were based upon hunting and gathering and limited agriculture in which the output was distributed by well-defined social claims. There must be enough to keep all within the group at a certain level of subsistence. Economics could be viewed as a network of activities aimed at providing for the groups in the most efficient ways possible. Perhaps of necessity, it was communitarian both in "production" and in "distribution." The primitive economic system is often termed "tradition-based."

From the emergence of civilizations in Egypt, China, India, and other areas of the world, there developed a system of economic coordination controlled by the command and ordering of the ruler. Economic tasks were assigned by the ruling person or dominant elite. The surplus of production over consumption was used to build vast temple complexes, mammoth fortifications, magnificent palaces, beautiful cities and also roads and irrigation systems to further advance wealth through commerce and production. The "command-based" system produced monuments to glorify the rulers and to cater to their luxurious consumption of goods. "Command-based" economics was a reflection of the centralized structure of society in which the rulers determine the means of the production of wealth and its distribution.

Marketplaces for the exchange of goods have existed for at least 3,500 years. Goods were bought and sold. Profits were made. But the transformation of marketplaces to a market economy (or capitalism) in "tradition-based" or "command-based" societies did not take place until traditions broke down and imperial rule was challenged. The imperial Roman society had massive slavery at the bottom and the ruling elite at the top. Feudal society was composed primarily of serfs and lords. Medieval feudal society broke down as a market network and a merchant class emerged. Now there were workers, landlords, and capitalists. The rulers of empires or nations and the traditions of peoples, formerly the coordinators of economic activity, gave place to a system in which individuals were to fend for themselves to improve their material well-being. The market itself would coordinate production and distribution. Mercantilism is viewed as a forerunner of capitalism although even it was controlled to a large extent by government monopolies.

In 1776 Adam Smith's *An Inquiry into the Nature and Causes of the Wealth of Nations* appeared. It is the foundational work for the understanding of modern capitalism. Smith saw a world where the production and distribution of all goods and services were to be left to market forces; where the level of wages was to be determined by the supply of and demand for labor (labor becomes a commodity); and where free competition would determine not only profit but also survival.

Adam Smith's world would reduce the rule of government to three areas: (1) national defense, (2) the protection of one individual from the injustice or oppression of any other, and (3) public works and public institutions necessary for the maintenance of society. Capitalism was to be freed from state control and entrusted to the market mechanism which itself is driven by the universal compulsion for material acquisition or betterment (profit). The only regulator would be competition. Economic activity would be severed from political or governmental control, hence the term laissez-faire capitalism.

The industrial revolution which transformed production in the eighteenth and nineteenth centuries fed the capitalist system. Wealth expanded exponentially in the mechanized and industrialized world.

The human cost of laissez-faire capitalism was the exploitation of workers—a mere commodity in the economic formula—men, women, and children, who often worked twelve-hour shifts, seven-day weeks, in mines, mills, and factories, for pay which hardly afforded minimal subsistence. A second human cost was the economic instability of recurrent cycles of depressions and recessions which resulted in widespread unemployment, crippling insecurity, and massive poverty.

The Great Depression of the 1930s led to the growth of the governmental role in moderating economic activities. After World War II governmental expenditures in the industrialized world dramatically increased for social security, education, health care and welfare. The remains of Smith's laissez-faire capitalism are the free market economy, retaining competition and the drive for wealth, but now constrained by the claims of a great variety of institutions of both the private and the public sector.

The Church's relationship with capitalism has been ambivalent from its rise. Before Pope Leo XIII's *Rerum Novarum* (1891), various popes approved private ownership of both personal and productive property, in opposition to the various forms of socialism which were arising in Western Europe. At the same time they called for Christians to forsake the extravagance of wealth and to commit excess goods to the poor.

Rerum Novarum strongly affirms the private right to own productive property, a basic tenet of capitalism, but criticizes the problems arising from it: poor working conditions, long hours of work, unjust wages, working conditions unsuitable for women and children, the neglect of employees who are sick, and the lack of provision for old age. To address these abuses, it affirms the right of workers to organize into unions to attain just wages to allow them to live in "frugal comfort." It also attacks "unchecked competition" which promotes greed and leads to the accumulation of wealth in the hands of a few.

Pope Pius XI's *Quadragesimo Anno* (1931) again strongly condemns socialism and affirms private property, but at the same time allows for state ownership of property which carries with it too much power to be left in the hands of private individuals. Neither capital nor labor are to claim all the profits in an economic enterprise, but they are to be equitably shared because both are necessary for the production of wealth. He condemned the domination of the state by economic interests as harmful to the common good. Free competition is a good which must be kept within just and definite limits by governmental authority. In Pius XI there is a favoring of the capitalistic system but it must be called to task for its excesses.

Pope John XXIII's *Mater et Magistra* is far less sanguine in its approval of capitalism, but it does express a preference for "widespread" private ownership which must not forget the social function of ownership. He would favor even greater intervention of the state to prevent private exploitation, but at the same time he would affirm the need for private initiative and decry any political tyranny.

Pope John Paul II's *Sollicitudo Rei Socialis* (1987) calls to task communism for its repression of freedom and lust for domination and capitalism for its all-consuming desire for profit and power. The result is the suffering of vast numbers of people. In *Centesimus Annus* (1991), written after the fall of Communism in the Eastern European countries and Russia, he castigates Communism not so much for its economic failure as its degradation of human dignity and human rights. He affirms a responsible free market economy, but cautions against greed and exploitation which characterize unlimited capitalism.

The U.S. bishops in *Economic Justice for All* (1986) call for a partnership between private economic forces and government in developing a free enterprise economic system with a conscience.

The Church's magisterial position seems to favor a limited, democratic form of capitalism over other systems. It sees capitalism as offering freedom and encouraging initiative both in production and marketing. It sees limited capitalism more in keeping with the demands of human dignity. At the same time, it sternly condemns capitalism's excesses and the evils they have caused in the world. There is a reluctant acceptance of a moderate capitalism perhaps because there is no other more acceptable economic system on the horizon.

CHARLES D. SKOK

See also COMMUNISM; ENCYCLICALS, SOCIAL; SOCIAL TEACHING OF THE CHURCH; SOCIALISM.

CAPUCHINS, FRIARS MINOR

See FRANCISCANS.

CARAVAGGIO, MICHELANGELO MERISI DA (1571–1610)

Although Caravaggio (b. 1571) had little lasting effect in Italy (outside Naples), he is generally regarded as the greatest Italian painter of the seventeenth century. After an apprenticeship in Milan, he came to Rome soon after 1590 and worked for the Cavaliere d'Arpino and for Cardinal de Monte. His early works represent still life and the human body with searching clarity and a tendency toward the erotic. But from the time of his first commissions (from 1599 to 1601, *The Life of St. Matthew,* S. Luigi dei Francesi; *The Conversion of St. Paul* and *The Crucifixion of St. Peter,* S. Maria del Popolo), he applied his highly original style almost exclusively to religious subjects. His bold and realistic human figures move dramatically from dark shadow (*chiaro-*

"The Deposition," by Caravaggio, 1602–1604, Pinocoteca, Vatican

scuro). While there is great nobility of composition, the figures themselves often show the splendor of ordinary people.

In 1606 Caravaggio fled Rome for Naples after killing a man, producing several works in his city of refuge. Going on to Malta, he was welcomed by the Order of St. John. He continued to be driven by a violent temper while his art, exemplified by *The Beheading of St. John the Baptist,* grew ever more concentrated, expressive, contemplative. He fled to Sicily in 1608 (after committing an assault) and again to Naples, where he was seriously wounded in a bar fight. He died of fever in 1610.

While Caravaggio's influence was great in Italy, especially outside of Rome, his greatest impact was probably in the north of Europe, particularly on Rubens and Rembrandt.

DAVID BRYAN

See also ART, CHRISTIAN.

CARDINAL

The term (from the Latin: *cardo,* "hinge") signifies the key clergy of a particular Church, though it is now used only in reference to the Roman Church, and through it, to the Universal Church. The cardinals were originally the seven (later fourteen) deacons, the parish priests, and the suburbicarian bishops of Rome. The cardinals acquired the rank of Roman princes and principal advisors of the pope.

DAVID BRYAN

See also COLLEGE OF CARDINALS; CURIA, ROMAN; PAPACY, THE.

CARMEL, MOUNT

A mountain in northern Palestine near the present-day Mediterranean port city of Haifa. It was the place where Elijah rebuked the prophets of Baal (1 Kgs 18), and demonstrated to the people of Israel the supremacy of Yahweh. Around the year A.D. 500 a church and a monastery were built there, and this is now considered the founding site of the Carmelite Order.

JOSEPH QUINN

See also CARMELITES.

CARMELITES, THE

The members of the Order of Carmel, popularly known as Carmelites, are a family of contemplative religious, both women and men, who have a distinct charism combining prayer and action and who call themselves, by privilege, the brothers and sisters of Our Lady of Mount Carmel.

Called by the rule of their order to be always conscious of the presence of God and "in allegiance to Jesus Christ," Carmelites combine a life of prayer with an apostolate consonant with their hermit calling. By making accessible to others the way of contemplative prayer they enable spiritually impoverished people of our time to find strength and hope. Secondly, by promoting devotion to Our Lady, whose Carmelite Scapular they wear, they mirror the love and reverence Jesus showed his mother.

Carmelite history begins in biblical times when the prophet Elijah lived on Mount Carmel, located near Haifa. His rallying cry, "With zeal have I been zealous for the Lord God of hosts," is the motto of the Carmelites and Elijah is considered the model and founder of the solitary life. Elijah's "double spirit" was passed on to his successor, the prophet and hermit on Carmel, Elisha. Carmelites today still perform the double office of solitaries who have a public mission.

In its beginning Carmel was more discernibly what it remains today: a community of eremitical celibates called together by the Spirit of the risen Lord. About 1206 the hermits of Mount Carmel, who lived in caves but gathered for the Eucharist and for meals in common, were given a rule by St. Albert, then patriarch of Jerusalem, which codified their way of life. Within a few years, British crusaders brought to Europe these Carmelites who then became known as friars since the order was classed with the mendicants.

The Rule of St. Albert is the common origin of two basic traditions. Carmel was a single order until the mid-sixteenth century. Since the Spanish saints,

Teresa of Jesus [Avila] and John of the Cross, established the Reformed Carmel in 1562, they and their followers have been called Discalced Carmelites (O.C.D.) and those who continued in the older tradition are now known as the Order of Carmelites (O.Carm.).

Scores of congregations and some secular institutes whose constitutions are based on its Rule of St. Albert have been affiliated to Carmel. Most numerous of all, the Secular Carmelites, primarily lay men and women, joined to the order through public promises, live the charism in their homes and the workplace.

Among Carmel's saints and Blesseds are Sts. Albert and Simon Stock, Sts. Teresa and John Mary Magdalen de Pazzi, Thérèse de Lisieux, and Teresa Margaret Redi, the martyred nuns of Compiégne in the French Revolution, Bl. Elizabeth of the Trinity; three young nuns slain in the Spanish civil war of 1936–1939, Maria Pilar, Teresa, and Maria Angeles; Titus Brandsma and Edith Stein, victims of the Nazis in the 1940s; a young Arab, Mary of Jesus Crucified; the Polish-Lithuanian, St. Raphael Kalinowski, and youngest of all at nineteen, the first canonized native of Chile, St. Teresa of Jesus of the Andes (Juanita Fernandez Solar). Others in Spain, in India, and Madagascar are candidates for canonization. All are models for the Christian of the third millennium in the following of Christ by a life of prayer and service to the Church.

JOSEPHINE KOEPPEL, O.C.D.

See also CONTEMPLATIVE ORDERS; INSTITUTE, SECULAR; RELIGIOUS ORDERS; THIRD ORDERS.

CARR, HENRY (1880–1963)

In 1897 Henry Carr left his home in Oshawa to come to St. Michael's College in Toronto. In 1900 he entered the Basilian Fathers, a religious community of priests centered in Toronto and working, in his time, in Canada and the United States (they are now in France, Mexico, and Colombia as well).

Even before his ordination in 1905, he took a principal role in changing the traditional classical course, offered in St. Michael's and similar institutions in Canada up to this time, into a high-school program which would better qualify students for entrance into the university. He then moved to bring the college, which already had some relationship with the University of Toronto, into the position of a federated college in Arts. The first high-school class, which he taught personally, matriculated in 1906, and most of these students then went on to graduate from the University of Toronto in 1910 as the first group trained at St. Michael's. The patterns of St. Michael's would become models for Basilian institutions in Canada and the United States and for Catholic schools and colleges throughout Canada.

As superior of St. Michael's from 1915 to 1925, and as head of the philosophy department there in later years, Carr established the practice of bringing outstanding Catholic scholars to the college. Men of the caliber of de Wulf, Windle, Phelan, Belloc, Noël, Gilson, Longpré, and Maritain came to teach there. Etienne Gilson, who first came in 1927, recognized the significant development achieved under Carr's leadership and proposed the establishment of a research and teaching institute which would study the Christian Middle Ages. When the Institute for Mediaeval Studies was established in 1929, Henry Carr became its first president, with Gilson as director of studies. Carr would continue as president of the Institute until 1935, even after his election as superior general of the Basilian Fathers.

As superior general from 1930 to 1942, Carr made relations with the Holy See a first emphasis. He brought the constitutions of the Basilians into shape to receive definitive approval from Rome in 1938. In the following year he was able to have the Institute of Mediaeval Studies designated as a Pontifical Institute, the only one, at that time, outside of Rome itself. Continuing to move along the paths he had pioneered, he greatly furthered the work of Basilians in high schools. During his time in office, the proportion of Basilians involved in this work increased from about 39 percent (36 men) in 1930–1931 to just under 50 percent (86 men) in 1941–1942. He also encouraged young Basilians to seek degrees which would enable them to work in the highest levels of scholarship. The first two were sent to Europe in 1930, and by 1934–1935 the list read: V. L. Kennedy, Rome; A. J. Denomy, Harvard; G. B. Flahiff, Paris; J. R. O'Donnell, Paris; L. A. McCann, Rome; T. V. Kennedy, Rome. Finally, he broadened the Basilian apostolate, which had been limited to schools, colleges and parishes, by undertaking work with the Mexican immigrants in Texas. This would eventually lead to the activity of the community in Mexico itself and in Colombia.

One of the basic ingredients in all that Father Carr undertook was his genius for friendship. He always insisted that friendship was vital in relations both within and without the Church. "Insist on rights," he said, "and you will get what you deserve—nothing. But act as a friend and be a friend among friends and the most cumbersome legal machinery will roll smoothly on." This lay behind his successes in working closely with secular universities in Toronto, in Saskatoon, and in Vancouver. From 1942 to 1949 he headed St. Thomas More College, a federated Arts college in the University of Saskatchewan. Moving to Vancouver in 1951, he began (at seventy-one years of age) a new career teaching in the University of British Columbia, and in 1956 became the first principal of St. Mark's College in affiliation with U.B.C. He died in Vancouver on 28 November 1963.

J. HANRAHAN, C.S.B.

See also CANADA, THE CATHOLIC CHURCH IN.

CARROLL, CHARLES (1737–1832)

Born in 1737, Carroll was a revolutionary leader, signer of the Declaration of Independence, and United States Senator. He began his education with the Jesuits in Maryland and for six years in the College de St. Omer in French Flanders. He continued his studies at Bruges and Paris and completed his legal studies in London. At the age of twenty-eight he returned to Maryland, and lived as a gentleman farmer but, as a Catholic, was debarred from political activity.

He favored and ardently promoted the separation of the American Colonies from England. Even though he was not a member of Congress at the time, he was chosen with Samuel Chase and Benjamin Franklin to visit Canada in February 1776 to promote a union between Canada and the Colonies. It was a doomed undertaking from the beginning. On 4 July he was elected a delegate to the Continental Congress, voted for the adoption of the Declaration of Independence on 19 July, and signed it on 2 August.

From then on, Carroll was prominent in Maryland politics and in the Continental Congress. He served in Congress from 1776 to 1778. He represented Maryland as a senator in the first Federal Congress (1789–1792). After 1800 he devoted himself mostly to family affairs and to the development of his estates in Maryland, Pennsylvania, and New York. Carroll, like his cousin Bishop John Carroll, was a firm believer in the separation of Church and state; and both were aware that what was viable in Europe was not feasible in America. When he died on 14 November, 1832, he was the wealthiest citizen of the United States and the last surviving signer of the Declaration of Independence.

JOAN GLAZIER

See also AMERICAN CATHOLICISM.

CARROLL, JOHN (1735–1815)

First Catholic bishop in the United States, born in Upper Marlboro, Maryland, on 8 January 1735, died in Baltimore on 3 December 1815, Carroll was the third of seven children of Daniel Carroll, an Irish immigrant, and of Eleanor Darnall, a French-educated woman whose family belonged to the Anglo-American Catholic gentry of Maryland. After initial schooling at home and at Bohemia Manor (a short-lived Jesuit school on the Eastern Shore), in 1748 at the age of thirteen Carroll left for France where he continued his education at St. Omer, a Jesuit college which had educated the sons of the English Catholic gentry since Elizabethan times.

In 1753 Carroll joined the Society of Jesus as a novice and spent most of the following twenty years as a student and then as a teacher at Jesuit houses in the Austrian Netherlands. Upon suppression of the Society of Jesus in 1773, Carroll left for England, then returned to America in 1774 after an absence of twenty-six years and took up residence at his mother's house in Rock Creek, Maryland. During the American Revolution, Carroll supported the patriot cause and, at the request of the Continental Congress, in 1776 he traveled to Montreal together with his cousin Charles, Benjamin Franklin, and Samuel Chase in a vain effort to persuade the French-Canadians to join the American side.

American independence created new problems and new opportunities for Catholics in the former colonies. The two dozen clergy (all ex-Jesuits) had ceased to have any corporate existence after the suppression of the Society of Jesus in 1773, and, after 1783, the vicar apostolic of the London District declined responsibility for the American missions. In an effort to organize the American clergy and to protect their property, Carroll devised a Constitution of the Clergy, the so-called "Whitemarsh Constitution," which was adopted by the American priests in 1784. At the same time the American clergy asked Rome to appoint as their leader Father John Lewis, the last Jesuit superior.

Instead, on the recommendation of Benjamin Franklin, in 1784 Rome appointed Carroll Superior of the Mission, the equivalent of a prefect apostolic. The following year Carroll sent to Rome the first offical report from the American Church. He estimated the number of Catholics as twenty-five thousand, one percent of the total population. For the next six years, as Carroll struggled to govern the nascent American Church, he came to see the need for episcopal authority. Earlier, he and most of the clergy had feared that the appointment of a bishop would provoke anti-Catholic bigotry. Now, the decline in prejudice against Catholics, and the need to confront unruly priests and lay trustees, persuaded the American clergy that the time was ripe for normal Church government. Consequently in 1788 they

Bishop John Carroll

petitioned Rome for the right to nominate a bishop and to select his see city. The following year Pope Pius VI granted both requests, and confirmed the appointment of John Carroll as first bishop of Baltimore.

The papal bull *Ex Hac Apostolicae* of 6 November 1789, erecting the Diocese of Baltimore, marks the formal beginning of the American hierarchy. Carroll himself was ordained a bishop on 15 August 1790, at Lulworth Chapel in England. Upon his return to the United States, to govern a diocese which included the whole country, Carroll held a synod in Baltimore in 1791 which issued the first canonical regulations for the new republic.

At Carroll's request, in 1808, Pope Pius VII established four new American dioceses in Boston, New York, Philadelphia and Bardstown, Kentucky, and he elevated Baltimore to the status of an archdiocese. In the meantime, the Louisiana Purchase of 1803 left Carroll with jurisdiction over the vast territory between the Mississippi and the Rocky Mountains until the appointment of an apostolic administrator in 1812.

One of Carroll's primary concerns was Catholic education. He supported the foundation of Georgetown College (1788), St. Mary's Seminary in Baltimore (1791), Visitation Academy (1799), St. Mary's College in Baltimore (1799), and Mount St. Mary's at Emmitsburg (1808). In the latter year Carroll encouraged Elizabeth Ann Seton to open a school for girls in Baltimore and later supported her efforts to establish a distinctively American community of sisters.

Throughout his episcopate Carroll was plagued by the presence in his diocese of eccentric and disreputable priests (most of them Irish)—"the wandering clerical fraternity," as he called them. They sometimes joined forces with the lay trustees of a local congregation to oust the legitimate pastor and thus to challenge episcopal authority directly. Such confrontations became especially bitter when they also involved ethnic antagonisms between priests and trustees of different nationalities. In both Norfolk, Virginia, and Charleston, South Carolina, Carroll faced protracted struggles with "lay trusteeism," which he left unresolved for his successors.

Historian James Hennesey, S.J., once described John Carroll as an "eighteenth-century bishop." His piety was of a solid and undemonstrative type which had little in common with the devotional romanticism of the nineteenth century. Likewise, Carroll's ecclesiology harkened back to a more restrained view of papal authority than the emotional ultramontanism of subsequent decades. Although Carroll never advocated an "independent" American Catholic Church, there can be little doubt that he became more conservative as he grew older. His earlier enthusiasm for a vernacular liturgy waned, and his plans for involving the local Church in the selection of bishops never got off the ground; likewise, his desire to afford the laity a role in Church affairs became less and less of a reality.

However, Carroll never faltered in his commitment to the American experiment in religious liberty and freedom of conscience. He embodied the enlightened principles of the Maryland Catholic colonial tradition and transposed them into the new world of the Immigrant Church.

THOMAS J. SHELLEY

See also AMERICAN CATHOLICISM; CATHOLIC HIGHER EDUCATION IN THE UNITED STATES; SOCIETY OF JESUS.

CARTHUSIANS

A religious order of great austerity dedicated exclusively to the contemplative life, the Carthusians were founded by St. Bruno in 1084 in the Chartreuse Mountains, a lonely branch of the French Alps. Remaining for the most part in their private cells, and dedicated to silence, the Carthusians follow a life similar to that of the early desert monks of Egypt and Syria while actually living together in a monastery and adapting much of the spirit of the Rule of St. Benedict. Their means to contemplation include renunciation of the world, solitude, mortification, working alone, and mental prayer. They meet together only for the Liturgy of the Hours and Mass, though, on the great religious festivals, they also share a meal. Once a week they walk together out-of-doors for a few hours and enjoy conversation. The rule of the Carthusians was approved by Innocent II in 1133 and has received but slight alteration to the present day. In medieval times their growth was enormous, and their example a powerful force for reform. The Carthusians were ejected from their first house, the Grande Chartreuse, at the French Revolution and made particular targets of persecution. Again driven from their home in 1901, when the anticlerical party came to power in France, they returned to the Grande Chartreuse in 1940. Their sole American foundation is on a high shoulder of Mount Equinox in Vermont. There are a few houses of nuns who also live the rule of Chartreuse.

DAVID BRYAN

See also CONTEMPLATION; MONK.

CASSOCK

(Ital. *casacca,* "overcoat") The ankle-length robe worn by Catholic clerics. The standard cassock for priests is black, though priests serving in tropical countries often wear white garb. Cassocks worn by bishops are purple, while those of cardinals are red and the pontiff's is white.

JOSEPH QUINN

See also VESTMENTS, LITURGICAL.

CASUISTRY

The intellectual process of applying moral principles to particular cases (Latin: *casus*). The term is used pejoratively when practitioners of casuistry argue a point too finely in order to arrive at a solution desired in advance.

DAVID BRYAN

See also THEOLOGY, MORAL.

CATACOMBS

The proper name of one underground cemetery, *Catacumbas,* on the *Via Appia* (now called San Sebastiano), became a generic name for the others after the eighth century because it was one of the few which continued to be known and visited after the others fell into disuse. The Latin *cymba* (from the Greek *kumbe*) means small boat; *Catacumbas* may get its name from an inn nearby called after a skiff.

Underground cemeteries were made possible due to a type of subsoil called *tufa granolare* produced in prehistoric times by volcanic activity around Rome. This *tufa* was strong, porous, and easily pliable—

Catacombs of S. Priscilla, Rome

perfect for underground burial grounds. Catacombs are also found in Naples, Sicily, Malta, North Africa and elsewhere.

Burying underground was due either to the fact that the surface had been used up for graves or because underground burial chambers (*hypogea*) had to be enlarged.

Since burial within the walls was forbidden by the Law of the Twelve Tablets (451 B.C.) these cemeteries are located along the main roads outside the walls.

Burial was by inhumation, a practice Christians inherited from the Jews. The corpse was placed in a rectangular opening carved out of the side of a corridor wall or room and was sealed with a marble slab or bricks covered with plaster and these were often decorated with inscriptions or frescoes—the beginning of Christian art. Unlike other ancient peoples Christians were not buried with precious mementos to the chagrin of the barbarian grave robbers who wreacked much damage on these graves.

Burials and even the ornamentation of tombs was due to the *fossor* (digger) who was a lesser cleric in charge of this corporal work of mercy.

The catacombs begin about A.D. 150 on the property of wealthy individual Christians. The property and administration passes to the Church as such around A.D. 200. How the Church acquired property at a time when Christians had no civil rights and were still persecuted is not clear but was due probably to the grace of the Roman government rather than to any law. Such catacombs were known to Roman authorities and therefore not useful for hiding. Because of their small chambers they were not normally the place to celebrate a community Eucharist. Though Christians were persecuted, their graves were protected by Roman law.

With the Peace of Constantine (313) the catacombs continued to be used up to ca. 450. After that time no more burials took place there but the tombs of the martyrs were still visited.

A period of decline began after 450 due to barbarian invasions and the subsequent translations of the bodies of the martyrs into Rome. Catacombs were occasionally stumbled upon but evoked no serious interest till the sixteenth century. Antonio Bosio (1576–1629) located many of the lost catacombs and left careful records of what he explored. Much of the early excavation and discoveries were marred by apologetic concerns and romantic ideas. A really scientific period begins in the nineteenth century with the work of G. B. de Rossi, the Father of Christian Archeology, who supplied scientific method and principles.

The art and inscriptions attest to a faith in eternal life and in the resurrection of the body.

The principal catacombs are Priscilla and Domitilla (begun before 150), and Callistus (ca. 200). All the lost catacombs have been found except one. There are thirty-five catacombs for Rome alone.

PAUL L. CIOFFI, S.J.

CATECHESIS

The word *catechesis* is rooted in the Greek verb *katechein,* to resound or to echo. In the New Testament the verb means formation in the way of the Lord, oral instruction, and a handing on of all that has been received in and through Christ. In the first centuries of Christianity catechesis centered on preparation for initiation into the Christian community within the catechumenate, i.e., the community of adults learning to become Christians. Catechesis took place in stages. It consisted of prebaptismal instruction that focused on God's action throughout history, on catechesis in and through the liturgy, and finally a postbaptismal catechesis (mystagogy) that was a reflection on the sacramental experience in terms of the Christian life. The goal of catechesis was conversion and growth in faith, expressed in worship and manifested in Christian life and witness. The conversion process was supported by the life, prayer, and witness of the Christian community.

When the catechumenate declined in the fourth and fifth centuries, catechesis shifted from adult initiation to infant baptism, from prebaptismal to postbaptismal instruction and from a biblical and liturgical context to a formation derived primarily from a Christian environment. Until the end of the fifteenth century catechesis remained oral and experiential but with the invention of the printing press and the proliferation of catechisms, catechesis was reduced to instruction, to memorization, and to children until the mid-twentieth century.

Vatican II, in defining catechesis as a ministry of the word placed both the word and its early meaning within the context of the Church's pastoral ministry. The *Decree on the Pastoral Office of Bishops in the Church* in 1965 (no. 14) states that the purpose of catechesis is to develop in believers, "a living, explicit and active faith enlightened by instruction." Throughout subsequent Church documents such as the 1971 *General Catechetical Directory* (GCD), the *Rite of Christian Initiation of Adults* (RCIA) in 1972, the 1977 Apostolic exhortation of John Paul II, *Catechesis in Our Time* (CT), and the *Code of Canon Law* in 1983, certain common understandings of catechesis emerge. Catechesis is a form of ecclesial action which leads both communities and individual members of the faithful to maturity of faith (GCD, no. 21). Catechesis is the responsibility of the whole community since faith is nurtured through the experience of Christian life (c. 773). The ultimate goal is conversion, a formation in faith that finds expression in a life lived in charity. Catechesis is a lifelong endeavor that is adapted to the age, ability and culture of the believer. It takes on varied forms and structures (GCD, no. 19) and is systematic or occasional. Catechesis involves four interrelated tasks: to proclaim the gospel message; to build up the community; to lead to prayer and worship; and to promote peace and justice. Catechesis continually aims to integrate liturgy, service, and the formation of community with the proclamation of the message in the process of catechesis.

CATHERINE DOOLEY, O.P.

See also CATECHETICS; CATECHISM; RELIGIOUS EDUCATION.

CATECHETICS

Catechetics is the systematic study of the history, nature, goals, principles, and process of catechesis. Catechetics is an interdisciplinary field drawing upon sources such as theology, biblical studies, learning theory, and social science for the development of norms and criteria to evaluate its activity. Catechetics and catechesis are often used interchangeably but catechesis is a pastoral ministry directed to conversion of life while catechetics is the objective analysis and critique of the process of catechesis.

An early treatise on catechetics is St. Augustine's *First Catechetical Instruction* which outines the nature and principles of catechesis and offers a practical methodology. Formal works on catechetics, however, began to appear only with the eighteenth-century Enlightenment. In the twentieth century catechetics emerged as an academic discipline when reflection on catechesis raised the issue of methodology and the need to find a more effective approach than memorization of catechism question and answer. Focus on method shifted to a more wholistic integration of method and message. More recent discussion centers on catechesis in the context of pastoral ministry.

Some of the first institutions of higher education which responded to the need for an academic study of catechetics at the graduate level were Lumen Vitae in Brussels (1946), Institut Supérieur Catéchétique in Paris (1951), The Catholic University of America (1937), University of San Francisco and Fordham University in the United States.

Professional organizations like the interdominational Association of Professors and Researchers in Religious Education (APRRE) and professional journals such as *Lumen Vitae, The Living Light, Sower, Catéchèse,* and *Catequesis Latinoamericana* contribute to ongoing discussion and development of catechetics.

CATHERINE DOOLEY, O.P.

See also CATECHESIS; CATECHISM; RELIGIOUS EDUCATION.

CATECHISM

The catechism is a concise summary of Christian doctrine usually written in question and answer format for easy memorization. The major divisions of the catechism are Creed, Sacraments, Commandments, and Prayer but the sequence of these elements will be arranged according to the theological approach of the author. With the invention of the printing press, catechisms, both Catholic and Protestant, proliferated and became the principal text for Christian education in most Church traditions over the centuries.

The following are a few of the most representative and influential.

The German Catechism (1529) and the *Small Catechism* (1529) of Martin Luther (1483–1546) popularized the method of question and answer. The *Small Catechism* for children and the uneducated, first published on posters, was unique in its ordering (Commandments, Creed, Lord's Prayer, baptism, confession and sacrament of the altar which reflected Luther's understanding of salvation), its arrangement of the creed in three articles instead of twelve, and the inclusion of woodcut illustrations. The *German Catechism* for pastors was based on Luther's own sermons and indicated how the catechism could be applied to the needs of the people.

The Heidelberg Catechism (1563) synthesized Reformed doctrine. The 129 questions considered the misery of the human person (exposed by the divine law); redemption of humankind (creed, justification, baptism, the Lord's Supper, and office of the keys), and the gratitude of humankind (commandments and prayer).

Catholic authors also successfully adopted the catechism genre. In Germany, St. Peter Canisius (1521–1597) produced three catechisms between 1555 and 1559: the large catechism for clergy; a brief one for children and a middle-sized text for youth. The sequence of the Canisian Catechisms is faith, hope, charity, the commandments of God and of the Church, the sacraments and Christian justice.

St. Robert Bellarmine's (1542–1621) catechism was widely used in Italy. The framework for the text is basically that of St. Augustine's treatise, *Faith, Hope and Charity*: those things a Christian must believe (the creed); must hope for (Lord's Prayer) and must do (commandments) to which Bellarmine adds a section on sacraments, the means to a Christian life. The catechism was suggested as a model for the universal catechism proposed at Vatican Council I (1870).

The Catechism of the Council of Trent for the Clergy (1566), popularly called the Roman Catechism, is a summary of Catholic doctrine written in expository prose for the use of the clergy in preaching and catechesis. It emphasized the importance of sacraments for Christian doctrine and life in its ordering of faith and the creed, sacraments, commandments and the Our Father.

Catechism of the Third Plenary Council of Baltimore (1885) and subsequent revisions was a standard sourcebook of Catholic doctrine in the United States for about seventy-five years.

Catechism of the Catholic Church (1993) is a compendium of Christian doctrine for bishops and all who are responsible for catechesis. The text is written in narrative form and has four main parts: the Apostles Creed (faith professed); the Sacraments (faith celebrated); virtues, beatitudes and commandments (faith lived); and prayer, particularly the Lord's Prayer (faith prayed).

CATHERINE DOOLEY, O.P.

See also BALTIMORE CATECHISM; CATECHESIS; CATECHETICS; REFORMATION, THE.

CATECHISM OF THE CATHOLIC CHURCH, THE

On 8 December 1993 Pope John Paul II presented the *Catechism of the Catholic Church* to the faithful in an official ceremony. It appears with an introduction from the Pope, an apostolic constitution, *Fidei Depositum,* which traces its origin and evolution. Requested by the Episcopal Synod of 1985, it was entrusted by the Pope to a commission of twelve cardinals and bishops, presided over by Cardinal Joseph Ratzinger, Prefect of the Congregation for the Doctrine of the Faith. Seven diocesan bishops (experts in catechetics) collaborated. In a central position was a gifted Austrian theologian, Christoph von Schönborn, O.P., now auxiliary bishop of Vienna. The collaboration of episcopates worldwide and of catechetical institutes was sought as the text went through nine successive revisions. The result of these labors is a remarkable achievement in providing a summary of Christian doctrine, as we see it, since Vatican II.

The plan differs from that of some well-known similar works, the Dutch Catechism issued by the episcopate of that country after the council, and quite recently the Catechism for Adults put out by the French bishops, and a similar work by the German hierarchy, these two in close collaboration with Roman authorities. The groundplan here is the four pillars: "the baptismal profession of faith, the sacraments of faith, the life of faith (the Commandments) and the prayer of the believer (the Our Father)." This distribution of materials has been quite flexible and has allowed for the inclusion of all the best insights of Catholic theology before and since Vatican II.

Thus, the first large section affords an opportunity to deal with problems arising in regard to faith, divine revelation, original sin, Christology, the theology of Mary, the Holy Spirit, and a number of themes which form the challenge of Christianity to the modern mind. The section on worship brings out splendidly the whole fresh and vital understanding of the liturgy. The treatment of the Eucharist, "source and summit of ecclesial life," is fully developed and admirable. Here, as throughout, there is a balance and depth of exposition, taking account of manifold mystery. Likewise in the treatment of Christian morality, the dignity of the human person is highlighted. The framework of the *Pater Noster,* taken as a special light on prayer, is rich and deeply suggestive of true piety.

The whole work benefits by the improved methodology in theological studies which preceded Vatican II, the revival of patristic studies, especially in France, Belgium, and the United States, the immense advance in biblical studies following Pius XII's encyclical, *Divino Afflante Spiritu,* and the importance attached to the history of theology. This is reflected in the ample use of sources, biblical, patristic, conciliar, papal (twenty-one popes are cited or mentioned), writings of saints, and liturgical, not excluding the Orientals. On the technical side the disposition of materials, regular summaries, and exhaustive indexes make this a most useful instrument of work. It is not a Roman imposition; it came out of the whole Church. The half million readers who, within five months, bought the first available translation, the French, indicate a special response.

MICHAEL O'CARROLL, C.S.Sp.

See also CATHOLICISM; VATICAN COUNCIL II.

CATECHUMENATE

The catechumenate is a formation process of unspecified length for those adults seeking incorporation into the Christian community. During this process the catechumen studies and prays with two groups. The first group consists of other adults who are also seeking the faith. The second group is made up of members of the faith community who assist the catechumen in his or her quest.

The catechumenate certainly existed in the Church prior to the First Council of Nicea (325). The period could last from several months to years. During this time the catechumen sought to grow in the Christian way of life. At the same time members of the community collaborated with the catechumen to effect this new way of life. Prayer, fasting, and rituals were regular elements in this formation process during which the catechumen and the community discerned the fittingness for incorporation into the Church.

Vatican II called for the restoration of the catechumenate, i.e., the Rite of Christian Initiation of Adults (RCIA). In 1974 the English translation of the rite appeared for use in the United States. The RCIA is broken down into four time periods and involves three transitional rites.

The first period is the precatechumenate. Its purpose is to promote conversion by means of evangelization. Once the person experiences initial conversion, the first transitional rite takes place, viz., the acceptance into the order of catechumens. The person thereby becomes a member of the Church as a catechumen.

The second and usually the longest period is the formation of the catechumen in the Christian way of life through catechesis. Catechesis involves, in addition to classroom study of doctrines, participation in the life of the believing community, particularly through the Sunday Liturgy of the Word, and involvement in the community's apostolic thrust. When the candidate has experienced a conversion in mind and action, the second transitional rite occurs, viz., election. This rite usually takes place around the beginning of Lent. Through it the Church acknowledges that God has selected the candidate for full initiation into its midst at the time of the Easter Vigil.

The third period is that of enlightenment and purification during the season of Lent with the community celebration of the scrutinies on the third, fourth, and fifth Sundays. The scrutinies are prayers begging healing and forgiveness for the elect (the new title of the catechumen). The third and most important transitional rite occurs at the Easter Vigil when the elect are fully incorporated into the Church as members of the order of the faithful through baptism, confirmation, and Eucharist.

The fourth period is the period of reflection by these new members of the Church during the fifty days of Easter. Together with the community these newly initiated members of the Church continue reflection on the significance of the Easter Vigil by participating in the Eucharist, meditating on the gospel, and engaging in works of charity.

JOHN F. CRAGHAN

See also CATECHESIS; EVANGELIZATION; SACRAMENTS OF INITIATION.

CATHARISM

See HERESY/HERETICS.

CATHEDRAL

(Lat. *cathedra,* "chair") The central church of a diocese, so named because it is the bishop's official "seat," or church, in which he is consecrated and,

St. Patrick's Cathedral, New York City

traditionally, where he ordains, confirms, and celebrates the liturgy of the Sacred Triduum. According to Church custom, cathedrals must be consecrated, and they are usually located in the principal city of the diocese. The cathedrals of Notre Dame in Paris, Chartre (also in France), and Hagia Sophia in Istanbul, Turkey, are among the world's most prominent works of architecture.

The first cathedral built in the United States was the Basilica of the Assumption in Baltimore, Maryland, established in 1790. Other historically and architecturally notable cathedrals in the U.S. are St. Patrick's Cathedral in New York City, St. Matthew's in Washington, D.C., and the Basilica-Cathedral of Saints Peter and Paul in Philadelphia, Pennsylvania.

JOSEPH QUINN

See also ARCHITECTURE, CHURCH; BISHOP.

CATHERINE OF SIENA (1347–1380)

Catherine (Caterina) of Siena was born in 1347, a twin and twenty-fourth of the twenty-five children of Lapa di Puccio Piacenti and the Sienese wool-dyer Giacomo (or Iacopo) di Benincasa. After a visionary experience early in childhood she adopted an increasingly fierce asceticism, and determined never to marry so that she might belong entirely to God. In her late teens she won entry into the lay Third Order of St. Dominic (up to then composed only of widows) and plunged into almost total seclusion in her parents' home. But when she was about twenty years old, her prayer led her to the realization that her love for God could no longer be divorced from service to others, a dramatic conversion. From work with the poor and sick of the city, her influence soon began to extend to civic and ecclesiastical spheres as the power of her personality and her gift for conciliation were recognized. Disciples, many her seniors and superior to her in education and status, were attracted to her circle. She found an ideal mentor, intellectually, spiritually, and politically, in the Dominican Raymond of Capua, who in 1374 was appointed by the Dominican Order (later confirmed by the pope) to be her confessor and the director of her public activities. In partnership with him she became deeply involved in attempts to mediate and resolve the growing tensions and rifts between the republics of the Italian peninsula and the papacy then resident in Avignon. Because these tensions, though basically political, threatened the unity of the Church, they represented for Catherine a religious crisis in which she felt compelled repeatedly to intervene. Her efforts took her to Pisa, Lucca, Florence, and eventually Avignon, where in 1376 she overcame the hesitancy of Pope Gregory XI to return with his curia to Rome. However, her own political naiveté when Raymond was not actually at her side often complicated matters, a realization that was a great psychological burden to her.

Catherine passionately promoted Gregory's projected crusade against the Turks, convinced that such a venture would not only unite the rebellious republics with the Pope in a common defense of Christian lands but would also bring converted Muslims into the Church as a leaven of needed reform.

"St. Catherine of Siena," detail, by Francisco Vanni, 16th century

After Gregory's death on 27 March 1378, a tumultuous election brought to the papal throne Urban VI, whose violent ways soon caused the majority of the cardinals to disavow him and elect an antipope, Clement VII, thus effecting the Great Western Schism. Catherine, however, vehemently supported Urban's legitimacy, even while urging him to moderation. At his invitation she moved with a number of her disciples to Rome for this cause in November 1378. By this time her health was failing under her relentless activity and asceticism. (Her early extremes of fasting had led to an inability to eat normally, which she regretted but was unable to reverse.) In addition, the apparent failure of her dearest exertions became a crushing weight which she felt even physically. Still she continued to preach and write, pray and fast in defense of the Church's unity until she was totally disabled early in 1380. She died on 29 April of that year.

Though unschooled, Catherine had learned to read during her years of solitude. Some time later she probably learned to write, but she almost always found dictation a more efficient vehicle for her prolific mind. Several of her disciples served as her scribes, and to them we owe the preservation of her letters, a book, and a collection of her prayers.

From the early 1370s until very near her death Catherine used letters prodigiously for counseling and to influence others in favor of her causes. Three hundred eighty-two of these letters have been discovered and published to date, addressed to a remarkably wide variety of her contemporaries: two popes, several cardinals and bishops, two kings and two queens, numerous lesser public officials, her religious and lay associates, her family and friends and disciples, and an assortment of others, including allies and opponents, a mercenary captain, a prostitute, a homosexual, and the prisoners of Siena. Unfortunately, the early compilers' purposes of edification and sometimes reasons of confidentiality led them to delete much of the personal content from the letters. But even so abridged they provide a window onto Catherine's evolving thought and personality and onto the history and culture of her age. They bear a particular added interest because her activity extended so far beyond the normal feminine bounds of her time and her status in Church and society.

During an eleven-month period in 1377 and 1378, in addition to her missions of mediation, Catherine composed a book since known as *The Dialogue* (because she cast it as a conversation with God). Her intent in writing it was to share with her disciples and others the insights into Christian life that she had gained from her prayer and experience.

Finally, during the last few years of Catherine's life, her scribes often recorded her words as she spoke aloud in ecstasy. Twenty-six such prayers have been preserved.

Though Catherine does not add any really new link to the theological tradition in terms of content, she does bring a refreshing new synthesis that is strongly pastoral. Always her intent is to exhort, to encourage, to instruct. She resorts for clarification not so often to conceptual argumentation as to everyday images, developing each over the years and interweaving them one with another. Hers is a theology that finds its source as much in experience and common sense as in the preaching she heard and the books she read. Catherine was canonized in 1461. In 1939 she was proclaimed patron of Italy with St. Francis of Assisi. In 1970 Pope Paul VI named her Doctor of the Church, a title she and Teresa of Avila are so far the only women to bear.

SUZANNE NOFFKE, O.P.

See also AVIGNON PAPACY; DOMINICANS; GREAT WESTERN SCHISM; WOMEN IN THE CHURCH.

CATHOLIC ACTION

On 30 March 1930, Pope Pius XI announced the official organization of Catholic Action, a spiritual and apostolic movement for laity which started in Italy. Eventually, under the personal direction and support of Pius XI, the movement spread to other countries around the Mediterranean. Basically, Catholic Action was the international organizing and consolidation of corporate and ecclesiastically recognized apostolic initiatives undertaken by laity throughout the world. It was one of the first great modern lay apostolic movements and gradually drew members from all over the world.

Catholic Action never claimed any monopoly on lay apostolic actions; other individuals and groups were free to foster their own approaches to encourage laity to be involved in the mission of the Church. What Catholic Action did was to give official recognition to some lay activities by granting a mandate to those who belonged. The implication was that Jesus entrusted his mission and ministry to his apostles, and the bishops as their successors shared their mission and ministry with laity who became instruments in the hands of the hierarchy extending their ministerial influence.

The Vatican Council discussed the possibility of extending the concept of Catholic Action, but decided to leave local Churches to foster lay ministry and dedication in ways they saw most appropriate for the local Church. The Synod on Laity (1987) suggested some kind of international organization of lay activities to attempt to consolidate the many lay movements that have developed since the council. This would not be a return to Catholic Action, since the theology of laity has now changed and the Church no longer sees laity as instrumental in the hierarchy's ministry but rather acknowledges they have specific ministry responsibilities of their own for the benefit of the whole Church.

LEONARD DOOHAN

See also CHURCH, THE; LAITY, THEOLOGY OF THE; MINISTRY.

CATHOLIC CHURCH IN AFRICA

See AFRICA, THE CATHOLIC CHURCH IN.

CATHOLIC CHURCH IN CANADA

See CANADA, THE CATHOLIC CHURCH IN.

CATHOLIC EMANCIPATION

See EMANCIPATION, CATHOLIC.

CATHOLIC HIGHER EDUCATION IN THE UNITED STATES

Catholic higher education is the term used in the United States to include research universities, four-year colleges and universities and two-year colleges. In 1993 there were 222 all together, serving some 620,000 students. (All data on the current state of Catholic higher education are taken from the Association of Catholic Colleges and Universities publication *Catholic Higher Education, an American Profile, 1993.*) These institutions were founded by various religious communities of men and women as well as by some dioceses; today, most of them have an independent legal status and are governed by boards of trustees which are predominantly lay.

In the main, they were extensions of high schools or academies and prep schools. With the exception of The Catholic University of America, they were all originally concerned with teaching young men or women as undergraduates. The history of these institutions parallels the development of American higher education in general. Because the United States has never had a Ministry of Education and, for the most part, has regarded education as a matter of state rather than federal regulation, the colleges and universities are answerable to fifty-one different state departments of education. There are no national examinations or assignments to places in the universities on the basis of such examinations. Instead there is a wide diversity: of some 3200 institutions, about half are state universities or community colleges (i.e., public) and about half are independent (i.e., private). Of the independent sector, some 800 are still Church-related to some degree, and, of that number, 222 are affiliated with the Roman Catholic Church. About 5 percent of these are research/doctoral universities; 10 percent are two-year colleges, and the rest are almost equally divided between liberal arts and comprehensive institutions.

The historical focus on young people meant that up until the end of the 1960s there was as much attention given to character formation as to intellectual growth and development of individuals—at least in the Catholic colleges. Today nationally over 50 percent of the students are "adult learners"—men and women over twenty-two when they begin their undergraduate studies. In our Catholic institutions the percentage in a recent survey was 36 percent. Thus, in both undergraduate and graduate programs the mix of students provides a campus culture of great variety in age as well as in race and ethnic background.

The Catholic colleges, as private independent institutions, are eligible for federal funding for student scholarships, loans, and other special programs. In some states they also receive low-interest loans for construction and/or direct institutional grants to help with the operating budget. These institutions are heavily dependent on the tuition which students pay, and so their leaders are constantly busy with an area of life unknown in other parts of the world—i.e., fundraising. Generally, Catholic colleges and universities do not receive financial support from the diocese in which they are located because whatever educational funding is available goes to the maintenance of elementary and secondary schools which are the direct responsibility of parish and diocese. Higher education, on the other hand, has traditionally been supported by the Church only to the extent of financial underwriting by the founding and/or sponsoring religious community, and the generosity of Catholic donors and individual bishops and priests.

From the beginning, the curriculum of the colleges was built on a solid foundation of liberal arts even as it attempted to meet the vocational needs of students. Preprofessional and professional education on the undergraduate level enabled the colleges to attract students to their classrooms who might otherwise have gone to state colleges. This was a major concern in the pre-Vatican II days when separate Catholic neighborhoods and organizations created a truly "Catholic" culture, and bishops worried about young people going too far away from it. Higher education in secular universities was considered a necessary evil in some instances but it was not to be considered a desirable place for young Catholics. However, the emphasis on ecumenism and a more positive view of the relationship between faith and the modern world articulated by Vatican Council II changed this attitude, leaving Catholic colleges and universities as only one option among many for the new generation. The tremendous changes in American society wrought by the civil rights movement, Vietnam, and the growing globalization of economics and politics also had an effect. Catholic colleges, in encouraging their students to participate in the various social movements, introduced them to the wider world of higher education. They now met with and came to know better the students and faculties in secular universities, finding common cause as they became involved in freedom rides and various antiwar activities.

At the same time, Catholic colleges and universities were judged eligible for most federal and state student aid programs provided they met the test of "independent" control. By 1970 most of them had an interest in becoming competitive with the institutions outside of the Catholic cohort, knowing that to do so would require higher academic standards and significantly improved financial resources. The move to independent boards of trustees, the stretching toward fellowships and faculty research grants, the switch from single-sex to coeducation by many of them, and the hiring of faculty from non-Catholic universities combined to make them less distinctive and more acculturated to American university life. The more they strove for educational goals that were identical with those of secular institutions, the more they were questioned about their own distinctiveness as Catholic colleges and universities.

The primary role of the Catholic university, as most recently emphasized by Pope John Paul II, is to mediate faith and culture. The development of highly credentialed faculties in the arts, the social sciences, and the natural sciences is essential for an understanding of cultures; in addition, the disciplines of theology and philosophy are seen as necessary partners in the dialogue by which the faith can be mediated to the culture. In 1990 the Apostolic Constitution, *Ex Corde Ecclesiae,* focused attention on this role of the Catholic University and challenged those responsible for the institutions to attend to the promotion of such dialogue.

Most of the Catholic colleges and universities in the United States do not have juridical bonds with episcopal authorities. Nevertheless, they are seen as an important part of the Church community, the place where the Church can do much of its serious and critical thinking. The education received in these many diverse institutions has provided the Church in America with thousands of leaders, both lay and religious, and has, at the same time, given the Church a voice within the higher education community in this country. Since 1899 the Catholic colleges and universities have had their own organization for the purpose of coordinating their actions, but they have also become increasingly visible leaders in the wider community of higher education. The diversity which they represent remains an important challenge to all institutions of higher learning for they are places where conversations involving insights based on religious faith suggest questions for the faculty in all disciplines, and debates on such issues can be carried on without embarrassment. In turn, the scientific and artistic currents in modern thought can enrich theological and philosophical speculation when the atmosphere is cordial and free.

Catholic higher education in the United States has benefitted from the absence of a centralized national educational program. It has been challenged by the achievements of other private and public institutions of higher learning in this country. Despite the many problems that all the colleges and universities have to face today, American institutions of higher learning remain one of the greatest educational ventures in the world. As part of this unique company, Catholic universities continue to search for the ways and means of fulfilling their role as both "university" and "Catholic."

ALICE GALLIN, O.S.U.

See also AMERICAN CATHOLICISM; EDUCATION, PHILOSOPHY OF.

CATHOLIC RELIEF SERVICES (CRS)

Catholic Relief Services is the overseas aid agency of the U.S. Catholic Conference. Its earliest forerunner was the Catholic Committee for Refugees and Refugee Children established prior to World War II by the bishops of the U.S. at the request of German bishops for the purpose of aiding refugees from Nazi persecution. In 1942, the bishops established War Relief Services—NCWC to promote and administer direct relief activities in Europe. The bishops launched special fund-raising appeals to provide support for the overseas relief, rehabilitation and resettlement programs of the War Relief Services. By 1955, it was evident that the programs of the War Relief Services were needed on a permanent basis in countries around the world. Consequently, the organization was renamed the Catholic Relief Services. By the 1960s, it had begun to expand its programs into Africa, Asia, and Latin America. The initial activities of CRS were restricted to emergency aid for victims of war, but the agency's current long-range policy is to work toward eradicating the root causes of hunger and abject poverty.

PATRICIA DeFERRARI

See also AMERICAN CATHOLICISM; NATIONAL CATHOLIC WELFARE CONFERENCE (NCWC).

CATHOLIC WORKER MOVEMENT

The Catholic Worker Movement, founded in 1933 by Peter Maurin and Dorothy Day, began as a newspaper "for the Catholic unemployed," and grew into a movement for nonviolent social change, based on gentle personalism.

Peter Maurin was born in 1877 to a farming family in the Languedoc region of France. He was educated by the Christian Brothers and became involved in Le Sillon, France's lay Catholic movement. He emigrated to North America in 1909, and worked as a homesteader, teacher, and itinerant laborer.

Dorothy Day was born in 1897, and came from a family of journalists. She wrote for the Socialist paper, *The Call,* and *The Masses,* covering strikes, poverty, and the struggle of women to get the vote. After the birth of her daughter in 1927, she converted to Catholicism, as she recounts in her autobiography, *The Long Loneliness.*

Dorothy Day's editor at *Commonweal* sent Peter Maurin to meet her, and he explained his synthesis of "cult, culture and cultivation." His points on faith, culture and "The green revolution," were written in free-form verse, called *Easy Essays.* Peter Maurin brought together the theories of radical thinkers with the teachings of the Church. He rejected both capitalism and state communism in forging a philosophy "so old it looks like new."

The first issue of *The Catholic Worker* was published on New York's Lower East Side 1 May 1933, and sold at a penny a copy to unemployed workers in Union Square. Issues through the years carried stories on strikes, poverty, racism, nonviolent campaigns and spiritual values, as well as columns from various houses and farms around the country.

As Peter Maurin wrote in *The Catholic Worker:* "The Catholic Worker believes in the Gentle Personalism of Traditional Catholicism. The Catholic Worker believes in the personal obligation of looking after the needs of our brother and sister. The Catholic Worker believes in the daily practice of the Works of Mercy. The Catholic Worker believes in Houses of Hospitality for the immediate relief of those who are in need. The Catholic Worker believes in the establishment of farming communes where each one works according to their ability and gets according to their need. The Catholic Worker believes in creating a new society within the shell of the old."

Peter Maurin had a three-part program of action. First, clarification of thought, through the newspaper and roundtable discussions. Second, the immediate relief of poverty through the practice of the works of mercy, with houses run in the same manner as hospices staffed by the clergy in the Middle Ages. These houses were to be operated on the parish level, at a personal sacrifice. The final part of Peter Maurin's plan was farm colonies or "agronomic universities," for a return to the land, manual labor, and self-support. The workers would become scholars and the scholars would become workers.

Houses were established around the country during the Depression. The number of houses has ebbed and flowed through the years, and now there are farms and houses around the U.S., Canada, and in other countries as well.

The houses are not run on any overall plan, but in response to local need. The movement is decentralist, and work is done on the local level, out of a sense of personal responsibility. Catholic Workers live in voluntary poverty, because, as Dorothy Day wrote, "By embracing voluntary poverty, that is, by casting our lot freely with those whose impoverishment is not a choice, we would ask for the Grace to abandon ourselves to the Love of others."

Seeing nonviolence as the way to bring about a personalist revolution, the Catholic Worker rejects violence and is opposed to war. This stand was difficult to maintain during the Spanish Civil War, and during World War II some houses closed rather than call themselves pacifist. But other Catholic Workers opposed the draft and war, and spoke out against militarism. Catholic Workers today are involved in resistance to nuclear weapons and military intervention around the world.

Along with the rejection of violence, the Catholic Worker advocates refusal to pay war taxes, because of the direct link between the huge sums of money spent on the military and the destitution of millions of people.

Catholic Workers generally take no money from government or institutions, but rather depend for support from individuals. Some Catholic Workers also support themselves with cottage industries, in the spirit of Peter Maurin's call to manual labor and rejection of technology. In the same spirit of decentralism, the Catholic Worker supports cooperatives, land trusts, worker owned businesses and homesteads.

These ideals can only be brought about through a life of faith, so above all else, in all it does, the Catholic Worker believes in the primacy of the spiritual. Inspiration comes from the Scriptures, the life and teachings of Christ, the teachings and sacraments of the Church and the spiritual weapons of fasting and prayer.

JENNIFER BELISLE

See also DAY, DOROTHY; MAURIN, PETER; PACIFISM; SOCIALISM.

CATHOLICISM

"Catholicism" refers to a particular experience of Christianity shared by Christians in Churches living in communion with the Church of Rome. In this sense, Catholicism involves a common heritage of faith and doctrine, life and worship, authority and ecclesial structure. In a broader sense, Catholicism is sometimes understood as including other Churches such as the Orthodox and those of the Anglican communion which share to a significant degree in the Catholic tradition.

The Greek adjective *katholikos,* meaning general, total, or universal, was first applied to the Church in the sense of the whole or universal Church by Ignatius of Antioch in his letter to the Smyrnaeans traditionally dated around the year A.D. 110. Ignatius wrote: "Wherever the bishop is, there his people should be, just as, where Jesus Christ is, there is the catholic church." Ignatius was arguing that just as Christ is the head and center of the whole Church, so the bishop is the head and center of the local congregation.

But as early as the third and fourth centuries the word catholic was being used more polemically to distinguish the great or true Church from heretical groups or movements separate from it. Augustine (d. 430), listing the true Church's characteristics, universal consent, authority, a succession in the priesthood from the seat of Peter, refers finally to "the name 'catholic' itself, which not without reason amid so many heresies, only this one Church has retained, so that, although all the heretics would like to be called 'catholics,' not one of them would dare answer a stranger's questions as to where the Catholic Church meets by pointing to his own basilica or house" (*Contra ep. Manichaei* 4,5; PL 42:175).

Augustine also contributed to the emergence of a third meaning of the word catholic; in the controversy with the Donatists the *ecclesia catholica* was understood geographically as referring to the Church spread throughout the whole world. Thus the word catholic has meant the Church in its fullness or totality; it has been used polemically for the true Church, and it has had a geographical or universal sense, for the Church present everywhere. Cyril of Jerusalem (d. 387) brought together several senses of the word when he described the Church as catholic because it extends to the ends of the earth, teaches all the doctrines necessary for salvation, instructs all peoples, heals every kind of sin, and possesses every virtue (*Catecheses,* 18).

But the Church has not been able to maintain unity and communion with all those who profess Christian faith, and so its catholicity has been diminished. After the division between the Eastern and Western Churches in 1054, the Churches of the East became known as "Orthodox," a word which had been used particularly in the East to describe those Churches which remained faithful to the teachings of the councils of Ephesus and Chalcedon. The Western Churches living in communion with and increasingly under the pope of Rome continued to be known as the Catholic Church, though its unity suffered a further loss through the sixteenth-century Reformation which gave birth to the Protestant Churches. After the sixteenth century it has become increasingly common to add "Roman" to the word Catholic, though that Church continues to refer to itself in its official documents simply as the Catholic Church. But with Christianity in fact divided, catholicity cannot belong only to Catholicism. The Catholic Church in its total membership constitutes roughly half of all Christians. Still, according to Catholic teaching, there is a fullness of catholicity which belongs to it (UR 4), even if there are elements of catholicity present in other Churches.

What then does it mean to be Catholic? It means first of all an inherently ecclesial way of experiencing Christian faith. The Church for Catholics can never be merely a sociologically understood religious institution. It has rather a deeply mystical, sacramental dimension, mediating for and through its members the mysterious divine presence. From at least the second century the Church has been described in maternal imagery because of its nurturing character, bringing men and women to new birth through baptism, instructing them through the word, drawing them to a deeper life in Christ through the sacraments.

A list of those things that Catholics would take for granted as characteristic of their tradition, though not always unique to it, would have to include the following: a sense for the historical uniqueness of their Church, a reverence for tradition, a hierarchical ministry and teaching authority, an incarnational theology, sacramentality, a strong liturgical tradition centered on the Eucharist, Mariology and the veneration of the saints, a rich tradition of spirituality and contemplative prayer, monasticism, religious orders, an appreciation of the religious value of art, a deep sense for the complementarity of faith and reason, a communal understanding of both sin and redemption, and thus, of the importance of community, a social doctrine based on the dignity of the human person, a commitment to missionary activity, and of course, the papacy. We will consider Catholicism in terms of its emphasis on mediating symbols and structures, its universality, and its comprehensiveness. Finally we will take a brief look at contemporary Catholicism.

Symbols and Structures of Catholicism

Catholicism means finding God's presence through an historical community of faith mediated by symbols and institutional structures which are understood as expressions of the fullness of the Church. At the root of this appreciation for symbol and structure is the doctrine of the incarnation so basic to the Catholic tradition, and hence, a sense for the divine immanence in creation. While it is necessary to use the language of both transcendence and immanence in speaking of God, an incarnational perspective stresses that in Jesus God has entered definitively into space and time and human history. This emphasis in turn grounds the sacramental principle, the view that the invisible divine presence is mediated by or disclosed through created realities and symbols. Knowledge of God is always a mediated knowledge; God is not experienced directly, in some kind of spiritual inwardness or personal revelation. Though it has a strong mystical tradition and recognizes the possibility of visions, Catholicism tends to be suspicious of an overly privatized faith experience; it has always emphasized the social and communal dimensions of faith carried by a living tradition and mediated by religious symbols, sacramental actions, and the structures of a Church which has developed historically from the communities of primitive Christianity.

Catholicism is not an otherworldly religion; it does not disdain the material world but sees in it traces of the divine. The Catholic imagination is sacramental. Compare the differences between the interiors of a typical Protestant and Catholic church. Catholics adorn their homes and institutions with religious art. Their churches are rich in sacred images, statues, crucifixes, and stained glass. Holy water fonts flank the doors and a red lamp burns before the tabernacle. Catholic liturgies, with processions, lighted candles, incense, sacred music, and vested ministers, appeal unabashedly to the senses. Bishops and popes dress in attire and symbols centuries old. Catholic devotional life has frequently taken over symbols, customs, feasts, and rituals from the cultures in which the life of the Church has become inculturated. Religious feasts and holidays celebrate the mysteries in the life of the Virgin Mary and the example of the saints.

The sacraments are ritual actions which make God's grace visible symbolically in the life of the community, sharing new life in the Spirit of Jesus, proclaiming the forgiveness of sins, healing the sick, celebrating faithful love in marriage and the presence of the risen Jesus in the Eucharist. The Eucharist stands at the very center of the Catholic tradition; the Catholic imagination has been deeply shaped by the experience of communion with the Lord and with one another in the breaking of the bread and the sharing of the cup. As the locus of these sacramental actions, the Church itself is a sacramental expression of the presence of Christ in the midst of the people gathered in his name.

Protestant Christians, nurtured in a tradition which stresses the sovereign freedom and transcendence of God, the one mediatorship of Christ, and the primacy of the word, are often suspicious of this Catholic emphasis on symbol, ritual, and the sacramental nature of the Church. They are even more skeptical about the importance Catholics attach to institutional structures such as apostolic succession, episcopal office, a teaching magisterium, and papal ministry. For many Protestants, following Calvin, the true Church is an invisible gathering of the elect. For Catholics the Church is always a visible, historical reality which has been maintained in its catholicity and apostolicity through its institutional structures.

Apostolic succession, the requirement that candidates for the episcopal office be admitted by those who have already been received into it themselves, makes visible the link between the Church and its ministry today and the original apostolic Church and ministry. Similarly, the bonds of communion (*koinonia*) uniting the members of the episcopal college with each other and with the pope, the Bishop of Rome, express and maintain institutionally the union of their Churches in the Catholic Church. The Church's official teaching office or magisterium, constituted by the bishops and pope together, protects the apostolic tradition by enabling the Church's faith to come to official expression. Though the magisterium cannot function independently of the whole Church, it teaches with authority (ordinary magisterium) and in certain limited circumstances can proclaim the faith of the Church infallibly, that is, without error (extraordinary magisterium). The papal ministry presides over the communion of the Church, symbolizing and safeguarding its unity. The preservation of the deposit of apostolic faith, ministry, and sacraments is an important dimension of the claim of catholicity.

Universality

Being a Catholic means having a sense for the universality of the Church. The Church cannot be reduced to the local congregation or to the sum of all the particular churches, but neither can it be a single, worldwide, monolithic institution. The *ecclesia catholica* means both the fullness of the Church as well as the communion of churches. The papacy, Catholicism's most obvious symbol, is not something derived from a particular church; according to the Second Vatican Council it belongs to the fullness of the Church (LG 14).

The catholicity of the Church is not just spatial or geographical; catholicity implies an inclusiveness towards Church membership. As a sign of reconciliation and communion in Christ, the Church must embrace all peoples, classes, races, and cultures as its birth on the feast of Pentecost suggests (Acts 2:5-11). From the earliest days, infant children of believing parents have been baptized into the Church. Today it is true that infant baptism is sometimes practiced indiscriminately in mainline Churches, Catholic and Protestant; this is a practice that needs some reexamination. But it is perfectly appropriate to baptize children when there is a Christian home, a "domestic church," in which they will be raised. The Church on earth also includes both saints and sinners. Protestant theology, again following Calvin, has sometimes held that the true Church consists only of the just or elect. Catholicism has stressed that the Church includes within itself all humanity, saints and sinners, rich and poor. The Catholic Church is a world Church. It is interesting to note that at the Extraordinary Synod of Bishops which met in Rome in 1985, 74 percent of the bishops came from countries other than those in Europe or North America.

The catholicity of the Church is also temporal. The Church embraces not just the baptized on earth, but the faithful departed as well. The doctrine of the communion of saints expresses the belief that those in the Church on earth enjoy some kind of fellowship with all those who have died in the Lord, the "saints," canonized or not, the holy ones of the Old Testament, and the souls in purgatory. The doctrine of purgatory grounds the Catholic practice of praying for the dead (cf. 2 Macc 12:44); it refers to the purification to be undergone for the "temporal punishment" due to sins already forgiven, in other words, for the damaging effects of sin. Whether that purification takes place here or hereafter is a matter of speculation.

Neither praying for the dead nor invoking the intercession of the saints has been understood by Protestant Christians; they do not find either practice warranted by the Bible. Furthermore, Protestants fear that invoking the saints might compromise the one mediatorship of Christ. But calling on the saints has been part of the Christian tradition since at least the third century, with roots that may go back to the middle of the second. As a practice which has its origin in the faith experience of Christian peoples over the centuries, the invocation of the saints remains today, particularly in certain cultures, very much a part of a popular religion which the Church has been willing to accept as part of the inculturation of the faith. At the same time, it has tried to guard, not always successfully, against the aberrations into which popular religion can descend. The honor and devotion shown for Mary, the mother of Jesus, holds a special place in the Catholic tradition. Mariology arises out of the interplay of imagination, popular faith experience, and theological reflection; imagination led to contemplation, to veneration, and to prayer. The Marian dogmas represent examples of doctrinal development within the Catholic Church rooted in the faith experience of Christian people over the centuries.

Comprehensiveness
The catholicity of the Church grounds Catholicism's appreciation for the comprehensive character of truth. The Greek *katholikos* originally meant whole or entire, as opposed to that which is partial or particular. Catholicism also has this comprehensive character; it is open to all truth. It is not the product of a single reformer or historical movement in post-New Testament Christian history. It does not find its identity in a single doctrine, confession, liturgical text, or theory of biblical interpretation. Thus it is able to include within itself a wide variety of theologies, spiritualities, and expressions of the Christian life. Catholicism is pluralistic in its approach to truth. Where the Reformation in the sixteenth century followed an "either/or" approach, Catholicism prefers to say "both/and." Not Scripture alone (*sola scriptura*), but Scripture and tradition, not grace alone (*sola gratia*), but grace and nature, not faith alone (*sola fide*), but faith and works.

Catholicism has a deep respect for what is referred to simply as tradition (as opposed to traditions). This is more than a respect for what is ancient. Tradition represents the faith experience of the Church, discerned, received, lived, and handed on; that tradition comes to official expression in the canonical Scriptures, in the creeds, the sacraments and liturgy of the Church, and in the teachings of the magisterium. The Scriptures are themselves a product of tradition; they are normative expression of the faith of the primitive Christian communities, and they remain today the norm for Christian faith and doctrine. At the same time, Scripture continues to be interpreted within the living tradition of the Church through the instrumentality of the magisterium. Tradition is never static; it is at once a normative and a dynamic reality which embraces the sense of the faithful (*sensus fidelium*), the scholarly work of theologians, the witness of various prophetic voices, and the pastoral leadership of the bishops.

Catholicism's both/and approach is evident in its theological anthropology. Protestant anthropology, heavily influenced by Augustine's theology and by Luther's soteriological interests, is pessimistic. Protestantism sees human nature after the Fall as totally corrupt. The image of God has been lost. Since the will was seen as being in a state of bondage, incapable of choosing good, any human cooperation with grace was denied. Justification through faith is entirely God's work; the merits of Christ are "imputed" to us, sin is covered over, not taken away. The Calvinist doctrine of predestination is an extreme form of this pessimism. Similarly, for the Reformers the intellect was blinded by sin, unable to know anything of God apart from Scripture. Luther, devoted to a "theology of the cross" (*theologia crucis*), emphasized what God has accomplished through the death of Christ; he rejected any kind of philosophical theology as a species of the forbidden "theology of glory" (*theologia gloriae*). Thus the emphasis on faith alone and grace alone. Without a sense for the complementarity of faith and reason and dependent on a Scripture principle which ultimately collapsed, undermined by the Enlightenment in the eighteenth century and the triumph of the historical-critical method in the nineteenth, Protestant theology has frequently been left with the alternatives of a philosophical rationalism or biblical fundamentalism.

While Catholic theology has not been entirely free of a similar pessimism regarding nature after the Fall, particularly when it has been influenced by Jansenism, its own theological anthropology is more optimistic. Because of the incarnation human nature is always graced nature; nature is damaged but not radically corrupted by original sin. Justification is God's work, but human freedom is always involved because persons must cooperate with God's grace. Justification is not merely a juridical act, nature is genuinely transformed by grace, the Johannine theology of the divine indwelling is taken seriously. There is no real discrepancy between faith and reason. Enlightened by faith, reason is able to ground the act of faith and attain a deeper understanding of faith's mysteries. Recognizing that truth is one, Catholic thinkers from the Scholastic theologians of the medieval universities to the systematic theologians of today have sought to integrate their faith with the knowledge that comes from philosophy and the sciences. The natural law tradition in Catholic philosophical ethics and moral theology reflects this confidence in the complementarity of faith and reason.

Thus Catholicism in principle is open to all truth, to whatever is genuinely human or naturally good. Even if the Church has occasionally inhibited the work of scientists who challenged what was understood as Church doctrine, it recognizes that science and the arts can also lead to God. The body is seen as sacred; rather than being opposed to spirit, it is the medium through which spirit expresses itself. The Spirit of God is active in all creation. In the twentieth century Catholic theology has increasingly returned to the patristic notion that human nature is intrinsically ordered towards the divine, and to a recognition of elements of divine truth in other world religions, without denying that the fullness of truth is revealed in Christ.

Catholicism's comprehensive approach to truth can also be seen in its ability to embrace and incorporate diverse expressions of Christian faith and life within a single Church. In the history of the Church various communities quite distinct in charism, spirituality, and mission have emerged; some of them, developing in the context of potentially divisive movements such as the monastic movement in the early Church or the evangelical awakening in the twelfth and thirteen centuries, might themselves have become schismatic. But in finding ways to accommodate these diverse communities within the Church, Catholicism has been able to provide for their members a way of living out their own particular vision of the Christian life. From these communities have come the different religious orders, some monastic and contemplative, others gathered for ministry. Their inclusion has enriched the Church with a number of different spiritualities, Benedictine, Franciscan, Ignatian, and nourished a long tradition of contemplative prayer. Other examples of this ability to preserve ecclesial unity while embracing diversity would include the Eastern Rite Catholic Churches, Eastern Churches with their own liturgical and canonical traditions living in communion with Rome, as well as the existence of numerous lay communities today such as the Catholic Worker, l'Arche, the charismatic covenant communities, and the Basic Christian Communities popular in many Third World countries.

Contemporary Catholicism

The Second Vatican Council (1962–1965), called by Pope John XXIII, initiated a process of renewal for Catholicism which will carry the Church into the third millennium. The debating and voting on the various documents which became the council's decrees took place on the floor of the Basilica of St. Peter's where the council "fathers," the 2,500 bishops and heads of the religious orders of men, were seated. But much of the real business of the council took place in the conference rooms, restaurants, and bars of Rome where innumerable conversations took place between the different groups gathered for the council, bishops meeting with one another, with their *periti* or theological advisors, with representatives of the Protestant and Orthodox Churches invited by Pope John, and with scholars and journalists. In occasionally reversing previously held positions, even positions taught by popes, the council illustrated the dynamic character of Catholicism. The sixteen documents which emerged from the council established the guidelines for Church renewal, still unfinished, in a number of areas.

Church Renewal. The Dogmatic Constitution on the Church (*Lumen Gentium*) represents an attempt to articulate a contemporary self-understanding of the Church which stands in marked contrast to the clerical and monarchical ecclesiology of nineteenth- and early twentieth-century Catholicism, often symbolized by a pyramid in which all authority descends from the top down. Among its most important teachings: chapter II described the Church as the People of God equipped with a diversity of gifts, both hierarchical and charismatic. Chapter III developed a collegial understanding of the episcopal office. Bishops are not to be understood as vicars of the pope, but as heads of local Churches; together with the pope, they have supreme authority over the Church and share in its infallible teaching office. The Church itself thus becomes a communion of Churches, as it understood itself in the first millennium, rather than a single, monolithic institution. Chapter IV turned to a theology of the laity, stressing that lay men and women share in the mission of the Church and in the threefold office of Christ as prophet, priest, and king. From this emphasis was to come the multiplicity of lay ministries in the postconciliar Church, and a new involvement of lay men and women in the Church's task of theological reflection.

Ecumenism. The Roman Catholic Church had been suspicious of the ecumenical movement since its beginning early in the twentieth century; Pope Pius XI in *Mortalium Animos* (1928) had forbidden Catholic participation, fearing that it would lead to an ecclesial relativism. Reversing this stance, Vatican II firmly committed the Catholic Church to the search for Christian unity. While the council understands the Catholic Church as a realization of the Church of Christ in its essential completeness or fullness (LG 14), it implies that the Church of Christ is also present in other Churches and ecclesial communities in various ways and recognizes that Christians from these Churches and ecclesial communities are already in an imperfect communion with one another through baptism. The Decree on Ecumenism (*Unitatis Redintegratio*) outlines the principles for Roman Catholic ecumenical involvement, encouraging personal conversion, dialogue between traditions, and joint prayer services, though it was more cautious about common worship (UR 8).

Religious Liberty. Again reversing previous papal teaching, the Decree of Religious Freedom (*Dignitatis Humanae*) proclaimed that human beings have a right to religious liberty, to worship freely according to the dictates of their consciences, rooted in their dignity as human persons (DH 4).

Social Justice. Perhaps the most significant shift represented by the Council was the turn towards the world, and especially, towards the poor. From its opening sentence, the Decree on the Church in the Modern World (*Gaudium et Spes*) called attention to the plight of the poor and the afflicted. In addition to stressing that great efforts had to be made to satisfy the demands of justice and equity (GS 66) and calling Christians to a new level of concern for the poor (GS 69), the decree addressed the subjects of marriage and the family, including the concept of responsible parenthood, the development of culture, the right of all to participate in political life, and the question of war and the arms race. *Gaudium et Spes* was to help inspire a host of contemporary socially conscious religious movements, among them, Latin American liberation theology, indigenous theologies in Africa and Asia, feminist theology, and the pastoral letters of the American bishops on peace and economic justice. But its roots are to be found in a rich tradition of Catholic social teaching which includes over the centuries thinkers such as Augustine, Aquinas, Suarez, von Ketteler, Maritain, and John Courtney Murray, as well as a tradition of papal social encyclicals reaching back over the last hundred years. From Leo XIII's *Rerum Novarum* (1891) on the rights of the working man, these social encyclicals have expanded in focus to embrace issues of development and economic justice between nations, technology and the arms race, the widening gap between the rich and the poor, and a critique of both communism and capitalism. At the heart of this social teaching and grounding its prolife stance is Catholicism's profound conviction of the preeminent value of every human person created in the image of God (GS 12).

The council began a process of renewal of ecclesial structures and life that remains unfinished. Efforts have been made to develop a less centralized, more collegial style of government, using instruments of collegiality, some new, others already in place. Episcopal conferences have led to much greater cooperation between bishops of a given country or region. Some have been particularly successful, such as the Latin American Episcopal Conference (CELAM), through its meetings at Medellín (1968), Puebla (1979), and Santo Domingo (1992), or the National Conference of Catholic Bishops (NCCB) of the U.S.A., with its pastoral letters, *The Challenge of Peace* (1983) and *Economic Justice for All* (1986), widely acclaimed both as teaching documents and because of the wide consultation which went into their preparation. Other efforts such as the international synod of bishops which serves in an advisory capacity to the pope could become more effective instruments. Contemporary Catholicism also faces many questions having to do with how authority is exercised in the Church. Many Catholics today find a growing disagreement between Church leaders and the laity on questions such as birth control, divorce and remarriage, clerical celibacy, and the ordination of women. They want to see the Church develop a more participatory style of government which would give lay men and women some say in the Church's decision-making processes, in the formulation of Church teaching, and in the selection of its leaders.

If Catholicism is understood as a tradition which expresses the fullness or completeness of the Church, both substantively and in terms of its extension, its catholicity is not yet fully realized. There are still millions of people in the world who have not heard the gospel and the body of Christ is still divided into Churches not in communion with each other. Thus the agenda for the future of Catholicism must include the carrying through of the renewal of its own structures of authority and governance which will make possible the inclusion of non-Roman Catholic communities as particular Churches into a more inclusive, more truly Catholic communion.

THOMAS P. RAUSCH, S.J.

See also ECCLESIOLOGY; ECUMENISM; MARKS (OR NOTES) OF THE CHURCH; VATICAN COUNCIL II.

CATHOLICISM, IRISH

Christianity was comparatively late in coming to Ireland. The principal reason for this was the fact that the island had never been incorporated into the Roman Empire. Nevertheless, the Irish did have links with the world of Rome, with Roman Britain in particular, by way of trading and raiding.

Through these contacts the first of the Irish became Christians. With one exception—St. Patrick—the process is undocumented. However, a number of figures venerated as founders of churches in the south and east of Ireland have traditionally been regarded as "pre-Patrician." The reality behind this tradition is almost certainly that they worked independently of Patrick, possibly but not necessarily before him.

Patrick remains unquestionably the greatest of the founding figures, but there is a growing agreement among historians that his mission was directed to the north and west of Ireland. The two short writings of his that have survived make best sense when read against this hypothesis. However, they provide neither dates nor places, and the annals record Patrick's death at various dates between 457 and 493.

Patrick may have been the last as well as the greatest of the missionaries. The transition to a Christian society was more gradual than legend depicted, but there is no evidence of violent resistance, and by the second half of the sixth century a confident Christian Church had emerged as social leader. Because the Western Roman Empire had dissolved into chaos, Irish Christianity established itself in great isolation, and in consequence adapted itself to a considerable degree to the patterns of civil society. The most distinctive feature of this society was that it was based on the extended kin group rather than on territorially-defined units. In consequence, the territorial ecclesiastical units of diocese and parish remained weak, while the strong unit was the monastery because it was more closely linked to the kin group.

This "monastic church" had many glories at a time which was elswhere truly "the Dark Ages"—in scholarship, book illumination, metalwork, architecture, and in the fearless missionaries it sent to a Europe ruled by terrible kings and even more terrible queens. Its internal weakness arose from the fact that it was too closely associated with civil power structures, so that it was all too easy for a monastery to become wealthy and just one unit among warring principalities. Externally, it suffered from the raiding Norsemen, who began their attacks in 795.

By the twelfth century the glories of the Irish monastic Church were over. The papacy had emerged from its problems as leader of a general movement of reform. This reform was established in Ireland by a number of saintly figures, the greatest being St. Malachy of Armagh. His main achievements were to restore the diocesan episcopate, introduce the Cistercians, and revitalize the older monastic centers by having them accept the Rule of the Augustinian Canons. This work was completed at the Synod of Kells in 1152, but before it could establish itself it was disrupted by the Norman invasion in 1169.

Everywhere except in Ireland the Normans brought centralized government. The island was so fragmented that complete conquest was difficult, and it was marginal to the interests of the Plantagenet kings of England. It settled down as a country of two cultures, Gaelic and Norman, with a Church *inter Hiberno* and a Church *inter Anglos.* The division was real even if inevitably a bit blurred at the edges, and it certainly did not lessen the problems that built up in Ireland as elsewhere in the later Middle Ages. When the Reformation came in the sixteenth century there was indeed much to reform.

In Ireland as in England the Reformation was initiated by "the King in Parliament." In Ireland, parliament meant the Anglo-Norman population to the exclusion of the Gaelic one. There appears to have been little opposition to accepting Henry VIII as Supreme Head of the Church in 1536. Opposition found a focus when the Mass was replaced by the Prayer Book Service in the reign of his successor, Edward VI. By now, Gaelic Ireland was beginning to face a war of conquest that escalated into genocide, and ended in the great land confiscations in Munster and Ulster. Yet by the 1570s there was in both Anglo-Norman and Gaelic Ireland a new generation, lay and cleric, quite consciously Counter-Reformation Catholic.

The Gaelic world was finally conquered in 1603, and finally despoiled shortly afterwards. The Anglo-Norman community, now firmly Catholic, still held its property and expected to retain the political power so closely associated with property. Seventeenth-century political thought had no answer to the dilemma of those who wished to give loyalty both to the pope and to a king who claimed supreme ecclesiastical authority. The "Old English," as this group now called itself, were crushed in disastrous wars in the middle of the seventeenth century, and in turn had their property confiscated.

The Irish were the only European people not to follow the religion of their civil ruler. The political and economic consequences had been disastrous. Yet the sheer weight of Catholic numbers made it possible to organize the Church on a diocesan and territorial basis. The diocesan Church drew further strength from the fact that its semi-furtive existence gave it something of the flexibility of a missionary Church, with—something not envisaged by Trent—a religious observance that was home-based to a degree quite unparalleled in Catholic Europe.

After the great confiscations Catholics in Ireland were, by and large, allowed to practice their religion provided they accepted the degradation that went with it. But they lived dangerously, priests and laity. The "Popish Plot" of 1678, fabricated to exclude the Catholic Duke of York from succession to the throne, saw the martyrdom of St. Oliver Plunkett. Yet laws designed to force out the Catholic clergy at the beginning of the eighteenth century were only very sporadically enforced. What the laity had most to fear for was what landed property remained to them, and in the eighteenth-century penal code it was only these laws against Catholic property that were really pressed home.

For a number of reasons it became possible to contemplate the repeal of the penal code towards the end of the eighteenth century. The laws against religious practice were repealed easily enough, for they had long been ignored; the laws against Catholic education with a little more reluctance; laws against Catholics acquiring land even more reluctantly, but in the end they too went. But there was a stubborn refusal to give political power to the Catholics, specifically the right to sit in parliament, even after the

Act of Union in 1800 had merged the Irish parliament into that of the United Kingdom at Westminster.

An Irish Catholic middle class had emerged from the Penal Code, its money for the most part made in commerce, its politics radical. However, had it got the right to enter parliament in 1800, it might well have blended into the British parliamentary scene. As it was, this right was not granted for thirty years, during which the Irish Catholics, led by Daniel O'Connell, developed the first formidable democratic movement in Europe. Priests and especially bishops became prominent in politics, because the political issue was seen as religious, because the clergy had emerged from the Penal Code as natural leaders, and because at the beginning the Church had the only effective organization in the country.

The Great Famine at mid-century naturally bore hardest on the Irish-speaking poor. After it, what has been called "the nation-forming class" consisted predominantly of peasant farmers, increasingly English-speaking, developing a rigorous religious observance that owed at least as much to a determination to preserve the family farm intact as to any precepts inculcated by the clergy, though these, under the leadership of the formidable Paul Cardinal Cullen, did develop a more anxious morality.

When Irish independence was achieved in 1921, land purchase had created a peasant proprietorship. The drive for separate statehood had come to be so closely associated with the Catholic religion and a commitment to revive the Irish language that the Protestant northeast successfully asserted a right to opt out. The Irish Free State (now the Republic of Ireland) was 95 percent Catholic, and it was inevitable that a Catholic ethos should dominate public life. This was encapsulated in the Constitution enacted in 1937, where a liberal idea was grounded in Catholic moral and social teaching.

It was only to be expected that such a society should be deeply disturbed by the great changes that began to show themselves in the 1960s, when the Catholic Church that emerged from the Second Vatican Council seemed more hesitant in its answers, and the questions were increasingly posed by an aggressive materialism. A radical challenge to what had been seen as the twin pillars of the nation, the Catholic religion and the Irish language, necessarily left a certain void of uncertainty.

PATRICK J. CORISH

CATHOLICITY

See MARKS (OR NOTES) OF THE CHURCH.

CATHOLICS IN POLITICS

Politics, according to a standard dictionary definition, is the art or science of government, and this, though simplified, will serve here, provided two things are kept in mind. First, the description may apply to regional or local as well as national government, and, increasingly nowadays, to the regulation of aspects of international relations. Second, it includes the realm of the relationship of citizens, individually and collectively, to the institutions of government: hence membership of political parties, the franchise, elections, and other incidents of participation in civil society.

The objective of politics is often characterized in Catholic teaching as the promotion of the common good, understood as the ensemble of conditions of social living which make for the human flourishing of each person. This gives rise to the question, what constitutes human flourishing? And the answer to this is to be found in one's view or vision of life.

It follows that the work of politics implies a morality, a conception of what it is to relate rightly to others and to the world around us. In the Christian vision this morality is ultimately religious, in that it is shaped by beliefs about God and about the divine design as this is disclosed in the revelation made in Jesus Christ. It is not therefore surprising that in the Christian vision, religion, morality, and politics are seen to be related.

In Roman Catholic theology some themes from the teaching of Vatican II are suggestive for the way in which these relationships may be perceived. The first is expressed in the words of *Gaudium et Spes* that "Christ did not bequeath to the Church a mission in the political, economic, or social order; the purpose he assigned it was a religious one" (GS 42). The second is that "[i]t is to the laity, though not exclusively to them, that secular duties and activity properly belong" (GS 43). The third is that there is an "autonomy of earthly affairs," by which is meant that "matter and society" have their own laws and values which are intrinsically worthy of respect (GS 36).

A fourth pertinent theme is that of religious freedom, which includes "the right of religious groups not to be prevented from freely demonstrating the special value of their teaching for the organization of society and the inspiration of all human activity," as the council's Declaration on Religious Freedom puts it (*Dignitatis Humanae* 4). This is an aspect of the more general position of the Declaration that no Church should be either particularly favored or discriminated against by the civil authority. The particular significance of this theme is usually considered under the rubric "Church and State."

The Church is the community of believers in Jesus as the Way, the Truth and the Life (John 14:6). Its raison d'être is to proclaim and bear witness to the gospel of Jesus, the Good News of a gracious God who wills the salvation of humankind and the liberation of the world from bondage to decay (Rom 8:21). Its perspectives are transcendent, its message addressed to humanity in all humanity's breadth and depth. The gospel is distorted when its import is reduced to a program for social or political reform.

Yet the Christian gospel has implications for life in the world. At its core is the notion that in Jesus God's reign is begun: that the love of God is abroad in the world, overcoming sin and offering the hope of salvation to all. The message resonates in the heart of the hearer who is thereby emboldened to turn again to God and to walk again in his ways. And this means working for justice and peace and truth and love, for these are the ways of God.

So is the reign of God given concrete form, and such is the calling of the Christian believer. This calling is lived first at the level of personal life: as parent or child or spouse, employer or employee, neighbor or friend, farmer or plumber or lawyer or priest. But it is lived also at the level of one's role in the polity; for we are also concerned about a common good, and this is the province of politics. The Christian vision of a reign of God's justice and peace and love can summon us forward and challenge us. God's reign is begun and we work toward its completion; and Christ's promise of its completion offers hope and a confirmation of the value of human effort to bring about justice and peace in the world.

Moreover, a community of Christians is as such a "presence" in society, with a capacity and an obligation to contribute to society's attempts to pursue the common good. The Churches as institutions retain an influential role, and their leaderships in particular are importantly placed to influence the course of public affairs. The development of a Catholic social doctrine in a series of papal encyclicals beginning with Leo XIII's *Rerum Novarum* is especially noteworthy in this context. And after Vatican II local Churches, through the medium of bishops' conferences, have been contributing to public debate on sociomoral matters. This is also the arena of liberation theology (or theologies), and of the concept of a political theology.

But the gospel also stands in judgment upon human endeavor. The form of the world is passing away, we have here no lasting city, the time is not yet come when God is all in all. It follows that even the noblest of human achievements is flawed, and there can be no absolutization of political or other social systems. The law does not always work justice, economies sometimes oppress and discriminate, government is not always for a common good. Christian faith and hope and love afford a basis for a critique. And of course the Church itself, in its institutions as in each of its members, is *semper reformanda.*

Active engagement in politics by Catholics may give rise to ethical problems, as when a Catholic is asked to vote for a measure contrary to Catholic morality. Such dilemmas are not peculiar to Catholics but they tend to achieve a prominence where Catholics are concerned both because of specific Catholic moral positions (as, e.g., on divorce or abortion) and because of a tradition in Catholicism of active hierarchical magisterium which makes claims of varying kinds and degrees upon the individual's conscience.

Of course it has never been a tenet of Catholicism that every sin should be a crime or that the law should try to enforce every act of every virtue. And a general guidance may be obtained if we transpose the teaching of *Dignitatis Humanae* so as to say that in moral as in religious matters people should not be made to go against their consciences, nor should they be restrained from behaving according to conscience, within the limits of the common good. But there remains the possibility of dispute concerning what the common good in a given case requires, nor is it always clear what the limits of tolerance should be.

One approach has been to invoke a distinction between personal moral belief and one's responsibility as legislator or voter to take account of the conscientiously held beliefs of others. This is helpful up to a point though it may be misleading. It is misleading if it suggests that there are two moral orders, the private and the public, the former subject to the latter so that conscience must yield to public purpose. It cannot justify the use of immoral means in the name of a public cause. Nor is it to be invoked as a cover for indifference or pusillanimity where the rights of others are imperiled.

Yet there is a difference between the task of the moralist and the art of the politician. The preacher or the prophet may, in the light of a moral vision, challenge a society to social or legislative reform. But the judgment of a measure's aptness bespeaks the experience and skill of the practitioner. It may be that a politician or citizen must from time to time be content with legislation which does less than justice to their personal moral conviction on a given issue.

Of course no one can rest content with what he or she believes to be wrong, and there remains a duty to work for reform by means of what John Courtney Murray called persuasion and pacific argument. A

Catholic approach will be informed by the principles and perspectives of *Dignitatis Humanae* and will respect also the legitimate autonomy of secular pursuits (GS 36). Where there is an irreducible conflict of moral conviction it may be helpful to consider the applicability of standard Catholic principles concerning cooperation in another's wrongdoing.

PATRICK HANNON

See also CHRISTIAN MORALITY; CHURCH AND STATE; MURRAY, JOHN COURTNEY; VATICAN COUNCIL II.

CAUSSADE, JEAN-PIERRE DE (1675–1751)

Jesuit spiritual writer. A renowned professor, preacher, and spiritual director, Caussade was deeply influenced by Fénelon, Bossuet, and St. Francis de Sales. His central theme is interior peace obtained by submission to God and his constant fatherly goodness. ("What God arranges for us to experience at each moment is the best and holiest thing that could happen to us.") In this he is faithful both to the Spiritual Exercises of St. Ignatius (the founder of the Jesuits), as taught by Louis Lallemant, and to St. Francis de Sales' idea of evangelical simplicity and docility. His principal works are (short titles) *Spiritual Instructions in the Form of Dialogues Concerning the Different States of Prayer* (1741), and the heavily edited and posthumous *Abandonment to Divine Providence* (1761).

DAVID BRYAN

See also CHRISTIAN SPIRITUALITY.

CELIBACY

The most striking difference between the Jewish way of life and the way of life of the followers of Jesus lies in the area of relationships between the sexes. Celibacy was not normally practiced by Jews, except possibly in the case of a prophetic call and, for a time, by priests engaged in the service of the Temple. Yet abstinence from marriage became an accepted way of life in the first centuries of the Church. If, like Peter, the apostles were married and Paul may have been widowed, the Christian tradition has taken for granted that Jesus remained single. It has also affirmed that, by the power of the Holy Spirit, he was born of a virgin, Mary of Nazareth.

This basic belief, and the expectation of the prompt return of the Lord that was shared by many in the first centuries of the Church, prompted Christian ascetics, both men and women, to live in solitude or to form communities of celibates dedicated to the exclusive search of God in this life. Reaction against the marriage customs of the Roman Empire, especially against the total submission of wives to their husbands in both Greek and Roman civilizations, were also at the origin of the invitation to Christian women to remain in a state of virginity, living in their family home and holding regular meetings under the bishop's guidance. This double movement toward celibacy and virginity reached a high point in the institution of monasteries for either sex. This institution was largely though not exclusively due to St. Basil and his sister St. Macrina in the East, to St. Augustine and St. Benedict in the West. As many of these monks were eventually chosen to be bishops, celibacy became an accepted feature of the episcopate.

With Augustine, however, another trend appeared. When he became bishop of Hippo he himself wished to continue in the monastic way that he had admired in others at the time of his conversion. He therefore lived in common with his priests and deacons. He thought that celibacy should not be reserved to monks, who, in their majority, were not ordained, but ought to be generalized among priests. Since Augustine had considerable influence over the Western Middle Ages, the norm that was eventually enforced in the Latin Church reserved ordination to unmarried men, while the Eastern Church preserved the older practice of ordaining married priests and married deacons, bishops being selected from among the unmarried. In the canonical collections of the Western Middle Ages priestly celibacy was considered an absolute requirement. This principle was carried to an extreme in the twentieth century, when the immemorial custom of Byzantine Catholic Churches was suspended in the U.S.A. and these Churches were forced by Roman decrees (*Ea Semper,* 1907; *Cum Data Fuerit,* 1929) to adopt the Latin rule of priestly celibacy in their American parishes.

It is frequently asserted today that the Latin norm is based on a false conception of sexuality and on an implicit or even explicit contempt for women. Quotations from the married priest Tertullian and from the ascetic St. Jerome give plausibility to the contention regarding women. The decisions of the Synod of Elvira, Spain, in the early fourth century, that married priests must renounce sexual relations, and the harsh treatment of married priests by the Synod of Fulda, Germany, in 742 (condemnation to two years in prison) give some substance to the accusations. But one cannot reasonably generalize from a few instances to the whole Church. There is no convincing evidence that either the patristic or the medieval Church ever taught that women are naturally inferior to men, even if this was the personal opinion of St. Thomas Aquinas. The fact that a number of abbesses had jurisdiction over priests, and the careers of remarkable women, from Hildegard of Bingen, through Jeanne d'Arc, to Catherine of Sienna suggest the opposite.

Enforcement of the rule of celibacy in the diocesan clergy, however, was never easy. All medieval reform movements had to deal with the problem, and they usually ended up by reinforcing the law. The rule of celibacy for the Latin clergy was strongly reaffirmed during the Gregorian reform, at the Synods of Mainz, 1075, Rheims, 1099, London, 1108, and many others. Married priests had to choose between marriage and the priesthood. The Second General Council of the Lateran (1130–1143) considered invalid the marriage of priests after ordination. Yet many priests throughout the Middle Ages lived openly with a concubine. Extreme measures, like banning them from officiating at their children's burials (Münster, 1280), or refusing a church funeral to their wives (Valladolid, 1322), had no lasting effect. At the time of the Renaissance, some bishops and cardinals kept a concubine, and in some cases more than one. In the sixteenth century, when Cardinal Pole was reconciling the clergy of England to the Holy See, he found that about one third had married during the reign of the Protestant Edward VI. The instructions he received from Pope Julius III (*Bulla Facultatum Extraordinarium,* 1553) assimilated their marriage to bigamy. This marriage was considered illicit, though valid, if they belonged to the diocesan clergy, and simply invalid if they were of the regular clergy. The former had to choose between their wives and the exercise of the priesthood. The latter were given no choice: they had to repudiate their wives if they wished to be in good standing in the Church.

The participants in the Council of Trent were aware of the problems connected with the celibacy of the clergy. It seemed evident that clerical celibacy could not be enforced on the sole basis of law. Some reforms were therefore instituted by the council (session 23, 1563) to encourage the creation of seminaries for the training of clerics. In the next century religious communities devoted to priestly formation came into being (Congregation of the Mission [Vincentians], 1617; Priests of St. Sulpice [Sulpicians], 1642; Congregation of Jesus and Mary [Eudists], 1643). They stressed the spiritual dimension of consecrated celibacy in the context of a life marked by ordination and devoted to the People of God. Following Cardinal de Bérulle and his disciple Philippe de Condren, the French school of spirituality found the reason for clerical celibacy in the nature of the priesthood as participation in the "states" of Jesus, including the celibate state. More recent theologies have justified celibacy as undivided devotion to God, or as a total gift of self to the Church and its people, or as implicit in "the poverty of the priest," or, more questionably, as being in harmony with an assumed complementarity of men and women.

The Code of Canon Law of 1918 assimilated clerical faults against chastity to sacrileges (c. 132, §1). This was often taken to mean that celibacy is implicitly vowed when the obligations attendant on ordination are accepted. More simply, the Code of 1983 specifies only that no one may be ordained unless he has "assumed the obligation of celibacy before God and the Church" (c. 1037).

Following Vatican II some problems that were not faced by the council emerged. In the light of psychoanalysis and depth psychology the basic health of vowing a celibate life was thrown in doubt. The capacity of canon law to suspend the natural right to marriage came into question. Awareness grew of the Church's prevalent "patriarchal" attitude toward women. Facing these questions the magisterium has reasserted the law. Yet many clerics have opted out of the active ministry and have married. Pope Paul VI was open to granting the necessary canonical dispensations. But a serious dearth of unmarried male candidates for ordination will eventually make it urgent to change the law of clerical celibacy.

GEORGE H. TAVARD

See also PRIESTHOOD, THE MINISTERIAL; VIRGINITY.

CELTIC ART

The Celtic peoples who dominated Europe from the fifth century B.C. were highly sophisticated metal

"Eight Circle Cross," Book of Kells, Dublin

workers (chiefly in gold and bronze), capable of decorating their jewelry, vessels, weapons, and other useful objects in incredibly minute detail, whether by inlay or *repoussé.* Their stylized designs, often, but not exclusively, geometrical or spiral, borrowed freely from every civilization with which they came in contact. While the metalwork of the Celts declined somewhat as the Celts were pushed westward by later migrations, their virtuoso decorative skills took a new form in the early Middle Ages in their exquisite illuminations of Christian manuscripts. Well known, too, are the standing stone crosses sculpted with a blend of pagan and Christian symbols.

DAVID BRYAN

See also ART, CHRISTIAN; KELLS, BOOK OF.

CENSORSHIP OF BOOKS

The prepublication censorship of books has a long history in the Church; but prior to the invention of printing in the fifteenth century, it was only exercised spasmodically. For instance, in 1260, the Franciscans were ordered to submit all books, intended for an outside readership, for the prior approval of their superiors. The first general legislation for the whole Church was promulgated by Innocent VIII in 1487, and succeeding popes and councils endorsed the prior censorship of books especially of those dealing with Scripture, doctrine, morality, spirituality, and Church history. With some changes and modifications, this practice lasted until the major revision of 1975 when the policy was streamlined and limited to biblical and liturgical texts; prayer books and catechisms; scholastic textbooks dealing with doctrinal and moral matters; and literature sold or given away in churches.

MICHAEL GLAZIER

See also IMPRIMATUR; INDEX OF FORBIDDEN BOOKS.

CENTERING PRAYER

Centering Prayer is a new name for a very ancient form of prayer. Its origins are found in the writings of John Cassian, a young Roman who went in search of a spiritual father. He found one in Abba Isaac, who was reputed to be the holiest and oldest and wisest father among the fathers in the Egyptian desert at that time, the end of the fourth century. John's quest had been a long one and he was filled with joy when the holy old man taught him how to find contemplative peace. Later John became himself a spiritual father, and a community of men as well as a community of women gathered around him after he returned to the West. For these disciples he undertook to write down what he had learned from the venerated father in the desert. A century later Benedict of Nursia wrote a *Rule for Monasteries* in which he recommended that his disciples turn to John Cassian and John's record of the conferences of Abba Isaac and others for deeper, richer spiritual teaching. Thus the teaching John received in the desert passed into the mainstream of Western spirituality.

We find it developed in the earliest spiritual writings we have in English. One in particular, that of a father who humbly hid in anonymity, became very popular and has held its popularity through all the following centuries. This little work, called *The Cloud of Unknowing,* written for one of the father's spiritual sons, is not easy to read because it does belong to a time long past. But the essence of the teaching is there with much wise counsel. This treatise and many others give witness to how widely this sort of contemplative prayer was practiced among the people. It was not the preserve of monks and nuns though they were the principal teachers. Because they were the teachers, when the monasteries were destroyed during the Protestant Reformation and the French Revolution, the practice of this form of prayer was largely lost. It is only in our times that it is again being widely taught and practiced among the faithful.

Traditionally this way of prayer has had many names: the prayer of quiet, the prayer of simple regard, the prayer of the heart, and others. It is prayer in the heart—the mind, the attention come down into the heart and abide quietly there. To achieve this Abba Isaac counseled John Cassian to be content with the poverty of a single simple word. The author of *The Cloud of Unknowing* pressed this further: Choose a simple word, a single syllable word is best, like God or love. He added: choose a word that is meaningful to you, the meaning being: I am all yours, Lord. This little word is fixed in the mind. It represents God and only God. It abides there keeping the mind and heart in God. Anything else that comes along is simply let go. This little word is the sole response, God is the sole care during this time of love. It is as simple as that.

To facilitate the teaching and practice of this very traditional prayer form it has been set forth in three simple points, with a bit of a preface and a final word: Sit quietly, eyes gently closed. (1) Be in faith and love to God who dwells within. (2) Take up a love word and let it be gently present, supporting being to God in faith-filled love. (3) Whenever, during the time of our prayer, we become aware of anything else, we simply, gently return to the Lord, with the use of our word. At the end of the twenty minutes, let the prayer word go and let the Lord's Prayer (or some other favorite prayer) quietly pray itself within.

If we begin to detail the rich fruits that flow from this little practice of love, there is much danger that we will vitiate the offering; we will begin to seek the fruits and turn our prayer into a project of the false self instead of it being a gift of purest love. If, in fact, we do this, we will frustrate ourselves. For when we begin to seek something for ourselves rather than giving ourselves in purest love to the Lord, we no longer truly center and the fruits will no longer be produced. In Centering Prayer we let go of the false self; we die to the false self to live to God. We find a new freedom. We no longer have to worry about what others think. We know how precious we are in the eyes of God. There is nothing to be sought outside now. All is within. We find everyone within the same Divine Center. We are all one. We come to everyone as our very self: Love your neighbor *as yourself.* We know we are one in God.

Centering Prayer is a deeply healing prayer. As we rest in the Lord, the free flow of thoughts and memories—of which we have virtually no awareness for our attention is set on the Lord even though our rational mind is still functioning—is washing away the hurts and pains, the scars and wounds, the psychological bindings of the past, the past deeply buried in our psyche and now allowed to freely flow up and out. "Come to me you who are heavily burdened and I will refresh you." Jesus is still the physician who comes to heal those who have need. In Centering Prayer we lay ourselves completely open to his healing ministry, not placing any of our limitations on what he can do. Our psychological defenses are all down. We are wide-open to the Lord. And little by little, as we faithfully center day after day, the healing goes on till we find in our lives a new freedom to love ourselves and everyone else, for now we see ourselves as one with everyone else, the beautiful one reflected in the eyes of the Beloved.

M. BASIL PENNINGTON, O.C.S.O.

See also CONTEMPLATION; MYSTICISM; PRAYER.

CÉZANNE, PAUL (1839–1906)

Cézanne was a French artist, who fused the techniques of Impressionism with solid forms to evoke the spiritual depth of simple subjects.

Paul Cézanne's father settled in the town of Aix-en-Provence in southern France and made his money exporting hats. With two children born out of wedlock, he bought respectability by buying the bank and a run-down eighteenth-century manor built for the governor of Provence. By 1848 when Paul was nine, all was in place, including the map of Paul's life.

Paul Cézanne, self-portrait, 1898–1900

The seeds of the struggle between Louis Auguste Cézanne and his sensitive son were planted long before Paul quit law school to study art. For years his consciousness absorbed the pure images and natural color all around him: a rough stone house barely rising out of a hill, the reddish-brown rocks of a quarry, peasant women scrubbing clothes on the banks of the Arc river. As he hiked about the woods and hills his artistic task was taking root—to sharpen those primitive images and fortify his own vivid perceptions of the enduring truth he saw, over against Louis Auguste's fixed pattern of success.

In the 1860s Cézanne studied painting, wandered the Louvre, and led the bohemian life in Paris. He practiced the art of the Young Romantic: sensuous, violent, imaginary, and restless. In *The Murder* a man leans over a woman holding her down, as another raises a knife to plunge into her. While his passions and rage poured onto the canvases, Cézanne craved approval from the official Salon. His paintings were rejected, and he was wounded. The art world's patterns of success were no less rigid than his father's.

The Impressionist Camille Pissarro recognized Cézanne's genius. A kind man, Pissarro took him home to his own family and worked with him, side by side. He taught Cézanne to stand humbly before nature and concentrate on the *motif,* the motive or germinal "idea accepted from the visible world" (R. Fry, *Cézanne: A Study of his Development,* New York: The Noonday Press, 1960, p. 35). From this point on, the "nucleus of crystallization," in Roger Fry's term, shifted outside of himself—the undisciplined texturing of the canvas with thick slabs of paint bowed to discipline. He now approached the canvas *consciously*—a contained space to be *shaped by* the external motif. The preconceived whole was made visible through replicating each distinct segment of color, "step by step, touch by touch." "In the end we find every person and every object presented to the eye in the simplest, most primitive fashion. . . ." (Fry, p. 26). No longer "struggling against the current of his genius" (Fry, p. 27), Cézanne captured the intense expression of his own face staring out from the canvas—without using a single defining line. The face, flesh, eyes, beard, coat emerge from *color alone.* But, in a sharp departure from the Impressionists' overall hazy effect, the form of the figure appears solid. Unconsciously he was cracking the rigid classical lines that had trivialized art into a mirror image of conventional perception. Cézanne, who craved the approval of his banker father and the official art world had embraced a priesthood: in his scrupulous devotion to the forms and the color that his purified vision perceived, he was laying the foundation for modern abstract art.

He withdrew to the isolated life of his home town. Before dawn he shouldered his easel and paints and walked—often for several hours—to the simple, primitive motifs: a rough stone chateau rising out of the trees and rocks, the mountain St. Victoire, a stone quarry. ". . . Here on the bank of the river, the motifs multiply, the same subject seen from different angles gives a subject for study of the most powerful interest and so varied that I think I could occupy myself for months without changing my place, simply bending a little to the right or left" (From a letter to his son, 8 September 1906, quoted in J. Rewald, *Cézanne, A Biography,* New York: Abrams, 1986, p. 259).

He painted people—not posed portraits of the great and wealthy, but whoever happened to be there—his father in a chair reading a newspaper, a housemaid sitting, hands askew, next to a coffee pot. He painted still lifes—arranging on a thick cover draped over a wooden table apples, onions, an old wine bottle. He violated the classical rules of perspective to make visible the grandeur of a simple subject. By heightening a rough peasant hand on the lap of a woman, framed by flowered wallpaper, he coaxed forth the deeper harmony underlying the appearances. "Painting is not a matter of copying the object slavishly," Cézanne later wrote. "It is a matter of discerning a harmony between many relations" (L. Venturi, *Cézanne,* Geneva: Skira, 1985, p. 126). This awed the poet Rilke. "It's as if every place on the canvas were aware of all the other places" (Rainer Maria Rilke, *Letters on Cézanne,* New York: Fromm, p. 80)." . . . all of reality is on his side: in this dense quilted blue of his, in his red and his shadowless green and the reddish black of his wine bottles. And the humbleness of all his objects: the apples are all cooking apples and the wine bottles belong in the roundly bulging pockets of an old coat" (Rilke, p. 29). ". . . He lays his apples on bed covers . . . and places a wine bottle among them or whatever happens to be handy. And . . . he makes his 'saints' out of such things; and forces them—*forces them*—to be beautiful, to stand for the whole world and all joy and all glory. . . ." (Rilke, p. 40).

At the heart of Cézanne's vision was a love for what endures beneath the clutter of passing fancy, of ornament. "Above all things I like the look of people who have grown old without doing violence to custom, surrendering to the laws of the time," he told a friend. "Look at that old café proprietor seated before his doorway, what style he has!" (Venturi, p. 126). To Rilke, this love of the enduring was "the beginning of holiness." As Cézanne aged, he embraced the Catholic Church. His simple habits included regular Mass and Sunday Vespers. "Once we have attained a certain age," he wrote to his niece, "we find no other support and consolation than in religion" (Rewald, p. 127).

In 1896 the aging and ill Cézanne slipped into the first exhibition of his paintings in Paris with his son. Cézanne's reaction: "And to think they are all framed!" A few years later Pablo Picasso called him "the father of us all."

PATRICIA O'CONNOR

See also ART, CHRISTIAN.

CHALICE

(Lat. *calix,* "cup") The cup or goblet used for the consecration of the wine in the celebration of the Eucharist. It is normally between eight and eleven inches tall, with a wide base, and a stem with a knob midway between the base and the cup. The cup is usually made of brass, sterling silver, or gold. Until recently, the inside of the cup was required to be gold-plated, regardless of which metal the rest of the chalice was made. Since Vatican II, however, chalices may be made of other solid materials deemed appropriate for worship in whichever country they are

Chalice by Rivir

used. Chalices are consecrated with chrism by a bishop.

JOSEPH QUINN

See also VESSELS, SACRED.

CHANCELLOR

Originally the record keeper and secretary of a bishop, the chancellor, from an early time, has been a key representative of, and administrator under, the bishop. The duties of the Roman chancery have now been largely absorbed by other officials.

DAVID BRYAN

See also DIOCESE.

CHANCERY

The office of the chancellor of a diocese.

DAVID BRYAN

See also CHANCELLOR; DIOCESE.

CHARISM

From the Greek for "free gift," this is Paul's term for graces of the Spirit given for building up the body of Christ. Paul treats the gifts in 1 Corinthians 12-14—mission, prophecy, wisdom, service—and claims they appear in healers, prophets, teachers, leadership, and tongue-speakers. Charisms were not much understood in medieval times: Christians' actions were spoken of as virtues, theological and moral. Theologically the Church was described as early as the nineteenth century as a "network of charisms." The recent emergence of the charismatic movement in the Catholic Church has stimulated reflection on the charisms. This broader vision gives the Catholic Pentecostal renewal a framework for understanding the extraordinary charismatic gifts of tongues, healing, and prophecy.

MARY BARBARA AGNEW, C.PP.S.

See also GIFTS OF THE HOLY SPIRIT; HOLY SPIRIT.

CHARISMATIC MOVEMENT

"Charismatic movement" is the general term for a surge of religious experience attributed to an outpouring of the Holy Spirit which arose in United States Protestantism in the nineteenth century and has appeared in mainline Protestant and Roman Catholic Churches in the second half of the twentieth.

While both Luther and Calvin had stressed the role of the Holy Spirit in justification, it remained for the Pietists and Wesley to make the work of the Holy Spirit a commonplace of their teaching. A key factor in this upsurge was the American Methodist Phoebe Palmer; as early as 1835, she was preaching full baptism of the Holy Spirit and the experience of a "second blessing." In 1843 her writings were issued as *The Way of Holiness,* a bestseller for a quarter of a century; by 1847 she had influential followers from Congregational, Presbyterian, Baptist, and Methodist clergy. In 1856, William Arthur's *Tongues of Fire* added to the interest in the topic by denying the common teaching that the extraordinary gifts of the Spirit had been withdrawn after the Church was founded, and called for their restoration in the Church. Thus, by 1890 Holiness Churches and revival movements were widely teaching a baptism in the Holy Spirit.

It was, however, in Kansas at the turn of the century, while praying that the Spirit would come upon them, that Charles Parham and a few students experienced the gift of tongues. A few years later some of the students led a three-year revival in Azusa, California, at which the gifts of tongues, prophecy, and healings were constant. Participants in revivals like these formed groups separate from their own Churches, which often could not accept their enthusiastic prayer style. The new groups regarded receiving the gift of tongues as necessary evidence of receiving baptism in the Holy Spirit; these include the Church of God (Cleveland, Tennessee), the Pentecostal Holiness Church, and the Church of God in Christ.

Besides those who broke from their own Churches, some Pentecostal Churches formed independently.

Most influential have been the Assemblies of God, organized in 1914, which moved away from the strict Wesleyanism of the earlier groups, and adopted different forms of Church government. Opposition from American Christians was strong; charges of fanaticism and schism-mongering, as well as derogatory names such as "holy rollers," were undergirded by the long held opinion that miraculous gifts of the Spirit had ended with the death of the apostles, no longer being needed for the foundation of the Church. This opposition continued until the 1940s, when an invitation to join what would become the National Association of Evangelicals was received as almost too good to be true. The wider contacts with fundamentalist and evangelical Christians which this afforded resulted in their forming the Pentecostal Fellowship of North America.

The contacts of the 1940s also brought cooperation between Pentecostals worldwide; in 1947 the first Pentecostal World Conference convened in Zurich. A periodical which resulted, *Pentecost,* carried editorials about non-Pentecostal Christians, and urged subscribers to work for Christian unity. David J. du Plessis, secretary of the Pentecostal World Conferences, furthered the effort from 1954 onward, attending the meetings of the World Council of Churches, speaking with Church leaders, and visiting hundreds of Christian churches of historic and Pentecostal character. He also cochaired ten years of dialogues with the Vatican's Secretariat for Promoting Christian Unity. Thus, from 1950 on, the larger Church became more aware of Pentecostalism's development around the world, a development which today ranks classical Pentecostalism as the largest Protestant denomination. Starting in 1951, the Full Gospel Business Men's Fellowship also gave Pentecostalism a basis for wider acceptance on the American scene.

Since 1960, this focus on the charismatic gifts has appeared in the mainline Protestant denominations, as well as the Roman Catholic Church. First known as "neo-Pentecostal," the more common term today is "charismatic." In the Catholic Church, the movement is known as the Catholic Charismatic Renewal; the shift from "Pentecostal" to "charismatic" reflects the fact that baptism in the Spirit and glossolalia are understood within the framework of the sacramental life of the Church, rather than as forces which serve to separate Catholic charismatics from other Church members. This broader understanding of charismatic activity was present also in the views of nineteenth-century theologians Adam Moehler and Matthias Sheeben, who wrote about the charismatic nature of the whole Church, as did Karl Rahner in the twentieth century.

In the broader context of a theology of charisms it might be argued that the religious fervor surrounding the Catholic parish mission, with its long lines at the confessional, invites comparison with the altar call and changed lives that resulted from the revivalist and Pentecostal experiences in Protestantism. Nevertheless, despite the worldwide growth of Pentecostalism, and its spread to mainline Protestantism in 1960, charismatic activity did not appear publicly in the Catholic Church until 1967, when participants in a retreat at Duquesne University experienced speaking in tongues and baptism in the Spirit.

Word of the event spread rapidly to the campuses of the University of Notre Dame and Michigan State University. Soon the "Catholic Pentecostal Movement" was flourishing and spreading, as summer students returned home. Leadership emerged in the formation of a National Service Committee, whose purpose was to share information and organize activities. The annual Pentecostal conference they organized drew 30,000 by 1976. Within the same nine years, a magazine, *New Covenant* was founded. The approval of the hierarchy was sought, and as membership grew, the National Service Committee prepared a series of preparatory experiences, the "Life in the Spirit" seminars. Joseph Cardinal Suenens attended the 1973 conference, and the 1975 conference, held in Rome, was greeted by Pope Paul VI.

As numbers increased, covenant communities and charismatic parishes developed at South Bend and Ann Arbor, and, without becoming separatist, the movement did become professedly reformist of Church life. In contrast to the Protestant leadership's hesitancy over the appearance of Pentecostal experience in its midst, the Catholic hierarchy's first formal response (1969) was positive. The beginnings were not, however, without difficulties. Warnings appeared that miracles and spiritual power are not to be equated with authentically Christian faith and morality. In the first enthusiasm a tendency to contrast negatively a deeply felt baptism in the Spirit in maturity with an arid confirmation in childhood resulted in a claim for sacramental status for the former.

After a period of rapid growth, membership in the movement leveled off in the late 1970s. The leadership's response to the situation began with suggestions of infidelity, but continued in a reevaluation of itself, finally calling, in the 1990s, for a "second generation" movement. Here again, the theological tradition of Catholicism provided resources for recognizing that religious experience is not itself spiritual maturity, and for acknowledging that if the Church is constituted by mutually supporting charisms, then extraordinary gifts of tongues, healing, and prophecy must not be exalted over less spectacular gifts of service. Similarly, the appointment of official Church liaisons for charismatic groups, while conferring recognition, also served to keep activities within recognizable Catholic Church patterns. Today, charismatic activity is present in active parish groups and covenant communities. The broadened character of the movement at its present stage is indicated in the statement of purpose of the movement's magazine, *New Covenant,* revised in 1980 to read: "a commitment to fostering renewal in the Catholic church, especially the charismatic, ecumenical, evangelistic and community dimensions of that renewal. . . ."

MARY BARBARA AGNEW, C.PP.S.

See also CHARISM; PENTECOSTALISM.

CHARITY

Charity is considered in Christian tradition either as the whole of authentic human communion with God and others, or more narrowly as one of the three theological virtues. In either case it is distinguished from a love of natural attraction, a love of needy desires, a love that simply clings to and aligns itself with the familiar, and from such responses as the instinctive care and protection of offspring. In contrast to all of these, charity is seen as a gift of grace empowering human beings to transcend their nature to share in the creativity and self-gift of God. It is an enhancement of human will to act, as it were, divinely.

Charity in Scripture

Scripture speaks primarily of God's love for human beings, and only secondarily of that love coming to fruition in human loving. The love of God is expressed first in creation, and then in a series of elections, of Abraham, of Moses, of the oppressed Hebrews, later of judges, kings, and prophets. In response to this, the people of Israel acknowledged as their first and most important commitment the precept, "You shall love the Lord, your God, with all your heart, and with all your soul, and with all your strength" (Deut 6:4). What this means is often described in terms of loyalty and fidelity, the analogy being used of marital fidelity. The Hebrews saw this as the worship of the one God and rejection of idols, the meticulous obeying of the commandments of the Law, the teaching of the tradition to their children, and if the occasion should arise, the confession of faith in the one God even at the cost of death by torture.

In the prophecy of Hosea, God is depicted as a persistent lover, wooing the chosen people, seeking their love, not their animal sacrifices. Amos 3 emphasizes that the love of God seeks reciprocity. In the prophecy of Jonah the love of God is shown as jealously protective of the loved one (Jonah 4, the parable of the shady gourd vine). Throughout the various images and analogies being used, there is a strong sense that God reaches out to extend friendship and fellowship to human beings, making them party to the divine purposes and the divine wisdom, and seeking a return of friendship and sharing of goals and wisdom.

In the New Testament this all becomes explicit and sharply focused both for the individual follower of Jesus and for the community of the believers. This is particularly true of the Johannine books of the NT. The First Letter of John, which is almost entirely about love (charity), emphasizes love as the totality of Christian life: "let us love one another, because love is of God; everyone who loves is begotten by God and knows God. Whoever is without love does not know God, for God is love" (1 John 4:7-8). The same passage also makes the point that such love is the gift of God who takes the initiative: "In this is love: not that we have loved God, but that he loved us and sent his Son as expiation for our sins" (1 John 4:10). Thus the gift in which the love of God has been offered is the person of Jesus who also becomes the model for the human response to God's love. This is further spelt out: "No one has ever seen God. Yet, if we love one another, God remains in us and his love is brought to perfection in us" (1 John 4:12).

When the New Testament quotes words of Jesus, there is the same emphasis that love is essentially the whole of the Law in which communion of the chosen people with God is expressed. This love has two inseparable facets: unqualified love of God and love of neighbor as being one with oneself (Matt 22:34-40). This is echoed clearly in the parable of the sheep and the goats in which Jesus identifies himself with all the needy, so that practical help to them is loving him, and loving him is loving the Father (Matt 25:31-46).

In the writings of Paul, this is expressed in equally practical terms, for instance in the famous passage: "Love is patient, love is kind. It is not jealous, is not pompous, it is not inflated, it is not rude, it does not seek its own interests, it is not quick-tempered, it does not brood over injury, it does not rejoice over wrongdoing but rejoices with the truth. It bears all things, believes all things, hopes all things, endures all things" (1 Cor 13:4-7).

Charity in Christian Tradition

In the Church Fathers this concern with practical charity is particularly connected with the Eucharist, and with the way the members of each local community support one another, as well as with the need for each community to be concerned for the welfare of other communities. This is very evident in the extant Letters of Ignatius of Antioch, probably to be dated around A.D. 110, who on his way to martyrdom is urging the young Churches along the way to be faithful to their calling. The concern with charity is likewise evident in another second-century document extant, the Didache, when it presents a catechesis distinguishing the way of death and darkness from the way of life and light to which Christians are called. Here, however, there is considerable concern with specific rules of morality, and this would later tend to obscure the centrality of charity in Christian life during the centuries of Christendom.

Nevertheless, this emphasis on charity as the essence of Christian life continued, and is noticeable particularly in some of the great sermons still extant from the fourth century, from authors such as St. Ambrose of Milan and St. Cyril of Jerusalem. But a systematic explanation of the centrality of charity in Christian life is given in the book, *The City of God,* written in the early fifth century by St. Augustine of Hippo. In this he sets out a painstaking argument from history, philosophy, and theology, to show why the world needs redemption and why authentic charity is the only way a society can survive in peace and well-being. He demonstrates that where each seeks his or her own without regard for others, there will always be conflict, disaster, fear, and suffering. Only when the saving power of divine love transforms human goals and desires, can human society hope for harmony and integration of all its parts.

In the medieval West, though the New Testament teaching was never lost, there was a certain turn to legalism, as when the Carolingian authors debated the justice of predestination, and when Anselm explained the incarnation and death of Jesus primarily in terms of the need to satisfy the justice of God. There was a further tendency to want to classify everything. This led to a focus on one particular passage in Paul: "So faith, hope and love remain, these three; but the greatest of these is charity" (1 Cor 13:13). Because Paul had been at pains to relativize everything else in order to draw these three to the center of Christian attention, it was rightly supposed that each of these three called for reflection and understanding. There was, therefore, an increasing desire to define each, and to distinguish them from one another.

In the thirteenth century, St. Thomas Aquinas, who made theological issues much clearer than anyone else, gave much attention in his *Summa of Theology* not only to definitions and distinctions, but also to interconnections of what have come to be called the three theological virtues (that is, those which relate directly to God). Thomas describes charity as consisting of friendship with God (obviously a gift of grace which must be initiated by God). He also makes the point that charity is a quality in a person's acting which corresponds to the indwelling of the Holy Spirit by which the person is acted upon. Charity is a specific virtue, although all other virtues depend on it, and although it is the most excellent (i.e., the most important) virtue in Christian life. Although people can act prudently or courteously or patiently without having charity, this would not be the graced activity of a life in the Spirit (II-II, q. 23, aa. 1-8). Although Thomas' teaching is argued in Scholastic categories, this is really the same message that Paul gave in 1 Corinthians 13, about the absolute centrality and inclusiveness of charity.

However, after the time of Thomas, two factors intervened to obscure this message. The late medieval period saw a great flowering of individualistic styles of piety, styles that tended to equate intimacy with God with withdrawal from other people and from problems in the society around the devout person. There was also a flowering of styles of mysticism which focused much more on contemplation than on charity. While this was going on in piety, the speculative theology of the universities was becoming more and more arid, preoccupied with small detail of definitions and distinctions, and more remote from the practice of the Christian life. This prompted, from the fourteenth century on, some first stirrings of the Reformation that was going to shake Europe in the sixteenth century.

Although the issues which the Reformers raised did not address the definition and place of charity in Christian life directly, the focus on faith in Christ as central and inclusive, and their insistence on a certain irrevocable destruction by original sin of the human power to do good, was an indirect attack on the careful medieval definitions and distinctions of the virtues. The response, therefore, in the theology incorporated in the documents of the Council of Trent, was to insist on the tradition in which faith was only one of three necessary theological virtues. This perpetuated the narrower definitions in a way which Thomas had tried to avoid.

A later complicating factor in this history is found in the emergence of moral theology as a separate discipline, developed particularly as a guide for confessors in judging the sinfulness, gravity, and species of acts, and calculating culpability as well as discerning what was genuine repentance. Although a parallel discipline of spiritual (sometimes named mystical and ascetical) theology also arose, there was a strong tendency to relate the latter only to those living religious life under vows and those in priestly orders or aspiring to them. Thus the catechesis of ordinary Christians tended to present a morality, or way of life, focused on the avoidance of specific sins, with faith, hope, and charity, like the other virtues, seen as the condition or state of avoiding sins against them. Many sample examinations of conscience were published according to which Christian life consisted essentially of a huge number of prohibitions and duties.

Charity in Contemporary Teaching

With the Second Vatican Council (1962–1965), two emerging strands in theological reflection were vindicated and placed at the center of Christian teaching. The first of these was largely due to one moral theologian, German Redemptorist Bernard Häring. Häring's central contribution was the insistence that Christian life was not in the first place a matter of knowing in great detail and plurality what actions were sinful, and then avoiding them. Rather, the Christian life is a matter of love, of charity, of coming to appreciate the love of God for us as personified in Jesus, and learning to live in that love in increasingly more intense, consistent, and practical ways. Häring drew this from the New Testament, and suggested that all the existing teaching in moral theology must at all times be subject to scrutiny by the light of the teaching of Jesus himself. This would affect catechesis, seminary theology, Vatican practice, and most of all the practice of the sacrament of penance from the perspective of both penitent and confessor.

While this focus has had a pervasive influence on moral theology, making charity the inclusive category, another aspect has also been brought to the fore by Vatican II. This is the social or community-building aspect. Charity is not only to be practiced in private life and one-to-one relationships, but is the essence of the redemption which the Church, the community of the believers, is called to bring into the world from Christ. It affects all aspects of human relationships and all the structures of human society from the local to the global. This means that concern for mass suffering of all kinds in the world is not an optional expression of the love of God but an essential one. While no individual can be practically engaged in the righting of all wrongs, the ending of all wars, the relief of all oppression, and the meeting of all needs, on the other hand no individual or group can claim to be living a truly Christian life while excluding the larger issues of human need and suffering from one's Christian concern and response.

The contemporary understanding of both the centrality and the social dimensions of charity implies a larger scale of engagement than was possible in earlier centuries. It implies much rethinking of priorities in catechesis and parish life, in lay activity and in the structures and functioning of the institutional Church. It also gives new insights on the inseparability of love of God from love of neighbor, and the relationship between the wider scope of charity and the coming reign of God.

MONIKA K. HELLWIG

See also FAITH; FRIENDSHIP; GRACE; HOPE; VIRTUE.

CHARLEMAGNE (ca. 742–ca. 814)

Charlemagne, or Charles the Great, born around 742, became the first emperor of the Holy Roman Empire when he was crowned in Rome by Pope Leo III on Christmas Day of the year 800. He had become ruler of the Franks in 771, and had aggressively extended his domain. At the request of Pope Hadrian I, he conquered Lombardy, and later campaigned against the Saxons and the Muslims in Spain. He had exceptional administrative skills, and was an unswerving advocate of ecclesiastical reform. He was also a highly cultured man with a studied knowledge of theology.

Charlemagne surrounded himself with highly competent advisors such as Alcuin, whom he commissioned to write against the Spanish Adoptionist heresy—which held that Christ, in his humanity, was only the adopted Son of God. He fostered the restoration of the hierarchy and Church discipline, and was responsible for unifying the liturgy. Charlemagne deserves a place in the history of education for initiating an intellectual renaissance during his reign. With his talented advisors Alcuin and Theodulf of Orleans, he used old and new statutes to decree that all monasteries and the houses of bishops should have centers of study. Later, he ordered that new schools be established. As a result of this educational crusade, Latin was restored as a literary language, many pagan and Christian classics were copied and preserved, and a more accurate orthography was established. He died around 814.

JOSEPH QUINN

See also CHURCH AND STATE; MIDDLE AGES, THE.

CHASTITY

See EVANGELICAL COUNSELS; VOWS.

CHASUBLE

(Lat. *casula,* "little house," from its mantle-like shape) The outermost garment worn by bishops and priests during the celebration of the Mass. Modeled after the outer cloak worn by Greeks and Romans in the later years of the Roman Empire, it is sleeveless and made of silk, velvet, or some other cloth appropriate for an ecclesiastical vestment. It represents the yoke of Christ, and is a symbol of the all-encompassing nature of Christian charity.

JOSEPH QUINN

See also VESTMENTS, LITURGICAL.

CHAVEZ, CESAR ESTRADA (1927–1993)

Migrant worker, union organizer and charismatic leader, Chavez was born in 1927 near Yuma, Arizona, where his parents—second generation Mexican immigrants—owned a small farm. Unable to meet mortgage payments, the family lost the farm and headed to California where they made an impoverished living following the sun and picking crops wherever work was available. Moving from place to place Cesar attended more than sixty-five schools but never graduated from high school. In 1939 his father found work as a union organizer at a dried-fruit packing plant in San Jose; and the lessons young Chavez learned stood him in good stead when—after serving two years in the navy—he joined Saul Alinsky's Community Service Organization helping Mexican-Americans to organize into a political force.

Cesar Estrada Chavez

In 1958 he quit and formed the National Farm Workers Association (La Huegla) in Delano. In its five-year strike, it battled the powerful corporations and wine growers of the San Joaquin Valley. The small laborer (five feet, six inches), with his reticent manner and inspiring dedication, won the world's attention and *La Causa* attracted volunteers from all over America. In 1968 the great boycott of table grapes won wide support from over seventeen million Americans. On 30 July 1970 the growers capitulated and agreed to bargain with the Farm Workers Union. Thereafter the union's successes were more spasmodic and limited. There were many reasons for this: it was difficult to organize and hold poor transient laborers; the more pliable and corrupt Teamsters Union was encouraged by the growers to compete with Chavez, who at times was suspicious of liberal non-Mexican supporters, and did not make full use of their talents and enthusiastic support.

Yet, Cesar Chavez did more than anyone in American history for the neglected farm workers. Edward R. Morrow had called the country's reluctant attention to the plight of the migrants in his documentary *The Harvest of Shame.* Chavez shamed the country into doing something about it. When he died in his sleep in San Luis, Arizona, on 23 April 1993 he was mourned not only by his wife Helen and eight children but by the nation who knew that a unique man had died, a poor man who lived the beatitudes.

JOAN GLAZIER

See also SOCIAL RESPONSIBILITY, FINANCIAL; SOCIAL TEACHING OF THE CHURCH.

CHESTERTON, GILBERT KEITH (1874–1936)

Author; London-born (in 1874) poet, journalist, essayist, novelist, critic, and artist, Chesterton was educated at St. Paul's School and the Slade School of Art. He began his career working in book publishing houses, and then turned to journalism—which provided him with the opportunity to demonstrate his remarkable writing skills. One of the many memorable literary creations of his novels is Father Brown, a Roman Catholic priest-detective modeled after his friend, Father O'Connor.

He was received into the Catholic Church in 1922, and thereafter vigorously defended Catholicism in his writings. Among his works are: *The Wild Knight and Other Poems* (1900), *Greybeards at Play* (1900), *Robert Browning* (1903), *G. F. Watts* (1904), *The Napoleon of Notting Hill* (1904), *Charles Dickens* (1906), *The Man Who Was Thursday* (1908), *All Things Considered* (1908), *Orthodoxy* (1909), *George Bernard Shaw* (1910), *What's Wrong with the World*

Gilbert Keith Chesterton

(1910), *William Blake* (1910), *Alarms and Discursions* (1910), *Appreciations and Criticisms of the Works of Charles Dickens* (1911), *The Innocence of Father Brown* (1911), *A Short History of England* (1917), *St. Francis of Assisi* (1923), *The Everlasting Man* (1925), *The Secret of Father Brown* (1927), *William Cobbett* (1925), *The Resurrection of Rome* (1930), *Chaucer* (1932), *Autobiography* (1936), and *The Paradoxes of Mr. Pond* (1936).

Chesterton contributed regularly to the *Eye Witness* (later the *New Witness*) newspaper, founded by his brother Cecil (1879–1918) and Hilaire Belloc and edited it under its new title, *G. K.'s Weekly,* from 1925 until his death in 1936.

JOSEPH QUINN

See also BRITAIN, CHURCH IN.

CHINESE RITES CONTROVERSY

The first Catholic missions to China started in the fourteenth century under the direction of Franciscans, like John of Monte Corvino. However, the consolidation of Roman Catholicism in China was achieved by the Jesuit missionary, Matteo Ricci (1582–1610) and his companions at the end of the sixteenth and beginning of the seventeenth centuries. The Jesuits attempted to integrate some Chinese practices into their missionary efforts, giving them a Christian interpretation. The Chinese rites controversy does not refer to any suggested acceptance of all ancient Chinese practices and rituals, but to three specific issues. These included some ceremonies in honor of Confucius, respect for ancestors, and the use of some important Chinese words describing God in the missionaries' catechetical vocabulary.

Pope Paul V gave the Jesuits some permissions, and in 1603 Ricci distributed a letter with his regional superior's approval, advocating the acceptance of ceremonies in honor of Confucius and all ancestors as an essential component of a successful missionary enterprise in China, believing neither were supersitious nor implied a recognition of divinity in Confucius or ancestors.

However, in 1693 Church authorities in China and Rome investigated the compatibility of these practices with Christian doctrine, and Pope Clement XI in 1715 eventually decided against the use of Chinese customs. The controversy remained until 1742, when Pope Benedict XIV reaffirmed Clement's decision.

Since the eighteenth century, several developments have given rise to further discussion of this issue. In 1932, Japan promoted the "worship" of Confucius, but local Church authorities interpreted this as a nonreligious ritual of respect for Confucius as a great moral teacher and allowed Christians to participate. In 1936, Pope Pius XI, the Pope of the Missions, urged adaptation and integration of oriental traditions into the Church. In 1939, Pope Pius XII interpreted many Chinese rites as licit, and gave directives that further interpretation could be made locally, thereby diffusing any prolonged discussion such as that which followed the work of Matteo Ricci. The Vatican Council II and later theologians developed the concept of adaptation and inculturation, opening the door once again to a reexamination of the issue of the Chinese Rites Controversy.

LEONARD DOOHAN

See also EVANGELIZATION; INCULTURATION; MISSIONS, CATHOLIC, THE MODERN PERIOD; RICCI, MATTHEO.

CHRISM

A mixture of oil and balsam (or balm) which is blessed by a bishop and used in the administration of baptism, confirmation and holy orders, and in the consecration of churches, altars, chalices, and patens. It is blessed by the bishop in the Chrism Mass, held during Holy Week (usually on Holy Thursday). Over the centuries, it was the Church's custom to use olive oil for chrism; in recent times, however, it has become acceptable to use vegetable, seed, or coconut oil.

JOSEPH QUINN

See also LITURGY; SACRAMENTALS.

CHRIST

See JESUS CHRIST.

CHRISTENING

The aspect of the baptismal ceremony in which the one baptized takes a Christian name. The tradition of adopting a Christian name in place of, or—as is now common—in addition to, one's own has been practiced by the faithful since the early centuries of the Church, when a newly baptized member of the Christian community would change his or her name to that of an apostle or an Old Testament figure. In

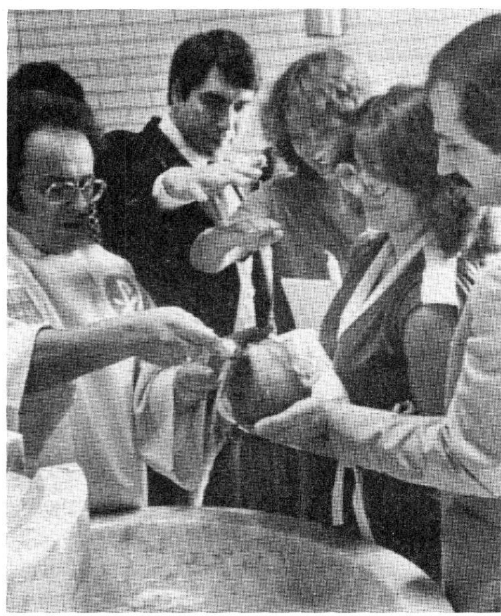

The sacrament of baptism

later centuries, it became common for parents to give their children the names of saints, martyrs, or Christian virtues. Although canon law required, for most of this century, that the name given a person at baptism be a Christian name (usually that of a saint), the present code stipulates only that the name conferred not be "foreign to a Christian mentality."

JOSEPH QUINN

See also SACRAMENTS OF INITIATION.

CHRISTIAN MORALITY

We should not take the expressions "Christian morality," "Christian ethics" for granted. The very conjunction of words seems to assume that doing ethics *as a Christian* is of significance. That is correct: the argument will be about precisely what significance. It is useful to note that the question of Christian ethics is part of a wider question, that of religious ethics. There are Muslim ethics and Jewish ethics and Buddhist ethics. To talk of religious ethics is to bring together two distinguishable strands of our experience, the religious and the ethical, and two languages, that of right, wrong, duty, and obligation and that of grace, justification, salvation, sin. There are many people who are explicitly nonreligious but who are sensitively moral: they often regard religion as inimical to morality, as a weakener of the moral sinews, as undermining human autonomy and encouraging a meretricious interest in reward. There are many others who find it difficult to see their ethical life as other than religious.

The relationships and interdependencies of religion and ethics are varied and subtle. So, the issue of Christian morality is many-faceted. In general one is asking how Christian faith bears on moral life. But that breaks down into different questions, all of them important. One might inquire whether faith affects the *notion* of morality or of *moral obligation.* One might ask whether and how the Christian story *interprets* the whole moral enterprise or supports it, or offers *motivation* for it, or provides an impulse to it: what difference does it make, for example, that one's God is intelligent, moral, loving, merciful—rather than arbitrary, capricious, self-indulgent? One might ask about the *significance* of moral life within Christianity, since the ethical strand receives a different emphasis from one religion to another: again, one might sharpen that by asking, for example, how it relates to a concept that is of importance to many religions, that of salvation. One might ask how the Christian story colors an understanding of the kind of *conduct* that is appropriate: one might sharpen this by seeking to compare it with the way of life espoused by some other religion or by some version of philosophical ethics.

The Christian understands morality within a particular religious story. It is a story about a deity who is creator, intelligent, purposeful, who has a care for the whole cosmos, who values individuals and seeks their true humanness. The Christian does it as one who has received love and forgiveness without measure and who experiences that as responsibility—as one who believes that the foundation of life is the love of God which is poured into our hearts (Rom 5:5), as one who is aware of the continuing presence of evil in history and the ongoing need for liberation, as one who sees a meaning and finality to things, who hopes in the eschatological promise of a final condition of justice and peace that hangs in judgment over every human state. This is the story we know. This is the only God we know. Christian belief and celebration have an inner impetus towards ethics, towards engagement with the other and with the structures in which we live. One cannot pray to the Christian God or celebrate the Christian Eucharist without being committed to the transformation of the world. And in the very engagement one might find more fully the meaning of the story.

Not all religions situate ethics so decisively. But one of the striking features of the Judaeo-Christian tradition is the prominence of ethics. That is the revelation which we have received. For the Christian, as for the Jew, religion is moral and morality is religious. That was something that was hammered home by the Prophets and that for the Jew was enshrined in the foundation document of the Decalogue. The people of God were to be a moral people. Not that this was achieved without struggle. It required the insistent prophetic proclamation to set the record straight: cult was not sufficient; moral concern was required. "Cease to do evil, learn to do good, seek justice, rescue the oppressed, defend the orphan, plead for the widow" (Isa 1:17ff.).

This is a staple element of daily Christian life. The New Testament tells us that love of other and love of God are inextricably intertwined, that what will matter in the end is how we have loved the other. But how we conceptualize that relationship or how it affects our notion of morality or of moral obligation is something about which we must be careful. It is a species of God-talk and perhaps the most recalcitrant part of it. It has been called "the theological frontier of ethics" (Maclagan) and been judged to present us with "a baffling semantic task" (Williams). Christians attempt to express it in various ways—ethical life as God's law or will, as imitation, liberation, kingdom, salvation, etc.

The basic metaphor of the tradition sees morality as the law of God. That especially invites misunderstandings. Many theologians have urged the need for great logical caution in using such language and have pointed to the shortcomings of the law-judgment forensic metaphor. The danger is of collapsing morality into religion, of failing to appreciate that morality, even for the Christian, has a relative autonomy and makes its own demand, *etsi Deus non daretur.* Rahner's model offers the best hope of giving due weight to moral experience and yet situating it in its ultimate context. It is not, he says, that one loves God and then—in accordance with the will of God—is disposed to do good to the neighbor. It is not that we have been commanded to love the neighbor and do so out of love of God. It is not that the love of God is the motive for love of neighbor. There is an even more radical unity between the two. The explicit love of neighbor is the primary act of love of God. God is the horizon of the moral act of love of the other and is implicitly sought in love of the other. Not to love the other is not to love God.

Everyday moral response is response to God. But how is one to *know* the right moral response? If we are believers in a theory of natural law we recognize that human beings have a capacity to decipher the moral way in some detail. But we do that within and in fidelity to our story. We do not make our choices in a vacuum. The horizon within which we make them is already established by our character. And that is a product of our worldview, our culture and environment, and of the particular manner in which they have shaped our individual lives.

In the search for the truth our religious myth ought to be significant. Beliefs about the way things are, about what is lasting or important bear on choice. They affect what we regard as worth choosing. Like all basic myths the Christian story gives us our stance towards the world and its creation, towards the value and significance of the human person, towards body, matter, spirit, towards the meaning and significance of history, towards life and death, towards what constitutes flourishing or perfection, towards success and failure. They are all matters that are the common coin of moralists and in various subtle ways they color our understanding of the whole moral project and enter into our concrete choices. Even within the Christian tradition itself one can easily detect how different attitudes towards these basic themes have affected moral understanding. Think how attitudes to body, matter, and spirit have affected moral positions on sexuality, how views about sexual (in)equality or about political authority and the God-given structures of society have affected moral positions on justice, or how the understanding of salvation has affected attitudes to moral engagement in the world.

In their daily struggle Christians will be enlightened by living with their tradition. We are not the first Christians. The discernment we engage in has been done since the beginning. We can learn by entering into the ethos-ethic dynamic of our predecessors in the faith, especially that of the formative time. They did in their own time and place what we try to do in ours. Entering into the ethico-mythical worldview of the apostolic Church will help to form our ethical sensibility. But it will not give us easy answers either as a community (Church) or as individuals. There can be no facile appeal to a revealed morality: the difficulties of mining the Bible for authoritatively permanent and universal moral rules are immense. The tradition commends general virtues and thrusts that are timeless but that will not absolve one from the search for practical judgments in the particularities of life—and it is worth remembering that many moral choices are highly personal and individual.

Much energy has gone into the question of whether Christianity has a specific morality. What is important for Christians is that they make their moral choices in fidelity to their story, that they allow the great value lines of the story to inform their choice. There is point to the question, however. Anyone who remembers that the document The Church in the Modern World, for example, sought to commend itself to all people of goodwill will see the point: are its moral implications meant to be transparent to all or do they depend on subscribing to the Christian story? The question of specificity has proved not to be a very manageable one. Much depends on what one understands by morality, by moral act, by norm, by moral content. Much also depends on the term of comparison: the question cannot really be asked without setting up some term of comparison; how does Christianity in its moral vision and in the practical implications deriving from this (presuming we could agree about this) compare with the vision and action guides of Buddhism or Islam or some particular brand of philosophical ethics? Christians are bound to find broad coincidences between their positions and some other moral systems, both religious and nonreligious—much will depend here on how closely the fundamental worldviews coincide. But it should not surprise anyone if there are aspects of Christian choice which do not recommend themselves to those who do not share the myth.

VINCENT MacNAMARA

See also ETHICS, BUSINESS; SOCIAL TEACHING OF THE CHURCH; THEOLOGY, MORAL; VIRTUE.

CHRISTIAN SCIENCE

See CHURCH OF CHRIST, SCIENTIST.

CHRISTIAN SPIRITUALITY

There has been an enormous groundswell of interest in Christian spirituality in the period following the Second Vatican Council. This is due in part to the council's clear affirmation of the universal call to holiness (*Lumen Gentium* nos. 40–41), which provided impetus to take stock of the gifts and responsibilities incumbent upon all the baptized. The extraordinary growth of interest in Christian spirituality is reflected in the increase in number of persons enrolled in courses in spirituality, in the commitment to a deep and sustained prayer life on the part of Christians of all walks of life, and in the growing number of participants in support/study groups focused on assisting participants to develop toward an ever more mature spirituality.

What is Christian Spirituality?

It is now more commonly understood that within the Catholic tradition there is not just one spirituality, but a great diversity. From a contemporary perspective it is important to recognize that not all spiritualities are Catholic. There are distinctively Protestant spiritualities, Jewish spiritualities, Islamic spiritualities, and so on. Beyond discussion of specifically religious spiritualities, there is much to be said about a Latin American spirituality, a Native American spirituality, an African-American spirituality, and some versions of feminist spirituality which may or may not have an identifiably religious dimension. These wider parameters must be kept in mind when treating the rather slippery reality described by the term "spirituality."

"Christian spirituality," refers to both a lived experience and a more scholarly or academic discipline. In the first instance, the term describes the whole of the Christian's life as this is oriented to self-transcending knowledge, freedom, and love in light of the ultimate values and highest ideals perceived and pursued in the mystery of Jesus Christ through the Holy Spirit in the Church, the community of disciples. That is to say, spirituality is concerned with everything that constitutes Christian experience, specifically the perception and pursuit of the highest ideal or goal of Christian life, e.g., an ever more intense union with God disclosed in Christ through life in the Spirit. Stated simply, Christian spirituality is nothing other than life in Christ by the power of the Spirit. At a second level, however, the term Christian spirituality refers to a scholarly or academic discipline, increasingly interdisciplinary in nature, which attempts to study Christian religious experience as such, and to promote its development and maturation.

Whether it be the lived experience or the discipline which attends to this subject, the particular focus of Christian spirituality is threefold.

First, Christian spirituality is concerned with the *human person* in *relation* to God. While this may be said to be the concern of any area of theology or religious studies, it is the specific concern of spirituality to focus precisely upon the relational and personal (inclusive of the social and political) dimensions of the human person's relationship to God.

Second, the focus of Christian spirituality is on the *full spectrum* of those realities that constitute the Christian life in relation to God. Christian spirituality does not stand alone, but exists in reciprocal relationship to biblical theology, systematic theology, moral theology, pastoral theology, and liturgical studies. What differentiates spirituality from, say, systematic theology or moral theology, is its focus on the *dynamic* and *concrete* character of the relationship of the human person to God in *actual life situations.* Moreover, this relationship is one of *development,* of *growth* in the life of faith, and thus covers the whole of life. Spirituality is concerned with religious experience as such, not just concepts or obligations.

Third, the focus in Christian spirituality in the postconciliar period is much wider than in previous generations. It is now more commonly recognized that insights from a great *variety of disciplines* can be rich resources for growth and development in the Christian life. Those concerned with Christian spirituality are attentive to insights from other disciplines (e.g., sociology, history, economics, especially psychology) as these may contribute to a fuller understanding of Christian spirituality. Additionally, the fruits of *ecumenical and interreligious dialogues* have greatly enriched contemporary understandings of Christian spirituality.

Currents in Contemporary Christian Spirituality

The enormous growth of interest in Christian spirituality especially apparent since the Second Vatican Council has been accompanied and further developed by a wide range of literature in the area of Christian spirituality. The range includes resources and research tools for those working in the academic field of spirituality, significant contributions in various scholarly journals, periodicals devoted to making the findings of scholarly research more accessible to an educated readership, and journals/magazines of a more popular/practical sort. It also includes an astonishing number of books published in the area of spirituality. These range from the scholarly and esoteric to the "pop," "thin," and "fluffy," from critical editions of the Christian classics and mystical treatises to self-help manuals for coping with grief or handbooks for living with integrity through separation and divorce. Contemporary writers in the field include priests, monks, nuns, religious, and laypersons, male and female, married and single. It would be impossible to provide here an exhaustive survey of the various types of contemporary spiritual writings, though it is important to note that there continues to be an abiding interest in particular spiritualities, and there is a great deal of writing on these, e.g., spiritualities of the priesthood, religious life, married life. Let it suffice to say that whether the subject be Christian spirituality more generally, or be it more specific or particular Christian spiritualities, there are some distinctive currents in the field of Christian spirituality as expressed in various writings, conference talks, workshop themes, titles of audiocassettes or audio-visual recordings. These currents in contemporary Christian spirituality may be outlined as follows: (1) There is a focus on a more holistic understanding of Christian faith and living, rooted in experience. (2) Great attention is given to the contextual and relational dimensions of spirituality, inclusive of affectivity, intimacy, and sexuality. (3) There is stress on the liturgical (*Sacrosanctum Concilium* nos. 1 and 10) and scriptural foundations of spirituality, as well as attention to the universal call to holiness, thereby undercutting the notion of a spiritual elite. Writing on particular Christian spiritualities for clergy and religious usually reflects this sensibility. (4) As in every age, there is attention to the search for the authentic self, the person one is created and called to be, but with greater appreciation for the complementarity of human development and spiritual growth. (5) In the quest for the authentic self, self-scrutinary and the development of critical consciousness vis-à-vis the sources of oppression and injustice go hand in hand. (6) This is related to the attempt to find ways of integrating prayer and action through forms of gospel living appropriate to the urgent demands of the age. (7) Among these urgent demands is the promotion of the full equality of women in Church and society, and the recognition of those who have been marginalized and, consequently, whose alternative experience has been rendered voiceless and insignificant by the dominant social-symbolic order in Church and society. (8) At the brink of the third millennium, more, but still insufficient, attention is being given to the appropriate Christian response in the face of the possibility of nuclear annihilation and the probability of ecological crises of proportions heretofore unimaginable. (9) There is a fuller recognition of both the riches and the shortcomings of the Christian tradition for answering the problems to be faced in the third millennium. (10) There is increasing attention given to the Trinity as the uniquely Christian understanding of God, stressing the relational and personal God disclosed in the person of Jesus Christ. This understanding of God as a communion of persons in relation has enormous consequences for a contemporary Christian understanding of God, the human person, and relations between and among persons both divine and human. A proper understanding of the Trinity, cognizant of its eminently practical implications, has profound ramifications for our understanding of Christian spirituality.

Ways of Understanding Christian Spirituality
One of the most important developments in post-conciliar reflection on Christian spirituality is the increasing attention being given to defining the precise nature, scope, and limits of spirituality, both as a lived experience and an academic or scholarly discipline. That is to say, there is deeper recognition of the importance of a clear and identifiable method for understanding Christian spirituality. What follows is one way among others for coming to a clearer understanding of Christian spirituality.

Whether one is concerned with Christian religious experience as such, or with a more academic or scholarly examination of Christian spirituality, it may be helpful to identify and consider seven focal points of investigation. Christian spirituality is concerned with the presence and activity of the Holy Spirit in persons: (1) within a culture; (2) in relation to a tradition; (3) in light of contemporary events, hopes, sufferings, and promises; (4) in remembrance of Jesus Christ; (5) in efforts to combine elements of action and contemplation; (6) with respect to charism and community; (7) as expressed and authenticated in practice. Such a framework can be used by those who are studying spirituality in a disciplined way, as well as by those who are simply attempting to come to a deeper understanding of spirituality, their own or others', past or present.

Whether one examines a scriptural or theological text, a legend of a saint or a painting of her with eyes turned heavenward, a type of religious vesture or sacred music, a kind of church architecture or sculpture, it is useful to attend to the object under consideration in view of these seven focal points. One might ask: What was the *culture* within which this depiction of the Last Judgment was painted? When considering a treatise on virtue, one might ask: What are the religious and theological *traditions* reflected, adhered to, departed from in this text? What are/were the significant *events, hopes, sufferings, and promises* of the age in which this score of sacred music was composed? How does the music reflect, nuance, or critique them? How is the *memory of Christ* expressed, or what is the dominant image of Christ being expressed, in this bronze or fresco? What is the view of the relationship between *contemplation and action* expressed in this stained glass depiction of Mary with book-in-hand? Or with Jesus in her arms? Or with hands folded in prayer? What is the understanding of *charism and community* expressed in the uniform attire of women religious prior to the Second Vatican Council? And what understandings of charism and community are expressed in the variegated attire of women religious today? How do these various understandings express themselves in different forms of *praxis,* then and now? This is a sample of the sort of questions that might be raised in trying to uncover the specific spirituality of person or group, past or present.

How might one work within this framework when considering a text or life of an individual of an earlier epoch? As an example one might focus on the life of Francis of Assisi in the early writings about him. In trying to understand Francis' spirituality, one could consider the way in which Francis remembers Christ, or try to uncover the predominant image of Christ that emerges in early Franciscan writings and devotion, e.g., the poor Christ crucified. By way of contrast one might then focus on what can be known of how Christ was remembered, or what image of Christ predominated, in the legacy of Dominic and his first followers. Whatever similarities there may be, there are significant differences in the way Christ was remembered by Dominic and the early Dominicans on the one hand, and by Francis and his followers on the other. And the practice (the seventh focal point of the framework) of the gospel appropriate to a Dominican, i.e., preaching, teaching, study, will be somewhat different from the practice appropriate to a Franciscan. This is due, at least in part, to the way Christ is remembered, or which image of Christ predominates, in each tradition. Said another way, there are distinctively Dominican and Franciscan spiritualities due to the fact that the central understanding of Christ that lies at the heart of each is quite different. One might then juxtapose these insights alongside what may be gleaned from a reading of the Ignatian sources in view of the question of how Christ is portrayed therein, attentive to what have been judged appropriate forms of practice that result from such a remembrance. What sort of spirituality is expressed and impressed by the dominant image of Christ as king in the Ignatian sources? How is such a spirituality to flourish in light of some contemporary modes of perceiving and being which are resistant if not outright hostile to the very notion of "royalty"?

Similar questions might be asked in trying to understand the spirituality of some twentieth-century figures such as Dorothy Day, Roger Schutz, Jean Vanier, Thomas Merton, or Chiara Lubich. The prevailing image of Christ in the writings of Thomas Merton is quite different from that in the writings of Jean Vanier. The latter is expressed and authenticated in the practice of living in community with mentally handicapped persons who, in their poverty and brokenness, disclose the presence of the living Christ whose grace is discerned in the weakness and poverty of our humanity, rather than in human strength, power, and achievement. What is the understanding of Christ that has led Roger Schutz to begin at Taizé a monastic community in the tradition of the Reformation, comprising both Protestant and Roman Catholic men whose vocation is to be a sign of reconciliation in a divided Church?

If one were to shift attention to a contemporary text such as the United States Catholic Bishops' pastoral letter on the economy, *Economic Justice For All,* with an eye to the spirituality expressed in its pages, it might be useful to consider the understanding of culture (the first focal point) operative therein. How is the Spirit at work within a culture shaped by materialism and consumerism? Where is the work of the Spirit in those economic systems that systematically impoverish one culture at the expense of another? How is the Spirit expressed and authenticated in the practice of the gospel amidst conflicts of impinging cultures replete with economic ambiguities? And how are the signs of the Spirit's presence and action to be discerned in the efforts of those who promote authentic human flourishing within contemporary North American cultures, but do so outside the parameters of any religious tradition or institution?

As another example of the attempt to understand a contemporary text, person or movement, when considering Christian feminist spirituality one might focus on the role of tradition (the second focal point) in women's spirituality. How has the Spirit been at work in those Christian traditions that have rendered the voices and experiences of women inaudible and insignificant? How has the Spirit enabled women to resist, critique, and/or reject those traditions by which they have been willfully and systematically excluded? Are there "spaces" within the Christian tradition that provided room for fuller participation on the part of women in the life and ministry of the Church? Where are such "spaces" being created today, and who is actively engaged in creating them?

Whether the focus be on the past or the present, using this framework enables one to attend to the crucial importance of practice as the expression and authentication of the Spirit's work (the seventh focal point). The practice appropriate to a person or group, past or present, will vary due to the way in which the Spirit is at work within a culture, in relation to a tradition, in response to the events, hopes, sufferings, and promises of an age, in view of different ways of remembering Jesus, in efforts to combine elements of action and contemplation, and with respect to diverse charisms and different constellations of community. Thus the practice of the Christian life, or spirituality, appropriate to the members of an enclosed monastic community of Cistercians will be quite different from that of the members of the Catholic Worker House due, in no small measure, to different peceptions of how action and contemplation are to be integrated. Similarly, the way that spouses and parents of young children strive to combine elements of prayer and action will be quite different from the ways appropriate to an aging widow. But it is crucial to see that whatever one's situation in life may be, the fullness of life in Christ entails the integration of prayer and action in response to the work of the Holy Spirit in human life, history, world, and Church.

Conclusion

This description has drawn attention to Christian spirituality as both lived experience and academic or scholarly discipline, to the precise focus of Christian spirituality, as well as to significant currents in Christian spirituality today. As lived experience, current trends in Christian spirituality give evidence of great vitality and maturation on the part of those who profess faith in Christ Jesus and live by the power of the Spirit. As an academic or scholarly discipline, spirituality is in a period of growth and development. Great effort is being made on the part of students and teachers in the field to clarify the limits, the scope, and the precise subject of Christian spirituality. Central to this task is the work of bringing methodological form to understanding and studying spirituality so as to facilitate its fuller development and maturation. It is in this vein that this examination has offered a way of beginning to understand Christian spirituality through careful attention to seven focal points in which the Holy Spirit's presence and activity may be discerned.

MICHAEL DOWNEY

See also HOLINESS; HOLY SPIRIT; SPIRITUAL LIFE; VIRTUE.

CHRISTMAS

See LITURGICAL YEAR, THE.

CHRISTOLOGY

See JESUS CHRIST; SOTERIOLOGY.

CHRISTOPHERS, THE

This is an international movement founded in the United States in 1945 by James Keller, a Maryknoll priest, and is dedicated to spreading the belief that each person has the responsibility to act positively and to overcome evil by doing good. Though it is nondenominational, it is steeped in the Judaeo-

Christian tradition of service to God and to one's neighbor, and it stresses the belief of how much good one person can do with God's help. The name, "christopher," is derived from the Greek words meaning "Christ-bearer," and the motto of the movement is "It is better to light one candle than to curse the darkness."

The movement is a loose association without meetings or membership dues, and it spreads its message through the mass media. The famous "Christopher News Notes" is a newsletter published ten times each year and sent to interested parties which explains some aspect of the Christian faith and gives concrete examples of people living this aspect of the faith in a specific, positive way. The Christophers also publish pamphlets in Spanish. In an effort to spread their message more widely, they produce radio and television programs, publish books, make videocassettes for children and adults, sponsor columns in many newspapers, conduct leadership courses, and publish materials for work with youth. They also honor various people living their message through an annual awards ceremony.

The Christophers have been successful in reaching millions of people through excellent productions and publications. Though they are not a Catholic organization in an exclusive sense, their message is definitely Christian. They use the Bible and Christian spirituality as a basis for this message.

ANTHONY D. ANDREASSI

See also LAITY, THEOLOGY OF THE; SPIRITUALITY, LAY; VOCATION.

CHRONOLOGY OF THE REFORMATION

See REFORMATION, CHRONOLOGY OF THE.

CHURCH AND STATE

This is the rubric under which prior to the Second Vatican Council the presence of the Church in the world was usually discussed in Catholic theology. It corresponds to an understanding of Church in which institutional features were predominant and in which the Church's relationship to society was envisaged in terms of its relationship to the institutions of the state. Specifically it evoked the issue of the recognition of Catholicism by constitutional and other secular law.

The apparent simplicity of the biblical "Render to Caesar what is Caesar's, to God what is God's" had in the history of the Church's relations with the secular arm proved deceptive. From the concept of a Holy Roman Empire, through the doctrine of the Two Swords, to the teaching of Leo XIII concerning the coexistence of two *societates perfectae,* there have been many mutations in both theory and practice concerning the proper relationship of the Church and civil society. Current doctrine is the teaching of *Dignitatis Humanae,* the Declaration on Religious Freedom of the Second Vatican Council.

The essence of the council's teaching is that in matters of religious belief and practice no one should be compelled to go against conscience, nor restrained from following conscience—within the limits of the common good. The common good is the ensemble of conditions of social living which make for the flourishing of each member of society according to his or her potential and with relative ease. Peace, justice, and public morality are taken to be touchstones of the common good's requirements.

The council bases this principle on the dignity of the human person and on the nature of the search for truth. Human dignity consists in the twin gifts of reason and freedom, the bases of personal responsibility and of the impulse and obligation to search for the truth, including religious truth. And the nature of the search for truth is such that people must be free to communicate with each other the truth which they have discovered or think they have discovered, so that they may help each other in the search. This freedom holds even when they are mistaken, even negligently or willfully so.

The philosophical grounding of the doctrine concerning religious freedom is enhanced by an appeal to the nature of religion, the characteristic acts of which are internal and voluntary and so not to be coerced. And these internal acts seek external expression also, including expression in community. Hence people should not be prevented from publicly expressing their faith, provided that the just requirements of public order are observed.

In support of its teaching the council also adduces some more precisely theological considerations. A key truth in Catholic teaching is that a faith-response is of its nature free. And this is reflected in the way in which Jesus himself preached his gospel, for he deliberately rejected the way of coercive imposition, allowing his message to draw his hearers by the power of its own truth. This too was the demeanor of the apostles; and "although in the life of the people of God in its pilgrimage through the vicissitudes of human history there has at times appeared a form of behavior which was hardly in keeping with the spirit and was even opposed to it, it has always remained the teaching of the Church that no one is to be coerced into believing" (DH 12).

The right to religious freedom should, the council says, be recognized by societies in such a way that it becomes a civil right. And it includes an entitlement "not to be prevented from freely demonstrating the special value of their teaching for the organization of society and the inspiration of all human activity" (4). This is an aspect of the right to bear public witness to faith through the spoken or written word. "However, in spreading religious belief and in introducing religious practices everybody must at all times avoid any action which seems to suggest coercion or dishonest or unworthy persuasion especially when dealing with the uneducated or the poor" (ibid).

A question which arises is whether the council's doctrine is applicable to morality as well as to religion. This is important because of an obvious pluralism in moral belief and practice in today's world. It might be answered that the council cannot have intended a sharp distinction between the two spheres and so must have envisaged its teaching as covering moral as well as religious truth in a strict sense of the latter expression. A better answer may be to say that the ultimate philosophical bases upon which the doctrine rests, the dignity of the person and the nature of the search for truth, hold in the moral as in the religious sphere.

Hence in formulating a Catholic theological response to the phenomenon of moral pluralism in modern societies it should be possible to take direction from the principles and perspectives of the Declaration. This is especially so as regards the sometimes difficult question of the embodiment of morality in law. In moral matters, as in religious, people should not be made to act against conscience, nor precluded from acting according to their consciences, subject only to the constraints required by the common good.

This of course raises the question, what is the common good? As indicated above, a standard Catholic description is that it is the ensemble of conditions of social living which enable the flourishing of each member of the community. The requirements of peace, justice, and public morality are touchstones of the common good, public order a precondition. Our principle then would be that freedom of moral belief and practice should be curtailed by law only in the interests of these values.

That, however, is a beginning and not the end of debate. The claims of "public morality" are obviously crucial and their specification often controversial. In seeking to define them Catholic theology joins a debate in Anglo-United States philosophy of law set in train in modern times by a celebrated exchange between the English judge Lord Devlin and H.L.A. Hart, then professor of Jurisprudence at Oxford. The latter's view, indebted to John Stuart Mill, is the "liberal" one that the law should restrain freedom only to prevent a demonstrable harm to others or, in a few matters, as an expression of a legitimate paternalism. Lord Devlin's standpoint is the more conservative: any society is held together by, inter alia, a shared morality which may be enforced by law where appropriate. It is worth remarking that a Catholic, as any other citizen, might hold either view.

Constitutional and legal questions concerning the relationship between Church and state and the embodiment of morality in law are however only one strand in a much wider discussion about the role of the Church in the modern world. An underlying theme is that of the presence of the Church in the secular arena, and especially the question of how the Churches and their leaderships may contribute to public debate about values. The Judeo-Christian inheritance is rich in insight into human nature and its flourishing, personal and communal. The challenge for the magisterium today is to find a stance and a style and an idiom which will enable them to commend that inheritance not only to Church members but to people of good will everywhere.

PATRICK HANNON

See also CATHOLICS IN POLITICS; RELIGIOUS FREEDOM; VATICAN COUNCIL II.

CHURCH IN AUSTRALIA

See AUSTRALIA, CHURCH IN.

CHURCH IN BRITAIN

See BRITAIN, CHURCH IN.

CHURCH OF CHRIST, SCIENTIST (CHRISTIAN SCIENCE)

Mary Baker Eddy (1821–1910), who founded the Christian Science Church, was a sickly woman with a severe back malady. In 1866 she was instantaneously cured as she read accounts of Jesus' healing in the Gospels, specifically Matthew 9:1-8. Mrs. Eddy's receptivity to this experience of healing was enhanced by her acquaintance with mental healer Phineas Parkhurst Quimby (1802–1866) who himself was a follower of eighteenth-century German physician, Franz Anton Mesmer.

These healings changed her life and she came to believe strongly that all sickness can be healed by belief and prayer. The latter became for her followers an acceptable alternative to medicine.

Within a few years she had written *Science and Health with Key to Scriptures* (1875) and with a small group of believers formed the first Christian Science community in her hometown of Lynn, Massachusetts, in 1875. The Christian Science Church was founded in Boston in 1879.

Christian Science represents a religious dimension of the Platonic legacy in much Western and Christian thought. That legacy insists that all reality is spiritual; ideas, not matter, finally exist. This philosophy was the basis of Mrs. Eddy's claim that mental power and prayer can change all forms of diseases.

At the heart of Christian Science is the conviction that God is Eternal Light, Perfect Mind, Unchanging Truth, Infinite Spirit, Divine Principle, and Ultimate Love. We are made in the image of God and so have the potential to realize all that perfection, truth, and light in ourselves. If we are in tune with the immutable spiritual laws of God, we will be healthy and whole just as God is. Our sickness and sin are expressions of an unreal picture (one of error and mistaken thoughts) of what human beings are meant to be.

One is helped by a Christian Science Practitioner who is trained by the Mother Church to assist in the healing of others by directed reading, counseling, techniques of positive thinking, and prayer.

A brief summary of Christian Science beliefs is found in this paraphrase from *Science and Health*: (1) The Bible is the inspired word of God and our sufficient guide for eternal life; (2) We acknowledge the oneness and infinity of God, Christ as His Son, the Holy Spirit as our Comforter, and man as made in the image of God; (3) We believe in the forgiveness of sin and acknowledge the spiritual understanding that evil is unreal; (4) Jesus' atonement reveals God's Love and our undying unity with God. We are saved through the "Galilean Prophet's" healing power and his overcoming of sin and death by his resurrection; (5) We wait and pray for that Mind which was in Christ; we desire to practice the Golden Rule and to be "merciful, just, and pure."

Christian Science is not a proselytizing religion, but Christian Science Reading rooms are available to the public in almost every major community. Here people can read the Bible, *Science and Health,* and a vast array of healing literature published by the Mother Church in Boston.

Sunday worship consists of reading from Scripture, Mary Baker Eddy's works, and a prescribed sermon for the day designed by the denominational headquarters. Music and testimonies of healing may also be heard on Sunday. Wednesday evening meetings include testimonies and prayer for healing. A Board of Lectureship authorizes lectures and speakers who address college audiences and other public forums.

Mary Baker Eddy was probably the first to use gender-inclusive language in Christian liturgy with her translation of The Lord's Prayer as "Our Father, Mother God. . . ."

Many non-Christian Scientists read the *The Christian Science Monitor,* one of the nation's most respected newspapers.

Christian Scientists do not keep membership rolls, so we do not have figures for assessing the number of Christian Scientists.

IRA ZEPP

See also FAITH; HEALING; PROTESTANTISM.

CHURCH OF JESUS CHRIST OF LATTER DAY SAINTS (MORMONS)

Joseph Smith (1805–1844), who founded the Mormons, was confused as a young man by the many denominational claims to Christian truth he heard. In his spiritual journey, he asked, "Are the Methodists right?" "What about the Presbyterians?" "Which one should I choose?"

A profoundly moving religious experience in 1823 helped answer his questions. An angel led Smith to discover a set of Golden Plates near Palmyra, New York. These tablets eventually became the Book of Mormon. The book, and subsequently the Church, was named after Mormon, a prophet who lived in America in the fourth century of this era. He compiled a book which contains the records of several "lost tribes" of Israel who Mormon believed came to this hemisphere from Jerusalem about 600 B.C. Moroni, Mormon's son, was the last prophet to write in the Book of Mormon, and was the same angel who appeared to Joseph Smith to tell him he was divinely chosen to restore God's Church to the "fullness of the everlasting Gospel."

As Joseph Smith assimilated the meaning of this vision, he found that neither Orthodox Christians, Roman Catholics, nor Protestants were acceptable versions of Christianity; they had all, to some degree, deviated from the purity of God's revelation in Jesus. The Mormons, therefore, were simply to return to the norms of the original Christian community. These "saints," or members of the Church, want to restore the gospel of Christ. The Church was founded in New York in 1830.

The new Church met with hostility and Smith migrated from New York State; and, after successive stops in Ohio and Missouri, he and his followers settled in Illinois. Here they met with severe persecution and Smith, himself, was killed in 1844.

After Smith's death, the Mormon community split into several factions. The largest group followed Brigham Young (1801–1877) to Salt Lake City, Utah, their present international headquarters. This group was known for its practice of polygamy which lasted from 1843 to 1890 when it was outlawed by the federal government. In Smith's view, singleness was virtually a heresy and salvation was directly linked to marriage.

The other main Mormon branch is the Reorganized Church of Latter Day Saints who consider themselves true successors of Smith's Church. It is headquartered in Independence, Missouri.

Some distinctive Mormon beliefs are: (a) The Book of Mormon is to read along with the Bible; (b) Adam and Eve are not responsible for our sin; (c) God's revelation continues today through the Elders of the Church; (d) missionary work for two years is required of all young men; (e) special emphasis on marriage and family (marriages last for eternity); (f) self-reliance; (g) Christ visited this hemisphere after his return to God, and America has a special place in the economy of God; and (h) because of their insistence that all human beings can trace their origins to Adam and Eve, Mormons probably keep the most accurate genealogical records in the world.

A striking distinction among Mormons is the belief that God was once a human being and achieved divinity and, likewise, we can become God. A Mormon saying goes like this: "What man is now, God once was; what God is now, man may become."

Mormons emphasize a healthy lifestyle—no caffeine, alcohol, drugs, or tobacco, and little meat. They stress modesty in speech and good grooming. Their worship service is typically a Protestant one. Millions of people have heard the concerts of the Mormon Tabernacle Choir for over fifty years. Some prominent Mormons are Ezra Taft Benson, George Romney, The Osmonds, and J. Willard Marriott, Jr.

There are about 8.5 million Mormons in the world and about 4.3 million in the United States.

IRA ZEPP

See also PROTESTANTISM.

CHURCH, THE

Origin and History

The four Gospels frequently present Jesus surrounded by a group of disciples who have dedicated themselves to him and learn from him. There are also several indications that Jesus expected them to continue as a group after his death. Thus he gives them teachings, ministries, rituals, mission, and the promise of the future direction of the Holy Spirit. After Jesus' death, apostles and missionaries spread his message and established communities throughout the Mediterranean world and beyond.

Paul describes the Church as God's building (1 Cor 3:10; 2 Cor 5:1), or Temple (1 Cor 3:16) in which God dwells (1 Cor 6:19; Rom 8:11). It is God's assembly—as Israel was in the desert (1 Thess 2:14; Gal 1:22; 1 Cor 1:2), only now it is the assembly of the saints (Rom 8:27; 1 Cor 6:1). Paul also describes the Church as a household (1 Cor 16:15) or family (1 Cor 4:14-15), mother (Gal 4:19), nurse (1 Cor 3:2), and spouse (2 Cor 11:2). He also develops several models of the Church: people of God (Rom 9:25-26; 2 Cor 6:16), a new creation (Gal 6:15), the body of Christ (1 Cor 10:16; 12:27).

Mark always presents Jesus in the company of his disciples; they are his new family (Mark 3:31-35), the house-church of the Lord, the boat of the Church (3:9; 4:1), the flock of God (Mark 6:34; 14:27), and the new Temple (Mark 14:58; 15:29). Mark's community believed Jesus had brought a new period of history and confided his message to them (Mark 1:15), and established a community on them as a foundation (Mark 10:14-15). Mark's central theme is the history of the kingdom, a kingdom that is communal, made up of the new People of God (Mark 4:1-34), and already present in the signs of the miracles.

Matthew's is the only gospel to use the word "church" (Matt 16:18; 18:17), and teachings on the Church influence his whole presentation. Thus, members of his community are they who hear "the message about the kingdom" (Matt 13:19), and have received "The knowledge of the secrets of the kingdom of heaven" (Matt 13:11), and who truly "seek first his kingdom and his righteousness" (Matt 6:33). These disciples will inherit the kingdom (Matt 5:3, 10; 25:34), replace those to whom it had previously been promised (Matt 21:43). This writer challenges followers to preach the gospel to the ends of the earth (Matt 10:7; 24:14; 28:20).

Luke is the only New Testament writer to give a second volume, presenting the life of the early Church. He portrays a growing self-awareness among the early disciples and a serious commitment to a community dimension of their faith-filled lives together (Acts 1:12-14; 2:41-47; 5:12-14). The apostolic Church that Luke describes saw itself as a community of those who were saved by God (Acts 2:47). The conditions for membership in this community were laid down by Peter: repentance, belief in Jesus, baptism, and reception of the Spirit (Acts 2:38). Their life together was maintained through ongoing fidelity to the Word (Acts 12:24; 19:20; 20:32) and Spirit (Acts 4:25; 5:32; 16:6), and included a joyful acceptance of the trials that accompanied life dedicated to the Lord (Acts 4:23-31; 14:22).

John sees the Church as a community of love, based on the Word, and guided by the Spirit. Membership implies rejection of the sinful world, a life centered on believing in Jesus, and love both of God and of neighbor. The Church is made up of a group of followers that Jesus can genuinely call his own (John 13:1). Jesus purifies them with his word (John 15:3), shares his friendship, entrusts them with confidence (John 15:15; 17:26), and empowers them to become children of God (John 1:12). Entry into life with the Lord in the community of the Church comes through a new birth to eternal life (John 3:3, 5). This new life as God's kingdom implies obedience to the commandments (John 14:21), acceptance of the words of Jesus (John 12:48), and a dedication to act in truth (John 3:21).

At first, the followers of Jesus were called disciples, and then "Christians" (Acts 11:26) but later referred to themselves with terms that had been used by the Jews as descriptions of the chosen place they held in God's plan: thus, the chosen assembly (*Qahal*), the chosen people, the family of the Lord. Two words arose in the cultures dependent on Mediterranean languages to portray the disciples' self-understanding: those dependent on the Greek world of the patriarch of Constantinople used the term (*kuriake oikia*) meaning family of the Lord, from which we get words like Church, *kirk, Kirche;* and those dependent on the Latin world of the pope at Rome used a term (*ecclesia*) that described the Church as the assembly of the Lord, from which we get words like *chiesa, église, iglesia.*

The Church believes that Jesus founded it upon the apostles, calling it to be one, holy, catholic or universal, and apostolic. Local communities gathered in union with other communities in the region under the leadership of their bishops; and bishops gathered their churches under the leadership of a patriarch. There were five great patriarchs—the leaders of Jerusalem, Antioch, Alexandria, Constantinople, and Rome—these were self-governing Churches (autocephalous). While they sought to maintain unity, divisions arose. In 861, the bishops of Rome and Constantinople divided over their different understandings of the relationship of the Holy Spirit to the Father and Son. While Rome claimed authority to make the change, Constantinople and the other Greek Churches began to describe themselves as Orthodox. The Great Schism (1378–1417) refers to the split in the Western Latin Church between those Christians showing allegiance to the Bishop of Rome, and those who showed allegiance to the bishop residing in Avignon. The sixteenth century witnessed the two divisions of Protestantism and Anglicanism at the time of the Reformation—it was from this time on that we have the denominalization of Christianity and the introduction of the term "Roman Catholicism." In 1889, a group of Catholics split from Rome over the teachings of the First Vatican Council (1869–1870), and referred to themselves as Old Catholics. In 1988, following their rejection of the teachings of the Second Vatican Council, a group of Catholics under the leadership of Bishop Levefre broke unity with Rome and started a traditionalist Church.

Church in the Teachings of Vatican II

In 1959 Pope John XXIII announced his intentions of calling an ecumenical council. This council opened on 11 October 1962 and concluded on 8 December 1965. There were four sessions, and some observers believe the participants moved through four moods or reactions—reckoning, direction, criticism, and maturity. Over twenty-six hundred bishops attended this twenty-first ecumenical council—first council of the world Church—more than any other council in Church history. Previous councils had often been called by a powerful group in the Church, eager to gain support for their agenda of reform, whereas Vatican II was called by one individual, John XXIII. Moreover, voting was frequently split. This lack of a powerful group, and split voting continued to show up after the council in divided reactions. Vatican II published sixteen documents, amounting to over two-thirds of all ecumenical conciliar documents in Church history. Central to all the teachings was the council's focus on the Church, especially in its two great documents, The Constitution on the Church (*Lumen Gentium*) and the Pastoral Constitution on the Church in the Modern World (*Gaudium et Spes*). These two documents act like the axis of the council and all other documents have some links with these two and must be read in light of these two.

Since the council the Church has been described in many ways with the help of images and models, some traditional and some new. Thus, the Church has been described as a mystery, the people of God, the body of Christ, the community of believers, a sign or sacrament for the world, the servant Church, the praying Church. The council participants seemed to go through three stages in their own appreciation of the nature of the contemporary Church, seeing the faithful as a community, in the heart of the world, to serve the world—these three dimensions of conciliar renewal emerged in the three sets of changes made to documents through the four sessions. Moreover, focuses of renewal can also be seen in the four journeys that John XXIII and Paul VI undertook during the council—Loretto-Assisi and simplicity, Jerusalem and the work for ecumenical unity, Bombay and concern for the poor, and New

York (United Nations) and the dialogue with the contemporary world.

The selection and arrangement of chapters in the Dogmatic Constitution on the Church (*Lumen Gentium*) reflects a new self-understanding on the part of the Church. Although originally it began with the hierarchy, after much debate the chapters were reordered to emphasize the Church as a mystery of God's love and the people of God which is ministered to by the hierarchical structures of the Church. The document then focuses immediately on the laity, then the religious, and their common final destiny.

The major understanding of the Church in the council's teachings is that the Church is the people of God, and all other understandings are secondary to this. Through baptism believers are reborn as a new community, God's chosen people, people of the covenant, the messianic people (LG 9:1-4). This people of God shares in Christ's offices of priest, prophet and servant-king (LG 10–12). All humanity is called to be part of this people of God (LG 13). In fact, while the council focuses on the Roman Catholic Church, it also recognizes the presence of God's grace in other Churches and ecclesial communities (LG 15).

Church and World in Mutual Service

While the Church's essential mission is to spread the kingdom, it is also immersed in the joys and pains of the world (GS 1:1), believes that the world although tempted to sin is good in itself (GS 36:2), and sees that part of its own mission is to intensify its service to the world (GS 2:1). The Church is a leaven in the world, witnessing to eternal values, helping society maintain the value of family life, supporting the dignity of human nature, promoting social unity, and urging its followers to fulfill their civic and political responsibilities as part of their Christian commitment (GS 40-43).

At the same time the Church gratefully acknowledges the help it receives from contemporary society; learning from past history, the work of science, culture, living exchanges between nations, economic and social progress, and the signs of the times (GS 44).

Christians acknowledge that it is their task to work for the betterment of the world, using it with detachment but transforming it into what it is capable of becoming in a vision under God. This implies the Church's collaboration with all people of good will, but also implies the Church's prophetic task of challenging society's injustice, by socially criticizing society's false values, denouncing injustice, and working to bring a Christian spirit to the creation of a better world.

One of the insights of the council was to complement the traditional emphasis on the universal Church with firm teachings on the centrality of the local Church (LG 26). This is where the greatness of the Church is best appreciated, where the people of God are seen in their strength. The strength is the foundation; so the vision of Church life is a local, grassroots one. The life, vitality and service of others is attained at the local level where every individual baptized Christian needs to accept responsibility for the Church.

Organization of the Church

Christians believe Jesus founded his Church on the twelve apostles. The original disciples of Jesus numbered more than twelve but the symbolic number Twelve reminded early Christians, many of whom were Jews, that Christian leaders replaced the twelve patriarchs of Israel's history. The Twelve carried authority among believers because they had seen the Lord, listened to his teachings, witnessed his resurrection, and gave testimony to his message of salvation. They were given authority to preach, teach, and heal in Jesus's name (Matt 10:1, 7-8; Mark 3:14; Luke 9:1-2). Among the Twelve, Peter held an undisputed position of leadership, he was the group's spokesperson, he received special teachings from Jesus, and was privileged to be present at special events in Jesus's life and ministry. Three of the Gospels give episodes in which Jesus singles out Peter for a position of authority over the rest of the community (Matt 16:17-20; Luke 22:31-34; John 21:15-19). This petrine primacy is accepted today by most mainline Christian Churches.

Again, most Churches believe that the authority Jesus gave to his apostles was handed on by them in an unbroken line traceable to Jesus and referred to as apostolic succession. However, some Christian Churches see this apostolic succession in the authority of elders or charismatic leaders. Episcopal Churches (Anglican, Episcopalian, Orthodox, Old Catholic, and Roman Catholic) see this authority handed from apostles to bishops in unbroken line to present-day bishops. Several of these Churches also believe Peter's primacy was handed on by him to his successors—all, like him, bishops of Rome. Thus, Churches like the Orthodox or Anglican accept a papal primacy of honor or love. Disagreement arises regarding the Western Church's papal primacy of jurisdiction or legal authority. Along with these areas of common faith regarding apostolic succession to authority and episcopal and papal authority must be included the orders of priesthood and deaconate (some Churches may refuse to use the term "priesthood" but still have a minister of word and sacrament ordained by episcopal authority). Thus, many Christians believe the Church has three orders or levels of authority for service in the Church—deaconate, ministerial priesthood, episcopacy. The pope is a bishop, but succeeding to the primacy of Peter, he is also head of the college of bishops as Peter was head of the college of the apostles.

The Roman Catholic Church accepts this basic structure but has developed other offices of authority. The pope is head of the Church with a universal authority. Bishops are leaders in their own particular Churches with authority over every aspect of their own dioceses. Groups of bishops gather in a region under the leadership of an archbishop. However, while an archbishop or metropolitan clearly holds a leadership role in the Greek Church, that is not so in Roman Catholicism. An archbishop may well hold a lot of authority in his region because of the importance of his diocese, or because of his experience, or because of his years as a bishop, but he cannot legally intervene in another diocese of his region.

Within a diocese each pastor holds authority in his parish and delegates that to other priests who minister with him. All ordained priests in a diocese form part of the presbyterate—a kind of college of priests who minister in the name of the bishop. Often priests of a region gather together to discuss common problems, and the leading priest of the region is called a dean—however, like an archbishop, he has no authority other than influence. Deacons are ordained to serve the bishop but generally end up serving the bishop by working locally under the authority of a pastor.

While historically all Church authority was an authority of service for the people, who originally chose their own leaders, it nevertheless developed into levels of power and control. The faithful, who were originally the objects of the service and the orders' reason for existence, gradually became passive communities called to obey the authorities. All bishops, priests, and deacons together now total about half of one percent of the Roman Catholic Church.

Over the centuries, however, other offices have developed, each with specified powers given it by the Code of Canon Law or by delegation from higher authorities. These are man-made positions of authority and can be changed. Thus, the pope is assisted by departments of the Vatican, called congregations, each headed by a cardinal. Cardinals are key advisers to the pope. Originally, all were leading laity of Rome, but now are bishops from all over the world. In addition to heading the sacred congregations, other cardinals are often administrators of major dioceses throughout the world. Part of the responsibility of cardinals (those under eighty years old) is to gather in Rome at the death of a pope to participate in a conclave to elect the next pope.

Since the Western Church of Rome developed along the lines of a political power, referring to itself as "a perfect society" with legislative, executive, and judicial authority, it chose to present itself as a sovereign nation with a monarch—the pope, ambassadors—the nuncios and apostolic delegates, government ministers—the congregations, a cabinet of leaders to work alongside the pope—the curia, and a personal assistant to the pope—the Vatican secretary of state. As a monarch the pope grants knighthoods and a wide variety of honorary titles.

At each national level the Roman Catholic Church has developed other positions of authority such as the national primate—generally the bishop of the first important diocese in a country. Sometimes this remains a powerful office, as in Poland; in other cases it is an honorary title from history, as in the United States. The bishops of each nation gather together in an episcopal conference to support each other and deliberate issues of common interest. Episcopal conferences are emerging as a major form of the collegial government of bishops, and except for a few divisive trends, are becoming a fine unifying force in the regional Church. There are also several consultive bodies established to foster the national life of the Church—councils for laity, national associations of religious, and various national organizations to facilitate the development of specific ministries.

At the diocesan level, pastoral councils have formed since the Vatican Council II, and at a parish level, parish councils. These bodies, like their national counterparts, are made up of elected and/or appointed members. However, all nonclerical bodies are always consultive in Roman Catholicism.

The Church Today

There is great interest in all aspects of the Church's life today. Even disagreements indicate interest and concern, and contrast with prior times of apathy. Nowadays, especially in countries like the U.S., there is a humanizing of structures in the Church—new decentralized and participatory structures are developing. There is less emphasis on the international aspects of the Church and more concern with local foundational expressions of Church life. Believers sense a need to live with a spirit of coresponsibility for their Church and this has led to new forms of discipleship. Appreciating more the importance of their own baptism, the faithful take a new approach to the importance of living the community vocation of the Church and their own personal vocation to holiness and ministerial responsibility.

In many countries we witness the increased education of laity and religious women—in the U.S., Roman Catholic laity are the most educated group in the nation. We also see greater stress on values that are part of the heart of lay life—social justice, the economy, peace, women's issues. Many are giving greater emphasis in their religious commitment to their own family life and to the interrelationship between religion and political and social life. Moreover, perhaps at no other time in the history of the Church have so many shown so much interest in prayer and spiritual movements. The Church today is fostering ministry between the vocations and this is leading to mutual appreciation of vocations and the development of new forms of leadership. The vision and values of the Church are rising up from the grassroots commitment of the faithful, whose patience and spiritual renewal are further signs of hope for the Church.

LEONARD DOOHAN

See also BISHOP; HIERARCHY; LAITY, THEOLOGY OF THE; PAPACY, THE; PRIESTHOOD, THE MINISTERIAL; VATICAN COUNCIL I; VATICAN COUNCIL II.

CHURCHES OF CHRIST

Known as the "Christian Churches" (Disciples of Christ, the Christian Churches/Churches of Christ, and the Churches of Christ), all three of these Christian groups were spawned by an early nineteenth-century American version of the Protestant Reformation. It was called the Restoration Movement which sought to "restore" the divided and often quarrelling Protestant denominations to the unity and simplicity of the New Testament Church and apostolic Christianity.

Among the prime movers in the Restoration movement were Barton Stone (1772–1844) and especially the Presbyterian father and son team of Thomas (1763–1854) and Alexander (1788–1866) Campbell who advocated non-creedal, locally autonomous Christian congregations which resembled as much as humanly possible the practice of the New Testament Church, including adult baptism by immersion and weekly observance of the Lord's Supper (understood to be a memorial meal). The new movement was simply called "The Christian Church."

The "Campbellite" restoration gave birth eventually to the Disciples of Christ. For the latter, Scripture is the final authority while there is considerable latitude in personal interpretation of the Bible. Disciples do not believe in original sin as a biological and human legacy from Adam. Nevertheless, they do recognize that all humans are sinful and in need of salvation. A strong belief in our free will (a reaction to Calvinist predestination) to accept or reject God's gracious offering of salvation is at the core of their understanding of human nature.

In 1968, they formed a national denominational structure and became in fact a mainline ecclesiastical body. Membership in this group is about 1.1 million.

In the early decades of the twentieth century, a large number of congregations began to move away from the Disciples' propensity to become a mainline Protestant denomination and in 1968 formally severed ties with the Mother Church. The group became known as The Christian Churches/Churches of Christ. They are "independent" Christian Churches similar in polity and practice to the Disciples. Their distinction is a refusal to become a national denominational body and to engage in ecumenical activity. There are also about 1.1 million members in this group.

The largest of the "Christian Churches" is the Churches of Christ which broke away early from the Disciples because the latter were not sufficiently replicating the purity of the New Testament Church. This new faction did not like the Disciples' addition of such things as Sunday schools and instrumental music. In every other major way, they agreed with the "Christian Churches" tradition, e.g., believers' baptism, weekly Lord's Supper, and local autonomy of congregations. A slogan which accurately represents this group is "Christians only, but not the only Christians." There are around 1.5 million members in this branch of the Christian Churches.

These three branches of the Restoration "tree" have been compared to the three aspects of contemporary Judaism. The Disciples are Reformed, the Christian Churches/Churches of Christ are Conservative, and the Churches of Christ are the Orthodox.

Most "Christian" Churches are in the midwest and south of the U.S., although there are congregations in every state and in at least a dozen foreign countries.

IRA ZEPP

See also ECUMENISM; PROTESTANTISM.

CIBORIUM

(Gk. *kiborion,* "cup") A vessel used to hold small Communion Hosts. It resembles a chalice, but is longer and has a lid. Also, it can refer to a dome-shaped canopy over an altar (otherwise known as a baldachino).

JOSEPH QUINN

See also VESSELS, SACRED.

CINCTURE

(Lat. *cinctura,* "girdle") The cord, belt, or girdle used to gather an alb at the waist. It is either white or the color of the day, and usually has a tassle at either end. The cincture is a symbol of chastity. The term also refers to the belt of an ecclesiastical habit.

JOSEPH QUINN

See also VESTMENTS, LITURGICAL.

CIRCUMCISION

The removal of the foreskin of the penis is a very ancient religious custom but its actual origin is uncertain. It existed in Egypt prior to 2400 B.C. and was probably an indication of priestly status. Both Arabs and Jews hold that Abraham introduced the rite among them. Circumcision appears throughout the Old Testament as a sign of association with Israel's covenant with God. In the New Testament, Christ was circumcised on the eighth day after his birth, as was the Jewish practice.

In the early days of the Church, circumcision became a debated issue. The matter was finally resolved by the Council of Jerusalem which ruled against the necessity of circumcision for Christians. From the sixth century to 1960, the feast of Christ's Circumcision was celebrated on 1 January in the Catholic liturgy.

MICHAEL GLAZIER

See also COVENANT; JUDAISM.

CISTERCIANS

On 21 March 1098, the saintly abbot of the thriving Benedictine Abbey of Molesme, Robert, led twenty-one of his monks into the inhospitable thickets of Citeaux to establish a new monastery where they hoped to follow Benedict of Nursia's *Rule for Monasteries* in all its fullness. The unhappy monks of Molesme, grieved at the loss of their holy leader, soon obtained a papal command for his return. The new struggling community continued until 1109 under the leadership of Alberic, who introduced the idea of lay brothers being accepted as full members of the monastic family, making it possible for the monks to be free to follow all the demands of the Benedictine Rule. Stephen Harding, who succeeded Alberic at the helm of the community, welcomed the dynamic Bernard of Fontaines, who came in 1112 with thirty relatives in tow. Thus began the saga of Citeaux.

Before Bernard died in 1153 he had not only founded the great Abbey of Clairvaux which would become a focal point for all of Christendom but he personally sent forth men to start sixty-five other houses while his brother abbots started another 235. Stephen and the other founders were determined to keep alive the pristine observance of the Rule which they had come to Citeaux to establish. To this purpose they created a *Carta caritatis,* a constitution which bound all Cistercian abbots to come to Citeaux annually for a general chapter. It also bound all the houses to a common observance and set up a system of visitation which respected the autonomy of each house but assured its fidelity.

The order continued to expand: by 1200 there were over 500 houses; on the eve of the Reformation, the records showed 742. In time geography began to defeat these model means of regularity which were eventfully adopted by all other religious orders. The decline in the number of recruits had its effect. But most destructive was the practice of the ecclesiastical and secular powers to give the abbatial office to clerics who had no interest in the well-being of the monastery, only in its revenues, leaving the monks without guidance and financial means. In some instances secular powers required the monks to take on active ministries, in others the monks did this on their own. There were repeated attempts at reform, most notably in the century after the Council of Trent.

In 1664 Pope Alexander VII recognized within the Cistercian Order two observances, the Common and the Strict, sometimes called the "abstinents" for their fidelity to Benedict's prohibition of the use of flesh meat in the monastic diet. Among these latter arose Armand Jean de Rancé, a commendatory abbot who underwent a conversion and brought about in his Abbey of Notre Dame de la Grande Trappe a renewal in the practice of monastic enclosure, silence, and manual labor, expressing a spirit of apartness from all worldliness and a dedication to prayer and penance. By the disposition of Divine Providence his was the one community that escaped complete destruction and dispersion at the hands of the French Revolution.

In the course of many and varied travels under the leadership of Augustine de Lestrange the community was able to establish foundations in Spain, Belgium, England, Italy and the United States. When the monks returned to re-establish La Trappe after the downfall of Napoleon, Vincent de Paul Merle remained in America to establish the first permanent Cistercian community in the New World which today flourishes in Spencer, Massachusetts: Saint Joseph's Abbey. Monasteries of the Common Observance continued in eastern Europe in many cases operating schools and pastoring parishes.

In 1892 Pope Leo sought to bring all the Cistercian houses back together into one order but pastoral responsibilities and national loyalties made it impossible for the Common Observance houses who were divided into many national congregations to unite with the Strict Observance who were at that time largely French and who had opted for the strict monastic heritage of the Cistercian founders. Thus the Pope recognized two Cistercian Orders, called today the Order of Citeaux and the Cistercian Order of the Strict Observance, popularly known as the Trappists. The Order of Citeaux suffered greatly under the communist onslaught, not only in eastern Europe but also in Vietnam, where it had a congregation of five houses. On the other hand, the Strict Observance began to flower on the eve of the Second World War and continued to grow until it had over a hundred houses located on all six continents. Only in Yugoslavia and China did its houses suffer at the hands of communism. With the renewal of the Second Vatican Council both orders have written new constitutions which retain the reforming features of Saint Stephen Harding, the general chapter (though no longer annual, usually every three years) and visitations by the superior of the founding abbey.

The Cistercian founders shied away from direct involvement with nuns. But ever since the Benedictine nunnery of Tart adopted the Cistercian usages in 1120, individual convents and whole congregations and federations of Cistercian nuns have sought ever closer alliance with the monks. Today the Strict Observance, besides many affiliated convents, has the rather unique situation in the Church of actually having sixty monasteries of nuns as fully part of the order and serving with monks on the general staff of the order in Rome.

The Cistercians have given to the Church many surpassing spiritual masters: the four "Evangelists" of Citeaux: Bernard of Clairvaux (1153), William of Saint Thierry (1148), Aelred of Rievaulx (1167), and Guerric of Igny (1163), as well as Isaac of Stella (1169), Gilbert of Hoyland (1172), and Adam of Perseign (1221) stand out among the early fathers. Their writings are available today in many languages. The Cistercian nunnery of Helfta in Saxony produced in the thirteenth century a rich vein of spirituality expressed especially in the writings of Saint Gertrude the Great and Saint Mechtild of Magdeburg. Through the centuries other Cistercians reached prominence and made their contribution right up to the twentieth-century spiritual masters: Thomas Merton and Thomas Keating. Simplicity, depth, and eminent practicality mark Cistercian spiritual doctrine as well as a very solid theological base drawn directly from the Scriptures and the Fathers of the Church.

M. BASIL PENNINGTON, O.C.S.O.

See also BERNARD OF CLAIRVAUX, ST.; MONASTICISM; MONK.

CITY OF GOD

See AUGUSTINE, ST.

CLARE OF ASSISI, ST. (ca. 1193–1253)

At the age of eighteen, Clare left her wealthy, noble family to follow a life of contemplation and simplicity inspired by the preaching of Francis of Assisi. Eventually Clare moved to the Church of San Damiano where she remained for forty-two years, establishing an enclosed order for women—the Poor Clares—whose members now number more than fifteen thousand.

Among the authentic writings of Clare we have her *Testament* and four letters to her friend Agnes of Prague. Although Clare would be the first to emphasize that her way of life grew out of her association with Francis, scholars today are also examining her life in its own right. In spite of the paucity of written data, her religious life is being recovered as a model of love, penance, and perseverance for women today.

Among the many notable attributes reflected in Clare's life, two stand out. The first was her unrelenting commitment to a life of utter poverty. She engaged in a lengthy contest with Church authorities who thought that such a radical, countercultural way of life was neither realistic nor feasible. Such a commitment witnesses to inner personal strength and confidence in her ability to uphold the poverty embraced by Francis, in its most radical form.

A second attribute was Clare's humility. Perhaps only a woman of such personal strength and commitment was able to speak of herself genuinely as an "unworthy" and "useless" servant of the Poor La-

"St. Clare of Assisi," by Simone Martini, Assisi

dies. The "hidden sweetness" of God's love for her in Christ enabled her to focus on others rather than herself. She not only recognized, but was awed by the gifts and virtues of other persons and the beauty of every created thing.

Clare's very name suggests the clarity and startling pureness with which she embodied the Franciscan ideal. She was canonized in 1255 by Pope Alexander IV and her feast day is celebrated on 11 August.

ELIZABETH DREYER

See also CONTEMPLATION; CONTEMPLATIVE ORDERS; FRANCIS OF ASSISI, ST.

CLEMENT OF ROME, ST. (fl. ca. 96)

According to the oldest succession list of Roman bishops (Irenaeus, *Against the Heresies* 3.3.3), Clement was the third successor to St. Peter in Rome. There was another tradition in the early Church that Clement was the immediate successor to St. Peter. Contradictory evidence suggests that Clement was one of a collegial leadership group in the Church of Rome, charged by the group to write to Corinth. We know almost nothing about his early life. Irenaeus wrote that Clement knew Saints Peter and Paul well. Origen (*Commentary on the Gospel of St. John* 6.36) and Eusebius (*Ecclesiastical History* 3.4.10) match him with the Clement whom Paul mentioned was his fellow worker in Philippians 4:3. This opinion is not confirmed by any other source or authority. The Pseudo-Clementines and Dio Cassius are not reliable in their reports that Clement was a member of the imperial family. There is also no confirmation that Clement was martyred. Two letters to the Corinthians were reported to have been written by Clement. The first one is genuine and is his main claim to fame. Clement wrote it around 96 in the name of the Roman Church to deal with factions that were raging in the Church at Corinth. The letter is a valuable source of information about the state of Christianity at the end of the first century. Around 170 it was read along with the Scriptures in church at Corinth. The so-called Second Epistle of Clement is, in fact, the earliest surviving Christian homily. It may have originated in Corinth, Rome, or Alexandria. Because of differences in literary form and style, the sermon's author is judged to be someone other than Clement. In addition to the so-called Second Epistle, there are several apocryphal writings claiming Clementine authorship that were in circulation in the early Church, including the Clementine Homilies, Clementine Recognitions, and two Greek excerpts (*epitomai*) from the Homilies. Feast day, 23 November.

JOHN DILLON

CLOISTER

In monastic architecture, a covered quadrangular walkway enclosing a monastery. Derivatively, the

Cloister of St. John Lateran, Rome

term refers to an area within a monastery or convent to which persons not belonging to the institution may not enter (and which the residents do not ordinarily leave).

DAVID BRYAN

See also MONASTERY; RELIGIOUS ORDERS.

CLOUD OF UNKNOWING, THE

The Cloud of Unknowing (written in the fourteenth century) presents itself as a practical book for those in the active life who are "nonetheless drawn by an inward stirring toward the secret spirit of God whose judgments are hidden" (Prologue). The author is clearly writing for people in all stations of life. He uses language and images that reflect the daily concerns of common people. The book is meant to be instructive and to lead the reader beyond the associations and sentimentality of childhood, or spiritual immaturity. The book has seventy-five short chapters, including a final one discussing signs that guide an individual in discerning whether or not she has been called by God to practice the spiritual work described in *The Cloud of Unknowing.*

The main authority of *The Cloud of Unknowing* is Dionysius' *Mystical Theology,* which the author acknowledges in the conclusion of his book. Nevertheless, *The Cloud* goes beyond Dionysius by combining negative theology with medieval love mysticism. In the apophatic tradition, the author maintains that the uncreated can never be known through the created, but it can be known through the failing of knowledge. "The truly divine knowledge of God is that which is known by unknowing" (ch. 71). Love, however, transforms this apophatic mysticism into a cataphatic orientation that speaks about God. Love leads to union with God. *The Cloud*'s doctrine of love, however, avoids sentimentality by defining it as "a radical commitment to God" (ch. 49). The experience of consolation, or absence thereof, makes little difference. The union of the spirit is grounded exclusively in the commitment of the will. Accordingly, the author constantly warns against premature ambitions toward ecstatic prayer: prayer and spiritual discipline must be vigilantly practiced. At the same time, within the practice of prayer, it is futile to resist distractions in contemplation (ch. 32). One must wait for God's rescue. In this way, *The Cloud* articulates clearly and precisely the principles of moral passivity and "pure love" that were adopted by the Quietist movement and that became the source of bitter controversy.

Although the author of the text remains anonymous, the book was clearly written by an Englishman, most likely a priest in a religious order. The text's style indicates that the author wrote in the northeast Midlands. Manuscripts of the author's works are rather numerous. The oldest dates back to the beginning of the fifteenth century.

Many of the words, phrases, and ideas of *The Cloud* are also found in Thomas à Kempis' *The Imitation of Christ* and in the writings of the Rhineland mystics. William Johnston further proposes that the themes and ideas of *The Cloud* suggest that the author belonged to the same spiritual tradition as the later Spanish mystic, St. John of the Cross.

The author of *The Cloud of Unknowing* composed another letter later in his life, *The Book of Privy Counseling*. This book is not directed to the general, spiritual reader but to one prepared for contemplative prayer. This letter's argument for replacing discursive meditation through "the faculties" with a state of inner quiet suggests strong parallels with Buddhist and Yoga methods, yet the author continually connects it with established Christian doctrine.

PATRICIA DeFERRARI

See also BRITAIN, CHURCH IN; MIDDLE AGES, THE; MYSTICISM.

COADY, MOSES MICHAEL (1882–1959)

He is known in Canada and internationally as a leader in the Antigonish Movement of adult education and economic cooperation. Coady was born in N. E. Margaree, Nova Scotia, in 1882. Having graduated from St. Francis Xavier University in Antigonish and worked as a local school teacher, he went to Rome to start studies for the priesthood. He graduated with doctoral degrees in philosophy and theology and was ordained in Rome in 1910. Returning to Nova Scotia, he became a teacher at St. Francis Xavier High School and later at the university.

In the 1920s, eastern Nova Scotia had been in a prolonged economic depression. Farmers and fishermen, receiving low prices for their products, were in a desperate situation. Cape Breton coal miners and industrial workers were also impoverished. A few local priests, including Coady's cousin, Fr. J. J. Tompkins, initiated adult education activity and started organizing local fishermen. As a result of a Royal Commission investigating the conditions in the fishery, Coady was hired in 1927 as part of a government initiative to organize workers in the fishing industry. A year later he was named as the first director of the extension department at St. Francis Xavier University. Working with a team of extension workers, he quickly developed an adult education and organizing method which led to the start up of consumer and producer cooperatives and credit unions in Eastern Nova Scotia and throughout the Maritime provinces.

Coady would start with a mass meeting in a specific community and follow up with ongoing study groups investigating issues of local economic concern. After a time of study, the group members would work together to organize local credit unions or cooperatives. Coady documented the history of the first decade of his work and explained his philosophy in his book *Masters of Their Own Destiny* (1939), which has been translated into several languages.

His overall vision was to develop "economic democracy" to complement political democracy. He sharply critiqued the capitalist economy of his day because it resulted in wealth and economic decision-making being restricted to a privileged few and left the masses with little or no say in their economic lives. Coady's priority was not primarily economic development, but rather full human development through adult education and grass roots self-help economic initiatives.

The Antigonish movement was rooted in the social Catholicism of the encyclicals of Leo XIII and Pius XI. However, following the Rochdale cooperative principles, these cooperatives were to be nondenominational. Eventually both Catholics and some Protestants became involved in the movement. Coady's spirituality was incarnational, embracing both the material and spiritual dimensions of life. For Coady, economic questions had a religious significance and economic cooperation was an aid to salvation. In many ways, Coady's approach of practical ecumenism, social justice, and empowerment of the poor as agents of social change prefigured *Gaudium et spes* and the post-Vatican II Catholic social justice movement. The Vatican officially recognized the Antigonish Movement in 1936 and Coady was personally honored by being named as domestic prelate by Pius XII in 1946.

Coady's influence spread throughout Canada as participants in the Antigonish movement were named to leadership positions in different dioceses and in the Canadian Bishops' Social Action Office first organized after World War II. Coady's leadership extended beyond Church circles. He served as president of the Canadian Association for Adult Education from 1949 to 1951.

After World War II, the Antigonish Movement developed an international reputation as missionaries and community activists came from all over the world to study the movement. In 1959, the year Coady died, the Coady International Institute was started in order to train Third World community leaders.

ROBERT McKEON

See also SOCIAL RESPONSIBILITY, FINANCIAL; SOCIAL TEACHING OF THE CHURCH; SOCIALISM.

COLLEGE OF CARDINALS

The principal clergy of Rome (see cardinal), the cardinals from an early date functioned as a college which, when met, provided the pope with his primary counsel and governed the Church when the Holy See was vacant. Since 1179 they have been the electors of the pope.

While the cardinals are still prominent advisors to the pope, they function now as his chief administrators, being the heads of the various congregations, tribunals, councils, and certain commissions of the Roman Curia. While residence in Rome is presumed, exception is made for key members of the various national hierarchies. Recent popes have thus striven to give the Church an international administration, and the number of cardinals (once limited to seventy) now passes 130.

DAVID BRYAN

See also CURIA, ROMAN; PAPACY, THE.

COLLEGES, CATHOLIC

See CATHOLIC HIGHER EDUCATION IN THE UNITED STATES.

COLLEGIALITY

The Vatican Council's teaching on the collegiality of bishops is found especially in chapter three of the Dogmatic Constitution on the Church (*Lumen Gentium*), which many theologians have claimed is the most important chapter in the council's teaching. Vatican Council I had emphasized the centrality of the papal office in the Church and had the intention of complementing this with teachings on the collegiality of bishops. Vatican Council II picked up on this topic and developed this teaching on collegiality which will have long-term impact on the Church, even though it will undoubtedly have transitional problems. The word "college" refers to the Twelve governing in cooperation with Peter, and applies this to the bishops as successors of the apostles governing the Church in union with the pope. One becomes a member of the college through the sacrament of episcopal consecration, which means that all bishops are members of the college and not just those who head dioceses (ordinaries). The college is not a creation of the pope but results from the sacrament. It is not a form of competition with papal primacy, nor even a diminishment of the latter, but a belief that bishops succeed to the roles of the apostles in union with the pope who succeeds to the universal responsibility of Peter. The bishops are college only with the pope, whereas the pope retains the role as universal pastor even without the college.

The council, speaking about collegiality, says that Peter and his successors have a prime place for the sake "of unity, of faith, and fellowship" (LG 18:3). "This college, in so far as it is composed of many, expresses the variety and universality of the People of God, but in so far as it is assembled under one head, it expresses the unity of the flock of Christ" (LG 22:4). Each bishop needs to live in unity with his flock, and then "in union with the pope represents the entire Church joined in the bond of peace, love, and unity" (LG 23:1). The bishops are not understood as distinct from the pope, but rather in the college of bishops the pope discovers his true self.

This central teaching was one of the most debated points in the council, many bishops (191) opposing the collegiality of the apostles with Peter, and a greater number (322) opposing the collegiality of bishops with the pope. This split vote in the council has continued in the different opinions that have developed since the council regarding the roles of bishops in relationship to the pope, and the importance of episcopal conferences.

Although Vatican II was the first council to present teachings on collegiality, bishops have always expressed the Church's faith in the collegial dimensions of their lives: ecumenical councils, regional synods, local meetings with a metropolitan, several bishops together consecrating another bishop and welcoming him into the college, pastoral letters from several bishops, and episcopal conferences.

The council's teaching on collegiality refers only to bishops governing in collaboration with the pope. Since the council, however, many Church leaders, especially Pope John Paul II, have applied the insight into collegial sharing to every level of Church life, claiming that the model of Church government is collegial.

LEONARD DOOHAN

See also BISHOP; CHURCH, THE; VATICAN COUNCIL II.

COLORS, LITURGICAL

The sequence of colors used for vestments and liturgical objects during different seasons of the ecclesiastical year. For the Roman Catholic Church, the sequence is as follows: white for feasts of Our Lord—excepting those of his passion—and of the Blessed Mother, for the Christmas and Easter seasons, and for feasts of saints other than the martyrs; red for Palm Sunday, for Good Friday, and for feasts of the apostles and evangelists—excepting John—and the martyrs; purple for Advent and Lent—excepting Gaudete Sunday (the Third Sunday of Advent) and Laetare Sunday (the Fourth Sunday in Lent), when rose vestments may be worn; green for Ordinary Time; and black for funeral Masses (for which purple and white are also allowed).

JOSEPH QUINN

See also LITURGY; VESTMENTS, LITURGICAL.

COMMANDMENTS OF THE CHURCH

In addition to the Ten Commandments tradition has accepted commandments or precepts of the Church as a help for believers to carry out their duties as members of the community. Although their number has varied over the centuries, the Third Plenary Council of Baltimore (1886) established six for all U.S. Catholics. However, the 1917 Code of Canon Law, the Second Vatican Council, and the new 1983 Code of Canon Law do not speak of commandments or precepts of the Church. Yet, the traditional six remain part of the Church's law, although spread out in the new 1983 Code. They are as follows: (1) to attend Mass on Sunday and other holy days of obligation (canon 1247); (2) to fast and abstain on certain specified days (canons 1249–1253); (3) to confess one's grave sins at least once a year (canon 989); (4) to receive Communion at least once a year, preferably during the Easter season (canon 920); (5) to contribute to the support of the Church (canon 222)—it is no longer just the support of the clergy; indeed, this canon now includes the obligation of social justice; (6) to observe the Church's laws concerning marriage (canons 1055–1165).

JOHN F. CRAGHAN

COMMON GOOD

The concept of the common good is based on the belief that we human beings are naturally members of society. We are not isolated individuals who choose to come together in society only because it is necessary to do so to protect individual rights and freedoms. Rather, individuals find their own meaning and identity and dignity as part of the larger community.

As a social being, every individual has the moral responsibility to work for the good of the community. The individual's own good is closely related to this common good; it is only when the right conditions of social life are established that individuals and social groups can flourish.

It is not enough to be morally sensitive and principled in one-on-one relationships and in dealings with other individuals. Moral responsibility includes the obligation to work for the social systems and conditions necessary for human fulfillment for all.

Understanding the Common Good

The common good is not a value easily understood in American culture. Because of the strong emphasis on individual rights and freedoms, the good of the community is often thought of as the good of many individuals. "The greatest good of the greatest number" is not, however, the same as the common good. The common good is the social order that makes possible and protects the good of all, the minority as well as the majority.

Resistance to the ideal of the common good sometimes comes from a fear of totalitarianism, which is often thought of as subordination of the individual to the good of the whole. But totalitarianism is not really a commitment to the good of the whole. It is, rather, a system devoted to the "good" or vision of particular persons or a particular party. Nor is it accurate to identify a desire to promote the common good with a denial of the importance of individual rights and individual dignity.

One way, in fact, of understanding the common good is to focus on individual human rights. As the American Catholic bishops expressed it in their 1986 pastoral letter on the U.S. economy, "The common good demands justice for all, the protection of the human rights of all" (*Economic Justice for All,* no. 85). To work for the common good is to work to protect the human rights of every individual. A commitment to human rights goes hand-in-hand with an emphasis on the common good.

On the other hand, there is a way in which a "rights" approach to social justice is often very different from a common-good approach. The claiming of rights can become a way of focusing on what an individual wants to satisfy his or her definition of the good life. Such a focus on personal goals might not foster the sense of an obligation to work for the good of the community. A commitment to the common good does entail a recognition that there are times when a member of the community has the responsibility to subordinate her or his own concerns and wishes to the good of the community.

In the understanding of property ownership, for example, a common-good orientation has led to a clear recognition that there are limits on what owners may legitimately do with what is theirs. Since everyone needs access to sufficient resources in order to meet basic needs, the "right" to use private property the way one wants is limited: we do not have a true right to more than we need when others do not have the necessities. The point is that there is a community dimension to ownership, there is a social responsibility to "private" economic behavior. Our economic activity should be placed in a context that recognizes the need to be focused on the common good as well as individual interests. Social responsibility means, in fact, that the good of the community often places limits on self-interest.

The Common Good and the Option for the Poor

In recent decades the fundamental or preferential "option for the poor" has become an important feature of Catholic social ethics. As the bishops stated in *Economic Justice for All,* "Decisions must be judged in the light of what they do *for* the poor, what they do *to* the poor, and what they enable the poor to do *for themselves*" (no. 24).

This emphasis on the poor has raised some questions about how a tradition that has long emphasized the *common* good can now be focusing so explicitly on only a *part* of society. The option for the poor is, however, implied by the commitment to the common good.

The very effort to promote the common good, to promote justice for all, and to protect the human rights of all, requires that the focus of attention be on those whose needs are not now being met. The common good is not achieved until all are able to share in and contribute to the social systems and conditions necessary for human fulfillment and human flourishing. An explicit focus on the poor is an essential step in efforts to understand the implications of the commitment to the common good.

LEONARD J. WEBER

See also SOCIAL RESPONSIBILITY, FINANCIAL; SOCIAL TEACHING OF THE CHURCH.

COMMON OF THE SAINTS

The sections of the Missal and the Liturgy of the Hours which contain the offices and Masses for saints who do not have their own complete office. It is divided into various classes, such as pastors, martyrs, and holy women.

JOSEPH QUINN

See also LITURGY.

"COMMONWEAL"

Commonweal was founded by Michael Williams (1877–1950) and the Calvert Associates in 1924 to convey to the general American public the insights that the venerable Catholic tradition and the best of contemporary Catholic thinking could bring to the questions of the day—social, political, religious, and cultural. It was to be nonparochial, independent and edited by lay people, to serve as a forum that would contribute to the successful resolution of many of our nation's important problems.

Accordingly, as its name implies, *Commonweal* has insistently championed the cause of social justice, national and worldwide. It deplored the use of the atom bomb and has called for disarmament, international cooperation, and all manner of agreements that contribute to international justice and peace. *Commonweal* has taken outspokenly critical positions against racism, anti-Semitism, McCarthyism, the Spanish Civil War, the war in Vietnam, the prevalence of poverty, and the inequitable distribution of wealth in this country and in the Third World. It consistently opposed the Reagan-Bush Latin American policy.

For years *Commonweal* pressed for Mass in the vernacular and other key liturgical reforms that were achieved by Vatican Council II. As the leading voice of the American Catholic laity, its editorials, articles, reviews, and poetry by distinguished contributors have won widespread acclaim. In recent years, *Commonweal* has been concerned with such issues as collegiality, ecumenism (the annual Graymoor Prize was established in 1991), authority in the Church, and the role of women and the laity in the post-Vatican II world.

In the course of its seven decades *Commonweal*'s recognition has grown nationwide. Originally a weekly, it became bi-weekly in 1974. Today its twenty-two yearly issues reach thousands of the country's sources of information and centers for discussion—universities, colleges, academies and high schools, and public libraries. It also reaches leading newspapers and magazines, and a number of other molders of American public opinion. It is welcomed for its well-substantiated but outspoken comment on issues of the day.

Among the editors over the years have been Michael Williams, George N. Shuster, Philip Burnham, C. G. Paulding, Edward S. Skillin, John Cogley, James O'Gara, William Clancy, Daniel Callahan, John Leo, Peter Steinfels, Wilfrid Sheed and Margaret O'Brien Steinfels.

Distinguished contributors to *Commonweal*'s pages have included G. K. Chesterton, Lewis Mumford, Walter Lippmann, Dorothy Day, Jacques Maritain, Thomas Merton, Richard Dana Skinner, Padraic Colum, Franz Werfel, Georges Bernanos, H. A. Reinhold, Evelyn Waugh, Nicholas Berdyaev, J. F. Powers, Virgil Michel, O.S.B., W. H. Auden, Robert Lowell, and Graham Greene among others.

EDWARD S. SKILLEN

See also AMERICAN CATHOLICISM.

COMMUNION, HOLY

The Eucharist is both celebration and sacrament. As sacrament, reception and consuming of the consecrated bread and wine is called Holy Communion. In Catholic practice Holy Communion is normally received during the liturgical celebration. However for the sick and the homebound, and for other practical considerations (including Sunday Eucharistic services without priest celebrants), Holy Communion can be received in other settings.

At the heart of Catholic teaching about the Eucharist as sacrament (cf. Council of Trent, Session 13, 21 and 22) is the understanding that through a sharing of the Eucharistic elements (bread and cup) the Christian shares more deeply in the life of Jesus Christ begun through faith and baptism.

Scriptural Teaching

The basis for this teaching is found in the classical text of St. John's Gospel (6:41-69 esp. 54ff.). The passage concerning the vine and the branches (John 15:1-8) is also cited in this context as well as John's First Letter (1 John 1:1-4). Paul develops the same theology in his First Letter to the Corinthians (1 Cor 10–14, esp. 10:16-18).

Many other passages could be cited showing how life in Christ which begins with faith, is celebrated in baptism, is renewed through the Bread of Life (Holy Communion), and is the foundation for good works performed out of love (Gal 5:6).

The early verses of John's sixth chapter describe life in Christ as grounded in faith. But at Capernaum Jesus draws his hearers beyond faith to sharing his life and resurrection through the Bread of Life, the Bread from Heaven that he will give "for the life of the world" (John 6:51). "Amen, amen, I say to you, unless you eat the flesh of the Son of Man and drink his blood, you do not have life within you. Whoever eats my flesh and drinks my blood remains in me and I in him. Just as the living Father sent me and I have life because of the Father, so also the one who feeds on me will have life because of me" (John 6:53 56-57).

The Christian Life As Communion with Christ

The Christian lives *in Christ* and *with Christ.* "I no longer live, it is Christ who lives in me" (Gal 2:20). This life in Christ must grow. Through sacraments and good works one identifies more and more closely with Jesus Christ, the risen Lord. One becomes more and more a member of his body. Christ lives in the Christian and continues his mission to the world.

Ascetical practice and contemplative prayer have seen in this communion with Christ the heart of Christian life. The purpose of prayer and contemplation is to deepen one's union with Christ and one's experience of this communion.

Theology

At the heart of Thomas Aquinas' exposition of the Eucharist as sacrament (largely endorsed by the Council of Trent) is the concept that the sacraments produce what they signify. The Eucharist symbolizes the sharing of food (with Christ). Thus fellowship, love, sharing of life are signified. In addition the Eucharist provides other secondary (spiritual) effects of food: refreshment, renewal, joy, etc.

The Thomistic view of sacraments stresses their efficient causality. Other opinions, such as Bonaventure's, see them more as "occasions" for God to touch human lives. The patristic view stresses incorporation (concorporation) into Christ (thus Cyril of Alexandria, John Chrysostom and Augustine).

Post-Vatican theology stresses the social dimension of communion. Because all Christians share one life in Christ they are bonded together by the Holy Spirit into the body of Christ. The Church is the body of Christ. As Paul reminds the Corinthians, they cannot say they do not need each other. Every member is necessary to the good health and happiness of the body (1 Cor 12:4-31).

Ecumenical implications of this theology of communion are readily seen. Indeed Vatican II (*Unitatis Redintegratio* nos. 3, 13, 14–18, 19–24, and *Lumen Gentium* nos. 8, 14, 15) stresses that all Christians are united in a communion with Christ. This communion with the Catholic Church is either perfect, almost perfect, or real though imperfect (among Catholics, with Orthodox or with other Churches/ Ecclesial Communions of the West respectively).

Ascetical/Spiritual/Liturgical Considerations

In the light of this teaching, the Eucharist as Communion assumes a central focus for the Christian life, ascetical practice and ecumenical relations. The importance of the Eucharist is universally recognized, especially in the light of recent renewal movements in the Catholic Church and all Churches (cf. World Council of Churches, *Baptism, Eucharist and Ministry,* esp. E nos. 19–26).

There are many aspects of the Eucharist as Holy Communion, e.g., the Eucharist and the forgiveness of sins, the Eucharist as the center of prayer, the Eucharist as source of unity, the Eucharist as viaticum, etc. The reader is referred to contemporary authors for these aspects of the Eucharist as Communion.

E. R. FALARDEAU, S.S.S.

See also ECUMENISM; EUCHARIST; SACRAMENTS.

COMMUNION OF SAINTS

History of the Term

Between the fifth and eighth centuries, perhaps in southwestern Gaul, an early Roman baptismal creed containing an article of faith in the *communionem sanctorum,* "communion of saints," was expanded into what is now called the "Apostles' Creed." The reality to which the words *communio sanctorum* refer is a rich treasure for the lives of Christians, but the history of the phrase is complex and its original meaning is ambiguous.

Sanctorum can mean either "of holy things" or "of holy ones." *Communio* translates the Greek word *koinonia*—an intimate "participation." Paul uses the word *koinonia* in referring to two profound and inseparable realities in the lives of Christians: their "sharing" in or union with the Holy Spirit (2 Cor 13:14) through baptism, and their "sharing" in or union with the Blood of Christ through the Eucharist (1 Cor 10:16). Though he does not use the term "holy things" to refer to the Eucharist or the other sacraments, he does use the term "holy ones" to refer to Christians themselves (1 Cor 1:2), for Christians are made holy in the Holy Spirit (Rom 15:16) bestowed on them in baptism (1 Cor 12:13).

The precise origin of the phrase which joins *communio* and *sanctorum* is not clear. The phrase was added to a creed recited in the West, but the term does not appear in Scripture, nor in any creeds of Eastern Christianity. Yet the varied levels of meaning contained in this phrase are prominent in Eastern Christian writings. Some Eastern patristic writers refer to the Eucharist as "holy things," while others speak of "communion" with the "holy ones," that is, with other Christians made holy by the Holy Spirit. Still others, such as Cyril of Alexandria, join in one statement all three elements: communion with one another through sharing in the Holy Spirit and the Eucharist: "Just as the flesh of Christ in the Eucharist makes us one body with him, so the Holy Spirit dwelling in us forges us into a spiritual unity. We are one through our communion in the sacred flesh of Christ and through our sharing in the one Holy Spirit" (*Commentary on John,* Bk. 11).

Though the precise phrase is not used, the *reality* of the "communion of saints" from this Eastern Christian perspective is the intimate sharing of Christians in the "good things" of salvation, especially the baptismal gift of the Holy Spirit (2 Cor 13:14) and the Eucharistic gift of the Lord's Body and Blood (1 Cor 10:16-17). Christians' "communion" with these blessings in turn gives them intimate "communion" with the triune God and one another as the one community of the Lord's body, the Church.

In the West, emphasis was more often on the communion of Christians with one another. A sixth century text incorrectly attributed to Augustine and influential for succeeding Western writers interpreted the phrase *communio sanctorum* to mean Christians' "communion" especially with those who have died in faith, a communion based upon sharing the same faith and hope. This stress on the *communio sanctorum* as communion or union with "holy ones" who have died continued in the West through key writers such as Bernard of Clairvaux and Peter Lombard. Thomas Aquinas, however, perhaps because of his own keen interest in the Eastern Fathers, preserved all the inseparable dimensions of the reality signified by the two words in the way that Eastern writers such as Cyril of Alexandria had used them.

After the Middle Ages, Western interpretation of the *communio sanctorum* continued to focus on the "communion" of Christians with the faithful who have died. Especially emphasized was the mutual help that Christians on earth and in purgatory give to one another by their prayer, while some writers in the first part of the twentieth century, such as Josef Jungmann, stressed the communion of saints as a mystical reality.

The Meaning of the Communion of Saints in the Lives of Christians

Little contemporary theological reflection has been devoted to the meaning and significance of the *communio sanctorum* for the lives of Christians today. Yet in the liturgical and theological texts of past and present there is much to glean about the rich and varied dimensions of this reality at the heart of the Christian life. It must be noted also that the ecumenical perspective opened up by Vatican II is of great import in interpreting past texts relevant to the "communion of saints." Vatican Council II affirmed that the Holy Spirit is at work wherever people labor to make life more human (GS 38), and that the Spirit's gifts "can be found outside the visible boundaries of the Catholic Church" (UR 3). These insights provide an entirely new context for understanding that, in the Holy Spirit, the communion of saints extends beyond the bounds of the Church to all persons of truth and love.

Gregory of Nyssa writes that Christians are united by the one same Holy Spirit bestowed in baptism. They thus "cleave together" to the one good given in Christ, forming one body, one Spirit (Gregory of Nyssa, *Commentary on the Canticle of Canticles,* Homily 15). The Third Eucharistic Prayer used in the Roman Rite today echoes these sentiments when it prays that those who are nourished by the Lord's body and blood may be "filled with his Holy Spirit and become one body, one Spirit in Christ." The Second and Fourth Eucharistic Prayers also make clear this intimate connection between the Holy Spirit, the Eucharist, and Christians bound to one another in the "communion of saints" precisely by sharing in the person of the Holy Spirit and in the Eucharist.

Cyril of Alexandria writes that the one same Spirit of the Father and the Son within Christians "commingles" them with God and one another (*Commentary on John,* Bk. 11). This intimate "commingling" is meant to be experienced in their marriages, family life, friendships, and care for others. Through their communion with the Holy Spirit and the Eucharistic Lord, they share intimately in the Trinity and thus enter into a bond that immeasurably deepens natural ties: "May you have communion with us, for our communion is with the Father and his Son Jesus Christ" (1 John 1:3). Eusebius tells of Origen's father, who would kiss the breast of his sleeping child, both as a gesture of love for his child, and, even more, as a gesture of reverence for the Holy Spirit who dwelt within his child (*Ecclesiastical History* VI, 2, 11). The love binding Christians to one another in the "communion of saints" thus undergirds and strengthens all other reasons for loving one another.

The Spirit's charity not only deepens the bonds of Christians with their loved ones, but also binds them intimately even to those whom they have not met. Early Christians such as Ignatius of Antioch (*Letter to the Ephesians,* no. 5) and Paulinus of Nola wrote about the bond they experienced with other Christians whom they knew only through letters or the word of others: "The Spirit reveals us to each other before we meet, and unites us in a love that anticipates our knowing one another" (Paulinus of Nola, *Letter Three to Alypius*).

This union through sharing in the one Holy Spirit is inseparable from communion with others through the Eucharist. Containing Christ himself, in whom the whole Church is united (Aquinas, *Summa Theologiae* [=ST] III, q. 67, a. 2), the Eucharist is the sacrament of love (ST III, q. 79, a. 4) and thus of the Church's unity (ST III, q. 67, a. 2; ST III, q. 79, a. 5). Because it joins Christians intimately not only to the Lord but also to one another (Aquinas, *Commentary on John* 6, Lectio 7), sharing the Eucharist together profoundly deepens the marriage covenants of Christians, as well as their family bonds, and all of their loving relationships (cf. ST III, q. 80, a. 4). The Eucharist also binds Christians with the entire Church community, living and dead (Aquinas, *Commentary on John* 6, Lectio 6). Through those physically present at the celebration, the Eucharist helps every person to whom Christians are related in the Spirit's love, even those who are physically absent (ST III, q. 79, a. 7).

The communion of saints also means that all of the good of Christians in some way belongs to and is shared with all, since charity makes each one's good common to all (John Chrysostom, *On the Perfection of Charity*; Rom 12:5). "The Holy Spirit unites the Church and communicates the goods of one member to another" (Aquinas, ST III, q. 68, a. 9, ad 2). The union of charity thus means that all share in the graces of the saints in heaven and of virtuous people on earth (Aquinas, *Sermon on the Apostles' Creed*) and that the material possessions of Christians are bestowed on them by God precisely so they may help others (Aquinas, ST II-II, q. 32, a. 5, ad 2). An early Christian writer urges, "Do not turn away from those in need; rather, share everything with your brothers and sisters, and do not say, 'It is private property.' If you have communion in what cannot perish [the Holy Spirit and the Eucharist], how much more so in the things that do perish [material possessions]" (Didache 4).

Even the good desires of Christians help others through the communion of saints. Those who find themselves unable to forgive can gain this grace through their communion with the whole Church, and thus with those whose charity has filled them with forgiveness (Aquinas, *Sermon on the Our Father*). There are other dimensions of the communion of saints as well. Aquinas writes that children who cannot receive the Eucharist through their own conscious desire receive it in some way through their union with the older members of the community to whom they are united by the Spirit's charity (Aquinas, ST III, q. 73, a. 3). Prayer for one another is also a way that the reality of the communion of saints becomes concrete in the lives of Christians. The God who is Trinitarian communion honors the prayer flowing from the love that binds human persons to one another (Aquinas, ST II-II, q. 83, a. 7).

Finally, not even death can sever the "communion of saints," for its bond uniting persons in God continues and immeasurably deepens after death. "Through the exchanging of spiritual goods" (LG 49), those on earth and those who have died mutually help one another through their love and prayer. "An immense stream of life" thus flows on earth and between heaven and earth (Cristoph Schonborn, "The 'Communion of Saints' as Three States of the Church: Pilgrimage, Purification, and Glory," *Communio* 15 (1988) 175). Those who have died do not leave their loved ones but are even more intimately with them, giving them the uninterrupted enjoyment of their presence which they could not give them before (Ambrose, *Funeral Oration on His Brother, Satyrus*). Cyprian writes movingly of this final dimension of the communion of saints: "A great number of loved ones await us in heaven. An enormous host is filled with longing for us. Their concern is only for us. To be in their presence, to be embraced by their arms—what immeasurable joy it will be for them and for us" (Cyprian, *Sermon on Death,* 26; Schonborn, p. 176). In the actual experience of this eschatological truth lies the fulfillment of the reality which the phrase "communion of saints" can only hint at now.

MARY ANN FATULA, O.P.

See also CHURCH, THE; GRACE; INDULGENCES; SAINTS.

COMMUNION SERVICE

In several Protestant traditions, the order of worship in word and sacrament is known as the service of Holy Communion. In Eastern Orthodox and Roman Catholic traditions, a Communion Service is an order of worship in which Holy Communion is distributed but the Eucharist is not celebrated. This kind of Communion Service originated in the Liturgy of the Presanctified Gifts, celebrated in the Byzantine tradition. This liturgy had developed to meet the popular desire for Communion on fast days, when the Eucharist was not celebrated. The Liturgy of the Presanctified is still celebrated in the Eastern Orthodox tradition as the office of vespers followed by Communion from the reserved Sacrament. This practice was not part of the tradition in the West, except on Good Friday. The structure of the Roman Rite is similar to that in the Byzantine tradition from which it was received. In 1973, the reformed rite of Distributing Holy Communion outside Mass was promulgated: greeting, penitential rite, celebration of the word of God, the Lord's prayer, sign of peace, "This is the Lamb of God . . . ," distribution of Holy Communion, postcommunion prayer, and benediction.

PATRICIA DeFERRARI

See also EUCHARIST.

COMMUNION UNDER TWO SPECIES

Until the twelfth century, it was the common and accepted practice for the faithful in most dioceses to receive Communion under the two species of bread and wine. By the thirteenth century, however, partaking of the chalice by the laity declined, and eventually it was restricted to the celebrant. However, there was minority dissent over the following centuries, and the Reformers of the sixteenth century stipulated that it was scripturally mandated and theologically correct to receive both bread and wine. This was subsequently adopted by all Protestant denominations. The question was discussed at the Council of Trent (1545–1563), which disagreed with the Protestant position that Christ was essentially present only in both the bread and wine. After Vatican II, the Catholic Church reverted to the custom of the early Church, and the faithful are now able to receive Communion under both species.

JOSEPH QUINN

See also EUCHARIST.

COMMUNISM

Modern Communism reached its maximum territorial expansion in the post-World War II years by encompassing the U.S.S.R., China, all of the Eastern European countries, Cuba, Vietnam, and Albania. In its attempt to bring the whole world into its ideological system, through operatives primarily from Russia and later China and Cuba, it fomented revolutionary movements in the underdeveloped nations of Latin America, Africa, and Asia. Communist parties were formed in almost all of the developed nations of the world which legally allowed them, and underground parties operated where they were illegal. The collapse of Communism in Eastern Europe in 1989 and subsequently in the U.S.S.R. has destroyed its power base and has discredited it as a potent international force for the organization of life in human society.

Modern Communism stems from the political and sociological philosophy of Karl Marx (1818–1883) and his collaborator, Friedrich Engels (1820–1895). Marx taught a "historical materialism," i.e., a determinist approach to the development of history based upon the material or natural needs of people. All the higher or spiritual human attitudes not only can be explained by practical accomplishments (praxis) but also can be reduced to human economic activities. Religion is an illusory expression and justification of the alienation people experience in the unjust socioeconomic conditions which encompass them. Oppressed and alienated people are driven to religion to protest the inhumanity of their lives. Religion, the "opium of the people," can do nothing to address the conditions which make religion necessary, because the issues are not spiritual but material, not religious but economic. Matter is the primary factor of all reality. The human mind and the human spirit are either the products of matter or nonexistent illusions.

Engels took the historical materialism of Marx and interpreted it by introducing the Hegelian idealistic dialectical process ("thesis," "antithesis," and "synthesis") but now seen only from the viewpoint of materialism; hence, "dialectical materialism." There are three key dialectical laws: (1) the union and struggle of opposites; (2) the transition from quantity to quality; and (3) the negation of the negation. These are the laws built into nature; their discovery gives a "scientific" view of all reality. It is a short step from those three laws to "class warfare" leading to the "dictatorship of the proletariat"; "revolution" overturning economic structures to workers enhancing their lives by enjoying "the fruits of their labor"; and the oppressed people arriving at the power to control their own destinies.

The development of Marxist theory into Communism has taken many different historical forms. Lenin (1870–1924) proposed the form most influential in the Russian Revolution of 1917. Revolutions do not happen spontaneously. They must be brought about by well-trained, highly disciplined, secret, well-organized professional revolutionaries. Revolution must be brought to workers from the "outside." The working class, on its own, would not have the vision necessary for long-range social change. Religion, an obstacle to revolution, must be eradicated. Class struggle is inevitable. Capitalism cannot be reformed; it must be destroyed by revolution and replaced by Communism. Joseph Stalin (1879–1953) implemented Leninist-Marxism in Russia through a ruthless eradication of all opposing forces. The Stalinist interpretation of Marxism in the Soviet Communist Party controlled the Soviet Union and became the model for international revolution and the export of Communism after World War II. Mao Tse-tung (1893–1976) gave a different face to Marxism by his stress on peasants, commune systems, decentralization of economic activities, and initiative from the masses of people, not the technological experts. The Cultural Revolution of 1966–1969 brutally enforced the equality of all by condemning any who were viewed as part of an intellectual, professional, economic, or even military elite.

Although Marxist Communism began as a social philosophy and movement to improve the lot of the working poor (the "masses," the "proletariat") in their struggle for a decent way of life, the Church has always opposed it from its inception to the present. The Church has maintained that Communism is wrong in its understanding of the human person and of society.

Communism denies the transcendent dimension of the human person and, therefore, the true dignity of the human person as sacred and called to communion with God—a God whose very existence is denied. Communism denies the right to private ownership of property and requires the common (in effect, government) ownership of all the means of production. Communism offers to the poor and oppressed the hope for a more humane life, but the salvation offered is limited to the temporal, the sociological, and the economic. It does not satisfy the deeper longings of the human heart. Communism conceives of human persons as mere cogs in the wheels of the system. Individuals are expendable. Their role is to facilitate and accelerate the inexorable development of the socioeconomic laws of its ideology leading ultimately to the "classless society." Any and all means may be used to bring this about. The Church maintains that this theory of historical necessity undermines the very foundations of morality.

Some aspects of the Marxist interpretation can be allowed as a method to address social issues ("class struggle" is a reality in many nations of the world, "alienation" in its Marxist sense is used by John Paul II, unrestrained capitalism has been condemned by all the modern popes, etc.), but Marxist Communism is widely seen as a failed system, especially since its fall in Eastern Europe in 1989. Empirically, it has not achieved what it has set out to achieve for people under its domination. Its hopes for oppressed and poor people have never been realized. It has substituted one domination for another. It has maintained its power primarily through military and police control. Those who have lived under its ideology have generally rejected it.

Communism offers an attractive alternative whenever social conditions of hunger, homelessness, joblessness, and poverty are present; whenever there are political realities of dictatorial control and systematic oppression; and whenever there is a pervasive hopelessness that conditions will not improve. The Church does not condemn communism's aspirations to overcome social and economic exploitation, to create a friendlier society, to value human work, to create more just economic and social structures, and to overcome conditions of inequality and underdevelopment. The Church has condemned its devaluation of the dignity of the individual human person, its atheistic philosophy, its historical and dialectical materialism, and the violence of its means to bring about change.

Communism has contributed to the extension of the understanding of history to include the significance of ordinary people in ordinary work. It has influenced the recognition of the importance of technical progress and economic development. But the general principles of the Communist laws of scientific historical materialism are flawed. They do not yield a consistent understanding of historical reality. The praxis of Communism has not produced the society, locally or internationally, which it had envisioned. But, nonetheless, Communism has been a major political and economic factor shaping the world of the twentieth century.

In the post-1989 world, Communism is viewed as having run its course as a vehicle of social change.

CHARLES D. SKOK

See also CAPITALISM; SOCIAL TEACHING OF THE CHURCH; SOCIALISM.

COMPOSTELA, ST. JAMES OF

See SANTIAGO DE COMPOSTELA.

CONCELEBRATION

This is the corporate celebration of the Eucharistic Liturgy by several bishops or priests in which one bishop or priest acts as the principal or main celebrant although all share in the Eucharistic Prayer and, of course, all consecrate the bread and wine. In the early Church it was common practice for several priests to share the prayers and ritual actions of the Mass. It is a practice that has taken various forms in different places in the Church's history.

Mass of concelebration

Concelebration in the early Church was often used as a way to honor a visiting bishop. On such occasions the visiting bishop was invited to be the celebrant while the other priests helped him in the reception of the offertory gifts and the distribution of Holy Communion. In the course of time in the Western Church the practice of "sacramental" concelebration fell into disuse, except at the ordination of bishops and priests. Today in the West and in most of the Orthodox Churches the main celebrant recites the Eucharistic Prayer aloud for all to hear while the other concelebrants say it in a low voice (although in a few Orthodox Churches the concelebrants remain silent). Concelebration is considered "sacramental" since all the concelebrants take part in the consecration, although a few theologians question the sacramentality of silent concelebration. A form of ceremonial concelebration in which the concelebrants simply "attend" the Eucharistic Liturgy has been abandoned.

The Second Vatican Council (1962–1965) revived the practice of "sacramental" concelebration on a wide scale in the Latin Rite. It can now be used at the Mass of the Lord's Supper on Holy Thursday, at councils, synods or bishops' conferences, and at other times deemed suitable by the local ordinary. Thus it can be used at conventual Masses, at the principal liturgy in churches when other Masses are not scheduled or needed, and at the meetings of priests. An individual priest may always opt to celebrate a Mass with a server (or even without a server for a "reasonable cause"), but in light of the restored understanding of the liturgy, many would rather concelebrate with a congregation present than celebrate a Mass without one.

The *General Instruction on the Roman Missal* gives the guidelines for concelebration (GIRM nos. 153–208). The present form of concelebration helps to convey well the collegiality of the ministerial priesthood and its relationship of leadership and of service to the universal priesthood of the faithful.

ANTHONY D. ANDREASSI

See also EUCHARIST; PRIESTHOOD, THE MINISTERIAL.

CONCILIARISM

Conciliarism is the assertion that a general council of the Church is the ultimate authority on matters of faith and Church order. In the early Church this understanding seems to have been the assumption underlying the great councils of antiquity. As the bishops of Rome gained power and respect, the Western Church tended to see the pope as ultimate authority while the East held out for a conciliar or collegial pattern of authority. Later, medieval canonists in the Western Church argued the question from the thirteenth century, and it became a matter of practical concern at the time of the Great Western Schism in the late fourteenth century. The issue has arisen again from time to time since.

MONIKA K. HELLWIG

See also GREAT WESTERN SCHISM; SCHISM.

CONCORDANCE, BIBLICAL

(Lat. *concordans,* "putting things in harmony") An index to the Bible which lists in alphabetical order the principal words used therein. It provides the context in which the term is used along with its exact location, and thereby enables the reader to find, and cross-reference, a particular text or reference. The English concordance compiled by Alexander Cruden (1701–1770) in 1737 is still considered the standard, and remains in popular use today. As there are many varying translations of the Bible, and each has its own concordance, an inherent limitation of any vernacular concordance is its reliance upon a single translation.

JOSEPH QUINN

See also BIBLE, ENGLISH VERSIONS OF THE; BIBLE, NEW TESTAMENT WRITINGS; BIBLE, OLD TESTAMENT WRITINGS.

CONCORDAT

Concordats are legal agreements between Church and state about matters of mutual concern, such as the rights of the Church, establishment of ecclesiastical jurisdiction, marriage laws, and education. About 150 such agreements have been negotiated since the Concordat of Worms in 1122, including concordats with Nazi Germany and Fascist Italy just prior to World War II. The intention was to protect the welfare of the Church; however, the governments in both countries broke the terms of the agreements many times.

PATRICIA DeFERRARI

See also CHURCH AND STATE.

CONCUPISCENCE

From the Latin *concupisco,* "desire something urgently," in Catholic tradition it means disordered, inappropriate desire. Based on common observation, the teaching about concupiscence is that we live in a condition in which we tend to act on impulse, following particular desires even when this will cause harm or disaster in the long run. Paul writes about the problem at length in Romans 5:12–7:25. Paul attributes the problem to the sin of Adam, and later tradition developed this idea. The disorderly desires are not only bodily cravings, but selfish strivings for whatever is contrary to the will of God, which means whatever is not ultimately ordered to God. The tradition about concupiscence led the medieval theologians to postulate that by "pure nature" human persons were not equipped for the destiny of intimacy with God to which they were called, and that God had therefore "originally" enhanced their nature with grace. This enhancement was lost, they maintained, by "original sin," leaving the human community in history burdened with concupiscence, and in need of a new order of saving grace. It was not claimed that grace eliminated concupiscence, but that it gave empowerment to transcend it. The Council of Trent, in the *Decree on Original Sin* (1546), defines concupiscence as "the inclination to sin," and insists on the one hand that this is real and universal but on the other hand that it does not force anyone to sin because human nature is not intrinsically corrupted (DS 1515).

MONIKA K. HELLWIG

See also ASCETICISM; ORIGINAL SIN.

CONDITIONAL ADMINISTRATION OF THE SACRAMENTS

The conditional administration of the sacraments is a concept which arises from the fact that the three sacraments that confer an indelible "character" on the soul (namely baptism, confirmation, and holy orders) are unrepeatable in the sense that they can be received only once. However, there may be cases where legitimate doubt exists whether a person has validly received one of these sacraments because of defective form or defective intention on the part of the minister. In such cases, it may be necessary to confer the sacrament again, not absolutely, but conditionally, in the sense that it is understood that the second administration is only operative if the first was ineffective.

ANTHONY D. ANDREASSI

See also SACRAMENTS.

CONFERENCES, EPISCOPAL

These are associations of all the bishops of one nation or, in some cases approved by the Holy See, of all the bishops of several geographically adjacent nations. Though these conferences have ancient precedents in the local and regional synods held in the early centuries before centralization of Church administration and authority, their present canonical status in the Catholic Church is unclear. The clearest definition of their role, composition and functions is in chapter III of the Decree on the Pastoral Office of Bishops in the Church, *Christus Dominus,* issued by the Second Vatican Council in October 1965. Even these, however, are very general, requiring the setting up of such conferences with central administrative offices, regular meetings, and common concerns with the pastoral situation of the region, and the power to make binding regulations for the whole region in certain liturgical and disciplinary matters.

MONIKA K. HELLWIG

See also BISHOP.

CONFESSION OF SINS

In the 1973 *Rite of Penance* confession of sins is one of the four "parts" of the sacrament of penance, together with sorrow for sin, satisfaction, and absolution. In the early Church there was little emphasis placed on this step in the reconciliation of sinners. Anyone who was known to have committed one of the capital sins (apostasy, adultery, or murder) was cut off from the Christian community. Prayers would be said for the conversion of the sinner and, if the sinner showed genuine repentance, members of the community would encourage the sinner in carrying out the years of penitential activity required before absolution could be given. There was little need for confession of the sin since it was already publicly known.

From the seventh century on, however, with the introduction of private penance, frequently repeated, the acknowledging of particular sins to a confessor grew in importance. This development reached its climax in the extensive teaching of the Council of Trent on the sacrament of penance.

When the faithful present themselves for the sacrament of penance, after a diligent examination of their conscience, they are required to confess every serious sin they have committed since their baptism which has not been previously confessed. The sins must be accurately named and the number of times each sin was committed must also be given. This form of the sacrament continued until the Second Vatican Council where it was decided to revise the celebration of this sacrament to express more clearly its nature and its effects.

The new *Rite of Penance* maintains the previous requirements about naming and giving the number of sins committed. The context of this avowal, however, is considerably altered. While the option of maintaining anonymity must be preserved, the setting should also permit the penitent to engage in a more personal dialogue with the priest, who greets the penitent with informal and friendly words and urges the penitent to have confidence in the mercy of God. Penitents are encouraged to make known to the priest their state in life, the time of their last confession, any difficulties they may be experiencing in living a fully Christian life, and "anything else which may help the confessor in exercising his ministry." Part of that ministry is to help the penitent to make a complete confession of all serious sins so that the priest may offer suitable counsel and encouragement.

The faithful are required to confess at least once a year, if they have committed a serious sin during that time. Those who have committed no serious sins need never go to confession, but they may choose to do so out of devotion and to participate in this sacramental expression of sinfulness and assurance of forgiveness.

Every liturgical celebration of the Eucharist begins with a penitential rite in which the worshiping community acknowledges its sinfulness and receives an assurance of God's merciful forgiveness. The new *Rite of Penance* contains an expanded version of this penitential rite, a communal celebration of penance with hymns, Scripture readings, a homily, litanies, and other prayers. In this communal form there is an opportunity for those who wish to make a private confession and receive individual absolution.

WILLIAM C. McFADDEN, S.J.

See also SACRAMENT OF RECONCILIATION.

CONFESSION, SEAL OF

See SEAL OF CONFESSION.

CONFESSIONS OF ST. AUGUSTINE

See AUGUSTINE, ST.

CONFIRMATION

See SACRAMENTS OF INITIATION.

CONFITEOR

(Lat., "I confess") A form of the Penitential Rite recited at the beginning of the Mass by the celebrant and the congregation. Its wording (text) is as follows:

"I confess to Almighty God, and to you, my brothers and sisters, that I have sinned through my own fault, in my thoughts and in my words, in what I have done and in what I have failed to do; and I ask blessed Mary ever virgin, all the angels and saints, and you, my brothers and sisters, to pray for me to the Lord our God."

The celebrant then responds:

"May Almighty God have mercy on us, forgive us our sins, and bring us to everlasting life."

This prayer of repentance originated in medieval times, when prayers of unworthiness (*apologiae*) were recited by the clergy as a testimony to their piety before the Lord during the procession to the altar. Though the prayer is not a substitute for the sacrament of reconciliation, its recitation is considered an appropriate preparation for Eucharistic celebration.

JOSEPH QUINN

See also EUCHARIST; SACRAMENT OF RECONCILIATION.

CONFRATERNITY

A lay association, canonically set up with ecclesiastical approval, whose members follow some spiritual regimen or engage in some form of apostolic work.

JOAN GLAZIER

See also LAITY, THEOLOGY OF THE; SODALITY.

CONFRATERNITY OF CHRISTIAN DOCTRINE (CCD)

The first society of Christian doctrine was established in Rome under Pius IV during the time of the Council of Trent (1545–1563). It was an organization formed to provide religious education for children and adults who had never taken part in any formal catechesis. Pius V supported the work and called for its establishment in parishes around the world. Pius X (1903–1914) was a strong advocate for the renewal and extension of the confraternity. His encyclical *Acerbo Nimis* (15 April 1905) mandated the establishment of the CCD in every parish to counteract the decline in religious knowledge and to provide religious education for children attending public schools.

In the United States, Edwin V. O'Hara, bishop of Kansas City-St. Joseph and organizer of the National Catholic Rural Life Conference, was a zealous supporter of CCD. He served as chairman of the episcopal committee of the CCD until his death in 1956 and established the national center at The Catholic University of America in 1935.

CCD is most widely known for providing religious instruction for elementary school children who do not attend parochial schools, but it actually includes catechesis at all stages of life and is involved with religious vacation schools, correspondence courses, high school and college sessions, and adult theological education.

PATRICIA DeFERRARI

See also CATECHESIS; CATECHETICS.

CONGREGATION FOR BISHOPS

This Roman administrative body handles various matters concerning bishops and their jurisdictions, military vicars, and the Pontifical Commission for Latin America.

DAVID BRYAN

See also BISHOP; CURIA, ROMAN.

CONGREGATION FOR CATHOLIC EDUCATION

This Roman administrative body superintends all institutes and works of Catholic education. The three general offices pertain to seminaries, Catholic universities, and Catholic schools below the college level. Its jurisdiction is particularly thorough in matters regarding seminaries, as well as with continuing education of priests, religious, and members of secular institutes. At the university level, the congregation concerns itself not only with pontifical universities, but with all higher faculties and institutes which depend on the authority of the Church. At lower levels, the congregation has a more general interest in cooperation with conferences of bishops and civil authorities.

DAVID BRYAN

See also CATHOLIC HIGHER EDUCATION IN THE UNITED STATES; CURIA, ROMAN; EDUCATION, PHILOSOPHY OF; SEMINARY.

CONGREGATION FOR DIVINE WORSHIP AND THE DISCIPLINE OF THE SACRAMENTS

This Roman administrative body superintends all matters concerning regulation and enhancement of the liturgy, especially of the sacraments, subject to the decisions of the Congregation for the Doctrine of the Faith. It handles, further, cases of the Privilege of the Faith, a type of marriage annulment involving nonsacramental marriages. Satellite commissions supervise the laicization of deacons and priests, and nullity of ordinations.

DAVID BRYAN

See also CURIA, ROMAN; LITURGY; SACRAMENTS.

CONGREGATION FOR INSTITUTES OF CONSECRATED LIFE AND SOCIETIES OF APOSTOLIC LIFE

In more familiar terms, this Roman administrative body has jurisdiction over institutes of religious, societies of apostolic life, third orders, and secular institutes. The congregation supervises the establishment and suppression of these types of institutes, and their general conduct in the light of their own rules and constitutions. The congregation is also concerned with the renewal and adaptation of institutes to contemporary circumstances, and promotes intercommunication between them.

DAVID BRYAN

See also CURIA, ROMAN; RELIGIOUS ORDERS.

CONGREGATION FOR ORIENTAL CHURCHES

This Roman administrative body concerns itself with Catholics who are members of the Eastern-rite Churches in communion with Rome, and with the affairs of the Churches themselves; it performs many of the functions which the entire Roman Curia handles for other Catholics.

DAVID BRYAN

See also CURIA, ROMAN; EASTERN CHURCHES.

CONGREGATION FOR THE CAUSES OF SAINTS

This Roman administrative body conducts the process of beatification and canonization of saints, and the preservation of relics.

DAVID BRYAN

See also CURIA, ROMAN; RELICS; SAINTS.

CONGREGATION FOR THE CLERGY

This Roman administrative body has jurisdiction over a wide range of matters concerning the clergy: (1) their rights and duties, including their life and discipline; (2) religious education conducted by the clergy, including preaching and catechizing; (3) the preservation and proper administration of the temporal goods of the Church. Under this congregation are the Pontifical Commission for the Preservation of the Artistic and Historic Patrimony of the Church, as well as the International Office of Catechetics.

DAVID BRYAN

See also CATECHETICS; CURIA, ROMAN; PREACHING; PRIESTHOOD, THE MINISTERIAL.

CONGREGATION FOR THE DOCTRINE OF THE FAITH

This congregation safeguards and promotes authentic Catholic teaching throughout the Church. It studies doctrinal matters and points of controversy, sponsoring extensive doctrinal studies when appropriate. It evaluates theological opinions and may reprove, after prior consultation with local bishops, those regarded as harmful to Catholic teachings. It similarly examines books, providing authors the opportunity to defend themselves.

DAVID BRYAN

See also CURIA, ROMAN.

CONGREGATION FOR THE EVANGELIZATION OF PEOPLES

This Roman administrative body directs and coordinates missionary work of all types. This includes promoting missionary vocations and indigenous clerical vocations, coordination of spiritual and financial support for the missions, the assignment of missionaries, establishing dioceses and other jurisdictional regions, including proposing candidates to serve as bishops and in other offices. The congregation promotes missionary cooperation through the Supreme Council for the Direction of Pontifical Missionary Works.

DAVID BRYAN

See also CURIA, ROMAN; EVANGELIZATION; MISSIONS, CATHOLIC, THE MODERN PERIOD.

CONGREGATION OF CHRISTIAN BROTHERS

The Congregation of Christian Brothers (CFC) (formerly the Christian Brothers of Ireland) was founded in 1802 by Edmund Ignatius Rice in Waterford, Ireland. Rice, a wealthy merchant, saw that English penal laws had reduced the Irish Catholic people to penury and ignorance, and so he sold his business and began teaching poor young people in Waterford. Soon others joined him, their work spread, and in August, 1808, Rice and six others took vows and formed a community of brothers. The brothers take the traditional vows of poverty, chastity, and obedience, and they also take a vow to work for the poor without hope of personal gain. In 1820 the congregation was given papal approval and Rice became the first superior general.

The congregation spread to other countries due to the requests from bishops who had to deal with waves of Irish immigrants fleeing the poverty and starvation of their homeland. In 1868 two brothers were sent to Australia where the congregation flourished. In 1876 they began a mission in Newfoundland, and soon after started schools in the British colonies, earning a reputation as respected educators. At the request of a New York pastor, the Reverend John Power, in 1906 the Christian Brothers came to the United States, and from New York they spread to other parts of the country. Today they administer numerous elementary and secondary schools and Iona College in New Rochelle, New York. They have two American provinces, with headquarters in New Rochelle, New York, and Chicago.

ANTHONY D. ANDREASSI

See also CATHOLICISM; IRISH; RELIGIOUS ORDERS.

CONGREGATIONALISM

Congregationalism is a Protestant denomination which traces its origins to dissenters from the Anglican Church in the sixteenth century. There is some evidence in England as early as 1550 of people praying together and celebrating the sacraments outside the established Church. After the Elizabethan religious settlement in 1559, these "dissenters" grew in number because of dissatisfaction with the shape of the Anglican Church. The "Separatists" or "Independents" were so displeased with the state Church that they chose to break away completely, choosing a more congregational form of Church polity. These early Congregationalists opted for the complete autonomy of each local congregation because they felt that this arrangement was more in keeping with the model of the early Church. They also rejected the notion of a clerical priesthood, believing instead that all Christians are priests. Since they considered Christ to be the sole head of the Church, they instituted a democratic church-order rejecting all forms of hierarchy. In 1582 Robert Browne authored a popular book on the tenets of "Congregationalism," which helped to spread the movement throughout England. These "Brownists" and "Separatists" soon became known as "Congregationalists" as they organized their separate Churches. When the Anglican Church began to persecute them, many went underground or fled to Holland, and eventually to America, to seek religious freedom.

The Pilgrims who arrived in Plymouth in 1620 were Congregationalists; however, non-Separatist Protestant dissenters also settled in Massachusetts around this time, and soon the two groups merged. Congregationalism spread throughout New England, establishing such prestigious educational institutions as Harvard College (1636) and Yale College (1701). After the Revolutionary War, Congregationalists played a prominent role in settling first the Northwest Territory and later the West. Education was always important for Congregationalists, and they were responsible for the founding of many colleges. During the early nineteenth century theological differences resulted in a split between the Unitarians and the "traditional" Congregationalists. During this period American Congregationalists developed an extensive foreign missionary apostolate. Both in the United States and abroad they worked hard for social reform, and in the U.S. were especially prominent in the abolitionist movement.

In the nineteenth and twentieth centuries, in both the U.S. and Britain, there have been numerous attempts by Congregationalists to unite with other Protestants, but these attempts have met with only mixed success.

ANTHONY D. ANDREASSI

See also ANGLICANISM; PROTESTANTISM.

CONNOLLY, THOMAS LOUIS (1815–1876)

The nineteenth century was an era of great prelates, zealous missionary activity, and theological challenge. During this time the population of North American cities was tripling and quadrupling with waves of immigrants, the Church was expanding, rooting, and taking shape, and pastoral needs were mushrooming. It was a period when the Church was being formed, for the most part, by missionaries, prelates and founders of religious orders. This was the century into which Thomas Louis Connolly was born.

Thomas Connolly was in turn Capuchin, missionary, bishop, founder of a religious order, statesman, leading member of the minority at Vatican I, and ecumenist. In almost every dimension of life Connolly left his mark; however, to friends and acquaintances he was above all, an Irishman.

Thomas was born to Anne Harte and Christopher Connolly in 1815 in Cork, Ireland. At this time Cork was still a thriving trading center and Thomas' father was a retailer. The Connolly house was known to the townsfolk by a sign which bore the inscription: "This world is a city with many a crooked street, And death the marketplace where all men meet. If life were merchandise that men could buy, The rich would live and the poor would die."

When Thomas was three, his father died, but fortunately throughout his formative years he came under the watchful eye of the Capuchins at the nearby friary. At sixteen, Thomas entered the Capuchin Order taking the name Frater Louis, and after studies in Rome and Lyons he was ordained. Within three years Connolly would be sent to Nova Scotia as chaplain to the newly appointed coadjutor bishop of Halifax, William Walsh, and would spend the remainder of his life serving the people and Church of Nova Scotia and New Brunswick.

When Connolly came to Halifax as a missionary in 1842, he arrived at a decisive moment both in Canada's ecclesiastical and political history. He was to make major contributions in both Church and society: in the Atlantic region in the area of Catholic education, in Rome at the First Vatican Council and in Canadian politics where he would earn the title "godfather of Canadian Confederation."

Connolly soon came to be recognized as a man of outstanding character—intelligent, well-educated, expert in business, kindly in manner, a notable preacher, and above all, he was zealous for religion. It is not surprising that in 1852 he was appointed to the vacant see in New Brunswick, and seven years later, to the vacant see of Halifax. His one obvious character flaw was his temper, which he readily recognized, owning that "with power in (one's) hands a temper is a dangerous companion."

One of the first problems facing Connolly on his arrival in Saint John was a cholera epidemic which left seventy children orphaned in the space of six weeks. It was essential to have sisters, first for the care of orphans, and then for education. Since no religious were available, Connolly, along with Honoria Conway, founded a congregation of Sisters of Charity, modeled on those recently founded by Elizabeth Ann Seton in the United States.

For Connolly education was key to preserving the faith of his people. To this end he worked indefatigably, raising money, building schools, and hammering out policies with boards and governments. He is credited with personally being responsible for a system of Catholic public education in New Brunswick and Nova Scotia which has been the mainstay of Catholic education until today. A sad note in all Connolly's efforts for Catholic education was that he did not have the heart or the means to provide a French Catholic education for the Acadians.

As bishop of Saint John and archbishop of Halifax, Connolly did not see himself only as a religious leader, but also as one called to have clear political ideals. He was a strong supporter of Canadian Confederation during those years when, in the 1860s, a North-South alliance between the provinces and the United States was a very real possibility. In 1867 four provinces united to form Canada; and while the British Act of Parliament was being formulated, Connolly was in England lobbying to ensure equity for Catholic education.

In 1869 the most significant Church event of the century took place, the First Vatican Council; it was here that papal infallibility would be defined. When Connolly arrived in Rome for this historic event, he was a relatively unknown missionary bishop, but he emerged eight months later a noted churchman. Personally, Connolly had always held the theological opinion of papal infallibility and he had never had reason to doubt his opinion. However, after just six weeks of research in Rome he found himself in a very different position. Connolly saw from his studies that it was virtually impossible to prove this position from either Scripture or tradition, and in addition, it was not essential that infallibility be defined at this time. Connolly, in conscience, had to change his stance, and he became one of the most ardent workers among the minority party at the council. Lord Acton, a historian and British member of parliament, named Connolly of Halifax and Kenrick of St. Louis as the two outstanding North American bishops of the minority at the Vatican Council. In the end, when the definition nevertheless was made, it was to the credit of the minority that the definition was neither too broad nor too imprecise. As for Connolly, he himself stated that he had always personally held the doctrine of papal infallibility though his theological difficulties never could be explained away; yet, he wrote: "I feel happy and as far as my own action in Rome is concerned tranquil, nay joyous in the inner kernel of my heart, as ever I have felt in my whole life."

When Connolly died in 1876, he was truly a churchman, a statesman, and a large-hearted man.

FAY TROMBLEY, S.C.I.C.

See also CANADA, THE CATHOLIC CHURCH IN; VATICAN COUNCIL I.

CONSCIENCE

We hear much about conscience in Christian moral life. People talk about consulting conscience, informing conscience, following conscience. We are told that in the end conscience rules and that one is entitled to appeal to and follow it. Conscience is made to appear like some special piece of equipment in addition to or apart from our general moral consciousness. If that is how we think of conscience then it is nearer to the truth to say that there is no such thing.

Far from being different from moral awareness our conscience is our moral awareness. At a basic level it refers to the fact that we experience the moral point of view. However strange and mysterious it may be, we know that life cannot be lived arbitrarily, that there are kinds of behavior that we should not indulge in, that being with others in the world makes claims on us. This is the constant undertow of experience. In the particularities of our daily lives we are continually faced with concrete decisions and we say that conscience—i.e., our own moral awareness—indicates the right response or struggles to know it. And, following action, we experience contentment that we have acted well, wonder whether we should have acted differently or reproach ourselves for rejecting the moral call.

But each of us, at any point of life, experiences conscience individually. We differ from one another in how we read the moral landscape, in what issues appear to us as moral issues, in how we interpret the moral claim, how we make judgments, how we weigh facts, whether we are emotionally touched by instances of exploitation or by opportunities for doing good. Confronting a moral decision is not just a rational but an affective issue. The lack of emotional response—of anger, fear, guilt, empathy—and the absence of imagination will constrict or deaden our sense of moral responsibility, our conscience. Normal emotions are as necessary for morality as is thought.

There is a personal history to the conscience of each of us. To some extent our conscience *is made* for us. We inherit the values, emphases, and prejudices of our culture, sex, and language. We imbibe in a subtle way the fears and insecurities of our parents. Already, as small children, we suffer wounds and lay down patterns of reactive response that are prepersonal. We take on emotional directions for which we were not responsible but which influence our choices over a lifetime. They influence not only what we want to do and are able to do but in the first place what we *see* and how we see it. They influence our moral point of view. To some extent *we make* and are responsible for the fabric of our conscience. Because, with whatever freedom we have, the daily choices that we make enter into the formation of character, contribute to our growth in moral sensitivity—or the opposite. It should be no surprise, then, if people disagree about moral judgment—and sometimes, because of its emotional implications for them, with great passion and persistence.

It is a human thing to want to know the truth, as Aquinas told us; it is something that draws us. But few of us would claim that we have an unalloyed desire to know it. Some part of us does not want to know—for the very good reason that knowing the truth for living imposes demands on us. To have an unrestricted openness to truth is to have achieved a self-transcendence. It implies a readiness to face the implications of knowing, a kind of holy indifference to what we may be called upon to do. So much in us—fears, prejudices, insecurities, anxieties, emotional needs—resists that. Seeing would make a demand on us to abandon the shell of our ego-defensiveness. The achievement of a limpid and authentic conscience, therefore, is a conversion. It is in part a matter of the resolution of the emotional fears that cloud our seeing, that imprison our empathy and imagination. That, if it occurs—and the hope is that it will be abetted by the great symbols of the Christian story—will allow a reeducation of our desires and a growth in freedom. It is this general level of character, our basic affection for truth and goodness, our heart-stance towards others, that is decisive for conscience. As Iris Murdoch says, it is what lies behind and in between actions and prompts them that is important.

Moral concerns in our tradition have been narrow, restricted roughly to the Ten Commandments. The emphases of these concerns often betray the time, the culture, the social status, and the sex of their formulators. In recent times, the understanding of moral responsibility has broadened to give more attention to issues of justice and discrimination, to a greater sensitivity to the rights of minorities, to environmental and feminist issues. Conscience awareness has meant a relativizing of the emphases of the past. It has also meant a healthy suspicion about the prejudices that covertly inform our moral judgments as individuals and as a community. And it has meant a realization that morality is not just about adherence to common rules but about responsible response to the rich uniqueness of our lives and situations.

Worldview bears on conscience judgment. Not all share the same worldview and so judgments will not coincide even where there is agreement about a fundamental moral theory. Not all will agree on what human flourishing, or common good, or a just society might mean. One version of worldview is religious story: there is a link between that and normative judgment. Much ink has been spilt on the manner in which Christian faith enters into moral judgments, on whether there is such a thing as a specific Christian morality and on what that might mean. The jury is still out on that question. What is more widely agreed is that our Christian tradition recognizes that the response of conscience is not just horizontal, intraworldly. It contains within itself a response to God, who is the horizon of our intraworldly choices. Moral response, therefore, is the place of our acceptance of the gift of God or our refusal of it. It is in this sense that it can be referred to as the voice of God. But saying that does not make the struggle to know the right response in the complexity of life one whit easier.

When we are engaged with conscience we are dealing with a most intimate and sacred dimension of human experience, something that involves one's humanness at a deep level. To force a person to go against her or his conscience is to do violence to them in a radical way. It asks them to act knowingly against their understanding of the true and the good, to deny the deep claim of their spirit. One who genuinely seeks to do the truth can only follow conscience because it is the only window one has on the truth. One must be allowed to do so. There have been unfortunate ages in which this was not accepted, when the shibboleth "Error has no rights" silenced all opposition and sought to crush personal conviction. Happily, that is something that Vatican II has repaired: conscience, it says, is the most secret core and sanctuary of a person and although it frequently errs it does not thereby lose its dignity (The Church in the Modern World, no. 16). It follows that "one is bound to follow conscience faithfully . . . is not to be forced to act in a manner contrary to conscience . . . nor be restrained from acting in accordance with conscience" (Declaration on Religious Freedom, no. 3).

The right to follow conscience seems to be diluted by insistence that one may do so only if one's conscience is informed, the insinuation being that conscience is informed only if one has accepted a particular piece of ecclesiastical teaching. The injunction to inform conscience can only be another way of saying that fidelity to the moral call entails a sincere effort, according to one's capacities, to find the truth. That will mean taking community wisdom and authoritative teaching, if such exists, seriously. But authority cannot make behavior right or wrong. In the end, one's obligation is to the truth: the attention to be given to tradition and authority depends on the likelihood of their offering the truth. It might be said, then, that a serious effort to be moral—informing one's conscience—involves giving due weight to whatever advice is available. "Due" because one will have more or less confidence in different forms or levels of Church teaching.

Conscience need not make cowards of us all. It is not a colonial governor sent to impose alien norms on us (Midgley). It is our own center at work in us. It is the call of our deepest selves to listen to the truth, to live in freedom, to be what we most want to be. It is, as Aquinas said, the light of God's countenance on us. It is a share in the divine wisdom.

VINCENT MacNAMARA

See also CHRISTIAN MORALITY; THEOLOGY, MORAL.

CONSCIENTIOUS OBJECTION

Conscientious objection is an act of dissent from a country's, institution's, or organization's policies or demands. As a statement of personal responsibility and integrity, it is based on an appeal to conscience in light of moral convictions, values, and principles that are integral to a person's character and relevant to a problematic situation or demand. Most often an act of conscientious objection is a response to a conflict or dilemma in which a person feels the appeal of two or more ethical demands, neither of which can be satisfied without neglecting or repudiating the other; for instance, the moral duty to serve one's country and contribute to the common good conflicts with the moral duty to respect life and not to kill. As an individual considers the values or disvalues involved in honoring each demand, he or she judges that one obligation is more primary and thus overrides the other. Still, because the neglected demand is substantial and is usually socially sanctioned, the individual appeals to conscience to explain why he or she feels a breach with customary, expected behavior is justified.

Acts of conscientious objection are motivated by the awareness that if one's behavior does not conform to his or her convictions, he or she will suffer not only shame and guilt, but also a loss of integrity, wholeness, and sense of self. Peace and harmony in one's life depend on heeding the demands of conscience; by contrast, knowingly to violate one's conscience leads to a divided and conflicted self. In the Catholic moral tradition there is an absolute obligation to follow conscience. This point was underscored in the Second Vatican Council's Pastoral Constitution on the Church in the Modern World (*Gaudium et Spes*). The council stressed the dignity of conscience, describing it as "the most secret core and sanctuary" of a person where he or she "is alone with God," adding that in the depths of conscience each person "detects a law" which binds him or her to obedience (GS 16). Nothing supercedes or overrides the authority of conscience because it is seen to reflect the demands of God. Similarly, no one, whether the state, the Church, or another person can usurp one's right and responsibility to act in conscience and should never coerce a person to act against conscience.

Conscientious objection is normally associated with a refusal to participate in military service, especially during time of war; however, it can be expressed in other ways, such as a refusal to take an oath, or more commonly, to pay taxes which would contribute to nuclear weapons, support a war, or fund abortions. In every case, an individual's refusal to participate in or contribute to certain actions is rooted in his or her unwillingness to cooperate in what they are convinced is evil. Applied to war, there are two types of conscientious objection. Universal or absolute conscientious objection, which is based in pacifism, is a refusal to participate in any war. Selective conscientious objection is a refusal to participate in particular wars because they are judged to violate just war criteria; for instance, either the war itself is seen to be unjust or the way it is being conducted is seen to be unjust. The just war tradition logically implies selective conscientious objection inasmuch as the latter illustrates how just war teaching presumes the immorality of war except under strictly prescribed criteria.

In the United States, exemption from military service for conscientious objectors was originally restricted to members of peace Churches, such as the Mennonites, Quakers, and Church of the Brethren. It was later extended to include all conscientious objection based on religious beliefs and today embraces those who oppose war for moral reasons as well. What matters is not whether the objection to war is religious, moral, or ethical, but that a person's convictions be sincere and deeply held.

Generally, the status of conscientious objection has been honored for two reasons. First, the state is obliged to respect an individual's conscience and should not force a person to act against conscience; this is why there is a strong presumption in favor of liberty of conscience. Secondly, loyalty to country does not supercede loyalty to conscience or loyalty to God. While every person has duties in justice to his or her country, each is also accountable to God and the moral law. Expectations of the state do not relieve a person of the responsibilities of conscience and the judgments each one has to make about the morality of situations and how he or she ought to respond. One's absolute moral duty is not to the state but to God. In this respect, conscientious objectors do not reject the state as such or deny its authority, but in their refusal to participate in certain undertakings remind the state that ultimate sovereignty lies not in the government, but in God and the moral law. For instance, Pope John XXIII's 1963 encyclical letter *Pacem in Terris* acknowledged the legitimate authority of the state, but insisted that it was subordinate to God and the moral order; thus, if a person was sincerely convinced that an action or law of the state was contrary to morality, he or she was not obliged to follow it (PT 51).

Nonetheless, conscientious objectors who are exempted from serving in wars are normally required to perform substitute or alternative service, either noncombatant work within the military or some service to society. The requirement of alternative service is based on fairness. If those who serve in war risk injury or death, it is only just that those who are exempted for reasons of conscience acknowledge the burdens others bear and prove the sincerity of their convictions by willingly accepting other ways of serving.

Recent Catholic social teaching has shown strong support for the right of conscientious objection. The Second Vatican Council's Pastoral Constitution on the Church in the Modern World (*Gaudium et Spes*) emphasized each person's responsibility for the common good (GS 75), but also challenged Christians to be "artisans of peace" (GS 77). The council praised those who renounced violence as a way to settle grievances and urged governments to provide legal support for the right of conscientious objection (GS 78–79). Similarly, the 1983 Pastoral Letter of the U.S. Bishops, *The Challenge of Peace,* acknowledged a government's right to require military service, but also supported exemptions for both absolute and selective conscientious objectors (*The Challenge of Peace,* 232–233). Too, the bishops stressed that both pacifism and conscientious objection flow from a gospel life of discipleship and an authentic witness to Christ. In "a world that is becoming increasingly estranged from Christian values," they argued, the witness against war and for peace is especially crucial (*The Challenge of Peace,* 276–277).

Ultimately, conscientious objection is part of the duties of good citizenship. People exercise patriotism and serve their country well when they grapple with questions about the morality of war. The challenge for the Church is to be the community of moral formation and reflection in which these questions can be raised and the setting in which Christians can be educated in the virtues of civic responsibility, of which conscientious objection is a vital part.

PAUL WADELL

See also CHRISTIAN MORALITY; PACIFISM; PEACE; THEOLOGY, MORAL.

CONSECRATION

The setting apart of a person or thing by ecclesiastical act, for a religious state or office, or for a particular use. When the word is used without qualification it generally means the consecration at Mass, whereby the bread and wine are changed into the Body and Blood of Christ.

JOAN GLAZIER

See also EUCHARIST; RELIGIOUS LIFE, ACTIVE.

CONSTANTINE (ca. 274–337)

Son of Constantius Chlorus, who was a soldier and ruler of Gaul, and of St. Helena. Detained at the court of Diocletian as a hostage, he escaped when Diocletian died and returned to Rome as its conqueror in 311, becoming the commander of the western part of the Roman Empire. Two years later, jointly with Licinius, emperor of the eastern part, he issued the Edict of Milan which lifted from the Christian Churches the classification of *religio illicita* once and for all, earning him great praise from Church leaders, especially Eusebius of Caesarea, the Church historian. Further military conflict with Licinius left Constantine the sole emperor of an empire that stretched all around the Mediterranean and northwards into much of Europe.

To maintain all this territory under one ruler was extremely difficult, and Constantine coopted the existing network of authority and communication of the Christian Churches as a kind of civil service. He began to mediate any doctrinal disputes that came to his attention (in spite of the fact that he was not particularly knowledgeable in such matters, and was not baptized until his deathbed) and considered himself the bishop of the bishops. In 325 he convened and presided over the first ecumenical council of the Churches at Nicea, at which the divinity of Jesus was defined and a common creed was officially promulgated. The symbiosis of Church and state that Constantine initiated has been called in retrospect the Constantinian Establishment and has had far-reaching consequences even into our own time.

"Constantine and St. Sylvester," fresco detail, 13th century, SS Quattro Coronati, Rome

Because of the difficulty of holding the empire together against hostile external forces, Constantine took up residence at Byzantium (in the European part of what is modern Turkey), rebuilt and extended the city, and renamed it Constantinople. His residing there left a power vacuum in the West which tended to be filled by the Patriarch of Rome from that time (except during brief periods when there was a strong Western emperor). This seems to have been the origin of the civil authority which the popes continued to claim for many centuries.

It is not clear what Christianity actually meant to Constantine himself. He declared Sunday as a public holiday, extended great generosity to Christians in the use of public buildings, titles, and privileges, and in supporting the construction of church buildings. But he scarcely lived as a Christian and he seems not to have abandoned the worship of the Unconquered Sun, nor a number of superstitious fears and practices. His patronage of the Churches was certainly helpful to those Churches in a material and practical way, but it also had great disadvantages, and the greater benefit may have been to Constantine's task of holding the empire together.

Although he did many unjust and cruel things in public life and was not edifying in private life, the Eastern Churches honor him as a saint for his one great gift of setting the Churches free from legal proscription and the ever-lurking threat of active persecution. He initiated the idea, if not the name, of Christendom.

MONIKA K. HELLWIG

See also CREEDS; ECUMENICAL COUNCILS.

CONSUBSTANTIAL

Of one and the same substance. In Church usage, the term refers to the belief that the Three Persons of the Blessed Trinity—the Father, the Son, and the Holy Spirit—are of the same essence and share the same nature. It was first employed at the Council of Nicaea (325) in relation to the divinity of Jesus.

JOSEPH QUINN

See also JESUS CHRIST.

CONTEMPLATION

The English term "contemplation" is rooted in the Latin *templum,* which refers to the space designated by a visionary with a divining rod. In addition to signifying sacred space, the term also came to refer to the actual observation made by the seer. It thus conveys the notions of "looking," "gazing," or a way of "seeing." The Greek origin of the term contemplation is *theōrein* which means to regard or to look at a spectacle or religious event. Some are inclined to trace the origins of the term back to *theos* (God) while others to *thea* (vision). Both the Latin and the Greek have given rise to common understandings of contemplation as speculative study, admiration of beauty, or beholding wisdom.

From a Christian perspective, contemplation is properly viewed within the context of prayer understood as the movement of the human heart in response to the divine initiative. In the history of Christian spirituality contemplation is often treated as a type of knowledge born of an experiential, connatural intuitive vision, in contradistinction to the systematic exercise of discursive reasoning more characteristic of traditional approaches to meditation. Writings on Christian life within the tradition often give emphasis to the distinctions between and among various types and degrees of contemplation, to the role of contemplation vis-à-vis ascetical practices and the pursuit of mystical union, as well as to the relation of contemplation to the "active life." While such distinctions may have been helpful to previous generations, the nuances and distinctions themselves tended to obfuscate the grace of contemplation given in baptism and the call of every baptized person to cultivate carefully the contemplative dimension of everyday living. The universal call to holiness so clearly affirmed in the documents of the Second Vatican Council (e.g., LG 40–41) requires fresh perspectives and new orientations rooted in the priority of the Word in the Scriptures, and in a deeper appreciation of the Church as the sacrament of the body of Christ.

A contemporary Christian approach to contemplation can do no better than begin with the Fourth Gospel. In the Gospel of John, vision and love are ineluctably related. God is seen through love. However, especially in chapters 14–17, this seeing is not just speculation, the mind's gaze upon some pure and unchanging truth. Seeing becomes a way of being. The disciple who sees Jesus and, through him, the One Jesus called "Abba," abides and lives in love. And living in love purifies the vision of God.

Similar insights are gleaned from the writings of Paul. Those who have faith in Christ and live in his light are bound together in a series of interlocking relationships with love as their source and end. It is love which makes of the disciples one body in Christ. To be "in Christ" is to live in communion with the body by both faith and charity.

The Johannine and Pauline perspectives lend to the central insight that the Christian's vision or knowledge of God is not primarily by thought but by love. This love is rooted in commitment to God, lived out in discipleship which in turn purifies one's knowledge of God apprehended first and finally by abiding, dwelling, living in loving communion with God and others.

Past perspectives in the history of Christian spirituality tended to highlight the speculative, indeed intellectual, dimension of contemplation. Far too often the contemplative life has been juxtaposed to the active life, assigning superiority to the former and inadvertently denigrating the latter. Thomas Aquinas argued persuasively for the advantages of the "mixed life," i.e., the life devoted to passing on to others the fruits of contemplation. But the contemplative life under religious vows within an enclosed monastery has, in practice, been viewed as the fullest expression of a life devoted to Christian prayer and practice.

Central to a proper understanding of contemplation is a thoroughgoing appreciation of the heart as the affective center of the human person. Contemplation may be properly understood as prayer of the heart. The heart does not refer to the region of "private," "individual" thoughts, feelings or emotions in contradistinction to other dimensions of the person. The term "heart" describes the deepest, most fundamental center of the self, and as such is found in Hebrew and Christian Scriptures and in the history of Christian spirituality to describe the whole person. The heart is the name for "affectivity," or the affective dimension of the person, the very openness of the human being to be touched by another, others, and God. As such, it is inclusive of communal and social realities. To have a heart is to possess the capacity to be in relation. Further, the heart describes human being's openness to relate to the real. It is the very being within human beings toward the good.

The Christian contemplative, then, is one who lives with the simple awareness of God's presence and action in human life, history, world, and Church. This awareness is not primarily at the level of thought or reason. It is a knowledge rooted in the love of Jesus Christ, increased in agapic praxis, and brought to fullness in purity of heart. This attentiveness or awareness of the heart is cultivated in receptivity, quiet, repose, recollection. It is in short supply in a world where people travel at breakneck speed, a culture of cacophany and clutter, an epoch in which instant communiqués have taken the place of interpersonal communication and communion.

From a contemporary Christian perspective, it is not useful to draw hard and fast separations between contemplation and action. The noble tension between action and contemplation is characteristic of any life in Christ by the power and presence of the Holy Spirit. To stress the differences between the "active life" and the "contemplative life" muddles this truth, and compounds the misguided spiritual elitism which the documents of the Second Vatican Council serve to correct. The draw of God's love is known in the depths of the human heart both in attentive awareness of the divine presence, and in active service through which one participates in the continuing redemptive mystery of Christ. Thus contemplation is not restricted to quiet moments of nondiscursive recollection. Nor is it always necessarily a private and isolated activity. Contemplation entails transformation of consciousness, a way of seeing with the eyes of the heart, which finds its fullest expression in interpersonal communion in and through communication with another, others, and God. The central Christian mystery of persons in loving communion, the Trinity, is known and loved not only in moments of quiet repose and reflective gaze, but also as this mystery is known in care and compassionate service of all those in need, especially the poor and the marginalized, the wounded and the weak, the last and the least. It is the same Christian mysteries contemplated in quiet moments of receptive prayer, as well as in those activities which heal the human family and build up the body of Christ. The contemplative sees that God is so intimately involved with every inch and ounce of creation that this necessitates an altogether different way of relating to others and to the world.

MICHAEL DOWNEY

See also PRAYER.

CONTEMPLATIVE LIFE

See CONTEMPLATION.

CONTEMPLATIVE ORDERS

Religious orders of austere life dedicated chiefly to religious contemplation. Among the means employed are silence, solitude, awareness of God's presence, meditation, prayerful reading (especially of the Scriptures), and the Liturgy of the Hours.

DAVID BRYAN

See also CONTEMPLATION.

CONTRACEPTION

This refers to all the various ways in which male–female sexual intercourse can be prevented from resulting in the conception of a new life. Specifically, contraception means all the ways in which the male seed can be stopped from fertilizing a female egg.

Contraception is to be distinguished, both morally and practically, from abortion. Contraceptive acts and the means employed in them seek to prevent a life from being conceived. Abortive acts and the means employed in them seek to terminate the life that has already been conceived. Contraceptive practices do not take life; abortive practices do. In addition, the means that are effective for contraception are of no use for abortion, while abortive means may or may not have consequences for future conception.

There is a variety of ways in which conception can be prevented; the most obvious and effective one being to abstain from heterosexual intercourse altogether. There are also physical (condoms), chemical (pills) and surgical (vasectomy, hysterectomy, tubal ligation) means to prevent conception, not all of which are equally effective or of the same duration. Because physical, chemical, and surgical means require some kind of human intervention into the natural, biological processes of the human body, such means have been described as artificial means of birth control or contraception. Those means of birth control or contraception which do not require some kind of manufactured device or other technological means of human intervention for their effectiveness are referred to as natural means of birth control. In this usage "natural" indicates the rhythms and processes of female biological nature.

The moral assessment of contraceptive attitudes and acts is directly dependent upon the meaning and value one ascribes to human sexual activity. Human heterosexual intercourse undoubtedly serves the purpose of propagating the human species. Hence one clear meaning of such activity is its procreative meaning. A clear value of such activity is a child. Until the twentieth century the Church taught that procreation was the primary end of human sexual activity and so the intention to procreate in the context of marriage was the primary and essential justification for such activity. Given that teaching, it was clear that all deliberately nonprocreative sexual activity failed of such an intent and was judged to be without moral justification. Contraception, both as a human purpose and as a human practice, was morally wrong. That view was commonly taught by Christian denominations through the first quarter of the twentieth century.

A number of historical and scientific developments reaching back into the eighteenth century and continuing to the present day conspired to call that clear and unanimous Christian teaching into question. Among those developments six will be briefly mentioned here. First, a more adequate scientific understanding of the human reproductive system, especially in the female, led to the technological development of effective, relatively safe and inexpensive, and easy-to-use contraceptive devices, culminating in a chemical means which has become the most common form of artificial birth control, the pill. The deliberate control of pregnancy became both effective and broadly accessible.

Second, a growing concern about overpopulation of the planet relative to the finite resources available and necessary to sustain human life provided strong motivation for limiting and controlling the number of births. Third, a growing sense of the dignity and capabilities of the human person put a new emphasis on the human responsibility to understand, control and direct natural processes toward consciously chosen human ends. Fourth, a growing interest in economic and social development led people to invest more of their energy and interest in public affairs and in working to improve the quality of life. This meant less time and energy for the creation and nurture of a family. In addition, as economic activity moved increasingly from the farm to the factory, large numbers of children ceased to be an economic blessing and became an expensive and time-consuming burden instead. This set of developments provided strong motivation for limiting the number of births.

Fifth, the growing awareness of the full humanity of women and the slow opening of new doors of opportunity for women's activity and fulfillment beyond the roles of wife and mother put additional strains on marriage and the family as the obvious end of human sexual activity. Sixth, a new appreciation of the essential importance of sexuality in personal identity and development enabled people to recognize more clearly the personal values of sexual intimacy, its capacity to deepen and strengthen the love and interpersonal union of the sexual partners, its capacity to foster personal sentiments of gratitude and caring and compassion. In short, sexual intercourse had a unitive meaning and value that was of major, if not primary, importance beyond the procreative meaning.

By 1965 almost all Christian denominations, including the Roman Catholic Church, had come to agree on at least two things about human sexual activity. One was that the unitive meaning and value of heterosexual intercourse was sufficient moral warrant for a married couple to engage in such activity. The other was that married couples had both the right and the duty to limit the size of their family to the number of children, given their real-life circumstances, they could care for responsibly. Responsible parenthood became an acceptable synonym for birth control.

Almost alone among the Churches, however, the Roman Catholic Church, at least in its official teaching, continued to insist that artificial means of contraception were contrary to reason and the moral law. Only natural means of family planning, and only for serious reasons, were judged to be morally acceptable. This teaching, while stated clearly and strongly, was greeted in many parts of the Catholic world with either dissent or with indifference. Statistical surveys indicated that Catholics practiced artificial contraception to the same degree in their sexual activity as non-Catholics, even while the techniques of natural family planning improved to an effectiveness rate of 95 percent or more for those capable of following these techniques faithfully.

The major reason for the Church's continued opposition to artificial contraception, in addition to the importance it accorded to past tradition on the subject, was the papal claim that the procreative and unitive meanings of human sexual activity were inextricably linked to one another and willed by God to be inseparable. The basis for this claim was an understanding of marital love, drawn from an understanding of the Divine Love, which saw the chief characteristic of such love to be total, unconditional, self-donation, of which the gift of self in sexual intercourse was understood to be both a sign and a concrete realization.

The argument put forth by Pope Paul VI in his encyclical letter, *Humanae Vitae* (On Human Life), and reemphasized and developed by Pope John Paul II in a number of different addresses, is both subtle and complex. Both popes, speaking as official teachers of the Church, have accepted the need for responsible parenthood, though neither saw the population problem to be as acute and urgent as some scientists seemed to think. Even so, the traditional Catholic moral principle that an evil means cannot justify a good end meant that neither pope would be swayed by predictions of dire consequences.

Furthermore, the position on birth control was closely related to the central importance accorded to the family in traditional Catholic social teaching. Human sexuality found its fulfillment in marriage and the marital relationship found its fulfillment in children. The well-being of the family, as the primary social unit and chief educator of children, was not a matter of private concern or of little social consequence. Both popes repeatedly warned against the dire, personal and social consequences of a contraceptive mentality and the widespread use of artificial contraceptive techniques. Only the practice of natural family planning, they argued, respected the mutual love, freedom, and human dignity of the couple.

What remains difficult and problematic about that teaching is why every single act of sexual intercourse must remain open to the possibility of procreation in a relationship that has already accepted and is living the marital vocation of parenthood. Despite the many advantages, both physical and personal, of natural family planning over artificial means of birth control, its practice is not easily disseminated or learned. Nor has it proven to be workable without a high degree of motivation on the part of both husband and wife. As a result, the techniques of the method, unfortunately, are not widely known nor commonly taught. In large parts of the Catholic world, therefore, and in all other sectors of society, the teaching on the immorality of artificial contraceptive practices has become something of a dead letter. The judgment about the morality of such practices was being left to the private domain of the individual conscience.

JAMES P. HANIGAN

See also SACRAMENT OF MATRIMONY; SEXUALITY; THEOLOGY, MORAL.

CONTRITION

Contrition—according to the Council of Trent as repeated in the *Rite of Penance* (1973)—is "heartfelt sorrow and aversion for the sin committed along with the intention of sinning no more" and is regarded as the most important act of the penitent.

Historically contrition was either perfect, based on the love of God, or imperfect, based on fear of punishment or some lesser motive. For centuries theologians inconclusively debated whether imperfect contrition sufficed to have serious sin forgiven in the sacrament of penance. The *Rite of Penance* opened a new approach and viewed a person's change of heart, *metanoia,* from a more positive scriptural viewpoint. It is a turning away from evil with remorse and contrition and turning to choose what conscience deems right. In his address on the new *Rite of Penance* on 3 April 1974, Pope Paul VI lucidly deals with the matter: "It is distinctive of contrition to add pure and more valid motives to the conscious regret of personal failure. These are the motives of seeing sin as an offense against God and as a sundering of ecclesial communion. . . ."

MICHAEL GLAZIER

See also REPENTANCE; SACRAMENT OF RECONCILIATION.

CONVENT

(Lat. *conventus,* "a gathering") The building or buildings in which a community of religious live. Though the term historically has referred to the residence of a community of religious of either sex, it is now generally accepted to mean a house of women religious. The term may also be used of the community itself.

JOSEPH QUINN

See also RELIGIOUS ORDERS.

CONVENTUALS, FRIARS MINOR

See FRANCISCANS.

CONVERSION

Conversion, from the Latin *conversio* "turning," "return," refers to the moment or process whereby one alienated from God is moved to a change from sinful choices and patterns of choices to new life in friendship with God.

The term "conversion" as such etymologically reflects the OT Hebrew *šûb,* "turn," "return," as in Hosea 6:1, "Come, let us return to Yahweh, for he has torn and he will heal us, has smitten and will bind us up." The "turning" image suggests that people have strayed off the true path, away from God, and need to change course and come back to God.

More generally, the notion is exemplified in the parable of the Prodigal Son (Luke 15:11-32): the young man "comes to himself" and resolves to arise and go to his father.

The notion is expressed also in the OT word *naḥămāh,* "repentance," and its NT correspondent *metanoia,* "change of mind" (or of "heart"). When Jesus begins his ministry, his message is the call to "repent and believe in the good news" (Mark 1:15). Both "repentance" and "conversion" describe a graced moment of change, in the life of the individual and of a people (cf. Jonah 3:8-10). The basis of the new life is the "good news" of God's forgiving love: hence the Marcan "repent and believe."

A cognate notion is the Pauline "reconciliation" (cf. Rom 5:10-11), a term which, however, has its own history. "Reconciliation" should not be simply identified with "conversion" or "repentance," but can be understood as the fruit of conversion. Turning back to God is the first moment in being reconciled with God and with one's neighbor; and God is the reconciler.

In the history of spirituality, the moment of "coming to oneself" that begins conversion was called in Greek *penthos,* "compunction." The image is of being pricked or pierced, namely by the painful consciousness of one's own sinfulness and spiritual need, with attendant feelings of shame and regret. The Desert Fathers saw *penthos* as being at the heart of one's relationship to God.

Though the term is often used to refer to a crucial, life-shaping moment, conversion is a constant in the believer's experience. God is *semper maior,* always greater, and one's relationship with God is a continual rediscovery of that truth, of one's own spiritual need, and of the ever-new call to new life in God.

J.P.M. WALSH, S.J.

See also CHRISTIAN SPIRITUALITY; REPENTANCE; SPIRITUAL LIFE.

COPE

(Lat. *cappa,* "cape") A long, cape-like vestment worn by clergy at certain liturgical rites, such as benedictions, processions, and solemn Liturgy of the Hours services. It is open in front—fastened at the breast by a metal clasp or flap—and reaches to the floor. It has a shield-shaped (attached) hood on the back, and may be adorned with embroidery. The cope is derived from the raincoat worn by men of the Roman Empire.

JOSEPH QUINN

See also VESTMENTS, LITURGICAL.

COPERNICUS, NICHOLAS (1473–1543)

Polish astronomer and mathematician; born 19 February 1473 at Torun, Poland; died 24 May 1543.

Orphaned at the age of ten, Nicholas was adopted by his uncle—a cleric and later bishop—Lucas Waczenrode. He was thus enabled to receive a broad education in subjects as diverse as the arts, canon law, mathematics and medicine, first at the University of Cracow and then at several major universities in Italy. Although he never became a priest, his uncle had him appointed a canon of the cathedral at Frauenberg, a post which allowed him to support himself while pursuing his interest in mathematics and astronomy.

A brilliant mathematician, Copernicus became increasingly perturbed by the complexity and awkwardness of the commonly accepted heliostatic view of the universe, according to which the earth sat motionless at the center of the heavens while the sun and planets raced around it daily. This system was a combination of the physics of Aristotle (378–322 B.C.) and the astronomical calculations of Claudius Ptolemy (fl. 150 B.C.) and it was commonly used to plot the positions of planets as well as for navigational and astrological purposes. Though cumbersome in its use of eccentric circles and epicycles to explain variations in planetary brightness, speed and position, the system did seem in accord with sense experience: it looks as though the sun moves and it does not feel as though the earth does.

Copernicus hoped to satisfy the needs of mathematical simplicity and harmony by divising a better scheme for charting and explaining the motion of the universe. He turned to a heliocentric or sun-centered system, advocated in ancient times by Philolaus (fl. 320 B.C.) and Aristarchus (fl. 280 B.C.). Copernicus was the first to combine the various elements into a true system and to work out in mathematical detail how planetary motions could be calculated based on it. His book, *De revolutionibus orbium coelestium* was published in 1543, literally days before his death.

Although the Copernican system was less complicated than the Ptolemaic, it still faced formidable obstacles to common acceptance. For one thing, since he described celestial orbits as perfect circles rather than as elliptical, Copernicus was required to sacrifice some of the gains in simplicity and to employ epicycles and eccentrics as did the Ptolemaic system. Secondly, there was no adequate physics at the time that could account for the perceived effects of a moving earth. This problem would not be solved until the seventeenth-century work of Galileo and, later, Isaac Newton. Finally, the suggestion that the Copernican theory might describe the real motions in the universe rather than being simply a useful mathematical device, seemed to go against a literal reading of various passages in Sacred Scripture. With Copernicus in ill health, final details of publication of his book in 1543 had been left in the hands of Georg Rheticus (1514–1574) and his friend Andreas Osiander (1498–1552), a Lutheran theologian. Osiander inserted an unsigned preface, wrongly assumed to be by Copernicus, that claimed the book was intended to be only a mathematical hypothesis and in no way claimed the reality of the heliocentric system. The book was dedicated to Pope Paul III and the confrontation between biblical literalists and the new astronomy was postponed until 1616 and Galileo's famous confrontation with the theologians.

JAMES R. LANGFORD

See also GALILEI, GALILEO; SCIENCE AND RELIGION.

COPTIC CHURCH

See EASTERN CATHOLIC CHURCHES.

CORPORAL

(Lat. *corpus,* "body") The piece of white linen cloth, measuring about twenty inches square, on which the bread and wine are placed and consecrated during Mass. Church custom dictates that the corporal be placed in the tabernacle beneath any vessel holding the Eucharist and, during Benediction or Eucharistic adoration, beneath the monstrance.

JOSEPH QUINN

See also EUCHARIST; LITURGY; RUBRICS.

CORPORAL AND SPIRITUAL WORKS OF MERCY

These are lists of good works, seven corporal (bodily) and seven spiritual, which have become traditional. At the heart of the Old Testament is a God of mercy who expects the Israelites to share mercy with each other and with the strangers in their midst. Isaiah 58:7, for example, already contains the nucleus of our "corporal" list. Christ seized the Israelite ideal and gave us a scene of the great judgment in which human beings are judged by their performance of six of our works of mercy (Matthew 25:31-46). Tradition rounds these out to seven by including, from Tobit 1:16-20; 12:12, the duty of burying the dead. Christ frequently reminds us that he himself has come "not to be served, but to serve." (Mark 10:45). The list of the spiritual works has been modeled after the corporal.

Corporal works of mercy: feeding the hungry, giving drink to the thirsty, clothing the naked, harboring strangers, visiting the sick, visiting the imprisoned, burying the dead.

Spiritual works of mercy: admonishing the sinner, instructing the ignorant, advising the doubtful, comforting the afflicted, bearing wrongs patiently, forgiving injuries, praying for the living and the dead.

DAVID BRYAN

See also CHRISTIAN MORALITY; CHRISTIAN SPIRITUALITY; MERCY.

CORREGGIO, ANTONIO ALLEGRI (ca. 1489–1534)

Born probably in 1489, Parma's great master of High Renaissance painting developed a style that anticipates the Baroque. His earliest known works are frescoes which show close contact with the works of Mantegna and Leonardo; in uniting their diverse styles he assured his own originality. His frescoes in the Camera di San Paolo, Parma (1518), recall the bottom-to-top perspective of Mantegna's *Madonna della Vittoria* and his Mantuan frescoes. Leonardo's influence shows particularly in the extreme softness of the *sfumato* style in which one color passes into another without linear boundaries (see especially *The Rape of Ganymede* and *Jupiter and Io,* works done for Duke Federigo II of Mantua about 1530, as well as *Saints Placid and Flavia*). He also shows the influence of Michelangelo and Raphael. Correggio was famed for the frescoes of the vaulted cupolas of S. Giovanni Evangelista (1520–1523) and the Cathedral of Parma (*The Assumption* 1526–1539) which represent an open sky filled with figures as seen from below. He was a master of illusion and foreshortening, a technique that gave his ceilings great ecstatic energy, but which he also applied to his altarpieces and mythological paintings. He died in 1534.

DAVID BRYAN

See also ART, CHRISTIAN; RENAISSANCE, THE.

COUGHLIN, CHARLES EDWARD (1891–1979)

A pioneer radio priest, Coughlin was born in Hamilton, Ontario, on 25 October 1891, and died in Bloomfield Hills, Michigan, on 27 October 1979. In May 1926 he was appointed pastor of Royal Oak, Michigan, where he built the Shrine of the Little Flower. A month later he launched his radio career as a religious broadcaster over station WJR in Detroit. By the 1930s, in Depression-torn America, Coughlin was devoting his Sunday afternoon radio talks to economic and social issues before a national audience that numbered between ten and forty million.

At first Coughlin strongly supported the New Deal policies of President Franklin D. Roosevelt ("Roosevelt or Ruin"), then broke with him in 1934 to organize the National Union for Social Justice. Disenchanted with both Democrats and Republicans ("a choice between rat poison and carbolic acid"), in 1935 Coughlin formed his own third party and later started a weekly newspaper, *Social Justice,* that was distributed outside many Catholic churches after Sunday Mass.

After the poor showing of his third party in the presidential election of 1936, Coughlin kept his promise to retire from the radio, but he resumed his weekly broadcasts a few months later, claiming that it was the dying wish of Bishop Michael J. Gallagher of Detroit. Coughlin became increasingly demagogic and anti-Semitic, publishing the notorious *Protocols of the Elders of Sion* in his newspaper. Catholic University Professor John A. Ryan commented that Coughlin's explanations were 50 percent wrong and his solutions were 90 percent wrong. Under pressure from the federal government (which threatened to prosecute Coughlin for wartime sedition), Archbishop Edward Mooney of Detroit silenced him in 1942, whereupon he confined his activities to his parish in Royal Oak where he remained as pastor until his retirement in 1966.

THOMAS J. SHELLEY

See also AMERICAN CATHOLICISM; ANTI-SEMITISM; SOCIAL TEACHING OF THE CHURCH.

COUNCILS, ECUMENICAL

See ECUMENICAL COUNCILS.

COUNCILS OF THE CHURCH

See ECUMENICAL COUNCILS; PONTIFICAL COUNCILS.

COUNSELING

Counseling is a helping process in which an individual, couple, family, or group meets with a specially trained professional for guidance in solving problems usually connected with life choices, relationships, or crisis situations. Counselors use psychological methods such as testing, structured interviews, and case history collecting to assist those who come to them for help. In contrast to a traditional view of counseling as giving advice or providing information, contemporary approaches to counseling focus more on enabling clients, the ones who have come for counseling, to find solutions themselves. Counselors enable clients to do this by attentive listening and sensitive responses to what clients say. In the context of a supportive counseling relationship, individuals are able to reflect on the various dimensions of the problem confronting them and come to a deeper level of self-understanding leading to a resolution of the difficulty. The counselor's expertise rests primarily in his or her ability to assist clients in acquiring a better perspective on the problem and their own self. Counseling is most effective with those who are willing to take responsibility for themselves, are capable of self-understanding, and are able to express themselves adequately.

Counselors carry on their work in a number of social settings including educational institutions, mental health agencies, social service agencies, and churches. Counseling centers on college campuses, for instance, assist students with personality problems, relational difficulties, and vocational and career choices. Counseling has also become highly specialized. Some counselors are trained to work with populations dealing primarily with one issue such as bereavement, marital or family dysfunction, addiction, or sexuality.

Although there are a number of schools or approaches to counseling, they generally seem to share a basic format and technique. Clients are typically seen for a series of weekly sessions lasting about an hour each. In these sessions the counselor seeks to facilitate both disclosure and understanding. Clients are encouraged to talk about the various aspects of the problem or situation which has brought them to counseling. A warm and accepting attitude on the part of the counselor creates an atmosphere where all thoughts and feelings can be shared. The counselor responds to the client's disclosure by at times reflecting back, summarizing, reformulating, and paraphrasing what has been said verbally or nonverbally. The counselor's empathic response which communicates that he or she can identify with and understand what the client is saying is crucial to the success of the counseling process. Gradually the client is able to gain a perspective and see steps to take to resolve the presenting problem.

Differences in approaches to counseling relate to both the focus which is maintained and the techniques employed. The most notable differences are between an approach to counseling rooted in the thought of Carl Rogers and an approach influenced by depth psychology. Counselors schooled in the Rogerian approach focus primarily on the present situation with minimal attention to the client's past and the influence of unconscious factors. A relationship in which the counselor expresses positive regard for the client is the most important factor contributing to the client's resolution of the difficulty which he or she faces. Counselors who are trained more in the depth psychology tradition tend to make use of analytic techniques. They typically are more interested in the unconscious and experiences from the past which bear on the current situation. They attend to whatever distortions may occur in the counseling relationship due to the clients transferring feelings and reactions directed originally to people in the client's past to the counselor.

Pastoral Counseling

Pastoral counseling is a structured process for helping individuals, couples, and families respond to a specific problem or concern in the light of a faith tradition. Typically a troubled individual will enter into an agreement to meet with a pastoral counselor over a certain period of time to resolve some identified problem. The distinctive features of pastoral counseling are the involvement of a minister or someone accountable to the Church as the helping professional and the use of a religious framework for illuminating the situation.

Some contemporary commentators have noted that ministers involved in pastoral counseling often forsake religious categories and embrace psychological ones as they set about a diagnosis of human problems. In pastoral counseling there should be place for a properly pastoral diagnosis which seeks to understand people and situations in light of such religious categories as vocation, faith, repentance, and awareness of the sacred. Some pastoral counselors explore what kind of image of God clients have. Research has shown that an individual's psychic image of God can have an important role to play in that person's psychic economy.

The factors leading up to the emergence of pastoral counseling as a specialized ministry are diverse. At the turn of the century researchers such as William James and Edwin Diller Starbuck began to use psychological concepts to understand religious experience and helped launch the psychology of religion. Early pioneers in the psychology of religion were interested in promoting religious development and so contributed to advances in religious education. Application of psychological concepts and approaches to the counseling work of ministers was an appropriate next step. Courses and books on pastoral counseling began to appear in the twenties and thirties. Anton Boisen along with others was instrumental in the mid-twenties in launching the Clinical Pastoral Education (CPE) movement. This movement promoted an intense program of supervised training for ministers and seminarians working with people in emotional distress. By the fifties and the sixties pastoral counseling was a flourishing enterprise in America with a number of training programs in existence and pastoral counseling centers established in various places. A professional association (American Association of Pastoral Counselors) emerged and professional journals (*Journal of Pastoral Care, Journal of Clinical Pastoral Work,* and *Pastoral Psychology*) began publication. While the movement started within American Protestant Churches and has developed there, it has had a significant impact on Roman Catholic seminary education in recent decades and has spread to other continents. The contemporary interest in spiritual direction both in the Catholic and Protestant Churches would be a related phenomenon.

Pastoral counselors use a variety of approaches and therapeutic strategies in working with clients which parallel approaches found in secular counseling and psychotherapy. Pastoral counselors are trained in grief counseling, marital and family counseling, crisis counseling, supportive counseling, and educative counseling. Some recent developments in the field include the use of hermeneutical theory to illuminate the process of pastoral counseling, the application of family systems theory to the understanding of congregational life, and an addition to the usual counseling strategies of "reframing," a psychotherapeutic technique which involves recasting and relabeling elements in a problematic situation.

RAYMOND STUDZINSKI, O.S.B.

See also CORPORAL AND SPIRITUAL WORKS OF MERCY; DISCERNMENT OF SPIRITS; SPIRITUAL DIRECTION.

COUNTER REFORMATION

See REFORMATION, THE.

COVENANT

Covenant is the traditional English translation of the Hebrew *bĕrît* and Greek *diathēkē*. It refers to any relationship of obligation, whether mutual or unilateral, between the partners who by oath enter into the relationship. This could be a "contract" between individuals (Gen 21:27; 1 Sam 18:3) or a "treaty" between peoples or kings (1 Kings 5:12; Hos 12:1).

As applying to a relationship between God and human beings, the term is found in the Hebrew Scriptures in various traditions. (1) In the Priestly source of the Pentateuch, God makes a covenant with Noah (Gen 9:8-17) and with Abraham (Gen 17:2-14). (2) In the Epic (JE) traditions, Yahweh makes a covenant with Abraham (Gen 15:17-21) and, at Sinai, through the mediation of Moses, with the people who experienced the liberation from slavery in Egypt (Exodus 19–24). (3) The Deuteronomic corpus centers on the Mosaic covenant as well. It is retrospectively described to the Israelites who are about to enter the Promised Land (Deuteronomy 5); its requirements are spelled out (Deuteronomy 6–26), and the people are instructed to bind themselves by oath to fulfill them once they have entered the land (27–31). (4) Traditions about David depict a covenant between Yahweh and the Davidic king: Yahweh promises that David's descendants will reign over Israel forever (cf. Pss 89; 132). (5) Jeremiah 31, in the context of the Babylonian Exile, speaks of a "new covenant" that will supplant and fulfill the Mosaic covenant.

The term "new covenant" was taken from Jeremiah and used to describe the sacrificial death of Jesus ("This cup is the new covenant in my blood," 1 Cor 11:25; Luke 22:20) and, more generally, the new relationship between God and humankind effected by that death. Hence, the writings the Christian community canonized came to be called the writings of the new covenant, which by an accident of translation (Latin *testamentum* rendering Greek *diathēkē*) are termed the writings of the "New Testament."

The seminal 1954 study of George Mendenhall, "Treaty and Covenant," and subsequent research based on it have shed much light on the nature and terminology of covenant in the OT. Mendenhall called attention to the similarities in format and language between pre-Israelite Hittite treaties and various OT passages treating the Mosaic covenant. The Hittite treaties, together with later treaties from the ancient Near East, follow a characteristic format: preamble, historical prologue, stipulations ("words"), provision for periodic renewal of the treaty, invocation of divine witnesses as guarantors of the treaty obligation, and sanctions for observance or nonobservance of the treaty provisions, called blessings and curses. These features Mendenhall and other scholars found in the Israelite covenant with Yahweh. Further, the central obligation of the ancient treaties was to "love," "know," "go after" (that is, follow or accept the leadership of) the ruler (the "suzerain") to whom the treaty partner (the "vassal") bound himself by oath. These similarities between the vocabulary and format of the ancient Near Eastern legal instruments and the Mosaic covenant between Yahweh and Israel suggest that the Israelites appropriated the forms of international law to describe their relationship to Yahweh: Yahweh was the suzerain, Israel the vassal. Their constitution as a people was based on their acceptance of Yahweh's rule and Yahweh's justice. Nor is the use of political language and forms metaphorical for a basically "religious" reality: the political language is inevitable, since covenant is what makes Israel a political entity, a people.

The discoveries the study of ancient Near Eastern treaties has yielded shed light also on the nature of the Israelite institution of prophecy. Prophets are messengers of Yahweh as covenant lord. Thus, they use the terminology and format of covenant to proclaim Yahweh's rule and the demands of his justice, and to indict king and people for infidelity to the covenant. The "historical prologue" of the treaties finds its counterpart in recitations of Yahweh's saving deeds (cf. Mic 6:3-5), as the blessings and curses serve the prophetic purpose of calling Israel back to fidelity to Yahweh's justice.

J. P. M. WALSH, S.J.

See also BIBLE, NEW TESTAMENT WRITINGS; BIBLE, OLD TESTAMENT WRITINGS; THEOLOGY, BIBLICAL.

COVENANT (BIBLICAL)

Covenant is the major biblical term for the relationship between God and God's people. Not exclusively a religious or theological word, "covenant" (*bĕrît* in Hebrew, *diathēkē* in Greek) is used to refer to agreements or alliances between people, leaders and subjects, and individuals. The secular background has been greatly illuminated by the discovery of treaty documents from the ancient Near East. A covenant between equals is called a parity treaty, whereas a covenant between a lord and a servant is a suzerainty treaty. The suzerainty treaties contain some recurrent elements: identification of the parties, a history of their relationship, the stipulations to be observed, provisions for preserving and reading the covenant, a list of human and divine witnesses, and blessings and curses.

In the biblical covenants God is always the lord and individuals or the people are the inferior party. To Noah God promises never to destroy humankind again by a flood (Gen 9:8-17). To Abraham God promises many descendants and the land of Canaan (Gen 15; 17). The gift of the Law to Moses on Mount Sinai is narrated in the "book of the covenant" in Exodus 19–24. Covenant language is also prominent in texts referring to the relationship between God and David's descendants (2 Sam 7). Whereas the covenants with Abraham and David are promises without conditions, the Sinai covenant and the book of Deuteronomy give many stipulations binding upon Israel if the covenant relationship is to continue.

The prophets repeatedly criticize Israel for breaking the covenant and urge a change of mind and action. They present God as the covenant lord calling the servants to account for their behavior in a covenant lawsuit (Mic 6:1-5). They interpret the fall of the northern kingdom of Israel in 701 B.C. and the destruction of Jerusalem in 587 B.C. as just punishments for the people's failures to live up to its covenantal obligations. And they express the hope for Israel's revival in terms of a "new covenant" (Jer 31:31-34) and an "everlasting covenant" (Isa 55:3).

Many of the key biblical terms (know, fear, love, serve, fidelity, justice, righteousness) and ideas (God as lord, God's mighty acts, laws and statutes, threats of punishments) reflect a covenant context. Likewise important features of ancient Israel's public worship—blessings and curses, calling on heaven and earth as witnesses, sacrifices and meals—suppose a setting in covenant ceremonies.

The covenant theme appears in the New Testament accounts of Jesus' Last Supper and his institution of the Eucharist (see Matt 26:28 par.). The "new covenant" is mentioned in Hebrews 8:7-13 and implied by 2 Corinthians 3. The traditional title for the collection of Greek writings sacred to Christians is the "New Testament (or, Covenant)." The adjective "new" in these expressions need not be taken as a rejection or dismissal of the "old" covenant. According to Christian faith, the one covenant made by God with Israel has been brought to its fullness through Jesus Christ. The covenant with Israel has not been revoked (Rom 11:29), and in the end "all Israel will be saved" (Rom 11:26).

DANIEL J. HARRINGTON, S.J.

See also ELECTION; THEOLOGY, BIBLICAL.

CREATION

The Creed professes that the one God, the Father almighty, is "the maker of heaven and earth, of all that is seen and unseen." This article of faith is rooted in the Bible. The opening pages of Genesis give us two stories of creation. The first, from the "priestly" tradition (Gen 1:1–2:4a), uses the seven-day scheme to describe how God brings everything into existence by the power of God's word. The creation of the man and the woman on the sixth day represents the summit of God's creative act. On the seventh day (the Sabbath) God is said to rest to indicate that the whole creation is destined for the glorification of God. The second, older account, from the "Yahwist" source (2:4b–25), contains a colorful story of God's creation of the man from clay and the woman from the man's rib and focuses on their privileged place in the Garden of Eden.

Both accounts employ the mythological framework to convey important truths of faith, namely, that God is the Lord not only of Israel but also of other peoples and of the whole universe; that the world is essentially good; that it is utterly dependent upon God and hence created out of nothing and not out of preexisting matter; that human beings, created in God's image and likeness, exercise dominion over the world but also bear responsibility toward it; and finally, that human beings must praise and trust in God because of God's creative act. Contrary to the Babylonian myths on which these accounts might have been drawn, there are in the first chapters of Genesis no monsters or demons that God defeats or imprisons. Creation is an action freely initiated by the almighty God and effected by God's word according to God's loving design.

This biblical teaching on creation is carried further by the the psalms, wisdom literature, and the prophets. Now that there was no longer the danger of confusing the doctrine of creation with the myths of the ancient Near East, the sacred writers could make use of the images of the old myths to paint God the Creator as the hero in a cosmic struggle against the beasts of Rahab and Leviathan, the personification of chaos. These monsters God crushed (Ps 89:11), pierced (Isa 51:9; Job 26:13) and shattered to pieces (Ps 74:13).

After the Exile, the editor of Proverbs not only affirms that God creates the world with wisdom, intelligence, and knowledge but goes on to personify Wisdom as the first work that God produced at the very beginning (Prov 8:22ff.). Wisdom was present when all things were created as the master artisan. She delighted in the universe before taking pleasure in the company of humanity. Similarly, the Book of Wisdom sees Wisdom as the craftsperson of the universe (Wis 8:6; 9:9). The same line of thought appears in the authors of the psalms who attribute creation to the personified Word and Spirit of God (Pss 33:6; 104:30).

Finally, in Deutero-Isaiah, God's creative act is intimately linked with God's redemption of God's people in history. Israel's return from exile and liberation from bondage are presented as a new creation. Creation is not just God's act at the beginning; rather it is God's continuing involvement in history on behalf of his covenanted people. God will create new heavens and a new earth (Isa 65:17; 66:22ff.).

The New Testament reiterates the Old Testament's teaching on creation, and at the same time a new light is shed on the meaning of creation by the event of Jesus Christ. On the one hand, creation is still regarded as the manifestation of God's power. There is also a polemical note against the pagan conception of the world. Paul had to turn the minds of the inhabitants of Lystra to the living God "who made the heaven and the earth and the sea and all that is in them" (Acts 14:15). At the Areopagus Paul rejected the cult of idols with an affirmation of God's creative act: "The God who made the world and everything in it, being Lord of heaven and earth, does not live in shrines made by human hands" (Acts 17:24). Indeed, for Paul, the fundamental sin consists in inverting the relationship between the Creator and creature, worshipping the creature rather than the Creator (Rom 1:25). Consequently, he constantly emphasizes the divine origin of creation (Rom 11:26; 1 Cor 8:6; 10:26; Eph 3:9; Col 1:16).

On the other hand, there is a totally new element insofar as God the Creator whom Israel worshipped is now revealed as the Father of Jesus Christ. What has been said about God the Creator is now applied to Jesus, "the one Lord through whom all things exist and by whom we are" (1 Cor 8:6). Since he is the Wisdom of God (1 Cor 1:24), he is "the reflection of God's glory and the image of his being" (Heb 1:3), "the image of the invisible God and the firstborn of all creatures" (Col 1:15). Since in him all things were created and now subsist (Col 1:16), he it is who "sustains the universe by his powerful word" (Heb 1:3). He is the Word, and "all things came to be through him, and without him nothing came to be (John 1:3). Furthermore, it is by and in him that creation will be brought to final fulfillment. It will be "a new creation" (Gal 6:15) which extends also to the universe, since God's plan is to bring all things under Christ as the one head (Eph 1:10), to reconcile all things in and with him (2 Cor 5:18ff.).

In the course of history, certain elements of the doctrine of creation were selected for emphasis, especially in response to heresies. Against the Gnostics, the Manichees, the Cathars, the Albigensians, and other dualistic sects, the Church affirms the fundamental goodness of creation, particularly of matter. With this teaching the Church also rejects every false asceticism which promotes flight from and contempt for the world. Against those who think that the world is a product of chance, or blind fate, or some necessary law, the Church teaches that creation springs from God's freedom and love and that God's purpose in creating the world is not to acquire further perfection but to share God's infinite being. Against pantheists who identify God with the world, the Church declares that God is ontologically distinct from the world and that the world is absolutely dependent on God. Against those who think that God needs some preexisting matter with which to create, the Church affirms that God creates the world from nothing (*ex nihilo*). This means that God is the sole and exclusive source of its being, truth, beauty, and goodness. Against deists who hold that God creates the world but deny God's active involvement in history, the Church affirms the existence of divine self-communication in revelation and grace and God's continuing providence over the world.

Contemporary theology of creation concerns itself with two issues: the relation between theology and natural science, and ecology. The conflict between theology and science began with Galileo's hypothesis of heliocentrism and was exacerbated by Darwin's theory of evolution. Four solutions have been offered to this conflict. The first considers the Bible and theology as confirming evolutionism insofar as God is believed to be actively present in the evolving process of the universe (classical liberal Protestantism, process thinkers, Teilhard de Chardin). The second rejects evolutionary theories by means of biblical faith in creation now reformulated as creation science (fundamentalist Christians). The third regards theology and science as two separate disciplines that do not contradict each other because they have different subject matters and methodologies (Karl Barth and many Roman Catholic theologians). The fourth argues that theology and science must engage in a mutually enriching and correcting dialogue (Karl Rahner and Wolfhart Pannenberg). In general, today many scientists recognize that science is far less objective than ordinarily thought and that it can no longer claim to offer a total interpretation of reality (the relativity theory of Einstein and the indeterminacy principle in the quantum theory of Bohr and Heisenberg). On the other hand, theology is no longer regarded as a purveyor of outmoded and unscientific notions about the world but a serious partner in dialogue with science, especially in epistemological issues.

Regarding ecology, some theologians have suggested that the biblical injunction to human beings to dominate the earth might have contributed to the exploitation of earthly resources and hence to the ecological crisis (Lynn White Jr.). Others have argued that a correct reading of the Genesis text would require human beings to be co-creators with God, managers or stewards of creation (Arthur R. Peacocke). Others have also pointed out that a harmful dichotomy has been drawn between nature and history, scientists being concerned with the former and theologians with the latter. To resolve the ecological crisis, the two areas of human existence must be linked together and brought to bear on sociopolitical praxis (Jürgen Moltmann and Sallie McFague). In general there is today a clear consciousness that human beings must respect the integrity of creation. As the *Catechism of the Catholic Church* has affirmed: "Our use of the universe's mineral, vegetable and animal resources must respect its moral dimension. Humanity's dominion over inanimate and living beings, granted by the Creator, is not absolute. It must be tempered by concern for the quality of life of our neighbor, including generations to come, and calls for a religious respect for creation's integrity" (no. 2415).

PETER C. PHAN

See also ECOLOGY/ENVIRONMENT; EVOLUTION; GNOSTICISM; SCIENCE AND RELIGION.

CREEDS

The earliest Christian creeds were simple affirmations such as "Jesus is Lord." These tended to be linked together in little hymns or recitations about Jesus, and were combined with a phrase or two about the heavenly Father. At baptisms, however, candidates were questioned about the Spirit, as well as about the Father and the Son. This produced the basic structure that we know today: A Trinitarian formula, whose second section is enriched by important affirmations about Jesus, while the third section, on the Holy Spirit, is enlarged with material on the fruits of the Spirit, such as the Church and the forgiveness of sins. (Candidates for baptism were questioned on the three sections separately, as is still done in baptisms and renewals of baptismal vows.) Such creeds were apparently common throughout ancient Christianity and one of them, the old creed used at Rome, was the immediate ancestor of Christianity's best known creed, the so-called "Apostles' Creed." This was certainly not composed at a meeting of Christ's apostles, but it does consist mainly of ancient phrases, most of which were already evident in the New Testament.

The second, or Christological, section of this creed is organized on the pattern of Christ's life: he was conceived and born; then suffered, died, rose, and ascended; he will be returning to judge. The early Church actually developed these affirmations in reverse order: Jesus will come again as King; Jesus is already the ascended Lord and Mediator; Jesus rose as the first born of the new creation; Jesus' suffering was his glory; Jesus' origin is of God and the Virgin. By meditating on the articles in this order we can better understand the power for living which each article contains.

The "Nicene" Creed, used now for many centuries at Mass on Sundays and solemnities, is a development of another of these earliest creeds, but in this case from somewhere in the eastern part of the Roman Empire. The title "Nicene" is valid in the sense that the faith of the Council of Nicaea (Christ is "one in being with the Father") is maintained. Otherwise, this creed would be better named the "Constantinopolitan" Creed, for we have here the creed adopted by the Council of Constantinople (A.D. 381) and promulgated by the Council of Chalcedon (A.D. 451). This creed is of the greatest ecumenical significance, for it is still accepted by Catholics, Orthodox, and the vast majority of Protestant denominations. Notable clarifications in this creed concern Christ and the Holy Spirit: The Christological section combines faith in Christ's origin from the Spirit and the Virgin (which is a feature of the "Apostles" and other Roman creeds) with the Eastern emphasis on Christ's eternal origin. This creed further teaches that the Holy Spirit, like the Son, is one in being with the Father, but it studiously avoids using this expression which had provoked a century of controversy. Instead, an equivalent is used: "with the Father and the Son he [the Spirit] is worshiped and glorified." Where the original creed said only that the Spirit "proceeds from the Father," Christians of the Latin rite have added "and from the Son." This has been a source of controversy between Catholics and the Churches of the East for a thousand years and the search for a solution is being vigorously pursued by theologians.

The Apostles' Creed

I believe in God, the Father Almighty, creator of heaven and earth.
And in Jesus Christ, his only Son, our Lord,
who was conceived by the Holy Spirit,
born of the Virgin Mary,
suffered under Pontius Pilate,
was crucified, died, and was buried.
He descended into hell.
On the third day he rose again from the dead.
He ascended into heaven,
sits on the right hand of God, the Father Almighty.
From thence he shall come to judge the living and the dead.
I believe in the Holy Spirit, the Holy Catholic Church, the communion of saints, the forgiveness of sins, the resurrection of the body, and life everlasting. Amen.

The Nicene (Constantinopolitan) Creed

We believe in one God
the Father, the Almighty,
maker of heaven and earth,
of all that is seen and unseen.
We believe in one Lord, Jesus Christ,
the only Son of God,
eternally begotten of the Father,
God from God, Light from Light,
true God from true God,
begotten, not made, one in Being with the Father.
Through him all things were made.
For us men and for our salvation
he came down from heaven:
by the power of the Holy Spirit
he was born of the Virgin Mary, and became man.
For our sake he was crucified under Pontius Pilate;
he suffered, died, and was buried.
On the third day he rose again
in fulfillment of the Scriptures;
He ascended into heaven
and is seated at the right hand of the Father.
He will come again in glory to judge the living and the dead.
And his kingdom will have no end.
We believe in the Holy Spirit, the Lord and giver of life,
who proceeds from the Father and the Son.
With the Father and the Son he is worshiped and glorified.
He has spoken through the Prophets.
We believe in one holy catholic and apostolic Church.

We acknowledge one baptism for the forgiveness of sins.
We look for the resurrection of the dead,
and the life of the world to come. Amen.

DAVID BRYAN

CREMATION

Cremation is the reduction of the body of the deceased to ashes by burning. The Church's long tradition, crystallized in the 1917 *Code of Canon Law,* stated: "The bodies of the faithful departed must be buried and their cremation is reprobated (c. 1203, §1); any request for cremation is to be disregarded (§2); those who make such a request are to be denied Christian burial (§3); and their ashes could not be preserved in a blessed cemetery (Holy Office, 19 June 1926).

Although cremation was practiced among the Greeks and Romans of the early Christian era, Christians buried their dead for three major reasons: (1) reverence for the body as a member of Christ and a temple of the Holy Spirit, (2) faith in its resurrection, and (3) a strong reaction against the burning of bodies by pagan persecutors as a taunt against belief in the resurrection. Christians, it seems, had some concern that resurrection would be impossible or at least more difficult if there were only ashes to be resurrected.

The Holy Office modified the tradition and law reprobating cremation 8 May 1963 (*De cadaverum crematione*). Cremation had been permitted only for the rapid disposal of bodies in time of pestilence, natural disaster, or other grave public necessity. Now it could be allowed for any sound reason, provided the request was not motivated by any denial of Christian dogmas, hatred of the Catholic Church, or a sectarian spirit. The major factors in the change arose from a renewal of the theology of resurrection and the increasing concern for the use of land resources for the burial of the dead.

The 1983 *Code of Canon Law* recommends burial but does not forbid cremation except when it is requested for reasons contrary to Christian teaching (c. 1176, §3). The 1989 Order of Christian Funerals in the instructions for the funeral rite makes provision for both cremation and the interment of ashes. The preference remains for traditional burial of the dead but, especially when cremation takes place after the funeral Mass with the body present, it has become an accepted practice in the Catholic Church.

CHARLES SKOK

See also DEATH; RESURRECTION OF THE DEAD.

CRITICISM, BIBLICAL

Biblical criticism involves textual, literary, and historical methods. It seeks to establish the best possible text, to understand the style and ways of communication, and to determine the origin and authenticity of the biblical writings. Vatican II's Constitution on Divine Revelation (DV 12) gave its approval in principle to biblical criticism, without endorsing everything said in the name of biblical criticism. Following Pope Pius XII's 1943 encyclical *Divino Afflante Spiritu,* the council encouraged biblical scholars to attend to the literary forms in which divine revelation is expressed, to look for the meanings intended by the biblical writers in their own historical situations and cultures, and to take into account the patterns of perception, speech, and narrative that prevailed at the time.

Textual criticism seeks to establish the text of a biblical writing. We no longer have access to the manuscripts written by the biblical authors. Rather, their works have been handed on by copyists through the centuries. The goal of textual criticism is to identify the errors and changes that have entered the manuscript traditions, and to get as close as possible to the autographs (original manuscripts written by the authors).

The initial step in textual criticism involves making an inventory of the manuscript evidence. The earliest complete manuscripts of the Hebrew Bible come from the tenth and eleventh centuries A.D. The most important manuscripts of the Greek NT come from the fourth and fifth centuries A.D. The OT manuscripts among the Dead Sea Scrolls and the NT fragments among the Egyptian papyri provide valuable evidence for the history of the text prior to the complete manuscripts. The ancient versions (Greek, Latin, Syriac, Coptic, Armenian, etc.) sometimes preserve significant textual variants. The second step involves deciding what was the original reading and explaining how the variant readings arose. The original reading must be consistent with the style and content of the document being studied as well as the rules of grammar and good sense. The rejected variants may have been unconscious errors (e.g., omitting words or phrases, confusing singular letters, including marginal comments) or deliberate changes ("correcting" grammar or style, harmonizing with parallel texts, removing "offensive" material).

Literary criticism is the systematic analysis of a text with regard to its words and images, characters, progress of thought or structure, form, and meaning. With the aid of biblical lexicons and concordances it is possible to situate the occurrence of a word or motif (e.g., love, covenant) in the framework of its historical development and thus better appreciate the individual uses. Attending to how characters interact within a story or to how an argument or story unfolds is essential for understanding what the biblical writers sought to communicate. They sometimes used forms of logic and discourse patterns (such as chiasmus ABA') foreign to readers today. The OT contains various literary genres: narratives, law codes, prophecies, psalms, collections of proverbs, love poetry, and visions. The NT presents stories of Jesus' words and deeds (Gospels), the exploits of some apostles (Acts), letters (Epistles), and visions (Revelation). Each book contains within itself smaller literary forms (e.g., parables, miracle stories, hymns, proverbs). Recognizing the forms that the writers chose is an indispensable step toward understanding their message.

Historical criticism has several aspects: charting the history of the text, placing the text in its historical context, and determining the shape of the events behind the text.

The literary analysis of biblical texts leads into historical study. Form criticism not only identifies the literary devices used in communication but also tries to determine the historical settings in which these forms arose and circulated. Source criticism establishes the presence of preexisting material incorporated in the final document. Redaction criticism investigates how the biblical authors used their sources to address the concerns of their audiences. With these techniques it is possible to chart the history of a text.

Historical study of biblical texts demands that they be read in light of what can be known of the cultures and historical conditions in which they took shape. Archaeological excavations and textual discoveries (e.g., Ugaritic texts, Dead Sea Scrolls) have greatly illuminated the material culture and spiritual atmosphere in which the biblical books were written.

The term "historical criticism" is sometimes used in a narrow sense to describe the effort to determine the exact shape of the events behind the texts (e.g., what really happened at Israel's exodus from Egypt or on the first Easter Sunday). Historical criticism also involves the circumstances in which the individual biblical writings arose: author, date, audience, language, purpose, content, structure, and theology.

DANIEL J. HARRINGTON, S.J.

See also BIBLICAL ARCHAEOLOGY; CANON OF SCRIPTURE; INSPIRATION, BIBLICAL; MANUSCRIPTS OF THE BIBLE.

CROSIER (CROZIER)

A pastoral staff, received by bishops and abbots at their installation as a symbol of their authority. In the Western Church the top of the crosier is curved like a shepherd's crook to symbolize that the authority is that of a shepherd who looks after the flock. The curved part of the crosier turns outward towards the community over which the bishop or abbot has authority. Other individuals who may have the privilege of carrying a crosier turn the curved part inward to indicate they make no claims to authority over the community. From the eleventh century, popes no longer used a crosier, until Paul VI (1963–1978) reintroduced its use in the form of a staff with a crucifix on top. Crosiers used to be very ornate and costly until the Vatican Council, when most bishops started using very simple wooden staffs.

Crosier, Vatican Museum

LEONARD DOOHAN

See also ABBOT; BISHOP.

CROSS

The most solemn and significant symbol of the Christian faith, as it represents the absolute sacrifice made by Christ—his willingness to perish as a common criminal in order to grant his followers the opportunity to gain salvation. Charged with treason, Jesus was executed by Roman authority in the brutal manner normally reserved for slaves and other non-Romans who had committed the most iniquitous of offenses.

It is likely that Jesus carried only the crossbeam to Calvary—his place of execution—as this was the common practice in Roman crucifixions; the vertical beam was fixed permanently at the crucifixion site, with the crossbeam being attached to it at the time of execution. The cross on which Jesus was crucified

Processional cross, Vatican Museum

was most likely in the shape of a lowercase "t" (the Latin cross) or a capital "T" (known as the Tau cross).

The victim of a Roman crucifixion was secured to a cross by rope—fastened around his arms, legs, and stomach—and sometimes (as in Jesus' case) also with nails. Although it is not mentioned in the New Testament, ancient Roman writers describe a peg, located at about the middle of the vertical beam, which supported the victim's body weight by acting as a seat. It was the practice of the Romans to strip criminals naked before crucifying them, and there is no evidence to suggest that Jesus was spared this added indignity. Victims usually died from hunger, thirst, asphyxiation, or trauma. The first Christian emperor, Constantine the Great (d. 337), abolished crucifixion as a form of punishment under the law.

JOSEPH QUINN

See also JESUS CHRIST; SUFFERING IN THE NEW TESTAMENT.

CRUSADES

The name given to nine armed expeditions sent by the Christians of the medieval West to liberate the holy places of Palestine from the Muslims. The term was often used more widely to describe any expedition against infidels, such as the Muslims in Spain, or against heretics like the French Albigensians or even against enemies of the popes. This article will restrict itself to the more common meaning of the word.

The notion of a crusade, a holy war, is both foreign and repulsive to the modern Christian mind, but it had a firm biblical pedigree. In the Book of Joshua the invading Israelites put to death everyone in the city of Jericho, except for the family of Rahab, and they do so at the command of the Lord. The Lord also stands behind the wars of the Judges and the campaigns of David. Indeed, the Lord not only encourages the Israelites but even fights for them; Deuteronomy 20:4 tells the Israelites "for the Lord your God is he who goes with you, to fight for you against your enemies, to give you the victory." Those who like to cite Isaiah 2:4, "they shall beat their swords into plowshares and their spears into pruning hooks," should recall Joel 3:10: "Beat your plowshares into swords and your pruning hooks into spears."

The Christian Book of Revelation tells of uncompromising war between the forces of good and evil, those of the lamb and those of the beast, and no mercy is shown to the enemy. No matter how unpalatable it may be to modern Christians, when read literally the Bible offers wide support for the notion of a holy war.

The First Crusade

In the seventh century the Muslim Arabs burst out of their desert world on a jihad or holy war to attack the civilizations of the Near East, specifically the Persian Empire, which they destroyed, and the Byzantine Empire, which halted their advance but not before the Arabs had taken from them the Holy Land, Egypt, Syria, and North Africa. The great ancient centers of Eastern Christianity, Jerusalem, Antioch, and Alexandria had been cut off from the empire, which lacked the strength to recover them.

After the first century of struggles and after the boundaries had been drawn, the Arabs and Byzantines settled down to an uneasy but generally peaceful coexistence. The Christian holy places remained in the hands of the Muslims, but the Byzantines were able to work out agreements which allowed pilgrims to visit Jerusalem and other sites in Palestine. The Arabs absorbed and transformed much of the ancient Near Eastern civilization, and Christian pilgrims, especially from Western Europe, were often astonished at the taste and quality of Arab life.

Islam was a strongly missionary religion, yet by the eleventh century the Arabs had lost much of their proselytizing energy. But the Islamic policy of equality for all believers, regardless of race, meant that as new peoples entered the Muslim fold, they did not feel bound to follow the Arabic lead. Indeed, it was not uncommon for the new converts to be disappointed at the laxness of the older groups of believers. In the eleventh century, a Central Asian nomadic people, the Seljuk Turks, converted to

Sunni Muslim faith, moved to the West, taking Baghdad in 1055. In 1071, they defeated the Byzantines at Manzikert, one of history's most decisive battles, and after that the Turks moved steadily into Asia Minor, thus giving it its modern name. Once again Islam confronted Christianity.

The Byzantine emperor, Alexius Comnenus (1081–1118), plagued with enemies on every side, asked the West for help against the Turks. Pope Urban II (1088–1099) knew the Western Catholics would not fight for the Byzantines, but he reckoned correctly that they would fight to liberate the holy places from infidels. At the Council of Clermont, France, in 1095, he urged the assembled Christian knights to take up the cross (Latin: *crux,* hence crusades) against the Muslims, promising a host of benefits both spiritual and temporal, including a rather ambiguous promise of remission of sins. The pope wanted to keep control of the crusade and did not invite Europe's crowned heads to go, and this first crusade was led by counts and dukes and a papal legate.

To Urban's surprise, his call was widely answered in France. Besides the genuine religious fervor, there were other reasons to motivate people: a sense of adventure, a chance for booty, and an opportunity for younger brothers to get their own land, something denied to them by the prevailing practice of primogeniture.

The First Crusade was an impossible task—recruiting, training, and transporting a Western European army to the Near East to fight in unfamiliar territory in a far different climate under leaders from different parts of the West. When the crusaders gathered outside Constantinople, the emperor Alexius was frightened at the size of the army, appalled at the crudity of the Western knights, and anxious to stop the pillaging of the suburbs with which the bored crusaders were occupying themselves. Alexius insisted the crusaders take an oath of allegiance to him, which most did, swearing to return the conquered lands to the empire. He then quickly transported the Western army across to Asia Minor (1097).

Overcoming logistic and tactical difficulties as well as their distrust and resentment of the Byzantines, the crusaders did the impossible. They defeated Turkish armies, captured the ancient city of Antioch in 1098, and on 15 July 1099, occupied Jerusalem. The crusading motto was *Deus volt,* "God wills it," and how could anyone doubt it?

But the great triumph was marred by a wholesale slaughter of the city's inhabitants, including Jews and even some indigenous Christians whose dress and language probably made them indistinguishable from the Muslims. This barbarous act made the crusaders infamous in the Islamic world and guaranteed that peaceful coexistence would be virtually impossible.

"The Siege of Antioch," manuscript detail, 13th century

Furthermore, the crusaders violated their oaths and promises to Alexius. Reasoning that since they had done the fighting, they should have the spoils, the crusaders—or Franks as they were widely known because most were French—created their own states. The Norman Bohemund of Taranto became Bohemund I, prince of Antioch, while Baldwin of Boulogne became Baldwin I, king of Jerusalem. These and the other Crusader States were collectively known as *Outremer,* literally, Overseas.

It did not take long before the political independence became ecclesiastical independence. The crusaders did not wish to have Greek bishops in their lands, and a Latin hierarchy was soon established with a Latin patriarch in Jerusalem. The emperor protested to both the crusaders and the pope, but to no avail. Soon the Byzantines found themselves battling the Franks, their erstwhile saviors, to get back their land. The battles were usually inconclusive but guaranteed that the Christians would rarely offer a united front to the Muslims. Complicating this were the frequent battles among the Westerners themselves.

Soon after the Franks established Outremer, Italian merchants from Pisa, Genoa, and especially Venice began to arrive. Since the Christians could not always count on reinforcements or new settlers journeying to Palestine via Asia Minor, they soon became dependent on the Italian fleets. The Italian city states would be major players in the history of Outremer.

The crusaders' enthusiasm for Jerusalem resulted in one of history's strangest phenomena, military-religious orders. A French knight, Hugh of Payens

(d. 1136), conceived the idea of an order of knights chivalrously dedicated to following a monastic life but also devoted to protecting the pilgrimage road to Jerusalem. King Baldwin II of Jerusalem granted them rooms in his palace, called the *Templum Salamonis,* and thus they were called the Templars. By 1128 this order had its own rule and was subject directly to the pope.

Similar to the Templars were the Hospitallers. Founded in 1170 by Italian merchants to provide a hostel for visitors to Palestine and responsible to a Benedictine abbey, the Hospitallers freed themselves from the abbey after the First Crusade and were directly under the pope's authority. By 1137 they had extended their mission to the defense of Outremer. Both orders were to outlast the Christian presence in the Holy Land.

The Second Crusade

Although most Crusader States were on the coast, one, Edessa, ruled by a Latin count, was far inland and even stretched east of the Euphrates. The Muslims, politically disorganized in 1099, united to attack a common enemy, and they retook Edessa in 1144. This shocked Christian Europe and frightened the Outremer Franks who always worried about their small size and population in what was, in effect, a Muslim sea. Help was needed from the West, and it soon came.

Since the holy places were in Christian hands and since there were Christian rulers in Palestine, the organizers of the Second Crusade could not offer land and booty as a prize, so the crusade's chief protagonist, the Cistercian abbot Bernard of Clairvaux, argued that the Muslim reconquest of Edessa resulted from the sinfulness of Christians, and, with the approval of his former pupil Pope Eugene III (1145–1153), he urged the Christians to go to the East as an act of penance. His preaching may have been too successful, because, contrary to the pope's wishes, the German emperor Conrad III and the French king Louis VII took the cross. With two monarchs on the crusade, the pope could not hope that his legate would be in charge.

The crusade (1148–1149) was a disaster. The undisciplined troops pillaged Byzantine territory in the Balkans, and the emperor Manuel I got the crusaders into Asia Minor as fast as he could to save his capital. After suffering a serious defeat, the Germans merged what was left of their army with the French. Bickering and jealousy made a unified command impossible. The Franks of Outremer wanted to be defended, but the new army decided instead to carry the war to the Muslims by attacking Damascus in Syria. Possibly aided by the treachery of the local Latin princes, the Muslims beat off the siege. Conrad returned home (1148), and Louis followed him a year later. Bernard of Clairvaux was widely blamed for the fiasco.

In the late twelfth century the leadership of the Near Eastern Muslims passed to Egypt where Salah ed-Din or Saladin, an ethnic Kurd, conquered the other Muslim states and, in 1187, led a united Islam against the Franks. Saladin was not a great general, but he was a great organizer. He had neutralized any potential Muslim allies the Franks might have, and he made peace with the Byzantines. His newly built Egyptian navy helped to keep the Italians at a distance. Outremer was isolated. The battle of Hattin in Galilee decimated Frankish strength, and on 2 October 1187, Jerusalem returned to Muslim hands.

The Third Crusade

This shocking event provoked the Third Crusade, the most famous and the most romanticized. Three monarchs took the cross, Emperor Frederick Barbarossa of Germany, King Philip Augustus of France, and King Richard Coeur-de-Lion of England. Frederick set out first, in 1189. His army raided Byzantine territory in the Balkans, and in 1190 crossed into Asia Minor. The Germans won a magnificent victory over the Turks, but, soon after, Frederick drowned trying to swim a river. Although some Germans continued on, most went home, and the leadership of the crusade passed to the two kings who departed for the East in July of 1190, urged on by the prophecy of the Calabrian abbot, Joachim of Fiore, who predicted victory for Richard in the East.

The Christians helped the Outremer Franks win the siege of Acre, and then Richard led the English to other victories while Philip returned home. But Saladin, although defeated, kept the English from Jerusalem, and when Richard heard that his brother John was dealing with the French behind his back, he had to leave for home in the fall of 1192. Richard became the stuff of legends, but, in fact, little had changed; the Muslims kept Jerusalem. Saladin died the following year, but by then Richard was in an Austrian prison, awaiting ransom, and could do nothing.

The Fourth Crusade

The undeserved name of Fourth Crusade is applied to the joint Frankish-Venetian expedition against Constantinople in 1203–1204. Pope Innocent III preached a new crusade, and a French army arrived in Venice in 1202, awaiting transportation. The French had promised the Venetian shipowners a larger amount than they could actually pay, so the Venetians struck a deal with them, guaranteeing the

Franks passage in return for the capture of Zara, an Adriatic city the Hungarians had taken from Venice. To the horror of the pope, a crusade attacked and sacked a Christian city. But worse was to come.

Alexius IV, a dispossessed Byzantine prince in exile in Venice, asked the crusaders for assistance in getting the imperial throne, promising the crusaders enormous amounts of money, help in attacking Muslim Egypt, and even the reunion of the Churches of Rome and Constantinople, in schism since 1054. The crusaders agreed to attack Constantinople, the Franks hoping for booty and the Venetians for a chance to drive the other Italian maritime cities out of the lucrative Eastern market. The crusaders successfully installed Alexius IV on the throne, but, when the local citizens revolted and murdered him, the crusaders realized the only way that they would get their payment was to attack Constantinople, which they captured on 13 April 1204. After a horrible bout of looting, murder, and rape, the crusaders decided to divide their spoils.

The Venetians got the trade concessions they wanted as well as some Greek ports and islands to protect their commerce. The Franks established a Latin Empire, complete with a feudal system and a Latin hierarchy. The pope was furious with the crusaders, but he could not pass up this chance to reunite Rome and Constantinople. Shamefully, he recognized the Latin Empire and agreed to a Latin hierarchy in Greek-speaking lands.

The Byzantines eventually got their empire back (1261), but it was so weakened that its demise was only a matter of time. Only skillful diplomacy and outside political events, such as the Mongol invasion, kept the Turks from putting it to an end.

Shortly after the Fourth Crusade was the Children's Crusade, a type of apocalyptic movement, led by a boy from Cologne named Nicholas who claimed in 1212 that God wanted him to liberate Jerusalem. Thousands of chidren followed him, and other groups soon formed. When the main group, 7,000 strong, arrived at Genoa they were shocked to find that the promised miracle did not occur; God did not enable them to walk across the water. Most of these children, along with another group which went to Marseilles, wandered home, although some perished and others were sold by unscrupulous merchants into slavery and prostitution.

The Fifth Crusade

The Fifth Crusade (1217–1221) was another disaster. Pope Honorius III (1216–1227) called it and sent his legate Pelagius to watch out for the Church's interests. The lay leaders were Duke Leopold VI of Austria and the Hungarian king Andrew II. Accepting their inability to take Jerusalem, the crusaders decided to invade Egypt in hopes of building a base to strike at the Holy Land. They captured the port city of Damietta in 1219, but an attack on Cairo in 1221 failed and even Damietta had to be abandoned. A noteworthy event in this crusade was the visit to Egypt in 1219 of Saint Francis of Assisi who got the crusaders' permission to visit the Egyptian sultan. The Muslim prince listened politely to Francis and, unconverted, sent him back to the Christian camp.

The Sixth Crusade

The Sixth Crusade (1228–1229) was unheroic but successful. The German emperor Frederick II, who maintained a palace in Sicily and who both knew and appreciated Muslim culture, visited Outremer and negotiated with the Muslims for the return of Jerusalem to the Christians. He claimed for himself the title of King of Jerusalem, but he did not stay long in the East, being forced to go home by political events in Italy. What others could not do by war, Frederick did by negotiation. In fact, Jerusalem was quickly reoccupied by the Muslims and then retaken by the Christians in 1239. In 1244 the Muslims retook it for good.

The Later Crusades

The saintly King Louis IX of France led the Seventh Crusade (1248–1254). Again the target was Damietta, again it was captured (1249), and again an attempt on Cairo failed (1250), resulting in the capture of Louis himself. He quickly negotiated a ransom, exchanging Damietta for himself. He went on to the Holy Land, established himself as leader of the Franks, negotiated the ransom of his army still in Egyptian captivity, and strengthened the fortifications of Outremer. Louis did not win new territory, but he did leave the Holy Land in a more stable situation when he returned home in 1254.

Soon after Louis's departure, the Mongol hordes invaded the Near East, capturing Baghdad (1258) amid unbelievable slaughter. The Muslims were in retreat on all fronts. The Franks were in a quandary, pleased to see their old enemies defeated but frightened at the Mongols. In 1260, in another of history's decisive battles, the Egyptian Muslims under the command of Baibars defeated the Mongols at Ain Jalud in Galilee, destroying the image of Mongol invincibility. Quite literally, Baibars saved Islam, which now went on the offensive against the Mongols, driving them out of the Near East.

The Franks had tried to remain neutral, giving Baibars free passage through their territory but not fighting alongside him. When he consolidated his power, he turned against Outremer, capturing city after city and effectively isolating the crusader strongholds. When Baibars took Jaffa, King Louis mounted the Eighth Crusade. He hoped to convert the Sultan of Tunisia and win his aid for an expedition to Palestine, so he sailed to Tunis, where he died in 1270. His troops returned home, and the Eighth Crusade ended without the Christian army even getting to the Eastern Mediterranean.

In 1271 the English Prince Edward (later Edward I) led the Ninth Crusade. He landed at the city of Acre and provided Outremer with some badly needed relief. But he left the next year after having concluded a truce with Baibars, which the Egyptian accepted in order to concentrate his efforts against the Mongols, Turks, and Armenians. There is an interesting footnote to this crusade. Accompanying Edward on the crusade was Tedaldo Visconti, archdeacon of Liege. For three years, since the death of Pope Clement VI in 1268, the cardinals had been wrangling over a successor. The local civic authorities had locked them in the papal palace, removed its roof, and then threatened to starve them out if they did not choose a pope. They chose Tedaldo, who returned to Rome to be consecrated as Pope Gregory X on 27 May 1272, reigning until 1276.

Gregory was a true crusader and tried again to interest Europe's nobility, but the tide had turned against crusades. The sultan Baibars died in 1277 but his son and then his grandson continued his policy of attacking Frankish possessions, until the last of them, Acre, fell in 1291. The age of the crusades was over.

Scholars differ as to whether the overall effects of the crusades were positive or negative, but there is no doubt of their influence. The West got to know the East and vice versa. The Fourth Crusade put an end to Byzantium as a great state, and several crusades strengthened the European monarchies against the pope. The Italian maritime cities, especially Venice, became Mediterranean powers. The military orders of the Templars and the Hospitallers came into being and established the basis of their power and, later, their wealth. And finally, it must be conceded, that in spite of all the bloodshed and futility, this was an age of high adventure. Some of the most colorful figures of the Middle Ages were involved in the Crusades: Frederick Barbarossa, Joachim of Fiore, Richard the Lionhearted, Saint Francis of Assisi, Saladin, and a host of lesser known figures. Wars for religion are rightly rejected by modern Christianity, but the Crusades captured a unique moment in the development of that faith.

JOSEPH F. KELLY

See also CHURCH AND STATE; MIDDLE AGES, THE.

CRYPT

(Lat. *crypta,* "vault" or "hidden cave") A vault or hidden recess, located underneath the main floor of a church, which serves as a burial place and, occasionally, as a chapel for devotional services. Christians of the early Church used crypts for worship, meetings, and the entombment of martyrs.

JOSEPH QUINN

See also ARCHITECTURE, CHURCH.

CULTS

The term "cult" has lately been used in popular parlance to refer to religious groups which use questionable recruiting and membership practices and exercise close control over members. Its original meanng, however, is the practices of worship such as sacramental rites, the veneration of saints, and pilgrimages to holy places. Since 1930 it has been used by social science to extend the continuum of "Church, sect, and denomination" as categories for the study of religious groups; its recent pejorative use is without objective foundation.

The negative use of the term "cult" derives both from long-term Christian hostility to sect-like groups as false religion, and from the strong anti-cult movement of parents seeking to reclaim sons and daughters whom they believe to have been deceitfully enticed into membership, and deprived of freedom. Most social scientists see them more positively: as a resurgence of religious searching triggered by the breakdown in the 1960s of cultural norms; as the result of increased awareness of Eastern religions and of the technologization of culture; and as a response to the secularization of religion. They are seen as similar to the originally sect-like Christian Science and the Church of the Latter Day Saints (Mormons), once considered quite controversial; in fact, U.S. Catholicism led a sect-like existence in the 1840s, in contrast to the mainstream Protestant culture.

Some characteristics of the new groups which set them off from mainline Churches are (1) strong charismatic leadership, (2) separation from the world, and (3) an orientation to bringing about deep religious experience; but the latter two are also features of the novitiate period of religious life, especially previous to Vatican II. Today, there are thought to be five hundred to six hundred such groups in the United States, with membership probably under 300,000; typically 90 percent of those who join a group remain for about two years. Some groups have splintered from mainline Churches; others have arisen around Asian spiritual leaders. Some groups are degenerate forms of a recognized denomination: Jim Jones' "People's Temple," which ended in mass suicide in Guyana in 1978, was once a highly praised congregation of the Christian Church (Disciples of Christ). The approaching millennium is said to be spawning new groups: Elizabeth Clare Prophet's Church Universal and Triumphant has retreated to a remote western area to await the end of the world.

When these groups become separatist and develop alternative social structures that occupy most of the members' time, they are less hampered by the checks that interaction with others provide, and are thus more easily prey to manipulative leaders. Despite the shocking cases of the People's Temple and David Koresh's Branch Davidians (1993), evidence does not support the argument that life in such a group is necessarily dangerous, nor that such groups are inherently prone to violence; but violence against these groups is not uncommon, and reports that they engaged in it or in child abuse have often proven to be rumors. Such deviations are contingent on many factors, however, and it is thus unfortunate that the psychology of such groups is not a popular area of research. While Freud wrote about the infectious nature of cohesive groups, and William James was critical of ignorance of the psychology of religious affiliation, their views have not been developed.

A study published by the Vatican's Secretariat for Promoting Christian Unity (*Sects or New Religious Movements,* 1986) reflects this sociological research, and attempts to account for the recent upsurge of new religious movements, and to offer a pastoral response. Prepared in answer to requests from Episcopal Conferences, and with the help of a worldwide questionnaire, it focuses on the origins of these movements, possible reasons for their success among Catholics, and on the pastoral problems that result when a family member joins such a group. While questionable recruitment and training techniques are mentioned, other factors are named: "needs and aspirations. . .not being met in the mainline churches. . .economic advantages, political interest. . .curiosity. . . ."; the "growing interdependence in today's world. . .the depersonalizing structures of contemporary society, largely produced in the West and widely exported to the rest of the world. . . ." These are interpreted as expressions of the human search for "wholeness and harmony . . .truth and meaning. . .values which. . .seem to be hidden, broken or lost. . . ." While its worldwide perspective on the variety of forces at work in the origin of these new movements prevents its drawing any simple conclusion, the study cites some practical recommendations of the Extraordinary Synod of 1985: stress on spiritual formation; the integration of evangelization and catechesis with an interpretive witness; interior and spiritual participation in the liturgy; dialogue among Christians which opens and communicates interiority; fostering concrete forms of the spiritual journey such as spiritual movements, popular devotion, attention to the word of God and witness to it. In short, the rise of new religious movements, "cults," is seen to be one more challenge to Vatican II's call for the renewal of Christian life in response to the signs of the times.

MARY BARBARA AGNEW, C.PP.S.

See also RELIGIOUS FREEDOM.

CURATE

A curate is an associate pastor or parochial vicar of a parish. The term is commonly used in English-speaking countries, especially Canada and England. Originally, the term referred to clergymen who had charge ("cure") of a parish. The curate was chosen by the "patron" and was admitted to the cure of souls by the bishop of the diocese.

PATRICIA DeFERRARI

See also PARISH; PASTOR.

CURÉ D'ARS (1786–1859)

Jean Vianney, the son of Matthew Vianney, a peasant farmer, was born at Darilly, near Lyons, on 8 May 1786, and grew up with very little education in the tumultuous years of the French Revolution. He helped his family by herding sheep, and was thirteen before he received his First Communion. Five years later he asked his father to help him get an education to become a priest. His father could not afford the expense, but when Jean was twenty he began to attend a "presbytery school" opened by the Abbé Balley in the neighboring village of Ecully. Jean was a very backward student and had the greatest difficulty mastering any subject or language, especially Latin.

Through an oversight he was not registered as a seminarian to exempt him from military service. On several occasions the authorities sought him but each time some minor event occurred preventing his marching off to war. At one stage he hid for eighteen months in a barn and worked on a farm to avoid being drafted. He is the patron of diocesan priests, and should also be the patron saint of conscientious objectors and military draft evaders. When he resumed his studies for the priesthood, he made little progress and a decision was made to dismiss him.

On appeal, "the most unlearned but the most devout seminarian in Lyons" was ordained on 12 August 1815, and was appointed curate to his old friend and teacher, the Abbé Balley who had lobbied for his ordination.

On the death of the Abbé in 1817, Vianney was made pastor or parish priest of the desolate and neglected village of Ars-en-Dombes with a population of 230. He was a rather complex person—full of understanding and compassion for the sinful and the sorrowful; at the same time he crusaded mercilessly against village dances and drinking and in the process created enemies. In the end, the Curé won the respect of the village; even those who judged him as a rigoristic spoilsport began to view him as an unselfish and saintly man. In 1824 he opened a small school to bring a little education to the village children, and three years later the famous La Providence was established, a shelter for homeless and abandoned children. No fees were requested or accepted, and no one was turned away. Slowly the village of Ars underwent a spiritual transformation; and its Curé underwent what seemingly were genuine demonic attacks. His name as a saintly and understanding confessor spread. By 1827 pilgrims began to come to share their sins and their woes with the emaciated little priest, and in a short time several hundred came daily to pray or confess at Ars. He heard confessions every day and often spent sixteen hours administering the sacrament with patience and common sense. The Curé was a wise spiritual director, encouraging the rich and the poor who flocked to him to cleave to the liturgy, the rosary, and other tried-and-true forms of devotion. He himself longed for a secluded life with the Carthusians or the Cistercians, but his dream faded and for forty-one years he lived a rigorous life avoiding promotions and honors. He remains an enigma and an inspiration. He had no intellectual gifts and knew little theology of any kind. He was just a simple peasant priest who lived and loved the message of the Gospels, took Christ at his word, and became a saint.

MICHAEL GLAZIER

See also SAINTS.

CURIA, ROMAN

Historically the Roman Curia was the Papal Court in which the College of Cardinals, sometimes organized into special commissions, advised the pope. Since the pontificate of Sixtus V (1585–1590), the Curia, still dominated by cardinals, has been the Church's permanent central administration whose decisions often have the authority of the pope. General reforms of the Curia were undertaken by Pius X (1903–1914) and by Paul VI (1967). The Curia now includes the Roman congregations (ten), tribunals (three), and pontifical councils (twelve), as well as lesser curial offices. The congregations (treated in separate entries elsewhere) are the Secretariat of State, and the Congregations for the Doctrine of the Faith, for the Oriental Churches, for Bishops, for Divine Worship and the Discipline of the Sacraments, for the Causes of Saints, for the Clergy, for Institutes of Consecrated Life and Societies of Apostolic Life, for Catholic Education (Seminaries and Institutes of Study), and for the Evangelization of Peoples. The tribunals (treated in separate entries elsewhere) are the Apostolic Penitentiary, the Apostolic Signatura, and the Roman Rota. See Pontifical Councils for a description of these bodies. Other offices are the Apostolic Chamber (administration of the temporal affairs of the Holy See when vacant), the Prefecture of the Economic Affairs of the Holy See (ongoing administration of the temporal affairs), and the Administration of the Patrimony of the Apostolic See (handles the estate of the Apostolic See). There are interdepartmental standing commissions dealing with appointments to local Churches, institutes of consecrated life in mission territories, and the formation of candidates to Sacred Orders.

DAVID BRYAN

See also COLLEGE OF CARDINALS; PAPACY, THE.

CURSILLO

The *cursillo de christianidad* or "little course in Christianity" is a movement of spiritual renewal which originated, with many variations, in Spain, and was finally streamlined and officially constituted in 1949. Essentially, the cursillo brings together, in a communal and convivial atmosphere, groups of clergy and laity—usually about forty—to deepen their personal awareness of and commitment to the presence and work of Christ in their everyday lives and surroundings.

When time and circumstance permit, participants may spend three days preparing for the cursillo (precursillo) and follow-up with another three-day reflective period (post cursillo). The three-day cursillo itself is usually held over a weekend beginning on Thursday evening and ending on Sunday evening. It is carefully planned to enable the participants to benefit from the program of Christocentric meditations, lectures, and discussions. The cursillo aims to let Christ invigorate and transform the personal and social lives of men and women in all areas of human work and activity. While the cursillo movement has had a significant success in Hispanic lands, its popularity in America—where it was established in 1957—has been limited.

JOAN GLAZIER

See also RELIGIOUS EDUCATION; RETREAT.

CUSHING, RICHARD, CARDINAL (1895–1970)

Archbishop of Boston (1944–1970), cardinal (15 December 1958), Richard Cushing was born in Boston on 24 August 1895, the son of a blacksmith, and died in Boston on 2 November 1970. Ordained a priest of the Archdiocese of Boston on 26 May 1921, Cushing earned fame as diocesan director of the most successful local office of the Society for the Propagation of the Faith in the United States. On 29 June 1939 he was ordained an auxiliary bishop of Boston and succeeded William Cardinal O'Connell as archbishop on 25 September 1944.

In contrast to his pompous and autocratic predecessor, Cushing was a gregarious and affable figure, popular with Catholics and non-Catholics alike. One of the last of the great "brick-and-mortar" prelates in the American Church, Cushing was responsible for the construction of eighty new churches, six hospitals, three colleges and a national seminary for older vocations, as well as for the introduction into his archdiocese of over sixty new religious communities of men and women. In 1958 he also established the Missionary Society of St. James the Apostle to enable American diocesan priests to volunteer for temporary service in Latin America.

Cardinal Richard J. Cushing

A close friend of the Kennedy family, Cushing delivered the invocation at the inauguration of President John F. Kennedy in January 1961, and he presided at the funeral liturgy for the slain president in November 1963. At the Second Vatican Council, Cushing made no secret of his inability to follow the Latin speeches, but, more importantly, he was a consistent champion of such progressive causes as ecumenism and religious liberty.

A forceful and energetic person with a deep gravelly voice, Cushing spent the last twenty years of life battling cancer, remaining active until his retirement in September 1970, two months before his death.

THOMAS J. SHELLEY

See also AMERICAN CATHOLICISM; MISSIONS, CATHOLIC, THE MODERN PERIOD.

CYPRIAN, ST. (ca. 200/210–258)

Bishop of Carthage. Even though details about his early life are sparse, Cyprian seems to have been born into a somewhat wealthy and socially prominent Carthaginian family. He became a rhetorician and embraced Christianity ca. 246. He was soon ordained a presbyter and in 248 or 249 was elected bishop of Carthage. Although most people were happy at his election, at least five Carthaginian presbyters were opposed to it perhaps out of jealousy at Cyprian's speedy advancement in clerical rank and responsibility. An edict of Decius demanding that everyone sacrifice to the gods was promulgated in the autumn of 249. Shortly after that Cyprian decided to go into hiding and to direct the Carthaginian Church by correspondence. He was able to return in 251. Many Christians had lapsed during the persecution but decided to be reconciled with the Church. Despite Cyprian's efforts to respond to all the pastoral problems presented by the lapsed, two other groups had established themselves in Carthage in 252: rigorists who followed Novatian of Rome and laxists who elected Fortunatus as their bishop. Cyprian had strained relations with Stephen I, Bishop of Rome over the question of whether heretics and schismatics could validly baptize. Stephen was a victim of the persecution of Valerian in 257, and a year later Cyprian was beheaded for the faith on 14 September. The corpus of Cyprian's letters (sixty-five by Cyprian and sixteen letters addressed to him) present significant information about a decade that is otherwise not well documented. The persecutions of Decius (250) and Valerian (257 to 258) and the expected persecution by Trebonianus Gallus (252 or 253) provide the background to most of the letters. Cyprian also wrote twelve treatises. Some are particularly significant for theological issues which they raise: *To Quirinus: Three Books of Testimonies* (before 250), a collection of Scripture texts topically arranged in three books; *The Dress of Virgins* (before 250), in which Cyprian praised virginity; *Concerning the Lapsed* (251) in which Cyprian presented conditions for the reconciliation of the lapsed; *The Unity of the Church* (251), in which Cyprian discussed the true unity of the Church in its relationship to the episcopate (in a second edition of this work Cyprian revised the fourth chapter to omit discussion of Petrine supremacy possibly as a result of his difficulties with Stephen I); *On the Lord's Prayer* (probably 251), in which Cyprian stresses the need of unity and concord; *Concerning Works and Almsgiving* (ca. 253), in which Cyprian urged Christians not to neglect their responsibilities to those in need. Feast day, 16 September (Catholic), 26 September (BCP).

JOHN DILLON

See also AFRICA, THE CATHOLIC CHURCH IN; FATHERS OF THE CHURCH.

CYRIL OF ALEXANDRIA, ST. (ca. 375–444)

Born of orthodox Christian parents, Cyril's maternal uncle was Theophilus, patriarch of Alexandria. Cyril accompanied his uncle to the Synod of the Oak (403), where Theophilus arranged for the condemnation of John Chrysostom. In 412 Cyril succeeded his uncle as patriarch of Constantinople and lost no time in attacking the Novatianists, the Jews, Neoplatonists, and the imperial prefect Orestes. Hypatia, a distinguished Neoplatonic philosopher and friend of Orestes, was brutally murdered by a mob. Even if Cyril was not directly responsible for her death, those who killed her were certainly his supporters. The big struggle in Cyril's life began after 428 when Nestorius, a famous Antiochene preacher, became patriarch of Constantinople. Nestorius supported Anastasius, one of his chaplains, who preached that Mary should not be called *Theotokos* (God-bearer) because she was only the mother of the humanity of Christ. The opponents of Nestorius soon received the support of Cyril, who objected to Nestorius for the first time in Paschal Letter 17 (429). Both sides appealed to Rome which decided against Nestorius in 430. Cyril was asked to communicate the decision of Rome to Nestorius. To the notice of condemnation Cyril added a letter containing Twelve Anathemas, which would not have been theologically acceptable to any Antiochene. Nestorius appealed to Emperor Theodosius II which resulted in the convocation of a general council at Ephesus in 431. Cyril took charge of this council and had Nestorius condemned before the Antiochene bishops arrived. On their arrival the Antiochene bishops held a separate council where they condemned Cyril. Theodosius II at first accepted both decisions but quickly reversed Cyril's condemnation. In 433 Cyril thought it opportune to make peace with the moderate Antiochenes. After the council Cyril was often moderate and conciliatory, quite amazing for a person whose methods and actions as a bishop often were rash, violent, and troublesome. He is remembered today for his contributions as a theologian. Influenced by Athanasius and the Cappadocian Fathers, Cyril expressed in a systematic way the classical teaching on the Trinity and the Person of Christ. At least in terminology his Christology does differ from that of the Council of Chalcedon (451). Cyril seemed to have used the term *physis* as almost the equivalent of *hypostasis* (person) and not in the sense of nature. Because of this terminology the Monophysites later claimed, with some justification, Cyril's authority for their position. Before the Nestorian controversy Cyril's writings were works against Arianism and scriptural exegesis. Once the Nestorian controversy began, this directly or indirectly influenced his writings. He wrote over one hundred letters, many exegetical works, including commentaries on John and Luke as well as on selected passages in the Pentateuch in *The Adoration and Worship of God in Spirit and in Truth* and the *Glaphyra;* several treatises on dogmatic theology; a long apology against Julian the Apostate; as well as about twenty sermons. Cyril was named a Doctor of the Church in 1882. Feast day, 9 June (East); 27 June (West).

JOHN DILLON

See also DOCTRINE, DEVELOPMENT OF; FATHERS OF THE CHURCH; TRINITY.

CYRIL OF JERUSALEM, ST. (ca. 315–ca. 386)

He is thought to have been born in Jerusalem. He was ordained as bishop of Jerusalem in 348. Since he was consecrated by Acacius, metropolitan of Caesarea, an Arian, Cyril was suspected of having made some concessions to Arianism before his ordination to the episcopate. However, soon after his ordination the Arians began to attack Cyril, because, even though he did not like the term *homoousios,* he did not support Arius. On three occasions he was exiled from his see. He was first exiled at a Council of Jerusalem in 357. He was able to return from Tarsus, his place of refuge, in the next year. Acacius of Caesarea banished him in 360. He was able to return in 362 when Julian the Apostate became emperor. His third exile lasted from 367 to 378 when the Emperor Valens forced him to leave

Jerusalem. During this last period of exile Cyril moved from a Homoeousian position to support the Nicene party. Cyril was among many Homoeousians who felt they were able to move over to the Nicene party as a result of the interpretation of *homoousios* provided at the Council of Antioch in 363 and later by Basil of Caesarea. He returned to Jerusalem after the death of Valens and worked to rebuild the Church which had fallen into moral decay and disunity. Gregory of Nyssa visited him in 379 and found Cyril's faith to be sound. He took part in the Second Council of Constantinople in 381. Cyril left a series of twenty-four *Catechetical Lectures* that he delivered either while still a priest or shortly after his ordination as a bishop (ca. 350). They are divided into two parts. The first consists of the *Procatechesis* (introductory lecture) and eighteen *Catecheses* (Lenten addresses to those who are to be baptized at Easter). The second part consists of the last five instructions, the *Mystagogical Catecheses* (instructions on baptism, confirmation, the Eucharist, and the liturgy of the Mass given during Easter week). Although some scholars have doubted that Cyril is the author of the *Mystagogical Catecheses,* most today would accept his authorship of them. The *Catechetical Lectures* are an important source of information about the catechumenate and the liturgy as it was celebrated in Jerusalem at the time. Cyril was named a Doctor of the Church in 1882. Feast day, 18 March.

JOHN DILLON

See also CATECHESIS; CATECHUMENATE; FATHERS OF THE CHURCH; LITURGY; SACRAMENTS.

CZESTOCHOWA

The shrine of the Black Madonna at Czestochowa, also called Our Lady of Jasna Gora, is the chief Marian sanctuary of the Polish people. The legend of this icon of Jesus and Mary maintains that it was painted by St. Luke on a tabletop made by Jesus himself, and that it was retrieved by St. Helena and

Our Lady of Czestochowa

brought to Constantinople in the fourth century. During the iconoclastic movement, the legends say, it was secreted in the forests of Poland and later taken to Czestochowa. At all events, in 1430 a great Gothic cathedral was built for the image. Subsequently, the fate of Poland itself was several times connected to the shrine. Even during the Second World War people made secret pilgrimages there in defiance of the Nazis, and these were repeated in even greater numbers after Poland was swallowed up by the Soviet Empire. The presence there of John Paul II, the Polish Pope, in June 1979, undoubtedly played a great part in the Polish overthrow of Communism ten years later and the subsequent defeat of Communism in Eastern Europe and the Soviet Union.

DAVID BRYAN

See also ART, CHRISTIAN; MARY, MOTHER OF GOD.

D

DALI, SALVADOR (1904–1988)

Spanish painter, born in 1904; first Cubist, then one of the surrealist school of Paris. Steeped in the literature of neurosis, and given to paranoid hallucinations himself, Dali aimed at representing the irrational and the horrifying so exactly as to achieve paintings having hallucinatory power. In these are combined nightmarish beings (such as giant ants) drawn in precise detail. In this period, too, Dali collaborated in the making of surrealist films. In his American period (1940–1955) Dali won great popularity with historicizing works, such as the *Last Supper,* in which rational and allegorical subjects tend to replace direct experience, though even these do not lack for macabre sensationalism. At the same time he experimented with the making of ceramics, jewelry, and sculpture. Often interviewed by the media, he became one of the most famous artists of his day. He died in 1988.

"The Sacrament of the Last Supper," detail, by Salvador Dali, oil painting, 1955

DAVID BRYAN

See also ART, CHRISTIAN.

DAMNATION

See HELL.

DANIÉLOU, JEAN (1905–1974)

Jesuit theologian, patristic scholar, cardinal (1969), Daniélou was born on 14 May 1905 in Neuilly-sur-Seine, near Paris, into a prominent, well-educated and devoutly Catholic family. He graduated from the Sorbonne in 1927 and earned a reputation in Parisian literary circles. He entered the Society of Jesus in 1929. During his theological studies he came under the influence of Henri de Lubac and Hans Urs von Balthasar, who initiated him into his lifelong study of the Fathers. He was ordained a priest on 24 August 1938.

Daniélou spent the whole of his life in Paris working as a scholar, prolific writer, teacher at the Institut Catholique, editor of *Etudes* and chaplain to university students. He is remembered especially for his original research on the mysticism of St. Gregory of Nyssa. As a theologian, Daniélou tried to answer the questions that contemporary secular culture posed for Christianity as Gregory had done for his time. Working with students, Daniélou tried to teach them how to be both authentically Christian and thoroughly at home in the modern culture. He also exercised influence over the young priests doing graduate work at the Institut Catholique.

In 1961 Daniélou wrote *Scandaleuse verité* as a warning of the impending crisis of faith. He studied the origins of the issues that were challenging the very roots of the Christian faith in the modern era. Pope John XXIII named him a *peritus* at Vatican Council II. He was ordained a bishop in 1969 and named a cardinal by Pope Paul VI a few days later. In the period after the council he was an outspoken critic of those who he felt were distorting both the gospel and the council. Such criticism earned him the label of "reactionary" in some quarters—an ironic development since not too many years earlier he himself had been regarded as "suspect" by some of the Roman authorities. Jean Daniélou died of a heart attack on 20 May 1974 in Paris.

ANTHONY D. ANDREASSI

See also PATROLOGY; VATICAN COUNCIL II.

DANTE ALIGHIERI (1265–1321)

One of history's supreme literary geniuses and author of *The Divine Comedy,* Dante Alighieri was born in Florence in 1265, and died in Ravenna in 1321. There he lies buried in a Franciscan church. His given name may simply mean "giving," or be a contraction for *durante* ("enduring").

The skimpy documentation of his life suggests that he was an only child who lost his mother when he was thirteen, his father when he was eighteen. The latter was a notary with some property and a middle-class background. Dante married Gemma Donati and had at least two sons and one daughter. (The male line died out in 1563.) There are no surviving documents in his hand, nor any certain portrait done from life.

As a youth Dante was an avid student and soon began writing prose and poetry. He soldiered for his native city in the crucial battle of Campaldino (1289). For two months in 1300 he was in effect the mayor of Florence. As such he made political enemies who came to power in 1301 and sentenced him to death in absentia the following year on the grounds of political corruption. The charge was always denied and never proven. Rejecting all compromise, he remained an exile for the rest of his life, possibly never seeing his wife again. He may have studied in Paris, which still has a Rue de Dante.

Dante Alighieri, detail, by Raphael, fresco painting, 1510, Vatican Museum

His writings include *La Vita Nuova* (a mix of poetry and prose), and a political treatise, *De Monarchia.* The latter attacked the political claims of the medieval papacy and was one of the first titles placed on the *Roman Index of Forbidden Books.* His masterpiece is the 14,233-line Italian poem which he called *La Commedia* and history has dubbed *Divina.* (Within the poem he does call it a sacred work on which heaven has set its hand.) Finishing it just before his death at fifty-six from malaria, Dante devoted many years of his maturity to this work "that has long kept me thin."

In his early youth Dante came to know at a distance a Florentine girl named Beatrice ("happy-making") Portinari, who married a Simone de Bardi and died at twenty-four in 1290. Stricken by her transcendent beauty and tragic death, he vowed in *La Vita Nuova* "to write of her what never yet was written of any woman."

He called his poem *La Commedia* because it has a happy ending: his own moral and spiritual conversion. It is not written in the Latin of scholars, but in the Florentine dialect of the vernacular Italian, of whose modern form Dante is considered the creator. His poem was meant to help the common person attain the true happiness of godly vision and conduct.

It is written in rhyme—the celebrated "terza rima," whose interlocking structure Dante was the first to make famous if he did not actually invent. The basic unit of this "triple rhyme" is three lines, of which the first and third lines rhyme, while the middle line will rhyme with the first and third lines of the following tercet (thus: aba/bcb/cdc. . .).

In Dante's poem each line contains eleven actual or elided syllables; thus each tercet contains thirty-three syllables, just as the three main sections of the poem each contain thirty-three chapters or cantos ("songs"). What has been called Dante's "triadomania" is a reflection of his belief in the foundational doctrine of the Trinity—God as Father, Son and Holy Spirit.

These three main sections are the *Inferno,* the *Purgatorio,* and the *Paradiso.* The *Inferno* has an introductory canto in addition to its basic thirty-three, so that the total is a perfect one hundred. The length of individual cantos varies from 115 to 160 lines; the average is 142. The three main sections are almost equal in length: 4,720; 4,755; and 4,758 lines respectively.

In essence *La Commedia* is the story of how three loving women (the Blessed Virgin, St. Lucy and Beatrice) befriend a sinful poet who is going through a mid-life crisis. The great pagan poet Virgil is engaged to guide Dante down through the nine shrinking circles of hell to a climactic vision of Absolute Evil (Satan); then up the seven shrinking circles of the mount of purgatory to the original Eden and a climactic vision of Goodness Incarnate in the person of Beatrice; this Beatrice then leads Dante across the nine expanding circles of the universe to a climactic vision of Absolute Goodness in the divine persons of the Trinity. A purified Dante then returns to earth to tell his story.

The journey takes place in April, 1300, from Good Friday to Easter Wednesday. In 1300, the Church celebrated its first "Holy Year," and Dante's life reached its theoretical midpoint of thirty-five. The Bible speaks of humanity's "three score years and ten," and the *Comedy* begins: *Nel mezzo del cammin di nostra vita*—"in the middle of the journey of our life." It ends with the poet's reintegrated personality now dominated by "the love which moves the sun and the other stars"—*l'amor che move il sole e l'altre stelle.* (All three main sections end with the word "stelle.")

Besides being a love story, the poem is a parable of political realities: corruption versus honesty; of moral realities: the freedom that comes from accepting just laws versus the self-slavery of lawlessness; and of mystical realities: individual self-absorption versus trusting surrender to the divine.

Outstanding in intellect, moral passion and emotional depths, Dante expressed himself through an astonishing range of poetic gifts. His was a "rhapsodic intellect," "a mind in love." He was the model for Rodin's "The Thinker." To his countrymen he is simply "The poet."

To John Ruskin he was "the central man of all the world." T. S. Eliot judged him and Shakespeare the two postclassical masters of Western literature—"there is no third." Thomas Carlyle called the *Comedy* Dante's "unfathomable heartsong"; Longfellow, "This medieval miracle of song." With understandable exaggeration, it has been termed Thomas Aquinas' *Summa Theologiae* set to music. Its most famous lines are "All hope abandon, ye who enter here," and "In His will is our peace." Yet no sensitive reader can ever forget this prophecy of the poet's painful exile: "You will learn how salty tastes another man's bread and how hard a road it is going up and down another man's stairs." Or this image of the beatific vision: "In God's depths I saw all the scattered leaves of the universe gathered together into one volume bound by love." Or this delicate intimation of the sin Francesca da Rimini and her brother-in-law Paolo were about to commit while reading of Lancelot and Guinevere: "That day we read no more." Or the poet's bemused view of the earth from outer space: "that little threshing floor that makes us so fierce." Or the chilling reason why those who never took a stand on moral issues groan so pitifully in the most disgraceful part of hell (but not the deepest or hottest part, as is sometimes incorrectly asserted): *Questi non hanno speranza di morte*—"These have no hope of death."

There are a number of good modern English translations: rhyming ones by Dorothy Sayers and John Ciardi; prose ones by Allen Mandelbaum, John Sinclair, Charles Singleton, and H. R. Ruse. Admirable general introductions are Thomas G. Bergin's "Dante"; Charles H. Grandgent's "Companion to *The Divine Comedy*"; and Helen M. Luke's "Dark Wood to White Rose: A Study of Meanings in Dante's *Divine Comedy.*"

JOSEPH GALLAGHER

See also MIDDLE AGES, THE.

DARK AGES, THE

The period from the fall of the Roman Empire in the West and the decline of classical learning (ca. fifth century) to the beginning of the medieval era in the eleventh century.

MICHAEL GLAZIER

DARK NIGHT OF SENSES

Throughout Christian history spiritual writers have suggested that individuals mature in the dedication of their lives to God through a series of stages; beginners (purgative way), proficients (illuminative way), and perfect (unitive way). They have also suggested that Christian development includes times of darkness and pain, in which individuals do not understand what is happening to their relationship to God and suffer from the misunderstanding. The Night of Senses is the transitional period between the stage of the beginners and that of proficients—it is also the transition from meditative prayer to contemplative prayer.

Described as the Night of the Senses, it refers to the purification of attachment to objects of sense. However, it does not refer to all objects of sense but to those objects that believers use to lead them to God. After all a person who is simply enthralled exclusively by objects of sense is generally not interested in religious matters. The Night of Sense is part of our deeper understanding of God.

While many spiritual writers have spoken about the Night of Sense, the Church's clearest understanding comes from the teachings of St. John of the Cross, a Spanish Carmelite reformer (1542–1591). The Night of Sense has two parts: an active night and a passive night. The former begins before the latter, but the latter continues after the former has ended.

The active Night of Sense consists in a remote preparation for Christian growth, consisting of appropriate virtues. These virtues enable the individual to control any attachments to sense objects that claim to portray God to us—since God is not like any image we have. The passive Night of Sense is the first stage of contemplative prayer in which we cease to pray discursively and receive a knowledge of God permeated with love, which comes in contemplative prayer—this purifies our understanding of God.

LEONARD DOOHAN

See also MYSTICISM; PRAYER; SPIRITUAL LIFE.

DARK NIGHT OF THE SOUL

Christian life, seen as a movement towards a deeper union with God, or better as a process whereby God draws us towards divine life, has often been viewed as moving through a series of stages—beginners, proficient, and perfect, corresponding to the purgative, illuminative, and unitive stages of life. Many spiritual writers have called the transitions between the stages of the proficients and the perfect as a dark night or a cloud of unknowing. St. John of the Cross, the Mystical Doctor, refers to this stage as the Dark Night of the Soul. Spiritual theologians and spiritual directors consider this stage as the decisive period of life.

Coming after a very religiously satisfying period that believers often resent leaving behind, the Dark Night of the Soul has two phases, an active night of spirit and a passive night of spirit. Both contribute to the purifying of our images of God. The insights into God gained in this period come primarily from contemplation, as the believer discovers that God is not the God one thought God was and that God does not act in the way we expect God to act. This takes place through the reeducation or redirection of the faculties of intellect, memory, and will that lead to a vision based on faith, hope, and charity.

The Dark Night of the Soul is the central experience of the journey of faith and the journey of love, both of which must be integrated into the believer's total direction of life to God. It is an experience of God based on knowledge but permeated by love and leads to a transformation of one's way of experiencing God. It is an experience of darkness and pain. Darkness—not because of the absence of light but because of the brightness of the illumination one gains into the knowledge of God. One is not blind in the darkness, but rather learns to see in a new way. The pain results from lack of understanding of what is happening to oneself in the contemplative experience, resentment at the loss of the former satisfying religious experience, and a feeling that friends and even God have abandoned one.

LEONARD DOOHAN

See also MYSTICISM; PRAYER; SPIRITUAL LIFE.

DARWINISM

The notion of evolution has been a feature of European thought at least since the Age of the Enlightenment, but Charles Darwin both popularized it and gave to it his own distinctive interpretation, first in *Origin of Species* (1859) and later in *Descent of Man* (1871). Darwin asserted that all species are mutable and have undergone repeated changes and adaptations to their environment. The species that have survived are those that have shown the greatest ability to adapt to new circumstances—a theory which quickly became known as "the survival of the fittest."

Darwinism provoked widespread criticism from religious leaders, especially fundamentalists, who saw in it an obvious challenge to the account of creation in the Book of Genesis. A more serious challenge to Christianity, however, was Darwin's explanation of the evolutionary process as entirely a matter of chance which owed nothing to Divine Providence. Social Darwinists appropriated these theories for their own purposes and concocted a pseudoscientific philosophy to assert that certain peoples and races were superior to others. At the end of the nineteenth century such theories won wide acceptance and provided a convenient justification for the new imperialism of that era.

ANTHONY D. ANDREASSI

See also CREATION; PROVIDENCE; SCIENCE AND RELIGION.

DAY, DOROTHY (1897–1980)

Dorothy Day was born on 8 November 1897, in Brooklyn, New York. Her parents, John Day and Grace Satterly Day, later moved to San Francisco with their four children. After the earthquake of 1906, the family relocated again, to Chicago, where another child was born.

In 1914, at age sixteen, Dorothy left home to attend the University of Illinois at Urbana. She worked as a domestic to support herself, and joined the Socialist party. After two years she left college and moved to New York City, where she found a job with *The Call,* a Socialist daily. She wrote about poverty from a radical perspective, taking a furnished room on the Lower East Side, and covering speeches by people such as Elizabeth Gurley Flynn and Leon Trotsky, as well as writing on strikes, poverty, and the women's suffrage movement. She went on to work for the Anti-Conscription League and, later, *The Masses.*

In 1917, at the age of twenty, Dorothy was arrested with suffragettes in Washington, D.C. Protesting their thirty-day sentences several of the women, including Dorothy, went on a hunger strike. They began to eat after ten days, and were released eight days later by order of the president. Her time in jail left a deep impression.

Dorothy Day

The next year, Dorothy began nursing in King's County Hospital, in Brooklyn. Her twelve-hour days wore her down—as she wrote later, "My work was to write, and there was no time for that where I was." After a year she left the hospital, and wandered in Europe. Eventually she returned to Chicago, and was again arrested, this time on a raid at an I.W.W. house, the radical International Workers of the World union.

In 1925, Dorothy moved into a beach house on Staten Island with her common-law husband, Forster Batterham, an anarchist and biologist. She was also drawn to prayer, not as the "opiate of the people," but as a way of thanking God for creation. She attended Mass, too, to the consternation of Forster. Dorothy and Forster conceived a child, Tamar Theresa, who was born in March of 1927. Forster had not wanted to bring children into what he saw as an evil world, and this, combined with Tamar's baptism, sent the couple their separate ways. Dorothy was baptized on 28 December 1927.

After her conversion, Dorothy felt isolated from her radical friends, and longed for a way to combine her faith and activism. By 1932, she was writing for *Commonweal* and *America,* two journals of Catholic thought. She was sent to Washington, D.C., in November to cover the Hunger March. On 8 December, the feast of the Immaculate Conception, Dorothy went to the National Shrine to pray "that some way would open up for me to use what talents I possessed for my fellow workers, for the poor."

When Dorothy returned to New York, Peter Maurin was waiting for her, sent by her editor at *Commonweal.* Peter began "indoctrinating" her, giving her a "Catholic outline of history," and repeating his program of action—roundtable discussions, houses of hospitality, and agronomic universities.

Together they founded *The Catholic Worker,* and Dorothy threw herself into the work of editing the paper and running the house of hospitality. The end of World War II brought new trials for the pacifist stand. Anyone who advocated peace or disarmament, as Dorothy and the Catholic Worker did, was labeled Communist. When Dorothy sided with striking gravediggers against the Archdiocese of New York, a member of the cardinal's staff told her to change the name of the paper or cease publication. She, however, felt it would be a scandal to the Church, and promised to be "less dogmatic, more persuasive," and publication continued.

In 1955, Dorothy, Ammon Hennacy and others refused to take shelter during compulsory civil defense drills, because they promoted fear of Russia and a sense of the inevitability of war, as well as a false sense of security from the destruction of war. The group was jailed, and repeated the protest the next year. By 1961, several thousand people joined in refusing to take shelter. Eventually the drills were stopped.

Dorothy spent years traveling, speaking and visiting Catholic Worker houses. She joined the United Farm Workers in California, and visited Cuba shortly after the Bay of Pigs invasion. She made pilgrimages to Rome, the first after the publication of *Pacem in Terris.* The second time was to bring "The Council and The Bomb" issue of the paper to the Second Vatican Council sessions. Dorothy joined a group of women on a ten-day fast in the hope that the council would issue a statement against war. The council, in *Gaudium et Spes* later condemned war "directed to the indiscriminate destruction of whole cities or vast areas with their inhabitants. . . ." It was to become part of *The Catholic Worker*'s continuing objection to war.

Dorothy spent her last years at St. Joseph House and Maryhouse, still located on New York's Lower East Side. By 1977 she was too weak to travel much. As she said, "The paper is in the hands of the young people, and the houses are strong. My prayer is, 'Now let thy servant depart in peace.'" She died on 29 November 1980 in Maryhouse. Her funeral was held at the Church of the Nativity and she was buried at Resurrection Cemetery on Staten Island. The legacy of the Catholic Worker Movement lives on.

JENNIFER BELISLE

See also CATHOLIC WORKER; MAURIN, PETER; SOCIALISM.

DAY OF ATONEMENT

See YOM KIPPUR.

DEACON

Diakonos in Greek means servant or minister. It has evolved to mean a specific kind of minister in the Church and, as such, has come to be translated as deacon. Ministries in the Church of the New Testament were quite diverse (1 Cor 12:27-31) and appear not to be uniform from place to place. *Diakonoi* are mentioned in the church in Philippi (Phil 1:1), although the word in this context may simply mean servants to describe generally the various kinds of ministers in that community. Paul, for instance, who is an apostle, calls himself and his coworkers *diakonoi* (2 Cor 6:4; 11:23), which means in this case simply ministers or servants of God or of Christ. *Diakonos* seems to be evolving towards the designation of a specific ministry in the early Church by the time of the Pastoral Epistles of Timothy and Titus, and is then more appropriately translated as deacon. 1 Timothy 3:8-13 lists the qualities of such ministers: that they not be deceitful, addicted to drink, or greedy; that they hold fast to faith that has been tested; that they be married but once, with a stable home and children. It is interesting that women may have held this office as well, since they are mentioned explicitly in the middle of these verses, though some think verse 11 refers to deacons' wives. Romans 16:1 also refers to the woman Phoebe as a *diakonos* of Cenchreae, though this earlier designation of ministry may not yet indicate the specific office of deacon as it evolved. In the biblical texts, the precise role of the deacons is unclear. In Philippi *diakonoi* are associated with the overseers and seem to have assisted them in administration. Acts 6:1-6 tells of seven disciples who are chosen for the distribution (*diakonia*) of food to the widows. They are designated for a formal ministry, indicated by the "laying on of hands," but the structures remain ambiguous. They are appointed to functions that will later devolve on deacons, but they may also have exercised other leadership functions as well. They are not specifically called deacons.

The office of deacon as mentioned in 1 Timothy emerged universally and with clearer definition by the second century as the expanding Church took on formal, hierarchical structures, and centered ministry around the Eucharist. In that context leadership of the local church devolved on a single bishop and deacons became his assistants. They undertook whatever the bishop assigned, but this was frequently the material care of the sick and the needy. In liturgy the deacons did not preside at Eucharist, but they assisted the bishop, sometimes preached, and often took Communion to the sick. By the seventh century the active and prestigious deaconate was gradually subordinated to priests who could represent the bishop in a local community and could preside at Eucharist. Eventually deaconate was discontinued as a permanent ministry and came to be simply a step on the way to celibate priesthood. The Second Vatican Council restored the permanent deaconate and opened it once again to married as well as celibate men. Debate now continues over the nature and the role of the deaconate and over whether women may be admitted into this ministry.

ANTHONY J. TAMBASCO

See also MINISTRY; SACRAMENT OF ORDERS.

DEACON, PERMANENT

The word "deacon" is derived from the Greek (*diakonein, diakonia*) for one who renders personal service, in particular a table waiter. Jesus makes clear that loving service of others is a hallmark of the disciples: "Let the greatest among you be . . . as the servant" (Luke 22:26), and in John this is made concrete when he washes his disciples' feet and declares: "I have given you a model to follow, as I have done for you, you should also do" (John 13:15).

In the New Testament this responsibility for loving service rested on "the Twelve," who had the ministry of leadership as well as preaching the word. So when a problem arose with the widows of Greek-speaking Jews being neglected in the distribution of food, seven men where chosen by the community at the behest of the Twelve, and the latter imposed hands on them for the service (*diakonia*) of charity to the poor. Although the Seven were not called deacons and their work expanded to include preaching and baptizing, the account in Acts 6:1-7 played an important part in the development of the diaconate in later centuries.

The first mention of deacons as holders of a particular office occurs in Philippians 1:1, where they are linked with overseers (*episkopoi*). Later in Romans 16:1-2, Phoebe, a woman, is referred to as a deacon (*diakonos*) of the Church in Cenchrae. But the clearest reference to the diaconate as a recognized office in the Church is found in the Pastoral Epistles, especially 1 and 2 Timothy, written around the start of the second century. There the office of deacon (*diakonos*) is open to both men and women it seems (1 Tim 3:11) and is distinct from that of the overseer (*episkopos*) and that of the elder (*presbyteros*) (cf. 1 Tim 5:17). The responsibilities of the deacon are not clearly specified in these passages, but must have included works of charity and especially service at the common meal (*agape*) and the Eucharist.

Through the next two centuries public worship (*leitourgia*) and service to those in need (*diakonia*) went hand in hand. The gifts not set aside for the Eucharist itself were available for the communal meal (*agape*), and what was left over was given to the sick, widows, and the poor under the supervision of a presbyter or deacon (Hippolytus 26, 1, 15). At the same time the office of deacon developed in very close relationship to the office of bishop (*episkopos*). Ignatius of Antioch wrote that deacons are entrusted with the service of Jesus Christ, and are fellow servants of the bishop (Magnesians 6,1). Hippolytus tells us that the deacon was ordained for service of the bishop (9, 1-2), and this included teaching, works of charity and assistance at liturgy including at some times preaching. The ministry of women deacons was directed specifically to women, in particular to the sick and to candidates for baptism.

By the fourth century, however, the diaconate was losing ground as a permanent order and becoming a transitional step to the presbyterate. Finally the Council of Nicaea (325) subordinated deacons to presbyters, signaling the end of the era of permanent deacons in the early Church. In the 1500s at the Council of Trent, the restoration of the diaconate as a permanent order was proposed but rejected by the majority. Only a few "political" deacons from powerful families remained in 1870 when the Papal States were dissolved and the practice was discontinued.

Interest in restoring the order of permanent deacon grew after World War II, especially in Europe, and theologians debated it up to the eve of Vatican Council II. The restoration was approved in *Lumen Gentium* (1964) by the council fathers and in 1967 Paul VI issued a *motu proprio* permitting national conferences of bishops to restore the diaconate. In 1971 the U.S. Bishops' Committee on the Permanent Diaconate published guidelines for the ministry of deacon with Rome's approval.

Under these guidelines, deacons must be thirty-five years of age, may be married or unmarried, but if unmarried or later widowed must observe the rule of celibacy. The deacon is ordained to serve the community in charity and justice, but, as for all the baptized, his ministry must be informed, structured, and given life by the word of God and the sacraments of the Church. Among the principal liturgical tasks of the deacon are (1) assisting bishops and priests at the Eucharist, (2) making intercessions and offering petitions for the people, (3) presiding in the absence of priest or bishop at certain liturgical celebrations, (4) administering baptism and officiating at marriages and funeral services, (5) proclaiming and preaching the word of God, and (6) blessing objects and persons within liturgical celebrations.

But the diaconal ministry is first and foremost a call to leadership in service (*diakonia*), as in the early Church. In his *motu proprio* Paul VI outlined this service as carrying out, in the name of the hierarchy, the duties of charity and of administration as well as the works of social assistance, guiding remote Christian communities in the name of the parish priest or bishop, and promoting and sustaining the apostolic activities of laypersons. In practice, deacons, some full-time and some part-time, are assigned to those tasks and responsibilities which best fit the needs of the community they serve and their own particular abilities or charisms. Today (1993) there are over 17,000 permanent deacons worldwide, with 11,000 of these in the United States alone.

JAMES HALEY

See also MINISTRY; SACRAMENT OF ORDERS; WOMEN IN THE CHURCH.

DEACONESS

New Testament Period

Diakonos in the NT refers to men and women in some official ecclesial capacity who provide the community with various forms of needed service or ministry (*diakonia*). The seven Greek-speaking members of the Jerusalem Church chosen by the community and appointed as deacons (Acts 6:1-6) were assigned practical tasks of serving at table and managing the community resources so that help would reach all needy widows. Stephen (Acts 6:8–7:60) and Philip (Acts 8:4-13, 26-40) suggest that deacons also interpreted Scripture, preached, baptized, engaged in theological debate, healed the sick, exorcised demons, and laid down their lives.

Paul describes his service to communities (*diakoneō,* 2 Cor 11:8 and Rom 15:31), when he refers to funds he provided. This is the same meaning given by Luke about many women during the public life of Jesus who provided service (*diakoneō,* Luke 8:3) to him and the disciples from their own wealth.

That women were acknowledged not merely as "helpers," but as actual leaders with authority and theological credibility in the early house churches is suggested by Priscilla, more dominant than her husband Aquila (Acts 18:1-3, 18-19, 26; Rom 16:3-4), Chloe, the community's moral guardian (1 Cor 1:11), Mary, the mother of John Mark and hostess of Peter (Acts 12:12), Lydia the hard-working laborer who hosted Paul (Acts 16:14-15, 40), and the series of women gratefully acknowledged by Paul (Rom 16:1-16). Since some of them are not linked with a family or spouse, it is likely they were known as autonomous leaders, e.g., Mary who "worked hard among you" (*kopiaō,* Rom 16:6, a term Paul also uses of himself in Gal 4:11).

Qualifications for the selection of bishops and deacons are given in a post-Pauline community (1 Tim 3:1-13). The characteristics, like those for deacons in Jerusalem (Acts 6:1-6) are inclusive of both married men and spouses, as well as single men and single women. These qualities do not seem equivalent with women's designation as formally enrolled widows devoted to community service (*chēras,* Acts 9:36-41; 1 Tim 5:3-16). These linguistic points are debated by scholars. When Paul greets the Philippians he distinguishes bishops and deacons (*diakonos,* Phil 1:1) from the rest of the community.

The existence of deaconesses undefined by married partnership in the first generation of the Church is indicated by Phoebe as deacon of the Church (*diakonos*) at Cenchrae, a port city near Corinth (Rom 16:1-2). Translations of the Greek as "servant," "minister" or "helper" have concealed her official status. As the likely carrier of Paul's epistle to Rome, she was regarded as a competent female leader and director (*prostatis,* Rom 16:2) who had the confidence of her community as well as Paul. Her probable task was to interpret Paul's long theological tract to the Church of Rome.

Grounds in the NT exist for reclaiming the historical foundation that women were officially acknowledged by some communities, and were authorized to undertake missionary activities, to preach, and to teach. Women administered funds, and also contributed their own wealth as patrons of local churches and missionary ventures. Women incarnated for the Johannine community its faith in Jesus Christ, e.g., the woman and the well (John 4:4-42), Martha and Mary of Bethany (John 11:1-44) and Mary Magdalen (John 20:1-2, 11-18).

Deaconesses in the Patristic Period

The *Didascalia Apostolorum* from a Syrian church dates from the middle of the third century and is the earliest testimony to an ecclesial office of deaconess. Women were appointed to assist in other women's baptisms, and to visit the sick and elderly in their homes. The *Apostolic Constitutions,* compiled about 370 to 380, developed some themes of the *Didascalia,* as well as part of the *Apostolic Tradition* of Hippolytus of Rome. The author of the *Constitutions* located deaconesses within the church's functions. She was a virgin or a worthy widow. She was subordinate to the male deacon but above other women in her relation to the bishop. Her service in the community, directed by the bishop, seems to have been adapted to changing pastoral practice and need, but her principal service seems to have been directed toward women. She was not authorized to teach in church or to baptize. Ordination rituals and prayers for deaconesses as well as deacons are found in Bk. VII of the *Apostolic Constitutions.* The bishop laid hands on her, invoked the Holy Spirit, and prayed a special blessing on her behalf. She was ordained after the deacon but before the subdeacon and lector. *Testamentum Domini* comes from the eastern part of Syria and dates from the late fifth century. It describes the role of deaconess in the liturgical assembly, and her relation to the bishop, presbyters, and deacons and subdeacons. The evidence of these documents indicates that deaconesses flourished in Greek-speaking and eastern parts of the Roman Empire, except Egypt, for six centuries.

As for the Latin Church in the West, scholars presently cannot find much evidence of an order of deaconesses in the first five centuries. There are signs of opposition to the practice in canon 25 of the First Council of Orange (441) which acknowledged deaconesses but forbade their actual ordination. In the sixth century, there were widow-deaconesses in Gaul; wives of deacons were called deaconesses. In the tenth century, pious organizations of laywomen were probably headed by a deaconess. These expressions are inconclusive about the Church's recognition of deaconesses in the West in the early centuries of the Church.

MARIE-ELOISE ROSENBLATT

See also LITURGY; WOMEN IN THE CHURCH.

DEAD SEA SCROLLS

The term "Dead Sea Scrolls" refers to a series of manuscript discoveries in the late 1940s and 1950s at various sites near the Dead Sea (then in Jordan, now in Israel). The largest manuscript discovery was at Khirbet Qumran, where ancient texts were found in eleven caves surrounding a central community complex. All the books of the Hebrew Bible except Esther are represented—in various states of preservation ranging from nearly complete texts (Isaiah) to mere scraps of text. There are also works of biblical interpretation: an Aramaic paraphrase or Targum of Job, line-by-line commentaries showing how prophetic texts were fulfilled in the community's life and history (Pesharim), and popular rewritings of biblical narratives (Genesis Apocryphon). And fragments of the original texts of 1 Enoch (Aramaic) and Jubilees (Hebrew) known previously in Ethiopic and other versions were found.

Another group of texts (almost all previously unknown) fall into the category of community rules: Manual of Discipline, War Scroll, Damascus Document, Temple Scroll, etc. There are also poetic works (Thanksgiving Hymns or Hodayot), liturgical texts, and Wisdom writings. Perhaps the most exotic of the Qumran discoveries was the Copper Scroll, which purports to be a map for discovering buried treasure.

Most of the Qumran texts can be dated confidently in the late Second Temple period (150 B.C. to A.D. 70). This confidence is based on archaeological excavation of the central building complex, analysis of the scripts in which the scrolls were written (paleography), historical allusions in the texts, and Carbon 14 testing.

The Qumran scrolls are generally understood to be the remnants of the library of a Jewish "monastic" community identified as Essenes. The Manual of Discipline portrays them as living a common life in matters of possessions and food, devoted to prayer and study, living in a highly structured and regulated manner, and awaiting the vindication they expected with the coming of God's kingdom. Some scholars contend that the central complex was a Jewish military outpost or that the library came from Jerusalem

"Thanksgiving" scroll from Shrine of the Book, Jerusalem

refugees fleeing the Romans in A.D. 70. But the Essene "monastery" hypothesis remains the most likely explanation. The community seems to have originated in response to the Maccabean seizure of the Jewish high priesthood and the Temple around 150 B.C. Indeed, the "Teacher of Righteousness," a major figure in some texts, may have been the rightful claimant to the high priesthood. The community of Essenes lived at Qumran from 150 B.C. to A.D. 70, with the exception of their dispersion after an earthquake in 31 B.C. for several years. They lived as a sect, cut off from the larger Jewish society, following a solar rather than a lunar calendar, and developing their own forms of worship and not participating in the rites of the Jerusalem Temple.

The Qumran discoveries are important on several levels. They provide the oldest texts of the Hebrew Bible, some one thousand years older than any other substantial manuscript. They also bear witness to a significant degree of textual diversity in the biblical tradition. They provide original texts for previously known works (1 Enoch, Jubilees) and texts for many previously unknown works. They give us the library of an ancient Jewish community and attest to the variety within Second Temple Judaism.

Reports about the discovery of NT texts at Qumran and about references to NT figures (Jesus, James, Paul, etc.) have no solid basis. Nor does there seem to have been any genetic relation between the Essenes and the early Christians. But the Qumran scrolls do offer some interesting parallels to early Christianity: interest in eschatology, community structures, ambivalence about the Jerusalem Temple, community of goods, biblical interpretation, rejection of remarriage after divorce, and so on.

Scrolls have been found at other sites in the Dead Sea area. Wadi Murabba'at has yielded Greek texts of the Minor Prophets, letters from the Jewish rebel

Caves at Qumran

Bar Kokhba, and the legal archive of the Jewish woman Babatha. These texts are from the second century A.D. The fortress at Masada destroyed by the Romans in A.D. 74 contained biblical texts, large parts of Sirach, and some texts found also at Qumran. Khirbet Mird was a Christian monastery of a later period.

The Dead Sea Scrolls were discovered in what was then Jordanian territory. An international team of scholars was chosen in the early 1950s to oversee their publication. In the meantime some other texts came into Israeli hands and were published. Most of the largest and best preserved manuscripts have been published for many years. Since 1967 Israel officials have overseen the project. Catholic scholars have been prominent in excavating Qumran (R. de Vaux) and publishing texts (J. T. Milik, P. W. Skehan, J. Strugnell). Stories about Vatican interference or a Christian coverup of embarrassing material are without foundation.

DANIEL J. HARRINGTON, S.J.

See also CANON OF SCRIPTURE; CRITICISM, BIBLICAL.

DEANERY

A subdivision of a diocese, comprised of several parishes and presided over by a dean. The dean, who is appointed by a bishop, is responsible for ensuring that liturgical and canon laws are faithfully observed by the clergy of his deanery.

JOSEPH QUINN

See also DIOCESE; PARISH.

DEATH

Death is one of the great mysteries of our existence. How we view death depends on how we view ourselves. The Greeks, for instance, thought of the human soul as immortal; at death, the soul merely shed its body and was thus freed from the "prison" of the flesh. The ancient Hebrews, on the other hand, thought of the human person as a unity: spirit and body joined together to make a whole. Consequently, in death, when the spirit separated from the body, the human person ceased to exist.

It was not until the second century B.C. that Judaism exhibited a clear belief in the resurrection of the dead. Even during Jesus's day, a group of Jews called Sadducees denied a belief in life after death. Christianity, however, following Jesus and the Jewish Pharisee tradition, has taught that death is not the last word; it is, rather, an invitation to a fuller life with God.

In the sixteenth century, the Council of Trent declared that death was a consequence of original sin; because Eve and Adam had disobeyed God, death came to them and to all their offspring. However, as the Second Vatican Council affirmed, human beings have been created by God "for a blissful purpose beyond the reach of earthly misery." Though we die, we live again and more fully in God.

Three types of relation to God in the life to come are described in Christian tradition as heaven, hell, and purgatory. Heaven is the state in which the human person is fully transformed into union with God. Hell, on the other hand, is separation from God. Though we are created by God, it is possible for us, through free will, to close ourselves off from God's love. It is possible for us to choose an isolated, selfish existence over union with the Divine. Purgatory, then, is the process through which our selfishness and egotism are cast off, that we might live more fully.

THERESA SANDERS

See also ESCHATOLOGY; HOPE.

DEATH AND DYING

God gives the gift of life to show forth his love for human beings. Human beings in turn show their love for God by respecting and fostering the gift of human life. Thus, it is not an act of responsible human love to willfully and directly end one's own life or the life of another. Suicide and euthanasia have always been denounced by Christians because these acts are a serious violation of love for God.

Although human life is a great good upon which many other goods depend, sacred Scripture and Church teaching make it clear that human life is not the absolute and ultimate human good. At times, the choice of another good may justify the indirect surrender of human life. In these circumstances, one does not choose death, but allows death to occur because another greater good is chosen directly. As Jesus approached death for example, he freely chose to do his father's will, knowing that violent suffering and death would follow as an indirect result of his choice. Martyrs surrender their lives when they choose to proclaim their faith in God, no matter what the consequences. Thus it is a tenet of Christian teaching that life may be surrendered indirectly, if efforts to continue life would not enhance one's ability to express love of God.

In the sixteenth century, as the possibility of prolonging life through medicine and surgery increased, theologians started questioning how much effort one should expend to stay alive (Daniel Cronin, *Conserving Human Life,* Braintree, Mass.: Pope John XXIII Medical-Moral Center, 1989 [orig. ed. 1956]). Thus, they sought to delineate the situations in which the use of medical and surgical procedures would or would not contribute to a person's ability to love God.

Through the centuries theologians developed a distinction to facilitate decision-making in regard to the use of medical therapy, surgical therapy, or pharmaceuticals. Theologians stated that the use of ordinary means to prolong life were a moral necessity. Using extraordinary means to prolong life, however, was not considered a moral necessity. Ordinary means to prolong life were defined as those means which would prolong life effectively and which would not impose an excessive burden. Extraordinary means to prolong life were those which were considered either not to prolong life effectively or which would impose an excessive burden upon the patient, his family, or upon society. Basically, effectiveness was discerned by considering whether or not the means in question would prolong life in quality and duration (Cronin, p. 88); thus if therapy would merely prolong a comatose condition, it was considered ineffective. Excessive burden was evaluated in regard to the physical, psychological, social or spiritual hardship that would result from the therapy. Even though therapy might be effective, it might still be morally optional if it imposed an excessive burden. Thus, two distinct criteria for removing life support were developed by theologians. Both criteria depended upon medical diagnosis and prognosis of particular patients. Hence, a decision that a particular means to prolong life is either ordinary or extraordinary cannot be made in the abstract. To say that a means to prolong life is inexpensive or readily available, does not indicate necessarily that it is an ordinary means to prolong life. Before a decision is made concerning moral necessity of prolonging life, the medical condition of the patient, as well as the nature and effect of the medical or surgical procedures, must be determined.

In light of the second criterion for removing life support, excessive burden, it is clear that the traditional teaching of the Church allows life support to be removed even if death is not imminent. In contemporary times, mainly because of the cases involving the removal of life support which have been settled in court in the United States, many physicians and ethicists assume that the death of the patient must be imminent and unavoidable before life support ethically may be removed. This assumption is erroneous. Medical therapy which is designed to overcome a serious pathology may be omitted if it imposes excessive burden, even if the therapy could help a patient avoid death.

The teaching of the theologians, especially in regard to the distinction between ordinary and extraordinary means to prolong life, was approved by the Church in 1957 and in 1980 ("Prolongation of Life," [11, 27, 57] *Issues in Ethical Decision Making,* Braintree, Mass.: Pope John XXIII Medical-Moral Center, 1976; Congregation for Doctrine of the Faith, "Declaration on Euthanasia," [5 May], *Vatican Council II,* Vol. 2, ed. Austin Flannery, O.P., Northport, New York: Costello, 1982, pp. 510–517). In 1957, Pope Pius XII applied the distinction to the removal of respirators from persons who would not benefit from continued therapy. In a statement which became an ethical benchmark for humanists, as well as Catholics, Pius XII made it clear that families and physicians who determine that continued respirator therapy is ineffective or imposes an excessive burden may remove the respirator. In so doing they would not be directly killing the patient but simply admitting that medical therapy was not an overall benefit for the patient. In 1980, when discussing the topic of euthanasia, Church teaching once again affirmed the traditional theological teaching concerning the use, withholding, and withdrawal of life support. But because the terms "ordinary and extraordinary" had become imprecise over the years, the document on euthanasia recommended that the terms proportionate and disproportionate be used when making decisions about life support.

Who has the right to make decisions concerning the use, withholding or withdrawal of life support? The final decision is the right of the patient, or the proxy of the patient often appointed by an advanced directive. However, the decision of the patient or proxy is to be founded upon medical knowledge provided by the attending physician. Particularly, it is necessary for the physician to give some indication of the burdens and benefits of a particular plan of therapy. Only when the benefits and burdens are known, can the patient or proxy make a valid decision about effectiveness, and the degree of burden which the therapy will impose. In this regard, it is important to note that the document on euthanasia states that the burden to the patient must be evaluated, but also the burden imposed upon the family or upon society.

In recent years, there have been contrary opinions expressed in the Catholic community in regard to prolonging life of persons in persistent vegetative state (PVS) by means of medically assisted hydration and nutrition (Committee for Pro-Life Activities, NCCB, "Nutrition and Hydration: Moral and Pastoral Reflections," *Origins* [9 April 1992], p. 705; Texas Bishops, "On Withdrawing Artificial Nutrition and Hydration," *Origins* [7 June 1990], p. 53). A person in this condition is diagnosed medically as having a dysfunctional cerebral cortex which cannot be healed. For this reason, some maintain that the therapy which prolongs their lives, artificial hydration and nutrition, is ineffective because it does not enable them to love God through cognitive-affective function, but only maintains human function at the vegetative level. Thus, this form of therapy is considered ineffective insofar as striving for the goal of life is concerned. Others maintain that life, even at the mere vegetative level should be maintained because it is a benefit to the person. Whatever the outcome of the debate, the ethical solution to the problem depends upon the interpretation of the criteria concerning effectiveness of the therapy. Many offer a solution to the problem of care for PVS patients based upon the criterion of excessive burden. This is an inaccurate approach to the problem.

The ethical use of pain medication often arises in cases of the dying. In sum, Church teaching allows the use of pain medication, even if death occurs more quickly, as long as the primary purpose of the medication is to relieve pain.

Too often when the topic of death and dying is discussed, the focus of attention is upon determining proportionate and disproportionate means to prolong life. When considering this topic from a Christian perspective however, the spiritual care for dying people should be emphasized. Thus, all persons should be provided the opportunity to prepare for their death. Spiritual support, through the sacraments and the presence of loved ones should be considered as ordinary or proportionate care for all who are dying.

KEVIN O'ROURKE, O.P.

See also ADVANCE DIRECTIVES FOR MEDICAL CARE; THEOLOGY, MORAL.

DECALOGUE

See TEN COMMANDMENTS, THE.

DEDICATION, CHURCH

The Dedication of Churches is the liturgical rite in which sacred buildings destined for divine worship are dedicated to God. The term, "church," is used principally to describe the people; however, since these people come together to hear the word of God and to celebrate sacred mysteries in a building, a house for the "church," the building itself takes on a sacred character.

Since the early Church possessed no permanent structures where the community could worship, we find no rite of dedication of primitive churches; however, by 314 Eusebius in his *Ecclesiastical History* describes the dedication of the basilica of Tyre. In this rite the building was dedicated solely by the celebration of the Eucharistic Liturgy without any additional rites. In the sixth century a letter from Pope Vigilius states that a church is to be dedicated by the celebration of the Mass, though a blessing with holy water may also be performed. During the Middle Ages the rite of dedication became more elaborate with multiple sprinklings with holy water and anointings of the altar and the walls. By the time of the publication of the Roman Pontifical (first published in 1485), the rites had become long and intricate, and it was this form that remained standard for the most part in the Church until this century. In 1961 the rite was considerably simplified and shortened, and in 1977 the Sacred Congregation of Sacraments and Divine Worship further reformed the rite of dedication again.

The present form of dedication represents a return to the ancient custom in which the celebration of the liturgy is seen to be the primary form of dedication, and the whole rite takes place within the Eucharistic Liturgy. In the Introductory Rite the people present the building to the bishop with the use of a sprinkling rite recalling the cleansing power of baptism. Then the bishop blesses the ambo where the word of God is proclaimed. The Litany of the Saints replaces the general intercessions, and there is the option to place relics beneath the altar. Next, the bishop offers the Prayer of Dedication where he announces to the people that the building is set apart for God. He then anoints the altar and walls with chrism, and then he incenses them along with the people. After the Liturgy of the Eucharist, the Blessed Sacrament is brought to the chapel of reservation. If Mass has already been celebrated in the church building before the dedication, a modified form of the above rite is used.

ANTHONY D. ANDREASSI

See also ARCHITECTURE, CHURCH; SACRAMENTALS.

DEFENDER OF THE BOND

An ecclesiastical office instituted by Benedict XIV in 1741 to defend the bond of marriage when nullity or dissolution was sought by one or both spouses. The Defender, appointed by the local bishop, also participated in cases where nullity of sacred orders was considered. In 1944 Pius XII, in an address to the Roman Rota, expressed concern that at times Defenders were overzealous and unfair in the exercise of their duties.

Under the New Code of Canon Law any person, clerical or lay, with qualifications in canon law, may be appointed Defender of the Bond who, today, works almost exclusively in the marriage tribunal where petitions for annulments have greatly increased.

JOAN GLAZIER

See also CANON LAW; DIVORCE; SACRAMENT OF MATRIMONY.

DEMON POSSESSION

See POSSESSION, DEMONIC.

DEMONOLOGY

Strictly, *demonology* refers to the "science" or study of demons, and, in a less accurate, more popular sense, the alleged practice of summoning, worshipping, and employing demons by means of ritual magic (sorcery). Since the latter is largely an item of fiction and is negligible in ordinary Christian life, nothing more need be said of it here.

Among the ancient Hebrews, as with almost all ancient peoples and so-called "primitive" cultures, belief in evil spirits or demons figured in folklore and ordinary religious belief, but was neither elaborate nor very important (see Deut 32:17; Ps 109:6; Isa 13:21; 34:14; 1 Sam 16:14, etc.). In later Judaism, largely under Persian, Greek, and other Middle Eastern influences, belief in the demons' power to affect human persons together with the practice of exorcism acquired increased importance in regard to accounting for and treating physical ills, social distress, and spiritual anxiety. Early Christianity inherited this tradition, which was developed and augmented by the Desert Fathers and Mothers and eventually reached heights of fantastic speculative elaboration, psychological obsession, and destructive practice in the late Middle Ages and Renaissance.

Ancient Hebrew belief included angelic beings later known as "Watchers" who fathered on human females the *nephilim* or "giants" of Genesis 6:1-4, as well as animal-like creatures such as *lilith,* the night-hag, and the *shadim* and *sairim,* who lurked in the wilderness or in dark, abandoned places (Deut 32:17; Ps 106:37; Isa 21:11; 34:14; cf. Rev 18:2). By the time of Christ, such demons had been spiritualized and organized under Satan (see Dan 8:10; 1 Chr 21:1). They assaulted human beings chiefly by means of possession, causing seizures, panic, destructive violence, blasphemy, and paralysis.

Although some references are metaphorical, New Testament authors took demons and "unclean spirits" seriously, considering them to be at least allied if not identical with fallen angels (Matt 25:41; Luke 10:18; 11:18; 2 Pet 2:4; Jude 6; Rev 12:4, 8; etc.). Like their Hebrew ancestors (Deut 32:17), they also considered pagan "gods" and mediumistic spirits to be demonic (Acts 16:16; 1 Cor 10:20-21; Rev 9:20). For such spirits, whether evil or not, lured believers away from the gospel (1 Tim 4:1; Rev 16:14; etc.) and thus opposed the Realm of God.

St. Paul interpreted demonic power and hostility in terms of fallen principles of the cosmos (Rom 8:38; 1 Cor 15:24; 2 Cor 11:14; Eph 1:21, etc.; Col 1:16; 2:15). He also affirmed that these envious spiritual but nonhuman forces had been subjected by God through the death and resurrection of Christ (1 Cor 6:3; 1 Pet 3:22; 2 Pet 2:10-11), whose victory will be fully manifest only at the end of time.

Doctrinally, the existence of demons has never been defined and is not, strictly speaking, an article of faith. Rather, like the existence of Satan, the reality of demons is presupposed in biblical writings and common belief. Pastorally, the Church continues to provide Christians all the resources of spiritual authority to withstand whatever powers of evil oppose the faith, including solemn exorcism when appropriate. Trying to confirm the existence, nature, and character of alleged demons from such practice is, however, fraught with risk.

Advances in medicine, psychotherapy, and pastoral counseling have rendered belief in the demonic origin of human and nonhuman suffering as well as natural disasters untenable to modern sensibilities. Nevertheless, recovering St. Paul's understanding of demonic agencies as sinful social structures (see Rom 8:35-39) as well as cosmic forces inimical to the reign of God (1 Cor 15:24, etc.) provides insight into the reality and power of the demonic in human experience. It also directs our efforts constructively towards alleviating suffering, healing of peoples, and restoring the living planet itself.

RICHARD WOODS, O.P.

See also EXORCISM; POSSESSION, DEMONIC.

DEMONS

See DEMONOLOGY; SATAN.

DEPOSIT OF FAITH

In the New Testament the Apostle Paul sends the following exhortation to Timothy: "Take as a model of sound teaching what you have heard me say . . . . Guard the rich deposit of faith . . ." (2 Tim 1:13-14). This metaphor of the faith as a *deposit* catches nicely the sense that it is something valuable that has been entrusted to another. From the beginning the Church has had the sense that one of its principal duties is to preserve unblemished "the faith which was once for all delivered to the saints" (Jude 3).

This deposit, of course, is not to be hidden in a napkin or buried in the ground by a fearful servant (cf. Matt 25:25; Luke 19:20). The faith entrusted to the apostles and by them to the Church is to be proclaimed at all times and in every place. As the saving message of the gospel is applied to new questions and new situations, its inner riches come to light. In this sense, the deposit of faith is like the treasure spoken of by Jesus out of which the householder brings "what is new and what is old" (Matt 13:52).

This dynamic sense of the Church's task in handing on the gospel message is expressed in the dogmatic constitution *Dei Filius* at the First Vatican Council. The teaching of faith revealed by God has not been proposed like a philosophical insight to be brought to completion by human ingenuity, but rather it has been entrusted to the Church as a "divine deposit," and it is to be faithfully preserved and infallibly expounded.

It is natural to think of this deposit as if it consisted of all the individual truths that have been revealed by God which are contained in the Apostles' Creed and in doctrines formulated by the Church over the centuries. This would, however, show too limited an understanding of how the deposit of faith was constituted and how it continues to function in the life of the Church. Faith is always a response to God's revelation in history, to all the ways in which God has acted to bring salvation to people. A believer is initially someone who trusts that it is truly God who is present and active in this history, truly God who guarantees the truth of the message of salvation, and truly God who calls for a personal response of faith. This is the deposit in its most basic sense, the foundational mystery at the heart of the Christian faith. Every particular truth is believed on the strength of this more basic truth. Every expression of the foundational mystery, whether in the Scriptures or in the formulations of creeds and catechisms, is a more or less successful attempt to give verbal expression to this ultimately transcendent reality.

The deposit of faith, then, is first and foremost God's saving presence in history. It will, of course, find expression in words, especially in the authoritative teachings of the hierarchy, but it cannot possibly be limited to them. The whole body of the apostolic traditions, customs, and practices constitutes further testimony to God's saving activity and continues to give witness to it in the whole life of the Church: in liturgical worship and in private prayer, in the enactment of sacraments and in the "sense of the faithful" under the guidance of the Holy Spirit. The bishops at the Second Vatican Council teach that the wealth of this tradition is to be found constantly enriching "the practice and life of the believing and praying Church" (Divine Revelation, no. 8). The council fathers wished to stress the fact that this sacred tradition as well as the inspired biblical writings have a common origin in God and tend toward the same end. Together, they form "one sacred deposit of the word of God." The teaching office of the bishops themselves is described as being in service to this expanded sense of the word of God, "teaching only what has been handed on," guarding and explaining the word of God faithfully. The teaching office "draws from this one deposit of faith everything which it presents for belief as divinely revealed" (no. 10).

WILLIAM C. McFADDEN, S.J.

See also DOCTRINE; DOGMA; TRADITION.

DESCENT OF CHRIST (INTO HELL)

This doctrine is bound up with a Semitic concept of a three-tiered world: (1) the heavens; (2) the earth; and (3) the underworld (see Phil 2:10). This underworld is called Sheol or Hades. When this underworld is called "hell," it is not a question of a place of punishment. Rather, it is the abode of the dead or a place where those confronting serious problems on earth (illness, loss of reputation, etc.) imagine themselves to be (see Pss 30:4; 40:3; Job 7:9; Isa 38:18). Against this biblical understanding of "hell" this doctrine asserts the reality of Jesus' death. Thus Jesus shared in the common lot of mortals by experiencing death. There are several New Testament texts that speak of Jesus' experience in this way (see Matt 12:40; Acts 2:27, 31; Rom 10:7; Eph 4:10).

Unlike all other mortals, however, Jesus did not go down into hell to remain there. Rather, the one who descended into hell ascended into heaven and indeed not merely for his own sake but for that of all humanity. Thus the descent into hell is bound up with the ascension of Jesus. The author of 1 Peter speaks of Jesus' going to the spirits in prison (3:19) but then adds: "who has gone into heaven and is at the right hand of God, with angels, authorities, and powers subject to him" (3:22).

By descending into hell and ascending from it, Jesus has begun the final assault on humanity's last enemy, viz., death (see 1 Cor 15:26). Thus Jesus becomes "the first fruits of those who have fallen asleep" (1 Cor 15:20) and "the firstborn from the dead" (Col 1:18). By passing from Sheol into heaven, Jesus impacts the entire cosmos in such a way that nothing lies outside his influence.

1 Peter 3:18-22 is unique among New Testament texts about Jesus' presence in the underworld by assigning to him an active role. Borrowing from the apocryphal First Book of Henoch, the author has Jesus preach to the spirits in prison (v. 19). These spirits are the fallen angels (see Gen 6:1-4) who have seduced humanity and influenced the reign of sin in the world. Through his passion and resurrection (1 Pet 3:18) Jesus has overcome these instigators of sin. His victory does not mean the conversion of these hostile spirits since they are incapable of conversion. It is, rather, their definitive subjection. The proclamation of the risen Christ to the disobedient spirits is a crucial element in the whole plan of redemption.

JOHN F. CRAGHAN

See also DEATH; PASCHAL MYSTERY.

DESIRE, BAPTISM OF

See BAPTISM OF DESIRE.

DESPAIR

Each life is marked by periods of crisis in which the meaning and significance of that life is questioned. At these times we seek the ultimate purpose and significance of existence itself and of *our own, individual existence.* "Why are we? What are we for? What awaits us after we die? Why love?" are questions that exemplify the struggle to find meaning again.

Typically we resolve this existential, spiritual crisis in one of two ways. We can achieve greater wholeness, purpose, and integration, or we can arrive at an intellectual, emotional, and spiritual state without significance, without purpose, and without hope. This is *despair:* When nothing matters, the lack of meaning fosters bitterness and contempt for ourselves, our universe, and whoever or whatever we believe created it. In despair there is no reason to be and no reason to go on. The will to live, the drive to uncover meaning, and the desire to live the challenge of living all wither away, and what remains is emptiness and denigration of oneself and the world. It is a profound state of being in which ultimate meaning becomes "there is no ultimate meaning." The life we are given is rejected and railed against, and we lose hope and purpose in the face of the ever-present possibility of our own deaths. Despair denies life, and denies the reasons we choose to live in spite of life's inevitable course.

PAUL MOGLIA

See also HOPE.

DETACHMENT

Detachment has always been a part of Christian spirituality, as it has of other religions. The word means "to cut oneself off from something." The practice of detachment as part of Christian asceticism referred to the desirability of cutting oneself off from every aspect of life that was viewed to be of no religious value. Thus, early monks detached themselves from food, social contacts, marriage, and family. Depending on what one thought was of no religious value, the notion of detachment enlarged or decreased. In times of dualistic approaches to religion when some religious writers and philosophers despised anything of a material nature as being of no religious value, the notion of detachment became of prime importance. After the Second Vatican Council taught the intrinsic goodness of the world and all temporal realities, simply to cut oneself off from them served no immediate purpose. They were good and could be integrated into one's totally God-directed life.

There still remains the necessity of detaching oneself from anything that leads us away from God—anything that is sinful. Moreover, it is still desirable to detach oneself from good values as part of a choice for something better: to choose celibacy for the kingdom without despising marriage, or to choose marriage as part of one's Christian commitment without despising celibacy. In general detachment has been viewed negatively and that is incorrect. To detach oneself from something seen as good in order to choose something that is viewed to be better is a necessary part of growth in Christian discipleship. However, to integrate all aspects of life into one great self-dedication to God, never absolutizing any value in itself, is a contemporary way of integrating detachment into one's life.

LEONARD DOOHAN

See also ASCETICISM; BEATITUDES; SPIRITUAL LIFE; VIRTUE.

DEUTEROCANONICAL BOOKS

This term applies to those books in the Bible whose place within the canon of Scripture was doubted or disputed, but are now accepted as part of the canon by Roman Catholics. Catholics, Protestants, and Jews all accept the same thirty-nine books in the OT. However, Catholics have forty-five OT books because they also include Tobit, Judith, Wisdom, Sirach, Baruch, and 1–2 Maccabees as part of the canon. They call the thirty-nine books protocanonical, and the disputed books, deuterocanonical. Protestants use the term canonical for the thirty-nine and apocryphal, which means "hidden" or "outside," for the deuterocanonical books. Some NT books were also disputed, and so Hebrews, James, 2 Peter, 2–3 John, Jude, Revelation are called deuterocanonical, although they are now accepted as part of the canon by all Christians. Thus, when Catholics use the term deuterocanonical today, they refer primarily to those additional OT books that are part of the canon of Scripture for the Catholic Church and were accepted as such by the Council of Trent.

A confusing element in the discussion is the fact that Catholics also use the term apocrypha but mean writings such as Gospel of Thomas, Acts of Paul, Epistle to Laodicians, Didache, and Shepherd of Hermas, which are not a part of Scripture but come from an early period. Protestants call these books pseudepigrapha.

HELEN DOOHAN

See also BIBLE, NEW TESTAMENT WRITINGS; BIBLE, OLD TESTAMENT WRITINGS.

DEVELOPMENT OF DOCTRINE

See DOCTRINE, DEVELOPMENT OF.

DEVIL

See DEMONOLOGY; SATAN.

DEVIL'S ADVOCATE

The devil's advocate is the popular name for the "promoter of the faith" in processes of beatification and canonization that come under the jurisdiction of the Sacred Congregation for the Causes of the Saints. Functioning after the manner of a prosecuting attorney, this official opposes the positions taken by patrons of a cause for beatification or canonization. Among other duties the promoter of the faith presents arguments against the very introduction of a cause and proposes any possible difficulties in the writings of a candidate. These and other specific procedures stem from the work of Prospero Lambertini, later Pope Benedict XIV (1740–1758). These various roles of the promoter of the faith explain the expanded use of devil's advocate as one who holds the wrong side or an indefensible cause, whether out of malice or for the sake of argument.

JOHN F. CRAGHAN

See also BEATIFICATION; CANONIZATION.

DEVOTIO MODERNA

This was a movement towards spiritual reform of the Church in the fourteenth and fifteenth centuries. Initiated by Geert Groote (1340–1384) in the Netherlands, the movement spread also to Belgium and northern Germany. It was sustained by Sisters and Brothers of the Common Life, communities of celibates who held their property in common, had a common life of prayer and study, earned their living by their own work, and in many ways lived like religious but without taking vows publicly acknowledged by the Church.

Although the lives of these groups living in community were strictly regulated, the main thrust of the movement was the practice of "inner devotion." The followers of the movement tried to maintain a state of recollection of God's presence at all times, and to avoid ambition whether for wealth, pleasure, honor, learning, or anything else. They tended therefore to be rather anti-intellectual, regarding the universities and the intellectual life of late Scholasticism as undesirably worldly. The inner devotion to God and the external activities of the person must be in harmony, hence much renunciation is required so that one is not distracted in pursuing the all-important "interior vision of God." Life is a constant struggle. One strives by self-denial and contempt for the world to imitate the life of Jesus Christ, especially in his passion. A key aspect of the life of Jesus on which the Devotio Moderna dwelt was his humility.

The Devotio Moderna has sometimes been seen as a source or forerunner of the Protestant Reformation for several reasons. It emphasized return to, and constant meditation on, Scripture, especially the Gospels. It was suspicious of the elaborate and philosophically based theology of the late Scholastic period. It was critical of clerical corruption and emphasized personal devotion in ways that might be considered individualistic. In these matters it anticipated the sixteenth-century Reformers. But in other matters, it had more in common with monastic traditions of spirituality.

The movement left quite a collection of devotional writings for posterity. Of these, the best known and probably the most influential is *The Imitation of Christ,* attributed to Thomas à Kempis (1380–1471).

MONIKA K. HELLWIG

See also IMITATION OF CHRIST; MIDDLE AGES, THE; SPIRITUAL LIFE.

DEVOTIONS

Devotions are prayers or pious exercises used to demonstrate reverence for a particular aspect of God or the person of Jesus, or for a particular saint.

For example, since the Middle Ages, many Christians have shown a devotion to the Sacred Heart of Jesus, a symbol of Jesus's love for humanity. This devotion gained popularity in the seventeenth century through the efforts of Saint Margaret Mary Alacoque, and in 1765 the feast of the Sacred Heart was proclaimed by the pope. Christians showed their devotion by the observance of an octave, or prayers said on the feast day and for seven days afterward.

Devotions to the saints have played a role in Christianity practically since its inception. For instance, many Christians demonstrate a devotion to Saint Jude Thaddeus, who is called the patron saint of lost causes. It is customary to make a novena (that is, to say certain prayers for nine days in a row) asking for Saint Jude's intercession and help. Christians may light candles or make offerings as part of their devotional practice.

Similarly, there are many devotions in honor of the Virgin Mary. To show their love and reverence, many Christians gather to pray the rosary. They may also sing hymns in praise of the Blessed Virgin, or perform ceremonies in which her statue is adorned or specially displayed.

During the Second Vatican Council, the practice of devotions was "warmly commended"; the council noted, however, that all devotions should be performed in accordance with Church law. Also, it is important to point out that though saints may be reverenced, they may never be worshiped. The goal of devotional practices should always be to further Christians' love of and commitment to God, who alone is worshiped.

THERESA SANDERS

See also BENEDICTION OF THE BLESSED SACRAMENT; EXPOSITION OF THE BLESSED SACRAMENT; HOLY HOUR; NOVENA; ROSARY.

DEVOUT LIFE, INTRODUCTION TO

See FRANCIS DE SALES, ST.

DIACONATE, THE PERMANENT

See DEACON, PERMANENT.

DIDACHE, THE

Also known as the *Teaching of the Twelve Apostles,* this is a compilation by an unknown author, most probably dating from the mid-second century. Its text was rediscovered in 1883, and subsequently it was widely researched and evaluated. The document is divided into three sections: moral, disciplinary, and liturgical; and it was valued only after the Bible by some of the Fathers of the Church. Its liturgical teaching recommends baptism by immersion when possible, and its Eucharistic Prayers are theologically and historically valuable. The Didache is generally grouped with the Apostolic Fathers, the earliest non-biblical Christian texts extant.

MICHAEL GLAZIER

See also APOSTOLIC FATHERS, THE; FATHERS OF THE CHURCH.

DIOCESE

A local church under the jurisdiction of a particular bishop, further divided into parishes.

MONIKA K. HELLWIG

DIRECTION, SPIRITUAL

See SPIRITUAL DIRECTION.

DISCERNMENT OF SPIRITS

When Pope John XXIII convoked the Second Vatican Council, he said he was taking to heart those words of Jesus on the need to discern the signs of the times (cf. Matt 16:3). That there are such signs presupposes that God is at work in history, revealing the divine plan, and that Christians of every age have an obligation to understand those signs and follow their lead. At the Last Supper Jesus promised to send the Holy Spirit to his disciples as a permanent gift, "the Spirit of truth . . . who will guide you into all the truth" (John 16:13). This passage into the truth, however, was not to be without opposition from the spirit of error, the Father of Lies, who would seek to lead the disciples astray. Hence, from the very beginning of the Church Christians were alerted to the need for discernment of spirits: "Do not believe every spirit, but test the spirits to see whether they are of God" (1 John 4:1). The test for John was a fundamental one: "Every spirit which confesses that Jesus Christ has come in the flesh is of God, and every spirit which does not confess Jesus is not of God" (1 John 4:3).

The Apostle Paul faced the same problem in the various communities he founded. He called attention to a special gift conferred on some members of the local Church, "the ability to distinguish between spirits" (1 Cor 12:10), and described it as one of the manifestations of the Spirit for the common good. When he himself writes more extensively on how to make this distinction, he develops a principle employed by Jesus in teaching the disciples how to recognize false prophets: "You will know them by their fruits" (Matt 7:16). Paul begins by drawing a distinction between "the works of the flesh" and "the works of the Spirit." The works of the flesh are things like anger and jealousy, selfishness and hatred. These are signs that the spirit of evil is at work. The works that testify to the activity of the Spirit, however, "the fruit of the Spirit," are such things as love and joy, peace and patience, kindness and faithfulness (Gal 5:22).

There has been a continuing need in the history of the Church for discernment in the matter of doctrine and of morals. That task has been confided to the teaching office of the Church. Another sort of discernment plays an important role in Christian spirituality. Those who serve as spiritual guides are regularly called upon to assist individuals in evaluating their interior life. This is a complex matter and it takes great skill to become a competent spiritual director. One of those who was deeply involved in this process was Ignatius Loyola. In his *Spiritual Exercises* he set down some "Rules for the Discernment of Spirits," guidelines for those who served as spiritual directors. Since the goal of the *Exercises* was to enable the one making them to respond freely to the call of God, an experienced director could be very helpful in enabling the retreatant to recognize various interior movements (thoughts, desires, feelings) and come to know which were from God and which from the evil spirit. Ignatius set great store by the experience of spiritual consolation in the souls of those who were making progress in the service of God. It is characteristic of the good spirit, he wrote, to encourage such persons through the experience of being drawn towards God and through felt increases in hope, faith, and charity. The activity of the evil spirit, on the other hand, may be recognized in an attraction to base and earthly things, a distaste for heavenly things, and a growing sense of being separated from God.

Because Ignatius was not only a skilled spiritual director but also a good teacher, he was aware of the importance of helping those being counseled to learn for themselves how to recognize and identify the interior movements in their souls. This ability is essential for anyone who wishes to become mature in forming their conscience and in responding to the promptings of the Spirit.

Following Vatican II, there has been heightened interest in discernment as religious communities and other apostolic groups have begun to practice a communal discernment. In a prayerful context and through honest exchange of views there often emerges a consensus about the signs of the times and the particular response God is asking of this community.

WILLIAM C. McFADDEN, S.J.

See also IGNATIUS OF LOYOLA, ST.; SPIRITUAL LIFE.

DISCIPLE

From the Latin verb *to learn,* a disciple is a student who accepts and follows a given teacher. The term is used about 250 times in the Gospels and Acts, but nowhere else in the NT. It is employed to designate one who accepts and follows a great leader or movement, as a general term for believers in Christ, and to refer specifically to one or more of the Twelve.

The term *disciple* is used to refer to anyone who accepts and follows a recognized master. In the NT one reads of disciples of Moses (John 9:28), of the Pharisees (Matt 22:16; Mark 2:18), and of Paul (Acts 9:25). Disciples of John the Baptist are mentioned in all four Gospels. Two of these disciples leave John in order to follow Jesus when they hear John refer to Jesus as the Lamb of God. John's disciples remain active, however, even after their leader is jailed (Matt 11:2; Mark 6:29).

Disciple is used much more frequently, however, for believers in Christ. A disciple of Jesus has a very definite lifestyle, usually seen as patterned or modeled after the life and ministry of Jesus. This conception of Jesus as model or example is often spoken about using the technical term *to follow* and its various equivalents (e.g., *to go after*).

Christ and his disciples enter Jerusalem, mosaic, 12th century, Palermo

In the Synoptic Gospels a disciple of Jesus is called to conversion of life, obedience, trust, and hope. Disciples are distinguished from others by their commitment to the person and work of Jesus. They are expected to leave behind their old ties and embrace the new family of Jesus (i.e., the Church). The call to follow Jesus carries with it the requirement to live a life of mutual service, to renounce power and prestige, and to trust in God. Following Jesus by leading your life in this manner may result in suffering and death at the hands of those hostile to Christianity. A disciple must be willing to suffer injustice rather than inflict it on others and to trust in God even in the face of suffering and death. The person who follows Jesus on his way will realize the need to fulfill the role of missionary and joyfully proclaim the saving message of and about Jesus to others.

John agrees with the Synoptics in many respects. Disciples are chosen by Jesus and must be willing to suffer and die for their faith as well as to engage in the missionary enterprise. John is especially concerned, however, to stress the importance of the disciple's faith. In this gospel, disciples are distinguished from others who reject the claims about Jesus' relationship with the Father. Disciples recognize Jesus in terms of traditional Jewish messianic expectations and in terms of his status as God's unique representative.

On occasion, the term *disciple* is used to refer to one or more of the Twelve. This occurs some two dozen times (e.g., Luke 9:54; John 6:8; 12:4), more than half of which are in Matthew. That members of the Twelve should be referred to as disciples is not surprising. They are, after all, committed to the person and work of Jesus and they fulfill all of the requirements, mentioned above, to be called disciples.

At times, however, Christians have used the term *disciples* in a restrictive sense to refer exclusively to the Twelve. In Matthew's Gospel, especially after chapter ten, there is a tendency to restrict the title *disciple* to the group of the Twelve. Matthew is the only NT book to speak of *twelve disciples* (Matt 10:1; 11:1; 20:17). That Matthew understands the term in a broader sense as well, is seen when the risen Lord appears on the mountain and commissions the eleven disciples to "make disciples of all nations" (Matt 28:16).

DENNIS SWEETLAND

See also APOSTLES; BIBLE, NEW TESTAMENT WRITINGS; SPIRITUAL LIFE.

DISSENT

See MAGISTERIUM.

DIVINE COMEDY, THE

See DANTE, ALIGHIERI.

DIVINE OFFICE

See LITURGY OF THE HOURS.

DIVINE PRAISES

A series of praises, beginning "Blessed be God," usually recited after Benediction of the Blessed Sacrament, but before the Host is replaced in the tabernacle. The greater portion is generally thought to have been compiled about 1779 by Louis Felici, S.J., to provide an "act of reparation" for the widespread sins of blasphemy and profanity.

Blessed be God.
Blessed be his holy Name.
Blessed be Jesus Christ, true God and true man.
Blessed be the name of Jesus.
Blessed be his most Sacred Heart.
Blessed be his most Precious Blood.
Blessed be Jesus in the most holy Sacrament of the Altar.
Blessed be the Holy Spirit, the Paraclete.
Blessed be the great Mother of God, Mary most holy.
Blessed be her holy and Immaculate Conception.
Blessed be her glorious Assumption.
Blessed be the name of Mary, Virgin and Mother.
Blessed be St. Joseph, her most chaste spouse.
Blessed be God in his angels and in his saints.

The praises of the Sacred Heart, Precious Blood, Immaculate Conception, Assumption, and St. Joseph are later additions.

DAVID BRYAN

See also BENEDICTION (OF THE BLESSED SACRAMENT).

DIVORCE

A divorce is a judicial declaration of a civil court which effects the legal dissolution of a marriage. It causes the marital relationship to cease in a legal sense, and releases husband and wife from their civilly enforceable matrimonial rights and obligations. The court may enjoin rights and duties of child custody, spousal support, and property division, but the marital relationship is ended.

The Church believes and teaches that marriage is permanent and indissoluble, a *lifelong* covenant and partnership. In the Church's view, all marriages have this essential character of permanence, both those which are "natural" (between non-baptized persons) and those which are sacramental (between baptized Christians). Because of this deeply held conviction about the indissolubility of marriage, the Church does not recognize that civil divorce terminates the marriage covenant. It has only civil effects. In other words, divorce does not affect the bond of marriage. The marriage bond endures despite a civil divorce.

The Church's commitment to the permanence of marriage is based on the words of Jesus: "What God has joined together, no human being must separate. . . . whoever divorces his wife . . . and marries another commits adultery" (Matt 19:6, 9; cf. also: Matt 5:31; Luke 16:18). St. Paul's comparison of marriage to Christ's union with the Church has also had a profound influence on this teaching (Eph 5:21-33).

Divorce has become a prevailing and widely accepted practice in many contemporary societies. It is so prevalent that we can be said to live in a divorce culture. The Church's position, in this context, can be accurately described as countercultural. The Church insists not only that divorce is wrong, that is, something which *should* not be done, but also that marriage is indissoluble, that is, divorce is something which *cannot* be done. Neither the parties nor the state have the power to sunder what God has joined.

This does not necessarily mean that to obtain a civil divorce is always morally wrong. There are situations, e.g., physical abuse of spouse or children, flagrant adultery, or failure of child support, etc., in which divorce may be morally justified, either as a practical necessity or as the lesser of two evils. In other words, to sue for divorce may or may not be sinful, depending on the circumstances, and to live as a divorced person does not imply a state of sin. The Church does not consider divorced persons to be excommunicated or unworthy of participation in the Eucharist. There is no canonical penalty attached to divorce.

The Church teaches that a person who has obtained a civil divorce is not free to remarry, since it holds that the bond of marriage endures even though separation and civil divorce have taken place. The Church permits divorced persons to remarry, while their spouses still live, only when their marriages have been annulled or dissolved by the authority of the Church. An annulment is a judicial declaration that the marriage was null and void from the outset for a good canonical reason. A dissolution of an unconsummated marriage or one involving a nonbaptized person involves an exercise of the Church's unique authority over marriage, and is relatively rare.

The Church reaches out pastorally in many ways to those whose marriages fail. It invites them to be reconciled and to resume full sacramental participation. It welcomes them to verify their freedom to marry by requesting a clarification of status through the annulment process. It assists them toward spiritual health and personal growth through groups like Separated and Divorced Catholics.

JAMES A. CORIDEN

See also ANNULMENT; SACRAMENT OF MATRIMONY.

DOCETISM

A heresy that held that Jesus Christ was not really human, but only seemed to have a body so that his human life was illusory. This was a way of thinking that occurred repeatedly in a variety of groups in the early Church. Arguments refuting Docetism are found as early as the letters of Ignatius of Antioch about A.D. 110.

MICHAEL GLAZIER

See also HERESY/HERETICS.

DOCTORS OF THE CHURCH

Since the time of Boniface VIII this is a title officially conferred by pope or general council to designate someone posthumously (and usually long after death) as wise, holy, and learned and a source, therefore, of sound teaching for the whole Church. In earlier centuries the title arose more spontaneously. Later, specific norms were laid down by Pope Benedict XIV: orthodoxy, personal holiness, learning, and explicit commendation by the highest Church authority. In theological discussion, particular respect is paid to the writings and opinions of those designated Doctors of the Church, because they are deemed to represent the Tradition in a noteworthy degree.

Among those counted Doctors of the Church, the earliest named are Saints Ambrose, Augustine, Jerome, and Gregory the Great, all representing the Western or Latin Church, to whom were added Basil the Great, Gregory of Nazianzen, John Chrysostom, and Athanasius of Alexandria, all of the Eastern or Greek Church. Those later declared Doctors of the Church include: Hilary of Poitiers, Cyril of Jerusalem, Cyril of Alexandria, Peter Chrysologus, Leo the Great, Ephraem of Syria, Isidore of Seville, John Damascene, Anselm of Canterbury, Bernard of Clairvaux, Albert the Great, Anthony of Padua, Thomas Aquinas, Bonaventure, Catherine of Siena, Teresa of Avila, John of the Cross, Peter Canisius, and Francis de Sales.

MONIKA K. HELLWIG

See also SAINTS; TRADITION.

DOCTRINE

Christians are united in faith by their acceptance of the *kerygma,* belief in the death–resurrection of Jesus the Christ (1 Cor 15:3-4). Although the *kerygma* is an expression of limitless Mystery, its appropriation by finite persons requires that its meaning be continually reinterpreted in light of the various historical and cultural situations in which the Church is incarnated. This is the process engaged in by the four evangelists, the Fathers, Mothers, and Doctors of the Church such as Sts. Irenaeus, Perpetua, Augustine, Thomas Aquinas, and Teresa of Avila, as well as by the various ecumenical and local councils of the Church, papal pronouncements, and encyclicals. The teachings enunciated in these various ways comprise the body of what is understood in the Church as doctrine. They are attempts to assist the Church in her ongoing struggle to remain faithful to the *kerygma.*

From these examples, characteristics of all Church doctrines may be derived. Doctrines are rooted in the Person of Christ, his words and deeds; they are faithful interpretations of the meaning of Jesus the Christ that are formulated in view of particular questions raised by particular ecclesial communities; each doctrine enunciates the truth but does not exhaust the truth; doctrines are shaped by the language, thought patterns, and concerns of the particular community or historical era in which they are formulated. From this it can be seen that the purpose of the whole complex of doctrinal expressions is to provide Christians with a worldview by means of which they may understand themselves in their relationship to the God of Jesus Christ, and to one another.

The vast majority of doctrines which shape Christian self-understanding have never been officially defined by the teaching office. Among such important but undefined doctrines are the importance of personal prayer and the imperatives to love one's neighbor and to be concerned for the poor. Since, however, members of the Church are the locus of sin as well as grace, it happens that not all teachings proposed to the community have been authentic. In such cases, the teaching authority of the Church has infallibly defined the parameters of authentic teaching. The most important examples are the pronouncements of the Christological and Trinitarian councils held during the first five centuries of Church history. Such infallibly enunciated doctrines are technically referred to as dogma.

From the earliest times, the Church has believed that its teachings are preserved by the Holy Spirit from error. This protection from error is recognized in the reciprocity that exists between those who exercise the office of teacher and those who recognize and receive such teaching. Thus, authentic doctrine is not extrinsic to the community but an expression of the community's insight into the meaning of the *kerygma.* To summarize, the primary function of Christian doctrine, even those infallibly defined, is to assist the community to live in fidelity to Christ. Therefore, they should be understood as helps to living life more fully rather than as defining juridical boundaries.

NANCY C. RING

See also DOCTRINE, DEVELOPMENT OF; KERYGMA.

DOCTRINE, DEVELOPMENT OF

Doctrinal development is the process whereby the teaching of the Bible in general, and the teaching of Jesus Christ in particular, has been interpreted ("developed") over the course of centuries to form the "official teaching" (doctrine) of the Church.

From a theological perspective, the problem of doctrinal development emerges from two premises: first, the teaching of Christ needs to be preached to all people of all times and all places; thus, Christ's teaching needs not only to be translated into different languages and expressed in different cultural settings, but also needs to respond to new questions and new problems; second is the belief that Christ was the "definitive revealer"—i.e., the fullness of revelation is given through Christ and no further revelation is to be expected; another way of expressing this belief is to say that revelation "closed" with the apostolic generation. Given these two premises, doctrine is understood (1) to develop in response to changing circumstances, (2) yet to do so without essentially changing the original revelation.

From an historical perspective, the Church has had to develop its "official teaching" (= doctrine) from the very beginning of its existence. For example, at the so-called "Council of Jerusalem" (Acts 15), the early Church needed to decide how Christians living in a pagan world should act in light of their belief in Christ; in other words, the teaching of Jesus needed to be developed to respond to a new situation. Similarly, at the First Ecumenical Council at Nicaea in 325, the bishops present had to decide how to describe the relationship of Jesus Christ and God the Father; in other words, the teaching of Scripture needed to be expressed in new terminology, which in this case became part of the Nicene Creed.

Although there have been many other instances of doctrinal development in the history of the Church, theologians first began to analyze the dimensions of doctrinal development in the nineteenth century. This theological investigation was undoubtedly influenced by the fact that the nineteenth century was a time of technological changes and scientific advances; for example, scientists like Charles Darwin saw evolution occurring in many fields. Simultaneously, there was renewed interest in the early Church, whose history showed the emergence of new doctrines to explain biblical teachings; theologians such as John Henry Newman began asking whether it was justifiable for the Church to amplify its "official teachings" if these doctrines were not explicitly in Scripture. In particular, the Roman Catholic Church proclaimed the "new dogmas" of the Immaculate Conception (1854) and the primacy and infallibility of the Roman Pontiff (1870); these dogmatic definitions led theologians to ask: Is the doctrine of the Church the same today as the teaching of the Bible, the teaching of Christ?

Three generic replies have been given to this question: "Yes" is the reply of "fundamentalists" who maintain that the Church has no *right* to teach anything that is not *explicitly* taught in the Bible; accordingly, fundamentalists generally reject the Marian and papal dogmas, since they are not literally mentioned in Scripture; in addition, fundamentalists frequently claim that the teaching of Scripture is immediately self-evident and applicable to today's problems and questions; thus, what is not explicitly taught by Scripture can never be a matter of "official Church teaching" but must be left to the individual to decide according to conscience.

"No" is the response of people who might be called "evolutionists" because they believe that the Church's teaching must continually evolve in response to new problems and questions. For example, evolutionists would see the papal dogmas as developing from the political crises of the nineteenth century in which the authority of the Church was seriously challenged; however, such dogmatic developments may in turn be modified or even erased by subsequent developments. In effect, evolutionists see Scripture as historically conditioned and in need of continual reinterpretation in light of changing circumstances. By implication, doctrines that were taught by the Church at one time in its history may need to be replaced by doctrines more appropriate to new circumstances.

Doctrinal development is not really a theological problem for "fundamentalists" who insist that doctrine should always be a restatement of what is explicitly taught in Scripture. Nor is doctrinal development a major issue for "evolutionists" who hold that doctrine is always evolving. Doctrinal development is a theological problem primarily for "developmentalists" who hold that the Church has the *right* and the *duty* to interpret the teaching of Scripture in response to new problems and new questions but without essentially changing the revelation given in Christ.

In effect, developmentalists reply both "Yes" and "No" to the question whether the Church's doctrine is the same as the teaching of the Bible. With fundamentalists, developmentalists agree that Scripture contains a universal message that is applicable in all circumstances, yet differ by maintaining that this message is not always explicit and so Scripture must be authoritatively interpreted. With evolutionists, developmentalists acknowledge that the teaching of Scripture is historically conditioned and so must be developed to deal with new problems and new questions, yet differ by insisting that such developments do not simply evolve in relation to new circumstances, but are authentic interpretations of the revelation given once and for all by Christ.

This *process* of interpreting Christian revelation—doctrinal development—has been explained by theologians in a number of different ways: (1) In some cases, the development of doctrine can be seen as a *logical* process; such is the case with the Church's teaching on the human will of Jesus: if Jesus is truly God and truly man, and if every man has a human will, then Jesus must have had a human will. This type of explanation is useful in those instances where doctrinal development is reducible to a logical pattern. While this type of explanation is very convincing, comparatively few cases of doctrinal development are so neatly logical. (2) In other cases, the development of doctrine seems to follow a *linguistic* process; for example, an idea that appears in Scripture needs to be explicated in new terminology. Such appears to have been the case with the scriptural description of the Word as being "with God" (John 1:1), which led to the expression in the Nicene Creed that the Word is "one in Being with the Father." However, if such a development appears merely semantic, it must be remembered that behind a change in words is a potential difference in meaning, and in fact, this formulation at Nicaea came only after lengthy debate. (3) Moreover, linguistic developments always occur as part of a more dynamic or *organic* process that is only partially expressible in words. Accordingly, theologians frequently compare the development of doctrine to human maturation with its interaction between heredity and environment. Just as an infant inherits his or her basic abilities, similarly the content of doctrine was essentially given through Christ. Yet just as an infant's inherited characteristics develop over the years, similarly the original doctrinal content has developed over the centuries. And just as it is possible to recognize "family features" as a youngster matures, similarly it is usually possible to see the resemblance of a doctrinal statement with a particular scriptural passage; for example, the doctrine of the Trinity can be seen in the gospel mandate to baptize in the name of the Father and the Son and the Holy Spirit (Matthew 28:19). (4) Yet not all cases of doctrinal development have such clear-cut antecedents; for example, Scripture does not provide such an obvious basis for the Marian dogmas of the Immaculate Conception and Assumption. In fact, the development of doctrine sometimes seems to have been more *circumstantial,* directly related to a particular situation in the history of the Church. For example, the early Christian community had to decide whether Gentiles who wished to become members needed to observe Jewish religious law; this question was decided when Peter received a vision which instructed him to welcome into the Christian community people of every race and nation (Acts 10:9-48).

In retrospect then, the *process* of doctrinal development can be seen to have followed at least four different patterns. Some doctrines seem to have followed one developmental process, while others have followed a different process; indeed, a specific doctrine may evidence more than one type of developmental process. While it is usually possible to describe the process after the fact, it is difficult to propose *criteria* for distinguishing genuine developments from erroneous interpretations: how does one *test* for genuine developments? (1) Perhaps the most convincing test is that of "logical sequence"—i.e., one can show that a particular doctrine can be "logically" deduced from a specific scriptural passage; however, this test is applicable to comparatively few doctrines, and even then such logic may become evident only after lengthy discussion. (2) In the case of linguistic development, one useful test is "preservation of type": does the new interpretation preserve the original meaning? While it may be evident that the basic meaning has been preserved, insofar as translations are usually only approximations, almost inevitably a new translation will include implications that are different from the original statement. (3) In regard to organic development, a useful test is "continuity of principles": for example, are the essential scriptural principles preserved in the process of development? However, in answering this question, it is not always easy to distinguish what is a matter of essential content and what is a matter of historically conditioned expression. (4) A similar difficulty arises in regard to circumstantial development, where what has developed may have little apparent resemblance to any specific passage in Scripture. Yet such a development may still be genuine, just as a small acorn may develop into a giant oak tree, even though they have little obvious resemblance.

Finally, while these theological criteria or "tests" can be useful in describing how specific doctrines have developed in the past, it is virtually impossible to use them to predict how any particular doctrine will develop in the future. Ultimately, the development of doctrine is part of the Holy Spirit's continuing guidance of the Church: if the Church is to interpret the revelation of Christ—a revelation given once and for all—without distorting its essential meaning, then the Church must be guided by the Holy Spirit.

Consequently, the Holy Spirit must empower the Church to distinguish authoritatively between genuine development and false teaching. In fact, it has sometimes taken the Church centuries to recognize officially that specific doctrines are authentic developments of the definitive revelation given by Christ. Moreover, in officially accepting such developments, the Church implicitly acknowledges that further developments are possible in the future.

JOHN FORD

See also DOCTRINE; DOGMA; ORTHODOXY; THEOLOGY, DOGMATIC.

DOGMA

Since the eighteenth century, the term "dogma" has been used for religious truth officially defined by the Church as divinely revealed.

From the origins of Christianity those exercising leadership within the community have accepted the responsibility of interpreting the meaning of God's revelation in Christ. They have done this for the purpose of engaging the minds and hearts of the followers of Christ in an existential encounter with truth. In New Testament writings as in the earliest documents of Christianity, such authoritative teachings were seldom referred to as dogma. The few New Testament and early Christian references to "dogma" allude to a particular decision of the community (Acts 16:4), Christian belief as a whole, or to the distinction between Christian and non-Christian beliefs. Throughout the medieval period, this situation prevailed. Even St. Thomas seldom referred to Christian beliefs as dogmas.

With the onset of modernity, however, Church leaders could no longer presume that the Christian worldview provided the framework for people's lives. Christian teachings came under attack by those proponents of the Enlightenment who reduced intelligible reality to the empirical and demonstrable. It was during this period of Church history that dogmatic statements began to attain the status and connotation that they hold today. In an attempt to respond to the prevailing culture, Church leaders promulgated the belief that revelation is a source of truth. Subsequently, they clearly defined particular Christian beliefs and did so in a propositional form that appealed to the intellect. In its further evolution, "dogma" came to refer to those statements explicitly set forth by the magisterium pertaining to divine, public, and official revelation, that is, Scripture and tradition. Indeed, a related development within the Church at this time was that of magisterial theology. This related development can be seen in the way Karl Rahner defines the current understanding of dogma as "A proposition which the Church explicitly propounds as revealed by God (DS 1972) in such a way that its denial is condemned by the Church as heresy and anathematized'' (CIC canon 751).

Today, dogma is understood as a very minimalist way of teaching. Contemporary dogmatic statements have as their purpose the elimination of error and the establishment of the parameters of belief. While this is a necessary function of authentic teaching, such statements are in no way commensurate with the totality of truth, Divine Mystery. Unless such statements are situated within the larger context of effective preaching and theological study, they seldom engage the heart in an existential commitment to Christian values. Because of this, they often contribute to the formation of legalistic and juridical mentalities.

Attention needs to be directed to the distinction between dogma and doctrine. Although these terms are often used interchangeably, dogma technically refers to a declarative statement that discloses revealed truth. Doctrines refer to explanations of how such truths may be understood. There may be several acceptable doctrines or explanations of a single dogma. It is on the level of doctrine, not of dogma, that the Church admits of pluralism.

NANCY C. RING

See also DOCTRINE, DEVELOPMENT OF; THEOLOGY, DOGMATIC.

DOGMATIC THEOLOGY

See THEOLOGY, DOGMATIC.

DOHERTY, CATHERINE DE HUECK (1896–1985)

Catherine de Hueck Doherty (nee Kolyschkine) was born in Nijni-Novgorod, Russia, 1896, and died in Combermere, Ontario, 14 December 1985, surrounded by the Madonna House community which she had founded. She was baptized and raised in the Russian Orthodox Church, but there was Roman Catholicism on her paternal Polish grandmother's side of the family. She was educated in a Catholic school in Alexandria, Egypt, during some of the most formative years of her young life. This "breathing with the two lungs of East and West" at an early age

Catherine de Hueck Doherty

would prove very significant for her future vocation in the Church.

Married in 1912, she and her husband Boris de Hueck were involved in the First World War. Escaping from the Red Peril, they enlisted in the abortive attempt of the White army to repel the Reds, only to flee again and make their way to England. Here Catherine made her profession of faith in the Catholic Church. Thus, before she was twenty-five, she had been exposed to war, hunger, exile, and had experienced the terrible consequences of anti-God doctrine. Having experienced the collapse of human ideologies, she would dedicate her life to the "restoration of all things in Christ."

Arriving in Toronto, Ontario, in 1921, she assisted refugees. In the early 1930s she established the first "Friendship House" to aid those hit by the Depression with food, clothing, and good Christian literature. She was one of the Catholic lay pioneers in teaching and seeking to implement the social encyclicals of the popes. She was instrumental in founding the *Social Forum,* the first Catholic newspaper in Canada dedicated to social issues.

In 1938 she established a similar house in Harlem, then Chicago and several other American cities, being one of the pioneers in interracial justice in America. Throughout the years she wrote numerous articles challenging clergy and laity to live the gospel in the social sphere.

Her first marriage having been annulled, in 1947 she and her second husband, Eddie Doherty, the famous newspaperman, came to Combermere, to help with the needs of the area by establishng a rural settlement house, and where the Madonna House community was founded and grew. This community, and the many books she wrote (including the world classic, *Poustinia*), are her greatest contributions to the Church in Canada.

Madonna House is one of the new communities of consecrated life, composed of priests and laypersons who promise the evangelical counsels of poverty, chastity, and obedience. All of Catherine's life and experience, all her writings, all that the Lord taught her throughout her long pilgrimage, flowed into the formation of this community. Its spirituality is a blend of Eastern and Western Christianity, and seeks to be a bridge of unity among all peoples. The Combermere community and its twenty-five missions have an outreach to the poor in material and spiritual resources. The community itself strives to be an expression of the living Church, a witness to the Trinitarian life of God.

Catherine had witnessed the destruction of Christian culture, both in Russia and in the West. She sought to make Madonna House a place where this culture could again be lived and experienced, and where people could come to drink from the wells of our great Christian traditions. The Madonna House community, and the worldwide influence of Catherine's teachings, is the crowning of her life's work, which the Lord has fashioned for the life and renewal of the Church and world today.

ROBERT WILD

See also CANADA, THE CATHOLIC CHURCH IN; CHURCH, THE; LAITY, THEOLOGY OF THE.

DÖLLINGER, JOHANN JOSEPH IGNAZ VON (1799–1891)

Church historian, theologian, he was born in Bamberg, Germany, on 28 February 1799. He was ordained a priest in 1822, did parochial work and then began teaching Church history at Aschaffenburg in 1823. In 1826 he received a doctorate from the University of Landshut, and then was appointed the professor of Church history at the University of Munich where he remained until 1873.

Döllinger authored some important historical works such as *Hippolytus and Callistus* (1853) and *Christentum und Kirche* (1860). He was critical of Protestantism and liberalism, claiming that they were not true to the tradition. He was conservative in his approach to theology, early in his career associating himself with Franz von Baader and Joseph von Görres, but the influence of John Henry Newman and Lord Acton helped to broaden his approach. He soon began to advocate more independence from Rome for the German bishops, the education of clerical students at universities rather than at separate seminaries, and he questioned the existence of the Papal States. He disliked the revival of Scholasticism (especially in its more reactionary form) and preferred a more historical approach to theology. The publication of the *Syllabus of Errors* in 1864 made him more distrustful of Roman authorities, and eventually one of his works was placed on the Index of Forbidden Books. The great crisis of his life came in 1870 when he rejected Vatican Council I's teaching on papal infallibility.

Döllinger was excommunicated by the archbishop of Munich in 1871 because of his radical views and then lost his professorship. However, he was befriended by King Ludwig II of Bavaria, and in 1873 he was named president of the Royal Bavarian Academy of Sciences in recognition of his past achievements. In these later years he became sympathetic to the Old Catholics, though never formally joining them. He continued to attend Mass though he stopped celebrating it, and he received the last rites from an Old Catholic priest before he died.

ANTHONY D. ANDREASSI

See also SYLLABUS OF ERRORS; VATICAN COUNCIL I.

DOMINIC, ST. (1172–1221)

Dominic de Guzman was born in Caleruega, Spain, ca. 1172, of a family of minor nobility. At an early age he was sent to school in Palencia in care of his uncle. During this period, he became noted for his studious and ascetical life. Around age twenty-four, Dominic joined the chapter of Augustinian Canons at the Cathedral of Osma, Spain, under the episcopate of Diego of Osma. His personal holiness, intelligence, and administrative abilities eventually commended him to his brethren who chose him as subprior.

In 1205, while accompanying Bishop Diego on a diplomatic mission to Denmark, which took them through southern France, Dominic became aware of the difficulties of the local Church in countering the preachers and growth of the Albigensian sects. He and Bishop Diego met with the officially delegated preachers, Cistercian abbots, and advised them to adopt simpler and poorer lifestyles to lend credence to their preaching, in the same way as the heretical preachers! When Diego returned to his diocese, Dominic remained to continue his itinerant preaching ministry. His ability to meet a wide variety of people, coupled with a zeal for preaching, organizational talent, and personal holiness attracted a small group of disciples.

With the help of the bishop of Toulouse, France, Dominic organized his followers into a group called "The Holy Preaching." Realizing the implications of his vision, he sought the approval of Popes Innocent III and Honorius III for his new work. By doing this, he was able to expand the focus of the group of preachers from a local area to the universal Church.

St. Dominic, detail, by Fra Angelico, San Marco, Florence

On 22 December 1216, Pope Honorius III issued a papal bull that, in effect, established an entirely new form of religious and apostolic life. The establishment of the Dominican Order, along with the newly founded Franciscans, marked the beginning of the movement of mendicant friars—mobile, unattached to one monastery, begging for food (instead of manual labor) and representing a new approach to apostolic ministry because they were exempt from control by the local bishop. Dominic's order was unique in receiving preaching as its officially designated mission.

Upon receiving approval of his order and mission, Dominic took the bold step of dividing the small group and sending them to the newly developing university centers, especially Paris and Bologna. By 1221, the fundamental structures of the order were in place and Dominic was traveling from house to house to encourage and strengthen the rapidly expanding number of friars. By taking on the additional mission of preaching a crusade in Lombardy in 1221, he became exhausted and fatally ill. He died on 6 August 1221, in Bologna, Italy, where he is buried. He was canonized in 1234.

R. B. WILLIAMS, O.P.

See also ALBIGENSES; DOMINICANS; MENDICANT ORDERS.

DOMINICAN SISTERS OF THE PERPETUAL ROSARY

The Dominican Sisters of the Perpetual Rosary are a diocesan, cloistered, contemplative institute of consecrated life in the Church. Founded on 20 May 1880, at Calais, France, by Damien Saintourens, O.P., then Director of the Association of the Perpetual Rosary for the Dominican Province of France, the congregation was intended to serve as a firm foundation and administrative center for the Perpetual Rosary movement, "a beautiful and notable example for the Associates of the Rosary," as the Founder recorded in his *Memoirs.* Mother Rose of St. Mary Wehrlé, a member of the contemplative Dominican monastery of Mauleon, France, formed the first postulants of the institute in the religious life and established foundations in Belgium, France, and the United States. She is regarded as cofoundress.

As members of the Order of Preachers, Perpetual Rosary Sisters proclaim the gospel by their way of life. They form a guard of honor for the Blessed Virgin Mary, succeeding one another day and night in the hourly praying of the rosary. The sisters profess perpetual vows of poverty, chastity, and obedience, consecrating themselves totally to God.

The sisters follow the monastic tradition, as defined by St. Dominic for the first contemplative sisters of the order. Their practice of silence and solitude fosters contemplative prayer and growth in the spiritual life. The Liturgy of the Word and the Eucharist is the center of their spirituality. As a continuation of the Eucharistic celebration the sisters pray the Liturgy of Hours together in choir. Each sister has at least one hour a day for private prayer. She also sets aside time for reading and pondering the Scripture and sacred doctrine.

The apostolate of the institute, intercessory prayer and contemplation of the mysteries of the rosary, the mysteries of Christian faith, serves the Church and the world. The communal life of the sisters witnesses to the presence of Christ's love in the midst of his people.

In common with all Dominicans, Perpetual Rosary Sisters follow the Rule of St. Augustine. Each community as an independent institute develops its own constitutions under the jurisdiction and protection of the local diocesan bishop. The prioress, elected by members of the community chapter, exercises the highest internal authority.

Since 1880, Perpetual Rosary monasteries have been founded in Belgium, France, Portugal, the United States, the Philippines, Japan, and Kenya.

JOANNA HASTINGS, O.P.

See also DOMINICANS; ROSARY.

DOMINICANS

In the broad sense, "Dominicans" refers to a "family" of friars (clerical and nonclerical—6700+), cloistered nuns (4400), professed sisters in apostolic congregations (36,000) and laity (70,000), all of whom consider St. Dominic to be their founder and inspiration. In a narrower sense, "Dominicans" refers to the Order of Friars Preachers (O. P.), founded by St. Dominic de Guzman and given official approbation by Pope Honorius III on 22 December 1216. Understood this way, the order is primarily clerical but it also includes nonordained friars called Cooperator Brothers.

The establishment of the Dominicans in the early thirteenth century occurred in a time of profound cultural transition in Europe from feudal to centralized forms of government (civil and ecclesiastical), from rural to urban economic structures, and from monastic schools to urban universities. In terms of popular religious expression, lay movements of preachers were having a broad impact.

The foundation of the order was the result of a need for mobile educated preachers, who imitated the early apostolic community (Acts 2:42-47) in their lifestyle and ministry, to counteract the preaching of various heretical sects, called Albigensians, in southern France. St. Dominic began by gathering a few associates for the preaching in the region around Toulouse, but his vision soon expanded to the concept of a new form of religious life which contrasted sharply in its flexibility and mission from the established and recognized monasticism of the time. He sought and obtained papal approval for his Order of Preachers and then made the bold decision to divide the small group and sent them to major urban and university centers beyond the confines of the original territory in southern France.

The Dominican Order has a number of unique characteristics, all of which were in place by the time of Dominic's death (1221). It is the only religious order in the Church which has received explicitly as its mission the ministry of preaching. Although the order adopted the Rule of St. Augustine in response to legislation by the Fourth Lateran Council (1215), it is primarily governed by constitutions which establish a system of democratic government from the local to the international level. This system of legislative power (local, provincial and general chapters) and elected executive authority (priors, provincial, and the Master of the Order) provides a balance of power between grassroots membership and the elected leadership. Structurally, the order is divided into territorial provinces, vice-provinces and regional vicariates.

Dominican life is a balance of apostolic work and contemplative community life. Study, prayer, vowed community life, and ministry must all be balanced (and in tension) with each other. The friars make a single vow of obedience to the Master of the Order according to the constitutions of the order and the Rule of St. Augustine. The commitment to lifetime study is another unique constitutional element.

From its beginnings, the Dominican Order has been dedicated to preaching and study, which has given it a missionary thrust and a continuing presence in academic settings, especially in philosophy, theology and Scripture. Its dedication to theological excellence led to accomplishments such as the *Summa Theologiae* of St. Thomas Aquinas and controversial involvement in the Inquisition. Well-known members besides St. Dominic include St. Thomas Aquinas, St. Albert the Great, St. Vincent Ferrer, St. Martin de Porres, (bl.) Fra Angelico, Pope St. Pius V, Girolamo Savonarola, and, in more recent times, Frs. M.-J. Lagrange, R. Garrigou-Lagrange, M.-J. Chenu, Yves Congar and E. Schillebeeckx.

The spiritual and apostolic ministry of the Dominican cloistered nuns, apostolic sisters, and laity has included such women as St. Catherine of Siena, St. Margaret of Hungary and St. Rose of Lima.

R. B. WILLIAMS, O.P.

See also MENDICANT ORDERS; PREACHING.

DONATISM

An heretical and schismatic movement centered in the Churches of North Africa in the fourth and fifth centuries. After the persecution of Diocletian, the last general persecution of Christians in the Roman Empire, some bishops were accused of handing over holy books on demand to the imperial authorities; their consecration of other bishops was contested and rival bishops were chosen in place of any whose line of succession was thus seen as invalidated. One of these rivals was the powerful Donatus the Great (d. ca. 355) for whom the movement was named. The group rallied many of the North African Christians to their cause because they claimed to be the authentic Church of the martyrs, a Church of the pure. They were schismatic because they set up a rival Church to the one acknowledged by the communion of bishops of the time. They are also recognized in retrospect as heretical because they based the validity of sacraments on the personal holiness and integrity of those who ministered or presided. This gave the occasion for the theology of sacraments worked out by Augustine of Hippo: the efficacy of sacraments does not depend on the personal qualities of the minister of the sacrament but on the holiness of Christ whose actions the sacraments essentially are. Likewise, the holiness of the Church is not dependent on the purity of the members (who will always be struggling and in need of continuous conversion) because the holiness of the Church is essentially that of Christ. Augustine was consistent in this and therefore would not allow those coming to his local Church from a schismatic community to be rebaptized because he acknowledged the validity of their baptism by schismatic ministers. In modern times this has provided an important basis for ecumenism.

MONIKA K. HELLWIG

See also AUGUSTINE, ST.; HERESY/HERETICS; SCHISM.

DOOLEY, THOMAS (1927–1961)

Doctor and author; born in 1927 in St. Louis, he attended the University of Notre Dame for two years before interrupting his studies to join the Navy medical service in which he served from 1944 to 1946.

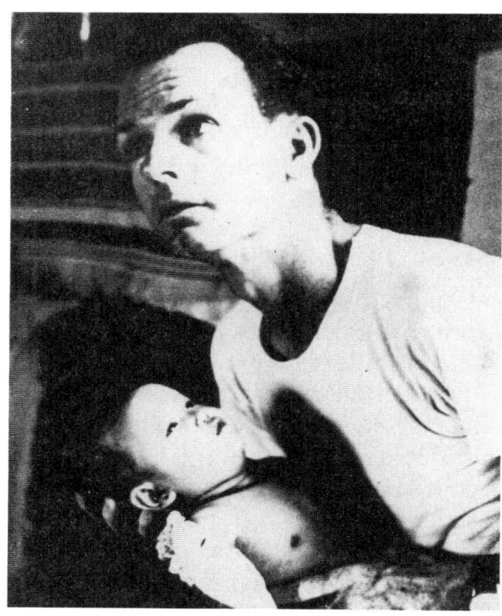

Dr. Thomas Dooley

After graduating from Notre Dame, he attended St. Louis University School of Medicine, receiving his M.D. degree in 1953. He became a medical intern on the U.S.S. *Montague*—stationed off the Vietnamese coast—and later worked in Haiphong, where he oversaw refugee camps housing an estimated 600,000 destitute, indigenous people fleeing the Viet Minh. Dooley's dedication and compassion inspired many. His experiences in Vietnam were recorded in his *Deliver Us from Evil* (1956), which became a best seller in the United States and made him a national hero.

With the help of Dr. Peter Comanduras, he founded in 1958 the Medical International Cooperation Organization (MEDICO), a relief agency for those stricken by war. MEDICO was later merged with CARE, Inc. Dooley donated all earnings from his books, as well as his substantial medical and organizational skills, to MEDICO. He died of cancer in New York on 18 January 1961, one day after his thirty-fourth birthday. Dooley's other books are: *The Edge of Tomorrow* (1958), *The Night They Burned the Mountain* (1960), *Dr. Tom Dooley, My Story* (1960), and *Dr. Tom Dooley's Three Great Books. Before I Sleep* (1961) is the story of his last days, told by those closest to him at the time.

JOSEPH QUINN

See also AMERICAN CATHOLICISM.

DOXOLOGY

[fr. Gk. *doxa* ("glory") and *logos* ("word")] A hymn or formula giving praise to God. "Glory to God in the Highest," sung or recited during Mass, is referred to as the greater doxology; "Glory be to the Father, and to the Son, and to the Holy Spirit," is known as the lesser doxology. There are also metrical forms of the doxology which have been added to various hymns.

JOSEPH QUINN

See also GLORIA IN EXCELSIS DEO; GLORIA PATRI; HYMNS.

DREXEL, BLESSED KATHERINE (1858–1955)

She was born in Philadelphia to Francis Drexel and Hannah Langstroth. (*His* father had been a Tyrolese

Mother Katherine Drexel

artist and musician.) In 1885, the twenty-seven-year-old Katherine inherited a fortune (her father had been a leading banker) and devoted it to the foundation and development of the Sisters of the Blessed Sacrament for the purpose of working among the Native Americans and the blacks. The congregation had forty-nine houses at the time of her death. Active in missionary endeavors, she developed teachers and catechists, built sixty-three schools, including Xavier University of New Orleans. She died in Pennsylvania at the age of ninety-seven. Feast day, 3 March.

DAVID BRYAN

DUCCIO DI BUONINSEGNA (fl. 1278–1318)

The greatest of the painters of the Sienese school, he flourished between 1278 and 1318. While almost nothing is known about Duccio's life or training, numerous panel paintings survive. Beginning with typically Byzantine models, Duccio seems to infuse them with a feeling for the nobility of the common people as preached by the Franciscans and Dominicans. This is brought out by the grace and uplifting

"Maestà," detail, by Duccio di Buoninsegna, oil painting, Uffizi Gallery, Florence

emotion of his lines and forms, all conveyed in gorgeous colors. Like Giotto, he could catch the essence of a narrative, when the conventions of the day permitted it, portraying various human relationships with a fine sense of drama. Best known is his two-sided *Maestà* for the great altar of Siena Cathedral. The front side presents *The Virgin and Child enthroned* surrounded by the angels and patron saints of Siena. The work was undoubtedly to serve the faithful as an icon, but accompanying panels on the life of Christ, together with others on the passion and resurrection (on the back) give scope to Duccio's narrative abilities. His style was supreme in the Sienese School for two centuries.

DAVID BRYAN

See also ART, CHRISTIAN.

DUE PROCESS

Due process is a fundamental right in English law and is enshrined in the Constitution of the United States. It guarantees that persons will not be deprived of life, liberty, or property without the observance of all pertinent legal procedures and safeguards.

The Church, particularly since the 1963 encyclical of Pope John XXIII, *Pacem in Terris,* has been increasingly responsive to the rights of the human person, rights which are not conferred by the Church or by governments but flow directly from human nature and which are "therefore universal, inviolable and inalienable" (no. 9). As a consequence, human persons are entitled to a juridical protection of their rights, "a protection that should be efficacious, impartial and inspired by the true norms of justice" (no. 27).

In 1967, the Synod of Bishops called for new administrative procedures to give greater protection to all those affected by administrative actions in the Church. To deal with cases where persons may feel that they have been treated unfairly, the National Council of Catholic Bishops, aided by the Canon Law Society of America, approved a set of arbitration procedures in 1969 which were subsequently ratified by the Holy See (see NCCB, *On Due Process,* rev. ed., Washington, 1972). The 1971 Synod of Bishops declared that, if the Church was to preach justice to others, court procedures in the Church itself should manifestly exhibit justice.

The 1983 Code of Canon Law specifies that all Christians have a right, if they are summoned before an ecclesiastical judge, that any judgment passed on them will be in accordance with the prescriptions of the law, applied with equity (c. 221, §2).

WILLIAM C. McFADDEN, S.J.

See also CANON LAW.

DUFF, FRANK (1879–1980)

Born into a middle-class family on 7 June 1879, he founded the Legion of Mary on 7 September 1921 and died on 7 November 1980. It was a long life, active to the end. Three nights before his death he attended an interfaith meeting; for the weekend he had planned a typical form of recreation, a cycling tour around Dublin bay; he died on the afternoon of Friday, while resting after a morning in which he had attended two Masses.

He entered government service after leaving high school, and helped in the changeover to native administration after the Anglo-Irish Treaty of 1921. His first contact with the lay apostolate was as a member of the St. Vincent de Paul Society. When the Legion of Mary came into existence he used his organizational experience from the older association. Membership implied attendance at a weekly meeting, reports on work undertaken, and study of the *Handbook.* This official text of the Legion was Duff's work. It was imbued with the spirit and letter of the book which had changed his life, Louis Marie Grignion de Montfort's *True Devotion to the Blessed Virgin Mary.* The ideas of this classic of Marian spirituality, especially the doctrine that Mary is the Mediatress of all graces, formed the essential fabric of legionary thinking. Distinctive in the new association was the set of prescribed prayers, at the beginning, middle, and conclusion of every meeting. The rosary was central in the program of prayer. Frank Duff was convinced that the call to the apostolate was intrinsic to Christian life. The Legion was prepared to undertake any form of the apostolate except the giving of material aid. At its inception work was centered on hostels to rescue and rehabilitate Dublin prostitutes, to provide shelter for the homeless, and a home for unmarried mothers. These hostels were to serve as a model for other cities with similar problems. Other activities fostered by the Legion were also apostolic: diffusion of Catholic literature, sessions for would-be converts, assistance to parochial activities, etc.

He was absorbed by the idea of the Church as Christ's Mystical Body when this reality was not widely appreciated within the Catholic community. His prayer and reflection also led him to deeper appreciation of the role of the Holy Spirit. The legionary promise was made not to Our Lady but to the Holy Spirit.

As the association took on worldwide dimensions, reaching 1,300 dioceses, the burden on Frank Duff increased. Contact with the different units involved enormous correspondence—the final estimate may be well over 100,000 letters. Expansion was principally the work of envoys, who reported regularly to the governing body, and through voluntary teams who had an umbrella title, *Peregrinatio pro Christo.*

Frank Duff had to contend with ecclesiastical opposition; he was singularly frustrated by supervision

Frank Duff

of his writing and in the suppression of two ventures which anticipated Vatican II—The Mercier Society for dialogue with Protestants, and The Pillar of Fire Society for dialogue with Jews.

Among his writings are: *Souls at Stake* (1948); *The Spirit of the Legion of Mary* (1956); *Miracles on Tap* (1962); *Mary Shall Reign* (1961); *Walk with Mary. Virgo Praedicanda* (1967); *The Woman in Genesis* (1976).

MICHAEL O'CARROLL, C.S.Sp.

See also LEGION OF MARY.

DUKE, ARCHBISHOP WILLIAM MARK (1879–1964)

As archbishop of Vancouver, William Mark Duke did more than any other to form the character of the archdiocese. The development of the Church in Canada generally took place in three stages: the missionary stage, an agricultural, familial and religious stage, which overlapped the first, and finally the development of the secular society built on the agricultural one. In British Columbia, where the missionary period was the time of the great work of the Oblates of Mary Immaculate, the second stage never really came about; with the completion of the railroad in 1886 the province moved rapidly into an urban and secular society. The Archdiocese of Vancouver was established in 1908, the first archbishop being Augustin Dontenwill, the third of the Oblate bishops of the area. On the day after his appointment, however, Dontenwill was elected superior general of the Oblates, a position which required him to live in Rome.

Archbishop Neil McNeil, 1910–1912, saw the need to face the rapid growth of population—the census of 1911 showed a non-native population more than five times as great as that of twenty years before—and the character of that growth, shown by the fact that seven out of ten adults were men. McNeil tried to promote settlement of Catholic families, but two things made his best efforts unsuccessful: he was moved to the See of Toronto after barely two years in office and in the following year the collapse of the boom in land values around Vancouver destroyed his investments. The third archbishop, Timothy Casey, 1912–1931, had been bishop of Saint John, New Brunswick. Vancouver was for him an alien and unhappy place. Hounded by debt and by illness, he was never able to give real direction to the archdiocese. It was left to his successor to do this.

Archbishop Duke was also from Saint John, having been ordained there by Bishop Casey in 1902. He came to Vancouver in 1928 as coadjutor, which gave him three years to observe the situation before he succeeded to office. He saw many needs.

The clergy needed reinvigoration and rejuvenation. To accomplish this Duke moved quickly to instill a strong spirit of discipline among the priests—not for nothing was he called "the Iron Duke"—using the spartan archbishop's palace he opened at the cathedral as a model and training ground. He recruited priests from elsewhere, and opened a seminary to train priests from the archdiocese itself, the first classes being held during his first year in office. Priests were needed to serve new parishes; of sixty-five parishes in the archdiocese today, thirty-eight were founded in Duke's time. He had a special concern for ethnic communities—most of the parishes he founded in Vancouver itself were for such groups—and for the needs of the rapidly growing suburbs.

Faced with the Great Depression in the first decade of his episcopate, he brought vigorous direction to the charitable efforts already underway by establishing, in one of his first acts, the umbrella organization of Catholic Charities. The hard times made the burden of debt on the archdiocesan treasury even heavier than it had been, but Duke's frugality and determination made them also times of new undertakings.

He saw the need and now the possibility to establish a family-based Church; by 1931 there were seventy-five women for each one hundred men, and by the end of Duke's time the proportion would be normal. It was urgent for the Church to develop its schools. With an increasing tempo, new schools were established and existing ones refurbished and enlarged. In British Columbia this had to be done without any aid from the government. The main thrust was for elementary schools, but several high schools and St. Mark's College at the University of British Columbia also testified to the archbishop's perseverance in his dreams. He died in Vancouver on 11 March 1964, just as Vatican II was ushering in a new time.

J. HANRAHAN, C.S.B.

See also CANADA, THE CATHOLIC CHURCH IN.

DUNS SCOTUS, JOHN (ca. 1268–1308)

A Scot, a Franciscan, a philosopher and theologian, who taught at Cambridge, Oxford, Paris and Cologne, he ranks among the most original and independent thinkers of his era. He disagreed with the teaching of Thomas Aquinas on a variety of issues. In the Thomistic system, reason and knowledge predominate; for Duns Scotus, love and will held pride of place. For Thomas, natural law rests on the mind of God; for Duns Scotus, it depends on the will of God and, consequently, is not immutable. Aquinas held that the beatitude of the souls in heaven was an intellectual vision of God; Dun Scotus held that this beatitude was purely an act of love. Scotus had a profound influence on the Franciscan attitudes and on centuries of Catholic thinkers down to the Reformation. Unlike Aquinas, Duns Scotus was an ardent proponent of the Immaculate Conception of Mary, and he was the first major theologian to take that stand without reservation.

MICHAEL GLAZIER

See also MIDDLE AGES, THE; SCHOLASTICISM; THEOLOGY.

DURROW, BOOK OF

See KELLS, BOOK OF.

E

EASTER

See LITURGY; PASCHAL MYSTERY.

EASTER VIGIL

See LITURGY; PASCHAL MYSTERY; VIGIL.

EASTERN CATHOLIC CHURCHES

Christianity arose in the context of one of history's greatest political entities, the Roman Empire. Despite the enmity of the Roman authorities to the new religious movement, the political, communication, and transportation system of the Empire provided the adherents of Christianity with the means to disseminate their message throughout the civilized world. With the death of Emperor Theodosius I in A.D. 395, the Roman Empire was divided into two empires, the Eastern Empire and the Western Empire. The term *Eastern Church* refers to those Christian Churches which trace their origins to one of the major metropolitan centers of the Eastern Roman Empire, namely Alexandria, Antioch, and Constantinople. The term *Eastern Catholic Church* specifically refers to the Churches which recognize the primacy of the Bishop of Rome.

While the Church had suffered earlier heresies and schisms, two fifth-century Christological controversies resulted in divisions of the Eastern Churches that remain today. The first dispute regarded the divine personality of Christ, defined at the Council of Ephesus in 431; opponents of this position, called Nestorians (after Nestorius, their leading advocate) broke communion with the rest of the Christian Churches and developed an independent ecclesial structure. The second dispute regarded the divine and human natures of Christ and was defined at the Council of Chalcedon in 451. Opponents of this position, known as Monophysites ("one nature") broke away and established their own independent hierarchies. During the period in which these disputes arose, the Roman emperors had assumed the role of protector of the Church and felt it was incumbent on them to maintain unity inasmuch as ecclesial divisions could also result in imperial divisions. It is ironic that the legalistic method adopted at both councils, i.e., an articulate definition of doctrine that could be agreed upon by everyone, perhaps contributed to the solidification of opposing positions and ecclesial divisions.

Those Eastern Christians who remained loyal to the Christological positions of the imperial court of Constantinople were known as *royalists* or *melkites* (after the Syriac term, *malek* = "king"). Eventually a division arose also within their ranks. With time the political division of the Roman Empire into East and West also became manifested in a "parting of ways" linguistically, culturally, and eventually ecclesiastically. The separation of the Eastern and Western Churches is anachronistically identified with the mutual excommunication of the Pope of Rome and the Patriarch of Constantinople in 1054.

"Christ and Saint Menas," Coptic icon, 6th century

The consequence of these heresies and schisms was that between the eleventh and sixteenth centuries, the great majority of the Eastern Churches were not in communion with the Roman Church. The few exceptions were the Maronites (whose origins are Antioch and modern-day Lebanon), Italo-Albanians in southern Italy and the island of Sicily, and Armenians in modern Lebanon and Syria who trace their union to Rome in the twelfth-century.

Formal reconciliations between Rome and Constantinople were reached at the Councils of Lyons (1274) and Florence (1431–1445), but were short-lived because of their unpopularity. The Catholic reform movement, officially initiated at the Council of Trent (1545–1563), resulted in enthusiastic missionary activities on the part of the Jesuits, Franciscans, Capuchins, and Dominicans. The arrival of Catholic missionaries to the Eastern Churches was usually welcomed by the bishops, clergy and laity of these Churches, who desired protection against the oppression of the agents of the Ottoman government. The Eastern Churches were assured that their communities would continue to exist if they accepted Catholic dogmatic positions and submitted to the authority of the pope. The patriarchs, bishops, and monasteries were also eager to have clerics attend Catholic colleges and universities in Europe, because centers of higher ecclesiastical studies had almost disappeared in the region. The Church of Rome appeared not only as richer and better organized, but also as eager to offer assistance to these Churches.

The Decree on the Eastern Catholic Churches (*Orientalium Ecclesiarum*), promulgated by Vatican Council II on 21 November 1964, opens with the statement that the Catholic Church treasures the traditions of the Eastern Churches as a patrimony of the Church of Christ. After emphasizing the equality of all the Churches of the East and West, the decree mandates the preservation and advancement of the various Churches and treats certain specific issues pertinent to the Eastern Churches. With regard to ecumenism, the Eastern Catholic Churches are given the special responsibility to promote the unity of all Christians, especially the Eastern non-Catholic Churches.

On 18 October 1990, Pope John Paul II promulgated the *Code of Canons of the Eastern Churches,* the common law of the twenty-one Eastern Catholic autonomous (*sui iuris*) Churches.

According to the *Code of Canons of the Eastern Churches*, Eastern Catholic Churches are categorized according to the status of their chief hierarchs. There are four categories: patriarchal; (cc. 55-150); major archiepiscopal (cc. 151-154); metropolitan and other Churches *sui iuris* (cc. 155-176).

The Catholic Church is currently comprised of twenty-two autonomous Churches (*ecclesiae sui iuris*) which enjoy a status of relative independent self-governance vis-à-vis the Roman Pontiff with whom they are in full communion and in whose person universal communion is realized. Only one of these Churches observes the Latin Rite; the other twenty-one autonomous Churches observe a specific rite derived from one of the five major Eastern traditions: the Alexandrian, Antiochene, Constantinopolitan, East Syrian (Chaldean) and Armenian.

The following is a list of the Eastern Catholic Churches, their hierarchical status and estimated population (G. Nedungatt, *The Spirit of the Eastern Code,* p. 62).

Traditions	Churches	Status	Membership
I. Alexandrian	1. Coptic	Patr.	166,953
	2. Ethiopian	Metr.	132,697
II. Antiochene	3. Syrian	Patr.	185,870
	4. Maronite	Patr.	2,176,152
	5. Syro-Malankara	Metr.	295,467

Traditions	Churches	Status		Membership
III. Armenian	6. Armenian	Patr.		142,853
IV. Chaldean	7. Chaldean	Patr.		628,250
	8. Malabar	Major Abp.		2,939,521
V. Constantinopolitan (Byzantine)	9. Belorussian	Ex. Ap.	(1940)	30,000
	10. Bulgarian	Ex. Ap.		15,000
	11. Greek	Ex. Ap.		2,300
	12. Hungarian	Ep.		252,840
	13. Italo-Albanian	2 Ep. + Monast.		61,597
	14. Melkite	Patr.		1,146,778
	15. Romanian	Metr. (in 1948)		1,562,979
	16. Ruthenian	Metr. 268,161		+ 461,555
	17. Slovak	Ep.		400,000
	18. Ukrainian	Major ABp.		4,194,900
	19. Krizevci	Ep.		48,770
	20. Albanian	Admin. Ap.		?
	21. Russian	2 Exarchates		?

JOHN D. FARIS

See also CHURCH, THE; EASTERN CHURCHES.

EASTERN CHURCHES

Bitter theological struggles and breaks of ecclesial communion followed the patristic councils of Ephesus (431) and Chalcedon (451). The origin of these schisms of the fifth century is found in the nonacceptance of the conciliar decisions by Churches that were culturally different from the majority present at these councils. Some of these Churches may not even have been informed that these councils were being held, due to their isolation at, or beyond, the extreme eastern frontier of the Roman Empire. The doctrine of Ephesus—that Mary should be called *Theotokos* (Mother of God) —was rejected by supporters of Nestorius, deposed by the council from his see as patriarch of Constantinople. These communities are often called Nestorian. The first Ancient Orthodox Churches are therefore the Nestorian or East Syrian Churches, originally located at the border of the Roman and the Persian Empires. Syrian-speaking rather than Greek-speaking, they were never familiar with Greek or Latin theology. There existed flourishing Nestorian communities in Arabia before the advent of Islam. As missionaries from East Syria brought the gospel to the Malabar Coast of India at an early time, the old Church of India was Nestorian, and China itself had thriving Nestorian communities, which however vanished in early modern times.

Partial reunions with the Bishop of Rome and acceptance of the Chalcedonian formulation gave birth to the Chaldaean Church in 1545 and 1552 (located mainly in Irak), and to the Syro-Malabar Catholic Church in 1599 (in Kerala, India).

Meanwhile, the doctrine of Chalcedon about Christ was rejected by other bishops and monks, who followed the Council of Ephesus II (449) that had been repudiated by most of the Greeks and all of the Latins. For the Chalcedonians the Lord Jesus existed in two natures, divine and human, united in the one person. The opponents of Chalcedon were called "Monophysites" by their adversaries because they espoused the formula of St. Cyril, *mia physis* ("one nature incarnate of the divine Logos") rather than the formula of "two natures" approved at Chalcedon. Widely popular in the patriarchates of Alexandria and of Antioch, this position became normative in many Churches of Egypt, West Syria, Ethiopia, and finally in Armenia. A large section of the Christians of India accepted this doctrine when West Syrian missionaries reached their area; these "Christians of St. Thomas,'' however, underwent many divisions and subdivisions in later times.

The second group of Ancient Orthodox Churches is thus made of a variety of rites. The Copts, originally of the patriarchate of Alexandria in Egypt, follow a liturgy of Alexandrian origin. They brought the gospel early to Nubia (the Sudan) and Ethiopia. The Jacobites—named after St. Jacob Baradaeus (ca. 500–578) who saved their Church from extinction in the persecution of Emperor Justinian (d. 665)

—were originally in West Syria (patriarchate of Antioch). Their liturgies are of basically Antiochene type. Located in the western and southern Caucasus mountains, the Armenians, or Armenian Gregorians—named after St. Gregory the Illuminator (d. ca. 325)—follow a liturgy of their own that has incorporated elements coming from the liturgies of Antioch, Jerusalem, and Byzantium.

Partial reunions with the See of Rome gave birth to Coptic (in 1552), Syriac (in 1662), Armenian (in 1740), Ethiopian (1839), and Syro-Malankar (in 1930, in Kerala, India) Catholic Churches.

In turn, Greek-speaking and Latin-speaking partisans of Chalcedon slowly grew apart in the following centuries. Greek was the language of the early Church Fathers. Yet theology began to develop in Latin in North Africa and Italy during the third century. Greek being progressively abandoned in the West, liturgies in the Latin vernacular were born locally, and came to be commonly used in the third and fourth centuries in North Africa, Italy, Spain, and Gaul. North African liturgies have been lost. The others were shaped by the practical concerns of the Romans. They generally exhibit the brevity that characterized the Latin language, some of their more solemn features deriving from Gaul. Thus the estrangement between the Greek and the Latin sections of the Church was in part the outcome of the successful inculturation of Christianity in the West. The Celtic liturgy and Church of Britain and Ireland were alive for some time as a third option that was neither Greek nor Latin; but they slowly gave way to Latin forms under the influence of the monks who were sent by St. Gregory the Great to evangelize the Anglo-Saxon invaders. The Synod of Whitby in 664 consecrated the Latinization of the British Isles.

Estrangement moved toward separation when opposite theologies developed concerning grace and freedom, original sin, the meaning and purpose of icons, the eternal origin of the Holy Spirit, the authority of the Bishop of Rome. Differences in discipline, the East practicing the ordination of married men, gave more visibility to these diverse theological leanings. Yet the schism was effective only in 1054, when the legate of Pope Leo IX, Humbert de Moyenmoutier, excommunicated the patriarch of Constantinople, Michael Kerularios. The patriarchs of Alexandria, Antioch, and Jerusalem supported their brother of Constantinople against the claims of universal primacy of the Bishop of Rome, patriarch of the West. Relations were further strained by political events, especially when, in 1203 and 1204, the fourth crusade assaulted and took Constantinople instead of liberating Jerusalem from Muslim rule. Unity was briefly restored at the Western councils of Lyon II (1274) and Florence (1439). But in 1453 Constantinople fell to the Turks. The Greek Church entered a period of isolation, that was not lessened by the success of Orthodoxy in the Russian Empire, when Moscow was considered, for a time, the "third Rome." The schism between Orthodox and Catholics has lasted until our day. By and large, Orthodoxy dominates in the lands of the former Byzantine Empire and in the zone of influence of Russia.

The Orthodox Church is organized along national and cultural lines. It is made of "autocephalous," self-governing, Churches. Honor is given to the ecumenical primacy of the patriarch of Constantinople, whose residence, the Phanar, is located in Istanbul in spite of recurring harassment by successive governments of modern Turkey. Several patriarchates have been added to the original four, the patriarch of Moscow having considerable influence because of the size and resources of the Russian Orthodox Church. The Orthodox Churches are doctrinally united by their recognition of the first seven ecumenical councils, their ecclesiology of communion between like-minded diocesan units, their cult of icons, and their general rejection of the Latin teaching about the procession of the Spirit "from the Father and the Son as from one principle." They use the same liturgies, though in various languages, Greek, Arabic, Old Slavonic, and several modern vernaculars.

Yet the differences between Ancient Oriental, Byzantine Orthodox, and Roman Catholic do not reside essentially in the specificities of distinctive rituals. A rite expresses a way of prayer, belief, and life. Orthodox prayer is centered in the perception of the divine presence in the icons that adorn churches and are displayed at home. Monasteries serve as spiritual and theological centers, as promoters of the conviction that the Holy Spirit proceeds from the Father alone, and as the nearly exclusive providers of unmarried priests who can be raised to the episcopate. Thanks to influential Russian mystics, Orthodox piety promotes an inner prayer of the heart that is focused on invocation of the Name of Jesus as Savior.

The chief Orthodox Churches are those of Greece, Russia, Rumania, Bulgaria, Albania, Cyprus, which all have extensive diasporas in North and South America and in Western Europe. Most of them have membership in the World Council of Churches. After Vatican II most have also been engaged in bilateral dialogues with the Catholic Church.

Unique is the Maronite Church—named after the holy hermit St. Maro (350–433)—in the mountains of the Lebanon. Originally non-Chalcedonian, of Antiochene origin and rite, it opted as a whole for communion with Rome and the Council of Chalcedon in 1181, during the second crusade, although it also submitted over the years to excessive Latinization. A similar pattern of reunion with Rome was followed in later centuries in many places, but never again by an entire Church. Byzantine Christians are therefore divided between an Orthodox majority and a number of Byzantine Catholic minorities. The forceful suppression by Stalin of several Byzantine Catholic Churches, especially in Ukraine (1945) and in Rumania (1948), brought new tensions to the relations between the Church of Rome and the Orthodox Church, all the more so as the breakup of the Soviet Union (1991) has allowed these Byzantine Catholic Churches to revive and to claim back their former buildings and properties.

The main Byzantine Catholic Churches are Italo-Greek, located in southern Italy, and never out of communion with Rome (sometimes called Italo-Albanian because of an influx of Albanian refugees after the fall of Constantinople), Ukrainian (Union of Brest-Litovsk, 1596), Ruthenian (1596), Melkite (in Lebanon and Syria, 1725), Rumanian (1701), Bulgarian (1860), most of them with diasporas in the Americas and in Western Europe. These Byzantine or Eastern Catholic Churches, both ancient and Byzantine, have often been called Uniate when they have an Orthodox counterpart, but the term has acquired a pejorative connotation. Each Church is headed by its own patriarch or at least by an archbishop major, who rules in keeping with the customs of his Church, under the primatial authority of the Bishop of Rome. Each of these Churches uses in principle the same liturgy as its Orthodox counterpart. Yet in most of them the original ethos inherited from the ancient patriarchates has been mitigated by contact with Latin piety and under the influence of the Scholastic theology of the West that has often been taught to their seminarians. In addition, a series of Roman decrees has forced the Eastern Catholic Churches in the U.S.A. to adopt the discipline of clerical celibacy, thus pushing them further toward Latinization.

GEORGE H. TAVARD

See also EASTERN CATHOLIC CHURCHES.

EASTERN MONASTICISM

See MONASTICISM.

EASTERN SCHISM

See SCHISM.

ECCLESIOLOGY

The term covers both doctrine concerning the Church and theological discussion of the nature, function, and structures of the Church. Taken from the Greek term *ekklesia,* "convocation" or "assembly," adopted into Christian Latin as *ecclesia,* meaning "Church," the word ecclesiology is recent in the history of theology. Some kind of reflection on nature, function, and structures of the Church has been going on since apostolic times. However, ecclesiology as a recognized theological discipline emerged rather slowly. In the fourteenth century, the existing patterns of Church government and sacramental practices raised a good deal of scholarly protest from William of Ockham, Marsiglio of Padua, John Wykliff and John Hus. In response to these protests, treatises *De ecclesia,* "On the Church," began to appear in the fifteenth century, largely justifying the status quo with theological arguments about the Church as essentially an institution instituted by Jesus who was credited with intending all the developments that had taken place in the Western Church. After the Protestant Reformation, these treatises were enhanced with further arguments that the Church in communion with Rome, and only that Church, was the true Church instituted by Christ and guided by the Holy Spirit. An attempt was made to set this out formally as official teaching at the First Vatican Council, but due to the warfare raging around the city of Rome, that council ended without completing its agenda, and left official statements only on the role of the pope. The Second Vatican Council reviewed ecclesiology quite radically in the light of Scripture and history.

MONIKA K. HELLWIG

See also CHURCH, THE; MYSTICAL BODY OF CHRIST; VATICAN COUNCIL I; VATICAN COUNCIL II.

ECOLE BIBLIQUE

This venerable intellectual center led the Church into modern biblical scholarship; and for over a century it has been in the forefront of the revival and expansion of higher biblical studies. The Ecole Pratique d'Etudes Biblique, usually called the Ecole Biblique, was opened in Jerusalem on 15 November 1892 and stands on the site of the martyrdom of St. Stephen. Its first director was the scholarly and saintly Marie Joseph Lagrange who mapped a new direction with his *Methode Historique,* his NT commentaries and the founding of the quarterly *Revue Biblique.*

The Ecole Biblique is under the direct supervision of the Dominican master general; and until recent decades its Dominican faculty was drawn from the members of the French and Canadian provinces. Its present faculty is more international and includes such scholars as Jerome Murphy O'Connor. The first issue of *Revue Biblique* (1892) outlined the ambitious program of the new foundation. From its inception it has paid special attention to field trips and archeological excursions, and the professionalism of its excavations has won international recognition. In 1920 the French government bestowed a unique honor and the Ecole Biblique was also made the "Ecole française archéologique de Jérusalem."

Apart from its specialized scholarly publications in all areas of biblical research, the Ecole Biblique has won popular recognition for its *Bible de Jérusalem,* which was widely translated and fostered a more sophisticated approach to popular scriptural studies. It played a special role in the work surrounding the Dead Sea Scrolls, and Roland de Vaux, O.P., became a leading explicator of the Qumran discoveries. The Ecole does not confer degrees on its students who are prepared to receive them from the Pontifical Biblical Commission, and they usually join seminary or university faculties. While the number of students is strictly limited, their training and research have enabled them to have a significant and formative influence in the Church. In *Divino Afflante Spiritu,* Piux XII praised the great contribution of the Ecole Biblique "while giving promise of much more."

MICHAEL GLAZIER

See also BIBLICAL ARCHAEOLOGY; CRITICISM, BIBLICAL; PONTIFICAL BIBLICAL INSTITUTE; THEOLOGY, BIBLICAL; VAUX, ROLAND DE.

ECOLOGY/ENVIRONMENT

Theologically, the environmental issue links with the theology of creation. Concern about the environment engages values such as reverence for creation, stewardship of the earth's resources, and responsibility towards our fellow inhabitants of a threatened planet. Ecology, in the sense of practical concern for our earthly habitat, is also about solidarity with generations yet to come.

Theology must keep in mind the seriousness of the issue. Environmental concern is about the survival not simply of this group or that, but the survival of our shared planet. Our concepts of the interdependence of all God's creation are re-shaped when we ask about the meaning of "increase, multiply, fill the earth and subdue it." "Subdue" must mean merciful stewardship rather than the "do-as-you-please" it has earlier been taken to signify.

The Churches have made some moves towards fostering an environmental responsibility. Stung perhaps by the charge that Christianity has been anti-ecological, the Churches have taken up the question. Thus, the World Council of Churches has endorsed programs towards "A Just, Participative and Sustainable Society" as well as towards "Justice, Peace and the Integrity of Creation." Likewise, Pope John Paul II in a message given on 1 January 1990 identifies the environmental issue among the foremost moral problems of the day.

It is not theology's task to draft descriptions of the problem. That has been admirably accomplished by those most directly affected by ecological breakdown in South America, Africa, and Asia. The task of theology is to explicate, in order to influence, the issues most likely to be suppressed in the *realpolitik* of the rich, powerful countries. One might reflect on Pope John Paul II's reminder that no solution can be found to the ecological problem if a solution to world poverty is not found (New Year's Day Message, 1990).

The principle that "the polluter must pay" makes bitter hearing to the polluters themselves. Yet the depredation of colonialism and the selfishness of neo-colonialism have caused most of the problems which every child can now enumerate: deforestation, waste pollution, and extinction of flora and fauna at an increasing rate.

Theological research brings us in the direction of a radical conversion to a "chastened anthropocentrism." This phrase, associated with Bernard Häring, does not signify denial that man/woman are special, created as they are in the image of God. To call this "specialness" in question would have far-reaching effects for human rights work and, indeed, for medical ethics. Yet, environmental awareness protests that there are other inhabitants on this earth. There is, to cite Leonardo Boff, a cosmic confraternity/sorority which was recognized by Francis of Assisi, Julian of Norwich, and other mystics. Their sensitivity reached to a God of compassion and a spirituality of brotherhood/sisterhood broader than the usual confines of Scholasticism.

There is the ever-delicate issue of population expansion. Despite pockets wherein human population is in decline, the global prospect still is for an expansion. Some will claim that the only responsible attitude is strict population control. Others will point to the possible racism inherent to this position. In essence, they will say, it makes poor people in Africa, Asia, and South America pay for the selfishness of North America and of Europe.

Environmental management is indispensable if policies are to be concerted and effective. The hegemony of powerful over powerless, of rich over poor, of men over women (in the main) is by no means new. The language of the scientific revolution heralded by Francis Bacon reflects the same logic. Bacon announced: "I come in very truth leading to you nature with all her children to bind her to your service and make her your slave."

We need a new and better logic. Without minimizing real conflict, without relapsing into facile romanticism, we need the logic of solidarity. Instead of the mindset of "being over" we need the mindset of "being with." Instead of power we should think of facilitation. Instead of wasteful aggrandizement we need frugal grace. To achieve this requires conversion, as much in ourselves as in others.

Certain forgotten traditions in Christianity, in Judaism, and in Buddhism contain helpful guidelines to the conversion needed. So, too, do some liberation movements, notably the movement which derives from feminist thought.

DENIS CARROLL

See also CREATION.

ECONOMICS

Economic theory attempts to model how real world economies operate by focusing on the self-interested behavior of individuals faced with scarcity. Economists are able to deduce from these models propositions such as higher wages will lead more people to work more hours, lower prices will entice them to buy more of a product, and higher taxes will be a disincentive for them to save and invest their incomes.

Economic theory's conception of the common good differs from that of Catholic Social Thought. Economic thought is rooted in an individualist conception of society. Society is seen as a collection of individuals who have chosen to associate because it is mutually beneficial. The common good is simply the aggregation of the welfare of each individual. Individual liberty is the highest good, and, if individuals are left free to pursue their self-interest, the result will be the maximum economic welfare.

By contrast, in Catholic Social Thought the common good is rooted in a communitarian vision of society. Because of this it emphasizes both the dignity of the human person and the essentially social nature of that dignity.

Modern economics is usually dated from the 1776 publication of Adam Smith's *The Wealth of Nations.* This book initiated a tradition in economic thought which continues today. The core of this theory is the model of competitive market capitalism which attempts to provide a rigorous demonstration that individuals, acting rationally to maximize their self-interest, will be led by the "invisible hand" of competition to produce those goods which people desire and to do so in the most efficient way. Thus, free individual choices are expected to overcome scarcity and result in the common good through the automatic adjustments of free exchange in markets.

But what prevents a market economy driven by the motive of self-interest from degenerating into a jungle, where the powerful oppress the weak? The economist's answer is simple—competition. If a producer tries to sell products at higher than the market price, consumers will buy from that firm's competitors. If a firm attempts to pay workers less than the going wage, they will be hired away by the firm's competitors. The result is that as each individual attempts to maximize his or her own well-being, society, the sum of these individuals, benefits. Thus, private profit and public welfare become reconciled through the automatic and impersonal forces of competition.

Economics has always attempted to do two things: (1) to explain how a market economy operates and (2) to show why it works so well. Thus, this economic theory is also a particular social philosophy. It is the "free enterprise" or "laissez-faire" tradition within economics. This was the dominant view of economics in both England and the United States until the 1930s, and became so again in the 1980s. It can be summarized under a few propositions:

(1) People are motivated primarily by self-interest, described best by Adam Smith as an "innate propensity to truck, barter, and exchange."

(2) A free market economy, through the forces of competition, converts that self-interested behavior into the common good by forcing profit-maximizing firms to produce what utility-maximizing consumers demand, and to do so in the most efficient way.

(3) A free market economy requires freedom of choice—of where to invest, of what job to take, of what product to purchase, and so on.

(4) Problems in the economy, including poverty, are due either to government interference with the free market or are the result of physical and human nature. The scarcity in physical nature requires time to overcome. The perversity of human nature—shortsightedness, lack of ambition, laziness—means some people will fail and thus be poor.

(5) Public authorities can and should do little besides enforce the rules of the game and provide those goods, e.g., defense, that the private sector is unable to produce.

(6) There is an inherent stability in the market economy, and since supply will create its own de-

mand, that equilibrium stability will generally be at a position of full employment. What may appear as destructive effects of market operation, the loss of jobs or industries, are transitory by-products of the markets' creativity in constantly forcing increases in efficiency and productivity.

(7) The propositions that hold for national economies hold in the international sphere as well. A regime of free trade through international markets with little government involvement will be most successful in improving world income.

From the 1930s until the 1980s the laissez-faire theory of economics was pushed to the margins of mainstream economics. Certainly a major factor in this eclipse was the Great Depression of the 1930s which fundamentally challenged the claims of that social philosophy, both on the causes of poverty and on the assumption of full-employment stability. Those who were thrown into poverty during the Depression had not changed overnight from thrifty and industrious workers to lazy and indolent loafers. Could the rash of bank failures, farm foreclosures, and business bankruptcies occur in an economy that was truly characterized by stability and efficiency? In addition it was becoming apparent that the theory could not account for two other major market failures encountered by actual economies: monopoly and externalities.

The market economy as it actually developed had an Achilles' heel: competition tended to self-destruct. It turned out to be a race with the winner getting larger and larger and the losers dropping out of the race. In economic theory competition was the key force ensuring that the market economy was efficient, so the decline of competition was a severe blow to the credibility of laissez-faire theory. This led to calls from economists outside the laissez-faire social philosophy for government intervention to restore competition through antitrust and pro-competition policies, or through the imposition of government regulation as a substitute for competition.

Externalities were the second free market failure that laissez-faire theory failed to address. An externality is a cost or benefit not included in the prices determined by the market. For example, a firm's cost of producing an auto might be $3,000. However, in producing the auto the firm dumps waste in the local river that will cost $500 to clean up. Thus, the true cost of producing the auto is $3,500. Instead the $500 becomes a cost to those who use the river for swimming, fishing, or drinking. As industrialization and population density increased during the growth of the U.S., so did externalities. And again, without government intervention the market failures were not corrected nor the external costs taken into account. Thus, economists developed amendments to economic theory that both accounted for these externalities and allowed for government intervention as a solution.

The most serious problem that plagues a free market economy is periodic recessions with their attendant unemployment. The New Deal-Keynesian economic consensus that emerged out of the 1930s created a new branch of economic theory called macroeconomics. This new economic theory analyzed how lack of aggregate demand (i.e., spending by consumers, business, and government) could make it impossible for firms to sell what they produced, resulting in recession and large-scale unemployment. This macroeconomic theory also embodied a program to overcome recessions and unemployment by utilizing government intervention in the form of monetary (changes in interest rates and the money supply) and fiscal policies (changes in taxes and government expenditures) to counteract deficient demand.

Economic theory today is composed of microeconomics—which uses the competitive model, initiated by Adam Smith, amended by analyses of monopoly and externalities; and macroeconomics which studies the economy as a whole—inflation, unemployment, economic growth. Economists have policy disagreements because they have different assessments about how well particular markets work and about the desirability of government intervention to make them work better.

CHARLES K. WILBER

See also JUST WAGES; SOCIAL RESPONSIBILITY, FINANCIAL; SOCIAL TEACHING OF THE CHURCH; SOCIALISM; VIRTUE.

ECSTASY

Generally applied to a mystical experience marked by a distinct consciousness of the Divine Presence. The body, overwhelmed by the divine action in the soul, becomes immobile; and sight, hearing, and the other senses cease to function. This differs greatly from a pathological ecstasy because in the mystical experience the person remembers everything that has taken place during the ecstasy, which is usually marked by intuitive knowledge of some religious truth.

JOSEPH QUINN

See also MYSTICISM.

ECUMENICAL COUNCILS

An ecumenical council for Roman Catholics is a gathering of the bishops of the entire Church meeting under the headship of the pope to determine the Church's doctrinal stance on particular matters, to correct disciplinary problems, and, at Vatican II, to make pastoral pronouncements. Councils have the authority to pronounce finally on a point of doctrine, although that does not mean theological investigation of a topic is over. For example, since the Council of Chalcedon in 451 it has been an article of the Christian faith that Jesus Christ is both divine and human, but theologians continue to investigate how he is both since conciliar statements are invariably bound up with the era in which they were produced. The philosophical worldview of the fifth century is not that of the modern age, and thus theologians must constantly try to deepen the Church's understanding of faith statements.

Councils function in the Roman Catholic Church as a means of bringing about agreement on an issue; but, in fact, councils can be controversial. The Church of England accepts as authoritative only the first four ecumenical councils, while the Orthodox communions accept only the first seven. During the Reformation, Martin Luther made it clear that the authority of popes and councils counted for nothing without the authority of Scripture behind them. The ecumenical movement has largely gone beyond these points of division, but, at some time, the various denominations will have to work out what role the councils will play. This article will accept the Roman Catholic position that there are twenty-one ecumenical councils.

Meeting in council has a long history in Christianity. In Acts 15 Luke portrays Jesus' earliest disciples meeting to discuss what, if any, obligations of the Jewish Law should be placed upon Gentile converts. Ca. 112 Ignatius of Antioch expected representatives from other Asian Churches to go to Antioch to elect his successor. Ca. 190 Pope Victor I called for synods of bishops to discuss the calculation of the date of Easter, the Quartodeciman Controversy, thus indicating that bishops of major sees had the right to call meetings and that membership in these was now limited to bishops. By the middle of the third century the annual meetings of the North African bishops had become a major force in a regional Church, expressing the doctrinal views of the Africans on such issues as the rebaptism of heretics. In sum, there were many councils before an ecumenical one had been called.

First Ecumenical Council at Nicea

The First Ecumenical Council was that of Nicea in 325. The Roman emperor Constantine (d. 337) had become a Christian and was disturbed about the havoc caused by the Egyptian priest Arius (d. 336) and his partisans, who claimed that the Son of God was actually a created being and there was a time when he was not. Arius' bishop, Alexander of Alexandria (d. 328), had condemned him, but the controversy had spread throughout the eastern half of the Roman Empire. The emperor then had an imperial idea: why not call a council of the bishops of the *oikumene,* that is, of the inhabited world, to settle this matter? On his own authority, the emperor called the First Ecumenical Council at Nicea, across the Sea of Marmara from his capital of Constantinople.

[Roman Catholic ecclesiology insists that only a papal summons or approval can make a council ecumenical; but, in fact, several early councils were called without papal authority or even papal knowledge. This does not change the need for papal authority for Roman Catholics, but one cannot read theology back into history.]

Few Latin bishops could attend, and the Greek bishops at Nicea struggled to refute Arius by scriptural citations, but he always had an answer. The emperor, at the urging of his theological advisor Hosius of Cordova (d. 357), suggested that the Father and Son were *homoousios,* of one substance (consubstantial), a term which Arius could not accept. Unfortunately, Greek theological terminology could be vague and *homoousios* could also be interpreted as saying the Father and the Son were numerically one. Many bishops had reservations about that and also about the use of a nonscriptural term. But they wanted to stop Arius, and so they adopted the term, and Arius stood condemned.

At the time no one knew what a watershed Nicea would be, but later generations saw Nicea as the touchstone of faith. Significantly, the bishops had used a nonscriptural term to explain a point of doctrine, thus freeing theologians from forcing their opinion into a biblical worldview which they had difficulty sharing. *Homoousios* was a theological, not a philosophical term, but once the scriptural bond had been broken, Christians felt free to adopt whatever terminology was necessary to express the faith, especially philosophical terminology.

Second Ecumenical Council at Constantinople

Many bishops had reservations about Nicea, and after the council many withdrew their allegiance, although they did not adopt the radical Arian position. For most of the fourth century a great theological controversy raged, with the Latin West solidly Nicene and the East divided. Led by Athanasius of Alexandria (d. 373) and the three Cappadocians, Basil of Caesarea (d. 379), Gregory of Nazianzus (d. 389), and Gregory of Nyssa (d. ca. 395), the Nicenes won the wavering bishops to their position. The emperor Theodosius (d. 395) called the Second Ecumenical Council at Constantinople in 381, which confirmed the Nicene faith and also added the important proviso that the Holy Spirit was also equal and divine in the Trinity. At Constantinople, the Council of Nicea was considered the mark of orthodoxy. This council also produced a creed, now known as the Nicene Creed, although its technical title would be the Niceno-Constantinopolitan Creed.

The Council of Constantinople had elevated the status of Nicea, but its own status was unclear. The bishop of Rome, Damasus I (366–384), was neither informed of nor invited to the council, although in 382 a Roman council accepted the council's dogmatic decisions. Since Constantinople had elevated the ecclesiastical status of the capital to second after Rome, Damasus rejected the disciplinary decisions—he did not want the status of the Roman Church to depend upon the secular status of the city, a very far-sighted observation. The Eastern bishops accepted all that Constantinople had done, but the Romans have always ignored those portions rejected by Damasus.

Third Ecumenical Council at Ephesus

In the fourth century there were two ecumenical councils and literally dozens of others, regional and local, but in the fifth century the situation changed. Theological problems demanded ecumenical councils, and the Third Ecumenical Council met at Ephesus in 431. The patriarchs of Alexandria used almost any means to promote the status of their see, and they resented the rising power of Constantinople as well as the theological prominence of Antioch. In 403 Theophilus of Alexandria engineered the deposition of John (later known as Chrysostom, "of the Golden Tongue"), an Antiochene monk who had become patriarch of Constantinople. In 431 a second Alexandrian, Cyril (d. 444), also had the chance to embarrass his theological and spiritual rivals.

In 428 the emperor Theodosius II (d. 450) appointed another Antiochene monk, Nestorius, to be bishop of Constantinople. Nestorius promptly attempted to eradicate heresy in the capital, including belief in the Virgin Mary as *Theotokos,* Mother of God. He claimed that she could only be *Christotokos.* To his many enemies, this implied that he was separating the one person of Christ into two, human and divine. The personally unscrupulous but theologically brilliant Cyril saw his chance. Nestorius the monk knew little of the ways of politics, and he never stood a chance against Cyril, who was quick to enlist papal support. Nestorius assumed that a council would vindicate him, and he asked the emperor to call one, which he did at Ephesus in 431.

Pope Celestine I (422–432) asked Cyril to be his representative. Armed with Roman support, Cyril arrived in Ephesus and stirred up the local populace against Nestorius, whom he convinced the council to condemn as the "new Judas." When the delegates from Antioch, who arrived late and after Cyril's council, heard what had happened, they called their own council and condemned Cyril. The Roman legates, coming even later, stood by the Alexandrian. The emperor stepped in, and, after much political machination, favored Cyril. Ephesus was a scandal and the Alexandrian's conduct despicable, but the council did affirm the unity of Christ by recognizing the title *Theotokos* and by furthering the Christological discussion which led to Chalcedon.

The Alexandrians and Antiochenes worked out a Formula of Union in 433 in which they agreed that Christ was one person with two natures, one human and one divine. But in 448 the Constantinopolitan monk Eutyches began to preach that Christ had two natures before the incarnation but only one nature (*Monophysis*) after the incarnation. His patriarch Flavian condemned this teaching, and Eutyches turned for help to Dioscorus of Alexandria, who saw yet another chance to humble Constantinople. He presided over the Second Council of Ephesus in 449 at which Flavian was condemned and deposed, while the legates of Pope Leo I (440–461) were denied a hearing. The infuriated pope gave the council its nickname, *latrocinium* or "robber council."

Fourth Ecumenical Council at Chalcedon

The emperor Theodosius II supported Dioscorus, but when he died accidentally in 450, his sister Pulcheria married a soldier named Marcian, and they ruled the empire. In 451 they called the Fourth Ecumenical Council at Chalcedon in Asia Minor. Pope Leo insisted that the bishops follow his views, and they did. Roman legates brought his *Tome,* as it was simply called, and the assembled Greek prelates agreed that it harmonized with the teachings of Nicea, Constantinople, and Ephesus as well as the theology of Cyril of Alexandria. No pope ever played so major a role in a primarily Eastern council. Chalcedon condemned Eutyches and deposed Dioscorus, but it also caused divisions in the Eastern Church which endure until today.

Fifth Ecumenical Council, Constantinople II

The Egyptian Monophysites resented Dioscorus' deposition, and they went into opposition to both the Chalcedonian Church and the emperors who supported it. Their movement soon spread to Syria and beyond. By the mid-sixth century hostile Monophysites dominated the eastern provinces of what was now the Byzantine Empire, the Western parts of the Roman Empire having fallen into barbarian hands. The emperor Justinian (527–565) had a Monophysite wife Theodora (d. 547), who mitigated his treatment of the heretics. In 553 the emperor decided to call the Fifth Ecumenical Council, Constantinople II, to reconcile the Monophysites and Chalcedonians.

Justinian used a clever ploy. He had to be faithful to Chalcedon, so he decided to condemn passages taken from the writings of three theologians the Monophysites loathed; thus this became known as the Three Chapters controversy. The emperor's armies had reconquered Rome and parts of Italy from the barbarians, and he expected papal support. When Pope Vigilius (537–555) refused, Justinian had him kidnapped and brutalized into signing the decrees of the council. All this failed, however, to pacify the Monophysites, and it generated a schism in the West where the notion of condemning as heretics men who had died in the peace of the Church was considered at best unseemly. Vigilius died on the way home to an uncertain reception, and the schism persisted until the early seventh century.

In the next century the Islamic tide swept over most of the Byzantine East, and many anti-Byzantine Monophysites gladly exchanged imperial rule for that of the religiously tolerant Arabs. The Constantinopolitan patriarch Sergius II (610–638) had meanwhile tried another tack to win back the fractious Eastern provinces, and that was Monothelitism, the notion that Christ had only one will since he, as a morally perfect human being, could not go against the divine will. The Chalcedonians saw this as a kind of back-door Monophysitism, and, led by Pope Martin I (649–655), they condemned it. The Byzantine Emperor Constans II (641–668), however, hoped that this formula might work, and he was furious at Martin, whom he had arrested and exiled in 653. The pope never returned to Rome.

Sixth Ecumenical Council, Constantinople III

The emperor's brutal treatment of the pope soured papal-Byzantine relations. When the new emperor Constantine III (668–685) recognized that the heavily Monophysite provinces were indeed lost to the Muslims, he decided to patch things up with Rome and thus called the Sixth Ecumenical Council, Constantinople III, in 680–681. Papal legates presided over the council, which condemned Monothelitism.

The Monophysite provinces were lost to Islam, but the Arabs wanted more, attacking Constantinople itself in 717 and 718. The general Leo the Isaurian successfully defended the city and then claimed for himself the imperial title, reigning as Leo III. The new emperor had a biblical aversion to idolatry, which he saw manifested in the many images (icons) in Eastern churches. Leo determined to cleanse the Church of this scourge, and in 730 he embarked on a policy of iconoclasm, literally the breaking of images.

Leo stands in a long historical tradition. The Church historian Eusebius of Caesarea (d. 339) had rebuked Constantia, sister of the emperor Constantine, when she asked for an image of Christ. Pope Gregory the Great (d. 604) had to defend the use of images as effective means of teaching illiterates against the criticisms of bishops who thought images were idolatrous. In later times, both Bernard of Clairvaux and many early Protestants opposed the use of images in worship.

These iconoclasts often had good reasons for their views. People could mistake the image for the reality; it is quite common for believers to think that God looks like them, for example, a white, middle-aged man. Furthermore, gross abuses abounded. There were icons which spoke, which wept, and which bled. Leo chose not to reform the abuses but eliminate the source.

His agents destroyed thousands of images, including many works of art. They were indifferent to the feelings of the people as well as to the piety which icons inspired. When iconodules (as venerators of icons were called) protested, they were abused, arrested, and even exiled. Upon Leo's death in 740, his son Constantine V (740–775) continued his policy and worsened it, executing sixteen iconodules in 766.

Seventh Ecumenical Council, Nicea II

Iconoclasm caused a rift between Constantinople and Rome, and the popes harbored iconodules. When the emperor died, his successor was too young to reign and the Empress Irene was regent, becoming co-emperor in 780. She was an iconodule, who worked to reverse previous policy. In 787 she triumphed at the Seventh Ecumenical Council, Nicea II, which legitimated the cult of icons, specifying that adoration was due to God alone but that icons could be venerated. The empress and her son, two papal legates, and over three hundred bishops acclaimed these decrees. Iconoclasm persisted, but it was never again a major threat.

Eighth Ecumenical Council, Constantinople IV

All ecumenical councils after Nicea II are recognized only by Roman Catholics, although the first of these was yet another Eastern council, the Eighth Ecumenical Council, Constantinople IV in 869–870. This resulted purely from ecclesiastical politics. The Constantinopolitan patriarch Photius had gotten his see in 861 when the emperor Michael III had forced his predecessor to resign. Pope Nicholas I (858–867) refused to recognize Photius and excommunicated him. When Michael III was murdered and replaced by Basil I in 867, Photius fell from power. The new emperor contacted the new pope, Hadrian II (867–872), about healing the schism. The pope agreed to the emperor's call for an ecumenical council at which three papal legates would preside. Constantinople IV met from October 869 to February 870. It condemned and deposed Photius, who, however, regained his see in 877, only to be deposed again, this time by an emperor, in 886.

The site of the council recalled the glories of the ancient councils, but this, in fact, was the last council to be held in the East. All subsequent councils were papal ones and were held in the West.

In the tenth and eleventh centuries, the papacy fell into a serious decline; the papal office became the prerogative of noble Roman families who blatantly played politics with it. In the eleventh century, the German emperors reformed the papacy by appointing worthy bishops from the ranks of their supporters, but this only transferred the papacy from the Roman families to the German emperors. Good emperors would appoint good popes, but would the emperors always have the papacy's interests at heart? Could they possibly avoid having political motives?

Ninth Ecumenical Council, Lateran I

A group of Roman reformers argued that the papacy must be free of lay interference, and, led by popes such as Leo IX (1049–1054) and Gregory VII (1073–1085), they struggled against vices of all sorts, including lay investiture, that is, the right of monarchs and nobles to invest bishops with the insignia of office. In 1122 Callistus II (1119–1124) concluded the Concordat of Worms by which the German emperor renounced his right to invest bishops but kept the right to maintain the empire's safety. The pope wanted the concordat ratified by a council which he called at the Lateran palace in 1123. The Catholic Church reckons this as the Ninth Ecumenical Council, Lateran I. Unfortunately, no acts or minutes of the council survive; scholars know of it from postconciliar documents. Three hundred bishops attended and dealt largely with disciplinary matters, ending their work in only twenty-three days.

Tenth Ecumenical Council, Lateran II

The Tenth Ecumenical Council, Lateran II, was just as short, meeting for three weeks in April of 1139. Innocent II (1130–1143) called it to end the schism of the antipope Anacletus II (1130–1138), "the pope from the ghetto," so-called because he was ethnically Jewish. Although Anacletus had died, many of his supporters were still alive, and Innocent faced the prospect of a continuing schism. But the major European powers as well as the greatest ecclesiastical figure of the day, the Cistercian abbot Bernard of Clairvaux, supported the pope. The approximately five hundred bishops at the council voted to force Anacletus' supporters to abandon all the signs of their office, croziers, palliums, and rings. The council also dealt with disciplinary matters, such as the enforcement of celibacy for clerics from the subdiaconate onwards; it likewise excommunicated some heretical groups.

Eleventh Ecumenical Council, Lateran III

The great German emperor, Frederick I Barbarossa (1152–1190), tried to assert imperial power in Italy by supporting an antipope, Victor IV (1159–1164), against Alexander III (1159–1181); when Victor died, Frederick supported Paschal III (1164–1168) and then Callistus III (1168–1178). The clearly German and political foundation for these antipopes prevented their wide recognition, and even in Germany Alexander was winning adherents. Pope and emperor were reconciled, and the Eleventh Ecumenical Council, Lateran III, met for two weeks in 1179. The pope wished to show the emperor how widespread his support was, and he did. This is the first council for which a list of participants survives as well as knowledge of the geographical range of their sees. Italians formed the largest number, but there were bishops from France, Germany, England, Scotland, Ireland, Spain, the Balkans, and even from the Crusader states in Palestine.

The bishops dealt largely with the disciplinary matters, the most important of which was the election of a pope. The council decreed that any candidate for the papacy must receive a two-thirds vote of the cardinals; they hoped by this to avoid future schisms. They also set requirements for the ordination of bishops (thirty years of age and birth within wedlock), and they condemned the heretical sect of the Cathari of southern France.

Twelfth Ecumenical Council, Lateran IV

The first three Lateran councils became ecumenical councils because they dealt with crucial matters facing the Church, albeit not so crucial as the Trinitarian and Christological councils of the first centuries. But the Twelfth Ecumenical Council, Lateran IV, was planned as an ecumenical council. The greatest of the medieval popes, Innocent III (1198–1216), invited the bishops to the council in 1213 "in accordance with the practice of the ancient fathers." In fact, the council did not open until 11 November 1215, and it had finished its work by 30 November.

Lateran IV had to face some sizeable challenges, including the persistence of the Cathar heresy, but its main concern was Church life. The bishops decreed that all Catholics must receive the sacraments of penance and Holy Communion at least once a year; these were part of the six commandments of the Church until Vatican II. The bishops insisted that bishops whose dioceses were so large that the ordinary could not teach many of the faithful in person should appoint teachers and preachers to represent them. The council also passed legislation regulating marriages, reforming abuses about relics, and, unfortunately, requiring Jews to wear a distinctive type of clothing and to stay off the streets during Holy Week.

The death of Innocent III less than a year after the council removed the personality most likely to enforce its decrees. The decrees made some difference, but the council was quickly overshadowed by political events. Jerusalem fell to the Muslims in 1244, the Mongols had entered Eastern Europe in 1241, the Greeks were threatening the Latin Empire of Constantinople, established by the Franks and Venetians during the Fourth Crusade (1204), and, most important to Innocent IV (1243–1254), the German Emperor Frederick II (1220–1250) was threatening the papacy's political position in Italy. Frederick was a strange man, a German and a Norman by blood but a Sicilian by temperament. King of Sicily from 1197, he preferred his southern domains to Germany. He was a remarkably cultivated man, sympathetic to Muslim culture, friendly to Jews, and determined to free his lands from papal interference. His admirers called him *stupor mundi,* the wonder of the world, but his enemies considered him the Antichrist.

Thirteenth Ecumenical Council, Lyons I

When Frederick tried to capture Innocent in 1244, the pope fled to his home city of Genoa, and then, unable to call a council in Italy, he went to Lyons and invited bishops to a council there. The Thirteenth Ecumenical Council, Lyons I, opened on 28 June 1245. It met in three sessions (28 June, 5 July, 17 July), ostensibly to deal with all the threats mentioned above as well as the need to reform the clergy, but its real achievement was Frederick II's deposition as King of Germany and Holy Roman Emperor. The deposition had an immediate effect. Frederick kept his throne, but a group of dissident nobles elected his young son Conrad IV in his place in 1246. Until his death in 1250 Frederick battled constantly to keep his throne.

Frederick was hardly an innocent victim of papal machinations, but one can still be disappointed at the blatant political nature of Lyons I, especially since it had so little effect on the other problems it had sought to address.

The papacy's concern with the Crusader States persisted throughout the century, and it resulted in a unique papal election. Pope Clement VI had died in 1268. For three years after his death, the cardinals wrangled over a successor. The local civic authorities locked them in the papal palace, removed its roof, and then threatened to starve them out if they did not choose a pope. Finally they chose Tedaldo Visconti, archdeacon of Liege, who at the time was in the Holy Land on crusade with the English Prince Edward (later Edward I). Tedaldo returned to Rome to be consecrated as Pope Gregory X on 27 May 1272, reigning until 1276.

Fourteenth Ecumenical Council, Lyons II

Not surprisingly, the welfare of the Crusader States was foremost in Gregory's mind, and he called the Fourteenth Ecumenical Council, known as Lyons II, which opened on 7 May 1274. The council's achievements were few, yet it is still well known because of one of history's "what ifs." Gregory wanted the best theological talent he could find to advise him, and so he invited the Dominican Thomas Aquinas. But Thomas, although aged only forty-nine, died on 7 March en route to the council, and historians can only wonder what influence he would have exercised if he had been there.

Gregory's experiences in the Holy Land made this a remarkably ecumenical council. He had seen firsthand the conflict of denominations, and he had heard much about the Mongols, so he invited the emperor of Constantinople, the king and primate of Armenia, and the Great Khan of the Mongols, who was rumored to be sympathetic to Christianity. Some Greek envoys arrived, and the council effected a reunion of two Churches. But it turned out that the Byzantine emperor had gone along with it only for political reasons, and the Greek hierarchy denounced the union. Mongol envoys also arrived, but their interest was an alliance with the West for an attack on Muslim Egypt. The real achievement of the more than two hundred assembled bishops was the reform of the papal election procedure, a reform intended to avoid future repetitions of the three years of wrangling preceding Gregory's election. Gregory also succeeded in browbeating the bishops into surrendering a considerable percentage of their revenues to support the defense of the Crusader States.

The reunion with the Greeks and the conversion of the Mongols did not take place, and by 1291 Acre, the last Christian possession in the Holy Land, had fallen to the Muslims. The papacy's attention turned from Palestine to Europe, where the growth of nation-states was threatening papal political power. When Boniface VIII (1294–1303) tried to assert his power against Philip IV the Fair, king of France, the king tried to have him kidnapped and tried for heresy (1302). The kidnapping failed, but the shock caused the aged Boniface to die soon after. His successor, Benedict XI (1303–1304), died suddenly, and, it was widely suspected that the French had poisoned him. His successor, Clement V (1305–1314) was a Frenchman and friendly toward Philip, whose overwhelming influence on the pope caused Clement to avoid Rome and settle in the town of Avignon, a papal city in southern France. The Avignon Papacy (1305–1377) had begun.

Fifteenth Ecumenical Council

Philip needed money for his wars, and he decided to expropriate the funds of the Knights Templar, a religious order originally founded to protect pilgrims to the Holy Land but one which had grown wealthy and powerful. His agents raided the houses of the French Templars and confiscated huge sums; Philip did this on the grounds that the Templars had given themselves over to perverse and diabolical practices. Europe was shocked, and the king sought to legitimize his actions by pressuring the pope to condemn the Templars. Clement was afraid to take this step alone, and so he called a council, the Fifteenth Ecumenical Council, which met at the French town of Vienne on 16 October 1311.

If Ephesus had been a circus, Vienne was a scandal. Clement invited only selected bishops, and the king's agents dominated the proceedings. Whether the Templars were guilty or not will never be known. Philip used ruthless and prolonged torture to get all the confessions he needed, and a commission appointed by Clement tried to hear the order's side. But the king won out, and the council condemned and suppressed the Templars. Even this did not satisfy Philip, who wanted the deceased Boniface VIII put on trial, but Clement managed to defer that.

The council tried to revive the idea of a crusade, but turned more profitably to the idea of evangelization instead, recommending that universities establish chairs in Eastern languages to facilitate missionary work among Jews and Muslims. There were also proposals for reforming the clergy, but little came of them. This most disappointing of councils ended on 6 May 1312.

Seven successive French popes resided in Avignon until 1377, when Gregory XI returned to Rome, where he died in 1378. In the popes' absence, Rome had declined considerably, and the anxious populace surrounded the papal palace, demanding that the cardinals elect an Italian, which they did—Urban VI. The new pope was a violent man who tried to reform the cardinals. Unaccustomed to such treatment, the cardinals fled from Rome, declared that they had elected Urban under threats and that his election was thus invalid, and elected a new pope, Clement VII. The new pope and the dissident cardinals returned to Avignon. Their action initiated the Great Western Schism.

Sixteenth Ecumenical Council

The rulers of Europe divided their allegiance and often bargained with the two popes, whose cardinals elected successors to them. An attempt to heal the schism, the Council of Pisa in 1409, only produced a third pope. Since none of the popes would resign nor would any pope's cardinals go over en masse to the other side, scholars and canonists concluded that only an ecumenical council could end the schism. Led by the German emperor Sigismund, clerical and lay leaders called the Sixteenth Ecumenical Council—and the most controversial—to meet at the Swiss city of Constance in 1414.

The popes *de jure* (in law) held the supreme power in the Church, but the Great Western Schism was a problem the popes had been unable to solve. Since the popes could not exercise the supreme power *de facto* (in fact), many concluded that they had no right to possess it *de jure.* Canonists argued for conciliarism, that is, the theory that the ecumenical council, not the papacy, holds the supreme power in the Church. The Council of Constance put this into force. Before ending the schism with an election of a pope acceptable to all Catholics, the council passed the decree *Sacrosancta* which declared that the council was the supreme authority, and this was followed by the decree *Frequens* which mandated the regular meeting of councils. In 1417 the council elected Martin V, thus ending the schism.

This council has always been a difficult one for the papacy. First, who called the council? The Roman pope was Gregory XII, the Avignonese Benedict XIII, and the Pisan John XXIII. John assumed that the council would support him, so he called the council, but his disreputable personal life soon caused his dismissal. Benedict refused to acknowledge the council's authority and was deposed. Gregory knew that he, too, would be deposed, so he agreed to resign, but only after he had called the council into session. The modern popes recognize

Gregory XII as the legitimate pope (as proved by later popes taking the names Benedict XIII [1724–1730] and John XXIII [1958–1963]), and so the modern popes can recognize Constance because Gregory called it.

Second, what about the conciliarist decrees? The popes have refused to recognize those decrees passed before the election of Martin V, so they can thus recognize Constance without accepting conciliarism.

Third, who elected Martin? When the council opened, John XXIII, an Italian, was counting on the large number of Italian bishops to support him, but representatives of other countries insisted that the voting not be done by the number of bishops but by the nations, that is, Italy, Germany, France, and England each had one vote. Countries like Hungary and Scotland were included with Germany and England, respectively. The cardinals as a group also had one vote. Since the election of Martin V was unanimous, one can say the cardinals chose Martin.

As if conciliarism were not enough, Constance also created another controversy. In Eastern Europe, many Bohemians followed the teachings of Jan Hus, who merged nationalism with reform. The Taborites, as the followers of Hus were called, had a wide following, and the Emperor Sigismund wanted the movement halted. Hus was invited to the council but feared for his safety. Sigismund gave him guarantee of safe passage, but the leaders of the council ignored this, arrested, tried, and burned Hus for heresy. This scandalous and loathsome act only exacerbated the situation in Bohemia.

Constance ended in 1418. In keeping with the decree *Frequens,* Martin called a council to meet in Pavia in 1423. The plague forced the transfer of the council to Siena, but low attendance gave Martin the chance to close the council in 1424.

Seventeenth Ecumenical Council

Again following the decree, Martin called the Seventeenth Ecumenical Council to meet at the Swiss city of Basle in 1431. The pope died three weeks after the council opened in July, and his successor, Eugene IV (1431–1447), had to deal with it.

Attendance at the council was very poor, and Eugene dissolved the council in December, but conciliarism asserted itself: the council refused to be dissolved. Attendance soon picked up, and the council participants insisted Eugene withdraw the bull of dissolution; the pope gave in although not until December of 1433. The conciliarists took charge, giving judgments and making appointments, and in every way trying to run the daily affairs of the Church. Eugene was helpless.

But help did arrive in an unanticipated way. The Byzantine Emperor John VIII Palaeologus realized that his empire could not hold out against the Turks without Western help, and he knew the price would be reunion of the two Churches. Naturally, he understood nothing about conciliarism, and so he contacted Eugene in 1437. The pope seized the opportunity for reunion and transferred the council to Ferrara in Italy to facilitate the meeting with the Byzantines. Most of those at Basle refused to go, thus starting a new schism, but this time with two councils. By 1439 the council had deposed Eugene and elected its own pope, Felix V, so now there were two popes and two councils.

But success lay with the pope. The council opened in Ferrara 1438, and in 1439 Eugene transferred it to Florence, where, on 6 July 1439, the two Churches were reunited. In fact, the reunion lasted only until the Byzantines arrived home. The Greek clergy rejected the union, preferring "the turban to the tiara." They got their wish in 1453.

As for the council, it stayed in session in Florence until 1443, moving then to Rome where it concluded in 1445.

The council of Basle continued to meet, transferring itself to Lausanne in 1443, getting progressively smaller and more disorganized. In 1449 "pope" Felix V resigned and the council ended. The papacy had won its victory over conciliarism.

Eighteenth Ecumenical Council, Lateran V

Basle-Ferrara-Florence-Rome was the last medieval council. The Eighteenth Ecumenical Council met in the Lateran from 1512–1517 on the eve of the Protestant Reformation, but Lateran V, which could have done much to prevent that event, was ineffective.

The Renaissance popes engaged in many political maneuvers, and their enemies often resorted to conciliarism as a means of attack, suggesting that if the popes would not reform the Church, a council should. Although usually a piece of propaganda, this threat became a reality when Louis XI of France called a council at Pisa in 1511. This council, which moved to Milan in 1512, invoked Constance to weaken the authority of Pope Julius II (1503–1513). The pope's supporters ridiculed the council as a *conciliabulum* (tiny council), but it did provoke Julius to call Lateran V.

The council met in Rome where the pope could control it; almost all the bishops there were Italians and the council's decrees were issued as papal bulls. The council attacked the French council, and most European monarchs sided with it. When Julius died, the French king reconciled himself to Leo X (1513–

1521). The council met until 1517, effecting a concordat with France and passing a number of reform decrees but conveniently ignoring the worst abuses. The council closed in March of 1517; seven months later in Wittenberg, Germany, a very different notion of Church reform took shape.

The Protestant Reformation started in eastern Germany but quickly spread to Switzerland, the Low Countries, Scandinavia, parts of eastern Europe, England, and France. About one-third of Catholic Europe left the Roman obedience. Neither Leo nor his short-lived successor Hadrian VI (1522–1523) nor Clement VII (1523–1534) acted with vigor to alleviate the situation; indeed, under Clement VII it was generally business as usual. But in 1534 a truly great pope appeared, Paul III (1534–1549). A vigorous, determined man, he strengthened the Catholic Church by appointing reformers to key positions, by instituting the Roman Inquisition in 1542, and by approving (1540) and supporting the Spaniard Ignatius of Loyola and his Society of Jesus. In spite of these deeds, Paul knew that only a council could deal with the most serious problems.

Nineteenth Ecumenical Council, Trent

Many minefields lay on the way to a council, including German and French politics and the fear of a revived conciliarism, and Paul was in office eleven years before he called the Nineteenth Ecumenical Council to meet at Trent in 1545.

The city of Trent was in Italy but in German imperial territory; Paul did not want his council to look like a purely Italian affair, although most bishops there were Italians. Bishops who were concerned about Protestant attacks wanted the council to deal with reform measures, while others feared that concentrating on reforms would only highlight and justify Protestant criticisms, and so these bishops favored passing doctrinal decrees. The papal legates presiding at the council decided to deal with doctrinal issues and pass appropriate reform decrees in association with them, for example, to clarify Catholic teaching on the Eucharist and to specify under what form it might be received. This wise decision helped to make Trent effective.

The first phase of Trent was from 1545 to 1547. The bishops dealt immediately with authority, the central question of the Reformation, by affirming that the revelation of Jesus Christ could be passed along in both "written Scriptures and unwritten traditions," a point completely unacceptable to the Protestants but one which enabled the bishops to formulate Catholic teaching on more than just the Bible. The bishops declined to approve vernacular translations of the Bible, thus playing into the hands of the Protestants who claimed the popes were afraid to have people read the Bible. The council also passed decrees on original sin and on justification as well as on the effectiveness of the sacraments, regardless of how they were administered.

An outbreak of the plague forced the transfer of the council to Bologna, where little was achieved and the council was suspended in 1548.

In May, 1551, the second phase opened under a new pope, Julius III (1550–1555). Protestant representatives came to Trent but insisted that they would accept the council's authority only if the principles of Constance, that is, conciliarism, were adopted. The gap between Catholics and Protestants had grown too wide, and the council rejected that condition. When a Protestant army advanced southward from Germany, the bishops took fright and decreed the suspension of the council.

Things looked bleak for the future of Trent, a point reinforced by the pontificate of Paul IV (1555–1559) who refused to recall the council. But Pius IV (1559–1564) determined to bring the council to a conclusion, and so he reconvened it in January of 1562. This phase saw the bishops finalize decrees on the sacrifice of the Mass, the use of the Eucharist, the calling of provincial synods, and the establishment of seminaries for the training of priests. When it closed in 1563, the Council of Trent had dealt with many of the abuses cited by the Protestant Reformers, and it had also met the desire of many Catholics for a true reform of the Church.

Trent was a great turning point for the Catholic Church, which was now seriously committed to reform. To be sure, much of the council's effectiveness depended upon how its decrees were carried out by the popes and bishops, but Trent had shown the way. Eventually and inevitably the work of Trent required updating, especially on the one issue on which Trent had not spoken, the nature of the Church, which became the main theme of the last two ecumenical councils, Vatican I and Vatican II.

JOSEPH F. KELLY

See also VATICAN COUNCIL I; VATICAN COUNCIL II.

ECUMENISM

The word, ecumenism, designates the movement that seeks to restore the unity of the divided Christian Churches. The desire for the mutual reconciliation of Christians goes back to the early Church, when the prayer of Jesus for the unity of his disciples became part of the gospel (John 17:11 and 21). Yet lasting schisms began as early as the fourth century (Nestorians and non-Chalcedonians versus

Chalcedonians). Other separations broke out in the eleventh century among the followers of the Christology of Chalcedon (Eastern Orthodox versus Western Catholics). The great divide between Catholics and Protestants followed in the sixteenth century.

From time to time attempts at reunion were made. Yet in its contemporary form the ecumenical movement originated in 1910 at an international conference of chiefly Protestant missionary organizations. It took shape between the two World Wars as two organisms: "Faith and Order," concerned with unity in doctrine, and "Life and Work," eager to promote joint action. A few Catholic theologians took an interest in it in the 1920s, especially when Cardinal Mercier, in Belgium, sponsored the Malines Conversations (1921–1926) between Catholics and Anglicans. In 1948 the two organizations united to form the World Council of Churches, in which Faith and Order remains an agency that is focused on growing together in the area of doctrine. Under the impact of the ecumenical movement, a number of Protestant Churches have taken practical steps toward reunion through progressive mergers, notably in South India, North India, Canada, Australia, and the U.S.A. Diverse forms of cooperation have also been tried. An agreement on Baptism, Eucharist, and Ministry (BEM), that was finalized at Lima in 1982 after many years of discussion in the Faith and Order Commission, was a hopeful achievement.

The immediate occasion for the start of the ecumenical movement was the scandal of rivalry between Christian missionaries and among Christian student organizations. The spiritual foundation was the desire to respond to the wish of Christ as formulated in Scripture, "That all may be one. . . ." The theological challenge made it clear that all Churches carry a weight of tradition even when they profess to follow Scripture alone, and that an organic reunion of Churches requires a conversion, *metanoia,* of both individuals and collectivities. The hope is that the fulfillment of the prayer of Christ and the restoration of Christian unity, as Christ wills it and by the means he will choose, cannot be stopped by temporary obstacles, however major these may seem to be at a particular moment.

Among Catholics, Pope Leo XIII anticipated the desire for Christian unity and set the tone for an official response to it: this God-given unity resides in the Catholic Church (encyclical *Satis Cognitum,* 1896). Pius X, who was chiefly concerned about theological Modernism, paid little attention to what happened in other Churches. Arguing that the Catholic Church has unity and therefore does not seek it, Benedict XV did not wish to be associated with any form of the movement. Pius XI was eager to obtain better relations with the Orthodox Church, and he at first encouraged the Malines Conversations. Yet he put an end to these at the death of Cardinal Mercier, and he did not authorize Catholic participation in meetings of Life and Work in 1925 (Stockholm) and 1937 (Oxford), and of Faith and Order in 1927 (Lausanne) and 1937 (Edinburgh) (encyclical *Mortalium Animos,* 1928). Pius XII ignored the feelings of both Protestants and Orthodox when he defined the Assumption of the Virgin Mary (1950), an action that provoked a wave of protests in many parts of the Protestant world. In the encyclical *Humani Generis* (1950), he also rejected notions regarding original sin and about angels that were widely accepted in Protestant theology.

Nonetheless, it was under Pius XII that the oldest ecumenical dialogue in existence, the unofficial Groupe des Dombes, began to meet in France in 1937. Pius XII himself prepared the ground for a broader ecumenical opening when he endorsed both the liturgical movement (encyclical *Mediator Dei,* 1947), and scientific exegesis (*Divino Afflante Spiritu,* 1943). The Holy Office also set down some cautious yet encouraging rules for Catholic participation in ecumenical conversations (Instruction, 1948). But it was John XXIII who threw the door wide open to extensive ecumenical activity in the Catholic Church when he called Vatican Council II and created the Pontifical Secretariat for the Unity of Christians. Paul VI took the first major steps toward applying the Catholic principles of ecumenism that were formulated at the council (decree *Unitatis Redintegratio,* 1965): he initiated the first bilateral ecumenical dialogues in which the Catholic Church is officially involved.

The decision of John XXIII had been heralded by growing attention to ecumenism by a small number of theologians. Yves Congar, O.P., was the outstanding pioneer. His extensive writings, on the disunion of Christians, on ongoing reform in the Church, on a theology of the laity, set the tone for a major ecumenical shift in Catholic theology.

As they were described by Vatican II, the Catholic principles of ecumenism are based on loyalty to the Catholic tradition and on trust that the yearning for Christian unity comes from the Holy Spirit who continuously guides the Church. They encourage friendship with those who today profess the Christian faith in other communions, concern for their spiritual welfare, knowledge of the history of their Churches, and a willingness to learn from them in theological and spiritual matters. Vatican Council II recommended that competent theologians take part in ecumenical dialogues. It trusted that, in spite of continuing divisions, prayer in common will contribute to mutual reconciliation. It promoted spiritual emulation as the proper attitude between divided Christians. And it recognized the bishops' authority to regulate such prayer and to invite the People of God to the appropriate conversion of heart.

The Secretariat (renamed, Council, by John Paul II) for the Unity of Christians was given permanent status by Paul VI. It is the agency of the Roman See to deal with ecumenical questions and to entertain friendly relations with other Churches. Shortly after Vatican II, the Secretariat negotiated a series of official bilateral dialogues with the main Churches of the Orthodox, Anglican, Lutheran, and Calvinist traditions. Similar dialogues were initiated later with Methodists, Disciples of Christ, and Pentecostals. At the same time, national dialogues with these and other Churches began in a number of countries, notably in the U.S.A., under the responsibility of the National Conferences of Catholic Bishops. Many dioceses opened ecumenical offices with the task of developing friendly relations at the local level.

The most striking results of these discussions have been the Final Report of the first Anglican-Roman Catholic International Commission (ARCIC-I), issued in 1981, and the study, Facing Unity (1980), in which Lutherans and Catholics envisaged several effective modes of reunion. In the U.S.A. a common statement by Lutherans and Catholics on Justification by faith (1985), and in Germany a study of the condemnations of Lutheran doctrine by the Council of Trent (1988) have been most significant. The Groupe des Dombes has also issued important documents, among them a study of conversion as a permanent need of the Churches (1991).

Besides such dialogues, ecumenical progress requires active relations with the WCC and its many agencies. While the Catholic Church is not a member of the WCC, meetings for information and cooperation bring together representatives of the WCC and of the Council for Christian Unity. Several Catholic theologians are full members of the Faith and Order Commission. At national and regional levels some Catholic dioceses have become members of Councils of Churches or, without formal membership, they have cooperated with such councils. Local clergy have taken part in ministerial associations that meet regularly.

A great deal of flexibility is needed to accommodate practical ecumenism to local and regional conditions. Yet there is a widening gap between cautious official directives and bold behavior at the grassroots level. In the U.S.A. ecumenism is taken for granted on many a college campus and it has been brought to the attention of a limited number of parishes. In many cases, however, individual Christians in all Churches have been impatient with the slow motion of clergy and magisterium. Eucharistic sharing is often practiced with no reference to official guidelines. And this is all the more likely to spread as most marriages, in the majority of American dioceses, are now "mixed," or, as they ought to be called, "ecumenical" marriages.

Some diocesan ecumenical offices are in fact quite inactive. Yet others have pioneered new ways to turn the minds and hearts of the People of God toward the hope that a reunion of divided Christians is not a utopia, while making sure that the base is neither too far ahead of the hierarchy nor lagging too far behind. Joint pastoral care has been carried out in a few places. Under careful pastoral supervision "covenants" have been passed between Catholic parishes and Anglican or Lutheran congregations. Their purpose is to bring the people of the two Churches into closer relations in all that may be done in common. In addition, the National Association of Diocesan Ecumenical Officers (Nadeo) has been engaged in surveys of ecumenical relations at the grassroots level, in close association with a similar organism in the Episcopal Church (Edeo).

Yet there are obstacles. As an unexpected effect of the ecumenical perspective, the belief of most Christians that their own Church has uniquely preserved some aspect of the Christian message and tradition has been strengthened by meeting with others. That this uniqueness could be lost in a reunion of Churches is a legitimate concern. But fear should not become unreasonable. Such a fear before the ecumenical opening of Vatican II has occasioned the "traditionalist" movement in some sections of contemporary Catholicism. The progress of ecumenical efforts has also been hampered by Leo XIII's denial of the validity of Anglican ordinations (apostolic letter *Apostolicae Curae,* 1896) and, more recently, by uncertainty as to the proper way of judging and receiving the agreed statements of ecumenical commissions. The Final Report of ARCIC-I has been received in Rome (Official Response by the Holy See, 1992) with less enthusiasm than in many National Conferences of Catholic Bishops.

Reaction against a rapprochement of the Churches with a view to their reconciliation cannot have the final word. Ecumenical involvement is at work at all levels in all the classical Churches of Christendom. In keeping with Vatican Council II, one may attribute this fact to the continuing guidance of the Holy Spirit.

GEORGE H. TAVARD

See also EASTERN CHURCHES; JOHN XXIII, POPE; MARKS (OR NOTES) OF THE CHURCH; PROTESTANTISM; VATICAN COUNCIL II.

EDUCATION

See CATHOLIC HIGHER EDUCATION IN THE UNITED STATES; EDUCATION, PHILOSOPHY OF.

EDUCATION, CATHOLIC

See CATHOLIC HIGHER EDUCATION IN THE UNITED STATES.

EDUCATION, PHILOSOPHY OF

Throughout history there has been a symbiotic partnership between education and philosophy; all approaches to education reflect a philosophy, and, as John Dewey often insisted, all good philosophy eventually becomes an approach to education. Their union is typically called "educational theory."

A theory of education is undergirded by many philosophical issues, but two seem particularly relevant, namely, the nature of the person (anthropology) and especially how people learn, and the nature of knowledge (epistemology) and especially its consequences for the person and society. The positions of the great philosophers of the West on these issues distinguish their particular contributions to the philosophy of education.

Plato (ca. 428–348 B.C.) was convinced that the human person has a deep desire (*eros*) to know and do what is good, and conversely, that reliable and certain knowledge leads to virtue and the happy life. Such knowledge, however, is not gleaned from life experience (this leads only to mere opinion), but rather from deductive reasoning in the mind alone. From logical dialectics that searches for foundational principles, we can reason our way to knowing the eternal Forms of all real knowledge (ideals of perfection like beauty, truth, justice, etc.) of which the transient and sensible world around us is but faint reflection. These Forms are already latent in our mind (as sight is present in the eye) by transmigration from previous lives. Though the prodding of experience may encourage these universal truths into consciousness, we "recollect" and recognize them through rational intuition and rigorous thinking. Only the rare few people come to such wisdom and they alone should govern the rest as philosopher kings. Thus, a focus on ideas ("idealism") rather than reality ("realism"), and elitism mark Plato's proposal for education.

Aristotle (384–322 B.C.) had more respect than his mentor Plato for human experience as a source of knowledge and thus as a basis for education. From life and reflection on it (*praxis*) we can come to practical wisdom (*phronesis*) that guides all affairs, personal and political; praxis is also the source of virtue and character formation. Aristotle likewise respected the skill of the artisan as a valid expression of knowledge. However, the highest knowledge is theoretical and comes from inner contemplation of eternal verities. Though he was convinced that knowledge should arise from and influence people's "being" and especially their ethic, educators often read Aristotle to encourage a separation of theoretical knowledge from practical wisdom and skills for life.

Augustine of Hippo (354–430), echoing his philosophical mentor Plato, located the primary source of knowledge within the person, arising from an inner sense of "truth" (though a gift of God rather than from transmigration). However, this potential knowledge is drawn out and brought to consciousness by education that actively engages people's faculties of reason, memory, and will, and by exposing them to the "wisdom of the ages" assembled in the seven liberal arts: the quadrivium of arithmetic, geometry, astronomy, and music; and the trivium of grammar, logic, and rhetoric. Thus Augustine favored education that encouraged the personal discovery and active engagement of students as well as rigorous study of disciplines of learning. For Augustine our eros for knowledge reflects our desire for God; its ultimate fulfillment and greatest wisdom is in loving God.

Thomas Aquinas (1225–1274), more partial to Aristotle than Plato, emphasized sense experience as our first source of knowledge; in his famous dictum "nothing is ever in the mind that is not first in the senses." Reason reflects on the data of the senses to bring us to understanding and judgment of ideas, and then to inform the will and shape our ethic of life. For Aquinas reason is both theoretical and practical. Though his anthropology was more positive and his epistemology more experiential than Augustine, in education Aquinas favored a didactic and teacher-centered style of teaching; inconsistent?

Though Martin Luther (1483–1546) wrote little explicitly about education, the Reformation movement he launched, with its emphasis on the "priesthood of all believers" and on the importance of everyone reading the Scriptures for themselves, encouraged education for all and universal literacy. Luther's turning to civic governments to replace the Church as primary educator initiated state-sponsored schools. And, the Reformation challenge to Church authority encouraged the confidence in critical reason that marked the whole Enlightenment movement and its emphasis on scientific inquiry unfettered by authoritarianism. Thus, the Reformation and Enlightenment movements greatly encouraged and influenced the spirit of the whole "public" education system of the Western world.

American public education was also much influenced by the philosophy of John Locke (1632–1704).

Locke was imbued with the spirit of the Enlightenment era, but rejected its metaphysics and rationalism, and favored a radical empiricism instead. Our mind at birth "is not a closet filled with innate ideas" but a "blank slate" (*tabula rasa*). Our senses are the primary and efficient cause of reliable knowledge, as we move from their data to concepts and then to general ideas that represent the external world. In education Locke logically emphasized learning from experience, and what would be "useful" over metaphysics. He emphasized education for character, but colored with a good deal of Puritan individualism.

The "Naturalists" posed a counterperspective to the Enlightenment quest for clear and certain ideas derived from a disembodied rationality (epitomized in Descartes, 1596–1650). They were also skeptical about the now-reigning emphasis on learning from books (becoming widely available with the printing press), and the concomitant emphasis on teacher-centered didaction. For example, John Amos Comenius (1592–1670) was convinced that everyone already possesses by nature the seeds of erudition, virtue, and piety. Thus, he insisted that education be based on "the method of nature," honoring the sequence of natural development and curiosity to nurture through sense experience and experimentation the learners' native capacities. He was likewise convinced that there is profound unity to all knowledge that can be the source of peace among all people, thus emphasizing the moral and social reform intent of education.

Perhaps the best known "naturalist" was Jean-Jacques Rousseau (1712–1778). With his classic text *Emile,* Rousseau rejected the excessive formalism and rationalism of eighteenth-century France and proposed that education honor the "natural" instincts, impulses, intuitions, and interests of children. He was convinced that we are born with a natural innocence that can be trusted to emerge if we don't interfere with it; education is simply to provide a tutor who encourages the personal observation and discoveries of the child.

Heinrich Pestalozzi (1746–1827) echoed these sentiments, though he was more realistic; he emphasized teaching children according to their natural process of development, in a community of love, with emphasis on play, shared activities, and self-discovery. Likewise, Friedrich Froebel (1782–1852), a student of Pestalozzi, founded the kindergarten movement to sponsor early childhood education that encourages children's holistic development according to their innate capacities and natural interests, leading eventually to personal consciousness and appropriation of their best "selves." In the twentieth century, Maria Montessori (1870–1952) kept alive and developed this "naturalist" emphasis in education.

Johann Friedrich Herbart (1776–1841) shared some of the naturalist sentiment (e.g., beginning with people's interests) but proposed a much more intentional dynamic for teaching. Drawing from the newly emerging science of psychology, Herbart claimed that education should respect the "apperceptive mass" of knowledge that people already possess (i.e., beginning with their conceptual structures and with what they already know), and then teaching should proceed through distinctive moments of preparation, presentation, association (of new knowledge with what students already know), generalization, and application. He was also convinced that education is essentially a moral enterprise ("virtue expresses the whole purpose of education"). Herbart founded the first teacher-training colleges and established many of the symbols of intentional pedagogy (e.g., the enduring "lesson plan").

John Dewey (1859–1952) and his educational philosophy has been called many things (instrumentalism, experimentalism, pragmatism, and reconstructionism), but his essential idea is consistent throughout. Dewey rejected what he called "the spectator theory of knowledge" and proposed that all knowledge arises from reflection on one's social experiences and interaction with the environment. Education, then, should be grounded in a "reconstruction of experience." However, the process of teaching must be intentionally organized so that people can have access through their own experiences to the "funded capital of civilization"; this is assembled in the disciplines of learning that have arisen from the experience and experimentation of people before us. Dewey proposed that all curriculum be structured according to the "organized intelligence" of scientific inquiry, moving from hypothesis intuited from experience, to experimentation, to reformulating the hypothesis. Truth is what is warranted by verifiable results and by its practical usefulness; "the hypothesis that works is the true one."

Other modern philosophies are also having impact on contemporary approaches to education. Existentialism in education eschews the quest for universal and certain ideas and gives priority instead to learning from individual existence and encourages contextual decision-making. Phenomenology likewise insists that all knowledge is grounded in our "life-world" of experience, and emerges from the "phenomena" of life as they present themselves to our consciousness. Marxist-inspired philosophies (e.g., critical theory) question the class bias in culturally dominant knowledge and call attention to the social interests that undergird it. Feminist epistemology highlights the gender bias of knowledge and education, and recommends a more relational and inclusive approach to education that respects "women's ways of knowing."

One can also detect a consistent philosophy undergirding Catholic education. It is drawn as much from Scripture and tradition as from philosophy. In general it emphasizes the uniqueness and dignity of the student, our ability to learn from both experience and critical rationality, from common sense and from rigorous scholarship. It emphasizes that knowledge should lead to an ethic and to formation of character that serves both the personal and common good.

THOMAS H. GROOME

See also CATECHETICS.

EJACULATORY PRAYER

(Latin: *ejaculari,* to toss or hurl quickly). The use of a short verbal prayer, sometimes called an "aspiration," which by occasional repetition can help one remain in the presence of God. Monasticism favored the psalm verse "God, come to my assistance; Lord make haste to help me." Well known is "My Jesus, mercy," or the "Jesus Prayer" of the Eastern Orthodox Churches: "Lord Jesus Christ, Son of God, have mercy on me, a sinner."

DAVID BRYAN

See also PRAYER.

ELECTION

The literal meaning of the word is "being chosen," and it is another word for the concept of vocation, namely, that people do not themselves determine what roles they will play in God's plan, because it is God who calls them to it. In the Bible this is very plainly stated both about the people of Israel and about individual patriarchs, judges, kings, and prophets. In the New Testament, Jesus calls the Twelve and the other disciples, and the early Christians refer to themselves as the elect. In later Christian thought the idea intrudes that if they are the elect there are others who are non-elect, and in St. Augustine of Hippo (early fifth century) this becomes a discussion of predestination to final salvation or the lack of it. In the Carolingian period the issue was much debated whether God could therefore be understood to predetermine that some human beings would be damned. The Church rejected this, but the idea emerged again with John Calvin.

MONIKA K. HELLWIG

See also AUGUSTINE, ST.; CALVIN, JOHN; GRACE; JUSTIFICATION; PROVIDENCE; SALVATION.

ELLIS, JOHN TRACY (1905–1992)

Priest-educator and historian, born Seneca, Illinois, 30 July 1905; died Washington, D.C., 16 October 1992. "As a priest-historian," said Ellis toward the end of his life, "I have lived for a half-century in two worlds, so to speak, the ecclesiastical and the academic." He entered the academic world first. Upon graduation in 1927 from the now defunct St. Viator College in Bourbonnais, Illinois, he won a Knights of Columbus fellowship to the Catholic University of America where he obtained a doctorate in history in 1930. After four years of teaching history in several small Catholic colleges, he began his studies for the priesthood as a candidate for the Diocese of Winona, Minnesota, whose bishop had agreed to allow him to continue his teaching career after ordination.

Declining an offer to attend the North American College in Rome, Ellis enrolled at the Sulpician Seminary (now Theological College) in Washington, D.C. Beginning in 1935, he also taught undergraduate history courses at the Catholic University of America and served for three years as director of the university's satellite summer program in San Antonio, Texas. After ordination to the priesthood on 5 June 1938, Ellis began full-time teaching at the Catholic University. Three years later he was asked to replace the ailing Peter Guilday as professor of American Church history, the field in which he was to make his mark as a scholar. That same year he also became acting secretary of the American Catholic Historical Association and managing director of the *Catholic Historical Review,* a post which he was to hold from 1941 until 1963.

In Ellis' own estimation the 1950s and early 1960s was the period of his most productive writing and publication. Without a doubt his masterpiece was the two-volume life of James Cardinal Gibbons which appeared in 1952 after three years of research and three years of writing. It not only set new standards for clerical biographies but quickly became the most reliable guide to a whole era in American Catholic history. His best-selling work was *American Catholicism,* a historical survey for the University of Chicago's History of American Civilization series, which was first published in 1956 and was reissued in a revised edition in 1969.

John Tracy Ellis

In addition to his own publications, Ellis opened up new areas of research in American Catholic history through the monographs of his graduate students, who included such talented scholars as Annabelle Melville, James Hennesey, S.J., and Colman Barry, O.S.B. With the help of his graduate students he also compiled an invaluable collection of source materials, *Documents of American Catholic History,* which went through four increasingly thick editions, the last of which (Michael Glazier, 1987), was a three-volume work of 1,175 pages.

In 1963 Ellis left the Catholic University of America for what was to be a one-year absence. Instead the charms of San Francisco induced him to spend the years 1964 through 1976 at the University of San Francisco where he enjoyed teaching history but regretted the absence of graduate students. In 1965 he published *Catholics in Colonial America,* the first volume of a projected multivolume history of American Catholicism which was never completed because, Ellis confessed, "the San Franciscans were too sociable and I was too weak."

Two of Ellis' shortest works were among the finest of his publications. In 1952 he created a stir throughout the American Catholic academic world with his provocative essay "American Catholics and the Intellectual Life," in which he chastised American Catholic scholars for "their failure to have measured up. . .to the incomparable tradition of Catholic learning of which they are the direct heirs." In his 1965 Boniface Wimmer lecture, "A Commitment to Truth," he made a moving appeal for honesty and integrity in the Catholic Church.

In 1976 at age seventy-one Ellis returned to the Catholic University of America, first as the initial occupant of the Catholic Daughters of America Chair of American Catholic History and then as Professorial Lecturer in Church History. He continued to teach and to direct graduate students until failing health forced him to retire from the classroom in 1989 (after fifty-nine years) and shortly thereafter to move to a nursing home. Even in retirement, however, he continued to write, finishing two forewords on his last birthday.

At his death the New York *Times* described him as the "dean of American Catholic historians," a title which he had held for as long as most American Catholics could remember. The list of his publications runs to over four hundred items, including more than a dozen books. He was the recipient of over twenty honorary doctorates and numerous awards, including the Laetare Medal from the University of Notre Dame. The *Times* also noted that Ellis' influence extended far beyond his chosen discipline. Throughout his long career he was an eloquent spokesman for academic freedom and for high scholarly standards in American Catholic higher education, and he was a fearless critic of cant and humbug wherever he found it. Above all else John Tracy Ellis was a devout Christian gentleman and a dedicated priest of the Catholic Church. His old-fashioned good manners and unpretentiousness, and his kindness and courtesy to high and low alike, were legendary.

THOMAS J. SHELLEY

See also AMERICAN CATHOLICISM; CATHOLIC HIGHER EDUCATION IN THE UNITED STATES.

EMANCIPATION, CATHOLIC

The process of rescinding the body of legislation, collectively known as the penal laws, which discriminated against Roman Catholics in Britain and Ireland from the sixteenth to the nineteenth centuries. In its final form this code forbade Catholics to acquire land, enter the professions or Parliament, to vote, open schools, or worship in public. By the 1760s religion had ceased to be a factor in international relations, a Jacobite invasion was no longer likely, Irish Catholics had been passive for seventy years, and in 1763 Great Britain acquired French Canada where arrangements had to be made to ensure the allegiance of a Catholic population. All this, together with the growing conviction in England that toleration was the mark of a civilized state, created an atmosphere conducive to relaxing the penal laws, some of which had long fallen into disuse. A Catholic Relief Act of 1778 permitted Catholics in Britain, who were relatively few in number, to be teachers and both to buy and inherit land; it also removed most of the penalties still theoretically enforceable against Catholic clergy. An Act of 1791 allowed Catholics to open public chapels and provided other reforms which left the right to be members of parliament the only major civic liberty denied to them because of their religion.

The American revolution persuaded the authorities in London of the need to mitigate popular grievances in Ireland, where Catholics formed the majority of the population, and they pressured the Irish Parliament into passing an Act in 1778 which extended similar benefits to Irish Catholics as their British coreligionists had been granted earlier that year. The emergence of an Irish Protestant patriotic movement favorably disposed to emancipation brought about the abolition in 1782 of remaining restrictions on landholding and the exercise of ecclesiastical functions. In reaction to the threat presented by the French revolution, Acts of 1792 and 1793 gave Irish Catholics the right to vote, take university degrees and serve in lesser public offices. They were still excluded from Parliament.

Following the union of Britain and Ireland in 1801 in a "United Kingdom" with a single Parliament the government put forward tentative plans for emancipation which envisaged state salaries for the Catholic clergy and acceptance by the pope of the king's right to a veto in the appointment of Catholic bishops. Some of the Irish bishops were intially inclined to accept the veto but quickly abandoned the idea when lay opinion, led by Daniel O'Connell, rejected any suggestion that the Irish Church should be subject to governmental control.

In 1823 O'Connell formed the Catholic Association, which even the poorest peasant could join for a subscription of a penny a month. O'Connell now faced the British authorities with the demand not for a concession but for the recognition of a civil right, the right of citizens not to be discriminated against because of their conscientious beliefs. O'Connell himself was elected a member of Parliament in 1828 and this finally forced the British government to abolish the antipapal oath required of members before they took their seats, which was the means by which Catholics had been barred from the legislature. The Catholic Emancipation Act came into force in 1829. It opened Parliament and all but a handful of the highest offices of state to Catholics throughout the United Kingdom—that is, in Britain as well as Ireland. It also contained gratuitously objectionable clauses against religious orders, which were destined never to be enforced, and it was accompanied by a measure disenfranchising some categories of voters without, however, applying a religious test.

LOUIS McREDMOND

See also BRITAIN, CHURCH IN; CATHOLICISM, IRISH; O'CONNELL, DANIEL; RELIGIOUS FREEDOM.

EMBER DAYS

The Wednesdays, Fridays, and Saturdays of four weeks of the year on which fasting, abstinence, and prayer were prescribed by the Church before Vatican II. They were observed during the weeks following certain Church feasts: the feast of St. Lucy (13 December), the First Sunday of Lent, Pentecost, and the feast of the Holy Cross (14 September). In 1969, the Roman calendar was revised and the responsibility for choosing appropriate dates and formats for the observance of Ember Days was delegated to local conferences of bishops. It is widely believed that Ember Days, long considered sanctification offerings for the four seasons of the year, were derived from the agricultural feasts of ancient Rome. They also have been closely associated with ordinations of the clergy, which were often held on Ember Saturdays.

JOSEPH QUINN

See also LITURGY.

ENCHIRIDION SYMBOLORUM

The full title of this work is *Enchiridion Symbolorum et Definitionum de Rebus Fidei et Morum,* that is, a handbook of symbols (creeds) and definitions about matters of faith and morals. The German theologian, Heinrich Joseph Denziger (1819–1873), compiled it in 1854; indeed, scholars generally refer to this simply as "Denziger." The ES was a collection of documents from the apostolic age (Clement of Rome) to the nineteenth century. It included (in Greek and Latin) excerpts from the teachings of the Church Fathers, theologians, ecumenical councils, and papal documents. Writing in an unecumenical age, Denziger hoped to make a case for Catholic positions with this collection. The work became enormously popular and has been expanded and re-edited literally dozens of times down to the present day.

JOSEPH F. KELLY

See also ORTHODOXY.

ENCYCLICAL

Encyclicals are circular letters written by the pope to convey timely teachings on matters of faith and morals. The New Testament example of an encyclical is 1 Peter addressed to the Churches of Pontus, Galatia, Cappadocia, Asia, and Bithynia (1:1). A letter detailing the martyrdom of Polycarp in 156 was addressed "to all the communities of the Catholic Church." That tradition of encyclical or catholic letters continued at least until Pope Martin VI in 649.

In 1740 Pope Benedict XIV revived "the custom of the ancient Popes" by writing an encyclical at the beginning of his pontificate. Including *Centesimus Annus* of Pope John Paul II in 1991, 285 encyclicals have been written. They are, with few exceptions, addressed to all the bishops of the Church or to bishops of a specific country. Sometimes the clergy and faithful and, since John XXIII's *Pacem in Terris* in 1963, "all people of good will" are included in the salutation.

Encyclicals are an exercise of the pope's authority as the "chief shepherd and teacher of the whole Church." Only if the pope clearly expresses that he is defining *ex cathedra* is the encyclical an exercise of his solemn and infallible magisterium, e.g., the definition of the Assumption of Mary as a matter of faith by Pius XII in 1950. Otherwise encyclicals are an expression of the ordinary papal magisterium, i.e., an authentic (authoritative) teaching safeguarding faith and morals, to which *obsequium* (various interpretations: assent, reverence, due respect, obedience, submission) is to be given because of the supreme and universal teaching mission of the pope under the guidance of the Holy Spirit.

CHARLES D. SKOK

See also AUTHORITY IN THE CHURCH; PAPACY, THE.

ENCYCLICALS, MAJOR, THE

Benedict XIV (1740–1758)
- 1755 *Allatae Sunt:* Aimed at missionaries in the Orient on the observance of Oriental rites.

Clement XIII (1758–1769)
- 1758 *A Quo Die:* A call for Christian unity.

Pius VI (1775–1799)
- 1775 *Inscrutabile:* Describes the pressing problems of the Church.
- 1791 *Caritas Quae:* Deals with the religio-political complications and the impact of the civil oath in France.

Gregory XVI (1831–1846)
- 1832 *Mirari Vos:* A condemnation of liberalism and religious indifference.
- 1834 *Singulari Nos:* Condemns the liberal ideas of F. de Lamennais.
- 1840 *Probe Nostis:* On the Propagation of the Faith.

Pius IX (1846–1878)
- 1849 *Ubi Primum:* On Mary's Immaculate Conception.
- 1864 *Quanta Cura:* Condemns the philosophical and religious errors of the age.
- 1870 *Respicientes:* Condemns the taking of the Papal States to achieve the unification of Italy.

Leo XIII (1778–1903)
- 1878 *Quod Apostolici Muneris:* On the deficiencies of socialism.
- 1879 *Aeterni Patris:* Calls for the restoration of Christian philosophical studies as expounded by Thomas Aquinas.
- 1885 *Immortale Dei:* Expounds the Christian constitution of states.
- 1888 *Libertas Praestantissimum:* On the meaning of Christian liberty.
- 1891 *Rerum Novarum:* Deals with the rights and duties of capital and labor in the light of conditions created by the Industrial Revolution.
- 1893 *Providentissimus Deus:* Encourages the professional study of Scripture and related science.
- 1897 *Divinum Illud Munus:* On fostering devotion to the Holy Spirit.
- 1901: *Graves De Communi Re:* Treats the meaning of Christian democracy.

Pius X (1903–1914)
- 1905 *Acerbo Nimis:* On the teaching of Christian doctrine.
- 1907 *Pascendi Dominici Gregis:* Condemns the teaching of the Modernists.

Benedict XV (1914–1922)
- 1914 *Ad Beatissimi Apostolorum:* An appeal to the great powers to end the war and seek peace.
- 1918 *Quod Iam Diu:* A plea for a fair and just settlement at the upcoming peace conference after World War I.

Pius XI (1922–1939)
- 1930 *Casti Connubii:* On the meaning of Christian marriage.
- 1931 *Quadragesimo Anno:* Issued on the fortieth anniversary of Leo XIII's *Rerum Novarum* whose teaching it confirms.
- 1937 *Mit Brennender Sorge:* On the trials of the Church in Nazi Germany.
- 1937 *Divini Redemptoris:* A condemnation of Communism.

Pius XII (1939–1958)
- 1943 *Mystici Corporis:* A major statement on the nature of the Church.

1943 *Divino Afflante Spiritu:* On promoting scriptural studies using the best historical and textual methods.
1946 *Deiparae Virginis Mariae:* Addressed to all bishops seeking views on making the Assumption of Mary a dogma of faith.
1947 *Mediator Dei:* A landmark statement on sacred liturgy.
1950 *Humani Generis:* An exposé of opinions which seemed adverse to the foundations of the Catholic faith.

John XXIII (1958–1963)
1961 *Mater et Magistra:* On a responsible approach to social progress.
1963 *Pacem in Terris:* A plea for peace based on love, truth, liberty, and justice.

Paul VI (1963–1978)
1964 *Ecclesiam Suam:* A statement on the true nature of the Church.
1964 *Magisterium Fidei:* On the mystery of the Holy Eucharist.
1967 *Populorum Progressio:* On the dignity and development of peoples.
1968 *Humanae Vitae:* A condemnation of artificial birth control.

John Paul II (1978–)
1979 *Redemptor Hominis:* On the dignity of humankind and on its redemption.
1981 *Laborem Exercens:* An analysis of the true meaning and dignity of work.
1986 *Dominum et Vivificantem:* A study of the Holy Spirit in the life of the people of God.
1987 *Redemptoris Mater:* On the role of Mary in the mystery of Christ and in the life of the Church.
1993 *Splendor Veritatis:* John Paul II worked on the longest encyclical in history for six years and addressed it to the bishops, not to the faithful in general. This moral treatise covers such subjects as the role of conscience, the intrinsic evil of certain actions, and the immutability of basic moral principles.

MICHAEL GLAZIER

See also ENCYCLICAL; JOHN PAUL II, POPE.

ENCYCLICALS, SOCIAL

The ordinary vehicle for papal social teaching is encyclicals. Although doctrinal encyclicals have moral and social consequences, encyclicals are termed "social" when they treat more directly economic, political, and cultural issues, actions, and problems which militate against the common welfare of people in society and which affect the dignity of human persons, families, communities, and nations. The tradition of major papal social encyclicals was a century old in 1991.

Pope Leo XIII, The Condition of Labor *(Rerum Novarum), 1891*

The Catholic Social Action movement of Germany, the pilgrimages of French workers to the Vatican, and the support of workers and their unions by the hierarchies of the United States and Great Britain influenced this landmark encyclical which sought "some opportune remedy . . . for the misery and wretchedness pressing so unjustly on the majority of the working class." Poor and working people were the victims of the unscrupulous business practices of the barons of the Industrial Revolution. Unacceptable remedies were socialism, class warfare, and liberal capitalism; acceptable remedies were the return to religion and morality, the inviolability of private property, and the proper intervention of the state on behalf of the workers who have the right to organize themselves into unions to achieve just wages and a dignified standard of life.

Pope Pius XI, Reconstruction of the Social Order *(Quadragesimo Anno), 1931*

The world was in the throes of the Great Depression. The social unrest from widespread unemployment and poverty led to the decline of democracies and the rise of dictatorships. QA condemns both communism and socialism. It calls for socially responsible ownership of property, an alliance between capital and labor by profit-sharing, cooperation between management and workers, state intervention to restrain greed and to promote justice, and the renovation of society through the application of the newly introduced principle of "subsidiarity"—that big business and big government must never arrogate to themselves the functions which can be performed efficiently and well by small business and local government. A healthy society is a multileveled organic society, not one characterized by the wealth of the few and the poverty of the masses.

Pope John XXIII, Christianity and Social Progress *(Mater et Magistra), 1961*

MM appeared at a time of great scientific and technological development, of racial and social upheaval, and of political change with the independence movements of developing nations. The awareness of the great disparity between rich and poor classes now expands to include the alarming disparity between rich and poor nations. The poor nations of the world are the victims of the Cold War between East and

West. The social teaching of the Church is "internationalized." The wealthy nations must aid the development of the poor, nonindustrialized nations and at the same time respect their cultures and refrain from political and economic domination.

Pope John XXIII, Peace on Earth *(Pacem in Terris), 1963*

PT was the first encyclical addressed to include "all people of good will." It rewrites the U.N. Declaration of Human Rights into the Christian context of Catholic social teaching. Against the background of the Cold War and the insatiable appetite of nations for armaments, it proclaims that true peace, based on the order established by God, can come about only if the mutual relations of the human family are restored "in truth, in justice, in love and in freedom." The social teachings of John XXIII were "constitutionalized" in Vatican II's The Church in the Modern World.

Pope Paul VI, The Development of Peoples *(Populorum Progressio), 1967*

PP places a theological foundation under social teaching and action by viewing them as a response to Jesus' proclamation of the reign of God in the world. Human development becomes a theological and moral imperative. The disparity between rich and poor nations must be addressed by placing the superfluous wealth of the rich nations at the service of the poor nations; otherwise the poor will succumb to the temptation of violent revolutions to address the inequities in social life. "The new name for peace is development."

Pope Paul VI, A Call to Action *(Octogesima Adveniens), 1971*

OA addresses the social problems of the "new poor," those migrating to the cities in the hope of a better life but entrapped in joblessness, homelessness, discrimination, and grinding poverty. A new principle for action is introduced: in the face of such widely varying situations of injustice, the pope should not be expected "to put forward a solution which has universal validity"; rather, Christian people are to analyze the "crying injustices" of their own countries in the light of the gospel, "draw principles of reflection, norms of judgment and directives for action from the social teaching of the Church," and take appropriate political action for the transformation of society.

Pope John Paul II, On Human Work *(Laborem Exercens), 1981*

LE criticizes both Marxism and capitalism for treating workers as mere means of production, reaffirms the papal teachings on the rights of workers to wages and benefits in keeping with human dignity, and adds the dimension of the subjective and spiritual value of work in the fulfillment of the human person.

Pope John Paul II, The Social Concerns of the Church *(Sollicitudo Rei Socialis), 1987*

SRS lays strong blame on the confrontation between liberal capitalism of the West and the communism of the East and the exploitation of the Southern Hemisphere by the Northern Hemisphere as major obstacles to the development of the poorer nations of the world. The problems are compounded by imperialism, neocolonialism, militarism, "wars by proxy," consumerism and waste. It calls for conversion of the "structures of sin" which are rooted in personal sin and the implementation of the social doctrine of the Church.

Pope John Paul II, On the Hundredth Anniversary of *Rerum Novarum (Centesimus Annus), 1991*

CA was written as Marxist communism collapsed in Eastern Europe and Russia. It remains critical of communism more for its degradation of human rights and human dignity than for its economic failure; it affirms a responsible free market economy; it cautions against greed and exploitation which characterizes unlimited capitalism; it praises democratic forms of government; and it reaffirms the dignity of the human person as the foundation of economic activity.

CHARLES D. SKOK

See also ENCYCLICAL; SOCIAL TEACHING OF THE CHURCH; VIRTUE.

ENCYCLOPEDISTS

The name given to the contributors to the *Encyclopedia,* a vast (thirty-five volumes) French work published between 1751 and 1780, although the bulk of the work was done by Denis Diderot and finished by 1772. Nothing like it had been imagined before; it required a consortium of four publishers and four thousand subscribers to sustain it financially. The *Encyclopedia* introduced the newly educated middle classes to the most advanced contemporary scholarship. Many of the articles dealt with science and technology and were famous for their illustrations; these furthered sales considerably. But Diderot and many other contributors, including Rousseau and D'Alembert, were generally supporters of natural religion and hostile to Roman Catholicism. Much of their hostility rested upon what they perceived to be the Church's support for a tyrannical aristocracy, a backward government, and rampant superstition among the illiterate. Although Diderot had to watch out for censors, he managed to slip in many pieces directly or indirectly inimical to the Church. Occasionally Church leaders and the French Jesuits tried to get the king to halt publication, but the popularity of the work and the immense investment put in by four prominent publishers kept the government at bay. Diderot struck out against superstition and the use of torture; he argued that the "Malefactor" (the title of an article) is the victim of heredity; he advocated a simple doctrine of good conduct in place of formal religious worship. The *Encyclopedia*'s emphasis upon scientific truth and rationalism as well as its anti-aristocratic and skeptical tone helped to undermine the support for the Church among French intellectuals; the close relation of the Church to the *ancien régime* and its crude attempts to censor the *Encyclopedia* only served to support Diderot's criticisms.

JOSEPH F. KELLY

See also RATIONALISM; SCIENCE AND RELIGION; THEISM.

ENLIGHTENMENT, THE

The term is generally applied to the ideas and ideals which characterized much of the intellectual life of the eighteenth century in Europe. It introduced religious toleration but downgraded religious belief, tradition, and authority in the intellectual pursuits, and emphasized reason as the path to truth and human well-being. Generally, the proponents of the Enlightenment sought to promote the moral and material welfare of society, but it was not a coherent movement and promoted a wide spectrum of secular aims, some of which were disdainful of Christian beliefs and practice. Many saw it as particularly anti-Catholic. However, the Enlightenment had significant achievements and had a formative influence on the Declaration of Independence and on the Constitution of the United States.

MICHAEL GLAZIER

ENVIRONMENT/ECOLOGY

See ECOLOGY/ENVIRONMENT.

EPHRAEM SYRUS, ST. (ca. 306–ca. 373)

Biblical exegete, Doctor of the Church, Ephraem was born in Nisbis in Mesopotamia to parents who were probably Christian. He was ordained a deacon, possibly by St. James of Nisbis, but it is disputed whether he accompanied James to the Council of Nicaea in 325. Syriac sources claim that it was through Ephraem's prayers that Nisbis was spared conquest by the Persians in 338. After the eventual fall of Nisbis to Persia in 363, Ephraem went to Edessa where he did much of his important work.

St. Ephraem the Syrian, fresco painting, Lesnovo

Ephraem is remembered for his scriptural exegesis, and he also wrote on ascetical, dogmatic and exegetical themes while drawing heavily from Scripture. He wrote in Syriac and mainly in verse, favoring a style that made frequent use of metaphor and repetition. His work included hymns for the different liturgical feasts and also didactic hymns which served as catechetical refutations of contemporary heretics, especially Marcion, Manes, the Arians and the Gnostics. He also helped to introduce hymns into public worship of the Church, and he is remembered especially for his Nisbian hymns and canticles for the seasons. His liturgical poetry influenced the development of Syriac and Greek hymnography. He had a strong devotion to the Virgin Mary, always defending her perfect sinlessness. Because of this, Ephraem is often used as an ancient witness of the Immaculate Conception.

In tradition, Ephraem was known as the "Harp of the Holy Spirit." He is revered for his ascetical life and for his biblical exegesis. Pope Benedict XV declared him a Doctor of the Church in 1920. In the East his feast is on 28 January. In the West his feast was formerly observed on 1 February; Benedict XV changed it to 18 June, and since the revision of the Calendar in 1969, it now stands on 9 June.

ANTHONY D. ANDREASSI

See also FATHERS OF THE CHURCH.

EPICLESIS

(Gk. "invocation") A prayer recited by the celebrant at Mass before or after the words of institution which asks the Holy Spirit to descend upon, and dwell within, the bread and wine of the Eucharist and in the congregation.

JOSEPH QUINN

See also EUCHARIST.

EPISCOPACY

See BISHOP.

EPISCOPALIANS

The history of the Episcopal Church begins with the Protestant (often called Tudor) Reformation in England which was triggered by the refusal of Pope Clement VII to grant King Henry VIII a divorce from Catherine of Aragon so he could marry Ann Boleyn. As a result, Henry soon declared himself the head of the Church of England and appointed Thomas Cranmer the first Archbishop of Canterbury in 1533. This dual function of the king forever linked the Anglican Church to the throne of England.

In historical perspective, it is safe to say that the separation of the Church of England from the Church of Rome was less over a royal divorce than over centuries' long uneasiness with what was thought to be unnecessary meddling in English affairs by the popes of Rome. That is why many scholars say that the English Reformation was more a political than a religious one.

The Anglican Church, therefore, resembles in many ways the "one, holy, catholic, and apostolic Church" in continuity with Roman and Eastern Christianity. The only real difference between Canterbury and Rome is that the former rejects papal authority.

The Church of England (Anglican) came to America with the early colonists in 1607. Their strongest settlements were in Virginia and in the southern colonies. Although many Anglicans were sympathetic with the revolutionary cause, others, especially clergy, were politically suspect because of their allegiance to the king.

To insure that the Anglican colonists would have an independent Church and would be able to rule themselves, the Anglican Church in America became the Protestant Episcopal Church in 1789. It remains today a member of the worldwide Anglican community.

It was "Episcopal" to denote its preference for bishops (the word in Greek for bishop is *episcopos*) and its continuity with the catholic tradition. It was "Protestant" to indicate its separation from papal authority.

Episcopalians pride themselves on being a bridge Church between Protestant theology on the one hand and catholic liturgy on the other. As a Church it has the unique capacity to include a variety of positions. It includes a "high" Church inclination to Catholic liturgy, the "low" Church emphasis on freer Protestant worship and a sermon, and the "broad" Church concerns of liberal social action.

There are no distinctively Christian doctrines which set the Episcopalians apart. They see themselves as an extension of the early Church affirming the theological statements of the Apostles' and the Nicene Creeds. They believe their priests are in apostolic succession from Peter, the first Bishop of Rome.

There is a trilateral authoritative structure in the Episcopalian Church—Scripture, tradition, and reason. All doctrines and Church practice must answer to these three criteria.

The unifying factor in the Episcopal Church, and the Anglican Church at large, is *The Book of Common Prayer* which contains collects, prayers for all occasions, and Bible readings for each Sunday in the Church year. The Prayer Book and its truly catholic (universal) Christianity allows Episcopalians the latitude to include conservative, middle-of-the-road, and liberal Christians.

The ministry of the Church is fundamentally one of word and sacrament, with an emphasis on the sacramental. A Roman Catholic legacy is that sacraments are understood to be channels of God's grace. There are two biblical sacraments—baptism, one's entry into the family of God and the Lord's Supper (called Eucharist or "thanksgiving," in which Christ is truly present) which is one's regular nourishment for the Christian life.

Many Episcopalians appreciate other "sacramental" acts such as confirmation (sacrament of the Holy Spirit), marriage (sacred unity by and before God), ordination (holy orders), confession (reconciliation with God), and healing (anointing of the sick).

The weekly Sunday service is called Morning Prayer with Eucharist. It is patterned after the Roman Catholic Mass. One may find there candles, incense, holy water, colorful priestly vestments, and stately music. Churches are often named after saints and theological themes, e.g., St. Thomas and the Church of the Ascension.

Episcopalians are governed by a triennial General Convention which consists of a House of Bishops, and a House of Deputies. The latter consists of lay and clergy members elected from all the dioceses. A diocese is a group of Episcopal parishes headed by a bishop.

The ecclesiastical order of the Church is based on the New Testament structure of bishops, priests, and deacons. The parish priest, usually called a rector, is assisted by a Vestry who are elected laity responsible for spiritual life and general administration of the parish. The Church Warden is a lay person who oversees the secular affairs of the congregation.

The Episcopal Church is one of the most liberal of Protestant denominations in terms of social issues, and one of the most conservative in terms of liturgy and Church tradition. Because of its catholicity and The Prayer Book, it has a broad appeal and an expansive ecumenical outlook.

There are about 70 million Anglicans in the world; this includes the 2.4 million Episcopalians in the United States.

IRA ZEPP

See also ANGLICANISM; PROTESTANTISM.

ERASMUS, DESIDERIUS (ca. 1467–ca. 1536)

The illegitimate son of Gerard of Gouda, he was born in Rotterdam, the Netherlands, around 1467. While a teenager, he was coerced by his guardians into becoming an Augustinian monk. But the bishop of Cambrai arranged for him to leave the cloister and become his secretary. The bishop recognized his unusual talents and encouraged him, after his ordination in 1492, to travel, study, and widen his intellectual horizons. Erasmus read the signs of the times and foresaw that Church reform, too long neglected, was a pressing necessity; the options were reform or upheaval. Today, he is viewed as the disciple of moderation and good sense in an age of extremes.

Erasmus traveled widely and had the ability to make and keep friends, among whom were Thomas More and John Fisher. He became well known and liked in English circles; from 1511 to 1514, he lectured on Greek at Cambridge, and he later dedicated one of his books to Henry VIII and Anne Boleyn. Archbishop Warham gave him the benefice of Aldington, and when he resigned it, he was given a pension for life. He was a patron to Holbein, by whom he was painted several times. His principal scholarly works include a new edition of the Greek New Testament (1516), followed by Latin paraphrases (1517–1524). He is more widely remembered for his earlier writings, such as *Encomium Moriae* (*The Praise of Folly*, 1511, a satire on theologians and Church dignitaries); *Enchiridion Militis Christiani* (1503), a simple book of spirituality which had a huge circulation in many translations;

Desiderius Erasmus, portrait by Hans Holbein, 1532

and *Institutio Christiani Principis* (*Education of a Christian Prince*). In 1520, he moved to Basel, Switzerland, where he worked as an editor at the publishing house of Johann Froben until 1527. During this period, he published some of his works on the Church Fathers and an edition of Aristotle. He saw the need for Church reform, but distanced himself from Luther, feeling that reform was possible without dividing the Church.

Erasmus was befriended by popes and princes, but maintained his respect for truth, tolerance, moderation, and independence. A man of great integrity and learning, he has had a lasting cultural influence over the centuries. He died around 1536.

JOSEPH QUINN

See also FISHER, JOHN, ST.; MORE, THOMAS, ST.; REFORMATION, THE.

ESCHATOLOGY

As a technical term, *eschatology* (from the Greek *eschatos* = the furthest, the last), is used commonly in theology to refer to the doctrine about the ultimate destiny of humanity and of the world.

Old Testament

The common handbook treatment of eschatology focused almost exclusively on the topics of death, resurrection, judgment, the end of the world, heaven and hell. It is commonly understood among exegetes today that, in this sense, eschatology is not an issue in the OT. Since the early 1960s, however, biblical theology has underscored the development of a future-consciousness throughout the centuries of biblical history. If this is seen as a form of evolving eschatological consciousness, then eschatology can be said to lie close to the heart of the revelatory process.

Viewed from this perspective, eschatology is closely tied to a theology of history. It reflects the sense that history is essentially incomplete until it finds its consummation in the aim God has set for it from the beginning. The issue for the OT is first of all the hope for the future of the nation. God's work with this people is not yet finished. But Israel's destiny is seen to be linked to that of the nations and eventually to that of the cosmos itself (Isa 2:2-4; 19:18-25; 56:6ff.; 60; Soph 3:9ff.; Zech 9:1-8). Thus, in the later prophets the future dimension of biblical faith becomes truly universal and eschatological in scope. It envisions not only the destiny of Israel but the destiny of all humanity and the world (Isa 65:17).

Since the fulfillment of God's promise lies in the future, its precise nature is not clearly known. Therefore the language with which the Scriptures speak of it is highly metaphorical and symbolic. The most common themes involved in it are: harmony, peace, reconciliation, justice, and fullness of life. Common metaphors are: new covenant, banquet, marriage feast, and kingdom.

It was against this background that the reflection of the wisdom literature raised the problem of individual destiny (Wis 2:3; 3:1-4; 9:15). The concept of an immortal soul available from the Greek-speaking world made it possible to think of some sort of personal survival after death in terms other than the shadowy existence of Sheol. This provided the basis for speculation on the problem of retribution and eventually on resurrection as a form of divine vindication for the just.

The apocalyptic reflections of the intertestamental period (from the beginning of the second century B.C.E.) radicalize the hope of the prophetic tradition. While the prophets for the most part hoped for an idealized future within history, apocalyptic raised the question of a future that transcends historical experience. It can be argued that it is only at this stage that the vision of Israel became truly universal and cosmic in scope. Because of its universality, this level of reflection raised also the possibility of a resurrection of the dead (Dan 12:2-3; 2 Macc).

While the OT does not end with a univocal vision of the future, it can be argued that the hopes and expectations of the centuries are drawn together in a symbol drawn from the experience of the Davidic monarchy and projected into the future. One looks to a future kingdom of God in which the divine promise, carried in the heart of the people for so many centuries, will be brought to full fruition.

The New Testament

These traditional hopes of the Jewish people were taken up by Jesus and reshaped in the light of his own experience of God and the events of his ministry. From this came the hope for the rule of God's tender, forgiving love; a rule which was beginning already in the experience of Jesus' ministry and yet was open to future fulfillment. Thus, the ministry of Jesus does not dissolve the sense of future hope, but keeps it open to yet deeper realization.

Certainly the great hopes opened up by Jesus' preaching and actions must have been devastated by the events of Good Friday. But, in the light of the Easter experience, new light is shed on the deeper meaning of those hopes. The confession of Jesus as the Christ was formulated in the categories of OT hope even though these categories had to undergo significant transformation in the process. And from this the specifically Christian vision of hope begins to emerge as a hope centered around the experience of Jesus as the risen Lord.

Early Christian reflections were not uniform. The Pauline tradition clearly reflects the shifting influence of apocalyptic thought in the early Christian community. The Johannine tradition reflects two patterns which may be described as "horizontal" and "vertical." The vertical pattern emphasizes the eschatological character of the present experience of the believer, while the horizontal pattern looks to a future "last-day" much as the broader biblical tradition had done. Of the canonical Christian Scriptures, only the Book of Revelation is structured completely as an apocalyptic text. Though the overall style of this book is emphatically apocalyptic, its central message, concentrated in the phrase "a new heaven and a new earth" (Rev 20:11-21:5), is unmistakably a message of hope.

Tradition

The development of eschatological thought continued after the writing of the Scriptures. As the Church moved more firmly into the world of the Greco-Roman Empire, it was confronted with a world of different categories and thought-patterns. As the influence of Hellenistic categories made itself felt, themes were set down for later development. Such themes include the idea of an immortal soul; the possibility of an interim period between individual death and the general resurrection; the practice of suffrages for the dead; the doctrine of limbo; the possibility of purgation beyond death.

Medieval eschatology indulged in extensive speculations about the nature of the separated soul, and the qualities of the resurrected body. Heaven was commonly thought of in terms of the doctrine of the beatific vision. The doctrine of purgatory, now viewed as a distinct, otherworldly place, was developed together with an elaborate system of suffrages and indulgences. In general, eschatology tended to become an elaborate description of the "other world." These themes may be seen as symptoms of the general tendency of medieval theology to focus more on the individual aspect of eschatology than was the case either in Scripture or in the patristic tradition. Collective symbols were not lost, but were emphasized less than those dealing with individual destiny.

These medieval developments played a significant role in the Reformation, particularly the theory of purgatory and the allied praxis of the Catholic Church. In general, the Reformation period and the baroque age saw little development in the area of eschatology that would move significantly beyond the medieval orientation.

From the period of Enlightenment, modern philosophical and scientific developments coalesced to highlight the human role in the shaping of history. This led to various forms of secularized eschatology reflected in immanentist philosophies of history and ideologies of progress. These eventually tended to focus on an immanent, worldly future and left no room for the action of God which had played so basic a role in the biblical tradition. Theological eschatology, then, tended to become isolated both from history and from cosmic reality and focused totally on that which awaits individual human beings in the afterlife.

Current Developments

Recent decades have seen a significant shift in theological eschatology. First, one can speak of a rediscovery of the eschatological dimension of the biblical tradition. Then, in the general rereading of the sources that characterized theological method in recent decades, a sense of the impoverished state of the eschatology operative in the modern era emerged. New insights led in the 1960s to discussions between Marxist philosophers and Christian theologians dealing particularly with the philosophy of history, the problem of hope, and the problem of the future.

The work of the Second Vatican Council reflects a significant shift in perspective. The text of the document on the Church (*Lumen Gentium*) reflects important insights of biblical eschatology in describing the Church and its mission. These are extended in the Pastoral Constitution on the Church in the Modern World (*Gaudium et Spes*). The latter document places the mystery of Christ emphatically in the context of a theology of history, affirming that Christ sums up the meaning of all history (no. 38). It goes on to describe human efforts to build a better world as a foreshadowing of the final age of God's kingdom. While the document cautions against identifying historical progress with the coming of the kingdom, it speaks of the positive significance such progress has in the overall picture (no. 39). Using language drawn from an understanding of the resurrection of Christ, the text suggests that the fruits of human endeavors will appear in a transformed state in the kingdom of God. It thus suggests that the relation between history and the kingdom is not one of simple continuity, but one of continuity together with radical transformation. Such an orientation, if pursued consistently, offers the hope of relating personal with social dimensions, present with future dimensions, and this-worldly with transcendent dimensions in a form of eschatology which retrieves the precious insights of the tradition and attempts to develop them in terms of contemporary social and cosmological theory.

After Vatican II, eschatology has provided inspiration for a number of movements: theology of the world, theology of revolution, and theology of liberation. All of these involve some reshaping of eschatology together with a new understanding of the Christian's relation to the world.

At the present time it is impossible to see any uniform approach to the problems of eschatology among theologians. But there is a broad consensus that a healthy development will call for a reshaping of the understanding of humanity in its individual, social, and cosmic dimensions. This will involve the rediscovery of the place of nature in history as well as the rediscovery of the meaning of salvation in the context of creation-theology.

ZACHARY HAYES, O.F.M.

See also DEATH; HEAVEN; HELL; HOPE; KINGDOM OF GOD; LIMBO; PAROUSIA; PURGATORY.

ESSENES

See DEAD SEA SCROLLS.

ETHICS

See ETHICS, BUSINESS; SITUATION ETHICS.

ETHICS, BUSINESS

Business ethics is a reflection on the moral values at stake in carrying out any form of business; that is to say, it is a reflection on the obligations an organization as a whole and its individual members have to respect human dignity and ecological integrity and to advance the common good.

As such, business ethics involves, first of all, a reflection on the values that define and drive an organization. These values are grounded in the basic responsibilities of an organization: (1) obligations to society—obligations not just to conform to the demands of the law but to contribute positively to the common good; (2) obligations to employees—obligations to provide an environment within which employees can carry out work in accord with their dignity; and (3) obligations to investors—obligations to protect the assets of the investors and provide them an equitable return on their investment. Based on these values, an organization determines its specific defining values in light of the nature of the business in which it is involved and from its past traditions.

Second, business ethics involves a delineation of the significance and implications of the organization's values (as enunciated through the process described above) for the various aspects of business: human resource issues such as hiring, promoting, firing, and downsizing; planning; finance; marketing; etc.

Third, business ethics involves a consideration of how decisions are to be made in situations where values are in conflict or where circumstances do not permit the full exercise of values. Such situations arise, for example, when the right of investors to a return on their investment has to be balanced against the right of employees to an appropriate wage; when the obligations of the organization to protect the environment have to be balanced against the pressures exerted by a competitive marketplace; or when the rights of employees to involvement in decisions affecting their work have to be balanced against the responsibilities of those in management.

THOMAS SCHINDLER

See also SOCIAL RESPONSIBILITY, FINANCIAL; SOCIAL TEACHING OF THE CHURCH; WORK.

ETHIOPIAN CHURCH

See EASTERN CATHOLIC CHURCHES.

EUCHARIST

The Eucharist is the central worship assembly of the Catholic community, consisting of prayers, Scripture readings, homily, and partial reenactment of the farewell supper of Jesus.

This article is addressed to Eucharistic practice, what it is and how it is influenced by doctrinal and theological perceptions. It begins by describing how the issues at stake in the present context of ecclesial awareness have emerged and looks for further understanding through a survey of how Eucharistic practice developed down through the centuries. Finally it takes up issues of importance for present practical developments in the celebration of the Eucharist.

Vatican II Renewal of Eucharist

In several of its documents, especially that on the liturgy, the Second Vatican Council stressed the central place which the Eucharist has in the life of the local and universal Church (SC 41, 42; DOL 1, 41). It laid down principles for a fuller and more conscious participation of all the faithful in Eucharistic action, pointing to the various ministries exercised in the course of its celebration. This was further developed in postconciliar documents, culminating in the 1975 edition of the Roman Missal (See General Instruction of the Roman Missal: DOL 208). In these documents, the Eucharist is presented primarily as memorial of the paschal mystery of Christ, the sacramental renewal of his sacrifice, and the table of his Body and Blood, of which all the faithful are invited to partake (SC 102; DOL 1, 102; General Instruction, ch. 1; DOL 208, 1391–1395). While the role of the priest to act in the person of Christ is kept to the fore, a development of community participation, and a promotion of various ministries such as that of reader, cantor, choir and liturgical planning, are espoused. Better instruction is fostered, and a catechesis on the sacrament which is intelligible to people today encouraged. More appreciation of cultural diversity in the celebration of the Eucharist is included in the general principles of the conciliar documents (SC 37–40; DOL 1, 37–40), as well as in the practice of the Roman Curia, as evidenced for example in the adaptations to the rite sanctioned for use in the Church of Zaire (*Notitiae* 24 [1988] 455–472).

New Testament Foundations

Eucharistic tradition has always looked primarily to the words of Jesus at the Last Supper as the foundation for belief and practice, whether the sacrament is named Eucharist, or Mass, or Lord's Supper, or simply Liturgy. The words however have been given different accentuation or put into different contexts. After the Reformation controversies of the sixteenth century, Tridentine Catholicism seemed to make only the priest's pronunciation of the words "This is my Body, this is my Blood" the focus of doctrine and practice, while Reformation Churches gave more attention to the words "Take and eat, take and drink," or to proclaiming the covenant given in Christ's Blood for the forgiveness of sins. Much of the effort in recent practice and theology has been to place these words in their larger context, in relation to the entire New Testament presentation of the sacrament.

Practice of Early Christians. While the difference between the accounts of the Last Supper given in Mark and Matthew on the one hand, and in Luke and Paul on the other, have long been noted, recent study has placed them in their different community and liturgical settings. Thus note is taken of what Luke in the Acts of the Apostles calls the "breaking of the bread," or of what Paul in 1 Corinthians calls the "Supper of the Lord." The community context of sharing the Eucharist is thus filled out, to include gathering together in house churches for instruction, prayer and mutual support, sharing the teaching of the apostles, practicing charity to the poor and the stranger, and building up communion in the one faith and charity through a diversity of ministries bestowed by the Spirit. At the same time it is noted that the Johannine narrative of Jesus's final meeting with his disciples is given dramatic expression in the washing of the feet and the command to the disciples to do likewise to each other. This mutual service is also a way of remembering Jesus Christ and it has to be a mark of any community which gathers for the liturgical celebration of the Lord's Supper in obedience to the memorial command.

Memorial Command and Ritual. Central to recent studies of New Testament origins is the perception that Jesus's memorial command places his action and the action of the Church in continuity with Jewish and Old Testament traditions of keeping memorial. The model for the Christian Eucharist is a kind of action in which memory is kept of a person or event through story, ritual, and blessing prayer. Through such ritual, the person or event remains alive in the memories, actions, and hopes of those who keep memorial.

Primary among memorial rites was the celebration of the Pasch. Although it is not clear whether Jesus in fact celebrated the paschal meal with his disciples on the night before his death, its events are presented in that way by the Gospels. He is seen to interpret elements of the rite and its blessings in order to show that paschal expectations are realized in his own death and that this opens a new eschatological hope for the future. The blessing and sharing of the bread and the cup were the elements of the rite which Jesus singled out, offering in these symbols his own Body and Blood for the forgiveness of sins and the nourishment of the community of God's kingdom which he inaugurated.

Early Christian communities remembered Jesus as Lord and Christ at this table, gathering regularly to do so, rather than just once a year. While various Scriptures were read, their principal narrative told of Jesus himself and the accomplishment of messianic expectations in his death and resurrection. In the blessing of bread and wine their prayer leaders invoked his memory, thus remembering him and asking that God remember them in his name. The gathering responded to the invitation to eat and drink of his Body and Blood at the table which was blessed.

The Presence of the Risen Lord. Even in ordinary circumstances, when a dead person is remembered there is a hope that there is still a communion in life between the living and the dead. In the Eucharist, Christians gathered in the assurance of Christ's resurrection and of the gift of the Spirit. Living now in communion with the Father and the Spirit he was still present among the disciples. The Body and Blood which Christians shared was thus the Body and Blood of the living Lord, sacrament of the death which he had endured, of the life to which he had been raised, and of the communion in him which made the community a new reality and an eschatological people.

Early Centuries

Assemblies. The size and nature of assemblies exercised an important influence on developments in Eucharistic practice. In the very early centuries, when local churches were quite small in size, the golden rule was that of one assembly on Sunday, under the presidency of the bishop. With the increase in numbers and a spread over more extended geographical areas, there were more assemblies and larger assemblies, with presbyters as well as bishops presiding.

The nature of the place of congregation also changed. Early small communities met in house churches, that is, in large rooms that were part of private homes, simply adorned with frescoes and the furnishings necessary to celebration. After the Constantinian peace, the Western Church developed the form of the basilica or large gathering place which it inherited from Roman culture. There the focus was on the practicality of gathering and celebrating and on the dignity of the people who gathered. The relation between the earthly Church and the living dead was represented in the presence of a martyr's tomb beneath the altar. Eastern Churches did more to enhance the symbolism of the building, through the use of light and of icons, so that the building itself became a reflection of the mystery celebrated within it. Some differences in ritual corresponded to the different focus and symbolism of the place in which the Eucharistic action took place.

Though the rule of the one Eucharistic assembly on the Sunday remained dominant for some centuries, increasingly allowance was made for weekday gatherings of members of the community. Relatively early mention is made of gatherings in cemeteries, for liturgies in commemoration of the dead buried there, some days or weeks after death, or on anniversaries of a death. In time, the celebration of the Eucharist was associated with the actual burial of deceased persons. In certain Churches, the special fast days called for Eucharist, though in others this would have been seen as a break of the fast. In short, there was no universal rule about the appropriate days or types of gathering outside Sunday, but more and more Churches allowed of weekday Eucharists for a variety of purposes.

Order of Service. The Eucharistic Rite developed in different local Churches in such a way that a common pattern emerged, even while there was room for considerable cultural diversity in expression. The common pattern was that of gathering, proclamation, and explanation of the Scriptures or word of God, communal prayer of intercession, offering of the gifts of bread and wine, Eucharistic Prayer, and Communion rite. The Eucharistic Prayer was one of commemorative thanksgiving and intercession, prayed with reference to the memorial command of the Supper Narrative. The blessing of this Eucharist was prolonged into the weekdays by the custom of allowing the faithful to take the Eucharistic bread home with them, for the sake of having this nourishment throughout the week.

Diversity from one Church to another showed in the particular choice of Scriptures to be read, in the texts and style of chant adopted, in the prayer texts composed, and in some ritual actions. After the fourth century, the differences between Eastern Churches and Western Churches increased. One important difference had to do with the invocation of the Spirit in the prayers of the East and the absence of such invocation in Western prayers. Joined with this was the fact that Eastern Churches used leavened bread, whereas the Western Church used unleavened. This reflected dissimilar understandings of the Church, of the presence of Christ in the liturgical gathering, and of the role exercised by the ordained minister.

Sacrifice of Remembrance. The sense in which the Eucharist is designated as a sacrifice can be understood from use of that term in early centuries. First the word was used to designate the whole Christian life, showing how true liturgy or worship is obedience to the gospel, as practiced by those who have been sanctified through Christ's redemptive death. Then it became customary to call the Eucharistic Prayer a sacrifice of thanksgiving, in which the true worship prophesied in Malachi 1:10 is fulfilled, since it is offered in thanksgiving for Christ's work, in the invocation of his name, and as a blessing of the first fruits of the earth, which thereby become the first fruits of the new creation, the Body and Blood of Christ. The table was thus called a sacrificial table and eventually the Eucharistic action as such was called a sacrifice, being sacrament of the sacrificial death of Jesus Christ.

It is only in relation to the Pasch of Christ, as its sacrament and memorial, that the Eucharist is called a sacrifice. As a memorial of Christ, it is salutary for those who make this memory and for those whom they remember as they remember Christ, especially the dead, for there is the assurance that God grants grace to those remembered in the pleading of Christ's Blood. In making memorial thanksgiving, in the profundity of their gratitude, by reason of their communion with Christ in his Body and Blood, the people make an offering of themselves to the Father, in Christ and in his Spirit. That is, they pledge themselves to that service of God and of the world which is the consequence of true faith and hope in Christ's Pasch.

Western Medieval Developments

Medieval Practice. In the latter centuries of the first millennium, increasing attention was given to the action of the priest in itself and to having Masses offered for particular intentions, especially for the dead. At the same time, for reasons not always easily discernible, the laity received Eucharistic Communion less and less frequently. In the end, in 1215, the Fourth Lateran Council felt obliged to prescribe annual Communion, at the time of Easter.

As some kind of compensation for infrequent Communion, various devotions to the consecrated sacrament emerged, such as gazing on the raised Host during Mass, praying to the reserved sacrament, or carrying it in procession for the reverence of the faithful. While to some extent these devotions fostered adoration of Christ's divinity, for the most part they proved to be alternate ways of developing an affective devotion to his passion and to his humble birth in the form of an infant from the Virgin Mary. Such other devotions as the Way of the Cross or setting up the Christmas crib went side by side with this fervent compassion with Christ in his birth, suffering, and death. Thus, instead of hearing the Scriptures in their own language (since the Mass continued in Latin) and of going to the Communion table, many women religious and laity participated in the Eucharist through prayers directed to the humanity of Christ who humbled himself for sinners in his birth and passion. Another mode of participation was to provide stipends to have Masses offered by priests for various intentions, thus providing a means of mediation for the living and the dead that had great importance in medieval society. Accounts are often given of superstitious practices or of exaggerations attached to these devotions, but sight should not be lost of their central attention to Christ's passion and to the work of his mediation.

Medieval Theology. Early medieval theology was an effort to resolve two dilemmas, one practical, the other doctrinal. The practical problem emerged from the separation between the sanctuary and the people and the lack of Latin which made it impossible for many to follow the rites. Expositors had recourse to allegorical explanations of the priest's actions, comparing his movements to moments in the drama of Christ's passion.

Doctrinally, problems were raised about the presence of Christ's Body and Blood in the sacrament. How could something be both the reality and the sign of the Body and Blood? How could Christ be present both in heaven and in the Sacrament? It was in facing such questions that the teaching on substantial presence and substantial change was worked out to explain the peculiar mode of being in sacrament, which is different both from physical presence and from purely spiritual figuration. Theologians were able to appeal to the terms and categories of Aristotle's philosophy which was just then gaining wider recognition. In the long run, this theological emphasis gave ground and support to Eucharistic devotions outside the time of the celebration of the Mass.

The high point of medieval Eucharistic theology was Scholastic theology, as passed down to us especially in the works of Thomas Aquinas and Bonaventure. Both used the new categories but the approach of Thomas was more intellectual, that of Bonaventure more affective. Thomas put emphasis on the difference between sacramental presence and physical presence and on the role of the Eucharist in bringing the faithful to a communion with Christ in the contemplation of the mystery of the Word whose incarnation and sacrifice won humanity's redemption. Bonaventure, for his part, underlined how the sacrament assures Christ's continuing presence in his Church, as promised in Matthew 20:18, and showed how the daily descent on the altar resembled the humble descent of the Word in the incarnation.

Reformation and Post-Reformation

Practice. In reaction against medieval development and in an effort to retrieve the preaching of the word and the practice of sacramental Communion, the Churches of the Reformation changed the ritual to one where it was clearly a celebration of word and Sacrament. They wanted it to be celebrated as a sacrament given to the faithful for the forgiveness of sins and the assurance of God's mercy in Christ, not as a sacrifice offered by the priest.

The Roman Catholic Church, for its part, standardized its rites and issued liturgical books and liturgical norms that regulated practice, with few exceptions, throughout the entire Western world. In reaction to Protestant demands, it reinforced the use of the Latin language and did not allow the giving of the chalice to the laity. It continued to advocate and foster a variety of devotions addressed to Christ present in the reserved sacrament. The post-Reformation period was more intransigent on these points than had been the Council of Trent, which while it did not make changes at that time allowed for some possible opening to such matters as liturgy in the vernacular or the offer of the chalice to the faithful.

Doctrine: Reformers and the Council of Trent. The teachings of the Reformers and the teachings of Trent on the nature of the Sacrament coincided with the problems about practice which divided Catholics and Reformers. Trent reiterated the teaching of substantial presence and substantial change, and hence was able to underline that permanence of Christ in the Sacrament which was the ground for Eucharistic devotion. Martin Luther and John Calvin, while affirming Christ's presence, gave more spiritually oriented explanations that related to the communion of the faithful which they wished to encourage. Today it is believed that these theologies, though indeed quite different, are not mutually exclusive, but at that time each party anathematized the teaching of the other.

On sacrifice, the Reformers insisted that the Eucharist is a sacrament to be consumed and not a sacrifice to be offered. In the Rite of Mass or Lord's Supper they allowed only for a sacrifice of thanksgiving and for the people's self-offering, but did not see these as belonging to the essence of the Eucharist. Catholic apologists and the Council of Trent affirmed that the Mass is not only a sacrifice of thanksgiving but that it is offered by the priest in the power of Christ as a sacrifice of propitiation, that is, one that benefits the living and the dead, for satisfaction for sin and the punishment due it, and for other necessities.

Though both parties taught the essential relation of the Mass to the Cross, as its memorial and representation, this common stance was obscured in the midst of the polemics about the sacrificial nature of the priest's action and about the relation between sacrament and sacrifice. This polemic dominated Eucharistic theology for the four centuries following the Reformation and the Council of Trent, as it also tended to determine sacramental practice, with the Protestant Churches giving primacy to the importance of the proclamation of the word and the Roman Catholic Church accentuating the offering of sacrifice and Eucharistic devotions outside Mass.

Present Approaches

Ecumenical Dialogue. In its appreciation of other Churches, not in full communion with the Roman Catholic Church, the Vatican Council included an understanding of what is expressed in their Eucharistic celebrations. While recognizing the full richness of Eucharistic celebration and doctrine in Eastern Churches, it also acknowledged the true Eucharistic realities present in those Churches to whose sacramental celebration the Roman Church is not presently ready to give full recognition (UR 22; DOL 6, 189).

In ongoing dialogue between the Churches, much has been learned about the nature of the Eucharist and its modes of celebration. Much progress has also been made in coming to agreement about the nature of the Sacrament, including positions on such controversial issues as Real Presence and sacrifice, and about the features necessary to its celebration (See *Baptism, Eucharist and Ministry 1982–1990. Report on the Process and Responses,* Faith and Order Paper No. 149, World Council of Churches, Geneva, 1990). As different Western Churches have revised their rites, a growing convergence has emerged in the manner of its celebration (See *Baptism and Eucharist. Ecumenical Convergence in Celebration,* eds. Max Thurian and Geoffrey Wainwright, Faith and Order Paper No. 117, World Council of Churches, Geneva, 1983), so that there is now greater similarity of practice on such matters as the proclamation of the word of God, the structure and content of the Eucharistic Prayer, the use of the chalice in the Communion of the congregation, and the frequency of celebration and of Eucharistic reception. While some Churches admit members of other communions to the Eucharistic table, the Roman Catholic Church continues to work towards that goal as a hope for the future, when the serious obstacles to the mutual recognition of Churches have been overcome.

Diversity within the Roman Catholic Church. Whatever the Church practices and teaches, it strives to be in continuity with the tradition received through the apostles and with doctrines and practices formulated throughout the ages. It is always open to new or fresh expression, but the new must augment or renew the old, not replace it with something unconnected. Transitions are not easy to make and there is an inevitable tension in times when more extensive changes seem desirable and are put into effect. At the present time of Eucharistic development, some wish to retain the aura of mystery and devotions that accentuate it, or to keep in sharp outline the difference between the priest and the people, thus underlining the aspect of sacrifice and mediation. Others focus more on congregational participation and the common Eucharistic table, thus reinterpreting in practice as well as in theory the nature of the sacramental sacrifice. In doctrine, there is a preference among some for repeating the tried and true formulas, but others prefer to use biblical language and images or to explain the Sacrament in more contemporary terms. Hence there is some polarization, not only between members of the same community, but between communities that give different accents to the manner of celebrating.

Central is the fact that the Eucharist is the sacramental memorial of the paschal mystery of Christ. It is only in relation to this that it is called either sacrament or sacrifice. It is also in this respect the sacrament of the Church, in which the bonds of its communion are constantly renewed. At the table of Christ's Body and Blood, the Church is itself manifested as his living Body in the Spirit and as his living sacrifice in the world.

Motivation for the practice of taking Communion at every Eucharist is provided by the need for this nourishment, by the nature of the Communion as a celebration of the communion of the Church in Christ, and by the call to partake fully in that paschal commemoration which is effected in the Eucharistic Prayer and at the Eucharistic table. The understanding of Christ's presence in the sacramental species is expanded by faith in his living presence in the gathering of the faithful, in the proclamation of the word, in the various ministries performed, and in the prayer of the ordained minister, proclaimed in Christ's name and in the name of the Church, his body. The editing of Church documents, however, shows some tension between the attention given to the presence in the community (SC 7; DOL 1, 7) and that given to presence in the person of the minister (compare SC 7; DOL 1, 7 and GIRM 2, 7; DOL 208, 1397). This tension is also apparent in approaches to celebration.

The aid given to remembrance of Christ's passion and of the mystery of his incarnation by devotions in the past is still sought by some in the revival of these devotions. For others, this memory is best renewed in actual celebration by a vivid recall of his life, teaching, ministry, and paschal mystery as these are recounted in the Scriptures, now expounded as living word, heard and pondered by all the faithful.

New Issues

As the Church reshapes its vision of its evangelical and ministerial role in society, and as communities come together on a new basis, several unexpected practical issues emerge for the celebration of the Eucharist.

Assembly. In the early Church, the local church was coextensive with the Eucharistic assembly. Indeed, the local church was, as it were, defined as the people who gather around the bishop for the celebration of the Sacrament. Other matters, such as the ordination of ministers, the appointment to services, the reconciliation of penitents, the preparation of catechumens, and the care of the needy, could be taken care of within that gathering. To some extent, this carried over into later centuries, as long as geographical boundaries clearly defined both the human community and the ecclesial community.

In today's world, there is, especially in urban areas, a different human and social basis for Eucharistic community. Membership of parishes and participation in the Eucharistic Rite are subject much more to voluntary subscription. Different models, therefore, more in the nature of those that serve intentional communities, provide the ground for Eucharistic assembly. This affects the distribution and conduct of roles within the liturgy.

While the ideal of full participation and of a distribution of ministries is fostered by official liturgical documents, the human elements at play have much to do with how that is realized. In some gatherings, the role of the priest as celebrant for the community stands out more strongly. In others, the need to coordinate the presidential role with other ministries is more desired, even in such matters as the preparation of the Eucharistic homily. As communities differ in their configuration, different models of leadership are called forth.

Women. Since they have been long held silent in the assembly, there is much to be reckoned with as women take on a more active part in community life, and in liturgical ministries. Questions of inclusive language, of ministerial garb, and of spatial arrangement affect their participation, either enhancing it or diminishing it. As long as the Roman Catholic Church professes that women cannot be ordained, while at the same time professing that this does not mean inequality, it is a great challenge to find ritual arrangement and practice which does not express inequality, despite what is said to the contrary.

Eucharistic Services without Ordained Presiders. For an increasing number of congregations, the Sunday Eucharistic assembly has to be conducted without an ordained presider. Rites suggested for this eventuality are at pains to provide directives which enhance the quality of the service, while also making it clear that such a service is distinct from a Mass (Congregation for Divine Worship, *Directory for Sunday Celebrations in the Absence of a Priest,* 2 June 1988, Washington, D.C.: USCC, 1988). The matter cannot be resolved simply on the basis of an a priori principle about the power of the priesthood. Where priests are unavailable, it is important to promote such assemblies, both for word and for sacrament. Having a Eucharistic service provides the community with its Christian identity, nourishes and challenges it in its Christian life with the word of God, and offers it the communion in the Body of Christ that makes it one in its own right and one with Churches around the world. The first principle of ordering is not therefore to differentiate it from a service with a priest. It is rather to enhance the symbols and rites of word and sacrament in such a way as to allow the community to come to the expression of its life as the Sacrament of Christ's Body, fed at the table of the word of God and of the Sacrament of the Lord. A layperson or persons de facto provide it with its presidency. Where this differs from the presidency of an ordained minister can appear only in practice and in what is signified about the communion of this particular Church and its sacramental being in the communion of all the Churches.

Eucharist and the Praxis of Freedom. Much has been written in recent theology (for example by Johannes B. Metz and Edward Schillebeeckx) about the dangerous and liberating memory of the passion of Christ. In the memory of Christ's passion, the memory of human suffering is contained and expressed. This gives special place to the memory of unjust suffering, of the victimization of human persons in the forging of societal goals. Within the memory of unjust suffering and of solidarity with the dead, there emerges however a memory of a deeper suffering that frames the human condition, a suffering of sinful state, of finitude, and of the insurmountable limits of communion with the Infinite God. The Christian community's testimony against unjust suffering, its solidarity with the dead, and its desire for the transcendent, are what give the underpinnings to its social ethic. These belong within the memory of Christ's Pasch, and hence have to color the language and the symbols whereby this is remembered within the liturgy, as well as the modes of addressing God in prayer. Eucharistic practice and social practice go hand in hand. The Church's liberating praxis falters without a good Eucharistic basis, and its Eucharist falters if its truth is belied in the behavior of its members.

In such a situation, better appreciation of the New Testament origins of the Eucharist, and of the ways in which Eucharistic thought and practice developed in past times, serves to put the present in perspective, tension perhaps giving way to a sense of legitimate diversity.

DAVID N. POWER, O.M.I.

See also CHURCH, THE; ECUMENISM; SACRAMENTS.

EUCHARIST, RECEPTION OF

In the Code of Canon Law there are certain minimum regulations with regard to the reception of Holy Communion which are listed below, but anybody wishing to live a full Christian life will want to do more than observe the minimum regulations. Vatican II's Constitution on the Sacred Liturgy, *Sacrosanctum Concilium* (hereafter SC) reminds pastors that in all liturgical celebrations "something more is required than the laws governing valid and lawful celebration" (11). The Vatican document, *Eucharisticum Mysterium,* "On the Worship of the Eucharistic Mystery" (hereafter EM) recommends that people take part in the celebration of Mass and receive Holy Communion whenever they "are setting out on a new state of life or a new way of working in the vineyard of the Lord . . . in order to dedicate themselves again to God and to renew their covenant with him" (36). It instances marriage, religious profession, renewal of baptismal vows, and adoption of a ministry in the Church. EM also recommends the "holy and salutary practice" of "frequent or daily reception of the Blessed Eucharist" (37). SC (55) strongly recommends (but see below also) that whenever one attends Mass one receives Holy Communion. This it describes as the "more perfect" way of taking part in the celebration of Mass. EM says that to receive Holy Communion at Mass is to take part "more fully" in the celebration of Mass (3, e). It also adverts to the need for "proper dispositions" in one receiving Holy Communion, instancing "personal devotion" (12). SC emphasizes the necessity of awareness and interior responsiveness in people taking part in liturgical celebrations, including the reception of Holy Communion, insisting that their minds "be attuned to their voices" and that they "co-operate with heavenly grace lest they receive it in vain" (11). It urges that when they take part in liturgical celebrations, people be "fully aware of what they are doing, actively engaged in the rite, and enriched by it."

EM states that on those who receive the Eucharist "sacramentally and spiritually, that is by that faith which operates through charity" the "gift of the Spirit is poured out abundantly, like living water" (38). Union with Christ is what this sacrament is meant to achieve, EM adds (38), and this is something which should be "prolonged into the entire Christian life" so that people's lives become "a continual thanksgiving under the guidance of the Holy Spirit." To help achieve this, "those who have been nourished by holy communion should be encouraged to remain for a while in prayer." This can be done, the 1980 "Instruction on Certain Norms Concerning the Worship of the Eucharistic Mystery," *Inaestimabile Donum* (hereafter ID) states "during the celebration, with a period of silence, with a hymn, psalm or other song of praise, or also after the celebration, if possible staying behind to pray for a suitable time" (17).

EM reminds us: "The Church has always required from the faithful respect and reverence for the Eucharist at the moment of receiving it" and continues: "With regard to the manner of going to communion, the faithful may receive it either kneeling or standing, in accordance with the regulations laid down by the episcopal conference. When the faithful communicate kneeling, no other sign of reverence towards the Blessed Sacrament is required, since kneeling is itself a sign of adoration. When they receive communion standing, it is strongly recommended that, coming up in procession, they should make a sign of reverence before receiving the Sacrament."

According to the Code of Canon Law, the minimum regulations (cc. 844, 912–923) governing the reception of the Blessed Eucharist by Catholics, other than those excommunicated or under interdict, or those "who obstinately persist in manifestly grave sin," are as follows: (1) Once one has received first Holy Communion, one is obliged to receive Holy Communion at least once a year, during paschal time or, for a good reason, at some other time. For "a good reason" read "any reason that is not frivolous." (2) It is "most strongly recommended" that Communion be received during Mass, but for a good reason one may receive Communion outside of Mass. (3) If one is aware of having committed grave sin one must go to sacramental confession before receiving Holy Communion. However, if on a particular occasion one has had no opportunity of confessing one's grave sin and yet has a sufficiently serious reason for receiving Holy Communion without having gone to confession, one must make an act of perfect contrition "which includes the resolve to go to confession as soon as possible." (An example of having "no opportunity of going to confession" would be if the only available priest was a friend to whom one would not wish to confess. A "serious reason" could be the need to receive Holy Communion on one's wedding day.) (4) Before receiving Holy Communion one must abstain from all food and drink for at least one hour beforehand. One may however drink water or take either solid or liquid medicine at any time before receiving Holy Communion. The rule does not apply to priests who have already celebrated Mass and need to celebrate again before an hour's interval has elapsed. Nor does it apply to the elderly, to those who are sick and those who care for them. (5) If one has already received Holy Communion one may communicate again on the same day, provided one does so while attending Mass. (6) If one is in danger of death, from whatever cause, one should receive Holy Communion as "viaticum"—a Latin term which means provision for a journey, in this case the journey to eternity. Viaticum should not be unduly postponed and should be administered while people are in full possession of their faculties. If one has already received Holy Communion it is "strongly suggested" that if one is in danger of death one should communicate again that same day, though without having to attend Mass. (7) If it is "physically or morally impossible" to receive the sacrament from a Catholic minister, one may receive Holy Communion from a non-Catholic minister in whose Church the Eucharist is valid, if "necessity requires or a genuine spiritual advantage commends it" and provided there is no danger of "error or indifferentism." "Moral impossibility" would occur if, for example, there was a psychological block, or if it would cause grave embarrassment.

AUSTIN FLANNERY, O.P.

See also EUCHARIST; EXCOMMUNICATION; SACRAMENTS; SUNDAY.

EUCHARISTIC DEVOTIONS

The heart of the Eucharist is its celebration in liturgy and its reception in Holy Communion. The Second Vatican Council in its Decree on Liturgy (*Sacrosanctum Concilium*) and subsequent documents (especially *Eucharisticum Mysterium*) indicates that while devotions surrounding the reserved Sacrament are legitimate, they must flow from the celebration and lead to the reception of the Eucharist. Such devotions must also be in tune with liturgical laws, in the spirit of liturgical seasons, and be guided by other rules of propriety (SC 13).

Eucharistic devotions include exposition and benediction of the Blessed Sacrament, adoration or prayer before the Blessed Sacrament, processions and Eucharistic congresses. Before Vatican II they also included the Forty Hours Devotion which are now replaced by the Annual Exposition of the Blessed Sacrament.

Devotions to the Blessed Sacrament are legitimate because the Eucharist is the abiding presence of Jesus Christ who is the priest who makes his self-offering on Calvary sacramentally present in the Eucharistic celebration and who continues to offer himself to Christians as the Bread of Life in Holy Communion and who prays "before the throne of God." Jesus Christ is the person adored and revered in the Eucharist. He is also the source of grace and the Spirit giving divine life to the Christian.

Exposition of the Blessed Sacrament is placing the host of the Mass in a receptacle (typically a monstrance which is made to hold the host aloft and make it visible to those who come to pray). Exposition of the Blessed Sacrament is encouraged, especially during the Solemn Annual Exposition (EM 60, 63).

However such expositions should be seen as connected with Mass, begin after the Eucharistic celebration and close with benediction of the Blessed Sacrament.

Exposition is forbidden during the time of Mass. This was a practice before the Second Vatican Council. The practice had been encouraged during the octave of the feast of Corpus Christi. This custom is entirely abolished and prohibited, the basic reason being it is a duplication of rites (EM 61).

Benediction of the Blessed Sacrament is a blessing (sign of the cross) with the monstrance or Sacrament following some time of prayer and devotion before the Blessed Sacrament. It may conclude Evening Prayer of the Hours. Exposition merely for the purpose of giving benediction after Mass is forbidden (EM 66).

Prayer before the Blessed Sacrament is encouraged because it includes the attitudes of adoration and thanksgiving (as well as reparation and petition) which characterize the Eucharistic celebration. It is thus a prolongation of the spirit of prayer which should fill the heart of Christians during the liturgy. It also prepares the Christian for reception of Holy Communion by deepening the union with Christ in the Holy Spirit which characterizes the reception of this Sacrament. This prayer deepens the intimate sharing of the life of Jesus Christ by Christians. They pray for the Church and the needs of their families and friends.

The appropriateness of this prayer is evident from the intimate union with Christ which flows from such prayer. Modern ascetical writers point out its

Eucharistic Congress, Philadelphia, 1976

usefulness as a center of focus for prayer, meditation, and contemplation.

Access to churches is encouraged to make such prayer possible; the reservation of the Blessed Sacrament for the sick is also encouraged.

Solemn Annual Exposition replaces the Forty Hours Devotion which was very popular before Vatican II. Forty Hours was a period of exposition of the Blessed Sacrament totaling forty hours. During this time parishioners made their confession and were given instructions on the Eucharist. A procession of the Blessed Sacrament and benediction usually closed these devotions.

The instruction *Eucharisticum Mysterium* encourages an annual celebration of the Eucharist with exposition of the Blessed Sacrament. This time in the parish should be an opportunity for instruction, reflection and prayer focused on the Eucharist (EM 63).

Eucharistic congresses are international, national, and regional events honoring Jesus Christ in the Eucharist. It is a time for instructional and inspirational events centered around the Eucharist. Conferences, celebrations, and devotions honoring Jesus Christ and his gift of the Eucharist are highlighted. It extends the kind of devotions we have been describing to a much broader and wider range of participants. Their rationale is the same and provides a greater awareness of the blessings which the Eucharist provides as celebration, Sacrament and abiding presence of the Lord. The highlight of such congresses are the solemn procession and final celebration of the Eucharist.

Eucharistic congresses began under the inspiration of Marie Marthe Emilia Tamisier (1834–1910). The first international congress was held in 1881 at Lille, France. It was such a success a Permanent Commission for International Eucharistic Congresses was established.

In 1893 the first International Eucharistic Congress outside Europe was held in Jerusalem. The first International Eucharistic Congress in the Western Hemisphere was held at Montreal in 1910. The international congresses were suspended during the First World War after the Congress in Lourdes in 1914. Pius XI attended the International Eucharistic Congress in Rome in 1922 and determined they should be held every two years. (They had been held annually in the early days.) At the present time they are held every four years.

Among the outstanding congresses was the International Congress of Bombay, India, in 1964. Pope Paul VI attended personally, rather than send a delegate *a latere*. It was the first time such a congress was held in a country where Catholics were in such a small minority. The fruits of the congress were outstanding and set a pattern for future congresses.

E. R. FALARDEAU, S.S.S.

See also DEVOTIONS; EUCHARIST.

EUCHARISTIC FAST, THE

See EUCHARIST, RECEPTION OF.

EUCHARISTIC PRAYER

The Eucharistic Prayer stands at the "heart" of the Eucharistic Liturgy. Also known as the Canon of the Mass in the Roman liturgy, the praying of it brings about the consecration of the bread and wine into the Body and Blood of the Lord. The earliest fully-formed extant Eucharistic Prayer is the one ascribed to Hippolytus of Rome in the *Apostolic Tradition* (ca. 215). For the most part a Eucharistic Prayer contains the following elements: introductory dialogue (between priest and assembly), preface, the "Sanctus," epiclesis (calling down of the Holy Spirit), anamnesis (the recalling of God's saving actions), narrative of the institution (the words of Jesus at the Last Supper as contained in Scripture), memorial acclamation, commemorations and intercessions, and the final doxology. (The order of these elements may vary.) In the Latin Church there was previously only one Eucharistic Prayer known as the Roman Canon. However, after the liturgical reforms initiated by the Second Vatican Council (1962–1965), several new Eucharistic Prayers were written and are now in use.

ANTHONY D. ANDREASSI

See also ANAPHORA; CANON OF THE MASS; EUCHARIST.

EUTHANASIA

Euthanasia, from the Greek for a "good death," generally refers to taking the life of a terminally ill person in order to escape the physical and mental pain that often accompanies the terminal stages of a fatal illness. The Vatican *Declaration on Euthanasia* (1980) defines it as "an action or an omission which of itself or by intention causes death, in order that all suffering may in this way be eliminated."

Discussions usually distinguish euthanasia by consent (voluntary or involuntary), intention (direct or indirect), and cause (active or passive). Passive euthanasia is the most confusing to understand. It entails a moral difference between ordinary and extraordinary treatment, and between killing and allowing to die.

Passive euthanasia is justifiable when it means withholding or withdrawing extraordinary (optional or disproportionate) means, i.e., treatment that offers no reasonable hope of benefit and/or is too burdensome to the patient physically, psychologically, or economically. Omitting such treatment allows the patient to die as a result of the fatal pathology running its natural course. By contrast, it is not justifiable to withhold or withdraw ordinary (required or proportionate) means, i.e., treatment which would not overly burden the patient while bringing relief or a cure. To omit such treatment is morally equivalent to direct killing.

The other moral difference distinguishing active and passive euthanasia is that between killing and allowing to die. "Killing" refers to a human agent being morally responsible for causing death. "Allowing to die" refers to withholding or withdrawing futile or burdensome treatment so that the fatal pathology can run its course and cause death. Advocates of active euthanasia see a descriptive difference but no moral difference between these ways of bringing about death. The Catholic moral tradition and other opponents of killing patients hold to a moral difference because it distinguishes deaths for which humans can be held responsible from those which are caused by nonhuman events. The distinction also has a social value in preserving the role of health care providers as ones committed to curing and caring but not to killing.

Recent efforts to legalize euthanasia have focused on voluntary, direct, active euthanasia. Advocates of euthanasia, such as the Hemlock Society, appeal to freedom in arguing that no one ought to be deprived of the right to have full control over one's body and one's life. The moral foundation for this position is that our bodies, our life, and our dying are our own and should be subject to our free control. The Hemlock Society claims that the law should recognize and sanction this right to ultimate self-determination. In their view, legalized active euthanasia would be the ultimate civil liberty for it would give control over one's dying and assure freedom from being helpless before technology.

Opponents of killing patients, such as the Catholic Church, argue theologically that euthanasia violates the sanctity of life and the sovereignty of God by assuming absolute ownership over life entrusted to us to make fruitful but not given to us as a possession to destroy when we so choose. Philosophically they argue that giving away freedom and life the way euthanasia does offends human dignity by giving away too much of what it means to be human. Also, they argue that legalizing euthanasia can threaten the common good.

Hospice is an active response to the movement to legalize active euthanasia. Hospice care tries to maintain the best quality of life for the dying while keeping the patient as free of pain as possible without prolonging dying or hastening death. The standards of care embodied in hospice make killing patients unnecessary and mistaken.

RICHARD M. GULA, S.S.

See also CHRISTIAN MORALITY; DEATH; SUICIDE; THEOLOGY, MORAL.

EVANGELICAL COUNSELS

The Evangelical Counsels are virtues recommended, rather than mandated, to achieve perfection in the Christian life. They are traditionally understood to comprise the virtues of poverty, chastity (i.e., celibacy), and obedience.

They are called "evangelical" because the call to their practice is found in the Gospels, and more generally in the NT, and because they represent a way of living out the gospel, the Good News of God's unconditional love and the possibility of the Christian's unconditional response to that love, sharing God's own life. They are "counseled" but not commanded to every Christian, because the NT passages which speak of them seem to envision a form of discipleship to which some but by no means all Christians are called. This has shaped the understanding of religious life in the Church, as a way of life to which only some are called, which satisfies a standard to which not every Christian is held, and which is a "higher" state of life than that which Christians not so called are required to lead.

The NT passages from which the notion of "counsels" is derived are principally but not exclusively three:

(1) In Mark 10:17-22 (cf. Matt 19:16-22; Luke 18:18-23), a young man asks Jesus what he must do

to inherit eternal life. Jesus responds by reminding him of the commandments; when the young man replies that he has kept the commandments all his life, Jesus tells him that "one thing is lacking to you: go, sell whatever you have and give to the poor, and you will have treasure in heaven, and come follow me." (In the Matthean parallel, Jesus tells the young man, "If you wish to be perfect, go, sell your possessions and give to the poor.") The young man goes away sad, "because he had many things." Jesus then gives a strong warning to his disciples: "How difficult it is for those who have possessions to enter the kingdom of God!" (Mark 10:23-25).

The story thus seems to envision two levels of response to God, keeping the commandments and—over and above that—embracing poverty; this last step will make one "perfect."

(2) In 1 Corinthians 7:25-35, Paul recommends that those who are unmarried remain so, though he does not require them to refrain from marriage ("I do not have a command of the Lord, I give my opinion [*gnōmē*]"). The reason for Paul's exhortation has to do with the "cares" or "anxieties" that distract married people from wholehearted response to God. Again, a form of life seems to be envisioned that is not for everybody but is objectively better.

(3) This Pauline passage has been read in the light of, and has influenced the interpretation of, Matthew 19:10-12, where Jesus speaks of "those who make themselves eunuchs for the kingdom of Heaven." The Matthean text explicitly pronounces this choice, of permanent abstention from sexual activity, something which is not for everyone: "not all can accept this word, but [only] those to whom it is given" (a theological passive: God is the giver).

There are no NT texts that specifically require the form of obedience to which vowed religious commit themselves; rather, such sayings as "Who hears you, hears me" (Luke 10:16), where "hear" can be taken as having the nuance "obey," have been accommodated to provide a gospel rationale for the structures of religious life, analogous to ecclesial structures of authority.

The Marcan story of the rich young man can be read as containing a teaching more nuanced than the one sketched above. The young man uses the word "good," and seems intent on being good; Jesus tells him that "only one is good, God," and his invitation to dispossess himself and become a disciple should be understood in the light of this problematic. The implication is that God's goodness involves that kind of self-dispossession, and until one shares in that totality of self-giving one will not understand true "goodness" or attain the fullness of eternal life. The Matthean term "perfect" recalls Jesus' exhortation in the Sermon on the Mount to "be perfect, as your heavenly Father is perfect" (Matt 5:48), where the context is forgiveness of one's enemy. Thus, these texts have an essential lesson for all Christians, not only those called to vowed poverty.

Similarly, the context for the Pauline and dominical teaching on virginity is the imminence of the kingdom (cf. 1 Cor 7:31, "the form of the world is passing away"). With the delay of the parousia, the urgency of the call to single-hearted service of God can be understood as entailing a variety of responses in different states of life, including of course marriage, as a way of living out discipleship.

Thus, all Christians are called to purity of heart and totality of commitment of the sort to which the rich young man and the Corinthian community are invited. The gift of self involved in living the evangelical counsels as a vowed religious, however, maintains in the life of the Church the indispensable dimension of eschatology. It serves as a witness to the centrality of God's claims in human existence, and as a reminder both that the kingdom is the true realm to which Christians belong (cf. Phil 3:20), and that Paul's teaching that "the form of the world is passing away" expresses a continual reality.

J.P.M. WALSH, S.J.

See also BEATITUDES; CHRISTIAN SPIRITUALITY; CORPORAL AND SPIRITUAL WORKS OF MERCY; RELIGIOUS ORDERS; SPIRITUAL LIFE; VOWS.

EVANGELIZATION

Evangelization is the proclaiming of the gospel, the Good News of salvation in Jesus Christ, to those peoples who have not yet heard it. Often the term evangelization is used in extended senses to include revival meetings to bring about personal commitment to Christ, preaching crusades to win people to a deeper faith in Christ, missionary endeavors to renew in Christian people the basics of lapsed faith, and even missions to convert Christians from one denomination to another. In this article the term evangelization is used in its basic sense of bringing the Good News to people who have not yet had access to it.

Jesus himself is the first evangelizer in his announcement of the reign of God. His disciples carried on that mission in behalf of the reign of God by proclaiming redemption and salvation in the very person of Jesus, the Christ, the Son of God, who was born of the Virgin Mary, suffered and died on the cross, and rose from the dead in glory. Jesus commissioned his disciples in Matthew's Gospel with the command: "Go therefore and make disciples of all nations, baptizing them in the name of the Father and of the Son and of the Holy Spirit, and teaching them to obey everything that I have commanded you" (28:19-20).

Evangelization takes place through the missionary activities of the Church. Those who have heard the Good News cannot but share it with others. The greatest evangelizer of the early Christian era was Paul who carried the gospel from its Palestinian beginnings in Jerusalem to the major cities of the Greco-Roman world. Peter, the foremost of the apostles, preached the gospel in Rome where he was martyred. Tradition has other apostles and disciples moving from Jerusalem in all directions, to be succeeded by missionaries from one generation to the next. The names of great evangelizers are familiar: Patrick to Ireland, Augustine to England, Boniface to Germany, Cyril and Methodius to the Slavs, and Francis Xavier to India. As European explorers discovered new lands and new peoples after 1492, missionaries accompanied them or soon after followed them to evangelize the native populations.

Pope John Paul II's encyclical *Redemptoris Missio* (7 December 1990) is subtitled, "The Permanent Validity of the Church's Missionary Mandate"—the Church must always be an evangelizing or missionary Church.

Three major approaches to evangelization can be identified. First, the "one-way transfer of riches." This often was the model of evangelization which took place after the great era of discovery. The sending Church possesses the truth; its evangelizing mission is to transmit it to those still in darkness. The sending Church possesses life-giving sacraments; its mission is to offer them to those struggling in their daily lives without them. The sending Church has the magisterial authority given it by Jesus Christ; its mission is to transmit the benefits of that authority to people unaware of it. This model tended to "colonialize" as well as evangelize. Although the motivation was to share the great treasures of the Christian faith, it did not recognize sufficient worth in the wisdom and culture already present in those being evangelized. It tended to suppress cultural practices which could have enriched faith and its practices by their incorporation.

Secondly, the "implantation-adaptation" model. The evangelization document of Vatican II, *Ad Gentes* (7 December 1965) modifies the "transfer of riches" approach by looking at evangelization in two phases. Implantation: the missionaries arrive, live among the people and preach the gospel; they learn the philosophy or religion of the people and offer corrections of its errors; they form a catechumenate for concrete instruction in and preparation for Christianity; they receive into the Church those prepared through the sacraments of initiation; the new church matures in Christian family life; it produces its own clergy; and eventually has a bishop from its own ranks. Implantation has taken place. Adaptation: as the new church becomes more stable and matures, it adapts itself more and more to the culture of its people; it allows for indigenous expressions of faith and practice; and it develops a character of its own. To moderate the process of adaptation, the bishop of the new church must take care to remain in union with other bishops and, above all, with Rome.

Thirdly, the model of "incarnation." Vatican II's *Ad Gentes* opened the way for this model by saying that the "sending Church" must also be a "receiving Church." The message of the gospel is enriched by the unique contribution of those to whom it is preached. Evangelization is a two-way process. The Apostle Paul wrote to the Romans that he not only would come to share his spiritual gift with them but that "we may be mutually encouraged by each other's faith, both yours and mine" (1:11). In this model, there is great sensitivity to the wisdom, the culture, and the religion of the people being evangelized. What is compatible with Christian faith and practice is to become part of an enriched expression of the Christian faith of the new church; only what is incompatible with Christian faith and practice must be exorcised. The salvation of the gospel of Jesus Christ becomes "incarnate" in the people in a new and unique way, enriching the whole Church.

The 1971 Synod of Bishops in Rome insisted that a "constitutive dimension" of the preaching of the gospel is "action on behalf of justice and participation in the transformation of the world." The Church's evangelizing mission for the redemption of the human race must include "liberation from every oppressive situation." That stance was re-affirmed by Paul VI in his Apostolic Exhortation, *Evangelii Nuntiandi* of 1974. Evangelization must not only proclaim the Good News of future salvation but also the Good News of the reign of God in our midst.

CHARLES SKOK

See also MISSION; MISSIONS, CATHOLIC, THE MODERN PERIOD.

EVIL

For Christians, "evil" may be both the easiest word to define and the hardest to understand. Evil can be defined as any action, tendency, state of affairs, or institution which is opposed to God's will.

A sin is an action opposed to God's will. Human beings freely choose to oppose God when they commit sin by willingly injuring themselves, others, and/or their friendship with God.

Original sin is the human tendency to oppose God's will. Each of us has inherited this tendency to commit actual sins.

Vice is an individual's developed tendency to sin. Vices are not inherited. Rather, we develop a pattern of sinning by committing actual sins. When confronted with circumstances similar to those in which we have sinned in the past, we tend to sin again. For instance, if lying has gotten us "off the hook" in the past, we can develop the vice of lying and tend to lie when we are "on the hook" in the present.

States of affairs that are opposed to God's will may include sufferings and social evils such as racism and exploitation. Suffering may include physical pains, feelings of "dirtiness," unwarranted shame, guilt or anxiety, etc. These may be evil not in that they result from sin or error, but in that an all-good God would not will creatures to suffer any of them. God might want us to learn from suffering and to work to overcome evils, and thus not will suffering to cease, but God's willing creatures' suffering seems inconsistent with divine goodness.

Social evils are communal vices. These states of affairs are not merely a sum of individual sins or vices of individuals. Rather, they are social practices or communal habits, i.e., patterns of belief and behavior, which make sinful actions more attractive, comfortable, or acceptable than they would otherwise be for the members of the community or society.

Institutions opposed to God's will are enduring, organized corporations, parties, governments, etc., whose purpose is to encourage sin and vice or to spread social evils.

Slavery provides a clear comprehensive example of the dimensions of evil. Forcibly enslaving another person is a sin; a slave-trading company operating in a legal system enforcing slavery exemplifies institutional evils; a society where slavery is tolerated is infected with a social evil for people are attracted to take (a sin) and hold (a vice) slaves in such a culture. In any culture, slavery is an evil; but in most cultures today, it is mainly an abstract, not a real, evil.

Yet two hundred years ago the evil of slavery issue was not clear at all. Real evil may not be apparent and apparent evil may not be evil at all. Understanding evil is most difficult, especially because human beings tend to think that our ways are all good, even God's ways, and so those who oppose us are evil. This tendency to self-deception, to fail to see the evil in us and the good in the other, may be the most visible evidence of original sin.

The reality of evils raises the "problem of evil": how can there be such evil in a world created and sustained by an all-powerful, all-knowing, all-good God? God has the power to rectify evils, knows what they are, and is opposed to them. How can evils exist? The options seem to be either that God does not exist, or that God does not have one of the "all-attributes," or that all apparent evil (including sin and vice) is really disguised good.

Theologians create theodicies to answer the question by explaining how God can allow evil in the world. Some say that all evils are really good; then slavery in all its forms is really hidden good, perhaps as proper punishment for sin, stimulus to do better, etc. Some say that God does not will evil, but tolerates it for some good reason (which may be unknown to us). Some say that God's power or goodness or knowledge is limited so that evils are unavoidable. Yet confronting such theories with real evils shows the hollowness of such explanations.

Philosophers create defenses to show that it is possible that evil is due to the abuse of freedom, and that God could either make people free or make them do good, but not both. Thus it is possible that there is a solution to the problem of evil beyond the three options, even if we cannot explain why God does allow evil in the world. While sufficient to deflect atheists' and agnostics' attacks, defenses are neither explanations of, consolations for, nor rectifications of evil.

Evil cannot be explained, only overcome. Evil is not primarily an intellectual or theoretical problem, but a practical one. We must learn how to recognize evil in all its forms, to exorcise it when we can, and to console and to minister to both its perpetrators and it victims.

T. W. TILLEY

See also THEOLOGY, NATURAL.

EVOLUTION

The significance of evolution in a religious context is complicated. Among other things, it is not so easy as might be supposed to state exactly what evolution is. To begin with what is most basic and least controversial, evolution is a name for the answer to a number of questions that arise in biology, the study of living organisms. For Charles Darwin, with whom the term "evolution" is always associated, the relevant questions included these: Why are the forms that living things take so diverse? Why are some kinds of organisms found only in certain places, rather than others? Why, at the places where they are found, have they got the shapes and characteristics they have? Why do certain sorts of plants and animals belong to certain times, rather than to others? Why is it possible to classify living things according to their observable similarities? Biological species are related in all these ways as well as others, despite their astonishing variety—why? Darwin's answer, which he called "descent with modification," was that species do not always remain identically the same over time; they are transformed, and the transformations do not differ essentially from the way in which pigeons were bred so as to preserve and enhance certain inherited characteristics, thereby permanently changing the anatomy of successive generations of individual birds. Since Darwin proposed his answer, two important scientific advances have occurred which modify it. On the one hand, the significance of fossils—what they are evidence *for*—is far more completely and accurately understood. On the other, discoveries in what today is called genetics have thrown light on how the "modifications" Darwin spoke of occur and are passed on.

Evolution, then, is a *hypothesis*—a possible way of understanding, in one comprehensive view, an enormous amount of factual evidence. And evolution is a *theory,* in the sense of an intellectual construction, that is concerned not simply with describing or classifying biological species, but with explaining *why* each species is such as it is, by proposing a general, unified account of how different species are related. As theory and as hypothetical, evolution is not a proven, demonstrated certainty. Although this fact is sometimes advanced in order to challenge the validity of evolutionary biology, it does no such thing. Modern science is not a matter of proof or demonstration, as those words apply to geometry or logic, and so there is no scientific statement that is utterly and unquestionably certain. Every science, in the sense of what a community of scientists knows, consists in hypotheses that have been proposed and that have been and continue to be confirmed or "verified" in so far as they account for more and more empirical evidence. Because there is so much that the theory of evolution does explain, biologists are virtually unanimous in accepting it. This is not to say that everything is settled. There are, in fact, unanswered questions and thus important debates within the biological-science community. Two of the more noteworthy are whether evolutionary change is always adaptive in relation to the environment of the evolving species, and whether it is always gradual and continuous or instead occurs by fits and starts. Neither of these, however, affects evolution as the basic explanatory principle of modern biology.

What then is the relevance of all this to religious, and especially Christian, belief and practice? Here it is possible only to mention very briefly a few of the more important points.

(1) In no way does the theory of evolution impinge upon the doctrine of *creation* in the proper theological sense of the word. That doctrine is not a story about the beginning of the world; it is a statement of the belief that each thing that exists does exist, and each event that occurs does occur, because God knows and wills its existence or occurrence. Creation, in other words, is not itself an event in time, something that happened once but has now finished happening. It is a relation of dependence, such that neither the universe as a whole nor any of its component parts is entirely self-explanatory. Biological evolution, for one thing, does not explain itself. The only complete explanation, the final answer to the question why things are as they happen to be, is that God creates them so.

(2) On the other hand, if the general account that modern biology gives of how life has evolved is an accurate account, then the biblical story of what happened "in the beginning" cannot be read as a statement of when and how biological species, including our own, came into existence. For those who take the Bible seriously, two alternatives present themselves. (a) The biological-science community must be wrong, and the available evidence, including the fossil record, can be explained equally well in a way that is compatible with the "literal" meaning of Genesis. Today this is the position of "creationism" or "creation science." (b) The primary meaning of the story in Genesis must be something besides an assertion about the origin of species. Historical scholarship suggests, for example, that the story as it stands represents a modification of much older traditions, and biblical theologians would argue that these traditions were altered by the ancient Hebrews in order to say something about the nature of their God and about the role of humankind in relation both to God and to other living things. The principle at work here—that Scripture is to be interpreted in light of the best knowledge available apart from Scripture—is nearly as old as Christianity itself, and today some such position on the meaning of the creation story in Genesis is taken by the great majority of Christians.

(3) Although "evolution" refers centrally to biological phenomena, the currently accepted theory is closely allied with genetics and so with biochemistry. From there the meaning of "evolution," at least in common parlance, has been extended to embrace the whole universe within one process of development moving from the so-called "big bang" through elemental particles to molecules to organisms to persons. Within this larger panorama, even more than on its own, biological evolution can seem to lend support to a materialist worldview. It is not just that "higher" species evolved from "lower" ones, on such a view, but that everything which exists has

"evolved" from physical matter. Ultimately, therefore, everything *is* material. A worldview of this kind does conflict with Christianity in so far as it denies the existence of spiritual realities, especially the human soul. Materialism, however, is far older than Darwin and is logically independent of the theory he introduced. Accepting biological evolution as an explanation of biological evidence does not, in itself, entail materialism, which is ultimately a philosophical, not a scientific, position. Vice versa, rejecting materialism on philosophical and theological grounds does not in itself imply a rejection of evolution.

(4) Essential to Darwin's theory, as originally formulated, was the notion of "chance variation," by which he seems to have meant an effect that does not stand in one-to-one correspondence with a cause. Such changes have no causal explanation; they simply happen. The later discovery that the occurrence of genetic mutations can be made statistically more probable does not do away with randomness or "chance" as intrinsic to biological evolution, and meanwhile quantum physics appears to have found that the very fabric of the universe is shot through with "chance." But the idea that "chance" is a reality that belongs to the world scientists study can lead in two diametrically opposed directions. (a) If there are objectively random factors in world-process, then the mechanistic view which early modern physics was thought to support is untenable. The universe is not a gigantic clockwork, running predictably until it runs down. Genuine novelty is possible, and sometimes actual; the future is not predetermined; human freedom can exercise a real effect; the possibility of miracle cannot be ruled out in advance. (b) If there is an objectively random component in things, then the universe is ultimately irrational. There is no rhyme or reason, no explanation for why anything occurs; it just does. The fact that humankind happens to have evolved is purposeless and meaningless, as is everything individual humans do. It will be obvious that the second of these views is not, and that the first is, compatible with Christianity. But again, neither of them is strictly speaking a scientific view. Evolution can be called in to support either one, but says nothing about which of the two is true. That is a question for philosophers and theologians rather than biologists.

(5) The idea of evolution can easily be, and has been, transferred from human life as *life* to human life as *human*. "Survival of the fittest," a phrase that Darwin himself borrowed from a political economist, takes on ethical implications in "social Darwinism" inasmuch as competition, conflict, and death come to be regarded as the mainsprings of human community in its social, political, and economic dimensions. Similarly, some exponents of contemporary sociobiology draw moral imperatives from what Darwin called the struggle for existence, contending that human attitudes such as altruism have evolved solely because they increase the likelihood of survival. Such quasi-scientific assertions do raise important questions about the foundations of morality in general and of Christian morality in particular; but, as with materialism, there is reason to think that these questions cannot be answered on genuinely scientific grounds alone.

(6) Finally, there is an important though highly general way in which the theory of biological evolution can affect Christian thought and practice with respect to nonhuman life. While there is certainly a way in which it is correct to speak of "higher" and "lower" species, it is also true that in light of evolutionary biology we cannot think of our own species as being so unique as to set us over against other forms of life. Evolution itself can be seen as a process that affects species, including humankind, not in isolation but in a network of interdependence with other species. From such an ecologically informed viewpoint the emergence of *Homo sapiens* is coming to be regarded less as a triumph over subhuman life and more as implying a responsibility for the flourishing of life as such.

CHARLES C. HEFLING

See also CREATION; CRITICISM, BIBLICAL; SCIENCE AND RELIGION.

EX CATHEDRA

See INFALLIBILITY.

EX OPERE OPERANTIS

(Lat. "by the work of the doer") A theological term which refers to the proper dispositions of the recipient and minister in the reception and administration of a sacrament.

JOSEPH QUINN

See also SACRAMENTS.

EX OPERE OPERATO

(Lat., "by the work done") A theological term which means that sacraments have their efficacy from Christ whose actions they are, and not from the qualities of the ministers of those sacraments.

JOSEPH QUINN

See also SACRAMENTS.

EXAMINATION OF CONSCIENCE

The examination of conscience is an aspect of the self-reflection characteristic of the human person. Plato declared that the unexamined life is not worth living (*Apology,* 38), and Seneca in his poetry exclaimed, "Is there anything more beautiful than this custom of examining the day in its entirety!" (*De Ira* III, 36) The examination of conscience is specifically self-examination in regard to the ethical and moral norms by which a person has chosen to live. It is given high priority not only in the Judeo-Christian tradition but also in Taoism and Islam. It was practiced in ancient India, Egypt, and in the Greco-Roman world. The philosophers, especially the Stoics, valued it. It is implied throughout the Bible, found in the teachings of the Mothers and Fathers of the Desert, and in the monastic tradition. St. Ignatius of Loyola (1491–1456) gave it first place in his list of spiritual exercises.

The examen as it is found in most manuals and prayer books came through the Devotio Moderna (fourteenth through sixteenth centuries), and has the following five points: (1) thanksgiving to God for the favors and graces of the day; (2) petition for God's light to see one's successes and failures; (3) examination of one's day in the light of chosen norms; (4) expression of sorrow; (5) resolutions for the future. Emphasis on an objective listing and judging of successes and failures, or virtues and sins, gradually made this exercise a distasteful, and eventually a superfluous one for many persons.

In 1956, Albert Görres, a German psychiatrist, suggested making the examen not so much by a conscious effort at moralistic self-evaluation, but more through a relaxed attentiveness to inner movements and feelings which are allowed to surface, or to be remembered. He saw the examen as a way of "finding God in all things," of discovering the unique action and call of God to each of us (Peter G. van Breemen, S.J., "The Examination of Conscience," *Review for Religious,* vol. 49, pp. 600–609).

In the wake of Vatican II (1961–1965) the examen was reevaluated, and more positive ways to make it were discovered. Emphasis on the uniqueness of the person, and a personal relationship with Jesus, and/or the mystical body of Christ made the examen more profound and meaningful. The use of the two great commandments of love of God and neighbor as the norm by which to order one's life and relationships simplified the examen, made it more positive and attractive. These adaptations are evident even in the revision of the rite of the sacrament of penance, which directs that the examen of conscience in preparation for the reception of this sacrament be made by comparing one's life with the life and commandments of Jesus (*Rite of Penance,* no. 15).

In 1972 George Aschenbrenner, S.J., wrote what has become in the United States a watershed article. It was entitled, "Consciousness Examen" (*Review for Religious,* vol. 31, pp. 14–21). Here Aschenbrenner, like Görres, proposed that the examen be a time of discernment of spirits, that one sift the deep spiritual movements of the day to discover in them the movement and call of God, and one's response. The appeal of this deeply interior, and personal way of making the examen sparked a new interest and devotion to it. To distinguish this interior and personal thrust of the examen from the objective, moralistic one, it is often referred to as the examination of consciousness or consciousness examen. In making the examination of consciousness, one may begin by asking God's light and help, then let memories of the various inner, spiritual movements of the day surface. As these come to consciousness, they are accepted just as they are. At times, it may be helpful to trace their source. In a response that springs more from love than from a judgmental attitude, prayers of thanksgiving and sorrow are made, and the path of conversion becomes a response to the movement of the Spirit.

Thanksgiving assumes a much greater role in the examen of consciousness as one becomes increasingly aware of the presence and action of God throughout the day. As a prayer, it takes on the character of Mary's *Magnificat,* "The almighty has done great things for me."

When the examen, in any variation, assists us in "finding God in all things" throughout our day, it becomes a prayer of such valuable intimacy with Christ that, like Ignatius of Loyola, we never exclude it from our day even though other forms of prayer may have to be shortened or omitted. In times when we experience the increased pressure of ministry or the weakness of ill health, we find the examen even more essential for the discernment of the spirits by which we are moved. At these times especially, the examen is important for our continuing to live the unique, radical, God-given meaning, the secret of unity and integration at the heart of our life (see, Herbert Alphonso, S.J., *The Personal Vocation,* Rome: Centrum Ignatianum Spiritualis, 1990).

FRANCES KRUMPELMAN, S.C.N.

See also CHRISTIAN MORALITY; CHRISTIAN SPIRITUALITY; SPIRITUAL EXERCISES OF ST. IGNATIUS OF LOYOLA.

EXCLAUSTRATION

A permission given by an appropriate major superior, allowing a member of his or her religious community to live outside the community for up to three years. For permissions beyond three years, the competent authority is the bishop for diocesan communities and the pope for pontifical institutions. The religious remains bound by his or her vows and profession in so far as these obligations are compatible with the new condition. In practice, exclaustration implies modification in the day-to-day practice of the vows of poverty and obedience, together with dispensation from the religious habit and most community obligations.

LEONARD DOOHAN

See also RELIGIOUS ORDERS.

EXCOMMUNICATION

Excommunication is a penalty imposed by the Church for grave reasons on baptized persons which separates those persons from the communion of the faithful and deprives them of the rights of membership in the Church, such as reception of the sacraments and Christian burial. Like all ecclesiastical penalties, excommunication is intended to call attention to the ways in which individuals in their thinking and in their actions come into conflict with the way of life contained in the gospel and taught by the Church. The ultimate goal of excommunication is to encourage someone to repentance and reconciliation with the community of the faithful.

The idea behind excommunication may be seen in the earliest pages of the Bible. When Cain murdered his brother Abel, the Lord drove him out from the human family as punishment for his crime (Gen 4:12). Religious authorities in Israel followed this example in separating from the people of God those who had seriously sinned. Later, formal disciplinary actions developed to expel offenders from the synagogue. A similar process was in use by the community of Qumran. The separation of serious offenders from Christian communities is associated with the power of binding and loosing conferred on Peter and the disciples (cf. Matt 16:19; 18:18). Paul exercised the same power when presented with the case of the man in Corinth who was living with his father's wife: "Let him who has done this be removed from among you" (1 Cor 5:2).

The best image of excommunication and its purpose is found in the practice of public penance in the early Church. As the community was assembled to celebrate the Eucharist, those who had seriously violated the Christian life (e.g., by apostasy, adultery, or murder) were required to leave the community at the offertory. The community continued to pray for them and they performed acts of penance until they were judged to be truly repentant and might be readmitted to the body of the faithful.

In current Church practice there are two forms of excommunication. In the first case, the penalty is incurred *automatically* (*latae sententiae*) whenever anyone deliberately and of set purpose performs an action to which this penalty has been attached. In the 1917 Code of Canon Law there were thirty-seven such automatic excommunications. As a result of directives issued by the Second Vatican Council, that number has been reduced in the 1983 Code to seven: (1) violation of consecrated bread and wine of the Eucharist; (2) physical attack on the person of the pope; (3) sacramental absolution of one's accomplice in a sexual sin; (4) consecration of a bishop without a mandate from the pope; (5) direct violation of the seal of confession by a confessor; (6) procuring of an abortion; and (7) apostasy, heresy, or schism. Permission to remove the first four of these excommunications is reserved to the Holy See.

The other form of excommunication is a specific judicial act pronounced by Church authority (*ferendae sententiae*). Two instances are mentioned in the current Code: (1) pretended celebration of the Eucharist or giving of sacramental absolution from sins by someone who is not a priest; and (2) violation of the seal of confession by an interpreter or others who have overheard a confession. This judicial action is taken because of the seriousness of the matter, often involving great public scandal, and because of the refusal of the offender to yield to the teaching authority of the Church. The two most recent examples in this country occurred prior to the Second Vatican Council. Leonard Feeney, after several years of obstinately refusing to moderate his rigoristic interpretation of the traditional teaching "Outside the Church there is no salvation," was finally excommunicated in 1953. In 1962, after many years of resisting Archbishop Joseph F. Rummell of New Orleans, three lay leaders refused to comply with the archbishop's orders to integrate racially certain Catholic schools and were formally excommunicated.

WILLIAM C. McFADDEN, S.J.

See also CANON LAW; SANCTIONS IN THE CHURCH.

EXEGESIS

For centuries this term meant the interpretation of the Bible in both method and meaning, but more recently scholars have used the term "hermeneutics" for the actual interpretation of a particular verse and exegesis for the practical application of what hermeneutics has discerned; that is, hermeneutics deals with the method of interpretation and exegesis with the meaning of the biblical text. Exegesis is properly a branch of theology. Like all branches of theology, it is carried out by believers for whom the interpretation of a biblical text has meaning for their faith or their moral life or their spirituality. Exegesis takes the Scriptures seriously, and while theology must inevitably go beyond the content of the Scriptures, all theology must at least be consonant with what is found there. Although exegesis rests upon the primacy of Scripture, it opposes a simple biblicism, that is, the notion that the Church can teach only what is in the Bible. Inevitably scholars sometimes disagree upon the results of exegesis, but modern ecumenical scholarship has generally removed the partisan elements from the discipline.

JOSEPH F. KELLY

See also CRITICISM, BIBLICAL; HERMENEUTICS.

EXISTENCE OF GOD

In the medieval era, a number of theologians sought to "prove" (Latin, *probare*) the existence of God. Anselm of Canterbury (1033–1109) formulated an "ontological argument" for the existence of God which goes roughly as follows: Given that God is that than which no greater can be thought, and given that real existence is greater than imaginary existence, God must exist really, not imaginarily. Thomas Aquinas (1224–1274) provided five ways to show the existence of God, from motion (a First Mover is necessary to set all things in motion), from causality (a First Cause is necessary to start the chain of efficient causation), from possibility and necessity (the basis for the existence of alterable beings is an unalterable Necessary Being), from the gradations in things (the good points to the better which points to the Best, the Source of such good), and from the governance of things (a world with beings who seek goals needs One who sets goals). Scholars disagree whether such arguments are independent philosophical attempts to prove to any reasonable person *that* God is (allowing revelation to show *what* God is), or whether they are reflections which probe our knowledge of God and thematize it.

Since the eighteenth century, few philosophers have found Thomas's proofs or ones similar to them cogent. David Hume's *Dialogues Concerning Natural Religion* (1779) is the centerpiece of a tradition of showing that such proofs are not cogent. Immanuel Kant also seemingly showed that ontological arguments have a fatal flaw, but also argued that God was a necessary postulate if morality was to be possible (*Critique of Practical Reason* [1788]).

A few recent philosophers have argued that the ontological argument is valid and does prove that God must exist. Some others have adapted William Paley's argument from the design of things in the world to a Designer (*Natural Theology* [1802]) by arguing that the best hypothesis to explain the universe we know is that it has a Designer and Creator. Few philosophers have found them convincing; some have claimed them inimical to religious faith.

In light of the failure of the arguments to prove the existence of God, some have been embarrassed by the claim of the First Vatican Council (1870) that God "can be known with certainty by the natural light of human reason from the things that he created" (DS 1785). But this does not necessarily mean that the Church endorses the soundness of arguments from motion, causality, or design. Rather, it is plausibly read to claim that created nature reveals something of what God the Creator is, not that arguments prove the *existence* of God to any rational person.

God's existence became a problem only in the modern era. For the medievals, God's existence is presumed—Anselm's argument occurs within a prayer addressed to God! For them, the arguments need only support the reliability of their presumption. For the moderns, God's existence is in doubt. The reality of other religions and the rise of modern atheism change the status of "God exists" from a presumption which only sound arguments could overturn to a proposition which is dubious unless there are sound arguments to support it. And even if they be sound, the arguments are not rhetorically strong enough to "prove" the existence of God when modern culture makes it a dubious proposition.

T. W. TILLEY

See also PHILOSOPHY AND THEOLOGY; THEOLOGY, FUNDAMENTAL.

EXISTENTIALISM

Either a point of view (expressed through literature, drama, and art) or an explicit philosophy which attempts to clarify what it means for us to exist as free, personal beings. Existentialism as a philosophy is often associated with the atheist writer Jean-Paul Sartre, but the term is also used with reference to other thinkers such as Gabriel Marcel, Miguel de Unamuno, José Ortega y Gassett, Karl Jaspers, and Martin Heidegger. The proximate ancestry of existentialism is sometimes traced to ideas of Friedrich Nietzsche and Soren Kierkegaard in the nineteenth century. And the remote ancestry is often located in the Protestant Reformation and even the teachings of Jesus.

Existentialist philosophers generally distinguish our uniquely human kind of "existence" from the reality of nonhuman natural objects. This difference consists primarily of the fact that human existence is characterized by individual *freedom*. Freedom, however, means more than just the faculty of free choice. It is a fundamental capacity to define, or "create" ourselves and the meaning of our lives (at least to some extent). Our identities are not given to us in a finished way, but we are required to fashion our own essence through the concrete decisions we make in life. The fact of freedom and the attendant responsibility for self-creation is the source of "anxiety" since this project remains forever unfinished. But "authentic existence" requires that we courageously accept our finite, never fully completed existence, together with the responsibility, guilt, and restlessness that inevitably accompany our freedom.

Existentialism has both atheistic and theistic proponents. Jean-Paul Sartre, the best known atheistic existentialist, held that we are *absolutely* free to define ourselves. *That* we exist has no explanation, and so our naked existence may appear "absurd." *What* we are, though, is the sum of our concrete actions, of what we have actually *done* with our existence. We typically flee from responsibility for our actions and lives into what Sartre called "bad faith," the inauthentic existence in which we strive unsuccessfully to have our identities given to us deterministically, in the passive manner typical of natural objects.

Sartre considered belief in God to be an egregious instance of "bad faith" inasmuch as it hands over to God the responsibility for our being. Especially in his early writings Sartre argued that theism leads us to deny our freedom rather than encouraging us to take responsibility for shaping our own lives out of an unintelligible existence. Reference to God, then, would be just another excuse for not accepting responsibility for ourselves.

A number of religious thinkers, while rejecting Sartre's atheism, value many of the insights of his existentialism, especially its resistance to determinism and its understanding of human existence as a project yet to be fulfilled. At its best existentialism, they suggest, is intrinsically neither theistic nor atheistic. It is simply a timely and insightful analysis of the human condition whose concepts and categories are useful to theology as the latter attempts to unfold the implications of a life of faith.

Paul Tillich, for example, looks upon existentialism as the "good luck" of theology. Through its analysis of anxiety and finitude, existentialism helps the theologian formulate the perennial human questions about fate, death, guilt, and the meaning of life in a manner that allows the revelatory answer of Christian faith to have a fresh significance in the twentieth century. In particular, existentialist articulation of the threats of emptiness and meaninglessness in our times is helpful to reformulating the relevance of religious faith.

Religious existentialists also emphasize human freedom, but, contrary to Sartre, they consider this freedom to be limited or finite rather than absolute. And unlike Sartre, who saw us as "condemned" to freedom, religious existentialists understand freedom as a gift granted us by the graciousness of a God who wills to have free dialogue partners in the form of human persons.

Existentialism has also had considerable impact on religious ethics. In the first place, it has helped moral theorists recognize that our moral actions are not unrelated to the "existential" situation or context in which they occur. Thus it has been a helpful corrective to a simplistic "essentialist" and absolutist moral theology that had removed moral theory from any consideration of the concrete life and circumstances of individual persons. And second, existentialism has pointed to the possibility that our individual moral choices may arise out of a much deeper existential "project," sometimes called a "fundamental option," for good or evil on the part of the moral subject.

Much twentieth-century theology, Protestant, Catholic, and Jewish has been deeply influenced by existentialist philosophy and literature. Today, however, there is some concern among a number of religious thinkers that an unqualified existentialism can fuel the exaggerated anthropocentrism (emphasis on the human) which in turn contributes to the devaluation and neglect of the nonhuman natural world. Since it makes such a sharp distinction between freedom and nature, existentialist theology often ignores the question of the relationship of God to the universe. Like many other philosophies, it is still considered a fruitful partner of theology—as long as it is used to clarify our situation, and not itself enthroned as a revelatory response to our deepest questions.

JOHN HAUGHT

See also PHILOSOPHY AND THEOLOGY.

EXORCISM

Part of the ministry of Jesus in establishing the kingdom of his Father was casting out demons and unclean spirits. In this he was performing an act of exorcism. This mission continues in the Church today. There is a series of exorcisms in the ritual for introducing catechumens into the Church. In the first stage of the initiation the celebrant breathes lightly on the candidate and prays: "Breathe your spirit, Lord, and drive out the spirits of evil: command them to depart, for your kingdom is drawing near." In the rite of baptism there is a prayer of exorcism just before the pouring of the water.

These ritual exorcisms are related to but must be distinguished from the phenomenon of diabolical possession. In the New Testament Jesus, the disciples, and Paul deal with an extraordinary manifestation of the power of evil, diabolical possession, in which a person's bodily movements and speech are under the control of the power of a demon.

In the history of the Church there have been instances of a similar nature. The Church tries to avoid attributing every unusual disorder to diabolical possession, but does not rule out the possibility that such cases do exist. In the 1983 Code of Canon Law there is provision for the carrying out of the special ritual of exorcism in the case of diabolical possession. The special and express permission of the local ordinary is required and is to be given only to "a presbyter endowed with piety, knowledge, prudence and integrity of life" (c. 1172).

WILLIAM C. McFADDEN, S.J.

See also CORPORAL AND SPIRITUAL WORKS OF MERCY; DISCERNMENT OF SPIRITS; HEALING.

EXPOSITION OF THE BLESSED SACRAMENT

The ceremonial presentation of the consecrated Eucharistic Host for the purpose of veneration. Devotions may be private—when the doors of the tabernacle are opened, or public—when the Host is displayed on a throne in a monstrance. The devotion was established in the fourteenth century, and has been practiced in various forms ever since. In the Roman Catholic Church, the public service—similar to that of the Benediction—is now held on the feast of Corpus Christi, or on other solemn occasions with the consent of the bishop.

JOSEPH QUINN

See also DEVOTIONS.

EXTREME UNCTION

See SACRAMENT OF ANOINTING.

F

FABER, FREDERICK WILLIAM (1814–1863)

English churchman whose name in religion was Wilfrid. Born in Yorkshire, he spent his childhood in Westmoreland and County Durham. At Oxford he fell under the influence of the High Anglican "Oxford Movement," then led by Pusey and Newman. As a Church of England clergyman, he came to know and adulate the elderly Wordsworth, who liked Faber's sermons but not his poetry. Faber supported the "New England" pressure group within the Tory party which called for a revival of the medieval ideal whereby the nobility would undertake to provide for "the poor masses." He joined the Catholic Church shortly after Newman in 1845, was ordained priest, and founded a quasi-monastic order which he merged in 1848 with Newman's recently established Birmingham Oratory. The Romantic lushness of his writings, his emotional fervor and unrestrained enthusiasm for Italianate forms of religious expression all irritated Newman, who was relieved when Faber departed in 1849 to set up the Oratorian house in London that eventually became Brompton Oratory. His Ultramontane attitudes, which alienated Newman further, led to several painful disputes between the two and between their foundations, but were much admired among the upper classes. Faber made numerous converts to Catholicism and his zeal won him warm approval of Cardinal Wiseman, archbishop of Westminster. Faber's genuine holiness inspired not only his devotional literature and preaching but the many hymns for which he was to be best remembered. These included "O purest of creatures," "Hark, hark, my soul," and "Faith of our fathers."

LOUIS McREDMOND

See also BRITAIN, CHURCH IN; HYMNS; ORATORIANS; OXFORD MOVEMENT.

FACULTIES

The permission granted to a clergyman by his ecclesiastical supervisor which enables the former to carry out his respective duties toward those to whom he ministers. The term is commonly associated with the authority needed by a priest to administer the sacrament of reconciliation; preaching and witnessing marriages also require faculties.

JOSEPH QUINN

See also PREACHING; PRIESTHOOD, THE MINISTERIAL; SACRAMENT OF ORDERS.

FAITH

In Christian usage, based on the Bible, faith has a range of meanings rather than one single meaning. It is sometimes used simply to designate a religious attitude in general, but more particularly it includes believing *in* the transcendent God or Jesus Christ as faithful and powerful to fulfill all promises, or believing *that* what has been revealed is true and what has been promised will come to be. The difference between these last two definitions is important. Believing *in* someone is a commitment of the will, the affections, and indeed of one's lifestyle, goals, and direction. Believing *that* something is true, or will happen, is both narrower and more precise, involving the intellect or understanding. The difference between these two meanings of the term has been important and troublesome in Christian history, causing profound misunderstandings.

In the New Testament, the Letter to the Hebrews deals with faith at great length, giving the famous definition that faith is the reality, or substance, or realization of what is hoped for, and the evidence or proof of what is not seen. It goes on to say that faith is a way of seeing reality which constantly relates it to God. A series of examples follows from the Hebrew Scriptures, mainly from the stories of the patriarchs. Abraham particularly is proposed as the model of faith because he responded to God's call as he heard it, no matter how unpromising the outcomes looked. In the Gospels Jesus is portrayed as constantly exhorting people to have more faith. In his sayings that almost always means they should not have such a limited notion of God's power, or so little expectation that God would help them. In all these biblical contexts faith emerges as a visionary way of living, with vivid awareness of God's presence, goodness, power, and immediate personal concern for even the least creatures.

In the Church Fathers of the early ages there is some evidence of efforts to fit this Hebrew concept of faith into prevailing Greek thought patterns. There was a tendency in the Greek apologists of the second century to link the idea of faith with the invisible or nonmaterial, living as they did in a cultural context which was sharply dualistic about mind and body, spirit and matter. The prevalence of Gnosticism (a salvation doctrine built on this dualism) led the Alexandrians, Clement and Origen, early in the third century to question the relationship between faith and knowledge. They concluded that there is a *gnosis* (knowledge) which is beyond faith, by which they seem to mean the mature outcome of a life dedicated equally to discipleship in practice and the pursuit of Christian wisdom in study and contemplation. Cyril of Jerusalem in the fourth century tried to shed more light on the matter, devoting one of his famous catechetical lectures to the topic of faith. In this he specifies that there is one kind of faith which has to do with giving intellectual assent to doctrines, and a second kind of faith which is a special gift of God's grace. This second kind of faith empowers the believer to live in a way that transcends ordinary human prudence because all is seen in the light of God's final triumph and vindication. Augustine of Hippo, who was certainly the most influential of the Church Fathers in shaping the doctrine and theology of the Western Church, preserves in his treatises on the Gospel of John the double meaning, describing faith as believing what is not seen, but also writing that one believes with the heart and can taste and savor with one's faith the dependability and divinity of Jesus. Of this faith the Second Council of Orange (529) insisted that it is a pure gift of God who bestows it on all who are baptized.

The great Scholastic writers of the medieval period were, on the whole, more preoccupied with the content of the faith (that which is believed) than with the act, virtue, or gift of faith, but they did reflect on the latter. That reflection was influenced by the fact that infant baptism was by this time the ordinary, almost the universal, way in which people entered the Church. As they were applying the teaching of the Second Council of Orange that God bestows this gift on all who are baptized, they had to find a way of describing faith that would show that infants were capable of receiving such a gift. This led to a certain sense that faith, like grace, is something not accessible to human experience and therefore known only by hearsay. The alienating effect of this view was counterbalanced by some profound insights most clearly expressed by Thomas Aquinas in the thirteenth century. In 1 Corinthians 13 Paul had written that in the last analysis what is important in a Christian life can be reduced to faith, hope, and charity. Thomas took up the tradition that these are three infused (graciously given) virtues received with grace in baptism, called theological because they relate directly to God. Distinguishing the three from one another, Thomas defines faith as a quality or habit of the mind inclining the latter to assent to God's self-revelation as truth. He distinguishes faith from hope and charity in part because these are primarily in the will rather than the intellect (ST Ia-IIae, q. 2, a.9).

This definition of Thomas Aquinas is very helpful if one remembers that it refers to one of two meanings that faith has in the New Testament. The Council of Trent endorsed this definition in its Decree on Justification (ch. 7), but this proved to be unfortunate because the decree was used polemically against Luther and other sixteenth-century Reformers who had written and preached about faith, understanding thereby the broader New Testament meaning. It caused much bitterness and arguing at cross-purposes because the Reformers insisted that it was faith in Jesus as Savior which alone, by God's grace, constituted the transition into the realm of grace, while the Catholic party insisted that a person was not in grace who had faith but no hope or charity. What had prompted the Reformers was a tendency in later Scholasticism to become entrammeled in arguments over fine points of definition and explanation of doctrine and to attach great importance to the intellectual aspects of believing correctly, while ordinary Christians were left bewildered and often anxious over the difficulty of knowing what was orthodox. Already in the fourteenth century, John Wykliff and John Hus led a movement back to the broader biblical idea of faith as belief in Jesus Christ and commitment to him. Among the sixteenth-century Reformers it was particularly Martin Luther who, on the basis of his studies of the letters of Paul, insisted that faith meant simply being open to God's gift of justification (grace) by putting one's trust not in one's own efforts but in the saving outreach of Jesus Christ.

It is clear that both sides, the Reformers and the Council of Trent, were right, each according to the appropriate definition. Catholic theology and doctrine until the Second Vatican Council consistently used the definition of faith as one of three theological virtues, incomplete without the complement of the other two. The First Vatican Council reaffirmed this. However, by that time (1869–1870), the issues preoccupying the council had turned to another aspect of the medieval discussion, namely, the relation of faith and reason. This had become urgently practical with the rise of modern science, the refinement of historical studies, and the progress and fecundity of modern philosophy. One of the important contributors to the discussion of the relationship of faith and reason in Catholic circles in the nineteenth century was John Henry Newman. Defending the concept of faith against those who claimed that reasonable people rejected faith, Newman pointed out that ultimate questions demand a response in which it is not possible simply to reason from facts by scientific standards of proof. Newman's solution, therefore, was to see faith as based on probabilities coming to focus for the individual through a certain moral response. Meanwhile, Vatican I was concerned to avoid fideism (excluding the role of reason altogether from faith in God) as much as rationalism (excluding all that cannot be explained or demonstrated by reason without recourse to religious authority). Vatican I, like the rationalist British and French philosophers to whose challenge the Church wanted to respond, was assuming a definition of faith in terms of believing that certain propositions were true. The Dogmatic Constitution on the Catholic Faith of that council states that because created reason is necessarily subject to God who created it, it must yield to God when God reveals, not because it can see the intrinsic truth of the revelation but simply because of the authority of God revealing. But God gives a basis for faith to be in harmony with reason by offering miracles and prophecies as proof that it is indeed God revealing (ch. 3), and faith and reason cannot be in contradiction because they are distinct in object and in principle (ch. 4).

Many believers of that time thought that the council statement had evaded key issues. The proper content of faith was defined as what was contained in Scripture and in the official teaching of the Church. Science was challenging the usual interpretations of texts such as the creation narratives; historical and archaeological study was challenging dating, genealogies, and so forth; literary and philosophical reflection was challenging many other accepted teachings and interpretations. Believers became aware that much human interpretation came between the self-revelation of God and the doctrinal formulations taught by the Church. This struggle was intensified among authors at the turn of the century who came to be clustered together by Church authority under the designation "Modernist."

The unresolved conflicts of the nineteenth and early twentieth century received an unexpected solution at the Second Vatican Council by the recognition that the more basic definition of faith has to do with believing *in* God and in Jesus Christ. The Dogmatic Constitution *Dei Verbum* (On Divine Revelation) of that council defines faith in terms of a response of entrusting oneself to God and being open to the self-revelation of God (5, 8). What is strongly implied is also that the reason for faith is not only extrinsic, namely, the authority of God revealing, but more importantly intrinsic, namely, the harmony and coherence attained in the practice of faith.

MONIKA K. HELLWIG

See also CHARITY; HOPE; REVELATION; VIRTUE.

FAITH HEALING

Faith healing is the practice of curing illness or relieving suffering. It can occur in two ways: (1) invoking divine assistance and (2) asserting the mind's or spirit's control over the body. This second way is often associated in the United States with Phineas P. Quimby and his healings in New England during the mid-nineteen hundreds. He influenced Mary Baker Eddy, the founder of Christian Science.

The Catholic tradition of faith healing follows the first way, i.e., seeking God's help, yet without precluding the use of modern medical science. It is grounded in the Scriptures, especially in the New Testament accounts of Jesus' healing ministry (see Luke 7:21). Such accounts often emphasize Jesus' compassion whereby he sees illness as a destructive and debilitating force. It is significant that Jesus commissioned his disciples to continue his healing ministry (see Matt 10:5-10; Mark 6:7-13; Luke 9:1-6).

Modern Catholic practice of faith healing involves at least four elements: (1) understanding healing as a divine gift; (2) perceiving disease as something very real; (3) accepting the use of reasonable medical assistance; and (4) seeing the human person as a whole, not merely a composite of body, soul, and spirit. It is worth observing that the charismatic movement in the contemporary Church accepts these four elements.

Part of the sacramental renewal stemming from Vatican II was the restoration of the anointing of the sick. The new rite understands the purpose of this sacrament as a sign and prayer for the return to physical health. The believer is thus not the sum of his or her parts but a total person who celebrates healing as a gift from the Giver of life.

JOHN F. CRAGHAN

See also CHARISMATIC MOVEMENT; SACRAMENT OF ANOINTING.

Adam and Eve, detail of mosaic, Palatine Chapel, Palermo

FALL, THE

The Fall is the standard term for the narrative meant to account for the human family's sinful condition and need for redemption. According to the narrative, Adam and Eve, our first parents, disobeyed God, and this sin—the original sin—and its effects were passed on, through generation, to all their descendants. The redemptive death and resurrection of Christ saved humankind from this sinful condition.

The constitutive canonical elements of this narrative are two: (1) the story of the sin of the first man and woman (Genesis 2–3), and (2) St. Paul's typology (Romans 5:12-21), almost certainly based on the Genesis narrative, of Adam and Christ.

(1) The story of "Adam and Eve" is part of a series of narratives and other traditions in the first section of Genesis. It follows the Priestly account of God's good creation (Genesis 1), and together with it forms the beginning of the protohistory of the human family (Genesis 1–11). There follow stories chronicling a human history that is increasingly, generation after generation, sinful and destructive. This protohistory is meant to provide a context for the call of Abraham (Genesis 12:1-3): through Abraham, Yahweh will reverse the destructive effects of sin, not just for the people (Israel) that will come from Abraham but for "all the families of the earth."

Thus, in its present context, the sin of Adam and Eve is the first moment in a history of sin leading up to the call of Abraham and the origins of the people Israel. This theological use of the story is attributed to the J or Yahwist source of the Pentateuch (tenth century B.C.).

The story thus used by the J writer may well have had an earlier existence in a different context. Categorized as a "wisdom tale," the story presents an original state of affairs, and an outcome wherein the Creator's intention is frustrated by human choice.

As the narrative unfolds, the man/human being (Hebrew *'ādām*), for whom the rest of creation is made, is alone, and other living beings are fashioned and brought to him as an adequate "help" (Hebrew *'ēzer,* a term otherwise mostly used for God as helper). None is found sufficient, so Yahweh-God forms from the man's rib "a help" adequate for him. This "help" is called *'iššāh,* "woman," connected by a popular etymology to the Hebrew word for male human being, *'îš*. The man recognizes her as "bone of my bone and flesh of my flesh," i.e., as being of the same nature as himself. Thus, the story presents the relationship of male and female as one of equality and equal dignity, in accordance with the Creator's intention. This narrative contrasts with the ancient Near Eastern view of woman as chattel property, subordinate to the male.

At the end of the story, however, is a condition of alienation of the man and woman from each other, from the soil, and from God, and the woman's subordination to the man. What brings about this sorry state of affairs is the couple's choice to be guided by the promise of the serpent, "You will be like gods" or "like God" (the Hebrew is ambiguous). For someone living in the Canaanite milieu of early Israel, the serpent—iconographically associated with one or another Canaanite goddess—might well have suggested the world of Canaanite religion, and thus have served as emblematic for the Canaanite vision of human existence, which focused on fertility and sheer survival, thus reducing woman to her reproductive function. The lesson of this tale, therefore, was cautionary: adhering to the Canaanite—as opposed to Yahweh's—vision of life entails a subordination of woman to man, a negation of God's creative intent. Thus, the story may well have been a polemic against Canaanite fertility religion. (An analogous story of disobedience and expulsion from God's presence is found in Ezekiel 28, especially vv. 12-19, and in Isaiah 14.)

Though this may well have been the burden of the Adam and Eve story in its original context, it came to play a part in a larger drama. In the last few centuries B.C., the story in Genesis 2–3 seems to have been the subject of speculative elaboration, and came to be seen as explanatory of the sinful condition of humankind. In the deuterocanonical writings, Sirach 25:24 and Wisdom 2:23-24 show this elaboration; the latter passage indicates an identification of the serpent with the devil. Later rabbinic writings reflect the same kind of speculation.

(2) In Christian tradition, the passage determinative of the standard understanding of the Fall is Romans 5:12-21, where Paul presents the salvific meaning of Christ's death and resurrection as a counterpoise to the sin of "Adam, who is a figure of the one who was to be" (v. 14). Through one man, sin and death came into the world (v. 12, cf. 15-18), but through one man, Jesus Christ (vv. 15, 17-18), and his obedience (v. 19), God's grace has abounded.

In following centuries, patristic meditation on these texts worked out a larger scenario which in rough outline involves an "original sin" (seen in the Genesis story) passed on to the whole human family; this sin is then taken away through the obedient suffering and death of Christ who rose from the dead; the fruits of this redemption are available to all who are baptized and thus reborn through participation in the paschal mystery. In this fully evolved account of the mystery, the serpent is identified with the devil, the mode of transmission of the original sin to the human race is specified, the cosmic drama of the entire scenario is highlighted, and so on. But though the elements of this scenario are found in Scripture, the final form of the doctrine of the Fall, like the term "Fall" itself, represents a development of Scripture rather than something derived from a plain reading of the canonical text.

That Israelite tradition expresses a conviction that sin was something entrenched in the life of the people and of the nations, there is no doubt (cf. e.g., Gen 6:5; Isa 1:4-6; Pss 51:1-5; 130:3; 143:2); but it is useful to note that this condition was not textually connected with the narrative of Genesis 2–3 until the latest period, and that terms like "original sin" come from a thought-world rather different from that of the Old Testament period.

J.P.M. WALSH, S.J.

See also ORIGINAL SIN.

FAST/FASTING

Fasting may be generally defined as refraining from eating and drinking out of a religious motive. In both the Old Testament and the New Testament fasting usually means total abstinence from food and drink for one day from morning until evening (see 2 Sam 1:12; Jonah 3:7; Acts 9:9). Fasting was part of the ritual for a holy war (1 Sam 14:34), a sign of mourning for the dead (2 Sam 3:35), and a reaction to calamity or distress (Joel 1:14). In times of calamity or distress the Israelites expressed a twofold religious attitude, viz., penance and supplication (see 1 Sam 7:6; Ezra 8:21-23). In the New Testament the most famous account of fasting is that of Jesus in the desert after his baptism. According to Matthew 4:2 Jesus "fasted for forty days and forty nights. . . ." According to Luke 4:2 he "ate nothing during those (forty) days. . . ." Whereas the Israelites in the desert wandering lost trust in God by demanding food and drink (Exod 16:1-4; 17:1-7), Jesus remained faithful to his Father by refusing to change a stone (Luke 4:3-4) or stones (Matt 4:3-4) into bread. Humankind lives not on bread alone.

In the Roman Catholic Church fasting is now understood as one full meal with an allowance for some food in the morning and evening—in effect, no eating between meals. It binds those from the ages of twenty-one to fifty-nine. Although fasting is obligatory on only Ash Wednesday and Good Friday, it remains a recommended penitential practice in general.

There is also the Eucharistic fast. The general norm in the new Code of Canon Law is that one who is to receive the Eucharist must abstain from all food and drink, with the exception of water and medicine, for at least one hour prior to the actual reception. The purpose of this legislation is to highlight the mystery of Christ as the one who sustains the faithful with his Body and Blood.

As a penitential practice, fasting is a means of solidarity with the hungry and the tempted. As developed in the accounts of Jesus' fast in the desert, this practice is intended to make the faithful aware of God's presence and to underline the need for trust and obedience. In the last analysis fasting is linked to fidelity.

JOHN F. CRAGHAN

See also ABSTINENCE, PENITENTIAL; LENT.

FATHERS OF THE CHURCH

A term which from an early date has referred to teachers or authentic witnesses of Christian tradition. Both in the Scripture and in the early Church, father was a term given to someone who provided spiritual formation through his teaching. In this sense Elijah was a father to Elisha (cf. 2 Kgs 2:12). Paul reminded the Corinthians that he became their father in Jesus Christ through the gospel (cf. 1 Cor 4:15). Polycarp was called the father of Christians by the crowds just before his death (cf. *Martyrdom of Polycarp* 12.2). Irenaeus (*Against the Heresies* 4.41.2), Clement of Alexandria (*Stromata* 1.1.2–2.1), and Origen (in Eusebius, *Ecclesiastical History* [hereafter *H.E.*] 6.14.9) all use the term father in this sense. The apostles and patriarchs are called forefathers in *1 Clement* 62.2. From the second century the term father was applied also to bishops (cf. *Letter of the Churches of Lyons and Vienne* in Eusebius, *H.E.* 5.4.2). Because of the doctrinal controversies of the fourth and later centuries, the term father was used particularly of those bishops who upheld, sometimes at great personal cost, orthodox teaching (cf. Basil, *Epistle* 140; Gregory of Nazianzus, *Oration* 33.5). It was also extended to ecclesiastical writers who, even though they might not be bishops, still were representatives of the tradition of the Church. Augustine considered Jerome to be among the fathers since he was a witness to the traditional teaching on original sin, even though he was not a bishop (cf. *Against Julian* 1.7.34). Vincent of Lérins also applied the term father to all ecclesiastical writers who in their own time and place maintained the unity of communion and faith and were accepted as approved masters (cf. *Commonitory* 3). The apocryphal decretal attributed to Pope Gelasius provided a list of works by the Fathers, including those of Prosper of Aquitaine, who was not a cleric.

According to the traditionally accepted criteria the Fathers of the Church were characterized by holiness of life, orthodoxy of doctrine, approval of the Church, and antiquity. The era of the Fathers is generally held to have been closed at the death of St. Gregory the Great (604), Isidore of Seville (d. 636), or the Venerable Bede (d. 735) in the West, and John of Damascus (ca. 749) in the East. Among Catholic theologians the authority of the Fathers has been thought to be infallible when they taught a doctrine unanimously. Even though the teaching of individual Fathers should not be set aside except for serious reasons, it is recognized that it could be in error. The rise of modern scholarship as well as the theological disputes that emanated from the Protestant Reformation have led to different opinions concerning the doctrinal authority that should be attributed to the Fathers. This has not called into question their importance for the formation of Christian theology. Tertullian and Origen and others who are not necessarily of unblemished orthodoxy are now generally numbered among the Fathers. The title Father of the Church is popular and broadly used.

The French ecclesiastical editor and publisher Jacques-Paul Migne (1800–1875) published two series on the Greek and Latin ecclesiastical writers: Patrologia Graeca, 162 vols. (PG [Paris, 1857–1866]) extends down through the Council of Florence (1439) and Patrologia Latina, 221 vols. (PL [Paris, 1841–1864]) ends with Innocent III (1215). Migne incorporated into his collection many editions published in the seventeenth and eighteenth centuries by the Benedictines of the Congregation of St.-Maur (Maurists). Even though there are many printing errors in the Migne editions and many of his editions have now been superceded (see below), PG and PL are still the standard means of reference and citation for most patristic authors. There is now a supplement to PL: Patrologiae Latinae Supplementum, ed. A. Hamman, 5 vols. (PLS [Paris, 1958–1974]). Migne's editions are gradually being replaced, particularly by volumes in the following series: Corpus Scriptorum Ecclesiasticorum Latinorum (CSEL [Vienna, 1866–]); Die griechischen christlichen Schriftsteller (GCS [Leipzig and Berlin, 1897–]); Sources chrétiennes (SC [Paris, 1942–]); Corpus Christianorum, Series Latina (CCSL [Turnhout, 1953–]); and Corpus Christianorum, Series Graeca (CCSG [Turnhout, 1977–]). Critical editions of Oriental Christian patristic literature can be found in Patrologia Orientalis (PO [Paris, 1907–1922]) and Patrologia Syriaca, rev. ed. (PS [Rome, 1965]). English translations of patristic writings can be found in several series: Ancient Christian Writers (ACW [New York/Mahwah, New Jersey: Paulist, 1946–]); the Ante-Nicene Fathers (ANF [Buffalo: Christian Literature, 1885–1896; repr. Grand Rapids, Mich.: Eerdmans, 1951–1956]); Fathers of the Church (FOTC [Washington, D.C.: The Catholic University of America Press, 1947–]); Nicene and Post-Nicene Fathers (NPNF [2 series of 14 vols. each; New York: Christian Literature, 1887–1894; repr. Grand Rapids, Mich.: Eerdmans, 1952–1956]); as well as volumes 1–9 of the Library of Christian Classics (LCC [Philadelphia: Westminster and London: S.C.M., 1953–1966]). English translations of several Greek and Syriac patristic authors have also been published by St. Vladimir's Seminary Press (Crestwood, New York).

JOHN DILLON

See also PATROLOGY; TRADITION.

FATHERS OF THE DESERT

The hermits and monks who lived in the Egyptian deserts in the fourth century were the precursors of monasticism. The names and achievements of many have been passed down the centuries: Paul is venerated as the first hermit; Anthony is regarded as the first monk; Palladius is viewed as the forerunner of monastic scribes. Their number was great by any standard. Anthony presided over five thousand monks in the Nitrian desert in northern Egypt. Some were hermits who lived alone and met only on Saturdays and Sundays for communal worship; others lived in small groups; and few were priests. There was no common rule, and aspirants were guided by older hermits or monks. Elders exercised limited authority, which was necessary to maintain some order and to curtail the extravagant feats of mortification which, at times, got out of hand. Custom became a dominant factor in the desert life, and when the hermits and monks were not praying or reading they were engaged in some crafts such as carpentry or weaving. In south Egypt, St. Pachomius decided to organize matters, and his monks began to live in monasteries under a common rule. The great founders of Eastern and Western monasticism derived their ideas and ideals from the hermits and monks of the Egyptian deserts.

MICHAEL GLAZIER

See also ASCETICISM; MONASTICISM; RELIGIOUS ORDERS; SPIRITUAL LIFE.

FATIMA

Fatima is a small town in the middle of Portugal. There in 1915 three young children, Lucia dos Santos, and her cousins Francisco and Jacinta Marto, aged eight, seven, and six respectively, saw a veiled figure. In the course of the following year they saw, on three separate occasions, a self-named angel, the Angel of Peace, who urged them to prayer, invoking each time the Hearts of Jesus and Mary. In 1917 the children witnessed between 13 May and 13 October the apparitions which are best known. The events took place on the thirteenth of each month, except for August, when it was on the fifteenth; the reason for the exception was the kidnapping of the children by a small-town official.

Basilica of Our Lady of Fatima, Portugal

During these six encounters the "lady," who would in the last apparition take the title Lady of the Rosary, was open to intimate, interpersonal dialogue. Certain ideas recur or are emphasized: the daily rosary, the Immaculate Heart of Mary, peace in the world. One day was heavy with meaning, 13 June. Our Lady on that day showed the visionaries hell, and told them that to save souls God wished to have devotion to the Immaculate Heart of Mary increase. If mortals did not cease offending God another and more terrible war would break out; the sign of the impending evil would be an unknown light appearing in the night. God was about to punish the world, to prevent which Our Lady would come to ask for the consecration of Russia to her Immaculate Heart. If her wish were heeded there would be peace. If not, Russia would spread her errors across the world, promoting wars, persecution of the Church, martyrdom of the good, and suffering for the Holy Father. Our Lady promised a sign to seal the authenticity of all she had said. On 13 October 1917 the promise was fulfilled. On that day a crowd of 50,000 saw the sun rotating in the heavens like a huge catherine wheel; then it left its orbit and plunged towards the earth. Some of the witnesses had been, before the event, noted sceptics. Besides the vision of hell and the exhortation to devotion to the Immaculate Heart of Mary, a third secret was communicated at Fatima.

Though known to the popes since John XXIII, it has not been disclosed.

The words about Russia were spoken in this remote spot four months before the Russian revolution. In 1929 Our Lady came to Lucia, now a nun in Spain, and requested the consecration. Her two cousins died in 1919, and a process is under way for their beatification. The shrine attracts large numbers of pilgrims, about three and a half million annually. An International Pastoral Congress took place there on the occasion of the seventy-fifth anniversary, in October, 1992. On 13 October 1991 a religious service was broadcast direct to Russian television screens, with government permission, from Fatima.

Three popes have honored Fatima. On the occasion of a broadcast for the twenty-fifth anniversary Pius XII consecrated the world to the Immaculate Heart of Mary. Ten years later in the encyclical *Sacro Vergente Anno* he consecrated Russia. Pope Paul VI went to the shrine in 1967 for the fiftieth anniversary, marking his visit with the apostolic exhortation *Signum Magnum,* and presenting the Golden Rose to the shrine. John Paul II went on pilgrimage to Fatima on the anniversary of the attack on his life, 13 May 1982; he went back in 1991 for the tenth anniversary.

MICHAEL O'CARROLL, C.S.Sp.

See also DEVOTIONS; MARY, MOTHER OF GOD.

FEAR

Often confused with anxiety, *fear* is actually an adaptive, psychophysiological mechanism which is activated in the presence of perceived threat. The psychological component of the reaction occurs in the form of a cognitive recognition of danger. Cognitive recognition can range from factual knowledge of an explicit, imminent event (e.g., a scheduled execution) to vague uneasy feelings arising from sensations processed preconsciously in the brain, that is, before the information has gotten to the brain's language centers. The physiological component occurs when the sympathetic nervous system is aroused. A perceived threat causes body tissues to secrete adrenalin, resulting in a rapid heart rate and corresponding increases in blood flow and oxygen supply to muscles and the brain. This cascading mechanism, commonly called the "flight or fight response," mobilizes people to take action in their best survival interest. Occasionally, this activation is inappropriate or excessive, and people respond to an emergency or a nonemergency in disorganized and self-destructive ways. This is what occurs when one panics or feels "petrified by fear."

In states of anxiety, on the other hand, no actual, observable threat exists. The sense of impending harm is vague and more likely related to feelings of shame and inadequacy within rather than to be a threat coming from outside. This is not to say that anxiety is necessarily less intense than fear. Anxiety can just as readily overwhelm and produce panic states. Fear, however, is a normal, necessary reaction in threatening situations which helps us generate the response needed to survive. Anxiety, while experienced by nearly everyone, does not have an adaptive role except as it helps us to identify problems within —often related to how we see and value ourselves.

PAUL MOGLIA

FEENEY, LEONARD (1897–1978)

Jesuit priest and poet, Feeney was born in Lynn, Massachusetts, on 15 February 1897 and died in Still Water, Massachusetts, on 30 January 1978. He entered the Society of Jesus in 1914, studied at Woodstock College and Weston College, and was ordained a priest in 1928. In the 1930s he became a popular Catholic writer, producing poetry, essays, short stories and biographies, and serving as literary editor of *America* from 1936 until 1940. He was also a college professor, popular lecturer and radio speaker, and president of the Catholic Poetry Society.

In 1943 Feeney became permanent chaplain at St. Benedict's Center for Catholic students at Harvard and Radcliffe, where he came to exercise great influence over some of the students. He also began to expound an extremely narrow interpretation of the axiom *extra ecclesiam nulla salus,* claiming that formal membership in the Catholic Church was necessary for salvation. In the words of historian Gerald Fogarty, S.J., St. Benedict's Center became an American Port Royal, "totally convinced that it alone represented the truth of Catholicism."

In 1948 Feeney refused an order from his Jesuit superiors to leave St. Benedict's Center. The following year he was dismissed from the Society of Jesus, and Archbishop Richard Cushing of Boston placed St. Benedict's Center under interdict. In the meantime, Feeney established a religious community of men and women for his followers at Still Water, Massachusetts. One ironic consequence of Feeney's intransigence was a decree from the Holy Office on 27 July 1949 formally stating that it was not always necessary "to be incorporated into the Church actually as a member" in order to be saved, a decree which repudiated Feeney's teaching on this point and actually improved relations between Catholics and non-Catholics. In October 1952 Feeney refused a summons from Rome, and only in 1972 were he and some of his followers reconciled to the Church.

THOMAS J. SHELLEY

See also AMERICAN CATHOLICISM.

FEMINIST THEOLOGY

Feminist theology is the study of God and the divine/human relationship with a starting assumption that women are equal to men.

Relationship to Feminism

Feminism as an ideological perspective assumes the following: (1) that women are equal to men; (2) that "patriarchy" refers to the father, or *pater,* functioning as the chief, or *archē,* in a society in which males dominate and are presumed to be superior to females; (3) that the superior status of men in patriarchal cultures has allowed them to possess more power than their female counterparts; (4) that this unequal distribution of power is inherently wrong; (5) that those who espouse feminism must work together to eliminate patriarchy and establish a more egalitarian society.

Though the general tenets of feminism are enumerated above, their philosophical and practical implications have led to differences among feminists (those who espouse feminism) and to the consequent categorization of feminists. Some wish to restructure society totally in a more egalitarian fashion; this has radical implications for family structure, economics, politics, etc. Others wish to maintain the current social system, changing only those aspects of it which currently put women at a disadvantage. While some feminists believe that men can also be feminists, others, for example, those who base feminism solely on women's experience, are not so inclusive. Most, but not all, feminists who do theology are moderate and inclusive in perspective.

Feminist theology is done by feminists. Theologians, both male and female, can do theology which is not feminist, but feminists, whether female or male, cannot do theology which is not feminist. They bring to the theological task their assumptions about the equality of women with men, their suspicions and questions about traditional theology which has been and continues to be done predominantly by men in a patriarchal culture, and their conviction that theology desperately needs to be (re)articulated in more egalitarian ways, in ways which include the experience of women.

Relationship to Liberation Theology

Feminist theology is considered by many to be a type of liberation theology. As a "branch" of liberation theology, it is based on the fundamental insight that the God of Israel and the God of Jesus Christ sides with the poor, and stands in solidarity with the marginalized and the social outcast. Though liberation theology is most often associated with Latin America, with Gustavo Gutierrez's groundbreaking *A Theology of Liberation,* with the bishops conferences at Medellin, Columbia (1968) and Puebla, Mexico (1979), and with the doing of theology by the economically poor, it is more broadly conceived to include the doing of theology by any marginalized individuals and/or groups, and understood to address unjust distribution and imbalance of power. Because of this broader definition, the term now embraces Asian and African theologies, as well as black, feminist and womanist theologies.

Feminist theology understands women as one of the groups which has been, as a consequence of patriarchy, structurally disempowered and marginalized. (The term "womanist theology" seeks to acknowledge the differences between the social location of most women doing feminist theology—First World, white, middle class, educated—and African-American and other minority women who are victims not only of sexism but also of racism, and often of classism.)

Relationship to Postmodernism

Latin American, African, and Asian liberation theologians frequently distance their work from postmodern consciousness because they believe that the daily struggle of the Third World's poor for mere physical survival has prevented their adoption of a "modern consciousness." And how can one be postmodern who has not yet been modern? On the other hand, feminist liberation theologians, most though not all of whom work in the First World, do claim a postmodern consciousness.

Such a consciousness rejects the assumption that it is humanly possible, let along desirable, to be totally objective. Further, it asserts that those who believe that total objectivity is possible and desirable, are denying their own subjectivity, including their own social location and the part that it plays in their own learning, perspectives, and theological interests. When a modern consciousness is held by a dominant group, i.e., males, their perspective on truth (on God, on appropriate social organization, etc.) becomes *the* truth, and they see no reason to tolerate, much less welcome, others' perspectives.

Having rejected the possibility of total objectivity, feminist theologians seek to bring to consciousness, their own and others, the subjectivity which affects their work. This subjectivity is heavily influenced by the particular social location of the theologian. They readily admit, for example, that the perspective of a white, middle-class, well-educated American male is likely to be different from that of an African-American, lower-class, poorly educated, female. Because the experiences are different the questions and concerns, including the theological questions and concerns, may very well also be different.

Feminist theologians often consider "women's experience" as the appropriate starting place for doing feminist theology. Because traditional "theology" was almost always "men's theology," the articulation of men's questions and yearnings concerning the divine/human relationship, they believe that women's experience has been omitted and/or disregarded. To compensate for this void, and to complement contemporary theology, feminist theologians wish to lift up, to emphasize, almost to privilege, women's religious experience.

An obvious example is the traditional understanding of pride as a potentially serious sin. Because patriarchal cultures have educated men to be assertive, to be dominant and dominating, to be in control of others (people and things), men's successful self-assertion may lead to pride. Theological writing has consequently warned of the dangers of pride. When one considers that patriarchal cultures have educated women not to be self-assertive but quite the contrary, to be dependent (on men), one realizes that women are much less likely than males to be guilty of pride. Theological writings which have warned of the dangers of pride have not been helpful to women but, in fact, have been damaging to them, because they have presumed an experience which most women do not have, blaming women for a quality they do not possess while being ignorant and insensitive to the real experiences of women. Many women's experience of God and of themselves has prompted an awareness that they must guard not against pride but against timidity and self-doubt.

Deconstructive and Constructive Moments

Feminist theologians understand their task to be *deconstructive* in so far as, suspecting a male bias within the tradition, they seek to identify and dismantle it. The sacred texts of Christianity—the foundational Old and New Testaments, the works of the "Fathers" of the Church, the later theological treatises—were almost all produced by men in a patriarchal culture. As a consequence, they are constructed as men would construct reality; they contain what men have determined to be important. Feminist theologians seek to point out this bias and to bring to full consciousness the patriarchal and sexist biases which have informed the tradition.

But feminist theologians do not believe that it is sufficient to deconstruct the tradition. They seek to *(re)construct* the tradition using a more egalitarian frame of reference. Among other things, this involves looking for and building on hints in the tradition of what is believed to be Jesus' fundamental call to a "discipleship of equals."

Feminist Biblical Studies

Because feminist biblical scholars believe that the Old and New Testaments were produced by men within a patriarchal culture, they are particularly concerned that the texts be interpreted, whenever possible, in ways which are not unnecessarily offensive to women. They recommend: (1) the acknowledgment, not the denial, of the patriarchal character of the texts' origins; (2) an effort to distance our contemporary culture from the culture which produced the texts, rejecting any attempts to justify the replication in our own culture of biblical prejudices against women; and (3) the encouragement of nonsexist and inclusive translations of the texts for use in liturgy. Certain texts, usually from the Old Testament, are judged by some to be so egregiously patriarchal that they should not continue to be read and/or prayed.

Examples of feminist biblical studies include works by Phyllis Trible and Elizabeth Schüssler Fiorenza, and contributions by forty-one female biblical scholars to the recently published *The Women's Bible Commentary* (eds. Carol Newsom and Sharon Ringe, Louisville, Kentucky: Westminster/John Knox Press, 1992).

Areas of Feminist Theology

Feminist theology is in its beginning stages. One reason for this is the fact that women were deprived of the opportunity for theological education until very recently. Nevertheless, the influence of feminists on theology is gradually being felt throughout the discipline.

The sampling below is clearly only a sampling; it does not pretend to raise all the feminist questions, nor to adequately indicate all the alternatives which feminist theologians have constructed, nor even to touch on all the areas of theology. It is meant merely to indicate how extensive are the implications for theology of the assumptions that women are equal to men and that, consequently, women's experience needs to be more adequately incorporated into the theological enterprise.

The Trinity. The Trinity has been, is, and will remain a Christian mystery. Theologians try to probe the mystery but can never fully exhaust it. Theological efforts to make the mystery more comprehensible can be found in the earliest centuries of the Church and continue into the present. Most recently a feminist theological effort (Catherine M. LaCugna, *God for Us. The Trinity and Christian Life,* San Francisco: Harper Collins, 1991) has tried to articulate the mystery anew, in a manner which, its author hopes, will make the mystery of the Trinity more accessible and meaningful to contemporary women and men. The effort is feminist in so far as it deliberately seeks to concretize the abstractions of traditional Trinitarian theology. Dependent on Scripture and incarnational theology, LaCugna is very attentive to personal relationships.

Christology. Can a male savior save women? This question has given rise to a reconsideration of the incarnation (i.e., Did God become "man" or "human"? And if God's intent was to become human, would it not have been more consistent with his revelation to come into the patriarchal culture of ancient Palestine as a "she" rather than a "he"? Could Jesus have been as effective had he come as a woman? What kind of hearing might he have received?).

Along with other branches of liberation theology, feminist theology emphasizes a Christology from below, a Christology which affirms that the humanity and life of Jesus are every bit as important as his divinity. Moreover, feminist theology pays particular attention to the gospel portraits of Jesus which depict him as demonstrating characteristics traditionally associated with women in patriarchal cultures (service, sensitivity to children, the inclusion of outcasts and identification with them) and which depict Jesus' attention to and respect for women. Moreover, feminist theology has searched the tradition to (re)discover theologians whose metaphors include feminine images of Christ, depictions, for example, of Jesus as mother.

Sacramental Theology. Did Jesus institute the sacrament of holy orders? If so, did he ordain only men (the apostles)? Have women been excluded from ordination to the priesthood in Roman Catholicism because of revelation or because of the continuing and determinative influence of patriarchal culture? What were the roles and spheres of influence of women in the early Church?

What is the power of the ordained minister in the sacramental life of the believing community? To what extent has sacramental theology been developed in ways which exclude the experience of women? For example, since the Eucharist is a meal, why have those who traditionally have been the preparers of food been excluded from "preparing" the Eucharist? These questions, their answers, to the extent that their answers can be learned, and the theological consequences of the answers are typical of the work of feminist theologians.

Moral Theology. Feminist theology emphasizes context and challenges all abstract reasoning that has led to theological judgments about right and wrong based solely on abstraction and/or male experience. It cautions that what the Churches teach as "divine" revelation about behaviors may be merely male/patriarchal perceptions of what is divine revelation. It challenges assumptions about power while recognizing the intricate link between sexuality and power in a patriarchal culture.

Mariology. The study of Mary has been deeply affected by feminist thought. Mary's identity in the Gospels is inextricably tied to her role as mother of a divine son. In patriarchal cultures generally women's identity is tied to the men in their lives, their fathers, their husbands, and their sons. Does the gospel portrait of Mary reinforce a patriarchal model? Further, is Mary portrayed in the biblical texts as submissive? Are women called by God to be like Mary, that is, to be submissive? Or rather, is she not like other prophets who accept their call? And if Mary is virgin and mother, and no other woman can be both a virgin and a mother, are women given a model which is impossible to achieve and are they consequently doomed to failure? Should all women aspire to be like Mary, that is, to be mothers?

Feminist theology has begun to wrestle with some of these questions and to (re)articulate and develop images of Mary which emphasize her importance in her own right, including that fact that she has represented and continues to represent, at least in popular piety, the "female face of God."

ALICE L. LAFFEY

See also MARY, MOTHER OF GOD; WOMEN IN THE CHURCH.

FENWICK, EDWARD (1768–1832)

Dominican friar, missionary and first bishop of Cincinnati, Ohio (1822–1832), Edward Fenwick was born in St. Mary's County, Maryland, on 19 August 1768, and died in Wooster, Ohio, on 26 September 1832. A member of an old Maryland Catholic family of English ancestry, Fenwick was orphaned at the age of six. He received his early education at the Fenwick Manor and later at the college conducted by the English Dominicans at Bornheim in the Austrian Netherlands. He entered the Order of Preachers and was professed on 26 March 1790. The French Revolution soon forced him to flee to England where he remained until 1804 when he left to

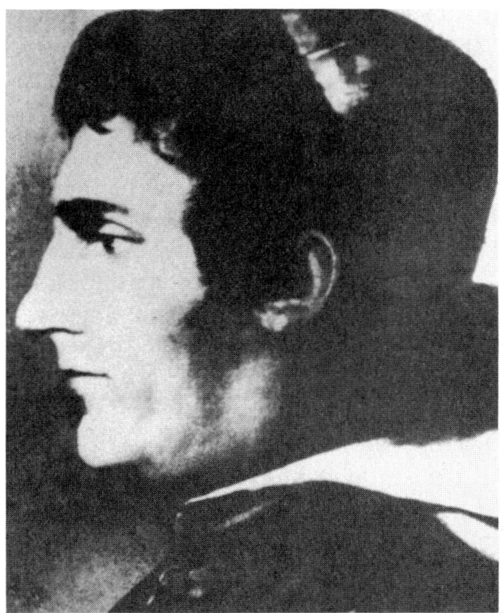

Bishop Edward Fenwick

establish a Dominican foundation in the United States.

On the advice of Bishop John Carroll, Fenwick went to Kentucky in 1805 where he established the motherhouse of the American Dominicans near Springfield in 1806. The following year he founded St. Rose's Church and Priory there, but then resigned as superior to devote his life to missionary work in Kentucky and Ohio. In 1821 he was appointed first bishop of Cincinnati and received episcopal ordination at the hands of Bishop Benedict Flaget in St. Rose's Church, Springfield, Kentucky, on 13 January 1822. In Cincinnati Fenwick built the new Cathedral of St. Peter in Chains (1826) and established a diocesan newspaper, the *Catholic Telegraph-Register.* In 1828 he was also appointed provincial of the American Dominicans for life.

THOMAS J. SHELLEY

See also AMERICAN CATHOLICISM; DOMINICANS.

FERIA

(Lat., "holiday" or "free day") In ecclesiastical usage, the term refers to a weekday on which no proper vigil is observed or feast celebrated. The traditional Church practice was to repeat the readings from the previous Sunday's Mass on ferial days; this is no longer done, however, as the current lectionary (composed in 1969) offers readings for each day of the year.

JOSEPH QUINN

See also LITURGY.

FEUDALISM

Feudalism was a way of governing and organizing society in much of Europe during the Middle Ages. It was a kind of pyramid of mutual obligations established originally by agreement or conquest. Thus a king (who had acquired that authority by conquest or heredity) would assign certain tracts of land to powerful men who became his vassals. That meant that in return for the land grant, the vassal had to equip and maintain a certain number of knights to fight for the king, and also had to make certain payments in kind. In order to have such payments and equipment available, each vassal of the king was also a local feudal lord who received payments in kind from the peasants of his tract of land. What a local feudal lord offered the peasants in exchange was protection against raiders as well as assignment of a plot of land from which the peasants could support their families after making the required payment to the lord.

Feudalism is connected with the Catholic Church in several ways. One is that many of the medieval bishops of western Europe were also feudal lords and vassals of kings because they held land grants. This caused considerable tension over the question of who had the authority to appoint bishops, and over the related question of what loyalty and obedience the bishops owed to secular sovereigns and how this could be reconciled with their loyalty and obedience to the pope.

A second connection between feudalism and the Catholic Church is that the institutional structures of the Church which developed in medieval Europe were in many respects modeled on the feudal system. Today, that means a general pattern of a pyramid of authority in which each owes obedience and loyalty to the one immediately above in the pyramid. That tends to mean that all the communication moves down the pyramid while all the attention is turned upwards. Decision-making and initiative tend to flow from the top or be seen as insubordination to lawful authority. Those who have examined the history of the structures in the Church and have considered our ecclesiology (theology about the Church) in the light of the history have questioned whether this is an appropriate development of the community of disciples as seen in the New Testament.

A third connection between feudalism and the Catholic Church may be seen in the veneration of saints and prayers to them seeking their intercession with God. It has been suggested that in the case of patron saints particularly (whether of individuals, parishes, cities, countries, or institutions) the pattern of protection in exchange for services, and of local intermediaries with higher or ultimate authority, is evident. This way of thinking and acting may well have seemed natural to Christians living in a feudal society.

MONIKA K. HELLWIG

See also CHURCH AND STATE; MIDDLE AGES, THE; PATRON SAINTS.

FIDEISM

Any of several doctrines advocated in the nineteenth century which asserted the supremacy of faith over reason in matters concerning the existence or nature of God. According to Fideists, divine revelation, received through faith, is the primary source and guiding force of all truth; hence, philosophy and other forms of human reason and judgment are by necessity secondary.

JOSEPH QUINN

See also PHILOSOPHY AND THEOLOGY; RATIONALISM.

FILIOQUE

See HOLY SPIRIT.

FIRST FRIDAYS

A devotional practice honoring the Sacred Heart of Jesus in which members of the Church observe the first Friday of each month by receiving Holy Communion. According to promises which it is claimed Jesus made to St. Margaret Mary Alacoque, those who follow this practice for nine consecutive months will be granted special graces such as final perseverance in faith and the consolation of Christ's love in their final hour.

JOSEPH QUINN

See also SACRED HEART OF JESUS.

FIRST SATURDAYS

The devotional practice of honoring the Immaculate Heart of Mary by receiving the sacrament of reconciliation, and—on the first Saturday of five successive months—receiving Holy Communion, reciting five decades of the rosary, and meditating on these sacred mysteries for at least fifteen minutes. These devotions are based on claims that the Blessed Mother, in apparitions at Fatima, Portugal, in 1917, promised to intercede for the faithful at their final hour in order that they might receive the grace of final perseverance and experience reconciliation with Christ.

JOSEPH QUINN

See also DEVOTIONS; FATIMA.

FISHER, JOHN, ST. (1469–1535)

English bishop and martyr. The son of a Yorkshire tradesman, he was ordained at a young age, acquired a high reputation for scholarship at Cambridge and was chosen as her chaplain by Lady Margaret Beaufort, mother of King Henry VII. With her help he established new colleges and courses of study in the university, of which he became chancellor in 1504.

St. John Fisher, by Hans Holbein

In the same year he was appointed bishop of Rochester, a small diocese in Kent. He shared the Renaissance interest in the Greek and Latin writers of antiquity and won the personal friendship of Erasmus, who admired Fisher greatly but confessed his discomfiture in the presence of so much holiness! Fisher in fact lived a life of remarkable simplicity and self-denial despite his personal involvement in the affairs of the royal family, which continued after the accession of Henry VIII in 1509. His sermons—among the first to be printed in English—were not at all academic but gently pastoral and full of homely images. His charity was of the direct kind, personally distributed at his palace gate. He collaborated with the King in repudiating the doctrines of Luther but when Henry sought to have his marriage to Catherine of Aragon annulled Fisher sided with the Queen, whom he counseled on the matter throughout the prolonged negotiations. When Henry married Anne Boleyn without papal dispensation, Fisher refused to acknowledge the right of Anne's daughter to succeed to the throne since he was required in making this acknowlegement to reject the authority of the pope and accept without qualification that the King was head of the Church in England. The King had him imprisoned in the Tower of London in 1534 at the same time as Sir Thomas More. Pope Paul III named him a cardinal, which infuriated Henry, and Fisher was now required to take the newly devised oath of supremacy, formally assenting to the King's claim. Fisher refused. He was put on trial, found guilty of treason and beheaded on Tower Hill. He was canonized in 1935.

LOUIS McREDMOND

See also ANGLICANISM; BRITAIN, CHURCH IN.

FITZSIMONS (OR FITZSIMMONS), THOMAS (1741–1811)

Born in Ireland in 1741, he came to Philadelphia as a youth and embarked on a mercantile career. In 1761 he married Catherine Meade, the daughter of a prosperous merchant, and thereafter his business activities widened and prospered. He was prominent in the Revolution and saw service in many important campaigns. As the war was ending, he lobbied strenuously to have arrears due to soldiers paid before demobilization. He served in the Pennsylvania legislature, but is best remembered as a member of the convention which framed the Federal Constitution in 1787, and was one of its signatories. He served from 1789 to 1795 in the House of Representatives. Thereafter he devoted himself mostly to business and charitable activities. He participated in the founding of the Bank of North America, and established the Insurance Company of North America. He was an active member of the Hibernian Society and liberally contributed to Catholic causes in Philadelphia. He died in 1811.

JOAN GLAZIER

See also AMERICAN CATHOLICISM.

FOCOLARE MOVEMENT

It was founded in Trent, Italy, by Chiara Lubich in 1943 and is approved as an association of the faithful. Vows are taken by a select group of 4000 key members who live in small communities, of which there are eighteen in North America. It has also developed an active youth section. Its members now number ca. 1,250,000 and they live a spirituality which fosters unity among the Churches and among all sections of society.

MICHAEL GLAZIER

See also INSTITUTE, SECULAR.

FORGIVENESS

See SACRAMENT OF RECONCILIATION.

FORTITUDE

See VIRTUE.

FORTY HOURS DEVOTION

A devotion in which the Sacred Host is exposed for the adoration of the faithful during part or all of forty hours, often with the participation of the clergy of nearby parishes. The present practice dates to the seventeenth century.

DAVID BRYAN

See also EUCHARISTIC DEVOTIONS; EXPOSITION OF THE BLESSED SACRAMENT.

FOUCAULD, CHARLES DE (1858–1916)

French nobleman who converted to Catholicism in 1886. Ordained to the priesthood in 1901. Today's followers of his way of life include the Little Brothers of Jesus, the Little Sisters of Jesus, the Union of Priests, and the Jesus/Caritas fraternity.

Charles de Foucauld ended his life a gentle "solitary" in a hermitage built into a rugged stone hillside in the Algerian Sahara. There he spent his days praying, responding to the basic needs of nomadic people in the area, and translating the tribal poetry of the Touareg into French. For years he had struggled inwardly to reshape the monastic life to more truly imitate Christ's response to each man and woman in his path. "I am a monk," he insisted, "not a missionary. Made for silence, not for preaching." A monk, yes, but one who eludes the common religious categories; a monk who practiced "contemplation in the streets." Charles de Foucauld will continue to baffle those set on framing his life strictly in such human constructs. His one central reality was Christ. His single defining principle: "Follow me. I am your rule. . . ." (Notes, 6 June 1897, quoted in Philip Hillyer, *Charles de Foucauld,* Collegeville, Minn.: The Liturgical Press, 1990, p. 86).

His journey to find Christ wound from France through Morocco and Syria, and back through centuries to Jesus' own village. A point of entry to his search is the ending of his military career. Charles, self-indulgent and cynical, defiantly thrust his mistress into the official regimental path. Next he became an explorer. Disguised as a Jew (to avoid attracting attention in an Islamic country), with a rabbi as his guide, he mapped a large uncharted segment of Morocco—on foot. For months he walked, unconsciously replicating Christ's own slow-paced and self-disciplined life and clearing away the room for an image to etch its way into his mind: Muslim villagers stopping their work throughout the day to turn devoutly toward Mecca and pray. Such simple reverence heightened his own emptiness and disgust with his bloated life, and brought him to his knees.

He joined the Trappists—first in France, then in a tiny monastery in Akbès, Syria. The Trappists gave him the discipline of a rule, a love for contemplative prayer, and a safe place to shed his old skin. In the poorest monastery he could find he planned to burrow contentedly inside "a huge enclosure, thick and high" (Hillyer, p. 99). The wandering adventurer now embraced the protective ideal of "enclosure."

But walls did not shut out the sight, one day, of a group of starving children in a hut with the body of their dead father. A new image crystallized in his mind: "I want a small monastery, like the house of a poor workman who is not sure whether tomorrow he will find work and bread, who with all his being shares the suffering of the world." His search now led to Jesus' own village, to "think his thoughts, speak his words, do his actions" (Hillyer, p. 81), and to Jerusalem. He wrote letters and recorded his impressions as a contemplative handyman like "Mary's workman-son." "The abbess . . . gives me the work I need to earn my bread, but I do it in my cell as and when it suits me. The convent is two kilometres from the town on the road to Bethlehem. I have a little boarded cell in a small enclosure right next to the cloister—from my window I see my much-loved Bethany and, beyond, the dark curtain of the mountains of the Jordan. I never go out except to the chapel, so I have been able to organize a hermit's life for myself and I deeply enjoy this marvelous solitude. . ." (Letter, Jan. 2, 1899, Charles de Foucauld, trans. Barbara Lucas [Maryknoll, New York: Orbis, 1979] 63).

He had stumbled on his true "guide," one that would steer his steps as surely in a "little boarded cell" as inside a walled enclosure "thick and high": a consciousness dedicated to imitating, minute by minute, the Master's Way. Once again Charles was being stripped—this time of the garments of centuries of abstract religious ideals which he had hungrily introjected. Once again he was starting over, this time to learn as a child in Nazareth. ". . . This life was enough for him, the Son of God, for many years," he wrote a fellow Trappist. ". . . it is as though you were five years old and learning to read, like a child. . . . Later he will take you to the desert . . . from there to Gethsemane . . . then to Calvary . . ." (Letter, 21 June 1898, Charles de Foucauld, *Meditations of a Hermit,* trans. Charlotte Balfour, London: Oates and Washbourne, 1981, p. 138).

His journal is richly textured with simple impressions of the village life of Jesus and his family. An entry for 21 December: "The Blessed Virgin and St. Joseph left Nazareth this morning to go to Bethlehem. They crossed the plain of Esdraelon and probably found food and shelter this night somewhere near Engannim towards Jenin or Zababda . . ." (Charles de Foucauld, *Meditations of a Hermit,* p. ix). He learned the physical demands on Jesus: "It was a life of fatigue, long journeys, long sermons, and days in the desert without shelter or shade . . . intemperate weather, nights without shelter, uncertain nourishment snatched when work permitted; all these mean suffering" (Charles de Foucauld, *Meditations of a Hermit,* p. 49). And he learned his habits: "Our Lord prays alone, and prays at night."

Nazareth was a time of incubation. The idealized Son of God became flesh, and the mind of Jesus became a window through which Charles might look freshly at the concrete world about him. Christ was there each time he hammered a nail to a piece of wood; he was as near as the Eucharist that shared the hut. Free of the Trappists' many rules, the Nazareth days provided Charles the simplicity, isolation, and silence for an important psychic event—the distilling of his own experiences and the varied images that had touched him, and their reassembly in his consciousness: the poor children in the hut with their dead father; the reverence of the villagers he met as he mapped Morocco; his rugged hiking in the desert and the mountains; the discipline of the monastic Rule; the Eucharist; the simple family life of Jesus.

Like the hidden pattern in an optical illusion, a plan slowly emerged: ". . . to found on the Moroccan border, not a Trappist house, not a big rich monastery . . . but a sort of humble little hermitage where a few poor monks could live on fruit and a little barley harvested with their own hands, in a narrow enclosure, in Penance and Adoration of the Blessed Sacrament, not going outside their enclosure, not preaching but giving hospitality to all comers, good or bad, friends or enemy, Muslim or Christian . . . (sharing) the very last mouthful of bread with any poor person, any visitor, any stranger, and (welcoming) every human being as a beloved brother" (Letter, 23 June 1901, Charles de Foucauld, *Inner Search: Letters (1889–1916),* Maryknoll, New York: Orbis, 1979, pp. 83-84). He trimmed the Rule of St. Benedict to fit Christ's formative village experience: ". . . similar to the Trappists, but poorer . . . none of those little external regulations that Trappists have scrupulously to obey, just a simple family life." No chanting of hours, only a few specific rules, regular manual work, prayer in the presence of Christ in the Eucharist. His vocation, he now saw, was to "preach the Gospel silently" while living his hidden life, "as did Mary and Joseph" (Hillyer, p. 86).

Returning to Beni-Abbès, a spot near the Moroccan border, living on bread and barley soup and sleeping on the ground, Charles built a simple home of palm trunks and mud, with a few tiny rooms and a chapel where he could lead "a life of prayer, at the foot of the tabernacle." In 1902 he ransomed his first slave: "a poor young boy who was snatched from his family four or five years ago." In 1905 he moved again to the isolated Saharan village of Tamanrasset to live the hidden life of Nazareth and to welcome poor and weary travelers to "share my feast."

Travelers did come to share his feast—tribal people, hot, hungry, weary from walking. But no one came to share his life. For nearly three years he was not permitted to say Mass, a hard trial for a man so devoted to the Eucharist. "I have often asked myself . . . would it be better to stay at Hoggar without being able to celebrate Mass, or to celebrate it and not go there?" The struggle led to a deeper grasp of holiness: "Formerly I tended to see on one side the *Infinite,* the Holy Sacrifice, and on the other the *finite,* everything apart from God, and was always ready to sacrifice anything to celebrate Holy Mass. But . . . from the time of the apostles the greatest saints have in certain circumstances sacrificed the possibility of celebrating to works of spiritual charity, in order to make journeys. . ." (Letter of 2 July 1907, quoted in Hillyer, p. 94).

During the last years of his life, still living without a single permanent companion, Charles spent hours each day meticulously compiling a French-Touareg dictionary and translating Touareg poetry. The images that had haunted him for years remained, scraped clean of their literal meaning: Nazareth was, as his spiritual director Abbé Huvelin had said, "wherever one worked with Jesus in humility, poverty, silence" (Hillyer, p. 78). Enclosure behind high walls had become an interior enclosure; silence was the conscious guarding of his inner quiet as he traveled to the isolated places where poor families needed him.

As he followed Christ each step of the way, from "the nest of Nazareth" to Calvary, "the boundary of God's will" quietly supplanted "the boundary of silence and solitude. . . ." But in his life of continuous change, one thing remained constant: Charles' need for and devotion to the Eucharist. It nourished him and kept him near his Lord. A footnote to his death suggests that his grasp of the Eucharist, too, had been distilled and purified. In an echo of World War I the gentle hermit was dragged outside, shot in the head, and his clothes stripped from him. When his friends found his body, knowing his love of "a life of prayer at the foot of the tabernacle," they searched the hermitage for the consecrated Host. They found the Host. But not in a *golden* tabernacle. Charles—who knew his Lord had slept in a desert—had hidden the Host, carefully, in the sand.

PATRICIA O'CONNOR

See also AFRICA, THE CATHOLIC CHURCH IN; CHRISTIAN SPIRITUALITY; CONTEMPLATION; HERMIT.

FRA ANGELICO (ca. 1400–1455)

Fra Angelico, born around 1400 as Guido di Piero, was apprenticed to a painter and by 1418 was undertaking work in Florentine churches, but none of it survives unless the Detroit *Madonna and Child* dates from this period. In 1422 Guido joined the reformed Dominicans at Fiesole and took the name of Fra Giovanni, by which he was known in his lifetime. It was the poet Corella who described him ca. 1468 as an "angelic painter"—hence the name Fra Angelico, by which he is universally known. By 1425 Angelico was working on *The Madonna and Child with Saints and Angels* which is still in San Domenico; later, he painted an *Annunciation* and a *Coronation of the Virgin* for the same church.

The *Madonna and Child with Saints,* completed in 1429 for the Convent of St. Peter Martyr, shows that in his figure-drawing and composition Angelico was then more under the influence of Masaccio than of Gentile da Fabriano or Lorenzo Monaco, though by 1433, when he was commissioned to paint a shrine for the Linen-Merchants' Guild, his personal style had matured. While in many of his pictures Angelico uses the same image of Mary, usually it is freshly composed with subtle variations, and in the altar panel for San Marco he introduces something iconographically new: the "holy conversation" scene, in which Mary speaks to relaxed groups of saints.

By 1440 Fra Angelico had moved to San Marco in central Florence. This monastery was the Medicis' gift to the Dominicans as a center for ongoing reform, where observance was to be strict, learning up-to-date and profound. Architecturally clean and modern, the monastery from the start used art as an aid to prayer and in fact every cell has its mural, though it is unlikely that Angelico painted more than four of them. The great *Chapter-Room Crucifixion* should be compared with the *Taking Down from the Cross* and the *Lamentation over the Dead Christ*—tranquil creations, all of them, of a contemplative who rose for midnight matins, and whose day was punctuated by the monastery bell calling the friars to the liturgical hours.

Fra Angelico, detail of fresco painting, by Signorelli, Orvieto Cathedral

In the *General Judgement* and *Coronation of the Virgin* Angelico marshals his crowds with powerful designs, assured figure-drawing and vivid color schemes whose opulent reds are harmonized successfully with blues of amazing intensity. In his handling of light and perspective he was advancing technical frontiers, so that when he left for Rome in 1445, Angelico was the leading artist in Florence. He died in 1455.

Angelico's surviving frescoes in the Vatican are a vigorous sermon to popes that the Church is a servant Church whose wealth is for distribution. While there have been periods in which his astonishing output of some two hundred paintings has been undervalued, popular appreciation of his saintliness has been constant, and Fra Angelico was formally beatified in 1982.

MICHAEL PRENDERGAST

See also ART, CHRISTIAN.

FRANCIS DE SALES, ST. (1567–1622)

He was the first of thirteen children born to noble and wealthy parents. After a happy and uneventful youth in 1582 he entered the College of Clermont which was directed by the Jesuits at the University of Paris. During his scholastic years he showed a keen interest in theology and led a well-planned spiritual life. Six years later he moved to the University of Padua and earned doctorates in civil and canon law. Against the objections of his father, he was ordained in 1592. In 1596 he volunteered to go with his cousin as a missionary to the Chablais, one of the eight states of Savoy. This was a tough assignment as the area had been impoverished by feuds and wars and the religious controversies, mostly as a result of the inroads of Protestantism, had put the Church on the defensive with many defections and wide discontent. Visiting hamlet after hamlet and working from dawn to dusk, Francis became known as a caring down-to-earth priest and a gifted preacher. He wrote and distributed pamphlets which refuted the positions and doctrines of the Reformers and offered instructions in a clear and interesting way. These were collected and published later as the *Controversies.* His administrative ability, pastoral zeal, and personal holiness attracted notice, and he was chosen to be bishop of Geneva in 1610. He was a hands-on prelate and personally got involved with the education of his clergy and of his flock. For twenty years he labored tirelessly and imaginatively, teaching, writing, and preaching. In his priestly life he preached over four thousand sermons and wrote some twenty-six books, two of which have become classics. The *Introduction to a Devout Life* has rarely been out of print since its publication in 1608; and *Treatise on the Love of God* (1616) is a spiritual masterpiece. Even as a bishop, he continued his work as spiritual director. Among those he guided was the saintly widow Jane Frances de Chantal with whom he founded the Visitation of Holy Mary, a contemplative order commonly known as the Visitation Nuns. Francis de Sales died in 1622 and in 1665 he was canonized by Pope Alexander VII. Various congregations have been founded under his patronage, including the Oblates of St. Francis de Sales, the Missionaries of St. Francis de Sales, the Salesians of Don Bosco and the Sisters of St. Joseph. He is the patron of writers and journalists.

MICHAEL GLAZIER

See also BISHOP; SAINTS; SPIRITUAL LIFE.

FRANCIS OF ASSISI, ST. (1181/1182–1226)

Born in Assisi to Pietro Bernardone and Lady Pica in 1181/1182, Francis was baptized Giovanni in his father's absence. His name was changed to Francis upon Pietro's return to Assisi from a successful business trip to France. Francis received a rudimentary education at the parish church of San Giorgio, but, as his biographers would point out, he appeared to be more interested in the good life and the advantages provided by a rising merchant family in the commune of Assisi. Francis fought in the battle of Collestrada in 1202, which pitted Assisi against Perugia, ending in defeat for Assisi and imprisonment for Francis. A period of sickness followed his release from prison. But after his recuperation, Francis again attempted to win the honor of knighthood and undertook an expedition in service of the pope, only to return to Assisi in obedience to what he considered to be God's will for him.

Francis himself would identify the turning point of his conversion with an encounter with a leper, which as he stated in his *Testament,* was God's doing, ultimately allowing Francis to overcome his revulsion for all that the leper was and stood for in an embrace which changed "bitterness to sweetness." From that moment on, Francis would make his home with the lepers and marginalized of the world, and there find Christ, the suffering, crucified Savior. Abandoning his family home and patrimony Francis took the gospel as his rule and life and he became a "herald of the great king." Around the year 1205/1206, he would find direction for his life in the voice of the crucified who spoke to him from a cross in the ruined church of San Damiano, instructing Francis to rebuild the church which was falling down around him.

St. Francis of Assisi, fresco detail, 13th century, Sacro Speco, Subiaco

Dedicating himself to rebuilding physically the church of San Damiano together with his service of the lepers, his simple lifestyle attracted attention, and soon others wished to associate themselves to Francis and his novel undertaking. Seeking explicit direction from the gospel, he and his brothers fell upon those passages wherein Jesus instructed his disciples to take nothing for the journey as they were sent on mission to preach conversion and the kingdom of God. Growing to a group of twelve, in 1209/1210, Francis and his brothers traveled to Rome to seek approval for their simple, poor gospel way of life from Innocent III. Giving the group oral approval for their rule of life, Innocent also gave them permission to preach penance.

From the moment Francis met his first brother, he would never again be alone, and the central axis of his simple lifestyle would be the relationship with his brothers and sisters given him by God. The Franciscan movement would continue to grow rapidly around Francis. Clare of Assisi became part of the Franciscan fraternity in 1212, herself directing the development of the Poor Ladies from the monastery of San Damiano where she would live the privilege of absolute poverty until her death in 1253. In addition to those brothers of Francis who would promise to live in poverty, chastity, and obedience in the First Order, men and women would associate themselves to the spirit and lifestyle of the Franciscans as members of the Third Order while living as married or single in the world.

Francis himself continued to lead and direct the Franciscan movement through his example and teaching. In addition to preaching locally, Francis took part in the mission of the order to nonbelievers. Seeking martyrdom, Francis traveled to Syria in 1219 where he came to the crusader camp at Damietta. There he attempted to discourage the impeding crusader's attack on the Muslim camp. Unable to stop the battle, he was a witness of the failed Fifth Crusade, which ended in the death of thousands. After the resounding defeat of the crusader army, Francis traveled to the camp of the Sultan, Melek-el-Kamel, where he spoke with him and witnessed to the Christian faith, but was unsuccessful in his attempt both to convert the Sultan and to achieve martyrdom for himself.

Returning to Italy in 1220, Francis then attended to some of the difficulties emerging within the growing Franciscan movement. In the next few years the Rule of the Friars Minor was discussed and finalized at the annual chapter meetings, with written approval of the final text being given by Honorius III in the bull *Solet annuere,* 29 November 1223. Francis resigned as general minister of the order and the final years of his life would be spent in prayer and preaching.

In December 1223, Francis was at the hermitage in Grecchio, where he would celebrate Christmas by reenacting the birth of Jesus at Bethlehem at midnight Mass with a cast of characters including both people and animals, in order to remember visibly and tangibly the poverty and humility of the incarnation. The following year, on 17 September, while in prayer on mount LaVerna, he would be marked in his flesh with the stigmata, the wounds of the crucified Christ appearing in his hands, feet, and side. Gradually growing weaker due to sickness and almost completely blind, he composed the *Canticle of Brother Sun* the following winter, in which he praised God with and in creation, inviting people to join in the hymn of praise with all of creation, their sisters and brothers, by living in peace and humility.

Francis would end his days at the little church of St. Mary of the Angels, the Portiuncula, where he died on the evening of 3 October 1226, and was buried the following day at his parish church of San Giorgio within the walls of Assisi. Pope Gregory IX canonized Francis on 16 July 1228, at the same time laying the cornerstone for the basilica of St. Francis, to which the body of Francis was transferred on 25 May 1230.

MICHAEL BLASTIC, O.F.M. CONV.

See also FRANCISCANS; MENDICANT ORDERS; PREACHING; RELIGIOUS ORDERS; STIGMATA.

FRANCIS OF ASSISI, ST., RULE OF

The definitive Rule of Francis was approved by Pope Honorius III on 29 November 1223 with the bull *Solet annuere,* bringing to an end the process of development of the text which began in 1209/1210. After the Lord gave Francis brothers, he states in his *Testament* that he was inspired by God to live according to the form of the holy gospel. This was written down very simply in a text which contained pertinent passages from the Gospels together with some simple, practical arrangements for fraternal life, and approved orally in 1209/1210 by Innocent III.

As the number of brothers grew and their mission took them throughout all of Europe and beyond to the nonbelievers, the text of the Rule developed and grew with the fraternity. An edition of the text of the Rule as it existed around the year 1221 is extant (referred to variously as the "Earlier Rule" or the *Regula non bollata*), containing twenty-four chapters. The final Rule approved by Honorius in 1223 is composed of twelve chapters.

Even in the various stages of textual development, the Rule always remained the same for Francis. Its nucleus consisted in a description of the evangelical lifestyle expressed in poverty and mobility, modeled on the concrete description of Christ's own sending of the apostles and disciples in the Synoptic Gospels. In the absence of fixed dwellings, the brothers were to find a home in their mutual love and support. They were to pray in churches along the way, and to preach according to the form of the Roman Church, and in addition, preach penance only with permission of the local clergy. All the brothers were to preach by example. The brothers were to supply their daily needs through manual labor and without provision for the morrow; failing this, they were allowed to beg for necessities. In addition to this general description of both the lifestyle and inspiration for the life of the Friars Minor, the Rule includes a chapter on the mission to nonbelievers, making the Franciscan Rule the first missionary rule and order in the Western Church.

MICHAEL BLASTIC, O.F.M. CONV.

See also FRANCIS OF ASSISI, ST.; RELIGIOUS ORDERS.

FRANCIS, ST., PRAYER OF

Lord, make me an instrument of your peace.
Where there is hatred, let me sow love,
Where there is injury, pardon,
Where there is doubt, faith,
Where there is despair, hope,
Where there is darkness, light,
Where there is sadness, joy.

O, Divine Master, grant that I may seek
not so much to be consoled as to console;
to be understood as to understand,
to be loved as to love,
for it is in giving that we receive,
it is in pardoning that we are pardoned,
and it is in dying that we are born to eternal
life. Amen.

This prayer is loved and recited by countless people on all continents. Its exact origin and date are disputed. Though it was not written by St. Francis, it is Franciscan in composition, spirit, and spirituality. It is one of the most popular Christian prayers, and is regarded as a spiritual treasure which, like the beatitudes, is an inexhaustible source for meditation and a touchstone for Christian living.

JOSEPH QUINN

See also FRANCIS OF ASSISI, ST.; FRANCISCANS.

FRANCIS XAVIER, ST. (1506–1552)

Francis was born in the family castle of Xavier in Navarre (now part of Spain) on 7 April 1506. In 1523 he went to the University of Paris where in 1529 he began sharing a room with the saintly Ignatius of Loyola. Having worldly ambitions, he resisted the appeals of Ignatius until 1533. On 15 August 1534, Francis, Ignatius and five others took private vows of poverty and chastity. They hoped to work in Jerusalem for the conversion of the infidel, but this being impossible they placed themselves under the pope. In 1540, six months before the Jesuits gained papal approval, Ignatius, responding to a request from the pope and the king of Portugal, sent Francis to the Indies.

Francis arrived in Goa on 6 May 1543. For two years he preached to the Paravas near Cape Comorin and set up catechists; then he worked in Cochin and Madras. He left India for the Moluccas (the Spice Islands), where he landed on 14 February 1546, where again he preached with great success. At Malacca he met Anjiro, a Japanese nobleman interested in becoming a Catholic, and Francis turned his attentions to Japan. With several other Jesuits he hired a pagan pirate to take them to southern Japan, landing on 24 June 1549. Through Anjiro he gained permission to preach Christianity there, but with only moderate success. Dressed poorly, Francis could not obtain audience with the emperor. He and his Jesuit companion then dressed in fine silk and brought a clock, crystal, wine, and a music box as gifts and soon obtained an interview with the daimyo of Yamaguchi who gave permission to preach Christianity in the empire. The Japanese wondered why the Chinese did not know of Christianity as most of their culture came from China; he decided to preach there. In 1551 Francis set out again for Malacca and India, but the ship was thrown off course by a typhoon and stopped at the desolate island of Sancian in the Bay of Canton. He returned to India where a letter from Ignatius appointed him provincial of the "Indies and the countries beyond." In September 1552 he returned to Sancian. There, trying to get transport to the Chinese mainland, he died of a fever on 3 December 1552. He was buried on Sancian, reburied in Malacca, and then in Goa, where his body remained largely undecayed till modern times. He was beatified in 1619 and canonized on 12 March 1622. He is patron of missionaries.

THOMAS M. KING, S.J.

See also IGNATIUS OF LOYOLA, ST.; MISSIONS, CATHOLIC, THE MODERN PERIOD; SOCIETY OF JESUS.

FRANCISCANS

The Franciscans take both their name and inspiration from Francis of Assisi (1181–1226). While the term "Franciscan" describes all those men and women of the first, second, and third (regular and secular) orders, this article is concerned with a description of the members of the first order: the Friars Minor, the Friars Minor Conventual, and the Friars Minor Capuchin.

All three branches of the Franciscan first order follow the Rule of Francis of Assisi which was approved by Pope Honorius III on 29 November 1223. The distinctions among the three branches of the first order arose as attempts to live, reform, and revitalize the charism of Francis in different historical contexts.

Even during the lifetime of Francis with the rapid numerical growth of the order and its wide geographic expansion, problems arose concerning structures intended to implement the prescriptions of the Franciscan Rule in regard to both ministry and poverty. The Rule itself does not describe concrete or exact structures but rather was intended by Francis to serve as a spiritual document. Francis intended the Rule to provide the motivation and spiritual values which would accompany and motivate an itinerant fraternity of men as they went about the world preaching the gospel by word and example. For Francis and his early companions in 1210 it was enough to say that the brothers should be "pilgrims and strangers in this world." For three to five thousand men in 1223, it was a much different situation. The ministers who became responsible for the large movement even before Francis' death sought more definite solutions to questions of poverty, ownership, and ministry which the Rule left vague. Francis himself, perhaps fearing that "life according to the form of the holy gospel" might be abandoned completely, wrote in his *Testament* that the Rule should not be interpreted or glossed but lived to the letter.

The inability to reconcile developments within the order concerning poverty and ministry with living the Rule to the letter led the officials of the order to seek papal interpretations of the Rule soon after Francis' death. Pope Gregory IX responded to the friars' request in September of 1230 with the bull *Quo elongati,* declaring that the *Testament* of Francis was not binding on the order since Francis had not consulted the order before it was issued, and proceeded to set the order on a juridical path of moderate security in terms of an interpretation of poverty which supported the development of a clerical ministry within the order. Gregory thus set a precedent of papal interpretation which would be used often throughout the thirteenth century and beyond in order to resolve internal disputes in the order concerning ministry and observance of poverty.

The mainstream of the order throughout the first century of its existence largely followed the lead of the papacy in both ministerial expression and the interpretation of poverty. The needs of the Church determined to a large extent the shape of Franciscan ministry—the Church needed dogmatic preachers able both to withstand heretics and to reap the fruits of personal conversion in sacramental confession. Hence, the Church's need for clerical preachers led at least in part to the transformation of the simple, itinerant brotherhood of Francis (open to both cleric and lay on an equal basis) to an educated clerical order with large convents in urban centers.

Parallel to this mainstream "conventual" community, was a smaller yet significant part of the order which resisted many of the implications of clericalization and held on to the more itinerant and rigorous lifestyle associated with the hermitages. It was in this context that a movement of renewal sprang up in the 1330s. At the hermitage of Brogliano a group of friars lived a generally contemplative life, rigorously observing the Rule of Francis without papal exemption and interpretation. While remaining juridically members of the one Franciscan Order, the observant movement grew independently of the community and spread throughout the world. Included in this movement were famous Franciscan preachers in the fifteenth century: Bernardine of Siena, John of Capistran, James of the March, and Albert of Sarteano. While they enjoyed some autonomy under the Vicar General of Observance, attempts to reunify the two groups failed. Pope Leo X issued his bull *Ite vos* on 29 May 1517, marking the official division of the friars minor into two distinct and autonomous groups, the Conventuals (O.F.M. Conv.) and the Observants (O.F.M.). In doing this, Leo created nothing new, but merely recognized the real division existing within the order.

This did not stop the movement of reform within the Franciscan Order from coming to concrete expression throughout the centuries: reform groups such as Recollects, Reformed, and Discalced, were eventually reunited into the Observants in 1898 by Leo XIII with his bull *Felicitate quadam.*

But shortly after the juridical division of the order in 1517, a significant movement of reform emerged which would eventually be shaped into the third autonomous Franciscan Order known as the Capuchins. Already in 1525 Friar Matthew of Basci desired to promote reform of the order. Again, this reform movement was associated with the hermitages and a greater emphasis on contemplative prayer understood as the most important source for an effective preaching ministry. Also, a return to the simplicity of the primitive observance of the Rule without papal privilege or interpretation in the manner prescribed by Francis in his *Testament,* that is, without gloss and to the letter, motivated these reformers who set down their principles in the *Albacina Document* in 1528. They received the name Capuchins from the small hood they wore on their habits. Their first constitutions were published in 1536, but they remained nominally under the general minister of the Conventuals until they became fully independent in 1619 with the right to elect their own minister general.

Throughout all the centuries of reform and division in the history of the Franciscan Order, the constant point of reference has been the charism and the Rule of Francis of Assisi. While remaining three distinct juridical orders, all follow the same Rule. The most recent history of three branches of the first order has tended to reverse the earlier historical tendency toward division, witnessing to a greater cooperation and coming together throughout the world in common projects from missions to schools. While differences between the Observant, Conventual, and Capuchin Franciscans do remain, they share the common foundation of evangelical life and brotherhood in the charism of Francis of Assisi.

MICHAEL BLASTIC, O.F.M. CONV.

See also FRANCIS OF ASSISI, ST.; RELIGIOUS ORDERS.

FRANCISCANS, THIRD ORDER OF

Addressing himself in a letter to "all who live in the whole world," Francis of Assisi outlined a Franciscan way of life for both clergy and laity who chose not to join either the Friars Minor or the enclosed monasteries of the Poor Clares. The life for these faithful men and women is described as a life of penance in the world, which expressed itself in participation in the sacramental life of the Church, love of neighbor, humility, almsgiving, simplicity, and prayer. The text of Francis' *Letter to the Faithful* served as the "rule of life" for these men and women through much of the century. Subsequent rules for the Third Order secular were promulgated by Pope Nicholas IV in 1289, Pope Leo XIII in 1883, and Pope Paul VI in 1978.

Among these men and women were also those who wished to live their Franciscan penitential life in community. These different groups followed the rule for seculars (that is, Francis' *Letter to the Faithful*), to which they added the distinctive note of a promise to live it together, in some form of common life. These communities came to be described as "Third Order Regular Franciscans." A variety of rules emerged. In 1521, Pope Leo X promulgated a rule for all the male and female communities, adding a new element—the profession of the three solemn vows of poverty, chastity, and obedience. Pope Pius X issued a new rule in 1927. Finally, on 8 December 1982, Pope John Paul II promulgated the new text of the "Rule and Life of the Brothers and Sisters of the Third Order Regular of St. Francis," with the bull, *Franciscanum vita propositum.*

MICHAEL BLASTIC, O.F.M. CONV.

See also FRANCISCANS; THIRD ORDERS.

FREEDOM, ACADEMIC

See ACADEMIC FREEDOM.

FREEMASONRY

In the eleventh century, the English masons established a trade and religious fraternity, with John the Baptist as its patron, to protect the secrets of their craft. It became active in educational and charitable fields until it was suppressed in 1546 by Edward VI. It revived and reorganized; and in London, in 1717, it originated the first Grand Lodge of Freemasons. In tune with the English social attitudes of the time, it was disdainful of Catholicism; but, while it held diluted religious beliefs, it was not atheistic. Freemasonry spread to continental Europe; and in France, Spain, Portugal, and the Italian states, it developed a virulent anti-Catholic and anticlerical stance. Latin Freemasonry—or Grand Oriental Freemasonry—became a powerful political and financial force, and drew the condemnation of Clement XII in 1738, and six other popes followed suit. Catholics were forbidden, under automatic excommunication, from joining the Freemasons.

During the pontificate of John Paul II, in 1983, the penalty of excommunication was dropped but the membership prohibition was confirmed, and local bishops were not empowered to grant dispensations. In America, England, and most non-Latin countries, Freemasonry is a social and philanthropic organization with minimum credal requirements or tenets. Nevertheless, the Vatican, with its long experience of the Latin Freemasonry, has not altered its opposition to and disapproval of all brands of Freemasonry. This attitude is shared by the Eastern Orthodox Church which forbids its members from joining the Freemasons under penalty of excommunication.

MICHAEL GLAZIER

FRIAR

A member of one of the mendicant orders founded during the Middle Ages, the most prominent being the Franciscans ("Grey Friars"), the Dominicans, ("Black Friars"), the Carmelites ("White Friars") and the Augustinians ("Austin Friars"). Other orders include the Trinitarians, Mercedarians, the Brothers of Saint John of God, and the Order of Penance.

"Friar" is a modern spelling for the Middle English "fryer," meaning "brother" and deriving from the Latin, *frater*. The term developed to distinguish the itinerant apostolic character of the new orders from the monastic orders in existence during the Middle Ages. Friars practice most religious observances associated with monasticism but do not restrict their allegiance to one monastery as monks do.

PATRICIA DeFERRARI

See also RELIGIOUS ORDERS.

FRIENDSHIP

The Christian appreciation of friendship has an interesting history. As natural a concept as it is, friendship was not readily received in the Christian tradition, and even as late as the twelfth century A.D. it was viewed with some reservation. The evaluation of the classical tradition of friendship by Christian authors is largely responsible for their hesitancy in discussing its place in the Christian life. Aelred of Rievaulx, for example, owes a debt to the classical friendship tradition, so evident throughout his treatise entitled *Spiritual Friendship.* In the work's prologue, Aelred recounts how much he was influenced by Cicero's dialogue, *De Amicitia.* He also notes, however, that, after a time, what most attracted him to Cicero's ideas on the subject had lost its appeal. Christianity is responsible for the change. Aelred claims that nothing which had not been sweetened by the honey of the name of Jesus or seasoned with the salt of Sacred Scripture interested him. He desired, rather, to discover what support for the classical tradition of friendship he could find in Sacred Scripture (see Aelred of Rievaulx, *Spiritual Friendship,* Cistercian Fathers Series, 5, Kalamazoo, Michigan, 1977, 45-47). In this regard he is not unlike early Christian authors, beginning with the New Testament, who aim at marrying the classical and biblical traditions on friendship. Were the development of the notion of friendship in Christianity placed on a trajectory beginning with the classical tradition, the growth of the idea would show appropriation of some of the classical elements with modification towards a greater spiritualizing of friendship as Christianity develops.

The Classical Tradition

The Greek and Roman classical tradition of friendship offers an embarrassment of riches. Plato's *Lysis* stands out as one of the first and foremost attempts at a serious treatment of the topic. Aristotle (*EN,* 8.1.1–9.12.3 [1115a–1172a]), however, has had the most influence on the subsequent development of the tradition. Eschewing Plato's more utilitarian view of friendship, Aristotle elevated the discussion of it to a new height. While acknowledging that there are three fundamental types, friendships of utility, pleasure, and virtue, Aristotle maintained that true friendship could only reside in virtue. His reasoned discussion of the nature and requirements of friendship laid the foundation for many of the ideas that became standard in later discussions of it. Friendship's highest form in the classical tradition was found between good people, considered to be equals, who shared in all things, including the use of one another's possessions, and who regarded each other for their own sakes. Aristotle characterized friendship of this type by agreement in all things, harmony, and mutual goodwill. Aristotle's disagreements with Plato on the nature of friendship were only the beginning of a fascinating conversation among philosophers, poets, and dramatists which was to follow.

The philosophical debate over the nature and function of friendship produced two results. First, by appealing to the tenets of friendship, philosophers indirectly catalogued the common ideas on the topic. Thus the distilled friendship tradition showed interest in the same general directions. Was friendship based on similarity or dissimilarity? Did it require equality? What was the place of reciprocity in friendship? Was attraction that could be judged in ethical terms responsible for friendship? Which had the greatest appeal, utility, pleasure, or virtue? Was a friend another self? What could friendship demand and what were its limits? Second, by attempting to answer these questions and others like them, philosophers created an ongoing conversation which not only distinguished their particular spin on the topic, but also expanded the horizons of the tradition to embrace the numerous life situations where they identified and applied the friendship tradition. So, in addition to its theoretical appeal, the popularity of the tradition in antiquity can be accounted for, in part, because its wisdom on the fundamentals of human relationships shed light on so many aspects of ancient life. Whether people were related intimately as in the family, or were linked more casually through commerce, patronage, or ἔϱωσ some appreciation for the essence of friendship, its nature and function, found an appropriate place in the discussion.

Particularly among philosophers, the ethical dimensions of friendship come to the fore. Differences of opinion among the philosophical schools paved the way for various interpretations of the tradition. Whereas Pythagoreans took literally the traditional maxim "Friends have all things in common," by sharing their actual goods, the Epicureans, known for their esteem of friendship, thought that common possession was impossible (Diogenes Laertius 10.11). Early Stoics understood friendship to symbolize the unity of the cosmos, while stressing the radical autonomy of individuals in it. Later Stoics shared the ideal of autonomy, but understood friendship rather broadly to encompass all people linked by common nature (Hierocles, *On Duties* 4.27.23; E. Elorduy, *Die Sozialphilosophie der Stoa*, Philologus Suppl. 28.3, Leipzig: Dietrich, 1936, pp. 160-180; L. Edelstein, *The Meaning of Stoicism,* Martin Classical Lectures 21, Cambridge, Mass.: Harvard University Press, 1966, p. 72).

Some of the cherished tenets of the classical tradition were enshrined in short maxims like "Friendship is equality," "Friends have all things in common," "One soul," or "A friend is another self." These were proverbial even in Aristotle's day (*EN* 9.8.2 [1168b]). To some extent the gnomic quality of these sentiments lent itself to use in a variety of ways. They appear in full discussions of friendship, as illustrative of principal ideas, and they show up in treatments of other topics where they lend support to the consideration of related matter. So, for example, Plutarch invokes such maxims in his treatise on the value of having many friends (*De amic. mult.* 96F), as well as in his discussion of brotherly love (*De frat. amore* 478D). So also do Cicero (*De Officiis* 51) and Seneca (*De Ben.* 7.12.3-5) use like maxims when they discuss the advantages and disadvantages of the patronage system in their works concerning the giving and receiving of benefits. Dio Chrysostom finds such friendship proverbs helpful when he exhorts people to harmony and cooperation within city life (*Ors.* 36.30.6; 38.46.5; 39.5.7). Thus the occasional appeal to the friendship tradition through the use of these maxims facilitated broader discussions. The use of friendship proverbs provided a shorthand way to draw on the tradition without having to launch into a full-blown discussion of every aspect of it.

Friendship in the New Testament

An interesting phenomenon occurs when Christian writers appropriate the classical tradition of friendship. On the one hand, they appeal to friendship and its conventions, while, on the other hand, they attempt to distance themselves from a complete identification with the classical tradition. Later Christian writers will explicitly criticize the Greco-Roman friendship tradition for its inattention to religion and will identify it closely with paganism. Early Christian authors show familiarity with and interest in some of the classical tradition, but discuss what appeals to them under the rubric of ἀγάπη rather than φιλία. So, for example, in the New Testament, the word "friendship" (φιλία) appears only once in James and "friend" (φίλος) occurs only in the Lucan and Johannine writings. The absence of these terms is striking, yet it does not argue against the influence of the friendship tradition on certain New Testament authors.

Paul, for example, knows about friendship and enmity, and the conventions associated with each, without ever using the words "friend" or "friendship." His preference for designations drawn from the language of family, such as "brother" and "sister," may prevent him from using the term "friends" directly. Still he associates aspects of the friendship tradition with the language of fictive kinship (A. J. Malherbe, *Paul and the Popular Philosophers,* Minneapolis: Fortress, 1989, p. 63; H.-J. Klauck, "Kirche als Freundesgemeinschaft? Auf Spurensuche im Neuen Testament," *Münchener Theologische Zeitschrift* 42 [1991] 10-13).

The situation at Corinth presented Paul with a series of problems which may be understood from the perspective of friendship, where he had to use its conventions in his own defense. Elsewhere in the Corinthian correspondence the friendship tradition helps him to solidify cohesion within the Christian community there. From 1 Corinthians 9:1-23, 2 Corinthians 1:13-24, 10-12 we learn how Paul's opponents became friends with his rivals in Corinth over the matter of Paul's refusal of Corinthian monetary aid. The coalition against Paul interpreted this decline of financial help as a gesture of enmity towards the Corinthians (P. Marshall, *Enmity in Corinth: Social Conventions in Paul's Relations with the Corinthians,* WUNT 2.23, Tübingen: J.C.B. Mohr (Paul Siebeck), 1987, esp. pp. 396-404).

In Galatians, Paul's knowledge of friendship is evident at 4:12-20 where he adopts that part of the classical tradition dealing with the ability to distinguish a true from a false friend (H.D. Betz, *Galatians: A Commentary on Paul's Letter to the Churches in Galatia,* Hermeneia, Philadelphia: Fortress, 1979, pp. 220-237). Chief among the elements noticed there is the theme of enmity, something which helps a person know who a true friend is. Paul's opponents in Galatia may have used this to their advantage by convincing the Galatians that Paul was not a true friend to them. This opened the way for them to preach their own version of the gospel and to draw the Galatians into friendship with them. Paul responded by exposing their strategy, and thus employing a more effective one in regaining the friendship of the Galatians (Marshall, *Enmity in Corinth,* pp. 152-156).

Commentators have noticed Paul's use of the idea that friends will die for one another in Romans 5:6-8. His interpretation and application to Jesus differs, however, in the note that Christ died for sinners and enemies of God (Klauck, "Kirche als Freundesgemeinschaft," p. 10). One finds, too, language and rhetoric associated with friendship in Romans 12:1–15:33: hospitality, mutual sharing, financial support, unity of affection and equality. Paul's exhortation to the Romans in this section of the letter benefits from his knowledge of the friendship tradition, which provides him with language and means for strengthening the community bond at Rome (B. Fiore, "Friendship in the Exhortation of Romans 15:14-33," *Proceedings of the Eastern Great Lakes and Mid-Western Biblical Society* 7 [1987] 95-103).

The letter to the Philippians provides a noteworthy example of Paul's appreciation of friendship. In Philippians Paul employs many features of the ancient friendly letter and invokes friendship themes, especially at 1:27; 2:2; 2:6-11; 2:30; 4:10-11 and 4:12-20. The letter's language appeals to mutual sharing and fellowship in the interest of promoting genuine community, where individuals put the interests of others before their own (J. T. Fitzgerald, "The Epistle to the Philippians," *The Anchor Bible Dictionary,* ed. D. N. Freedman, New York: Doubleday, 1992, 5:320). The example of Christ's self-effacing death in the hymn in 2:6-11 is a model of virtuous friendship designed to counter self-assertion among community members (L. M. White, "Morality Between Two Worlds: A Paradigm of Friendship in Philippians," *Greeks, Romans, and Christians: Essays in Honor of Abraham J. Malherbe,* eds. D. L. Balch, E. Ferguson, and W. A. Meeks, Minneapolis: Fortress, 1990, 205-207). An interesting tension between self-sufficiency and dependence on others is noticed in chapter 4, where Paul invokes friendship language to explain why he is unable to accept further financial aid from them. This may be a response to the trouble he faced in Corinth over a similar matter. In the end he shifts the focus from his friendship with the Philippians to their friendship with God (4:18-19), who replaces Paul in this regard. Therefore he justifies his own self-sufficiency by making it a means of facilitating a friendship between the Philippians and God (M. Ebner, *Leidenlisten und Apostelbrief: Untersuchungen zu Form, Motivik und Funktion der Peristasenkataloge bei Paulus,* FB, Würzburg: Echter, 1991, 331-364).

Luke has a special fondness for friendship and, unlike other New Testament authors, is not shy about using the word "friend" (Luke 7:6, 34; 11:5 [bis], 6:8; 12:4; 14:10, 12; 15:6, 9, 29; 16:9; 21:16; 23:12; Acts 10:24; 19:31; 27:3). Only Luke has the Parable of the Persistent Friend (11:5-8) and even the peculiarly Lucan Parable of the Prodigal Son employs classical friendship traditions.

Luke's use of friendship shows familiarity with the Greco-Roman tradition, as well as an interest in the social and ethical implications of friendship in his day. Luke modifies the classical tradition for his community when he challenges the reciprocity ethic which was taken for granted in the society conventions of his day. Since friendship had the capacity for uniting and dividing individuals, its function cannot be divorced from its status-specific nature. If equality were the glue of friendship, the issue of who could be friends was significant. The practical norm restricted friendship to social equals, where power and influence were important commodities of relationship. The high value of reciprocity in these friendships only served to reinforce social divisions in Greco-Roman society. Luke envisioned an alternative for Christians. If they could be friends with one another, social divisions could be overcome. Friendship is a vehicle for equality between people within the Christian community, who outside of it would be prevented from being friends by societal conventions. In view of this Luke's encouragement for his community involves a call for social lowering on the part of upper-status Christians. This fits with his concern for the poor and expectation of detachment from wealth and possessions on the part of the rich.

Luke's challenge to the reciprocity ethic is grasped in redacted sections of his gospel. Luke 6:34-35a, for example, joins classical friendship language to the Christian tradition of love of enemies, and the special Lucan theme of doing good and lending without expectation of return. Luke 14:13-14 echoes these sentiments and specifically exhorts Christians, "But when you give a feast, invite the poor, the maimed, the lame, the blind, and you will be blessed, because they cannot repay you. You will be repaid at the resurrection of the just." The thought is carried over to Acts 20:35 where Paul proclaims, "It is more blessed to give than to receive."

In the early chapters of Acts the theme of friendship figures prominently among the members of the Jerusalem community. Both summaries describing the life of the community (2:44-47; 4:32-37) employ friendship maxims, interpreted with the help of language from the LXX (see Deut 4:29; 6:5; 15:4). The Jerusalem community is presented as being of one heart and soul and as having all things in common. The image of Barnabas, a person of relative status as a landowner, bowed before the apostles, fishermen of lower status, is as powerful as the words Luke uses to show how property was disposed among Jerusalem Christians. The story of Ananias and Sapphira (5:1-11), following upon the second summary underscores the proper attitude towards possessions and friendship which Christians should aspire to, as does the stress on harmony and togetherness in related material in the first five chapters of Acts. Luke's interest in promoting an effective friendship among Christians of varying social status is confirmed by other examples in Acts where individuals of higher status help those of lower status, and where both groups form κοινωνία, Christian fellowship based on the equality of friends (11:29; 12:12; 13:1; 16:15, 40; 17:12; 20:33-35) (A. C. Mitchell, "The Social Function of Friendship in Acts 2:44-47 and 4:32-37," *Journal of Biblical Literature* 111 (1992) 255-272).

Like Paul and Luke, John adapts the friendship tradition to the needs of the community he writes for. Φίλος in the Fourth Gospel refers to Jesus's relationship with other human beings (3:29; 11:11; 15:14-15), including the negative use by the crowd in 19:12 where Pilate's alleged friendship with Jesus is opposed to his friendship with Caesar. The verb φιλεῖν applies to Jesus's friendship with humans and with God (5:20; 11:3, 36; 20:2; 21:15, 16, 17 [bis]). It also carries the meaning of reciprocity between God and human beings who have befriended Jesus (16:27; cf. 15:23). Enmity is included in John's use of φιλεῖν in 15:19; the world's hatred is directed against those who belong to Jesus (cf. 7:7; 17:14). Φίλος in 3 John 15 may refer to a group of Christians allied with Gaius or simply to Johannine Christians in general (Klauck, "Kirche als Freundesgemeinschaft," pp. 1–2).

An important friendship theme for John is the self-sacrificing love that marks the true friend. In the classical tradition, the friendship ideal reached a high point in the idea that friends would die for one another (Plato, *Symposium* 179B, 208D; Seneca, *Ep. Mor.* 1.9.10; Lucian, *Toxaris* 36; Epictetus, *Diss.* 2.7.3). The influence of this sentiment on John 15:13, "No one has greater love than this, to lay down one's life for one's friends," is inescapable. Echoes of this theme are found in John's image of the Good Shepherd, who lays down his life for the sheep (10:11, 15, 17-18) and in 1 John 3:16 where community members are encouraged to do the same for one another. Interestingly, in John, love of enemies does not accompany love of friends. Perhaps this is due to the historical situation of the Johannine community's difficulties with synagogue leaders (see John 9:1-40; 12:42-43; R. E. Brown, *The Community of the Beloved Disciple: The Life, Loves, and Hates of an Individual Church in New Testament Times,* New York: Paulist, 1979, pp. 42, 43, 65; J. L. Martyn, *History and Theology in the Fourth Gospel,* Nashville: Abingdon, 1979, p. 47; D. Rensberger, *Johannine Faith and Liberating Community,* Philadelphia: Westminster, 1988, pp. 79, 128).

Yet another use of the friendship tradition by John appears in 15:15, "I do not call you servants any longer, because the servant does not know what the master is doing; but I have called you friends, because I have made known to you everything that I have heard from my Father." Free sharing of information between friends is part of classical friendship tradition (see Aristotle, *EN* 8.11.6; Cicero, *De. Amic.* 6.22) connoting that the friend is really another self (cf. Klauck, "Kirche als Freundesgemeinschaft," p. 5).

Friendship in Early Christian Literature

A clear preference for spiritual friendship among Christian writers emerges in the early patristic era. The concept is used to describe the Christian's relationship with God (L. Vischer, "Das Problem der Freundschaft bei den Kirchenvätern," *ThZ* 9 (1953) 173–200).

Irenaeus, in the second century A.D., speaks of friendship with God (*Ad. Haer.* 4.13; 5.14, 17) as does Justin Martyr (*Dial. cum Trypho.* 28) who adds the notion of friendship with Christ (*Dial. cum Trypho,* 8).

Clement of Alexandria finds the classical tradition helpful for describing Christian love. In *Stromateis* 2.9 the definition of love as "harmony in what pertains to reason, life, and manners, or, in brief, fellowship of life" echoes earlier definitions of friendship in Greek and Roman authors. He speaks, too, of the three basic types of friendship, and like Aristotle he places the highest value on virtue-friendship (2.19). The classical stress on likeness in friendship affords Clement the opportunity to base the Christian's friendship with God on a firm foundation. Drawing on the biblical tradition that humans are created in the image and likeness of God. Clement is able to ground friendship with God in the principle of likeness and what friends have in common (*Strom.* 6.14; 7.11).

In the third century, Origen, too, knows the friendship tradition and shows similarities to Irenaeus and Clement in his use of it (Vischer, *Das Problem,* p. 174). It is the Word of God which invites Christians to friendship (*Contra Cels.* 8.1) and once invited, all those who live by the precepts of Jesus are elevated to friendship with God (*Contra Cels.* 3.28). Interpreting John 15:15, "No longer do I call you servants . . . but I call you friends," Origen claims that when the crowds, hearing the preaching and teaching of Jesus, came to wisdom about him, he no longer remained their Lord, but became their friend (*Comm. in ev. Joannis,* 1.201-202). Wisdom and friendship with God go together as helps for the Christian life (*De Orat.* 27.14) and prayer is a powerful means of securing that friendship (*De Orat.* 10.2). But friendship with God requires a moral commitment on the part of the Christian, and Origen is clear that anyone who is in "either a state of sickness or mental alienation" cannot be a friend of God (*Contra Cels.* 4.18-19). Likewise, any form of servility has the same effect (*De Orat.* 29.8). So also, to sustain friendship with God one must have ordered priorities. When Origen comments on the petition for "supersubstantial bread" in the Our Father (Matt 6:11; Luke 11:3) he paraphrases Proverbs 15:17, "It is better to be invited to friendship and grace than to a fatted calf with enmity" (*De Orat.* 27.6). Like classical authors he knows the function of enmity in defining friendship. Commenting on Luke 14:26 and John 12:25 about hating one's life in order to save it, Origen claims that it is through such hatred that one becomes a friend of God (*Exhortatio ad Martyr.* 37.44). And again, in a discussion of the enmity placed between Eve and the serpent, he observes that it is through this very enmity that God was able to establish the possibility of friendship with Christ, since one cannot be a friend of two opposites (*In Jeremiam* 20. 7. 55-65). So Origen speaks of the joys of friendship with God, but knows of its fragility and the need to tend it carefully in one's spiritual life.

Building on the classical, biblical, and patristic legacies of friendship, Christian writers in the fourth century make notable efforts at situating elements of the received wisdom on the topic within a high ascetic ideal, that understands friendship among Christians to be a true gift of God. Augustine, Jerome, Basil the Great, Gregory of Nazianzus and John Chrysostom found a wealth of information among the classical Greek and Roman theories of friendship, that helped them to distinguish among various levels of love, which were subordinated to its ideal form in Christianity. The role of grace in the formation and maintenance of friendships emerges to the fore in such writers, to the point where God is instrumental in bringing people together as friends, and friendship in God becomes the equivalent of virtue-friendship in the classical tradition (M. A. McNamara, O.P., *Friendship in Saint Augustine,* Studia Friburgensia 20, Fribourg: The University Press, 1958 pp. 196-197; C. White, *Christian Friendship in the Fourth Century,* Cambridge: Cambridge University Press, 1992, pp. 63, 72, 78, 102–106, 155, 196, 219, 221). Thus in moving closer to a more spiritual form of friendship, akin to what one finds in the monastic tradition, as evidenced in the thought of Aelred of Rievaulx, Christian authors of the fourth century found important ways to supplement, and at times transform, the classical ideal with the biblical and patristic interpretations of Christian love (G. C. Meilaender, *Friendship: A Study of Theological Ethics,* Notre Dame: University of Notre Dame Press, 1981, pp. 16–22).

ALAN C. MITCHELL, S.J.

See also CHARITY; CHRISTIAN SPIRITUALITY; MYSTICAL BODY OF CHRIST; VIRTUE.

FRUITS OF THE HOLY SPIRIT

See HOLY SPIRIT.

FUNDAMENTAL OPTION

See SIN.

FUNDAMENTAL THEOLOGY

See THEOLOGY, FUNDAMENTAL.

FUNDAMENTALISM

Fundamentalism is a contemporary movement within Protestant evangelical Christianity. "Evangelical" is an umbrella term for Protestant groups who adhere to conservative doctrine and practice, hold the Bible as directly authoritative, emphasize the importance of being "born again" by trusting in Christ, and display a zeal for evangelism. "Fundamentalists" are evangelicals who militantly oppose modern, liberal culture. They stress the separation between themselves and the secular world, often forbidding their members to play cards, smoke, or dance. The term "Pentecostals" refers to Christians who may be either simply evangelicals or fundamentalists, but who emphasize such gifts of the Holy Spirit as speaking in tongues, prophecy, and healing.

Fundamentalism arose in the first decades of the twentieth century as a response to certain intellectual and cultural trends. First, in the eighteenth century, Enlightenment thinkers had challenged the authority of religious teaching by stressing the importance of reason instead. These thinkers separated "natural religion," or religious truths available to any reasonable person, from "revealed religion," or truths that rested on the authority of the Bible or the Church. They then dismissed such "revealed" knowledge as the divinity of Jesus and the Trinitarian nature of God. What could not be demonstrated rationally was discarded.

Second, Christian authority had been further eroded by philosopher Karl Marx's famous claim that religion is the opium of the people, and that in order to be free, human beings had to break the religious bonds that were oppressing them. Similarly, philosopher Ludwig Feuerbach had argued that religion arises from the needs and wishes of human beings rather than from the existence of a God.

Third, modern science, especially the evolutionary theories of Charles Darwin, appeared to challenge traditional biblical teachings. Science relied on purely natural knowledge, not on the supernatural knowledge that was revealed by Scripture, and it left little room for divine interventions.

Fourth, in the late nineteenth century, scholars began applying historical and literary methods of interpretation to the Bible; that is, they began investigating the Bible as they would any other work of literature. The conclusions of this kind of criticism challenged longstanding beliefs about the person of Jesus and the origins of the Hebrew Bible (Old Testament) and the New Testament.

Last, philosophers began to suggest that truth is not fixed and absolute, but relative to history and culture. Thus what once had been thought of as moral and religious certainties were suddenly thrown into question; perhaps what had been true in one place and time was true no longer.

Fundamentalism developed in response to and as a critique of these movements. Between 1910 and 1915, a series of paperback volumes called *The Fundamentals: a Testimony of Truth* was published by a group of Bible teachers and evangelical leaders. It is from this series that the term "fundamentalism" is derived. The twelve volumes were written as a defense of Christian faith against the onslaught of modern culture, and they are often summarized in five points known as the five fundamentals: the inerrancy of Scripture, the virgin birth of Christ, the substitutionary theory of atonement, the literal resurrection of Jesus from the dead, and the literal return of Jesus to the world at the second coming.

Fundamentalists stress that the Bible must be inerrant (that is, contain nothing that is not true) because it is divinely inspired. This inerrancy extends not only to matters of faith and doctrine but to matters of history, science, and geography as well. The Bible is seen as a book of facts more reliable than any modern textbook.

It follows, then, that the Bible is correct when it says that Jesus was born of a virgin named Mary. But the real importance of Jesus's miraculous birth is that it is testimony to his status as the Son of God; it is evidence for his uniqueness. Further evidence for Jesus's divine status comes from the miracles performed by him, such as raising Lazarus from the dead and walking on water. These miracles, like the virgin birth, are to be understood as historical events.

The theory of substitutionary atonement refers to a belief that Jesus died as a substitute for human beings. That is, because of original sin, human beings deserved death; however, Jesus took that death upon himself, and in doing so spared them from their just punishment. Fundamentalists affirmed this theory in contrast to some more liberal Christians who thought of Jesus as a moral teacher who saved people by showing them how to live an upright and virtuous life.

Likewise, some Christian theologians interpreted Jesus's resurrection to mean simply that Jesus's message lived on after his death, or that faith in Jesus as the Son of God continues in Jesus's followers. In contrast, fundamentalists affirmed that Jesus rose bodily from the dead and appeared in literal bodily form to his disciples: and, further, that he would come bodily to earth again to bring earth's history to its ultimate culmination.

This last of the five fundamentals, emphasis on the second coming, reflects fundamentalism's roots in the millenarian movements that became popular in the nineteenth century. "Millennialists" are Christians who look forward to the thousand-year reign of Christ on earth described in the Book of Revelation, the last book in the New Testament (see Rev 20:1-5). However, millennialists differ as to how they think this reign will come about. Some, called "Postmillennialists," believe that there will be a period of a thousand years during which the Holy Spirit will be poured out and the world will be Christianized. Jesus will come to earth only after (thus "post") this period.

Others, called "Premillennialists," maintain that the coming of Jesus will take place before (thus, "pre") the thousand-year period. They are more likely to emphasize a sharp break between the world as it is today and the world as it will be under Christ. God's kingdom, they maintain, is wholly discontinuous with history as we know it.

Many fundamentalists are premillennialists. They look forward to the return of Jesus, then to the "secret rapture" of believers who will be taken up to meet Christ in the air, to a following seven years of turmoil and strife (from which believers will be spared), and finally to the Last Judgment. All fundamentalists profess belief in a literal heaven and hell and in the existence of Satan.

Fundamentalism has other roots besides millennialism. It was also influenced by the Keswick holiness movement, a British teaching that stressed yielding to Christ as a way of achieving personal victory over sin. Further, it was greatly influenced by the turmoil caused by World War I; some fundamentalists interpreted the war as a struggle between Christian civilization and satanic forces.

Perhaps the most famous event in the history of fundamentalism was a trial held in Dayton, Tennessee, in 1925. The "Scopes Monkey Trial," as it came to be called, crystallized the differences between fundamentalist Christians and the secular culture they were fighting against. In January of that year, the Tennessee legislature had passed House Bill 185; this bill affirmed the story of creation as set forth in the Bible's Book of Genesis, and it disallowed teaching in the public schools any theory that human beings had descended from lower orders of animals. Soon after, the law was challenged by high school biology teacher John Thomas Scopes.

Scopes's trial became a media event, with lawyer Clarence Darrow acting for the defense, and populist William Jennings Bryan acting as prosecutor. Though Scopes was found guilty of teaching evolution, fundamentalism was attacked and ridiculed in the national press, particularly by famous journalist H. L. Mencken. Popular sentiment turned as fundamentalism was portrayed as backward and anti-intellectualist.

However, Protestant fundamentalism was far from dead. It experienced a resurgence in the 1970s and 1980s, and it continues to be an important force in American religion and politics.

It is important to point out that Protestant Christianity is only one of the many traditions in which fundamentalist strains have emerged. Fundamentalism can be broadly defined as any militant movement which seeks to protect what it sees as religious truths from the encroachment of modernity. In that sense, fundamentalism can be said to be present within Catholicism as well.

Nevertheless, there are important differences between Protestant fundamentalist and Catholic approaches to Scripture. Traditionally, Catholicism has acknowledged four levels of scriptural interpretation: literal, analogical, moral, and anagogic, or mystical. The literal meaning of the Bible has not been thought to be the only possible meaning.

Further, since the Second Vatican Council, Catholic biblical scholars have utilized a variety of tools to study biblical texts, including literary criticism and historical analysis. Rather than trying to protect the Bible from these modern methods, they have sought to use the methods to understand the Bible more fully. In general, these scholars contend that the Bible is primarily a statement of faith in Jesus rather than an objective report of historical facts.

THERESA SANDERS

See also CRITICISM, BIBLICAL; PROTESTANTISM.

FUNERAL

There are three services connected with a Catholic funeral. First, the vigil service, traditionally known as the wake, is usually celebrated in a funeral home where the body is in an open or sealed casket. The second and major service is the Funeral Mass. At the entrance to the church, the celebrant sprinkles the casket with holy water as a reminder of the deceased's baptismal participation in the death and resurrection of Jesus. The casket is then placed in front of the altar. The varied selection of readings available for the Liturgy of the Word and the Eucharistic Liturgy resonate with hope in Christ. At the conclusion of the Mass, the casket is incensed and blessed again with holy water, and the prayer of commendation is recited. Then the last journey of the body to its grave begins (unless the body is to be cremated) and, at the graveside, the final prayer service for the dead takes place.

JOAN GLAZIER

See also CREMATION; OFFICE OF THE DEAD.

G

GALILEI, GALILEO (1564–1642)

Galileo Galilei, Florentine philosopher, physicist and astronomer; born 15 February 1564 in Pisa, Italy; died 8 January 1642.

The son of a musician, Galileo received his early education at the monastery school at Vallombrosa before enrolling at the University of Pisa. Financial problems forced him to withdraw from the University during his fourth year, but he continued to study and began to write treatises on scientific topics. Thanks to the influence of a patron, Guidobaldo del Monte, Galileo was appointed to lecture in mathematics at the University of Pisa in 1589.

Although he taught traditional mathematics and science, he was not afraid to challenge some tenets of the prevailing philosophy and physics of Aristotle. This, coupled with the fact that he had never graduated, made him many enemies on the faculty. In 1591 he resigned and a few months later was appointed to the chair of mathematics at the University of Padua, a post he was to hold for eighteen years.

It was at Padua that Galileo became deeply interested in astronomy. Throughout most of recorded history, it was accepted that the earth was fixed in its place as the center of the universe. This geostatic view received philosophical support in the physics of Aristotle (378–322 B.C.) and the observational, mathematical calculations of Ptolemy (fl. 150 B.C.). Moreover, it seemed to accord with ordinary sense experience: the sun does seem to move and the earth does not. Several challenges to an earth-centered universe had been offered, in ancient times by the Pythagoreans, in the fourteenth century by Cardinal Nicholas Oresme and a century later by Cardinal Nicholas of Cusa. But the strongest advocacy of a heliocentric or sun-centered universe came from Nicholas Copernicus (1473–1543) whose book *On the Revolutions of the Heavenly Spheres* pictured the earth as a planet that moved around the sun, as well as on its axis. Thanks to an unsigned preface actually written by Andreas Osiander, it was thought that Copernicus intended his system only as a mathematical hypothesis, not as a model portraying the actual motions in the universe.

Although the Copernican system was less cumbersome than Ptolemy's in the number of motions it needed to use to describe the heavens, it still needed important astronomical corrections and a new physics before it could claim widespread allegiance.

Having learned of the invention of a telescope, Galileo constructed several of his own and turned them on the heavens with immediate and far-reaching results. In 1610 he published *The Starry Messenger,* announcing that the moon is not a perfect sphere, that the Milky Way is a multitude of stars and that the planet Jupiter has its own moons. Fame was quick in coming; Galileo was appointed philosopher and mathematician to the Grand Duke of Tuscany. But opposition was also forthcoming. The university Aristotelians challenged Galileo's findings and their Copernican implications. They

Galileo, 1624

objected that the Copernican universe contradicted common experience, violated all of the known laws of physics, and, if true, would need confirmation in the form of a stellar parallax. Finally, to anyone proposing that the Copernican system was real and not simply a mathematical hypothesis, opponents began to appeal to the authority of Sacred Scripture which seemed clearly to support a geostatic universe.

Galileo continued to make discoveries such as the phases of Venus and the existence of sunspots and, when the Jesuit astronomers at the Collegio Romano confirmed them, Galileo was much encouraged and publicly endorsed the Copernican system in his *Letters on Sunspots* in 1613. Interest in the growing controversy came to focus less on science and more on the scriptural difficulties raised by the new system. Scripture states that "God fixed the earth on its foundation, not ever to be moved" (Ps 103:5) and "The sun rises and the sun goes down, then it presses on to the place where it rises" (Eccl 1:5). Why would it be a miracle for Joshua to command the sun to stand still if it never moved anyway? (Josh 10:12-13).

Though not a theologian, Galileo was drawn into a theological controversy and wrote two lengthy letters on the relationship of the Bible and science. In 1615 a Carmelite priest, Paolo Foscarini, published a book explicitly attempting to reconcile the Copernican system with Scripture and the issue quickly became one of authority. The conservative climate of the Counter Reformation and the strong directives of the Council of Trent regarding nonauthoritative interpretations of Scripture led Cardinal Robert Bellarmine to warn against considering the Copernican system as real unless and until a scientific demonstration could be produced, at which time a nonliteral reading of the texts involved could be admitted. Galileo was on better footing when he argued that the Bible did not intend to teach science but even he mistakenly conceded some precedence to the literal sense of Scripture over unproved physical arguments to the contrary.

When the matter seemed to be getting out of hand, Pope Paul V ordered the Congregation of the Holy Office to investigate. On 19 February 1616, two propositions, clumsily worded summaries of Galileo's views, were sent to a committee of eleven theologians. They responded that the positions were "philosophically foolish," "absurd" and "formally heretical" in one case and "erroneous in the faith" in the other. Thus, on 5 March 1616, the Congregation of the Index suspended Copernicus's book until it could be rendered more hypothetical, and forbade all books that attempted to reconcile the heliocentric system with Scripture. It is small consolation to note that the decision of the theologians and the decree of the Congregation of the Index, though approved by Pope Paul V, did not fall under the infallible teaching authority of the Church; they were still erroneous decisions and they were used again in 1633 to confront Galileo after the publication of his book *Dialogue on the Two Great World Systems.* This time, Galileo was summoned to Rome by the Holy Office, charged with vehement suspicion of heresy for holding that the Copernican astronomy is not contrary to Scripture, and made to kneel and abjure his views. He was sentenced to house arrest until his death in 1642, four years after publication of his masterful *Discourses on Two New Sciences.*

The whole unfortunate matter was a complex web of issues, intellectual currents, religious concerns and powerful personalities. Though it is unfair to infer from the Galileo case that the Church is an enemy of science, freedom of thought and progress, the fact remains that even Pope John Paul II's 1979 and 1989 acknowledgments of Galileo's bad treatment at the hands of the theologians, fails to specify or retract the theological errors involved in the matter or the role of two popes in its outcome.

JAMES R. LANGFORD

See also CONGREGATION FOR THE DOCTRINE OF THE FAITH; COPERNICUS, NICHOLAS; ORTHODOXY; SCIENCE AND RELIGION.

GALLICANISM

The term describes a variety of theological theories which, in one way or another, sought to curtail papal power. It is generally, and for good reason, associated primarily with France, but civil and ecclesiastical authorities in other countries also sought to dilute papal authority in various areas. Josephism in Austria is an example.

Proponents of Gallicanism in France held that the king had a special role in Church matters, and that the papacy should not interfere with the temporal and civil matters of the French. In 1516, Leo X, in the Concordat of Bologna, granted the king the right to nominate bishops and fill other high ecclesiastical offices. In 1663, the Sorbonne published a declaration which sought to minimize papal authority, and this was adopted by the Assembly of French Clergy in 1682, in the formula called the Four Gallican Articles. Though the king and clergy agreed to withdraw the articles three years after their papal condemnation in 1690, the teaching of the articles was widespread in France through the following century. The definition of papal primacy and infallibility at Vatican I in 1870 was devastating to the Gallicanism movement.

JOSEPH QUINN

See also PAPACY, THE; PRIMACY OF THE POPE.

GAUDETE SUNDAY

(Lat., "rejoice") The Third Sunday of Advent, named after the opening antiphon of the Introit *Gaudete in Domino semper* ("Rejoice in the Lord always"), as it signals the approaching joy of the Christmas celebration. On this day, rose-colored vestments may be worn in place of the traditional violet vesture of the Advent season. In recent times, Gaudete Sunday has become known simply as the Third Sunday of Advent.

JOSEPH QUINN

See also ADVENT.

GENERAL ABSOLUTION

Absolution comprises the words and actions of an ordained minister who while extending his hands over a penitent, proclaims the mercy of God and the forgiveness of sin. While tracing the sign of the cross over a penitent he prays: ". . . through the ministry of the Church may God give you pardon and peace and I absolve you from your sins in the name of the Father and of the Son and of the Holy Spirit." Absolution is "general" when the forgiveness of sin is declared over a number of penitents at the same time. The present norms for general absolution are based on the Instruction of the Apostolic Penitentiary (25 March 1944) which permitted general absolution in the time of war, and the Pastoral Norms issued by the Congregation for the Doctrine of the Faith in 1972 which expanded the opportunities for use of general absolution to situations of grave necessity. Both documents were revised by the publication of the *Code of Canon Law* in 1983.

In the revised 1973 Rite of Penance of the Roman Ritual general absolution is one of the three recognized forms. Certain restrictions, however, are placed upon its use and individual, integral confession (Form I) remains the ordinary way for the faithful to reconcile themselves with God and the Church (c. 960). General absolution is allowed in circumstances where there is danger of death or where there are not enough confessors for the number of penitents resulting in the deprivation of the reconciliation of the sacrament or of Communion for a long time (understood as one month by the U.S. Conference of Catholic Bishops). Permission by the diocesan bishop for general absolution is not based on the number of penitents but on whether confessors are available and whether the rite can be celebrated in a proper way (c. 961).

To participate in general sacramental absolution, the penitent must have sorrow for sin, resolve to change one's life, and intent to rectify whatever injury the sinfulness may have caused to others. Moreover, penitents with serious sins who receive general absolution must intend to confess individually the grave sins which could not be confessed at the time of general absolution (c. 962). This individual confession should take place as soon as there is an opportunity to do so and before receiving general absolution again unless prevented by some just cause, for example, lack of confessors, remoteness of the area, physical disability, or imprisonment (c. 962). This requirement indicates the priority of individual confession over general absolution and the need to retain confession of serious sins as a part of penance and as a manifestation and completion of conversion within the Church.

Rite for Reconciliation of Several Penitents with General Confession and Absolution (Rite III), begins with an introductory rite of song and opening prayer, followed by the Celebration of the Word of God. The third part is general confession in which penitents indicate sorrow by kneeling or bowing their heads, then praying a common act of contrition and the Lord's Prayer. The priest then prays one of the two forms of the prayer of forgiveness while extending his hands over the whole assembly. The rite concludes with proclamation of God's mercy and goodness and a closing blessing.

CATHERINE DOOLEY, O.P.

See also ABSOLUTION; SACRAMENT OF RECONCILIATION.

GENERAL CONFESSION

"Confession" refers both to the sacrament itself and to the act of admitting personal sin to the confessor, which is one of the necessary elements in the matter of the sacrament. "General confession" and absolution, by which a group of individuals express contrition for their sins and receive sacramental pardon, is permitted only under restricted conditions (c. 961). For a general absolution to be valid, the penitents must have contrition for their sins and intend to confess serious sins individually.

"General Confession" may also refer to the repetition of some or all of the previous confessions of one's life. Such confession is obligatory when it is known for certain that previous confessions were invalid. Sometimes people make general confession when they enter a new state in life, such as marriage, the pronouncement of religious vows, or holy orders.

PATRICIA DeFERRARI

See also SACRAMENT OF RECONCILIATION.

GENERAL INTERCESSIONS

See PRAYER OF THE FAITHFUL.

GIBBONS, JAMES, CARDINAL (1834–1921)

Ninth archbishop of Baltimore (1877–1921), cardinal (1886), James Gibbons was born to Irish immigrant parents in Baltimore, Maryland, on 23 July 1834, and died in Baltimore on 24 March 1921. In 1837 his parents returned to Ireland where James lived until 1853 when his widowed mother came back to the United States and settled in New Orleans. After studies at St. Charles Seminary, Ellicott City, and St. Mary's Seminary, Baltimore, Gibbons was ordained a priest of the Archdiocese of Baltimore on 30 June 1861.

During the following sixteen years he rapidly ascended the ladder of ecclesiastical preferment. He spent six weeks as a curate, then served for four years as a local pastor. In 1865 he became secretary to Archbishop Martin J. Spalding of Baltimore, who made Gibbons assistant chancellor the following year and found him of great assistance at the Second Plenary Council of Baltimore (1866). In 1868 Gibbons was named vicar apostolic of North Carolina, a missionary diocese of fifty thousand square miles with seven hundred Catholics and three priests.

In 1869 through 1870 Gibbons attended the First Vatican Council where he was the youngest of the seven hundred bishops present. In 1872 he became administrator; then (in 1873) bishop of Richmond, while retaining responsibility for the vacant vicariate apostolic of North Carolina. Selected by Archbishop James Roosevelt Bayley of Baltimore to be his coadjutor with right of succession in May 1877, Gibbons arrived in Baltimore five months later as the ninth archbishop after Bayley's sudden death.

During his forty-three years in Baltimore, Gibbons acquired a prominence and influence equaled by no other Catholic bishop in American history. Indeed, after Gibbons' death, the apostolic delegate warned Rome that no U.S. prelate should be allowed to enjoy such power in the future. One reason for Gibbons' influence was the fact that his diocese included the national capital with the result that the federal government looked to him as the natural leader of the Catholic Church in the United States, especially before the establishment of the Apostolic Delegation in 1893. From 1886 until 1911 Gibbons was also the sole U.S. cardinal. Moreover, Gibbons' irenic and even ecumenical temperament endeared him to many non-Catholics. His famous book of popular apologetics, *The Faith of Our Fathers* (1876), while totally orthodox, contained hardly a word that was offensive to Protestants.

In the last decades of the nineteenth century Gibbons was intimately involved in the highly publicized quarrels that divided the American hierarchy over such issues as German-American nationalism, the parochial school system, Catholic membership in "secret societies" and the celebrated McGlynn Affair. As the unofficial primate of the U.S. Church, Gibbons generally attempted to act as a mediator between the two episcopal factions, although his personal sympathies usually inclined him to favor the positions of such "Americanist" friends as Archbishop John Ireland and Archbishop John Keane.

An innately cautious person, Gibbons once attributed his success to "masterly inactivity." The historian of the Archdiocese of Baltimore, Thomas Spalding, states that, in his own archdiocese, Gibbons' "accomplishments of all forty-three years would hardly need a sheaf of paper for their telling." His biographer, John Tracy Ellis, admits that it was not Gibbons' nature to inaugurate bold new ventures. However, Ellis also points out that on occasion Gibbons responded splendidly when decisions were thrust upon him. For example, Gibbons did not favor the convening of the Third Plenary Council of Baltimore in 1884, but he presided over it as apostolic delegate in masterful fashion. Likewise, he was unenthusiastic about the creation of the Catholic University of America, but, once it was established in his diocese in 1887, he became one of its staunchest supporters. In preventing a Roman condemnation of the Knights of Labor in 1887, the initiative probably stemmed from Bishops Ireland and Keane,

Cardinal James Gibbons

but it was Gibbons alone who signed the crucial memorandum that stayed Rome's hand and forestalled the alienation of large numbers of workers from the Catholic Church in the United States. He told the Roman authorities: "The dignity of the Church demands that we should not offer to America an ecclesiastical protection for which she does not ask, and of which she believes she has no need."

Historian Marvin O'Connell sees the key to Gibbons' remarkable career in the fact that he "was a persuadable man, never afraid to change his mind when circumstances dictated it." Says O'Connell: "Gibbons was above all else a realist. He indulged in no visions, he dreamed no dreams. That does not mean that he was without idealism or lofty moral purpose. It does mean, however, that he took the world as he found it, and that he accepted the people he had to deal with as they were, and not as he might have liked them to be."

Stung by Pope Leo XIII's condemnation of "Americanism" in 1899, Gibbons assured the Pope that his fears of an "Americanist" heresy were unfounded. A decade earlier, upon taking possession of his titular Roman Church as a cardinal, he had boldly defended the advantages to religion of the American system of separation of Church and state. It was a conviction which he never lost. A month before he died he declared that he was "more and more convinced that the Constitution of the United States is the greatest instrument of government that ever issued from the hand of man." In recognition of Gibbons' many contributions to American public life, his friend, former president Theodore Roosevelt, told him in 1917: "Taking your life as a whole, I think you now occupy the position of being the most respected, and venerated, and useful citizen of our country."

One of Gibbons' last contributions to the American Church was the crucial support that he gave to the establishment of the National Catholic War Council in 1917 and of its successor organization in 1919, the National Catholic Welfare Council (later Conference). True to form, Gibbons did not initiate either move, but he welcomed both developments as evidences of the growing maturity and professionalization of the American Catholic Church. It was also a mark of his greatness that he could so graciously relinquish his role as the dean of the American hierarchy to make way for a more collegial episcopal structure.

THOMAS J. SHELLEY

See also AMERICAN CATHOLICISM; CHURCH AND STATE; RELIGIOUS FREEDOM.

GIFTS OF THE HOLY SPIRIT

The gifts of the Holy Spirit are the seven spiritual gifts given to Christians by the Holy Spirit. They are: wisdom, understanding, counsel, strength, knowledge, piety, and fear of the Lord. The teaching on this has its basis in both Sacred Scripture and the tradition of the Church. The Book of Isaiah 11:2 speaks of the Spirit and the promised gifts (six in the Hebrew and seven in the Septuagint) that will be given to the one who will "come forth from the stump of Jesse." In the New Testament Jesus is the fulfillment of this prophecy, and he has given the Spirit to his Church, thus giving to many the gifts of the Spirit (although the NT makes no specific mention of "seven" gifts).

It was not until the second century A.D. that Justin Martyr wrote of the seven gifts that come to Christians who receive the Spirit. The Latin Fathers theorized how these gifts work and relate to one another. St. Augustine described how these seven gifts work in the soul of the recipient. Later, in the Middle Ages, St. Thomas Aquinas developed the most complete theology surrounding the seven gifts, distinguishing them from the other virtues. He saw them as qualitatively different and superior to the moral and theological virtues. Moreover, he regarded the Holy Spirit, not the human person, as the actuator of these gifts in each individual.

Contemporary theology has said little about the "seven" gifts of the Holy Spirit, preferring instead to discuss all the gifts of the Spirit. Vatican II's *Lumen Gentium* does not refer to the Isaian list at all, opt-ing instead to speak of St. Paul's description of the gifts of the Spirit found in his First Letter to the Corinthians (1 Cor 12:4-11).

ANTHONY D. ANDREASSI

See also HOLY SPIRIT; SPIRITUALITY, LAY.

GILL, ERIC (1882–1940)

British sculptor, illustrator, typographer, and engraver, Gill was born in 1882. A Catholic convert, he advocated, in numerous writings, a return to medieval ideals of art, particularly in his rejection of the modern emphasis on realism, and in this he appealed to G. K. Chesterton and his circle. In religious sculpture, his style is simple and direct, usually in low relief (exemplified by his *Stations of the Cross* in London's Westminster Cathedral). He is now best known as a designer of alphabets. He died in 1940.

"Madonna and Child, with children," illustration by Eric Gill, 1925

DAVID BRYAN

See also ART, CHRISTIAN; BRITAIN, CHURCH IN; CHESTERTON, GILBERT KEITH.

GILLIS, JAMES MARTIN, C.S.P. (1876–1957)

A Paulist editor and author was born on 12 November 1876. He was the second of the four children of James Gillis, a machinist originally from Montreal, Quebec, and Catherine Roche of Cambridge, Massachusetts. After attending the Boston Latin School, the younger James enrolled at Saint Charles College in Ellicot City, Maryland, graduating *summa cum laude* in 1896. Gillis studied philosophy for two years at St. John's Seminary in Brighton, Massachusetts, and then entered the Paulist novitiate. He continued his studies at Saint Thomas College, the Paulist house of studies affiliated with The Catholic University of America in Washington, D.C. He was ordained in 1901 at the Church of St. Paul the Apostle, New York City. He received his S.T.L. in 1903 and taught at the Catholic University for a year.

After three years of service on the Chicago Mission Band from 1904 to 1907, Father Gillis was appointed professor of dogmatic theology and Church history, as well as novice master and superior of Saint Thomas College until 1910. From 1910 to 1922 he was assigned to the New York Mission Band. In 1922 he succeeded John J. Burke, C.S.P., as the editor of the *Catholic Word,* a position he would hold until 1948, and it was in this capacity that he became a nationally renowned figure. From 1948 until his death in 1957 he served as contributing editor.

Gillis was an outspoken champion of the Catholic Church and its position on many issues of the day, including communism, fascism, and social justice. Although he supported Franklin D. Roosevelt's election in 1932, he became an ardent critic of what he perceived as the President's abuse of the emergency powers he received from Congress in 1933. Gillis vigorously opposed Roosevelt's running for an unprecedented third term, and created controversy when he endorsed Wendall Wilke in a *Catholic World* editorial shortly before the election.

While on vacation in 1920 Gillis read, and was horrified by, several accounts written by soldiers who fought in World War I. He repudiated his former position supporting the American war effort and became a pacifist. Later he seriously critcized what he perceived to be an inherent contradiction between President Roosevelt's stated desires for peace and his actions in support of the Allies prior to U.S. entrance into the Second World War.

Father Gillis also wrote a weekly syndicated column, *Sursum Corda,* from 1928 to 1955, of which there are over 1,300 installments; he spoke regularly on the Paulist radio station WLWL from 1925 to 1937, as well as on the *Catholic Hour* radio broadcasts from 1930 to 1941. Between 1923 and 1943 he published 17 pamphlets. He was also the author of several books, including *False Prophets* (1925); *The Catholic Church and the Home* (1928); *The Ten Commandments* (1931); *Christianity and Civilization* (1932); *The Paulists* (1932); *This is Our Day* (vol. I, 1933; vol. II, 1949); *So Near is God* (1953); *On Almost Everything* (1955); *This Mysterious Human Nature* (1956); and *My Last Book* (1957).

Father Gillis received numerous honorary degrees. In 1951 he became the first American to receive an honorary doctorate in sacred theology from the Angelicum College in Rome. In 1952 he was awarded the *Pro Ecclesia et Pontifice* decoration.

He died on 14 March 1957, and was buried in the crypt of the Church of Saint Paul the Apostle in New York City. His papers are stored in the Paulist Fathers Archives in Washington, D.C. In 1958 James F. Finley, C.S.P., published *James Gillis, Paulist,* as a memorial biography.

NICHOLAS M. CREARY

See also AMERICAN CATHOLICISM.

GILSON, ETIENNE (1884–1978)

Etienne Gilson was an historian of philosophy, especially of the medieval period and of the thought of Thomas Aquinas; b. Paris, 13 June 1884, d. 19 September 1978.

His two major accomplishments were: author of many writings, both books and articles, on the thought of the medieval period; one of the founders (in 1929) and the director of the Institute of Mediaeval Studies, at Toronto, Canada, with one of the finest libraries in the world. He was also a very fine literary stylist, noted for his clarity and simplicity. In 1946 he was elected a member of the French Academy. A bibliography of his works contains over one thousand entries.

Neither Gilson nor Maritain was taught philosophy at Catholic schools. Gilson was a product of the Sorbonne, where he later taught, and became acquainted with the medieval thinkers through his early studies of Descartes. From the very beginning of his career he began to produce notable and unusual works. Even his first work, a thesis on Descartes for the Sorbonne, was remarkable and in his very readable style. After military service in the First World War, the young professor produced two works which he was continually revising throughout his life. The first (in 1919) was a brief summary of the thought of St. Thomas. After years of revisions it appeared in English as *The Christian Philosophy of St. Thomas Aquinas* (1956). The thought of St. Thomas is also presented in a work written especially for use in colleges and called, *Elements of Christian Philosophy* (1960). The second presented a general view of medieval philosophy under the title of *The Philosophy of the Middle Ages* (1922). This led to his final general history of the period, now written in English, *History of Christian Philosophy in the Middle Ages* (1955). This is generally regarded as an indispensable work, and is nonacademic in style. As for individual thinkers, there are books on *The Philosophy of St. Bonaventure* (1924), *Introduction to the Study of Saint Augustine* (1929), and *Duns Scotus* (1952).

Since the popes, particularly from Leo XIII on, had encouraged a return to the study of the great Scholastics, and especially to the genuine thought of Thomas Aquinas, Gilson wanted to determine exactly what this genuine thought was. He found that many of the so-called Thomistic manuals of philosophy were seriously defective. In metaphysics, some were even denying a key Thomistic notion, the real distinction between essence and existence in all things except God. In epistemology, the theory of knowledge, others were posing the problem with the same presuppositions as Descartes and those who came after him. This was not only at variance with Aquinas, it also made any Thomistic resolution of the problem impossible.

Gilson's work as an historian gives his exposition of Aquinas a different flavor from that of Maritain. For Maritain, Aquinas is "the Apostle of modern times." His Aquinas speaks a modern language, wants to deal with modern philosophers and discuss the problems of the day—and even develop itself indefinitely. Gilson, on purpose, does not wish to go beyond the text of Aquinas; he wants to consider him in his thirteenth-century milieu, and to understand him in relation to the currents of thought in the thirteenth century. Gilson would say that studies of his kind are necessary before one can attempt to further the doctrine and apply it to one's own time.

Gilson was much preoccupied with the influence of revelation on philosophy and the notion of Christian philosophy. This was especially true in his great work, *The Spirit of Mediaeval Philosophy* (1932), which so enlightened the young Thomas Merton. He admitted the great debt of medieval thought to the Greeks, especially Aristotle, but he illustrated by concrete examples that the Christian thinkers did not take over these ideas without deepening these very ideas and making changes so great that the Greeks would no longer recognize them. He showed that revelation had presented certain ideas that, once accepted by faith, could be seen to be also attainable by reason, and could become part of a philosophy based on reason. Yet, prior to revelation these ideas remained, as a matter of fact, undiscovered by the philosophers. These ideas included those about God, freedom, nature, chance, providence, moral and physical evil, and others. So, revelation was aiding reason and enabling it to do what in fact it did not do before revelation. He also found that modern philosophy could not be fully understood in isolation from medieval thought, for the modern philosophers, who tried to isolate themselves from revelation and theology, took over unawares a host of ideas and attitudes inherited from the Middle Ages.

During the latter part of his career Gilson wrote several books on art, no doubt influenced by one of his daughters, who was a painter. His *Painting and Reality* (1957) was originally lectures given at the National Gallery of Art in Washington. A readable intellectual autobiography is his *The Philosopher and Theology* (1962). For a detailed biography see *Etienne Gilson* by Laurence K. Shook (1984).

THOMAS GALLAGHER

See also MIDDLE AGES, THE; PHILOSOPHY AND THEOLOGY.

GIOTTO DI BONDONE (ca. 1267–ca. 1337)

A master of early Italian painters and the headwaters of the Florentine school, Giotto was born around 1267. Working in fresco, he virtually founded modern painting by adding to his Byzantine models a concern for giving his figures real shapes occupying real space with real emotions. His work is marked by a noble simplicity of composition, combined with human feeling and imagination. Works of Giotto survive all over Italy, but these doubtless represent a small fraction of his output.

"The Virgin and Child Enthroned with Angels and Saints," by Giotto, Uffizi Gallery, Florence

His power can be appreciated in his scenes from the life of Christ, and of Saints Joachim, Anne, and Mary, in the Arena Chapel, Padua (ca. 1313). His *Life of St. Francis* and *Lives of St. John the Baptist and Evangelist* (after 1320) from S. Croce, Florence, are perhaps his best representatives. To him also belongs the design (later somewhat modified) for the marvelous campanile of the Cathedral of Florence. He died around 1337.

DAVID BRYAN

See also ART, CHRISTIAN; MIDDLE AGES, THE.

GLORIA IN EXCELSIS DEO

(Lat. "Glory be to God on high") Known as the greater doxology at Mass, it is the opening refrain of the Latin version of the hymn "Glory to God in the Highest"; it is sung or recited after the Penitential Rite by the congregation, the choir, or both. The date and authorship are unknown, though it was used in morning prayers as far back as the fourth century.

JOSEPH QUINN

See also DOXOLOGY.

GLORIA PATRI

(Lat., "Glory be to the Father") Known as the lesser doxology at Mass, it is a short prayer of praise to the Trinity, and derives its name from the prayer's opening phrase. The full text reads: "Glory be to the Father, and to the Son, and to the Holy Spirit. As it was in the beginning, is now, and ever shall be, world without end. Amen." It is normally recited along with the entrance and Communion verses at Mass, and at the end of the psalms in the Liturgy of the Hours. Its recitation at the end of the psalms dates back to the fourth century.

JOSEPH QUINN

See also DOXOLOGY.

GLOSSOLALIA

From the Greek, *glossa,* tongue, and *lalia,* speaking or giving forth sound, this term is rather ambiguous. Two quite distinct experiences are described in the New Testament. The first, as reported in Acts 2:4-11, asserts that the confusion of tongues of the Tower of Babel was reversed at Pentecost when the apostles spoke in their own language but were heard and understood by people of many nations, each in their own language. However, in the repeated references in 1 Corinthians 12–14, Paul seems to be referring to enthusiastic babbling unintelligible even to those of the same language as the speaker, but understood as a manifestation of religious ecstasy. Paul respects this phenomenon but is at pains to keep it within bounds at Christian assemblies and to make it quite clear that it is charity, not ecstasy, which constitutes the core of Christian conversion.

Until recent decades, the topic of glossolalia was nothing but an interesting point in NT interpretation. Since the beginning of the twentieth century, claims to have experienced glossolalia arose occasionally among Protestant groups that came to be known as Pentecostals. From late in the 1960s some Catholic groups in the U.S.A. also began to claim this for their members. On the whole the official Catholic attitude to the phenomenon has been extremely cautious, both for Paul's reason cited above, and because psychological illness can also manifest itself in that way. However, the teaching of the Catholic Church does not prejudge claimed occurrences of glossolalia.

MONIKA K. HELLWIG

See also CHARISM; CHARISMATIC MOVEMENT; GIFTS OF THE HOLY SPIRIT.

GNOSTICISM

Gnosticism is both a way of interpreting reality and a message of salvation, which was particularly influential in the second Christian century. As a way of interpreting reality it is dualistic: it divides human experience into a good or real realm of spirit and a bad or illusory realm of matter. These two realms are understood as coming from different sources, always at enmity with one another, whereas in biblical, Jewish, Christian and Muslim interpretations of reality, there is only one source or creator of all that exists, both material and spiritual, and the whole of creation is good.

As a message of salvation, Gnosticism proposes escape from the body and all material constraints by a kind of introspective meditation in which one becomes aware of oneself as essentially spirit trapped accidentally in a body. Gnosticism has had many forms, some including an elaborate mythology, but the dualism and the promise of escape into pure spirit are common to these many forms.

Since its origins in or before the second century, Gnosticism has been rejected and condemned by the Churches although many Christians have found it attractive. It has been condemned because in addition to opposing the doctrine of creation, it was an elitist teaching about salvation: some people were seen as "spirituals" who would certainly be saved, others are "psychics" who could be saved with help from teachers of truth, and yet others were designated "carnals" for whom there was no hope at all and who could do nothing about it. A third reason for the Church's rejection of this doctrine is that it preached salvation by self-absorption in introspective meditation, rather than by charity moving out in concern for others.

Gnostic ideas have never quite died out in the Church. They reappeared as a challenge from the Manichaeans in the time of Augustine of Hippo. In the Middle Ages, such ideas were brought to the Western Church by the Crusaders, their advocates being named Bogomils, Cathari, or Albigensians. Less distinctly in later centuries the tendency has frequently recurred to see all matter as evil, not to take the world and its needs seriously, to distrust sexuality, to be concerned about saving souls out of the world rather than about the redemption of the world. These are all manifestations of recurring Gnostic assumptions.

MONIKA K. HELLWIG

See also AUGUSTINE, ST.; CREATION; MANICHAEISM.

GOD

The word "God" can be used as both a common noun and a proper name. As a common noun, a "god" is an object of worship and faith, and an irreducible center of meaning, power, and value. The biblical prohibition of idolatry, "Thou shalt not have strange gods before me," is one example of this usage.

A person who worships or has faith in many gods is a *polytheist.* In ancient Greece and Rome, for instance, all the gods and goddesses had their own temples. Each was invoked for specific different human activities, e.g., Mars for war, Venus for love, Ceres for agriculture. Each had power over and gave meaning to a different part of life.

In the modern world, polytheists do not worship such personified forces, but impersonal and abstract ideas. They worship "money," "power," "sex," etc., divinizing them by making these irreducible centers of meaning and value in their lives. Modern polytheists gives ultimate allegiance to none of them, but use them and are used by them at different times and places.

A person who worships one god, but recognizes that there are others' gods, is a *henotheist.* In the ancient world, some worshiped only the god of their own tribe or group, but recognized that other tribes worshiped other gods and that these gods were also real and powerful. Early Israelites were henotheists, indicated, for instance, in the contests between the gods and their prophets, such as the one depicted in 1 Kings 18.

In the modern world, unbridled patriotism is a prime example of henotheism. Whenever individuals or societies sacralize national symbols, whether inviolable flags or mottos like "blood and soil," and also permit nothing to be more important than the nation and its symbols, they are henotheistic.

Jews, Christians, and Muslims are properly *monotheists,* people who have faith in and worship one and only one god as supreme creator, the sovereign power of the universe, the ultimate and only proper object of worship, and the irreducible center of meaning and value of whatever is.

Monotheists often use the word "god" as a proper name in invoking their god, e.g., "Oh God, our help in ages past. . . ." This usage may be as ancient as monotheism. It is so common that it is sometimes difficult to see other uses of the word "god."

For monotheism, because God creates and sustains the world, whatever is, is made by God, and is thus good. Everything has value because it is valued by God. The creation myths in Genesis underscore this goodness of the creator's world.

Monotheism must be distinguished from deism and pantheism. The deists' god creates the world and leaves it alone, while monotheism generally accepts the doctrine of providence or other ways of talking of God's immanent action within and for the world. Pantheism denies God's transcendence of the world; the pantheists' god is equally everywhere and everything.

Most Christians differ from other monotheists in that they believe in and worship a triune and incarnated God. The doctrine of the Trinity highlights the personal presence of God in creation, redemption, and sanctifying sustenance of the world. The doctrine of the incarnation means that the god Christians worship, while distinct from the world, became truly present in the world in an actual human being, Jesus of Nazareth, called the Christ, whose life and death effectively redeem the world.

Christians who minimize the distinctions between the three persons in God may approach the unipersonal monotheism of Judaism and Islam. While the other monotheistic traditions also see God as both transcendent of and actively immanent in the world, the doctrine of the incarnation strongly distinguishes Catholic and Orthodox (and many Protestant) doctrines of God from them.

Traditionally, monotheists also regard God as infinite or unlimited in perfection; hence, God is all-powerful, all-knowing, all-good, totally free, and depends on no other for existence or perfection (aseity). God is simple and eternal (not composite), and is thus unchangeable and immutable both as God and in relation to the world. God alone is holy; any other holiness is derivative from divine grace. Philosophers and theologians have proffered numerous explanations of these divine attributes.

The prohibition of idolatry applies in the contemporary world as in the ancient. Adherents of biblical religion all too easily fall into idolatry by making other "gods" the centers of our lives, whether those gods are money, power, the nation or other, lesser deities. Faith in and worship of God requires us to have no strange gods before us.

T. W. TILLEY

See also FAITH; THEOLOGY.

GODPARENT (SPONSOR)

Godparent (*patrinus* in Latin) is an office and ministry in Christian initiation. Ancient custom of the Church as well as the norms of current Church law insist that a candidate for baptism have a godparent. The godparent is not necessary for the validity of the sacrament; hence, if a godparent cannot be found (e.g., when baptizing in an emergency situation), the requirement does not bind.

Sometimes *patrinus* is translated as "sponsor"; the liturgical books, however, distinguish between *sponsor* and *patrinus*; the former stands as witness to the candidates' moral character and qualifications upon admission to the catechumenate; the latter accompanies the candidate from the day of election. The same person may serve in both capacities, but this is not necessary.

While Church law is fulfilled by having one godparent (either male or female), convention in many cultures has called for two, a male and a female, especially in infant baptism. The Code of Canon Law allows this selection of two godparents, providing that one be male and the other female, a godfather and godmother.

The godparent, especially in adult baptism, has a significant role to play prior to the baptism. The godparent helps in the spiritual preparation of the candidate; he or she is expected to give good example, showing the candidate how to put the gospel into practice, and to sustain the candidates in moments of hesitancy and anxiety. In the Rite of Election the godparent affirms the candidate's suitability to the community.

At the baptism itself, the godparent presents the candidate, accompanies him or her to the font, assists there as necessary, and presents the candidate with a candle lit from the paschal candle.

At the baptism of an infant, the godparent, together with the parents, presents the candidate, publicly declares his or her readiness to help the parents in their duty as Christian parents, and, together with the parents, renounces sin and professes the Church's faith in which the infant is to be baptized.

Godparenthood gives rise to obligations that endure. A godparent of the adult candidate is obligated to help the initiated one persevere in the Christian life. In infant baptism, the godparents, as occasion offers, are to help the parents so that the baptized child will come to profess and live the faith.

The qualifications for a godparent include these: (1) The choice of godparent belongs primarily to the candidate or, in the case of infant baptism, to the parents. If the choice is not made for some reason (e.g., in the event of an emergency), the parish pastor or minister of baptism is to designate the godparent. (2) The person chosen must be at least sixteen years old. An exception can be made for a just cause in a particular case by the parish pastor or minister of baptism. (3) The godparents must be fully initiated Catholics (i.e., they have been baptized in the Catholic Church or received into it, have been confirmed, and have received the Eucharist). They must not be presently bound by any imposed or declared penalty (e.g., excommunication or interdict). The pertinent canon provides also that the godparent must "lead a life in harmony with the faith and the role to be undertaken." If a prospective godparent is not from the parish where the baptism will take place, pastoral practice in the United States asks that a certificate be obtained from his or her parish pastor indicating that the qualifications are met. The Ecumenical Directory (1993) permits a Christian of the non-Catholic Eastern Churches to serve as godparent, together with a Catholic godparent. Other non-Catholic Christians (e.g., Protestants), however, are not eligible to serve as godparents. Together with a Catholic godparent, though, they may serve as a "Christian witness" of the baptism. Non-Christians are not eligible to serve in either the ministry of godparent or "Christian witness." (4) The canon expressly disqualifies the mother or father of the candidate from serving as godparent. This is especially appropriate in the case of infants and children, because parents already bear a primary responsibility for their spiritual formation.

Church law previously restricted the designation as godparents of men or women religious or those in sacred orders, but this constraint is eliminated in the 1983 Code of Canon Law.

Under the 1917 Code, a "spiritual relationship" arose by virtue of baptism between the candidate and the minister and between the candidate and the godparent. Unless dispensed, this relationship impeded marriage between those thus related. This impediment is dropped in the 1983 Code.

A godparent (*patrinus*) is required for the sacrament of confirmation, insofar as possible. If the sacraments of initiation are celebrated together, the same person serves throughout the rite as godparent. The obligation of the confirmation godparent is to see that the confirmed person acts as a true witness to Christ. The qualifications are the same as for the baptismal godparent, and the Code expresses a preference that the one who performed the role of godparent at baptism likewise serve in that role for confirmation.

If the godparent cannot be present for the ceremony of initiation, a proxy is generally understood to be permissible.

ROBERT C. GIBBONS

See also LAITY, THEOLOGY OF THE; SACRAMENTS OF INITIATION.

GRACE

Grace is at the heart of the Christian understanding of human existence, for it concerns the mystery of the relationship of humanity to God revealed in Jesus Christ. The doctrine of grace lies embedded in the Scriptures and underwent development through the course of Christianity's history. That development crystallized in a theological anthropology, a Christian understanding of the human person considered from both an individual and a social perspective. As a crucial element in a theological anthropology, the doctrine of grace is fundamental to Christian life.

Definition

Grace refers to God's benevolence to human beings. In face of sin God's grace appears as redemptive pardon and healing; in face of human finitude, it is empowerment to live humanly and enter interpersonal communion with God eternally. Protestantism has tended to stress the former, Catholicism, the latter, though these two horizons are not opposed and can be fused. The long history of the doctrine of grace has dealt with many issues. From this history emerged a theological anthropology and an interpretation of the meaning of God's relationship to human beings revealed in Jesus Christ. From the time of Augustine (354–430) Christianity has insisted on the gratuity and priority of grace. Sinful human beings, strapped by a moral impotence to love God in and above all things else, cannot save themselves. Salvation is the work of God mediated through the grace of Christ, a sheer gratuity in view of sinful humanity's betrayal of God and of itself. Augustine, however, opened the door to a profusion of opinions and quarrels, e.g., concerning the relationship between grace and human freedom, between providence and the human struggle in history.

Scripture

But long before Augustine the seeds that were to generate a doctrine of grace lay sewn in the Scriptures. The Scriptures tell the story of God's grace and the wholeness (salvation) it offers to human beings and their world. A word-study of Hebrew and Greek terms associated with the reality of grace would show them converging in the idea that God acts for the salvation of human beings. Employing a myriad of images and symbols, the Jewish and Christian Scriptures show God at work dealing graciously in varied ways with humankind and its world. But the galaxy of graces find a controlling center in the conviction that God is steadfast love that pours itself out upon human beings. Jesus, as manifestation of that self-emptying love, is himself grace and pours into human hearts the grace that is his Spirit (Rom 5:5). In this Trinitarian pattern grace effects human salvation, which is variously portrayed as being reborn, being adopted as a child of God, receiving the gift of God's Spirit, or being formed in the image of Christ. No one symbolic representation dominates in the Scriptures. Yet one basic experience permeates the fund of Christian symbols for grace: salvation, freedom from sin and death, and reconciliation with God, comes from God in and through the Christ, who pours out God's Spirit upon the world. God's indwelling Spirit is the source of faith, hope, and love; the Spirit liberates from enslavement to sin, assists in prayer, enlightens minds, draws hearts, and heals the fragmented self. For "the fruit of the Spirit is love, joy, peace, patience, kindness, goodness, faithfulness, gentleness, self-control" (Gal 5:22). To different ones the Spirit imparts different gifts, but all are bound by the Spirit into the one body of Christ (1 Cor 12–13).

These rich biblical symbols were in time distilled into more general, technical, and theoretical concepts of grace. These distillates indicate that grace is an analogous notion layered with multiple meanings. Grace in all its distinctiveness and complex richness is the heart of Christianity. Grace is salvation, completeness, wholeness for the human person, and according to the Christian Scriptures such completeness comes only with participation in the life of God. Human beings are called to union with God, beginning here and now, for God in sheer love communicates God's very self to every human as an innermost constitutive element. In a word, grace *is* God's communication of God's self to all human beings; grace is the Holy Spirit's presence within and influence upon human beings.

This self-giving by God is utterly free and gratuitous, unowed, and totally unconditioned by human merits or achievements. Love is always uncoerced, a surprising gift. God's gracing is not an afterthought, a corrective contingency plan following upon a world run amok; God creates because God intends from the start to engage free beings in loving interpersonal communion. Anticipating every human being born into the world is God's loving self-communication. Humanity is the event of God's absolute and forgiving self-gift. Within each one is the perduring presence of God as Spirit and offer of love and the free human being will accept or reject this offer in and through choices made amidst the concrete circumstances of his or her world. One remains free to say "yes" or "no" to God. Normally, this will not be done explicitly, but implicitly in acceptance or rejection of concrete values. Because every decision is constitutive of the person, acceptance or rejection of concrete values includes a movement into or a spurning of the horizon against which they are perceived, absolute goodness, God. The extraordinary, therefore, is encountered in the ordinary; biography and history are the medium of divine/human dialogue.

Augustine of Hippo

While the effects of grace are manifold, in his war against Pelagianism Augustine stressed the universality of human sinfulness so as to highlight the absolute necessity of medicinal grace. Pushing Paul's metaphor in Romans 5 to the breaking point, Augustine insisted that in Adam all had fallen from the divine plan, according to which all human powers were to be subject to reason and pressed into service of God. After the Fall human appetites ran riot in rebellion against reason and reason's God. Christ rectified this state of things. Those believing in him and following him could, with the gift of God's Spirit, be restored to virtuous lives. Still, they would always experience the aftereffects of sin, the rebellion of the appetites. Augustine, therefore, saw grace as liberating human beings from the bondage of egoism, empowering their freedom by giving them the capacity to love the supreme good, and drawing them toward it. Grace is the Spirit at work in fallen humanity, whose freedom is enslaved by habits of sin and concupiscence. Weakened by the ravages of sin, "our hearts are not in our power" and our lives are disordered; all are devoid of true freedom because incapable of the love that makes for authentic freedom, the love that transcends self. Only grace, God's Spirit, can free fallen humanity from the "cruel necessity of sinning" and by loving it render it lovable and capable of loving. "What have you that you did not receive?" (1 Cor 4:7). The Spirit makes freedom possible, then expands freedom and opens one to values beyond the self and ultimately to supreme value, God. In today's language, grace, God's Spirit, effects human self-transcendence.

Thomas Aquinas

In the thirteenth century, Thomas Aquinas (ca. 1225–1274), drawing his armature from Aristotelian metaphysics, took a teleological approach to grace as he attempted to move from symbolism to finely hammered theory. All beings exist for the purpose to which they are oriented and to which their capacities are proportioned. The nature of a being, its principle of operation, determines how it acts and the kind of acts it will perform, given its powers and faculties. Natures are proportioned to their end and elicit acts that conduce to that end. For Thomas, human beings are called to a super-natural goal, union with God triune, which outstrips the capacities and actions of any created nature. A special gift of God, grace, must supply a new, super-natural "nature" outfitted with new powers of faith, hope, and love that elevate, empower, and incline one to enter into interpersonal relationship with God here and in eternity. Hence the entrance of the term "supernatural" as common currency.

Life finds fulfillment through actions played out in the here and now, but actions motivated by supernatural powers lift up and perfect "natural" human powers by inserting them into a higher integration. Grace, therefore, effects a new way of being by launching one into a new orbit of communion with the triune God culminating in beatifying face-to-face vision. Grace as elevation and empowerment became a benchmark for Catholic theology. Grace is gratuitous, not merely because human beings are sinners, as Augustine had it, but primarily because it projects them into a realm transcending their own order of being. For Thomas, grace is medicinal, healing the wounds of sin, as it was for Augustine. But more, it is elevating, transposing life into a new key. As with the incarnation or the beatific vision, earthly existence had to become "supernatural," exceeding the proportions of any created nature. In each case, incarnation, vision, the here-and-now life of the believer, God is sharing God's very self with human beings. This re-creation of the sinner's hardened heart is God's greatest work, greater even than creation, said Thomas, and it is effected by grace as a new habitual orientation of the person toward God, who alone can sate the heart's desire.

Martin Luther

In the sixteenth century Martin Luther (1483–1546) revived Pauline and Augustinian thinking and took up the cudgel against the idea that anyone can earn salvation by doing good works. Grace is not within human control; salvation is not a human achievement. All is grace, God's first call and every step on the way to salvation. Yet Luther conceived grace less in terms of God's Spirit than in terms of God's Word, Jesus Christ. Nothing human beings can do can ever sunder the bonds of sin. God's justifying word of forgiveness, acceptance, and healing love is embodied in the Christ, who is himself, therefore, God's grace. One is justified by an imputed, alien justice, the justice of Christ. Acceptance of God's grace-filled Word is by faith; one must cling to God in Christ. With this forensic justification of the sinner comes inner transformation by a mystical nuptial in which one takes on the qualities of Christ with whom one is now united. To Luther's credit, he gave the dynamics of grace a personal cast. Liberation from sin's bondage occurs only within the context of interpersonal union with God. Faith is not mere intellectual assent, but a clinging to God, a surrender fired by hope and love.

The justification of the unjust is not, however, in Luther's mind, the end of human fallenness. Forgiveness cannot wholly remove the vestiges of past sinfulness nor eliminate the possibility of future sin. As with Augustine, graced human beings are convalescent. Indeed, they are at once just and sinful, torn by concupiscence and temptation, to which they inevitably yield. Nonetheless, God's graceful Word effects an acceptance of human beings as they are, despite their sin. For Luther, people are thereby freed from the frustration of attempting to prove their worth to God by their good lives, forever an impossible dream.

Perhaps Luther put his finger on the most basic effect of grace. If human beings are lovable, it is not, ultimately, because of their achievements, but because God has accepted and loved them first in all their misery. All is grace. Note the variations in stress. Augustine and Thomas view grace at work within human freedom, transforming and empowering it; Luther minimizes freedom so as to make room for the absolute gratuity and priority of God's justifying forgiveness. For Luther, grace is God's forgiving Word incarnated in Christ; human justification is always by the justice of another, of God in Christ. Both accents are needed and are not at all Church-dividing.

Council of Trent

The Council of Trent (1546–1547), however, undertook to state synthetically the Catholic understanding of grace in a way that would counter what it perceived to be the imbalances in the Reformers' teaching. Trent affirmed both free will and the necessity and gratuity of grace while denying predestination to damnation. And it insisted on a Catholic realism over against what it wrongly took to be Protestantism's legalism; grace is a real, inner transformation of the sinner, not merely an extrinsic declaration that the sinner is now considered just. Trent, in accord with biblical imperatives and common sense, also affirmed the necessity of performing good works, which, done under grace, merit eternal life, not of themselves, but because of Christ. God crowning human merits is God crowning God's own gifts.

Trent notwithstanding, divisions in the Church deepened. No matter how nuanced either side might attempt to be, it could not be heard above the polemical din of charge and countercharge, Catholics being accused of semi-Pelagianism, Protestants, of antinomianism. Out of this regrettable history and the materials it afforded came the standard Catholic texts on grace which prevailed until the mid-twentieth century. These texts were given to reified abstractions, such as "pure nature," to preoccupations with "actual grace," divine foreknowledge and its compatibility with human freedom, and the importance of merit, and to dense technicalities concerning the metaphysical status and classification of various graces. These emphases fostered the image of grace as an entity intermediate between the soul and God and possessed in measured quantities contingent upon one's merits. The connection of grace with salvation appeared extrinsic and arbitrary. As a result, Catholic piety tended to be schizoid, with the human agent operating on two levels because endowed with two ends, one natural, and attainable by human efforts, the other, supernatural and attainable solely by actions elevated by grace to a new order. Thus the religious and the secular became two zones separated by an impenetrable wall. Not until the mid-twentieth century would more appropriate priorities and emphases be reestablished.

Nevertheless, if one dug deep enough beneath these post-Tridentine layers one could still find the buried mother lode. The whole drift of Christian thinking had been and still was to view grace as effecting human transformation by bestowing upon human beings a share in God's own life beginning in this world and growing to completion in eternal life. "We are God's children now; it does not yet appear what we shall be, but we know that when he appears we shall be like him, for we shall see him as he is" (1 John 3:2). "He has given us his precious and very great promises, so that through them you . . . may become participants of the divine nature" (2 Pet 1:4).

Grace is sanctifying, divinizing, and therefore, paradoxically, humanizing. To be what we are we must be more than we are. Aquinas spoke of grace as a new, infused supernatural quality of the soul that raises one to participation in the life of God. Luther also affirmed as much in more personalistic terms. As heated iron glows like fire because one with the fire, he said, so too the soul takes on the qualities of the Word of God with which it has become one. Or again, it is, said Luther, like a man marrying a poor harlot who is recreated by his love, raised to a new level. "It is no longer I who live but Christ who lives in me" (Gal 2:20). God's presence is a power at work within human freedom as it falteringly emerges from potentiality to ever fuller responsibility. Grace as offered and accepted initiates a dialogue between divine and human freedoms. Human faith, hope, and love are drawn out by God's creative love. Still, the sin/grace tension rankles. There can be no absolute Yes or No to God while "the death dance in our blood" surges on. Ignorance, concupiscence, temptation within and without, preclude absolute disposition of the self. There are pockets of the self we will not surrender.

Further Questions

Of course, the doctrine of grace tows a large raft of problems in its wake. Human life is effort, growth, development through intelligence, judgment, and responsible choice, all of which are the gift of grace. One grating problem that follows is the determinism of grace, or better, the mystery of the two freedoms. How to sustain both the primacy of God's free grace in all salutary human acts and the modern experience of human freedom as creativity? The problem, more acute now because modernity sets a premium on autonomy, is a perennial. To hold both ends of the chain, Augustine distinguished operative and cooperative grace. God operates preveniently, without us, plucking out the heart of stone, replacing it with a heart of flesh that we might love; but when we do love and act lovingly, God cooperates with our good will to initiate and sustain its good intention and performance. Aquinas argued that God always acts upon creatures in accord with their nature. Freedom is the nature of the human person. Therefore God acts within, not against human freedom. The human agent is no mere passive instrument in the hands of God, but becomes a free, self-initiating person.

We can add to this that mechanistic metaphors must yield to personalistic models. The love of others is absolutely needful to us if we are to become free. Such love draws us out but we remain free; in fact, the grace of such love gives us freedom. The paradox of love is that it at once necessitates or compels and frees. Thus grace and freedom are not competitive; grace presupposes and perfects the human elements. Both/and replaces either/or. Divine and human freedoms operate on different levels, are complementary, and mutually needful. Crippled by sin, fragmented by finitude, yet destined to union with God, human beings need the redeeming, gracing God; a God who is love, on the other hand, knows the compulsion to love and the need of a free response from the other. God sustains human freedom in being, heals it, transforms it, and empowers the self-transcendence that in turn transforms its own world and its history. All is the work of grace and freedom; and free one cannot be unless graced. One can live and love only because one has been loved.

Contemporary Catholic Teaching

These last remarks lead us to the social dimensions of grace, which, like sin, cannot be reduced to its significance for the individual. But first, note some of the reversals and retrievals introduced by the theological renaissance in twentieth-century Catholicism. From the thirteenth century on grace came to designate primarily "created grace," called sanctifying grace, a habitual disposition or quality of the soul infused by God, the "new nature" Aquinas spoke of. God, who is "uncreated grace," was also said to be present and indwelling the graced person. This is now reversed: grace is seen primarily as uncreated grace, God's own self-communication, and secondarily as created or sanctifying grace, the change effected in the person by God's self-gift, the reality resulting from and corresponding to God's very real presence and action in the human heart. Secondly, from Augustine on, stress rested on the scarcity of grace, its transient character, and its rarity or absence beyond the pale of Christianity. Now, on the basis of God's universal salvific will grace is seen to be abundant. God is abidingly present and persistently inviting all to the banquet. All of life, even in its most secular corners, is embraced by the presence of God offering Godself to human beings. Thus the walls erected between Church and world, between Christianity and other religions, between the sacred and the secular, collapse. Distinction is not separation. There is a kingdom of grace outside the Church.

Thirdly, twentieth-century theology has jettisoned the extrinsicism of Baroque theology. The offer of grace is now viewed as a constitutive element in the human condition and no longer as an alien and transient element super-added from without to a self-sufficient, closed human nature. God is the heart's home. Humanity is a desire for the God of grace, who perfects and completes the human person. This God of grace is not remote, but near in hidden closeness and forgiving intimacy. Fourthly, contemporary theology maintains, contrary to Baroque theology's position that grace, because supernatural, cannot be experienced, that grace can be experienced. Grace cannot be known directly as grace, but it can be known indirectly in experiences of self-transcendence, in the heart's restlessness, in endless dissatisfaction with possessions and achievements, in love's unshrinking acceptance of responsibility. At the term of such transcendence one intuits the presence of the infinite, the ineffable, a reality beyond one's disposal, the holy mystery that lures one. Finally, there is now a burgeoning ecumenical consensus on the doctrine of grace. Lutheran-Catholic dialogues have thawed the frozen positions occupied by both parties since the sixteenth century. Despite differences of idiom, stress, and theme, the two communities have reached substantive agreement concerning grace.

The Social Dimension

The ecumenical discovery of buried common ground is momentous; equally momentous is the awakening of sensitivity to the social character of grace. This macro-dimension arises with modern awareness that human beings have emerged from a far distant past and are moving into an uncharted future. Such historical consciousness highlights change, relativity, and an awareness that social and cultural institutions and structures are not immutable givens determined by nature but malleable forms created by human freedom. Also accompanying modernity's historical consciousness is a new concern about the meaningfulness and direction of the collective human project within history. Past theologies of grace tended to focus on ontological analyses of the individual and his or her private concern about eternal life, thus minimizing the import of the historical process and slighting its corporate dimension. The contemporary theology of grace offers a corrective by calling attention to the social, historical, and eschatological aspects of grace, which is a retrieval of a more biblical perspective. There is a continuity between history and the end-time; the kingdom is aborning now. The purposiveness of human creativity and the goal of history fuse. To think otherwise is to evacuate history with its collage of tears and laughter, its striving and its small victories of any meaning at all. The fusion of humanity's creativity and history's goal is not negation of traditional thought but expansion of its insight that grace is the seed of glory. The doctrine of grace necessarily carries sociopolitical implications, concerning as it does human life in its totality.

Because human beings are social, the question of the relationship of grace to social life must arise. By analogy with personal sin we now speak of social sin; the correlative analogous reality is social grace. The reality of social grace assumes great importance in a world where the dehumanizing power of social sin presses upon individuals and groups. A theology that views grace solely in terms of the individual is inadequate and concedes the sociohistorical world and its structures to sin and meaninglessness.

Social grace, like social sin, is elusive, but surely it involves the institutionalization of the dynamics of grace. Any group or institution is the social embodiment of grace to the extent that it fosters human development and the common good. The Church is but one example. Other institutions may function similarly (and often better than the Church) across the entire register of human existence. Grace is incarnated not merely in the personal lives of individuals but also in their collective life, which is more than the sum of their individual lives, and in their institutional patterns. Thus, structured social arrangements objectively mediate God's grace insofar as they nurture the lives of individuals and groups in their self-transcending concern for justice, truth, and human solidarity. Human beings freely create and sustain a grid of institutions; the institutional network is not a brute given. Good institutions that enhance the common good derive from the energies of graced and organized groups concerned with providing a social milieu that promotes the common welfare.

In this we see the subjective side of social grace. Institutions, however, are objective realities. Society's web of institutional arrangements precedes and conditions the exercise of personal freedom. The values of a society are sedimented in its institutions. People shape institutions; institutions shape people. They permeate all of life and, as noted above, beget within us a "second nature" that spontaneously embraces the culture's values and approved modes of behavior. To the degree that these social structures impel self-transcendence in concern for the well-being of others, they are objective channels of grace. And as with individuals, so with institutions; no institution is purely sinful or purely graceful, though some may appear so. The categories of social sin and social grace, therefore, despite their elusiveness, throw light on dimensions of our social world that were heretofore generally left dark and provide us with a critical eye to take the measure of the world we are creating.

Finally, an important corollary following upon all this: grace always incarnates or sacramentalizes itself. The presence and power of grace, Christ's Spirit, becomes palpable primarily in the humanity of Jesus, but continues to take flesh in the persons, events, and social structures of our many worlds. All reality is symbolic of God, but especially other persons, individually and collectively, are sacramental mediations of grace. The God of grace is first encountered not on the threshhold of another world, but in the midst of everyday routines, and uncommon joys and tragedies. "The just man justices/keeps grace: that keeps all his goings graces/Acts in God's eye what in God's eye he is—Christ/For Christ plays in ten thousand places/Lovely in limbs, and lovely in eyes not his/To the Father through the features of men's faces" (G. M. Hopkins).

Within this social context we return to the question of the divine purpose inscribed in human freedom with all its creative and destructive potential. Given our analysis of social grace, it seems that the purpose of freedom here and now, under the influence of grace, is the creation of a system of graced social structures. This is the trajectory of the effects of grace: forgiveness of sin, empowerment of freedom in self-transcending love, communion with God that affords freedom a creativity it would not have if left curved in on itself. All of these effects inextricably intertwine with love of and service to the neighbor.

Given, however, the increasing solidarity and complex interdependence of modern social life, love of neighbor cannot be reduced to a superficial civility. Love of neighbor necessarily bears a sociopolitical dimension. Hence participation in the creation of just, life-promoting institutions is now as never before one of life's demands. Today, a new phenomenon, the massive public suffering that marks modern culture, throws into question the meaningfulness of human history. The meaningfulness of our humanity is by no means an objective given. With the help of grace meaningfulness must be forged by human freedom in the fires of everyday struggle. The dynamics of grace draw human freedom into a twofold struggle: first, to resist social sin and evil; secondly, to join in the construction of social systems that embody and mediate grace. The logic of Christian life is not in escape from the world. Nor is it in passing time while looking to another life in another realm. Life is not merely prelude to the real thing. Rather, the logic of Christian life is responsibility, making one's own God's intention for human freedom: constructive works of love and justice in the world to counteract the dehumanizing forces of evil, sin, and death. Resistance to social sin and construction of structures that may be mediations of social grace are essential to Christian life, not optional "extras." For grace is a dynamic impulsion to action, not merely the measure of a reward to be reaped in a future life. Holiness is gauged in terms of active love, not in terms of quantity of grace. Christian concern is not with accumulating merits, but with bringing forth the fruits of grace in sacrificial love.

For Christianity the ultimate goal of history is the kingdom of God, an elusive eschatological symbol not susceptible of easy translation. At very least it is a way of living in accord with God's rule and will, which implies an order of justice and compassion, hence peace. God's kingdom comes to be in a new way in the life of Jesus, who embodies the kingdom. The kingdom values manifest God's intention for human history, for the end of history throws light on what history should be moving toward in any given era. That the purpose of human freedom is the creation of graced social structures is thus coherent with Christian eschatology. The symbol of the kingdom points to a continuity between the historical process and the end-time. Life, to be meaningful, must participate under the influence of grace in the building of the kingdom. For if human choices have no bearing whatever upon construction of the final reality, then the creativity of human freedom is ultimately irrelevant, even meaningless, which seems contrary to the creative intention of God.

Catholic theology, especially, has always tied final union with God to works of grace in human life. What is accomplished in love by graced people in their own small acre of the world contributes to establishment of the final reality, the kingdom. Even though the power of evil and the destructiveness of time are more manifest than the effects of grace as one traces the features of history, the resurrection of Jesus grounds the hope that God's grace will be and already is eschatologically victorious. "Where sin increased, grace abounded all the more" (Rom 5:20).

To sum up, the divine destination of human beings to communion with their God precedes creation itself. From the beginning human existence is created as an orientation to transcendent mystery. God's offer of self-communication was to embrace and contextualize all of human existence. God's Spirit is abidingly and personally present to and in dialogue with human freedom. The effect of the Spirit's graceful presence is acceptance and forgiveness of sinful human beings, the opening up of ambiguous human freedom to ego-transcending love, a new creation and a new history. Everything accomplished by freedom informed and carried by grace will be transformed into definitive, perduring reality, the kingdom. The old dichotomies between spiritual and material, religious and secular, eternal and temporal, supernatural and natural fade. There is no pure nature; nor was there ever. Nothing is purely secular. For every nook and cranny of life is permeated with the offer of God's Spirit and all of one's decisions and actions, in whatever sphere, and the whole tidal pull of one's life, consciously or not, is toward acceptance or rejection of the gracing God. The eternal is in the temporal. The quotidian and the religious do not inhabit separate enclaves but suffuse each other. If one has eyes to see and ears to hear, the humdrum is transformed into poetry and poetry into revelation. All is grace. Evil will surely thrive, but all the more will grace abound in depths and heights yet undreamt of.

STEPHEN J. DUFFY

See also SALVATION; SOTERIOLOGY.

GRAIL, THE HOLY

The legendary cup used by Jesus at the Last Supper. The quest for it has wrought many myths and legendary stories—a popular one being that Joseph of Arimathea brought the grail to England in A.D. 64; this story gave rise to numerous medieval romances, particularly those associated with the fabled King Arthur. Such legends, however, were never seriously considered by Church authorities.

JOSEPH QUINN

See also MIDDLE AGES, THE; VESSELS, SACRED.

GREAT WESTERN SCHISM

This refers to the period (1378–1417) in which there were several claimants to the papal throne. Previous popes had been in exile from Rome and maintaining a court in Avignon in France since 1309. In 1376, Gregory XI set out on his return to Rome, dying soon after. Many devout Christians, including St. Catherine of Siena who had persuaded Gregory to come back to Rome, expected to see the end of a scandalous period in the history of the papacy. What happened was even worse than the "Avignon exile."

In 1378, a conclave (a meeting of cardinals to elect a new pope) was held in Rome. The cardinals were not free because there was rioting in the streets and those in the conclave were threatened by civic leaders if they did not elect a Roman. Moreover, not all the cardinals were present. Some had stayed in Avignon. By deceiving the rioting crowds about their intentions, the cardinals managed to elect an Italian (not, however, a Roman) who had maintained connections with the Avignon court. They quickly notified the Christian rulers of Europe, including Emperor Charles IV, of the identity of the new pope who took the name of Urban VI.

Urban VI was a reformer, but a ruthless, arrogant, and undiplomatic one. Some thought he was mentally ill. As the cardinals found it more and more difficult to cooperate with him, the French cardinals issued a proclamation that his election was invalid because made under threat of grave bodily harm to the electors. They now declared that he had been deposed. A number of cardinals moved to a safe place (the Italian town of Fondi) where they elected a cardinal from Geneva who took the name of Clement

VII. Because Urban VI still had a considerable contingent of supporters who thought his election valid and his deposition invalid, this initiated (in the same year 1378) a schism in the Western Church between the supporters of the two popes—a schism which lasted thirty-nine years. Actually, however, while scandalous, and difficult for princes and bishops, this schism did not affect ordinary Christian people very much.

It might have been expected that when one of the rival popes died this would solve the problem. Urban, however, had returned to Avignon and named twenty-nine new cardinals drawn from many nations, rejecting the proposal for a general council of bishops of all the local Churches to resolve the schism, but raising an army of mercenaries to reinforce his claims by military campaigns. He died in 1388, possibly by poisoning. Fourteen Roman cardinals, who had considered him the legitimate pope, now elected a pleasant and sensible Neapolitan cardinal who took the name of Boniface IX. As soon as he was elected, Clement VII excommunicated him and Boniface reciprocated. However, some cardinals who had supported Clement because Urban was so scandalous, now had nothing against Boniface and went over to his side. He was a shrewd negotiator and rejected proposals for a general council because he hoped to make it worthwhile to Clement VII to abdicate his claim to the papacy. Unfortunately, Boniface greatly increased the medieval scandal of selling benefices and indulgences.

Meanwhile, Clement VII died in 1394, and again there were hopes of ending the schism. The Avignon cardinals held a conclave and agreed that whoever among them was elected would abdicate as soon as the majority of cardinals thought it appropriate. They elected a Spaniard who took the name Benedict XIII, who refused to abdicate but hoped to negotiate with Boniface IX to end the schism. In response, the French Church withdrew the revenues it contributed to popes of the Avignon succession, followed by a similar withdrawal by most of the Spanish Church, and by withdrawal of allegiance by many of the hitherto Avignon cardinals. Eventually, Benedict was besieged and was imprisoned for some years, escaping in 1403. The following year his rival Boniface IX died, to be replaced by another Roman pope who took the name of Innocent VII and died after two years.

The next Roman pope came from the Venetian nobility and took the name Gregory XII. Again, this promised an end to the schism. Gregory contacted Benedict XIII, proclaiming that he was prepared to renounce his title, and arranging a meeting to negotiate the end of the schism. However, the intervention of several European rulers threatened violence and treachery and the negotiations came to nothing. Finally, some of the princes and some of the cardinals agreed that only a general council could resolve the schism. Under the authority of the cardinals, a council met at Pisa in 1409, both popes disassociating themselves from it, and each calling his own rival council. The Council of Pisa deposed both popes, declared the Holy See vacant, and supported the cardinals in their election of the humbly born but much traveled Greek Franciscan, Peter of Candia, archbishop of Milan, who took the name Alexander V.

Unfortunately, this did not resolve but rather aggravated the problem. Because supporters of Gregory and Benedict did not accept their deposition, there were now three rival popes. Battles were fought over the claims by armies of mercenaries. Alexander had taken up residence in Bologna, but entertained a delegation from Rome urging him to take up his see by residing there. He hesitated and some months later died, leaving the suspicion he had been poisoned.

When Alexander died so suddenly in 1410, the cardinals who had backed the Council of Pisa elected a Neapolitan who was frankly immoral, rapacious, and ambitious, had been an adventurer, not to say pirate, and had extensive military experience. He took the name John XXIII (not to be confused with the saintly twentieth-century pope who took that name). John returned to Rome briefly but had to flee again and, under political and military pressure, called a council to meet at Constance in 1414. John hoped this council would confirm the decisions taken at Pisa five years previously. That would have excluded his rivals and left him the rightful claimant. This did not happen. The council demanded the abdication of all three rival popes and, meeting resistance, declared a general council superior in authority to the pope. John was persuaded by various kinds of pressure to declare the Council of Constance infallible and to ratify its deposition of the popes.

A conclave, consisting of twenty-two cardinals and thirty representatives of the five nations which had engineered the Council of Constance, met in 1417 and elected a cardinal of the famous and prestigious Colonna family, who took the name Martin V. This successfully ended the schism because support for the other two rivals petered out quickly. The real grounds for the schism had been political and were resolved by diplomacy among the five nations. In retrospect, the papal line of succession is traced in this period through the "Roman" line that followed Urban VI, according to the official listing by the Catholic Church.

While ending the schism, however, the events of the Council of Constance and the subsequent conclave did not resolve the question whether a general council is superior in authority to the pope. Conciliarism, which claimed so, has continued to have a history in the Church, though disavowed frequently since.

MONIKA K. HELLWIG

See also AVIGNON PAPACY; ECUMENICAL COUNCILS; PAPACY, THE.

GRECO, EL (DOMENIKOS THEOTOKOPOULOS) (1541–1614)

A great master of the Spanish painting, though of Cretan origin and Italian training. Born in 1541, he was a man of wide culture, and was in demand as an architect and sculptor, though little survives of his work in these areas. Possibly trained in Byzantine icon painting (one specimen has been discovered), his work shows the influence of the Venetian painter Tintoretto and, according to tradition, of Titian himself. (Venice was a natural choice for El Greco, as the city then had the control of Crete.) He worked for a time in Rome and was influenced by the works of many Italian masters, including Michelangelo, though it is known that he was critical of the latter. He was in Toledo by 1577 and lived there for the rest of his life. While never enjoying imperial patronage, he was very popular among the clergy and religious orders for whom he produced many religious paintings (*Christ stripped of his Garments* is generally considered the greatest) as well as portraits. It was in Spain that he developed his unique style, and particularly his elongated figures, which express mystical feelings, if not ecstasies, of his own, as well as the intense religious emotion he encountered in his new country. The uniqueness of his work precluded his founding a school, and his work suffered from obscurity for two centuries after his death in 1614.

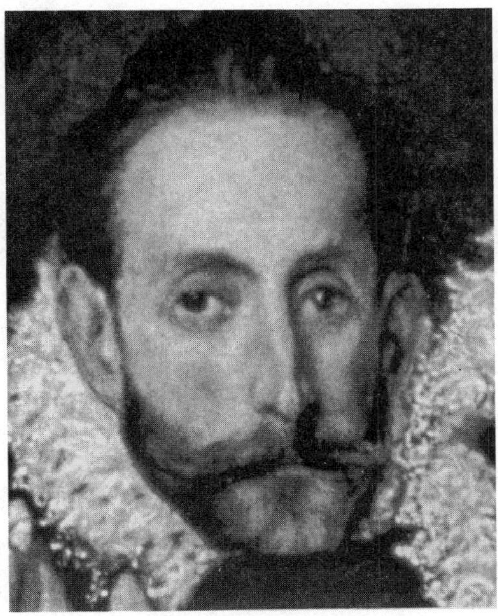

El Greco, self-portrait, detail of painting "The Burial of the Lord of Orgaz," 1586–1588

DAVID BRYAN

See also ART, CHRISTIAN; MICHELANGELO BUONARROTI; RENAISSANCE, THE.

GREEK CHURCH

See EASTERN CATHOLIC CHURCHES.

GREENE, (HENRY) GRAHAM (1904–1991)

Author (born in 1904), educated at Berkhamsted School, under the watchful eye of his father, the headmaster, and later at Oxford University—where he wrote his first published work, *Babbling April* (1925), a collection of verse. From 1926 to 1930, he was on the staff of *The Times,* a journalistic experience which tempered his literary style. He became a Catholic in 1926; married in 1927; and five years later published *Stamboul Train* (1932), the success of which led him to devote his life to writing.

Greene's novels established him as a literary giant. They have had a wide and ongoing influence, and Greene offers a hint to their unique play on salvation, damnation and grace with a quotation from *Bishop Blougram's Apology:* "Our interest's on the dangerous edge of things / The honest thief, the tender murderer, / The superstitious atheist. . . ."

His novels include: *England Made Me* (1935), *The Power and the Glory* (1940), *The Heart of the Matter* (1948), *The End of the Affair* (1951), *The Quiet American* (1955), *A Burnt-Out Case* (1961), *The Honorary Consul* (1973).

His writing has a taut and haunting approach, "the appalling strangeness of the mercy of God." He spent some years in the British secret service; and was an inveterate traveler. His first-hand experience of people and places gives an exceptional vitality to the work of this superb literary craftsman. He viewed some of his works as "entertainments," and these include *The Confidential Agent* (1939), *Loser Takes All* (1955), *Our Man in Havana* (1958), and *The Third Man* (1950), which was made into a memorable film by Carol Reed.

As a playwright, he is best remembered for *The Living Room* (1953), *The Potting Shed* (1957), and

Henry Graham Greene

The Complaisant Lover (1959). His autobiographical *A Sort of Life* (1971) and *Ways of Escape* (1980) give a variegated insight into one of the great writers of this century. He died in 1991.

JOSEPH QUINN

See also BRITAIN, CHURCH IN.

GREGORIAN CALENDAR

The name given to the calendar established by Pope Gregory XIII (1572–1585) in order to reform the Julian Calendar, imposed upon the Roman world by Julius Ceasar in 46 B.C. The Julian Calendar was based upon a solar year of 365.25 days with three years of 365 days and a fourth year having an extra day (Leap Year). Because the year is actually eleven minutes and fourteen seconds shorter than 365.25 days, there was a deviation of approximately three days every four centuries between the calendrical and astronomical times; by 1582 the deviation had grown to ten extra days. The Gregorian Calendar "fixed" this deviation by eliminating ten days in October; the night of 4 October led directly into the morning of 15 October. Further deviation from the solar year, which the papal astronomers now knew to be 365.2422 days, was accounted for by the provision of dropping three days from the calendar every 400 years. The pope enacted a decree stating that years ending in two zeroes would not be leap years unless the first two digits were divisible by four, for example, the year 2,000. Acceptance of the Gregorian Calendar was slow. France, the Netherlands, Poland, and the Catholic states of Germany adopted it within four years of its completion. By 1700 England and its colonies accepted the reform, albeit with some civil disturbances; Sweden held out to 1752 before accepting the new calendar. The Orthodox countries did not accept it until the twentieth century. By this time there was a discrepancy of thirteen days between the Gregorian and the Julian Calendar, which the Orthodox followed. The accuracy of the Gregorian Calendar is not perfect; changes in the length of the solar year and laws of physics account for some of its shortcomings. Ironically yet fittingly, only time will tell how long this new calendar will govern the world's measurement of time.

JOSEPH F. KELLY

See also JULIAN CALENDER; LITURGY.

GREGORIAN CHANT

Also called Plainsong or Plainchant, it is a plain, monodic, and purely vocal chant used in musical worship. In its modern form, it is printed in square notes on a four-line staff and its scales, known as modes, run from D, E, F, and G. It has no definite rhythm. Probably derived from chants sung in ancient Jerusalem or Antioch, it is recognized as the oldest chant still in use.

Some chants were compiled and arranged in the sixth century, and this is believed to be the work of Pope Gregory I (ca. 540–604), after whom the chant is named. Many, however, were composed in later centuries. Much credit for the revised present form is due to the Benedictine monks of Solesmes (in northwest France), who, in the latter half of the nineteenth century, began restoring the authentic texts. Since the introduction of the vernacular—

Page from a Lombard Graduale

effected by Vatican II—the use of the Gregorian chant has declined greatly. The majority of Gregorian chant music is gathered in two sources: the *Graduale* for the Mass, and the *Antiphonale* for the choir Offices. It has also been gathered in the *Liber Usualis*.

JOSEPH QUINN

See also LITURGY; MUSIC AND WORSHIP.

GREGORY VII, POPE (1073–1085)

Hildebrand was born of a poor Tuscan family and was schooled by the monks in Rome. Deciding to serve the Church, he held a number of high offices, became the mentor of several popes, and was given delicate missions up and down Europe. Chosen pope by acclamation, Gregory fearlessly undertook the reform of the Church. Among his chief targets were simony (the sale of Church appointments), violations of clerical celibacy, and lay investiture (appointment of bishops by lay rulers). In his contests with kings and princes, Gregory was fortified by his conviction that the pope has authority even over earthly rulers, and may even depose them if necessary, not to obtain political advantage over them, but to help insure the eternal salvation of king and subjects alike. Being in awe of none, Gregory met huge opposition in France, England, and, particularly, from the Germanies, led by King Henry IV. When the latter convened a synod which deposed the Pope, Gregory, nothing daunted, excommunicated Henry and released his subjects from their allegiance. Vulnerable in this situation, Henry proclaimed his conversion and went barefoot to Canossa to submit. Gregory, though very suspicious of Henry's repentance, at length felt his pastoral duty was to take Henry at his word. It was not long, however, before Henry was again trading in abbeys and bishoprics against his oath at Canossa. Within three years Gregory had determined that he must again excommunicate, and even depose, the king. Henry in turn deposed Gregory, arranged the election of antipope Clement III, and, four years later, invaded Rome. Although Gregory died a fugitive from Henry, his reforms, carried on by Urban II, did much to revive the Church. Feast day, 25 May.

DAVID BRYAN

See also CHURCH AND STATE; MIDDLE AGES, THE; PAPACY, THE.

GREGORY XVI, POPE (1831–1846)

Bartolomeo Alberto Cappellari, a lawyer's son, entered a Camaldolese monastery at eighteen. After ordination, he became a professor of science and philosophy. He was made an abbot in 1805 and, in 1807, procurator-general of the Camaldolese. While a professor, he was also a consultant to several congregations, sat on committees to examine prospective bishops, and was vicar general of the Camaldolese. He was made a cardinal and Prefect of the Propaganda in 1826, becoming active in the fostering of the Catholic missions. Both Leo XII and Pius VIII made use of his talents in particular matters and he was elected pope in 1830.

The new Pope was a strict monk and a scholar suspicious of modern political trends and of the effects of technology (he banned railroads in the Papal States). In matters of doctrine, he rebuked the premature attempts of Lamennais, a Catholic liberal, to reconcile Catholicism to the spirit of the French Revolution. His relations with various nations were generally strained, as he denounced anticlericalism in Spain and Portugal, revolutionary fervor in Poland, antipapal laws in Switzerland, the persecution of Catholics in Russia, and Prussian interference with Catholic marriages.

Gregory reorganized the hierarchy and attempted to reinvigorate the practice of religious vows. As former Prefect of Propaganda, he had great interest in the missions, creating many missionary dioceses and vicariates under Roman control. In Rome itself, he built museums (Etruscan, Egyptian, Christian antiquity) and generally supported the arts and sciences.

Decades of poor management of the Papal States led to rebellions which began immediately upon Gregory's election and ran intermittently throughout his pontificate. Conditions in the Pope's domains were such as to require the intervention first of Austria, then of France. The cost was high: The admission that the Papal States needed foreign peacekeepers was very damaging, and the financial burden was heavy. While Gregory used his energy to denounce the specious philosophy of the French and subsequent revolutions, his subjects looked enviously at the better management that such revolutions seemed to produce. And, on Gregory's death, it became clear how far the financial affairs of the Church itself had been mismanaged. The stage was now set for the total loss of the Papal States (1870) to the revolutionary movement in Italy.

DAVID BRYAN

See also CHURCH AND STATE; PAPACY, THE.

GREGORY OF NAZIANZUS, ST. (ca. 330–ca. 390)

Known in the East as Gregory the Theologian. His parents (Gregory of Nazianzus the Elder and Nonna) and sister and brother (Gorgonia and Caesarius) are honored as saints today. Gregory was born at Arianzum not far from Nazianzus in Cappadocia. He met Basil of Caesarea when they both were students of rhetoric in Caesarea in Cappadocia. Gregory later studied in Caesarea in Palestine and Alexandria. When he went to Athens to complete his studies, he renewed his friendship with Basil who was also studying there. After baptism in 358 Gregory spent some time with Basil at the monastic community Basil had established on the river Iris in Pontus when they collaborated on the *Philocalia,* an anthology of Origen's works. Gregory reluctantly agreed to be ordained to the priesthood ca. 362 by his father, then serving as bishop of Nazianzus, who wanted his help for the pastoral care of the diocese. After ordination Gregory fled from Nazianzus, but soon returned to assist his father. In 372 Basil, as metropolitan of Caesarea, ordained him as bishop of Sasima, as part of his strategy to outmaneuver Anthimus, the Arian bishop of Tyana. Gregory accepted episcopal consecration with great reluctance and never went to his episcopal see. Instead he stayed and helped his father at Nazianzus until the elder Gregory died in 374. Soon after that he went to Seleucia in Isauria to begin a life of contemplation. In 379 the small Nicene party in Constantinople begged Gregory to come to the capital to reorganize the Church there. Gregory resided in the house of a relative which he consecrated as the Church of the Anastasis. By his many eloquent sermons delivered over the next two years he advanced the cause of the Nicene faith in the capital and prepared the way for the triumph of the Nicene position at the Second Council of Constantinople in 381. Because certain bishops at the Council of Constantinople objected that his appointment as patriarch of Constantinople did not follow regular canonical procedure, he resigned before the year was over. He returned to Nazianzus and then to the family estate at Arianzum where he died. Gregory's writings consist of *Orations, Poems,* and *Letters.* Gregory delivered five of his *Orations* (27-31: known as *The Five Theological Orations*) in Constantinople in the summer of 380. In them he discussed the attributes of God, the unity of nature in the three divine Persons, the divinity of the Son, and the divinity of the Holy Spirit. *Oration* 2 (entitled *In Defence of His Flight to Pontus*) served as a model for John Chrysostom's *Six Books on the Priesthood* and Gregory the Great's *Pastoral Rule.* He composed his poetry (about 400 poems) near the end of his life at Arianzum. Three of his Letters (101, 102, and 202: known as the *Theological Letters*) are important pieces against Apollinarianism. Gregory was named a Doctor of the Church along with Athanasius, Basil the Great, and John Chrysostom by Pius V in 1568. Feast day, 25 January and 30 January (East); 2 January (West).

JOHN DILLON

See also DOCTORS OF THE CHURCH; FATHERS OF THE CHURCH; TRINITY.

GREGORY OF NYSSA, ST. (ca. 335/40–ca. 395)

Gregory was born into a devout and distinguished Christian family. He was educated to a large extent by his elder brother Basil (the Great). After being a lector in the Church, Gregory married and became a rhetor. In 371 Basil ordained him as the bishop of Nyssa. Basil became disappointed in Gregory's performance as bishop: he sometimes lacked tact in dealing with people; other times he was not firm when firmness was required; on other occasions he was careless about financial matters or inept in dealing with ecclesiastical politics. This gave his enemies the opportunity to depose him from his see for two years on the false charge of misusing Church funds. After Basil's death in 379, Gregory became prominent in the struggle against Arianism. In 380 he traveled to Sebaste (modern-day Sivas, Turkey) to supervise the election of a new bishop and found himself elected to that post which he held for a short time. Later his youngest brother Peter became bishop of Sebaste. Gregory took a prominent part in the Second General Council of Constantinople in 381. He attended a synod on Constantinople in 383 and preached the funeral orations of the Princess Pulcheria and the Empress Flacilla there in 385. By the time of his death which occurred shortly after he participated in a synod in Constantinople in 394, he was an important and revered figure in the Eastern Church. Gregory was a profound and original thinker whose knowledge of Middle Platonism and Neoplatonism helped him in expressing authentically Christian theological and mystical concepts. His major dogmatic works include *Against Eunomius,* the *Antirrhetic against Apollinaris,* the treatise *That There Are Not Three Gods* addressed to Ablabius, and the *Great Catechism* (a comprehensive presentation of the principal Christian doctrines for catechists). His exegetical works include the *Life of Moses, On the Witch of Endor, On the Lord's Prayer, On the Beatitudes,* as well as homilies on Ecclesiastes and the Song of Songs. Among his ascetical works are *On Virginity* and the *Life of Macrina.* Many of Gregory's orations, sermons, and letters survive as well. Feast day, 9 March.

JOHN DILLON

See also FATHERS OF THE CHURCH; MYSTICISM.

GREGORY THE GREAT, ST. (ca. 540–604)

A member of a wealthy aristocratic family which already counted two popes: Felix III and Agapetus I, Gregory was the son of a senator. Gregory received an excellent education and entered into public service: ca. 572 to 574 he was prefect of Rome. When his father Gordianus died, Gregory sold his property and gave the money to the poor. He also established six monasteries in Sicily and one in Rome (St. Andrew on the Caelian Hill). He entered the latter as a monk in 574/575. He was not destined, however, to remain in monastic seclusion. He was ordained a deacon by Benedict I or Pelagius II and sent by Pelagius II in 579 as *apocrisiarius* (ecclesiastical deputy) to Constantinople where he stayed until 585 or 586. He was not able to obtain much relief from the imperial court for Rome and Italy which had been plagued for years by invasions from the Lombards. Upon his return to Rome, Gregory resided once again at his monastery but continued to advise Pelagius II on important ecclesiastical matters. In 590 he was elected to succeed Pelagius II as bishop of Rome. Although he had been reluctant to accept the papacy, he responded firmly and decisively to the problems at hand. Because the emperor's representative offered little help when the Lombards were threatening Rome in 592 to 593, Gregory himself negotiated peace terms with the latter. By default he became civil ruler of Italy: appointing governors, raising armies, negotiating treaties. Gregory also reorganized the vast papal estates by appointing overseers who were directly accountable to him. His administrative actions enabled him to provide relief for those who were starving. All of these measures mark the beginnings of the papal state. Gregory also exercised an effective oversight of the Church in the West with northern Italy, Spain, and Gaul particularly benefitting from his actions. Gregory was also concerned for the conversion of England, and so he arranged for Augustine, prior of the monastery of St. Andrew on the Caelian Hill, along with forty other monks, to sail to England in 596. Five years later Melitius and Paulinus brought additional missionaries. In his relations with the imperial court at Constantinople, Gregory often had to yield to the emperor in matters of Church policy, but he successfully maintained the primacy of the Roman see. He objected strongly to the title Ecumenical Patriarch for the archbishop of Constantinople.

Gregory, the first monk to become pope, favored monasticism and granted specific privileges to monks that freed them to a certain extent from jurisdiction by local bishops. He was a prolific writer and his writings reflect his study and synthesis of St. Augustine of Hippo adapted to the needs of his audience. His correspondence during his pontificate numbers more than 850 letters which address a wide variety of topics. Gregory wrote in 591 *Pastoral Care* which sets out his thoughts about a bishop being a shepherd of souls. It was regarded as a handbook for bishops in the Middle Ages. Gregory's *Dialogues* (ca. 593) which set forth the life of St. Benedict and other Italian saints reflect the credulity of the times. Gregory commented on the Scripture before and during his time as bishop of Rome. Surviving exegetical works by Gregory include *Homilies on the Gospels* (590–591), *Homilies on Ezekiel* (593), *Homilies on the Song of Songs* and part of a *Commentary on 1 Samuel.* Gregory began while in Constantinople and finished in 595 the *Moralia,* a commentary on Job in the literal, mystical or allegorical, and moral sense which became a standard work on moral and ascetical theology in the Middle Ages. All during his pontificate Gregory suffered from ill health, and at the end of his life he was not able to walk. Viewed as a saint immediately after his death, Gregory was proclaimed a Doctor of the Church (along with Ambrose, Jerome, and Augustine) by Boniface VIII in 1295. Feast day, 3 September.

JOHN DILLON

See also DOCTORS OF THE CHURCH; FATHERS OF THE CHURCH; PAPACY, THE.

GRIEF

Just like contemporary Middle Easterners so too our ancestors in the faith were not psychologically-minded but positively anti-introspective. Certainly they were aware of internal emotions and experiences but believed that these were entirely inaccessible to human scrutiny. "The Lord does not see as mortals see; they look upon the *outward appearance,* but the Lord looks upon the heart" (1 Sam 16:7).

Biblical Roots

Our biblical ancestors experienced grief, the human emotional response to loss or disappointment but in a very different way than we, their Western descendants. When the Lord struck the child conceived in David and Bathsheba's adultery, David prayed, fasted, and lay prostrate on the bare earth day and night on behalf of the child.

After a week, the child died. David rose, washed and anointed himself, and changed his clothes. Then he went to worship in the house of the Lord and returned home to eat. To his bewildered servants and attendants he explained that while the child lived, God might have spared him. But now that the child is dead, of what use is grief (fasting) in moving God?

"Can I bring him back again? I shall go to him, but he will not return to me" (2 Sam 12:22).

Two Middle Eastern cultural peculiarities should be noted. One, grief is a publicly demonstrated emotion deliberately intended to engage or affect others. Our ancestors were strongly group-oriented. Two, this culture was and is intensely present-oriented; it is unable and unwilling to think about the future. When the present cause or reason for grief is ended, so too is the emotion.

Catholic Practice

Since the Enlightenment, Western believers have become very individualistic and very introspective. For contemporary Catholics, the behavioral sciences such as psychology and counseling have assumed central importance in belief and practice. These are undeniable gifts from God, but modern Catholics should resist trying to analyze our long-deceased, non-introspective ancestors in the faith, to guess their Myers-Briggs Type or their Enneagram number.

Contemporary believers in the United States do best to follow the advice of Paul to first-century Christians in Thessalonika who were grieved because relatives and friends were dying before the imminently expected return of the Lord. "We do not want you to grieve like others who have no confidence [hope]" (1 Thess 4:13).

Grief: The Western Process

Because Western culture has an exceptional capability for introspection and a refined sense of the future dragging behind it a fleeting sense of the present (witness our digital calculation of time in nanoseconds), it has analyzed the human emotion of grief as a process.

C. Murray Parkes proposed one very useful description of the stages in the process of grief. These stages should not be sharply distinguished from each other. They frequently overlap, especially as a person is in transition from one stage to another.

Given Western culture's emphasis on individuality and distinctiveness, certain aspects of these stages differ from person to person. Still, it is possible to identify and name four stages in the process.

Numbness and Denial. The first and common response is shock and denial. A person refuses to believe the tremendous and tragic loss that has just occurred. The loss seems to drain the person of all sensation. This stage may last for five to seven days.

Yearning. As wave after wave of emotion follows upon the experience of loss, the mind unconsciously tries to recapture the loss. The deceased, the destroyed home, the broken marriage relationship—these cannot be lost! There is an intense longing and yearning for what has been lost.

Confusion sets in, and many physiological symptoms may emerge. This stage may last a few weeks, perhaps even longer.

Disorganization and Despair. At this point, a grieving person will frequently resume functioning rather well, but complete honesty will reveal an underlying sense of aimlessness and loss of future orientation. This stage can extend from a few months to a year or more.

Reorganization of Behavior, "Back to Normal." When a personal sense of optimistic planning for the future returns, a Western believer knows that the condition has returned to normalcy. Even so, the healed person may suffer "anniversary reactions" or occasional pangs of loss stirred by a photo, or something else.

Experts agree that for believers, theological or spiritual maxims which may sound trite and useless in the depths of grief, are nevertheless the sure foundation of confidence. God does care and has a reason which "reason may not know."

JOHN J. PILCH

See also DEATH.

GUADALUPE

On 9 December 1531 a Mexican peasant, Juan Diego, on his way by Tepeyac, a hill outside the city of Mexico, saw a beautiful lady who told him that she was the Virgin Mary, Mother of God. She told him to bear a message to the bishop of the diocese, requesting to have a church built in her honor. The bishop, Msgr. Zumarraga, a Franciscan, was perplexed, even after a second vision in which the request was repeated. He asked the visionary to seek a sign which would convince him. The sign which Our Lady gave Juan Diego when he next saw her was flowers, including Castilian roses blooming on stony ground in mid-winter. Juan Diego wrapped them in his cloak made of woven cactus grass. The day was 12 December. He went to the bishop's home and opened his cloak and the flowers fell to the ground. The bishop and those with him then saw on the cloak the image of a young girl, surrounded by rays of light. This is Our Lady of Guadalupe, venerated for centuries, center of unparalleled interest, curiosity and piety.

The image has been publicly exposed, as have few similar religious objects, in churches first built in modest proportions, eventually in a basilica, and later in a large modern church.

Our Lady of Guadalupe

The effects of the Guadalupe event have been vast and varied. It began the conversion of the Mexican Aztecs. Within two generations eight million were converted to Christianity.

Scientific experts from MIT have brought optometry to bear on the image, disclosing in the eyes reflections of those present when it was first seen. The fabric also survived a terrorist bomb blast from a few feet away, which shattered every window in the basilica. Also, it should have disintegrated into dust, as all woven grass does, many years ago.

MICHAEL O'CARROLL, C.S.Sp.

See also DEVOTIONS; MARY, MOTHER OF GOD.

GUARDIAN ANGELS

See ANGELS.

GUARDINI, ROMANO (1885–1968)

Philosopher of religion, pioneer in the liturgical movement, priest, he was born in Verona, on 17 February 1885. At the age of one he emigrated with his family to Germany. While studying at the University of Tübingen, he first developed his love for the liturgy after experiencing the liturgical celebrations at the Benedictine abbey of Beuron. Despite parental opposition, Guardini decided to enter the priesthood and was ordained in May, 1910. After a brief stint as a parish priest, he continued his studies at Freiburg, and he began teaching at Bonn in 1920 and then at Berlin (1923–1939) where he held the chair of "professor of philosophy of religion and Catholic world-view." After the war he taught briefly at Tübingen and then at Munich (1948–1963).

While a parish priest, Guardini began to question antiquated liturgical practices and to see the importance of preaching in the public worship of the Church. In 1915 he began working at a youth center at Burg Rothenfels on the Main River where he influenced thousands of young people, inculcating in them a love for the liturgy, and the spiritual life, and academic excellence. Here he began to implement liturgical changes by moving the altar away from the wall, seating people around it on three sides, and making frequent use of the *missa cantata.* During this time he began visiting the Benedictines at Maria Laach, was influenced by their liturgies and began working with Dom Odo Casel. In 1939 the Nazis closed the youth center and removed him from his teaching position at Berlin.

Guardini was a leader in the renewal in Catholicism and the liturgical movement between the two wars, and he wrote *The Spirit of the Liturgy* (1918) to stir up a liturgical spirituality in people. As a university professor of philosophy he tried to show the relevance of the Christian faith to the realities of the modern world. Though he was not a systematic theologian, writings like *The Church and the Catholic* (1922) helped to influence the theology of Josef Jungmann and Karl Adam. Guardini is especially remembered for *The Lord* (1937), his life of Christ, although he also wrote on education, art, literature, and meditation.

Plagued with scruples as a youth, Guardini suffered from poor health and severe bouts with depression throughout his life. Though never encouraged by the hierarchy, his thought and work anticipated much of the teaching of Vatican Council II (1962–1965). He died in Munich on 1 October 1968.

ANTHONY D. ANDREASSI

See also LITURGICAL MOVEMENT, THE.

GUILT

Guilt is a focus of concern both in theology and psychology. In theology guilt is seen as rooted in some violation of a person's relation to God. Such guilt may generate guilt feelings which may be an appropriate response to the perceived violation. Psychology has given primary attention to guilt feelings which are at times inappropriate or disproportionate responses and not necessarily related to any wrongdoing.

Theologically guilt is a free decision to evil. To feel guilty in a theological sense is to find oneself feeling personally responsible before God and others for the evil which was intended or has been done out of one's freedom. Conditions for real, theological guilt include knowledge and freedom. To the extent that knowledge is lacking or freedom is in some way impaired, guilt is lessened. Theological guilt can be further seen as having both an inward element and a social element. The inward element has to do with the awareness that an individual has of personal wrongdoing. Psychology is helpful in sorting out unauthentic guilt feelings from a true consciousness of guilt. Often in a given instance there is a mixture of both authentic and unauthentic guilt. The social element of guilt pertains to the consequences which result from someone having posited the evil act. Here it is common to speak of juridical guilt which implies there is a penalty to be paid or compensation to be made. Juridical guilt may remain after the wrongdoer has dealt with the inward element through a process of repentance.

Guilt as a psychological reality has been discussed by Freud and a host of other psychologists. Freud saw guilt feelings as arising when there was tension between a strict superego, the internalized authority of parents and other significant figures, and the ego, the executive agency of the personality. The sources of such guilt were the dread of authority and more specifically a fear of the loss of love of those on whom one depends.

According to Melanie Klein's formulations, the life of every infant is replete with both gratifications and frustrations. The normal infant responds to frustrations with a desire for retaliation; in other words, he or she would like to respond to the sources of frustration by punishing the inflicting party. The infant is here struggling with the raw emotions of love and hate and will only gradually learn to mitigate the hate with more powerful feelings of love. Infants project their own aggressive feelings onto others and consequently begin to fear they will be treated in the same punishing way they wish for others. In the course of infant development, the child senses that the "good mother" who provides food and the "bad mother" who frustrates the child's desire for immediate satisfaction are one and the same person. The child begins to sense its mother is a whole person in which it finds both good and bad. It senses, too, that the very one on whom its well-being depends is the same one whom it has wished to destroy. The child would have liked to have taken this food-provider into itself and so avoid frustration. But now the child begins to feel concern for the mother and goes through a period of anxiety related to the feeling of almost having lost or destroyed the mother on whom it depends. An experience of guilt over such possible damage signals the ability to tolerate the ambivalence of conflicted feelings of love and hate directed to the same object. This guilt is dealt with through reparation and various restitutive gestures.

In sorting out guilt which has more a psychological origin from guilt in the strict theological sense, it is helpful as Glaser has suggested to distinguish between the conscience and the superego. Conscience, in psychoanalytic terms, is seen as an ego function which is acquired through healthy appropriation of the values and norms of the society of which the individual is a part. As such, it intends to invite a person to love rather than to command a person to observe some rule. It is other-directed, value oriented, and dynamic in the sense that it looks at the nuances of a particular situation. The experience of guilt which conscience engenders is proportionate to the value at stake.

In contrast, superego is a more primitive agency which censors behavior in terms of past commands. It tends to induce guilt which is often disproportionate to the value at stake. It is more static and does not pay attention to the nuances of situations. It simply enforces past commands of authorities in a blind fashion.

In the average individual guilt is an ambiguous experience inasmuch as it can respond to a genuine violation of a value or norm as well as to commands internalized during childhood development and still operative in the dynamic unconscious. As Rahner has correctly pointed out, guilt is truly a borderland between theology and psychotherapy, an area where both ministers and psychotherapists may have vital roles to play.

RAYMOND STUDZINSKI, O.S.B.

See also SIN; THEOLOGY, MORAL.

GUTENBERG BIBLE

This forty-two-line Latin Bible was printed in Mainz between 1452 and 1456. It was the foremost achievement of Johann Gensfleisch zum Gutenberg (ca. 1399–1468), a Mainz goldsmith, who is generally (but inaccurately) regarded as the inventor of printing. In fact, at that time printing from wooden blocks had been practiced by the Chinese for over a thousand years. Gutenberg's distinctive contribution was the invention and manufacture of movable types for each letter of the alphabet, types which could be locked together to produce a printed page, and could then be broken up and used again. A crucial element in Gutenberg's success was also the invention of ink that would adhere to the metal types. In the opinion of H. S. Steinberg, "it is no exaggeration to describe Gutenberg's invention as Germany's most important single contribution to civilization."

Thanks to Gutenberg's invention, it now became possible and financially practical to edit and correct a text and then to produce thousands of identical copies of the same work. Once the principle of mass production became established, other applications eventually followed such as the publication of mass-circulation daily newspapers. "Thus," says Steinberg, "Gutenberg can also be acclaimed as the progenitor of the periodical press."

ANTHONY D. ANDREASSI

See also BIBLE, ENGLISH VERSIONS OF THE; MIDDLE AGES, THE.

H

HABIT

Habit is an internal quality of a person that develops through repeated actions. Many human physical activities such as speaking are habits; however, habit has a specific meaning in theology. Aristotle in his *Nichomachean Ethics* writes on the nature of habits and describes how both good and bad habits are formed. Aquinas took Aristotle's analysis and used it to describe habitual virtues in Christian morality. The Christian who repeatedly performs a certain "good" act will build up a "habit" within the self. Thus, one will begin to act almost spontaneously in doing this virtuous action. One will have little trouble in repeating this virtuous act after it has become habitual. This type of habit is "acquired" in that the person must perform this virtuous action many times before it becomes habitual. It requires a positive act of the will. Acquired habits are to be distinguished from "infused" habits, the habits formed in the person by grace, namely, the theological virtues of faith, hope, and love.

ANTHONY D. ANDREASSI

See also VIRTUE.

HABIT, RELIGIOUS

The common, nonliturgical attire of members of religious orders—normally comprised of a tunic, belt or girdle, scapular, hood for men and veil for women, and a mantle. Traditionally worn by monks, friars, and nuns, habits vary in type among orders (some orders no longer require them, while others have modified theirs), and are either white, black, or brown in color.

JOSEPH QUINN

See also RELIGIOUS ORDERS.

HAGIOGRAPHY

This derives from two Greek words, *hagios* (holy) and *graphe* (writing) and recounts the lives of holy people, that is, the saints. It began in the second century with the *Martyrdom of Polycarp,* an Asian bishop of Smyrna martyred ca. 156; a Christian witness wrote an account of his death. Even this early work shows what became traditional literary devices, stressing the parallels between Polycarp's death and that of Jesus. As the number of martyrs began to mount, a specific type of hagiography, the *acta martyrum* (acts of the martyrs) became increasingly popular, emphasizing the affective element; that is, the reader should be moved to imitate the saint. When the persecutions ended, the monks replaced the martyrs as the most revered of Christians, and the fourth century saw the composition of the two most influential hagiographies, the *Life of Saint Antony* by Athanasius, dealing largely with the saint's thaumaturgical abilities and his struggle with the devil, and the *Life of Martin of Tours* by Sulpicius Severus [amazingly written (395) before Martin had died (397)], a brilliant propaganda piece which popularized monasticism in the West. Many medieval hagiographers followed these leads but concentrated upon the miraculous. Historians must discount the biographical value of these works, but they do provide an insight into medieval piety, since saints often stood between the common people and their oppressors, both human and demonic. When the Protestant Reformers attacked the cult of the saints as nonbiblical and superstitious, the Jesuit Jean Bolland (1596–1665), embarrassed by the deplorable state of hagiography, reformed the discipline, founding a society (now called the Bollandists) to produce critical editions of the lives of the saints and to distinguish between authentic and inauthentic biographical elements. The Bollandists' multivolume *Acta Sanctorum* contains the lives of the saints and their periodical (from 1882) contains learned articles on hagiography. In general, modern hagiography follows the conventual scholarly methods for writing biographies.

JOSEPH F. KELLY

See also SAINTS.

"HAIL MARY"

The best known intercessory prayer in Catholicism, the Hail Mary begins with the angel's salutation of Mary (Luke 1:28), and adds Elizabeth's blessing (Luke 1:42). A litany-response, expanding on the usual "pray for us," was added in the late Middle Ages, reaching its present form in the sixteenth century. The Hail Mary is the characteristic prayer of the rosary and of the Angelus, and enjoys many other privileged positions in public and private prayer.

Though addressed to Mary, the Hail Mary is Christ-centered. Not only does the prayer explicitly bless "the fruit of thy womb, Jesus," but the prior phrase, "Blessed art thou among women," is a Jewish birth-blessing meant to praise the mother for the child. Additionally, the words "Hail . . . full of grace," have echoes of Spirit theology, while the final petition implies ongoing prayer to the Father. Hence the Hail Mary is a participation in the mystery of the Trinity.

The Greek expressions translated "Hail . . . full of grace" are rich in allusions to Mary's spiritual joy and repeated divine favor. "Mother of God," from the third section, is the equivalent of the Greek *Theotokos* (God-bearer) which became popular as a result of the councils of the fourth and fifth centuries which upheld the human and divine natures of Christ.

Hail, Mary, full of grace,
the Lord is with thee.
Blessed art thou among women
and blessed is the fruit of thy womb, Jesus.
Holy Mary, Mother of God,
pray for us sinners, now and at the hour of our death. Amen.

DAVID BRYAN

HALLINAN, PAUL J. (1911–1968)

First archbishop of Atlanta (1962–1968), Hallinan was born in Painesville, Ohio, on 8 April 1911 and died in Atlanta on 27 March 1968. A graduate of the University of Notre Dame and of St. Mary's Seminary in Cleveland, he was ordained a priest of the Diocese of Cleveland on 20 February 1937. After five years as a curate at St. Aloysius parish in Cleveland (where he excelled in youth work), Hallinan volunteered as an army chaplain in 1942, spending the next two-and-a-half years in the South Pacific.

Upon his return to Cleveland in 1946, he began a long association with the Newman Apostolate among Catholic university and college students, first as part-time chaplain at Cleveland College, then from 1947 to 1958 as director of Newman Hall at Western Reserve University. He also became active in Newman work on the national level, from 1952 to 1954 serving as national chaplain of the National Newman Club Federation and as president of the chaplains' association.

On 28 October 1958 (the day that Angelo Cardinal Roncalli was elected pope), Hallinan was ordained bishop of Charleston, South Carolina, a diocese where Catholics numbered a mere 30,000 in

Archbishop Paul J. Hallinan

a general population of 2,370,000. Anti-Catholic bigotry was still a potent force in the state as Hallinan discovered during the presidential campaign of John F. Kennedy in 1960. A more pressing issue, however, and the cutting edge of the civil rights movement at the time, was school integration. In a pastoral letter in February 1961 (issued together with the bishops of Savannah and Atlanta), Hallinan promised to integrate Catholic schools "no later" than the public schools. It was a prudent decision which won the approval of Southern moderates like newspaper editor Ralph McGill.

When the Diocese of Atlanta was raised to the status of a metropolitan see in 1962, Hallinan was selected to be the first archbishop. Like Charleston, the new archdiocese contained only a minuscule Catholic population, 33,000 Catholics in a general population of 2,150,000, with half of the twenty-nine parishes concentrated in Atlanta and its suburbs. From the day of his installation, 29 March 1962, Hallinan was an activist archbishop, involving himself in community affairs, supporting moderate civil rights leaders (such as Dr. Martin Luther King Jr.), integrating Catholic schools and hospitals, and establishing an excellent rapport with Protestants and Jews. He also managed to find the time to complete his doctoral dissertation and to receive a Ph.D. degree in history from Western Reserve University in 1963.

The Second Vatican Council proved to be a great learning experience for Hallinan as it was for many United States bishops. The only American prelate elected to the conciliar liturgical commission, Hallinan relied heavily upon Monsignor Frederick R. McManus for advice, and he strongly supported the progressive features in the proposed schema of the Constitution on the Sacred Liturgy. Endorsing the use of the vernacular at Mass, Hallinan said: "The liturgy of the Church must be public, but this can have real meaning for our people only if they can understand enough of it to be part of it." After the promulgation of the liturgical constitution in December 1963, Hallinan told the people of his archdiocese: "Gradually we will all come to wonder how we really worshipped God in any other way."

On 17 October 1963 at the English College in Rome, Hallinan took part in a meeting of representatives from various English-speaking countries to discuss the possibility of common liturgical texts. It was an historic occasion, which would later give rise to the formation of ICEL, the International Commission on English in the Liturgy. In later sessions of the council, Hallinan spoke in favor of the Declaration on Religious Freedom, and he submitted written interventions asking for a more explicit condemnation of racial discrimination and for an enhanced role for women in the Church, including the right of women to act as deacons.

Early in 1964 Hallinan suffered a severe attack of hepatitis from which he never really recovered. Despite his weakened condition, he spent the last four years of his life trying to promote what he called "the vital center" in an increasingly polarized Church and country. As chairman of the Bishops' Committee on the Liturgy he fought extremists on both the left and the right as he sought to implement the conciliar reforms in the United States. He took the same stance with regard to the civil rights movement, supporting the Selma march of 1965 but denouncing Black Power advocates of violence.

For Hallinan as for many Americans in the 1960s the most difficult issue was the Vietnam War. Together with his auxiliary bishop, Joseph Bernardin (who actually wrote the text), in October 1966 Hallinan issued a pastoral letter on the war, offering a qualified endorsement for American intervention in Vietnam but warning that "a Christian simply cannot approve indiscriminate bombing, methodical extermination of people, nuclear arms designed for 'overkill' or disregard for non-combatants."

After January 1968 Hallinan's health deteriorated rapidly, and he died three months later at the age of fifty-seven. If he had lived longer, under Pope Paul VI he might reasonably have expected promotion to a more important see with the possibility of becoming one of the most influential figures in the American hierarchy. As it was, during his nine-and-a-half years in Charleston and Atlanta, he helped to hold American Catholics together and to pull them through a period of bewildering changes in both Church and society.

THOMAS J. SHELLEY

See also AMERICAN CATHOLICISM; VATICAN COUNCIL II.

HANUKKAH

Hanukkah or the feast of the Dedication derives from the purification of the Temple by Judas Maccabeus on the twenty-fifth Kislev (early December) in 164 B.C. Three years earlier by way of championing Hellenism versus the sectarian ethos of the Jews, the Seleucid king Antiochus IV Epiphanes had sacrificed to Zeus Olympios within the Temple.

Like the feast of Tabernacles (*sukkōth*), Hanukkah is prolonged eight days and characterized by rejoicing. The synagogue service includes the chanting of Psalm 30 and the Hallel (Pss 113–118) and the reading of Numbers 7:1–8:4 on the dedication of the altar in the wilderness. But the most dramatic feature of Hanukkah is the lighting of the candles or lamps, one for each day of the feast. 2 Maccabees alludes to the lighting of the lamps within the Temple at its purification by Judas Maccabeus (2 Macc 10:3). The Mishnah urges that lamps be lit at the front of each house.

To the Jewish historian Josephus, Hanukkah was the festival of light (*Ant.* 12:323-325). The sudden liberation of the Jewish religion was like a light appearing amidst the darkness of despair. After Mattathias, Judas Maccabeus had led the campaign. In swift succession he defeated the generals of Antiochus and then purified the Temple. Thus even after the later destruction of the Temple Hanukkah could and did endure, a symbol of Jewish courage.

In the New Testament Jesus is said to have preached in the Temple at the feast of the Dedication (John 10:22). To the evangelist the allusion was appropriate. For according to the Fourth Gospel Jesus is the new Temple (John 2:19-21) whom the Father consecrates (John 10:36).

THOMAS BUCKLEY

HAYES, HELEN (1900–1993)

Helen Hayes won a special place in the heart of America, and when she died on St. Patrick's Day 1993 a sense of loss and sadness befell the land. She won Emmy, Tony, and other awards for her theatrical performances; and she won two Oscars. Universities vied to honor her; and President Reagan gave her the nation's highest civilian award, the Presidential Medal of Freedom. This graceful lady with the winsome smile had a theater named for her, and a pink rose was called the Helen Hayes. She was aptly called The First Lady of the American Theater.

Helen Hayes was born in 1900 in Washington, D.C., the only child of a poultry and pork salesman, Francis Van Arnum Brown and Catherine Estelle Hayes, a disappointed actress and the great-niece of the Irish singer, Catherine Hayes. As a child, Helen showed an unusual interest in acting and her mother took in washing to get her a good education. She graduated from the Sacred Heart Academy in Washington and went on at the age of twenty to star on Broadway in the mediocre play, *Bab.* For the next sixty years, Helen Hayes became an essential part of the New York theater; among her memorable triumphs were *Mary of Scotland* (1933); *Victoria Regina* (1935); *Harriet* (1943); *The Glass Menagerie* (1948, 1956, 1961); *A Touch of the Poet* (1958); and *Harvey* (1970).

Helen Hayes was a woman of the theater and she disliked Hollywood. Though she was awarded Oscars for her performances in *The Sin of Madelon Claudet* and *Airport,* she turned down countless film offers. She also curtailed her work on television despite her applauded success in *The Snoop Sisters* (1972); *Murder is Easy* (1983); and *Murder With Mirrors* (1985). She performed comedy, mystery, and drama with warmhearted grace. In 1979 Notre Dame University awarded her the Laetare Medal for her many contributions to Catholic culture.

She married playwright and humorist Charles McArthur; and Mary, their only child, was born in 1930. Their happy marriage was darkened when Mary, a novice actress of nineteen, died of polio in 1949. Charles McArthur buried his grief in drink and died an alcoholic seven years later. She tells the harrowing story in her best-selling autobiography *My Life in Three Acts* (1990). Helen Hayes brought grace and greatness to the American theater, and she is an American legend.

JOAN GLAZIER

HEALING

According to one's viewpoint, modern Western believers are blessed or cursed with a knowledge of science. Those who view science as a blessing use it for understanding faith. Those who view science as a curse believe that it destroys "blind" faith which alone suffices.

The science of medical anthropology identifies *sickness* as a human reality which can be viewed in two ways. Sickness viewed as *disease* is an abnormality in the structure or function of human organ systems. Sickness viewed as *illness* is the uniquely personal perception, experience, and interpretation of socially disvalued states including but not limited to disease. In general, health professionals tend to see "diseases" while ordinary lay people tend to see "illnesses."

A therapist who takes effective control of disordered biological and psychological processes by means of surgery, medications, or other strategies is said to *cure* disease. In contrast, a therapist who provides personal and social meaning for the life problems created by sickness is said to *heal* illness. Medical anthropologists note that cure is rather rare, but healing takes place always, infallibly, 100 percent of the time. These scientific distinctions help a modern Western believer to understand Catholic practice.

Sacraments of Healing

Following the opinion of St. Bonaventure, many scholars believe that all the sacraments—not just anointing of the sick—have healing and life-giving power. In the sacraments, Christ gives power to regenerate, to confirm, to forgive, to nourish, to sanctify human love, to ordain for sanctification, to restore to physical well-being or at the very least to relieve and comfort the dying.

Electing to ignore the distinctions of medical anthropology and the insights of contemporary sacramental theology, some theologians turn intellectual somersaults to avoid stating that sick people are "infallibly healed" and sometimes "truly cured" in a scientific sense by the sacrament of anointing. Medical anthropologists recognize the truth of the maxim: "all healing is faith healing" which explains why some sick people are sometimes mysteriously "cured" as well.

Liturgical purists caution against ordinary lay people anointing the sick with consecrated or blessed oils, or even simple olive oil. The fear is futile. The sick believer welcomes remedy from whomever and wherever it comes, recognizing that God often acts in unexpected ways through unanticipated means.

Modern Healing Ministries

Quite in accord with contemporary interpretation of the Bible and understanding of tradition, many Catholics engage in a variety of healing ministries that are distinct from but inspired by the modern understanding of the sacraments. Most if not all such ministries are recognized by scientists as an attempt to restore meaning to human life, as a process that can affect more than physical, physiological, or psychological ailments.

Some familiar contemporary healing ministries include or specialize in the healing of memories, dealing with anger, building self-esteem, searching for wholeness or wellness, learning to forgive, and pursuing holistic approaches to life, health, and spirituality.

Other avenues for seeking healing include varieties of prayer, devotion, and pilgrimage to particular saints believed to specialize in healing or curing specific ailments. St. Lucy, for instance, is a patroness of eyesight. These Catholic practices are rooted in the Mediterranean social institution of patronage which views God as a *patron* and the saints as *brokers* who intervene on behalf of sick and ailing *clients.*

Americans prefer a direct approach to God but in a crisis human beings will try any and every reputedly effective remedy even if borrowed from cultures with contrasting or conflicting values.

In the final analysis, practice follows belief which confirms the maxim: "All healing is faith healing." Scientists may call such healing "the placebo effect" but none will deny its reality.

JOHN J. PILCH

See also SACRAMENTS.

HEALTH CARE

See ADVANCE DIRECTIVES FOR HEALTH CARE.

HEALY, TIMOTHY S. (1923–1992)

President Bill Clinton, a graduate of Georgetown University, described him as "the epitome of the merging of faith and intellect, a walking demonstration that there need be no conflict between the two." Timothy S. Healy died unexpectedly at Newark Airport on 30 December 1992. Those who knew this scholarly Jesuit thought that he would have appreciated his place of departure as Healy was God's standby, a traveling man who was ready to move anywhere at a moment's notice to answer the call to serve.

He was born in Manhattan in 1923, the son of a Texas mother and an Australian father. He received degrees from Woodstock College, Fordham University, Louvain, and Oxford University. Healy began his academic and administrative career at Fordham, where he was professor of English before becoming executive vice president. He moved to become vice chancellor of City College of New York in turbulent times and he helped to launch a most controversial "open admissions program" accepting thousands of minority students, some of whom had to begin with remedial courses. He faced his critics, and quietly recalled: "It was so simple at CUNY. There were no agendas, no politicking. Your task was clear: educate the poor." And that's what he did. Healy's thirteen-year tenure as president of Georgetown, the nation's oldest Catholic university, cut new furrows. He labored tirelessly to put the university on a firm financial foundation, improve the facility, reached out to students, and spoke out when needed against political meanness and bigotry. When he compared Jerry Falwell's Moral Majority to the Ku Klux Klan, he meant it. "Whether hatred comes wrapped in white sheets or the Scripture, it is still a denial of man and his works." He angered many when he went to El Salvador to bestow an honorary degree on Archbishop Oscar Romero, who was later murdered by military rightists. And three years later, he riled many liberals when he awarded an honorary degree to Jeanne Kilpatrick, Ronald Reagan's ambassador to the United Nations.

In 1989 the nation was surprised when Healy became president of the New York City Library, the world's largest circulating and research library. Prominent writers and journalists, including Norman Mailer, Jimmy Breslin and Gay Talese, thought the appointment of a Jesuit created a disastrous conflict of interest. But within months the open exuberance of this cultured and brilliant administrator made citizens and critics realize that Timothy S. Healy was a man apart who really believed that his hometown library was "the people's university."

MICHAEL GLAZIER

See also CATHOLIC HIGHER EDUCATION IN THE UNITED STATES; SOCIETY OF JESUS.

HEAVEN

In Christian theology, this term designates the condition of final fulfillment for created reality which is to be found in the definitive relationship of creation with God.

Old Testament

In the OT the term *heaven* is used in a variety of ways. In the archaic cosmology of the early OT period, it designated the vault of the sky which was understood to be the highest region above the earth. In earlier periods of OT history, this was understood to be the dwelling place of God. Later reflection led to the awareness that heaven and earth could not contain God, and the physical heavens came to be seen as a symbol of divine transcendence over the world and its history.

The prophetic tradition came to see a parallel between the first creation as described in Genesis (1:1ff.) and the eschatological renewal which was to come through the future action of God. God would create a new heaven and a new earth in which the age-old hopes of Israel would be brought to fulfillment (Isa 65:17; 66:22).

New Testament

The imagery of the OT and intertestamental period is the point of departure for understanding the NT usage. The traditional imagery is given a specifically Christian interpretation in as far as heaven came to be associated explicitly with Jesus Christ. Not only does the Word of God come from heaven to take on flesh in Jesus (John 3:13); but after the resurrection, Jesus ascends to heaven to sit at the right hand of God (Matt 26:64; Mark 14:62; Luke 22:69; Acts 7:55). From heaven Jesus begins to exercise his definitive role as Lord and Messiah, and from there he will appear again as judge at the end of time (Mark 8:38; 14:62; 1 Thess 4:16; Heb 9:28).

The rich imagery of the NT suggests that heaven involves a fullness and maturity of life in the presence of God. One specific mark of the NT is the transformation of the OT hopes into the notion of the vision of God (Matt 5:8; 1 Cor 13:12; 2 Cor 3:18; 5:7; 1 John 3:2) and the reunion of the faithful around Jesus, the unique Son of God, who leads his brothers and sisters to the Father (Matt 11:27).

The Tradition

The ancient creeds of the Church often include an explicit article affirming belief in eternal life (DS 3–5; 15; 19; 21; 22). While official magisterial teaching is relatively sparse, the theological tradition developed the understanding of heaven at times with great elaborateness and in terms that can hardly find an equivalent in the biblical texts. The idea of the *beatific vision* eventually becomes one of the most common technical terms for the heavenly condition. This is understood in at least two distinct ways in the period of High Scholasticism. The Thomists saw it in more intellectual terms (in seeing God, one is beatified) whereas the Scotists saw it more in terms of a radical love (in joy of loving God, one sees).

At the present time, most theologians are inclined to emphasize that heaven is an expression for the realized fulfillment of human beings as individuals and of humanity as a whole together with the world whose destiny is bound to human destiny. This is seen as the implication of the resurrection of Jesus Christ which is understood to embody the fulfillment of humanity in all its dimensions and to be the anticipation of the future of creation.

ZACHARY HAYES, O.F.M.

See also ESCHATOLOGY; SALVATION.

HEBREW

"Hebrew" (*'ibrî*) is used in Scripture in a double sense.

(1) The word is applied to Abraham (Gen 14:13), to Joseph (e.g., Gen 39:14, 17), and to Israelites (in the narrative of the sojourn in Egypt, Exodus 1–7; in the account of the struggle with the Philistines, 1 Samuel 4–14). In legal contexts (Exod 21:2; Deut 15:12), the term recurs in connection with servitude.

In all but the last of these usages, the context in which the word is used has to do with the view other peoples take of the persons so designated, as if it is their characterization of them; and the peoples involved in these contexts rule or seek to rule the persons so designated.

This circumstance has led to speculation that the term is not, as might otherwise be thought, a gentilic or ethnic designation (a view that might be sustained by the genealogy found in Genesis 10:21, 24-25; 11:14-17) of the people Israel and their forebears in Canaan and in Egypt.

In 1962, George Mendenhall ("The Hebrew Conquest of Palestine," *Biblical Archaeologist* 25:66-87) suggested that the OT word translated "Hebrew" might represent the Israelite form of the common ancient Near Eastern term *'apiru,* found notably in the Amarna Letters (fourteenth century B.C.). In Mendenhall's understanding, based on the ancient extrabiblical texts, *'apiru* is not an ethnic or racial designation but rather refers to the political status of persons vis-à-vis the established political order, something like "outsiders," "dissidents," or "rebels." Such persons have "withdrawn," or are perceived to have withdrawn, from "the network of procedures and obligations" that constitutes membership in a political entity.

This understanding of the extrabiblical term *'apiru,* and its application to the Israelite traditions listed above, form the basis for the theory that early Israel consisted of the underclass of the land of Canaan who, by affiliating themselves to the nascent political movement called "Israel," became *'apiru* from the kings of Canaan. Hence, "the 'Hebrew' Conquest of Palestine."

(2) Hebrew is also the term for the language spoken and written in ancient Israel, and so is the language of the Hebrew Scriptures. It belongs to the family of languages called Semitic, the linguistic divisions of which conventionally are said to follow a quadrant-based geographic grid: Northeast, Southeast, Southwest, and Northwest Semitic, corresponding respectively to the languages of ancient Mesopotamia, Ethiopia, Arabia, and the Levant. Northwest Semitic is categorized under the general headings of Aramaic and Canaanite; Hebrew is a Canaanite language, along with (among others) Ugaritic, Phoenician, and Moabite. The differences between the Hebrew spoken in ancient Israel and the languages of their Canaanite neighbors were not much more significant than the dialectical differences attested in the linguistic usage of Israelites themselves (cf. Judg 12:5-6).

The Hebrew Scriptures show continuous evolution in the language, from the earliest texts (Exodus 15; Judges 5), which date from around the twelfth century, to the latest, second-century ones (the Hebrew portions of Daniel). In the last hundred years, extrabiblical discoveries (notably the fourteenth-century texts from Ugarit, various Israelite and non-Israelite inscriptions from pre-exilic times, the Dead Sea Scrolls) have greatly helped to clarify the stages of development of the language and its usage at each stage.

After the Exile, the vernacular of Jews came to be Aramaic, the international *lingua franca* of the Persian Empire, though Hebrew perdured as the language of prayer, learning, and the evolving collections of books that later became the canonical Hebrew Bible. The restored use of Hebrew, however, accompanied the rise of nationalistic sentiment in the time of the Hasmonaeans and of the movements that led to the Jewish revolts of A.D. 66–70 and 132–135.

Hebrew survived as a learned language for Jews throughout the postbiblical millennia. As part of the Zionist movement of the late nineteenth and twentieth centuries, Hebrew became the spoken language of Jews who returned to the Holy Land; this modern Hebrew differs in significant respects from biblical Hebrew.

J.P.M. WALSH, S.J.

See also BIBLE, OLD TESTAMENT WRITINGS; BIBLICAL ARCHAEOLOGY.

HECKER, ISAAC THOMAS (1819–1888)

American Catholic evangelist and founder of the Paulist Fathers, Hecker was born in New York City on 18 December 1819, the fourth son of John Hecker and Caroline Friend. His father, a skilled metalworker, had operated his own brass foundry in lower Manhattan. John and Caroline separated in 1830 and Isaac's older brothers, John and George, went to work as bakers. By 1840 the brothers had become quite wealthy, owning a series of bake shops and a flour mill. The family's improved circumstances freed young Isaac to pursue an education, and shortly after, he came under the influence of Orestes Brownson who was a frequent house guest. A private mystical experience in the summer of 1842 deeply troubled Hecker. At the recommenda-

Isaac Hecker

tion of Brownson, Hecker joined the Brook Farm Community in West Roxbury, Massachusetts, in January 1843, where he came under the tutelage of George Ripley and Ralph Waldo Emerson. Initially attracted to the Episcopal Church, he was baptized a Roman Catholic on 2 August 1844 by Bishop John McCloskey. His decision to become a Catholic brought an end to his spiritual disorientation and formed the paradigm of what would become his life's work: the conversion of Protestant America.

Hecker joined the Redemptorist Order in August 1844, and was sent for studies to Belgium. He was ordained a priest by Nicholas Cardinal Wiseman on 23 October 1849 in London, England. Returning to the United States in March 1851, he joined his fellow Redemptorists, Clarence Walworth, Augustine Hewit, and in time, Francis Baker and George Deshon in the creation of an English language mission band, preaching in Catholic churches throughout the east coast of the United States. Hecker's particular interest in non-Catholics led to his writing *Questions of the Soul* (1855) and *Aspirations of Nature* (1857). These works made Hecker a national apologist for a developing American Catholic Church. A growing dispute over the nature of their missionary work led Hecker and his companions to separate from the Redemptorists in 1858. With the blessing of Pope Pius IX and the permission of Archbishop Hughes they founded the Paulist Fathers in New York City on 10 July 1858. Clarence Walworth resigned following Hecker's election as superior, and returned to his home diocese of Albany, New York.

As the leader of a new religious community, Isaac Hecker was now free to develop his evangelical outreach to non-Catholic America. In October 1862, Hecker inaugurated a series of platform lectures in New Haven, Connecticut. Renting a local lyceum, Hecker invited Protestants to come and hear the story of his conversion to Roman Catholicism. He continued these public lectures sporadically until the winter of 1869. Hecker believed that if he could present the case for Roman Catholicism in a nondefensive manner and in an open forum of public inquiry, non-Catholics would seriously consider his arguments and join him as a Catholic. In April 1865 he began *The Catholic World,* a monthly journal that sought to demonstrate the compatibility of Catholic thought with American culture. In 1866, he founded the Catholic Publication Society that would in time become Paulist Press. In 1872, Hecker raised funds to purchase a New York newspaper and transform it into a national Catholic daily. Increasing health problems prevented him from completing the project. He continued to edit *The Catholic World* and in his latter years enthusiastically advocated the idea of a national Catholic university. The Catholic University of America was opened the year after his death.

Beginning in 1871 Hecker experienced chronic bouts of exhaustion, headaches, and extreme nervousness. These episodes increased throughout the 1880s. Following his sixty-ninth birthday, he died at the Paulist mother church in New York City on 22 December 1888.

Isaac Hecker is buried at the Church of St. Paul the Apostle in New York City. His papers and personal effects are kept at the Paulist Archives in Washington, D.C. In addition to his early works and his articles for *The Catholic World,* he published *The Church and the Age* (1887) and left an unfinished manuscript, *God and Man.* Notable biographies include: David O'Brien, *Isaac Hecker: An American Catholic* (1992); John Farina, *Isaac Hecker: The Diary* (1988) and *An American Experience of God* (1981); Vincent Holden, *Yankee Paul,* and Walter Elliott, *The Life of Father Hecker* (1891).

PAUL ROBICHAUD, C.S.P.

See also AMERICAN CATHOLICISM; EVANGELIZATION.

HELL

A common name for the condition of those who fail to reach that final communion with God which is understood in Christian theology to be the final positive destiny of humanity.

Old Testament

The teaching of the Hebrew Scriptures concerning the fate of the dead is not clear but undergoes development through the centuries of Jewish history. The early idea of an underworld involved neither joy nor punishment; it was simply the place to which all the dead were consigned. Only later did the tradition develop the idea of two distinct places in the other world; one for the good and one for the evil. This development is related to reflection on the problem of retribution and the attempt to gain some insight into the problem of evil. In intertestamental Judaism, such reflection gave rise to the concept of a particular place of punishment in the afterlife.

New Testament

Christian writers presuppose and utilize the Jewish traditions. In the Synoptic Gospels, the idea of punishment after this life is accompanied with the imagery of fire, darkness, worms, howling, and gnashing of teeth, etc. (Matt 3:12; 5:22; 5:29ff.; 10:28; 13:42-50; 18:9; 23:15-33; Mark 9:43ff.; Luke 13:28).

Paul speaks of eternal destruction and banishment from the face of God (2 Thess 1:9; Rom 9:22; Phil 3:19), and of the tribulation and distress that will be the lot of those who do evil (Rom 2:9).

In line with its tendency to see salvation as the fullness of life mediated through the Son, the Gospel of John is inclined to speak of punishment as the exclusion from the fullness of life (John 2:19; 8:24; 10:28).

Apocalyptic imagery is used frequently in the NT. The place of punishment is a lake that burns with fire and sulphur (Rev 21:8). Hell is a place of the nether gloom of darkness reserved for the wicked (2 Pet 2:17). Jude 6–7 uses the images of eternal chains, nether gloom, and eternal fire.

Such graphic language is best understood in metaphorical terms. As such, it is not a description of otherworldly places, but a reminder of the basic possibility that human beings can fail to realize the ultimate point of their existence.

Teaching of the Magisterium

From numerous ancient Christian creeds and councils we may conclude that the official teaching of the Church affirms a punishment after death for those who die in the state of mortal sin. This punishment, which begins immediately after death, will be in conformity with the evil works of the persons involved. Since official Church teaching has never judged that any particular person has in fact been condemned to hell, theologians read this tradition to mean that the Church's teaching implies the possibility of eternal loss without making any judgment concerning the actual fate of any individual person.

The Synod of Constantinople in 543 condemned the views of the followers of Origen concerning the final restoration and universal reintegration (*apocatastasis*) of all created reality, including the demons and evil persons (DS 411). This condemnation has led the main line of Roman Catholic theology to an open understanding of the final outcome of history. One may hope for universal salvation, but one may not see any necessity for affirming it without raising difficult questions about the nature of human freedom and its relationship to God. Thus, the traditional language of hell holds before us the negative possibility of human freedom.

ZACHARY HAYES, O.F.M.

See also APOCALYPSE; ESCHATOLOGY; SIN.

HERESY/HERETICS

The Greek word *hairesis* originally meant a sect, and the word thus came to mean the teaching of a particular group as distinct from the teaching of the Church at large. Heresy is a word both widely used and misused, and one way of defining it is to say what it is not. Technically heresy must involve a conscious and deliberate deviation from a formally and publicly promulgated teaching by an authoritative organ of the Church. In this sense, heresy must be distinguished from heterodoxy, which is simple disagreement from what is widely believed. For example, in the New Testament period there were Christians who disagreed with the prevailing teaching, but since Christian teaching was still in a state of formation, one cannot call these Christians heretics. Indeed, one could make the case that Paul's teaching was heterodox since his view that Christians need not follow the Jewish Law was not one which was widely held until he changed the Church's thinking on this point.

Likewise, heresy is not something which can be imposed on someone *ex post facto;* that is, if someone held a view which later Christians rejected, such a person cannot rightly be called a heretic. Most third-century Christian theologians considered the Son of God to be subordinate to the Father in the Trinity, a view condemned as heretical in the fourth century. It is historically inaccurate and morally inappropriate to label the third-century theologians as heretics because they did not anticipate fourth-century developments.

Finally, heresy must be distinguished from speculative theology. The theologian starts with the data of revelation and then investigates these data. Often the theologian will reach a conclusion at variance with the prevailing magisterial teaching, but this is not heresy since the theologian is voicing a theological opinion and expects to dialogue with other theologians on that point. A noteworthy feature of the Second Vatican Council (1962–1965) was the presence, as consultors, of several theologians who had been accused by some Vatican groups a decade or so before of holding heretical or at least questionable views; the council recognized these men as the pioneers they were.

Heresy is a clear phenomenon by the fourth century. By then the Christians had determined the canon of the Old and New Testaments, so the basics of scriptural revelation were established, and the practice of holding an ecumenical council to determine the faith of the Church had begun at Nicea in 325. For all Christians, deviation from the Scripture is heresy, although such deviation depends upon the type of exegesis involved. For example, most fundamentalists would consider much Roman Catholic and mainline Protestant exegesis heretical. The role of the ecumenical councils varies—some denominations accept the authority of the first four councils, others of the first seven, others of none, while Roman Catholics accept the authority of all twenty-one. Within the Catholic Church, other instruments have been used to judge heresy, specifically the papacy, which has often delegated its authority to papal congregations or offices, such as the Inquisition.

Recently the treatment of heresy has become more pastoral. A heretic is one who deviates from the teaching of the Church and so is in danger of being cut off from the Church. In the past, ecclesiastical officials would often condemn and excommunicate such a person. Today heresy is seen as a wound in the body of Christ, something which must be healed; just as an individual will not amputate a limb which aches, so the Church will not cut off from the body of Christ one of its members, unless there is no other choice.

Similar to this is the sense of ecumenical understanding. No Catholic today would call Protestantism a heresy. Both Catholics and Protestants recognize there were real if unfortunate causes for the Reformation of the sixteenth century, and this tragic rending of the body of Christ was in many ways unavoidable. Indeed, not just ecumenism, but also fair play and Christian charity demand that both sides recognize the existence of separated brethren rather than of heretics.

There have been many heresies in the history of the Church; what follows is a brief list of those which have had the greatest impact on Church life.

Arianism

In the fourth century an Egyptian priest named Arius (d. 336) taught that in the Trinity, the Son of God is inferior to the Father, that the Son is a creature, and that there was a time when the Son was not. Arius drew upon his own interpretation of Scripture as well as upon third-century Christology, but it was clear that he had carried matters too far, effectively denying the divinity of the Son. The Roman Emperor Constantine (d. 337) called an ecumenical council, the first one, to meet at Nicea in 325. This council condemned Arius and proclaimed that Father and Son are *homoousios,* that is, of one being.

Because Greek theological terminology was often vague, some theologians and bishops thought that the council had declared that there was no numerical difference between Father and Son, that both were one person. For a half-century after the council Arianism remained a potent force, and a second ecumenical council, Constantinople I (381), had to be called. It was this council which taught that the Holy Spirit is *homoousios* with the Father and Son.

Nestorianism

Just as Arianism had impelled the Church to clarify its Trinitarian teaching, so Nestorianism did for Christology. This heresy is named for Nestorius, bishop of Constantinople (428–431), who was accused by Cyril of Alexandria of having so emphasized the distinction between the divine and human in Christ that he had considered the human Christ and the divine Son of God to be two persons. The third ecumenical council, Ephesus (431), condemned and deposed Nestorius, but the issue was not settled. Instead it led to the next heresy.

Monophysitism

If Nestorius had separated the human and divine too much, Eutyches (d. 454) eliminated the distinction, claiming that there were two natures before the incarnation of the Son but only one nature (*monophysis*) after it. Dioscorus, the bishop of Alexandria supported Eutyches, but the Council of Chalcedon condemned both in 451 and taught that Christ is one person with two natures, one human and one divine. In effect, Chalcedon clarified the Christology which Ephesus had left unsettled.

But there was a price to pay. The disciples of Nestorius and Dioscorus did not just go away; on the contrary, they continued to teach and proselytize so effectively that, just prior to the Muslim invasion of the Near East, most of the Byzantine Empire's Near Eastern provinces were Monophysite, with sizeable groups of Nestorians in Syria. Both groups survive today, albeit in small numbers.

While the Eastern theologians dealt with the Trinitarian and Christological issues, Western theologians concerned themselves with sin. Augustine led the way. His attacks on Manichaeism, a dualistic religion which posited a good being and an evil one, raised the question of good and evil in a new way. But Manichaeism was a minor movement, and Augustine's real struggle lay elsewhere.

Pelagianism

Pelagius (d. ca. 420) was a British monk who taught in Rome. He claimed that human beings can discipline themselves so effectively that they could be saved by their own free will, independent of divine grace. In fact, he stressed that this was a rare occurrence, but it was possible. But Augustine, who had considered himself poised on the brink of hell and saved only by God's gratuitous intervention, saw Pelagius' teaching as destructive of God's grace.

Augustine claimed that thanks to the corruption of human nature caused by original sin (he was the first to use the phrase), we are born damned, unable to do anything perfectly good. God chooses to give his grace to those whom he has chosen to save, and God knew before he created the world whom he would save. Although Augustine defeated Pelagianism and made Christians aware of the necessity of divine grace for salvation, he himself drifted into *predestinationism* and weakened the case for free will. Although Augustine is a Father of the Church and Pelagius is a condemned heretic, the bishops and teachers of the Church have had to walk a fine line between the two positions.

In the early Middle Ages in the West, after the fall of the Roman Empire, there were no major heresies. There were people holding heretical views, but the low state of education in the West made serious heresy something for the textbooks. Things were different, however, in the Byzantine East, where the learned tradition had continued unbroken. Yet the most important Byzantine heresy came not from theologians and scholars but from an emperor.

Iconoclasm

The Eastern Church had a long tradition of venerating icons, that is, images of God, Christ, Mary, and the saints. Theoretically, the icons were supposed to point beyond themselves to the persons they portrayed, but inevitably some of the icons themselves were seen as holy objects and thus were venerated. Supporters of icons made an important distinction, that icons could be venerated yet only the person to whom they pointed could be worshipped.

But distinctions are often lost in popular worship, and by the eighth century the veneration of icons included the fantastic and the superstitious. There were icons which spoke, which wept, which bled; regrettably Byzantine Church leaders did little to check that sort of thing. Convinced that icons led to idolatry and concerned that their veneration prevented Jews and Muslims from converting to Christianity, the emperor Leo III (717–741) issued an edict in 726 calling for the destruction of icons. Iconoclasm, as the policy was called, met strong resistence, and Leo resorted to persecution of his opponents.

Iconoclasm was resented by the public and denounced by Western Church leaders, and when a venerator of icons, the Empress Irene, came to the Byzantine throne, the policy was reversed. Allied with Pope Hadrian I (772–795), she called the seventh ecumenical council, Nicea II, in 787. The council defended the veneration of icons and condemned iconoclasm.

In the ninth century in the West, there was an intellectual revival called the Carolingian Renaissance (named after Charlemagne [d. 814]), and Carolingian theologians discussed several issues, including predestination and the real presence of Christ in the Eucharist. These discussions were largely academic in nature and based upon patristic teachings. Although the word heresy was used freely, no new heresies emerged.

In the two following centuries, the Western Church sank into an intellectual despond, which persisted until the twelfth century and the rise of Scholasticism which reinvigorated theological life. But by then a new type of heresy had arisen.

Catharism

In the early Church, heretics were often theologians and bishops, who enunciated a particular theology rejected by the Church at large. Beginning in the High Middle Ages and lasting until the Reformation, heresies tended to start from the bottom, to reflect the discontent of the lower socioeconomic groups. The Cathars, who were located most prominently in southern France and northern Italy, were descendants of the Manichees. They were dualists who saw an unending struggle between two principles, one good, one evil, and they considered the union of body and soul to be a "mixed state," caused by the devil. They rejected things of the flesh, which meant they also rejected Christ's incarnation, marriage, the resurrection of the flesh, and even the eating of animal products. They moved on to reject the sacraments and the doctrine of hell. They tried to lead lives of evangelical poverty, and, in the eyes of the people, they contrasted favorably with bishops who often came from the nobility. Frequently they were confused with other groups which favored evangelical poverty, such as the Waldensians; even St. Francis of Assisi was suspect of Cathar ideals because of his own commitment to poverty.

But poverty was not the real issue; the condemnation of the material world was. Christianity has always seen this world as a theater of divine activity, especially in the creation and the incarnation, and, after several local councils had condemned the Cathars, the twelfth ecumenical council, Lateran IV, did so in 1215. If only that had been the end of it.

In 1208 a papal legate in France had been assassinated by the Cathars, so Pope Innocent III (1198–1216) agreed to a crusade against them. Led by the French noble Simon de Montfort, this decade-long crusade (1208–1218) centered on the Cathar stronghold of Albi and is known as the Albigensian Crusade. De Montfort spread destruction and massacre throughout much of southern France, and thousands of innocent people died. So did Catharism; it is unknown after the fourteenth century.

Jan Hus

The Cathars' heresy had social overtones; that of Jan Hus had national ones. Hus (ca. 1372–1415) was a priest in Prague. He became acquainted with the teaching of John Wycliffe (d. 1384), an English theologian who had argued that only clergy in the state of grace could own property and that the civil authority could deprive clergy not in that state of their property. Hus was concerned at what he considered Western depredations in Bohemia, and he argued against clerical immorality and misuse of power. By 1407 he had been denounced at Rome, but many Czech nobility and people supported him, seeing the papacy as an agent of predatory German and Austrian nobles. Hus' cause became a national one.

In 1414 Hus was invited to the sixteenth ecumenical council, Constance. He feared for his life, but the German emperor Sigismund gave him a safe conduct. When he arrived in Constance, the leaders of the council ignored the safe conduct, tried and convicted him for heresy, and had him burned at the stake on 6 July 1415. For the Czechs, Hus became both a martyr and a national hero. The Hussite movement persisted to the end of the Middle Ages. This link of heresy and nationalism prompted some German admirers of Luther to call him "the Saxon Hus."

After the Reformation, most heresies in the Catholic Church were academic or political. For example, *Gallicanism* was the contention of Louis XIV (1643–1715) and other French kings that the French Church could act largely independently of the papacy, a view supported by a sizeable number of French bishops. *Josephism* was basically the same thing, except that the advocate was Joseph II (1765–1790) Hapsburg of the Holy Roman Empire. But one heresy of this age did reach out to embrace a wider circle.

Jansenism

A Belgian priest named Cornelius Jansen (1585–1638) wrote a book called *Augustinus* which emphasized the need for a special and irresistible grace from God for salvation. Since this grace was irresistible, the overtones of Jansenism were both predestinationist and deterministic. Jansen's theological opponents were the Jesuits, and the essayist Blaise Pascal (1623–1662) won over the anti-Jesuit forces in France to the Jansenist side. The debate raged for decades until Clement XI condemned Jansenism in 1713. The heretics' unquestioned moral rigorism made them very popular, and Jansenist ideas survived the condemnation.

Modernism

The only "heresy" which has had significance for twentieth-century Roman Catholics is Modernism, a name given less to a movement than to an attitude which emerged in the late nineteenth century. The Modernists were theologians who accepted the advances in biblical exegesis and Church history taken for granted by liberal Protestants; furthermore, they rejected the overrationalism of contemporary Scholasticism. Reacting against Pius IX's condemnation of the modern world in his *Syllabus of Errors* (1864) and fearful that Roman Catholic theology would become hopelessly outdated, the Modernists hoped that Leo XIII (1878–1903) would support them. Leo did not condemn them, but he kept his distance. His successor, Pius X (1903–1914) believed that modern biblical and historical criticism would undermine much Roman Catholic doctrine as well as the foundations of the papacy (the Modernists had doubts about the traditional founding of the Church by Jesus himself). In 1907 Pius condemend the Modernists, and in 1910 he obliged all Roman Catholic priests to take an oath against Modernism, a requirement just recently lifted since many of the attitudes of the Modernists are now accepted by contemporary Catholic scholars.

JOSEPH F. KELLY

See also ECUMENICAL COUNCILS; MAGISTERIUM; ORTHODOXY.

HERMENEUTICS

The term "hermeneutics" derives from the Greek verb *hermeneuō,* which means "interpret." The term can include the whole process of interpretation described under "Biblical Criticism." Or it can be used more narrowly to refer to what one does with the text after it has been subjected to literary and historical analysis. In the latter sense hermeneutics concerns the significance and appropriation of a text for a person or a group today.

The NT presents Jesus as the authoritative interpreter of the OT (e.g., Matt 5:21-48; Mark 10:2-9), the one who determines what the OT text really means. Matthew, Paul, and other NT writers found Jesus to be the key that opened up the OT Scriptures. In patristic times the Alexandrian interpreters such as Clement and Origen looked for the spiritual or allegorical meaning in OT and NT texts, whereas the school of Antioch represented by John Chrysostom insisted on the literal sense as the basis for any spiritual interpretation. The medieval interpreters distinguished four senses in a Scripture text: literal (what happened), allegorical (the hidden theological meaning), anagogical (the heavenly sense), and moral (the relevance for the individual's behavior). Though heavily dependent on medieval exegesis, Luther put forward some important principles of interpretation: the clarity of Scriptures, the importance of a historical understanding, Scripture as the criterion for judging the Church, and preference for those books that best "promote Christ." The rediscovery of classical texts in the Renaissance led to the development of historical criticism; i.e., the effort to understand ancient texts in their ancient setting and to determine what the ancient authors were trying to say to their original audiences.

Much of contemporary biblical scholarship is historical criticism. But individuals and communities today still want to know what this text means for them. Hermeneutics (narrowly defined) concerns the move from the ancient text to its meaning in the present. For some people the move presents no problem. Fundamentalists assume a perfect continuity between the world of the Bible and our world, and use the Scriptures as a quarry of answers to today's questions. Spiritualizers and modern allegorizers and deconstructionists treat the Bible as a collection of symbols or archetypes, providing raw material for positions already reached. But most Christian interpreters recognize the differences between the biblical world and today, and revere the Bible as in some true sense the Word of God. They seek analogies between the experience described in the biblical text and their own situation. Their chief mode of interpretation is analogy, i.e., finding parallels between the text and their lives. Or they may draw universal lessons from particular texts. Or they may spiritualize biblical references to blindness (into spiritual blindness) or idolatry (into making created things into divine beings). Or they may engage in narrative recreation of a biblical scene and place themselves in it ("Were you there when they crucified my Lord?"). These are the kinds of moves that preachers make in actualizing biblical texts for their communities.

The interaction between the text to be interpreted and the interpreter has been called the "hermeneutical circle" by the German philosopher Hans-Georg Gadamer. An interpreter necessarily brings to every text a set of prejudices or pre-understandings, including the tradition in which the interpreter stands and the presumption that the text has continuing validity (a "classic"). The challenge is to distinguish true and false (distorting) prejudices. A "horizon" is the range of vision that includes everything that can be seen from a particular vantage point. Understanding happens in the fusion of horizons between text and interpreter. Interpretation involves sharing the common meaning so that there is an interplay between the text and the interpreter. By the fusion of horizons interpreters change or are changed, and so application is an integral part of interpretation.

The French philosopher Paul Ricoeur has also made important contributions to hermeneutical theory. In contrast to the concerns of historical critics Ricoeur contends that the goal of the interpretive task is not to recover the genius of the author, or the situation of the original audience, or the one correct interpretation. Rather, according to Ricoeur, the very act of writing produces an alienation or distancing, whereby the text becomes an object to be interpreted, free from the writer's intention and the concrete situation, and open to anyone who can read. Thus a text is open also to many readings (multivalence), since it transcends its situation of production and is read by people in different sociocultural settings. Each reader stands in relation to the kind of world that the text presents. We understand ourselves in front of the text, and so the text is the medium through which we understand ourselves (appropriation).

DANIEL J. HARRINGTON, S.J.

See also CRITICISM, BIBLICAL; INSPIRATION, BIBLICAL.

HERMIT

One who lives a solitary life for the sake of a more intense communion with God.

MONIKA K. HELLWIG

HERR, DAN (1917–1990)

Dan Herr (11 February 1917 to 28 September 1990) was a publisher, writer, and lecturer. Born in Huron, Ohio, Herr was christened Daniel Joseph, but known professionally by the Dan of his byline. He studied at St. John's College in Toledo, and on its closing transferred to Fordham College in the Bronx, from which he was graduated in 1938. Herr went to work at the New York *Daily News* as a copy boy at sixteen dollars a week. Three years later he was in the U.S. Army, where he served with distinction during World War II in the South Pacific and Caribbean theaters, moving from private to major and winning the Silver Star and Purple Heart.

On discharge, Herr freelanced as a writer out of New York City, his work appearing in the *Saturday Evening Post, Life, Coronet,* among other magazines. The Catholic press at the time was attracting many talented veterans matured beyond their years by military experience, and Herr saw his future there. He placed an advertisement of availability in *The Priest,*

Dan Herr

and was invited by John Tully in 1948 to join the Thomas More Book Shop in Chicago, a modest enterprise with a book club and the literary magazine *Books on Trial.* Herr speedily transformed the operation, giving the magazine a less inquisitional name, *The Critic,* and, after succeeding Tully in 1951, broadening the scope of operations to include book publishing, newsletters, audiocassettes, symposia, lectures, and a religious art center. The expanded entity was incorporated in 1949 as The Thomas More Association.

Over the years, Herr became for many the arbiter of taste in American Catholic publishing. He delighted in controversy, and was quick to speak his mind, particularly regarding the Catholic press, becoming in time its severest critic. "With apologies to Churchill," he wrote of Catholic-press editors, "never have so many worked so hard to put out a product that is read by so few." He subsequently maintained there was nothing wrong with the Catholic press that a paper shortage wouldn't cure. Many sensed, however, that Herr played the curmudgeon, and that behind the mask was a man of charm, wit, intelligence—and commitment to Catholic publishing.

With Joel Wells, Herr compiled several Catholic-press anthologies. His own books included *Stop Pushing!* (New York, 1961) and *Start Digging!* (Chicago, 1987). He received the Pere Marquette Award from Marquette University, 1957, and an honorary doctor of letters degree from Rosary College, 1967. Herr died in Chicago, and was buried at Wood National Cemetery, Wood, Wisconsin.

JOHN DEEDY

HESYCHASM

Hesychasm is a method of interior prayer practiced especially in the Eastern Church. It begins with a system of breath control, with the chin resting on the breast and the eyes focusing on the navel. As the person breathes in deeply, he repeats "O, Lord Jesus Christ, Son of God" and as she slowly exhales, she intones, "have mercy on me, a sinner." This exercise stills the mind and heart, thereby preparing it for an experience of divine light. Hence, its practitioners are sometimes called "Taborites," after Mount Tabor, the place of Jesus' transfiguration.

The earliest reports of hesychasm date from the fifth century. St. Anastasius, the founder of the laura on Mt. Athos, permitted only five of the holiest monks in each community of 120 to attempt practice of the ascetical discipline. The Justinian Code and the Council in Trullo warned against false and excessive versions of such ascetical practice. In the fourteenth century, Gregory Palamas (d. 1359) gave hesychasm theological foundation by distinguishing between two concepts of God: the transcendent, incomprehensible, uncreated Being and the experience of God's goodness shared with human beings in creation and sanctifying grace. Palamas was challenged by Barlaam of Calabria, and the matter became the occasion of much theological controversy in the fourteenth century. In 1351, hesychasm was recognized as an official doctrine of the Orthodox Church.

PATRICIA DeFERRARI

See also CONTEMPLATION; MYSTICISM; PRAYER.

HIERARCHY

Hierarchy is a term that literally means "holy origin," or "sacred order," and refers to the ordering of ministries in the Church, an ordering that believers consider is traceable to Jesus. In practice it refers to deacons, priests, bishops, and pope. However, deacons are not really subordinate to priests but form a distinct ministry that serves the bishop. Bishops receive the fullness of the priesthood but are not sacramentally subordinately ordered to the pope. Rather the pope is head of the college of bishops; first among equals, and as the Bishop of Rome who succeeds Peter in holding a universal ministry.

Historically, hierarchy referred to the shared authority structures of the Church; the Lord sharing his authority with Peter and his successors, the apostles with their successors (LG 20:1), the presbyters and their successors in the priesthood who serve the community and receive their authority from the bishop, the deacons—a ministry established by the apostles—and their successors who serve the bishop. These three orders are believed to be divinely ordained. Subjectively, hierarchy refers to the people who hold these ministries—men considered to be sharing in the personal authority of Christ the head of the Church.

The Lord's authority continues in the Church through those members who receive the charism of sharing in the Lord's authority through apostolic succession, and represent the unity of their Churches with the universal Church. In history, the hierarchical structuring of the Church sometimes followed the political hierarchies of the day, such as those of the empire, with the unfortunate emphasis on power instead of service.

Although historically "hierarchy" referred to authority structures seen as a way of sacramentally portraying the unity of the Church, Vatican II reinterpreted the concept to refer to a hierarchy of service (LG 18). Bishops are servants of the people (CD 16; LG 20:4), modeling themselves on Jesus (LG 27:3); so too priests (PO 12:6; 15:3). In fact, the council sees the hierarchy of priestly ministry as interrelated with the priesthood of all believers (LG 10:2). The conciliar change has helped move the Church away from too objective an understanding of office and power, leading us all to an appreciation that service is the essential virtue of the Church, the sacrament of the self-emptying of the Lord.

One becomes a member of the hierarchy through the sacrament of orders in the case of bishops, and through the sacrament and canonical mission in the case of priests and deacons. All orders demand unity with the universal Church seen in the bishop, or pope as head of the college. In addition to the three orders traceable to the New Testament, and found in Roman Catholicism, Eastern Orthodoxy, and Anglicanism, some Churches have added other orders. The Roman Catholic Church itself has added other minor orders such as the subdeaconate and acolyte. It has also developed an elaborate hierarchy of jurisdiction: pope, Curia, cardinals, legates, nuncios, apostolic delegates.

The hierarchy portrays the Church's shared authority and shared sense of service and unity. A gift of the Lord, it sacramentally manifests the nature of the Church.

LEONARD DOOHAN

See also BISHOP; CHURCH, THE; PAPACY, THE.

HIERARCHY OF TRUTHS

In the Old Testament and in the writings of the rabbis attempts were regularly made to provide handy summaries or "cores" of the Law. The best-known of these is probably the succinct formula of Hillel: "What is hateful to you, do not do to your neighbor; that is the whole Torah, while the rest is commentary thereof." When Jesus was asked what he thought was "the great commandment in the law," he cited two, Deuteronomy 6:5 and Leviticus 19:18, the commandments to love God and one's neighbor. He then concluded: "On these two commandments depend all the law and the prophets" (Matt 22:40). It was characteristic of Jesus' teaching to keep a clear focus on what he called the "weightier matters of the law, justice and mercy and faith," even as he commended lesser observances (Matt 23:23).

With the rise of the ecumenical movement in this century it became necessary for all the participants in an interfaith dialogue to make the same sort of distinction between what was of the greatest importance in the faith of each and what was less so, if the dialogue was to be fruitful. Mindful of this fact, the bishops at the Second Vatican Council in the Decree on Ecumenism reminded Catholic theologians engaged in ecumenical dialogue that they "should remember that in Catholic teaching there exists an order or 'hierarchy' of truths, since they vary in their relationship to the foundation of Christian faith" (no. 11).

The individual Catholic would also do well to keep in mind this idea of the hierarchy of truths. This is not meant to suggest that a believer may stand before the body of Catholic truths and decide whether to accept one and reject another. The believer really stands before God who reveals the truths of the faith in their totality and serves as the guarantor of their believability. Rather, it is the case that, even though all these truths are revealed and all are to be believed, not all are of equal significance. The relative significance of a doctrine is not determined by its presence in the New Testament or by its being infallibly defined as an article of faith. In the passage cited above, the bishops clearly state that the hierarchy of truths is determined by the relationship of a particular doctrine to the foundation of Christian faith, the mystery of Christ. Consequently, the divinity of Christ and the work of redemption hold a higher ranking in the faith than the veneration of the saints or the bodily assumption of Mary into heaven. Not only does the mystery of Christ provide a norm for the relative importance of teachings, it also helps the believer to receive and understand all the less important truths in the light of their relationship to this foundational mystery.

Few believers, however, have the time or the inclination to seek the highest intelligibility of each and every teaching, and they accept much of the substance of the faith through an implicit faith in the Church's teaching office. In this case, awareness of the hierarchy of truths frees the believer to give the greatest attention to the "weightier matters" in the gospel message.

WILLIAM C. McFADDEN, S.J.

See also DOCTRINE; DOGMA; MYSTERY (OF FAITH).

HILARY OF POITIERS, ST. (ca. 315–ca. 367)

Hilary was born in the early part of the fourth century. Between 350 and 353 he became bishop of Poitiers. After the synod of Béziers (356) where Hilary opposed the activities of those in Gaul who favored Arianism, Emperor Constantius exiled him to Phrygia for four years. While in Phrygia he came into contact with the Homoeousians. From this he saw that it was necessary to watch out not only for Arianism but also Sabellian Monarchianism and that it was possible to profess an orthodox belief in the Trinity without having to make use of the Nicene term *homoousios.* Influenced by these experiences, Hilary wrote between 356 and 360 *On the Trinity* and *On the Councils.* In 359 he defended the cause of orthodoxy in the Council of Seleucia. While in Constantinople in 360 he tried to debate Saturninus of Arles, a pro-Arian spokesman in Gaul. He was soon allowed to return to Gaul but was not restored to his see. Because Gaul was under the control of Emperor Julian the Apostate, he was able to rally the anti-Arians at the Council of Paris in 361. A moderate course of action was recommended against those who had been forced to endorse a pro-Arian formula at the Synod of Ariminum (Rimini) in 359. Hilary was also successful in promoting a doctrinal line that respected the concerns of both Homoousians and Homoeousians. In 364 Hilary was in Milan working with Eusebius of Vercelli to attempt to expel Auxentius, an Arian who had been bishop there since 355. Nothing more is mentioned about Hilary. According to Jerome, Hilary died in 367. Hilary also wrote *Fragmenta historica,* and commentaries on Psalms and Matthew. Hilary was also the first-known hymn writer in the Western Church. Known as the Athanasius of the West, Hilary was proclaimed a Doctor of the Church in 1851. Feast day, 13 January.

JOHN DILLON

See also DOCTORS OF THE CHURCH; FATHERS OF THE CHURCH; HERESY/HERETICS; HYMNS; TRINITY.

HILTON, WALTER (?–1395)

Walter Hilton (?–1395) was an English mystic of the fourteenth century. Although he wished to remain anonymous, he very quickly became a famous spiritual director. Nevertheless, little information about his own life has survived to the present. It is not known where or when he was born. Historical evidence suggests that Hilton studied canon law at Cambridge before entering a life of solitude. In a letter written between the years 1375 and 1380 to his friend, Adam Horsely, on the advantages of religious life (*De utilitate et prerogativis religionis*), Hilton indicated that he was living a solitary life but was beginning to see its limitations. A few years later he became a regular canon of St. Augustine. He died at Thurgarton Priory in Nottinghamshire, England, in 1395.

Hilton's fame as a mystical theologian derives primarily from his book, *The Scale of Perfection,* although his writings include other works, such as *The Goad of Love* (an original adaptation into English of the *Stimulus Amoris*) and his *Commentaries on Psalms 90 and 91. The Scale* is a very clear and comprehensive treatise on the interior life. It was especially valued by the English Carthusian communities. *The Scale* was translated into Latin in 1400 and printed by Wynkyn de Worde in 1494; more than ninety manuscript copies are still extant.

The Scale consists of two essays. The first is addressed to an anchoress and the second contains the well-known "Christocentric additions." In this second treatise, Hilton rejects the idea that perfection of spiritual life can only be achieved in the cloister. In times of turmoil and social unrest, the Christian must not retreat but must adapt the Church's spiritual teaching to life in the world. In his translation and adaptation of *Stimulus Amoris,* Hilton writes, "I shall tell you where Jesus your spouse is, and where you can find him—in your sick brother who is lame or blind or afflicted with any other disease. Go to the hospital and find Christ there."

PATRICIA DeFERRARI

See also BRITAIN, CHURCH IN; MIDDLE AGES, THE; MYSTICISM; SPIRITUALITY, LAY.

HINDUISM

Hinduism is perhaps the world's oldest living religion with nearly 800 million adherents, the vast majority of them in India. Unlike most religions, it does not have a founder (such as Buddhism) or a historical crisis which gave it initial momentum (such as the Exodus from Egypt).

It simply evolved beginning about 2500 B.C. in the Indus Valley of India and by a millennium later had appropriated elements of the culture and Vedic religion Aryans had brought with them from southern Asia. Indeed, the first Hindu gods and scriptures were from the Vedic tradition.

Hindus had a penchant for gods but out of what might otherwise be construed as rampant polytheism (according to tradition there were 333 million gods) emerged a trinity of primary deities: Brahma the Creator, Vishnu the Preserver, and Shiva the Destroyer. The function of Shiva is not a negative one; it allows Brahma to re-create the universe. Vishnu has had several avatars or incarnations, e.g., Krishna, Rama, and Buddha.

In addition to these major gods, there is another level of deities with specific duties—Indra, the storm god, Agni, the god of fire, Lakshmi, goddess of wealth, and Saraswati, goddess of wisdom. Many Hindu gods have female consorts, e.g., Krishna and Radha, Shiva and Parvati, and Rama and Sita. A third level consists of village gods found in abundance in small rural communities throughout India.

Behind and beyond the plethora of deities is the all-pervading impersonal divine reality called Brahman which unites all existing things. Brahman is not a separate supreme being, but an Absolute Cosmic Consciousness of which everything is a part.

Brahman in each devotee is called Atman or Divine Self. The goal of every Hindu is to realize more fully the Atman, at the expense of the individual ego, until he or she is free from the wheel *(samsara)* of birth and death.

One is assisted in this journey to freedom *(moksha)* by performing acceptably one's *dharma* (religious duty). The law of *karma* (what you sow you reap) determines the progress and regress of the human soul through a number of cycles of redeath and rebirth until it escapes the bondage of *samsara* and becomes one with the Infinite.

This Brahman-Atman unity is the source of Hindu ethical concern, especially *ahimsa,* the philosophy of non-injury. In fact, the traditional Hindu gesture of *namaste* (hands held together in front of the body) is the acknowledgment of the divinity in each of us.

Various yogas or disciplines are available to help the Hindu achieve *moksha.* You choose the one most appropriate to your inclination and ability. If you are a reflective person, interested in learning, you choose Jnana yoga. If, on the other hand, you are a deeply pious person given to devotion to God, you would choose Bhakti yoga. Those who are action-oriented and who delight in work, are devotees of Karma yoga. Finally, if you are particularly inclined to meditation or contemplation, Raja yoga would be your path.

One of the attractive features of Hinduism is its capacity to include. There is hardly anything it is not. A further illustration of this is the variety of goals available to people depending on what they want to accomplish in a given lifetime. There are quite legitimate, though lesser goals of Desire called pleasure *(kama)* and work *(artha)* and higher goals of Renunciation called *dharma* (righteous behavior) and *moksha* (ultimate release).

"Vishnu," Chola period, Central Museum, Madras

These paths and goals are experienced as one passes through certain stages of life and assumes the responsibility found in each. They are the stages of student (ages 1 through 20), householder and family responsibility (ages 20 through 40), forest dweller or retirement from family duties (ages 40 through 60), and finally, sannyasin (the hermit stage) in which one is devoted to the holy life and complete renunciation until physical death. When death occurs, the soul migrates, depending on one's *karma,* to another level of reality either closer to or further away from ultimate freedom.

Consistent with its inclination to provide many avenues for the believer, there are many Hindu scriptures. The oldest is the Vedas made up of a collection of chants, hymns, rituals, and some religious speculation. In addition, the Upanishads (800–400 B.C.) stress philosophical monism, the Brahman-Atman unity, and the oneness behind the diversity of Hindu gods and goddesses. Finally there is the Mahabharata (500–200 B.C.) which contains the popular Bhagavad-Gita.

Hindu social life for centuries was structured along caste lines. Even though it has been unconstitutional since 1948, the psychosocial impact of the caste legacy remains. The origin of caste is unknown, but it is likely the Aryans brought with them an informal class structure of priests, warriors, businessmen, and manual laborers. These groups *(varnas)* became known respectively as Brahmins, Kshatriyas, Vaisyas, and Sudras. In time, the castes were designated by birth *(jati)* and one was bound to one's caste in every way. In addition to the formal caste structure, there appeared another large group who had no caste and were known as the Untouchables. Much of what was considered ethically and socially appropriate was determined by one's caste obligation and duty.

There has been a great deal of ferment in the last century and a half in India. Such reform programs as Brahmo-Somaj (Society of God) led by Ram Mohun Roy, the Ramakrishna Movement, and Gandhi's Indian National Congress were instrumental in the abolition of caste and India's political independence from Great Britain. It must be noted as well that a strong vocal minority of Hindu fundamentalism has surfaced in the past decade.

Hinduism's final appeal may be its capacity to hold together apparent contradictions such as desire and renunciation, affirmation and denial of the world, duty and freedom, and monotheism and polytheism. It refuses to exclude, to polarize, and to divide.

One of the most representative stories in Hinduism is the Wish-Fulfilling Tree which grants you whatever you desire. When, after all your wants are fulfilled, you ask, "Is having every wish granted all there is to life?", you begin to appreciate Hinduism.

IRA ZEPP

See also ASCETICISM; MYSTICISM; SPIRITUAL LIFE.

HISPANIC SPIRITUALITY

See SPIRITUALITY, HISPANIC.

HISTORICAL JESUS

See QUEST FOR THE HISTORICAL JESUS.

HOLINESS

Preliminary Considerations

Holiness designates the state of being put aside or set apart for specifically religious purposes. It also connotes that which is consecrated to God. The term "holiness" is rooted in the Old English *hâlignes* which describes something without blemish or imperfection due to injury. "Holy" is the English for the Greek *hagios* and the Hebrew *qds.* Both the Greek and the Hebrew carry the sense of setting aside or separating something for the purposes of consecration.

Contemporary understandings of the holy have been influenced considerably by Rudolf Otto's *The Idea of the Holy* which describes the holy as *mysterium tremendum et fascinans.* Otto's investigations draw attention to the fear, wonder, shock, amazement, and astonishment evoked by the holy. The holy elicits both awe and fascination because it is different from the ordinary or profane. The holy is that which is of the realm of transcendence. It pertains to the ultimate, and so is first and foremost a term used in reference to God. But by extension the term holiness can be applied to that which is related to the ultimate. Persons, communities, nations, places, time, and objects, when understood in terms of their relationship to the source of the ultimate, may be designated "holy" insofar as they manifest the holy. They, like the holy, are distinguished from the ordinary. They are set apart, consecrated (Lat. *consecrare, sacer,* sacred). Holiness and its cognates "sanctity" and "saint" are dependent notions deriving their significance in relation to God.

Biblical Perspectives

In the Hebrew Scriptures it is God who is holy, separate, in that God is not to be identified with the limited, finite order. Though God creates, God is other than the fruit of the creative act. There is a nonidentity between God and the creature and creation. But people, actions, places, times, and objects may be holy by association with God. Indeed the history of Israel is a history of a holy people, a people called and set apart by God. God's call to holiness is followed by God's judgment upon a people who fail to live in holiness. Israel must learn again and again what is required if they are to live in a way that is holy and blameless (Mic 6:8).

The Hebrew Scriptures describe God as the Holy One, and rely on various synonyms for the holiness of God, e.g., glory = Hebrew *kabod;* Greek *doxa.* Israel's oldest hymn of praise proclaims that God is majestic in holiness (Exod 15:11); a holiness discerned primarily in and through God's saving activity in the history of this people. The Psalmist and Isaiah speak of God as the Holy One (Isa 1:4; 5:19; Ps 99). In Isaiah's description of the court of heaven, angelic voices echo in acclamation: "Holy, holy, holy" (Isa 6:3).

The holiness of God becomes an extended quality by reason of proximity to God. The term "holy" is ascribed to specific places where God has appeared, or sites where God was worshiped and adored, e.g., the burning bush renders the ground holy (Exod 3:5) and Bethel is consecrated as a holy place (Gen 28:11-22). The Temple in Jerusalem was the holy place par excellence (1 Kgs 8:10-11). Objects set aside for Temple usage were designated holy and could not be used in ordinary life. Specific persons, especially the priests, were judged to be holy. Very few were permitted to enter those parts of the Temple wherein sacrifices and other ritual activities were conducted. Ritual observances were judged to be holy, e.g., those of the Sabbath (Gen 2:3) and other feasts (Lev 23). The name of God is itself holy (Lev 20:3). Certain times were understood to be holy, specifically the Exodus and covenant, and their annual celebration through festival and holy days. Indeed the whole history of Israel is itself holy, rooted in the experience of God's presence and activity in their past, present, and in the future which God has promised them. Israel itself is a holy nation, and this requires obedience to God's commandments, constantly turning from evil and sin. Specific ethical and ritual laws are enshrined in the Holiness Code (Lev 18–26). These are to be adhered to if the holiness of Israel is to be upheld: "You shall be holy; for I the Lord your God am holy" (Lev 19:2). The word of the prophets was judged to be holy, and the text of the Scriptures was understood as holy. Indeed every action for the glory of God was seen as holy.

This Old Testament understanding of holiness as otherness and setting apart or aside should not be understood in too spatial or too cultic a sense. There are at least three distinct and identifiable strands in Old Testament views of the holy. The priestly understanding of holiness emphasizes separation, purity, and segregation for cultic purity and practice. The prophetic view places strong accent on the relationship between worship, social justice, and conversion of heart. And the sapientiel current or wisdom tradition stresses personal integrity and moral uprightness of life in adherence to God's providential plan for humanity.

The New Testament understanding of holiness is rooted in the traditions of Judaism and builds upon them. Holiness reaches its climax in the person of Jesus the Christ. He fascinates those he encounters, and draws them to himself in love and compassion. Yet he is also a cause of amazement, wonder, and astonishment. In some he elicits fear and trembling. Jesus addresses God as "Holy Father" (John 17:11) and in the the Lord's Prayer he praises God the Father with the words "hallowed be thy name," petitioning God to be active in the world and in human life. Jesus is called holy numerous times because of his singularly important relationship to God. And he is said to be holy because of his actions (Matt 11:4-6). The demonic spirits recognized Jesus as the Holy One of God (Mark 1:24). Peter does also (John 6:69). At the Annunciation, the angel promises Mary that the Holy Spirit and God's power will make the child holy (Luke 1:35). The followers of Jesus refer to Jesus as holy after his death and resurrection (Acts 3:14; 4:27, 30). The Book of Revelation does as well (3:7).

The Holy Spirit is the continuing presence and power of Jesus in the account of Luke and in Acts. For Paul, the Holy Spirit sanctifies and teaches (Rom 15:13, 16; 1 Cor 2:13). In the Fourth Gospel, the Holy Spirit guides and strengthens the beloved community in their adversity (John 14:26). Christian people are God's holy people. The Holy Spirit enlightens, enlivens, guides, and heals Christians so that they may grow in the fullness of holiness which Jesus reveals in his own life and teaching. The holy is disclosed supremely in Jesus' self-sacrificial love. The Christian beholds God's glory first and foremost in Jesus' washing feet, and in his service to the wounded and the weak, the last and the least.

In early Christian understandings, holiness is not primarily a place, building, or thing. Because of the destruction of the Temple in A.D. 70, and because Gentile Christians had moved away from its practices, the holiness of the Temple was gradually deemphasized. The Temple nonetheless serves as a singularly important metaphor for a Christian understanding of holiness (1 Cor 3:17; 6:19). Holiness resides in a people, the body of Christ, who celebrate Christ's abiding presence in word and sacrament. The Church is a holy people, "holy ones," "saints" (Rom 1:7; 1 Cor 1:2) who await Christ's coming again in the fullness of time. Believers consecrate one another as holy, thereby becoming a corporate presence for the sanctification of the whole world. They are a holy nation (1 Pet 2:9) and are exhorted to be holy because God is holy (1 Pet 1:16). Through the continuing presence and power of the Holy Spirit, Christian life derives from God, indeed is participation in the very life of God, and so is holy. Believers must therefore avoid everything that is evil and sinful, and anything that would compromise the life of God within which constitutes them as temples of the Holy Spirit.

Historical Developments

In the New Testament and in the earliest Christian communities, holiness of life in and through the presence and power of the Holy Spirit came to be emphasized far more than priestly and cultic practices. Holiness was envisioned primarily as the fullness of life in Christ by the presence and power of the Holy Spirit. Christians were to be distinguished, marked as a people apart, by faith, hope, and love. Paul addresses Christians as saints or holy ones, inclusive terms extending the Jewish notion of a people chosen by God. Only later is the term applied in a restricted sense to those who were explicitly remembered in the liturgy because of the exemplary Christian lives they lived.

The historical development of Christian understandings of holiness can only be properly understood in light of the question of precisely what constitutes holiness of life. Various historical and theological factors have gone to shape views of holiness that have prevailed throughout Christianity. Perhaps none has been more important than the dominant image of God in various historical periods.

The holy person has often been understood as the one who, by virtue of a "higher calling," is set apart and above others for nobler purposes. He or she is set apart geographically or enclosed behind cloister walls, distanced from the everyday concerns of life "in the world," and from the ordinary pursuits of domestic and civil life. This notion of holiness as pertaining to those set apart may properly be understood to be grounded in a particular understanding of a God who dwells in light inaccessible, in solitary simplicity, unmoved by the events of human history and, because unchangeable, remains altogether unmoved by human pain and suffering. Such a notion of God as unaffected by the pains and possibilities of human development is in part the cause of a notion of holiness in which people flee the city and turn their backs on the world for the purposes of responding to the "higher" calling to live for God alone; a God whose being is understood to be removed and unaffected by the triumphs and tragedies of human life and history.

The holiness of God is understood here to be mirrored most perfectly in the Christian who is self-sufficient, who lives alone, and who remains unaffected by, or indifferent to, the actual historical circumstances that involve the great number of human beings. Such an approach to God gave rise to forms of Christian life that focused on the solitary quest for personal holiness by means of the inner journey through self-scrutiny and personal sanctification. Even though the monastic life (from *monos* = alone) gives particular attention to the requirements of community living, monasticism is properly understood as the solitary life pursued with others.

The monastic life became the model for most forms of the religious life in later centuries, even for religious sisters and brothers in "active" congregations, e.g., communities of nursing sisters or teaching brothers. From early Christian centuries, virginity and celibacy developed as superior forms of life. Celibacy in particular was understood as a form of the solitary, holy life that precluded sexuality, marriage, and active engagement in affective relationships. Holiness among the laity was often understood as derivative and lesser because of the priority given to virginity and celibacy. Models of holiness abounded, to be sure. But these exemplars engaged in excessive mortification, denial of pleasure, penance for sexual peccadillos. There is a dearth of models of Christian holiness who have led exemplary lives through the challenges of marital and family life; the uncertainties of rural and farm life with its daily struggles for making ends meet; tough choices about the proper usage of the goods of the earth; the chaste exercise of sexuality for single adults; responsibility for care of the earth; the rigors of education and study; disciplined care and exercise of the body (proper nutrition, balanced diet, integration of leisure and work); the burdens and exhaustion of too much work.

Even though there have been numerous exceptions to this predominant model of holiness, it has had a singular influence throughout Christian history. The holy person generally has been understood as the one with the "higher calling" to the religious life bound by vows of poverty, chastity, and obedience, or to the priesthood with its discipline of clerical celibacy. Both of these had as an intrinsic component abstinence from sexual relations and the foregoing of marriage and children. Religious life and priesthood have been regarded as the true Christian expressions of the life of holiness, and therefore "higher" than marriage and the single life.

Contemporary Perspectives

The Second Vatican Council has had inestimable influence on understanding Christian holiness in the contemporary Church and world. This is due in large measure to the understanding of holiness articulated in chapter five of *Lumen Gentium* (the Dogmatic Constitution on the Church), entitled "The Call of the Whole Church to Holiness." Here holiness is not accidental but essential to the life of the Church and each of its members. All are called to holiness of life, which is first and finally found in charity. Holiness is not just an ideal but a living reality in the Church. It is both gift and task. It is given by grace but also sought after by ongoing participation in the sacramental life of the Church and in its mission to be sacrament in and to the world. This entails ongoing conversion to a life of grace, and the avoidance of all that would compromise this gift. In this view there is greater recognition that the holiness of the Church will be worked out in marriage and in celibacy, through choices at home and in the workplace, in the classroom and in factories, in the range of human relationships including those with people of other races and classes, and among the poor, the wounded, the weak, the last and the least.

The awareness of the importance of human relationships and of community has been one of the distinguishing features in contemporary perspectives on Christian holiness. This must be seen in view of contemporary theological efforts to recover the centrality of the doctrine of the Trinity. Such efforts correct understandings of God as abstract and removed, unaffected by human life and history. From the perspective of a revitalized Trinitarian theology, God is understood first and foremost as a communion of persons, divine and human, in loving relation. God is God with us and for us in loving communion. Such an understanding of God implies that Christian holiness is more properly understood within the context of relationship. Holiness does not reside primarily with those who feel called apart or set apart to pursue nobler and loftier purposes, and who remain unmoved by daily concerns and the contingencies of life in the world. Christian holiness is realized by living in Christ by the presence and power of the Spirit who enables us to be for others in relationships of mutuality, reciprocity, and equality without subordination, grounded in the *perichoresis* of the three divine persons of the Trinity.

In this view, setting aside self-preoccupation and self-absorption in order to live in rightly ordered relations with others and God becomes the real task of Christian holiness. We find the fullest expression of Christian holiness not in standing apart from the affairs of human life and its concerns, but by entering into personal communion with the God who is for us. This entails being in communion with all human persons and with the whole of creation.

Here it must be recognized that contemporary understandings of holiness draw attention to the holiness and sanctity not just of human life, but of all creation. Even within a specifically Christian framework it must be recognized that Jesus offered his life not only for the salvation of those who believe, but for the whole world. And the Holy Spirit who enlightens, enlivens, guides, and heals human hearts also renews the face of the earth.

Conclusion

Above all else Christian holiness entails living in faith, hope, and love, exemplified to such an extraordinary degree in the lives of some persons that they are called saints. These are the ones who have gone before us in faith, embodying the heritage of the Christian life. They serve as signs of our common future, inviting us to the fullness of Christian life as something always to be more fully realized. And they open up new possibilities by demonstrating that Christian holiness is possible in vastly different cultures, social milieux, and historical periods.

One of the more pressing needs in the life of the Church today is for models of Christian holiness truly representative of the quite diverse forms of life in which people actually live. The great majority of those who are canonized saints are men. Most were celibate. Of the women canonized, the great majority were virgins, or were consecrated by formal religious vows. Married women who have been canonized were often widowed rather early in life, or separated from their husbands, and later became foundresses of religious congregations. There are relatively few "persons of color" who have been canonized as saints. In short there is a great measure of imbalance in the communion of saints, at least in terms of those canonized. But the communion of saints extends beyond those who have been formally recognized by canonization. And it includes children, women and men, married, single and celibate, people from vastly different socioeconomic strata and vastly different walks of life who have lived lives of faith, hope, and love in extraordinary measure, thereby demonstrating that Christian holiness is possible in *this* way of life.

MICHAEL DOWNEY

See also CHARITY; CHRISTIAN SPIRITUALITY; GRACE; SAINTS; VIRTUE.

HOLISTIC SPIRITUALITY

The word, "holistic," comes from the Greek word *holos* which means whole, entire, complete. Those who prefer to spell the word "wholistic" base their choice solely on the English language. The Greek word begins with an *omicron* (o) pronounced with a hard breathing (') which is always transliterated with an "h" and never a "wh."

This minor skirmish over spelling reflects different viewpoints. Those who prefer "wholistic" say the alternate spelling is too easily confused with "holy." Devotees of the wholistic approach are interested in wholes rather than parts and believe that the notion of "holy" or "holiness" has no necessary connection with wholistic philosophy.

Those who prefer to spell the word "holistic" are sometimes linguistic purists but more often people who believe that "the holy" and holiness however understood should be part of any all-embracing or holistic philosophy of human life and experience.

The word, "holistic," was first used in a 1926 book, *Holism and Evolution,* by a former prime minister of the Union of South Africa, Ian Christiaan Smuts (1919–1924). He observed that everything in nature tends to form wholes, and in nature any whole is far greater and much more complex than the sum of all its parts.

Smuts affirmed that evolution is "nothing but the gradual development and stratification of a progressive series of wholes, stretching from the inorganic beginnings to the highest levels of spiritual creation. Wholeness, healing, holiness—all expressions and ideas springing from the same root in (the English) language as in experience—lie on the rugged upward path of the universe." This is the core belief of holism.

Smuts applied the idea to politics (the British Empire; the League of Nations). About a generation later, some nutritionists borrowed the word to propose an alternative approach to health, healing, and medicine. The medical establishment in the United States generally dismisses "holistic health" as quackery. Very recently in the United States, the word has been used to describe new approaches to understanding and living "the spiritual life."

Spirituality

In the Judaeo-Christian Scriptures, the human person alone among all the creatures on earth was brought to life by the spirit-breath of God. "Then the Lord God formed an Earthling from the dust of the ground and breathed into its nostrils the breath of life. And the Earthling became a living creature" (Gen 2:7). In this perspective, the human person is an "inspirited body" or an "embodied spirit." Spirituality, therefore, is an approach to human living that pays serious attention to the spirit, human and divine. Spirituality can be defined as a way of life that is based on an experience of God (or transcendence) and shaped in response to that experience.

Through the centuries of Catholic tradition, some have glorified the body and its strength, beauty, or marvelous complexity and ignored the spiritual dimension of life. Others have devoted exclusive attention to the human soul or spirit and ignored, despised, or abused the human body. As a result, some spiritualities have tended to focus exclusively on the soul considering the body an impediment to perfection.

In the contemporary United States, psychology has become for some Catholics a surrogate spirituality. As one commentator noted: "I have long felt that what we call a spiritual truth can be validated *only* if we can legitimately turn it into a psychological truth." All of these attitudes are far from holistic.

Biblical Basis for Holistic Spirituality

Jesus' response to a question intending to shame him expresses the fundamental basis for holistic spirituality: "Love the Lord your God with all your heart, and with all your soul, and with all your strength, and with all your mind; and love your neighbor as yourself" (Luke 10:27). Each individual should respond to the experience of God with total and undivided love and commitment.

Early Christians took two paths toward achieving this commitment. The Synoptic Gospels emphasized an ascetic approach: taking up one's Cross and following Jesus; selling all to gain the pearl; gaining one's life by losing it. John, in contrast, reflects a mystical approach. A believer should become a branch in the vine, offer no obstacle to the flow of divine energy in creation. Even John's vocabulary ("be in" or "abide in") reflects a mystical or unitive mentality.

In Paul we find both approaches. Sometimes he uses athletic-ascetic imagery (running the race, fighting full strength and no shadow boxing), and at other times he speaks of the need to be "in Christ" in order to be someday "with Christ." All of this and more fits into a holistic spirituality.

An American Holistic Spirituality

John Carroll, America's first bishop, was a child of the American Revolution, and nothing was clearer to him than that "it was his task to incarnate the church in a world that was distinctively new." Generations of American Catholics have continued to this day to work at making this vision a reality. This is certainly true in the realm of spirituality. Americans have developed varieties of holistic spiritualities to better suit the American spirit. Wellness spirituality is but one among many.

Wellness spirituality is a way of life based on the experience of God mediated through American culture and shaped in distinctively personal response to that experience. It is a lifestyle that views and lives life as purposeful and pleasurable. It seeks out life-sustaining and life-enriching options to be chosen freely at every opportunity. It sinks its roots deeply into spiritual values and specific religious beliefs, classical spiritual traditions, and contemporary God-given insights into creation in all its manifold aspects.

Wellness, a holistic spirituality, attends to and respects every dimension of human life. It recognizes the spirit as the integrating force of all these dimensions: physical, psychological, mental, emotional, and many others.

Patterned after the Franciscan heritage emphasizing primacy of the will, wellness spirituality cherishes and promotes human freedom and enlightened free choices. This explains why wellness spirituality takes on many different forms. The classical Latin proverb (Terence; Cicero) cherished by the medieval Scholastics: "there are as many opinions as there are individuals" (*quot homines tot sententiae*) aptly describes the American pluralistic penchant for diversity in holistic spirituality.

JOHN J. PILCH

See also HEALING; SPIRITUAL LIFE.

HOLOCAUST (NAZI)

The Holocaust is the term used to refer to the systematic genocide of the Jewish people by the Nazis during the years 1933 through 1945. This "final solution" continues to be an ongoing concern since it raises innumerable questions about the ethical and religious values of the West.

The motivation of the Nazis and the means employed distinguish the Holocaust from other mass murders and forms of perverse brutality. With regard to motivation, the Holocaust was based on Nazi racist philosophy according to which the Jews (together with gypsies, homosexuals, etc.) were considered subhuman. Concerning the means employed, the Holocaust ran the gamut of dehumanizing cruelty from shootings to gas chambers and death camps. By the end of World War II the extent of the slaughter became known. Some six million Jews were dead, among them more than one million children. Europe's ancient Jewry had vanished. In Poland alone some three million Jews perished.

This unprecedented inhumanity has led to a number of upsetting questions for Christians in general and Catholics in particular. What made this atrocity possible in the very heart of Western culture? Why were there not more efforts to rescue the victims? Did Christian anti-Semitism help to make the Holocaust possible? How is one to explain the silence of the various Christian Churches? How is one to interpret the role of Pope Pius XII? What lessons are to be learned from the Holocaust, so that it will not happen again?

The Catholic Church has taken some steps to respond to these questions. In the conciliar declaration on non-Christian religions, *Nostra Aetate* (1965), the Church speaks of the positive elements in the Jewish-Christian relationship. Two other Vatican statements have built upon *Nostra Aetate.* They are the 1975 Guidelines for the Implementation of *Nostra Aetate* and the 1985 *Notes for the Correct Presentation of Jews and Judaism in Catholic Preaching and Catechetics.* In the latter document there is the directive that catechesis should help in understanding the significance for the Jews of the extermination during the years 1939 through 1945. Other positive signs of Catholic response to the questions

The entrance to Auschwitz-Birkenau

of the Holocaust are Pope John Paul II's visit to Auschwitz in June, 1979, his address to the United Nations Assembly in October, 1985, and his historic visit to Rome's main synagogue in April, 1986.

JOHN F. CRAGHAN

See also ANTI-SEMITISM; JUDAISM; MARTYRDOM; VATICAN COUNCIL II.

HOLY DAYS

The feast days of the Church which are observed by attendance at Mass and, if possible, rest from servile work (i.e., needless work or chores which would hinder the intended physical and spiritual rejuvenation). In the United States, there are currently six holy days: Solemnity of Mary, 1 January; Ascension of Christ, forty days after Easter; Assumption of the Blessed Mother, 15 August; All Saints' Day, 1 November; Immaculate Conception of the Blessed Mother, 8 December; and Christmas, 25 December. Special Masses are to be offered in each parish on these days.

JOSEPH QUINN

See also LITURGY.

HOLY GHOST FATHERS AND BROTHERS (SPIRITANS)

The evangelization of the "poor" is the purpose of this clerical religious congregation which comprises clerics and consecrated laymen. According to their rule (ch. 1, par. 4) these "Spiritans" as they are often called "go especially to peoples, groups and individuals who have not yet heard the message of the Gospel or who have scarcely heard it, to those whose needs are the greatest and to the oppressed." They also "willingly accept tasks for which the Church has difficulty in finding workers."

Founder: *Claude-Francis Poullart des Places (1679–1709)*

The Spiritans were founded in Paris on 27 May 1703 in the era of Louis XIV when the first community assembled on the feast of Pentecost. Renouncing a title to noble status and an immense family fortune, the young founder, aged twenty-four, perhaps the youngest founder of a religious congregation in the history of the Church, assembled with a group of poor students who, despite their very limited means, wanted to become priests. Although he was only a clerical student himself, he did not hesitate to demand a commitment from all members of this unusual "Seminary of the Holy Spirit" that they "would always serve in preference in posts for which the Church with difficulty found volunteers." The project flourished steadily. Although not a religious institute from the beginning, the young society adopted a community way of life in which the practice of the evangelical counsels was fostered. Claude himself was ordained in 1707. But his premature death in 1709 nearly marked the end of the young congregation. Although his first two associates also died within a year, the young students managed to keep his dream and his seminary alive. Eventually the majority committed themselves to serve on the foreign missions. When the revolutionary government suppressed the seminary in 1793, some 800 Spiritans were serving in France and its colonies. But the society managed to rise again and to survive the persecution in the very difficult years after their restoration in 1805. It was granted full religious status with the approval of its rule and constitutions in 1855.

In 1848 the convert Jew Francis Libermann became superior general and the society was renewed and transformed into a dynamic force for the evangelization of Africa. Born at Saverne, France, in 1802, Libermann became a Christian on Christmas Eve 1826. Despite the fact that he had a serious epileptic condition, Libermann was ordained in 1841. In the same year he founded his Congregation of the Holy Heart of Mary for an apostolate among the blacks, especially the slave population of Haiti and Reunion. Within a year he sent the first members to the Two Guineas, an area stretching along 5,000 miles of Africa's western coast. Like des Places' society, that of Libermann was not a religious institute. However, both the founder and first members attached much importance to community life. In practice the evangelical counsels were observed, even if not under public vow. In 1848, with the encouragement of the Holy See, Libermann's society was suppressed. Its members joined the Congregation of the Holy Ghost and Libermann was elected its eleventh superior general.

The Congregation and its Work

Both des Places and Libermann saw their apostolate in response to the needs and signs of the times. They did not tend to act in terms of blueprints or preconceived notions. By and large this open-ended apostolic concern has determined their congregation's commitments over the years. Libermann himself moved beyond Haiti and Reunion to Mauritius, Australia, Africa, and a wide variety of apostolates in France. Since his time the congregation has undertaken work in every continent and in many of the islands of the Atlantic and Pacific Oceans. This work has ranged from first evangelization in Africa, to orphanages in France, to schools in Ireland, and Duquesne University in Pittsburgh, U.S.A. But it has always been undertaken as part of the Church's apostolate with pride of place given to evangelizing the poor in accordance with the vision of the founders.

The story of its successes and failures is well told by Henry J. Koren, C.S.Sp., in his general history *To the Ends of the Earth,* Duquesne University Press, Pittsburgh, 1983. During three centuries his account embraces epic struggles with despotic governments and even more despotic revolutionaries, in wars and disasters of every type. He describes some members close to the remote borders of Tibet or clinging to tiny footholds in Africa dreaming of their many successors who would reap the harvest they had planted. They reached North America in 1732, the year George Washington was born. Some years later they traveled the matted jungles and strange waterways of South America as they grew to a worldwide congregation of some thirty-five nationalities working in fifty-five countries.

Today (1992) the total is 3295 (down from 4237 in 1974) of whom 42.6 percent are in Europe, 37.1 percent in Africa, 13.7 percent in North America and the Caribbean, 0.3 percent in Asia and 0.6 percent in Oceania. Some 538 members are in formation of which 80 percent are in the Southern Hemisphere and, significantly, 72 percent in Africa.

SEAN P. KEALY, C.S.Sp.

See also MISSIONARIES (OR MISSIONERS), COMMUNITIES OF.

HOLY HOUR

An hour of continuous devotion to the Holy Eucharist, which is either exposed on the altar or reposed in the tabernacle, through prayer and meditation. Its inspiration is found in Jesus' rebuke to the apostles in Gethsemane: "Can you not watch one hour with me?" In a personal vision St. Margaret Mary Alacoque (1647–1690) was instructed by Christ to practice this special act of piety as part of the Sacred Heart Devotion. It has been supported by numerous popes throughout the ages. Public Holy Hours are designated and arranged by a priest or director, while private Holy Hours may be observed at any time. Traditionally, the latter have been made on Thursday or Friday evenings.

JOSEPH QUINN

See also EUCHARISTIC DEVOTIONS.

HOLY OFFICE

See CONGREGATION FOR THE DOCTRINE OF THE FAITH.

HOLY OILS

Used in Old Testament times to anoint priests, prophets, and kings, and in the apostolic age to anoint the sick (Mark 6:13), holy oils have been consistently used by the Church in the administration of sacraments. The three oils presently used—holy chrism, the oil of catechumens, and the oil of the sick—have traditionally been made from either pure olive oil or, in the case of holy chrism, olive oil mixed with balsam; they may now be drawn from any plant. They symbolize spiritual nourishment and divine countenance, and are now used in the public administration of baptism, holy orders, and the anointing of the sick.

Holy oils are normally blessed on Holy Thursday by the bishop at his cathedral, after which they are distributed to the local parishes. When not in use, the oils are kept in vessels in an ambry.

JOSEPH QUINN

See also BLESSING, CHRISM; SACRAMENTS.

HOLY ORDERS

See SACRAMENT OF ORDERS.

HOLY ROMAN EMPIRE

A major political configuration of kingdoms, duchies, principalities, and free cities in Europe from the ninth to the nineteenth centuries. It was established in A.D. 800—with the coronation of Charlemagne by Pope Leo III—for the purpose of unifying the former western domain of the ancient Roman Empire, on which it was modeled. Spanning much of central and western Europe, it included the kingdoms of France, Germany, and Italy. The title of emperor lapsed in 924 but was restored by Pope John XII in 962, when he crowned Otto I of Germany Emperor. Otto I's successors were of the Saxon, Salian, and Hohenstaufen dynasties. From the thirteenth century until 1806, when the empire was abolished by Napoleon I, the office of emperor was held by the Hapsburgs of Austria, with one exception. The eighteenth-century French author Voltaire once remarked that it was "neither Holy, nor Roman, nor an Empire." Indeed, its rulers were often in conflict with the Church, it was Teutonic rather than Roman, and it was an empire only in theory.

JOSEPH QUINN

See also CHARLEMAGNE; CHURCH AND STATE.

HOLY SEE

Technically, it is the see of the pope, Bishop of Rome. However, the term usually refers to the authority, jurisdiction, and functions of government exercised by the pope, with the assistance of the Roman Curia, in administering the affairs of the Church around the world. The Curia's functions are delineated by canons 330–367 and in *Pastor Bonus,* the apostolic constitution (28 June 1988) of John Paul II. It consists of various congregations, tribunals, councils, and administrative bodies including the Congregation for the Doctrine of the Faith, the Congregation for Sacraments and Divine Worship, and the Secretariat of State.

MICHAEL GLAZIER

See also CURIA, ROMAN; PAPACY, THE.

HOLY SEPULCHER

The name given both to the tomb in which Jesus is buried and the church which stands on the traditional site of his death, burial, and resurrection. The church stands in the northwest quarter of the Old City of Jerusalem. The Roman Emperor Constantine I the Great (313–337) first excavated the hill of Calvary where Christ was crucified, and he built the original Church of the Holy Sepulcher (also called the Church of the Anastasis or Resurrection) on this site. In his construction, he attempted to enclose both the place of Jesus' cross and the place of his tomb. This first church was completed and consecrated in 336. It stood until 614 when Persian invaders burnt it to the ground. Between 616 and 636 an abbot named Modestus led the effort to build a new church, which stood until the eleventh century when the Muslim caliph Hakim had it destroyed. To re-

Church of the Holy Sepulchre

place it, ca. 1130 the crusaders built a new and much larger church, which stood until 1310 when it was partially rebuilt. In 1808 the medieval church partially burned down, and the present Church of the Holy Sepulchre dates largely from the rebuilt church of 1810. Several Christian sects share the church, including the Armenian, Coptic, Greek Orthodox, and Roman Catholic Churches. Scholars continue to debate whether the church actually stands over the place of Jesus' death and burial; future archaeology may hold the answer. But it must be noted that there are no convincing arguments against this location, nor does any other location have a strong claim to be the site. Regardless of the archaeological niceties, the present site of the Holy Sepulcher has been a sacred place since the fourth century and has played a significant role in the Christian presence and witness in Palestine.

JOSEPH F. KELLY

See also PILGRIMAGES.

HOLY SPIRIT

The Holy Spirit is the "Lord and Giver of Life" (2 Cor 3:6; John 6:63; Nicene-Constantinopolitan Creed), the third divine Person in whom believers are joined to the triune God and to all to whom God's love binds them. As the source of transformed life in Christ (Rom 8:2, 6, 9; Gal 5:16, 25), the Holy Spirit is at the heart of Christian existence. The very name "Christian" (from *christos,* "anointed") designates those anointed by the risen Lord with the same Spirit who transformed the human existence of Jesus. Christian life is thus "life in the Spirit." Through the Holy Spirit, believers intimately share in the Spirit-permeated life of the risen Lord and are transformed into a new creation. Becoming "one body, one Spirit in Christ," they are formed into the community of the Church called to self-giving love in the world, especially to those most in need.

The following article develops these themes by reflecting first on the Spirit in Scripture and tradition, tracing the broad outlines of key scriptural, patristic, and medieval insights on the Spirit, including the meaning of Pentecost and the gifts and fruits of the Spirit. The second part of the article reflects on the Holy Spirit in modern Catholic thought and life by considering historical developments until the present time; the Holy Spirit at work in the lives of Christians through the sacramental economy; and the Holy Spirit leading the Church into the future.

The Holy Spirit in Scripture and Tradition

The Spirit in Scripture. "The flesh profits nothing; only the Spirit gives life" (John 6:63). These words voice the conviction of Scripture and tradition about the absolute centrality of the Holy Spirit for believers. In the Hebrew as well as Christian Scriptures, human effort without God is often termed "the flesh"; unaided human endeavors, like cut grass, quickly wither and die (Isa 40:6). But wherever true power surges, wherever new life springs up and with vitality endures, wherever there is anything kind and good in human life, the Spirit of God is actively present.

The Hebrew word for spirit, *rûaḥ*, means also "wind" or "breath." Israel found an illuminating image for God's creative power or *rûaḥ* in the desert wind bringing life-giving rain to the earth. The *rûaḥ* of God hovered over the abyss (Gen 1:2) and by the power of this creative breath accompanying God's Word or *dabar,* all of creation came to be. Hebrew scriptural authors also found a striking symbol of God's life-giving power in the breath within living persons, a life-breath that comes from God and returns to God at a person's death (Gen 2:7; Ps 104:29-30; Job 34:14-15).

The "Spirit of God" was also the creative power which came upon chosen members of the Israelite community, such as the judges, to achieve powerful deeds (Judg 6:34; 1 Sam 11:6; Judg 13:25; 15:14). Wherever life was vigorously manifested, God's mighty *rûaḥ* was felt to be at work. Thus the enthusiastic, ecstatic states of the early prophetic bands were attributed to the power of the "breath" of God which no human force can manipulate or control (1 Sam 10:10). It was in this Spirit's anointing, therefore, that prophets proclaimed God's life-giving word to the people (Mic 3:8; Ezek 2:2).

With the prophet Ezekiel a profound new way of envisioning God's creative *rûaḥ* appeared. In the wake of Israel's destruction and exile in Babylon, Ezekiel prophesied the joyous return of the people to their homeland in the remarkable image of a nation being raised from the dead. Through the power of the Spirit of God who alone gives life, the people who had been devastated like a skeleton's dry bones would rise and live again, returning from the death of their exile to a whole new life in their homeland (Ezek 37:1-14). "I will put MY Spirit within you and you shall live" (Ezek 37:14). Far from being simply a transitory power given to certain individuals to perform a mighty deed or to speak a powerful word, the Spirit of God is envisioned by Ezekiel as placed deep within the *entire* people as *interior* power to transform their hearts: "I will give you a new heart and put a new spirit within you. I will put *my* spirit *within* you" (Ezek 36:26, 27).

As they reflected on these and other passages of the Hebrew Scriptures relating to the Spirit of God, early Christians discovered in their own lives the fulfillment of Joel 2:28: "In the last days I will pour out my Spirit upon all flesh" (Acts 2:17). These disciples of the risen Lord experienced an overwhelming new life within and among them. They identified the source of this life as the same Spirit of God who permeated the human existence of Jesus and in whose power he was raised from the dead.

Among the Christian Scriptures, the writings of Paul, Luke, and John focus in a particular way on the central role of the Holy Spirit in Christian life. For Paul, the Holy Spirit is at the very heart of Christian belief and life (Rom 8:1-11; Gal 5:16-26). This Spirit is Christ's own Spirit (Rom 8:9; Phil 1:19; Gal 4:6), in whose power he was raised from the dead (Rom 8:11). The same Spirit who transformed the human existence of Jesus now dwells in those baptized into Christ, leading them to him (1 Cor 12:3). Freed to live a whole new life of love in the power of the Spirit (2 Cor 3:17; Rom 7:6), Christians become "Spirit-permeated" (1 Cor 2:13-15): "You are not in the flesh, you are in the Spirit, if the Spirit of God dwells in you" (Rom 8:9).

For Paul, therefore, human life without the Holy Spirit is no life at all; it is devoid of power, sweetness, hope. He terms unaided human efforts the "flesh," whose pitiful "works" result in strife, anger, jealousy, dissension, envy, drunkenness, carousing, enmity, immorality (Gal 5:19-21). But the Holy Spirit of life poured out by the risen Lord gives human persons the power to live in a totally different way, with a joy, peace (Rom 14:17), and freedom (Gal 5:13, 16, 22-23) that infinitely surpass what merely human efforts could accomplish or imagine. The Spirit unites believers so intimately with Jesus that in the Holy Spirit they have a whole new power to pray (Rom 8:26), addressing the first divine person with Jesus' own intimate, familiar name, *Abba* (Gal 4:6). No longer strangers and slaves filled with the spirit of fear, Christians are transformed by "the Spirit of sons and daughters" (Rom 8:15, 16).

Paul stresses that the Spirit's intimate activity does not form isolated individuals but a community of people in loving relationship, united to the triune God and one another in the "communion (*koinonia*) of the Holy Spirit" (2 Cor 13:14) with the triune God and one another. By the Spirit they are baptized into the one body of Christ, the Church, and drink of the one Spirit (1 Cor 12:13). In this body of Christ, each member is important; the Spirit gives to each one his or her own gifts and service in fostering the growth of the entire body (1 Cor 12:4-11). Infusing all the gifts is the Spirit's own charity (Rom 5:5; 1 Cor 13:1-13) by which Christians are called to give themselves to others in unselfish love and service (Gal 5:13). Even now, the Holy Spirit is the "guarantee" of the joy of heaven, where what is mortal will be "swallowed up by life" (2 Cor 5:4, 5) and human beings will share fully in the Spirit-permeated existence (1 Cor 15:42-44) of the risen Christ.

The evangelist Luke envisions the Holy Spirit as the eschatological Gift in answer to all of God's promises (Acts 2:38). From the moment of his conception, Jesus himself was filled with the Holy Spirit (Luke 1:15, 35). With the other evangelists (Mark 3:10-12; Matt 3:16; John 1:33), Luke depicts the Holy Spirit descending on Jesus at his baptism so that he lived his entire life in the power of the Holy Spirit (Luke 3:22; 4:1, 14): "The Spirit of the Lord is upon me, for the Lord has anointed me to bring good news to the poor" (Isa 61:1; Luke 4:18). And at his death, the Spirit of life gloriously transformed Jesus' human existence. This same Spirit, who is the entire treasure of the Father's heart (Luke 11:13), is now lavished on believers by the risen Lord (Acts 2:1-47; Acts 10:38).

To encounter the risen Lord in faith, therefore, is to experience "Pentecost," the outpouring of his Holy Spirit of love. The word *Pentecoste,* meaning "fiftieth," is a Greek word applied to the Hebrew Shabuoth or "Feast of Weeks," a harvest festival beginning with the feast of Unleavened Bread and continuing for seven weeks. For Luke, the feast of Weeks symbolized the abundant life in the Spirit which the early community experienced as a result of the Spirit's outpouring by the risen Lord. The number "seven" symbolizes fullness; one more than seven times seven connotes inconceivable plenitude. Luke envisions the risen Lord's outpouring of the Spirit upon the Church as the new "Pentecost."

Adopting this perspective from Luke, the Church throughout the centuries has joyously celebrated the resurrection of the Lord during one long "feast" beginning on Easter Sunday, and culminating fifty days later on the "Great Sunday" of Pentecost. Pentecost is thus the fulfillment of the entire paschal mystery, the birth of the Church in the Spirit. The entire Acts of the Apostles, Luke's second book of his two-part work, recounts the joy and power of this Spirit filling the Church and spreading its boundaries to the ends of the earth.

In the Gospel of John also, the giving of the Spirit is seen as the culmination of the paschal mystery; at the very moment of his death, Jesus "handed over his spirit" (John 19:30). The author of John envisions the Holy Spirit descending and remaining on Jesus so that he might bestow the same Spirit on his disciples (John 1:33; 7:37–39). The Holy Spirit is the Paraclete ("Counselor," "Advocate"), given by the risen Lord to be with and for his disciples. The Spirit is also the "Spirit of truth" dwelling within them and leading them into the fullness of truth (John 14:16-17; 15:26; 16:7-15).

Patristic Understanding of the Holy Spirit. During the following centuries, Christians' experience of living in the power and intimacy of the Holy Spirit drew them to articulate in a public way the personal identity of the Spirit as the Giver of Life within and among them. For the words of Ezekiel 36:26-27 had taken on a profound, new meaning for the early Church: "I will give you a new heart and put a new spirit within you. I will put *my* Spirit within you."

Under the Holy Spirit's inspiration, early Christians began to recognize that the peace, joy, and forgiveness they felt, the loving communion with God and one another which they experienced, were not the fruit of an impersonal power but of Someone, the Holy Spirit, Giver of life (John 6:63). They grew to realize that the impersonal images of the Spirit in Scripture—breath, wind, fire, water, dove, gift, promise—hint at the Holy Spirit's identity as a divine Person. Just as human beings cannot live without breath, water, or warmth, without freedom, truth, or love, they cannot live without the Holy Spirit. Even more, this Spirit does not receive life as a creature does but rather gives life as only God can do (2 Cor 3:6; John 6:63).

For a half-century after the Council of Nicaea's profession of faith in the divinity of Jesus (A.D. 325), the Church continued to struggle with Arian and semi-Arian interpretations of the philosophical term used at Nicaea, *homoousios,* "one in being." At the same time the Church had to respond to other Arians, termed Pneumatomachians or "Spirit-fighters," who did not believe in the divinity and personhood of the Holy Spirit.

In proclaiming the divinity of Jesus, Eastern Church Fathers had argued, "If Christ is not God, we are not saved." Now, in defending the divinity of the Spirit, they again spoke from the depths of their own experience: "If the Spirit is not God, we are not divinized." Through their baptism they were filled with the joy and power of God's own life—which Eastern Christians call "divinization." This experience, as well as the liturgical practice of praying "in" the Spirit and of worshipping the Spirit with the Father and the Son, impelled bishop-theologians such as Athanasius and the "Cappadocians"—Basil the Great, Gregory of Nazianzus, and Gregory of Nyssa—to defend the personal identity and divinity of the Spirit.

Under the leadership of Gregory of Nazianzus, the Council of Constantinople (A.D. 381) proclaimed the Church's belief in the Holy Spirit, "Lord and Giver of Life." The Nicene Creed had professed belief simply "in the Holy Spirit." Avoiding the technical philosophical language that had occasioned so many debates after Nicaea, council fathers at Constantinople affirmed the Church's belief in the divinity of the Spirit by adding to the Nicene Creed words drawn from Scripture, "Lord and Giver of life" (2 Cor 3:6; John 6:63).

For the centuries preceding Constantinople, the Church had struggled with the issue of whether the Holy Spirit is something or Someone. This ambiguity stems from the New Testament itself. The Holy Spirit is often referred to by an impersonal pronoun, since the word for spirit, *pneuma,* is a noun of neuter gender in Greek. But other New Testament texts, especially in the Acts of the Apostles and chapters 14 through 16 of the Gospel of John, refer to the Holy Spirit with words and pronouns that are personal (Acts 13:2; 16:6-7; John 14:26; 16:7-15). After four centuries of theological struggle surrounding the personal identity of the Holy Spirit, the Council of Constantinople solemnly proclaimed the Church's belief in the Holy Spirit not as a personification of God's power, but as third divine Person, transcending all that human beings mean by "person."

In the West, Augustine of Hippo developed a pneumatology (theology of the Spirit) drawn from Neoplatonic insights which helped him to illumine the profound meaning of Romans 5:5: "God's love has been poured into our hearts through the Holy Spirit who has been given to us." These words inspired Augustine to reflect on the Holy Spirit as the divine Person who is the Father's and Son's Love for one another in person, their Embrace and Delight, their Joy and Gift in person. This same Spirit has been given to believers as the intimate bond of love uniting them to God and to one another (Augustine, *On the Trinity* 5.15; 6.10; 19.36, 37; see also Hilary, *On the Trinity* 2:1; Aquinas, ST I, q. 38, a. 2). Because Scripture affirms that both the Son and Spirit proceed from the Father, Augustine also tried to illumine how the Spirit is distinct from the Son: as their love in person, the Spirit proceeds from both the Father "and the Son" (in Latin, *filioque*).

In the eleventh century, the *filioque* was inserted into the Nicene-Constantinopolitan Creed recited at Rome. Eastern Christians viewed this as a nonscriptural tampering with the Creed, a subordination of the Spirit to the Son and a denigration of the Father's unique identity in the Trinity. The *filioque* thus became a key reason, among many other political and theological factors, for the eventual schism between Western and Eastern Christians in 1054. Ironically, this tragic break in Church unity centered on differing theologies of the Spirit who is source of the Church's love and unity.

Medieval Theology of the Spirit, Gifts and Fruits. Thomas Aquinas developed a theology of the Spirit as well as the gifts and fruits of the Spirit which has influenced theological thinking in the West until the present time. With Augustine, he stressed the Holy Spirit's personal identity as the Father's and Son's Love and therefore Gift (ST I, qq. 37, 38). As the person of Love, the Spirit is the heart and soul of the Church, giving its members life, and intimately uniting them to God and to one another as the one body of Christ (ST III, q. 8, a. 1, ad 3).

It was also in the cherished gift of friendship that Thomas found intimations of the Holy Spirit's personal identity. Just as intimate friends console and delight the hearts of their loved ones, the Holy Spirit, the Comforter, fills believers with delight and security in God even in difficulties (Aquinas, *Summa Contra Gentiles* IV, 22, 3). Christians are meant not only to use the Spirit's power and gifts in their lives, therefore, but even more to enjoy the Holy Spirit, to delight in the Holy Spirit's closeness as one delights in the presence of an intimate friend (ST I, q. 43, a. 3). They are meant to draw their every breath from the Spirit of life within them (*Commentary on Galatians* 5, Lectio 7) and thus to flourish according to the Holy Spirit's purposes rather than the confines of their own narrow plans.

Thomas' theology of the Spirit is intimately linked to his understanding of the "seven gifts" (Isa 11:2-3) and "twelve fruits" (Gal 5:22-23) of the Spirit. With other medieval theologians, he accorded great importance to the gifts and fruits as essential means of experiencing the profound difference that the Holy Spirit makes in human lives.

Isaiah 11:2-3 describes the future messianic king as endowed with wisdom, understanding, counsel, knowledge, fortitude, and fear of the Lord. The Greek translation of the Hebrew Scriptures, the Septuagint, duplicates "fear of the Lord" with the translation, "piety," thus bringing the list of qualities to seven, symbolizing plenitude. St. Paul does not use this list of "seven gifts," but he does urge Christians to live in the power of the Spirit (Gal 5:16, 25), and to be led and moved by the Spirit of God (Rom 8:14). Thomas considers how, in baptism, the Spirit gives to believers certain habits which enable them to do precisely this. The "seven gifts of the Spirit" dispose believers to follow the Holy Spirit's leading promptly, easily, gladly, inspiring and anointing them with the power to live in a way that surpasses all that human effort alone could do (ST I-II, q. 68, aa. 1-8).

Wisdom is the gift to know God and the things of God by an intimate union with them through the familiarity of love (ST II-II, q. 45, a. 2). The gift of understanding enables believers to penetrate to the very heart of the truths of faith and to understand more deeply their meaning (ST II-II, q. 8, a. 6). The Spirit's gift of knowledge gives an intuitive, sure judgment in discerning the truth from error about created reality (ST II-II, q. 9, a. 1). Counsel perfects human prudence and enables believers to know intuitively what should be done in certain situations (ST II-II, q. 52, a. 2). In the gift of fortitude the Spirit bestows an inner confidence that conquers fear and empowers believers to face difficult situations with God's own strength and courage (ST II-II, q. 139, a. 1). Piety gives an affection and familiarity with the Father, intensifying desire to give God glory and to do good to all people (ST I-II, q. 68, a. 4, ad 2). Finally, the gift of fear of the Lord tempers lust for pleasure, drawing the human heart to revere God and lovingly to avoid all that is displeasing to God (ST II-II, q. 19, a. 9).

Paul stresses that in giving believers communion with the risen Lord, the Holy Spirit fills them with the Spirit's own joy and peace (Rom 8:6; 14:17). In the Epistle to the Galatians he contrasts qualities that are the "fruit" of the Spirit with the "works of the flesh" stemming from unaided human efforts (Gal 5:16-17). In doing so, he lists nine attributes that characterize Christian life in the Spirit: love, joy, peace, patience, kindness, goodness (generosity), faith (faithfulness), gentleness, and self-control (Gal 5:22-23). The Vulgate has duplicate words in Latin for some of the Greek words and so adds to the above list modesty, continence, and chastity. These twelve "fruits" represent the manifold good effects of the Holy Spirit in the life of believers. In reflecting on these fruits (ST I-II, q. 70), Thomas Aquinas comments on how the Spirit's peace and joy especially fill us with contentment, since they flow only from love. For what we do out of love, we do most willingly, with the greatest freedom and delight (Aquinas, ST II-II, q. 23, a. 2). The fruits of the Spirit of love thus transform the human heart, changing fear and anxiety into growing security, inner directedness, trust, and self-giving to others.

The Holy Spirit in Modern Catholic Thought and Life

Historical Background. The writings, homilies, commentaries on Scriptures, and baptismal instructions of early Christian writers, especially the Eastern Fathers of the Church, are permeated with the sense of the Holy Spirit active in the life of the Church. This focus on the centrality of the Holy Spirit has been maintained in the life, liturgy, and theology of the Eastern Christian Churches until the present time. For many reasons, the same has not been true for Western Christianity. After the tragic schism of 1054, the Western Church lost contact with many sources in Eastern Christianity that would have kept alive an awareness of the Spirit in Christian life, liturgy, and theology. In addition, the plague that decimated Europe in the fourteenth century had disastrous effects in the life of the Western Church, including the repopulation of monasteries and ranks of the clergy with ignorant and unworthy candidates. The sacraments often became empty ritual as they were divorced from the Spirit-filled proclaiming of the word essential to their reality.

In the context of these and other debilitating factors, the Church that was meant to be the community of God's people animated by the Holy Spirit not infrequently became in the West an institution with leaders guided by desire for power and wealth rather than the Spirit of God. Thus the way was opened for the Protestant Reformation of the sixteenth century.

During the sixteenth to the first part of the twentieth century, writers who were steeped in the Scriptures, patristic writings, and liturgical texts kept a focus on the Holy Spirit that was often lost to the Catholic Church in the West. Mystics such as the sixteenth-century Carmelite John of the Cross experienced the intimacy of the Spirit as the "living Flame of Love" in the depths of the those surrendered to God, and writers such as the seventeenth-century Jesuit Louis Lallemant stressed the need for docility to the Holy Spirit as the essence of the spiritual life. During the nineteenth century theologians such as Cardinal John Henry Newman, Cardinal Henry Edward Manning, and Matthias Scheeben wrote of the fundamental importance of the Holy Spirit in the Christian life. In 1897 Pope Leo XIII published an encyclical on the Holy Spirit, *Divinum Illud Munus,* in which he spoke of the Holy Spirit as the "soul" of the Church, a theme drawn from Augustine and Thomas Aquinas. Pope Pius XII later developed this motif in his 1943 encyclical on the Church as the Mystical Body of Christ (*Mystici Corporis*).

In the years preceding Vatican II, twentieth-century writers such as Dom Columba Marmion, O.S.B., Yves Congar, O.P., Louis Bouyer, and Archbishop Luis Martinez, whose own lives were fed by the study of Scripture, liturgy, and the Fathers of the Church, continued to emphasize the central role of the Holy Spirit in the Church, thus preparing the way for the remarkable event that would be the Second Vatican Council. In 1959 Pope John XXIII announced that he would convoke an ecumenical council. In urging prayer for the outpouring of the Holy Spirit in a new Pentecost on the entire Church through this council, Pope John used words echoing themes stressed by writers such as Dom Columba Marmion.

The Holy Spirit Encountered Today in the Sacraments. The texts of Vatican II (1962–1965) are not as permeated by a pneumatology as council observers such as the Orthodox Nikos Nissiotis and others urged. Nevertheless, they do call the Church to a new awareness of the centrality of the Spirit in the lives of Christians. The Constitution on the Church, for example, affirms that it is the whole People of God and not simply the clergy who are "anointed" by the Holy Spirit through their baptism (LG 12; PO 2). The Holy Spirit pervades the Church and accomplishes a profound "communion of the faithful," distributing to all believers various gifts and ministries to build up the body of Christ (UR 2; LG 12, 13; AA 3). Every member of the Church is called in this way to let the Holy Spirit permeate his or her life. Indeed, lay people are urged to do all that they do in the Spirit of God, to live their entire life with its every dimension, including "family and married life, daily work and relaxation" in the Holy Spirit (LG 34).

The Constitution on the Sacred Liturgy emphasizes that it is precisely through the sacraments that Christians can grow most deeply in this life of the Spirit, for "the liturgy is the summit and source of the Church's activity" (SC 10; see also LG 50). The liturgical renewal initiated by the council thus highlights the central role of the Holy Spirit in the sacaments as the Church's participation in the Lord's death and resurrection. It is through the invoking of the Holy Spirit on the elements of the sacraments that earthly realities like water and oil, bread and wine are transformed to mediate God's presence and grace. The Spirit is also invoked upon those who celebrate these sacraments so that their hearts and lives may be transformed as well.

Baptism, the fundamental sacrament of initiation, plunges believers into the mystery of the Lord's death and resurrection, intimately uniting them to the triune God and to the community of the Church as members of the Lord's body: "By one Spirit we were all baptized into one body, and all were made to drink of one Spirit" (1 Cor 12:13). In the early Church, the process of sacramental initiation included baptism, anointing with chrism, with the laying on of hands by the bishop, and the reception of the Eucharist. Through a complex series of factors, these components of initiation eventually came to be separated. The Council of Trent (1545–1563) acknowledged seven sacraments, thus officially identifying confirmation as a distinct sacrament. In the Vatican II Rite of Christian Initiation of Adults the central role of the Holy Spirit in the initiation process is asserted and the intimate relation of baptism, confirmation, and Eucharist is reclaimed.

Through confirmation, believers are united intimately with Jesus and his Church in the gift of Pentecost. Joined with the entire community, the bishop prays for those to be confirmed "that the Holy Spirit may act in the depths of their spirit and make them like Jesus Christ." While extending his hands over each candidate, the bishop invokes the Holy Spirit on each of them. The Spirit is again invoked as the foreheads of those being confirmed are anointed with chrism: "Be sealed with the Holy Spirit" (cf. Eph 1:13). Through baptism and confirmation believers thus are "stamped" in their inmost being with the very Spirit of God, so that they belong completely to God. Two differing theological attempts to explain the meaning of confirmation today focus on its nature as a sacrament either of "initiation" or of "maturation." This latter approach stresses that it is an outpouring of the Spirit to "confirm" or strengthen Christians to live the Christian mission of Pentecost, witnessing in the world to the risen Lord.

The final sacrament of initiation, the Eucharist, is the fulfillment and culmination toward which all the other sacraments are directed. The liturgical renewal begun by Vatican II has restored in the Western Church the central place of the twofold *epiklesis* or invoking of the Spirit upon the bread and wine to transform them into the Body and Blood of Christ, and on the people to form them into "one body, one Spirit in Christ" (Eucharistic Prayer III; see also Eucharistic Prayers II and IV). The Holy Spirit thus bears a special relationship to the Eucharist as the sacrament of love and the Church's unity, since the Eucharist joins believers intimately with the person of the Lord whose one body Christians are (Thomas Aquinas, ST III, q. 79, a. 4; III, q. 67, a. 2).

In order to grow as the one body of Christ in the Spirit, the Church has need of structure, authority, and the service of leadership. Those called to ordained ministry exercise this ministry of liturgical and evangelistic leadership in and for the Church. Since this ministry is a specific expression of the call to service inherent in baptism and confirmation, Vatican II situates ordained ministry within the vocation of all the baptized to share in the priesthood and ministry of Jesus. Those ordained enter into a sacred covenant with the Church community to represent publicly the risen Lord and to witness to him in his paschal mystery. Precisely because their prime responsibility is to foster the community's life in the Spirit, the heart of the sacrament of orders is the invoking of the Holy Spirit upon candidates through the laying on of hands by a bishop. The Vatican II Decree on the Ministry and Life of Priests emphasizes that the service of those ordained will be fruitful in the Church in the measure that they grow in the "life of the Spirit," becoming increasingly led by the inspiration and guidance of the Holy Spirit (no. 12).

The liturgical rewewal begun by Vatican II is inspiring a renewed awareness of the centrality of the Holy Spirit in the celebration of the other sacraments as well. Because forgiveness is the fruit of love, the Holy Spirit of love is bestowed "for the forgiveness of sins" through the sacrament of reconciliation: "Receive the Holy Spirit; those whose sins you shall forgive, are forgiven" (John 20:22-23). In the sacrament of marriage, a couple is made "one flesh" in the union of the Holy Spirit. Through this sacrament they enter into and publicly express their deepened covenant in the Holy Spirit with the triune God, one another, and the whole Church. Finally, in the sacrament of the anointing of the sick, the Holy Spirit is invoked over the sick and dying as Healer, Consoler, and the One in whose power death is transformed into an act of love. Each sacrament in this way is a particular means of deepening the communion of the Church, strengthening Christians' bond in the Spirit with the triune God and one another, and of impelling them to love and service in the world. From their sacramental celebrations in and with the Church, Christians' experience of the Holy Spirit's transforming power is meant to permeate the whole of their daily lives.

The Holy Spirit Drawing the Church into the Future. "What is the greatest need of the Church today?" To this urgent question Pope Paul VI responded, "the Holy Spirit." For it is the Holy Spirit, he continued, "who animates and sanctifies the Church, who is her divine breath, the wind in her sail, the principle of her unity, the inner source of her light and strength, her support and consoler, the source of her charisms and songs, her peace and joy, the pledge and prelude of her blessed and eternal life." On 6 June 1973, a year after he spoke these words, Pope Paul VI called the whole Church to deepened study of and submission to the Holy Spirit as the indispensable fulfillment of all that Vatican II had begun. On Pentecost, 1986, Pope John Paul II recalled these words of Paul VI and issued the encyclical *Dominum et Vivificantem* ("Lord and Giver of Life"), publicly placing the Church under the guidance of the Holy Spirit as it faces the third millennium.

The emphasis of John XXIII, Paul VI, and John Paul II on the importance of the Holy Spirit for the Church reflects what is happening in the "grass roots" of the present-day Church. The liturgical, theological, and pastoral renewal fostered by Vatican II continues to inspire a reclaiming of the centrality of the Holy Spirit in Catholic belief and practice today. The Rite of Christian Initiation of Adults (RCIA), in which the Holy Spirit's role is fundamental, has become a growing force of renewal in the Church. The Vatican II's affirmation of the call of all the baptized to use the gifts bestowed on them by the Spirit to build up the body of Christ has resulted in increasing involvement of lay people in varied ministries in the Church.

The Holy Spirit is also inspiring the renewal of the Church through such means as Scripture and prayer groups, parish renewal programs, Marriage Encounter, Cursillo, and the charismatic renewal. In 1975 Paul VI publicly acknowledged the charismatic renewal as a gift of the Holy Spirit in and to the Church, drawing attention to how informed involvement in this renewal fosters conversion to the risen Lord; personal experience of the closeness and power of the Holy Spirit; intimacy with the triune God; renewed desire for Scripture, the sacraments, and prayer; deeper understanding of the mysteries of the faith; and loving communion with and service to others.

Impelled by their own experience of the Holy Spirit in their lives, a growing number of theologians such as Cardinal Léon Suenens, Yves Congar, O.P., Hans Urs von Balthasar, Louis Bouyer, J. M. R. Tillard, O.P., Walter Kasper, Heribert Mühlen, Kilian McDonnell, O.S.B., George Montague, Francis A. Sullivan, Edward O'Connor, C.S.C., and Luis Bermejo, S.J., have, by their scholarship, encouraged renewed awareness of the Christian life as life in the power of the Holy Spirit.

A growing conviction about the centrality of the Holy Spirit in the Church today is also fostering a deepened commitment to work for the Church's unity, which only the Spirit can give, in the bond of peace (Eph 4:3). Vatican II opened Catholics to a new ecumenical awareness of Church unity as a mandate of Jesus which can and must be achieved only in the power and love of the Holy Spirit. What the Holy Spirit accomplishes in other Christian communions and in other religions can be true gifts to the Catholic Church, for the Spirit's gifts "can be found outside the visible boundaries of the Catholic Church" (UR 4, 3). The council thus opened the Church to a global perspective when it affirmed that the Holy Spirit is at work wherever people pursue the tasks of goodness and truth that make life more human (GS 38).

This reclaiming of the centrality of the Holy Spirit in the Church has served also to relate Catholic belief and life even more closely to contemporary issues of a global nature. Before Vatican II, writings on the Holy Spirit often stressed the activity of the Spirit in the individual "souls" of Christians. But in the different historical, cultural, and social contexts of today, writings on the Holy Spirit include a focus on the Holy Spirit as immanent Creator who forms communities of equals and inspires activity related to social justice, ecumenical, and ecological concerns.

History shows that the Church is able to meet complex challenges in the measure that the concrete persons who comprise the Church experience the Holy Spirit's power in their own lives. The twelfth-century sequence composed by Stephen Langton and used today for the Church's liturgy of Pentecost gives poetic expression to many of the preceding insights of Scripture, tradition, and contemporary theology on the Holy Spirit who alone "gives life" (John 6:63). The beauty of this Sequence makes it an especially fitting prayer for Christians seeking deeper experience of the power and presence of the Holy Spirit in their lives. The Sequence beseeches the Holy Spirit, without whose power human effort is fruitless, to come as the One who cares for the poor and lifts those who have fallen. For the Holy Spirit is the divine Person who is Strength for the tempted, Comfort for the sad; the Spirit is Rest for the weary, Refreshment for those discouraged, Healing for the wounded, Consoler of those troubled, and Joy for those without joy. Echoing the sentiments of Scripture, the Sequence acknowledges that everything good and sweet in human life, everything infused with love and kindness and truth, is the fruit of the Holy Spirit whose closeness and transforming power every person is meant to know by experience.

Luke presents Jesus as urging his disciples to ask constantly for the Holy Spirit (Luke 11:5-13). Those who do pray for a deepening of the Holy Spirit's presence in their hearts and lives can expect to experience the Person of the Holy Spirit as the source of their inner security, peace, and joy; as the bond of love in their marriages, families, and friendships; and as the power of their self-giving in the Church and in communion with those to whom God's love joins them, especially the poor and weak of the world. In this way, through the love of those whose lives are filled with the Spirit's tenderness and power, the entire cosmos is meant to be filled with the transforming presence of the Holy Spirit who is "Giver of Life."

MARY ANN FATULA, O.P.

See also GRACE; TRINITY.

HOLY THURSDAY

Also called Maundy Thursday, this is the Thursday before Easter, on which the Church commemorates the farewell supper of Jesus as institution of the Eucharist. The principal Mass is celebrated in the evening and may include a ceremonial footwashing in remembrance of the example Jesus set—and instructed his apostles to follow—at the Last Supper. Holy oils are blessed by the bishop on this day in a morning Mass held at the diocesan cathedral.

JOSEPH QUINN

See also HOLY WEEK; TRIDUUM, EASTER.

HOLY WATER

Water which is blessed by a priest and used by the clergy as a sacramental for blessings, dedications, the Rite of Sprinkling at Sunday Mass, and for baptismal renewal (by dipping one's fingers in the holy water and making the sign of the cross) upon entering a church. Besides ordinary holy water, there are also baptismal holy water (used with chrism in the administration of baptism) and Easter water, which is blessed for use in the paschal season.

JOSEPH QUINN

See also SACRAMENTALS.

HOLY WEEK

The week preceding Easter, in which the Church commemorates the passion of our Lord. Palm Sunday recalls Christ's entry into Jerusalem, while Holy Thursday marks his institution of the Eucharist. Monday, Tuesday, Wednesday, Good Friday, and Holy Saturday are days of meditation on the passion of Jesus. The Easter Vigil, held either on Saturday evening or in the pre-dawn hours of Easter Sunday, initiates the joyful celebration of Christ's resurrection. Holy Week is considered the focal point of the ecclesiastical and liturgical year.

JOSEPH QUINN

See also PASCHAL MYSTERY; TRIDUUM, EASTER.

HOLY YEAR

"Jubilee Year," a year for special pilgrimages to Rome. Originating in a plenary indulgence granted by the pope and celebrated at the turn of each century, it is

"The Holy Door," St. Peter's Basilica, Rome

now observed every twenty-five years (1950, 1975, etc.) These are the only occasions when "The Holy Door" in St. Peter's Basilica in Rome remains open. The indulgence is named from the Hebrew "jubilee" (year of liberation) which was observed on the fiftieth year.

DAVID BRYAN

See also PILGRIMAGES

HOMILY

See LITURGY OF THE WORD.

HOMOSEXUALITY

Homosexual behavior has consistently been declared immoral by the Roman Catholic Church on the basis of certain passages in the Bible and a moral tradition supported by natural law reasoning. Since 1975, due to the rise of scientific study of human sexuality, developments in biblical studies, and the renewal in moral theology mandated by the Second Vatican Council, there have been significant changes in Church teaching with respect to the nature of homosexual behavior and the pastoral care of homosexual persons. The most recent Church teaching, however, continues to affirm that homosexual behavior is always objectively disordered, and as a result never morally acceptable.

In the opening chapters of Genesis the creation of the sexes by God is presented as having a twofold purpose: men and women are meant to come together in a one-flesh unity of life (Gen 2:24) and to beget children (Gen 1:28). In sharp contrast, all the men in the sinful city of Sodom are depicted as threatening homosexual rape on the two visitors given hospitality by Lot (Gen 19). In addition, the Holiness Code in Leviticus decrees that, if a man lies with a man as with a woman, both shall be put to death (20:13).

The Gospels report no teaching whatever of Jesus on the subject of homosexuality. When sending his disciples to preach the kingdom, he does refer to Sodom, but his focus is on Sodom's failure of hospitality. Paul in one place argues that pagans, even without the biblical revelation, ought to have honored the true God but they turned instead to idolatry. As a consequence of this primary disorder, God gave them over to sexual disorder as well, both women and men exchanging natural relations for unnatural ones (Rom 1:24-27). Paul also includes in a list of vices to be avoided two activities which have been taken to refer to homosexual acts (1 Cor 6:9-10; see also 1 Tim 1:9-10).

These relatively few passages in Scripture condemning homosexual acts found support in natural law reasoning. Since sexual activity was seen to be ordered to procreation and the continuance of the human race, any form of sexual activity other than heterosexual intercourse was judged to be against nature and a clear violation of right reason. This teaching constituted the unchallenged tradition of the Church until modern times.

In the latter part of the nineteenth century researchers began to study sex in a scientific way. Gradually, a new concept, "sexuality," emerged which embraced all the aspects of the human person affected by being male or female: biological, psychological, sociological, cultural, and spiritual. Sexuality unfolds dynamically over a person's lifetime and is subject to constant modification. Alfred Kinsey's studies showed that in terms of behavior it is simply not the case that males and females are either homosexual or heterosexual. Some indeed are exclusively heterosexual or homosexual, but others may, for a time at least, be predominantly one and incidentally the other or equally responsive in both ways.

Kinsey's studies led to a new distinction between sexual acts and sexual orientation. Sexual orientation refers to the object of someone's erotic interest, to what someone experiences as sexually arousing. This orientation is present, the attraction is experienced, even though the person has never engaged in sexual activities. This distinction yielded a new and more precise definition of a homosexual person: someone who in adult life has a stable erotic attraction to persons of the same sex. There have been a number of theories to explain the origin of this orientation, but it is generally agreed that the person does not deliberately choose it. He or she discovers its presence and it cannot be wished away or changed into a heterosexual orientation by counseling.

The bishops at the Second Vatican Council never dealt directly with the question of homosexuality. They did, however, forcefully proclaim the dignity and fundamental equality of all human persons as created in God's image and redeemed by Christ. On that basis they concluded that every type of discrimination based on sex, race, color, social condition, language, or religion, is contrary to God's will and should be eliminated (Church in the Modern World, no. 12, no. 29). They also called for the renewal of moral theology with proper attention being given to new knowledge coming from the social sciences and to the experience of conscientious persons.

An example of taking empirical sciences into account may be found in the *Declaration on Certain Questions concerning Sexual Ethics,* issued in 1975 by the Vatican Congregation for the Doctrine of the Faith (CDF). In its opening sentence the declaration makes its own the opinion of contemporary sexologists: "The human person is so profoundly affected by sexuality that it must be considered as one of the factors which give to each individual's life the principal traits that distinguish it" (no. 1).

In treating of homosexuality, the congregation accepts also the idea that there are some homosexuals whose sexual orientation is fixed and unchangeable. Some people had been proposing that, given the central importance of sexuality in defining a person, those who are definitively homosexual should be encouraged to enter into a sincere communion of life and love analogous to marriage. The congregation's decision is that these homosexuals should be treated with understanding and their culpability judged with prudence, but that homosexual acts, since they are necessarily nonprocreative, violate the objective moral order and can in no case be approved (no. 8).

In 1976, the National Conference of Catholic Bishops devoted a section to homosexuality in their pastoral reflection on the moral life, "To Live in Christ Jesus." They follow the scientific opinion that one's sexual orientation need not be thought of as deliberately chosen: "Some persons find themselves through no fault of their own to have a homosexual orientation." Before giving their judgment that homosexual activity, as distinguished from the homosexual orientation, is morally wrong, the bishops do a very instructive thing. They apply to homosexuals the teaching of the Second Vatican Council on the dignity and fundamental equality of all persons, declaring that homosexuals "should not suffer from prejudice against their basic human rights" and they specify three of those rights: "a right to respect, friendship and justice." In addition, the bishops teach that homosexuals deserve to play an active role in the Christian community.

The Washington State Catholic Conference in 1983 addressed the matter of justice in "The Prejudice against Homosexuals and the Ministry of the Church." The bishops responded to concerns of parents about homosexual teachers in schools: "There are those who think that gays and lesbians inevitably impart a homosexual value system to children or that they will molest children. There is no evidence that exposure to homosexuals, of itself, harms a child. . . . Accordingly, there is no need to make efforts to screen out all homosexually oriented persons from our educational system."

Some Scripture scholars, interpreting the relevant texts in the Bible, advanced the argument that the condemnations of homosexual behavior are best understood as rejections of male prostitution, particularly in connection with what the biblical authors judged to be the idolatrous practices of other religions. In any case, these texts interpreted in their ancient contexts do not envisage what is meant today by the term "homosexuality" and therefore cannot legitimately be cited as condemning it.

Moral theologians began proposing a Catholic approach which would be faithful to the traditional teaching about the two goals of sexuality, heterosexual love and procreation, and yet respond to our better understanding of the nature of homosexuality. Since a change of orientation is out of the question, homosexuals should be invited to embrace the highest Christian ideals available to them: either celibacy, if they feel called to follow this form of Christian witness, or a permanent and exclusive partnership of life and love.

In 1986, however, the CDF sent a letter to the bishops of the world on "The Pastoral Care of Homosexual Persons" which had been personally approved by the pope. Despite the fact that "increasing numbers of people today, even within the Church, are bringing enormous pressure to bear on the Church to accept the homosexual condition as though it were not disordered and to condone homosexual activity" (no. 8), the congregation declares that the Church cannot alter its traditional teaching. The new exegesis which claims that the moral injunctions of the Bible are so culture-bound that they are not applicable to modern life is described as "gravely erroneous" (no. 4). The CDF also notes that some persons have recently been giving an overly benign interpretation to the homosexual orientation, calling it neutral or even good. The truth is, in the judgment of the CDF, that this inclination is "essentially self-indulgent" (no. 7) and, while not sinful, is a "tendency toward an intrinsic moral evil and thus the inclination itself must be seen as an objective disorder" (no. 3). Those who find themselves to be homosexual must be treated with understanding and compassion, but they must never be led to believe that they may act on their sexual inclinations. They should accept the fact that they are called to a life of celibacy. The bishops are encouraged to establish authentic pastoral programs which will assist homosexual persons through sacraments, prayer, witness, counsel and individual care to lead chaste lives in the Christian community (no. 15).

Other Christian Churches have been wrestling with this issue as well. Generally, the Churches recognize that homosexuals have long been the victims of unjust discrimination and support initiatives to guarantee their civil rights. The Churches have also for the most part welcomed homosexuals as members of their congregations. To date, however, no major Christian Church has given official approval to homosexual acts. All continue to affirm the traditional teaching which limits sexual activity to the bonds of heterosexual marriage.

WILLIAM C. McFADDEN, S.J.

See also CELIBACY; SACRAMENT OF MATRIMONY; SEXUALITY.

HOPE

To long for a more just, peaceful, and compassionate world and to allow an imagined future to guide our behavior is distinctively human. Hope is the capacity whereby we begin to move reality towards a desired future in spite of the difficulties involved. The biblical hope in God sustains and transforms this natural human instinct and ability.

The Old Testament Hope in Yahweh

The basic pattern of biblical hope is this: because of what God has done in *the past* and because God is faithful in *the present,* God's promises for *the future* will be fulfilled. The liturgies of Advent highlight this aspect of the experience of Israel. To be a people of hope implied confidence, freedom from fear, courage, strength, joy, trust, yearning for God, and waiting patiently (Prov 14:26; Isa 2:5; 7:4; 12:2; 32:11; 35:3-4; 40:25-31; 41:13ff.; Bar 5:9; Zeph 3:15ff.). For Israel God is father, rock, rampart, shelter, shield, fortress, refuge, lamp, light, shepherd, liberator, and Savior. God is just and faithful. Hope is justified by God's name, God's word, and God's loving-kindness. The hope of the people and the reliability of God are tested and strengthened by sickness and poverty, by affliction and sin, by what seemed like desertion by God (Qoheleth, Job). God who helps in time of distress will finally put an end to all distress (Isa 25:9; 51:5; Jer 30:16f.; Mic 7:7).

Initially Israel's hope is *collective.* The people receive the promise and are the subject of hope. They look forward to a promised *reign of God,* a kingdom of peace, truth, honor and justice, a land of fertility and plenty, a paradise of fine foods, a time when creation will be in harmony, a place whose way of life will be mercy and faithfulness, a moment when the Lord will dress the wounds of the people (Pss 72; 85; 96; Bar 5:1-9; Isa 2:5; 11:1-10; 25:6-10; 30:19-21, 23-26).

Towards the end of the OT period faith in the resurrection and in life beyond death became part of the hope of Israel (Job 19:25-29; Isa 25:8; Sir 48:11; Wis 2:23; 3:1-9; 2 Macc 7:9-14; 12:43-46). Yahweh's justice will be seen on a day when this world's injustices are set right, the just being raised to life and the wicked to judgment.

The hope of Israel became more spiritual and interior particularly as a result of the Exile. The promised Messiah, initially a king like David, will be the Servant of Yahweh (Second-Isaiah) and Son of Man (Daniel). This eventually becomes a promise that God will be among the people as their King and Shepherd (Pss 96–98; Ezek 34). In their deepest reality the promises guaranteed by God will mean shared life with God (Pss 26:8-9; 27:13-14; 73: 25-28).

The New Testament Hope in Christ

While repeating the OT pattern, the hope of Christians is "better" because enacted on "better promises" (Heb 7:19; 8:6). Because of what God has done in Christ in *the past,* we look to the full revelation of God's glory in *the future* which gives Christian living in *the present* its distinctive qualities of courage, enthusiasm, and confidence (1 Cor 9:24; Phil 1:9-10; 1 Thess 4:1). The kingdom of God is already come while we look forward to its consummation, the appearing of Christ in glory (Luke 21:27; 1 Thess 5:9-10; Titus 2:13; 2 Thess 2). The basis for the better hope of Christians is the resurrection of Jesus since the risen Lord is the source, guarantee, and term of our hope (1 Cor 15). Our new life is hid with Christ in God. It is already ours and yet we hope for it (Rom 8:24-25; 1 Cor 13:12; 2 Cor 4:17-18; 1 Tim 1:1; 1 Pet 1:3; 3:15).

This mystery is present in the Eucharist: Christ who *died, is* risen and *will* come again (Luke 24:30-35; 1 Cor 11:26; 1 John 3:2; Heb 12:18ff.). Hope itself is an eschatological blessing flowing from the presence of Christ and the Spirit (Matt 12:21; 28:20; John 14:15-17; Rom 8:24; 15:12; Gal 5:5; Eph 1:11f.; 2:12; Col 1:4f., 23; Titus 1:1-3; 3:7).

Christian hope is realistic. While looking to future glory it knows that the way is hard that leads to life. But because it *is* hope it sets out, confident that Christ will not desert those who follow his way. Hope does not remove the difficulty of the way or the horrors of suffering and death, of failure and sin, of disappointment and loss. But it does encourage us to face the demands of love, the continual dying to ourselves to which baptism calls us.

Death is faced with hope because Christ has conquered death. The resurrection is victory over death and not a bypassing of it. The hope of personal immortality is certain because the resurrection of Christ guarantees the resurrection of all (Col 1:27; 1 Cor 15; Acts 23:6; 24:15; 26:6).

Christian life is a pilgrimage (1 Pet 1:3-21; Heb 6:18-20; 10:23; 12:1-4; 13:8; Rev 19-20). Because of persecution and the delay of the parousia (Col 1:23; Rom 8:18-23; Heb 10:19-25; Jas 1:2-4) we must wait, be on our guard and not grow weary as we watch for what is promised (Rom 8:24-39; Gal 5:5).

Our hope of sharing the glory of God's kingdom includes the hope that that kingdom will begin to be realized in this world. Christians hope for liberation from all that hinders the fullness of life. Far from justifying a turning away from this world, hope is the basis of all Christian involvement in education and health care, in development work and in the promotion of social, economic, and political progress.

Saint Thomas Aquinas on Hope

For Aquinas hope (*spes*) is a *passion* moving us towards future good things which are difficult but not impossible to attain. These good things are the *ob-*

ject of hope and so is the agency through whose assistance our hope will be realized. The highest good for which we can hope is our complete fulfillment. This is the possession of God attained only with God's help. God is thus our eternal happiness and the agency through whom we seek and find that happiness. The hope which seeks God through God's help is the *theological virtue* of hope. The virtue of the pilgrim Christian, it enables us to cling to God as a friend who is present and ready to help even though we are still distant from God.

To love others is to hope for their good as other selves says Aquinas. God's justice is a mode of God's mercy which is the *primary root* of all God's works. In virtue of theological hope we hope for the salvation of all since we are called to show mercy and love to all. Hope charts a course between despair and presumption, recognizing that if we are not yet there we are on the way. The virtue of ongoing youthfulness, hope makes us confident without being arrogant and humble without self-contempt. Hope makes prayer possible and teaches us the *fear of the Lord.* This medieval theology of hope is recounted in poetic form by Dante (*Paradiso, Canto* XXV).

Some Modern Writers on Hope

For **Ernst Bloch** (1885–1977) human life is a constant experience of "not-yet," an impulse towards what is lacking. Anguish arises from socio-economic alienations which can be removed by human intelligence. More fundamental than anguish (*contra* Heidegger), hope carries us towards "ultimate perfection" in a dialectical ascent of faith and risk, of uncertainty and concern. The destiny of individuals is to be incorporated in "the soul of future humanity."

Bloch's secular messianism moves between atheism and humanistic pantheism. Through **Jurgen Moltmann** Bloch's emphasis on the revolutionary potential of hope passed into liberation theology. For Moltmann, Christian hope is directive, uplifting and critical. It revolutionizes and transforms the present. Hope is born in the point of contradiction where suffering, evil and death meet the future of Jesus Christ who is raised. Yahweh has *future* as his essential nature (Exod 3:14) and *becoming, freedom* and *promise-making* as key attributes.

Only thus can history be real and not simply the unfolding of a reality "already there." The future is the real category of historic thinking. It makes risk and hope possible. All other categories are made contingent by the resurrection. Human beings know their true selves in the face of a call from God and in the light of a mission which sees the world as transformable. For Moltmann hope is motion not locus, dynamic not static, tension towards the future not peace in the present. Unlike Bloch he believes that hope is established by a promise-making and faithful God.

Hans Urs von Balthasar (1905–1988) writes that because we are all under the judgment of Christ we can hope that all will be saved. We do not *know* either that all are saved (the view that is termed *apocatastasis*) or that some are damned. The gospel calls us to a decision with irrevocable consequences but as Christians we have *hope* and not *knowledge* about the outcome of the judgment. Augustine thought he knew that some are damned, an error which threw sacred history out of balance and had unfortunate consequences for the history of theology.

The testimonies of saints and mystics witness to another view. Because God's love is stronger than any resistance to it hope for all is permitted. Paul's wish to be cut off from Christ for the sake of Israel expresses a recurring Christian insight (Rom 9:3; Gal 3:13). His descent into hell means that hell too belongs to Christ. Charity requires me to love unreservedly which is possible only if I continue to hope for the salvation of all. Von Balthasar cites Edith Stein saying that, while it is possible to remain perpetually closed to God's love, the likelihood of this is "infinitely improbable." Divine freedom can "outwit" human freedom without neutralizing or destroying it. There are no limits to God's love which is the basis of our hope and the most serious thing that exists.

VIVIAN BOLAND, O.P.

HOPKINS, GERARD MANLEY (1844–1889)

As late as 1946 the *Encyclopedia Britannica* contained no entry for Gerard Manley Hopkins, who was born near London on 28 July 1844, and died in Dublin on 8 June 1889. The latest edition finds him recognized as "one of the great poets of the English language." His work stands "among the most original, powerful and influential accomplishments of his century." It has exerted "marked influence on such leading 20th-century poets as W. H. Auden, T. S. Eliot, Stephen Spender and Dylan Thomas."

When he died at forty-four of typhoid fever, Hopkins left behind virtually no published poems, and not that many unpublished ones. His mature, completed poems number forty-six, of which thirty-four are brief sonnets. Fortunately Hopkins had for an Oxford classmate and devoted friend a future poet laureate of England, Robert Bridges. At first Bridges slipped some of Hopkins' easier poems into

Gerard Manley Hopkins, portrait by Rita McKenzie

anthologies. In 1918, he published the first collected edition, whose 750 copies took ten years to sell out. The second edition (1930), however, found a literary climate much readier to appreciate the power, beauty, word-magic as well as the emotional, intellectual and spiritual depths of the poems.

The eldest of nine children—one of whom became an Anglican nun and two of whom were illustrators for *Punch* magazine—Hopkins was born into a literary and artistic High Church family, and might well have become a painter or a musician. He won youthful poetry prizes before entering Oxford at eighteen. Three years later, to the "terrible" distress of his parents, he "went over" to Rome under the guidance of Oxford's John Henry Newman, who received him into the Church. The future cardinal's writings had potently swayed the brilliant, ascetic, high-strung, depressive and soul-searching youth.

Two years later, he joined the English Jesuits. As for poetry: "What I had written I burnt before I became a Jesuit and resolved to write no more, as not belonging to my profession, unless it were the wish of my superiors." Some copies, nevertheless, survived this burning.

Seven years later, while studying theology in Wales, Hopkins read about five Franciscan nuns exiled from Germany who drowned in a shipwreck in the Thames. His superior casually remarked that someone should write a poem on the subject. Hopkins felt authorized to produce the 35-verse, 280-line "Wreck of the Deutschland," a dazzling meditation on the mystery of suffering. So dauntingly original was this poem, however, that the Jesuit *Month* "dared not publish it." Some critics now regard it as the greatest twentieth-century poem of the nineteenth century.

Ordained a priest at thirty-three, he preached in London, taught at several schools, and did parish work in Chesterfield, Oxford, Liverpool, and Glasgow. He confessed that the poverty he encountered among Irish Catholic immigrants would have tempted him to become a communist. His last assignment was as Greek professor at Dublin's University College.

Prone to perfectionism, overexertion, fatigue, and depression, he felt himself a failure as both preacher and teacher. Various scholarly projects fizzled out. As "Time's eunuch," he could "not breed one work that wakes." He apparently now felt he had permission to write more poetry in his minimal spare time. But he always felt uneasy about doing so—even more uneasy about the vainglory of possible publication. He lived to see only a few, minor items printed in obscure journals.

As a scrupulous priest, a frustrated artist and an Englishman in nationalistic Dublin, he found his depression deepening: "I think that my fits of sadness, though they do not affect my judgment, resemble madness." ("O the mind, mind has mountains; cliffs of fall/ Frightful, sheer, no-man-fathomed.")

During those five, final Dublin years, he composed what Bridges called "the terrible sonnets"—the one "written in blood" was probably: "Not, I'll not, carrion comfort, Despair, not feast on thee." Hopkins once wrote: "I have long been Fortune's football and I am blowing up the bladder of resolution big and buxom for another kick of her foot." But, spoken in the presence of his now-reconciled parents, his dying words were: "I am so happy, I am so happy." Without a marker, but with his name inscribed among others on a large Celtic cross, Hopkins is buried in the Jesuit plot of Dublin's Glasnevin Cemetery, featured in Joyce's *Ulysses.*

Yet, "good grows wild and wide,/ Has shades, is nowhere none." So there had been joyous poems too, sung in praise of nature ("There lives the dearest freshness deep down things;"), bodily beauty, and "God's better beauty, grace." In his experimentation with language, his responsiveness to nature and his religiousness, he resembled his American contemporary Walt Whitman. "I always knew in my heart Walt Whitman's mind to be more like my own than any other man's living. As he is a very great scoundrel, this is not a pleasant confession." The two men also shared a special sensitivity to masculine grace, though there was no breath of scandal in the priest's case. Still, the priest found "mortal beauty—dangerous . . . Those lovely lads. . . ."

At the technical level, Hopkins revived an old English practice of not giving a line of verse a definite number of syllables, but of permitting any number of unstressed syllables between a fixed number of stressed syllables or beats. He called this Sprung Rhythm and defended it as "the native and natural rhythm of speech." He also reveled in the ancient Anglo-Saxon and Welsh poetic practice of heavy alliteration ("consonant chiming"): "Down in dim woods the diamond delves! the elves'-eyes!"; ". . . the Holy Ghost over the bent/ World broods with warm breast and with ah! bright wings."

He also coined the word "inscape," modeled on the words landscape and seascape, where "scape" is from the Dutch word for "shape." The inscape is therefore the inshape, the inner form and identity of a bird, a tree, a flower or any other creature. In all such inscapes, Hopkins revered a unique revelation of the divine. ("The world is charged with the grandeur of God./ It will flame out, like shining from shook foil.") In his sonnet "The Windhover," Hopkins famously sees in a hovering falcon an epiphany of the loveliness and power of Christ. The experience of such an inscape Hopkins termed an instressing.

He had his eccentricities, but Hopkins impressed some very demanding people who knew him. Fellow poet and convert Coventry Patmore confessed he "seldom felt so much attracted toward any other man." Most movingly, an agnostic friend of his Oxford days, Mowbray Baillie, had a special reason for regretting his doubts about life after death: "I want somewhere, somehow to meet Gerard Hopkins again." More than a century after his death, the poet can still be memorably met through his poems, which include some of the "immortal diamonds" of our tongue. In 1975 a plaque was dedicated to him in the Poets' Corner of Westminster Abbey.

W. H. Gardner has produced annotated editions of Hopkins' writings, as well as a two-volume biography. An excellent, more recent biography was published by Robert Martin.

JOSEPH GALLAGHER

See also NEWMAN, JOHN HENRY, CARDINAL; SOCIETY OF JESUS.

HOSPITALLERS OF ST. JOHN OF GOD

An order of religious brothers and priests engaged in healthcare and its related fields, they were founded in 1552 by St. John of God, a Portuguese soldier and shepherd. After hearing a sermon preached by St. John of Avila, John of God experienced a religious conversion, and as a result of which he founded this order dedicated to caring for the sick and the poor. The order was given papal approval in 1572, and St. John of God was canonized in 1690. The order adopted the Rule of St. Augustine and a monastic habit. The brothers take a vow of service to the sick in addition to the customary vows of poverty, chastity, and obedience. The motto of the Hospitallers is, "*Caritas,*" since their charism compels them to see the person of Christ in each sick person whom they serve.

The order spread quickly in Europe where many of the brothers were excellent surgeons and doctors. They were especially known for their fine rural hospitals where the brothers were pharmacists and made visits to the homebound. The order also had clerical members who acted as chaplains to the sick and the poor. In the seventeenth century the Hospitallers set up hospitals in South America where their kindness and service to the sick played a key role in the conversion of many of the native peoples. The order suffered greatly in the aftermath of the French Revolution and were expelled from some of their institutions. They were able to recover from this, and by the middle of the twentieth century they had over 2,500 members. They came to the United States in 1941, and in 1993 were represented in California in the Archdiocese of Los Angeles and the Diocese of San Bernadino, and in the Diocese of Camden, New Jersey.

ANTHONY D. ANDREASSI

See also CORPORAL AND SPIRITUAL WORKS OF MERCY; RELIGIOUS ORDERS.

HOUSELANDER, CARYLL (1901–1954)

An outstanding English spiritual writer, some of whose books have approached classic stature. She was formally received into the Catholic Church when she was six years old and later wrote of her early childhood in *A Rocking Horse Catholic.* She attended a convent school near Birmingham for her religious education, and although she had no formal theological training, she displays in her writings a remarkable grasp of psychological and theological insights.

In her early twenties she left the Church for a number of years and during that period fell in love with an espionage agent in London. The relationship ended when the agent married another woman. Her pilgrimage in faith thereafter took on greater intensity, revealed clearly in her writings and in her very active life spent helping others.

During World War II she worked in the censor's office and as a fire-warden during the bombings. One of her first major works, *This War Is the Passion,* (1941), emphasizes the place of the Church in the world, the need for asceticism and the building of the kingdom of God here and now in all of human life.

She thrived on giving herself to the marginalized, particularly abused children. Her therapy was simply to love them back to life. A London doctor, referring to her unusually deep piety and her very obvious idiosyncrasies, called her "a divine eccentric." The main focus of her life was to see and act out the presence of Christ in every person. Frank Sheed, her publisher, maintains "she wrote the plainest prose, deeply emotional, totally unsentimental, taking us to the depths in Christ and Mary and ourselves."

Among her titles other than those mentioned were *The Reed of God, The Comforting of Christ, The Dry Wood, Guilt, The Risen Christ, Stations of the Cross,* and *The Flowering Tree.*

JOHN McHALE

See also BRITAIN, CHURCH IN.

HUGUENOTS

A nickname which was applied—and was quickly accepted by all parties—to describe the French followers of John Calvin. They played a major dissenting role in French life especially during the sixteenth and seventeenth centuries. The Huguenots attracted many educated and wealthy followers and within two generations they numbered about 13 percent of the French population. They were fiercely independent and for over thirty years (1562–1594) they were locked in civil war with the Catholic majority. The struggle was marked by terrible atrocities on both sides, including the Massacre of St. Bartholomew in which over six thousand Huguenots were slaughtered in Paris and other cities on 23 and 24 August 1572.

This led many to support the movement for religious toleration and eventually led to the end of the French religious wars when on 13 April 1598 Henry IV signed the Edict of Nantes. This granted the Huguenots free exercise of their religion, except in certain locations and, among other concessions, provided a state subsidy for the support of their troops and clergy. With frequent infringements this uneasy settlement lasted until the Edict of Nantes was revoked by Louis XIV on 18 October 1685. Troops were quartered in Huguenot homes and many were forced to renounce their faith. Over 300,000 fled to Holland, Prussia, England, and America.

A greatly reduced Huguenot community lived on, without official recognition as a Church, until Napoleon granted them both recognition and religious equality in 1802, when they numbered about 430,000. In an atmosphere of freedom their influence and numbers grew substantially, and in the nineteenth century their evangelical, missionary, and educational activities increased. However, after decades of revival, the Church was internally rent by fierce theological and administrative problems, and today the Huguenots have more historical than contemporary importance.

MICHAEL GLAZIER

See also CALVIN, JOHN; PROTESTANTISM; REFORMATION, THE.

HUMAN RIGHTS

To say that someone's basic or fundamental human rights are being violated is to make a most serious charge. Few terms in our contemporary vocabulary express the kind of moral commitment and passion implied by an appeal to human rights.

Especially since World War II, it has become increasingly clear that respect for the dignity of each individual is the essential foundation of a just and caring society. The language of human rights is used to express this obligation to respect human dignity.

Perhaps the most basic implication of acknowledging that we all have certain fundamental rights is that we do not have to earn respect. We are to be respected just because we are human. Respect for human dignity means that all of us, regardless of our power, our race, our abilities, our achievements, can make binding claims upon others and upon the society in which we live. We can make a legitimate claim that our fundamental freedoms be respected and that our essential needs be met. There is something fundamentally and morally wrong when they are not.

Despite the nearly universal recognition of the importance of human rights, there is sometimes a tendency, especially in the United States, to identify human rights with Constitutional rights or with civil rights and liberties. It is easy for Americans to emphasize those human rights that are most compatible with the American tradition—the civil/political rights. There is, however, another dimension to human rights that needs equal recognition in order to protect and promote human dignity: the rights that are usually called social/economic human rights.

In the Catholic tradition, the full range of human rights was systematically articulated by Pope John XXIII in *Pacem in Terris.* A similar understanding of these basic rights, though not expressed in a religious context, is found in the United Nations Universal Declaration of Human Rights.

Civil/Political Human Rights

Respect for human dignity requires that individual freedoms be protected, that individuals not be subjected to interference by others when seeking to live according to their own beliefs and when seeking to participate actively in society. Fundamental human rights include, therefore, such rights as to speak one's opinion and to advocate in public (freedom of speech, freedom of assembly), to worship according to one's own beliefs (freedom of religion), to be treated as a criminal only after due process has been followed (freedom from arbitrary arrest).

These civil/political human rights are asserted, primarily, over against government. Protecting these rights means protecting individuals from excessive governmental control over or involvement in the lives of citizens. Thus, the United States Constitution was immediately amended, in the Bill of Rights, to include many of these protections against government.

Civil/political rights are negative rights or claims. In recognizing that everyone is entitled to having these rights respected, we acknowledge the justice of claims not to be unduly restrained. These human rights claims are not that others *do* something to ensure that human dignity is respected; they are claims that others *not do* something.

In the American tradition, in which our national statement of rights was articulated in a revolutionary era in which the primary concern was about excessive governmental interference, these civil/political rights have received the most emphasis. They are, however, only part of the meaning of human rights.

Social/Economic Human Rights

Respect for human dignity requires more than individual freedoms. It seems empty to argue that someone who is lacking the basic necessities of life, who is homeless and hungry, is living a life of dignity as long as she or he is free to speak and worship without interference. Everyone has a basic human right to have material needs met.

The American Catholic bishops, in *Economic Justice for All,* identify key social/economic human rights and stress their importance: "First among these are the rights to life, food, clothing, shelter, rest, medical care, and basic education. These are indispensable to the protection of human dignity. . . . Any denial of these rights harms persons and wounds the human community. Their serious and sustained denial violates individuals and destroys solidarity among persons" (no. 80).

Society has a moral obligation to see to it that social/economic human rights are protected just as society has an obligation to see to it that civil/political human rights are protected. But social/economic rights are not negative rights; they cannot always be protected by simply not interfering. They often require active efforts to structure the economic and social systems to guarantee access to employment, to health care, to education, and to guarantee that everyone has food and shelter. This may require a more active role by government than would be suggested by an emphasis on only civil/political human rights.

Human Rights, Misfortune, and Injustice

"Bad things" happen to human beings all the time. Some of these things are unfortunate, when someone is harmed or suffers as a result of factors beyond human control or responsibility (some illnesses, storms, accidents). Sometimes these things are injustices, when someone suffers because legitimate expectations regarding the behaviors of others are not met (such as robbery, racial discrimination, toxic contamination of the environment).

The virtuous person seeks to respond as well as possible to others who are suffering. When someone suffers from a misfortune, we should respond (as individuals or through agencies and institutions) to attempt to relieve the suffering. When someone suffers from an injustice, the appropriate response is not only to try to relieve the suffering but also to attempt to prevent future occurrences. When legitimate expectations regarding human society are not being met, it is part of the moral responsibility of all of us to try to bring about a change.

The clear identification of and commitment to respecting human rights is a way of recognizing our responsibility as members of a society. If someone is arrested simply because she or he speaks politically unpopular opinions, that is a violation, an injustice, and not merely an unfortunate event. It is not enough to comfort and relieve the suffering of the individual. When there are unemployed, poor, and homeless persons, the situation is not merely unfortunate and it is not enough simply to assist the individuals to have food and a place to sleep. In Catholic social ethics, it is clearly unjust and not merely unfortunate that poverty exists when there are enough resources to meet the essential needs of all.

The attempt to identify and explain human rights is a recognition of an obligation on the part of individuals and society to seek to protect and respect everyone's dignity. The political and economic institutions are to be structured in a way that recognizes the fundamental importance of both social/economic human rights and civil/political human rights.

LEONARD J. WEBER

See also ANTHROPOLOGY, CHRISTIAN; SOCIAL TEACHING OF THE CHURCH; VIRTUE.

HUMANAE VITAE

One English translation of this encyclical of Paul VI, issued 25 July 1968, is entitled "The Transmission of Human Life." It is popularly known as the "birth control" encyclical.

Birth control or contraception is not a new matter. There were written descriptions of means to prevent conception as early as 1900 B.C. in Egypt (John T. Noonan, *Contraception*). The arguments regarding contraception over the centuries have had a variety of cultural, philosophical, and theological settings. There is no clear biblical foundation for the condemnation of contraception. The Old Testament had a strong bias in favor of procreation to perpetuate the family lines of the People of God. Contraception was not a major issue. The New Testament, in a radical departure from Old Testament teaching, exalts virginity. It also maintains the good of marriage and the proper conduct of husbands and wives in marriage. There is a value assigned to procreation, but there is no clear teaching on contraception.

St. Augustine (d. 430) laid the theological foundations for the tradition of the Western Church regarding contraception. In his younger life, he was a follower of the dualistic Manichean philosophy which devalued all sexual activity because it was not "spiritual." But if intercourse were to take place, according to the Manichees, procreation must be avoided either through the use of nonfertile periods or by early withdrawal. For the Manichees, contraceptive prostitution was preferable to marriage with procreation. The Christian Augustine's rejection of Manicheism was sharp and definitive. The first "good" of marriage is offspring; the purpose of marriage is the procreation of children. Following the earlier Stoic philosophy of the purposes of acts, he taught that intercourse can be allowed for no other purpose.

Although arguments arose over the centuries modifying and challenging the Augustinian position, the Church's stance remained firmly in opposition to contraception. By the early 1800s birth control had became more and more widespread, particularly in the industrialized West. There were now arising proponents of birth control, primarily because of concerns regarding poverty and population growth. The typical response of Rome to those advocating any form of contraceptive practice was that such propositions were "scandalous, erroneous, and contrary to the natural law."

In 1930 the Lambeth Conference of the Anglican Church, which previously condemned contraception in the Conferences of 1908 and 1920, allowed contraception if there was a "morally sound reason for avoiding complete abstinence." Pius XI response to a growing acceptability of contraception was his encyclical, *Casti Connubii,* 31 December 1930, in which he stated: "Assuredly no reason, even the most serious, can make congruent with nature and decent what is intrinsically against nature." Any use of marriage "deprived of its natural power of procreating life violates the law of God and nature," and those who do such things are "stained by a grave and mortal flaw."

The discussion of birth control and the disputed and permitted means of birth control had continued unabated into the time of the Second Vatican Council. The bishops of the Second Vatican Council debated the issue in their preparation of The Church in the World (*Gaudium et Spes*), 7 December 1965. The council reaffirmed the previous teaching of the Church: "Of their nature marriage and married love are directed towards the begetting and bringing up of children." But a new dimension was added in the phrases translated variously "without prejudice to the other purposes of marriage" or "while not making the other purposes of matrimony of less account." The procreative purpose of marriage was upheld, but the unitive or love aspect of the marriage relationship was made of equal importance. This embodied a major shift. What had been looked upon as primary and secondary purposes of marriage now are viewed as purposes without a specification of priority. The council document went on to encourage parents in their "special mission" and offered guidelines to them in discharging their task of procreation "with human and Christian responsibility." The council stated: "The Church reiterates that there cannot be a true contradiction between the divine laws of transmitting life and of promoting genuine married love." The bishops were about to propose concrete solutions to the apparent dilemma, but the intervention of Paul VI led them to state only that "it is not permitted to daughters and sons of the church who rely on these principles to take steps for regulating procreation which are rejected by the teaching authority in its explanation of divine law."

The intervention of Paul VI was the beginning of *Humanae Vitae.* John XXIII had established a commission of six members to study population, family, and births. Paul VI expanded it to fifteen members by May of 1964. On 23 June 1964, he directed the commission to make an extensive and careful investigation of the birth control issue, and, once their work was completed, he himself would pass judgment. The commission was expanded to fifty-two members from nineteen countries. There were nineteen theologians, fifteen demographers or economists, twelve doctors, and six married laity. There were five women among them. The first plenary meeting was held in March of 1965, before the promulgation of *Gaudium et Spes.*

The commission did not come to a consensus. Paul VI received the report of the commission and was faced with "passing judgment." On 25 July 1968, he issued *Humanae Vitae.* The key teaching regarding birth control is stated: "Nonetheless the Church, calling men [and women] back to the observance of the norms of the natural law, as interpreted by their constant doctrine, teaches that each and every marriage act must remain open to the transmission of life." There is a call for responsible parenthood, as the council insisted, but responsible parenthood must be exercised in relationship to the objective moral order established by God according to a correct hierarchy of values: duties of husband and wife toward God take priority over duties toward themselves, family, and society.

The only form of birth control allowed is the use of infertile periods because "God has wisely disposed natural laws and rhythms of fecundity which, of themselves, cause a separation in the succession of births." The use of any other forms of contraception, except intercourse during infertile periods, is forbidden.

The major development of the encyclical declares the two meanings of the conjugal act: "the unitive meaning and the procreative meaning." In marriage these two meanings are never to be separated. John Paul II has written extensively upholding that principle. The marriage act must always be an act of love and the marriage act must never exclude the procreation of children.

Humanae Vitae immediately became a source of contention in the Catholic world. There were questioning and even rejection of its teachings by many theologians. Many pastors do not make birth control an issue in their ministerial practice. Sociological data reveal that approximately 80 percent of practicing Catholics of childbearing age in the United States do not follow the Church's official and authoritative teaching. Conferences of bishops in many areas of the world wrote pastoral letters as guides towards its interpretation, allowing a greater weight to the judgment of conscience, at least in certain cases, than the encyclical provides for.

Humanae Vitae arose out of Vatican II's *Gaudium et Spes* and must be interpreted in light of the council. Both are landmark documents in the development of the moral doctrine on contraception. *Humanae Vitae*'s moral positions are clear, but not without nuance. Its issuance triggered healthy theological and popular discussions on the role of ordinary magisterial teaching and the application of moral principles in the formation of conscience. It also provoked a reexamination of different understandings of natural law. On a practical level, the acceptance or "reception" of the moral position of *Humanae Vitae* by Catholic people has at best been problematic. The development of doctrine, dogmatic or moral, is a fact in the history and life of the Church. *Humanae Vitae,* as were *Casti Connubii* and *Gaudium et Spes* before it, is an important step in that development.

CHARLES SKOK

See also SACRAMENT OF MATRIMONY; SEXUALITY.

HUMANISM

Belief in the dignity of human persons and the human species, usually in the face of efforts to deny or diminish their value. The modern origins of humanism are associated with early Renaissance figures like Petrarch, Ficino, and Mirandola, and with Erasmus and Thomas More in the sixteenth century. However, the remote roots of humanism (at least in the West) extend deeply into the cultural worlds of ancient Greece and the Bible.

Humanism today may be either secular or religious. Secular or atheistic humanism is premised on the conviction that the world accessible to ordinary human experience and to science is all there is to reality. It insists that there is no transcendent realm of values, and that within the secular world the human species is the supreme instance of value. Secular humanism generally maintains that belief in God robs us of our own dignity and creativity. By directing our attention toward the worship of God, theism allegedly distracts us from the task of developing our human powers and from cultivating a sense of our specifically human nobility. Belief in God retards our ability to make "progress" ethically, aesthetically, emotionally, scientifically and economically. Classical expressions of this kind of humanism are those of Ludwig Feuerbach, Karl Marx, Friedrich Nietzsche and Sigmund Freud. Derivative versions of their outlook persist today among many intellectuals, some of whose ideas may be found in the periodical *The Humanist.*

Humanism, however, is not necessarily atheistic. A powerful strain of humanism, for example, runs throughout the Christian tradition. Christian humanism perceives a special dignity in human persons, rooted in their relationship to God. Unlike secular humanism, Christian humanism denies that universal ethical values can be appropriately cultivated without reference to a transcendent order. And it maintains that our human dignity comes from our being created in the image of God and in our being eternally cared for by the infinite love of God.

In response to the atheist claim that theism robs us of a sense of our freedom, Christian humanism, following St. Augustine, claims that true human liberty is attained by way of our participation in God's freedom. Today Christian theology maintains that we gain an appropriate sense of our human nobility especially in our obedience to and imitation of a self-emptying God through a life of emancipating love. At the same time an increasing number of theologians are aware also that an exaggerated humanism can lead to an ecologically dangerous neglect of the inherent value of the nonhuman natural world.

JOHN HAUGHT

See also CREATION; EXISTENTIALISM; PHILOSOPHY AND THEOLOGY.

HUMILITY

Humility is the virtue by which the human person sees that all the good things that one possesses are from God, and thus rightly understands and acts according to this relationship with God. The Hebrew and Christian Scriptures contain the recurring theme of how all good things come from God making the human person utterly dependent upon God. In the Bible one responds to this fact by continually praising and thanking God for God's greatness and unbounded generosity. In the New Testament Jesus is always conscious of his subordinate position to God the Father, and he acts accordingly. Because of Jesus' great charity, he humbled himself in the utmost way by dying for the children of his Father, humanity. In the New Testament the humble person is open to grace and becomes a player in God's salvific plan. God will raise up the humble forever.

By contrast, pride is the desire to be independent of God and to seek after one's own goods and end. Sin has its basis in pride in that the proud person does not seek God but other ends. Apart from the theological (and supernatural) virtues of faith, hope, and charity, humility is the supreme moral virtue in that it enables a person always to seek God as the most important goal. Humility allows the human person to realize relationship to God and others. In other words, humility is the rejection of all self-centeredness. St. Augustine saw it as the foundation of all human virtues, and St. Thomas Aquinas believed humility to be more important than any other moral virtue except justice. It is the virtue that allows a person to see the good in oneself and in others as ultimately coming from God. It leaves no room for jealousy or pride but instead calls for thanks and praise to God who gives all good things.

ANTHONY D. ANDREASSI

See also VIRTUE.

HUS, JAN

See HERESY/HERETICS.

HYMNS

The hymn is poetry in a given meter and in stanza form, with text addressing a sacred topic or written as a prayer, and with a strophic musical setting. Ephesians 5:18 refers to "psalms and hymns," and Philippians 2:6-11 and Colossians 1:15-20 quote sections of Christological hymns; such pieces can be regarded as precursors of what is defined here as the hymn. Early contributors were Ephrem the Syrian, Ambrose of Milan—with whom Latin hymnody begins, Prudentius, and Venantius Fortunatus. The Eastern Church developed its own musical-poetic forms, notably *kontakion, kanon,* and *troparion.*

Under Benedict in the sixth century, monastic Office in the West, and considerably later the Roman Office as well, acquired a prescribed hymnody. The Latin monophonic hymn thus developed within the context of Office and liturgical year, although it also played a role in services like processions and devotions. Hymn collections with musical notation date from about 1000 onward; by this time, there were two distinct major repertoires of hymns, differing in age and/or region of origin. In general, earlier hymns have a rather small melodic range; later compositions exhibit bolder intervallic movement and marked melodic direction; among textual characteristics, one constant is that the final stanza is usually a doxology. By the fourteenth century, hymn settings often featured polyphonic versions of verses in alternation with the monophonic. Gradually, the polyphonic hymn assumed an independent life and would continue to be composed for centuries.

Among new musical-poetic forms of the Middle Ages was the sequence, which eventually spawned the vernacular hymn based on the sequence text; numerous such hymns acquired immense popularity. Still, Latin hymns continued to be composed throughout medieval times; the many prominent hymnists included Rabanus Maurus and Thomas Aquinas. During the Renaissance, the Latin hymn began its decline, epitomized by the humanist-inspired "revision" of Office hymns in the seventeenth century.

With the Reformation, singing in vernacular language became an integral part of the central act of worship, whether word service or Eucharist. Martin Luther wrote new hymns, and translated texts and skillfully adapted melodies of great Latin hymns, incorporating musical features common in his time. By contrast, John Calvin insisted on the use of biblical texts; this gave rise to the metrical Psalter in which psalms are versified, set to a melody with a fixed rhythmic pattern, and sung only in unison at worship. The metrical Psalter was important in the music of England's ecclesiastical reforms.

Modern hymnody in English begins in the eighteenth century with Isaac Watts and the Wesley brothers, John and Charles. During the nineteenth century, burgeoning interest in liturgy restored to use earlier hymns of East and West, many translated by John Mason Neale. This interest culminated in the landmark collection, *Hymns Ancient and Modern* (1861, and subsequent editions). Even to contemporary times, fascination with hymnody and creation of new hymns flourish in the traditions born of the sixteenth-century reform movements.

Among Roman Catholics, after the Reformation—and in Germany, already early in the seventeenth century—both vernacular and Latin hymns found a place in certain types of Eucharistic celebration. In the nineteenth century, the Caecilian Movement advocated excellence in, as well as the restricted liturgical use of, vernacular hymns. The best legacy of the quite barren eighteenth-nineteenth century period is a number of hymn tunes of enduring quality.

Since Vatican Council II, the vernacular hymn repertoire of Roman Catholics has been enriched by new compositions and by the hymns of various ecclesial and cultural traditions. Presently, within the Office, hymns remain normative; at Eucharist and other rites, hymns are used alongside musical compositions in other forms. The heritage of hymns endures, treasured both for the texts, often deeply inspired by Scripture; and for the music, composed specifically to be sung by the worshipping community in praise of God and God's works.

JOAN HALMO

See also LITURGY; LITURGY OF THE HOURS; MUSIC AND WORSHIP.

HYPOSTATIC UNION

Hypostasis means individual or person, and the hypostatic union is the union of two distinct natures of God and man in the person of Jesus Christ, who is true God and true man, consubstantial with the Father according to his godhead and consubstantial with us according to his humanity. The doctrine, elaborated and clarified by Cyril of Alexandria (d. 444), was formalized in the Definition of Chalcedon (451) and accepted by the Church.

JOAN GLAZIER

See also ECUMENICAL COUNCILS; JESUS CHRIST.

I

ICON

The name icon may be used for all images but is more properly applied to the flat paintings venerated instead of statues in the Eastern churches. The painting of icons reflects the influence of the post-Iconoclasm Byzantine painters. Icons play a more significant and intimate role in the Eastern churches than statues do in the West; and the icon of the saint of the day is usually put on display. They are prominent in processions; and icons of Jesus and Mary receive special reverence and veneration in the liturgy.

MICHAEL GLAZIER

"Christ the Savior," 14th century, Mount Athos

See also EASTERN CHURCHES; SACRAMENTALS.

ICONOCLASM

In the seventh and eighth centuries religious and political controversies about the veneration of icons disturbed the Eastern Empire. At times these disputes reached a tense and abrasive level, sometimes augmented by the hostility of heterodox movements such as the Monophysite heresy which slighted the humanity of Christ and by the Paulicians who regarded all matter as evil and abominated the veneration of icons. At times the excessive attention to icons exacerbated a volatile situation. The controversy crested when Emperor Leo III, the Isaurian (717–741), issued an edict ordering the destruction of all images on the pretext that they were idolatrous and were an obstacle to the conversion of Jews and Muslims. The patriarch Germanus was deposed in 730 after he appealed to the pope; and a persecution, especially against the monks who defended the veneration of icons, made a settlement impossible. St. John Damascene wrote his defense of icons and his condemnation of iconoclasts, and Pope Gregory III condemned Leo's actions in 731.

Leo died in 741 and his son, Constantine V, continued his father's iconoclastic policies and called the Synod of Hiera which the patriarchs of Antioch,

Jerusalem, and Alexandria, as well as the pope, boycotted. The persecution worsened; many monks were martyred while many of the secular clergy compromised. This persecution lessened under Constantine's son, Leo IV (775–780). But on his death, the empress Irene withstood the opposition of the army and reversed the policy. Her actions and negotiations with Pope Hadrian I led to the Second Council of Nicea (787) which mandated the return of icons to the churches and condemned iconoclasm.

The army resented the actions of the council and in 814 elected Leo V the Armenian, a general, emperor, and the persecution was resumed. Opponents were persecuted, often with great severity, or exiled. After the assassination of Leo in 820 the persecution continued in milder form under Michael II, but when his son Theophilus succeeded him in 829 the crusade against the veneration of icons assumed a fanatical ferocity. When he died in 842, his widow Theodora reversed the iconoclastic policies completely, and ordered icons to be venerated in all churches. She gave her full support to celebration of a feast in honor of the icons on the First Sunday of Lent in 834; and since then the feast, called the "Feast of Orthodoxy," has been celebrated in the Eastern Church.

MICHAEL GLAZIER

See also EASTERN CHURCHES; IMAGES, VENERATION OF.

IGNATIUS OF ANTIOCH, ST. (EARLY SECOND CENTURY)

Bishop of Antioch in Syria (modern-day Antakya, Turkey). He called himself Theophorus which can mean either "one who bears God" or "one who is borne by God." According to Eusebius (*Ecclesiastical History* 3.22) Ignatius followed Evodius as bishop of Antioch. Not much is known about his life except that he made a journey guarded by ten soldiers (whom he called leopards) from Antioch to Rome. At Smyrna (modern-day İzmir, Turkey) he was welcomed by Polycarp as well as by Christians from other neighboring Churches. While at Smyrna he wrote letters to the Christian communities at Ephesus, Tralles (modern-day Aydin, Turkey), Magnesia, and Rome. In his letter to the Christians at Rome he asked them not to deny him the opportunity of giving his life for Christ by interceding on his behalf with the authorities. From there he was taken to Troas where he wrote letters to St. Polycarp as well as to the Christian communities in Philadelphia (modern-day Alaşehir, Turkey) and Smyrna. These seven authentic letters show someone who deeply desired to imitate Christ. He strongly upheld both the divinity and humanity of the Lord as he warned his readers to avoid any thought that Christ did not have a human nature or that he did not suffer. Ignatius also wrote that the Eucharist was the medicine of immortality and everlasting life in Jesus Christ. To be in communion with the bishop, the responsible teacher of the faithful, was the best safeguard against error and heresy. Only with his authority might baptism, Eucharist, or marriage be celebrated. Ignatius's letters give the first evidence of a three-tiered hierarchy: monarchical bishops, priests (presbyters), and deacons. Ignatius makes special mention of the Church of Rome as that "which also presides in the region of Roman territory," although he does not mention the Bishop of Rome. Traditionally Ignatius was thought to have been martyred in the Colosseum in Rome during the reign of the Emperor Trajan (98 to 117). Feast day, 17 October.

JOHN DILLON

IGNATIUS OF LOYOLA, ST. (1491–1556)

Ignatius was born in 1491 in the Basque province of Guipuzcoa, Spain; he was the youngest of thirteen children and baptized Inigo—later changing his name to Ignatius. Serving as page to the treasurer of Castile he assisted at the royal court. On 20 May 1521, while serving under the duke of Najera, the French stormed the fortress of Pamplona, and Ignatius rallied the defending Spaniards. A cannon ball damaged both his legs, the town surrendered, and Ignatius was carried to the family castle of Loyola where he underwent painful surgery to straighten his legs. Though he seemed about to die, he began a slow recovery. To pass the time he read two devotional books and underwent a radical conversion: he would serve as knight of Christ rather than any earthly king. He set out on pilgrimage to Jerusalem, confessing and dedicating himself at the monastery of Montserrat. He delayed nearby to write in his journal at Manresa, where he suffered greatly from depression and scruples. Till then he thought only of doing great external works, but now he became aware of "interior things, like humility, charity, patience and discretion." Here he began writing *The Spiritual Exercises,* a guide for a month of prayer. Early in 1523 he resumed his pilgrimage and arrived in Jerusalem that September. Refused permission to stay, he returned to Barcelona and began street-preaching and studying elementary Latin. Being uneducated he soon had difficulties with the Inquisition. So he began seven years of studies at the University of Paris.

In Paris he met Francis Xavier and five other recruits whom he directed in his Spiritual Exercises;

St. Ignatius of Loyola

together they took private vows on 15 August 1534. They decided to work in Jerusalem for the conversion of the infidels, or, if this were impossible, they would place themselves at the disposal of the pope. Because the Turks were in the Adriatic they could not get to Jerusalem, so, calling themselves the *Compania de Jesus,* they went to Rome where their rule of common life was approved by Pope Paul III on 27 September 1540. Ignatius was elected superior and for fifteen years lived in Rome governing the new Society and writing extensive letters. In Rome he finished writing the Jesuit Constitutions in 1551, preached and gave *The Spiritual Exercises.* The Jesuits were joined by many recruits and soon were established in Portugal, Spain, France, the Low Countries, and Germany. Ignatius sent other Jesuits to Africa, the Indies, and the New World. Long suffering from stomach problems, he died of a fever on 31 July 1556. At the time of his death there were almost one thousand Jesuits. He was beatified in 1609 and together with Francis Xavier was canonized by Pope Gregory XV on 12 March 1622. His body is interred in Rome at the Church of the Gesu. Jesuit schools became an important part of the Counter Reformation, and their missions soon extended throughout the world.

THOMAS M. KING, S.J.

See also REFORMATION, THE; SOCIETY OF JESUS.

I.H.S.

A monogram for the name of Jesus, derived from the Latin transliteration of the first three letters of his name in Greek. In the past, it has been erroneously interpreted as an acronym for *Iusus Hominum Salvator* ("Jesus, Savior of Men").

JOSEPH QUINN

See also JESUS CHRIST.

ILLIG, ALVIN ANTHONY (1926–1991)

Paulist publisher and evangelist was born in Los Angeles, California, on 17 August 1926. His parents, Joseph Illig and Kathernina Metz, were immigrants who left Alsace-Lorraine in 1913. They eventually settled in Los Angeles in 1917 where Joseph began a construction company. Alvin was the third of their four sons. Educated in local parochial schools, he then attended the minor seminary for the archdiocese of Los Angeles. Inspired by the vocation of Walter Patrick Burke, a young Paulist who was a friend of the family, Illig entered the Paulist novitiate on 6 August 1945. After studies at St. Paul's College, near the campus of the Catholic University of America in Washington, D.C., he was ordained a priest by Bishop Fulton J. Sheen on 1 May 1953, at the Paulist mother church, St. Paul the Apostle parish in New York City.

Illig had hoped to work in the Catholic missions following his ordination, but was assigned instead to the Paulist Press. As a seminarian, Illig had created a Catholic national news service and demonstrated great organizational and business acumen. Illig spent the next twenty years of his priestly ministry at the press and participated in its transformation from a distributor of pamphlets and tracts into one of the largest publishers of Catholic hardbound and paperback books in the United States. Beginning as an editor of the Paulist magazine *Information,* he created the National Catholic Reading Distributors, an organization that would supply some five thousand Catholic parishes with a variety of Catholic periodicals by 1960. At the end of the Second Vatican Council, he helped launch the ecumenical series CONCILIUM in 1965. The publishing boom in theology ended in the early 1970s. Illig then turned his attention to developing The American Library and Education Service Company to distribute books and audiovisual materials to schools and libraries. Initially quite successful, ALESCO was criticized as a Catholic incursion into the public schools. At Illig's request, Paulist Press sold the company in 1973, and Illig retired from Catholic publishing.

In search of a new direction for his ministry, Illlig went to Denver in May 1973 to develop a communications project for the diocese. He moved on to Pascagoula in January 1974 to devise a program of evangelization along the Mississippi Gulf Coast.

Alvin Illig

Drawing on the marketing skills he learned in his years in publishing, he organized door-to-door visitation, directed a phone campaign, and purchased radio ads and billboard space. His initial success in evangelization was expanded in March 1974 into "Operation Share," a program developed across the Diocese of Natchez-Jackson. In September 1975 Illig moved his base of operations to Washington, D.C. with the permission of Archbishop Baum. In September 1976 he founded the Paulist Office of Evangelization. In November 1977 he became the first director of the National Conference of Catholic Bishop's Office for Evangelization. A professional marketer and communicator, Illig used his position at the National Conference of Catholic Bishops to educate the national Church on the need for evangelization, and his Paulist Office of Evangelization to experiment with local and regional programs for the unchurched. In 1980 he launched his most popular program, *Share the Word,* a Bible study for Catholics. The series reached almost one quarter of a million subscribers by 1986. Illig was a significant influence in the national Church's growing awareness of the unchurched and alienated, and a critical catalyst in the development and dissemination of new forms and approaches to evangelization. He died of colon cancer 2 August 1991. The bishop's November 1992 national plan for evangelization, *"Go and Make Disciples"* is dedicated to his memory.

Illig is buried in Los Angeles, California. His papers, video- and audio-tapes, and newsclippings about his life are kept at the Paulist Archives in Washington, D.C. He was a contributor to Dean Hoge's *Converts, Dropouts and Returnees* (1981), and Ken Boyack's *Catholic Evangelization Today* (1987) and *The New Catholic Evangelization* (1992).

PAUL ROBICHAUD, C.S.P.

See also AMERICAN CATHOLICISM; EVANGELIZATION.

ILLUMINATIVE WAY

The illuminative way is the intermediary stage between the purgative and unitive ways—all three being stages of a journey to union with God in prayer that brings knowledge permeated by love. Having left the stage of beginners, and not yet having arrived at the stage of the perfect, this is the stage of the proficients. During this stage God illumines the believer's mind with a knowledge-love of God and divine ways. The believer passes through a dark night, for the illumination is so bright that one cannot see (like looking into the headlights of an oncoming car). During this stage a person learns to see God in a different way; finding that God is not as we thought God was and that God does not act as we thought God would act. An individual discovers that knowledge of God is not accumulated through personal efforts but is a gift received with open and empty hands. The illumination is always of knowledge permeated by love.

LEONARD DOOHAN

See also CHRISTIAN SPIRITUALITY; THEOLOGY, PRACTICAL.

IMAGES, VENERATION OF

An image gives the beholder a moment's intuition into a reality that is beyond itself, and the image is never identified with the reality of which it is only a shadowy portrayal. Some images simply point to a reality; thus signs in an airport are images, as are flags of nations. However, some images evoke responses in those who behold them; thus a particular flag may well evoke patriotism, or a club's emblem an identification with the club's values. In the context of religion images evoke responses that should lead to greater appreciation of values at the heart of faith. When these images lead beyond themselves they foster religious response, but they can also become ends in themselves and then, as idols, block entry into deeper appreciation of religion. People of the First Testament believed that no image could portray the divine nature; rather, images falsely gave the believer the impression of knowing the unknowable, and so the veneration of images was prohibited (Exod 20:4-6). Some leaders of the early Church followed the First Testament's prohibition—thus in 726 the Emperor Leo III ordered the destruction of images, as did Leo V in 814, and others allowed the veneration of images that led believers to glimpse into divine realities, believing that all reality was purified and ennobled by Christ's incarnation. In 787 the Second Council of Nicaea approved the veneration of images. Some of the leaders of the Reformation opposed the veneration of images, whereas the Council of Trent reaffirmed the value of this practice. Today the Church supports the veneration of images as a way of cultivating the devotion of the faithful. All images for public veneration must be approved by the local bishop, and all veneration is referred to the one whom the image portrays and not the image itself.

LEONARD DOOHAN

See also ICONOCLASM.

IMITATION OF CHRIST

The term is used both for a central theme in Christian spirituality and as a particular book title. As a continuing theme in Christianity, the following or imitation of Christ is a comprehensive definition of Christian life as discipleship. It consists of trying to be and act like Jesus. However, in different historical periods, the emphasis has been on different aspects of the life and death of Jesus as we know them from the Gospels. In the letters of Paul in the New Testament, imitation of Jesus focuses on his death and resurrection. However, in Paul this does not relate to physical death or to a quest for suffering; it means dying to selfish ways to live in a community that gives witness to the new life of the resurrection. In the first Christian centuries, following or imitating Christ also meant a quest for the reign of God by changing relationships among people.

Submerged for centuries by the dominant pattern of worship of Christ, imitation of him came to the forefront again in the twelfth century with various lay movements including the early Franciscans. Here the emphasis was on following the way of life of Jesus during his public ministry—his poverty, simplicity of life and teaching, his association with the poor and disgraced and so forth. In the fourteenth and fifteenth centuries this was carried on by the Brethren and Sisters of the Common Life and in the spirituality movement known as the Devotio Moderna ("modern piety"). Their emphasis was like that of the early Franciscans but with special focus on rejecting any useless quest for learning, especially any theology not strictly related to personal piety.

A contemporary concern with imitation of Christ, as found for instance in liberation theology, focuses on trying to understand his manner of life and actions in the cultural, religious, political, and economic context of his time and place—something that must be learned from sources outside the New Testament, in order to understand the Gospels better. This approach focuses on the plight of the Jews under Roman occupation and the oppression and mass poverty of the people.

Out of the period of the Devotio Moderna came a number of books entitled *De Imitatione Christi,* the most famous and influential of which to this day is that attributed to Thomas à Kempis (1380–1471). It nourished the piety of many Catholics until the liturgical and biblical renewals endorsed by Vatican Council II and continues to provide spiritual reading and inspiration to more conservative Catholics. By modern standards it is a very small volume though it collects what were originally four *libri* (books). The first of these gives general advice about "following Christ and despising the vanities of this world" (much of it about living in community with others). The second concerns "the inner life." The third, "the Book of Inward Comfort," is much the longest, and contains many rules for discernment. The fourth and final "book" is a "devout exhortation to Communion" and is a guide to Eucharistic piety of the individualistic manner of the time.

MONIKA K. HELLWIG

See also DEVOTIO MODERNA; SPIRITUAL LIFE.

IMMACULATE CONCEPTION

The Immaculate Conception is the belief that Mary, the mother of Jesus, was graced by God in such a way that she was preserved from sin from the first moment of her existence. "Immaculate" thus refers to the absence of sin or stain, and "Conception" refers to Mary's very beginning. This belief has nothing to do with the sexual manner of Mary's conception, nor with the way in which she later conceived her own child through the overshadowing of the Holy Spirit (the virginal conception of Jesus). Rather, it points to God's graciousness to this woman as she came into the world sinless or "full of grace."

In 1854, after consultation with the world's bishops, Pope Pius IX declared this belief to be a dogma of the Catholic Church. In the words of the decree, the Blessed Virgin Mary "was, from the first moment of her conception, by the singular grace and privilege of almighty God and in view of the merits of Jesus Christ the Savior of the human race, preserved free from all stain of original sin" (the bull *Ineffabilis Deus*).

The Immaculate Conception is celebrated with a liturgical feast day on 8 December, ranked as a solemnity. In the United States this is a holy day of obligation, partly because this country is dedicated to Mary under the title of the Immaculate Conception.

The idea of the Immaculate Conception has had a long and controversial history. The belief is not found explicitly in Scripture, although the dogmatic definition calls upon certain texts which seem implicitly to support it. These texts include the angel Gabriel's greeting to Mary as "full of grace" (Luke 1:28); her cousin Elizabeth's tribute "blessed are you among women" (Luke 1:42); and the promise made to Adam and Eve after the Fall that the serpent's head would be crushed (Gen 3:15). The belief was also unknown throughout the early Christian centuries, although the way theologians set up Mary's contrast to Eve, the one obedient and bringing in life, the other disobedient and bringing in death, set minds working in this direction.

Influenced by Eastern Christianity, parts of western Europe introduced a feast of Mary's conception beginning in the ninth-tenth centuries. Opposition to this feast brought the doctrine under critical discussion for the first time.

Theologians such as Anselm, Bernard, Aquinas, and Bonaventure objected that the Immaculate Conception seemed to detract from the belief that Jesus Christ was the universal Savior. If Mary was not touched by sin, they argued, then she did not need the Redeemer, and this would violate the deepest Christian sense that Christ came to save the whole human race. These theologians were willing to allow that Mary was sanctified in the womb, but they argued that she had to be touched by original sin for at least one instant in order to be redeemed by Christ.

This objection was answered by Duns Scotus (d. 1308) and his idea that Christ can save human beings in two ways. In one, he rescues from sin those already fallen. In the other, he preserves someone from being touched by sin to begin with. This is uniquely the case with Mary, whose being conceived without original sin demonstrates Christ's redemptive power. Given this reasoning the Council of Trent deliberately excluded Mary from its decree on original sin, and taught in its decree on justification that she was free from sin throughout her entire life.

In the following centuries a number of Marian apparitions encouraged this belief. In 1830 in Paris, Catherine Labouré had a vision of Mary standing on a globe with rays of light streaming from her hands, surrounded by the words, "O Mary conceived without sin, pray for us who have recourse to thee." A medal was struck with this design; known as the miraculous medal it was worn by Catholics everywhere as a devotional custom. In 1858 Bernadette Soubirous in Lourdes also saw a vision of a lady who, when asked her name, said "I am the Immaculate Conception." The place of this encounter became and remains a center of pilgrimage where the sick in particular are welcomed, some being cured in waters welling up from a natural spring.

The religious meaning of the Immaculate Conception centers on the victory of God's grace, freely given in Christ. Sin is universal and the whole human race is in need of salvation. Through his life, death, and resurrection, Jesus Christ mediates the saving mercy of God to all sinners prior to any merits or deserving works on their part. Belief in Mary's original sinlessness celebrates God's victory over the powers of sin as this woman comes into the world. To the Catholic imagination it is fitting that she receive God's free and abundant grace because of her role as the faith-filled mother of Jesus. Her yes to God brought Christ into the world, through whom the ancient sin is overturned. That God generously graces Mary, enabling her living union with God from her beginning even while not removing her from the sufferings of history, is congruent with divine mercy. It also symbolizes the good news that in the life of every human being, grace is more original than sin.

ELIZABETH A. JOHNSON

See also GRACE; MARY, MOTHER OF GOD; ORIGINAL SIN.

IMMACULATE HEART OF MARY

The Heart of Mary has been widely represented in religious art, especially in the twentieth century, and is identified with Mary's maternal love which overflows in her concern for the Church. Many religious orders, as well as churches and nations, are dedicated under this title.

References to Mary's heart became increasingly frequent until, in the Middle Ages, prayers and treatises explicitly treating this subject began to appear. The devotion began to be more prominent after St. John Eudes and others linked it to the devotion to the Sacred Heart of Jesus in the seventeenth century. The first Masses in honor of the Heart of Mary were permitted in 1648. Pius VII (1805) authorized the cult itself, and Mass texts were designated for it in 1856. Devotion to the Immaculate Heart of Mary was enhanced when the visionaries of Fatima reported that Mary had mentioned it in an apparition. The festival was universalized in 1944 with a new Mass and office to be celebrated on 22 August (a week after the Assumption). It was reduced to an optional memorial after the Second Vatican Council. Feast day, 22 August.

DAVID BRYAN

See also DEVOTIONS; FIRST SATURDAYS; MARY, MOTHER OF GOD; SACRED HEART OF JESUS.

IMMACULATE HEART OF MARY, SISTERS, SERVANTS OF THE

Founded in Monroe, Michigan, in 1845 by Louis Florent Gillet, C.SS.R., in collaboration with Mother Theresa Maxis and Sr. Ann Shaaf, of Baltimore, and Theresa Renauld of Grosse Pointe, Michigan. Mother Theresa, the first U.S.-born African-American woman to become a religious, had already pioneered in founding the Oblate Sisters of Providence. From the original foundation in Monroe, two independent congregations were formed in Pennsylvania, one centered in West Chester, the other in Scranton. All three groups were committed to the apostolate of education as their primary contribution to the work of the Church.

Established as the Sisters of Providence, the congregation in 1847 changed its title to the Sisters, Servants of the Immaculate Heart of Mary. The Young Ladies Academy, as the first school was called, opened on 13 January 1846, and initiated a work that eventually expanded across the U.S., into the Caribbean and Latin American lands, and into Africa.

The first two missions outside Michigan were established in Susquehanna and Reading, Pennsylvania. A conflict of episcopal jurisdiction, among other things, resulted in 1859 in a separation of the Pennsylvania houses from the foundation in Monroe. Survival of the institute in Monroe was dependent on several factors, but primarily on the clarification of the rule of episcopal jurisdiction. This was accomplished in 1861; the rule was given papal approval in 1920.

In 1992 the Monroe congregation totaled 884 professed members and 67 associates. The sisters serve in 54 dioceses of the U.S. and are present in 9 Third World countries. They are also coworkers in the Detroit Archdiocesan Pastoral Team in Recife, Brazil. The congregation conducts Marygrove College (Detroit) and St. Mary Center (Monroe), a multipurpose facility housing agencies engaged in human services.

In response to the renewal called for by the Second Vatican Council (1962–1965) and the emerging pastoral needs of the later 1960s and 1970s, I.H.M. sisters moved into a variety of ministries. The three congregations have continued to serve educational needs in schools, but many of the members are now committed to various forms of pastoral ministry, spiritual development, mental/physical health care, social services, and services to the marginalized.

The houses of Susquehanna and Reading served as centers for the Immaculate Heart missions in the northern and southern parts of Pennsylvania until 1864 when Reading became the motherhouse for the eastern I.H.M.s. This motherhouse was transferred to West Chester County in 1872 but moved to Immaculata in 1966. The membership of the Immaculata congregation totals 1,553, working in 9 states, and in Peru and Chile. The congregation conducts Immaculata College, 35 high schools, and 128 elementary schools. It also directs a one-day nursery and a school for visually-impaired children.

In 1868 the Diocese of Scranton was formed. In 1871, since the I.H.M.s were working in Susquehanna and Pittston (formerly in the Philadelphia Diocese), Bishop William O'Hara invited them to stay in the diocese; twelve did so and formed a new congregation with a motherhouse in Scranton. The congregation now totals 773 professed sisters serving in 34 states, Peru, and British Columbia, Canada. They also conduct Marywood College (Scranton), two hospitals, and an Educational Enrichment Institute (Immaculata).

In 1965 a Tri-I.H.M. Immaculate Heart of Mary Education Conference was approved by representatives of the three congregations assembled at Marywood in Scranton. Its primary objective is "to strengthen the spirit of cooperation and unity among the three congregations."

CLAUDIA CARLEN, I.H.M.

IMMORTALITY

The God of the Bible by nature must always exist and so may be said to possess immortality (1 Tim 6:16). The gods of other religions also cannot experience death and, in fact, the gods in Homer were simply referred to as "the immortals" since this was the single most important characteristic that set them apart from human beings. The mortality of humanity, however, has never been in question. Its inevitability and finality are dramatically underlined in the epic of Gilgamesh, the story of a powerful king in Mesopotamia in the third millennium B.C. When he lost his dear friend Enkidu to death, Gilgamesh undertook a perilous journey to win back the life of his friend but finally had to accept his powerlessness in the face of death.

And yet, the burial customs of the earliest cultures testify to at least the hope, if not the conviction, that there may be life for human beings beyond the grave. The Greeks pictured a life in the underworld, but it is a shadowy and insubstantial sort of existence, hardly worthy of being called immortality. Plato's philosophy, though, established a new direction in Greek thought. Immortality belongs to the nature of the soul, a spiritual substance which antedates being joined to a material body and survives its separation from the body at death. Plato's arguments for the immortality of the soul, based on its ability to grasp eternal truth and goodness, proved to be very appealing to Augustine and later Christian theologians.

The Old Testament writings speak of an abode of the dead similar to that of the Greeks (Ps 88:3-12), but this shadowy survival is of little consequence until many centuries later there develops the idea that those who sleep in the dust of the earth shall awake either to everlasting life or everlasting contempt (Dan 12:2). One of the incentives for such a belief was the need to provide a suitable reward for the virtuous and punishment for the wicked. Jesus sided with the Pharisees against the Sadducees in affirming belief in a life beyond this age "in the resurrection" (Mark 12:18-27), and indicated in one of his parables that this life begins immediately after death. The rich man who ignored the needs of the poor man at his gate ended up in Hades in torment, while the poor man Lazarus was carried by angels after his death to rest in the bosom of Abraham (Luke 16:22-23). According to Jesus, the God of Abraham, Isaac, and Jacob "is not God of the dead, but of the living" (Matt 22:32). And so, when the good thief crucified with Jesus asked to be remembered, Jesus replied, "Today, you will be with me in Paradise" (Luke 23:43). This "today" is taken to mean that there will not simply be a general raising of the dead at the end of time, but that each individual passes into a new state of being immediately after death.

On what transpires after death, which remains always beyond our experience, the Church speaks very soberly, affirming only what is necessary to be faithful to the revelation it has received. The Church cannot teach the view of Plato, which identifies the soul as the essence of the self and understands the death of the body as liberating the soul from a supposedly unworthy association with matter. On the other hand, the Church cannot teach that the dead remain in some suspended state until the general raising of the dead at the second coming of Christ. According to Church teaching, in fidelity to the picture presented in the Bible, a human being must be understood as a unitary reality, a fusing together of a spiritual element and a material element. At death the spiritual element, which is endowed with consciousness and will, survives and begins the new life of intimacy with God, or of eternal separation from God, or else undergoes a process of purification prior to entering fully into communion with God. This spiritual element has been traditionally referred to as the soul, but in Christian faith it must be understood as essentially incomplete unless it is joined to a resurrected or glorified body.

WILLIAM C. McFADDEN, S.J.

See also DEATH; ESCHATOLOGY; HEAVEN; HELL; PURGATORY.

IMMOVABLE FEASTS

The earliest immovable feasts were probably commemorations of the martyrs observed in Asia Minor from the second century and in Rome from the third. Later other saints were honored, mostly on the dates of their deaths. By the fourth century Christmas and Epiphany were widely observed on a fixed date, and later other feasts of the Lord and of Mary were added. Some examples of current immovable feasts celebrated on a specific day of a particular month, are: the Solemnity of Mary, Mother of God on 2 February, the Solemnity of St. Joseph on 19 March, the Annunciation on 25 March.

MICHAEL GLAZIER

See also LITURGY.

IMPRIMATUR

Prior to 1975, the diocesan censor granted a license, known as the *imprimatur,* to books that did not contravene Catholic teaching on faith and morals. The revised norms for the granting of the *imprimatur* strictly mandate that it should only be granted to books in conformity to official Church teaching. But presently only the following require an *imprimatur:* official biblical and liturgical texts and their translations; catechisms and prayer books; scholastic textbooks dealing with doctrinal and moral matters; and literature sold or given away in churches.

MICHAEL GLAZIER

See also CENSORSHIP OF BOOKS.

IN VITRO FERTILIZATION

In natural reproduction, one ovum is released into the fallopian tube each month at mid-menstrual cycle. During intercourse, millions of spermatozoa are deposited in the vagina. Many of them swim through the uterus, but only a few dozen reach the ampullary end of the fallopian tube where contact may be established with an ovum released from the ovaries. When a sperm penetrates an ovum, fertilization occurs. The resulting embryo remains in the fallopian tube for two or three days and then enters the uterus, where it implants and grows over the next nine months.

The process of In Vitro Fertilization (IVF) with Embryo Transfer (ET) bypasses the fallopian tubes and effects fertilization through technology. Thus, IVF is not a cure for sterility. Rather than cure sterility, it simply bypasses the natural acts of human intercourse resulting in a method of human generation which separates through technology the unitive and generative aspects of sexual intercourse. In IVF the ovum is removed from the ovary immediately before ovulation and is placed in a culture medium contained in a petri dish along with sperm from the husband or another man (John Biggers, "In Vitro Fertilization and Embryo Transfer in Human Beings," *New England Journal of Medicine* 304 [5 February 1981], no. 6, p. 336). If the ovum is fertilized in the petri dish, it is transferred to the uterus. After a number of days it may implant and if so, it matures over the next nine months. Thus the process of IVF with ET has four distinct stages: the induction of ovulation, the retrieval of the ova, fertilization, and transfer of the embryo.

To date, IVF and ET have not been very successful. Only 5 percent of the procedures result in live births, although the results seem more encouraging if more than one procedure is attempted. Each attempt at fertilization costs anywhere from $10,000 to $15,000 and is usually not covered by private health insurance or HMOs. "Long term follow-up on the babies that are created is simply non-existent. All we know about them is their pregnancy status. According to Robert Lee Hots, author of *Designs for Life,* and figures from IVF clinics around the world, IVF produced twice as many spontaneous miscarriages, five times as many babies with spina bifida, six times as many with transposition of the heart and a rate of still births and deaths in the first month of life that is three times higher than normal. And these are babies of relatively wealthy parents with access to pre and postnatal care" (Barbara Rothman, "Not all that Glitters is Gold," *Hastings Center Report* [July-August 1992] 511).

Most Americans, using a pragmatic method of ethical evaluation accept IVF as ethical as long as the gametes are from husband and wife. But the Church looks not only at the result of IVF, generation of a baby, but also the process by which generation is effected. Hence, when evaluating in vitro fertilization and embryo transplant, the Church returns to the basic notions of human sexuality: that the family is the goal of human sexuality and that the unitive and procreative aspects of the act of generation must not be separated in the process of generation by a deliberate human act. To act otherwise is to act contrary to the natural and moral order revealed by God. Moreover, the Church in a document issued in 1987 follows a moral method that stipulates that every human act has its own morality and that the intention does not justify an immoral act. "The desire for a child is a good intention, but the good intention is not sufficient reason for making a positive moral evaluation on in vitro fertilization between spouses" (Congregation for the Doctrine of the Faith [CDF], "Instruction on Respect for Human Life in Its Origin and on the Dignity of Procreation," *Origins* 16 [19 March 1987], no. 40, pp. 697-709). Thus the moral goodness or badness of a human act or a series of human acts may not be subsumed or overlooked by evaluating only the intention of the person or the consequences of a series of human actions.

The aforementioned document of the Church discusses the morality of Artificial Insemination (AI) and surrogate motherhood, as well as, IVF. Four principles summarize the teaching of the Church in regard to these procedures:

Human procreation must take place in marriage. "The procreation of a new person, whereby the man and the woman collaborate with the power of the creator, must be the fruit and the sign of the mutual self-giving of the spouses, or their love, and of their fidelity. The fidelity of the spouses in the unity of marriage involves reciprocal respect of their right to become a father and mother only through each other" (p. 704).

Using the sperm or ovum of a third party is not acceptable. "Recourse to the gametes of a third person, in order to have sperm or ovum available, constitutes a violation of the reciprocal commitment of the spouses and a grave lack in regard to that essential property of marriage which is its unity. . . ." (p. 705). Moreover, this form of generation "violates the rights of the child; it deprives him of this filial relationship with his parental origins and can hinder the maturing of his personal identity" (p. 705).

Generation of new person should occur only through an act of intercourse performed between husband and wife. ". . . [F]ertilization is licitly sought when it is the result of a conjugal act which is per se suitable for the generation of children to which marriage is ordered by its nature and by which the spouses become one flesh. . . ." (p. 706). "Spouses mutually express their personal love and in the language of the body which clearly involves both spouses' meaning and parental ones. . . ." (p. 706). "It is an act that is inseparably corporal and spiritual. It is in their bodies and through their bodies that the spouses consummate their marriage and are able to become father and mother" (p. 706).

The fertilization of the new human person must not occur as the direct result of a technical process which substitutes for the marital act. "Conception in vitro is the result of the technical action which presides over fertilization. Such fertilization is neither in fact achieved nor positively willed as the expression and fruit of a specific act or the conjugal union" (p. 707).

Two methods of fertilization, Tubal Ovum Transfer, (TOT) and Gamete Intrafallopian Transfer (GIFT) have been advanced as merely assisting the natural process, not substituting for it. Thus they are purported to be in compliance with the teaching of the Church (Machelle Seibel, "A New Era in Reproductive Technology," *New England Journal of Medicine* [31 March 1988] 828). Both involve methods to retrieve ova similar to that of IVF. The sperm is collected after natural intercourse from a perforated condom. TOT and GIFT differ from IVF because both sperm and ova are deposited in the woman's body, and if the process is successful, fertilization occurs therein. Whether or not these processes are morally in accord with Catholic moral tradition is disputed. Does the retrieval and capacitation of a sperm and ovum and placement within the woman's body merely facilitate the natural generative process or does it substitute for the conjugal act? To date the Church has not evaluated these forms of generation but several theologians have offered opinions pro and con in regard to these procedures.

KEVIN O'ROURKE, O.P.

See also BIOETHICS; SEXUALITY; THEOLOGY, MORAL.

INCARDINATION

Refers to the enlistment of a cleric under the jurisdiction of an ordinary, i.e., the affiliation of a priest to his diocese. Normally, such enlistment is permanent, although transfers are possible under restricted conditions. (The term derives from Latin, *cardo,* "hinge"; *incardinare,* "to hang on a hinge.")

PATRICIA DeFERRARI

See also PRIESTHOOD, THE MINISTERIAL; SACRAMENT OF ORDERS.

INCARNATION

Every Sunday, in hundreds of lands and languages, Christians gather for the celebration of the Eucharist and profess their common faith. In the ancient Creed, dating from the fourth century, we confess that, for us and our salvation, God's eternal Word by the power of the Holy Spirit took flesh of the Virgin Mary: became incarnate. This incarnation of God in human flesh is the central and defining mystery of our Christian faith, the "place" where God and humanity meet in the "wondrous exchange" which the liturgy joyfully celebrates.

Whatever we confess concerning the reality of God, the Holy Trinity, we know only because God's only-begotten Son became flesh and revealed the Father to us and sent the Holy Spirit upon us. Whatever we acknowledge of the wondrous salvation God has wrought on our behalf, we experience only because the Word became flesh and established his dwelling among us (John 1:14). Hence to affirm the

Nativity scene, 1520, South Tyrol

mystery of incarnation is not merely to profess doctrine, but to practice discernment: to recognize the glory of God on the face of Jesus Christ. And to assent to incarnation is not merely to utter a formula, but to undertake the following of Christ: living out our adoption as sons and daughters which the incarnation alone makes possible (John 1:12).

The incarnation of God's Word in Jesus Christ is the unsurpassably unique instance of God's self-gift to the beloved creature with whom God has freely and graciously entered into covenant. It might, then, be instructively contrasted with "inspiration." By the inspiration of the Holy Spirit individuals are empowered to speak and act in God's name on behalf of the people. But in incarnation God himself speaks and acts in unique fashion: assuming personally the humanity of Jesus Christ. This singular union of the divine and the human has received in the Church's tradition the designation "hypostatic union," because it affirms faith's conviction that the humanity of Jesus is united inseparably to the person or "hypostasis" of the Word, the second person of the Trinity. Jesus himself becomes God's own personal word and deed in our midst: Emmanuel, God with us.

God comes in the person of the Son of God and takes on human flesh. But "flesh" here means the taking on of human life in its entirety. Thus incarnation does not merely concern the conception or birth of the Savior, but the entire redemptive history of the Word made flesh. Moreover, it is human life in all its grandeur and vulnerability that is assumed. As a result, inseparably connected with the understanding of incarnation, is the recognition of the *kenosis,* the self-emptying of God into human form, even unto death. This "incarnational kenosis" is celebrated in the great Christological hymn of St. Paul's

Letter to the Philippians, where, referring to Jesus Christ, Paul exclaims: "Though he was in the form of God, he did not count equality with God something to be held tightly, but emptied himself, taking the form of a servant.... And being found in human form, he humbled himself still more, becoming obedient unto death, even death on a cross! (Phil 2:6-8).

There is, in all this, an inescapable and irreducible "scandal of particularity" that stands at the very threshold of belief. God's revelation and the fulness of God's presence dwells bodily in Jesus Christ, in his concrete existence and identity (see Colossians 2:9). In this one, crucified and raised, are hidden "all the treasures of wisdom and knowledge" (Col 2:3); for Jesus Christ in his own person is "the power of God and the wisdom of God" (1 Cor 1:24). Confronted with the concrete particularity of the Good News of Jesus Christ, that God's salvation and truth come uniquely through him, believers can only stammer: "Lord, I believe; help my unbelief!"

Moreover, part of what the full realization of incarnation entails is that in this concrete existence believers discern the very principle and pattern of God's action in creation itself. Through the Word of God, made flesh in Jesus Christ, "all creation came to be" (John 1:3). Hence the mystery of incarnation is at once personal and cosmic: in Jesus Christ "all things have been created...and in him all things hold together" (Col 1:16, 17). To enter into the mystery of incarnation is to enter deeply into the meaning and destiny of created reality itself which finds in Christ its origin and fulfillment.

This discernment of faith leads to a life of discipleship that is both intensely personal and also concretely universal, even cosmic, in scope. It is utterly personal because defined by an intimate and ongoing relation with the person of Jesus Christ. In the words of John's Gospel: We are the branches of the vine who is Jesus Christ, without whom we can do nothing (John 15:5). The life of discipleship depends, from start to finish, on being with Jesus Christ, learning from him, abiding in Christ, in a union more intimate than that between husband and wife (see Eph 5:32).

But Christian discipleship is also singularly universal in that the mission of discipleship transcends ethnic and racial divisions by the Lord's mandate to "make disciples of all nations" (Matt 28:19) and even embraces concern for the whole creation, destined to be transfigured in Christ. In the magnificent vision of the Apostle Paul: "Creation itself waits with eager longing for the revelation of the children of God" (Rom 8:19). Hence the contemporary sensitivity for social justice and environmental stewardship finds in incarnational faith its ultimate justification and motivation.

Faith in the incarnation, therefore, cannot be restricted to past occurrence or reduced only to dogmatic statement. The Church believes that the incarnation is a permanent reality, continuing in Jesus Christ's real presence in word and sacrament, in worship and witness. "Where two or three are gathered in my name, I am there in their midst" (Matt 18:20); for "behold I am with you always, even to the consummation of the world" (Matt 28:20). And the affirmation of the mystery of incarnation always bears a "mystagogic" intent: it summons us to participate more fully in the very mystery we confess.

Thus the writings of the New Testament ever exhort the faithful to enter more deeply into the mystery of Christ. In the words of the Letter to the Ephesians: "May Christ dwell in your hearts through faith...and may you comprehend with all the saints the breadth and length and height and depth of the love of Christ" (Eph 3:17, 18). And by so entering and appropriating the mystery, they discover in Christ their own involvement in incarnation: for the mystery finds its completion in "Christ in you, the hope of glory" (Col 1:27).

This "christening," this transformation of the Christian in Christ, is effected by the Holy Spirit which the risen Christ pours out upon his disciples. In a real sense, then, the giving of the Spirit may be considered the completion of the incarnation, the fulfillment of Jesus' mission and of God's saving plan for humanity. The mission of the Spirit is now to transform and to incorporate all created reality into Christ. In the splendid benediction that begins the Letter to the Ephesians, the ultimate goal of God's saving will is proclaimed: "to recapitulate all things in Christ, everything in heaven and on earth" (Eph 1:10). The Holy Spirit works this gathering up of all into Christ, creating the one body of redeemed humanity: Love's body.

In a famous passage of his poem, *The Four Quartets,* T.S. Eliot muses: "The hint half guessed, the gift half understood, is Incarnation./ Here the impossible union/ Of spheres of existence is actual,/ Here the past and future/ Are conquered, and reconciled. . . ."

The believer confesses that the foundation stone which God himself has laid is the incarnation of his only Son. And upon this foundation God is raising up in the Spirit the temple of God's presence whose living stones are the lives of those called through Jesus Christ to be God's own adopted daughters and sons.

ROBERT P. IMBELLI

See also CREEDS; JESUS CHRIST.

INCENSE

(Lat. *incensum,* "something burned") Aromatic gum or resin, in granulated or powdered form, which gives off a fragrant smoke when it is burned. This smoke symbolizes prayer rising to God (Ps 141:2; Rev 8:3-5) and, in a liturgical context, the sacredness of a person or object. Its use long restricted to High Mass, incense may now be burnt at any Mass, particularly during the entrance procession, the Gospel procession, at the Preparation of the Gifts and the elevations following the consecration, and during the recessional. It is also used in the Benediction of the Blessed Sacrament, and may be burnt as part of the Rite for Dedication of a Church and during the rite of commendation and farewell at the close of a funeral Mass.

JOSEPH QUINN

See also SACRAMENTALS.

INCULTURATION

A relatively new term in theology, inculturation refers to the efforts of Christianity to be truly catholic by adapting its message to new cultures. Sometimes words such as "accommodation," or "contextualization," or "indigenization," are used to convey a twofold movement of the faith—incarnating its values in new cultures, and "baptizing," or Christianizing the culture's own values, drawing them into Christianity's worldview.

Inculturation describes the relationship between faith and cultures around the world. This relationship is not something over and done with in some grandscale adaptation, but is rather the ongoing interaction of faith and culture to the advantage of both. The Church's efforts to bring Christ's healing to the whole world are based on the mystery of the incarnation. Inculturation leads to pluralism, unity, and mutual enrichment between Church and world.

The challenges of inculturation were introduced into the Vatican Council documents and later appeared in the writings of Pope Paul VI, and especially in major documents of the Society of Jesus. Pope John Paul II used the word "inculturation" for the first time in a major Church document in his letter on catechetics in 1979. Inculturation challenges the Church to become multicultural. This raises difficulties for many regarding what is perennial and unchanging in the Church's history and in prior forms of incarnating the gospel. A further question regards what is enriching in diverse cultures and so to be integrated with the gospel, and what should be transformed by the spirit of Christianity.

LEONARD DOOHAN

See also EVANGELIZATION.

INDEFECTIBILITY

Because Jesus is the victorious, definitive, and eschatological Word of God and because of his abiding presence in the Church through the gift of his Spirit, the Church, which is founded by him, is said to be indefectible. That is to say, it is guaranteed to remain in existence and to be maintained in fidelity to Christ's teaching and in grace until the end of time. This indefectibility is of course not predicated of individual Christians who can always fall from truth and grace, but of the Church as a whole. It is the consequence of the Church's apostolicity and holiness. Indefectibility is larger in scope than infallibility, though the latter is implied by the former. The Church's permanence in the truth and apostolic faith logically entails that it be able to express its faith in doctrines that are true (though not necessarily adequate) and binding on its members. Finally, it is connected with Vatican II's teaching on the infallibility of the whole People of God in its belief due to its "supernatural sense of faith" (*sensus fidei, sensus fidelium,* and *consensus fidelium*). (See *Lumen Gentium,* no. 12.)

PETER C. PHAN

See also CHURCH, THE; INFALLIBILITY; MARKS (OR NOTES) OF THE CHURCH.

INDEX OF FORBIDDEN BOOKS (*INDEX LIBRORUM PROHIBITORUM*)

The banning of books, barring any and all access to them, has a long secular and religious history. It was intermittently resorted to by the early popes and councils. For instance: the Council of Nicea banned the works of Arius, and Pope Anastasius banned some of the works of Origen. After the Reformation, book banning, by Catholics and Protestants, became standard practice. In 1564 Pius IV issued ten "Rules for the Index" and in 1571 Pius V created the Congregation of the Index, and for more than four hundred years Catholics were forbidden, under threat of excommunication, to read books listed in *Index Librorum Prohibitorum.*

The *Index* listed a wide and varied selection of titles which the Roman officials viewed as a danger to the faithful including theologians. In the course of time, the *Index* became an object of ridicule in Protestant and other circles and an embarrassment to many Catholics—especially when the *Index* banned such works as Pascal's *Pensées,* most of the writing of Voltaire and Zola and all the love stories of Dumas, *père* and *fils.* Fortunately, Paul VI, a sensitive and highly cultured man, put an end to the *Index Librorum Prohibitorum* in 1966.

MICHAEL GLAZIER

INDULGENCES

In his apostolic constitution *Indulgentiarum Doctrina* (1967), Pope Paul VI defines an indulgence as "the remission before God of the temporal punishment due to sins whose guilt has been forgiven" (Norm 1). To understand the Church's doctrine and practice of indulgences, one must place them in the context of the sacrament of penance. Sin has a double consequence. Mortal sins break our communion with God and deprive us of eternal life. The remission of this eternal punishment is effected by the forgiveness of guilt and by the restoration of our communion with God. Besides this eternal punishment, there is another, called the temporal punishment, brought about by both mortal and venial sins. This temporal punishment consists in the disorderly and often painful attachment to creatures which hampers our full communion with God. It must be purified on this earth through works of mercy and of love as well as through prayer and penance or after death through a process called purgatory.

In the ancient Church, confessors, that is, those who have borne great sufferings in the persecutions, could reduce penance imposed upon repentant sinners. In the sixteenth century the scandalous abuse of indulgences was one of the causes that brought about the Reformation.

By granting indulgences the Church applies, by virtue of the communion of saints, to those who are rightly disposed and who fulfill the prescribed conditions the treasury of merits of Christ and the saints and in this way removes totally or partially the temporal punishments ("plenary or "partial" indulgences). Pastorally, it is important to stress the necessity of personal conversion of mind and heart when discussing indulgences today.

PETER C. PHAN

See also REPENTANCE; SACRAMENT OF RECONCILIATION; SIN.

INDULT

(Lat. *indultum,* "a concession") Special permission granted to someone by the Holy See to deviate from the common law of the Church. Synonymous with dispensation, privilege, or faculty.

JOSEPH QUINN

See also CANON LAW.

INDWELLING OF THE HOLY SPIRIT

See HOLY SPIRIT.

INFALLIBILITY

Etymologically, infallibility means inability to err. It does not mean freedom from sin or moral perfection. Despite its negative tone, it implies something positive about the Church: by virtue of the abiding presence of Christ who is the definitive and unsurpassable Word of God and of the assistance of the Holy Spirit who is Christ's eschatological gift, the Church is "the pillar and foundation of truth" (1 Tim 3:15). As a consequence, it is preserved from definitively falling away from the truth of Jesus Christ.

This gift of truth is given to the Church as a whole. Vatican I (1870), which defines papal infallibility in its dogmatic constitution *Pastor Eternus,* says that the pope possesses "the infallibility with which the divine Redeemer willed his Church to be endowed in defining the doctrine concerning faith and morals." Vatican II (1962–1965) affirms that "the whole body of the faithful who have an anointing that comes from the holy one (cf. 1 John 2:20 and 27) cannot err in matters of belief. This characteristic is shown in the supernatural appreciation of the faith (*sensus fidei*) of the whole people, when, 'from the bishops to the last of the faithful' they manifest a universal consent in matters of faith and morals. . . .The People unfailingly adheres to this faith, penetrates it more deeply with right judgment, and applies it more fully in daily life" (*Lumen Gentium,* no. 12). In this sense the Church is also said to be indefectible.

This gift of infallibility in *believing,* however, would remain ineffective, so the Catholic Church holds, unless there were concrete organs by which the truth of Christ can be infallibly *taught.* Infallibility in teaching, then, refers to the exemption from error of certain authoritative persons or organs in the Church in their definitive formulations of doctrines. These organs can exercise this charism of infallibility in two ways, extraordinary and ordinary. In the ordinary way, the bishops, even though taken individually they are not infallible, do proclaim infallibly the doctrine of Christ when "even though dispersed throughout the world but preserving the bond of unity among themselves and with Peter's successor, in their authoritative teaching concerning matters of faith and morals, they are in agreement that a particular teaching is to be held definitively and absolutely" (*Lumen Gentium,* no. 25).

The extraordinary or solemn way can be exercised in two modes. First, when the bishops, assembled in an ecumenical council, act as teachers and judges for the universal Church in matters of faith and morals. Secondly, when the pope, head of the episcopal college, defines *ex cathedra (Petri)* (from the chair of

Peter). According to Vatican I, four conditions must be fulfilled: (1) the pope must act as supreme pastor and teacher of all Christians; (2) he must use his supreme apostolic authority, i.e., as successor of Peter; (3) the subject matter of his teaching must concern faith and morals, i.e., a doctrine expressing divine revelation; (4) he must expressly indicate that the doctrine is to be held definitively by all.

Such definitions are said by Vatican I to be "irreformable of themselves, not because of the consent of the Church" (*ex sese, non autem ex consensu ecclesiae*). This phrase must be understood in the context of Vatican I's rejection of one of the articles of Gallicanism (1682) which asserted that papal definitions are infallible and hence binding only if they are subsequently ratified by the Churches. Vatican I rejected the subsequent ratification of the Church as the source of papal infallible teaching; rather, the source, it said, is the assistance of the Holy Spirit. Hence, it ruled out further appeal to a higher authority.

The fact that papal definitions are "irreformable of themselves, not because of the consent of the Church" does not mean that they can dispense with Scripture and tradition, with the faith of the Church, and with the universal episcopate. In fact, the pope cannot teach any new doctrine and he is morally obliged to take the necessary means to ascertain that his definition indeed conforms with the Christian revelation. In this regard Vatican II affirms that "the assent of the Church can never be lacking to such definitions on account of the same Holy Spirit's influence, through which Christ's whole flock is maintained in the unity of faith and makes progress in it" (*Lumen Gentium,* no. 25). Furthermore, the irreformability of infallible teachings only means that their basic contents cannot be reversed in future developments. It does not rule out the possibility and necessity of reformulation and even reconceptualization of these teachings.

Finally, on what subject matters can infallible teaching be exercised? Vatican II affirms that "this infallibility with which the divine Redeemer willed his Church to be endowed in defining a doctrine of faith and morals extends as far as the deposit of divine revelation, which must be religiously guarded and faithfully expounded" (*Lumen Gentium,* no. 25). Theologians often distinguish between the primary object and secondary object of infallible teaching. The former includes whatever has been revealed for the sake of our salvation, whether explicitly or implicitly, whether written or handed on (the "deposit of faith," "matters of faith and morals"). The latter includes whatever has not been revealed but is necessary for a proper safeguard and exposition of the deposit of faith. It is a dogma of faith that infallibility can be exercised on the primary object, whereas it is theologically certain that infallibility can also be exercised on the secondary object.

In current ecumenical dialogues, the doctrine of infallibility has received extensive attention. In general, it may be said that most Churches do not have difficulty with infallibility in believing. With regard to infallibility in teaching, some Churches accept the infallibility of an ecumenical council. The majority of Churches, however, have objections to papal infallibility as Vatican I defined and Vatican II reaffirmed it. Recently, some Roman Catholic theologians began questioning the validity of this doctrine either on philosophical grounds or on the basis of the doctrine's alleged lack of biblical foundation or on the argument that the bishops at Vatican I were deprived of sufficient freedom to express their opposition to the doctrine. Others accept the teaching of papal infallibility but suggest that it should not be imposed on non-Catholic Christians either because Vatican I taught it without consulting other Churches or because it does not belong to the core of the Christian faith.

PETER C. PHAN

See also AUTHORITY IN THE CHURCH; ECUMENICAL COUNCILS; PAPACY, THE; VATICAN COUNCIL I.

INFANCY NARRATIVES, THE

Each year Christian churches erect nativity scenes at Christmas time and each family tells and retells the events surrounding the birth of the Lord. From childhood every Christian knows the story of where Jesus was born, and those who were present: Jesus, Mary and Joseph, the angels, shepherds, and magi.

For centuries the infancy accounts of both Matthew and Luke were accepted as strict history. New insights into the New Testament, however, and new studies have modified the understanding of the origin of Jesus without taking away the fundamental meaning of the birth of the Lord.

Three periods of scholarship can be distinguished in the understanding of the infancy narratives. In the history of scholarship, the first period of interest in the infancy narratives began to separate the birth material from the material narrating the ministry of Jesus. The latter dealt with the teachings of Jesus and the events of his life as an itinerant preacher. The material comes to us from people who were witnesses from the baptism in the Jordan to his crucifixion and resurrection (Acts 1:21-22). But who was responsible for the story of the birth? In the past some have speculated that the source was the testimony of Joseph or Mary. Today most will find no evidence for such speculation.

Discovering the testimony behind the stories became more difficult when the infancy narratives were subject to biblical criticism. This is the second stage in scholarship. Matthew and Luke actually tell two different stories of the origin of Jesus which agree in very few details and present many contradictions.

The final stage of scholarship concentrates not on the historicity of the narratives nor their origin but on the theology that they present. What did these early chapters of Matthew and Luke mean to the early communities and what do they mean to subsequent generations of Christians?

The infancy narratives represent the last part of the gospel tradition to develop. Mark does not offer us an account of the origin of Jesus. John has in its place the hymn to the preexistence of the Word of God. Compared with the third-century *Proto Evangelium Jacob* and the *Infancy Story of Thomas the Israelite Philosopher,* the accounts of Matthew and Luke are only in the incipient stage of development. The infancy narratives are also late in origin since no mention of the actual origin of Jesus appears in the earliest preaching about Jesus. The preaching in Acts speaks only of the ministry of Jesus from baptism to resurrection. Galatians 4:4 makes mention that Jesus was "born of woman" but this hardly can be seen as a story of origins. Paul also refers to Jesus as being "descended from David according to the flesh" (Rom 1:3). This contrasts Jesus as Son with power according to the Spirit. What Paul says differs significantly from Matthew and Luke.

The first two chapters of Matthew are the overture to the gospel in which the evangelist gathers together various themes that will be played out as the gospel unfolds. Matthew tells us who Jesus is and the goal of his life. He is Son of David and Son of Abraham; he is in continuity with Old Testament salvation history (genealogy in Matthew 1:1-17); he is born of Mary by the Holy Spirit and is called Jesus, Savior, Emmanuel, God with us. His destiny in life will be persecution unto death and he will be restored to life through the intervention of God his Father. The passion narrative in the body of the gospel with the death of Jesus by a cruel ruler is anticipated by the efforts of a cruel king to put him to death at his birth (Matt 2:16-18). The universalism of the command to proclaim the gospel to all nations is anticipated in the coming of the Magi to worship the newborn infant (Matt 2:1-12).

Structure of the Matthean Infancy Account

The first two chapters of Matthew can be divided into six sections:

1. Genealogy (1:1-17)
2. Birth (1:18-25)
3. Adoration of the Magi (2:1-12)
4. Flight into Egypt (2:13-15)
5. Slaughter of the Children (2:16-18)
6. Return from Egypt (2:19-23)

These six sections can be further grouped together into two major units: The genealogy which has its own divisions and the birth sequence which contains five biblical citations. The first section (1:18-25) contains reference to Isaiah 7:14: "Behold a young woman shall conceive and bear a son and shall call his name Emmanuel." The adoration of the Magi refers to Micah 5:1-3: "But you O Bethlehem, Ephrathah, who are little to be among the clans of Judah. . . ." The flight into Egypt refers to Hosea 11:1: "When Israel was a child I loved him and out of Egypt I called my own." The slaughter of the children refers to Jeremiah 31:15: "A voice is heard in Ramah, lamentation and bitter weeping. Rachel is weeping for her children; she refuses to be comforted for her children because they are not."

The final reference is the return from Egypt: "He shall be called a Nazarene"; although Matthew says it was spoken by the prophets, no such reference can be found in the Old Testament. The infancy narrative of Matthew must be understood in light of the Old Testament.

Midrash

Once scholars recognized the relationship between Matthew and certain Old Testament stories or events, they faced the question of the literary nature of the infancy narratives. "Midrash" means an interpretation and comes from the Hebrew word *darash,* to dig or to search. Today most scholars assume that Matthew used the midrash form in his infancy narratives. Midrash attempted to apply the lessons and laws of the Scriptures to the contemporary audience. The rabbis applied the narrative material of the Scriptures to the lives of the congregation. They instructed, offered edification and, sometimes, offered a literary embellishment and application of the text (*derash*).

Matthew did something similar. He combined certain Old Testament texts and interpreted these texts in the light of the actual ministry and ultimate fate of Jesus to create for us stories about the origin of Jesus. The evangelist wrote theologically and not historically, seeking meaning and not wishing to narrate specific events.

The Genealogy

Genealogies establish continuity, legitimacy, relationship, and historical frameworks. By beginning his gospel with a genealogy, Matthew established the continuity of Jesus with the Old Testament tradition. He affirmed the legitimacy of Jesus as Messiah from the line of David. He explained the relationships among individuals who ultimately were under the provident control of God. Finally, by this genealogy he established the historical framework which reached its completion in the coming of Emmanuel.

Much has been written on the Matthean genealogy trying to understand its significance for the evangelist. Primarily, Matthew wants to emphasize the origin of Jesus in the People of God and sees him as the fulfillment of Old Testament salvation history. Since Matthew has a community of both Jewish Christians and Gentile Christians, he begins his story of Jesus by proclaiming that he is Son of David and Son of Abraham. As Son of David he fulfills the Jewish expectations; as Son of Abraham, in him all nations of the earth will be blessed (Gen 22:18). In this way, Matthew pleased both his Jewish Christians and his Gentile Christian community.

Of special interest are the four women named in the genealogy: Tamar, Rahab, Ruth, and indirectly Bathsheba (the wife of Uriah). Some see these women as sinners: Tamar was a seductress and pretended to be a prostitute (Gen 38); Rahab was a prostitute (Jos 6); Ruth may have sinned with Boaz (Ruth 3:6–9:14); Bathsheba was an adulteress (2 Sam 11,12). Others emphasize their Gentile connection. Perhaps the principal reason for their inclusion is their position in the history of salvation. They represent discontinuity. Something irregular or extraordinary was associated with the union with their partners. Yet, this union continued the blessed line of the Messiah. God chose them as special instruments in the history of salvation. They may even foreshadow that special and extraordinary role of Mary recorded in this gospel. The genealogies unite Jew and Gentile in Jesus; they establish continuity with the history of Israel and proclaim that God in his providence controls history and makes use of the irregular and extraordinary to fulfill his purpose.

The Birth Story

Matthew explains the conception of Jesus through supernatural intervention. The primitive tradition affirmed that Jesus was born of a very young woman in the first stage of her marriage. Matthew takes up this tradition and accentuates the divine activity in the birth of the Lord by alluding to his conception by the Holy Spirit. He gives a Christian formulation to the tradition and interprets the origin of Jesus by reference to Isaiah 7:14: "Joseph son of David, do not fear to take Mary your wife, for that which is conceived in her is of the Holy Spirit; she will bear a son, and you shall call his name Jesus, for he will save his people from their sins. All this took place to fulfill what the Lord had spoken by the prophet: 'Behold a virgin shall conceive and bear a son and his name shall be called Emmanuel, which means, God with us'" (Matt 1:20-23).

The child is the presence of God among us, Emmanuel. In 1:25, Matthew further expands his virginal conception tradition by affirming that Joseph "did not know his wife" until the birth of Jesus. This statement leaves open the question whether or not Joseph and Mary had subsequent sexual relationships and other children. In any case, this verse emphasizes the traditional belief in the virginal conception of Jesus. The son of Mary is the Son of God because of his supernatural conception.

Adoration of the Infant Jesus 2:1-12

The mention of wisemen from the East (no number is given) and the star emphasizes the importance of the birth of Jesus and the universality of his message. Matthew takes his framework from the testimony of Balaam, a magus from the East who is supposed to curse Israel and instead blesses it: "A star shall rise from Jacob and a scepter from Israel" (Num 24:17). Gentiles came from the East and recognized the presence of God while the Jews fail to see in Jesus the fulfillment of their history and hopes.

The Flight into Egypt 2:13-15a

"Out of Egypt I have called my son" (Hos 11:1). The story calls to mind the origin of Moses when the Pharaoh attempted to destroy a rival. Like Israel, God's Son, Jesus, will undergo an Exodus from Egypt and return to the Promised Land. Innocent children will die to preserve the Messiah but only that later the innocent Jesus might die to save his people from their sins.

Slaughter of the Children 2:16-18

The massacre of the children of Bethlehem, although not beyond the character of Herod, has no foundation in history. Herod who killed his wife and at the time of his death ordered the execution of several hundred people to ensure that the land would be in mourning, might well have thought of a massacre of children. But if Josephus, the Jewish historian, and no great friend of Herod, makes no mention of such an event we can presume that the story comes from the thought of Matthew. At the birth of every great person, according to ancient Near East legends, evil forces or people seek to destroy those persons before they can accomplish their destiny. It happened to

Moses, and Matthew tells us that Jesus experienced the same fate.

Return from Egypt 2:19-23

In these verses Matthew links Jesus with Nazareth at the very beginning of the gospel with the citation: "He shall be called a Nazarene." Matthew knew the tradition that Jesus grew up in Nazareth and must somehow place Jesus in Nazareth as a child. He accomplished his task by using the above citation. However, no such passage can be found in the Old Testament.

Historicity of the Infancy Account

We can conclude from the analysis of the first two chapters of Matthew that Jesus was born towards the end of the reign of Herod. His mother was Mary and people presumed his father was Joseph. He was brought up in Nazareth. The rest of the narrative comes from the use of the Old Testament to illuminate the fuller meaning of the origins of Jesus.

Christology of the Infancy Narratives

Matthew presents a rather sophisticated Christology which centers on Jesus as Son of David and Abraham, and king. He must be the legal son of Joseph since through Joseph he is related to David. Joseph gives Jesus his name. As the ideal David he will shepherd his people.

The birth of Jesus also fulfills the divine plan of salvation. Matthew incorporates in his account the wonderful story of the virginal conception, the great sign of God's intervention. Jesus comes to us as God's gift, not due to humanity in any way. The Magi and star highlight the universality of the mission of Jesus and the plan of God: salvation for all, Jew and Gentile alike. Matthew further presents Jesus as the new Israel and the new Moses. All of these themes will become part of the fabric of the gospel as Matthew unfolds his understanding of the Jesus tradition. Old Testament stories of Israel and Moses and Balaam have been reworked into a unified anticipation of the passion and resurrection of Jesus. The cast of characters is the same: the secular ruler, the priests and scribes. All are against Jesus who has God with him. God saves Jesus at his birth and brings him back to life after his crucifixion. In the process those who should have recognized Jesus fail to see him as Emmanuel while Gentiles come to adore. The Matthean infancy narrative is not only the gospel, the Good News, but the good news in miniature. Perhaps this explains why this story is so well known and has such a powerful appeal. In the origin of Jesus, people have come to recognize the presence of God in the form of a child waiting to be recognized by people of faith.

Luke

Luke also has his stories of the origin of Jesus but differs considerably from Matthew. He mentions a census under Quirinius which requires Joseph and Mary to go to Bethlehem where Jesus is born in a manger because there is no room for them in the inn. Matthew, as we have seen, gives no details of how Joseph and Mary came to be in Bethlehem. Nor does he give any details about the birth of Jesus.

In Luke, shepherds guided by an angel find Jesus in the manger and praise God. Matthew narrates the coming of Magi from the East, guided by a star. They come to worship and offer gifts not in Jerusalem but in Bethlehem. Herod hears of the Magi and he sends them to Bethlehem to learn and report to him about the infant. Warned by an angel of the treachery of Herod, the Magi return to their own country instead of reporting to Herod. An angel then warns Joseph and he flees to Egypt with his wife and child where they live until Herod's death. When Joseph hears of the death of Herod, he returns to Nazareth instead of Bethlehem. Luke has no mention of Egypt but instead describes how the child is brought to Jerusalem for the ritual of circumcision. Afterwards the holy family returns to live again in Nazareth.

Stages of Development

The first two chapters of Luke are the result of a two-stage literary development. In the first stage Luke created two parallel accounts: One containing the annunciation narratives for John and Jesus (Luke 1:5-25 and Luke 1:26-45, 56); the other, the birth-circumcision-naming narratives for John and Jesus (Luke 1:57-66; and Luke 2:1-12, 15-27, 34-40). Later, Luke added to this balanced literary creation the four canticles which probably predated Luke: The *Magnificat,* which Mary proclaims (Luke 1:46-55); the *Benedictus,* spoken by Zechariah (Luke 1:67-79), the *Gloria,* sung by the angels (Luke 2:13-14) and finally the *Nunc Dimittis* uttered by Simeon (Luke 2:28-33). These hymns were probably composed by Jewish Christians and formed part of their prayer tradition before the composition of Luke's Gospel. At the same time that Luke added these canticles, he also added the pre-Lucan account of the boy Jesus in the Temple, astounding the elders with his wisdom (Luke 2:41-52). This particular account has its origins in some popular tradition of preministry marvels attested in John 2:1-11 and in particular in the apocryphal gospels which seem to delight in stories about the boy Jesus performing wonderful miracles.

Jesus and John

Luke patterns the annunciation of the birth of John in the same manner as the annunciation of the birth of Jesus. How much history is involved is debatable. Perhaps the dating in the reign of Herod the Great and the names of the parents of John are historical details. The actual presentation of Elizabeth and Zechariah, however, are modeled after two famous Old Testament accounts of births to barren parents: Elkanah-Hannah in Samuel's birth (1 Sam 1–2) and Abraham-Sarah in Isaac's birth (Genesis 17–18). Luke utilized the theme of barrenness, and the Old Testament annunciation pattern of the birth of any great figure, as a bridge of continuity between the history of Israel and the history of Jesus's life and ministry.

In the Jesus half of the annunciation account (Luke 1:26-56), Luke reworked the pre-gospel annunciation of the birth of Jesus as the Davidic Messiah used by Matthew: "He will be great, and will be called Son of the Most High; and the Lord God will give him the throne of David his father and he will reign over the house of Jacob forever" (Matt 1:32-33). And like Matthew, Luke will add the proclamation of the divine sonship of Jesus through the power of the Holy Spirit: The angel declares to Mary: "The Holy Spirit will come upon you and the power of the Most High will overshadow you; therefore the child to be born will be called Holy, the Son of God" (Luke 1:35).

While some scholars have questioned the presence of the belief in a virginal conception of Jesus in this account, a comparison between these two annunciation events will highlight the superiority of Jesus over John. If the birth of John was marvelous because of the barrenness of his parents, the birth of Jesus was more marvelous since it was through the power of the Holy Spirit and not through the ordinary means of human conception.

Luke then turns to the birth-circumcision and naming of these same individuals. The first section which describes the birth, circumcision, and naming of John originally closed with a summary statement of his growth (Luke 1:80), which included two elements taken from the synoptic ministry of John: He was "strong in spirit," and he was "in the desert."

The birth-circumcision-naming of Jesus is more complex. Luke has added the Temple scene (Luke 2:22-39) built around two Jewish practices: the consecration of the first-born and purification after birth. This section originally closed with a description of Jesus' youth in Nazareth (2:39-40) as a transition to his later ministry (Luke 3:21).

In all probability the census described in Luke 2:1-5 is a Lucan device without historical basis. Luke probably knew a tradition that the birth of Jesus was associated with the end of a Herodian rule and he confused Herod the Great (died in 4 B.C.) with his son Archelaus (deposed in A.D. 6). We do have a record of a census in A.D. 6 and Luke utilized this historical event as a means of bringing Mary and Joseph to Bethlehem.

The appearance of angels to shepherds to announce the birth of Jesus is a typical annunciation form in which Luke utilized Isaiah 9:6 (describing a newborn child who is to be heir of the throne of David), and Isaiah 52:7 (describing the messengers who bring the good news of salvation). In fulfillment of the Old Testament prophesy, the angels announce the Christian proclamation of Jesus as Savior, Messiah, and Lord. The presence of shepherds also foreshadows the outcasts who will recognize Jesus and believe in him.

The Temple scene in Luke utilizes the model as found in Malachi 31:1: "The Lord whom you seek will suddenly come to his temple," and Daniel 9:24, which speaks of the anointing of a most holy one whom Luke sees as Jesus. The angelic announcement met the expectations of Israel and now in the Temple the *Nunc Dimittis* of Simeon reaches out to the Gentiles: "Lord . . . my eyes have seen your salvation . . . a light of revelation for the Gentiles."

Finally, his parents present Jesus at the age of twelve in the Temple for Passover and his wisdom astounds the elders. His parents do not understand him because they do not yet have the Easter faith in Jesus as God's Son. The insertion of this account here enables Luke to show the continuity from the infancy of Jesus as God's Son, through the boy Jesus in the Temple, to the resurrected Lord.

Historicity of the Infancy Account

This account, like that of Matthew, is not concerned with history. Whatever historical elements are present are incidental and inconsequential. In these chapters on the origin of Jesus Luke narrates a powerful literary composition, based principally on passages of the Old Testament with a set theological perspective. Luke has reflected, along with the broader Christian community, on the life of Jesus. The reflection takes place by using literary forms current and acceptable and part of the Old Testament tradition. In reading this narrative, like that of Matthew, the Christian community must progress in its understanding of the origin of Jesus. The thinking will move beyond the stage when every detail was accepted as historically accurate, to the position of asking: what does Luke wish to state theologically in his record of the origins of Jesus?

Old Testament Comparisons

Certainly his wide use of the Old Testament to construct most of the actual material demonstrates a continuity between the Jewish messianic tradition and the origin of Jesus. Although the gospel is directed primarily to Gentiles, the historical Jewish roots of Jesus and Christianity are not forgotten. Moreover, the use of particular passages of the Old Testament will highlight the particular theology of Luke. He often alludes to the Old Testament but does not quote the passages in detail. The reader can compare specific sections of the Gospel of Luke with Old Testament traditions to understand just how carefully Luke utilizes parts of the Jewish tradition.

Luke 1:26-33 compare with Zeph 3:14-17
Luke 1:32-33 compare with 2 Sam 7:16, 26
Luke 1:35 compare with Exod 40:34-35
Luke 1:39-44 compare with 2 Sam 6:2-11
Luke 1:46-55 compare with 1 Sam 2:1-10
Luke 2:1-14 compare with Mic 4:7–5:5
Luke 2:34 compare with Isa 8:14

Christology of the Infancy Narratives

Luke proclaims that Jesus is Lord and Messiah (Acts 2:32, 36). His origin is in the hands of God alone for almighty God gives Jesus to the world as Savior. Throughout his public ministry the poor and the outcast find acceptance in Jesus. At his birth the powerful are not present but only the poor shepherds who recognize him and praise God.

Mary

The chief character in this narrative is Mary. She has given herself to God and God has responded to her faithfulness by calling her to become the mother of his Son. Mary as the model of faith in the ministry of Jesus, lives as the model of faith in his origin. She trusts in God through the words of the angel and once she has given birth to Jesus, she will offer his presence to the shepherds.

Luke depicts her kindness in his story of the journey to her cousin Elizabeth. Luke presents Mary as unmindful of her own needs but more concerned about the needs of Elizabeth. She makes the arduous journey. Luke also has her declaration of faith by having her speak the *Magnificat.*

Whatever historical memories the early Church retained of Mary, they must have contained the image of a woman of great faith and great kindness. She does not figure in the public ministry of Jesus other than one who has heard the word of God and kept it. Here in the infancy narratives she has responded to the word of God and has lived that faith in a kind and loving way. In the ministry of Jesus someone informs him that his mother and brothers are outside. Jesus responds: "My mother and brothers are those who hear the word of God and keep it" (Luke 8:21). Later when a woman proclaims: "Blessed is the womb that bore you and the breasts that nursed you" (Luke 11:27b), Jesus responds: "Blessed rather are they who hear the word of God and keep it" (Luke 11:28). Mary bore Jesus in her womb because she was one who had heard the word of God and had kept it.

Theology

Luke even has a foreshadowing of the passion. Simeon declares that Jesus will be the cause of the fall and rise of many in Israel (Luke 2:34) and a sword will pierce through the soul of his mother (Luke 2:35). The author foreshadows the ministry of Jesus with acceptance and rejection in these opening chapters; the call to the outcasts is also present; the need for faith and hearing and keeping the word of God is present in the response of Mary. The overshadowing of the Holy Spirit, who figures prominently in the gospel, explains the origin of Jesus. Luke has taken his principal theological themes and gathered them together into an account of the origin of Jesus. Christians should read these chapters and ask themselves continually: What is the author saying about the meaning of Jesus? In doing this, the unfolding of the origin of Jesus will take place as the sign of God's salvation offered to all through faith.

JOHN F. O'GRADY

See also BIBLE, NEW TESTAMENT WRITINGS; CRITICISM, BIBLICAL.

INFANT BAPTISM

By the end of the second century children were among candidates for the reception of baptism, although in the fourth century adult baptism was still quite common. However, by the fifth century the practice of infant baptism was universal in the West. In the sixteenth century the Church faced the Protestant reformers and their varied views on infant baptism. While the council fathers at Trent (1545–1563) emerged strong on the issue of baptizing infants, they did not address the central issue, viz., the practice of infant baptism did not engage persons in conversion to Christ. However, at Vatican II (1962–1965) the Constitution on the Liturgy called for the revision of the rite of baptism of infants and greater awareness of the roles of both parents and godparents. In 1969 there appeared the *Roman Rite of Baptism for Children.* In this document infants are understood as children up to the age of reason.

The new rite accentuates the role of the parents. They present the child and publicly ask for its baptism. They (or at least one parent) renounce Satan, profess the faith of the Church, and promise to raise the child in that faith. They also sign the child with the sign of the cross, carry the child to the font, and receive a blessing.

The new rite also underlines the role of the sponsors. Each child may have a godfather and a godmother. As occasion demands, they must be willing to assist the parents in raising their child to profess the faith and to demonstrate that faith by a Christian life.

JOHN F. CRAGHAN

See also FAITH; SACRAMENTS OF INITIATION.

INFUSED VIRTUES

Infused virtues are those "powers" of the soul, namely, faith, hope and charity, which are directly imparted to ("poured into") the soul of a person by God. They are not acquired by repetition or habit as are other virtues, such as prudence or justice. The infused virtues (also known as the theological or supernatural virtues) redirect the person's freedom and powers fully toward God by the presence of supernatural grace. They give the person the possibility of sharing in the divine life, but the recipient must cooperate with the grace given by these virtues. To realize the full effect of the infused virtues, the recipient must develop and perfect the other virtues and seek to live a life free from sin.

ANTHONY D. ANDREASSI

See also VIRTUE.

INITIATION, CHRISTIAN

See SACRAMENTS OF INITIATION.

INQUISITION, MEDIEVAL

The Medieval Inquisition was established by Pope Gregory IX in 1231 to investigate and adjudicate persons accused of heresy. The name Inquisition derived from the method of procedure adopted by the Pope whereby a particular official was charged with the duty of inquiring into and trying alleged heretics. In the flowering of the High Middle Ages in the thirteenth century the common heritage of all social ranks in western Europe was Roman Catholicism, which, it was felt, was necessary not only for the ecclesial community but for the body politic as well. Hence when the Albigensian sect arose teaching that marriage was evil, that all oaths were forbidden, that mortals had no free will and therefore could not be held responsible for their actions, that religious suicide was good, that civil authority had no right either to punish criminals or to defend the country militarily, it seemed in the medieval view of the average person to strike at the very base of society. Thus heretics disassociated themselves not only from the religious community but from the political and social community as well. They had declared themselves rebels.

The crime of heresy was defined as a deliberate denial of some article of revealed truth of the Catholic faith, and a public and obstinate persistence in that error. Since both the Albigensians and the Waldensians claimed to be Christian, to the extent that their teachings differed from the Roman Church they were considered to be heretics in the popular mind. On the other hand since neither the Jews nor the pagans purported to be Christian, they were not accounted heretics.

In order to bring order and legality to the procedure of dealing with heresy which in southern France was growing steadily, while in Germany, particularly, there was the tendency for mobs to burn alleged heretics forthwith, Pope Gregory IX created an extraordinary court of exception to inquire into alleged heresy. The purpose was to discover the beliefs of those differing from Catholic teaching, and to instruct them in the orthodox doctrine. It was hoped that persons with erroneous beliefs would see the falsity of their opinion and would return to the community. Thus success was achieved and all was well. If, however, they persisted in their heresy, it was felt that it was necessary to protect the community from the infection and they were handed over to the civil authority for they had violated civil law as well and the state would now enforce its own code.

Upon arrival of the inquisitors in a town the people were assembled to listen to a sermon explaining the teachings of the faith. They were then requested to tell of any words or actions they knew of that were contrary to the faith. Those accused were then called before the inquisitorial commission and questioned about those matters. After questioning the accused the inquisitor came to a decision and conveyed this to the local bishop. If the bishop and the inquisitor agreed on the appropriateness of the sentences, a general assembly was convened on a given Sunday and the inquisitor delivered a discourse covering the main articles of the faith, stressing those beliefs which had come under attack by the local heretics. Then the sentences were read out to all those present including the ones receiving the verdicts. The penances handed down were both spiritual and physical: the spiritual were excommunication, interdict, and suspension; the physical were pious works, visiting churches, pilgrimages to various shrines, almsgiving, presence at church functions wearing signs of penitence and subjection to ritual flagellation, wearing crosses of different colors in public, fines, confiscations, destruction of buildings, imprisonment.

If, however, an individual, after having relapsed, refused to repent, the church, recognizing its failure, declared that person a heretic, withdrew its support and "abandoned" him or her to the secular authority, which proceeded to apply its own law, which at this time was burning at the stake.

The Church permitted appeals from the inquisitor and the bishop to the Pope—which was used many times. Further the Church considered imprisonment a medicinal penalty whereby convicted heretics might have time to meditate on their errors and might hopefully return to the Catholic faith. At the same time she protected the faithful from being corrupted by heretical doctrine. This was a major change for the times, for the civil authority had prisons only for custody before trial, whereas the Church introduced prisons for detainment after the verdict. The secular authority did not; capital punishment was the prevailing law.

ALBERT C. SHANNON, O.S.A.

See also CHURCH AND STATE; HERESY/HERETICS; MIDDLE AGES, THE; ORTHODOXY.

I.N.R.I.

(Lat. *Iesus Nazarenus Rex Iudaeorum,* "Jesus the Nazarene, King of the Jews") The initials of the Latin inscription which Pontius Pilate ordered to be placed on the cross above Christ's head. Describing Jesus as a claimant to the Davidic throne, and therefore a rebel against Roman rule, it followed the Roman custom of inscribing the crime for which the person was being crucified. It was written in Hebrew, Greek, and Latin. In portrayals of the cross before the thirteenth century, the inscription either was written out fully or omitted.

JOSEPH QUINN

See also CROSS; PASSION NARRATIVES.

INSPIRATION, BIBLICAL

The Jews considered their Scriptures as the Word of God (Exod 24:4; 34:27; Jer 30:2; 36:2; Mic 1:1), and when Christians inherited these writings they too believed them to be the Word of God (Matt 22:31; Mark 7:13; John 10:35; Acts 1:16; 4:25; 28:25). The Church from the times of the Fathers and throughout history has always believed that both Old and New Testament contained God's Word and were written under the inspiration of the Holy Spirit.

The term "inspiration" is not found in the Bible, but the reality certainly is. In the Old Testament the Spirit of God descends on individuals and on the whole people (Isa 11:2; Joel 2:28), and in the New Testament both individuals and the whole Church are filled with the presence of the Holy Spirit (Luke 1:35; 2:27; Acts 2:4; 6:5; 10:19, 44). In the Bible we find people who are inspired to act (pastoral inspiration), others who are inspired to speak (oral inspiration), and others who write about the first two (scriptural inspiration). Biblical inspiration is a combination of all these three.

God reveals self and the way of salvation in history that culminates in the revelation of Jesus. The Christian Scriptures do not reveal a list of abstract truths to be believed or obeyed but a living person, Jesus, with whom humanity is called to establish a relationship of love, imitation, and faithful obedience to his Word. We know of God's revelation to us in the actions, words, and writings of the early Christian community or those who represented it—thus, revelation is God active in history, and inspiration is when God calls and moves ("inspires") people to tell others about the revelation.

Inspiration is a gift to the community even though individuals may act, speak, or write on the community's behalf. Through the gift of biblical inspiration the original revelation is preserved and prolonged for the benefit of future generations. The result is that the Bible teaches truthfully and without error those truths which are necessary for our salvation. This does not mean that the Bible is free of mistakes. There are mistakes about geography, history, science, and so on. But inspiration assures us that it is truthful in those matters which prolong God's revelation and which are necessary for our salvation.

There is a clear difference between what God inspired people to reveal and how they do it. Inspiration is the result of divine and human interaction. God uses peoples' gifts, leaves their individuality intact, and sometimes conveys teachings in spite of their failures. God inspires some people, like the prophets Jeremiah and Agabus, to act out the truths God wishes to reveal (Jer 18:1-4; Acts 21:10-11). At other times individuals preach a truth with faithfulness and love, as in the case of Peter (Matt 16:16), or with disbelief, as in the case of Caiaphas (John 11:49-51). When God inspires individuals to convey

God's revelation in writing they do so using a variety of writing styles and literary techniques. Thus, although inspiring people, God accommodates self to them, and when we wish to read the inspired word we too will need to respect the individuals who presented them, adjusting to their strengths and weaknesses, their culture and conditioning, their styles and compositional forms.

LEONARD DOOHAN

See also BIBLE, NEW TESTAMENT WRITINGS; BIBLE, OLD TESTAMENT WRITINGS; REVELATION; THEOLOGY, BIBLICAL.

INSTITUTE, RELIGIOUS

A religious institute is a society in the Church of men or women who profess public vows (perpetual or temporary) of poverty, chastity, and obedience and who share a common life and worship of the Lord. The canonical term, "Religious Institute," was used in the documents of the Second Vatican Council (1962–1965) to describe any religious order, society, or congregation taking public vows. Members of religious institutes differ from members of societies of apostolic life in that the latter do not take public vows.

ANTHONY D. ANDREASSI

See also RELIGIOUS ORDERS; VOWS.

INSTITUTE, SECULAR

The canonical definition is: "a secular institute is an institute of consecrated life in which the Christian faithful living in the world strive for perfection of charity and work for the sanctification of the world especially from within" (c. 710 of the 1983 Code of Canon Law).

The members remain laypersons or diocesan priests (c. 711); they are not considered religious in the technical sense. Nevertheless, they commit themselves in some binding way to the evangelical counsels (c. 712), and do not withdraw from the world of ordinary affairs but are very much engaged in it (c. 713). They are committed to celibacy though they often live in their own homes.

Secular institutes arose to meet situations in which the restrictions on vowed religious would interfere with the work or life to which a band of devout people have dedicated themselves. The secular institutes are a modern phenomenon but do correspond to the virgins living in their own homes in the early Church.

MONIKA K. HELLWIG

See also LAITY, THEOLOGY OF THE; RELIGIOUS ORDERS.

INTERCOMMUNION

A relationship between denominations which permits the members of one Church to receive Holy Communion in another. For non-Catholics to receive the Eucharist in a Catholic Eucharist certain conditions, described very generally by the Code of Canon Law (c. 844) and applied with slight variations in particular regions and dioceses, must be present. Though Catholics are not ordinarily permitted to receive Communion in churches of other denominations, intercommunion between Catholic and Eastern Orthodox Christians is acceptable.

This term can also refer to an agreement between two Christian Churches in which each grants membership privileges to members of the other.

JOSEPH QUINN

See also ECUMENISM.

INTERPRETATION, SCRIPTURAL

See ALLEGORICAL MEANING OF SCRIPTURE; CRITICISM, BIBLICAL; LITERAL MEANING OF SCRIPTURE.

INVESTMENT RESPONSIBILITY

See SOCIAL RESPONSIBILITY, FINANCIAL.

INVINCIBLE IGNORANCE

A type of ignorance held in moral theology to be exempt from moral consequence due to its involuntary and irretrievable nature.

JOSEPH QUINN

See also THEOLOGY, MORAL.

IRELAND, JOHN (1838–1918)

First archbishop of St. Paul, Minnesota (1888–1918), Ireland was born in County Kilkenny, Ireland, on 11 September 1838, and died in St. Paul on 25 September 1918. John Ireland's parents emigrated from Ireland in 1849 as a result of the Great Famine, eventually settling in St. Paul in 1852. When young Ireland expressed an interest in the priesthood, the French-born bishop of St. Paul, Joseph Crétin, sent him to his own *alma mater,* the seminary in Meximieux. Ireland's eight years in France made him an ardent Francophile, fluent in the written and spoken language.

Upon returning to the United States, Ireland was ordained a priest of the Diocese of St. Paul on 22 December 1861 by Crétin's successor, Bishop Thomas Grace, O.P. After nine month's duty as a Civil War chaplain, Ireland served as curate and

Archbishop John Ireland

then rector of the St. Paul Cathedral. In 1875 he was unexpectedly named vicar apostolic of Nebraska, but Bishop Grace prevailed upon Rome to cancel the appointment and instead to make Ireland his coadjutor. Upon Grace's resignation, Ireland succeeded to the see on 31 July 1884 and became the first archbishop of St. Paul on 15 May 1888.

Both as priest and prelate, Ireland was an intensely active individual, leading admirers to call him "the consecrated blizzard of the Northwest." The range of his interests was remarkable. Even as a young priest he campaigned against alcoholism and he remained a lifelong champion of the Catholic Total Abstinence Society. While coadjutor bishop, he worked with his Protestant friend, Canadian-born railroad tycoon James J. Hill, to organize a Colonization Bureau, which bought 380,000 acres of prairie real estate to establish agricultural colonies for Catholic immigrants.

According to his biographer, Marvin O'Connell, "Ireland's most striking physical characteristic was the timbre of his voice, honeyed thunder sometimes and sometimes a throaty growl, but always dominant, clear and loud, a wonderfully vibrant and resonant instrument that carried to the farthest corner of the largest hall." At the Third Plenary Council of Baltimore in 1884, Ireland delivered a memorable oration on "The Catholic Church and Civil Society" in which he stressed the natural affinity of the Catholic Church and American civilization. It was a theme to which he often returned, most notably in 1893, when he declared: "I preach the new, the most glorious crusade, the Church and the Age. Unite them in the name of humanity, in the name of God."

Ireland's optimism made him one of the leaders of the liberal or "Americanist" wing of the American hierarchy. Together with his friends, James Cardinal Gibbons and Bishop John Keane, in 1887 Ireland helped to avert a papal condemnation of the Knights of Labor. He was also instrumental in obtaining Roman approval for the charter of the Catholic University of America, an institution which he had helped to establish.

Perhaps Ireland's most acrimonious dispute with his fellow bishops occurred over the question of parochial schools. While recognizing the value of such schools, Ireland questioned the practicality of the decision of the Third Plenary Council of Baltimore to create a comprehensive parochial school system financed entirely by the laity. In 1891 pastors in Stillwater and Faribault, Minnesota (in Ireland's archdiocese), worked out an agreement with the local school boards whereby the school boards assumed most of the financial responsibility for the parish schools in return for a limited degree of state supervision. Ireland supported the arrangement, but conservative bishops protested that it would undermine the parochial school system. In 1892 Rome gave a qualified approval to the so-called Faribault-Stillwater plan, but protests from militant Protestants led to the abrupt termination of the experiment.

One of Ireland's most attractive traits was his defense of the rights of American blacks. His seminary was one of the few to accept black candidates for the priesthood, and in 1890, Ireland said: "Let the Negro be our equal before the law." Unfortunately, he did not show a comparable sensitivity for the ethnic pride of European Catholic immigrants, especially German-American Catholics who clung to the language and customs of their homeland. Moreover, when German Catholic leader Peter Cahensly complained of the treatment of German-American Catholics, Ireland mendaciously depicted him as an agent of the German Imperial government. Even more deplorable was Ireland's attitude to Eastern-rite Catholics. He was instrumental in preventing the introduction into the United States of married Eastern-rite clergy with the result that an estimated 225,000 Eastern-rite immigrants left the Catholic Church for the Russian Orthodox Church.

Alone of the American archbishops, Ireland favored the appointment of an apostolic delegate in 1893, thinking that he could use papal authority to buttress his own "Americanist" views. His tactics backfired when after 1895 the delegate, Archbishop Francesco Satolli, allied himself with Ireland's conservative opponents. Pope Leo XIII's condemnation of "Americanism" in 1899 was widely regarded as a rebuke of Ireland and his friends. The previous year Ireland had also lost influence in Rome when he was unable to prevent an American declaration of war on Spain. After the war Ireland served on the commission which settled the dispute over Church property in the Philippine Islands.

Shortly before his death, Ireland completed two magnificent cathedrals in the Twin Cities of Minneapolis and St. Paul. They stand as fitting monuments to the dynamic churchman and patriot who symbolized the contribution of the Catholic Church to the American Republic during an era of unprecedented growth. Cardinal Gibbons eulogized him as "the man who had contributed perhaps more than any other to demonstrate the harmony that exists between the Constitution of the Church and the Constitution of the United States."

THOMAS J. SHELLEY

See also AMERICAN CATHOLICISM; AMERICANISM; CHURCH AND STATE.

IRENAEUS, ST. (ca. 130/40–ca. 200)

Little is known about his life. Possibly he was a native of Smyrna (modern-day İzmir, Turkey) since he wrote to Florinus that as a boy he heard Polycarp (as reported in Eusebius, *Ecclesiastical History* 5.20.5-7). He lived at Rome for a time but later became a presbyter in Lyons in Gaul. This Christian community sent him (ca. 177) to Pope Eleutherius in Rome to request toleration for the Montanists in Asia Minor. On his return Irenaeus became the successor to Bishop Pothinus who had died as a martyr during the persecution that had swept through Lyons while Irenaeus had been away. The last event in Irenaeus's life which can be dated was a letter which he wrote to Pope Victor in Rome (189 to 198) in which he admonished Victor that peace, unity, and love should prevail in his dealings with the bishops in Asia over the question of when Easter should be celebrated. Not until the sixth century is there any report that Irenaeus died as a martyr. Only two of Irenaeus's works have survived. An Armenian version of *The Demonstration of the Apostolic Preaching* was discovered and published early in the twentieth century. This work is an apologetic treatise that draws heavily upon the Old Testament. His main work, *Exposé and Overthrow of What Is Falsely Called Knowledge*—but commonly called *Against the Heresies,* is a detailed attack upon Gnosticism. Part of it survives in the original Greek. The whole text survives in a literal Latin version, and sections of it also exist in Syriac and Armenian. Because the Gnostics claimed that their secret traditions could be traced back to the apostles, Irenaeus decided to oppose them by exposing this to be false and by showing, moreover, that what he taught could be traced back to the apostles. To this end he emphasized the canon of Scripture, the episcopate, and the religious and theological tradition as it had developed to that point. He insisted on the unity of Father and Son in the work of revelation and redemption. Irenaeus borrowed (but further developed) from St. Paul the notion of recapitulation. Paul wrote in Ephesians 1:10 that God summed up all things in Christ. Irenaeus expanded Paul's notion in this way: humankind which had fallen in the sin of the first Adam was restored to communion with God by the obedience of Christ, the second Adam. For Irenaeus recapitulation also meant that the previous revelations of God were summed up in the incarnation. *Against the Heresies* is also valuable because of its information on the Gnostic systems which has generally been upheld in the modern discovery of Gnostic literature. Feast day, 28 June.

JOHN DILLON

See also DOCTRINE, DEVELOPMENT OF; FATHERS OF THE CHURCH.

IRISH CATHOLICISM

See CATHOLICISM, IRISH.

ISIDORE OF SEVILLE, ST. (ca. 560–636)

Doctor of the Church, teacher and writer, he was born in Seville to a noble Hispanic-Roman family from Cartagena. He was educated by his brother Leander, a monk, who introduced him to a life of scholarship. Isidore succeeded Leander as archbishop of Seville ca. 600, and he worked diligently to convert the Visigoths from Arianism to Catholicism. He laid the foundation of Church organization in Spain by convoking numerous councils and synods including the councils of Seville in 619 and Toledo in 633, which called for the establishment of cathedral schools—almost two hundred years before Charlemagne's call for them. An ardent believer in the importance of education, he helped to found schools all over Spain, in which not only theology, but also medicine, liberal arts, and law were taught.

Isidore is best remembered today for his writings. His famous, *Etymologies,* is a quasi-encyclopedia containing information on grammar, rhetoric, history, theology and other topics. The information is presented as etymologies, and the data are often wrong—an indication that the Dark Ages were descending upon Western Europe. His major historical work, *Chronica Majora,* is an amalgamation from other historians and attempts to cover the period from creation to A.D. 615 with specific references to Spanish history. He also wrote a history of the Goths, some biographies, a summary of Christian doctrine, monastic rules for men and women, and an edition of the Mozarabic missal and breviary. Bede thought highly of Isidore, and many medieval library catalogues gave him a prominent place. Thus he shares with St. Gregory the Great the title, "Schoolmaster of the Middle Ages." Isidore always prized the ascetical life and charity to the poor. He died on 4 April, the day still observed as his feast. He was canonized in 1598, and Pope Benedict XIV declared him a "Doctor of the Church" in 1722.

ANTHONY D. ANDREASSI

See also FATHERS OF THE CHURCH.

ISLAM

Of the major world religions, it is the fastest growing and one of the largest with approximately one billion adherents. Its chief population centers are in Indonesia (161 million), Bangladesh (100 million), Nigeria (100 million), and India (100 million). The vast majority of Muslims are non-Arabic, but the majority of Arabs are Muslim. There are approximately 4 to 5 million Muslims in the United States.

Islam is pronounced with the accent of the second syllable: i-SLAM. The word literally means submission, obedience, or surrender. The word Islam, however, is derived from *Salam,* the Arabic word for peace. So a more profound meaning of Islam is "peace through submission to the will of Allah."

Islam is the name of the religion. The religion is not, as with Christianity, Buddhism, and other world religions, named after its founder. It is incorrect to call Islam "Muhammadanism." Muslims believe God, not Muhammad, founded their religion. Muhammad played a crucial role in the formation of Islam, but he is secondary to Allah and the Quran in terms of importance and status. Muhammad is not divine nor an incarnation of God, nor is he worshiped in any way.

A Muslim or Muslima is one who practices Islam, that is, one who is surrendered to God. You become a Muslim, not by birth, but by confession of the *Shahadah*: "There is no God but God and Muhammad is the Prophet of God," and by practicing the good deeds prescribed by the Quran. Entrance into Islam is not conditioned by a religious experience, the reception of sacraments, or belief in theological formulae.

Islam is less a religion, as many Westerners generally understand the word, and more of a way of life. Politics, art, education, daily routine, diet, and many social customs are guided by Allah and are infused with the spirit of Islam. Because of this, Islam is not easily reduced to cultural forms, social systems, or psychological states. It is a way of life, confidently embracing this world and a preparation for the afterlife, just as confidently embracing the other world.

Beyond the simplicity of the Islamic core, that is, the *Shahadah,* a righteous life, and the Five Pillars of faith, there is as much a heterogeneity in Islam as you find in any religion. Diversity exists from country to country, from America to Algeria to Arabia, from India to Indonesia. There are progressive Muslims as well as liberal and conservative ones.

The Role of Abraham

Islam's history begins with Abraham, usually considered the world's first monotheist who lived about eighteen centuries B.C. He is, as well, the common parent of the great monotheistic religions, Judaism, Christianity, and Islam. Abraham's willingness to sacrifice his son is the prototype of submission (Islam). He is the tribal ancestor of Israel and Arab people by way of two women, Hagar and Sarah, and two sons, Ishmael and Isaac.

Abraham's new God made a covenant with him and promised that his family and descendants would be many and blessed. His wife, Sarah, was past childbearing age, and did not believe God could fulfill the promise for progeny. So she encouraged Abraham to take another wife, her Egyptian maid Hagar.

Abraham and Hagar had a son who was named Ishmael, that is "God hears" or "The Lord has given heed"—presumably to Sarah's incapacity to have children. Soon after, another son was miraculously born to Sarah. This son was Isaac, who figures

Dome of the Rock, Jerusalem

prominently in the Hebrew tradition. Because Sarah feared, perhaps out of jealousy, that Ishmael, the first-born and legitimate heir to God's promise, might compete with Isaac for this heritage, she, with Abraham's consent, forced Hagar and Ishmael out of the household. They were banished to fend for themselves in the wilderness of Paran which Muslims believe was the desert area near Mecca. Islamic tradition has it that Abraham sought out Hagar and her son and built in Mecca the Kaaba, the world's first monument to monotheism.

Religion in pre-Islamic Arabia was noted for its animism and polytheism. Along with these pagan religions were small communities of Jews, Christians, and Zoroastrians, especially in western and southern Arabia. In addition to these religious expressions were the Hanif, the pure ones, who sought to preserve the monotheism of which Abraham's God was the prototype and whose name was Allah.

It was the worship of Allah, admittedly alongside other deities, that eventually provided the framework for Muhammad to make his radical monotheism understood by his fellow Arabians.

Life of Muhammad

Muhammad ibn Abdullah was born in Mecca about 570 to a young couple of the Qurasyh tribe and Banu Hashim clan. This Arab boy whose name means "highly praised one" did not see his father who died two months before his birth. Upon his mother's death, he became a foster child (at age six) under the care of his grandfather. After the latter's death, Muhammad was adopted by an uncle, Abu-Talib. By his early teens, Muhammad was traveling with his uncle's caravans to northern Arabia and Syria. He was so earnest, dependable, and sincere that they nicknamed him al-Amin, "the one who can be trusted."

His reputation soon reached a wealthy widow and local business woman by the name of Khadija. She hired him to work with her trading company and eventually to supervise her commercial enterprise. Khadija was most impressed with his business acumen and his responsible leadership.

Their relationship eventually shifted to a more personal one and although Khadija had been married before, had several children, and was fifteen years his senior (Muhammad was twenty-five at the time), she asked him to marry her. During their marriage of twenty-five years, they had six children, two boys who died in infancy, and four girls. Of the four daughters, only Fatima, the youngest, survived the father.

The most important moment in Muhammad's life came at age forty around the twenty-seventh of the month of Ramadan. His religious quest found him frequently meditating in a cave on Mt. Hira. During one of these visits, he heard a voice say, "Recite in the name of thy Lord and Cherisher who created man of a clot of congealed blood! Proclaim!" (Quran 96:1-2). This was his vocation from Allah and he called this experience the "Night of Power—better than a thousand months . . . peace until the rising of the dawn" (97:3, 5).

Since he was illiterate, his first reaction was shock and reluctance. But when he realized it was the voice of the angel Gabriel who had talked to Moses and to the Virgin Mary and after his wife assured him it was an authentic divine revelation, he went again and again to Mt. Hira to hear the voices and to recite the words Allah was revealing to him. He memorized these words, then recited them to his friends who wrote them on any piece of scrap material they could find. Over a period of twenty-three years, until his death in 632, Allah, through the angel Gabriel, communicated the words of the Quran to Muhammad. For Islam, this is the greatest of miracles—that an illiterate, ordinary camel-herder from Mecca could be the source of such wisdom, could remember it, and above all could recite it in such exquisite Arabic verse.

So at age forty, Muhammad launched a new career. He began to teach and proclaim God's word with a fervor seldom seen among the founders of world religions. Khadija became his first convert. His next two converts were people he knew well—a cousin, Warakh, and Zaid, a slave he had freed and adopted as a son. A few of the early converts were merchants and persons with some standing in Mecca, especially Abu Bakr of the Umayad clan, but most of his first followers were from the lower classes.

However, within a year or so, his family and tribe withdrew support from Muhammad and virtually disowned him. The entire Meccan community became hostile because his message threatened them in several major ways. It meant they had to forego worship of many gods; this resulted in a subsequent loss of revenue from the sales of idols representing the hundreds of deities enshrined in the Kaaba. Furthermore, his ethical demands and call for social justice challenged their self-interest. His insistence on shifting primary kinship loyalty from the tribe to the new Muslim community (*Umma*) raised the level of ridicule to fever pitch. Rejection by Muhammad's family and friends resulted in a conspiracy to kill him.

With his life in danger, Muhammad made his famous "flight" or migration to Medina. This Hegira

(*Hijra* in Arabic) was made on 16 July 622 and was such a decisive move that the Muslim calendar is dated from that activity. It was not Muhammad's birth, as in Jesus' case, which divided history, but his migration to Medina.

Why did the Hegira divide history? Why was it such a defining moment for Islam? Professor I. Abu-Rabi of Hartford Theological Seminary suggests three reasons: (1) Historically and politically, it meant the creation of a strong Islamic state to which Muslims could now belong. They were no longer stateless persons. They had moved from *Dar al-Harb* (House of War) in Mecca to *Dar al-Islam* (House of Peace) in Medina; (2) From a religious point of view, it meant that Muslims could freely practice their new faith and legislate for their own needs; (3) In a symbolic sense, Muslims were willing to sacrifice their former tribal and clan loyalties for their new family identity in Islam. Relation to God had priority over past relationships. It is for these reasons that all years since the migration are "A.H."; (After Hegira).

Meccan armies tried to prevent Muhammad from returning to his hometown, but in 630 he and his troops entered Mecca and the first pilgrimage was made to the Kaaba. A year or so after this spiritual and political success, Muhammad developed a high fever and became deathly ill. On 8 June 632, he died in the arms of his wife, Aisha. His last words were reputed to be: "Rather God on High and Paradise."

Muhammad married several women after Khadija's death, mostly out of mercy and for their social and economic welfare. He did have one other child by a Coptic woman, a son, Ibrahim, who died at eleven months. Fatima, his youngest daughter, married Muhammad's nephew, Ali. They had two sons, Hasan and Husayn.

The spread of Islam after Muhammad's death has no parallel in history. Within twenty years, Islam expanded north of Arabia to Damascus and Jerusalem, east to Persia, west to Egypt, and further on to the northern coast of Africa. By 715, the new religion had reached Spain; Muslim armies were finally stopped in southern France at Tours in 732.

Beliefs of Islam

Oneness of God. The central affirmation of Islam is the *Shahadah*: "There is no God but Allah and Muhammad is the prophet of Allah." The foundation of Islam is the uncompromising unity and oneness of God, called *Tawhid* in Arabic. Allah is beyond distinction and division and has no equal or associate. While God is the Creator of all, God is not called Father or Mother (both imply relationship) nor is God part of a trinity (which implies a plurality of gods). God's primary attribute is Mercy. Each chapter (*sura*) in the Quran begins with the *Bismallah*: "In the name of God, the Merciful, the Compassionate." A secondary, but very important attribute of God's nature is justice. The moral ground of the universe provided by God is the basis for a just and moral Islamic social order. Other qualities attributed to God are Light and Sovereignty.

The Divinity of the Quran. Al-Quran literally means "the Recitation" and was revealed directly from Allah to Muhammad. It is the infallible Word of God, a transcript of an Eternal Book, a perfect copy of original heavenly verses, the very essence of God in our midst. What Jesus is for the Christian, the Quran is for the Muslim—God in historical form.

Muhammad: The Seal of the Prophets. He is not a savior, redeemer, mediator, messiah, or divine Son of God; he is the *Rasul*—someone not only who speaks on behalf of God, but one who is called and sent by God to bring a special revelation. His message combined the oneness of God, an ethical imperative, and the coming divine judgment. Muhammad supersedes all previous revelations and prior prophets. Jesus is considered the most significant prophet in the Quran next to Muhammad, but Jesus is only one in a succession of prophets, of which Muhammad is the culmination. Just as Christians seal the canon of Scripture, that is, no more books will be added to the Bible, Islam seals forever the canon of prophethood with Muhammad.

The Wisdom of the Law. Islam legislates for the personal and social dimensions of life in the hopes of providing an infallible and helpful guide for Muslims. This law is called *Shariah* and has four components: Quran (Scripture), Hadith (Tradition), Ijma (Consensus), and Qiyas (Reason). The first two are the most important and the most utilized. While the Quran is the Word of God and the primary authority for Muslims, the Hadith contains the words, teaching, and deeds of the Prophet. These extra-Quranic activities and sayings of Muhammad were collected into a body of tradition called *Sunna,* which means "example" or "Path" or "custom." Often Sunna and Hadith are used interchangeably when they refer to an act or word of Muhammad. Hadith is the most frequently used word and second only to the Quran in importance.

The Inevitability of Last Judgment. Except for the theme of monotheism, the Quran speaks more of the coming Day of Judgment than any other topic. Muhammad spoke of the Day when accounts would be settled and when scales would be balanced—A Day of Judgment when everyone will be accountable to God. The righteous arrive at the Garden of Bliss (heaven) and the unrighteous go to the "Fire," a place of punishment. For Islam, resurrection and Judgment Day are practically the same idea and refer to the same event, that is, we are raised from the dead to be present at Judgment Day.

The Nature of Human Beings. Human beings are not original sinners or original saints. As a result of our actions, we become either. Sin is not who we are; it is what we do. Sin is disobeying God and forgetting our responsibility to God. There is no need for a savior or redeemer in Islam and so atonement is unnecessary. The only way we are "saved" is by our sincere repentance and an improved life. So people are relatively good, radically free, and capable of change. Allah respected men and women so much that he made them his "vicegerents" (2:30), his deputies and representatives (*Kaliph* in Arabic).

The Protection of the Angels. These invisible beings are assigned particular tasks by God to protect us, to record our good and bad deeds, and to encourage us through life.

Five Pillars of Islam (the Practice of Islam)

Shahadah (Witness to the Faith). "There is no God but God, and Muhammad is the Prophet of God." The confession is so basic that to say it is sufficient for conversion and makes a Muslim a Muslim. The vertical dimension of this confession is the affirmation of the oneness of God; the horizontal dimension states that Muhammad is the Prophet of God which provides us with guidance for ethical life. The Muslim's goal is to be able to make this witness perfectly.

Salah (Prayer). This is a prescribed liturgy which includes bodily movement, saying of prayers in Arabic, and recitation of the Quran, all of which are preceded by ritual ablution. Prayers are said five times a day—at dawn, noon, mid-afternoon, sunset, and at night. These daily acts of worship have the effect of sanctifying the whole day. The weekly noonday prayers on Fridays are a communal Salat, directed by an Imam.

Sawm (Fasting). It is primarily observed in the month of Ramadan. This month is chosen for personal and spiritual renewal because it was in the last ten days of Ramadan that Muhammad experienced his "Night of Power," receiving from Allah his first revelation. From sunrise to sunset for the entire month one is to fast from food, drink (including water), gambling, sexual activity, and all sensuous pleasures. Total abstinence reminds the Muslim that his or her life is one of sacrifice and dependence on God.

Zakat (Almsgiving). It is a tax of 2½ percent of one's annual savings, after personal and business expenses. This provides a kind of social security system and an organized welfare program which help a Muslim society share its wealth and maintain an equitable society. An early Muslim saying suggests how the last three pillars are related: "Prayer carries us half way to God; fasting brings us to the door of His praises; almsgiving procures for us admission."

Hajj (Pilgrimage). Once in a lifetime, if health and material means permit, a Muslim is expected to make a religious journey to Mecca. This ultimate act of worship includes a three-day ritual and allows the pilgrim to reenact the founding of Islam and to renew links with Abraham, Hagar, Ishmael, and Muhammad. The crowning experience is the circling of the Kaaba, a cube-shaped building in the middle of the courtyard of the Grand Mosque in Mecca.

The present Kaaba is about forty feet long, thirty-three feet wide, and fifty feet high. It is covered with a black cloth with verses from the Quran embroidered on it in gold thread. The four corners of the Kaaba coincide with the four cardinal points of the compass. This sacred precinct, including the city of Mecca, is *haram*; it is forbidden territory for non-Muslims.

At this physical and spiritual center of Islam, all pilgrims experience the egalitarian nature and radical unity of their faith. Muslims from around the world—all classes, colors, nationalities, and races—are there in the same dress, performing the same rituals. There is no rank or privilege in this holy place because we are without rank before Allah.

As part of their sacred journey, many pilgrims go to Medina to visit Muhammad's Tomb and the Prophet's Mosque. If possible, they also will visit the "Fartherest Mosque" (Al-Aqsa) in Jerusalem to celebrate Muhammad's "Night Journey" to heaven.

Jihad. It is so central in the practice of Islam and is so imperative to the life of the Muslim, that *jihad* is considered by some Muslims a *de facto* sixth pillar. The essential meaning of *jihad* is the spiritual, psychological, and physical effort we exert to be close to God and to achieve a just and harmonious society. The word literally means "striving" or "struggle." Professor David Kerr, an Islamic scholar, says there are four aspects of *jihad*: *jihad* of the tongue, in which Muslims speak about their faith;

jihad of the hand, in which the faithful put their religion into action by good works; *jihad* of the heart, which makes their faith real as a spiritual force in their lives; and *jihad* of the sword, in which Muslims defend their faith when it is under attack.

It is important to note that the Quran does not call for aggressive war (2:190). The specific laws which determine a genuine *jihad* are very similar to the "just-war theory" in Christianity. Practically speaking, however, a true *jihad* is rarely invoked. Certain Muslim factions, in the name of self-interest, will engage in political struggle and call it *jihad*, but no individual or group can arbitrarily wage *jihad*. Only the state, through its leaders—the Caliph or Imam—can authorize a Holy War.

Divisions in Islam (Sunni and Shiite)

These divisions in Islam are not along conservative or liberal lines, but arose out of some practical questions after Muhammad's death. "Who will be our leader?" and "How shall leadership be determined?" Supporters of Ali (Muhammad's son-in-law and cousin) were certain the Prophet's successor should be someone in the family. With just as much certainty, friends of Muhammad led by Abu Bakr wanted someone who most exemplified the spirit and character of the Prophet.

Ali's group was called Shiites, literally "partisans" of Ali. Abu Bakr's contingent was called Sunnis, that is, those who followed the example or the custom of the Prophet. About 90 percent of Islam is Sunni, the remaining 10 percent (Shiite) reside in and around the Middle East.

Sufism is the mystical dimension of Islam. It is not a sect nor a division because both Sunnis and Shiites can practice Sufism. Sufis are the "inner dimension" of Islam, the personal, esoteric, inward path (*Tariqa*) as compared with the exoteric, public, outward observance of the Shariah. Sufis often live in non-monastic communities with a spiritual leader (Sheik) and like many theistic mystics, stress the Heart as the seat of comprehension. Sufi mysticism is often called the "path of love"; some observers claim that Sufis have a "love affair" with God. Perhaps the greatest of Islam's poets, al-Rumi, was a Sufi as was the most extraordinary of its theologians, al-Ghazzali.

Islam and Women

A discussion of women and Islam must appreciate the historical context of social class and country in which Islam arose and, above all, the Quran. It is more accurate to say what a particular country does not permit women to do than to say what Islam permits or forbids. There is a good deal of diversity and flexibility in the roles of women as one moves from patriarchal cultures of the Arab states to the democratic countries of the West to the matriarchal societies of Indonesia and sub-Saharan Africa. Admittedly in the Quran, as in every divine text of major world religions, one finds a reflection of cultural devaluation of women.

However inadequate these teachings and practices seem to be to the Western reader and to an increasing number of Islamic women, the Quran was a virtual champion of women's rights in the seventh century. Much of what the Quran advocates for women was not seen in the West until approximately a hundred years ago. Many Muslim women of this century are reclaiming rights and a status given them by the Quran, but which was whittled away during the last fourteen hundred years. It is clear in the Quran that there is religious equality of men and women before God and intellectual equality in society (4:124).

Although the Quran allows the limit of four wives per husband, polygamy was never encouraged in the Quran. Monogamy is the Islamic ideal and preferred state. The husband is permitted additional wives only on the condition that he is able to treat each wife equally, fairly, and justly, and only if the family, as a unit, will not suffer by the addition of wives (4:3).

Islam and Jesus

The Quran calls Jesus a Word from God, a Messiah and Prophet, but not the Eternal Logos, Divine Son of God, or Savior. He helped deliver people from the bondage to religious law by the commandment to love; it is believed he performed miracles, including healing the sick and raising the dead; furthermore, he was a faithful teacher of monotheism. Jesus did not die on the cross, but was taken up into heaven by God before his death (4:157-159). Since Islam has no need for a doctrine of atonement, there is no need to have a redemptive sacrifice. For the average Muslim, Jesus is an example of sanctity and piety and someone who embodied true Islam. For this reason he is accorded more honor and deference than all the other prophets who preceded Muhammad. Islam sees as authentic the religion *of* Jesus and is inspired by that, but not the Church's religion *about* Jesus.

Summary. The heart of Islam is *continuity, certainty,* and *balance.* It is not a new religion, but a renewal and restoration of the religion of Jesus, Moses, and Abraham—the original religion God planned

J

JANSENISM

An austere and rigorous movement rooted in the five propositions formulated by Cornelius Jansen (1585–1638) in his *Augustinus* (1640). It postulated that human nature was thoroughly flawed by original sin, and that, without a special grace, the following of Christ is impossible. Furthermore, this grace is irresistible; thus a certain determinism—limited only by its noncoercive nature—is paramount in humanity's dealing with God, who chose only some to be saved. Basically, the Jansenist teaching was akin to Calvin's doctrine of predestination.

Initially, the movement was led by Jansen's friend Saint-Cyran, and was centered in the convent of Port-Royal, located southwest of Paris. After Saint-Cyran's death in 1643, Antoine Arnauld (1612–1694) became its leader. The five propositions were condemned by Innocent X in 1653; the Jansenists countered that the condemned propositions were heretical and did not represent Jansen's real teaching. Alexander VII issued another condemnation in 1656, and, in 1668, the Jansenists made a qualified submission. The bull *Unigenitus,* issued in 1713 by Clement XI, made a final condemnation, which led to the subsequent persecution of the Jansenists in France. The strict and morally rigorous movement lingered on, and continued to have an influence on moral and spiritual writing in France, Tuscany, and the Netherlands.

JOSEPH QUINN

See also PROVIDENCE.

JEHOVAH'S WITNESSES

The Jehovah's Witnesses are a religious group tracing its origins to the millennarianist Charles Taze Russell. Originally known as the Russellites, in 1931 Joseph F. Rutherford, Russell's successor, renamed the sect the Jehovah's Witnesses while the legal name of the group was the Watch Tower Bible and Tract Society and International Bible Students Association. The Witnesses believe that the present world is under the control of Satan, and that one day there will be a re-creation of all things during the course of a new millennium. At that time, all people will be given a second chance of salvation. There will be a final judgment, and the just, numbering exactly 144,000, will reign forever with Christ. The Witnesses reject the Christian belief in the Trinity and the divinity of Christ, and instead profess a modified, Arian Christology. They proclaim the "Armageddon," when Christ will come again and defeat Satan definitively.

The tenets of the organization are strict. All baptized members are expected to spend time each week performing missionary work. They are also supposed to attend prayer meetings and Bible study sessions several times each week. Since Witnesses believe themselves to be members of a theocracy, they reject participation in such civic activities as voting and military service. The movement is tightly centralized and autocratic. Members are given exact interpretations of the Bible and no contrary opinions are tolerated.

In the 1930s and 1940s the sect grew rapidly through aggressive proselytizing. Today the Witnesses have about one million active members with a smaller group of about 35,000 who work full-time for the movement. There are about 450,000 Witnesses in the United States where the sect has its headquarters in Brooklyn, New York. The Witnesses publish the magazines *The Watch Tower* and *Awake!* which have a combined circulation of about ten million. In recent years, despite efforts to attract blacks and Hispanics, the growth of the Jehovah's Witnesses has slowed considerably.

ANTHONY D. ANDREASSI

See also MILLENARIANISM; PROTESTANTISM.

JEROME, ST. (ca. 347–419/20)

Born at Stridon, a fortress on the border between Dalmatia and Pannonia (in what was formerly Yugoslavia), Jerome studied in Rome where he was baptized in 366. In Trier he learned about monasticism and then moved on to Aquileia where he lived an ascetical life with friends for a time. Jerome's younger brother Paulinian as well as a younger sister later followed his example in taking up the ascetical life. He traveled to the East ca. 372. While staying in Antioch, he intently studied Greek. Then he moved on to the Syrian desert where he lived as a hermit at Chalcis for a few years. During that period of time he studied Hebrew. When Jerome returned to Antioch, he was ordained a priest by Paulinus and attended the lectures given by Apollinarius of Laodicea. Jerome accompanied Paulinus to the General Council of Constantinople in 381 and then went with Paulinus and Epiphanius of Cyprus to Rome in the hope of getting the support of Pope Damasus I for Paulinus in his controversy with Melitius. Jerome became the secretary for Damasus I and became the spiritual director for a group of Roman noble women, including Paula and Eustochium. Unfortunately because Jerome had a sarcastic wit and could be self-centered and touchy, he tended to kindle animosity wherever he went. After the death of Damasus and the election of his successor Siricius in 384, Jerome, under a cloud of suspicion, traveled in the East and established in Bethlehem in 386 a double monastery for men and women. Jerome then devoted the remainder of his life to study and writing. Jerome, who worked to produce as accurate a biblical text as was possible based on the original languages, is known first of all for his translations and revisions of the books of the Bible (the Vulgate). Jerome composed many commentaries on the biblical books in which his knowledge of philology and topography helped to shape his interpretation of the text. He also translated and updated the *Chronicle* of Eusebius and prepared a catalogue of Christian writers (*On the Lives of Illustrious Men*), partially based on the *Ecclesiastical History* of Eusebius. Jerome also translated works by Origen and Didymus. Jerome produced controversial works against the followers of Lucifer of Cagliari, Origenism, and Pelagianism, and others. Often he could be violent and abusive in these works. Jerome's letters have attracted wide interest because of his talent in this genre. Notable letters include those on virginity, widowhood, monastic life, the clergy, funeral eulogies, as well as exegesis. His correspondence is valuable for its historical importance as well as its personal interest. Jerome's views on the perpetual virginity of Mary, celibacy, and monasticism were influential in the Middle Ages. Jerome anticipated the Reformers in urging that the Church accept the Hebrew canon of Scripture and thus reject the deuterocanonical books. He was named a Doctor of the Church along with Ambrose, Augustine, and Gregory the Great in 1295. Feast day, 30 September.

St. Jerome, fresco by Domenico Ghirlandaio, 1480, Church of Ognissanti, Florence

JOHN DILLON

See also DOCTORS OF THE CHURCH; FATHERS OF THE CHURCH.

JERUSALEM IN THE TIME OF JESUS

For pilgrims, travelers, tourists, Jerusalem is an exciting adventure. It is an impressive emotional, religious, aesthetic, architectural, historical, and "people" experience. Whether coming eighteen miles from Jordan River to the east, following the way the early Israelites approached, or coming from the Mediterranean Sea ports of Joppa or Caesarea, thirty-eight miles to the west, it is an ascent, a going up to Jerusalem (Pss 122, 125). It is an arduous journey, on foot or by donkey; it is a dangerous journey because of robbers and bandits along the routes. The ascent is through rocky ravines, boulder-covered hills, barren desert land and over dry, dusty reddish dirt paths or roads, climbing to the city at 2500 feet above sea level. Yet Jerusalem sits among higher mountains on every side.

The first view of the city evokes joy of mission accomplished and dream fulfilled. The rare beauty of Jerusalem comes from its mountain height and the surrounding valleys, against a clear sky, in a fortress-like position. A city built entirely of stone, surrounded by immense walls anchored in bedrock and towers reaching into the sky.

YERUSHALEM (founded by Shalem god) URUSALIM (foundation of peace). Jerusalem called: "Holy Mountain of Jahwe" (Isa 27:13); "Mountain house of Jahwe" (Isa 2:2); "Mountain of divine assembly" (Isa 14:13); "City of God" (Ps 46:4); "Zion" (Isa 24:23); "Holy City" (Ps 48); "City of David" (1 Chr 11:7); "City of Judah"; "Mount Moriah" (2 Chr 3:1); "Center of the earth and navel of the world" (Ezra 5:5). These names reverberate with Jerusalem's history and significance, rooted in religious and national life of a people.

Origin and Growth

Ancient Jerusalem, dating to ca. 3000 B.C., was a small Canaanite settlement rather isolated on the eastern watershed between the Mediterranean Sea and the wilderness of Judah. A town was born there because a gushing spring, Gihon, at the foot of the ridge of Ophel in the Kidron Valley is the only source of water in the entire area.

The city was captured from the Jebusites by King David ca. 1000 B.C. Bringing the ark of the covenant to Jerusalem, he consolidated it into a metropolitan royal city and religious cultic center, the capital of Israel (2 Sam 6). Solomon built a royal palace and the first Temple, symbol of the presence of God among his people in the city (1 Kgs 6–8). The city was destroyed in 586 B.C. by the Babylonians, rebuilt by Zerubbabel in 515 B.C. and destroyed by the Greeks. The present city manifests the ambitious and pretentious building program of Herod the Great, Idumean king of Israel from 37–34 B.C.

The city rests on a limestone shelf shaped like a tongue or a V, with boundaries of two valleys—the Kidron on the east and the Hinnom on the west. Expansion is possible only to the north. Another valley, the Tyropaean valley ("Vale of the cheesemakers") divides the city into two parts, separating the western hill, or upper city from the eastern hill or lower city.

Model of Jerusalem at the time of Jesus

Jerusalem is a splendid city, likely the most cosmopolitan and famous in the Near East. It covers about 450 acres and its population is estimated at 100,000 including the suburbs. During pilgrimage time of feasts the population doubles and since Jerusalem is very compact and crowded, lodging is sought in nearby villages such as Bethphage and Bethany.

Herodian Jerusalem

Jerusalem and the entire country experienced great prosperity and development under Herod. Peace in the Roman Empire led to more pilgrims from the Diaspora coming to Jerusalem, and increase of wealth, enabling Herod to build monumental and grandiose structures to beautify and to fortify the city.

Most outstanding and elaborate buildings were strategically planned by Herod. In the southwest corner of the city, immediately upon entering the city through the western gate, rises the Royal Palace. It is about six city blocks square with three striking towers named after his wife, Miriam, his brother, Phasael, and his friend, Hippicus. This is government headquarters and the administrative center. Its two complexes are surrounded by parks and gardens, and inside are apartments, banquet halls, and quarters for an army garrison.

The Antonia Fortress in the northwest corner, attached to the wall of the Temple for its protection, Herod dedicated to his patron, Mark Anthony. He also built a theater, an amphitheater, and a hippodrome within the city; he dug cisterns and reservoirs underground to cope with scarcity of water and perhaps constructed aqueducts.

Herod's greatest efforts however went into the building of the Temple which is his greatest achievement. The Temple Mount dominates the view of Jerusalem, is the main attraction of the city, and is the primary target of pilgrims and visitors. Once inside the western gate they proceed along a wide stone-paved road with columns and arcades on either side housing various shops. The Temple lies straight ahead.

The Temple Mount

The Temple Mount is the focal point of Jerusalem and is the center from which everything radiates. Located in the southeast corner of the city at its highest point, it covers seventy-five acres, one-sixth of the entire city. It is the religious center of cultic worship, the national center of Jewish solidarity, and the center of social and political affairs. It unites the sacred and the secular. It is the heart of the city and the entire country.

One of the largest artificial structures in the ancient world, the Temple Mount is a man-made platform foundation of rock which can easily hold 300,000 people. On top of this vast area reached from the street via ramps and steps, rises the Temple with its 150 feet high facade of gold and marble gleaming and visible from great distances. The Temple faces east. It is reached by way of outer and inner courts designed to safeguard the purity of the enclosed sanctuary. A concentric quadratic system indicates that as one approaches the Temple, the demands of ritual purity increase. Porticoes with white columns supporting a cedar roof surround the entire complex. The largest are the Royal Portico on the south and Solomon's porch on the east.

The outer court is the court of the Gentiles to which all pagans are admitted. Entrance into the inner court is forbidden and it is protected by a fence with thirteen gates each displaying a warning: "No foreigner is allowed within the balustrade surrounding the sanctuary and the court encompassed. Whoever is caught will be personally responsible for his ensuing death." Jews ascend fourteen steps to the terrace surrounding the Temple, where there is first the women's court containing four golden bowls and lamps. Next, the court of the Israelites where men with a sacrifice enter the gate of Nikanor to approach the priests. The altar of sacrifice is fifty feet square and twenty-five feet high. It is flanked by preparation tables and the bronze purification basin.

The Temple

The Temple faces east. The ground plan is traditional and similar to temples in the Near East—a long room, entered from the short side, divided into three rooms, one leading into the other: vestibule to sanctuary to Holy of Holies. Twelve steps lead to the entrance and to the doors in front of which stands a golden trellis over which is a golden vine, symbol of Israel. Inside, the solid gold seven-branch candlestick burns with oil. The smallest room, a cube, symbol of perfection, is entered only by the high priest once a year on the Day of Atonement.

This is the sacred place where God's presence dwells for Jews, where parents present their children, bring their first fruits, are judged; where pilgrims gather from Israel and from the Diaspora. There is also a sacred time, when three great annual feasts are celebrated. Passover (Pesach) for one week in spring; Booths or Tabernacles (Sukkot) after the fall harvest; Pentecost (Shabuot) to celebrate the first fruits (Lev 16 and 23; Num 28–29). The Temple is the gathering place *par excellence* (Isa 14:13; Mic 4:2).

The first Temple was built by Solomon and became the royal shrine and capital, symbol of God's presence among his people and in the city. Destroyed by the Babylonians in 586 B.C. (2 Kgs 6–7; 2 Chr 3–9), the Temple was rebuilt by Zerubbabel in 515 B.C. (Ezra 3) and destroyed by the Greeks. This Temple was built by Herod the Great in 20 B.C. and dedicated in 10 B.C., though not yet completed. The monumental wonder incorporates the finest of Hellenistic and Roman style. Ten thousand workers were employed, plus 1000 priests to direct ritual observance of all construction. Wagon wheel ruts are still visible in the wide, stone-paved street leading to the Temple, for 1000 wagons were used to haul stone quarried in Jerusalem and on the outskirts of the city.

Special characteristics of Herodian buildings and walls are enormously huge stones, carefully hewn, fitted together without mortar or cement, and having a smooth border or edge to create light and shadow. Stones in the Temple measure up to 42 feet in length and can weigh 100 tons. How large stones were raised to high places is difficult to explain.

Personnel, furnishings, upkeep of the Temple require an annual tax to be paid by every Jew in Israel and in the Diaspora. The Temple area contains many boxes for freewill offerings.

City Tour—Upper City

After the highlight of a Temple Mount visit, other points of interest are suggested to experience the city. Well-defined streets in a grid system give easy access to sites. From the Temple there is a stone-arched roof columnade or bridge that connects the upper city with the Temple in the lower city. Below on either side are shops for changing money and purchasing items for services.

The upper city or western hill area which contains a substantial community, is the wealthy residential part of Jerusalem, home of the aristocratic families of royalty, high priests, landowners and bankers. Two- or three-story houses, spacious and luxurious, are filled with expensive furnishings, have mosaic floors and colorful frescoes on plastered walls; there are courtyards, baths and ritual baths, stone balconies with terraced ledges to grow flowers and grapevines. People are elegantly dressed and have servants to cater to their needs. The air is pleasant here, with a westerly wind, so that smoke and smells of the lower city and Gehenna, the garbage dump area, do not reach this quarter.

Lower City

Across the Tyropaean Valley lies the lower city, with the homes of the poor which are small, often one-room houses where large families live, rolling out their mats at night, sleeping on the floor. Cooking is done outside, and animals are in pens attached to the house. This is also the commercial area where all the action is. It is the hub and lifeline of Jerusalem, the market, or bazaar where buying and selling takes place on the streets.

The visitor is inundated with peculiar smells, sounds, and sights every step of the way. There are pungent odors of food being cooked over open fires, of spices arrayed in clay pots and bags, of blacksmith coals burning, the acidic odor of hides in tanning vats, the pleasant odor of bread and pastries baking, the sweet perfumes, oils, ointments, soap, drifting into the air.

On right and left are colorful stacks of oranges, fresh almonds, red pomegranates, purple figs, plums, olives, grapes, corn, and chick peas. Meat hangs on hooks and animal parts are displayed. People are weaving baskets and carrying water in pitchers and jugs of water from the Gihon spring now brought into the city by Hezekiah's Tunnel.

Voices of merchants yelling bargains, people haggling over prices, the sound of sheep, goats, chickens, and doves join donkeys braying. Hammers hitting chisels to chip and mold stones, carpenters cutting wood, and coppersmiths and silversmiths hammering metal, bombard the visitor. This is the shopping center for all of Jerusalem. Tailors are near the gates and weavers are near the Dung gate. This is what gives the ordinary people a livelihood; this is their daily life where they intermingle and communicate, share and grow.

Overview from the Mount of Olives

The best panoramic view of Jerusalem is looking down upon the city. Exit via the eastern gate, past the Antonia fortress and Temple wall, cross the Kidron Valley and climb the slopes full of olive trees to the summit of Mount of Olives, the highest point in the area, ca. 2700 feet above sea level. This lookout affords a better and more comprehensive understanding of Jerusalem and its surroundings: the skyline with ramparts and towers of royal, public, sacred, military buildings. One sees clearly that ridge upon which the whole city rests, jutting out between the Kidron Valley on the east and Hinnom Valley on the west, and how they meet. The fertile Kidron Valley has date palms, almonds, roses, pomegranates, figs, and olives. In the sides of the Kidron Valley are beautiful mausoleums and tombs built by Herod and royal families. White tombs in cemeteries on the slopes of Mount of Olives are numerous. There is a road that leads to Bethphage and Bethany. On a clear day Moab, across the Jordan River is visible; also, one of Herod's winter palaces, the Herodian near Bethlehem, the road to the hill country and Galilee, the road to Jericho.

Before re-entering the city by the east gate there is Bethesda, or the Sheep Pool in the northeast corner just outside the walls. It is a famous shrine dedicated to a Semitic or Hellenistic divinity and attracts many people seeking cures in the water. A walk around the walls of the city (Ps 48) to see the various gates is also rewarding.

Jerusalem climate is pleasant because of the altitude. Eight months of clear skies, with December and January the months of the most rain. The western sea breeze cools in the hot summer, and early mornings and evenings are always fresh without humidity.

Cosmopolitan Life and Economy

Jerusalem is predominantly Jewish but as the capital city, religious, intellectual, political, and social center, it is the most cosmopolitan city in the Near East. Hellenistic influence is strong and there are many resident merchants. From Lebanon, cedar wholesalers; from Tyre, glass blowers and fish merchants; from Egypt, grain and corn merchants; from Babylonia come linen and fabric merchants. Romans are numerous as administrators, army personnel, architects, and engineers. As the center for religious studies and locus of religious movements, Jerusalem also attracts scholars and students.

The cost of living is high because virtually everything must be transported up to the city from the outside. Herod imposes high taxes upon all residents and upon everyone in Israel. All Jews are supposed to spend one-tenth of their income in Jerusalem.

Besides the very rich and royal, there are the middle-class craftsmen, merchants, priests. But the poor abound and beggars, blind, lame, lepers, are in need of charity. Most scribes and teachers are subsidized for their life is dedicated to study only, not work (Sir 38:24-39).

LUKE STEINER, O.S.B.

See also BIBLICAL ARCHAEOLOGY; JESUS AND POLITICS; JESUS CHRIST.

JESUITS

See SOCIETY OF JESUS.

JESUS AND POLITICS

"Regardless of what anyone may personally think or believe about him" Jesus, according to Jaroslav Pelikan's *Jesus through the Centuries* (New Haven, Conn.: Yale University Press, 1985, p. 1) has been the "dominant figure in the history of Western culture for almost twenty centuries." On the other hand the historical reality of Jesus, to quote the title of a recent study by John P. Meier, was that of *A Marginal Jew* (New York: Doubleday, 1991). According to Meier, Jesus attracted little attention from Jewish and other historians in the first two centuries—he was brutally put to death by the authorities of his time, had abandoned the conventional social and economic structures of society, was out of tune with the convictions of the serious religious of his day, had a knack of alienating everyone who was anybody and was a layman from a country with no hold on the levers of power guarded so closely by the urban ruling elite.

Granted the dominance of the figure of Jesus in Western history, even a cursory reading of books like Pelikan's shows that the tendency of people in every age is to create their own image of Jesus. Thus George Tyrrell accused Harnack of looking down the deep well of history to discover the reflection of his own "liberal Protestant face." Likewise Albert Schweitzer in his classic *The Quest of the Historical Jesus* could say of Ernest Renan's very popular *Life of Jesus* (1863) that "the gentle Jesus, the beautiful Mary, the fair Galileans who formed the retinue of the 'amiable carpenter' might have been taken over in a body from the shop-window of an ecclesiastical art emporium in the Place St. Sulpice."

The problem particularly in politics is that when Jesus becomes a person who simply adds sublimity and nobility to any or every cause does he really stand for anything at all? (See J. L. Houlden, *Jesus A Question of Identity,* London: S.P.C.K., 1992, p. 113). The fact, as Houlden points out, is that the images are contradictory: "Jesus the freedom-fighter and Jesus the super-emperor; Jesus the overthrower of authority and Jesus its Legitimator; Jesus the friend of the poor and powerless and Jesus the endower of the powerful and established."

For the larger part of Christian history, there was agreement on the story described by the Synoptic Gospels, deepened by the spiritual portrayal of John. Admittedly, the first four to five centuries were marked by controversies. However, official statements of belief were provided by the great councils of the Church and widely accepted. The Christian communities have continued to read the Gospels in both public and private, confident that they provide authentic portraits of Jesus and a standard or canon against which all limited models and interpretations can be measured.

The current wave of books about Jesus with their wide range of hypotheses are often described as the Third Quest for the Historical Jesus. This contrasts with the first quest which emerged to prominence with Reimarus in the 18th century and the new or second quest started by Käsemann in 1953.

For James H. Charlesworth (*Jesus Within Judaism,* London: S.P.C.K., 1988, pp. 26ff.) research on the historical Jesus is demanded because mutually incompatible portraits of Jesus are claimed by widely differing groups—he is pictured as a Marxist providing the blueprint for an economic and social reform, as a Black Messiah who stood against Rome, an exploitative white nation, as a liberator who proclaimed that God's kingdom belongs to the poor and as the Prince of Peace who shows the way for nuclear disarmament. Charlesworth is dissatisfied with the terminology "the quest for the historical Jesus" which suggests that "we are in a dark room fumbling about trying to find the door." He finds a better analogy in "a dimly lit room" in which we constantly bump into things that compel us to bend down and examine them. He insists that we are not on a quest. His thesis is that Jesus is a historical man who must be seen within Judaism rather than in some kind of philosophical or existential framework. Previously we were "lost in a wasteland of history" due to a lack of sources from pre-70 Judaism. Today since the 1940s we have hundreds of pre-70 Jewish documents (OT Pseudepigrapha, the Dead Sea Scrolls, the Nag Hammadi Codices, Josephus) and phenomenal archaeological discoveries—he discusses in ascending order of importance the seven most significant archaeological discoveries for Jesus research: the excavation of first-century synagogues in Palestine and what seems to have been Peter's house in Capernaum; the walls and gates of Jerusalem; the Temple Mount in Jesus' time; the pool of five porticos; the Praetorium where Jesus was tried; the bones of a man named Jehohanan who had been crucified; the growing proof of the site of the crucifixion. We must remember that the historian at best can only provide relative probability but not certainty—therefore "any talk about searching for the pure facts (*bruta facta Jesu*) or Jesus' precise words (*ipsissima verba Jesu*) is imprecise, imperceptive and impossible."

Charlesworth sees a paradigm shift in Jesus Research from Bultmann's "almost nothing" approach. He quotes E. P. Sanders' (*Jesus and Judaism,* Philadelphia: Fortress, 1985, p. 2) remarks that the dominant view today "seems to be that we can know pretty well what Jesus was out to accomplish, that we can know a lot about what he said, and that those two things make sense within the world of first-century Judaism." Sanders attempts to describe Jesus without the lenses of contemporary piety. He begins not with Jesus' sayings but with his symbolic action against the Temple. This provoked a reaction from the Jewish leaders who then handed Jesus over to the Romans. But he insists that Jesus was no political revolutionary—the fact that his disciples were not arrested is evidence for this. The Romano-Jewish establishment recognized that Jesus was not a political revolutionary. But they were determined to get rid of him because they were afraid of a popular uprising.

In my overview, *Jesus and Politics* (Collegeville, Minn.: Glazier, 1990), the five main options open to the Jews in the complicated political world of Jesus' day are discussed: opportunistic Herodians, rich aristocratic Sadducees, Essenes, Pharisees, Zealots. Much of the modern discussion has centered on the "cover-up" theory of the Gospels for an originally zealot or zealot-sympathizing Jesus. The dominant view is to reject the zealot-sympathizing Jesus. The danger in this position is that one proves too much and produces a politically harmless Jesus, a gentle Jesus, meek and mild, a soothing baptizer of the status quo.

In *Conflict, Holiness and Politics in the Teachings of Jesus* (New York: E. Mellen, 1984) and *Jesus A New Vision* (San Francisco: Harper, 1987) Marcus Borg finds a Jesus who is both deeply spiritual and deeply political. He criticizes the exclusion of politics in most mainstream biblical scholarship. There is a tendency to restrict politics to the Zealot party with the implication that religion and politics were separate realities in the ancient Mediterranean world. Further he blames the influence of R. Bultmann for attributing only individualistic characteristics to Jesus. A model such as Jeremiah, Moses, or Elijah shows the inseparable interpenetration of religion, holiness, and politics in Jesus' career in such aspects as the centrality of the Temple, the Sabbath, and the coming judgment on Israel. For Borg Jesus was a Jewish holy man or sage in addition to being a prophet announcing the breaking of the numinous into everyday reality. His healings and exorcism are historically credible and indicative of his spiritual power. Jesus' radical and even subversive concern for holiness led to conflicts with the other Jewish groups. In fact, the Jewish resistance to Rome was centered on their search for holiness. Jesus saw that Israel with its popular expectations was on a collision course with Rome. He warned them that revolution would lead to military and social disaster—this according to Borg is the meaning of the so-called eschatological passages. Jesus challenged the dominant politics of holiness and called for a politics of compassion in which Israel would be centered on God rather than the triple snare of wealth, honor, and religion. Instead of a politics which divided between pure and impure, Jew and Gentile, observant and unobservant, righteous and sinner, male and female, Jesus called for the life of the spirit, the relativization of social distinction and the way of peace, not violence. The following comments of Borg (*Conflict,* pp. 229f.) are quite incisive: "In particular, Jesus' conflict with the Pharisees centered upon the adequacy of the quest for holiness as a program for Israel's national life; his choice of terrain upon which to do battle concerned those subjects (table fellowship, Sabbath, Temple) important to Israel's survival and integral to her quest for holiness. . . . Jesus ministry concerned what it meant to be Israel in the setting of Israel's conflict with Rome."

One is left finally with the problem of moving from Jesus' to our own very different political world. R. Bauckham in *The Bible in Politics* (London: S.P.C.K., 1989) makes the interesting contrast between the OT which largely addresses Israel as a political state and the NT which is addressed to a politically powerless group within the Roman Empire. In an interesting chapter in his book *What is the Bible?* (London: S.P.C.K., 1991, pp. 110ff.) called "A Political Gospel?" John Barton asks how can the Bible contribute to modern political life if the situations of the Old and New Testaments are so different from each other and from our own. He notes for example the use of the Exodus model in Liberation Theology. It was used long before by black Americans, by Afrikaners in South Africa, and by the Civil Rights movement in the 1950s and 1960s. He concludes on a note of caution that the Bible offers "relatively little guidance on questions of political conduct"—there are for example "no laws in the Bible that say one should break out of slavery or that authentic human existence is possible only when people refuse to be slaves and assert their human dignity." But he wisely concludes that the Bible is not "the be-all and end-all of the Christian faith." All too often it is twisted to ignoble ends. Other sources are also needed.

SEAN P. KEALY, C.S.Sp.

See also BIBLE, NEW TESTAMENT WRITINGS; JESUS CHRIST.

JESUS CHRIST

Jesus of Nazareth was named "the Christ" (from the Greek *Christos,* the translation of the Hebrew "Messiah," meaning the Anointed One) on the basis of his resurrection from the dead. Early on the title became part of his name. Matthew 1–2 and Luke 1–2 tell us that Jesus was born in Bethlehem of Judea near the end of Herod the Great's reign (died 4 B.C.) and grew up in Nazareth of Galilee.

Jesus in History

Jesus of Nazareth was baptized in the Jordan River in the land of Israel about A.D. 27. John's baptism was offered to those who wished to belong to God's elect and thus be protected from the impending divine judgment on Israel. Jesus' personal motives for undergoing John's baptism are unknown. But the event signaled the beginning of his own public ministry. After a time of purification in the desert, Jesus, having left his home in Nazareth, began a ministry of teaching and healing. He was active principally in Galilee but appeared in Judea as well and in the area of the Twelve Cities. John's Gospel places him in Jerusalem at the beginning of his ministry as well as at the end; the three Synoptic Gospels have him in the capital only at the end of his life.

Jesus' relation to the God of Israel came to its most profound expression in his calling God *Abba* and in the central role of the kingdom or reign of God in his public preaching. While *Abba,* as a way of directly addressing God, may not have been unique to Jesus in his day, it was highly unusual and seemed to express the extraordinary closeness of God to him. The kingdom of God is a symbol in the OT, but there it has nothing like the frequency and future orientation recorded of Jesus in his ministry. The symbol expressed the divine project of salvation, aimed in a special way at the poor and outcast. This reign was already breaking into history in Jesus' preaching, exorcising, and healing, but was expected in its fullness at a time that Jesus never specifically named.

Jesus' ministry was aimed primarily at the "lost sheep of the house of Israel" though he did respond to the needs of Gentiles who requested his aid. He healed many who were sick in mind, spirit, and body, and exorcised demons. The precise nature of this last activity is unclear in our present-day medical terms. Jesus' approach to physical ailments was that of a first-century Jew. He taught with compelling authority, although he had not been trained in rabbinical circles.

With regard to miracles, some scholars would distinguish between healing deeds and "nature miracles" such as the multiplication of loaves and fish (Mark 6:30-44) and Jesus' walking on water (Mark 6:45-52). A principal source for interpreting the latter class of miracles is the OT. For example, Exodus 16 (the manna in the desert) illuminates the story of Jesus' feeding the multitude; and Psalm 77:19 and Job 9:8 (texts which refer to God's walking on the water) offer theological perspective in reading the story of Jesus walking on the water. In any case, it is apparent that not only historical reminiscence but also the early community's faith in the exalted Jesus are at work in the formation of the miracle traditions.

Jesus' teaching sought to return to the core of the Law's purpose and to reduce the burden of the interpretive tradition, the fence around the Law. He redrew boundaries of the pure and impure in a way that offended some Jews and encouraged others. He preached a message of divine compassion and mercy, the acceptance of which spelled salvation and the rejection of which meant spiritual disaster. One characteristic manner of teaching was the parable. Not an allegory (in which there are point-to-point correspondences between the story and the subject of instruction), a parable, as told by Jesus, portrayed a kind of world-reversal and, as the parable unfolded, the reactions to it revealed the hearts of those listening to it. In their original settings, the parables were remarkably provocative ways of speaking about what the in-breaking reign of God looked like when expressed in thoroughly human terms.

Jesus called men and women to discipleship, a different way of acting from most Jewish teachers, who expected prospective students to take the initiative. The people most resistant to his teaching were those "good" fellow Jews who sought to let their righteousness protect them from the new grace that Jesus offered. People brokenhearted in their guilt and those who were like "children" seemed most open to the gift of divine acceptance he preached. He related publicly to women in ways that did not respect the traditional boundaries of his day (Luke 7:36-50; 8:1-3), thus implying that service of God's reign, as it was breaking in through Jesus' ministry, was transforming the customary lines of distinction.

Jesus gathered about himself a community of disciples. An inner core was called the Twelve, a name that referred symbolically to the twelve tribes of Israel. In the light of Jesus' preaching of the inbreaking reign of God, the name seemed to suggest that the community gathered around Jesus would be the eschatological (end-time) community of Israel.

During his ministry Jesus made enemies. The Gospels portray the Pharisees, Sadducees, scribes and elders as his chief opponents. It may well be that the animosity and self-righteousness of the Pharisees are overdrawn by gospel writers; this is due in part to the conflict between early Jewish-Christians and Pharisees, who were the only surviving Jewish "party" after the Roman destruction of Jerusalem in A.D. 70.

It is probable that the chief Jewish protagonists at the time of Jesus' arrest and trial were some of the Sadducees, the priestly class intimately associated with the Jerusalem Temple. Their position was secure only if the Roman occupiers supported their legitimacy. The increasingly excited crowds Jesus drew, the fear that he was another messianic pretender, and Jesus' provocative act of symbolically interrupting the normal activity of the Temple in temporarily suspending the currency exchange would have profoundly concerned the priests in their delicate relationship with the Romans. They would not have had a difficult time persuading some Roman officials that Jesus posed a grave danger to the civil-religious "peace."

The actual trial of Jesus is difficult historically to reconstruct, but the sign over the cross suggests that he was executed by the Romans as a messianic pretender. The mode of execution was reserved in those times for slaves and for those who violated the "pax romana," the religio-political hegemony of the Romans. The form of execution treated the victim as subhuman, attacking the very dignity of the individual. Roman citizens understood crucifixion as literally an obscene event, i.e., one which ought to occur off the stage of civilized life. The final legal responsibility for Jesus' death lay with the Roman governor, Pontius Pilate.

The stories of the Last Supper and the Agony in the Garden give expression to the freedom with which Jesus went to his death as a service of God and people in full continuity with his ministry. Soon after Jesus died (ca. A.D. 30) and was buried, several events occurred. His tomb was discovered to be empty, and disciples reported his appearances on several occasions. The narratives of the empty tomb and of the appearances that we find in the Gospels underwent much development to acquire the form and content they now have; thus, precise historical reconstruction of the earliest Easter events is not possible. Jesus' own passage from death to new, transformed life in God was in principle unobservable, and the canonical Gospels show awareness of that.

"The Redeemer," oil painting by El Greco, 1610–1614, Museo del Prado

There is a pattern that shapes many of the appearance narratives: Jesus appears on his own initiative to disciples who knew him before his death; at first they do not recognize him; he gives a sign or signs that make it possible for them to recognize him; he offers them companionship; he sends them on mission; he returns to "heaven" or the realm of God's eschatological future. Not surprisingly, this pattern contains the principal elements of Christian discipleship.

What God did for Jesus at Easter is called various names by the New Testament: resurrection, exaltation, glorification; his being constituted Lord and Christ; his becoming the first fruits of those who have fallen asleep. Catholic faith teaches that God raised all of Jesus into the divine glory, and thus the tomb was empty.

Jesus through History

Early Christians began to pray to Jesus and to worship him in the power of the Holy Spirit. Much of this activity no doubt preceded theory about its significance. Terms such as "Lord" were addressed to Jesus, although such language had been reserved among Jews for the one God (e.g., John 20:28). It became imperative that this activity be interpreted and articulated in the light of traditional Jewish monotheism.

Foundational to the discussion was the question of salvation. If Christians experienced Jesus as offering them the two fundamental gifts of salvation that God alone could offer, namely, the forgiveness of sins and participation in the divine life, what did this imply about Jesus' being? There was never doubt about Jesus' humanity during his earthly life. But after Easter, Christians experienced this humanity as mediating to them divine gifts, and mediating them as *his* to give.

At the First Ecumenical (General) Council of Nicea (in present-day Turkey) in 325, the Church affirmed that the Word which became flesh in Jesus is all that God the Father is except that the Word is not the Father ("one in being, or consubstantial, with the Father"). Thus, the full divinity of Christ was affirmed. The relation of the divine Word to the Father and to the Holy Spirit occupied the energies of preeminent theologians of the fourth and fifth centuries, with reflections by the Cappadocian Fathers (Gregory of Nyssa, Gregory of Nazianzus, and his brother, Basil) a high point of patristic theology.

Successive councils defined additional Christological truths. The Council of Ephesus (431) determined that Christ's humanity is worthy of full worship insofar as it is united to the divine Word, and declared the orthodoxy of Mary's title as *theotokos* (God-bearer or Mother of God), not simply *Christokos* (mother of the human Christ).

The Council of Chalcedon (451) affirmed the oneness of the person of Christ in two distinct, unmixed, indivisible and inseparable natures, divine and human, and his consubstantiality with us human beings ("like us in all things but sin"). The Nestorians and the Monophysites lined up against each other over whether Christ is best thought of as possessing two natures or one. After Chalcedon, the one person of Christ would be identified as the person of the divine Word of the Trinity ("neo-Chalcedonianism").

The magisterium made additional Christological decisions of a fundamental kind in the following centuries, many of them occurring before the eighth century. However, Chalcedon provided the fundamental pattern for future developments until criticism of the pattern arose among some Protestant theologians in the last century and some Catholic thinkers in this century.

From early on, Jesus was viewed by Christians as the one in whose name all can be saved. Over the centuries, beginning with the NT, he was called by many titles, most of which expressed some aspect of his saving significance: Christ (Messiah), Lord, Savior, Pioneer of Faith, Reconciler, the Lamb of God, Victim or Sacrifice for sin, Expiator of sins, Protector from God's wrath, Vicarious Satisfier for sins, Mediator between God and humans, the Teacher, the Healer, the Peace-Maker, the Lord of the Cosmos, and the Liberator.

Down through the centuries, Christian thinkers have regularly employed the understanding of human relations accepted in their own cultural context as a key to expressing the nature of Christ's salvation. For example, in the feudal period, the liege lord as symbol and source of the integrity of society helped Anselm of Canterbury interpret Christ as making satisfaction to God for the dishonor done to the integrity of creation by sin. John Calvin viewed Jesus' saving death in the light of penal law that sought to hold society together in a tumultuous time. Present-day interpretations lean more to therapeutic healing and forgiveness, to an evolutionary understanding of the world, or to emancipation of the oppressed from destructive social structures.

The Eastern Churches have emphasized a "descending Christology." Christ is the exalted Son of God, King of creation and High Priest of the heavenly liturgy in which the Church's historical liturgy participates "in a glass darkly." The Western Churches have emphasized much more the temporal, historical character of the Christ-event, and the humanity of Jesus in its distinction from the divine (although Western Christians' popular piety can at times involve a crypto-Monophysitism, which views Jesus' human nature as suffused by the divine and transformed by it into something more than human). Recently, many Western theologians have been developing various forms of an "ascending Christology" which interprets Jesus in his human movement toward death and resurrection.

Jesus and Contemporary Concerns

In coming to Jesus in public worship and personal prayer, and acting in his name in explicit ministry and in deeds of loving service, Christians relate to Jesus as one whom they confidently trust will be able to respond to their human issues and concerns. A partial listing of the Christological concerns of contemporary Catholic theologians mirrors some of the most pressing concerns of our culture: Jesus' genuine humanity, his knowledge and self-consciousness, his freedom, his role in evolution, his liberating role in social structures, his identification with the oppressed, his relation to women and their struggles for equality, his saving role in relation to other world religions, and his relationship to the inner word of God at work invisibly and inaudibly in people's hearts (the Holy Spirit).

The constant concern of the Church's tradition has been to do justice to both the divine and human reality of Christ, as well as to his personal unity. Catholic Christology has ordinarily developed within the perspective of Chalcedon: two natures in one (divine) person. The divine person, the Second Person of the Trinity, is traditionally affirmed as the bearer of the human nature, creating it and uniting in that very act of creation to the divine person. The divine nature or principle of operation acts in and through the human nature, respecting the limits of that nature while making it the "real-symbol" of the eternal Word. More recently, attempts have been made to reverse the Chalcedonian model, and to think of Jesus as first of all a human person (in the ordinary, twentieth-century meanings of the term) so that the divine nature becomes personal (again, in the ordinary sense of the term) through the incarnation, while the divine Word creates and provides the divine root for the human person. This latter view has drawn some adherents, but has also been the object of official Vatican criticism.

No major contemporary Catholic theologian has ever maintained that during his earthly life "Jesus did not know who he was." Many theologians, however, do find it helpful to distinguish levels of human consciousness, such as explicit, focal consciousness, and implicit, background awareness. Such a distinction allows one to affirm that Jesus' human, conceptual knowledge of himself developed with the aid of the culture in which he was immersed, and that his deeper, preconceptual awareness was richer than he would have articulated during his lifetime.

That Jesus was free is a preeminent NT affirmation. Paul's letters speak of this freedom in terms of "obedience," a term which summarizes for Paul the entire course of Jesus' life in relation to *Abba.* The challenge begins when one tries to conceptualize the freedom of someone who was truly tempted like us but never sinned (Heb 4:15). One strand of the theological tradition would maintain that he could not sin, while others would be content to say that he was able not to sin, and that his ability not to sin developed more and more in his life into a concrete impossibility of sinning against God.

Jesus is the first of the New Humanity. The laboring universe is destined by God in Christ to come to full "issue," to the full stature of Christ, provided it cooperates with the purifying, unifying, and divinizing grace interiorly at work in its evolution. There are times when suffering, for all its darkness, is the price of synthesis and growth. But this fruitful suffering as passage to greater life must be contrasted with the dead-end waste that is formal sin, which is lethal disobedience to the law of growth at work in God's project, the emerging universe of loving personal subjects.

In his relating to individuals in his ministry, Jesus was dealing with social roles and structures as well as individuals. His own human consciousness at the time lacked the differentiations which have been developed only in modernity (e.g., sociology, social psychology, theories of culture). But in a way appropriate to his time, his ministry was social-structural as well as interpersonal. His criticism of teachers and other religious authorities, his exorcisms and healings, his telling of parables, his preaching the (public) reign of God, his formation of alternative community, his denunciation of a cultic situation that would lead a widow to give up her sustenance (Mark 12:41-44)—all these aspects of his ministry and teaching have social and structural implications that our age is learning to value and highlight.

Can the human, male Jesus do justice to women's concerns? It is true that within his own patriarchal context, Jesus was an exception, an individual who related to women in a countercultural way. Yet contemporary feminists—both men and women—ask that deeper question. The tradition maintained that on the creaturely level what was essential to salvation was Jesus' human nature as human. His individualizing characteristics (male, Jew, first-century, a certain height, with eyes of a specific color, etc.) were not soteriologically significant in their individuality; any human being has to have such characteristics. Today, some maintain that Jesus' maleness is positively significant, with the inference that women cannot adequately represent him in the Church's Eucharistic Liturgy. Others draw a negative conclusion, affirming that a male cannot adequately mediate between God and women. Theologians who want to be open to women's concerns and faithful to the Christian tradition find in the New Testament's portrayal of Jesus as God's Wisdom a fruitful source for a renewed Christology directed to both men and women, since wisdom is personified as feminine in Jewish tradition. They focus on the humanness, rather than maleness, of Jesus as theologically significant.

The topic of Christ and world religions is a particularly controversial one. Vatican II inaugurated a new age with its affirmation that God's grace and salvation are found in other Churches and religions although the true Church of Christ "subsists in the Catholic Church" (LG 8). Theologians supportive of the council's position would affirm that Jesus Christ is the inclusive and constitutive Savior of all humankind, whether or not people are explicitly conscious of that fact. Christ is inclusive in that *de facto* he offers salvation to all. Christ is constitutive in the sense that there would be no salvation available to the human race if the Christ-event had not occurred. Some Catholic theologians take a more controversial position. Going beyond the council, they affirm that Christ is inclusive and normative, but not constitutive of salvation. That is, Christ excludes no one from salvation, and is the prime exemplar of the salvation process, but other ways of salvation do not derive their efficacy from the Christ-event. The Vatican has expressed objections to this approach.

One of the most promising developments in recent Christology has been the exploration of the relationship between Jesus and the Holy Spirit. Jesus could say in a most emphatic way: "The Spirit of the Lord is upon me" (Luke 4:18). The Spirit represents the interior, universal, persuasive power of God at work in human history, and is thus the friend and guardian of authentic human freedom, as well as the source of that freedom's purification and divinization. If Jesus represents God come among us in particularity (a first-century Jewish male of the tribe of David, founder of the Church), the Spirit is about breadth (and breath), unboundedness, silent prayer, and prophetic power. The Spirit is the source of institutional reform and refreshment as well as of loving unity among those who are different, with divine respect for the differences.

BRIAN O. McDERMOTT, S.J.

See also ECUMENICAL COUNCILS; SALVATION HISTORY; SOTERIOLOGY.

JESUS, NAMES OF

See NAMES OF JESUS IN THE NEW TESTAMENT.

JESUS PRAYER, THE

When Orthodox Christians desire to take their life in Christ more seriously, they go in search of a spiritual father or mother. As disciples they ask, "Father/Mother, give me a word of life." The most common and popular word (word is used here in a broad sense—it may be a single word or a phrase or a sentence) is: "Lord Jesus Christ, Son of the living God, have mercy on me a sinner."

The disciple is told to do perhaps ten *komvoschinion* and fifty prostrations. This means that the disciple is to stand before the icon, looking into the face of Christ—Byzantines find a real presence in the icon—with a prayer cord (*komvoschinion*) in hand. As each knot passes through the fingers, the disciple repeats the word received from the spiritual guide. When one has gone round the cord ten times, has recited the word one thousand times, the prostrations will begin, again reciting the word as one falls to the floor. The prostration might be the little *metonia* or the great. For the little *metonia* one goes down on one's knees, touches knuckles to the ground and bows deeply. For the great *metonia,* the disciple prostrates full length.

The repetition and especially the repetition with prostrations is to allow the word to sink deeper and deeper into the disciple, forming the heart. The classical way the Fathers express this is "to bring the mind down into the heart."

When evening comes the disciple goes to see the spiritual guide and "manifests one's thoughts." The disciple will share with the guide the thoughts that came to consciousness as the word was recited and the prostrations were made. On the basis of this manifestation the elder judges the disciple's progress and, as appropriate, modifies the "obedience." The elder might increase or diminish the number of *komvoschinion* or the number of prostrations or might modify the word itself. If the manifestation indicated that the disciple was very conscious of sinfulness and much in need of purification and enlightenment, the spiritual guide might give the command simply to say: "Lord, Jesus, be merciful to me a sinner." If the disciple is moving more fully toward enlightenment, the prayer might be: "Lord Jesus Christ, Son of God"—the prayer becoming more simply one of adoration. Eventually the prayer comes to be one simple word: "Jesus." That is enough. The prostrations come to rest in one prolonged one. Or perhaps the disciple will simply stand before the icon or sit in a quiet, composed manner, achieving an ever greater stability of mind, body, and spirit. The word becomes rarer as the mind stills more and more. The disciple has found the holy rest of contemplation.

Ordinarily speaking, this process moves along most expeditiously if the disciple can abide with the elder or is able to come each evening for the manifestation. When this is not possible, then the fine honing of the prayer moves along less sensitively. The disciple comes to the guide when possible and the elder gives what direction the manifestation calls for. The goal of this practice is a purity of heart that enables one to be simply before the eyes of God, totally revealed, so pure, so clear, that no thought mars the surface. The undistorted image, reflecting the Divine One of whom it is the image and absorbing

The following selection of classical works of art depicts an overview of the life of Jesus Christ. These works, rendered by masters throughout the centuries, portray the grandeur and lofty ideals upheld by such gifted individuals. They were moved to express their inspired visions of the author of Christianity through their own creative imaginations, and in accordance with the aesthetic idiom of their own time and place.

PLATE 1 The Adoration of the Magi
Fra Angelico ca. 1400–1455; Filippo Lippi ca. 1406–1469

Plate 2

Plate 3

PLATE 2
The Annunciation
Alessandro Botticelli 1445–1510

PLATE 3
The Visitation with Saint Nicholas and Saint Anthony Abbot
Piero de Cosimo 1462–1521

PLATE 4
The Nativity
Book of Hours, Rouen Workshop, ca. 1500

PLATE 5
The Flight into Egypt
Vittore Carpaccio ca. 1465–1526

PLATE 4

PLATE 5

Plate 6

Plate 6
The Presentation of Child Jesus
Book of Hours
ca. 15th century

Plate 7
The Holy Family with Mary Magdalen
El Greco 1541–1614

Plate 8
The Baptism of Christ
Master of the St. Bartholomew Altar ca. 1475–1510

Plate 9
The Marriage Feast at Cana
Juan de Flandes ca. 1496–1519

Plate 7

Plate 8

Plate 9

Plate 10

Plate 10
The Healing of the Paralytic at Capernaum
Workshop of Dirk Vellert ca. 1520–1525

Plate 11
Christ Blessing the Children
Lucas Cranach, the Elder 1472–1553

Plate 12
The Calling of the Apostles Peter and Andrew
Duccio di Buoninsegna ca. 1255–1318

Plate 11

Plate 12

Plate 13
The Return of the Prodigal Son
Bartolomé Esteban Murillo 1617–1682

Plate 14
The Raising of Lazarus
Jacopo Robusti Tintoretto 1518–1594

Plate 15
The Temptation of Christ
Titian ca. 1488–1576

Plate 13

Plate 14

PLATE 15

Plate 16
Christ Presenting the Keys to St. Peter
German, 14th century

Plate 17
Christ at the Sea of Galilee
Jacopo Tintoretto 1518–1594

Plate 18
Christ and the Woman Taken in Adultery
Max Beckmann 1884–1950

Plate 19
Christ Driving the Money Changers from the Temple
El Greco 1541–1614

Plate 16

Plate 17

Plate 18

Plate 19

PLATE 20

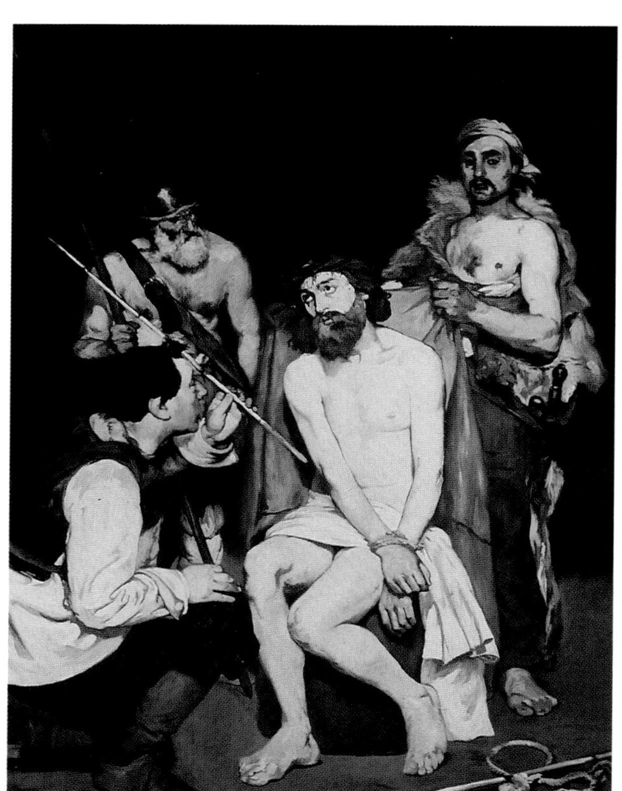

PLATE 21

PLATE 20
The Sacrament of the Last Supper
Salvador Dali 1904–1989

PLATE 21
The Mocking of Christ
Edouard Manet 1832–1883

PLATE 22
White Crucifixion
Marc Chagall 1887–1985

PLATE 22

Plate 23

Plate 24

Plate 25

Plate 23
Pietà with Saints John the Baptist and Catherine of Alexandria
Master of the Saint Lucy Legend
15th century

Plate 24
The Risen Christ Appearing to the Virgin
Francesco Solimena 1657–1747

Plate 25
The Supper at Emmaus
Diego Velazquez 1599–1660

Plate 26
Pentecost
Book of Hours
ca. 15th century

Plate 26

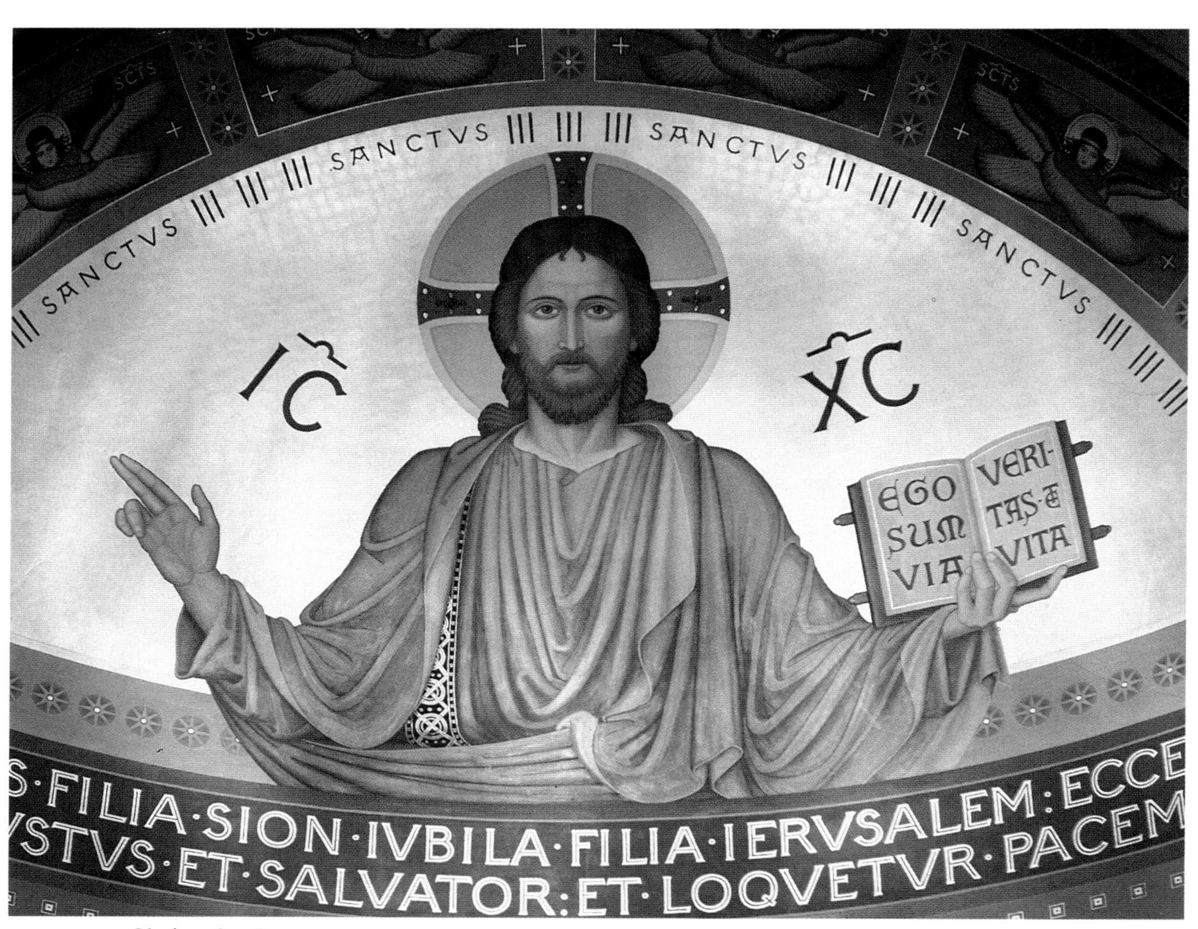

PLATE 27 Christ the Pantocrator
Clement Frischauf, O.S.B., 1869–1944

all the love that comes forth from the Source. A total and perfect communion of love.

M. BASIL PENNINGTON, O.C.S.O.

See also EASTERN CHURCHES; MYSTICISM; PRAYER; SPIRITUAL DIRECTION.

JOHN XXIII, POPE (1958–1963)

Whatever may be history's final verdict on the popes of the twentieth century, it will surely recognize the pivotal, crucial role of Angelo Giuseppe Roncalli, who on 28 October 1958, became John XXIII. For it is not too much to say that he changed the course of the Church. The great agency of change which he initiated, but whose completion he did not live to see, was of course the Second Vatican Council (1962–1965). But in word and action, in his very appearance as seen on television and a thousand press photographs, he had already made his mark as a *different* kind of pope: certainly different from Pius XII, but also from previous pontiffs still remembered. And in making this strong personal impact, he may paradoxically have begun the demythologization of the papacy, a process which his successors—assuming they wished to—could not arrest. One thinks then of "Good Pope John" not only in his Church, nor even among the whole Christian community, but in the world "out there"—not that he would have put it like that. The phrase "the World his parish," however sentimental, is not in fact inappropriate.

Born on 25 November 1881, the fourth child in a poor peasant family, devoutly and traditionally Catholic, at Sotto il Monte a few miles from Bergamo in northern Italy, it is not fanciful to say that at any early age he was made aware of wider horizons. This was due to his great-uncle Zaverio, a "humble but convinced apostle" of the infant Catholic Action movement which had already struck roots in the diocese of Bergamo. And although his years (1893–1900) of formation at the diocesan seminary—one of the "new" Counter-Reformation foundations established by St. Charles Borromeo—were conventionally pious, even rigorist, he was not unaware of new developments in the local Church. Bishop Camillo Guindani pioneered a remarkable campaign of social action, a foretaste perhaps of that Christian democracy whose realization lay still far in the future, but which drew encouragement from Leo XIII's *Rerum Novarum.*

In 1901 he left Bergamo to enroll as a scholarship-holder in the *Collegio Romano* where he remained, apart from a year's military service, until 1905 when he returned after ordination as secretary to the new

Pope John XXIII

bishop, Radini Tedeschi. He was already something of a hero to Roncalli who knew and admired his work in the *Opera dei Congressi.*

This was the Rome-based coordinating body of social action and a focus for Catholic "progressive" thinking. As such it fell a victim of Pius X's purge of all institutions and individuals seen to be carriers of the "Modernist" plague. Radini Tedeschi's appointment was then a mark of disfavor, but Bergamo was a congenial place of exile, and both bishop and secretary found ample opportunity for their chosen apostolate. Don Angelo also made the acquaintance of the saintly and erudite Cardinal Andrea Carlo Ferrari, archbishop of Milan, towards whom Pius was continually and quite unpleasantly hostile. But he became another hero of the future John XXIII who would introduce the cause of his beatification.

Familiarity with the archiepiscopal palace led him to the discovery of documents detailing the post-Tridentine proceedings of Ferrari's illustrious predecessor, St. Charles Borromeo in the diocese of Bergamo: editing the *Acta* of the great Counter Reformer was to be Roncalli's lifework as a scholar. And faith and scholarship met in his model of historical writing, the sixteenth-century Oratorian Cesare Baronius in whose work science and orthodoxy coexisted without conflict.

Roncalli became professor of Church history in Bergamo in 1906, and the following year he commemorated the third centenary of Baronius' death with a lecture on "Faith and Scientific Research." It was a courageous but cautious statement, in the aftermath of the two papal salvos against Modernism, the decree *Lamentabili* and the encyclical *Pascendi.* He avoided censure, but sailed close to the wind in an article endorsing Radini Tedeschi's strong support of a strike in 1909 at Ranica near Bergamo. In retrospect, this defense of the Church's "intervening in politics" is particularly remarkable for its prophetic statement that "Christ's *preference* goes to the disinherited, the weak and the oppressed. . . ." In general, while loyally supporting his bishop in a range of enterprises, he steered clear of papal displeasure and reprimand, but, it must be admitted, by, on at least one occasion, a statement of personal explanation which was less than admirable (a not uncommon and perhaps understandable proceeding in times of witch-hunt).

This grey period ended with the death of Pius X as well as of Radini Tedeschi, and the new darkness of the War of 1914–1918. Roncalli was called up in May 1915 as a hospital orderly, then served as a chaplain. His experiences left him with the conviction that "war is the greatest evil."

The immediate postwar years brought new duties, new contacts, new ideas. Don Angelo served as warden of a student hostel, seminary chaplain, and, from January 1921, National Director of the Propagation of the Faith. This made him a member of the Curia with the title of Monsignor, as well as sending him abroad to study the organization of missionary activity elsewhere in Europe. Then, at the beginning of 1922, Benedict XV, successor of Pius X and active patron of evangelization in a changed world, died and was himself succeeded by Achille Ratti, Pius XI.

The Italian political scene was also changing, and not for the better. The foundation of the Partito Popolare Italiano (PPI) by Don Luigi Sturzo in 1919, with Vatican blessing, was greeted (not least by Roncalli) as the dawn of a new age of true Christian Democracy. But following Mussolini's seizure of power in 1922, it appears that the Vatican decided to drop, first Sturzo (succeeded for some months by the young Alcide de Gasperi), and then the PPI as a whole, after the Fascist landslide in the elections of April 1924. The following September, on the tenth anniversary of the death of Radini Tedeschi, Roncalli preached a sermon which was a lament for Italy's stillborn democracy. It was a gentle but firm and brave challenge to Fascism and to the new Vatican policy.

It met with no immediate response, and Roncalli's work in the Curia was supplemented by lecturing in patristics at the Lateran. But in February 1925 he was appointed "apostolic visitor" to Bulgaria, and Pius XI personally decided he should be ordained archbishop. His appointment was however fairly generally regarded as an exile in Limbo: the post would have no official diplomatic status (until 1931 when it became that of apostolic delegate). Still, it began a career of nearly thirty years in which he represented the Roman Catholic Church and the Holy See in several very diverse situations. And his very lack of diplomatic training gave much of his work a certain pastoral aura, as among the Bulgarian "uniates" and in the relief of human distress without reference to creed or tradition. Both creed and tradition were nevertheless of continuing concern, and expressed not least in his liturgical and ecumenical awareness—this latter of especial significance for future developments.

The Lateran Pacts signed in 1929 included a concordat which gave the Italian state a role in episcopal appointments. Roncalli's name was widely canvassed as successor to the see of Milan, but in the event the Benedictine Ildefonso Schuster was appointed—a politically "reliable" man. Don Angelo remained in Sofia until 1935 when he moved to Istanbul as apostolic delegate to Turkey and Greece. His farewell to Bulgaria was a moving occasion: he had become widely respected and admired. Militantly secularist Turkey and aggressively Orthodox Greece provided fresh challenges.

The accession of Pope Pius XII in March 1939 was the occasion of a small but unprecedented ecumenical victory, when the apostolic delegate was able to welcome the Ecumenical Patriarch Benjamin I at the *Te Deum* held in Istanbul: on the following day, when Roncalli called at the Phanar, the Patriarch embraced him warmly with the kiss of peace. But war, not peace, soon became a major preoccupation: Turkey declared for neutrality, but the German ambassador von Papen (a Catholic) was immensely active on the diplomatic front, and among those he courted was the Pope's man, who for his part liked to think of himself as "God's Consul," in the service of peace and of all war's victims.

His success in this role was only partial: it could hardly have been otherwise. As ever, he remained on good terms with the most unlikely people and while considered somewhat naive by many—not least in certain Vatican quarters, and not for the first time—his courage and goodwill were never in doubt. Perhaps his most positive achievement was in saving the lives of many thousands of Jews ("I am Joseph, your brother"), and indeed facilitating their passage to Palestine—despite his own (and the Vatican's) coolness towards the idea of an Israeli state. And, in the dark year of 1944, he delivered a Pentecost sermon in which he insisted that "in the light of the Gospel" the logic of religious division "did not hold," and pointed out that "Catholic" should be a unifying, inclusive term, not a mark of exclusive distinction. A remarkably prophetic vision.

In December 1944 he was suddenly sent as nuncio to Paris. It was an appointment which in normal times would be the "plum" posting in the Vatican service, but circumstance had rather made it a very hot potato. His predecessor Valerio Valeri was unacceptable to de Gaulle as having been too close to the Vichy regime, and Pius XII had agreed to his withdrawal only under pressure. The new nuncio had to cope with the thorny problems of alleged collaborationist bishops, the new "priest worker" movement, and the financing of church schools—all this in the aftermath of occupation and liberation, in a country now seen by many as a *pays de mission.* There were many tightropes to walk: he trod delicately and on the whole surely—there were few tumbles. His natural sympathy for Christian democracy made him at ease with the new Catholics in power—Bidault, Teitgen, Schumann, even de Gaulle himself who was never the easiest to get on with. And he shared an openness to the modern world expressed by Cardinal Suhard of Paris and the new breed of French clergy who supported him, as well as Suhard's successor Maurice Feltin, president of Pax Christi. But he could do little to defend those theologians including Chenu and Congar who were censured and disciplined by the Pope of *Humani Generis.*

He once declared that "the maintenance of peaceful relations between Church and State" was the primary object of the Nunciature. By this criterion he was more than successful; indeed his outreach extended to a brief term as Vatican observer to UNESCO, and his *congé* in February 1953 took the form of a dinner-party at which the president of the national assembly, the prime minister, and seven of his predecessors were guests.

His departure from Paris followed elevation to the College of Cardinals—his red biretta was conferred by President Auriol, assuming the old privilege of "Catholic princes"—and nomination to the metropolitan see (or "Patriarchate") of Venice. It was his first pastoral appointment, and, after some initial regrets at leaving Paris, he took to it with considerable enthusiasm. He was, as might be imagined, a very popular choice. Over his study door he placed the words *Pastor et Pater,* which expressed his idea of authority, and in his relations with those outside his flock he said that he would stress "what unites rather than what divides." This did not please those Christian Democrat politicians who (with Vatican backing) were firm in their opposition to any "opening to the Left": but it enabled him to welcome the Italian Socialist Party when they held their thirty-second Congress in Venice in February 1957. This irenicism displeased, even enraged many, but it survived their criticisms. And its spiritual corollary found expression in the Patriarch's developing ecumenical enthusiasm, mainly in relation to the Eastern Churches, but also to those of the Reformation. In this as in so much else his years in Venice were a preparation for what was to come. On 12 October 1958 he left for Rome to attend the funeral of Pius XII and to take part in the conclave which would follow. It would be rash to suggest that neither he nor the Church of Venice had any inkling that he might not return.

He was in fact elected on the twelfth ballot on 28 October, the fourth day of the conclave. (The only serious opposition seems to have been the Armenian Cardinal Agagianian). On signifying his acceptance, he announced that he would be called John—the first, as has been said, of his many surprises. Just an hour after the traditional "white smoke" had signified that the papal vacancy had been filled, the announcement of his name was greeted with great enthusiasm by the crowd in St. Peter's Square. Then the new Pope appeared and gave his blessing *urbi et orbi.*

On the following day he broadcast his first radio address. Having given a special greeting to those suffering from persecution (under Communist regimes) which were "in open contrast with the rights of man," he went on to adumbrate two major concerns: unity in the Church (with especial regard to the Orthodox and all separated from "this Apostolic See"), and peace in the world "among all men of good will." And at his coronation on 4 November (feast of St. Charles Borromeo) his homily was all on his desire to be a good shepherd and a brother among brothers. He used the same language to the press—he had already asked the *Osservatore Romano* to drop all pompous locutions and flowery epithets when referring to or quoting him. And later he "took possession" of his cathedral of St. John Lateran, not as "a prince, a ruler," but as a "priest, a father, a shepherd."

Indeed the new Pope took his "basic" title of Bishop of Rome very seriously: he was careful to pay pastoral visits to parishes, and saw to it that St. John Lateran became the diocesan center in fact as well as by dedication. He had a genuine affection for Rome's citizens, especially the poor: his Christmas visits to the Regina Coeli prison and the Bambin' Gesù children's hospital were more than gestures. But he was not blind to the darker sides of Roman life, and saw the city as mission territory. Hence, when on the feast of the Conversion of St Paul, 25 January 1959 he proclaimed the convening of an ecumenical council, he also announced two other projects: the renewal of canon law and, more immediately, a synod for the diocese of Rome, the first in history.

The synod was duly held and its decrees published on 29 July 1960. Although the Pope had taken a close interest in its preparation, and hoped it would be a valuable "practice run" for the council, it was a disappointing affair and far from progressive in tone or substance. One of the few bright spots, due to the Pope's personal initiative, was a decree dealing with "priests under censure or other penalties": they were to be shown charity and friendship by their (ex-) colleagues and given spiritual and material assistance. But the synod as a whole did not appear to augur well for the council. Nor did *Veterum Sapientia,* a eulogy of the Latin language and a strong directive to its use, not only in liturgy but in teaching, which was issued in the Pope's name but was the work of Cardinal Antonio Bacci, the Curia's great Latinist.

Indeed the first four encylicals issued in the second half of 1959 had been equally conservative. The first, *Ad Petri Cathedram,* seemed cool on ecumenism, and the others—*Sacerdotii Nostri Primordia* on the centenary of the Curé d'Ars; *Grata Recordatio* on the Rosary; and *Maximum Illud* in commemoration of the Pope's old patron Benedict XV as "Pope of the Missions"—had little impact. Not until *Mater et Magistra* appeared in July 1961, was what may be justly called his social radicalism unambiguously revealed and proclaimed. "Catholic social teaching" took an enormous leap forward, and could no longer be quoted as a theological underpinning for right-wing politics. Not unnaturally, the encyclical was less than warmly received by Italian conservatives in Church and state, but it gave great encouragement to those Christian Democrats—like Fanfani and Moro—who sought the long-delayed "opening to the left."

And any apparent foot-dragging on the ecumenical front ended with the establishment of the Secretariat for the Promotion of Christian Unity under the leadership of the Jesuit biblical scholar and former confessor to Pius XII, Augustine Bea (created cardinal in January 1960). Bea picked a brilliant team, as varied in nationality as in talent and background—two of them Americans: the Paulist Thomas Stransky, and the Jesuit orientalist John Long. The Secretariat was the dynamo which ensured that the council would firmly commit the Roman Catholic Church to the aim of Christian unity.

On Christmas Day 1961 Pope John issued the apostolic constitution *Humanae Salutis* convoking the council. He stressed that it must be at the service not alone of the Church but of the world, where the Spirit was still at work, if we would only follow Christ's command to read "the signs of the times." And he prayed "for the return of unity and peace" among all Christians. A month before he had celebrated his eightieth birthday: greetings received included one from Nikita Khrushchev (duly acknowledged), not altogether as unexpected as first appeared—it is now clear that there had been some discreet, "unofficial soundings."

The actual date of the council, 11 October, was announced only in February 1962. The intervening months were full, as the Pope kept in close touch with the proceedings of the Central Preparatory Commission, but refrained from interfering. He did however take a particular interest in the development of ecumenical contacts which would lead to the presence of observers from the "separated" Churches, and indeed personally met a number of Church leaders—following the historic visit of Archbishop Fisher of Canterbury in December 1960. He was also impressed and influenced by the views of the council to be expressed in diocesan pastoral letters by Cardinal Suenens of Belgium and, an old friend, Cardinal Montini in Milan: they were to become his close advisers. His immediate personal preparation for the council however was a pilgrimage to Loreto and to Assisi (for 4 October, the feast of St. Francis)—the latter emphasizing his concern for peace and for the poor.

The first conciliar assembly, the greatest gathering in the history of the universal Church, with its lengthy and splendid Tridentine liturgy, was however made most memorable by the presence of the "Pastor and Father" and his thirty-seven-minute address which was a manifesto for the age of renewal. A patriarch indeed, but one who evoked also the biblical image of the mother hen with her brood—not least those who had gathered in from afar off and whom he happily and proudly surveyed from his place among them. The observers from Eastern Europe were especially welcome, though the absence of the Greeks was painful. The Russians missed the opening but arrived the next day.

That night he spoke with great warmth to half a million people in St. Peter's Square. The following day he met the statesmen and diplomats who represented nearly eighty nations at the council, then the observers, and finally some twelve-hundred journalists—with the promise of an openness which, in the event, was but slowly and even grudgingly fulfilled.

The council session continued until 8 December. It was, contrary to previous expectations, to be only the first of four. But it was to be the only one of the pontificate. For some time now the Pope had known that he was very seriously ill, and that his ultimate contribution to the council and to the Church would be his own private, physical pain. Perhaps his final word on his great objective was "At the day of judgement we won't be asked whether we realized unity, but whether we prayed, worked and *suffered* for it."

That was in December 1962: again there was an exchange of messages with Krushchev, and in the following February, the Ukrainian metropolitan Josef Slipyj was released from a Soviet labor camp, and came to Rome. Less than a month later the Pope received Khruschev's daughter Rada and son-in-law Alexis Adzhubei. Their visit marked the papal acceptance of the Balzan Prize—awarded for "his activity in favor of brotherhood between all men and all peoples, and his appeals for peace and good will in his recent diplomatic intervention (*sc.* in the Cuban missile Crisis)."

But Pope John's final and greatest gift to world peace was his last encyclical, *Pacem in Terris,* issued on Maundy Thursday 1963. The months of April and May were a time of almost constant suffering, but he continued aware and as active as possible. He was assiduous in study of new council texts as they were prepared, and even left the Vatican on a number of occasions—to pay a historic visit to the Italian president in the Quirinale on 11 May and, two days later, to bless the foundation stone of a new Slav college. He received guests, including five Polish bishops on 20 May, but by 23 May, was reconciled to not going to Monte Cassino as planned. On the last day of May, he received the doctor's final, terminal verdict.

The end came on the morning of Whit Monday, 3 June: members of his family were among those at his bedside. It is for once true to say that the whole world mourned the passing of one whom they saw to be a great and good man.

Every moment of his life in the Church and the world is well-documented in his *Journal* (kept since boyhood), and in the personal documentation compiled by his friend and secretary Loris Capovilla. His spirituality is articulated with an unusual blend of confidence and humility and firmly rooted in God's word in Scripture and liturgy. It is too much to speak of "spiritual masters," although he was deeply influenced by thinkers and teachers from Augustine to Benedict to Ignatius of Loyola to Francis de Sales, and was especially the follower and disciple of Charles Borromeo. Among contemporary figures he owed much to the Benedictine Lambert Beaudoin, a pioneer in the ecumenical, social, and above all liturgical movements.

His relations with Vatican officialdom were always respectful and he maintained good relations with those with whom he disagreed, and who thought him naive and ineffectual. Some may have come to recognize that they were mistaken.

SEAN MacREAMOINN

See also CHURCH AND STATE; ECUMENISM; VATICAN COUNCIL II.

JOHN CHRYSOSTOM, ST. (ca. 347–407)

Born in Antioch in Syria (modern-day Antakya, Turkey), John was raised by his widowed mother Anthusa, as his father Secundus, a civil servant, died while he was still an infant. John received a good education and showed great promise for a distinguished career in law or government. He decided, however, on serving the Lord. He was baptized and spent about three years studying the Scriptures. Melitius, bishop of Antioch, appointed him as a lector ca. 371. Because he desired to flee from the world and seek God alone, John spent four years in the countryside under the direction of an old Syrian monk and two more years living alone in a cave while he memorized Scripture. Because his health broke down from his ascetical observances, John had to return to Antioch. He was ordained a deacon in 381 by Melitius and a priest by Flavian, Melitius's successor in 386. Melitius assigned John the task of preaching regularly in the churches of Antioch. Over the next twelve years (386 to 397) John preached his famous homilies on Genesis, Matthew, John, Romans, Galatians, 1 and 2 Corinthians, Ephesians, Timothy, and Titus. His preaching showed keen insight in the spiritual meaning as well as practical application of the text. However, he insisted that the text should be interpreted literally and not allegorically. During this same period he preached the *Homilies on the Statues,* a series given after the statues of the Emperor Theodosius and the imperial family were knocked down by a mob after a new heavy tax had been imposed. While Bishop Flavian was in Constantinople to ask the Emperor's pardon, John proclaimed twenty-one sermons in which he both encouraged the crowds who had come to hear him and rebuked them for their sins which had brought down God's anger upon them. In 398, John was forced to accept the position as patriarch of Constantinople. He threw himself into reform of the city where clergy, the court, and the people had become lax and self-indulgent under Nectarius, the previous bishop. Although things seemed to go fairly well during the first two years he was in office, John did not prove adept at the ecclesiastical politics of the capital city. Theophilus, bishop of Alexandria, had resented his appointment as patriarch of Constantinople. Though John began on good terms with the Empress Eudoxia, she began to suspect that some of Chrysostom's criticism of opulence and luxury was directed to her. At the Synod of the Oak (403) Chrysostom was summoned to defend himself before thirty-six bishops selected by Theophilus who were all his enemies. He was condemned on a series of fabricated charges including Origenism and making slanderous remarks against the Empress. Chrysostom was promptly deposed from office and banished to Bithynia but recalled at the request of Eudoxia herself. He soon caused offense to Eudoxia by an indiscrete reference to her in a sermon. His enemies saw their opportunity and procured Chrysostom's banishment on the charge of unlawfully assuming again the duties of a see from which he had been canonically deposed. Even though he received the support of the people of Constantinople, the pope, and the entire Western Church, he lived out his last days in exile. At first he was sent to Cucusus in Armenia where he lived for three years. Then his enemies decided to send him to Pityus (Colchis) on the eastern end of the Black Sea. He died before reaching this destination in a forced march in severe weather that was designed to kill him. Thirty years later his body was brought back to Constantinople. Early in his career John wrote six books *On the Priesthood,* a classic description of the duties of a Christian minister. Several generations after his death he received the name Chrysostom (golden-mouthed) because of his reputation as a preacher. Considered the greatest preacher in the early Church, he was widely read in the Middle Ages. He was named a Doctor of the Church in 1568. Feast day, 13 November (East); 13 September (West).

JOHN DILLON

See also DOCTORS OF THE CHURCH; FATHERS OF THE CHURCH; PREACHING.

JOHN OF DAMASCUS, ST. (ca. 650 [or 675?]–ca. 749)

Born of a wealthy Christian family of Damascus, he followed his father as chief representative of the Christians to the caliph. He resigned his post (ca. 716) to enter the monastery of Mar Saba (St. Saba) near Jerusalem, where he became a priest. He resided there until his death. When Emperor Leo III decreed that images should be destroyed, John composed his *Apostolic Discourses* in which he reasoned ably and effectively for the veneration of images. The emperors were unable to stop him because he was residing in Muslim territory. His most important work is the *Fount of Knowledge,* of which the third section, *The Orthodox Faith,* summarizes the teaching of the Nicene and Post-Nicene Fathers on the main Christian doctrines: particularly, Trinity, creation, and the incarnation. He also discusses topics like baptism, veneration of the cross, and the resurrection of the dead. *The Orthodox Faith* has had great influence in both the East and the West. His other great work, the *Sacra parallela,* is a compilation of scriptural and patristic texts on the moral and ascetical life. John also wrote a commentary on the Pauline Epistles as well as a number of homilies. Topics he covers in them include Holy Saturday, the Transfiguration, and the birth and death of Mary. Leo XIII named John of Damascus a Doctor of the Church in 1890. Feast day, 4 December.

JOHN DILLON

See also FATHERS OF THE CHURCH; IMAGES, VENERATION OF.

JOHN OF THE CROSS, ST. (1542–1591)

Born Juan de Yepes at Fontiveros in Castile, St. John was the youngest son of the gentleman merchant, Gonzalo de Yepes, and the poor weaver, Catalina Alvarez. In honor-conscious Spain, such a cross-class marriage often had serious consequences. Gonzalo was disinherited for marrying beneath his station and was unable to support his family in economically depressed Castile. The family's desperation increased when Gonzalo died, probably in 1544. Children in tow, Catalina undertook several arduous journeys to seek help; none provided more than temporary respite. The family finally settled in Medina del Campo in 1551. There, an orphanage accepted John as a boarding student. In 1556 the administrator of the town hospice gave him work nursing the sick poor and collecting alms for the institution. While living at the hospice, he attended classes at the nearby Jesuit school, completing his studies in 1563.

Turning aside offers from other religious orders, in 1563 he entered the Carmelite Order as Fray Juan de Santo Matía. He studied at Salamanca and was ordained priest in 1567. That same year, he met the future St. Teresa of Avila (1515–1582) who was in Medina to establish her second reformed (Discalced) convent for women. Teresa was also looking for Carmelite men to inaugurate a reform of the friars. John, about to transfer to the austere Carthusians, decided instead to join the reform. In 1568, he and a companion formed the first Discalced community for friars in the backwater of Duruelo, embracing the demanding regimen of contemplative prayer and total poverty Teresa had already introduced among Carmelite women. There he took a new name, John of the Cross.

John was no sedentary contemplative. Fervently committed to the extension of the reform and a

St. John of the Cross, oil painting by Joaquin Canedo, 1795

skilled administrator and spiritual director, he was one of Teresa's most trusted and beloved allies. As rector of the College of the Discalced at the University of Alcalá (1571–1572), he oversaw the formation of young friars. From 1572 to 1577 he was confessor and spiritual counselor to the nuns of the Convent of the Incarnation in Avila where Teresa was prioress. Throughout these years, he traveled widely to establish and nourish the growing Discalced movement.

The reform had its detractors. John quickly became a target for Carmelites working to suppress it. After the anti-reformist general chapter at Piacenza in Italy (1575), the visitor general sanctioned John's seizure and imprisonment. In December of 1577, the bold abduction occurred. At the priory of Toledo, he was confined under indefinite sentence to a six-by-ten windowless cell. After nine months of brutal treatment, he made a daring escape to Andalusia. During his imprisonment he had composed the greater part of the poem, "Spiritual Canticle." In the years immediately following, he wrote the theological commentaries, *Spiritual Canticle, Ascent of Mount Carmel* and *The Dark Night.*

When the Discalced were granted independent provincial status in 1580, the sometimes violent opposition subsided. John continued his service by establishing a college at Baeza. He was its first rector (1579–1582). In the year of Teresa's death (1582), he became prior at Granada. While serving there, he was also appointed vicar-provincial of Andalusia (1585). It was during this period that he composed, in a two-week burst of creativity, his other major treatise, *Living Flame of Love* (1585). In 1588, he was prior at Segovia and was appointed definitor at the first general chapter of the Discalced.

His relations with the Discalced vicar-general, Nicolás Doria, turned sour when John opposed Doria's plans concerning the governance of the Discalced nuns. He also disapproved harsh disciplinary measures enacted against Teresa's old friend and lieutenant, Jerónimo Gracián. In 1591, amid a campaign of defamation, John was removed from office and ordered to Andalusia, where he underwent further humiliations. That same fall, he contracted a serious fever. Transferred to Ubeda for medical care, he died in December, after three months of terrible suffering.

John's writings rank among the most authoritative of all Christian spiritual literature. Arising from his own mystical experience and from his skillful direction of gifted souls like Teresa's, his poems and treatises describe the loving relationship between God and the soul and provide guidance for those undertaking the contemplative journey. With the sensibilities of a poet and the acuity of a Thomist, he maps out the phases through which the soul grows able to respond in pure love to a God who is *beyond* our senses, understanding and imagination.

John's mysticism is *apophatic* ("negative"), stressing God's essential unknowability by human intellect. Only through "unknowing" and the purification of attachment to all creatures and concepts can the soul apprehend the "no-thing" (*nada*) that is God. This necessary stripping involves a series of purifications John calls "nights." During the nights of the *senses* (active and passive), the soul is led to that radical freedom in which alone the pure love of God can take root. During the nights of the *spirit,* faith itself is purified. The soul suffers intensely, yet the love of God is present to it through the beginnings of infused contemplation: that "dark" but dawning true knowledge of God. Then the soul comes to the bright day of transforming union. This unitive stage is described in spousal imagery as mystical betrothal and marriage.

John also treats phenomena such as voices and visions commonly experienced by proficients in the mystical life. With unsparing candor and psychological insight he describes the effects of spiritual experience and the delusions that await the unprepared, the unaccompanied, and the self-involved. Wisely he enjoins a fundamental reserve about all forms of religious sensationalism.

Small in stature (Teresa once called him and a Discalced companion "a friar and a half") and large in intellect (Teresa named him "little Seneca"), John was a man of unfailing integrity. Indefatigably given over to the good of the reform, the Church and the souls entrusted to his care; hard with himself but generous with others, he was canonized in 1726 and declared a Doctor of the Church in 1926. His liturgical commemoration falls on 14 December.

MARY LUTI

See also CARMELITES; CONTEMPLATION; MYSTICISM; SPIRITUAL LIFE.

JOHN PAUL I, POPE (26 AUGUST–28 SEPTEMBER 1978)

Albino Luciani was born into a poor working-class family at Forno di Canale near Belluno, Italy, on 17 October 1912. He was ordained a priest in 1935 and completed doctoral studies at the Gregorian University in Rome. Afterwards, he worked as a parish priest in his home parish and at Agerdo, and then became the vice-rector of the seminary in Belluno in 1937 where he also taught for ten years. While still at the seminary, he was named vicar general of his diocese, and he was involved in coordinating catechetics for a local Eucharistic conference in 1949. In 1958 John XXIII named him bishop of Vittorio Veneto where he demonstrated impressive pastoral leadership. During Vatican II (1962–1965) he served on the doctrinal commission for the Italian bishops. In 1969 his appointment as patriarch of Venice was attributed to his popularity and wide-based local support.

While patriarch of Venice, he was active in ecumenical dialogues, including the Anglican-Roman Catholic International Commission (ARCIC). During his time in Venice he became an outspoken critic of communists, although he had formerly maintained a good working relationship with them. In fact, his own father had been an active socialist. Between 1972 and 1975, he was president of the Italian Conference of Bishops, and on 5 March 1973 he was made a cardinal by Paul VI. A strong defender of *Humanae Vitae* and generally conservative in his approach to theology, Luciani also eschewed ecclesiastical pomp and was fiercely committed to the poor. He also supported the suggestion that the wealthy Churches of the first world should give one percent of their income to the poorer Churches of the Third World.

A dark horse at the first conclave of 1978, he received considerable support from cardinals who favored him because he was not a curial insider. After his election as pope, he chose the name, John Paul, as a sign of both the progressiveness of John XXIII and the cautious tradition of Paul VI. He dispensed with the traditional papal coronation, and instead chose to be invested with the archiepiscopal *pallium* on 3 September 1978. At the beginning of his brief pontificate, he told the cardinals of his desire to go forward with the work of Vatican II, but he stressed to them also the importance of discipline in the lives of the priests and the faithful. He died of a heart attack on Thursday, 28 September, at about 11 P.M.—having only reigned for thirty-three days. Some journalists claimed foul play, but these accusations were spurious at best. A man of humble origins who shied away from the traditional display of power, he received an overwhelmingly favorable reception. One can only speculate what the character of his pontificate might have been if he had lived longer.

ANTHONY D. ANDREASSI

See also PAPACY, THE.

JOHN PAUL II, POPE (16 OCTOBER 1978–)

Karol Wojtyla was born on 18 May 1920, in Wadowice, Poland. His mother died when he was young, and the young Karol was reared by his father. In 1938 they moved to Krakow which gave Karol the opportunity to study at the Jagiellonian University where he wrote poetry and was involved in drama. After the beginning of World War II, he continued studying and acting, though secretly, while working as a laborer. Early in the war his father died, and in 1942 Karol began his studies for the priesthood though he had to do this in underground fashion also. When the seminary was reopened after the war, he was able to complete his theological studies and was ordained a priest on 1 November 1946. He was

Pope John Paul II

then sent to Rome where he earned a doctorate at the Angelicum University writing his dissertation on the question of faith in St. John of the Cross. He returned to Poland where he was engaged in pastoral work while continuing studies toward another doctorate, and working with university students. In 1954 he began teaching Christian ethics and moral theology at the Catholic University of Lublin, wrote much and was widely published.

In 1958 Wojtyla was named an auxiliary bishop of Krakow, and in 1964 he was named archbishop of the historic see at the age of forty-three. He was a member of the Preparatory Commission for Vatican Council II (1962–1965) and showed great interest in working on the question of the Church and religious liberty. He was an important voice for the Polish bishops during the council and worked hard for the implementation of the conciliar decrees in Poland. He was a staunch champion of the rights of the Church in communist-dominated Poland, and as such he soon became an international figure, traveling and speaking widely. Pope Paul VI recognized his service to the Polish Church by making him a cardinal in 1967. By the time of the second conclave of 1978, Karol Wojtyla was a well-known and respected figure to many of the cardinals, and he was elected pope by an overwhelming majority of them at the relatively young age of fifty-eight. He was the first non-Italian pope since Adrian VI (1522–1523). He was not crowned with the traditional papal tiara but was simply invested as "Universal Pastor of the Church" on 21 October 1978.

Since his election, John Paul II has traveled throughout the world in order to show the universality of his office and ministry. In each of his visits he makes a point of visiting and addressing a wide variety of groups including bishops, priests and religious, laity, and even non-Catholics and non-Christians. He takes particular delight in meeting young people, the sick, and the poor. As supreme pastor and teacher, John Paul has issued numerous letters and encyclicals including *Centesimus Annus* (1991), a major statement of Catholic teaching on social justice, on the occasion of the one-hundredth anniversary of Pope Leo XIII's encyclical on labor, *Rerum Novarum.* In 1983 he promulgated a new edition of the Code of Canon Law. He makes it a priority to meet with world leaders both on his visits abroad and at the Vatican, and he speaks openly, and sometimes critically, of the world's problems and the responsibilities of world leaders. Interested greatly in the Church's commitment to the poor, he has been quite critical of the defects and excesses of both communism and capitalism. He also has continued the policy of Pope Paul VI in making the college of cardinals more representative of the whole Church.

On the whole, Pope John Paul II has been tireless as spiritual leader of the world's Catholics. Due to much of his own hard work, charisma, and popular style, he has made the papacy an important presence in the modern world.

ANTHONY D. ANDREASSI

See also PAPACY, THE.

JOHN THE BAPTIST

The New Testament texts concerning John the Baptist reflect a very rich and diverse tradition which was developed within the context of his own ministry as well as those of Jesus and the early Christian Church. Except for a brief reference in the works of the Jewish historian Flavius Josephus (*Ant.* 18.5.2 nos. 116-119), these are the only literary sources that are available for an understanding of his person and work. That the Gospel of Thomas or other noncanonical works offer any help in this matter has not been convincingly demonstrated. Of course, since we are dealing with gospel material, we must take into consideration the dynamic of the Christian proclamation which pervades that collection, and even allow, perhaps, for a previous filtering of the historical record by the use of the tradition among the followers of the Baptist himself. Any attempt at separating the various strands of tradition, therefore, is fraught with difficulty and must proceed with utmost caution. There will necessarily be a degree of uncertainty in any reconstruction that follows.

It is surely significant that, in the New Testament, the ministry of John is always associated with that of Jesus. While the tradition uses a number of different models or images to describe John, nowhere does he stand alone or apart from Jesus and the gospel of the Church. John is the one who prepares for, reveals, gives witness to, and even inaugurates its proclamation. With all its diversity, this portrait of John can provide us with access to the process of discernment which begins with the remembrance of his prophetic activity in the wilderness of Judea and culminates in the Fourth Gospel's portrayal of the Baptist as a witness to its own Christology. At the same time, it invites us to hear his call for repentance and to respond as did his own contemporaries and those in the early Church who took up his challenge.

John as Prophet and Evangelist

Perhaps the earliest model used to understand the work of the Baptist was that provided by the text of Isaiah 40:3 and used within the context of his own

St. John the Baptist, detail of oil painting, by Duccio di Buoninsegna, Uffizi Gallery, Florence

ministry: "A voice cries out: 'In the desert prepare the way of the Lord! Make straight in the wasteland a highway for our God!'." As we have it now, this reference to Isaiah is found only in Mark 1:2-4 par. as part of an adapted and expanded citation of Scripture which has already taken on Christological implications, and in John 1:23 where it is placed in the mouth of the Baptist himself. It may also stand behind the Christian summary of his preaching which we find in both Mark 1:7-8 and Q (Matt 3:11 par. Luke 3:16) as well as in John 1:26-27 which makes explicit the Christological implications of the earlier citations of Isaiah: "One mightier than I is coming after me . . . he will baptize you with the Holy Spirit (and fire)."

This same Isaiah text was used by the Qumran community to justify its own withdrawal to the desert, not far from the place where the Fourth Gospel tells us that John was baptizing (John 3:23). Although it is not likely that John was a member of the Qumran group, the Isaiah text was ready at hand to lend support to a ministry that was challenging and provocative. John's call from the wilderness was a powerfully symbolic word to all of Israel; an invitation to return to its roots in the desert, there to take part in a ritual baptism in the waters of the Jordan, and thus stand purified for the visitation of its Lord. In the spirit of Isaiah, it was an announcement of grace and, as Matthew would have it, a joyous proclamation of the coming of God's kingdom (Matt 3:2). His call for repentance was a call for recognition that the vision (of God's coming) which he proclaimed was true; that indeed he had the authority to proclaim his message as the word of God itself. It is clear from both the New Testament and from Josephus, that his words did not fall on deaf ears!

At the same time, the tradition provides us with a text that reflects another aspect of John's preaching: "You brood of vipers!. . . Do not presume to say to yourselves, 'We have Abraham as our father'. . . (for) the ax is already laid to the root of the tree!" (Matt 3:7-10; par. Luke 3:7-9). This portrait of John as an apocalyptic prophet of imminent judgment differs markedly from the remainder of the Baptist tradition, but, in the mind of many exegetes, it is more likely than the rest to represent his actual preaching. That may be the case, but there is a possibility that this tradition finds its home not in the ministry of John, but in the reaction of those Christian missionaries who saw the rejection of their own preaching as a continuation of the history of persecution suffered by the prophets since the time of Jeremiah (Acts 7:51-53). This is not to deny that such a pronouncement might reflect the dark side of John's proclamation (see Matt 3:12 par. Luke 3:17). But there is reason to believe that, as it now stands, it has been exaggerated by the new circumstance of the Christian preachers, under whose influence it has become a radical image of judgment and curse hurled at those who had not accepted their (his) call to repentance.

He is Elijah!

Matthew suggests the likely situation that the Pharisees and Sadducees were among those who could not accept John's call to repentance. For these upholders of the status quo, John was not a prophet at all, rather he gave every sign of being possessed by evil spirits. After all, what authority would the son of a rural priest have had for such a call to conversion on the part of all Israel? Who did he think he was? The charge of demon possession that was leveled against him (Matt 11:18; par. Luke 7:33) was an attempt on their part to undermine his reputation as a prophet and thus neutralize any influence he would have had among the people. In first-century Palestinian society, any such challenge to John's honor would have been met by an equally aggressive countermove by those who had chosen to follow him.

Of course, not the least of these was Jesus. He had been baptized by John and, according to the Fourth Gospel, had joined him in his ministry (John 3:22; 4:1), and had even drawn his first disciples from among his followers (John 1:35-51). His high regard for John certainly stands at the background of the scene in Matthew in which he proclaims him as the greatest of all prophets, "the Elijah who is to come" (Matt 11:14). In its present context in Matthew's

Gospel, Jesus' statement represents a Christian reflection on the role of John in salvation history. In its simplest form, however, it would have been a straightforward comparison of John to Elijah, the prophetic troublemaker of Israel. As such it would have served as a response to the charges made against his honor. Its position as a word of Jesus would certainly account for the predominant use of this imagery in the remainder of the tradition, for once this image of John as Elijah had entered the tradition about the Baptist, it was to serve as the most fruitful model for the developing Baptist theology which would later take place within the Christian movement after the death and resurrection of Jesus.

John as Precursor and Witness to the Messiah

According to the tradition reflected in Acts 2:36, the proclamation of the crucified Jesus as Lord and Messiah was an Easter event. This same connection between his divine sonship and his resurrection can be seen in the primitive confession of faith found in Romans 1:3-5: "Jesus . . . (was) made Son of God in power according to the spirit of holiness by (his) resurrection from the dead." It was in light of this proclamation that the problem of John's relationship to the *Kyrios Iesous* would be posed in a radically new way, for it presented a challenge to their memory of the history of John and of his baptism of Jesus. This can be seen to be reflected at one level in the scene that Matthew has added to the narrative of the baptism of Jesus, where John protests, "I need to be baptized by you, and yet you are coming to me?" The answer of Jesus in this instance seeks a solution in the overall notion of conformity to the will of God: "Allow it for now, for thus it is fitting for us to fulfill all righteousness" (Matt 3:14-15).

A second, and perhaps more satisfying approach was to be found in the affirmation of the Church's remembrance of the Baptist's history. John had come before Jesus; his way had surely prepared the way of their Lord. Through an expansion of the Elijah image which was applied to him during his own lifetime, and its association with the original Isaiah preaching of John, the early Church was able to present an understanding of John which was in line with their own recognition of Jesus as Messiah and true to their remembrance of the way things were. This was possible by their assimilation of the texts of Malachi 3:1 and Exodus 23:20 to Isaiah 40:3, and the application of the resultant John-Elijah model in a way not previously found in Jewish tradition.

This developed image of John as Elijah is found primarily in the Gospels of Mark and Matthew. Perhaps the ambiguity of the model accounts for its seeming avoidance on the part of Luke and the forceful denial of any such relationship by the Fourth Gospel (John 1:21-23). There John's role is to witness to the Messiahship of Jesus. This image is first introduced in John 1:6-8, "There was a man named John sent by God, who came as a witness to testify to the light, so that through him all men might believe—but only to testify to the light, for he himself was not the light." John is presented as subordinate to Jesus, "A man is coming after me who ranks ahead of me because he existed before me" (1:30). His role is to testify to Jesus, "the one who comes from heaven . . . who speaks the words of God" (3:31-36). While it may be that this development of the tradition was prompted by an unwillingness of some followers of the Baptist to accept the Messiahship of Jesus in preference to that of John, the evidence for this is not strong. It is clear, however, that the testimony which John gives is the testimony of the Church, who has seen and can testify "that (Jesus) is the Son of God!" (1:34).

The feast days of John the Baptist are 24 June and 29 August.

CARL R. KAZMIERSKI

See also BIBLE, NEW TESTAMENT WRITINGS.

JOSEPH, ST. (IN THE NEW TESTAMENT)

Through the legal paternity of Joseph, Jesus was called the Son of David. Matthew traced Joseph's ancestry through Jacob back to Solomon (1:6, 16), and Luke traced it through Eli to Nathan (3:23, 31). Jesus' contemporaries regarded Joseph as the legal father of Jesus (Luke 4:22; John 1:45; 6:42), though the Gospels affirm that Jesus was conceived not by Joseph but by the Holy Spirit (Matt 1:18; Luke 1:35). Joseph worked as a *tektōn* (Matt 13:55), usually translated "carpenter" but probably better understood as "builder" or "artisan." Joseph is a major character only in Matthew 1–2. Puzzled by Mary's pregnancy, Joseph goes through with marriage to her when reassured by an angel in a dream that it is part of God's plan revealed in the Scriptures (1:18-25). In response to subsequent divine communications in dreams, Joseph along with Mary and Jesus eludes Herod's plan to kill Jesus (2:12), flees into Egypt (2:13), and returns to Nazareth (2:19-20). Matthew portrays Joseph as a "just man," the model of openness to and trust in God. Because Joseph is absent from Jesus' adult life in the Gospels, it is often assumed that he had died by then and so may have been relatively old when he married Mary. The gospel references to the "brothers and sisters" of Jesus (Matt 12:46-50; 13:55-56; Mark 3:31-35) have sometimes been explained as Joseph's children from a previous marriage that ended in his wife's death. In later apocryphal gospels (*Protevangelium of James, Infancy Gospel of Thomas, Story of Joseph the Carpenter,* etc.), Joseph plays even more prominent and often fantastic roles.

DANIEL J. HARRINGTON, S.J.

See also INFANCY NARRATIVES, THE; SAINTS.

JOSEPH, ST., DEVOTION TO

Popular devotion to St. Joseph has grown greatly in the last two centuries. But in the early centuries, he seems to have had little impact on Christian devotional or artistic life. Historians have noted that, in the eighth and ninth centuries, Joseph received wide recognition and veneration among the Copts in Egypt, and devotion among the Crusaders—who built a church in his honor in Nazareth—indicates that the foster father of Jesus had found a place in the spiritual life of the West. The preaching of the Franciscans, especially of St. Bernadino of Siena (1380–1444) spread the cult of St. Joseph, and Sixtus IV, a Franciscan, mandated that the feast of St. Joseph be universally celebrated. The solemnity of St. Joseph is now celebrated on 19 March. In 1870, Pius IX declared Joseph patron of the Universal Church. In 1956, the feast of St. Joseph's Patrocinium, a universal feast since 1847, was abolished and replaced by the new feast of St. Joseph the Worker on 1 May. This feast was reduced to an optional memorial in 1969, with the reminder that it could be celebrated on any country's labor day, regardless of the date.

In recent decades, devotion to St. Joseph has taken on a new impetus. Joseph, the artisan of Nazareth, has been popularly designated as the patron of real estate, whose intercession is widely sought in the selling of houses.

JOSEPH QUINN

See also SAINTS.

JOSEPHISM

See HERESY/HERETICS.

JUBILEE YEAR

See HOLY YEAR.

JUDAISM

Jewish self-understanding has undergone many changes over the course of centuries. Periods of communal decline have generally been followed by new expressions of political, cultural, and religious creativity. Certainly Jewish history has not been marked by stagnation as some scholars have claimed. As one surveys the march of the Jewish people through history, what is especially striking is their continued capacity for adaptation to new circumstances. This has not always come easily, but generally it has come.

Even during the biblical era, the time from the initial coming together of the disparate tribes into a peoplehood entrusted with a covenantal mandate until the conclusion of the Maccabean Wars (ca. 150 B.C.), Jewish religious understanding and expression experienced numerous changes. A major reinterpretation of the meaning of the original covenantal tradition is to be found, for example, in Deuteronomy. And in the prophetic literature there is significant re-evaluation of the relationship between cultic worship and justice. And in what was already the post-biblical period for Jews the wisdom writings followed by the Pharisaic-rabbinic movement transformed Jewish faith and communal life in some fundamental ways. This transformation made it possible for the community to survive, and at times even to prosper, in a primarily diaspora situation without the Jerusalem Temple and its priesthood which had been integral to its religious and social life for several centuries.

The medieval period created new problems for Jews. Persecution became commonplace in Christian nations. But it also produced, especially in Spain, some new opportunities for unprecedented efforts to relate Jewish theology and philosophy to the Christian and Islamic traditions. With the coming of the modern era and the emergence of democratic, pluralistic societies, Jews began to share in the cultural and political life of their societies to a degree previously unknown. This period was also marked by the rise of new Jewish religious movements as first Reform Judaism came on the scene in Germany and spread to other parts of Europe and to North America, followed by Conservative Judaism and most recently the Reconstructionist movement. The latter two branches both represented efforts to bridge the gap between classical Orthodox Judaism and its Reform counterpart.

In the twentieth century two events have exercised a profound impact in shaping Jewish consciousness: the annihilation of six million Jews by the Nazis (called Shoah or Holocaust) and the re-establishment of an independent Jewish national homeland by the United Nations in 1948. Though Jews are hardly in agreement on the ultimate significance of these two events, they have become central in one way or another for nearly all of them. And while the Jewish community certainly does not regard Israel as compensation for the horror of the Shoah, many Jews do speak of an interconnection between the two realities. On occasion theological language of death/resurrection (imported from Christianity) is used to describe the relationship between the two.

As we reflect on the many sweeping changes that have transformed practices and social structures in world Jewry, we notice the persistence of several major themes that have continued to shape communal identity in the midst of otherwise profound changes. The first of these pervasive themes is *covenant/peoplehood.* It has both a universalist side as well as a particularistic dimension. The universal aspect is to be found in chapter nine of Genesis where God is said to have forged a covenant with all humankind after the great flood (Gen 9:9-11). God set a rainbow in the sky as the permanent sign of this pact with the human family. The more particularistic side follows upon the narrative of the covenant with all humankind through Noah and his sons. God now turns to Abraham and promises the patriarch that he would become the father of a great and numerous nation and that the land of Canaan would remain its perpetual possession. Finally, at Mount Sinai, God seals a special covenantal relationship with the entire people of Israel. The twenty-fourth chapter of Exodus describes the actual covenant-making ceremony which included a sacrifice.

As presented in Genesis, the special covenant between Abraham and Israel does not invalidate the earlier covenant with Noah. Rather, it imposes a set of new responsibilies upon the Israelite people in the areas of worship and ethics in particular. It also gives them a distinctive mission—to bring the knowledge of the one loving God to all of humankind. In return Israel received an assurance of special blessings and protection if the mission is faithfully pursued. But the special covenant with Israel also included a warning that failure to fulfill its obligations would bring dire consequences for the community, though the promise was given of divine faithfulness to Israel till the end of days, come what may (a promise recalled by St. Paul in Romans). Though sinfulness would be punished, the basic bond would remain intact forever.

The meaning and expression of the Sinai covenant took on varied forms in the course of history. Within the Bible itself we find reinterpretation in the later prophets such as Hosea where marriage imagery begins to replace legal terminology as well as in Deuteronomy and Ecclesiasticus. During the Pharisaic-rabbinic period a growing sense of personal intimacy with a Father God was added to covenantal understanding and the family meal became more and more the center of covenantal reaffirmation. Faithfulness to Torah in worship and in deed became the keystone of preserving Jewish covenantal existence during the centuries Jews lived as minorities among the peoples of Europe, the Middle East, North Africa, and the Americas. Some Jews, especially in Poland, developed a new covenantal piety called Hasidism rooted in a direct, mystical encounter with the Creator God.

The Enlightenment produced new possibilities for Jewish life outside the confines of the ghetto. This political liberation led some Jews to begin to view any notion of a special relationship between God and Israel as obsolete. In recent years various efforts have emerged to refocus attention on the centrality of the covenant. Both Conservative and Reconstructionist Judaism, albeit in differing ways, have tried to restore the covenantal notion of Jewish peoplehood to its earlier centrality. And even some in Reform Judaism which tended to emphasize a fairly individualistic interpretation of Jewish life have begun to stress anew a sense of peoplehood. The various strains of Zionism, some of which have a deeply religious base, have moved the biblical land tradition, intimately tied to covenant and peoplehood, to center stage after its virtual abandonment by most of Reform Jewry. And the Shoah has sparked a profound theological debate whether the experience demands the final renunciation of the covenant or in fact summons Jews to make covenant central to the rebuilding of Jewish identity in a post-Shoah age.

Torah is the second central theme of Jewish identity. The term is difficult to translate, being in fact far more complex and extensive that the usual English equivalent "law." In its widest sense "Torah" signifies a deed performed in conformity with the obligations of the covenant as defined by leading Jewish teachers. More narrowly, it includes all Jewish religious writings, including the Hebrew Scriptures, the Talmud, the Responsa literature, rabbinic commentaries, and so forth.

Traditional Judaism regards the Torah as God's revelatory gift to the Jewish People. It represents the very embodiment of God's word and God's presence. Hence Torah scrolls are kept in the ark (or tabernacle) and are carried in procession, much as Catholics have traditionally done with the Eucharist. For traditional Jews everything within the Torah is from God, especially the teachings found in the Pentateuch.

The newer Jewish movements have all moved away from rigid Torah interpretation to some degree. Some parts of Reform Judaism virtually abandoned it, or left it entirely to personal interpretation. There is now generally a greater appreciation of the

Torah tradition within Judaism, but intense debates continue about how far it can, and should, be reinterpretated in light of contemporary scientific knowledge and social changes. The ordination of women rabbis is but one example of such a continuing dispute.

The third major continuing component of Jewish identity—*land*—is closely related to the covenantal tradition. It was part of the original covenantal grant. Important sectors of Reform Judaism did turn against this tradition for a time, opposing the growth of the Zionist movement which successfully recreated a Jewish political state in Palestine. But that opposition has now practically disappeared, even though arguments continue regarding the exact meaning of the land tradition. But few Jews today deny its centrality. And for many, land assumes within the covenantal framework a theological significance equal in importance to peoplehood and Torah. It is seen as integral to the concreteness of the Jewish understanding of religious existence.

The enhanced, positive understanding of Judaism that has developed in recent decades has generated fundamental reconsideration of Christianity's classical understanding of its relationship to the Jewish People. This process began in earnest in Europe right after World War II. Pope John XXIII and Vatican Council II gave it official endorsement in the conciliar declaration *Nostra Aetate.* Chapter four of that document repudiates the historic deicide charge, the basis for the patristic notion that Christians had replaced Jews in the covenantal relationship, and re-emphasized (quoting St. Paul) the enduring covenantal bond between God and the People Israel and hence between Jews and Christians today. Further Vatican statements in 1975 and 1985, as well as numerous statements from Pope John Paul II, have re-emphasized these points and expanded on them. While we have a long way to go in fashioning a fully developed theology of the Church's relationship with the Jewish People, it is clear that such a theology must be rooted in a sense of deep Christian-Jewish bonding and in an understanding of how profoundly and constructively the Jewish biblical tradition, as well as parts of Second Temple Judaism, impacted the teachings of Jesus and St. Paul.

JOHN T. PAWLIKOWSKI, O.S.M.

See also COVENANT; ELECTION; THEOLOGY, BIBLICAL.

JULIAN CALENDAR

The name given to the calendar established by Julius Caesar to reform the lunar calendar used in the Roman Republic. By 46 B.C. there was a three-month gap between the Roman calendrical equinox and the astronomical or actual equinox. Caesar, ever the practical man as well as dictator and *pontifex maximus* (chief priest), utilized the services of the Alexandrian astronomer Sosigenes and added sixty-seven days between November and December, thus making 46 B.C. a year of 445 days. To make sure the old discrepancies did not creep back in, Caesar abandoned the lunar calendar and substituted a solar one. Sosigenes had calculated that a solar year was 365.25 days, a remarkably accurate estimate for that age, but since no working calendar could include a quarter of a day, Caesar decided to set the year at 365 days and to add one more day every four years (Leap Year). In 44 B.C. the Romans renamed the month Quintilis as July in Caesar's memory. The Christians adopted the Julian Calendar, but they faced the difficulty of reconciling their earliest festivals, based upon the Jewish calendar, with the Julian one; this was especially true of the feast of Easter, hitherto determined by the date of Passover. The Easter Controversy set West against East, with the latter favoring Jewish dating and the former favoring Roman dating. The feast of Christmas depended completely on the Julian Calendar; it replaced the feast of the birthday of the Unconquered Sun (*Sol Invictus*) which fell on the winter solstice, dated to 25 December in the third century. Since Sosigenes had miscalculated the length of the year, which was eleven minutes and fourteen seconds shorter than 365.25 days, the Julian Calendar deviated from astronomical time by approximately three days every four centuries. By 1582 the deviation had grown to ten days, which led another Roman *pontifex maximus,* Pope Gregory XIII (1572–1585) to reform the calendar. His reformed calendar, known as the Gregorian Calendar, is the one commonly in use today.

JOSEPH F. KELLY

See also GREGORIAN CALENDER; LITURGY.

JULIAN OF NORWICH (1342/1343–ca. 1416)

Most of what is known about Julian's life is drawn from *Revelations of Divine Love,* the only extant sample of her writing. There are no empirical data giving evidence of any enduring *cultus* to her, local or otherwise. Her reputation for holiness seems to be based solely on her writings, with the one exception of a brief reference to her by Margery Kempe of Lynn, who notes Julian's expertise in giving good counsel.

By Julian's own account, she was born toward the end of 1342 or the beginning of 1343. In mid-May of 1373, she suffered a grave illness that brought her so close to death that she received the last rites of the

Church. Two days later, however, she recovered. During the course of that day, she received sixteen revelations which she later recognized as true gifts from God. Some time after that experience she began living as an anchoress in a cell attached to the church of Saints Julian and Edward at Conisford, Norwich, where she took for herself the name of that saint, as was the anchorite custom.

At that time, Norwich was a lively center of world trade, a converging point for many languages and cultures from around the world. As an anchoress, however, Julian lived apart from this teeming activity in her cell attached to the church. She devoted her life to prayer, both contemplation and the recitation of the psalms or the Offices of the Church. She also set aside time every day to provide comfort or advice for those who came to see her.

During her many years as an anchoress, Julian wrote two versions of her showings. The first was relatively short and was limited to a descriptive account of what she had experienced that day she recovered from her illness. Approximately twenty years later, she wrote a much longer text that elaborated on the experiences and reflected on their meaning. This second version demonstrates not only her literary talents but also her stature as a mystical theologian capable of correlating her experiences with Scripture and the teaching of Christian tradition.

Julian's revelations fall into three different categories. The first, which speaks of seeing "the red blood running down from under the crown, hot and flowing freely and copiously, a living stream, just as it was at the time when the crown of thorns was pressed on his blessed head," represents what is traditionally termed an "imaginative vision." Five other revelations are of this same type. "Locutions" or what Julian calls "words formed in my understanding" comprise a second category. The third group is made up of intellectual visions, or what she calls "spiritual vision" and about which Augustine had written in *The Literal Meaning of Genesis* and which Teresa of Avila and John of the Cross would discuss in detail two hundred years later (see Dupré and Wiseman, *Light from Light*). In the first "shewing," the figure of Christ on the cross became alive in front of her eyes. Six other showings concerned Christ's passion. Eight dealt with other spiritual truths, and the final showing concerned the indwelling of the Trinity in the soul. Both versions are written in the first person and adopt a narrative tone that is informal and conversational. *Revelations* deals with the knowledge of God and of human beings: what people are in the mercy and grace of God and what they are in sinfulness and weakness.

Many have debated the source of Julian's theology. She is clearly indebted to St. Paul and to St. John. She is very much concerned with sin and damnation, which seem to contradict divine love and goodness and her underlying belief that all shall be well in Christ. Julian says that her writings are for all Christians, yet she is especially concerned with the "little and the simple—those who for love hate sin and dispose themselves to do God's will." This intention is reflected in the title of the first printed edition of the shorter version of *Revelations,* "Comfortable Words for Christ's Lovers." Julian did not think of herself as a theologian or a professional expert of any kind. She says that she was illiterate, suggesting that her book was dictated to a scribe, yet her style is impressively clear and concise. Some modern commentators have proposed that a review of *Revelations* might also suggest that Julian wrote especially for women who are experiencing situations of hopelessness or helplessness. Whether or not this is true, her writings are accessible and of interest to a wide-ranging audience, including non-Christians. Indeed, she has become a rather prominent figure in dialogues between Christians and Buddhists in Asia, especially in discussions of the nature of compassion, love, and humanity (see Pelphrey, "Preface," *Christ Our Mother*). She died around 1416.

PATRICIA DEFERRARI

See also BRITAIN, CHURCH IN; KEMPE, MARGERY; MIDDLE AGES, THE; MYSTICISM; WOMEN IN THE CHURCH.

JUNGMANN, JOSEF (1889–1956)

Born in 1889, Jungmann devoted his life to researching and disseminating the history and theology of Catholic worship. The reform of the liturgy at Vatican II was, in good measure, the harvest of Jungmann's pioneering work, and his influence on those who drafted the Constitution of the Liturgy. A Jesuit scholar, he taught at Collegium Canisianum in Innsbruck, Austria, for many years. He was an indefatigable lecturer in Europe and America, and his literary output was massive. Among his works which were translated into English are *The Eucharistic Prayer* (1956); *The Early Liturgy* (1959); *Handing on the Faith* (1959); *Pastoral Liturgy* (1962); *The Place of Christ in Liturgical Prayer* (1965); *The Mass* (1976); and *Christian Prayer through the Centuries* (1978). He died in 1956.

JOSEPH QUINN

See also LITURGICAL MOVEMENT, THE; LITURGY; VATICAN COUNCIL II.

JUST WAGES

During the nineteenth century the dominant economic philosophy in Western Europe and North America was that wages should be determined by the law of supply and demand. The worker was said to be free to accept or reject the market price for labor; the employer had fulfilled his or her moral obligation by paying the wage agreed to. In this approach, there was no recognition of other moral criteria for determining just wages.

Modern Catholic social ethics has contributed to the extensive attention that has been given this century to the issue of just wages and salaries. It was the harsh reality of poverty and the exploitation of workers that initially led to a re-examination of the starting point for determining just pay. The ethical reflection continues today, still focused on poverty but also now focused as well on the issue of maximum salaries and on the issue of discrimination in compensation practices.

Minimum Wages

Ethical thinking about what is an acceptable minimum wage has, for the most part, rejected a pure market standard (whatever someone is willing to work for) and has insisted that wages paid must, at a minimum, allow the worker to live in dignity. As this principle was expressed in 1989 by the Commission of the European Community in their "Social Charter," "Workers should be paid wages sufficient to support a decent standard of living for themselves and their family." In Catholic documents, this principle has often been called a "living wage" or a "family wage." Full-time employment should be compensated in a manner sufficient to meet ordinary family needs adequately.

It should be noted that the ethically acceptable minimum wage is not necessarily the legally defined minimum wage. It should not be assumed that the U.S. federally mandated minimum wage is always legislated at a level sufficient for someone to satisfy his or her essential needs and those of dependents.

In considering whether compensation is sufficient to meet the needs of individuals and families, increased attention is presently being given to benefits, especially health care insurance. Access to health care is one dimension of a decent standard of living. Unless a comprehensive system of financing health care for all is provided in a given country, it is difficult to see how an employer who does not provide health care benefits (or wages clearly sufficient for employees to purchase such coverage) is meeting the ethical standard for minimum compensation.

Maximum Salaries

The gap between the incomes of the rich and the poor in the United States is great and has been growing in recent years. This raises serious questions about justice; such a difference reflects the uneven distribution of power in society. As the American Catholic bishops said in *Economic Justice for All,* these inequalities "suggest that the level of participation in the political and social spheres is also very uneven" (no. 184). Unequal distribution of income is "detrimental to the development of social solidarity and community" (no. 185). One reason, then, for being concerned about very unequal compensation is the impact upon levels of participation in the economic and political life of the nation.

As a way of trying to address the concern for disparity of wealth and income, some have suggested that standards be established in an organization regarding the gap between the highest paid and the lowest paid. What ratio is accepted (whether, for example, 30–1 or 15–1 or 3–1) makes for a very different application of this approach, of course. It is not yet clear where these efforts to apply ethical standards to maximum salaries will lead.

Equal Pay and Comparable Worth

In addition to a needs standard of fair wages (enough for a decent livelihood), another standard that has acquired widespread support is the equality standard. This principle is primarily designed to prevent wage discrimination based on such factors as gender or race. "Equal pay for equal work" means that individuals who are doing similar work within the same organization should be paid according to the same wage scale. (An unfortunate interpretation of the "family wage" tradition had suggested to some that a woman did not need to be paid as much as a man because the man was thought to have the responsibility to support the family.)

Making sure that pay levels are equal in similar job categories does not, however, address the question of very different rates paid to different jobs or occupations. The gender gap—women earning considerably less than men—is partly the result of the fact that women often work in job categories that are lower paid than those job categories which employ mostly men.

"Comparable worth" is an attempt to address this sort of wage disparity. The argument is that individuals who are doing work that is comparable in terms of skills, responsibility, working conditions, and effort should be paid comparable rates. Where comparable worth policies have been implemented, wages have been significantly increased in many jobs that have been traditionally held by women.

LEONARD J. WEBER

See also ECONOMICS; HUMAN RIGHTS; SOCIAL TEACHING OF THE CHURCH.

JUST WAR

The just war tradition is a body of moral wisdom and a framework for moral reasoning designed to assist a community in discerning when the normally authoritative presumption against war may no longer apply. The criteria associated with just war teaching define the conditions in which violence, which is generally proscribed, may be morally justified and even necessary. The purpose of the just war doctrine is twofold. First, it is a reminder that war is always a moral matter, never simply a political or economic one, and should never be endorsed without serious self-examination and reflection; in this respect, the just war teaching serves to hold societies and individuals morally accountable. Secondly, even though the just war doctrine can approve certain wars as legitimate, it functions to limit and restrain even justified violence; thus, even legitimate war is an exceptional practice that ought to be mourned.

Although distinct from pacifism, just war teaching shares with pacifism the strong conviction that nonviolence has moral priority over violence. Because the obligation not to injure or harm others (the duty of nonmaleficence) is intrinsically binding, any recourse to violence must be stringently justified; in every instance, the priority of peace and nonviolence is presumed and the burden of proof is on the one who wants to resort to war. The moral priority of peace and nonviolence remains unless it can be shown that short of war values central to humanity would be lost. Traditionally, just war teaching has accepted that the presumption against war may be overridden for equal or more pressing moral duties such as protecting the innocent or restoring peace.

Historically, the just war tradition was preceded by pacifism. Prior to A.D. 312, from the persecution of the Church to the time of Constantine, pacifism was normative for Christianity. War was prohibited for Christians first because of the danger of idolatry in military service (soldiers might be asked to offer sacrifices to the emperor), and secondly because killing, even of an aggressor, was judged a direct violation of Jesus's command that Christians love their enemies and overcome evil with good.

With the accession of Constantine, however, the Church was no longer a persecuted sect but had attained official status within the Roman Empire. An alliance was forged between the empire and the Church in which the emperor was to safeguard the well-being of the Church and the Church was to defend and support the interests of the empire. During this period of close relationship between the Church and society, Christianity's commitment to pacifism declined and the first outlines of just war teaching appeared, specifically through Ambrose and Augustine. The close identification of the interests of the empire and the interests of the Church, particularly against the invading barbarians, prompted Ambrose to argue that war, even for Christians, could be justified.

It was Augustine, however, who offered a more fully developed teaching on the justification of war. He argued that instead of violating Jesus's commandment of love, violence could be a requirement of Christian love if it were necessary to protect one's neighbor, especially the innocent and the weak, from unjust harm. In a sinful and imperfect world, Augustine reasoned, violence is sometimes necessary to restrain evildoers and insure a relative justice and peace. Augustine acknowledged the moral priority of nonviolence because he believed God meant men and women to live in peace with one another; however, because of original sin he also believed such peace was constantly beset by conflict. Amidst such turmoil and chaos, Christians were obliged to protect their neighbors from unjust attack even if doing so required violence.

As the just war doctrine developed, eight criteria for guiding its application emerged. These are rigorous conditions which must be satisfied for war to be morally justified. Too, they function to insure that the presumption in favor of peace and against war can be overriden only for extremely serious reasons. The first seven criteria are used to determine the right to go to war (*jus ad bellum*), and the final one determines right conduct within war (*jus in bello*). Both are relevant because a country that might be justified in resorting to war could be unjustified in the means it employed; or, conversely, it could fight by justifiable means a war it never should have undertaken. The seven criteria that determine whether a war could be just are: (1) just cause, (2) competent authority, (3) last resort, (4) comparative justice, (5) proportionality, (6) right intention, and (7) probability of success.

Just cause is the most basic of the criteria for legitimating a particular war. Traditionally, just cause has included protecting people from unjust attack, restoring rights that have been wrongly taken away, and defending or restoring a just political order. The criterion of last resort demands that if there are nonviolent ways of restoring justice and protecting the innocent, they must be pursued. War is justified only after all peaceful alternatives have been attempted and failed. Comparative justice reminds both sides of a conflict that neither one is absolutely just. Proportionality implies that even a war which has just cause cannot be pursued if the evils to be suffered through the war significantly outweigh the goods which might be gained. Right intention refers to the purpose or objective of war. Even for just cause, war is legitimate only when the abiding intention for undertaking it is not hatred or vindictiveness, but a better and more just peace.

Right conduct within war (*jus in bello*) is guided by the principle of proportionate means and discrimination. Proportionate means demands that conduct within war be ruled by justice and measured to the peace to be restored. The principle of discrimination forbids direct and intentional attack upon noncombatants in war. Noncombatants would include enemy military who are wounded or have surrendered.

The just war doctrine is an important part of the Catholic moral tradition; however, in recent years, given technological advances and nuclear weapons, the principles of this teaching have prompted many to ask if war can ever be just. This question was raised by the U.S. Bishops in their 1983 pastoral letter, *The Challenge of Peace: God's Promise and Our Response.* The bishops affirmed the just war doctrine and then used its criteria to argue that under no circumstances could they foresee even limited nuclear war to be justified. Following the tradition, they concluded that the burden of proof is on those who claim restricted nuclear war could be just.

Finally, given the danger that just war teaching could be abused as a rationalization for war, a crucial question is that of competent authority. Whose responsibility is it to apply the just war criteria in a conflict situation? In the past, governments and political leaders were seen as the legitimate authorities for determining the rightness of a war. Many today, however, are reluctant to make the state the sole arbiter of the just war teaching because governments are prone to use the doctrine to legitimate their desire to go to war. In this respect, the Church must be a community of moral formation and deliberation in which the just war teaching can be discussed, refined, and applied. It is only within such a community dedicated to peace that the just war tradition's strong presumption against violence can be sustained.

PAUL WADELL

See also PACIFISM; PEACE; PROPORTIONALITY; SOCIAL TEACHING OF THE CHURCH.

JUSTICE

See VIRTUE.

JUSTIFICATION

In Catholic theology "justification" refers to the event in which God changes human beings from a state of injustice or sin to a state of righteousness or grace before God. This change is brought about by God through human beings' grace-filled faith in the incarnation, life, death, and resurrection of Jesus Christ through whom human beings are reconciled to God. Justification must be seen within the larger context of God's salvific will for human beings in Jesus Christ. It is the free gift of a loving God, a gift which human beings cannot earn and which they can lose by their unfaithfulness. This free gift is first of all the self-communication of God to human beings through the presence of the Holy Spirit (uncreated grace). It is also the resulting transformation of human beings through the presence of that self-communicating God (created grace). This transformation is not something that can be known with certainty but must be worked out in hope and love, and with "fear and trembling" (Phil 2:12).

The term "justification" is derived from the Latin *iustificatio/iustitia* which is a translation of the Greek term *dikaiosunē* and indirectly of the Hebrew terms *ṣedeq* and *ṣ^edāqā*. All of the terms mean "justice" or "righteousness." The Hebrew verb *ṣādaq* means "to be just"; its causative form (*hiṣdîq*) (Greek: *dikaioō*) means "to justify," "to declare righteous," "to acquit." In the Old Testament all were basically forensic terms connected with legal actions in which a judge or a tribunal declared or found someone just or innocent of a charge (Deut 25:1). It was important, however, that the judgments reflected reality, that the just be found innocent and the guilty condemned; otherwise justice was perverted (Prov 17:15). The attribute of justice or judging justly was applied especially to God (Isa 50:8; 1 Kgs 8:32; Ps 103:6), and human beings were expected to act and judge justly because of God (Deut 6:25; Isa 1:27). In postexilic Judaism, God's righteousness was connected particularly with the faithful vindication of his covenant relationship with Israel (Isa 51:4-5) and, at Qumran, with the forgiveness of sins (*Rule of the Community* 11.2-3, 12).

In the New Testament the Greek terms *dikaiosunē* and *dikaioō* were used in a variety of ways consistent with their use in the Old Testament. The terms first appeared in creedal summaries now imbedded in other New Testament documents (e.g., 1 Cor 6:11; Rom 4:24-25). In the Gospel of Matthew, the term "justification/righteousness" was used to refer to

God's salvation (5:6; 6:33) as well as the proper human response to that salvation (5:10; 6:1). For later Christian theology and theological controversies, however, the most important uses of the terms are found in the letters of Paul and in the Letter of James and concern the notion of "justification by faith." While the term "justification by faith" is pre-Pauline (Gal 2:15-21), Paul certainly sharpened the meaning of the term, especially by contrasting it with justification through the observance of the Mosaic Law. Through his own conversion experience (Gal 1:15-17; Acts 9:1-19) Paul became convinced of two things: (1) his experience of the risen Jesus was so central that nothing else could be of equal value, even the observance of the Mosaic Law; and (2) the gospel of the risen Jesus had to be preached to the Gentiles. Paul emphasized that justification was a free gift of God for both Jews and Gentiles and took place by faith in Jesus Christ *apart* from the observance of the Mosaic Law (Gal 2:15-21; Rom 3:21-31). For Paul justification by faith rather than by observance of the Mosaic Law served to break down the barrier between Jewish Christians and Gentile Christians. For Paul justification by faith as a free gift of God was central, but he also used a number of other significant concepts and images to understand the same reality: salvation (2 Cor 7:10), expiation of sins (Rom 3:25), reconciliation of sinners to God (2 Cor 5:18-20), adoption (Gal 4:5), freedom (Rom 8:1-2, 21), sanctification (1 Cor 1:2, 30), glorification (Rom 8:30), and a new creation (Gal 6:15; 2 Cor 5:17). Toward the end of the first century A.D. Paul's contrast between justification by faith and justification *by observance of the Mosaic Law* was turned into a contrast between justification by faith and justification *by human works or human actions in general.* This misinterpretation of Paul provoked the reaction found in the Letter of James (2:14-26), in which the author of the Letter of James inveighed against the notion that faith without subsequent works is enough. For him "faith without works is dead" (2:26); the Christian must have both faith and the actions which follow from faith.

For much of the patristic period, justification was neither a central nor a controversial notion. It appeared primarily in connection with the liturgy of Christian baptism and its interpretation. In baptism previous sins were forgiven, and the baptized became participators in the life of Christ. In the Greek East the latter was emphasized, often through the notion of "divinization" (*theōsis* or *theopoiēsis*) while in the Latin West the former received more emphasis.

The interpretation of justification became much more important and contested in the Latin West primarily because of the Pelagian controversies and Augustine's (354–430) role in the controversies. In the early fifth century, the British ascetic Pelagius began to teach that Christians should and could strive for and achieve perfection in this present life. In opposition to Pelagius, Augustine emphasized that perfection was impossible to achieve through human efforts. The differences between the two were rooted in different anthropologies. For Augustine, human nature and human freedom were much more deeply flawed by original sin than Pelagius allowed for. In addition, Augustine, through his interpretations of Paul, emphasized that justification was by grace alone (*sola gratia*), that is, human beings were transformed by a gift of God and not as the result of human efforts toward perfection. Augustine emphasized the importance of the practice of the virtues, especially that of love; but for him it was crucial to understand that even acts of love were the result of God's grace. Human beings after the forgiveness of their sins in baptism were transformed by God's grace; but, because concupiscence (the tendency to sin) remained, the transformation was slow and never finally achieved in this present life.

In the medieval period, discussions of the doctrine of justification were primarily attempts to interpret the legacy of Augustine. While medieval theologians such as Thomas Aquinas (1225–1274) emphasized the primacy of grace, there was also great interest in the various stages and ways in which human beings were transformed by grace. By the end of the medieval period these discussions often became bewilderingly complex, especially under the influence of nominalism, and their emphasis on the human response to or reception of grace set the stage for the Reformation debates of the sixteenth century.

During the Protestant Reformation the doctrine of justification became a major point of contention between Roman Catholics and Protestant Reformers such as Martin Luther (1483–1546) and John Calvin (1509–1564). The Reformers went beyond Augustine's conviction that salvation was by "grace alone" to emphasize justification by "faith alone" (*sola fide*). Like Augustine, they appealed to passages in the letters of Paul (especially Galatians and Romans). Sinners are justified before God by faith in Christ alone; their "works" are pleasing in God's sight only "on account of Christ" (*propter Christum*). The Reformers turned away from the Augustinian and medieval model of justification as a progressive transformation to the view that justification was in some real sense complete once it had been "imputed" or attributed to the sinner. The believer, however, remained simultaneously a righteous person and yet still a sinner (*simul justus et peccator*). Only this imputed and still "alien righteousness" (*iustitia aliena*) of Christ exposed human sinfulness for what it was in its totality. The Protestant Reformers were reacting in part against trends in the late medieval period. They saw the late medieval emphasis on the human response to grace as a form of Pelagianism or "works-righteousness," in which human beings in effect achieved righteousness rather than received it as a free and unmerited gift of God. The Reformers also found in justification by faith alone the answer to Luther's anguished question "How do I find a gracious God?" For them this question and its subsequent anguish were also rooted in the late medieval tendency to ascribe salvation partly to human effort. Justification by faith alone was meant to console anxious consciences terrified by their inability to perform the good works supposedly necessary for salvation.

The Catholic response was stated in the Decree on Justification (1547) by the Council of Trent. Like the Reformers, Trent affirmed both the universal reality of human sinfulness (original sin) and that the justification of human beings was by faith in Christ, that is, it was a free gift (grace) of God which human beings could not merit. Trent went on to affirm, however, against what they took to be the Reformers' position, that faith was not a "living" faith unless hope and charity were also added to it. These were, according to Trent, also gifts of God infused in the believer as a result of faith and baptism. While agreeing with the Reformers that justification always had to be seen as an act of God, Trent insisted that justification was a real, although incomplete, transformation of the believer. Justification was not simply "imputed" but represented a real change in the believer. Because of this Trent rejected the notion that the believer was at once both a righteous person and yet still a sinner (*simul justus et peccator*). While concupiscence remained after baptism, it was not as such sinful but only a tendency to sin.

During the next four hundred years both Catholic and Protestant Churches continued to refine their own positions, often over against caricatures of each other's positions. In the latter part of the twentieth century and especially since Vatican II, Catholics and Protestants have come to see that their conceptions of justification are not nearly so far apart as was once thought. They have come to understand that, because of the polemics of the sixteenth century and their aftermath, both Catholics and Protestants have failed to grasp the positive values of each other's interpretations of the doctrine of justification. While there continues to be significant differences at least in emphasis, both Protestants and Catholics have come to see the close similarities of many of their positions on justification. Both Catholics and Protestants agree that because of original sin all human beings stand in need of justification. They agree that justification is a free gift of God in Jesus Christ and that this free gift which is received in faith and trust cannot be merited. They also agree that justification effects the inner renewal of the believer and leads to good works. There are, however, still significant differences at least in emphasis. In general, Protestants continue to see "justification" as a more central or organizing principle than do Catholics. Catholics and Protestants also tend to evaluate differently the human situation both before and after justification. Protestants emphasize more the pervasiveness of the *effects* of original sin, and so they see less human receptivity for and cooperation with justification than do Catholics. After justification Catholics tend to emphasize the extent to which believers can be transformed by grace and can become capable of good works. These good works, while always performed through God's grace, can be meritorious. Protestants, while admitting that believers can perform good works, are suspicious of the language of transformation as well as of speaking of any rewards for good works as "merited." While granting that these differences in emphasis are still significant and that they result in different religious sensibilities, it is an open question whether they still need be seen as Church-dividing issues.

THOMAS TOBIN, S.J.

See also GRACE; REFORMATION, THE; SOTERIOLOGY.

JUSTIN MARTYR, ST. (ca. 100–ca. 165)

Born of pagan parents in Flavia Neapolis, a city established by Vespasian near the ruins of the ancient Shechem (modern-day Nablus). Justin's search for truth moved him to investigate the schools of the Stoics, Peripatetics, Pythagoreans, Platonists and to become a Christian (between 130 and 135). During the reign of Antoninus Pius (138 to 161) Justin moved to Rome where he opened a school. Tatian was one of his students. Justin was strongly opposed by Crescens, a Cynic philosopher. Between 148 and 161 he wrote his *Apologies* addressed to Antoninus Pius and his *Dialogue with Trypho,* the oldest existing Christian apology against the Jews. Justin was the first Christian thinker who tried to reconcile faith and reason. Justin taught that God's saving plan was made manifest in Christ the Logos. He held that elements of truth could be found in pagan thinkers because in every person there was a "seed of the Logos," which came from the Seminal Word

(*Logos spermatikos*). Christians, on the other hand, knew the incarnate Word. The reason the Word became flesh was to teach people the truth and to redeem them from the power of the demons. Justin's stress on the transcendence of God led him to what would be a Subordinationist doctrine of the Son, although his theological intention was orthodox. Being well aware of St. Paul's contrast between Christ and Adam, Justin was the first author who also contrasted Mary with Eve. His eschatology strongly emphasizes the second coming of Christ and is chiliastic. In addition to these concerns Justin also responded in his *First Apology* to charges of immorality that had been leveled against Christians. The *First Apology* is also an important witness to second-century liturgical belief and practice (particularly in regard to baptism and Eucharist). Justin and six companions were denounced as Christians. When they refused to offer sacrifice, they were scourged and then beheaded, probably in 165. An authentic account of their martyrdom, based on an official court report, survives. Feast day, 1 June.

JOHN DILLON

See also FATHERS OF THE CHURCH.

K

KATAPHATIC/CATAPHATIC THEOLOGY

A theology that makes positive statements about God in contrast to a negative theology (apophatic) which tells us what God is not.

MICHAEL GLAZIER

See also APOPHATIC THEOLOGY; PRAYER; SPIRITUAL LIFE.

KAVANAGH, PATRICK (1905–1967)

One of the most respected modern Irish poets was the son of a small farmer and shoemaker. After working on the farm for some years, he moved to Dublin in 1939, penniless but hopeful. "Looking back, I see that the big tragedy for the poet is poverty. I had no money and no profession except that of a small farmer. . . . On many occasions I literally starved in Dublin." His work includes *The Ploughman & Other Poems* (1936); *A Soul for Sale* (1947); his searing rural novel *Tarry Flynn* (1948). His most memorable poem is *The Great Hunger* (1942) which contrasts the realistic and raw life of poverty, frustration and humdrum desperation of an Irish peasant with the fanciful, idealized, pleasant life of the Irish literary revival. In 1952 he and his brother Peter founded *Kavanagh's Weekly,* a controversial newssheet which had a brief and turbulent life. Kavanagh became an Irish "character"; but his hard-drinking and iconoclastic ways did not detract from his deep poetic sensitivity. Here is one of his short poems titled "To A Child."

Patrick Kavanagh

Child do not go
Into the dark places of the soul,
For there the grey wolves whine,
The lean grey wolves.

I have been down
Among the unholy ones who tear
Beauty's white robe and clothe her
In rags of prayer.

Child there is light somewhere
Under a star,
Sometime it will be for you
A window that looks
Inward to God.

MICHAEL GLAZIER

See also CATHOLICISM, IRISH.

KEARNEY, JOHN (1865–1941)

Born in County Tipperary, Kearney was educated in Blackrock College and in the novitiate and seminary of the Holy Ghost Congregation in France. Ordained a priest, he was assigned to the teaching staff of Blackrock College, specializing in scientific subjects. He devoted his talent as musician to Church music. After some years he suffered a health breakdown with nervous effects. Restored to fairly good health, he was appointed rector of the senior seminary. It was a time when recruitment to the congregation was rapidly expanding. Exemplary and dedicated, he strictly upheld the seminary rules of the time, training a whole generation of missionaries (including bishops) and educators who marked the life of the Church in Ireland, several African states, Brazil, and the West Indies. Not powerfully intuitive, Kearney's influence was through his own self-discipline, and through unfailing delivery of daily lectures on spirituality. He was called on to preach retreats and used the material of all his lectures as the substance of spiritual books. The first, *The Meaning of the Mass,* met a response that encouraged Burns and Oates to seek further titles which the industrious priest, with the help of seminarist typists, was eager to provide: *My Yoke is Sweet; Treasure in Heaven; You Shall Find Rest.* All appeared in his seventies.

MICHAEL O'CARROLL, C.S.Sp.

See also CATHOLICISM, IRISH.

KELLS, BOOK OF

Illuminated manuscript of the four Gospels, dating from the early ninth century, now exhibited in Trinity College, Dublin, Ireland. It is known to have belonged to the monastery of Kells, forty miles from Dublin, in the early eleventh century. Despite much scholarly dispute, there is no compelling reason to doubt that it was written and illustrated in the monastery itself. By the ninth century, Kells ranked as the chief foundation in Ireland of the Columban community founded by the Irish St. Columba (or Columcille) in the sixth century, which eventually had houses in Ireland, Scotland, and Northern England. The art of manuscript illumination developed by these monks was among the outstanding glories of the Celtic Church. The Book of Durrow, written on vellum, almost certainly at the monastery of Durrow in County Offaly, Ireland, about A.D. 670, was the first "manuscript de luxe" in this tradition. Its features include "carpet pages" of abstract design and initial letters made up of elaborate interlacing to introduce important parts of the sacred text. Four colors are tastefully intermingled in these illuminational elements.

Representation in Durrow is handled with restraint, although dramatically in the symbols of the four evangelists (man, lion, ox or calf, and eagle). In Kells it proliferates on virtually every page, with lively pictures of little human forms or heads, birds, rabbits, cats, and dogs sprinkled through the handsome Irish "majuscule" (large-letter) script. Careful examination shows that these elements are not randomly used but achieve an overall balance on the page, especially if a line needs to be filled out or an error of transcription has to be rectified. Nine colors are deployed in the book and often the legs, tails, or wings of the creatures depicted are elongated and transformed into interlacings to exquisite effect. Whole pages of Kells are given over to beautifully complex designs of initial letters and, as in Durrow but now with far more exuberance, to the symbols of the evangelists. A full-page Virgin and Child with attendant angels, hieratic in style like all the major figures in the book, is said to be the earliest representation of the Blessed Virgin in a Western manuscript.

"The Book of Kells," detail, Gospel of Matthew

Details on this and numerous other pages provide extensive information about the clothing, ornaments, buildings, flora and fauna typical in the ninth century Celtic world of Ireland and Northern Britain. The artwork reflects Mediterranean and Eastern influences as well as Viking elements which had begun to arrive in Western Europe about this time, but its primary patterns can be traced to the decoration of the bronze and enamel artifacts of the pre-Christian Celts. The Gospel text used is the Latin Vulgate of St. Jerome.

LOUIS McREDMOND

See also ART, CHRISTIAN; CELTIC ART; MANUSCRIPTS OF THE BIBLE.

KEMPE, MARGERY (ca. 1373–ca. 1439)

Margery Kempe was born in the medieval port of King's Lynn in Norfolk (known as Bishop's Lynn in Margery's day) around 1373. Her father, John Brunham, was a very prominent figure in the political scene of Lynn. He served as mayor five times and was one of the town's two members of parliament. He was also an alderman of the Trinity Guild, coroner, justice of the peace, and chamberlain. When she was about twenty years old, Margery married John Kempe, a burgess. At this point in her life, Margery was very much concerned with appearances and status and was quite ambitious. She took up two trades, brewing and then a horsemill; however, both of these businesses eventually failed. After the birth of her first child, Margery also suffered an attack of insanity. By her account, this madness was healed by a vision of Christ seated on her bed, telling her, "Dowtyr why has thou forsakyn me and I forsoke never the."

After this vision and the failure of her businesses, Margery turned to prayer and penance. She developed traits that remained with her the rest of her life, namely, frequent sobbing and weeping and continual thinking and talking of God and heaven. Sexual relations with her husband no longer interested her, yet he insisted on his rights and she remained with him until about her fortieth year. Finally, in 1413, having borne fourteen children, Margery separated from her husband.

Margery adopted the life of a pilgrim and traveled to many English shrines and holy people, including Julian of Norwich. During these travels, she encountered a great deal of criticism and even threats to her life. She was frequently accused of being a Lollard even though she was very clearly orthodox in her devotion to the sacraments, her observance of fasts and her pilgrimages—all of which were questioned in Lollard writings. At one point, upon return from traveling abroad, she was even jailed on this charge. Margery was examined by Church authorities in both Leicester and York. Even though she was cleared in both places, in each instance she was asked to leave the diocese.

Margery traveled to the Holy Land in 1414. On her way home from Palestine, she spent six months in Italy, where she encountered some of the same difficulties she had experienced in England. Two years later she visited Santiago de Compostela. She returned to her husband in 1425 and nursed him until his death in 1431. A couple of years later, she visited Norway and Danzig. She herself died around 1439.

The Book of Margery Kempe is the oldest extant autobiography in English. It gives vivid accounts of Margery's travels, temptations, and mystical experiences. At the same time, it provides a marvelous picture of medieval life. Because Margery was illiterate, as she indicates at several points in her *Book,* she had to dictate her story. She describes this effort in the Proem and in chapter 89. The first attempt to dictate it was a disaster. The text was unintelligible. After some time and effort, she succeeded in having it rewritten by a priest. She then added the last ten chapters. For centuries, all that was known of her work were extracts from the more devotional sections originally published by Wynkyn de Worde towards the beginning of the sixteenth century in a seven-page quarto pamphlet. In 1934, however, a manuscript of the complete book was found in the Butler-Bowden family and since then several editions of it have been made available to the modern reader.

Despite her illiteracy, Margery demonstrates a working knowledge of several significant spiritual books. In her own book, she describes her conversations with various learned people of her day and her requests to have people read books to her. In particular, in chapter 58, she mentions the Bible and commentaries on it, St. Bride's book (refers to the Swedish visionary), Hilton's book (probably *The Scale of Perfection*), Bonaventura's *Stimulus Amoris* and *Incendium Amoris* (a guide to the spiritual life, written in Latin by Richard Rolle of Hampole in the fourteenth century but often wrongly attributed to Bonaventura). While these works are prominent in Margery's thought, other influences are also evident, such as Mary of Oignes (d. 1213), Angela of Foligno (ca. 1249–1309), and Dorothea of Montau (1347–1394).

PATRICIA DeFERRARI

See also BRITAIN, CHURCH IN; JULIAN OF NORWICH; MIDDLE AGES, THE; MYSTICISM; SPIRITUALITY, LAY; WOMEN IN THE CHURCH.

KEMPIS, THOMAS À

See IMITATION OF CHRIST.

KENNEDY, JOHN F. (1917–1963)

Thirty-fifth president of the United States, a descendant of Irish immigrants whose children had prospered in the United States, Kennedy was born in Brookline, Massachusetts, on 29 May 1917, and was assassinated in Dallas, Texas, on 22 November 1963. His father, Joseph P. Kennedy, was a Harvard graduate, successful businessman, prominent Democrat and ambassador to Great Britain. His mother, Rose (Fitzgerald) Kennedy was the daughter of a former mayor of Boston. An older brother, Joseph, Jr., was killed in World War II, leaving John the oldest of three surviving sons.

John Fitzgerald Kennedy

After graduation from Harvard and service in the U.S. Navy in World War II, Kennedy entered Massachusetts politics, serving as a congressman (1947–1952) and as a United States senator (1952–1960). In 1956 he came close to receiving the Democratic nomination for vice president. Nominated for president in 1960, he defeated Richard Nixon by less than one percent of the popular vote to become the first Catholic president of the United States. Kennedy's religion was a major issue in the campaign; he confronted it directly by saying: "I am not the Catholic candidate for president, but the Democratic Party's candidate who happens to be a Catholic." Some Catholics complained that he reduced religion to a purely private matter. His tragically brief administration was short on legislative substance, but he brought to the White House an elegance of style unmatched in recent years.

THOMAS J. SHELLEY

See also AMERICAN CATHOLICISM; CHURCH AND STATE.

KENOSIS

Kenosis is the noun form of a Greek root meaning "empty." It never appears as such in the New Testament, but has become the customary term for referring to the action of Christ Jesus described in Philippians 2:7 in which the same Greek root appears. Paul is urging the community at Philippi to be of one mind and offers them the model of the Lord who *emptied himself* for their sake. This self-emptying took place in three stages: (1) though equal to God in rank, he put that aside in order to become a human being; (2) though worthy of the highest honor as a human being, he humbly took on the role of a slave; (3) though innocent, out of obedience to his Father he gave himself up to death on the cross. Paul says his joy would be complete if each member of the Church at Philippi would put on this *kenotic* mind of Christ.

WILLIAM C. McFADDEN, S.J.

See also HUMILITY; JESUS CHRIST.

KERYGMA

Kerygma has the general meaning of proclamation. In the Greek Old Testament (the Septuagint) the cognate verb usually refers to a prophetic or priestly proclamation (see Isa 61:1; Exod 32:5). Such proclamation generally focuses on the declaration of an event. In the New Testament kerygma embraces the following: (1) the content of Christian proclamation (Rom 16:25; 1 Cor 1:21); (2) the activity of proclamation itself (1 Cor 2:4; 15:14); (3) the office or task committed to a preacher or herald (Titus 1:3). In its Christian sense kerygma is the proclamation of the crucified and risen Jesus as God's final and definitive act of salvation (1 Cor 15:3-5).

Although the English New Testament scholar, C. H. Dodd, limited the kerygma to the public proclamation of Christianity to the non-Christian world, a study of Luke-Acts demonstrates that Dodd's understanding of kerygma was too restrictive. For Luke the kerygma of Jesus involves the training of the disciples to hand on his message (Luke 10:16). At the end of the Third Gospel, Jesus commissions the disciples to preach repentance for the forgiveness of sins (Luke 24:47). In Acts the disciples boldly proclaim the word (Acts 4:13, 29, 31). With regard to the content of the kerygma, Luke observes that the person of Jesus and his proclamation fulfill God's plan announced in the Old Testament (Luke 4:18-21; 7:22).

Kerygma overlaps with the literary form of a gospel. All four Gospels reflect the concern of the evangelists to teach believers the very core of the kerygma. By presenting Jesus' words and works against the backdrop of the mystery of the Cross and its consequences for discipleship, Mark achieves his synthesis of the kerygma. By carefully constructing five great sermons that highlight the message of Jesus for his community, Matthew offers his sense of the kerygma. By employing the journey motif to undergird the meaning of Jesus' death and resurrection, Luke presents his understanding of the kerygma. By developing the gradual revelation of Jesus' glory from Cana to the empty tomb, John unfolds his perception of the kerygma. Hence kerygma is intimately linked to the very heart of the fourfold message of the Good News.

JOHN F. CRAGHAN

KINGDOM OF GOD

The term "kingdom of God" originates within the Jewish Scriptures with early references to Yahweh as king (Deut 33:5) with an eternal reign (Exod 15:18). Israel becomes God's chosen people and experiences Yahweh acting on her behalf (Exod 15:11-13). The kingdom of God is an integral part of Israel's faith, and after the period of monarchy and of exile, Israel's hope focused on a future king from the line of David and a restoration of the kingdom. This eschatological emphasis offered hope to the people. Later writings refer to the final, universal, and eternal kingdom and contain apocalyptic imagery (Dan 7:13-28). Because of this emphasis in Judaism, people were ready for Jesus' preaching of the kingdom of God and the insights he offered.

The Synoptic Gospels contain most of the New Testament sayings and teachings on the kingdom, with scant references in John (3:3, 5; 18:36), and some in Acts and various letters. In Mark's Gospel, Jesus begins his public ministry by announcing that the kingdom of God is at hand (Mark 1:15) and later refers to its imminence (9:1), as do other writers (Matt 2:2; 4:17; 10:7; Luke 10:9; 17:20). The kingdom (*basileia* in Greek), also called the reign of God, or the kingdom of heaven (Matt 13:33), has future dimensions as well (Matt 25:34). The parables of Jesus emphasize the kingdom as both present and future (Mark 4; Matt 13), using many images including those of mustard seed and leaven to convey the gradualness of growth and universal significance of God's reign. The gospel writings also speak of Christ as king (Matt 2:2; Mark 15:2; John 19:12), the kingdom of the Son of Man (Matt 16:28), and the kingdom as unending (Luke 1:33). The theme of the kingdom of God was the centerpiece of Jesus' preaching.

Characteristics of the kingdom include an aura of mystery (Matt 13:11; Mark 4:11; Luke 8:10), an otherworldly character (John 18:36), an association with the parousia (Matt 16:28) and eternal life (Mark 9:43), a relationship to righteousness (Matt 5:10), peace, and joy in the Spirit (Rom 14:17). In the Lord's Prayer, disciples pray for the coming of the kingdom (Matt 6:10; Luke 11:2), and in the celebration of the Lord's Supper anticipate its fullness (Luke 24:30). While the kingdom is not the product of human endeavor, disciples wait patiently while seeking it (Matt 6:33), and then receive it like children (Mark 10:15).

Membership in the kingdom requires conversion, and participation is open to all, especially the poor, lowly, and suffering (Matt 5:3, 10; 19:14; Mark 10:14; Luke 6:20). The Gospels stress childlike qualities (Matt 18:3; Mark 10:15; Luke 18:17) and a life of active obedience as requirement for the kingdom (Matt 7:21).

In the emerging theology of New Testament writers we see that the kingdom is made real in the present in some way, while the fullness of God's reign remains in the future. This perspective allows for social justice teaching in these writings as opposed to the lack of such emphasis in Jewish apocalyptic literature. As we live in anticipation of the fullness of the kingdom, we have a responsibility to create a world more in keeping with the values of the reign of God. A radical inbreaking of the kingdom occurred with Jesus' preaching, his death was a step in its development, but the new era will be fully realized in his second coming and the completion of God's salvific action.

Within the NT the community of believers or Church becomes a sign pointing to the kingdom—the kingdom being a more inclusive reality, open to all. After biblical times, the understanding of the kingdom developed and preaching shifted from the kingdom to the Church's proclamation of Jesus as Lord.

In Church history leaders emphasized various aspects of the kingdom, such as the relationship between kingdom and Church, the earthly and heavenly kingdoms, and the role of world involvement in relation to the kingdom. The Second Vatican Council acknowledged the need for creating a new world order while recognizing that the final kingdom will result from God's action. This integration of social justice and faith in the Catholic understanding of the kingdom of God offers reasons for world involvement and reasons for hope.

HELEN DOOHAN

See also SALVATION; SALVATION HISTORY.

KNIGHTS OF COLUMBUS

Overview

The Knights of Columbus, founded in New Haven, Connecticut, by Father Michael J. McGivney, is an international Catholic fraternal insurance society with over 1.5 million members located in the United States, Canada, Mexico, the Philippines, and Puerto Rico. It has a three-tiered structure: supreme, state, and local councils; there are also Squire Circles for youths between fourteen and eighteen years of age. The initiation ceremonies are rooted in Catholicism and include a Columbian component. The three degrees are Unity, Charity, and Fraternity, with Patriotism infused into the Fourth Degree founded in 1899. The vast majority of members are in the third degree.

At the end of 1991 there were 9,810 local councils, 1,900 Fourth Degree assemblies, 1,100 Squire Circles. The insurance program, which was placed on an actuarial basis in 1902, is valued at almost $25 billion, a figure that makes the order in the top 4 percent among the 2,400 life insurance companies in North America.

Though the Church permitted Catholics to join the order and though there are chaplains in every council, assembly, and circle, the Knights of Columbus is not an officially approved Catholic society; instead it is an organization of Catholic laymen. The order influenced the foundation of Columbian women's societies, the Daughters of Isabella and the Catholic Daughters of the Americas.

History

The order traces its origin to 2 October 1881, when a group of men met in the basement of St. Mary's Church, New Haven, to discuss the formation of a fraternal death-benefit society. Convened at the request of Father Michael J. McGivney, the twenty-nine-year-old curate of the parish, this meeting eventually led to the 29 March 1882 incorporation of the Knights of Columbus. By rooting their fraternalism in the great navigator, the Knights were asserting their Catholic legitimacy in a New England society frequently subjected to fits of anti-Catholic hysteria. In this sense the *Santa Maria* was the Catholic countersymbol of the Puritan's *Mayflower*. Columbianism was the organizing principle of their sense of American Catholic peoplehood. Columbus represented the Catholic baptism of the nation and was perceived as transcending old-world loyalties allowing the order to mediate Catholic assimilation into American society.

The spirit of Columbianism gained national momentum during the Quadricentennial of Columbus's landfall in 1892, the year the order instituted Boston's Bunker Hill council, the first in Massachusetts. The Columbian celebrations were so popular that the order opened its ranks to noninsurance, associate members, so that it could accommodate the thousands eager to infuse Columbian themes into their American Catholic identity. Its promotion of Catholic patriotism and the American-Catholic heritage established the order as the foremost Catholic anti-defamation society.

With a strong economic base, rising membership and committed leadership, the order has sponsored a wide variety of programs to serve its members, the Church and society. The erection of the national monument to Columbus, unveiled on 8 June 1912, was strongly supported by the Knights. The movement to make Columbus day a national holiday was promoted by the order. Its many cultural programs included a K of C chair in American History and a $500,000 endowment fund at the Catholic University of America (1907), a K of C edition of the Catholic Encyclopedia (1910), the funding of the microfilming of valuable manuscripts of the Vatican library to be housed at St. Louis University's Pius XII Library (1951). The order has funded several history projects: the Racial Contribution series that includes W.E.B. DuBois's *Gift of the Black Folk;* the composition of its own centennial history (1982), a Quincentennial revised edition, and a six-volume history on the bicentennial of the appointment of the first bishop in the U.S. Catholic anti-defamation projects included sponsoring lectures on Catholic social thought of *Rerum Novarum* and other areas of apologetics (1900–1920), the establishment of a Commission on Religious Prejudices (1914–1917), the anti Ku Klux Klan activity in the 1920s, the protests against anti-Catholicism in Mexico (1910–1940), and prosecution of anti K of C and anti-Catholic libel suits from the 1920s to the 1960s.

The volunteer efforts to improve society include a social service campaign in World War I which entailed deploying thousands of secretaries in "K of C Huts" or recreation centers in army camps in the United States, Europe, and Asia; the order also sponsored a postwar reconstruction program in education and in employment centers for veterans. Contemporary volunteerism totals over a million man-hours in programs for the mentally and physically handicapped, for the homeless, and for prolife activities.

Three Supreme Knights have made their marks on the order's history over the past forty years. Luke E. Hart (1953–1964), of St. Louis, Missouri, the first full-time occupant of the office—the Supreme Secretary had been the only full-time administrator prior to 1953—had been the chief legal officer, (i.e., Supreme Advocate) since 1919. He modernized the insurance program, diversified the order's investments, and led the order to adopt the Catholic advertising program, originating in St. Louis, and to fund several other projects including the campanile at the National Shrine of the Immaculate Conception.

John W. McDevitt, of Malden, Massachusetts, was State Deputy of his home state during a crucial period. As Supreme Knight from 1964 to 1977, McDevitt led the order's racial integration program, its adaptation to the changes of Vatican Council II within the context of a strong loyalty to the Church authority. His administration is also identified with prolife activities in the wake of Roe v. Wade. One of the order's most significant projects during this period was its response to the Vatican's need for modernizing its radio and television communications.

In answer to a 1921 request from Pope Benedict XV, the Knights have sponsored five recreation centers—playgrounds—in Rome. For over sixty years Count Enrico Galeazzi, an architect and engineer of enormous influence in Church and civic affairs, was director of these centers and the Knights' agent in Rome. During the administration of Hart, McDevitt, and Dechant, Galeazzi was a valuable liaison between the Vatican and the order.

Under the leadership of Supreme Knight Virgil C. Dechant (1977–) of western Kansas, the order responded to the Vatican's communications' program, its projects for new chapels in the crypt and restoration of the facade of St. Peter's Basilica, and the Pope's private charities in the form of a $20 million Vicarius Christi fund which yields an annual gift of approximately $2 million. The order has extensively funded programs in education, vocations, Marian devotions, prolife, medical-moral research, natural family planning, history and restoration projects, and the 1988 establishment of the North American Campus of the Pontifical John Paul II Institute for Studies on Marriage and the Family in Washington, D.C. Dechant continues the modernization of the insurance program and the professionalization of the order's personnel. Between 1981 and 1991 the order's assets grew from $1.5 to $3.5 billion. According to a fraternal survey of all societies, the Knights of Columbus on the local, state, and international levels contributed $93.5 million and 41.4 million volunteer man-hours of service in 1991. Between 1981 and 1991, the Knights volunteerism entailed $681.4 million and 219.3 million man-hours of service.

Originating in an obscure meeting in the basement of an Irish-American parish church, the Knights of Columbus have evolved into a major force as a Catholic fraternal insurance society serving the interests of Church and society.

CHRISTOPHER J. KAUFFMAN

See also AMERICAN CATHOLICISM.

KNIGHTS OF MALTA

The Sovereign Military Order of the Hospital of St. John of Jerusalem, of Rhodes and of Malta (Knights of Malta) was founded by Master Gerard (d. 1120) in a hospice in Jerusalem as a religious community caring for the sick following the rule of St. Augustine. The order received papal approbation in 1113, and it soon became engaged in military activities as it helped defend Christian pilgrims to the Holy Land against Islamic attacks. The order grew quickly, acquiring land and opening hostels for pilgrims, and it began taking on a chivalric character with the appointment of knights and sergeants-at-arms in its organization. All members of the order were monks who took the three traditional religious vows.

After the failure of the Crusades, the order received possession of the island of Rhodes where it established an independent state and organized a navy to patrol the seas against Muslim aggression. Later the Knights were forced to leave Rhodes, and in 1530 the Emperor Charles V gave them some lands in the West including the island of Malta. From this strategic island, the Knights were able to ward off Islamic excursions into Europe. The Reformations and the French Revolution deprived the order of its vast temporal possessions and political influence. The order went into decline, and first the French (1798) and later the British (1801) invaded Malta, ending the Knights' control of the island.

After much political intrigue and a series of moves, the Knights set up their headquarters in Rome in 1834. Since they are no longer engaged in military work, their constitutions have been updated to meet modern conditions. Today the members of the order are divided into four classes including professed religious, titled laity, and laity who are not nobility. They are present in over one hundred countries and engage in charitable works, especially those related to the sick. Some nations including the Holy See still recognize the Knights of Malta as a sovereign political entity. The Grand Master of the order is a cardinal and must be of noble birth.

ANTHONY D. ANDREASSI

See also CORPORAL AND SPIRITUAL WORKS OF MERCY; RELIGIOUS ORDERS.

KNOCK SHRINE

On the evening of 21 August 1879, for some hours, fifteen people of different ages reported that they saw an unusual vision in the village of Knock, in County Mayo, in the west of Ireland. The location was the end wall of the village church. Against it were seen an altar on which stood a lamb, and in the background moving figures which seemed like angels. To the right of the altar were three figures identified as Our lady (in the center and crowned), St. Joseph on her right, inclining slightly towards her, and on her left St. John the Evangelist, holding a book in his right hand.

An episcopal commission was established to examine the witnesses. No authoritative judgment was given. In 1936 a second commission was set up and its findings sent to Rome. No decision was made known. The movement of piety stirred by knowledge of the apparition had waned. For fifty years no bishop visited Knock.

A new phase opened in 1936. Two lay apostles, Mr. Justice and Mrs. W. D. Coyne, founded the Knock Shrine Society and the *Knock Shrine Annual.* Local bishops were increasingly supportive, and favors were received from the popes: John XXIII sent a ceremonially blessed candle; Paul VI sanctioned official crowning of the statue of Our Lady; John Paul II visited the shrine on 30 September 1979, the centenary year, and he offered the Golden Rose to the shrine and raised the newly built church to the rank of basilica. For decades prior to this, the energetic parish priest of Knock, Monsignor James Horan (d. 1986), slowly saw his dreams come true—the shrine of Knock grew, and millions of pilgrims began to come from all over the English-speaking world. Some came to seek help for their problems; all came to pray. The Mass and the rosary are—and were from the beginning—the spiritual pillars of the shrine of Knock.

MICHAEL O'CARROLL C.S.Sp.

See also DEVOTIONS.

KNOWLEDGE OF GOD

Our knowledge of God arises out of the experience which occurs when we respond in faith to divine revelation. That experience is conditioned by the beliefs we inherit from the religious traditions which nurture us and is generated by God's action upon us and our reaction to God. We formulate our knowledge of God in creeds or other statements.

Knowing God is not simply having beliefs or knowing propositions about God, any more than knowing a friend is knowing propositions about her. We come to know our friends by their sustained interaction with us which reveals who they are to us. We then reflect on that interaction. Similarly, we come to know God by faithfully responding to and reflecting on God's action upon us. The experiential interaction which reveals God to us is primary, the formulated beliefs are derivative. We know God first. We know about God second.

The Second Vatican Council highlighted Scripture and tradition as the key means through which God reveals. The First Vatican Council also teaches that God "can be known with certainty by the natural light of human reason from the things that he created" (DS 1785). Some theologians claim that all people have at least an "unthematized" or "inchoate" knowledge of God, which can be developed into explicit and articulate (but always partial) understanding of God.

The Christian tradition has two paths for articulating what we know of God, the way of negation and the way of perfection. In the former, we say that God is not, e.g., not a body, not limited, etc. This talk can guide those who seek to know God by turning them away from what God is not. It also sets limits on what we can properly say of God. In the latter, we indicate what God is by using the imperfect goods we know in this world, e.g., justice, beauty, love, power, as a way of understanding the infinite perfection of God as perfect justice, absolute Beauty, all-encompassing love, and irresistible power. These paths guide those who seek to know God by showing them how the experiences they have and what they already know can be occasions for recognizing and responding to God's action and for understanding that divine action.

Our tradition conditions our expectations of how God acts. Scripture, doctrine, the created world, worship, and other people provide the gracious means through which we come to experience and know the revealing God. Our tradition also guides us in our interpretation of our experience with God, especially in the formation of creeds like the Nicene Creed. Hence, to construe Jesus Christ whom we experience through word and sacrament as merely divine or merely human is to misunderstand the truly human, truly divine Christ we experience.

Our knowledge of God can have numerous sources, for the ways in which God revealingly interacts with us and in which we can respond to God are manifold—if we only have the eyes to see.

T. W. TILLEY

See also MYSTICISM; THEOLOGY.

KNOWLES, DAVID (1896–1976)

English Benedictine, scholar and historian was educated at Downside, Cambridge University and Sant' Anselmo in Rome. He was a gifted historian and the finest stylist among historians writing in English in this century. His monastic life at Downside was rather complex, and this cultured monk was often difficult to live with and uncompromising in his demands. He eventually went his own way and incurred canonical suspension, but his position was later regularized. Nevertheless, he cherished the Benedictine ideal and his booklet *The Benedictines* (1929) is regarded as a classic, a nearly perfect exposition of Benedictine life. He is universally respected as the greatest authority on pre-Reformation monasticism and his *magnum opus, The Monastic Order in England; a History of its Development from the Times of St. Dunstan to the Fourth Lateran Council, 943–1216* (Cambridge 1940; 2nd ed., 1963) and his *The Religious Orders in England* (Cambridge 1956, 1957, 1959) established him as a historian of the first rank. He had a brilliant academic career and in 1954 was appointed Regius Professor of Modern History at Cambridge, a post which he held until his retirement in 1963.

MICHAEL GLAZIER

See also BENEDICTINES; BRITAIN, CHURCH IN.

"KNOW-NOTHINGS"

The popular name for an anti-Catholic secret society and political party (the American Party), which flourished in the United States in the mid-1850s. The name is derived from the Know-Nothing practice of saying "I know nothing" when asked about the organization. Historians trace the origin of the movement to the Order of the Star Spangled Banner, a secret society founded by Charles B. Allen of New York in 1849. Real expansion began in 1852 when Allen relinquished the leadership to James W. Barker. That same year the election of Democrat Franklin Pierce as president provoked widespread resentment against the immigrants who had voted for him in large numbers. Barker capitalized on this anti-immigrant sentiment and the breakdown of the traditional party system to make the Know-Nothings briefly a potent political force.

In 1854 they elected seventy-five congressmen and gained control of several state governments, mainly in the northeast and the border states. In Massachusetts the Know-Nothing legislature appointed a Nunnery Committee to investigate conditions in convents. While professing to be anti-immigrant and agitating for a twenty-one-year naturalization period, the Know-Nothings were in fact anti-Catholic. "Only one force held the members of the Know Nothing party together," said historian Ray Allen Billington, "and that was their hatred for the Catholic Church."

Like many American organizations of that era, the Know-Nothings came to grief over the slavery question. In June 1855, when their National Council refused to condemn the existence of slavery in the territories or in the District of Columbia, most northern Know-Nothings abandoned the movement. The grand finale came in the presidential election of 1856 when Know-Nothing candidate Millard Fillmore won a mere 25 percent of the popular vote and the electoral vote of only one state—Maryland. It was a defeat from which the Know-Nothings never recovered and they were soon swept away in the growing national debate over slavery.

ANTHONY D. ANDREASSI

See also AMERICAN CATHOLICISM.

KNOX, RONALD ARBUTHNOTT (1888–1957)

His mother died when he was four, and his evangelical father became the bishop of Manchester, and was a most devoted parent and steadfast friend. Knox won a Balliol scholarship and went up to Oxford in 1906. He was a brilliant student and, on leaving Balliol in 1910, was elected fellow at Trinity. In 1912 he was ordained priest in the Church of England, and began his work as chaplain in Oxford. During this time he became curious about the claims of the Bishop of Rome and, after a period of painful doubt,

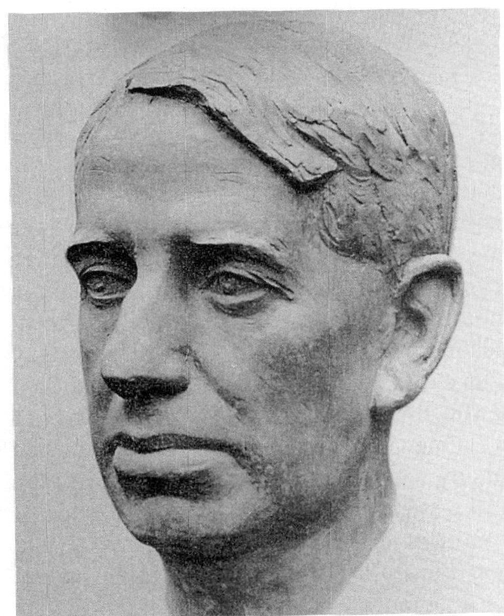

Ronald Arbuthnott Knox, terracotta by Arthur Pollen

he was received into the Catholic Church in 1917; and in 1919 was ordained a priest. From 1926 to 1939 he was Catholic chaplain at Oxford, and he wrote prolifically and became known as a satirist, wit, and apologist. In 1939, the bishops of England commissioned him to make a new translation of the Bible from the Vulgate. His translation of the New Testament appeared in 1945; the Old Testament in 1949; and the whole Bible in one volume was published in 1955. Initially "The Knox Bible" was well and widely received; but within twenty-five years it had lost its popularity because he had been required to translate from the Vulgate and not from the original languages. Knox deserves to be remembered also for some of his other literary accomplishments such as: *A Spiritual Aeneid* (1918), *The Belief of Catholics* (1927), *Essays in Satire* (1928), and *Let Dons Delight* (1939).

MICHAEL GLAZIER

See also BIBLE, ENGLISH VERSIONS OF THE; BRITAIN, CHURCH IN.

KOINONIA

A term in New Testament Greek for sharing and being sensitive to the needs of others, as well as for the relationships, associations, and Christian communities in which such sharing is practiced. In 1 Corinthians 10, St. Paul designates the "cup of blessing" shared by Christians as a *koinonia,* and this is reflected by our use of the Latin equivalent (*communio,* "communion").

DAVID BRYAN

See also BASIC COMMUNITIES; COMMUNION, HOLY.

KOLBE, MAXIMILIAN, ST. (1894–1941)

A prevailing Jewish proverb explains that people can recognize that night ends and day begins when one can look on the face of any man or woman and see that it is one's sister or brother. Father Maximilian Kolbe, looking on the face of a fellow prisoner about to die in the empire of death at Auschwitz, a town west of Crackow in southern Poland, at the hands of the Nazis, wakened to one of those heavenly days that cannot die on the eve of the Assumption, 14 August 1941. One of the inmates in the prison had escaped and, by the rules fixed by the captors, ten were to die in reprisal. One Polish soldier selected as one of the victims cried out in agony: "What will happen to my family?" Father Kolbe stepped out of line and volunteered to take his place "because he has a wife and children" and, upon being accepted as the substitute, was executed by a lethal dose of carbolic acid in his left arm. The next day his remains were cremated. That day, long to be remembered, resulted in the canonization of Father Kolbe on 10 October 1982 *as a martyr,* with the man whose life he saved witnessing the ceremony.

St. Maximilian Kolbe

St. Maximilian Kolbe was baptized in the Church of the Assumption of our Lady (and was to die on the eve of that feast) in Zdunska-Wola, Poland, shortly after his birth on 7 January 1894, with the name of Raymond, but was given the name Maximilian Maria when he made his profession in the Franciscan community. He was somewhat of a rascal as a teenager but had the sensitivity to be upset when, one day, his mother said: "Raymond, what is to become of you?" He sought the intercession of the Blessed Mother and made the resolve to enter religious life where he showed talent in mathematics, physics, and astronomy, and even envisioned space flight and sketched many plans for rocket ships. He designed a spacecraft and applied for a patent on it, even though the idea of space travel was not taken too seriously in the early days of the present century.

Just before his ordination in Rome in 1918 he felt called to combat religious indifference and for this purpose he founded the Knights of the Immaculata with the thought that the miraculous medal would be an ideal means to gain other souls for Christ. Each member was to dedicate himself to Mary Immaculate and was charged to work for the salvation of all souls, particularly the enemies of the Church. He traveled extensively to promote the publishing apostolate which was the outgrowth of this pious institute.

Throughout his life deplorable health plagued this saintly man, suffering as he did from repeated attacks of tuberculosis. This outstanding servant of God distinguished himself throughout his life by his living belief in God's divine providence and by his unshakable hope and supreme love of God and neighbor. Those who testified in the canonization process believe that his successful career as a priest was due to his extraordinary calmness in the many storms that characterized his life.

JAMES McGRATH

See also HOLOCAUST (NAZI).

KULTURKAMPF

After the definition of papal infallibility, a repressive anti-Catholic movement began in Germany. It was chiefly inspired by Bismarck, who feared that Catholicism would be inimical to German political unity. In 1871 Bismarck introduced a series of anti-Catholic laws and suppressed the Catholic department of the Prussian Ministry of Public Worship. Shortly thereafter, the Jesuits were expelled and all Catholic schools and seminaries were placed in the control of the state. The conflict heightened and the German envoy to the Vatican was withdrawn and Pope Pius IX strongly condemned the persecution in the encyclical *Quod Nunquam* (7 February 1875). As a retaliation, all religious orders were expelled from the country and financial aid to the Church was stopped. Bismarck's bullying tactics united the German Catholics as never before, and he came to realize that he had made a major miscalculation. To gain Catholic cooperation against social democracy, most of the laws were gradually revoked and a concordat with Leo XIII marked the end to the repression.

MICHAEL GLAZIER

See also CHURCH AND STATE.

KYRIE ELEISON

(Gk., "Lord, have mercy") An invocation which, together with *Christe Eleison* ("Christ, have mercy") makes up a prayer formula that is now sung or recited as part of the Penitential Rite at the beginning of the Eucharistic celebration, often in the vernacular. It is the only remaining Greek prayer in the Latin Mass, into which it was incorporated in the sixth century.

JOSEPH QUINN

See also EUCHARIST.

L

LA SALETTE

On 19 September 1846 it was reported that the Blessed Virgin appeared to two children in southern France as they were herding cows on a mountain above La Salette. Melanie Mathieu-Calvat, age fifteen, and Maximin Giraud, age eleven, were startled by the appearance in a globe of brilliant light of a beautiful lady resplendently attired but weeping. She gave them a message addressed to "all her people." There was only one appearance of Our Lady to the children but great devotion to Mary sprang up and several popes have approved the cult found there.

This shrine does not enjoy the fame or draw the numbers of the faithful as do the better-known shrines at Lourdes and Fatima.

JAMES McGRATH

See also DEVOTIONS; FATIMA; LOURDES.

LABOR UNIONS

See UNIONS, LABOR.

LABOREM EXERCENS

Taken from the first two words of the text, "engaged in work," this is the title of a papal encyclical letter of John Paul II issued in September 1981, to commemorate the ninetieth anniversary of the groundbreaking encyclical letter of Pope Leo XIII, *Rerum Novarum.* Also known in the English-speaking world by the title, *On Human Work,* the letter continues the line of thought of the social encyclicals issued since 1891, reflecting on questions of social justice, more particularly those concerning the rights and needs of people as workers and producers. It uses an analysis of working situations which was first offered by Karl Marx, though entirely in harmony with the doctrine of creation in which John Paul II situates the discussion.

The main argument concerns the dignity of human beings as workers which is seriously threatened by ways of thinking in the economic sphere which treat labor as simply a factor of production, concealing the reality that labor is not an entity in itself, but an abstract way of referring to human persons and the work they do. The work that people do is supposed in God's order to be good for them, the workers themselves, in enhancing their human lives. It is supposed to be helpful in this way for workers as individuals, good for their families, and good for the quality of life and relationships in society. In pursuing this ideal, the encyclical rejects both the profit motive as dominant in uncontrolled capitalism and the collectivization of strict Marxist theory, as working against the enhancement of human lives at the three levels specified. However, the text clearly claims the priority of labor over capital on biblical and theological grounds. In practice this means that the dominant consideration must be the quality of life of the workers and not the maximizing of profit, and this is proposed as foundational to social morality. The encyclical further pursues this principle in relation to employment practices, the problems of large, impersonal corporations, not only wages but fringe benefits, the functions and limits of trade unions, the special questions relating to agricultural workers, and the issues concerning migrant and immigrant workers. A final section concerns the spirituality of work as founded upon Christology.

MONIKA K. HELLWIG

See also JUST WAGES; SOCIAL RESPONSIBILITY, FINANCIAL; SOCIAL TEACHING OF THE CHURCH; WORK.

LABOURÉ, CATHERINE, ST. (1806–1876)

Zoé Labouré was born to peasant farmers at Fain-les-Moutiers in the Côte d'Or on 2 May 1806. She was never formally educated. Her mother died when she was eight, so Zoé had the responsibility of helping to raise her siblings when her older sister, Louisa, left to enter religious life. In 1830 her father allowed her to enter the Sisters of Charity of St. Vincent de Paul at Chatillon-sur-Seine. Taking Catherine as her religious name, after her postulancy she was sent to a convent on the Rue du Bac in Paris.

Soon after her arrival in Paris Catherine received several visions of the Virgin Mary in the convent chapel. In one vision she saw a picture of the Virgin standing on a globe surrounded by the words, "O Mary, conceived without sin, pray for us who have recourse to thee." On the reverse side there was a large "M" with a cross, two hearts, and two crowns. Catherine was told to have a medal cast with these images on it. She believed that those who wore this medal would have the special protection of the Virgin Mary under the title of her Immaculate Conception. These visions ended in September, 1831. Shortly thereafter, she received permission from her spiritual director, Fr. Aladel, to ask Archbishop Quelen of Paris for permission to follow the commands of her visions. He allowed it, and in June, 1832, the first medals were made. Catherine remained anonymous throughout the official investigations of her visions, and they were finally approved in 1836. The popularity of the medals grew quickly, and it soon became known as the "miraculous medal."

Catherine spent the rest of her life doing menial labor in a Catholic hospice and spoke of her visions to no one except her spiritual director. A few months before her death, however, she revealed the content of them to her superior. She died on 31 December 1876, and her popularity grew quickly with many miracles ascribed to her. She was canonized by Pope Pius XII in 1947, and her feast is celebrated on 28 November.

ANTHONY D. ANDREASSI

See also MIRACULOUS MEDAL.

LACOMBE, ALBERT (1827–1916)

The circumstances surrounding the family situation of Father Albert Lacombe had a unique impact on both his early life and his ministry as a missionary priest in western Canada.

Born on 28 February 1827, he descended from a line of colonists who had come to settle on lands inhabited by North American Indians. Among his ancestors, on his mother's side, was a woman who as a young girl was abducted from her home near Ville-Marie (Montreal), by a group of Algonquin natives belonging to the Ojibway tribe. Her family never gave up the search and she was discovered one day when an adventurous uncle, who was a *coureur de bois,* penetrated an Indian settlement. The chief of the tribe had taken her unto himself and had fathered her two sons. The young mother and the boys were returned to her family. Young Albert was born in the very house where the abduction had occurred.

The Indian and French blood which coursed in his veins marked him as a Métis, a race marginalized by both natives and whites. Father Lacombe understood the problem, and although he loved all peoples, there would always be a special concern in his heart for the Metis nation.

He was ordained to the diocesan priesthood in 1849, at the age of twenty-two, and he ministered for a while in eastern Canada. But his was a free spirit, adventurous and restless, and when he heard the pleas of Bishop Alexandre Taché, O.M.I., and Bishop Joseph Provencher for help in the mission territory of the west, he offered his services. He was first stationed at Pembina (now in the United States) in the diocese of St. Boniface. He learned the Saulteaux language, went on buffalo hunts, and generally shared much of the way of life of the Indian people whom he deeply loved. Nonetheless, he missed the strong Christian family atmosphere in which he had grown up, and felt the need for a more disciplined way of life. He returned to Montreal in 1851 for a period of spiritual renewal. His need for community led him to join the Congregation of the Missionary Oblates of Mary Immaculate, a religious order of priests and brothers dedicated to ministering to the native peoples. After pronouncing his first vows in 1856 he returned to the western missions and felt strengthened by the companionship of his fellow Oblates.

By the 1870s, infiltration by white people had altered the Indian way of life. The buffalo had all but disappeared and many were thereby deprived of what had been their mainstay in terms of food, shelter, clothing, and general livelihood. Epidemics became rampant, and the numerous deaths left behind a large number of homeless children. Father Lacombe took an active part in negotiations with the Canadian government in search of solutions to the plight of his flock. He was involved in treaties six and seven but would have wished for a different solution than the creation of Indian reservations in 1882 and 1883, which he felt placed too many restrictions on the Indian people.

In 1860 the town of St. Albert, Alberta, was named after him. He founded the first Roman Catholic parish in the province of Alberta, now St. Mary's Cathedral Parish in Calgary. By 1864, he had organized farming districts and initiated his people to the cultivation of their fields. He was an influential peacemaker during the troubled times surrounding the Riel Rebellion in Manitoba, in 1869 to 1870, and took an active part in the establishment of the first Roman Catholic schools.

He won the trust of his ecclesiastical superiors, and the bishops did not hesitate to delegate him to speak for them on critical issues such as dialogue with the newly arrived Ruthenians. In 1879 he was delegated by Bishop Alexandre Taché, who was not well, to replace him at the general chapter of the Missionary Oblates. He was able to convince the bishops of St. Boniface, St. Albert, and Prince Albert to collaborate with him in setting up a corporation for the creation of a Métis colony in St. Paul, Alberta. The project held out until 1909, when it reverted back to the federal government, and the land was opened up to settlers for the establishment of homesteads. In 1907, Bishop Emile Legal chose him as his companion to attend the first Catholic Congress of the New World. He was for a time vicar general of the bishop; he saw his special powers as further means of helping his flock.

Father Lacombe was also held in high regard by the laity. He counted as one of his lifelong friends and supporters millionaire Patrick Burns. The latter placed two hundred acres of choice agricultural land at his disposal, for the erection of a home where the elderly could end their days in a beautiful natural setting, and orphans could have ample open-air space for their play. The institution officially opened in 1910 and at Mr. Burns' insistence it was named the Lacombe Home. It consisted of a residence for the aged and orphans, regardless of color or creed, as well as a school where the children would be initiated to trades and to cultivation of the land.

He considered it important to maintain an ongoing relationship with government officials, always with a view to helping the native people. Officials of the Canadian Pacific Railway made him president of the company for a day, and awarded him two lifetime passes which he generously shared with whoever had need of them. He was widely known as "The Man of Good Heart" and as "The Big Chief of the Prairies."

Father Lacombe died on 12 December 1916 at the age of eighty-nine in the Home which he had founded and had entrusted to the Sisters of Providence of Montreal.

LINA GAUDETTE, S.P.

See also CANADA, THE CATHOLIC CHURCH IN.

LAETARE SUNDAY

The fourth Sunday, or midpoint, of Lent, which is meant to provide a slight relaxation of the Lenten discipline (e.g., rose vestments are worn in place of the more severe violet, flowers are permitted on the altar). The term is from the Latin text of the Introit at Mass: *Laetare Jerusalem* ("Rejoice O Jerusalem").

DAVID BRYAN

See also GAUDETE SUNDAY; LENT.

LAFARGE, JOHN (1880–1963)

Jesuit priest, editor, social activist. Born in Newport, Rhode Island, 13 February 1880, died in New York City 24 November 1963. He was the third son of artist and writer John LaFarge and of Margaret Mason Perry LaFarge, a descendant of Benjamin Franklin and granddaughter of Commodore Oliver Hazard Perry. After receiving his A.B. degree from Harvard in 1901, LaFarge studied at the Canisianum Seminary of the University of Innsbruck, Austria, where

John LaFarge, S.J.

he was ordained a Roman Catholic priest by the prince-bishop of Brixen in 1905. That summer he entered the Jesuit Order at St. Andrew-on-Hudson, Poughkeepsie, New York. After teaching briefly at Canisius College, Buffalo, New York, and Loyola College, Baltimore, Maryland, he went to Woodstock College, Woodstock, Maryland, to review his philosophical and theological studies until 1910, when he began a missionary career, first on Blackwell's Island in the East River of New York City, and then in rural parishes of southern Maryland, where he served as a country pastor for fifteen years at Leonardtown, St. Inigo's and Ridge, where he founded the Cardinal Gibbons Institute, an agricultural school for blacks. From 1926 until his death, he was associated with *America* magazine in New York City, including two years (1942 to 1944) as executive editor and four years (1944 to 1948) as editor in chief. A patrician intellectual, he early interested himself in interracial matters, working for interracial justice through foundation of Catholic Interracial Councils, their *Interracial Review,* and the Catholic Laymen's League, made up of black Catholics come together to plan a combined program of spiritual training and race-relations investigation. In 1958, at a convention in Chicago, the National Catholic Conference for Interracial Justice was formed under LaFarge's inspiration. He also collaborated with Dr. Thomas Wyatt Turner in foundation (1924) of the Federated Colored Catholics. Apart from his pioneering work in race relations, LaFarge was also instrumental in such organizations as the Liturgical Arts Society (1933), the St. Ansgar's Scandinavian Catholic League (1910), the National Catholic Rural Life Conference (1923) and the Catholic Association for International Peace (1927). Towards the end of the pontificate of Pius XI (1922–1939), he was one of a group of Jesuits consulted on preparation of a never-published encyclical on the unity of the human race. His life is perhaps best summed up in the comment that he was "the persistent voice of reason and justice in a time of apathy and racism."

JAMES HENNESEY, S.J.

See also "AMERICA"; BLACK CATHOLICS; SOCIAL TEACHING OF THE CHURCH; SOCIETY OF JESUS.

LAGRANGE, MARIE-JOSEPH (ALBERT) (1855–1938)

He was a French Dominican biblical scholar. Born on 7 March 1855 in Bourg-en-Bresse, he took a law degree before entering the Dominicans in 1879. After ordination in 1883, and graduate study in Vienna, he founded the Ecole Biblique, the first modern Catholic school of biblical and archaeological research, in Jerusalem on 15 November 1890. His approach to the Bible was moderately critical, supporting, for example, source criticism of the Pentateuch with evidence from the field: geographical, archaeological, and epigraphic (=inscriptional). His historical method intended to combine document and monument. He also taught the need to pay attention to the different types or genres of literature to be found in the Bible, law, wisdom, prophecy, praise as well as history. This view cost him Church favor during his lifetime but has since been confirmed in a papal encyclical. At first (1890–1903), Lagrange focused on the Old Testament, and received encouragement from Leo XIII. But under Pius X (1903–1914), he fell into disfavor. To avoid controversy he switched to New Testament studies. In 1892 he founded the *Revue Biblique;* in 1900 the monograph and commentary series *Etudes Bibliques.* Both continue. A prolific author, he produced over 30 books, 248 articles, and more than 1500 major book reviews. In addition to fullscale commentaries on *Judges* (1903), *Mark* (1911), *Romans* (1916), *Galatians* (1918), *Luke* (1921), *Matthew* (1923), and *John* (1925), he produced works on the NT canon, messianism, intertestamental Judaism, textual criticism, patristics, historical method, apologetics, and a widely translated life of Christ. In 1935 he returned to France, and in 1938 he died at 83. He has since been reburied in the Basilica of St. Stephan, Jerusalem.

Marie-Joseph Lagrange, O.P.

His steady commitment to truth and scholarship combined with obedience to Church authority and an exemplary religious and devotional life earned him victory and vindication soon after his death.

This came in 1943, with the encyclical *Divino Afflante Spiritu* of Pius XII. It was Lagrange's own students: Eugene Cardinal Tisserant, Bishop Bruno de Solages, Fr. Jacob Voste, O.P., the layman Jean Guitton, together with Augustin Bea, S.J., who fought for this triumph. The story of Lagrange's struggle and belated success has become the basic model for Catholic intellectual life in the twentieth century, a pattern for other pioneers who came after him. The manuscript of his completed commentary on Genesis (except for the first two hundred pages, up to chapter six) was burned after his death, a great loss to Catholic scholarship. Since the decree on divine revelation at the Second Vatican Council, which limited the extent of biblical inerrancy to matters pertaining to salvation, and which emphasized a biblically centered theology, it may be said that Lagrange's spirit has become the dominant force in Church theology today. The cause of his beatification is in active process.

BENEDICT T. VIVIANO, O.P.

See also CRITICISM, BIBLICAL; ECOLE BIBLIQUE.

LAITY, THEOLOGY OF THE

Origin and Meaning of the Term Laity

The word "laity" comes from the Greek words *Laos Theou,* meaning "People of God," and manifested the early Christians' conviction that they were successors to the Jews as God's chosen people. Originally the word had a very positive meaning, often used instead of "the elect," or "the holy ones," or "disciples." There were no vocational distinctions in the New Testament, and Jesus preached to followers who were neither priests nor religious, and even as the Church developed such distinctions they were not as clearly defined as they are today. Church structures and authority differed from place to place, and laity often played key roles in the Church's life—in missionary work, preaching, leadership, catechetical instructions, and even in administering the sacraments, presiding at the Eucharist, and establishing monastic life. Like any organization, the early Church evolved gradually, establishing authoritative structures, common devotional rituals, and specialized ministries. Already by the end of the first century the word "laity" was being used as a description of the common people by Clement of Rome (*Letter to the Corinthians,* 40). They were presumed to be merely recipients of the clerical hierarchy's guidance. By the second century the Church had a clearly organized hierarchy and priesthood, and laity had become second-class citizens (Origen, *In Jerem., hom.* XI, 3; Clement of Alexandria, *Strom.* III, 12, 90, 1; V, 6, 33, 3; *Paed.* III, 10, 83, 2).

In early decades after the death of the apostles, many Christians bore witness to their faith in Jesus through martyrdom. However, with the passing of the period of persecutions many dedicated individuals bore sacrificial witness to the Lord in life as a hermit, and as these hermits began to gather together in monastery-like groups their lifestyle became the model of holiness. Laity who had become secondary to the hierarchy then became second class to the religious—the former viewed laity as passive in contrast to Church leaders, and the latter presented them as profane in contrast to the holiness of the monks. As the centuries passed the Church's dialogue with the Roman Empire, especially with the Emperor Constantine (317), led to a consolidation of its hierarchical structures and resulting increased passivity among the laity. Later, the magnetic influence of the monastic movement further diminished the religious significance of lay life; the former were challenged to spirituality, the latter only to morality. The laity's loss of position and dignity in the Church can be symbolically seen in the screen that separated them from clergy during the liturgy, and the monastery and convent cloister and grille that kept their negative influence away from religious life.

There were always lay renewal movements, outstanding lay saints—like Catherine of Siena, and Church leaders who worked to help laity in their Christian growth—like Francis of Sales (1608, 1616). Outstanding laity have been present to every period of history, including our own—men and women like Friedrich von Hügel, Frank Duff, Jacques Maritain, Dorothy Day, and Jean Vanier. However, a major change takes place with the renewal of the Second Vatican Council (1962–1965).

Vatican II and the Laity

There were a few lay observers to the council, including some from the United States, but no laity actively participated in the deliberations or voting. Nevertheless, the council set in motion a serious dialogue between the various vocations in the Church. It recognized a fundamental equality of all members of the Church, based upon the sacraments of initiation and a common sharing in the threefold mission of Jesus—priest, prophet, and servant-king. It proclaimed that everyone has a personal vocation that is manifested in diversity of ministries, and a rich variety of charismatic gifts. Moreover, it insisted that all the baptized participate in the saving mission of the Church, and urged clerical ministers both to recognize the rightful freedom of laity and to utilize their gifts for the benefit of the whole Church and world. One of the very important teachings of the council was to declare that temporal realities are good in themselves. This undid the results of many negative trends in Church history and led to the possibility of stressing the importance of family, work, civic and social life as part of one's Christian growth. The main teachings on lay life appear in the Dogmatic Constitution on the Church, especially chapter four, and in the Decree on the Apostolate of the Laity.

Laity were the great beneficiaries of the council. However, the council's texts still left a few problem areas for laity—deficiencies that would be addressed in the years that followed. Laity were defined by their secular quality—they are Christians who live in the world (AG 15:8); the world is still viewed as evil; the hierarchy seem to have a complete monopoly on Church life (GS 3); laity are still presented as dependent on the clergy who assign duties and responsibilities; and laity are viewed as instruments in the ministry of the hierarchy. The council gives little clarification to the religious importance of laity's daily work and does not develop the specifics of their ministry.

Lay life can never be the same after the Vatican Council II for while some details were left unanswered it changed the direction of the Church and focused its attention on new priorities. Both the new direction and changed priorities centered on values of lay life. In the course of conciliar deliberation a new direction emerged as the participants moved through three major attitudinal changes during their four years in Rome. These changes—seen in the amendments to the documents—were like a great Church conversion experience and stressed the community aspects of the Church's life, the need to incarnate or bring the Church to birth in the concrete circumstances of everyday life, and the realization that as Church we are in the world to serve the world. Community, incarnation, and service became three great focuses of the council's teachings. In additional areas of deliberation the participants moved from one emphasis to another: from Church as institution to Church as mystery; from hierarchy to collegiality; from obedience to coresponsibility; from flight from the world to involvement to change it; from office to charism; from individual to community. These changes did not exclude the former but the pendulum swung to the latter in each case, and like the new direction stressed values of lay life.

The Mission of Laity in Vatican II

The decree on the apostolate of the laity begins with this very clear statement: "The laity have a proper and indispensable role in the mission of the church" (AA 1), thus claiming that laity have a mission which is exclusive to them and that no one else can fulfil. The council recognizes the diversity of gifts and ministries in the Church, stressing the laity's participation in Christ's priestly, prophetic, and servant-kingly offices (AA 2:2). Every believer has the right and duty to use charisms for the benefit of the whole Church and the good of humankind (AA 3:3). Moreover, the laity's apostolate is so necessary, both within the Church and in service to the world, that without it the work of the clergy will frequently be ineffective (AA 10:1). The council launched a major challenge to laity, urging them to contribute with all their effort to the Church's life (LG 33), reminding them of their responsibility (LG 33:3), urging them to use their initiative (GS 43:4), and inviting their cooperation (AG 36).

The council describes each lay person as "a living instrument of the mission of the Church herself" (LG 33) and teaches that lay mission has two focuses; involvement in the world and its transformation, and involvement in the Church and its growth. While leaving details to changing conditions of local Churches and individuals, the council calls laity to realize that there are a series of needs to which they should respond. Regarding the world involvement of laity the council urges them to dedicate their lives to evangelization: to spread the gospel by the witness of a good Christian life (LG 31:3-4), joining action on behalf of the gospel to their profession of faith (LG 35:3). In addition to good living, their work of evangelization should include the sharing of the word of God with nonbelievers in the hope of bringing them to the faith, and with believers to strengthen their faith (AA 6:3). The council also teaches that it is the laity's mission to influence the local environment of civic and social life by bringing a Christian spirit to organizations, institutions, and associations (AA 7:2). This will require education, initiative, and conscience formation. A further part of lay mission toward the world and its development is their charitable activities on behalf of the needy. This personal responsibility to strive for justice and love is a sign of the fruitfulness of faith (GS 21:6). A major area of lay mission in the mind of the council is in family life. While the council's use of "family" refers primarily to the traditional family unit, it also uses the concept in a broad way and refers to the married, widows, single people, and young people. The council teaches that laity's development of family life is their principal responsibility and contributes to the resolution of one of the most urgent problems facing humanity today (AA 11:1). The council calls laity to develop their own family spirituality and to make their families into schools of holiness (LG 35), of social virtues (GE 3), of ministry (LG 35), and of the social defense of family values (GS 52). Laity should make their families into the domestic Church (LG 11) and gather with other families for mutual support (AA 11:6). The council stresses that one of the laity's principal responsibilities is the ministry of social outreach, insisting that it "is so much the duty and responsibility of the laity that it can never be properly performed by others" (AA 13:1). This social mission of laity includes cooperating for justice in regulating economic and social affairs (AG 12), defending the dignity of the human person (GS 26), cultural developments (GS 53), education (GS 60:1), involvement with the media (IM 13), and participation in politics (GS 75; AA 14).

In addition to the council's emphasis on the laity's mission of world involvement, one of the great impressions made on readers of the documents is the insistence on the laity's responsibility within the community of the Church. The council frequently refers to three specific duties: liturgical participation (SC 11), community building (GS 92:1), and a sense of coresponsibility for the life of the local Church (AA 10:2). In the latter case the council calls laity to offer their special competencies to the parish, to help in the administration of church goods, to share responsibility for catechetical instruction, and to participate in various pastoral commissions and diocesan councils.

Vatican II's Key Components of Lay Life

Laity are not a segment of the Church; rather, they make up over 98 percent of the whole Church. So it is not appropriate to simply distinguish between clergy, religious, and laity, for there are many different vocations for laity—varied states of life in which laity live out the fundamental call of the council to be people of the Church at the heart of the world and people of the world at the heart of the Church. What is special to laity is the same as what is special to clergy or religious, for there is equality and common dignity regarding the essentials of Christian discipleship.

Baptismal vocation is a common calling for the Lord's disciples. The council challenged all Christians to rediscover their baptismal vocation, even representing priestly ordination and religious profession as intensifications of this calling. Through their baptism laity become Church and are called to live as a community of faith. This conciliar focus on baptismal equality restores the dignity of lay life and challenges the laity to integrate baptismal awareness and dedication into every aspect of life.

The sacramental life of the Church is the common source of grace and spiritual growth. The council moved away from any elitist approach to spirituality such as was present in history and focused on the sacraments as the basis of all spiritual growth. It declared that the nature of spiritual growth is the development of charity, and that the source of spiritual growth is the Holy Spirit. It is not saintly individuals who make the Church holy but a holy Church that makes individuals holy because they participate in its life.

The council stressed an understanding of the Church that included a vision of community life. This implied participatory styles of government and collaboration in ministry. Lay participation in all dimensions of Church life now contributes to a contemporary image of the Church at all levels of Christian life—family, work, parish, Church committee work, parishes, and dioceses. These efforts to build community stress the importance of lay life and lay contributions to the Church.

The council taught that the Holy Spirit blesses all the faithful with a variety of gifts, or charisms, that benefit the Church and world. Each one has the right and duty to use these charisms, for without each other's charisms the faithful remain incomplete as a believing community.

One of the special teachings of the council was to refocus attention on the priesthood of all the baptized. This led to the contemporary emphasis on the universal call to integrate a dimension of ministry into one's life, thereby calling laity to appreciate a new perspective on their own baptismal priesthood. This led to two trends among laity: a growing awareness that service of others is a necessary part of baptismal dedication, and a realization that in these years God is calling many laity to make the service of others a career commitment.

Thus, the history of laity has had many ups and downs, from the New Testament's equality and universal call to holiness and ministry, through the times of second class citizenship and neglect, to the rebirth of challenge in the teachings of the Second Vatican Council.

LEONARD DOOHAN

See also CHURCH, THE; MINISTRY; VATICAN COUNCIL II.

LAMENNAIS, FELICITÉ ROBERT DE (1782–1854)

De Lamennais came from a socially prominent family in Brittany. His readings in the French writers of the revolutionary period caused him to lose his faith while still a teenager, but his older brother Jean, a priest, converted him back to Roman Catholicism. He became extremely conservative on ecclesiastico-political matters. His first book, *Reflections on the State of the Church* (1808), attacked the simplistic belief in the power of reason, which, de Lamennais believed, led to rationalism and atheism. He advocated a stronger role for the Church in political affairs, a view which forced him to flee France during Bonaparte's brief return from Elba (1815). In the next year de Lamennais became a priest, and he again turned to writing. His book *An Essay on Indifference in Matters of Religion* (1818) stressed the importance of belonging to an ecclesiastical community in order to avoid doubt and even ignorance; truth can be provided only by authority. Monarchists and Ultramontanes applauded these views, which only became stronger over time. De Lamennais believed that Roman Catholicism was the rightful religion of all peoples, that (following Wycliffe) Catholics did not have to obey rulers who did not govern as Christians, and that the world would be better off if the pope were the political leader of Christendom. Since de Lamennais believed that European governments routinely oppressed the Church, he began to argue (1829) for the separation of Church and state and the freedom of the press. He believed that people achieved true freedom within the Church, but his views were poorly received in Rome, which had concordats with several European governments and which considered freedom of the press an invitation to atheists and anarchists to attack the Church. He suddenly found himself considered a liberal, and his old enemies among the Gallicans took advantage of this to discredit him and his newspaper, *L'Avenir,* for opposing the concordat between France and Rome. De Lamennais was convinced the pope would understand what he meant by freedom, and, in the last issue of *L'Avenir* (1831), he asked the pope to lead a crusade for freedom. He went to Rome to plead his case, but Gregory XVI refused to meet him; in 1832 Gregory published the encyclical *Mirari Vos* which condemned too much freedom in religious matters as leading to indifferentism. De Lamennais submitted, but in 1834 in his book of poems, *Words of a Believer,* he took his doctrine of freedom further, denying the Church a role in politics. The encyclical *Singulari Nos* condemned the book, and de Lamennais left the Church. Now free of the Church, he soon freed himself from Christianity, publishing books which denied the idea of a supernatural order as well as most Catholic doctrine. He served in the revolutionary parliament of 1848, but left in 1852 when the antirevolutionary reaction set in. Much of what de Lamennais proposed is now accepted by Catholics, including freedom of the press and the separation of Church and state, but his views were simply too advanced for his day.

JOSEPH F. KELLY

See also CHURCH AND STATE; RELIGIOUS FREEDOM.

L'ARCHE

The French term meaning the Ark, Noah's Ark, "l'Arche" is the name of a worldwide community of handicapped and nonhandicapped persons founded in 1964 in Trosly-Breuil, France, by the Canadian Jean Vanier.

Son of Georges Vanier (d. 5 March 1967), nineteenth governor-general of Canada, and Pauline Archer Vanier (d. 23 March 1991), Swiss-born Jean Vanier (b. 10 September 1928) first embarked on a career as a naval officer, and later studied philosophy at l'Institut Catholique de Paris. After finishing his doctorate, Vanier taught philosophy for a brief time at Saint Michael's College in Toronto. At the age of thirty-five, following a long period of searching for his path in life, Vanier's vocation became clear. French Dominican Thomas Philippe (d. 4 February 1993) was serving as chaplain at le Val Fleuri, a large residential facility in Trosly-Breuil for men with mental disabilities. He invited Vanier to create a small "foyer," or place of welcome for some of the men of "le Val." On 4 August 1964 Vanier welcomed Raphael and Phillipe, two men with mental handicaps, to live with him. He christened the dilapidated little home "l'Arche." Like Noah's Ark, Vanier intended l'Arche to be a place of refuge, diversity, and hope. Within a short time, more handicapped men and women came to l'Arche. "Assistants," the nonhandicapped persons who live in community with the handicapped, began to come from different regions of France and then from different parts of the world.

From a small and seemingly insignificant gesture of welcome and hospitality in an obscure village just north of Paris, the communities of l'Arche have spread throughout the world. There are now approximately one hundred communities in the International Federation of l'Arche. "Faith and Light," also founded by Vanier, is an even larger network of support communities comprised of handicapped persons, their families and their friends who gather in different parts of the world for retreats, conferences, or periods of rest and renewal. Even though Vanier is no longer primarily responsible for leading l'Arche or Faith and Light, his inspiration continues to have a singularly important and formative role. Thomas Philippe, considered the cofounder of l'Arche by many, has also had a considerable influence in the life and spirituality of l'Arche.

Vanier's key insight is that the handicapped person is the teacher of the clever and the strong. The handicapped person is endowed with rich qualities of heart: compassion, mercy, forgiveness, celebration, simplicity. In their poverty and woundedness, persons with mental handicaps reveal the heart of Jesus. It is in and through them that we meet Jesus. Further, it is in and through the handicapped person that we find our own humanity, what it means to be a human person created in God's image.

In l'Arche, handicapped and nonhandicapped persons live, work, and pray together in the spirit of the beatitudes. Work, usually comprised of simple, manual tasks, varies according to the capacities of each. The type of work done depends upon availability and locale: gardening is often done in rural communities; subcontract work for factories is sometimes done in urban settings. The shape of each l'Arche community differs, sometimes considerably so. But the single most important feature of this form of community is that the clever and the strong do not function primarily as caregivers or helpers. Rather, the nonhandicapped persons "live with" handicapped persons in a spirit of the beatitudes, open to receive the gift of the handicapped person. And what is this gift? In the community of l'Arche, the essential poverty of each one of us is disclosed through the conspicuous weakness and woundedness of the person with a mental handicap. It is the basic humanity of each one, the person we are called to be, the true self, that is manifest in the shared life of l'Arche. Community, thus, becomes a place of pardon and of celebration.

The membership of l'Arche includes persons of different religions, languages, and races, often within the very same household. Some assistants come to live in l'Arche with the intention of spending a lifetime, and they stay a week. Others come for a weekend visit, and decide to put down roots in a l'Arche community. Many who stay in l'Arche for a long time make a covenant, "l'Alliance," through which they commit themselves to live in solidarity and communion with the poor and wounded.

Originally Christian, indeed Roman Catholic in inspiration, l'Arche is founded on the principle of the dignity and sanctity of the handicapped person. Today, many members of l'Arche are active in Catholic Church life and practice. Others are disaffected with religion. Some are decidedly agnostic. Others are avowedly atheist. In Britain and Ireland, Roman Catholics and Christians of different Protestant traditions live, work, and pray together as members of the same community. In India, Christians and Hindus join together in life, work, and prayer. The ecumenical and interreligious character of l'Arche poses distinctive problems and possibilities. What binds them all together is the belief in the dignity and sanctity of persons with disabilities. This conviction is the raison d'être of the communities of l'Arche throughout the world.

Because l'Arche is not a canonical religious community, it does not have benefit of some of the advantages that membership in a religious institute affords. But its noncanonical status does have advantages. For example, l'Arche is able to establish new communities in countries where Christians or Catholics identified with Church institutions or structures may be suspect or unwelcome. Further, there is a greater measure of freedom in developing the charters, constitutions, and forms of life in l'Arche. Because l'Arche is not formally a "Church-related" organization, the communities are eligible for financial assistance from governments and grants agencies, which they might not be otherwise. Without government assistance, many of the communities could not continue because of lack of funds.

The great majority of l'Arche communities have deep links and bonds of affection with local bishops and Church leaders. In many instances the communities are enriched by the participation of vowed religious women and men, and by the sacramental ministry of priests associated with the communities. But l'Arche is a lay community and, as such, encounters both the problems and challenges, as well as the grace and freedom that this entails.

MICHAEL DOWNEY

See also CHRISTIAN SPIRITUALITY; CORPORAL AND SPIRITUAL WORKS OF MERCY.

LAS CASAS, BARTOLOMÉ DE (1474–1566)

The son of a merchant who had accompanied Columbus on his second journey to the New World, he himself went to Hispaniola (Haiti) at the age of eighteen. He aided the Spanish government there and was given an *encomienda* (land with Indian inhabitants). He evangelized as layman and was ordained ca. 1512, probably the first priest ordained in the Western Hemisphere. After taking part in the bloody occupation of Cuba (1513), he received more land, this time with Indian serfs. About this time, he had a conversion and began to work on behalf of the Indians but with few results. Realizing he had to change official policy, he went to Spain in 1515. By this and other visits to the home country, he won approval for an audacious experiment, the founding of towns of free Indians, but poor planning, local resistance, and an Indian revolt in 1522 destroyed the experiment. Las Casas left civic life and joined the Dominican Order (1523). He continued to work on behalf of the native peoples, but he now did so with his pen. In 1537 his book *De unico modo* ("The Only Way") advocated peaceful evangelization. The *Historia apologetica,* written over several years, defended the abilities of the Indians to govern their own lives, a refutation of the common European view that they were merely brutal savages. A pamphlet, *The Destruction of the Indians* (1542), denounced the greed of the colonists but went beyond the facts in its accusations. His masterpiece, *The History of the Indians* (1562), offers a detailed account about what he experienced in New Spain with emphasis upon the harsh treatment, exploitation, and enslavement of the native peoples and with a warning that God would exact a price from the Christians for their behavior. As his writings gained acceptance, Las Casas worked to change the lot of the Indians. In 1542 and 1543 Spain published the *New Laws,* mitigating the treatment of the Indians and outlawing their enslavement. Las Casas became bishop of Chiapas, Mexico, in 1544 and discovered the difficulty of enforcing the laws even in his own diocese. His devotion to the indigenous led Las Casas to advocate a tragic policy, the importation of black slaves from Africa to replace the Indian workers lost to the colonists. That a man like this could do such a thing testifies to the low status in which Africans were held in Europe. In 1551 Las Casas, now seventy-seven, retired from his diocese and returned to Spain, but at the time of his death, at age ninety-two, he was pleading with King Philip II for equitable treatment of the natives of Guatemala. His lifelong struggle for the native peoples of the Americas earned Las Casas the title "Defender of the Indians."

JOSEPH F. KELLY

See also DOMINICANS; HUMAN RIGHTS; MISSIONS, CATHOLIC, THE MODERN PERIOD; SLAVERY.

LAST SACRAMENTS

See SACRAMENT OF ANOINTING.

LATERAN TREATY, THE

This treaty established Vatican City as a sovereign state, without any qualification, on 11 February 1929. It was a final settlement of the Roman question. The Holy See gave recognition to the Italian state with Rome as its capital; and the state recognized "the Catholic and Apostolic Religion as the sole religion of the State." A concordat, attached to the treaty, stipulated that the state would recognize marriages performed in accordance with canon law; would provide religious instruction in the schools; would grant freedom to Catholic action, provided it avoided political activities. It also decreed that the bishops would take an oath of allegiance to the king of Italy before taking possession of their dioceses.

JOAN GLAZIER

See also PAPACY, THE; PAPAL STATES.

LATTER DAY SAINTS (MORMONS)

See CHURCH OF JESUS CHRIST OF LATTER DAY SAINTS (MORMONS).

LAW

Law is a vehicle that regulates human conduct in necessary matters concerning the common good. As such its content encompasses normative articulations, whether written or unwritten, regarding the values and obligations and rights—not merely of individuals as independent entities—but, rather, of their welfare as members of society, as well as the welfare of society in general. Insofar as laws regulate matters of necessity for society and the members thereof, they are obligatory norms of action. Such laws are ordinarily enacted by the directive judgment of those in positions of authority, whether elected or appointed, in relation to the common good. When properly formulated and implemented, laws ordinarily serve the social order as an alternative to the employment of force for furthering the common good. Thus the four basic functions of law in relation to the common good of society include the ability to command what is good, to forbid what is evil, to permit what is indifferent, and to coerce in certain limited circumstances.

In the Christian dispensation, law is generally divided into categories of eternal law, natural law and positive law. Eternal or divine law is that determined by God for all ages for the good of all material and spiritual reality. While the origin, meaning, and content of natural law have been the subject of considerable controversy, the notion of natural law as it has survived through the centuries is that of a rule of action implicit in the nature of things or a rule of conduct that emanates from human nature as rational. In Christian thought, natural law is considered that portion of divine or eternal law which applies to human beings, whereas divine law in its entirety is regarded as that which governs the whole of creation including the universe and humanity and all creation, whether material or spiritual, animate or inanimate. Positive law, on the other hand, is that which is enacted by human beings for the good order and governance of people in society, and it is divided into a variety of subcategories including international law, public law, private law, economic law, procedural law, and the like. In general, positive law is understood as a legitimate, external norm of action providing stability and order in necessary aspects of societal relations.

Catholic thought considers authority—or that moral power able to engender unity of action toward good—as related to law in that all authority originates ultimately in God and that divine positive law as enunciated in Scripture has normative authority as does the content of natural law which is rooted in the essential nature of things. Catholic thought also considers positive law as related to divine law and to natural law in that legitimate, humanly enacted positive norms of action must be in keeping with right reason and must have the intent of fostering or of attaining some morally good purpose. Law is also related to justice—or that fundamental disposition to render to another what is due—in that it gives specification to the obligation for and the boundaries of just actions in particular circumstances.

Some Christian legal theories place greater emphasis on the will (Duns Scotus and William of Ockham) than on reason (Thomas Aquinas and Francisco Suarez), while legal theorists of other persuasions attempt to ground natural law and law itself primarily in the social nature of mankind (John Locke and J. J. Rousseau). Still other legal theorists reject the idea that any objective norms are knowable from either natural or positive law (Immanuel Kant and Georg Hegel), or they reduce all legal norms primarily to the utilitarian good of the largest majority (Jeremy Bentham) or to the observable historical evolution of basic patterns of choice known as custom (Friedrich von Savigny).

ELIZABETH McDONOUGH, O.P.

See also COMMON GOOD; NATURAL LAW; VIRTUE.

LAW, CANON

See CANON LAW.

LAWRENCE OF BRINDISI, ST. (1559–1619)

Priest, Doctor of the Church, Cesare de Rossi was born at Brindisi in the kingdom of Naples in 1559 to a prominent family. Educated by the Conventual Franciscans and then at St. Mark's college in Venice, he joined the Capuchins in Verona and took the name of Lawrence. He studied at the University of Padua excelling in languages and biblical studies, and began a successful preaching campaign through northern Italy. He was named the definitor general of the Capuchin Order in 1556, and was assigned to work for the conversion of the Jews by Pope Clement VIII (1592–1605). He was sent to help preach against the rising tide of Protestantism in Germany and while there set up provinces in Austria, Styria and Bohemia. In 1602 he was elected minister general of the Capuchins. While in this position he was asked to help the Germans ward off the advancing Turkish armies. He became a chaplain and advisor to the German forces and was credited with helping to win the victory. While on a political mission to Philip III of Spain, he established a Capuchin house in Madrid. Later he was sent to Munich by the Holy See as an envoy and continued his preaching and mediation of political disputes.

In 1618 he retired from public life to a friary at Caserta, yet again he was called upon by the Neapolitan rulers to mediate a dispute between them and the king of Spain. After an arduous journey, he accomplished the wishes of the Neapolitans; soon after his return home, he died on 22 July 1619.

Lawrence is remembered best for his commentary on Genesis, his writings against Lutheranism, and a large corpus of his sermons. He was canonized by Pope Leo XIII in 1881 and named a Doctor of the Church by Pope John XXIII in 1959. His feast is celebrated on 21 July.

ANTHONY D. ANDREASSI

See also FRANCISCANS; REFORMATION, THE.

LAY SPIRITUALITY

See SPIRITUALITY, LAY.

LAY TRUSTEEISM

As the American Revolution succeeded and the former colonies were freed from English law, Catholic parishes were presented with a new situation and new opportunities. In the spirit of the new republic and in keeping with civil statutes, when a Catholic parish was incorporated, Catholic laymen were recognized as its legal administrators or trustees.

This congregational model of church organization had the merit of involving laymen intimately in the management of parish affairs, but it opened up the possibility of abuse. In any case, the congregational model was in conflict with the hierarchical model of parish governance favored by the Catholic Church. Through most of the nineteenth century the hierarchy worked to gain control of parish governance and by the Third Plenary Council of Baltimore in 1884 lay trusteeism had come to an end.

The story begins with a New York state law in 1785 which, following a custom familiar in Protestant churches, gave adult males authority to elect trustees to oversee the management of the operations of a church. Catholic laymen who had purchased the land, built the church, and paid the salary of the clergyman thought it in keeping with their trusteeship to hire the pastor and, if they so deemed, to terminate his services for a variety of reasons, including lack of eloquence in the pulpit.

Though the system often worked well with all parties acting in a cooperative manner, over the years there were, perhaps inevitably, a number of severe tests of ecclesiastical control. Pius VII was moved in 1822 to send a letter to the trustees of St. Mary's church in Philadelphia, directing their attention to the fact that in the Catholic Church the appointment of pastors and the management of church property is under hierarchical, not lay, control. In a separate letter to the archbishop of Baltimore the Pope directed him to limit the powers of lay trustees and ensure the freedom of bishops and priests to exercise their proper roles in the church.

In their attempts at limiting the excesses of lay trusteeism, American bishops found they were not without resources. The First Provincial Council of Baltimore in 1829 reminded bishops that they might require the handing over of the deed to the property before consecrating a new church.

The increase in the number of clergy during the nineteenth century fostered the establishment of parishes by individual priests. The emergence of the "brick and mortar pastor" signaled the decline of the trustee system. Though the laity were called upon to contribute extensively and expensively to the building up of the parish, they no longer enjoyed the authority of trustees in the appointment of the clergy or the management of church property.

WILLIAM C. McFADDEN, S.J.

See also PARISH; PARISH COUNCIL; PASTOR.

LECTIONARY

See LITURGICAL BOOKS.

LEEN, EDWARD (1885–1944)

Holy Ghost Father, missionary, lecturer, spiritual writer, Edward Leen was born in Abbeyfeale, County Limerick, and educated in Rockwell College, University College, Dublin, and the Gregorian University, Rome. His academic career was marked by the highest honors. He served for a while in Nigeria with his former Rockwell teacher, Joseph Shanahan, and returned in 1922 to Blackrock College, where he was dean of studies and president. Thereafter he seconded Shanahan's missionary foundation, the Sisters of the Holy Rosary, an institute which grew rapidly in the Irish missionary age of the thirties and forties.

Influenced by the writings of John Henry Newman and J. B. Terrien, and greatly encouraged by his publisher, Frank Sheed, he became a popular and influential spiritual writer. Among his books are: *Progress through Mental Prayer* (1935), followed by *In the Likeness of Christ* (1936), *The Holy Ghost and his Work in Souls* (1937), *Why the Cross* (1938), *The True Vine and its Branches* (1938).

MICHAEL O'CARROLL, C.S.Sp.

See also CATHOLICISM, IRISH; HOLY GHOST FATHERS AND BROTHERS (SPIRITANS); SHANAHAN, JOSEPH; SHEED, F. J. (FRANK).

LÉGER, PAUL-ÉMILE (1904–1991)

Paul-Émile Léger was born in 1904, 25 April, in the industrial town of Valleyfield, Québec. He spent his childhood in the border village of St. Anicet where his father was manager of the general store. He studied in Petit Séminaire at St. Thérèse de Blainville and in the St. Sulpice Grand Séminaire of Montreal. Ordained a priest in May 1929, he traveled the same year to Issy-les-Moulineaux, near Paris, and joined the Society of St. Sulpice. In 1933, he became a missionary in Japan, working as a parish priest and teacher of philosophy in an intermediate seminary.

In the summer of 1939, Léger returned to Canada. After teaching for a year at the seminary of philosophy in Montreal, he left St. Sulpice in 1940 to go back to his original diocese of Valleyfield as general vicar and rector of the cathedral. In April 1947, he rejoined the St. Sulpice Society and became rector of the Canadian College in Rome.

Three years later, he was named to replace Mgsr. Joseph Charbonneau as the head of the Archdiocese of Montreal. He proved himself a dedicated leader and an apostle of charity for the poor, and for neglected children, men, and women, never hesitating to denounce the evil and corruption in society. Soon after his arrival, he founded the "Foyer de charité" for the poor and rejected sick people; in 1957, he established St. Charles-Borromée Hospital for the handicapped. With an alarmist fear of Masonry and Communism, and with a conviction of the supremacy of the Church over the state and of the spiritual over the material, he sponsored many campaigns against materialism, pornography, prostitution, obscene literature, and alcohol abuse. He led action in favor of prayer (Rosary at the radio) and public morality, observance of Sunday, and housing for poor families. His most impressive campaign was the Great Mission during Lent 1960. In all those actions, he succeeded in interesting the general population, influencing public opinion, and engaging members of various Catholic or professional associations and even public authorities in his projects, always with success and great publicity.

With the opening of the Vatican Council II (1962–1965), he played a prominent role with such key personalities as Cardinals Liénard, Suenens, Frings, and Döpfner, Patriarch Maximos, and Jesuit Bea. With the collaboration of his theologians Pierre Lafortune and André Naud, he prepared and delivered refreshing, clear, pertinent, and well-documented declarations on liturgy, revelation, bishops, sanctity, ecumenism, religious freedom, Jews and non-Christians, marriage, and the training of priests. He has been considered by specialists as one of the few to have borne witness to, as wrote René Laurentin (France), a "liberated language and thought" and one whose interventions have been most influential.

After the council, a new task was to be achieved: to realize the gains of Vatican II. But Léger never succeeded in being entirely comfortable with the new model of community church which replaced the pyramidal and authoritarian model in which he was deeply rooted. The evolution of his thought was not deep enough to inspire in him a new kind of leadership. In November 1967, he left Montreal for Africa. He devoted the rest of his life to activities where he was at ease, and began a new life in the field of international care for lepers, the handicapped, and the poor. He finally returned to Montreal in 1979, where he died 13 November 1991.

DENISE ROBILLARD

See also CANADA, THE CATHOLIC CHURCH IN; VATICAN COUNCIL II.

LEGION OF MARY

One of the largest lay associations founded in the twentieth century, the Legion of Mary took its origin in a meeting of St. Vincent de Paul workers and associates in Dublin on 7 September 1921. Present with priest Michael Toher was Frank Duff who attracted many followers. The group undertook social and charitable work and quickly acquired a separate identity. Its spirituality was influenced by the treatise of St. (then Blessed) Grignion de Montfort on *True Devotion to the Blessed Virgin Mary,* his thesis on Mary's universal mediation of grace. The structure was firmly drawn, with a nomenclature taken from the Roman Legion; the local unit was a *praesidium,* with the next highest grouping a *curia* and so on to the supreme governing body, the *consilium.* A weekly meeting, with prescribed prayers, was the life of the body. Frank Duff, well-read in spirituality, especially in French works, nourished the growing organization, setting out ideals, counsel, and regulations in the *Handbook of the Legion*—soon to be translated into every major language in the world. He clarified the universal call to holiness and developed a dynamic spirituality of the Holy Spirit.

The objective of the Legion was apostolic work of any kind save material assistance. Pioneer works of spiritual rescue were Sancta Maria Hostel for prostitutes, Regina Coeli Hostel for unmarried mothers, Morning Star Hostel for homeless men. The Legion quickly spread outside Ireland to other countries beginning with Scotland. It reached the U.S.A. in 1931, and entered France during the war. Meanwhile, a vast expansion was to carry the organization to Australia, Africa, and Asia. In English-speaking countries the Irish diaspora offered the means of communication.

A system of specially commissioned envoys developed and proved very successful: Edel Quinn was the best known of these and she worked in East Africa. There she left a reputation for sanctity which is under consideration by Church authorities in view of her beatification. Alfie Lambe's envoyship to Latin America may have a similar outcome. Names with a similar aura are Hilda Firtel in Germany, and Pactia Santos and Joaquina Lucas from the Philippines. The Philippines and South Korea at the present time have seen a true efflorescence of the Legion. The Legion had gained a firm foothold in China, and there it had its first martyrs in the ferocious anti-Catholic drive of the Mao Tse-tung years.

An influential ally in the theological arena during the fifties and later was a young auxiliary bishop of Malines-Brussels, Leon Joseph Suenens, (later cardinal), who was destined to a play a great role in Church life up to, during, and after Vatican II. His books on legionary spirituality and his life of Edel Quinn were a considerable help. More powerful was the support coming directly from the papacy; every pope since Pius XI has fully endorsed the organization.

Statistics are not easily available. The organization exists in some two thousand dioceses across the Catholic world and has certainly more than one million active members who work in a great variety of apostolic fields.

MICHAEL O'CARROLL, C.S.Sp.

See also CATHOLICISM, IRISH; DUFF, FRANK; QUINN, EDEL.

LENT

Lent is the forty-day period of fasting and prayer that Christians observe in preparation for the celebration of Easter. For the first three centuries, the period of fasting before Easter varied from a few days to a week. However, the Council of Nicaea in 325 mentioned a period of forty days of preparation, and by the end of the fourth century, a forty-day fast before Easter (called *quadragesima* in the West) was commonly observed in both the East and the West. The Lenten fast may have originated in the fast mandated for the candidates preparing for baptism at Easter, and the number forty may have its origins in the forty-day fast observed by Moses, Elijah, and Christ. The Eastern and the Western Churches differed as to the computation of the forty days. The East fasted for seven weeks omitting Saturdays (except Holy Saturday) and Sundays resulting in thirty-six days of fasting. The West observed six weeks of fast, but omitted only Sundays, which also amounted to thirty-six fast days in all. However, local customs differed greatly as to the actual observance of the Lenten fast. In the West in the seventh century the period from Ash Wednesday to the First Sunday of Lent was added to the original six weeks, achieving a total of forty days.

Initially the fast was severe allowing for only one meal each day (to be taken in the evening) and forbidding the consumption of fish and flesh-meat, and in some places, even dairy products. Beginning in the ninth century, however, the fast was relaxed to allow fish and eggs, and the meal was moved up to an earlier part of the day. In the last few centuries meat has been permitted except on Fridays, and the emphasis on the meaning of Lent has shifted. For centuries the popular understanding of Lent centered on physical suffering. Vatican Council II (1962–1965) shifted the emphasis to the spiritual preparation for the paschal mystery of Easter and broadened the focus to include other forms of penance and increased prayer and works of charity. The three aspects of Lent—prayer, fasting, and almsgiving—are not ends in themselves, but means to prepare the Christian to celebrate the resurrection of the Lord. Lent helps to remind Christians of their sinfulness and the need to return to their baptismal innocence.

ANTHONY D. ANDREASSI

See also LITURGY.

LEO XIII, POPE (1878–1903)

Vincenzo Gioacchino Pecci was born into a military family at Carpineto in 1810, and was educated by the Jesuits in Viterbo and Rome. He was ordained in 1837, worked in the Papal States, and spent three years as nuncio to Brussels. In 1846 he was made bishop of Perugia and seven years later was made a cardinal priest of S. Crisogono. In 1877 Pius IX,

Pope Leo XIII

who had had some disagreements with him, brought him back to Rome. On the death of Pius in 1878, he was elected pope on the third ballot. He was almost sixty-eight and many regarded him as an "interim pope"—but he outlived most of the cardinals at the conclave and reigned for twenty-five years as Leo XIII. Leo was a man of wide culture, deep faith, and great confidence. He reached out to seek understanding with the modern world. He fostered education on all levels; encouraged the study of astronomy and natural science at the Vatican; and opened the Vatican archives and library to all qualified researchers. He strongly supported the study of St. Thomas with his encyclical *Aeterni Patris* (1879) and his personal participation and interest in Thomistic studies was one of the distinguishing features of his pontificate. With his encyclical *Providentissimus Deus* (1893) he cautiously encouraged critical and scholarly biblical studies.

He made strenuous diplomatic efforts to reach peaceful accommodations with hostile governments, and moved to end the *Kulturkampf*, the anti-Catholic movement in Germany initiated by Bismarck during the papacy of Pius IX, so that by 1887 most of the discriminating laws were repealed. His move to normalize relations with France was more delicate. Many Catholics, particularly the clergy, aligned themselves with the royalists. Leo, despite the blatant anticlericalism and pervasive secularism of the Third Republic, pleaded with French Catholics to accept the republican form of government. Leo also faced thorny problems in dealing with the Italian government. At first, he had hoped that France and Austria might, for their own interests, back the restoration of the papal possessions. When that did not materialize, he softened his stance and allowed Italian Catholics to participate in local, but not in national, political affairs. He succeeded in getting subsidies for Catholic schools in Austria, Hungary, Germany, Belgium, and the Netherlands.

His approach to the Anglican and Orthodox Churches did not advance the hopes of reunion; and the bull *Apostolicae Curae,* declaring Anglican orders invalid, created consternation in England. Despite his goodwill and good intentions, Leo was uncomfortable with democracy, which he felt should have no place in the governing structures of the Church. He did not fully appreciate the dynamics of democracy in America's pluralistic society; his condemnation of Americanism—a practical movement initiated by some Catholic leaders to make the Church an acceptable part of the American milieu without any compromise of essentials—surprised many and created more confusion than solutions. Leo XIII was a towering international figure who brought more prestige to the papacy than any pope since the Middle Ages. He had the advantage of working on a spiritual level, unburdened with the problems of the lost Papal States, which were usually badly administered and were a constant distraction and often a scandal.

He is rightly remembered as "the pope of the workers"; his social teaching was the great challenge both to the works of Karl Marx and to the unbridled capitalism advocated by the proponents of laissez faire. Since the 1840s, the working class and intellectuals had begun drifting from the Church which seemed almost oblivious to the industrial revolution and the multiple social problems to which it gave rise. In 1891 Leo issued his landmark social encyclical *Rerum Novarum,* which outlined the rights and responsibilities of the family and of private property against the intrusion of the state. He cogently stated that labor is not a commodity, and outlined the rights of workers to just remuneration. The encyclical stressed the responsibility of the state to intervene, when necessary, to prevent the exploitation of workers and to protect their right to form unions. The encyclical received universal attention but not universal acceptance. Many Catholic employers and many Church leaders were slow to accept the implications of Leo's social manifesto. The great Dublin strike of 1913 is ample witness to this. For over a century *Rerum Novarum* became the inspiration for needed social legislation and for the involvement of Catholics in the trade union movement and in the political life of many countries.

MICHAEL GLAZIER

See also CHURCH AND STATE; ENCYCLICALS, SOCIAL; PAPACY, THE.

LEO THE GREAT, ST. (d. 461)

Born perhaps at the end of the fourth century, Leo became a deacon in the Church at Rome where he influenced popes to act against Nestorianism and Pelagianism. While he was on a diplomatic mission in Gaul in 440, he was elected pope. He devoted himself totally to his duties as bishop of Rome: preaching, promoting the liturgy, encouraging religious life, opposing heresies. In other parts of the Western Church, notably Gaul, Africa, and Spain, he exercised such jurisdiction as he felt was necessary to promote orthodoxy, peace, and good order. To this end he obtained a rescript from Emperor Valentinian III that recognized his jurisdiction over the western provinces of the Roman Empire.

Eutyches appealed for Leo's help after Bishop Flavian removed him as archimandrite of a large monastery in Constantinople for his teaching that Christ incarnate had only one nature, a teaching which appeared to deny the full humanity of Christ. After studying the matter carefully, Leo wrote his famous Tome (Letter 28) to Flavian in 449 which condemned Eutyches and set forth what would become a classic Christological statement that there were two distinct natures in the person of Christ. Naming it a "robber council" (*latrocinium*), Leo refused to accept the decisions of a council convened in Ephesus in 449 by Emperor Theodosius II which rejected his Christological position and rehabilitated Eutyches. In October 451 the Fourth General Council of Chalcedon (modern-day Kadiköy, Turkey) accepted with respect Leo's Tome. Leo's courage in the face of impending disaster from barbarian invasions helped to restrain violence and bloodshed. In 452 Leo was part of an imperial delegation that persuaded Attila to remove the Huns who were destroying northern Italy. In 455 Leo was able to persuade Gaiseric not to massacre the inhabitants or burn the city when the Vandals took Rome. Leo's surviving works include 143 letters and 96 sermons. His sermons cover the Church year and are an important source for the study of liturgy. He was named a Doctor of the Church in 1754. Feast day, 18 February (East); 10 November (West).

JOHN DILLON

See also DOCTORS OF THE CHURCH; ECUMENICAL COUNCILS; FATHERS OF THE CHURCH; LITURGY; PREACHING.

LEONARDO DA VINCI (1452–1519)

Born in 1452, Leonardo da Vinci was a master of Renaissance painting, a scientist, and a philosopher. After the manner of many painters and sculptors of the Italian Renaissance, he engaged in a wide range of studies helpful to his art. He was a minute student

"Virgin and Child with St. Anne," by Leonardo da Vinci, Louvre, Paris

of nature, including human and animal anatomy, rocks, folds of garments, optics, geometry, and perspective. He experimented with oil painting. While he was rooted in the fifteenth-century's discoveries in the area of artistic technique, he was never satisfied with them. Leonardo's interests ranged wider than any of his contemporaries, spilling over into philosophy, physics, and engineering (he sketched plans for numerous inventions), and he was in demand as a specialist in weaponry and defense works.

Leonardo's tremendous gift for painting was recognized immediately and spread from Florence across Italy and Europe. (He worked also in Milan, Venice, and Rome, dying at the court of France in 1519.) He aimed at representing his subjects in the action which would best express their emotions, a trait already evident is the unfinished *Adoration of the Magi* (1481) and especially in the much damaged *Last Supper* (Santa Maria delle Grazie, Milan, ca. 1495–1497). This painting also is original in focusing on an exact moment in the story of the Supper: Christ's announcement that one of his disciples would betray him. These features of Leonardo's art amount to a new concept of the artist himself: one who penetrates to the depths of reality and conveys it successfully to the serious beholder. The artist is no mere craftsman; he moves with the penetration of the philosopher and the inspiration of the poet. In addition to motion and expression, Leonardo's work is characterized by complexity, excellence of composition (overall and in detail) and convincing modeling through light and shade as seen, for example, in *Mona Lisa.* His studies from 1503 to 1505 for paintings of the Madonna and Child with St. Anne broke new ground for group subjects. He also worked in sculpture and architecture, though nothing survives which is certainly attributable to him.

DAVID BRYAN

See also ART, CHRISTIAN; RENAISSANCE, THE.

LIBERALISM

Liberalism refers to a dominant *spirit* of the nineteenth century which combined features of Renaissance humanism, Enlightenment rationalism, Kantian neo-rationalism, strains of Hegelian idealism and German romanticism, among others. It created an atmosphere and temperament that prized openmindedness, intellectual honesty and rigor, individual liberty rooted in the exercise of rational will, devotion to truth wherever found and wherever it might lead, and above all, tolerance of others (and their ideas and beliefs) born of humility in oneself.

In politics this spirit required that states, constitutions, laws, social formations, and the like, must respect, protect and promote individual liberty—or face defiance, reformulation or rebellion. In religion, where one strain of the Christian tradition had always affirmed that God is the source of all truth and that the believer—however unknowing and sinful—is called to pursue the unity of all truth, this *liberal spirit* challenged believers to embrace the vital substance of their Christian faith while at the same time accommodating the intellectual, artistic and scientific accomplishments of modern culture. Implicit in nineteenth-century liberalism was the conviction that there is "unity in diversity" in the search for truth in philosophy, religion (theology), and science.

If the search entailed a common quest for unity, the diversity of discovery and expression required a distinctive method: open, nondogmatic, dialectical, critical in both approach and temper. Uncompromising critical examination of all the sources of the faith became the expectation; unquestioningly accepted "truths" of the faith became the target. This point of collision, "Lord, I believe; help thou my unbelief," joined with the claim that "Christian" language coupled with "wish" is further from the "Christian faith" than the denials of an "honest" atheist (W. Herrmann).

Friedrich Schleiermacher's *On Religion: Speeches to Its Cultured Despisers* (1799) shows the development of this liberal thrust in his forceful apologetic against skepticism. The true grounding point of religion, especially Christianity, is to be found in "affectation" and the "feeling of dependence," not in rational proofs, appeal to miracles, and claims for the authority of Scripture or Church dogma. Joining Kant's critical philosophy—with its removal of God from the phenomena of human experience and knowing—with his Moravian pietistic background, Schleiermacher laid out a theology centered in the distinctive religious consciousness of Jesus, the "God-filled man" who is able to communicate his "essential God-consciousness" to others.

Schleiermacher's shift of theological concern to Jesus' consciousness gave credence to the liberals' claim that the *real* Jesus was hidden behind the Jesus of scant biblical record and excessive theological projections. St. Paul became an object of assault for having converted the life and works of Jesus into a rigid, authoritarian Christology. Finally, through the work of liberal theologians like Ferdinand Christian Bauer and Albrecht Ritschl the historical "person" of Jesus became the primary object of the "quest" for truth in liberal theology. Claiming that no external authorities of the faith are normative, since all are human interpretations of Jesus' redemptive activity, their emphasis turned to applying the methods of historical, critical research to Jesus' distinctive religious experience, his ethico-religious example (Ritschl), and his faithfulness to God's commandments (Harnack). In pursuit of the "Jesus of history" they drew away from the "Christ of faith" as it had been couched in Pauline and Johannine language, in dogmatic formulation, Catholic and Protestant, and in apocalyptic projections.

If biblical criticism was a threat to the doctrines of inspiration and inerrancy of Scripture in Protestantism, it was no less threatening to Roman Catholicism, where the radical challenges to biblical authority of the "Modernists" amounted to attacks on the authority of the Church and its tradition. The condemnation of "Modernism" by Pius X in 1907 was to thwart the serious appropriation of historical-critical method in Roman Catholic scholarship for nearly a half century.

Two other cardinal developments in liberal theology of the nineteenth century have carried forward into the twentieth century: respect, bordering on accommodation, for science, with the result that the advance of scientific understanding required abandonment of the biblical earth-centered universe and mounting urgency for the Churches to engage social reality to critique its injustices, to correct its wrongs, and to effect a restructuring of society to approximate more closely what was understood to be the "kingdom of God on earth." The first, coupled with intense biblical criticism, has led to sustained examination of the function of myth and symbol in religious expression; the latter has extended to the Social Gospel movement, Troeltsch's concern for a Christian ethic to base a social criticism, the fight for racial justice, and theologies of liberation.

JAMES W. THOMASSON

See also MODERNISM; PHILOSOPHY AND THEOLOGY; SCIENCE AND RELIGION.

LIBERATION THEOLOGIES

Liberation theology is a new theological method that arose in the 1950s in conscious opposition (a) to the intellectualism and fideism of earlier European theology and (b) to the criticism of Christianity by Immanuel Kant and Karl Marx. Liberation theology seeks to recover the Christian commitment to transforming the world, being part of and making a contribution to the kingdom of God, and social justice. Of crucial import is the belief that Christian faith is mediated by concrete historical experience. The context in which one does theology significantly shapes the method, content, and structure of theology. The form of faith itself is influenced by the historical situation in which it is mediated. Since theology has been done largely within the Euro-American historical context, the influence of this context is often assumed to be normative for theology. Hence, perspectives (however important, valid, and useful) from other cultures and contexts are dismissed or suppressed (i.e., marginalized). Because these liberation theologians speak with and on behalf of specific communities, one should expect that there will be differences among them. Therefore, it is appropriate to use the plural and to speak of liberation theologies.

Following some general remarks appropriate to various liberation theologies regardless of their distinctive point of view will be a closer examination of the more popular types in existence today. Examined first will be those liberation theologies that developed in response to specific types of oppression: (1) Latin American liberation theology, in response to poverty; (2) feminist theology, in response to sexism; (3) black theology, in response to racism. This will be followed by an examination of those liberation theologies developed to enable marginalized cultures to voice their faith in ways specific to their context and experience, and thus overcome *cultural imperialism,* and also to contribute to the faith of the universal Church. Discussed in this section will be: (4) Native American theology; (5) Asian theology; (6) *Minjung* theology; (7) African theology; (8) South African theology.

Response to Earlier Theological Methods

Liberation theologians see traditional understandings of faith as inadequate because they did not inspire active engagement in the service of the kingdom of God. Some earlier theologies saw faith as a merely passive virtue by which human beings accept and rely upon God's promises. Liberation theologians claim that faith cannot exist without commitment to the implementation of the gospel. In fact, it is the experience of "faith working through love" (Gal 5:6) that helps to determine the concrete form of faith in any given time and place. Faith includes transforming the world according to the word of God.

Some earlier theologies place the hope of salvation solely in the future when God will miraculously intervene in history. Liberation theologians see the kingdom of God as presently existent and operative, and see faith as a force actually promoting the cause of justice and liberation. The separation of faith from good works in some theologies has spawned an immoral neutralism with regard to political systems. The Bible, on the other hand, suggests to liberation theologians that people of faith animated by selfless love should be involved in the work of reconciliation and social justice on earth.

Liberation theology, therefore, is a dialectical interweaving of theory and practice, contemplation and action. Older theologies, with their undialectical approach, tended to stress the intellectual component of faith at the expense of the emotional. The primary focus of some earlier theologies was the immediate relationship of the soul to God in a contemplative union that could best be achieved through relative detachment from the world. For liberation theologians, however, faith is neither primarily intellectual nor a passive waiting upon God's own decision to act. On the contrary, faith seizes the initiative and reshapes the world by its God-given power. It begins with the active commitment to a specific struggle for liberation and includes critical reflection upon the communal practices in which one is engaged.

This dynamic view of faith is very biblical. The NT forbids us to look upon the kingdom of God as exclusively future. Thus, it supports the contention of liberation theologians that the kingdom, in a provisional manner, is present and operative within history. Faith does not simply protect us from the world; it remakes that world. In John's Gospel one reads that "whoever lives the truth comes to the light" (John 3:21). Truth is to be done, not just thought; and the doing of truth is a condition of believing it.

Response to Kant and Marx

Kant believed that what made one truly human was free will. Christianity was seen in a negative light because, according to Kant, it demanded blind faith that was neither free nor responsible. He attacked Christianity, charging that it keeps people from thinking (e.g., one must believe everything), caring (e.g., one thinks only of heaven), and behaving morally (e.g., one acts selfishly, either in anticipation of a reward or in fear of punishment). The orthodox Christian response to Kant pointed out that free and responsible thinking is a necessary component of faith, that the Christian is expected to care deeply and passionately about life on earth, and that not even spiritual selfishness is acceptable. The roots of liberation theology, therefore, can be found in the orthodox Christian response to Kant.

Marx attacked religion as the opiate of the people. Christianity, he said, merely gave the illusion of freedom and responsibility. Marx believed that Kant was wrong in presupposing that people are free. Some people are not able to be free and responsible because they live in conditions which make it impossible. One is not free if one does not have enough to live on or if someone is forcing you to act in a certain way. Since two-thirds of the human race live in a situation of poverty, oppression, and degradation, most people are not free to make their own decisions and, therefore, cannot be held responsible for their choices. You cannot have free and responsible decisions unless the society in which you live allows this to happen. The orthodox Christian response was that our choices are limited because of original sin, that baptism requires Christians to fight against the evil effects of original sin, and that the Christian tradition insists upon political activity and concern for justice. The roots of liberation theology, therefore, can be found in the orthodox Christian response to Marx.

Liberation Theology in General

Liberation theologians often speak about faith as the *historical praxis of liberation.* It is historical because the word of God comes to us through a specific historical situation, which mediates the word of God to the believer. Any act of faith, therefore, must correspond to the actual historical situation in which it is made. When liberation theologians speak of historical context or social location they are not referring to something particular to the individual; they are assuming that this perspective is shared by others in a specific class or group. This method normally sees the word of God as mediated especially by the cry of the poor and the oppressed. Thus the Bible and the documents of the magisterium have to be read in relation to one's own particular reality and practice. The canonical texts do not become revelation until they are read in correlation with the signs of the times in which the particular group reading them lives.

Praxis refers to those human activities which are capable of transforming reality and society, and thus making the world more human. It is the action that is directed to changing economic and social relationships. Liberation theologians argue that Christians must not accept an oppressive situation. They believe that the word of God is distorted whenever it is accepted without a commitment to working toward transforming the world into the kingdom of God. Those authentically committed to the kingdom will be involved in the struggle to subvert the existing social order, with its institutionalized injustice, and to establish on earth a just society. It is not inevitable that oppression exist. Oppression experienced by individuals is often produced by cultures, societies, and institutions. Even if the present situation is beyond individual control, societies can be changed and ought to be changed.

The word *liberation* suggests a re-creation, the freedom to realize one's potential to the fullest. Its goal is to empower individuals and groups to challenge and change unjust structures. It includes, but is not confined to, political and socioeconomic transformation. Liberation theologians sometimes distinguish three levels: (1) political and social liberation of oppressed nations and social classes; (2) liberation of humankind in the course of world history; and (3) liberation from sin and total reconciliation in communion with God through Jesus Christ. Liberation theologians fight against the charge of sociopolitical reductionism, while emphasizing the inseparability of total liberation from social, economic, and political factors.

It would be a mistake to see liberation theology as fostering utopian illusions about the future. These theologians are aware that we will never, by our own actions, fully insert the kingdom of God into historical time. They argue, however, that with the biblical concept of the kingdom as our goal we will creatively find new ways of provisionally realizing within history signs and anticipations of the promised kingdom. Liberation theologians conclude that it is the responsibility of Christians to protest against unjust social structures and to work for the transformation of society in order to produce greater justice for all.

Cautions

While many insights of liberation theology deserve high praise, one ought to be aware of some often heard cautions.

Liberation theologians must remain aware that faith is a personal response to a call from God and not just a reaction to a particular historical situation. They must also try to do justice to the religious significance of a personal faith that, for one reason or another, fails to achieve appropriate expression in actual conduct and social involvement. Not to do this runs the risk of minimizing the dimension of interiority in the life of faith.

While liberation theologians are commended for following John XXIII and Vatican II in trying to find God in the "signs of the times," they must be careful not to romanticize or idealize the poor. Jesus may come to us in the poor and the oppressed, but he may be found elsewhere as well. In the NT, no class is presented as a paragon of virtue; all are admonished to examine their motives and to repent.

Liberation theologians should be praised for urging all Christians to take seriously the obligation to work for a better political and social order. They must remember, however, that no one social or economic system is endorsed by the gospel itself.

Summary

Liberation theologians see the kingdom of peace and justice not simply as a remote ideal for which Christians long, but as already at work transforming the world. In Jesus the kingdom of God has entered into history. Christians participate in the work of the kingdom insofar as they engage in actions which promote the healing and reconciliation of the broken world. Faith, therefore, involves more than intellectual assent, more than hope in what God will do without us. Liberation theologians argue that faith, correctly understood, involves active participation in the work that God is doing, the task of bringing forth justice to the nations. Christian faith requires that one collaborate with God to reshape the world in love and justice.

Liberation theologians speak with and on behalf of specific communities. Because communities differ among themselves, there are differences among liberation theologies. Sometimes these communities are the victims of wide-ranging types of oppression (e.g., poverty, sexism, racism) while at other times the oppression is manifested in a specific region (e.g., *Minjung,* Native American).

Liberation Theologies that Respond to Specific Types of Oppression

Latin American Liberation Theology. Usually seen as the starting point for liberation theology, Latin American liberation theology begins with the experiences of a people who have been poor, oppressed, and exploited for centuries. As a result of the colonial activities of Spain and Portugal, a society grew in which a very few wealthy people owned most of the land and property. Because they were interested in preserving and expanding their wealth and privilege, Latin America developed an export economy. An enormous part of the land which could be cultivated for the local economy was dedicated instead to producing goods for export. The Church, for the most part, was seen as on the side of the rich who oppressed the poor. The motives for this are not always clear. Perhaps Church figures were motivated by selfishness and greed, or perhaps they saw this position as a means to the end of vast numbers of conversions.

The tension that existed in the past between the people of Latin America and their Spanish and Portugese conquerors has abated to a large extent. The tension that exists today is between these people and the United States which is viewed as a new colonial power. The United States, like the Church in the past, is seen as on the side of the rich. It supports the status quo which involves exploitive and corrupt regimes controlled by the rich and powerful for their own selfish concerns.

At the Second Vatican Council in the early 1960s, the Church started talking about the widespread need for social and economic reforms. Many of the local clergy in Latin America abandoned the rich and started working with and for the less fortunate.

Latin American liberation theology attempts to empower the poor and oppressed so that they will fight for alternatives to the present unjust structures of society. When the experiences of the poor and exploited people of Latin America are heard, the faith of wealthy and powerful Christians will require them to respond. A solidarity will result among all Christians and work can begin to refashion the world according to the vision of the kingdom of God.

Feminist Theology. Feminist theologians remind us that the experience of women in ancient cultures and throughout most of human history has been significantly different from that of men. Women have been seen as representing a lower level of human existence than men and, therefore, have been subordinate to them. Sexism has led to socially tolerated, condoned, or approved violence toward women and has restricted the opportunities of women to exercise social and political rights, privileges, and powers. Feminist theology seeks to empower women to fight against the unjust structures of society. It stresses the full human dignity of women and gives voice to the experiences of this long oppressed group. Society needs to hear what women have to say because in determining what is normative the experiences of half of the human race have been ignored. Feminist theologians believe that if women are treated as equals in reshaping the world, a more peaceful and just society will result.

In various locales a more culturally specific theology has developed around women's issues. An example of this is *Mujerista* theology. Emerging in the late 1980s, *Mujerista* theology is rooted in and has as its source the experience of Hispanic women. *Mujerista* theologians conclude that Hispanic women are so marginalized that they have virtually no way of influencing the societies in which they live. Their goal is to challenge the oppressive structures of society which refuses to allow them full participation while preserving their distinctiveness as Hispanic women. From their special vantage point as an oppressed minority, Hispanic women are able to envision a new social situation in which there will be peace and justice for all. Movement toward this objective will take place when Christians understand that solidarity with the oppressed and among the oppressed is the heart of Christian behavior.

Black Theology. In this theology, that emerged in the late 1960s, it is the experience of the black community's struggle for justice in white North America that serves as the basis of theological reflection. The faith of this community led its members to fight to make the dominant white power structure of the United States accountable to the ideas of justice and democracy articulated in the Declaration of Independence and the Constitution. In addition to calling the country back to its roots, black theology endeavors to envision and work for a model for society in which the contributions of its excluded minorities are recognized.

Black theology believes that God is found in those who are exploited and humiliated because of their color. While it is true that these people are also poor and oppressed, black theology argues that they are victims of injustice primarily because of their color. It is God who sustains these oppressed people and empowers them to fight against their oppressors. As blacks in the United States become better acquainted with their history and tradition they become proud of their roots and more aware of their human dignity. This leads quite naturally to their desire for justice as they seek to take their rightful place in society.

Some argue that God has taken on the condition of the oppressed and identified with them to such a degree that one ought to speak of God as being black. Solidarity with the poor and oppressed, then, can be spoken about as becoming black with God. When this kind of language is used the radical nature of the conversion required to become identified with the victims of society becomes more apparent.

God does not view in a neutral fashion a situation in which oppression exists; God sides with the oppressed and against the oppressor. Obedience to God, therefore, requires a commitment to fight for social justice, not meek submission to oppression.

More Culturally Specific Liberation Theologies

Native American Theology. The Christian theology of Native America, that emerged in the 1970s, believes that God spoke to generations of Native People over the centuries. Therefore, the traditions of these people that have been kept alive for several generations cannot be ignored. On the contrary, they form the common experience of a people out of which their theology flows. While the voices of these early Native American men and women were not necessarily Christian, their experience of God formed them and shaped their communities. These traditions continue to be passed on from generation to generation. When one says that the Native Americans of today interpret the Bible in light of their own context one must realize that this context includes centuries-old stories of God's revealing acts among the Native American people. As they encounter Christianity, Native Americans realize that much that appears in Native American tradition was confirmed and much was challenged in the teaching of Jesus.

Native American theologians believe that the rediscovery and authentication of their ancient traditions will provide a focal point for the reunification of Native People and a vantage point from which to critique Western colonialism. While these theologians are interested in criticizing unjust structures and in social transformation, their immediate goal is the empowerment of Native Americans. The necessary changes will take place only after Native Americans become more conscious of their human dignity and proud of their heritage.

Asian Theology. Christian theologians in Asia speak from cultural traditions and historical environments nourished by centuries of pain and suffering and steeped in Asian philosophical systems and religious systems. They believe that traditional Western theologies built their systems on how the Christian West looked at humanity and world history. These theologies taught that revelation cannot be inherent in Asian existence and history and that God works only tangentially within Asian cultures.

Asian theologians, recognizing the revelatory significance of their context, seek a deeper knowledge of their own Asian traditions. They want to become better acquainted with the stories, poems, and songs of their ancestors that speak of their hopes and fears, joys and sufferings, and their encounter with the divine. Asian theology is born when these theologians meet the heirs of these ancient traditions in their present-day life and history.

As with other liberation theologies, the focus here is with the poor and oppressed who are struggling for the recognition of their human dignity and for full participation in society. Those who suffer in Asia, as those who suffer elsewhere, yearn for a better future. Asian theologians believe that the best way to bring God's saving love and power into sharper relief is to be aware of their own context. The Asian experience of human existence has been different than that of Western Europeans. Therefore, the Asian experience of God and their understanding of faith will be different. What unites this theology with other liberation theologies is its belief that faith, correctly understood, involves working for social justice.

Minjung *Theology. Minjung* theology was formed and developed out of the religious, social, and political experience of the Korean people. The context from which this theology comes has been influenced by several different religious traditions, including native shamanism. While the Korean people have inherited a single racial and linguistic tradition, their cultural and religious experiences are grounded in diverse traditions.

Emerging in the 1970s, *minjung* theology stands in contrast to Western theology in general. It is neither analytical nor dialectical, but rather synthetic and dialogical. It seeks the truth about reality in relationships rather than in dichotomy. Therefore, *minjung* is a theology of stories and narration. Myth-making is essential to *minjung* theology. In its early stages, *minjung* theology focused on transformation, blending social awareness and analysis of the Korean society with the Christian tradition. Recently it has taken a different turn and now focuses on transforming theology itself. Much attention has been given to analyzing and interpreting the basic assumptions of Christian faith from the Korean social and cultural point of view.

While *minjung* theologians tend to avoid precise definitions of terms, it is fair to say that those they seek to speak for are the oppressed, exploited, and alienated in society. The response of the hearer to the myths and stories of this tradition is expected to be a deep feeling for and solidarity with the situation of the oppressed. It is hoped that this will lead to the transformation of the social and political structures of Korea.

African Theology. African theologians believe that their experiences of being human in the world and of God have been ignored by European-centered theologies. In the socio-political-economic sphere the wealthy nations of the world have paid little attention to the collective voice of Africa. The result has been that the wealthy nations have oppressed Africa and plundered it for their own selfish purposes. The experience of Africa is the experience of the poor and oppressed. These theologians argue that the voice of Africa must be heard on the international stage if the world is to become more peaceful and just. Once the people of Africa appreciate their own self-worth, they will begin to demand equal treatment in worldwide secular and religious decision-making bodies. All peoples will benefit when the lost voice of Africa is heard.

Black South African Theology. Black South African theology emerged in the late 1960s in response to the brutal repression of apartheid and the private notion of faith promoted in the dominant white Churches which supported the prevailing racial and economic status quo. In this context, to have faith in Jesus is to oppose apartheid. This faith and its commitment to social justice challenges the distortions of a white faith that is rooted in cultural and economic privilege and continues to justify apartheid.

In a context of violence and death, faith is shaped by the spirit of resistance. Faith in Christ requires one, often at great personal risk, to denounce the present unjust and repressive social structures in South Africa and to provide a context in which a vision of a new society based on peace and justice can be shaped.

DENNIS SWEETLAND

See also OPTION FOR THE POOR; THEOLOGY; THEOLOGY, SYSTEMATIC.

LIGUORI, ALPHONSUS, ST. (1696–1787)

Alphonsus Mary de Liguori was born at Marianella on the outskirts of Naples on 27 September 1696. His father was a young officer in the navy, his mother, Anna Caterina Cavalieri, a lady of intense, almost cloistral, piety. Alphonsus, the eldest of eight children, was educated privately at home and then in the University of Naples where he read law. On the completion of his studies he practiced successfully at the Naples Bar. In 1723, following a decision which went against him in an important lawsuit, he determined to fulfill a long-cherished desire to become a priest. His decision was confirmed by reflection on the gospel maxim "what doth it profit a man if he gains the whole world and suffers the loss of his soul" as he attended the sick poor in one of the largest hospitals in Naples. He was ordained at the end of 1726 in his thirty-first year, which makes him a patron of those whose call to the priesthood comes to them rather late in life.

In his adolescent years he suffered considerably from scruples; his early years as a priest were a period of intense suffering in this regard. The early years of his pastoral ministry were spent among the uneducated poor of Naples and in preaching popular missions and retreats throughout the entire Bourbon Kingdom. To cater for the spiritual welfare of the pastorally neglected people of the countryside he founded a missionary society, the Congregation of the Most Holy Redeemer or Redemptorists (cf. The Redemptorists). Widely recognized as the foremost missionary preacher of his day, Alphonsus was appointed Bishop of St. Agatha of the Goths in 1762. For thirteen years he guided his diocese in a programme of pastoral renewal until ill-health forced him to retire in 1775 to his monastery at Pagani between Naples and Salerno. His final years were saddened by internal difficulties in his missionary society and by increasing harassment from the Bourbon authorities which resulted in the Naples section of his Congregation being disowned by the pope. He died at Pagani on 1 August 1787.

Besides his preaching and episcopal ministries he devoted himself throughout his life from his first years as a priest to writing books on moral, dogmatic, spiritual and devotional theology; he has over a hundred titles to his name. His main work, his moral theology, chartered a middle course between the rigidity of the Jansenists and the laxity of their opponents. His dogmatic writings vindicated the authority and infallibility of the papacy, clarified the way for the proclamation of the doctrine of the Immaculate Conception in 1854, and promoted devotion to the Sacred Heart of Jesus. His devotional writings on prayer, visits to the Blessed Sacrament, the Way of the Cross, conformity with the will of God, the incarnation and passion of Jesus Christ, devotion to the Mother of God, the priesthood and the religious life, determined Catholic devotional practice worldwide right up to the present time. He was canonized in 1839, declared a Doctor of the Church in 1871, and made patron of confessors and moral theologians in 1950. In 1992 Pope John Paul II declared that "St. Alphonsus is a gigantic figure not only in the history of the Church but for the whole of humanity as well. Even people who would not seem close to him in the sense of having followed his vision still see in him the teacher of the Catholic soul of the West. He did for modern Catholicism what Augustine accomplished in ancient times."

FREDERICK JONES, C.SS.R.

See also REDEMPTORISTS.

LIMBO

As a technical theological term, it designates the place or temporary condition of those who have died without the conditions necessary for entrance into heaven but also without the sort of personal guilt necessary for purgatory or for condemnation to hell. The concept of *limbo* is essentially a theological postulate which has provided a way of discussing the possibility of salvation for people who, through no personal fault, have not had any explicit experience of Jesus Christ or of the Church.

Traditional theology has distinguished the *limbo of the Fathers* and the *limbo of infants.* The first designates the presumed state of the just who have preceded Christ in history and hence could not have known him. The second refers to the state of children who have died without baptism but without having committed any serious, personal sin. It was not clear how one could think of these as being in heaven since they died in the condition of original sin. On the other hand, and despite the authority of Augustine, it was not clear how they could be consigned to hell since they had never had the opportunity to commit a serious, personal sin.

The issues involved in any discussion of the matter are: the universal salvific will of God, the universal need for salvation, and the relation of salvation to the person and work of Jesus Christ and hence also to the Church. Since *limbo* is a temporary condition, theologians who maintain it as a theory must find some way to bring it to an end.

The teaching of early theologians shows a considerable range of viewpoints on the matter, and there is no dogmatic definition of the magisterium with respect to it. Much medieval and post-Reformation discussion revolved around such ideas as a "desire for the Church," a "baptism of desire" or a "baptism by blood." One could think of those who preceded Christ in history as having a "desire to do what God wishes them to do" without having an explicit knowledge of the concrete form salvation would take in the person of Christ and the Church. Thus, one could speak of an implicit desire for the Church and for baptism.

Though one could hardly speak of a desire in the case of the infants of Bethlehem (Matt 2:16), one could think of a baptism by blood. In the case of children dying without baptism after the coming of Christ, the prayer and desire of a child's parents or of the Church might be seen as a vicarious baptism of desire (Cajetan). In the nineteenth century, H. Klee and H. Schell suggested that, in some way, death itself might be seen as an extra-sacramental means of attaining heaven even in the case of children. For Klee, this involved the claim that the child attained the use of reason in the moment of death and was capable of making a choice either for or against God. Schell, on the other hand, emphasized the suffering of death itself more than the element of choice. Such speculation anticipates aspects of contemporary theology in making the concept of *limbo* unnecessary.

At the present time, where the question is dealt with, the discussion is situated in the context of a theology of death. Some have suggested that the personal decision necessary for salvation is made at some point after death. This decision may take place either soon after death or at the time of the Last Judgment. In the latter case, *limbo* remains on the eschatological map until the end of history at which time it will cease to exist. But when death itself is seen as the moment of final choice even in the case of children, the concept of *limbo* becomes unnecessary, and it simply disappears from the map of the other world. This view seems to be the most common one today.

ZACHARY HAYES, O.F.M.

See also DEATH; ESCHATOLOGY.

LITERAL MEANING OF SCRIPTURE

Biblical criticism seeks to establish the plain meaning of Scripture—what and how the text itself communicates (by the tools of philology and the methods of literary criticism), and what and how the biblical authors spoke to their original audiences (by historical criticism). Concern with the literal meaning of Scripture was characteristic of the Church Fathers associated with Antioch in Syria (Theodore of Mopsuestia and John Chrysostom) and Jerome. This approach to biblical interpretation emphasizes the historical reality of biblical revelation and insists that any allegorical or fuller sense be based on careful analysis of what the text says.

DANIEL J. HARRINGTON, S.J.

See also ALLEGORICAL MEANING OF SCRIPTURE; CRITICISM, BIBLICAL.

LITTLE OFFICE OF THE BLESSED VIRGIN MARY

A liturgical prayer of the Church modeled after the Liturgy of the Hours, though shorter. First appearing in the tenth century, the Little Office flourished in the religious orders. It was retained in the reforms of Pius V and Pius X, but was made completely nonobligatory by the latter. In our century it has been popular with various third orders, and with certain new orders of women, and has many adherents among the laity. Revised and enriched in 1953, a new edition by John E. Rotelle (1988) rearranges the office after the analogy of the revised Liturgy of the Hours.

DAVID BRYAN

See also LITURGY OF THE HOURS.

LITURGICAL BOOKS

"Liturgical books" may refer to any collection of texts used during liturgical celebrations. More commonly, the phrase refers to the official books prepared for use by priests, ministers, readers, and others who have special roles in the liturgical assembly. The pope gives official approval to the basic Latin edition of each book (known as *editio typica*). The conferences of bishops approve the vernacular versions to be used in the churches of their own territory, although this approbation is subject to review by the Roman See.

The most commonly known and used liturgical books in the Roman Rite are the Lectionary and the Roman Missal (also known as the Sacramentary). The Lectionary contains the Scripture readings, including the Gospels, which are required for Mass, for the celebration of sacraments and for other ritual occasions, such as the dedication of a Church. It also includes the intervening chants, that is, responsorial psalms and gospel acclamations. The current edition also gives extensive general instruction about the theology of the Word proclaimed at liturgy and about the principles guiding the selection of texts in the present Lectionary.

The Roman Missal (*Missale Romanum*) includes the introductory instructions and prayer-texts for the celebration of Mass in the Roman Rite. The revised liturgy of Mass, corresponding to the directives of Vatican II, was promulgated by Pope Paul VI in 1970. The Roman Missal provides three proper "presidential prayers" for each Mass (Opening Prayer, Prayer over the Gifts, Prayer after Communion), the Entrance and Communion Antiphons, and the complete Order of Mass.

PATRICIA DeFERRARI

See also LITURGY.

LITURGICAL MOVEMENT, THE

In his book, *Liturgical Piety,* Louis Bouyer defines a liturgical movement as, "the natural response arising in the Church to the perception that many people have lost that knowledge and understanding of the liturgy which should belong to Christians, both clergy and laity, and, in consequence, have lost the right use of the liturgy also."

This definition accurately describes the Roman Catholic liturgical scene during the nineteenth and twentieth centuries. The Council of Trent in the latter half of the sixteenth century had imposed a strict central control on the Roman Rite in reaction to the chaotic state of the liturgy in the several centuries preceding the Reformation. While this control served an immediately useful purpose, the long-range effect was debilitating. Joseph Jungmann in his history of the Mass of the Roman Rite says of the post-Tridentine period: ". . . the forces of further evolution were often channeled into the narrow bed of a very inadequate devotional life instead of gathering strength for new forms of liturgical expression." The modern liturgical movement, then, came as reaction to the paralysis resulting from the post-Tridentine era.

While it is always difficult to trace the exact beginning point of any movement, there is general agreement that contemporary liturgical reform can be traced in origin to Prosper Gueranger (1805–1875) and his influence as abbot of the Benedictine monastery of Solesmes in France. Through his writing and daily liturgical celebration, Gueranger attempted to restore the liturgy to an earlier, purer form, involving active participation especially in the beauty of the chant. Though later research showed the inevitable limitations of Gueranger's historical scholarship, the influence of Solesmes spread through Germany and Belgium during the remaining years of the nineteenth century with the help of other Benedictine monasteries.

Only in the early twentieth century, however, did the movement begin to expand beyond the monastic community to influence the liturgical life of the laity. Outstanding for his leadership in this transition was Lambert Beauduin (1873–1960) of the Benedictine abbey of Mont-César in Belgium. By his writing and teaching Beauduin reached diocesan clergy and, through them, larger numbers of lay people.

Official recognition of the growing liturgical movement had begun to appear in the very first years of the twentieth century. Pope Pius X published a *motu proprio* on 22 November 1903 expressing the conviction which would serve as the charter for those involved in liturgical reform: that the primary and indispensable source of the true Christian spirit is active participation in the liturgy of the Church. Pius X reinforced his position with subsequent decrees on frequent Communion (1903) and on first reception of Communion at an early age (1910).

To complete the picture of the liturgical movement in Europe prior to 1925, we would have to include mention of the contribution of theological research and publication which accompanied the movement and would prove its firm grounding in the decades ahead. Johann Adam Möhler (1796–1838) led the field of patristic research at the University of Tübingen and moved away from the Counter Reformation stress on the structural and hierarchical elements of the Church to a sense of the Church as life in Christ, of the Church as the body of Christ.

The early twentieth century would see the work of the scholars of the Benedictine abbey of Maria Laach, Ildefons Herwegen (d. 1948) and Odo Casel (1886–1948). Casel's *The Mystery of Christian Worship* set out new directions in attempting to understand the very nature of Christian liturgy as the living presence of Christ in the worship of the Christian people. This German scholarship was complemented by the creative pastoral initiatives of Pius Parsch (1884–1954) and the Augustinian monastery of Klosterneuberg in Austria. Parsch's several-volume liturgical commentary, *The Church's Year of Grace* (originally published in German in 1929) would have far-reaching effect in nourishing the growing number of dedicated apostles of the liturgical movement in both Europe and North America. Parsch especially emphasized the importance of Scripture in the celebration of liturgy.

The liturgical movement as it had grown in Europe met the young American Benedictine priest, Virgil Michel (1890–1938), during his travels there in 1924 and 1925. Michel was so impressed by the pastoral possibilities of the movement for his native American Catholicism that he convinced the religious superiors at his monastery in Collegeville, Minnesota, to let him carry the best of the European movement across the Atlantic and to turn the Abbey of Saint John the Baptist in Collegeville into the focus for what was to become the American Catholic Liturgical Movement.

When Dom Virgil returned to Collegeville in the summer of 1925, he had been in touch with the best of the European currents in the movement: solid roots in theology, vital connection with the spiritual maturity of all Catholics, and great potential for increasing the social awareness of those participating in liturgy. In the amazingly short period of thirteen years, Michel established the structures at Collegeville which would help popularize the liturgical movement throughout American Catholicism, among them The Liturgical Press and the journal, *Orate Fratres* (later *Worship*). This pioneer worked so hard, in fact, that he burned himself out in the cause and died at the age of forty-eight. While a number of other pioneers, themselves either European or American by birth, had bridged the Atlantic from the European foundations of the modern movement to its American adaptations, Virgil Michel more than anyone would deserve credit as the founder of the American Catholic Liturgical Movement.

The task set for themselves by Michel and the other early liturgical reformers was formidable. Pius X's "active participation in the liturgy of the Church as the primary and indispensable source of the true Christian spirit" was hardly understood by American Catholics, let alone practiced. Even though by the 1920s frequent Communion was becoming more common, there was still a sense of distance between the people and the action of the Mass. People saw the Mass and sacraments as a holy drama being enacted before them for their benefit and ultimate salvation but had no understanding that what they witnessed in a spirit of reverential awe should be participative drama, to engage their bodies, their voices, and their hearts. They did not know themselves as the body of Christ worshipping the Father.

The distance between the people and the altar deprived them of their sense of being one in the body of Christ. Their silence and the variety of private devotions to which they gave themselves during a Mass expressed and fostered a sense of individualism and, therefore, of less responsibility for one another as members of the one body.

Obviously there was need for teaching; the early American liturgical reformers knew this well. *Orate Fratres,* founded in 1926, and the publications of The Liturgical Press set the theological tone for liturgical renewal in a popular and convincing style. This was enough to win over a small but steadily increasing group of religious, diocesan priests, and educated laity during the late 1920s and through the 1930s. Meanwhile, the rediscovered concept of the Church as the Mystical Body of Christ was elaborated in the theological journals of the same period, enlightening the faculties and students of the nation's seminaries. Far from yet reaching the vast numbers of American Catholics during this time, the reawakening began to form those who would, in their turn, form others.

One notable example of such education was the volume *Christian Life and Worship* by Gerald Ellard, S.J. (1894–1963), originally published in 1933 and in subsequent editions until 1963. This book, intended as a college text, laid out a vision of Christian life as life in the body of Christ with the Mass and the sacraments integrated into that vision. The steady sales of the book over a thirty-year period up to the Second Vatican Council indicate its formative influence over more than a generation of educated Catholics.

A landmark event came in 1940 with the first of what were to become the National Liturgical Weeks, annual meetings where those interested in liturgical renewal could come to be enlightened and encouraged. They often needed more encouragement than enlightenment. Like any new movement to change the status quo, the liturgical movement was looked upon with at least suspicion if not hostility. Those who attended these annual meetings from the beginning in 1940 to the zenith of their popularity in 1964 found hope and courage to return to the indifference of their local environments.

The 1940s saw many more local efforts to bring Catholic congregations in parishes and schools into the mainstream of liturgical piety. While the rituals of Mass and sacraments remained themselves unchanged, measures were introduced to encourage participation in the services. Joseph Stedman's *My Sunday Missal,* first published in 1932, now became more popular in use along with similar weekday missals and other such aids to help people follow along with the action of the Mass. The pamphlet *Community Mass: Missa Recitata* (1938), invited the actual vocal participation of the worshipping congregation in the Latin responses usually prayed by the Mass servers alone. Justine Ward and Georgia Stevens had founded the Pius X Institute of Liturgical Music in 1916 and by the late 1930s and early 1940s there were enough teachers to train interested congregations in singing the Mass ordinary in Latin chant. The American Liturgical Movement was under way!

During the same decade two papal encyclicals were published by Pius XII: *Mystici Corporis Christi* on the Church as the body of Christ in 1943, and *Mediator Dei* on the liturgy in 1947. These documents summarized much of the development already described and put an official seal of approval on the efforts to renew Catholic liturgy and spirituality.

In the summer of 1947, Michael Mathis, C.S.C., began the first summer session in the program of liturgical studies at the University of Notre Dame, offering a master's degree with several summers' study. Many of this summer faculty came from Europe with the best and latest of liturgical scholarship. This part-time program drew students from all over the country and eventually evolved into the present year-round doctoral program at Notre Dame.

After the publication of *Mediator Dei,* those interested in liturgical reform began to press for change in the rites themselves. The Vernacular Society was formed in 1946. The publication of Joseph Jungmann's definitive history of the Roman Mass just after World War II had made it evident that the Mass had a long history of change through the centuries and that the Missal of Pius V in the wake of the Council of Trent had given an impression of stability (even rigidity) which was actually quite out of character with the preceding sixteen centuries.

The official changes in the liturgy began with major adjustment in the services of Holy Week, first in 1951, then in 1955. Whereas the practice of the *Missa Recitata* or Dialog Mass had previously been left to the initiative of the local parish, the Congregation of Rites in 1958 published an instruction encouraging active participation by the congregation in the prayers of the Mass and in the singing of vernacular hymns.

Even with the help of this gradually growing interest in liturgical reform, American Roman Catholics found themselves caught off guard by the sweeping changes in their worship mandated by the Second Vatican Council in its decree on the liturgy of 4 December 1963 and in subsequent decrees and instructions, especially those of the next ten years. Those local congregations fortunate enough to have pastors or teachers knowledgeable in the background and meaning of the changes were able to begin the adjustments with profit. While thirty years later most American Catholics are satisfied and even enthusiastic about the results of liturgical change, those early days of the late 1960s and early 1970s witnessed widespread confusion and, in some quarters, hostility.

Over the years the Roman Catholic Liturgical Movement had counted on the talent and generosity of its leaders. In addition to those already mentioned, others stand out as well: Ade Bethune, Godfrey Diekmann, O.S.B., Clifford Howell, S.J., Martin Hellriegel, Maurice Lavanoux, Frederick McManus, Hans Ansgar Reinhold, Mary Perkins Ryan, and Gerard Sloyan. Through the written and spoken word and through the arts these teachers patiently and successfully sowed the seeds of liturgical renewal; others build on their efforts today.

The liturgical movement has certainly achieved its goal of reordering worship to a condition more faithful to its nature as expressing the heart of Christian life. The roots of the movement were grounded in nineteenth-century Europe. The American pioneers of the movement saw to its faithful transplanting and cultivation in American soil. American Catholics have begun to experience the first fruits of renewal but now realize the length of the process in which they are engaged. The reordered worship has only begun to reveal its possibilities as "the primary and indispensable source of the true Christian spirit."

J. LEO KLEIN, S.J.

See also LITURGY; MICHEL, VIRGIL GEORGE; PIUS V, POPE; PIUS X, POPE; VATICAN COUNCIL II.

LITURGICAL MUSIC

See MUSIC AND WORSHIP.

LITURGICAL YEAR, THE

Also designated the Liturgical Cycle or the Church year, this term refers to the pattern of feasts and seasons which occurs every year. It is celebrated primarily in the liturgy (the formal community worship of the Church) but is also reflected in observances and devotional customs which may vary from place to place and time to time.

The Shape of the Year

The basic pattern is built around two major feasts and their surrounding seasons: Easter and Christmas, in order of their importance. The order of their importance is not, however, the order of their placement in the calendar, because the calendar to some extent follows the chronological sequence of events in the earthly life of Jesus, while also maintaining continuity with the festivals of the year in the Jewish calendar by which Jesus himself lived. This gives us a complicated pattern. In practice it is complicated further by the fact that over the centuries feasts of saints were added, interweaving a "sanctoral cycle" with the liturgical cycle proper.

The calendar of the liturgical year begins on the first Sunday of Advent. This is not always the same date on our secular calendar, because it is determined by counting back four Sundays from Christmas, 25 December. Thus although there are always four Sundays of Advent, there are not always four full weeks, depending on the day of the week on which 25 December falls. Advent leads to the feast of Christmas, which is celebrated for an octave (that is, eight days) ending with the Solemnity of Mary, Mother of God, which is also the feast of the Naming of Jesus, on 1 January. Still in the Christmas season are two more Sundays, the feast of Epiphany (or manifestation) and the feast of the Baptism of the Lord (in the Jordan by John the Baptist, initiating the public ministry of Jesus). Another Christmas-related feast, the Presentation of the Child Jesus in the Temple, occurs later, on 2 February, outside the Christmas season proper, because custom had placed it there.

The greatest feast of the Christian year really has two seasons, the preparatory one of Lent and the continuing one of Eastertide, also known as Paschaltide. The dating of this two-part season is even more complicated than that of the first Sunday of Advent. It begins by establishing the date for Easter, and then counting back six and one-half weeks for Lent. Easter Sunday falls on different dates of the secular calendar because it is celebrated on the first Sunday following the first full moon after the spring equinox. This unusual dating system is based upon the one traditionally used by Jews in determining the date for Passover (because the Gospels and the Eucharist link the death of Jesus to the date and the theme of Passover). The season of Lent culminates in Holy Week, recalling the challenge, arrest, trial, passion, and death of Jesus, traditionally a time of intensified prayer and quiet reflection for the whole Christian community.

Beginning with the nighttime Easter Vigil, the Paschal Season lasts for seven weeks, includes the feast of the Ascension, and culminates with Pentecost (meaning "fifty after") which is the Sunday commemorating the birth of the Church when its early leaders were empowered by the Holy Spirit. This season more than others is constructed to match exactly the time frame of the New Testament accounts of Jesus, in this case of the community's experience of the appearances of the risen Christ among them, and his definitive commissioning of them to carry on his work.

These two major festivals and the seasons surrounding them do not occupy all the available weeks of the year. There is a gap of varying lengths from year to year between the end of the Christmas season and the beginning of Lent, and there is always a long period after Pentecost before another liturgical year begins with a new Advent. These two periods together make up what is known as Ordinary Time. There is a series of Sundays with their appropriate readings which begins in January, is interrupted for close to fourteen weeks, and then continues to the next Advent.

The way the seasons of the year are celebrated in the liturgy is by a complex rotation of Scripture readings, by texts in the Eucharist and the Liturgy of the Hours which are appropriate to the occasion, by the color of liturgical vestments and church appurtenances, by appropriate music, church decoration or lack of it, and occasionally by special ceremonies. The selection of Scripture readings to be used at the Eucharist is large and complex since the changes of the Second Vatican Council. There is a three-year cycle of readings to be used on Sundays, and a separate two-year cycle for weekdays, covering the entire New Testament and much of the Hebrew Scriptures (or Old Testament).

The Purpose and Theology of the Liturgical Year

The continual repetition of the Liturgical Year is based on the expectation that as Christian individuals and communities mature in their prayer and their Christian lives they will be receptive at progressively deeper levels to the meaning of the mysteries being celebrated. Thus the Church year celebrates in the Advent season the hope and forward thrust towards a fulfillment of God's promises that is yet to come, and the readings focus on the grounds for such hope. The Christmas season celebrates the incarnation, that is, the presence of the divine among us in the midst of our history, giving new hope and energy and calling for a response of trust and generosity. The Lenten season recalls who we are as creatures, demands discernment about our relationships, values, expectations, and actions in the world, and stresses the radical nature of the choices to be made and the efforts and renunciations integral to those choices.

The focus of the year is Holy Week and Easter, because in these the community rehearses, so to speak, the central mysteries of the redemption: the ultimate act of self-gift of Jesus that reverses human self-centeredness, and the vindication of that act by the transcendent God in the resurrection of Jesus in which human possibilities are transformed with new life. Finally, Pentecost refocuses attention on the continuing presence of the divine in the world through the Holy Spirit that sustains that new life in the community of believers which is the Church.

It is the main concern of the celebration of Ordinary Time to keep this focus on the gift and continuing task of the believing community alive in the experience of Christians in their daily lives. In fact, it is particularly in Ordinary Time that the pattern of the week emerges as continuing celebration of the mysteries of redemption, with every Sunday a resurrection feast and every Friday recalling the redemptive death of Jesus and what it means in terms of the unfinished confrontation with forces of evil.

The History of the Liturgical Year

The history of the Church year is complex, drawing on Jewish, pagan, and early Christian events and customs, and often converting an existing feast or observance into Christian usage and meaning. It is the pattern of the week, rather than that of the year, which has been common to all Christians throughout the ages and in all places. The festivals and seasons that now shape the Christian year developed differently in various churches and only very gradually were welded into the present pattern.

Evidence of a paschal celebration, other than the weekly observance, does occur among the Christians of Asia Minor towards the end of the second century. It seems to have begun as a *triduum* (three-day observance), spread into a Holy Week, and become joined with what may have been an independent tradition of a forty-day fast. This forty-day fast was connected with the final period of preparation before baptism, and baptism became linked with the paschal celebration, as it is today. Early testimonies about the Easter feast seem to show that it was celebrated for fifty days, and early references to Pentecost are not to the one culminating feast but to the whole period.

There is no doubt that the Nativity, or Christmas, feast is of later origin (some testimonies date from the fourth century) and that it does not reflect the calendar date of the birth of Jesus. Observed in the Eastern Churches on 6 January, it came to be celebrated in Rome on 25 December. Although the evidence is much disputed, there seems to be some connection with the winter solstice, pagan worship of the unconquered sun, and pagan winter festivals. As the Eastern and Western strands became mingled, a sequence emerged in which both 25 December and 6 January were integrated into the Christmas celebration as Nativity and Epiphany (birth and manifestation, respectively). Since the Vatican II postconciliar adjustments, Epiphany may be celebrated on the Sunday preceding 6 January whenever the latter falls on a weekday.

The accumulation of additional feasts of Jesus and of Mary, some connected with mysteries from the life of Jesus recorded in the Gospels, and some arising in relation to shrines, events in Christian history, and emerging devotions, not to mention the accumulation of feasts of saints assimilated into the universal calendar from local origins, finally rendered the calendar so cluttered that the main feasts and themes were obscured. There was, therefore, a drastic pruning after the Second Vatican Council, based on careful historical, theological, and pastoral studies, leaving a much simpler pattern.

Devotional Customs of the Liturgical Year

Besides the official liturgical celebration of the feasts and seasons, pious customs have grown up locally and often spread to the universal Church. These include the Advent wreath, a wreath of evergreens hung in the house or placed on a table with four candles attached, three purple and one pink. Each Sunday of Advent one candle is added to the number lit, the pink one being the third (for Gaudete or "rejoice" Sunday). On Christmas eve the candles are changed to four white ones. Each time the candles are lit, some Scripture is read aloud and a Christmas carol or Advent hymn is sung.

Probably the most common devout custom connected with Christmas is the giving of gifts. Although this has been much commercialized in modern times, some parishes have attempted to refocus the custom by asking for specific gifts for needy families at Christmas. Since medieval times, there has also been the custom of setting up a nativity scene patterned on the description in the infancy narratives of the Gospels of Matthew and Luke, a custom whose origin is attributed to St. Francis of Assisi. Finally, adopted from pagan Germanic sources, the Christmas tree has been adapted to Christian usage and meaning. A tradition which seems to stem from England is the custom of going from house to house with lighted candles, singing Christmas carols. Through the Christian centuries there has probably been more music composed for and about Christmas than for any other feast or season.

Many penitential customs have been connected with the Lenten season in the past—pilgrimages, the recitation of "stations of the cross" while walking from marker to marker in fourteen stages commemorating incidents in the passion of Jesus, either in a church or out-of-doors, special devotions including Benediction of the Blessed Sacrament and rosary, and so forth. More familiar in recent times, though certainly less devout, is the pre-Lenten celebration of Mardi Gras ("fat Tuesday") with a carnival ("farewell to meat") of partying. The origin of it was in the stricter observance of Lent as a time of strict fast and abstinence from meat.

Customs connected with Easter have featured the wearing of new clothes to express appreciation of newness of life and hope, the presenting of colored or chocolate eggs, especially to children, also to symbolize the birth of new life, the enshrining of palm leaves brought home from the Palm Sunday procession and of candles brought home from the Easter Vigil. In more traditional societies it is also the custom to place bright spring flowers at the graves of relatives.

Popular piety through the ages has superimposed its own Marian cycle in which May and October are honored in a special way as Marian months with processions, small shrines and altars on which statues of Mary are surrounded by flowers, and other devotional practices. Popular piety has also added processions and pilgrimages to many summer feasts, and novenas (nine-day prayers) to the feasts of a number of saints. Though not officially incorporated into the Liturgical Year, such pious practices are not condemned or rejected by the Church.

MONIKA K. HELLWIG

See also ADVENT; LITURGY; PASCHAL MYSTERY; PENTECOST.

LITURGY

Since Vatican II the word "liturgy" has become a common term in the Roman Catholic Church, as well as in Lutheran and Episcopal communions, when referring to church services. Any religious community's official public worship is its "liturgy." Using the word "liturgy" itself, however, expands the community's understanding of what is involved in public worship.

Implications of the Term

Originally a Greek term, *leitourgia* meant service done for the common good, whether of a political, religious, or pragmatic nature. Any service performed for the sake of others—serving in the army or caring for the destitute—would have been considered as "liturgy." In time, however, the word "liturgy" came to be used in an exclusively religious sense, and took on Christian usage as well.

Extant sources, in fact, use the word in an exclusively religious context, so liturgy has come to connote only religious service done for the sake of others, or more properly, public worship. Instead of public service, it became "divine" service done for the sake of others. This dimension of liturgy had not been emphasized in the centuries leading up to Vatican II.

An expectation was that restoring the word "liturgy," would also restore the concept that liturgy is not self-serving, but outwardly directed. When people go to public worship, they do it for the other people, to support them in faith.

This restored sense of liturgy as service for the sake of others gives each member a role. Liturgy is no longer something that is thought of as solely the priest's domain. While the priest functions as the principal celebrant of the liturgy, all those participating in the service are celebrants, in the same way that all those at a dinner party celebrate, not just the host.

Finally in doing something together, people become something together. When they work together on an important project, for example, or for a corporation, people tend to take on a corporate identity.

Scope of the Liturgy

In the Roman Catholic Church today, then, "liturgy" would include celebrations of the seven sacraments, Liturgy of the Hours, Eucharistic worship outside Mass, rites of profession, blessings, and the rituals of the Order of Christian Funerals.

In the Eastern Churches the word "liturgy" was used exclusively in reference to the Eucharist (*The Divine Liturgy of St. John Chrysostom,* for example).

In the West, however, the word virtually disappeared from usage until the mid-nineteenth century when it became the subject of research, and was popularized by the growing liturgical movement.

Occasionally the word "liturgy" is misused. For example, it is often misused as a contemporary synonym for "Mass." To say that "liturgy" will be at 4 P.M., is equivalent to saying that we will eat at 4 P.M. It is not clear whether we will be having a late lunch, high tea, cocktails and hors d'oeuvres, or supper. Similarly, "liturgy" is a generic term emcompassing all forms of the Church's official public worship.

Not all public church services are "liturgy." Stations of the Cross, public recitation of the rosary, and novenas, for example, are private devotional practices often prayed in common. None of these devotional practices is part of the Church's official public worship, but they have a special dignity and place in the spiritual life of Catholics.

By emphasizing that liturgy is *official* we mean that its texts and ritual elements have been approved by competent authority, ultimately the Holy See, for use on specific occasions. Each of the ritual books carries an official decree of promulgation from the Congregation of Divine Worship. No papal pronouncements to date, however, have ever specifically defined the meaning of the term "liturgy"; rather, they have either emphasized what liturgy is not, or described how liturgy functions.

In *Mediator Dei* (20 November 1947) Pius XII corrected faulty notions about and uses of the term "liturgy." Reacting to usage that equated liturgy with rubrics, he wrote "it is an error . . . to think of the sacred liturgy as merely the outward or visible part of divine worship or as an ornamental ceremonial. No less erroneous is the notion that it consists solely in a list of laws and prescriptions according to which the ecclesiastical hierarchy orders the sacred rites to be performed." Liturgy, he emphasized, while including rubrics, is not limited to them. According to *Mediator Dei* and the rites themselves, liturgy includes both rubrics and the ritual action of celebrant and assembly.

Sacrosanctum Concilium (1963), promulgated by the Second Vatican Council, does not define "liturgy" either. Instead it describes the action of liturgy and its place of prominence in the life of the Church: "The liturgy is thus the outstanding means by which the faithful can express in their lives, and manifest to others, the mystery of Christ and the real nature of the true Church" (SC 2).

Rightly, then, the liturgy is considered as an exercise of the priestly office of Jesus Christ. In the liturgy, by means of signs perceptible to the senses, human sanctification is signified and brought about in ways proper to each of these signs: in the liturgy the whole public worship is performed by the Mystical Body of Jesus Christ, that is by the Head and his members (SC 7). While *Sacrosanctum Concilium* makes it clear that liturgy "does not exhaust the entire activity of the Church" (SC 9), it also concludes that liturgy is "the summit towards which the activity of the church is directed; at the same time it is the fount from which all her power flows" (SC 10).

Following the directives of the Second Vatican Council, all of the liturgical books have undergone a process of revision in the years since the council's conclusion in 1965. They restored Eucharist to its place of prominence as the central expression of worship. At Eucharist the community gathers together to "do this" in memory of Jesus. In doing so it keeps before our eyes both the paschal mystery, the Church's mission on earth, and our communal yearning for the peace and unity of the heavenly banquet. Drawn into this holy communion are believers of the past, present, and future. For these reasons, all the other expressions of liturgical prayer stand in relationship to Eucharist.

The rituals which form the Rite of Christian Initiation of Adults, as well as the Rite of Baptism for Children, find their completion in the assembly gathered for Eucharist. Beginning at the door of the church, with the presbyter asking, "What do you want?" all of the stages in the process of full incorporation into the community are celebrated in the midst of the assembly. Catechumens are sent from the assembly to celebrate the Rite of Election with the diocesan bishop. The scrutinies are celebrated in the midst of the assembly on the third, fourth, and fifth Sundays of Lent. Finally, the celebration of the sacraments of initiation takes place at the principal celebration of a major feast, usually the Easter Vigil, Pentecost, or Epiphany.

For those who are incorporated in stages, that is, baptized in infancy, confirmed and Eucharistized at a later time, the Eucharistic assembly is also locus of celebration, as reflected in the revised rites.

The Church's ministry and rites of pastoral care for the sick and dying, while not ordinarily celebrated at Eucharist, have Eucharist as their focus. By bringing Holy Communion to the sick and homebound, deacons and Eucharistic ministers are actually extending the Eucharistic assembly to include those unable to be physically present. At the same time, the needs of the sick and dying are raised in prayer before God and the community during the general intercessions at Eucharist.

By continuing the Church's ministry of reconciliation through prayer and celebration of the rites of penance, the community works toward restoring the unity of the Eucharistic assembly, disrupted by sin and alienation. The penitential rite at the beginning of the Eucharistic celebration and the kiss of peace which precedes the communion procession, both have reconciliation as their intent.

The Church teaches that Christian marriage mirrors the union of love Christ has with the Church. Thus, marriage becomes an icon for the community. The celebration of this union is most fully expressed in the context of the Eucharistic Liturgy, although the rite of marriage may also be celebrated outside Mass.

Rites of ordination to the diaconate, presbyterate, and episcopacy also form part of the Church's liturgy, along with rites of installation to various liturgical ministries. All of these are focused on leadership roles within the Church and are celebrated at the Eucharistic assembly. Related to these are rites of religious profession. While these do not incorporate one into the clerical state, or of themselves indicate the assumption of a leadership role within the Church, religious vows establish an official, public relationship of service between the vowed religious and the ecclesial community, and are normally celebrated at the Eucharistic assembly.

Increasingly, groups of people gather to celebrate the Liturgy of the Hours, the official daily prayer of the Church. Consisting of psalms, canticles, and intercessory prayer, the Liturgy of the Hours draws the community together at the rising of the sun and its setting, in an endless chorus of praise.

Eucharistic worship outside Mass, formerly limited to "benediction," has been broadened in focus in the reform of Vatican II. This liturgical celebration now includes both a proclamation of the word, and time for silence, adoration, and praise before the reserved Eucharist.

The Church's liturgy also includes various blessings, recently made available in the Book of Blessings. The Book of Blessings has two parts: one set of blessings for household or family use; the other to be used as part of priestly ministry. The intention is to bring the prayer of the Church to all the corners of one's life.

The final aspect of the Church's liturgy is its ministry to those who have died, using the Order of Christian Funerals. The Order of Christian Funerals contains various rites by which the Church accompanies the deceased and grieving family and friends from the moment of death, through the wake and funeral, to committal of the body to its final resting place.

As explained earlier, although the foregoing are the official texts of the liturgy, more is required than words to bring the texts to life in the Church. When we emphasize the *public* character of liturgy, we mean that the presence of the assembly, as well as the faith of the assembly—the believing action of the community—are of prime importance. This was clearly stated by the bishops at Vatican II when they declared that "full, conscious, active participation of all the faithful" (SC 14) is an "aim to be considered before all else."

Liturgy as Ritual

Human beings have an innate propensity for ritualizing the significant moments and experiences of their lives. Defined by the renowned anthropologist, Victor Turner, as "an organized pattern of words, symbols and actions which the members of a community use to interpret and enact for themselves, and to express and transmit to others their relation to reality," ritual taps into the depths of human consciousness. Entered into deeply and enacted in faith, ritual even has the power to transform us. Using words, symbols, and actions, we highlight an event to such an extent that we engrave it deeply on our memories and thereby make it available for us to reexperience periodically.

This need to worship is linked to our understanding of the present and appreciation for memory. Worship is what human beings do when they sense the presence of someone or something that they do not want to miss. They savor that presence. In worship the community gathers together. They pause, leave aside their everyday concerns, and savor the presence of Jesus. They savor that movement of Jesus in dying and rising. They savor the mystery.

Liturgy is basically an exercise in remembering. Browsing our fingers through the pages of the Scriptures for the basis of our faith, the sights and the sounds of the difficult times come alive for us. The fears and the triumphs of the people come alive for us. The faith and the love that makes us who we are are found in those pages. It is in such remembering that liturgy draws its meaning. And we move from word to action. Liturgy is, therefore, both word and action—the Liturgy of the Word and the Liturgy of Eucharist, which is the action that flows from the word.

In a communal context, ritual is a social drama which embodies the experiences of the community. Ritual is the form that "full active conscious participation" takes in the liturgy. Of themselves, rituals are "corporate symbolic activity" which have the possibility of forming and transforming the individual and community over and over again.

When the community gathers for Eucharist, for example, they recall the Last Supper, but focus particularly on the death and resurrection of the Lord which ultimately gave meaning to the Last Supper. The gathered assembly stands, almost two thousand years later, in a long line of people who have been nourished at the same banquet table. They have come from many walks of life, across centuries, through times of war and times of peace, all drawing strength from the one Lord and Savior.

Christian liturgy, however, is even more than a celebration of a mystery which is not only past and present, but it is future as well. Theodore of Mopsuestia, (350–428) had a unique way of approaching sacred rituals which has come to be known as his doctrine of the "two ages." Whereas anthropologists view rituals as a means for plunging us into primordial time, Theodore saw them as rare opportunities for enjoying the future.

Liturgy, as ritual, involves words, symbols, and actions. We have discussed the words, as official texts, at length. Symbols and actions, however, are also significant elements, and involve the assembly directly, while the words involve them only indirectly.

Symbols are multivalent in that they can communicate one reality at one time, and another reality later. They can also have different meanings for different people. When words fail us, symbols do not.

The liturgy involves both universal and communal symbols. Universal symbols are those so deeply rooted in humanity that they cut across time and place, communicating to people of all times and places. These are the most powerful symbols available to us when they are used appropriately. Water, for example, is a universal symbol—communicating death, life, rebirth, and cleansing. Used in its fullest expression in baptism, we see the candidate buried with Christ in the waters, and rising, reborn, to live a new life. A trickle of water hardly communicates the same reality as immersion does.

Communal symbols are those developed by a community for use at a particular time and place. The crucifix, for example, is a communal symbol. To the believing community it is a powerful symbol—worn, venerated, covered, carried in procession, decked with flowers. Outside the believing community, it is at best a gruesome decoration.

Postures and processions, signings and singing—all these actions are important elements that enhance our celebrations of the Church's liturgy, and enable the community to express its faith, while handing that faith on to others.

Ultimately, liturgy is prayer, enabling the community as a whole, and individual members as well, to deepen their relationship with God. This relationship is nurtured by private prayer, but expresses itself most eloquently in times of public celebration.

Cycles of the Liturgy

There is also an underlying rhythm to our lives as Christians, with a cycle that is framed by the Liturgical Year. Through the cycle of feasts and seasons the Church recalls the story of salvation, and offers us the opportunity to savor again and again the mysteries that weave their way out of the pages of Scripture and into our daily lives, and to journey with Jesus along the way he marked out for us.

Advent begins the Liturgical Year in a posture of waiting. Compressing four thousand years of waiting for the Messiah into the four weeks of Advent might seem, at first glance, to be disproportionate. Liturgical celebrations, however, are never intended to be literal reenactments of the mysteries. Rather, they are symbolic representations of those events in the life of Jesus and the life of the community that shape us, both as followers of Jesus and as members of his community.

Christmas and Easter are the two feasts that the Church celebrates with an octave. We know that Christians began to celebrate the feast of Christmas in the year 354, and the oldest liturgical calendars show us that they followed Christmas day not only with an octave, but also layered upon it the feasts of those who died in witness to Jesus—St. Stephen, St. John the Evangelist, and the Holy Innocents. In the Middle Ages, these came to be seen as a guard of honor.

The Church uses the expression "ordinary time" to refer to those Sundays of the Liturgical Year that are outside the official seasons. Several of these Sundays occur between the end of the Christmas season, and the beginning of the Lenten season, although the bulk of them extend from the close of the Easter season to the end of the Liturgical Year.

Lent is the Christian community's forty-day preparation before moving into the holiest season of the Liturgical Year. As more and more parishes begin to have active catechumenates and celebrate the stages of the Rite of Christian Initiation of Adults, members of those communities will have even more opportunities to see the varied ways in which the Lenten season weaves in and out of daily life, renewing us in its path.

The Lenten season draws to a close as we come to celebrate Holy Thursday, and begin our commemoration of those momentous events in the life of Jesus that marked his death and resurrection.

The Church commemorates the Lord's crucifixion and death on Good Friday in a ritual that is stark and low-key. No Masses are celebrated until the resurrection, but on Friday the community gathers together to remember and to pray. This day's ritual has four separate parts, and it is unlike other rituals we experience. This adds to our spiritual discomfort with the day as well as the event in Christ's life.

The ministers enter in silence and some or all of them prostrate themselves on the floor before the altar, while the rest of the community kneels in prayer. Prostration is a very dramatic posture for prayer, for it literally and figuratively communicates one's total submission to God.

At the conclusion of this prayer, the Liturgy of the Word begins, and the community begins to relax with this more familiar form of worship. The readings focus on the passion of Jesus, as it was prefigured in the Hebrew Scriptures and took place in history, recounted in the Gospel of John.

The intercessions which follow the homily on this day are very elaborate, becoming a ritual in themselves. Different groups of people are singled out for prayer. The celebrant announces the intention and asks the community to kneel in silent prayer. Then we all stand as the celebrant prays aloud in our name. This is repeated for each of the nine groups of people for whom we pray.

After the intercessions, a veiled cross is carried in with great solemnity. The priest or deacon who carries the cross pauses three times, uncovering a portion of the cross and announcing in song, "Behold the wood of the cross, on which has hung the salvation of the world." Each time the community responds, singing, "Come, let us adore." A parallel action is used at the Easter Vigil, when the paschal candle, symbolizing the risen Christ, is carried into the church. The ritual continues as each member of the community is invited to come forward to venerate the cross.

The reserved Eucharist is distributed to conclude the commemoration of Good Friday. The community prays the Lord's Prayer and comes forward in procession to receive Communion as at any other time. After the concluding prayer, the celebration ends in the silence in which it began.

The highlight of the liturgical year is the Church's celebration of Easter, beginning with the great vigil of Easter. In the darkness of Jesus' death and the dying day, centuries ago the Christian community gathered together on Holy Saturday night. The catechumens had spent the entire day in prayer and fasting, but were joined in these last hours of preparation by the entire community. This was the night of memory, and as the hours passed, the community would read again the story of their salvation. From Scripture they read and reflected on the stories of Adam and Eve, Abraham and Sarah, Moses and Miriam, as the community recalled God's faithfulness and mercy down through the ages. Echoing the praise of their ancestors, the community sang the songs of David throughout the night.

Today the community gathers for the Easter Vigil in a very similar fashion to listen to the story of our salvation. Like our Christian ancestors we are bombarded today with a complex of symbols in the ritual that come with such rapid-fire succession as to stun the most seasoned of us. This bombardment, however, is part of the festival atmosphere, not unlike the mood at a fireworks display.

Easter is an eight-day feast. Liturgically, each of those days is treated as a Sunday. The paschal candle is lit, and the strains of the Gloria sing out day after day, as the Church tries to absorb the profound mystery we encountered at the Easter Vigil. In some countries Easter Monday is a holy day of obligation; in others a national holiday. Here in the United States we slip back into business-as-usual with hardly a backward glance.

The Easter Season is the Church's honeymoon. Even beyond the octave of Easter, the community continues to revel in the mystery that is our salvation. It is appropriate and necessary that this take time. The mystery is simply too awesome to be appreciated in a few days.

JULIA UPTON, R.S.M.

See also EUCHARIST; LITURGICAL YEAR, THE; LITURGY OF THE HOURS; SACRAMENTS.

LITURGY OF THE HOURS

This liturgy acknowledges the power of nature inherent in certain times of day and in the seasons, consecrating these special times to God in comparatively short services of divine praise. It is liturgical prayer in the strict sense: a public act of the whole Church and a continuation through time of the Eucharistic praise.

"Sacred time" is attested in the oldest documents of civilization in the Near East, where sunrise, noon, sunset, and nighttime, in particular, were recognized, along with annual seasons and festivals, with various hymns being rendered to this or that god. Israel borrowed these practices from her neighbors, adapting them to the service of the One Lord in Jerusalem. The Book of Psalms was the prayer book and hymnal of Jerusalem, and it is still the core of our Christian Liturgy of the Hours. The Jewish sect of the Pharisees deserves credit for insisting that lay Israelites, even if resident in distant towns, could join the services in various ways.

The first Christians, most of them Jews, continued to observe the Hours in Jerusalem and from afar. After the destruction of the Temple (A.D. 70), they carried similar practices throughout the evangelized world. These developing Christian traditions, which were a way of living the biblical command to "pray constantly," were not modeled in detail on the Jewish services, and they contained many new hymns thanking God for Jesus of Nazareth. It was soon noticed, besides, that the Hours coincided with key Christian events. Thus morning was the time of the resurrection; midmorning corresponded to the Pentecost event; the crucifixion, and the reception of the Gentiles (Acts 10), had occurred at noon. Midafternoon was associated with the death of Christ, while evening spoke of Passover and the Lord's Supper.

The early Christian history of the Hours is obscure, but we know that the daily celebration of the principal hours (morning and evening) was very common, while the lesser Hours were also well-known, all being chiefly a work of the laity. Monasticism, also a lay movement, gave this liturgy further form and impetus. With the decline of the classical languages, the Hours belonged less to the people and more to monks, nuns, and clergy, though, amazingly, Evening Prayer (Vespers) continued in certain parishes even to modern times. The Second Vatican Council called for the restoration of the Liturgy of the Hours to the people generally; subsequently the services were somewhat recast (with, for example, a monthly journey through the psalms, rather than a weekly).

While the restoration has been of considerable value in religious orders, in which nonmembers sometimes participate, it has made little impact on the Church as a whole. While the full services are too long for most people, even abbreviated rites have not become popular. This may have more to do with modern life, which is clock-driven and alienated from nature and its cycles, than with any grave defect in the revised rites. Little has been done by parishes, but it could be argued that success will depend on the laity taking responsibility, as in antiquity, for the Hours. If one prays alone, a simple approach may make the best foundation, since the basic thing is simply consecrating the various times, something we already do if we pray upon arising, over meals, and at bedtime.

In the Latin Rite, the hours observed are Morning Prayer, Midmorning Prayer, Midday Prayer, Midafternoon Prayer, Evening Prayer, and Night Prayer, with particular emphasis on Morning and Evening. Night Prayer is often observed privately. Additionally there is the Office of Readings, in which extracts from the Bible and subsequent Christian authors are read after appropriate psalms. While this is observed at any convenient time, it can also be a night vigil comparable to those of the early Christians and to the "matins" of monasticism. Taking account of modern pressures, the revised rites suggest that only one of the three "daytime" hours need be observed. It may still be recommended, however, that all the hours be at least noticed, so that they may call forth from us some brief expressions of praise.

DAVID BRYAN

LITURGY OF THE WORD

"The Mass is made up of two parts, the Liturgy of the Word and the Liturgy of the Eucharist. They are so closely connected with each other that they constitute but one single act of worship" (GIRM 8).

The Liturgy of the Word is preceded by what are known as the "Introductory Rites" of the Mass: the Antiphon at the entrance, the Greeting, the Penitential Act, the *Kyrie,* the *Gloria* and Collect, which "serve as an opening, introduction and preparation" (GIRM 24).

"The most important part of the Liturgy of the Word consists of the readings from sacred scripture and the chants occurring between them. The homily, the Profession of Faith (Creed) and the Prayer of the Faithful develop and conclude it" (GIRM 33).

The Scripture readings "reveal the mysteries of redemption and salvation" to the faithful and give them "spiritual nourishment" (GIRM 33). Through them "God himself speaks to his people, and Christ, present in his word, proclaims his Gospel" (GIRM 9). It follows that "all who are present should listen to them with reverence. The word of God in the Scripture readings is indeed addressed to people of all times and can be understood by them; yet its power to influence people is increased if it be given a living explanation by means of a homily which should be ranked as an integral part of the liturgical action" (GIRM 9). On Sundays and holy days there are two readings before the Gospel, on other days there is only one. The Responsorial Psalm after the first reading "should be sung, normally" (GILM 20), or "recited in a manner conducive to meditation on the word of God'' (GILM 22). The Alleluia (or, during Lent, verse) before the Gospel ''should be sung'' (GILM 23) and if not sung "may be omitted" (GIRM 39).

The congregation "should sit during the readings which precede the Gospel, during the Responsorial Psalm" and during the homily, and should stand during the Creed and the Prayers of the Faithful. Local hierarchies may, however, adapt these regulations to "the sensibilities of their own people" (GIRM 21).

The most important of the Scripture readings is the Gospel: "The liturgy itself teaches that the greatest reverence is to be shown towards the reading of the Gospel, for it assigns to the Gospel more particular marks of honor than it does to the other readings. The minister deputed to announce it prepares himself for his task by prayer or seeks a blessing; the faithful, by their acclamation ["Glory to you, Lord"], recognize that Christ has come to speak to them, and they stand erect while listening to his Gospel. Marks of honor are also paid to the book itself" (GIRM 35).

It is recommended that the Book of the Gospels be carried from the altar to the ambo "preceded by ministers with candles and incense or other symbols of veneration. . . . The faithful stand and, acclaiming the Lord, pay honor to the Book of the Gospels" (GILM 17).

The chant after the first reading, which may be said or—more appropriately—sung, is known as the Responsorial Psalm, or Gradual. "Normally it is taken from the Lectionary, for the texts in it have been chosen so as to have some bearing on the particular reading" (GIRM 36). The Alleluia and verse are said or—again, more appropriately—sung during all seasons except Lent. During Lent a verse replaces the Alleluia. Everbody stands, "the choir or the entire congregation taking up the singing after the cantor's intonation" (GILM 23).

"The homily is part of the liturgy and is strongly recommended, for it is a source of nourishment for the Christian life. Ideally its content should be an exposition of scripture readings or of some particular aspect of them, or of some other text taken from the Order or the Proper of the Mass for the day, having regard for the mystery being celebrated or the special needs of those who hear it" (GIRM 41). A homily is obligatory on Sundays and holy days of obligation and is "recommended" on other days, "especially on the weekdays of Advent, Lent and Eastertide" (GIRM 42).

"The Liturgy of the Word should be celebrated in a way that favours meditation. Any kind of haste is to be totally avoided, for it impedes recollection. Dialogue between God and his people, with the help of the Holy Spirit, requires short periods of silence . . . during which the heart opens to the word of God and a prayerful response takes shape. Such moments of silence can appropriately be observed just before the commencement of the liturgy of the word, for example, after the first and second readings and after the homily" (GILM 28).

"The purpose of the Profession of Faith (or Creed) [said or sung on Sundays and solemn feasts] is to express the assent and response of the people to the scripture reading and homily they have just heard, and to recall to them the main truths of the faith, before they begin to celebrate the Eucharist" (GIRM 43).

"In the Prayer of the Faithful (also called General Intercession or Bidding Prayer) the people exercise their priestly function by praying for all humankind. It is desirable that a prayer of this type be normally included . . ." (GIRM 45).

On Sundays and holy days "There are three readings at each Mass: the first from the Old Testament, the second from an apostle (that is, from one of the epistles, or from the Acts of the Apostles or the Apocalypse, depending on the season) and the third from the gospels. This arrangement illustrates the unity of the two Testaments and of the history of salvation. A more varied and wider selection is achieved on Sundays and holydays by presenting the readings over a three-year period, thus ensuring that the passages are repeated every four years" (GILM 66).

The readings are arranged in two different patterns. The first pattern is that of "semicontinuous reading," which means that extracts from a particular book of the Bible are taken in order until the entire book is covered. The other pattern is that of "harmonization," meaning that, for example, a passage from the Old Testament is chosen on a particular day because it harmonizes with the passage from the the New Testament, especially from the Gospels, selected for that day. "Another kind of harmony is found between the readings at Mass in Advent, Lent and Paschal-time, those seasons which have a particular importance and character" (GILM 67). On the thirty-four Sundays "through the year" (i.e., the Sundays outside of Lent, Eastertide, Advent, and Christmastide), "which do not have a distinctive character of their own, the apostolic and gospel passages are arranged in semicontinuous sequence, while the Old Testament passages are chosen to harmonize with the gospels" (GILM 67).

"The weekday readings have been arranged as follows: Every Mass has two readings: the first reading from the Old Testament or from an apostle (that is from the epistles or from the Apocalypse and from the Acts of the Apostles during Paschal time), the second reading from the gospels. The annual Lenten cycle is arranged according to special principles, which take into account the season's baptismal and penitential character. . . . There is a one-year cycle of the gospel readings on weekdays and it is repeated each year. The first readings, however, are arranged in a two-year cycle, read on alternate years, the first on odd-numbered years, the second on even-numbered" (GILM 69). There are special readings for the feasts of our Lord and our Lady and for more important feasts of the saints, and there are special readings for ritual Masses, Masses for various needs and occasions, votive Masses, and Masses for the dead.

AUSTIN FLANNERY O.P.

See also BIBLE, NEW TESTAMENT WRITINGS; BIBLE, OLD TESTAMENT WRITINGS; EUCHARIST; READING THE BIBLE.

LIVING WILL

See ADVANCE DIRECTIVES FOR MEDICAL CARE.

LOGOS

This is a Greek term for "utterance," "pronouncement," "word." Among the Greek philosophers, especially the Stoics who influenced early Christian thought greatly, the term had come to mean the ordering principle of the universe, reflected in a small way in human intelligence. At the same time, Judaism during the period of Christian beginnings took very seriously the *memra,* "word," by which God acted in creation, reflecting the narrative about God's speaking in Genesis 1. The prologue to John's Gospel, which certainly intends to draw a parallel with that creation story, also opened the way for subsequent Christian writers to make a synthesis of the Hebrew *memra* and the Greek *logos,* with the preexistence of Jesus identified with both these concepts. Justin the Martyr, writing in Rome in mid-second century is particularly explicit about this identification, intending thereby to show pagan intellectuals how reasonable was the Christian faith, recognizing the fruition and fulfillment of ancient traditions of wisdom as they converged in the person and impact of Jesus. A little later in the second century Athenagoras, writing in Athens, makes the case that it is not unreasonable for the monotheistic Christians to speak of God having a son, because what they mean by this is thought or utterance, a *logos.* He expects his listeners and readers to recognize the reasonableness of this from their own philosophically shaped understanding. At the beginning of the third century, Origen of Alexandria incorporated this way of explaining Jesus into his *Peri Archon,* "on First Principles," the first Christian attempt at a philosophically based systematic theology. Since that time the notion of *logos* has been used constantly in Trinitarian theology and is implicit in the models of Trinity proposed by St. Augustine of Hippo.

MONIKA K. HELLWIG

See also CREATION; JESUS CHRIST; TRINITY.

LOISY, ALFRED FIRMIN (1857–1940)

Sprung from farming stock, he was educated at the Institut Catholique in Paris. He was ordained priest in 1879 and, between that and his excommunication in 1908 by Pius X, Loisy had a controversial academic career. He adopted the historical-critical method, then popular with Protestant biblical scholars, and came to believe that the Church had to modernize her teaching. After three years as a professor of Scripture at the Institut Catholique, he was dismissed in 1890. In 1902 Loisy published *L'Evangile et L'Eglise,* a novel defense of Catholicism against Harnack who sought to base Christianity on the historical Jesus apart from later doctrinal developments. Loisy held that Christianity rested on the faith of the Church which broadened and expanded under the guidance of the Holy Spirit. A series of condemnations, led by the archbishop of Paris, fell on Loisy. But Rome made no move until 1903 when Loisy published an account of the controversy and published *La Quatrième Évangile.* Both books were placed on the Index of Forbidden Books and Loisy made an act of submission. But his book attacking the papal decree *Lamentabili,* which condemned Modernism, and the publication of the second volume of *Les Évangiles Synoptiques* (two volumes, 1907 to 1908) brought his excommunication. After his break with the Church, Loisy wrote profusely but his flow of opinions came to be regarded as conjectural and rather erratic.

MICHAEL GLAZIER

See also CRITICISM, BIBLICAL; MODERNISM.

LONELINESS

It is a fact of life that as individuals we are all separate from each other. Loneliness occurs when we experience that separateness so profoundly that we feel broken off from the continuity of humanity—even the one with whom we are most intimate. *Loneliness* is our experiencing that we are all we have. We have no others and no one has us. We are apart from each other, different, distinct, unconnected. And we do not feel a part of each other.

Most of us do not feel lonely despite knowing our individual lives are separate. So what produces the experience of loneliness? In loneliness, we perceive that we are always separate, as if we have been cut adrift to wander the world. We also become afraid that we are not enough, that we are inadequate. Our self-perceptions can repulse us, leading us to reject who we are. We cannot be at home with ourselves because what we find in the "home" which is "the us," is not enough for us. We discover we are all we have, and we will not do. We need more. Without connection, without belonging, we feel empty and afraid.

We can do much to avoid loneliness. We can busy ourselves, phone people, create more obligations than time to fulfill them, distract ourselves with situations or background noise. Avoiding the experience, however, does not change the reality: We are alone.

Alternatively, aloneness does not always bring with it feelings of loneliness. Being *by* ourselves can be an experience of being *with* ourselves as well, not lonely without company, but alone keeping our own company. In solitude we find ourselves at home, discovering and being intimate with our truest self. While alone, we can see more clearly who we are, what is good about us, what is bad about us, and what simply *is* about us. We do not have the distracting otherness of the world. Without schedules, work, obligations, or even the emotional tugs of those we love, we are left facing ourselves to see, understand, and forgive. We can appreciate who we are, unburdened by what, how much, and how well we do. In aloneness we can be self-intimate and nourish this most fundamental of relationships. Loneliness can lead to despair, but it can also lead back to ourselves, delineating a path for future growth.

PAUL MOGLIA

LONERGAN, BERNARD, S.J. (1904–1984)

Bernard J. F. Lonergan is considered by many the outstanding Catholic philosopher of the twentieth century. Born in Buckingham, Quebec, on 17 December 1904, Lonergan attended Loyola College in Montreal from 1918 to 1922. On 29 July 1922, he entered the Society of Jesus at Guelph, Ontario, where he did his novitiate and early Jesuit training. In 1926 he was sent to study philosophy at Heythrop College in Oxfordshire, England. While in England, he obtained a degree in classics at the University of London. After teaching at Loyola College in Montreal from 1930 to 1933, he was sent to study theology at the Gregorian University in Rome. He was ordained to the priesthood in Rome on 25 July 1936. With the exception of a tertianship year in Amiens, France (1937–1938), he remained in Rome until the beginning of the war in 1940 when he returned to teach in Montreal and Toronto. During his last two years in Rome he wrote his doctoral dissertation on the development of the notion of operative grace in the writings of Saint Thomas.

In his early student days Lonergan reacted against the Suarezian Scholasticism he was taught and considered himself a "nominalist." He rejected the intuitive view of knowledge as some kind of a "seeing

Bernard Lonergan, S.J.

the nexus" between concepts. He had an early interest in modern logic and methodology and, after reading John Henry Newman, Plato and Augustine, he developed a notion of human understanding as "immanent act." In Rome he was introduced to a sympathetic account of Saint Thomas Aquinas through the Jesuit writers, Peter Hoenen, Joseph Maréchal and Bernard Leeming. His "intellectual conversion" to a "critical realism," which he later claimed took place during this time in Rome, was the result of his own creative assimilation of Newman's emphasis on assent, Augustine's notion of *veritas,* Maréchal's emphasis on judgment and Leeming's teaching on the one *esse* in Christ. He had moved from a view of knowing as intuitive to an understanding of human knowing as discursive with the decisive element coming in the act of judging.

In the early 1940s, after publishing his doctoral dissertation in *Theological Studies,* Lonergan wrote a series of articles on Aquinas' notion of *verbum,* the procession of the "inner word" from the act of understanding. In the late 1940s and early 1950s he focussed on the dynamics of scientific method and in 1957 published his classic work, *Insight: An Essay on Human Understanding.*

In 1953 Lonergan returned to Rome to teach theology at the Gregorian University, where he remained until 1965. During that time he published several Latin texts on the Trinity and on Christology. He also began to focus on the nature of historical consciousness and scholarship especially as this new awareness influenced theological methodology. In 1972 he published *Method in Theology* in which he distinguished the eight "functional specialties" involved in the doing of theology: research, interpretation, history, dialectic, foundations, doctrines, systematics and communications. The first four specialties concern hearing the word of God out of the past; the second four concern taking a stand in the present, on the basis of one's conversion, and speaking the word of God towards the future.

Between 1965 and 1975 Lonergan was the research professor of theology at Regis College in Toronto. In 1971 to 1972 he was Stillman Professor at Harvard University. Between 1975 and 1983 he was the Visiting Distinguished Professor at Boston College. During this time he returned to an early interest in economics, specifically the analysis of the patterns of the circulation of money in an exchange economy. That work, *An Essay in Circulation Analysis,* will be published among the twenty-two volumes of *The Collected Works of Bernard Lonergan* now being published by the University of Toronto Press.

During his lifetime Lonergan received seventeen honorary doctorates as well as the John Courtney Murray Award from the Catholic Theological Society of America (1972). He was a member of the International Theological Commission (1969–). He was named Companion of the Order of Canada in 1970 and Fellow of the British Academy in 1975.

On 26 November 1984, Lonergan died at the Jesuit infirmary at Pickering, Ontario. Since his death a number of "Lonergan Centers" have been established in various parts of the world. There is a yearly "Lonergan Workshop" at Boston College. Various *Festschriften* have been dedicated to his thought as well as a quarterly journal, *Method: Journal of Lonergan Studies.* The Lonergan Research Institute in Toronto contains the archives on his life and thought and is currently collaborating with the University of Toronto Press in publishing *The Collected Works of Bernard Lonergan.*

Lonergan always sought to address the underlying foundational questions confronting religious people in their communication with modern and contemporary culture. Inevitably those questions lead to the need to realize the levels of our own consciousness and to know "what we are doing when we are doing it."

RICHARD LIDDY

See also PHILOSOPHY AND THEOLOGY; SCHOLASTICISM; SOCIETY OF JESUS.

LORD, DANIEL ALOYSIUS (1888–1955)

Jesuit, teacher, author, composer and evangelist, he was born in Chicago on 23 April 1888 and received his early education in Catholic schools. He entered the Society of Jesus in 1909 and was ordained in 1923. He was a talented and innovative teacher and had a splendid rapport with youth. He revived the moribund Sodality movement and helped to establish the Sodality magazine *Queen's Work* in 1933. From 1935 he was a tireless traveler promoting the Sodality movement and various forms of Catholic action. Lord was the prolific author of thirty books, sixty-six booklets and three hundred pamphlets, fifty plays and six musicals, and besides wrote a syndicated column *Along the Way.* While his literary work is long forgotten, his pamphlets had a massive readership all over the English-speaking world and had extraordinary influence especially on young Catholics. While dying of cancer, he embodied his fortitude and cheerfulness in his memorable last book *Cancer is My Friend.*

MICHAEL GLAZIER

See also AMERICAN CATHOLICISM; CATHOLIC ACTION; SODALITY.

LORD'S PRAYER, THE ("OUR FATHER")

Every religious culture down the centuries has had its own rituals and prayers. Christians are no exception, and the "Our Father," the earliest and most distinctive, is shared by all Christian denominations. The two Gospels in which it occurs, Matthew and Luke, present the "Our Father" in the context of teaching on prayer (Matt 6:9-13; Luke 11:1-13). Though the other two Gospels, Mark and John, do not have the complete "Our Father," phrases from it occur in both, especially in the context of the prayer of Jesus at his passion (see Mark 14:36, 38; John 12:27, 28; 17:11, 26). Luke's version is shorter than Matthew's having only five petitions. Matthew has seven and it is his rendering which has been used in the liturgy down to our own time. The doxology at the end, "for thine is the kingdom, the power and the glory. . . ." comes from its use in the early liturgy. It is to be found in the Didache (the Teaching of the Twelve Apostles), a document of the early Church later than the New Testament. Each age has made the "Our Father" its own; many of the great saints down the centuries such as St. Cyprian (see *Prayer of the Church,* Week 11 of the Year) and St. Teresa of Avila have shown how the "Our Father" can be adapted to each succeeding culture. This continues to be done in our time: for instance the beautiful commentary of Simone Weil evokes the hardship of continental Europe during the Second World War, while a recent book presents the "Our Father" in the light of present-day ecological preoccupations (see N. Douglas-Klotz, *Prayers of the Cosmos—Medita-*

tion on the Aramaic Words of Jesus, Harper & Row, 1990).

As well as being the essence of Christian *prayer,* the "Our Father" is a summary of Christian *teaching.* Luke's account starts directly with the special Aramaic word for "father," *Abba,* which is better translated by the more intimate "Dad" or "Daddy" (see Matt 11:25; Mark 14:36). The addition of "who art in heaven" in Matthew comes from his Jewish background where "heaven" was a substitute to avoid using the name of God. The intention is not to make God remote but to suggest that the overall parenthood of God makes us brothers and sisters of one another on earth (Matt 23:9). This is made explicit in the petitions which follow, all of which point out that our response to God is shown by the way we exercise responsibility for one another.

"May your name be sanctified" asks us to question the kind of God we believe in; knowing the name of someone in ancient times meant experiencing the person. In many parts of the Bible *profaning* God's name implied dishonoring not just God but God's people (see Lev 18:21; Amos 2:6-7). "Your kingdom come" and Matthew's addition of "Your will be done" are petitions asking that the justice and peace of God, spoken about and acted out by Jesus in his lifetime, may become a reality in our world. In many ancient manuscripts of Luke's Gospel the petition "May your Holy Spirit come down on us and cleanse us" was added; it is only through the action of the Spirit that we can bring about God's good pleasure, God's will, for the world.

"Give us this day our daily bread" is open to many different interpretations. At an obvious level it is a prayer for the physical food necessary for survival (see Matt 6:25-34). It is to be prayed not only for ourselves but for all those in need of daily sustenance. There is a good tradition in the Bible which this petition highlights, and which our Western world has perhaps lost sight of, that we should only satisfy the needs of each day and not store up for the future (see Exod 16:4-31). But desire for bread in the Bible also often referred to a hunger for wisdom (see Prov 9:1-6); and this aspect is present in the "Our Father." Bread as signifying the Eucharist was also a meaning given to the phrase from earliest Christian times, indeed already in the Gospel of John (see John 6). In our own day, however, with the occurrence of widespread famine, Maslow's hierarchy of human needs makes us realize the impossibility of hungering for God's word on an empty stomach; the primary meaning is again uppermost.

"Forgive us our trespasses as we forgive those who trespass against us." One of the outstanding features of the expectation of the coming of a Messiah in the Judaism of the first century was that he would bring a great outpouring of forgiveness (see Joel 3:1-3). Forgiveness is not easy as is brought to our attention acutely in so many troubled spots of the world. Forgiveness is gift, to be prayed for, but ultimately we are called upon to be as magnanimous as God in the way we exercise it.

"Lead us not into temptation but deliver us from evil." In times of persecution the greatest temptation for the early Church was to reject Jesus and the *Abba* he had spoken about. The evil we ask to be delivered from may be different; it includes today the threat of the extinction of our world. We need courage to live out the Christian life (see Acts 4:29-30); this courage should be characteristic of all those who, as the liturgy puts it, "dare to say Our Father."

CELINE MANGAN, O.P.

See also ESCHATOLOGY; PRAYER.

LORD'S SUPPER

See EUCHARIST.

LORETO, HOLY HOUSE OF

This is the *Santa Casa,* the reputed Holy House of Nazareth in which Mary was born, the house in which, according to legend, she was hailed by an angel, where the Word was made flesh. Pious stories exaggerate that the home was made into a church by the apostles and then St. Luke made a statue of Mary for it. When the Latin kingdom of Jerusalem fell around the year 1290 angels supposedly conveyed the house from Palestine to Fiume in Yugoslavia. And strangely even the date of that "translation" is given in legend as 10 May 1291. Because the Holy House was not properly venerated at that station, the angels carried the edifice to a wood in the vicinity of Recanati, Italy, just south of Ancona on the Adriatic Sea. Here again pilgrim attention was not paid to it and on 10 August 1295 the legend says that it was transported to a hill in that same area. Still failing to attract veneration the Holy House was moved the fourth time by angels to Loreto, Italy, where it achieved its final resting place on 2 December 1295. The statue of Mary, allegedly crafted by St. Luke, was destroyed in a fire in 1921 and subsequently replaced by a copy. The Loreto basilica, with three naves, was built between 1468 and 1587.

JAMES McGRATH

See also DEVOTIONS.

LOURDES

Lourdes is the most frequented shrine of Our Lady in Europe, drawing many more than five million pilgrims annually. It is also one of the greatest healing centers of the world, with on average an authenticated first-class miracle every two years, besides thousands of cures which may not be submitted to the Medical Bureau, or may lack formal documentation. It has been honored by popes, notably by Pius XII who declared a Marian Year from 1957 to 1958, and by John Paul II who visited the shrine in 1983. Its origin is in the apparitions granted to a poor child of the village, Bernadette Soubirous.

It is reported that in 1858 between 11 February and 25 March she saw, on eighteen occasions, a very beautiful lady who gave her different messages. She told Bernadette to uncover a flow of water, which would have healing effects; the lady charged her to ask for a church to be built nearby; she showed regard for Bernadette's privacy, entrusting her with three secrets which she should divulge to no one—the child said that she would not even tell them to the pope; she promised to make Bernadette happy "not in this world but in the next"; finally, on the day of the last apparition, she disclosed her identity: "I am the Immaculate Conception." Four years earlier, on 8 December 1854, Pius IX had solemnly defined this dogma. Bernadette possessed a sturdy, tenacious, utterly humble character; she had a sharp tongue, and was disconcertingly honest. Within four years, after rigorous examination, the apparitions were declared authentic on the basis of her testimony and the occurrence of miracles. She was canonized in 1953.

St. Bernadette Soubirous, 1858

Lourdes was the seat of the International Mariological and Marian Congresses in 1958, the occasion of Pius XII's last public broadcast on Our Lady, 17 September; and it was the scene of the International Eucharistic Congress in 1981. Before the Second World War a triduum of Masses was held there for peace, with the approval of Pius XI; his legate was Cardinal Pacelli. A feature of the Lourdes cult is the permanent custom of organizing pilgrimages on a diocesan basis in many countries. The Medical Bureau is open to all qualified medical personnel, irrespective of creed; its findings are reviewed by an international jury composed of experts in medical science and Church law.

MICHAEL O'CARROLL, C.S.Sp.

See also DEVOTIONS.

LOVE

See CHARITY.

LUBAC, HENRI DE (1896–1991)

Born 20 February 1896 in Cambrai in northern France, de Lubac entered the Jesuits in 1913. He was ordained in 1927 and in 1929 became professor of theology and history of religion at the Catholic University of Lyons; soon he was also serving on the Jesuit faculty at Fourviere.

He authored about forty books in theology and religious history. In 1938 he published *Catholicism,* his first major work, a study that emphasized the social and historical dimensions of the Church, evident in his claim that "a supernatural unity supposes a previous natural unity, the unity of the human race." He continued along the same lines with *Corpus Mysticum* in 1944. In the same year he published *The Drama of Atheist Humanism*—probably his best-known work. When he published *Surnaturel* in 1946 (with an imprimatur from 1942), some conservative theologians objected. In August of 1950 came "the lightening bolt of *Humani Generis*"—a papal encyclical warning of the dangers of modern and evolutionary thought. He was no longer allowed to teach and his books were banned in many places. He took it with quiet patience writing in 1953, "It is possible that many things in the human aspect of the Church disappoint us. . . . Patience and loving silence will be of more value than all else. . .the Church never gives us Jesus Christ in a better way than in the opportunities she offers us to be conformed to his passion." He was not fully rehabili-

Henri de Lubac

tated until Pope John XXIII nominated him *consultor* for a preparatory commission for Vatican II, and he then served as *peritus* throughout the council. By then he was long co-editor of *Sources chrétiennes* (critical editions of patristic texts) and was publishing his monumental four-volume *Exégèse médiéval* (1959–1964); this told of four senses of Scripture and of their unity being broken in the late Middle Ages.

In 1941, 1951, and 1953 de Lubac wrote several studies of Buddhism differentiating its mysticism from the Christian; yet he would say that apart from the incarnation and redemption that "Buddhism is without doubt the greatest spiritual fact in human history." In 1962 he wrote the first of five studies defending his Jesuit friend, Pierre Teilhard de Chardin. In 1969 he wrote of crisis in the Church following Vatican II and soon was regarded as a conservative voice. In 1965 he continued his earlier theme of the supernatural claiming that a human being's desire for God is "the evidence of a promise, inscribed and recognized in the being's very self." He became a fervent admirer of Pope John Paul II; in 1980, when the Pope was speaking at the Catholic Institute in Paris, he noticed Fr. de Lubac in the audience and said, "I bow my head before Fr. de Lubac." The Pope made Fr. de Lubac a cardinal in February, 1983. The cardinal continued to write and stay active in Church affairs until shortly before his death in Paris on 4 September 1991.

THOMAS M. KING, S.J.

See also GRACE; SOCIETY OF JESUS.

LUTHER, MARTIN (1483–1546)

The pivotal character in the sixteenth-century Reformation drama called Protestantism, Martin Luther was a young German Augustinian friar, who marshaled a humbling experience of faithful trust in the gracious forgiveness of a merciful and righteous God, coupled with a violent protest against abuses of the practice of indulgences, into a "protest" that condemned the worldliness and moral decline of the popes and clergy, challenged the sacramental and penitential systems of the medieval Church, grounded apostolicity in "the true treasure" of "the holy Gospel of the glory and grace of God," and eventually issued into a radical schism in the body of Roman Christianity.

Born into the lower-middle-class family of a German miner, Luther received an early education at schools in Magdeburg and Eisenach, where association with devout families helped strengthen a burgeoning religious faith. In 1501, at the pleasure of his father, he entered the University at Erfurt to study law. No doubt some of the shape for his later thought was derived from classical study of Virgil and Cicero and readings of the nominalist philosophies of Biel and Occam.

While at Erfurt, Luther had the first of two experiences that had tremendous impact on his young life. During a violent thunderstorm, he was driven to the ground by a bolt of lightning, a terrifying experience for a young man filled with doubts and troubled by thoughts of being an unworthy sinner at the hands of a wrathful God. "St. Anne, help me," he said. "I will become a monk." This was not an uncommon reaction to such a frightful experience. The abiding medieval belief was that an individual could accrue credit from God for performing good works, and certainly there could be no more meritorious a deed than renouncing the sinful world and entering a monastery. With that, over the angry protest of his father, he joined the Observant order of Augustinian Eremites in Erfurt.

Little relief came to Luther. Fearful of the wrathful God, he sought the refuge of a gracious God, troubled by the growing sense that his faithful devotion to his monastic duties and serious effort to perform "good works" were failing to appease God. Looking back he wrote: ". . . and I returned to confession very often, and thoroughly performed the penance that was enjoined unto me; yet for all this my conscience could never be fully certified, but was always in doubt." By 1507 he records the spiritual trauma of the Mass, where he encountered the crucifixion as condemnation of his unworthiness.

Seeking to intervene in Luther's personal suffering and redirect his energies, his spiritual counselor,

Martin Luther, painting by Lucas Cranach, 1529, Uffizi Gallery, Florence

Vicar General Staupitz, urged Luther to study Scripture and prepare to lecture at the new university at Wittenberg. In 1512 Luther received his doctorate of theology from Wittenberg and spent the period from 1513 to 1517 lecturing on Psalms, Genesis, and particularly Paul's Epistles to the Galatians and Romans. Late in this period Luther had a second encounter that altered his thinking and provided a centering point for his personal and theological reflections. In a tower of the monastery he suddenly felt the powerful presence of God—not destroying him, but affirming. His mind was driven back to a passage in Paul, Romans 1:17, where before he had been thwarted by the phrase "in it the righteousness of God is revealed." This had always been interpreted for him as the harsh condemnation of sinful, unrighteous man by the God who is righteous. Now Luther found in the conjuncted phrase—"he who through faith is righteous shall live"—the key to a different understanding of God.

The content of this "revelation" was to provide the foundation for a movement that would strike at the base of the entire medieval ecclesiastical and sacramental/penitential system: no human acts can merit forgiveness of sins, nor is grace a supernatural quality infused into the soul. Forgiveness lies in the faithful, trustful acceptance of the gracious God, who was actively present in the life, death, and resurrection of Christ, reconciling the world to himself. Thus, righteousness is unredeemed by merit or indulgence, but is purchased by the grace and mercy of God at Calvary. This righteousness is the "Good News" of the gift of God in the gospel, which is the true "treasure" of the Church, entrusted to the "living witness" or priesthood of all believers who trust in and commune with the forgiving God. In short, justification is solely by faith (not works) and solely through Scripture (not sacramental rituals of the Church): justification *sola fidei, sola Scriptura.*

Initially, for Luther, this was the treasure to be rediscovered by the Church through its own cleansing. Nowhere was the need of reform more obvious than in the exaggerated practice of indulgences, which originally had been instituted as a practical concession for satisfaction of penalties imposed by the earthly Church for the temporal punishment of sins. By the late Middle Ages this practice had been vulgarized to include remission of punishment in purgatory, and even remission of sins themselves. With the permission of the dean of the theological faculty, on 31 October 1517, All Saints' Day, Luther posted his ''ninety-five theses'' on the door of the Castle Church, inviting disputation.

It is clear at first that Luther opposed the excesses, not the practice as intended, of indulgences. Reform, not revolution, was perhaps a naive expectation. By challenging accepted, even endorsed, practices of the institution, he questioned its authority. Initially the papacy reacted only mildly. At the Heidelberg Disputation, however, Luther outlined his "theology of the Cross," to which Johannes Eck later rejoined with public denunciation, "the heretic!" By the Leipzig debate of 1519 Luther had moved toward a total rejection of the medieval view of Church and sacraments: monasticism, the sacrificial Mass, penance, works of merit, indulgences, the pope (now called Antichrist), all were perversions of the grace of God given freely in Christ. On 6 October 1520, all this was rolled together in *The Babylonian Captivity of the Church.* On 10 October Luther received the papal bull *Exsurge Domini,* condemning his views and giving him sixty days to submit to the Church's teaching authority. Instead, on 10 December 1520, Luther and his supporters staged a bonfire outside the gates of Wittenberg, burning the bull, along with a copy of canon law. Finally, at the Imperial Diet of Worms he defended his writings and declared his total reliance on apostolic witness and the "voice" of conscience: "Here I stand, I can do no other."

With that declaration made, reconciliation with the Roman Church was no longer desirable or possible. In its draft version of *Decretum Romanum Pontificem,* 3 January 1521, Luther was excommunicated. The division of Christendom was realized.

Luther was escorted to Wartburg Castle by his followers, under whose protection, amid attempts to capture him and bring him to trial for heresy, he spent better than twenty years, preaching, writing biblical commentaries and catechisms, teaching, and overseeing the halting development of this new "community of the faithful." His exploration of God's grace and humanity's faithful, trusting confidence came to an end on 18 February 1546.

JAMES W. THOMASSON

See also PROTESTANTISM; REFORMATION, THE.

LUTHERANS

Lutherans trace their heritage to the spiritual struggle of the Protestant Reformer, Martin Luther (1483–1546). After Luther had become an Augustinian monk, ordained a priest, and received a doctorate in theology, he became a professor at the University of Wittenberg.

During his extensive studies he discovered a disparity between the teaching of Scripture and the teaching of the Church. He was particularly disturbed by the Church's sale of "indulgences" or payment for decreasing one's time in purgatory. This was combined with his own personal anguish in seeking a gracious God. He was told by the Church that his salvation depended on his good works and what he could offer God. But Luther knew he was too sinful to offer God anything in exchange for his salvation.

All the tension Luther experienced within the Church and within himself was resolved when he read in Romans 1:17: "The just shall live by faith." It is alleged that Luther was so moved by this verse that he inserted *sola* (alone) after the word "faith" in his Latin Vulgate.

This was Luther's conversion, his enlightenment, the answer for which he had long struggled. Now he knew his salvation depended not on what he could offer God, but on what God had offered him in Jesus Christ. Following Luther's lead, Lutherans tend to emphasize the saving work of Christ, the second person of the Trinity.

Luther's new insight was the beginning of the Protestant Reformation. Luther wanted to debate the issues of indulgences, how we are saved, and what this meant for papal authority. That is why he nailed his ninety-five theses on the door of the castle church at Wittenberg on 31 October 1517.

The ensuing debates caused great turmoil in the Church and Luther was finally asked to recant his position at the Diet of Worms in 1521. He refused to do so with the famous reply: "I neither can nor will recant anything, since it is neither right nor safe to act against conscience. Here I stand. God help me. Amen." His teaching was then condemned and he was excommunicated.

Soon after his break with the Roman Catholic Church, a papal decree referred to the followers of Luther as "Lutherans." He, however, wished his followers to be called "Evangelicals," a word from the Greek meaning "good news," or "gospel." That is why today a synonym often used for Protestantism in Germany is "The Evangelical Church."

Luther's theological protest against medieval Catholicism five hundred years ago forms the basis of Lutheran belief today. It became, as well, the core of what it means to be a Protestant.

(1) Scripture is the Christian's sole authority in matters of faith and life, not the pope or the councils (the teaching of the Church). (2) Christians are saved by grace, not by works; this is what Luther called justification by faith. It is important to note that Luther did not juxtapose faith and works as later Protestants did. He said, "Just as the sun is bound to shine, a person of faith is bound to produce good works." So a better way of stating Luther's position is "faith not without works." (3) A person cannot only deal with God directly, but is expected to be a priest (a "Christ") to the neighbor. This is what he meant by the "priesthood of all believers." A summary of Luther's beliefs and the official standard for Lutheran doctrine is the Augsburg Confession, written in 1530 by Luther's friend, Philip Melanchton.

In contrast to Calvin's theocratic model, Luther advocated the "doctrine of the Two Kingdoms." In the realm of the gospel and Christian teaching, the Church is to rule; in the area of politics and matters of the state, the civil magistrate rules. God is present in both realms to make the entire society a more just and peaceful one.

Lutheranism spread rapidly throughout Europe, especially in Scandinavia, the Baltic nations, as well as in Germany and its surrounding countries. From a historical perspective, it must be said that the success of the Reformation was due, in no small measure, to the rising nationalism of the time and the cooperation of princes who saw in Luther's religious reform an attempt to gain political independence from Rome.

While the first Lutherans came to America in the seventeenth century, the first organization of American Lutherans was in 1748 in Philadelphia by Henry Melchiŏr Muhlenberg (1711–1787), the "father of American Lutheranism." A fine liberal arts college in Pennsylvania is named for him. The denomination's first theological seminary was founded in Gettysburg, Pennsylvania, in 1826.

For several generations, Lutherans were ethnically defined since many had come from state churches in Europe. But in the nineteenth century two branches emerged which attempted to transcend national identity—The American Lutheran Church led by Samuel S. Schmucker and The Lutheran Church of America led by Charles P. Krauth. About the same time, The Lutheran Church, Missouri Synod, was formed by Carl F. W. Walther. He wanted to preserve the German heritage of his community and to retain a strict confessional adherence to the Book of Concord, the standard of Lutheran orthodoxy.

In the early seventies, a major split occurred in the conservative Missouri Synod and the Association of Evangelical Lutheran Churches was formed. Then in 1987, the three main non-Missouri Synod branches mentioned above united to create the present Evangelical Lutheran Church of America. There are about seventy million Lutherans in the world and approximately nine million in all American denominations. Over five million belong to the ELCA which was formed in 1987.

Lutheran worship centers around the pulpit (God's invisible Word of preaching) and the altar (God's visible Word of the sacrament). In contrast to Presbyterians, who believe that Christ is symbolically present in the Lord's Supper, Lutherans believe in *consubstantiation,* that is, the Real Presence of Christ in the elements of bread and wine.

The Lord's Supper and baptism are the two sacraments, but there is a major emphasis placed on confirmation. Lutherans and Episcopalians are the two most liturgical of Protestant denominations; each faithfully follows the cycle of the Church year with its accompanying lectionary.

Some of the most well-liked Protestant music was produced by the Lutheran tradition as illustrated by Bach's chorales and many hymns of Lutheran pietism. Luther's own "A Mighty Fortress is Our God" is a kind of "national anthem" of Protestantism.

A number of Lutheran Churches form a synod, which is an official policy-making body. Local churches follow the "congregational" model and call their pastors; they are seldom appointed by a higher agency. The Lutheran emphasis on education is found in its strong parochial school system and the many colleges it established.

IRA ZEPP

See also LUTHER, MARTIN; PROTESTANTISM; REFORMATION, THE.

M

McAULEY, CATHERINE (1778–1841)

Catherine McAuley (1778–1841), foundress of the Sisters of Mercy, was born in Dublin, 29 September 1778 to James McGauley, a Catholic, and Elinor (Conway) McGauley, the first of three children. The others were Mary and James. Contemporaries describe Catherine as a little above average height, attractive with animated blue eyes, ash-blond hair, with large hands and square-tipped fingers. After her husband's death (20 July 1783), the much younger Elinor changed the surname to McAuley. Outliving her husband by fifteen years, indifferent to Catholicism, she maintained an active social life and spent the inheritance. Dying in 1798, she left little money or property.

Mary and James went to live with a Protestant relative of their mother, William Armstrong. Catherine chose the house of a Catholic uncle, Dr. Owen Conway, whose daughter Ann was a friend. Conway, a surgeon, was given to drink and gambling. The eventual financial strain on the family moved Catherine to rejoin her sister and brother in the Armstrong household. There she endured taunts about her Catholic faith, which fostered in her the value of ecumenical respect as well as a desire to learn more about her faith. Prejudice against Catholics had taken the form of penal laws between 1695 and 1731. They were not finally withdrawn until 1829.

In 1799 she met friends of the Armstrongs, William Callaghan and his wife who were childless. He was Protestant and she was Quaker. They had returned from India in 1785 after he had amassed a fortune as a pharmacist. In 1809, she went to live with the Callaghans in Coolock House, their country residence three miles outside Dublin. They were tolerant of her desire to attend Mass and do charitable works for the poor of Coolock parish. Often challenged to defend her Catholic beliefs by Protestant relatives and guests, she sought instruction from several priests: Fr. Andrew Lube, Fr. Thomas Betagh, vicar general to Archbishop Troy, Fr. Edward Armstrong, and Fr. Daniel Murray, later archbishop of Dublin.

Mrs. Callaghan died at seventy-eight in 1819, having converted to Catholicism. Her husband also converted; when he died in 1822, he made Catherine his principal heiress and sole executor of his property. She sold Coolock House in 1828. It was the Callaghan inheritance that funded the first foundation of the House of Mercy at Baggot Street in Dublin (24 September 1827). The congregation's patronal feast of our Lady of Mercy is celebrated by its link to this event. From 1827 to 1830, the house served as a residence for women, a school, employment agency, orphanage, and living quarters for Catherine's companions, who attended daily Mass at the Carmelite monastery on Clarendon Street.

Past forty, Catherine's energy was absorbed by a succession of deaths and her care for children. When Ann Conway Byrne, her first cousin, was dying of tuberculosis in 1821, Catherine adopted Ann's six-month-old baby, Teresa. After Ann's death in 1822,

Catherine adopted the oldest child, also named Catherine, and took in the two other siblings, Antoinette and James, to live at Baggot Street. Catherine's sister Mary died in 1827, and her physician husband in 1829, leaving five children in the care of Catherine; her beloved eldest niece, Mary Teresa, died in 1834; her niece Catherine died in 1837 after a one-year profession as a Sister of Mercy.

Catherine's work for the poor of Dublin attracted both companions and a succession of volunteer socialites. So that stability would be given her work, Archbishop Daniel Murray (1768–1852) and Dr. Michael Blake, vicar general and later bishop of Dromore, encouraged her to establish a religious community. She and two companions, Anna Maria Doyle and Elizabeth Harley, entered the Presentation Convent at St. George's Hill in Dublin on 8 September 1830. After fifteen months, including the novitiate, they professed vows on 12 December 1831, and immediately returned to Baggot Street. This is regarded as Mercy Foundation Day.

Over the next few years, Catherine was to adapt the Presentation Rule, based on the Rule of St. Augustine, for her own sisters, adding chapters on visitation of the sick and protection of distressed women. On 23 January 1832 the first seven of her companions were received as Sisters of Mercy at Baggot Street. One of these, Frances Warde (1810–1884) established the first foundation in the U.S. in Pittsburgh (1846), and was the recipient of many letters of the foundress. The final version of the rule was confirmed by Rome on 6 June 1841.

From 1831 to 1841, Catherine made foundations at Tullamore (1836), Carlow (1837), Cork (1837), Charleville (1836), Booterstown (1838), Limerick (1838), Naas (1839), Bermondsey, London (1839), Galway (1840), Wexford (1840), Birr (1840), and Birmingham (1841). She died of tuberculosis at Baggot Street on 11 November 1841. Her death was noted in Irish papers, as well as in London and New York. She was declared Venerable by Pope John Paul II on 9 April 1990, the first Irish woman to be so declared.

MARIE-ELOISE ROSENBLATT

See also CATHOLICISM, IRISH; CORPORAL AND SPIRITUAL WORKS OF MERCY; RELIGIOUS ORDERS; SISTERS OF MERCY.

Mother Catherine McAuley

McCARTHY, JOSEPH R. (1909–1957)

United States senator from Wisconsin, McCarthy was born in Grand Chute, Wisconsin, on 14 November 1909, to a Catholic farm family of German-Irish origin, and died in Washington, D.C., on 2 May 1957. Elected to the U.S. Senate as a Republican in 1948, McCarthy first attracted national attention in 1950 with a speech alleging Communist infiltration of the U.S. Department of State. As a member and later chairman of the Senate Committee on Government Operations and of its Permanent Subcommittee on Investigations, McCarthy used Senate investigative hearings to make highly publicized charges of Communist influence in the U.S. government.

In the early 1950s McCarthy was one of the best-known and most controversial figures in American politics. Critics accused him of abusing his senatorial immunity to make reckless accusations such as his claim that the Democrats had been guilty of "twenty years of treason." McCarthy's defenders, among them numerous Catholics sensitive to the Communist threat at the height of the Cold War, were apt to accuse McCarthy's critics of "anti-anti-communism."

McCarthy's career reached a climax in 1954 with his televised investigation of the U.S. Army for allegedly concealing evidence of Communist espionage activities. The hearings alienated not only Democrats and the liberal media, but also many Republicans, including President Dwight D. Eisenhower. In December 1954 the Senate voted to censure McCarthy whereupon his influence declined abruptly until his death three years later.

THOMAS J. SHELLEY

See also COMMUNISM.

McKENZIE, JOHN L. (1910–1991)

John L. McKenzie was one of the foremost leaders of the American Catholic biblical movement which brought sound scholarship to the attention of the

Catholic community between 1950 and 1970. Born in 1910, he was educated at St. Louis University, at Weston College, and ordained a priest in 1939. In his early teaching years at the Jesuit theologate at West Baden, Indiana, he began to use and adapt the principle of literary forms to the Catholic approach to Scripture and theology as the encyclical of Pius XII, *Divino Afflante Spiritu* (1943) had encouraged.

As an early member of the Catholic Biblical Association he shared that organization's objective not only to foster sound and deep scholarship but also to present it to nonprofessionals in a way that would have an impact on the public life of the Church. *The Two Edged Sword,* published in 1956, was probably the first important Catholic book which shared this new scholarship on the theology of the Old Testament with the American public. It was followed by *The Bible in Current Catholic Thought* (1962) and *Myths and Realities: Studies in Biblical Theology* (1963). McKenzie was showing himself as a scholar who could communicate broad and important truths to serious readers not only Catholic but ecumenical. As the culmination of many years of research at West Baden, he published *The Dictionary of the Bible* in 1965. This proved an instant success, went through many editions and remains a standard reference today. As a tribute to his leadership, McKenzie was elected president of the Catholic Biblical Association in 1963 and in recognition of his ecumenical influence he was the first Catholic elected president of the nonsectarian Society of Biblical Literature in 1967.

Much of this was engulfed in controversy as McKenzie, Bruce Vawter, Roland Murphy, and Patrick Skehan used their influence in the Catholic Biblical Association to validate the claims of biblical scholars to pursue the program laid down by Pius XII against intense conservative academic forces within the American Catholic Church. The problem was the right of biblical scholars to pursue legitimate means of developing new understandings of Sacred Scripture within the framework of inspiration and also to publish the results to a general audience. Between 1961 and 1965 McKenzie and others succeeded in establishing this position as accepted and in influencing Vatican Council II in its declarations on Divine Revelation and Religious Freedom. Later Catholic scholars such as Raymond Brown, Joseph Fitzmyer, etc., have had to continue to fight a running battle, but their ability to influence the American Catholic Church as a whole has depended largely on McKenzie's stand. It was honest in its approach—and often very aggressive.

After the sixties most of McKenzie's writings were more sharply polemic and had less impact on the movement. He died on 2 March 1991 in Claremont, California, where he had retired as a priest of the Diocese of Madison, Wisconsin.

JAMES A. FISCHER, C.M.

See also CRITICISM, BIBLICAL; THEOLOGY, BIBLICAL.

McKILLOP, MARY (1842–1909)

Mary McKillop, an Australian candidate for canonization, is one of the creative founders of Catholicism in that country. The eldest of eight children of Scots immigrants, she supported the family by teaching when her father's business failed, although she had conceived a desire to try a vocation to the religious life. Contact with a remarkable but erratic priest, Julian Tenison Woods, showed her how this might be possible in colonial society. Together they founded the Sisters of St. Joseph of the Sacred Heart in 1866.

The Josephites, as they came to be called, were teachers of the poor, living in poverty close to the lives of those they served. Wherever there was need, in mining towns, bush settlements and city slums, they were to be found, their convents humble cottages and tenements. Unlike the European religious orders which relied on dowries and centered themselves on grand buildings, Josephites were as mobile as gypsies. Thus they fitted well into emerging Australian society, moving in when needed and moving out when the need evaporated. The new institute attracted many postulants, membership being soon numbered in hundreds, then thousands, until it became the largest body of religious women in Australia. Its foundation coincided with the withdrawal of state aid to Church schools. The bishops decided to preserve and expand the Catholic school system, relying on the Josephites and other, mainly Irish, orders for teachers. In this they succeeded; so that by the end of the nineteenth century the vast majority of Australian Catholic children were enrolled in Catholic schools, many of them in the hands of Josephites. For the next century it remained true that most Catholics had their grounding in religion from nuns in parochial schools.

Mary McKillop envisaged her foundation as an Australia-wide unit to ensure homogeneity over the vast continent. Some bishops, however, wanted to control the Josephites in their own dioceses and when McKillop resisted they moved against her. Her own bishop in Adelaide (South Australia) excommunicated her for alleged insubordination and elsewhere her order was extruded or forbidden entry. She took her case to Rome and moved headquarters to Sydney, where she could expect protection from Cardinal Moran. In 1888 Rome definitively approved of her concept of central extra-diocesan leadership, leaving McKillop free to direct expansion as she saw fit.

Roman rewriting of the Josephite rule angered Tenison Woods, who believed his ethos of extreme poverty had been watered down. He blamed McKillop for this and their intimate friendship was thus abbreviated. Her cause for canonization was introduced in 1973; the process proceeds smoothly. Mary McKillop's sufferings in a patriarchal Church have made her a heroine to modern Australian feminists.

R. EDMUND CAMPION

See also AUSTRALIA, CHURCH IN; MORAN, PATRICK FRANCIS.

McNABB, VINCENT (1868–1943)

Dominican priest, theologian, preacher, and apostle of poverty. He was born in 1868 in Portaferry, County Down, in Northern Ireland. His father was a sailor, his mother a dressmaker, and Vincent was the tenth of eleven children. He entered the English province of the Dominicans in 1885, and after ordination embarked on a career of prayer, study, and work for the poor. His interest in literature, art, history, and social justice brought him in contact with such public figures as Hilaire Belloc, Bernard Shaw, Eric Gill and G. K. Chesterton who revered him as a crusading associate and an unforgettable personality: "Nobody who ever met or saw or heard Father McNabb has ever forgotten him." While he was a master of economic theories, he was rather impractical in their application, believing that the industrial revolution was a human disaster and that industrialism tended to create a servile society and should be abandoned. He fostered a return to the land and to subsistence farming.

The impractical economist was a very practical theologian and spiritual writer. He wrote over thirty books, living his dictum "produce as much as you can, consume as little as you need." The following brief selection of his books shows the range of his intellectual pursuits: *The New Testament Witness to St. Peter; The Catholic Church and Philosophy; Infallibility; The Church and Reunion; Frances Thompson and Other Essays; The Path of Prayer.*

Clad in Dominican habit and wearing army boots, Vincent McNabb avoided public and private transport and became a well-known figure as he walked the streets of London. He preached on street corners and in Hyde Park where he became known for his wit and wisdom. He was the happy ascetic who slept on the floor and owned only four books: the Bible, the *Summa Theologiae,* the *Dominican Constitutions* and his breviary. He died of throat cancer on 17 June 1943 and his memory is fresh and cherished among English Catholics.

JOAN GLAZIER

See also BRITAIN, CHURCH IN; DOMINICANS.

MAGISTERIUM

The Latin word *magister* means "master," not only in the sense of "teacher" but also in the broader sense of someone possessing authority or mastery in a particular field. St. Thomas spoke of two kinds of magisterium in the Church, that of bishops based on their role as prelates and that of theologians based on their scholarly competence. In contemporary Roman Catholic theological usage, magisterium refers almost exclusively to the teaching office of the pope and bishops or to these men themselves.

Vatican II declares that "the task of giving an authentic interpretation of the Word of God, whether in its written form or in the form of Tradition, has been entrusted to the living teaching office of the Church alone. Its authority in this matter is exercised in the name of Jesus Christ. Yet this Magisterium is not superior to the Word of God, but is its servant. It teaches only what has been handed on to it. At the divine command and with the help of the Holy Spirit, it listens to this devotedly, guards it with dedication and expounds it faithfully. All that it proposes for belief as being divinely revealed is drawn from this single deposit of faith" (*Dei Verbum,* 10).

According to the Roman Catholic belief, this pastoral teaching authority of bishops is both legitimate and necessary. Legitimate, because the bishops are the successors of the apostles, receiving their mandate to teach the truths of salvation in the name of Christ as authorized witnesses and as "judges of faith" (*Lumen Gentium,* 25). Necessary, because without this authorized witness we would not be able to know what God has revealed to us.

There are two ways in which this authoritative teaching is exercised with different results and corresponding obligations of assent on the part of believers. First, there is the extraordinary or solemn way, which can be carried out in two modes: either by an ecumenical council with the pope as its head or by the pope personally (*ex cathedra*). In these cases, the teaching is an infallible dogma to which the faithful are required to give an irrevocable assent of faith.

Secondly, there is the ordinary way. Again, it can be carried out in two modes. First, by the universal magisterium, when dispersed throughout the world, the bishops propound with moral unanimity a doctrine related to faith and morals "to be definitively held" (*Lumen Gentium,* 25). Mere *de facto* universal agreement is not sufficient. There must be an explicit intention to bind the faithful to the teaching proposed. In this case we also have an infallible teaching to which an assent of faith is demanded. Secondly, by the ordinary nondefinitive magisterium, when the pope, an individual bishop, or conferences of bishops exercise their day-to-day teaching office. Such teaching is authoritative (sometimes called "authentic," that is, taught in the name of Christ), but not infallible.

The response called for by this last kind of teaching, which constitutes the bulk of Catholic doctrines, is said by Vatican II to be "a ready and respectful allegiance of mind," a "loyal submission of the will and intellect (*religiosum obsequium*)" (*Lumen Gentium,* 25). It is not easy to specify exactly the meaning of the term *obsequium.* Ladislas Orsy suggests that it is, like the expression *communio* used by Vatican II, a "seminal locution," that is, a broad expression which conveys an intuitive insight into the truth but does not define it and requires further development. In general it may be said that *obsequium* describes an attitude of respectful trust and docility toward the Church's teaching office, a willingness to question one's own opinions and to make every effort to understand and accept the teaching of the magisterium. This attitude is said to be religious because ultimately it is based on one's love for Christ and his Church, and not on the reasons one can perceive justifying the teaching.

Is there then no possibility of legitimately "dissenting" from the ordinary, noninfallible teaching of the magisterium? First of all, the term "dissent" is not a theologically helpful term to describe a legitimate disagreement a person may have with a particular teaching of the nondefinitive magisterium. It is too negative and too broad. It insinuates more than just an intellectual disagreement, suggesting a bellicose and closed posture. Secondly, because noninfallible teachings can and often have an organic relationship with the core of the Christian faith and may acquire in the course of time a binding force, it is simplistic to say *tout court* that it is always permissible to dissent from noninfallible ordinary magisterium.

This does not however mean that disagreement (even public) from nondefinitive magisterium is always illegitimate and that it should always be construed as disobedience or lack of loyalty to the Holy See. The *obsequium* mentioned above does not simply require respect and submission to the teachings of the magisterium but also the duty to examine them critically and, if necessary, to express reservations and disagreement without rebelling against authority. Such a disagreement is legitimate and even necessary if the truth is to be discovered or better formulated. The American National Conference of Catholic Bishops has laid down three conditions for licit theological disagreement: "The expression of theological dissent from the magisterium is in order only if the reasons are serious and well-founded, if the manner of the dissent does not question or impugn the teaching authority of the Church and is such as not to give scandal" (*Human Life in Our Day,* 1968).

PETER C. PHAN

See also AUTHORITY IN THE CHURCH; INFALLIBILITY.

MAGNANIMITY

(Lat. *magnus,* "great" + *animus,* "spirit" or "mind") A virtue which prompts a person to act charitably and honorably toward others; it is associated with generosity, kindness, and moral fortitude. A gift of grace, it arises from an individual's consciousness of the ultimate sanctity and worth of every person, and consequently is immune to worldly judgment and criticism.

JOSEPH QUINN

See also VIRTUE.

MAGNIFICAT

The hymn attributed to Mary (but to Elizabeth in a few manuscripts) in Luke 1:46-55 is traditionally known by the first word in its Latin translation *Magnificat* ("magnifies"). In it Mary rejoices that she is to be the mother of Jesus and interprets his conception as an instance of how God raises up the lowly and puts down the proud, powerful, and rich, and of how God deals with Israel. The hymn is a pastiche of OT allusions and phrases (see Hannah's song in 1 Sam 2:1-10), and thus typical of Second Temple Jewish hymnody.

DANIEL J. HARRINGTON, S.J.

See also BENEDICTUS; HYMNS; MARY, MOTHER OF GOD; NUNC DIMITTUS.

MAJOR ORDERS

See SACRAMENT OF ORDERS.

MAJOR SUPERIOR

One who has general authority over a religious congregation. Among those accorded the title of major superior are abbots and superiors of entire religious institutes or their component provinces.

JOSEPH QUINN

See also RELIGIOUS ORDERS.

MANICHAEISM

This complex heresy originated with Manichaeus (or Manes) who was born in Persia ca. 216 and died there in 260. He was deeply influenced by Persian Gnosticism and Pauline teaching and developed very complicated systems, some of whose heretical tenets caused recurring religious controversies for over a thousand years. His basic dualistic teaching rested on a supposed primeval confrontation between light and darkness, between the Spirit of God and a Spirit of Evil. He postulated that there are two eternal first principles: a Spiritual God, the source of all good, and the Spirit of Evil, generally equated with matter, that was the cause of all evil.

The Manichaeans rejected the Old Testament and rejected anything in the New Testament which did not conform to their basic beliefs. As the body was evil, sexual abstinence was mandated, marriage was condemned and the bearing of children was an abomination. The sect advocated severe asceticism which included vegetarianism. Despite its austere mode of life and its convoluted and eclectic creed—with so many different elements drawn from a variety of sources from astrology to metaphysics—Manichaeism attracted adherents through many centuries in many cultures, the most famous of whom was Augustine of Hippo in his youth. It had a profound influence on later heresies such as Catharism and Abigensianism.

MICHAEL GLAZIER

See also ALBIGENSES; GNOSTICISM.

MANIFESTATION OF CONSCIENCE

A voluntary practice of revealing one's conscience primarily to get spiritual guidance. It is usually performed with a priest, but sometimes a nun or a layperson is preferred. Canon law forbids a religious superior to demand a manifestation from a subject.

MICHAEL GLAZIER

See also CONSCIENCE; SPIRITUAL DIRECTION.

MANNING, HENRY EDWARD, CARDINAL (1808–1892)

English cardinal, born in Hertfordshire. His father was a banker and member of Parliament. Henry took a first in classics at Oxford and after ordination in the Church of England he served as rector of a rural parish in Sussex. He married but his wife died in 1837. In 1840 he became archdeacon of Chichester. As a prominent figure in the High Anglican "Oxford Movement," he stressed the Church's right to exercise control over matters of faith and discipline. Newman's conversion to Catholicism in 1845 distressed him greatly because he thought it a betrayal which would do serious injury to the Church of England.

Five years later, however, the "Gorham Case" went to the heart of Manning's priorities. An Anglican bishop had refused to employ a clergyman on the ground that his beliefs were heretical. The bishop's decision was reversed by the judicial committee of the Privy Council, that is, by a lay court. For Manning this meant that Anglican doctrine was being determined by an authority other than the Church itself. This he could not accept and in 1851 he became a Catholic. Cardinal Wiseman, archbishop of Westminster, facilitated his speedy ordination as a Catholic priest and sent him to Rome for theological studies. When he returned he founded an order called the Oblates of St. Charles whose members were diocesan clergy living in community.

Wiseman made full use of Manning's administrative competence but it was as a spokesman for ultramontane attitudes that the new convert was most prominent. His instinct to protect ecclesiastical independence spurred him not only to argue in defense of the pope's right to rule the Papal States, then being fiercely criticized by European liberals and coming under recurrent military assault from Italian nationalists, but also led him to champion the inflexible theology favored in Rome. Manning's views were shared by Wiseman, Father Faber of the Brompton Oratory, and the journalist, W. G. Ward, and received powerful support from Monsignor George Talbot of the Roman Curia. At the opposite pole of English Catholic opinion were Newman and the historian, Sir John (later Lord) Acton, men whose spirit of inquiry, insistence on the rights of the laity, and stress on the development of doctrine were considered by Manning and his friends to be dangerously unorthodox, above all when they touched on contemporary issues of interest to the Church like the government's educational policy.

Manning's identification with extreme papalism intensified when he succeeded Wiseman as archbishop of Westminster in 1865, an unexpected appointment said to have been the personal decision of Pope Pius IX. In 1870, at the First Vatican Council, Manning was among the leaders of the majority who urged that papal infallibility be defined as dogma, but the definition adopted by the council was more cautiously phrased than he would have wished. He was made a cardinal in 1875. He never overcame his suspicion of Newman, which intensified when Newman's coolness on infallibility became apparent. Manning made a genuine attempt at rapprochement shortly after he became archbishop but it collapsed when each of the two churchmen had to agree that he found the other incomprehensible.

As an advocate of social reform, Manning ranks high among the practical philanthropists of the Victorian era as well as among the socially conscious contributors to the mind of the Church on the eve of *Rerum Novarum.* His concern for the working classes—demonstrated in his promotion of the temperance movement, denunciation of child labor and other protests at the excesses of capitalism—was acknowledged by his appointment as a member of the royal commissions on housing the poor in 1885 and education in 1886. His successful intervention in the London dock strike of 1889 was long remembered with gratitude by the dockers for whom he achieved a wage increase, and his demand that the Irish peasantry be treated with justice was untypical of a man coming from his conservative background. Only on the education of Catholics was he less than perceptive. He ensured the continuance of a Church prohibition against the attendance of Catholics at Oxford and Cambridge universities, yet failed in his efforts to establish a viable Catholic university in London; he founded a number of primary schools but made little headway in providing secondary institutions.

LOUIS McREDMOND

See also BRITAIN, CHURCH IN; NEWMAN, JOHN HENRY, CARDINAL; OXFORD MOVEMENT.

MANNIX, DANIEL (1864–1963)

Daniel Mannix, archbishop of Melbourne (Australia), became famous as the articulator of Australian Catholics' rejection of British imperial hegemony. His career before he went to Melbourne in 1913 gave no premonitions of his tempestuous life there. The son of tenant farmers, he was a product of the Irish national seminary, Maynooth, who stayed on to become an admired professor of moral theology. In 1903 he became seminary president, in which role he entertained successive English kings, thus attracting the scorn of Irish nationalists.

When Rome ordered him to Melbourne he obeyed, taking as his episcopal motto that of the late Cardinal Moran (*Omnia Omnibus*)—a clue, perhaps, that he intended to take on Moran's role of public advocacy. In Melbourne he quickly attacked the denial of state funds to Church schools as of a piece with early persecutions of Catholics. The wider community began to notice the new bishop.

It was World War I which made Mannix into a national figure. He was not against Australia's involvement in the war but, along with other Catholic bishops, and unlike some Protestant leaders, he did not project war service as a sacred duty, almost sac-

Daniel Mannix

ramental in its soul-cleansing potential. Troop losses on the Western Front led the government in 1916 to propose conscription of men for military service. The referendum on this proposal split the Australian electorate. On the side of conscription, were those who saw Australia as integrally part of the British Empire, linked to Britain by ties of kinship, honor, and obligation. For the most part, the British Empire people were middle class, conservative and Protestant. Those who said no to conscription tended to be workers, Laborites and Catholic. The leader of the anti-conscription cause was T. J. Ryan, a Catholic lawyer who was Australian Labor Party premier of the Queensland state government.

Mannix said little during the 1916 referendum campaign. Failure to win this campaign, however, prompted the government to try again in 1917, deliberately using anti-Catholicism as a political technique. Mannix became a major target. He was thus cunningly promoted by government supporters into a leader of the opposition. Realizing the exasperated feelings of his own constituency, Mannix did not refuse the challenge. Witty, sarcastic, argumentative open-air oratory delighted the thousands who mobbed him wherever he appeared. He became a hero to the underclass, a powerful articulator of their yearnings for an Australian identity separate from the hegemony of the British Empire. He wrote nothing and spoke off the cuff, sometimes to his later embarrassment. Upper-class Catholics disapproved and complained, but the Vatican would not move against a bishop so secure in his people's affections. Catholic critics of his politics, especially if they were from Melbourne, soon felt his displeasure.

In 1920 Mannix made his *ad limina* visit to Rome, traveling via U.S.A. Irish America took him to its bountiful heart. More mass meetings, more scalding oratory. He was given the freedom of New York City. Lloyd George's British government, its Black and Tan mercenaries bogging it deeper in the quagmire of Ireland, watched Mannix's American triumph with cold eyes. When his ship entered British waters it was intercepted by the Royal Navy, Mannix was arrested and put ashore at Penzance in Cornwall. He was forbidden to visit Ireland or the major Irish centers in England, but they could not keep the crowds away from someone who now had an international reputation.

Opponents hoped he would stay overseas but his return to Australia saw renewed adulation for this living icon. In the last twenty years of his episcopate, he sponsored a secret Catholic political apparatus, known as The Movement. Catholics criticized this as an unacceptable involvement of the Church in politics and the electorate rejected it as undemocratic. Nevertheless, The Movement survived because it could claim to speak with the authority of Mannix.

R. EDMUND CAMPION

See also AUSTRALIA, CHURCH IN; MORAN, PATRICK FRANCIS.

MANUSCRIPTS OF THE BIBLE

While original texts of the Old and New Testament are not available, early manuscripts of the biblical text and ancient fragments allow scholars to understand the history of translation and of interpretation. Ancient writers used papyrus, made from a plant, cut into strips, glued together, and joined into scrolls as long as thirty-five feet. The text was written on these scrolls in parallel columns without punctuation. From the beginning of the second century A.D. codices were used. These looked more like a book and were easier to handle. Parchment made from animal skin or vellum replaced papyrus until paper was used in the Middle Ages. The oldest manuscript of the entire Bible comes from the fourth century, but earlier NT fragments and segments of the Jewish Scriptures offer a wealth of material for study and comparison.

The following are among the most important manuscripts:

Hebrew Texts of Old Testament

Discoveries in Qumran in 1947 uncovered manuscripts representative of 250–175 B.C. such as the Isaiah Scroll. The importance of the Qumran manuscripts is that the Hebrew texts can be compared to later Greek translations. The Masada manuscripts

"Wedding Feast at Cana," manuscript detail, Egbert Codex, ca. 980, Trier

represent another ancient collection. Manuscripts from the postbiblical period include Samaritan Pentateuch, Origen's Second Column, and the later Cairo Prophets (A.D. 895), the oldest extant Hebrew manuscript. Discovery of storage places (geniza) for manuscripts that outlived their usefulness give us texts like the Cairo Geniza Manuscript of Sirach from the eleventh century.

Greek Versions of the Old Testament

The most important and earliest is the Septuagint (LXX) from the second century B.C. and used in apostolic times by the writers of the NT. Pre-Christian fragments are available as well as second- and third-century revisions and translations. Papyri from as early as the second and third centuries are in the Chester Beatty and Freer Collections. The Great Uncial (block letters) Codices from the fourth to tenth centuries are carefully preserved manuscripts of LXX. The oldest are Codex Vaticanus and Codex Sinaiticus from the fourth century and Codex Alexandrinus from the fifth.

Other Versions of the Bible

Some early Aramaic translations or targums (last centuries B.C.) add to our understanding of the Jewish Scriptures. The Vulgate by Jerome (A.D. 389), a Latin translation from the Hebrew Bible rather than the Greek text is most important for the Catholic Church. Syriac, Coptic, Ethiopic, and Western Asian versions show the transmission of the Scriptures throughout the known world.

Greek Texts of the New Testament

The oldest texts are the great Uncial Codices of the fourth and fifth centuries. The Codex Vaticanus contains the NT minus Hebrews 9:14ff., Pastoral Letters, Revelation; the Codex Sinaiticus contains the entire NT; the Codex Alexandrinus has NT minus Matthew 1–24; John 7–8; 2 Corinthians 4–12. The Codex Bezae contains much of the NT in both Greek and Latin. Less important codices are also available from this period. The Chester Beatty and Rylands Papyrus collections contain fragments of the NT from the second to the eighth centuries. In addition to manuscripts, citations from the NT by the second-century Fathers of the Church offer insight into the development of Scripture, and new discoveries continue to uncover ancient fragments and manuscripts from the biblical period.

HELEN DOOHAN

MARCIONISM

A heresy, or series of heresies, named after Marcion (d. ca. 160), a native of Sinope in Pontus, who, according to Hippolytus, was the son of a bishop. In 140 he went to Rome, and over the next years he formulated a rather intricate corpus of doctrines. He was excommunicated in 144, and communities of his adherents spread rapidly through the Empire. His success drew refutations from such eminent bishops as Irenaeus of Lyons. Marcion's aim was to expurgate all Jewish elements from Christianity.

According to the Church Fathers, Marcion maintained that Christ was a manifestation of the Good God who was opposed by the Creator God of Law revealed in the Old Testament whom Marcion called the Demiurge. Marcion rejected all of the Old Testament and most of the New Testament except ten letters of Paul and an edited recension of Luke. Matter was evil and he rejected the resurrection of the body. Baptism was denied to those living in matrimony. The death of Jesus was the work of the Demiurge. Marcionism and its convoluted doctrines and severe moral code survived for five hundred years.

MICHAEL GLAZIER

See also HERESY/HERETICS.

MARGARET MARY ALACOQUE, ST.

See DEVOTIONS; FIRST FRIDAYS; SACRED HEART OF JESUS.

MARIAN YEAR

A year honoring the Blessed Virgin Mary and marked by special events, prayers, penance, and papal indulgences. Pius XII proclaimed 1954 a Marian year to observe the centennial of the definition of the dogma of the Immaculate Conception, while John Paul II made the fourteen months ending on the feast of the Assumption 1988 a Marian year, in part as a preparation for the third millennium of Christianity. Marian years are a modern phenomenon patterned after the traditional Holy Year.

DAVID BRYAN

See also HOLY YEAR; MARY, MOTHER OF GOD.

MARIE OF THE INCARNATION, O.S.U. (1599–1672)

A happy girl, married woman, parent, widow, mystic, business manager, nun, missionary, foundress, educator, writer—Marie of the Incarnation was all of these. She established the first school and the first convent in North America. A Quebec Ursuline, she enjoys the unique title of "Mother of the Church in Canada."

Daughter of devout parents, she was born to Florent and Jeanne Guyart, on 28 October 1599 in Tours, France. Her entire life was marked by a dream she had at the age of seven, a dream in which Jesus asked her "Will you be mine?" and she replied enthusiastically "Yes!"

At fourteen, Marie wanted to join the Benedictines, but her parents thought she was too vivacious for the cloister. Three years later they prevailed upon her to marry Claude Martin, a master silkworker. He died when she was nineteen, leaving her with an infant son, Claude, and with crushing debts. Shortly thereafter she became the manager of her brother-in-law's flourishing transport company. For ten years, her long and busy days were combined with a profound mystical union with God. Marie experienced several visions of the Trinity during this time and in 1627 when she was twenty-eight years old, entered into a "mystical marriage"—an overwhelming sense of oneness with Christ.

In 1631, when her son Claude was barely twelve, she entered the Ursuline monastery in Tours. After an initial joyful period, Marie's spirits plunged into extreme depression, grief, and anguish. Having spent ten years in exercising a great deal of responsibility and authority, she suddenly found herself having to conform to an exacting routine with novices about half her age. But, most painful of all, her son Claude often appeared at the grille weeping and shouting for his mother. In 1633, Georges de la Haye, S.J., became her director, advised her to write her spiritual autobiography, and arranged for Claude to be admitted to a Jesuit school.

Following her profession, she dreamed of a strange and beautiful land and became filled with a profound apostolic longing. That yearning was fulfilled on 1 August 1639, when after a series of extraordinary events and an extremely difficult three-month

Atlantic voyage, Marie, along with two companions and a laywoman, Madame de la Peltrie, set foot on the dock of the Quebec settlement. Within a week they had settled into a little house near the quay and had started a boarding school with six Indian and two French boarding students.

Here in Quebec, Marie labored for the remaining thirty-three years of her life, enduring extreme hardships of every kind, including a fire which completely destroyed their monastery in 1650. Besides tending to the many practical concerns of the sisters and boarders, teaching classes, hosting numerous visitors—Indians, settlers, officials, clerics, soldiers, and merchants—she wrote dictionaries in Algonquin and Iroquois as well as a Huron catechism. A prolific writer, she wrote some three thousand letters, many of them to her son Claude who became a Benedictine abbot in Marmoutier, France.

Marie died on 30 April 1672. The Ursuline monastery of Quebec still stands today, the first of a vast network of Catholic schools across North America, and *alma mater* of many thousands of women who have received their education there over the past 354 years.

Marie of the Incarnation was declared "Blessed" by John-Paul II on 22 June 1980.

TERESITA KAMBEITZ, O.S.U.

See also CANADA, THE CATHOLIC CHURCH IN; URSULINES.

MARIOLOGY

The branch of theology which has as its subject the Blessed Virgin Mary. The word was first used in the seventeenth century by Nigido Placido (d. 1650). Though from early and medieval times works had occasionally appeared dealing entirely and solely with Our Lady, St. Thomas Aquinas and the Scholastic theologians treated theological themes on Mary within the framework of the incarnation. Francis Suarez (d. 1617), first author of a systematic Marian theology, still adhered to the context of the mysteries of Christ, while his near contemporary, St. Peter Canisius (d. 1597) had composed a very large independent work on the "Incomparable Virgin Mary." Spiritual authors and theologians devoted books to Our Lady, St. Louis Marie Grignion de Montfort and St. Alphonsus Liguori foremost among them. This was accepted practice in the nineteenth century and the first six decades of the twentieth, when most major theologians and spiritual writers wrote a book on Mary. Vatican II did not issue a separate document on Mary, but dealt with her primarily in the Dogmatic Constitution on the Church (*Lumen Gentium*), and this set the pattern for postconciliar writings on Our Lady.

MICHAEL O'CARROLL, C.S.Sp.

See also MARY, MOTHER OF GOD.

MARITAIN, JACQUES (1882–1973)

Philosopher, religious thinker, and humanist, Jacques Maritain was born in Paris 18 November 1882 and died in Toulouse 28 April 1973. His significance is on two levels. First, on a general cultural plane, where he helped start or gave impetus to ideals and aims now regarded as obviously desirable, but at that time were suspect by many, such as, ecumenism between Western and Eastern Churches, religious liberty, the teaching of Christians about the Jews, human rights, the role and importance of the laity in the Church, a humanism aided by religion instead of at war with it. In general he encouraged a religious revival among intellectuals and an intellectual revival among the religious. The second level is the more narrow frame of philosophical thought, especially that of Thomas Aquinas. Maritain's express aim was to take the thought of Aquinas out of its cultural ghetto and medieval trappings and place it in the marketplace of current ideas to contribute to solving the problems of the day. In addition, he aimed to deepen doctrines already formulated and to enrich this philosophy with new directions and insights. He was awarded the Grand Prize of Literature from the French Academy (1961), and the French National Prize For Letters (1963). He was invited to Rome for the closing days of the Second

Jacques Maritain

Vatican Council and received from Pope Paul, as the representative of the intellectual class, the "Message To Intellectuals."

It was while studying at the Sorbonne that he met a fellow student and his wife-to-be, Raïssa Oumansoff. She was Jewish and had emigrated from Russia to Paris with her parents and her sister Vera. Soon after their marriage the couple read a work by an author unknown to them, *The Woman Who Was Poor,* by Leon Bloy. A friendship developed between Bloy and the Maritains and this led to their joining the Church in 1906.

A few years after this Maritain started the study of Thomas Aquinas. From the beginning his topics and problems were current rather than historical studies. For example, his first book (1914) was on the contemporary philosopher, Henri Bergson—translated years later as *Bergsonian Philosophy And Thomism.* In addition to his writing, he taught, especially at the Institut Catholique.

He was asked by certain ecclesiastical authorities to produce a course of philosophy for use in the French seminaries. Several volumes were planned, only two were completed. There was a work on logic and another (1920) later translated as *An Introduction to Philosophy.* In this same year (1920) appeared the astonishing *Art And Scholasticism.* It showed how fruitful the philosophy of Aquinas could be if really made use of by another philosopher of wide culture and in sympathy with modern art and the creative process.

Although his personal motto at this time was "Woe to me if I do not Thomisticize," he never confused faith with philosophy or theology or thought that the Church imposed the doctrine of Aquinas on anyone. If the Church wanted the doctrine of Aquinas taught it was to give its members a chance to see what it actually was, to examine it and accept what truth they could find in it.

His first real effort in political philosophy was occasioned by the Church's censure of a group called *Action française.* The censure deeply offended many Catholics, and to help soften the controversy he produced *The Primacy of the Spiritual* (1927), translated as *The Things That Are Not Caesar's.*

The time between the two world wars was one of several lecture tours to North America and important writings. In the United States, the University of Chicago was hospitable, and he also scheduled brief courses at Toronto, at the Institute of Mediaeval Studies, invited by Gilson. This period saw two important works. The first was in political philosophy, *Integral Humanism* (1936). He tried to show that a Christian could indeed be a humanist and even more of a humanist than others, and that, since the social structure of the Middle Ages was over and done, a new kind of relationship must be found for the coexistence of the Church and society. The other major work was *The Degrees of Knowledge* (1932). This was a difficult and technical work, and aimed to contrast the different approaches taken by modern science, philosophy, and the highest degree of knowledge, that of the mystics.

Jacques, Raïssa, and Vera came to the United States in January of 1940 for a lecture tour by Jacques, but due to World War II a return to France was impossible. New York City became their home until early in 1945. Cut off from his usual income, Maritain had to make it up by his writing and teaching. In addition to lecture tours, he gave courses at Princeton and Columbia Universities.

Several important books also appeared in this period. *Ransoming the Time* (1941) was a collection of essays on such matters as "Human Equality" and "The Mystery of Israel." *The Rights of Man and Natural Law* (1943) tried to balance the rights of the person with the demands social life can make on him. In the same year he delivered the Terry Lectures at Yale University, published as *Education at the Crossroads.* This was written for a general audience and contains so much of a very humane psychology, and an appreciation of human values and aspirations that it was quite an astonishing success, and a revelation for many. (Many of both Gilson's and Maritain's most popular and influential works were first given as lectures, later published, at non-Catholic institutions. One gets the impression that they were not in much demand at the Catholic colleges.)

Things greatly changed when he agreed to be the French Ambassador to the Holy See. This kind of work was uncongenial to the philosopher, and it was chosen more as a matter of duty. Many facts are yet to become known about the issues and problems of his ambassadorship. While ambassador, Maritain became friendly with Monsignor Montini, the future Paul VI, who was then working under Pius XII. Years before, Montini had translated into Italian an early work of Maritain, *Three Reformers: Luther, Descartes, Rousseau* (1925). A product of this stay in Rome was the short but important work in metaphysics, *Existence and the Existent* (1947). It described the existentialism of St. Thomas and tried to deepen and clarify certain basic Thomistic doctrines and relate them to current philosophies.

He resigned his ambassadorship in 1947 and accepted a professorship at Princeton University. He was to remain in the United States, living at Princeton, until 1960. This period produced some of his most outstanding works. His most important, or second most important, contribution to political philosophy was the Walgreen Foundation Lectures, given at the University of Chicago, *Man And The State* (1951). Here we have a justification of the democratic form of government; refinements on the rights of human beings and Church and state relationships; and the problem of a world political society. Then there were the Mellon Lectures in the Fine Arts, given at the National Gallery of Art, in Washington, *Creative Intuition In Art And Poetry* (1953). Other lectures, also given at the University of Chicago, appeared as *Reflections On America* (1958). These were delivered in "ordinary language" and in a nontechnical style, but still contained a philosophical depth. It became one of his most widely read books. There was also a large work, for those already familiar with ethical thought, called *Moral Philosophy: An Historical and Critical Survey of the Great Systems* (1960).

Life at Princeton was ended by the death of his wife, Raïssa, in 1960. Vera had died the year before. He was now in his late seventies. Wondering what to do, he was offered living quarters in Toulouse, with the Fraternity of the Little Brothers of Jesus. They are a society of contemplatives, living in the world of the poor, and receiving their inspiration from Charles de Foucauld (d. 1916). Maritain always saw himself as a philosopher and was concerned that because he had to consider some theological themes due to special circumstances, his true significance, if any, would be missed. Still, his last works are theological in many ways—all of them introducing efforts to deepen customary teaching, rather than conflict with it. *God And The Permission of Evil* (1963) was the one work he was personally least displeased with. In 1966, in the wake of the Second Vatican Council, he wrote kind of a testimony of his faith and philosophical outlook, *The Peasant Of The Garonne: An Old Layman Questions Himself About the Present Time.* It had some fiery passages and some general disapproval of certain rejections of what were for centuries regarded as the teachings of the faith and philosophical certitudes. There was much more in this book, as if it were a compendium of his favorite themes. Despite this, and because of his rejection of the current euphoria for change, it was harshly criticized and misunderstood by many who had previously supported him and thought they had understood him. But then he expected this.

On The Grace And Humanity of Jesus (1967) tries to throw light on the grace of Christ and the psychology of the soul of Christ, bringing in the notion of a "supraconsciousness." Lastly, there was *On The Church Of Christ: The Person Of The Church And Her Personnel* (1970). Before his death he did become a member of The Little Brothers of Jesus.

As is usually the case with seminal thinkers, there are always some who regard you as suspect, and would like your work to be censured. Even Gilson, with his historical studies, was not immediately received at his true worth. More so with Maritain, who dealt with more pressing issues. He was often treated with hostility as treading in dangerous waters, but had enough supporters to protect him. A great deal is known about the private lives of him and his wife. Gilson suggested to Raïssa that she write a volume of her memoirs. This she did, in *We Have Been Friends Together* (1942), and it was so popular it was followed by *Adventures In Grace* (1945). After her death a spiritual diary was found, and this was also published as *Raïssa's Journal* (1974). See also, *Our Friend, Jacques Maritain,* by Julie Kernan. He was gifted with an attractive and calming physical presence which greatly contributed to his influence. His devotion to his wife is well-known, so much so that on their gravestone, at his wish, there is in the middle, in large letters, "Raïssa Maritain" and down in the right corner, in smaller letters, is found "and Jacques." His collected writings are now in the course of publication, in France. They are expected to comprise some fifteen volumes of over one thousand pages each.

THOMAS GALLAGHER

See also CATHOLICISM; GILSON, ETIENNE; PHILOSOPHY AND THEOLOGY; THOMISM.

MARKS (OR NOTES) OF THE CHURCH

This term has come to refer to four constitutive characteristics that define what is really the Church of Christ. These characteristics are: unity, holiness, catholicity, and apostolicity. The earliest example of this list of qualities occurs in the Nicene Creed as completed at the Council of Constantinople in 381.

The meaning of the mark of unity is that to be fully itself the Church must maintain harmony and union among its members. Overcoming of prejudices and factions belongs to the essential task of the Church. It is supposed to be "a seed of unity" for the whole human community (LG 9) and cannot really fulfill this if not united within itself.

The second characteristic, holiness, is self-evident as a necessary condition for the task of reconciling the human community to God. Holiness applies to the members of the Church as well as to its official activities. Derived from the person and actions of Jesus, holiness can nevertheless not be taken for granted but must really characterize the persons and activities if the Church is to fulfill its purpose.

Universality (catholicity) as a mark of the Church means non-elitism, or being open to all. It does not necessarily mean that all human beings must belong, or that Christians must earnestly entice others away from their traditional religions or personal convictions. It means rather that the Church must make everyone welcome, excluding no categories (racial, linguistic, cultural, economic, etc.). Whether this leaves Church membership still a "small flock" among the world's large populations is not important as long as the Church is doing and being what it is called to do and be (LG 9).

Apostolicity refers to continuity with the mission and ministry of the apostles. In the early centuries, this continuity was sought primarily in the teaching and the carrying on of the authentic life and worship. After the sixteenth century reformations, Catholic use of the term apostolicity focuses on the validity of holy orders and the succession of bishops by accepted standards of consecration.

It is clear that the marks of the Church are proposed in the first place as ideals to be striven for. However, since the fifteenth century, they have been used in a polemical way, to insist that it is only by union with, and acceptance of, the pope as head of the universal Church that all four marks can be realized. That means that the discussion of the marks of the Church was used, until Vatican Council II, mainly to claim that other Christians were not in the true Church. Since that council there has been a return to an eschatological appeal (pointing out what the goal is) in the citing of the four marks.

MONIKA K. HELLWIG

See also CHURCH, THE; HOLINESS.

MARMION, JOSEPH COLUMBA, O.S.B. (1858–1923)

Joseph Columba Marmion, born in Dublin on 1 April 1858, was one of nine children of an Irish father and a French mother. He was educated at Belvedere College and Holy Cross Seminary, Clonliffe, both in Dublin. For his theological studies he was sent to the Irish College in Rome and enrolled in the College of Propaganda. Ordained on 16 June 1881, he returned to Ireland and was assigned to the parish of Dundrum, a Dublin suburb. Within a short time he became a philosophy professor at Clonliffe. On 21 November 1886 and with the permission of his bishop, he entered the Benedictine Abbey at Maredsous in Belgium, since there were no Benedictine monasteries in Ireland at the time. As a novice he was given the name Columba in honor of one of the greatest Irish monks.

In 1899 a small group from Maredsous established a priory on Mont César in Louvain. The first superior and later abbot was Dom Robert de Kerchove who chose Dom Columba as his prior. Abbot Robert was tall, thin, and serious with the lean features of an ascetic; Prior Columba was plump, cheerful, and lively. University students spoke of them as "Shrove Tuesday and Ash Wednesday." Both were deeply spiritual men. The abbot, however, wished his monks to limit their activity to the confines of the enclosure, whereas the prior was incessantly driven, both by his apostolic zeal and his desire to respond to human needs beyond the abbey. Prior Columba was appointed spiritual director and theology professor for the young monks who came to Mont César to prepare for ordination. During his years there he acquired a widespread reputation as a distinguished preacher, retreat master, and spiritual director.

Joseph Columba Marmion, O.S.B.

In 1901 Dom Columba was postulated as abbot of Maredsous to succeed Dom Hildrebrande de Hemptinne who had been named abbot primate by Pope Leo XIII. Under obedience to his own abbot at Mont César, he agreed on 29 September to be the abbot of Maredsous. During the First World War Abbot Columba left Belgium, which was overrun by the German army, and went to England and later to Ireland in an effort to establish a house of refuge for his dispersed monks. Distressed by his absence from his own monastery, he returned to Maredsous in May 1916. He aged prematurely as abbot, especially during the war years. In many ways he was not an effective administrator, but he was a great master of the spiritual life. After a brief illness he died on 30 January 1923.

The substance of Dom Marmion's spiritual doctrine, especially that contained in his retreat conferences, theological lectures, and sermons, has been collected mainly from the notes of those who heard him preach and teach. For readers today his style appears dense and theoretical, dull and perhaps even boring. Those who heard him, however, readily gave him attention because his voice was familiar and straightforward, and his lectures contained many examples and stories from real life. Apart from his letters, these have generally been omitted from his published works.

Dom Marmion's publications reveal a doctrine that is profoundly biblical and liturgical, one that is rooted in the mystery of Christ, above all as it is set out in the Pauline epistles. Christians belong to Christ as members of his body; hence they are adopted children of God. They are grafted into the very life of the Blessed Trinity. All of God's dealings with humanity are a consequence of the divine goodness and mercy. Holiness is not a human achievement; it is the Father's work in us through the Son and in the power of the Holy Spirit present in human hearts and operating in human lives. Sanctification, however, requires human consent and free cooperation. It consists in being by grace what Jesus Christ is by nature, a child of God. This is the basic message of *Christ, the Life of the Soul.*

Christ in His Mysteries, which follows the outline of the liturgical year, consists of reflections on the major feasts celebrating the historical life of Jesus, the mystery of redemption and the gift of Christ's Holy Spirit sanctifying all who respond to Christ in faith. It was this work which led Dom Lambert Beaudouin to describe Dom Marmion as a "theologian of liturgical spirituality."

Christ, the Ideal of the Monk is focused on the virtues of Christ proposed for the imitation not only of Benedictine monks but every religious and indeed every Christian. It is a manual of spiritual life. *Christ, the Ideal of the Priest* sets out the life and teaching of Christ as a special model for ordained ministers who continue the Lord's work of pastoral care, leading people to God through Christ. *Sponsa Verbi* is addressed to nuns as brides of Christ.

Approximately seventeen hundred of Dom Marmion's letters are extant, most of them unpublished. Some have been issued in part or whole in a short treatise on *Union with God.* He shied away from the term "spiritual director." Writing to an English nun, he said, "I am the mortal enemy of what is called direction. The Holy Ghost alone can form souls." Dom Marmion's message is concerned with the most essential teachings of Christianity. It is simple and unsentimental; hence it has lasting value.

R. KEVIN SEASOLTZ, O.S.B.

See also CHRISTIAN SPIRITUALITY; LITURGICAL MOVEMENT, THE; LITURGICAL YEAR, THE; LITURGY.

MARONITES

See EASTERN CATHOLIC CHURCHES.

MARRIAGE

See SACRAMENT OF MATRIMONY.

MARRIAGE ENCOUNTER

Marriage Encounter is a worldwide movement which aims at the spiritual renewal of married couples and through them of families, parishes, and society. It was founded by a Spanish priest, Gabriel Calvo, in the early 1960s and came to the United States a few years later. The popularity of the movement arises from the success of a weekend of exercises directed by a team composed of a married couple and a priest who have "made the weekend" themselves and who wish to share the experience with others. The presentations made by the team members do not take the form of lectures or exhortations but are an open sharing of their experience as people seeking, often struggling, to grow in intimacy with each other and with God. This style of presentation is intended to encourage each of the participating couples to reflect honestly and without fear on their present lives, first individually and then through dialogue on the life they share as a couple. The movement from I to We, from personal prayer to prayer as a couple, is further expanded as the couple is directed to consider their marriage in the context of God's plan through prayerful reflection on a series of texts drawn from the Bible. The weekend experience is designed to initiate a continued dialogue between the spouses and to continue to promote their spiritual growth through regular meetings with other couples.

WILLIAM C. McFADDEN, S.J.

See also RETREAT; SACRAMENT OF MATRIMONY.

MARRIAGE TRIBUNAL

The tribunal (or court) is the agency of the diocesan curia which exists to prosecute or vindicate the rights of persons, to declare juridic facts, or to impose/declare Church penalties. In practice the great bulk of tribunal work involves broken marriages, i.e., declaring the juridic fact of whether or not a broken marriage was ever, in fact, a true or valid marriage. Hence, we commonly speak of tribunals as "marriage tribunals" (although tribunals by law are able to perform a variety of judicial services).

When people celebrate a marriage, the Christian and civil community presume the juridic fact that the union is valid. The procedures of the tribunal aim at discovering whether or not this presumption is to be upheld. The merely civil effects of a marriage are decided by a civil court.

Officers

The judge of each tribunal is the diocesan bishop. He must appoint a judicial vicar who shares the bishop's ordinary power to judge. The diocesan bishop may appoint assistants for the judicial vicar, known as adjutant judicial vicars. All these must be priests. In addition, he may appoint others known simply as diocesan judges who may be clerics or laypersons.

The bishop also appoints one or more defenders of the bond who are to propose and clarify whatever can be reasonably adduced against the nullity of a marriage. He also appoints one or more promoters of justice who may intervene in marriage cases when the public good is involved. These two officials may be clergy or laypersons.

All the officers mentioned above must have at least a licentiate degree in canon law.

Every marriage case is to be judged by a collegiate tribunal of three judges, one of whom may be a layperson. The episcopal conference, however, may permit the bishop to entrust marriage cases to a single clerical judge if a collegiate tribunal cannot be established. The defender of the bond must always intervene. The promoter of justice would intervene to challenge the validity of a marriage only in cases of marriages whose nullity has become public. In practice such an intervention is most rare.

Parties

The spouses themselves (or the promoter of justice) are able to challenge the presumed validity of a marriage. The party approaching the tribunal is the petitioner, and the other party is the respondent. Normally, the presumed validity can be challenged only while both parties are alive. Each party may appoint one or more advocates who are trained in canon law and approved for this service by the bishop. Each may also appoint one procurator who substitutes for the party through the tribunal process.

Competent Tribunal to Judge

Unless the marriage is reserved for judgment to the Apostolic See (as when, for example, one party holds the highest civil office in a state), the tribunals competent to judge a marriage are: (1) the tribunal of the place where the marriage was celebrated; (2) the tribunal of the place where the respondent lives; (3) the tribunal of the place where the petitioner lives, if both parties live in the same episcopal conference and if the judicial vicar of the respondent consents after hearing the respondent; (4) the tribunal of the place where de facto most of the proofs will be collected, if the judicial vicar of the respondent consents after asking if the respondent has any objections.

Procedure

A marriage trial begins when the petitioner presents a petition (called a libellus) to the tribunal, which requests the services of the tribunal to judge the validity of the marriage. After the judge accepts the libellus, he cites the respondent. The respondent has the right to be informed of the libellus and to take full part in the tribunal's proceedings. If the respondent refuses to reply or to take part in the trial, the procedure may proceed nonetheless.

After the respondent has been contacted, the judge determines firmly the grounds on the basis of which the tribunal will study the marriage. Possible grounds include, on the part of one or both parties: an intention against children or permanence or fidelity, forced consent, lack of sufficient use of reason, serious lack of discretion concerning the essential matrimonial rights and duties, incapacity to assume these essential obligations due to psychic causes, etc.

Next the judge gathers proofs aimed at overturning the presumed validity of the marriage. Proofs commonly may include: the declarations of the parties, documents, witnesses, and experts' evaluations. If full proofs are not present from other sources, the judge may evaluate the declarations of the parties by using witnesses who attest to the parties' credibility (commonly called "character witnesses").

In cases of impotence or defect of consent due to mental illness, the judge is to employ one or more experts, unless it is obvious from the circumstances that this would be useless.

The defender of the bond, the advocates, and the promoter of justice (if taking part in the trial) have the right to be present during the examination of the parties, the witnesses and the experts; further, they as well as the parties themselves have the right to inspect the judicial acts even if they are not yet published for review.

When the proofs have been collected, the judge must permit the parties and their advocates to review the acts of the case. The judge may decree, however, in order to avoid very serious dangers, that a given act is not to be shared with anyone, provided the right of defense remains intact. If the parties wish to add nothing further, the judge decrees that the case is concluded. He then asks the petitioner, the respondent and the defender of the bond to offer written observations. These may be shared among the parties and the defender, and rejoinders may be offered.

The judge(s) then makes the decision, based on the acts of the case and the proofs presented. The decision is given in a written sentence. If a single judge makes the decision, he writes the sentence. If a collegiate tribunal makes the decision, one of judges (called the ponens) writes the sentence. The judges must achieve moral certitude that the presumed validity of the marriage is to be overturned. Otherwise the decision must be in favor of the presumption. The publication or announcement of the sentence can be made either by giving a copy of the sentence to the parties or their procurators, or by sending a copy to them. The sentence concludes the process in the first instance tribunal.

Appeal

Both the parties and the defender of the bond have the right to appeal to the second instance (appeal) court the decision of the first instance tribunal. The appeal suspends the execution of the first decision. The appellate tribunal, which follows the same procedure as the first instance tribunal, may consider the case only on the grounds proposed in the first instance. If new grounds are introduced, the appellate court acts as a first instance tribunal.

If the parties or the defender of the bond do not select to appeal the first instance decision declaring the marriage null, the judge of the first instance must send the sentence ex officio to the appellate court. The appellate court may confirm the first decision without delay by a decree, or may admit the case to an ordinary full examination resulting in another sentence.

If the second tribunal confirms the first sentence, whether by decree or sentence, the parties are able to enter a new marriage. The appellate tribunal may, however, attach to the sentence or decree a prohibition preventing one or both parties from remarrying. Normally, this may be imposed if there is serious doubt that the party is unwilling or unable to enter a new valid marriage.

The declaration of the nullity of the marriage, as well as any prohibitions of future marriages, is to be entered in the parties' baptismal and marriage registers.

JOHN RENKEN

See also ANNULMENT; CANON LAW; SACRAMENT OF MATRIMONY.

MARTYR

See MARTYRDOM.

MARTYRDOM

Martyrdom signifies submission to death as a testimony to one's faith. Literally, "martyr" means *witness* [to the faith] (Rev 17:6). Christianity finds the roots for its concept of martyrdom first, in heros in the Bible like Eleazar and the Maccabees (2 Macc 6:1–7:42), and the deacon Stephen (Acts 6:8–8:1), and second, in philosophers, such as Socrates, who died for their teachings. The value of martyrdom is in its conformity to the death of Jesus (Rev 1:5) whose vicarious suffering benefitted all of humanity.

Martydoms in earliest times often resulted from mob violence, e.g., Stephen (ca. A.D. 33) and James the Apostle (ca. A.D. 62). Christians of the second and third centuries believed that the dead had to wait until the Last Judgment to experience heaven; however, martyrs were an exception because they died like Jesus who already is in heaven. Consequently, the Church had to mitigate enthusiasm for and provocation of martyrdom.

During the third century, Roman officials engaged in organized, legalized persecution. Sometimes they required Christians to hand over the Scriptures to be burned and at others times they ordered them to sacrifice to Roman divinities or be martyred.

With the legalization of Christianity under Constantine (312), martyrdom declined, but whenever religion became politicized, there were martyrs. Some died for their doctrinal stands, e.g., Catholic and Protestant martyrs of the Reformation. Missionaries and their converts were also martyred when the introduction of Christianity followed the flag of a conquering nation, e.g., the North American martyrs in French territories in the 1600s. Sometimes Christians were martyred when Christianity seemed a threat to the religious system of a missionized area, e.g., Japan from 1596 to 1598. Since the 1940s the designation of individuals as "martyrs" has been complicated by the issue of politics. The key question has been: did the "martyrs" die for their faith in a politicized setting or for their politics in a situation with religious overtones? Dietrich Bonhoeffer and Franz Jaegerstatter in Nazi Germany, Martin Luther King, Jr. in the U.S., and Archbishop Oscar Romero in El Salvador are examples.

The cult of martyrs has been a concern of the Church since the the time of Polycarp (ca. 155). Christians venerated their relics as a locus of divine power. Believers desired to be buried near them so that they could rise with the holiest Christians on Judgment Day. Relics are still placed in altars.

Christians have always written accounts of the martyrs' deaths to inspire one another. Critical questions about this sort of hagiography have included the historicity of the accounts versus their conformity to literary conventions, and the extent to which these stories reveal the leadership of women in ancient Christianity such as Blandina in Lyons (177) and Perpetua and Felicity in Carthage (203).

Since Vatican II, there has been a revival of interest in the cult of martyrs and of saints generally. Pastoral agents are once again using hagiographical materials in catechesis and preaching.

MAUREEN A. TILLEY

See also DEATH; SAINTS.

MARTYROLOGY

An official list of Christian martyrs and saints. The first martyrologies—from the fourth century and earlier—were calendars which named the martyr under the date of his or her feast day. Later martyrologies, notably that attributed to Usuard, included short biographies of the martyrs, the writings of Church Fathers, and writings on Church history. The Roman Martyrology, a revised version of Usuard's, is regarded as the official martyrology of the Church; it was issued in 1584 by Pope Gregory XIII.

JOSEPH QUINN

See also MARTYRDOM; SAINTS.

MARY, MOTHER OF GOD

An immense literature has appeared in the present century, from the twenties on, dealing with the Blessed Virgin Mary. There was a decline during the decade immediately after Vatican II, but gradually writers and publishers returned to the theme. The great centers of research and reflection, Marianum in Rome and Dayton, Ohio, had if anything grown in quality. The two scientific reviews of Marian theology, *Marianum,* a work of the Servites and collaborators, and *Ephemerides Mariologicae,* directed by the Spanish Claretians, adopted the methodology and approach supported by the council, as did Marian theologians with established reputations, notably Fr. Gabriele Maria Roschini, O.S.M., and Fr. René Laurentin. The Regensburg *Marienlexikon,* a monument of scholarship, internationally based, when completed will be a scholar's charter in this area.

The council was a watershed, setting its seal on a method which had been tested. Marian theology is based on direct analysis and interpretation of the Bible, enlightened by accurate reading of the Fathers. With expansion of the ecumenical movement, a priority of Vatican II, this approach was especially welcome. Marian theological societies, especially the French, and interfaith biblical research groups in the United States, have pooled the intellectual resources of the different Christian communions in fruitful dialogue. Pious accretions of dubious value, groundless suspicions, have been rigorously scrutinized.

The Bible

Certain Old Testament texts are validly interpreted as a foreshadowing of the Virgin Mary, principally Genesis 3:15 and Isaiah 7:14, with some attention also to Micah 5:3. The Fathers of the Church were almost unanimous in applying Isaiah 7:14 to Our Lady. Certain recurring themes have also been studied to elicit from the sacred Jewish writings intimations of the future heroine of humanity. With the present-day enormous interest in the Jewishness of Jesus Christ, the evidence here will be viewed and evaluated most profitably.

In the Semitic mentality, corporate personality was a ready concept and often given a single name. Thence arose the meaningful title "Daughter of Zion," eventually applicable to Mary of Nazareth. The council adopts the idea, though biblical scholars differ as to how it may be justified. Significant too is the superior role of the king's mother in the Davidic kingdom (cf. 1 Kings 1:16, 19). When the true spiritual messianic kingdom was instituted we find that Mary's name was changed, something which never happened in Sacred Scripture without a serious reason affecting personal vocation. She is now the "Mother of Jesus" (Acts 1:14, but especially John 2:1; 19:25, 26), the first person in the new community, retaining her maternal character towards its members. She thus realized what was forecast in the Davidic kingdom, forecast typologically.

The New Testament passages relating to Mary have been the object of intense examination in recent times. They are chiefly contained in the infancy narratives, the first two chapters of Matthew and Luke, the latter especially; the Johannine accounts of the miracle of Cana and of Jesus' words from the cross (John 19:25-27); episodes and statements by Jesus reported from his public ministry by Matthew, Mark and Luke—they relate to brief appearances of the Mother during this phase of the Son's life; the narrative of events immediately preceding Pentecost; and the mysterious portrait in Revelation 12 of the woman clothed with the sun and her assailant, with the cosmic duel in which he was vanquished by the Archangel Michael. The apocryphal gospels are treated separately.

The New Testament testimony to Mary is quantitatively slight, but replete with theological insights.

The virgin birth has always been read in the infancy narratives of Matthew (1:18) and Luke (1:27, 34, 35). The Annunciation is the starting point in Christian salvation history, the beginning of the Christ event. Jesus' messianic mission opens to discernment, awaiting later fulfillment obviously, in the context of Mary's personal decision, manifest in the Temple mysteries.

The reflection of the ages has gradually perceived the validity of a Marian interpretation of Revelation 12 as, increasingly in our time, her presence at Pentecost stimulates thought about her special relationship with the Holy Spirit.

The New Eve

The Fathers of the Church initiated the reflection which, through the ages, would create a fully convincing theology of Mary; at critical moments the teaching authority intervened. Already in the second century three writers representing a wide geographical area of belief had the intuition of Mary as the New Eve: Justin Martyr, Irenaeus, and Tertullian. They did not derive the "rudimental idea" as Newman called it from the Pauline teaching on Christ as the new Adam, which might seem to suggest that there was a partner on the model of the first parents. The concept was reached from a comparison of the Lucan Annunciation narrative with the story of Eve's sin in Genesis: the tempter, the woman's failure, the sequel all redeemed by Mary's faith and obedience in the word of the angel. The parallel and antithesis which permeates patristic works was expressed in a way never surpassed by Irenaeus, who drew the conclusion that Mary by her faith and obedience was a "cause of salvation to herself and the whole human race." St. Jerome used the pithy phrase, "death through Eve, life through Mary."

The richness of the intuition has ensured its appeal to theologians through the ages, to St. Bernard and to Newman. It was taken up by Vatican II. From the Genesis story and language two other elements would be integrated with it: "Mother of the living" (Gen 3:20) was transferred from Eve to Mary, who later would be styled "a helper like himself" (Gen 2:18).

Virgin Mother

The Fathers, being unanimously convinced of the Marian sense in Isaiah 7:14 which had been quoted by Matthew (1:23) in his account of the conception and birth of Jesus (according to the Septuagint version), solidly established the doctrine of Mary's virginity. A threefold sense was seen in this attribute: virginity before the conception of Jesus, in the moment of his birth, and ever afterwards (*virginitas ante partum, in partu, post partum*). The title "ever-virgin" (*aei-parthenos*) was from early times current in the East, where most of the constructive doctrinal thinking about Mary took place. Pride of place goes to Alexandria, then the intellectual capital of the Roman Empire, home of great doctors, Origen, Athanasius, Cyril. Virginity in the moment of Christ's birth meant miraculous preservation of the Mother's bodily integrity.

Mother of God

Profound reflection was active from earliest times on Jesus Christ. The word Logos used about him by St. John challenged Greek-speaking intellectuals. How to see his claims to Godhead, his manifest humanity in the perspective of the Holy Trinity—how to understand the Holy Trinity? Much debate and widespread heresy ended with the Council of Nicaea (A.D. 325) which declared that Christ was the eternal Son of the Father, "consubstantial" with him. The hero of the day was St. Athanasius (d. 373).

Thereon a further question arose: What was the plenary relationship of Mary to Christ who is God? A new center of thought was now rivaling Alexandria, Constantinople. From there came the answer that Mary was Mother of Christ (*Christotokos*, Christ-bearer). She could not be called *Theotokos* (God-bearer), a term already used in Alexandria, at least from the fourth, probably the third century; it was of Egyptian origin. Again argument and controversy were ended by a council. Held at Ephesus (A.D. 431), it was dominated by St. Cyril of Alexandria (d. 444) and fully vindicated the title *Theotokos*, now destined to a fixed place in the thought-process, liturgy, hymnography, and even popular prayer of the East. It is in the papyrus preserved in the John Rylands Library, Manchester, the earliest form of the prayer still addressed to Mary, "We fly to thy patronage," dated fourth, probably third century. Mary is the Mother of God because motherhood is related to the person and in Christ the person is divine. A further Council at Chalcedon (A.D. 451) fully expounded the relationship of human and divine in Jesus Christ, one person, two natures; the mental categories of the time were adopted. This time Pope Leo the Great (d. 461) had the central role.

Mother of Humanity

All Mary's privileges, all her significance in the whole plan of salvation, all the glory she gives to God, spring as from a mysterious, satisfying source from her divine motherhood. Two of her privileges, the Immaculate Conception and the Assumption are considered separately. Her spiritual motherhood of humanity, basic to Catholic and Orthodox belief in practice, questioned with varying emphases by Protestants, grew as a belief or conviction through converging factors. The deep sentiment of the faithful, which Newman, with a scholarly memory of its triumph in the Arian heresy, valued so highly, pointed this way from early times. They invoked Our Lady. This invocation was also expressed in the liturgy, where the East led the way; the feasts of Mary were the occasion of prayer to her. Homiletics increasingly stressed Mary's power with God; hymnography first in the East and later in the West played its part; witness the most perfect hymn to Mary *Theotokos,* the *Akathistos.* The four great Latin hymns were later, *Salve Regina, Alma Redemptoris Mater, Regina Coeli, Ave regina coelorum.*

Then came the Latin Middle Ages, a great age in Marian doctrine and piety, rivaling the early flowering in the East of the fourth and fifth centuries. The hymns give the tone. Great contemplative teachers like St. Anselm of Canterbury (d. 1099), mighty charismatic teachers and preachers like St. Bernard (d. 1153), supported by a host of others made the twelfth and thirteenth centuries a glowing world of Marian piety, where art in statuary, painting, stained glass, and architecture made Western Europe a vibrant community animated by a sense of Mary. The great thirteenth-century doctors, Thomas Aquinas (despite his faltering on the Immaculate Conception), Bonaventure, and above all Duns Scotus supplied the intellectual framework.

Mediation

The search for a coherent theory underlying belief in Mary's spiritual motherhood sends us back to the biblical data. The words from the cross, "Behold your Mother" (John 19:27) would be with time supported by appeal to Revelation 12:17, "Then the dragon was angry with the woman, and went off to make war on *the rest of her offspring,* on those who keep the commandments of God and bear testimony to Jesus." The spiritual motherhood is theologically rooted in the divine motherhood; Mary's fiat to the incarnation involved her role in regard to all who would be one with Jesus, the fruit of her womb.

Did this fiat and all that she did and endured as its consequence constitute her a Mediatress along with her divine Son? The title has been applied to Mary in the East since the fifth century, in the West from the ninth. It is sometimes thought that its greatest exponent is St. Louis Marie Grignion de Montfort (d. 1716) along with St. Alphonsus Liguori (d. 1787). Not so. The most complete synthesis on the subject came from the Orthodox writer Theophanes of Nicaea (d. 1381) who brought to a climax the thinking on these lines of the whole Palamite school. This should nullify the occasional sentiment that talk about Mary's universal mediation is due to Latin, possibly Celtic enthusiasm. It was strongly advocated by the great apostle of the Holy Name of Jesus, St. Bernardine of Siena (d. 1444).

In the present century the important name is Desiré Joseph Cardinal Mercier (d. 1926). He was influenced by De Montfort's book on *True Devotion to the Blessed Virgin Mary* and he launched a crusade to have her universal mediation recognized in the liturgy and in the official teaching of the Church. Benedict XV granted the Mass and Office; Pius XI set up three commissions to examine the definability of the dogma, Roman, Spanish and Belgian. Theologians of exceptional caliber worked in these bodies.

No papal act took place, though Pius XII used the word Mediatress in his vast Marian corpus eight times. In the forties and fifties a gigantic literature appeared on one specific aspect of Mary's mediation, her role in the redemption. She was commonly given the title Co-redemptress, to which rigorists objected, contending that it made her the equal of Christ, as opponents to her universal mediation constantly invoked the Pauline text on "One Mediator" (1 Tim 2:5). The response to the first objection is that St. Paul speaks of Christians as "co-workers with Christ"; as to the second it is true that those united with Christ in his Mystical Body participate in his mediatorial functions of prophet, priest, and king. Mary does so preeminently.

The question was raised at Vatican II. A first-draft text was explicit on Mary's universal mediation. This had been put back for redrafting after the vote in the assembly decided to treat of Marian theology in a chapter of the Constitution on the Church. It is an irony of history that Mercier, protagonist of Mary's universal mediation, had, in the Malines Conversation, shown himself the first Catholic ecumenist since the Reformation, wherein the council was in his spirit, but it was to ignore his formidable campaign on behalf of Mary's universal mediation.

The ecumenical outlook of Vatican II was narrow because sufficient attention was not given to the Orthodox who have beautiful Marian liturgies, striking iconography, and through the ages great theologians of Mary. A fully committed member of Faith and Order, one of the parent bodies of the World Council of Churches, Sergey Bulgakov (d. 1944), was of this company. Author of important works on Our Lady, he refused any kind of doctrinal compromise about her dignity and power.

The debate on Mary's mediation within the council left the essential question open. Agreement could only be reached on a statement that the "Blessed

Virgin is invoked in the Church by the titles of Advocate, Helper, Aid-giver, Mediatress." The bare affirmation of fact was strengthened somewhat by the context and by a reference to the experience of the Church which commends it to the hearts of the faithful; mediation was explained on the analogies of divine goodness shared with humanity and participation in Christ's priesthood. But the hard core of opposition to the very word Mediatress was active even to the last day of the conciliar debate in September, 1964: Cardinal Alfrink, speaking for 150 bishops, asked that the word be deleted from the text. Did these people know that an International Mariological Congress in 1950 had sent a Votum to the Holy See asking for a declaration on Mary, "universal Mediatress of God and men"? The question has been reopened by John Paul II in his encyclical *Redemptoris Mater.* There is in the encyclical a lengthy treatment of Mary's maternal mediation. "Mary" the Pope tells us "entered in a way all her own, into the one mediation 'between God and men' which is the mediation of the man Christ Jesus."

Mary and the Church

Two approaches to the theological study of Mary came to prominence before and during the council: Church-type and Christ-type. One emphasizes the profound resemblance between Mary and the Church, the other her similarity with her divine Son. A Father of the Church, St. Ambrose (d. 397), spoke already of Mary as the type of the Church. True, to grasp this intuition fully we have to get away from the institutional image which influences much of our thinking; we have to see the communion, the inner spirit which makes the Church, the phases of its existence, pilgrim on earth, oriented towards eschatological glory. Vatican II teaches that "the Mother of God is a type of the Church in the context of faith, charity and perfect union with Christ"; St. Ambrose is invoked. Again it says: "[The Church] imitating the Mother of her Lord, and by the power of the Holy Spirit, preserves with virginal purity and integral faith, a firm hope and a sincere charity."

Since theology dealing with mystery is manifold in its approach, another aspect of Mary's relationship with the Church kept recurring in the conciliar debates, her maternal role. It too was challenged, but Paul VI, in his final address to the third session, speaking at length of the council's Marian doctrine—one third of his discourse—authoritatively proclaimed Mary Mother of the Church; he was thinking of a substantial minority dissatisfied with the final text: "Therefore, for the glory of the Blessed Virgin and our consolation, we declare most holy Mary Mother of the Church, that is of the whole Christian people, both faithful and pastors, who call her a most loving Mother, and we decree that henceforth the whole Christian people should, by this most sweet name, give still greater honor to the Mother of God and address prayers to her." The office is ultimately rooted in the divine motherhood.

Mary and the Holy Spirit

This theme has become increasingly prominent in recent decades. A reproach to the Fathers of Vatican II, formulated bluntly by a Greek Orthodox theologian, Nikos Nissiotis, said in effect that the impact of their documents in his world would be negligible if they did not speak more fully and cogently of the Holy Spirit. Neglect of the Spirit has been a defect in the Latin Church. Efforts were made during the last session and then by Paul VI, but above all by John Paul II to meet the demand. Marian theologians found it congenial to do so in the context of Mary's destiny and role in salvation history. Initial hesitation between the charismatic movement and the Marian trends were overcome in 1975 when two congresses were held in Rome at Pentecost, the International Mariological and Marian Convention and the World Assembly of the Catholic Charismatic Renewal. Paul VI had agreed to have, as the theme of the Marian congress, Mary and the Spirit.

Many problems arise. By what title is the relationship between the Paraclete and the Mother of divine grace best expressed? Saints, notably St. Louis Marie Grignion de Montfort and St. Maximilian Kolbe, and Popes Leo XIII, Pius XII, and John Paul II, used the term "Spouse." Early Fathers of the Church and seventeenth-century writers spoke of Mary as Spouse of the Father; M. J. Scheeben spoke of her as Spouse of her divine Son. In every case we must retain the idea of divine transcendence. Sergey Bulgakov thought that Mary after her fiat had the Spirit within her in the full force of the Annunciation, "her human personality seems to become transparent to him and to provide him with a human countenance. . . ." Others have spoken of Mary as the personification of the Spirit, a term to be carefully nuanced. St. Luke makes a point subtly; he does not deem it necessary, after the Annunciation, to introduce any action or word of Mary by a reference to the Spirit, as he does with Zechariah, Elizabeth, and Simeon. He assumes that the Spirit dwelt in her inseparably.

Much will be clarified with attention to the three capital moments, the sanctification of Mary in the instant of her conception by the Spirit, the descent in the incarnation, and the presence at Pentecost, birthday of the Church.

The Spirit is also the source, in the perpetual mission from the Father and the Son, of the vast and varied manifestations of the divine given to the contemporary Church in the person of Mary: apparitions, locutions, diverse phenomena within but not of the natural order, apparent solar changes, change in the color of religious objects and similar things. Mary does not leave heaven or the Holy Trinity, her close relationship with the Spirit of her divine Son does not cease; rather, it is effective on our behalf. The images of geography or of mathematics are not helpful in dealing with Marian piety. Mary, like her divine Son, is not bound by time and space, nor when we give to her do we take from him.

For some time within the Catholic Church interest and some controversy has and still centers on papal response to a private revelation, but Fatima is one with far-reaching effects. There Our Lady foretold a request that she would one day ask for the consecration of Russia to her Immaculate Heart, to secure the world from war and many evils. Has it been done? Partial responses were made, but John Paul II on 25 March 1984 achieved completion.

Yet another stirring of piety within the faithful, already closely scrutinized and supported by theologians is the devotion to the two Hearts, that is of Jesus and Mary. A symposium in Fatima in 1986 examined the different aspects of the ideal, with thorough research supporting their conclusions and experts on hand to match each demand. John Paul II encouraged the work by a formal letter and an address when the findings were submitted to him. To the theology of the Hearts the Pope has added a dimension from his own training in phenomenology. To integrate it fully into theology will demand a loosening of the Graeco-Roman categories which have ruled thinking, often to advantage. Have we an example of progress in doctrine through the "contemplation and study of believers who ponder these things in their hearts (cf. Luke 2:19, 51)" . . . of "the intimate sense of spiritual realities which they experience," as Vatican II taught (DV 8)? The Mother of God continues to arouse the deepest response from the human mind and heart.

MICHAEL O'CARROLL, C.S.Sp.

See also AKATHISTOS HYMN; CHURCH, THE; DEVOTIONS; JESUS CHRIST; THEOTOKOS.

MARYKNOLL

Maryknoll is the popular name of two related communities dedicated to universal mission. Authorized by the U.S. hierarchy, Maryknoll was founded in 1911 with the approbation of the Holy See. Canon law required separation into two legally and finan-

Maryknoll, New York

cially independent entities of Society and Congregation. The Catholic Foreign Mission Society of America (Maryknoll Society) is an Institute of Apostolic Life composed of non-religious priests and lay brothers. The Maryknoll Sisters of St. Dominic is the official title of the congregation of women religious. Both groups have Associates: (priests, brothers and laity, and sisters, respectively) formally contracted for short-term missionary service abroad. Headquarters and training centers for both are at Maryknoll, (Ossining) New York.

The Maryknoll charism stresses sensitivity to contemplation-in-action; sacrifice in witness to the kingdom; and openness to insights of other cultures and peoples in understanding the gospel message. Missioners developed the charism with a spirit of adaptability to meet diverse needs for pastoral, medical, educational, and social programs at both community and institutional levels. The Society's main purpose is pastoral work in overseas areas, subject to the Congregation for the Propagation of the Faith. The Maryknoll Sisters, recently placed under jurisdiction of the Congregation for Religious, give priority to ministry abroad, while also engaging in missionary work within the U.S. Church. A cloistered community of sisters was formed in 1933.

Maryknoll's first mission was undertaken in China in 1918. Missions were later established throughout Asia, among Asian migrants and Afro-American peoples in both Hawaii and the U.S.A. In 1942, as response to new understandings of mission, to include strengthening local churches and pastoral formation of indigenous leaders, work was begun in Latin America. In the post-World War II decades, membership grew rapidly, enabling expansion to East Africa (1946); restoration and extension in Asia; and new missionary commitments in other countries. Today, the Congregation and Society work independently and collaboratively in more than thirty countries in Asia, Africa, Latin America, the Middle East, the Pacific Islands, and the United States.

From the beginning, the charism included providing mission education and fostering global awareness. *Maryknoll* (the Society-sponsored monthly magazine) and its Spanish edition *Revista*; and literature, films, school curriculum materials, and parish programs have served to keep the urgency of Mission before the U.S. Church. Since 1970, Orbis Books has made theological thought and experiences of Christian practice from the local churches around the world available in English, and fostered dialogue on missiological concerns. The School of Theology and the Mission Institute at Maryknoll, New York, offer graduate level cross-cultural training programs in Scripture, theology, and mission studies, attracting both U.S. and international faculty and students.

With Vatican Council II emphasis on the vocation of the laity, a program was established in 1975 to recruit and train lay men and women for short-term missionary service. By 1990 lay missioners constituted 10 percent of the Maryknoll family. At the direction of the Holy See, a fully independent Associate organization is currently being developed (1993).

Maryknoll has continued to pioneer new missionary efforts in the Middle East, Southern Africa, and the countries of the Indo-China peninsula; and since the 1980s, has returned to China to offer educational and social services. In all their ministries, Maryknoll missioners try to exercise a "preferential option for the poor" and marginalized peoples. Maryknoll seeks to develop indigenous elements, as well as global dimensions of justice and peacemaking, within Christian spirituality. In an emerging World Church, Maryknoll remains committed to the formation of local leadership (clergy, religious, and lay) to enable self-sustaining communities of faith among all peoples everywhere.

JANET CARROLL, M.M.

MASS OF THE CATECHUMENS

The initial part of the Mass, from the entrance antiphon to the offertory, so named because in the early Church it was the section of the Eucharistic celebration in which catechumens (adults preparing for baptism) could participate, a practice being reestablished in the Rite of Christian Initiation of Adults. It is now known as the Liturgy of the Word, while the second part of the Mass is referred to as the Liturgy of the Eucharist.

JOSEPH QUINN

See also RITE OF CHRISTIAN INITIATION OF ADULTS (RCIA).

MASS OFFERINGS

The practice of Mass offerings (stipends) is so familiar to Catholics that it may come as a surprise to hear that theologians today are raising serious questions about it.

The Traditional System

The emergence of this system in the eighth century was deeply influenced by the understanding and practice of the Mass at the time, and practice tended to give rise to theology. In the eighth century the priest alone, in effect, offered the Mass; the congregation were largely spectators. Also the laity had ceased to bring bread and wine as gifts to be offered during the Mass and gave money instead. These facts led to the practice of the Mass stipend proper. Jungmann describes it as an offering paid in advance to obligate the priest to offer a Mass exclusively for the intention of the donor.

Today we see important difficulties in this system. (1) The idea that a Mass stipend once accepted by a priest excludes him from offering a particular Mass for another similar intention derives from the belief that the fruits of the Mass are in practice limited. Questions surround this exclusivity. (2) The ideas that the priest alone offers the Mass, that the congregation is largely passive, and that the priest has control over some of the Mass's fruits are severely questioned today. (3) Questions are raised also about the practice of the donor not being present at the Mass in which the intention he or she wants prayed for is remembered. (4) The medieval theory of the fruits of the Mass, which explained how a Mass can benefit a particular intention, is today left aside and that is a step forward. But this does not really change the system itself, where the real problems are. (5) The legal view of a Mass stipend as a payment for a service rendered and as involving a legal contract is widely questioned in our day.

Theological Rethinking

It is today's theology of the Eucharist that really gives rise to significant rethinking in regard to Mass stipends. Four main points are made.

(1) The 1983 Code of Canon Law dropped the word "stipend" and uses "offering" instead. This implies that a Mass offering is a gift to the priest, not a payment for a service rendered. Hence, a minimum offering should not be asked or set. Also, it is better to see the obligation a priest incurs when he accepts a Mass offering as one in fidelity rather than in justice. The idea of a legal contract is not helpful here.

(2) Official Church teaching today indicates two main beneficiaries. By giving a Mass offering the

donor benefits by his or her closer participation in a particular Mass. It is recommended, then, that donors be present at the Mass being offered for their intention. The second one to benefit by a Mass offering is the priest-celebrant (or local Church) who gets the offering.

But Church teaching today does not claim that the intention the donor wishes remembered at Mass gets any special graces beyond those available to all the intentions prayed for in the Eucharistic Prayer and the Prayer of the Faithful. The idea that the priest has control of a portion of the fruits of the Mass is also abandoned. Only God gives grace inside or outside the Mass.

(3) It follows from this that there is no theological justification for and no point in maintaining that a Mass should be offered exclusively for one intention. One may offer Mass for many intentions, as the 1991 Vatican document states.

(4) Contemporary Church teaching, unlike medieval theology, states that the Christian assembly with the priest presiding offers the Mass, not the priest alone. Hence, all the petitions mentioned in the Eucharistic Prayer and the Prayer of the Faithful are offered by the assembly. Clearly the same holds for the intentions requested by particular donors of Mass offerings.

Pastoral Implications

The most basic thing is that priests and people be re-educated about the nature and use of Mass offerings.

More specifically, the best way to incorporate the intentions to be prayed for into the Mass is to insert them into the Prayer of the Faithful.

Also, the *Missa pro Populo* (Mass for the People) that parish priests are obliged to offer every Sunday and holy day is in reality redundant. Every Mass in a parish, especially on Sundays and holy days, is offered for all the parishioners and indeed for the whole Church.

The so-called diocesan Mass offering, i.e., the minimum amount to be given as a Mass offering, is here seen to be inappropriate, since free gifts may not be demanded. In one case, however, it will be needed, namely, when a lump sum is given "for Masses" and the number of Masses is not specified (c. 950). Using the new multi-intentional Mass, such a diocesan Mass offering would be needed to specify how much the single offering for the priest-celebrant should be.

The New (1991) System

In 1991 the Vatican approved a new system of multi-intentional Masses or collective Mass intentions, which allows the practice of offering one Mass for many intentions. This practice is seen as an exception to the traditional one and its use is limited by three conditions: (1) the donors must consent to combining their intentions in one Mass; (2) the time and place of this Mass must be made public; and (3) such a Mass may be celebrated only twice a week in any place of worship.

No one is obliged to use either the old or the new system of Mass offerings. But the new system seems to avoid the weaknesses of the older one as described earlier and, thus, to be theologically well grounded. It will, however, yield less money for the priest over a period than the present system, because the priest-celebrant may keep only one offering from any one multi-intentional Mass he celebrates (c. 951, § 1).

WILLIAM COSGRAVE

MATERIALISM

A diverse group of philosophical and practical outlooks which maintain that "matter" is all there is to reality and that there is no spiritual or transcendent realm beyond the sensible universe. "Materialism," in everyday usage, often signifies a hedonistic attitude toward life. Thus a "materialist" would be one whose life is devoid of ethical and spiritual concerns and whose existence is given over to the unnecessary acquisition and consumption of "material" things. Materialism, in this sense, can function almost as the religion of a culture at times.

As a philosophical position, "materialism" means any understanding of the universe that denies the existence of nonmaterial dimensions of reality. Its historical roots are complex, but in the West it is the product especially of ancient Greek atomism, Cartesian dualism and seventeenth-century mechanics. In antiquity Democritus and Lucretius thought all things were made up of indivisible material entities (atoms) which come together in various configurations in the void. And although Rene Descartes (1596–1650) carefully distinguished mind (*res cogitans*) from matter (*res extensa*), subsequent philosophy has often absorbed the former into the latter, giving rise to a materialist "monism of matter." In addition, the mechanics of Newton, beginning in the late seventeenth century and continuing almost to the present century, conceptualized cosmic reality, outside of an occasional reference to the human soul, in terms of mindless, quantifiable "matter."

Numerous modern scientific thinkers have taken this Cartesian-Newtonian matter to be the only and ultimate reality. Because of its appeal to so much scientific thought, Alfred North Whitehead called this modern way of conceiving the universe "scientific materialism." Scientific materialism, which is not a scientific but a metaphysical position, holds that matter as understood by physics (the totality of mass and energy) is the bedrock of all reality. Correspondingly all phenomena, including life and mind, can be exhaustively understood in terms of a mindless and lifeless material base. Scientific materialism has been the ideological backbone of numerous presentations not only of modern science but also of intellectual culture in general. Materialist metaphysics has been extraordinarily influential in shaping the modern political world, especially in the "dialectical" form given to it by Marx and Engels.

Materialism is obviously incompatible with religions such as Christianity. As Whitehead has shown, however, scientific materialism is logically flawed since it originates in the confusion of the measurable with the concrete. Our scientific notions of "matter" are the product of our abstracting from the mysterious complexity, value and beauty of the natural world, most of which slips through the net of our scientific methods. Science, of course has every right to make its mathematical abstractions. Materialism, however, results from mistakenly identifying the scientifically useful mathematical abstractions of science with the concrete world. Thus much of modern intellectual history is the unfortunate and emaciated product of a materialist "fallacy of misplaced concreteness."

Today developments in relativity and quantum physics have dissolved the hard "brickyard" materialism of classical physics and continue to "soften" our understanding of physical reality. It is risky for theology to draw too many conclusions directly from developments in physics, but the implicit challenge by the new physics to an older scientific materialism, upon which so much of the modern intellectual opposition to religion has been based, is not without consequences for theology.

In spite of the anti-materialist developments in physics (a science which was formerly the stronghold of materialism), scientific culture is still deeply influenced by materialist assumptions and methods. In the biological sciences, for example, discovery of the role of amino and nucleic acids (which are made up of chains of atoms) has led biologists of the stature of Francis Crick and James Watson to profess that all of life is in principle *completely* explicable in terms of chemistry and physics. And some neuroscientists now conjecture that even what we call "mind" can be—at least in principle—fully specified by chemical analysis of the constitution of the brain and the central nervous system. Arguing that nature has evolved without any sharp breaks from matter, through life, to mind, materialists claim that all phenomena, even those that we used to think of as nonmaterial, are reducible to, and fully understandable in terms of chemistry and physics.

It is not helpful for theology to counter this position simply by postulating a separate, nonmaterial principle (life, mind or soul) which allegedly exists alongside the chemical and physical aspects of things in a manner unrelated to them. After all, it is no longer possible plausibly to deny that life does indeed have a molecular makeup or that mind has a physiological basis. If the chemistry of the cell breaks down, we know that life ebbs away. And if the chemical integrity of the brain is disturbed, then mind is likewise impaired. Dualistic and vitalistic efforts to salvage the apparent independence of life and mind from being absorbed in matter have been justifiably rejected, in part because they still concede too much to materialism as far as understanding the inanimate world is concerned.

However, to admit that life and mind have a molecular constitution is not to say that they are *reducible* to phenomena that chemistry and physics can ever fully understand all by themselves. Michael Polanyi has clearly shown, for example, that while the reliable chemical processes in the cell or brain are *necessary conditions* for the successful functioning of living and thinking beings, they are not *sufficient conditions.* Life and mind are the result not only of chemical activity, but also of orderings and patternings which are logically extraneous to the chemistry itself. Life and mind are as much a product of *organization* as of brute "matter." A purely materialist explanation cannot account for the organizational coefficient in living matter, such as the specific sequence of nucleotides in a DNA chain. Chemistry may specify how different atoms or molecules bond with one another, but what is most important in living beings is the informational arrangement, or specific *sequence,* of the nucleotides (ATCG) in DNA. If this arrangement were chemically determined then it would be invariant, and then there would be only one kind of DNA molecule, whereas in fact there are millions. There is more to the cell than can be understood by chemistry and physics alone.

It would be a mistake for theology to bring a "god-of-the-gaps" kind of explanation into yet unexplored, mysterious regions of cellular activity. And theology can fully support purely chemical analysis of living and thinking tissue. But we are becoming more aware today that things are made up not only of matter and energy, but of matter plus energy plus *information.* The new science of information, together with developments in the scientific understanding of "chaos" and "complexity," is beginning to render more and more questionable the reductionist materialism of the past. These awakenings in science, of course, do not lead directly to the confirmation of any religious view of reality. But since scientific materialism has been the philosophical foundation of most modern critiques of the idea of God, the new challenges to materialism are not without theological significance.

JOHN HAUGHT

See also CREATION; PHILOSOPHY AND THEOLOGY.

MAUNDY THURSDAY

See HOLY THURSDAY.

MAURIN, PETER (1877–1949)

Peter Maurin was born in Oultet, France on 9 May 1877. His parents, Jean and Marie Maurin, were farmers whose ancestors had cultivated the same piece of land in the Languedoc region for one thousand years. They kept sheep, grew vegetables, and made cheese and bread. The family recited the rosary and read from the Bible daily, and attended Mass in the village.

At fourteen, Peter left home to study at St. Privat, a Christian Brothers school. The brothers selected Peter for further training, in the hope of his entering the order; in 1893 he began his novitiate in Paris. He took his first vows in 1895, teaching in various schools for the next seven years.

In 1902 the secularization of France led to the closing of religious schools. Peter left the Brothers and became involved in Le Sillon, a French Catholic social movement founded by Marc Sangier. Le Sillon wanted to combine Catholicism with the new Democratic republic, through public meetings, cooperatives, and hospices. In 1908 Peter Maurin left the movement because it had become less spiritual, more political.

Peter served three times in the military reserves, but by 1908 he had decided that he could no longer in conscience do so. Partly to avoid conscription, partly to start a new life away from Le Sillon and France, Peter emigrated to Canada in 1909.

He worked a homestead in Saskatchewan until his partner died the next summer; he then traveled around, harvesting wheat, digging ditches, and quarrying stone. In 1911, he moved to the United States, still wandering from place to place as a laborer. In 1925 he taught French in New York State, deciding at the age of forty-eight that work was a gift, to be given without price. His students supported him in various ways.

Peter Maurin

During this time Peter was developing his ideas on how to apply Catholic social teaching to contemporary life. He approached the Third Order of St. Francis as a group to support his ideas, but they declined, so he struck out on his own. He would travel down to New York City from Mt. Tremper, where he worked as a caretaker at a Catholic boys' camp, and preach to political radicals and the unemployed in Union Square, staying at flophouses on the Bowery.

Peter wanted to start a newspaper, and meeting journalist, Catholic convert, and fellow radical Dorothy Day made this a possibility. As Dorothy wrote, "We were to popularize this program for immediate needs, which in itself would be the seed for a long range program, a green revolution, by publishing a paper for the person on the street."

The first issue of *The Catholic Worker* was published on 1 May 1933, and distributed on the street in Union Square. Peter wanted to give people a vision "of a society where it is easier for people to be good." He believed that involuntary destitution could be countered with voluntary poverty, like that of St. Francis. Problems of society could be relieved by the practice of the works of mercy out of a sense of personal responsibility. In his essay "Back to Christ, back to the land," Peter outlined his critique of industrialization, and his solution—the "return to a society where agriculture is practiced by most of the people."

Unemployed workers came to help, sleeping on the floor of the apartment where they published the paper, and eating from a communal pot. The first House of Hospitality was on Charles Street; later, it moved to Mott Street. By 1936 the circulation had risen to 150,000.

Houses opened around the country during the Depression. However, the Spanish Civil War and the U.S. entry into World War II were to be some of the Catholic Worker's hardest trials. Dorothy insisted that "there must be a disarmament of the heart," and that the Catholic Worker is a pacifist movement. Houses closed and the circulation of the paper fell by half.

In the spirit of the green revolution, a farm was started—first on Staten Island and later near Easton, Pennsylvania. Peter hoped to teach by example as well as word, and divided his time between manual work, discussion, and prayer. He also spent time traveling, speaking around the country to scholars, Catholic Workers, and in churches.

By 1947, Peter was too ill to travel much or work the land. He told Dorothy he could no longer think, and spent his last years in near-silence, still embracing voluntary poverty. On 15 May 1949 Peter Maurin died, and his body was brought from the retreat house in Newburgh to the house on Mott Street. The funeral was held at Transfiguration Church, and Peter was buried in St. John's Cemetery, Queens, wearing a donated suit, in a donated grave.

JENNIFER BELISLE

See also CATHOLIC WORKER MOVEMENT; DAY, DOROTHY; SOCIALISM.

MAY DEVOTIONS

Special prayers and devotions seeking the intercession of the Blessed Mother during the month of May. The tradition of honoring Our Lady and invoking her mercy during May extends back to the sixteenth century. It was sanctioned and indulgenced by Pope Pius VII, and subsequent pontiffs—such as Leo XIII and Pius XII—issued prominent documents on the veneration of Mary which supported May devotions in the universal Church. The feast of the Visitation is celebrated on 31 May. The month is named after "Maia," a Roman goddess, and there is no historical relationship between it and the Blessed Mother.

JOSEPH QUINN

See also DEVOTIONS; MARY, MOTHER OF GOD.

MEDALS, RELIGIOUS

Flat, coin-shaped disks bearing the image of Christ, the Blessed Mother, a saint, a shrine, or a sacred mystery. They are made of metal, wood, or plastic, and are usually worn around the neck. Medals are customarily blessed by the Church, and are intended to increase the piety and devotion of the wearer or carrier. The discovery of many medals in the catacombs attest to their ancient usage in the Church.

JOSEPH QUINN

See also IMAGES, VENERATION OF; SACRAMENTALS.

MEDIATOR

Mediator (Lat. "one who goes between") denotes a person who intervenes between two others in order to effect a reconciliation. In the OT, Moses, Abraham, and others act as mediators between human beings and God in order to end an impasse or rupture in the relationship between them. Jesus Christ is the mediator *par excellence* between fallen humanity and God the Father. His life, death, and resurrection bridged the gap between God and humanity caused by the sin of Adam. This is a central belief of the Christian faith which is attested to by both Sacred Scripture and the lived tradition of the Church.

ANTHONY D. ANDREASSI

MEDIATRIX (MEDIATRESS)

See MARY, MOTHER OF GOD.

MEDITATION

The term "meditation" derives from the Greek *melete,* meaning "care," "study," "exercise." The Latin word *meditatio* conveys the sense of preparation and practice. In the context of Christian life and practice, meditation is one form of prayer within a larger schema that includes *oratio* (vocal prayer), and *contemplatio* (sometimes called pure prayer, or "prayer of the heart" in the desert tradition). Ordinarily viewed as more advanced than vocal prayer, which includes such practices as praying the Liturgy of the Hours, saying the rosary alone or in common, reciting the Creed, and making novenas to the Sacred Heart or to a saint, meditation may be understood as a preparatory practice that disposes one for the gift of contemplation. Though hard and fast distinctions do not always hold, it is useful to consider contemplation as a less active, indeed more receptive, mode of prayer.

In the history of Christian spirituality, *oratio, meditatio,* and *contemplatio* are often viewed as finding their fullest fruition in the experience of mystical union, the highest expression of prayer. In mystical experience, the human person and God are altogether present one to another, so that the mystic echoes the words of St. Paul: "No longer I, but Christ who lives within me" (Gal 2:20).

Today there is a clearer recognition that the distinctions between and among the stages or degrees of prayer, as well as a hierarchy among them, is not as clear as was once thought. It is more helpful to consider the various types of prayer as distinct moments in the life of prayer. Meditation may or may not give way to contemplation. And at the threshold of mystical experience one may be inclined to pray using short, ejaculatory, vocal prayers. Further, it may be that one continues long and lovingly in simple meditation on Christ's cross throughout the course of a lifetime. If there is no movement to a more contemplative form of prayer it does not necessarily mean that the authenticity of prayer is any the less. As with all expressions of prayer, meditation is not simply a means to a higher end. Meditation is in itself a real participation in Christ's mysteries.

Meditation is ordinarily understood as mental prayer involving the systematic reflection on a Christian mystery like the passion of Christ or on a scriptural passage such as Mark 8:27-30 in which Jesus elicits Peter's confession of faith. In most approaches to meditation since the sixteenth century, the powers of the mind are called upon to serve as impetus to affection and practical resolution. For example, in meditating on the passion of Christ one would imagine the depths of Christ's pain and suffering on the cross and, in so doing, be moved to enter more completely into Christ's redemptive love. One would thereby be led to strengthen one's commitment to self-sacrificial love and solidarity with all those who suffer in the hope of the resurrection. In meditating on Peter's confession of faith, one might be drawn to scrutinize the regions of uncertainty and doubt within oneself and to make a firmer resolution to live by faith and in more authentic Christian discipleship. When meditating on the parable of the Prodigal Son (Luke 15:11-32) one might see again the unrestricted forgiveness that lies at the heart of the gospel, accept it in greater measure, and offer it in turn to others as an expression of the gift of forgiveness received.

What distinguishes meditation from other forms of prayer is that it is primarily discursive in nature. This distinction has been strongly emphasized in practices of meditation that have been highly influential in Christian spirituality since the sixteenth century. The Ignatian approach, for example, is particularly noteworthy because of its attention to the importance of the imagination in prayer, and to apostolic action for the greater glory of God in which one's prayer is expressed and authenticated. This approach has also emphasized the important practice of the examen, or the examination of conscience, by which one scrutinizes one's intentions and activities over the course of a day or week, or some other specified period of time. Examination of both positive and negative motives and actions in one's life is to be undertaken in view of the mystery of God's mercy and compassion, which enables one to resolve firmly to reorient one's intentions and actions by the power of God's grace.

Practices of Christian meditation such as these have real merits, particularly for those whose imagination is rich or who are inclined to cultivate the imagination and intuition in the life of prayer. It is also well-suited to those who are busy, active people, or whose energy is devoted to apostolic work, because it requires concentrated time and energy given to quiet and recollection on a regular basis. It is no surprise that such an approach to meditation has been very familiar to generations of apostolic religious women and men, especially prior to the Second Vatican Council. It is to be lamented that many formed in this approach to prayer practiced it as the only mode of prayer appropriate to their way of life when, in fact, the potential and grace for other expressions of prayer were clearly manifest in their lives.

One of the difficulties with certain practices of meditation is that the concern for practical resolution and firm amendment often gives way to preoccupation with measurable results and identifiable changes in one's motives and behavior. Too, there is often a tendency toward voluntarism, a willful activism in the practice of meditation itself so as to assure that one is following the correct procedure in prayer in order to ascertain the desired results. Further there is the problem faced by those who attempt to meditate but seem to have no natural inclination or capacity for it. The gift and task in such a situation is to come to recognize the other forms of prayer for which one is more naturally suited, and to develop in the practice of meditation rooted in those bases.

Contemporary practices of meditation, often influenced by practices of the Christian East and the age-old wisdom of East Asian religions, give greater emphasis to the importance of quiet, receptive, listening in meditation. As an example of the former, there is a renaissance of interest in the regular, slow, silent repetition of the "Jesus Prayer": "Lord, Jesus Christ, Son of the living God, have mercy on me." As an example of the latter, there is a groundswell of interest in Zen and the way it can enhance Christian meditation. East and West meet in the growing number of people who have adopted the practice of saying a "mantra" such as "Maranatha" or "Jesus,

Mercy" regularly, repeatedly, silently. The purposes of all such Christian meditation is to focus one's energy, center one's spirit, attend to the presence and action of the Holy Spirit, so that one might be prepared to receive God's grace and mercy in fuller measure, and in so doing, give praise and glory to God.

With the Second Vatican Council's emphasis on the universal call to holiness there has been a deepening awareness that all the baptized are called to a life of prayer. Consequently there has been a resurgence of interest in various forms of prayer among people of all walks of life. It is to be lamented that most practices of meditation remain focused on the individual. What is needed is a deeper appreciation of the need and potential for practices of communal meditation so that a community of faith might enter more fully into Christ's mysteries through meditation. Periods of meditation provide opportunity to focus a community's energy, to "center" the community as a community so that all that is done individually and communally springs from hearts quieted and at rest in the love of the Holy Spirit dwelling within.

As an example of such approach to meditation, making the Stations of the Cross, ordinarily done on one's own, might provide occasion for the larger community to enter more fully into meditation on the passion, death, and resurrection of Christ. In so doing, a community might be awakened as a community to a deeper sense of the suffering of the human family with whom and for whom Christ died, entering thereby into his solidarity with victims and his ongoing ministry of justice. Whatever is done in this regard, it is most important to relate more closely those practices of meditation ordinarily done by individuals and in private, to the communal celebration of the sacraments and to the proclamation of the word in worship.

MICHAEL DOWNEY

See also CONTEMPLATION; JESUS PRAYER, THE; MYSTICISM; PRAYER.

MEISTER ECKHART (ca 1260–ca. 1329)

Meister Eckhart was a Dominican mystic, living and preaching in Germany about the same period that Dante was alive and writing in Italy. Eckhart wrote in both German and Latin and was well known in his own day for his spectacular sermons. Today he may very possibly be the most quoted Christian mystic.

Johannes Eckhart was born around 1260 in one of two villages called Hoccheim near Erfurt. His father was steward of a knight's castle in the Thuringian forest. Eckhart entered the Dominican Order at Erfurt in his mid-teens. He began his theological studies in 1280 at Cologne, where Albertus Magnus had been teaching prior to his death in that same year. Although Eckhart most probably did not study under Albertus Magnus himself, Eckhart was clearly influenced by him and by the writings of Thomas Aquinas, who had died in 1274 and whose writings were entering into prominence at that time. Eckhart became a bachelor of theology at Paris in 1293 and wrote commentaries on Peter Lombard's *Sentences.* From 1302 to 1303, he lectured at Paris. During that time he received his master of theology degree and was henceforth known as "Meister" Eckhart.

Eckhart was a well-respected member of the Dominican Order and held several positions of authority in it. In 1294 he became prior of the house of his order at Erfurt and vicar of the vicariate of Thuringia. From 1303 until 1311 he served as provincial of the Dominican province of Saxony. In 1307, he also assumed the duties of vicar of Bohemia. It was during this middle, and very active, part of his life that Eckhart wrote *The Book of Divine Comfort,* which provides a rather comprehensive view of his theology. The book is said to have been written for the queen of Hungary, who had suffered several tragedies.

Eckhart returned to Paris in 1311 and remained there until 1313, at which time he accepted a professorship in theology at Strasbourg. In Strasbourg, Eckhart became especially active as a preacher and spiritual director. He was highly respected by the Dominican and Cistercian nuns, Beguines and others. He also made some enemies, however, particularly the archbishop of Cologne, a Franciscan by the name of Heinrich von Virneberg. The archbishop appointed two theologians to investigate Eckhart. In 1326, they presented Eckhart with two lists of suspect propositions drawn mostly from his sermons. Eckhart passionately defended himself in his "Justificative Report" and argued that he had always been faithful to the Church. In 1327, he appealed to the pope. He died around 1329 in Avignon while awaiting the verdict of the papal commission. On 27 March 1329, Pope John XXII promulgated *In agro dominico,* which condemned twenty-eight propositions, representing barely a quarter of the propositions included in the original lists. Although Eckhart's works were seldom copied after his condemnation, he clearly influenced German speculative mysticism. Indeed, the works of Tauler, Henry Suso, John Ruusbroec and others reflect concern with many of the same topics that preoccupied Eckhart.

Eckhart's theology stresses both the total transcendence of God and God's total immanence. God is beyond being, as in the Neoplatonic tradition, yet God is defined as *esse simpliciter,* Being as such, the ultimately real beyond all names. Eckhart took apophatic theology to its logical conclusion going beyond the Persons of the Trinity. The innermost reality of the Godhead is indistinguishably one. At the same time, Eckhart's theology of the Image is arguably one of the first important Trinitarian spiritual theologies in Latin Christianity and clearly influenced the Trinitarian mysticism in the Rhineland and Flanders. In fact, his doctrine of the birth of the Son in the soul and his effort to present the creature as eternally present in the divine Image of the Son (see especially his sixth sermon) received more criticism from the Cologne and Avignon commissions than did his apophatic assertions.

Eckhart emphasizes spirituality of the intellectual type as developed by Pseudo-Dionysius. Eckhart believed that the most elevated part of the soul was in essence intellectual. This part of the human person is united with God and is the seat of the divine life, of the truly contemplative life, where the spirit reigns. The birth of the Word takes place in this uncreated essence of the soul (see his commentary on St. John).

PATRICIA DeFERRARI

See also DOMINICANS; MIDDLE AGES, THE; MYSTICISM; SPIRITUAL LIFE.

MELKITES

See EASTERN CATHOLIC CHURCHES.

MEMORARE

The *Memorare* is a late medieval prayer of uncertain authorship asking the intercession of Mary. It is known first from manuscripts of the late fifteenth century.

This is the popular translation: Remember, O most gracious Virgin Mary, that never was it known that anyone who fled to your protection, implored your help or sought your intercession, was left unaided. Inspired with this confidence, I fly to you, O Virgin of virgins, my Mother; to you do I come, before you I stand, sinful and sorrowful. O Mother of the Word Incarnate, despise not my petitions, but in your mercy hear and answer me. Amen.

DAVID BRYAN

See also DEVOTIONS; PRAYER.

MEMORIAL (COMMEMORATION)

The term refers to the lowest category of feast in the calendar of the Church. It represents two types of memorial: those which must be observed ("obligatory"), and those which do not require a proper observance ("optional").

JOSEPH QUINN

See also LITURGY.

MENDICANT ORDERS

Literally this means congregations of religious who beg. The Franciscans and Dominicans are the best known. In fact they were founded as begging friars, but in the course of time the emphasis was on poverty and frugality as a personal way of life, and on the refusal of fixed revenues for the communities. Even this last proved impracticable if the members were to study and teach and preach.

From the beginnings in the twelfth century, the mendicant friars were distinguished in other ways from the older, monastic communities. Though they took vows and formed permanent communities, they did not follow a prescribed *horarium* (daily schedule), and were not bound to a particular place. They were intended to be itinerant preachers, able to follow apostolic needs wherever they arose. In the thirteenth and fourteenth centuries, they were prominent in the universities of Europe, though this had not been foreseen at the foundations. In the era of colonial expansion, the mendicants often went as missionaries alongside the colonial forces, sometimes defending the rights of indigenous populations. In the upheavals of the sixteenth-century Reformation, the friars, especially the Dominicans, were at the forefront of Catholic defense and counterreformation.

These communities had aptly arisen in the twelfth century. With the new urbanization then taking place in Europe, mendicancy by the homeless and needy was a new and shocking phenomenon. It was new because under the feudal structure of the countryside no one was unemployed or homeless. Everyone succeeded to plots of land, crafts, or other services which ran in the family. Correspondingly, everyone had a place to stay (though it might be crowded), a livelihood (though it might be skimpy), and a definite, recognized place in society (though it might be lowly). When people moved into the newly established town centers, they had to find their own way. The traditional structures of economic and social relationships were not provided. Some flourished in the competition but others failed and had to turn to begging in a most humiliating and desperate situation. The mendicant friars (like some other Christian individuals and groups) looked at this development in the light of the gospel. They saw Jesus living an itinerant life and identifying with the poorest, and they committed themselves in discipleship to do likewise.

MONIKA K. HELLWIG

See also DOMINICANS; FRANCISCANS; MIDDLE AGES, THE.

MERCIER, DESIRÉ JOSEPH (1851–1926)

Archbishop of Malines, cardinal (1907), scholar, he was born near Waterloo, in Belgium, on 21 November 1851. He studied at the seminary in Malines, was ordained a priest in 1874 and received a licentiate in theology from the University of Louvain in 1877 where he began teaching philosophy in the same year. After Pope Leo XIII's (1878–1903) encyclical *Aeterni Patris* (1879) calling for the restoration of the study of Thomistic philosophy in light of modern scholarship and scientific study, Mercier helped to set up the chair of Thomistic philosophy at the University of Louvain. With Pope Leo's support, Mercier established the Institut Supérieur de Philosophie, a school founded expressly for education in all areas of philosophy. In 1894 he was named president of the Institut and then established the *Revue Néo-Scholastique,* an international journal highlighting the thought of this institute.

Mercier disliked the attitudes of some Catholics who claimed that philosophy was merely an apologetic for dogmatic theology. Instead he wished to place philosophy on the same level as other university disciplines maintaining that it must always be open to questioning, inquiry, and new research. As far as he was concerned philosophy had to deal with the issues raised not only in theology but also in all the other sciences. Consequently, Mercier believed wholeheartedly in the need to study human experience, which in turn led him to take a deep interest in modern psychology. In his zeal to prove the hylomorphic unity of the human person he employed data from biology, neurology, and physiology, and he stressed the need for Catholic philosophers to be open to the use of data from all sciences.

In 1906 Mercier was named archbishop of Malines, where he worked hard at his pastoral duties, showing a particular concern for the needs of his priests. As primate of Belgium and a cardinal (1907) he sought to coordinate the work of the Church in all of Belgium. During World War I he became an international figure by championing the rights of his people against the German occupation forces. Looking beyond the needs of his own Church, he was also active in ecumenical dialogue between Catholics and Anglicans and Orthodox Christians. He died in Brussels on 23 January 1926.

ANTHONY D. ANDREASSI

See also ECUMENISM; PHILOSOPHY AND THEOLOGY; THOMISM.

MERCY

Mercy is the willingness to help those in need simply because they are in need. Like all that pertains to God's goodness, mercy is both a much sought after gift and a life-giving action. The scriptural tradition tells us that people in need cry out for God's mercy (Matt 15:22), and give praise when they recognize the presence of that mercy (Luke 1:58, 78).

Mercy is always connected with the divine presence and power. It is God who shows mercy, who is merciful. God's mercy manifests itself in a faithful, loving kindness that reaches out to save those in need. The Hebrew Scriptures speak frequently of the *hesed* of God (Hos 6:6). God is praised as loving, kind, faithful, and constant in helping the people. In other words, God is merciful.

The ground for both understanding and expecting God's faithful mercy is the covenant. Because it is grounded in relationship/covenant, mercy is an ongoing/constant activity. God is not merciful once, in some dramatic act, and then forgetful of the people. Fundamental to mercy is constancy. God saves, helps, and continues to help (Isa 54:10). The relationship established by the covenant between God and people enables the people to look to God for constant mercy. While one never earns mercy, experience teaches those who are in relationship with God to expect it.

Jesus is the revelation of God's mercy. Mary sings of his forthcoming birth as the manifestation of God's mercy on the people (Luke 1:50). As Jesus walks among the people, they recognize God's presence and cry out for God's power: "Son of David, have mercy on us" (Matt 9:29). And when God's mercy rises within the compassion of Jesus, people are healed. The blind see, the lame walk, the suffering know they are loved.

Because God is lovingly merciful, God's people are called to be expressions of that mercy. Relationship with God always implies relationship among people. Mercy is the loving kindness and faithful service we owe each other as members of God's people. Those who know God are called to be merciful with each other (Luke 10:37). This is particularly true for the leaders of the people. They are measured by the quality and constancy of their mercy—especially toward those most in need. They are rebuked for their lack of mercy, for the burdens they lay upon the people.

The merciful belong within the kingdom of God. The Gospel of Matthew tells us that Jesus declared the merciful blessed and promised them that—as they showed mercy toward others—God would act mercifully toward them (Matt 5:7).

Often we think of mercy as a form of pity or institutionalized charity. It can echo with a notion of superiority. The superior one, the more powerful one, does a good deed or forgives the debt of the inferior one. In truth, mercy springs from the passion of love. Love for the other urges both God and God's people to act in kindness and tenderness, to heal and to save.

JULIANA M. CASEY, I.H.M.

See also CORPORAL AND SPIRITUAL WORKS OF MERCY; VIRTUE.

MERCY, SISTERS OF

See SISTERS OF MERCY.

MERCY, WORKS OF

See CORPORAL AND SPIRITUAL WORKS OF MERCY.

MERICI, ANGELA, ST. (1474–1540)

Foundress of the Ursuline Order in 1535, Angela Merici was born some sixty years before in Desanzano, Italy. She worked where she was needed, lived where provision was made for her, and prayed with a passionate love of God. Yet despite her obscure simplicity she was referred to as "La Santa"—and the small group of young women whom she had gathered to found her first company under the patronage of St. Ursula was soon to spread over the face of the earth.

MAGDALEN O'HARA, O.S.U.

See also RELIGIOUS ORDERS; URSULINES.

MERIT

Merit is the goodness of a human act that entitles the agent to a recompense or reward. There are numerous scriptural references to God in both the OT and NT where people are rewarded for performing good things for God. Tertullian introduced the term "merit" into theology, and it was developed by other Fathers such as Cyprian. Augustine believed that strictly speaking the human person cannot demand or claim anything from God out of justice for one's good deeds. The human person can only merit what God has already freely given to humanity. The Protestant Reformers rejected the Catholic teaching on merit, or, at least, what they conceived to be the Catholic teaching on the subject at that time. The Council of Trent (1545–1563) responded to their objections by admitting that a person cannot work for or merit justification and the salvation it gives. Nevertheless, Trent also affirmed that a person can cooperate with God's grace by doing good deeds, and thus share in God's just rewards.

ANTHONY D. ANDREASSI

See also GRACE; JUSTIFICATION; SALVATION.

MERTON, THOMAS (1915–1968)

Life

Merton was born in Prades, France, on 31 January 1915. His Episcopal father (from New Zealand) met his Quaker mother (from New York) while both were studying art in Paris. Shortly after birth Merton was baptized "Tom," but his parents gave him little religious education. When he was one year old they moved to New York where soon John Paul, a younger brother, was born. Tom's mother taught him to read before he entered school, and he remained an avid reader all his life. She died when he was six; then he traveled with his father till placed in boarding schools in France and England.

While studying at Cambridge he got into unidentified trouble (it seems he fathered a child). He then returned to New York to live with his mother's family and attend Columbia University, from which he would receive his bachelor's and master's degree in literature. He had considered himself an atheist until as an undergraduate he read Etienne Gilson's *The Spirit of Medieval Philosophy.* He was further influenced by writings of Aldous Huxley, Jacques Maritain, Leon Bloy, and the poetry of William Blake and Gerard Manley Hopkins ("they sang me into the Church"). He was rebaptized Catholic on 16 November 1938. He soon began an application to enter the Franciscans and taught at the Franciscan college, St. Bonaventure's (now University), in upstate New York.

Merton met Catherine de Hueck and briefly considered working at Friendship House, an outreach house in Harlem, but instead decided to enter the Trappists (Order of Cistercians of the Strict Observance). He entered the monastery of Gethsemani in Kentucky on 10 December 1941—three days after the Japanese bombed Pearl Harbor. The abbot gently encouraged Merton's long-time interest in writing. He published a book of poems and wrote two biographies before completing his autobiography, *The Seven Storey Mountain.* Appearing in October

Thomas Merton

1948, it quickly became a bestseller; it has been translated into fifteen languages and sales are estimated at three-and-a-half million. He soon followed with *Seeds of Contemplation* which was translated into fourteen languages. He continued writing on Christian spirituality, *The Ascent to Truth* and *No Man is an Island;* but in the early 1950s he broadened his interest to include Eastern spirituality with a particular interest in Zen. He became restless with the common life of the monastery and requested transfer to a monastic congregation that allowed more solitude. Some limited modifications of schedule were made for him, and in 1955 he began serving as novice director.

In 1958, after being distant from world events, Merton developed an interest in social causes, notably race relations, the politics of Latin America, and later U.S. military actions in Vietnam. This brought a change in his popular image: he lost some former readers and gained some new ones. Though he was not an absolute pacifist and publication of his pacifist writings were restricted, many leading opponents of the Vietnam War quoted him and visited him at Gethsemani. In 1965 he finished his work as novice director and obtained permission from Cistercian authorities to spend most of the day at a hermitage on the monastery grounds (in recent times there had been no Cistercian hermits). From the time of his entrance until 1968 Merton rarely left the monastery—save for hospital stays in Louisville with nervous stress, allergy, and back problems. But with Vatican II he took several trips within the U.S. and then left to attend monastic conferences in Calcutta and Bangkok. After presenting a paper in Bangkok on 10 December 1968, he was found dead in his room, electrocuted by the faulty wire of an electric fan. He is buried in the monastic cemetery at Gethsemani.

Merton wrote about fifty books—it is difficult to give an exact number as some essays are duplicated in different collections and some book-length manuscripts have appeared only as articles. He wrote poetry and prose, a play and a novel, letters and journals, essays and satires, biographies and an autobiography. His writings considered contemplation and spirituality, monastic history and life, contemporary art and literature, liturgy, pacificism, racism, Eastern religion and consumerism. Twenty-five years after his death his books continue to sell. Most of his original papers are kept in the archives of The Merton Study Center at Bellarmine College, Louisville, Kentucky.

Spiritual Teaching

Central to the thought of Merton is the radical denial of the self; this refers to the reflective self known in the Cartesian *cogito.* This self is considered an illusion created by the deceptive forces that pit one person against another in competition. Merton insisted we must lose this artificial self in order to discover our true self ("person") in Christ. In Christ we will discover our person united in love with the persons of all other people. Sometimes Merton would call this awareness (infused) contemplation or the "transcendent experience"—for by it we transcend our individual selfhood. In contemplation we find our person—what can never be known in reflection. It is a timeless identity that simply is. Much of Merton's interest in Zen writers came from their radical and unequivocal denial of all selfhood.

In telling of contemplation as the life of God infused in us, Merton set his understanding in opposition to those who regard contemplation as a warm, oceanic feeling of bliss. He found such bliss sometimes recommended in spiritual literature, but he considered it only psychological regression (he allowed something similar might be involved in the early stages of Christian mysticism). Yet the experience can leave one bogged down in feelings of sweetness and ego-peace, while nothing transcendent to the self is involved. So he warned that spiritual directors must be careful "*not* to confuse this narcissistic self-awareness with true mystical contemplation." Merton would also oppose Aldous Huxley and others who had claimed that mystical states can be had with drugs. For Merton insisted true mysticism involves "a direct spiritual contact of two liberties [God's and our own]." In true mysticism God is not known as an 'object' or as the "one in everything." Rather one contacts the biblical "I AM"; it is the free presence of Another and so it depends not on chemicals but on the freedom of the divine Other.

Merton would also distinguish true mysticism from what some psychologists speak of as a "peak experience": this he saw as only "a heightening and intensification of our personal identity" that enables us to feel exhilarated and good about ourselves. But the self-aware subject would remain self-aware and not transcend the self at all. Should the ego claim the transcendent experience as its own, Merton would see this as the "crowing glory of egohood and self-fulfillment"—that is, the crowning glory of illusion.

Merton believed that the "transcendent experience [infused contemplation]" is found in the Christian, the Jewish, the Buddhist and the Sufi traditions. Christians would tell of it when they would speak of putting on the mind of Christ; other traditions would tell of the "(I) AM," the Atman, the Pneuma, etc. To arrive at this awareness one must turn one's ego-consciousness inside out so that one becomes a desert, a nothing, a void. Because Zen Buddhist writers insisted most strongly on a radical self-emptying, Merton had more interest in them than other writers on Asian religion. Zen Buddhists do not speak of a personal God, yet Merton found them "very germane and close to our own *approaches* to inner truth in Christ." It is their "approaches" that resemble the Christian approaches: they too insist on the radical denial of self. But in opposition to the Buddhists Merton continued to insist on the personal nature of God. This is evident in his continued insistence that contemplation is love and in the spontaneous prayer he offered shortly before his death; though leading a prayer for many nontheistic, Asian monks, he did not soften his theism. His considerable interest in Asian religious texts drew him to Asia, but he would explain: "I am not very open to Hindu religion, as distinct from philosophy."

Merton has told of three forms of contemplation: the metaphysical, the natural, and the infused. All are in opposition to the Cartesian *cogito.* Metaphysical contemplation would put us in touch with Being apart from the division between subject and object. Then, natural contemplation would involve a loving gaze upon an objective truth or beauty (such as a good liturgy); here there would be some division between subject and object. Then, infused contemplation would involve a radical entrance into God apart from all selfhood; one would disappear from this world.

The value of freedom runs through all the writings of Merton. He would speak of God as Freedom or Liberty, and our freedom is the image of God within us. Yet people in the modern world are estranged from their freedom and caught in a frantic activism. His autobiography begins with the claim, "Free by nature, in the image of God, I was nevertheless the prisoner of my own violence and my own selfishness in the image of the world in which I was born." His autobiography then tells of his journey from the prison of compulsive behavior to the monastery, where he found the "sweet savor of liberty" within "the four walls of my freedom."

Social Teaching

Merton had had an interest in social issues (racial justice and world peace) while a student in Cambridge and Columbia. Later, in writing on the same issues as a monk, he tried to bring the activists of the sixties the perspective of one "halfway between in and out of the action." He warned pacificists against antagonistic forms of protest that drove the opposition only further into its "patriotism." He was suspicious of all group movements and wanted each individual to "stand on one's own two feet." This required "a lucid reason, a profound religious faith and, above all, an uncompromising and a courageous spirit of self sacrifice." His earlier writings had spoken of contemplation as a monastic ideal that required considerable withdrawal from the world. But eventually he would see contemplation as necessary for anyone who wanted to live freely and sanely in the world. He would see people crowded together, yet alienated from themselves and one another with minds full of propaganda and slogans; so he came to consider solitude essential to any true human community and silence necessary for meaningful speech.

Monastic Teaching

Merton wrote abundantly on monastic issues and Catholic liturgy. In general he favored the monastic reforms that followed Vatican II, but he insisted on retaining both discipline and asceticism to free the monk from slavery to his appetites. But he came to believe that the formalisms of monastic life can bring about another form of servitude. Personally, he found it increasingly difficult to assist at community office, but he wanted Latin and Gregorian chant to remain. He had an interest in Asian religions, but he did not think Christian and non-Christian monks could form a common monastic community. During the twenty-seven years of his monastic life, he changed from being a world-denying ascetic to being a world-affirming Christian involved in the events of his time.

THOMAS M. KING, S.J.

See also AMERICAN CATHOLICISM; MONASTICISM; MYSTICISM.

MESSIAH

Messiah, from the Hebrew *māšîaḥ,* "anointed," is a title applied to various figures, especially kings, in the Hebrew Scriptures; the title is applied in the New Testament to Jesus in the form *christos,* its standard translation in the Greek OT.

In ancient Israel, anointing—smearing oil on the skin—was a symbolic act or ritual that was thought to imbue the person of the one anointed with a power inhering in the oil (cf. Ps 109:18). The ritual was used when one undertook an office, by way of consecrating him, in his inmost being, to that task. Priests were anointed (Lev 8:12, 30); prophets were anointed (1 Kgs 19:16); and kings were anointed (1 Sam 10:1; 16:13; 1 Kgs 19:15-16; 2 Kgs 9:6).

Hence, the word *māšîaḥ* served as a title for the king in Israel. The prophet Samuel refers to Yahweh's "anointed one" (1 Sam 12:3, 5) and means Saul, who was then king; cf. also 1 Samuel 24:6, 10. In Psalm 89:20, Yahweh says of David, "With my holy oil I have anointed him."

In the Dynastic Oracle (2 Samuel 7), Yahweh promises eternal kingship to the "seed" of David: a line of kings descended from David will sit on the throne of Israel forever. The Davidic king would be a son to Yahweh, and Yahweh would be a father to him (7:14; cf. Pss 2:7; 89:26). The promise of everlasting kingship was unconditional (but cf. Ps 132:12). The title "anointed one" was of course applied to the Davidic king: cf. Psalm 2:2.

With the Babylonian Exile (587–539 B.C.), however, the kingly rule of the House of David ended; nor, after the Exile, was there a restoration of the dynasty. This state of affairs continued under successive Persian, Greek, and Roman rule; the Hasmonaean kings (160–37 B.C.) were not of the House of David.

Thus, in the time of Jesus, there was an expectation, based on the Dynastic Oracle and cognate traditions about the Davidic king, that the Lord would "raise up the seed" of David, the anointed one: the "Messiah," or "Christ."

In the Gospels, this expectation is seen in various reactions to John the Baptist (Luke 3:15; John 1:19-20) and to Jesus (cf. Luke 4:41; 9:20). The expression "son of David" (Matt 21:9) can be understood in this light, and so also "Son of God" as understood by the crowds and the disciples. Mark, followed by Luke and (except for 16:17-19) Matthew, shows Jesus strenuously rejecting the title of Messiah, until the trial scene (14:61-62), when there can be no misunderstanding of the nature of his messiahship. That Jesus is the Messiah, however, is indicated in the evangelists' own comments (e.g., Mark 1:1) and in the baptism and transfiguration scenes, where the voice from heaven identifies Jesus in the words of Psalm 2:7 (Mark 1:11; 9:7; Matt 3:17; 17:5; Luke 3:22; 9:35).

The Gospels (and Acts) reveal a full development in understanding of the term. It is no longer merely a royal title; the OT passages about the messianic son have been transformed in meaning. The title is the focus for an understanding of Jesus as one designated by God as God's own Son. This fuller meaning, however, still includes the core notion of kingship. 1 Corinthians 15:24-28 reflects this understanding; but for the most part Paul seems to use *christos* as a name rather than as the messianic title.

Other titles from the Hebrew Scriptures aggregated to the title of Messiah: notably the "servant of the Lord" (Isa 42:1; 52:13–53:12); and "savior," a term used in Judges 3–9 for the leaders Yahweh raised up to govern early Israel. In the person of Jesus, these and other originally disparate titles came together, mutually illuminating and enriching their meanings as understood in the light of Jesus: "This Jesus whom you crucified, God has made both Lord and Messiah" (Acts 2:36).

J.P.M. WALSH, S.J.

See also CHRISM; JESUS CHRIST; MISSION.

MEŠTROVIĆ, IVAN (1883–1962)

A Croatian sculptor, imprisoned by Nazis in 1941. After the war, Meštrović lived in exile to protest the communist regime. He exhibited in major European capitals and the New York Metropolitan Museum. His collections are in Split, Zagreb, Syracuse University, and the University of Notre Dame.

Meštrović spent his childhood in Otavice, a mountain village of a few stone houses. The land was rugged, harsh and poor—and he fell deeply in love with it. He tended sheep, heard ballads of folk heroes, and from his father, a mason, learned to carve figures from the stone he found in the fields. When he was fifteen the villagers pooled money to send him to Split as apprentice to a stonecutter. Though he later lived in Vienna, Paris, Rome, London, Syracuse, New York, and finally settled at Notre Dame University, his heart remained in Croatia. ". . . I always heard deep within myself a whisper saying: 'My poor, small homeland, in the entire world you are the greatest and the dearest to my heart.' This feeling enabled me to accomplish a few things of value in my life. No matter how far fate has blown the frail tree of my life across foreign lands, its roots have always sucked nourishment from that little barren clod of soil from which it sprung" (Interview in *Hrvatska Revija* [September

Ivan Mĕstrović

1953], quoted in L. Schmeckebier, *Ivan Meštrović: Sculptor and Patriot,* Syracuse: Syracuse University Press, 1959, p. 4).

Meštrović became the giant among Croatian artists. The land that was Yugoslavia is sprinkled with his monuments and heroic sculptures of legendary figures in marble, bronze, wood and granite. ". . . the moral of (our) legends is simple and clear: to fight to death against oppression and cruelty . . . the whole of our country is an altar for this faith. . . ." (Milan Curčin, *Ivan Meštrović: A Monograph,* quoted in Schmeckebier, p. 21). His art was an altar for another faith—a simple religion that also sprang from his roots. "We peasants who have learned to follow the plow . . . hope that the harvest time will give us wheat, or at least enough grain for seed. We must have faith." (Schmeckebier, p. 3). As his heroic art projects the legends he heard as a child, his religious art is a shaft to the piety he learned from his mother, the intense and dignified piety of primitive village life: *Pietà, Job, My Mother at Prayer.* Some figures crouch in pain. Many are roughly chiseled. All distill a strong peasant faith.

His monumental statues overshadow a small chapel above the sea in Split—a twelfth-century stone cloister. In an echo of his childhood work on the stone houses of pious peasants, in his early thirties Meštrović began to carve scenes from the life of Christ to decorate the chapel walls. From time to time he packaged a crate containing a large wood relief and mailed it home to his chapel—a gift to the people of Croatia. He finished the last of the thirty panels at age seventy-one.

The constancy of his image of the stone chapel as he shifted from place to place is a window to his creative consciousness: "That other eye . . . the eye of the soul . . . is much more important than the body's eye . . . even before the sculptor lays his chisel to the rough stone . . . he sees within it the figure he wishes to make. . . . He sees the figure not only in rough outline but precisely and in detail from all sides . . . the creation is already completed, in its total harmony, without the hand or the eye taking part. All that remains for the sculptor is to draw the statue out of the material and reveal it to the physical eye" (Schmeckebier, pp. 45–46).

Meštrović's life was a continual wrestling with blocks of stone to reveal the images he saw at the core, images planted in his mountain village. "I have the feeling that my best work will remain forever hidden and unhewn in the pure granite which lies at the heart of the mountain" (Schmeckebier, p. 2).

PATRICIA O'CONNOR

See also ART, CHRISTIAN.

METHODISTS, UNITED

Methodism began as a revivalist movement within the Church of England under the leadership of John Wesley (1703–1791). Wesley was an Anglican priest who felt the Christianity of his mother Church lacked the vitality of true godliness.

While students at Oxford University, John, with brother Charles (1707–1788) and friend, George Whitefield (1714–1770), formed the "Holy Club." Their purpose was to establish certain rules and disciplines, be in regular prayer and Bible study, and to visit society's unfortunate. They were so "methodical" in their devotion that they were derisively called "Methodists" and the name stuck.

Moravian pietists from the continent, with their centerpiece of heartfelt religious experience, greatly influenced Wesley's journey to a living relation with Christ. Indeed, it was at a Moravian meeting in London in May, 1738, that Wesley "felt his heart strangely warmed" and where he found that personal reality of Christ he was seeking.

Wesley called his religious experience the "witness of the Holy Spirit." Some scholars say that Wesley completed the "trinitarian emphases of the Protestant Reformation"—Calvin with God the Father, Luther with God the Son, and Wesley with God the Spirit.

John Wesley did not want to start a new Church or to deviate from theological and ecclesiastical tradition. His message was a simple one—New Testament Christianity, love for God and neighbor, personalized faith, and social concern.

Wesley and his colleagues formed bands or small classes in the Church to practice their newfound experience of Christ, to unite what he said had been long divided, "knowledge and vital piety." Wesley's experiential religion was no substitute for creeds and theology; he took these for granted and assumed their importance. He wanted to recapture the power and vitality of a Spirit-filled faith.

Wesley embodied in his preaching and teaching four main elements, often called the Wesleyan quadrilateral, which form the authoritative base for thinking about faith and life: (1) *Scripture,* especially the New Testament; (2) *tradition,* retention of catholic liturgy and Reformation theology; (3) *experience,* a personal validation of faith and a pragmatic adjustment to what seems to work in a given situation; and (4) *reason,* a rational and logically thought-out religion and polity. The latter was an Enlightenment legacy.

Wesley articulated the meaning of his experiential religion in a threefold theological framework: (1) justification by faith, or what God does for us in forgiveness (the gift of grace); (2) conversion or regeneration, the result of the personal appropriation of that gift; and (3) sanctification, or what God does in us as we grow in holiness and Christian perfection.

John and Charles Wesley had preached in Georgia in 1735, and Methodism came to America in the middle of the eighteenth century with Francis Asbury, Thomas Coke, Philip Embury, and Robert Strawbridge. They were all circuit-riding preachers who went to out-of-the-way places to proclaim a gospel available to the ordinary person. Their successors, a century later, conducted camp meetings and revivals which changed the lives of many persons. Very few of those early preachers were Calvinist; most of them espoused the free will tenets of Arminianism.

Early Methodism was known as a singing Church; Charles Wesley wrote over six thousand hymns, many of which found their way into the American hymnal. These hymns were often paraphrases of Biblical passages and became a way for the congregation to sing the Scripture.

Methodists soon outnumbered the Baptists as they grew rapidly, not only in the middle and southern colonies, but beyond the Appalachians, as well.

The fledgling movement formally organized itself as the Methodist Episcopal Church in Baltimore, Maryland, in 1784 and produced two bishops, Francis Asbury and Thomas Coke. Within fifty years, two separate denominations had split off from the original body as it became more acculturated to the American scene. In 1830, the Methodist Protestant Church became a democratic reform in its elimination of bishops and by allowing lay people to vote on Church matters. In 1845, The Methodist Episcopal Church, South, was formed over the divisive issue of slavery. In 1939, these three branches merged to form The Methodist Church. A further merger took place in 1968, when the Evangelical United Brethren, a Protestant group with a long German pietist heritage and a symbiotic relation with Methodism, joined with the Methodists to become the United Methodist Church.

In terms of doctrine, United Methodism is a typical mainline denomination; it is not fundamentalist, nor liturgical, nor ideological. It is a moderately liberal Church, stressing dynamic preaching, warm fellowship, and a practical faith. Its history is replete with a strong social witness in matters of race, peace, labor relations, and human rights. Over a hundred colleges and universities illustrate its commitment to higher education. United Methodists have contributed a great deal, also, to the ecumenical success of American Protestantism. Methodism ordained its first woman in 1956 and today over a third of its seminary students are women.

Worship can vary from the relatively liturgical to the informal and free. There are two sacraments: baptism, which is initiation into the Church, and the Lord's Supper, which is held quarterly and, increasingly, on a monthly basis. Most members believe in Christ's symbolic presence in the Supper.

United Methodists are governed by a General Conference which meets every four years and is composed of bishops (elected for life), and clergy and lay delegates, elected by their respective Annual Conferences. There are seventy-two Annual Conferences which are made up of a number of districts. Clergy are appointed to their "charges" (parishes) by a bishop.

There are several smaller Methodist bodies, e.g., Wesleyan Methodists and Evangelical Methodists as well as several large black Methodist denominations, such as the African Methodist Church, the African Methodist Episcopal Zion Church, and the Christian Methodist Episcopal Church.

There are about twenty-five million Methodists in the world; this includes nine million United Methodists in the United States, making them now the second largest Protestant group in that country.

IRA ZEPP

See also ANGLICANISM; PROTESTANTISM.

MICHEL, VIRGIL (GEORGE), O.S.B. (1890–1938)

Author, editor, founder of the American liturgical movement, Virgil Michel was also a philosopher, pioneer in catechetics and religious education, social philosopher and activist for "social regeneration."

Educated at St. John's Prep and St. John's University (Collegeville, Minnesota), he received a B.A. in Latin in 1909. He entered the novitiate at St. John's that year, professed solemn vows in 1913, and was ordained in 1916. He was awarded a Ph.D. in English at the Catholic University in Washington D.C. in 1918, having completed a dissertation on the essays of Orestes Brownson. Concurrently with his studies in English, he followed courses in philosophy and languages as well. Returning to St. John's, he taught English and philosophy and served in various administrative roles in the Prep School and the University for six years.

From the leadership at St. John's, his work with the wide-ranging thought of Brownson and his own study program, these early years laid a foundation for the intense and fruitful work of the remaining years of his short life. However, the decisive experience was a year and a half (1924–1925) of study in Europe. His association with the Benedictine liturgist and ecumenist Lambert Beauduin in Rome, his experience in numbers of European abbeys where the liturgical revival was alive, and (at the University of Louvain) studying the philosophy of St. Thomas Aquinas as open, vital, and relevant to today (in contrast to his experience in Rome where Thomism had been presented as a rigid, closed and lifeless system)—these experiences reinforced his native gifts and the interests nurtured at St. John's.

By the time he returned to St. John's in the autumn of 1925, he had already proposed to Abbot Alcuin Deutsch the fundamental outlines of what he called "the liturgical apostolate." More importantly, perhaps, he had formulated (and perceived the interrelations of) the essentials in his vision of that apostolate. He focused on *life* rather than structure, without minimizing institution. Consequently he would emphasize interiority rather than externalism regarding person, Church, liturgy, all aspects of spirituality; correlatively, given his emphasis on "the sacramental principle" pervasive in his vision, he underscored the importance of authentic embodiment of mystery in liturgy or any aspect of human life. Deeply responsive to the dignity and inviolability of the human person as well as the person's existential need for genuine communion and community, he would oppose both individualism and collectivism in all their expressions. Living very much in the present, deliberately a man of his time and hence sensitive to the "signs" and needs of his age, he was at the same time a man who reverenced the living tradition, the best of the past that can continue to communicate life in present and future.

Virgil Michel, O.S.B.

Michel nurtured that vision throughout his life and it was operative in all his efforts for the liturgical apostolate. At the heart of that apostolate were the image of the Church as the Mystical Body of Christ, and the motto of the movement: *Instaurare omnia in Christo* (Eph 1:10). Michel judged that the body of Christ, among all the biblical images of the Church, best communicated the reality and fullness of relation to Christ and to one another. It most effectively called forth the participation of every member in worship and in daily life, and it focused on the mystery of life and growth *in Christ.* On this foundation, Michel and his associates sought to realize the motto which they translated: "To bring all things under the headship of Christ." Progressively Michel saw the full implications of that goal.

In 1926 he established The Liturgical Press and soon published his translation of Lambert Beauduin's booklet, *La pieté de l'Église* as "Liturgy, the Life of the Church." *Orate Fratres* (now *Worship*) began publication in 1926 with a richly diverse group of associate editors including several lay persons and two women. Readers were informed about developments here and abroad, pastoral concerns were addressed, participation invited. Michel wrote extensively on the Mystical Body and the liturgical movement in many other periodicals as well during these years, and in 1937 published *The Liturgy of the Church.*

Beginning in 1929, with the collaboration of Sister Jane Marie Murray, O.P., his efforts to redirect and vitalize religious education resulted in texts for elementary, secondary and college levels. The earliest was a series of guides to supplement existing texts for grade schools. This was followed by *The Christ Life Series* (eight volumes) in 1934–1935, and then by texts for high schools. His own more advanced texts, *Our Life in Christ* and *The Christian in the World,* were published later. In each of these the unifying themes were the Mystical Body of Christ and the liturgy as the life of that Body, a life with the power to transform all aspects of human existence. The primary references in each were to Scripture and liturgical texts.

Following an extended illness (1930–1933) Michel saw more clearly the necessity of extending the transformative power of liturgical worship to the social, political and economic arenas. Between 1935 and his death in 1938, he organized (cooperating with the Central Verein) an Institute for Social Study, a monthly gathering for young men from parishes around the state to discuss social questions. The principal lectures were published as *The Social Problem* (four volumes, 1936–1938). He also published a widely-used series of nine pamphlets on various social questions in 1936, and *Christian Social Reconstruction,* a study of the social encyclicals.

His vision led him to support Peter Maurin, Dorothy Day, Catherine de Hueck and their apostolates as well as many similar movements inspired by them. (Reflected here were Michel's pioneer and sustained support of the laity and of women.) He was drawn into interracial concerns and the decentralist movement, and played a significant role in the Catholic Rural Life Movement. He valued his experience with the Catholic co-operative movement in Nova Scotia in 1938. And his interest in the Personalist movement of his time culminated in translation of Emmanuel Mounier's book as *A Personalist Manifesto* in 1938.

Perhaps Michel's most notable contribution to the liturgical movement was his vigorous application of Pope Pius X's dictum—"active and intelligent participation in the liturgy of the Church is the primary and indispensable source of the true Christian spirit"—to the entire field of social justice. As a consequence, the annual national Liturgical Weeks, which began in 1940, two years after Michel's death, consistently made this application one of their explicit concerns.

Given Michel's ecclesial and liturgical focus (and his continued communication with Beauduin), commitment to ecumenical concerns was inevitable. He corresponded extensively with Orthodox and Anglican leaders, was invited to participate in dialogues, and contributed ecumenical articles and reviews to *Orate Fratres* throughout the years of his editorship.

Similarly, his love of a "living" Thomism perdured. He wrote frequently for such periodicals as *The New Scholasticism,* critiqued the social order in the light of Thomistic teaching, translated Martin Grabmann's study of Thomas under the title *Thomas Aquinas: His Personality and Thought* (1927; reprinted 1963), and continued to value G. Contenson's seventeenth-century commentary on Thomas, *Theologia mentis et cordis* (nine volumes).

Music and art were also continuing interests. To choose but one illustration: Mrs. Justine Ward, founder of the Pius X School of Liturgical Music in New York, was one of the original associate editors of *Orate Fratres.* His support of worthy liturgical art was also evident in that first issue: Eric Gill and David Jones of England designed the cover. Michel corresponded with leaders in both fields, and unfailingly encouraged the best work.

This broad range of interests and activity was condensed into a few years: 1926–1930, 1935–1938. Bishop (later Cardinal) Muench remarked on the risk of sacrificing depth to breadth, but said Michel avoided the danger: "Philosophy gave his thinking unity, social economics gave it modernity, and liturgy gave it life." Michel was less an innovator than a synthesizer and communicator: studying the best sources available to him, reflecting on their application to the American scene and the American Church of his time, he sought to communicate the fruit of this study to all who might become a leaven in the Church's life in this country. In so doing he anticipated, by a generation, a great deal of the spirit and teaching of Vatican II.

JEREMY HALL, O.S.B.

MICHELANGELO BUONARROTI (1475–1564)

A Florentine, born in 1475, one of the greatest of Renaissance artists, equally at home in painting, sculpture, and architecture. Michelangelo made his reputation as a sculptor (Rome, *Bachus, Pietà* [completed by 1500]). During another stay in Florence (from 1501 to 1504) he executed the gigantic *David.* He did several *tondi* (round paintings), and began the cartoon of a huge fresco (the *Bathers,* depicting an incident in the Battle of Cascina) commissioned for the Council Hall of the newly established Florentine Republic. (The work was a pendant for a similar project given to Leonardo; neither was finished.) In this project, Michelangelo asserted the nude human body as the all-sufficient vehicle for expressing human nature and character in various situations.

Yielding to a demand by Pope Julius II, Michelangelo gave up the completing of *The Battle of Cascina* in order to begin the Pope's tomb, a project which was to drag on intermittently for forty years. Then he turned his hand to the frescoes in another project

Michelangelo, portrait bust by Schüler

for Pope Julius, the ceiling of the Sistine Chapel (1508–1512). Depicting life before the Law, the gigantic plan combines the Histories, Prophets, Sibyls, and Ancestors of Christ in an arrangement which may be compared only with the structures of the very greatest works of art, such as the *Aeneid,* which stand at the head of their respective genera. The individual representations combine nobility of composition with Florentine grace, the whole depicted in glowing, but carefully shaded, colors only recently restored to something like their original effect. The work, as a whole and in its parts, instantly conveys the feeling of the human seeking the divine. Michelangelo was immediately acclaimed as the greatest of living artists (this while Raphael was working next door and Leonardo was still alive); indeed the idea of "artist" had, in fact, been redefined.

Michelangelo immediately resumed working on Julius' tomb between 1513 and 1515, but, on the accession of a Medici pope (Leo X) who had known him from youth, he returned to Florence to work on the façade of the Medici church (San Lorenzo). Wasting four years on this stillborn project, he next (1520) began the planning of the Medici funerary chapel. This, as well as the Laurenziana Library, were great successes, though much of the statuary for the chapel was never completed. Several years after 1527 were tumultuous and minimally productive, due to the political fall and resurrection of the Medici. In 1534 Michelangelo returned to Rome for the remaining thirty years of his life.

His somber *Last Judgment* (1536–1541, commissioned by Paul III) has been said to reflect the embattled atmosphere of the times (the sack of Rome and the growing Protestant revolt) and a developing pessimism in Michelangelo himself. Here he gave the greatest possible emphasis to the nude figure as the essential vehicle of painting. While this idea was widely received, not all were convinced, and many of Michelangelo's figures were "clothed" after his death. Paul III, however, rewarded the artist with commissions for the frescos in his own chapel between 1532 and 1550: the *Conversion of Paul,* and the *Crucifixion of Peter.*

Michelangelo's great power is evident, also, in architecture, particularly in the construction of the new St. Peter's to which he now, at age seventy-five, increasingly gave his energy. His personal piety, which motivated all of his last works, only grew more intense as his life advanced. He did a *Pietà* intended for his own tomb, and the unfinished *Rondanini Pietà* in which the bodies of Jesus and Mary actually merge at points, and the grief which is humanity's fate rides on the crest of Michelangelo's own brooding emotion. He died at age eighty-nine in 1564 while engaged on the *Pietà.*

DAVID BRYAN

See also ART, CHRISTIAN; LEONARDO DA VINCI; RAPHAEL; RENAISSANCE, THE.

MIDDLE AGES, THE

The era from the end of the eleventh century to about the end of the fifteenth century. It reached its cultural zenith in the thirteenth century with the contributions of Thomas Aquinas, Bonaventure and Albert the Great.

MICHAEL GLAZIER

MIDRASH

(Hebrew, Aramaic: "Search, study") A Jewish and Jewish-Christian method of commenting on specific passages in sacred writings by comparing them with other materials from the same or other texts. In legal texts, the opinions of various rabbis may be cited, while narrative texts are often illuminated by quotations, examples, and stories, particularly of a moralizing nature. The role of midrash in the New Testament, and other early Christian writings, is important, though difficult to assess. While midrashic commentators were not governed by the concerns of modern history writers, they had their own principles and were not simply governed by free invention or fantasy.

DAVID BRYAN

See also CRITICISM, BIBLICAL.

MIGNE, JACQUES-PAUL (1800–1875)

French priest, publisher and printer, who sought to make basic theological research material available at reasonable prices. His output was prodigious, and he is deservedly remembered for his *Patrologiae Cursus Completus* (The Complete Course of the Teachings of the Fathers of the Church) which included *Patrologia Latina* (Collection of the Latin Fathers) which was published in 221 volumes between 1844 and 1864. He supplemented this with the works of the major Latin ecclesiastical writers from earliest time down to Innocent III (1198–1216). His great *Patrologia Graeca* (Collection of the Greek Fathers) appeared between 1857 to 1866 in 161 volumes. He also published the works of Greek Christian writers down to the Council of Florence (1438–1439). Migne's contribution to Christian scholarship deserves greater recognition.

MICHAEL GLAZIER

See also FATHERS OF THE CHURCH.

MILLENARIANISM

A millennium is literally a period of one thousand years. Symbolically, it connotes an indefinite period of peace and fulfillment, usually following lengthy periods of suffering. This symbolic meaning may be rooted in the biblical notion that human beings because of sin cannot live to be one thousand years old. In Genesis 5 all of the just from Adam to Methuselah die before reaching that symbolic number of years.

In ancient Jewish apocalyptic literature there are several references to a millennial kingdom which will be established by the Lord after a series of cosmic disasters. The Psalmist's idea that a thousand years in the sight of the Lord "are but as yesterday when it is past" (Ps 90:4) becomes in 2 Peter 3:8 a sign of God's forbearance and mercy in delaying the destruction of the world ("with the Lord one day is as a thousand years") so that all might have a chance to repent. Millennial thinking received a strong impetus in Christianity from the prophetic vision described in Revelation 20. Satan will be bound in chains and cast into a bottomless pit. During this time the martyrs (and possibly all those who died in the faith) will be raised to life and will reign with Christ for a thousand years after which human history will come to an end and all things will find their consummation in the world to come. It is not specified that this thousand-year reign will be on earth, but popular traditions have so interpreted it and have elaborated this passage in various ways into a loosely related set of teachings known as *millenarianism* (after the Latin word for one thousand) or *chiliasm* (if the Greek root is used).

The development of millenarianism was checked for many centuries due to the influence of Augustine who developed a spiritual interpretation of Revelation 20 as referring to a kingdom established at the time of the resurrection of Christ. In this interpretation the "first resurrection" of Revelation 20:5 is actually the new life conferred in baptism and Christ's thousand-year reign coincides with the life of the Church in this world until the second coming.

Since the sixteenth century new life has been given to millenarianism by a number of religious groups (Anabaptists, Seventh-day Adventists, Mormons, Jehovah's Witnesses, etc.) which all have in common an interest in the end-times, especially with the idea of a sudden return of Christ to deliver the faithful from the tribulations of this world. In the United States those who are called premillenarianists believe Christ will return to reign on earth with the saints before the end of time, while postmillenarianists believe the saints alone will reign for a thousand years after which Christ will come to inaugurate the world to come.

The Holy Office has not favored millenarianist thinking, even in its more moderate forms, proscribing in 1824 a version that had gained some popularity in Latin America, a judgment repeated in 1941, declaring that it cannot be safely taught as Catholic faith that Christ will return to reign visibly on the earth prior to the final judgment at the end of time.

WILLIAM C. McFADDEN, S.J.

See also ESCHATOLOGY; SALVATION HISTORY.

MINISTER

(Lat., "servant") The term is used of those who serve in liturgical and pastoral engagements of the Church. These include the clergy and lay people such as lectors, cantors, and acolytes at the liturgy, and those who serve the needs of the community, such as youth ministers. Though the Second Vatican Council permitted substantially greater flexibility in the designation of lay persons as ministers, the title assumes an appropriate degree of liturgical or pastoral training.

Among certain religious orders, the title is given to a cleric in a position of authority. The head of the Franciscan Order, for example, is the minister general, while the assistant to the rector (or second in charge) of a Jesuit community is the minister.

JOSEPH QUINN

See also LAITY, THEOLOGY OF THE; LITURGY; SACRAMENTS.

MINISTRY

Ministry derives from a Greek word, *diakonia,* which connotes offering a service to others or attending to their needs. Until recently "ministry" was mostly associated with the work of the Protestant communities and it came into popular Catholic usage in recent decades when more and more men and women decided to offer their services to the Church, complementing the work of those in the priesthood and religious life.

The essence of ministry is service, and that is the motivating factor for anyone attracted to one of a great variety of ministries. Every ministry is rooted in a charism and each Christian derives from baptism some charisms which lead to ministry; each ministry performs some public service for the community to further the kingdom of God. "There are varieties of gifts but the same Spirit, and there are varieties of service (ministries) but the same Lord, and there are varieties of working, but it is the same God who inspires them all in every one" (1 Cor 12:4-6). Today, ministry could also be considered in a more informal, interpersonal way, as when we offer support to others by our daily words and acts of mutual kindness and encouragement.

Jesus interpreted his life and work as a service: "The Son of Man has not come to be served but to serve—to give his life in ransom for the many" (Mark 10:45). And that was the test and criterion of the work of all who followed him. Since the beginning of the Church ministries arose to meet the needs of the community—as they did in every subsequent age. Paul saw his own ministry as preaching the "Good News" of righteousness by faith together with reconciliation through the Cross and resurrection of Jesus. And he pointed to the community endowed with a great variety of gifts and services with a multiplicity of ministries such as prophesy, teaching, preaching, healing, speaking in and interpreting tongues, distinguishing of spirits, etc. All are gifts of the Holy Spirit and are given for the building up of the gathering (*ekklesia*) or the community.

In the first Christian centuries when the Church spread to all corners of the known world, the need for leadership and administration arose, and the ministry of leadership evolved in diverse ways in different cultural religions. Structures became more defined; we read Ignatius of Antioch (d. 125) stressing that the welfare of each Church called for an *episcopos* (an overseer or bishop), *presbyteroi* (elders) and *diakonoi* (ministers). However, then and afterwards, the ministries of leadership and administration went hand in hand with the charismatic offices of apostle, prophet, and teacher.

Century after century a plethora of ministries arose to meet the needs of the people in changing times. During the persecutions the ministry of confessors/martyrs arose, and their courage and fidelity were inspiring examples for a suffering people. Later, monastic communities often ministered to liturgical, spiritual, and educational needs. With the rise of the cities in the eleventh and twelfth centuries a variety of new ministries arose to meet urban needs: nursing the sick, housing and feeding the poor, burying the dead during frequent plagues. During the twelfth and thirteenth centuries, the rise of the mendicant orders led to a needed revival of preaching and to an enlivened call for reform in the head and members of the Church. From the late Middle Ages to the post-Reformation era, new ministries catered to all areas of education, and new conditions called for vast changes and innovations to meet and serve the spiritual and material needs of the times.

Even in bleak periods the Spirit moved the waters. From the beginning of the nineteenth century, through Vatican I (1869–1870) and its aftermath, right up to Vatican II, the official Church eschewed all contact and dialogue with new democratic, nationalistic, and economic movements. And its condemnatory attitudes, coupled with a restrictive ecclesiology, tended to treat all ministries from a confining clerical viewpoint. Yet it was a period of unprecedented missionary expansion, and new congregations, many dedicated to the education and medical care of the underprivileged, mushroomed; and the laity bore Catholic witness in the trade union movement and in other social and economic struggles. Many lay ministries—such as the Catholic Worker Movement and the Legion of Mary—flourished despite clerical disapproval.

A new era was ushered in by Vatican II (1962–1965), with its fresh view of the nature of the Church and the mission of all its members and with the updating and reform of many aspects of Catholic life. A new day arrived for the laity for whom new ministries sprouted in the liturgical, missionary, educational, and administrative fields. The role of women changed, but many felt there were still miles to go. An unforseen phenomenon, without precedent in history, cast all questions and debates in a new and uncertain context: priests and religious left the ministries in large numbers, and vocations to the priesthood and religious life dried up. It is a new era; and the Spirit will lead God's people to new ministries and to changes which Vatican II did not even consider.

MICHAEL GLAZIER

See also LAITY, THEOLOGY OF THE; MINISTER; PRIESTHOOD, THE MINISTERIAL.

MINOR ORDERS

The four minor orders were the primary and preparatory ministries received by a candidate for the priesthood. They were porter, lector, exorcist, and acolyte, and were clearly distinguished from the major orders of deacon, priest, and bishop. In 1207 Pope Innocent III added subdiaconate to the list of major orders, though the Eastern Church did not follow this change.

The earliest extant reference to the minor orders occurs in a letter from Pope Cornelius to Fabius of Antioch in 252. Here subdiaconate was still considered a part of the minor orders. The conferral of minor orders was substantially different from the conferral of major orders. The West followed the directives found in the *Statua Ecclesiae Antiqua* (ca. 500). The rite consisted of a blessing and a handing over of instruments proper to each office. Over the course of time the liturgical functions of those invested with minor orders were taken over by priests, and the minor orders themselves became steps toward the priesthood for students in seminaries. In 1972 Pope Paul VI in *Ministeria Quaedam* abolished the minor orders and replaced them with the ministries of lector and acolyte, which are not considered orders at all.

ANTHONY D. ANDREASSI

See also SACRAMENT OF ORDERS.

MIRACLE

In the modern Western tradition a miracle is an event that breaks through or surpasses the laws of nature. The Bible assumes a broader definition expressed by the terms "sign" and "wonder," which refer to those extraordinary occurrences that allow one to surmise that God is at work. Biblical miracles include unexpected recoveries from illness, reversals in battle, and sudden storms.

In the Old Testament the Exodus from Egypt is surrounded by miraculous events (the ten plagues) and results in Israel's liberation from bondage and the journey to the Promised Land. The Exodus taken as a whole and in its parts was looked upon as the work of God and thus is the great sign in the Hebrew Scriptures. Moses performed signs in Pharaoh's court (Exod 7:8-13), and at Joshua's word the sun is said to have stood still (Josh 10:12-13). But the most spectacular miracle workers of the Old Testament are the prophets Elijah and Elisha whose exploits are recounted in 1 Kings 17–2 Kings 13.

The Gospels present Jesus as a healer and exorcist, as transcending the laws of nature (walking on water, stilling a storm, etc.), and restoring dead people to life (Lazarus, the son of the widow of Nain, Jairus' daughter). His resurrection from the dead is the New Testament counterpart of the Exodus as the great sign of God's power. The oldest gospel traditions connect the mighty works performed by Jesus to his preaching of the kingdom of God (Luke 11:20/Matt 12:28; Matt 11:21-22). Even Jesus' opponents admit his power as a miracle worker. They contest only the source of his power: Was it from God or Satan? (Matt 12:22-24). Jesus' miracles generally respond to human needs, demand faith on the part of the recipients, and serve a didactic purpose. Jesus acts by means of his own power (not simply as a mediator), and his miracles are signs that in him the reign of God is breaking into the present age.

In antiquity miracles were associated with the Jewish rabbi Hanina Ben Dosa, Apollonius of Tyana, Alexander the Great, and many other extrabiblical figures. Throughout Christian history great saints such as Francis of Assisi performed marvelous actions that were regarded as miracles. Miracles have been verified, after careful scrutiny, to have occurred at such holy places as Lourdes and Fatima. Canonized saints are acknowledged officially to have been instruments of God's power manifested by miracles. Before their canonization at least two miracles, granted through their intercession, are required. Christian miracleworkers reflect the holiness and power of God and Jesus his Son.

Philosophical skeptics regard miracles as impossible but Catholic theology contends that miracles can and do take place. Some of the philosophical objections arise from an outmoded and mechanistic view of nature. Nevertheless, even believers should maintain a cautious prudence about the extent to which God works miracles directly or indirectly (through secondary causes).

The miracles narrated in the Gospels are often adduced as proof of Jesus' divinity, on the grounds that only God could do what Jesus did. Current Catholic theology following the biblical tradition, however, looks on Jesus' miracles primarily as signs pointing to his identity as the one sent from God and as manifestations of God's reign breaking into the present.

DANIEL J. HARRINGTON, S.J.

See also CANONIZATION; CRITICISM, BIBLICAL; THEOLOGY, BIBLICAL; SAINTS.

MIRACULOUS MEDAL

An oval medal bearing the image of the Blessed Mother. In November of 1830, Our Lady appeared to St. Catherine Labouré, a Daughter of Charity of St. Vincent de Paul in Paris, and revealed the medal's design. On the front side, Mary is shown standing on the globe of the earth, with arms outstretched and rays of light emanating from her hands; the words "O Mary, conceived without sin, pray for us who have recourse to thee" and the year "1830" are inscribed along the periphery. The reverse side portrays the "M" of Mary at the base of the cross of her Son; below this are depictions of the Sacred Hearts of Jesus and Mary. Around the edge, twelve stars—possibly symbolic of the "crown of twelve stars" written of by St. John (Rev 12:1)—are engraved. The medal is called miraculous because of the numerous miracles associated with it. It is regarded by the Holy See as an object through which devotion to Mary may be practiced.

JOSEPH QUINN

See also DEVOTIONS.

MISHNAH

See TALMUD.

MISSIOLOGY

See EVANGELIZATION.

MISSION

In its general sense mission refers to the sending of someone to do something on behalf of another. In Catholic usage the word has three particular applications. In the first place the term is used for the redemptive task of Jesus and of the Church in the world. In the second place it refers to the official designation of individuals or congregations to carry the Good News and saving presence of Christ in his Church beyond the boundaries of present membership. In this case the term is often, but not always, used territorially, as in the term "the foreign missions." A third use applies the word "mission" to an intensified period of preaching and pastoral activity among those already Church members, as in "parish mission." This usually involves a team of preachers coming from outside for a week or so, holding devotional services with long sermons and instructions, making themselves available for the sacrament of penance if ordained, and possibly visiting homes of parishioners. Parish missions of this post-Tridentine type are less frequent since Vatican II when lay participation in parish life, worship and ministry has been far more active, and adult education, RCIA, bible studies, and prayer groups are going on continuously.

MONIKA K. HELLWIG

See also EVANGELIZATION; MISSIONARIES (OR MISSIONERS), COMMUNITIES OF; MISSIONS, CATHOLIC, THE MODERN PERIOD.

MISSIONARIES (OR MISSIONERS), COMMUNITIES OF

Since apostolic times, missionaries have left home and country to bring the gospel to people who knew not Christ. The apostles and Paul set examples and left no doubt that evangelization was a focal facet of the Church's mission, answering the call of Jesus to teach all peoples (Matt 28:19; Luke 24:47). Missionary work became an accepted part of the vocation of the early religious communities, and in the eighth and ninth centuries we see Irish and English monks working to Christianize Europe. Such activity greatly increased with the arrival of the mendicant orders, the Franciscans and the Dominicans, in the thirteenth century. Until the Reformation missionaries usually followed the colonizers, and, apart from preaching the gospel, they were a moderating influence on the methods of colonization.

With the foundation of the more active orders, such as the Jesuits, the Redemptorists and the Passionists, missionary activity increased greatly and regular communities were established in mission territories. In time, congregations such as the Holy Ghost Fathers, the White Fathers, the Scheut Fathers and others were established for the sole purpose of bringing the gospel to pagan regions, especially in Asia and Africa. In this century congregations, whose members are canonically secular priests, have played a distinctive role in Catholic missionary activities. Among these are: the Maryknoll Missionaries; the Mill Hill Fathers; and the Society of St. James the Apostle, founded by Cardinal Cushing of Boston. Many other religious congregations, such as the Kiltegan Fathers and the Columban Fathers, train their members to spend their lives as missionaries in Africa, Asia, or, more recently, in South America.

This century saw the spectacular rise of a plethora of congregations of women religious—such as the Medical Missionaries of Mary and the Maryknoll Sisters—devoted exclusively to education and medical work in mission territories. They have changed the face of Catholic missionary activity, and they foreshadowed the expanding role of women in the Church. And, more than ever before, associations of lay men and women are becoming an accepted part in Catholic missionary work. Such groups come from all countries where Catholicism is concerned and vital; among their growing number are the Maryknoll Lay Missionaries working in sixteen countries; Lay Mission Helpers/Mission Doctors, helping in eight countries; and the Jesuit International Volunteers, now in six countries.

MICHAEL GLAZIER

See also MISSION.

MISSIONS, CATHOLIC, THE MODERN PERIOD

The foundation of the Congregation for the Propagation of the Faith (Propaganda) in January, 1622, ushered in a new era in Catholic missions. This article surveys the areas under Propaganda's direction up to Vatican II.

Prior to Propaganda's foundation, missionary activity was the preserve of the great religious orders who had received missionary mandates and special papal indults for their work. The traditional mendicant orders had been joined in this work by the Society of Jesus (Jesuits) founded in 1534.

Rome's writ did not account for much in these colonies where royal patronage held supreme. In the overseas dominions of Spain and Portugal, missionary activity was controlled by directives from Madrid and Lisbon.

Propaganda would face the political opposition of Spain and Portugal and the intransigence of missionaries on site, exempt religious for the greater part, who did not take kindly to the intrusion of what was perceived to be, and was in fact, a centralizing agency for the development and control of missionary activity worldwide.

Propaganda's first secretary, Francesco Ingoli, undertook a survey of the missions which led him to the conclusion that the papal concession of royal patronage had outlived its usefulness and should be replaced by mission mandates directly originating with Propaganda as instrument of the papacy's missionary responsibility. The agent of the new missionary approach would be vicars apostolic, immediately dependent on Rome for their missionary mandate and jurisdiction, enjoying the same rights in their missions as residential bishops.

Spain and Portugal did not surrender easily; their South American territories never came under Propaganda while Portuguese padroada in the Far East was hotly contested for centuries. Propaganda supervised those countries where the Catholic hierarchy was not yet established or where, if it was established, the life of the Church was considered to be in its infancy or in a period of regression. Asia and Africa with some exceptions, North America and those European countries where the Protestant Reformation had been successful would come under its control. The United States of America remained under Propaganda until 1908. In 1627 Propaganda opened its own seminary in Rome, Collegium Urbanum, for the training of missionaries. A polyglot printing press, with possibly the greatest range of fonts then available, was also put into service.

In 1659 three vicars apostolic were appointed to the Far East, the first expression of Propaganda's new approach. They were also the beginning of a new missionary organization, the Parish Foreign Mission Society. What was unique to this society was that it was composed of secular priests devoted exclusively to missionary work. Originating in the combined efforts of the French clergy and laity, it set up a missionary seminary to support the newly erected missionary vicariates in the Far East. Formally erected in 1660 the Paris Foreign Mission Society would be the model of missionary work for years to come.

While the Parish Foreign Mission Society and others modeled on it would be the wave of the future, the older established religious orders continued to deploy personnel both in areas subject to Propaganda and the Spanish and Portuguese colonies. The annals of Jesuit missionary enterprise in these decades are superb. They began a unique public relations effort in popularizing and gaining financial support for their missions: *"Lettres edifiantes et curiesuses."*

Tragically, Jesuits and Dominicans were pitted against each other in the celebrated Chinese Rites controversy. The Jesuits Alessandro Valignano and Matteo Ricci applied the concept of cultural accommodation in their work, an approach first mooted by St. Francis Xavier. This approach became a source of division, initially between Jesuit and Dominican, and soon divided the Catholic world. The controversy was officially closed by Pius XIV in 1742 with the most stringent prohibitions against the use of certain rituals in honor of Confucius and family ancestors. A cloud was cast over the possibility of accommodation and inculturation which remained for the next two centuries.

The suppression of the Jesuits by Pope Clement XIV in 1773 removed with one stroke a cadre of what was best and bravest in mission history. While European religio-political considerations were dominant in the decision, especially the power of the Bourbons, the success of the Jesuits in South America had made many enemies. When the French Revolution followed (1798) a mission era came to an end.

Phoenix-like, a new beginning arose from the bloody ruins of the French Revolution and the despotism of Napoleon, who had dissolved Propaganda in 1808 and suppressed the missionary societies the following year.

The restored monarchy in the person of Louis XVIII re-established the Parish Foreign Mission Society, the Seminary of the Holy Spirit, and the Congregation of the Mission (Vincentians or Lazarists) in 1815 and 1816. It is arguable that more important was the founding of the Association for the

Propagation of the Faith in 1822 by Pauline-Marie Jaricot. With its publication *Nouvelles des Missions* changed to *Les Annales de la Propagation de la Foi* in 1825, not only was the literary tradition of the Jesuit "*Lettres edifiantes et curiesuses*" continued but the association tapped into new financial support among the middle and artisan classes, replacing the traditional papal and aristocratic sources now greatly depleted.

While Propaganda was re-established in 1817, it only came to exercise its crucial and decisive role in the direction of Catholic missions with the appointment of Cardinal Cappellari as prefect in 1826 and his election as pope some four years later as Gregory XVI (1830–1846).

Propaganda gave formal support to the new Association for the Propagation of the Faith, recommending it to all the bishops of the world. While Rome had some reservations that the Association might favor French-directed missions to the disadvantage of others, its suggestion that Rome should make proposals as to the distribution of various monies was rejected. A certain tension remained between Rome and Lyons, the Association's French headquarters; eventually the headquarters was removed to Rome in 1922.

In an attempt to deny any lingering state or royal patronage, missions technically under Portuguese bishops, frequently unappointed or absentee, were now placed under Propaganda and given to new missionary societies. Seventy new mission jurisdictions were erected and placed under the control of missionary societies headed by clerics immediately dependent on Propaganda. Propaganda favored the new missionary societies as being more in tune to its ways as against the older orders "with their entrenched traditional allegiances and territorial interests."

Ironically, France now attempted to create its own royal patronage abroad. Its first attempt was in Senegal and it would seek to extend an honorary protectorate in the Near and Far East. Rome insisted that the Seminary of the Holy Spirit founded by the French monarchy for the provision of priests in the colonies should be joined to the new missionary congregation founded by Fr. F. Libermann, again showing its preference for the new societies.

As Spain and Portugal began their decline as world powers, Britain and Holland expanded worldwide as did France. Britain expanded into the Indian subcontinent. Gregory XVI reorganized the Church in India with a view to limiting the exercise of Portuguese patronage to the old diocese of Goa, Cranganore, Cochin, and Mylapore. The vicariate of the Old Mogul was renamed Bombay and new ones, Madras and Bengal, erected. These were headed by Irish clergy, regular and secular, who as British subjects were acceptable to the British administrators. The movement of Irish clergy to India was part of a wider missionary interest and activity that occurred in Ireland after the granting of Catholic Emancipation (1829).

Irish clergy were appointed to head up missions throughout the English-speaking world, missions directly dependent on Propaganda: North America, West Indies, Australia, New Zealand. Many saw it as providential that a predominantly Catholic nation within the British Empire should be called upon to provide missionaries to the English-speaking world. All Hallows College, Dublin, opened in 1842 as a seminary devoted exclusively to the foreign missions. In time it concentrated on providing priests for those areas of the English-speaking world where the Irish had emigrated as a result of the famine. Five other Irish seminaries staffed by the secular clergy to provide for home and foreign missions became in time almost exclusively geared to foreign missions. A country with no political power had thrust on it a major spiritual vocation: "upon this country the obligation devolved in a most special manner of preaching the gospel to the many missions who acknowledged the Rule or speak the language of Great Britain" an 1849 report noted.

The nineteenth-century scramble for Africa gave rise to new international missionary societies, Missionaries of Africa (White Fathers), African Missionary Society (SMA) and the Spiritans or Holy Ghost Fathers (C.S.Sp.). French in origin, they would establish provinces outside of France and in time became responsible for vast missionary areas in Africa. The Irish C.S.Sp. province would direct the West and East African missions. Significantly, all of these new societies saw the absolute need of having missionary sisters as coworkers.

French dominance of the Catholic missions was challenged by Holland, Germany, and Ireland. Benedict XV's encyclical on the missions, *Maximum Illud* (in 1919), took to task the slowness in advancing indigenous clergy to the episcopate and the setting up of the local Church. It was interpreted as a veiled critique of French missionaries in the Far East. Benedict felt that love of the fatherland could work against the setting up of the kingdom of God abroad. On the other hand national feeling gave rise to specific national missionary societies. Examples from the English-speaking world: Maryknoll in the U.S.A. and in Ireland the Maynooth Mission to China (St. Columban's Missionary Society) and St. Patrick's Missionary Society. All were sprung from mission interest among the secular clergy.

In 1957 Pius XII in his letter *Fidei Donum* appealed to the older European American dioceses to release some of their clergy for temporary work on the missions. Cardinal Cushing of Boston responded the following year by founding the Society of St. James which would train secular clergy for work in South America. With the closure of mainland China to Catholic missionaries, many societies that hitherto had concentrated their personnel there, now began working in South America, Maryknoll and the Columbans (Maynooth Mission to China) being two examples. There was a widespread feeling that South America had been neglected. Even societies still working in Africa began to take up areas of South America. There was a sense of crisis about the future of the Church there.

The Catholic missions were and are funded by four pontifical associations: Society for the Propagation of the Faith which is organized nationally with directors in each diocese; Society of St. Peter for the training of local clergy; Missionary Union of Clergy and the Association of the Holy Childhood. Individual missionary societies have their own financial programs. Some national hierarchies have additional programs; the U.S. bishops have a collection for South America; Germany has Misereor for grants covering a wide area of mission work; Ireland has Trocaire (Mercy) for social development programs.

Accurate statistics from missionary personnel are difficult to come by. Between 1822 and 1963 the Parish Foreign Mission Society had sent 3,816 priests overseas. In 1976, Ireland had 2,353 priests, 3,122 religious sisters and brothers, and 328 lay missionaries working in Africa, Asia, South America, and Oceania (excluding Australia and New Zealand).

Vatican II would accelerate the indigenization of the hierarchies in the missions. The movement towards multimissionary groups working alongside local diocesan clergy, twinning relations between North American and European dioceses with mission ones, would become common. Some dioceses would send entire mission teams—priests, sisters, brothers, married and single laity—to their mission partners.

The older national hierarchies became conscious that their fellow countrymen on the mission were a very worthy expression of the home Churches' faith. The pastoral letter of the United States Bishops, *To the Ends of the Earth: A Pastoral Statement on World Mission* (1986), expresses a new understanding of mission; that the Church in its very nature is missionary.

In 1967 the Congregation for the Propagation of the Faith had its name changed to the Congregation for the Evangelization of Peoples. The name change bespoke a new era, a new opportunity and mood.

Since Vatican II *Ad Gentes* (The Missionary Activity of the Church), two vital papal encyclicals have been issued: Paul VI's *Evangelii Nuntiandi* (Announcing the Gospel) in 1975, and John Paul II's *Redemptoris Missio* (Mission of the Redeemer) in 1991. These emphasize the permanent priority of missions in the context of the overall evangelization responsibility of the Church.

Both pontiffs in their pastoral journeys overseas highlighted the missions in very dramatic fashion. Their teachings, while continuing to emphasize the importance of mission *ad gentes* (to the nations), examine the new frontiers opening in modern cities and many Christian countries needing reevangelization.

COLMAN M. COOKE

See also EVANGELIZATION; MISSION.

MITER

(Gk. *mitra,* "turban") The liturgical headdress worn by bishops, abbots, cardinals, and the pope. It is shield-shaped, usually of silk or linen, and often ornamented with gold embroidery; two fringed lappets hang down from the back. There are three types of miters—the precious, the golden, and the simple—

Miter, 14th century, Sixt, France

each worn according to the liturgical season or occasion. The simple miter is always white, and is worn when the prelate presides or assists at a funeral, during Lent, and on Good Friday. The miter is believed to be derived from the headdress of the high priest of the Temple in Jerusalem and the civil head garment worn by high-ranking officials of the Roman Empire.

JOSEPH QUINN

See also HIERARCHY; VESTMENTS, LITURGICAL.

MIXED MARRIAGE

The expression "mixed marriage" refers generally to a marriage between a Catholic and a non-Catholic. More precisely, in the canons of the Church, a mixed marriage is a marriage between a Catholic and another Christian, that is, one who is a baptized member of a Church not in full communion with the Catholic Church, e.g., Protestant or Orthodox. A marriage between a Catholic and a non-Christian, for example, a person of the Jewish, Muslim, or Hindu religions, or with a nonbeliever, is referred to as "disparity of cult," implying a greater and deeper religious difference.

From the earliest times the Church has discouraged mixed marriages. Church councils in the third and fourth centuries forbade marriage with Jews or heretics. After the Protestant Reformation mixed marriages became a more widespread concern because of their higher incidence in religiously mixed regions. The Church reacted with very severe prohibitions. However, the Church's discipline permitted exceptions, and, gradually, in religiously pluralistic countries, the exceptions became quite commonplace.

The reasons for the Church's negative posture towards mixed marriages are the foreseen danger to the faith of the Catholic partner and the children of the marriage, and the difficulties posed to the marriage partnership by the diverse religious and moral values of the two traditions. In other words, one partner might convert to the faith of the other or become religiously indifferent, or conflict might arise over issues such as Church attendance, family prayer, religious formation of children, abortion, birth control, or divorce.

The Church continues to discourage mixed marriages for these same reasons, but, in practice, routinely permits its members to enter into marriage with those of other Churches or faith traditions. The Church's disciplinary canons prohibit mixed marriages (cc. 1086 and 1124), but the local bishop is empowered to grant permission for the mixed marriage or a dispensation from the impediment of disparity of cult, provided that there is a just and reasonable cause for doing so, and provided that the following conditions are fulfilled: (1) that the Catholic party state that he or she will avoid the danger of falling away from the faith, and will do all in his or her power to have the children baptized and brought up in the Catholic Church; (2) that the other partner is informed of the promises required of the Catholic party, so that he or she is aware of the Catholic's obligations; (3) that both parties to the marriage are instructed about the essential ends and properties of marriage, and that neither party exclude them; the "ends" of marriage means that the marital partnership of the whole of life is ordered to the good of the spouses and the procreation and education of offspring (c. 1055), and the "properties" are unity and indissolubility, that is, fidelity and permanence (cc. 1125, 1055 and 1056).

It should be noted that "to do all in one's power" to baptize and rear children in the Catholic Church is a carefully crafted and nuanced expression of the obligation. It states a duty, but implies limits, a duty which is important, but measured. It means to do what one can, within reason, in this situation, with this partner, to see to the appropriate religious upbringing of the children.

Technically, although the procedure is the same, the action which the bishop takes is different depending on whether the Catholic's proposed marriage partner is a baptized Christian or a nonbaptized person. In the former case, the bishop is simply permitting a marriage which is prohibited, while in the latter situation he is granting a dispensation (which is a relaxation of the law in a particular case) from the invalidating impediment of disparity of cult. The difference is based on the Church's perception of greater danger and more serious potential problems in marriages between Catholics and non-Christians.

The Church's attitude and practices about mixed marriage, while still negative, were much mitigated after the Second Vatican Council. In the council, the Church formally acknowledged the spiritual value of other Churches and religions, and this compelled a modification in the rules for mixed marriage. The Church's ongoing ecumenical involvement will undoubtedly cause further changes in its mixed marriage discipline in the future.

Meanwhile, the Church enjoins upon its pastoral leaders a special solicitude for the families of mixed marriages (c. 1128). They should be nurtured and helped in their conjugal and family lives by their local parish or faith community.

Some see in the mixed marriage experience a very positive and precious ecumenical opportunity. The couple and their family can be a miniature model of the close and loving relationship which should exist between the faith traditions. Their marriage and family life can provide a living example of successful striving for unity in Christ.

JAMES A. CORIDEN

See also SACRAMENT OF MATRIMONY.

MODERNISM

Towards the end of the nineteenth century several theologians, Scripture scholars, and philosophers were open to contemporary processes for elucidating the meanings of revelation, tradition, faith, and dogma. Groping for a fresh apologetic that would vitalize Catholic culture, these scholars, intellectuals, and Church leaders were drawn to a developmental model of the Church in the world, one that was promoted by the theology of John Newman, the science of Charles Darwin, and the contributions of contemporary Protestant thought and scriptural exegesis.

The reigning theological synthesis in the Church was Neo-Scholasticism which is grounded in an essentialism that excluded the historical character of all human thought. Hence, the foundations of Christian faith, revelation, and dogma are immutable; they transcend historical time. Accordingly the Church is the repository of the eternal truths; new understandings of tradition are not derived from inductive methodologies of the scientist and historian but rather logical deductions derived from Aristotelian notions of abstracting from the particular the universal, immutable truths. Because the new apologetics explored the role of human experience, the immanence and transcendence of God, and the historicity of revelation, tradition, and the articulation of dogma, there was no common rhetorical ground for a dialogue between the two conflicting worldviews.

Modernism was a pejorative term coined around 1905 by Neo-Scholastic theologians who identified their synthesis of reason and revelation with orthodoxy. Maurice Blondel was suspect but never condemned for his notion of immanence central to his work, *L'Action.* However, Lucien Laberthonière, an Oratorian priest who worked with Blondel and elaborated on his thought, was condemned as a Modernist. Another French philosopher, Edouard LeRoy, was considered a Modernist for urging the renovation of the edifice of dogma on the basis of lived experience rather than deductive reasoning.

The most significant Modernist was the scriptural scholar Alfred Loisy, whose work *The Gospel and the Church* (*L'Evangile et L'Eglise*) placed the Church as historically conditioned in the post-apostolic age. Hence, there is a vast period of time between Jesus of the synagogue and the origins of the Church.

Another significant Modernist was the Anglo-Irish Jesuit George Tyrrell, who concentrated on the experiential basis of revelation and the metaphorical character of religious language. The generalist scholar, responsible for developing a self-styled network among several putative Modernists was the Austro-Scot Friedrich von Hügel. Among the sociopolitical Modernists were the Italian reformers R. Murri and E. Buonaiuti.

Modernism reached the intersection of "all the heresies" in 1907 when it was condemned by the papal encyclical *Pascendi Dominici Gregis,* preceded by the papal decree *Lamentabili.* Among the errors listed are "the principle of immanence and symbolism" (Tyrrell); "the church and the sacraments have been found mediating Christ" rather than identified with Christ's presence. "To the laws of evolution everything is subject under penalty of death—dogma, Church, worship, the books we revere as sacred, even faith itself."

Modernism was primarily a European phenomenon, but as a spirit of liberal reform it was manifested in the United States. Among the scientists and theologians who promoted evolution as a vital force were the scientist Holy Cross priest-scholar John Zahm and the Sulpician theologian James Driscoll. Scripture scholars, such as the Sulpician Francis Gigot and priest-scholars Henry Poels and Charles Grannon at The Catholic University of America, were writing and teaching ideas congenial to the historical criticism of the Bible, e.g., the non-Mosaic authorship of the Pentateuch. Most of the American and many European scholars of the new apologetics contributed articles to the advanced theological journal *The New York Review,* founded at St. Joseph's Seminary at Dunwoodie, New York. Subtitled *A Journal of Ancient Faith and Modern Thought,* the *New York Review* commenced publication in 1905 and was abruptly terminated by order of the Apostolic Delegate in 1908. Approved by Archbishop James Farley, the journal published such articles as "The Spirit of Newman's Apologetics" by Wilfred Ward; "Consensus Fidelium" by George Tyrrell; and "Catholicity and Free Thought" by George Fonsgrive. James Driscoll, editor of the journal, had corresponded with Alfred Loisy and was eager to translate his work into English. Francis Patrick Duffy, later known as the World War I chaplain of the Fighting Sixty-Ninth, as late as 1907 quoted George Tyrrell. Duffy's article on "Does Theology Serve Religion?" was a lengthy analysis on the defects of Neo-Scholastic theology in elucidating religious truths to contemporary readers. Duffy admired Tyrrell's attack upon the arid mathematical logic of the theological manualists: "For such persons, religion has the same kind of interest as the multiplication tables and no more. . . ."

Edward Hanna, who later became archbishop of San Francisco, was instructed by Vatican authorities to explain his views published in an article for the *Review,* "The Human Knowledge of Christ." Because he had invoked a developmentalist notion of Christ's self-awareness, some officials at the Vatican doubted that Hanna should be elevated to the episcopate. It was the investigation of Hanna that highlighted the controversial character of the *Review* and led to its demise.

Driscoll, Duffy, Hanna, Gigot, and others do not entirely fit Pius X's definition of Modernism. However, in the sense that they were promoting a new apologetic informed by modern ideas of experience, evolution, and historical criticism, they were in opposition to the Neo-Scholastic synthesis upon which *Pascendi* was based. In that sense they were Modernists.

There were only three self-proclaimed American Modernists; John R. Slattery, William L. Sullivan, and Thomas J. Mulvey. The latter two were associated with *The New York Review.* Mulvey, a priest of the diocese of Brooklyn, had written a book-review article, but Sullivan, a Paulist priest who left the Church in 1910, had published an article in the *Review* which extolled the positive significance of Americanism. Later, he would represent the convergence of Modernism and Americanism, a theme that was particularly evident in his published *Letter to His Holiness Pius X.*

John R. Slattery, superior general of the Josephite Fathers when he left the priesthood in 1903, was disillusioned with the Church's slow pace at breaking down its own racism. As a Josephite, long committed to ministry of African-Americans, Slattery also articulated an Americanist vision and a Modernist critique of the Vatican's entrenchment in Neo-Scholasticism. Slattery ultimately became an agnostic while Sullivan became a Unitarian minister. Mulvey entered into a life of relative obscurity.

Americanism and Modernism stressed the need for a new apologetic derived from an historical understanding of the significance of the Church's adaptation to the spirit of the age. Modernists were in accord with the Americanist enterprise while many Americanists were in touch with European scholars associated with Modernism. Though both extolled a free Church in a free society and opposed the Neo-Scholastic synthesis, Americanism was a movement among priests and bishops while Modernism never achieved a unified strategy aimed at specific goals.

The anti-Modernists were certainly unified in the Vatican and perceived the conspiracy to be of such large proportions that the Vatican instructed local dioceses to form Vigilance Committees to censor any ideas resembling Modernist thought. An anti-Modernist oath was required by every priest as a symbol of his commitment to orthodoxy as it was articulated in the idiom of Neo-Scholasticism. The Americanist and Modernist impulse to fashion a new apologetics continued to have an impact as some of its adherents entered missionary movements at home and abroad; second-generation Americanists were associated with the National Catholic Welfare Council, where they promoted moderate reforms in an American-styled activist Church. Anti-Modernism and anti-Americanism finally withered away as the Second Vatican Council promoted a developmental model and apologetics suitable to the needs of local cultures.

CHRISTOPHER J. KAUFFMAN

See also AMERICANISM; LOISY, ALFRED FIRMIN; TYRRELL, GEORGE; VATICAN COUNCIL II.

MONASTERY

The fixed abode of a community of monks. The name is sometimes popularly extended to the residents of communities who are not monks, such as Franciscans, Dominicans, and Passionists.

JOAN GLAZIER

See also MONASTICISM; MONK.

MONASTICISM

General Notion

Monasticism in the broader, more popular sense is a term that designates a way or state of life followed by those (monks, nuns, monastics) who either alone or in community systematically order their whole existence to achieving a goal which they perceive to be their ultimate concern, i.e., that which they believe to be the "sacred" or the "holy." In this sense monasticism is a phenomenon that appears in some form in almost every religion known by the history and comparative study of religion.

In this broader meaning, therefore, anthropologists will speak of "monastic" groups of holy men and women such as the Essenes of early Judaism, the *sannyasis* of Hinduism, the *bhikkus/bhikunis* of Buddhism, and even the *sufis* of Islam. Within Christianity as well the term will be broadly applied to all who follow a specialized religious vocation, including canons regular (Augustinians), mendicant friars (Dominicans and Franciscans), and members of religious societies such as the Jesuits. This article will be primarily concerned with those Christian movements that historians call monastic in a more technical and juridical sense of the term, although admittedly, the distinction is not clear-cut nor, in some cases, easily determined.

Origins of Christian Monasticism in the East

Christian monasticism, as a distinct movement within the early Church is first most clearly revealed in the second half of the second century, about the time the major persecutions of the Church are coming to an end. The principal spark that sets the movement ablaze seems to be the writing of St. Athanasius, the bishop of Alexandria, Egypt (ca. 296–373), entitled *The Life of Antony.*

In this work (soon translated into Latin), Athanasius states that the hermit who was to become known as the principal founder of Christian monasticism, St. Antony of the Desert (ca. 251–356), was motivated by the gospel injunction of Matthew 19:21, "If you wish to be *perfect,* go, sell what you have. . . . Then come, follow me." In time, this invitation to seek perfection was seen to be best achieved by a radical following of "the evangelical counsels," i.e., dedicating one's life to imitating Christ in his obedience, his celibate chastity, and his poverty. Perseverance in cultivating these virtues was soon to become the object of solemn (public) promises or vows.

According to Athanasius, Antony fled into the Egyptian desert to give himself over entirely to this struggle for evangelical perfection. He attracted many and soon the deserts of the eastern Mediterranean world (Egypt, Syria, Asia Minor) were populated by those who came to imitate him. Thus the Christian monastic phenomenon became a major feature of the Church's life.

The phenomenon soon manifests two forms that will be lasting characteristics of the life. Antony himself is the hermit, following the *eremitic* form of monastic life. His later contemporary, St. Pachomius (ca. 290–346), appears in the Thebaid region of the Egyptian desert with a way of living that places the emphasis on the common life the monk has with his fellow-monks, the forerunner of what becomes the *cenobitic* (*koinos bios,* common life) form of monastic life. In this latter form it is promoted with great success in Asia Minor by St. Basil the Great (ca. 330–379), whose rule is still the primary basis for those who follow the religious life in the Church of the East. His writings have great influence on the formation of monastic life in the West.

Origins of Monastic Life in the West

In Europe the beginnings of the monastic movement is given a strong sudden impetus in a manner corresponding to Athanasius' *Life of Antony* in the East: St. Martin of Tours (ca. 316–397) gains the traditional reputation as the first monk in the West by reason of the popularity of the book, the "Life of Martin," written by his friend, Sulpicius Severus shortly after Martin's death. After several years of living as a hermit, Martin took up residence in 361 at Ligugé, France, where gradually a group of monks gathered around him to live a semi-eremitic life.

Another very early monastic tradition also appears at the turn of the fourth/fifth century in a monastery found by St. Honoratus on the island of Lerins near Cannes. Lerins became not only a monastic center but an intellectual, cultural, and ecclesiastical center as well. From it many smaller and basically autonomous monastic houses arose, especially up and down the Rhone Valley.

Two other early fifth-century figures must also be noted as major influences on later monastic development: John Cassian of Marseilles (ca. 360–435) and St. Augustine of Hippo (354–430). Cassian's *Conferences* and *Institutes* reflect his experiences of many years spent in the East and constitute the major source of Eastern influence on the West, whereas St. Augustine in Roman Africa is the theological and spiritual source of several works of monastic legislation. He is the principal and most influential promoter of the cenobitic form of monastic life in the West. In his view, the exercise of charity within the brotherhood has a *practical* primacy of place over the person's search for individual perfection.

The Rule of St. Benedict

It is now recognized that the Rule of St. Benedict is only one among many in existence in the sixth century when it was written at Monte Cassino, Italy. Its outstanding characteristics of discretion and moderation, in conjunction with unique historical circumstances, led to its gradual adoption by the early ninth century as a dominant, almost exclusive rule for European monasteries, earning for Benedict of Nursia (ca. 480–540) the title of "the Patriarch of Western Monasticism." The basic facts concerning his life are to be found in only one source, the second book of the *Dialogues* of St. Gregory the Great (ca. 540–604), another "Life" of an outstanding monastic figure that exerts enormous influence on subsequent tradition.

Benedict's Rule, drawing freely from earlier authors (especially Basil, Cassian, Augustine, Caesarius of Arles, and the anonymous *Regula Magistri*), places great stress on the cenobitic character of the monastic life. It requires from entering candidates promises (later solemnized and legalized as vows) of obedience, stability, and *conversatio morum* (a much

Abbey of Cluny, reconstruction, ca. 1157

discussed phrase commonly translated today as "the monastic way of life," but cf. Phil 3:20, "citizenship" or "commonwealth"). The tradition that stresses the evangelical counsels of poverty and chastity seems implicitly presupposed within the Rule but is not mentioned explicitly.

As a literary genre, the monastic rules written during this era intend to be a codification of practical and specific customs and usages prevailing in a particular house, regulating or directing the lives of those who are living in that house. The genius of Benedict's Rule seems to be that in great part it admits of a more generalized adaptation to a larger number of varying circumstances. Its spiritual teaching, presented basically as the motivation for the particular practices, is to be found primarily in the Prologue and in the first seven of its seventy-three chapters. It is a Pauline-Augustinian view of the Christian (monk) imitating Christ's humility and obedience against Adam's pride and disobedience.

Later Monastic Developments

While the monastic movement in Europe was generally developing in a way that would lead to the gradual ascendancy of the Benedictine cenobitic form of observance, another powerful influence appeared in the late sixth and early seventh centuries in the form of Celtic monasticism in Ireland, Scotland, and England. St. Columban (ca. 543–615) and his followers, following the pilgrim-monk ideal of Celtic practice, traveled extensively throughout the continent, founding numerous monasteries which, however, during the Carolingian reforms of the late eighth and early ninth centuries adopted the Rule of St. Benedict as their norm.

From about the end of the eighth century until the beginning of the thirteenth century the monastic influence upon mainstream cultural and social European history is so extensive that these years are often justly referred to as the Benedictine centuries. During this time some rather substantial modifications in monastic institutions took place, the most outstanding of which may be briefly glimpsed in the principal collective reform movements that occur periodically. These often begin in a single monastery and then radiate from it as a center to form a grouping of satellite monasteries with common ideas about how the monastic charism is to be realized at a particular time in history.

Thus, for example, the foundation in 910 of the monastery of Cluny in France led to a Cluniac "order" that for a time constituted the most powerful reforming influence in the Church of its time. In the eleventh century the founding of the Camaldolese and Carthusian Orders represented a more eremitic and strictly contemplative life style. In 1098 the monastery of Citeaux, soon to become the motherhouse of the Cistercian Order, was founded. In 1662 a reform of that same order led to the formation of the Cistercian Order of Strict Observance, the Trappists. Later developments led to the formation of monastic congregations, over twenty of which now form the Benedictine Confederation with its administrative headquarters at the Collegio di Sant' Anselmo, Rome.

The first Benedictine monastery in the United States was founded in 1846 by Boniface Wimmer. This monastery, later to be St. Vincent's Abbey, Latrobe, Pennsylvania, was to become the motherhouse of numerous daughter houses that today form the American-Cassinese Benedictine Congregation. In 1851 Sister Benedicta Riepp and two other nuns from St. Walburga's Convent in Eichstätt, Bavaria, established the first U.S. Benedictine monastery for women, St. Mary's, Pennsylvania. It too became the source of other U.S. foundations.

In 1854 monks from Einsiedeln, Switzerland, founded St. Meinrad's Archabbey in Indiana, the first of what was later to be the Swiss-American Congregation. Swiss Sisters from Rickenbach arrived in Missouri in 1874 and soon after other monasteries for women of Swiss origin formed into congregations. Today monasteries of other congregations (English, Ottilian, Belgian, Camaldolese, Sylvestrine) are also to be found in the U.S.

DONALD GRABNER, O.S.B.

See also ABBESS; ABBEY; ABBOT; MONASTERY; MONK; RELIGIOUS LIFE.

MONK

A man who by taking vows binds and commits himself totally to the monastic life. In the Eastern Churches all male religious are monks; in the Western Church, only members of the following orders are monks: Benedictine, Camaldolese, Vallambrosan, Sylvestrine, Olivetan, Cistercian, and Carthusian.

JOAN GLAZIER

See also BENEDICTINES; MONASTICISM; RELIGIOUS ORDERS.

MONOPHYSITISM

See HERESY/HERETICS.

MONSIGNOR

(Ital. *monsignore,* "my lord"—distinct from feudal usage) An ecclesiastical title of honor bestowed on priests and prelates by the pope. All bishops and archbishops are entitled to it, but it is used more commonly to distinguish certain priests whose faithful and abiding service to the Church has gained them approbation from the Holy See. Monsignori may wear distinctive vestments similar to those of bishops.

JOSEPH QUINN

MONSTRANCE

(Lat. *monstrare,* "to show") The sacred vessel used for exposing the Blessed Sacrament for veneration, as during solemn Benediction or other ceremonies of Eucharistic devotion. It has a wide base, a stem with a knob, and a glass enclosure through which the Host (in its lunette) may be viewed. The enclosure is usually framed with ornamental rays of silver or gold.

Monstrance

JOSEPH QUINN

See also BENEDICTION (OF THE BLESSED SACRAMENT).

MONTANISM

This schismatic sect was started by a second-century Phrygian, Montanus, who with Prisca and Maximilla and some ardent followers claimed the gift of prophesy which involved special inspiration of the Holy Spirit and a new revelation. They forecast the imminent end of the world and urgently awaited the second coming. The sect followed a strict moral and ascetical code, mandating rigorous fasting, forbidding second marriages to the widowed, and ordering its followers not to flee for safety during persecutions. The Montanists also denied the power of the Church to forgive sin. They survived, fragmented and doctrinally divided, for over two hundred years.

The sect is best understood as one of the many apocalyptic groups which sprang up in the early Christian era and appeared, to a lesser extent, in later centuries. Montanism is also remembered for winning the allegiance of Tertullian, the brilliant third-century North African apologist, who was attracted by its theological rigorism and its ascetical severity.

MICHAEL GLAZIER

See also HERESY/HERETICS; SCHISM.

MONTE CASSINO

The principal monastery of the Benedictine Order was founded by St. Benedict in 529. He and his sis-

Monte Cassino, aerial view

ter, St. Scholastica, were buried there. It was destroyed by the Lombards ca. 585, by the Saracens in 884, by the Normans in 1046, and by the Americans in 1944, but was once again restored and reconsecrated by Paul VI in 1964. It was designated an Italian National Monument in 1866 with the monks acting as guardians.

JOAN GLAZIER

See also BENEDICTINES.

MONTESSORI, MARIA (1870–1952)

Born in 1870, Montessori was an Italian physician and educator who developed an educational system based on utilizing a child's creative abilities and innate desire to learn.

The first woman in Italy to graduate in medicine from the University of Rome (in 1894), Montessori began her career as an assistant doctor at the university's psychiatric clinic. There she worked with mentally handicapped children, and became interested in their learning difficulties. She began to devise a system which emphasized the use of simple materials to help the children develop complex skills. For example, she had her students work with numbered beads to familiarize them with mathematical concepts, and small pieces of wood designed to encourage left-to-right reading movements.

Innovative methods such as these, stressing individual effort and freedom rather than uniformity and discipline, would form the foundation of her system. Those who applied them found that young children, typically between three- and six-years-old, would not tire as easily. Nor would unruly students become restless and lose their focus, as they had in other educational settings.

Montessori herself was a lifelong student. While holding a chair in anthropology at the University of Rome from 1904 to 1908, she furthered her studies in philosophy, psychology, and education. She also lectured in pedagogy at the university from 1900 to 1907.

In 1907, she opened the first Children's House, a school dedicated to teaching the poor children of Rome; the success of this school led to the opening of similar ones soon after. Montessori spent the next forty years traveling throughout Europe, India, and the United States lecturing, writing, and instituting teacher-training programs. She left Italy permanently in 1934, due to her opposition to Fascist rule. She lived temporarily in Spain and Sri Lanka, and eventually settled in The Netherlands. She died in 1952.

Montessori's teaching methods are described in the following works: *The Montessori Method* (1912); *The Advanced Montessori Method* (1917–1918); *The Secret of Childhood* (1936); *Education for a New World* (1946); *To Educate the Human Potential* (1948); and *The Absorbent Mind* (1949).

Maria Montessori

JOSEPH QUINN

See also EDUCATION, PHILOSOPHY OF.

"THE MONTH"

Catholic monthly review published by the English Jesuits. It was founded in 1864 to examine historical and contemporary questions in the light of Catholic values. Apologetics, theological speculation, literary critique, and sociological research each predominated in the journal for a time; in the later nineteenth century it featured a fiction section. The refusal of *The Month* in 1876 to publish "The Wreck of the Deutschland," the greatest work of the Jesuit poet, Gerard Manley Hopkins, was invoked in later years to criticize both the journal and the Jesuits—perhaps unfairly, given the complexity of Hopkins' use of language even for sophisticated readers. In the years immediately preceding the Modernist crisis of 1907 *The Month* came under strong criticism from the Jesuit Generalate in Rome, where it was thought to be excessively liberal. Ironically, in the later part of the century *The Month* would carry much research material on Modernism as well as on the life and writings of Hopkins. After the Second Vatican Council it took on the task of explaining attitudes prevalent in various local Churches. Liberation theology, the Churches of Eastern Europe under communism, and the role of religion in the Northern Ireland troubles were subjected to repeated examination, generally from a questing and progressive perspective. On British public policy *The Month* stressed the need to measure economic theory and business practice by ethical standards. It also dealt in depth with questions related to marriage, education, and the numbers lapsing from active membership of the Church.

LOUIS McREDMOND

See also BRITAIN, CHURCH IN; SOCIETY OF JESUS.

MORAN, PATRICK FRANCIS (1830–1911)

Patrick Francis Moran was the dominant prelate in nineteenth-century Australian Catholicism. Orphaned at the age of eleven, he was given into the care of his uncle Paul Cullen, later to be the accepted leader of the worldwide Irish Church. The young orphan went to Rome, absorbing there a deep, but clerical, culture. All his life he pursued antiquarian interests, his best publications being collections of documents. Ordained priest in 1853, he remained in Rome as vice-rector of the Irish College and adviser to the papal curia. Returning to Ireland in 1866 as Cullen's secretary, in 1872 he became bishop of Ossory (Kilkenny), where he gained a reputation for canonical exactitude. He was a pattern Cullenite bishop.

In 1884 Leo XIII appointed him archbishop of Sydney and the next year made him a cardinal. The pope knew Moran from his Roman days, had been one of his doctoral examiners, and admired his talents. The cardinalate was a paternal gesture to New World Catholicism as well as a recognition of the importance of the Irish there. Moran's arrival had ended the pioneering English Benedictine oversight of Australian Catholicism. Moran and his fellow bishops, all from the same mold as he, stressed the identification of being Irish and being Catholic. Previously, St. Patrick's Day had been a lay, unchurched celebration; now it was taken over by clerics and made a Church feast day. Irish saints and devotional practices found a new home in Australia. Irish blood ran in the veins of most Catholics, who therefore welcomed this Hibernian emphasis. It gave them focus and cohesion in what they felt to be an unfriendly society.

Almost since the foundation of Australia as a white society in 1788, Catholics had been one-quarter of the population. They were the biggest single bloc standing out from the British Protestant monocultural majority. Moran's insistence on their Irish identity had a creative influence on the development of an Australian national sentiment away from the hegemony of the British Empire. For, encouraged by him, Catholics translated their love of Ireland into love of Australia.

His pastoral initiatives, such as the Manly seminary, cultural congresses, and a quarterly for priests, the *Australasian Catholic Record,* were on a national scale, never merely diocesan. He argued publicly for the federation of the then separate Australian colonies and stood for election to the convention which prepared a commonwealth constitution. Although defeated, his candidature showed his Australianity, as did his advocacy of an independent defense and foreign policy for Australia.

Moran saw himself as a civic leader with a duty to speak out on public affairs. Famously, he sided with the emergent trade union movement and the young Australian Labor Party. During the national maritime strike of 1890, he was cheered by a parade of strikers and their supporters. When criticized by conservatives for his pro-Labor stance, he replied that Australian "socialism" was sanitized and acceptable. Most Catholics were working people, which partly explains Moran's advocacy. But he also found reasons for his actions in traditional Church social teaching. When Leo XIII published *Rerum Novarum* in 1891 Moran was quick to claim it as validation of his own positions. His incursions into public affairs were treated seriously by the press and community leaders.

His death in 1911 put a stop to such public episcopal engagement from Sydney. In a pique over rejection of a favorite as his auxiliary bishop ten years earlier, Moran had nominated a pious nonentity, Michael Kelly, as his coadjutor with the right of succession. For the last ten years of his life, he regretted this choice. Kelly's reluctance to comment on public matters became a Sydney tradition.

R. EDMUND CAMPION

See also AUSTRALIA, CHURCH IN.

MORE, THOMAS, ST. (1478–1535)

English lawyer, scholar, and martyr, born in London. He grew up in sophisticated surroundings. His father was a judge; so also, until he became Archbishop of Canterbury, was Cardinal John Morton to whose entourage More was attached as a boy. After studying Greek, the Scriptures and other subjects at Oxford, More trained to be a lawyer at the inns of court in London and was called to the bar (i.e., licensed to practice as an advocate) in 1501. He vacillated for a time between making his career in the Church or as a civil lawyer. Having chosen civil law, he soon became one of the two under-sheriffs of London, an office involving many legal duties. He made a favor-

St. Thomas More, portrait by Holbein

able impression on Cardinal Wolsey and King Henry VIII, whom he served successively in a number of important appointments which could loosely be described as government ministries: these included the posts of Master of Requests, Treasurer of the Exchequer, and Chancellor of the Duchy of Lancaster. He was also a member of Parliament and for a time Speaker of the House of Commons.

Following the death of his first wife, More married again. An enduring image of his family circle has come down to us in the biography written by his son-in-law, William Roper, and in drawings by Holbein. The Mores were a lively, argumentative, intellectual group of people, among whom the questions of the day were discussed with insight and even humor. More was far ahead of his time in favoring the education of women to the same level as men. His daughter, Roper's wife Margaret, was unusually accomplished for a woman of her time, especially in her knowledge of the classics. More himself ranked with the most distinguished of Renaissance thinkers, breaking new ground with his imaginative *Utopia,* in which he described the degree of perfection to which society might be brought in a state built solely on natural law and philosophy.

Like his friend Erasmus, More believed with some passion in the unity of Christian Europe based on a common civilization and he deplored the warfare between European princes which weakened that unity in the face of the threat from Islamic expansion under the Turks. Luther's revolt and the subsequent religious divisions between Christians he found particularly deplorable because they went to the heart of what Christians until now had shared in common. His personal Catholic faith, deeply held and unwavering, strengthened these convictions and made it inevitable that he would be unable to concur in King Henry's repudiation of papal authority.

In 1529 Henry named More to be Lord Chancellor in succession to Wolsey, who had been dismissed when he failed to obtain the pope's approval for the King to divorce Catherine of Aragon. More tried to avoid the appointment but had to accept when the King agreed not to involve him in the divorce proceedings, on which More's opinion differed fundamentally from that of Henry. When the clergy declared the King to be supreme head of the Church of England in 1532, More resigned the chancellorship. He was summoned in 1534 to swear that he recognized the infant daughter of Henry and Anne Boleyn as heir to the throne. He was ready to do this, since Parliament had so decided, but like Bishop John Fisher of Rochester he declined to take the oath in the form in which it was worded because it also obliged him to reject the spiritual authority of the pope. He was thereupon imprisoned in the Tower of London.

Parliament then passed a body of legislation under which it became high treason, punishable by death, to refuse to acknowledge the King's title as Head of the Church. More remained silent when again asked to make this acknowledgment. He went on trial charged with treason and despite a skillful defense was found guilty. He was beheaded on Tower Hill, declaring on the scaffold that he went to his death as "the King's faithful servant, but God's first." He was canonized in 1935.

LOUIS McREDMOND

See also ANGLICANISM; BRITAIN, CHURCH IN.

MORMONS

See CHURCH OF JESUS CHRIST OF LATTER DAY SAINTS.

MORTAL SIN

See SIN.

MOSAIC

Mosaic, the adjectival form of the name Moses, is applied to (1) the covenant mediated by Moses between Yahweh and Israel at Mount Sinai; (2) the bodies of law contained in the Torah or Pentateuch; and (3) the five books of the Torah itself, as indicating their authorship.

(1) In Exodus 19–24, Moses is the intermediary between Yahweh and the refugee slaves who have been brought out of Egypt in the Exodus. The refu-

"Moses Receives the Tablets of the Law," manuscript detail

gees become a people, Israel, by entering into a covenant with Yahweh. After a theophany at Sinai, the mountain of God, Moses proclaims Yahweh's "words and judgments," commonly called commandments or laws, and the people swear an oath, sealed by blood sacrifice and by a meal, to obey and perform these laws. The event is recapitulated in the Book of Deuteronomy, where Moses recalls to the Israelites what their forebears experienced at the mountain of God. Owing to Moses' mediating role in this covenant, it is called the Mosaic covenant.

(2) The laws contained in Exodus, Leviticus, Numbers, and Deuteronomy are communicated to the people by Moses, and so these laws, including those enunciated after the Sinai covenant proper (Exodus 19–24), are termed Mosaic. Thus, they are given the authority of Moses, and more importantly are linked with the formative relationship with Yahweh called covenant. No aspect of life in Israel could be seen apart from that relationship with the God of the Exodus and the liberating and mediating function of his servant Moses (cf. Exod 14:31).

(3) Traditionally in Judaism and Christianity, until the beginnings of biblical scholarship in the last few centuries, it was taken for granted that Moses was the author of the Pentateuch. The textual basis for this assumption is found in Deuteronomy 31:24, ". . . Moses finished writing the words of this *tôrāh* in a book, to their end." Readers identified "this *tôrāh*" with the Pentateuch itself (the "five books of Moses"). More likely, however, the verse refers to the "words" (i.e., commandments) of the covenant, beginning with the "ten words" or decalogue, together with the other covenantal stipulations. Moses inscribes these covenant commandments in a book, "book" being a faulty translation of the technical term *sēper,* "account" or "listing." The reference is to the tablets of the covenant. Thus, the *literary* question of the authorship of the Pentateuch is far from settled by Deuteronomy 31:24.

That the Pentateuch, as the record of Yahweh's formation of the people Israel, can claim Mosaic *authority,* however, can be strongly argued, for the reasons sketched above under (2).

J.P.M. WALSH, S.J.

See also CRITICISM, BIBLICAL; PENTATEUCH.

MOUNT ATHOS

See ATHOS, MOUNT.

MOVABLE FEASTS

Yearly ecclesiastical feasts, the observance dates of which are determined by the Church calendar or some other cycle not related to the secular calendar (e.g., Easter—celebrated on the first Sunday after the first full moon following the spring equinox; and Pentecost—celebrated fifty days after Easter). They are also called "movable observances."

JOSEPH QUINN

See also LITURGY.

MOZARABIC RITE

Also called the Rite of Toledo, it is the form of Latin liturgy practiced on the Iberian Peninsula (comprising Spain and Portugal) from the earliest years of the Church through the eleventh century. Closely related to the Gallican and Celtic rites, it varies from the Roman Rite in several key ways: the formulas for Mass vary from day to day; catechumens and penitents are dismissed before the Liturgy of the Eucharist; and chants of Moorish influence are sung. It is now celebrated exclusively in a chapel in the Cathedral of Toledo. The Mozarabic marriage ceremony has been used in recent times in Spanish South America, and there is renewed interest among liturgists in incorporating Mozarabic elements into an indigenous Spanish Mass.

JOSEPH QUINN

See also RITES.

MURILLO, BARTOLOMÉ ESTEBAN (1617–1682)

The principal painter of Seville during the seventeenth century, Murillo was born in 1617. He originally followed the grand style of Zurbarán, another Sevillian, as can be seen in a group of eleven paintings he did for the Franciscans between 1645 and 1656. Murillo's mature work shows knowledge of

"The Immaculate Conception" by Murillo, detail, Prado Museum, Madrid

Rubens, van Dyck, Titian, and Barocci, and he eventually eclipsed Zurbarán with his own style (*estilo vaporoso*), noted for soft and merging colors and designs. His religious works concentrate on popular devotional subjects full of sentiment (most frequently *The Immaculate Conception*). His secular works favor sentimental scenes of peasant children, but he was also in demand as a portrait painter, a *genre* in which he also excelled.

DAVID BRYAN

See also ART, CHRISTIAN; ZURBARÁN, FRANCISCO.

MURRAY, JOHN COURTNEY (1904–1967)

Theologian. Born 12 September 1904 in New York City, son of Michael and Margaret (Courtney) Murray, died in New York City, 16 August 1967. After graduation from Xavier High School, Manhattan, he entered the Jesuit Order in 1920 and spent the next four years as a novice and student of classics at St. Andrew-on-Hudson, Poughkeepsie, New York. From 1924 to 1927 he studied philosophy at Weston College, Weston, Massachusetts, an academic division of Boston College, from which he received a B.A. (1926) and M.A. (1927). After three years teaching Latin and history at the Ateneo de Manila High School in the Philippines, he studied theology from 1930 to 1934 at Woodstock College, Woodstock, Maryland, where he was ordained priest on 25 June 1933 by Archbishop Michael J. Curley of Baltimore. Graduate studies in systematic theology followed at Rome's Pontifical Gregorian University, which awarded him the S.T.D. in 1937. From then until his death he was a member of the pontifical faculty of theology at Woodstock. He became editor in chief of the journal *Theological Studies* in 1941 and retained that position until his death. In 1951 to 1952 he held an appointment as visiting professor of medieval philosophy and culture at Yale University, and from 1966 until his death, he directed the John LaFarge Institute in New York City, a center for interreligious and interracial dialogue.

In the late 1940s, Murray was a leader in efforts to upgrade the level of theological courses in Catholic colleges, but gained initial prominence on the national theological scene through the literary debate in which he engaged until 1954, largely in the pages of *Theological Studies,* with Monsignor Joseph Clifford Fenton, professor at the Catholic University of America and editor of *The American Ecclesiastical Review,* Francis G. Connell, C.Ss.R., also of Catholic University, and Monsignor George Shea of Darlington Seminary in New Jersey. The issues were religious freedom and the limits of toleration; separation of Church and state; and whether an "ideal" relationship between the two could be, or ever had been, realized. Murray based his analysis of these themes on his reading of the social and political thought of Pope Leo XIII. Another theme was the limits of ecumenical cooperation. His adversaries, with strong Roman support from Cardinal Alfredo Ottaviani, Secretary of the Holy Office, held to what they considered traditional Catholic stands in the line of thinking of popes such as Gregory XVI, Pius IX, Pius X, and Pius XI. For them union of Church and state was an ideal, from which deviation was to be tolerated only when the ideal was practically unachievable, while ecumenical cooperation in the contemporary sense of the term was impossible for the "one true Church." After a series of confrontations and a requirement that writings on Church-state questions be submitted for Roman Jesuit censorship, Murray withdrew from the arena. His earlier articles were gathered and edited for Sheed and Ward by Philip Scharper, and appeared as *We Hold These Truths* (1961).

Murray remarked that he had been "disinvited" to attend the first session of the Second Vatican Council as a *peritus* or "expert," but, at the insistence of Cardinal Francis Spellman of New York, he was listed among the *periti* in April, 1963, and functioned in that capacity until the council ended. He was entrusted with rewriting the Declaration on Religious Freedom, and the final conciliar document, *Dignitatis Humanae* (7 December 1965), bears his strong impress. He contributed an introduction to the document in the collection edited by Walter M. Abbott, S.J., *The Documents of Vatican II* (1966),

John Courtney Murray, S.J.

and further reflections on the whole subject in *Problems of Religious Freedom* (1965) and *Religious Liberty: An End and a Beginning* (1966). An analysis of Murray's conciliar contribution by a former student using his council notes is Richard J. Regan, S.J., *Conflict and Consensus: Religious Freedom and the Second Vatican Council* (1967).

Murray, although a thoroughgoing Scholastic philosopher, was aware of the danger of archaism, the naive appropriation of formulas phrased in the concepts of past ages, and he was made alert to the importance of new data, and shifts in historical context and circumstances through his contact with Canadian Jesuit Bernard Lonergan, who promoted the idea of "historical consciousness" in contrast to the "essentialism" or "substantialism" of earlier theologians. In this approach, both were indebted to the British historian R. G. Collingwood, *The Idea of History* (1946) and other post-Enlightenment writers. During the 1950s Murray wrote on nuclear deterrence. Not a classic "cold warrior," he worried about what he saw as a national moral contraction in society. His positions have been reported on in William A. Au, *The Cross, the Flag and the Bomb: American Catholics Debate War and Peace 1960–1983* (1985). Believing that war and maintenance of the balance of power were realitities to be faced, Murray focused on responsible use of power and the moral limits of the use of force. For him, Soviet Communism marked apostasy from civilization, and he thought that only a power-oriented approach would work. He took issue with the "idealistic internationalism" of Pope John XXIII's encyclical, *Pacem in Terris,* and wanted a policy for limited nuclear war. Questions have been asked about Murray's views: did he lack critical perspective on United States capitalism? on the Cold War? Did he have a bias for liberty at the expense of justice? for United States social and economic arrangements and a lack of appreciation of contrary views?

Charles Curran has suggested that on some of these points Murray was more the natural law philosopher than the theologian (following in this his model, Leo XIII), but Curran admits that Murray did call for a more dynamic understanding of the natural law, and in this was influenced by his appreciation of the growth of historical consciousness (Charles E. Curran, *American Catholic Social Ethics: Twentieth-Century Approaches* [1982]). Leon Hooper has seen as crucial to Murray's thought his understanding of a radically social view of human dignity, which led him to religious ecumenism, the realization for the need of freedom within as well as for the Church, and the overriding necessity to achieve a renewed American consensus in both Church and society, the result of civic discourse among morally mature adults (J. Leon Hooper, S.J., *The Ethics of Discourse* [1987]).

The great achievement of Murray's life was Vatican II's Declaration on Religious Freedom, of which Bishop Donald Pelotte wrote, "More than anyone else, Murray was responsible for the best parts of the Declaration." For German Bishop Walter Kampe, Murray's "concern about civil rights and specifically, religious liberty," was "the American contribution to the Council." Even hardshell opponent Paul Blanshard conceded that Murray had built "verbal bridges to the modern world."

During the final two years of his life, Murray applied his theological principles of freedom to critical social, political, and moral problems of the times like racial discrimination, censorship, abortion, the population explosion, war and the antiwar movement, and the Christian-Marxist dialogue. He was one of two members of a presidential commission to advocate the legitimacy of selective conscientious objection to military service. In every discussion, his basic conviction was that freedom was the first truth about human beings, a positive value both personal and social, and to be respected, even at the cost of tolerating error and evil.

In mid-June, 1967, Murray suffered a serious heart attack. He had two earlier attacks in 1964 and had been hospitalized with a collapsed lung in Rome during the council's final session. He died suddenly in a taxicab in Queens, New York, while returning to Manhattan from a visit with his sister. An olympian, urbane man, generally thought of as aloof—his friends attributed it to shyness—formidable in debate and equipped with a sesquipedalian vocabulary and a dry sense of humor, Murray was a giant in his generation of American Catholic theologians. President Lyndon B. Johnson commented that his life "transcended the barriers of nation, race and creed." Speaking for the Holy See, Archbishop Giovanni Benelli paid tribute to him as one who "never stinted in his service of God, the Church and the Society of Jesus." For Charles Curran, Murray's "creative genius has made him the most oustanding Catholic theologian in the United States in this century."

JAMES HENNESEY, S.J.

See also CHURCH AND STATE; RELIGIOUS FREEDOM; SOCIETY OF JESUS; THEODICY; VATICAN COUNCIL II.

MUSIC AND WORSHIP

The Terms

Many terms have been used over the centuries to describe the music employed in the Church's worship. The most common of these are: Church music, liturgical music, religious music, and sacred music. Although often used interchangeably, these are not synonymous. The ancient designation *Church music* has come to denote virtually any music employed within worship during the history of the Christian Churches. *Liturgical music* is a more recent term, infrequently employed in the literature before this century. It came to prominence in the 1960s as a specific term for music integral to the reformed liturgy of the Roman Catholic Church after the Second Vatican Council. *Religious music* is a popular label for any music that is perceived to have an explicit or implicit religious theme, from Christian rock to Hindu chants. *Sacred music* is both the preferred term in universal documents of the Roman Catholic Church for music composed for "divine worship" as well as a generic term for religious music, especially that which is considered art music.

Joseph Gelineau (b. 1920) has been very influential in redefining Roman Catholic worship music in the West since the Second Vatican Council. It is especially his emphasis on liturgical music as music *of* the liturgy and not merely occurring *in* the liturgy which is pivotal for an adequate understanding of this term. In view of Gelineau's insight, liturgical music can be defined as that music which unites with the liturgical action, serves to reveal the full significance of the rite and, in turn, derives its full meaning from the liturgical event and not simply from its liturgical setting. The ability of this term to emphasize the fundamental link between music and the liturgy recommends its usage, and underscores the ambiguity of the more generic term sacred music. Some would suggest that the term *Christian ritual music* is preferable even to the term liturgical music because it captures the ritual essence of both our music and our worship. While Christian ritual music is sometimes preferred by specialists, liturgical music is the more common term.

The Relationship Between Music and Liturgy

The change in terms and the need for even further clarification in language is indicative of a more fundamental change that has taken place in the thinking about the relationship between music and worship over the last century. Key to this change was a 1903 declaration of Pope Pius X which noted that music was "an integral part of the solemn liturgy." The same document also noted that music was the "handmaid of the liturgy" and stressed the "active participation" of the faithful in the liturgy. These various statements, brought together in a papal document, contributed to new ways of thinking about the relationship between music and liturgy and the people's role in both. Such developments would eventually lead to assertions about the normativity of musical liturgy, and the ritual nature of liturgical music.

At the time that Pius X proclaimed the integral relationship between music and worship, many Roman Catholics were experiencing worship without music. When music was employed, it was often performed by the choir and not by the assembly. In a 1909 speech to the Congress of Catholic Action held in Belgium—which some consider to be the beginning of the liturgical movement in this century—Dom Lambert Beauduin popularized Pius X's call for the active participation of the faithful. As this call spread throughout Europe, strategies for implementation developed. One important strategy was the musical participation of the assembly in worship.

The musical result of this call and resulting strategy was not only a revival in Gregorian chant but the first step toward reintegrating the song of the assembly into the liturgy. Over the next few decades there evolved various liturgical forms—especially in Germany and France—which called for sung participation in the vernacular and, contrary to previous directives, were allowed by Rome. These included various forms of the "Low Mass" at which the people assisted with prayers and songs in the vernacular, as well as forms of the "High Mass" sung by the assembly both in Latin and in the vernacular.

Decades of experimentation in Europe and the United States, as well as the accompanying scholarly and popular writing, prepared the way for a series of official documents in the 1950s, 1960s, and 1970s that progressively redefined the relationship between music and liturgy. In 1955, for example, Pius XII issued *Sacred Music* which made great strides in emphasizing music's overall contribution to the liturgical action. In 1963 the Fathers of the Second Vatican Council approved the Constitution on the Sacred Liturgy [= SC]. Chapter 7 of this document outlined basic principles for music in the reformed liturgy, reiterating Pius X's position that music was to serve the liturgy and forms a necessary or integral part of the liturgy. According to this document, the basic reason for music's integral role in worship is its ability to unite with and serve the liturgical text. SC further recognized music's power to serve not only the word but also the whole of the ritual action. The distinction between solemn, high, and low Mass disappeared in the first edition of the *General Instruction of the Roman Missal* (1969). The 1972 document of the United States Bishops, *Music in Catholic Worship,* further eliminated the distinction between the ordinary and the proper parts of the Mass and outlined a new priority for singing the various elements at Mass.

The cumulative effect of the experimentation, writings, and official documents about music in the twentieth century was not only the affirmation that music should be an ordinary part of Roman Catholic worship, but the further awareness that music-making itself was worship. From this perspective, music is understood not simply as a pleasant yet dispensable adornment of more essential elements. Rather, music is understood as an ordinary, constitutive element of the ritual. The liturgy and its music are not two separate ritual entities, with distinct purposes and principles that can arbitrarily be separated, but are best understood as distinguishable facets of a single event. Roman Catholic worship after the Second Vatican Council is conceived as a fundamentally lyrical, musical event. Music provides something critical to our worship, that cannot be achieved with any other art form. From this perspective, musical liturgy can be considered normative.

The Functions of Music in Worship

While there might be widespread agreement about the need to integrate music into worship, and even agreement about the normativity of musical liturgy, there is yet enormous diversity in the types of music employed in worship as well as in the ways such music is utilized, and the effects of such music. This diversity may be explained, in part, by the often unspoken presuppositions people have about music's function in worship. While by no means an exhaustive listing, the following categories are one way to think about the different functions music fulfills in worship. These categories are not necessarily mutually exclusive, and often a piece of music fulfills two or more functions simultaneously.

The Aesthetic Function. There is an ancient tradition in Judaeo-Christianity for connecting the holy with the beautiful. That tradition asserts that God deserves the most beautiful works of art that humankind has to offer. The tradition further asserts that, besides being ultimate good or ultimate truth, God is ultimate beauty. From this perspective, it is appropriate—even necessary—to employ the most beautiful music possible in worship, as proper homage to God and as an appropriate reflection of God's own beauty.

The Diversionary Function. This capability is best explained by contrasting it with the enjoyment function. While the latter has as its purpose the inducement of pleasure, the diversionary function takes a different tack, and serves to eliminate boredom or monotony in the rite. Especially in transitional moments—like the collection—or at times of limited or imperceptible ritual action, music can serve as a temporary diversion in the rite.

The Emotional Function. As in other moments of our lives, there are some ritual moments when hope or joy or some other emotion is so profound that it cannot be expressed in words alone. At such times, music allows and even enables the community to express its feelings. A joyful organ postlude at the close of a marriage ceremony, or the saddening strains of a loved one's favorite hymn during the funeral liturgy help the community to express those human emotions that are an ordinary part of all worship.

The Enjoyment Function. Closely related to the previous two functions, is music's role as a source of enjoyment in worship. While some may believe that worship music is not supposed to be enjoyable—much less entertaining—in actuality, much worship music is chosen, at least in part, because it is pleasurable to hear or to perform.

The Involving Function. One of the basic premises of Christian worship, embraced again by the Roman Catholic Church after the Second Vatican Council, is that everyone at worship—including the assembly—is an important participant. In many of our rituals, however, there are a limited number of specialized tasks that need to be performed, some of which require particular gifts and/or training, such as preaching and prayer leadership. Music-making, especially singing, is one of the few ritual acts that can consistently and repeatedly involve all worshippers actively in the liturgy.

The Mood-Setting Function. Worship is capable of addressing a wide range of human experiences and emotions. These emerge in festival and ordinary time, in regular Sunday worship and once-in-a-lifetime gatherings such as weddings or funerals. Music is one of the ritual elements that enables a community not only to express but also to perceive the mood or ethos of the celebration, as well as its level of festivity.

The Movement-Enhancing Function. Like any ritual event, worship entails not only the speaking or singing of texts, but also requires a wide range of gestures and movement. Some of these, like processions, are clearly related to the dance in their regular rhythmicity. Music, an art form closely allied to the dance, has a special ability to support and facilitate such movements.

The Revelatory Function. While many people have religious experiences outside of worship, worship also is a place where believers encounter God. Such encounters can be aided or even triggered by the setting, an appropriate word, or a special ritual gesture. Music is one of those elements which not only facilitates religious experiences, but can actually mediate such experiences. Thus it is not only while listening to music in worship that some people experience God, but it is precisely through the music that such experiences occur.

The Text-Enhancing Function. Judaeo-Christianity takes texts seriously, and believes that God speaks through sacred words. Another belief in Judaeo-Christianity is that individuals and groups can speak directly to God through sacred words, which God is expected to hear. The sacredness of certain texts, and their power to mediate between God and the community, often requires an extraordinary quality of utterance and manner of performance. Music is a treasured vehicle for underscoring the sacredness of certain texts, and for highlighting their power.

The Liturgical Application

While it is possible for music to function many ways in our worship, there are consequences of these many functions. These consequences are related to an ancient principle of Christian worship which asserts that our prayer is foundational for our belief (the Latin maxim is *lex orandi, lex credendi*). This principle was reaffirmed in new language by SC which declares that the liturgy is the fount and summit of the Church's life: "The liturgy is the summit toward which the activity of the Church is directed; at the same time it is the fount from which all the Church's power flows" (SC 10). Thus, our worship both expresses and shapes our faith.

From this principle, it follows that music—as an integral element of worship—is an important vehicle for expressing and shaping our faith. Music has the power to express and shape faith because it is a dynamic symbol. Every symbol has this expressive-creative quality about it: the raising of our flag can express our national identity, but also can stimulate and renew that identity; the giving of a ring can both express one's love for another and also heighten and increase the love.

It should be noted that the expressive-creative ability of music, like that of other symbols, does not rely solely upon the conscious intention of the leader or participants in the symbolic event. Rather, the expressive-creative ability of every symbol is related to the participants and the nature of the symbol itself. For example, a man might want to express his love to a woman by giving her roses. The hoped-for effect from the roses should be delight and gratitude. The roses, however, were the favorite flower of the woman's recently deceased mother. Thus, instead of evoking delight or gratitude, they evoke grief and sorrow. The ambiguity of all symbols, including music, requires attention, therefore, not only to our intentions or hoped-for effect, but also to the symbols themselves and to the way they function.

Our previous list of some of the functions of music in worship underscores the ambiguity of the musical symbol. A music leader might select a piece of music for one hoped-for effect, while the music might achieve something completely different or even contradictory. For example, one might employ popular styles of worship music in order to increase the participation of the assembly. It is possible, however, that the music—which might sound like the top 40—communicates that worship, like one's favorite radio station, is essentially entertainment. On the other hand, one might select music that is beautiful according to "classical" standards, as proper homage to God and as an appropriate reflection of God's own beauty. Such music—often performed only by specially trained musicians—might communicate that authentic worship is performed only by the trained specialists, while ordinary people look on.

While there is no perfect solution to this dilemma, the U.S. bishops have offered useful guidelines for addressing this issue in their statement *Music in Catholic Worship* (=MCW, 1972). This document acknowledges the symbolic nature of worship in general, and liturgical music in particular. It further suggests that there is a three-faceted decision which respects the symbolic nature of worship, the symbolic nature of music, and people's experience of both. This is the liturgical-musical-pastoral judgment.

According to this judgment, one must respect the nature of the liturgy, the nature of the music and people's experiences of both. Liturgically, for example, SC calls for the active participation of the people (SC 14), and asserts that music has an important text-enhancing as well as ritual-enhancing function (SC 112). Musically, it is important to employ music of quality (MCW 26), but to distinguish quality judgments from stylistic judgments (MCW 28). Thus, the question is not whether to employ folk-style music or music written in the style of Mozart, but the quality of each according to its particular style. Pastorally it is necessary to recognize that people of different cultures, ages, geographic locations, etc., have different musical tastes and musical needs. These must be respected in order to enable people to enter into the liturgy, and pray as they are able.

Employing this musical-liturgical-pastoral judgment will not yield the same musical decisions in every place, nor completely resolve the continuous dilemma resulting from the various functions of music in worship. This three-faceted judgment can, however, provide communities a framework in which to address this dilemma with integrity.

EDWARD FOLEY, O.F.M. CAP.

See also GREGORIAN CHANT; LITURGICAL MOVEMENT, THE; LITURGICAL YEAR, THE.

MYSTERY (OF FAITH)

In common parlance, mystery denotes something hidden, beyond human ken, that can be known only if it is revealed by a superior power. Vatican I in its dogmatic constitution *Dei Filius* (1870) asserts against rationalism that "apart from what natural reason can attain, there are proposed to our belief mysteries that are hidden in God, which can never be known unless they are revealed by God." The council goes on to say that "even when they (i.e., the mysteries) have been communicated in revelation and received by faith, they remain covered by the veil of faith itself and shrouded as it were in darkness as long as in this mortal life 'we are away from the Lord; for we walk by faith, not by sight' (2 Cor 5:6-7)."

This heavily intellectualist understanding of mystery, while not incorrect, needs to be complemented by a more biblical and sacramental approach. According to Scripture, mystery refers to the plan or design God intends for humanity and the world. It is, as Ephesians 1–3 puts it, God's plan to sum up all things in Christ, to unite Jews and Gentiles through the Cross so as to form a new person and to reconcile them both to God. And since this plan is carried out by Jesus, the mystery is said to be "Christ in you, the hope of glory" (Col 1:27).

This biblical usage of mystery was continued in patristic times, only this time it is placed in the context of sacramental celebrations. Where Greek Fathers used the word *mysterion,* their Latin counterparts used either *mysterium* or *sacramentum.* Both baptism and Eucharist are called "divine mysteries." It is by means of the sacraments that the faithful are initiated into God's eternal plan of salvation realized in history by Christ.

Contemporary theologians such as Karl Rahner attempt to place mystery in the midst of human existence. Mystery is not something left over after everything else is known and hence obscure and dark and not relevant to us. Nor is it a series of propositions whose meaning is now unfathomable but will be made clear in beatific vision. Rather it is that by which everything is known and loved, the condition of possibility of our knowing and loving. It is the horizon toward which we transcend ourselves in knowledge and freedom. This act of self-transcendence is called "transcendental experience," an experience which is at the heart of human existence. It is, in other words, God as the incomprehensible. There are, therefore, not many mysteries. On the contrary, there is but one selfsame mystery, namely, God, who communicates Godself to us as Word and Spirit, in the incarnation and in grace, in history and in the beatific vision.

PETER C. PHAN

See also FAITH; REVELATION.

MYSTICAL BODY OF CHRIST

A term less common since the Second Vatican Council because the term People of God was preferred in the Dogmatic Constitution on the Church (*Lumen Gentium*). More common in the middle decades of the twentieth century, the expression is based on a metaphor frequently used in the letters of Paul in the New Testament (e.g., 1 Cor 6:15; 10:14-17; 12:12-30). What the metaphor is intended to express is the intensity with which the community of believers share the life of Christ and therefore share life with one another. The adjective "mystical" was introduced to stress that it is the life of grace that is shared in the risen Christ. When the term was reintroduced in the 1930s and officially acknowledged by Pope Pius XII in the encyclical letter, *Mystici Corporis* (1943), it was a first step towards a less juridical definition of the nature of the Church. The ecclesiology built on this term came to be linked with the liturgical movement because of the continuity of vocabulary and thought between this encyclical and one four years later, *Mediator Dei.* However, as biblical, patristic, and liturgical scholarship progressed and was more widely diffused, it became clear that although mystical body of Christ was a good and serviceable metaphor, it had limitations and needed the balance of other images, also drawn from Scripture.

MONIKA K. HELLWIG

See also CHURCH, THE; EUCHARIST; GRACE.

MYSTICISM

Scriptural Considerations

The terms "mysticism" and "mystical" (Greek *mystikos*) do not appear in the New Testament. The meaning of both terms in later usage derives from the term "mystery" (Greek *mysterion*), rooted in *myein* (Greek meaning "to close," e.g., the mouth or the eyes) which conveys the sense of something secret, hidden, or not readily accessible. Prior to the Middle Ages, the concept of a purely personal spiritual experience ordinarily associated with mysticism was largely unknown in Christian spirituality. And the substantive "mysticism," referring to a separate kind of activity or higher type of religious experience, was nonexistent.

In the history of Christian spirituality, mysticism has often been viewed as the highest expression of Christian prayer, the apex of the Christian life. In recent centuries mysticism has been associated with extraordinary phenomena such as the stigmata, levitation, visions, locutions, raptures, and healing powers. But such a view, prevalent especially since the seventeenth century, has tended to eclipse the earlier meanings of Christian mysticism. Contemporary developments in the study of Christian spirituality and mysticism have recovered the early biblical sense of the term "mystery." From this vantage, a proper understanding of mysticism entails nothing more or less than life in Christ. It is the full, conscious participation in the Christian mysteries. But however it is conceived within the Christian tradition, there is no strict equation between the mystical and the religious. The difference lies in that the mystical experience is subjectively and objectively more direct, even at times immediate.

New Testament perspectives on mysticism are rooted in the Semitic understanding of mystery rather than in the diverse Greek mystery religions. The Old Testament literature does not present a view of mystery as something altogether obscure and unknowable. Rather, mystery refers to a plan, specifically God's plan of salvation. In early Christian usage it describes the divine plan of salvation, previously undisclosed, now made manifest in the person of Jesus the Christ. Though the Synoptics and John develop this understanding of mystery, it is Paul who gives it greatest emphasis. In the Pauline view, God's plan is that Gentile as well as Jew be saved in Christ. This mystery, or divine plan, is so central to Pauline thought that it may be said to encapsulate for him the entire range of the gospel message.

Historical Developments

Writers during the patristic period keep this understanding of mystery to the fore. In patristic scriptural exegesis the focus was on discerning the unfolding plan of God rendered present in Christ and his saving mysteries. This presence was not limited to Scripture. Christ's mysteries revealed in Scripture were celebrated sacramentally. Further, for the early Fathers of the Church, it is Christ's presence in the sacraments, preeminently baptism and Eucharist, which is *the* Christian mystery. Participation in the sacraments thus constitutes the mystical life. And the height of participation in the Christian mysteries is union with Christ, to live "in Christ," so that Christ may be all in all.

This biblical and patristic understanding of mystery and mysticism is eclipsed by later developments. Beginning in the early Middle Ages, there are signs of a movement away from earlier meanings. In the twelfth century, there was an emergent awareness of the importance of the individual in Church and society. Though this must be distinguished from the "turn to the subject" in twentieth-century philosophical and theological reflection, the focus on the individual's own self-awareness and self-consciousness is one of the distinctive features of the age. Its influence is seen, for example, in the life and writings of Bernard of Clairvaux, who emphasizes the role of *cor, cordis affectus* in the Christian life. For Bernard and others in the early Cistercian tradition, the personal and affective dimensions of the individual's life play a central role in one's prayer. Though the proper focus in prayer here remains on the person of Christ, as well as upon Mary and the the saints, there is much greater attention to the ways in which the emotions or affections are aroused, stirred up, and ordered properly in the life of prayer. In later centuries the higher stages of prayer came to be viewed not so much in terms of union in Christ, but as that union is felt and experienced within the soul.

The personal and experiential elements of mysticism are also enunciated in the theology of Thomas Aquinas (d. 1274). He understood mysticism as the knowledge of God through experience. In Aquinas as well as in other medieval theologians there is recognition that the mystic's knowledge of God is distinct though not unrelated to the knowledge of God in and through faith. Without prejudice to the complexity of the issue, faith and theological reflection give access to knowledge *about* God, while mystical experience opens one to knowledge *of* God, in much the same way that poetry might inform one about the experience of love whereas the experience of being in love provides one with a different kind of knowledge of love precisely through the experience of it. It is this personal knowledge in and through experience that is to the fore in various understandings of mysticism throughout Christian history, even those of more systematic theologians like Thomas Aquinas for whom sober faith and reason are foundational to Christian life and practice.

Later writers in the Christian West emphasize the mystical difference more strongly. Within the same Dominican tradition as Aquinas, the writings of Henry Suso in the fourteenth century portray mysticism as a state of consciousness clearly surpassing ordinary Christian experience. A definitive move toward a modern understanding of mysticism is taken in the fifteenth century in Jean Gerson's definition of mystical theology as the experiential knowledge of God through the embrace of unitive love. But it is not until the sixteenth century, with the Spanish mystics Teresa of Avila and John of the Cross, that the modern Christian view of mysticism as experiential knowledge of God in and through love reaches classical formulation. On the heels of the centuries-long theological quibble over whether faith or love has priority in Christian life and prayer, the mystic John of the Cross boldly maintains: love knows.

The Spanish mystics Teresa and John maintain that extraordinary phenomena do not constitute the core of the mystic's experience. Both insist that such experience takes place and is authenticated in total self-abandonment to God in Christ through faith and love. And both advise caution in the face of raptures, locutions, and visions, which are no guarantee of authentic mystical experience. But because of the attention Teresa gives to extraordinary phenomena in recounting her own religious experience, particularly in the "sixth mansion" of her *Interior Castle,* she bolsters, perhaps inadvertently, the emergent understanding of mysticism as rare and extraordinary. And because of her vivid description of the various states of her interior life, she furthers a view of mysticism in which the psychology of the individual Christian is front and center. This attention to human psychology is also found in the life and legacy of another Spaniard, Ignatius of Loyola, which may explain the strong appeal of his *Spiritual Exercises* in the latter part of the twentieth century, a period unrivaled in its fascination with personalities and the psychology of the individual.

Understandings of the mystical life as altogether different from the ordinary Christian life of baptism held sway from the seventeenth century well into the twentieth. The early biblical and patristic understanding of mysticism was eclipsed in the process. In the first part of this century, the works of Augustin-François Poulain and Adolphe Tanquerey were highly influential in the lives of vowed religious and priests. Poulain's *The Graces of Interior Prayer* stresses the essential difference between the mystical life and the ordinary Christian life. The mystic's experience is not only that of the fullness of life in Christ, but constitutes a different kind of experience altogether. In this view, since the mystical life is superior to the ordinary life of grace, a higher form of Christian life available to very few, the spiritual life became the province of an elite, and the higher forms of mystical union reserved for the elite among the elite, *la crème de la crème.*

This approach to mysticism was seriously challenged even prior to the Second Vatican Council. Dominican theologian Reginald Garrigou-Lagrange argued persuasively that the mystical life is the full flowering of the ordinary life of grace. In this view, all baptized Christians are called to the fullness of life in Christ Jesus. In principle, no baptized Christian is excluded from the full flowering of the life of grace and Spirit. All Christians are mystics, at least potentially, insofar as each and every one participates in Christ's mysteries through baptism and the ongoing sacramental life of the Church and its mission.

Contemporary Perspectives

With the Second Vatican Council, spiritual and mystical elitism was dealt a fatal blow. The council articulated a call for Church reform and renewal rooted in personal and interior renewal nourished above all by word and sacrament. Such renewal of life is not only the responsibility of those who are ordained, or those committed to the evangelical counsels. It is the responsibility of all the baptized. All who are baptized into Christ are called to holiness. The manifestations of Christian holiness will vary because of the diversity of charisms given by the Spirit. But it is the one and same holiness to which all are called (*Lumen Gentium* 40–41). And Christian holiness is none other than this: To live "in Christ." And to live in Christ is to experience Christ's mysteries in and through word and sacrament. To this fullness all are invited by the grace of baptism.

In the second half of the twentieth century, two Roman Catholic writers have been most significant in recovering the original significance of mysticism, emphasizing that it is the full flowering of the life of grace and prayer. The German Jesuit theologian Karl Rahner (5 March 1904 to 30 March 1984) is judged by many to be the most important mystical theologian of the twentieth century. Perhaps no one has written more persuasively about the "mysticism of everyday life." Rahner's abiding theological concern was with the fundamental, universal human experience of the mystery of God who draws all human beings into communion. Christian or not, God addresses each human heart. And all persons must affirm or deny the divine initiative in their inmost being. Rather than treating mystical experience as a form of heightened consciousness among a rare few, Rahner's concern was in describing the "mysticism of the masses," or "mysticism in ordinary dress," insisting that mystical experience "is not specifically different from the ordinary life of grace as such."

If Karl Rahner is judged by many to be the most significant mystical theologian of the century, Thomas Merton (31 January 1915 to 10 December 1968) is arguably its most significant spiritual writer. Merton was not a theologian in the sense in which the term is ordinarily understood today. Nonetheless, he did articulate a "sapiential theology," resonant with early patristic theologies and with other theological currents in which the nature of religious experience is kept to the fore. From his Cistercian monastery in rural Kentucky, this Trappist monk, author, poet, and social critic wrote in such a way as to make available to a wide readership the riches of the Christian and monastic traditions of prayer. He affirmed that every baptized Christian was called to a life of deep contemplative prayer, and that the contemplative life could not be confined to the monastic enclosure. Monastic life is no guarantee of mystical grace. The graces of contemplative life and mysticism are available outside as well as within the monastery. Further, as Merton's own vocation led him to raise a prophetic voice in the face of the most pressing social issues of his age, he grew more insistent on the crucial importance of lay Christians who are deeply committed to a life of contemplative prayer while living "in the world" and working for social transformation in light of the gospel. Merton and Rahner shared the conviction that if Christians are to be an effective witness to the gospel in the twenty-first century and beyond, they must be at once mystical and political.

Without doubt, the ongoing work of Bernard McGinn stands as a high watermark in the study of Christian mysticism in the latter part of the twentieth century. Professor of historical theology and the history of Christianity at the Divinity School of the University of Chicago, McGinn's efforts have been devoted to the study and teaching of the Western Christian mystical tradition and to the herculean task of writing a multivolume history of Christian mysticism. Persuaded that mysticism is the acme of the spiritual path, he views the mystical tradition from the vantage of the "consciousness of the divine presence" rather than that of "union," the category which has governed many traditional and contemporary interpretations of mysticism. McGinn describes mysticism as the experienced presence of God. This shift from "union" to "presence" as the governing category for understanding Christian mysticism has distinct advantages. As but one example, the metaphor of union has usually been accompanied by images and metaphors such as "ascent," "mountain," and "ladder," which ordinarily connote higher and lower stages, i.e., a hierarchy, in the mystical journey. McGinn's governing category of the "consciousness of the divine presence" allows for a rich array of metaphors to describe the mystical experience. Such metaphors include the birth of the Word in the soul, ecstasy, radical obedience to the divine will discerned in the present moment, deification, and vision. These and other metaphors allow for vivid descriptions of various types of mystical experience, while at the same time avoiding the hierarchical language that has often accompanied accounts of mystical union.

Friend and foe of the mystical tradition agree that however it be understood, mysticism is not synonymous with religion. But the precise nature of the mystic's experience has been and remains the subject of controversy. At the heart of this matter is the issue of whether the mystic has "direct," "immediate" experience of God. Some affirm that all experience, even and especially that of the mystic, is mediated through language, culture, tradition and so on. Others insist that the mystic's experience transcends categories of language, culture, and tradition, i.e., it is ineffable. McGinn's contribution is instructive in that he navigates the middle ground between these two approaches. He suggests that the mystic's experience is one of mediated immediacy. That is to say that language, culture, tradition, and other factors prepare the mystic for the consciousness of the divine presence which is subjectively and objectively direct, even at times immediate. And language, culture, and tradition are the means through which the mystic attempts to communicate the consciousness of the presence of God to others, however ineffable it may be said to be.

Questions about the precise nature of mystical experience have led to increased discussion as to whether or not the mystic's experience is essentially the same throughout quite diverse religious traditions. In the twentieth century, the probings of Thomas Merton, Abhishiktananda (Henri le Saux), Hugo Lassalle, and Bede Griffiths have contributed significantly to exploring the possibility of transcultural, transreligious mystical experience. Ewert Cousins has treated mysticism in terms of the depth dimension of all human experience, suggesting that such transcultural and transreligious mystical experience is possible. Others such as Bernard McGinn maintain that even though the mystic's experience is direct or immediate, it can only be properly understood in view of the linguistic, cultural, and religious factors which shape the experience and thereby constitute it as distinct from other experiences shaped in their turn by very different languages, cultures, and traditions.

Christian Mysticism and the Trinity

As the fullest expression of Christian life and prayer, mysticism has been understood, for the most part, in terms of unmediated union with God. The individual soul meets and gradually and progressively is united with the one God. The goal of the mystical journey is the immediate experiential apprehension of the deepest recesses of divine life. The mystic is usually a solitary, often eccentric figure, someone not in any way like the ordinary Christian. Classical approaches to mystical experience affirmed that the mystical life was not the normal outcome of the baptismal call to the life of holiness and the pursuit of virtue. The mystical life was judged to be an extraordinary life, made possible by special graces. But the very notion of an immediate experience of God can undercut the importance of God's saving acts in human history wherein God's providential plan for human beings and for the whole world is at work, mediated in and through the Incarnate Word, and in the concrete work of the Holy Spirit who brings about the reordering of all of creation.

An approach to mysticism rooted in a proper understanding of the Trinity requires attention to the panoply of human experiences in history, world, culture, personal relationships, and Church, wherein God's presence and action are discerned. The experience of God's presence is to be found in every form of communion: affective, sexual, familial, artistic; the intellectual pursuit of truth, the apprehension and pursuit of the good, the appreciation of the beautiful. All forms of authentic communion are potential avenues for the consciousness of the presence of the triune God.

At this juncture it may be useful to draw attention to the question of whether and to what degree Christian mystics are Trinitarian. The mystical writings of Catherine of Siena, the Victorines, and the Rhineland mystics in the West, and the Cappadocians, Maximus the Confessor, and Gregory Palamas in the East, to name just a few, clearly represent an approach to the Christian mysteries informed by the symbols and narrative of the Christian tradition. On the other hand, the *Cloud of Unknowing,* or the writings of Pseudo-Dionysius, Thérèse of Lisieux, or especially Meister Eckhart, do not obviously exhibit the symbols of Christian faith. Since the affirmation of God as triune is central and essential to Christian faith, the question arises as to why so many mystical writings seem to rely so little on Trinitarian symbolism. It is conceivable that there is a particular way that mystics perceive the basic truth that the doctrine seeks to articulate, but that it is expressed in a way that requires skillful and careful translation. Or, it may be that the prevailing Christian doctrine of God had by a certain historical point so marginalized the Trinitarian dimension (because of its esoteric and speculative character) that Christian mystics gravitated toward a more generic understanding of the one God. Whatever the reason, it is crucial to affirm that Christian mysticism is a path through God's saving activity in and through history, in which God is revealed through Jesus Christ and the Holy Spirit. Thus it is to be expected that Christian mystical experience in some way or another reflects the particularities of symbols and events important in Christian faith.

The altogether Trinitarian character of Christian mysticism provides occasion for looking at perhaps the most fertile ground for the growth and development of Christian mysticism in the future. What has heretofore been assumed to be the loftiest, most abstract and ethereal Christian doctrine, the Trinity, is after all the most practical. The doctrine of the Trinity is the specifically Christian way of speaking about the mystery of God. It is the summation of Christian faith. The Trinity is the Christian naming of God as personal and relational. God exists in a loving communion of persons. Taken as the point of entry and the destination of Christian mystical life, the Trinity gives rise to an understanding of participation in the Christian mysteries attained through participation in communion of persons both human and divine, and through the perfection of these relationships in self-donation, mutuality, and reciprocity, rather than in an ever more pure gaze of the solitary mind's eye toward some eternal verity. The revitalization of the doctrine of the Trinity is the most effective strategy for correcting those approaches to spirituality and mysticism that dabble in self-preoccupation, self-absorption, self-fixation. Because it is personal, relational, and communal, Trinitarian mysticism naturally connects with the ethical and social demands of Christian life in the Spirit, which is now seen from the perspective of the increase of communion of persons in mutuality and reciprocity, rather than as individual sanctification achieved by a journey inward. The recovery of the Trinity as the most practical of Christian mysteries has the widest-ranging implications for Christian mysticism today and for generations to come.

MICHAEL DOWNEY

See also CHRISTIAN SPIRITUALITY; HOLINESS; PRAYER.

MYTH

Myth represents transcendent reality in a narrative which uses familiar terms analogously. Myths usually intend to motivate rather than inform. For many people, myth has a negative connotation. A myth is a falsehood, a fairy tale, an untrue depiction of reality. This negative appreciation becomes more intense whenever myth is connected with faith or religion or the Bible. To speak of faith or of the Bible in terms of myth is to deny their truth, say some.

There are good reasons for such an understanding. Myth has long been relegated to the realm of "stories," and stories have been held to be fictional accounts of unreal characters living idealized lives. Myth had nothing to do with fact or with reality.

Recent studies have shown, however, that myth is often more truthful than fact. Myths help us to understand reality and our place within that reality. A myth is a narration (story) that seeks to express a truth that is often too big for our own words, for logical discourse. Myth says what we can't get our minds around, like: who we are, how we got here, what life means.

All societies have myths that account for their origins and their meaning. The cultures that produced the biblical tradition used myth in order to express their understanding of what God had done in their midst.

The stories of creation and of the Exodus are gripping and larger than life, for they contain the meaning of life. The inspired authors of the Scriptures understood that God had acted in creation, in freeing the people from Egypt. They knew that their identity as God's people sprang from that action. They knew each person's reality was grounded in his or her relationship with this God and with these people. Their way of telling this, of letting others know, is the way of myth.

Myth differs from ordinary language in that it uses story and it appeals to the imagination and to the intuition. We know a story is true. We don't need to analyze, dissect, compare. We just know. Myth lets us know. It does not tell us lies or falsehood. It imparts to us the truth of who we are and for what we stand, and it lets us see that God is in the midst of all.

JULIANA M. CASEY, I.H.M.

See also CRITICISM, BIBLICAL; MIDRASH.

N

NAG HAMMADI

Also spelled Naj Hammadi, this is a town on the West Bank of the Nile River, in which a collection of thirteen codices containing numerous texts, commonly called the Nag Hammadi Library, was discovered in 1945. These texts date from the second and third centuries A.D. They are written in Coptic, the language of the Egyptian natives, that is, those outside the Alexandrian area, but scholars think the original language of most of the texts was Greek, although they cannot say where these works were originally composed nor by whom. Although scholars believe that a number of religious groups are represented in the texts, the bulk of them belong to Christian Gnostic groups. This makes them of great value because, until this discovery, scholars knew of the Gnostics largely through citations of their works by the Church Fathers, whose interest was often to refute the Gnostics rather than to explain their positions. Texts such as *The Gospel of Thomas, The Secret Teaching of John, The Apocalypse of Peter,* and *The Treatise of the Three Natures* are typical examples of Gnostic literature in the ancient world. They contain homilies, secret revelations, prayers, and exegesis; they are also occasionally prolix, elitist, and anti-Semitic, regrettably common traits among the Gnostics. Because Nag Hammadi lies close to the ancient Egyptian monastery of Chenoboskion, scholars think that some fourth-century Christian monks were willing to read these rather heterodox works, which would explain how they were copied and preserved.

JOSEPH F. KELLY

See also GNOSTICISM; PATROLOGY.

NAMES OF JESUS IN THE NEW TESTAMENT

When we name someone or something, we give it meaning. To say what a thing is is to say how we understand it to be. The same is true of persons; how we name them is how we say who they are. Our answer, the name we give, may not be the true name, the full meaning, but it is ours.

The Christian Scriptures contain several names for Jesus Christ. These names represent attempts to answer the question that haunted the early Christians: "Who do you say that I am?" (Mark 8:27-30; Matt 16:13-23; Luke 9:18-22). The names and images used of Jesus seek to answer that question in ways that are meaningful and helpful for the early communities. Jesus is called the Christ, the Word, the Messiah, the Son of God, the Son of Man. Significant images such as Light, Way, Truth, Good Shepherd, are also applied to him.

The Scriptures contain names that were probably given to Jesus during his time of ministry as well as names or titles given to him after the experience of the resurrection. Passage of time and growth in understanding are reflected in the various titles given to Jesus. The dynamic of this development is reflected in the encounter between Jesus and the Samaritan woman in John 4:7-30, 39-42. At first, she calls Jesus "a Jew." As their conversation progresses, she names Jesus "Sir, prophet, the Christ." Finally, the people who come to Jesus on her witness declare that he is "the Savior of the world."

Understanding both the dynamic of naming and the meaning of the names is a complicated business. It is not clear which—if any—of the names for Jesus were used by Jesus himself. Further, several of the names have multiple meanings.

The term "Lord," for example, was a title of respect ("Sir, mister") in Aramaic. In another (apocalyptic) context, "Lord" referred to the eschatological judge or messiah. In the Greek-speaking world, "Lord" (*Kyrios*) referred to God, and it is sometimes used for both God and Jesus in the Christian Scriptures (cf. Phil 2:6-11).

The terms "Son of Man" and "Son of God" are two important titles. "Son of Man" is placed on the lips of Jesus and refers to Jesus' earthly ministry, the coming passion, Jesus' role as judge and Savior at the end of the aeon. Questions have arisen as to whether Jesus actually used this title of himself. Some scholars say that he did, and that the title was simply a way of referring to oneself in a self-effacing manner. Others insist that "Son of Man" has roots in Jewish apocalyptic traditions and that the early Christian community, after Easter, applied this eschatological title to Jesus.

"Son of God" also has multiple meanings and roots in pre-Christian Judaism. It refers to one who has been called by God to accomplish a particular and important role within the history of salvation. Son of God connotes closeness of relationship to God even though it does not imply direct parent-child relation. Its use in the Christian Scriptures appears to have been of post-Easter origin. That is, believers recognized in the risen Christ the one who mediated God's fullness of salvation. His role is now an eschatological one, connected with the final coming of God.

In sum, the many names given to Jesus in the Christian Scriptures are indications of a growing and dynamic faith among the early Christians. Recognizing that Jesus had been raised from the dead by God, that he was what he had claimed to be, that he was more than anyone had thought he was, believers strove for ways to express that. They used titles they knew from earlier traditions, they applied them to Jesus, they gave them new meanings. All of this may cause some difficulties for later interpreters. It also allows us to take comfort in the realization that the full meaning of Jesus the Christ is always beyond our limited human understanding.

JULIANA M. CASEY, I.H.M.

See also JESUS CHRIST; MESSIAH.

NANTES, EDICT OF

See HUGUENOTS.

NARRATIVE THEOLOGY

See THEOLOGY, NARRATIVE.

NATIONAL CATHOLIC WELFARE CONFERENCE (NCWC)

The National Catholic Welfare Conference succeeded the National Catholic War Council (1918–1919) on 20 February 1919. It was an agency of the archbishops and bishops of the United States established to "organize, unify and coordinate Catholic activities for the general welfare of the Church." It operated until 1967 when its activities were assumed by the United States Catholic Conference and the National Conference of Catholic Bishops.

PATRICIA DeFERRARI

See also AMERICAN CATHOLICISM.

NATIONAL CONFERENCE OF CATHOLIC BISHOPS (NCCB)

After the Second Vatican Council, the United States bishops reorganized the National Catholic Welfare Conference as two separate associations, the National Conference of Catholic Bishops (NCCB) and the United States Catholic Conference (USCC). The NCCB emphasizes internal Church concerns, whereas the USCC focuses on the Church's work in society.

The staff of both organizations operate under the direction of the General Secretariat, which consists of a General Secretary, who is elected by the bishops to a five-year term, and three Associate General Secretaries. NCCB and USCC offices are located in Washington, D.C.

The standing committees of NCCB include: Bishops Welfare and Emergency Relief; Black Catholics; Church in Latin America; Doctrine; Ecumenical and Interreligious Affairs; Evangelization; Hispanic Affairs; Marriage and Family Life; Migration; Pastoral Research and Practices; Religious Life and Ministry; Selection of Bishops; Vocations; Women in Society and in the Church.

PATRICIA DeFERRARI

See also AMERICAN CATHOLICISM; BISHOP.

NATURAL LAW

Natural law generically describes ethical theories that determine what is right or wrong on the basis of the common humanity that all human beings share. A brief overview of the philosophical and jurisprudential aspects of natural law helps to understand better the theological discussion about natural law and its effects on society.

Most of the classical moral philosophers in the Western tradition adopted some sort of natural law theory. In ancient times Stoics maintained that the moral life involved living in accord with nature understood as the entire natural order. Despite so many appeals to nature and natural law as the criterion of morality, natural law philosophers have not agreed on the meaning of the criterion of nature nor on all the content norms proposed on the basis of a natural law theory. In modern times many contemporary philosophers have challenged a natural law approach for a number of different reasons—the very diversity among natural law thinkers themselves, cultural relativism, evolutionary development, antifoundationalism, and the naturalistic fallacy of trying to go from the "is" to the "ought." Other philosophers continue to defend a natural law approach but often with a "thin" concept of the human good which avoids claiming too much as based on a common humanity. In jurisprudence, legal positivists and others reject the natural law contention that human civil law and legislation must be based on natural law.

In theological ethics Roman Catholic thought has traditionally appealed to natural law to determine how Christians and all others are to live, but some Anglicans and Protestants have proposed their own version of natural law. In this context natural law involves three distinct but overlapping considerations—the strictly theological, the philosophical, and the legal.

From the theological perspective natural law involves the question of the sources of moral wisdom and knowledge for the Christian and the Christian Church. Does the Christian find moral wisdom only in Scripture and in Jesus Christ or also in human reason and experience? Natural law approaches assert that the Christian, Christian ethics, and the Christian Churches can find moral wisdom through human reason and on that basis can be in dialogue with all humankind. Historically Roman Catholic natural law theory has defended the role of reason to arrive at moral knowledge on the basis of its reflection on human nature. Orthodox Christianity affirms a natural law common to all based on the image of God in all humans, but the natural law provides only for a minimal social existence. Many Anglicans, Methodists, and some in the Reformed tradition have given some role to the natural law or its equivalent.

The primary theological justification of natural law rests on the doctrine of creation. God has created human nature and human reason so that human reason can discover how human beings should act by reflecting on their own human nature. Supporters of natural law or the more generic use of reason in moral theology also appeal to Romans 2:14 which asserts that the Gentiles who do not have the Law (the Mosaic Law) do by nature what the Law requires. The Roman Catholic understanding sees the natural law as a participation of the divine plan or law in the rational creature. God has formulated a plan for the world and has given human beings reason so that reflecting on the human nature made by God they can discern how God wants us to act in this world.

Many Protestants in the Lutheran tradition, some in the Reformed tradition (Karl Barth), Evangelicals, and the sects or left wing of the Protestant Reformation have strenuously opposed natural law invoking the emphasis on Scripture alone, insisting that sin has grievously affected both human nature and human reason, and maintaining that one can never go from the human to the divine but must start with God and God's revelation. Mainline Protestants who do not accept the natural law on theological grounds usually still find some basis for a common social morality for all human beings.

Before the Second Vatican Council (1962–1965), Roman Catholic ethics and official hierarchical teachings were based almost exclusively on a Neo-Scholastic natural law theory thereby recognizing a morality common to all human beings and capable of dialogue with all others on the basis of human reason and a shared human nature, but such a morality lacked any explicit Christian dimensions. The Second Vatican Council called for a greater incorporation of Scripture, faith perspectives, and explicitly theological themes in Christian ethics and life. The majority of mainstream Christians today are debating the question about the exact relationship of faith and reason in morality and how Christian and human morality are related. Many Roman Catholic theologians, while recognizing a greater role for faith and strictly theological appeals, still maintain that Christian faith does not add any unique content to morality, especially in the understanding of social ethics in our pluralistic world. However, some Roman Catholic theologians today insist that faith calls for some different content in the moral life of the Christian.

The more philosophical aspect of the natural law question concerns the meaning of human nature and of human reason. The Roman Catholic teaching and tradition have consistently identified their approach as a natural law theory dependent on the work of Thomas Aquinas. Human reason can discern the plan of God by grasping the specific ends toward which we tend by nature—the ends we share with all living substances (the conservation of one's own being); with other animals (the procreation and education of offspring); and the ends that are proper to human beings (to know the truth about God and to live in human society). On the basis of these generic ends reason can discern (usually by deduction) the principles that should guide the moral life. Later Neo-Scholastic theologians developed this role of natural law, insisting on its universality and immutability and the need to observe the God-given finalities of all the human faculties and powers. Official Catholic hierarchical teaching has employed the natural law theory to develop its moral teaching in all areas including social, biomedical, and sexual morality.

Revisionist Catholic moral theologians have dissented from the official Church teaching on many sexual questions such as contraception, sterilization, masturbation, artificial insemination, and the principle of double effect. Such ethicists criticize the Neo-Scholastic natural law theory because of its physicalism (identification of the human moral act with the physical structure of the act), classicism (emphasis on the eternal, immutable, universal, and unchanging), and naturalism (failure to give primary significance to the personal). Alternative ethical theories have been proposed based on other philosophical approaches (e.g., transcendental, pragmatic, relational, liberationist, linguistic, praxis-oriented), but many theories constitute a revision and not a rejection of natural law. Today in Catholic theological ethics a pluralism of methodologies exists although all continue to give an important role to human reason.

The hierarchical teaching office of the Roman Catholic Church continues to employ the Neo-Scholastic natural law method in its official documents and teaching although that method has been modified somewhat in the area of social morality. Some theological ethicists continue to defend the Neo-Scholastic natural law approach in sexual and medical ethics. Others (e.g., Germain Grisez and John Finnis) propose their own revision of natural law insisting on the existence of a number of basic human goods that one can never directly go against. Grisez, Finnis, and their school generally use their revised natural law method to defend the existing hierarchical Church teachings in sexual and biomedical ethics.

Discussion continues in Roman Catholicism about the third aspect of natural law—the relationship between natural law and civil law and legislation. Thomas Aquinas (d. 1274) understood civil law to be based on natural law either by accepting the conclusions of the natural law (murder is a crime) or by making specific what the natural law leaves unspecified (vehicular traffic uses the left or the right side of the road). However, no exact equation exists between natural law and human civil law or between sin and crime. Civil law embraces only those acts that relate to the common good of the community. Likewise the legislator must take into account human reality and not suppress all vices but only the more grievous vices from which the majority are able to abstain, especially those which are harmful to others.

As the twentieth century progressed, Roman Catholic natural law thought has recognized the growing importance of freedom and the legitimacy of democratic political structures thus affecting its understanding of the relationship between law and morality. The Declaration on Religious Liberty of the Second Vatican Council (no. 7) enshrines the principle of free constitutional government; freedom is to be respected as far as possible and curtailed only when and insofar as necessary. The state should and must intervene to protect the public order which includes an order of justice, of public peace, and of public morality. Disputes both in theory and in practice continue about the relationship between law and morality with abortion being the primary practical issue in many countries.

CHARLES E. CURRAN

See also PHILOSOPHY AND THEOLOGY; THEOLOGY, MORAL.

NATURE

In its general sense nature is a term that designates the known or unknown characteristics that define or classify anything. It is in this sense that philosophical theology has discussed the nature of God. It is also in this sense that Catholic dogma speaks of the two natures of Christ. Finally, it is this sense that grounds the Catholic tradition of "natural law" ethics. Most commonly, however, the term nature has been used in an elusive sense that opposes it to grace. Augustine of Hippo, in line with the Pauline idea of the flesh (not body, but human being acting apart from God) lusting against the Spirit, defended the absolute need of God's intervention by grace against Pelagius and his followers. Pelagius maintained that the help people need from God in order to act rightly and live well is already given to them in creation in the gift of free will. Augustine maintained that after the "sin of Adam" it is not possible to be in harmony with God except by special "healing grace." Centuries later the debate was still going on in the medieval West, and gave rise to a classification in which it was assumed that God created people in a state of "pure nature" but immediately enhanced this with grace which was however lost by sin. This meant that in fact in history people are born not in a state of "pure nature" but in a state of lost grace and therefore distorted nature, requiring to be restored to balance by redeeming grace. Further discussion concluded with the understanding that "pure nature" had never actually existed. In contemporary theology the sharp opposition between nature and grace has been nuanced in many ways, but interest has focused more on the relationship between nature and person and on the realization that nature is not static but always in a state of becoming. This has important consequences, especially in moral theology when "natural law" is invoked.

MONIKA K. HELLWIG

See also CREATION; GOD; GRACE.

NERI, PHILIP, ST. (1515–1595)

Born in Florence in 1515, he was the son of a notary. He was educated by the Dominicans of San Marco, whose teachings and example nurtured and inspired his fledgling faith. At eighteen, he was sent to San Germano to live and work with a childless relative who, it was assumed, would make Philip the heir to his business. Shortly into his apprenticeship, however, Philip experienced a mystical transcendence of sorts (which he would later call his conversion), and became disaffected with wordly ambitions.

He left for Rome, where he was taken in by a Florentine customs official who provided him with a room and the basic necessities of life; in exchange, Philip taught his host's two young sons. During his two-year stay here, he led a simple and austere life, devoting the majority of his free time to prayer. In 1535, Philip ended this period of sabbatical and undertook the study of philosophy and theology. After three years he decided to give up his studies and dedicated himself fully to charitable works and the moral instruction of the Roman people. In this manner, Philip sought to help bring about the re-evangelization of Rome, a task which would become his life's work.

Though he spent his days in active service to the sick, the needy, and the inquisitive, Philip devoted his evenings to prayer, often in the catacomb of St. Sebastian on the Appian Way. It was there, in 1554, that he is said to have had an experience of divine rapture which caused his heart to enlarge physically. In 1548, Philip co-founded the Confraternity of the Most Holy Trinity, which cared for needy pilgrims and convalescents; in 1575—the year of the Jubilee—the group assisted 145,000 pilgrims. He was ordained in May 1551, after which he went to San Girolamo, joining a community of priests there. Philip soon became recognized as a gifted confessor, and scores of penitents came to him for guidance. In order to further their faith, he held informal spiritual conferences for men and boys; these were often followed by visits to the Seven Churches of Rome or attendance at Vespers and Compline. The conferences became the impetus for the Congregation of the Oratory, named after their meeting room at San Girolamo. In 1545, the congregation was approved by Pope Gregory XIII.

Philip had become by this time one of the most popular figures in Rome, and his counsel was sought by popes and cardinals as well as by the common people. In his later years, both the rich and the poor of Rome venerated him as a saint. He died in 1595 and was canonized in 1622. Among the notable biographies on St. Philip are: *St. Philip Neri and the Roman Society of His Times,* by Abbé Louis Ponnelle and Abbé Louis Bordet, translated by Fr. R. F. Kerr, 1932; a biography by Cardinal Capecelatro (English version, 1926); and a life sketch by Fr. V. J. Matthews, 1934.

JOSEPH QUINN

See also ORATORIANS.

NESTORIANISM

See HERESY/HERETICS.

NEUMANN, JOHN NEPOMUCENE, ST. (1811–1860)

Born in Prachatitz, Bohemia, the third of six children, John grew up with the idea of becoming a missionary to America, but entered the diocesan seminary at Budweis in 1831, finishing at the archiepiscopal seminary at Prague University. With his ordination indefinitely postponed due to a surplus of priests in Bohemia, he decided to pursue his first inspiration. He was ordained in New York City (1836), and served with characteristic energy the next four years trudging from village to village in the wilds of western New York where there were many German-speaking Catholics. In 1840, he joined the Redemptorist Order at St. Philomena's in Pittsburgh (his younger brother was already a member) and became (1842) the first Redemptorist to take vows in the United States. He continued to be very popular among German-speaking Catholics, serving in Baltimore, Ohio, and Virginia, becoming rector of St. Philomena's in 1844. He was chosen vice regent of his order, and later vice provincial (1847), becoming superior of all American Redemptorists at the age of thirty-six. In this position he put the Redemptorists in the forefront of the parochial school movement in America.

In 1852, Neumann was consecrated fourth bishop of Philadelphia. He reorganized the diocese, founded a preparatory seminary, built some eighty churches and many schools. He brought a number of teaching sisterhoods into the diocese, and organized the schools into a diocesan system. He visited each parish annually, and introduced the Forty Hours Devotion to the diocese. He was much loved by the clergy for his fatherly concern in their regard.

Though famous as an administrator, Neumann was respected for his pastoral zeal, his charity, his preaching, and for the practice of his faith. Possessed of boundless energy, he was patient and kind. Well educated, frequently published, intelligent (he spoke six languages), he was yet humble. Stories of his sanctity began to emerge after his death, and many testified to the value of his intercessory prayer. His surviving spiritual manuscripts and journals added to the testimony. He was canonized in 1977 by Pope Paul VI, the first American male to receive that honor. Feast day, 5 January.

DAVID BRYAN

See also AMERICAN CATHOLICISM.

NEW ZEALAND, CHURCH IN

Christians first arrived in New Zealand soon after the year 1800, and the first Anglican missionary arrived in 1814. In 1836, when the Holy See created the vicariate apostolic of western Oceania and entrusted it to Marist missionaries from France, New Zealand had 100,000 Maoris (the native New Zealanders) and a mere one thousand Europeans, mostly British. The first Marists reached New Zealand in 1838, and by 1843 there were twelve missions among the Maoris.

Many Irish Catholics in the British Army were sent to New Zealand to enforce the government position in land disputes with the Maoris (1859), and these were later joined by Irish miners from Australia. Continued outbreaks of violence, finally put down in 1871, left the missions in shambles, and these were revived only in 1881. The Maoris are now largely Christian, and 20 percent of them are Catholic. There are now six dioceses: Wellington, Auckland, Palmerston North, Hamilton, Christchurch, and Dunedin. While the population of New Zealand is small (3.5 million), Catholics form a significant minority of all New Zealand Christians (15 percent), while 24 percent are Anglican, followed by Presbyterians (18 percent), Methodists (5 percent), and others.

DAVID BRYAN

See also CATHOLICISM.

NEWMAN, JOHN HENRY, CARDINAL (1801–1890)

John Henry Newman, English author, Anglican clergyman, and Roman Catholic cardinal, was born in London on 21 February 1801 and died in Birmingham (England) on 11 August 1890.

Newman was the oldest of six children born to John Newman and his wife Jemima (Foudrinier). Newman grew up in a middle-class family that regularly worshipped in the Church of England and read the Bible at home. At the age of seven, Newman was sent to a boarding school at Ealing, where he was a precocious student. Shortly before his sixteenth birthday, Newman entered Trinity College, Oxford, which awarded him a scholarship.

Before going up to Oxford, Newman experienced "a great change of thought" which he later described as "making me rest in the thought of two and two only absolute and luminously self-evident beings, myself and my Creator." After this "first conversion," he made a commitment to Christianity and considered himself "predestined to salvation."

His future career, however, remained uncertain. His family wanted him to study law; personally, he was attracted to the clergy. But before deciding on either vocation, he had to pass the examinations for his bachelor's degree. Trinity College regarded him as its outstanding student and expected him to pass with first-class distinction; in fact, he broke down during his oral examination and was granted the degree without honors.

During the following months, Newman made two important decisions: to prepare himself for ordination, and to apply for the most prestigious fellowship at Oxford. After successfully competing in a week-long exam in the spring of 1822, Newman was elected a Fellow of Oriel College, where he came into contact with John Keble, Edward Pusey, and Richard Hurrell Froude, his later coworkers in the Oxford Movement.

Two years after his election to Oriel, Newman was ordained a deacon in the Church of England and began assisting in the parish of St. Clement's in Oxford. His parochial work taught him the important lesson that theological theories need to be tested in pastoral practice.

Newman was ordained an Anglican priest in 1825 and the following year, agreed to become a Tutor of Oriel College. This new responsibility posed a question of conscience for Newman: should a priest be a teacher of undergraduates? After considerable reflection, Newman came to the conclusion that a tutor has a pastoral responsibility in caring for his students' spiritual formation, as well as for their educational development.

Cardinal John Henry Newman

His pastoral view of the tutorship soon led to a conflict with the new Provost of Oriel, Edward Hawkins. Newman wanted to concentrate his efforts on the more promising students; Hawkins wanted all students treated equally. After a polite but sharp argument, Hawkins refused to assign any more students to Newman, who would have to wait a quarter century for another opportunity to put his educational ideals into practice.

Meanwhile, freed from his responsibilities as tutor, Newman had time to pursue a project that he had planned at the time of his ordination: to study the writings of the Fathers of the Church. From this study came his first book, *The Arians of the Fourth Century* (1833), which emphasized the development of Christian doctrine in the early Church.

Newman also began publishing the *Plain and Parochial Sermons,* which he delivered as Vicar of St. Mary's Church in Oxford, a position to which he was appointed in 1828. St. Mary's also provided the setting for a series of theological presentations, which he eventually published as *Lectures on the Prophetical Office* (1837) and *Lectures on Justification* (1838).

During the winter of 1832–1833, Newman joined his Oriel colleague, Hurrell Froude, on an extended voyage to the Mediterranean. Newman welcomed this opportunity to see the places about which he had read in classical, biblical, and patristic literature. The trip, which included a visit to Rome, brought Newman into first-hand contact with Roman Catholicism.

Yet the trip was almost the end of Newman's life; in Sicily, he came down with a severe fever. Once recuperated, he felt that he had been spared by Divine Providence for a future work in England. On the return voyage, he expressed his newly found sense of mission in his most famous hymn, "Lead Kindly Light."

Newman arrived back in England on 9 July 1833; a few days later, John Keble preached a sermon against the "National Apostasy," which Newman considered the "start" of the Oxford Movement. Newman responded to what he felt was a providential call for the reform of the Church of England by beginning a series of *Tracts for the Times.*

At first, the *Tracts* were received favorably by many of the clergy and educated laity. However, as the *Tracts* became more Catholic in tone and content, opposition increased. Matters came to a head in 1841, when Newman published "Tract XC," which attempted to show that the "Thirty-Nine Articles" of the Church of England were compatible with Roman Catholic dogma. When this tract was condemned by many Anglicans, Newman agreed to stop publication of the *Tracts.*

Newman also decided to move to Littlemore, a village about three miles from Oxford, where he established a monastic-like retreat for himself and his followers. For the next four years, Newman pondered his future. On the one hand, he was dismayed that the Church of England had apparently repudiated its Catholic heritage. On the other hand, he felt that the Roman Catholic Church was guilty of many exaggerations both in dogma and in practice. He asked himself: Where is the Church of Christ today?

To answer that question, Newman began studying the way that doctrine has developed. His *Essay on the Development of Christian Doctrine* (1845), expressed his conviction that the doctrines of the Roman Catholic Church are legitimate developments of the teachings of the Church of the apostles.

In October, 1845, Newman resigned his Oriel Fellowship and was received into the Roman Catholic Church. This decision separated him from his friends at Oxford and even from his own family. He wondered what to do in the future. After a year of theological studies in Rome, he was ordained a Roman Catholic priest on 30 May 1847.

Newman then returned to England to establish an Oratory, a community of diocesan priests committed both to intellectual endeavors and to pastoral ministry. Two Oratories were established—one in London, the other in Birmingham; Newman chose to reside in the latter city, where he devoted much of his literary efforts to the task of explaining to his Anglican contemporaries his reasons for becoming a Roman Catholic.

In 1851, Newman was invited to become the first rector of the Catholic University of Ireland, which the Irish hierarchy had decided to establish in Dublin. Newman quickly accepted this opportunity to put into practice the educational ideals that he had advocated as a Tutor at Oriel. To gain support for the new university, he prepared a series of lectures and essays, that eventually were published as *The Idea of a University.* However, in spite of his dedicated efforts, the university did not grow as expected; in 1857, Newman decided to resign as rector.

Newman was subsequently asked to assume the editorship of *The Rambler,* a journal founded by Catholic laymen to discuss theological and ecclesiastical questions. These discussions irritated the English bishops who were on the verge of condemning the publication, when Newman agreed to serve as editor in an attempt to save it. Instead, the publication of his essay *On Consulting the Faithful in Matters of Doctrine* (1859) resulted in his removal from the editorship and his denunciation to Rome. Since these charges against him were made secretly, Newman was unable to reply.

Newman's most successful project at this time was the establishment of the Oratory School at Birmingham, where he helped prepare youngsters for college. Then unexpectedly in 1864, an Anglican clergyman and well-known author, Charles Kingsley, publicly impugned Newman's honesty. Newman replied in his *Apologia pro vita sua,* which proved to be a huge literary and apologetic success. The accusations that Newman had been deceitful during his Oxford years were at last laid to rest. Moreover, the way in which he expressed his indebtedness to the Church of England for his personal spiritual development restored his standing among the English public and reestablished his friendship with Keble, Pusey, and other participants in the Oxford Movement.

In 1870, Newman published *An Essay in Aid of a Grammar of Assent,* a philosophical and theological treatise, which examined the way a person assents in daily life and in religious matters. By showing that human assent is really motivated by a "convergence of probabilities," Newman hoped to answer those who maintained that no assent is legitimate unless it is based on unquestionable proof.

The year 1870 also saw Newman fearful that the First Vatican Council's proposed definition on infallibility would create serious problems for Catholic intellectuals. Once the dogma was defined, however, he found that its wording allowed a moderate interpretation; however, he was disturbed that influential people like Archbishop Manning extended the scope of infallibility to a wide variety of papal pronouncements.

In 1874, William Gladstone, four-time prime minister, claimed in *Vatican Decrees in Their Bearing on Civil Allegiance* that Roman Catholics could no longer be regarded as loyal citizens, since they were bound to obey the pope. Newman replied in a *Letter to His Grace the Duke of Norfolk* that Roman Catholics are bound to obey the pope in religious matters, but must obey the government in civil matters. In this book, Newman pointedly rejected the ultramontane exaggeration of infallibility advocated by Manning; for Newman, infallibility is a charism that is exercised only rarely and only in regard to matters of revelation.

Newman's *Letter* was his last major publication. His subsequent literary efforts consisted of writing essays, editing his previously published works, and preparing his manuscripts for a future biographer. In 1878, he was named an Honorary Fellow of Trinity College and returned to Oxford for the first time in a third of a century.

The year, 1878, also saw the election of a new pope, Leo XIII, who decided to elevate Newman to the cardinalate, an honor usually bestowed only on bishops of important dioceses and curial administrators. For Newman, the "red hat," which he received from the pope on 15 May 1879 was a welcome vindication of his intellectual service to the Church.

Newman returned to England to a hero's welcome, not only from Roman Catholics, but also from Anglicans. His final years were spent in quasi-retirement at the Birmingham Oratory. On 10 August 1890 he received the last sacraments and died the following day. He was buried in a simple grave at the Oratorian cemetery at Rednal on the edge of Birmingham.

JOHN FORD

See also ANGLICANISM; DOCTRINE, DEVELOPMENT OF; OXFORD MOVEMENT.

NICENE CREED

See CREEDS.

NORBERTINES

Also known as Premonstratensians or Canons Regular of Prémontré (O. Praem.), the Norbertines are an order founded by St. Norbert of Xanten (ca. 1080–1134) in 1120 in Prémontré, France. Adopting the Rule of St. Augustine, the Norbertines blended both contemplative and active religious life. (St. Norbert himself emphasized preaching rather than parochial work.) The order spread quickly over practically all of Europe. Indeed, around 1250 there were some five hundred abbeys or priories in France, Germany, Austria, Switzerland, Hungary, Spain, Greece, Palestine, Poland, Portugal, the British Isles, and the Scandinavian countries. During this period the Norbertines were particularly noted for their hospices where they aided the sick and the poor and housed and fed pilgrims.

The Norbertine communities shared in the reverses that affected the Catholic Church in Europe from the sixteenth through the nineteenth centuries. In 1893 the first Norbertines came from Berne Abbey in Holland to North America at the invitation of the bishop of the Diocese of Green Bay. In 1924 this American foundation attained abbatial status, becoming St. Norbert Abbey in De Pere, Wisconsin. In addition to this abbey there are two other abbeys in the U.S.: Daylesford Abbey in Paoli, Pennsylvania, and St. Michael's Abbey in Orange, California. Counting priests, seminarians, and brothers, there are some two hundred Norbertines in the U.S.

The Norbertine Order is made up of three parts: (1) the first order, comprising priests, clerics, and brothers; (2) the second order, consisting of canonesses and sisters; and (3) the third order, composed of lay men and women who participate in the works and benefits of the order. Norbertine life places great emphasis on the liturgy, especially the Eucharist and parts of the Liturgy of the Hours. Norbertine apostolate has generally developed according to the needs of the area where their houses are found. In the U.S. the Norbertines have been especially involved in education as well as parochial ministry. An example of their educational achievements is St. Norbert College, a coed institution of some 1800 students located in De Pere, Wisconsin.

JOHN F. CRAGHAN

See also AUGUSTINE, ST., RULE OF; RELIGIOUS ORDERS.

NORTH AMERICAN MARTYRS

Between 1642 and 1649, eight French Jesuits were martyred by the Indians. Isaac Jogues and Jean de Brébeuf have been the subjects of many studies and biographies. The eight were canonized by Pius XI in 1930.

René Goupil (1606–1642) had been a Jesuit novice, but after ill health forced him to leave, he became a successful surgeon. In 1638 he went as a lay assistant to work among the Jesuit missions in New France, being assigned to the Sillery mission (near Quebec City) and to the Hôtel Dieu (hospital) de Quebec. Two years later he was assigned to the Huron Indian mission. In 1642, while traveling there with Isaac Jogues, he was captured by a group of Iroquois, the worst enemies of the Hurons. For two months he was tortured and mutilated, finally being tomahawked to death at Ossernenon (now Auriesville, New York) as Jogues looked on.

Isaac Jogues (1607–1646) came from a prosperous family and studied with the Jesuits in his home city (Orléans), joining the Society of Jesus in 1624. Requesting assignment to New France in 1636, he became a highly successful missionary to the Hurons. While returning to his mission after a visit to Quebec, his party was captured by the Iroquois and taken to Ossernenon where, as mentioned above, he witnessed the death of Goupil. Despite the regime of tortures and mutilations to which he was subjected, he raised an outdoor cross and preached Christianity, baptizing sixty children during the winter. His escape and return to France was eventually brought about by the Dutch Protestants who had founded Fort Orange (Albany).

In France, Jogues was received as a hero and was honored by Pope Urban VIII, but, again at his own request, he returned to New France in 1644. A peace was concluded with the Iroquois in 1646, and Jogues, with Jean de la Lande, was sent to bring the treaty to Ossernenon. Captured by a war party of the Mohawks, Jogues was tomahawked and beheaded, with de la Lande winning the same crown the next day.

Jean de la Lande (d. 1646) went to New France, becoming a lay assistant with the Jesuits at Quebec. As mentioned above he and Isaac Jogues were captured by the Mohawks in 1646. Jean was tomahawked and beheaded at Ossernenon on 19 October, the day after Fr. Jogues' martyrdom.

Antoine Daniel gave up a law career to enter the Society of Jesus as a college teacher and theologian. With three other priests he came to North America to join the Jesuit missions, first in Acadia (Nova Scotia, 1632) and Quebec (1633). Most of his work (from 1634 on) was in the Huron country, except for two years when he directed a successful school for Huron boys at Quebec. He was martyred (4 July 1648) by the Iroquois at the Indian village of Teanaustaye (near modern Hillsdale, Ontario).

Jean de Brébeuf (1593–1649) attended the university at Caen in his native Normandy and ran his parents' farm until joining the Jesuits in 1617. Despite a bout with tuberculosis which threatened to prevent his becoming a priest, Jean was ordained and, in 1625, sent to New France at his own request. He was a missionary in the Huron country for twenty-four years, though with much opposition from merchants and from the Huguenots. He compiled a dictionary of the Huron language and wrote a Huron catechism. When the English took Quebec and ejected the Jesuits in 1629, Jean returned to France to become treasurer of the Jesuit college at Eu. He returned to the missions when England restored Canada to the French (1633). Brébeuf remained with the Hurons, even when the medicine men were blaming the missionaries for the smallpox epidemic of 1637. He was transferred to Quebec in 1640, but returned to the Hurons in 1644. Five years later he was captured by the Iroquois, the bitter enemies of the French and Hurons, at St. Marie, near Midland, Ontario, at Georgian Bay. After the massacre of the villagers, Brébeuf and his companion, Gabriel Lalemant, were tied to stakes and submitted to one of the cruelest martyrdoms ever recorded. He was known for holiness, and famed among the Indians for his courage (seven thousand of whom he converted to Christ).

Gabriel Lalemant (1610–1649), who had two uncles who were priests, entered the Jesuits in 1630, was ordained in 1638, studying and teaching until 1646. Then, in pursuit of a dream to enter the mission field in New France, he joined his fellow Jesuits in Canada, though poor health prevented his moving out to the Huron country for two years. He then became assistant to Jean de Brébeuf, but was martyred with him after only one year of service (see above).

Charles Garnier (1605–1649), a son of the Treasurer of Normandy, was born and educated in Paris, joining the Jesuits there in 1624. After teaching at the college at Eu, Garnier was ordained in 1636 and, with three other priests, sent to New France the following year to be missionaries among the Huron. He died twelve years later in an Iroquois attack on St. Jean, where he had been sent after Fort St. Marie had been abandoned. He encouraged his flock to flee and was the first to be felled by incoming bullets, after which he was tomahawked.

Noël Chabanel (1613–1649) joined the Jesuits in 1630 and was sent to the Huron country in 1643. Father Chabanel, who had been a brilliant professor of rhetoric, understood that he was not suited for life among the Hurons, and found it impossible to learn their language. Still, he was determined to be faithful to his missionary calling, even if, God willing, he should be a martyr. He went so far as to take a special vow committing himself to remain. He was the assistant of Father Charles Garnier, but was not in the village during the Iroquois attack. He was killed the next day by a lapsed Huron Catholic. Feast day, 19 October.

DAVID BRYAN

See also CANADA, THE CATHOLIC CHURCH IN; MARTYRDOM; SOCIETY OF JESUS.

NOVENA

(Lat. *novem* "nine" and *noveni* "nine at a time") A period of public or private prayer lasting nine days—either consecutively or once weekly for nine weeks—to mark an important occasion, obtain a particular grace, or offer up a special intention. The prayers are often devotions to a saint or a particular virtue of Christ, such as mercy. Novenas originated in the seventeenth century; many have been supported and indulgenced by the Holy See—notably that observed before Pentecost. The nine-day period is symbolic of the nine days between Christ's ascension and Pentecost when Mary and the apostles waited for the coming of the Holy Spirit.

JOSEPH QUINN

See also DEVOTIONS.

NOVICE

A person undergoing a period of formation (novitiate) in order to prepare for membership in a religious community. The novitiate lasts between twelve and twenty-four months, during which the novice wears the dress and adopts the rule of the community, and submits himself or herself to the authority of the superior. A novice is expected to spend prescribed periods of time in the house of novitiate and perform works consistent with the apostolate of the community. Temporary vows of poverty, chastity, and obedience are made upon the completion of the novitiate. A novice may leave, or be dismissed (without incurring canonical penalty), at any time.

JOSEPH QUINN

See also RELIGIOUS ORDERS.

NOVITIATE

See NOVICE.

NUN

A member of a religious community of women living under the vows of poverty, chastity, and obedience. Strictly speaking, nuns are distinguished from sisters by taking "solemn vows" rather than "simple vows."

PATRICIA DeFERRARI

See also RELIGIOUS ORDERS.

NUNC DIMITTIS

The hymn attributed to the old man Simeon in the Jerusalem Temple in Luke 2:29-32 is often referred to by the first two words in its Latin version *Nunc dimittis* ("Now dismiss"). Recited over the infant Jesus by a prophetic figure, the hymn is a pastiche of phrases from Isaiah 40–55, which celebrated Israel's return from the Babylonian Exile in the sixth century B.C. Jesus is identified as the salvation (Isa 40:5) to be seen by all peoples (Isa 52:10), the light to the Gentiles (Isa 42:6; 49:6), and the glory of Israel (Isa 46:13).

Text of the Nunc Dimittis (Luke 2:29-32)

"Master, now you are dismissing
your servant in peace,
according to your word;
for my eyes have seen your salvation,
which you have prepared in
the presence of all peoples,
a light for revelation to the Gentiles
and for glory to your people Israel."

DANIEL J. HARRINGTON, S.J.

See also BENEDICTUS; HYMNS; MAGNIFICAT.

O

O ANTIPHONS

The antiphons sung before and after the *Magnificat* on the seven days preceding Christmas Eve. Each begins with the exclamation "O" (hence their name) and invokes Christ by an Old Testament symbol. The antiphons are sung in Gregorian chant. They are as follows: 17 December—*O Sapientia* ("O Wisdom"); 18 December—*O Adonai* ("O Sacred Lord"); 19 December—*O Radix Jesse* ("O Root of Jesse"); 20 December—*O Clavis Davidica* ("O Key of David"); 21 December—*O Oriens* ("O Radiant Dawn"); 22 December—*O Rex Gentium* ("O King of Nations"); 23 December—*O Emmanuel* ("O God with Us").

JOSEPH QUINN

See also ADVENT; GREGORIAN CHANT.

O SALUTARIS HOSTIA

(Lat., "O Saving victim") A short hymn which comprises the final two verses of the devotional song *Verbum supernum prodiens* ("The heavenly word issuing forth"), attributed to St. Thomas Aquinas. It is customarily sung during Benediction.

JOSEPH QUINN

See also BENEDICTION (OF THE BLESSED SACRAMENT); HYMNS.

OBEDIENCE

See EVANGELICAL COUNSELS; VOWS.

OBERAMMERGAU

Oberammergau is a small Bavarian town which was saved from the ravages of the plague in the early seventeenth century. In gratitude, the townspeople vowed in 1633 to perform a play about the passion and death of Jesus Christ, which has been performed every ten years since then. It developed continually into something larger and more elaborate and drew large crowds from many countries. It takes about nine hours and is performed in a large open-air theater. About seven hundred actors take part and consider it a kind of religious worship. The major roles for actors became a legacy in certain families, passing from parents to children.

Although built around texts from Scripture, the text and tableaux also incorporated many elements of later Christian piety. In the nineteenth century, music was added, and continuous small additions and alterations were made to improve style and content.

While this Passion Play has been very inspirational for Christians from far and wide, it had carried over from the seventeenth century some blatantly anti-Semitic elements. Prompted by reflection on the Nazi Holocaust and by contemporary scholarship and ecumenism, an international group of scholars suggested amendments to correct the anti-Semitism carried over uncritically from earlier times. Changes were made in 1980, the special performance in 1984, and again in 1990, leaving the play much more accurate historically by the excision of anti-Semitic references, texts, and characterizations.

MONIKA K. HELLWIG

See also PASSION NARRATIVES.

OBLATE

(Lat. *oblatus,* "offered") A member of a religious community who has offered himself or herself to the monastic life or a similar form of religious ministry. In the first centuries of the Middle Ages, the term referred to children pledged by their parents to a monastery, where they received their upbringing. In subsequent years, laity who lived in or near—and offered themselves and their property to—a monastery were known as oblates. In modern times, a number of orders have "oblate" in their title—such as Oblates of Mary Immaculate.

JOSEPH QUINN

See also LAITY, THEOLOGY OF THE; RELIGIOUS ORDERS.

O'BROIN, LEON (1902–1990)

Irish patriot, gifted historian, lay apostle, O'Broin was a Dubliner who came to early manhood in the years of Irish independence. He served in the first national army of his country, then entered government service where as a lawyer he rose to be the administrative head of the Department of Posts and Telegraphs, to which was also subject Radio Eireann, later Radio Telefis Eireann. In government service he met and worked with Frank Duff, later joined the Legion of Mary, and was editor of its periodical, *Mary Legionis.* A bilingual writer, Irish and English, he gained a reputation for well-researched monographs. In time O'Broin became a founder member of three societies which drew on a large interfaith membership in Dublin: The Mercier Society for dialogue with Protestants, the Pillar of Fire Society for dialogue with Jews, Common Ground for dialogue with writers and artists. He read papers at all three. The two societies fostering religious dialogue had immense success, but they were then subjected to restrictive ecclesiastical vigilance and were finally suppressed. Common Ground did not long survive them.

Leon O'Broin

O'Broin had an international reputation, being a member of the European Broadcasting Union and the International Telecommunications Association. He was an ideal choice as representative of the Legion of Mary to the Second International Congress on the Lay Apostolate summoned by Pius XII. Because of his personal qualities and cultural finesse he influenced the personal lives of many. His life ended in a debilitating illness which he bore with exemplary faith and fortitude.

MICHAEL O'CARROLL, C.S.Sp.

See also CATHOLICISM, IRISH; DUFF, FRANK; LEGION OF MARY.

O'CONNELL, DANIEL (1775–1847)

Irish political leader. He was the eldest son of Morgan O'Connell of Carhen, County Kerry, but was adopted by his childless uncle, Maurice "Hunting Cap" O'Connell, who lived in nearby Derrynane on the wild Atlantic coast. Daniel was educated in France, where he saw the revolution firsthand and recoiled from its violence. Upon his return home he studied law and became a barrister (a courtroom attorney), as which he quickly acquired a formidable reputation. His first venture into politics was to oppose the Act of Union, which abolished the Irish parliament in 1800 and amalgamated Ireland with Great Britain in a single "United Kingdom," but he soon threw himself into the struggle for Catholic emancipation. He virulently attacked the government's attempt to secure Catholic acceptance of emancipation subject to allowing the king a veto in the appointment of bishops.

O'Connell eventually concluded that direct action was likely to be more effective than mere lobbying. Instead of trying to negotiate concessions, he moved the argument to the higher ground of what today would be called civil liberties: "The right of every man to freedom of conscience," he said, was "equally the right of a Protestant in Italy or Spain as of a Catholic in Ireland." To promote this cause he

Daniel O'Connell

founded the Catholic Association in 1823, which everybody could join for the subscription of a penny a month and which was dedicated to achieving emancipation by political means. Both the principle declared and the concept of popular democracy chosen to force a reluctant government to implement it were of major significance for they showed that a Catholic could espouse the values of the revolution while rejecting its methods, that the Church and the revolution—God and liberty—could be reconciled. This was the greatest achievement of O'Connell's career and the most important outcome of the emancipation campaign.

Following the victory won in 1829 (see *Emancipation, Catholic*), O'Connell, now known as "The Liberator," took his seat in Parliament and proceeded quickly to build up an Irish party whose support was wooed by English politicians. O'Connell used this advantage shrewdly to extract acknowledgment from the Whig government of the full citizenship shared by all the people of Ireland. Judgeships and other state appointments were now conferred on Catholics as well as Protestants, municipal administration was taken out of the control of closed monopolies, a tax levied for the support of the established (Anglican) Church was abolished in its most discriminatory form. Nor did O'Connell confine his promotion of human rights to rights for the Irish. He spoke up for English Jews and when offered the backing of men who owned slaves in the West Indies if he would drop his support for the abolition of slavery, he spurned them, saying, "May my right hand forget its cunning and my tongue cleave to my mouth if to help Ireland—even Ireland—I forget the Negro one single hour."

O'Connell never abandoned his first political objective of gaining self-government for Ireland by securing repeal of the Act of Union. He deliberately suspended his demand for repeal as long as a relatively friendly government held office in London from which he could extract urgently needed reforms, but when a Tory administration returned to power in 1841 he revived his campaign for restoration of an Irish Parliament, under which the only link with Britain would be the monarchy common to both islands. He formed a Repeal Association modeled on the Catholic Association of the 1820s and organized huge "monster meetings" attended by hundreds of thousands to show the extent of support for repeal.

Unlike the romantic pressure group, Young Ireland, which grew up within the repeal movement, he rigorously refused to approve of any resort to arms or even lawbreaking: when the government proscribed a "monster meeting" planned for Clontarf outside Dublin in 1843 O'Connell at once called it off. He was jailed for conspiracy, but the government was unable to sustain its case and O'Connell had to be released. Famine, however, was soon spreading through Ireland. Incipient senility and a bruising break with the Young Irelanders further weakened O'Connell's grasp on popular leadership and in 1847 he died in Genoa as a pilgrim on his way to Rome.

Irish Catholic triumphalism as much as English prejudice did immense injury to the memory of O'Connell in the century after his death. So far from being merely a sectarian hero or rabble-rouser, O'Connell was essentially a man imbued with the best values of the Enlightenment wedded to a profound Catholic faith: a novel, indeed unique, combination until he showed that rightly understood it involved no contradiction. The lesson was read by thoughtful believers in Europe who sensed the many truths behind the superficial anticlericalism of liberal propagandists. From France came Montalembert, Tocqueville and Beaumont (who wrote a still readable and reliable assessment of O'Connell's Ireland) to see the Irish developments firsthand. Lamennais and Lacordaire acknowledged their debt to O'Connell. So, later, did the more cautious Germans, von Ketteler, Görres and Döllinger; and likewise Rosmini and Ventura in Italy. The Catholic Church took longer to absorb the message: not until John XXIII would it fully accept that human rights as democratic society understands them are the concomitant of God-given human dignity. Or as Lacordaire put it in 1848, preaching the panegyric on O'Connell in the cathedral of Notre Dame in Paris, "To deny the rights of man is to deny the rights of God ... the rights of God and human rights form a unity ... liberty is a work of virtue, a holy work and therefore a work of the Spirit."

LOUIS McREDMOND

See also CATHOLICISM, IRISH; HUMAN RIGHTS; RELIGIOUS FREEDOM.

O'CONNOR, FLANNERY (1925–1964)

Southern American writer of fiction. Novels: *Wise Blood, The Violent Bear it Away*. Stories: *Everything that Rises Must Converge*. Non-Fiction: *Mystery and Manners* (essays), *The Habit of Being: Letters of Flannery O'Connor*.

In one of her letters Flannery O'Connor tells of a dinner party at which the hostess was a "Big Intellectual," who "departed the Church at the age of 15." "We went at eight and at one I hadn't opened my mouth once, there being nothing for me in such company to say ... Having me there was like having a dog present who had been trained to say a few words but overcome with inadequacy had forgotten them." The conversation turned to the Eucharist, which was, the hostess suggested, a "pretty good" symbol. "I then said, in a very shaky voice, 'Well, if it's a symbol, to hell with it.' That was all the defense I was capable of but I realize now that this is all I will ever be able to say about it, outside of a story, except that it is the center of existence for me; all the rest of life is expendable." (Sally Fitzgerald, ed., *The Habit of Being: Letters of Flannery O'Connor,* New York: Random House, 1980, pp. 124–125). Both her faith and her fiction start here.

Flannery O'Connor's faith was anchored in the Judeo-Christian tradition: "... all my own experience has been that of the writer who believes, in Pascal's words, in the 'God of Abraham, Isaac, and Jacob and not of the philosophers and scholars.' This is an unlimited God ... who has revealed himself specifically. It is one who became man and rose from the dead. It is one who confounds the senses and sensibilities, one known early on as a stumbling block. There is no way to gloss over this specification or to make it more acceptable to modern thought. This God is the object of ultimate concern and he has a name." (F. O'Connor, *Mystery and Manners,* eds. Sally and Robert Fitzgerald, New York: Farrar, Straus & Giroux, 1969, p. 161).

While her own faith was grounded in sacrament, she wrote for an audience which denied sacrament because it no longer recognized the sacred. A sharp challenge for a woman who believed one should only write about things "of the gravest concern ... and

Flannery O'Connor

for me this is always the conflict between an attraction for the Holy and the disbelief in it that we breathe in with the air of the times." (Fitzgerald, ed., *The Habit of Being,* p. 349). Sacrament, for her, meant grace coming through matter, through the concrete, observable world of the people around her who spoke with a Georgia dialect, who were innocent of grammar, who lived in small towns. That world was largely unredeemed and it bred evil. To render the impact of Christ's redemption, she had to make the evil believable. "When we think about the Crucifixion we miss the point of it if we don't think about sin" (Fitzgerald, ed., *The Habit of Being,* p. 143).

To *make* the point, she used the technique of distortion: *sharpening* evil to make it visible to readers who no longer believe in sin. At the close of "A Good Man is Hard to Find" a demented murderer and a garrulous old woman are standing on the edge of a woods where two other men have just led her son, daughter-in-law and grandchildren. The criminal calls himself "The Misfit," he tells her, "because I can't make what all I done wrong fit what all I gone through in punishment."

"There was a piercing scream from the woods, followed closely by a pistol report ... There were two more pistol reports and the grandmother raised her head like a parched old turkey hen crying for water and called, 'Bailey Boy, Bailey Boy!' as if her heart would break." The Misfit calmly talks about Jesus. As the grandmother grows disoriented, he ponders whether Jesus was raised from the dead. "'Listen lady,' he said in a high voice, 'if I had of been there I would of known and I wouldn't be like I am now.'

His voice seemed about to crack and the grandmother's head cleared for an instant. She saw the man's face twisted close to her own as if he were going to cry and she murmured, 'Why you're one of my babies. You're one of my own children!' She reached out and touched him on the shoulder. The Misfit sprang back as if a snake had bitten him and shot her three times through the chest. Then he put his gun down on the ground and took off his glasses and began to clean them. . . ." (F. O'Connor, "A Good Man is Hard to Find," *Flannery O'Connor, The Complete Stories,* New York: Farrar, Straus & Giroux, 1971, pp. 131–132).

Flannery O'Connor explains: "There is a moment of grace in most of the stories, or a moment when it is offered, and is usually rejected. Like when the grandmother recognizes the Misfit as one of her own children and reaches out to touch him . . . This moment of grace excites the devil to frenzy" (Fitzgerald, ed., *The Habit of Being,* p. 373). As Christ's standing in front of the Sanhedrin and acknowledging that he was God's son stirred the rage that led to his crucifixion, so the grandmother's startled recognition that The Misfit is "one of my own children" roused him to fury. Violence is a tool to shock a world grown deaf to the truth. For the hard of hearing, Flannery insisted, "you have to shout."

She defined her writing sharply against any intellectual, pietistic or sentimental approach: ". . . the writer . . . (calls) up the general and maybe the essential through the particular, but this general and essential is still deeply embedded in mystery. It is not answerable to any of our formulas. It doesn't rest finally in a statable kind of solution. It ought to throw you back on the living God. Our Catholic mentality is great on paraphrase, logic, formula, instant and correct answers. We judge before we experience and never trust our faith to be subjected to reality because it is not strong enough" (Fitzgerald, ed., *The Habit of Being,* p. 516). Through writing fiction she subjected her own strong faith to reality. Her vocation as an artist demanded that her moral sense coincide with her dramatic sense, to "penetrate the concrete world in order to find at its depth the image of its source" (*Mystery and Manners,* p. 157). To be true to her vocation she had to be true to the nature of fiction: "When fiction is made according to its nature, it should reinforce our sense of the supernatural by grounding it in concrete, observable reality" (*Mystery and Manners,* p. 148).

Her life, like her fiction, was rooted in a concrete world. In 1951, sick with lupus, the disease that had killed her father, she settled on her mother's Georgia farm. And there she stayed until her death at age thirty-nine, raising peafowl, observing the farm hands, and writing letters to her many friends. Her letters shift easily from philosophy ("I have sent you *Art and Scholasticism.* It's the book I cut my aesthetic teeth on . . .") to the latest news from the farm ("I have bought us a new refrigerator—the kind that spits the ice cubes at you, the trays shoot out and hit you in the stomach, and if you step on a certain button, the whole thing glides from the wall and knocks you down. . . .") (Fitzgerald, ed., *The Habit of Being,* p. 175).

Aptly titled *The Habit of Being,* the letters catch the flavor of her days, her comic sense of life, and the price Flannery paid for her faith, "every step of the way." "What people don't realize is how much religion costs. They think faith is a big electric blanket, when of course, it is the cross (Fitzgerald, ed., *The Habit of Being,* p. 354). To a friend struggling with intellectual questions of faith she wrote: "You will have found Christ when you are concerned with other people's sufferings and not your own" (Fitzgerald, ed., *The Habit of Being,* p. 453). Her last letter testifies that she took her own advice. A friend in New York was receiving anonymous phone calls. Flannery wrote back: "Don't take any romantic attitude toward that call. Be properly scared and go on doing what you have to do, but take the necessary precautions. And call the police . . . Don't know when I'll send those stories. I've felt too bad to type them. Cheers" (Fitzgerald, ed., *The Habit of Being,* p. 596). She died six days later. Her mother found this letter next to her bed—and mailed it.

Whether in violent stories or blunt letters to the friends she loved Flannery O'Connor always wrote about "felt life" "from the standpoint of the central Christian mystery: that it has, for all its horror, been found by God to be worth dying for" (*Mystery and Manners,* p. 146).

PATRICIA O'CONNOR

See also AMERICAN CATHOLICISM.

OCTAVE

(fr. Lat. *octavus,* "eighth") The liturgical practice of commemorating a Church feast over a period of eight days, beginning with the feast day itself. The eighth and final day is known as the octave day. The Church celebrated numerous octaves before the Second Vatican Council; currently, only those of Christmas and Easter are observed. During an octave, the feast being observed takes precedence over any other feast which may occur.

JOSEPH QUINN

See also LITURGY.

OFFICE OF THE DEAD

The Office of the Dead is one of the most ancient Offices in the Roman Breviary (Liturgy of the Hours). Some think that it may even have originated before the pontificate of Pope St. Gregory the Great (590–604). Its structure is Roman in style without Gallican or monastic influences. It resembles most closely the Office for the last three days of Holy Week, and it contains no hymns or introductory orations, in marked contrast to the monastic and Gallican Offices. Its structure and celebration have varied over the years, and in its current form, it resembles the other Hours in possessing its own selections of psalms, scriptural and nonscriptural readings. The Office of the Dead is often prayed in common at the funeral liturgies and wakes of religious and clergy, and there is a growing appreciation for it among the laity.

ANTHONY D. ANDREASSI

See also LITURGY OF THE HOURS.

OLD CATHOLICS

This is a designation for a loose affiliation of Christian Churches in Europe which have separated themselves from the Roman Catholic Church but do not consider themselves in the Protestant tradition. They achieved a degree of unity at the Union of Utrecht of 1889.

The Old Catholics originated in 1724 when a group of Catholics and three bishops in Utrecht separated themselves from Rome because of their support for the French Jansenists. Quite independently of them, in the late nineteenth century a small group of German Catholics broke away from the Catholic Church when they rejected the definition of papal infallibility and papal primacy at Vatican Council I (1870). There were also sympathetic groups in Switzerland and Austria who were dissatisfied with Rome for these and other reasons. Since they failed to attract any Catholic bishops to their movement, these groups sought apostolic succession from the older Church of Utrecht. In 1889 they came together as an association when they formed the Union of Utrecht and formulated a common doctrinal statement. In the U.S.A. a group of dissident Polish Catholics also broke away from Rome over the issue of Polish nationalism in the American Church to form the Polish National Catholic Church in 1897. Later they formally subscribed to the teachings of the Union of Utrecht and received apostolic succession from the Old Catholic bishops.

Most Old Catholics today subscribe to the declaration of faith drawn up at the Union of Utrecht in 1889. They accept the teachings of the first eight ecumenical councils of the Church, reject the deuterocanonical books of the Old Testament accepted by the Roman Catholic Church, and do not require priestly celibacy. They also reject the Catholic teaching on transubstantiation and the sacrificial nature of the Eucharist, the veneration of saints, the necessity of auricular confession, and the intercessory role of the Virgin Mary.

In 1925 the Old Catholics recognized Anglican orders and agreed to intercommunion with them in 1932. However, the Orthodox Churches will not allow intercommunion with them and view them as schismatics from Roman Catholicism. Other small ecclesial bodies which call themselves "Old Catholics" are not recognized by the "official" body or association of Old Catholics.

ANTHONY D. ANDREASSI

See also CATHOLICISM; SCHISM.

OPTION FOR THE POOR

The *preferential option for the poor* was institutionalized at the episcopal conference at Medellín (1968), enthusiastically endorsed at Puebla (1979), and confirmed as a principle for the whole Church by Pope John Paul II in his encyclical *Laborem Exercens* (1981).

The option for the poor recognizes that the evangelical commitment of the Church, like that of Christ, should be a commitment to those most in need. When we draw near to the poor in order to accompany them and serve them, we are doing what Christ taught us to do.

We ought to side with the poor because Scripture tells us that this is what God does. In the OT, especially in the Exodus event, God is seen as saving the oppressed and establishing them as God's people. God liberates them from oppression and poverty simply because they are poor and oppressed, not because they are better or more moral than others.

The objective of the preferential option for the poor is to proclaim Christ the Savior. The evangelization of the poor is a messianic sign which looks to liberation from all the sufferings and enslavements of human existence. The poor are enlightened about their dignity and helped in their efforts to liberate themselves from all forms of oppression.

DENNIS SWEETLAND

See also MERCY; POOR, THE; SOCIAL TEACHING OF THE CHURCH.

OPUS DEI

The multinational organization known as Opus Dei (the Work of God) was founded in Madrid in 1928 by Msgr. José María Escriva de Balaguer. He had gathered and inspired a small group of priests and laypeople who, as members of Opus Dei, made a commitment to live highly disciplined and exemplary Christ-centered lives. Under the spiritual direction of Escriva, their numbers and influence grew; and in 1950 Opus Dei received Vatican approval as a secular lay institute. While membership is open to Catholics in all walks of life, most of its members are educated, middle-class professionals. It has about 75,000 lay members, 1300 priests and over 350 seminarians. While it claims to have members in over 80 countries, its membership is predominately European, 40 percent of whom are Spanish. In recent years, Opus Dei has been subjected to widespread criticism as "the conservative, elitist and elusive Roman Catholic organization." Much of the criticism has originated from former Opus Dei members and some of it may not have been justified. But matters are not helped by the aura of secrecy that surrounds the activities of the organization. Pope John Paul II has taken a personal interest in Opus Dei and has given it his enthusiastic approval and active backing. In 1982 he elevated the secular institute to the Prelature of the Holy Cross and Opus Dei; and in 1992, the Pope exercised his prerogatives and had Msgr. Escriva, who only died in 1975, beatified.

MICHAEL GLAZIER

See also INSTITUTE, SECULAR.

"ORATE FRATRES"

See "WORSHIP."

ORATORIANS

Members of the Congregation of the Oratory, formed by St. Philip Neri in 1564 and sanctioned by Pope Paul V in 1612. St. Philip's Oratory, named after the oratory at San Girolamo in Rome (where Philip and a community of fellow priests held their first meetings) is comprised of societies of secular priests and brothers living in community without public vows. The individual oratories, or houses, were independent until 1942, when they were consolidated into a confederation. The superior of each house is elected every three years. Oratorians exercise their apostolate through prayer, popular preaching, the sacraments, and instruction—particularly of the young.

JOSEPH QUINN

See also INSTITUTE, SECULAR; NERI, PHILIP, ST.

ORDERS

See SACRAMENT OF ORDERS.

ORDINARY, LOCAL

An ecclesiastic who possesses the established jurisdiction of a particular office; this authority pertains to his rights of teaching, governing, adjudicating, and administering the sacraments. The title applies to the pope and all diocesan bishops; vicars, abbots, and other major superiors of religious communities of men; prelates or prefects with regional jurisdiction and their respective deputies; and, when a see is vacant, the vicar capitular or administrator.

JOSEPH QUINN

See also ABBOT; BISHOP.

ORDINATION

See SACRAMENT OF ORDERS.

ORIGEN (ca. 185–ca. 254)

Eusebius (*Ecclesiastical History* 6) gives details of Origen's life. Probably born in Alexandria, Origen came from a Christian family. His father Leonides was martyred in 202 during the persecution of Septimius Severus. Bishop Demetrius appointed Origen as head of the Catechetical School after Clement fled Alexandria. He began to lead a very ascetical life: fasting, spending long nights in prayer, voluntary poverty, even castrating himself (taking Matthew 19:12 in too literal a sense). The first part of his teaching career (203 to 230) was very successful. Eventually he lectured to the advanced students in theology, philosophy, and Scripture, while also attending for a time the lectures on philosophy and literature of the Neoplatonist Ammonius Saccus.

In 215 or 216 Origen traveled to Palestine where the bishops of Jerusalem, Caesarea and other cities invited Origen, though not a priest, to preach. Demetrius of Alexandria objected to this breach of ecclesiastical discipline and ordered him to return to Alexandria. In 230 Bishops Alexander of Jerusalem and Theoctistus of Caesarea ordained him to the priesthood when Origen stopped at Caesarea on his way to Greece. As a result of this Demetrius removed him from his teaching responsibilities and the priesthood owing to the irregular nature of his ordination. Origen then left Alexandria for Caesarea in Palestine where the local bishop invited him to establish a school of theology. For the next twenty years Origen continued his teaching, preaching, and literary activity.

During the Decian persecution in 250, Origen was imprisoned and tortured in the hope that he might apostatize. His sufferings in prison broke his health, and he died soon afterward.

Origen was a most productive author. His chief work on biblical criticism was the *Hexapla,* an edition of the Old Testament in which the Hebrew text, the Hebrew text transliterated into Greek characters, and four Greek versions (Aquila, Symmachus, Septuagint, and Theodotion) were laid out in parallel columns. It represents the first attempt to establish a critical text of the Old Testament. He wrote scholia (brief explanations of difficult passages), commentaries, and homilies on every book of the Bible. He preferred to look beyond the literal meaning of the text to find its moral, dogmatic, or spiritual meaning. Between 220 and 230 he wrote *First Principles,* the first treatise to investigate various aspects of Christian theology in a systematic way. Two ascetical works by Origen, the *Exhortation to Martyrdom* and *On Prayer* were widely read in Christian antiquity. His *Against Celsus* is a very important apologetical treatise against a formidable opponent of Christianity. Celsus was a philosopher who systematically attacked Christianity in order to show the reasonableness of paganism in the *True Discourse.* Origen took up each of the arguments raised by Celsus in the eight books of the *Against Celsus* and presented a philosophical case for Christianity in a calm and dignified manner.

Origen defended the unity of God, but also held that the Son was eternally generated from the Father. The Holy Spirit is also eternal, but it is not clear in Origen how the Holy Spirit is related to the Father and the Son. For Origen the Son can only be divine in a lesser sense than the Father: the Son is God but the Father is absolute God.

One of his most controversial theories was that of the preexistence of souls. All spirits were created equal. As they exercised their free wills, some fell into sin and so became demons or souls imprisoned within bodies. Death did not in the end decide the fate of the soul which may become an angel or a demon. This process of ascent or descent will go on until finally angels, humankind, and even devils share in the grace of salvation. After his death and especially in the fourth and sixth centuries, some theologians attacked the more daring parts of his teachings with the result that many of his writings were burned. In the course of the disputes on Origenism (various theories enunciated by or attributed to Origen), his teachings have often been misrepresented. Since we no longer have original texts, it becomes difficult to reconstruct his authentic thought. There has been a rediscovery and clearer understanding of Origen's spirituality and exegesis in the twentieth century with the result that Origen's surviving works are widely read today.

JOHN DILLON

See also DOCTRINE, DEVELOPMENT OF; FATHERS OF THE CHURCH; THEOLOGY, SYSTEMATIC.

ORIGINAL SIN

Original sin as an explanation of evil is a central topic of Catholic teaching. It is not explicitly found in Old or New Testaments, but there was sufficient biblical background for it to be proclaimed a doctrine of faith by the Council of Trent. It is presented there as a personal actual sin on the part of the first man, resulting in the loss of the state of original justice or holiness, wounding the human nature passed on to his descendants, darkening their understanding and weakening their will, and leaving them subject to pain and death. This teaching stresses that original sin is a condition of guilt found in all human beings (except Mary the mother of Jesus) prior to any personal act of sin on their part. It also defines that it does not consist in concupiscence, since this remains after justification by grace. Essentially, original sin is the lack of that sanctifying grace or holiness which God intended for, and offered to humanity in the person of Adam. But it is more than a mere lack or absence, a kind of natural defect. Church teaching insists on calling it a sin on the part of our first parent and says that it is passed to his descendants by propagation or generation, and not merely by imitation. Original sin is a mystery of faith, not simply because of the difficulty of understanding it in today's scientific and democratic culture, but because it belongs in the context of grace, which is the mystery of God's self-communication and self-gift, totally unmerited, wholly gratuitous.

The common understanding of this dogma may have left a negative streak in the Church's psyche, but the motivation of the teaching was quite positive, namely, to stress, with the revealed Word of God, that Jesus came as the Savior of all humankind, that in him evil has been overcome, and through him we are intrinsically restored to the status intended for us in creation itself, that of sons and daughters of God, sharing his Spirit and life. The Old Testament has no explicit teaching about a primordial sin whose effects were passed on to later generations of the human race, but throughout Jewish history humanity's inherent sinfulness and its need for salvation were continually recognized. The Gospels give no indication of original sin or its effects. When St. Paul stressed the universality of sin he traced it to its source in Adam, and spoke of it as a state or condition of human nature itself, into which we are born, and from which sinful actions come forth. It was Paul's strong teaching in Romans 5:12-19, contrasting Adam and Christ, that led later theology to read Genesis 3 as a description of the first sin, the fall of humanity.

The traditional understanding of original sin is faced with serious criticism in today's culture. (1) In spite of the obvious evils in the world, it is generally accepted that human nature is basically sound and good. Individual and social evils are seen as unfortunate consequences of civilization which can be eliminated by human effort, without need of any deeper evil, such as original sin, to explain them. (2) Likewise, people today see concupiscence and death as part of the natural order of things, understandable and acceptable, and see no need to link them to humanity's original sinfulness. The traditional teaching was strongly and negatively colored by Augustine's linking of original sin with the *libido* in the parents' lovemaking, through which the sin is transmitted, and this strikes a false note when measured against the experience of good people today. (3) The modern democratic mind finds it difficult to accept that the whole human race should be punished for a sin of its first parent, whether the descendants are seen as potentially present in him as parent or representatively and morally present in him as their head. (4) Most of all, in the light of what science has to say of human origins, it is extremely difficult to accept the traditional teaching of a cataclysmic sin at the dawn of human history, with the implication that the dogma almost requires one to opt for monogenism (i.e., the human race originating from a single couple).

Despite these difficulties, the doctrine remains a dogma of Catholic faith that cannot be ignored or watered down. The Council of Trent defined it in terms of the culture and theology of its time, with all the limitations of Augustine's genetic model, but mere verbal repetition will not keep its truth alive today. To make it meaningful and credible in today's scientific culture, theologians have attempted to distinguish between the substance of the teaching and its formulation, with the reminder that the latter of necessity will always be culturally conditioned. It would seem that the substance of Christian faith in this area can be summarized in the statements: that Christ is at the very center of the divine plan, that all human beings have a basic need of the redemption he brought about, and this need is antecedent to any act of sin on their part, or even mere exposure to a sinful environment.

It is now more clearly recognized that the biological, legal, pathological, and botanical models used by Augustine to describe how our human nature became tainted by *original sin* (he first coined the term) are nothing more than metaphors, poetic exaggerations to describe a sinful state about which he personally felt very strongly. Unfortunately, Augustine's poetic license was translated by Scholastic theology into metaphysical abstraction and soon the common understanding was of an historical sequence of events, with our first parents being created in grace, endowed with preternatural gifts (clarity of mind, strength of will, freedom from pain and death), failing the test of obedience through their sin, losing their privileged state and thus needing the redemption of Christ. But it is now recognized that Genesis 3 is not a literal description of an historical first sin, but an ingenious psychological description of all sin, telling us nothing of what happened at the beginning of human history, but reminding us of what is happening all the time in our sinful existence. It needs to be read not in the past tense, but in the continuous present. The dogma of original sin gives no details about our historical, physical origins, but stresses the flawed state of our basically good human nature as intended and created by God, and sets that in the context of Christ's saving grace. Modern theology is more inclined to link the theology of grace with the theology of creation, focusing on the divine plan as a whole, and bypassing the problems raised by a narrow concern with origins.

In spite of the criticisms mentioned above, modern human beings, even as nonbelievers, can understand and accept the reality symbolized in the myth of the fall. Only an incurable optimist could fail to recognize the seemingly inevitable mixture of good and evil in all human existence, both individual and social. Even our best motives are mixed and even our highest ideals can be ambiguous. Mysterious forces in our subconscious can be directed to both good and evil. St. Paul speaks of these opposing forces and the tension they create, and links this with sin. The Second Vatican Council refers to the same human experience, pointing out that "man is unable to overcome the assaults of evil successfully, so that everyone feels as though bound by chains" (Church in the Modern World, 13). In this sense modern theology would claim that "to be human is to be situated in a sinful world, to be affected by it even before personal choice becomes possible, to be the product of a sinful human history, and to have an inherent predisposition to sin." This approach avoids the crude notion of a sinful human nature inherited from a sinful first parent, but it also runs the risk of reducing original sin to a matter of external contagion from a sinful environment.

There is no doubt that every human being is born into a sinful world and is not only affected, but also *infected* by that fact. The embryo and the growing fetus can be harmed by its parents' chemical addictions. The young child can be emotionally warped by siblings and elders, and all human beings can be deformed by unjust and inhuman social structures. The forces of evil are of human making, and yet they seem to involve a greater and more mysterious power. In this sense, to be human is to be in need of salvation, because side by side with this dark side of our nature there is the picture of the ideal human being revealed and promised in Christ, in whose image we were created. The doctrine of original sin is a foil to proclaim that where sin abounds, grace does more abound, that in Christ there is the fullness of forgiveness and healing. Indeed recent theology extends the work of Christ beyond the human family to embrace the whole of creation, echoing St. Paul's words about "nature groaning for its salvation."

A novel and exciting development in theology is the stress, not only on God's responsibility *for* creation, but his involvement *in* creation, and also humanity's physical, chemical, and biological roots in the material world which is not only its garden, but in a certain sense its womb. This awareness of the continuing development of the universe and of our human culture goes beyond the notion of a fixed, static human nature passed on from one generation to the next, and opens up horizons for a growing, developing nature that can imperceptibly make progress or also suffer setbacks. It is not for theology to invade the field of biology or anthropology, but in this wider context it is not inappropriate for the theologian to speculate about the stages that preceded hominization, and to glimpse perhaps the beginnings of original sin at the various points in cultural development when the gain from a significant leap forward also involved a certain loss. Ambiguity and the tension between good and evil would seem to have deeper roots than the first sin of the mythical couple who are credited with founding our race. Theological reflection needs to look at evolution, but it is doubtful if any theory can do full justice to the mysterious reality symbolized by original sin. Much more study is needed. But the abiding certainty of Catholic faith is that the forgiving, healing grace of Christ is a much more powerful and far-reaching reality.

SEÁN FAGAN, S.M.

See also SALVATION; SIN; SOTERIOLOGY.

ORTHODOXY

From two Greek words, *orthos* meaning straight or correct, and *doxa* meaning opinion, orthodoxy means holding the right beliefs according to official Church teaching. Christians of the earliest centuries seem to have been more concerned with orthopraxis (living and acting rightly) than with orthodoxy. However, even in the second Christian century when some particularly egregious religious ideas were being promoted, bishops like St. Irenaeus were at great pains to demonstrate that they were heterodox (other than the received teaching of the Churches). Orthodoxy became an issue in the Churches in an entirely new way and on a universal scale at the beginning of the fourth century when the Arian dispute (whether Jesus is truly divine) prompted the emperor Constantine to initiate a series of ecumenical councils which issued definitions, creeds, and condemnations. The consequence of this development was the excommunication and schism not of individuals or factions but of whole clusters of local churches. Eventually orthodoxy disputes were concerned not only with major doctrines of the faith but with words in the creeds such as the *filioque* ("and from the Son" concerning the procession of the Holy Spirit) and with the proper date for Easter, two issues which divided the Churches of East and West into a millennium-long schism which has never been healed. In the sixteenth century orthodoxy disputes arose again in the Western Church over teachings concerning the sacraments, the vocabulary of "justification" and "faith" and so forth, dividing the Western Churches into Catholic and Protestant, roughly into south and north.

In the Catholic Church the touchstone of orthodoxy is the magisterium, the official voice of the Church as embodied in the bishops and councils, but especially in the pope. As the pope does not deal personally with all issues that arise, a commission was set up by Pope Gregory IX in 1233, which came to be known as the Inquisition. Originally intended to correct heretical opinions by expounding the official teaching and inviting profession of faith, it often fell into the control of ignorant and unscrupulous people. As guardian of Catholic orthodoxy, this office continued for many centuries under the name "The Holy Office" and is succeeded in our time by the Congregation for the Doctrine of the Faith.

The content of Catholic orthodoxy is less easily defined, consisting of Scripture as interpreted in creeds, formal definitions, ordinary agreed teaching and tradition, and the cumulative body of papal and episcopal writings and pronouncements. Because this is a large and amorphous body of teachings, it is generally agreed that there is a "hierarchy of truths," that is to say that some teachings or articles of faith are more central and important than others.

The term Orthodoxy, with a capital letter, more usually refers to the communion of Orthodox Churches comprising mainly Greek and Slavic groups. Among these there is a feast of Orthodoxy commemorating the overthrow of the iconoclast heresy.

MONIKA K. HELLWIG

See also CREEDS; DOCTRINE; DOGMA; HIERARCHY OF TRUTHS; MAGISTERIUM.

ORTHOPRAXIS

From the Greek words, *orthos* meaning straight or correct, and *praxis* meaning action or deed, the term orthopraxis as used in contemporary theology asserts that acting according to the gospel of Jesus Christ is more important than, and is prior to, having the right beliefs. This is related to the Marxist concept of *praxis* as the engagement with reality about us from which we shape our understanding and our theories. Although the term is a twentieth-century one in theological usage the idea is as old as Christianity, and has long been proposed in the phrase, "imitation of Christ." This notion appears in the letters of Paul in the New Testament and is suggested in the Gospels in the sayings of Jesus. The term orthopraxis is particularly important in the writing of the liberation theologians of Latin America.

MONIKA K. HELLWIG

See also CHRISTIAN SPIRITUALITY; IMITATION OF CHRIST; LIBERATION THEOLOGIES.

L'OSSERVATORE ROMANO

In July 1861, four Catholic laymen began publication in Italian of *L'Osservatore Romano.* Pope Leo XIII bought the newspaper in 1890 and it became known as the "official newspaper of the Pope." Currently, the daily paper prints official news or announcements under the heading *Nostre Informazioni.* It also publishes the official policies and the social and political attitudes of the pope. Its staff of reporters investigate foreign events as well as news in Rome. It has weekly editions in French, Spanish, Portuguese, German, Polish, and English.

PATRICIA DeFERRARI

See also VATICAN.

OTTAVIANI, ALFREDO, CARDINAL (1890–1979)

Alfredo Ottaviani was born on 29 October 1890 in the Trastevere section of Rome, where in his childhood and early education he witnessed the confrontation between a strong anticlerical movement and a popular Catholic religiosity. After ordination from the Roman Seminary in 1916 and advanced studies in canon law and philosophy, he became a professor of the former at the Apollinaris in Rome and of the latter at the Urbaniana. His chief publication was the *Institutiones Iuris Publici Ecclesiastici,* which became a standard work in the field.

Cardinal Alfredo Ottaviani

In 1926 he began a career in the Roman Curia that would last for fifty years, serving in various posts in the Congregation of Propaganda, the Secretariate of State, and the Holy Office, where he served as assessor from 1935 to 1953, when he was named a cardinal and became pro-secretary. During this time the Holy Office took various measures against political and theological movements such as the "*nouvelle théologie*" in France (Chenu, Congar, de Lubac, Teilhard), against the ecumenical movement, the priest-worker movement, any sort of rapprochement with communists, and attempts to question the ideal status of the Catholic confessional state (Maritain, Murray).

In Italian politics, particularly after the Second World War, Ottaviani represented a right-wing stance that was fiercely anti-communist and anti-liberal and convinced that the Church was involved in a mortal struggle over the very nature of civilization. His doctrinal and political intransigence was considered typified by his motto, *Semper idem,* and by the title of one of his books, *Il Baluardo,* "The Bulwark."

The election of Pope John XXIII in 1958 brought to the papal throne a man who did not share Ottaviani's theological and political orientations.

Their differences over Italian and international politics became public knowledge. The doctrinal texts prepared for Vatican II by Ottaviani's theological commission were designed to confirm the major magisterial statements of modern popes as the only appropriate response to a modern and apostate society and culture. Pope John's opening speech at the council rejected this vision of the council's work, and many people thought he was referring to people like Ottaviani when he criticized "prophets of doom" and instead called the council to a positive and pastoral rather than a negative and dogmatic magisterial task. The official doctrinal texts were severely criticized during the first session of the council, and Ottaviani became the symbol of what a new spirit in the Church wished to oppose. The Cardinal and his line had even less strength when Paul VI succeeded to the papacy, and he was unable to prevent the new doctrinal orientation of the conciliar texts nor the series of reforms which followed from them.

In the postconciliar period Ottaviani was critical of the liturgical reforms and particularly disturbed by the doctrinal and disciplinary confusion that followed the council. On the eve of the announcement of the reorientation which Paul VI wished to give to the Holy Office, henceforth to be called the Congregation for the Doctrine of the Faith, Ottaviani submitted his resignation, accepted by the Pope in January 1968. In the last decade of his life, he continued to exercise the role he gladly described as that of *un carabiniere della Chiesa,* "a soldier of the Church." He died on 3 August 1979.

JOSEPH A. KOMONCHAK

See also CONGREGATION FOR THE DOCTRINE OF THE FAITH; VATICAN COUNCIL II.

"OUR FATHER"

See LORD'S PRAYER, THE.

OXFORD MOVEMENT

An effort initiated at Oxford University in the 1830s which sought to restore traditional Catholic principles to the Church of England (or the Anglican Church). Its proponents—including John Keble, John Henry Newman, R. H. Froude, Edward Pusey, and William Ward—were concerned that liberal theology was undermining the Church of England's fundamental doctrines (namely its divinity, the apostolic succession, and the Book of Common Prayer as a rule of faith) and that Church life itself was becoming stagnant. *Tracts for the Times,* a series of essays written by the movement's leaders, specified its teachings and objections; a number of these were censured or condemned by the established Church. Many of the movement's strongest adherents—Newman and Ward among them—converted to the Catholic Church, greatly compromising the movement's vitality. Despite its seeming lack of success, the Oxford Movement is credited with transforming, and restoring the religious life to, the Church of England; renewing interest throughout the country in Catholic doctrine and practice; and inspiring the incorporation of traditional Catholic elements into the Anglican liturgy.

JOSEPH QUINN

See also ANGLICANISM; NEWMAN, JOHN HENRY, CARDINAL.

OZANAM, ANTOINE FREDERIC (1813–1853)

At the age of twenty, while studying law and literature in Paris, he and some friends founded the Society of St. Vincent de Paul (originally called the Conference of Charity), an association of layfolk who committed themselves to devote some regular time to alleviate the suffering of the destitute and the poor. Ozanam chose an academic career and in 1839 published a very erudite and original study of Dante. In 1841 he began to teach foreign literature at the Sorbonne and he also taught rhetoric at the College Stanislas. In 1846 he began research, in Italian libraries, on early Franciscan poetry and six years later he published a comprehensive work on the subject. During these years Ozanam made his work for the Society of St. Vincent de Paul his top priority, and interest in social justice fostered his friendship with Montalembert, Chateaubriand and Lacordaire, who held that the Church's offical policies should not be anchored to moribund conservatism which was becoming progressively divorced from the needs of the working middle class and the poor. As a result, Ozanam was subjected to bitter criticism especially when he joined Lacordaire in 1848 to found *Ère Nouvelle* to propagate their ideas on social justice and structures. Ozanam's increased apostolic work did not prevent him from writing his most respected work *La Civilisation chrétienne chez les Francs* (1849), a study of the Church's educational influence on the Teutonic tribes. He devoted the last five years of his short life to ministering to the poor and guiding the expansion of the Society of St. Vincent de Paul.

JOAN GLAZIER

See also CORPORAL AND SPIRITUAL WORKS OF MERCY; LAITY, THEOLOGY OF THE; ST. VINCENT DE PAUL, SOCIETY OF.

P

PACIFISM

Pacifism usually means a refusal to resort to arms and to take part in warfare. This course of action generally rests on religious grounds, but not necessarily so. Pacifists often appeal to the writings of the New Testament to find the inspiration for their resistance to violence, especially warfare. Although this appeal is not without its scriptural difficulties, Jesus' forgiveness of enemies, his compassion, and his refusal to defend himself through the use of violence provide the basis for the pacifist course of action.

Prior to the Constantinian period Christians usually did not take part in warfare. Origen was of the opinion that the prayers and discipline of Christians contributed more to the Roman Empire than the military exploits of soldiers. With Augustine the Church's attitude toward violence was linked to the just war theory. For Augustine the use of force by legitimate authority was a lawful means for dealing with evil when other means failed. He separated the individual morality of the gospel from the social morality dictated by the common good. However, throughout the Middle Ages there were movements, e.g., the Franciscans and the Waldenses, that urged nonparticipation in warfare. In the seventeenth and eighteenth centuries the Anabaptists and the Society of Friends promoted the same attitude. It is from these movements that the so-called peace Churches, e.g., Mennonites, Quakers, the Brethren, have emerged.

Given the threat of nuclear warfare, the pacifist movement has grown within all Churches. In the United States Dorothy Day and *The Catholic Worker* link pacifism with social spirituality. Thomas Merton taught a contemplative foundation for nonviolence. Martin Luther King, Jr. caught the imagination of an entire country by his gospel of social equality through nonviolence. Outside the United States Mahatma Gandhi laid the international basis and inspiration for pacifism on truth spoken with compassion.

Church documents also speak positively of pacifism. *Pacem in Terris,* encyclical letter of Pope John XXIII, issued April 1963, was a radical assertion of the necessity and possibility of outlawing war completely in the nuclear age. "The Church in the Modern World" from Vatican II, although it employed just war teaching, praised those who renounce the use of violence. *The Challenge of Peace: God's Promise and Our Response* (1983) of the United States Conference of Catholic Bishops teaches two distinct moral options available to Christians, viz., pacifism and just war.

In addition to religiously oriented pacifism there is another phenomenon today, viz., the nonviolence movement. This movement underlines the need for careful strategy and organization as well as an insistence on social justice. The bonding of pacifism and nonviolence emphasizes the role and significance of human justice in the context of history. This union also removes the stigma of sectarianism from pacifism and unites people of a variety of backgrounds in a common cause.

JOHN F. CRAGHAN

See also PAX CHRISTI; PEACE.

PAGANISM

Paganism is a term derived from the Latin *paganus* which originally had no religious meaning but simply meant one who dwelt out in the countryside, not in the city. As Christianity in the early centuries tended to spread from city to city around the Mediterranean, those who lived in the countryside were more likely to be untouched by the new faith and to retain their allegiance to Greek, Roman, Egyptian, or local gods. The term never included members of the other monotheistic traditions, such as Jews and Muslims.

The term paganism is seldom used today, except when dealing with the historical past. When still used in the history of religions or in missiology, the term now applies to those who do not follow any of the great world religions.

MONIKA K. HELLWIG

See also LIMBO; MISSIONS, CATHOLIC, THE MODERN PERIOD.

PALLIUM

A circular band of white woolen material, two inches wide, with two hanging strips, marked with six purple crosses. By ancient custom, it is worn by the pope as a symbol of the plenitude of his episcopal power which he shares with archbishops, each of whom receives a pallium. (On very rare occasions the pope bestows a pallium on a bishop as a special honor.) The pallium is made from the wool of lambs and is blessed on the feast of St. Agnes at the church of St. Agnes fueri le mura; and it rests for a night on the tomb of St. Peter before it is sent to a new archbishop.

MICHAEL GLAZIER

PAPACY, THE

At present, "pope" is the common designation of the Bishop of Rome, but it was more widely used in the early Church. Indeed, it was only used exclusively of the Bishop of Rome from the ninth century.

The popes have traditionally claimed St. Peter as the first of the Roman bishops and that their authority over the Church at large derives from the commission given by Jesus to Peter in Matthew 16:18-19: "You are Peter and upon this rock I will build my church and the gates of hell shall not prevail against it. I will give you the keys of the kingdom of heaven, and whatever you bind on earth will be bound in heaven and whatever you loose on earth will be loosed in heaven." Orthodox and Protestant apologists have always claimed that the papalist interpretation of these verses is exaggerated. Clearly this verse will be a center of ecumenical discussion for years to come, but from the fourth century to the sixteenth its papal character was widely accepted in the Western Church.

From the earliest days of the Church, Rome was an important community. Paul wished to go there, and if chapter 16 is indeed part of the Epistle to the Romans, then Paul was clearly dropping names in order to ingratiate himself to the Roman community. As the eponymous capital of the empire, Rome had immense prestige, and it is not surprising that the Christian community there attained an immediate significance.

A factional dispute in the Church of Corinth ca. 95—proof that the Corinthians had changed little since Paul's day—occasioned a fraternal letter from the Church of Rome. Clement, the traditional third successor of Peter, wrote the letter, not in his own name but in that of the Roman community. (References in later Greek authors refer to Clement's authorship.) This has led scholars to suggest that the Church structure in Rome was collegial, although in the second century a clearly episcopal Church structure had emerged.

Some second-century popes are unknown except for their names, but papal history emerges ca. 160 when Pope Anicetus (ca. 155–ca. 166) was visited by a Greek bishop, Polycarp of Smyrna, to discuss how to determine the date of Easter. Significantly, the two men agreed to disagree. Yet by the end of the century, Victor I (189–198) was threatening to excommunicate those bishops who differed with Rome on the calculation of the date of Easter. The other bishops, including those following the Roman way, were shocked at Victor's intemperance, and he apparently backed down. Unfortunately, scholars do not know what convinced Victor that he could take such harsh unilateral action nor why he abandoned the conciliatory approach of Anicetus.

The controversial Callistus I (217–222), on his own authority, relaxed penitential and marriage regulations for the Romans, much to the chagrin of the traditionalists and rigorists, who chose history's first antipope, Hippolytus (d. 235). Callistus did not try to extend his authority beyond Rome but clearly felt comfortable exercising it within his own jurisdiction.

Evidence that a Roman ideology had been building comes from the pontificate of Stephen I (254–257). In a debate with the African episcopacy and its leader, Cyprian of Carthage, Stephen invoked the authority of the primatial see of Peter and Paul. Scholars do not know how Stephen developed this theory, but its application was unsuccessful. The Africans resisted, and a serious breach was avoided only by Stephen's death, possibly as a martyr.

The situation changed drastically in the fourth century when Constantine I (306–337) became emperor and, after giving the Christians freedom to worship, converted to the faith about 319. The popes now had to deal with emperors who intervened in Church affairs not to persecute but to help; occasionally those being helped saw the emperor as a manipulator if not an outright tyrant. This was also the century of the great theological controversies and the first ecumenical councils, although the popes were for the most part on the sidelines. But they nonetheless were able to increase their authority considerably.

In the late second century the theologian Irenaeus of Lyons enunciated a theological method which would last until the Enlightenment, namely, Scripture and tradition. That is, Christian truth can be found in the Scriptures and in the teaching of those bishoprics which could trace their origins back to the time of the apostles and which had remained orthodox. To give an example of such a bishopric, Irenaeus chose Rome, giving a list of the Roman bishops from Peter to Eleutherius (ca. 174–189). (This list has proved to be invaluable since it alone names some of the earliest popes.) Thus an apostolic foundation raised high the prestige of a see. Importantly, all the apostolic sees but one lay in the East, and Rome's double apostolic foundation (Peter and Paul) soon raised it to the chief see of the West. Furthermore, fourth-century evidence proves that with the exception of the Africans, most Western, Latin bishops accepted this notion.

This notion enabled the popes to play a significant role in the affairs of the day even though they did not always play a direct role. For example, the popes insisted that the decrees of an ecumenical council must have their approval. The Greek bishops who attended the councils did not really believe that, but every side in a theological dispute was anxious to get Roman support because that guaranteed Western support, and thus papal influence grew. The Western bishops, on the contrary, acknowledged the need for papal approval.

Damasus I (366–384) considerably heightened papal prestige by physically remaking Rome into a Christian city, claiming that the new founders of Rome were Peter and Paul, replacing Romulus and Remus. But in the fourth century the references to Paul decrease as the Petrine foundation was mined incessantly. Siricius (384–399) claimed that when he spoke officially, the still-present St. Peter was speaking through him, and Innocent I (401–417) wrote to other bishops in Peter's name. The Easterners resented this but the Westerners accepted it. It was also in the late fourth and fifth centuries that the popes

View of St. Peter's Basilica

began the practice of encouraging other bishops to send questions and especially controverted matters to Rome for settlement, an effective way of making Rome the judge of the West. Siricius, Innocent, and the other popes were also emphatic proclaimers of Rome's headship of all the Churches, not just those in the West.

Leo I the Great (440–461) epitomized the ancient papacy. He personally convinced Attila the Hun to spare Rome after the imperial army had fled, and his Christology was accepted by the ecumenical council of Chalcedon in 451, a signal victory for the papacy in theological matters. As schism rent the East, Rome became more and more a bastion of strength and resilience.

When the Western Roman Empire fell to the barbarians in the fifth century, the popes now had a monumental task in front of them, the conversion of entire barbarian peoples, but the popes were hindered by the Eastern or Byzantine Empire which considered Rome to be a provincial city on the western frontier, subject to Constantinople. Byzantine officals treated the popes in a condescending manner or worse. The emperor Justinian (527–565) had Pope Viligius (537–555) kidnapped and brutalized into approving the decrees of the emperor's Second Council of Constantinople (553).

This intolerable situation was alleviated by Gregory I (the Great) (590–604) who, although loyal to the Byzantine emperor, turned Rome's face to the West. He worked with local bishops to convert the barbarian Visigoths in Spain; he tried to convert the Lombards in Italy; he had preachers root out vestiges of paganism in rural Italy and Sardinia; he tried to stop simony in France; and he sent a Christian mission to the pagan Anglo-Saxons in Britain. While not everyone welcomed the pope's initiatives,

Gregory raised the prestige of the papacy among the Western peoples and guaranteed Rome the spiritual leadership of the Christian West.

For another century and a half the popes balanced the needs of the West with the demands of the East, but the East had changed drastically. The rise of Islam had cost the Byzantine Empire the provinces of Egypt, Palestine, and Syria, and the great ancient Christian cities of Alexandria, Antioch, and Jerusalem were in Muslim hands. The Eastern emperors could no longer exercise dominance in Rome.

When the Muslim threat had been stopped, a new empire arose in the West. With the assistance of Pope Zachary (741–752) in 751, Pepin the Short overthrew the king of France and established his own dynasty. His son Charlemagne (768–814) built a gigantic northern European empire and made clear his intent to dominate the papacy. Pope Leo III (795–816) crowned Charlemagne emperor of the West in 800, a gesture which was to aid the papacy centuries later when the popes were to claim that they and they alone could crown an emperor. It is also in the eighth century that the Italian territories known as the Papal States came into being as Pepin and other French rulers gave land in Italy to their papal ally. This gift would prove to be a burden since it forced the popes to be secular rulers with all the attendant problems.

In the ninth and tenth centuries the papacy was seriously weakened, becoming virtually the exclusive property of aristocratic Roman families, and some truly scandalous wretches occupied the papal throne. But in the eleventh century a group of reformers turned the papacy's prestige into a spiritual weapon to reform the Church at large.

Leo IX (1049–1054) battled against clerical incontinence and simony. He brought to Rome a group of younger reformers who became his curia. When the Byzantines interfered with Church appointments in southern Italy, Leo sent envoys, led by the canonist Humbert, to Constantinople where the anti-Latin patriarch Michael Cerularius argued with the envoys about Latin practices and papal claims of primacy in the Church. Neither side would budge, and in 1054 the envoys and the patriarch exchanged excommunications, technically inaugurating the schism which endured until 1965.

Nicholas II (1058–1061) attempted to limit the influence of outsiders, especially noble laypersons, on the papacy with a decree restricting the election of popes to the cardinal bishops, a group of suburban bishops whose functions till then had been largely liturgical.

But the real reform lay with Gregory VII (1073–1085). One of Leo's young reformers, he came to the papacy with experience and a determination to rid the Church of undue lay influence. He chose to fight over lay investiture, that is, the right of a lay lord to invest a bishop with the symbols of office. This struggle lasted fifty years, and in the end the papacy won—and not just on the question of lay investiture. Although the lay lords showed their willingness to oppose the papacy (Gregory ended his days in exile), the popes had shown that they could unite the Church behind them and could lead a powerful reform movement. Abuses remained, but a structure now existed to deal with them.

The popes of the twelfth and thirteenth centuries were not saints, but they were mostly intelligent, competent men who furthered their office. They strengthened their administration, established a bureaucracy, and encouraged canon lawyers to formulate the rights of the Church vis-à-vis the lay lords. The overall impression is of spiritual concerns being pushed to the background by legal and administrative ones. The size and complexity of the medieval papacy naturally produced abuses, and many of those fought by the Gregorians appeared again, especially simony. To meet the needs of the ever-growing papal state, the cardinals repeatedly chose popes whose governing abilities came first. Innocent III (1198–1216) treated kings and emperors as inferiors (he actually excommunicated John of England), and he arranged his own appointment as regent and guardian for the future German emperor Frederick II (1220–1250). Innocent was the most politically powerful of the medieval popes, and he set the standard for his successors. Politically active popes were so taken for granted that when the cardinals fortuitously elected a saintly hermit to be Celestine V (1294), the ensuing confusion forced the pope to resign after only five months in office.

But the papal concern for administration produced some very solid results. The popes supported a new educational institution, the university, and they also supported two new reforming religious orders, the Dominicans and the Franciscans, even against the opposition of some bishops. Church government became more ordered and responsible; ecumenical councils (I–IV Lateran, I–II Lyons) were common. The popes also supported the Crusades, but the dominance of those wars by European royalty guaranteed that the papal voice in practical matters was small.

Boniface VIII (1294–1303) witnessed and largely provoked the change in lay–papal relations. He took seriously the papal claims to absolute power over all members of the Church, but by this time some European countries, especially France, had become unified nation-states, consumed by their own nationalism and not willing to be ordered about by an international figure like the pope. The French king, Philip IV (1285–1314), opposed Boniface at every turn and drove the pope to his death by an attempted kidnapping. The pope received sympathy but no real assistance; the other European rulers were as anxious as the French to be free of papal authority.

From 1305 to 1377 the popes resided at Avignon, a papal city but French in location and character. The French monarchy dominated the Avignonese popes. The papacy's bureaucracy grew as did its wealth, and Avignon, the "Babylon of the West" as the poet Petrarch called it, seriously lowered papal prestige. When Gregory XI died in Rome in 1378, a disputed election produced two popes, one in Avignon and one in Rome. The European rulers supported the pope who offered them more; their cynicism was evident when a council called at Pisa in 1409 to end the schism produced a third pope.

The Great Western Schism produced the worst administrative crisis the popes ever faced. The popes claimed to have supreme power in the Church, yet here was a supreme problem which they were unable to solve. This situation led many people to wonder that if the popes were unable to exercise this power *de facto,* should they have it *de jure?* The answer was No, and it produced conciliarism.

Conciliarism is the theory that the supreme authority in the Church resides in an ecumenical council. The Council of Constance (1414–1418), organized by lay lords and dissident bishops, formulated this theory and put it into practice, dismissing the claims of the three popes and electing Martin V (1417–1431). Naturally enough the popes opposed conciliarism and fought it steadily but diplomatically. When the Byzantines, realizing that only the West could save them from the Ottoman Turks, asked Eugenius IV (1431–1447) for a reunion of the Churches, he called a council at Ferrara in 1438 in defiance of the then sitting council of Basel. The council of Ferrara-Florence (an outbreak of plague forced the council to move) was a triumph for the pope and marked the end of the conciliar movement.

But conciliarism had raised many hopes of a true Church reform, hopes dashed by Eugenius but also by his successors, the so-called Renaissance popes whose often lurid personal lives created such scandal. These popes had little or no interest in reform, and when the inevitable happened, the reformers were Martin Luther, Ulrich Zwingli, John Calvin, and the other Protestants. The Reformation made the question of authority the central one, claiming that *sola Scriptura,* Scripture alone, was the authority for Christians. They accused the papacy of having built an enormous ecclesiastical structure with no scriptural foundation, and antagonism for the papacy was a hallmark of Protestant polemics until the ecumenical age. The popes responded by stressing their authority. Led by Paul III (1534–1549), they established the Roman Inquisition, approved the new Society of Jesus, and called the Council of Trent (1545–1563) which was always under papal control. By what historians call the Counter Reformation, the popes succeeded in reforming the Catholic Church, abolishing the worst abuses, clarifying Roman Catholic teaching on matters such as the sacraments, and encouraging new forms of piety. But the Protestants did not return to the Roman fold.

In the post-Reformation period, the popes had to rely upon the efforts of the Catholic princes to win back Protestant lands; this policy resulted in such horrors as the Thirty Years War. But the popes were routinely outmaneuvered by such politicians as the Frenchman Cardinal Richelieu, and papal influence was increasingly confined to ecclesiastical matters. The Enlightenment of the eighteenth century treated Roman Catholic belief as one step ahead of superstition, while the French Revolution was genuinely anti-Catholic. In response to these pressures, the popes often aligned themselves with the most conservative and reactionary movements in Europe. Napoleon claimed to restore papal prestige, but when he took the crown from the hands of Pius VII (1800–1823) to crown himself emperor in 1804, the low political status of the papacy was made clear to all.

Emphasis on the political fortunes of the popes can obscure the continuance of papal administration in the centuries after Trent, as well as the successful missionary programs in the Western Hemisphere and Asia, the controlling of heresies like Jansenism, and the struggle to keep the Church free from rulers like Louis XIV of France (1643–1715) and Joseph II Hapsburg (1765–1790) of the Holy Roman Empire. Yet there can be no doubt that papal influence upon larger political and intellectual movements declined, as the popes strove to find a new role throughout the nineteenth and twentieth centuries.

JOSEPH F. KELLY

See also CHURCH, THE; HIERARCHY; HOLY SEE.

PAPAL STATES

Beginning with the endowments of patronage of Constantine (d. 337), the Church was generously endowed over the years and became a substantial landholder. The holdings grew greatly during the reign of Pepin the Short (751–768), the Papal States were established, and the pope became a political power whose involvement in secular affairs for the next millennium was taken for granted as a necessity to preserve and further the spiritual mission of the Church.

The territorial holdings of the papacy reached their greatest dimensions at the beginning of the sixteenth century when the Papal States covered the duchies of Parma, Piacenza, Modena, Romagna, Urbino, Spoleto, and Castro; the Marches of Ancona; the provinces of Bologna, Perugia, and Orvetano; and the papal French possessions of Avignon and Venaissin. The dual role of the papacy as a spiritual leader and as a secular power, with armies and all the political and military obligations, faced questioning and challenges in the post-Reformation world. It lost much by its enmeshment in the politics, alliances, and wars of Europe; and the Enlightenment and the French Revolution presaged the beginning of the end for the Papal States. In 1791 the French annexed the papal possessions of Avignon and Venaissin. The instability of Europe during the era of Napoleon followed by the upsurge of nationalism put the papacy on the defensive but still holding firm to the tenet that secular sovereignty was essential to the papacy's spiritual mission and independence.

The popular demand for the unification of Italy doomed the Papal States with their discontented inhabitants. Prior to 1860, the papal territories covered 15,774 square miles with a population of over 3,000,000. When in 1860 the kingdom of Italy annexed the last of the States—Romagna, the Marches of Ancona, and Umbria—the pope was left with the city of Rome and the province of Latio, and these were lost to Italy in 1870. For a decade the pope had lived with the protection of French troops who were hastily withdrawn at the start of the Franco-Prussian War. With their departure, the end was inevitable. In 1871 the Italian government passed the Law of Guarantees which offered the pope sovereignty over the Vatican, the Lateran, and the country residence of Castel Gondolfo; an annual pension of 3,500,000 lire (equivalent to the income from the Papal States); full religious and diplomatic freedom; and other less important concessions. Pius IX refused the offer and became "the prisoner of the Vatican." The impasse continued until 1929 when Pius XI and Mussolini reached a settlement with the Lateran Treaty.

JOSEPH QUINN

See also CONSTANTINE; LATERAN TREATY; PIUS IX, POPE; PIUS XI, POPE; VATICAN.

PARABLES, THE

A parable is a short discourse that makes a comparison. The Greek word used in the New Testament and from which we get our English word "parable"—*parabolē*—referred to a much broader range of verbal expression than we denote with our word. Besides a story with an implied comparison, *parabolē* in the ancient world could mean metaphor, type, symbol, proverb, riddle, wisdom saying—almost any figurative use of language. Drawing on the tradition of Greek rhetoric, however, Western writers have usually used the word "parable" to mean some kind of elaborated comparison, especially the brief stories Jesus told.

The parables of Jesus participate in a venerable Jewish tradition that is rooted in the Hebrew Scriptures. Two Old Testament parables in particular serve as prototypes for Jesus' parables. In 2 Samuel 12:1-4, the prophet Nathan confronts David by telling the story of the Poor Man's Lamb. When David hears the story only on the surface level, Nathan explains that the point of the parable is a surprising second meaning: David's murder of Uriah and taking of Uriah's wife, Bathsheba. Another Old Testament example of a story with a hidden meaning is Isaiah's Vineyard Song (Isa 5:1-7). The first six verses present the landowner complaining about his vineyard's failure to produce good fruit and his consequent abandonment of the vineyard. Verse 6 explains the allegorical meaning: vineyard refers to Israel and Judah; its fruitlessness represents Israel's and Judah's injustice, spelled out in detail in verses 8-13 (the land-grabbing and self-indulgence of the rich and powerful).

The Synoptic Gospels show Jesus working with this tradition creatively, usually as a way of teaching his challenging revision of popular notions regarding the expected apocalyptic kingdom of God.

To focus on how Jesus' parables "work," it has become customary to sort them into three categories: similitudes, parables in the strict sense, and example stories.

(1) A *similitude* is a parable that briefly narrates or alludes to a typical occurrence from daily life. Usually told in the present tense, a similitude makes an implied or explicit comparison between the common occurrence and a spiritual reality. Examples: the Seed Growing Secretly (Mark 4:26-29), the Mustard Seed (Mark 4:30-32; Matt 13:31-32; Luke 13:18-19), the Lost Sheep (Matt 18:12-14; Luke 15:3-7), the Fishnet (Matt 13:47-50).

(2) A *parable in the strict sense* is a parable whose form is a story about a fictitious, once-upon-a-time event. Examples: the Sower (Mark 4:3-9; Matt

13:3-9; Luke 8:5-8); the Wicked Tenants and the Landowner (Mark 12:1-11; Matt 21:33-43; Luke 20:9-18); the Unmerciful Servant (Matt 18:23-35); the Prodigal Son (Luke 15:11-32).

(3) It has been observed that some full-story parables comprise a subset commonly called *example stories.* These are parables that present not an analogy but a specific case of human behavior that is meant to be imitated or avoided (that is, a good example or a bad example). Most commentators find only four example stories in the Synoptic Gospels, all of them in Luke: the Good Samaritan (Luke 10:29-37), the Rich Fool (12:16-21), the Rich Man and Lazarus (16:19-31), and the Pharisee and the Tax Collector (18:9-14). Note that in each of these stories, the point is literally the behavior displayed in the narrative. In parables like the Unjust Steward (16:1-8) and the Persistent Widow (18:1-8), however, the human behavior is not presented for direct imitation (or avoidance) but as an analogy.

Are we breaking fresh ground today in our understanding of the parables of Jesus? Yes, especially in two areas: (a) the social and cultural setting of first-century Palestine and (b) the way each of the Synoptic evangelists has refashioned and incorporated the parables to serve the pastoral and theological purposes of his gospel.

A close study of the cultural context has made us aware that Jesus' preaching about the kingdom of God must be understood against the current expectations of an imminent inbreaking of God's reign as this is imaged in Jewish apocalyptic writings shortly before the New Testament period. Jesus puts a new "spin" on these expectations by proclaiming in his parables that the apocalyptic kingdom of God is both more imminent and more immanent than was popularly thought. For example, in a culture whose imagery included grandiose symbols of earthly kingdoms (see the cosmic tree representing Nebuchadnezzar's kingdom in Daniel 4; or the majestic cedar representing postexilic Israel in Ezekiel 17:23), Jesus dared to compare the coming kingdom of God to a humble, non-kosher plant, the mustard bush, as if to say that the presence of the kingdom might be more a part of ordinary life than people had expected. Or, in a culture where yeast was a conventional symbol for the subversive power of evil (see Mark 8:15, "the leaven of the Pharisees" or 1 Cor 5:16, where Paul associates leaven with sexual misconduct), Jesus boldly used it as an image of the kingdom. A third example of how our knowledge of the culture of the times can nuance our appreciation of the original impact of a parable: when we read the Good Samaritan (Luke 10), it helps to know that Temple officials such as the priest and the Levite were forbidden by purity laws even to come close to a dead body (the apparent condition of the mugging victim) and that a Samaritan on the road between Jerusalem and Jericho was an ancient enemy in hostile territory.

Attending to the parables in the Synoptic Gospels brings out the distinctive contributions and emphases of each evangelist.

Mark transmits around a dozen similitudes (e.g., the Patch, 2:21; New Wine and Old Wine Skins, 2:22; the Divided House, 3:23-26; the Doorkeeper, 13:34-37) but he has only two full-blown parables: the Sower (4:3-9) and the Wicked Tenants (12:1-11). The latter is especially notable in its affinity with Old Testament tradition: in the story of the Wicked Tenants, Jesus improvises upon and contemporizes the theme of Isaiah's Song of the Vineyard (Isaiah 5, discussed above) and thereby confronts the oppressive officials of his day much as the prophet Nathan did with respect to David (2 Samuel 12) a thousand years before. In a gospel whose special emphasis is the rejection and victory of Jesus as Son of God, it is fitting that this parable should figure so importantly. In this context it is easier to understand the allusion to Isaiah 6:9-10 at Mark 4:12; it interprets Jesus' failure as parabolic teacher by drawing a parallel between his prophetic career and that of Isaiah.

Matthew and Luke repeat both of Mark's parables and virtually all of his similitudes (the sole exception, the Seed Growing Secretly [4:26-29], unique to Mark). In addition, Matthew and Luke share some parabolic material not found in Mark (material usually ascribed to the Q source): five similitudes (the Two Builders, a variant of the Mustard Seed, the Leaven, the Lost Sheep, and the Faithful or Unfaithful Servant). But the great majority of the parables of Matthew and Luke are special to each of those gospels.

Since Matthew transmits most of the sayings of Jesus in the format of five major speeches, it is not surprising that most of the stories of Jesus in his gospel also occur in those speeches. The third speech (Matthew 13) is an expansion of Mark 4 and contains seven parables. The fourth speech (Matthew 18, on Church order) gives us two, the similitude of the Lost Sheep and the parable of the Unmerciful Servant. And the fifth speech (Matthew 24–25, the eschatological discourse) presents four (the Faithful or Unfaithful Servant, the Ten Maidens, the Talents, and the Sheep and Goats similitude in the Last Judgment scenario). In each case, the parables are thoroughly integrated with the theme of the particular speech. Matthew's warning against complacency and Jesus' call to joyful decisiveness in the light of the final judgment are conveyed by the parables of chapter 13. The hard sayings about fraternal confrontation and possible excommunication at the center of Matthew 18 are given a sensitive pastoral context by Matthew's framing them with parables about care and forgiveness (the Lost Sheep and the Unforgiving Servant). And the parables Matthew adds to the Farewell Discourse of chapters 24–25 all promote the theme of using well the time between Easter and the second coming.

Luke, on the other hand, uses the special parabolic traditions available to him in quite another way. Virtually all of them appear in his Central Section, his ten-chapter expansion of that journey to Jerusalem (Luke 9:21–19:44), a journey involving only a single chapter in Mark's Gospel, chapter 10. With singular artistry, Luke usually provides an appropriate narrative setting for the telling of the parables. For example, the Two Debtors (7:41-43) is part of Jesus' confrontation of Simon the Pharisee at the dinner party; the Good Samaritan story is Jesus' response to the lawyer's impertinent request for a definition of "neighbor"; Jesus tells the Rich Farmer example story (12:16-21) in response to a request for his intervention in a family financial squabble. Perhaps the most important setting of all is that of Luke 15: when Jesus is again charged with legal impropriety in his table fellowship with tax collectors and sinners, he defends his behavior with three parables—the similitudes of the Lost Sheep and the Lost Coin, and the famous parable of the Father and the Two Lost Sons (the Prodigal Son). Attending to the setting and literary unity of Luke 15 highlights a number of elements: that the tax collector and sinners are imaged as the lost sheep, the lost coin, and the runaway son; that God is imaged first as a male shepherd, then as a female householder, then as the compassionate father; that the Pharisees and scribes are figured as the resentful elder brother of the runaway; and that the table fellowship is, by these three stories, interpreted as mirroring and extending divine compassion.

A comparison of the ways Luke and Matthew transmit the story of the Great Feast demonstrates well how each evangelist brings the parabolic tradition into the service of his respective gospel. In Luke 14, Jesus tells the story at a dinner party at the home of a leading Pharisee. As is typical in the Third Gospel, the story comes in response to a concrete situation. Here it is the idle beatitude of one of the dinner guests: "Blessed is the one who will dine in the kingdom of God" (14:15). Jesus proceeds to tell the story of a man giving a dinner party to which none of the invited guests come, each of them begging off with a patently empty excuse. The angry host then proceeds to invite the poor, crippled, blind and lame of the town. Learning that there is still room, he sends his servant to gather people in from the highways and hedgerows. In the narrative context of the Third Gospel, this parable is clearly a defense of Jesus' ministry, where the poor and the marginal respond to Jesus' kingdom invitation and the privileged invitees resist with lame excuses, e.g., that Jesus heals on the Sabbath and eats with the unclean.

Matthew passes on the same tradition in a different setting and with other emphases (see Matt 22:1-14). In this gospel, Jesus tells the parable of the Great Feast in the Temple precincts right after speaking the parables of the Two Sons (21:28-32) and the Wicked Tenants (21:33-43). The audience is the admiring crowds and the chief priests and the Pharisees. Matthew transforms the parable into an allegory that turns out to be a kind of mini-history of Israel. In Matthew's version, the host is a king. The banquet is a wedding feast for the king's son. The excuses of the guests are summarized briefly. The single servant becomes two groups of servants. The refusal of the invitation escalates into murder of the messengers. The anger of the host also escalates, finding expression in murderous revenge against the invitees and the burning of their city! And in Matthew the story does not end with the gathering of the marginal people. He adds the epilogue about the king surveying the guests and expelling one who had refused to put on a wedding garment (customarily provided by the affluent for their guests). In this allegorical elaboration of details, Matthew has firmed up the association between the host and God (king). By turning the single servant into two waves of rejected messengers, he has (as in the two sendings of servants in 21:34-36) thereby represented God's messengers the prophets (see 23:37). The punitive burning of the city alludes to the Romans' destruction of Jerusalem in A.D. 70. The final scene about expulsion of the man without the wedding garment is a cameo representation of the final judgment. In thus allegorizing the parable of the Great Feast, Matthew has joined it with the other parables in his gospel that evoke the powerful imagery of the last judgment to wake up a complacent community (see the explanation of the Weeds among the Wheat [13:36-43], the Net [13:47-49], and the climactic parables of Matthew 25—the Ten Maidens, the Talents, and the scenario of the judgment of the nations).

The Gospel of John contains no parables in the usual sense of the term. Instead, the Fourth Gospel emphasizes key metaphors (Jesus as word, lamb, light, life, bread, way, gate, Temple, water source) and features several extended allegories (the sheepfold gate and the shepherd, John 10; the vine and the branches, John 15).

DENNIS HAMM, S.J.

See also BIBLE, NEW TESTAMENT WRITINGS; THEOLOGY, BIBLICAL.

PARACLETE

See HOLY SPIRIT.

PARADISE

See HEAVEN.

PARISH

(Gk. *paroikia,* "dwelling near") Traditionally, a community of the faithful in a designated territory within a diocese. Each parish has a pastor as its steward and is assigned its own church. Though territorial by custom, parishes may also be defined by rite, nationality, or language.

JOSEPH QUINN

See also DIOCESE.

PARISH COUNCIL

A group of parishioners who assist the pastor in the administration of a parish. The formation of such groups was first suggested at Vatican II, in the context of increasing the involvement of the laity in pastoral affairs. They are consultative in nature—their decisions and recommendations not binding upon the pastor, but serving rather to inform him of the parish's needs.

JOSEPH QUINN

See also PARISH; PASTOR.

PARISH PRIEST

See PASTOR.

PAROUSIA

This Greek term means "arrival" or "presence" and refers to the ceremonial arrival of a ruler to a city where he is greeted with honors. The people anticipate this joyful occasion with their preparations. Within the New Testament writings, the term refers to the coming of Christ in glory or the second coming, an event anticipated by the early Christians as the culmination of Christ's work.

While the Jewish Scriptures contain references to the "day of the Lord" and focus on the radical intervention of God in their history, it is the Book of Daniel (7:13ff.) that provides the imagery that New Testament writers use to portray the events of the last days. They affirm that the Son of Man will come and live in hope that God will bring the fullness of the kingdom with the ultimate victory of Christ.

Early writings evidence the Christian's belief that this coming of the Lord was imminent, indeed within their lifetime (1 Thess 4:17). However, even Paul seems to modify his view (2 Cor 4:14) emphasizing the reality of the event rather than the immediacy or time of its occurrence, and encouraging Christians to prepare for their union with the Lord in glory by a life of holiness (1 Thess 3:13; 2 Thess 1:10).

The Synoptic Gospels describe the parousia in various episodes, frequently using Son of Man terminology (Mark 8:38; 14:62; Matt 16:27; 24:27, 30 37, 39; Luke 9:26; 18:8; 21:27), seeing the event as future, but affecting Christian life. The context of Jesus' sayings changed in the biblical writings as the theology of the end-times developed. Usage of the apocalyptic imagery of Daniel with signs preceding the end continued. The Johannine writings contain few references to the parousia, possibly because of John's unique understanding of the resurrection. The Book of Revelation, with its apocalyptic perspective, offers testimony to this epiphany of Jesus within a liturgical context (Rev 22:20), and emphasizes the protection of Christians in the intervening period (Rev 3:11). Some writings, such as Galatians, Philemon, and 2–3 John, display little interest in the parousia.

However, the early Christian community placed their faith and hope in the coming of Christ in glory. While some were convinced of the nearness of the end in the early period, indefiniteness regarding time contributed to an atmosphere of anticipation and hope, which are the attitudes of Christians today. The biblical imagery of the last days, a literary device used to convey faith convictions, contributes to the drama of the writings. However, it is the new age and hope in the culminating victory of Christ that remains the essence of Christian belief.

HELEN DOOHAN

See also APOCALYPSE; ESCHATOLOGY.

PARSCH, PIUS (1884–1954)

Pius Parsch was born on 18 May 1884 in Olmütz, in what used to be the Austrian province of Moravia. In 1904 he became a Canon of Saint Augustine at Klosterneuburg near Vienna and took the name Pius in honor of Pope Pius X with whom he shared a deep love for the Bible. He studied for the priesthood in his own monastery and was ordained in 1909. Some of the money he received as an ordination gift he used to buy the nine volumes of Prosper Guéranger's *L'Année liturgique* (*The Liturgical Year*). This already indicated a direction his future work would take. For four years after ordination he ministered as a curate in a Vienna parish and studied for a doctorate in theology. Once he received the degree he returned to his monastery to teach pastoral theology to the novices. This ministry led him to undertake a more careful study of the psalms and the breviary.

In May 1915 he became a chaplain in the Austrian army. Working with the soldiers he became aware of their psychological and religious needs and came to realize how little they knew about the Mass. Frequently he gave a running commentary on the parts of the Mass while another chaplain was celebrating the liturgy. That experience, along with a tour of duty with the troops in the Ukraine where he saw how the Eastern-rite Christians participated fully in the Church's worship, inspired him eventually to publish a High Mass leaflet missal. Hence he became the founder of the modern missalette.

After the war ended he returned to his monastery and his work with the novices. For Easter Sunday, 1919, he produced his first High Mass leaflets which were regularly published under the title *Lebe mit der Kirche* ("Live with the Church"). That same year he organized Bible Study groups among the people. Weekly meetings were held with special attention given to the life of Christ in the Gospels. By 1922 the groups shifted their attention to the Mass and other parts of the liturgy as the sacramental celebrations of the mystery of Christ. He gave so-called "Mass demonstrations" for the people, explaining the parts of the Mass while a lector read the Mass prayers in German. In this way he encouraged the development of the dialogue Mass.

Not far from the monastery of Klosterneuburg is a small chapel dedicated to St. Gertrude. It was there that the members of Father Parsch's study groups gathered on Ascension Thursday, 1922, for their first sung and dialogue Mass. The Kyrie, Sanctus, and Agnus Dei were sung by all; the Gloria and Credo were recited. The lessons and prayers were read in German by a lector while Father Parsch read them in Latin. The offertory procession was revived and the sign of peace was shared by all. Each Saturday at St. Gertrude's there was a preparation for the Sunday Mass. The community thus anticipated many of the practices that were to become widespread in Europe especially after World War II.

In Vienna Father Parsch extended his ministry to many parishes by giving "Liturgical Weeks" in

Pius Parsch, O.S.A.

which he explained the Mass and taught the people how to participate more fully. These conferences developed into the *Seelsorgeinstitut,* "Pastoral Institute," held at regular intervals in Vienna under the direction of Dr. Karl Rudolf. The Institute raised the level of pastoral ministry in parishes, so that its methods were adopted in many dioceses throughout Europe. Its special aim was to make the parish an organic community rather than an ecclesiastical administrative district which it often was in the past. This involved emphasis on the sacramental basis of family life, making parents conscious of their religious responsibilities at home, and training lay men and women to minister in the Church. Special Masses for children and teenagers were celebrated and proper training was given to altar servers.

The name Father Parsch gave to his ministry was *Volksliturgisches Apostolat,* "Popular Liturgical Apostolate." It highlights his main concern, which was not research or monastic or cathedral liturgical forms but rather the active participation of ordinary people in the celebration of the mystery of Christ. Because he concentrated on the popular aspects of the liturgy, his explanations were at times superficial and have been corrected by modern research. His efforts sometimes met with opposition and misunderstanding, especially in the earlier years of his ministry. Wild rumors periodically circulated in certain European areas about the "goings-on" at the Klosterneuburg chapel of St. Gertrude. Father Parsch, however, was not deterred. He regularly ended his personal correspondence with the words, "*mit sanfter Zaebigkeit,*" "with gentle doggedness."

Father Parsch was a prolific writer. Books and pamphlets, mostly written by himself, issued from the *Volksliturgisches Apostolat* press which he founded. In October 1926 he published the first issue of *Bibel und Liturgie,* a magazine which continues in existence at the present time. While he lived, most issues carried one or more of his articles. The title of the magazine underscores his aim: to show that the Bible and the liturgy are essentially complementary. He came to this understanding through his own biblical training and teaching and his realization that people could be brought to an appreciation of the liturgy only by understanding the Bible. His inexpensive Bible translations and biblical workbooks pioneered an interest in the Bible among ordinary lay people.

Among his principal works are *The Church's Year of Grace, The Liturgy of the Mass, The Breviary Explained,* and *Seasons of Grace.* There is no doubt that Pius Parsch's spirit and work have exercised a major influence on the popular liturgical movement throughout the world. He has helped give Christian spirituality the focus it needs on both the Bible and the liturgy. He died at Klosterneuburg on 11 March 1954.

R. KEVIN SEASOLTZ, O.S.B.

See also LITURGICAL MOVEMENT, THE; LITURGICAL YEAR, THE; LITURGY.

PASCAL, BLAISE (1623–1662)

French moralist, theologian, mathematician, and scientist. As versatile a scientist as he was a writer, he invented the calculating machine, the syringe, and the wheelbarrow. He has, therefore, had as much influence on everyday living as he has had on the intellectual life. Born in 1623, he was attracted to Jansenism in 1646 and made a full commitment in 1654, when he attached himself to the convent of Port-Royal. His literary fame was established by a series of polemical letters, known as *Lettres Provinciales,* written in 1656 and 1657, which primarily attacked the casuistry of the Jesuits. But he is best remembered for his *Pensées* ("Thoughts"), an uncompleted defense of the Christian religion published eight years after his death. This fragmentary work has had a wide influence on thinkers over the last three centuries. The notion that it is prudent to believe in God's existence, since little can be lost if there is no God and eternal happiness can be gained if there is one, is known as "Pascal's wager." He died in 1662.

JOSEPH QUINN

See also APOLOGETICS; SCIENCE AND RELIGION.

PASCHAL MYSTERY

"Christ our Passover has been sacrificed." Paul wrote these words to the Church at Corinth (1 Cor 5:7) in the course of an exhortation to believers to live incorruptible lives. Behind Paul's allusive use of the Passover metaphor to interpret Jesus's death on the cross lies his own traditional Jewish religious understanding of God's graciousness to Israel. Beyond Paul's words, later generations of Christians would elaborate on the theme of *the paschal mystery* to speak of the meaning of what God had done in Christ. This article will consider, first, the biblical foundations for the theme in the New Testament; second, the development of the theme in homilies and other writings that have survived from the early centuries of the Church; and finally, the contemporary retrieval of the theme in the twentieth century theological writings and the documents of Vatican II.

Biblical Foundations

When Paul called Christ "our Passover," he was writing to the Christians at Corinth during the Jewish season of Passover (cf. 1 Cor 16:8) about the year A.D. 56. The traditional Jewish celebration of the Passover season lasted fifty days, a week of weeks, culminating in the fiftieth day celebration or Pentecost. First generation Christians were fully aware that the crucifixion, death, and resurrection of Jesus had occurred at the time of the Jewish Passover. The whole set of images associated with the annual Jewish liturgical memorial (celebrating Israel's going out from the land of Egypt and God's conferring of the covenant at Sinai) made "Passover" a fruitful metaphor for Jewish Christians like Paul to use in interpreting the meaning of God's act in Christ.

In the passage cited above, Paul is recalling the ritual practice of removing fermenting agents like yeast or leaven as part of domestic preparation for the Passover. His purpose is to suggest that faithful Christians should get rid of whatever was the source of corruption in their lives (1 Cor 5:7-8; cf. Exod 12:17-20). Paul's insight was not idiosyncratic. The local Church in which the Gospel of John was composed also used the Passover frame throughout its narrative of Jesus's passion. For example, the writer associates Jesus imaginatively with the slaughtered lamb of the Passover by noting that none of his bones were broken, thereby honoring what the Law prescribed for the Passover offering (John 19:31-33; cf. Exod 12:46). Further, in the Book of Revelation, the description of the heavenly victory celebration opens with the declaration "I saw a Lamb standing, a Lamb that had been slain" (Rev 5:6).

While the paschal framing of the mystery of Christ clearly derives from the apostolic period, it in no way exhausts the earliest Christian explorations of the meaning of God's action in Jesus of Nazareth. So "the mystery of Christ" is a more fundamental concept in the Pauline writings than is the particular image "Christ our Passover" that underlies the theme "paschal mystery."

The Letter to the Ephesians (Eph 1–3) offers an extended, although not systematic, reflection on "the mystery of Christ" apart from any explicit paschal framing. The mystery is multifaceted. It is God's secret plan for the world's salvation, concealed from the beginning of the world but now manifested through the blood of Christ. The mystery is that God is now welcoming those who were not God's people, those who were strangers and aliens under the terms of the first covenant. The mystery is God's choosing to reconcile everything in the heavens and on the earth. The mystery is that Christ's body on the cross has put to death all the world's old enmities. The mystery is the richness of God's mercy in the face of human sin. The mystery is that salvation is God's gift freely available to all those who believe.

Both the words *paschal* and *mystery* are English words derived from the Greek language in which the New Testament was originally written. The English adjective paschal was coined from the Greek *pascha,* a word itself coined by Greek-speaking Bible translators in the third century B.C. Coining the new word to translate the Hebrew *pesach* was necessary because neither classical nor conversational Greek (nor, later, Elizabethan English) had a word to name the foundational religious events recorded in the Bible. The annual Jewish festival of *pesach* plays off the poles of the journey from bondage in Egypt to freedom in the Promised Land, a journey begun when the angel of death passed over the houses of the Israelites whose doors had been marked with the blood of the lamb. It was that blood which effectively delivered them from death (Exod 12:21-36). Christians would appropriate variations of those same themes to speak of the Christ event.

Mysterion had general associations with the worldview of Platonic philosophy long before New Testament writers used this Greek word to speak of what God was doing in Christ. In the Platonic scheme, sensible realities are understood to participate in and to point to invisible heavenly realities. This symbolic understanding, that the created world perceptible to the senses requires contemplation in order to be understood spiritually, was in the course of time also extended to the spiritual interpretation of historical events. Chronologically prior events came to be perceived as preparation for or foreshadowing of future events; promise awaited fulfillment. Something of this hermeneutical approach is evident in the New Testament writings, when, for example, Jesus is presented as the new lawgiver completing the work Moses had begun (Matt 5–7).

For the first Christians, belief in "the mystery of God—namely Christ" (Col 2:2) evoked communal contemplation of that mystery, in order to understand the religious importance of what they had seen and heard. Typology was a common approach to the interpretation of religious texts in the ancient world. The process of uncovering religious meaning by a sustained communal exploration of *type* (the passover event) and *antitype* (the Jesus event), lies at the origins of the Christian concept of the paschal mystery.

Early Christian Explorations of the Paschal Mystery

A century after Paul's passing allusion to "Christ our Passover," Melito, the bishop of Sardis in Asia Minor (present-day Turkey) preached a homily "On the Pasch," that has survived to the present. In its day this Easter homily was circulated widely, not only in Greek but also in Syriac and Coptic. But only in the last century have scholars rediscovered the ancient text and translated it for modern readers. Melito does not use the phrase "paschal mystery," but he celebrates with great eloquence the meaning of Christ as the fulfillment of the earlier redemptive act of God. His strategy is to compare and contrast type and antitype.

Melito composed his reflection "On the Pasch" about 165, at a time when the local Churches of the eastern mediterranean world were divided over when to celebrate Easter—on the day when the Jewish Passover fell or on the Day of the Lord, the Sunday, following the Jewish Passover. Theologically, the tension involved various understandings of the relationship between the passion of Jesus and his glorification as the risen Christ. The vision of the Gospel of John, for example, sees Jesus's dying on the cross as the moment of his ascent to the Father and his glorification, so that passion and glorification are inseparable. In this view, the time of Jesus's dying is the time of his glorification; accordingly, the annual celebration of the mystery of Christ ought to coincide with the actual day of Passover. Others tended to take a chronological rather than a theological approach to interpreting events: the Friday passion is viewed as distinct from the Sunday resurrection and glorification.

Melito's homily does not take up the calendar question directly. But he is concerned with interpreting for his assembled hearers the liturgical reading from the Book of Exodus, "how the lamb was sacrificed, how the people were saved." His point of departure is the declaration, "the sacrifice of the Lamb, and the celebration of the Pasch, and the letter of the Law, have been fulfilled in Christ" (L. Deiss, ed., *Springtime of the Liturgy,* Collegeville, Minn.: The Liturgical Press, 1979, p. 100). Melito's eloquence is brought to bear on the meaning of the lamb, the blood of the lamb, the death of the firstborn, the delivery from slavery to freedom, and a whole myriad of other related themes.

Melito is not a solitary witness to the paschal interpretation of Christian faith. Elsewhere in the second and third centuries Christian homilists, catechists, and teachers, were also interpreting the initiation of Christians within the paschal frame. Just as the blood of the paschal lamb marked the doorposts of those who were destined for salvation in Egypt, so now the sign of the cross marks the foreheads of those destined for baptismal salvation through the blood of Christ. The Hebrew people's eating of the paschal lamb foreshadowed the messianic banquet to which all the baptized are invited, and which the Christian Eucharistic meal, too, anticipates. The early sacrificial understanding of the Eucharistic Liturgy also drew on the imaginative identification of Christ with the Lamb.

The paschal motif in all its many variations gained a measure of authority in these early generations as a way of understanding the mystery of Christ. The Easter celebration was the Christian pasch. The paschal interpretation of the mystery of Christ was and continues to be theologically fruitful for Christian believers, as we shall consider momentarily. But with hindsight the twentieth-century Church also recognizes that the promise/fulfillment scheme of interpretation, with its dependence on sharp contrasts, provided one of the seeds of Christian anti-Semitism for the spiritually, intellectually, and morally ungifted. To be effective with the argument that the new pasch had replaced the old, such Christians had to negate the legitimacy of Jewish celebrations of the Passover festival paralleling Christian paschal celebrations generation after generation—sometimes negating the very legitimacy of Jewish communal life itself.

Poetic insight and rhetorical genius in praise of the pasch gave way to more systematized treatments of the paschal theme in third-and fourth-century biblical commentaries. Two principal approaches to the theme of the paschal character of salvation emerged as biblical and liturgical commentators focused on either chapter twelve or fourteen of the Book of Exodus and developed typologies accordingly. The image at the heart of Exodus 12 is the lamb slaughtered and the blood of the lamb as the source of the people's salvation. This starting point evoked reflections on the passion of Christ in his suffering humanity. In the era of early Christological debates, it provided a way of confronting Docetist and even Arian errors that denied the human dimension of the deed of salvation. Exodus 14 focused on the Israelites' passing through the waters of the Red Sea, waters of death miraculously becoming waters of new life.

Both typologies evoked much fruitful mystagogical catechesis, the reflective teaching that fourth-and fifth-century bishops offered the newly baptized in the weeks after their Easter initiation. The theme of the passage through the waters generated a full-blown mystagogy of the many biblical types of the waters of baptism: the waters of creation, the deluge, the crossing of the Jordan into the Promised Land, and so on. The theme of the lamb slain, the redeeming blood, and the paschal meal supported mystagogical reflection on the Eucharist as a celebration of Christ's sacrificial death. It also evoked an expanded mystagogy of biblical types, drawing on the narrative of the sacrificial blood that sealed the first covenant at Sinai and on themes associated with Jewish temple sacrifices.

By the end of the fifth century, the Church's great bishop-teachers like Ambrose of Milan, Theodore of Mopsuestia, John Chrysostom of Antioch, and Cyril of Jerusalem had effectively focused the Church's attention on the way in which the faithful had access to the mystery of Christ, which was the one mystery of salvation. In Ambrose's words, *ubi ecclesia est, ibi mysteria sunt* (*De mysteriis,* 27). Wherever the Church is gathered to celebrate the Eucharist and baptism, there can be found the mystery of salvation.

The Jewish pasch served for centuries as a privileged, if not exclusive, *type* for the theological interpretation of the Christian life and liturgy. It did so because the Passover narrative provided an imaginative frame for dealing with central doctrinal themes: the saving value of the death of Christ and redemption by his blood, and the way in which believers participated in these.

Twentieth Century Retrieval of a Theology of the Paschal Mystery

From the ninth to the twentieth centuries, theological reflection took a sharp turn away from the early biblical and liturgical theology of the mystery of Christ recalled here. This theology drawn from the Church's liturgical celebration was displaced by the more abstract Scholastic sacramental theology identified at its best with the work of Thomas Aquinas and at its worst with a mechanized and objectified understanding of sacramental liturgy. Then in the early decades of the twentieth century the Benedictine monk Odo Casel of the German abbey of Maria Laach began the work of retrieval of the Church's more ancient liturgical theology of the mystery, which he characterized as "paschal."

Recovery. The context for Casel's work had been established two or three generations earlier, when European scholars had inaugurated a renewal of interest in the writings of the early Fathers of the Church as well as a renewed interest in early forms and understandings of the liturgy. The liturgical and patristic movements were contemporaneous with renewed ecclesiological reflection that emphasized the inner mystery of the Church more than its mere institutional form. These revivals, taken together, provided the remote preparation for the achievement of the Second Vatican Council (1962–1965). Our concern here is more narrow: renewed interest in theological reflection on the Christian pasch.

Casel, editor of the scholarly journal *Jahrbuch für Liturgiewissenschaft* and himself familiar with the achievements of nineteenth-century scholarship, ventured to advance liturgical theology by offering an original interpretation of the doctrine of the mysteries (his *Mysterienlehre*). He based his work on his reading of chapter six of Paul's Letter to the Romans ("Are you not aware that we who were baptized into Christ Jesus were baptized into his death? . . .); he read Paul in the spirit of the ancient liturgical catechesis, homilies, and commentaries on the pasch available to him. The controversy sparked by Casel's unfamiliar theological method and the resistance to his unfamiliar assertions about the nature of the Church's liturgical acts eventually led to the still-unfinished theological reconsideration of the sacramental activity of the Church. But, at the end of the twentieth century, many of the ideas that Casel had proposed in the face of strong opposition have become familiar and are now recognized as fully traditional.

Casel declared that the mystery of salvation celebrated in the Church's liturgy was more than a past historical event whose fruits or benefits were made available to the baptized through the mediation of the priest. Rather, he argued, the saving activity of the risen Christ continues; and each time the Church gathers for worship it is participating here and now in the dying and rising of Christ. Without such a real presence of the mystery (*Mysteriengegenwart*), the worshipping Church is disconnected or alienated from the living source of its salvation.

The immediacy of Paul's teaching about the baptized believer's share in the death and resurrection of Jesus provided the basis for Casel's bold reconsideration of the workings of the sacraments of the Church. In his view, the Church's liturgical action effects more than the personal Real Presence of Christ; it effects the whole assembly's participation in Christ's journey through death to life. For Casel, a true theology of the liturgical mysteries had to begin with a belief in the continuing presence of God's saving deed in the whole Christ, head and members.

Development. Casel never developed a satisfactory theoretical account of how this doctrine of the presence of the mysteries was to be understood. Other theologians subsequently took up the challenge of more systematic reflection on the matter. Edward Schillebeeckx, for one, (*Christ the Sacrament of the Encounter with God,* Dutch, 1960; English, New York: Sheed and Ward, 1963) suggested that in the sacraments there is "a presence in mystery" because "in Christ's historical redemptive act there already was an element of something perennial, an enduring trans-historical element which now becomes sacramentalized in an earthly event of our own time in a visible act of the church" (p. 56). For Schillebeeckx, this "transhistorical element" is to be found in the *living relationship* (emphasis added) within which Christ stood before God in his entire human life, "his very sonship realized in human form," so that "all the mysteries of the human life of Christ endure forever in the mode of Glory" (p. 58). Accordingly, in his judgment, the sacraments, as mediators between Christ and the Church, "must be situated not immediately between the historical sacrifice of the Cross and our twentieth-century situation, but rather between the Christ who is living now and our earthly world" (p. 62).

Cypriano Vagaggini (*Theological Dimensions of the Liturgy*) identified the positivist-historical mentality of the twentieth century and the abstract conceptualism of Western Neo-Scholastic theology as two sources for the contemporary difficulty with appreciating the fact that the paschal mystery is at work at the center not only of liturgy but all of Christian life (pp. 252 ff.). Contrary to the prevailing mentality, the passion, death, and resurrection of Christ are not three past events but one saving mystery. The mystery perdures because the Church exists within the mystery and celebrates the mystery sacramentally in its liturgical actions. In sum, says Vagaggini, the paschal mystery is "the whole and integral Christian mystery" viewed in its central point "toward which all tends and from which all is derived: Christ's passage from death to life and his communication with the world." That communication with the world comes in the Church's sacramental celebration of Christ's pasch.

In much of the theological discussion of the perduring presence of the paschal mystery and the liturgical celebration of the mystery, only limited attention has yet been given to the working of the Holy Spirit of Christ poured out on the Church. More recently, theologians have begun to explore the doctrine of the Holy Spirit in the Church as the foundation for all ecclesial life and worship. A fuller theological exploration of the doctrine of the Holy Spirit clearly has implications for further reflection on the perduring presence of the paschal mystery of salvation, about which Odo Casel wrote so passionately.

Conciliar Teaching. Twentieth-century exploration of the paschal character of Christian life and worship is affirmed both in the 1963 Constitution on the Sacred Liturgy (*Sacrosanctum Concilium*) and also in the reformed Roman liturgical books called for by the conciliar constitution. The ancient Latin Easter proclamation (the *Exsultet*) had kept alive the Church's paschal consciousness—calling Easter night the *festa paschalia*—with its exclamation "This is the night. . .in which the true lamb is slain. . . ." So the centrality of the paschal motif in the liturgy constitution is far from novel. In its theological introductory chapter, the constitution asserts that Christ redeemed humanity and gave perfect glory to God "by the paschal mystery of his blessed passion, resurrection from the dead, and glorious ascension. . ." (SC 5); and it affirms that from the day of Pentecost onward "the church has never failed to come together to celebrate the paschal mystery. . ." (SC 6).

English translation of the liturgy after the council and the development of additional new prayers made the ancient theme more prominent. Many worshippers heard it for the first time. The traditional Latin Easter preface had called Easter the night/day *cum Pascha nostrum immolatus est Christus,* "when Christ our Pasch is sacrificed." The phrase is retained in all five prayers of the expanded collection of prefaces for the Easter season in the revised Roman Missal. Paschal imagery is heightened throughout the liturgies of Lent ("when we prepare to celebrate the paschal mystery with mind and heart renewed"—Roman Missal, Preface 8), on Good Friday ("by shedding his blood for us, your Son, Jesus Christ, established the paschal mystery"—Opening Prayer), through the day of Pentecost ("Today you sent the Holy Spirit on those marked out to be your children. . .and so you brought the paschal mystery to its completion"—Roman Missal, Preface 28). The time from the evening celebration of the Lord's Supper on Holy Thursday through the Easter Vigil is named the paschal triduum (=three days), and is called "the culmination of the entire liturgical year" (General Roman Calendar, 1969).

But the paschal language and imagery is not limited to the prayers for the forty days of Lent and the fifty days of Easter, as though the paschal mystery was a seasonal motif and not the one mystery of salvation. A preface for the Sundays of Ordinary Time praises God, whose "gift of the Spirit, who raised Jesus from the dead, is the foretaste and promise of the paschal feast of heaven" (Roman Missal, Preface 34). During the course of the year, the adult Christians are called to "[join] the catechumens in reflecting on the value of the paschal mystery and. . . reviewing their own conversion'' *(Rite for the Christian Initiation of Adults,* Introduction, p. 4). In fact, even when explicit paschal language is not used, the liturgy regularly strikes the paschal chord. During the Christian funeral liturgy the Church praises God because "Though the saving death of your Son we rise at your word to the glory of resurrection"—Roman Missal, Preface 80).

Integrating Liturgy and Life. The recovery of the paschal nature of the one Christian mystery has also provided late twentieth-century theologians with a conceptual vehicle for exploring the connection between life and worship. The Christian community gathers weekly to participate sacramentally in the mystery of faith, namely this: that salvation is the gift of God for those who, in communion with the Lord Jesus, die to themselves in order to live for God. But every sacramental celebration of the paschal mystery ends with a rite of dismissal, a dispersal of the Church into the larger society.

Christians are sent to live the one mystery of Christ and so give witness to the world of God's plan for its salvation. That one paschal mystery, within which faithful Christian people live daily, in its turn provides the foundation for the Church's weekly (even daily) sacramental celebration of salvation. Orthodoxy or correct worship of God is intimately bound to orthopraxis or authentic witness to the gospel of Jesus expressed in works of justice, love, and mercy in the course of daily life in whatever society the Christian people find themselves.

This perception of the connection between orthodox worship and Christian orthopraxis has been conceptualized in the formulation *the Eucharist makes the Church and the Church makes the Eucharist.* What does the formula mean? At least this. The weekly liturgical celebration of the mystery of Christ's death and resurrection forms the Christian religious imagination or "the Christian spirit." Week by week, believers learn to contemplate the presence of the mystery of Christ's dying and rising in the great and small events of ordinary life and in the natural rhythms of things. From a paschal perspective, illness, poverty, injustice, hunger, social disorder, exploitation, environmental degradation, and other forms of diminishment, but also efforts toward reconciliation, fidelity, forgiveness, and human courage in the face of adversity, not only invite but even require of the Christian people some suitable response in the Spirit of Christ Jesus.

If the sacramental celebration of the paschal mystery is efficacious, then the Church of Jesus Christ is always being realized in history. The Church is always being born and reborn. The community of believers takes shape in particular ways in particular times and places. For example, in our day, in those places where Christians, individuals or communities, long experienced themselves as passive and dependent and understood themselves as life's "victims," faithful paschal celebration may result in greater courage, confidence and solidarity in the face of adversity. But where established and prosperous Christians, individuals or communities, have prided themselves on their achievement, the paschal faith may be an invitation to self-emptying.

According to this perception of the relationship between the liturgy and life, the reverse is also true. Sometimes particular Churches at particular moments in history are caught up in a "cycle of decline," and the inauthenticity of their lives as Christians has steadily weakened their capacity to celebrate the paschal mystery as the power for salvation. The impoverishment of the liturgical celebrations in such Churches simply feeds the cycle of decline. The weak cling to their weakness and lose hope; the proud lack love. So it is that good celebrations strengthen faith where it is strong, and poor celebrations may further weaken the faith and love of those who have little to begin with. Breaking out of such a cycle of decline is itself a gift of God's grace to the Church.

In their attempts to develop an integral paschal theology that connects liturgy, life, and doctrine, many liturgical theologians have gone far beyond Odo Casel's beginning reflections on the presence of the mystery. Nevertheless, the Church remains indebted to him for his recovery of an ancient Christian perception of the one mystery of salvation. Without his readiness to grapple with the contemporary significance of ancient texts, despite the resistance of those who had forgotten the heritage of the past, the Church would be less confident than it is about the paschal character of its faith.

MARY COLLINS, O.S.B.

See also EUCHARIST; LITURGY; TRIDUUM, EASTER; VIGIL.

PASSION NARRATIVES

The designation "passion," found in the NT itself only in Acts 1:3 ("his passion"), refers to the suffering and death of Jesus. The sections of the four Gospels which recount the last days, crucifixion, death, and burial of Jesus are called passion narratives (hereafter, PN). The precise extent of the PNs is in dispute. Does it begin with the entrance of Jesus into Jerusalem (Mark 11:1-11 and parallels), with the anointing of Jesus (Mark 14:3-9 and par.), or with the Last Supper tradition (Mark 14:22-25 and par.; cf. 1 Cor 11:23)? Does it conclude with the burial of Jesus (Mark 15:42-47 and par.) or with the empty tomb stories (Mark 16:1-8 and par.)? For practical purposes, scholars consider the PN proper to be Mark 14–15; Matthew 26–27; Luke 22–23; and John 18–19. Christian reflection on the significance of these first-century events is rooted in the earliest Christian *kerygma* and perdures to the present as these events are commemorated by Christians liturgically every year during Holy Week. This article will examine the topic according to the following categories: (1) origins; (2) genre; (3) the respective PNs of Mark, Matthew, Luke, and John; and (4) historical issues.

Origins

The earliest NT references to the suffering and death of Jesus are not found in lengthy narratives but in short, kerygmatic traditions about the Last Supper (e.g., 1 Cor 11:23-26), the crucifixion (Acts 13:28-29), and other liturgical and hymnic formulations (e.g., Rom 6:5-11; Phil 2:8). The PNs themselves likely developed from oral historical reminiscences about the fate of Jesus, which were then collected at an early date into a coherent continuous narrative influenced by liturgical celebration of the events they commemorate. Scholars have debated inconclusively whether such stories circulated in independent pieces, such as a betrayal story, a denial story, a crucifixion story, etc., or in the form of a full-length narrative. Some credit Mark's Gospel, the earliest of the canonical Gospels, with creatively stitching together independent traditions into the present sequential narrative. Other scholars have sought to reconstruct a pre-Markan PN which may have been a source for the details of the account. Such reconstructions remain hypothetical and debatable. Scholars are agreed that none of the PNs are strictly historical accounts of Jesus' fate. Rather, each one is a unique theological interpretation of history based upon a common historical event: that Jesus of Nazareth was betrayed, denied, and abandoned by his disciples, and crucified at Jerusalem during the governorship of Pontius Pilate. (For an analysis of each PN see D. Senior, *The Passion Series,* 4 vols. [Collegeville, Minn.: The Liturgical Press, 1984–1991].) J. D. Crossan (*The Cross That Spoke,* San Francisco: Harper & Row, 1988) has proposed that the PN of an apocryphal gospel, "The Gospel of Peter" (ca. 150), antedates the versions found in the canonical Gospels, but this position has not won wide acceptance.

Asserting that the PNs are primarily theological rather than historical literature is not to deny the basic historicity of the events they seek to portray. Other factors besides liturgical settings influenced how such events were remembered and preserved in the Christian tradition for later generations. One of the most important influences in this process was the OT. The evangelists used the OT to help interpret the meaning of Jesus' passion (D. J. Moo, *The Old Testament in the Gospel Passion Narratives,* Sheffield, England: The Almond Press, 1983). One thematic influence is seen in the traditions about the suffering "righteous person" who is wrongly persecuted by enemies but is vindicated by God (Wis 2, 4 and 5). A similar feature of the OT tradition is the anonymous figure of the "suffering servant" (Isa 52:13–53:12). Still further interpretational perspectives were found in the prophetic literature (e.g., Zech 9–14) and the psalms of lament (especially, Pss 22 and 69). At times, these references are made by direct quote and at other times by allusion, but a primary motif is that the passion of Jesus occurred as a fulfillment of the OT Scriptures.

Genre

This OT influence has led some scholars to suggest that the genre of the PNs is that of OT tales about persecuted righteous men and women who are vindicated by God when they uphold their righteousness and innocently suffer persecution and even death (G. W. E. Nickelsburg, *HTR* [1980] 73:153–184). Tales such as the stories of Joseph (Gen 37, 39–45), Susanna (Dan 13), Esther (Esth), and the virtuous mother and her seven sons (2 Macc 7) contain many similar elements to the PNs of Jesus' suffering and death. But, like most of the canonical gospel material, the PNs appear to be *sui generis,* especially because of the special divine status accorded to Jesus. Despite the influence which such OT stories may have had in shaping the PNs, the story of Jesus' passion, death, and resurrection transcends the genre of traditional martyrdom tracts.

The basic plot of each of the four PNs remains the same. Jesus of Nazareth is rejected by the Jewish leaders who perceive him as a serious threat to their authority. The leaders contrive a plot against Jesus which involves one of his own closest followers, Judas Iscariot, who is persuaded to betray him into the hands of the authorities. Jesus is consequently arrested in the Garden of Gethsemane, deserted by his disciples, put on hasty trial, sent to the Roman authority, Pontius Pilate, condemned to death by crucifixion, and hastily buried. Within this basic framework, each gospel tells the story in a unique fashion, heightening certain details, making additions or deletions, and recasting the story for the evangelist's own audience. The remainder of the article will summarize the main lines of each PN.

Mark 14–15

Mark's PN is a concise sequential narrative. The extended PN would include the entry into Jerusalem (beginning at Mark 11:1), but the PN proper begins with the preparations for the Last Supper. Mark's version may be divided into the following three distinctive segments, each consisting of numerous subscenes: (1) Anointing and Last Supper (14:1-31); (2) Gethsemane, Arrest, and Trial (14:32–15:20); (3) Crucifixion, Death, and Burial (15:21-47). In the first section Mark begins the passion of Jesus at a time of two days prior to "Passover and the Feast of Unleavened Bread" (14:1), the fourteenth day of the month of Nisan. The precise dating of the events of the passion is not consistent in the Gospels. Whereas the Synoptics basically follow Mark's dating, the Fourth Gospel relates Jesus' death to noontime on the Day of Preparation (John 19:31), the time of the slaughter of the Passover lambs.

Mark's PN is intimately tied to and prepared for by earlier sections of the Gospel. Of tantamount importance is the motif of the secret identity of Jesus ("messianic secret") as the suffering Son of Man and the royal Messiah, and its concomitant theme of the misunderstanding of the disciples. Though demons in the Gospel know Jesus' identity (e.g., 1:24, 34; 3:11), the disciples do not properly know him (especially the portrait of the disciples in 8:22–10:52). Those who do recognize him are commanded to silence (e.g., 1:25; 3:12; 5:43; 7:36; 8:30). In Mark, the disciples misunderstand or simply cannot understand Jesus, his teachings, and his deeds. This theme reaches a climax when his own disciples betray, deny, and abandon him. Despite the threefold predictions of violent death which Jesus makes in the course of his ministry (8:31; 9:31; 10:33-34), the disciples fail to comprehend the necessity of the Cross in his life and in theirs (8:32-35). In the PN the disciples' failure reaches its nadir. Mark notes baldly: "they all forsook him and fled" (14:50). Unique to

Mark is the story of the unnamed young man who flees naked (14:51-52), symbolic of the utter abandonment Jesus experiences. The characters in the story thus do not understand that Jesus' identity is intimately bound to his suffering and death on the cross. Only in the climactic exclamation of the centurion (a non-Jew) at the cross is Jesus' true identity revealed for what it is: "Truly this man was the Son of God!" (15:39; cf. 1:1, 11; 9:7).

Tied to this motif is the ironic aspect of the royal nature of Jesus' messiahship. Mark does not explicitly use the title "King" of Jesus in his Gospel until chapter 15, when the strong royal theme shines through as the title appears six consecutive times (15:2, 9, 12, 18, 26, 32) in a series of three mockeries that climax in the centurion's confession (15:39). The ones who mock Jesus in his passion are inadvertently acknowledging, without knowing or believing, the true identity of Jesus as the King-Messiah, Son of God, and suffering Son of Man. Thus, the cross for Mark is the climactic revelation of Jesus' true identity and the climax of the whole Gospel. The cross alone reveals the true identity of Jesus as the messianic king who must suffer.

Mark's PN, as do other parts of the Gospel, tends to heighten human aspects of Jesus' fate. Jesus truly experiences an agonizing time in Gethsemane, praying that the "hour" of his suffering will be taken away (14:35-36). When betrayed by Judas with a kiss and arrested, Jesus offers no resistance but surrenders to the will of his Father and the fulfillment of Scripture (14:49). When he is crucified, his words from the cross (a quote from Psalm 22:2) constitute a cry of dereliction which echoes the depth of human suffering he undergoes: "My God, My God, why have you forsaken me?" (15:34).

Several other aspects of Mark's PN are noteworthy. Mark has a penchant for small curious details, such as the naming of the sons of Simon of Cyrene (15:21, perhaps because they are known to the community) and noting the hours of Jesus' crucifixion as between 9 A.M. and noon (perhaps reflecting liturgical practice rather than pure history). Already Mark's succinct narrative shows a tendency developed much further in the other Gospels to lessen (but not exonerate) Pilate's guilt and to stress the guilt of the Jewish leaders in connection with Jesus' crucifixion, in particular the chief priests and scribes. Although Mark's PN concludes with the burial of Jesus and the significance of the Cross, the message is nonetheless one of hope because of Jesus' promise to the disciples at the Last Supper to precede them to Galilee (14:28). At the empty tomb, once the resurrection has been announced, this message of hope is given to the frightened women (15:7).

Matthew 26–27

A close comparison of Matthew's PN with Mark's reveals that they are similar in both structure and content. Matthew follows Mark very closely in this section of the Gospel. Despite this, Matthew's PN has its own distinctive emphases which must be viewed within the context of the whole of the Gospel.

Several factors weigh heavily in viewing Matthew's PN from a different perspective. Matthew does not have (as Mark does) a developed motif of the secret of Jesus' identity, nor is the Cross alone the great climax of the Gospel. Rather, the climax of the whole Gospel is in the commission scene (28:16-20), and only Matthew explicitly mentions the resurrection at the moment of Jesus' death (27:53). Matthew focuses on the passion, death, and resurrection of Jesus in one great, climactic sweep, and not just the passion itself. Nor does Matthew portray the disciples in quite as negative a fashion as Mark, who emphasizes their lack of understanding. In Matthew they acknowledge Jesus' identity explicitly (14:33). Neither does Matthew envision the cross as the only place where Jesus' true identity is revealed, for Matthew has an infancy narrative (1–2) and resurrection and appearance narratives (28) which affirm Jesus' divine origin and sacred identity. Indeed, the infancy narrative functions like an overture to the PN by means of the contrast which is established between those who wish to kill Jesus, and thereby reject him as God's Son, and those who accept him. The contrast is found in the figures of Herod and the Magi (2:1-12). The king (along with the religious leaders) rejects Jesus and seeks to destroy him (2:16-18), while pagan (Gentile) astrologers acknowledge his royalty with lavish gifts and even "worship" him (2:11). This pattern of rejection or acceptance culminates in the PN. The crowds, who throughout the Gospel are ambivalent toward Jesus, ally themselves to the Jewish leadership and reject him (27:25).

Although all the Gospels associate the notion of "the fulfillment of Scripture" with the PN, Matthew makes it a prominent motif which stretches from the infancy narrative through the PN. This is accomplished by means of fulfillment citations, often employing the formula, "this happened to fulfill what was spoken through the prophet(s) . . ." (e.g., 1:22-23; 2:5-6, 15, 17, 23; cf. 26:31, 54, 56; 27:9-10). Jesus' fate, as it is worked out in the PN, is seen as a fulfillment of the divine will of his heavenly Father. Jesus is thus not a victim of a miscarriage of justice but an obedient and faithful Son who fulfills his Father's will for the sake of the forgiveness of sins (26:28).

Another theme in the Matthean PN is that of Jesus being "with" God's people. In the infancy narrative Jesus is described as "Emmanuel, God-with-us" (1:23; cf. 18:20; 28:20). In the PN he is contrasted with the disciples. In two places Matthew adds a tiny phrase where Mark has none: 26:38, "Remain here and watch *with me*" (cf. Mark 14:34 "remain and watch"), and 26:40, "So you could not watch *with me* one hour?" (cf. Mark 14:37). Their inability to be "with" Jesus in his hour of suffering contrasts greatly with Jesus' promise to be with them even in times of persecution (10:26-42).

Unlike Mark, Matthew views Jesus' passion as the time of ultimate temptation for God's Son. The hour of the Cross is a time of temptation in the passion, not a time of glory. Matthew makes a subtle connection with the temptation scene (4:1-11) in which Satan tempts Jesus as the Son of God. Twice in the PN Matthew adds the term "Son of God" on the lips of those who mock him, echoing the temptations of Satan: 27:40 "If you are the Son of God, come down from the cross . . ." (cf. Matt 4:3, 6 and Mark 15:30, and Matt 26:43). Just as he vanquished evil at the beginning of his ministry, so Jesus, as God's Son, is victorious over evil in his critical hour (26:45).

A further and more unfortunate emphasis in Matthew is the expression throughout his passion account of anti-Jewish sentiment in connection with the decrease in the responsibility of Pilate. Clues to this theme appear throughout Matthew in places where it is indicated that Israel rejects its Messiah (2:1-12, 22; 11:20-24; 21:33-43). This feverish anti-Jewish sentiment peaks in the PN in three ways. First, Matthew adds the unique story of Judas' demise (27:3-10; cf. Acts 1:16-19) in which Judas returns to the chief priests the money paid for the act of betrayal. The money is labeled "blood money" for the sake of "innocent blood." Only Matthew mentions the amount of this paltry sum (26:15, "thirty pieces of silver"), derived from Zechariah 11:12 where it is the payment made to the irresponsible shepherd.

Second, Matthew adds a note of Jesus' innocence through the special story of Pilate's unnamed wife (27:19) who has a dream that recognizes Jesus as an "innocent man." Just as Gentiles (the Magi) at the beginning of Jesus' life recognized his innocence, they do likewise in his passion. Third, another Matthean addition to the passion in 27:25 fully implicates the Jews in the death of Jesus, as the crowds ("all the people"), and not just the leaders, shout out in response to Pilate's gesture of washing his hands: "His blood be upon us and on our children!" Despite the unfortunate misuse of this line through history improperly to justify violent acts of anti-Semitism, this line may be taken in ironic fashion as a way to include even the rejectors of Jesus under the salvation achieved by shedding his blood for all people (26:28).

In contrast to Mark, Matthew portrays Jesus in a more dignified fashion throughout the PN, in keeping with a tendency to emphasize Jesus' special divine attributes as God's Son (2:15; 3:17; 17:5). Thus, Jesus' passion is set in motion by his own words (26:2) reiterating the threefold passion predictions (16:21; 17:22-23; 20:18-19). Even the name "Jesus" is used more frequently throughout the narrative, a reminder of the salvific effect of his death (1:21). In contrast to Mark's simple description that Jesus "breathed his last" (Mark 15:37), Matthew says that Jesus "gave over his spirit" (27:50), denoting Jesus' free gift of his life as a fulfillment of his Father's will. The response to Jesus' death is also heightened. In place of the lone centurion's expression of Jesus' identity (Mark 15:39), Matthew describes "the centurion and those with him" (27:54, probably symbolic of the coming of the Gentiles to faith) who react not to the manner of Jesus' death but to the awesome cosmic events which accompany it (27:51-53). As at birth Jesus' death is accompanied by apocalyptic events which confirm his cosmological significance.

Luke 22–23

Whereas Mark and Matthew are closely paralleled in the passion account, Luke's version is so different that some scholars have suggested the evangelist used a special source other than Mark or Matthew. Two unique aspects of Luke's account include lack of any formal night hearing (22:54) or actual Jewish death sentence against Jesus, and a separate hearing before Herod (23:6-11).

The disciples come across less harshly in Luke than in either Matthew or Mark. They remain faithful to Jesus in his trials (22:28) and in Gethsemane they fall asleep only once (rather than three times), not because of human frailty but because of sorrow (22:45; cf. Mark 14:37-42; Matt 26:40-46). They may even be alluded to at the cross (23:49), if they are meant to be counted among the male acquaintances of Jesus who are present. Luke also leaves out any reference to their fearful desertion of Jesus. Even Judas's betrayal is attributed to the greater evil of Satan and the powers of darkness (22:3, 53), and Peter's betrayal is made a more poignant scene of sorrowful human frailty: "And the Lord turned and looked at Peter, and Peter remembered the word of the Lord . . ." (22:61).

For Luke, Jesus dies as an innocent martyr whose death ironically brings reconciliation even to those who persecute him (22:32, 51; 23:34, 40-43). The theme of Jesus' innocence, used for apologetic as well as theological purposes, is strongly stressed by Luke even more than Matthew, for no less than three times in short succession does Pilate declare Jesus innocent (23:4, 15, 22). This judgment is confirmed by the acknowledgment of one of the criminals crucified with Jesus, who says, ". . . for we are receiving the true rewards of our deeds, but this man has done nothing wrong" (23:41). Not even the Jews can produce false witnesses against Jesus (cf. Mark 14:56; Matt 26:59), nor is there a scene of mockery by the Roman soldiers (cf. Mark 15:16-20; Matt 27:27-31). Furthermore, the confession of the centurion ("Truly this man was innocent!" 23:47) stands in contrast to both Mark and Matthew where the confession is a dogmatic profession of Jesus as the Son of God.

Some scholars have questioned whether Luke, in contrast to Mark and Matthew, sees much atoning value to Jesus' death. Unlike Mark and Matthew, who in the Last Supper accounts record the words "This is my blood of the covenant which is poured out for many" (Mark 14:24; Matt 26:28; Matthew adds "for the forgiveness of sins"), Luke leaves out these words and consequently reduces the atoning value of Jesus' passion. Other factors mitigate this observation. Only Luke includes the words "This is my body given up for you" in the words over the bread (22:19) and uses the explicit term "*new* covenant in my blood" (22:20). Further, the various acts of healing, reconciliation, and salvation which Jesus performs in the midst of his passion (22:51; 23:12, 28, 34, 43) indicate that his death has powerful atoning value, even toward his persecutors. Jesus' hearing before Herod also ironically results in a friendship between Herod and Pilate (23:12).

Another significant part of Luke's view is the connection of the Cross with Paradise. Jesus says to the one criminal crucified with him and who defends his innocence: "Today you will be with me in Paradise" (23:43). For Luke, the Cross represents the victory of Jesus over the powers of darkness (22:53) and prepares the way for the mission of the Church which is pursued in Luke's second volume, the Acts of the Apostles. Indeed, one of the functions of the Lukan PN is to serve as a model for the endurance of persecution and trials which later disciples undergo. Stephen's martyrdom (Acts 7:54-60) and Paul's sufferings (16:19-24; 17:5-9) and trials (18:12-15; 23:23-30) contain parallels to Jesus' fate.

John 18–19

If Luke's PN is the most unique among the Synoptic Gospels, John's is nonetheless the most distinctive of all the canonical passion accounts. It is the shortest account and it may be the most familiar one to many Catholics. John's PN is always read in the liturgical service of Good Friday. The other three are read in the liturgical calendar only once every three years on Palm/Passion Sunday. Being the most dramatic of the PNs, John's account has influenced both Christian art and popular Catholic piety through the centuries.

Although chapters 18–19 constitute the heart of John's PN, many details particular to the passion story are found scattered throughout chapters 10–17. John's distinctive PN must be seen in the context of Johannine Christology, a portrait that is different from that in the Synoptics. The passion can only be understood in the context of a Jesus who is the preexistent Word of God, who comes down from heaven and dwells with humans, performing his ministry of signs and instruction, and then being exalted, by means of the Cross, and returning to the glory from which he came (1:1-18). Jesus is not only preexistent but also omniscient (cf. 2:25; 6:6; etc.) and one who is fully in charge of his own destiny. He is the Good Shepherd who surrenders his own life freely: "I lay down my life and I take it up again; no one takes it from me" (10:17-18). Jesus offends the high priest with his self-assurance (18:20-22) and even gives Pilate cause for concern when he asserts, "You have no power over me" (19:8-11). With regard to his betrayer, Jesus is the one who gives him permission during the Last Supper to go out and do what he must do (13:27-30).

Other factors enhance and develop this general theme of Jesus being in charge of his own destiny. For example, in place of the three passion predictions found in the Synoptics, John has three sayings about Jesus' return to the Father (7:33-36; 8:21-23; 13:33) and three sayings about the necessity of the Son of Man being "lifted up" (3:14; 8:28; 12:32-33). The latter expression is loaded with Johannine double entendre, referring both to a lifting up in sacrifice and in glory.

Another theme that finds its culmination in the PN is the contrast between light and darkness (1:1-9; 3:19-21). That darkness is the time of evil deeds is dramatically confirmed when Judas leaves the supper to fulfill his role as the betrayer: ". . . and it was night" (13:30). John also heightens the effective irony at the arrest of Jesus by adding the notice that Judas and the band of soldiers (the Roman cohort, mentioned only in John's account) and some officers of the chief priests come to arrest Jesus "with lanterns and torches." Judas, the one who has chosen the darkness, needs artificial light because he cannot see the true light that stands before him. Unlike the arrest scene in the Synoptics, we do not see a picture of a Jesus who is grieving over his fate and praying to be released of his duty. On the contrary, there is no "agony in the garden" in John (cf. Luke 22:44). Instead, Jesus boldly embraces his fate. In response to Peter's drastic action of cutting off the slave Malchus's ear to protect him, Jesus says: "Put your sword into its sheath; shall I not drink the cup which the Father has given me?" (18:11). Other elements contribute to this deliberate portrayal of Jesus in the response of those who come to arrest him. When Jesus responds "I am [he]" to the statement that the crowd seeks Jesus of Nazareth, "they drew back and fell to the ground" (18:6). This is part of the Johannine use of the OT expression "I am." The captors unwittingly respond in a devout manner to Jesus' self-presentation as "I am," the divine name revealed to Moses (Exod 3:14).

John also enhances the culpability of the Jewish people with regard to Jesus' death. He uses the generic expression, "the Jews" (cf. 18:12, 14; 19:20) throughout the Gospel and also explicitly refers to the Pharisees in the plot against Jesus (18:3; cf. Matt 27:62).

If John has heightened some of the drama of the passion and intensified the picture of Jesus with a veil of divinity, he has also artistically shaped other traditions in the PN. R. E. Brown has demonstrated the elaborate staging of the Roman trial (18:28–19:16) which portrays Pilate's "shuttling" back and forth between Jesus, who is inside the praetorium, and the Jews, who remain outside the building for fear of ritual contamination before the Passover feast (*John XIII-XXI,* AB 29A, Garden City, New York: Doubleday, 1970, p. 859). John has also moved the position of the scourging and mockery scene to the center of the Roman trial (19:1-3). Rather than being a part of the sentence carried out against Jesus, it becomes a prelude to the climactic exaltation of the Cross. John has even left out the detail of having the purple cloak (a sign of royalty) stripped off Jesus once it is put on him during the mockery. Jesus goes to his moment of glory, not as an innocent martyr, but as a royal king at his enthronement. Jesus is not simply meek and silent but the one in control of his destiny. In the trial Jesus dialogues eloquently with Pilate about the nature of his kingship and the nature of truth. On the way to the crucifixion, there is no Simon of Cyrene to carry the cross. Jesus carries his own cross. The term *christos* is never used in John's passion (unlike Mark, Matthew, and Luke), but the importance of the kingship theme, already prominent in Mark, takes precedence. The titulus hung upon the cross is portrayed as a universal announcement of enthronement, directed to all the world, for "it was written in Hebrew, in Latin and in Greek" (19:20) and said: "Jesus of Nazareth, the King of the Jews" (19:19). Even the burial scene adds to this royal theme by having Nicodemus (19:39-40; cf. 3:1-15) come and anoint the body of Jesus with "about a hundred pounds" of myrrh and aloes, wrapping it in linen and spices, enough ritual and materials fit for a king.

John's account is rich in other symbolism as well, such as Passover. Jesus is proclaimed by John the Baptist as the "Lamb of God" (1:29, 36), and only John makes it plain that Jesus died at noontime on the Day of Preparation ("the sixth hour," 19:14), when the Passover lambs traditionally began to be slaughtered. Other Passover allusions, which thus make a connection with Jesus' death as the new paschal event, are the reference to "hyssop" (19:29; cf. Mark 15:36 and Matt 27:48, "reed") and the unique Johannine reference to Jesus' bones not being broken (cf. Exod 12:46; John 19:36). Although some scholars dispute whether these Passover allusions are really significant, they are nonetheless a factor in the complex network of Johannine symbolism.

Other symbolic items in the Johannine PN are high priest symbolism (19:23-24, the "unseamed garment") and the importance of the crucifixion as life-giving (19:34, "blood and water" from Jesus' side; cf. the "living water" symbolism in John 4:13-14). Even more important, however, is the connection at Jesus' death with the Holy Spirit, the Paraclete. John 7:39 (cf. 20:22) makes the clear connection that the Holy Spirit can only be given to the disciples after Jesus' glorification, which is achieved by the Cross. Jesus, who was handed over (*paredōken,* 19:16) to be crucified, then hands over (*paredōken,* 19:30) his spirit, not with a lamenting outcry (Mark 15:34/Matt 27:46) but with the consummative expression, "It is finished!" (19:30).

Two more symbols present in the account of John are the personages of the "beloved disciple" and Jesus' own mother (19:26). They do not stand as the women in the Synoptics (from afar) but at the foot of the cross. For John's community, the Beloved Disciple represents the ideal or true disciple. Interpretations about the symbolism of Jesus' mother vary. Some relate her with the OT themes of the New Eve (Gen 2–4) or Lady Zion (Isa 49:20-22; 54:1-7) who brings forth after birth pangs a new people in joy. Others prefer to see her as a symbol of the Church.

In sum, the Jesus of John's PN dies not abandoned and alone, maltreated and completely humiliated, but as the sovereign king who is ironically victorious over the world that does not recognize him.

Historical Issues

The variegated richness of these four PNs is testimony to the power of the gospel to evoke diverse theological insights from the same historical foundations. But such a theological appreciation of the PNs does not resolve the many historical issues about Jesus' passion and death which remain unanswered. Scholars continue to explore questions about the sources, origins, and genre of all of the PNs. Difficult historical issues such as the role of the Jewish leaders in the trial of Jesus, the date and exact nature of the Last Supper meal, the date of the crucifixion, the nature of the charges against Jesus, etc. continue to be explored by biblical scholars even as recognition of the theological value of the PNs abides. (See R. E. Brown, *The Death of the Messiah,* 2 vols.; Garden City, New York: Doubleday, 1994).

RONALD D. WITHERUP, S.S.

See also BIBLE, NEW TESTAMENT WRITINGS; JESUS CHRIST; PASCHAL MYSTERY.

PASSIONISTS

A religious institute, officially entitled the Congregation of the Passion of our Lord Jesus Christ (*Congregatio Passionis Jesu Christi*), (C.P.), and founded by Paolo Francesco Danei (St. Paul of the Cross, 1694–1775) in Italy in 1720. Under the sponsorship of Francesco M. Arborio di Gattinara, bishop of Alessandria, Paul wrote the rule and constitutions for the institute. He received papal approval for the rule and constitutions of the community in 1741 from Pope Benedict XIV. The congregation received final approval from Pope Clement XIV's bull *Supremi Apostolatus,* 16 November 1769.

The spirit of the congregation is one of prayer, penance, solitude, and apostolic ministry. The Passionists take the traditional vows of poverty, chastity, obedience, as well as a special vow to keep alive in the People of God the memory of the passion. The members (priests and brothers) of this institute are called to a contemplative-apostolic spirituality. This is achieved through a serious commitment to living in community as well as a vigorous apostolic ministry. This latter is especially attained through the preaching of the word of God, in retreats and parochial missions, and by teaching people to pray.

In this century, the age of martyrs, Passionists, in fidelity to the gospel and in loyalty to serving God's poor, have proclaimed without measure the passion gospel of justice and love. Many priests, brothers, and students have done this at the price of their own lives. Those who have given their lives are: in 1929, in China, Walter Coveyou, Godfrey Holbein, and Clement Seybold; in 1936, in Spain, Innocent Arnau, Nicephoros Diez and the Damiel Martyrs (thirty-one priests, brothers, and students); in 1946, in Palestine, John Salah, an Arab Passionist; and most recently, in 1988 in the Philippines, Carl Schmitz was martyred in service to the B'laam peoples.

Among its membership, three have been canonized: Sts. Paul of the Cross, Gabriel Possenti, and Vincent Mary Strambi (which number does not include Sts. Gemma Galgani and Maria Goretti). Several have been declared blessed: Innocent Arnau, Dominic Barberi, Isidore De Loor, Nicephoros Diez and the Damiel Martyrs, Charles Houban, and Bernard Mary Silvestrelli. And even still more have been declared "Servants of God" by the Church.

The Second Vatican Council has had a profound influence on the renewal and development of the Passionists. The congregation has researched and reflected upon its founder and his charism. This has led to a deeper appreciation of the import of the "memory of the Passion," "option for the poor," and the 1984 revision of its *Constitutions.* Since Vatican II the congregation has witnessed growth and expansion in Africa, India, Indonesia, Korea, Japan, Latin America, and the Philippines. In January 1992, Passionists numbered 2,579 members.

In 1771, Paul of the Cross with Mother Mary Costantini of Jesus Crucified, founded a community of contemplative Passionist nuns. Other groups of men and women share the Passionist community charism of promoting the memory of the passion in today's world. A community of Passionist sisters was established in England in 1852; the Passionist Sisters of St. Paul of the Cross were instituted in Italy in 1872; the Congregation of the Daughters of the Passion of Our Lord Jesus Christ and the Sorrows of Mary were constituted in Mexico in 1892. The Brothers of the Passion were planted in Zaire in 1944. The Missionaries of the Passion (a secular institute) was launched in Sicily in 1980.

KENNETH O'MALLEY, C.P.

See also MISSIONS, CATHOLIC, THE MODERN PERIOD; PAUL OF THE CROSS, ST.

PASSOVER

Passover (*Pesaḥ*) is the most important feast on the Jewish calendar being rivaled only by the Day of Atonement. It is significant also to the religious expression of Christianity.

As a rite originally practiced by shepherds, Passover harked back to a period long prior to Israel's emergence as a nation. The springtime sacrifice of a young animal was meant to secure the well-being of both shepherd and flock. Its blood, smeared on the entrance to the tent, would ward off evil. This ritual was appropriated in Israelite tradition to interpret the deliverance of the Hebrew people on that historic night when judgment was visited upon their Egyptian taskmasters.

Woven into the traditions connecting Passover with the Exodus would be provision for what was originally a distinct festival, that of Unleavened Bread (*maṣṣôth*). Like Passover the festival of Unleavened Bread was a spring festival. Probably taken over from the Canaanites, it marked the beginning of the barley harvest. It would be connected with the Exodus for, once in the Promised Land, the harvest would fulfill for the Israelites the hopes voiced on the night of their going forth from Egypt.

The feast of Unleavened Bread was a pilgrimage feast. The Passover, however, was largely a family feast and kept in each village and home (Exod 12:21-27). In the springtime month of Nisan, on the evening of the full moon, a lamb would be slain and its blood sprinkled over the lintels of the door to the house. That same night the meat would be roasted and consumed with bitter herbs and unleavened bread. This was to be observed throughout the generations (Exod 12:42). Thus was Israel summoned to acknowledge that the divine intervention which had redeemed the people from slavery in Egypt was also to be redemptive of succeeding generations.

Not until the time of Josiah (640–609 B.C.) and Deuteronomy were the feasts of Passover and Unleavened Bread combined into one observance. The Passover then became a pilgrimage feast and was to be kept in Jerusalem. Thus the observance persevered to the destruction of the Temple in A.D. 70, when all sacrifice including that of the paschal lamb ceased. In its absence greater emphasis would be laid upon the Passover meal or *Seder*. The lesson of the deliverance from Egypt was not to be lost on the Jews when they faced renewed oppression (Pes 10:5).

In the New Testament it is Jesus who as the new Passover sacrifice, delivers not only Jews but all men and women from the thralldom of sin and death. According to the Synoptic Gospels even as he celebrates his last Passover, Jesus commences the immolation which would be consummated on the cross (Mark 14:12-26; Matt 26:17-30; Luke 22:7-38). Though in the Letter to the Hebrews Jesus' sacrifice is said to supersede that of the Day of Atonement, in the Fourth Gospel it is the Passover which affords the point of comparison (John 1:29, cf. Isa 53; also, John 19:14, 36). In another Johannine work the lamb which was slain also recalls the paschal lamb (Rev 5:6, 9, 12; 12:11). Early in the Church's life Paul alludes to the sacrifice of Christ as that of "our Paschal Lamb" (1 Cor 5:7).

THOMAS BUCKLEY

PASTOR

(Lat., "shepherd") A priest who is entrusted with the pastoral care of the parish community. His chief responsibilities are: ensuring that the Gospel is proclaimed in his parish through preaching; affirming the primacy of the Eucharist in the life of the community; and meeting the community's sacramental needs. The pastor also exercises authority over the administration of parish finances, and represents the parish in legal matters. Pastors are appointed by the bishop.

JOSEPH QUINN

See also PARISH.

PASTORAL ADMINISTRATOR

A pastoral administrator, in the canonical sense, is a priest who has care of a parish in the absence of the pastor. The term is also used in a popular sense to refer to situations in which laypersons or nonordained religious administer a parish, although canon law does not use the term "administrator" when a layperson has charge of a parish. This situation would only occur in rare cases when there is a severe dearth of priests. When a diocesan bishop does appoint a layperson as administrator of a parish, he or she works jointly with a priest who is expected to come periodically to celebrate the sacraments, although the administrator may be given the power to preach, to baptize, and to witness marriages.

ANTHONY D. ANDREASSI

See also PARISH; PASTOR.

PATEN

(Lat. *paterna,* "a dish") A saucer-like dish which holds the bread to be consecrated at Mass; it is usually gilded or silver-plated and must be large enough to cover the chalice. Patens traditionally are blessed by a bishop or his delegate.

JOSEPH QUINN

See also VESSELS, SACRED.

PATER NOSTER

See LORD'S PRAYER, THE.

PATRICK, ST. (fl. FIFTH CENTURY A.D.)

''Apostle of Ireland.'' Scholars differ over Patrick's dates, arguing that he began his mission either ca. 432 or ca. 456 and that he died either ca. 461 or ca. 493. A remarkably clear outline of his life, however, emerges from his own writings, the authenticity of which is undisputed. His *Confessio* and earlier *Letter to the Soldiers of Coroticus* were composed in a crude form of late Latin since, as he himself explained, he was ''the most unlearned of men'' and had become accustomed on his mission to speaking the language of the Irish. The *Letter* reprimands a British chieftain for killing and kidnapping Irish Christians. The *Confessio* tells how Patrick came to undertake his mission and defends his work among the Irish against criticism voiced by a group of churchmen who had denigrated him because of an unspecified offense which he committed in his youth.

From these writings we learn that Patrick's father, Calpurnius, was a wealthy Romano-British municipal councilor and a deacon in the Church at some time during the prolonged collapse of the Roman Empire; his grandfather was Potitus, a priest. Patrick spent a carefree and less than pious boyhood at the family villa near a place called Bannaven Taberniae, the location of which is unknown other than that it was near the coast of Britain. Raiders from the sea took him captive at the age of 16, together with his father's servants, and carried him to Ireland. There he worked as a slave for six years tending animals ''in the woods and on the mountains.'' He underwent a personal conversion and would rise before dawn to pray ''even in times of snow or frost or rain.'' He eventually escaped and after various adventures settled down in Britain with his relatives. In a dream he saw ''a man called Victor'' who brought him letters from Ireland, one of which was headed ''the voice of the Irish''; as he started to read it he seemed to hear the people who lived ''near the Western Sea'' calling out ''we ask you, boy, come and walk among us again.''

At least twice more Patrick became intensely aware of what he believed to be this urging by the Holy Spirit to return to Ireland, where it would be his duty "to spread out our nets so that a very great multitude might be caught for God and that there might be clergy everywhere to baptize and preach to a people in need and want." Preparation and ordination were necessary, of which he tells us little, but it was as "bishop of this mission" that he came back to the Irish and never left them thereafter. He would not, he wrote in old age, "consider leaving them and going to Britain. . . . God knows how I yearned for it, but I am tied by the Spirit. . . . I am afraid of undoing the work which I have begun."

Patrick described graphically what he did in Ireland, telling of "the many baptisms I performed" and "how the Lord ordained through my unworthy person so many clergy." He refused to take credit for this, saying that it was through God's grace that "in Ireland a people who had in their ignorance of God always worshipped idols and unclean things" had become "a people of the Lord," and "the sons and daughters of Irish chieftains" were seen to be "monks and virgins dedicated to Christ." It was not easily achieved. Patrick speaks of the taunts, imprisonment and robbery he had to endure as he traveled around the country preaching the gospel. Yet he continued to see himself as a mere agent through whom God accomplished the conversion of Ireland. "My only prayer to God is that it may never happen that I should leave his people which he won for himself at the end of the earth.'' The stress typifies Patrick: it is God who acts, the missionary merely bears witness.

From other records and traditions of reasonable authenticity, Patrick's own narrative can be expanded a little. It seems that his boyhood slavery was spent first "near the Western sea" in what is now Mayo and then on Slemish mountain in the present northern county of Antrim. The ship on which he escaped almost certainly brought him to Gaul (now France) where, then or later, he lived for a time in several monasteries, perhaps at Auxerre and Tours and on the Provençal island of Lérins in the Mediterranean. There is good reason to suppose that he came under the influence of St. Germanus of Auxerre both in Gaul and in Britain, where Germanus came to preach against the heresy of the British-born theologian Pelagius. Pelagius contended that we could attain salvation by our personal unaided efforts without divine assistance. Patrick's repeated emphasis on God's grace and God's support for all that he did can be read as conscious rejection of Pelagianism, traces of which he may have come across in Ireland among a small Christian community whose bishop had been a missionary named Palladius.

Palladius, who is thought to have been sent by Pope Celestine I, does not appear to have been very successful and some authorities suggest that when his mission collapsed Patrick was sent in his place. It has also been argued that the annalists confused Palladius with Patrick so that the Patrick of Irish tradition is in fact a composite figure. This remains unproven. So does Patrick's legendary association with places of pilgrimage such as Croagh Patrick in Mayo, Lough Derg in Donegal, and Saul in County Down, where he is supposedly buried. The best-loved stories about him tell how he lit the Easter fire on the Hill of Slane in defiance of druidic custom, how he used the shamrock to elucidate the mystery of the Trinity for the High King, and how he banished the snakes from Ireland: all of these, sadly, must be considered pious inventions thought up long after his death. It is reasonably certain, on the other hand, that he established his see at Armagh, close to Eamhain Macha, the chief fortress of the kings of Ulster. What has never been doubted is that it was the man called Patrick, the author of the *Confessio* and the *Letter,* who carried out the massive work of implanting the Christian faith so widely and deeply in Ireland that the Irish became the second Christian nation (after Ethiopia) outside the ambit of ancient Rome.

LOUIS McREDMOND

See also CATHOLICISM, IRISH; MISSIONS, CATHOLIC, THE MODERN PERIOD; PATROLOGY.

PATROLOGY

Formerly synonymous with patristics, which refers to the study of ancient Christian writers who were accepted as witnesses to church life and teaching. This period ended in the West with the death of Isidore of Seville in 636 and in the East with the death of John of Damascus in 749. Patristics studies the thought of these "Church Fathers," particularly regarding doctrinal issues.

Currently, "patrology" refers more commonly to a systematically laid out manual on patristic literature.

PATRICIA DeFERRARI

See also FATHERS OF THE CHURCH.

PATRON SAINTS

It has long been customary to give a person a saint's name at baptism so that the baptized person will invoke the help of the patron saint to intercede with God. Churches, dioceses, countries, and other civic and ecclesiastical bodies are also put under the patronage of saints. The United States of America has Mary under her title of Immaculate Conception as its patron.

The practice of selecting patrons dates back to the earliest centuries of Christianity. In the catacombs the burial places of Christians indicate they had chosen the names of the apostles and early martyrs. Angels too were chosen as patrons. The practice developed of choosing a patron or protector for almost every circumstance of life. There is a list of patron saints published to cover almost every group, life situation, and illness.

JAMES McGRATH

See also SAINTS.

PATRON SAINTS OF OCCUPATIONS, PLACES, AND COUNTRIES

The patron saints for various occupations, places, and countries usually arose from popular devotion. Those who were formally chosen by Church authorities are rather few, and dates of designation are given in parentheses.

Patron Saints of Occupations

Accountants: Matthew
Actors: Genesius
Advertisers: Bernardine of Siena (20 May 1960)
Alpinists: Bernard of Montjoux (or Menthon) (20 August 1923)
Altar servers: John Berchmans
Anesthetists: Rene Goupil
Anglers: Andrew
Animals: Francis of Assisi
Archers: Sebastian
Architects: Thomas, Apostle
Armorers: Dunstan
Art: Catherine of Bologna
Artists: Luke, Catherine of Bologna, Bl. Angelico (21 February 1984)
Astronomers: Dominic
Athletes: Sebastian
Authors: Francis de Sales
Aviators: Our Lady of Loreto (1920), Thérèse of Lisieux, Joseph of Cupertino

Bakers: Elizabeth of Hungary, Nicholas
Bankers: Matthew
Barbers: Cosmas and Damian, Louis
Barren women: Anthony of Padua, Felicity
Basket-makers: Anthony, Abbot
Beggars: Martin of Tours
Blacksmiths: Dunstan
Blind: Odilia, Raphael
Blood banks: Januarius
Bodily ills: Our Lady of Lourdes
Bookbinders: Peter Celestine
Bookkeepers: Matthew
Booksellers: John of God
Boy Scouts: George
Brewers: Augustine of Hippo, Luke, Nicholas of Myra
Bricklayers: Stephen
Brides: Nicholas of Myra
Brushmakers: Anthony, Abbot
Builders: Vincent Ferrer
Butchers: Anthony (Abbot), Luke

Cabdrivers: Fiacre
Cabinetmakers: Anne
Cancer patients: Peregrine

Canonists: Raymond of Peñafort
Carpenters: Joseph
Catechists: Viator, Charles Borromeo, Robert Bellarmine
Catholic Action: Francis of Assisi (1916)
Chandlers: Ambrose, Bernard of Clairvaux
Charitable societies: Vincent de Paul (12 May 1885)
Children: Nicholas of Myra
Children of Mary: Agnes, Maria Goretti
Choir: Dominic Savio (8 June 1956), Holy Innocents
Church: Joseph (8 December 1870)
Clerics: Gabriel of the Sorrowful Mother
Communications personnel: Bernardine
Confessors: Alphonsus Liguori (26 April 1950), John Nepomucene
Convulsive children: Scholastica
Cooks: Lawrence, Martha
Coopers: Nicholas of Myra
Coppersmiths: Maurus

Dairy workers: Brigid
Deaf: Francis de Sales
Dentists: Apollonia
Desperate situations: Gregory of Neocaesarea, Jude Thaddeus, Rita of Cascia
Dietitians (in hospitals): Martha
Dyers: Maurice, Lydia
Dying: Joseph

Ecologists: Francis of Assisi (29 November 1979)
Editors: John Bosco
Emigrants: Frances Xavier Cabrini (8 September 1950)
Engineers: Ferdinand III
Epilepsy, Motor Diseases: Vitus, Willibrord
Eucharistic congresses and societies: Paschal Baylon (28 November 1897)
Expectant mothers: Raymond Nonnatus, Gerard Majella
Eye diseases: Lucy

Falsely accused: Raymond Nonnatus
Farmers: George, Isidore
Farriers: John the Baptist
Female domestic servants: Zita
Firefighters: Florian
Fire prevention: Catherine of Siena
First communicants: Tarcisius
Florists: Thérèse of Lisieux
Forest workers: John Gualbert
Foundlings: Holy Innocents
Fullers: Anastasius the Fuller, James the Less
Funeral directors: Joseph of Arimathea, Dismas

Gardeners: Adelard, Tryphon, Fiacre, Phocas
Glassworkers: Luke
Goldsmiths: Dunstan, Anastasius
Gravediggers: Anthony, Abbot
Greetings: Valentine
Grocers: Michael

Hairdressers: Martin de Porres
Happy meetings: Raphael
Hatters: Severus of Ravenna, James the Less
Headache sufferers: Teresa of Jesus (Avila)
Heart patients: John of God
Homemakers: Anne
Hospital administrators: Basil the Great, Frances X. Cabrini
Hospitals: Camillus de Lellis and John of God (22 June 1886), Jude Thaddeus
Hunters: Hubert, Eustachius

Infantry: Maurice
Innkeepers: Amand, Martha
Invalids: Roch

Jewelers: Eligius, Dunstan
Journalists: Francis de Sales (26 April 1923)
Jurists: John Capistran

Laborers: Isidore, James, John Bosco
Lawyers: Ivo (Yves Helory), Genesius, Thomas More
Learning: Ambrose
Librarians: Jerome
Lighthouse keepers: Venerius
Locksmiths: Dunstan

Marble workers: Clement I
Mariners: Michael, Nicholas of Tolentino
Medical record librarians: Raymond of Peñafort
Medical social workers: John Regis
Medical technicians: Albert the Great
Mentally ill: Dymphna
Merchants: Francis of Assisi, Nicholas of Myra
Messengers: Gabriel
Metal workers: Eligius
Military chaplains: John Capistran (10 February 1984)
Millers: Arnulph, Victor
Missions, Foreign: Francis Xavier (25 March 1904), Thérèse of Lisieux (14 December 1927)
Missions, Black: Peter Claver (1896, Leo XIII), Benedict the Black
Missions, Parish: Leonard of Port Maurice (17 March 1923)
Mothers: Monica
Motorcyclists: Our Lady of Grace
Motorists: Christopher, Frances of Rome
Mountaineers: Bernard of Montjoux (or Menthon)
Musicians: Gregory the Great, Cecilia, Dunstan

Notaries: Luke, Mark
Nurses: Camillus de Lellis and John of God (1930, Pius XI), Agatha, Raphael

Nursing and nursing service: Elizabeth of Hungary, Catherine of Siena

Orators: John Chrysostom (8 July 1908)
Organ builders: Cecilia
Orphans: Jerome Emiliani

Painters: Luke
Paratroopers: Michael
Pawnbrokers: Nicholas
Pharmacists: Cosmas and Damian, James the Greater
Pharmacists (in hospitals): Gemma Galgani
Philosophers: Justin
Physicians: Pantaleon, Cosmas and Damian, Luke, Raphael
Pilgrims: James the Greater
Plasterers: Bartholomew
Poets: David, Cecilia
Poison sufferers: Benedict
Police: Michael
Poor: Lawrence, Anthony of Padua
Poor souls: Nicholas of Tolentino
Porters: Christopher
Possessed: Bruno, Denis
Postal employees: Gabriel
Priests: Jean-Baptiste Vianney (23 April 1929)
Printers: John of God, Augustine of Hippo, Genesius
Prisoners: Dismas, Joseph Cafasso
Protector of crops: Ansovinus
Public relations: Bernardine of Siena (20 May 1960)
Public relations (of hospitals): Paul, Apostle

Radiologists: Michael (15 January 1941)
Radio workers: Gabriel
Retreats: Ignatius Loyola (25 July 1922)
Rheumatism: James the Greater

Saddlers: Crispin and Crispinian
Sailors: Cuthbert, Brendan, Eulalia, Christopher, Peter Gonzales, Erasmus, Nicholas
Scholars: Brigid
Schools, Catholic: Thomas Aquinas (4 August 1880), Joseph Calasanz (13 August 1948)
Scientists: Albert (13 August 1948)
Sculptors: Claude
Seafarers: Francis of Paola
Searchers of lost articles: Anthony of Padua
Secretaries: Genesius
Security personnel: Peter of Alcantara
Seminarians: Charles Borromeo
Servants: Martha, Zita
Shoemakers: Crispin and Crispinian
Sick: Michael, John of God and Camillus de Lellis (22 June 1886)
Silversmiths: Andronicus
Singers: Gregory, Cecilia
Skaters: Lidwina
Skiers: Bernard of Montjoux (or Menthon)
Social workers: Louise de Marillac (12 February 1960)
Soldiers: Hadrian, George, Ignatius, Sebastian, Martin of Tours, Joan of Arc
Speleologists: Benedict
Stenographers: Genesius, Cassian
Stonecutters: Clement
Stonemasons: Stephen
Students: Thomas Aquinas
Surgeons: Cosmas and Damian, Luke
Swordsmiths: Maurice

Tailors: Homobonus
Tanners: Crispin and Crispinian, Simon
Tax collectors: Matthew
Teachers: Gregory the Great, John Baptist de la Salle (15 May 1950)
Telecommunications workers: Gabriel (12 January 1951)
Television: Clare of Assisi (14 February 1958)
Television workers: Gabriel
Tertiaries (Secular Franciscans): Louis of France, Elizabeth of Hungary
Theologians: Augustine, Alphonsus Liguori
Throat ailments: Blase
Travelers: Anthony of Padua, Nicholas of Myra, Christopher, Raphael
Travel hostesses: Bona (2 March 1962)

Universities: Blessed Contardo Ferrini

Vocations: Alphonsus

Weavers: Paul the Hermit, Anastasius the Fuller, Anastasia
Wine merchants: Amand
Women in labor: Anne
Women's Army Corps: Genevieve
Workingmen: Joseph
Writers: Francis de Sales (26 April 1923), Lucy

Yacht sailors: Adjutor
Young girls: Agnes
Youth: Aloysius Gonzaga (1729, Benedict XIII; 1926, Pius XI), John Berchmans, Gabriel of the Sorrowful Mother

Patron Saints of Places and Countries

Alsace: Odilia
Americas: Our Lady of Guadalupe, Rose of Lima
Angola: Immaculate Heart of Mary (21 November 1984)
Argentina: Our Lady of Lujan
Armenia: Gregory Illuminator

Asia Minor: John, Evangelist
Australia: Our Lady Help of Christians

Belgium: Joseph
Bohemia: Wenceslaus, Ludmilla
Borneo: Francis Xavier
Brazil: Nossa Senhora de Aparecida, Immaculate Conception, Peter of Alcantara

Canada: Joseph, Anne
Chile: James the Greater, Our Lady of Mt. Carmel
China: Joseph
Colombia: Peter Claver, Louis Bertran
Corsica: Immaculate Conception
Czechoslovakia: Wenceslaus, John Nepomucene, Procopius

Denmark: Ansgar, Canute
Dominican Republic: Our Lady of High Grace, Dominic

East Indies: Thomas, Apostle
Ecuador: Sacred Heart
El Salvador: Our Lady of Peace (10 October 1966)
England: George
Equatorial Guinea: Immaculate Conception (25 May 1986)
Europe: Benedict (1964), Cyril and Methodius, co-patrons (13 December 1980)

Finland: Henry
France: Our Lady of the Assumption, Joan of Arc, Thérèse (3 May 1944)

Germany: Boniface, Michael
Gibraltar: Blessed Virgin Mary under title, "Our Lady of Europe" (31 May 1979)
Greece: Nicholas, Andrew

Holland: Willibrord
Hungary: Blessed Virgin, "Great Lady of Hungary," Stephen, King

Iceland: Thorlac (14 January 1984)
India: Our Lady of Assumption
Ireland: Patrick, Brigid and Columba
Italy: Francis of Assisi, Catherine of Siena

Japan: Peter Baptist

Korea: Joseph and Mary, Mother of the Church

Lesotho: Immaculate Heart of Mary
Lithuania: Casimir, Bl. Cunegunda
Luxembourg: Willibrord

Malta: Paul, Our Lady of the Assumption
Mexico: Our Lady of Guadalupe
Monaco: Devota
Moravia: Cyril and Methodius

New Zealand: Our Lady Help of Christians
Norway: Olaf

Papua New Guinea (including northern Solomon Islands): Michael the Archangel (31 May 1979)
Paraguay: Our Lady of Assumption (13 July 1951)
Peru: Joseph (19 March 1957)
Philippines: Sacred Heart of Mary
Poland: Casimir, Bl. Cunegunda, Stanislaus of Cracow, Our Lady of Czestochowa
Portugal: Immaculate Conception, Francis Borgia, Anthony of Padua, Vincent of Saragossa, George

Russia: Andrew, Nicholas of Myra, Thérèse of Lisieux

Scandinavia: Ansgar
Scotland: Andrew, Columba
Silesia: Hedwig
Slovakia: Our Lady of Sorrows
South Africa: Our Lady of Assumption (15 March 1952)
South America: Rose of Lima
Spain: James the Greater, Teresa
Sri Lanka (Ceylon): Lawrence
Sweden: Bridget, Eric

Tanzania: Immaculate Conception (8 December 1984)

United States: Immaculate Conception (1846)
Uruguay: Blessed Virgin Mary under title "La Virgen de los Treinte y Tres" (21 November 1963)

Venezuela: Our Lady of Coromoto

Wales: David
West Indies: Gertrude

MICHAEL GLAZIER

PAUL VI, POPE (21 JUNE 1963–6 AUGUST 1978)

Giovanni Battista Montini was born to middle-class parents in Concesio, near Brescia, northern Italy on 26 September 1898. His father was an influential lawyer who controlled the local newspaper and his mother was active in charitable causes. From an early age he showed an interest in books and learning. Because of poor health he was turned down for military service in World War I. He attended the local diocesan seminary as a day student and was ordained a priest on 29 May 1920, and the following year he began graduate studies in Rome.

Pope Paul VI

In 1922 he began working in the papal secretariat of state while also serving part-time as a chaplain to Catholic university students, who were then being harassed under the Fascist regime. He demonstrated his lifelong love for learning by publishing some of the conferences given to the university students. In 1937 he became assistant to the secretary of state, Eugenio Pacelli. When Pacelli was elected pope in 1939, Montini continued to work with him as a director of internal Church affairs, and in 1952 he was promoted to pro-secretary of state.

In 1954 Montini was named archbishop of Milan, a move which was widely interpreted as a sign of the Pope's displeasure with him. Here he poured himself into pastoral work while trying to establish the credibility of the Church with the industrial workers. While in Milan he also devoted his efforts to ecumenism. In 1958 the newly elected John XXIII made him a cardinal. Montini was involved in the preparations for Vatican Council II though he was not as eager as some other bishops. After Pope John's untimely death during the early stages of the council, Montini was elected pope on the fifth ballot in the largest papal conclave ever. He chose the name, Paul, as a symbol of an outward-looking papacy.

Paul continued the work of the council and brought it to a successful conclusion and began the difficult task of implementing its work. He carried through the application of the conciliar changes in the liturgy despite criticism from both the left and the right. Paul believed strongly in the importance of ecumenical dialogue and met with the archbishop of Canterbury, Michael Ramsey, and with the Ecumenical Patriarch, Athenagoras I. He traveled extensively, visiting the United Nations in New York where he stirred the General Assembly and the world with his cry, "No more war!" He was the first pope to visit Manila and Bogota. His encyclical, *Progessio Populorum,* demanded social justice for the world's poor. He reformed the Roman curia, abolished the old papal aristocracy, and dropped much of the pomp still associated with his office. He also greatly increased the number of non-Italian cardinals in order to make the college more reflective of the whole Church. An example of his evenhanded approach to Church affairs was the fact that he replaced the Holy Office with the Congregation for the Doctrine of the Faith and then placed the very conservative Cardinal Ottaviani in charge of it. His 1968 encyclical, *Humanae Vitae,* forbidding artificial birth control, was probably the most controversial act of his pontificate.

Some observers believed that after 1968 Paul became more conservative in his approach to Church reform. He reacted strongly against those who he felt were going too far and too fast in this area, though he never allied himself with the intransigent right. He died at his summer residence, Castelgondolfo, on 6 August 1978. Paul VI had presided over and guided the Catholic Church through some of the most momentous changes that it had ever experienced.

ANTHONY D. ANDREASSI

See also PAPACY, THE; VATICAN COUNCIL II.

PAUL OF THE CROSS, ST. (1694–1775)

Missionary, mystic, spiritual director, and founder of the Passionists, Paolo Francesco Danei was born in Ovada, near Genoa, in the Piedmont region of northern Italy, 3 January 1694, and died in Rome 18 October 1775. He was the second of sixteen children born to Anna Marie Massari and Luke Danei, a merchant of cloth.

Paul's early education was at a school for boys in Cremolino, Lombardy. In 1709 he left school and returned to Castellazzo, where he received a calling to serve God. In 1715 he joined the army of the Venetian Republic to serve for a short time as a chaplain during the Turkish War. In 1720, in a vision, he saw himself clothed in the habit which was to become the distinctive garb of his congregation.

After a series of mystical experiences and under the guidance of Francesco Arborio di Gattinara, bishop of Alessandria, Paul was prompted to found a congregation dedicated to preaching the memory of the passion. On 7 June 1727 he was ordained, with his brother John Baptist, by Pope Benedict

St. Paul of the Cross

XIII. He conducted his first mission at Grazi's Ferry in 1730 and his last in the Basilica of Santa Maria in Trastevere, Rome, at the age of seventy-five. Proclaiming the word of God through retreats and parochial missions was the most dynamic vehicle Paul knew to keep the memory of the passion alive in the hearts of people. He was especially courageous for his times in that he actually invited the laity to participate in the preaching of the word of God.

On 10 April 1747, at the first general chapter in the Retreat of the Presentation on Mount Argentaro, Paul was elected general of the congregation, a position he held until his death in 1775. He also founded a community of nuns. Paul is recognized as a master of the mystical life and spiritual director. Over three thousand of his estimated ten thousand letters, which deal mainly with spiritual direction and ascetical and mystical theology, are in existence. His treatise on *The Divine Nativity and Mystical Death* is one of the greatest documents in the Christian tradition on the mystical life. He is unique for his time in that he taught that all Christians are called to the same holiness of life, regardless of their state in life.

The body of St. Paul lies in the basilica of SS John and Paul, Rome. He was beatified on 1 May 1853, and canonized on 29 June 1867. His feast is celebrated 19 October in the universal calendar, and 20 October in the United States.

KENNETH O'MALLEY, C.P.

See also PASSIONISTS.

PAUL, ST.

Apostle to the Gentiles

The Apostle Paul is a unique first-century figure whose life and experience embrace the Jewish, Hellenistic and Christian worlds. The earliest sources for the events of Paul's life are his own letters and Luke's Acts of the Apostles which reflects Church interests some twenty to thirty years after Paul's death. A number of details emerge from these sources: Paul was born in Tarsus in Cilicia (Acts 9:11; 21:39; 22:3), inheriting Roman citizenship (Acts 16:37-38; 22:25-29; 23:27), a Hebrew of the tribe of Benjamin (Rom 11:1; Phil 3:5), and a Pharisee educated fully in the Law (Phil 3:5-6; Gal 1:14; Acts 23:6; 26:5), under Gamaliel in Jerusalem (Acts 22:3). Paul was extremely zealous as a Pharisee and became a persecutor of the Church (1 Cor 15:9; Gal 1:13; Phil 3:6), but was later converted by a profound experience of the Lord (1 Cor 15:8-10; Gal 1:15-16). Paul made four missionary journeys which Luke describes in detail: the first missionary journey in Acts 13:1–14:28, the second in 15:30–18:22, the third in 18:23–21:17, and the journey to Rome in 27:1–28:16. While any chronology is tentative because biblical writings rarely offer exact dates, Paul was probably born before A.D. 10 and died about 64. Several historically documented facts (Acts 18:12-17; 23:26; 24:27) enable scholars to date Paul's conversion between 34–37, his major journeys between 46–63, and his letter-writing between 50–60.

After witnessing the stoning of Stephen (Acts 7:54–8:3), Paul set out for Damascus and experienced a profound conversion on his way to the Syrian city. Of all the events of his life, the Damascus experience is most important for an understanding of Paul and his mission. In addition to Paul's own references to his conversion (Gal 1:11-17; 1 Cor 9:1; 15:8-10; Phil 3:4-11; Rom 1:5; 2 Cor 4:1; 5:16), Luke gives us three distinct accounts based on a single tradition (Acts 9:1-19; 22:4-16; 26:12-18). These accounts emphasize Paul's experience of Christ as risen Lord, his call to be an apostle, and his mission to the Gentiles. The event is transformational for Paul's understanding of Christ and of Christ's relationship to believers, providing the seeds for Paul's theology and ecclesiology.

The person Paul emerges from these sources, and his letters reveal his dynamic personality (Gal, 2 Cor, Phil) and contribute to our understanding of the development of the early Church. In his letters he responds in different ways to situations and communities, but with passion and concern, appreciating conflict, struggle, and diversity as means of clarifying the Christian response. The Corinthians acknowledge that he is a poor speaker but a prolific writer (2 Cor 10:10), while Luke portrays him as an excellent speaker throughout the Acts of the Apostles and never mentions his writing. Luke also conveys a more ideal picture of the apostle and the early Church than does the historical Paul in his letters. Sometimes the perspective of Paul and Luke differ, but the apostle always emerges as a dedicated and tireless missionary.

From the letters we receive glimpses of the colorful personality of Paul who is, at times, filled with anguish, affliction, tears, and pain (2 Cor 1:4; 6:4-6), beside himself (2 Cor 5:13), fighting within and without (2 Cor 7:5), but also bold (2 Cor 1:12), humble (2 Cor 10:1), boastful (2 Cor 11), and filled with feelings of warmth and tenderness (Phil 1:7-8; 2:12; 4:1; 2 Cor 2:4). Joy and hope permeate his correspondence (Phil 1:4; 2 Cor 2:4; 4:16; 7:16). To understand Paul's writing we must understand the complexity of the person, since the person and message go hand in hand. With his religious tradition within Judaism, his growth and development in the Greek world of his day, his knowledge of Hebrew, Aramaic, and Greek, Paul was well-prepared for his mission to interpret the gospel message for the Gentile communities.

The Churches Paul Founded

Paul's preaching of the gospel led to the establishment of communities of believers or Churches. These believers responded to the proclamation of faith (kerygma) that emphasized fulfillment of Scriptures in the death and resurrection of Jesus, the presence of the risen Lord through the power of the Spirit, belief in the second coming of the Lord in glory (parousia), and a call to repentance and baptism. Since Paul's conversion was to an already existing Church, he received elements of the kerygma from those who were believers before him (1 Cor 11:2; Gal 1:9; Rom 6:17). On the other hand, his conversion offered him key insights into the radicalness of the Christian response and into the implications of the abiding presence of Christ within the believing community.

Paul took the gospel into the Gentile world, needing to interpret the message of Jesus, originating in Palestine, to an audience primarily influenced by Greek ways. Antioch in Syria was a favorite starting point for travelers who could journey all the way to Rome by land and sea routes. Using these routes of trade and commerce and earning his living by his trade of leather working (Acts 18:3; 1 Thess 2:9), Paul embarked on his missionary journeys to the cities of the Roman Empire. Unlike Jesus who worked primarily in the rural areas of Palestine, Paul was an urban missionary, taking the gospel to highly populated areas. He established Churches in places like Philippi, Thessalonica, Corinth, and Ephesus, and developed a vast network of coworkers and missionaries to work in different ways in the spread of the gospel. Luke mentions these places and people in the journey sections of Acts; Paul mentions local leaders and Christian colleagues who work for the sake of the gospel in the introductory and concluding sections of his letters and offers extensive greetings to important coworkers in Romans 16.

Since the communities Paul founded usually met in large homes of believers, these house-churches became the usual places for celebrations and worship in this early period. Paul was particularly concerned about the relationship of these Gentile communities to the Jerusalem Church, and since the latter was suffering in times of famine, he took up a collection for the needy in Jerusalem as a sign of unity and of concern (1 Cor 16:1-3). He also traveled to Jerusalem (Gal 2:1-10; Acts 21:16-26), engaged in discussion with Peter (Gal 1:18-19), and challenged the Jewish wing of the Church in matters of Gentile interests (Gal 2:7-21). He became an articulate spokesperson for believers living outside Palestine.

A fascinating aspect of Paul in the establishment of Churches was his unique approach to each of the communities. He understood their situation and background such as the social stratification in Corinth (1 Cor 1:26-29), was aware of pagan influences as in Thessalonica whose people turn away from idols (1 Thess 1:8-10), and formed an ongoing relationship with the communities through visits and letters. In fact, we see Paul affirming communi-

St. Paul, mosaic detail, Palatine Chapel, Palermo

ties in Philippi, confronting communities in Galatia, and attempting to sort out a difficult relationship in Corinth. The growth and development of these Churches is a primary interest of the apostle as he preaches and travels in response to his call.

Paul's Writings and Missionary Work

In this early period of Church life, missionaries like Paul preached the Good News in synagogues, marketplaces, and forums or simply in response to the gathering of the crowds. Paul also utilized his work of tent-making and leather work as another opportunity for the preaching of the gospel. In fact some have called him a part-time missionary, since he continued to support himself as he traveled for the sake of the gospel. When visits became increasingly difficult, Paul revealed his creativity by using letters as a substitute for his apostolic presence. These letters followed the typical form of the day and Paul made use of the element of thanksgiving, particularly in 1 Thessalonians, in order to affirm Christians in their faith. Within the body of the letter, he spent considerable time on the theological understanding of Christ and the gospel, following this section with exhortations that challenged believers in their lived response. These exhortations are culturally conditioned in that they reflect first-century customs. Paul followed a pattern in his letters, so that the Galatians recognized his omission of the thanksgiving in his letter to them.

Only seven of the letters attributed to Paul undisputedly come from the historical figure, namely 1 Thessalonians, Galatians, 1–2 Corinthians, Romans, Philippians, and Philemon. Scholars question the authenticity or authorship of 2 Thessalonians, Colossians, and Ephesians because of style, language, and theology. Most conclude that the Pastoral Letters of 1–2 Timothy and Titus belong to a later period because of the development of Church life that they reflect. Since Paul lived in cultural centers like Damascus, Tarsus, and Antioch, his letters incorporated elements from this world such as preparations for the coming of the emperor that Paul uses as a basis for his description of the second coming or parousia (1 Thess 2:19), images of the olympic games that serve as an analogy for persevering in Christian life (Phil 2:16; 3:14; 1 Cor 9:24-27), and reflections on the Stoic ideal in our approach to suffering and adversity (Phil 4:12). He used diatribe or discourse (Rom 2:1-29; 1 Cor 9), as well as political, commercial, and legal terms from the Greek world.

Paul's writings are filled with biblical images and categories such as flesh/sin, old/new Israel, Torah, obedience, and he accommodated or interpreted scriptural passages as the rabbis of his day (Deut 25:4 in 1 Cor 9:9). While his Jewish background gave him familiarity with apocalyptic thought, resurrection, and afterlife, Paul reinterpreted these traditions in light of God's action in Christ. In many ways, the age of transition into which Paul was born, prepared the way for the acceptance of his message of hope. His writings frequently reflect the struggles of the times and they offer a glimpse into the yearnings and aspirations of humankind in the middle of the first century.

Paul's ministry within the local communities seemed to follow a pattern. He handed on the *tradition* while respecting the culture and religious heritage of various groups. His emphasis on a faith *community* based on mutual love, freedom, and equality in Christ was the starting point for Churches that created an alternative environment in a world influenced by patriarchy. To facilitate communal growth, Paul engaged in dialogue with the Churches and utilized various *forms of sharing* so that both he and Christians could discern the appropriate gospel response in such new and diverse situations. These Churches were very human communities in that they frequently experienced conflict, had different interpretations of the message, and appreciated a variety of apostolic approaches. These potential obstacles, faced by Paul and his coworkers, turned into opportunities for *building up* the faith community. Communal responsibility, utilization of spiritual gifts, discernment of direction, and a collaborative spirit among all enabled the Church to develop and to spread in this early period. Although Paul was frequently strong and directive in his leadership approach, he seemed to encourage participation by the community so that it could assume responsibility for its life. Paul's emphasis in the early period was on local Churches and, from these beginnings, the seeds of a universal Church grew and developed.

Surprisingly, Paul's apostolic effectiveness had little to do with the length of time spent in the local community. A brief stay in Thessalonica yielded fine results, while eighteen months in and four letters to Corinth did little to establish a workable rapport between missionary and local Church. However, Paul continued in his service to the Churches no matter what their response to his own interventions. In Philippi, the first community he founded on European soil, he could share deeply, and they supported him throughout his imprisonment and suffering.

A key factor in the development of the early Church was the number of coworkers engaged in the spread of the gospel. Since Christianity was a missionary movement, many individuals, particularly among the wealthier Christians, traveled from place to place. Others became the local leaders who gathered the community together for worship and service. Most of the names we read in Acts and Paul's letters belong to laity, married couples, outstanding women, with little reference to religious leaders or to priests, groups who were known for their abuses rather than their upright life in the first century.

The apostle and other missionaries attempted to live out the principle of equality in their relationships within their communities (Gal 3:28). When Paul addressed issues within these Gentile Churches, he offered guidelines or principles that the community could apply to situations at hand. In a major section of 1 Corinthians, Paul addresses concerns regarding food to idols (1 Cor 8:8-9), the Lord's Supper (1 Cor 11:17-34), marriage and celibacy (1 Cor 7), in ways that allowed the community to discern its own appropriate response. In the instance of celibacy, when Paul offered a strong personal opinion, he presents it as such to the Church (1 Cor 7:25).

Paul's writings reflect his vision of community with its emphasis on love, Christian responsibility, ethical choices, and freedom in Christ. The variety of issues that surface in the letters become the foundation for Paul's theological reflection and offer a glimpse into the life and world of Paul and the early Church. Later writers in the Pauline tradition would develop these insights, set new directions, and reinterpret the message and mission of Paul.

The Theology of Paul

Within twenty years of the death of Christ, Paul wrote letters to communities that contain the earliest Christian theology available to us. Uncovering this theology is no easy task, since Paul did not systematically develop different topics. Rather, his theology, embedded in the letters, reflected the issues and concerns of each of the communities, and gave the Churches ways of understanding their faith in response to their unique situations. Contemporary scholars attempt to make sense out of this early, at times conflicting, theological reflection as in Paul's letters to Galatia and to Rome which provide an interesting example. While Galatians contains the theology of Romans in seed, particularly in regard to the Law and salvation history, these letters present two seemingly contradictory theological perspectives. In Galatians, Paul stressed discontinuity with Jewish roots in light of the community's abandonment of the gospel (Gal 3), but in Romans he spoke of continuity with the Jewish tradition (Rom 4) in light of Jewish Christians' return to the Gentile Roman community after expulsion under Claudius (A.D. 49). Paul addressed two difficult situations in two very different ways while maintaining the radical difference Christ makes—the centerpoint of his theology.

In other letters we see the development of Paul's theology from resurrection/parousia in early letters, to death/resurrection in the major correspondence, and from a beginning understanding of Church as local church to a fuller understanding of Church as universal. Paul's Christology and ecclesiology developed along parallel lines so that later letters and interpreters emphasized the cosmic influence of Christ and the Church.

Paul's theology contains language, images, and influences from the Jewish and Hellenistic world, so that understanding its meaning presents difficulty for the modern reader. A requirement is awareness of how these influences, his conversion, early Church tradition, and his apostolic experience influence his theology. In addition, Paul's task was interpreting the gospel message for new times and circumstances, rather than repeating past traditions or beliefs. He set in motion a theological task that is still ours today.

Primary in Paul's theology was his understanding of God's action in Christ and of the radical difference Christ makes for humankind. This Christology, a direct result of his conversion experience, influenced Paul's understanding of God's plan, salvation history, justification, Church, and Christian life. God now acts *through* Christ, Christians are baptized *into* Christ, identify with the redemptive acts *of* Christ, and draw on the abiding presence and power of the Lord since they are *in* Christ. Because of this union, Christians witness to a new life in the Spirit and become a new creation.

Justification by faith, well within the early Jewish tradition, now becomes justification by faith in Christ. The Cross and resurrection transform sin and death so that glory is ours in Christ. To convey his understanding of Church and his conviction that Christ and Christians share the same Spirit, Paul described the community as the body of Christ (1 Cor 12:12-30), a unique insight of the apostle. Paul understood that a new era has begun for humankind in Christ and that God forms a new people of God, fulfilling all promises in and through Christ.

While Paul's theology developed in dynamic and interactive situations in this early period, the challenge of recovering his understanding offers new opportunity for assessing later theological developments.

Paul's Unique Contributions

Paul made a significant contribution to the Christian movement by his proclamation of faith in Jesus as risen Lord. His conversion occurred in the midst of apostolic activity as a zealous Pharisee, and his understanding of Christ changed. This religious experience affected Paul's view of reality and resulted in various contributions to the development of the early Church.

Paul described himself and his call in terms of the biblical prophets and offered a prophetic voice to a Church that was sorting out its relationship to its Jewish roots. Not only did he speak God's word of comfort and hope, but he challenged communities and religious leaders to expand their ideas regarding Gentile admission to the faith community, thus reinforcing a universal dimension to the Christian movement early in its development. He confronted the influence of patriarchy by working with women, respecting their leadership, and offering alternatives to hierarchical approaches within the households of faith. Rather than affirm the tenets of Judaism, he interpreted the gospel message for the Gentiles of his day. As a prophetic voice he spoke for the outsiders such as women, slaves, and Gentiles, rather than identify with priests, religious, and civic leaders.

Paul understood the gospel message as one of freedom and equality in Christ. This equality opened new possibilities for the community of faith as Christians affirmed gifts of the Spirit rather than allow sexual distinctions guide choices for specific roles and responsibilities in the Church. Paul used the principle of equality in his challenge to Philemon and demonstrated, perhaps inadvertently, how Christians could change society by creating communities that live by different values. In his collaborative efforts, Paul worked with women, praised their ministry, acknowledged their apostleship, and respected their leadership.

Paul focused on a community of mutual love and service to reflect the relationship between Christ and Christians, emphasizing the abiding presence of the Spirit. Paul was convinced that the gospel transformed all life in practical and concrete terms. Local communities, the basic units of ecclesial life, were dynamic and relational Churches. He found little security in buildings or hierarchical structures; rather, his letters attest to the preorganizational life of the Church with the spiritual gifts shared by all. While Paul deals only with the beginnings of the Christian movement, he reminds us that the gospel challenged the patriarchal structures and values of both society and religion.

Paul was a great missionary and the first theologian whose writings are preserved for us. His theological reflection resulted from his apostolic encounters and were in touch with the issues and concerns of communities of the day. We find little abstraction in Paul's theology, but instead, a functional approach that emphasizes meaning *for us.* Because of this slant, Paul educated believers as he challenged them to grow and to change. In fact, a theological development spanned his letters, with exhortations based on Christian principles. Paul emphasized the gift of faith offered to everyone with believers' task being acceptance and obedience. Christian life becomes a radical response to the gift of God offered in Christ.

Paul developed an understanding of the way Christians ought to live by his unique approach to spirituality. He seemed to advocate an apostolic and ecclesial spirituality, one that enables us to reach out in service as members of the faith community. The apostle offered an insight that response to need within the community was an expression of authentic spirituality. Believers become a sign of Christ's love to the world around them. Mutual responsibility and mutual concern create the fabric of a well-lived faith. This spirituality offered a challenge to all believers, not just to select religious leaders, and Paul became an early spokesperson for this dimension of gospel response.

The Apostle Paul certainly emerges as a leader in the early Church and, because of his own writings, we can reconstruct his interactions with various Churches and individuals. He held his own with other religious leaders and communities, confronting and challenging both on important issues. In the unique situations of the Churches, Paul attempted to guide, persuade, or convince communities, choosing approaches that would achieve the desired result. As a leader, he sometimes became too personally involved in the results of his ministry, as in Corinth, compromising his ability to lead effectively. However, we also see a dynamic in Philippi that is mutually supportive and engaging. Paul's unique leadership contribution was his ability to foster unity in diversity, respecting pluralism as a characteristic of a community in transition. With his unique approach to each situation, Paul proved effective in most situations. His faith convinced him that the power of Christ could be reflected in earthen vessels (2 Cor 4:7). Paul offered principles and guidelines that communities adapted to their own situations, and since all share the Spirit of the Lord, he encouraged discernment by the community.

A Christian leader knows the gospel and reinterprets its core message for new times and places, understands the tradition and has a sense of history, and has a vision of Church that respects the contributions of all. In addition, the Christian leader reads the signs of the times that reflect the deepest aspirations of humankind, understands the needs of people, and develops a viable spirituality that integrates all dimensions of life. Effective leaders utilize a variety of leadership responses, knowing full well the effect of their particular choices on the followers. Paul was such a leader in a Church searching for its identity in relation to Judaism.

Paul's letters represent the earliest written accounts of the gospel message interpreted for Gentile communities in the middle of the first century. The apostle emerges as a great missionary and theologian whose insights have affected the development of the Church throughout the ages. As we move towards the twenty-first century, Paul's vision, perspective, spirituality, and leadership can enlighten us in our struggles to live out our response to the message of Jesus.

HELEN DOOHAN

See also APOSTLE; PETER, ST..

PAULINE PRIVILEGE

The Pauline privilege is a principle that deals with the marriage of an unbaptized couple, one of whom becomes a Christian. The scriptural basis for this teaching is 1 Corinthians 7:10-16. While Paul affirms the commitment of partners in marriage as a teaching "from the Lord," he also addresses the question of a union between Christian and non-Christian. The conversion and baptism of one partner in a marriage situation occurred in the early Church. If the partners were content, then separation was not a question, for Paul believed that the Christian partner could influence and sanctify the relationship. However, he identifies another situation, that of an unbeliever who refuses to live with, or who separates from, the Christian partner. In this instance, the Christian is no longer bound to live with the unbeliever, and is free to remarry since God wills that we live in peace.

The Pauline privilege became part of the canonical legislation of the Church in 1199, was clarified in the 1917 Code of Canon Law, and exists in the present code (canon 1143). The canon states that when two unbaptized people have married and one has later been baptized, a subsequent marriage by the baptized partner is recognized by the Church if the unbaptized partner has abandoned the marriage. In Church teaching, as in Paul's time, the decision is made in favor of the faith commitment of the baptized partner.

The Church has used the Pauline privilege since the sixteenth century, particularly in the missionary expansion of the Church, allowing the convert to remarry if an unbaptized spouse does not also become a Christian. It addresses particular marriage problems in the contemporary Church as well. Just as Paul interpreted the teachings of Jesus for the situation in Corinth, so too, the Church interprets the Scriptures for culturally different situations.

HELEN DOOHAN

See also MARRIAGE; PETRINE PRIVILEGE.

PAULINES

The popular name for the Society of St. Paul for the Apostolate of Communications (SSP), a religious congregation of priests and brothers who work in book publishing, radio, film, and television.

Founded in Alba, Italy, in 1914 by Reverend James Alberione, the Paulines work in twenty-six countries. In the English-speaking world they are most active in America where they run Alba House and Alba Communications; and in England and Australia they operate St. Paul Publications. They are the largest international Catholic publishing organization.

MICHAEL GLAZIER

See also BORRANO, FRANCIS XAVIER; INSTITUTE, RELIGIOUS.

PAULINUS OF NOLA, ST. (ca. 353–431)

Born in Bordeaux of an aristocratic family with estates in Aquitania and Italy, Paulinus was educated by Ausonius. After becoming governor of Campania in 379, Paulinus lived the cultured life of a wealthy landowner.

Various factors may have led Paulinus to withdraw from the world: the influence of his Spanish wife Therasia, the violent death of his brother and dangers to his own life, his infant son Celsus's death, and the encouragement of Delphinus and Amandus of Bordeaux, Martin of Tours, and Ambrose of Milan. Paulinus was baptized in 389 by Bishop Delphinus of Bordeaux and ordained a priest in Barcelona in 394. He and Therasia disposed of their immense riches and settled near the tomb of St. Felix in Nola (near Naples) to enter into the monastic life. From the monastery Paulinus corresponded with many important Christian figures of his day: fifty of his letters are extant. Twenty-nine poems can certainly be attributed to Paulinus. Many of his poems were written for the feast of St. Felix (14 January) and present valuable testimony about religious and popular customs of the time. He was ordained a bishop of Nola probably in 409 (but certainly before 413). Feast day, 22 June.

JOHN DILLON

See also FATHERS OF THE CHURCH.

PAULISTS

The Society of Missionary Priests of St. Paul the Apostle (C.S.P.) was founded in New York City by Isaac Thomas Hecker in cooperation with Augustine Hewit, George Deshon, and Francis Baker. All were converts and former Redemptorist priests who had been part of a missionary group taking care of German immigrants. Father Hecker and his companions felt that the Redemptorists should found an American house which would cater to the unique needs of the American milieu.

In 1857, with the approval of three bishops, Isaac Hecker went to Rome to present his idea to his Redemptorist superiors, but they expelled him for coming without the requisite permission. He appealed to the Holy See and, aided by Cardinal Alessandro Barnabo, his case got the attention of Pius IX. Hecker and his companions were released from their Redemptorist vows, and the Pope advised them to start a new congregation.

In 1858, Isaac Hecker and his associates drew up a preliminary Program of Rule that Archbishop Hughes approved. Instead of the traditional vows, they took solemn promises, and the new society made the conversion of America the reason for its existence. From the beginning the Paulists stressed the quality and professionalism of their members rather than enlisting large numbers. To overcome anti-Catholic prejudice they advocated discarding unessential foreign and Roman traditions and trappings and encouraged the rapid Americanization of all immigrants.

They established houses in Toronto and Johannesburg, and, to cater to American residents and visitors in Rome, took charge of Santa Susanna's Church. But the Paulists have never forgotten that America is the primary arena of their activities. Over the decades they have used the printed word with great proficiency. Hecker, a practical visionary, founded *The Catholic World* (now *The New Catholic World*) and the Paulists quickly became specialists in the publication and distribution of pamphlets and instruction material. Today Paulists are found as chaplains on secular college campuses; they are pioneering activists in ecumenical activities, are in demand for retreats and parish missions, and are engaged in all forms of communication. Under the direction of Kevin Lynch, C.S.P., the Paulist Press became one of the largest and most influential publishing organizations in the English-speaking world.

MICHAEL GLAZIER

See also AMERICAN CATHOLICISM; HECKER, ISAAC; ILLIG, ALVIN; INSTITUTE, RELIGIOUS; SHEERIN, JOHN.

PAX CHRISTI

(Lat., "peace of Christ") An international Catholic organization dedicated to promoting peace among nations through constructive dialogue on social, scientific, and theological issues. Created in 1945 for the purpose of reconciling the French and German peoples (principally through prayer), it soon expanded its mission to include the peaceful resolution of all international conflicts. Its monthly publication, *Pax Christi,* serves as a forum for dialogue on issues of peace and war—though it does not advance particular positions.

JOSEPH QUINN

See also PEACE.

PEACE

Peace is the integrity, harmony, well-being, and happiness experienced when the reign of God is fully acknowledged in human affairs. Peace is central to the biblical tradition. It is promised and hoped for, given and longed for, absent and yet always present. Often understood as the cessation of hostilities, the end of war or conflict, peace is a much larger and more encompassing reality. One incident in the Gospels offers a clue: a woman with a hemorrhage, hearing about Jesus and all that he has done, approaches him in search of healing. "If I can just get near him," she thinks, "if I can just touch his clothes, I will be healed." She does get near him, she does touch his clothing, she is healed. As with all biblical healing, she gets more than she had hoped for. Jesus turns and speaks with her. He tells her that her faith has healed her, and that she is to go in peace: she is made whole (Mark 5:25-35; Luke 8:43-48).

This incident tells us that peace is connected with the divine. Peace appears when God is near. The healing of the woman shows us that peace heals, it is present when people are made whole. Peace is not a static concept, not an abstract idea. It is, rather, a condition of wholeness in which one lives. We "go *in* peace," rather than "have peace." Peace requires effort, and it marks the arrival of God's reign.

Peace as a powerful symbol of the reign of God is not unique to the Christian Scriptures. Both the longing and the hope for peace permeate the Hebrew Scriptures. Peace expresses the fullness of relationship, the safety and security of life lived in union with the creator and with each other. Relationship is at the heart of peace. Peace is the result of God's action, it is the fulfillment of God's dream. The Hebrew Scriptures tell us that God's peace is integral to God's covenant. Right relationship with God results in right relationship with each other and with all of creation (Hos 2:14-23). Joined in covenant with God, God's people are also one with each other. In the love and justice that flows in such holy union, peace flourishes (Ps 85:10-11). It "flows like a river" (Isa 48:18). When the longed-for Messiah comes, peace will come with him, and Isaiah tells us that one of the Messiah's names will be Prince of Peace (Isa 9:6).

The Christian Scriptures build upon this hope and declare that, in Jesus, God's kingdom has arrived. Because this is true, peace, too, has come. We are told that John the Baptist will prepare the way for the one who will "guide our feet in the way of peace" (Luke 1:79). The angels who announce Jesus' birth cry that there is "Peace to all of good will" (Matt 2:13-14). Jesus' use of peace as a result of healing is not by accident. His saving presence, his action to make whole are presence and action that free peace among the people. We are in peace when we receive God's presence. When women and men recognize and embrace the saving presence of Jesus, when their lives give witness to this presence, they become peacemakers and are known to be the children of God (Matt 5:9).

As the resurrection was evidence of Jesus' identity and God's activity, so too it was marked by the gift of peace. At his last meal with his friends, Jesus promises a peace the world cannot give (John 14:27). When the risen Christ returns to these friends, he greets them with one word, "Peace" (see John 20:19-29). The promised gift is given in the reality of resurrection.

Only God can give this peace, for peace is of God. Political machinations, manipulation of power, wishful thinking . . . none of these produce true peace. Peace is gift and, as such, always comes from the giver. This does not mean that the biblical tradition calls for passivity or defeatism. On the contrary, intense and consistent activity is called for. This activity, however, reverses what we normally would do. This activity is attentiveness and obedience to the ways and wonders of God's working among us. It is acceptance of and fidelity to the covenant established in Jesus' blood (see Eph 2:13-22). We will have peace, we are told, when we attend and accept; when we recognize the risen Christ in our midst.

JULIANA M. CASEY, I.H.M.

See also KINGDOM OF GOD; SALVATION; SALVATION HISTORY.

PECTORAL CROSS

(Lat. *pectoralis,* "of the breast") A cross, usually of precious metal, which is suspended from the neck by a chain or silken cord and worn over the breast; it may be ornamented with precious stones. It is worn by abbots, bishops, archbishops, cardinals, and the pope.

Pectoral cross, by Frank Kacmarcik, 1992

JOSEPH QUINN

See also HIERARCHY.

PELAGIANISM

See HERESY/HERETICS.

PENANCE

See SACRAMENT OF RECONCILIATION.

PENTATEUCH

Deriving its name from the Greek *pentateuchos* meaning "five scrolls," the Pentateuch encompasses the first five books of the Old Testament. Called after their Greek names they are Genesis, Exodus, Leviticus, Numbers, and Deuteronomy. Because it contains all the legislative codes of the Old Testament, the Pentateuch is known as the Law or Torah (1 Chr 16:40; 22: 12; 2 Chr 23:18; 30:16) and traditionally attributed to Moses. Though the Torah had become the principle of Jewish life when the Pentateuch achieved its final form after the Exile, much else than provision of law in the first five books of the Scripture inspired and sustained the Jewish people. There was the narrative about God, heroes, and the people. In time, through the Diaspora and then, through the diffusion of Christianity, the narrative would afford hope to the Gentiles also.

The Pentateuch begins with the creation of man and the universe and concludes with the death of Moses. In the prehistory to Israel, the author traces the creation, the Fall of man and his deepening corruption. There follows the flood and then God's covenant with Noah and through him, with all humanity. But God would achieve his purpose through a people he chooses to be his own. The call of Abraham and the patriarchal narratives follow the prehistory of Israel in Genesis.

The birth of the nation is told in Exodus. Once delivered of their Egyptian taskmasters the people followed Moses through the wilderness to the Promised Land. But first, within the wilderness of the Sinai, God enters into covenant with his people. Besides the Decalogue whose observance would be the people's acknowledgment of their God, Exodus contains the Code of the Covenant (Exod 20:22-23:33). Behind the Law lies the figure of Moses. His presence pervades this book and that of Numbers. Between Exodus and Numbers is interposed Leviticus with its cultic legislation.

Deuteronomy or the "second law" reasserts and reinterprets the Law even as in the name of Moses it eloquently appeals for loyalty to the covenant. With the end of Deuteronomy the Pentateuch concludes. It does so by recounting Moses' vision of the Promised Land just before he dies. Moses looms heroically in the Pentateuch but it is God and his mercy which makes the story so enduring a source of hope. God, who is the creator, is compassionate to an enslaved people whom he calls to be his own, that through their messianic hope and its fulfillment he might invite all peoples to enter with him into an everlasting covenant.

Though the Pentateuch has been traditionally attributed to Moses, he cannot be regarded as its author in the modern sense of the word. The final redaction of the Pentateuch would be achieved only after the prophet was dead for some centuries. The origin and inspiration of the Pentateuch can be ascribed to Moses but its thrust and development to others. Thus provisions of the Law were reinterpreted in the light of Israel's movement from a nomadic to an agrarian and more settled life; from a tribal confederation to a kingdom. In the case of both law and narrative, the broad cohesion of the Pentateuch notwithstanding, the inconsistencies, the repetitions, and the linguistic diversity can best be explained by the conflating of sources. Hence in the nineteenth century such scholars as W. de Wette, K. H. Graf, and especially J. Wellhausen, proposed the documentary hypothesis. Wellhausen identified four major strands entering into the composition of the Pentateuch. Each has its own perspective and literary characteristics. The J or the Jahwist source was distinguished in the first instance by its name for God, "Yahweh." It is thought to have derived from the court at Jerusalem in the tenth or ninth century B.C. With a universal perspective J describes first the creation of man and the universe. Towards man God wears a human face. Yet man sins, and with compelling realism J recounts the Fall of man and its tragic consequence: crimes of blood and an insatiable thirst for vengeance (Gen 4:1-16, 23-24). Its accounts of the patriarchs are lively and colorful.

E or the Elohist source is also distinguished by its name for God, "Elohim." It is thought to have arisen in the northern kingdom a century after the Jahwist source. When Samaria fell in 722 B.C., it was brought south to Jerusalem and fused with J. Beginning with Abraham, E's narrative parallels that of J though in recalling the heroes of old, E's style is the more sober and its approach the more moralistic. The anthropomorphisms of J are wanting in E. God communicates with men in dreams and through the medium of angels.

The priestly source, P, is dated from the late fifth century B.C., not long prior to the final redaction of the Pentateuch. P also begins with creation and because of its distinctive style and formulaic language P is more easily delineated than J or E. P affords Genesis a certain chronology. Its use of the *tôtlēdôt* or genealogies enhances the text's orderly development. But the primary interest of P is Israel's cult and the tabernacle. To the priestly source the tabernacle was the prototype of the Temple and its description derived from the Temple. P relates the theophany which transpired at the dedication of the tabernacle (Lev 9:24) when fire signaled the descent of the *Shekinah* or divine presence upon Israel.

Prior to the fusion of P with the J and E sources, Deuteronomy is introduced to the developing Pentateuch. Since the time of W. de Wette (1805) Deuteronomy has been associated with "the book of the law" (2 Kgdms 22:8) found in the Temple during the reign of Josiah (640–609 B.C.). Though appearing elsewhere in the earlier books of the Pentateuch but infrequently (e.g., Exod 12:24-27; 13:3-6; 15:26) this concluding text exhorts the people with a distinctive and eloquent style. They are to be loyal to the covenant and thus choose life (Deut 30:15-20). D calls for centering cult in the Holy City even as Jeremiah preached against idolatry and the high places abroad. Loyalty to the one God (Deut 6:4), to the one covenant, and to the one cult and sanctuary is the leitmotif of the Deuteronomic strand. Loyalty to the covenant becomes the norm by which the Deuteronomistic historian will judge the successive kings of Israel and Judah.

For all that the documentary hypothesis was well received by scholarly opinion, it is today being subjected to revision. The sources J, E, D, and P were themselves compilations. This is true of the legislative parts of Deuteronomy (Deut 12-26) where the older Code of the Covenant is recalled and modified (e.g., Deut 12). The Code of the Covenant itself (Exod 20:22–23:33) contains some norms appropriate to a nomadic life; others, to an agrarian or more settled life. The priestly legislation contains both ancient and more recent provisions. The latter would be appropriate to the situation where the Pentateuch achieved its final redaction. And woven into the broader narratives were older oral and written traditions. Couched in such literary forms as genealogies, ritual, valedictories and last blessings, folk tales and saga, the traditions could be isolated and their nature and intent examined.

To substantiate such older traditions as relate to the deliverance from Egypt and the Sinaitic covenant scholars have sought to establish their historical background. And to the investigation of ancient Near Eastern history and literature, archaeology has been especially helpful. But results of enquiry initially asserted with confidence must often be subjected to further enquiry and revision. The date of the Israelite movement into Canaan is a case at point. Nevertheless, the patriarchal narratives, the deliverance from Egypt, and the covenant relationship of God with his people acknowledged at Sinai, all are recounted against an historically credible background.

As to the documentary hypothesis itself, most twentieth-century scholars have found it persuasive in its broad outlines. But that too is being reevaluated. The Elohist as a distinct source of the Pentateuch is being increasingly questioned and perhaps more significantly, the J source is being dated later and, by a few, made dependent upon a Deuteronomistic redactor (e.g., H. Schmid [1976] and R. Rendtorff [1983]). The P source remains the clearest. Most recently J. Blenkinsopp (1992) ascribes P to the Babylonian Diaspora. D was then amalgamated with P to afford substance to a powerful call to Israel, a call enhanced by renewed emphasis on the Mosaic constitution and the restoration of the Temple.

Early in the twentieth century the Pontifical Biblical Commission (1906) asserted that Moses was substantially the author of the Pentateuch even while conceding that subsequent modifications could have been made to his work. In 1948, however, in a letter to Cardinal Suhard, archbishop of Paris, the commission went further in its acknowledgment of recent biblical research and allowed for a progressive development both of the Mosaic laws and the narrative of the Pentateuch.

To conclude the Pentateuch, the name of Moses is evoked. At a time critical to the nation's very survival, the Exile in Babylon and the tentative and uncertain movement toward restoration, the priestly source recalls the death of the nation's founder. The appeal of the Deuteronomist had been voiced and then, according to the account, Moses dies. That the provenance of Deuteronomy and of the priestly source is far removed from the life and death of Moses apparently does not derogate from his authority. His inspiration could be summoned to rally Israel in its darkest hour. Moses' birth and rescue as an infant may smack of a folk tale but his name rings authentic as do those of his wives who are recalled in spite of the prohibition of marrying non-Jews (Deut 7:3; Ezra 9:1-15; Neh 10:28-30, 13:3, 23-30).

The influence of the Pentateuch through history is beyond measure. To the nascent Church Jesus was the prophet whom God raised up like unto Moses (Deut 18:15; cf. John 1:21, 6:14; Acts 3:22-23). In the Fourth Gospel Jesus is said to be the fulfillment of "the law and also the prophets" (John 1:45). In Matthew Jesus is the new Moses setting forth a new law in the Sermon on the Mount (Matt 5–7).

More recently in these late years of the twentieth century, to Martin Luther King the struggle of the blacks was a later chapter in the story which began when Moses stood in Pharaoh's court centuries before and cried, "Let my people go." (*Where Do We Go from Here?* [1967]). And from the threshold of outer space, on Christmas Eve, 1968, while amidst the stars and constellations above, the astronauts of Apollo 8 radioed to earth, "In the beginning God created the heavens and the earth. . . ."

THOMAS BUCKLEY

See also BIBLE, OLD TESTAMENT WRITINGS; CRITICISM, BIBLICAL.

PENTECOST

The Solemnity of Pentecost celebrates the descent of the Holy Spirit upon the early Church as recorded in Acts 2. To understand the significance of the feast it is important to recall that, in early Christianity, the Sunday celebration of the Eucharist was always a sort of Easter, a commemoration of the resurrection of Jesus Christ from the dead. It was not until the second century that various Churches began to celebrate an annual Easter as well. Even then, the Easter observance expanded quickly into a season embracing fifty days. Thus, ironically, the Season of Easter was actually called Pentecost (Greek: "fifty"). Only from the early fourth century was there a special festival called Pentecost assigned to the fiftieth day and commemorating the events of Acts 2 (the Descent of the Spirit). In the same century most Churches began also to distinguish the feast of the Ascension from that of Pentecost, celebrating the ascension on the fortieth day from Easter in accord with Acts 1:3.

The Old Testament speaks of a festival of the first fruits of the grain called "Ingathering," "Harvest," or "Weeks" (because it was seven weeks after Passover). Seven weeks are fifty days, hence the New Testament called the festival Pentecost, the name adapted by Christians for their own festival. Originally, then, the Christian Pentecost took little from the Jewish festival except its position on the calendar. Its meaning for Christians was determined principally from the fact that, according to Acts 1:4, 5; 2:1-47, there occurred on the festival of Pentecost the decisive outpouring of the Holy Spirit which inaugurated the mission of the Church.

The Pentecost episode in Acts portrays the disciples of Jesus as able, by the infusion of the Spirit, to preach ecstatically and convincingly to people of all nations in each nation's own tongue. This, some think, reverses the "babble" of languages and nations that has been our lot since the day when people tried to build a tower to heaven (Gen 11:1-9). More importantly, it is both a foretaste of the successes of the Church's ministry, and an improvement of the Old Testament situation in which inspired prophets often spoke ecstatically but unintelligibly. The celebration of Pentecost, then, should ideally empower each generation to new beginnings in the Christian ministry. At the same time, the festival undoubtedly provides occasion to celebrate all the "gifts of the Spirit," which may be said, generically, to embrace anything surprising: new beginnings, unexpected powers, courage and wisdom beyond the ordinary, love, and the like. Traditionally one cites the "Gifts of the Spirit" based on Isaiah 11:2: wisdom, understanding, knowledge, fortitude, counsel, piety, fear of the Lord. In celebrating the fruits of the Spirit, we may accommodate the Old Testament idea of Pentecost as a festival of first fruits.

Some have thought that the Pentecost narrative once centered on an appearance of the risen Christ which may have been removed in Luke's account because he had already narrated the ascension. While this is very uncertain, it remains true that Jesus the Lord should not be omitted from the festival of Pentecost. The Spirit which descended is the same Spirit by which Jesus lived, the Spirit he had promised to release after his death. This way of understanding the festival would also draw on the early practice of celebrating the victory of Christ through the whole of a united Easter season of fifty days.

DAVID BRYAN

PENTECOSTAL CHURCHES

Following the American Civil War, certain Methodist revivals produced what came to be known as the Holiness Movement. This new religious activity stressed that entire sanctification could be achieved immediately by the believer's reception of the Holy Spirit.

Mainline denominations, e.g., Lutherans and Presbyterians, stressed justification as an act of God *for* us which changes our status before God. The Holiness people, following the Methodist model, talked about sanctification as an act of God *in* us which alters our nature. Sanctification was also called "perfection" and implied a high standard of ethical behavior and adherence to pure doctrine. Denominations produced by the Holiness Movement were The Church of God (Anderson, Indiana), The Church of the Nazarene, and the Salvation Army.

This same Holiness Movement also gave rise to the twentieth century Pentecostal Movement. Of course, this movement traces its origin to the first Pentecost when the Holy Spirit came upon the disciples with power and the gift of tongues and the Christian Church was born.

Modern Pentecostalism was inspired by the work of Charles Fox Parham (1873–1937), a Kansas preacher who linked salvation and holiness with the Baptism of the Spirit accompanied by glossolalia, e.g., ecstatic unintelligible speech or more commonly, speaking in tongues. The most important event in the formation of the movement was the three-year revival in 1906 at Azusa Street in Los Angeles by W. J. Seymour. The largest and most visible Pentecostal group to emerge from this revival was the Assembly of God, founded in 1914.

Pentecostals have several central beliefs which put them in the fundamentalist camp: Scripture infallibly inspired by God; Jesus as the sinless eternal Son of God; human beings as naturally sinful and saved only by the substitutionary death of Christ; bodily resurrection of Jesus; Christ to return soon; and baptism by immersion upon a public confession of Christ as Savior and Lord.

On the other hand, the following unique and defining beliefs of Pentecostal churches often separate them from fundamentalist Christians: Baptism of the Spirit and speaking in tongues. This practically means that the authority for the Pentecostal is the inspiration of the Spirit ("God spoke to me this morning") and for the fundamentalist it is the Bible ("God says in the Scripture"). In addition, the Spirit brings certain gifts of healing and prophesy (see 1 Corinthians 12) and fruits such as love, joy, and peace (see Galatians 5). In each case, the Pentecostal personally experiences internal confirmation of God's presence.

Pentecostal worship services are intensely emotional experiences led by a fiery preacher intent on bringing hearers to repentance and conversion. All of this results in the cultivation of a deeply spiritual life.

Pentecostalism is not only a denomination; in the last thirty years it has also become a dimension in many mainline Churches, sometimes called the charismatic renewal. The emphases are typically Pentecostal ones: inner experience of the Spirit, speaking in tongues, gifts of healing, tightly knit fellowship, and an emotionally satisfying religious life.

The energy provided by the Spirit issues in enthusiasm and activist missionary work here and abroad. Membership in this country numbers 1.3 million while there are about 18 million Pentecostals worldwide.

IRA ZEPP

See also "BAPTISM IN THE HOLY SPIRIT"; CHARISM; HOLINESS.

PEOPLE OF GOD

See CHURCH, THE.

PERSONALITY

No specific, universally accepted definition of *personality* exists. It is a hypothetical construct employed to help us organize, categorize, systematize, understand, and interpret individual behavior. At its core are two notions: uniqueness and consistency. First, every individual has or exhibits a constellation of thoughts, emotions, and behaviors which allows for identification of each person as distinct from any and all other persons. This identification is made by both the person him- or herself, and by others who know the individual. In this way, one's *personality* is perceived as unique, or at least as having unique attributes and manifestations. Second, each individual's thoughts, emotions, and behaviors manifest themselves in similar ways over time and in spite of varying circumstances. In fact, it is this general sameness of presentation which allows for recognition of what the individual personality attributes are and how they exist in combination within the individual. Persons whose personalities lack this consistency are considered to be underdeveloped or malformed and to have abnormal personalities.

This construct does not deny that people change. Individuals grow and develop, shrink and regress. But they change in ways characteristic of the constellation of traits associated with their identities. People change, by analogy, much in the way a river changes. Its flow, volume, chemistry, and temperature constantly vary. At times, given certain conditions and circumstances, even its course and direction can change so it is not recognizable as the same river. Still, we identify it and call it by the same name. Depending on precipitating events and conditions, people's behavior, quality of thought, and prevailing emotional state or mood can vary widely; in spite of this, their personalities remain. What is known about their identities is assumed not to change substantially. That which singles out and identifies the individual as that individual and no other is what is termed his or her "personality."

Multiple theories, some complementary and some competing, exist in the field of "personality psychology." These can be roughly grouped into four categories. Approaches termed "existential, humanistic, phenomenological, interpersonal, and personological" tend to understand *personality* as the relatively consistent pattern of interactions between an individual and the individual's world. These explore the typical ways individuals attempt to make meaning in their lives and make sense of their world.

A second group of approaches termed "psychoanalytic, psychodynamic, and ego psychology" see *personality* as the interplay among an individual's conscious decision-making process, reduction and satisfaction of his or her unconscious needs and biological drives, and the survival needs of society at large.

A third group of approaches, referred to as "trait theories, type theory, and biologically-based theories" understand *personality* as the enduring responses to external stimuli as regulated by inborn or neuronal and neurochemical activity. These approaches emphasize our being the end-products of our own biology, struggling to survive in particular environments.

The fourth group, "social learning theories and behaviorism," approaches *personality* as the enduring response repertoire of the human organism as evidenced by overt behavior which has been influenced by previous experience and learning. These approaches emphasize the adaptational pattern people exhibit over their lifetime while de-emphasizing the focus of the other three groupings namely: relating to others and making meaning in the world; resolving unconscious and biological drives in the real, public world; and neuronal and glandular reactivity.

PAUL MOGLIA

PERSONALITY TYPE

Carl Gustav Jung, a Swiss psychiatrist whom Sigmund Freud had handpicked to be his successor, constructed a theory in the early part of this century describing how personality develops over one's lifetime. Jung sought to understand how one becomes a complete individual, unique and *differentiated* from any and all other individuals. Based on his clinical observations, Jung postulated the existence of several personality dimensions which together made up the behaviors, feelings, and thoughts which typify each unique individual. While we are born with basically the same dimensions, we *individuate* over time, that is, become more of who we uniquely are, through developing preferences within these dimensions. For example, we come to prefer our right or left hand to write with, prefer to walk in or stay out of the rain, prefer to be part of smaller or larger social gatherings, prefer a map or verbal directions in finding our destination, or prefer setting our own goals at work or having our boss set them for us.

Human beings live, survive, and grow by taking in information and making decisions about that information. For Jung, we all have our preferred mental process for *perception,* that is, how we take in information: we can be oriented toward using the five senses in recognizing that something is (*sensation*), or we can be oriented toward feeling a hunch about what that something is (*intuition*).

We also have mental preferences for *judgment,* or how we come to conclusions about what is perceived. Once we take in information, we may tend to *think* about the data, evaluating them logically and objectively, or we may tend to *feel* about them, evaluating them affectively and personally.

Jung further maintained that each of us will have an innate preference between *perception* and *judgment.* Whichever is our inborn preference becomes the primary cognitive function, orienting all the others, while the nonpreferred function, be it perception or judgment, becomes the secondary cognitive function, helping us achieve balance within our personality.

If the primary tendency is to function using perception, the secondary tendency will be to function using judgment. In this case, perception will be more utilized, trusted, emphasized, and influential in our relationships, work, avocations, creativity, etc., but judgment will provide the potential for balance in the way we make choices and respond to stimuli. Balance or *psychic equilibrium* is not automatically developed, however, and any of us can overuse our innately preferred function and/or underuse our secondary function.

People with underdeveloped perception often jump to conclusions. They may not wait until the facts are in, or may be inflexible when exposed to other points of view. People with a perception preference, but who have underdeveloped judgment are overcautious and wait until they are 100 percent certain before making decisions.

Another dimension of personalty for Jung is our preference for directing psychological energy: toward the world within ourselves or toward the world outside ourselves. *Extraverts* invest their energy in the world outside themselves. They understand life more through acting in it than through thinking about it, more through social and environmental encounters than through reflection and introspection. They go after information and experience, and often learn by trial and error. Others describe extroverts as social, visible, practical, and pragmatic. *Introverts* spend their energy more in their private domains of sensing/intuiting, thinking/feeling, and judging/perceiving. They harbor information and experiences and review them in order to understand and incorporate them. They experience the public world as less present and less personally significant. Their psychological anchor comes from within themselves, and they often learn by insight and self-discovery. Others describe introverts as private, solid, self-contained, and as knowing themselves well.

Isabel Briggs Myers and Katharine Briggs took Jung's theoretical descriptions of these eight inborn tendencies (introversion/extraversion, sensing/intuiting, judging/perceiving, thinking/feeling) and identified sixteen personality types. When people speak of "personality type" in a technical sense, they are likely referring to Jung's typology of personality which Myers and Briggs developed in the form of their widely used personality instrument, the *Myers-Briggs Type Indicator* or *MBTI* or simply, *the Myers-Briggs.*

The merits of using the Myers-Briggs lie primarily in helping persons of one personality type understand persons of the other fifteen personality types. Most of us tend to unconsciously assume that other people think, feel, behave, and are motivated much in the same way as we ourselves are. Most of us also have experiences which demonstrate that these assumptions are more often wrong than right. Understanding that many differences among people are simply differences in the way people are predisposed to invest themselves (extravertedly or introvertedly), deal with the outer world (judging or perceiving), come to conclusions (thinking or feeling), and perceive data (sensing or intuiting) can greatly enhance our ability to understand and reconcile differences.

Because we differ in how and what we perceive, and in our conclusions about what we perceive, we also differ in our corresponding interests, values, motivations, and reactions. *Personality type* becomes one way to categorize and systematize these differences, in effect forming *a* taxonomy of human experience.

Using the four Jungian dimensions of personality, the Myers-Briggs assigns letters to both poles or preferences manifested in each dimension. For whether one directs oneself more to the outer, public or inner, private world, it uses *E* (extraversion) and *I* (introversion). For whether someone uses data which comes more from the five senses or uses data coming more from a sixth, having-a-hunch sense, it uses *S* (sensing) and *N* (intuition; "N" is used because "I" is already used for introversion). For whether someone trusts reason or emotions more in making judgments about what is perceived, it uses *T* (thinking) and *F* (feeling). And for dealings with the outer world, it uses *J* (judgment) when someone prefers either thinking or feeling, both judgment-oriented processes, and *P* when someone prefers sensing or intuition, both perception-oriented processes. The four dimensions are bipolar with two tendencies each. This yields sixteen possible personality types which the four letters of the preferences identify.

What follows is a brief synopsis of traits characterized by each personality type and identified by the four-letter code (The *Manual: A Guide to the Development and Use of the Myers-Briggs Type Indicator* by Isabel Briggs Myers and Mary H. McCaulley, Palo Alto, Calif.: Counseling Psychologists Press, 1985, greatly expands on the descriptions given here):

ESTP. Extraverted, Sensing, Thinking, and Perceiving. Conservative in values, but adaptable and tolerant. Interested in getting to the point. Tend not to worry and are usually good at solving problems as they arise. Best with manipulation of real things as in sports and mechanics.

ESTJ. Extraverted, Sensing, Thinking, and Judging. Pragmatic and practical, and good at getting the job done; better at organizing and directing others. Low interest in things that do not have practical meaning or application. Others often consider ESTJs as natural administrators.

ESFP. Extraverted, Sensing, Feeling, and Perceiving. Equally at home with people or things when common sense and practical abilities are needed. Outgoing, gregarious, accepting, with wide interests and enjoyments. Always in on the action or the goings-on of a group. Others describe ESFPs as active, energetic, fun to be with, and friendly.

ESFJ. Extraverted, Sensing, Feeling, and Judging. Most interested in things which directly affect others. Need environmental and interpersonal harmony to feel good, and are often able to accommodate enough to foster it. Team player, popular, reliable, talkative, and well-liked. At risk for doing nice things for others to a fault.

ENFP. Extraverted, Intuitive, Feeling, and Perceiving. Energetic, creative, high-spirited, and highly adaptable. Often impress with ability to improvise and develop rapid responses to seemingly any problem. Warm, enthusiastic, and willing to help anyone. Often gifted in ways which allows for pursuit of nearly any interest.

ENFJ. Extraverted, Intuitive, Feeling, and Judging. Equally accepting of and responsive to praise and blame, and able to interact with groups easily and tactfully. Aware and sensitive to others' feelings, always taking them into account in reacting to situations. Others describe ENFJs as responsible, sympathetic, responsive, and likable.

ENTP. Extraverted, Intuitive, Thinking, and Perceiving. Great at debate, will argue both sides of a question for the fun of it. Good at many things, aware, outspoken, and ingenious. Better at taking on the new rather than carrying on the old. Always seem to be involved in new projects. Others describe ENTPs as quick thinking, stimulating in conversation, and creative.

ENTJ. Extraverted, Intuitive, Thinking, and Judging. Active leaders who are direct and frank though not without compassion and understanding of different points of view. Verbally strong, would be good at public speaking, panel discussions, talk shows. Unusually knowledgeable and like adding to fund of knowledge. Run the risk of acting more confidently than warranted in some circumstances.

INTP. Introverted, Intuitive, Thinking, and Perceiving. With relatively few, but sharply circumscribed interests, have dislike of chit-chat and social gatherings. Reserved, self-contained, and quiet. Enjoys science, the theoretical, and solitary intellectual activities. Tend to be at their best when logic and analysis are called for.

INTJ. Introverted, Intuitive, Thinking, and Judging. Self-determined and stubborn, sometimes missing the main points for details. Critical and independent thinkers with determination to follow plans to their full purpose. Can be both appropriately and inappropriately skeptical. Others often see them as inventive and original.

INFP. Introverted, Intuitive, Feeling, and Perceiving. Interested in ideas, learning, education, and their own projects. May have a great love or dedication which is not made apparent until INFPs trust the other person. Take on too much, but still are usually successful at meeting commitments. Not deliberately unsociable, but often preoccupied with projects of interest to the point of appearing unsociable.

INFJ. Introverted, Intuitive, Feeling, and Judging. Independent of the crowd while concerned for their welfare and the common good. Respected and esteemed for unwavering principles and effort. Diligent, dedicated, and persevering. Clear about their convictions.

ISFP. Introverted, Sensing, Feeling and Perceiving. Enjoy today, taking whatever time is needed to complete tasks. Rarely hurries or overexerts. Prefer following to leading. Others describe ISFPs as kind, modest, friendly when approached, but also as reserved, quiet, and sensitive. Avoid arguments and discord. Not interested in persuading or being persuaded.

ISFJ. Introverted, Sensing, Feeling, and Judging. Solidly stable force in a group or on a project; will often undertake aspects of a task others shun. Thorough, conscientious, detail-oriented, and reliable. Not technically inclined or interested, yet perceptive. Others describe ISFJs as loyal, dedicated, willing to do their part; quiet, and considerate.

ISTP. Introverted, Sensing, Thinking, and Perceiving. Described more often as thinking and analyzing than as feeling and supporting. Appear detached, but are also curious and observing and interested in pragmatic organization and the logic in positions, situations, and policies.

ISTJ. Introverted, Sensing, Thinking, and Judging. Self-determined and self-satisfied, make up their own mind and follow it. Hard to distract, dissuade, or discourage. Pay attention to details and concentrate well so that things will run well. Others describe ISTJs as serious, successful, respected, logical, well organized, and reliable.

The dynamics of the trait interactions, which include their direction and strength, are complex. When taken into account, they describe the sixteen personality types in richer, more detailed, and more helpful ways than the synopses here suggest.

The Myers-Briggs is widely used and has many applications beyond empirical verification of Jung's personality theory (e.g., to analyze motivations in learning, how to reward employees, why team communication seems blocked, which college major or profession might be more rewarding, why one group does not seem to understand where the other group is coming from, to help couples value their differences and similarities). Religiously affiliated institutions often use the Myers-Briggs, even more than they do the concept *personality type,* as means to resolve group conflict and understand group process and differences. Identification of *personality type,* and utilization of the Myers-Briggs to that end, continues to prove useful in many other settings as well.

Despite its application and sophistication however, the concept of *personality type* has important limitations as does the use of the Myers-Briggs. Firstly, personality traits vary in salience and strength over time. Preferences change, motivations change, interests change, and our ability to meet our own needs change in the course of normal growth and development. Our lived experience of our own personality type is more fluid than fixed. *Personality type* is not equivalent to *person* or even *personality.* To the extent *personality type* (and the Myers-Briggs) helps us understand people we otherwise would not understand, its use is appropriate, valuable, and welcomed. But individuals are not types and should never be reduced to such.

Secondly, the sixteen types are rarely found in pure form, and they neither represent nor are they intended to represent every trait found in every personality. There are more kinds of personalities, especially "abnormal" personalities and "abnormal" tendencies in otherwise "normal" personalities, than either *personality type* or the Myers-Briggs covers or is intended to cover. Outside of organizational development, clinical psychology seldom uses the technical concept *personality type* and psychiatry's use is rarer still. The term has not proved useful for understanding particular problematic behaviors or most maladaptive character traits. Other psychological instruments like the Minnesota Multiphasic Personality Inventory–2 (MMPI-2) and the Millon Clinical Multiaxial Inventory–II (MCMI-II) have much greater utility in those instances. While useful for sorting people into a specific number of stereotyped groups (the personality types), the Myers-Briggs has minimal usefulness in clinical and mental health settings.

In spite of Jung's personal genius and encyclopedic knowledge, and in spite of years of theorizing, researching and refining both theory and instrument, *personality type* stands as one example of how we remain more complex and complicated than our ability to measure and describe ourselves.

PAUL MOGLIA

PETER CHRYSOLOGUS, ST. (ca. 380–449/58)

Born at Imola in Emilia, he was named archbishop of Ravenna sometime between 425 and 429 (but before 431). Details of his life are contained in the *Liber Pontificalis Ecclesiae Ravennatis,* a ninth-century work full of historical errors by Abbot Agnellus. In 448 or 449 Eutyches wrote to Peter to appeal for help after Flavian, bishop of Constantinople, had deposed him as archimandrite of a large monastery. Peter urged Eutyches to submit to the decisions of Leo, Bishop of Rome, on the matter. His authentic writings include a letter and 183 sermons. His homilies give an excellent picture of the liturgy as it was celebrated in his day as well as of life in Ravenna as the Western Roman Empire was coming to an end. In his preaching he attacked paganism and was anxious to promote authentic Christian teaching and living. Peter acknowledged the primacy of the Bishop of Rome. He died between 449 and 458, probably on 3 December 450. From the ninth century he has had the epithet Chrysologus (Gk. Golden-worded), presumably to make him a Western counterpart to John Chrysostom (Gk. Golden-mouthed). Chrysologus was named a Doctor of the Church in 1729. Feast day, 30 July.

JOHN DILLON

See also DOCTORS OF THE CHURCH; FATHERS OF THE CHURCH.

PETER DAMIAN, ST. (1007–1072)

Doctor of the Church, monk, reformer, cardinal, he was born in Ravenna to a poor family. Orphaned as a child, he was reared by an older brother who was a priest and who made it possible for him to receive an education in rhetoric, grammar and law at Faenza and Parma. While a lay teacher and living an ascetical life, he decided to join the Camaldolese Benedictines at Fonte Avellana in 1035. There he lived a severe life practicing great personal penances and strict fasting while observing a regular round of liturgical and private prayer. He continued his learning by his arduous study of the Scriptures and the Church Fathers. In 1043 he was elected abbot of the monastery, and he then founded five new hermitages, always insisting on the importance of solitude and the renunciation of all worldliness. Though compassionate on penitents, he was noted for his strictness in spiritual matters with both priests and bishops.

Peter began to influence the Church in a larger context when he spoke out against ecclesiastical abuses at local synods in Italy. He rejected simony and clerical marriage and supported a reformed papacy to guide the Church through this dark age. In 1057 he was made bishop of Ostia and a cardinal, and he became a key figure in the Gregorian reform movement. He spoke out against the antipopes and traveled throughout Europe preaching reform. After repeated requests, Pope Nicholas II (1058–1061) allowed him to return to Fonte Avellana.

In addition to his contributions to the Gregorian reform, Peter also helped to influence monasticism by teaching the supremacy of the eremetical life over the cenobitical. He wrote much on the Eucharist and in support of clerical celibacy. He was so strongly opposed to simony that he denied the validity of the sacraments administered by unworthy priests. Also a poet, his most famous work is a hymn in honor of St. Gregory. Peter Damian died on 22 February 1072 after having helped with problems in the Church in Ravenna. Though never "officially" canonized, his memory was celebrated locally, and in 1828 Pope Leo XII extended his feast to the whole Church and made him a Doctor of the Church.

ANTHONY D. ANDREASSI

See also GREGORY VII, POPE.

PETER, ST.

This article focuses on Peter in the New Testament. It summarizes the conclusions of the following outstanding ecumenical discussion: R. E. Brown, K. P. Donfried, and J. Reumann, eds., *Peter in the New Testament,* Minneapolis/New York: Augsburg/Paulist, 1973. This study draws an extremely useful distinction between (1) the role of Peter in his lifetime (before A.D. 65) and (2) the evolution of his image in New Testament writings after his death (the so-called Petrine trajectory). Regarding the first point, i.e., the historical Peter, it is helpful to speak of (1) Peter during the ministry of Jesus and (2) Peter in the life of the early Church. For the former the principal source is the Gospels; for the latter the main sources are the letters of Paul and the Acts of the Apostles.

Prior to receiving the name of Peter, the first apostle was called Simeon in Hebrew (see Acts 15:14) and Simon in Greek (Matt 16:17; John 1:42). One cannot know for certain whether the change to Peter took place during the ministry or after the resurrection (note the different contexts in Matt 16:18; Mark 3:16; John 1:42). However, this change must have occurred early since Paul regularly refers to him as Kephas, not Simon (1 Cor 1:12; Gal 1:18). ("Kephas" is a grecized form of the name derived from Aramaic *kêpā'* meaning "rock"; *Petros* is a Greek masculine name derived from *petra* meaning "rock.")

It is clear that Peter was one of the first called by Jesus who would follow him (Matt 4:18-20; Mark 1:16-18; Luke 5:1-11; John 1:40-42) and remain active after the resurrection. In this group Peter was very prominent—indeed in all four Gospels he is the disciple mentioned the most. He is often associated with other significant disciples, such as James and John, in the Synoptics (Mark 1:16-20, 29-31; 5:37; 9:2; 13:3), and the Beloved Disciple in the Fourth Gospel (John 13:23-24; 20:1-10; 21:7, 20-23). It is probable that Peter made a confession of Jesus as the Messiah (Matt 16:16; Mark 8:29; Luke 9:20; but see John 6:69). However, this confession was most likely inadequate. According to Matthew 16:23 and Mark 8:33 Jesus had to rebuke Peter for the limitations of his confession—a point that argues in favor

St. Peter, sculpture detail, Vatican

of the historicity of the event. When one considers the account of Peter's denial of Jesus during the passion (Matt 26:69-75; Mark 14:66-72; Luke 22:55-62; John 18:15-18, 25-27), one may reasonably conclude that Peter misunderstood Jesus—at least to some degree.

In the time of the early Church Peter figures prominently. He received an appearance of the risen Jesus, most likely the first such appearance (Luke 24:34; 1 Cor 15:3; perhaps Mark 16:7). Perhaps it was this experience that contributed to Peter's stature in the early Church. In the city of Jerusalem and the environs Peter was the most important of the Twelve. For example, he functioned as spokesperson for the Twelve (Acts 2:14-41). It is not inconceivable that this function impacted Peter's role as spokesperson during the time of Jesus' ministry. However, there is no clear testimony about a special authority Peter enjoyed over the others. The apostles in Jerusalem send Peter and John to Samaria (Acts 8:14). Acts further depicts Peter and John acting practically as a team (3:1-26; 4:1-31). Peter also served as a missionary. While Paul limits Peter's missionary activities to the circumcised (Gal 2:7), Acts shows Peter as the chief protagonist in the baptism of the first Gentile Cornelius (10:1-48). Other texts imply that Peter was influential in predominantly Gentile areas (1 Cor 1:12; 1 Pet 1:1). On the question of observance of the Jewish Law Peter supported a middle position. James, "the brother of the Lord," (Gal 2:12) and Paul (Gal 2:11) represented the more conservative and liberal positions, respectively.

The trajectory of the images of Peter affords a variety of perspectives, some rooted in the historical Peter, others dependent upon the ideal Peter. A first image is that of Peter as the great Christian fisherman/missionary. The miraculous catch of fish in Luke 5:1-11 and John 21:1-14 depicts a successful missionary undertaking. A second image is that of Peter as the shepherd. Here Peter is seen as the model pastor whose first obligation is to provide for the sheep (John 21:15-19). Two other images linked to that of pastor are those of the ideal presbyter/elder concerned with the care of the flock (1 Pet 5) and the holder of the keys of the kingdom (Matt 16:19; see Isa 22:15-22). A third image is that of Peter as the martyr. John 21:18-19 reveals a martyr who follows the example of the Good Shepherd who lays down his life for the sheep (John 10:11). Peter's death ca. A.D. 65 is the ultimate form of witness (1 Pet 5:1). A fourth image is that of Peter as the recipient of special revelation. In addition to the appearance of the risen Jesus to Peter there is one along with James and John in which Peter experiences the Transfiguration (Matt 17:1; Mark 9:2; Luke 9:28; see also 1 Pet 1:16-18). A fifth image is that of Peter as the confessor of the Christian faith. Thus in Matthew 16:16 Peter acknowledges Jesus to be not only the Messiah but also the Son of the living God. Thus Peter is the "rock" of the Church against which not even the powerful forces of the underworld can prevail. A sixth image linked to the fifth is that of Peter as the guardian of the true faith against false teaching (2 Pet 1:20-21; 3:15-16). A seventh and final image is that of Peter as sinner. A pertinent example of this is his denial of Jesus during the time of the passion. But the sinful Peter underwent rehabilitation (John 21:15-17). Ironically the weak Peter becomes the tower of strength for others (Luke 22:32).

JOHN F. CRAGHAN

See also APOSTLE; PAUL, ST.

PETRINE PRIVILEGE

The Petrine privilege or privilege in favor of the faith is the dissolution of a nonsacramental marriage between a baptized person and an unbaptized person. The pope can grant this dissolution under certain conditions. The "Petrine" privilege is actually a misnomer derived from the "Pauline" privilege. In the latter it is a question of the dissolution of a marriage between two nonbaptized persons.

Use of the Petrine privilege is linked to the so-called Helena case. This was a petition from the bishop of Helena, Montana, to the Holy See in 1924 for the following case. In 1919 an unbaptized non-

Catholic man married a non-Catholic, specifically Anglican woman, in an Anglican ceremony. In 1920 the man obtained a civil divorce from the woman. However, the man later wanted to accept the Catholic faith and marry a Catholic woman. By this time the Anglican woman had already remarried. Pius XI approved the petition and granted the dissolution of the natural bond of the first marriage. It was granted "in favor of the faith," viz., the intention of the man to become a Catholic.

JOHN F. CRAGHAN

See also PAULINE PRIVILEGE.

PEYTON, PATRICK (1909–1992)

He became known to millions as "The Rosary Priest" who crusaded for fifty years promoting the family rosary all over the world. Patrick Peyton was born into poverty in a thatched cottage in Carracastle, Mayo, Ireland. In 1928 he emigrated, for economic reasons, to America where he eventually joined the Congregation of the Holy Cross. As a seminarian he contracted tuberculosis and attributed his recovery to Mary's intercession. After his ordination he founded the Family Rosary Crusade and traveled from parish to parish across America.

He soon realized that he could bring his message to a much larger audience by use of the mass media. In 1947 he founded the Family Theatre in Hollywood and won the active support and participation of Bing Crosby, Natalie Wood, Ronald Reagan, Loretta Young, Jimmy Stewart and many others prominent in the entertainment world. His prize-winning weekly radio dramatic show entertained Americans for twenty-two years. Each week's drama closed with Fr. Peyton's famous slogan: "The family that prays together, stays together." With the arrival of television the Family Theatre, under Fr. Peyton's direction, brought memorable programs into American homes. These included such award winners as *Hill Number One* with Jimmy Dean and Raymond Burr. Patrick Peyton was a man of great courtesy who read widely and had an unusual appreciation of modern communications technology. But he was above all a priest of deep spirituality who won the friendship, respect, and support of Grace Kelly, Helen Hayes, Bob Newhart, Mother Teresa and many others who participated in his films on the mysteries of the rosary. They felt that this big sensitive Irishman was a person apart, a man living at ease in two worlds.

JOAN GLAZIER

See also ROSARY.

PHARISEES

The Pharisees were an observant and influential group of Jews prominent in Palestine especially from the second century B.C. to the first century A.D. Their name most likely derived from the Hebrew word *pĕrûshîm* ("separated ones"). At some times in their history they appear to have been a social-political movement having influence over both rulers and the common people, while at other times they seem to have been a religious sect or a Hellenistic school promoting a way of life. Their chief interests according to the Mishnah were eating food in a state of ritual purity, tithing and agricultural offerings, rules about raising crops, keeping the Sabbath and festivals, and clarifying marriage laws. According to Josephus, they insisted on free will, the resurrection of the dead, and judgment resulting in rewards and punishments. The Gospels present them as the chief opponents of Jesus, emphasizing careful observance of the Law and the traditions surrounding it, seeking popular respect and influence, and sharing common meals (perhaps in their view thus replicating the Temple cult in ordinary homes). Paul was a Pharisee before his experience of Christ on the Damascus Road (see Phil 3:5; Acts 23:6). The vigorous criticisms of the Pharisees (and scribes) in Matthew 23 probably reflect the formative role of the Pharisees in reviving Judaism after the destruction of the Jerusalem Temple in A.D. 70.

DANIEL J. HARRINGTON, S.J.

See also BIBLE, NEW TESTAMENT WRITINGS; JUDAISM.

PHILOSOPHY AND THEOLOGY

Philosophy and theology have had a long, close relationship because both deal with ultimate realities. In the Western world, philosophy began in Greece through the principal figures of Plato and Aristotle. Philosophy, meaning etymologically "love of wisdom," described the search of the philosopher to penetrate behind the appearances of everyday life and beyond the knowledge that science renders us to the ultimate realities. Once these were penetrated, a person knew "wisdom" and the way things really were.

The areas of philosophy developed out of the subject matter considered and the methods used. Hence to look at the world and how it was structured is the work of *cosmology;* to examine the universals and their relations behind science is the work of *metaphysics;* to know what makes up a human being is the work of *anthropology;* to render the way we know is *epistemology;* to explain the limits of communication is *linguistics;* to explain the actions of freedom in relation to right and wrong is *ethics*. While these are the main branches of philosophy, many other types of "philosophy of . . . (e.g., God, art, history, society . . . etc.)" have developed which correspond to changes in human consciousness, newly acquired skills in science and technology, improved or new methods of examining human concerns through new disciplines such as psychology, anthropology, and the social sciences.

Christianity found the various critical powers of philosophy helpful to explain and express its own understanding of faith. Two great syntheses of theology and philosophy occurred which have dominated fifteen hundred years of Catholic theology: the first in the fifth century with St. Augustine's use of the Platonic current of thought and, the second, in the thirteenth century with St. Thomas Aquinas' use of Aristotle as well as Arabian and Jewish thought which became Scholasticism. Many philosophies today deal with the problem of the limits of knowledge (Kant), verifiability of truth (Wittgenstein), and adequate theories of interpretation (Habermas).

The main difference between theology and philosophy rests not upon the methods but upon what is admitted as evidence. Philosophy accepts universally verifiable evidence able to be subjected to the powers of critical reason; theology accepts the particular, singular, and unrepeatable experience of divine revelation in history and continually verified in Christian faith. While accepting of the critical thinking of philosophy, Christian theology rests its "wisdom" upon the event of Jesus' life, death, and resurrection as the revelation of God's love for us and our call to love one another.

J. J. MUELLER, S.J.

See also THEOLOGY, FUNDAMENTAL; THEOLOGY, SYSTEMATIC.

PIETÀ

(Italian, "pity") In painting or sculpture, the word refers to an image of the Virgin, seated, receiving the dead Christ on her lap. The most famous is that of Michelangelo at St. Peter's, Rome.

DAVID BRYAN

See also ART, CHRISTIAN; MICHELANGELO BUONARROTI.

PILGRIMAGES

A pilgrimage is a journey to a sacred shrine or sanctuary for a religious purpose. The Old Testament mentions pilgrimages to such shrines as Bethel and Dan as well as pilgrimages for the festivals of Unleavened Bread, Pentecost, and Booths. Christians made pilgrimages to venerate places significant in the life of Jesus, e.g., the Church of the Holy Sepulcher in Jerusalem, areas linked to the saints, especially the martyrs, e.g., the tombs of Peter and Paul in Rome, and sites famous for their miracles. In modern times Marian apparitions have given rise to pilgrimages, e.g., to Lourdes, France, and Fatima, Portugal. On these occasions pilgrims seek God's help, often for cures from illness and disease and frequently through the intercession of a particular saint. Pilgrims also perform acts of penance for past sins or thanksgiving for favors received.

St. Peter's Square

Pilgrims often bring votive offerings to the shrine, e.g., a reproduction of a healed limb or a tablet recounting an escaped danger. Usually pilgrims make gifts of money or kind at the shrine. In modern times, for example, the shrine of Mary in Czestochowa, Poland, was regarded as one of the richest in the world.

Prayer and penance figure prominently in pilgrimages. Usually pilgrims pray kneeling. One of the very common penitential practices is the climbing of a high staircase on hands and knees. Frequently pilgrims participate in an all-night vigil at the shrine itself or nearby. Appropriately, the reception of the sacraments, specifically reconciliation and the Eucharist, is characteristic for pilgrims who have reached the goal of their journey.

JOHN F. CRAGHAN

PILGRIMS

See PILGRIMAGES; PURITANS.

PINAMEN, MISHTA (1873–1962)

Pinamen's story is one of courage, faith, and service. Pinamen, daughter, wife, mother, widow, catechist, and leader of her people, stands as a testimony to native peoples, to people of the north, and to all Christians called to hope through pain and struggle. Pinamen McKenzie was a Montagnais woman of Canada's north. She lived her whole life in the traditional ways of her native people, hunting and trapping, relying on God's providence, subject to all kinds of disease, knowing strong family ties and sharing loyalty to her band.

Pinamen was born 3 February 1873 in Betsiamits, an Indian village in Quebec on the lower North Shore of the St. Lawrence River. She was the third of ten children, and though she was physically unattractive, she possessed an extraordinary goodness. Until the age of twenty she cared for her father who was in need; only then did she marry, which was at a late age according to the customs of her people.

Pinamen and her husband, Jerome Fontaine, were blessed with four daughters, but in 1911 her husband died and Pinamen was left with the responsibility of caring for her family. She remained in Betsiamits until all her children were provided for. Then in 1921 Pinamen moved to the village of Sheshatshit near Goose Bay in Labrador where her daughter, Anne Philomena, was living. This was to be a turning point in Pinamen's life. For the remaining forty-one years of her life, Pinamen devoted herself to the poor, to children, to prayer, and to helping the Church.

The native people of Sheshatshit were poverty- and disease-ridden, illiterate, and subject to famine. Pinamen recognized her mission. She began to care for the sick, visiting them in the hospital, praying beside their beds, or gathering the children outside, beneath the windows, where she would lead them in singing hymns to gladden those within. Mary-May Osmond, the secretary at the hospital, says: "She was always there with the sick and the dying, praying at their bedside, night and day."

Soon Pinamen became aware of the many poor in the region and she began to beg for them. Often she was seen carrying sacks of things she had solicited. These begging trips took Pinamen around the North West River area which meant she had to cross the river either by canoe in the warm season or by dog sled in the winter. A story illustrates the simplicity of this child of nature. One time as she was making one of these long excursions by foot, feeling the fatigue, the heat of the day, and the pain of her arthritic knee, Pinamen settled down in the high grass beside the roadside for a siesta and, not expecting anyone to be around, she pulled up her skirts and exposed her aching limbs to the comforting rays of the sun. This daughter of St. Francis was only doing "what the doctor had advised her to do."

During the winter months Pinamen lived in a tent. This woman was never idle: she washed, mended, resoled moccasins, or prepared skins for tanning. Often she was left to guard the campsite and on such occasions she would sit on a cushion at the door of the tent, her working materials beside her and her hands in perpetual motion.

Pinamen was known by her people as a woman of faith and prayer. Inside a tent, walking in the village, even at work, "Pinamen prayed unceasingly," we are told by her relatives. Each morning she was the first in church, whether it was summer or the bitter cold of the Labrador winter. Frequently she came on snowshoes, following in the tracks of a Good Samaritan who might accompany her. Since the chapel was cold and damp, and took time to warm up, Pinamen would stand on the hot air grate in front of the tabernacle and pray long and fervently.

In addition to her daily round of prayer and her spiritual and corporal works of mercy, Pinamen was teacher of her people. Her teaching consisted of all she had learned herself during her years in Betsiamits: creed, commandments, sacraments, angels, Mary, the Mother of our Savior Jesus, the Catholic Church and the hierarchy under the pope, the "great Chief," as well as the prayers she had learned. Pinamen knew by heart the fifteen mysteries of the rosary, a few psalms and litanies and many prayers of her own choice. Two of her daughters testify: "As soon as Mother entered our homes, she began to teach our children." Another daughter says: "Whenever I meet people in my travels, they invariably tell me: 'It was your mother who taught me to pray, to know and to love God'."

For more than twenty-five years in the absence of a priest, Pinamen kept the faith alive in this remote region of Canada's north. It was Pinamen who reestablished the Church's liturgical seasons: Advent, Christmas, Lent, Easter, Pentecost. "She was our priest in those days," say the people of Sheshatshit. A cousin says: "Yes, Pinamen explained our religion, but above all, she showed us how to live it." "It was she who planted the faith in our hearts," says Mrs. Joseph McKenzie. Until a resident priest came, Pinamen was leader and guide of the Catholic community.

When a resident priest, Father Joseph Cyr, O.M.I., finally came to Sheshatshit in 1947, he found a people of faith. Pinamen continued her faith-filled life of service but now she could add to her duties daily Mass and Evening Prayer.

It is no surprise that when the federal and provincial governments constructed a million-dollar school in Sheshatshit in 1968, a petition was supported by the whole population that it be dedicated to Pinamen. Today this school stands as a testimony to Pinamen, the forerunner of education in a remote part of Labrador.

When Pinamen McKenzie died on 21 June 1962, she had earned the title of *Mishta,* a title of love and respect given this humble native woman by her own Montagnais people. Mishta Pinamen, "Great and Dauntless Pinamen."

MARCEL MONGEAU, O.M.I.

See also CANADA, THE CATHOLIC CHURCH IN; EVANGELIZATION.

PIUS V, POPE (1566–1572)

Michele Ghislieri, of a poor family from Bosco, entered upon the life of a shepherd until he joined the Dominicans at fourteen. The future pope became a teacher of theology and philosophy, a master of novices, an inquisitor, and a prior. When his great administrative talents began to be noticed, he was made commissary general of the Roman Inquisition. Zealous, ascetical, devoted to evangelical poverty, he was promoted and consecrated a bishop, and finally a cardinal, by Paul IV. Always a reformer, he opposed the nepotism of Pius IV and, after the death of the latter, was unanimously chosen pope.

During his short reign, Pius V continued to live the ascetical life and brought simplicity to the etiquette of the papal court. He vigorously enforced the reforms of the Council of Trent in the face of much opposition, revitalizing religious orders, limiting the granting of indulgences, insisting that all clerics live in the places which provided their incomes. He completed the Roman Catechism of 1566, and reformed the liturgies of the Mass and the Hours, reforms which were generally in effect until Vatican II in our own times. He gave the Church a new edition of the works of St. Thomas Aquinas, proclaiming him to be a Doctor of the Church. His charities were great, and he was often found visiting the sick in hospitals.

Pius opposed the spread of the Reformation with great energy, and was severe with heretics in the Papal States. He established the Congregation of the Index in order to supervise the burgeoning power of the printing industry, then only a little over a century old. His international policies were often naive and counterproductive. His order for the excommunication and deposition of Elizabeth I, for example, only served to make conditions difficult for English Catholics. Yet he also promoted unity among Christian monarchs in the face of the advancing Turks and lived to see the victory of Lepanto and the end of Turkish power in the Mediterranean. If Pius was severe and narrowly focused, he was at the same time a great and honest reformer of the sort much needed in his time. Feast day, 30 April.

DAVID BRYAN

See also CHURCH AND STATE; PAPACY, THE; REFORMATION, THE.

PIUS VII, POPE (1800–1823)

Barnabà Chiaramonte was born to a noble family at Cesena, in Emilia, and became a Benedictine at fourteen. The future pope was successively a theology professor, abbot of San Callisto, bishop of Tivoli, and then of Imola, where he was made a cardinal. Chiaramonte was sensitive to contemporary thought, declaring, for example, that there was no necessary conflict between the Church and the new democratic forms of government then emerging in America and France. Elected pope in 1800, most of Pius' pontificate was taken up with the disasters brought about by Napoleon. The latter had restored the Church in France and many surrounding states, but increasingly usurped control over it. Pius' participation in Napoleon's coronation did nothing to improve relations. Napoleon subsequently thought he merited Pius' backing in his military ventures, but, when this was not forthcoming, a French army entered Rome (1808). Pope Pius, after excommunicating those responsible (without naming the emperor), found himself under arrest. After four years of detention, while he was sick and separated from his advisors, Pius agreed to still more concessions, including the surrender of the Papal States to France, which he would later revoke. He was able to return to the Vatican only in 1815 after the fall of Napoleon.

Pius' courage during six years of captivity earned him much respect and sympathy. The Congress of Vienna restored the Papal States which Napoleon had annexed. In his remaining five years, Pius fostered the arts and sciences; significantly, he restored the Jesuit Order.

DAVID BRYAN

See also CHURCH AND STATE; PAPACY, THE.

PIUS IX, POPE (1846–1878)

Giovanni Maria Mastai Ferretti was born at Senigallia (Ancona), Italy in 1792. His family was of the lower nobility with moderate reform and cultural interests. He was an epileptic, but with few health difficulties he studied theology at the Roman College and was ordained in 1819. He worked in an orphanage for some years and spent two years (1823 to 1825) with the apostolic delegation in Chile where his interest in the missions was born. He became archbishop of Spoleto in 1827, was transferred to Imola in 1832, and made cardinal in 1840. He did impressive pastoral work and was regarded as a tolerant and liberal prelate with an understanding of the nationalist trends of the times. He was elected pope in 1846, taking the name Pius IX.

Pius introduced limited reforms to the Papal States and was regarded as an apostle of liberty. This hasty opinion waned when he showed that he was no democrat. He insisted that neither he nor the Papal States would be active participants in a united Italy. Revolutionary unrest made him flee Rome for Gaeta in the kingdom of Naples. With the help of French troops, Pius returned to Rome and was henceforth regarded in popular and political circles as a "reactionary and maladroit." Pius came to regard the anticlerical and nationalist forces that despised him as sworn enemies of religion. The loss of papal territories—Romagna and Marches in 1860—stiffened his stand. Rome fell to Italian forces on 20 September 1870 and the temporal power of the Pope came to an end. Refusing all offers of compromise or accommodation, Pius IX came to regard himself as the prisoner of the Vatican.

Italian unification and territorial problems played an everyday role in his pontificate. But Pius' political disappointments and failures were balanced by his spiritual and pastoral accomplishments. He reestablished the hierarchy in England and Wales (1850) and in the Netherlands (1853); and he also erected 206 new dioceses and vicariates apostolic. During his pontificate, missionary activity expanded, and popular devotions flourished, especially after the definition of the Immaculate Conception of Mary in 1854. Many new religious congregations were founded, and vocations to the priesthood and religious life increased. Pius was a man of deep spirituality but, with the advance of revolutionary ideas and the political upheavals that overtook Europe, he decided to make no compromise with the changing world. He was viewed outside the Church as the epitome of reaction; and his uncompromising theological spirit is embodied in his Syllabus of Errors (condemning eighty propositions) and the encyclical *Quanta Cura* (1864), both of which gave no quarter to modern philosophy, religious and political liberalism, rationalism and other philosophical and theological issues which he felt were incompatible with tradional Catholic teaching.

The most important achievement of his pontificate was the definition of papal infallibility at the First Vatican Council (1869–1870) which he had summoned. While this had immediate adverse reactions such as the Old Catholic schism and the *Kulturkampf* in Germany, it increased, consolidated, and centralized spiritual authority in the papacy. Though controversy still surrounds the actions of Vatican I, it marked a new course for the Church, no longer encumbered with temporal possessions and political problems. Pius IX died in 1878 after reigning longer than any pope in history.

MICHAEL GLAZIER

See also MODERNISM; PAPACY, THE; PAPAL STATES; SYLLABUS OF ERRORS; VATICAN COUNCIL I.

PIUS X, POPE (1903–1914)

The second of ten children, Guiseppe Sarto was born in the village of Riese in Venetia in 1835. His father worked as a postman and messenger and there were no luxuries in the Sarto home. He was educated at the College of Castelfranco and attended the seminary of Padua where he was a diligent but very average student. After ordination in 1858 he spent seventeen years in pastoral work, and was made chancellor of the Treviso diocese in 1875. He was ordained bishop of Mantua, serving from 1884 to 1893; then, as cardinal-patriarch of Venice for the next decade. In this priestly and episcopal work, he was primarily a gifted spiritual leader with a great interest in making the liturgy the formative center of Catholic life and of religious education.

At the conclave that followed the death of Leo XIII, Cardinal Rampolla del Tindaro led in the first three ballots and was on the verge of being elected pope when the disapproval of Emperor Franz Josef of Austria was announced. Rampolla then withdrew and Sarto was chosen and took the name Pius X on

Pope Pius X

4 August 1903. One of the first steps of the new pontiff was to issue the constitution *Commissum Nobis,* which finally put an end to the interference of any government, by veto or otherwise, in the election of a pope. When, in 1905, the French government effected the separation of Church and state, Pius moved again to put an end to government interference in the selection of bishops and in Church affairs. His stand stripped the French Church of much of its wealth, but it gave it independence. Pius had few diplomatic skills but had a reforming instinct. He is best remembered for restoring the frequent reception of the Eucharist, a practice that had been in decline since the Middle Ages and his 1910 decree *Quam Singulari* called for the early reception of the Sacrament by children. He initiated the reform of Church music and promoted the restoration of Roman plainchant. Pius inaugurated the revision of the breviary; he promoted the daily reading of the Scriptures; and established the Pontifical Biblical Institute in 1903. He also entrusted the Benedictines with the revision and correction of the Vulgate text of the Bible. He opened up a new era in religious instruction and called for setting-up the Confraternity of Christian Doctrine in every parish. He issued two encyclicals on Catholic Action, but had no enthusiasm for ecumenical activities. Pius lifted the ban on Catholic participation in Italian political life; and he reorganized and consolidated the Roman Curia with the apostolic constitution *Sapienti Consilio* in 1908. He initiated the preparation of the Code of Canon Law, an arduous task which was not completed until 1917. Pius' pastoral concern was global; he had a special concern for the Indians in Brazil; he took a personal interest in the problems of the Church in North America; and the Church's missionary vocation was paramount in all his hopes and work.

Yet the career of this man of great personal holiness and pastoral commitment is clouded in many ways. Since the beginning of his pontificate, there was conflict between the theological defenders of Thomism, revived by Leo XIII as the Church's preferred theological and philosophical system, and those who argued that it was foolhardy for the Church to close itself to all the intellectual discussions, advancements, and movements in scriptural, theological, philosophical, scientific, and other fields of modern scholarship. Pius was primarily a rigorous cleric with narrow intellectual perimeters. In 1905 the term "Modernism" was coined to describe the heresies and conspiracies which supposedly beset the Church. In reality, Modernism was an umbrella which covered a variety of disparate movements and opinions. Some of the proponents of the new ideas, such as Alfred Loisy and George Tyrrell moved to positions which were unorthodox. But there was no unified movement or planned conspiracy. The defensive and preventive measures inaugurated or justified by the decree *Lamentabili Sane Exitu* (July 1907), by the encyclyical *Pascendi Dominici Gregis* (8 September 1907), and by the motu proprio *Sacrorum Antistitum* (1 September 1910) were radical. An anti-Modernist oath was formulated for all priests and clerical teachers. Sodalitium Pianum, directed by Msgr. Benigni, a system of informers protected by a promise of anonymity, was set up for all dioceses. Advances in theological, biblical, and philosophical studies were stultified. Catholic intellectual life suffered greatly until the advent of a new era with Vatican II. Innocent men were betrayed, blacklisted and at times silenced. The worst aspects of this sad chapter were terminated on the election of Pius' successor, Benedict XV, in 1914. His name was later found on a list of suspected Modernists.

Yet, no matter how harshly history judges the anti-Modernist crusade, Pius X will be venerated for his sanctity and the many salutory changes he brought to the life of the Church which he loved. He was canonized by Pius XII in 1954.

MICHAEL GLAZIER

See also COMMUNION, HOLY; MODERNISM; ORTHODOXY; PAPACY, THE.

PIUS XI, POPE (1922–1939)

Achille Ambrogio Damiano Ratti was born in Desio, near Milan in 1857. He was ordained in 1878, and he became an expert in paleography and in library administration. In 1918 he was sent as apostolic visitor to Poland and was made nuncio the following year. He displayed exceptional diplomatic finesse, and was created a cardinal and appointed archbishop of Milan in 1921. A year later he was elected pope. He saw the rise of Fascism and its leader, Benito Mussolini, to whom he gave limited and qualified support. In 1929, the Lateran Treaty was signed and the final settlement of the Roman Question was reached. The papacy recognized the Kingdom of Italy and, in return, the full sovereignty of the Vatican State was recognized. It was agreed, among other things, that the papacy would evermore be neutral in military and diplomatic conflicts, and, in future, the pope would intervene in such affairs as head of the Church, not as head of a state. The papacy also received compensation for waiving all claims to the former Papal States—but this was far less than the compensation turned down by Pius IX in 1861. Catholicism was to be the recognized religion of Italy; the Church was given certain rights in education; and a church marriage was to precede a civil marriage for Italian Catholics.

Pius also negotiated the end of religious persecution in Mexico. In 1933 he signed an agreement with the new Nazi regime in Germany, but this was violated and Pius denounced Nazism in March 1937 in a vigorous encyclical *Mit Brennender Sorge* ("With burning anxiety"). He also denounced the upsurge of anti-Semitism in Mussolini's regime and condemned all forms of racism. He was deeply disturbed by the rising popularity and power of Communism, considering it the most pernicious enemy of the Church. This led to the Vatican's support of General Franco during the Spanish Civil War.

Pius also expressed his commitment to social and economic justice in his major encyclical *Quadragesimo Anno,* issued to commemorate the fortieth anniversary of Leo XIII's *Rerum Novarum.* Piux XI died in February 1939, and is remembered as a competent but not as an outstanding pope.

MICHAEL GLAZIER

See also CHURCH AND STATE; COMMUNISM; ENCYCLICALS, SOCIAL; LATERAN TREATY; PAPACY, THE.

PIUS XII, POPE (1939–1958)

Born into the Roman upper class, Eugenio Pacelli, the future pope, had a brilliant academic career. As a priest and prelate he was closely linked with the papacy. Named nuncio to Bavaria, eventually becoming nuncio to Germany, he was consecrated bishop by Benedict XV on 13 May 1917. In Germany he succeeded in negotiating concordats with Prussia, the bulwark of German Protestantism, and with other states. Returning to Rome to become Secretary of State in 1930, Archbishop (soon Cardinal) Pacelli shared Pius XI's concerns with dictatorships of different kinds in Europe and Russia and with the Spanish civil war. The future pope traveled more than any of his predecessors in the office of Secretary of State, to France, the United States, the Argentine, Hungary. The German Nazi government was a constant anxiety in Rome. We now know that Cardinal Pacelli continually protested by letters to the Foreign Ministry, sending one lengthy memorandum, a complete indictment of the persecution suffered by the Church. Why then did he sign a concordat with the Nazi regime? The answer was given in the encyclical *Mit Brennender Sorge* (1937) written by the Cardinal and the German cardinals and issued by Pius XI. It was a serious indictment of racism and its evil consequences, and the German hierarchy and representative lay people thought it would afford some legal support in their trying situation.

Pope Pius XII

In the first months after his election Pius labored to avert war. When it began, he worked incessantly to relieve the sufferings of its victims. That he did this on a vast scale for the Jews has been documented by Jewish scholars Jeno Levai, David Herstig, and especially Pinhas Lapide who, in his book *The Last Three Popes and the Jews,* shows that Pius saved 860,000 Jewish lives, more than all governments and agencies.

Pius was, in the life of the Church, immensely creative. Of his many encyclicals and pronouncements three were of capital importance: *Mystici Corporis Christi* (1943) on the Church; *Mediator Dei* (1947) on the liturgy; and *Divino Afflante Spiritu* (1943) on the Bible. He encouraged the missions, and he held two international congresses on the lay apostolate and gave full status to secular institutes.

Pius XII was especially a Marian Pope. He consecrated the world to the Immaculate Heart of Mary, 31 October 1942, defined the dogma of the Assumption, 1 November 1950, proclaimed the universal queenship of Mary, 1 November 1954, declared a Marian Year for the centenary of the dogma of the Immaculate Conception from 1953 to 1954, and for the centenary of Lourdes from 1957 to 1958, addressed many Marian congresses and institutes, supported every valid form of piety or apostolic endeavor, and canonized Marian saints, Louis Marie Grignion de Montfort, Anthony Mary Claret, Catherine Labouré, and Bernadette Soubirous.

MICHAEL O'CARROLL, C.S.Sp.

See also HOLOCAUST (NAZI); PAPACY, THE.

PLAINCHANT

See GREGORIAN CHANT.

PLANNED PARENTHOOD

See CONTRACEPTION.

PLATO (428–348 B.C.)

A Greek philosopher (428–348 B.C.) and a disciple of Socrates. He established a school on the outskirts of Athens near the grove sacred to Academus (hence known as the Academy which had a continuous life until its dissolution by Justinian in A.D. 529). Plato's philosophy is idealistic and dualistic insofar as it sharply divides reality into the illusory world of sense and the real world of "ideas" or better still "forms." Plato's literary legacy consists of his *Dialogues* whose literary artistry, philosophical depth, and moral seriousness are unrivaled. His thought has profoundly influenced Western thought as well as Christian theology, both Greek (e.g., Clement of Alexandria and Origen) and Latin (e.g., Augustine). Even Thomas Aquinas, who adopted Aristotle's philosophy, was heavily influenced by Plato. In mysticism his influence is no less extensive, especially in the writings of Pseudo-Dionysius.

PETER C. PHAN

See also APOPHATIC THEOLOGY; AUGUSTINE, ST.; PHILOSOPHY AND THEOLOGY; PLATONISM.

PLATONISM

Platonism is the philosophical system based on the thought of the Greek philosopher Plato (428–348 B.C.). Greatly influenced by his mentor, Socrates, Plato founded his own school, the Academy in Athens, and he summarized much of his work in the *Dialogues.* Platonism is best known for its "theory of ideas." Plato postulated a world of eternal, nonchanging and incorruptible forms or ideas. The world of sensible corruptible objects somehow "participates in" these forms in an imperfect way. Platonism teaches that the human soul is eternal, and that learning results when the soul remembers or "reminisces" its former life when it was united with these eternal ideas. Material objects give a shadowy impression of the forms they reflect, and the soul begins with them in its remembrance of the forms. The goal of the human person is to become like God (The Form of the Good). The person needs education, formation, and life in a well-ordered society to attain its end.

Platonism survived beyond the death of its founder, and it affected later philosophers including Plotinus (ca. 205–270). St. Augustine (A.D. 354–430) was affected greatly by Platonism, which influenced much of his thought and writings. Augustine's acceptance of Platonic thought had a profound impact on the medieval Scholastics, at least as great, if not more, than the influence of Aristotle. The Renaissance revived interest in Platonism, and it has continued to influence philosophers of many schools into the twentieth century.

ANTHONY D. ANDREASSI

See also AUGUSTINE, ST.; BONAVENTURE, ST.; DUNS SCOTUS, JOHN; ORIGEN; PHILOSOPHY AND THEOLOGY.

PLUNKETT, JOSEPH MARY (1887–1916)

Irish revolutionary born in 1887, he was the son of George Noble Count Plunkett, the distinguished antiquarian, art connoisseur and papal count. He was educated by the Jesuits and attended University College, Dublin, before he was sent on medical advice to live for several years in Italy and North Africa. He was of a poetic, even mystic, bent of mind and when he returned to Ireland in 1911 he became involved in the literary ferment of the time with his friend, Thomas MacDonagh, a university lecturer who taught him Irish. In addition to the writing and theatrical activities in which he became immersed, Plunkett also threw himself wholeheartedly into the separatist politics of the Irish Republican Brotherhood and the Irish Volunteers. In 1915, during the First World War, he went to Germany and the United States to secure support for an Irish insurrection against British rule. On his return he was ad-

Joseph Plunkett

mitted to the inner group of the I.R.B. by whom an armed rising was being planned: MacDonagh and Patrick Pearse were also members of this group and together with Plunkett they formed the core of intellectuals and poets who gave a rarified sense of high purpose to the Rising which broke out in Dublin on Easter Monday, 1916. Plunkett was very ill at the time, having just been discharged from hospital after an operation on his throat, but he joined Pearse in the General Post Office, the headquarters of the Rising. He also signed the Proclamation of the Irish Republic, which ensured that when the Rising collapsed he was sentenced to death by a British court martial, as also were Pearse, MacDonagh, and other leaders. On the night before his execution in May, 1916, he was allowed to marry his fiancée, MacDonagh's sister-in-law Grace Gifford, in the chapel of Kilmainham jail. A volume of his poems published by his sister shortly after his death included his most memorable composition, inspired by St. John of the Cross, the verses beginning "I see His blood upon the rose. . . ."

LOUIS McREDMOND

See also CATHOLICISM, IRISH.

POLYCARP, ST.
(TRADITIONALLY ca. 69–ca. 155)

Bishop of Smyrna (modern-day Izmir, Turkey) and one of the Apostolic Fathers. Polycarp was a leading figure in the Christian Church in the middle of the second century in Asia Minor who strongly opposed the Docetists, Marcionites, and Valentinian Gnostics. He is known to us from a letter written to him by Ignatius of Antioch as well as his letter to the Philippians and the account of the martyrdom of Polycarp. Irenaeus (according to Eusebius, *Ecclesiastical History* [hereafter *H.E.*] 5.20.6) said that when he was a boy he heard Polycarp speak of his relationship with John (the Apostle or Elder?) and others who had seen the Lord. Eusebius (*H.E.* 4.14.1) said that Polycarp was in Rome during the pontificate of Anicetus (ca. 154 to ca. 166) and discussed with Anicetus the date on which to observe Easter. The Church in Rome observed Easter on a Sunday, while the Churches of Asia Minor were accustomed to celebrate it on the fourteenth day of the Hebrew month Nisan (no matter what day of the week it would be in a given year). As a result of their meeting Anicetus did not change the Roman observance, but he had no problem with Polycarp continuing to observe Easter, the Christian passover, on 14 Nisan. Soon after his return to Smyrna, a persecution of Christians broke out. Polycarp went into hiding outside the city, but was betrayed by a slave and arrested. Proclaiming that he had served Christ faithfully for eighty-six years, Polycarp refused to disavow his faith in Christ and was burnt to death. The traditional date of his martyrdom is 23 February 155 or 156, but since Eusebius places it during the reign of Marcus Aurelius (161 to 180), some scholars would prefer to date his martyrdom in 167. Feast day, 23 February.

JOHN DILLON

PONTIFICAL BIBLICAL INSTITUTE

The closing decades of the nineteenth century, and the first years of the twentieth, saw the rise of several Catholic enterprises to meet the revolution in biblical and related studies. Among these were the Dominican Ecole Biblique in Jerusalem; the Benedictine Biblicum Studium in Montserrat; the Pontifical Biblical Commission; the Franciscan Studium Biblicum in Jerusalem; and the Jesuit Pontifical Biblical Institute, which was an idea of Leo XIII but came into existence under the aegis of Pius X in 1909. Originally this new institution of higher scriptural studies was an independent expansion of the Cursus Superior in Biblical Studies at the Gregorian University and only doctors of theology were accepted as full-time students. In 1916 it was allowed to give the baccalaureate and the licentiate in the name of the Pontifical Biblical Commission; and in 1928 it was designated to give all normal degrees in its own name.

In 1932 it expanded its program to study the ancient Near East and it has made significant contributions to that field. In 1927 the Institute opened a branch in Jerusalem and its expanded work included excavations; the editing of a Greek NT; and the publication of Hebrew and Greek dictionaries. Its distinguished publications include reviews such as *Biblica* and *Orientalia.* It also publishes scholarly monograph series including *Analecta Biblica* and *Analecta Orientalia.* The first decades of the Institute made lasting contributions to philology and Oriental studies rather than to biblical studies. This was due in part to the caution and conservatism of many on its faculty. This was changed during and after the rectorate of Augustin Bea (1930–1949) who also influenced the writing of the encyclical *Divino Afflante Spiritu.* Today, graduates of the Pontifical Biblical Institute are in the vanguard of Catholic biblical studies all over the world.

MICHAEL GLAZIER

See also BEA, AUGUSTIN, CARDINAL; BIBLICAL ARCHAEOLOGY; CRITICISM, BIBLICAL; ECOLE BIBLIQUE; THEOLOGY, BIBLICAL.

PONTIFICAL COUNCILS

The Roman Curia includes twelve pontifical councils which foster and promote various elements of Church life.

Pontifical Council for the Laity: Composed mainly of lay people, the council is concerned with lay participation in the life and apostolate of the Church.

Pontifical Council for Promoting Christian Unity: regulates, promotes, and coordinates Catholic ecumenical groups; studies the nature of ecumenism and implements the obtained results; undertakes dialogues with other Churches and ecclesial communities; sends Catholic observers to other Christian gatherings, and receives their observers; handles relations with individual members of other ecclesial communities. The council includes the Commission for Religious Relations with Jews.

Pontifical Council for the Family: concerned with the pastoral care of families with a view to their educative, evangelical and apostolic missions, including promoting the sanctity of life and responsible procreation. Members are lay people from various cultures the world over.

Pontifical Council for Justice and Peace: concerned with promoting gospel values and the social teaching of the Church.

Pontifical Council *Cor Unum:* provides information and coordinating services for Catholic aid and human development organizations worldwide.

Pontifical Council for Migrants and Travelers: concerned with pastoral assistance to migrants, nomads, travelers, and tourists.

Pontifical Council for the Apostolate of Health Care Workers: promotes works of study, formation, and action among the various international Catholic organizations in the health care field.

Pontifical Council of the Interpretation of Legislative Texts: gives authentic interpretations of the universal laws of the Church.

Pontifical Council for Interreligious Dialogue: promotes studies and dialogues with non-Christians; includes the Commission for Religious Relations with Muslims.

Pontifical Council for Dialogue with Non-Believers: studies the nature of atheism; promotes dialogue with non-believers.

Pontifical Council for Culture: facilitates contacts between the gospel message and the diverse cultures of the world.

Pontifical Council for Social Communications: studies modern instruments of social communication with a view to injecting the message of salvation, and of human progress, into civil culture and mores.

DAVID BRYAN

See also PAPACY, THE.

PONTIFICAL MASS

A Pontifical Mass is a solemn Eucharistic Liturgy celebrated by a bishop or abbot. The rite calls for participation by two deacons and a priest in addition to the other liturgical ministers. When the celebrant wishes to achieve the maximum solemnity, he presides at his throne; otherwise, he uses a faldstool. When a bishop celebrates a Pontifical Mass with his priests and people, this liturgy gives visible expression to the unity of the Church.

ANTHONY D. ANDREASSI

See also ABBOT; BISHOP; EUCHARIST.

POOR CLARES

See CLARE OF ASSISI, ST.

POOR, THE

References to the poor abound in the biblical tradition. The texts often tell us more about God than about poor people themselves. God, the Scriptures tell us, does not ignore those who are in need. God calls the people to care for each other, especially the poor among them. Basic to any understanding of the biblical teaching about the poor is the recognition that, while the poor are precious in God's eyes, their poverty is not.

Because God desires the fullness of life for the people, poverty stands as a sign that God's will is not yet fully accomplished. God's people, especially the leaders, are charged with care for the poor. They are to see to the needs of those who cannot care for themselves, who have no access to the goods of society (Ps 72:4). People who belong to a faithful and loving God who hears the cries of the poor (Ps 12:5) and acts to save those in need, must be and act in ways which reflect their belonging to this God. They, too, must act to save those in need.

The Scriptures do not intellectualize about the poor. They are not spoken of as hypothetical "cases," but as real human beings with real needs. The poor as a significant social group appear after the Exodus when the Promised Land is occupied and some people begin to have more than others. The rulers and those who profit from the status quo try to hide the presence and problems of the poor. The prophets, however, speak to make the poor visible. They are precious to God (and hence to the leaders) *because* they are needy, because they must depend upon God for their lives. The God revealed in Scriptures is one who cannot turn from those in need. The needy, therefore, are constant call and invitation to the mercy of God, the compassion of God's people.

The poor are vital to Jesus' proclamation of the kingdom. The beatitudes tell us that the poor are blessed because the kingdom of God is theirs (Luke 6:20). The reign of God, ushered in by Jesus, reverses values and turns worlds upside down. The unimportant become important, those who have nothing now have everything. They have the kingdom.

One particular group of poor has a special and important part in the biblical tradition. These are the *anawim,* the remnant, the people who survived both oppression and chastisement and who learned to rely totally on God. Created by God and protected by God, the remnant looked to God for salvation. According to the prophets, it is the *anawim* who would return to Israel, and it was from this group that the Messiah was to come (Mic 5:2-8).

The poor within the biblical tradition are challenge in that they remind us of the responsibility people of faith have for one another. They are special challenge to those who are leaders among the people—today's judges and "kings." The poor are also revelation. They tell us of a God who chooses to be close to the ones in need, the little ones. Their salvation is witness to God's fidelity. Their help is our hope.

JULIANA M. CASEY, I.H.M.

See also BEATITUDES; CHARITY; MERCY; SOCIAL TEACHING OF THE CHURCH.

POPE

See PAPACY, THE.

POPES AND ANTIPOPES, CHRONOLOGICAL LIST OF

until ca. 64	St. Peter
	Linus
	Anacletus
fl. ca. 96	Clement I
	Evaristus
	Alexander I
ca. 117–ca. 127	Sixtus I
ca. 127–ca. 137	Telesphorus
ca. 137–ca. 140	Hyginus
ca. 140–ca. 154	Pius I
ca. 154–ca. 166	Anicetus
ca. 166–ca. 175	Soter
175–189	Eleutherius
189–198	Victor I
198–217	Zephyrinus
217–222	Callistus I
217–ca. 235	*Hippolytus
222–230	Urban I
230–235	Pontian
235–236	Anterus
236–250	Fabian
251–253	Cornelius
251	*Novatian
253–254	Lucius I
254–257	Stephen I
257–258	Sixtus II
259–268	Dionysius
269–274	Felix I
275–283	Eutychianus
283–296	Caius
296–304	Marcellinus

308–309	Marcellus I
310	Eusebius
311–314	Miltiades
314–335	Sylvester I
336	Mark
337–352	Julius I
352–366	Liberius
355–365	*Felix II
366–384	Damasus I
366–367	*Ursinus
384–399	Siricius
399–401	Anastasius I
402–417	Innocent I
417–418	Zosimus
418–422	Boniface I
418–419	*Eulalius
422–432	Celestine I
432–440	Sixtus III
440–461	Leo I
461–468	Hilarus
468–483	Simplicius
483–492	Felix III (II)
492–496	Gelasius I
496–498	Anastasius II
498–514	Symmachus
498, 501–505	*Laurentius
514–523	Hormisdas
523–526	John I
526–530	Felix IV (III)
530–532	Boniface II
530	*Dioscorus
533–535	John II
535–536	Agapetus I

536–537	Silverius
537–555	Vigilius
556–561	Pelagius I
561–574	John III
575–579	Benedict I
579–590	Pelagius II
590–604	Gregory I
604–606	Sabinianus
607	Boniface III
608–615	Boniface IV
615–618	Deusdedit *or* Adeodatus I
619–625	Boniface V
625–638	Honorius I
640	Severinus
640–642	John IV
642–649	Theodore I
649–655	Martin I
654–657	Eugenius I
657–672	Vitalian
672–676	Adeodatus II
676–678	Donus
678–681	Agatho
682–683	Leo II
684–685	Benedict II
685–686	John V
686–687	Cono
687	*Theodore
687	*Paschal
687–701	Sergius I
701–705	John VI
705–707	John VII
708	Sisinnius

*Indicates antipope

708–715	Constantine
715–731	Gregory II
731–741	Gregory III
741–752	Zacharias
752	Stephen II
752–757	Stephen II (III)
757–767	Paul I
767–769	*Constantine
768	*Philip
768–772	Stephen III (IV)
772–795	Hadrian I
795–816	Leo III
816–817	Stephen V
817–824	Paschal I
824–827	Eugenius II
827	Valentine
827–844	Gregory IV
844	*John
844–847	Sergius II
847–855	Leo IV
855–858	Benedict III
855	*Anastasius Bibliothecarius
858–867	Nicholas I
867–872	Hadrian II
872–882	John VIII
882–884	Marinus I
884–885	Hadrian III
885–891	Stephen VI
891–896	Formosus
869	Boniface VI
896–897	Stephen VII
897	Romanus
897	Theodore II
898–900	John IX
900–903	Benedict IV
903	Leo V
903–904	*Christopher
904–911	Sergius III
911–913	Anastasius III
913–914	Lando
914–928	John X
928	Leo VI
928–931	Stephen VIII
931–935	John XI
936–939	Leo VII
939–942	Stephen IX
942–946	Marinus II
946–955	Agapetus II
955–964	John XII
963–965	*Leo VIII
964–966	Benedict V
965–972	John XIII
973–974	Benedict VI
974 & 984–985	*Boniface VII
974–983	Benedict VII
983–984	John XIV
985–996	John XV
996–999	Gregory V
997–998	*John XVI
999–1003	Sylvester II
1003	John XVII
1004–1009	John XVIII
1009–1012	Sergius IV
1012–1024	Benedict VIII
1012	*Gregory
1024–1032	John XIX
1032–1044	Benedict IX
1045	Sylvester III
1045	Benedict IX [for the second time]
1045–1046	Gregory VI
1046–1047	Clement II
1047–1048	Benedict IX [for the third time]
1048	Damasus II
1048–1054	Leo IX
1055–1057	Victor II
1057–1058	Stephen X
1058–1059	*Benedict X
1059–1061	Nicholas II
1061–1073	Alexander II
1061–1072	*Honorius II
1073–1085	Gregory VII
1080, 1084–1100	*Clement III
1086–1087	Victor III
1088–1099	Urban II
1099–1118	Paschal II
1100–1102	*Theodoric
1102	*Albert
1105–1111	*Sylvester IV
1118–1119	Gelasius II
1118–1121	*Gregory VIII
1119–1124	Callistus II
1124–1130	Honorius II
1124	*Celestine II
1130–1143	Innocent II
1130–1138	*Anacletus II
1138	*Victor IV
1143–1144	Celestine II
1144–1145	Lucius II
1145–1153	Eugenius III
1153–1154	Anastasius IV
1154–1159	Hadrian IV
1159–1181	Alexander III
1159–1164	*Victor IV
1164–1168	*Paschal III
1168–1178	*Callistus III
1179–1180	*Innocent III
1181–1185	Lucius III
1185–1187	Urban III
1187–1191	Clement III
1191–1198	Celestine III
1198–1216	Innocent III
1216–1227	Honorius III
1227–1241	Gregory IX
1241	Celestine IV
1243–1254	Innocent IV
1254–1261	Alexander IV
1261–1264	Urban IV
1265–1268	Clement IV
1271–1276	Gregory X
1276	Innocent V
1276	Hadrian V
1276–1277	John XXI
1277–1280	Nicholas III
1281–1285	Martin IV
1285–1287	Honorius IV
1288–1292	Nicholas IV
1294	Celestine V
1294–1303	Boniface VIII
1303–1304	Benedict XI
1305–1314	Clement V
1316–1334	John XXII
1328–1330	*Nicholas V
1334–1342	Benedict XII
1342–1352	Clement VI
1352–1362	Innocent VI
1362–1370	Urban V
1370–1378	Gregory XI
1378–1389	Urban VI
1378–1394	*Clement VII
1389–1404	Boniface IX
1394–1423	*Benedict XIII
1404–1406	Innocent VII
1406–1415	Gregory XII
1409–1410	*Alexander V
1410–1415	*John XXIII
1417–1431	Martin V
1423–1429	*Clement VIII
1425–1430	Benedict XIV
1431–1447	Eugenius IV
1439–1449	*Felix V
1447–1455	Nicholas V
1455–1458	Callistus III
1458–1464	Pius II
1464–1471	Paul II
1471–1484	Sixtus IV
1484–1492	Innocent VIII

1492–1503	Alexander VI	1605	Leo XI	1769–1774	Clement XIV
1503	Pius III	1605–1621	Paul V	1775–1799	Pius VI
1503–1513	Julius II	1621–1623	Gregory XV		
1513–1521	Leo X	1623–1644	Urban VIII	1800–1823	Pius VII
1522–1523	Hadrian VI	1644–1655	Innocent X	1823–1829	Leo XII
1523–1534	Clement VII	1655–1667	Alexander VII	1829–1830	Pius VIII
1534–1549	Paul III	1667–1669	Clement IX	1831–1846	Gregory XVI
1550–1555	Julius III	1670–1676	Clement X	1846–1878	Pius IX
1555	Marcellus II	1676–1689	Innocent XI	1878–1903	Leo XIII
1555–1559	Paul IV	1689–1691	Alexander VIII		
1559–1565	Pius IV	1691–1700	Innocent XII	1903–1914	Pius X
1566–1572	Pius V			1914–1922	Benedict XV
1572–1585	Gregory XIII	1700–1721	Clement XI	1922–1939	Pius XI
1585–1590	Sixtus V	1721–1724	Innocent XIII	1939–1958	Pius XII
1590	Urban VII	1724–1730	Benedict XIII	1958–1963	John XXIII
1590–1591	Gregory XIV	1730–1740	Clement XII	1963–1978	Paul VI
1591	Innocent IX	1740–1758	Benedict XIV	1978	John Paul I
1592–1605	Clement VIII	1758–1769	Clement XIII	1978–	John Paul II

MICHAEL GLAZIER

PORRES, MARTIN DE, ST. (1579–1639)

Born in 1579 in Lima, Peru, to a Spanish knight (John de Porres) and a former slave from Panama (Anna by baptism). At the age of twelve, Martin's mother apprenticed him to a barber-surgeon. Three years later, however, he was admitted to the Rosary Convent of the Friars Preachers at Lima, and subsequently became a professed lay brother.

He readily assumed responsibility for many duties—including those of barber, surgeon, wardrobe-keeper, and infirmarian—yet he did so, in the words of a fellow lay brother, "with great liberality, promptness, and carefulness, without being weighed down by any of them."

Martin also cared for the poor and sick of urban areas, helping to establish an orphanage and foundling hospital. He was put in charge of distributing the convent's daily alms of food to the impoverished, and he also accepted the responsibility of caring for the destitute slaves who had been brought to Peru from Africa. His protegé, Juan Vasquez Parra, described him as a practical and efficient administrator of the provisions he collected. He dedicated himself to meeting the physical and spiritual needs of those entrusted to his care, supplying them with blankets, shirts, and candles, and offering up his prayers for them.

Among his close friends were St. Rose of Lima and Blessed John Massias, also a Dominican lay brother in Lima. When Martin died on 3 November 1639, he was carried to his grave by prelates and noblemen. He was beatified in 1837 and canonized in 1962. In the U.S. and elsewhere, St. Martin is recognized as the patron saint of work for interracial justice and harmony. Among the biographical and devotional works on him are those by S. Fumet (1933, in French) and J. C. Kearns (1950).

JOSEPH QUINN

See also CORPORAL AND SPIRITUAL WORKS OF MERCY; DOMINICANS.

POSSESSION, DEMONIC

Among world religions, *possession* refers to the condition of a person, animal, place, or object believed to be under the control of a spirit, demon, ghost, witch, etc. Such control may be total or partial, continuous or intermittent, physical or psychological, and is regarded variously as harmful, beneficent, or even desirable. Christian teaching has generally attributed possession only to demons or Satan, regarding it as a manifestation of the power of evil in human experience but not necessarily the consequence of personal sin. Traditionally, possession is permitted by God in order to demonstrate the victory of grace and faith over the realm of evil in a way dramatically suited to times and places.

Early Hebrew belief recognized demons as part of creation, focusing on their ability to frighten, injure, or even kill the unwary. Under later Canaanite, Babylonian, and other Mesopotamian influences, psychological possession gradually came to prominence. By the time of Christ, exorcism—the ritual expulsion of demons or the liberation of the possessed person from their external control—had also acquired a prominent place in Jewish religious practice.

Although Jesus and his disciples cast out demons, the term *ekballein,* "to expel" (Matt 8:16; Luke 11:14), rather than *exhorkizein* was used of them in the Gospels. The practice was regarded as part of the healing ministry (Mark 1:34; Luke 6:18; 8:12; and also Acts 10:38, where the word *iaomai,* which also means "to heal," is used).

In early Christian practice, ritual exorcism was included in sacramental baptism, although "possession" in this respect was considered external and symbolic as well as collective. In liturgical practice, mentally disturbed persons (*energumenoi*) were placed under the care of ministers who came to be called "exorcists." The community routinely prayed for its "possessed" members, but they were not subjected to long rituals of exorcism such as those developed in the Middle Ages and Reformation era.

In recent centuries, belief in demons and other spirits has been progressively eroded by the development of science, medicine, and a dominant secular worldview. Instances of possession and exorcism have almost disappeared from Western civilization. But even as early as the sixteenth century, the likelihood that a supposed occurrence of possession was caused by suggestion, fear, social expectations, or other unknown physical or psychological factors, led to the distinction between true and false possession (pseudopossession). Today, despite the persistence of possession phenomena and the practice of exorcism among non-European peoples and among certain pentecostal and evangelical sects, true possession is considered so rare as to be clinically and pastorally negligible.

Conversely, pseudopossession occurs both randomly and in situations where it is accepted as an item of belief, whether or not accompanied by the practice of exorcism. Such instances include misinterpretations of neurophysiological conditions such as Tourette's syndrome and epilepsy, and alterations of consciousness occurring in trance states. The latter may be either voluntary, e.g., the practices of mediumship and theriomorphism (the acquisition of animal characteristics) among shamans, medieval berzerkers, Mau Mau terrorists, etc.; and transformations of personality in Voudouan, Macumban, and other rituals; or involuntary, e.g., hypnotic phenomena and dissociation states such as "cinematic neurosis"—imitative behavior induced when some highly suggestible persons are exposed to convincing portrayals of, e.g., fictional possession behavior or violent criminal activity in motion pictures, television, theatrical presentations, print media, etc.

Certain psychopathological reactions such as obsessive-compulsive disorders, schizophrenia, and multiple personality disorder can also mimic possession states, as can the effects of brain tumors or lesions, and the ingestion of drugs (e.g., LSD, peyote, mescaline, psilocybin, and other psychotropic agents), anesthetic reactions, and the side-effects of certain tranquilizers. Psychological dissociations resulting from involvement in séances, automatic writing, Ouija boards, etc., are commonly interpreted as possession states, especially in evangelical circles. So-called social "manias," riots (including those at sporting events), and mob violence may also display certain characteristics traditionally associated with possession.

Although some evangelical and especially pentecostal traditions continue to affirm the reality of true possession and foster the practice of public exorcism, as a whole Protestantism has tended to reject both possession and exorcism. In the Roman Catholic Church, the minor order of exorcist and the ritual of exorcism were suppressed after 1971, although both Catholic and Orthodox tradition continues to accept the possibility of possession and has admitted the practice of exorcism under normally strict control.

Paradoxically, while *demons* can be dismissed as elements of folk-belief and religious fantasy, especially as causes of physical and mental diseases once regarded with superstitious dread, the undeniably *demonic* element in human experience—the capitulation of individual and social control to forces beyond our awareness and will—testifies to the enduring reality of possession. It is to this dimension of the spiritual life that the ministry of Christian healing must address itself in the future.

RICHARD WOODS, O.P.

See also ANTHROPOLOGY, CHRISTIAN; DEMONOLOGY; EXORCISM.

POSTCOMMUNION

A brief prayer recited by the priest at Mass after the administration of Holy Communion. It is essentially a request that the Eucharistic celebration bring forth the graces associated with the Blessed Sacrament. The congregation participates in the prayer by responding "Amen."

JOSEPH QUINN

See also EUCHARIST.

POSTULANT

A candidate for membership in a religious order in a preliminary period of testing prior to acceptance into the novitiate. The length of postulancy varies according to the order and the circumstances of the candidate, but normally lasts several months, during which the candidate lives at a religious house of the community in which he or she would be professed.

JOSEPH QUINN

See also RELIGIOUS ORDERS.

POVERTY, EVANGELICAL

See EVANGELICAL COUNSELS; VOWS.

PRAXIS

A Greek word meaning deed or action, praxis is used in contemporary philosophy and theology in a special sense drawn from the thought of Karl Marx. It is not simply another word for practice. Practice is action based on an existing theory or doctrine applied to a particular case or situation. Praxis is engagement with reality out of which theory or doctrine is drawn. Marx was concerned with ready-made theories distorting perception of facts, and called this ideology. He wanted people to become conscious of the ideologies that distorted their perception of their own situation and experience. In contemporary theology, especially the political theology of J. B. Metz and the liberation theologies of Latin America, there is a strong awareness that some theological positions and creedal interpretations can function as ideologies in this pejorative sense, that is to say, they can be accepted in a way that distorts the truth of experience. Hence a constant plea from these theologians to acknowledge that praxis is the foundation of all theories and doctrines, and that the experiences of living Christian life in deep and practical commitment to redemptive activity in the world is the appropriate praxis to give rise to a true Christian theology.

MONIKA K. HELLWIG

See also CHRISTIAN SPIRITUALITY; LIBERATION THEOLOGIES; THEOLOGY, SYSTEMATIC.

PRAYER

Prayer is the expression of personal relationship to God. It is lifting of mind, heart, and soul to God. Prayer demonstrates loving consciousness of God and a purposeful opening of self to life shared in God. Prayer leads one into the presence and reality of God.

Prayer is association with the one in whom all "live, and move, and have being," out of whom, and in whose image humankind was formed, who is the fulfillment of life's journey. How much God loves and how much God gives are discovered and recalled in prayer. Here is found that something, that some place within self which will always call for exploration, that center which is home to God.

Prayer demonstrates that God is always present to each person, even when that person is absent to God. It makes visible the inexhaustible depths of God's presence within every aspect of daily life and within each being, illustrating that every person is an existence of God, a presence of Christ, a sacrament to the world. Prayer reveals and underscores the reality that no one is ever alone.

Christian prayer is Trinitarian, relationship to Father, to Son, and to Holy Spirit. It is dynamic, living, an ever-changing expression of self in and with each Person of the Holy Trinity, a sharing in the very life of God.

All prayer requires personal presence: mind presence and heart presence. It involves use of intellect, management of time, and focus of attention. With deepest confidence and love, spiritual communion with God is sought.

Types of Prayer

Prayer is universal. All are drawn to pray. Since the days of primitive humankind, prayer has been experienced as a hunger, a cry of the heart to make sense of this world. The sensation, then realization, of God's presence invites response; a call to speak to God, to acknowledge human dependence on God.

Recognizing the existence of God is prerequisite to prayer and is a prayer in itself. Humankind is naturally disposed to revere what is perfect, to rely on the supreme, to cherish what is good. Prayer is attentiveness to God, Divine Perfection, Supreme Being, Everlasting Goodness. Thinking about, waiting for, and meeting God are all manifestations of prayer. Putting aside the business of daily life to offer a space of time and attention to God is prayer, as are focusing total attention and awareness toward God's ever-present love, considering one's frailty before God, longing to absorb the light and love of the one who is light and love. Simply possessing the hope of being heard reveres God and is prayer. The human experience incites a turning toward God in petition, in gratitude, in adoration, and in reparation.

Petition. Petition is perhaps the oldest and most common movement behind prayer. Human dependence upon God provokes pleas for courage and assistance and bountiful life. Seeking God's intervention is itself homage, an act of confidence venerating God's benevolence and power as the source of all that is good.

Personal needs and desires bring requests of God for good health, security, and comfort for self, relatives, friends, and others. In times of threat or pain or loneliness, God's intercession or aid is sought. Personal gifts and spiritual blessings are requested. As such, humanity concedes its own smallness, shortcomings, weaknesses; and comes to God for grace, strength, forgiveness.

Petition strengthens kinship with God, recognizes that one is never alone. In petition, human dependence on God is accepted, and hopeful awareness of God's mercy and extravagant giving are embraced.

Gratitude. Gratitude, thanksgiving for innumerable gifts from the source, also inspires prayer. God's response to petitions is recognized and the recipient expresses heartfelt thanks. Unexpected "gifts" are bestowed, joys generated by the most common events of human existence. God is comprehended as "giver" of inexhaustible favors. In childlike appreciation, prayer responds to the wonders and joys of daily life by acknowledging and exhibiting appreciation to the one who has provided all.

Adoration. Adoration is the expression of fervent and devoted love, an offering of reverent homage to God's supreme dominion, and recognition of humankind's absolute dependence. Adoration is the deep worship due God alone. It venerates the absolute excellence of God and offers unconditional submission.

To adore is to praise God from the very depths of being, celebrating God's reality and presence. It is joyful awareness of personal relationship with the divine, God's life within individuals, and, reciprocally, personal life in God. Prayer of adoration imparts faith, hope, and love, and becomes a prayer of abandonment, an experience of poverty, of kenosis, of being emptied out; a prayer of unlimited expectations and yet no expectations.

Reparation. Bringing requests and hope for pardon before God is another type of prayer. The humble recognition of one's faults, sincere sorrow for using God's gifts offensively, and the desire to be reunited with his perfection further glorify God.

Forms of Prayer

Christian prayer takes many forms. Prayer is, paradoxically, both the most public and the most personal activity of human life.

Public Prayer. The most public common prayer resides in liturgical prayer: celebration of Mass, the sacraments, Divine Office, Benediction of the Blessed Sacrament. These public prayers of the Church recognize Christ as presider and are offered through him, with him, and in him. Public prayer unites individuals and prayer communities as the body of Christ. Community prayer, seeing and hearing the sincere prayer of others, nurtures personal devotion. Shared prayer has strength: the voices of many combine into one voice and one heart praising God.

Eucharist, the source and summit of Christian life and primary public Christian prayer, is also the most personal, the most intimate relationship. The call to holiness is principally rooted in Eucharist. In the prayer of Eucharist resides the personal presence of Christ manifest to each individual in a unique way. Christian daily prayer gravitates toward Eucharist as its center, and flows outward from Eucharist as its source. The Eucharist is the ultimate Christian prayer. "This is my body given for you. This is my blood shed for you." All Christian prayer begins and ends in the Eucharistic Prayer. Lives lived in Eucharist overflow with spiritual gifts and are compelled to share with those in need. Individuals enveloped in the Eucharistic Prayer become Eucharist themselves, feeding the hearts of all they encounter with Jesus' own life.

Scripture is the well-spring of Christian teaching. Here, God speaks! God communicates with each individually and specifically. The Bible continually provides a new message because each moment is new and accompanying personal needs are new. It is Scripture, the word of God, that is the reality and depth of prayer. The word imbeds itself in heart, mind, and soul releasing insight as seeds to mature in their own time. Reading and reflecting upon Scripture leads to discovery of self and life in God.

The *Divine Office* is a public prayer of the Church consecrating the entire day and night to the praise of God. Because the Church cannot gather daily in the ceaseless adoration that God deserves, monastic traditions have frequently included recitation of the Divine Office several times a day. Contemporary prayer of the laity also embraces the Divine Office not only as a source of devotion and a strengthening of personal prayer, but in the name of the entire Church on behalf of all humankind.

Tre Ore, the Trinity Prayer or Three Hour Prayer, is group prayer which includes elements of both public and personal prayer forms. The *Tre Ore* is comprised of one hour of adoration in silence before God, one hour of writing to record insights, and one hour of sharing those reflections with others. It is a prayer espousing Jesus' pledge that where two or three are gathered together in his name, he is there; something special happens. Here individuals gather to amplify their individual prayer, to bring out the best in one another, and to be united to and for one another and all others in God. It is recognized that to grow in prayer, one needs another person to help one be faithful, to respond to personal grace, with whom to celebrate the life within.

Personal Prayer. God is experienced by each individual in a singular way. This personal prayer integrates faith with daily life through recitation, spiritual reading, listening, mental prayer, and journaling.

Recitation is a common mode of personal prayer. Dedicating time and centering thoughts on God with memorized prayers, the rosary, litanies, or the Way of the Cross reverence God. These focus time and energy, rendering one present to God and inviting God's response.

Spiritual reading or *lectio divina* feeds and nourishes Christian prayer with the word of God. For some this method entails the complete reading of the Bible, book by book, each year. Others supplement or substitute the continuous reading with the reading of one or another book to coincide with phases of the liturgical year. Still others employ scholarly study of the Bible, integrating historic vision and traditional understanding toward serious understanding of the word.

In its monastic origin, *lectio divina* is a spiritual exercise fostering a life of prayer, and is maintained as a basic element of all spirituality. Such reading calls for special attentiveness and sacred motivation.

Listening is imperative to discover God's will. The "dialogue" of prayer implies a readiness to listen. Each prayer journey calls for constant openness to God's word. Spiritual listening requires eliminating self-interests and living sincere abandonment to God's will.

Mental prayer is any interior act of the mind and heart that unites one to God. It glorifies God and provides focused, reflective attention which draws and invites God's presence. Life within self is awakened to look at the outer world with wonder, excitement, and reverence. Thus, the creative act of God ever continuing in the world is intensely realized.

Recollection is the frequent recall of God's presence within self and a centering of attention on God's life within. It is a striving never to lose sight of God's proximity, even in the midst of the most absorbing matters.

Meditation is mental prayer in which the intellect and reasoning predominate. It is exercised by consciously placing oneself in the presence of God with an attitude of faith, adoration, and abandonment. The exercise of meditation is normally focused, guided by written material such as a Scripture passage, notes from spiritual reading, or inspirational thoughts. Meditation brings serenity and inner peace into daily commotion and aims to enrich one's relationship with God.

Affective prayer is a prayer form intermediate to meditation and contemplation intended to increase sharing in the mystery of Christ. Unlike meditation, it encompasses little or no reasoning. Devout affections predominate, and the heart is engaged to a greater degree than the mind. Affective prayer is distinguished from contemplative prayer because it involves numerous emotions.

Contemplation is heart, soul, and being affectionately gazing upon God. It is characterized by its simplicity of affection. Contemplation may be *acquired,* actively exercised as a simplified affective prayer, or *infused,* passively received as affections bestowed upon the contemplative by God. Contemplation bonds one's spiritual life with the reality of Divine Life. In contemplation one "knows" God and experiences the absorption of self into God, conforming to God, united with God.

Examen of consciousness entails an inventory taken in the presence of God. It can be an assessment of life and Christian practices or can focus on a specific time period, distinctive virtue, particular fault, or a precise point. The goal of an examen of consciousness is knowledge of oneself aimed at perfection and life in God.

Journaling (keeping a prayer journal) is another personal interactive prayer process. Writing cherished passages from readings and recording insights and reflections represent an entering into the mind and heart of Christ. Journaling facilitates discovery of self and relationship with God. It provides an avenue into prayer, an openness to contemplation, a celebration and remembering, a discovering, a centering. It "maps" one's prayer journey.

PERSONAL IMPACT

Discovering Self. In prayer, in relationship with God, one unavoidably develops a relationship to oneself as well. In all of creation there can be no direct experience of anything closer to God than one's own self. The closest proximity to God is experienced through life as self, as the singular being each individual is meant to be, in God's image and likeness. This reality provides the most personal sacrament of God and of Christ for humankind: the gift of oneself. The mystery of God dwelling within, the different forms of prayer, all of the sacraments, the whole of Scripture are to foster belief and life in that cumulative presence that is in each life, in one another, in God.

Prayer is not a thing, not words, not an action. It is life always evolving, always dynamic. Each person is a personal prayer. One's prayer is self at the deepest level of being. Prayer involves all that comprises identity. The exercise of faith, hope, and love has a very personal effect. Prayer unfolds not simply theological virtues that in some way reach out to God with the mind, but the reality that the deepest effect is within self. In prayer, it is the believer who is transformed and who becomes the vision that God gives, the prophecy that God utters.

Prayer is the deepest means of being present to oneself. The more one is present to God, the more present one becomes to self. Prayer demonstrates that to be present to God is to step deeper into oneself and into God's indwelling presence.

Overflow of Presence. Mary's *Magnificat* is the best paradigm, a wonderful pattern for personal prayer. Mary is fully present to herself. She does not hesitate to say "*My* soul," "*My* spirit," "all generations will call *Me* blessed." Out of her presence to herself, she was present to what God has done, is doing, will do. And in her presence to God she became present to the poor, the hungry, Israel, God's servant. The Prayer of Mary, the *Magnificat,* raises the question: If prayer doesn't lead us to the hidden Christ in the poor is prayer truly Christian?

The contemplative prayer of the ordinary Christian of our day is also Trinitarian. Silent adoration of the Father creates an ever-deepening capacity for the Son, the Word of God. When the Word is deeply experienced, one is compelled, through the Holy Spirit, to share him with others. Contemplation is the activity of the Holy Spirit drawing all into God.

Becoming One's Belief. In the maturation of one's prayer journey is encountered the most radical kind of prayer, a prayer that is believing and hoping and loving so deeply that the believer *becomes* that which is believed. There comes a time of personal experience of self as God's "light" in this world. A realization of the autobiographical nature of Scripture calls the faithful to answer the question, "Who is Jesus?", with the boldness of saying "I am." And each dares to believe Christ's promise that his followers can do even greater things than he has done. Prayer brings the knowledge that God exists, and that he loves and knows each individual by name. In prayer one finds that the power of God's heart and God's compassion resides within self.

Carrying God's Presence. Prayer draws the faithful into service as ambassadors for Christ, as his fellow workers. Personal relationship to God demonstrates that only within God can humankind be free and at peace. Christ alone can give the freedom, the hope, the faith, and the joy he so wishes everyone to know and experience. It is the recognition of Christ's presence within that makes one deeply Christian—that makes each individual one who is sent to create the presence of Christ among others. Through prayer is received an unlimited capacity to carry his presence, to open one another to his reality in all. Each one has a prayer that has never been prayed before. Each has a mysterious gift of prayer—for self and for others.

Praying Always. In a truly Christian life, there is no moment, no act which is not prayer. One's whole life becomes prayer. Prayer penetrates the entire day every day. In this fashion, prayer is a hope, an expectancy, a conscious awareness of his real presence. Life in prayer is life doing the work of Christ, is awareness that everything is gift and grace, is recognition of others as a presence of Christ.

The Lord's Prayer

Christian prayer is simply the prayer of Jesus internalized. Only Jesus can teach his prayer. How well the Lord's Prayer is known! Perhaps too well, in that it can be recited as words without being present to its reality. At times, it is good to pray it in reverse:

Deliver us from evil—the reality that surrounds humankind on all sides, that is amplified by the media every hour. *Lead us not into temptation*—it is easy to be seduced with the world, flesh, and devil. *Forgive us our sins as we forgive one another*—but people cannot forgive and be forgiven if You are not present, so . . . *Give us our daily bread*—personal faith, love, joy, one another. Because it is only in You, and with You, and through You that one can . . . *Do your will on earth as it is in heaven.* And in being faithful to Your word each day *thy kingdom comes*—in each mind and heart and overflows into the world. Then and only then is Your *name hallowed*—Your presence recognized and reverenced, *You who are in heaven*—the heaven created by Your indwelling presence in each heart. And You are called *Our Father*—because all have become brothers and sisters in the body of Christ, risen from the dead.

The Lord's Prayer represents all prayer. Every word focuses on God's glory, yet with a simplicity that is within the reach of all. The task of prayer is to lead one into presence, into readiness, into availability, into continuous consciousness of the One who has made a home within each person.

EDWARD FARRELL

See also CHRISTIAN SPIRITUALITY; CONTEMPLATION; MEDITATION; MYSTICISM.

PRAYER OF THE FAITHFUL

Also referred to as General Intercessions, these are the intercessory prayers offered during Mass in which the celebrant and congregation pray for a series of intentions, normally grouped in the following sequence: the needs of the universal Church and of civil authorities; the salvation of the world; the healing of the sick, liberation of the oppressed, and salvation of the deceased; and the needs of the local community. This litany of intentions is recited by a deacon or lay minister, and the congregation responds to each with a solemn invocation such as "Lord, hear our prayer."

JOSEPH QUINN

See also BIDDING PRAYERS; EUCHARIST.

PRAYER OVER THE GIFTS

The prayer recited by the priest at Mass following the offering of the bread and wine. It asks that the sacrifice of the Mass be acceptable and pleasing to the Lord in order that divine favor might rest upon the Church. Some versions also invoke the transubstantiation of the bread and wine.

JOSEPH QUINN

See also EUCHARIST.

PREACHING

Preaching falls into four categories. (1) *Pre-evangelization* is directed at the nondisposed nonbeliever and attempts to show how the gospel responds to the deepest needs of the human heart. (2) *Evangelization* is directed at the disposed nonbeliever and attempts to bring about an inner conversion in those preevangelized (Acts 2:14 ff.; 3:12 ff.; 10:34 ff.). It evokes a practical course of action: Repent and be baptized (Acts 2:38). (3) *Catechesis* is directed at the maturing believer and aims to deepen the moral and doctrinal teaching of the gospel already received. (4) *Mystagogical preaching* is directed at those initiated into and already formed in the faith and invites them as a liturgical assembly to enter more deeply into the very paschal mystery which the liturgy contains. This type of preaching like evangelization is also kergymatic in nature: i.e., it proclaims an event; it does not elaborate an intellectual doctrinal argument.

The term "sermon" applies to the first three forms and these usually occur outside the liturgy and are not related to the biblical readings of the liturgy, while the fourth is properly preached only in a liturgical context and in Roman Catholic parlance is called the *homily* to which Vatican II gives "pride of place" among all forms of preaching (DV 24). The roots of the word suggest familiar conversation as opposed to formal rhetoric.

While a homilist may from time to time feel the need to pre-evangelize, evangelize, catechize his congregation on a specific point within the liturgy these are not the normal tasks of the homily.

When the SC (no. 52) used the word "homily" it did not just mean any form of preaching in connection with the conferral of sacraments. It had in mind a very specific type of preaching with a unique purpose.

Vatican II returned to a premedieval tradition which sees the homily not as an interruption of but as *integral to the liturgy.* The homily's very position—between the Scriptures and Sacrament—indicates its distinctive purpose: i.e., what Jesus announces in his word (the cure of a paralytic or calming of a storm, etc.) he fulfills in the Sacrament. Every pronouncement, parable, and miracle of Jesus was ultimately a promise of the Spirit to be released by his glorification. This communication of the Spirit occurs in the Eucharist. The word itself, proclaimed and preached, involves a real presence of the risen Lord (SC 7; EM 9).

Like the evangelist the homilist proclaims that the marvels of the history of salvation are occurring *now* and that through the liturgy we are being inserted into that history: "*Today* this Scripture has been fulfilled in your hearing" (Luke 4:21).

The homilist, of course, must make use of the tools of biblical criticism in order to get at the literal meaning of the text without which he cannot exhort with confidence. But biblical exegesis is not the goal of the homily.

Fulfilled In Your Hearing (U.S.C.C., 1983) takes us beyond what the SC (nos. 35, 52) presented as the object of the homily when it states that the purpose of the homily is not merely to explain the Scriptures but to so use the Scriptures that they shed light on the meaning of human existence (20, 29). While Catholic preaching has become more biblical, homilists have not yet fully grasped this correlative factor.

A homily doesn't normally teach; nor is it moralistic. It should produce the awareness "The Lord is *again* doing marvels for us." Its inner dynamic should lead the congregation by means of the scriptural and preached word to "lift up (their) hearts" and "give thanks to the Lord our God" through the Sacrament about to be celebrated.

PAUL L. CIOFFI, S.J.

PRECENTOR

See CANTOR.

PREDESTINATION

See PROVIDENCE.

PREFACE

(Lat. *praefatio,* "A saying beforehand") A prayer of praise and thanksgiving to God which follows the Liturgy of the Word at the Eucharist. It is recited by the celebrant—in one of its many variations—between the opening dialogue ("Lift up your hearts . . .") and the praise of the Sanctus ("Holy, holy, holy Lord . . .").

JOSEPH QUINN

PRELATE

(Lat. *praelatus,* "one set before") A cleric with ecclesiastical jurisdiction by reason of his rank or office. The former includes all bishops, cardinals, and the pope. Prefects, vicars apostolic, abbots nullius, prelates nullius, and apostolic administrators also are prelates by virtue of their office, but cease to be so if they are not bishops when they give up their respective office. The higher officials of the Roman Curia are regarded as prelates, as are those with jurisdiction over religious institutes or societies of apostolic life (e.g., abbots and provincial superiors). Honorary prelates, or monsignori, are granted the title by the pope as a means of recognizing their service to the Church.

JOSEPH QUINN

See also HIERARCHY; MONSIGNOR.

PRESBYTERIANS

John Calvin (1509–1564), a second-generation Protestant Reformer, was born a French Catholic and converted to Protestantism in 1533. He moved to Geneva, Switzerland, where he came under the influence of Ulrich Zwingli (1484–1531) who had provided, in his Reformed movement, a Protestant alternative to Luther. The Reformed tradition was motivated less by Luther's interest in personal salvation and more in Christians obeying God's will as found in the Bible.

Calvin continued the work of Zwingli and became the systematic theologian of the Reformation with the writing of his *Institutes of the Christian Religion,* probably the most important doctrinal statement in all Protestantism.

John Knox (1505–1572), a Scottish Reformer and Calvinist, actually started what is called Presbyterianism. The latter became a significant force behind the Puritans and the Non-Conformists of seventeenth-century England.

"Presbyterianism" came to America in the 1600s by way of the Dutch Reformed Christians who founded New Amsterdam (New York) and the Puritans who landed at Plymouth Rock. The Middle Atlantic states of New York, New Jersey, Delaware, and Pennsylvania eventually contained the most Presbyterians.

Within a century they were making sizable contributions to the educational, political, and economic life of the colonies. Presbyterians were almost always highly educated and were so active in political resistance to England in pre-Revolutionary America that the House of Commons called the revolution "a Presbyterian Rebellion." At least fourteen of the signers of the Declaration of Independence were Presbyterians.

Francis Makemie, who came to the colonies in the late 1600s, became known as the "father of American Presbyterians" because of his important leadership in organizing the newly arrived immigrants from Scotland, Ireland, England, and Holland.

In due time, along with other Protestant denominations, Presbyterians divided over the issue of slavery—one group becoming the Presbyterian Church, United States, the southern branch, and the other becoming the United Presbyterians in the United States, the northern branch. In 1983, both united to form the Presbyterian Church in the United States of America (PCUSA), now the fourth largest Protestant denomination in America with over 3.5 million members. Smaller Presbyterian bodies, e.g., The Reformed Presbyterian Church, tend to be more conservative than the mainline larger liberal denomination.

Presbyterians take theology very seriously, as the Calvinist tradition would suggest. Like the Lutherans, they are a creedal and confessional Church; the Westminster Confession is their normative guideline for doctrine.

Calvin's distinctive emphasis among the Reformers was the "sovereignty of God"; that sovereignty is found in God's revelation in Christ and in the Bible. From this emphasis on the power and freedom of God emerged the doctrine of predestination or election. Because people are sinful and every dimension of human life is "depraved" we are powerless to effect our salvation. That belongs entirely in the hands of a sovereign, holy God, argued Calvin. This God selects those who will be saved as well as those who will be damned independent of human freedom. This rather harsh doctrine was Calvin's attempt to show how important it was to give *God* credit for our salvation. Jonathan Edwards (1703–1758), a famous American Calvinist preacher, reflected this sterner fabric of Calvinism in his sermon "Sinners in the Hands of an Angry God." Today Presbyterians have modified the more severe elements of this doctrine while retaining the centrality of God's sovereign power and appreciating the mystery of God's saving work. Presbyterians tend to stress the first person of the Trinity.

Another implication of the sovereignty of God was Calvin's attempt at theocracy in Geneva. He was determined that all of life—political, social, religious, economic, and recreational, would be ruled by God. Furthermore, Calvin was so afraid that something else would come in between the worshiper and that sovereign God that he was forced to destroy the "idols" of religious art, stained glass, ritual, priestly garments, and organ music. Of course, most Presbyterians today have regained an appreciation of many of these essential aspects of religious life.

The Presbyterian worship service is dignified and orderly, with an emphasis on the sermon, which is a rational, teaching discourse intended to interpret the Bible for the edification of the believer. The community of faith is important for Presbyterians because people finally come to know the truth of the Bible by associating with God's people who worship, study the Bible, and live according to the will of God found in Scripture.

Presbyterians are typically Protestant with a belief in the Trinity, the authority of the Bible, salvation by grace, and the traditional Christian creeds. They believe in infant baptism and observe the Lord's Supper as a Memorial Meal rather than a meal in which Christ's Body and Blood are present.

The Church's name is derived from the presbyterian polity it practices. This model is based on the New Testament order of *presbyteros,* Greek for "elder." There are teaching elders who are the ordained clergy. There are also ruling elders, lay people elected by the congregation who form a Session who supervise the spiritual life of the local congregation. In addition, a Board of Deacons administers necessary works of charity and the Trustees are in charge of the property.

A number of Sessions make up a Presbytery; a number of the latter comprise a Synod. Every year a General Assembly reviews and sets policy for the entire denomination. A local congregation "calls" its minister with the aid of the Presbytery.

IRA ZEPP

See also PROTESTANTISM; REFORMATION, THE; THEOCRACY.

PRICE, THOMAS FREDERICK, M.M. (1860–1919)

Thomas F. Price, a cofounder of Maryknoll, was born in Wilmington, North Carolina, in 1860. Following studies at St. Mary's Seminary in Baltimore, he was ordained in 1886, becoming the first native North Carolinian diocesan priest. For twenty-five years he was a traveling missionary serving U.S. Catholics and appealing to non-Catholics. In 1897 he founded a national Catholic magazine, *Truth.*

Thomas F. Price, M.M.

With his sister, Catherine, a religious, he founded an orphanage near Raleigh, where he also established a center for priests and seminarians recruited for missionary service. In 1911 Price joined Fr. James A. Walsh in organizing the Catholic Foreign Mission Society. Appointed Superior of Maryknoll's first mission to China in 1918, he died in Hong Kong the following year. Price's spirituality was marked by missionary zeal, openness to martyrdom, and a mysticism in which union with Christ was experienced through a profound relationship with Mary and Bernadette of Lourdes.

JANET CARROLL, M.M.

See also MARYKNOLL.

PRIDE

See CAPITAL SINS.

PRIESTHOOD, THE MINISTERIAL

The term "ministerial priesthood" combines two related but different notions: priesthood and ministry. The distinctively Christian understanding of priesthood is rooted in the person and destiny of Jesus. From an early date his life and especially his death were understood in sacrificial language. His love, obedience, and fidelity constitute the perfect sacrifice which brought forgiveness and reconciliation to the world. The Letter to the Hebrews speaks of the risen Christ as the great high priest who once and for all entered into the heavenly temple where he continues to intercede for us.

Through faith and baptism all Christians receive Christ's Spirit and become members of his body. Together they form a "holy priesthood" called "to offer spiritual sacrifices acceptable to God through Jesus Christ" (1 Pet 2:5). Included in such sacrifices are all aspects of Christian life: worship and prayer, love and mutual service.

The word ministry is rooted in the New Testament term for service, *diakonia.* Jesus, who came not to be served but to serve, is the model of Christian ministry. In the broadest sense ministry refers to the whole range of services by which the community of faith is built up. The ordained ministry is a particular form of ministry, an officially recognized form that is blessed and graced by a special sacrament.

NT authors speak of those who exercise leadership in the Church as *episcopoi* or overseers, as presbyters or elders, as teachers and prophets, as pastors and deacons. Nowhere, however, do they call them priests. This may have been because of a fear of confusing the Christian ministry with the priesthood of Judaism or of paganism. It may also reflect a sense of how profoundly the life of Jesus transformed the very notion of priesthood.

In the course of the second century the traditional Catholic division of the ordained ministry into episcopacy, presbyterate and diaconate became the norm. At the end of the same period the word priest began to be used for the bishop. Later it was extended to the presbyterate. In the medieval period the presbyterate is seen as embodying what Catholics understand by the ministerial priesthood. The emphasis is on the Eucharist. In Scholastic theology the priest is above all someone who is empowered through ordination to offer the Eucharistic sacrifice.

At the Reformation, Luther and others, while emphasizing the importance of the ordained ministry, rejected the priestly understanding of it. Luther restricted the word priesthood to Christ and to that sharing in Christ's priesthood that belongs to all the faithful. In response, the Council of Trent (1545–1562) insisted on the priestly quality of the ordained ministry. It drew a parallel between the Old and New Testaments. Just as God called Aaron and his descendants to be priests of the first covenant, so at the Last Supper Jesus ordained the apostles priests and entrusted to them the sacrifice of the Eucharist.

The emphasis on the priestly quality of the ordained ministry brought in its wake a distinctive image of the Catholic priest. He was a man set apart, a celibate, a religious person called to render present in his life and in his liturgical activity the sacrifice of Jesus. Although priests had many other pastoral and liturgical responsibilities, the theology and spirituality they were given throughout the post-Tridentine period focused on the Mass.

Vatican II marked a shift in the Roman Catholic understanding of the ministerial priesthood. Prior to the council, a number of bishops and theologians, especially in Western Europe, were concerned not only that the traditional theology was one-sided in comparison with the teaching of the NT, but that it was also insufficiently evangelical. The inroads of secularization in France in particular required a greater emphasis on preaching and on missionary outreach. The first task of bishops and presbyters, such people affirmed, is to proclaim the gospel, to draw people to faith and to the community of faith. Nor was preaching to stop there. The centrality of faith to Christian life demands that ordained ministers make the strengthening and deepening of faith one of their primary concerns. On this point, modern needs were leading people back to the NT. There the most important tasks of the apostles as well as of local Church leaders were preaching and teaching.

In developing its understanding of the ministerial priesthood, Vatican II appealed to the practice and theology of the early Church. There the emphasis was on the bishop rather than on the presbyter. The communities were more like present-day parishes than dioceses, and each was led by a bishop. He preached and presided at the Eucharist and at the other sacraments. Together with the presbyters and deacons, he tried to respond to the social and spiritual needs of the community. The office was a pastoral one, an office of religious leadership which, given the nature of Christianity, involved teaching and liturgical functions. The model was Christ, the Good Shepherd. In and through the bishop, the risen Christ was thought to continue his pastoral, priestly and prophetic activity in the midst of the community.

In defining for the first time the sacramental nature of the episcopacy, Vatican II placed the bishop at the center of its theology of the ordained ministry. In spelling out the content of such ministry, it had recourse to the traditional threefold office of Christ as priest, prophet, and king or shepherd. All three areas pertain to the ordained ministry, at both its episcopal and presbyteral levels. At both levels the council emphasized its corporate nature. To be ordained as a presbyter is to become a member of a local presbyterium or community of presbyters who are called to collaborate with the bishop in serving the local Church.

The insistence of Vatican II on the breadth of tasks involved in the ordained ministry has led to some confusion. People have tended to stress one or other of the elements and to play down the remaining two. Some have insisted on pastoral leadership, others on preaching and teaching, and others, finally, on the idea of priesthood. Clearly all three belong together even if in practice individual presbyters, especially those belonging to religious orders, might in their ministry focus on one or the other of them.

The emphasis at the council on the priesthood of the faithful and on the importance of the active participation of all the baptized in the life and mission of the Church, has, in the eyes of some, undermined the identity of ordained ministers. In response, recent statements of the magisterium have tended to stress the distinctiveness of the priesthood. The priest is said to represent in a special way Christ, the head and shepherd of the Church, and to be called, particularly in the sacraments, to act in his person and in his name. The emphasis on the relation of the ministry to Christ needs to be balanced by an awareness of its relation to the community as a whole. In the liturgy ordained ministers also act in the name of the Church. The Christological approach, moreover, needs to be balanced by a pneumatological one. All ministerial functions, as indeed the whole life of the Church, are carried out under the impulse and in the power of the Spirit. One of the tasks of ordained ministers is precisely to foster and coordinate the many gifts and ministries that the Spirit inspires within the community for its well-being.

Since Vatican II there has been considerable debate about both the ordination of women and the requirement of celibacy for the ministerial priesthood. The latter question is a disciplinary one. The official rationale for the present law is that there is a particular affinity between the ministerial priesthood and celibacy. Among the many arguments of those who favor a change, emphasis has recently been given to current needs. The centrality of the Eucharist to Church life demands that sufficient numbers of priests be available to provide for it. If the law of celibacy is a hindrance here, it should be changed.

The magisterium of the Roman Catholic Church maintains that it is unable to ordain women to the ministerial priesthood because of the practice of Jesus, the apostles, and the Church throughout the ages. This continuing tradition is interpreted as an indication that the present practice is rooted in the divine will. When theological arguments are offered in explanation, use is made of marital imagery to describe the relation between Christ and the Church. It is suggested that the nature of this relationship gives a sacramental significance to the masculinity of Christ that can only be maintained by an all-male priesthood. Both the appeal to tradition and the argument from symbolism are rejected by large numbers of theologians and of the faithful. The debate will clearly continue.

The model of the ordained ministry operative at Vatican II reflects in many ways the responsibilities of a diocesan bishop or of a parish priest. In them one most easily sees the coming together of the teaching, priestly, and pastoral offices. At the present, the precise meaning of the ministerial priesthood of members of religious orders, especially of those who are only tangentially related to the pastoral ministry, is somewhat unclear. Some efforts have been made to address this issue, but they have not as yet been able to establish any consensus.

In order to make the above overview of the teaching of Vatican II on the ministerial priesthood complete, one would also have to consult what the council said on such topics as liturgy, the laity, charisms, and the role of the Church in the modern world. Because the ordained ministry is an ecclesial office, a service dedicated to the well-being of the Church, everything that touches on the nature and mission of the Church has implications for its understanding and exercise.

DANIEL DONOVAN

See also MINISTRY.

PRIMACY OF THE POPE

The primacy of the pope, the quality of being *first,* which according to Catholic teaching belongs to the Bishop of Rome, developed over many centuries. This doctrine is rooted in the New Testament description of Peter, the growing importance of the Church of Rome in the early centuries, and reached its fullest expression in the First and Second Vatican Councils.

The Gospels describe Jesus as choosing a group of twelve disciples to carry on his ministry after his death. To one of them, named Simon, Jesus gave the surname of Peter or Rock (Mark 3:16) and said that upon this rock he would build his Church (Matt 16:18). Simon Peter is the most frequently mentioned disciple in all four Gospels, appears first in every list of the Twelve, and is shown acting as their spokesman, both during the earthly ministry of Jesus and in announcing the resurrection of Jesus, as described in Acts 1–15. Jesus prayed for Simon Peter that his faith might not fail so that he might strengthen his brothers (Luke 22:32), and he is the one who received from Jesus the threefold command to feed the Lord's sheep (John 21:15-17).

Peter ended his days as a martyr for the faith in Rome and from the beginning the Roman Church held a unique position. Ignatius of Antioch wrote of it as "presiding in love." It was a symbol of the unity in faith of the Churches spread over the Mediterranean world, and served as a norm of orthodoxy in settling disputes which arose between local Churches. The culmination of centuries of leadership may be found in the papacy of Leo I (440–461), who was the first pope to declare expressly that the Bishop of Rome succeeded to the fullness of power conferred on Peter by Christ.

The practical implications of this primacy continued to develop in the life of the Church over the centuries. The most detailed exposition of the primacy was fashioned at the First Vatican Council. The bishops were concerned to vindicate the authority of the pope as independent of any other human power, secular or ecclesiastical, and as universal in its scope. They taught that the Roman Pontiff holds supreme authority over each and all Churches, all pastors and faithful, not only in matters of faith and morals, but also in those pertaining to discipline and government.

Unfortunately, the political situation in Italy in 1870 did not permit the council to continue with its planned treatment of the role of the other bishops in preaching, teaching, and governing in the Church. This task was taken up at the Second Vatican Council, which reiterated the teaching of Vatican I on the nature of papal primacy, but helpfully located it in the context of a collegial exercise of authority by all the bishops in the Church. The entire episcopate, including the Bishop of Rome, succeeds as a college to the college of the apostles under the leadership of the pope as successor to Peter, the head of the apostolic college. The college of bishops holds supreme authority in the Church but only in relation to the pope, who is "pastor of the universal Church."

WILLIAM C. McFADDEN, S.J.

See also APOSTOLIC SUCCESSION; PAPACY, THE; PETER, ST.

PRIOR

Refers to the superior in some religious houses. Benedictines and Cistercians recognize three kinds of prior: the claustral prior, who is second in command in an abbey, the simple or obedientiary prior, who is superior of a dependent priory and who is selected by the motherhouse abbey, and the conventional prior who is the independent superior of an independent priory.

PATRICIA DeFERRARI

See also RELIGIOUS ORDERS.

PRIORESS

Refers to the superior of a community of women religious. Her role approximately corresponds to that of a male prior. In the Roman Catholic Church, strict use of the term refers only to convents with papal approval and whose members have taken solemn vows.

PATRICIA DeFERRARI

See also NUN.

PRIORY

Denotes the houses of most monastic orders governed by a prior or prioress. Priories of some orders, particularly Benedictine, may be either conventual (that is autonomous with the right to elect their own superior) or simple (i.e., dependent on an abbey).

PATRICIA DeFERRARI

See also RELIGIOUS ORDERS.

PRIVATE PROPERTY

The concept of property refers to the social rules governing the allocation of material resources (tangible or corporeal objects such as land and manufactured goods) and immaterial resources (intangible or incorporeal goods such as stocks and shares, profits, rents, copyrights and patents). Private property systems resolve the question of allocation by establishing a juridical relationship of ownership between persons (individual or legal persons such as corporations) and material and immaterial objects. In both common and civil law systems, legal title to property generates property rights which confer direct and immediate authority over the possession, use or management, enjoyment, and disposition of property. Although these "incidents" of ownership may vary across societies (e.g., social rules may limit the power of transmitting property rights in inheritance), and be combined in various ways (e.g., the differing rights of landlord and occupant), they distinguish regimes of private property from regimes of common property (e.g., national parks or reserves) or collective property (e.g., socialized means of production). Legal systems of private property, moreover, may distinguish the original and derivative acquisition of property rights; correlative immunities, powers, privileges, and liabilities; personal and real property (realty); movable and immovable property; and goods of production and consumption.

Private Property in Scripture

The Scriptures recognize private property yet subordinate property claims to God's salvific purposes. The Deuteronomist depicts Israel as God's "private possession" (Deut 7:6-8); the land is a divine inheritance preserved in covenantal fidelity to the Torah (Gen 24:35; 30:30; Deut 4:1-5; 8:7-20; 11:8; 28:11-14). Psalm 37 describes those who possess the land as the "meek" who "wait for the Lord" and "the righteous" (Ps 37:9-11, 29). Lest any Israelite be deprived of the blessings of the land (Lev 25:23-34; Deut 4:40; Josh 14:9; 1 Kgs 21:3), the Torah provides for the right of redemption of patrimonial land (Lev 25:25-28); the general remission of debts in the Sabbath or fallow year (Exod 23:10-11; Lev 25:1-7; Deut 15:1ff., 12ff.); and the restoration of the land to its original owners or their heirs in the Jubilee Year, the culmination of seven Sabbatical years (Lev 25:8ff.). The Prophets recall Israel to the demands of covenant fidelity and condemn those who "turn aside the needy from justice and rob the poor of my people of their right" (Isa 10:1-3; 1:11ff.; 3:14ff.; Jer 6:18-21; 7:4-7; 22:13-17; Ezek 16:49; 22:29; 45:9ff.; Hos 4:1-3; 6:6; Amos 5:21-27; Mic 6:6-8).

In the New Testament, Jesus announces the eschatological Jubilee in his messianic proclamation of "good tidings to the poor" (Luke 4:16ff.; 7:22; Isa 61:1ff.). The imminence of the "day of the Lord's favor" demands trust in the loving providence of God and the renunciation of "unrighteous mammon," for in Jesus' reign, the "meek shall inherit the land" (Luke 12:22-32; 16:9; Matt 5:4; 6:25-34), as "a people to be God's personal possession" (1 Pet 2:4-10). Jesus' parables condemn the "deceit of riches" and the idolatry of covetousness (Matt 6:24; 13:18-23; 19:16-26; Mark 4:13-20; 10:17-31; 12:41-44; Luke 8:11-15; 12:16-21; 16:13, 19-31; 18:18-30; 21:1-4). The disciples are to imitate Jesus who though "rich in faithful love" (Eph 2:4-5) "became poor, so that by his poverty (they) might become rich" (2 Cor 8:9; cf. Matt 6:2-4, 20-21; Luke 6:30; 11:37-44; 12:33-34; Acts 9:36-43; 10:2-4, 31; 24:17, 1 Cor 7:30). The primacy of the great command of love (*agapē*) inspired the primitive, voluntary "communism" of the early Jerusalem Church (Acts 2:44-45; 4:34-35; 5:1-11), and the generosity of the Churches of Macedonia (Acts 11:29-30; 24:17; Rom 15:26-28; 1 Cor 16:1-4; 2 Cor 8-9; Gal 2:10).

Property in the Church's Tradition

The theme of faithful stewardship of the earth's riches (Matt 25:14-30; Luke 16:1-15; 19:12-27; 1 Cor 4:7) is elaborated in the patristic period (cf. Basil, *Hom.* I in Ps 14.5; John Chrysostom, *Hom.* in 1 Tim 11, *De Lazaro,* 2.4, 6ff., *Hom.* in Rom 11.5; Ambrose, *In Psalm.* 118.8.22; Augustine, *In Joann. Ev.* 50.6, *Enarratio* in Ps 147, 12; Gregory the Great, *Regulae pastoralis liber,* pars III, ch. 21). In the words of Clement of Alexandria, the "poor in spirit" regard property as a divine gift administered "for the sake of the brethren" (*Quis div. salv.* 16:3) for "it is monstrous for one to live in luxury, while many are in want" (*Paedagogus* 2, 119, 2-120, 5). Those who would imitate the divine munificence, writes Cyprian, must be "common and just in gratuitous bounties" (*De unit. ecc.* 25), since those who hoard their treasures are but "robbers and thieves": in Basil's words, "the bread which (they) withhold belongs to the poor" (*Hom. in illud Luc.*: "Destruam . . ." 1; cf. also, Chrysostom, *Hom.* XII on 1 Tim 4). Gregory Nazianzen attributed the origin of private property to the "envy and quarrelsomeness" of the Fall, a motif recurring in Franciscan theology and the writings of Zwingli and Melancthon (*Hom.* XIV, 25). Nature's "common right," wrote Ambrose, was usurped by greed into "a right for a few" (*De off.* 1.18.132; cf. *De Nabuthe Jez.,* 53ff.).

Augustine's belief that private property was an institution of positive rather than divine law was systematically elaborated in the writings of Thomas Aquinas (*In Joann. Ev.* 6.25-26, *Ep.* 93.12.50). The natural law, for Thomas, decreed the common finality of external goods and the general "right" (*dominium*) over their use; private property rights arise as a "positive" specification "added to natural law" for our benefit and perfection. Distinguishing the incidents of "care and disposition" and "use," Thomas argues that the private "care and disposition" of external goods are "legitimate," and "indeed necessary for human life" inasmuch as (1) persons are more likely to care for what they possess themselves, (2) "human affairs are more efficiently organized if the proper care of each thing is an individual responsibility," and (3) "peace is better preserved" if persons are content with their own property (ST II-II, q. 66, arts. 1, 2, 6; cf. q. 57, a. 3). With respect to the "use" of property, Thomas contends that one "should not possess external things as one's own alone, but for the community, so that one is ready to share them with others in cases of necessity" (ST II-II, q. 66, a. 2; cf. ST I-II, q. 94, a. 5; ST II-II, q. 32, a. 5; *De Regimine Principum,* Bk. 1, chs. 15, 17). The positive right to private property thus presumes the natural obligation of securing the "common good" of the community; indeed, Thomas admits that "in cases of necessity everything is common property" (ST II-II, q. 66, a. 7). The Thomistic heritage was transmitted in the Renaissance through the writings of the Spanish Scholastics, Francisco de Vitoria, Luis de Molina, and Francisco Suárez.

Modern Church Teaching on Property

With the eclipse of the medieval ideal of the common good in modernity, various justifications were offered for the institution of private property, i.e., the right-based arguments of John Locke and G.W.F. Hegel and the utilitarian arguments of Jeremy Bentham and J. S. Mill. Recurring to the earlier natural law tradition, modern Roman Catholic social teaching offered a *via media* between the "liberalistic individualism" of laissez-faire capitalism and the revolutionary criticism of Karl Marx (*Divini Redemptoris,* 29). Leo XIII's *Rerum Novarum* denounced the socialization of the means of production, yet recognized the natural right of the industrial proletariate to just remuneration and retention of the fruits of labor (RN, 43–47; cf. 3, 5-10, 20, 32-33, 40). "The utter poverty of the masses" was to be ameliorated through a broad dissemination of the natural right to (consumptive and productive) property (RN, 1, 22, 33, 47). Pius XI's *Quadragesimo Anno* defended the institution of private property as a bulwark against undue restrictions of personal liberty and as an effective means of satisfying basic human needs (QA, 45–51). For Pius XI and his successor, Pius XII, the accumulation of wealth and property "remains subordinated to the natural scope of material goods and cannot emancipate itself from the first and fundamental right which concedes their use to all" (AAS 33, 198–199; cf. QA, 49, 57–58, 61, 78–80, 114–115; Pius XII, *La Solennità,* 31–33).

Like his predecessors, John XXIII derives the right to private property from "the fruitfulness of labor," while affirming the common finality of material goods (MM, 112, 119). *Mater et Magistra* defends the right of private property as "a safeguard" and "stimulus" for "the exercise of liberty" and "the rights of the human person" (MM, 109–112). Yet the *personal* right to property presupposes the correlative *social* duty of ensuring not merely a broader, but a more equitable distribution of property rights so that all "in the community can develop and perfect (themselves)" (MM, 73–74, 112–115). In *Pacem in Terris,* John insists that the right to private property is qualified by other universal human rights deriving from the inherent "dignity of the human person" (PT 9, 21–22, 60, 63, 84, 139; cf. MM, 65, 75, 77, 92–93, 97, 104, 120).

The Pastoral Constitution on the Church in the Modern World of Vatican II reaffirms that private ownership, as an "expression of personality," represents "an extension of human freedom" offering an "incentive" for persons to fulfill their "function and duty" in "society and in the economy" (GS 71). Yet property's "social quality," deriving "from the law of the communal purpose of earthly goods," subordinates private property rights to the global common good (GS 69–71). In his encyclical, *Populorum Progressio,* Paul VI treats of property rights in terms of "integral" development: ownership must foster the good "of the whole (person)" and of "every (person)," especially the victims of "oppressive social structures" originating in the "abuses of ownership" and "power" (PP 14, 21–24, 26, 48–49; cf. also OA *[Octogesima Adveniens]* 43–44; *Justice in the World,* ch. 1).

In *Laborem Exercens,* John Paul II argues that "the only legitimate title" to capital is that it "should serve labor," promoting the "solidarity" of laborers and of the poor (LE 32–37, 63–69; SRS 28–31, 39). *Sollicitudo Rei Socialis* insists that the right to property bears a "social mortgage" deriving from the priority of the "subjectivity of human labor" over capital (LE 52–58; SRS 42). John Paul thus recognizes not only the legitimacy of labor unions and of socializing certain means of production, but of workers' participation in policy-formation, management, and ownership (LE 64–69, 94–10, 102). With the demise of European communism, *Centesimus Annus* commemorates the centennial of *Rerum Novarum* by reaffirming "a society of free work, of enterprise and of participation" in which "the economic sector is . . . circumscribed within a strong juridical framework which places it at the service of human freedom in its totality" (CA 35, 42; cf. 6, 11–13, 19, 24, 30–43, 48, 61). For further reference, see Jeremy Waldron, *The Right to Private Property* (Oxford: Clarendon Press, 1988); Martin Hengel, *Property and Riches in the Early Church,* trans. John Bowden (Philadelphia: Fortress Press, 1974); Justo González, *Faith and Wealth* (San Francisco: Harper and Row, 1990); Donal Dorr, *Option for the Poor,* rev. ed. (New York: Orbis Books, 1992).

WILLIAM O'NEILL, S.J.

See also ENCYCLICALS, SOCIAL; SOCIAL RESPONSIBILITY, FINANCIAL; SOCIAL TEACHING OF THE CHURCH.

PROBABILISM

Probabilism is a moral system which addresses the question whether one is free from or bound to obey a law when there is serious doubt if the law exists or if it applies to one's situation, and when this doubt cannot be resolved through further study. Probabilism establishes a presumption in favor of freedom provided that there are serious reasons in favor of freedom from the law and that the application of the law to this situation is not certain.

WILLIAM C. McFADDEN, S.J.

See also THEOLOGY, MORAL.

PROFESSION OF FAITH

A profession of faith is an outward expression of the Christian faith. In the Eucharistic Liturgy, the profession of faith is the "symbol" of faith (creed) which verbally expresses the basic tenets of the Christian faith. The Church has officially used three professions of faith: the Athanasian Creed, the Apostles' Creed, and the Nicene Creed. Each has a particular emphasis and was composed as a response to different theological questions or disputes. The Nicene Creed, a compilation of creeds from the church of Caesarea, the Council of Nicaea (325), and the Council of Constantinople (381), is used in the Latin Church at Mass on all Sundays and solemnities and is considered to be an integral part of the liturgy.

ANTHONY D. ANDREASSI

See also CREEDS.

PROFESSION, RELIGIOUS

See RELIGIOUS LIFE, ACTIVE.

PROOF OF THE EXISTENCE OF GOD

See EXISTENCE OF GOD.

PROPHECY OF SAINT MALACHY

St. Malachy was born in Armagh in 1094. He held several important ecclesiastical and monastic positions in Ireland, including that of archbishopric of Armagh. He was a friend of Bernard of Clairvaux and helped to introduce the Cistercians to Ireland. Malachy died at Clairvaux, and Bernard wrote his life. He was canonized in 1199. Malachy always had close ties to Rome. He introduced the Roman Liturgy to Ireland, he asked Pope Innocent II (1130–1143) to grant the pallium to the archbishops of Cashel and Armagh, and he served as papal legate in Ireland. This allegiance to Rome may explain his place in the so-called *Prophecy of Saint Malachy,* first published in Venice in 1595, in which Malachy prophesies about Pope Celestine II (1143–1144) and his 111 successors. Supposedly Malachy was in Rome when he had a vision of the popes who would rule to the end of time. Malachy composed an account of this and gave it to Innocent II to console him by assuring him of the continuance of the papacy in spite of contemporary difficulties. The popes were given mystical titles and characterized by some trait or by an allusion to their families or places of birth. The papal names include some taken by popes who reigned in subsequent centuries, such as Pius IX and Leo XIII. The *Prophecy* provides specific information up to 1590 but then becomes (understandably) rather ambiguous. This forgery had nothing to do with the historical St. Malachy.

JOSEPH F. KELLY

See also CATHOLICISM, IRISH; PROPHECY/PROPHET.

PROPHECY/PROPHET

In the Hebrew Bible the common term for a prophet is *nābîʾ* which may mean either "called" or "calling." The usual translation of this word in the Greek Old Testament is *prophētēs,* i.e., one who speaks for or on behalf of another. Prophets, therefore, are those who communicate in various ways God's message to the community of faith.

Early biblical prophecy includes such figures as Moses (Num 11:24-30), Deborah (Judg 4:4), and Abraham (Gen 20:7). Though different from the later literary prophets (e.g., Isaiah—see below), such early prophets do suggest inspired persons or those under special divine protection.

Ecstatic prophecy emerges around the time of the monarchy in Israel and continued thereafter. One hears of Samuel presiding over a band of prophets in a frenzied state (1 Sam 19:20-21), of Saul stripping himself of his clothes and entering an emotional state (1 Sam 19:22-24), of Elisha falling into a state of seizure at the sound of music (2 Kgs 3:15), etc. Scholars continue to debate the degree to which ecstaticism played a role in later prophecy. However, it is clear that the sixth-century B.C. prophet Ezekiel describes himself as seized by the "spirit" and the "hand of Yahweh."

Classical prophecy is usually associated with that line of fearless spokespersons that left such an impact on the religion of Israel. Such classical prophecy emerges in the eighth century B.C. in Israel in the persons of Amos, Hosea, Isaiah, etc. It is commonplace to designate these spokespersons as the literary prophets since their names are associated with the body of prophetic literature that forms the conclusion of the Christian Old Testament (see Bible, Old Testament Writings). W. Brueggemann speaks about two dimensions of the prophetic office, particularly among the classical prophets. The first is the criticizing dimension. God's spokespersons must tell it the way it really is, i.e., they must denounce evil and attempt to win back their audiences from the clutches of royal business as usual. The second is the energizing dimension. These spokespersons must also tell it the way it can be, i.e., they have to provide the possibility of hope for their disillusioned and despairing hearers.

"The Prophet Isaiah," by Michelangelo, fresco detail, Sistine Chapel, Vatican

Prophecy is also a reality in the New Testament. Both men and women functioned as prophets in the Churches (Acts 21:9; 1 Cor 11:4-5). According to Paul, prophecy is a gift of the Spirit given to individuals for the good of the community (1 Cor 12:10, 28-29). A later interpreter of Paul, the author of Ephesians, sees prophecy as fundamental to the very structure of the Christian community (Eph 2:20; 3:5). It is hardly surprising that Jesus is perceived to be a prophet (see Luke 4:16-30; 7:16). He is God's spokesperson who communicates his Father's message of concern, exemplifying both the criticizing and energizing dimensions of that office.

Prophetic Books according to Roman Catholic Canon: Isaiah; Jeremiah; Lamentations; Baruch; Ezekiel; Daniel; Hosea; Joel; Amos; Obadiah; Jonah; Micah; Nahum; Habakkuk; Zephaniah; Haggai; Zechariah; Malachi.

JOHN F. CRAGHAN

See also BIBLE, NEW TESTAMENT WRITINGS; BIBLE, OLD TESTAMENT WRITINGS.

PROPORTIONALITY

The principle of proportionality has to do with the relationship between actions and their consequences. It is an element in the just war theory, although as a moral principle it is not limited to that concern. It states that there must be a proportion between the evil produced by the war and the evil hoped to be avoided or the good hoped to be attained. In the context of self-defense it means that the evil brought about by the means of self-defense should not be greater than the evil brought about by the aggression. With regard to the use of nuclear and/or other weapons, even in a just war the United States Conference of Catholic Bishops in *The Challenge of Peace: God's Promise and Our Response* (1983) invokes the principle of proportionality. Accordingly the advantages achieved by the use of these means must not be disproportionate to the harms reasonably anticipated to follow from their use.

JOHN F. CRAGHAN

See also CHRISTIAN MORALITY; JUST WAR; THEOLOGY, MORAL.

PROTESTANTISM

Protestantism is that form of Western Christianity that does not recognize papal authority. It accentuates the role of the Bible and grace in Christian life. The term derives from the "Protestatio" of the German princes and free cities to the Diet of Speyer in 1529. They protested the decision to uphold the edict of the Diet of Worms that would have led practically to the abolition of the Lutheran territorial Churches. One should note the positive dimension of the term "Protestant," viz., "to witness, testify."

The roots of Protestantism are earlier than Martin Luther's posting of the ninety-five theses in 1517. John Hus of Bohemia (ca. 1369–1415) took issue with papal authority and strongly reacted to the neglect of the Bible and the doctrine of grace. Indeed Hus had been influenced by John Wycliffe of England (ca. 1329–1384) who championed the superior authority of the Scriptures over the papacy. However, the permanent Protestant cause occurred in the sixteenth century. Martin Luther in Germany, John Calvin and Ulrich Zwingli in Switzerland, and Reformers in the Netherlands, Scotland, and especially in England, broke with Roman Catholicism. Today the term "Protestant" embraces not only Lutherans,

Calvinists, Anglicans/Episcopalians, but also later groups such as Methodists, Baptists, etc.

As Protestants did away with papal authority, they underlined the role of the Bible. The translation and distribution of Bibles were central to the Protestant cause. Most Protestants took the Good News of Jesus as the very core of their biblical tradition. God's gift to humanity culminates in Jesus' atoning death and life-giving resurrection. It is faith, not good works, that justifies the Christian.

In the area of institutions Protestants tend to divide up power, although Anglicans/Episcopalians and some Lutherans have retained the office of bishop. Generally it is the local congregations that enjoy most authority. Indeed, in some Protestant traditions local congregations are totally independent. Although laity and clergy possess the same status before God, clergy have a special status because of preaching and administering the sacraments.

Sunday morning is the traditional time for Protestant worship. In general, Protestants favor a more word-oriented form of service that culminates in the preached word. Protestant communities are singing churches where the laity share in the singing of hymns. The Lord's Supper or Eucharist and baptism are the only "sacraments" recognized by Protestants. Their liturgical calendar focuses on Christmas, Easter, and Pentecost, with little concern for feast days honoring the saints.

JOHN F. CRAGHAN

See also CALVIN, JOHN; LUTHER, MARTIN; LUTHERANS; PRESBYTERIANS; REFORMATION, THE.

PROVIDENCE

Providence is a central Christian belief. Vatican I expresses it as follows: "God protects and governs by his providence all those things he created, 'reaching from end to end powerfully and ordering all things well' (cf. Wis 8:1). 'For all things are naked and open to his eyes' (Heb 4:13), even those that will occur through the free action of his creatures."

This belief has its own difficulties in our time. In part this is due to some elements traditionally associated with the belief, such as the view of Augustine and many of his followers that God predestines some to eternal life by an absolute decree and lacks such a decree for others before any consideration of their merits or demerits. In part it is due to the view of many scientists that what order there is in the physical world has come about simply by chance. Many difficulties come from experiences of evil, personal or social, such as the Holocaust, or from the sense that belief in God's providence has instilled in the poor a passivity and in the wealthy a complacency, leading them to view their states of life as God's design and will. Practically speaking, many Christians are influenced by a view our culture widely accepts, namely, that our human future depends, for better or worse, on our own or our society's cleverness and choices, not on God's design. This is due to a modern historical consciousness that is at least in practice largely naturalistic, i.e., many act as though only the human is operating in history—human agents, goals and resources. In our fragmented world, a large design in history is difficult to see.

Scripture

There is belief in a divine providence outside Jewish and Christian traditions, e.g., in Stoicism and Neoplatonism and in other religious traditions. Our Christian understanding of God's providence depends first of all on a recovery of the biblical message. The word is a translation of a Greek word (*pronoia*) that is used only several times of God in the OT (Job 10:12 [LXX]; Wis 6:7; 14:3; 17:2) and means God's plan or foresight. But the reality it expresses is found throughout the OT, and its meaning is gradually illuminated by the way God actually governs Israel. For example, the Exodus experience, covenant, and entrance into the Promised Land were seen as the result of God's care and design for the people. God's design was shown also in the Law and in the words God gave the prophets for particular critical circumstances. The prophets had to correct false interpretations of God's care or providence (see Jer 7:4; Ezek 18). The experience of the Exile led to a deeper understanding of God's ways. Deutero-Isaiah expressed God's creative activity more clearly than his predecessors, and so also God's care as embracing all peoples (Isa 44:7). And this may have contributed to the editing of the first chapters of Genesis to proclaim that God has a covenant with and cares for all peoples (Gen 9). After the Exile, the Book of Job showed that the mystery of God's providence was not sufficiently understood by the Deuteronomic code (Deut 7:9-13; 11:26-28). And apocalyptic literature, particularly Daniel, acknowledged that in the present age the powers of evil seemed to be prevailing; Jews were being killed *because* they were faithful to God. But it promised that in the age to come God will give the kingdom, a universal and eternal kingdom of justice, to one like a Son of Man, and those who were faithful would rise from the dead (Dan 7; 12:1-3). God's design or providence will prevail. Confidence in God's fidelity led to doxology: "the plan of the Lord stands forever" (Ps 33:11). God's providence is a mystery of faith to be trusted in all circumstances, not an object of sight.

In the NT Jesus proclaimed God's loving care and providence, using the beauty of the field and the birds of the air to illustrate it (Matt 6:25-34). He proclaimed this as a more intimate mystery by constantly speaking of God as "Father." He, however, experienced the darkness from which the apocalyptic message had earlier come. In the midst of the seeming triumph of evil, he spoke of himself as the Son of Man who, though about to be put to death, would rise from the dead and be vindicated (e.g., Matt 8:31). Human opposition will not thwart God's designs for Jesus, or for the kingdom of God and the faithful.

The apocalyptic message is an essential part of God's providence. Providence is usually ascribed to God as creator. But the NT ascribes it also to God as redeemer through Jesus specifically as by his death, resurrection, and exaltation he has been made Christ and Lord (e.g., Rom 1:3; Acts 2:36). This means that he is given the functions of God to save and judge—to achieve God's purposes in history over all that opposes these purposes. The first Christians may well have initially thought Jesus would be Lord when he comes again at the parousia, for the word "salvation" initially meant what he would give at that event (e.g., 1 Thess 1:10; 5:9; Rom 5:10; 10:9, 13). But they quickly realized that what Jesus would do when he came again he is already doing *in part* through sending the Holy Spirit, through sharing with his disciples an anticipation of the messianic banquet in the Eucharist, through sending them to proclaim the Good News and thus give people an opportunity for salvation, through being with his disciples in the Church. There is a sense then that God's providence is being exercised from the *future* by Jesus who has gone into the fullness of the kingdom and acts on and through his disciples from there. This is not counter to God's providence as source of creation and history, but rather fulfills and liberates creation and history from the powers of evil that hold sway. Already such powers are being thrust back. There are already within history partial instances of that salvation and that judgment (e.g., the destruction of Jerusalem in A.D. 70) that Jesus will exercise when he comes again. In what is generally recognized as his theology of history (Rom 9–11), Paul shows some elements of *how* God will bring his designs to fulfillment through his gifts of grace that are deliberately "frustrable" or resistible and in spite of the opposition of human beings.

Some Reflections on Providence in Christian History

Several key reflections on this theme in history are the following. Augustine had a great influence on later thought concerning that part of God's providence that is called predestination. In his writings against the Pelagians, he so stressed that our faith and good works come from God's grace that he ascribed human salvation to an absolute decree of God—predestination. In this he misinterpreted Paul's teaching (see Rom 8:28-30), who meant by predestination that God gives the fulfillment of baptism when God justifies the sinner; Paul meant this as encouragement to all believers, and he realized that those who were predestined could still fall and become castaways (Rom 11:20-22). Predestination is a gift that can be resisted (see Farrelly, *Predestination, Grace and Free Will,* Washington, D.C.: Newman Press, 1964, Council for Research in Values and Philosophy). Many in the West, both Protestant and Catholic followed Augustine in his views, and these views contributed to an anti-Christian spirit in the modern age.

A second element of Augustine's and, later, Thomas Aquinas' interpretation of God's providence or design to save is found in what is called the "exitus-reditus" (creatures coming from God and returning to God) context of theology. Influenced by Plotinus, Augustine saw all stages of being coming from God, and our return to God by God's grace as a turn from domination by the external to the internal, from body to spirit and hence to God. The incarnation—God becoming human so that in turn human beings could become divine by grace—became more the model of our return to God than the earliest Christian perspective on the parousia and the present influence of the exalted Christ. This reflected a measure of influence by the Greek cyclical view of history upon Christianity that was perhaps helpful for a largely agricultural society. But in our period of historical consciousness, it is important to understand our return to God as an opening of ourselves to the coming kingdom of God as the fullness and liberation of history rather than as an interior ascent that too easily supports those Christians who resist needed historical change.

A third element of reflection on providence in Christian history is found in the Enlightenment and its consequences. In the seventeenth century Newtonian physics showed people the order of the physical world, and this led many to interpret God's design more by this than by Scripture. It led also to a deism that viewed God as establishing the universe and its natural laws in the beginning, but then removing Godself from guidance of the world. Particularly in the eighteenth century, there emerged modern historical consciousness and so the sense that historical forms of government and society were human creations, a sense followed by the American and French revolutions toward the end of that century. And in the nineteenth century, there was a heightened sense of the centrality of freedom as the human goal (e.g., in Hegel), and a gradually widespread revolt against God as limiting human autonomy. Moreover, Darwin's view of evolution undermined for many a sense that nature reflects God's design. Atheistic humanisms developed from these tendencies, and in the twentieth century achieved great power in new paganisms such as Nazism, Communism, and American naturalism—all of which are heresies against Christian belief in providence, and all of which have sacrificed multitudes of human beings to gain some vision of an earthly paradise.

A Contemporary Theology of Providence

Three central elements of a contemporary theology of providence are the following. In the first place, we need to give central importance to what we find in the NT's understanding of the apocalyptic nature of the kingdom of God and Jesus' Lordship—a matter that is given primacy in their own ways by some futurist eschatologies of our time (e.g., Pannenberg, Moltmann). Also, in relation to this, there has recently been a new recognition that Jesus' ministry to mediate the kingdom of God included a strong concern to address such questions as poverty and the political peace of Jerusalem, to the extent of making efforts to overcome systemic social and economic injustice. This was integral to the kind of salvation he sought to bring about, not as a substitute for final salvation but as a partial instantiation of it in the present. By emphases such as these, political and liberation theologians have sought to correct some interpretations of providence that led to passivity among the poor and acceptance of systemic injustice among the rich, as though men's and women's current states in life could be accepted uncritically as coming from God.

Secondly, we must have a Christian anthropology that integrates modern historical consciousness. God acts providentially with human beings in accord with their nature. Even in nature lower than humans the existence of purpose is being more widely accepted; some even speak of the anthropic principle, namely, that from its first moments the universe seems to be oriented toward the evolution of human beings. With human beings God achieves God's purposes through time, in accord with their personal and the social character, as a lure operating through their constitutive human good that is historically conditioned and by appealing to their freedom. In part this means that God has given history into our hands to shape as cocreators. For better or worse human beings are responsible for the historical future of themselves and their societies, even to the point of possibly destroying the world by a nuclear cataclysm. God's providence uses human agency and holds human agency responsible to a moral order that respects the dignity of the individual person and seeks his or her integral development. The court of history is in part God's court, as a partial anticipation of that final assize in which all will see that God has been faithful and just in history, and that God's providential design has triumphed.

Thirdly, God's providence should be seen as a Christian mystery—though other religions have some sense of this too—that we should respond to by belief, trust, and action. While some of our experiences offer reassurances of the reality of God's care, others can lead us to doubt it; we are called to have Christ's dispositions (Luke 24:46) in all circumstances. This belief does not detract from human creativity but calls it forth both to discern God's plan to some extent as it is pertinent to us, accepting the insecurity of our limited knowledge, and to cooperate with it.

M. JOHN FARRELLY, O.S.B.

See also CREATION; KINGDOM OF GOD; THEOLOGY, PROCESS.

PROVINCE

An ecclesiastical province is a group of dioceses headed by a metropolitan archbishop. Normally such dioceses border each other. In the U.S., most ecclesiastical provinces follow the geographic boundaries of the states and include all dioceses within a state.

A religious province is a territorial division of a religious order under the jurisdiction of a provincial superior.

PATRICIA DeFERRARI

See also ARCHBISHOP; BISHOP.

PROVINCIAL

Major religious superior of a regional division or province within a religious institute. He or she is responsible to the superior general of the institute and has authority over the houses in the region. The provincial is normally elected by the provincial chapter, subject to approval by the superior general, and serves a term for a specified number of years, never for life. The provincial's chief function is to oversee the administration of the province and supervise the religious life of the houses.

PATRICIA DeFERRARI

See also RELIGIOUS ORDERS.

PRUDENCE

See VIRTUE.

PSALMS

The psalms are the prayer book of ancient Israel and the spiritual patrimony of the Christian Church. They reveal how Israel responded to the words and deeds of God. While some psalms clearly derived from settings outside the sanctuary, the majority seem to have been composed originally for liturgical purposes. This was the insight of S. Mowinckel who insisted that the "I" of the psalmist corresponds to the "we" of the community.

Words and Meanings

The Greek verb *psallein* means to pluck or pull. In the context of musical instruments it signifies playing a stringed instrument with the fingers. In the Greek Bible it means singing to a harp. *Psalmos* is, therefore, a song sung to the accompaniment of a harplike instrument. While *psaltērion* (in English Psalter) is such a harplike instrument, it also denotes a collection of psalms.

The Hebrew title for this book in rabbinic and later literature is *t*^{e}*hillîm,* i.e., praises. Just as the Greek terminology implies the musical setting of the psalms, this Hebrew title amply suggests the theological thrust of Israel's prayer.

Numbering

The Hebrew Psalter contains 150 songs. Owing to a different separation of certain psalms the corresponding number in the Greek Psalter (the Septuagint) is different. The rule of thumb is that the numbering in the Greek Psalter (later followed by the Latin Vulgate) is one digit behind the Hebrew. The translation of the psalms adopted here, viz., the revised text of the *New American Bible,* follows the Hebrew numbering. It is worth noting that many traditional English translations of the psalms are frequently a verse number behind the Hebrew text since they do not consider the superscriptions (see below) as a verse.

Superscriptions

The superscriptions are titles or notes that stem from pre-Christian Jewish tradition. They provide information about authorship. For example, seventy-three psalms are linked to David, although the actual dating of such psalms is exceedingly difficult. The superscriptions also provide notes about the nature of a particular psalm, e.g., Psalm 4 is to be sung to the music of stringed instruments. The superscriptions may also indicate the mode for singing, e.g., Psalm 69 is to follow the melody of "Lilies." Still other superscriptions focus on liturgical use, e.g., Psalm 30 is a song for the dedication of the Temple. Finally some titles seek to supply historical background, e.g., Psalm 51 reflects David's prayer after his adultery with Bathsheba.

Formation

In its present form the Psalter is divided into five books after the manner of the Pentateuch or the five books of Moses. They are: (a) 1–41; (b) 42–72; (c) 73–89; (d) 90–106; (e) 107–150. Each book ends with a doxology or expression of praise (41:14; 72:18-19; 89:53; 106:48). Psalm 150 serves as the doxology for the fifth book as well as for the Psalter as a whole. However, this division is clearly an artificial arrangement since the psalms are a collection of collections. For example, Psalms 42–49, 84–85, 87–88 are psalms of Korah, Psalms 73–83 are psalms of Asaph, and Psalms 120–134 are psalms of ascents. Psalm 40:14-18 (from Book One) is almost identical to Psalm 70 (from Book Two).

Parallelism

The chief characteristic of Hebrew poetry is parallelism, i.e., a balancing or rhyming of thoughts. Although scholars continue to debate the nature of Hebrew poetry and discuss the refinements of parallelism, it seems useful to focus on three traditional types of parallelism. The first is synonymous parallelism, i.e., the second line balances the first in meaning. For example, "When Israel came forth from Egypt, the house of Jacob from an alien people" (Ps 114:1). The second is synthetic parallelism, i.e., the second line develops or expands the first. For example, "For the Lord is the great God, the great king over all gods" (Ps 95:3). The third is antithetic parallelism, i.e., the second line is in opposition or contrast to the first. For example, "The Lord watches over the way of the just, but the way of the wicked leads to ruin" (Ps 1:6).

The Rhythm of Life and Different Types of Psalms

The American biblical scholar W. Brueggemann has pressed the question of the function of the psalms. Thus he investigates the use Israel made of these prayers. He concludes that there are different types or genres of psalms that are appropriate for different stages in the rhythm of human life. The first stage is orientation. In this stage the person does not experience any devastating shocks or upsetting blows. A sense of security, harmony, and balance characterizes this stage. The second stage is disorientation. In this stage the person experiences the loss of the stability found in orientation. A feeling of devastation, despair, disillusionment typifies this stage. The third stage is reorientation or new orientation. In this stage the person overcomes the disaster of disorientation. A sense of newness, grace, and gift sums up this stage. Although one has regained the balance of orientation, it is only as a result of dealing with and working through disorientation.

To be sure, this rhythm of life approach does not exhaust the richness of the psalms. However, it may serve as a useful way for discussing many, but not all, genres or types of psalms.

Hymns or Psalms of Descriptive Praise. Hymns or psalms of descriptive praise envision an ongoing situation or condition. They offer praise to Yahweh because Israel's God regularly and consistently provides for the needs of God's people. Such care and concern are demonstrations of God's ongoing creation. This is clearly the world of orientation.

The structure of these psalms is relatively simple. In the introduction the psalmist declares his intention to praise God or he may invite others to join in the praise. In the main section the psalmist provides motives for such praise. In the conclusion the psalmist usually restates the elements of the introduction. For example, in Psalm 113 the psalmist begins with the invitation to praise the Lord. As motives for praise, the psalmist cites God's ongoing care for the poor and the barren woman. The psalm concludes with: Hallelujah, i.e., praise Yahweh. (For other examples of this type of psalm see Pss 8; 19; 29; 65.)

Psalms of Trust or Confidence. These psalms probably evolved from the laments. At a time of disorientation protestations of trust or confidence were the reasons for God to act on behalf of the psalmist. As independent psalms, these compositions attest to a world of stability and balance. One senses here the God who is completely reliable. Some common motifs are the security of the child on its mother's lap (Ps 131:2), intimacy with God (Ps 16:9-11), and exclusive attachment to God (Ps 125:1-2).

Psalm 23 is a familiar example of this type of psalm. There are two main images: (1) shepherd and (2) host. As shepherd, the Lord sees to the flock's needs of water, pasture, and protection against wild animals. As host, the Lord entertains the psalmist by meeting all the rubrics of hospitality, e.g., anointing the head with oil. (For other examples of this type of psalm see Pss 11; 62; 91; 121.)

Wisdom Psalms. Wisdom psalms reflect on the possibilities and the problems of living before God. They also offer advice on how to live that life. Hence they are related to such wisdom books as Job, Proverbs, and Ecclesiastes/Qoheleth. These psalms portray the world of orientation. They present a black and white world where virtue is always rewarded and evil punished. They inculcate such virtues as responsibility and diligence. Their hallmark is fear of the Lord, i.e., a profound respect for God's person that carries over into action.

Psalm 1 is a good example of this kind of psalm. It opens with a beatitude, an expression of the enviable state of the person described: "Happy those who do not follow the counsel of the wicked. . . ." The psalmist offers images of both the righteous and the wicked. Like a tree planted near streams of water the righteous constantly thrive, prospering in all their endeavors. However, the wicked are like chaff driven by the wind, unable to survive judgment. The concluding verse captures the thrust of the wisdom mindset: "The Lord watches over the way of the just, but the way of the wicked leads to ruin." (For other examples of this type of psalm see Pss 34; 37; 112; 128.)

Royal Psalms. The royal psalms are prayers linked to the Davidic dynasty in Jerusalem. They celebrate key events in the lives of David's successors, such as marriage and coronation. Although not all royal psalms belong to the stage of orientation, several of them do. They depict the stability and security that the king as God's agent was to effect for the people.

Psalm 72 is a good illustration of the orientation thrust of the royal psalms. Composed for either the coronation or the anniversary of the coronation of the king, this psalm opens with a prayer for judgment and justice that the king may govern wisely. The psalm prays that the king will provide fertility: "like rain coming down upon the fields, like showers watering the earth." There is the florid court language longing for the prosperity of the time of David and Solomon. However, the special objects of the king's rule are the poor and the needy. Where there is justice, there is equilibrium. (For other examples of this type of psalm see Pss 2; 45; 101; 132.)

Laments. The lament is the most common type of psalm in the Book of Psalms. It speaks to the situations of pain, frustration, and disillusionment in which a person (individual lament) or a community (communal lament) is involved. The psalmist underlines the poignancy of the catastrophe that has led to this state of disorientation.

The lament has a consistent structure: (1) address to God with an introductory cry for help; (2) the lament itself; (3) expression of trust or confidence; (4) petition; (5) vow to praise God—this last element is often an anticipation of God's action on behalf of the petitioner.

Psalm 22 is a well-known example of the (individual) lament. It opens with the address and lament: "My God, my God, why have you abandoned me?" There are frequent expressions of trust or confidence, such as God's concern for the psalmist since the moment of birth. The petitions are linked to images that capture the disorientation of the psalmist, e.g., "Deliver me from the sword, my forlorn life from the teeth of the dog." At the end there is the stated intention to praise God, hence an anticipation of God's help: "Then I will proclaim your name to the assembly; in the community I will praise you." (For other examples of the lament see Pss 3; 39; 42–43; 44; 58; 69; 74; 85.)

Thanksgivings or Psalms of Declarative Praise. This type of psalm speaks to the needs of reorientation or new orientation. It praises God, not for ongoing and regular providence, but for something concrete and specific that the psalmist has recently experienced. Here the accent is on newness and God's capacity to surprise.

The structure of both the individual and communal thanksgiving or psalm of declarative praise is the following: (1) introduction or call to praise/thank; (2) an account of the newness that the Lord has brought forth; (3) a conclusion that is usually a renewed call to praise/thank.

Psalm 30 is a good illustration of this psalm type. It opens with an expression of praise: "I praise you, Lord, for you raised me up. . . ." The psalmist then recounts God's marvelous intervention in terms of healing and deliverance from the nether world. Later on the psalmist describes his downfall as one of complacency that led to terror. The author then depicts the transition from disorientation to reorientation: "You changed my mourning into dancing; you took off my sackcloth and clothed me with gladness." The psalm concludes with the psalmist's intention to praise God forever. (For other examples of this type of psalm see Pss 40; 73; 118; 124.)

JOHN F. CRAGHAN

See also BIBLE, OLD TESTAMENT WRITINGS; CRITICISM, BIBLICAL; THEOLOGY, BIBLICAL.

PUNISHMENT, CAPITAL

See CAPITAL PUNISHMENT.

PURGATIVE WAY

The first stage in the spiritual life is called the stage of beginners or the purgative way. It is a time when one actively prepares oneself for a deeper relationship with God by purifying oneself of anything that can block growth in that relationship. Prayer in this period moves from vocal prayer to occasional meditation to habitual meditation. At the same time the believer purifies his or her life of sin through a commitment to virtue. As prayer simplifies and virtue increases, an individual readies himself or herself to receive the gift of God's self-revelation and love in contemplative prayer.

LEONARD DOOHAN

See also SPIRITUAL LIFE; THEOLOGY, PRACTICAL.

PURGATORY

The doctrine of purgatory expresses the traditional belief in a process of purification after death. According to this tradition, a person who has died in the state of grace may be freed through this process from every form of residual guilt or punishment and thus be made ready for entrance into his or her heavenly fulfillment in the presence of God.

The idea of purgatory is situated within the context of the *communion of saints.* The latter term expresses the sense of a human solidarity reaching beyond death and the related idea that the departed can be aided by the prayers and good works of those living on earth.

Scripture

While scriptural support for this doctrine remains ambiguous, it can be said that Scripture does not contradict the doctrine. The principal texts cited in this context are: 2 Maccabees 12:38-46; Matthew 5:26; 12:32; and 1 Corinthians 3:11-15. While these texts certainly do not suggest anything of the elaborations of the later doctrinal tradition, they do allow for the possibility that some sins may be forgiven in the next world.

History of Doctrine

It is clear that the Fathers used language about purgation. But the idea of purgatory as a particular place in the other world seems to be a creation of Western Christianity and is dated in the late twelfth century (cf. J. Le Goff, *The Birth of Purgatory,* Chicago, 1984). Once this idea arrived on the scene, it was possible for medieval theologians to develop the theology of purgatory in terms that would remain familiar into the twentieth century. Thus for centuries Roman Catholic theology has commonly conceived of a purgation after death which is carried out in a specific place and for a time proportionate to the number and quality of sins in this life. The connection between purgatory, penance, confession, indulgences, and the "power of the keys" was elaborately developed in late medieval theology. Over the centuries, the doctrine of purgatory has been a point of controversy between Roman Catholics and the Eastern Orthodox as well as between Roman Catholics and Protestants.

Teaching of the Magisterium

The doctrine is affirmed by the Second Council of Lyons (1274) and the Council of Florence (1439), and by the Council of Trent (1563). The teaching of the Council of Trent may be summarized in the following points: (1) There is purgation after death; (2) those involved in this purgation may be aided by the prayers and good works of the faithful, particularly by the sacrifice of the altar. While urging the bishops to see that a sound understanding of purgatory is fostered among the people, the council instructs them to avoid the more difficult questions which do not contribute to piety. According to the recommendation of the council, everything that savors of idle curiosity, superstition, or moneymaking is prohibited.

More recently, the doctrine on purgatory is presupposed by the Second Vatican Council in its Dogmatic Constitution on the Church, no. 51. It has been reaffirmed by Pope Paul VI in his *Credo of the People of God* (1968) and by the "Letter on Certain Questions Concerning Eschatology" (1979) from the Congregation for the Doctrine of the Faith.

Theological Reflection

The limited nature of the official teaching leaves much room for theological reflection on the mystery of purgation. Today it is commonly seen as an aspect of the encounter with God in death. This in turn is thought of more in terms of maturation than in terms of paying a debt. Such speculation stands within the framework of theological possibilties set out by the Church's official teaching though specific formulations may be problematic.

ZACHARY HAYES, O.F.M.

See also ESCHATOLOGY.

PURIM

Purim celebrates the deliverance of the Jews through the intercession of Esther when the Persian ruler, Xerxes (486–465 B.C.) had sanctioned a pogrom of the Jews. Purim is so called because the king's vizier Haman had cast lots (Akkadian *pūrū*) to arrive at the date of the proposed massacre.

The date of the Book of Esther, however, is uncertain. It is more historical romance than history. It appears to reflect rather the bitter second-century persecution of the Jews by the Seleucid king Antiochus IV (175–163 B.C.). But according to the Book of Esther, a pogrom was instituted earlier in Persia by Xerxes' vizier, Haman, of the race of Agag, typically enemies of the Jews (Exod 17:14, 16). It was thwarted by Esther.

That deliverance was observed by a festival which was originally largely secular. Exchange of gifts, banquets and amusements, and a measure of buffoonery characterized Purim. Thus it was thought to be initially connected with a Persian New Year festival. Later the feast fell under the influence of the carnival and introduced a masquerade of its own. The religious element of the feast consisted in reading the scroll or the Book of Esther. Purim is also a time for almsgiving.

With the eventual collapse of Persia and the ensuing diffusion of Hellenism the Jews would be challenged anew. Their deliverance at that time from the Hellenizing monarch Antiochus IV in the second century B.C. is celebrated at Hanukkah—a feast whose origin is much different from that of Purim but which like Purim is one of encouragement.

THOMAS BUCKLEY

PURITANS

This is the name given to religious sectaries who were originally members of the Church of England but who later formed an independent group. When Henry VIII led England out of the Catholic Church, many English Christians anticipated a reformed Church based solely on biblical teachings, but Henry and his daughter Elizabeth I had every intention of keeping the Church under royal control. The dissidents wished to "purify" the Church and so earned the appellation "Puritans." When the Stuart monarchs replaced the Tudors, the Puritans' situation declined. James I and Charles I kept control of the Church and relied upon bishops; they also permitted some practices which the Puritans thought smacked of Roman Catholicism. Since Charles I (1625–1649) tried to dominate Parliament, the Puritans turned to that body and soon gained great influence there.

In 1642 civil war broke out between Parliament and the king. Oliver Cromwell, a rigid Puritan, soon became the leading Parliamentary general. After a series of brilliant victories, he felt strong enough to ignore the non-Puritan elements in Parliament, and in 1649 the "saints," as the Puritans regarded themselves, took over that body. The saints controlled the government but found it impossible to govern. Their criterion for political worthiness was moral fitness—as judged by the saints. This appalling self-righteousness alienated non-Puritans, but it also split the Puritan camp. Power corrupts even saints, and as the saints now had power, they fought over it. As parties developed, the right to judge others' moral fitness became increasingly difficult to put into practice. Furthermore, these splits caused some of the saints to doubt their own righteousness. But Cromwell had no doubts. God had called him and his army to save the state. In 1653 he used his army to dissolve Parliament. While his soldiers were barring the doors after the members had been expelled, Cromwell picked up the speaker's mace, the symbol of civilian authority, and asked, "What shall we do with this bauble?" Cromwell ruled as Lord Protector from 1653 until his death in 1658; the Puritans, who had fought for freedom against an oppressive monarch, had now delivered England into the hands of a military dictator. Richard Cromwell succeeded his father, but popular dissatisfaction with the Puritan government and his own poor leadership drove him from office in 1660, opening the way for the restoration of the monarchy. Puritan influence in England declined steadily after this.

Some Puritans, believing the Church of England could never be reformed, left England for North America in the early 1600s; they settled in what are now Connecticut and Massachusetts. These groups are known to Americans as the Pilgrims. When the saints tried to establish a theocracy in New England, factions again arose, and one dissident leader, Roger Williams, left Massachusetts to found a colony in Rhode Island (1636). The American Puritans never gained the political prominence the English saints did, but they did significantly influence other American Protestant denominations. They also gave Anglophone America its earliest literature, the feast of Thanksgiving, and witch trials; thanks to Nathaniel Hawthorne, the Puritans are the best known of the early colonists of the United States.

JOSEPH F. KELLY

See also BRITAIN, CHURCH IN.

Q

Q DOCUMENT

The collection of Jesus' sayings thought to have been used independently by Matthew and Luke is designated by the letter Q (deriving from the German word *Quelle* meaning "source [of sayings]"). The Q source is a hypothesis based on comparison of the Synoptic Gospels: Where Matthew and Luke coincide and Mark has nothing or something very different, there is Q. The source is thought to have existed by A.D. 50 in Greek as a collection of Jesus' sayings (like Proverbs, Sirach, Gospel of Thomas, etc.) with no infancy or passion narratives.

DANIEL J. HARRINGTON, S.J.

See also CRITICISM, BIBLICAL.

QUADRAGESIMA

See LENT.

QUAKERS

See SOCIETY OF FRIENDS.

QUEST FOR THE HISTORICAL JESUS

The quest for the historical Jesus is the attempt to recover the facts about Jesus by using the tools of modern historiographical research. The history of the quest in Enlightenment and liberal German Protestant circles was first chronicled by Albert Schweitzer in *The Quest of the Historical Jesus* (1910). In the late eighteenth century H. S. Reimarus sought to peel away the ecclesiastical wrappings to get back to the simple historical figure of Jesus. During the nineteenth century some German Protestant scholars took a rationalist approach to miracles and so explained away most of the NT miracle stories. D. F. Strauss proposed a mythical interpretation as an alternative to the supernaturalist approach of the Churches and the rationalism of the Enlightenment. Schweitzer himself focused on eschatology as the setting for Jesus' life and teaching about the kingdom of God.

The major developments in the quest during the twentieth century include the following: the distinction between the Jesus of history and the Christ of faith, the parables as a privileged entry into Jesus' own teaching about God's kingdom, the development of criteria for determining what Jesus said and did, and the increasing interest in trying to locate Jesus within Judaism. Scholars today show special interest in Jesus as a wisdom teacher and poet, as a philosopher (something like the Cynics), and as an apocalyptic prophet.

The criteria that scholars have developed to ascertain what in the Gospels definitely comes from the historical Jesus include the following: dissimilarity or discontinuity (with regard to Judaism and early Christianity), multiple attestation (in several sources), Palestinian coloring (language, customs, etc.), and coherence (fits with what can be established by the other criteria).

The historical existence of Jesus of Nazareth is as well (or better) established as that of any ancient figure. One can say with great certainty that Jesus was raised in Nazareth, was baptized by John the Baptist, gathered disciples, preached and healed in Palestine, went up to Jerusalem about A.D. 30, and was crucified under the Roman governor Pontius Pilate. There are, however, some obstacles to writing a modern scientific biography about Jesus: The ancient sources mix fact and interpretation (as other ancient biographies did), and make claims about Jesus' origin, significance, and destiny that transcend the limits of human biography. One practical problem is chronology: Mark (followed by Matthew and Luke) has a one-year public ministry and one journey up to Jerusalem, whereas John has a three-year public ministry and several visits to Jerusalem. Which chronological framework does one choose?

The criteria listed above also allow us to get a sense of the major concerns in the teaching of the earthly Jesus: the coming kingdom of God when God's sovereignty will be acclaimed by all creation; the relation of intimacy with God as Father now available to all through Jesus; a special concern for "marginal people" (poor, lame, sinners, tax collectors); and a free attitude toward the traditions surrounding the Law and the Jerusalem Temple. Jesus was perceived as enough of a threat by the Jewish leaders and Roman officials to have him crucified as a political revolutionary.

The so-called historical Jesus is really the historian's Jesus; that is, the Jesus reconstructed out of literary fragments by historians. The object of Christian faith is not merely the historian's Jesus but rather the risen Jesus—the one who says "I died, and behold I am alive for evermore" (Rev 1:19). Following the Gospels, the Catholic Church assumes a continuity between the Jesus portrayed in the Gospels and the risen Lord: "The sacred authors . . . told us the honest truth about Jesus" (DV 19). That basic continuity extends backward from the Gospel texts, through the complex transmission of the Jesus tradition and the earliest witnesses and formulas of faith, to Jesus of Nazareth. While admitting the complexity of the Jesus tradition, Catholic theology contends that the tradition is basically reliable and allows us to hear the voice of Jesus, and that behind the tradition there is the strong personality of Jesus of Nazareth who is also the risen Lord.

DANIEL J. HARRINGTON, S.J.

See also BIBLE, NEW TESTAMENT WRITINGS; CRITICISM, BIBLICAL; JESUS CHRIST.

QUIET, PRAYER OF

Quiete in Latin means "at rest," and the prayer of quiet describes that stage in the life of prayer when a person is "at rest." It specifically refers to the passivity of the faculties of will, imagination (or memory), and intellect. After all the activity and efforts to grow in the spiritual life made by dedicated individuals during the stage of the beginners, the prayer of quiet becomes the transition to (some people would say the first stage of) the passive prayer of contemplation. It is said that the faculties are passive, but they are passive regarding every object except God; regarding God they are active. The prayer of quiet is a significant stage in prayer when one wants, hopes for, and thinks only about God, and one's faculties are not distracted by any other objects.

LEONARD DOOHAN

See also CHRISTIAN SPIRITUALITY; CONTEMPLATION; PRAYER.

QUIETISM

Quietism comes from the Latin word *quiete,* meaning "at rest." Quietism refers to the tendency to emphasize passivity in the spiritual life. Spiritual life is a combination of God's grace and work within us and our efforts. Over Church history some religious movements have stressed human activity more than God's (Pelagianism), and other movements have stressed God's transforming action and played down the importance of human activity (Quietism). Exaggerated emphases in either direction have led to condemnations by the Church. Since in the later stages of spiritual life the believer receives God's transforming grace in passive contemplation, the question arises what is the best way to prepare for these later stages—by action, even the action of meditational prayer, or by passively waiting for God's union? Does one earn this by good actions or does one wait in emptiness aware that one can do nothing to earn this transforming gift of God?

Throughout Christian history, several movements have emphasized union with God by renouncing human effort. In the fifth century Eutychians rejected the importance of works, claiming union with God is attained by indifference (*apatheia*). The influential writer Pseudo-Dionysius stressed that letting go led to absorption in God. In the thirteenth century, the Brethren of the Free Spirit renounced deliberate effort as a way to union with God in prayer and urged passivity. In the fourteenth century the monks of Mount Athos developed a passive preparation, a psychological technique (Hesychasm), to prepare for union. All these movements showed signs of quietism, a word that describes a seventeenth-century spirituality in France (based on the writing of a Spanish priest M. de Molinos). While quietism correctly stresses the need for passivity, it can degenerate gradually from the acceptance of passivity to the uselessness of action, to the conclusion that whatever one does has no consequence in spirituality, and finally to the conviction that the perfect cannot sin, or that whether one sins or not is not relevant in spiritual growth.

Exaggerations at either end of the spectrum are inauthentic. Quietism reminds us of the importance of putting our own efforts into perspective and increasing our awareness that God's work within us is primarily what really leads us to growth.

LEONARD DOOHAN

See also ASCETICISM; SPIRITUAL LIFE.

QUINN, EDEL (1907–1944)

Edel Quinn, lay apostle, missionary to Africa, was born in 1907 in a village near the town of Kanturk, County Cork, Ireland. Her father was a bank official, which meant changing residence until finally the family settled near Dublin. Eldest of her family, she took work as secretary in a business house managed by a Frenchman, who expressed the wish to marry her. She refused, as she had already thought of a dedicated life. In her early twenties she joined the Legion of Mary, so impressing those in high office, especially Frank Duff, that she was put in charge, after some time, of a branch (praesidium) dealing with prostitutes. But she felt a higher call and had arranged to enter the Order of Poor Clare Sisters when grave disease struck. In 1932 tuberculosis condemned her to eighteen months in a sanatorium. It was a time of purification, of deepening spirituality, time certainly not lost. Returned to health, she was back at Legionary work, and did an extension stint in England and was ready for a larger assignment in Wales. Then her great moment came. In 1936 Bishop J. W. Heffernan, C.S.Sp., of Nairobi, had asked the Legion authorities to send him someone to launch the association in his diocese.

In the next eight years she accomplished a remarkable apostolate as a Legionary envoy and had the support of Archbishop Anthony Riberi, delegate apostolic in Nairobi. She had a recurrence of ill-health, during which a campaign of prayer for her recovery was launched from the Legionaries in Dublin. Her apostolic activity is summarized in their appeal to

Edel Quinn

members everywhere for support: "That mission began in November, 1936 with the landing of Miss Quinn at Mombasa, and continued with but little sickness (though she was far from robust) until last year. Her journeying brought her through the towns and villages, the jungle paths and swamps of Kenya, Uganda, Tanganyika (now Tanzania) Nyasaland (now Malawi) and out to Mauritius in the Indian Ocean. Everywhere she found the devoted Bishops, missionary priests and nuns anxious to try this new machinery which seemed likely to be of help to them in their work. Praesidia to the number of many hundreds, and Curiae sprang up and prospered. They took to the Legion with facility. Then was a new and delightful thing seen, the African people themselves co-operating ardently, successfully, perseveringly in the work of evangelization."

She recovered then, but within a short time illness befell her again. She died on 12 May 1944. The cause for the beatification of Edel Quinn has been introduced and is making satisfactory progress.

MICHAEL O'CARROLL, C.S.Sp.

See also DUFF, FRANK; LAITY, THEOLOGY OF THE; LEGION OF MARY.

QUMRAN

See DEAD SEA SCROLLS.

R

RABBINIC LITERATURE

The term "rabbi" was (and is) an honorific title for a teacher of the Jewish Law. The ancient collections of the teachings of the rabbis constitute rabbinic literature, and the Judaism shaped by these rabbis and the literature that preserved their teachings is called rabbinic Judaism.

The earliest rabbinic collection is the *Mishnah,* put into shape in Palestine about A.D. 200. The Mishnah's teachings are arranged in tractates that in turn constitute six Orders: Seeds, Torts, Festivals, Women, Purities, and Holy Things. The central concern is how one practices Judaism; it is not a "theology" book. Neither is it a commentary on Scripture; indeed, some tractates prescind from Scripture almost entirely, though others stay fairly close to Scripture. The ancient teachings not included in the Mishnah are gathered in the *Tosefta* ("additions"), which is like the Mishnah in structure and date. The *Talmuds* comment on, update, and expand the Mishnah. The Palestinian or Jerusalem Talmud was edited around A.D. 400. The Babylonian Talmud, which was put into form around A.D. 500, has traditionally been the more authoritative version in Jewish life.

The *Targums* are Aramaic paraphrases of the Hebrew Bible. Prepared for use in Jewish liturgy, the Targums are somewhat free translations that adapt the biblical text to more "refined" theological views (e.g., with regard to God's anger or action in the world) and add popular traditions to the text by way of expansion. There is a Targum of Job among the Dead Sea Scrolls. The most important Targums of the Pentateuch are Onqelos, pseudo-Jonathan, and Neofiti 1. The historical and prophetic books are treated in Targum Jonathan. The Targum traditions for the Writings are more fluid.

The *Midrashim* are anthologies of comments on Scripture—some arranged like a modern verse-by-verse biblical commentary, others taking the shape of homilies gathered together. The so-called tannaitic midrashim (Mekilta, Sifra, Sifre) are roughly contemporary with the Mishnah. The other collections (Genesis Rabbah, Exodus Rabbah, etc.) are later. The *Hekhalot* literature (3 Enoch, Hekhalot Rabbati, etc.) contains Jewish mystical writings.

For Catholics rabbinic literature is important because it has exercised such a strong formative influence on Judaism throughout the centuries. For further progress in the new relationship between Catholics and Jews that has emerged since Vatican II it is essential that these writings be understood and appreciated sympathetically.

In NT scholarship there is a long tradition of using the rabbinic writings for understanding Jesus and early Christianity. But there are some serious methodological problems. The earliest work seems to be the Mishnah at about A.D. 200. How much (if any) of the rabbinic tradition goes back to Jesus' time or to before the destruction of the Second Temple in A.D. 70? Is there a genuine historical continuity between the Pharisaic and rabbinic movements? How representative and authoritative was rabbinic Judaism in its own time? What kind of circulation did the rabbinic movement and ideas have? How and when did the rabbis gain their dominance? These serious questions have made NT scholars today more cautious than their predecessors in appealing to rabbinic parallels.

DANIEL J. HARRINGTON, S.J.

See also CRITICISM, BIBLICAL; JUDAISM.

RACISM

In one sense "racism" can be said to be a modern phenomenon. In other ways it is probably as old as humankind itself. The noted historian John Hope Franklin once remarked that he knew of no society totally free from this social disease. The tendency to cast other groups, particularly minorities in an unfavorable light, has been a persistent characteristic running through civilization as such. Anti-Semitism, for example, a historic form of racism, was commonplace in Greco-Roman society well before the onset of the Christian era.

The modern age, however, has seen racism take on some significantly new dimensions. For one, a biological dimension has sometimes been added which has reduced certain groups to innate inferiority. During the Nazi period such groups were either destined for total annihilation as in the case of the Jews and the Roma and Siti peoples (often known incorrectly as "Gypsies") or perpetual subjugation as in the case of the Poles. Secondly, racism became imbedded as never before in the social, economic, and political structures of nation states. Apartheid in South Africa is one example, but so are the various attempts to impose particular tribal hegemony in other African states such as Kenya. And certainly in the United States systemic racism, directed primarily at African-Americans, continues to separate supposedly equal citizens into distinctly unequal groups as the Kerner Commission Report demonstrated. The persistence of the Klu Klux Klan and the emergence of the "skinheads" and other fascist groups show that racism remains imbedded in the fabric of North America and Europe.

The American Catholic record on racism is mixed at best. Slave ownership, for example, was not unknown in Catholic circles as the examples of the diocese in Charleston, South Carolina, and the Maryland Jesuits bear witness. The Catholic hierarchy basically distanced itself from the abolitionist movement and only a few individual Catholics took a strong anti-slavery position. The official Catholic position during the time of the great national debate on slavery in America was that slavery as a principle of social organization was not in itself sinful, though in 1839 Pope Gregory XVI had reiterated the Church's condemnation of the slave trade. The leading American theologian of the period, Bishop Kenrick of St. Louis, said that "Since such is the state of things (slavery being the status quo) nothing should be attempted against the laws nor anything be done or said that would make them bear their yoke unwillingly" ("Catholic America," *St. Anthony Messenger,* [January 1976] 16).

After the Civil War the Second Plenary Council of Baltimore (1886) came to grips with the problem of four million newly emancipated slaves. Bishop Martin Spalding, serving as apostolic delegate, took a deep interest in the African-American apostolate, suggesting that special prefects apostolic be appointed for African-Americans. His proposal did not carry the day, but nine decrees were adopted which focused on a new outreach to the African-American community. The question of segregated parishes, however, was left to the judgment of local legislation. Unfortunately, little in fact came of these decrees as racism both among clergy and laity vitiated their intent. Bishops in the Southern states appealed for workers and funds, but their calls largely went unanswered. Most religious orders, with a few notable exceptions such as the Josephites, shied away from ministry to African-Americans for fear of alienating their white constituency. And most dioceses were reluctant to accept African-Americans as candidates for the priesthood. Thus the noble legislation of the Council of Baltimore remained dormant.

A major breakthrough on the racial front in American Catholicism did not occur until 1947. It was in that year that Cardinal Ritter of St. Louis ended all racial segregation in the Catholic schools of his archdiocese. Ritter's action was duplicated the following year by Archbishop Patrick O'Boyle of Washington.

During this period there also developed in several areas of the country new groups specifically dedicated to the eradication of racism within and without the Catholic Church. A Jesuit, Fr. John LaFarge, who wrote extensively on racism for *America* and other journals, provided the spiritual and theological framework for this organizing effort. These local councils eventually coalesced into an umbrella national organization called the National Catholic Conference for Interracial Justice. NCCIJ was quite active in the historic meeting in Chicago on Religion and Race which solidified interreligious support for the newly emergent civil rights struggle as well as in organizing the famous March on Washington at which Dr. Martin Luther King delivered his memorable "I have a dream" speech. Catholic clergy, sisters, brothers, and lay people also became significantly involved in the marches organized by Dr.

King and his movement as well as other local efforts to end racial discrimination.

Another important effort in the attempt to eradicate racism within Catholicism came in the late fifties and early sixties. A group of researchers at St. Louis University carefully studied the most widely used literature, social studies, and religion texts in parochial schools and CCD classes. This Catholic study was part of a broader interfaith endeavor that involved similar self-studies on Protestant and Jewish materials.

The results of the St. Louis studies proved very disturbing. It became clear that Catholic teaching and Catholic life were being presented almost exclusively through the narrow lens of white, northern European culture. Any student who did not totally fit this mold would likely be left with the feeling of an "outsider" in the Church. Specifically, the texts involved in the study exhibited little concern for the political, social, and economic discrimination which was the lot of many, if not most, of the minorities to some degree. While the tensions prevalent today had not yet surfaced, they existed. Hence it is unfortunate that Catholic students of a generation ago were not being prepared to cope with the challenges presented by American social discrimination. If they had, perhaps some of the problems facing us today would not have become so intense. When minority groups charge the Church with failing to come to grips with the social and economic inequalities in American society based on racial differences, the seeming indifference of Catholic social studies materials to these inequalities certainly tends to confirm their judgment. The social studies texts, as well as the religion texts (which showed a strong strain of anti-Semitism), did not prepare students to become leaders in the struggle against racism in America. As a result of these studies, Catholic textbook publishers in America made major changes in the text and context of their educational materials.

The Catholic effort to combat racism has persisted into our own day, a sign that the problem still afflicts both the Church and the larger society. A Vatican document on racism issued in February 1989 by the Pontifical Commission for Peace and Justice declared that "Harboring racist thoughts and entertaining racist attitudes is a sin." It went on to cite specifically apartheid in South Africa, discrimination against foreign workers in Western Europe, and the recurrence of anti-Semitism (including some forms of anti-Zionism) as particularly disturbing problems connected with racism. It also went on to warn against the potential for the resurgence of a new form of the deadly myth of eugenic racism which stood at the heart of Nazism.

A decade earlier, in November 1979, the American bishops released a Pastoral Letter on Racism entitled *Brothers and Sisters to Us. . . .* This document began with the bold assertion that "racism is an evil which endures in our society and in our Church. Despite apparent advances and even significant changes in the last two decades, the reality of racism remains. In large part it is only the external appearances which have changed." It was this letter in particular that began to focus Catholic attention on the problems of "institutional racism" whereby African-Americans, indigenous peoples, Hispanic and recent Asian immigrants are subjected to systematic discrimination in terms of employment, housing, cultural expression, educational opportunities, and even faith expression in organized Church settings, particularly the liturgy. It urged a concerted effort by local, regional, and national Church bodies in dealing with this reality of racism. For this to happen, the bishops recognized that a profound conversion was necessary on the part of many in the Church.

Efforts have also been made at addressing the problem of institutional racism by such groups as NCCIJ and Project Equality (originally founded by NCCIJ and now an interreligious effort). The latter tries to use the considerable purchasing power of religious institutions to combat racism by insuring that goods and services are obtained from minority-controlled firms and that other vendors are committed to affirmative action. NCCIJ, on the other hand, has recently turned its attention in a special way to lack of minority employment within the Church. It released a report in January 1993 which clearly shows that most Church institutions have a long way to go in the area of minority employment. In response to its report NCCIJ has developed a pilot program on minority hiring which it has begun to implement in a number of American dioceses, including Seattle, Milwaukee, Cleveland, and Pittsburgh.

Given the ambiguous record of Catholicism on racial matters and the new challenges that are emerging, it is clear racism will remain a challenge for Catholicism for the forseeable future. It will continually need to remind itself of the prophetic words of the 1979 Pastoral Letter: ". . . let the Church proclaim to all that the sin of racism defiles the image of God and degrades the sacred dignity of humankind which has been revealed by the mystery of the Incarnation. Let all know that it is a terrible sin that mocks the cross of Christ and ridicules the Incarnation. For the brother and sister of our Brother Jesus Christ are brother and sister to us."

JOHN T. PAWLIKOWSKI, O.S.M.

See also ANTI-SEMITISM; BLACK CATHOLICS; SOCIAL TEACHING OF THE CHURCH; VIRTUE.

RAHNER, KARL (1904–1984)

Karl Rahner (1904–1984) has been called the greatest Catholic theologian of the twentieth century, and it is sometimes said that he tried to do for his age what Thomas Aquinas did for the Church in the thirteenth century. Whether one agrees with these assessments or not, they can give some indication of his importance in theology and of his impact on the life of the Catholic Church in the twentieth century. It is a century which has seen radical changes both in theology and in the Church, changes in which he played a very influential role. A look at the Church before and after Rahner can provide some measure of his influence and importance.

The Church into which Rahner was born in Freiburg, Germany, in 1904 was the Church of Pius X, and still very much the Church of his predecessor and namesake Pius IX and the First Vatican Council (1870). Pius IX had published his "Syllabus of Errors" in 1864, condemning a host of modern ideas he considered false, and Pius X led the struggle against the inroads of this modern thinking into the Church and the dangers of what was called "Modernism." When Karl Rahner entered the Jesuit Order in 1922 at the age of eighteen and began his study of philosophy and theology, Rome's harsh and relentless struggle against Modernism was still being waged vigorously. By contrast, the Church in which Rahner died in 1984 was the Church of the Second Vatican Council (1962–1965), a Church pursuing the program of *aggiornamento* introduced by John XXIII to bring the Church "up-to-date" in the modern world. The path that led from the fear of "Modernism" through the Second Vatican Council to a deliberate and conscious attempt to "modernize" the Church was and is a very controversial path. Rahner's influence in moving the Church forward can be seen at certain crucial points along the way.

Karl Rahner

He exercised this influence as professor of theology from 1937 until 1971 in three different universities, and through the prolific writing he did during this period and right up until the time of his death in 1984. He began his teaching career in the Jesuit faculty of theology at the University of Innsbruck (Austria) from 1937 until 1964, a tenure that was interrupted when the Nazis closed the Jesuit college in 1939 until it was reopened in 1948. In April, 1964, Rahner moved to the University of Munich to succeed Romano Guardini in the chair of the philosophy of religion. Desiring to return to the teaching of dogmatic theology, Rahner accepted his last teaching position at the University of Münster in April, 1967, and remained there until his retirement from teaching in 1971.

Rahner's books and articles and their translations into a host of languages amount to thousands of titles. His two early and more philosophical works, *Spirit in the World* (1939) and *Hearers of the Word* (1941), appeared in English in 1968 and 1969 respectively. His major theological articles were collected into the twenty-three volumes of *Theological Investigations,* published in English from 1961 until 1992. Rahner's most systematic synthesis of his theology appeared in English as *Foundations of Christian Faith* in 1978. He also published many more pastoral works such as sermons, prayers, and meditations. Among the many works he helped to edit should be mentioned the six volumes of *Sacramentum Mundi* (1967–1969), and the *Quaestiones Disputatae* series which began in 1958 and reached its 101st volume shortly before his death.

Rahner's teaching and writing bore immense fruit through his participation in the Second Vatican Council. He played only a minor role in the preparatory work, being named an advisor to the commission on the sacraments in 1960. But when both Cardinal König of Vienna and Cardinal Döpfner of Munich chose him as their theological advisor, the way was opened for his appointment as an official *peritus* or expert for the theological work of the council. His discussions with various bishops' conferences and collaboration in the drafting of many conciliar documents made him one of the most influential theological voices at the council.

Without suggesting that John XXIII's program for the council of *aggiornamento* or modernizing was simply an acceptance of the Modernism mentioned earlier, it did, nevertheless, call for a new way of seeing the modern world and modern history through the eyes of the Church. The earlier way saw the Church as the sole possessor of that truth which was of ultimate and salvific significance and as the single repository of that grace by which this salvation could ordinarily be attained, and saw the world merely as the recipient of these supernatural goods. The new way came to expression in Vatican II's Pastoral Constitution on the Church in the Modern World (*Gaudium et Spes*) when it said that the Church has to read "the signs of the times" (no. 4) because the Spirit who leads the Church also "fills the earth" (no. 11), and the grace with which the Church is blessed is at work in the hearts of "all men of good will" (no. 22). The Church is related to the modern world not only as teacher, but also as listener and learner. Coming to expression here is a new way of seeing the relationship between the natural or secular world and the supernatural world of grace, a new understanding of which Karl Rahner was one of the chief architects.

In his 1950 encyclical *Humani Generis* Pius XII was highly critical of the new approach to this question associated with the "new theology" in France because it did not seem to safeguard the gratuity of God's grace. Rahner suggested that the offer of grace could be an intrinsic element universally present in all creation and still be utterly gratuitous if God freely created nature in the first place to be the embodiment of grace. Then grace is not something added to nature from without, but nature's deepest truth and innermost supernatural dynamism. The world comes into contact with God's grace not in the first instance through contact with the Church, but through contact with its own deepest self. When the Church proclaims this truth and lives in this grace, it becomes the visible sign or sacrament of grace in the world, not its exclusive purveyor.

The implications of Rahner's understanding of grace are many and fruitful. God's grace and revelation have been present in all times and places creating the possibility of supernatural faith for all peoples. Non-Christian religions are not simply false religions, but possible mediations of this grace in the world. Moreover, the offer of God's grace is universal not only in the sense of all people, but also in the equally important sense that this grace is not confined to the religious realm or one compartment of life, but pervades all the dimensions of human life, both individual and social. Every human situation, however "secular" or "worldly," offers a possible encounter with God and the call to his kingdom. Contemporary movements striving for a more just social, economic, and political order are aspects of the liberating power of God's grace to free people here and now from the power of evil.

When grace is seen in this universal way and salvation is understood as pertaining to here and now as well as hereafter, encompassing the material as well as spiritual realm of God's creation, it follows that the Church exists not for itself, but for the sake of God's universal kingdom. Its members are not merely passive recipients of supernatural goods dispensed by the clergy, but all are active participants in the Church's mission to continue Jesus' proclamation of the kingdom. Hence the need often expressed by Rahner to develop Church structures that are less autocratic and more democratic to facilitate this active participation, and to give voice to the Spirit at work in the life and experience of all the members of the Church. Such an understanding does not make the Church and its sacramental life less important, but stresses the active rôle of every Catholic in enabling the Church to be the visible and tangible sacrament of God's universal call to salvation in all the dimensions of human life and history.

Rahner's use of the notion of sacrament or symbolic causality to explain the relationship of the Church to the prior reality of grace also finds fruitful application in his theology of Jesus or Christology. When God freely utters God's eternal Word outwards in God's creative act of self-communication, what comes to be is the humanity of Jesus as the real symbol of the eternal Word. In Jesus the Word of God is expressed in human flesh and history, and his history becomes the supreme moment in the single human history of God's gracious offer of union with Godself. It became the supreme moment because of the fullness of God's offer and the fullness of Jesus' response. Jesus was and is the man who throughout his life and especially in his death lived his human life as God's son so perfectly that in him the Son of God became man and man became the Son of God. Divine life, that is, the eternal relationship between the Father and the Son, became flesh in the human life of Jesus of Nazareth. In him God's offer of salvific union with Godself was realized in history, so that because of Jesus this offer is now final and irrevocable.

It is in this sense that Rahner understands Jesus as the absolute and universal Savior. The fullness of the union with God offered and achieved in him is unsurpassable, not relative to some possible closer union, and this union is the end for which universal human history was created from the beginning. He is, then, the final cause of the world's salvation as well as its symbolic cause. Unlike other ways of understanding how Jesus is the cause of salvation, which see his life and death as in some way having an effect on God, Rahner sees the effect on the world and on history. God's offer of grace was unconditional, dependent for its fulfillment only on human acceptance, the acceptance which Jesus accomplished in his life and death and which came to fulfillment in his resurrection and exaltation.

Rahner's entire effort in understanding God, grace, Jesus, and the Church is to preserve the primacy of grace and God's salvific initiative while at the same time safeguarding the autonomy of God's creation and human freedom. The initiative is always God's, but God works with and from within creation, not by breaking into it from without in mythological fashion. For this reason Rahner's theology has rightly been called a theological anthropology: statements about God always entail statements about the human because God has freely entered into relationship with the latter and Christian theology is always about both parties in this relationship. Christian theology is therefore always Trinitarian: God in God's sovereign freedom is the utterly transcendent source and creator of all things (Father), who is at the same time not distant from God's creation but immanent within it in God's gracious self-communication (Spirit), which self-communication must be freely accepted in the flesh of human life and history (Son). The Trinity is the single mystery of Christian faith, the Trinitarian mystery of God with us.

Against the charges of the modern world, then, that believing in God is an alienating escape from history because it denigrates human concerns and destroys the autonomy of human freedom, Rahner wanted to "modernize" theology by showing that in affirming God Christian faith simultaneously affirms the world and human history, endowing time with eternal significance. The incarnate God of Jesus Christ is a God who must be found in the world or not at all, for since the incarnation, indeed since the beginning of creation, "God and the world are never identical, but neither are they ever separate." Rahner insisted, then, on the unity of the love of God and neighbor and the unity of our innerworldly and eschatological hopes, and spoke of the theology of "everyday things," for it is the ordinary affairs of life that present the challenge of Christian faith to share in the sonship of Jesus by sharing in his life, death, and resurrection.

Karl Rahner was also acutely aware that the Second Vatican Council was the beginning, not the end, of the Church's efforts to be the sacrament of God's grace in the modern and post-modern world. The challenge, as he expressed it, was for the *Roman* Catholic Church to become the Roman *Catholic* Church, that is, a truly universal Church in both senses in which he understood the universality of grace. It must shed the exclusive trappings of European culture to allow Christian faith to find roots and come to expression in all the cultures of the world. Secondly, it must discover God's Spirit at work in every genuine effort to humanize the world both in our individual and in our social lives. For Christians should be the true humanists of our age, believing that humanizing the world is the very process of its divinization or sharing God's life, thereby moving it forward towards the final and eternal kingdom of God's justice and peace.

WILLIAM V. DYCH, S.J.

See also THEOLOGY, FUNDAMENTAL; THEOLOGY, SYSTEMATIC; VATICAN COUNCIL II.

RAPHAEL (RAFFAELLO SANZIO) (1483–1520)

Italian painter and architect representing, more than any other, the ideals of the High Renaissance. From his father, Giovanni Santi, he learned not only the rudiments of painting, but was also given his first exposure to the broad range of renaissance humanism. Born in 1483 and orphaned at age eleven, his earliest commissions are in the style of Perugino, whose pupil he became. Still in his late teens, he seems to have traveled widely in Tuscany and Umbria, and, upon arriving in Florence (1504), he immediately began to absorb the achievements of Leonardo and Michelangelo. A series of small Madonnas from this period utilized Leonardo's Virgin and Child with St. Anne (itself an original solution to the compositional problem of a child with more than one adult). His *Maddalena Doni* is a portrait after the style of Leonardo's *Mona Lisa,* while his *Deposition* (1507) shows the influence of Michelangelo. Immensely popular from an early age, his style embodies formal perfection, clarity, and humanity, while his subjects generally exhibit the highest ideals of Christianity combined with tranquility and well-being. In this he differs from Leonardo and Michelangelo who often give us scenes of complex tension and emotion.

Raphael took up residence in Rome in 1508, remaining there for the rest of his life. Commissioned by Julius II, he immediately adapted to the large-scale requirements of the papal apartments (e.g., *The School of Athens,* 1509–1511; Michelangelo was then working on the ceiling of the Sistine Chapel). His style now acquired the balanced classicism of ancient Rome, then being revived.

Henceforth he would be in great demand for all manner of projects, including portraits and architecture (he succeeded Bramante as architect to St. Peter's, though little of his architectural work sur-

Raphael, self-portrait, 1506, Pitti Palace, Florence

vives intact). Much of Raphael's painting at this time was entrusted to his students for completion. The *Sistine Madonna* (1512–1513) is an exception. Here we find, in the manner of Leonardo and Michelangelo, that mother and child are absorbed in profound thoughts, as though looking forward to the passion itself (which even the cherubs are contemplating). The lesser figures, the Pope and St. Barbara, represent the priesthood and the peoples of the earth (St. Barbara is clothed in what we now call earth colors). Together they implore the aid of the Madonna and her child, thus giving the painting much of the power of an icon.

Raphael died at the early age of thirty-seven in 1520 while working on his *Transfiguration,* which was completed by his assistants. At his death he had the personal friendship of princes and cardinals. With Leonardo and Michelangelo, and a very few others, he had changed the world's perception of artists from that of craftsmen to men of genius ranking with the greatest of theologians and philosophers.

DAVID BRYAN

See also ART, CHRISTIAN; LEONARDO DA VINCI; MICHELANGELO BUONARROTI.

RATIONALISM

A theory postulated by certain philosophers of the Enlightenment and humanists of the Renaissance which argued that religious truth—including those aspects held to be divinely revealed or inspired—is subject to intellectual cognition and discernment. This mode of thinking placed reason firmly ahead of faith, and rejected the more authoritarian and dogmatic teachings of the Church in favor of philosophical criticism. Thinkers associated with this polemic include René Descartes, Immanuel Kant, and G.W.F. Hegel.

JOSEPH QUINN

See also ENLIGHTENMENT, THE.

READING THE BIBLE

The Bible is actually a collection of books; therefore, readers might approach it as a library from which they select first one book, then another, according to their differing tastes or needs. The books of the Bible originated in a variety of cultures, and historical periods, and are of diverse literary styles. These characteristics, along with the purpose of the author in writing, are taken into consideration both in the choice of reading, and in efforts to discover the inspired message of each book.

Once an interest in reading the Bible is sparked, sustaining it is of prime importance. This is best served by the selection of books and/or passages which capture the attention, and nourish the spiritual life. A guide for beginning to read the Bible might be: Read what is interesting and helpful; pass over what is not.

For many, the short, fascinating books of religious stories, such as Ruth, Tobit, Judith, or Esther provide easy entry into the Old Testament. Or, history buffs may be drawn first to the more ponderous, historical books of Samuel, Kings, Chronicles or Maccabees. Reading some of the shorter prophetic books (Jonah, Micah, Amos, Haggai) before attempting the longer ones (Isaiah, Jeremiah, Ezekiel) may be advantageous. Though the psalms are prayers, reflective reading of them can foster both a familiarization with their style and content, and the use of a growing number of them for prayer.

Either the Gospel according to Mark, or the Acts of the Apostles is a good place to begin reading the New Testament. Mark's fast-paced account is the shortest of the Gospels. It focuses on the words and actions of Jesus, with little attempt to theologize about them. The Acts of the Apostles gives the broad strokes of the spread of the Church in the Mediterranean world, as well as moving details of the lives and conflicts of the real people who came to be called Christian. With Acts as a basis, one could then go to the Gospels, which flowed out of the Church's faith accounts of the life of Jesus; and to the epistles of Paul, Peter, James, and John.

Since the invention of the printing press, and the spread of literacy, the habit of reading the Bible, known in monasteries as *lectio divina,* has increasingly become a hallmark of devout Christians. The progress in Scripture studies promoted among Roman Catholics by Pius XII (*Divino Afflante Spiritu,* 1943), and the renewal initiated by Vatican II (1962–1965) have successfully encouraged Roman Catholics to read and study the Bible.

There is a type of reading of the Bible that might be called reflective and receptive. Here, readers do not analyze or seek the meaning of the text. Instead, the words and images are simply taken in, and allowed to be stored in the subconscious. From there they influence thoughts, decisions, and actions. The Book of Job, Isaiah 40–66, the Gospels, and epistles are examples of books that lend themselves to this receptive, relaxed reading.

Familiarity with books of the Bible which readers find attractive will lead them gradually to those which were initially less inviting. There is no need to rush to get through everything. Some books may never be read in their entirety, but will serve as reference books to which one goes from time to time for specific information. Readers will become increasingly aware of the interrelation of books. They will see that later books draw on earlier ones, and that several books may draw on similar oral traditions.

In reading the Bible one seeks more to be formed than informed; to be grasped by God rather than to grasp ideas; to be challenged, consoled, strengthened, and encouraged; to be transformed by the Spirit of God speaking words of life in the words of Scripture; in short, to take on the mind and heart of Christ.

Resources

Many questions about a text are answered in the footnotes and introductions included in some editions of the Bible. Cross-references often help to clarify or situate a passage, and to direct readers to other biblical books they may find interesting. Reading the same book or passage in different editions or translations of the Bible often provides helpful nuances. In doing this kind of comparison of translations, readers often discover a favorite version of the Bible.

A few editions of the Bible contain their own glossary as well as maps of places mentioned. When these are not included, a one-volume dictionary of the Bible may serve as a handy resource. Groups which study, discuss, and pray the Bible assist members in understanding and living out the Scripture message. These and the many attractive and effective programs for Bible study available in parishes and dioceses are intended as supplements to the private reading of the Bible in which we discover that to us as to Moses, God speaks as a person to a friend (see Exod 33:11).

FRANCES KRUMPELMAN, S.C.N.

See also BIBLE, ENGLISH VERSIONS OF THE; BIBLE, NEW TESTAMENT WRITINGS; BIBLE, OLD TESTAMENT WRITINGS; THEOLOGY, BIBLICAL.

REAL PRESENCE

This term refers to the presence of Jesus Christ in the Eucharist. The word real indicates the presence is not merely figurative or metaphorical. The Lord Jesus is really and truly present in the Eucharist.

This assertion is based on the scriptural statements, especially in John 6:48ff., that Jesus is the Bread of Life, the true bread come down from heaven for the life of the world (John 6:51).

The Fourth Lateran Council (A.D. 1215) reaffirmed its teaching on the Eucharist against medieval denials, especially by Berengar of Tours. More specifically the Council of Trent (A.D. 1545–1564) declared that after the consecration of the bread and wine "Our Lord Jesus Christ, true God and man, is truly, really, and substantially contained under the perceptible species of bread and wine" (Session XIII, chapter 1, DS 874). The council further explains that this presence is not "only in a sign or figure, or by his power" (Session XIII, canon 1, DS 883).

This presence of the person of Jesus Christ (God and man) is the basis for the Council of Trent's encouragement of Eucharistic Devotions such as processions, adoration of the Blessed Sacrament, prayer before the Eucharist, exposition of the Blessed Sacrament.

Many of the Reformers did not categorically deny the presence of Jesus Christ in the Eucharist. However, they felt the emphasis on the Real Presence which gave rise to many of the devotions of the Middle Ages led to many abuses, superstitions and false emphases. Luther preferred to emphasize the cosmic presence of Christ and companation (i.e., that the bread and wine remain along with the presence of Christ). Calvin stressed the spiritual nature of the communion with Christ in the Eucharist and thus preferred to emphasize the symbolic nature of the presence of Christ. Zwingli and other Anabaptists, at the other end of the spectrum of the Reformation, stressed that the sacraments were signs of God's love or occasions of God's grace. Zwingli denied any efficient causality in the sacraments. He stressed, rather, the importance of faith in the recipient.

The World Council of Churches in *Baptism, Eucharist and Ministry* (1982) was able to work out a convergence on the teaching about the Eucharist. It emphasizes both the real change that occurs in the

Eucharistic elements and the importance of real change in the recipient of the Eucharist, i.e., the challenge of the Eucharist to Christian attitudes toward the world and its many social problems.

E. R. FALARDEAU, S.S.S.

See also COMMUNION, HOLY; EUCHARIST.

RECOLLECTION

See CONTEMPLATION; PRAYER.

RECTOR

In the Roman Catholic Church, a rector is a priest who has care of a church that is neither a parish church nor a church affiliated with a religious community. The term also applies to the priest in charge of a seminary and to the local superior of certain congregations such as the Jesuits.

PATRICIA DeFERRARI

RECUSANTS

(Lat. *recusare,* "to refuse") Persons in England who, between the reigns of Elizabeth I (1558–1603) and George II (1727–1760), refused to attend the services of the Church of England, which at that time were mandated by civil law. The majority were Catholics, some of whom were martyred for their obstinacy; others were imprisoned, stripped of property and/or voting rights, disqualified from holding office, or fined. Laws concerning recusants were enforced inconsistently, and under the Catholic Relief Act of 1791 recusancy ceased to be a crime.

JOSEPH QUINN

See also BRITAIN, CHURCH IN.

RED MASS

A votive Mass of the Holy Spirit, so named from the red vestments worn during its celebration and from the red gowns traditionally worn by judges in the Middle Ages. Today such Masses are usually celebrated at the opening of councils, synods, etc. to invoke the Holy Spirit, source of wisdom, understanding, counsel, and fortitude. Catholic judges in England also assemble at Westminster Cathedral to celebrate the Red Mass. Since its inauguration in the United States on 6 October 1928 at old Saint Andrew's Church, many groups of Catholic attorneys continue to celebrate it annually.

PATRICIA DeFERRARI

See also INSTITUTE, RELIGIOUS; SEMINARY.

REDACTION CRITICISM

See CRITICISM, BIBLICAL.

REDEMPTORISTS

The Redemptorists are a religious congregation of missionary priests dedicated to the popular preaching of the Word of God. Soon after his ordination to the priesthood, St. Alphonsus Liguori (1696–1787) became aware of the pastorally neglected state of the ordinary country folk throughout the kingdom of Naples. His desire to work for these neglected souls was confirmed by a visit to an abandoned shrine of Our Lady in the mountains above the city of Scala on the Amalfi peninsula where hundreds of shepherds and their families gathered to hear him preach. At the same time a contemplative nun in the Visitation Convent at Scala, the Venerable Maria Celeste Crostarosa (1696–1755) saw in vision a new missionary congregation to be headed by the young Liguori. Having consulted widely in Naples and after placing himself under the guidance of Bishop Falcoia of Castellamare, Alphonsus succeeded in inaugurating his missionary society on 9 November 1732 under the title of the Missionaries of the Most Holy Savior. The success of his efforts was finally guaranteed some seventeen years later when his society was approved by Pope Benedict XIV in 1749 with a new title, the Congregation of the Most Holy Redeemer, or simply, the Redemptorists.

Roman approval, however, brought Alphonsus and his missionary society into conflict with the antireligious and anti-Roman policies of the Bourbon kings of Naples and their prime minister, Bernard Tanucci. The congregation survived precariously, being on the verge of suppression all during the lifetime of Alphonsus. Foundations in Rome and in the Papal States, free from Bourbon influence, finally assured its survival. In 1784, that restless hermit from Moravia, the future St. Clement Mary Hofbauer, entered the congregation in Rome. Ordained the following year, he left with the blessing of the existing superior general to establish the Redemptorists in Vienna and then in Warsaw in Poland. Despite enormous difficulties the congregation continued to expand into Switzerland, Germany, France, Belgium, Holland, England, and Ireland. In 1832 the first Redemptorists set sail from Europe for the United States, establishing themselves in Pittsburgh, New York, Philadelphia, and Rochester. The first provincial superior of the Redemptorists, John Neumann, became the fourth bishop of Philadelphia in 1852 and in 1977 was the first member of the American hierarchy to be canonized.

From the second half of the nineteenth century the Redemptorists have exercised considerable influence in the life of the Church, particularly in the areas of moral and dogmatic theology as well as in determining the direction of popular devotional practice, not least in the area of devotion to the Mother of God under the title of Our Lady of Perpetual Help. Their theologians assured widespread acceptance of the theological positions adopted by their founder who was declared a Doctor of the Church in the immediate aftermath of the First Vatican Council in 1871. Important ecclesiastical figures such as Cardinal Deschamps, archbishop of Malines, Cardinal Van Rossum, prefect of Propaganda Fide, as well as theologians like Marc, Wouters, Aertnys, Damen, the American Connell and post-Vatican II, Bernard Häring, assured a high profile for the Congregation. In the course of the one hundred and forty years since the reorganization of the congregation in 1855 under a superior general in Rome, Clement Hofbauer, Gerard Majella, and John Neumann have been raised to the honors of the altar. Fathers Peter Donders, apostle of the lepers in Surinam, and Gaspar Stanggassinger have been declared Blessed while the causes of several others have been introduced.

The first American superior general, Father William Gaudreau, was elected in 1954. During his period of office the Redemptorists faced the challenge of renewal initiated by the Second Vatican Council. The rule outlined by Crostarosa and modified by Alphonsus was remodeled and a new impetus was given to the traditional apostolate of preaching the Word of God to those most in need. Today (1992) the congregation has some six thousand members divided into forty independent provinces.

FREDERICK JONES, C.SS.R.

See also LIGUORI, ALPHONSUS, ST.; NEUMANN, JOHN NEPOMUCENE, ST.; RELIGIOUS ORDERS.

REFORMATION, CHRONOLOGY OF THE

1494 Reforms of Savonarola in Florence

1499 foundation of University of Alcala, Spain

1509 Erasmus: *The Praise of Folly*

1510 first priest ordained in America: Bartolome de las Casas, defender of Native Americans

1512 Fifth Lateran Council (to 1517)

1516 Erasmus: New Testament in Greek and Latin

1517 31 October: Luther's ninety-five theses

1518 Luther summoned to Rome

1519 Charles V elected Holy Roman Emperor
Luther's disputation with John Eck
Zwingli begins Reformation in Zurich

1520 bull of Leo X, *Exsurge Domine,* calling Luther to submit, burned by Luther
Luther's *Address to the Christian Nobility of the German Nation*
beginning of Anabaptist movement

1521 Luther excommunicated
Diet of Worms. Luther placed under Imperial ban

1522 Turks occupy Belgrade
Luther's translation of the New Testament into German
Polyglot Bible published by University of Alcala

1523 Zwingli presents his reforming program to the government of Zurich

1524 Peasants' uprising in Germany
founding of Theatine order

1525 founding of Capuchin Franciscans by Matteo Bassi

1526 Diet of Speyer: tolerance of Lutherans left to conscience of rulers
Battle of Mohacs: Turks defeat Hungarians, take Buda

1527 Sack of Rome by imperial troops
Diet of Västeras (Sweden): seizure of Church lands
Henry VIII seeks annulment of marriage to Catherine of Aragon
first Protestant university at Marburg

1528 Papal recognition of Capuchin Franciscans

1529 Second Diet of Speyer: revocation of tolerance of Lutheranism. Protest of the free cities and Lutheran princes
Marburg colloquy between Luther and Zwingli
Luther: *Greater and Smaller Catechisms*
Turks threaten Vienna

1530 Diet of Augsburg: *Augsburg Confession;* Diet calls on Lutherans to submit on pain of war

1531 founding of Schmalkaldic League of Protestant states
death of Huldrych Zwingli in the second war of Kappel

1532 Peace of Nuremberg: legal recognition of Protestants until a general council

1534 Henry VIII declared supreme head of Church in England

Anabaptists declare "New Jerusalem" in Münster

completion of Luther's translation of Bible into German

foundation of Society of Jesus by Ignatius of Loyola

1535 founding of Ursuline order

trial and execution of Thomas More

1536 Paul III calls a general council (which meets in 1545)

establishment of Lutheranism in Denmark and Norway

Calvin takes part in reform in Geneva; *Institutes of the Christian Religion*

dissolution of the monasteries in England

1537 *Report of a Select Committee on Reforming the Church* submitted to Paul III

publication of first Catholic hymnal

1538 Calvin expelled from Geneva

formation of the Catholic League of German princes

1539 Colloquy of Worms: attempt at theological reconciliation of Lutherans and Catholics

the "Six Articles": doctrinal statement of religion imposed by Henry VIII

1540 Papal approval of Society of Jesus (Jesuits)

1541 Calvin returns to Geneva: *Ecclesiastical Ordinances* summarize structure of Church

Ignatius of Loyola completes *The Spiritual Exercises*

Colloquy of Ratisbon between reformers and papal representatives

John Knox leads Calvinist Reformation in Scotland

1542 Paul III introduces Roman Inquisition

"New Laws" declare equality of Spanish and Indians in Americas

1543 Paul III issues Index of prohibited books

1544 founding of University of Mexico

1545 first meeting of Council of Trent (sessions 1–8) (to 1549)

1546 death of Martin Luther

war of Charles V against Protestant states

1547 Battle of Muhlberg: victory of Charles V against Protestants

death of Henry VIII; accession of Edward VI

1548 Diet of Augsburg: "Augsburg Interim" gives Protestants disciplinary concessions

Francis Xavier founds Jesuit mission in Japan

1549 promulgation of *Book of Common Prayer* with Lutheran view of Communion

1551 Thomas Cranmer: "Forty-two Articles"

Second meeting of Council of Trent (sessions 9–16) (to 1552)

foundation of Collegio Romano by Jesuits

foundation of University of Lima

1552 revision of *Book of Common Prayer,* with Zwinglian view of Communion

1553 accession of Queen Mary in England: attempted restoration of Catholicism

1555 Peace of Augsburg. Rulers determine religion of states

Abdication of Charles V; accession of Philip II

1558 accession of Queen Elizabeth I in England. Act of Supremacy makes her supreme governor of Church of England. Act of Uniformity establishes *Book of Common Prayer* for worship

1560 Protestantism established by Parliament in Scotland

1562 Huguenot wars in France (to 1598)

Third meeting of Council of Trent (sessions 17–25) (to 1563)

Teresa of Avila begins further reform of Carmelite Order

1563 the Thirty-nine Articles defined by the Convocations of Canterbury and York

1564 death of John Calvin

founding of Congregation of the Oratory in Rome by Philip Neri

1566 *Advertisements* of Matthew Parker, Archbishop of Canterbury, enforce uniformity in Anglican liturgy. "Puritans" react

1567 revolt of Netherlands against Spanish rule

1568 founding of first house of Discalced Carmelites by John of the Cross

first Jesuits arrive in Peru

1569 Spanish Inquisition extended to Americas

1570 excommunication of Elizabeth I of England

1571 penal legislation against Catholics in England begins

battle of Lepanto: Turks defeated

1572 first Jesuits arrive in Mexico

St. Bartholomew's Day massacre: two thousand Huguenots killed in France

1593 Sweden adopts Augsburg Confession

1598 Edict of Nantes grants toleration to Huguenots in France

1599 Matteo Ricci founds first Catholic church in Nanking

1600 persecution of Catholics in Sweden under Charles IX

1608 establishment of Reductions in Paraguay by Jesuits

Francis de Sales: *Introduction to the Devout Life*

formation of the Evangelical Union of Protestant states

1609 formation of the Catholic League

1618 beginning of Thirty-Years War

1620 Battle of White Mountain: victory of Catholic League

foundation of Plymouth Colony by Puritans

1625 foundation of Sisters of Mercy by Vincent de Paul

1629 Edict of Restitution of Church lands in Germany

1635 Cardinal Richelieu allies France with Protestant Sweden

1641 Catholic rebellion in Ireland

1642 Puritan revolution in England; beginning of civil war

1648 Peace of Westphalia ends Thirty-Year War. Reformed Churches recognized

RICHARD VILADESAU

See also REFORMATION, THE.

REFORMATION, THE

The Notion of the Reformation

The Latin term *reformatio* (from *reformare,* to renew, give new form) was frequently used in Middle Ages to designate attempts to change both the Church and society. With regard to the Church, the idea implied a turn away from worldliness and a purification of doctrine and practice. It was sometimes linked to a hope for a general "rebirth" ("renaissance"). There had been a number of significant reform movements throughout the Middle Ages; but the word has come to refer especially to the Reformation of the sixteenth century in its various aspects. Like earlier attempts at purification, this movement originally implied no intent of division of the Church; but when Rome condemned the Reformers and the latter concluded that Roman Church was not only corrupt in practice but was in theological error, the reform eventually led to the separation of large parts of Christianity from communion with Rome and with each other. The term as used here includes also the effort to reform the Catholic Church from within. The "Catholic Reformation" (sometimes called the "Counter Reformation") of the sixteenth and seventeenth centuries was in fact a continuation of the impetus to reform that existed already before Luther, which was intensified and given focus (especially theologically) as a reaction against Protestantism.

Background and Causes of the Reformation

A number of factors contributed to the eruption and rapid success of the Reformation. Conditions in the Church and society were probably not worse than in some previous periods. It was the particular combination of these conditions with a new social and intellectual environment that made the Reformation possible.

The Condition of the Church. The Church at the beginning of the sixteenth century stood in great need of purification and reform at every level. The Renaissance popes frequently lived more like secular princes than like spiritual leaders. Their personal lives were sometimes scandalous. Their position as rulers of the Papal States involved them in warfare and political intrigue. Their political and artistic projects (like the refurbishing of the Vatican by Italy's leading artists and the building of the new St. Peter's Basilica) demanded the expenditure of enormous amounts of money. The Roman Curia, the central administrative body of the Church, was top-heavy, inefficient, and corrupt; positions were frequently sold to raise funds for a depleted papal treasury.

Most bishops came from the nobility, and had little contact with their flocks. In many places, secular rulers had control of the appointment of bishops and the disposition of other Church offices; they used them to reward their relatives and friends with lucrative positions. Some episcopal sees in the Holy Roman Empire were also princedoms, combining in the bishop the spiritual and secular rule over vast territories.

Frequently bishops and pastors had multiple "benefices" from which they drew income without attending to their pastoral responsibilities or even residing in the place, while the actual care of parishes was left to poorly paid and ill-educated curates. Celibacy was poorly observed; it was common for clergy to have concubines or common-law wives. Discipline in the monasteries was lax. Preaching was neglected, especially by the secular clergy. Not surprisingly, popular religion was riddled with superstition and theological misunderstanding. Much devotion centered around relics (some of them false) and their shrines. The "Real Presence" in the Eucharist was often understood in a materialistic way, and the sacrament was seen more as something to be adored than to be received.

The Political and Social Situation. The political and economic structure of Europe was in a state of change at the turn of the sixteenth century. The recent discovery of America had not yet had an appreciable effect; but increased trade and the growth of a money-based economy were changing the nature of economic power. In England, France, and Spain, the authority of the central government was increasing. Monarchs attempted to curb the rival power of the Church by controlling Church appointments and limiting the outflow of money to Rome (causing the papacy to depend more on the German states, which lacked a powerful central authority). They resisted traditional Church privileges, like the freedom of clergy from secular jurisdiction. In the Holy Roman Empire, on the other hand, there was great instability: the emperor, the great territorial rulers, the lower nobility under them, and the free cities all sought to increase their power at the expense of the others. Meanwhile, the eastern borders of the empire were constantly threatened by the military expansion of the Turks. On the local as well as the national and territorial levels there was expansion of civil power: town councils began to take over education, public morality, and the care of poor, all at one time the domain of Church institutions.

The Intellectual Climate. The Renaissance movement of humanism (literary culture based on the study of Greek and Roman classics) challenged the accepted authorities of the Middle Ages. Christian humanists like Erasmus of Rotterdam studied biblical languages and attempted to produce reliable editions and translations of the Scriptures. Erasmus's influential book *The Praise of Folly* (1509) ridiculed the abuses in the Church and its decadent Scholastic theology. Erasmus also deplored the superstitions of popular piety, and called for a return to the simple and pure religion of the Gospels. The use of the recently invented printing press allowed for the widespread dissemination of such ideas.

Philosophy and theology were largely dominated by Nominalism, a theory that mistrusted the ability of the human mind to reach universal truths, and emphasized concrete individual things. This tendency favored the development of the empirical sciences; on the other hand, it divested philosophy of any knowledge of the being or substance of things, and reduced it to a study of logic. Without a philosophical doctrine of "substance," Scholastic Eucharistic theory ("transubstantiation") was undermined. Deprived of the support of rational knowledge of the divine nature, theology tended to voluntarism—the view that God's will, rather than intelligibility, is primary. Moral precepts—even that of love itself—were then seen as the revelation of God's arbitrary will or "law," rather than as intrinsically good. The practical result was frequently legalism. Luther's ideas both reflected and reacted against this type of theology, in which he was educated.

Early Attempts at Reform. Attempts at reforming the Church were not lacking. In Bohemia, Jan Hus attacked clerical abuses and the authority of Rome, denied the doctrine of transubstantiation, and called for Communion under both species for the laity. (Hus was burned as a heretic in 1415.) The Dominican Girolamo Savonarola in 1494 established a puritanical theocracy in Florence; he condemned the worldliness of the pope and called for his deposition. (Savonarola was burned in 1498.)

In the wake of the schism of 1378 through 1417 (during which there were two and sometimes three claimants to the papacy) the Councils of Constance (1414) and Basle (1431) attempted to change the structure of Church authority by calling for frequent councils and affirming their superiority over the pope ("conciliarism"). Subsequently several popes attempted (without great success) to reform the Roman Curia, and in 1513 an ambitious program of reform was presented to Leo X.

The most successful reforms were carried out at the grassroots level. Many houses of the religious orders, especially of the preaching friars, were purified in their observance. Some of these would later become centers of resistance to Protestantism. In Germany there was a series of reforming bishops, who were sometimes joined by local rulers in their efforts at reforming clergy and religious. In France, provincial councils initiated a reform of the secular clergy.

In the Low Countries and north Germany the movement of the Devotio Moderna ("modern way of devotion") formulated a new kind of religious life, modeled on the example of Christ, and initiated communities of laity living together without vows.

The most comprehensive disciplinary reform occurred in Spain, through the combined efforts of the monarchy and the hierarchy. The Spanish Inquisition (which was directly under the control of the king, with no appeal to Rome possible) was introduced in 1481 to ensure orthodoxy. The energetic Franciscan Cardinal Ximénez (Grand Inquisitor and primate of Spain, 1495–1517) enforced the observance of poverty on monks and friars and dissolved communities that resisted. He obliged pastors to reside in their parishes, to expound the Scriptures, and to instruct children. To train clergy and theologians he created the University of Alcalá, which became a center of the humanistic and reforming ideas of Erasmus. It produced a Spanish translation of the Gospels and epistles (1512), and later a critical edition of the Bible in Hebrew, Greek, and Latin.

Martin Luther and the Beginnings of the Reformation in Germany

The Controversy over Indulgences. "Indulgence" originally referred to the reduction or cancellation of certain ecclesiastical penalties. By the sixteenth century it had come to be understood as the remission of the temporal punishment due to sin (in purgatory), granted by the pope from the treasury of the merits of Christ and the saints, in view of some good work performed by the indulgence seeker. In 1517 Pope Leo X permitted the proclamation of an indulgence in the territories of Archbishop Albert of Mainz; the "good work" required was a contribution toward the building of St. Peter's basilica. (The faithful were not told that half the contributions were to go to Albert to pay the debt he incurred for his "installation fee" as archbishop.) Albert and the preachers of the indulgence made extraordinary claims for it: remission not only of punishment, but of sin itself; or, for souls in purgatory, immediate release, without repentance on the part of the contributor. It was easy for uneducated people to think that they were "buying" grace.

On 31 October 1517, the Augustinian monk Martin Luther, a pastor and professor of theology at the University of Wittenberg, sent to the archbishop and others copies of his "Ninety-five Theses," in which he attacked the sale of indulgences on pastoral and theological grounds. This attack quickly raised other issues, especially that of the authority of the pope. By 1518 Luther was under suspicion of heresy. In 1519, in a public disputation, the theologian John Eck drove Luther to agree with some of the positions of the condemned heretic Jan Hus, and to deny the infallibility not only of the pope, but also of Church councils.

Development of Luther's Theology. Even before the indulgence controversy, Luther's personal struggles had led him to conclude that human beings cannot win assurance of salvation by their own efforts to conquer sin, but only by accepting God's grace through faith. This insight, founded on his reading of the Scriptures, was to become the basis of his doctrine of "justification by faith alone." His conflict with Rome led him to develop the position that the Scriptures are the sole normative authority for the Church. On this basis, he eliminated doctrines and practices that he thought had no basis in Scripture.

At the start, Luther's message was principally a denunciation of abuses and a call for a more spiritual Church. His views were regarded sympathetically by many, including some bishops, because of his spiritual message and because of nationalist German opposition to Roman power. Even his more radical positions were at first not totally beyond the pale of theological discussion (for example, papal infallibility was only defined in 1870, and the Renaissance popes themselves had disputed the authority of councils). As time went on, however, Luther more explicitly attacked not only abusive practices, but also Church doctrines. In his *Address to the Christian Nobility of the German Nation* (1520), he called upon the secular princes to reform the Church. He emphasized the priesthood of all believers and identified the papacy with Antichrist. In other writings he denied the theory of transubstantiation and reduced the sacraments first to three (baptism, Eucharist, and confession) and then to two (eliminating confession).

The Formal Condemnation of Luther. Rome reacted slowly to Luther for fear of alienating his protector, Duke Frederick the Wise of Saxony. But in 1520 Pope Leo X issued the bull "Rise, O Lord," (*Exsurge Domine*), calling on Luther to submit; Luther burned it publicly. In 1521 Luther was formally excommunicated. At an Imperial Diet (assembly of territorial rulers) at Worms, he was declared an outlaw (the "Edict of Worms").

The Growth of the Reformation

Development of Lutheran Church Practice. The Elector Frederick the Wise protected Luther, shutting him in the castle at Wartburg, where he completed his translation of the New Testament into German, making it accessible to common people.

Meanwhile, his movement gained momentum. In his absence, the first "evangelical" congregation was formed in Wittenberg. The practical implications of Luther's ideas were thought out and began to be implemented. Priests, and shortly afterwards monks and nuns, were permitted to marry. Convents and monasteries were closed. The obligation of confession was eliminated. Communion was given under both species. On his reappearance, Luther himself contributed to a new Church structure, producing a new formula for the Mass in 1523.

Expansion of the Reformation in Germany. The Reformers used the vernacular language to reach the people with their ideas, publishing many tracts that were disseminated throughout Germany. They emphasized interior religion, rather than outward forms; freedom in the spirit, rather than the law; and utter dependence on grace rather than works. They also attacked and satirized the abusive practices and the doctrines of Rome. The new ideas received widespread popular support, especially in the cities. Aside from genuine religious conviction, there were sometimes reasons of self-interest involved in the acceptance of the reforms; for example, the nobility were eager to appropriate Church lands and properties.

The Political Course of the Reformation in Germany. Many territorial rulers who had not been present at Worms considered its decree illegal. The Diet of Speyer in 1526 concluded that it was impossible to enforce the Edict of Worms, and allowed the territorial rulers to deal with the reform movement according to their consciences until a Church council could be convened. The Holy Roman Emperor Charles V, who was also king of Spain, was preoccupied with threats from both France and the Turks, and was unable to proceed forcefully against the Lutheran movement. Instead, the Catholic emperor found himself at war with the pope, who as an Italian prince was an ally of France. The emperor's German Lutheran troops under the Spanish duke of Alba sacked Rome in 1527.

In 1529 the Catholic majority at the Second Diet of Speyer revoked the toleration decreed in 1526. The Lutheran princes and free cities protested—whence arose the name "Protestant" (those of the Zwinglian and Calvinist tradition prefer "Reformed").

In 1530 Charles V called another diet at Augsburg, at which the Lutherans presented their position in a moderate document written by Philip Melanchthon known as the "Augsburg Confession." The effort at conciliation failed, largely through misunderstandings, and the Lutherans were given six months to submit, on pain of war. In response they formed the Schmalkaldic League (1531) to resist.

Because of new threats from the Turks, the Emperor was forced to the Peace of Nuremberg (1532), which granted legal recognition to the Lutherans until a Church council could be called. In 1536 Pope Paul III called a council (which began in 1545). In 1538 the Catholic League was formed to oppose the Protestant alliance. But the emperor was forced again to grant tolerance to the Protestant states in order to gain their aid in fighting the Turks. In 1546, after concluding peace with France and an armistice with the Turks, Charles declared war against the unsubmissive states. Despite his military victory, the emperor was unable to impose religious uniformity immediately. The "Augsburg Interim" (1548) temporarily allowed the Protestants a married clergy and Communion under both species.

When it became apparent that Charles was seeking not only the return of Catholicism, but also an increase in imperial power, he lost the support even of the Catholic territorial rulers, and the hope of a Catholic restoration was lost. In the Peace of Augsburg (1555), the principle was established that each state of the empire should be Lutheran or Catholic according to the religion of its ruler; but ecclesiastical rulers whose territory had become Protestant lost their lands. Zwinglians, Calvinists, and members of other sects were not included in the Peace; it would be nearly a century before they would receive legal recognition at the Peace of Westphalia (1648).

Divisions in the Continental Reformation

Although all the Reformers agreed in condemning abuses in the Church and in opposing the authority of Rome, they differed in their theology and their ideas about Church structure and practice. Differences soon arose among the Reformers associated with Luther. His colleague Andreas Karlstadt taught a more radical view of the separation of flesh and spirit, and held that art and music should be eliminated from the Church. Meanwhile, in other parts of the empire an independent reform movement began to appear.

The Churches that eventually differentiated themselves represent three main traditions: (1) the Lutheran or "Evangelical," which became the state religion in parts of Germany and in the Scandinavian countries; (2) the Reformed, stemming from Zwingli's and Calvin's reforms in the Swiss cities; (3) the Anabaptist, the direct source of the Mennonites and Hutterites and an indirect inspiration for the later Quakers, Baptists, and Congregationalists. The reformation in England merged elements from these tendencies in a national Church to form the Anglican tradition.

Thomas Müntzer and the Peasants' Uprising. One of Luther's strongest critics among the Reformers was Thomas Müntzer, who believed that the political rule of God could be established on earth. He accused Luther of watering down the gospel and of subservience to the established rulers. In 1524 the peasants in central Germany rebelled. In 1525 Müntzer joined them and became their spiritual leader, linking their cause to his theology. Luther disapproved the use of violence in the service of the gospel. He condemned the peasant uprising and called on the nobles to crush it. The peasants were defeated and Müntzer executed.

Ulrich Zwingli. The secular priest Ulrich Zwingli, a humanist and follower of Erasmus, in 1523 proposed a program of reform to the city council of Zurich. Zwingli rejected the use of images and music in church and the interpretation of the Mass as a sacrifice. His ideas were accepted and imposed on the city by the political authorities. The Zwinglian branch of the Reformation was characterized by strict collaboration of Church and state, both of which were to be under the rule of God ("theocracy"). Zwingli was killed in 1531 in a war against the Catholic Swiss cantons. The expansion of his ideas into other allied cities, including Geneva, set the stage for John Calvin.

The main issue that divided Luther from Zwingli was the interpretation of the Eucharist. Luther denied the theory of transubstantiation, but affirmed a Real Presence of Christ. Zwingli (at his most extreme) thought of the Eucharist simply as a memorial of Christ's death. Luther and Zwingli were brought together for a colloquy at Marburg in 1529. Luther found Zwingli theologically and politically radical, and thought that union with him would hurt chances of concord with the emperor. No substantial agreement was reached on the issue of the Eucharist. It became the source of a vehement controversy that permanently divided the two traditions.

In liturgical practice Zwingli was more radical than Luther. His Communion service was performed without an altar or vestments. He introduced other services that consisted only of a sermon and prayers.

The Anabaptists. The Anabaptists were originally followers of Zwingli who wanted a quicker and more radical reform. They insisted that baptism should be performed only in adulthood, as the sign of personal commitment to Christ (hence the name "Anabaptists," or "rebaptizers," since they did not acknowledge infant baptism and performed the ceremony anew for those who had received it). They renounced violence and saw membership in the Church as a completely voluntary personal decision; hence they preached religious liberty and the total separation of Church and state. They were persecuted by the Zwinglians and Lutherans as well as by Catholics. A crisis occurred when the city of Münster, converted to the movement, was declared the "New Jerusalem" and communism and polygamy were introduced. Catholics and Lutherans joined to capture the city and execute the leaders of the movement. Persecution intensified.

A Dutch ex-priest named Menno Simons gave further direction to the Anabaptist movement by emphasizing nonviolence and withdrawal from society. Many of the Mennonites, as his followers were called, eventually migrated to America.

Another group, called Hutterites after their leader Jakob Hutter, formed communes in Moravia. Later, when persecuted, they also migrated to America (where today they are called the Amish).

John Calvin and the Expansion of the Reformed Tradition. The lawyer and humanist John Calvin fled his native France after his adoption of reformation principles. In Basle in 1527 he published the first edition of his *Institutes of the Christian Religion,* a systematic presentation that eventually became the standard text of Reformed theology. Passing through Geneva in 1536, he took part in its Reformation. Expelled in 1538 because of conflict with the civil authorities, he returned in 1541 and was the primary inspiration and authority in the city's attempt to reform both Church and society.

Calvin agreed with Luther on justification by faith and the authority of Scripture. On the Eucharist he took a position somewhere between Luther and Zwingli: there is a real communion with the risen Lord through his universal spiritual presence, although there is no bodily presence of Christ in the sacrament. Although like Zwingli he rejected the use of material aids to worship, he was not quite so severe: he permitted the singing of psalms (which became an important part of Reformed worship) and the use of a plain cross, but not the crucifix or other images.

The characteristic feature of Calvin's thought was his emphasis on the doctrine of predestination. He thought that the "elect" could be discerned by their external profession of faith, strict Christian behavior, and participation in the sacraments (baptism and Eucharist). Moreover, the elect were to establish God's kingdom not only in the Church but in society. This did not mean ecclesiastical rule over the state, but rather that both Church and state were to be ruled by God's word, as in ancient Israel. Civil authorities therefore also had a divinely ordained place in ordering society according to Christian principles, and collaborated with the Church's ministers in maintaining correct faith and morals. The city of Geneva became the model of such a society.

After the Peace of Augsburg (1555) Lutheranism was preoccupied with internal disagreements. Calvinism (which was not included in the peace) became the most dynamic force of the Reformation. It was the basis of John Knox's reform in Scotland and of the Puritan movement in England. It also became the dominant form of the Reformation in the Netherlands, and an important factor in their struggle for independence from Spain.

Calvinism spread quickly in France. The Huguenots (as French Protestants were called after about 1560, when Calvinism began to be the dominant form) were supported by some of the prominent nobility. The question of religion became enmeshed with a struggle for political power. In 1562 began the French "Wars of Religion" that lasted, with uneasy intervals of peace, until 1598. In that year King Henry IV, himself a former Huguenot, proclaimed the Edict of Nantes, which conceded freedom of worship throughout France. Unlike the Peace of Augsburg, which allowed territorial rulers to determine the religion of their subjects, the edict gave freedom of conscience to all. It thus implied that the political unity of the nation was possible without religious unity.

The Reformation in England

Henry VIII and the Break with Rome. The influence of Lutheranism was already felt in England in the 1520s. King Henry VIII opposed it with a defense of the Catholic doctrine of the sacraments, for which Pope Leo X granted him the title "Defender of the Faith." But when Henry was unable to obtain from the Pope an annulment of his marriage to Catherine of Aragon, he decided to take matters into his own hands. A series of Acts of Parliament, culminating in the Act of Supremacy (1534), declared the King to be the supreme head of the Church of England. The new archbishop of Canterbury, Thomas Cranmer, declared the desired annulment. Sir Thomas More and John Fisher, bishop of Rochester, were beheaded for refusing to acknowledge the royal supremacy over the Church (both were later canonized). In 1536 Henry dissolved the monasteries of the kingdom and seized their properties. Apart from the question of authority, the teaching and practice of the Church remained essentially Catholic; the "Six Articles" of 1539 retained clerical celibacy and the doctrine of transubstantiation.

The Book of Common Prayer. Protestant leanings dominated the English Church during the reign of Henry's successor, Edward VI. *The Book of Common Prayer* (1549; revised, 1552), the new order of worship for the Anglican Church, espoused first a Lutheran and then a Zwinglian view of the Eucharist.

The Catholic Restoration. Under Queen Mary, the daughter of Catherine of Aragon, an unsuccessful attempt was made to reestablish Catholicism in England. John Foxe's *The Book of Martyrs,* describing the persecution of Protestants, greatly influenced public feeling and increased hostility to Catholicism. Exiles on the Continent, especially in Geneva, experienced new ideas and models of Church structure. Some began to feel that the Reformation in England had not gone far enough.

The Reign of Elizabeth I. Protestantism was restored on the accession of Elizabeth I (1558). The Act of Supremacy made her supreme governor of the Church of England, and the Act of Uniformity reestablished worship as it had been in the first years of Edward VI. The new edition of the *Book of Common Prayer* used more ambiguous language with regard to Communion, leaving the question of the Real Presence unsettled. The official Church strove for uniformity of practice, while leaving room for wide divergence of theological opinion. The Church's legislative body, the Convocation, in 1563 issued the "Thirty-nine Articles," a basic statement of classical Protestant doctrine.

The implication of Catholics in plots against the Queen, the revolt of Catholic nobles in the north (1569), the attempt of Philip II of Spain to invade England with his armada, and the bull of Pope Pius V excommunicating Elizabeth and releasing her subjects from obedience to her (1570), all made Catholics automatically suspect of disloyalty. In 1571 began the penal legislation against Catholics. By 1585 it was high treason for a Catholic priest to remain in England. Between 1577 and 1603, 123 priests were executed, as well as some 60 men and women who had sheltered them.

The Puritans and Separatists. The Anglican liturgy as restored under Queen Elizabeth included the use of vestments and other liturgical practices that seemed to some too close to Catholicism. These "Puritans," as they were called (at first derisively), desired a more radical form of Protestantism. The Puritan movement included various strands. Some questioned the episcopal form of Church government, favoring councils of clergy (Presbyterianism). Some urged separation from the Church of England. Some eventually left England for more tolerant Holland and then for America to establish a holy commonwealth on Calvinist lines. The movement eventually evolved into a potent political force that would divide England in civil war (1642–1649).

Other groups of dissenters at the end of the sixteenth century would eventually separate from the established Church. Several eventually became major denominations in America: the Congregationalists, Baptists, and Quakers.

The Catholic Reformation or "Counter Reformation"

The Catholic Reformation was both a continuation of pre-Lutheran efforts at internal reform of the Church and an attempt to meet the challenge of Protestantism.

Attempts at Reconciliation. From the start of the Reformation Catholics were divided between a policy of reconciliation and confrontation.

Several dialogues were held between the Lutherans and Catholics, most importantly at Worms (1539) and Ratisbon (1541). The Catholic representative, the humanist Cardinal Contarini, like many others in the Church, agreed with the Reformers that abusive practices in the Church, including those in the Roman Curia, had to be ended. Like the emperor, he also hoped for theological conciliation. Agreement was actually reached on the doctrine of justification by faith, but the talks broke down on the issue of transubstantiation.

Luther was suspicious of such efforts at reconciliation. They also met with opposition from conservative forces in Rome, which on the whole preferred the path of militant opposition. There were also political obstacles: German Protestant rulers did not want to give up Church property they had appropriated, and the French king Francis I, who was the Pope's ally, did not wish to see the empire united.

Reforms in Religious and Clerical Life. The effort to reform the church from within centered largely on eliminating abuses among the clergy and religious. Several new orders appeared that aimed at reestablishing the credibility of the ascetical life. The Capuchins (founded 1528) were a reformed order of Franciscans. They were devoted to poverty and to pastoral charity, especially work in hospitals and preaching. The Ursulines (1535) were an order of women who originally lived at home, worshiped with the parish, and lived lives of charity and social concern. Most significant was the Society of Jesus, founded by the Spanish Basque Ignatius of Loyola in 1534 and approved by the pope in 1540. The Jesuits formed the forefront of the counteroffensive against Protestantism, carrying a militant and spiritually renewed Catholicism into education, the missions, pastoral activity, the arts, and politics.

The hierarchy and secular clergy were also the object of reforming efforts. In 1536 Pope Paul III appointed a commission to write a memorandum on reform. Its report recommended abolishing absenteeism in parishes and dioceses, and denounced the misuse of episcopal authority, the avarice of cardinals, and extreme claims for the papacy.

The Council of Trent (1545–1565). From the start of the Reformation there were appeals for a general Church council to address the doctrinal and practical issues it raised. The popes, however, remembering the Councils of Basle and Constance, were afraid that a council might limit their authority. If there were to be a council, they wished it to be held in Rome, under close papal supervision. The emperor and German princes wanted the council in Germany. The French opposed anything that would settle the turmoil in the empire. A council was called in 1536 by Pope Paul III; it began to meet in 1545 in the city of Trent (chosen because although in Italy it was still part of the empire).

The emperor wished the council to deal primarily with practical matters, to reform the Church and make certain disciplinary concessions to the Lutherans. In accord with the pope's wishes, however, definition of doctrine dominated the council's deliberations. Lutheran representatives were invited to the council. On their arrival in 1551 they insisted that deliberations should start again from the beginning; the bishops refused. All hope of a council of reconciliation was lost; Trent instead defined Catholic teaching in opposition to the theology of the Reformers.

Doctrinal Clarification. The council's teachings were framed in a polemical context, and therefore emphasized those aspects of doctrine that seemed challenged by Reformation theology. But the decrees were carefully worded to permit diverse opinions within the general framework of their teaching. As contemporary ecumenical dialogue has shown, they left a great deal more room for possible agreement, once misunderstandings were eliminated, than was sometimes realized in the hostile climate of the following centuries.

The council taught that the truths and practices of the Church have as their source both the Scriptures and non-written apostolic tradition (without clearly defining what this tradition contains). It also defined the canon (list of inspired books) of Scripture, including in the Old Testament not only the Hebrew Bible, but also the Greek "apocrypha."

With regard to the central question of "justification," or how salvation takes place, the council insisted that mere trust in God's mercy is not sufficient. We must freely "cooperate" with grace through love in order to be saved; that is, God's freely given grace must truly change us interiorly. It insisted that no one is "predestined" by God to reject grace.

The council enumerated and discussed seven sacraments (while the Protestants recognized only two or three). It taught that in the Mass the one sacrifice of Christ is truly present (but not repeated), and reaffirmed the doctrine of transubstantiation in the Eucharist.

Disciplinary Reform. It was obvious to all that reforms were needed in Church life; but there were disagreements about their kind and extent. The Spanish bishops, for example, thought that it was a matter of divine law that bishops should reside in their dioceses; but Rome employed many bishops in the central administration of the Church. On the other hand, the Catholic princes of south Germany thought that the Church should be flexible in certain matters of practice demanded by the Lutherans, like a married clergy and Communion under both species; Rome was generally against concessions (although in 1564 Pius IV did give permission for Communion under both species in many parts of Germany).

The disciplinary decrees of Trent became the main source of Catholic Church practice until the Second Vatican Council. A major focus was the fostering of a well-educated and pure clergy. The council for the first time created a system of regular education for candidates for priesthood, instructing that a seminary should be established in every diocese that did not have a university.

The council described the office of bishop in terms of pastoral responsibility, including preaching, and gave bishops more power of supervision in their dioceses, removing many of the exemptions that had previously limited episcopal authority. It abolished the office of "quaestor" or purveyor of indulgences. It called for synods of clergy.

Other reforms were aimed at doctrinal orthodoxy and uniformity of practice. A new edition of the Index of condemned books was issued (1564). The success of Luther's catechisms inspired Rome to produce its own (1566): it was intended not for children or parents, but for the clergy. The first draft was revised by Charles Borromeo, archbishop of Milan. He also aided in the production of a new, clearer, and simpler breviary (1568), from which many nonscriptural readings were removed. Against the Protestant preference for the language of the people, Trent decided that the Mass should normally be celebrated in Latin, and a new Roman Missal (1570) established its ritual.

The full implementation of the council's decrees took time. The council was solemnly received in Spain in 1564 and in southern Germany (but not by the emperor) in 1566, but in France not until 1615. The Roman Inquisition had no power outside Italy; secular rulers would not permit its interference with their authority. It was difficult to ensure that bishops would be pastoral and spiritual men when many episcopal appointments remained in the hands of kings, who frequently used them for political purposes.

Spirituality and Devotional Practice. The spirituality of the Catholic Reformation emphasized doctrinal orthodoxy, moral purity, asceticism, and mysticism.

While many of the Renaissance popes had been causes of scandal, Pius V (Pope, 1565–1572; canonized in 1712) set an example of asceticism and morality. He limited luxurious living in the papal territories and imposed penalties for simony, blasphemy, sodomy, and concubinage. He reformed the Roman Curia and tried to force bishops residing in Rome to return to their dioceses. He forced secular priests to wear distinctive clerical dress (influenced by the black costumes of the Spanish court) and to shave their beards, while forbidding physicians and academic doctors to wear the biretta.

Traditional forms of piety were revived and extended. Frequent confession and Communion were encouraged, and the first printed Catholic hymnal appeared in 1537. Since the Mass remained in Latin, however, spirituality was generally more individual and personal than liturgical. While previously the reservation of the Eucharist had been somewhat haphazard, now elaborate tabernacles appeared in churches, emphasizing the enduring Real Presence. The modern form of Benediction with the Blessed Sacrament also took shape during this period.

Spirituality reflected the idea of the triumph of God's grace. Mysticism, the experience of intense immediate union with God even on earth, flourished in such figures as Teresa of Avila and John of the Cross. There was a new devotion to the humanity of Jesus, and an emphasis on affection, emotion, and the use of imagination in prayer. The idea of human cooperation with grace was expressed in the devotion to Mary and the saints. The Spanish theologian Suarez developed the idea of a collaboration of Mary in the work of redemption.

The use of art and music reflected the idea that God attracts the soul by beauty, sweetness, and grandeur. Churches were lavishly decorated, and the new Baroque style in art inculcated a sense of glory and triumph. Church music was influenced by the spirit of mysticism, and strove to elevate the soul by its ethereal beauty.

Accompanying the renewal of clerical and religious life was a new emphasis on spirituality for the laity. The Spiritual Exercises of Ignatius of Loyola gave rise to the practice of retreats for laypersons as well as religious. The Jesuits preached a life of devotion that is accessible and attractive to all, while their scholars like Robert Bellarmine (d. 1621) defended the intellectual credibility of the Catholic tradition. Francis de Sales (bishop of Geneva, 1602–1622; canonized 1665) in his *Introduction to the Devout Life* (1609) and *Treatise on the Love of God* (1616) taught that contemplative prayer is possible for all and that all laypersons should have a spiritual director to aid them on the path of perfection, to which all are called.

A major expression of the vigor of the Catholic Reformation spirit was the expansion of missionary activity. The first priest ordained in America, the Dominican Bartolomé de las Casas, energetically took up the defense of the native peoples against exploitation. His spirit was followed by others, especially among the Jesuits, who established special settlements for the protection of the natives. Missionaries like Francis Xavier and Matteo Ricci carried Christianity to Asia.

The Political Counter Reformation. During the second half of the sixteenth century militant Catholicism began to reclaim some areas from Protestantism. In Germany, the prince-bishops enforced Catholicism within their territories, where the people frequently had embraced the Reformation. In Poland, where Protestantism was originally strong, the kings gradually suppressed it.

In 1618 the Protestant nobility of Bohemia revolted against the emperor, drove the Jesuits from the country, and offered the crown to the Calvinist Elector of the Palatine, Frederick V. This marked the beginning of the Thirty Years War, which started as a religious struggle between the Catholic and Calvinist states of the empire. Imperial successes eventually brought into the conflict other Protestant states, which feared the forced reconversion of all Germany to Catholicism and the return of all ecclesiastical lands to the Church (as demanded by the Edict of Restitution, 1629).

The war lost its religious character when in 1635 Cardinal Richelieu allied France with Protestant Sweden against the German Empire and the pope refused to condemn the alliance. The Peace of Westphalia in 1648 reestablished the terms of the Peace of Augsburg, but now extended recognition to Calvinists as well as Lutherans and ensured some toleration of religious minorities within states.

Effects of the Reformation

The Reformation is frequently referred to as the beginning of the modern age. Along with the Renaissance, the scientific revolution, and the European discovery of America, it changed the consciousness of the Western world.

The most obvious effect of the Reformation was the division of Western Christianity and a long history of misunderstanding and hostility between the separated Churches. On the positive side, it led to a much-needed purification of Church life and clarification of doctrine. Religion became more personal and individual. Both Protestant and Catholic reformed spirituality emphasized the inner encounter with God. Religious culture was profoundly changed. The Protestant Churches introduced congregational singing; Catholic spirituality found expression in Baroque art and music.

Secular culture was also affected. Luther's translation of the Bible profoundly influenced the development of the German language. His teaching that each person has a vocation directly from God aided in the emergence of lay culture, separate from the realm of the sacred. The decline of ecclesiastical power and the loss of Church lands aided in the formation and strengthening of the new nation-states of Europe. Although it was not intended by the Reformers, the principle of freedom of conscience emerged from the necessity of compromise in the religious wars.

In the Catholic Church, the reaction against Protestantism frequently resulted in defensiveness and narrowness of perspective. Fear of heresy led to theological uniformity and the loss of the theological pluralism that had characterized earlier ages. Authority was emphasized, and Church structure became increasingly centralized in Rome. At the same time, the Catholic Church has gradually absorbed many of the positive insights of the Protestant Reformers, and in the contemporary era has come to acknowledge their contribution. The Second Vatican Council explicitly refers to the Church as "always in need of reform."

RICHARD VILADESAU

See also CALVIN, JOHN; LUTHER, MARTIN; PIUS V, POPE; PROTESTANTISM.

REGINA COELI

See MARY, MOTHER OF GOD.

REIGN OF GOD

See KINGDOM OF GOD.

RELICS

A relic is an object kept and reverenced as a memorial of a holy person. Relics include the bodily remains of such persons (for example, bones or teeth) as well as objects that once belonged to them or which they touched (for example, clothing).

Veneration of relics plays a role in several religious traditions, including Buddhism, and it has been part of Catholic tradition since the early days of the Church. Its origins in Christianity probably lie in the ancient practice of celebrating the Eucharist on the tombs of martyrs. Since the martyrs had died in imitation of Jesus himself, they were considered to be especially blessed by God; they and their possessions were thus highly honored.

Veneration of relics has enjoyed widespread popularity, particularly in the Middle Ages. The Crusades increased this popularity, as objects from the Holy Land were brought back to Europe by returning armies. Relics were and still are often kept in magnificent containers called reliquaries.

Such popularity sometimes led to abuse. Superstition attributed magical powers to the relics; further, a veritable traffic developed in which bones of the saints were bought and sold. And, frequently dealers sold inauthentic relics, defrauding their buyers.

Because of these abuses, Protestant Reformers opposed the veneration of relics. Catholics continue the practice however, as a way of remembering and making present the lives of holy men and women. Today, a relic must be certified as authentic by a Church authority, and relics may not be bought or sold for money. Further, a distinction is maintained between venerating and honoring, on the one hand, and worshiping, on the other. Relics are venerated and honored, but only God is worshiped.

THERESA SANDERS

See also MARTYRDOM; SAINTS; VENERATION OF SAINTS.

RELIGION, VIRTUE OF

St. Thomas Aquinas (ST II-II, q. 81–100) describes this virtue as a supernatural, infused, moral habit that inclines us to give to God the worship that is due him as Supreme Being and as Creator and Lord of the universe. Suarez (*De Religione, Opera Omnia* vv. 13 and 14) treats this virtue immediately after the theological virtues of faith, hope, and charity. Aquinas treats it under the moral virtue of justice.

But God is not simply Lord. He is also Father, Son, and Spirit. Through grace the Christian shares in the divine life, is an adopted child and part of God's family. Thus the virtue of piety also comes into play in our relationship with God. Justice can never be fully satisfied where human beings are concerned (Christ is an exception) but piety can supply the human need.

The virtue of religion was more fully appreciated in a time when the relationship between sovereign and subject was part of the culture. In a more democratic world full appreciation of this virtue is more difficult. Nevertheless the liturgical movement has restored some sense of one's obligation to worship God.

Religion has been called "the inner life of worship." This is because its principal act is the interior submission to God as Lord. Devotion is another interior act of the virtue of religion and is closely connected with love. Because we are body and soul, exterior acts of the virtue of religion are also very important. They are the outward expression of the inner dynamic of religion. Adoration, prayer, gestures and sacramental worship are important exterior acts of the virtue of religion.

While the Thomistic view of this virtue seems better suited to the age of kings, its inner logic and appropriateness can be appreciated in every age.

The Second Vatican Council emphasized the importance of worship especially in its Decree on the Liturgy (*Sacrosanctum Concilium*). The heart of the liturgy and of the Christian life is the offering of the Eucharistic sacrifice. Summit and source of both Christian worship and apostolic life, the liturgy is the ritual offering (and source) of the Christian's prayer, life and works (SC 10).

Since the life of Christ is summarized and recapitulated in his self-offering on Calvary, the Christian's life reaches its zenith in the personal and corporate offering of the body of Christ which is the Church, the assembly of believers together with Jesus Christ, their head.

In an age of individualism and self-gratification, the virtue of religion is an antidote to self-centeredness. Emphasizing the theocentric nature of all existence, it stresses that human beings begin to reach their full potential when they place God at the center of their lives. It recognizes the supreme value of prayer as openness to grace and salvation. Thus human beings are free to become fully who they are: children of God.

E. R. FALARDEAU, S.S.S.

See also CHRISTIAN SPIRITUALITY; PRAYER; VIRTUE.

RELIGIOUS EDUCATION

Religious education takes place when teachers in a school offer courses in religion or religious studies. But religious education is not confined to school classrooms. Long before the advent of universal schooling, religious-minded people have been concerned about making sense of their own religious experience. Insofar as they have brought religion and reflective thought together, they can be said to have engaged in religious education.

Jews have been debating the meaning of their Scriptures from time immemorial. Though they seldom call this work religious education, it surely merits that title, since it involves an interplay of religious text and imaginative debate. The work of theology can also be regarded as a work of religious education, since it involves the critical examination of the sources and practice of a living religion. Parents of every religion have taught their children to reverence God and to respect human values, a daily exercise not just of family life but also of religious education. Now that people are painfully aware of the conflicting claims of the major world religions, and of how these claims have fueled the fires of global conflict, it seems likely that a kind of cross-religion religious education will become even more necessary in the future, if the world is ever to know a real peace.

Three major styles of religious education have been created during almost two thousand years of Christian living.

Initiation as Religious Education

The catechumenate is a procedure for initiating interested people into Christian worship and a life of discipleship. The perennial value of catechumenal initiation is the main reason for the success of the RCIA in recent times. Because the life of faith is complex, those who wish to share it fully need a long period of preparation before they are initiated, and then further enlightenment after initiation. The catechumenate can be likened to a faith-apprenticeship or even to a series of pre-service and in-service courses for professionals. The rituals, doctrines and moral standards of professed Christians are hard to assimilate and people need time to ask what they mean and to relate them to daily life. Indeed, a similar challenge confronts every cultural inheritance. Culture is quite complex and people need time to rehearse it, to live it out and above all to try to comprehend its deepest meanings. To that extent, cultural initiation inevitably demands an educational moment in which one looks at it in depth to see what is hidden from view.

This is what happened in the culture of faith, during its early years. In the hands of teacher-bishops the catechumenate was not just a process of initiation into the mysteries, but also a profoundly reflective or educational experience. Most bishop-initiators were great teachers, great educators. Cyril of Jerusalem gave three hours of daily instruction during Lent. He explained to his potential converts the shape of Christian discipleship by relating it to the Creed. He interpreted the Scriptures for them in relation to Christ and Christian living, and helped them grasp the symbolic power of the rituals in which they were sharing. John Chrysostom prepared his neophytes for baptism through image-filled instructions which still excite the religious imagination. When Augustine of Hippo wrote a letter to his deacon Deogratias, giving practical advice as to how he could teach the elements of the faith more effectively, it was not his intention to compose a major work of educational theory. But this is what happened. *De Catechizandis Rudibus* (*The First Catechetical Instruction*) is primarily an analysis of the complex process of teaching the faith to beginners. But modern educational theorists will sense there many echoes of their own concerns about pupil readiness and motivation, teacher burnout, key attainment targets and core curriculum.

Socialization as Religious Education

During the period of persecution, only those gifted with courage and community support undertook the onerous program of catechumenal initiation. Once Emperor Constantine made Christianity legal, the numbers seeking baptism grew considerably. Large buildings had to be built to facilitate the crowds of neophytes and the increasing number of the faithful. During all this time, the normal seekers of Christian initiation were adults who wished to leave behind their pagan culture and break with their national religion. Matters changed dramatically with the conversion of the pagan tribes of northern Europe. Since their numbers were so great, it was not possible to prepare them all adequately before baptism. Instead, they were baptized in the hope that further instruction would be available later on through regular liturgical practice. This hope was not always realized. As Latin remained the liturgical language, while more and more people began to speak the new European languages, the active conscious liturgical participation of earlier days began slowly to be replaced by a more routine and passive liturgical style. The educational value of an active participation in a vernacular liturgy was gradually lost. But this educational value was often found instead in powerful paraliturgies and morality plays. These were areas where the medieval religious imagination revealed its depth and its educational power.

Once Christianity became the religion of the masses, a new educational dynamic was inevitable. No longer was adult baptism the norm for initiation. No longer did people have to break with family and culture to become a new creation as Christians. The reverse was true. By virtue of being born into a Christian family, people were now socialized into the faith. One learned the faith as one learns one's mother tongue, by immersion in the world of faith from birth. In practice, this meant that family life became central in religious education. People first learned to pray at home. Parents and godparents were truly the first teachers of their children in the ways of faith. The advantages of this system were obvious. Religious education was part of living, part of one's overall culture. The drawbacks were equally real. Parents were themselves educated largely through participation in a liturgy that made them mostly passive attendants. In educating their own children, they often taught acceptance and obedience rather than creativity and initiative.

If it were not for the work of artists and builders and sculptors, religious education might have been a very dead experience indeed. The liturgy was inadequate to its educational role and parents were often ill-equipped for the onerous task of teaching their children the faith at home. But, once one walked out into the streets and into the countryside, one was immersed in a whole culture which was shot through with Christian values and incarnated a Christian perspective on life. Since communal life was entirely pervaded by religion, learning the faith took place as it were by osmosis. As one moved about in this milieu, one was being educated through one's eyes and ears. This should not be called informal religious education, as if to suggest it somehow lacked form or shape. It was highly structured; it simply followed the structure of the imagination rather than the form of rational thought.

Instruction as Religious Education

Initiation of the catechumenal kind is primarily liturgy. In other words, it is ritual work. Only in a secondary or indirect sense does it have educational outcomes, in which the practitioners' minds, hearts, and imaginations are stretched. The same can be said of the socialization process that characterizes the era of Christendom. This is primarily community living. Only indirectly has it an educational component of meaning-making and intellectual stimulation. Both initiation and socialization are forms of education by immersion in rich human experience. When we look at religious instruction, however, we are dealing with a direct educational encounter with religion. Here the heart of the process is deliberately to seek educational objectives related to religion. However, the manner of seeking them is by drawing back from or distancing oneself from the full riches of the religious experience and by attending instead to textual or other secondary representations of religion.

Religious instruction has taken many forms during the centuries. For Clement of Alexandria, it consisted of study circles for well-educated, Greek-speaking adults who were taught the meaning of Christian living by relating it to significant elements of classical Greek culture. In the cathedral schools of medieval times religious instruction was offered to young boys aspiring to the clerical state, by a textual analysis of elementary question-and-answer-type catechisms. Martin Luther wrote his own question-and-answer-type *Small Catechism* and offered it to householders so that they could teach their children and servants the meaning of the faith as interpreted by the Reformers, and wean them away from the errors of papal religion. When the fathers of the Council of Trent authorized a major catechism for parish priests, the hope was that these pastors would immerse themselves in its contents as they prepared their weekly sermons, and make selective use of its contents by taking account of the needs of their listeners and by adapting the material accordingly. With the development of schools for young people, and more recently, with the worldwide pattern of schooling for all between the ages of six and sixteen, a new kind of religious instruction has emerged. This is "timetabled religion," in other words, the study of religion as a subject alongside other academic disciplines in a comprehensive school curriculum.

Critics of this form of religious education have often described it as indoctrination. By that they have meant the passing on of information about religion and of religious concepts, without due regard for pupils' freedom and without allowing their critical dialogue with the material. Clearly indoctrination is not education. However, to refuse religious instruction a place in schools because it is necessarily indoctrinatory, is simply to beg the question. Religious instruction given by well-trained and experienced religion teachers draws upon a range of carefully devised educational strategies for engaging pupils creatively, imaginatively, and intelligently with religious experience and religious discourse. Concept formation, concept extension, discussion, role-play, storytelling, experience-tradition are some of the rich methodologies for making sense of religion in life. Often the prophetic dimension of religious education is given great scope during such religion classes. The critical faculties of pupils are sharpened by careful reflection on the hidden agendas of ordinary life. This kind of religious instruction by critical appropriation is not only not indoctrination but, by the way it operates, is in fact a necessary challenge to much of the subtle cultural indoctrination that masquerades as common sense today.

Gabriel Moran (*Religious Education as a Second Language*) has identified four universal values at the heart of all education, namely, work, community, literate knowledge, and leisure. I should like to apply this insight now to the three major styles of religious education. The main religious educational value of Christian initiation derives from its being a work experience, a liturgical work of art, a spiritual and physical work of great beauty and of great value. Like homemaking, it is a priceless work for which no pay is offered. To retain its perennial educational place within the Church, it needs to be done by a genuine community of people, who have the leisure to waste time with new members and the wit to appreciate the human value of literate knowledge. The central religious educational value of socialization into a Christian milieu is that this process is a building of human and religious community. Immersion in community life is its own justification, but to prevent its being a stifling immersion, the socialization model of religious education needs to attend with passion to the critical mode of religious instruction. Clearly this requires a modest leisure and the readiness to work at making sense of the rich experience. Religious instruction is the form of religious education that gives primacy to schooling and the literate knowledge achieved there. But schooling and literate knowledge will thrive only in an atmosphere of hard intellectual work and an environment that treasures the leisure dimension of human experience.

Perhaps the hope for the future of religious education is to experiment with new forms of educational practice in the leisure mode. The voices of mystics and artists and retreatants and retired people and spiritual gurus will need to be heard more in the future.

PATRICK M. DEVITT

See also CATECHESIS; CATECHETICS; SACRAMENTS OF INITIATION.

RELIGIOUS FREEDOM

The issue of religious freedom has a long and difficult history in the Roman Catholic Church and has been influenced by various historical, political, and juridic contexts (Joseph Lecler, S.J., *Toleration and the Reformation,* New York: Association Press, 1960). In turn, the theory and practice of religious freedom has further affected the areas of ethics (Hans Küng and Jürgen Moltmann, *The Ethics of World Religions and Human Rights,* Philadelphia: Trinity Press International, 1990), ecumenism, missions, and relationships with non-Christian religions. Tertullian, for example, argued in A.D. 212 before the Roman Proconsul Scapula that freedom of worship and the practice of religion must be undertaken freely and not under pressure. The Edict of Constantine (A.D. 313) ensured freedom for Christians and all others to practice the religion they espoused. By 380, however, Emperor Theodosius required that the Catholic faith was to be the religion of his empire. After centuries of dispute, the Roman Catholic Church seriously endeavored to face the issue squarely. The Second Vatican Council's declaration, *Dignitatis Humanae* (On Religious Freedom), publicly issued by Pope Paul VI on 7 December 1965, provided a balanced modern teaching on the subject. It was set more immediately in the context of the post-Reformation period and specifically against the Enlightenment and the eighteenth- and nineteenth-century interpretations of the question.

While Catholics had enjoyed exemption and favor in modern European countries where Church and state were united, often Muslims and Jews within Christian Europe experienced proscriptions in the practice of their religion. Similarly, in Islamic countries, Christians were restricted in their religious expression. At the time of the Reformation, one of the first juridical and theological treatments of religious freedom was framed in the context of the Spanish missions. In the argument over the rights of indigenous people in Spanish colonies, Dominican friar Bartolomé de las Casas (1474–1566) stressed two significant ideas in his seven point reform program: (1) War, which was contrary to the spirit of the gospel, was not a "fitting" means of evangelization. The example of a Christian life and preaching with gentle words were more effective; (2) The right of a Spanish sovereign in the New World could not be claimed to the detriment of the individual freedom of Indians. Neither the Crown nor missionaries could force Native Americans to convert to the religion of the conqueror. Both points emphasized persuasion rather than coercion as a method of evangelization. The context for religious freedom in this case revolved around the best way to make the original inhabitants good vassals of the King and Queen.

After Luther's break with the Roman Catholic Church in 1521, the political implications of religious freedom were felt all over Europe. The Augsburg Settlement (1553) and the Peace of Westphalia (1648), in effect, established the principle that the religion of the ruler was to be the religion of the people (*cujus regio, ejus religio*). Even in this divided Christendom, the assumption of Church establishment, a political system based on a unity of faith, remained the ideal.

Enlightenment thought, which played such a significant role in the formation of the United States of America, the French Revolution and Thomas Paine's, *The Rights of Man,* entertained ideas often at odds with the established religion. While the eighteenth-century *Encyclopédie* contained an amazing collection of knowledge in a wide spectrum of learning, many contemporaries, especially Jesuits and the Jansenists, interpreted as anticlerical and secular the work's critique of poverty, intolerance, and abuses in the religious and political systems. Among the ideas expressed in this ecclesiastically censured work were freedom of the press and a denial of papal power in the area of secular governance and temporal affairs. In the wake of the wrenching experience of the Church in the French Revolution, Hugues Félicité Lamennais (1782–1854) wrote apologetic material aimed at addressing religious indifference, laying a foundation for a religious basis for a civil society, and attempting a renewal of Christianity. He questioned the congruence of nation and religion and supported a Gallican position on the relationship between the spiritual and temporal power of the Church, that is, a Church independent of Bourbon rulers. After the 1830 revolution in France, he edited *L'Avenir,* a newspaper which became the voice of Catholic liberalism. Contributors, such as Gueranger, Lacordaire, and Montalembert, advocated freedom of the press, a complete separation of Church and state, popular sovereignty, and religious liberty. These views, as well as other ideas raised by Catholic liberalism, were censured by Pope Gregory XVI in *Mirari Vos* (15 August 1832). Among the points raised by the pontiff, who was experiencing the gradual loss of the Papal States, was a disclamation of any collaboration with those who sought political and religious liberty. A similar condemnation came with Pope Pius IX's *Quanta Cura* (8 December 1864) and the Syllabus of Errors. Ten sections of fallacies were condemned, among them those relating to the rights of the Church (the Perfect Society) and the state, the temporal power of the papacy, modern liberalism, and the exaltation of human reason to the detriment of the acknowledgement of revelation. Though Leo XIII agreed with some of Pius IX's points, Leo acknowledged a legitimate and healthy civil and political freedom as well as democratic governments (Roger Aubert, "Religious Liberty from 'Mirari vos' to the 'Syllabus,'" *Historical Problems of Church Renewal,* Glen Rock, New Jersey: Paulist Press, 1965).

In the twentieth century, political and religious factors around the world, such as the growth of democratic governments, the adoption of the Universal Declaration of Human Rights by the United Nations General Assembly (10 December 1948), and the declaration of the freedom of religion by the World Council of Churches in 1948 and 1961, indicated a gradual global support for the principle of religious freedom. By the time Pope John XXIII called the Second Vatican Council (1959), these realities, as well as a developing theology undergirding religious freedom, helped shape the official acceptance of a less polemic pastoral and theological position on the issue.

Vatican II signified an important shift in position in official Roman Catholic teaching on religious freedom. The decree originally was a chapter in the document on ecumenism. Without adequate time at the second session to deliberate the issues, a new, larger committee, under the direction of the Secretariat for the Promotion of Christian Unity, prepared a text for the next session of the council. The document was voted upon at the end of the fourth session.

Removing a restriction which had prohibited discussion of the subject ten years earlier, the council fathers held a full and open discussion of the issues. In dispute were two perspectives from which to understand the problem. One view saw the Church, in possession of the one truth, having the sole right to exist as the state religion. Error had no rights and could be tolerated only as a second-best situation. Only those in possession of the truth (i.e., the Roman Catholic Church) had a right to religious freedom. Allowance for the presence of other religions or for a separation of the Church and state was interpreted as indifferentism toward religion and neutrality or hostility toward the Church on the part of governments. The obligatory Catholic state was the ideal, the "thesis." Other forms of Church/state relationship were tolerated as the "hypothesis." This position was that of Cardinal Ottaviani and the Italian and Spanish bishops. Among the committee members preparing the document, Cardinal Browne, Dominican Master General A. Fernandez, and Archbishop M. Lefebvre fell on this side of the discussion. A second, newer, position affirmed religious freedom as a civil and human right, with sanction by civil law. It acknowledged the growth of governments, many of them democratic, which had inscribed in their constitutions freedom for religious witness and practice and an immunity from constraint to act against conscience. This allowed for the freedom of the Church in its mission and for the rights of the human person, whose expression of faith required a free act. This position was supported by the United States bishops and committee members Cardinal Frings, Bishops DeSmedt and Willebrands, Father P. Pavan, and Dominicans

Jerome Hamer and Yves Congar. The latter position was accepted in the final document (Alberic Stacpoole, *Vatican II Revisted, By Those Who Were There,* Minneapolis: Winston Press, 1986). An important architect of the declaration was U.S. Jesuit John Courtney Murray (1904–1967), who had meticulously examined the issue and who had been silenced earlier for his position on the role of Church and state (Donald E. Pelotte, S.S.S., *John Courtney Murray, Theologian in Conflict,* New York: Paulist Press, 1976). The decree, voted upon in the fourth session of the council, was passed with 2308 "yes" and 70 "no" when the document was formally promulgated.

Against the background of a constitutional order of society, the key issues in *Dignitatis Humanae* revolved around the rights of the human person and the bases for the principles of religious freedom as found in revelation. The declaration stated several general principles of religious liberty. Because of the dignity of the human person, human beings have a right to religious freedom and thus are immune from restriction of their conscience in the practice and witness of their religion. People should be able to act according to their consciences, whether in private or in public. Religious communities have the freedom to govern themselves according to their norms, provided that "the just demands of public order are observed" (par. 4). The responsibility for establishing and maintaining religious freedom belongs to all persons, but especially to the government and the Church, because of their duty toward the common welfare of all. All religions have the right to assemble for educational, cultural, charitable, or social purposes. People should be able to pursue truth through communication and dialogue and to act upon truth. The exercise of religious freedom is bound by the moral law, wherein all are to deal with others in justice and charity. However, "society has the right to protect itself against abuse committed on the pretext of freedom of religion" (par. 7). The document then noted the presence of the principle, though not the actual words, of religious freedom in Scripture. Citing the example of Christ, who refused to be a political messiah or to command belief from those in his time, and a similar witness of the apostles, the document stated that this pattern was to be the Church's own. This especially respected the nature of the act of faith, which presupposes a person's free choice. In the judgment of this document, the role of the Church in society becomes more stable and the Church is able to fulfill its religious mission where religious freedom is observed in word, in law, and in practical application (par. 13). The document concluded by noting that religious freedom was a principle found in many national constitutions and international documents, a fact that the council fathers greeted with joy and recognized as one of the "signs of the times" (par. 15; see also, John Courtney Murray, ed., *Religious Freedom,* New York: P.J. Kennedy & Sons, 1965).

Dignitatis Humanae moved the focus of the argument from the strong nineteenth-century papal concern of an embattled Church to a more developed appreciation of the rights of the human person. All the Vatican documents, but this one particularly, displayed a shift of tone from that of the Syllabus of Errors, which had assumed a paternalistic attitude toward Church members. The document on religious freedom, partly because of its temper and content, immediately received a favorable response from non-Catholics, who had found the Church often defensive and unwilling to approach the times in a favorable light. Significant in this document, addressed to all persons of the world, is the recognition of the validity of the search for truth among all those of other faiths. The themes of *Dignitatis Humanae,* sounded earlier in Pope John XXIII's *Pacem in Terris* (pars. 14, 34, 35), were subsequently carried forward in the Vatican's *Ostpolitik,* and in several of Pope John Paul II's writings. Further discussion of the implications of religious freedom for ecumenism and world religions has opened the question of religious freedom into a discussion of religious pluralism and the role of Christ and Christianity in a context of several religious and social cultures throughout our world (Leonard Swidler, ed., *Religious Liberty and Human Rights in Nations and in Religions,* Philadelphia: Ecumenical Press, 1986). Still to be addressed because it was excluded from conciliar deliberations is the issue of religious freedom within the Church.

ANGELYN DRIES, O.S.F.

See also FAITH; RELIGION, VIRTUE OF; VATICAN COUNCIL II.

RELIGIOUS LIFE

Christian discipleship embodied by women and men religious constitutes a state of life which Vatican Council II affirmed as belonging to the life and holiness of the Church. Traditionally religious included members of cloistered and contemplative communities, monastic orders and active apostolic institutes. They distinguish themselves as persons who take vows, live in community according to a specific constitution or rule of life, and are generally called sisters, brothers or priests. Religious in the broad sense include secular institutes (those who make vows or promises but do not live in community), societies of apostolic life (who live in community but do not make public vows), consecrated virgins and the newly organized non-canonical groups.

Vocation

A vocation to religious life is rooted in the basic call to Christian life through baptism. It is a specific way of living out one's baptismal commitment. The initial stage of religious formation immerses the individual in a life of prayer, study, and daily living of religious life. During this time both the individual and the community mutually discern the authenticity of one's call.

Profession

After a period of initial formation (varying in length from five to fifteen years) the individual is confirmed in the vocational call and makes a public profession of the vows of chastity, poverty, and obedience according to the constitution or rule of the particular institute. This religious profession is an act of permanent commitment to God in religious life.

Charism

Vatican Council II recognized religious life as a charism or gift for the building up of the Church. This charismatic element is most clearly distinguished from the institutional dimension of the Church at the time of the beginning of the various orders in the spontaneous, flexible, and prophetic leadership of the founding persons. They often challenged existing Church structures and provided new and alternative ways of community, prayer, and service. Every religious community is identified by its specific charism or "community spirit," such as education for the poor or health care for the most abandoned. Each generation receives, clarifies, deepens, and shares the charism in ways appropriate for the culture and time. The charism embodies the deepest values of the group, and becomes criterion for decision-making and is a source of unity. The variety of charisms in religious orders witnesses to healthy and creative pluralism in the Church.

Religious Life Before and After Vatican Council II

The renewal of Vatican II called for the updating of religious life. The mandate directed religious to return to their roots in the following of Christ and living the gospel, to recapture the original spirit which inspired the foundation of the institute and to adapt to the contemporary world. All members were encouraged to participate in the renewal process.

In the time following Vatican II religious life went through radical upheaval. Many members left their orders. Yet signs of new life are appearing; new forms of membership, new ways of living community, new expressions of vows in contemporary life and new ministries are emerging as needed for the twenty-first century.

As a result of the renewal process the differences in women's and men's experience of religious life became apparent. A contemporary reading of Church history reveals that the norms for religious life were influenced by the social and cultural roles and expectations for women and men of those times.

Essential Elements Today

Religious life is rooted in a personal call to follow Christ in service to the people of God. It requires fidelity to the community charism as an expression of the mission of Jesus to bring about the reign of God. It requires a life of prayer and the development of a personal and communal spirituality as foundational for community life and apostolic action. The public witness of religious life is expressed in vowed lives of service and commitment as a prophetic and sacramental presence in the world.

MARY GARVIN, S.N.J.M.

See also EVANGELICAL COUNSELS; MONASTICISM; VOW.

RELIGIOUS LIFE, ACTIVE

Religious life is often described according to three types; contemplative, monastic, and active. Active religious are characterized by their apostolic and charitable activity. Contemplative life refers to those religious who have given themselves exclusively to God in solitude, silence, prayer, and penance. Monastic life, part of the ancient tradition of the Church, values stability, prayer, work, and separation from the world within the monastic community. This community understood as family is self-reliant, self-contained, and self-governed.

Regrettably in the Church's past a harmful dichotomy polarized interior life and apostolic activity. Human life taken up with created things was separated from the contemplative life which was concerned with the things of God. Or active life was concerned with external activity in contrast to the interiority of prayer and worship. Even in the last century a division was made in the statement of purpose of many religious institutes. The *primary* purpose was the personal sanctification and salvation of the members and the *secondary* purpose was the work of the apostolate . . . the active life. Since Vatican II the Church acknowledges each expression of religious life as contributing to the whole life of the Church.

Vatican Council II names religious "active" when apostolic activity is of the very nature of religious life. Their religious consecration is lived out in action. The apostolic work is entrusted to them by the Church and is carried out in the name of the Church. The diversity of lifestyle of active religious is necessitated by the diversity and needs of various apostolic commitments. The basis of apostolic life is a contemplative spirit which presumes a life of union with God expressed in service of neighbor. The motivation for an active religious is the imitation of Jesus desiring to participate in his mission: teaching the people, healing the sick, releasing those bound, feeding the hungry and proclaiming the reign of God.

MARY GARVIN, S.N.J.M.

See also EVANGELICAL COUNSELS.

RELIGIOUS ORDERS

Usually three kinds of religious institutes are distinguished: (1) religious orders; (2) religious congregations; and (3) secular institutes. In religious orders, e.g., the Norbertines, members take solemn vows and live a common life. In religious congregations, e.g., the Redemptorists, members take simple vows and live a common life. In secular institutes, e.g., the Ladies of Nazareth, members pledge to observe the evangelical counsels of poverty, chastity, and obedience but do not necessarily live a common life. Besides these three categories there are societies of common life, e.g., the Sulpicians, in which members live together but do not necessarily take sacred vows. It is worth noting that the new Code of Canon Law (1983) does not distinguish between simple and solemn vows.

There is also a distinction between apostolic and monastic institutes. Apostolic institutes, e.g., the Redemptorists, assume various ministries for the Church, e.g., extraordinary preaching, and are not restricted by obligations of stability or cloister. Monastic institutes, e.g., the Benedictines, dedicate themselves to the praise and worship of God. Members of such institutes usually belong to one monastery and pray the Liturgy of the Hours in common, while also engaging in certain apostolates, e.g., education.

Religious institutes are either diocesan or of pontifical right. Diocesan institutes are subject to the local diocesan authority. Institutes of pontifical right relate to the Holy See, especially to the Congregation of Religious and Secular Institutes.

A common feature of all religious institutes is the permanent commitment of members to a life of poverty, chastity, and obedience. Each institute has its own rule or constitutions. They spell out the particular charism of the institute that derives in some measure from the original vision of the founder or foundress. Thus these rules or constitutions elaborate the way in which members will lead their life and carry out their mission in the Church.

JOHN F. CRAGHAN

See also CONTEMPLATION; INSTITUTE, SECULAR; MONASTICISM.

RELIQUARY

A repository for sacred relics. They are commonly made of precious metals, with rich ornamentation;

Reliquary of an unknown saint, ca. 1160–1170, Maastricht

their size and shape vary according to the enclosed relic. Relics exposed for public veneration must be enclosed in a reliquary. Most modern reliquaries are fairly small and closely resemble a monstrance.

JOSEPH QUINN

See also DEVOTIONS; SAINTS.

REMBRANDT HARMENSZ, VAN RIJN (1606–1669)

Dutch painter, draftsman and etcher, hailed as one of the very greatest artists. Coming from the shop of an obscure painter, Rembrandt possessed virtuoso technique from an early age. He was introduced in 1624 and 1625 to the early Baroque style by Pieter Lastman of Amsterdam. Perhaps at this time he came in contact with the style of Caravaggio with its

"Old Self-Portrait," by Rembrandt, oil painting, 1669, The Hague

dark shadows which became so much a characteristic of Rembrandt's work. He worked in Leyden, his home town, from 1625 to 1631, and demonstrated that he could easily convey a sense of physical reality.

Returning to Amsterdam, he opened shop as a portrait painter, and his *Anatomy Lesson of Dr. Tulp* guaranteed that his next ten years would be prosperous and busy. He married the wealthy Saskia van Uylenborch in 1634, and they lived in fame and high style until 1642. This was the year of his famous group painting, *Night Watch,* but it was also the year of Saskia's death. He was unable to straighten out his financial affairs without Saskia; meanwhile his tremendous abilities and psychological insights bewildered his typical portrait clients. By 1656 he had descended to near ruin.

Rembrandt's financial struggles improved somewhat when he and his son began to live with Hendrickje Stoffels (though this enraged the stricter Calvinists among his fellow citizens). He began to paint landscapes and greatly expanded his interest in religious art. He stands virtually at the head of the tradition of sacred art in Protestantism. Always a painter of portraits, Rembrandt increasingly suffused these with the psychological and spiritual power which in other painters tended to appear only in religious or dramatic works. His intense introspection (there are sixty self-portraits), combined with personal tragedy and increasing loneliness, contributed to the depth of insight evident in his work. More to satisfy himself than anyone else, he eventually learned to integrate these elements into portraiture so skillfully as to be accepted by his clients.

Surviving Hendrickje and his son, Rembrandt died in 1669 as one of the most prolific painters in history. He was a famous teacher, and his legacy was continued by many devoted admirers, guaranteeing his unrivaled position in painting.

DAVID BRYAN

See also ART, CHRISTIAN.

RENAISSANCE, THE

The word, renaissance, means rebirth. The age of the Renaissance was perhaps the greatest creative period in history, and is generally understood to cover the fourteenth, fifteenth, and sixteenth centuries. Prompted by renewed interest in the classical culture of the ancient world, it ended the theocentric Middle Ages and was the beginning of the modern world. It was an era of immense artistic achievement which fostered a revival of classical literature, and witnessed a tendency toward a more secular and utilitarian approach to politics and society. The Renaissance fostered humanism, lauding the human reason and its creative activity without necessarily relating its endeavors to the supernatural. The secular spirit gradually superceded the otherworldly spirit of the medieval centuries. Art, music, drama, architecture, and literature received new appreciation and encouragement; and few other ages portray such innovative genius. Despite its secularism, the Renaissance also put subsequent centuries in its debt with the works of Dante, Petrarch, Shakespeare, Cervantes, Leonardo da Vinci, Michelangelo, Erasmus, Galileo, Gutenberg, and others in every area of human achievement.

MICHAEL GLAZIER

See also REFORMATION, THE.

RENAN, JOSEPH ERNST (1823–1892)

A native of Brittany, he studied for the priesthood at Paris in 1838 where he realized that he was learning what he contemptuously called "a schoolgirl's theology" (*théologie des demoiselles*), a situation which did not improve when he went to the seminary of Saint-Sulpice, leaving unordained in 1845. He began to study German theology and Hebrew, and in 1852 he established his scholarly reputation with a book on Averroism. In 1860 the Emperor Napoleon III sent him to the Middle East on an archaeological mission, and while there he got a firsthand look at what he would call "the fifth gospel," the land of Palestine. This trip helped him to focus many of his thoughts about the Bible. He returned home and in 1862 became professor of Hebrew at the Collège de

France, a position he lost in 1864 as a result of his great book, *Vie de Jésus,* published the year before. Unable to reconcile the contradictions in the Bible, Renan decided that it lacked supernatural qualities and was just another ancient document and should be treated as such. The Jesus of the theological textbooks disappeared from his pages to be replaced by a likeable if rather naive Jewish peasant preacher, wandering around the countryside with some illiterate disciples and a bevy of women devotees. This peasant let events get ahead of him, drawing the wrath of the authorities and unable to back down from what he had said. The book caused a sensation and a scandal, shocking conservative sentiment; its superb style guaranteed it a wide audience. It contributed little to the "quest for the historical Jesus" because Renan did not understand the complexities of the gospel narratives, but it awakened the French to a new, nonsupernatural reading of those narratives.

JOSEPH F. KELLY

See also CRITICISM, BIBLICAL.

RENUNCIATION

Renunciation is the verbal rejection of the devil by a Christian at baptism. The *Apostolic Tradition* of Hippolytus (ca. 215) contains a formula of renunciation in which the one about to be baptized "renounces Satan, his service and his works." Later, in the Western Church, the renunciation developed into an interrogation between the celebrant of baptism and the catechumen. In Jerusalem, in the fourth century, the practice developed of facing west during the renunciation and facing east when professing the creed as a symbol of the newly baptized person's conversion.

ANTHONY D. ANDREASSI

See also CATECHUMENATE; RITE OF CHRISTIAN INITIATION OF ADULTS (RCIA); SACRAMENTS OF INITIATION.

REPARATION

Reparation is the act of making amends to another for a damage inflicted or crime perpetrated. In moral theology, reparation denotes the restitution given to one against whom some wrong has been committed. For certain crimes (such as murder or calumny) there can be no "exact" restitution; however, there are compensations, some of which are detailed in the OT. In devotional theology, reparation refers to the means (prayers, penances, good works) by which a person tries to make amends to God for the sins committed against God. Reparation plays a particularly important role in the cult of the Sacred Heart, in which a person seeks recourse to the Sacred Heart of Jesus for sins which reject the perfect love of Jesus which finds its fulfillment in the Eucharist.

ANTHONY D. ANDREASSI

See also REPENTANCE; SALVATION.

REPENTANCE

Repentance is the rejection of one's own sinfulness and a turning to God for forgiveness. Prophets in the OT called the people to repent when they broke the covenant and sinned against God. In the NT Jesus called people to a complete change of heart and mind (Gk. *metanoia*) and to live a life in complete service of God. Repentant persons confess their past transgressions against God, express sorrow for them, and resolve to change their ways. The Christian tradition has also recognized the need for penance or reparation on the part of repentant persons "to make up" for their sins in the sense of associating themselves more intimately with the atonement achieved by Jesus through his death and resurrection.

ANTHONY D. ANDREASSI

See also SACRAMENT OF RECONCILIATION; SIN.

REREDOS

A reredos is any architectural or artistic decoration behind an altar adjacent to a wall. When the liturgy called for the priest to celebrate Mass with his back to the congregation, reredos consisted simply of paintings or symbols on the wall around and above the altar. Later, in the Middle Ages, they became

"Virgin and Child with St. John the Baptist and St. Andrew," by Taddeo di Bartolo, altarpiece, 1363, Siena

much more ornate and included silk hangings or jeweled metalworks. The most common reredos were wooden panels, sometimes in the form of a triptych, with paintings depicting saints or biblical scenes. Also popular were carved stone images depicting similar images. If there were no window above the altar, a reredos might dominate the entire wall. After the liturgical reforms initiated by the Second Vatican Council (1962–1965), altars were moved away from walls in order to be freestanding, thus obviating the need for a reredos.

ANTHONY D. ANDREASSI

See also ARCHITECTURE, CHURCH.

RESERVATION OF THE BLESSED SACRAMENT

Reservation of the Blessed Sacrament is the custom of keeping the Eucharistic elements (usually the Body of the Lord, but on some occasions, the Precious Blood too) after the conclusion of the Eucharistic Liturgy. As early as the second century Justin Martyr mentions the reservation of the Eucharist, and from the second through the fourth centuries there are references to this practice in the writings of both the Fathers and in other Church writers. When liturgies were infrequent or difficult to attend, Christians began the practice of keeping the Eucharist in their homes or even carrying it on their persons. Hermits continued this custom until as late as the fourteenth century. At the time of Constantine in the fourth century, when public churches were first erected throughout the Roman Empire, churches became the normal place for the reservation of the Blessed Sacrament. Local customs differed, however, and the place of reservation varied from the sacristy, a pyx suspended over the altar, to an ambry in the wall. Eventually the tabernacle on an altar became the normal place of reservation in the Catholic Church. Normally only the Body of the Lord is reserved; however, the Eastern Church developed a custom for Communion for the sick by dipping the host in the Precious Blood and allowing it to dry before reservation.

Originally reservation developed simply to have Holy Communion apart from a Mass; however, as time progressed, the practice of prayer before the reserved Sacrament became commonplace. Lambert Beaudin, the Belgian monk who was one of the leaders of the modern liturgical movement, said of Eucharistic reservation: "One did not reserve the blessed sacrament in order to adore it, but because it was reserved, it was adored."

ANTHONY D. ANDREASSI

See also EUCHARIST.

RESPONSORY

A liturgical chant, consisting of a full or partial psalm, which is sung or recited between readings at Mass (e.g., the Responsorial Psalm) and in the Liturgy of the Hours.

JOSEPH QUINN

See also LITURGY.

RESTITUTION

See REPARATION.

RESURRECTION OF CHRIST

"I believe in . . . the resurrection of the body and life everlasting." The closing statement of the Apostles' Creed expresses a basic conviction of our Christian faith. For us, this earthly life is not the be-all and the end-all. For us, death—for all its seeming finality—does not speak the last word. For us, God must have the last word. We look to new life beyond death, a life in which we will be, wholly, what we are destined to be: children of God. "Beloved, we are God's children now; it does not yet appear what we shall be . . ." (1 John 3:2).

A creedal formula is all very well. The crucial question is: what do we make of it? Orthodoxy is not in formulas but in right understanding of our faith. It surely must be that it is not the parroting of a creed but a grasp of its meaning that matters. Mainly on the basis of Scripture, one may indicate how we, in our day and in our way, might get behind the formula to the truth it speaks.

Judaism and Resurrection

A fascinating feature of the religious history of Israel is the fact that not until near the beginning of the second century B.C. was there any notion of an afterlife. Of course there was Sheol—but that is nothing other than the grave where all, good, bad, and indifferent, ended up indiscriminately. Perhaps no one better than the plain, blunt Qoheleth has drawn so poignant a picture: "There is no work or thought or knowledge or wisdom in Sheol to which you are going" (Eccl 9:10). It is this that explains his otherwise scandalous statement: "For the fate of the sons of men and fate of beasts is the same; as one dies, so dies the other. They all have the same breath, and man has no advantage over the beasts, for all is vanity. All go to one place; all are from the dust, and all turn to dust again" (3:19-20). The point he makes—and how effectively he makes it!—is that death is the great leveler. He is thoroughly biblical in his conviction that humankind is the summit of God's cre-

"The Resurrection," manuscript, 15th century, Master of Osservanza

ation, standing apart from and above all other creatures (Gen 1–2). And yet there is the inescapable fact that man and beast meet in death—for Sheol is a place of darkness and gloom, away from the sight of God.

Until recently it was assumed that belief in an afterlife emerged for the first time in Judaism about the middle of the second century B.C.—the Maccabean era. This was because the first explicit biblical reference to resurrection and blessedness beyond death occurs in Daniel 12:2-3. Today we tend to acknowledge that the belief had emerged half a century earlier—which does not substantially change the picture. What does appear clear is that belief in resurrection and life beyond death evolved in an apocalyptic environment. The Book of the Watchers—chapters 1–36 of a composite Jewish writing known as 1 Enoch—is now dated to the end of the third century B.C. The introduction to it, the brief chapters 1–5, is a parable on the lot of the wicked and the righteous. The perspective is beyond death: "And to all the righteous he will grant peace. He will preserve the elect, and kindness shall be upon them. They shall all belong to God and they shall prosper and be blessed; and the light of God shall shine upon them" (1:8). "To the elect there shall be light, joy and peace, and they shall inherit the earth. To you, wicked ones, on the contrary, there will be a curse" (5:7).

Resurrection of the Body

Resurrection of the body could be, and was, understood in different ways. In general one might say that there was a popular notion and a more sophisticated one. A good instance of the former is found in the Jewish apocalyptic writing, 2 Baruch (A.D. 100–120): "For the earth will surely give back the dead at that time; it receives them now in order to keep them, not changing anything in their form. But as it has received them so it will give them back. . . . For then it will be necessary to show those who live that the dead are living again. . . . And it will be that when they have recognized one another . . . then my judgment will be strong. Then both [wicked and righteous] will be changed, these into the splendor of angels and those into startling visions and horrible shapes" (50:2-4; 51:5). The concern here is recognition. If transformation were to follow at once on resurrection, how should we know one another? This text solves the problem: there are two stages. We first appear, warts and all. Then, when we have had a good look at one another, we will be transformed—for better or worse. Jesus and Paul had to contend with such crass notions of resurrection.

God of the Living

The Sadducees were a priestly and aristocratic party whose theology was conservative and traditionalist. They were not prepared to accept the newfangled doctrine of resurrection. The pronouncement story of Mark 12:18-27 (parr.) contains their objection to it and Jesus' reply. The case they present—designed to show that belief in resurrection leads to absurdity—is based on the law of levirate marriage (Deut 25:5-10). The law was in abeyance but could be invoked in theological argument. Jesus' rejoinder is that the Sadducees did not understand the power of God who is capable of achieving something beyond human imagining and, in particular, make resurrection-life something notably different from life on earth. That is the point of the punch line: "For when they rise from the dead, they neither marry nor are given in marriage, but are like angels in heaven" (Mark 12:25). The statement represents a more sophisticated (as opposed to a popular) notion of resurrection: it will effect a radical transformation.

In vv. 26-27 Jesus turns to the fact of the resurrection. In Exodus 3:6 Yahweh declared: "I am . . . the God of Abraham, the God of Isaac and the God of Jacob." By the time of Moses the three patriarchs had long been dead. And yet, because their God is always God of the living, the patriarchs must, though dead, be destined for life; they will be raised to life. He had named himself their God, he had made promises to them which could not fail, promises which death could not annul. Their hope of resurrection lay in fellowship with God. By standards of modern exegesis this rabbinical-style argument is hardly convincing. Yet the reason for life beyond death adduced here is congenial to modern men and women. "Proofs" for the immortality of the soul, presupposing a questionable dichotomy between "soul" and "body," are not helpful. For the Christian the real ground of immortality lies in fellowship with the risen Lord and with the living God. Paul has said it all: "thanks be to God who gives us the victory [over death] through our Lord Jesus Christ" (1 Cor 15:57).

Paul

In 1 Corinthians 15 Paul energetically defends the reality of resurrection from the dead. The Corinthians, more precisely the Greeks among them, envisaged the human person as made up of two distinct and separate parts: soul and body. In their view the essence of personality was concentrated in the soul. Furthermore, the soul was immortal, the body ephemeral and mortal. There was no point in the raising of the body, no sense in resurrection from the dead. Paul's Hebrew anthropology is quite different. The human being is one, not an amalgam of two parts. The Hebrew words (and the corresponding Greek words in the New Testament) regularly translated "body," "flesh," "soul," "spirit" are all different *aspects* of the one whole human being. The difference in outlook has been summed up rather neatly in the observation that the Hebrews conceived of the human as an animated body; the Greeks conceived of the human as an incarnated spirit.

It is clear that Paul, by insisting on the resurrection of the *body,* is stressing the reality of a true and integrated human life beyond death—it is no partial existence. Of this he is convinced. But he is coping with a reality wholly beyond his experience. Wisely, he does not really attempt to describe the nature of the risen state; he is content to insist that the resurrection-body is very different from the human body that we know; it belongs to a new order (vv. 35-41). Throughout, Paul is striving to find words to express his faith-conviction of a reality beyond his ken. Due allowance must be made for the difficulty involved. What is undoubted is that his understanding of life beyond death—immortality—is Christocentric. It is because of the resurrection of Jesus, because of our union with the Risen One, that Christians will live with God beyond death. God is source of life and Jesus, as the presence of God for us, is where we can find life. It seems to be Paul's view that life can only be "with Christ"; if one is not "in Christ" then one does not have life. Clearly, this "in Christ" must be widened into "in God." God, the Living One, offers life and offers life *to all.* To say "Yes" to God is to win life; to say "No" is death.

We have noted that resurrection of the body is a Jewish idea—and in Hebrew thought human existence could never be the existence of a disembodied soul. We have seen that Jesus and Paul were at pains to insist that the "body" of one who lives beyond death is a transformed body—very different from our earthly body of flesh and blood. This is the early Christian view, the New Testament view. Resurrection of the body, in the sense of a body conjured up from the grave, is no part of our Christian faith. "Resurrection of the body" is an assertion of our belief in life beyond death. We are faced with a reality outside of our earthly experience—but it remains human reality.

One may venture an alternative to the, until now, received way of stating the matter of resurrection. Our life is lived in two phases. Death is transition: it marks the end of the earthly phase and is the opening to new life. At death *I,* leaving behind my body of flesh and blood—for good—enter upon a new way of living my *whole* humanness. The whole "I" is involved, not part of me. This view is no denial of resurrection of the body; it is forthright avowal of what ''resurrection of the body'' means. What might otherwise ask too much of my credulity can be shown to make good sense.

The Risen Lord

When, in 1 Corinthians 15, Paul energetically defends the reality of resurrection from the dead, he starts by appealing to the resurrection of Jesus. It is clear, from the New Testament as a whole, that Christians were, from the first, convinced that the crucified Jesus was not held by death. In Jewish faith and prayer, God is he who "makes the dead live." Jewish faith and hope looked to a resurrection of the righteous at the end of time. What the first Christians asserted was that, in the person of Jesus of Nazareth, this divine act had taken place. Jewish expectation was eschatological: resurrection was an event of the end-time. Christians had asserted that an eschatological event had taken place in time. If one can put it so, the resurrection of Jesus is an event at once eschatological and historical. In essence it is a spiritual event, beyond our world of time, and yet it has impinged on our world of time.

Paul uses the verb *ōphthē* to state that Christ appeared to Cephas, to the other witnesses listed, and to Paul himself (1 Cor 15:3-8). The word can be rendered "he showed himself." It means that the risen Jesus manifested himself as present in some fashion so that Paul, and the others, can say, "I have seen the Lord." What is involved is a divine initiative leading to a real experience of the presence of the Lord and a firm conviction of the reality of this presence. Something had happened to these men and women which they could only describe by saying that they had "seen the Lord," that the Lord had "shown himself" to them. The phrase did not refer to some general Christian experience but rather to a particular series of occurrences confined to a limited period. Such occurrences, on the threshold of ordinary human experience, just would not submit to precision of detail. Only symbol and imagery, not literal prose, could tell *this* story.

The Narratives

Six gospel passages serve as sources for our knowledge of the resurrection: Mark 16:1-8; Matthew 28; Luke 24:13-49; John 20; John 21; Mark 16:9-20 (and to these should be added Paul's text in 1 Cor 15:5-8). In this group we may distinguish two types of narrative: those of the post-resurrection appearances and those of the finding of the empty tomb. The narratives of the post-resurrection appearances were composed to ground Christian faith in the risen Jesus and to justify apostolic preaching. The nature of such appearances makes it obvious enough that the Gospels cannot agree where and to whom Jesus appeared. This diversity does not seriously affect the historicity of the events; it is a product of the way in which the stories were told and preserved. A basic pattern is followed when Jesus is said to appear. The disciples are together and are apprehensive. Jesus appears, is at first unrecognized, and ends by giving a solemn command, which includes the commission to carry to humankind the Good News of Jesus and his gift of salvation. Each gospel witness stresses some particular appearance or some significant aspect of one, and each evangelist has presented his material in the light of his own theological interest.

The Tomb

The empty tomb figures in our earliest gospel version of the resurrection story. Mark relates that the women—Mary Magdalene, Mary the mother of James, and Salome—intent on anointing the body of Jesus, came to the tomb early on the first day of the week. To their surprise they found the great stone already rolled back (16:1-4). Entering the tomb they were amazed to find a young man, dressed in white, sitting there. He said to them, "Do not be amazed; you seek Jesus of Nazareth, who was crucified. He has risen, he is not here; see the place where they laid him" (16:5-6). The "young man" plays the role of *angelus interpres,* of interpreting angel, a feature of apocalyptic. The women were faced with the riddle of an empty tomb; he explains why the tomb is empty. It is a neat literary way of presenting, as economically as possible, the fact of the empty tomb and the reason of its emptiness.

John has preserved two versions of the women's visit to the tomb—John 20:1-3 and 20:11-13. Underlying the first of them (vv. 1-2) would seem to be the earliest form of an empty tomb narrative in any gospel. Thoroughly Johannine is 20:3-10. At Mary Magdalene's disturbing news (v. 2) Peter and "the other disciple" hurry to the tomb. In the tradition, Peter's companion was unnamed. John has introduced him as the Beloved Disciple so that his coming to faith might interpret the significance of the empty tomb. The encounter with Mary Magdalene (20:14-16) has a special significance. She is bidden, by the risen Lord, to "go to my brethren"; and her message was: "I have seen the Lord." The story is all the more remarkable because our earliest account of resurrection appearances ascribes the initial appearance to Cephas (1 Cor 15:5). Despite that, the later Johannine picture emphatically gives the honor to Mary Magdalene. An important strand of gospel tradition proposes a woman as the privileged person who had first met the risen Lord; the assertion is taken up in the "longer ending" of Mark (16:9).

Apologetics

A constant feature of the resurrection narratives, with the exception of Matthew 28 (but note 28:17), is that the Lord is not at once recognized (Luke 24:16, 37; John 20:14-15; 21:4); it required some word or some familiar gesture of his to make him known. This is an effective way of making the point that Jesus had not returned to life as before but had passed beyond death to *new* life with God. He is Jesus—and yet he is different. The appearance stories are heavily laden with theological and apologetic motifs.

At the appearance of Jesus to the eleven and the two who had hurried back from Emmaus, "they were startled and frightened and supposed that they saw a spirit" (Luke 24:36). Jesus invites them to see and handle his hands and feet and he eats in their presence (vv. 39-43). The apologetic concern is obvious: Jesus shows that he is the same person whom the disciples had known prior to the crucifixion. The assertion that he invited touching of his (wounded) hands and feet and that he ate before them is, in the apologetic of the time, a firm Christian rejection of any challenge to the reality of the new life of their Lord (see John 20:25-27; 21:9).

In Matthew, the sealing and guarding of the tomb (27:62-66) is clearly a Christian counter to a Jewish charge that the body of Jesus had been stolen by his disciples, who could then claim that he was risen and had been seen by them. The Christian retort was that the Jews and Romans had conspired to prevent just that eventuality but that God had had his way despite their efforts. And they went on the attack by claiming that the accusation of grave-robbery was, in the first place, a lie propagated by the Jewish authorities precisely to cover-up the embarrassing fact of resurrection (28:11-15). All of this is a technique—acceptable at the time—of rebutting an accusation that is *known* to be false. An intriguing point is that the obvious counter to resurrection, that the body is still in the tomb, seems not to have been made. At any rate, these later details—guarded tomb, display of wounds, eating—are apologetic arguments, not hard facts. The hard fact is the Christian conviction that the Lord *is* risen.

The Lord of Life

It is evident from our Gospels that the resurrection of Jesus is not at all the resuscitation of a corpse in a sense of a return to earthly life. The resurrection of Jesus means his rising to life beyond death. The risen Jesus lives a life that transcends earthly life; he has broken out of the confines of time and place. The risen Jesus was present to his disciples in a new and unfettered manner. And not only to his original disciples; he is present, potentially, to all men and women through time and history. This abiding presence is implied in Matthew 28:20: "I am with you always, to the close of the age." He is the same Jesus of his earthly life, but now transformed. Paul can declare: "The last Adam [Christ] became a life-giving Spirit" (1 Cor 15:45), living a Spirit-life now and no longer a life of flesh. Christians came to understand that "eternal life" is life with God and with the risen Jesus. That conviction is enshrined in the promise to the "good thief": "Truly, I say to you, today you will be with me in paradise" (Luke 23:43). Instead of trying to situate or describe "paradise" it is more profitable to recall the comment of Ambrose: *Vita est enim esse cum Christo: ideo ubi Christus, ibi vita, ibi regnum.* Life means living with Christ. Where Christ is, there too is life and there is the kingdom. Now the creed *has* meaning for me: "I believe in . . . life everlasting."

WILFRID J. HARRINGTON, O.P.

See also BIBLE, NEW TESTAMENT WRITINGS; RESURRECTION OF THE DEAD.

RESURRECTION OF THE DEAD

Resurrection in the OT involves many complex themes. Yahweh "raises up" (the causative form of the verb *qûm,* "rise, arise") many figures: saviors (Judg 3:9); prophets (Deut 18:18); the "seed" of David (2 Sam 7:12); the poor (1 Sam 2:8). These usages indicate various forms of Yahweh's saving activity: providing leaders, lifting up the oppressed.

That Yahweh raises or delivers from the realm of death is a commonplace in the Psalms (e.g., Pss 6:4-5; 13:3; 16:9-10; 18:4-5, 16; 22:29; 23:4; 30:3; 49:15; 103:4; 116:8-9; 118:17-18), but probably in the sense that he rescues from mortal danger and from the power of death over human beings (cf. Hos 13:14).

In certain passages, however, there is mention of Yahweh's deliverance from a death already undergone. Ezekiel's vision of dry bones—"Can these bones live?" (37:3)—asserts Yahweh's power to restore life even when every trace of life has been erased: "I am opening your graves and I will bring you up from your graves, O my people" (v. 12). Yet the meaning of this vision is expressed in what comes next: "and I will bring you back to the land of Israel." Restoration from exile is spoken of in the imagery of restoring to life.

In Isaiah 26:19, a passage dated to the fifth century B.C., there is mention of an awakening from death: "Your dead shall live, their corpses shall arise. Awake and sing for joy, O dust-dwellers. For your dew is a radiant dew, and the earth will give birth to the shades." This answers v. 14: "The dead do not live, shades do not arise." Again, this seems to be imagery for restoration of Israel's good, despite the seeming finality of disaster, like that of death.

Two passages from the second century B.C., however, reveal a clear belief in resurrection. Dan 12:2 speaks of resurrection (using the same word, *qîṣ,* "awake," as in Isaiah 26:19): "Many of those who sleep in earth's dust shall awake, some to eternal life, some to shame and eternal confusion." The following verse uses ancient imagery to describe subsequent life in the divine presence, in the heavenly court.

2 Maccabees 7 (vv. 9, 11, 14, 23, 29; cf. also 14:46) asserts the certainty of resurrection for those who faithfully accept death at the hand of the persecutor, but with the expectation that God will restore their bodies for eternal life, apparently on earth.

The theology underlying both these passages is that of the movement within Palestinian Judaism that formed later Pharisaism. It is characterized by a strongly marked apocalyptic imagination. Within the apocalyptic thought-world, assurance of a future life, despite the apparent triumph of wicked persecutors, is central. God is faithful: this conviction gets expressed in vivid imagery, derived from, or at least using, the proto-apocalyptic passages in Ezekiel and Third Isaiah quoted above.

In any case, NT passages reveal that by the first century B.C. belief in resurrection was widespread, though not universal, in Palestinian Judaism: cf. Mark 12:18-27 (Matt 22:23-33; Luke 20:27-40); Acts 23:6-9. In his discussion of the resurrection of Jesus in 1 Corinthians 15, Paul seems to presuppose an established scenario of general resurrection, and seeks to explain how Jesus' resurrection accords with that expectation.

It is important to stress that belief in resurrection represents a re-imagining, within the vivid thought-world of apocalypticism, of God's powerfully life-giving fidelity, and that both the theological conviction and the imagery that expresses it are continuous with the whole of earlier Israelite tradition.

J.P.M. WALSH, S.J.

See also DEATH; ESCHATOLOGY; RESURRECTION OF CHRIST.

RETREAT

Retreat, in the religious sense, is a withdrawal from ordinary activities for an extended time of communion with God in prayer, reflection, and other spiritual exercises. Laity, religious, and clergy all make retreats, and usually go to a retreat house or some other place of solitude to do so. If such a lengthy interruption of schedule is not possible, a retreat in daily life is made by setting aside a period of time each day for exercises of the retreat.

The Christian retreat of any length or format imitates both the forty days of prayer and fasting of Jesus in the desert before he entered into his public ministry, and his frequent withdrawals to the desert for solitary communion with God.

In the early Christian era, the desert, mountains, and other remote areas were the ordinary places for long, uninterrupted periods of prayer. Later, spaces in monasteries and convents were reserved for those seeking solitude and prayer. In the late sixteenth century retreat houses began to be established. They multiplied rapidly, and their growth in number and variety continues today.

Though most retreats involve a community of people, interaction with the community varies according to the format of the retreat. The three general formats are: preached, directed, and private. In preached retreats, there is a group leader who, in two or three conferences each day, suggests topics for reflection. This person also leads prayer, and talks with retreatants privately as requested. In directed retreats, each person meets with a guide who, according to the needs or wishes of the retreatant, suggests Scripture passages or other suitable material for prayer and reflection, and often, methods of prayer which seem best suited to further the goals of the individual. Private retreats are made without a leader or guide.

Silence, some degree of solitude, and at least a minimum of ascetical practices are traditional aspects of any retreat, even those for youth. For the most part, Scripture, especially the New Testament, provides the content of retreats. The liturgical period of Lent, with its emphasis on ascetical practices and the public and private prayer that prepares for the celebration of the paschal mystery, has long been regarded as the retreat of the whole Church.

Many enter into retreat in order to make a serious decision in a spirit of profound prayer and dependence on the guidance of God, or to prepare for a solemn commitment. Those who make annual retreats hope for an encounter with God and their deeper selves which will lead to conversion, greater inner purification, and spiritual maturation.

The classic manual for retreat directors is the *Spiritual Exercises* of St. Ignatius of Loyola. Ignatius (1491–1556) began to write the manual after his mystical illumination at Manressa (1521), and intended it to serve as a guide for others in the experiences of their own inner journey. For thirty days of the Exercises, retreatants note their spiritual experiences, learn to discern their origin, and through prayer and discernment come to a clearer realization of and surrender to God's great plan of salvation in Christ Jesus. In the four Weeks of the Exercises, retreatants first consider creation, repentance for sin, and redemption. They then contemplate the life of Christ, his passion, and finally his resurrection. This structure mirrors the three traditional ways of perfection: the purgative, the illuminative, and the unitive.

Ignatius and his early followers always used the format of the directed retreat when giving the Exercises. Later, in order to accommodate the large numbers of people who desired to make the Exercises, Jesuits and others began to give them in preached retreats. Today both formats are used.

In annual preached, directed, or private retreats of a week or so, and in shorter retreats for specific groups, selected elements of the *Spiritual Exercises* are often used. A retreat might be designed instead around a theme from Scripture or from some spiritual writing which seems best suited to the needs and goals of the group or individuals involved. For example, the Dominican Parable retreat is based on the daily Scripture readings assigned in the Lectionary of the Roman Missal. Those who make charismatic retreats depend on the guidance and gifts of the Holy Spirit for content. They use freely the charismatic gifts, such as healing and prophecy, for the good of all. In Cursillos an overview of Catholic teachings and practice is given, and community is formed by discussions in small groups. In most retreats, but especially in those considered holistic, there is an emphasis on and practice of a healthful lifestyle in regard to food, relaxation, and exercise.

A listing of retreat houses can be found in diocesan and parish offices.

FRANCES KRUMPELMAN, S.C.N.

See also LENT; MEDITATION; PRAYER; SPIRITUAL LIFE; SPIRITUAL EXERCISES OF ST. IGNATIUS OF LOYOLA.

REVELATION

Revelation names the divine initiative in God's self-communication to humanity. For the Judaeo-Christian tradition revelation means God's self-disclosure in the history of Israel and in the life, death, and resurrection of Jesus of Nazareth. The normative testimony to this divine revelation is the Bible.

Thomas Aquinas defined revelation as truths disclosed by God for our salvation. This rather cognitive approach to revelation became the common understanding among Catholic theologians. Correlative to this perception of revelation as divinely communicated truths expressed in doctrines is the understanding of faith (human response to revelation) as primarily belief. This "truths-belief" paradigm led people to conceive of revelation as "information from the Beyond" to be accepted on the authority of God revealing through the mediation of the ecclesiastical magisterium. At times a rigid adherence to this "orthodoxy" became most divisive in the Church. The idea that revelation, so understood, ended with the last apostle and was stored in a "deposit of faith" rendered revelation something static, past, and closed. This traditional Catholic approach led to much unfortunate misunderstanding at the time of the Reformation when Martin Luther recovered the more biblical portrayal of faith as radical trust in God's self-revelation as promise.

At Vatican II, the Catholic Church returned to this biblical understanding of revelation as primarily an *event* of divine self-disclosure. Biblical theologians have discovered and appropriated the more precise meaning of the revelation of the divine name, Yahweh, in Exodus 3:14—instead of the rather abstract translation, "I am who am" (the so-called "metaphysics of Exodus"), the word, Yahweh, means a *promise:* "I will be (for you) who I will be" or "I will be there for you." God's "mighty acts" of salvation for the people, Israel, were experienced as partial fulfillments of the divine Name which is promise. For Christians the definitive fulfillment of the divine promise is Jesus of Nazareth. Revelation is no longer understood primarily as "statements about God from God." Such doctrinal formulations are seen now as secondary to the more fundamental recognition that revelation is the *self*-disclosure of God.

As the human face of God, Jesus reveals the divine Mystery. Contemporary theology insists that philosophical notions of God must no longer be allowed to dictate to God's personal revelation in Jesus. As the definitive fulfillment of the theomorphic anthropology of Genesis 1:26, Jesus is *the* Image of God (2 Cor 4:4). Thus, our God is "Jesus shaped," and that is the Good News of Christianity. Thanks to the biblical scholarship of the twentieth century we now have significant knowledge about Jesus of Nazareth. This knowledge informs contemporary attempts to construct a *theo*centric Christology wherein the fundamental issue is not the divinity of Christ but the kind of God disclosed by Jesus in his words, deeds, and destiny. It was this new, liberating vision of God that led to Jesus' rejection, not directly his claims about himself. The appropriation by Christians of this vision of God shaped by Jesus is one of the most important events in the contemporary life of the Church. We have come to recognize the fact that for too long we have been under the tutelage of Greek metaphysics for our God-talk. And it is somewhat uncanny that this recognition is concurrent with contemporary philosophical deconstructive critiques of the metaphysical tradition, the central feature of which was the conflation of "God" and "Being." As disciples (in the literal sense of that word) of Jesus we must *begin* our talk about God from Jerusalem, because Jesus provides us with *the* criterion, *the* yardstick for evaluating all forms of speech about the living God. For Catholics this insistence that we begin from Jerusalem does not terminate dialogue with Athens. Philosophical notions may be employed as conceptual frameworks for further clarification of God's self-deed in Jesus, but no philosophical notion of, for example, divine immutability or impassibility may mute God's incarnate Word in whose becoming and in whose suffering is revealed the God who becomes our God through love—a love that entails suffering and death. The theology behind all of the liberation movements of our time is not the Absolute Being of the philosophers but the self-giving, passionately loving God of Jesus.

When we turn to the dynamics of revelation, the model of personal self-disclosure through events becomes most suggestive. In the revelatory event God takes the initiative, but this divine lead must be *received* by human beings—there must be a receptive hermeneutics on the part of the addressees of revelation. The human expression of God's word of address is necessarily limited by the linguistic resources of the ones addressed, and these linguistic resources are never merely private; they are the living tradition of a concrete community. In other words the reception of revelation is always historically contextualized in accord with the given potential of linguistic expression, a potential always defined by the given social, political, cultural, and religious circumstances of the addressee. The process of discernment of the divine purposes in revelatory events is simultaneously God's gift and human response. Revelation and faith are correlative. In this human response (faith) the primary linguistic carriers of the revelatory event are generally more akin to poetry than to precise prose, since it is in the poetic mode that language finds its highest possibilities. Accordingly, primary religious language will always be symbolic or metaphorical and usually cast in the genre of narrative or story. Indeed, narrative holds pride of place in the expression of revelation precisely because this genre is most appropriate to human beings *as essentially temporal beings.* Human beings become themselves in and through time; from time they make history, and history is the stuff of story. For the Christian, revelation takes place when the story of Jesus becomes the Christian's story. This is how faith becomes real—faith becomes the personal skill of the disciple for living a Jesus-shaped life.

One can illustrate the dynamics of revelation from Jesus himself. The focal symbol for all of Jesus' preaching and teaching was the kingdom of God, a symbol with a long history in the traditions of Israel. At the time of Jesus this symbol had taken on strong eschatological overtones. Many were awaiting the arrival of the kingdom of God as a final act of divine salvific intervention on behalf of the people of the covenant. As a symbol, the kingdom of God is a circumlocution for God's "being there" for us. Through those superb extended metaphors known as the parables Jesus explicated the revelatory potential of the kingdom of God as symbol. God is graciously disclosed to the human imagination in the extraordinary, even extravagant, twists in the plot of the parable. The revelatory power of these stories was in turn enhanced by the deeds of Jesus on behalf of others—these works of Jesus can most properly be understood as symbolic actions. His words interpreted his deeds, and his deeds illustrated his words.

With God's vindication of what Jesus said and what Jesus did at Easter, Jesus himself becomes *the* revelatory symbol for the Christian community. While Jesus disclosed the meaning of the symbol, kingdom of God, in his parabolic words and lifestyle, Christians find in him *the* parable of God for us. For us Jesus is *the* revelatory symbol, disclosing at once the meaning of God and the meaning of humanity. Indeed, Jesus reveals God in and through his humanity which is the supreme "imaging" of God. One becomes a disciple when the revelatory power of the symbol, Jesus, transforms one's imagination to the extent that everyone and everything is seen *through* Jesus Christ (Phil 2:5).

Divine self-revelation does not lead to our comprehension of God. God remains the ineffable Mystery beyond all human words and concepts. Disclosure entails concealment. It is not that God wants to hide something from us. But God remains the "hidden God" precisely because God is *personal.* Just as we can never fully comprehend the persons we know and love because, as persons, their freedom is directed to an open future, *a fortiori* the Personal God whose freedom is inscrutable Promise remains concealed in every divine disclosure, even in the ultimate historical epiphany of God, Jesus of Nazareth.

If Jesus is *the* historical embodiment of God, this event cannot be merely a fact of the past. Jesus is "once," but "once and for all" (Heb 7:27). What occurred in Jesus must be repeated and represented for every new generation of his disciples. The power of Christian revelation must be vitally effective in every age, in every "today." It is the mission of the Church, the People of God, to witness to the revelatory power of Jesus through word and sacrament. But this mission is radically dependent for its ongoing efficacy on the presence in the Church of the divine Power, the Spirit of God who has become the Spirit of Jesus. This divine empowerment, this divine bearer of the memory of Jesus is the deepest meaning of what Catholicism has appropriately named "tradition." Tradition is the living (Spirit-inspired) memory of Jesus in the Church. Tradition is the lived faith of the People of God. Tradition is the mysterious core, the vivifying center of the Church, the temple of the Holy Spirit. Without this divine presence no one can recognize Jesus as God's self-deed. With this divine presence the recognition of Jesus that is known as faith becomes the skill of the disciple for translating the memory of Jesus into deeds done unto the final consummation of the kingdom of God which remains "not yet."

According to the Epistle to the Hebrews (11:6) no one can be saved without faith. But since God wills the salvation of all (1 Tim 2:4), then faith must be a universal possibility in response to some general revelation. This general revelation has been understood in many ways. The testimony creation offers to its Creator is a theme of Romans (1:20). There is also the more mystical testimony to the inner presence of God in all human beings, a silent presence of the Ineffable One which is really what enables people to recognize God in the special revelations of the great religious traditions. When Vatican II officially acknowledged the major world religions *as religions,* it acknowledged this "original" divine revelation as well. With this new appreciation of the world religions the Roman Catholic Church has in principle extended the need for ecumenical conversation beyond the Christian pale. As Catholics we are Christocentric, but we are not Christomonist. While we witness to Christ in our dialogue with people of other religions, we should expect to learn more about the God of Jesus who is Promise for all people.

Further developments in the theology of revelation should be expected as theologians explore the consequences of the rather recent turn to language as the key to understanding human existence. One of the most important of these consequences currently under exploration is the pragmatics of religious language. The power of the God revealed focally by Jesus, a God whose interest is our interest, whose concern is our concern, becomes efficacious in our world through empowering us. This divine empowering (the Holy Spirit) happens through a transformation of the human imagination, which is our potential to become images of Christ, the Image of God (Rom 8:29). The imagination is not a "faculty" alongside other "faculties" such as intellect and will. It is the basic human ability to live life in consciousness and freedom. The range of potential for any human being is defined by the scope of the imagination. For the Christian, faith, which names our acceptance of God's self-revelation, is identical with a new imagination wherein the divine disclosure and human trust are fused to produce the disciple of Jesus for whom everything is possible (Mark 11:22-24). Divine revelation is not information but a gift that entails a command to *do* the truth.

MICHAEL J. SCANLON, O.S.A.

See also FAITH; THEOLOGY, FUNDAMENTAL; THEOLOGY, SYSTEMATIC.

REVELATIONS, PRIVATE

Private revelations are communications by God to an individual which are not part of divine ("public") revelation as contained in Scripture which ended with the death of the last apostle. By their nature private revelations add nothing new to the revelation already given by God to the Church. Traditionally ecclesiastical authorities have used extreme caution in treating claims of private revelations. Such revelations must be in agreement with the teaching of the Church to be considered authentic. They may call the person to do something extraordinary, but this "vocation" may not be seen as an eschatological fulfillment of the work or person of Christ. Private revelations may call an individual to preach or live the gospel in a special or unique way; however, this call and its content must be harmonious with the message of the gospel as taught by the Church.

ANTHONY D. ANDREASSI

See also APPARITIONS; REVELATION.

RICCI, MATTHEO (1552–1610)

Sent to Rome at the age of sixteen to pursue legal studies, he turned instead to the Jesuits, beginning his studies in 1572 at the Roman College where he specialized in mathematics and astronomy. Fulfilling a dream to be a missionary, he went to Goa (1578) and was ordained there (1580). In 1582 he finished his theological training and relocated to the Portugese colony of Macao to join Pompilio Ruggieri, S.J., in a mission to China. To be more acceptable to the Chinese, the Jesuits abandoned their clerical robes (1583) and dressed like Buddhist monks. In 1585 they dedicated their first church in China. Ricci quickly found out that the Chinese were fascinated by his scientific knowledge, which they could not emulate, and educated Chinese flocked to see his prisms, clocks, and especially his World Map. Seizing the initiative, Ricci began composing books in Chinese (he would eventually write twenty), spreading his reputation and making the Chinese willing to listen to his religious teachings. In 1589 he shed the Buddhist garb, which Confucian scholars resented, and literally reached for the top, moving to the large cities, dressing like a Chinese scholar, and demanding and receiving the social stature of a great scientist. In recognition of this, his Jesuit superior appointed him head of the Chinese mission in 1597, and in 1601 the emperor summoned him to Beijing. The summons recognized his scientific abilities, and, in the capital, Ricci had to maintain his scientific work, even at the expense of his missionary endeavors. He believed that only by being as Chinese as possible and by impressing his hosts could he win the respect necessary to convert them. In fact, he went beyond this, frequently trying to reconcile Christianity and Chinese culture by adapting the former to the latter. In spite of his prestige, few nobles or intellectuals actually converted, and Ricci's hopes of converting the masses by converting the elite faded. He died in 1610, and after his death Italian critics accused him to the popes of going too far in accommodating Catholicism to the Chinese, a criticism eventually endorsed by Pope Clement XI (1700–1721). But posthumous condemnation cannot sully the reputation of this Jesuit missionary who remains, in Chinese eyes, the most respected foreigner ever to visit their land. His principle of inculturation was later justified as necessary in missionary outreach.

JOSEPH F. KELLY

See also INCULTURATION; MISSIONS, CATHOLIC, THE MODERN PERIOD; SOCIETY OF JESUS.

RICE, EDMUND IGNATIUS (1762–1844)

Educationalist and founder of the Irish Christian Brothers. Born in 1762, the son of a relatively prosperous tenant farmer near Callan, County Kilkenny, he received a good education, first at home and later in Kilkenny city, after which he was apprenticed to his uncle, a wealthy ship chandler in Waterford. He married in 1785 but his wife died in childbirth four years later. Rice then abandoned the social life which he had much enjoyed and increasingly devoted himself to the education of poor boys, whose Catholic faith was under threat from the lure of cheap schooling offered by zealous Protestant evangelists. When his uncle died in 1794, he inherited the business but soon retired from trade to concentrate on teaching. Inspired by the work of the Presentation nuns who were setting up schools for the girls of poor families, Rice decided to build and open a school in Waterford himself, which he did with the support of the local bishop in 1803. To help him in his work, Rice recruited a number of young men, mainly of the same solid commercial background as his own. This enabled him to set up schools elsewhere in County Waterford, in Cork, Dublin, and England. The community developed first as a diocesan congregation under the control of the bishop in whichever diocese it happened to be working and later, in 1820, as a Pontifical Institute or religious order, formally entitled "Brothers of the Christian Schools of Ireland" but popularly known as "the Christian Brothers," with Rice as their superior general, an office which he held until 1838. The brothers spread rapidly, both in Ireland and throughout the English-speaking world. Their highly organized system of education owed much to the independent spirit of their founder and first members, derived from their experience of responsibility in business. This would have considerable influence in the development of Irish education. As early as Brother Rice's time and for long afterwards, the brothers stood apart from state schemes preferring to organize their schools in the way they knew best, eventually producing their own textbooks and undertaking the provision of secondary schools with much success. The same spirit made them the promoters of a nationalist spirit in their pupils, but this was after the death (in 1844) of Edmund Rice who concentrated always on strengthening the boys' commitment to the Catholic faith and qualifying them in the harsh conditions of his day for secure and satisfying employment.

Ignatius Rice

LOUIS McREDMOND

See also CATHOLICISM, IRISH; CONGREGATION OF CHRISTIAN BROTHERS.

RIEL, LOUIS (1844–1885)

Born in St. Boniface, Manitoba, in 1844, Louis Riel was of Métis ancestry, a member of the French-speaking, Roman Catholic mixed-blood community. As a young man, Riel was sent to the Sulpician Seminary in Montreal but never completed his studies. He returned west in 1868, and became president of the provisional government during the Red River Insurrection of 1869 through 1870. Afterwards, Riel was forced to flee and live in the United States. On 8 December 1875, he underwent a mystical spiritual experience while attending Mass in Washington, D.C., and became convinced that he was the prophet of the New World. He formulated a new Catholicism that was highly personalized and self-glorifying. Riel appropriated the name "David" as well as the titles "Prophet, Priest-King, Infallible Pontiff."

He was later committed to an asylum where he experienced numerous revelations. Released in January 1878, Riel traveled in the United States and, in 1883, began to teach school at St. Peter's Mission near Great Falls, Montana. The following year, a delegation from the territorial district of Saskatchewan arrived at the mission to ask Riel to return with them to Canada and assist in redressing their grievances. Riel was regarded as a hero and savior by the Métis whose society was being overwhelmed by the disappearance of the buffalo and the advance of civilization.

In the meantime, Riel again underwent intense spiritual experiences and, upon his return to the district of Saskatchewan, the Oblate missionaries were suspicious of his motives. As time passed, Riel's religiosity became more evident and unorthodox. On 18 March 1885, Riel seized the church at Batoche and announced that Rome had fallen. The following day, the Exovedate or governing council was formed and Riel was officially proclaimed a prophet "in the service of Jesus Christ" with the right to direct the clergy. Ignace Bourget, the Ultramontane bishop of Montreal, was designated pope of the "Catholic, Apostolic and Vital Church of the New World." Other reforms instituted by Riel included a lay ministry and a Saturday Sabbath as well as significant doctrinal modifications.

This religious fervor coincided with military action against the Dominion of Canada. After the suppression of the North West Rebellion, Riel was charged with treason, found guilty and executed on 16 November 1885. Riel's prophetic role had posed a serious threat to the Oblates and their influence over the Métis population and they retaliated by denouncing him as an apostate who was insane. This allegation of insanity was designed to undermine Riel's prophetic figure among the Métis and cast doubts on his spirituality.

Riel indigenized Catholicism, something which orthodox Oblate missionaries had never succeeded in doing. As a result of his attempt to rejuvenate the Catholic faith with new ideas that were meaningful to the Métis in the crisis which their society faced, Riel became a religious outsider within the mainstream of Catholicism and was denounced as a heretic. Riel, however, should be regarded as manifestation of that unique and creative response that results from the release of the Word. Within the context of inculturation, Riel is the cutting edge of the gospel.

RAYMOND HUEL

See also CANADA, THE CATHOLIC CHURCH IN.

RIGHT TO DIE

See EUTHANASIA.

RIGHT TO LIFE

See ABORTION; CONTRACEPTION; EUTHANASIA; HUMANAE VITAE.

RIGHTEOUSNESS

See JUSTIFICATION.

RIGHTS, HUMAN

See HUMAN RIGHTS.

RITE OF CHRISTIAN INITIATION OF ADULTS (RCIA)

The Rite of Christian Initiation of Adults (often called the catechumenate) is a process for incorporating unbaptized adults into the Christian faith and community in the Catholic Church through the sacraments of baptism, confirmation, and Eucharist. The process includes periods of evangelization called the precatechumenate; instruction in the faith called catechumenate; immediate preparation for the sacraments known as purification or enlightenment, usually coinciding with Lent; the celebration of the sacraments of initiation, normally at the Easter Vigil; and a period of reflection on the Easter experience and bonding with the Christian community called the mystagogia. The rite was instituted as a result of the decrees of the Second Vatican Council calling for the revision of the rite of baptism and the restoration of the catechumenate for adults. The new rite was prepared by the Congregation for Divine Worship and published with the approval of Pope Paul VI in 1972 for translation and implementation by national episcopal conferences. A provisional translation was approved for use in the U.S. in 1974, and the official edition of the rite approved in 1986 by the U.S. Catholic Conference.

The adult catechumenate developed in the first centuries of the Christian era in response to the circumstances of the Church in the Roman Empire and the rapid spread of the Christian faith. On the one hand the intermittent threat of persecution made apostasy a not infrequent occurrence, and on the other, the lack of a formal process of catechesis in many places contributed to the growing problem of heresy. As a result, Christian communities began to establish basic criteria for receiving baptism and extended the period of formation for prospective converts. By the early third century Hippolytus writes of stages of initiation and examination of the candidates to determine their suitability for the sacraments at the Easter Vigil, including a period of evangelization and inquiry, a three-year catechumenate for instruction and testing of the faith, a period of election and immediate preparation for the sacraments, full initiation at the Easter Vigil, and a period of reflection on the Easter mysteries celebrated in the sacraments.

With its emergence from the time of persecution (313) and its establishment as the official Church of the Roman Empire (396), the Church began to experience a massive influx of converts, with many joining for the political advantage that ensued. And often such converts chose to remain catechumens, with no serious intention of joining the community until the approach of death. As a result, the catechumenate process of earlier centuries fell into decline, though it continued in some form and in certain places into the Middle Ages. Another factor in this decline was the increasing practice of infant baptism, motivated in part by the doctrine of original sin as developed by St. Augustine (ca. 400). As infant baptism became common, the rite of water baptism was separated from anointing with chrism (chrismation or confirmation) which came to be reserved to the bishop in the Latin Rite Churches, with Eucharist deferred until after the latter. In the early twentieth century, the papal decrees allowing children to receive Eucharist at the age of reason, usually preceding confirmation, further obscured the original order of the rites of initiation.

Thus the institution of the RCIA in the last two decades is an attempt to restore sacramental initiation (at least for adults and some children) to its form in the early Church. The impetus for this restoration has come not only from liturgical research, but from the growth in understanding of the human person, and the human condition in society provided by modern disciplines such as psychology and sociology, and from the exigencies of the historical situation for the Christian Church in the modern world.

The RCIA from this latter perspective is a response to the realities of modern life: the rise of a neopagan culture on the one hand, in which the need for exemplary witness of the Christian faith is seen as critical to its survival; and, on the other, the breakdown of a sense of community in society and inevitably in the Church requiring extraordinary measures to counteract.

The RCIA attempts to meet these challenges by first of all calling each parish to be a welcoming community, reaching out to those seeking deeper meaning and reasons for faith and hope in their lives. The stages are celebrated publicly at Sunday Mass, and members of the community serve as catechists and sponsors for those accepting the invitation to "come and see."

As in the early Church, the process begins with evangelization—the year-round effort to welcome the stranger and to respond to his or her need for a caring, believing community. Those who respond are received into the precatechumenate or inquiry stage, where they share their stories with members of the RCIA community, and learn the basic beliefs of the Christian faith. When they are deemed ready to take up a serious investigation of the faith and teachings of the Catholic Church, they are enrolled in the catechumenate for whatever length of time is deemed necessary. They normally then participate in the celebration of the Word each Sunday with the community, and are dismissed after the homily for reflection on the Word and further instruction in the faith. At the appropriate time, usually at the beginning of the Lenten season, those who are deemed ready for sacramental initiation by witness of their sponsors and the consent of the community are formally received in the Rite of Election by the bishop or his representative. They enter the period of Enlightenment, in which they are prayed for by the community and are presented with the Church's Creed and the Lord's Prayer as the basic documents of the faith.

Then, ideally at the Easter Vigil, the elect become full members of the Catholic Christian community through the sacraments of baptism, confirmation, and Eucharist, celebrated in the midst of all who have gathered to commit themselves once again to the risen Lord. The newly baptized, or neophytes, then enter a period of reflection on the experience of the Easter mysteries, called mystagogia, and so begin the process of full assimilation into the community in which they are called as witnesses in turn to their newfound faith in Christ.

The Rite of Christian Initiation of Adults is meant primarily for the unbaptized, but has been adapted also for those who have been baptized in another Christian denomination and are seeking full communion with the Catholic Church through confirmation and Eucharist. The same process now often includes baptized but uninstructed Catholics, who are seeking full sacramental initiation in the Church. Finally, the RCIA is being adapted in many places for the initiation of children of catechetical age into the faith community, especially those whose parents are being welcomed at the same time.

The critical factor in the success of the RCIA remains the experience of the Church as a caring community of faith, beginning at the parish and diocesan levels and extending to the universal Church. This is often problematic, especially in large traditional parishes where many members remain anonymous or somewhat alienated from the communal experience. Without a vibrant faith community the rite can deteriorate into mere formalism, concealing the basic mission of the apostolic Church to "make disciples of all nations, baptizing them in the name of the Father, and of the Son, and of the Holy Spirit" (Matt 28:19).

JAMES HALEY

See also CATECHESIS; SACRAMENTS OF INITIATION.

RITES

"Rite" has three principal meanings: (1) the order of service for a particular sacrament or other liturgical event; (2) a ritual process that includes several such rites (e.g., the Rite of Christian Initiation of Adults); or (3) the patterns of worship of a particular Church (e.g., Roman Rite). There are nine rites in the Catholic Church: Latin or Roman, Byzantine, Armenian, Chaldean, Coptic, Ethiopian, Malabar, Maronite, and Syrian.

PATRICIA DeFERRARI

See also CATHOLICISM; EASTERN CHURCHES.

RITUAL

Ritual can be understood as a social symbolic process; that is, it develops within a community and uses gestures, objects, words, and sounds as symbols to communicate, create, criticize, and transform meaning. Ritual meaning is always performative. Because ritual is so multidimensional, its study spans most traditional disciplines within the human sciences, including anthropology, sociology, and psychology. Interest in ritual studies developed primarily after Vatican II as people involved in liturgical reform began to recognize liturgy as a form of ritual action.

In a second, more restricted sense, "ritual" refers to a book, a collection of rites other than Eucharist or Liturgy of the Hours over which a priest presides (e.g., the Roman Ritual).

PATRICIA DeFERRARI

See also LITURGY.

ROGATION DAYS

In Western Christendom, certain days in early summer were commonly prescribed days of prayer and fasting. "Major Rogation" was 25 April and was a Christianized version of the pagan observance of Robigalia, which involved processions through cornfields and prayers for the preservation of the crop from mildew. The feast of Saint Mark, also on 25 April, was a later institution. "Minor Rogations" were observed on Monday, Tuesday, and Wednesday before Ascension Thursday.

In 1969 the Roman Catholic Church replaced Rogation days with periods of prayer for the needs of humanity, the fruits of the earth, and the work of people's hands. The observance of these periods may occur at various times throughout the year and is decided by the conference of local bishops.

PATRICIA DeFERRARI

See also LITURGY.

ROGERS, MARY JOSEPHINE, M.M. (1882–1955)

Mary Josephine Rogers, one of the three founders of Maryknoll, was born in Boston, Massachusetts, in 1882. After graduating from Smith College in 1905, she obtained a teacher's certificate from Boston Normal and taught science in the Boston schools.

Mary Josephine Rogers, M.M.

On a teaching fellowship back at Smith, a Protestant colleague urged her to form a Mission Study Club for Catholic students. Seeking missionary materials, she corresponded with Fr. James A. Walsh at the Propagation of the Faith office in Boston. Her burning zeal for mission, which had been awakened during student and faculty years at Smith, found new expression in collaboration with Walsh, as translator and author of mission publications.

In 1912, her missionary vocation was fully realized when she joined the foundation at Maryknoll, giving leadership to the women providing auxiliary services for the Catholic Foreign Mission Society. When the women were separated as a canonically recognized religious congregation in 1920, Rogers was chosen superior. Elected Mother General at the first General Chapter in 1925, she led the congregation until retirement in 1946. Her spirit and leadership as foundress remained a vibrant influence in the community until her death in 1955.

JANET CARROLL, M.M.

See also MARYKNOLL.

ROMAN COLLAR

An upright white linen neckband worn by the clergy, usually with a black clerical shirt or a rabat. A distinctively ecclesiastical garment, it is customarily worn outside the church or rectory.

JOSEPH QUINN

See also PRIESTHOOD, THE MINISTERIAL.

ROMAN INQUISITION, THE

Paul III established the Roman Inquisition in 1542 primarily to combat Protestantism. It was governed by a commission of six cardinals called the Congregation of the Inquistion, who were authorized to protect the faith throughout the Catholic world, but Julius III ruled that its actions should be confined to Italy. Under successive popes, with the notable exceptions of Paul IV (1555–1559) and Pius V (1566–1572), the Roman Inquisition usually operated with restraint; and when the threat of Protestantism ebbed in Italy, it became the watchdog for the purity of the faith. It is remembered for its condemnation of the Copernican system and of Galileo (1616 and 1632). The best known victim of the Roman Inquisition was the Dominican philosopher Giordano Bruno who was burned at the stake in 1600.

When Pius X reorganized the Curia in 1908 the word "Inquisition" was dropped as its purposes had evolved and changed and it was renamed the Holy Office with a mandate to guard Catholic orthodoxy. In 1965, Paul VI, with more reformist attitudes, renamed it the Congregation for the Doctrine of the Faith.

The history of the various epochs of the Inquisition—Medieval, Spanish and Roman—has ever been the subject of polemical controversy; and, all things considered, that history is a sad and very regrettable chapter in the life of the Church.

MICHAEL GLAZIER

ROMAN MISSAL

See LITURGICAL BOOKS.

ROMAN RITE

The Roman Rite is the style of celebration of the Eucharist and other liturgies that developed in ancient Rome. This style of liturgy, later influenced by both Spanish and Gallican liturgical traditions, became the most common form of liturgical worship for the Western Church by the twelfth century. In 1570 Pope St. Pius V promulgated the Roman Missal which made the Roman Rite the official liturgy of the Western Church, although a few local rites were allowed to continue. The Roman Rite (also known as the "Latin Rite") is marked by its simplicity and brevity, unlike liturgies of the Eastern Churches, which are much more elaborate and expansive and stress the repetition of words and gestures. Another distinguishing feature of the Roman Rite is the use of unleavened bread at Mass. Vatican Council II (1962–1965) changed much of the Roman Rite by simplifying many of the rubrics and eliminating numerous medieval accretions. Two of the most obvious changes was that Latin gave way to the vernacular of each local Church, and Communion under both species became more common whereas previously it was rare to nonexistent.

ANTHONY D. ANDREASSI

See also LITURGY.

ROMAN ROTA

This tribunal within the Roman Curia is the ordinary court for cases appealed to the Holy See. It is best known for handling cases concerning the validity of marriages.

DAVID BRYAN

See also ANNULMENT; CURIA, ROMAN.

ROMERO, OSCAR ARNULFO (1917–1980)

Oscar Romero was archbishop of San Salvador, El Salvador, from 22 February 1977, until 24 March 1980. He is remembered for his bold preaching and decisive leadership of the San Salvador archdiocese, which led to his assassination, regarded by many as a martyrdom.

He was born on 15 August 1917, in Ciudad Barrios, a village in the mountains of eastern El Salvador. At the age of thirteen, he entered the minor seminary in the city of San Miguel, and in 1937 he went on to the major seminary in San Salvador. A few months later, he was sent to the Latin American College in Rome to study theology at the Gregorian University. He was ordained in Rome in April of 1942, at the age of twenty-four, while preparing a doctoral thesis in ascetical theology. In 1943, however, he returned to San Miguel, without finishing the doctorate.

Father Romero achieved great recognition in San Miguel as a pastor, radio preacher, editor of the Catholic paper, and promoter of lay organizations. Many persons, however, viewed him as harsh and perfectionistic; he also noted these traits in himself in his retreats, and he gradually overcame them in later years.

Archbishop Oscar Romero

In 1967, he was appointed secretary general of the Salvadoran bishops' conference, moving to San Salvador. In 1970, he was ordained an auxiliary bishop to the archbishop of San Salvador.

Changes were sweeping the Catholic Church in the years after the Second Vatican Council, which ended in 1965. Bishop Romero, totally dedicated to the love and service of the Church from his youth, supported the council but found the readjustment difficult. As an auxiliary bishop, he avoided the meetings of the San Salvador clergy, who saw him as hostile to the type of pastoral work that flowed from the council and from the 1968 assembly of Latin American bishops in Medellín, Colombia. As editor of the archdiocesan weekly from 1971, he showed clearly his suspicions of the way the Church was going.

In late 1974, Bishop Romero was made bishop of the rural diocese of Santiago de María. He plunged into pastoral work as he had done in San Miguel, visiting all parts of his diocese. Here he became more aware of the hardship and injustice that characterized the lives of the peasantry. On 21 June 1975, the rural police massacred five peasants in his diocese, and he visited their families and celebrated Mass for them; he protested vigorously to the local commandant and to the president of El Salvador, but cautiously avoided public statements.

By 1976, pressure for land reform was building in El Salvador from the growing peasant organizations and from the country's two universities and many of the clergy. The national congress passed a timid reform law, and Bishop Romero held a seminar on the new law for his clergy. But protest from the land-owning class effected the law's repeal after a few months. In the archdiocese of San Salvador, meanwhile, several rural parishes were using a new sort of pastoral approach emphasizing small Christian communities, in which the members became accustomed to meeting and discussing matters vital to their lives, including the social inequality under which they lived.

At this time, the government and prominent leaders in El Salvador persuaded the Vatican to choose Bishop Romero to replace the retiring archbishop of San Salvador, and he was installed on 22 February 1977. Unrest in some rural areas had recently brought about alarm among the country's oligarchy and swift government reaction against the peasant movement. Several foreign priests were deported, and the communications media, owned by the oligarchy, openly attacked the Church's work among the peasantry and the priests who carried it out.

On March 12, gunmen ambushed and murdered a rural pastor, Rutilio Grande, S.J., as he was on his way to say Mass. Shocked by the event and urged by his clergy and others to take firm action, Archbishop Romero reacted vigorously, closing all Catholic schools for three days of reflection and protest and canceling all Masses one Sunday except for one in the square before the cathedral, which about 100,000 persons attended.

Tension with the government and the oligarchy, angered by what they saw as the new archbishop's betrayal of them, continued. During his three years as archbishop, six priests were killed, as were many lay people, especially members of the small communities. Four of the other five bishops generally allied themselves with the government and the oligarchy, and eventually Archbishop Romero and Bishop Arturo Rivera Damas, who succeeded him in Santiago de María, found themselves isolated from the others. The papal nuncio also sided against the archbishop, who journeyed to Rome four times in three years to explain to the Pope and his Curia the situation in El Salvador and how he was trying to follow the Church's teaching about the rights of the poor and oppressed. He explained the apparent change in himself as a development of his desire to be faithful to God and to the gospel, which demanded a new "pastoral fortitude" in the circumstances he encountered as archbishop.

A chief source of his conflict with the government and the oligarchy was his preaching, in which he commented boldly on the sufferings of the people. His lengthy Sunday homilies, broadcast on the archdiocesan radio to the whole country, were the program most listened to in El Salvador. He himself became clearly the country's most respected and popular figure. Although his enemies were powerful, they were few, and support for him grew among persons far beyond the borders of El Salvador, leading to his being nominated for the Nobel Peace Prize and receiving honorary degrees from Georgetown University and the University of Louvain. At the assembly of Latin American bishops in Puebla, Mexico, in January and February of 1979, which he attended as a consultor of the Pontifical Commission for Latin America, he was among the most sought-after delegates for interviews by the press.

Archbishop Romero was assassinated by a rightist death squad while he was preaching at Mass in the chapel of the cancer hospital where he resided. He was buried in the San Salvador cathedral. The archdiocese has introduced the cause of his canonization.

JAMES BROCKMAN, S.J.

ROSARY

The rosary is the best known private devotion in the Catholic Church and Christianity's most popular method of meditation. The use of key prayers (Our Father, Hail Mary, Doxology), which are repeated with the aid of a string of beads, focuses the meditator, increasingly opening him or her to the Real. The meditator, further, keeps in mind fifteen scenes (mostly biblical) called "mysteries," all illustrative of the principles of rosary meditation.

The rosary swept Europe only some five hundred years ago, but it uses meditative techniques which can be documented from the dawn of recorded history. People placed themselves in the Presence (gods, spirits, ancestors) and cultivated a state described by terms such as Waiting, Seeking, or Searching. The Sought One was then repetitiously addressed by name or title, to which were added words of blessing and petition.

The Search became a favored element in the contemplative life of Israel (without being recognized as such) and was part of the messianic spirituality of many Jews at the time of Jesus. The writings of Luke (the Gospel and the Acts), in particular, sketch scenes containing elements of the Search, scenes which are today the mysteries of the rosary.

Luke's powerful scenes were popularized by Christian art, hymns and festivals, while early monasticism continued the Search. In the late Middle Ages the custom of Searching by the use of repeated acclamations such as "Our Father" and "Hail Mary" received a new popularity. At the same time, and almost accidentally, Luke's ever-popular "mysteries," were added to produce a meditative device of great power. The Dominican Order took the lead in popularizing the rosary, and came to attribute its discovery to St. Dominic. In recent centuries the rosary has been repeatedly urged by Church authorities. Group recitation of the rosary, while not so clearly an instrument of meditation, has also been widely promoted, especially for family prayer.

The fifteen mysteries of the rosary fall into three divisions, called "chaplets," of five mysteries each. Each mystery accompanies the recitation of one Our Father, ten Hail Marys, and the Doxology. The ten Hail Marys enhance the quality of the Our Father, which remains the key prayer of the rosary. The "Joyful Mysteries" are the Annunciation, Visitation, Nativity, Presentation, and Finding (of the child Jesus). The "Sorrowful Mysteries" constitute a single great mystery, the passion of Christ. They are the Agony in the Garden, the Scourging, the Crowning with Thorns, the Carrying of the Cross, and the Death of Jesus Christ. The "Glorious Mysteries" are the Resurrection, Ascension, Pentecost, the Assumption of Mary, and the Crowning of Mary as Queen of Heaven and Earth. The last two are not derived from Luke, but from the prayer life of Christians; they sharpen our appreciation of prayer as a means of meditation. That Mary is "assumed" means that she is the disciple most "awake," most suitable to hear us tell our prayers. With her as listener, we develop the art of praising God and Christ to a *third person.* The "Crowning" signifies the traditional "queenly" role: Mary carries our prayers to Jesus, her Lord and ours, absorbing them into her own and leaving aside whatever may be unworthy.

DAVID BRYAN

See also DEVOTIONS.

ROSH HA-SHANAH

Rosh Ha-Shanah or the Jewish New Year occurs just prior to the great autumnal observances of the Day of Atonement and Tabernacles. It is observed on the first day of the seventh month, the month of Tishri. This follows the calendar which the Jews began to observe during the Babylonian ascendancy. Of obscure origin, the feast probably derived from an ancient harvest festival. While looking back with joyful thankfulness, it looked forward to the coming year with some anxiety. Thus apprehension of divine judgment and petition for mercy were woven into the observance. To the rabbis, Rosh Ha-Shanah became a day of judgment.

Featured in the liturgical observance of the New Year are readings and prayers, including three series of benedictions relating first to God as sovereign, then to God as mindful of creation and his covenant, and finally those relating to the sounding of the shofar especially at theophanies in Israel. And frequent sounding of the shofar would characterize the New Year feast. To Philo, it is the festival of trumpets (*De Specialibus Legibus* II:188). Though the traditional summons to battle, on the New Year the trumpet sounds an appeal to God as peacemaker and peacekeeper throughout the universe (*De Specialibus Legibus* II:192). But Israelite prophecy had long urged the cosmic resonance of the trumpet blast. It would signal the Day of the Lord (Joel 2:1; Zeph 12:16). And similarly, in the New Testament (Matt 24:31; 1 Thess 4:16; 1 Cor 15:52; Rev 8:6; 11:15).

Preaching repentance and the coming judgment, John the Baptist probably began his ministry near the New Year observance in the fall of the year.

THOMAS BUCKLEY

ROUAULT, GEORGES (1871–1958)

A French expressionist painter whom Jacques Maritain called "The greatest religious painter of our time."

Rouault was born in a cellar during the bloody street fighting that crushed the Paris Commune. His father, a cabinet maker, taught him to respect a craft. His grandfather took him strolling along the banks of the Seine, rummaging through bookstalls for artists' prints. In the Paris streets Rouault saw the faces of the poor—prostitutes, clowns, prisoners—twisted into roles that mocked their pain.

At fourteen Rouault was apprenticed to a restorer of stained glass. His task was to repair damaged pieces from the windows of medieval cathedrals. It was slow work. During those long hours his consciousness was being shaped—not by the classicists' forced ideal of form and line, nor the impressionists' pursuit of the play of light in nature, nor the naturalists' despair in a pitiless world. The shaping was taking place unconsciously through focused attention on those roughly carved pieces of glass through which light had illuminated deep reds and blues for hundreds of years. The hours of handling chunks of dark glass rimmed in lead stirred a connection to the old cathedrals.

While Paris spawned a secular art of vibrant color, Rouault studied Rembrandt. In his early twenties he met Gustave Moreau, a teacher who understood him. "You love art that is grave, sober and essentially religious," Moreau told him, "and everything you do will bear this seal" (Guiseppe Marchiori, *Rouault,* New York: Reynal/Morrow, 1967, p. 6). Rouault plunged into a period of savage painting of dwarfs, clowns, acrobats—the street faces that haunted him—in shapeless layers of color heightened by thick black strokes. The brutality shocked

Lithograph by Georges Rouault

critics and cost him a valued friendship with Leon Bloy. "I have . . . seen your sole and sempiternal canvas," Bloy wrote him in 1907, "still the same old slut or clown . . . each time the effect gets worse . . . you are attracted solely by ugliness and you are obsessed with it . . . if you were a man of prayer . . . you would never be able to paint these vile pictures" (Marchiori, p. 9).

Rouault *was* a man of prayer. To be true to his inner vision, rooted in faith, he had to shatter the calcified ideals of beauty (Jacques Maritain, *Rouault,* New York: Abrams, 1954, p. 8). "I am seeking not beauty," Rouault wrote, "but expression" (Marchiori, p. 8). Fortunately for the sensitive Rouault, the writer André Saurès understood him. "You have seen too much of the world through your spirit of revolt and anger," he wrote in 1913, ". . . you had to deliver yourself of it . . . you have emerged from the dark suburbs, basements and confounded places inhabited by monsters. You must not go back" (Marchiori, p. 15). On another occasion he told Rouault not to stay in hell. "It is enough to pass through" (W. A. Dryness, *Rouault: A Vision of Suffering and Salvation,* Grand Rapids, Mich.: Eerdmans, 1971, p. 86).

But human suffering was the spur to his creative life: "I believe in suffering," he wrote, "it is not feigned in me. It is my only merit" (Maritain, p. 28). In an isolated studio where he withdrew for many years Rouault distilled an artistic vision that fused his "journey through hell" with "a faith in redemption" (Maritain, p. 8), and a medieval reverence for harmony. Jacques Maritain, who knew him, believed that Rouault's creative force sprang from "spiritual inwardness taming and lifting a ferocious art of the human abysses" (Maritain, p. 32).

Throughout his life Rouault remained a stumbling block to the modern temper: in the wasteland of broken images he was redeeming sacred art. As he aged he painted images of Christ—mocked and crucified. A mute dignity glows through the oil colors as subtly as light through the opaque reds and blues of stained glass. The "ferocious art" had ripened into masterpieces of serenity. But the inner harmony of his art is hidden to any viewer who stands close to the paintings. Like the relationship among many distinct pieces of the old cathedral windows, it appears only by meditating on the whole from a distance.

In its maturity Rouault's art expressed as much compassion for a king as for a clown. "The trouble with me . . . is that I can never leave anyone in his 'spangled suit.' Even if he is a king or an emperor, it's the *soul* of the man facing me that interests me . . . and the greater he is and the more glorified on the human plane, the more I fear for his soul. To extract the whole of one's art from the expression of a broken-down old acrobat (or horse for that matter), is either mad pride—or, if one is capable of it, sheer, perfect humility" (Marchiori, p. 27).

PATRICIA O'CONNOR

See also ART, CHRISTIAN; CATHEDRAL.

RUBRICS

Rubrics (Lat. for "red") are the directions and explanations for celebrants found in liturgical books. The name is derived from the fact that originally these directives were printed in red to distinguish them from the text. Rubrics can be found in the introduction to a liturgy, explaining its nature and purpose, and throughout the actual liturgical text, detailing actions to be performed or materials to be used. Some rubrics are preceptive and admit of no variation, while others are suggestive and leave the words, actions, or general mood to be set to the discretion of the celebrant.

ANTHONY D. ANDREASSI

See also LITURGY.

RULE OF ST. AUGUSTINE

See AUGUSTINE, ST., RULE OF.

RULE OF ST. BENEDICT

See BENEDICT, ST., RULE OF.

RYAN, JOHN AUGUSTINE (1869–1945)

Born in 1869 of Irish immigrant parents in Vermillion, Dakota County, Minnesota, John Ryan was educated at the local Christian Brothers high school where he showed an unusual curiosity about labor and social problems. At home his interest was fostered by reading *The Irish World* and *The American Industrial Liberator.* After he entered St. Paul Seminary in 1892, he was deeply influenced by the social opinions of Archbishop John Ireland and by Leo XIII's *Rerum Novarum.* After ordination in 1898, Ryan did four years of postgraduate studies in moral theology at Catholic University. He titled his doctoral thesis *A Living Wage: Its Ethical and Economic Aspects.* On returning to Minnesota, he taught moral theology, ethics, and economics at St. Paul Seminary until 1915 when he was invited to join the faculty of Catholic University. Over two decades his lectures on moral theology, industrial ethics, and sociology at Catholic University had a lasting impact on students, many of whom graduated to teach and carry the Ryan social messages to many parts of America.

John Augustine Ryan

In 1919 Ryan wrote a pamphlet which was adopted as their own by the bishops of the Administrative Committee of the National Catholic Welfare Conference. It was titled *Social Reconstruction: A General Review of the Problems and Survey of Remedies,* and when published on 12 February 1919 it caused a furor. It cogently argued for minimum wage legislation; unemployment, health, and old-age insurance for workers; an age limit for child labor; legal enforcement of labor's right to organize; the need for a national employment service; and a call for a comprehensive public housing program. It was an unexpected bombshell for the business community. The reaction of Stephen C. Mason, president of the National Association of Manufacturers, was typical. "... a careful reading of this pamphlet will lead you to the conclusion we have reached, namely, that it involves what may prove to be a covert effort to disseminate partisan, pro-labor union, socialistic propaganda under the official insignia of the Roman Catholic Church in America." Ryan's proposals became the American Catholic social agenda for most of the twentieth century.

In February, 1920, the N.C.W.C. started its Social Action Department and John A. Ryan was appointed its first director; and for the next quarter century it became his forum. He became "the Catholic labor priest" and his social conscience and erudition won him respect from friends and some foes. He lectured widely, and many of his books became standard texts which educated more than a generation. Among his better known works are: *Distributive Justice; Social Reconstruction; The Catholic Church and the Citizen; A Better Economic Order;* and, in collaboration with Joseph Husslein, he wrote *The Church and Labor,* a work that had a widespread impact. When Pius XI issued *Quadragesimo Anno,* one of the Church's focal social encyclicals, Bishop Shahan, the Rector of Catholic University, voiced the sentiments of many when he remarked, "Well, this is a great vindication for John Ryan."

Franklin D. Roosevelt's New Deal changed the face of America; and its social programs were a dream come true for John A. Ryan. He was a strong supporter of Roosevelt's crusade and was appointed one of the three members of the important Industrial Appeals Board of the National Recovery Administration. He gave the benediction at the President's second and fourth inaugurations. But the eyes of John A. Ryan were not on the centers of power, but on the nameless poor and the countless working men and women who deserved a fairer deal and a better life. And John A. Ryan, one of the clarion voices for social justice in this century, spoke for them all his life. He died in 1945.

JOAN GLAZIER

See also AMERICAN CATHOLICISM; SOCIAL TEACHING OF THE CHURCH.

S

SABBATH

Derived from the Hebrew word for "cease, stop," the term Sabbath refers to the observance of the seventh day of the week (Saturday) as a day of rest and religious observance by Jews. According to Genesis 2:3 the Sabbath was made part of the very structure of God's creation. The Sabbath commandments in the Decalogues appeal to different theological roots: creation (Exod 20:11), and Exodus (Deut 5:15). In NT times the chief topic of controversy was what constituted "work" on the Sabbath day of rest. Jesus appears to be respectful of the Sabbath rest but having the authority to do what more strict observers would not allow (see Matt 12:1-14; Mark 2:23–3:6; Luke 13:10-17; John 5:1-18; 7:19-24). The term "Sabbath" is also applied in some circles to the Christian observance of the first day of the week (Sunday) as the memorial of Jesus' resurrection. Sunday seems to have originally been a day of worship. But from the fourth century on Church leaders often applied the OT Sabbath commandment to the observance of Sunday as a day of rest.

DANIEL J. HARRINGTON, S.J.

See also SUNDAY; TEN COMMANDMENTS, THE.

SACRAMENT OF ANOINTING

The ritual for the anointing of the sick was revised in accordance with Vatican II, and appeared in Latin in 1972. It describes how to celebrate the sacrament in different circumstances. A person may be anointed outside Mass or during Mass. A large number of people may be anointed in one celebration, for example in a hospital or place of pilgrimage. The following is a description of the anointing of one person outside Mass.

The priest greets the person who is sick and the other people who are present; he may sprinkle holy water. He says some words by way of introduction to the rite. The sample introduction in the ritual is based on the Letter of St. James. There is a penitential rite, like that at the beginning of Mass.

A passage of Scripture is read, usually one which shows Jesus consoling and healing. This may be followed by a brief period of silence. The priest may say a few words of explanation, bringing out the connection between the reading and the situation of the person who is sick.

Everyone takes part in a litany-type prayer, which may be shortened or adapted.

The priest, in silence, lays hands on the head of the person who is sick, a gesture imbued with sentiments of caring and of trust in the Holy Spirit.

Then the priest says a prayer over the oil. Ordinarily the oil has been blessed by the bishop on Holy Thursday, and the prayer said by the priest is one of thanksgiving. It is Trinitarian in form, recalls the work of salvation, and prays that God may ease the sufferings and comfort the weakness of the person who is sick.

In case of true necessity, the priest himself may bless the oil. (A draft of the rite, which appeared in 1970, would have allowed the priest to do the blessing whenever it seemed pastorally appropriate.) In blessing the oil, he may use a prayer based on an old text which goes back at least to the sixth century, but which has been modified to bring in a reference to Christ, through whom God is healing the world. It prays, "God of all consolation, you chose and sent your Son to heal the world. Graciously listen to our prayer of faith: send the power of your Holy Spirit, the Consoler, into this precious oil, this soothing ointment, this rich gift, this fruit of the earth. Bless this oil and sanctify it for our use. Make this oil a remedy for all who are anointed with it; heal them in body, in soul, and in spirit, and deliver them from every affliction." Alternatively, the priest may use a modern formula, which however does not revel in the rich juiciness of the oil in the same way that the ancient prayer does.

The priest anoints the head of the person who is sick, saying, "Through this holy anointing may the Lord in his love and mercy help you with the grace of the Holy Spirit." He anoints the person's hands, saying, "May the Lord who frees you from sin save you and raise you up." After each anointing, all present say, "Amen."

Depending on local customs and various circumstances, the priest may anoint other parts of the body, without repeating the words. Down through the ages, rituals have given different directives about the anointing. Some specified the parts of the body to be anointed. Others said to anoint the place which is hurting most. The ritual of 1614 had seven anointings: eyes, ears, nostrils, mouth, hands, feet, loins. The Code of Canon Law of 1917 abandoned the anointing of the loins and made the anointing of the feet optional.

The priest says a special prayer for the person who is sick. Different options are provided, corresponding to different situations. Besides prayers for general use, there are prayers to suit the situation where the person is infirm due to old age, or in great danger, or about to receive viaticum, or dying. The English language ritual adds prayers for one who is about to undergo surgery, for a child, and for a young person.

Then comes the Lord's Prayer, followed by a blessing unless Communion is to be received immediately.

This rite of anointing calls for some comments to be made about the meaning of the anointing, the person who is anointed, and the person who does the anointing.

The Meaning of the Anointing

What does the anointing mean? In the Bible, anointing with oil has many shades of meaning. As regards the custom of anointing the sick, the New Testament shows us the sick being anointed by the Twelve (Mark 6:13) and by the presbyters of the Church (Jas 5:14). It is good to recall that the olive tree has a very special place in the culture of Mediterranean peoples. There was even a Jewish tradition which said that the tree of life in the Garden of Eden was an olive tree. Admittedly the ritual no longer insists on olive oil, though it does demand vegetable oil. Oil is a powerful symbol of health and healing and strength; it is also a sign of beauty and dignity and sacredness.

If we read through all the texts associated with anointing, we see that their main message is one of faith in the healing power of Christ. They do not precisely delimit the effects of anointing, but speak of Christ as the one who brings complete healing to the whole person. An ancient Egyptian prayer for the blessing of oil, that of Serapion of Thmuis, prays that the oil may be "a means of removing every disease and every sickness, of warding off every demon, of putting to flight every unclean spirit, of banishing all fever, all chill, and all weariness; a means of grace and goodness and the remission of sins, a medicament of life and salvation, unto health and soundness of soul and body and spirit, unto perfect well-being."

It is true that, as regards the words which accompanied the anointing itself, the medieval Church settled on "May the Lord forgive you by this holy anointing and his most loving mercy whatever sins you have committed by the use of your sight (touch, etc.)." This formula, focusing on the forgiveness of sin, continued in use until it was changed under Pope Paul VI. But, even while it was in use, the ritual still contained prayers for healing, even for bodily healing.

The words which now accompany the anointing (quoted above) preserve the reference to the forgiveness of sin, but put it in a subordinate clause. They pray that the person may be filled with the Holy Spirit, and that the Lord may save and raise the person up. The Latin verb which is translated as "raising up" (*allevare*) was chosen because it had a wide range of meanings: lifting up, alleviating, cheering up. It evokes those New Testament texts in which sick people were raised up (Mark 5:41-42; Acts 3:7; Jas 5:15).

There is no need to narrow down the meaning of the sacrament, but it can be useful to search for the typical case around which we can arrange our thinking. For example, in thinking about baptism we take as the typical case an adult being converted and joining the Church. In reconciliation we think of an adult who has sinned seriously being reconciled to

God and Church. As regards anointing, it may be good to take up the idea expressed in the General Introduction to the ritual where it says, "Those who are seriously ill need the special help of God's grace in this time of anxiety, lest they be broken in spirit and, under the pressure of temptation, perhaps weakened in their faith." The experience of illness or old age can bring with it a feeling of alienation from the life of the Church and the life of faith. One of the effects of illness can be that a person's place and role and even basic human dignity no longer seem assured. A great step is taken when the person who is sick realizes that he or she has a place and a role in the community, and can give invaluable witness to the dignity of the human person. The sacrament may be seen as celebrating this healing, in which the person's alienation gives way to reinsertion into the life of the Church. A development of this theme, done with great respect for the person who is sick, may be found in Empereur's *Prophetic Anointing,* especially in the chapter on anointing as a sacrament of vocation. Of course practice does not have to be suspended while theologians are trying to agree on the typical case. There is no question of saying that the typical case is the only case, and people will continue to be anointed in many different situations.

In the typical case, it is presupposed that a process of healing has led up to the anointing, just as a process of conversion leads to adult baptism and a process of repentance leads to the sacrament of reconciliation. The sacrament is a sign of the life of the Church, in its healing dimension. It is not in competition with the work of healing which is being done in different ways, by friends and neighbors, by the Christian community, by different forms of medicine and counseling, and, in them all, by the Lord Jesus. It is a sign and a celebration of all this work. As with all the sacraments, if the reality signified is not experienced outside the rite, it will hardly be experienced in the celebration—though it is true that a good liturgy can help a person to see what is actually happening outside the celebration.

Sometimes the moment of celebration is the moment when the person experiences healing in mind or body. Some authors think it is only a lack of faith which prevents some of us from expecting this to happen. But perhaps these authors are drifting away from seeing the sacrament as a sign of life, and thinking of it as a method of healing, perhaps even in competition with the wider world of healing and care.

In emphasizing that anointing is a sign, there is no intention of saying it is an empty sign. What is said about sacraments in general may be said here too. In the celebration of the sacrament, the healing initiative of God acquires a particular kind of visibility in the Church.

James 5:15 speaks about the prayer of faith. It is important for the sacraments to be celebrated in an atmosphere of prayer, expressing a humble reliance on God. An attitude which concentrates on power and efficiency is ill-at-ease with the actual liturgy.

The Person Who Is Anointed

Who should be anointed? The basic text is James 5:14-15, which tells us that those in the community who are sick should send for the presbyters of the Church, who will anoint them with oil in the name of the Lord and pray over them. The prayer of faith will save them, the Lord will raise them up, and, if they have committed any sins, they will be forgiven. In this text we see a picture of someone who is ill enough to be confined to bed, but well enough to be able to send for the presbyters and to expect recovery.

Some people's attitude to anointing is still marked by the fact that in the course of time anointing became very closely associated with the deathbed. This probably happened when it became common to postpone the sacrament of penance until the end of life. In the fifth century, Pope Innocent I said anointing should not be administered to sinners before reconciliation. When reconciliation was postponed, the anointing too was postponed. But when reconciliation as it were escaped from the deathbed, the anointing was left there. In the Middle Ages, theologians reflected on what was current practice, and explained the sacrament on the assumption that the person was in imminent danger of death. The sacrament was called "extreme unction," "last anointing." Duns Scotus (ca. 1300) held that the person should be so far gone as to be incapable of further sin. In practice, there was a tendency to leave the anointing until the very last moment. At the time of the Reformation, Luther contrasted the picture we see in James with the then current practice of the Church. Calvin too spoke disparagingly about anointing people who were practically dead. Some of the participants at the Council of Trent wished to canonize the medieval practice and say that only those who are at the point of death should be anointed, and this was incorporated into a preliminary draft. However, the text which finally appeared said that the sacrament is for the sick, especially for those who are in danger of death—in other words, the council avoided an exclusive statement. But in fact practice did not change very much. Even the Code of Canon Law of 1917 said that this sacrament should not be administered to anyone except in danger of death. Pope

Pius XI felt obliged to tell priests not to be too scrupulous about this. Vatican II took an important step in preferring to call it "anointing of the sick" rather than "extreme unction," and in choosing to use a softened phrase and speak about a person who "begins to be in danger of death." The Code of Canon Law of 1983 uses an even softer expression, speaking about those who "begin to be in danger," but omitting the word "death." Neither of these texts uses the word "only"—they are not absolutely exclusive.

The English language ritual speaks about "those of the faithful whose health is seriously impaired by sickness or old age," deliberately avoiding the word "dangerously." In fact, pastoral practice is very definitely focusing on serious illness, and there is a welcome swing away from the idea that anointing is the last rite. Indeed, Holy Communion administered as viaticum (food for the journey) is coming back into its own as the traditional last sacrament.

There are some questions about the possible extension of the use of the sacrament. The ritual says that anointing may be administered to children who are sick if they have sufficient use of reason to be strengthened by it. Perhaps this reference to the use of reason reflects the medieval explanations of the sacrament as a remedy either for venial sin or for the effects of sin. If the emphasis is placed on the healing power of Christ in the community, then it can be argued that a child should be anointed, as a sign of gentle care and Christian hope. This is especially true if the child's family do not regard anointing as the last rite.

On another level, some authors suggest that it would be better to concentrate on the subjective state of the person rather than on the particular kind or degree of illness which produces the state. They suggest, for example, that it would be appropriate to anoint anyone who is really hurt by the realization of human vulnerability and mortality. For example, the family of someone who is terminally ill might need this healing sacrament, and a person going through a mid-life crisis might benefit from it.

As regards mental illness, the English language ritual mentions that some forms of mental illness should be regarded as the kind of serious illness which justifies the administration of this sacrament.

The Person Who Does the Anointing

There are also some questions about the minister of the sacrament. James 5:14 speaks about calling in the presbyters (elders) of the Church, and this presumably means presbyters in the sense of local leaders or officeholders. Nonetheless, it is obvious that there was a time when the oil was taken home and applied by lay people. Innocent I (d. 417) witnesses to this. Caesarius of Arles (ca. 470–542) was worried because people were resorting to all sorts of charms and spells, and urged them to come to the church, receive the Eucharist, and take home the holy oil to anoint themselves and their loved ones. Bede (ca. 673–735) also witnesses to this custom. Some authors would argue that when done by lay people this was not a sacramental anointing—but such a conclusion seems to be something of an anachronism. Others would say that we are faced here with a case of extraordinary ministers of the sacrament. It is probably best to say that such a use of the sacrament was once regarded as an ordinary part of Christian life.

Trent, looking to James and to current practice, and no doubt influenced by the sacramental formula's reference to the forgiveness of sins, said that the priest is the only proper minister. Some authors think the present discipline ought to be maintained. Others say that at the time of Trent anyone suggesting a change would have been challenging the whole tradition and authority of the Church, and that this broad consideration is all we need to worry about. Still others take "proper" to mean "ordinary" and say that it does not exclude the possibility of extraordinary ministers, deacons or even nonordained. There is some force in the argument that the ministry of a full-time hospital chaplain would be most appropriately centered in the anointing of the sick, even if the chaplain is not a priest.

Since Vatican II, we have come a long way towards realizing that the sacrament of anointing is a liturgical celebration, not just a perfunctory application of oil. Normally there will be a number of people present and joining in the celebration. More often than not, nowadays, the person who is sick will take an active part in the proceedings. The sacrament is a sign of care for the sick and an assertion of the dignity of the person. It is a celebration of the healing mystery of Jesus the Christ.

PHILIP GLEESON, O.P.

See also SACRAMENTS.

SACRAMENT OF EUCHARIST

See EUCHARIST.

SACRAMENT OF MATRIMONY

Since the great fourth-century bishop-theologian, Augustine of Hippo, the Catholic Church has held that there is a sacrament in marriage between Christians. Since the thirteenth-century theologian, Thomas Aquinas, it has held that a marriage "in the Lord" is as much sacrament as the great sacraments of baptism and Eucharist. In the twentieth century, it has acknowledged that the sacrament in marriage rests specifically in the marital relationship between the spouses. This essay considers in turn those two interrelated realities, marriage and the sacrament of marriage.

Marriage

Every reader will have been to a wedding. It may have been a wedding presided over by a judge, it may have been a wedding presided over by a religious minister. It was always a solemn and joyous occasion. For a valid marriage, however, only one moment of the wedding counts, the moment of giving consent in these or similar words. "I, William, take you, Margaret, for my lawful wife, to have and to hold, from this day forward, for better, for worse, for richer, for poorer, in sickness and in health, until death do us part." When Margaret declares her intention in the same words, they are pronounced "husband and wife." If that moment of free consent is missing or in any way flawed, there is no wedding and the intended marriage is said to be null. A subsequent declaration of its nullity could be given in that canonical process called annulment.

The wedding of William and Margaret is conducted according to laws not of their making, laws rooted in the Roman Empire. In Roman law, a marriage is created by mutual consent, not by sexual intercourse, as in the northern European tribes. Both the Roman and the northern answers had long histories; in twelfth-century Europe, there were brilliant proponents of both opinions. In mid-century, the lawyer Gratian of Bologna proposed a compromise solution which combined both views. Consent initiates a marriage; subsequent sexual intercourse completes or consummates it. This compromise settled the debate and it is still today enshrined in the *Code of Canon Law* that governs marriages in the Roman Catholic Church (c. 1061). For the purposes of this essay, we note only this single implication: when William and Margaret have given their consent one to the other, they are not yet definitively and indissolubly married. Their marriage *becomes* indissoluble in the eyes of their Church only after its human consummation.

We ask now what *is* the marriage to which William and Margaret consent and which they make indissoluble by consummation? Again, a Roman definition, found in the emperor Justinian's *Digesta* (23,2,1), has dominated the Western answer. "Marriage is a union of a man and a woman, and a communion of the whole of life." Though this definition is simply a description of how marriage was lived in Rome, it has controlled all subsequent judgments about marriage in the West. The bedrock is that marriage is a communion embracing the whole of life. That phrase, "the whole of life," is ambiguous, open to two different but connected interpretations. It can mean as long as life lasts, and then implies that marriage is a lifelong commitment. It can mean everything that the spouses have, and then implies that nothing is left unshared between them. Over the years, both meanings have been so interwoven that marriage is looked upon as the communion of a man and a woman embracing the sharing till death of all their goods, material or spiritual. In the freshness of their love, William and Margaret certainly approach it in that way. Their mutual love impels them to promise marital communion in everything "until death do us part."

It has become fashionable to be cynical about the marital promise "until death do us part," not only because divorce statistics make a mockery of it but also because, so it is argued, unconditional promises covering a period of forty years are just not possible. To promise I will do something next week is one thing; to promise I will do it forty years from now, when so much will have changed, is quite an impossible other. Only those marital promises that are made on the condition that there be no change in either spouse, so the argument runs, can be made with any binding moral weight. The Catholic Church, correctly, disagrees.

The claim that the marriage vow "until death do us part" is somehow impossible is false. It is perfectly possible for William and Margaret to commit themselves unconditionally, for commitment is a statement of their present, not of their future, intention. Love is not an airy sentiment, but an act of the will wishing well to another. It is not true that either William or Margaret is helpless when and if one or the other changes or wavers in marital commitment. It is entirely possible that principles, freely chosen and willingly embraced now, can continue to be freely chosen and willingly embraced fifty years hence in substantially changed circumstances. History is full of examples. I cite only one, the prisoner of conscience.

Contemporary history has made heroes of many such prisoners, Steve Biko, Nelson Mandela, Andrei Sakharov. They have all followed the example of honor set by the Roman Cato. When offered life, freedom and the friendship of Caesar, and asked to name his terms, Cato replied thus. "Bid him disband his legions, restore the empire to liberty and submit to the judgment of a Roman Senate. Bid him do this and Cato is his friend." Like any other human, Cato valued life and liberty. He valued, however, not just *any* life. He had opted for the life of honor and, from that moment of freely-chosen commitment, life without honor was no longer a real option for him. The principles of the life he had chosen, and to which he willed to be faithful, did not permit it. A similar declaration has been made for centuries by married women and men, who have freely chosen unconditional love and honor, and who have willed to be faithful to them "for better, for worse, for richer, for poorer, in sickness and in health, until death do us part."

Love and marriage are a lot like a flower garden. It is never enough to plant the seeds and then to sit back and wait for the flowers to grow. The seeds must be lovingly watered and fed, the garden must be assiduously weeded, if a beautiful garden is to grow. So it is with love and marriage. If they are to grow into a thing of beauty, they must be weeded and watered by lovers and spouses. William and Margaret must work unceasingly to nurture and sustain their marriage, for old, unnurtured marriages are a lot like old, unnurtured gardens; they simply go to seed, promise and love and honor notwithstanding.

One final consideration completes this section. We ask about the purposes or the ends of marriage, not now what marriage *is* but what is it *for?* In both the Western and the Catholic traditions, marriage is held to have two purposes or ends. These ends are consistently articulated, from Augustine to the twentieth century, as they are in the 1917 *Code of Canon Law.* "The primary end of marriage is the procreation and nurture of children; its secondary end is mutual help and the remedying of concupiscence" (c. 1013, §1). The *Code* did not invent this hierarchy of ends; it merely repeated it from a long history. William and Margaret should be aware, however, that the twentieth century has brought a significant change.

The Second Vatican Council met each fall from 1962 to 1965 to consider the teachings of the Catholic Church. Among the many questions raised and answered was the one that concerns us presently, namely, the ends of marriage. In its Pastoral Constitution on the Church in the Modern World, the council teaches that both marriage and the marital love of the spouses "are ordained for the procreation and education of children, and find in them their ultimate crown" (GS 48). Given Western intellectual history, there is nothing surprising there. There is something surprising, however, in the council's approach to the primary-secondary ends terminology.

Despite insistent demands to reaffirm the traditional, hierarchical terminology, the council refused to do so. Indeed, the commission that prepared the final formulation of the pastoral constitution was careful to explain explicitly that the text cited above was not to be read as suggesting a hierarchy of ends in any way. The council itself taught explicitly that procreation "does not make the other ends of marriage of less account" and that marriage "is not instituted solely for procreation" (GS 50). The intense debates that took place at the council make it impossible to claim that the refusal to speak of a hierarchy of ends in marriage was the result of anything less than deliberate choice.

All possible doubt was removed in 1983 with the publication of the revised *Code of Canon Law.* The Church in the Modern World had described marriage as an "intimate partnership of married life and love . . . rooted in the conjugal covenant of irrevocable personal consent" (GS 48). The *Code* picked up this description and repeated it, declaring that "the marriage covenant, by which a man and a woman establish between themselves a partnership of their whole life, and which of its very nature is ordered to the well-being of the spouses and to the procreation and upbringing of children, has, between the baptized, been raised by Christ the Lord to the dignity of a sacrament" (c. 1055, §1). These two documents sum up the Catholic essence of marriage. It is a partnership of love for the whole of life, ordered equally to the well-being of the spouses and to the generation and nurture of children. The discovery of this essence concludes this section and leads us into the next, for when such a marriage is between two believing Christians, the Catholic Church teaches, it is also a sacrament.

Sacrament

In the Bible there is an action called a prophetic symbol. Jeremiah, for instance, buys a potter's earthen flask, dashes it to the ground before a startled crowd, and proclaims the meaning of his action. "Thus says the Lord of hosts: so will I break this people and this city, as one breaks a potter's vessel" (19:11). Ezekiel takes a brick, draws a city on it, builds siegeworks around the city and lays siege to it. This city, he explains, is "even Jerusalem" (4:1) and his action "a sign for the house of Israel" (4:3). He takes a sword, shaves his hair with it and divides the hair into three bundles. One bundle he burns, another he scatters to the wind, a third he carries around Jerusalem shredding into even smaller pieces, explaining his action in the proclamation: "This is Jerusalem" (5:5).

The prophetic explanations clarify for us the meaning of a prophetic symbol. It is a human action which proclaims, makes explicit and celebrates in representation the action of God. Jeremiah's shattering of the pot is God's shattering of Jerusalem.

Ezekiel's action is not the besieging of a brick but, again, God's overthrowing of Jerusalem. The prophetic symbol is a representative action, a sensible action which proclaims and reveals in representation another, not-so-obvious action. It is a representative symbol.

Self-understanding in Israel was rooted in the great covenant between the god Yahweh and the people Israel. It is easy to predict that Israelites, prone to prophetic action, would search for such an action to symbolize their covenant relationship with Yahweh. It is just as easy, perhaps, to predict that the symbol they would choose is the marriage between a man and a woman. The prophet Hosea was the first to speak of marriage as prophetic symbol of the covenant.

On a superficial level, the marriage of Hosea and his wife Gomer is like many another marriage. But on a level beyond the superficial, Hosea interpreted it as a prophetic symbol, proclaiming, making humanly explicit and celebrating in representation the covenant communion between Yahweh and Israel. As Gomer left Hosea for other lovers, so too did Israel leave Yahweh for other gods. As Hosea waits in faithfulness for Gomer's return, as he receives her back without recrimination, so too does Yahweh wait for and take back Israel. Hosea's human action is prophetic symbol of Yahweh's divine action. In both covenants, the human and the divine, the covenant relationship has been violated, and Hosea's actions both mirror and reflect Yahweh's. In symbolic representation, they proclaim, reveal, and celebrate not only Hosea's faithfulness to Gomer but also Yahweh's faithfulness to Israel.

Contemporary feminist theologians rightly object to the reading of the story of Hosea and Gomer which gives Hosea, and all husbands, the role of the faithful God, and Gomer, and all wives, the role of faithless Israel. The story is not such a linear allegory; it is a parable whose meanings remain always to be discovered anew in each changing circumstance. One meaning is a clear meaning, not so much for Gomer and Hosea as for their marriage. Not only is marriage a universal human institution; it is also a religious, prophetic symbol, proclaiming, revealing and celebrating in the human world the communion between God and God's people. Not only is it law, it is also grace and redemption. Lived into as grace, lived into in faith as we might say today, marriage appears as a double-tiered reality. On one tier, it presents the mutual love of a man and a woman; on another it prophetically and symbolically represents the mutual love of God and God's people. This double-tiered view of marriage became the Christian view, found for instance in the Letter to the Ephesians (5:21-33). Jewish prophetic symbol became Christian sacrament.

The classical Roman Catholic definition of sacrament, "an outward sign of inward grace instituted by Christ," can now be more fully explicated. A sacrament is a prophetic symbol in and through which the Church proclaims, reveals, and celebrates in representation that presence and action of God which is called grace. To say that a marriage between Christians is a sacrament is to say, then, that it is a prophetic symbol, a double-tiered reality. On one tier, it proclaims, reveals, and celebrates the intimate communion of life and love between a man and a woman. On another, deeper, less obvious tier, it proclaims, makes explicit, and celebrates the intimate communion of life and love between God and God's people and between Christ and Christ's people, the Church.

A couple entering any marriage say to one another, before the society in which they live, "I love you and I give myself to and for you." A Christian couple entering a specifically sacramental marriage say that, too, but they also say more. They say "I love you as Christ loves his Church, steadfastly and faithfully." From the first, therefore, a sacramental marriage is intentionally more than just the communion for the whole of life of this man and this woman; it is also representation of the communion between Christ and Christ's Church. It is more than just human covenant; it is also religious covenant. It is more than law and obligation and right; it is also grace. From the first, God and God's Christ are present as third partners in it, gracing it and guaranteeing it.

The presence of grace in its most ancient and solemn Christian sense, namely, the presence of the gracious God, is not something extrinsic to sacramental marriage. It is something essential to it, something without which it would not be *Christian* marriage at all. Christian, sacramental marriage certainly proclaims the love of William and Margaret. It also proclaims, reveals, and celebrates the love of God and of the Christ they confess as Lord. It is in this sense that it is a prophetic symbol, a sacrament, both a sign and an instrument, of the gracious presence of Christ and of the God whom God reveals.

In every symbol there are, to repeat, two levels of meaning. There is a foundational level and, built on this foundation, a symbolic level. The foundational level in a sacramental marriage is the loving communion for the whole of life between a man and a woman who are disciples of Christ and members of his Church. The symbolic or sacramental level is the representation in their communion of the communion of life and love between Christ and this

Church. This double-tiered meaningfulness is what is meant by the claim that marriage between Christians is a sacrament. In a truly Christian marriage between believing Christians, the symbolic, sacramental meaning takes precedence over the foundational meaning in the sense that the steadfast love of God and of Christ is actively present as the model for the love of the spouses. In and through their love, God and God's Christ are present in a Christian marriage, gracing the spouses with their presence and providing for them models of steadfast and abiding love.

There is one, concluding question for this essay. When the Catholic Church claims that *marriage* between baptized Christians is a sacrament, what meaning of the word *marriage* is intended? In ordinary language, the word is ambiguous. Sometimes it refers to the wedding ceremony, in which William and Margaret freely commit to one another "for the purpose of establishing a marriage" (c. 1057, §2). Sometimes it means the marriage and the life that flows from their wedding commitment, the communion of life and love that lasts until death. Both these common meanings of the word *marriage,* the second more important than the first, are intended in the Catholic Church's teaching that marriage is a sacrament. Margaret and William, and all married believers, need to be convinced that their lasting married life together is more significant as sacrament of the mysterious presence of God and God's Christ than their quickly-done wedding ceremony.

MICHAEL LAWLER

See also ANNULMENT; SACRAMENTS.

SACRAMENT OF ORDERS

The rites of ordination were revised in accordance with Vatican II. They appeared in Latin in 1968; a second Latin edition appeared in 1989. This article describes the rites and discusses some questions which they raise.

The Ordination of a Bishop

A bishop is usually ordained on a day when a large number of the faithful can be present. Besides the presiding bishop (the principal consecrator), there are at least two other consecrating bishops.

The ordination takes place after the reading of the gospel. A hymn is sung, usually the *Veni, Creator Spiritus.* A presbyter addresses the principal consecrator, saying, "Most Reverend Father, the church of N. asks you to ordain this priest, N. [the bishop-elect], for service as bishop." If the candidate is to be a nonresidential bishop, then it is "our holy mother the Catholic Church" who asks for him to be ordained. The mandate from the Holy See is read, and all present give their assent to the choice.

The principal consecrator gives a homily. A sample is included in the ritual. It says Jesus sent forth the twelve apostles filled with the Spirit, to preach, sanctify and govern; the apostles selected helpers, and passed on the gift of the Spirit by the laying on of hands; and the work continues through the succession of bishops. Jesus, who is priest, prophet and pastor, is present in the bishop, whose attitude should be one of service and love. Each bishop, as a member of the college of bishops, should be concerned not only for his own diocese but for all the Churches.

The bishop-elect is then questioned, and expresses his resolve to discharge his duties faithfully. He promises obedience to the pope. He lies prostrate during the litany of the saints.

The principal consecrator lays hands on the head of the bishop-elect in silence. All the bishops follow suit.

The principal consecrator places the open book of the Gospels on the head of the bishop-elect, and two deacons hold it over his head during the prayer of consecration. This ancient ritual appears in Eastern sources around the year 400.

The principal consecrator says the prayer of consecration. It is based on the Apostolic Tradition of Hippolytus of Rome, dating from the beginning of the third century. It replaces the prayer in use before Vatican II, which made a lengthy comparison between the hierarchy of the Church and the priests of the Old Testament. In a pattern which is typical of prayers of blessing and consecration, it acknowledges God's plan of salvation, and, in particular, God's plan to provide rulers and priests for God's people. It then asks God to send down the Holy Spirit. All the consecrating bishops join in saying the essential words, "So now pour out upon this chosen one that power which is from you, the governing Spirit whom you gave to your beloved Son, Jesus Christ, the Spirit given by him to the holy apostles, who founded the Church in every place to be your temple for the unceasing glory and praise of your name." The prayer then goes on to ask that the new bishop may be a faithful shepherd and high priest.

There follow some secondary rites, dating from medieval times. The bishop's head is anointed with chrism, and he is given the book of the Gospels, a ring, a mitre, and a crozier.

If the new bishop is ordained in his own church, he usually goes to the presidential chair. He receives the kiss of peace from all the bishops present, and may preside at the Liturgy of the Eucharist.

The Ordination of a Presbyter

The ordination of a presbyter follows a similar pattern. There is a difficulty in translating Latin texts about the presbyterate, because in ordinary English we use one word, "priest," to translate both *presbyter* (elder, senior) and *sacerdos* (sacrificer—a cultic term, equivalent to the Greek *hiereus*). In the New Testament, the cultic term is never applied to individual Christian ministers. Later, it was applied to the bishop. By the Middle Ages it was regularly applied to the presbyter, and the meanings of the two terms tended to blend into each other.

The candidate is called forward by the deacon. A presbyter, designated by the bishop, says that holy mother Church asks the bishop to ordain this man, and declares that "After inquiry among the people of Christ and upon recommendation of those concerned with his training, I testify that he has been found worthy." The bishop then says he chooses this man for priesthood in the presbyteral order. All present give their assent.

The bishop gives a homily. The sample homily in the ritual presents the order of presbyters as coworkers of the order of bishops, sharing in the threefold ministry of prophet, priest and pastor. The candidate is questioned and he expresses his resolve to be faithful to his duties. He promises obedience. The litany of the saints is sung.

The bishop, in silence, lays hands on the head of the candidate. Then all the presbyters lay on hands.

The bishop says the prayer of consecration. It is the ancient Roman prayer, going back to the fifth or sixth century, and included in the Roman Rite since then. It was slightly modified in 1968, to bring out the missionary role of the presbyter. It was extensively modified in 1989. It has the usual shape: thankful acknowledgment of God's providence and care, and an invocation of the Holy Spirit. In saying this prayer, the bishop recognizes that God is the author of human dignity and of all gifts, and that, in order to form a priestly people, God provides various ministers of Christ by the power of the Holy Spirit. God gave Moses seventy wise men to help him govern the people. God communicated Aaron's priestly role to Aaron's sons, so that the sacrifices of the Law might be offered. God sent the Son into the world, as Apostle and Priest, who offered himself to the Father through the Holy Spirit, and who gave the apostles a share in his mission. God gave helpers to the apostles, so that the work of salvation might be proclaimed and enacted throughout the whole world. Having thus acknowledged God's care for the Church, the bishop asks God to give him the helpers he needs in the exercise of the apostolic priesthood. He then says the essential words, "Almighty Father, grant to this servant of yours the dignity of the priesthood (*presbyterii dignitatem*). Renew within him the Spirit of holiness. As a coworker with the order of bishops may he be faithful to the ministry that he receives from you, Lord God, and be to others a model of right conduct." The 1989 text spells out some of the ways in which presbyters collaborate with the episcopacy, by preaching the gospel, by dispensing the mysteries of baptism, Eucharist, and reconciliation, by the care of the sick, and by praying for the Church and the whole world. The prayer of consecration ends by looking forward to the final gathering together of all peoples in the kingdom of Christ.

The presbyter's stole is rearranged and he is clothed in the chasuble. The bishop anoints the presbyter's hands. At the offertory of the Mass, the bishop gives him the bread and wine, saying that they are the gifts of the people, and admonishing him to imitate the mystery which he celebrates. The newly ordained presbyter concelebrates Mass with the bishop, joining in the central part of the Eucharistic Prayer.

The Ordination of a Deacon

The ordination of a deacon also follows a similar pattern. The candidate is called forward by the deacon. A presbyter says that holy mother Church asks the bishop to ordain this man, and gives public witness to the candidate's suitability, using the same formula as for a candidate to the presbyterate. Then the bishop says that with the help of God he chooses this man for the order of deacons. All present give their assent.

The bishop gives a homily. The sample homily speaks of the deacon as one who helps the bishop and presbyters in the ministry of word, sacraments, and the administration of charity. It puts forward Jesus Christ himself, who came to serve, not to be served, as the model which the deacon should follow.

If the candidate is unmarried, he makes a commitment to celibacy. Then he is questioned and expresses his resolve to fulfill his duties. A promise of obedience follows. The litany of the saints is sung, while the candidate lies prostrate.

The bishop, in silence, lays his hands on the head of the candidate. No one else lays on hands.

The bishop says the prayer of consecration. It goes back to the fifth or sixth century. It was however heavily modified in 1968: a comparison with the Levites of the Old Testament was played down; the seven helpers of Acts 6:3 were introduced; Christ was put forward as the primary example of one who serves; and the prayer no longer expresses the hope that the deacon will go on to a higher rank. In 1989 a few slight modifications were made.

Like all such prayers, it acknowledges God's care for the Church, and prays that the candidate may be filled with the Holy Spirit. The essential words are, "Lord, send forth upon him the Holy Spirit, that he may be strengthened by the gift of your sevenfold grace to carry out faithfully the work of the ministry." It prays that the deacon may "excel in every virtue: in love that is sincere, in concern for the sick and the poor, in unassuming authority, in self-discipline, and in holiness of life."

The deacon is vested with stole and dalmatic. He is given the book of the Gospels, with the words, "Receive the Gospel of Christ, whose herald you now are. Believe what you read, teach what you believe, and practice what you teach."

The newly ordained deacon brings the offerings for Mass to the bishop, and assists him at the altar. He may administer the chalice at Communion.

Comments and Questions

All the rites begin with a presentation which implies that everyone agrees to the ordination. A whole process has gone before, and the community has had time to express its opinion. The process is open to further regulation and development.

In the New Testament we see the selection of ministers ascribed to the community (Acts 6:3); to Paul and Barnabas (Acts 14:23); to prophetic discernment (1 Tim 4:14). Exegetes discuss to what extent these texts describe what happened in the earliest days of the Church, and to what extent they are colored by the milieu in which they were written. In the Didache (written perhaps in the first century), the community is told to choose for itself bishops and deacons. In the *Apostolic Tradition* of Hippolytus of Rome (early third century), the one who is to be ordained bishop has been chosen by all the people.

Even today there are dioceses in the Latin Church where the chapter of canons elects a candidate for the episcopacy, and the pope confirms or rejects the election. In most dioceses of the Latin Church, however, the bishop is appointed by the pope. The papal delegate has a role to play in the process of gathering information, and consults individuals in secret. Of course the pope, the Bishop of Rome, is elected by the assembled cardinals. In Eastern Rite Churches, election by the clergy is still common; in those Eastern Rites which are in union with Rome, the election is in many cases done on the basis of a list of candidates approved by Rome.

So the process leading to ordination varies from time to time and from place to place. Perhaps, at least in some parts of the world, a more open process in the choosing of a bishop might be a good thing. As regards presbyters and deacons, it might help if some better way were found to show that the candidates go forward with the support and blessing of the Christian people. After all, in the old ordination rite, the bishop used to say (in Latin), "But as the judgment of one person, or even of several, may, perhaps, be mistaken or led astray by partiality, it is well to ascertain the general opinion. Freely declare, therefore, what you may know of the conduct or character of these men. . . ."

The central gesture in the ordination rites is the laying on of hands. In the New Testament, in the context of the establishment of officeholders, a laying on of hands is attributed to the apostles (Acts 6:6—though the text is slightly ambiguous); to the presbyters (1 Tim 4:14); to Paul (2 Tim 1:6). Again there is the exegetes' question about whether we are being told exactly what happened in the earliest days of the Church or whether we are looking at a later theologizing of the ministry. A laying on of hands is common in Christian prayer, and seems to go particularly well with an invocation of the Spirit. There is some dispute about whether, in the context of appointment to office, the idea of transmitting power is present in this biblical gesture. In the Middle Ages the focus was very much on power. In particular, ordination to the presbyterate was seen as the transmission of the sacerdotal power to consecrate the Eucharist and forgive sin. Many theologians thought that the essential rite was the giving of the bread and wine to the presbyter, with the words, "Receive the power to offer sacrifice to God, and to celebrate Mass, both for the living and the dead, in the name of the Lord." There was so much concentration on this aspect of things, that, in the Middle Ages, episcopal consecration was generally not regarded as part of the sacrament of orders, and the diaconate had become little more than a step on the way to the presbyterate. Pope Pius XII removed any lingering doubts about the gesture by declaring that the essential rite is the laying on of hands. Vatican II stated that episcopal consecration confers the fulness of the sacrament of orders.

The ordination prayers themselves are an expression of need and a grateful acknowledgment of the way in which God cares for the Church and provides it with ministers. They take for granted the familiar arrangement of bishop, presbyter, and deacon. Is this arrangement fixed for all time? Do certain declarations of the Council of Trent mean that the present system is unalterable or simply that it is in faithful continuity with the apostolic Church? The three terms, *episkopos* (bishop, overseer), *presbyteros* (elder, senior) and *diakonos* (minister, server), occur in the New Testament, and refer to local leaders or officeholders. However, in the New Testament, bishop and presbyter are not clearly distinct. It is in Ignatius of Antioch (early second century) that we first see a clear description of a system in which a local Church is governed by one bishop who is sharply differentiated from the presbyters and deacons who are under him. It is generally assumed that this system was adopted by all the Churches at varying times during the second century. Is the Church free to make changes to the pattern? For example, many dioceses nowadays are served by a group of bishops, although only one is officially the bishop of the diocese. Perhaps it would be possible for the Church officially to ordain several people as the bishops of a diocese, governing it as a team of equals, with, no doubt, a first among equals.

Similar questions about what should be regarded as fixed can be asked about the Latin Church's practice of ordaining only celibate people to the presbyterate, with a few carefully controlled exceptions. In this case it is clear that the Church is free to change, and the question is whether or not it should. Those who advise against change point to the values of the present system, and thank God for presbyters who choose celibacy for the sake of the kingdom. Those who recommend change say that God is in fact raising up Christian leaders who preach the Word, lead the people in prayer, and hold communities together, but who happen to be married men. They say we should thank God for such leaders, and ordain them as presbyters, so that the place they occupy in the life of the community can be reflected in the place they occupy in the celebration of the Eucharist.

The debate about the practice of not ordaining women follows similar lines. Some say this is the way God wants things to be, and that we should try to appreciate the wisdom of God's plan. Others say God is providing the Church with women leaders who do most of the things associated with the ordained ministry and who bring a welcome new dimension to the work; they wonder why this gift of God is not celebrated in the sacrament of orders.

The answers to ecumenical questions tend to diverge in the same way, with one side saying ordination by a bishop is absolutely necessary for the institution of a presbyter and for the validity of the presbyter's Eucharistic ministry, while the other side is reluctant to assert that God does not raise up the ministers needed by Christian communities even outside what we regard as the normal order of things. This debate touches on almost every possible controversy about Church and sacraments.

Whatever may be the questions and arguments, the ordained ministry exists as a service to the Church and in the Church. The ordained minister must always be seen in relation to others—in relation to Jesus Christ, the model of all service, in relation to other ministers ordained and not ordained, in relation to the whole Church. This way of thinking is now solidly embodied in official documents. Only by living the reality of ministry in and for the Church will the questions be resolved.

PHILIP GLEESON, O.P.

See also BISHOP; DEACON, PERMANENT; PRIESTHOOD, THE MINISTERIAL.

SACRAMENT OF RECONCILIATION

Popularly called confession and officially titled penance (in Latin, *poenitentia,* which literally means repentance or conversion), this sacrament is founded on Jesus' call for repentance, his forgiveness of sinners, and his command that his followers forgive one another. Down through history, liturgical rites of reconciliation have at times been occasions for genuine conversion, and at other times they have been legalistic barriers to the experience of God's forgiveness. Regardless of the Church's rites, however, Christians have always been expected to live morally upright lives and to ask for and give forgiveness whenever it was needed.

The earliest known Christian practice designed to induce repentance was apparently adapted from the Jewish practice of "binding and loosing" (restricting a person from normal dealings with a community, and later lifting the restriction). This practice is mentioned in two of Paul's letters to the Corinthians, but it is unknown whether any liturgical rite accompanied it. The earliest evidence of a rite of repentance and reconciliation comes from the second century, when Christians who renounced their faith during persecution asked to be readmitted to the Church. *The Shepherd of Hermas,* written probably in Rome, envisioned the possibility that unfaithful Christians might be readmitted to the fold if they approached the bishop and did works of repentance (fasting, praying, almsgiving, etc.) to show that they could live up to the most rigorous demands of the gospel. By the third century, Hermas' vision found itself being put into practice throughout the Roman Empire. The process of public reconciliation culminated in a rite presided over by the local bishop, and it was permitted only once in a person's lifetime.

In time, the privilege of public repentance was extended to others who had ostracized themselves from the Christian community (for example, those who had committed murder or adultery) lest they die unreconciled with Christ. During the same period, for sins that were not flagrant violations of public morality, Christians simply asked God's pardon whenever they began the Eucharist, just as they do today during the penitential rite at the beginning of Mass.

What started out as a means of reunification to people who were alienated from the Church, however, eventually became so legalistic that this practice itself caused alienation from the Church. During the fourth century, the number of sins requiring public reconciliation went up, the harshness of the penances increased, and works of penance were required even after readmission to the Eucharist. Penances became perceived less as aids toward moral conversion and viewed more as penalties due for sins committed. People who were guilty of public sins preferred to abstain from the Eucharist until very late in life (when they might reasonably expect clemency from a bishop) because if they relapsed after having been publicly forgiven they were not allowed to seek liturgical reconciliation a second time. Thus the number of people who actually sought public reconciliation went down and the liturgical practice fell into disuse.

In the meantime, a quite different practice was developing in monasteries, where novices in the religious life confessed their faults to older monks who were assigned to them as mentors. In fifth-century Ireland, monks carried this practice beyond the monastery walls and made confession available to the recently converted tribespeople in the hope of gradually converting them from their unchristian ways. In contrast to the older practice, this mode of reconciliation was administered by a priest (or even by a layman, for not all monks were priests) rather than by a bishop, it could address hidden sins as well as publicly sinful behavior, and it could be repeated as often as needed. Just as in the older practice, however, works of repentance needed to be performed prior to readmission to the altar.

During the ensuing centuries, this new practice was carried by missionaries throughout northern Europe and it eventually made its way into Mediterranean areas, where it was occasionally denounced by bishops as an unauthorized departure from traditional Church procedure. The popularity of private, repeated confession to a priest gradually overcame episcopal opposition, however, and by the eighth century it was well on its way to becoming an accepted means of repentance and forgiveness in the Church. For a long time, works of repentance continued to be performed before priests would grant assurance of God's forgiveness, but pastoral considerations increasingly led priests to declare that people's sins were forgiven even before they had performed all the penances required. Similar considerations led priests to grant penitents absolution from any unfinished penances in the event of death, and eventually priests found themselves granting absolution from the sins as well, instead of simply assuring penitents of God's forgiveness as earlier confessors had done.

Thus by the twelfth century the normal process of sacramental reconciliation in the Church was confession to a priest, absolution from sins, and performance of penance (commonly the recitation of prayers). The format had become rather juridical, for the priest had to judge the truthfulness and sincerity of the penitent before granting absolution and imposing the penance. The tendency toward legalism was increased by the fact that penances were no longer activities performed prior to being forgiven by the priest, so they were perceived as penalties due for sins rather than as aids toward moral conversion. The sacrament was thought to be effective not because it brought about a change in people's moral behavior (as it had earlier) but because the priest spoke in God's name when bestowing forgiveness on the penitent.

This somewhat magical interpretation of the sacrament was challenged by the Protestant reformers of the sixteenth century, who also argued that the sale of indulgences implied that God's forgiveness could be bought. The Council of Trent, convened to counteract the Reformation, conceded the second point and forbade the selling of indulgences. Nonetheless, the council insisted that the sacrament, properly understood and devoutly practiced, was a true means of receiving God's forgiveness and growing in spiritual perfection.

From then to the twentieth century, Catholic practice and theology of penance changed very little. Catholics were required by Church law to confess their sins to a priest at least once a year, and they were also required to go to Communion at least once during Easter time, so many Catholics combined these two obligations into what was popularly referred to as the "Easter duty." An expansion of religious devotion in the eighteenth and nineteenth centuries gave some Catholics the desire to receive the Eucharist more frequently—perhaps once a month—which also increased the perceived need for more frequent confession. When Pope Pius X in 1910 said that children should be allowed to make their First Communion as early as the age of seven, they were prepared for the Eucharist by learning how to go to confession. Penance was understood to be necessary for the remission of mortal sins, and it was recommended for the remission of venial sins before going to Communion. One could not enter heaven with a mortal sin on one's soul, and unconfessed venial sins needed to be cleansed in purgatory.

Through the mid-1960s parish priests regularly heard confessions on Saturday afternoons, and confession lines in churches were a common sight. Then, within a decade, new ideas about sin and forgiveness (and a clearer understanding of many old ideas) led to a drastic decrease in the number of Catholics who regularly went to confession. Scripture scholars pointed out that in the Bible sin is more the breaking of a relationship (with God and with other people) than the breaking of a law. Moral theologians noted that to commit a mortal sin requires a deliberate rejection of God—which most people do not do when they disobey God's commandments or the Church's rules. Developmental psychologists suggested that seven-year-olds did not have sufficient self-awareness to commit a mortal sin. And even canon lawyers pointed out that any Catholic who was not in mortal sin could not be refused the Eucharist. As a result, Sunday Communion lines lengthened and Saturday confession lines dwindled.

In 1973 a revised rite of penance was promulgated by Rome, in accordance with the directive of the Second Vatican Council that all the sacraments be examined and reformed according to scriptural and liturgical principles. Individual confession can now take place face-to-face as well as in the traditional confessional, the use of relevant Scripture passages is encouraged, and it is now permissible to focus on particular concerns instead of reciting a long list of sins. A second form of the rite allows for a communal preparation for confession, usually in the shape of a liturgical service of Scripture readings, reflections, responses and hymns. A third form of penance permits people in emergency situations to receive a priest's absolution without having to confess their sins individually first.

Despite the changes, the Catholic drift away from confession (at least in Europe and America) was not halted, and many do not avail themselves of the sacrament except in times when they feel a need for a priest's guidance and assurance. In light of recent history this is a drastic reversal in practice, but in light of earlier history it is not an extraordinary departure from the norm. During the first four centuries very few Christians went through the process of liturgical penance, and for most of medieval and modern times the majority of Catholics went to confession only once a year.

Nevertheless, some explanation of the sudden change is called for. One has already been suggested, namely, that the Catholic theological and psychological understanding of sin has changed to the point where confession to a priest is no longer viewed as necessary or even desirable. The concept of sin has also been broadened to include social sin, which is injustice perpetrated not by any single individual but by society—by social forces, structures and conditions. It is difficult to imagine confessing and being forgiven for racism, militarism, pollution, or such in any way that would be meaningful.

Referring to the rite as the sacrament of reconciliation also highlights structural shortcomings of the ritual as it is presently constructed. The ancient format of the sacrament actually effected reconciliation between a Christian community and its ostracized members. Likewise, the early monastic form of confession encouraged genuine reconciliation between sinner and community through works of repentance that led to a change in heart and, at times, apologies and restitution to an aggrieved party. The legalistic understanding of penance which developed during the Middle Ages and survived into modern times ritually effected reconciliation with God and brought a certain amount of emotional relief from the fear of punishment. Having abandoned a legalistic attitude toward sin, however, many Catholics feel less need for a church ritual to become reconciled with God. In addition, the present structure of the rite is rather individualistic and the rite does not of itself foster reconciliation between members of the community.

Although pastorally sensitive priests can enhance the basic ritual with penances that address real life situations (for example, instructing a husband to apologize to his wife), the fact remains that absolution is given before any human reconciliation has taken place, and that the reconciliation is curiously celebrated before it occurs—not to mention that it is celebrated by only one of the persons involved. And although liturgically sensitive ministers can create penance services which truly promote moral self-awareness, conversion and growth, the fact remains that such changes of heart are private affairs which may or may not have any long-lasting effects.

The theology of any sacrament entails reflection on the experience of participation in the ritual in the light of Scripture and tradition. Thus any realistic understanding of penance today has to have conversion of the individual and reconciliation with God as its primary focus, and in fact this has been the focus of the rite and its theology since the Middle Ages. The experience of being forgiven, of being loved and accepted by God, has coincided precisely with Christ's gospel call to repentance and the Church's tradition of forgiving sins in God's name.

There is, nonetheless, both in the Scriptures and in tradition a solid basis on which to build other rituals of repentance and other celebrations of reconciliation. Biblical repentance is not primarily a matter of inner remorse but a matter of changed behavior. Although sudden conversion is possible, most deep changes in people take time, guidance and support. Moreover, when the conversion is solidified, both the individual and the community have something to celebrate. If a liturgical process such as that which has already been devised for the Rite of Christian Initiation of Adults were designed for this sacrament as well, it would reintroduce genuine, community-supported change as an important focus of this sacrament. In fact, the North American Forum for the Catechumenate has developed a program based on the ancient Order of Penitents for persons who are returning to active membership in the Church, but there is nothing in principle which prevents the same type of process from being used to support other transitions from death to life and from life to fuller life. Twelve-Step programs do it all the time.

Along these same lines it is possible to envision that persons who are having difficulties in relationships, especially within families, might find support within their Christian community to work through the difficulties, to overcome their estrangement, to reconcile their differences, and to reestablish the respect and love they once had for each other. Although our society's penchant for privacy would probably make people unwilling to ritualize their initiation into such a reconciliation process, our culture's approval of success would make it possible to celebrate successful reconciliations. Evangelicals and charismatics have developed ways to testify about and applaud real changes in people's relationships with God and with one another.

Moving into a wider circle of Christian involvement and responsibility, it can be argued that a Church which calls itself an instrument of God's reconciliation ought to be actively involved in mediating disputes between individuals and between groups in society. Some churches already offer Christian mediation services for individuals, and some social programs already try to bring people together and reduce tensions between groups, so this is not beyond the realm of possibility. Catholics have yet to recognize, however, that these real experiences of working toward and achieving social harmony and group cooperation are genuine instances of reconciliation which could be beneficially celebrated.

Although such ceremonies would take us far from the experience and theology of the confessional, they would be quite at home in the setting and understanding of the Gospels. When Jesus called people to repent he was asking them to change their lives (Mark 1:15), to live as daughters and sons of a loving Father (Matt 6:9-15), and to allow God to reign in their hearts and in their relationships (Mark 7:6-13). Jesus told his followers to forgive one another (Luke 17:3-4), to care for one another and to love one another (John 15:9-17), and it is impossible to follow these commands of the Lord without being reconciled with one another. Moreover, Jesus made it clear that the Good News of God's love transforming the heart and establishing the kingdom was meant to be spread by word and deed (Luke 10:1-11), for his followers were to be like salt to the tasteless earth and like light in a darkened world (Matt 5:13-16), working for peace (Matt 5:9), challenging the way things are (Luke 12:49-53), and bringing a salvation that begins in this life and continues into the next (Mark 10:29-30). Finally, such salvation from sin is to be celebrated, as is clear from the way that Jesus likened the kingdom to a banquet (Matt 22:1-10) and from the way that Jesus rejoiced at the conversion of sinners (Luke 19:1-10).

Clearly there is more to the New Testament theology of forgiveness and reconciliation than can be fit into a confession box. The way is open to develop new processes that will satisfy the human need for forgiveness and to create new rites that will celebrate the divine gift of reconciliation.

JOSEPH MARTOS

See also SACRAMENTS.

SACRAMENTAL THEOLOGY

See SACRAMENTS.

SACRAMENTALS

Sacramentals are sacred signs, such as the sign of the cross, medals, holy water, Stations of the Cross, etc., that put the believer in touch with God's grace in Christ. As such, they acknowledge the new creation and redemption achieved by Christ. They differ from sacraments in several ways. The number of sacramentals is not limited, the Church institutes them, and they attain their effect through the intercession of the Church. Laypersons can also administer some of the sacramentals, e.g., the distribution of ashes and parents' blessing of their children.

JOHN F. CRAGHAN

See also BLESSING; SYMBOL.

SACRAMENTARY

A liturgical book comprised of the prayers and directives for Mass, and various sacramental formulas; it does not include the Scripture readings for the Mass, which are collected in the lectionary. Sacramentaries were used in many countries up to the thirteenth century, but were gradually replaced by Missals—particularly the Roman Missal, which included the sacramentary, the lectionary, and the (Roman) gradual. Prescribed by the Second Vatican Council, the current sacramentary renders the prayers for Mass in the vernacular.

JOSEPH QUINN

See also EUCHARIST.

SACRAMENTS

The Catholic Church officially recognizes and celebrates seven sacraments: baptism, confirmation, and Eucharist; marriage and ordination; penance/reconciliation and anointing of the sick (see separate entry for each of these). Sacraments are defined (Code of Canon Law 840) as "signs and means by which faith is expressed and strengthened, worship is rendered to God and the sanctification of humankind is effected, and they thus contribute in the highest degree to the establishment, strengthening and manifestation of ecclesial communion." The "signs" referred to in this definition are rituals or ceremonies of worship celebrated by a community of Christians gathered together. There are of course many such, but those clustered under these seven names have a special, public or official character, and are rooted in the traditions of the Church from early times.

In contemporary practice, Catholic life is focused around the Eucharist, more particularly the regular Sunday gathering of the whole community for Eucharist, with a three-year cycle of Scripture readings and commentary thereon, prayers and hymns, and the reenactment of the actions of Jesus over bread and wine at the Last Supper, followed by a symbolic meal in which these are consumed by the members of the congregation.

Newcomers, whether children or adults, are initiated into the community of believers by instruction, baptism (pouring of water or immersion in it), confirmation (anointing and laying on of hands), and first full participation in Eucharist. Two callings are particularly acknowledged by sacramental celebration: marriage and sacramental ministry to the Churches. Although there is a sacramental wedding ceremony, witnessed officially by a representative of the Church, it is clearly understood that the actual sacrament in this case is the mutual commitment of the spouses to each other. This is seen as representing concretely, in particular, the redemptive harmony made possible in the world by the mutual commitment of Christ and his followers (Eph 5:31-33). Ministries in the Church are many, but those more subject to hierarchic control are sacramentally celebrated. This involves ordination to diaconate and priesthood, and consecration of bishops, all included in one designation as the sacrament of orders. Finally, two kinds of alienation are recognized and countered by a sacramental reconciliation: sinful behavior and attitudes by Church members are countered by a ritual of conversion known as the sacrament of penance or reconciliation; and isolation from the community and its gathering for worship by life-threatening illness is met with a sacrament of anointing of the sick.

History of Sacraments

The early Church developed sacramental worship out of its Hebrew roots, as exemplified in the actions of Jesus. They did not number these celebrations, and they gave simple narrative explanations. After the emergence of the Church from persecution in 313, and its rapid increase in members, status, and wealth, the rituals of worship became far more elaborate, and so did the (still narrative) explanations. We have some examples of the latter from the fourth century, e.g., the *Mystagogical Catechesis* of Cyril of Jerusalem. We also have some descriptions of the ceremonies of that time, e.g., *Egeria's Pilgrimage.*

With the transition from the ancient civilization of the Mediterranean to the new barbarian Christianized nations, and the increasing separation between Eastern (Greek, Syriac, Coptic, etc.) and Western (Latin-based) Churches, the Church of Western Europe lost much of the continuity of story and symbolism in the sacraments. Consequently, new questions were asked about what the sacraments were supposed to accomplish and what were valid or invalid celebrations. A note of legalism was introduced, and the focus of attention was on the prescribed ritual words and gestures and on the things used. It was no longer on the worshipping community. Moreover, in the celebration the people had become more and more passive and the actions of the presiding priest more secret and incomprehensible. This led to many abuses of a superstitious kind, culminating in the protests that led to the Protestant Reformation.

From the sixteenth century, the Holy See has exercised detailed central control over sacramental worship, issuing official texts, rubrics, qualifications of presiders, etc. However, until the Second Vatican Council (1962–1965), the celebrations were in Latin, the people continued to be rather passive, the Scripture readings were few and often presented without commentary, and the sacramental piety that was promoted was individualistic. Vatican II mandated reforms, which were gradually carried out, to recover texts and gestures which really conveyed the meaning of the symbolism, and which allowed the congregation very active communal participation. Also mandated and later realized was a three-year inclusive cycle of Scripture readings, and the requirement of a homily on the texts of the day at every Sunday Eucharist.

Theology of Sacraments

As mentioned above, the early theology of Christian worship was narrative and simple. It linked stories and people from the Bible with the actions of the rituals, always in order to illuminate the ideals and issues of Christian life for the believers. In the fifth century some specific questions arose about celebrations presided over by leaders who were in schism from and in defiance toward the mainstream leadership of the local Churches. In response, St. Augustine of Hippo introduced the legal concept of validity. He linked validity to the action by and for the community, rather than the goodness or acceptability of the leader. His reason was: sacraments are actions of Christ himself in the Church, so that they have the authority and authenticity of Christ, not of the presider. This led indirectly to the paying of more attention to faithful following of rubrics, than to genuine worship and commitment of the people.

Medieval sacramental theology of the Western Church moved in the Carolingian era to a preoccupation with the nature of the change in bread and wine at the Eucharist, leading in turn to preoccupation with what kind of efficacy or effect the sacraments had. By the twelfth century (when counting and classifying was the order of the day), the question of how many sacraments there are was answered by a consensus that there are seven, though it was not at first agreed which seven they were.

Following on this was the attempt to justify the enumeration and selection of the seven by citations from Scripture to show that Jesus himself "instituted" these seven specifically. When the Reformers of the sixteenth century questioned this, and maintained that there was scriptural evidence for baptism and Eucharist only, the Council of Trent (1545–1563) elaborated an official sacramental theology. The council's canons on the sacraments stated: that Jesus instituted these seven sacraments; that they are necessary for salvation; that they "contain the grace which they signify" and "confer that grace on those who place no obstacles in its way;" that baptism, confirmation, and orders "imprint a character on the soul" which is permanent, so that these sacraments cannot be repeated; that all sacraments must be conferred by a designated minister, who intends to do what the Church does, and who follows the rubrics. To these a later session of the same council added some further specifications. Subsequent papal teachings from time to time reiterated this understanding of sacraments.

Acting on modern historical, biblical, and liturgical scholarship, Vatican II refocused the official sacramental theology in a radical way. It sees the sacraments as the worship of the community, and not only as something done for the congregation. It links the sacramental action not only to the person of Jesus Christ in a timeless way, but also to the teaching and redeeming actions of Jesus. Moreover, it places great emphasis on the faith of the community and on the growth of that faith by meditating on Scripture. Likewise, it emphasizes the exemplary character of sacramental celebrations, symbolizing what should be happening in everyday life as redemptive transformation (SC 5–12).

The Sacramental Principle

Sacramental behavior is much more widely diffused than the seven sacraments named by the Catholic Church. All religious traditions have symbolic expressions for their understanding of the meaning of human life, and enact rituals that express their convictions and their ideals. These enactments are intended to foster what they represent, and indeed usually do so. Even in secular life there are rituals using flags and other emblems in order to consolidate national or group loyalty. There are rituals for birthdays which promote family solidarity and relationships. Handshakes, salutes, kisses, and embraces have a similar type of symbolic/effective quality.

In the Catholic community, sacramentality in the broad sense is also found in the display of crucifixes and images of saints, in the use of holy water and rosaries, in the sign of the cross and genuflections and pilgrimages, in the building and visiting of churches and shrines, in the wearing of medals, and so forth. In all of these the sacramental principle is at work. The sacramental principle is the reality of our relationship with God. Given the confusion of the world of human experience in a history distorted by consequences of sin, we do not spontaneously see and experience everything in relationship to God. There are moments of breakthrough, special memories and associations that help. These must be treasured, reflected on, recalled, celebrated to open the awareness of the divine in our lives to ever wider circles of experience, and to learn progressively to respond to the divine. In this broad sense, sacramentality is pervasive.

MONIKA K. HELLWIG

See also EUCHARIST; LITURGY; SACRAMENT OF ANOINTING; SACRAMENT OF MATRIMONY; SACRAMENT OF ORDERS; SACRAMENT OF RECONCILIATION; SACRAMENTS OF INITIATION.

SACRAMENTS OF INITIATION

In the early Church, men and women became Christians by being baptized and chrismated, and by celebrating the Eucharist, during which they received the Body and Blood of Christ for the first time. As time passed in the Western Church, the unity of these three sacraments of baptism, confirmation, and Eucharist disintegrated, especially due to the rise and predominance of infant baptism. Confirmation, originally bestowed at the time of the water-rite of baptism, gradually became delayed due to the absence of a bishop. Eventually even first Eucharist was separated from baptism because of the reluctance to give the Body and Blood of Christ to infants. All this resulted in what is frequently called the "disintegration of the primitive rite of initiation."

In the post-Vatican II Church, the complex structure of rites comprising the three sacraments of baptism, confirmation, and Eucharist is known as "the sacraments of initiation." Actually, that terminology is quite recent, being first used at the end of the nineteenth century. The phrase "sacraments of initiation" quickly caught on among liturgists and then was gradually embraced by theologians in general. Finally, the 1983 Code of Canon Law stated quite clearly that "The sacraments of baptism, confirmation, and the Most Holy Eucharist are so interrelated that they are required for full Christian initiation" (c. 842, § 2).

Baptism

The word *baptism* comes from the Greek *baptizein,* meaning "to dip." The followers of Christ were dipped or immersed into the water which had been mystically sanctified due to the fact that Jesus had gone down into the waters of the river Jordan and allowed himself to be baptized by John the Baptist. Jesus' baptism by John, frequently called the "Jordan Event," became the prototype of all Christian initiation. "After Jesus was baptized, he came up from the water and behold, the heavens were opened, and he saw the Spirit of God descending like a dove coming upon him. And a voice came from the heavens, saying, 'This is my beloved Son, with whom I am well pleased'" (Matt 3:16-17). This event revealed primarily two things. First, the presence of the Holy Spirit; secondly, the status of divine sonship. The same would be true for the baptism of those who would follow Christ: first, their baptism would be essentially an event of the Holy Spirit, an anointing with the Spirit; secondly, their baptism would make them "other Christs," sons and daughters of God.

The first distinguishing feature of early Christian baptism, then, was life in the Spirit. The ritual act of baptism was a type of birth, birth into the life of a community of followers of Christ who lived in the Spirit. Becoming a Christian meant rubbing shoulders with Spirit-filled men and women, and indeed, having that Spirit rub off on one's self. Baptism inaugurated a journey, a spiritual journey of life in the Spirit which would come to its completion with the coming of Christ, when pledge would give way to reality. The Spirit given at baptism was the sign of much more to come: "But the one who gives us security with you in Christ and who anointed us is God; he has also put his seal upon us and given the Spirit in our hearts as a first installment" (2 Cor 1:21-22).

As time went on in the life of the Church, this emphasis on the Spirit unfortunately subsided. At times a tug of war began between those who claimed to possess the Spirit and the institutional Church. How could the Spirit be measured? How could one be sure that one was leading a life in the Spirit? This pull was symbolized in the antithesis between "water" versus "the Spirit" in the baptismal situation. The Church began to want to control her sacramental situation, and this was done by an emphasis on correctly pouring the water and reciting the proper baptismal formula. At times this resulted in a neglect of concern for the gifts of the Spirit.

A change likewise took place as to the second element of the baptismal event, the status of becoming "another Christ." In the early Church it was the baptized woman or man who was considered to be "another Christ." By baptism one put on Christ, and became a member of the body of Christ, the Church. But as time passed, this notion of being "another Christ" was predicated, not of the baptized woman or man, but of the ordained member of the Church, the priest. This clericalization of the Church had great effects on the theology of baptism, and it is only in recent times, in the post-Vatican II period, that theologians and teachers are insisting on an earlier theology that underscores what unites, rather than what divides, the baptized members of the body of Christ, the Church.

The foregoing has emphasized the early Church's understanding of baptism as rooted in the metaphor of birth-life (John 3). Another understanding, prevalent especially in the Western Church, was built upon the metaphor of death-life (Rom 6). The classical statement of this theology was expressed by St. Paul: "We were indeed buried with him through baptism into death, so that, just as Christ was raised from the dead by the glory of the Father, we too might live in the newness of life" (Rom 6:4). In the West, this dying and rising with Christ imagery of baptism would prevail. In that context, an unfortunate dichotomy sometimes arose from the imagery of going down into the baptismal bath (tomb) on the one hand, and the coming up from the pool on the other. The forgiveness of sin aspect of baptism was predicated of the first (descending) action, while the bestowal of the Spirit was predicated of the second (ascending) action. This was unfortunate in that often the effect of baptism was limited only to the forgiveness of sin aspect, while the aspect of bestowal of the Spirit became more and more identified with the separate sacrament of confirmation. The ideal theology was that of an earlier period which saw forgiveness of sin to be a result of the gift of the bestowal of the Spirit. According to that theology, the two aspects were part of the one reality.

This type of dichotomy between forgiveness of sin and bestowal of the Spirit grew when the two sacraments of baptism and confirmation were separated. Furthermore, once infant baptism became the norm and adult baptism a rarity around the beginning of the sixth century, the stage was set for the total acceptance of such thinking. Baptism was seen more and more exclusively in terms of washing away sin, especially original sin. Original sin in turn was seen progressively as blocking the way to salvation. Pope Innocent III remarked in the early thirteenth century that were it not for the grace of baptism, the vast number of children who died daily would perish eternally. It was no wonder then, granted the very high rate of infant mortality during the Middle Ages, that parents wanted their infants baptized as soon as possible after birth. That practice of baptizing as soon as possible brought an end to the custom of limiting the celebration of baptism to the great baptismal feasts of Easter, Pentecost, and Epiphany.

Probably the greatest effect of the rise of infant baptism and the demise of adult baptism was the cessation of the ancient catechumenate. Earlier, when adults were being baptized, the catechumenate, normally lasting for three years, served as a period of preparation and gradual entrance into the Christian community, culminating in the reception of the initiation sacraments at the Easter Vigil. It was a period not only for instruction, but for moral improvement. The catechumens were exhorted to frequent prayer and fasting; they were to hear the word of God; they were to learn what it meant to be a Christian and how to live as a Christian. The catechumenate was punctuated by a series of marvelous rituals, marking the various stages of development of the catechumens.

After the sixth century, with the demise of adult baptism, the catechumenate lived on in a modified way, but now, not for comprehending adults, but for infants. It was no wonder, then, that the rites of the catechumenate lost their force, and were open to misunderstanding or even to total confusion or extinction. Multiplication of ritual often took over in the rites of infant baptism, attempting to fill the void of understanding, once the subjects of the actions were no longer comprehending adults.

Even in mission lands, where it was a question of adult converts, the traditional catechumenate was not used. Fortunately, in modern times there were calls for the renewal of the ancient catechumenate. This came especially from the Congregation for the Propagation of the Faith. In the early twentieth century, Africa saw a widespread renewal of the practice of the catechumenate especially through the influence of the White Fathers. In 1955 the renewal of the Holy Week liturgy brought with it the return of baptizing at the Easter Vigil, and a separation of the preliminary steps for baptism was permitted.

Then there followed a number of experimental rites around the world which restored the liturgical catechumenate. Finally in 1963 the Constitution on the Sacred Liturgy of Vatican II mandated: "The catechumenate for adults, divided into several stages, is to be restored and put into use at the discretion of the local Ordinary. By this means the time of the catechumenate, which is intended as a period of well-suited instruction, may be sanctified by sacred rites to be celebrated at successive intervals of time" (no. 64). This mandate was accomplished in 1972 with the appearance of the *Ordo Initiationis Christianae Adultorum,* with a provisional English translation entitled *Rite of Christian Initiation of Adults* being approved in 1974. The final edition for use in the dioceses of the United States of America was confirmed by the Apostolic See and appeared in 1988. The rite included the "National Statutes for the Catechumenate." These statutes mandated that children of catechetical age should not "receive the sacraments of initiation in any sequence other than that determined in the ritual of Christian initiation" (no. 19), that is: baptism, confirmation, Eucharist.

The 1988 rite complemented the 1972 *Ordo* by adding a number of rites, modelled on the original

RCIA, for already baptized but uncatechized people. This was an attempt to answer a great pastoral problem of whether to separate or put together catechumens and candidates for full communion in the one formation process. In this regard the "National Statutes for the Catechumenate" mandated: "Those who have been baptized but have received relatively little Christian upbringing may participate in the elements of catechumenal formation so far as necessary and appropriate, but should not take part in rites intended for the unbaptized catechumens" (no. 31).

Confirmation

As mentioned above, confirmation was originally bestowed at the time of the water-rite of baptism. This was due to the intrinsic link in apostolic times between the forgiveness of sins and the imparting of the Holy Spirit. Indeed, in the eyes of many scholars, the problem of confirmation as a sacrament separate from baptism is a post-New Testament problem.

Nevertheless, as early as Tertullian (ca. 200) we find the gift of the Spirit being attributed to the imposition of hands which is separate from the waterbath with its anointing. The classical Roman pattern is seen in the *Apostolic Tradition* of Hippolytus (ca. 215) where the bishop completes the presbyteral postbaptismal anointing by laying on his hand, anointing, and sealing the forehead of the candidate. A major influence in the Western pattern of initiation is found in the mandate of Pope Innocent I (ca. 416) when he wrote to the bishop of Gubbio that presbyters may anoint the baptized with chrism but they are not to sign the brow with the oil, "for that is reserved to bishops alone when they deliver the Spirit the Paraclete." This separates Western practice from the Eastern pattern of initiation. The West will insist on the presence of the bishop for the administration of confirmation (causing a separation of baptism and confirmation since bishops cannot be omnipresent), while the East would see the presence of the bishop in the chrism consecrated by him (thus saving the unity of baptism and chrismation).

In some places in the Western Church the presbyteral postbaptismal anointing was seen to be enough. Indeed, when laws were enforced insisting on the necessity of the Roman pattern with its complementary episcopal involvement, one began to seek a meaning for this second required anointing. Some thought it gave the grace to preach to others. The theme that came to predominate was "strength for the battle." The traditional welcoming kiss of the confirming bishop was even changed into a symbol of spiritual combat, with the bishop striking the candidate's cheek.

Perhaps the greatest change of pattern was the episcopal anointing's being delayed in some places until *after* (often a week after) the Communion of the baptized. This fracturing of the proper order of the sacraments of initiation served as a strong proof of the disintegration of the primitive rite of initiation.

Another proof was the growing practice of the refusal to give the Eucharist to newly baptized infants in the West. In 1215 the Fourth Council of the Lateran stated that Communion was not obligatory until one reached the "years of discretion." In 1562 the Council of Trent abolished the practice of infant Communion, stating that baptized infants had no need of Communion since they were incapable of losing their baptismal grace.

Confirmation, then, stood on its own. This caused the interval between baptism and confirmation to lengthen. For a long time the attitude at least in theory was that infants should be confirmed as soon as possible after baptism. The trouble, however, was that infant confirmation came to be increasingly uncommon in practice, due to the negligence or indifference of both clergy and parents. At first, councils tried to deal with this problem by setting an age-limit for confirmation, and by setting up penalties for those who did not comply. Different ages were established in various areas (e.g., 1, 3, 5, 7), the intention being to keep the interval between baptism and confirmation as short as possible. The maximum was the age of seven. What happened in practice, however, was that the maximum age ended up becoming the norm.

This age of seven predominated in Roman documents from the eighteenth century onward, but always allowing earlier conferral in danger of death. At the end of the nineteenth century Pope Leo XIII wrote to the archbishop of Marseilles that children need the grace of confirmation even from their tender years, as it prepares them to receive the Eucharist. The 1917 Code of Canon Law stated: "Although the administration of the sacrament of confirmation should preferably be postponed in the Latin Church until about the seventh year of age, nevertheless it can be conferred before that age if the infant is in danger of death or if its administration seems to the minister justified for good and serious reasons" (canon 788). In 1932 the Sacred Congregation for the Sacraments stated that it was more in conformity with the nature of the sacrament of confirmation that children should not come to First Communion until they had received confirmation, and in 1952 the Commission for Interpreting the

Code of Canon Law denied to local bishops the power to defer confirmation until children were ten years old. They considered it too long a delay.

The present legislation concerning the age for confirmation is found in the *Rite of Confirmation*: "Adult catechumens and children who are baptized at an age when they are old enough for catechesis should ordinarily be admitted to confirmation and the eucharist at the same time as they receive baptism. With regard to children, in the Latin Church the administration of confirmation is generally delayed until about the seventh year. For pastoral reasons, however, especially to implant deeply in the lives of the faithful complete obedience to Christ the Lord and a firm witnessing to him, the conferences of bishops may set an age that seems more suitable. This means that the sacrament is given, after the formation proper to it, when the recipients are more mature" (no. 11).

This last sentence has opened up the door to a great variety of practices as to the age for confirmation. In some places confirmation is given at the time of First Eucharist (thus safeguarding the traditional order of the sacraments of initiation), while in some places confirmation is given to adolescents (arguing that this is a justifiable modern development). It is interesting to note that the 1983 Code of Canon Law makes no mention of conferring confirmation "at a more mature age." It states: "The sacrament of confirmation is to be conferred on the faithful at about the age of discretion unless the conference of bishops determines another age or there is danger of death or in the judgment of the minister a grave cause urges otherwise" (canon 891).

Underlying the great diversity of practice as to the age of confirmation lies a parallel diversity of understanding as to the meaning of the sacrament. Some theologians identify the sacrament with a distinct moment of the life cycle, thus urging the conferral of confirmation at a later age, even at the time of adolescence. Others will underscore the unity of the initiation process, and urge the traditional order of baptism, confirmation, Eucharist. This latter group would argue that until the unity of the primitive rite of initiation is restored, the current state of the sacrament of confirmation is a "practice in search of a theory."

Eucharist

The Eucharist is the apex of the initiation process. This is most graphically seen in the adult rite. During their formation period, catechumens long ever more intensely to participate in the Eucharist actively and fully. Indeed, many directors of RCIA programs use this longing as the major indicator as to when a catechumen is ready to enter the ranks of "the elect" on the First Sunday of Lent.

The *Rite of Christian Initiation of Adults* describes the newly baptized's first sharing in the celebration of the Eucharist: "Finally in the celebration of the Eucharist, as they take part for the first time and with full right, the newly baptized reach the culminating point in their Christian initiation. In this Eucharist the neophytes, now raised to the ranks of the royal priesthood, have an active part both in general intercessions and, to the extent possible, in bringing the gifts to the altar. With the entire community they share in the offering of the sacrifice and say the Lord's Prayer, giving expression to the spirit of adoption as God's children that they have received in baptism. When in communion they receive the body that was given for us and the blood that was shed, the neophytes are strengthened in the gifts they have already received and are given a foretaste of the eternal banquet" (no. 217). This culminating point in their Christian initiation is not merely the act of receiving Holy Communion. Rather it is first and foremost joining themselves, under the leadership of the ordained presider, to the once-and-for-all sacrifice of Christ which takes place at Mass. It is saying "yes" to one's baptism. It is offering one's life in union with Christ who offered his life for us. This is well described by the Constitution on the Church of Vatican II: "For all their works, prayers and apostolic undertakings, family and married life, daily work, relaxation of mind and body, if they are accomplished in the Spirit—indeed even the hardships of life if patiently borne—all these become spiritual sacrifices acceptable to God through Jesus Christ (cf. 1 Pet. 2:5). In the celebration of the Eucharist these may most fittingly be offered to the Father along with the body of the Lord" (no. 34).

It is in that context of actively offering at Mass that the newly baptized receive Communion for the first time, and continue to do so week after week, year after year. This helps us to understand why the United States Bishops termed the Eucharist "the repeatable sacrament of initiation" (1978 *Statement on Christian Commitment*). It exemplifies the teaching of Thomas Aquinas that the Eucharist is the summit of the spiritual life and the goal of all the sacraments.

The spiritual journey begins at baptism. We are baptized but once, confirmed only once; but we celebrate (and receive) Eucharist time after time, Sunday after Sunday, year after year. In this sense, the sacraments of initiation of baptism, confirmation, and first Eucharist are means to an end. We are initiated in order to live a Eucharistic life, to "be built into a spiritual house to be a holy priesthood to offer spiritual sacrifices acceptable to God through Jesus Christ" (1 Pet 2:5).

Finally, this process of Christian initiation is renewed and revitalized by lives of service. Having been incorporated into the Christ who came to wash the feet of others, the baptized carry out Christ's command to remember him, not only by liturgical action but by Christian love. To put it another way, baptismal-Eucharistic spirituality is not something only for the moments of Mass. It is the hallmark of the entire Christian life, a life marked by giving one's self in memory of Jesus who gave of himself, who washed the feet of others.

GERARD AUSTIN, O.P.

See also EUCHARIST; INFANT BAPTISM; SACRAMENTS.

SACRED ART

See ART, CHRISTIAN.

SACRED HEART OF JESUS

Devotion to the Sacred Heart of Jesus is a fairly prominent feature of modern Catholicism. It is mainly in European civilization that the heart has become the symbol of the great love of Christ. (Even in the Bible, the heart is regarded as the seat of knowledge, rather than of love.) The devotion is traceable to medieval mystics such as Juliana of Norwich, Frances of Rome, and St. Bonaventure. In the sixteenth century it was fostered by the Carthusians and, later, the Jesuits. St. John Eudes (seventeenth century) provided a theological basis, and the apparitions to St. Margaret Mary (1673–1675) gave focus, especially as regards the need for reparation for sin. A Mass and office were authorized in 1765 (becoming universal in 1856). The Solemnity of the Sacred Heart is celebrated on the Friday after Corpus Christi; hence June is the month of the Sacred Heart.

DAVID BRYAN

See also DEVOTIONS; FIRST FRIDAYS; IMMACULATE HEART OF MARY; JESUS CHRIST.

SACRED HEART, RELIGIOUS OF THE, (R.S.C.J.)

St. Madeleine Sophie Barat (1779–1865, canonized 1925) and her first companions made their first consecration in Paris, 21 November 1800, under the direction of two Jesuits, Joseph Varin and her brother, Louis Barat, with the aim of spreading devotion to the Sacred Heart of Jesus especially through the education of girls. St. Rose Philippine Duchesne (1769–1852, canonized 1988) and three companions came to Missouri, diocese of Louisiana, in 1818. Their first foundation at St. Charles, Missouri, closed after one year but reopened in 1828, was the site of her death and now of her national shrine. The *Life and Letters* (ed. Maud Monahan; New York: Longmans Green 1922) and other writings of Janet Erskine Stuart (1857–1914), sixth superior general, are well known.

The aim of the Society as set forth in the constitutions of 1815 (whose pontifical approval in 1826 constituted the Society an institute of pontifical right) is to glorify the Heart of Jesus by four principal means: education of children in boarding schools; free education of the underprivileged in day schools; retreats; other forms of contact related to our work. The new constitutions of 1982 express this aim as participation in the mission of the Church "by making known the revelation of God's love, whose source and symbol is for us the Heart of Christ . . . through the service of education which is our way of continuing the work of Christ" (1982 *Constitutions,* no. 3).

Today the Society of the Sacred Heart carries on its mission with 4500 members in 42 countries on 6 continents, with its motherhouse in Rome. The 600 members of the United States Province, with provincial house in St. Louis, operate the Network of Sacred Heart Schools and serve in other schools and in higher education, in work with the poor, and in a variety of other ministries.

CAROLYN OSIEK, R.S.C.J.

See also EDUCATION, PHILOSOPHY OF; RELIGIOUS ORDERS.

SACRIFICE

Sacrifice has many and varied meanings, often somewhat negative in tone, e.g., doing something difficult, depriving oneself, or destroying something good as a sign of homage or to make up for sins. These negative ideas have tended to overshadow the more positive notion of sacrifice in the Bible: a gift to God that effects communion and moves one out of sin. The story of Abraham and Isaac (Gen 22) shows that Israel rejected human sacrifice from the beginning and substituted animals in their rituals. Understanding precisely how such sacrifices worked has been debated. Until recently much emphasis was put on more negative ideas of sacrifice and thus on sacrifice as a "giving up." Thus, the essence of Hebrew sacrifice was seen to be the killing of the animal. In this view the animal represents the worshipper(s). Its destruction represents their total self-effacement before the all-powerful God and/or their just punishment for sin. This view brings implicit as-

Sacrifice of Abraham, mosaic detail, Palatine Chapel, Palermo

sumptions that creatures must placate God and/or that divine anger must be overcome by the punishment of sinners. Thus, sacrifice has often been associated with atonement, but atonement seen as propitiating or satisfying divine wrath.

More recently, emphasis has shifted to understanding sacrifice as a "giving" or offering of self in a quest for union or reunion. The essence of sacrifice is not in the killing of the animal, but in its offering. Life is seen in the blood (Lev 17:11). Releasing blood from the animal enables the releasing of life for union with God. As in the other view, blood represents human life. Only now the shedding of blood is not for submission or punishment, but as an offering of life to be joined with God. Naturally, in releasing blood an animal dies, but killing is not the essence of sacrifice. Implicit in this view is not a God to be placated, but a God who graciously provides sacrifice as a means for union and for overcoming the alienation of sin. Sacrifice is still associated with atonement, but atonement is now understood as expiating or removing sin by being reconciled or becoming "at-one" with a merciful God. In the New Testament the concept of sacrifice has been spiritualized. Christ's life, death, and resurrection achieve adoration and reconciliation, so we are saved "by his blood" (Rom 5:6-11). Because of this, every Christian can now offer his or her life as a living sacrifice offered for worship and reconciliation (Rom 12:1).

ANTHONY J. TAMBASCO

See also CROSS; EUCHARIST; REPARATION.

SACRILEGE

Disrespectful treatment of a person, place or thing that is considered holy or is dedicated to worship.

MONIKA K. HELLWIG

SACRISTAN

The person appointed for the care of the church sacristy and its contents (e.g., sacred vessels and vestments). The term also refers to the custodian of the church building.

JOSEPH QUINN

See also PARISH.

SACRISTY

(Lat. *sacristia,* fr. *sacrum,* "holy," "sacred") A room adjoining a church or chapel wherein sacred utensils, vessels, and vestments are kept, and where the celebrant of a liturgy dons his priestly garb. The sacrarium (or piscina) also is normally kept there.

JOSEPH QUINN

See also VESSELS, SACRED; VESTMENTS, LITURGICAL.

SADDUCEES

The Sadducees constituted a Jewish religious and political movement (or movements) in Palestine from the second century B.C. to the first century A.D. Their name may derive from the Hebrew word *ṣaddîkîm* ("righteous ones"), or from Zadok who was the high priest under David (see 1 Kgs 1:26). In the ancient sources the term is ambiguous. It sometimes describes a conservative group of priests and their supporters (as in the Dead Sea Scrolls—*Damascus Document* and 4Q MMT). It sometimes applies to an aristocratic and Hellenizing priestly group in Jerusalem. Josephus says that the Sadducees denied the immortality of the soul, attributed all human activity to free will, and rejected other traditions beyond the Pentateuch. In the New Testament the Sadducees are active at the Jerusalem Temple (Acts 4:1; 5:17; 23:6) and are said to reject belief in angels and spirits (Acts 23:8) and in resurrection (Acts 23:8; Mark 12:18). They are often allied (improbably) with the Pharisees as the chief opponents of Jesus (Matt 3:7; 16:6).

DANIEL J. HARRINGTON, S.J.

See also BIBLE, NEW TESTAMENT WRITINGS; BIBLE, OLD TESTAMENT WRITINGS; JUDAISM.

SAINTS

The early Church called all the faithful "saints." The term is taken from the Latin, *sancti,* which means "holy ones." They were holy simply because they had entered into close relationship with the risen Christ by becoming members of the community of followers of Jesus.

As the community of disciples became larger and older and in many cases less fervent, it became more usual to call only exceptional people saints, and only after they had died, and especially if they had died as martyrs. For many centuries people were recognized as saints by popular acclaim without any formal process. Gradually, however, bishops claimed some authority to decide who might be honored as a saint. Since the twelfth century, the Western Church has acknowledged that canonization (designation of a saint) requires papal authorization. The present process is very elaborate and hemmed about with rules and requirements. It is, however, generally acknowledged that many who have not been canonized were probably more virtuous and dedicated than those who were.

What the Church looks for in venerating a saint is not a faultless or sinless life, but a passionate and single-minded dedication to prayer and good works that makes this person an exemplary model of heroic virtue in some respect. Thus the saints are the heroes of Christian tradition.

Saints are venerated by the observance of feasts in their memory in the calendar, by shrines, churches, and other institutions named after and dedicated to them, by asking for their intercession with God, and by having pictures and statues of them in homes, churches, schools, and elsewhere.

The reason for the invocation of saints to ask their intercession is the doctrine of the communion of saints, that is, the belief that there is communication with the dead by prayer, and that those who have gone before can also pray efficaciously for the living.

MONIKA K. HELLWIG

See also CANONIZATION; COMMUNION OF SAINTS; HOLINESS.

SALESIANS, THE

Officially known as The Society of Saint Francis de Sales and also as Salesians of Don Bosco (S.D.B.), this religious congregation was founded by St. John Bosco (canonized on 1 April 1939) in 1859. Its constitution was approved by the Holy See on 3 April 1874. The society comprises priests, clerics, and lay brothers (called coadjutors). Its main mission is the education of youth, especially the poor ones. The Salesians are also well known for their publication of religious educational materials and their missionary work, especially in South America, Africa, and Asia.

St. John Bosco

PETER C. PHAN

See also INSTITUTE, RELIGIOUS.

SALVATION

A theology of salvation for today needs to take into account the fact that the human community faces a crisis it has never had to face before. One dimension of this crisis is the dawning awareness that our exploitation and abuse of the earth is doing irreparable damage to other living creatures, and to the life-support systems of our planet. A second aspect of this crisis has to do with injustice in the distribution of the earth's resources. A minority of the earth's population control and use most of the wealth, while others suffer in poverty, and this inequality is undergirded and maintained by the structure of trade and international debt. A third interrelated dimension of our current context is the awareness of the patriarchal oppression of women, and the movement towards an emancipation of both women and men, which holds a promise of new possibilities for life on this planet.

As Christian believers of today ask about the meaning of salvation, they face all the ancient fundamental questions—about sin and forgiveness, the suffering of the innocent, death and life beyond death, and the meaning of who they are and what they do before God. But they also ask: what does salvation in Jesus Christ have to do with the ecological crisis, global injustice, and the relationship between women and men?

Salvation from God in Jesus of Nazareth

The great event of salvation in the history of Israel was God's deliverance of the Jewish community from Egypt and covenant with them at Mount Sinai. This was not only a religious but also a political reality. It involved both the liberating action of God and human participation. The God of Israel was Savior and Redeemer, a God who acted in history, and the experience of this God's saving actions continued to open up new promises of future salvation to come from God.

The Gospels tell of a child born within this community whose name was Jesus, a name which means "God saves" (Matt 1:21; Acts 4:12). Luke's Gospel has Mary rejoice in God her "Savior" (1:47), Zechariah blesses God for the coming of salvation (1:69, 71, 77), the angels announce the birth of a "Savior who is Christ the Lord" (2:11), and Simeon declares, as he holds the infant in his arms, that his eyes have seen God's salvation (2:30).

Jesus' ministry was a constant witness to God as Savior, above all through his preaching of the reign of God, and his practice in the light of this coming reign. In Jesus' words and deeds God's salvation was already a matter of experience as the sick were healed (Mark 3:4; 5:23, 28; 6:56) sins were forgiven (Luke 7:50; 19:9) and the disciples were rescued (Matt 8:25; 14:30). The word "save" or "salvation" occurs eighteen times in the healing stories of the Synoptic Gospels, often in the phrase "your faith has made you well (saved you)" (Mark 5:34; 10:52; Luke 17:19).

Jesus' healings make it abundantly clear that salvation is a matter not only of the strictly "religious" areas of life, but that it involves liberation from all that oppresses and enslaves people, and human wholeness in all its dimensions. When Jesus ate with outcasts and sinners, when he ministered among the peasants of Galilee, when he challenged religious and social patterns of exclusivity, domination and self-righteousness, and replaced them with ones based upon compassion, and when he involved women and men in a radically inclusive community of disciples, God's coming salvation was already present and being made manifest.

In the human and limited actions of Jesus, as he "went about doing good" (Acts 10:38), God's final salvation was already partially anticipated. Yet final salvation was still to come and could come only from the hand of God at God's time (Mark 13:32).

Jesus' ministry in fidelity to God and in love "for others" led to his death in fidelity to God and "for others." Jesus' death expressed the radical nature of his commitment lived out "for others." This death seemed like a total failure and abandonment by God. But the disciples had their lives transformed in joyful, liberating encounters with Jesus risen from the dead. In these encounters they experienced God's vindication of Jesus and were convinced that in his life, death and resurrection, God's salvation had taken hold irretrievably in our world.

What, perhaps, was only implicit for the disciples during the ministry of Jesus—that here God's salvation was breaking in upon our world—was now unambiguously explicit. In the light of the resurrection Jesus was clearly recognized for what he was—Salvation coming to us from God.

Early Christian Theologies of Salvation

In and through the resurrection, it became apparent to Jesus' disciples that in him, in his life, death, and exaltation, divine love had been poured out into the brokenness of our human history, bringing grace and forgiveness, healing and liberation. They found in him a radically new experience of God's presence, releasing women and men from guilt and failure, from self-sufficiency, anxiety and isolation and freeing them for compassion, love, and inclusive community. Hope opened up in the face of defeat and death itself no longer had the last word.

This experience was too big for any one theology, and the disciples used a variety of images and metaphors to try to express what God had done in Jesus. Many of them, like the image of the Suffering Servant of Isaiah 40–55, were taken directly from the disciples' Jewish tradition. Some were influenced by contemporary Hellenistic culture. As Joseph Fitzmeyer has pointed out, in the letters of Paul alone, we can find ten different images to describe the effects of the Christ-event: justification, salvation, reconciliation, expiation, redemption, freedom, sanctification, transformation, new creation, and glorification. Each image expresses an aspect of the meaning of Christ for Paul. No one image is completely adequate.

Only three of these images can be pursued here.

Justification (*dikaiōsis*) is a key theological concept for Paul. The basic image is drawn from a court of law, and expresses the idea of *acquittal* or *vindication* before a judge's tribunal. Paul builds on his Jewish heritage, where justification or righteousness could describe the right relationship between God and God's people, particularly in the context of the covenant. When Paul speaks of Christ justifying us he means that because of God's action in Christ—apart from the observance of the Mosaic Law—we can stand before God acquitted and free. This justification comes by grace, as God's free gift, and through faith (Rom 3:21-26; Gal 2:16-21).

The image at the base of the word "salvation" (*sōtēria*) is that of a *rescue* from harm of any kind. This word was used within Judaism to describe God's deliverance of Israel, and it was also used in Greek culture to describe a divine or human rescuer. For Paul, we are "saved" by the Cross of Christ (1 Cor 1:18, 21; 15:2; 2 Cor 2:15), but salvation also has a future dimension and will not be complete until we share the fullness of resurrection life (1 Thess 2:16; 5:8-9; 1 Cor 3:15; 5:5; Rom 5:9-10; 8:24).

"Redemption" (*apolytrōsis*) has the primary meaning of *buying back* above all of someone who had fallen into slavery. Behind it stands the belief in God as Israel's *gô'ēl* (Exod 6:6-8). The *gô'ēl* is the member of a family who buys back an enslaved or captive relative. When Paul uses the language of redemption he is suggesting that in Christ's death and resurrection God acts to "buy" us back from sin and evil and to take us into a new relationship (1 Cor 1:30; Rom 3:24). He never takes the metaphor literally, so we do not find him specifying to whom the debt is paid. There is a bodily aspect of redemption, since we await "the redemption of the body," and a cosmic aspect as the whole of creation waits to be set free from bondage (Rom 8:19-23).

Each of these theologies of salvation is a metaphor taken from a different aspect of life, seeking to express what finally escapes adequate expression. The diversity of metaphors and theologies for salvation in the early Church witnesses to the vitality of the experience of God's saving action in Jesus.

In patristic times this vitality continued, with a lively appreciation of, and debate about, the saving work of Christ. St. Irenaeus of Lyons (ca. 115–200) saw the redemption in cosmic terms, as a restoration of all things in Christ, which following Ephesians 1:10 he spoke of as *recapitulation.* St. Athanasius (ca. 295–373) is a prominent representative of a theology of *deification*: the divine Logos was made truly human so the human beings might be made divine—by grace and adoption.

During the patristic era there were some who took the concept of redemption too literally, and ended up in speaking of the death of Jesus as a price paid either to God or the devil. In opposition to such theological mistakes, St. Anselm of Canterbury (1033–1109) worked out a theology of salvation as "satisfaction." Influenced by medieval notions of right order and just and legal relationships, he saw sin as an objective injuring of right order and a massive insult to God's honor. Because God is just this cannot be ignored. How can this wrong be put right? Only one who was divine could offer satisfaction for such an offense against an infinite God, and only one who was human could offer satisfaction for human sin. Satisfaction could be offered, then, only by one who is God incarnate.

Anselm's carefully worked out theology has sometimes been misrepresented in popular teaching, with God pictured like some powerful ruler who demands compensation for offenses in suffering and blood. This badly distorts the God revealed in Jesus. It is also unfaithful to Anselm's insights which have had a lasting influence on both Catholic and Protestant theology.

Contemporary Theology of Salvation

Gustavo Gutierrez is a key figure in the contemporary theology of salvation. Doing theology from the side of the poor of Latin America he asks the question: what relationship is there between salvation in Jesus Christ and the historical process of liberation?

Gutierrez finds three interrelated levels in a theological approach to liberation: (1) political liberation; (2) the broader movement of full human liberation; (3) liberation from sin for communion with God. These three levels are all part of one single salvific process. Jesus Christ is the Liberator whose saving action embraces all dimensions of human existence. The three levels are distinct and each is necessary. They must not be collapsed into one another. Yet they are interrelated so that one cannot exist fully without the others. Human political actions which are truly liberating can be understood in this theology as a partial and limited realization of God's salvation, although they are not all of God's salvation.

This kind of theology has had an impact not only in Latin America, but in the theology coming from Asia and Africa, and in feminist and black theologies of liberation. It has also influenced European theology as is evident, for example, in Edward Schillebeeckx's major contribution to the theology of salvation. The magisterium has engaged with some of the themes of this theology. Pope Paul VI, for example, in his 1975 work on evangelization, wrote that a theology of liberation must envisage the whole human person, in all his or her aspects, right up to and including openness to the divine. The Sacred Congregation for the Doctrine of the Faith in its two "Instructions" of 1984 and 1986, has entered into dialogue with liberation theology, raised some critical questions, and affirmed fundamental insights of this theology.

The ecological crisis has forced theologians to ask about the relationship between the whole of creation and salvation in Jesus Christ. This has meant reevaluating, and building upon, the insights of Teilhard de Chardin and Karl Rahner, and the contributions of process and feminist theologies. An ecological theology will seek to go beyond anthropocentrism to a theology of salvation which embraces all creatures. The cosmology of the late twentieth century, and the insights of relativity and quantum theory call for a theology which can show the relationship between salvation in Jesus Christ and an expanding, evolutionary and interrelated universe.

By way of summary, it can be said that a theology of salvation must situate human liberation, including individual, ecological, interpersonal, political and religious dimensions of liberation, within the context of the redemption of all creation (Rom 8:21; Col 1:20). In schematic form, a theology of salvation would involve:

God's Creative and Transforming Engagement with the Whole Universe. God's salvation in Christ embraces the formation of great clusters of galaxies and the interactions of subatomic particles, and touches every plant, insect, animal, and human being, and every ecosystem on earth.

God's Self-offering in Grace to Human Beings, and the Invitation to Them to Participate in the Work of Salvation. God's liberating grace, and our call to participation, involve all the dimensions of human existence: our interrelationships with other persons and our life in community; our participation in social and political structures and our engagement in transforming action aimed at justice and peace; our relationship to other living creatures, ecosystems, the earth and the universe; our relationship to our selves, our bodies, minds and feelings; in and through all of this, our relationship with the living God.

Who Can Be Saved? The World and the Church

Christianity began with a conviction that salvation came through faith in Jesus Christ, and baptism into the Church. When the question was asked whether the Church was necessary for salvation the answer was yes—and the slogan was "outside the Church no salvation." This was incorporated into the teaching of the Fourth Lateran Council of 1215 and Pope Boniface VIII's *Unam Sanctam* of 1302. However, this slogan was understood as referring to those who had heard the gospel of salvation, and willfully and sinfully rejected it.

This axiom was not understood as solving the question about God's salvation of people of good faith who had either never heard the gospel, or never heard it adequately presented. The Christian community always preserved the conviction that God's action could not be confined to the boundaries of the visible Church. One way that theologians attempted to give expression to this conviction was through a theology of "baptism of desire." The Second Vatican Council has provided a remarkable clarification of this issue. It teaches unambiguously that grace and salvation operate beyond the visible limits of the Church. The Constitution on the Church states: "Those who through no fault of their own, do not know the Gospel of Christ or his Church, but who nevertheless seek God with a sincere heart, and, moved by grace, try in their actions to do his will as they know it through the dictates of their conscience—those too may achieve eternal salvation. Nor shall divine providence deny the necessary assistance to those who, without any fault of theirs, have not yet arrived at an explicit knowledge of God, and who, not without grace, strive to live a good life" (par. 16). The Pastoral Constitution on the Church in the Modern World teaches that the Holy Spirit offers to all people "the possibility of being made partners, in a way known to God, in the paschal mystery" (par. 22).

As Karl Rahner has pointed out, we need to think of God's salvation as coextensive with world history. Every human being stands before the offer of God's grace, an offer that can be rejected or accepted through fidelity to conscience. Furthermore, in contemporary Christian theology, it is argued that other religious traditions may be a means of grace and salvation, and it is a matter of ongoing discussion as to how this insight relates to the Christian conviction that Christ is universal Savior.

In a world where, through the action of the Holy Spirit, salvation is offered to all people, the Church can be understood as the sacrament of God's saving action in the world. According to the documents of Vatican II, the Church is the "universal sacrament of salvation" (LG 48; GS 45; AG 1). The Church is the sign and instrument of universal salvation. It is called to express and signify God's universal salvation, and, as God's instrument, to help to bring about the salvation of the whole world.

Already—Not Yet

How are our actions and experiences connected to God's final salvation? Schillebeeckx suggests that we may see in our lives "fragmentary anticipations" of God's reign. In our everyday experiences that "all is grace," we already experience partial anticipation of final salvation. Our earthly actions aimed at human liberation can be understood as a part of salvation coming from God, even though they also include elements of human weakness and sin. We cannot simply identify our human projects with God's salvation. This would be idolatry. Our projects are historically conditioned and limited, and always subject to distortion from human frailty and sin. God's final eschatological salvation, although present within our experience in a partial and anticipatory way, nevertheless transcends our experience and our actions, and cannot be foreseen or controlled.

But we can be confident that our actions aimed at justice, peace, and love have meaning in terms of God's final transformation of all things in Christ. The resurrection teaches us that even what looks like terrible failure can have final meaning. Cleansed of sinful elements and transfigured in Christ, our contributions do matter in terms of God's new creation. As Pope John Paul II has said with regard to our human actions and efforts, in God's final salvation, "nothing will be lost or will have been in vain" (*On Social Concerns,* 48).

DENIS EDWARDS

See also ESCHATOLOGY; GRACE; SALVATION HISTORY; SOTERIOLOGY.

SALVATION HISTORY

Salvation history is an idea rooted in the Bible. It is the interpretation of everything that has happened, is happening, and is yet to be, in relation to God as creator, judge, and Savior. It is a narrative theology: it interprets the meaning of human life by telling a story beginning with things coming into existence by God's command (including the special origin of human beings), and continuing with explanations of what went wrong and how the world and its people are being rescued and will one day be fully in harmony with the creator and with one another.

Salvation history constructs a framework which is outside observable history and interprets a particular line of observable history within this framework. The framework is God's act of creating, enhancing by grace, and ruling of creatures, God's intervention with a promise of salvation, the giving of the Law on Sinai, the sending of the divine Word in Jesus and of the Spirit in the Church, and the drawing together of all things for good. The observable history is the actual sequence of events in Jewish history, in the life, death, and impact of Jesus, and in the Christian experiences of subsequent centuries. There are many rehearsals of this story sequence in Scripture, interpreting events not in terms of natural, economic, strategic, or political causality, but in terms of God's judgment and interventions. The Liturgical Year is built around the salvation history theme, and the Easter Vigil is a short, intensive version of it.

One of the most interesting short accounts of salvation history is that written by St. Augustine of Hippo in the fifth century in his *First Catechetical Instruction* (*De rudibus catechizandis*). In the twentieth century the salvation history idea was rediscovered as a structure for catechesis because there are strong foundations for it in Scripture, liturgy, and the writings of the Church Fathers. The movement for a kerygmatic (proclamation) theology also looked to the story form of salvation history as providing a structure for the developing of a new systematic theology. Christian art and literature have made extensive use of the salvation history story line and symbolic figures.

MONIKA K. HELLWIG

See also CATECHESIS; THEOLOGY, BIBLICAL.

SAMARITANS

In the Old Testament the Samaritans were those who resided in the district of Samaria (2 Kgs 17:29). In later Jewish history and in the New Testament the term describes an ethnic-religious movement independent of and at odds with the Jerusalem Temple and its authorities. The cultic center of the Samaritans was (and is) Mount Gerizim at present-day Nablus. In Matthew 10:5 the Samaritans are equated with Gentiles, and Jesus and his disciples observe Jewish custom by avoiding Samaritan territory as they journey up to Jerusalem. The surprise of Jesus' parable in Luke 10:25-37 is that the good neighbor turns out to be a Samaritan. Likewise, it is surprising that the only healed leper who comes back to thank Jesus was a Samaritan (Luke 17:11-19). Jesus' willingness to converse with the Samaritan woman in John 4 is also presented as shocking. The Samaritans continue to exist as a religious movement. They hold to the Pentateuch as their Scripture and maintain the tradition of the Passover sacrifice and other distinctive customs.

DANIEL J. HARRINGTON, S.J.

See also BIBLE, NEW TESTAMENT WRITINGS; BIBLE, OLD TESTAMENT WRITINGS; JUDAISM.

SANCTIFICATION

See HOLINESS.

SANCTIONS IN THE CHURCH

Penalties, as a response to serious external transgressions of Christian discipline, have existed since the early centuries of the Church. Applying to community members within the prominent boundaries of

Christian social life, penalties involved a strong notion of self-condemnation because of generally assumed expectations for Christian behavior. Community leaders were responsible for the establishment and application of penalties which obtained only for serious, external transgressions that had social repercussions. Such penalties were considered necessary to defend Church integrity, to convert offenders and to militate against compromise under persecution. By the fourth century deprivation of union with the community appeared as the earliest form of what is now excommunication and was employed for offenses such as apostasy, idolatry, murder, and adultery. Automatic penalties, in which the offender was supposed to consider himself excluded from communion, began to appear by the fifth century. Penalties and penal procedures were expanded in the ninth century, developed significantly after Gratian (ca. 1140), and reached a peak in the era of canonist popes (ca. 1200–1350). The Council of Trent (1545–1563) published extensive penal procedures, and in the next century (1627) Urban VIII promulgated a list of transgressions resulting in penalties. Pius IX revised this list in 1869, but there was no single codified source of penal legislation prior to the Code of Canon Law of 1917. This contained over two hundred penal canons in a section entitled "Crime and Punishment" (*De delictis et poenis*).

The 1983 Code contains only eighty-nine penal canons (cc. 1311–1399) in a section entitled "Sanctions in the Church." These now encompass penal remedies (c. 1339), penances (c. 1340), penal precepts (c. 1319), censures (cc. 1331–1335), and expiatory penalties (cc. 1336–1338). Penal remedies include a warning (*monitio*) or correction (*correptio*), while penances include acts of religion or piety or charity. A penal precept is a formal command to do or to omit something to which the threat of a penalty is attached for noncompliance. Censures include excommunication (c. 1331), interdict (c. 1332) and suspension (cc. 1333–1334), with the last applying only to clerics (deacons, priests, or bishops). Excommunication restricts participation in liturgical functions or exercise of ecclesiastical power. Interdict is a limited excommunication applying only to liturgical participation. Suspension removes or limits the specific powers of a cleric (such as preaching, etc.). Expiatory penalties apply to clergy and laity and affect the possession or exercise of any ecclesiastical power or function.

Sanctions can also be distinguished according to: (1) their purpose; (2) the manner incurred; (3) the manner of application, (4) their specification, and (5) their duration. Regarding purpose, a sanction can be medicinal or expiatory. Medicinal penalties (also called censures) are intended to reform the offender, while expiatory penalties are intended to repair harm done to the common good. Thus, medicinal penalties cannot validly be applied unless preceded by a warning and opportunity for the offender to reform (c. 1347, §1). Once the offender is truly repentant and at least promises to repair any harm done, remission of a medicinal penalty cannot be denied (c. 1358). However, expiatory penalties—because they repair harm to the common good—do not require a warning prior to application and need not be remitted even if the offender has repented. Regarding the manner of incurring a penalty, they may be automatic or imposed (c. 1314). Automatic penalties (*latae sententiae*) are incurred by the very fact of an external transgression of the law itself and can be declared or nondeclared depending on whether there has been only an external transgression or whether this has been followed by a formal declaration by an ecclesiastical authority (such as the bishop). Imposed penalties (*ferendae sententiae*) always require the intervention of an ecclesiastical authority. Regarding application, penalties are divided into those which can apply (*potest*) or must apply (*debet*) in particular circumstances. Regarding specification, penalties are determinate if the law itself names the penalty (such as excommunication) or indeterminate if the law simply indicates there is a penalty without naming the type. Regarding duration, penalties may be perpetual or definite or indefinite. Penalties are indefinite if they apply until certain conditions are fulfilled, while definite penalties terminate after the expiration of a specified period of time. A perpetual penalty, such as dismissal from the clerical state, has no provision in law for its expiration or remission.

Although the Church may appear inordinately concerned with penalizing recalcitrant members, there is an entirely mitigated approach to sanctions in the current Code compared to former legislation. A new canon (c. 1341) cautions against hasty application of penalties and indicates clearly the threefold purpose of ecclesiastical sanctions as repairing scandal, restoring justice and reforming offenders. This canon requires competent authorities to employ penal remedies, penances or other means of pastoral solicitude before considering penal action. Although there are two procedures for the application of penalties—administrative (c. 1720) and judicial (cc. 1721–1728)—the law clearly favors judicial procedure (c. 1342, §1) and also requires preliminary procedures before any penalty can be applied, whether administratively or judicially (cc. 1717–1719). Canon 1321 indicates no one is liable to a penalty unless a law is transgressed and the action is gravely imputable by reason of deliberate violation (*dolus*) or failure to preclude violation (*culpa*). Although imputability is presumed after an external transgression, one is not liable to a penalty if the matter appears (*appareat*) otherwise. There are extensive excusing and mitigating circumstances in which a penalty is not applicable or must be tempered (cc. 1322–1324), and there is extensive judicial discretion which permits the lessening or moderation or excusing of a penalty in particular circumstances. There is also a three- or five-year statute of limitations from the actual offense which terminates application of most penalties and, even if any penalty is duly applied, recourse or appeal against it automatically suspends its effect until a higher authority decides the case (c. 1353).

In sum, then, sanctions in the Church today are primarily about the tolerable limits of *communio,* just as they were in the early years of Christianity. Moreover, for penalties to have any practical meaning, it is obvious that the body ecclesiastic must have some identifiable boundary—with an inside, an outside and a periphery—and that the *communio* within that body ecclesiastic must be both worthwhile and desirable to its members, thus engendering a certain voluntary compliance with the system of sanctions for the purpose of restoring everyone to full participation.

ELIZABETH McDONOUGH, O.P.

See also CANON LAW.

SANCTUARY

Originally meaning simply "shrine," or "holy place," the word has now come to mean the center of ceremonies in a church building. While the Orthodox Churches continue to use the icon screen to mark off the sanctuary, the Western custom of erecting an "altar rail" in the same position is now disappearing.

DAVID BRYAN

See also ALTAR.

SANCTUARY, RIGHT OF

Based on the idea that a sacred place was not of this world, and therefore not subject to the powers of this world, church sanctuaries or precincts came to be places of refuge from enemies or even from secular justice. The concept has been revived in modern times for the benefit of refugees who have crossed an international boundary illegally.

DAVID BRYAN

See also CHURCH AND STATE; MERCY.

SANTIAGO DE COMPOSTELA

One of the chief pilgrimage sites of Christianity, Santiago de Compostela ("St. James of Compostela") is located in the hills of northwest Spain.

Main facade of the cathedral of Santiago Compostela

Although St. James the Apostle (St. James the Greater) was beheaded and buried in Jerusalem, local tradition maintains that he had evangelized the region around Compostela and that his body was re-interred there in 830. While these traditions are not confirmable by scholarship, the papacy has promoted the shrine.

DAVID BRYAN

See also PILGRIMAGES; SAINTS.

SATAN

Belief in a chief or principal spiritual agency hostile to both God and human beings emerged in late Judaism mainly under the influence of Persian beliefs to which exiled Jews were exposed during the Babylonian Captivity. Before that, in both Jewish folklore and Scripture, Satan (Hebrew, "the Adversary"; in Greek, *diabolos,* "accuser") was considered to be a member of the heavenly court (cf. 1 Chr 21:1; Job 1:6; Zech 3:1; etc.) permitted by God to test the faith and perseverance of human beings or to inflict punishment on wrongdoers. As a creature, Satan was not considered equal to or even opposed to God.

Jesus described his ministry as a direct assault on the realm of Satan—the sway over the world of deception, hatred, injustice, oppression, and illness of body and mind. Satan is shown in the Gospels as trying to tempt Jesus away from his mission as well as opposing Jesus even through his disciples, e.g., Judas and Peter (Luke 22:3; 22:31; and John 13:27). From the earliest times, Christians maintained that Jesus' death and resurrection definitively destroyed the power of Satan over humanity, although Satan continues to tempt and afflict human beings in order to lead them away from God.

Many late Jewish beliefs which interpreted Satan as a great but fallen angel commanding other fallen spirits as well as demons were incorporated into Christian teaching. Such notions, developed by theologians and spiritual writers throughout the patristic era, the Middle Ages, the Reformation period, and into modern times, often led to exaggerated attributions of power to Satan and demons, consequent fear of supernatural evil, and eventually to atrocities committed against non-Christians, religious dissidents, and women and men suspected of witchcraft, i.e., worship of Satan. But as the metaphorical and mythical elements associated with Satan were more clearly identified by critical scholarship in recent times, belief in and fear of the devil diminished except among fundamentalists and extreme traditionalists.

While the existence of Satan has never been solemnly defined as an article of faith or found mention in official creeds, both Scripture and traditional Christian teaching presuppose the reality and limited power of the devil as one of the sources of evil in human experience, history, and even the world of nature. Events within the twentieth century, including repeated global warfare, the development of weapons of mass destruction, racial hatred and the attempted annihilation of ethnic minorities, materialism and consumerism coupled with indifference to the poor, sick, and suffering, and the systematic despoliation of the planet by industrial overdevelopment, testify to the enduring presence, power, and mystery of evil transcending individual and collective human malice. Demonic in scope and destructiveness, such sinful social structures and forces can rightly be regarded as contemporary manifestations of the kingdom of Satan.

Thus, fundamental Christian teaching regarding the devil's primary activity centers on both temptation and our need to recognize the transcendent aspects of both temptation and sin. Similarly, effective resistance to the power of evil has been held to rely on faith in Christ, prayer, moral vigilance, spiritual development, and wholehearted dedication to works of justice and love.

RICHARD WOODS, O.P.

See also ANGELS; DEMONOLOGY.

SATISFACTION

See SALVATION.

SAVONAROLA, GIROLAMO (1452–1498)

Born to a prominent family in Ferrara, he was a very serious young man, apparently concerned about the deplorable state of the Church from an early age. He entered the Dominican Order at Bologna in 1475 in spite of parental opposition; in the order he began to practice a severe asceticism. In 1482 he was sent to the priory of San Marco in Florence, where he attracted crowds and attention with his fiery sermons, frequently denouncing the immorality of the citizens but also that of the local clergy. He left Florence in 1484 but returned again in 1490. In the following year he became prior of San Marco; simultaneously he began preaching in the Duomo (the Florentine cathedral) and his heavily attended sermons made him a power in the city. More and more his sermons had prophetic and even apocalyptic qualities; significantly, some of his predictions came true. Lorenzo di Medici, head of the family which ruled Florence, died in 1492, and in 1494 the French king Charles VIII invaded Italy, deposing the Medici from power. Savonarola seized the moment and established what can only be called a theocratic democracy. But the pope, Alexander VI (1492–1503), of the notorious Borgia family, resented the French. When Charles returned home, the Pope, prodded by the preacher's enemies, turned on Savonarola, demanding that he come to Rome to explain his prophecies (1495). Savonarola refused to leave Florence, citing the danger to himself. Alexander forbade him to preach. Although the contrast between the ascetic friar and the Borgia pope brought Savonarola some sympathy, he could not stand up to papal power. Alexander excommunicated him in 1497. He ignored the excommunication, but when the Franciscans joined his enemies, he lost the support necessary to maintain his position. Arrested and tortured, he confessed that he did everything for personal gain. Condemned to death, he retracted his confession and was hanged. His body was burned. Some of his sermons and theological works survive.

JOSEPH F. KELLY

See also DOMINICANS; PREACHING; PROPHECY/PROPHET.

SCANDAL

A scandal is a snare or a stumbling block which causes someone to fall. To give scandal in this sense is by word or example to tempt another to sin. Thus, Jesus warns it would be better to be cast into the sea with a millstone around one's neck than to scandalize any of his followers (Luke 17:1). Not all scandal, however, is to be avoided. Jesus knew that his preaching of the gospel would be a stumbling block to many and he declared all those blessed who would not be scandalized at him (Matt 11:6). Paul preached Christ crucified even though this was a scandal to those who were looking for a glorious and powerful Messiah (1 Cor 1:23). One should be careful not to give the first kind of scandal, but it is much more important to give the second kind of scandal, i.e., to speak and act in the truth even in the face of opposition.

WILLIAM C. McFADDEN, S.J.

See also THEOLOGY, MORAL.

SCHISM

The word "schism" comes from a Greek word meaning "to tear." It refers to any split or division within an organized group.

More specifically, a schism occurs within Catholicism when one group refuses to live in communion with the rest of the Church, or refuses to recognize the authority of the pope.

There have been several schisms within Catholic history. For example, in the fourth century, one group of Christians called Donatists refused to accept the authority of a bishop who they thought had acted immorally. The Donatists ordained their own bishops instead, thus separating themselves from the larger Church.

In the eleventh century, a schism developed between what are now called the Roman Catholic and the Eastern Orthodox Churches. Roman Catholics recognized the authority of the Bishop of Rome (the pope). Eastern Orthodox Christians, however, assigned preeminence to the bishops of Constantinople, Jerusalem, Antioch, and Alexandria, as well as to the Bishop of Rome, and they felt that final authority rested only in a council of the whole Church. This and several other differences caused a breach between East and West; in 1054, the pope and the bishop of Constantinople excommunicated each other. Though there still exists a division between the two Churches, in 1965 Pope Paul VI and the Eastern Patriarch Athenagoras formally lifted the anathemas (declarations that the other is accursed and under the judgment of God) that had been set down in 1054.

Other schisms include the fourteenth-century Avignon papacy and Martin Luther's break from the Church in the sixteenth century.

THERESA SANDERS

See also CALVIN, JOHN; GREAT WESTERN SCHISM; LUTHER, MARTIN.

SCHISM, WESTERN

See GREAT WESTERN SCHISM.

SCHOLASTICISM

A system of thought and an intellectual approach associated with the scholars of the medieval universities. It sought a better understanding of revealed truth by using disciplined philosophical method. The forebears of Scholasticism were Augustine and Boethius whose commentaries on Aristotle and Porphyry introduced medieval scholars to the use of logic. In the ninth century, John Scotus Erigina made clear distinctions between the authority of Scripture, the main source of our knowledge of God, and the rational exploration and explication of revealed truth. In the eleventh and twelfth centuries, the use of the dialectic in theological discussion became accepted with some reservation. Abelard made a fundamental contribution to the methodology and shape of Scholasticism by the unrestrained use of the dialectical method in its totality. The Arabic commentators, Avicenna and Averroes, introduced the work of Aristotle to the West, and the Augustinian theologians were less than enthusiastic. The bridge between the Aristotelian and Augustinian approaches was built by Thomas Aquinas, whose *Summa Theologiae* was the greatest achievement of Scholastic theology. With his intellectual genius, Thomas lucidly drew the lines between revelation and reason, and showed how they enhanced each other. By the end of the thirteenth century, Scholasticism was in decline; and by the sixteenth century, many held it in disrespect. Yet, a lingering veneration for the authentic teaching of Aquinas survived among scholars. In the end of the nineteenth century, a revival of Scholasticism in the form of neo-Thomism took root, and dominated Catholic theological studies until recent decades.

MICHAEL GLAZIER

See also MIDDLE AGES, THE; PHILOSOPHY AND THEOLOGY; THEOLOGY.

SCIENCE AND RELIGION

The relationship between science and religion is extremely complex. There is no simple way to define either "science" or "religion," and moreover the meanings of both terms have changed, sometimes profoundly, in the course of time.

Although the basic meaning of "science" is simply "knowing" or "knowledge," contemporary usage applies it chiefly to physics, chemistry, and biology (the "natural sciences"), and by extension to disciplines such as sociology, psychology, and anthropology (the "human sciences"). "Political science" and the like seem to be sciences by courtesy only. Implicit in this usage is the assertion that the primary instances of knowing are the *modern* disciplines that investigate nature, which arose in Europe beginning in the seventeenth century. Their rise has been called, with good reason, the most significant event in Western history since the advent of Christianity, and it is their relationship with Christianity that has, ever since, been a matter of sometimes heated discussion. Although much could be learned by including non-Western science and non-Christian religion, this article must remain within what have by now become the traditional boundaries of the topic.

The rise of modern science did not make it an entirely new topic. Many of the questions that now belong to "religion and science" extend and transpose questions that had long been discussed under the more traditional rubric of "faith and reason." In that older context, the main lines of the problem can be stated without much ado. It is a matter of determining, on the one hand, which truths are or can be arrived at by exercising the "natural" powers of human reason, and which truths belong, on the other hand, exclusively to "supernatural" revelation and can therefore be known only by the supernatural power of faith. Given this distinction of ways in which truth is knowable, difficulties arise only insofar as a truth belonging to one category appears to contradict a truth belonging to the other. Even then, the difficulty is easy to resolve by making the apparently similar but in fact quite different assumption that there are two disparate kinds of "truth." The more usual view, however, at least in Catholic thought, has been the one taken by Thomas Aquinas. Thomas held that truth is one, because God, who is Truth itself and the source of all that is true, is one. From this it follows that any apparent contradiction between the contents of revelation and the achievements of reason must be *only* apparent; it cannot be real. Either the reasoning will turn out to have been mistaken, or revelation will turn out to have been misunderstood. Showing where the mistake or the misunderstanding lies may be difficult, but it is always possible in principle.

This approach has more than historical interest. Many would hold that it is along just these lines that issues of science and religion today can best be dealt with. But adopting such a position is not as straightforward as it might seem, for at least four sets of reasons.

(1) Both science, in the broad sense of investigating the world, and religion, in the equally broad sense of worship and devotion, are conscious activities that individual men and women deliberately engage in. Yet neither of them is a solitary pursuit. Each has social roots, institutional forms, political implications. The question of truth, whether scientific or religious, is not a question that is asked in a vacuum, apart from these other considerations. What a scientist or a religious believer holds to be true is as much influenced by history, culture, and language as is anything else that he or she does or thinks or says.

(2) A distinction needs to be drawn between genuinely scientific procedures and findings on the one hand, and on the other hand the simplified, popularized, and often seriously inaccurate presentations that give a wider public its picture of science. What a particle physicist means by an electron, for example, bears little resemblance to an account of it such as might appear in a newsmagazine. Similarly, the meaning of terms in theology, where by "theology" is meant a specialized, technical reflection on religion, must be distinguished from inflated or diluted meanings that may be current in everyday speech. Creation, for example, in the proper sense of the word, has very little to do with the commonsense notion of making or fabricating.

(3) In any conversation between religion and science there is always a third party, whether or not invited or even acknowledged—philosophy. Its presence as a distinct voice may be hard to detect. For one thing, the difference between philosophy and science has not always been clear; what now is called science used to be called "natural philosophy," as it was by Isaac Newton. For another, there is a sense in which Christianity may rightly be called a philosophy. For yet another, Christian theology in general and Catholic theology in particular have had a long and intimate association with a particular philosophy, namely Aristotle's—so intimate that attacking (or defending) Aristotle has at times been considered tantamount to attacking (or defending) Christianity itself. It is of course true that Aristotelianism enjoys no such status today, but that does not mean that philosophy as such can be ignored. It still has a mediating role to play. The very basic question of what it is to "do" science is neither a scientific nor a theological question. It is a philosophical question, and the same is true of what it is to "do" theology. Answering these questions does not automatically resolve all the rest, but unless they are answered the others never will be.

(4) It is true that individual scientists have sometimes gone out of bounds, by arrogating to science the final word on what does and does not exist, what is and what is not real, what the human mind can and cannot know. Likewise, it is true that individual theologians have sometimes gone out of bounds, by

pronouncing on questions of empirical fact. Even more destructive, however, have been those apologists of science who have used its achievements to attack ecclesiastical pretensions, and those apologists for Christianity who have used what they took to be its beliefs as a bulwark against the onslaught of modernity. The fact that both science and Christianity can become weapons of ideological conflict makes it all the more difficult to address on its own merits the question of their respective claims to truth.

All four of these complications contribute to what has long been the conventional wisdom on religion and science, namely that from the seventeenth century onward the history of their relationship has been a history of irreconcilable opposition. On this view the condemnation of Galileo and the hostile reaction to Darwin are only the most notable battles of a ceaseless war, in which science has slowly triumphed over the dogmatism of the Christian Church. While such an oversimplified account would now be rejected by nearly all historians of science, it nevertheless continues to exert a strong influence on the way many people perceive science in relation to Christianity.

The case of Galileo illustrates how complicated the real issues, as contrasted with their popularizations, can be. The question was not simply whether the earth travels around the sun or *vice versa.* Galileo not only championed the sun-centered system proposed by Copernicus; he also insisted that he had demonstrated its correctness. In fact, however, none of his "proofs" were valid, much less decisive. He was right, in other words, but not for the reasons he claimed he was. Moreover, by resting his arguments on supposedly demonstrative proofs, Galileo was in effect maintaining that the new, heliocentric world-system fit the definition of science espoused by Aristotle, for whom science was *true and certain* knowledge of things through their *necessary* causes. So, paradoxically, although Galileo did break with Aristotelianism on particular scientific questions, his philosophical view of what constitutes scientific knowing as such was thoroughly traditional.

The same view lies behind Newton's famous statement, "I do not put forth hypotheses." It is a true statement, inasmuch as Newtonian physics does not include any entities which are hypothetical in the sense that there is no empirical evidence for their existence. But it is a misleading statement too, inasmuch as Newton did propose hypotheses in the sense of intellectual constructions that explain the observable evidence. In itself, his highly mathematical theory of gravitation, for example, is a hypothesis—a hypothesis which, as it happens, is *confirmed* by every falling body as well as by the orbits of the planets. It is not, however, true of necessity, in the sense that no other explanation is possible; nor is it complete, as has become evident since Einstein.

Increasingly, in the twentieth century, the Aristotelian ideal of science as true and certain knowledge of necessary causality has been replaced by a view that better fits the facts of what scientists actually do, the view, namely, that scientific laws are hypotheses that happen to be verified. But the older view held sway for perhaps two hundred years, with profound effects on the way in which not just the solar system but everything else came to be conceived. If scientific laws, especially the laws of motion, are necessarily true—if it is impossible for them to be other than they are—and if these laws are somehow attached to discrete blocks of "matter," whether particles or planets, then the behavior of those blocks, alone or in combination, is determined from the outset. The whole universe operates as one great machine. Its every movement can in principle be predicted, because each must occur as it does, according to the relevant laws, and not otherwise.

This mechanistic view of things would seem to rule out most of what Christianity has said about God's interaction with the universe, and atheistic conclusions were in fact drawn from it. Not by everyone, though. In the English-speaking world, especially, the pursuit of science could be, and was, regarded as a kind of intellectual praise. God, that is, could be known through the "book of nature" in a way that complemented the "book of Scripture." The lawfulness of the world seemed to many, including Newton, to lend support to belief in an intelligent Lawgiver. The universe, in other words, could be thought of as *designed* and so as evidence for God as its designer. It is true that the God who figures in the argument from design is something less than the God of the Bible; having planned the universe and set it in motion, he has nothing else to do. Divine "interference" in general, and miracles in particular, were not surprisingly pushed into the background.

With Darwin's theory—better, his hypothesis—of evolution by natural selection, the argument from design suffered a severe blow. Evolution says nothing, one way or the other, about the Christian doctrine of creation, understood in the strict sense. It does affect the way the seven-day cosmogony in Genesis is to be interpreted, but that is a minor problem compared with its other implications. Randomness, in the form of "chance variations," plays a central part in Darwin's explanation of the origin of biological species, and in so far as randomness is unintelligible it seems to contradict the idea of an intelligent Designer. Moreover, the idea that "higher" species emerge from "lower" ones leads logically to a materialist worldview for which the spiritual qualities of the human species, morality and intelligence itself, become mere accidents preserved because of their survival value. On the other hand, "chance variation" did, at least implicitly, undercut the mechanistic worldview that dominated the eighteenth century, although it was not until the advent of quantum physics that randomness began to be regarded as an intrinsic component of the objective universe.

Meanwhile, where religion is concerned, the most significant development in modern times has been an increasing recognition that religion is not, or at least not in the first instance, cognitive. Emphasis on the noncognitive—on religious experience, on feeling and conscience, on conversion and existential decision—began with Schleiermacher and has only slowly been assimilated by Catholicism, first with the modernists and more sweepingly since the Second Vatican Council. In this new context, the terms in which the question of science vis-à-vis religion must be framed are not what they were when modern science was young. If conversion is basic, then God is in the first instance the Other to whom one is oriented in the experienced mystery of love and awe. The question then becomes how to integrate that experience with one's cognitive knowledge of the world. Questions about the existence and attributes of God certainly do not disappear, but they do get postponed. Religious faith does not depend on answering them; rather, answering them plays a part in *understanding* what one believes.

In light of all this there seem to be three broad ways in which the spheres of science and religion can be related.

Separation

The simplest approach is to argue that Christianity says nothing about the external world of nature, and that science says nothing about the interior realm of personal existence. The two are separate but equal. This view can involve a drastic separation of mind from matter, of body from soul, of the "objective" from the "subjective," and for that reason it is highly questionable both from a philosophical standpoint and from that of Christian doctrine, the doctrine of the incarnation in particular.

Complementarity

Positions that stress the "complementarity" of science and religion often do no more than name the problem without solving it. The argument, for example, that a comprehensive view of things requires both a scientific and a religious "perspective" or "model" seems insufficient unless it goes on to show that the two are really compatible, and how. This further step can be taken by proposing that religion goes beyond science, which asks questions of fact, to ask questions of meaning and value. But unless religious answers can draw support from the world as scientifically understood, meaning and value will themselves be little more than a halo gratuitously added to the factual world.

God as Makeshift

Though perpetually derided, the "God of the gaps" approach is perpetually tempting. On this view, some particular item in the world, some event or type of event, is singled out because science has not yet explained it, and God is introduced as its explanation. Much of what has been written about "the new physics" tends in this direction. It is not a fruitful direction, first, because gaps in the scientific account may well be filled with explanations that are perfectly natural, making a supernatural explanation superfluous; and second, because the idea of God as *an* agent, in the sense of one among many things that cause events in the world to happen, is not what Christianity has meant by *God.*

If none of these approaches appears to be entirely satisfactory, the conclusion to be drawn is that in its most basic form the question of religion and science is the question of how the God who is the focus of religious worship is best conceived—a question on which there is little if any agreement at the present time. The criteria for this "best" conception will presumably come from various sources, especially from Scripture, tradition, and experience. But one of the chief criteria, where the tradition is that of Catholic Christianity, will be that of intellectual coherence. Hence philosophy, the third partner in the conversation, will continue to make its voice heard.

CHARLES C. HEFLING

See also EVOLUTION; GALILEI, GALILEO; PHILOSOPHY AND THEOLOGY.

SCRIBES

Scribes were originally those who wrote legal documents—a task that demanded literacy and knowledge of the laws. Since in ancient Israel the Torah was the law either in fact or theory (depending on the period), the scribes were also the keepers and interpreters of the Jewish religious tradition. By 200 B.C. the scribes in Israel seem to have constituted a guild of religious intellectuals (see Sirach), though not bound to a particular political program or religious stance. In the New Testament they appear frequently with other groups: elders, high priests, Pharisees, etc. The references to the "scribes of the Pharisees" (Mark 2:16; Acts 23:9) suggest that scribes could belong to other Jewish parties also. The scribes are generally portrayed as siding with the opponents of Jesus and of the early Christians, and are paired with the Pharisees as the objects of Jesus' vigorous denunciation of hypocrisy in Matthew 23. The scribes' emphasis on the knowledge of the Jewish Law (Torah) and on study contributed to the revival of Judaism after A.D. 70 under the rabbis.

DANIEL J. HARRINGTON, S.J.

See also BIBLE, NEW TESTAMENT WRITINGS; JUDAISM.

SCRUPLES

An irrational anxiety that one may have sinned, or may not have adequately confessed, performed penance, completed a duty, or the like. Most authorities recognize that a mental or emotional disturbance is involved. Frequently afflicted persons will not believe that they have really been absolved or forgiven; they may compulsively repeat confessions (in which sexual matters often predominate) and penances. In addition to expert spiritual direction, psychological counseling may be indicated. Without these cautions, the sacrament of reconciliation may serve to intensify the problem.

DAVID BRYAN

See also CHRISTIAN SPIRITUALITY.

SEAL OF CONFESSION

In the early Church the confession of serious sins was a public matter so the issue of confidentiality did not arise. Gradually, however, from the fifth century on, the practice emerged of private confession. The seal of confession developed as a way of encouraging penitents to confess their sins freely by assuring them of total secrecy. Whatever is told in confession is, as it were, sealed. The confessor is bound by canon law under the gravest obligation not to violate this seal "by word or in any other manner or for any reason" (c. 983, §1), not even to save his own life. The obligation continues even after the death of the penitent and binds not only the priest but all others who either deliberately or accidentally come to know what a penitent has revealed in confession.

WILLIAM C. McFADDEN, S.J.

See also SACRAMENT OF RECONCILIATION.

SECRETARIAT OF STATE

The Secretary of State serves as the pope's most immediate assistant in the care of the Church. The Section for General Affairs aids in the pope's daily administration by coordinating the work of the Roman Curia, drafting papal documents, and supervising the Vatican Press Office, the Central Statistics Office, and the journal *Acta Apostolicae Sedis.* The Section for Relations with States supervises all relations with civil governments, especially those of a diplomatic nature.

DAVID BRYAN

See also CURIA, ROMAN; PAPACY, THE.

SEMINARIAN

A person who attends a theological college, or seminary, as a candidate for the priesthood. Seminarians are given a liturgical foundation for their spiritual lives, an understanding of Church history and theology, and an opportunity to contemplate and celebrate the sacred mysteries of the Church.

JOSEPH QUINN

See also PRIESTHOOD, THE MINISTERIAL.

SEMINARY

See SEMINARIAN.

SEPARATION OF SPOUSES

The Code of Canon Law admits two sorts of separations of spouses: with the marriage bond enduring, or with its dissolution.

Separation with the Bond Enduring

Spouses have the right and the duty to preserve married life unless a legitimate cause excuses them. One cause permitting separation is adultery. Although it is recommended that an innocent spouse, moved by charity and a concern for the family's good, pardon an adulterous partner, he or she has the right to sever conjugal living, unless the innocent spouse has expressly or tacitly condoned the adultery, has consented to it, has given cause for it, or has also committed adultery. Tacit condonation exists if the innocent spouse, aware of the adultery, continues voluntarily to live with the adulterous partner in marital affection. Such tacit condonation is presumed if the innocent spouse continues conjugal living for six months without recourse to ecclesiastical or civil authority. If the innocent spouse does separate, he or she must bring a suit for separation before the competent diocesan authority, who is to decide if the innocent spouse can be led to forgive the adultery and not prolong permanently the separation.

Other reasons for separation are a partner's causing serious danger of spirit or body to the other spouse or children or otherwise rendering common life too hard. Such actions give the other partner a legitimate cause to petition for a decree of separation from the local ordinary, or even to separate on his or her own authority if there is danger in delay. When the reason for the separation ends, conjugal living is to be restored unless ecclesiastical authority decides otherwise.

The innocent spouse can always laudably readmit the other partner to conjugal life, in which case the former renounces the right to separate.

After any separation of spouses, suitable provision is to be made for the support and education of children.

The procedure to be followed for a separation with the bond enduring is found in canons 1692–1696.

Dissolution of the Marriage Bond

The Code teaches that a ratified and consummated marriage cannot be dissolved by any human power or for any reason other than death. A marriage is called ratified if it is celebrated between two baptized persons, Catholic or otherwise. A marriage is called consummated after the parties have performed the conjugal act together in a human fashion.

This means that a marriage can be dissolved if it is *not* ratified, that is, if one or both partners is not baptized. This also means that a marriage can be dissolved if it is *not* consummated.

The Church recognizes five possible dissolutions of the marriage bond:

Dissolution of a Non-Consummated Marriage. A non-consummated marriage between baptized persons or between a baptized and an unbaptized person can be dissolved by the Roman Pontiff for a just cause, at the request of both parties or of one of them, even if the other is unwilling. The procedure to be followed for such a dissolution is found in canons 1697–1706.

Dissolution by the Pauline Privilege. A marriage entered by two unbaptized persons can be dissolved by the so-called "Pauline Privilege," based on an Paul's teaching in 1 Corinthians 7:12-15. This dissolution is granted in favor of the faith of the party who has received baptism. The spouse of that party must depart. The baptized person's new marriage itself dissolves the union with the spouse who has departed. The nonbaptized partner is considered to have departed if he or she does not wish to cohabit with the baptized party or does not wish to cohabit in peace without insult to the Creator unless, after having received baptism, the baptized party gives the spouse reason to depart.

For the baptized spouse to enter a new marriage, the non-baptized partner must always be asked whether he or she wishes also to receive baptism, and whether he or she at least wishes to cohabit in peace with the baptized spouse without insult to the Creator. These questions are to be asked after the baptism. The local ordinary, however, can permit them to be asked before the baptism or even to dispense with the questioning if it is evident to him that such cannot take place or would be useless. The questions are normally asked by the local ordinary of the baptized partner but, if this cannot be done, a private interrogation by the baptized spouse suffices. In either event, there must be proof of the questions asked and the answers given.

The baptized partner has the right to enter a new marriage with a Catholic (1) if the other spouse answered negatively to the interrogation or it was omitted, or (2) if the other spouse at first peacefully cohabited without insult to the Creator and then departed without a just cause.

For a serious reason, the local ordinary can permit the baptized spouse to enter a new marriage with a non-Catholic, baptized or not.

Dissolution of Polygamous Marriages. After receiving baptism, a person with several simultaneous non-baptized spouses can keep one while dismissing the others if it is difficult to remain with the first spouse. Marriage is to be celebrated anew with this spouse according to the legitimate form. The local ordinary is to care for sufficient provision for the dismissed spouses according to the norms of justice, Christian charity and natural equity, after considering the moral, social, and economic situation of the region and of the persons involved.

Dissolution in Captivity or Persecution. A non-baptized person who, after receiving baptism in the Catholic Church, cannot restore cohabitation with a non-baptized spouse due to captivity or persecution can contract another marriage, even if the former spouse has been baptized in the meantime, provided the couple has not consummated their marriage after both received baptism.

Dissolution by the "Privilege of the Faith." A marriage entered by a baptized person and a non-baptized person can be dissolved personally by the Roman Pontiff, in virtue of his vicarious power. Such a dissolution is called the "Petrine Privilege" or, popularly, "In Favor of the Faith." Three things must be proven for the favor to be granted: (1) the non-baptism of one of the spouses during the whole marriage; (2) the non-use of marriage after the baptism perchance of the party previously not baptized; and (3) the promise (*cautio*) of the non-Catholic of the new marriage that the Catholic can freely practice the faith and baptize and educate the children as Catholics. The provision for this dissolution is not contained in the Code of Canon Law, but is found in an 1973 instruction from the Congregation for the Doctrine of the Faith, *Ut notum est.* These norms remain operative.

JOHN RENKEN

See also ANNULMENT; SACRAMENT OF MATRIMONY.

SEPTUAGINT

"Septuagint" is the term used to describe the Greek translation of the Hebrew Bible, made for the benefit of Jews living in the dispersion in Greek-speaking countries. The translation is probably the one made in Alexandria in the third century before the birth of Christ. The term "septuagint" is the Latin word for seventy, and the translation is sometimes represented by the Latin numerals LXX. Tradition suggested that the translation was accomplished by six representatives of every Jewish tribe ($6 \times 12 = 72$). Later the 72 was modified to suggest the 70 elders who worked with Moses (Exodus 24:1, 9) or to link the LXX with the authority of the Sanhedrin's 70 members.

Having completed the Hebrew Bible, the translators then added several religious books which had only been preserved in Greek. The Septuagint was the translation used by early Christian missionaries in the preaching of the gospel, and they used not only the books of the Hebrew Bible but also the additional ones in Greek. When conflict developed between Christians and Jews, the latter, gathered in council in Jamnia, rejected the Bible used by Christians—the Septuagint—claiming all sacred books must be written in the sacred language of Hebrew. This decision did not change the Christians' missionary practices. However, during the Reformation, Martin Luther, desiring to establish a secure list of the books of the Bible, accepted the decision of the Council of Jamnia, and thereby rejected all those books written in Greek. These books are now known by Protestants as the Apocrypha and by Catholics as deuterocanonicals. This is the reason for the differences between the Roman Catholic and Protestant Bibles.

LEONARD DOOHAN

See also BIBLE, MANUSCRIPTS OF THE; BIBLE, OLD TESTAMENT WRITINGS.

SERENITY PRAYER

God, grant me the
Serenity to accept the
things I cannot change;
Courage to change the
things I can;
and Wisdom to know the
difference.
Living one day at a time;
Enjoying one moment
at a time;
Accepting hardship as
the pathway to peace.

Taking, as He did,
This sinful world
as it is, not as I
would have it.
Trusting that He will
make all things right
if I surrender to His
will.
That I may be reasonably
happy in this life,
and supremely happy with
Him forever in the next.

This relatively new prayer was composed by Reinhold Niebuhr (1892–1971), one of the great Christian spokesmen of this century. His fearless voice for social justice, his deep faith, and his theological versatility are reflected in his many writings. But it is ironic that he will be remembered by millions for his Serenity Prayer which, though written in a few hours, reflects his mature and sterling spirituality. The first twenty-five words of the prayer are recited by people of different faiths all over the world and they have been adopted by many groups, such as Alcoholics Anonymous, as an essential part of their programs. During World War II, the prayer was widely distributed to troops by the United Services Organization.

JOSEPH QUINN

See also PRAYER.

SERMON

See LITURGY OF THE WORD.

SERVER, ALTAR

Also referred to as a Mass Server, this is a person who assists the priest at Mass and at other liturgical celebrations. Normally wearing a cassock or alb, the server contributes to the Eucharistic celebration by carrying the cross, candles, and incense during the opening and closing processions, bringing the bread and wine to the altar, and attending the priest or deacon at the proclamation of the Gospel.

JOSEPH QUINN

See also LITURGY.

SETON, ELIZABETH ANN, ST. (1774–1821)

Elizabeth, the first person born in America to be canonized, came from colonial English stock well connected in the Episcopal Church and in New York society. Born at New York City, she was the daughter of Richard Bayley, professor of anatomy at King's College, and Catherine Charlton, whose father was rector of St. Andrew's (Episcopal) Church, Staten Island. Though her mother died when Elizabeth was very young, her father educated her and successfully shaped her character. Even as a child she showed great sympathy for the poor, earning the nickname "the Protestant Sister of Charity." Her youthful writings are deeply spiritual.

She married William Magee Seton, a successful merchant, in 1794, and continued her works of charity, becoming one of the founders of the Society for the Relief of Poor Widows with Small Children. But she was soon to know poverty and tragedy herself. Her husband lost his fortune and, soon after, his health. The family took up residence with friends in Italy, a Catholic family, hoping that the change might halt William's rapid decline. He died (1803), and Elizabeth, twenty-nine years old, spent the first months of her widowhood with her Catholic friends, gradually convincing herself of the merits of the Catholic faith.

Returning to New York (she had five children), Elizabeth acted on her desire to become a Catholic, despite great opposition from her spiritual adviser and friend, Dr. Henry Hobart. Her ostracism by her family and friends was nearly complete. Desperate, she planned to move her family to Catholic Montreal, but accepted a surprising invitation by the rector of St. Mary's Seminary, Baltimore, to open a school there. In 1809 the farseeing Elizabeth, with four companions, left Baltimore to found a religious community and a school for poor children near Emmitsburg, Maryland, the beginning of the Catholic parochial school system in the United States. Elizabeth trained teachers, wrote textbooks, translated religious books from the French, wrote spiritual treatises, and counseled the other sisters. Together, they visited the poor and sick throughout the vicinity of Emmitsburg. In 1812, John Carroll, the archbishop of Baltimore, approved their rule of life,

St. Elizabeth Ann Seton

which was a modification of St. Vincent de Paul's rule for Sisters of Charity. Elizabeth was elected superior; she and eighteen other sisters took vows on 19 July 1813. They were the first religious community formed by Americans for Americans. In the remaining seven years of her life, Mother Seton saw the order grow to some twenty communities spread through the various states. She was canonized by Pope Paul VI in 1975, the first American-born saint, her community numbering in the thousands throughout the Americas and the world. Feast day, 4 January.

DAVID BRYAN

See also AMERICAN CATHOLICISM; RELIGIOUS ORDERS.

SEVENTH-DAY ADVENTISTS

The title of this denomination reveals its two main emphases—worship on the seventh day of the week and the belief in the imminent second coming of Christ.

Although formally organized as a Church body in 1863 at Battle Creek, Michigan, their roots lay in an American spiritual revival which followed the turn of the millennium in 1800. The leader of the revival was a Baptist farmer-preacher from New York State named William Miller (1782–1849). He was fascinated with biblical prophecies, especially those in Daniel and Revelation. As a result, he calculated the world would end and Jesus would return on 22 October 1844.

After a period of disappointment at Jesus' failure to appear, a small group of Adventists, inspired by

Ellen Gould White (1827–1915), believed that Christian indifference to the Sabbath was the reason for the delay of the return of Christ. So there was formed the Seventh-Day Adventist Church, the largest of the adventist Churches which include the Mormons and Jehovah's Witnesses. James White, Ellen's husband, and Joseph Bates were cofounders of this main adventist denomination.

In addition to their deeply held beliefs about Sabbath observance and Christ's expected return (for which there is no longer a timetable), the Bible is the infallible word of God and the sole authority of the Adventists' life and faith. They believe in salvation by grace, substitutionary atonement, believer's baptism, a combination of footwashing and Lord's Supper (based on John 13), and in an afterlife which is a "sleep in Christ" until, upon his return, we will all be resurrected in glory.

While conservative in doctrine, they have an "open communion" for all Christians and do not feel they have an exclusive hold on salvation.

Seventh-Day Adventists are very health conscious; many of them are vegetarians and refrain from drugs, tobacco, and alcohol. Their numerous hospitals in the U.S.A. and elsewhere are highly respected.

The Seventh-Day Adventists are a democratically organized Church with primary attention paid to the local congregation. A number of congregations can form a conference which has the power to appoint clergy. Clergy participate in an equal salary plan regardless of the size of church they serve.

The World Headquarters is in Washington, D.C., with the chief officer of the Church being a president who is elected every five years. There are over 6.5 million Seventh-Day Adventists in the world, and about 750,000 in North America.

IRA ZEPP

See also BAPTISTS; HEALING; PROTESTANTISM.

SEXAGESIMA

[Lat., "the sixtieth" (day before Easter)] The second Sunday before the beginning of Lent (on Ash Wednesday); also the eighth Sunday before Easter. Prior to the Second Vatican Council, it was observed as part of a transitional pre-Lenten "subseason." In 1969, the term was suppressed in order to distinguish more clearly the Lenten season.

JOSEPH QUINN

See also LITURGY.

SEXUALITY

In its primary and most precise sense, this refers to the state or condition of being sexual. Sexuality is a creature's mode of being in the world as a female or a male. It includes the structural (anatomical), functional (biological), and behavioral characteristics of living beings who reproduce themselves by heterosexual interaction with others of their species, which characteristics serve to distinguish them as either male or female.

When applied to human beings, sexuality specifies who and what one is as a human being, rather than what one does or how one acts. To be human is to be either a male or a female, to be a sexual being with certain kinds of structural, functional, behavioral characteristics as essential components of one's nature. Sexuality is, therefore, a fundamental aspect of one's personal identity, not merely an anatomical or biological designation. One is, in all one's relationships and in all forms of one's self-expression and activity, sexual. There are no generic, a-sexual or non-sexual human beings.

Given this broad but precise meaning of sexuality as an integral and essential aspect of human personal identity and selfhood, it is not difficult to understand the importance of sexuality to human well-being and wholeness. The ability to accept and care for oneself, as well as to accept and care for others, requires the acceptance and healthy integration of one's own sexuality and the sexuality of others into one's total personal orientation to the world. Problems with the acceptance and integration of sexuality are often at the root of psychological disorders and not infrequently the cause of interpersonal and social conflicts, as well as of actions that violate the rights of others such as rape, incest, voyeurism, and other forms of sexual abuse.

Human sexuality, in addition to what a person is in terms of anatomical and biological nature, that is female or male, also takes in one's gender ascription that comes from one's social culture. Gender designates what it means to be masculine or feminine and refers to the virtues, the behaviors, the social roles that a particular society or culture holds to correspond appropriately to males and females. Closer analysis of human sexuality also allows us to distinguish sexual orientation, sexual desire, sexual attraction, and specifically sexual acts as essential aspects of human sexuality.

Biological nature is the most readily understood of these aspects of human sexuality. Males produce sperm; females produce eggs. Males ejaculate; females ovulate, lactate, and menstruate. Males are not bound to particular temporal and physical manifestations of their sexuality other than the changes that come at puberty and the diminishment in sexual energy that comes with age. Females know the monthly menstrual cycle from puberty through menopause. Males have a direct but distant physical connection to the children they father; females bear their children in the womb for nine months, give birth with hard, often painful physical labor, and nurse their young for a considerable time thereafter.

It seems plausible to think that the different bodily experiences of their sexual natures which males and females so evidently have would produce quite different psychologies in males and females, so fitting them more to some social roles than others. One might expect that attitudes, emotions, modes of perceiving, evaluating, judging, and acting would be quite different in men and women as a result of their different biological natures. That is to say, we might assume, as people have assumed for centuries, that biology determined in important ways one's gender as masculine or feminine and so the appropriate social roles of the two sexes.

While there is some evidence to suggest that there may be some innate tendencies toward masculine and feminine differences, gender seems to be far more a result of culture than of biological nature. A man cannot escape being a biological male with all that means, but he can avoid the characteristic attitudes and behaviors his society designates as masculine. A woman will inevitably manifest the structural, functional, and behavioral characteristics of female biological nature, but she may or may not manifest the characteristics her society labels feminine. Gender, then, seems to be, in large part, a matter of cultural and social nurture rather than a matter of nature.

It was also thought for many centuries that biological nature determined one's sexual orientation. Males are attracted to females; females are drawn to males. For the most part this heterosexual orientation is, in fact, the reality of human and animal life. But homosexuality, the orientation of the individual's sexual desires, attractions, fantasies, to members of the same sex as oneself, is not an insignificant reality. Estimates of the number of human persons in society whose sexual orientation is overwhelmingly or predominantly homosexual are notoriously difficult to evaluate. The number seems to vary from society to society and to be different for males and females. An estimate of about 10 percent of the male population and 3 percent of the female population of the United States having a predominantly homosexual orientation seems to be the most reasonable guess we can make today.

Sexual orientation, however, remains a little-understood reality. What is known about it is that it is not a freely chosen matter nor can one simply choose to change the sexual orientation one finds oneself to have. What causes sexual orientation to be what it is, whether it is due to nature or nurture, or some combination of the two, is a matter of considerable debate. The available evidence inclines more and more toward the side of nature. Furthermore, for a variety of psychological and social reasons, sexual orientation is often not easily discovered.

Human sexuality manifests itself in human consciousness not only in an awareness of one's biological nature and of society's instruction on what constitutes masculine and feminine ways of living. It also manifests itself in the form of sexual desires and sexual attractions. Sexual desires have their origin in the biochemical processes of the human body. They appear in consciousness as urges seeking satisfaction, as an appetite clamoring for the pleasure that will satiate it. Such desires arise most clearly at puberty. They can vary greatly in individuals in intensity, frequency and duration, and seem to have quite different rhythms in males and females. Human beings can learn to stimulate such desires in themselves and others to some degree; they can also learn to discipline, control and direct these desires, to use the energy these desires afford in ways of their own choosing. Every society known to us has developed ways to control and direct human sexual desires, with more or less success, to serve what the society understood the purpose of these desires to be.

Human beings also experience their sexuality as attracting them to specific persons, as drawing them to seek not merely the satisfaction of a bodily urge but a more intimate, more personal union with a specific other. This experience of sexual attraction, when it is intense and of some duration, is what the culture generally means by being in love. Such attractions are mysterious to human beings for they are clearly not freely willed in their origin, though human beings are free to pursue the attraction or to run away from it. It is the mysterious nature of such an attraction, one suspects, that often leads people to attribute its origin to fate or destiny or even to God, though there is no good or necessary reason for doing so.

Finally, the nature of human sexuality impels human beings to perform sexual acts, to seek the satisfaction of their sexual desires, to pursue and nurture the intimate personal union to which sexual attraction draws them, to achieve the fatherhood or motherhood their sexuality makes possible. In all these ways human beings seek the fulfillment of their human nature, seek the goods promised by their sexuality which can be summarized as pleasure, love and children. In short, they seek happiness. The human questions about sexuality in its multiple dimensions and aspects are how to understand it and how to order it so that it will realize its promise.

Every sexual ethic is nothing more than an attempt to answer these questions. The traditional teaching of Christianity can serve as an illustration of this claim.

God created human beings as male and female and saw that it was very good. Sexuality, then, in its fullness, is a good gift of God. Its two primary purposes are procreation and the mutual comfort, support, and fulfillment a man and a woman can be to each other. The pleasure involved in sexual activity is also a gift of God, but never one to be sought for its own sake or in isolation from the other two ends. Sexuality finds its human fulfillment in the creation of the social unit known as the family. Like all things human, sexuality is subordinate to and at the service of the kingdom of God and the common good of the human community. People, then, may find or be called to channel their sexual energy, not into directly sexual actions, but into activities of service to the community, celibacy for the sake of the kingdom of God.

Finally, like all things human, sexuality is deeply affected by the disorder introduced into the world by sin. This disorder touches every dimension and aspect of human sexuality and confronts human beings with the personal and moral challenge to learn to be sexual and act sexually in truthful and responsible ways. The amount of sexual disorder and abuse in human history and in our personal lives makes clear that this is no easy challenge.

JAMES P. HANIGAN

See also ANTHROPOLOGY, CHRISTIAN; SACRAMENT OF MATRIMONY.

SHALOM

See PEACE.

SHANAHAN, JOSEPH (1871–1943)

When Fr. Joseph Shanahan, C.S.Sp., went to Nigeria at the beginning of the century there were some thousands of Catholics in the country. Today there are eight million with a fully established local Church and the largest seminary in the world. The capital role in this achievement is generally accorded to the bishop. He concentrated on education and catechetics and in a short time saw the beginning of change. His education was almost entirely in France. He was ordained priest on 22 April 1920 in Blackrock College, taught for a while in Rockwell College, and left for Africa in 1902.

As the need for priestly ministry increased with the new interest in the Catholic faith, Shanahan, with contacts in Maynooth, the Irish national seminary, persuaded volunteers to obtain leave of their dioceses to come out and work with him. This was after he had been ordained first vicar apostolic of Southern Nigeria in 1920. He attracted a number of young women volunteers in nursing, education, and homemaking. One of them was Marie Martin, foundress of the Medical Missionaries of Mary. The others were to form the nucleus of Shanahan's own religious foundation, the Missionary Sisters of the Holy Rosary.

A number of the priest volunteers from secular dioceses were permanently released and in time formed St. Patrick's Missionary Society; they resemble the Society of St. Columban, which also had a Maynooth connection, and had China as its initial area of work. Meanwhile the Church in Nigeria was growing fast in numbers and spirit. Many other religious congregations entered the area to meet the need for clergy and religious. Native sisterhoods arose, and missionaries went out to evangelize other countries. Bishop Shanahan resigned in 1931 and was succeeded by Msgr. (later Archbishop) Heery, his coadjutor. After some years in Blackrock College, he accepted Bishop Heffernan's invitation to go to Nairobi. There his last years were spent as chaplain in a Carmelite convent. He died on Christmas Day, 1943.

MICHAEL O'CARROLL, C.S.Sp.

See also AFRICA, THE CATHOLIC CHURCH IN; HOLY GHOST FATHERS AND BROTHERS (SPIRITANS).

SHEED, F. J. (FRANK) (1897–1981)

Born in 1897, Frank Sheed was an Australian writer, lecturer and publisher. He graduated from Sydney University, and went on to law school. In 1920 he came to London. In 1926 he married Maisie Ward and they founded Sheed and Ward Publishers (U.S. branch opened 1933).

The intellectual approach to religion of the Ward family and other speakers of the Catholic Evidence Guild in London was a revelation to this devout traditional Catholic, and Sheed decided not to practice law but to teach the faith as a career, in order to share with others the truths Christ died to give us. He studied theology and learned public speaking through training as a CEG outdoor speaker, but at a time of intellectual excitement in the Church all over Europe he wanted to publish the work of some of the major Catholic thinkers of the day—not only Chesterton, Belloc, Knox, Dawson, etc., but continental writers whose work was not available in English. Most important was to ensure that Catholics themselves understood the Church's teaching, and his own writing and speaking were directed as much to them as to the non-Catholic world.

His major books (all written in response to perceived needs) included *Map of Life, Nullity of Marriage, Communism and Man, Theology and Sanity, Society and Sanity, The Church and I, God and the Human Condition, To Know Christ Jesus, Is It the Same Church?, What Difference does Jesus Make?, Genesis Regained.* His many translations included St. Augustine's *Confessions* and the *Letters* of St. Thérèse of Lisieux.

Uniquely for a layman, he received a doctorate in theology from the Roman Congregation of Seminaries and Universities (conferred at Lille University in 1957).

He continued writing and lecturing to within a month of his death in 1981, six years after that of his wife. He was survived by two children and seven grandchildren.

ROSEMARY SHEED

See also BRITAIN, CHURCH IN; WARD, MAISIE.

SHEEN, FULTON J. (1895–1979)

University professor, radio and television personality, and prelate, Fulton J. Sheen was born in El Paso, Illinois, on 8 May 1895, and died in New York City on 9 December 1979. Baptized Peter, he adopted the maiden name of his mother, Delia (Fulton) Sheen. Ordained a priest of the Diocese of Peoria on 20 September 1919, Sheen pursued graduate studies at the Catholic University of America, the Sorbonne, the Collegio Angelico in Rome, and at the University of Louvain where he earned a Ph.D. and the prestigious *agrégé en philosophie* in 1925.

After a year of pastoral work in Peoria, Sheen joined the faculty of the Catholic University of America where he taught theology and the philosophy of religion from 1926 until 1950. He was a prolific writer, producing nearly seventy books. In addition to his university teaching, Sheen embarked on a second career as a public speaker and preacher. A gifted orator, his sermons regularly drew capacity crowds to St. Patrick's Cathedral in New York City. In 1930 he began his Sunday afternoon broadcasts on the "Catholic Hour," eventually reaching a weekly audience of four million over NBC radio. In 1951 he inaugurated a television series called "Life Is Worth Living" which proved to be even more popular than his radio broadcasts, reaching an estimated audience of thirty million each week. Still another reason for Sheen's prominence was the role that he played in receiving into the Catholic Church a number of prominent converts such as the journalist Heywood Broun and Clare Booth Luce.

Bishop Fulton J. Sheen

In 1950 Sheen entered upon still another career when he moved to New York and accepted the position of national director of the Society for the Propagation of the Faith. Sheen was very successful in raising funds, but he became embroiled in a bitter row with Francis Cardinal Spellman over the financial policies of the organization. One consequence of the conflict with Spellman was Sheen's disappearance from the pulpit of St. Patrick's Cathedral. In 1951 Sheen was made an auxiliary bishop of New York, and in 1966 (at the age of seventy-one), he was appointed bishop of Rochester, New York, a pastoral and administrative post for which he had neither training nor experience. After three unhappy years in Rochester, Sheen resigned his see, was made a titular archbishop, and retired to New York City where he continued his writing and preaching until his death ten years later.

John Tracy Ellis, a close personal friend, said that "with the sole exception of a strain of vanity over his prowess as a public speaker it would be difficult to think of any serious defect in the man." Moreover, said Ellis: "In his hey-day almost literally millions called his name blessed for the religious inspiration, the kindling of renewed hope, and the spiritual enrichment that he brought to their lives" [*NCE,* XVIII:475]. Since his death, Sheen has become a cultural icon for some conservative American Catholics who are nostalgic for a type of preconciliar Catholicism which they—rightly or wrongly—identify with him.

THOMAS J. SHELLEY

See also AMERICAN CATHOLICISM.

SHEERIN, JOHN BASIL (1906–1992)

Paulist editor and ecumenist, Sheerin was born in Brooklyn, New York on 12 October 1906. His father, Francis Sheerin, was a baker who had immigrated from Ireland and married Margaret Daugherty in 1896. John Basil, their third son, was one of eight children. He attended local parochial schools in Brooklyn, enrolled at Fordham University in 1924, and graduated from Fordham Law School in 1930. After two years he became disillusioned with the practice of the law. Sheerin, who had begun to publish his writing, was persuaded to join the Paulist Fathers through the influence of James Martin Gillis, Paulist editor of *The Catholic World.* Sheerin entered the Paulist novitiate in 1933 and was ordained a priest on 16 June 1937.

Initially assigned to teach English at the Paulist House of Studies in Washington, D.C., he served briefly on the Paulist mission band in New York in 1944, and was named director and superior of the Paulist Information Center in Boston in 1945. In 1947 James Gillis invited Sheerin to become his assistant editor. He succeeded Gillis as editor of *The Catholic World* the following year, beginning a distinguished editorial career at the journal that would continue until 1972. In 1956 Sheerin began a nationally sydicated column, *Sum and Substance,* which he continued to publish until 1982. During his years as a journalist Sheerin contributed numerous articles to a variety of Catholic periodicals including *America, Commonweal,* and *The American Ecclesiastical Review.*

John Sheerin, C.S.P.

A strong advocate in the pages of *The Catholic World* for reconciliation between the Churches, his career as an ecumenist began in 1957 when he and theologian Gustave Weigel were named Vatican observers at the Faith and Order Conference of the World Council of Churches in Oberlin, Ohio. He continued to serve as a Vatican observer to the Central Committee of the World Council until 1963. His particular concern for Catholic-Jewish relations led to his appointment in 1974 as a general consultor to the U.S. Bishops Secretariat for Catholic Jewish Relations. In attendance at the Second Vatican Council, initially as a journalist, and then as the moderator of the American Bishop's Press Panel, he was named a *peritus* to the Fourth Session in 1965 in recognition of his work in ecumenical affairs.

Sheerin was an early supporter of the civil rights movement, and together with Martin Luther King Jr. and Abraham Heschel was a founder of Clergy and Laity Concerned, serving on the national steering committee to organize religious leaders in opposition to the American prosecution of the war in Vietnam. His antiwar position was uncompromising although he strongly disagreed with the tactics of Philip and Daniel Berrigan. He was equally critical of the American hierarchy for their failure to take a stand in opposition to the war. In 1973 he published *War, Peace and the Young Catholic,* a guide for Catholic conscientious objectors.

He retired from all activity in 1982 and began a ten-year battle with Alzheimer's disease. Sheerin died on 13 January 1992 and was buried at the Paulist Novitiate in Oak Ridge, New Jersey. His papers are kept at the Paulist Archives in Washington, D.C. In addition to his numerous articles, Sheerin was the author of *The Sacrament of Freedom* (1961), *Christian Reunion: The Ecumenical Movement and American Catholics* (1966), and *Never Look Back: The Career and Concerns of John J. Burke* (1975).

PAUL ROBICHAUD, C.S.P.

See also AMERICAN CATHOLICISM; CONSCIENTIOUS OBJECTION; ECUMENISM.

SHEPHERD OF HERMAS, THE

The second-century treatise derives its name from Hermas to whom an angel in the form of a shepherd is supposed to have revealed most of its contents. Hermas, a liberated Christian slave, became a rich merchant who later became impoverished. He claims to be a contemporary of Clement of Rome, and is numbered among the Apostolic Fathers. Some scholars attribute the work to a brother of Pius I and date it between 140 to 155. It was regarded as Scripture in the Eastern Church in the second and third centuries. The treatise is divided into three parts: Five "Visions" in which a woman, as representative of the Church, appears to Hermas; twelve "Mandates" in which Hermas expounds on Christian virtues; ten "Similitudes" in which Christian principles are presented under various images. The treatise preaches penance and forgiveness.

MICHAEL GLAZIER

See also APOSTOLIC FATHERS, THE; APPARITIONS; FATHERS OF THE CHURCH; PROPHECY/PROPHET.

SHROUD, HOLY

The Holy Shroud of Turin is a long, narrow piece of linen (about fourteen feet by three and a half feet) claimed to be the burial cloth of Jesus. It bears the images of the front and the back of a bearded, male body about five feet, eleven inches tall, with bloodied wounds and marks of crucifixion, all imprinted on the cloth because it appears to have been folded lengthwise to cover the front and back of the corpse resting in horizontal position. The clearly ascertainable history of the Shroud begins only in the mid-fourteenth century in Troyes, France, where it was first displayed, though two bishops in that city insisted at that time that it was not the burial cloth of Jesus. About a century later it was given to the House of Savoy and put in the cathedral of Turin in northern Italy, where it is still kept, though under the aegis of the Vatican since 1983. While it was only infrequently displayed publicly over the past two centuries, the issue of its authenticity came to the fore with the recent involvement of the scientific community to date and explain its origins.

Researchers are convinced that the image on the Shroud is not painted or stained into the linen or transposed by some kind of scorching from a statue. While some use this mystery to indicate a miraculous imprinting from the resurrection of Jesus, the evidence may indicate no more than that the technique or method of creating the image was known in the past but lost in the present. The bloodstains on the cloth appear genuine, and the formation of the image may have involved a human corpse, but the stains raise suspicion in that they are all very precise without smearing and indicate blood flow from head toward foot rather than the called-for flow vertically downward from a reclining body. The anatomical features of the body image also raise problems. The face and hands stand out, reflecting artistic emphasis rather than the expected emphasis from chest, toes, and buttocks that would protrude to contact the Shroud more forcefully. Also, the hands extended and folded to cover the genitalia represent artistic reverence for Christ but require that the arms be too long in proportion to the body and that they be awkwardly positioned, since they would fall to the side of a body at rest. Material in the Shroud includes pollen from the Near East not known in France in the fourteenth century. This may indicate origins in Palestine, but doesn't necessarily date it to Jesus, though it may also mean simply that such material was left in the Shroud through contact with pious pilgrims. In 1988 carbon dating was done of a corner piece of the Shroud independently in England, the United States, and Switzerland. All results agreed on dating the origin of the Shroud between A.D. 1260 and 1390. Conclusions are 95 percent certain that this relic is the product of the pious devotion of the Middle Ages.

ANTHONY J. TAMBASCO

See also RELICS.

SIGN OF THE CROSS

A ritual gesture in the form of a cross by which a person confesses faith in the paschal mystery and the Holy Trinity. In the Roman Rite, a person touches the fingers of the right hand to the forehead, below the breast, the left shoulder and the right shoulder, while saying, "In the name of the Father, and of the Son, and of the Holy Spirit." The sign is used in certain sacramental rites, such as baptism and the Eucharist, and to bless people and objects. It is also commonly used to begin or end prayers of personal devotion, such as the rosary or grace at meals. Historically, the practice can be traced back as early as the third century, when Tertullian (ca. A.D. 230) reported its use as a personal gesture of piety to sanctify the actions of daily life.

PATRICIA DeFERRARI

See also CROSS; TRINITY.

SIN

Sin is the word used to describe moral evil when seen in the context of religion, as distinct from ethics or civil law. The Christian ideal is to do everything as done to the Lord, so shortcomings are considered as against a divinely given law, as grieving the Holy Spirit. Sin is often defined as the free and deliberate disobedience of a creature to the known will of God, so it is primarily a religious and theological reality, a symbol which expresses our alienation from God. As a symbol it was subject to historical and cultural development, from biblical times to the present day. The cultural conditioning of past centuries was so strong that the word sin has almost become trivialized in today's secularized world. The popular press often uses it in reference to sexual misconduct, but never applies it to economic oppression or the abuse of power. Within the Christian community, preachers claim that there is a loss of the sense of sin, but the reality may well be that the meaning of the word has changed. The catechism definition was clear and workable within the framework of stable, classical culture. But the radical cultural change of recent decades has produced Christians who are more questioning and critical, less passively accepting of rules and regulations binding "under pain of sin," especially mortal sin with its implication of eternal punishment. If they use the word sin they would like it to make sense in the light of modern experience and without the legalism inherited from the past.

In the Catholic tradition sin was very much related to confession, with a special focus on guilt. Confessors were trained to measure the degrees of sin, and there was a serious obligation to confess all mortal sins according to number and species. Examination of conscience meant checking infidelity to the laws of God and of the Church. All sin was ultimately disobedience, to God and to one's lawful superiors, and a strong emphasis on obedience became a feature of Catholic life. The healthy fear of sin as displeasing to God could often degenerate into a crippling and scrupulous fear of self and a doubting of one's own self-worth. Preoccupation with law and measurement and a kind of lust for certainty left people ill-equipped to live creatively with tension or to keep a balanced Christian attitude in ambiguous situations. The scandal of "good-living" Christians supporting an unjust social system, even economic exploitation and cruel repression, raised questions about the primacy of obedience. Liberation theologians have warned us of the harm done to the Christian message by preaching patience and submission to the victims of unjust social structures. Poverty and oppression are nowadays seen as manifestations of sin. The one-sided emphasis on private morality and otherworldly piety contributed to the gap between the concept of sin and the realities of everyday life.

Today's Christians have a different vision of the world and an understanding of their faith more in line with Vatican II theology. They not only reject the legalism of the past, but they have also benefited from the developments of psychology and sociology. The change began even before the council and reached a certain peak in the publication of Bernard Häring's *Law of Christ,* which still spoke of God's law, but explained it as a law of love. The starting-point was no longer the sinfulness of the creature needing pardon, but the incredible love of God our Father and Mother who treasures each of us infinitely, and sees in each one of us the image of Jesus the Son. Twenty-five years later Häring wrote a totally new summary of moral theology with the significant title *Free and Faithful in Christ.* The central insight here is that we are most like God in our freedom, that we are created to be free, to grow and develop into the fullness of the maturity of Christ. We do this by saying Yes to the world, to life, to our neighbor, and in and through all of this, to God. To say No is to sin, to alienate ourselves from the world, from life, from our true selves, from our brothers and sisters in the human family, and ultimately from God who created us for life, for friendship and love. If the glory of God is the human person fully alive, sin can be seen as anything that violates our human dignity, anything that restricts or blocks freedom, in ourselves or others.

The negative forces and actions that offend human dignity and lessen human freedom are seen as bad, as evil, as realities to be avoided, to be fought against, but they are not moral evils until associated with deliberate human action, the outcome of free human choice. Since sin is moral evil, all that is said of moral evil applies to sin, but is understood in a wider context. It is seen in the context of Christian faith in a God who is love, a God who is not indifferent to how we live our lives and treat our brothers and sisters, how we care for the universe God created as our home.

Biblical Background

As a religious reality, the understanding of sin is rooted in its biblical background. King David's sins of adultery and murder were certainly against a fellow human being and the order of society, but in the moment of conversion he acknowledged them as sins against God. This is reflected in the psalm, "Against you, you only, have I sinned and done what is evil" (Ps 51:4). The Old Testament describes sin as iniquity, guilt, rebellion, disorder, abomination, a lie and folly, but it is always clear that it involved more than the mere transgression of a law. It was seen as a break in the love-relationship with God, a failure to live up to the dignity and destiny intended for us by God. This basic insight is central to an understanding of sin, and any meaningful developments in the concept must remain within this context of faith. The Jewish people, our ancestors in the faith, continually experienced the presence of God in their history, and in that sense *knew God* as a wife knows her husband and is known by him. But their response was often one of infidelity, provoking God to complain with all the heartbreak of a deserted husband or wife: "My people, why do you turn away from me without ever turning back? I listened carefully, and you did not speak the truth. Not one of you has been sorry for his wickedness. . . . Everyone keeps on going his own way . . ." (Jer 8:5-7). This is the essence of sin, each one going his own way, seeking his own private ends regardless of others, forgetting that we are members of one family, parts of a greater whole.

The Old Testament seems to be the story of Israel's infidelities, a history of sin, but it is equally the story of God's continual, never-ending forgiveness and love. No matter how often or how far God's children go whoring after false gods, God is always there gently drawing them back to forgive and heal them. The New Testament does not enter into details about sin, but presents Jesus as the incarnation of God's love capable of overcoming sin and death. His healing miracles are signs of his mission. He drew sinners into fellowship with himself, restored their dignity, and assured them of full status in his Father's house. The Pauline letters have the most developed treatment of sin, with the word occurring sixty times. They stress the results of sin: a hardening of the heart, a dulling of the moral sense, and a kind of death, because sin is the denial of life, and the sinner dies to his better, potential self each time he sins. Paul is concerned about personal sin and individual responsibility, but the major emphasis is on sin as something universal, something in which all human beings are involved. It is a power which has us in its grip, so that we are captured by it and become "slaves of sin." It seems to be a state or condition of human nature itself, into which we are born, and from which sinful actions come forth. But Paul equally affirms our freedom in the face of sin, repeatedly assuring us that we can resist and overcome it by Christ dwelling in our hearts, by his spirit taking possession of us (Rom 8:1-17).

Original Sin

Since death was seen as a result of sin, and death is universal, Paul argued to the universality of sin, which he used as a foil to emphasize the new life brought by Christ. In contrast to Christ the source of life, he painted Adam as the cause of our sinful condition. This sinful condition into which all humans are born was described by later theology and Church teaching as *original sin,* and Genesis, chapter 3, was thought to be the biblical foundation for it. But scholars now admit that the third chapter of Genesis tells us nothing about what happened at the beginning of time, but is the story of what is happening all of the time. Instead of describing an historical first sin, it presents an ingeniously simple picture of what every sin really is: the human self-assertion of those who want to be God, who want to go their own way in deciding what is right and wrong. There was no Garden of Eden, but instead a beautiful picture of how God meant us to live, in harmony with ourselves and the surrounding world, in partnership with others, not ashamed of being fully known because we have nothing to hide, and enjoying intimacy with God walking with us in the Garden. Sin means saying No to all of this, and thus becoming alienated from our true selves, from our closest companions, from our environment which now seems hostile, and most of all from God, from whom we hide in guilt and shame. This kind of approach speaks to the condition of today's Christians. It makes sense of their experience, but especially it gives them consolation and hope. Our story begins, not with sin, but with God's infinite and intimate love, which we can never lose. Sin is something that happens along the way. In a sense it is statistically normal.

We can see our own personal struggle in the Genesis story, but we can also glimpse something of the universal sinful condition Paul describes when we look at the evil in the world: corruption, exploitation, torture, millions who die for lack of the simplest necessities, and the evil in ourselves: the aggression, hatred, vengeance, fear, and so many other forces that prevent us from reflecting the glory God intended. It is difficult to believe that the evil in the world is the result of one person's fault at the beginning of history. The genetic model developed by Augustine to explain the propagation of original sin is not credible in today's culture, particularly his bias against human sexuality. We need to remember that his theory is not part of Catholic faith. Theologians are looking for more meaningful models. Some link it to evolution, so that original sin is something flowing from the contingency and fallibility of human nature itself, part of the slow process of becoming human. This would mean that even the darker side of our nature has the potential for holiness, that anger and aggression and other primal instincts are not evil in themselves. The faith-core of the doctrine of original sin is that without grace no human being can rise to the level of existence God planned for us. Even with grace we will continually fail, because we are free, and grace will always respect our freedom. It is significant that the new rite of baptism no longer emphasizes liberation from original sin as the primary purpose of the sacrament, but initiation into the Christian community, incorporation into the holy body of Christ.

Personal Sin

It needs to be stressed that what theology calls original sin is not on the same level as the personal sins flowing from our own responsibility. Our personal sins can add to the general climate of sinfulness in the world and can poison the moral and physical atmosphere into which children are born, but we are responsible for them ourselves. We are the perpetrators of them rather than the victims of them. To cope with them, and to avoid them, we need to know what they are. The OT has several catalogues of sins (Deut 27:15-26; Amos 2:4-8; 8:4-6; Hos 4:2; Ezek 18:5-20). Jesus himself gives an abbreviated version of the Decalogue (Matt 10:18-19), and gives further examples of sinful behavior in his description of the Last Judgment (Matt 25:41-46). The NT has other lists (1 Cor 6:9-10; Gal 5:19-21; Rom 1:24-32; 1 Tim 1:4-11; 1 Pet 4:2-5; 2 Pet 2:12-22).

Degrees of Sin

It was always recognized that some sins are more serious than others. The early Church described idolatry, apostasy, murder, abortion, and publicly known adulterous relationship as "crimes, grave sins, capital sins," not so much because of the degree of personal guilt, but rather because they caused scandal and serious injury to the Church. The First Letter of John speaks of a deadly sin, one which leads to death, which probably refers to the "sin against the Holy Spirit," final impenitence, the attitude of one who simply refuses forgiveness. Later centuries refined the measuring process to produce the two categories of mortal and venial sin. Serious matter, full knowledge and full consent were necessary for mortal sin, and a lack of fullness in any of these three dimensions reduced the sin to venial. A sin was called "mortal" when it was serious enough to kill the life of the soul (leaving the sinner without sanctifying grace), and "venial" when it was less serious and could be easily forgiven (from the Latin *venia*).

This division was logical and was meant to be helpful to a penitent preparing for confession, but in practice it gave rise to considerable worry and anxiety and often led to scrupulosity. One of the confessor's duties was to help the penitent measure the gravity of his guilt. It is now realized that in the past moral theology and pastoral practice were too act-oriented. The biblical notion of sin and some insights from modern psychology have helped to change the focus, so that morality is now more person-centered. To know how one stands in terms of moral goodness more is needed than a simple check of single acts. It is a question of the whole pattern of our lives, the basic or fundamental option arising from the depth of conscience and directing our decisions and actions.

Though OT and NT make clear that individual actions can be sinful, the emphasis is more on sin as a basic attitude, a state of sinfulness, so that mortal sin is now seen as a state of mind and will, a way of life amounting to a total rejection of God, a condition of total selfishness, or in modern terms, a false fundamental option. Nowhere in the NT do we get a list of individual mortal sins meriting the punishment of hell or needing confession and special absolution, but the various sin-lists are warnings and indications as to the kind of behavior that can lead to the state of mortal sinfulness, to spiritual death. This is the area of mortal sin. But it does not follow that all the others are "only venial." As serious illness can lead to death, these so-called venial sins can be serious enough to lead to a break in our fundamental option towards God, to a change that is mortal. This newer approach may mean fewer individual mortal sins than earlier moralists assumed, but it need not lead to laxity. Today's Christians realize that it is no longer easy to determine mortal sin by "objective" criteria of the material action, though it remains true that certain kinds of behavior are seriously harmful. There is need for a new language and catechesis to avoid the one-sided, act-oriented approach of the past. Modern, educated and critical people are not helped in the formation of Christian conscience by misleading terms such as "objective sin," "intrinsic evil," obligation "under pain of sin." An action considered in the abstract may be bad, or evil, but only in a premoral sense; it cannot be labeled moral evil or sin until the whole person is considered in the context of understanding, intention, foreseen possible consequences and all the other circumstances that are required to assess moral responsibility. In the case of obligation, the law may stipulate a penalty to be paid for infringement, but it cannot be asserted in the abstract and absolutely that it is a sin to break the law, though it may well be a bad thing, an evil. It is essential that we keep a clear distinction between the objective and subjective dimensions.

Rahner, Häring, and other theologians remind us that it is not so simple to give clearcut answers to people whether they have committed mortal or "only" venial sins. The emphasis on person-centered morality should free us from an obsessive effort to find the borderline between mortal and venial sin, and free us too from the centuries-old misconception that in sexual morality everything is considered as "grave matter," with the automatic assumption of mortal sin.

New Sins

When sin was considered primarily as disobedience, examination of conscience, especially in preparation for confession, was simply a matter of checking our record in terms of the commandments of God and of the Church, and our duties of state. But when the concept of sin is broadened to include all the ways in which we can say No to God by saying No to life, to the world, to ourselves and others, it is not so easy to draw up a list. When sin is seen as the refusal to grow in humanity and into the likeness of Christ, how do we measure? When it is seen as inhumanity, as a violation of the dignity of the human person, how do we recognize what counts as sin? In how many ways can we be inhuman, to ourselves and to others? Honesty and justice are easily measured in one-to-one personal relations, but more difficult to assess in the world of corporate business. Simple business decisions taken for economic advantage can have disastrous social consequences, putting whole towns of people out of work. Sins of omission can also be extremely serious. Our basic option for the kingdom of God, for love, justice and peace, with a special concern for the poor and deprived, may be quite genuine and sincere, but are we not sinning in some sense when we allow this to atrophy through inaction, indifference? How many inhuman regimes in history have come to power through the inaction of good Christians who failed to see that politics is about the common good? The Nazi experience is only one example.

Pope John Paul II alerts us to the dehumanizing, and therefore sinful, effect that unjust and oppressive social structures can have on whole populations in his encyclical *Centesimus Annus:* "The decisions which create a human environment can give rise to specific structures of sin which impede the full realization of those who are in any way oppressed by them. To destroy such structures and replace them with more authentic forms of living in community is a task which demands courage and patience" (no. 38).

A further area for examination of conscience has been highlighted by women theologians who point to forms of sin which may be more peculiar to women than pride or the hunger for power: triviality, distractibility, and diffuseness; dependence on others for one's own self-definition; tolerance at the expense of standards of excellence; sentimentality, gossipy sociability, and mistrust of reason—in short, underdevelopment or negation of the self. For many women self-denial, giving up oneself, not wanting to have any real self, which often seem like virtues, are the real sins, because they are saying No to their own God-given self-worth.

The searchlight of conscience should not avoid the sins of the Church. If we seriously accept the Vatican II concept of the Christian community as both saved and sinners, we need to admit, accept, and repent of the sins that are committed by the Church and its officials against human freedom and human dignity, sins that are all the more serious for being done in the name of God. In the Gospels, the real sinners for Jesus were those members of the religious establishment who blinded themselves to his message, who arrogantly behaved as though God were their own private possession. Those who have great influence and authority in the Church have a heavy responsibility in how they use it. Does their leadership and administration free people to grow into the fullness of the maturity of Christ, or do they prefer to keep people passive and subservient? Do they listen to lay women and men who have the authority of knowledge and experience, and involve them in the common search for deeper truth, especially moral truth in the areas of sexuality, marriage, biotechnology? Are they insensitive to the suffering caused to conscientious dissenters by harsh treatment and sometimes injustice in official procedures? It is no service to the credibility of the Church to pretend that its structures and officials are beyond question.

If the Church wishes to awaken a healthy and fruitful sense of sin, it needs to abandon the legalism of the past and free itself from doctrines, practices, and structures which prevent the development of mature and free conscience. Sin is still important, but it should not be either trivialized or exaggerated. Most of all, it needs to be seen always in the context of God's infinite love and never-ending forgiveness and healing. A basic truth of faith is Paul's assurance that "Where sin increased, God's grace increased much more" (Rom 5:20). Indeed, when Paul reminded us that "all things work towards good for those who love God," Augustine added: "Yes, even sin."

SEÁN FAGAN, S.M.

See also CHRISTIAN MORALITY; ORIGINAL SIN; THEOLOGY, MORAL.

SIN, CONFESSION OF

See CONFESSION OF SIN.

SIN, ORIGINAL

See ORIGINAL SIN.

SISTERS OF MERCY

The Sisters of Mercy are a worldwide religious community of women, numbering over 15,000, who are devoted to serving the mission of the Roman Catholic Church. The initials "R.S.M." stand for "Religious Sisters of Mercy." Their foundress, Catherine

McAuley (1778–1841), an Irish woman, inaugurated the Institute in Dublin on 12 December 1831. The special talent or charism of the Sisters of Mercy is rooted in the gospel's portrayal of Jesus whose public ministry of teaching and healing gave evidence of his compassion for the poor, the sick, and the marginalized. The compassion of a merciful God is a constant theme throughout the OT and NT. Sisters of Mercy follow the example of Catherine, whose practical service for the needy and poor was marked by resourcefulness and a special concern for women. In addition to vows of chastity, poverty, and obedience, sisters make an additional vow to serve "the poor, the sick and the ignorant," to respond to those whose economic, health, and educational needs press most critically on society for relief.

This spirit was evident in Catherine's first institution. She used a large inheritance from her benefactors to finance her charitable works. The House of Mercy, which opened on Baggot Street in Dublin (24 September 1827) served a variety of needs. It provided housing for poor women from the country who came to Dublin to work. Economically vulnerable, they were often exploited by employers. Religious education and training in domestic skills were provided. Orphans and children of the poor were given shelter. In this house McAuley and her companions gathered for prayer; they went out to visit the sick in hospitals and the bedridden poor in their homes.

The establishment of the Sisters of Mercy was encouraged by Daniel Murray (1768–1852), archbishop of Dublin. The mobility needed to perform her services to the poor challenged Catherine to propose a rule which would free her community from the strictures of cloister. She chose to model her rule on that of the Sisters of the Presentation, founded by Nano Nagle. In this community she and two companions made their novitiate and took simple vows on 12 December 1831.

The newly established Sisters of Mercy used the chapter on "union and charity" as its guide until revisions of the Presentation Rule were completed. Catherine's original vision of expansion included autonomous foundations, all following the same rule, with Sisters united by a close spirit of friendship and charity. They came to be called the "walking nuns" because they were visible on the streets. The institute and its rule received formal approbation by Pope Gregory XVI (6 June 1841). At the time of her death (11 November 1841) Catherine had established twelve Mercy foundations in Ireland and two in England. These latter (Bermondsey, London, 1839, and Birmingham, 1841) were the first convents built in England following the Protestant Reformation. In 1854, Mercy Sisters from Ireland and England went to serve as nurses during the Crimean War.

The first American foundation was Pittsburgh (1843) by Sr. Frances Warde (1810–1884). The first in Australia was Perth (1846), with Adelaide later (1880) and New Zealand (1849). Sisters from Ireland had also settled in New York (1846) and San Francisco (1854). Buenos Aires (1856) was the first in South America; first in Central America was Belize (1883), followed by Jamaica in the Caribbean (1890) and Mafeking in South Africa (1897). The pattern of expansion was sometimes prompted by invitations of local bishops to attend the needs of the burgeoning population of poor communities created by emigration of laborers and their families in the nineteenth century. Sisters of Mercy opened schools, hospitals, and programs for the poor.

Especially after Vatican II, with a papal call for missionary outreach, U.S. regional communities started establishing new missions in Latin America and the Caribbean, forming ties with other Sisters of Mercy already in the area, as well as other religious communities.

In 1965, all U.S. congregations of Mercy, eighteen independent congregations and nine provinces, were affiliated within the Federation of the Sisters of Mercy of the Americas. The larger number of nine provinces had earlier been linked as the Sisters of Mercy of the Union (1929). In 1991, the Holy See approved the consolidation of the twenty-five regional communities in the U.S. as the Institute of the Sisters of Mercy of the Americas. At the inaugural event (20 July–4 August 1991) in Buffalo, New York, Doris Gottemoeller was elected the first president of the Institute. Its central office is in Silver Spring, Maryland.

Sisters of Mercy are centered in English-speaking countries and do not maintain a head office in Rome. Several hundred live and work in Spanish-speaking countries, in Central and South America, and the Philippines. Missionary work also involves projects in other countries. Around the world, there are nine institutes or federations of Mercy congregations. Sisters of Mercy of the Americas (7,400), Ireland (3,900), Australia (2,400), Great Britain (1,000), New Zealand (500), Newfoundland (200), South Africa (60), and Philippines (45).

Representative of service commitments in other countries, the "spiritual and corporal works of mercy" of the Sisters of Mercy in the U.S. include the sponsorship and co-sponsorship of 7 health care systems with 111 facilities in more than 100 cities, making them a leading health care provider. They sponsor 18 colleges and universities, in addition to

40 secondary schools. Forty percent of members are engaged in education, about 20 percent in health care, 16 percent in social work and housing, 9 percent in administration of parish services, with others in a diversity of works. These include congregational administration, geriatric care, political action, advocacy for women and children, staffing of shelters, soup kitchens, spiritual direction, art and music, counseling and prison ministry.

MARIE-ELOISE ROSENBLATT

See also McAULEY, CATHERINE; CATHOLICISM, IRISH; CORPORAL AND SPIRITUAL WORKS OF MERCY; RELIGIOUS ORDERS.

SITUATION ETHICS

Situation ethics is an understanding of morality which argues that the goodness or badness of an act is determined not by the kind of act itself, but by the context and circumstances in which the act is situated and by the intention of the agent. A reaction against legalism and moral absolutism, situation ethics emerged in the aftermath of World War II and was most prominent in the 1960s. It was strongly influenced by French existentialism and, to a lesser extent, postwar German nihilism.

In general, situation ethics rejects traditional notions of objectivity in ethics, especially ones founded on a natural law morality which attempts to anchor moral claims in a static, unchanging human nature. It saw such an essentialist ethic as being inadequate to the complexities and challenges of modern life. In place of universal norms and principles, the cornerstone of situation ethics is the individual conscience, unrestrained by law or custom, using its freedom to determine what ought to be done here and now. In this respect, the responsible moral agent is not one who takes refuge in the false security of moral codes and rules, but who risks the burdens and ambiguities of freedom as he or she struggles to live responsibly in the world. In 1952, Pope Pius XII condemned situation ethics as contrary to Catholic moral teaching. He charged it with encouraging moral relativism, subjectivism, and individualism.

Although there were many different versions of situation ethics, some secular and some religious, most held that there was one sovereign principle which ought to be determinative in helping a person decide what ought to be done. For instance, the most prominent and influential proponent of situation ethics in the United States, Joseph Fletcher, reduced all moral principles to love. Love was the only moral absolute, the only universal and always relevant principle of Christian ethics. In every instance, Fletcher argued, one is obliged to do whatever is most loving. Other principles and rules may illumine a situation and offer guidance, but only love is intrinsically good and binding. Similarly, Fletcher made law subservient to love. Laws were to be heeded if they served love; however, when laws conflicted with love, love overruled law.

At its best, situation ethics recognized that adequate moral analysis demands looking at more than the physical act itself. It worked to broaden the scope of moral evaluation by including in the description of an act not only the kind of act involved, but also the circumstances surrounding it, the intention of the agent, and the foreseeable consequences. In this respect, its criticism of moral absolutes and traditional notions of intrinsically evil acts reflected not a slide into relativism and subjectivism, but a realization that moral appraisal involves a whole complex of factors traditional morality often overlooked. Thus, more moderate forms of situation ethics did not reject moral principles and rules, but tried to discern their relationship to the equally important factors of circumstances, context, and situation.

There are several positive contributions of situation ethics which need to be noted. First, historically, the development of situation ethics represented a shift from a rigidly deductive method of moral reasoning in which all conclusions were derived from universal general principles, to an inductive method in which moral obligations emerged from history, experience, and relationships. This is often described as the move from a classicist worldview to one marked by historical consciousness. In the first, moral truth is universal, absolute, and unchanging. Fixed moral principles yield eternally valid conclusions. There is little room in the classicist worldview for exceptions or modifications in light of varying historical or cultural factors. By contrast, the historically conditioned worldview stresses the provisional nature of human knowledge. It begins not with abstract principles, but with concrete, particular experiences. Unlike the deductive method of the classicist worldview, its conclusions are often tentative and open to revision in light of new evidence and experiences.

Secondly, situation ethics recognizes what is distinctive to ethics as a practical, instead of theoretical, science. It appreciates that ethics deals with concrete, particular actions that ought to be done in the complex, unique circumstances of life. Moral absolutism misconstrues what is unique to moral reasoning because it forgets that the moral good is always specific, concrete, and contingent, a matter of deliberation and studied reflection. The responsible moral agent is not someone who unthinkingly follows laws and rules, but one who apprises a situation carefully, weighs the values at stake in it, and decides prudently.

Third, situation ethics appreciates that the singlemost important criterion in ethical assessment ought to be the overall good of persons. Determining this demands looking not only at the physical act itself, but seeing it in relation to circumstances, intentions, and consequences. Circumstances are all the factors surrounding an act that are morally relevant because they affect the meaning of the act, sometimes changing the nature of an act. An appreciation of circumstances enables one to see how the setting or context of an act must be incorporated into its moral meaning. To abstract an act from its circumstances is not only to misunderstand what an act is, but also to forget that the moral quality of an act in some way is derived from its circumstances. Similarly, adequate moral assessment must pay attention to the intention of the agent because it is the intention which gives birth to an action, shapes it, and directs it to its end. Consequences must also be incorporated into the evaluation of an action because often it is only in light of foreseeable consequences that one can ascertain whether a particular action will serve or hinder human well-being.

Fourth, more moderate forms of situation ethics acknowledge the important but limited role of moral rules and principles. They recognize that rules are made to apply to a wide array of situations. The rules presume that the situations are similar in morally relevant ways, but it is sometimes the case that there are important moral differences among them. Rules and laws are formulated generally and cannot capture every morally relevant difference. They must admit of exceptions because they are not perfectly adequate to the complexities of life. In its rejection of legalism, situation ethics does not dismiss rules and principles, but calls attention to their limits. They do not of themselves disclose the truth, but are helpful in discovering it. In this respect, situation ethics echoes Thomas Aquinas's remark that the more concrete and particular the situation, the less perfectly will the rule or principle apply (ST, I-II, q. 94, a. 4). Too, in its rejection of legalism and extreme moral absolutism, situation ethics is related to the Catholic tradition of casuistry, a method of moral decision-making made popular by the Jesuits in the sixteenth and seventeenth centuries. Casuistry was a case method of moral evaluation which said the moral good could be determined neither by rules nor circumstances alone, but by each interacting with the other.

Fifth, situation ethics has a deep respect for the role of individual conscience and responsibility in moral decision-making. Although this emphasis on conscience could lead to subjectivism and relativism, its concern is to make room in moral analysis for personal insight, intuitions, and discernment as people struggle to fathom the call of God and the working of the Spirit in their lives. It stresses that every moral obligation cannot be captured in a preexisting rule or law, but sometimes is the result of an inner conviction about what a situation demands or what God might be asking one to do.

Despite its strengths, there are several significant weaknesses to situation ethics. First, its tendency to reduce all moral principles to one is simplistic. Morality is too rich, complex, and varied to be guided adequately by a single sovereign principle. Different principles call attention to different dimensions of the moral life which cannot be overlooked. Secondly, the opposition it establishes between persons and rules forgets that moral rules and principles are not meant to oppress or harm persons, but to protect them; a legitimate moral principle does not destroy human well-being but preserves it. Third, situation ethics has a high estimation of a person's capacity to discern adequately what a situation involves and to calculate the consequences of an action. It presupposes and depends on an individual's ability to see clearly the values and disvalues present in a situation, how they are related, and what a fitting response would be. Its relative optimism about human nature and its moral capacities overlooks human finitude and minimizes the effects and presence of sin, especially original sin and how this can be manifested in rationalization and self-deception. Finally, while situation ethicists appreciate what is unique and morally relevant to situations, they fail to see the continuities and similarities among situations which moral rules and principles address.

PAUL WADELL

See also THEOLOGY, MORAL.

"SLAIN IN THE SPIRIT"

The relatively modern expression for a phenomenon of Pentecostal and charismatic prayer services where believers, singly or in groups, fall backward into the arms of an usher in an apparent "faint," which may last from a few seconds to hours. Subjects report deep spiritual effects and a general euphoria. In Catholic circles, it is more generally known as "resting in the Spirit." Sociologists of religion prefer to name it as "possession trance"; scholars within the charismatic tradition acknowledge that it may have a double source: the action of God and autosuggestion or response to peer pressure. Defenders of the authenticity of the experience point to scriptural warrants (e.g., Matt 17:1-6; 28:1-4), the ecstasies recorded in the passions of early martyrs, and entries in Wesley's *Journals,* but evidence for the Spirit's presence in the phenomenon is inconclusive.

MARY BARBARA AGNEW, C.PP.S.

See also CHARISMATIC MOVEMENT; PENTECOSTALISM.

SLAVERY

The social institution of slavery enabled one person to acquire ownership and free disposition of another person. It conjures up images of cruel treatment of powerless individuals according to the whim of their master. In the biblical world, however, slavery had a broad range of meanings from oppressive bondage to a secure but dependent condition as part of an extended family. A slave might be a skilled and trusted manager of a master's affairs, and it was customary to refer to an officer of the royal court as a slave of the king. In the Hebrew Scriptures a single word is used to refer to all these various situations and so it is often not completely certain what precise meaning the author wishes to give the term. When it describes someone subjected to a harsh and demeaning way of life, the word is usually translated into English as "slave," and when it signifies someone who belongs to and is dedicated to a master, it is rendered "servant."

For example, in Egypt the Israelites were said to be slaves. After their liberation, they belonged to God, and so God refers to them as "my servants" (Lev 25:55). Prophets like Jeremiah (25:4) and Amos (3:7) were called servants, too, as was the mysterious figure in Isaiah 40–55, who is referred to as the Servant of the Lord.

A similar broad range of meanings is associated with the Greek word *doulos* used by the New Testament authors. The term "slave" has acquired such offensive overtones that the Greek word is usually translated "servant," possibly with some loss of the meaning intended by the author. For example, the early Christian hymn quoted by Paul in Philippians makes the point that in his incarnation Christ gave up every honor which belonged to him by right and "emptied himself, taking the form of a *doulos*" (2:7). The meaning is best kept here by using the word "slave." This may also be the case in John's Gospel when Jesus performed the task of a slave by washing the feet of his disciples. He wished to teach them the lesson that, if he their master washed their feet, they should wash the feet of one another, since "a slave is not greater than his master" (13:16).

Sometimes the text makes it quite clear that the author intends the meaning "slave." Jesus is described as responding to signs of ambition among his disciples by declaring: "Whoever would be great among you must be your servant (*diakonos*) and whoever would be first among you must be slave (*doulos*) of all" (Mark 10:43-44).

Pauline letters present the picture of the gospel being preached in the Greco-Roman world where the institution of slavery was unquestioned. Paul calls himself a slave (or servant) of Jesus Christ (Rom 1:1) and of God (Titus 1:2), and tells slaves who became Christians that they have been "bought with a price" and each has become a freedman of the Lord (1 Cor 7:22-23), whereas, if their master becomes a Christian, he becomes a "slave of Christ" (1 Cor 7:22). In saying this, Paul made it plain that he considered one's social status of no consequence in comparison with one's relationship to God in Christ, in whom there is "neither slave nor free" (Gal 3:28). Consequently, he could urge slaves to be obedient to their masters and masters to treat their slaves with kindness (Eph 6:5-9; Col 3:22).

But the language of master/slave is not suitable for expressing what is dearest to Paul's heart. For that he shifts to the couplet slavery/freedom. He refers to life under the Law as slavery (Gal 4:24) and distinguishes "the spirit of slavery" from "the spirit of sonship," for all are children of God, "and if children, then heirs, heirs of God and fellow heirs with Christ" (Rom 8:15-17).

Paul so loves the language of freedom that he goes on to express his belief that "creation itself will be set free from its bondage to decay and obtain the glorious liberty of the children of God" (Rom 8:21).

And yet, the institution of slavery persisted for many centuries. The slave trade which began in the sixteenth century resulted in over fifteen million black Africans being transported to the Western hemisphere to provide cheap labor in agriculture and mines. This practice was gradually eliminated during the nineteenth century and, finally, in 1948 the United Nations General Assembly adopted as part of the Universal Declaration of Human Rights the following principle: "No one shall be held in slavery or servitude; slavery and the slave trade shall be prohibited in all their forms." The evil so dramatically shown in slavery, however, continues to exist in other guises: economic bondage, forced labor, exploitation of children, and the "domestic slavery" of women.

WILLIAM C. McFADDEN, S.J.

See also HUMAN RIGHTS.

SMITH, ALFRED E. (1873–1944)

Governor of New York and presidential candidate, Alfred Emmanuel Smith was born on the lower east side of Manhattan on 30 December 1873 and died in New York City on 4 October 1944. Forced to leave school at the age of thirteen because of his father's death, Smith joked that he was a graduate of the Fulton Fish Market. He entered Tammany Hall politics in 1895 as a server of jury notices and was elected to the New York State Assembly in 1903 where he built a reputation as a supporter of progressive social legislation. After serving as sheriff of New York County and chairman of the board of Alderman of New York City, Smith was elected governor of the state in 1918. Defeated for reelection in 1920, he was again elected governor in 1922, 1924, and 1926. His administrations were noteworthy for administrative reform, aid to education and social services, and support of low-rent housing and public recreational facilities.

Alfred E. Smith

Unsuccessful in obtaining the Democratic nomination for president in 1924, Smith won his party's nomination in 1928—the first Catholic to do so—but went down to overwhelming defeat at the hands of Herbert Hoover in a campaign marred by widespread anti-Catholic bigotry. In a famous 1927 *Atlantic Monthly* article (ghostwritten by Father Francis P. Duffy of World War I fame), Smith declared his commitment to religious liberty and freedom of conscience. In the 1930s Smith became disenchanted with the domestic policies of Franklin D. Roosevelt but supported his foreign policy in World War II. In recognition of Smith's role as an exemplary Catholic layman, the University of Notre Dame awarded him the *Laetare* medal in 1929, and Pope Pius XI made him a papal chamberlain in 1939.

THOMAS J. SHELLEY

See also AMERICAN CATHOLICISM; CHURCH AND STATE; RELIGIOUS FREEDOM.

SOCIAL JUSTICE

See SOCIAL TEACHING OF THE CHURCH.

SOCIAL RESPONSIBILITY, FINANCIAL

An important aspect of social responsibility, i.e., taking responsibility for the common good, is recognizing the way in which our actions, often without our being aware of their social consequences, affect the common good. Thus, for example, when making decisions about where to bank, what products to purchase, or what stocks to invest in, we tend to consider such things as convenience, percentage of return, and price. But, we tend not to take into account the impact, for example, that the lending policy of a bank has on a community or the presence of a company in a poor country has in supporting unjust economic structures.

Taking social responsibility into account in banking, purchasing, and investing does not mean that there are not other types of responsibility at stake as well. Those charged with investing and banking the funds of an organization have a fiduciary responsibility to insure that the funds are safe and offer an appropriate return. Those charged with purchasing products have responsibility to buy goods that are effective and appropriately priced. But, whatever actions are taken have social implications; and social responsibility means factoring those implications explicitly in whatever decisions are made.

Factoring social responsibility in decisions about banking, purchasing, and investing does not mean that an individual or an organization should be involved only with banks and companies that have perfect records. At issue is working in a less than perfect world to advance the cause of justice incrementally. Nor does factoring social responsibility into decisions mean that an individual should be involved in every cause. It is important that energies be focused on a limited set of issues.

Acting out of a concern for the social responsibility of a bank or business can take different forms: (1) bringing concerns to their attention through letters or face-to-face discussions; (2) limiting or ruling out involvement because of concerns related to social responsibility.

Acting out of a concern for social responsibility can take many different forms in investing: (1) bringing concerns to a company's attention through letters or face-to-face discussions; (2) taking social concerns into account in voting proxies; (3) sponsoring or co-sponsoring stockholder resolutions; (4) setting up criteria to identify companies or areas of the economy in which no investments will be made and/or present investments sold.

Taking social responsibility into account in investing can also take the form of alternative investments. Alternative investments are loans made either directly or through intermediaries to groups involved in community development (e.g., through construction of low-income housing or developing of minority businesses) who are unable to gain access to capital through normal channels.

THOMAS SCHINDLER

See also SOCIAL TEACHING OF THE CHURCH.

SOCIAL TEACHING OF THE CHURCH

In its popular sense, the social teaching of the Church is that body of teaching or collection of teachings on the human person and the human community derived primarily from conciliar, papal, and episcopal documents. In its broadest sense, it also includes the writings of theologians and other scholars who develop, comment on, and draw applications from that teaching.

The basic Christian ethical question is: "How ought human beings, gifted and graced by God in Christ, to live their lives as individuals and in society?" Christian social teaching advances beyond simply "living in society" to the "building of a more just society." It deals with the equitable, just, and peaceful organization of society in its major components (global, international, and national) and its smaller components (regional, provincial, and local). Church authorities promulgate social teaching in the face of political, governmental, economic, and cultural policies and practices which undermine and threaten a Christian understanding of personal dignity, family life, religious conduct, and purposeful living in community and society.

Modern social teaching is dated from Pope Leo XIII's *Rerum Novarum* in 1891. Drawing upon the philosophy of Thomas Aquinas, he places the foundation of social teaching in the proper metaphysical understanding of the human being, created by God, not only rational and free, but also by nature social. From this can be deduced what is worthy or unworthy of human beings in their relationship to God and to one another in a well-ordered society. Rights and duties flow from the correct understanding of the human person: ownership and management's concern for the safety and welfare of workers, the payment of a just wage, and the provision of means for living in "frugal comfort"; the workers' right to organize into unions to secure their proper needs and dignity; and the state's obligation to protect the rights of workers in securing the common good. These are specific conclusions from general natural law principles.

The social teachings of pre-Vatican II popes were based primarily upon a metaphysical or essentialist social philosophy. Both an antipathy against and a distrust of empirical social sciences were present because of their claims to be philosophies in their own right, but information from social sciences, critically examined, was not excluded. The proper philosophical understanding of the human being, interpreted authentically by the magisterium of the Church, would yield the foundational principles for a more just and humane society. There was very little drawn from the scriptural and theological tradition of the Church.

Vatican II, corrective of longstanding Platonic-Augustinian dualism and its harsh dichotomies, developed a dialogical approach toward the understanding of the human person and the world. The source of human dignity is in the human person's "call to communion with God" (19). The growth of Christ's kingdom contributes to earthly progress and the better ordering of human society contributes to the kingdom of God (39). The foundation for social teaching is now solidly theological. The 1971 Synod of Bishops states: "Action on behalf of justice and participation in the transformation of the world fully appear to us as a constitutive dimension of the preaching of the Gospel, or, in other words, of the Church's mission for the redemption of the human race and its liberation from every oppressive situation." An embodiment of the theological bases of social teachings is liberation theology in Latin America, Africa, and Asia.

The key theological themes of the modern social teaching of the Church are solidarity, personalism, and subsidiarity.

The foundation of solidarity is the doctrine that the one God is the Creator of all that exists, above all, the Creator of the one human family. Humanity is one in sin and one in the redemptive grace of Christ. In the solidarity of the human species, all are brothers and sisters. As Ambrose (397) taught, it is not right that what God intended as the common possession of all should be made the possession of a few. Thomas Aquinas (1274) affirmed the right to own property, but in human need property becomes the possession of all. The right of individuals to own property has been constantly affirmed. Communism and socialism have been condemned for denying that right. But human solidarity may also call for public ownership of certain types of productive goods and it demands the recognition of a "social function inherent in the right of private ownership." Human solidarity, above all, requires the addressing of not only the inequities between rich and poor, but also between rich and poor nations and between the developed and developing nations. The solidarity of the human species demands, as John XXIII taught, that every nation seeking its own common good also seek a "universal common good." The "unity of the human family" makes the social question worldwide.

Flowing from the theme of solidarity is the preferential option for the poor, a concept developed by the bishops of Latin America and incorporated into papal social teaching. The poor, wherever they are in the world, are equal members of the common human family and therefore must have access to all the means necessary for living in human dignity. The very presence of the poor in the midst of any people is a sign of the rupture of the bonds of solidarity.

Another corollary of solidarity is the principle of participation not only in political life but also in economic life. Unrestrained access to a secret ballot in free elections is a primary sign of political participation; the implementation of the right to suitable and gainful employment which enables people to take control of their own lives is the primary sign of adequate participation in economic life.

A second theme is a personalism delineated by Pope John XXIII in *Peace on Earth* (1963) and developed in Vatican II. All human persons, as children of God in the world, have personal, social, and instrumental rights which must be secured to live according to the standards appropriate to human dignity. Political, social, and economic institutions are to be judged by what they do to and for people. The U.S. Bishops' pastoral letter, *Economic Justice for All* (1986) echoes Vatican II's teaching that the human person is "the source, the center, and the purpose of all socio-economic life." Pope John Paul II's *On Human Work* (1981) teaches that the chief value of labor is that it is done by a human person. The dignity of work should be sought primarily in its "subjective dimension."

The third major theme is subsidiarity. Initiated as a social justice principle by Pope Pius XI, subsidiarity became a governing principle in the teaching of John XXIII for the balancing of the universal common good and individual and community rights: "Just as it is wrong to withdraw from the individual and commit to the community at large what private enterprise and endeavor can accomplish, so it is likewise unjust and a gravely harmful disturbance of right order to turn over to the greater society of higher rank functions and services which can be performed by lesser bodies on a lower plane. For a social undertaking . . . ought to aid the members of the body social, but never destroy or absorb them."

Subsidiarity is a basic principle of social teaching with a solid foundation in the theology of the Christian biblical and patristic tradition. Subsidiarity calls for the maximization of participation in decision-making at every level of society. Human beings tend to be more responsible in smaller organizations than in larger; they tend to cooperate more closely in smaller units (the village, neighborhood, tribe, family) than in larger; and they tend to be more creative and efficient as they undertake enterprises which are more immediately their own. The formation of small ecclesial communities is an example of the effectiveness of the principle of subsidiarity when even the poor become "empowered to take charge of their own future and become responsible for their own economic advancement."

John Paul II's *On Social Concern* reintroduces the term "social doctrine." Theologians question the use of that term if it means a body of teaching built up by the papal magisterium of the Catholic Church over the last hundred years. Theological analysis prefers the development of themes which have arisen because of the need of the Church to apply gospel teachings to social situations.

Paul VI stated: "In the face of such widely varying situations it is difficult for us to utter a unified message and to put forward a solution which has universal validity. Such is not our ambition, nor is it our mission." This allows an active role for local regions and local communities in analyzing the objectivity of their situation, "to shed on it the light of the Gospel's unalterable words and to draw principles of reflection, norms of judgment, and directives for action from the social teaching of the Church."

There is a developing but not yet unified core of papal social teachings. It is the responsibility and the competence of the local Churches, listening to those teachings and at the same time addressing their own unique needs, to search for the best means to bring about their various and complex implementations. The social teachings of the Church offer a forum for dialogue between Catholics and the people of the larger society around them to seek the means to pursue equity, justice, and peace for all the peoples of the world.

CHARLES D. SKOK

See also ENCYCLICALS, SOCIAL; VIRTUE.

SOCIALISM

Socialism is the term used for a variety of political and economic systems or movements which favor the social nature of human beings over their individuality and which emphasize duties toward people as members of a community or social body over personal independence and individual freedom and private gain. In this broad perspective there is a certain affinity of Christian social movements and Christian social doctrine to at least certain moderate forms of socialism.

Socialist movements have arisen historically as a criticism of the inequities in society caused by unrestrained laissez-faire capitalism or the opulence of royal or ruling classes with the resulting poverty of the masses of people. Although some socialist movements were Christian in origin, more often their leaders were atheistic and anti-Christian, protesting not only the social situation of the time but also the Church as a presumed accomplice in an acquiescence to those unjust conditions.

Socialism has received severe condemnation by the Church. Pope Leo XIII saw socialism as an all-encompassing system which takes away the God-given right of individuals to own property by giving common ownership to the state. This would cause the sources of wealth to dry up, industriousness and talent to lie unused, and misery to become the condition of all. By supplanting the role of parents in the lives of children, the state, intruding into family life itself, would threaten the very existence of the family. Socialism is condemned as against the law of nature.

Although Pope Pius XI issued a strong condemnation of unrestrained free competition in capitalism and its economic domination, and softened Leo XIII's right to private property by allowing state ownership of certain forms of property, he issued an even stronger condemnation of Communist socialism with its merciless class warfare and its abolition of all private ownership. He acknowledged less radical forms of socialism and praised some of its goals, but he still condemned it as hostile to religion and false in its conception of human nature and human society. Socialism's vision was limited too much to material well-being in this world attained by imposing a system of collective or governmental ownership of the means of production and distribution of goods and services, without a regard for God, the religious and spiritual nature of people, and a sufficient concern for individual freedom. He concluded that no one could be a sincere Catholic and a true socialist at the same time.

Later developments in Church documents are much more open to mitigated forms of socialism. Pope John XXIII calls for state intervention, according to the principle of subsidiarity, to address imbalances in the economy and to remedy the differences in economic prosperity among various peoples. The state must play its part in securing the common good of all, not just the advantage of the few. Too much state control stifles creativity and enterprise; too little state control leads to exploitation and poverty. John XXIII's term is "socialization." All people desire to enjoy the results of the "multiplication of social relationships" brought about by economic and cultural development. They want to have access to and share in the services and advantages of education, health care, housing, leisure, recreation, and all the goods of society. Vatican II continued John XXIII's view of "socialization." Economic life should mitigate social inequalities, not exacerbate them.

A Christian form of socialism would demand a balance between autonomous and active collaboration of individuals and groups and timely intervention and direction on the part of public authority. The dignity of the individual human person with personal rights and duties must always remain in place; at the same time the common good and the common welfare of all must be sought. The collectivity must not be exalted over the individual nor must individuality be exalted over the collectivity. Society does not exist for itself but for its members, nor do its members exist only for themselves but for society in its common good.

Marxist Communism, constantly condemned by the Church, has fallen in Russia and Eastern Europe. Its radical, atheistic socialism as a philosophy and political system has been inextricably discredited. Catholic social teaching has the task of shaping a new "socialization" upon the sound principles of the Christian understanding of the dignity of the human person as a full participant in the politics, economics, and culture of human society.

CHARLES D. SKOK

See also ENCYCLICALS, SOCIAL; SOCIAL TEACHING OF THE CHURCH.

SOCIETY OF FRIENDS (QUAKERS)

The Society of Friends was formed by George Fox (1624–1691), a devout English nonconformist who was dissatisfied with what he perceived to be the inauthentic piety of the Churches of his day and their propensity to fight wars in the name of religious truth. He lived during the Thirty Years War which was fought in Europe and the Puritan Revolution in England led by Oliver Cromwell.

The word "Quaker" was originally a pejorative title and derived from the fact that George Fox and some of his closest followers would "quake" at the word of God.

Fox's own intense religious experience in 1646 convinced him that an Inner Light, a Voice of God, a Divine Spark, dwells within each person. This distinctive Quaker belief had several implications for Fox's alternative vision for sixteenth-century English Protestantism; it was, in general, a third way between Roman Catholicism and Protestantism. Furthermore: (1) It provided a source of spiritual assurance for the believer. (2) It suggested a more positive view of human nature than the prevailing Calvinist notion of human depravity. (3) The Inner Light gave a sense of mystical immediacy between the person and God and bypassed the regular religious channels of authority, e.g., revelation, Church, and Bible. (4) With its focus on the God within, Quakers developed a simple pattern of devotion and worship which excluded hymns, ritual, sacraments, clergy, and other external religious expression. The interior life was given priority and legitimacy. (5) The Inner Light of God in each person radically democratized membership in the Quaker meeting as well as beyond it. All people were equal, other religious points of view were tolerated, and every individual was treated with dignity. (6) Finally, there is a direct line from this spirituality to their extraordinary concern for peace, justice, and social equality. It is not permissible to take another's life if God resides in that life. Nonviolence, conscientious objection to war, and a quiet witness for peace are at the center of Quaker Christianity. As a result, most people hear about Quakers through the relief work and pacifist activity of The American Friends Service Committee.

Quakers have had an influence on American history out of all proportion to their size. William Penn (1644–1718), a Quaker, founded the state of Pennsylvania on the basis of the Friends' notions of freedom of conscience and religious toleration. Everyone was free to worship God according to his or her own beliefs. Penn got along well with the American Indians as depicted in each of the Quaker-Preacher artist Edward Hicks' "Peaceable Kingdom" paintings.

John Woolman (1720–1772), another Quaker, was part of the underground railroad, and spoke out against slavery. Quakers, historically, have also been strong supporters of women's rights.

Quaker worship reacts against any formal approach to God and is a silent meeting with worshipers speaking only when moved by the Spirit. Their meeting houses are plain and simple as compared to the "steeple houses" of traditional denominations. Quakers tend to make decisions by a process known as the "sense of the meeting." It is a consensual method for decision-making rather than the usual majority/minority vote in which often some people feel slighted.

Quakers have founded several fine colleges, among them Swarthmore and Haverford, and continue to produce inspiring writers such as famous twentieth-century mystics Rufus Jones, Douglas Steere, and Thomas Kelly. There are about 250,000 in the world and approximately 110,000 in the United States.

IRA ZEPP

See also CHRISTIAN SPIRITUALITY; HUMAN RIGHTS; PACIFISM.

SOCIETY OF JESUS (JESUITS)

In 1534 St. Ignatius of Loyola, a Basque and former soldier, gathered in Paris with St. Francis Xavier and five others to take private vows of poverty and chastity. They hoped to work in the Holy Land, but, this not being possible, they went to Rome and put themselves at the disposal of the pope. As their numbers increased, Ignatius submitted to the pope a summary of their ideals: they would not chant a common Office; they would work for the advance of souls in Catholic doctrine and life; they would vow to go anywhere in the world at the pope's behest. On 27 September 1540, Pope Paul III issued the bull *Regimini militantis ecclesiae,* canonically establishing the Society of Jesus.

Ignatius was elected first "general" in 1541 and set about writing constitutions. These and his *Spiritual Exercises* would later serve as models for the constitutions and spirituality of many religious congregations. Soon Jesuits were established in the major cities of Italy and spread through Portugal, Spain, France, Germany and the Low Lands. The Jesuits first became involved in education in Messina, Sicily, and in 1551 opened the Roman College—soon to be called the Gregorian University. When Ignatius died in 1556 there were 938 Jesuits and Jesuit missionaries had traveled to Japan, Malaysia, India, the Congo, and Brazil. Ignatius was succeeded by Diego Laynez and then St. Francis Borgia. By 1580 there were 5000 Jesuits with 144 colleges.

In their preaching and mission work Jesuits made wide use of the printing press, religious art, music, drama, baroque architecture, and invented the lantern slide. Kircher, Boscovich and Clavius were distinguished mathematicians. In Europe, Jesuits became confessors to kings and Jesuit schools were centers of the Counter Reformation. North America had Jesuit explorers like Kino and Marquette and martyr-saints like Isaac Jogues and John de Brébeuf. At the court of the Chinese emperor, Valignano and Ricci adopted Chinese ways with great success (later largely undone in a controversy over modifications in liturgy). In North and South America Jesuits organized large numbers of Indians into almost one hundred thriving communities (largely undone as European powers coveted the land). In 1759 Portugal confiscated Jesuit property and expelled 1100 Jesuits, while others died in prison. They were expelled from France in 1764 and Spain in 1767. Under pressure from the Bourbons and the Jansenists, Pope Clement XIV signed a brief suppressing the order in 1773. An inconsistent policy of promulgation and enforcement led to much confusion. Catherine the Great refused promulgation in White Russia and Pius VI approved of the situation in 1801. Former Jesuits began renewing their vows and Pius VII restored the Society in 1814.

A movement away from monarchy and Church authority had transformed Europe and the new Jesuits did not easily adjust. But they flourished in the United States where presently there are twenty-eight Jesuit-related colleges or universities (notably: Georgetown, Fordham, Boston College, Loyola, and Marquette). In 1964 there were almost 36,000 Jesuits worldwide. With the changes in the Church and religious life started by Vatican II, Jesuit numbers have diminished to about 25,000. Noted recent Jesuits would include Gerard Manley Hopkins (poet), Pierre Teilhard de Chardin (paleontologist and philosopher), Karl Rahner, Bernard Lonergan, and Henri de Lubac (theologians). Others have been active as social reformers.

Supreme Jesuit authority is vested in a general congregation—which meets only to elect a new general or deal with other matters of great moment. The general serves for life, has extensive power, and is the only elected officer. Training today involves a two-year novitiate followed by perpetual vows, two years of philosophy, two years of active work (mostly teaching), and four years of theology. The Jesuit motto is *Ad Majorem Dei Gloriam*—To the Greater Glory of God.

THOMAS M. KING, S.J.

See also BELLARMINE, ROBERT; CATHOLIC HIGHER EDUCATION IN THE UNITED STATES; FRANCIS XAVIER, ST.; HOPKINS, GERARD MANLEY; IGNATIUS OF LOYOLA, ST.; LONERGAN, BERNARD, S.J.; LUBAC, HENRI DE; NORTH AMERICAN MARTYRS; RAHNER, KARL; RICCI, MATTEO; SPIRITUAL EXERCISES OF ST. IGNATIUS OF LOYOLA; TEILHARD DE CHARDIN, PIERRE.

SOCIOLOGY OF RELIGION

The sociology of religion studies religion as a social phenomenon: its social cohesion and internal organization and its relation to the society in which it exists.

The Paradox of the Sociology of Religion

Inspired by a secular faith in science and evolution, nineteenth-century sociologists (A. Comte, K. Marx, H. Spencer) entertained a reductionist understanding of religion: they saw religion as an irrational human projection at odds with scientific reason. Even in the twentieth century, important sociologists (E. Durkheim, M. Weber, P. Berger, B. Wilson) maintained the so-called theory of secularization: they saw a contradiction between traditional religion and modern rationality, and hence believed that the spread of industrialization would inevitably secularize society. M. Weber, though secular in outlook, lamented the decline of religion.

The paradox of the sociology of religion is that some of the same thinkers also recognized important social functions exercised by religion: stabilizing, developing, and even reforming society. A. Comte and E. Durkheim argued that the Christian religion would eventually be replaced by a secular form of worship, celebrating the values to which modern society was committed. This positive evaluation of religion is pursued in Talcott Parsons' sociological synthesis that recognizes the integrating role of religious values, in Andrew Greeley's analysis of the success of American religion organized in denominational form, and in Robert Bellah's hypothesis of American "civil religion." In a similar vein, Peter Berger's social theory proposes that to be stable society needs "a sacred canopy" and that as traditional religion declines, this sacred service will be rendered by social science or, worse, by secular ideologies.

The Christian Reaction to the Sociology of Religion

In the nineteenth and early twentieth century Christian theologians reacted negatively to the sociology of religion. They objected to the scientific-positivistic study of humans and their society. They disagreed with the evolutionary perspective. They rejected the use of the scientific method (valid for the natural sciences) in the study of human beings, that is to say the quantification of the human data, the assumption that there were discoverable, necessary laws of human behavior, and the aim of making infallible scientific predictions. Christian thinkers defended human spirit and human freedom, and affirmed the transrational reality of God.

With Max Weber at the turn of the century and with his followers, sociology became more modest, ceased imitating the natural sciences, and developed an appropriate methodology that respected human freedom and did not reduce religion to a human projection. The first major (Protestant) theological study of Christian history that used Weber's sociology of religion was done by Ernst Troeltsch, whose historical work has demonstrated that implicit in the teaching and spirituality of every Christian community throughout the ages were a social ethic and an outlook on society. In the thirties, the Catholic sociologist, Gabriel Le Bras, the founder of *la sociologie religieuse,* engaged in sociological research of French parish life in order to propose to the Church more adapted forms of pastoral ministry.

In the United States

Since the dominant sociology in the United States up to World War II reflected a positivistic and evolutionary stance, American Catholics engaged in what they called "Catholic sociology," which reflected a concept of the human and a vision of society taken from Catholic social teaching. In 1940 they founded the American Catholic Sociological Society and *American Catholic Sociological Review.* When, in the 1950s the important American sociologist, Talcott Parsons, produced a functionalist sociology that acknowledged the irreplaceable social function of culture and religion, Catholics began to shed their aloofness, studied the sociology of religion in cooperation with secular scholars, and abandoned the idea of a Catholic sociology. In 1960 they renamed their society, Association for the Sociology of Religion (ASR) and their review, *Social Analysis.* Since then Catholics have produced important studies in the sociology of religion. What Catholic scholars bring to the sociology of religion is a special sensitivity toward the phenomenon of religion and an experiential knowledge of what it means to be a member of a religious community.

Of great importance is the role sociology has begun to play in Catholic and Protestant theology. Sociology provides theologians with a critical understanding of their own social context and that of their Church, and sociology reveals to them the social implications present in all expressions of religion, including doctrine, liturgy, and spirituality.

GREGORY BAUM

See also CHURCH AND STATE.

SODALITY

An alternative name for a confraternity. Sometimes one and sometimes the other name is used in the official titles of these lay associations, but sodality is more often used for an association connected with Our Lady (Children of Mary).

JOAN GLAZIER

See also CONFRATERNITY; LAITY, THEOLOGY OF THE.

SON OF GOD

See NAMES OF JESUS IN THE NEW TESTAMENT.

SON OF MAN

See NAMES OF JESUS IN THE NEW TESTAMENT.

SOTERIOLOGY

Etymologically, soteriology means the doctrine of salvation. In Christian theology, it concerns Jesus' accomplishment of God's saving plan for humanity. In the recent past, this doctrine of Christ's work was separated from the doctrine of his person (Christology). Contemporary theology has overcome this dichotomy and tends to elaborate Christology and soteriology as two sides of the one reality. In other words, Jesus is who he is because of what he did, and what he did he did in virtue of who he is. As a consequence, Jesus' saving activity is not restricted to his incarnation but is extended to his entire life, from his infancy to his public ministry to his death and resurrection.

One of the fundamental presuppositions of soteriology is that the human situation is in need of salvation and that such a need must be explicitly recognized (though not by everyone in the same way). This need is derived not simply from the finite and limited character of human existence but primarily from the guilt which humans incur because of their sinful acts. Another presupposition is that humans cannot save themselves from their sinful condition by their own efforts. Rather, the initiative and the power to save lie with God exclusively.

Scripture uses different images to describe God's saving work in Christ. It speaks of "redemption" or "ransom" from the domination of sin, the Law, death, and the "principalities and powers" (Rom 3:24; 1 Cor 1:30; Eph 1:7; Col 1:14; Heb 9:15). Another expression is "reconciliation," that is, restoration of union and peace between humans and God, among humans themselves, and between humans and the cosmos (Rom 5:10; 11:15; 2 Cor 5:18; Col 1:20). Christ's redemptive act is also described in liturgical terms such as "sacrifice" offered to God the Father (Eph 5:2; 1 Cor 5:7; Heb 9:25), "expiation" for our sins (Rom 3:25); shedding of the "blood of the new covenant" for many (Matt 26:28 and parallels; Acts 20:28; Rom 5:9; Eph 1:7; Col 1:20; Heb 9:12, 14; 10:19; 13:12, 20; 1 Pet 1:19; 1 John 1:7; Rev 5:9). Another general term for this redemption is "salvation," that is, making whole and sound.

Among the many effects of redemption is liberation from the slavery of sin (Eph 1:7; Col 1:14; Titus 2:14; Heb 9:12), of the Law (Gal 3:15; 4:5; Rom

8:1), of the devil (John 16:11); new creation and rebirth (2 Cor 5:17; Gal 6:15; Eph 4:24; John 3:1); justification (Rom 5:1); becoming adopted children of God and possession of the Spirit (Gal 3:2; Rom 8:12-17); peace, joy, life, light, truth (Gal 5:22-24).

This biblical doctrine of salvation was further developed by the Fathers of the Church. Some, like Irenaeus, speak of Christ's saving work as "recapitulation," that is, as a historical process that moves toward a climax in which Christ becomes the head of a new humanity and stands in solidarity with his sisters and brothers. Others, like Clement of Alexandria, compare Jesus to a teacher who saves us by delivering us from darkness and ignorance and giving us a new revelation and knowledge. Still others, such as Athanasius and the Cappadocians, describe Christ's redemption as a divinization of the human nature insofar as in his incarnation the Logos restores to our corrupted nature the immortal image of God. Finally, others (e.g., Gregory of Nyssa) depict the redemptive process in mythic language as a cosmic struggle between God and Satan in which the body of Christ is used as a bait to trick the devil into defeat.

In the Middle Ages, St. Anselm of Canterbury (ca. 1033–1109) offers an influential model to understand redemption. Sin, for him, is an offense against God's honor which the sinner must restore. But because sin is an infinite offense (its gravity is measured by the dignity of the person offended), God's honor can be satisfied by no one except an infinite person (the worth of the satisfaction is measured by the dignity of the offerer). And yet it is human beings that must perform the satisfaction, though they are unable to do so. Anselm concludes that the person who does the satisfaction must be a God-Man. In this sense, Christ, by his obedience even unto death on the cross, presented a fully adequate, infinite reparation for humanity's infinite offense against the holiness and justice of God who freely accepted the Son's vicarious satisfaction in the name of sinful humanity. Peter Abelard (1079–1142) proposes what has been called the exemplarist theory of redemption, according to which Jesus did not die to appease the anger of God but to inspire human beings through an example of faithful love. Thomas Aquinas (1225–1274) accepted the basic elements of Anselm's satisfaction theory, though he modified it by emphasizing the human agency in Jesus' saving work and by replacing the metaphysical necessity of the incarnation and satisfaction with one of convenience.

Luther (1483–1546) highlighted Jesus' role as the representative of all humanity; in his suffering and death, Jesus willingly accepted in our stead the divine punishment for sin which we deserve. This view of redemption as Jesus' free acceptance of God's punishment for sin was reiterated and extended by Calvin (1509–1564).

Contemporary soteriology is more conscious of the plurality of metaphors by which to understand the saving work of God in Christ and holds that no one of them should be used as the exclusive paradigm to construct a Christian soteriology. It is also aware of the historical conditioning and theological limitations of such dominant modes of interpreting the salvific meaning of Jesus' death as Anselm's satisfaction theory. Karl Rahner (1904–1984), for instance, pointed out that Anselm's theory is unsatisfactory at least in five respects. First, its starting point is the categories of Germanic law (e.g., offense, satisfaction, dignity of the offended, dignity of the satisfier) and these cannot easily be given a personalist interpretation which would make sense to contemporary people. Second, it does not explain how a moral action can be regarded as compensation for an offense against God when this action is already absolutely due to God and is God's gift. Third, it does not make clear why the satisfaction had to be carried out in Jesus' death rather than in any other moral action of Jesus. Fourth, it does not make plain that the initiative comes from God and God's saving will, so that the Cross is the effect and manifestation of God's gratuitous love and not its cause. Finally, in this theory, the connection between Jesus' expiation and many other effects of redemption such as the resurrection of the body and the transfiguration of the cosmos, is at best extrinsic.

Furthermore, contemporary soteriology does not restrict Christ's saving work to his death on the cross but extends it to his entire life, from his incarnation to his resurrection. Besides uniting Christology and soteriology, contemporary theology (e.g., political theology, liberation theology, and feminist theology) also sees salvation not simply as liberation from sin, original and personal, but also as emancipation from all forms of oppression such as economic deprivation, gender discrimination, and political subjugation. In addition, ecological theology extends the effect of Jesus' saving work beyond humanity to include the earth and the cosmos itself.

Finally, some theologians (e.g., Jürgen Moltmann and Hans Urs von Balthasar) suggest that the event of the Cross must be located in the inner life of the Trinity itself. Whereas Moltmann tends to deny God's immutability, von Balthasar affirms it but at the same time suggests that the Cross is to be situated in God's Trinitarian life itself. He views God's inner life as a drama of the eternal self-emptying of the three divine Persons. The Father gives himself to the Son; the Son surrenders his being back to the Father in love; and the Spirit is totally given to the Father and the Son. In this self-emptying, there is, according to von Balthasar, a moment of "God-lessness," and the Cross is rooted in this "God-lessness" of the Trinitarian life. On the cross, as the representative of our sinful humanity, Jesus experienced the total abandonment of God, but at the same time, he died in absolute obedience to the Father. In this way, he accomplished salvation for all.

Like any other theme of Christian theology, contemporary soteriology has undergone extensive reconstruction. While maintaining fidelity to the Christian past, it attempts to respond to current challenges to make the ancient doctrine once more intelligible and transformative to people of today.

PETER C. PHAN

See also JESUS CHRIST; SALVATION.

SOUL

In the Western philosophical tradition the soul is the spiritual principle that inhabits (Plato) or informs (Aristotle) the body. The immaterial part survives after death and either exists immortally or inhabits a new body (reincarnation). The biblical words for "soul" (*nepeš* in Hebrew, *psychē* in Greek) have a broader range of meaning. In the Old Testament "soul" can refer to the breath of life (Gen 2:7), individual persons (Gen 46:18), or the seat of desire or emotion (Ps 42:1). Likewise in the New Testament "soul" describes life (Matt 2:20) and persons (Acts 3:23), as well as what survives after death (Luke 9:25; 12:4; 21:19; 1 Pet 1:19). In Paul's writings the soul is sometimes contrasted with both the body and the spirit (*pneuma*) as an aspect of the person not yet fully under God's grace. The early Jewish and New Testament writers generally looked forward to the resurrection of the whole person and not just the immortality of the soul (but see Wis 3:1-4; 9:15).

DANIEL J. HARRINGTON, S.J.

See also ANTHROPOLOGY, CHRISTIAN.

SOUTANE

See CASSOCK.

SPALDING, JOHN LANCASTER (1840–1916)

First bishop of Peoria, Illinois (1877–1908), Spalding was born in Lebanon, Kentucky, on 2 June 1840, and died in Peoria on 25 August 1916, a descendant of English Catholics who had emigrated to St. Mary's County, Maryland, in the seventeenth century. One of the first graduates of the American College in Louvain, Spalding was ordained in Belgium on 19 December 1863. Upon return to the United States, he served in several pastoral assignments in his home diocese of Louisville, then spent five years in New York City writing the biography of his uncle, Archbishop Martin J. Spalding of Baltimore. He was assistant pastor of St. Michael's Church in Manhattan when, in 1877, he was named the first bishop of Peoria where he built a new cathedral, 140 churches, and 58 schools during the next 31 years.

Spalding became a national figure because of his interest in such causes as the Irish Catholic Colonization Association, serving as president of the organization's board of directors. He was the guiding spirit behind the foundation of the Catholic University of America in 1887, but refused an offer to become the first rector. He was a strong advocate of parochial schools and of education for women, and a prolific writer on educational topics. An ardent patriot, he delivered a courageous defense of American political institutions in Rome in 1900 shortly after the papal condemnation of "Americanism." In 1902 and 1903 President Theodore Roosevelt appointed him to an arbitration committee which ended a bitter coal strike. Spalding suffered a stroke in 1905, resigned his see three years later and was made titular archbishop of Scythopolis. John Cardinal Glennon of St. Louis described him as "the one Catholic who has best understood the American mind."

THOMAS J. SHELLEY

See also AMERICAN CATHOLICISM; AMERICANISM.

SPANISH INQUISITION, THE

The Medieval Inquisition had an active history in Spain during the thirteenth century; but then the ongoing struggle against the Muslims occupied the energies of the Iberian peninsula until the last decades of the fifteenth century when the victory over the Moors was almost complete. Attention then shifted to the Jewish community which was viewed as an obstacle to religious unity. Anti-Semitism was not rampant, but occurred periodically. In the end of the fourteenth century Henry III of Castile and Leon began to pressure Jews to convert, and that policy became the norm thereafter. To avoid persecution, many Jews converted, but many were only nominally Christian and these were called Marranos. The merger of Aragon and Castile after the marriage of Ferdinand and Isabella (1469) marked the beginning of the persecution of the Jews as a threat to Christian Spain. In 1478 Sixtus IV acceded to a royal request to establish the Spanish Inquisition, and in 1483 he granted permission for the appointment of a grand inquisitor, who was named by the government and received ecclesiastical jurisdiction from Rome. The first grand inquisitor was Dominican Tomás de Torquemada (1420-1498) whose fanatical zeal carved him a place in history. During his tenure, over two thousand were burned at the stake. Gradually the control of the Inquisition passed to the civil power, especially during the reign of Philip II. An edict of 31 March 1492 gave all Jews the choice of conversion or banishment. The Muslims, who had converted to Catholicism, were known as Moriscos and were the next group to receive the scrutiny of the Inquisition. Owing to the vigilance of the institution, Protestantism made no inroads in Spain.

The intolerance that marked the activities of the Inquisition was not confined to Jews, Muslims, and Protestants. Catholics who did not share the inquisitor's view of orthodoxy also fell under suspicion. Ignatius of Loyola was arrested twice as a suspected heretic, and the archbishop of Toledo, the Dominican Bartolomé de Carranza, was jailed for seventeen years.

The jurisdiction of the Spanish Inquisition spread to the colonies, and its domestic and overseas activities lasted, in diluted fashion, until it was finally suppressed in 1834.

MICHAEL GLAZIER

See also INQUISITION, MEDIEVAL; ISLAM; JUDAISM; ORTHODOXY; ROMAN INQUISITION, THE.

SPELLMAN, FRANCIS, CARDINAL (1889–1967)

Archbishop of New York (1939–1967), cardinal (1946), Spellman was born in Whitman, Massachusetts, on 4 May 1889, and died in New York City on 2 December 1967. A graduate of Fordham College and of the North American College, Spellman was ordained in Rome on 14 May 1916 as a priest of the Archdiocese of Boston. Upon his return to Boston, however, Spellman's relationship with William Cardinal O'Connell was difficult from the beginning, resulting in his assignment to such positions as archivist and circulation editor of the diocesan newspaper.

In 1925 Spellman secured an appointment as director of the Knights of Columbus playgrounds in Rome and as an attaché of the Vatican Secretariat of State. During his second Roman stay, which lasted from 1925 until 1932, Spellman continued his earlier practice of cultivating important figures, most notably Eugenio Cardinal Pacelli, who became Secretary of State in 1930. In 1931 Spellman won plaudits for his role in the successful publication in Paris of Pius XI's anti-Fascist encyclical, *Non Abbiamo Bisogno.* The following year he was appointed auxiliary bishop of Boston and was ordained a bishop in St. Peter's basilica.

Cardinal O'Connell reacted to Spellman's promotion with disdain, assigning him as pastor of a debt-ridden church in Newton Center (where he proved to be an able administrator). For the next seven years Spellman managed to endure this difficult situation with O'Connell, always careful to observe the proper ecclesiastical amenities. Meanwhile, he attended to his Roman connections and solidified his growing friendship with Joseph P. Kennedy through whom he gained access to the White House. In 1936 Spellman achieved national prominence (and overshadowed the apostolic delegate to the U.S.) when he escorted Cardinal Pacelli on his tour of the United States and arranged a meeting between Pacelli and President Franklin D. Roosevelt at Hyde Park.

Upon the death of Patrick Cardinal Hayes of New York in September 1939, Spellman was widely rumored as a possible successor. At first he was not optimistic about his chances, but his prospects improved dramatically six months later with the election of Pacelli as Pope Pius XII. On 24 April 1939 the Holy See formally announced Spellman's appointment as the sixth archbishop of New York. The first person (outside his family) to whom Spellman told the news was President Roosevelt.

In New York Spellman moved quickly to reorganize the finances of the archdiocese; in his first year alone he saved $500,000 in interest payments by refinancing the $28,000,000 debt with the help of Boston banks. He also modernized the administrative structure by introducing such centralized agencies such as the Archdiocesan Building Commission and a central purchasing organization. After World War II, Spellman embarked on a major expansion of the Catholic educational system, spending over $500,000,000 to construct or renovate over 370 schools. He created a system of diocesan high schools and completely refurbished the badly neglected diocesan seminary. He also vastly expanded the social services of the archdiocese, spending over $92,000,000 on hospitals and other institutions.

A national figure even before he became archbishop of New York, Spellman was the best known American Catholic prelate of his era. His friendship with Pius XII gave him influence in Rome unmatched by any other American bishop. He played a major role in the negotiations that led to the announcement by President Roosevelt on 24 December 1939 that he would send a "personal representa-

Cardinal Francis Spellman

tive" to the Holy See. As military vicar of the Armed Forces, Spellman became a familiar figure to many Americans in World War II and came to personify Catholic patriotism and commitment to the war effort. Every year from 1942 to 1966 he made a Christmas visit to American troops in all parts of the world.

In the postwar world Spellman was a vociferous foe of Communism both at home and abroad. He blamed Communist influence for a strike at Catholic cemeteries in 1949, which he broke by using seminarians as substitute gravediggers. That same year he became involved in a controversy with Mrs. Eleanor Roosevelt over public aid to Catholic schools. He accused the former first lady of "conduct unworthy of an American mother"—a remark for which he later apologized.

A poor public speaker (and worse singer), Spellman rarely preached in his own cathedral, but, in 1956 he attracted banner headlines when he condemned a popular film from the pulpit of St. Patrick's Cathedral. On the other hand, he showed great pastoral leadership in responding to the influx into his archdiocese of large numbers of Puerto Rican immigrants, organizing a comprehensive Spanish Apostolate to care for their spiritual needs.

After the death of Pius XII in 1958, Spellman's influence in Rome waned. He played a prominent role at Vatican Council II where he generally supported the conservative side, especially in matters of liturgical reform. However, Spellman defied facile ideological categorization. He was responsible for the presence at Vatican II of Fr. John Courtney Murray, and he strongly supported the Declaration on Religious Liberty and the council's statement on the Jews. Earlier he had shown himself surprisingly receptive to modern Catholic biblical scholarship, defending two of his own priests, Myles Bourke and Patrick Skehan, from attacks by ecclesiastical obscurantists. He also defended the right of priests and religious to take part in civil rights demonstrations.

The turmoil in both the country and the Catholic Church in the late 1960s left Spellman bewildered and depressed. Upon his return from a Christmas visit to the troops in Vietnam in 1966, he declared that "total victory means peace," but such statements no longer brought the automatically favorable responses that they had produced in World War II. A few months later antiwar demonstrators (including several sisters) were arrested for disrupting the Sunday liturgy at St. Patrick's Cathedral. It was a sad end for Spellman. An intensely ambitious man who had wedded his ambition to the service of both his Church and his country, Spellman must have felt increasingly alienated from both when he died in St. Vincent's Hospital on 2 December 1967.

THOMAS J. SHELLEY

See also AMERICAN CATHOLICISM; CHURCH AND STATE; JUST WAR; RELIGIOUS FREEDOM.

SPIRITUAL DIRECTION

One of the most effective ways for individuals to experience the truth about themselves before God and others, is that of spiritual direction. It is practiced in various religious traditions; for example, the *guru* in the Hindu tradition helps the person grow into self-abandonment. Within the Christian tradition, direction has a history stretching back to the earliest Christian communities. The Churches of the East have a long and rich tradition of spiritual direction. While the form and accent have changed in various generations, the purpose remains basically the same: to help the person put on the mind and heart of Jesus Christ, under the guidance of the Holy Spirit (cf. Phil 2:5). To put on the mind of Christ involves a deepening of one's personal relationship with God, lived out in faith, hope and charity in everyday life. Hence spiritual direction is concerned with all relationships in an individual's life, prayer, and way of loving.

There are many dimensions to what is called spiritual direction, but it is about living the Christian life in faith, hope and love to the depth and fullness of which the person is capable. In the past twenty or so years, more has probably been written about spiritual direction than in all the previous centuries put together. Numerous centers for preparing people for this ministry have opened. The number of people seeking direction has multiplied. All of this seems to reflect a felt need on the part of many individuals. As has happened throughout the centuries, people are searching.

Augustine, in the fourth century wrote in his famous *Confessions* "my heart is restless until it finds rest in you" (I.1). Deep within each person, there is a profound longing for "the other." At the heart of the Christian experience is an experience of faith. Prayer is an expression of faith in Christ that, through the power of the Holy Spirit, draws the person into the encounter with God, into an experience of the love of the Father. In Christ we hope and trust in this merciful and compassionate God, who is "slow to anger and rich in mercy" (Exod 34:6).

When someone asks another for accompaniment on the inner journey, it is within this context of faith, hope and love, which means that the whole of one's life and being is involved. Prayer, recognition of one's own strengths and weaknesses, trust in God, and relationship with others are all part of the story, all part of the journey inward. Before all else though, it is important to remember that the first and most important director in the life of each person is the Holy Spirit, who brings each one "into the truth" (John 14:17); recalls all that Jesus has said and teaches all things (14:26), witnesses to Christ (15:26), shows the world about sin and the truth (16:8-11), and leads all Christians to the complete truth (16:13). In spiritual direction one person asks another for help in listening and responding to the inner promptings of the Holy Spirit.

We receive spiritual direction through the Holy Spirit in different ways. Above all we are instructed in the liturgy, by the word of God, by people we encounter, by secular events, by the insights we obtain in solitary or communitarian prayer. Everybody needs spiritual direction, even if no director is involved.

Various terms have been used to express the pastoral relationship set up between two people in spiritual direction. For some, the term itself is quite repugnant unless understood in the sense of accompaniment. However, "spiritual direction," has been and remains that most commonly used. The expression "soul friend" (a translation of the Irish, *anamchara*) corresponds for some people to the experience. "Spiritual guide" is another term sometimes used, but most people return to that of spiritual direction and therefore to the use of the words director and directee.

Spiritual direction is a form of prayer based in Scripture, the word which makes us Christ's disciples, brings us into the truth and sets us free (John 8:31-32). Because the Holy Spirit is the first director, the purpose of spiritual direction is to help one become more attuned to the Spirit at work in all circumstances of one's life so that one may grow closer to Christ.

Scripture itself offers models of spiritual direction. The Gospel of Matthew reflects a tradition among the Jewish rabbis who taught that God was present when two met to discuss the Torah: "for where two or three meet in my name, I am there among them" (Matt 18:20). In the Old Testament, the author of Ecclesiasticus writes of false friends and advisers. He concludes: "Have constant resort to some devout person, whom you know to be a keeper of the commandments, whose soul matches your own, and who, if you go wrong, will be sympathetic" (Eccl 37:12-15). The idea of approaching someone who will be sympathetic is present also in Paul's writings. He likens supporting and helping others spiritually, to the act of giving birth (Gal 4:19). On another occasion he writes: "Like a mother feeding and looking after her children, we felt so devoted to you" (1 Thess 2:7-8). There is a reminder here of Christ's own tenderness and sympathy (see Heb 4:15-16).

It is also helpful when considering the question of spiritual direction, to reflect on John the Baptist. The whole purpose of his life was to point out Christ to his disciples. "As John stood there with two of his disciples, Jesus went past and John looked towards him and said 'Look, there is the lamb of God' and the two disciples heard what he said and followed Jesus" (John 1:35-37). This act of pointing out Christ, of witnessing to his presence, is the essential role of the spiritual director. We read further in John what may be considered the basic attitude of the director: "It is the bridegroom who has the bride; and yet the bridegroom's friend who stands there and listens to him is filled with joy at the bridegroom's voice. This is the joy I feel and it is complete. He must grow greater, I must grow less" (John 3:29-31). Contained in these texts are the basic elements underlying the faith experience of spiritual direction. On the part of the one seeking direction there is the encouragement to go to someone who is known to be experienced in living Christian values; while the director should be someone who witnesses to Christ through his or her life.

Throughout the centuries, various Christian writers have reflected on the experience of spiritual direction. Perhaps one of the best known is Ignatius of Loyola (1491–1556). In his *Spiritual Exercises* he offers clear guidelines to all involved in the art of spiritual direction. Basically Ignatius proposes that as one makes the decision to follow Christ more fully in one's life, one needs help to distinguish what is of the Lord and what is not. Because we are each of us blind and find it is easy to deceive and delude ourselves, spiritual direction can be of help to us in sifting through experience. The description of the movements of the spirit is important to both the director and directee, in their search together for the way forward on the inner journey, and so Ignatius advises openness on the part of the one being directed (no. 17).

In the Ignatian tradition the place of spiritual direction is central to the experience of making the *Spiritual Exercises* which is meant to be a turning point experience, a moment of conversion, in the life of the exercitant, which will continue for the remainder of the retreatant's life. Therefore the role of the director is very important.

According to Ignatius the director must always be kind and gentle as well as firm (no. 7). Clearly both the director and the directee have an important part to play in this listening to the Spirit.

A contemporary of Ignatius, the Dominican novice director, John of the Cross, O.P. (d. 1565), describes the director as a person who is known to be a friend of God, practiced in the spiritual life, as well as prudent and humble. This is not unlike the advice found in Ecclesiasticus and also John 3. The director should be someone close to God and experienced in the spiritual life. This makes sense. If someone decides to climb a mountain, it is normal to go with another who has already made the climb.

William Barry, S.J., in his book *Spiritual Direction and the Encounter with God,* speaks of the experience of what is called discernment of spirits as that of being "in tune" or "out of tune" with God's action in one's life (76–77). This is a helpful way of expressing it. The purpose of spiritual direction is to help another "be attuned to the one action of God, to his will" (78).

For Teresa of Avila (1515–1582), the great reformer of Carmel, being at one with the will of God is essential in the spiritual life. Because this is so important to her, both in her *Autobiography* and the *Interior Castle,* she writes of the need for the director to be learned and prudent, experienced and holy. But, she advises, if such a person cannot be found, then approach someone who is virtuous and learned. Teresa had suffered at the hands of poor directors and felt that reasonable knowledge and humility on the part of the director were really essential qualities.

Her companion in the Carmelite reform, St. John of the Cross (1542–1591), in his writings on the spiritual life, has important things to say on the topic of spiritual direction. He was influenced in his early years by both Dominicans and Jesuits. He himself was an experienced spiritual director for all types of people. (Most of his writings were intended for enclosed Carmelite nuns, but his experience was very broad.) He wrote in his book *Living Flame of Love* that for the inner journey, the director needs to be experienced, wise and discreet; ("discreet" in this context meaning able to discern the Spirit at work). He himself directed people in the way of detachment. Often misinterpreted, this detachment does not so much mean a rejection of people and things (good in themselves), but rather a profound focusing of all one's affectivity, thoughts, and will on God. The key question then, for those embarking on the inner journey becomes: "where is your heart?" In other words, where is the focus of affectivity and attention in the person's life? John of the Cross proposes the way of love, a way which would be echoed centuries later by the French Carmelite, Thérèse of Lisieux.

John of the Cross, perhaps more than any other of the great spiritual writers, gives help both to directees and directors. He explains in detail the stages through which people journey in their search for God and how the different prayer experiences are part of that inner journey. He has a clear sense of where the directee is heading and at the same time he has a profound understanding of the variety of ways in which the Spirit leads each individual, realizing that "God raises each one by different ways" (*Flame,* pp. 3, 59).

Because of the activity of the Holy Spirit it is essential that the director is able to exercise the gift of discernment of spirits (*discretio spiritum*), a charismatic gift of the Holy Spirit. All gifts and charisms including those needed for growth in the spiritual life, are for the good of others. John teaches that when the directee "continues loving and feeling love with humility and reverence of God, it is a sign that the Holy Spirit is at work within" (*Ascent,* II, pp. 29, 11). The director needs to know how to recognize such signs, and to offer encouragement.

In the seventeenth century, St. Francis de Sales (1567–1622) stands out as a spiritual director. Although both Ignatius and John of the Cross directed people from all walks of life, Francis is known especially for encouraging lay people to enter into the inner, spiritual journey. His *Introduction to the Devout Life* is a beautiful example of spiritual guidance. He is famous for his letters of direction, especially for the way in which he helped people come to a profound knowledge of God's love and mercy.

In the eighteenth and nineteenth centuries in France particularly, it was fashionable for people to have a spiritual director. It was usual for this person to be a priest and direction was almost always linked with the practice of sacramental confession. It is this link with the sacrament that has continued well into the present century and has meant that spiritual direction has been considered the prerogative of the priest. By the time of Vatican II, the practice was virtually limited to priests despite the fact that in past centuries both lay men and women were well known for the spiritual help they gave others. (One of the most well known, deserving much more than a mention, is St. Catherine of Sienna [1347–1380]).

Since Vatican II, there has been a growing realization that spiritual direction depends both on knowledge and the giftedness of the Holy Spirit, and is not limited to priests. Many people are being gifted by the Spirit with the experience, wisdom, and discernment needed to help others on their inner journey, a point made in the new *Catechism* (no. 2690).

To sum up: First, spiritual direction is concerned with seeking God's will, within the whole context of the individual's life. For both the director and directee, this is the "aim" of their meeting. Direction explores the circumstances of the person's life only in as much as this helps the directee move more deeply into the experience of the encounter with God. While in spiritual direction the person may experience personal help and learn much, this is not the main purpose of the coming together of director and directee. Spiritual direction is not predominately informative.

Secondly, spiritual direction is not primarily therapeutic and neither is it a personal counseling session although healing will possibly be experienced by the individual, as the Holy Spirit leads to a discovery of personal truth and subsequent freedom in Christ. Counseling centers on helping clients reach wholeness, making full use of their resources, and is focused on the psyche. Spiritual direction looks rather to Christ in the search for wholeness and healing, while using the giftedness of the individual. A certain knowledge of counseling and its techniques is very important, but the spiritual director is not normally trained to be a counselor as such. The goals of the spiritual director and of the counselor are different and do need to be distinguished.

Thirdly, spiritual direction is not essentially advisory, although at times a director might offer helpful suggestions. Spiritual direction is a form of prayer, a particular way in which people witness to and share their faith in Christ.

There are many forms which spiritual direction may take. The most satisfactory is one-to-one encounter. This may not be often, depending on the directee's needs at a time. Frequent regular direction may be a luxury not available to many. Those who cannot find a spiritual director can trust in the Lord that if they try to remain faithful, he will not allow them to go far astray. There can be times when some contact with a spiritual director is necessary, for instance in some personal vocational or faith crisis. Again, some people are very good at direction by letter; others quite definitely are not gifted in this form of direction.

There are those who criticize spiritual direction as being too self-focused, but because it is a form of prayer, the fruit of the Spirit should be evident in the life of the individual: growth in humility, that is the truth about oneself, and in love. As with all gifts of the Spirit, these gifts of wisdom, discernment, humility and so on, are given freely to individuals, but they are always given for the good of others. It is the same Spirit that Christ promised would teach all things, remind us what Christ has said, and lead to witnessing to Christ, that is at work in the heart of the experience of spiritual direction.

The prayer of St. Francis of Assisi expresses so well the attitude of heart with which we make this journey inwards in the company of another: "Most high and glorious God, illumine the darkness of my heart. Give me right faith, firm hope, perfect love and profound humility. Give me, Lord, wisdom and discernment to understand your truth and holy will."

TERESA CLEMENTS, D.M.J.

See also FRIENDSHIP; SPIRITUAL LIFE.

SPIRITUAL EXERCISES OF ST. IGNATIUS OF LOYOLA

A text outlining a four-week set of meditations written by St. Ignatius of Loyola, the founder of the Jesuits. The text developed out of the mystical experiences and interior struggles Ignatius had in 1522 at Manresa, Spain, but he kept rewriting the text until his death in 1556. The purpose of *The Exercises* is "to help the exercitant conquer one's self and regulate one's life so that decisions will not be influenced by any inordinate attachment." The meditations are made under a director with much attention to feelings of consolation and desolation; they are generally made away from home and in silence, but can be made during one's ordinary life. The intended four weeks are often shortened.

The First Principle of the text affirms: We are created to praise, reverence, and serve God our Lord, and by this means to save our soul. Everything else is created to help us attain this end, and is to be so used or so avoided. The First Week of *The Exercises* centers on the commandments, sin, and repentance; it ends with confession. The Second Week centers on the life of Christ; the Third centers on his passion and death; the Fourth on the risen Christ. During the Second Week there are key meditations on The Kingdom (Christ seen as an earthly leader summoning his followers), on The Two Standards (Christ's poverty and humility is opposed to Satan's riches, honor, and pride), on The Three Classes (only the third class is free). The final contemplation tells of God dwelling and working in the elements, plants, animals, and humans. *The Exercises* includes instruction on prayer and rules to interpret spiritual movements, instructions on almsgiving, dealing with scruples, and thinking with the Church. The apostolic spirituality of *The Exercises* has been the basis of Jesuit training and is fundamental to the spirituality of many congregations of religious. *The Spiritual Exercises* is a basic text in many religious congregations and most Catholic retreat houses.

THOMAS M. KING, S.J.

See also IGNATIUS OF LOYOLA, ST.; SOCIETY OF JESUS; SPIRITUAL LIFE.

SPIRITUAL LIFE

Christians refer to the growth of their commitment to religious matters as their spiritual life. This term, spiritual life, is a carryover from times when religious people thought negatively of material things, presuming they made no contribution to a God-directed life. Thus, spiritual life seems to imply that material is not good, just as interior life—another way of referring to spiritual life—seems to imply that exterior is not good. Since the Vatican Council II's teaching on the intrinsic goodness of temporal realities, believers' discipleship must integrate every dimension of life as part of one's commitment to God. One can direct one's family or professional life to God just as easily as one can direct one's liturgical life to God. On the other hand one can be self-centered in the use of liturgy just as easily as one can in the abusive use of money. So, spiritual life refers to a Christian's efforts to direct his or her whole life to God.

Spiritual writers and mystics have traditionally taught that one's spiritual life evolves through a series of identifiable stages: beginners—who strive for virtue and for the removal of false values and whose prayer is a form of meditation; proficient—those who have purified their senses and have received the gift of contemplative prayer, a period of notable renewal of life; perfect—those who have purified their faculties of intellect, memory, and will through faith, hope, and charity, and encounter God in the prayer of union.

The Vatican Council moved away from any elitist approach to spiritual life—such as we often had in history—and insisted that the source of spiritual life is sacramental life; that the true nature of spiritual growth is the daily development of the life of charity; that the center of all spiritual enrichment is the life of the Holy Spirit within us; and that Christians are called to be holy by participating in the life of a Holy Church. The council launched a universal call to holiness, making growth in spiritual life a part of every Christian's daily responsibility.

LEONARD DOOHAN

See also HOLINESS; MYSTICISM.

SPIRITUAL WORKS OF MERCY

See CORPORAL AND SPIRITUAL WORKS OF MERCY.

SPIRITUALISM

This is the belief that living human beings can contact the spirits of the dead. Although ordinarily average human beings cannot do so, they can use the assistance of a medium, literally one who stands in the middle between the living and the dead. Spiritualists believe that humans consist of a material body, an immortal spirit, and a soul which gives form to the spirit and, after death, vests the spirit in a semi-material body so that the spirit can appear to the living. The spirit of the deceased lives in a spirit world but can still maintain contact with the material one. A medium can sense the vibrations in this world caused by a spirit. If people wish to contact a deceased person, almost always someone known to them, the medium will gather them together in what is called a séance. The medium asks all present to focus their thoughts on the deceased, who then announces his or her presence, for example, by making rapping sounds on the wall or by moving or levitating some object in the room in which the séance occurs. Often the deceased will speak to those present via the medium; some mediums claim the power to "materialize" the deceased, that is, those present will see the deceased in bodily form.

Spiritualism began in 1848 when two sisters, Katherine and Margaret Fox of Hydesville, New York (near Rochester), heard inexplicable knocking sounds in their house. Convinced these sounds were attempts by spirits of the dead to contact them, the sisters worked out a "code" of sorts to decipher the messages. They next publicized their case via lecture tours in which they demonstrated some psychic phenomena to sizeable audiences. The fad of séances caught on in the United States and spread to Great Britain in the 1850s. In 1863, Andrew Jackson Davis, who had written about spiritualism, founded a Spiritualist Sunday school in Buffalo, New York, which lasted until 1872. In 1893, spiritualists founded the National Spiritualist Association, now called the National Spiritualist Association of Churches. There are also other spiritualist organizations.

Spiritualists see their doctrine as a religion, and their beliefs can claim an affinity with some biblical and Christian elements, for example, the Witch of Endor (1 Samuel 28) and the belief that the saints can intervene in human affairs. But Christian sects reject these associations. The Witch of Endor was not working on God's behalf, and Deuteronomy condemns spiritualism (18:10-12), so a biblical foundation is weak at best. As for the intervention of saints, denominations which accept that believe that it results from prayer or divine grace, not from the power of a medium. Furthermore, people at a séance can ask the deceased about anything, including material gain; the saints cannot be invoked for such purposes. Lastly, the occasional exposure of prominent mediums as frauds has weakened any possible links between spiritualism and Christianity. Indeed, some Christians would link spiritualism with demonic agency, but most Christians simply think it wrongheaded.

JOSEPH F. KELLY

SPIRITUALITY

See CHRISTIAN SPIRITUALITY; SPIRITUALITY, HISPANIC; SPIRITUALITY, LAY.

SPIRITUALITY, HISPANIC

C.P.M. Jones wisely states that "in spirituality, there are ultimately no 'rules of the game', even those laid down by the saints, but only 'tips of the trade', freely offered to be freely available, to those who need them, sometimes permanently and sometimes in a passing stage of development" ("Liturgy and Personal Devotion," *The Study of Spirituality,* eds. Jones, Wainright, and Arnold, New York: Oxford, 1986 p. 6). The following article offers tips, hints, and possible ways for understanding Hispanic spirituality "to those who need them." The first tip concerns the term "Hispanic"; second is an attempt to define spirituality from the Hispanic perspective; third, characteristics of Hispanic spirituality; and finally spiritual issues facing the Hispanic community.

Hispanic or Latino or . . .

Both the terms "Hispanic" and "Latino" are problematic in that they refer to a diverse people. Alan Deck Figueroa demonstrates why both must be used with caution. "For the purpose of dividing Hispanic communities into more workable grouping, one might conceive of them in terms of five historical and geographical divisions: (1) Those whose origins are to be found in Middle America, especially Mexico; (2) Central Americans; (3) The Caribbean people (Cubans, Puerto Ricans, and Dominicans); (4) The Andean peoples and (5) the Borderlands peoples of the American Southwest and California" ("Hispanic Catholics: Historical Explorations and Cultural Analysis," *U.S. Catholic Historian* 9 [Winter/Spring 1990] 138).

The Hispanic people are diverse not only in their geographic and cultural background but also in their identification within the Hispanic community itself. Some Southwestern Hispanic families trace their histories to this land before the United States existed. Other Hispanics have disassociated themselves from the Spanish language, Hispanic culture and community for a vast array of reasons. They are foreigners among their own. There are others who see themselves as a new race of people—a U.S. Hispanic *mestizo,* a blend of the peoples of the past formed by the realities of the present. The diversity of the Hispanic community is its strength insofar as it reflects and incorporates many different peoples into one.

There are points of convergence that help to unite the Hispanic community. The most basic point is one of common origin: from the painful birthing act of the sixteenth-century Spanish conquest, a new life issued forth. The religious spirit of the indigenous pre-Columbian/African people grafted with the Christian faith of the Spanish evangelizers roots Hispanic spirituality.

Another point of convergence is what we might call the *mestizo* (Virgil Elizondo, *The Future is Mestizo,* New York: Crossroad, 1992) way of mixing various experiences to form a "third way." Life is not seen as black or white, either-or, one or the other, but as "perhaps," "maybe," "possibly this way." This perspective, this pattern of living, shapes the Hispanic spiritual reality.

There is one other point that is important to make when defining the Hispanic community. Formerly this community was universally thought to be Roman Catholic. With the successful evangelization by various fundamentalist and evangelical denominations, Roman Catholicism can no longer be presumed. Yet even here the dynamic of *mestizaje* (mixing) that is characteristic of the Hispanic community cannot be underestimated. Though we will continue to use the term "Hispanic" in this article, in reality we are speaking about a new *mestizo* spirituality that is blended from all these experiences. Let us consider our second tip, how the Hispanic community defines spirituality.

Attempting a Definition

Definitions of spirituality can seduce us into believing that we can fully comprehend a religious experience. By attempting to define Hispanic spirituality, we may be tempted to think that we can control—even dominate—our relationship with God. The challenge at hand is to articulate in understandable categories something of the spiritual pattern that is etched in the Hispanic person while acknowledging that the ways of the Spirit are beyond definition and our control. Three persons attempt a definition.

Ricardo Ramírez places spirituality *within* the mystery of the human person. He writes, "Spirituality for any group of people refers to the 'inner space' or internal spiritual processes that allow people to come in touch with themselves as 'believing.' It refers to the area of life where the divine spirit touches the human spirit, where the redemption happens as the person recognizes the transcendent in his or her own life. . . .For Hispanics, this faith experience that is at the heart of spirituality touches not only the spiritual. . .but is also one that affects their total lives. . . .It brings (Hispanic) people in touch with the past spirituality of their ancestors" ("Hispanic Spirituality," *Social Thought* 9 [Summer 1985] no. 3, p. 6).

This "inner space" emphasis becomes a dynamic of seeking, searching, and stretching oneself in ways that define the Hispanic person's relationship with God and with the community. The word to emphasize in this definition is *touch*—something characteristic of Hispanic spirituality.

Alan Deck Figueroa speaks of spirituality ". . . as encompassing all those ways in which the Christian faithful pursue and deepen their life of faith in Christ within the Christian community" (140). *All those ways* carries a sense of inclusivity. Whatever puts a person *in contact* with the Christ of their life is included in a definition of spirituality. This means suspending judgments about traditional, cultural, popular religious expressions that from an outsider's (non-Hispanic) point of view might be considered superstitious, uninformed, or overly pietistic. It also means assessing and valuing familial patterns of prayer, even if they are practiced in English. Deck clearly states that this inclusivity requires "a sense of awe and contemplation in the face of the mystery of God" ("Hispanic Catholics," p. 141). Both Ramírez and Deck regard popular religious expressions as keys for entering into a relationship with the God of our lives.

Rosa Maria Icaza's definition, based on the *National Pastoral Plan for Hispanic Ministry* (United States Bishops, November, 1987), identifies spirituality as "the orientation and perspective of all dimensions of a person's life in the following of Jesus, moved by the Spirit, and in continuous dialogue with the Father" ("Spirituality of the Mexican American People," *Worship* 63 [May 1989] 232). Once again the theme of inclusivity lights the way as Icaza affirms *the orientation and perspective of all dimensions of a person's life.* There is a dialogue of life, an interaction of people, an emotional interchange that motivates the relationship between the Hispanic person, God, and the community at large. Icaza says "It seems, then, that for Hispanics, spirituality is translated into the love of God which moves, strengthens and is manifested in love of neighbor and self." Love binds a people together no matter how diverse they may be. This common experience of the Hispanic community, being loved by God, fashions us into *El Pueblo de Dios,* the People of God.

General Characteristics

Touch, inclusiveness, love of God, self and neighbor translate into specific characteristics of Hispanic spirituality. Using the *Pastoral Plan,* Rosa Maria Icaza delineates these characteristics: (1) A basic and constant aspect is a sense of the presence of God. (2) God is found in the arms of the Virgin Mary. She is at the heart of spirituality. (3) "The seeds of the Word" in pre-Hispanic cultures are still cultivated. (4) Spirituality is expressed in popular devotions and in the use of symbols and gestures. (5) It is also expressed in behavior revealing gospel values, such as prayer and hospitality, endurance and hope, commitment and forgiveness. (6) Faith is kept alive at home through practices in daily life and particularly during the principal seasons of the liturgical year. (7) All celebrations are seen as communal and most of them include prayer, sharing of food, and singing/dancing/reciting or composing poetry. (8) Finally Hispanics seldom pray for themselves but regularly for others. They often request others to remember them in their prayers.

I would add the following clarifications: (9) Hispanic spirituality is "touchable," incarnational. Body, soul, and Spirit are seen as one. Oftentimes this is referred to as "fiesta," where all that is contained in life (including death) is embraced and celebrated. This unity of body, soul, and Spirit is what makes sense of healings—physical, emotional, and spiritual and those who administer them, the faithhealers of the Hispanic community, curanderos, santeros, etc. (10) Spiritual intimacy relates and reveals us to one another thus forming familial and extrafamilial relationships between ourselves and with God. (11) There is a personal and communal sense of sin, culpability, and evil. (12) Hispanic spirituality is related to four sacramental moments: baptism, Eucharist (specifically in First Communion), marriage and anointing (inclusive of the funeral rites of the Church and Hispanic community). (13) Oral traditions, namely *dichos* (sayings), popular songs and traditional sacred religious hymns, shared family religious histories, dramas, and festivals form Hispanic wisdom literature. (14) Contemplation and mysticism are characteristic marks of Hispanic spirituality. "The sense of mystery and awe, of contemplative and mystical interiority are part of the Hispanic soul" (German Martinez, O.S.B., "Hispanic Culture and Worship: The Process of Inculturation," *U.S. Catholic Historian* 11 [Spring 1993], no. 2, p. 88).

These characteristics come to life and become the language of prayer when they are expressed "rite-fully" in the diversity of Hispanic popular religiosity. "The fundamental expression of that spirituality is popular devotion (popular religiosity), not the refined asceticism, profound mysticism, or elaborate spiritualities of great writers, mystics, and saints" (Deck, p. 141).

Issues Facing Hispanic Spirituality

Mestizaje is only achieved at great price. As was true in the sixteenth century, the birthing of a U.S. Hispanic *mestizo* spirituality requires great sacrifice. Though there are many concerns, three specific issues suggest approaches for the future.

(1) "A core spiritual issue facing each and every Hispanic, whether he or she be of Mexican, Cuban, Puerto Rican, or other Latin American extraction, is how to relate to the dominant culture and to one's culture of origin" (Juan-Lorenzo Hinojosa, "Culture, Spirituality, and United States Hispanics," *Frontiers of Hispanic Theology in the United States,* Maryknoll: Orbis Books, 1992, p. 155). Hispanics, be they Spanish speaking only, bilingual, or English-speaking only face the constant influence of the dominant culture as well as the influence of other racial and ethnic groups. Each group has its own spirituality, popular expressions of prayer and experiences of God. *Mestizaje* means mixing: not assimilating or disappearing but blending with these other spiritual realities. *Mestizo* spirituality is expressed best in *mestizo* liturgy, a form of prayer that allows the Hispanic faith experience to be heard, seen, touched, smelled, savored, and embraced by those at prayer.

(2) Popular religiosity is a living language of prayer that will continue to evolve into new ways, forms, and expressions. Popular religious practices based on "what has always been" may not necessarily be appropriate for the future. One example of this is the experience of Hispanic popular religious practices celebrated in English. The change in language, from Spanish to English, affects the silent "inner spaces" of life. The "touch" that is felt between the community, God, and one another is lived out in a new way. The language of prayer, as it develops and changes will continue to be an issue in the spiritual life of the Hispanic community.

(3) The third issue is the simple acknowledgement that Hispanic spirituality does indeed exist. Can we, Hispanic and non-Hispanic alike, accept and affirm it as an authentic school of spirituality, as much as the Ignatian, Franciscan, Teresian or any other school of spirituality? This school of spirituality is more easily found in pilgrimages of faith, in Good Friday living stations of the cross, in the Hispanic rites of marriage, in all that makes life holy and acknowledges the Presence of God.

Hispanic spirituality touches the center of life, the heart of the Hispanic community. It offers "spiritual tips" to the larger United States Catholic community and the opportunity to testify to the diversity of God's life. "Since the spiritual crisis of modernity is rooted in the loss of the symbolic, the transcendent and the communal characteristics of Hispanic spirituality, Hispanic wisdom, can make an important contribution to the renewal of the spiritual wealth of the American Churches searching today for a new post-modern experience faith'' (Martinez, p. 91).

ARTURO PÉREZ RODRIGUEZ

See also SPIRITUAL LIFE.

SPIRITUALITY, LAY

Preliminary Considerations

The term "lay spirituality" refers to the spirituality of the baptized. Lay spirituality is nothing more or less than life in Christ by the presence and power of the Holy Spirit. It is rooted in membership in a people (*laos*), nurtured by ongoing celebration of Christ's mysteries in word and sacrament, and brought to completion by loving discipleship through which the baptized participate in Christ's ongoing paschal mystery in Church and world. Common understandings of the term "lay" as unlettered or nonprofessional can muddle the fundamental dignity of all the baptized who make up a holy people, the People of God (*laos theou*).

Ecclesial Foundations

A proper understanding of lay spirituality takes seriously the image of the Church as the People of God who together constitute a sacrament of God's redemptive presence *in* and *to* the world. Such a view of lay spirituality, informed by the documents of Vatican Council II (especially LG 40–41), does not relegate laypersons to the life of the Church *ad extra,* to quotidian life "in the world," while particular spiritualities, i.e., those of priesthood, monastic and religious life, are relegated to the life of the Church *ad intra.* Further, such a view poses serious challenges to any notion of a spiritual elite, which has often been inadvertently fostered by many approaches to particular spiritualities in the history of Christianity. All too often the "common" spirituality of the baptized has been understood as lesser than particular priestly, religious, or monastic spiritualities. The former has often been thought to derive from latter, as seen in efforts to apply the wisdom of the Rule of Benedict to life "in the world," or in the efforts of members of various Third Orders to adhere to a mitigated rule of life based upon that of the Franciscans, Dominicans, or Carmelites. But it is rather more the other way around. Specific spiritualities such as Franciscan, Benedictine, or Ignatian are only properly understood if they are seen as specifications or distinctive manifestations of the baptismal spirituality to which all are called by virtue of their membership in God's people. In that sense, they are derivative of baptismal spirituality. Said another way, all authentic Christian spirituality is *ipso facto* lay spirituality. All the baptized, whatever their situation in life, are called to the fullness of life in Christ by the presence and power of the Holy Spirit as this is discerned in and through membership in God's people, the Church.

The documents of the Second Vatican Council have given shape to an understanding of all Christian spirituality as first and finally a spirituality of word and sacrament. The Eucharistic Liturgy is described as the source and summit of Christian life (SC 10). In the Liturgy of Word and Sacrament, the identity of the Church as the body of Christ *in* and *to* the world is expressed and impressed.

A Spirituality of Word and Sacrament

Christian spirituality may be understood as Christian faith in practice. It is the living of the gospel in a particular form of discipleship to which one is invited by grace and Spirit. It is in the proclamation and hearing of the word, and in celebration of Christ's mysteries in sacrament that the Christian community discerns the contours of the reign of God, the hallmarks of life in Christ by the presence and power of the Holy Spirit. In this view, the sacraments of the Church are not isolated moments that can be restricted to certain times and places, e.g., in the church on Sunday. Both the New Testament and the documents of Vatican II, as well as the history of Christian spirituality, emphasize the strong connection between liturgy and life, sacrament and living. What believers perceive and pursue as the highest values and purposes in human life they express in worship. Proclaiming and hearing the word together with the celebration of Christ's mysteries in sacrament is expressive of how Christians hope to live their lives, of what they understand to constitute life "in Christ." That is to say that in word and sacrament, Christians can discern practical implications, the contours of how one is to conduct oneself in the wider spheres of life. Clues to the ways in which Christians are to live may be discerned in the Scriptures and in the traditions of the different Christian communities. Indications are found in the teachings of the Church. For Roman Catholics, the magisterium plays a central role, to be sure. An informed, formed conscience is a vital dimension in the quest for living a good Christian life. But for those whose tradition is marked by a strong sacramental worldview as is the Roman Catholic tradition, what is said and done in word and sacrament expresses the deepest convictions of a people regarding how they are to live in relationship with others and God. Said another way, a Roman Catholic Christian spirituality is necessarily a sacramental spirituality. And a sacramental spirituality is nurtured and shaped by the constant proclamation and hearing of the word.

In the sacrament of baptism, one is initiated into a people of the covenant through incorporation into Christ's death and resurrection. Such initiation calls for a new way of life based in the covenant. This is a way of life rooted in love and fidelity, rather than law or obligation. It is shaped by a sense of responsibility to God and to others, rather than by preoccupation with obligations and requirements. This responsibility springs from belonging to God's people through baptism. It is expressed in a way of life in which prayer, devotions, and ascetical practices such as abstinence and fasting, as well as the other practices ordinarily associated with the "spiritual life," are integrated in a life project of purifying relationships. Shaped and strengthened by the words and work, meaning and message of Jesus in the Scriptures, authentic baptismal spirituality entails participation in the mystery of persons in communion. Baptized "in the name of the Father, and of the Son, and of the Holy Spirit," the spirituality of the baptized is altogether Trinitarian. It is a way of life in communion with persons—human persons and divine persons. It matures through the daily response to the call to relate rightly to another, others, and God.

The sealing of the Spirit in confirmation is the sacramental act by which a person and the whole community of the baptized recognize and submit to the attraction of life in the Spirit. Confirmation signals abandonment and submission to the presence and power of the Spirit. One abandoned to the sway and power of the Spirit is led to live according to the Spirit, not according to the flesh. The lives of those baptized into the body of Christ bear the fruit of peace, patience, kindness, long-suffering, gentleness, faithfulness, single-hearted love of God and neighbor. The absence of the Spirit is recognized in hatred, jealousy, envy, greed, lust, and despair.

As the central expression of the Church's call and commitment to communion and justice, the Eucharist comprises the heart of a Christian spirituality. Divisions and failure to share signal a failure to discern the body of the Christ. Unwillingness to share in life as well as in the Eucharist, self-preoccupation, self-absorption, and self-indulgence all constitute a failure to discern God's presence in the breaking of the bread and the blessing of the cup. Those who share at the Eucharistic table enjoin themselves to live in accord with a covenant spirituality that stems from membership in God's people: to live according to the Spirit and not according to the flesh (Romans 8).

The willingness of Christians to share extends beyond those gathered at the table. It must include all who constitute the human family, especially the poor and wounded, the last and the least, and all whom Jesus promised will hold pride of place in the reign of God anticipated in the Eucharistic meal. As participation in a ritual meal of communion and justice, the Eucharist does not permit distinction of persons: divisions, separations, and distinctions of persons based on race, class, sex, handicap, status, and rank are decried. In the Eucharistic Liturgy, the baptized express a willingness to work toward overcoming such divisions, factions, and distinctions so that Christ may be all in all (Gal 3:27-28). To celebrate the Eucharist implies that we live our lives motivated by a vision of communion and justice. To break bread and bless the cup is to live in the memory of Christ's passion and death. It is to have died with him. To have died with Christ is to live for God and for the coming of God's reign wherein the power of love will prevail over all evil.

In celebrating the sacrament of penance, Christians express a new vision of reality. They live within the perspective of God's mercy and forgiveness. The lordship of Christ and the empowerment of the Holy Spirit are the criteria by which judgments and decisions are made. Compassion is the hallmark here. Judgments about one's own life and the lives of others are made in light of a consciousness of sin and grace in the events of human life. As a result, the lives of the rejected and the scorned, the outcast and the forgotten, those judged to be worthless and burdensome by the criteria of efficiency, productivity, and propriety, come to be seen from the perspective of God's mercy and forgiveness. In light of the consciousness of sin and grace, the wounded, the weak, the little, the fragile and the poor are viewed as disclosing God's grace and mercy, which touches us in the depth of our need. Those who respond to God's love and attraction become the clearest signs of God's reconciling love in our world. Life itself becomes an echo of the testament of Paul: In our weakness is God's strength (2 Cor 12:9-10).

Through the sacrament of anointing, the Christian community lives in remembrance of Christ's healing ministry. As such, Christians are called upon to care for the sick and dying, to struggle against illness, suffering and depersonalization. In celebrating the sacrament of anointing, the community expresses a new perspective on suffering, illness, and death which enables Christians to live in the hope and with the confidence that nothing escapes the grasp of God's healing and compassion in Jesus Christ.

In the sacramentality of marriage, the entire Christian community as well as the two persons united live out of a vision of God's personal, loving fidelity. Christian marriage is thus the model par excellence of love and fidelity, and provides a new way of living from the perspective of God's self-sacrificing love and faithfulness to the divine promise. The relationship between the two persons united in marriage as well as their relationships with others, are all seen in light of the value of God's fidelity to the person and to the human community. The couple thereby becomes a sign of God's own loving fidelity through union with one another, as well as in their dealings with others in the human and Christian communities. Particularly through the bearing and rearing of children, fruit of faithful union and invitation to a more inclusive love, the couple gives expression to the values of self-sacrificing love and fidelity to promise. These are values by which the whole Church is enjoined to live.

The value of service to the human and Christian communities modeled on Christ's own service is expressed in the sacrament of ordained ministry. It is rooted in the Church's care of the various needs of the community throughout the ages and in remembrance of Christ's own life and ministry. Whatever advantages or disadvantages one may care to point out, the discipline of clerical celibacy has been and remains an invitation to, and expression of, faithful service to the community. All ministry—ordained and lay, undertaken by persons married and single—aims at giving concrete expression to the value of self-sacrificial love motivated by a new vision of reality shaped by Christ's own servanthood and faithfulness to God's promise unto death.

Conclusion

Informed by the perspectives shaped by the Second Vatican Council, hard and fast separations between lay spirituality and other more particular spiritualities are difficult to sustain. Each baptized Christian is called by grace and Spirit to the fullness of life in Christ Jesus. Those baptized into his body are called to rightly ordered relationships with another, others, and God. The contours of such rightly ordered relationships are discerned in the word and the work, the meaning and message of Jesus, whose mysteries are celebrated in word and sacrament. Prayer, devotions, ascetical practices, and other disciplines ordinarily associated with the "spiritual life" are brought to fruition as we grow in ever-deepening communion of persons, both human and divine. Whether the relationships be those of a family, or workers on the job, between spouses or members of a support group, among sisters in a monastic community or parishioners in an urban diocese, among college students or volunteers in the Catholic Worker soup line, the baptized are called to participate in the Trinitarian life of God in Christ through the Holy Spirit precisely in and through being in loving relationship.

MICHAEL DOWNEY

See also CHRISTIAN SPIRITUALITY; LAITY, THEOLOGY OF THE.

SPONSOR

See GODPARENT.

ST. VINCENT DE PAUL, SOCIETY OF

It was originally called the Conference of Charity when founded by Frederic Ozanam, a twenty-year-old student in Paris in 1833. He and his friends felt the need to make a personal commitment to work with the poor. Ozanam became a respected scholar, but is primarily remembered for his apostolic dedication. The Society's program of spiritual and corporal works of mercy has attracted men and women in all continents, and besides its person-to-person assistance to the sick and the poor it manages stores to cater to the needy and participates in rehabilitation work and other social services. It has now over sixty-six thousand members in America, working in some five thousand parishes across the country.

JOAN GLAZIER

See also CORPORAL AND SPIRITUAL WORKS OF MERCY; OZANAM, ANTOINE FREDERIC.

STATIONS OF THE CROSS

A series of fourteen pictures or carvings portraying incidents in Christ's journey from his condemnation by Pilate to his being laid in the tomb. They are arranged around the inside walls of churches and chapels, but are also to be found in other settings such as along wooded paths near shrines. In the devotion of the Stations, an individual or group passes from station to station reciting prayers and meditating on each incident, or at least on the passion of Christ in general. It is thought that the Stations originated as a way that those unable to travel might follow the pilgrimage route in Jerusalem, the "Via Dolorosa," and the plenary indulgence attached to the pilgrimage is also given to those who prayerfully make the journey of the fourteen stations. Many texts have been written for use during the Stations, but that of St. Alphonsus Ligouri probably remains the most popular. A further custom is the singing of a stanza of the medieval hymn *Stabat Mater* ("By the Cross her Station Keeping") between each station.

DAVID BRYAN

See also DEVOTIONS; PASSION NARRATIVES.

STEIN, EDITH (1891–1942)

Edith Stein (Sr. Teresa Benedicta of the Cross, O.C.D.), the German Discalced Carmelite nun, well-known phenomenologist, lecturer, and martyr at Auschwitz, was born 12 October 1891, in Breslau, Germany, which is now Wroclaw, Poland. She was educated in primary and secondary schools in her hometown and attended Breslau's University before beginning the study of philosophy under Edmund Husserl in the University of Göttingen in 1913. She earned her doctorate, *summa cum laude,* under Husserl in Freiburg in 1916 and served as his assistant until 1918. She translated into German the English writings of John Henry Cardinal Newman, and the Latin "Disputed Questions" of St. Thomas Aquinas.

Her studies in phenomenology had convinced her she could no longer support the atheism she had laid claim to in her sixteenth year. Witnessing the spiritual strength drawn from the Cross of Christ by her friend, Anna Reinach, when her philosopher-husband Adolf Reinach was killed in World War I, Edith Stein knew she would have to become a Christian. She was uncertain whether to seek her spiritual home in the Lutheran or the Catholic Church. In the summer of 1921, she read the life of St. Teresa of Avila and found in that saint's response to God the answer to her quest. Edith was baptized in the Catholic Church on New Year's Day, 1922. In consideration of her beloved mother's welfare, she postponed entering the Carmelite Order although she felt called to that form of contemplative religious life from the moment she chose to become a Catholic Christian.

Edith Stein

In obedience to her spiritual guides, she taught from 1923 to 1931 at the Dominican sisters' college for girls in Speyer. She also gave lectures throughout Germany, Switzerland, and Austria on topics of particular interest and assistance to women. Her final teaching assignment was at the Pedagogical Institute in Münster. Her activity there and as lecturer-at-large was curtailed by the Nazi prohibition of any form of professional employment by anyone of Jewish ancestry.

Edith took this curtailment as justification for entering Carmel at last. On 15 October 1933, three days after her forty-second birthday, she was received into the Discalced Carmelite family at the monastery of Cologne, Germany. There, at her own request, she was given the name of Teresa Benedicta of the Cross.

Edith Stein made her profession on Easter Sunday, 21 April 1935. She was as generous in her observance of the daily life of a Carmelite as she had been in the various duties of teacher and lecturer. To her sisters, she was a warm-hearted, kind, and considerate companion with a full quota of human qualities and shortcomings which made religious life in community challenging, at times astringent, but joyful just the same. Because of her ability to adjust to community life without sacrificing her common sense, it was very hard for the sisters to accept her transfer to the Carmel of Echt, Holland, on the last day of 1938. The persecution of the Jews by the Nazis had escalated alarmingly and Edith worried that her presence in the community would bring Nazi reprisals on her sisters.

But Holland, where Sr. Teresa Benedicta found a new home in the Carmel of Echt, fell to the Nazis by 1940 and the danger to Edith and the nuns was simply transferred to another country. The Dutch Catholic hierarchy and the leadership of several Protestant denominations officially protested the mistreatment and persecution of the Jews in Holland by a pastoral letter read in all the churches on Sunday, 26 July 1942, after a telegram of protest had been utterly ignored by Seyss-Inquart, commander of the occupation forces. The following Sunday, 2 August, in reprisal for the pastoral protest, the Nazis arrested hundreds of Catholics who were of Jewish descent, particularly priests and religious, among them Edith Stein and her sister Rosa who were arrested at the Carmel in Echt.

The processing of these prisoners of the Nazis was deliberately speedy, and they were transported, via Amersfoort and Westerbork camps, to Auschwitz where Edith Stein was killed (according to Red Cross investigations) on 9 August 1942.

On 1 May 1987, Pope John Paul II added her to the number of the Blessed at a public ceremony in Cologne, Germany. Her writings, translated into many languages, are studied on all the continents and her canonization process continues.

JOSEPHINE KOEPPEL, O.C.D.

See also BEATIFICATION; CONTEMPLATIVE ORDERS; JUDAISM; PHILOSOPHY AND THEOLOGY.

STERILIZATION

Sterilization is a surgical procedure which renders a person incapable of conceiving children. Differing from impotency which signifies that a person is unable to engage in sexual intercourse, sterilization does not prevent a person from engaging in sexual intercourse but it does prevent a generative act of sexual intercourse. From a moral perspective, sterilization is either *direct* or *indirect.* Direct sterilization implies that the principal purpose of the surgical procedure is contraception. Contraceptive sterilization for a man is called a vasectomy; in this procedure the vas deferens is severed thus preventing semen from being deposited in the womb during intercourse. In the case of a woman, contraceptive sterilization is usually accomplished through a tubal ligation; the fallopian tubes being severed or tied, thus preventing the ovum from uniting with the sperm during intercourse. Tubal ligation and vasectomy are common forms of contraceptive birth control in most industrial countries. Latest statistics indicate that about twenty million people have been surgically sterilized in the United States. *Indirect* sterilization occurs when the direct purpose of the surgical procedure is to circumvent or remove an existing pathology or to restore health. For example, removal of a cancerous uterus or radiation of diseased testicles resulting in sterilization constitute indirect sterilization because sterility is not the principal procedure.

Indirect sterilization is not morally objectionable because it is beyond the intention of the person. On the other hand, because direct sterilization is a form of contraception, it is intrinsically unethical and contrary to the Principle of Totality and Integrity. Moreover, it sacrifices a basic human function without the necessity of preserving life (R. Lawler and others, *Catholic Sexual Ethics,* Huntington, Indiana: *Our Sunday Visitor,* 1985, pp. 10–44).

As a form of birth regulation, the chief disadvantage of direct sterilization is that it freely deprives the human person of a basic human capacity. Individuals so deprived do not at the time want any more children and often report subjective satisfaction with the results. Nevertheless, the ability to reproduce, even when not actually used, relates the individual to the community and its future. The sense of power, of life, and of belonging that this engenders is reflected in the religions and philosophies of all cultures, as the Old Testament testifies by treating sterility in man or woman as a curse. The efforts of Indira Ghandi in India, politically disastrous to her regime, to enforce a sterilization program on a people of ancient culture illustrate both how tempting this method is to governments seeking a simple and permanent solution to the problem of population control and how deeply it is resented and feared where this sense of the human meaning of complete sexual power is still alive among the otherwise powerless.

The highly technological culture in the United States is singularly insensitive to deep human needs, which are unconscious or suppressed by cultural influences. Simply because most sterilized persons respond on a questionnaire that they experienced only a feeling of relief and freedom as a result of their surgery is not necessarily a reliable indication of its deeper consequences. Social and psychological research on such effects is still very superficial, and the present ecological crisis warns of the gradual long-term risks of what at first appeared to be harmless and effective technologies.

In sum, in keeping with its tradition of moral discernment, the Church teaches that direct contraceptive sterilization is immoral. But there is some dispute concerning the distinction between direct and indirect sterilization. For example, if a woman would experience serious renal or cardiac dysfunction if she becomes pregnant in the future, may she have a tubal ligation now to avoid a future pathology arising from pregnancy? This question has practical consequences for Catholic hospitals in the U.S. because the Ethical and Religious Directives for Catholic Health Care Facilities in the U.S. prohibit performance of contraceptive sterilization in Catholic hospitals. The National Conference of Catholic Bishops (NCCB) in the United States sent the question concerning the distinction between direct and indirect sterilization to the Holy See and received the following response. "Not-with-standing any subjectively right intention of those whose actions are prompted by the prevention of physiological or mental illness which is foreseen or feared as a result of pregnancy, such sterilization remains absolutely forbidden according to the doctrine of the Church" (Congregation of Doctrine of the Faith, "Statement on Sterilization," Washington, D.C.: NCCB, 1978).

Underlying the statement of the Holy See concerning sterilization is the traditional interpretation of the principle of Totality and Integrity. According to the traditional application of this principle, surgery may not be used to excise or damage a part of the body unless (1) the continued presence or functioning of a particular organ causes serious damage to the whole body; (2) the harm to the whole body cannot be avoided except by the surgery, which gives promise of being effective; and (3) one can reasonably expect that the negative effect will be offset by the positive effect.

KEVIN O'ROURKE, O.P.

See also BIOETHICS; SEXUALITY; THEOLOGY, MORAL.

STIGMATA

The term "stigmata" is the plural of the Greek noun "stigma," meaning mark or tattoo, and is used to refer to the marks of the wounds suffered by Christ in his crucifixion. Some individuals, known as stigmatists, have been recipients or sufferers of marks like these. For most stigmatists, great pain accompanies this phenomenon, which is usually external and visible and may include profuse bleeding. Invisible yet painful stigmata may also occur, as with St. Catherine of Siena. The experience is generally believed to be a sign of favor by the Lord and an indication of personal holiness. There are approxi-

"Stigmata of St. Francis," oil painting by El Greco, 1585–1595, Escorial Monastery

mately three hundred recorded cases, perhaps the most famous being St. Francis of Assisi.

PATRICIA DeFERRARI

See also CROSS.

STOLE

A liturgical vestment made of a long strip of cloth, several inches wide, which is worn by deacons, priests, and bishops; a deacon wears it over his left shoulder (like a sash) and underneath his dalmatic, while a priest or bishop wears it around his neck (allowing it to hang straight down in the front) and under his chasuble. It is worn at Mass, while administering the other sacraments, and when preaching. Its color corresponds with the liturgical color of the day or season.

JOSEPH QUINN

See also VESTMENTS, LITURGICAL.

SUB TUUM

This ancient prayer is translated thus: *We fly to thy patronage, O holy Mother of God; despise not our petitions in our necessities; but deliver us from all danger, O ever glorious and blessed Virgin.*

For centuries it was considered a medieval prayer. But the publication in 1938 of a fragment of papyrus, purchased in 1917 by John Ryland Library in Manchester, led scholars to identify it as a third-century composition. This is the first known prayer to Mary which expresses belief in her intercession. Consequently it is reasonable to assume that belief in Mary's intercessory power was part of an older tradition.

MICHAEL GLAZIER

See also MARY, MOTHER OF GOD.

SUBDEACON

See MINOR ORDERS.

SUBSIDIARITY, PRINCIPLE OF

The term is taken from the Latin, *subsidium*, which had the general sense of help or support and the military meaning of an additional force reserved as a backup. In Catholic usage the term means that larger organizational structures and higher authorities are by nature a backup force to supply what individuals and smaller or voluntary groupings cannot do. The implication is that they should not usurp functions that can be handled by the latter. The principle is based on the dignity, freedom, and responsibility of the human person before God. The principle has been discussed explicitly since the pontificate of Pius XI when the Church turned its attention to Soviet Communism, Fascism, and the Nazi regime in Germany. In these cases it was clear that these totalitarian states were taking control of so many aspects of human life that they threatened to eliminate private life altogether, reducing people to puppet-like cogs in the state machine. In the pontificates of Pius XII and Paul VI (and implicitly in that of John XXIII) the question was raised whether the principle of subsidiarity ought not also to apply to the Church itself. The documents of Vatican II which dealt with Church structure and function, such as *Christus Dominus,* the decree about bishops, incorporate this principle, and it was intended to be integrated into the new *Code of Canon Law.* The Church, however, had structured itself for so many centuries on the pattern of the Constantinian Empire that the process of decentralization of what is more appropriately done locally, informally, or individually is inevitably conflictual and slow.

MONIKA K. HELLWIG

See also SOCIAL TEACHING OF THE CHURCH.

SUFFERING IN THE NEW TESTAMENT

The New Testament reckons with the inevitability of human suffering in this present evil age: James 1:2 says "*when* you meet various trials," not *if,* and Acts

14:22 says that "through many tribulations we must enter the kingdom of God." The assumed ultimate cause of human suffering is the Fall (Gen 3:14-19; cf. Rom 8:18-25).

Because of the Fall, some suffer oppression at the hands of others, both human and nonhuman. Just as the Hebrews in Egypt prior to the Exodus suffered at the hands of the Egyptians, and Jesus suffered in the days of his flesh at the hand of his human oppressors (Heb 2:10; 1 Pet 2:21), so Christians suffer in the present world because of other fallen humans (1 Pet 4:4; Heb 10:32-34; Acts 5:41; Rev 17:6; 18:24). When oppressed, Christians are (1) to make sure their suffering is for righteousness sake (1 Pet 3:17; Matt 5:10-12); (2) not to add to the pool of suffering by their reactions to it (Matt 5:38-42; Rom 12:14, 17, 19-21; 1 Pet 2:21-25); (3) to recognize that suffering for Christ is as much a spiritual gift as is faith (Phil 1:29) and is to be embraced with joy (Acts 5:41; Heb 11:26); (4) to try to change the oppressive situation, if there is an opportunity, for oneself (1 Cor 7:21b) and for others (Phlm 15–17). Christians can act this way because God is ultimately their vindicator (Matt 5:10; Phil 4:5; 1 Pet 4:5).

In agreement with both Jewish and Greco-Roman cultures, early Christians believed still other suffering is due to nonhuman fallen beings. 1 Corinthians 12:7; Luke 9:38-39; 13:16; Acts 10:38; 19:11-12 speak of suffering due to Satan and his evil spirits. The power of Jesus is viewed either as a remedy for or as sustenance within such pain.

Others suffer as a consequence of their sin (Mark 2:1-12; John 5:14; Jas 5:13-18). Jewish (Deut 30:15-20; Ezek 18) and Greco-Roman (Hierocles, *On Duties: How to Conduct Oneself towards the Gods* 1.3.53-54) cultures also took this position. The criticisms leveled against this position by Jesus (Luke 13:1-5; John 9:1-2) were not against it as such but only against its being absolutized. It is not the only explanation for suffering, but it is an explanation for some suffering.

Given the nature of the biblical God, such suffering was believed to have a redemptive aim (1 Cor 11:31-32; Heb 12:5-11; Jas 5:13-18; 1 Pet 1:7; Rev 3:19 has the risen Christ say to the Laodiceans: "Those whom I love, I reprove and chasten; so be zealous and repent"). The roots of this belief lay in the Jewish Scriptures (Deut 8:5—"Know then in your heart that, as a man disciplines his son, the Lord your God disciplines you"; Prov 3:11-12—"My son, do not despise the Lord's discipline or be weary of his reproof, for the Lord reproves him whom he loves, as a father the son in whom he delights"; 2 Macc 6:12-15 says the calamities that befell the Jews were designed to discipline the people. To punish immediately is a sign of great kindness. "For in the case of the other nations the Lord waits patiently to punish them until they have reached the full measure of their sins; but he does not deal in this way with us, in order that he may not take vengeance on us afterwards when our sins have reached their height"). Presupposed in this position is the assumption that the sufferer has strayed from the right path either consciously or unconsciously, knowingly or unwittingly. The pain is the discipline necessary to correct this misdirection.

Still others suffer even though they have not sinned. The hardships are understood as a test that builds endurance and character, just as training does for an athlete (Rom 5:3-4; Jas 1:2-18). The roots of this perspective are in ancient Greece (Sophocles, *Oedipus at Colonus* 7). It flowered in first-century A.D. Stoicism (Seneca, *On Providence* 1.5 says: "God does not make a spoiled pet of a good man; he tests him, hardens him, and fits him for his own service"; Epictetus, *Discourses* 1.xxiv.1-3 says: "When a difficulty befalls, remember that God, like a physical trainer, has matched you with a rugged young man. What for? . . . So that you may become an Olympic victor; but that cannot be done without sweat").

It found its way into Hellenistic Judaism in 4 Maccabees (63 B.C.–A.D. 70). There, one of the Maccabean martyrs, on the point of death, says: "We, vile tyrant, suffer all this for our training in divine virtue" (10:10). The narrator says of them: "Truly divine was the contest in which they were engaged. On that day virtue was the umpire and the test to which they were put was a test of endurance" (17:11-12). In this Jewish text, suffering is understood not as a correction of misdirection but rather as conditioning that results in increased strength, enabling the victor's prize. It is the Stoic view of suffering espoused by Seneca and Epictetus but in a Jewish framework with a Jewish view of virtue (obedience to God and the Law). It sees suffering as training, as producing endurance, as endured out of hope, and as a blessing in which to rejoice. It is this Jewish appropriation of the Stoic view that is closest to Romans 5:3-4 and James 1:2-18 in the New Testament. There Christians suffer, not as a correction to their misdirection, but as conditioning that builds endurance and character, that is, deep-rootedness in God.

It is this view of suffering that is associated with Jesus in Hebrews (2:10; 5:8; 12:2) and in Luke. In both, Jesus' sufferings constitute the way along which he moved to glory. Through them he learned obedience and had his faith completed. This does not imply that Jesus was a sinner and needed his misdirection corrected. Hebrews states the belief held in common with Luke: Jesus "in every respect has been tempted as we are, yet without sin" (4:15). Jesus' suffering was not the correction of his misdirection but was the arena in which his development was enabled, as an athlete's skill is developed in the stress of training.

Still others suffer, not as a correction of their misdirection or as conditioning to develop their endurance, but as a contribution on behalf of others. This was a view found both in the Greco-Roman world (Seneca, *To Lucilius on Providence*) and in ancient Judaism (Gen 50:15-21; Isa 53:2-12; 2 Macc 7:37-38). Joseph, sold into slavery by his jealous brothers, rose to prominence in Egypt. When his brothers came to Egypt for food in a famine and discovered who he was, they were fearful for their lives. Joseph, however, responded to their fears, saying: "As for you, you meant evil against me; but God meant it for good, to bring it about that many people should be kept alive, as they are today" (Gen 50:20). Joseph's suffering benefitted others. Isaiah says of the suffering servant: "But he was wounded for our transgressions, he was bruised for our iniquities; upon him was the chastisement that made us whole, and with his stripes we are healed" (53:5). His sufferings were a contribution to others. One of the Maccabean martyrs concludes his speech with these words: "I, like my brothers, give up body and life for the laws of the fathers, appealing to God to show mercy soon to our nation . . . and through me and my brothers to bring to an end the wrath of the Almighty which has justly fallen on our whole nation" (7:37-38). Their deaths are for others' benefit.

It is in this context that one can understand the New Testament's comments about the suffering of Jesus (Gal 1:3-4; Mark 10:45) and Paul (2 Cor 1:6; Col 1:24). When Jesus gives his life a ransom for many and when Paul rejoices in his sufferings for his Church's sake, it is not a correction of their misdirection or a strengthening of their spiritual prowess but rather a benefit they are bestowing upon others.

Although the New Testament assumes the inevitability of human suffering, it does not countenance a pathological desire for suffering *per se.* For example, like ancient Judaism, it frowns upon a lust for martyrdom. Hence the Gospels depict Jesus' desire to avoid death, if that be God's will (Mark 14:35-36), and 2 Corinthians 12:7-10 refers to Paul's threefold prayer for deliverance from his thorn in the flesh. Suffering may be inevitable in a fallen world but one does not go looking for it.

The New Testament teaches that the ultimate resolution of the mystery of suffering is not intellectual; it can never be satisfactorily explained. It is rather devotional; one confronts God in prayer, asking for what one desires—escape from suffering—but then accepting what God gives as his will for one, whether that be deliverance from or sustenance in the pain (Mark 14:32-42; 2 Cor 12:7-10). This solution, of course, has its roots in the Jewish Scriptures (Job; Psalms). The various views of suffering in the New Testament are more strategies for a proper response to suffering than an explanation of it.

CHARLES H. TALBERT

See also BIBLE, NEW TESTAMENT WRITINGS; CHRISTIAN SPIRITUALITY.

SUFFRAGAN BISHOP

The bishop of a diocese which is part of an ecclesiastical province that is supervised by an archbishop known as the metropolitan archbishop.

JOAN GLAZIER

See also BISHOP.

SUICIDE

Suicide is uncoerced, intentional self-killing. It must not be confused with the willing surrender of one's life in self-sacrifice, such as in defending another unjustly attacked, in delivering health care to the highly infectious sick, or in witnessing to one's faith in persecution. In these instances, one does not will one's death but accepts it as an inevitable result of doing what one feels called to do to serve justice, mercy, or faith.

In health care, refusing "ordinary" means of treatment is considered suicide. Refusing "extraordinary" means is not suicide but more accurately understood to be humbly accepting the inherent limitations of the human condition and letting a fatal pathology run its course (see "euthanasia"). "Assisted suicide" is a related concept which emphasizes helping someone to take one's own life by providing the means and knowledge of how to do it.

Even though suicide generally carries negative moral connotations, not everyone agrees that suicide is always immoral. Three principles have shaped the discussion for and against suicide.

The principle of autonomy upholds the freedom of each person to pursue one's own goals without the interference of others. It supports the right to commit suicide for those who are capable of rational deliberation and acting on those deliberations as long as the person's actions do not affect the freedom and interest of others. However, autonomy does not support suicide if the person's freedom is impeded by some incapacity, such as the influence of drugs or alcohol, the emotional strains of crises in life, or coercion. In such cases, others may interfere with attempted suicide in order to prevent the person from harm.

The principle of utility looks to the impact of an action on the interests and welfare of all concerned. Thus, the fact that one has certain obligations to others in the community, or that others love the one contemplating suicide and value that person's contribution to the community are to be considered in determining whether the suicide is justified. To the extent that one has no dependents or outstanding obligations, and that others perceive the person to be plagued with an untreatable condition which only death can relieve, then utility would justify suicide. However, the negative impact of grief, guilt, and deprivation to dependents and society generally brought on by the suicide could render the suicide unjustified by utility.

The Catholic moral tradition rejects the arguments from autonomy and utility in support of suicide. The Catholic tradition opposes suicide by appealing to the principle of the sanctity of life and its related principles of the sovereignty of God, human stewardship, and the prohibition against killing. The religious argument claims that life has been given to us to use and to make fruitful, but that it ultimately belongs to God and so is not for us to end when we so choose. To take one's own life violates God's sovereignty over life, attacks human dignity, and is an offense against the proper love of self. In this view, acts of suicide are objectively immoral. However, the degree of culpability for suicide depends upon the state of mind in which the act is done.

Recent studies which have paid attention to the social and personal circumstances surrounding suicides show that they are not often voluntary acts and so, while they may be mistaken and morally wrong, they are not always blameworthy. Ecclesiastical law does not withhold Christian burial from one who has committed suicide and many legal jurisdictions are moving toward decriminalizing attempts at suicide.

RICHARD M. GULA, S.S.

See also DEATH; DEATH AND DYING.

SULPICIANS

A part of the great reform movement which developed in France during the seventeenth century, the Company of Priests of St. Sulpice was founded in 1641 by Jean Jacques Olier during his pastorate of the parish of St. Sulpice in Paris. Never intending to form a "religious congregation," he gathered around himself a group of diocesan clergy totally dedicated to the formation of priests. Wishing to be close to those whom they serve, the Sulpicians to this day do not take vows. Rather, they remain diocesan priests released by their bishops so that they might carry out this mission of formation, bound to one another by priestly charity and dedication to the education of the clergy. They devote themselves to this task primarily through the discernment of vocations and the initial and ongoing formation of priests. This devotion finds its institutional expression in founding and directing seminaries.

The Sulpician approach to seminary education is marked by five essential characteristics: (1) Responsibility is collegially exercised by the rector and faculty; (2) Faculty and students engage in a common life, in French a *communauté éducatrice,* which assists the discernment of priestly vocations by the development of an atmosphere wherein personal initiative, responsibility, and service to others are encouraged and evaluated; (3) Seminarians are progressively initiated into a personal spiritual life, most importantly through spiritual direction; (4) There is a great concern for the spiritual freedom of the candidates, especially through guarding the confidentiality of the spiritual direction relationship; (5) The entire program is marked by the constant search for union with Christ wherein the various aspects of priestly formation (intellectual, spiritual, communal, and pastoral) are integrated into a coherent unity.

While never attempting to impose a particular spirituality upon the candidates for priesthood entrusted to their care, the Sulpicians nonetheless have a distinct spiritual tradition. Grounded in the spirituality of the French School, especially as formulated by Father Olier, they center their spiritual lives on union with Jesus Christ. As he exhorts them in the *Pietas Seminarii,* a work which summarized this spirituality at the time of the founding of the first Sulpician seminary, "the first and final end of this Institute will be to live wholly for God in Christ Jesus." Animated by the Holy Spirit, they are to be priests marked by an apostolic spirit of ministerial service. In addition to seminary formation, this service includes parochial ministry, continuing education of the clergy, and expert assistance of bishops on the local and national level. This apostolic spirit is nurtured by contemplative prayer, sustained by the Eucharist, constant reflection upon the word of God, and devotion to the Virgin Mary.

The apostolic spirit of the Sulpicians is also expressed in the missionary character of the Society. During Father Olier's lifetime, the Sulpicians arrived in Canada, and he himself aspired to join them in Montreal. With the approval of Bishop John Carroll, the Sulpicians founded St. Mary's Seminary in Baltimore, the oldest Catholic seminary in the United States, in 1791. At the present time, the Sulpicians direct seminaries on five continents.

Since the Second Vatican Council, the Sulpicians have been at the forefront of seminary reform. They have taken the initiative in modernizing seminary life and have sought to provide a strong theological education which finds its final expression in an integrated spiritual life. Although small in number, the Sulpicians continue to exert an important influence on the life of the Church through their ministry of priestly formation.

DAVID D. THAYER, S.S.

See also SEMINARIAN.

SUMMA THEOLOGIAE

See THOMAS AQUINAS, ST.

SUMMERHILL, LOUISE (1916–1991)

Louise Summerhill was born in Aberdeen, Scotland, and emigrated with her family at age seven to Gananoque, Ontario. At age seventeen, she began receiving instruction in the Catholic faith, and was received into the Catholic Church. She then attended Loretto Abbey, Toronto. In 1937, at age twenty-two, she married Stephen Summerhill who also converted to Catholicism; they had seven children. Summerhill died 11 August 1991 at the age of seventy-five after an illness of several months.

Summerhill founded Birthright on 15 October 1968 in Toronto, Ontario, Canada in a faith-filled response to the Omnibus Bill passed in the Canadian legislature in 1967. This bill made abortions legal if performed in designated hospitals and approved by the hospital's abortion committee. Her faith-filled action blossomed, and today there are over 650 Birthright centers spread throughout the world, of which eighty spread from coast to coast in Canada. Birthright International Headquarters remains in Toronto (761 Coxwell Avenue, M4C 3C5).

Birthright, a comprehensive pregnancy support service offering alternatives to abortion, is nonjudgmental, nonmoralistic, interdenominational, independent, and nonpolitical. It receives no government funding, and does not get involved in lobbying of any kind. Its pastoral focus is to bring practical, emotional, and psychological help to the pregnant woman in distress.

Louise Summerhill often quoted from Scripture in describing her work in Birthright, because she realized the importance of faith and prayer in her work. She believed that it was by God's grace that Birthright ever got off the ground.

Summerhill always maintained that "the essence of Birthright is love." This conviction was rooted in her taking to heart St. Paul's message in 1 Corinthians 13:1, "If I have all the eloquence of men or of angels, but speak without love, I am simply a gong booming or a cymbal clashing." More important than saving millions of babies, trying to get the laws of abortion changed, or trying to convince others of her views, was the Christian stance of unconditional love. This unconditional love was an actual, incarnational love for real human beings, part of community, and the body of Christ. St. John says, "God is love and anyone who lives in love lives in God, and God lives in him" (1 John 4:16). In the community of Birthright, God is present, often frail, weak, and in pain. The Birthright volunteer is present to suffer with and taste the tears of the woman in distress due to an unplanned pregnancy. In this interaction, compassion is born. We have a strange God indeed who chooses broken people to build a community of shared love and life—a Church in miniature. Says Summerhill, "The love of God surpasses all knowledge, and here is the secret of the success of Birthright. We are, indeed, a community of love." This community of love lived out God's preferential option for the poor and voiceless.

Summerhill, though a convert to Catholicism, always stressed the interdenominational aspect of Birthright. It was Summerhill's firm conviction that when we died, God would not ask us which Church we belonged to but say: "Come, you whom my Father has blessed, take for your heritage the kingdom prepared for you since the foundation of the world. For I was hungry and you gave me food; I was thirsty and you gave me drink; I was a stranger and you made me welcome; naked and you clothed me, sick and you visited me, in prison and you came to see me" (Matt 25:34-37). When the volunteers at Birthright listen to women's stories, give out maternity clothes and layettes for the infants, coach a woman in labor, provide food and shelter, they are doing true missionary work of humble service. This humble service leaves its indelible mark, and there is no need for direct proselytizing or preaching of the gospel.

Over the years, Summerhill received many honors on behalf of Birthright: The Christian Culture Award from Assumption College in Windsor, Ontario, in April, 1988; The Temple Award for Creative Altruism from the Institute of Noetic Sciences in December, 1988; the Canadian Volunteer Award in February, 1990. She also received honorary degrees: a Doctor of Humane Letters from Molloy College,

Long Island, New York; a Doctor of Laws from St. Joseph College, Rensselaer, Indiana; a Doctor of Sacred Letters from St. Michael's College, University of Toronto, Ontario. She was posthumously honored with the National Physicians for Life Award and the St. Joseph College Award accepted on behalf of Birthright by the codirector of the Birthright center in Johnstown, Pennsylvania.

Jesus said, "It is never the will of your Father in heaven that one of these little ones should be lost" (Matt 18:14). Summerhill took this message to heart in founding Birthright as an alternative to abortion. She thus became co-creator with God, the Creator and Nurturer of all things on earth.

ANITA ALLSOPP

See also ABORTION.

SUNDAY

(Lat. *Dominica,* "The Lord's Day") The first day of the week, known to Christians as "the day of the Lord" (Rev 1:10) and "the day to break bread" (Acts 20:7). In New Testament times it replaced the Jewish Sabbath as the day to worship God and refrain from work. Leaders of the early Church established Sunday as the day to recall the descent of the Holy Spirit at Pentecost, and to honor God's creation. Its greatest theological significance is as the Church's weekly commemoration of Christ's resurrection.

The principle of abstaining from work on Sundays (cf. Exod 20:8-11) was formalized in the fourth century by ecclesiastical legislation (Council of Elvira, ca. A.D. 306) and civil decree (by Constantine in 321). Between the sixth and thirteenth centuries, attendance at Mass also was mandated by Church and civil law, the latter of which stipulated harsh penalties for noncompliance. At Vatican II, the Church reiterated its requirement that the faithful attend Mass on Sundays, as the Eucharistic celebration remains its chief act of worship. The current *General Norms for the Liturgical Year and the Calendar* states that "Sunday must be ranked as the first holy day of all" (no. 4).

The Mass of the Sunday may be superceded only by solemnities or feasts of the Lord. The appropriate observance of Sunday is summarized in the present Code of Canon Law, which stipulates that the faithful are to "abstain from those labors and business concerns which impede worship to be rendered to God, the joy which is proper to the Lord's Day, or the proper relaxation of mind and body" (canon 1247).

JOSEPH QUINN

See also LITURGY.

SUPEREROGATION, WORKS OF

This term, now seldom used in Catholic circles, comes from the Latin, *erogatio,* a payment due, and the prefix *super,* above. Used formerly in moral theology, it referred to good works not strictly required, such as the vows of religious congregations, and particular apostolic and charitable activities. The term was used commonly in the pre-Vatican II era in moral theology in part because there had been a rather sharp distinction between moral and spiritual theology. Moral theology tended to be minimalist, that is to say, to define the minimum requirements for avoiding personal sin. Reflection on the living of a Christian life beyond that minimum became the concern of spiritual theology, which tended to be seen as the concern of vowed religious and exceptional people but less necessary for the whole laity making up the Church.

The developments of Vatican II brought a clearer awareness of the vocation of the laity to holiness and apostolate, based on a return to Scripture and the consciousness expressed in the writings and liturgy of the early Church. In this light a Christian can never be satisfied with the observance of explicit commandments, but must constantly discern what must change in one's own attitudes, relationships and expectations and in those of one's society so that the reign of God in all human affairs may be more fully welcomed. Thus conversion is a continuous task and has no blueprint. In that context it is not helpful to speak of works of supererogation as though only minimal avoidance of actual sin were required by the Christian life for most people. It is more appropriate to speak of a call to holiness and apostolate for all, within which there is an unlimited variety of particular vocations.

MONIKA K. HELLWIG

See also MERIT; THEOLOGY, MORAL.

SUPERNATURAL

Used both as a noun and adjective, the term literally means "above nature." Nature here is understood to comprise not only the material cosmos (minerals, plants, and animals) but also human beings and angels. The divine, which is at the top of this hierarchy of beings, is regarded as supernatural with respect to the other realities.

In Christian theology, the term is used to describe the absolutely free, gratuitous, and undeserved character of God's gift of self to us in the incarnation of the Son and in the sanctifying grace of the Spirit which culminates in the beatific vision. Unfortunately, since the sixteenth century, some theologians, in order to defend the gratuitous character of God's self-communication, devised the concept of "pure nature." In this two-tiered universe, pure nature refers to the hypothetical condition in which human beings have their own end and pursue it with their own means apart from grace; grace is then seen as a superstructure imposed upon nature and paralleling it with its own end and means. This theological construct (which can be called "supernaturalism" and is a reaction to naturalism and rationalism) obscures the fact that "nature" is not a closed system but dynamically open to and tending toward the divine, that humans have a "natural desire" for God, that their hearts are restless until they rest in God (Augustine), and that grace operates not apart or above nature but in, through, and with it.

PETER C. PHAN

See also GRACE; NATURE.

SURPLICE

A loose white linen vestment which has wide sleeves and extends to the waist; it is sometimes embroidered at the hem and sleeves. The surplice is worn by all clergy (over their cassock or religious habit) when administrating sacraments, in choir, or during processions, and by laypersons when ministering at liturgical functions or in the choir.

JOSEPH QUINN

See also VESTMENTS, LITURGICAL.

SUSO, HENRY (1295–1366)

Henry Suso was born at Constance on 21 March, probably in the year 1295. His father was Count Heinrich von Berg and his mother was a very pious woman of the Süse family (latinized as Suso, Seuse in the modern German). Henry took his surname from his mother out of veneration for her.

Through special exemption and with a donation to the order from his parents, Henry entered the Dominican community at age thirteen, two years younger than Church law normally allowed. The circumstances surrounding his admittance to the order troubled Henry for many years. He was afraid that he was destined for hell because his entrance into the order had been secured through the sin of simony, the exchange of material goods for spiritual profit. It was not until he was consoled by Meister Eckhart ten years later that he was able to let go of the guilt, an indication of the powerful influence Eckhart had in Suso's life.

When Henry received the Dominican habit, he took on the ascetic and devotional practices of the life with rather mediocre conviction. Several years later, however, he experienced a "conversion" that marked the start of a life of very extreme austerity, prayer, and solitude. Indeed, his ascetic practices, as recorded in his autobiography, *The Life of the Servant,* bordered on masochism. Henry also received considerable education. He studied at Constance, most likely at Strassburg. Once he completed the normal course of studies, Henry was chosen to continue theological studies at the general house of studies at Cologne, a tribute to his intelligence and previous academic success. During at least part of the time that Suso was in Cologne, he studied with Meister Eckhart. In 1326 Henry returned to Constance and the post of lector. He directed the studies of the younger members and provided lectures for the rest of the community as well.

Suso had an active preaching ministry. He served as spiritual mentor to Dominican nuns and to the Friends of God in Switzerland and the Upper Rhine region. He served as prior of the Dominican friars at Constance from 1343 until 1344 while he was in exile at Diessenhoven for supporting the papal cause over the claims of Louis of Bavaria. During these years Suso suffered physical hardship as well as persecution and betrayal by friends. Around the year 1347 he was transferred to Ulm where he died in 1366.

Henry Suso is commonly acknowledged as one of the three great male mystics of early medieval German mysticism, along with his teacher, Meister Eckhart, and his contemporary, John Tauler. These three Dominicans lived and taught during a period of great political and religious turmoil in Europe. The Holy Roman Empire had been seriously weakened by the collapse of the Hohenstaufen dynasty in 1254 and the subsequent nineteen-year delay in reestablishing rule. Chivalry was declining due to the deteriorating economic status of the knightly class and the rise of towns. The continuing struggle between emperor and papacy only exacerbated the social and moral decline. Natural calamities, such as famines, floods, and plagues added to the instability of the period and the tendency toward apocalyptic thought.

Amid this political and social upheaval, there was a reawakened spirituality, a religious "turning inward." Practitioners of this spirituality included members of religious orders, particularly the mendicant orders, men called beghards and women called beguines, and even large numbers of laypersons. One current within this stream of religious practice was the brothers and sisters of the Free Spirit. This was not a formal organization, but rather a loose association of people with similar beliefs. Nonetheless, they were seen by Church authorities as a heretical group and several of their teachings were condemned by the Council of Vienne (1311–1312). They were accused of teaching that one could attain a state in this life wherein it is impossible to sin, hence requiring no further concern for practices or disciplines of any kind. This state arose from the annihilation of the soul in the nothingness that is God. Both accusers and accused have alleged that Meister Eckhart was the source and authority for their beliefs. As a student and admirer of Eckhart, Henry's life and writings were shaped by this controversy.

Around the year 1327, Suso wrote the *Little Book of Truth* to counter the arguments of the Brethren of the Free Spirit. He gave a systematic, speculative treatment of mystical questions, such as God's being, Unity and Trinity, creation and incarnation, human freedom and responsibility, and union with God while preserving personal identity. *Little Book of Eternal Wisdom,* written about a year later, is often judged to be Suso's masterpiece. It is a practical book "intended for simple persons who have bad habits to crush" (Prologue) and enjoyed continual popularity until the appearance of the *Imitation of Christ.*

The first part of Suso's autobiography, *The Life of the Servant,* records his spiritual growth, and the second part instructs his student, Elsbethe Stägel, in how to advance in the spiritual life. In fact, the origin of the book lies in correspondence between Suso and Stägel. Suso used her notes of their conversations and included some of the letters.

Suso's teaching is more cautious than Eckhart's at the same time that it is shaped by the affective mysticism of Bernard and Bonaventure. Imitation and contemplation of Christ's sufferings were basic elements. For the most part, his teaching is psychological, practical, and ascetical. He illustrates his points by alluding to his own experiences.

PATRICIA DeFERRARI

See also DOMINICANS; MIDDLE AGES, THE; MYSTICISM; SPIRITUAL LIFE; SPIRITUALITY, LAY.

SYLLABUS OF ERRORS

This was the appendix to the letter *Quanta Cura* issued by Pope Pius IX in 1864. It condemned eighty theses (or statements) attributed to modern thinkers. These theses formulated positions ranging from pantheism, deism, rationalism, socialism, communism, and secret societies to claims that revelation is continuous, that Scripture and theology should be studied with scholarly methods, that Christian doctrines underwent historical development and so forth.

Many Catholics and many thoughtful Christians of other Churches were dismayed by the wholesale condemnations which lacked real understanding of modern developments and their foundations. The Syllabus of Errors had the effect of polarizing liberal and conservative elements in the Church. The conservative elements were dominant and continued to be so at the First Vatican Council which followed in 1869 and 1870, and defined papal infallibility.

Most of the theses condemned were later considered in a more nuanced way, distinguishing positions that had been clustered together, considering more carefully terms used, and looking seriously at the grounds on which certain positions were founded. Thus several Roman documents on biblical studies culminated in the dogmatic constitution *Dei Verbum* of Vatican II and in the uses made of Scripture in the other documents of that council. Likewise, a far more careful and discerning attitude to Church-state relations and to modern social and political developments is reflected in the council's documents on the Church in the world (*Gaudium et Spes*) and on religious liberty (*Dignitatis Humanae*).

Occasionally the term Syllabus of Errors is also applied to the sixty-five theses attributed to Modernism and condemned by Pope Pius X in *Lamentabili* in 1907.

MONIKA K. HELLWIG

See also PIUS IX, POPE; VATICAN COUNCIL I; MODERNISM.

SYMBOL

The word "symbol" is derived from a Greek word that means "to throw together" or "to juxtapose." It has come to have a variety of meanings in contemporary theology, philosophy, art, and psychology, and no easy summary of these meanings is possible. Broadly, however, a symbol is a sensible reality (e.g. an object, word, or drawing) that represents another reality not directly perceivable or expressed. For instance, the love two people share might be symbolized by an exchange of wedding rings.

Symbols need not imitate what they represent (as a picture of an apple imitates a real apple); nevertheless, most symbols do have a natural relationship to what they stand for. For example, in Christian baptism, water is used to symbolize a new spiritual life and the washing away of sin; both these meanings are directly related to the everyday functions of water.

Thus symbols are less arbitrary than signs. Signs can be created at will, and they bear no intrinsic relation to what they represent. One could change the shape or color of a traffic sign, for instance, without changing the meaning of the sign itself.

Symbols have played a role in Catholic tradition since its inception. Some ancient symbols survive today; the cross still signifies the power of Jesus as the Christ, and the lamb and the fish continue to serve as symbols of Jesus as well.

The most original Christian symbol, however, is Jesus himself. As the Word of God in human form, Jesus makes visible the invisible God.

The word "symbol" is also a traditional equivalent for "creed."

THERESA SANDERS

See also CREEDS.

SYNOD OF BISHOPS

On 15 September 1965, in the document, *Apostolica Sollicitudo,* Paul Pope VI called for the establishment of the Synod of Bishops as a "permanent consultative body of Bishops for the Universal Church subject directly and immediately to Our authority." The nature and purpose of this assembly of bishops was described in the Vatican II document *Christus Dominus:* "Bishops chosen from different parts of the world in a manner and according to a system determined or to be determined by the Roman Pontiff will render to the Supreme Pastor a more effective auxiliary service in a council which shall be known by the special name of Synod of Bishops. This council, as it will be representative of the whole Catholic episcopate, will bear testimony to the participation of all the bishops in hierarchical communion in the care of the universal Church" (CD 5).

The pope is the president of the Synod and has authority to assign its agenda, to call it together, and to give it deliberative power. While the importance of the Synod is evident, its actual significance remains unclear. Some argue that the synod is an extension of papal primacy, in other words, its role is purely advisory. Others maintain that the synod is an exercise of the collegial dimension of the episcopal office. An examination of the history of synods so far serves only to highlight this ambiguity. Some papal documents reflect none of the concerns of the gathered bishops whereas others, in particular Paul VI's *Evangelii Nuntiandi,* clearly incorporated the work of the bishops.

PATRICIA DeFERRARI

See also BISHOP; PAPACY, THE.

SYNOPTIC GOSPELS

The word "synoptic" means "sharing a common view" or "seeing at a glance." The Gospels attributed to Matthew, Mark, and Luke give a common view of Jesus' public ministry (different from John's Gospel). A Gospel "synopsis" presents these three (or four) texts in parallel (usually vertical) columns, thus allowing the user to see the common features and differences at a glance.

The first three Gospels present a common view of Jesus' public ministry: association with John the Baptist, gathering disciples and instructing them, ministry of teaching and healing in Galilee, journey up to Jerusalem, brief activity in Jerusalem, passion (arrest, trial, suffering, death), and empty tomb. These Gospels portray Jesus as a teacher and healer, and use the same titles for him (Son of Man, Son of David, Son of God, Lord, etc.). At some points the verbal similarity between two or three Gospels is so great that it cannot be explained as coincidence or due even to oral tradition.

Despite their many obvious similarities the Synoptic Gospels differ in their structures, purposes, and theological emphases. Mark begins Jesus' story as an adult, whereas Matthew and Luke tell about the events surrounding Jesus' birth. Jesus' modest teaching activity in Mark is expanded greatly by five speeches in Matthew (chs. 5–7, 10, 13, 18, 24–25) and by Luke's long travel narrative (9:51–19:44). The risen Jesus appears to his followers in Jerusalem (Luke 24) and Galilee (Matt 28).

Matthew wrote for a largely Jewish-Christian community to show that Jesus brought to fullness God's promises to Israel. Mark wrote for Gentile Christians under the pressure of persecution and presented Jesus as their suffering Messiah. Luke wrote for fairly wealthy Gentile Christians and portrayed Jesus as a good example, a prophet, and a martyr faithful to his own principles.

The *Synoptic Problem* concerns the relation between the first three Gospels. Some sayings or episodes appear in all three Gospels; some are in two; some are only in one. The many similarities in content and wording indicate that there is some organic relation. What is it?

Augustine thought that Matthew was the first Gospel, Mark was a poor copy of it, and Luke used both Gospels in writing his own. In the late-eighteenth century J. J. Griesbach modified Augustine's theory: Matthew was first, Luke came second, and Mark is a combination of the two.

The most widely held explanation is the Two Source theory. According to it, Mark was the earliest complete Gospel (about A.D. 70). When Matthew and Luke set out (A.D. 85–90) independently to revise Mark, they both had access to a collection of Jesus' sayings known now as Q (put in form in the 50s) and to special traditions (M for Matthean, L for Lucan). This explanation is regarded as the most economical and satisfying solution today. But there are some problems, especially the so-called minor agreements (where Matthew and Luke agree against Mark). There are more complicated and comprehensive explanations available. Some also contend that remnants of the early Jesus tradition can be found in the apocryphal gospels (Gospel of Thomas, Gospel of Peter, etc.). But most NT scholars work on the basis of the Two Source theory.

DANIEL J. HARRINGTON, S.J.

See also BIBLE, NEW TESTAMENT WRITINGS; CRITICISM, BIBLICAL; Q DOCUMENT.

SYNOPTIC PROBLEM

See SYNOPTIC GOSPELS.

SYSTEMATIC THEOLOGY

See THEOLOGY, SYSTEMATIC.

T

TABERNACLE

(Lat. *tabernaculum,* "a tent") The receptacle in which Hosts for Holy Communion are reserved in churches and chapels. They are usually constructed of wood, stone, or metal, and are round or rectangular in shape. A tabernacle normally contains a ciborium for consecrated Hosts, a lunette (or luna) —which holds a large consecrated Host for use in exposition and Benediction—and a corporal. It is located in the middle of the sanctuary or in a side chapel, and a sanctuary lamp is kept nearby to call attention to the presence of the Blessed Sacrament.

The tabernacle derives from the portable shrine built by the Israelites (under the direction of Moses) to house the Ark of the Covenant (Exod 25-31; 35-40), which they considered the manifestation of God's presence during their years in the desert. The Jewish people continue to honor God's faithfulness to them during this period by celebrating the eight-day feast of Tabernacles each year.

JOSEPH QUINN

See also ARCHITECTURE, CHURCH; EUCHARIST.

"THE TABLET"

Catholic weekly journal carrying news and comment, published in London, where it was founded in 1840 by Frederick Lucas, a Quaker lawyer who had converted to Catholicism. He believed that Catholics should speak openly and without undue concern for either the political establishment or the Protestant ethos of Victorian Britain. The paper reflected his own opinions, which were radical, influenced by Benthamite principles and endorsed by Daniel O'Connell. He thereby made *The Tablet* suspect to the conservative Catholic gentry and influential clerics like Bishop (later Cardinal) Nicholas Wiseman. In 1849 he transferred the paper to Dublin where he used it to advance a number of Irish nationalist causes and the Catholic University then being established by John Henry Newman. Lucas was elected a member of Parliament for the Irish county of Meath and Pope Pius IX later thanked him for his parliamentary endeavors on behalf of the Church but added "I am afraid the editor of *The Tablet* sometimes exceeds the bounds of patience and escapes from the kingdom of moderation."

When Lucas died in 1854 his more cautious successor brought the paper back to London and altered its tone to reflect the tory politics and ultramontane ecclesiastical attitudes then common within the English Catholic establishment. In 1868 Father Herbert Vaughan, founder of the Mill Hill Missionaries, bought the paper. He made it the platform for extreme views in favor of papal infallibility during the First Vatican Council but was pragmatic in politics, supporting whichever party seemed for the time being best disposed towards Catholic requirements, especially in education. Vaughan became bishop of Salford (Manchester) in 1872 and was later to be cardinal archbishop of Westminster. *The Tablet* accordingly fell under episcopal control and remained so until 1936.

Throughout most of this period the paper's lay editors steadily enhanced its reputation as an authoritative source of information and analysis on political, literary, and other developments. On Church affairs it generally reflected the official Roman attitudes voiced by the hierarchy but a courteous scholarship in argument now ensured that intellectual reasoning replaced the vituperation of its earlier days. It was able, for example, to support the condemnations of Modernism without unnecessary denigration of the Modernists. But it had its critics. Irish Catholics deplored its opposition to Home Rule (i.e., an independent Parliament for Ireland) and the editor's explanation that he was "against applying political remedies to economic and social evils" betrayed an ideological conservatism which showed itself on other subjects also, such as the paper's long resistance to women's suffrage.

In 1936 a consortium of laymen bought *The Tablet* from the diocese of Westminster and appointed one of the group, Douglas Woodruff, as editor. He took the paper to new heights, especially in its coverage of foreign affairs. It was soon rumored that the British Foreign Office supplied all British embassies with *The Tablet,* considering it indispensable reading for diplomats. These standards survived unaffected by the Second World War, but its impressive reportage of the Second Vatican Council disguised Woodruff's distress over developments in the Church to which his essentially conservative nature could not reconcile itself. Tom Burns, who succeeded him in 1967, reversed this stance, championing progressive views on Church affairs and also promoting a more perceptive approach to Irish questions—a subject never irrelevant for English-speaking Catholics and of particular importance with the onset of paramilitary violence in Northern Ireland.

A serious decline in circulation followed the emergence of the new liberalism in religious commentary. Traditionally minded readers objected to the paper's trenchant criticism of the "birth control" encyclical, *Humanae Vitae,* and were distressed by the ecumenical emphasis in its response to the canonization of the Forty Martyrs of England and Wales. The conciliar vision, however, began to make its own converts and circulation was already climbing again when John Wilkins took over as editor in 1982. His more radical stance on political questions—matching the openness on religious issues which he inherited—brought a dramatic doubling of sales within seven years and confirmed the place of *The Tablet* in the forefront of forward-looking Catholic publications throughout the world.

LOUIS McREDMOND

See also BRITAIN, CHURCH IN; CHURCH AND STATE; VATICAN COUNCIL I; VATICAN COUNCIL II.

TAIZÉ COMMUNITY

This ecumenical, monastic center was founded by Roger Schutz (b. 1915), who felt the need for some form of monastic life within Protestantism. In 1940, he bought a large house in Taizé (located in southeast France) and this became, until 1942, a refuge for persecuted Jews and other displaced persons. He and his companions were forced to leave France in 1942, at which time they moved to Geneva and joined Max Thurian and his companions in a communal life with ecumenical dimensions. In 1944,

Brother Roger Schutz

Schutz returned to Taizé and resumed his monastic life. Five years later, the first seven brothers were solemnly professed. In 1952, the Rule of Taizé was drawn up, outlining a simple way of monastic living. Since the end of World War II, Taizé has become a religious attraction for many young men, and has earned widespread renown for its ecumenical work and appealing spiritual apostolate.

JOSEPH QUINN

See also ECUMENISM; MONASTICISM; PROTESTANTISM.

TALBOT, MATT (1856–1925)

He was born in the Dublin slums and died in poverty after a life which has inspired legions. As a boy he went to work as a messenger and by the age of thirteen was a confirmed alcoholic. By seventeen he was selling his scant possessions, even his boots, to buy a drink. For the next ten years drink became the focal factor in his life, and gradually even his drinking friends avoided him. By 1883 he was deserted and destitute and he came to the realization that he was an unwanted outcast and a drunkard. He took the pledge for three months and began to attend daily Mass at 5:00 A.M. Slowly his lifestyle changed; he went to bed at 10:30 P.M., rose at 2:00 A.M. to pray; four hours later he went to Mass and from there he went to work at 8:00 A.M. His unskilled job in a lumberyard was poorly paid; his quiet and tolerant demeanor won the respect of his fellow workers; and he shared his meager earnings with the hungry and the hopeless. Over his years of work, penance, and prayer, Matt Talbot—who could hardly spell—kept a spiritual journal which reflected the biblical basis of his spirituality. In 1925 he died of a heart attack in Granby Lane near the Dominican church in Dublin where he attended daily Mass. All over the English-speaking world he is now venerated as the uncanonized patron of alcoholics.

MICHAEL GLAZIER

TALMUD

The Talmud (from the Hebrew word for "to study") is the spiritual and intellectual center of Jewish life. In its broader sense, the term refers to two texts: the Mishnah, the first written summary of the Oral Law, and the Gemara, known as the Talmud in its more restricted sense.

Ancient rabbis taught that Moses received revelation in two forms, written and oral. Leaders of each generation faithfully transmitted this "Oral Torah" to their successors. The conversations, teachings, and conduct of Talmudic scholars were also committed to memory and occasionally recorded in brief notes. These texts became the object of study in their own right, called *talmud* in Hebrew and *gemara* in Aramaic.

The foundation of Talmudic study is the Mishnah ("recitation" or "recapitulation" of the Oral Torah), although these statements also provide a deeper understanding of all Halakhic statements and the Torah in general. The Mishnah is divided into six Orders, each concerned with a broad area of Jewish life. Each statement of the Mishnah is subject to several questions. Sometimes complicated problems arise, which might be left unresolved for generations. In the past, if an individual scholar did succeed in finding a solution, the solution would be attributed to him (only men studied the Torah) and recorded in the Talmud. The Talmud is thus a living dialogue among several generations of scholars.

Towards the end of the fourth century, the Babylonian scholar Rav Ashi began to put the Talmud in written form to protect it from being lost or forgotten. The final editing was completed during the following century-and-a-half. This text is known as the Babylonian Talmud and has served as the foundation of Jewish law and practice since its completion. A shorter, less comprehensive version had been compiled a century or two earlier. It is known as the Jerusalem or Palestinian Talmud and is barely half the size of the Babylonian Talmud.

PATRICIA DeFERRARI

See also JUDAISM.

TANEY, ROGER BROOKE (1777–1864)

Fifth chief justice of the United States Supreme Court (1836–1864), Taney was born on 17 March 1777 in Calvert county, Maryland, to an old Catholic family of considerable means, and died in Washington, D.C., on 12 October 1864. A graduate of Dickinson College, Taney practiced law in his native state and was elected to the Maryland Senate in 1816 as a Federalist, but broke with the Federalists to endorse Andrew Jackson in the presidential election of 1824. He served as attorney general of Maryland from 1827 until 1831, when Jackson appointed him attorney general of the United States in which office he gave Jackson strong support against the Bank of the United States. As a consequence, when Jackson nominated Taney as secretary of the treasury in 1834, the Whig-dominated Senate rejected his name—the first time in American history that the Senate had rejected any cabinet nomination.

Judge Roger Brooke Taney

Upon the death of Chief Justice John Marshall in 1835, Jackson nominated Taney for the post of chief justice of the United States Supreme Court. He won Senate confirmation in 1836 and served until his death in 1864. Taney was a staunch defender of fugitive-slave laws, and, unfortunately for his reputation, he is best remembered today for writing the majority opinion in the *Dred Scott* case of 1857 in which he declared that slaves were property and not citizens. The first Catholic to hold the post of chief justice, in 1806 Taney married Anne Phoebe Key, sister of the author of "The Star Spangled Banner." A son died in infancy, and his six surviving daughters were reared as Protestants.

THOMAS J. SHELLEY

See also AMERICAN CATHOLICISM.

TANTUM ERGO

The final two verses of St. Thomas Aquinas' hymn *Pange Lingua.* It has long been prescribed for singing at Benediction. A modern English translation begins with the line "Down in adoration falling," while a more traditional version begins "Therefore, we before Him bending."

JOSEPH QUINN

See also HYMNS.

TARGUM

Early in Jewish history, Hebrew was the language of the people of Israel but after the Exile (587 B.C.) the majority of the people gradually adopted Aramaic, the common language of commerce and diplomacy. Consequently the people were unable to understand the Hebrew biblical readings in the synagogues, and needed Aramaic translations. That is the origin of the targums. The first reference to these Aramaic translations is found in the Book of Nehemiah (8:8): "[Ezra] read from the book, from the law of God, translating and giving the sense, so that the people understood the reading."

On Sabbaths and feast days, there were Hebrew readings from the Pentateuch, or the Law, and from the Prophets. A translator (called *meturgeman*) gave an Aramaic translation after each verse of the Pentateuch reading. He did the same after every three verses read from the Prophets. These translations, called targums, aimed to give the people an understanding of the texts in a way to make them applicable to their lives. In the course of time the paraphrastic translations evolved into a semistandard format, and they became part of the oral tradition and memory of the Jewish people. Liturgical practices tend to become standardized and so the targums gradually assumed a fixed pattern and were eventually written down. In recent years targumic studies have received deserved attention from Jewish and Christian scholars, and a complete translation of all the extant targums is being published by The Liturgical Press.

MICHAEL GLAZIER

See also BIBLE, OLD TESTAMENT WRITINGS; CRITICISM, BIBLICAL.

TAULER, JOHANNES (ca. 1300–1361)

Johannes (John) Tauler was born in Strasbourg around the year 1300. His father was a fairly wealthy burgher in the town. Strasbourg had about twenty thousand inhabitants and was a center of commerce and trade, as well as a place of learning. Tauler entered the Dominican novitiate in 1314, the year that Meister Eckhart visited the Dominicans in Strasbourg. It is not known whether Tauler came to know him there. It appears, however, that Tauler's later status as disciple of Eckhart was achieved more through study than personal acquaintance. Tauler completed his studies at the Cologne general house of studies, where he became friends with Henry Suso. They both became involved with the spiritual movement of the region known as the Friends of God and were soon leaders in the movement. The Friends of God included men and women from all levels of society who wished to cultivate a life of interior prayer.

Tauler was primarily a preacher, not a writer. What has survived from him are his sermons, which were recorded largely from memory by those who followed his teaching, most often nuns of the Dominican houses in Rhineland where he ministered, and members of the Friends of God. His sermons were widely circulated along the Rhine and in Low Countries, first in handwritten form and later in printed editions. The first printing was at Leipzig in 1498 followed by a reprinting at Augsburg in 1505, an edition which reached Martin Luther. Tauler's sermons acquired truly international influence only after being translated into Latin in 1548. From this Latin edition, which included pseudo-Taulerian works, portions were translated into the various local languages of Italy, Spain, and France.

Tauler's style is plain and direct, quite different from that of his teacher, Eckhart. Tauler speaks of being between the two extremes of time and eternity. This experience gives rise to an anguish, a suspension between heaven and earth, sublimity and humility, knowledge and non-knowledge. Progress in this state requires imitation of Jesus Christ, an imitation which stresses his humanity and which makes his passion and suffering the model to be followed. This stress on imitating Christ marks a clear distinction between Eckhart and Tauler.

Although Tauler praised the active life, he also reminded those called to the contemplative life that they must find and maintain a true passivity. To receive the Eucharist's richest blessings one must be detached both from the world and even from oneself in order to allow God to act within oneself. The contemplative must go into God as the Persons of the Trinity enter into one another and then come out again from God, renewed and enriched by the union. In this understanding, Tauler parallels Ruusbroec's Trinitarian mysticism. He died in 1361.

PATRICIA DeFERRARI

See also DOMINICANS; MIDDLE AGES, THE; MYSTICISM.

TE DEUM

The opening words of an ancient Latin hymn of praise and thanksgiving, *Te Deum Laudamus* ("We praise thee, O God"). Its authorship is disputed; some scholars attribute it to St. Niceta of Remesiana (d. A.D. 414), while others posit that it derives from ancient liturgy. Regardless, its early use in the Divine Office is evidenced in the Rule of St. Benedict (ca. 540). The hymn is sung at the end of the Office of Readings (of the Liturgy of the Hours) on Sundays, solemnities, and other feasts.

JOSEPH QUINN

See also HYMNS.

TEILHARD DE CHARDIN, PIERRE (1881–1955)

Marie-Joseph Pierre Teilhard de Chardin was born on 1 May 1881, the fourth of eleven children. Through his father, Emmanuel, he developed an interest in natural history and through his mother, Berthe-Adele de Dompierre d'Hornoy, a personal devotion to the Sacred Heart. After attending the Jesuit *collège* at Mongre, he entered the Jesuit novitiate on 20 March 1899. From 1905 to 1908 he taught physics and chemistry at the Jesuit *collège* in Cairo and did original geological research in the Fayum before going to England to study theology. He was ordained on 24 August 1911 and the following year began studying geology in Paris under Marcellin Boule. In December 1914 he was drafted into the French army and served, mostly as stretcher-bearer, in several major battles of the First World War including Champagne, Verdun, and the Second Battle of the Marne. During his military service he developed all the major lines of his thought and began writing the many religious and philosophic essays that would later bring him fame.

Following the war Teilhard finished his doctoral studies and taught briefly at the Institut Catholique in Paris before going to China in the Spring of 1923 to assist another Jesuit geologist, Emile Licent. On returning to Paris in the fall of 1924 he learned that a paper he had written for private circulation had been taken from his desk and sent to Rome. The paper saw the story of Adam and Eve as parable and not literal history; Church authorities required Teilhard to sign an agreement not to write or say "anything contrary to the Church's 'traditional' position on Original Sin" and accept other restrictions on publishing anything in philosophy or theology. In the spring of 1926 he returned to China and wrote *The Divine Milieu,* a devotional work that he hoped would assure authorities of his orthodoxy. He submitted the text for Church approval, but censors never rendered a final verdict. He continued to write essays and circulate them privately. In 1929 the expedition on which he was geologist found a well-preserved skull of Peking man (the first fire-user who lived in Asia about 400,000 years ago) and Teilhard wrote abundantly of the skull and related finds. He soon gained considerable scientific recognition for his work on the geology of China and excavations in India and Burma. He traveled widely and spoke at geological conferences in the U.S. and Europe.

In June of 1940, while living in Beijing, he finished *The Phenomenon of Man,* his best-known work. He stayed in Beijing through the Japanese occupation, returning to Paris in the spring of 1946.

Pierre Teilhard de Chardin

There his essays had been mimeographed and he found himself a minor celebrity—this brought new difficulties with Church authorities. In October 1948 he went to Rome hoping to obtain permission to publish *The Phenomenon of Man.* Permission was refused and he was required to continue his scientific work away from France. He relocated in New York. In 1951 and 1953 he made trips to South Africa and became convinced that the human species had originated in Africa—not in Asia, as was then widely believed. He died suddenly on Easter Day, 10 April 1955 and is buried at the Jesuit cemetery at Poughkeepsie, New York. With permission of his Jesuit superior he had willed his religious and philosophical essays to a friend who after his death proceeded to publish them in thirteen volumes. These had considerable influence both within and outside of the Church. The Vatican issued a "warning" concerning them in 1962, but many observers have seen his influence on Vatican II, especially in the pastoral constitution *Gaudium et Spes.* In 1981 the Vatican Secretary of State wrote a letter in his praise calling him "a man seized by Christ in the depths of his being." His scientific writings have been collected in ten volumes and a dozen volumes of his letters have appeared.

Philosophic and Religious Thought

Teilhard has told of being aware of two strong attractions; one was for the impersonal world of matter known by science, and the other was for the revealed Word of God known by faith. At one time they were like two stars dividing his allegiance. Eventually he reconciled the two by seeing evolution as the process by which the material world was rising in spirit: what once was the impersonal world of matter had become reflectively conscious as ourselves. At the same time he was influenced by passages from the Pauline letters, especially a passage that told of God descending into the lowest parts of the earth so that rising from there he might fill all things (Eph 4:9-10). Teilhard wrote that this and similar passages gave the incarnation a cosmic and universal meaning.

Thus, the revelation told of God descending into the world of matter, and science told of matter rising into spirit. The two stars were coming together. The Pauline letters spoke of Christians uniting to form the (mystical) Body of Christ; other Pauline texts would see all creation involved in the process, so that God might become all things in all things (1 Cor 15:28; Eph 1:23; Col 3:11). Christ was thus presented as the one in whom all things held together (Col 1:17). Teilhard would view evolution as the process by which all the elements of matter became increasingly interrelated until eventually they would form a sort of single organism. This he took to be the body of Christ, a body that would finally be animated by a single divine soul. Evolution was the process by which the universe is becoming Someone; conversely it is the process in which God is becoming incarnate. Because of a strong sense for the divine omnipresence, Teilhard spoke of the world as holy and saw elements of his thought resembling the teachings of the pantheists. But in opposition to the pantheists he insisted on a personal God, the God revealed in Jesus. Drawing on John 3:16 he dedicated *The Divine Milieu* "To those who love the world."

Teilhard believed this positive outlook was more in keeping with the sense of progress in the modern world, a world that looks to a common human future with dedication and enthusiasm. But he also believed the modern world needed Christian faith with its teaching of an afterlife and a personal God. Otherwise, Teilhard believed, accounts of an impersonal human future ending in total death (the entropy, or death of the universe that is predicted by science) would lead increasingly to widespread despair. Teilhard believed that when peoples saw they were going nowhere (as science seemed to show), they would either turn to faith or stop striving, and the age-old process of evolution would self-abort in widespread discouragement. He wanted to give hope to the world.

The theology of Teilhard would see the creation, incarnation and redemption as ongoing processes with the fullness of the universal Christ as their goal: "Across the immensity of time and the disconcerting multiplicity of individuals, one single operation is taking place: the annexation to Christ of his chosen; one single thing is being made: the mystical Body of Christ." If one becomes aware of Christ as the goal of creation, one will see one's own work in a different way: Christ will be seen "at the tip of my pen, my spade, my brush, my needle—of my heart and my thought. By pressing the stroke, the line or the stitch, on which I am engaged, to its ultimate natural finish, I shall lay hold of that last end towards which my innermost will tends." Teilhard would speak with enthusiasm of the coming unity of nations, for this would make the world more organically one: "The age of nations is past; it remains for us now, if we do not wish to perish, to set aside our ancient prejudices and build the earth."

Teilhard is best known for this positive view of creation and the theology of human work, growth and achievement. Yet he wrote abundantly of diminishment, failure and death. He would see action and passivity, growth and diminishment, attachment and detachment as two natural phases of a single process. We have communion with Christ through all the deeds of our life; but the kingdom of God is not of this world, so our communion will be complete only with our death. He prayed that death itself might be an act of communion. His reflections on the Mass would see the growth and development of the world symbolized in the bread; while the diminishment and death were symbolized in the wine.

Some writings of Teilhard were largely scientific and others largely devotional. Most of his essays tell of the world needing Christian faith and Christians needing faith in the world. He considered this his mission. Many theologians and scientists have praised his work, but others have criticized him for confusing the disciplines and mixing poetry with prose.

Influence

From the early sixties to the early seventies Teilhard had an immense popular following. His theology led other theologians to see the world as an ongoing and interrelated process. He influenced theologians (notably Henri de Lubac and liberation theologian Juan Luis Segundo); some philosophers of science (notably Ian Barbour and Thomas Berry) have continued his thought. His mystical teaching concerning love of the world gave a new orientation to Catholic spirituality: Thomas Merton, "The real importance of Teilhard is his affirmation of the holiness of matter." Scientists specializing in evolution (Julian Huxley, Ashley Montague, Sol Tax) have written in his praise. Mortimer Adler has listed *The Phenomenon of Man* as one of the Great Books of the twentieth century. Teilhard has been quoted by politicians, social activists and environmentalists; U Thant, Secretary General of the U.N., has told of the importance of his influence. Even during the height of the cold war limited editions of his works were available in Soviet countries. He became a fictional character in Morris West's *Shoes of the Fisherman,* in William Blatty's *The Exorcist,* and in Romain Gary's *The Roots of Heaven.* His texts have been set to music and inspired painters and sculptors. Flannery O'Connor and Thornton Wilder have told of his influence; the architect, Paulo Soleri, named the central building of his city the Teilhard Cloister. In 1980 Stephen Jay Gould accused Teilhard of complicity in the Piltdown fraud (a phoney human fossil presented to the world in 1912 and revealed as a hoax in 1953). But Piltdown experts have rejected the claim: J. S. Weiner, who led in uncovering the hoax, "rubbish"; Kenneth Oakley, "completely untrue"; Charles Blinderman, "flimsy." Though Teilhard's popular following has diminished, there are still many Teilhard discussion groups and Teilhard newsletters are published in New York, London, and Paris.

THOMAS M. KING, S.J.

See also EVOLUTION; MYSTICISM; SCIENCE AND RELIGION; SOCIETY OF JESUS.

TEKAKWITHA, BLESSED KATERI (ca. 1656–1680)

Tekakwitha's mother was a Christian Algonquin who had been raised among the French at Three Rivers, Canada, but was captured by the Iroquois and married to a chief of the Mohawk. Tekakwitha was born at the Indian village of Ossernenon (Auriesville), New York, (where two Jesuit priests, St. Isaac Jogues and St. Jean de la Lande, had suffered martyrdom in 1646). An epidemic of smallpox took the lives of her parents and a younger brother, and left Tekakwitha nearly blind with her face heavily pocked. She was converted to her mother's religion by Fr. Jacques de Lamberville, a Jesuit missionary, in 1676 and was accordingly ostracized by her relatives and the other Indians, and subjected to much abuse. Fearing for her life, she fled Ossernenon and made her way through the wilderness to the Christian Indian village of Sault Ste. Marie on the St. Lawrence near Montreal. On Christmas of that year (1677) she received her First Communion and began a life marked by holiness and great austerity. Two years later she dedicated herself exclusively to Christ by a vow of chastity. She died the following year at the Indian village of Caughnawaga; she was twenty-four.

Blessed Kateri Tekakwitha

During the thirty-five years after her death, the missionaries who had known her best recorded the details of her life and attested to her virtues. She was known as the "Lily of the Mohawk," and the faithful have, for three centuries, credited her with many miracles. She was beatified in 1980 by Pope John Paul II. Memorial, 14 July.

DAVID BRYAN

See also CANADA, THE CATHOLIC CHURCH IN.

TEMPERANCE

See VIRTUE.

TEMPLARS (KNIGHTS TEMPLAR)

In 1118 Hugh de Payens and his companions took a vow to protect pilgrims journeying in the Holy Land; ten years later the Council of Troyes approved their rule and thus one of the two main medieval military orders came into being. The order quickly increased in numbers, activities, influence, and wealth, becoming a trusted and powerful banking institution. Charges, including heresy and sodomy, were leveled against the order mainly by those who, like Philip the Fair of France, coveted its great wealth. The accusers won the day when at the Council of Vienne (1312), Clement V had the Templars suppressed. While history has exonerated the order of all major accusations, its pursuit of wealth nevertheless compromised its original purpose and ideals and held the seeds of its eventual demise.

JOSEPH QUINN

See also CRUSADES; KNIGHTS OF MALTA.

TEMPLE OF JERUSALEM

Although David was anxious to build a temple (2 Sam 7:1-7; 1 Chr 22:8-10), it was his son Solomon who actually undertook and completed the construction of the First or Solomonic Temple. He chose the eastern hill of the then city of Jerusalem (2 Chr 3:1) that his father had conquered from the Jebusites. It is possible that this site stood about fifty yards north of the Dome of the Rock. It required about seven years to complete the construction (1 Kgs 6:37-38). Solomon obtained the wood and skilled labor from Hiram, king of Tyre; he got the necessary stones and unskilled labor from the areas around Jerusalem (1 Kgs 5:15-32).

The First Temple was modeled on Syro-Phoenician prototypes. Rectangular in form, it was a stone structure with interior wall panellings of exquisite carved cedar wood (1 Kgs 6:15-18). Measuring 105 feet long, thirty feet wide, and forty-five feet high, the edifice was divided into three sections. The first section, the Ulam or atrium, was fifteen feet long. The second section, the Hekal or Sanctuary, was sixty feet long. It contained the altar of incense, the table for the loaves of proposition, and ten candlesticks. The third section, the Debir or Holy of Holies, was thirty feet long and thus was a perfect cube. This most sacred part housed the Ark of the Covenant near or on top of which were two gold-plated wooden cherubim. Their wings reached from wall to wall and ascended halfway to the ceiling (1 Kgs 6:19-28). Around the building was a so-called inner court that was later enlarged into both an upper and a lower court (1 Kgs 6:36). In the court in front of the Temple were the altar of bronze (1 Kgs 8:64) and the Sea of bronze (1 Kgs 7:23-26).

As the national shrine, the Temple figured prominently in Israel's self-understanding. It was God's house and, therefore, God's dwelling among his people. At its dedication God's taking possession of his house was symbolically represented by means of a cloud (1 Kgs 8:10-11). The Temple expressed God's election of Israel as his own people, but, in a special way, his election of the city of Jerusalem and the Davidic dynasty (1 Kgs 8:16; 2 Kgs 19:34). However, as the prophets had made abundantly clear, this divine dwelling was not an absolute guarantee of well-being for the nation (Jer 7:1-15; 26:1-15).

Realizing that the transcendent God could not be circumscribed by a physical building, Israel's theologians taught that only God's name dwelt in the Temple (1 Kgs 8:17, 29). God actually lived in heaven but he heard the prayers uttered in the Temple (1 Kgs 8:30-40). However, name was synonymous with person. Where God's name was, so also was his person, though not in a manipulative way.

Eventually the Temple became the only legitimate place of worship in Israel. This was the teaching of Deuteronomy 12:5: ". . , you shall resort to the place which the Lord, your God, chooses out of all your tribes and designates as his dwelling." When the core part of the Book of Deuteronomy was discovered in the renewal/restoration of the Temple in 621 B.C., King Josiah (640–609) used the find to continue his cultic and political reforms. This law of the one sanctuary clearly enhanced Josiah's bid for independence.

In 587 B.C. the Babylonians destroyed the First Temple. After the return from exile efforts to rebuild were slow. Eventually, however, the Second Temple was completed in 515 B.C. most likely on the same lines and proportions as the First Temple. Although some who remembered the First Temple mourned at

Scale model of Temple of Jerusalem

the sight of the rebuilt sanctuary (Ezra 3:12-13), its status and magnificence continued. (From 515 B.C. to A.D. 70 the Second Temple was the unique place of worship for all Israel.) In 169 B.C. Antiochus IV Epiphanes plundered the Second Temple and further profaned it in 167 B.C. by forbidding legitimate sacrifice and foisting the worship of Zeus Olympios (1 Macc 1:46-47; 2 Macc 6:1-5). In 164 B.C. however, under Judas Maccabeus the Second Temple was purified (1 Macc 4:36-59). Its rededication became the occasion for Hanukkah or the Feast of Dedication.

In 20 B.C. Herod the Great (37–34) began a grandiose restoration of the Second Temple. The construction of its precincts was finished long after Herod, viz., ca. A.D. 63 (ironically it was some seven years before its destruction). Under Herod a large part of the Temple Mount was taken up with courts. There was the Court of the Gentiles that non-Jews were permitted to enter. There was the Court of the Women that marked the limits of access for Jewish females. There was the Court of the Israelites for Jewish men. Finally there was the Court of the Priests that surrounded the Temple proper. In A.D. 70 the Romans under Titus besieged Jerusalem and destroyed the Second Temple.

JOHN F. CRAGHAN

TEN COMMANDMENTS, THE

"Ten Commandments" translates the Hebrew "ten words" found in Exodus 34:28; Deuteronomy 4:13; 10:4. They are also traditionally known as the Decalogue. According to Deuteronomy the expression refers to the commandments in Deuteronomy 5:7-21 that speak of the two stone tablets (see Deut 5:22). In Exodus 34:28 the expression is not original since the number of commandments in Exodus 34:14-26 is actually twelve, not ten. Finally the expression is applied to the commandments given in God's appearance on Mount Sinai (see Exod 20:3-17).

The Bible also has incomplete texts or summaries of the Ten Commandments (see Lev 19:3-4, 11-13; Ps 15:3-5; Hos 4:2). It is from such series that the Ten Commandments evolved and except for those dealing exclusively with obligations toward Yahweh reflect ancient tribal wisdom. Hence the young were to learn them from their elders who endeavored to provide for the good of the tribe. These series were considered an enumeration of death sins, i.e., they deal with those crimes that are so grave that they jeopardize the community itself.

The legal form of the Ten Commandments is important. It is a series of apodictic laws, i.e., laws that obligate a person directly. They require the person to perform (or refrain from performing) a specific action that the lawgiver regards as desirable (or harmful). These apodictic laws evince two forms: (a) third person, e.g., "No one shall be put to death on the testimony of only one witness" (Deut 17:6) and (b) second person, e.g., "You shall not have intercourse with your father's wife" (Lev 18:8). Although exceptional in the ancient Near East, these apodictic laws are characteristic of Israel. Furthermore, the second-person forms, insofar as they express the fundamental religious attitude of a community, are unique to Israel.

The second-person singular forms create an atmosphere of intimacy. It is Yahweh who speaks directly to the individual. Even though murder and adultery were already forbidden in the ancient Near East, the biblical commandments by reason of their formulation are actually new laws. In the introduction (see Exod 20:2; Deut 5:6) Yahweh presents himself as the liberator of slaves who now constitute his covenant people. As a result, Yahweh assumes and transcends the office of the tribal elders. Israel is urged to keep these commandments, not only because these prescriptions promote the good of the tribe, but also because this God has intervened decisively in their lives.

The present arrangement of the Ten Commandments in the Book of Exodus demonstrates their prominence. In the first stage of the tradition the fear experienced by the people at Sinai (Exod 20:18) was a direct result of God's appearance in Exodus 19, particularly the violent storm (Exod 19:16b-17, 19). As a result, the people asked Moses to receive the entire revelation (Exod 20:19). In the second stage of the tradition owing to the significance of the Ten Commandments the people received this basic law from God directly (Exod 20:1-17). Their fear on this level applies only to the legislation of the Covenant Code (Exod 20:22–23:19) that Moses is deputed to hear and then communicate afterwards. The arrangement in this second stage clearly attests to the importance of the Ten Commandments since, unlike the Covenant Code, God revealed them directly to the whole people.

There are differences in the formulations of the Ten Commandments in Exodus 20:3-17 and Deuteronomy 5:7-21. For example, in Exodus 20:11 the motivation for keeping the Sabbath is creation, while in Deuteronomy 5:15 it is the Exodus. To the list of those forbidden to work on the Sabbath (Exod 20:10) Deuteronomy 5:14 adds the ox and ass. Deuteronomy 5:16 adds to the commandment of honoring one's parents (Exod 20:12) the following: "as the Lord, your God, has commanded you." The most striking difference is the order of not coveting the house and wife of one's neighbor. Exodus 20:17 reads: "You shall not covet your neighbor's house. You shall not covet your neighbor's wife." However, Deuteronomy 5:21 reads: "You shall not covet your neighbor's wife. You shall not desire (a different Hebrew verb) your neighbor's house."

Various faith communities have adopted either the enumeration of Exodus or that of Deuteronomy. Roman Catholics and Lutherans follow Deuteronomy, while Jews, Eastern Orthodox Christians, and Protestants other than Lutherans follow Exodus. These communities preserve the number "ten" in a variety of ways. For Jews the first commandment is the introduction, "I, the Lord, am your God" etc. Their second commandment is the prohibition of *both* false gods *and* images. Their tenth commandment is the prohibition of coveting *both* the house *and* wife of one's neighbor. For Eastern Orthodox Christians and Protestants other than Lutherans the first commandment is the prohibition of false gods. Their second commandment is the prohibition of false images. Their tenth commandment is the prohibition of coveting *both* the house *and* wife of one's neighbor. For Roman Catholics and Lutherans the first commandment is the prohibition of false gods. The prohibition of false images is either included in this first commandment or suppressed in the enumeration. Their second commandment is the vain use of God's name. Their ninth commandment is the prohibition of coveting the wife of one's neighbor. Their tenth commandment is the prohibition of coveting the house of one's neighbor.

Text of the Ten Commandments

Exodus 20:2-11	*Deuteronomy 5:6-15*	*Traditional*
I am the Lord your God, who brought you out of the land of Egypt, out of the house of slavery.	I am the Lord your God, who brought you out of the land of Egypt, out of the house of slavery.	I am the Lord your God.
I. You shall have no other gods before me. You shall not make for yourself an idol, whether in the form of anything that is in heaven above, or that is on the earth beneath, or that is in the water under the earth. You shall not bow down to them or worship them; for I the Lord your God am a jealous God, punishing children for the iniquity of parents to the third and the fourth generation of those who reject me, but showing steadfast love to the thousandth generation of those who love me and keep my commandments.	You shall have no other gods before me. You shall not make for yourself an idol, whether in the form of anything that is in heaven above, or that is on the earth beneath, or that is in the water under the earth. You shall not bow down to them or worship them; for I the Lord your God am a jealous God, punishing children for the iniquity of parents to the third and the fourth generation of those who reject me, but showing steadfast love to the thousandth generation of those who love me and keep my commandments.	You shall not have strange gods before me.

Exodus 20:2-11	*Deuteronomy 5:6-15*	*Traditional*
II. You shall not make wrongful use of the name of the Lord your God; for the Lord will not acquit anyone who misuses his name.	You shall not make wrongful use of the name of the Lord your God; for the Lord will not acquit anyone who misuses his name.	You shall not take the name of the Lord your God in vain.
III. Remember the Sabbath day, and keep it holy. Six days you shall labor, and do all your work; but the seventh day is a Sabbath to the Lord your God; you shall not do any work—you, your son or your daughter, your male or female slave, your livestock, or the alien resident in your towns; for in six days the Lord made heaven and earth, the sea, and all that is in them, but rested the seventh day; therefore the Lord blessed the Sabbath day and consecrated it.	Observe the Sabbath day, to keep it holy, as the Lord your God commanded you. Six days you shall labor, and do all your work; but the seventh day is a Sabbath to the Lord your God; in it you shall not do any work—you, or your son or your daughter, or your male or female slave, or your ox or your donkey or any of your livestock, or the alien resident in your towns, so that your male or female slave may rest as well as you. Remember that you were a slave in the land of Egypt, and the Lord your God brought you out from there with a mighty hand and an outstretched arm; therefore the Lord your God commanded you to keep the Sabbath day.	Keep holy the Sabbath.
IV. Honor your father and your mother, so that your days may be long in the land that the Lord your God is giving you.	Honor your father and your mother, as the Lord your God commanded you; that your days may be long, and that it may go well with you, in the land that the Lord your God is giving you.	Honor your father and your mother.
V. You shall not murder.	You shall not murder.	You shall not kill.
VI. You shall not commit adultery.	Neither shall you commit adultery.	You shall not commit adultery.
VII. You shall not steal.	Neither shall you steal.	You shall not steal.
VIII. You shall not bear false witness against your neighbor.	Neither shall you bear false witness against your neighbor.	You shall not bear false witness against your neighbor.
IX–X. You shall not covet your neighbor's house; you shall not covet your neighbor's wife, or donkey, or anything that belongs to your neighbor.	Neither shall you covet your neighbor's wife.	You shall not covet your neighbor's spouse.
	Neither shall you desire your neighbor's house, or field, or male or female slave, or ox, or donkey, or anything that belongs to your neighbor.	You shall not covet your neighbor's goods.

JOHN F. CRAGHAN

See also BIBLE, OLD TESTAMENT WRITINGS; LAW; THEOLOGY, MORAL.

TERESA OF AVILA, ST. (TERESA OF JESUS) (1515–1582)

Teresa de Ahumada was born near Avila to a Castilian family whose *hidalguía* (minor nobility) had been purchased from the Crown to conceal Jewish origins. She was the third of ten children of Beatriz de Ahumada, second wife of Alonso Sánchez de Cepeda; two children from Alonso's first marriage completed the well-to-do home. Teresa's childhood was happy, marked by strong bonds with her brothers and a precocious if conventional piety. There were tensions, however. A 1520 lawsuit opened to public scrutiny her family's social pretensions as *conversos* with "tainted" lineage, leaving them vulnerable to dishonor and ostracism. Beatriz died in 1528 amid worrisome signs that the family's wealth was rapidly declining. In 1531, Teresa was sent to a convent school after a flirtatious incident by which, according to Spain's exacting codes of behavior, she compromised the family's honor. After eighteen months, she fell ill.

She convalesced in the home of an uncle who had a pious spirit and a fine library. One of few literate women in her day, Teresa read eagerly, soon discerning a vocation to religious life. She secretly entered the Carmelite Convent of the Incarnation in Avila in 1535, professing in 1537. Another illness forced her to leave in 1538. Resting again at her uncle's house, she learned the prayer of "recollection" by reading the *Third Spiritual Alphabet* (Francisco de Osuna). After brutal medical treatments at Becedas, she returned to the Incarnation still desperately ill. Recovery took nearly three years.

Exhausted and depressed, Teresa gave up mental prayer. After her father's death (1543), she tried again but found it mostly dry and frustrating. In 1554, a reading of St. Augustine's *Confessions* and an encounter with an image of the suffering Christ broke through the obstacles. To resolve her questions about the authenticity of the visions she began experiencing in 1559, she consulted numerous confessors. Generally ignorant about the mystical life and fearing the Inquisition, they declared her deluded. She finally found understanding from certain pious laypersons, ascetics and clergymen whose credibility helped establish hers. During this period she aided her directors' discernment by writing intimate communications that became her spiritual autobiography, *The Book of her Life* (1562).

Teresa grew unsatisfied with life in the overcrowded Incarnation. Although not lax, the Rule provided no period of contemplation. Economic ties between religious institutions and noble houses confined nuns mostly to routine forms of piety, like perpetual prayers for benefactors. The same preoccupation with caste and the glaring inequities found in the world obtained within convent society. Nuns engaged in distracting social concourse and were consumed by dynastic interests. Teresa believed these conditions hindered interior liberty, genuine community, and the imitation of Christ.

St. Teresa of Avila

She envisioned a small house where a few nuns could lead an unencumbered life of total poverty and contemplative prayer consonant with earlier Carmelite tradition. Opposition from the order and civil officials threatened the project, but by 1565, she had succeeded. While at this house (St. Joseph's) during 1565 and 1566, she composed *The Way of Perfection* to instruct the first Discalced nuns and devised constitutions to regulate community life. She also wrote meditations on verses of the biblical text, Song of Songs (1559).

Teresa's times were marked by ecclesiastical reform (Protestant and Catholic), religious wars, foreign conquest and exploration. To further Catholic reform, she wanted to offer the Church holiness as a remedy for its internal weaknesses, an antidote to heresy, and a support for preachers, theologians, and missionaries. She conceived the nuns' vocation as essentially apostolic: participation in mission at home and abroad through a hidden life of prayer and fidelity. Thus, in 1567 she requested authorization from the prior general to open additional houses.

For fifteen years Teresa traveled almost ceaselessly. Despite violent opposition from other Carmelites, competing royal and papal interests, the red tape of bishops, bankers, and benefactors, and an appalling lack of health, Teresa established fourteen houses for women. With St. John of the Cross, Jerónimo Gracián and others, she inaugurated a reform of Carmelite friars and supervised the organization of an independent province for the Discalced (1580). All the while, her spiritual life deepened (she experienced "spiritual matrimony" in 1572), and somehow she found time to write. Along with lesser works, she composed a chronicle of the reform, *Foundations* (1573–1574), and her most mature work, *The Interior Castle* (1577). Most of her voluminous correspondence also comes from these years.

Teresa's spiritual teachings derive mainly from her own discerned experience and have a *kataphatic* ("affirmative") emphasis. Incarnational and image-centered, her mysticism is anchored in the humanity of Christ and in the notion of friendship with God, fostered by attending to God's presence in the soul through prayer. Comparing growth in prayer to ways of watering a garden, Teresa leads the soul from exhausting effort to total receptivity to God's initiative. She describes interiority as a many-roomed castle. Wending its way through the "mansions," the soul is purified and led lovingly towards the center where union with God, or spiritual matrimony, occurs.

Teresa's account of spiritual growth embraces a variety of religious experiences and takes seriously God's freedom to deal with souls in unpredictable ways. Humorous and pragmatic, she recommends spiritual companionship, prudent discernment, solid virtues (especially humility), and the Church's traditional means of grace to all who travel the way of perfection. She insists that contemplation is not an end and that spiritual attainment is measured not by private ecstasy or unusual experiences, but by sacrificial love of neighbor.

After inaugurating the last foundation (Burgos), Teresa died at Alba de Tormes on 4 October 1582. A woman of vibrant intelligence, warm relationality and a strong sense of justice, Teresa was canonized in 1622. Her holy example and sound theology broke the barrier of gender: in 1970 Pope Paul VI named her a Doctor of the Church. Her liturgical commemoration falls on 15 October.

MARY LUTI

See also CARMELITES; CONTEMPLATION; MYSTICISM; SPIRITUAL LIFE.

TERTULLIAN (ca. 160–ca. 225)

The traditional account of Tertullian's life and career (which has come under a great deal of questioning by scholars in recent years) indicates that he was born in Carthage of pagan parents; that he studied literature and rhetoric; he may have been a lawyer (but probably should not be equated with Tertullian the jurist); in middle age he became a Christian; even though Jerome says he was a priest, there are indications that he remained in the lay state; eventually he became a Montanist and died after living a long life. It is hard to infer much about Tertullian's life from any autobiographical statements that Tertullian provides in his writings because they are written in a very rhetorical fashion. We do not really know when he was born or when he died, but we can date some of his treatises between 196 or 197 and 212. He authored many apologetic, controversial, moral, disciplinary, and ascetical works in Latin (and a few in Greek). In the *Apology* (written ca. 197 and often considered his masterpiece), Tertullian attacks pagan superstitions and defamatory remarks about Christian morality as he goes on to make the case that Christians are good and upright citizens who are neither enemies of the state nor of the human race. To present and defend orthodox Christian doctrine against Gnostic threats, Tertullian wrote his controversial works. He discussed Christian belief about Scripture and tradition (*The Prescription of Heretics*); God and creation (*Against Hermogenes*); Christ (*On the Flesh of Christ*); the soul (*On the Soul*); the creation and resurrection of the body and final judgment (*The Resurrection of the Flesh*). In his moral and disciplinary works (particularly *The Shows, The Chaplet, Concerning Idolatry*) Tertullian urged Christians to separate themselves from the world in order to avoid contamination from the idolatry and immorality found therein. Two of Tertullian's ascetical works (*On Repentance* and *On Modesty*) are very important for penitential practice in the early Church. Tertullian is the first notable Christian author to write in Latin, and he was very creative in adapting Latin to express theological concepts. Despite becoming a Montanist, Tertullian was a popular writer in antiquity and the Middle Ages: Cyprian (according to Jerome) considered Tertullian to be his master. Because of his influence on language and thought Tertullian has been called the Father of Latin theology.

JOHN DILLON

See also AFRICA, THE CATHOLIC CHURCH IN; APOLOGETICS; FATHERS OF THE CHURCH.

TEXTUAL CRITICISM

See CRITICISM, BIBLICAL.

THEISM

Belief in a personal God who is active in the world. It differs from atheism that does not believe in God and from deism that believes in a God who is not active in the world. Sometimes theism focuses on natural theology and is seen as a philosophical foundation for theology based on revelation. In the seventeenth century, theism sought to identify a view of God that was common to all world religions.

LEONARD DOOHAN

See also PHILOSOPHY AND THEOLOGY; THEOLOGY.

THEOCRACY

Theocracy means government by God and refers to an institutionalized form of government based on the revealed teachings of God as implemented through God's representatives. The best-known historical example for contemporary Westerners would be Israel, governed in earlier times by prophets and in later times by the high priest and Sanhedrin—although restricted by kings and the Romans. These representatives of God claimed to build the nation on the Law of God. In recent times, the Ayatolla Khomeni established a theocracy in Iran, as Muhammed, the founder of Islam had done in Medina.

LEONARD DOOHAN

See also CHURCH AND STATE.

THEODICY

The term was originally used to postulate the existence of God in view of the existence of evil; and it was so used by the philosopher Leibnitz in 1710. However, its meaning was broadened to encompass the knowledge of God through the use of human reason alone (natural theology). The validity of such rational knowledge of God was solemnly confirmed by Vatican Council I (1869–1870). In the U.S.A. the term is generally given the narrower meaning.

MICHAEL GLAZIER

See also EVIL; GOD; PHILOSOPHY AND THEOLOGY; THEOLOGY, NATURAL.

THEOLOGICAL VIRTUES

See VIRTUE.

THEOLOGY

The etymology of the word theology is "talk" or "discourse" (*logos*) about "God" (*theos*). The word was first used by the Greeks centuries before Christianity began and, because the Greeks used it to speak about "pagan" gods, Christians neither readily adopted the word nor agreed on its meaning when they did use it. By the eleventh century Anselm of Canterbury helped the term become universally acceptable and provided a Christian definition that underpinned Scholastic theology and is still considered classic. He defined theology as "faith seeking understanding" (*fides quaerens intellectum*). The definition does not preclude reason but clearly acknowledges that faith, the lived relation between God and humanity, grounds the starting of theological reflection, or as Anselm states, "understanding." In Anselm's definition, faith is a knowledge that finds illumination through reasoned understanding.

The task of theology begins with the faith experience of committed believers in community in relation to God, and seeks to articulate it explicitly by understanding everything this relationship signifies, means, and implies. It is open to truth wherever it is. Any definition of theology falls short of complete, however, if it is thought to be only an exercise of reasoning upon faith. Faith seeks understanding so that understanding can contribute to a living, growing faith that makes a difference in life.

Christian theology goes beyond "talk about God" in the abstract and focuses upon the concrete historical event of the revelation of God as expressed by the Jesus Event (his life, death, and resurrection). It is the Jesus Event through which the founding revelation and continuing relation of Christian believers, as leaven in humanity, to God is normatively interpreted. The Jesus Event, therefore, is the central Christian revelation through which we continue to be graced by God's salvation and from which Christians proclaim God's enduring love for all people. Christian theology, by constitutive necessity, expresses a threefold integral and dynamic love relationship: Jesus' relation to God and us, God's relation to Jesus and us, our relation to God and Jesus. It is from these interrelationships that the various areas of theology are generated.

Theology is not an exclusive but an inclusive discipline that involves a public claim about the truth of this revelation for all humanity, namely that we are sisters and brothers of the same God. Just as no one person or culture can encompass, let alone claim to interpret, the totality of human experience, so no person, culture, or system can encompass or claim to interpret the totality of theology. Theology necessarily requires a collaborative or team effort with many specialties, fields, and methods. It also recognizes its historical limitations and cultural restrictions.

Theology has a threefold responsibility in this social setting that can be compared to a series of ever-widening yet always related concentric circles. First, theology is responsible to the faith of the individual; second, it is responsible to the faith community and the tradition it represents; third, it is responsible to all of humanity, even those who do not believe, because it claims a truth about humanity as related to God and to one another. The fundamental understanding of Christian revelation is that God loves everyone and extends salvation to everyone. Any truth about humanity is not for private use and certainly no revelation from God can be withheld from humanity; it must be proclaimed to all. Still, theology remains humble in that the reality of God with us exceeds complete and comprehensive human understanding, even of theology.

The practitioner of the discipline of theology is the theologian who is trained in various specialties and represents a service to the wider Church. The theologian can never claim exclusive rights to the doing of theology. Just as a surgeon practices medicine operating on torn ligaments in a patient's knee, so too does a parent practice medicine by pouring antiseptic over a child's bleeding knee. Just as a theologian practices theology by studying the meaning of the resurrection, so too does a friend who talks about death with one who is dying. Theology embraces a process of faith seeking understanding that begins anew in every human person and then finds some of its understandings formulated into specified areas or disciplines, as do all disciplines. Both the doctor (an M.D.) and the theologian (a Ph.D. or S.T.D.) go beyond the ordinary practice open to most people. They specialize in the accumulated knowledge about how and why treatments work, while continuing a never-ending search for new and better understandings. The specialists may not be the ones who pour the antiseptic or sit with the dying friend, but they are the ones who know when and why to suggest these "treatments" and where to look for new ones.

The comparison between medicine and theology is an apt one. Both seek the health of the individual and the community. Medicine's domain is physiological; theology's domain is spiritual. Both seek health which is the theological word "salvation." The word "salvation" comes from the Latin "to save" or "to be safe," "to have well-being." "Well-being" means "being well" on all levels of human living and foremost, for theology, is our living relation with God through Jesus the Christ. The theologian helps us to "live well" with God in the fullness of life.

As our understandings are gathered, ordered, systematized, and explained, recognizable areas of theology emerge. It is important to remember that theology did not float down ready-made from heaven; it is a product of human understanding, never a substitute for faith. Theology is a fallible enterprise that continues to correlate the past and present revelation of God in the threefold relation of God, Jesus, and us. Theology, thus, always remains time-bound, historical, reformable, fallible, and human. At the same time, theology serves faith by being a place of remembering, of challenging easy or impartial understandings, of including the voiceless, of seeking and explaining in open and accessible understandings what we know of God and why. Theology is the self-articulated understanding of its journey with God.

Theology, like the believing community, never stands still but continually develops. Just as the world of theology from Anselm's day to ours has changed vastly, so too has the task of theology. Contemporary theology is marked by four significant influences: (1) the advent of historical consciousness which has contributed the idea of change, development, and contextual specificity; (2) the return to and use of Scripture as privileged source of theology; (3) the development of new methods of interpretation (hermeneutics), especially those coming from physical and social sciences; and (4) the rapid interconnectedness of the world into a new global consciousness.

The current divisions of theology, though dependent upon the method chosen and continually undergoing change, always reflect both the act of human understanding and its relationship to the integral and dynamic moments of believing. Three clear moments exist which can be covered by three general categories: the coming to faith called *fundamental* (or foundational) theology, the coherent and unified beliefs as a whole system with their hierarchy of truths called *systematic* (or dogmatic) theology, and the many dimensions of lived faith called *practical* (or pastoral) theology. While various divisions exist according to the theological presuppositions at work, nevertheless the three moments described above will remain in some form. Still, more divisions exist.

Theology can be categorized by both (1) its areas of study and (2) its methods. If one examines the areas or fields (1), one finds the experience of God, revelation, faith and conversion the area of *fundamental* (or *foundational*) theology; the designation of the main faith beliefs such as God as one and triune is *dogmatic* theology; the ordered coherency of the various topics in the entirety such as the meaning of the symbols of incarnation, death, and resurrection in Christology is *systematic* theology; the study of the Church is called *ecclesiology;* the study of sacraments is *sacramental* theology; the study of the fulfillment of the kingdom of God is *eschatology;* prudential actions about how to live the faith are gathered up under the general topic of *practical* theology and include the principles of right and wrong actions which is *Christian ethics* (or *morality*); the study of different gifts by which we live the faith is *spirituality;* and the study of different religions and their faith experiences in relation to Christianity is *ecumenism.* These areas are always connected to the sources of Scripture scholarship and the discipline of history, which can have their own theological positions and then are designated *biblical* theology and *historical* theology.

If one were to examine theology by the various methods that it uses (2), one would find another way of designating theologies. Some contemporary examples of the many possibilities are: the corpus of theologies as the search for the divine within the human capacity is *transcendental* theology (K. Rahner and B. Lonergan); concern for the lived gospel message in its social context, especially the poor, is *liberation* theology (G. Gutierrez) and in Europe often, but not exclusively, referred to as *political* theology (J. Metz, E. Schillebeeckx); a balance of human experience, Christian message, and language mutually critiquing one another as *correlational* (D. Tracy); concern for the experience of women and their articulation of the faith experience is *feminist* (R. Reuther); and a variety of methods that provides a theory of interpretation because of developments in linguistic, rhetorical, or critical theories that go under the general title of *hermeneutical* theologies.

J. J. MUELLER, S.J.

See also ANSELM, ST.; AUGUSTINE, ST.; RAHNER, KARL; THOMAS AQUINAS, ST.

THEOLOGY, BIBLICAL

This term designates a new area of theology that has developed in response to modern biblical criticism. Biblical criticism gathers the basic data (various and varied texts, archaeological information, knowledge of many languages and their development, etc.), places those texts in their times (historical, cultural, social, and anthropological criticisms), and tries to understand the development of the texts in their oral and written traditions (form, redaction, and composition criticisms). These are all necessary steps, with their own data, that are required for a full and correct understanding of every biblical text. Because the biblical texts belong to and within a believing community, the texts finally must be interpreted through the lens of the historically lived experience of faith. To understand and articulate the experience of faith and the faith experience in the biblical texts for our time is the responsibility of biblical theology.

Vatican II in the document *Verbum Dei* recognizes that even in the composition of the biblical texts, faith was operating within the communities and with layer after layer present from eyewitness to oral to written form. For example, the four Gospels are not identical in themes emphasized but reflect the favored stories and even slightly different twists to the same stories as the communities understood them, loved them, and retold their already developing meaning before being finally written down as a text. While differences in concerns and emphases and even theologies are present in the biblical texts, nevertheless they render a unified testimony of authentic expressions of the same Christian faith, recognized historically by their inclusion in the canon of Sacred Scripture. Other "gospels" were not included.

The biblical theologian has three demands: to stand as a necessary bridge between the rapidly expanding terrain of the Scripture scholar and the reflective tradition of two thousand years by the systematic theologian; to combine both the area of scriptural scholarship and the core of our faith tradition; and to present the various respective theologies of the biblical texts as accurately as possible. The field is never static but is always dynamic as "good news" always is. Just as the faith experience develops in relation to the contemporary situation, so too do insights from the present day allow us to see and hear dimensions of the texts in new ways which call upon biblical theologians for their expertise. For example, in the globalization of the world taking place, people from the poorer and dependent countries have come to understand and articulate the demand of the gospel to reach out to total human liberation, recognizing the entire human realms including ecological, racial, social, and spiritual dimensions of humanity. They have come to grasp a fullness of the preaching of Jesus not readily seen before and articulated "from below" as constituent of any global Christianity. Sacred Scripture, as generally affirmed and particularly experienced, thus has a double edge which operates both as a privileged source of our faith and as a continual norm in the present about how to find and respond to God. The biblical theologian serves to render that faith as source and norm for the believing community.

Outstanding theologians such as Karl Rahner (*Foundations of Christian Faith,* 1978) have argued for its place within the method of theology, and Edward Schillebeeckx in his two monumental books *Jesus: An Experiment in Christology* (1979) and *Christ: The Experience of Jesus as Lord* (1980) demonstrated biblical theology at its best.

J. J. MUELLER, S.J.

See also CRITICISM, BIBLICAL; THEOLOGY.

THEOLOGY, DOGMATIC

A branch of theology whose task is to organize and synthesize the data of Holy Scripture and Tradition in order to expound coherently and systematically the doctrines of the faith, with the aim to perceive their truth and understand their meanings more profoundly. Vatican II, in the decree on the training of priests (*Optatam Totius*) affirms: "The following order should be observed in the treatment of dogmatic theology: biblical themes should have first place; then students should be shown what the Fathers of the Church, both of the East and West, have contributed towards the faithful transmission and elucidation of each of the revealed truths; then the later history of dogma, including its relation to the general history of the Church; lastly, in order to throw as full a light as possible on the mysteries of salvation, the students should learn to examine more deeply, with the help of speculation and with St. Thomas as teacher, all aspects of these mysteries, and to perceive their interconnection" (no. 16).

PETER C. PHAN

See also THEOLOGY; THEOLOGY, SYSTEMATIC.

THEOLOGY, FUNDAMENTAL

The overarching designation within theology that examines the foundations of faith itself. (Hence it is sometimes referred to as *foundational* theology.) It examines the conditions and authenticity (the how, why, and what) of the "coming to believe" which is called in the widest sense conversion. It necessarily treats the revelation of God and the meaning of that disclosure and its consequences for individuals and humanity. Topics such as faith, revelation, God, grace, and human nature are the main relationships examined. Fundamental theology interacts with and uses the advancements of scientific, philosophical, linguistic, historical, and cultural data in its exploration and explanations. What makes its area of understanding different is not in its methods but the acceptance of faith as a stance from which it interprets reality. Because fundamental theology is always historically and culturally conditioned, no one explanation will be sufficient and final but always developing and searching for more complete and adequate understandings. Thus theology always pulsates with the best of human knowledge. When the term "fundamental theology" is used, it is most helpful to ascertain the specific methods and use employed by the specific theologian.

J. J. MUELLER, S.J.

See also PHILOSOPHY AND THEOLOGY.

THEOLOGY, MORAL

Moral theology belongs to the area of "practical theology" which logically follows from systematic theology. Moral theology examines the responsible behavior involved in the practice of Christian living in its relationship to following God within this world's situations. Today, the term "moral theology" is gradually and more commonly being referred to as "Christian ethics." The reason is that "moral" theology was considered as confessionally determined and therefore restricted to a particular ecclesial community only. The word "ethics" which is a more philosophically based word stresses both starting points other than faith and an applicability to all of humanity that can be examined by anyone. The term "Christian ethics" signifies that the insights, values, and judgments into human behavior derive from a Christian perspective while, at the same time, it is inclusive of all human persons. In so doing, moral theology has stepped out of any exclusivist ecclesial framework into a secular and global context in its claims for truth about humanity. Therefore, moral theology or Christian ethics has moved to the public arena, without apology yet willing to listen to others who differ, with sound anthropological values and insights derived from its faith experience.

Moral theology is a relatively recent development whose history explains its contemporary changes. In the patristic period, prescriptions about life were given as instruction for baptism and Eucharist; in the Middle Ages prescriptions were penances given in the sacrament of reconciliation; in the thirteenth century when theology entered the lecture halls, the trend continued as Thomas Aquinas addressed topics of morality but did not see morality as a separate discipline; only with the Council of Trent in the Reformation atmosphere of the sixteenth century did a fully blown discipline of morality arrive which was confessionally divided between Catholics and Protestants.

For the last several centuries, moral theology has been challenged especially and even driven by the rapid advances in science. Today the challenges for moral theology come from the macro and micro levels. On the macro or global level, and even here it might be best to say the cosmic level, moral theology attends to such questions as ecology, cultures, society, population, wealth and poverty, distribution and uses of limited resources, war and peace, racism and sexism. On the micro level, and more particularly right now spearheaded by technologically developed nations yet with universal implications for humanity, scientific advances in extremely specialized areas such as medicine take the limelight because the capacity and ability to manipulate life itself is now possible: the manipulation and splicing of the genes of life themselves, control over conception and birthing, transplants, death and dying issues (e.g., nutrition, extraordinary means, terminating life), allocation of limited resources and its cost, and the responsibility of scientific research itself.

Moral theology has always been an issue-driven discipline which divides into two categories: general principles called fundamental morals, and specific issues called special morals which consists of many divisions (e.g., business ethics, social ethics, ecological ethics, medical ethics, sexual ethics, etc.). In both categories its concern is behavior, including formation of conscience, freedom to choose, sufficient data, and the lived understanding of faith both personally and communally within a rich tradition of religious experience. The situation or circumstances within which Christians find themselves is always a limiting condition that requires new adaptation of Christian values.

For the Christian, the central question is "How do I do the loving act in this situation?" The balancing of goods and evils, the tradeoffs that are required for the greatest good, the minimizing of evil consequences, and the willingness to deal with the mystery of finding God in these actions makes morality as much an art as a science. Human living and loving is a mystery; the Christian understands this mystery as one always focused upon God and asking the central question of how to love as God loves us in Christ? How to proceed in complicated and sometimes resisting circumstances, to remain in solidarity with all human persons, and to bring to life an inclusive love of God to all that is done, is the challenge of the Christian that moral theology embraces.

J. J. MUELLER, S.J.

See also CHRISTIAN MORALITY; THEOLOGY, PRACTICAL; THEOLOGY, SYSTEMATIC.

THEOLOGY, MYSTICAL

See MYSTICISM.

THEOLOGY, NARRATIVE

This theology concerns itself with the disclosive and transformative power of story. It is a recent area that responds to the wider critical examination of literary forms and their role in the proclamation of the faith experience. Linguistic and literary criticisms have presented the irreducible communication that a narrative or story gives by the nature of its own structure. A narrative, such as the Gospels, tells the story of Jesus the Christ in matter and form that is indissoluble and must be taken on its own terms. No amount of critical abstraction can remove the reality that it communicates through narrative. The gospel narrative, in this case, proclaims the deepest truth about ourselves and God, with a transformative power and a meaning that is only grasped in and through the structure of narrative itself. Unlike a story whose point we understand and discard, the gospel narratives hold us in a truth never-ending, and a reality ever-unfolding. Narrative theology acts as a corrective reminder of the necessity of hearing the story on its grounds, fresh, irreducible, multilayered, filled with symbols, and powerful. It communicates reality unlike logical or abstract propositions. At the same time, narrative theology probes the continued use of story and storytelling as a form of communication of faith and theology.

J. J. MUELLER, S.J.

See also SALVATION HISTORY; THEOLOGY, BIBLICAL.

THEOLOGY, NATURAL

Natural theology refers to the effort to show the reasonableness of belief in the existence of God and to clarify the attributes of God by means of human reason alone. It also examines the limited character of human knowledge of God. Theodicy, a branch of natural theology, deals with the fact of evil in the world and attempts to reconcile this fact with reasonable belief in an all-knowing, all-powerful and loving God.

"Natural theology" became prominent during the Enlightenment, when people sought ways of avoiding devastating religious wars. Its original purpose was to provide a common ground in certain basic questions about God in order to promote tolerance. Romans 1:20, "since the creation of the world his [God's] invisible nature, namely, his eternal power and deity, has been clearly perceived in the things that have been made," provided scriptural justification for the project. The success of the new empirical sciences, also based on reason, gave added impetus to the study of natural theology. At this same time, some scholars attempted to demonstrate the existence of a "natural religion," a core of religious beliefs or experiences common to all religions and accessible to all people through reason. The overwhelming diversity of actual religions, however, eventually discouraged this particular attempt at "natural theology."

PATRICIA DeFERRARI

See also THEOLOGY.

THEOLOGY, PRACTICAL

This term designates the understanding of the lived faith experience in its pastoral dimension. It completes systematic theology by incorporating the abstract reflection process and testing its applicability in the lived practice of the faith. It also raises questions for how to proceed, what is prudent, what needs to be done and in what order, what can be accomplished, how one can respond. The areas of Christian ethics, spirituality, worship, and pastoral practice are topics within this overarching category of theology. Practical theology is an equal partner with fundamental and systematic theologies in raising the questions of what must be examined by theology. These three areas, fundamental, systematic, practical, taken together form the overarching categories within which the other topics and methods find their unity.

J. J. MUELLER, S.J.

See also THEOLOGY, MORAL.

THEOLOGY, PROCESS

This term designates a theology that has switched from static categories of rest as the basis of everything to the dynamic categories of change, or process, as the basic reality. Process, however, is only one important category; relations, or relationships, are equally important. The more correct designation of the theology is "process-relational theology." The "philosophy of organism" constructed by Alfred North Whitehead is the principle source and dialogue partner. While process theology generally, but not universally, uses the insights of Whitehead in its interpretation of faith, alternative sources are also used. The Jesuit scientist Teilhard de Chardin provided an entirely new way of conceiving the theological enterprise, incorporating evolutionary and processive categories. In the United States such philosophers such as William James and subsequently Charles Hartshorne also offer additional positions not truly Whiteheadian. Process theology has brought attention to change (process) and relationships (structure) as the basic ingredients of life itself. One of its strongest contributions is that it offers an entirely new cosmology, based on scientific discoveries of relativity physics and quantum mechanics with its indeterminacy principle, which points to a new conception of a relational God. Or, as Whitehead described it, "a fellow sufferer who understands."

J. J. MUELLER, S.J.

See also CREATION; PHILOSOPHY AND THEOLOGY.

THEOLOGY, SYSTEMATIC

This area of theology examines the various teachings, or doctrines, of the faith community. The various parts of the faith come together in this area to make up a whole, or a system, that requires criteria of coherence in relationships and ordering, and adequacy with respect to faith and its consequences. The hierarchy or centrality of doctrines, sometimes called *dogmatic* theology, can be and often is included within this area depending upon different theological methods. It includes topics about God as triune, creation, sin, the meaning of the Jesus Event with its symbols of incarnation, Cross, and resurrection, the understanding and dimensions of Church, sacraments, Mary, and saints. Systematic theology is one of the main categories of theology and is integrally related to *fundamental* and *practical* theologies.

J. J. MUELLER, S.J.

See also THEOLOGY; THEOLOGY, DOGMATIC.

THEOTOKOS

Literally "God-bearer," the Greek word is the ancient Eastern title for Mary, Mother of God. It is cherished in different contexts, doctrinal and liturgical principally. It also featured in popular prayer. It is found in the vocative case in the most ancient prayer to Our Lady, the original form of the *Sub tuum,* "We fly to thy patronage. . . ." The manuscript evidence for this is the papyrus in the John Rylands Library, Manchester. This papyrus is at latest from the fourth century, possibly the third. In the development of dogma it is deeply significant. A scholar has reconstructed the prayer to read thus: "Under your mercy we take refuge, Mother of God, do not reject our supplications in necessity. But deliver us from danger (You) alone chaste, blessed." The Latin *Sub tuum* varies slightly. What is important is that the prayer nourished belief in Our Lady's divine maternity, so that Newman, who prized highly the "sentiment of the faithful," could maintain that "the spontaneous or traditional feeling of Christians had anticipated the formal ecclesiastical decision." He was speaking of the Council of Ephesus (431) where *Theotokos* was at the center of the debate, as *homoousios* had been, in regard to Christ, at Nicaea (325).

At Ephesus the capital text was a letter from St. Cyril of Alexandria, which contained these words: "Now the Word's being made flesh is nothing else than that he partook of flesh and blood in like manner with us, and made our body his own, and proceeded man of a woman without having cast away his divinity. . . . That is what the expression of the

"Coronation of the Virgin," apse mosaic in Santa Maria Maggiore, 1294, Rome

exact faith everywhere preaches; this is the mind we shall find in the holy Fathers. In this sense they did not hesitate to call the holy Virgin God's Mother (*Theotokos*). . . ."

Research has been active in regard to the origin of the word *Theotokos*. Texts showing use of the title from Hippolytus of Rome (d. 235) and Origen (d. 254) are controverted. At present the first certain literary use of the title is attributed to Alexander of Alexandria in 325. Thereafter it is found widely, once with St. Cyril of Jerusalem, more often with St. Athanasius and the Alexandrians and the Cappadocians—even Arians like Asterius the Sophist used it.

MICHAEL O'CARROLL, C.S.Sp.

See also MARY, MOTHER OF GOD.

THÉRÈSE OF LISIEUX (1873–1897)

Thérèse, born in Alençon, France, lived most of her short life in the old Norman town of Lisieux, where she entered the Carmelite monastery at age fifteen. She became known after her death through her autobiographical *Story of a Soul*, a collection of three manuscripts: a series of memories written at the request of her sister (then her prioress) Pauline; a letter to her sister Marie; and comments on her life in the convent written during her last summer alive. Thérèse wrote in a disarmingly simple, concrete style. But while editing her work, her sisters scraped away many of her blunt words and injected their own pious phrases—distorting Thérèse's personality. Since 1947 when the original manuscripts were opened, all publications—including her complete correspondence and the extensive and scholarly, *Derniers Entretiens* (Paris: Desclée de Brouwer-Editions du Cerf, 1971) which chronicles her final illness and conversations—are meticulously true to original sources. Through her spontaneous thoughts and reactions the autheutic Thérèse comes to life as realistic and lively, as a brief excerpt from the drama played out during the last few months of her life testifies.

In the summer of 1897 Sister Thérèse of the Child Jesus and of the Holy Face was dying. Three of her natural sisters—also Carmelite nuns—hovered about her infirmary bed with visions of the glory of death. "You will probably die on July 16, the feast of Our Lady of Mount Carmel, or on August 6, the feast of the Holy Face," Pauline said. "Eat 'dates' as much as you want," Thérèse quipped. "I no longer want to eat any. . .I have been too much taken in by dates" (John Clarke, O.C.D., trans., *St. Thérèse of Lisieux, Her Last Conversations,* Washington: ICS, 1977, p. 83). Stage imagery did not fit the slow suffocation of tuberculosis. "You prefer to die rather than live?" Pauline prompted. Thérèse was weary of Pauline's fishing for mystical sentiments. "I don't love one thing more than another; I could not say like our holy Mother St. Teresa (of Avila) 'I die because I cannot die.'" She wanted, simply, "what God prefers and chooses for me" (Clarke, p. 183). The word Thérèse repeated continually was *maintenant, now.* "*Now* I want to be sick all my life if that gives pleasure to God. . . ." "I'm like a little child, very little. I'm without any thought, I suffer from minute to minute" (Clarke, p. 170).

In August, according to Pauline: "She was no longer able to perform bodily functions except with terrible pains. If we placed her in a seated position to ease the suffocation after a long coughing spell, she thought she was sitting 'on iron spikes.' She begged prayers because, she said, the pain was enough 'to make her lose her reason.' She asked that we not leave poisonous medicines for external use within her reach. . . . Besides, she added, if she hadn't any faith, she would not have hesitated for one instant to take her life" (Clarke, pp. 162-163, footnote). This image does not quite fit the "little flower" of the haloed holy cards. To grasp Thérèse's Way we must listen, not to the haloed abstractions her sisters grafted onto her from stories of The Saints, but to her own human "stammerings."

Thérèse was only fifteen when she passed through the cloister door that locked behind her with an iron bolt and an iron rule. Glad to escape the clutter of French life (she once learned to dance quadrilles), she liked the stark monastic bed of board and straw with a brown wool spread, she liked the silence broken by the call to Morning Prayer, as it had been in Teresa of Avila's day, with clappers. But she did not like the monastic ideal of perfection. Rooting out her "faults" and "weaknesses" day after day stirred up more and more fear until she finally grasped that the *ideal,* not her weakness, was the problem. By the time she died she had cut a simple, concrete path to God which shed centuries of layers of pious thoughts, gothic prayers, and abstract ideals. She found a shaft to the heart of Christ: the unadorned words of Scripture. Words from the passages of Isaiah and Tobit and the psalms and his own words that unveiled the intimacy he knew with his Father.

During that last summer alive she wrote her experiences in a child's copybook, in a startlingly fresh voice: "I wanted to find an elevator . . . (to) raise me to Jesus, for I am too small to climb the rough stairway of perfection. I searched, then, in the Scriptures for some sign of this elevator. . .and I read. . . *Whoever is a LITTLE ONE, let him come to me.* But wanting to know, O my God, what you would do to the *very little one* who answered your call, I continued my search and this is what I discovered: *As one whom a mother caresses, so will I comfort you; you shall be carried at the breasts, and upon the knees they shall caress you.*"

". . . The elevator which must raise me to heaven is Your arms, O Jesus! And for this I had no need to grow up, but rather I had to remain little. . ." [Thérèse Martin, *Story of a Soul,* Washington: ICS, 1976, pp. 207-208).

"Remain little," each moment, free of any human role or projected ideal. Remain connected with Christ, not kneeling at his feet—but in his *arms.*

In the world to which Thérèse was born Christ was present on a distant altar, the faithful lowering their eyes while the Host was elevated. She suffered the agony of adolescent girls—"scrupulosity"—a crippling anxiety that common reactions were sins. The education of the day, as Gustave Flaubert so powerfully demonstrated in *Madame Bovary,* had little to do with shaping a critical consciousness. Rather, it instilled "received ideas"—romanticized images, ingested whole and divorced from an authentic experience of life. To her father Thérèse, with the long blond curls tumbling down her back, was "the little queen"; to her sister Pauline, "the little rosebud of the rosebush of my affection" that would open "to the very gentle Sun of the Child Jesus' Love" (Pauline to Thérèse, LC 5, 20 December 1882, *General Correspondence, Vol. I,* Washington: ICS, 1982, p. 154). To her sister Marie she was, even at thirteen, "the baby", unable to do her own hair. In Rome, at age fourteen, Thérèse said "I felt born in my heart a *great desire* to suffer" (*Story of a Soul,* p. 9). "My heart was beating hard when my lips touched the dust stained with the blood of the first Christians" (*Story of a Soul,* p. 131). She dreamed of dying a martyr, like Joan of Arc.

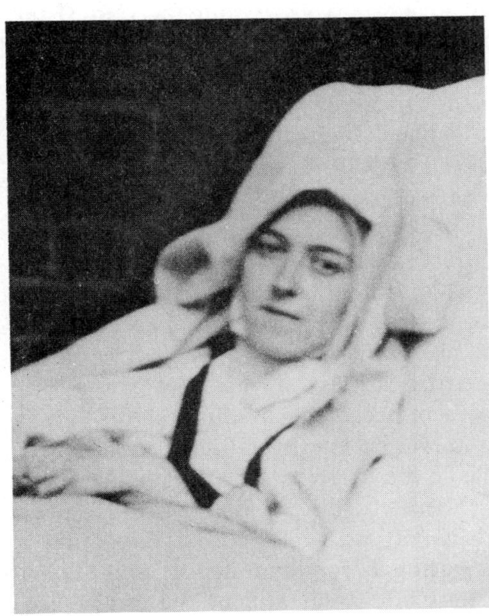

St. Thérèse of Lisieux

One person in her life stands out in relief against this backdrop. Her mother, Zelie, practiced a living faith, purged of romantic sentiment. She was realistic, practical, and ran a cottage industry from their first home—making Alençon lace. When she gave birth to Thérèse in the winter of 1873 she had already seen four of her children die. A week later Zelie walked alone all night to a farm to bring a wetnurse back to save her baby. Thérèse spent the next fifteenth months on the farm, growing tanned and healthy, and being wheeled into the fields in a wheelbarrow. She never lost her love of wild cornflowers. The "sunny years" ended sharply when she was four and a half, and was lifted up to her mother's coffin to kiss her.

After Zelie's death Thérèse was bombarded with contradictions and harsh realities: at nine, her "second mother" left home to enter the cloistered Carmelites, and a cold image seared into Thérèse's mind: "*My Pauline,* behind the *grille!*" (*Story of a Soul,* p. 60). The loss sparked an hysterical illness with hallucinations. At twelve she made a school retreat: "What the Abbé told us was frightening. He spoke about mortal sin and he described a soul in the state of sin and how much God hated it. He compared it to a little dove soaked in mud, and who is no longer able to fly" (Jean-François Six, *La Veritable Enfance de Thérèse de Lisieux, Nevrose et Saintete,* Paris, Éditions du Seuil, 1972, p. 201). Flooded with dissonant images, Thérèse left school and spent hours at a time alone in an attic decorated with religious objects, flowers, and mementos of

Pauline. Her cocoon failed to shield her: the cloister swallowed her *third* mother, her sister Marie, "The only support which attached me to life!" (*Story of a Soul,* p. 91). The year after she entered the cloister herself, her gentle father was committed to a mental hospital. She could not visit him. "That day I didn't say I was able to suffer more!" (*Story of a Soul,* p. 157). Her sense of the sacred was now stripped of romantic feelings, ideals, and sentiments. "Sanctity does not consist in saying beautiful things," she wrote to her sister Céline, "it does not even consist in thinking them, in feeling them! . . . it consists in *suffering* and suffering *everything*" (Thérèse to Céline, LT 89, 26 April 1889, GCI, 557, 558).

She was only sixteen years old. As her letter suggests, a critical change had taken root in her. She had begun to read, and reflect, on her own. In Thomas à Kempis' *The Imitation of Christ* she read: "Make room for Christ, and deny entrance to everything else." Mastery of her own emotions and habits led her out of "the very narrow circle in which I was turning, without knowing how to come out" (*Story of a Soul*, p. 101). The sickly, frightened, indulged Thérèse had stumbled on the ancient practice of detachment. Embracing a hidden life, she strictly discounted other peoples' opinions of her—whether sisters, prioress, priest, or bishop—as well as the lofty sentiments attributed to saints. Moment by moment she turned from the heroic ideal back to earth: ". . . I don't understand the saints who don't love their family . . ." (Clarke, 46-47).

With her discovery of the poet/mystic John of the Cross Thérèse entered another level of understanding: the painful purging of the soul—the "dark night"—was merely a prelude to intimate love: "Beneath the apple tree/ There I took you for My own,/ There I offered you My hand,/ And there I restored you . . ." (John of the Cross, *The Collected Works of St. John of the Cross,* trans. Kieran Kavanaugh, O.C.D., Washington: ICS, 1979, p. 413). Scripture nourished the love she'd found. In an Old Testament, hand-copied by her sister Celine (the nuns had none available to them), Thérèse read and reread the most personal and intimate passages until she knew them by heart. "You permitted me to be bold with you," she wrote in the child's copybook as she lay dying, "you have said to me as the father of the prodigal son said to his older son: *EVERYTHING that is mine is yours.* Your words, O Jesus, are mine, then, and I can make use of them to draw upon the souls united to me the favors of the heavenly Father. . . . O my Jesus, it is perhaps an illusion but it seems to me that you cannot fill a soul with more love than the love with which you have filled mine. . . . I dare to ask you '*to love those whom you have given me with the love with which you loved me. . .*'" (*Story of a Soul,* p. 256). "Those you've given me." She meant the words literally. She treated the people around her with as simple and direct a love as Christ had treated her.

In the final months of her life she corresponded with a young seminarian named Maurice Bellière. The letters show a sharp shift away from the patronizing words and distant stance Father Pichou, her own spiritual director (in earlier years) had adopted with her, a stance that deflected an authentic relationship: ". . .Were you not well pampered to receive the blessing of the Holy Father?. . .oh! pampered in all ways? I was quite touched by seeing your crown of white roses blessed by the venerated Patriarch, and posed on the white hair. . . " (Père Pichon to Thérèse, LC 146, 16 February 1891, CG II, 632]. Thérèse bluntly told Pauline, "Father Pichon treated me too much like a child" (Clarke, p. 73).

She did not repeat the mistake. "Remaining little" also meant detaching from the formalism and distance that sprang from idealized religious roles: seminarian, Carmelite nun. She took a real interest in the details of Maurice Bellière's life—giving him the freedom to open to her the shame that crippled him. Thérèse challenged his shame and led him, step by step, to respond to her simply: "My dear little brother."

"My pen, or rather my heart, refuses to go on calling you 'Monsieur l'Abbé'. . ." (Thérèse to l'Abbé Bellière, LT 224, 25 April 1897, CG II, p. 974). "I must confess that in your letter there is one thing that pains me, it is that you do not know me as I am in reality . . . believe me, I beg you, the good God did not give you a *great* soul for your sister, but one that is *very small* and very imperfect" (Ibid, p. 975). "How I must bore you," he wrote to her, "distract you. . .I speak of myself to excess. . .I am a wretch. . ." (l'Abbé Bellière to Thérèse, LC 186, 7 June 1897, CG II, pp. 1011 and 1013). "O, my dear little Brother, please never think you 'bore me or distract me' by speaking much about yourself. Would it be possible for a sister not to take an interest *in all* that touches her brother? . . . Don't think you can frighten me with talk of 'your best years wasted'. . . . I know there are saints who spent their lives in . . . astonishing mortifications . . . what of it? 'In my Father's house there are many dwelling places.' Jesus has told us so, which is why I follow the way He traces for me. I try to be occupied with myself in nothing. . ." (Thérèse to l'Abbé Bellière, LT 247, 21 June 1897, CG II, pp. 1020-1021). Expecting a formal, inspirational correspondence with Sister Thérèse of the Child Jesus and of the Holy Face, Maurice Bellière was startled to find a real human being beneath the veil. He was curious about her name, but apologized for the "indiscretion." "I find your question perfectly natural," she wrote back, giving details of her family life. She begged him to be simple with God and with her, too. "I am your *sister*" (Thérèse to l'Abbé Bellière, 26 July 1897, p. 1053).

On Good Friday of 1896 Thérèse first coughed up blood. That same night she was invaded by the "thickest darkness." It seemed that a voice was mocking her and death would bring "not what you hope for but a night still more profound, the night of nothingness" (*Story of a Soul,* p. 213). Though the fog of inner darkness never lifted, it never touched her *trust.* This was rooted in the ancient Hebrew sense of faith—not dogmatic conviction, but personal trust in Yahweh. She had only to "remain little" and God would uphold her "from instant to instant." Watching Thérèse suffer night sweats, high fever, vomiting of blood, and laboring to breathe tormented her sister Pauline. "Don't be disturbed," Thérèse told her. "If I can't breathe, God will give me the strength to bear it. I love him! He'll never abandon me" (Clarke, p. 115). Eight weeks later she died, with the same trust. "God is not going to abandon me, I'm sure. . . ." she said the day she died. "He has never abandoned me" (*Story of a Soul,* p. 205). She was twenty-four years old.

A nice footnote rounds out the story of the romantic child who wanted to die a martyr like Joan of Arc. Joan was finally canonized in 1920, in a modest Vatican ceremony. When Thérèse was canonized, five years and one day later (1925), an old ceremony of outlining St. Peter's in torches was revived for her—and a million people jammed the hilltops of Rome to see the sight of the Great Dome illuminated for *Saint* Thérèse.

PATRICIA O'CONNOR

See also SAINTS.

THIRD ORDERS

Members of third orders (tertiaries) are divided into two classes, secular and regular.

Secular third orders contain members of the lay branch of a religious order. While living a normal secular life, they strive to participate in the spiritual and apostolic work of their particular order. These third orders originated in the thirteenth century, and their members follow a specific rule and spiritual regimen. They usually wear a scapular under their clothing and wear the habit of their order on special occasions. A person may not belong to more than one third order at the same time. There are Augustinian, Carmelite, Dominican, Franciscan, Premonstratensian, Servite, and Trinitarian third orders.

Regular members of a third order take simple vows and live a religious life, following a particular rule. They engage in a great variety of apostolic work: teaching, nursing, etc. At present, the most active are the Dominican, Franciscan, and Carmelite regular third orders.

JOSEPH QUINN

See also LAITY, THEOLOGY OF THE; RELIGIOUS LIFE, ACTIVE.

THOMAS AQUINAS, ST. (1225–1274)

Thomas D'Aquino was the youngest son born to a family of minor nobility at Roccaseca, Italy, in 1225. At a very early age, his family gave him as an "oblate" to the Benedictine monastery at Monte Cassino with the hope that he might eventually become abbot. When the monastery was nearly suppressed by Frederick II in 1239, the monks recommended that Thomas be sent to Naples to study at the university. There he came into contact with the newly established Dominican Order (1216) in the person of John of St. Julian who encouraged his interest in the order.

Around 1242 to 1243, against the wishes of his family, Thomas received the Dominican habit. When the order attempted to send him to study in Paris in 1244, the D'Aquino family kidnapped him and confined him in a family castle at Montesangiovanni. Although the captivity lasted till 1246, Thomas could not be persuaded to give up his decision to become a Dominican and, possibly with the help of his mother, he escaped from confinement. The Master of the Order, John of Wildeshausen, took him to Paris to begin studies, where he came under the tutelage of the famous Dominican scientist-theologian, Albert the Great. When Albert moved to Cologne in 1248, Thomas moved with him. It was Albert who recognized the rare genius within the large, taciturn Italian friar and encouraged him in his studies.

In 1251, Thomas was sent back to Paris as a candidate for the position of Master of Theology. This position required that all candidates lecture as "bachelors" on the Bible and on the Sentences of Peter Lombard, the leading theological "textbook" of the time. Thomas fulfilled these requirements in such an outstanding way that, in 1256, he was given his "license" to teach as a Master in Theology at an age far younger than customary. It was during this period of "regency" that Thomas was first involved in the attacks on the new mendicant religious orders from the so-called "secular" Masters on the faculty.

St. Thomas Aquinas, oil painting, S. Caterina, Pisa

For the next three years, he taught at the University of Paris as one of two Dominican Masters of Theology. As a Master, he was required to teach from biblical texts, hold public debates on theological topics and preach in the university church.

Around 1260, Thomas was recalled to the Roman Province of the order. He was appointed "lector" or official teacher at the Dominican priory in Orvieto till 1264, and in 1265 was assigned to establish a Dominican house of studies in Rome. At the same time, he lectured at the papal court in Viterbo. In 1268, he was once again assigned to the University of Paris, this time in response to a renewed attack on the mendicant orders by the Secular Masters, which included their rejection of the use of the philosophy of Aristotle as a foundation for Christian theology—a use which Albert and Thomas had pioneered.

In 1272, Thomas was recalled by his province to Naples to establish a house of studies. On 6 December 1273, he underwent an experience, partly physical, partly spiritual, which left him unable to teach or write further. While traveling to the Council of Lyons in March 1274, he became ill and died at the Benedictine abbey of Fossanova. He was canonized in 1323.

Contribution of St. Thomas Aquinas

Even though he was a famous and influential theologian in his own lifetime, Thomas Aquinas was to become one of the true giants of Christian theology in the Western Church and one of the most influential thinkers in history. His literary output was prodigious, despite his many duties, and his relatively premature death at age forty-eight/forty-nine. Some of it exists in his own writing and some in the notes of students or in the form of dictation to secretaries. The works include scriptural commentaries, a commentary on the Sentences of Peter Lombard, lectures and commentaries on the works of Aristotle, collections of academic disputations on philosophical and theological topics, special essays on particular issues such as the right of mendicant orders to exist, and a kind of theological compendium called the *Summa Contra Gentiles,* which, in part, was a response to a need for a theological reference work for missionaries.

Thomas' most famous and influential work, however, is the *Summa Theologiae* which he wrote or dictated over a period of seven years beginning in 1266 and left uncompleted at the time he ceased writing in December 1273. The *Summa Theologiae* is an effort to present in a systematic and global fashion all of Christian theology ("sacred doctrine") in response to what Thomas saw as a need for a reference work for "beginners." The result was a profound synthesis of Christian theology which not only utilizes Scripture and the Church Fathers, but also the philosophy of Aristotle as its foundations.

The *Summa Theologiae* is organized into three major parts. (Later students were to divide the second part in such a way that the work popularly falls into four parts [Prima pars, Prima-secundae, Secunda-secundae, and Tertia pars].) The first part treats of God as the source and creator of all being; the second part considers human beings and their return to God; the third part treats of Christ and the sacraments as the means whereby human beings return to God. The three parts treat a total of 512 questions containing 2669 "articles." A sample of the many riches of the *Summa Theologiae* might include the famous "five proofs for the existence of God" (I, q.2, a.3), the treatise on law (I-II, qq. 90–97) and the treatise on the Eucharist (III, qq. 73–78).

Thomas Aquinas' fame has been celebrated in the Church in addition to his canonization in 1323. In 1567, Pope St. Pius V proclaimed him a "Doctor of the Church" and gave official sanction to the title "Angelic Doctor" by which he is generally known. In 1880, Pope Leo XIII proclaimed St. Thomas Aquinas the patron of all Catholic educational institutions. The *Summa Theologiae* continues, even today, to be a profound and authoritative statement of Catholic theology.

R. B. WILLIAMS, O.P.

See also ARISTOTELIANISM; PHILOSOPHY AND THEOLOGY; THEOLOGY, SYSTEMATIC; THOMISM.

THOMISM

"Thomism" is a term used broadly to describe efforts to base philosophical or theological thought on the writings and insights of St. Thomas Aquinas. Since these efforts extend from the period immediately following the death of St. Thomas Aquinas up to the present day, a single monolithic definition of Thomism is not practicable.

Viewed from the perspective of the history of philosophy, Thomism may be seen as a periodic renewal of interest in the writings of St. Thomas Aquinas. The renewal known as Neo-Thomism in the nineteenth century resulted in the official adoption (by Pope Leo XIII in the encyclical *Aeterni Patris*) of the teachings of St. Thomas Aquinas as a true and perennial expression of Roman Catholic doctrine. Most of the influential theologians of the Second Vatican Council were thoroughly trained in Thomistic philosophy and theology. Understandably, the Dominican Order, to which St. Thomas Aquinas belonged, has been a consistent champion of Thomistic thought.

From the viewpoint of systematic philosophy and theology, Thomism in all its various forms, takes as its starting point the writings of Aquinas. These, in the form of commentaries on Aristotle or on Scripture, recorded lectures and academic debates, and especially the *Summa Theologiae,* represent the profound genius that inspires continual interest in his works. A fundamental characteristic of Thomism is the acceptance of Aristotelian (and to some degree, Platonic) philosophy as the basis of Christian philosophy and theology. Although this use of Aristotle as a way of bringing reason to bear on nature and faith was extremely controversial in the thirteenth century, it now suffers from criticism that it fails to cope with scientific discoveries in the nineteenth and twentieth centuries.

At the same time, Thomism's profound respect for the compatibility of human reason with the gift of faith is a great strength in the effort to understand Catholic faith in our own time.

Thomism upholds the objectivity of certain values that also are realized through faith and revelation. Thus nature and grace, reason and faith, work together in the process of living out Christian life.

Thomism also suffers from widespread (albeit unofficial) rejection within Roman Catholicism of the Scholastic approach to theology in favor of existential and phenomenological schools of thought of more recent origin. Nevertheless, the insights of St. Thomas Aquinas seem to transcend the structural difficulties of Scholasticism and continue to attract attention and respect from Christian and non-Christian philosophers and theologians. For this reason, Thomism in its many forms will continue to be a part of the Western Roman Catholic theological heritage.

Prominent Thomistic philosophers and theologians in modern times include Jacques Maritain and Etienne Gilson.

R. B. WILLIAMS, O.P.

See also PHILOSOPHY AND THEOLOGY; THEOLOGY, SYSTEMATIC; THOMAS AQUINAS, ST.

THOMPSON, FRANCIS (1859–1907)

Born in 1859 into a Catholic family in Preston, Lancashire, he intended to become a priest, but he and his superiors decided that he lacked a vocation. He then decided to follow his father's profession and enter a medical school, but failed to qualify. He became addicted to opium and lived a destitute life until he furtively brought some poetry he had written to the attention of Wilfred Meynell, the publisher of *Merry England.*

Meynell and his wife Alice, a distinguished essayist and poet, took Thomas under their loving and patient care and encouraged his writing career, despite his inability to rid himself of his drug addiction. He published three volumes of verse (1893, 1895, 1897), and published literary criticism in *Merry England, The Academy,* and the *Athenaeum.* He also wrote a mediocre life of St. Ignatius of Loyola. His poetry conveys his deep religious convictions and his mystical views of reality. At times, his writing is overly ornate, but nevertheless he demonstrated a superb mastery of the English language. Thompson is chiefly remembered as the author of *The Hound of Heaven,* which has been in print since its first publication, and *The Kingdom of God,* which illustrated the mystical bent of his poetry. He died of tuberculosis and drug addiction in 1907. After his death, his poetry enjoyed great popularity, and the royalties, which he bequeathed to the Meynells, made their lives more comfortable in their declining years.

JOSEPH QUINN

See also BRITAIN, CHURCH IN.

THURIBLE

(Gk. *thuos,* "burned offering") The metal vessel used for the ceremonial burning of incense at liturgical services. It is suspended on a chain, (or chains) which allows it to be swung during incensations at Mass, at the Liturgy of the Hours, or at Benediction.

JOSEPH QUINN

See also LITURGY.

TIARA

The ceremonial headdress of the pope. It is approximately fifteen inches tall, bulbous in shape, and made of silver (or gold) cloth ornamented with precious stones. Three golden coronets—symbolizing the pontiff's universal episcopate, his supremacy of jurisdiction, and his temporal influence—encircle the crown, which is surmounted by a small cross. Before Vatican II, the tiara was worn at nonliturgical ceremonies (e.g., during the proclamation of a dogma or a canonization); after the council, Paul VI (1963–1978) stopped wearing it, and, though it is still permitted, no pontiff has worn it since.

JOSEPH QUINN

See also PAPACY, THE.

TITHES AND TITHING

Tithing, the practice of offering tithes, or one-tenth of one's annual income, as a religious observance is an ancient practice, probably cultic in origin, and not limited to Israel. Deuteronomy prescribes tithing grain, wine, oil, and the firstlings of the herd or flock each year (14:22-23). In the time of Jesus, some Pharisees were so observant that they tithed even the smallest herbs. He approved of this act of piety but declared that it does not exempt someone from also observing the weightier matters of the law, such as justice, mercy, and faith (Matt 23:23).

There is no law prescribing tithing in the New Testament, but Paul argues that, just as those in Temple service receive food from the Temple, in the same way according to a command of the Lord "those who proclaim the gospel should get their living by the gospel" (1 Cor 9:14).

In the 1983 Code of Canon Law the principle is laid down that the faithful are obliged to assist the Church by providing what is necessary for divine worship, apostolic and charitable works, and the decent sustenance of its ministers (c. 222). In addition to financial support, the faithful may offer their time and their talents. While the Church has the right to require this support (c. 1260), it is more fitting that such offerings be made freely, as in regular Sunday collections or in response to authorized appeals for special purposes.

In some countries a tithe or Church tax is collected annually by the civil government.

WILLIAM C. McFADDEN, S.J.

See also ALMSGIVING; MINISTRY.

TITHES AND TITHING, BIBLICAL APPROACH

A tithe is a tenth of one's income and tithing is the practice of contributing this amount to the support of religious institutions or of the needy. The practice had precedents among the ancient Near Eastern cultures and had a secular version as a tax for the support of the king (Gen 14:20; 1 Macc 11:35). Even this royal tax may have had a sacred dimension insofar as the king was responsible for the religious institutions. Nevertheless, many biblical texts command tithing directly for religious purposes, though the procedures seem to have varied over the centuries. One might offer grain, fruit, other produce, wood, oil or livestock. Sometimes money was required. One could substitute money for material tithes, but had to add a further 20 percent (Lev 27:30-33). Numbers 18:21-32 gives the tithes to the Levites, but requires that they in turn tithe to the priests. Deuteronomy 14:22-29 tells the Israelites to bring their tithes to the sanctuary but to eat them in God's presence, except for every third year when they are to offer them for the Levites and for the poor and needy. Nehemiah commands that tithes be brought to the Temple for the support of priests and Levites, but under the care of trustworthy men (10:36-40; 12:42-47). In the New Testament Jesus acknowledges tithing, but criticizes those who substitute it for "the weightier things of the law" (Matt 23:23). The Church still encourages tithing as acknowledgement that the earth is the Lord's and that possessions must be shared especially for the service of the Lord and for the needs of the poor.

ANTHONY J. TAMBASCO

See also SOCIAL TEACHING OF THE CHURCH.

TITIAN (TIZIANO VECELLIO) (ca. 1485–ca. 1576)

Born around 1485, Titian is the great master of the Venetian school. He studied under Gentile and Giovanni Bellini, and was much influenced by Giorgione, as can be seen in the early work *The Three Ages of Man* (ca. 1512). After the deaths of his mentors, Titian dominated Venetian painting for sixty years. To precision and nobility of form, Titian added a use of color which enabled him to express natural bodies and objects with an unrivaled power (already seen in *The Assumption of the Virgin,* Church of the Frari, 1516–1518). He expressed his virtuosity in numerous mythological works, notably for Alfonso d'Este of Ferrara (e.g., *Bacchus and Ariadne,* 1522–1523). Titian was in demand all over Europe beginning with the imperial house of Charles V who was his personal friend and ennobled him in 1533. In the emperor's service he developed his art of portraiture and was soon in demand in Urbino, Venice, and elsewhere as a portrait artist. In mid-life he began to develop the art of the female nude in the tradition of Giorgione, and a trip to Rome strength-

Titian portrait by Agostino Caracci, engraving

ened his sense of classicism. About the same time he began to be influenced by Michelangelo. Philip II favored Titian's erotic mythologies (e.g., *The Rape of Europa,* 1562). In Titian's late years he almost invented impressionism in favoring color over lines (*Christ Crowned with Thorns,* 1570). It was widely said that he was losing his powers, but this charge is refuted by the *Pietà* he designed for his own tomb, a work of incredible majesty and emotional power. He began an artistic revolution of immense influence, and died around 1576.

DAVID BRYAN

See also ART, CHRISTIAN.

TONSURE

(Lat. *tondere,* "to shear") The centuries-old Church custom of shaving a lock or circle of hair from the top of the head. Originating in the fourth and fifth centuries as a monastic observance, it became (in the Middle Ages) an official rite signifying a layman's admission to the clerical state. The practice was suppressed officially in 1972 by Pope Paul VI.

JOSEPH QUINN

See also SACRAMENT OF ORDERS.

TORAH

The Hebrew root of the word "Torah" means teaching or instruction. In one sense, it refers to the first of the three component parts of the Hebrew Bible: *Torah* (the first five books of the Christian "Old Testament"), *Nev'im* (Prophets), and *Ketuvim* (Writings). In another sense, Torah refers to the whole Hebrew Bible. In its deepest sense, however, Torah is more than that, it is revelation and the entire activity of Jewish study throughout generations. Torah establishes *Halakhah* (practical law) and provides guidance in fulfilling the commandments, but its ultimate purpose reaches beyond that. It provides a comprehensive worldview that reveals the essential relationship of all things to Torah and also to each other. The Torah is believed to be God's own word and as such eternally "original." It lives in the hearts and minds of its students; thus, for the tradition, Torah demands interpretation and study in each generation.

Opening page of Ahavah Mishnek Torah, ca. 1400, Italy

PATRICIA DeFERRARI

See also BIBLE, OLD TESTAMENT WRITINGS; TALMUD.

TORQUEMADA, TOMAS DE (1420–1498)

A nephew of the distinguished theologian Juan de Torquemada, he entered the Dominican Order. After finishing his theological training, he became prior of the convent of Santa Cruz in Segovia and confessor to the Spanish royal treasurer. This contact helped him to become in 1474 confessor to Their Catholic Majesties, Ferdinand V and Isabella I, a post he held for twenty-two years. His influence in Spain became enormous. The Spanish Jews (Marranos) and Moors (Moriscos) did not figure in the royal couple's plans for a Catholic Spain, and in 1478 the monarchs received permission from Pope Sixtus IV to establish the Inquisition in their kingdom; Torquemada helped to compose the royal request. The first inquisitors were unsuccessful, and in 1482 Torquemada became one of eight Dominican inquisitors. In 1483 Isabella persuaded the pope to name him Grand Inquisitor. Torquemada quickly organized the Inquisition into five regional tribunals and appointed himself as the court of appeals. He also published the *Ordinances* which established the procedures to be used by the Spanish Inquisition for three centuries. Torquemada unleashed the Inquisition upon Moors, Jews, witches, apostates, heretics, and anyone else suspected of threatening the state or Church; approximately two thousand people were burned to death and many more punished in other ways. Many Spaniards sent complaints to Rome, but the king and queen stood behind the Grand Inquisitor. In 1492 he advised the expulsion from Spain of Jews who refused to convert, advice taken by the royal couple. Torquemada succeeded in purging dissidents from Catholic Spain, but he did so by a savage persecution of innocent people. Indeed, the Inquisition's obsession with preventing dissidence guaranteed that Spanish intellectual life would be stifled and would fall behind that of Italy and northern Europe in the sixteenth and seventeenth centuries.

JOSEPH F. KELLY

See also CHURCH AND STATE; ORTHODOXY; SPANISH INQUISITION, THE.

TRADITION

Etymologically tradition means "handing on" or "transmission." It can mean either the process of transmission itself (often written with the capital "T") or the content of what is transmitted (written with the small "t"). The latter can be used in the singular (the content in general) or in the plural (the distinctive traditions of each Christian denomination in particular).

It is universally agreed that no society, secular or religious, can be constituted or survive without some tradition. Without being rooted in a tradition one loses both the moorings of one's present identity and the directions for one's future. But one's attitude to tradition cannot simply be acquiescence and repetition. St. Paul's injunction: "Test everything; retain what is good" (1 Thess 5:21) is valid in this regard. Jesus himself displayed the same critical attitude toward his Jewish traditions. On the one hand, he followed many teachings and practices of his religion; on the other hand, he replaced rabbinical interpretations of the Law with his own ("You have heard that it was said. . . . But I say to you") and broke many of the Jewish ritual laws, e.g., those concerning the Sabbath and food observances.

For Christianity, which is a historical religion, tradition assumes a special importance. Besides the Sacred Scripture there is a body of traditions which are normative for all Christians. Against the Gnostics who claimed to possess a secret knowledge which alone leads to salvation, Irenaeus and Tertullian argued that there is a public postscriptural tradition located in the consensus of the Churches founded by the apostles, in particular the Church of Rome established by Peter and Paul. This consensus was termed the "rule of faith" or the "rule of truth," a principle distinct from though not independent of the Scripture, by which the orthodoxy of beliefs is measured. This rule of faith is embodied most fully in the creeds and later in the teachings of ecumenical councils. The normativity of tradition is solemnly affirmed by the fifth ecumenical council (Constantinople II, 553): "We rightly confess the doctrines that have been transmitted to us by the divine scriptures and the teaching of the holy fathers, and by the definitions of the one and selfsame faith made by the four holy councils" (canon 14). Again the seventh council (Nicaea II, 787) states that anyone who "rejects the ecclesial tradition, written or unwritten" is to be anathematized (canon 4).

One central issue regarding tradition is its relation to Scripture. Scandalized by many abusive traditions of the Catholic Church at their times, the sixteenth-century Reformers set forth "Scripture alone" as the formal principle corresponding to the material principle of "justification by faith." In reaction to this position, the Council of Trent (1545–1563) taught that the gospel, "the source of all saving truth and rule of conduct" is "contained in the written books and unwritten traditions" and that the council itself "receives and venerates with the same sense of loyalty and reverence all the books of the Old and New Testaments . . . together with all the traditions concerning faith and morals."

In contemporary ecumenical dialogues, the differences between Roman Catholic and Protestant positions regarding the relationship between Scripture and tradition have been largely overcome. For one thing, the historico-critical research in biblical studies has shown that before the composition of the Scripture, in particular the Gospels, there had been oral traditions which were later selected, synthesized, or explained according the needs of the Churches. Indeed, the canon of the Scripture itself was established by postscriptural tradition. For another, historical studies on the Council of Trent's phrase "the written books and unwritten traditions" has shown that the post-Tridentine interpretation of it as meaning two separate, parallel, and independent sources of revelation is unwarranted. Some

Roman Catholic theologians have argued that for the Council of Trent Scripture and tradition are identical in content though different in form and that therefore tradition is only formally, not materially, independent of Scripture.

Vatican II, in its Dogmatic Constitution on Divine Revelation (*Dei Verbum*), did not settle the issue of how Trent should be interpreted. However, it strongly insists on the unity of Scripture and tradition: "Sacred Tradition and sacred Scripture, then, are bound together, and communicate one with the other. For both of them, flowing out from the same divine well-spring, come together in some fashion to form one thing, and move towards the same goal. . . . Hence, both Scripture and Tradition must be accepted and honored with equal feelings of devotion and reverence" (no. 9). The council goes on to say: "Sacred Tradition and sacred Scripture make up a single sacred deposit of the Word of God, which is entrusted to the Church" (no. 10). As to the contents of tradition, Vatican II declares: "What was handed on by the apostles comprises everything that serves to make the People of God live their lives in holiness and increase their faith. In this way the Church, in her doctrine, life and worship, perpetuates and transmits to every generation all that she herself is, all that she believes" (no. 8).

Though there is widespread agreement today among the Churches about the necessity of tradition for a correct understanding of Scripture as well as about the necessity of tradition to be in conformity with the Scripture, there is no consensus as to how the authenticity of traditions is to be gauged. It may be said in general that Jesus Christ himself, as he is attested in the Scripture, is the criterion by which traditions are to be judged. Or appeal can be made to St. Vincent of Lerins' threefold criterion of universality, antiquity, and consensus. In the concrete, however, the question of whether a particular doctrinal or moral tradition is in fact in conformity with Jesus Christ or whether it has in fact been believed "everywhere, always, and by all" still needs to be decided. Who in the Church is authorized to make such a determination? The Roman Catholic Church declares that "the task of giving an authentic interpretation of the Word of God, whether in its written form or in the form of Tradition, has been entrusted to the living teaching office of the Church alone," even though "this Magisterium is not superior to the Word of God, but its servant" (no. 10). Obviously not all the Churches agree on this point. Despite these serious divergences, ecumenical unity has been considerably strengthened by the universal agreement that tradition is essential for the life of the Church and that it is a living, developing force. Or as a terse aphorism has it, "Tradition is the living faith of the dead, traditionalism is the dead faith of the living."

PETER C. PHAN

See also AUTHORITY IN THE CHURCH; MAGISTERIUM; ORTHODOXY.

TRANSUBSTANTIATION

The term refers to the change which takes place in the bread and wine of the Eucharist making them the Body and Blood of Jesus Christ. The term began to appear around the twelfth century and was popularized by Peter Lombard in his *Sentences.* The Fourth Lateran Council used the term in speaking of the Eucharist and the Council of Trent defended the doctrine against attacks by the Reformers.

The Council of Trent was careful to point out that the Scholastic interpretation of the change in the Eucharist was not part of the doctrine. It stated simply that such explanations were appropriate to interpret the kind of change the Church was talking about (Session XIII, chapter 4, DS 877). Unfortunately this distinction is not always clear in popular (and even theological) explanations.

Since the Council of Trent the doctrine of transubstantiation has been the object of bitter polemic between Catholics and other Christians. More recently, thanks to the ecumenical movement, a more irenical spirit has prevailed. The Scholastic interpretation of the doctrine is seen as *one* interpretation of the Church's teaching.

After Vatican II a number of theological efforts to express Church teaching in contemporary language and philosophy (especially existentialist) have been attempted. Such terms as transfinalization, transignification, etc., have been used. In response to these attempts the Holy See has emphasized the *real* (or ontological) change which occurs in the Eucharist through the words of consecration.

E. R. FALARDEAU, S.S.S.

See also EUCHARIST.

TRAPPISTS

See CISTERCIANS.

TRENT, COUNCIL OF

See ECUMENICAL COUNCILS.

TRIBUNALS, ROMAN

See APOSTOLIC PENITENTIARY; APOSTOLIC SIGNATURA; ROMAN ROTA.

TRIDUUM

(Lat. *tres,* "three" + *dies,* "days") A three-day period of prayer observed privately or publicly in preparation for a major feast (especially Easter), solemnity, or special occasion (e.g., First Holy Communion or confirmation). It also may be observed as a request for a particular grace.

JOSEPH QUINN

See also LITURGY.

TRIDUUM, EASTER

The three-day period which commemorates the final three days of Christ's life on earth. It begins with the Evening Mass of the Lord's Supper on Holy Thursday, culminates in the Easter Vigil, and concludes with the evening prayers (or Vespers) on Easter Sunday. During the triduum, the faithful are called to bear in mind solemnly Christ's passion and death, and to celebrate joyfully his resurrection on Easter Sunday.

JOSEPH QUINN

See also LITURGY; PASCHAL MYSTERY.

TRIDUUM, PASCHAL

See PASCHAL MYSTERY; TRIDUUM, EASTER.

TRINITY

The doctrine of the Trinity sums up the Christian understanding of the mystery of God. What is ultimately distinctive about Christianity is its understanding of God as tri-personal. The confession of three persons in one God is the outcome of extended reflection on the full implications of the mystery of Christ: the God revealed in the life of Jesus is Father, Son and Spirit.

At present a renaissance is taking place in Trinitarian theology. This renewal has been prompted by a variety of influences: the turn to human experience and liberating *praxis* in contemporary theology, dissatisfaction with the classical formulae of the Trinity, the renewal of Christology in the latter half of the twentieth century, and the emergence of Christian feminist theology.

The classical doctrine of the Trinity had become for many more a mathematical problem to be solved than a living mystery of persons to be experienced. As a result the Trinity assumed a life of its own divorced from human experience, practical living, and the story of salvation. The highly technical language of one nature, two processions, three persons, four relations gave the impression of providing inside knowledge to a privileged few who understood the inner nature of God. As a consequence the doctrine of the Trinity became marginal in the lives of many Christians. Indeed, Karl Rahner once wrote that if the Trinity was proved false, most theology books could remain virtually unchanged.

In spite of these negative observations it must be pointed out that the Trinity lies at the very heart and center of Christian faith: it tells us something extremely important about the nature of the Christian God, it retrieves the relational dimension of personal identity and historical reality, it sums up the Christian story of salvation, it structures the whole of Christian worship, and it intimates the eschatological destiny of humanity and the cosmos as one of transformed communion within diversity.

The seeds of the Christian doctrine of the Trinity are to be found in the life, death, and resurrection of Jesus, the post-Easter experience of the Spirit, and the worship of early Christian communities. However, it was not until the fourth century that these seeds were to flower into a full-blown coherent doctrine.

Of particular significance in the life of Jesus is the experience of God as *Abba* and the resulting self-understanding of Jesus as Son. Equally important in the life of Jesus is the drama of the Cross which arose out of Jesus' radical commitment to the coming reign of God the Father. Closely connected to the Cross is the outpouring of the Spirit through the exaltation of Christ. Reflection by the early Church on the experience of Jesus and the God encountered in the person of Jesus as well as the ongoing experience of the newness of the Spirit of Jesus in the world gave rise to a series of Christian insights which paved the way for the Christian doctrine of the Trinity. These insights include the affirmation that Jesus is the Christ (Mark 8:29; John 20:31), who is the Lord (Rom 10:9; Acts 2:36; 16:31; Phil 2:11), the Son of God (Rom 1:3-4; Gal 4:4; Mark 1:1; Matt 3:17; John 3:35-36), the Word made flesh (John 1:14). In addition, the Christian declaration that God is love (1 John 4:16), the soteriological claim that Jesus is the Savior of the world (Luke 2:11; John 4:42; Acts 4:12), and the Christian liturgical practice of addressing God through Christ in the Spirit also lie behind the Christian doctrine of the Trinity. Thirdly, the strong sense of Jesus as the mediator between God and humanity (1 Tim 2:5), and therefore as mediator of creation (1 Cor 8:6; Col 1:15-16; John 1:1-3), of salvation (Eph 1:7; Titus 3:4-7) and of the worship of God (Eph 5:20), is also an important element in the development of a Trinitarian consciousness in the early Church. The weaving together of these Christologies, theologies, soteriologies, and liturgies issued in the full-blown doctrine of the Blessed Trinity in the fourth century.

A number of questions came to the fore in the second century as the early Church encountered the world of Hellenistic culture and theology. If Jesus is the eternal Word of God incarnate, how can this be reconciled with the absolute unity and transcendence of God in Greek thought? What is the relationship between Jesus as the Logos of God and the atemporal monotheistic God of Middle Platonism? Is Jesus an emanation of the eternal God and therefore subordinate to the one God? What is the relationship between God the Father at the center of the life of Jesus and the Christian proclamation of Jesus as the eternal Word of God made flesh?

These questions came to a head with Arius who sought to safeguard the integrity of Greek theology alongside a recognition of the divinity of Jesus. For Arius, Jesus, though very close to God the Father, ends up as second in importance to God the Father and therefore never fully equal to the Father. The influence of Middle Platonism with its strong emphasis on the absolute unity of God prevails over the biblical claim that Jesus is the eternal Word of God made flesh. Thus we find the followers of Arius insisting that "there was a time when he (Christ) was not." In effect Arius was unable to accept that the eternal God had personally entered into the historical condition of humanity in Jesus of Nazareth.

In response to Arius the Council of Nicea (325) asserted that Jesus is of one substance/being with God the Father (*homoousios*) and not simply of similar substance (*homoiousios*) with God the Father. Nicea affirmed explicitly the absolute unity between God and Jesus. In doing so the Council of Nicea broke the hold of Hellenistic thought on popular belief and upheld clearly the divinity of Jesus and the full mystery of the incarnation of God in Jesus. It was at this dramatic moment in history that Christology moved doctrinally in the direction of a Trinitarian theology. The way was now open for the full flowering of the doctrine of the Trinity because what was affirmed of Jesus at Nicea would be in effect affirmed of the Holy Spirit at the Council of Constantinople (381), though Constantinople did not apply the word *homoousios* to the Spirit. The Nicean-Constantinopolitan Creed describes the Spirit as "the Lord and Giver of life, who proceeds from the Father, who together with the Father and the Son is adored and glorified."

The price paid for this defense of the full mystery of Christ was a certain shifting of theology towards ontology, i.e., the development of ontological expressions of the doctrine of the Trinity. The technical terms of person, nature, substance, relation, energy, procession now move to the center of the stage to account for the activity of God as Father, Son and Spirit in the economy of salvation.

After the Council of Nicea the Cappadocian theologians from the East sought to synthesize the biblical and ontological understandings of the mystery of God as Triune. The Father and the Son and the Spirit share one and the same divine nature and yet each person is distinct and different in virtue of their relationship with each other. This dynamic relationship involves the outward movement of the Father through the Son in the Spirit to humanity and the return movement of humanity back to God the Father through Christ inspired by the Spirit. The unity of God within diversity of persons was described by the Greek term *perichoresis*—a technical expression which involved at least the idea of a cyclical movement, a revolving action, and a mutual indwelling of divine persons in the one single mystery of God.

On the other hand, the Latin theology of the West, largely influenced by Augustine, developed psychological analogies, with special emphasis on the psychology of the human soul as the image of God to explain the life of the Trinity: lover, beloved, love; memory, understanding, will. Augustine in his highly influential treatise *De Trinitate* emphasizes the one divine substance of the Godhead so much that at times the distinctiveness of the three persons appears to be blurred, though this is not his intention. Further, it was Augustine who formulated the axiom that "all actions of the divine persons are one" so that it is the Trinity that creates, the Trinity that redeems, and the Trinity that sanctifies. Yet, Augustine does not wish to do away with the existence of the three divine persons who have "relations of opposition" to each other.

In subsequent centuries these theologies of the West and the East are developed into elaborate systems with varying degrees of success. In the East the focus continues on the internal relations of the three divine persons with a tendency to collapse the economic Trinity into the immanent Trinity, or as it is sometimes called the essential Trinity, who gradually becomes separated from the history of salvation. In the West the emphasis is placed on the individuality of the three persons with the attendant danger of communicating a kind of tri-theism.

It is against this background that the renaissance in Trinitarian theology in the latter half of the twentieth century has come into being. The contemporary debate about the Trinity is not unlike the debate of the early centuries of Christianity. The underlying issue in patristic times and in the present is one of inculturation. How can the Christian understanding of God revealed in Christ be expressed in a language and culture that is living? The relationship between Christian faith and culture then and now is a two-way, mutually critical relationship.

Part of the difficulty today concerns our understanding and interpretation of the contours of contemporary culture. Many would hold we are at present in the midst of a significant paradigm shift in the way we understand the self, society, and the cosmos, and that this has a direct bearing on the way we express and understand the mystery of the Trinity today. Another difficulty at present is the challenge to retrieve an inclusive nonpatriarchal reading of the revelation of God in Christ Jesus out of the biblical tradition.

In developing new ways for understanding the Trinity, account must be taken at least of the following cultural shifts. On the one hand there has been a shift from a mechanical view of the world to an organic understanding of creation. Secondly there has been a movement from individualism to an understanding of the human person as radically relational. Further, there has been a development from a largely patriarchal understanding of the Judaeo-Christian Scriptures to an inclusive understanding of the Scriptures. And finally, there has been a very significant shift from a philosophy of being and substance to a philosophy of process and becoming. These shifts are best understood in terms of balancing influences rather than polar opposites. What, then, will be the shape of Trinitarian thinking in the light of these theological and cultural shifts?

On the one hand the retrieval of the doctrine of the Trinity from the Judaeo-Christian tradition suggests other models complementary to the reigning model of God as Father, Son and Spirit. Some (e.g., J. Moltmann) talk today about the need to move from the Father-Son-Spirit sequence to Father-Spirit-Son and Spirit-Son-Father sequences so as to avoid the twin dangers of monarchianism and subordinationism and to capture the important reality of *perichoresis* within the life of the Trinity. Others (e.g., Elizabeth A. Johnson) suggest a retrieval of the Trinitarian God in the female imagery of Wisdom (*Sophia*) who is with and for the world as the creative Wisdom of God bent over the world, present in Jesus as the personal wisdom of God, and continuing to be with us in the liberating Spirit of Wisdom: Spirit-Sophia, Jesus Sophia, Mother-Sophia. Still others suggest the possibility of talking about the Trinitarian God as one who creates, redeems, and sanctifies provided the personal relationships that obtain between Father, Son, and Spirit can be seen to obtain with equal force between the divine activities of creating, redeeming, and sanctifying. Another voice (e.g., Anne E. Carr) highlights the need to restate the relationships between Father, Son, and Spirit in terms of radical equality, mutuality, and communion within diversity.

On the other hand in the light of these proposals the doctrine of the Trinity as retrieved from the Christian tradition might begin to offer a critique of modern liberal anthropologies of autonomy and individuality by highlighting the insufficiency of the isolated human subject. Likewise the Christian doctrine of God as Trinity could begin to act as a countercultural reality to the existence of so much atomism in contemporary society, without however pretending to possess in any way a social doctrine for the ordering of society. Thirdly, the doctrine of the Trinity might begin to be held up as a model of the kind of relationships that should obtain between rich and poor, female and male, sheep and shepherds within the Christian community.

In conclusion, we must highlight the need to keep before us in any reconstruction of the doctrine of the Trinity at least two basic theological principles. The first of these principles states that all doctrines of the Trinity are subject to the limitations that attach to the principles of analogy and apophatic theology. The temptation to suppose that the Trinity images adequately the holy mystery of the hidden God must be resisted as much in Trinitarian theology as it is in all other aspects of Christian theology. The God revealed in Jesus Christ as Father, Son, and Spirit continues to be incomprehensible to the human mind. In the words of Augustine, "If you have understood, then what you have understood is not God." Similarly Aquinas reminds us that we can know that God is but not what God is. The second principle that should guide Trinitarian discourse and praxis is that every doctrine of the Trinity must be earthed in the reality of Jesus, the crucified and risen One. Trinitarian theology must continually be controlled by the historical economy of salvation revealed in Jesus of Nazareth and so in this way continue to serve the twin realities of Christian soteriology and liturgy.

DERMOT A. LANE

See also GOD; HERESY/HERETICS; THEOLOGY.

TRINITY SUNDAY

The first Sunday after Pentecost. A feast of the Church since 1334, its purpose is to honor the Holy Trinity. St. Thomas Becket (1118–1170) first celebrated the feast in the Church of Canterbury, of which he was archbishop. Under Pope John XXII, it began to be observed by the universal Church.

JOSEPH QUINN

See also LITURGY.

"The Virgin and Child with Saints," by Hans Memling, oil on panel, 1475–1480, National Gallery, London

TRIPTYCH

(Gk. *triptukhos,* "threefold") Three adjoining panels on which a devotional painting is portrayed. The large central panel usually depicts the focus of the work (e.g., an event in the life of Christ or the Blessed Mother), while the side panels show secondary figures, such as worshiping angels. This term can also refer to a hinged tablet comprised of three leaves on which are written the names of persons to be memorialized in the liturgy.

JOSEPH QUINN

See also ART, CHRISTIAN.

TRISAGION

The Trisagion (Gk. "holy three times") is the short chant, "Holy God, holy and mighty, holy and immortal, have mercy on us," which originated in early liturgies of the Eastern Church. The oldest extant citation of it is in the *acta* of the Council of Chalcedon (451). The chant was sung in the Eastern Church in both the Eucharistic Liturgy and in the Liturgy of the Hours. It found its way into the Western Church through the Gallican liturgy, and it first appeared in the Roman Rite sometime in the eleventh century during the Reproaches of the Good Friday liturgy where it remains today.

ANTHONY D. ANDREASSI

See also HOLY WEEK.

TYRRELL, GEORGE (1861–1901)

A convert to Catholicism, he became a Jesuit and a popular confessor and spiritual writer. His friend, Friedrich von Hügel, introduced him to continental writers who were later called Modernists. Tyrrell developed an antagonism toward Scholasticism and stressed the centrality of personal religious experiences. His writing drew the disapproval of his Jesuit superiors who, while opposing his request for laicization, expelled him from the Society of Jesus. He vehemently opposed *Pascendi,* Pius X's encyclical condemning Modernism, and was excommunicated. His posthumous work *Christianity at the Cross-Roads* posited Christianity as the possible basis for a universal religion.

MICHAEL GLAZIER

U

ULTRAMONTANISM

A theological movement which, principally in the last three centuries, argued for a strong papacy whose voice and decisions would be decisive in matters of doctrine and authority. It was primarily a European movement, and the term (which means "beyond the mountains," referring to the Alps, beyond which lay Rome) was embraced in the seventeenth and eighteenth centuries by those opposing Gallicanism and Josephism. It became widely accepted that only a strong papacy could protect the Church against oppressive civil laws and heterodox movements.

In the nineteenth century, Ultramontanism became a major element in French theology and politics, and liberal reformers such as the early de Lamennais, Montalambert, and Lacordaire felt that a strong papacy would foster a Catholic revival and prevent the restoration of Bourbon autocracy after the Congress of Vienna (1814–1815). Rome, however, was less than sympathetic toward their liberal and democratic ideas. On the opposite end, conservatives such as Joseph de Maistre and his followers saw a strong papacy as a bulwark against liberalism and an ally of the established order in France and Europe. De Maistre's influencial polemical work, *Du pape* (1819), helped to attract adherents to the Ultramontane cause and his conservative ideas.

The tide turned completely during the pontificate of Pius IX, from 1846 to 1878, whose policy was to appoint bishops with Ultramontane views in order to encourage the Ultramontanist work of the Jesuits. Vatican I (1869–1870), with its definition of papal infallibility, marked the greatest advancement of the Ultramontane cause, which, for the following century, went almost unchallenged. Vatican II (1962–1965), with its richer theology and ecclesiology, saw the Church as communion and fostered a collegiality and ecumenical spirit which moderated the rigidity of some Ultramontane views of the nineteenth century.

JOSEPH QUINN

See also LIBERALISM; PIUS IX, POPE; SYLLABUS OF ERRORS; VATICAN COUNCIL I.

UNBAPTIZED, FATE OF

See LIMBO.

UNIONS, LABOR

The Roman Catholic tradition recognizes the right of workers to form unions and to bargain collectively for fair wages and proper working conditions. Unions can be an important factor in dealing with the inequalities of power that exist between management and employees. They can be a significant means for realizing the positive dimensions of work—for establishing solidarity and community among workers and for providing workers a voice in their work. As an intermediary social organization, unions can make a substantial contribution to the common good through, for example, the ongoing education and the retraining of workers.

Among the activities of unions, strikes play a significant role in bargaining with management. As a last resort, strikes are a legitimate means of pursuing justice for employees.

While unions can provide and perform important social functions, they are not the only means of achieving these ends. Unions can help establish solidarity among workers and give them a voice; but there are other ways of accomplishing this as well. Each situation must be evaluated on its own merits to determine the most appropriate means to realize the positive dimensions of work. The final judgment about the most appropriate means rests with the employees.

As a major social institution, unions have obligations to society. Efforts by government and business to break unions and prevent people from joining unions are not ethical; but unions themselves must act in ways that benefit and empower workers and contribute to the common good.

THOMAS SCHINDLER

See also LABOREM EXERCENS; SOCIAL TEACHING OF THE CHURCH; WORK.

UNITARIANISM

While Unitarianism as a creedal formula achieved prominence as a practiced denomination within Protestantism in correlation with liberal theology of the nineteenth century, its presence in early biblical formulations, in monarchial forms of early Christian theology, and in sixteenth-century protests of Michael Servetus and later the Reformed Church of Transylvania is well documented.

In simplest form the Unitarian creed stresses the undivided unity and unqualified morality of a sovereign, majestic God. It finds in the earliest biblical witness testimony to the oneness (sometimes called "uni-personality") of God, and, thus, rejects the classical Nicene doctrine of Trinity. In the Calvinistic notion of predestination Unitarians find a target for their protest against any concept of God that allows the interpretation that God is immoral or violates individual conscience or rational standards of morality. In the "modernist" temper of late nineteenth- and early twentieth-century discussion of the relation of science and religion, Unitarianism assumed the posture first established by seventeenth-century Rationalism: the dogma of orthodoxy must be scrapped, because it is incompatible with the joint tests of critical reason and rational morality.

The "unitarian creed" was suppressed in medieval Christendom. Even in the early stages of the Reformation, when Lutherans, Calvinists, and spiritualizing Anabaptists commonly opposed Roman Christianity, there was little tolerance for anti-Trinitarian thought. As Spaniard Michael Servetus was executed in Geneva for his heretical denial of the divinity of Jesus, Calvin opined: "He who has trampled under foot the majesty of God is worse than a brigand who cuts the throat of a wayfarer."

It is with Servetus and Anabaptist Ludwig Hetzer that the unitarian doctrine first appeared in full theological and liturgical expression. The name Unitarian was in public usage by Bishop Francis David, Reformed Church of Transylvania, in 1569. By 1580 a group of Socinians, influenced by Italian lay theologian Fausto Sozzini, had taken control of the Minor (Reformed) Church of Poland and Lithuania, converting it to a fellowship of unitarians and evangelical rationalists.

Unitarianism found its safest ground in Germany, Poland, and Lithuania, where the tolerance secured for reforming Lutherans was extended to the wide range of reform and reconstructionist groups. However, it found in Calvin's strict theological constructs the antithesis to shape its own rationalist thought.

While Calvin emphasized the doctrine of the Trinity, some of his followers so separated the personal being of Father and Son that they seemed to differ even in temperament and character (much as early heretic Marcion had separated the Gods of Old and New Testament). Against this the Unitarians proclaimed the radical unity of God in its Arian simplicity. Drawing from French and Italian humanism, as well as the Platonic "Demiurgos," they represented Christ as the adopted Son of God, whose function was as the secondary ruler of the universe. The central claim of traditional Christianity, Catholic and Protestant—the incarnational presence of the divine Christ—was rejected as antirational, unscientific, and essentially immoral.

Likewise, the Unitarians rejected such traditional doctrines as original sin, the Lutheran doctrine of the total depravity of human nature, infant damnation, the Calvinist teaching on predestination, the wrathful judgment of the righteous God, even traditional views of atonement as effecting change in the nature of humanity. Such doctrines, they thought, violated New Testament teaching and rational morality. The role of Jesus was twofold: (1) he exemplifies the righteousness, holiness, and goodness that Christian living requires; (2) he testifies to the merciful goodness and moral perfection of God.

These strains were combined in the Socinian Racovian Cathechism (1605), where the three "functions" or "offices" of Christ's life—prophet, priest, and king—provide the ground for a systematic theology and a set of ethical instructions. By 1770, we find Englishman Josef Priestly offering a reasoned apologetic for Unitarianism, entitled *An Appeal to the Serious and Candid Professors of Christianity.*

By the nineteenth century Unitarianism, like the general liberal theological development, was attracted to a "scientific worldview" and a heightened awareness of individual and social responsibility. James Martineau in England and William Ellery Channing and Thomas Parker in the United States protested early nineteenth-century Protestant and Catholic orthodoxies. At the same time they rejected liberalism's efforts at retrieving the "kernel" of the gospel to dress it up in the clothing of modernity. For them scientific method was the starting point for enlightened, responsible inquiry.

As to religious interests, primary concern was with general religious perspectives that would be compatible with scientific understanding and could serve as the basis for moral devotion. Gradually, the Unitarian pendulum swung away from any distinctively Christian affirmation toward a broadly reverential "ethical humanism," concerned with fostering moral sensitivities in individual and society alike.

Today Unitarianism is dispersed between its many historical interests, some wings maintaining a token Christian orientation, others functioning as ethical societies, still others connecting with intellectual interests like Universalism, scientific study of religion, and ethical rationalism.

JAMES W. THOMASSON

See also LIBERALISM; PROTESTANTISM; REFORMATION, THE; SCIENCE AND RELIGION.

UNITIVE WAY

This is the final stage in the spiritual life as described by the mystics who have experienced it. After the stage of beginners in which one purifies one's life from sin and one's prayer through simplicity, a person enters the stage of proficients, which is a period of purification of our knowedge-love of God through an illumination received in contemplative prayer. This illumination is attained by engaging in—or better, allowing God to draw us through—a journey of faith and a journey of love. Mystics sometimes refer to three parts of the unitive stage: spiritual courtship, spiritual engagement, and spiritual marriage. This period of transformation and loving union is beautifully described in "The Living Flame of Love," a poem by St. John of the Cross.

LEONARD DOOHAN

See also CHRISTIAN SPIRITUALITY; MYSTICISM; PRAYER.

UNITY OF THE CHURCH

See MARKS (OR NOTES) OF THE CHURCH.

UNIVERSITIES, CATHOLIC

See CATHOLIC HIGHER EDUCATION IN THE UNITED STATES.

URBI ET ORBI

"To the city (Rome) and to the world." This Latin phrase refers to a blessing given by the pope from the balcony at St. Peter's, Rome. Especially noted by the media is the first such blessing of a new pope.

DAVID BRYAN

See also PAPACY, THE.

URSULINES

Founded in 1535 by Angela Merici, this is the oldest teaching order of women in the Church. Originally, it was a society of virgins living in their own homes and devoting their lives to catechetics and care of the sick. However, at the suggestion of St. Charles Borromeo, Paul III in 1544 mandated community life and simple vows for the new society. In 1612 Paul V allowed the Ursulines in Paris strict enclosure and solemn vows, but directives of Vatican II eliminated these edicts. The Ursulines have made a significant and global contribution to Catholic education and have given the Church saints and mystics including Marie Guyard (''Marie of the Incarnation''), who brought the Ursulines to Quebec.

MAGDALEN O'HARA, O.S.U.

See also MERICI, ANGELA, ST.; RELIGIOUS ORDERS.

USURY

In the ancient world a borrower was required to pay back the original loan plus an additional charge called usury. The term then corresponds to what in the modern world is called interest. In today's usage, usury always refers to interest rates which are exorbitantly high and go beyond the limits established by law. For the sake of clarity, usury will be used here only in its original sense of a charge added to a loan, and will be used interchangeably with the more familiar term interest.

In the Old Testament Jews were permitted to lend at interest to foreigners, but not to fellow Jews (Deut 23:19-20). In the same way, debts might be exacted from foreigners, but the debts of Jews had to be forgiven every seven years by law (Deut 15:2). This is testimony to their care for their less fortunate neighbors. It is also a recognition of the often grim situation of a debtor, unable to pay off interest charges, much less the principal of a loan, and as a result losing all his property.

This lofty ideal of sharing one's resources freely within the people was not always observed, of course. In the time of Nehemiah an outcry arose from the people against their fellow Jews who had been charging such high interest on loans during a time of famine that poor Jews were being sold into slavery to pay off debts. Nehemiah accused the usurers of wrongdoing before the assembled people and prevailed upon them to return the people's lands and goods (Neh 5:1-13).

Opposition to usury also arose among the Greeks, even though it was a common practice and regulated by law. Plato and Aristotle argued that by its very nature money was "sterile" and that it was therefore a violation of the law of nature to demand interest on loans.

There is little on the subject in the New Testament. In the parable of Talents it is taken for granted that with proper management the money entrusted to the servants will be increased. The slothful servant was roundly criticized by his master: "You ought to have invested my money with the bankers, and at my coming I should have received what was my own with interest" (Matt 25:27). Jesus is using current business practice as an example to his followers to be industrious in the service of God, but his compassion goes out to those in debt. Followers of Christ should not only not wish to profit from someone who is forced into debt, but should be willing to forgive the debt entirely. In the Lord's Prayer Jesus taught them to pray to the Father: "Forgive us our debts as we also have forgiven our debtors" (Matt 6:12). In Luke's narration of the Sermon on the Plain Jesus urges his followers to be free from attachment to earthly goods. He goes much further than a prohibition of usury. He counsels them to "lend, expecting nothing in return" (Luke 6:35). This particular text will be cited with great frequency in Christian tradition as justifying the total prohibition of taking interest on loans.

Usury was condemned by the early Fathers, at the Council of Nicaea and subsequent councils, by a number of popes, and by theologians in the Scholastic tradition. In the Roman Catechism, composed by order of the Council of Trent, usury is described as a "most grave crime" and is equated with murder. Clearly, the passion with which usury was denounced in the Church for over a thousand years was based on the experience of human misery that resulted from excessively high interest rates. The arguments, however, employed to combat usury proved too much. They were derived from a too literal reading of Luke 6:35, from an analysis of the nature of money as "sterile" which had become anachronistic with the rise of a market economy, and finally from fidelity to the centuries-long tradition of condemning usury.

By the end of the sixteenth century bankers and entrepreneurs had amply demonstrated the productive nature of money and credit. It taxed the ingenuity of theologians to find a way to approve moderate, regulated interest rates without seeming to contradict the formal teaching of the Church that usury is a grave violation of divine and natural law. They succeeded by leaving intact the previous teaching about the intrinsic nature of money, while showing that there were a good number of extrinsic reasons which entitled a lender to charge interest, e.g., as compensation for the risk of investment, since the return varied with the success or failure of the venture, and since part or all of the invested capital might be lost.

This proved to be a serviceable solution. Over the next few centuries the official teaching of the Church about usury remained in force but was increasingly obsolete. Finally, in *Quadragesimo Anno* (1931) Pius XI noted approvingly that investment is able to provide increased opportunities for employment and so is to be considered "an act of real liberality particularly appropriate to the needs of our time" (no. 51). According to the 1983 Code of Canon Law, it is even required of church administrators that they invest for profit funds not needed to pay expenses (cc. 1283, § 6; 1305).

The history of the condemnation and subsequent approval of usury has value far beyond the issue itself. It is a cautionary tale and should serve as a permanent warning against simply repeating a teaching without examining the changing historical situation to which it is being applied. More positively, it is a vivid demonstration of the importance to the Church that its official teachings appropriately reflect all the various expertises which are present in the People of God.

WILLIAM C. McFADDEN, S.J.

See also SOCIAL RESPONSIBILITY, FINANCIAL; SOCIAL TEACHING OF THE CHURCH; VIRTUE.

V

VANIER, GEORGES-PHILÉAS (1888–1967) AND PAULINE (1898–1991)

Georges-Philéas Vanier, born Montréal, Québec, Canada, 23 April 1888, eldest son of Philéas Vanier, a businessman, and Margaret Maloney; died, Ottawa, Ontario, Canada, 5 March 1967; and Pauline, née Archer, born, Montreal, 27 March 1898, only daughter of the Honorable Charles Archer, justice of the Superior Court of Quebec and Thérèse de Salaberry; died Compiègne, France, 23 March 1991.

On 29 September 1921, Georges and Pauline Vanier were married in the cathedral in Montreal. He was a much decorated war hero, she a lively, outgoing, young woman with high religious ideals. They would have five children (Thérèse, b. 1923; Georges, b. 1925; Bernard, b. 1927; Jean, b. 1928; Michel, b. 1941) and they would develop as an exceedingly close-knit couple, enjoying, despite their very different and strong personalities, an unusual spirit of harmony and understanding.

"We always think of them together," became a phrase often repeated by their many friends over the years, and not least during the seven years (from 1959 to 1967) when Georges was serving as governor general of Canada. They formed a striking couple; he, a tall and impressive man who moved with great dignity and composure; she, stately, tall, and ever elegant, with eyes shining over a brilliant smile, radiating vitality and personal concern. He wrote to her every day whenever he was away from her, and throughout the forty-six years of their public life together, they seemed to be the perfect partnership: Pauline, compassionate, sympathetic and warm, complementing the quality of Georges' unconditioned dedication.

They were much together, too, in the decision to found the Institute of the Family, which bears their name and has continued since 1965 to aid parents in need of counsel and to help deepen public understanding of the importance to society of the quality of family life. They wanted "more people to find in their families, the warmth and delight we found ourselves."

It was together as well that they worked for refugees and the dispossessed. In the Paris of late 1939 and in the Algiers of 1944, Georges' concern was to find new homes in Canada for the victims of Nazi brutality, particularly the Jews. Later, in 1944—within days of the liberation, Georges was the first foreign diplomat to return to Paris—Pauline helped to strengthen his influence on the French government by becoming a daily presence at the Gare d'Orsay, where in her Canadian Red Cross uniform she greeted the trains of the returning deportees. In their own apartment, she welcomed tortured underground fighters, wounded soldiers, and orphaned children. "Her loving, sympathetic ear," one young person later recalled, "and her simple, practical approach, were our only hope of sanity and peace in a world of upheaval." Georges made it a point to visit Buchenwald and to broadcast an indignant and moving reaction back to Canada. "Tonight," commented one newspaperman, "you put Christ on the airwaves." Later, in 1956, he took responsibility for Montreal's committee of welcome for the victims of the Hungarian Revolution, and became a familiar sight among social workers as they worked (successfully) to find places for them.

The Vaniers also prayed together. It was at Pauline's urging that on Good Friday, 1938, Georges attended a sermon by the celebrated Jesuit spiritual director, Robert Steuart, and underwent a spiritual experience that gave new direction to his life. He resolved to attend Mass every day. After 1944 he and Pauline began to set aside a daily half-hour of prayer, and to read to each other out of the same spiritual books. They shared a remarkable devotion to the Sacred Heart and to St. Thérèse of Lisieux, and they each developed a marvelous way in ordinary conversation with their friends of passing from everyday matters or business subjects to profound truths of the spirit. "Have you ever seen the Vaniers at prayer?" asked a noted Canadian journalist in 1967. "They are utterly wrapt. Their whole heart and minds are in deep communication with God. Some say God is dead. How absurd. If God is dead, with whom are the Vaniers talking?"

Much of the spirit in the Vanier couple, as in their achievements and concerns, is common to each one. Yet they were very different people.

As a boy Georges was a gentle, intelligent, and serious student whose tastes were literary and whose close friends were older than he was. He was devout, too, committed to daily recitation of the rosary—a practice he continued all his life. He was brought up in both English and French and completed his undergraduate studies at Loyola College, Montreal, and his law degree at Laval University there in 1910. He was called to the Quebec Bar in 1911.

At the outbreak of the Great War, he was among the first to enlist, in November 1914, in the new "22nd French-Canadian Battalion," which became the Royal 22nd Regiment in 1920, and in which he rose to be commanding officer from 1926 to 1928, and honorary colonel in 1952. He served with outstanding courage and was decorated for bravery under fire four times. He was also twice wounded in action, his second set of injuries, in August 1918, necessitating during a period of intense and prolonged suffering the amputation of his right leg above the knee. Major Vanier's experience of the war years affected him all his life, and intensified his clear, firm, outspoken and unswerving faith in God's help and in the protection of Our Lady. It also strengthened his extraordinary sense of public duty.

In 1927 Colonel Vanier was appointed to the Canadian delegation at the League of Nations in Geneva, and soon began to play there a leading role in what was essentially the emergence of Canada's presence in international diplomacy and politics. He served on the Preparatory Disarmament Commission from 1927 to 1931, and at the London Naval Conference in 1930. In 1931 he became military attaché at the Canadian High Commission in London. His reputation grew as a peacemaker who sought justice, and in 1939, he became minister to France; then, in 1942, minister to all the Allied governments in exile. As such he followed the Free French to Algiers in 1944, and to Paris as ambassador, 8 September 1944. He continued there for almost a decade until January 1954.

Throughout these years, bearing and raising children, Pauline had worked with him. Born to privilege and wealth, she had learned from her parents that this was something entrusted to her for others. Her mother, who was directed in her prayer life by the Jesuit preacher Almire Pichon, also spiritual director of Thérèse of Lisieux, had an active faith that inspired her daughter with her own lifelong confidence in God. In the early 1930s Pauline began to retire periodically to the Carmelite convent at Hitchins, near London, and joined with friends around Farm Street Church in regular prayer groups. She learned from the Carmelites and from Fr. Steuart to find God in her family at home, and to take him with her in the rush of her social rounds. It was her duty, he advised her, to be as *mondaine* as diplomacy required. Later, during the years she served as chancellor of the University of Ottawa from 1965 to 1972, she was often closely observed by students. One confided once: "She shows that being religious can be fun."

Major-General Vanier was installed as governor general of Canada on 15 September 1959. His years in office were turbulent ones for the country. A difficult economic situation, a succession of minority governments, and the rise of violent separatism in the Province of Quebec made his task difficult and delicate. Yet he won the admiration and affection of Canadians by his deft and diplomatic handling of problems, and by his concern, manifested in his inspiring messages and in his wide travels across the county, for the poor and the humble, for youth, and for spiritual values. Pauline's own tremendous spiritual energy won equal respect. Her encouraging kindness and self-deprecating laughter seemed to give a truly heightened sense of self to everyone who met her.

Five years after her husband's death, Madame Vanier decided to return to France to support her son, Jean, at "L'Arche" (the Ark), the headquarters near Paris of the worldwide movement he had founded in 1964 for the care of the mentally disadvantaged. There again, her small home became a refuge for those in need of her love: for the handicapped, certainly, but also for the young volunteers from around the world, often emotionally overextended in their eagerness to help, and mostly for the young mothers among them, who carried, as she did with her husband for so long, the double burden of serving others and of raising a family.

In 1989, the archbishop of Ottawa set up a committee charged with studying the grounds for introducing Georges Vanier's cause for beatification. After Pauline's death, the same committee undertook the study of her cause as well. The couple is, after all, together again.

JACQUES MONET, S.J.

See also CANADA, THE CATHOLIC CHURCH IN; L'ARCHE.

VASECTOMY

See STERILIZATION.

VATICAN

The popes have made the Vatican their principal residence since their return to Rome after their sojourn in Avignon (the Babylonian Captivity, 1309–1377). The present state of Vatican City is the smallest sovereign state in the world, comprising only 108.7 acres. It was established by the Lateran Treaty in 1929 which also mandated the extraterritorial rights of Vatican City to the basilicas and other buildings in Rome and to Castel Gandolfo, the summer residence of the popes.

The Basilica of St. Peter is the focal point of Vatican City. Built between 1506 and 1626, it is the mother church of Catholics and the largest church in Christendom. The normal resident population of Vatican City is about one thousand, and over four thousand work there. The eyes of the world turn to the Vatican, not for its great libraries or fabulous art collections, but because it is the home of the Bishop of Rome, the spiritual leader of Catholics.

JOAN GLAZIER

See also HOLY SEE; LATERAN TREATY; PAPACY, THE; PAPAL STATES.

VATICAN COUNCIL I

On 8 December 1869, Pope Pius IX solemnly convened the First Vatican Council, the twentieth ecumenical council in the Church's history. A lengthy agenda faced the seven to eight hundred cardinals, patriarchs, archbishops, bishops, and heads of male religious orders assembled for the solemn opening, but events beyond their control were to ensure that only a fraction of it would be completed. The council, which was held in the basilica of St. Peter, Rome, was interrupted on 1 September 1870, leaving behind much unfinished business.

On 6 December 1864, Pope Pius IX had announced his intention to summon an ecumenical council, having sounded a number of bishops, and he appointed a Central Preparatory Commission the following March. Theological subcommissions were given the task of preparing draft documents for the council, dealing with the following subjects: dogmatic theology, discipline, religious communities, apostolic missions and the Eastern Churches, politico-ecclesiastical matters, and ceremonial.

On 29 June 1868, the Pope, in the "bull" *Aeterni Patris,* formally summoned to the council patriarchs, archbishops, bishops and abbots, and all others entitled to take part. Separate communications were sent to Orthodox and Reformed Churches, inviting them to look upon the council as an opportunity for returning to the true fold, but these did not elicit a positive response.

Aeterni Patris stated that the objective of the council was "to provide a remedy for present evils in Church and society." It went on: "the ecumenical council, after the most careful consideration, is to determine what is to be done in these calamitous times for the greater glory of God, for the integrity of belief, the splendor of worship, the eternal salvation of humanity, the discipline and the solid instruction of the secular and religious clergy, the observance of ecclesiastical laws, the reform of morals, the Christian education of youth, and peace and universal concord."

Even though the preparatory subcommissions had produced a total of fifty-two draft documents for discussion at the council, only six of them reached the council floor and of these only two were adopted, after extensive revision. One was the constitution *Dei Filius:* "The Son of God," which was solemnly promulgated on 24 April 1870. It contained four chapters and dealt with (1) God, the creator, (2) the possibility of knowing God and the need for revelation, (3) the nature of faith, and (4) knowledge derived from faith and knowledge acquired by reason. The other document promulgated by the council was the constitution *Pastor Aeternus:* "The Eternal Pastor," which defined the infallibility of the pope.

The bull *Aeterni Patris* had made no mention of the infallibility of the pope, which at the time had been the subject of intense debate. However, on 6 February 1869, an article in the semiofficial Jesuit-edited publication, *Civiltà Cattolica,* had expressed the hope that the council would be short and that the infallibility of the pope would be defined by acclamation, without debate. The *Civiltà Cattolica* article set off alarm bells for the governments of several European countries, who feared that the definition of the pope's infallibility might upset the balance of Church-state relations. Initially some governments considered bringing pressure to bear on the council, but in the event they refrained.

It is tenable that before the council the majority of Catholics would have approved of defining papal infallibility, but there is no way of knowing this, since the majority of Catholics did not then, as they do not now, write or speak publicly on such matters. Such Catholic views on the topic as were given public expression ranged from outright opposition, on the one hand, to the wholehearted approval voiced by the English theologian and convert, William George Ward, on the other. It was Ward's opinion that every papal pronouncement ought to be declared infallible. In between were many who, while believing that the pope's infallibility should be defined, were not clear as to the range of pronouncements to which it should extend. And there was a minority who thought the definition inadvisable, for differing reasons. Among them were some who felt that it was unhelpful to treat papal infallibility in isolation from the infallibility of the Church.

In the event papal infallibility became the dominant theme at the short-lived council. It is reckoned that more than three-quarters of the participants were in favor of definition, while those against it amounted to roughly one-fifth. In between was a group who were undecided.

In January 1870, some 500 bishops signed a petition to have the teaching defined. A counterpetition was signed by only 136 bishops. A text was prepared and was debated in the council between 13 May and 13 July. More than 150 of the participants spoke, most of them in favor of definition.

A formula was devised which the majority of the assembly accepted as an accurate expression of the nature and extent of papal infallibility and on 18 July, at a solemn session presided over by Pius IX, the constitution *Pastor Aeternus,* which contains the definition of papal infallibility, was adopted by 433 votes to 2. Sixty-two participants in the council who had reservations of various kinds about the advisability of defining infallibility or about the wording of the definition left Rome the day before the solemn session. All of them subsequently accepted the definition. The two bishops who had voted against it, Luigi Riccio of Caiazzo, Italy, and Edward Fitzgerald of Little Rock, Arkansas, U.S.A., accepted it as soon as it was passed and joined in the *Te Deum.*

The constitution *Pastor Aeternus* consists of a prologue and four chapters: (1) the institution of the primacy of the pope; (2) its continuation; (3) its extent; and (4) the definition of papal infallibility.

The following is a translation of the definition of infallibility: "with the approval of the sacred council we teach and define as divinely revealed dogma that the Roman Pontiff, thanks to that divine assistance promised him in blessed Peter, when speaking *ex cathedra*—that is, when, as pastor and teacher of all Christians and with his supreme apostolic authority, he defines a teaching on faith or morals to be accepted by the universal Church—is endowed with that infallibility which the divine Redeemer wished his Church to have when defining a teaching on faith or morals. For this reason, such definitions of the Roman Pontiff are irreformable of themselves, and not by the consent of the Church."

The council continued, with only some one hundred taking part, until 1 September 1870, during which time nothing much happened. The Italian invasion of the States of the Church began a week later and Rome surrendered on 20 September. Pius IX suspended the council indefinitely on 20 October and it was never re-convened.

The foremost opponent of papal infallibility, the German historian Johannes J. I. von Döllinger, was excommunicated for refusing to accept the definition, as was his friend Johann Friedrich. Both became identified with the Old Catholic Church in Germany, but Friedrich left it when it ceased to uphold clerical celibacy.

On the other extreme, in the words of Douglas Woodruff, William George Ward was "deeply upset at the influence of the moderate party at Vatican Council I and was further distressed when the all-embracing definition of papal infallibility that he hoped for was not forthcoming."

AUSTIN FLANNERY, O.P.

See also ECUMENICAL COUNCILS; INFALLIBILITY; THEOLOGY, DOGMATIC; VATICAN COUNCIL II.

VATICAN COUNCIL II

On 25 January 1959, in the monastery of St. Paul Outside the Walls, Rome, Pope John XXIII announced his intention to summon an ecumenical council. The announcement took everyone by surprise and it is doubtful whether many perceived its momentous significance. The *Osservatore Romano* published a resumé of the Pope's address the following day, in the course of which one read: "In the mind of the Holy Father, the ecumenical council is being called, not only with a view to the building-up of the Christian people, but also as an invitation to the separate communions to seek unity, for that is what many souls long for, nowadays, in all parts of the world."

On 17 May 1959 (the feast of Pentecost), Pope John set the preliminary preparations for the council in train by appointing an "ante-preparatory commission" composed of a number of highly placed members of the Roman Curia, under the presidency of Cardinal Domenico Tardini and with Monsignor Pericle Felici as secretary. The commission's task, which took almost a year to complete, was (a) to consult various categories of persons in the Church as to what should form the council's agenda, (b) to copy, summarize, classify, and coordinate the replies received and (c) to suggest how the labor might be divided in the next stage, the preparation of the council's agenda.

All Catholic archbishops and bishops were consulted, as were Roman congregations, male superiors general of religious orders, and the faculties of theology and canon law in Catholic universities.

On 5 June 1960 (again, the feast of Pentecost), Pope John (motu proprio, *Superno Dei Nutu*) established ten preparatory commissions and two secretariats, all of them responsible to a central commission. It was to be their task to prepare the council's agenda. He also established a commission for ceremonial, an administrative secretariat, and a secretariat of the central commission.

In his encyclical, *Ad Petri Cathedram* (29 June 1959), Pope John said that he had Church unity particularly at heart and he hoped that one day other Christians would return and that there would be one fold and one shepherd. The principal aim of the ecumenical council would be to "promote the growth of the Catholic faith and a salutary renewal of morals amongst Christian peoples, to bring ecclesiastical discipline up to date, according to the needs of our times." He hoped that this spectacle of truth, unity and charity would, of itself, be seen by other Christian communions as an invitation to unity.

By the following December, a total of 728 persons had been appointed to the commissions and secretariats, 48 of them cardinals, 215 patriarchs, archbishops or bishops, 217 prelates, 240 priests and religious, and eight lay people. The majority (71 percent) of these were European, with smaller numbers from North and South America (16.3 percent), Africa (3.1 percent), Asia and Oceania (9 percent, including bishops of European nationality). And the council itself when it did assemble would prove to be European-dominated.

The remits of the ten commissions were: Theology, Bishops and the Government of Dioceses, the Discipline of Clergy and Laity, Religious, the Discipline of the Sacraments, the Sacred Liturgy, Studies and Seminaries, the Eastern Churches, the Missions, the Apostolate of the Laity. The remits of the two secretariates were: (1) Press, Radio and Television, (2) Christian Unity.

The potential importance of the Secretariat on Christian Unity was not immediately obvious to many in 1960, but it became increasingly clear that the Pope had invested in it no small proportion of his hopes for the council. And it quickly began to attract the interest of individuals in other Christian Churches. The executive secretary of the World Council of Churches' New York office, Dr. Roswell P. Barnes, said that the establishment of the Secretariat was the major ecumenical event of 1960 and the Most Reverend Geoffrey Fisher, retired archbishop of Canterbury, welcomed it as "an exciting advance."

The Pope, as he explained in *Superno Dei Nutu,* had more in mind for the Secretariat than merely to help prepare the council's agenda. He saw its role also as helping Christians "separated from this Apostolic See" to "follow the work of the council and more easily to find the way of attaining that unity for which Jesus Christ prayed so ardently to his heavenly Father."

On many different occasions during the run-up to the council the Pope wrote and spoke about it, outlining his hopes for it and asking prayers for it. The words "we pray" and "we hope" peppered addresses and writings. Thus, in a letter to the clergy of Venice (23 April 1959) he said "we pray and hope that the council will, before all else, restore the spectacle of the apostles gathered together in Jerusalem . . . a unanimity of thought and prayer with Peter and centered on Peter."

The First Session

The first session of the council opened on 11 October 1962 and was attended by 2,450 churchmen, out of a total of 2,908 who were entitled to attend. Some bishops were too old or too infirm to attend, and the majority of bishops in Communist countries were refused permission to travel. Only 5 of Poland's 70 bishops were granted permission, for example, and only 3 of Czechoslovakia's 15. Restrictions were eased somewhat in subsequent sessions, 27 Polish bishops being permitted to attend the second session.

The other major Christian Churches had been invited to send "observers" to the council, who would be free to attend all sessions, but not to speak or vote. Thirty-five attended the first session and their numbers increased in subsequent sessions. The Pope's address at the opening of the council did

Vatican II in session

much to establish its mood. He decried "the prophets of doom," who could find nothing but falsehood and evil in the modern world. He spoke of the Church's duty to "hold fast to the sacred heritage of truth received from the past." However, he added: "Our duty is not limited to the mere custodianship of this precious treasure, as though antiquity were our sole concern. Rather should we set about meeting the needs of our own age, energetically and courageously. . . . What is expected . . . is progress towards a better understanding of doctrine and a formation of conscience which is in more perfect accord with authentic teaching, itself studied and expounded with the help of modern means of research and in modern literary forms. . . . The substance of the ancient doctrine, the *depositum fidei,* is one thing, its presentation is another."

He went on to say that the Church has always been opposed to error and has often condemned it "with the greatest severity. Nowadays, however, the Spouse of Christ prefers to use mercy rather than severity. She aims to meet the needs of the day by showing the validity of her teaching rather than by issuing condemnations."

While the Pope's ecclesial and theological agenda appealed to the majority of the council fathers, there was a powerful minority, centered on a group of curial cardinals, who saw the Church's needs somewhat differently. Among them, it was said at the time, were both the "prophets of doom" of whom the Pope had spoken and those who saw the issuing of "condemnations" as very much part of the Church's task. It became commonplace to describe the temper and viewpoint of the minority as "conservative" and those of the majority—for it soon became clear that they were a considerable majority—as "progressive." The terminology did full justice to neither side, but it was serviceable.

On 13 October, two days after the start of the council, the conciliar majority asserted its right to determine how its business should be run. The council had been asked by the administrative secretariat to elect the "conciliar commissions" whose task it would be to shepherd the various draft documents through the council, amending them in accordance with the mind of the council. However, it appeared that the council fathers were expected to choose the conciliar commission members exclusively from among the preparatory commissions. Such a list, it was felt, was too narrowly confined to the traditions of the Roman universities and too dominated by curialists to be representative of the universal Church. At the motion of Cardinal Achille Liénart, bishop of Lille, the council adjourned and the elections were postponed until 16 October, allowing more time for reflection. "Cardinal Liénart's gesture . . . largely determined the later development of the council. It was the first conciliar act . . . ," Yves Congar, O.P., wrote later.

On 20 November, there came a second assertion of the majority viewpoint. A draft document on revelation, entitled "The Two Sources of Revelation" had come under heavy fire from many council fathers. At issue was the relationship between Scripture and tradition and it became clear that a substantial body of opinion was opposed to the proposed draft document. When the matter was put to a vote, there was a very large majority in favor of rejection, but their numbers did not reach the required two-thirds majority. Next day it was announced that in accordance with the wishes of the majority and in order to rescue the council from a procedural impasse, the Pope had ordered the withdrawal of the draft document and the preparation of a replacement drawn up by a new commission, representative of both sides to the dispute.

The existence of divergence of opinion in so august an assembly as an ecumenical council was grist to many a journalist's mill and, at the very least, it helped them to enliven their reports, sometimes to the detriment of accuracy. For this they were sometimes criticized, but in fairness it must be said that journalists and writers in periodicals contributed enormously to the dissemination of an understanding of the conciliar event, and even to the education of the council fathers. Radio and television networks and major newspapers all had their correspondents in Rome during the council and coverage was very extensive. Some newspapers, like the *New York*

Times, published translations of all council documents as soon as they appeared.

The first session of the council was a lean period in terms of productivity. No documents were published at the end of the first session; the council was still to some extent finding its feet. The draft constitution on the liturgy was discussed from 22 October to 13 November. On 14 November it was approved by 2,163 votes in favor, 46 against, and 7 abstentions. Draft documents on the media, Church unity and the Church were discussed and the first session closed on 8 December.

Pope John's health had been in decline since late November and by the month of May, 1963, it had become clear that he was soon to die. His private secretary, Monsignor Loris Capovilla, was later to reveal that as he lay dying, he said: "This bed is an altar. An altar needs a victim. I am ready. I offer my life for the Church, for the continuation of the ecumenical council, for the peace of the world and for the union of Christians."

Pope John died on 3 June, and on 21 June Cardinal John Baptist Montini was elected pope, taking the name Paul VI. In his first radio address a day later, Pope Paul announced, "The main duty of our pontificate will be the continuation of the Second Vatican Council."

During the period between the first and second sessions of the council the various conciliar commissions continued working. They revised the draft documents, or schemas (schemata), as they were called, in accordance with the pastoral needs of the Church, as outlined by Pope John in his address at the first session. It was decided to limit the scope of the council to matters of more general interest, leaving detailed matters and matters of less moment to the commission for the revision of the Code of Canon Law and to the commissions which were to be established after the council. It would be for them to write, as it were, the fine print of certain council documents. A new commission was established to coordinate the work of the council and to direct the work of the commissions. The revised schemas were sent to all the council fathers, who were asked to send their comments on them within a specified time. Pope Paul issued revised regulations about the running of the council, correcting procedural and organizational defects which had become obvious during the first session. He appointed four moderators, Cardinals G. Agaginian, G. Lercaro, J. Döpfner and L -J. Suenens, who would take turns at chairing the conciliar discussions. This proved to be a considerable help: the four were more sensitive and sympathetic to the range of opinion in the Church than were many of the curial cardinals. The Pope also established a more effective press committee and, to a considerable extent, lifted the veil of secrecy which had been the bugbear of journalists hungry for news and with demanding deadlines to meet.

The Second Session

Pope Paul opened the second session of the council on 25 September 1963, with an address in which he asked the council (1) to set out its understanding of the nature of the Church and of the role of bishops, (2) to renew the Church, (3) to restore Christian unity and (4) to initiate dialogue with the modern world. It was during this session of the council that the "Constitution on the Sacred Liturgy" was promulgated, as was the "Decree on the Media," or, to give it its official title, the "Decree on the Means of Social Communication."

At this session, too, it was decided not to produce a special document on Our Lady, but to include the council's teaching on her in the Dogmatic Constitution on the Church. For some, it seemed a downgrading of Mary, but the majority accepted that it gave more theologically correct and more fitting expression to her relationship to her Son and to the Church.

For the rest, progress was made in discussion of the draft documents on the Church, on bishops and on ecumenism, though some expressed disappointment that treatment of the Church's attitude to non-Christians, and especially to Jews, and discussion of religious freedom were postponed until the third session.

The Third Session

Pope Paul opened the third session on 14 September 1964, by concelebrating Mass with twenty-four of the bishops. The highlight of the session came at the end, on 21 November, when three council documents were promulgated, one of them being the council's foundational "Dogmatic Constitution on the Church." Insights gained during discussion of this document had already begun to find expression in other conciliar documents still in preparation. The other documents promulgated on 21 November were the "Decree on the Catholic Eastern Churches" and the "Decree on Ecumenism." On the same day, Pope Paul proclaimed our Lady "Mother of the Church" and it was announced that the Eucharistic fast was being reduced to one hour. It was during the third session that the problem of artificial contraception was declared off-limits to the council fathers, the Pope having appointed a special commission to study the matter and report directly to him. The special commission was subsequently to recommend a change in the Church's teaching, but Pope Paul reiterated the prohibition of artificial birth control in his famous encyclical "On the Regulation of Births," *Humanae Vitae,* issued on 25 July 1968. A number of problems with regard to marriage, and mixed marriages especially, were discussed with no great unanimity of viewpoint. At the suggestion of the moderators the matter was left to the judgment of the Pope. Three documents on mixed marriages were issued after the council: "An Instruction on Mixed Marriages," *Matrimonii Sacramentum,* 18 March 1966; "Marriage between Roman Catholics and Orthodox," *Crescens Matrimoniorum,* 22 February 1967 and "Apostolic Letter on Mixed Marriages," *Matrimonia Mixta,* 7 January 1970. Discussion of the remaining eleven council documents continued during the course of the third session. At its close, the Pope concelebrated Mass with twenty-four bishops in whose dioceses were Marian shrines.

The Fourth Session

Pope Paul opened the fourth and final session of the council on 14 September 1965, with a concelebrated Mass. He announced that he was establishing a Synod of Bishops as a means of continuing the collaboration between pope and bishops which had obtained during the council. He also asked the council fathers not to discuss the celibacy of priests but to submit their views on the subject to him in writing. After the council he issued an encyclical letter on priestly celibacy, *Sacerdotalis Caelibatus,* 24 June 1967, reiterating the current teaching. Towards the end of the final session the remaining eleven documents were promulgated. On 28 October: the "Decree on the Pastoral Office of Bishops in the Church," the "Decree on the Up-to-date Renewal of the Religious Life," the "Decree on the Training of Priests," the "Declaration on Christian Education," the "Declaration on the Relation of the Church to non-Christian Religions"; on 18 November: the "Dogmatic Constitution on Divine Revelation," the "Decree on the Apostolate of Lay People"; on 7 December: the "Declaration on Religious Liberty," the "Decree on the Church's Missionary Activity," the "Decree on the Ministry and Life of Priests," the "Pastoral Constitution on the Church in the Modern World."

On the same day, Pope Paul VI and Patriarch Athenagoras I expressed their regret for the excommunications and the offensive words of which each side had been guilty, so many centuries before, in 1054.

Pope Paul proclaimed a special jubilee to be celebrated in all dioceses of the world from the following January to May, thus encouraging Catholics to take the council to heart. He also established a number of commissions to see to the implementation of certain conciliar documents. He established a papal commission on the media and made permanent three hitherto temporary secretariats.

The Sixteen Council Documents

The council documents comprise four constitutions, nine decrees, and three declarations. One does not want to push this too far, but it can be said that the constitutions are documents of greater moment, containing matters of greater theological substance than do the decrees, which have more to do with promulgating practical reforms. Declarations, while important, contain less theology and do not promulgate practical reforms. Finally, when reading the council documents it is well to bear in mind that the overall purpose of the council was pastoral.

The originals of the council documents are in Latin and the documents are frequently referred to by the first two, or more, words of the Latin original. Such Latin titles of documents are in no way intended to be descriptive of their contents. Thus, for example, the "Constitution on the Sacred Liturgy," while, quite correctly, it is referred to by that more descriptive title, is also referred to, equally correctly, as *Sacrosanctum Concilium*—literally ''the sacred council''—which tells us nothing about its contents. The same holds true of Vatican documents whose originals are in other languages.

All the conciliar and postconciliar documents mentioned in this article are contained in *Vatican II: Conciliar and Post Conciliar Documents* and *Vatican II: More Post Conciliar Documents,* edited by Austin Flannery, O.P., The Liturgical Press, Collegeville, Costello Publishing, Northport, New York, and Dominican Publications, Dublin.

The Four Constitutions

"Constitution on the Sacred Liturgy," *Sacrosanctum Concilium,* issued 4 December 1963. This is the document which had the most immediate and palpable effects on the lives of Catholics, lay and clerical. The aim of the liturgical reform which it set in train—in fact, "the aim to be considered before all else" (no. 14)—was to ensure that Catholics would no longer be present at the celebration of the Eucharist and at other liturgical celebrations "as strangers or silent spectators. On the contrary, through a good understanding of the rites and prayers they should take part in the sacred action, conscious of what they are doing, with devotion and full collaboration" (no. 48). The more theologically reflective portions of the constitution provide the theoretical underpinning for this grand design, while the rest is intended to facilitate its achievement or is a more detailed implementation of it. A large number of documents, too many to list here, was issued after the council to guide the implementation of the liturgical reform. The more important of them are contained in the two volumes referred to above.

"Dogmatic Constitution on the Church," *Lumen Gentium,* issued 21 November 1964. The opening paragraph explains that in the constitution the Church "proposes for the benefit of the faithful, and of the whole world, to set forth, as clearly as possible, her own nature and universal mission." The "nature and universal mission" of the Church is explained by telling the Bible's story of the sending of God's Son into the world, his death and resurrection and his establishment of his kingdom. From the Bible too are taken the images of the Church which offer insights into its nature: a sheepfold, a field, a building, a temple, a spouse, a body: Christ's body. Leaving the images to one side, the constitution invites us to see the Church as, to begin with, a gathering of people, the "people of God" (ch. 2), who "acknowledge" God and "serve him in holiness" (no. 9). All of this people share to differing extents and in different ways in Christ's own priestly, kingly, and prophetic offices. They are joined by fraternal/sororal or cousinly bonds, as it were (such phrases are not used), to other Christians who are not Catholics and, to a much lesser extent—as to distant relatives, one might say—to members of non-Christian religions, especially Jews and Muslims. The Church is also an organization; it is "hierarchical," a sacred organization, in which there are officeholders: bishops, united with the pope (no. 22), priests and deacons. The members of the Church who are neither officeholders nor religious (chapter 6 is on religious), are laity (ch. 4). All members of the Church, officeholders, religious and laity, are called to holiness (ch. 5). However long they may live and whatever their achievements, they are pilgrims, people in transit (ch. 7), on their way to join their brothers and sisters in heaven, with whom they are already to some extent one, especially in the liturgy. The final chapter sets out in detail "the role of the Blessed Virgin in the mystery of the Incarnate Word and the Mystical Body, and the duties of the redeemed towards the Mother of God" (no. 54).

"Dogmatic Constitution on Divine Revelation," *Dei Verbum,* issued 18 November 1965. In this document the council "sets forth the true doctrine on divine revelation and its transmission. For it wants the whole world to hear the summons to salvation, so that, hearing, it may believe . . ." (no. 1). "Sacred scripture," the constitution adds later, "is the speech of God as it is put down in writing under the inspiration of the Holy Spirit. And Tradition transmits in its entirety the word of God which had been entrusted to the apostles by Christ Jesus the Lord and the Holy Spirit" (no. 9). To interpret the word of God authentically is the task of the teaching Church, which must see itself as the servant of the word of God (no. 10). The document goes on to describe the inspiration of Scripture and how Scripture is to be interpreted (ch. 3), the Old Testament (ch. 4), the New Testament (ch. 5) and the Bible in the Church's life (ch. 6), which chapter encourages all Catholics, and especially clergy and religious, to read the Bible frequently and prayerfully (no. 25).

"Pastoral Constitution on the Church in the Modern World," *Gaudium et Spes,* issued 7 December 1965. The constitution deals with the relation of the Church to the world and to the men and women of its day, displaying an openness towards the world which the Church had not known for a very long time. It must be borne in mind when reading the constitution that the "day" in question was the mid-1960s. Much has changed since then and not all statements about the world as it was then are true of the world of today. Thus, for example, the description of state-sponsored atheism in article 20 has lost much, though by no means all, of its relevance with the collapse of Soviet Communism, which few could have foretold in the mid-1980s, never mind the mid-1960s. However, the gospel insights and the Church teachings which the council endeavored to apply to the world of its "day" have by no means lost their relevance.

The constitution opens with the much-quoted statement that the Church takes on itself the "joy and hope, the grief and anguish of the people of our time, especially of those who are poor or afflicted in any way." After an Introduction on the situation of humankind in the world today, the constitution is divided into two parts. The first, more theoretical, part is entitled "The Church and the Vocation of Humankind" and deals with the dignity of the human person (ch. 1), the human community (ch. 2) human activity in the universe (ch. 3) and the Church's role in the modern world (ch. 4). The second part deals with "some more urgent problems." Of particular interest is the first chapter, "The Dignity of Marriage and the Family." There follow chapters on the development of culture (2), economic and social life (3), the political community (4) and peace (5).

The Nine Decrees

"Decree on the Means of Social Communication," *Inter Mirifica,* issued 4 December 1963. The decree deals in general terms with the press, the cinema, radio and television, and on how they can be used for the betterment of humanity, noting that they can also be used in very detrimental ways. It outlines the moral principles governing the proper use of the media. In accordance with the decree's directive, the "Pastoral Instruction on the Means of Social Communication," *Communio et Progressio,* was published on 29 January 1971.

"Decree on the Catholic Eastern Churches," *Orientalium Ecclesiarum,* issued 21 November 1964. The decree set down "some guiding principles" for the Eastern Churches in communion with Rome, asserting the value of their rites and their entitlement to their own liturgies and their ecclesiastical disciplines. It stated that members of separated Oriental Churches may be admitted to the sacraments of penance, the Eucharist and the anointing of the sick in Catholic Churches and that Catholics may request these sacraments "from non-Catholic ministers in whose Church there are valid sacraments, as often as necessity or true spiritual benefit recommends such action, and access to a Catholic priest is . . . impossible" (no. 27).

"Decree on Ecumenism," *Unitatis Redintegratio,* issued 21 November 1964. In this decree the council "set before all Catholics guidelines, helps and methods" (no. 1) by which they can respond to the call for the restoration of Christian unity, which it described as "one of the principal concerns of the Second Vatican Council" (no. 1). The decree deals, in successive chapters, with "Catholic Principles on Ecumenism" (1), "The Practice of Ecumenism" (2), "Churches and Ecclesial Communities separated from the Roman Apostolic See" (3). After the council, more detailed guidelines were issued in the "Directory Concerning Ecumenical Guidelines," which was published in two parts. The first part, *Ad Totam Ecclesiam,* was published on 14 May 1967, and the second part, subtitled "Ecumenism in Higher Education," *Spiritus Domini,* on 16 April 1970. The "Directory for the Application of Principles and Norms on Ecumenism" was issued on 25 March 1993.

"Decree on the Pastoral Office of Bishops in the Church," *Christus Dominus,* issued 28 October 1965. The decree sets out in three chapters "the pastoral functions of bishops" (no. 3). The first chapter deals with individual bishops in relation to the universal Church, for which they bear joint responsibility. It touches on their right to take part in ecumenical councils, the service they can render in Synods of Bishops, and their relationship to the Holy See. The second chapter deals with bishops in their own dioceses, while the third deals with collaboration between bishops in synods, councils, and episcopal conferences. It deals also with ecclesiastical boundaries and with interdiocesan collaboration. Further guidelines were issued after the council in "Norms for Implementing Christus Dominus," *Ecclesiae Sanctae* II, issued 6 August 1966.

"Decree on the Up-to-date Renewal of Religious Life," *Perfectae Caritatis,* issued 28 October 1965. In effect, the decree instructs each religious order and congregation to carry out its own mini-Vatican II, after the council. The decree deals "only with the general principles of the up-to-date renewal of the life and discipline of religious orders" (no. 1). It instructs religious to return constantly to the "sources of the Christian life and to the primitive inspiration of the institutes" and to adapt their institutes to "the changed conditions of our time." It discusses the different forms of religious life, the vows, common life, and prayer. It states that it is for "the competent authorities [in religious institutes] . . . and especially for general chapters to establish the norms for appropriate renewal and to legislate for it" (no. 4), within the guidelines of the decree and of the other conciliar documents, especially *Lumen Gentium.* Further guidelines were provided after the council in the "Norms for Implementing the Decree on the Up-to-date Renewal of Religious Life," *Ecclesiae Sanctae* II, 6 August 1966. Other documents on the implementation of the decree are to be found in the two volumes mentioned earlier.

"Decree on the Training of Priests," *Optatam Totius,* issued 28 October 1965. The decree "solemnly affirms the fundamental importance of priestly training" and "lays down certain fundamental principles" with regard to it (no. 1). It covers priestly training in different countries, the fostering of vocations, seminaries, spiritual training, the revision of the program of studies, pastoral training and later studies.

"Decree on the Apostolate of Lay People," *Apostolicam Actuositatem,* 18 November 1965. The decree sets out "the nature of the lay apostolate, its character and the variety of its forms" and it gives "fundamental principles and . . . pastoral directives for its more effective exercise" (no. 1). In six chapters the decree deals with the vocation of lay people to the apostolate (1), the objectives to be achieved (2), the different fields (3) and forms of the apostolate (4), relations between lay apostles and the hierarchy and clergy (5) and training (6). The decree ends with an "exhortation" to respond to the call of Christ to the apostolate.

"Decree on the Church's Missionary Activity," *Ad Gentes Divinitus,* issued 7 December 1965. The decree outlines "the principles of missionary activity. It wishes to unite the efforts of all the faithful, so that the people of God, following the narrow way of the cross, might everywhere spread the kingdom of Christ" (no. 1). Its six chapters cover doctrinal principles (1), missionary work itself (2), newly formed churches (3), missionaries (4), the organization of missionary activity (5) and cooperation between missionaries (6). Further guidelines were issued after the council: "Norms for Implementing the Decree on the Church's Missionary Activity," *Ecclesiae Sanctae* III, 6 August 1966.

"Decree on the Ministry and Life of Priests," *Presbyterorum Ordinis,* issued 7 December 1965. It was because of the "increasingly difficult role assigned to priests in the renewal of Christ's Church" (no. 1) that the decree was issued, "with the aim of giving more effective support to the ministry of priests and making better provision for their lives in the vastly changed circumstances of the pastoral and human scene" (no. 1). After a first chapter describing the role of the priesthood in the Church's ministry, the decree goes on to discuss the ministry of priests (ch. 2), the life of priests, including a section on celibacy, and a section on helps for the priest (ch. 3).

The Three Declarations

"Declaration on Christian Education," *Gravissimum Educationis,* issued 28 October 1965. The declaration accepts the importance of education and people's right to it, including young people's right to moral education. The Church is obliged to educate its children both in its own schools and in schools which it does not control. Parents must have true freedom, recognized by the state, in their choice of schools. The declaration insists on the importance of the contribution to be made by Catholic schools and it stresses that Catholic colleges and universities should operate according to the highest academic standards and that at non-Catholic educational establishments provision should be made for the spiritual and intellectual formation of Catholic students.

"Declaration on the Relation of the Church to non-Christian Religions," *Nostra Aetate,* issued 28 October 1965. This short document asserts that partial answers to the great questions about human origin and destiny are given by Hinduism and Buddhism and "other religions which are found throughout the world" (no. 2). The Church "rejects nothing that is true and holy in these religions" (no. 2) and "has a high regard for the Muslims. They worship God, who is one, living and subsistent, merciful and almighty, the Creator of heaven and earth, who has also spoken to humanity" (no. 3). The declaration goes on to speak of the spiritual ties between Christianity and Judaism. Since "Christians and Jews have such a common spiritual heritage, this sacred Council wishes to encourage and further their mutual understanding and appreciation" (no. 4). Neither all Jews of his time nor any Jews today can be held responsible for Christ's death. The declaration asserts that "the Church reproves, as foreign to the mind of Christ, any discrimination against people or any harassment of them on the basis of their race, color, condition in life or religion" (no. 5). Further guidelines were issued after the council: "On Dialog with Unbelievers,'' *Humanae Personae Dignitatem,* 28 August 1968.

"Declaration on Religious Liberty," *Dignitatis Humanae,* issued 7 December 1965. The introductory section of the document is headed "On the right of the Person and Communities to Social and Civil Liberty in Religious Matters" and the body of the document is in two chapters: Chapter 1, "The General Principle of Religious Freedom," and chapter 2: "Religious Freedom in the Light of Revelation." The essence of the declaration's teaching is summed up in the first chapter: "The Vatican Council declares that the human person has a right to religious freedom. Freedom of this kind means that all men and women should be immune from coercion on the part of individuals, social groups and every human power so that, within due limits, nobody is forced to act against his/her convictions, nor is anyone restricted from acting in accordance with his/her convictions in religious matters in private or public, alone or in association with others" (no. 2).

AUSTIN FLANNERY, O.P.

See also CHURCH, THE; DOCTRINE; ECUMENICAL COUNCILS; MAGISTERIUM; VATICAN COUNCIL I.

VAUX, ROLAND DE (1903–1971)

Roland Etienne Guerin de Vaux was born in Paris 17 December 1903, of a family of finance inspectors for the French government. He attended the College Stanislas for his secondary studies, and then received a licence-es-lettres from the Sorbonne, specializing in history. After his priestly formation at the seminary of St. Sulpice (at Issy, on the outskirts of Paris), he was ordained for the archdiocese on 29 June 1929. His main professor of exegesis was J. J. Weber, the future archbishop of Strasbourg. That September he entered the Dominican novitiate at Amiens, making simple profession of vows 23 September 1930. While waiting the three set years to take his solemn vows and to begin his public ministry, he pursued his historical research in Orientalism at the Saulchoir (Kain, Tournai, Belgium). This terminated in a book on Latin Avicennism in the twelfth and thirteenth centuries (1934). Having been recruited by Paul Synave for the Ecole Biblique et Archéologique in Jerusalem, he left for Palestine immediately after final vows in September 1933. There he spent the rest of his life, until his premature death at the age of sixty-eight, 10 September 1971.

At the Ecole, after two years of further study under Lagrange, Vincent, and Abel, and acquiring his Roman Scripture license in 1935, he became a professor and taught biblical history and archaeology from the fall of 1935 to the spring of 1971. He also taught Assyrian from 1935 to 1940, after which he was replaced by R. J. Tournay. From 1946 to 1949 he taught the exegesis of OT historical books on which he later published short commentaries. It may be said that he had been trained to be a historian and he trained himself to be an archaeologist, though he was helped in this by his friendships with Vincent, W. F. Albright, K. Kenyon, B. Mazar, and many others.

Since archaeology is a practical discipline, he learned it by doing. Up till 1946, his excavations were modest practice digs: the uncovering of a Byzantine mosaic church floor at Ma'in in Jordan in 1937 (with Savignac); an Arab caravanserai at Abu Gosh (biblical Kireath Jearim) with Steve in 1944 (final report 1950); a Byzantine shrine to John the Baptist at el-Ma'mudiyeh near Hebron in 1945 and 1946. Thus prepared, he tackled Tell el Far'ah in Samaria. He devoted nine seasons to this site, from 1946 to 1960. The site had been identified by Albright with biblical Tirza, the first capital of the northern kingdom of Israel, before Omri transferred it to Samaria. De Vaux accepted this identification, but was not able to prove it absolutely (preliminary reports in the *Revue Biblique*). Here he was in his element.

De Vaux became a figure of international renown as a result of the discovery of the Dead Sea Scrolls in the caves near Wadi Qumran in 1947 (and due to the romantic descriptions of him by Edmund Wilson in his popular book on the scrolls). He was involved in three ways. First, he helped negotiate with the Bedouin who had found them to acquire the scrolls for the Palestine Archaeological (Rockefeller) Museum. Second, he excavated the site of the production of the scrolls, as well as at Wadi Murabba'at and Ain Feshkha (1949–1958), and published the results in preliminary reports in the *Revue Biblique* and in a book (but not the final reports nor the pottery). Third, he became the editor in chief of the team for the publication of the fragments. All this should have been under the direction of G. L. Harding, but he was so busy with the administration of the Jordanian Department of Antiquities that he left most of the work on Qumran to de Vaux. De Vaux was succeeded as editor by his colleague P. Benoit.

After Tirza and Qumran, de Vaux participated in the excavations of Jerusalem directed by K. M. Kenyon, from 1961 to 1963. His sector was the el-Khatuniyeh quarter south of the el-Aqsa mosque, later taken over by Benjamin Mazar. When he decided that the Ecole should resume excavations after the shock of the Six Day War, he enthusiastically supported J. Prignaud's first season at Tell Keisan near Akko in 1971 but was too infirm to direct it. He was always in his element on a dig.

De Vaux served as editor of the *Revue Biblique* from 1938 to 1953, as director of the Ecole from 1945 to 1965, as prior of the Dominican community from 1949 to 1952, as consultor of the Pontifical Biblical Commission from 1956 till his death. He was named a master of sacred theology in 1958, a member of the Académie des Inscriptions et Belles-Lettres in 1952, of the Legion of Honor in 1953, and of the British Academy in 1961. He received nine honorary doctorates. From 1964 to 1965 he was visiting professor at Harvard and during that time gave over 130 lectures throughout the U.S.

He was the author of at least thirteen books and over one hundred articles. Among his most successful works was the *Jerusalem Bible* project (1956), for which he served as general and OT editor and translator and commentator on Genesis, 1 and 2 Samuel, 1 and 2 Kings. This work was translated into many languages. Another was the two-volume *Ancient Israel: Its Life and Institutions* (1958–1960, Eng. 1961), which related archaeological finds to the biblical text in a helpful way and covered the social institutions of Israel under four headings: family, state, military, religion. It remains a useful text, uncluttered with notes, but with a detailed bibliography at the end, dated in part by Lévi-Strauss on kinship patterns and by others on the origins of Passover. In a follow-up work on sacrifices (1964), he went deeper into one aspect of Israelite religion. His Schweich lectures on the archaeology of Qumran, while not settling every question, firmly fixed the stratigraphy and dates of inhabitation of the site. No coins were found from later than A.D. 70. (This dating grieved G. R. Driver but stands as the common opinion.) He also was able to relate the ink found in the inkwells in the scriptorium of the community to the ink found on the scrolls in the neighboring caves. It was more difficult to get the international team of scholars to publish their batches of fragments promptly. The last years of his life were devoted to composing a projected three-volume history of Israel. Here, however, his health and his luck began to desert him. He was only able to complete the first volume on the Canaanite setting, the patriarchs, the sojourn in Egypt, the Exodus, Sinai, and the settlement in Canaan (1971). A part of the second volume, on the period of the Judges, was published posthumously (1973), after being reconstructed from his notes by François Langlamet. This work represents an excellent synthesis of the state of research on the early history of Israel up to 1970 and contributes an acute judgment, but from a historicist bias. The scholarly consensus turned to a more skeptical approach soon after the work appeared. He is remembered as a charming, witty, dynamic, enthusiastic teacher and colleague, with a sound archaeological judgment.

BENEDICT T. VIVIANO, O.P.

See also BENOIT, PIERRE MAURICE; CRITICISM, BIBLICAL; DOMINICANS; ECOLE BIBLIQUE; LAGRANGE, MARIE-JOSEPH.

VEILS

The three veils used to cover the gifts in the celebration of the Divine Liturgy of the Byzantine Rite (also known as the Mass of the Oriental Rite). They are the chalice veil, the veil over the diskos, and the aer, which is laid over both.

JOSEPH QUINN

See also EASTERN CHURCHES.

VELAZQUEZ (VELÁSQUEZ), DIEGO RODRIGUEZ DE SILVA Y (1599–1660)

Born in 1599, Velazquez is recognized, now and in his lifetime, as the greatest Spanish painter. He was trained by Pacheco in his native Seville (from 1613 to 1618), and married Pacheco's daughter. Already with the *Immaculate Conception* he established his unique style of solid naturalism combined with full control of light and shade. He very early interested himself in *bodegones* (domestic scenes incorporating still lifes) which, in his hands, became serious works of art and feeling. Much of his early work was religious, but it was his portrait of the poet *Luis de Congora* (1622) that brought him to the attention of Philip IV, whose Court Painter he became. Henceforth he was to develop mainly as a portrait painter. Keenly observant, he achieved great realism and character delineation in settings which demonstrated absolute mastery of form, space, and light. His most superb painting is perhaps that of *Pope Innocent X* (1650), made on one of two trips to Italy during which he further developed his breadth of vision. He increasingly developed a freedom of technique in which he concentrated on reproducing what the eye

Velazquez self-portrait, detail of "Las Meninas"

sees, rather than what the mind knows to exist, and in this way anticipated impressionism. *Las Meninas* (1656, a portrait of the Infanta Margareta Teresa with her attendants), unites many complex elements and is a fine example of Velazquez' ability to bring convincing reality to the canvas. He died in 1660.

DAVID BRYAN

See also ART, CHRISTIAN.

VENERABLE

See BEATIFICATION.

VENERATION OF SAINTS

Saints are venerated in the Catholic Church by feast days in their honor, by representation in pictures and statues, by the telling of their life stories, by prayers for their intercession with God, and in some cases by shrines and pilgrimages dedicated to their remembrance.

The title "saint" is correctly reserved to embrace those brothers and sisters of Christ recognized by the Church, either traditionally as was the custom in the early Church or by formal canonization in modern times, as being in heaven and, accordingly, worthy of honor by the rest of the faithful. There is no rule so general which does not admit of some exception and so even in the use of the term "saint" we find certain angels referred to as Saints: Michael, Gabriel, and Raphael.

The saints, Christ's closest friends, lead us to God and are the visual aids indicating how to live our faith. Literally they took Christ's primal commandment of love of God and neighbor with utter seriousness, understood it profoundly and bent every effort in their lives to carry it out. These individuals whom we call saints forged ahead to meet God's command resolutely, completely, and without reservation, and remain in our memory to give us new hope in this dreary world. Holiness, which is the object of Christian search, is concerned with the development of charity and hence there is little, if any, difference between a saint of ancient and modern times in this regard. The manner in which charity, love, unfolds is different as well as is a likeness to the saints as reflected in the Christian conscience in our day.

Believers, in contemplating the lives of the saints, feel a mysterious attraction which the lives of these individuals continue to the present to exercise upon us to the end of our days. Many assertions about the saints have been exaggerated beyond reasonable belief, and many superficial and boring lives of the saints have been written, but it is the life of a saint itself which shows the key to spiritual growth in keeping the commandment of love.

A saint may be defined as a person of heroic virtue. These are the persons who have done the ordinary things of life out of an extraordinary love of God. In civil society hero-worship exists, has existed, and will continue to exist universally among peoples. The veneration of heroes, the outward expression of reverent feeling, is transcendent admiration of great people and is found in every sphere of human activity.

Veneration of the saints, respect mingled with awe of these spiritual giants, is a recognition of the supernatural excellence of those who substituted their own ideas for those of Christ and are declared by the Church to be now in heaven and, as a consequence, are constituted as intercessors with God for the other members of Christ's Church. In Catholic practice the esteem for the saints takes the form of praise and then imitation of the virtues of the saint and also of soliciting the intercession of the saint. Statues are not worshiped but have the same function as a photo of a loved one, an instrument to bring back vivid representations.

JAMES McGRATH

See also CANONIZATION; DEVOTIONS; SAINTS.

VENI CREATOR SPIRITUS

(Lat., "Come creating Spirit") A hymn to the Holy Spirit traditionally sung during the conferral of holy orders, at confirmation, at councils and synods, and at church dedications. Its authorship has not been determined, though it has been variously attributed to Rabanus Maurus, St. Ambrose, St. Gregory the Great, and Charlemagne.

JOSEPH QUINN

See also HYMNS.

VENIAL SIN

See SIN.

VERSICLE

The first of two short exclamatory lines—usually taken from a psalm—recited or sung antiphonally at a liturgy. It is directly followed by the response (the second line).

JOSEPH QUINN

See also LITURGY.

VESSELS, SACRED

The various vessels used in liturgical celebrations. They include the chalice, paten, ciborium, pyx, capsula, and the lunette—these are of special importance since they come into direct contact with the Blessed Sacrament. Other common liturgical vessels are cruets, lavabo dish, thurible, boat, and aspergillum.

JOSEPH QUINN

See also LITURGY.

VESTMENTS, LITURGICAL

Liturgical vestments are the outer clothing worn by the different ministers at a liturgy in the Catholic Church and in some other Christian Churches. The vestments used today have their origins in the fashions of the Greco-Roman world. Men's clothing consisted of a long tunic with a rope at the waist (alb and cincture) and a large mantle worn over it (chasuble). In the early Church the clergy wore this ordinary vesture at liturgies. Even as late as the fourth century, liturgical vesture was of the same type as everyday clothing, though usually of a better quality.

The fall of the Roman Empire (487) led to changes in secular dress, but the Church retained the clothing of this earlier period in its liturgy, and thus the vestments acquired symbolic value. Between the tenth and thirteenth centuries other vesture was introduced such as the use of the surplice by priests as a substitute for the alb at some liturgies, and the use of the mitre and gloves by bishops. In the Middle Ages many of the vestments became more ornate and made of heavier materials. Because of their cumbersomeness, they were designed to be tapered and tight-fitting. This style prevailed until the nineteenth century when there was a movement back to the earlier type of vestments, thus introducing the distinction between "Roman" (close-fitting) and "Gothic" (flowing) vestments.

Since the major liturgical reforms initiated by Vatican Council II (1962–1965), many of the liturgical vestments have been simplified and some have been completely discontinued. Priests today normally wear an alb, stole, and a chasuble at Eucharistic Liturgies, and deacons wear an alb, stole, and a dalmatic. The bishop wears these same vestments along with his miter. Other nonordained ministers at a liturgy wear either an alb or surplice (over a cassock), depending on the local customs. Copes and humeral veils are still worn at certain liturgies. The color of vestments is still regulated by the Church to mark the various seasons and feasts of the liturgical year.

ANTHONY D. ANDREASSI

See also LITURGY.

VIA MEDIA

See ANGLICANISM.

VIANNY, JEAN, ST.

See CURÉ D'ARS.

VIATICUM

(Lat., "provision for a journey") The Holy Communion given to those facing life-threatening circumstances in order that they may be imbued with God's grace on their journey into eternal life.

JOSEPH QUINN

See also EUCHARIST.

VICAR

(Lat. *vicarius,* "a substitute") A cleric who substitutes for another in the exercise of an ecclesiastical office. The vicar may act in the name of (and with the authority of) the incumbent cleric, as stipulated by canon law. A vicar general acts in the name of the bishop throughout the latter's diocese; an episcopal vicar may do the same but only in a particular section of a diocese.

JOSEPH QUINN

See also BISHOP; DIOCESE.

VICAR OF CHRIST

A vicar is a person who acts in the place of and under the authority of another: a deputy. The term "Vicar of Christ" refers to the pope, who acts as Christ's representative on earth.

In the fifth century, Pope Leo the Great referred to himself as the "Vicar of Peter." For the next seven centuries this title was commonly used to describe the pope; it emphasized his connection to the apostle and thus his authority in the Church.

At the end of the twelfth century, however, Pope Innocent III (1160–1216) adopted the title Vicar of Christ. The term itself was not new; it had been used informally for centuries by priests and bishops and even kings to describe their function as servants of God. But Innocent's use of the title to describe himself signaled a shift in how the papacy was viewed.

The twelfth and thirteenth centuries were a turbulent time marked by power struggles among kings and emperors. Each ruler sought to assert and justify his own authority. But the term Vicar of Christ expressed a claim to a more universal authority; by calling himself Christ's deputy, Innocent III sought to set himself above merely political rulers. His power, the title suggested, came not from human beings but from God. Therefore, all human beings, regardless of their nationality or class, were subject to him. Innocent declared, "No king can reign rightly unless he devoutly serve Christ's vicar."

Thus the shift from the term "Vicar of Peter" to the term "Vicar of Christ" coincided with a consolidation of the power of the medieval papacy.

THERESA SANDERS

See also CHURCH AND STATE; MIDDLE AGES, THE; PAPACY, THE.

VIGIL

(Lat. *vigil,* "alert") The day or evening preceding a particular feast, on which prayer services—comprised of readings, psalms, and silent prayers—are observed as a preparation for the feast. The most prominent vigil throughout the history of the Church has been that for Easter; the Church also continues to observe solemn vigils for Christmas and Pentecost.

JOSEPH QUINN

See also LITURGY.

VINCENT DE PAUL, ST. (ca. 1580–ca. 1660)

Born into a peasant French family around 1580, he lived in an age when the alleviation of widespread poverty and appalling social conditions in urban areas was dependent mostly on private charity, as the governments paid scant attention to them. At the age of twenty-five, he was captured by pirates, and for two years he worked as a slave in Tunisia. From 1613 to 1625, he served as chaplain and tutor to the

St. Vincent de Paul accepting the chains of the galley slave

household of Count de Gondi, general of the galleys. During this period, he constantly sought the betterment of the cruel and abusive conditions endured by prisoners sentenced to serve in the galley ships; when he was appointed chaplain-general to the galleys in 1619, he helped improve those conditions.

Vincent also spent time with the poor and slum dwellers of Paris during this time, and in 1625 he founded the Congregation of Priests of the Mission (popularly known as Lazarists, after the priory of St. Lazare, where Vincent had his headquarters). This charitable congregation was composed of secular priests who took religious vows, and its purpose was to minister to the rural poor. Eight years later, he and St. Louise de Marillac founded the Sisters of Charity, whose work all over the world has become an inspiration to people of all faiths. The sisters were the first congregation of women without enclosure devoted to the care of the sick and the poor.

Two centuries later, when French scholar Frederic Ozanam (1813–1853) founded a lay organization to serve the poor, he almost spontaneously, and appropriately, named it The Society of St. Vincent de Paul. He died around 1660.

JOSEPH QUINN

See also CORPORAL AND SPIRITUAL WORKS OF MERCY; INSTITUTE, RELIGIOUS; OZANAM, ANTOINE FREDERIC; ST. VINCENT DE PAUL, SOCIETY OF.

VIRGIN BIRTH

This term usually refers to the miraculous conception of Jesus in the womb of Mary without sexual intercourse. The accompanying belief is that Mary remained a virgin thereafter. Roman Catholic tradition has formulated the belief in a statement that Mary was a virgin before, in, and after the birth of Jesus. Biblical texts speak explicitly only of Mary's virginal conception of Jesus and only in Matthew 1:18-25 and Luke 1:26-38. Several texts that speak of "brothers and sisters" of Jesus (e.g., Mark 6:3) appear to refute the belief in Mary's perpetual virginity after the birth of Jesus, but these are generally explained either as cousins (perhaps raised in the home of Jesus), or as stepbrothers and sisters through a previous marriage of Joseph.

Because of the awkward explanations of these latter texts and because the virginal conception is mentioned only in the infancy texts and appears unknown in all the other New Testament traditions, scholars have raised the question of whether the teaching on Mary's virginity refers to historical fact or is rather a theological symbol conveying a truth of faith of a different order. Catholic tradition weighs heavily in the direction of historical fact, but the argument may be moot. Whether history or symbol, the event still means the same; it is a question of whether God planted the symbol first in a historical event or only in the writing of the evangelists. In either case, the virginity of Mary should be understood as saying something about Christ more than about Mary. It is a sign of the uniqueness of Christ, of a new creation in Christ and of a redemption that is God's work and not ours. It should not denigrate marriage or human sexuality, especially women's sexuality, and should not imply that Jesus needed such a conception in order to avoid original sin or in order to be truly divine. Emphasis should be placed on the theological level and not on the biological.

ANTHONY J. TAMBASCO

See also INFANCY NARRATIVES, THE; MARY, MOTHER OF GOD.

VIRGINITY

The practice of perpetual sexual abstinence, formally professed by religious in a public vow. The voluntary abjuration of one's sexual engagement is held by the Church to be a means by which personal sanctity and holiness may be furthered, and a life consecrated to God in the service of humanity expressed. The scriptural foundation for a life of sexual abstinence can be found in the example and words of Jesus (Matt 19:10-12; Luke 20:34-36), as well as in the teaching of Paul (1 Cor 7:1-9).

JOSEPH QUINN

See also VOWS.

VIRTUE

Virtue (Lat. "force") is a habit of good behavior which enables us to do what is right with increasing ease, joy, and consistency, in response to God's offer of and invitation to covenant love. As Gregory of Nyssa says, "the aim of the virtuous life is to become like God" (*The Beatitudes,* vol. 1, trans. H. C. Graef, *Ancient Christian Writers* 18 [1954] 89). We shall first briefly examine the place of the virtues in Christian life; secondly, present the four cardinal virtues and the three theological virtues, according to the classical distinctions, and thirdly, explore some current developments with regard to the meaning of the virtues in Christian life today.

The Place of the Virtues in Christian Life

The practice of virtue is related to ongoing openness to the action of God in our life, to conversion of heart. Thomas Aquinas speaks of the virtues as bringing about a "modification of the subject" (ST I-II, q. 49, a. 2). While good actions certainly depend on our effort, virtue is a gift of the Spirit. From the Spirit comes the "force" (Gk. *dynamis*) or "power from on high" (Luke 24:49) which makes us "rich in hope" (Rom 15:13) and strengthens us inwardly, so that "Christ may live in our hearts through faith" until "planted in love and built on love", we may one day be "filled with the utter fullness of God" (Eph 3:16-19). Growth in virtue is an essential aspect of spiritual growth.

While the idea of four key virtues was found in Stoic philosophy, these virtues were regarded as acquisitions by one's own efforts. By contrast, the Christian view is that they are gifts of the Spirit. Based on the Book of Wisdom, Clement of Alexandria speaks of four, namely, prudence, justice, fortitude and temperance: "If it be uprightness you love, why, virtues are the fruit of her labors, since it is she who teaches temperance and prudence, justice and fortitude: nothing in life is more useful for human beings" (Wis 8:7). St. Ambrose is the first to give them the name "cardinal" (Lat. "hinge"), since on them, like hinges, the whole moral life hangs, and all other virtues may be regrouped around them.

The Four Cardinal Virtues

Prudence may be defined as the virtue which disposes us to discern in every circumstance our true good and to choose the right means to accomplish it (*Catechism of the Catholic Church,* no. 1806). Prudence is called the *auriga virtutum* ("pilot of the virtues"): it guides our judgment and conscience and leads the other virtues in indicating to them rule and measure. It is related to prayerful reflection and discernment and involves bringing God's word to bear on our life decisions, under the influence of a growing faith, hope, and love.

Justice is the virtue which indicates the constant and firm will to give to God and to others what is their due. Justice, faithful love and mercy are closely related biblical concepts. Justice is traditionally considered as having three basic forms: commutative justice (relations of people with one another), distributive justice (relations of society to individuals) and legal justice (individuals in relation to the common good). Since Vatican II, social justice has assumed a key role and the 1971 Synod of Bishops declared that "action on behalf of justice and participation in the transformation of the world fully appear to us as a constitutive dimension of the preaching of the gospel" (*Justice in the World,* no. 6). Inspired by the strong biblical themes of the Exodus event and justice for the oppressed, liberation theologians call for justice that extends to concrete social, economic and political circumstances.

Fortitude strengthens our resolution and our ability to resist temptation and overcome obstacles in the pursuit of good and in the following of Christ: "In the world you will have hardship, but be courageous: I have conquered the world" (John 16:33). Acts of fortitude, usually described as endurance and risk, must be informed by prudence. Endurance is an active form of witness to Jesus Christ as the many martyrs of the Church testify. The virtue of fortitude is needed as we endeavor to respond with hope and perseverance to the many obstacles we experience from within ourselves and without, on our journey to God.

Temperance (Lat. "moderation") enables us to moderate our appetites and control our passions, to acquire a certain equilibrium in the use of created goods: "We must be self-restrained and live upright and religious lives in this present world" (Titus 2:12). The NT also calls it "sobriety," "self-control," "modesty." The focus is on the development of the whole person, in a holistic manner, rather than on the body as the enemy of the spirit, and indeed, each person is called to discover, through prayer, experience and ongoing effort, a sense of equilibrium which will ground a healthy spiritual and moral life.

The Three Theological Virtues

The four human or moral virtues are rooted in Faith, Hope and Love, also called "virtues" by Gregory the Great. These latter are described as theological virtues because they are infused by God in us, enabling us to enter into relationship with God who is infinitely trustworthy and lovable, and to whom we are invited to commit our whole life and future (DV 5). They have God as their "origin, motive and object" (*Catechism of the Catholic Church,* no. 1812) and all three have both a personal and a communitarian dimension.

Faith, made possible through the working of the Holy Spirit (2 Cor 3:16-18), is a free, reasonable and total response through which we confess the truth of God's self-revelation, obediently commit ourselves to it, and entrust our future to God. The believer is called not only to "keep" the faith but also to "profess" it, to "witness" to it and to "spread" it (*Catechism of the Catholic Church,* no. 1816).

Hope enables us to look beyond our present, incomplete existence to desire and anticipate the full coming of God's final reign and the liberating resurrection of all creation and to wait for it with "persevering confidence" (Rom 8:18-25). Hope is grounded in the promise of Christ: "Let us keep firm in the hope we profess, because the one who made the promise is trustworthy" (Heb 10:23). Far from being a passive waiting for God's definitive coming, hope calls us to be responsible for the world, to work for more justice and peace here and now (GS 39) and make our own "the joy and hope, the grief and anguish" of our brothers and sisters (GS 1).

Love, the primary virtue, enables us to share in the divine love which is the inner life of the Trinity: "I have made your name known to them and will continue to make it known, so that the love with which you loved me may be in them, and so that I may be in them" (John 17:26). It is the fulfillment of the greatest and the "new" commandment of Jesus to love one another just as he has loved us (John 13:13-34). The qualities of love, the first of the theological virtues, are described by Paul in 1 Corinthians 13. This "perfect bond" (Col 3:15) binds together all the other virtues and indeed, without love, no virtue really counts (Bernard Häring, *Free and Faithful in Christ,* vol. 1, New York: The Seabury Press, 1979, p. 6). Love is the greatest of the theological virtues; it is also, for Augustine, the heart of all virtues: "So that temperance is love, keeping the self entire and uncorrupt for the beloved. Courage is love, bearing everything gladly for the sake of the beloved. Righteousness is love, serving the beloved only, and therefore ruling well. And prudence is love, wisely discerning what helps it and what hinders it" (*On the Morals of the Catholic Church,* I,15.25, PL 32:1322).

The Meaning of the Virtues in Christian Life Today

In some contemporary trends of moral theology virtue has reemerged as an important theme. Since the moral agent is more than the sum of his or her acts, and since the acts derive their moral quality from the character of the agent, moral theologians have stressed the necessity of virtues in the moral development of the person. As means to forming virtues and character, various elements have been suggested: story (Stanley Hauerwas and Alasdair MacIntyre), tradition (Edward Shils and Daniel Callahan), liturgy (Paul Ramsey), spirituality (Bernard Häring), imagination (Daniel Maguire and Philip Keane), and aesthetics (von Balthasar).

BRÍD LONG, S.S.L.

See also CHRISTIAN SPIRITUALITY; THEOLOGY, MORAL; THEOLOGY, PRACTICAL.

VIRTUES, MORAL

See VIRTUE.

VISIONS

See APPARITIONS.

VISITATION ORDER

Founded in 1610 by St. Francis de Sales and St. Jane Chantel. Originally, its members only took simple vows and only novices were enclosed while professed sisters went out on works of mercy. In 1618 the congregation was approved as an order, whose members would be enclosed and live a contemplative life. Each house is independent under the jurisdiction of the local bishop. One of its members was St. Margaret Mary Alacoque, whose visions were responsible for the great increase in devotion to the Sacred Heart.

JOAN GLAZIER

See also FRANCIS DE SALES, ST.; RELIGIOUS ORDERS.

VOCATION

Vocation, from Latin *vocare,* "to call," a notion with OT antecedents but stemming immediately from NT, especially Pauline, thought, refers to God's invitation to share in God's own life through grace; and, in common usage, to a particular state of life or occupation in which one's acceptance of that invitation can be lived out.

In the Gospels, Jesus calls the sons of Zebedee (Mark 1:20), and the other disciples (Mark 3:13; 6:7), to be his followers. More generally, he describes his purpose as that of "calling" sinners to repentance (Mark 2:17). There is a nuance of "invitation" in this usage, since the Greek word we translate "call" is the ordinary term used to summon or invite someone to a feast (Matt 22:3-4, 8; especially Luke 7:39; 14:7-10, 12-13, 16-17, 24; and John 2:2; 1 Cor

10:27; Rev 19:9), a usage familiar from the Roman Eucharistic Liturgy Communion Service: "Happy are those who are called to his supper."

Paul in his letters makes frequent use of the term. He describes himself as "called an apostle" (Rom 1:1; 1 Cor 1:1), comprising one of two meanings, and likely both at once: Paul is named or termed an apostle (like those named by Jesus); and he is called to be an apostle. But in Paul's mind all Christians have received a call. Cf. Romans 8:30, "Those whom he predestined he also called, and those whom he called he also justified." Paul seems to think of this call as the beginning of Christian life, the moment of conversion to the gospel: Rom 9:24; 1 Cor 1:9; 7:15, 17-18, 20-22, 24; Gal 1:6; 5:8, 13; 1 Thess 2:12; 4:7; 5:24; etc.

It is likely that Galatians 1:15, "[God] set me apart before I was born and called me through his grace," echoes Isaiah 49:1. Paul understands himself and his life according to the pattern of the servant of the Lord: "Yahweh called me before I was born; while I was in my mother's womb, he named me." In OT usage, "call" in the sense of inviting to and designating for a work is mostly found in Isaiah 42–54. Elsewhere in the OT "calling" means naming; but often the name indicates God's purpose, so the notion is in that sense cognate with NT usage. We speak of the call of Abraham, or of Moses, but (except for Isa 51:2), that seems to be NT usage; cf. Hebrews 11:8.

God's "call" of the Christian, then, is understood after the model of Jesus' calling of the disciples, and is influenced by Pauline usage of the term. Historically, "vocation" has been a term restricted to a calling to embrace the religious and/or priestly life; but every form or state of life that allows one to serve God and neighbor as a follower of Jesus can be seen as a vocation.

J.P.M. WALSH, S.J.

See also CHRISTIAN SPIRITUALITY; RELIGIOUS ORDERS; SACRAMENT OF MATRIMONY; SACRAMENT OF ORDERS; SACRAMENTS OF INITIATION.

VON BALTHASAR, HANS URS (1905–1988)

A native of Basel who originally studied German literature and philosophy, he entered the Society of Jesus in 1929 and did his theology in Germany and spent four years at Lyon (from 1933 to 1937), being ordained in 1936. He was on the editorial board of the journal *Stimmen der Zeit* from 1937 to 1939 and next became a chaplain at the University of Basel. In 1940 he met Adrienne von Speyr (1902–1967), a medical doctor who, by age thirty-eight, had been married, widowed, contemplated suicide, married again, and had several mystical experiences, including visions. Von Speyr was a Protestant, but, after von Balthasar and she became friends, she soon converted to Roman Catholicism. Von Balthasar became her confessor, a task he carried out until her death, and he testified to her experience of the stigmata of Jesus in 1942. In 1945 the two friends founded the Johannesgemeinschaft, a secular institute. This founding caused von Balthasar difficulties with his order, and he eventually left the Jesuits (1950). He also founded a publishing house, the Johannesverlag, which published works of the Church Fathers but also sixty volumes of von Speyr's writings, many of which she had dictated to him. Von Balthasar remained devoted to her cause, even after her death, supporting publication of her works and encouraging others to know them. Her strong mysticism resonated with his own interest in the spiritual life.

Von Balthasar had been a student with Jean Danielou, and scholars such as Erich Przywara and Henri de Lubac also influenced him. All were patristic scholars, and von Balthasar studied many of the Fathers, especially those who wrote on the spiritual life, including Origen, Gregory of Nyssa, and Augustine. He shared this interest with other theologians of his generation, such as Karl Rahner who wrote some early articles on Clement of Alexandria and Origen. Although he knew and appreciated the Scholastics, von Balthasar believed that theology had to deal with the various manifestations of God's revelation, in the incarnate Christ but also in the human senses. He once titled a book on Christian pluralism *Truth Is Symphonic,* suggesting both the outer sounds and the inner harmony. ". . . the humiliation of the servant (Jesus) only makes the concealed glory shine more resplendently, and the descent into the ordinary and commonplace brings out the uniqueness of him who abased himself." This passage appears in an essay entitled "Revelation and the Beautiful," a title von Balthasar thought would "startle the reader"—as it probably did. The passage illustrates how he combined revelation (the incarnation) with the virtues (humility and service to others) with daily life (ordinary and commonplace) with the mystical (glory, descent). His was a new voice which many did not want to hear; significantly, he was not invited to be a *peritus* (theological expert) at Vatican II. But his reputation grew after the council until his death. His works now await the judgment of history.

JOSEPH F. KELLY

See also INSTITUTE, SECULAR; LAITY, THEOLOGY OF THE; SOCIETY OF JESUS.

VON HÜGEL, BARON FRIEDRICH (1852–1925)

Born in Florence, he was the eldest son of Carl Alexander Anselm, Baron von Hügel and Elizabeth née Farquharson, a Scottish Presbyterian convert to Catholicism. In 1867, after an eclectic education, he came to live in England and three years later he contracted typhus and became deaf. Shortly thereafter he underwent a profound spiritual crisis, which gave him a compassionate insight into the religious problems of others. He was sympathetic to the progressive and cultural forces in the Church and became a steadfast friend of Alfred Loisy and George Tyrrell. In 1905 he founded the London Society for the Study of Religion, and came into contact with the religious leaders of his age.

The Mystical Element of Religion as studied in Catherine of Genoa and her Friends (1907) was his first major work; and his significance as a thinker and writer was established with *Essays and Addresses on the Philosophy of Religion* (published in two series in 1907 and 1909) and by *The Reality of God* (published posthumously in 1931).

His correspondence shows him as a wise and gifted spiritual counselor and as a dependable and understanding friend to many. He is remembered as a cultured intellectual with a deep sense of time and history and with a profound and unswerving loyalty to the Church which he felt was ever in need of reform and deserved better than the status quo.

MICHAEL GLAZIER

See also MODERNISM; MYSTICISM.

VOW

A vow is a conscious, free promise made to God, which has as its object a moral good that is both possible and better than its omission. Those entering religious life take vows of poverty, chastity, and obedience.

A public vow is accepted in the name of the Church by a legitimate superior. The 1917 Code of Canon Law distinguished between solemn vows, taken by members of religious orders, and simple perpetual vows, taken by members of congregations. The revised Code refers to solemn vows but does not discuss their distinction from simple vows (cc. 1191–1198). Instead, the Code classifies vows as perpetual or temporary.

PATRICIA DeFERRARI

See also INSTITUTE, SECULAR; RELIGIOUS ORDERS.

VOWS

Vows are solemn promises made freely to God to do some task or to live according to a certain way of life. Vows can be private, made individually to a confessor or a bishop, or public such as those made by members of religious communities. By profession of religious vows an individual dedicates one's life to God and the service of God's people through a public commitment which is liturgically celebrated. The traditional vows of religion are poverty, chastity, and obedience. However, vows of stability, obedience to the pope, zeal, service to the poor, or commitment to a certain apostolic project are also part of some religious professions.

Chastity

Chastity or consecrated celibacy for the sake of the reign of God is a charism or gift of God. This vocation to discipleship is an invitation to live one's life exclusively for God in a lifestyle that supports this commitment. Although one freely chooses not to marry, have children or actively engage in sexual activity, it is a positive choice recognizing human sexuality as a gift of God. A celibate commitment as a freely chosen adult Christian lifestyle witnesses to a personal relationship with God and service of God's people. Chastity for love of God lived out in religious celibacy is part of the continuing tradition of the Church.

Poverty

Voluntary poverty lived out in imitation of Christ witnesses a life of active dependence on God. Jesus is the one who became poor that we may become rich (2 Cor 8:9), the one who emptied himself (Phil 2:7), the one who surrendered to the reality of being human in life and death.

Poverty, traditionally understood, means that all resources are held in common. One asks for what one needs. The expectations of common life presume that work and resources are all shared according to need and ability. Vowed poverty characterized by a simple lifestyle, leads one to be poor in fact and spirit and recognizes that all possessions are gifts from God. Poverty requires one to participate in a world of work and to share material goods and personal gifts of mind and heart with one's community and all God's people. Vowed poverty witnesses to hospitality, detachment, service to the poor and commitment to justice.

Obedience

The teaching and example of Jesus who came to do the will of God is the inspiration for religious obedience. Obedience is not a denial of one's will but commitment to gradual growth in union of one's will with God's will.

Through obedience one commits one's whole being to search for and act according to the will of God as it is revealed in the situations of human life. It presumes personal freedom and responsibility. For religious the context for obedience is religious community which designates those persons who become mediators of God's will. Through faith, religious recognize the manifestation of God's will for them through community membership, community leaders and persons in authority, community documents and rules, chapters and constitutions, community charism and corporate mission.

In Church tradition obedience has found various expressions. For some, obedience is listening and learning from spiritual guides or directors. Others stress obedience to authority to insure order and discipline in community life and effectiveness in apostolic assignments. Others recognize the value of obedience as cooperation for the common good. Generally Church tradition reflects two major expressions of obedience. One tends toward the hierarchical, when leadership is exercised from the top down with strong emphasis on superiors. The other, a more communal model, emphasizes decisions made in community through consensus and enunciated in chapters of elected delegates.

MARY GARVIN, S.N.J.M.

See also EVANGELICAL COUNSELS; RELIGIOUS LIFE.

VULGATE

This Latin version of the Bible dates from the fourth century, and its uniqueness lies in the fact that Jerome translated the Jewish Scriptures from the Hebrew Bible rather than from the Greek Septuagint. The Vulgate includes deuterocanonical books and the New Testament, offering a translation of the Bible for the people of western Europe and north Africa who spoke Latin.

Jerome worked on the Gospels in A.D. 383–384 in Rome at the request of Pope Damasus. He used excellent Greek manuscripts, and while Jerome gets credit for translating the rest of the NT, his influence on the other books is unclear. In 389, Jerome began translating the OT Hebrew text into Latin, breaking with the tradition of using the Greek and giving us an understanding of the Jewish Scriptures in Syria and Palestine before the first century. However, he did underline messianic themes from a Christian perspective, going beyond the Jewish interpretations of texts (Isa 45:8; 62:1-2). His work progressed with completion of Samuel, Kings, Job, Psalms, and Prophets by 392; Ezra and Nehemiah by 394; Proverbs, Canticles, Ecclesiastes by 398, Pentateuch, Joshua, Judges, Ruth, Judith, Esther, Tobit by 405. Jerome did not intend to include 1–2 Maccabees, Wisdom, Sirach, and Baruch, since as a Scripture scholar, he considered them noncanonical. These translations of the deuterocanonical books in the Vulgate were done by other translators and preserved by the Church, so that the Vulgate becomes the basis for the canon of Scripture for Roman Catholics.

Early manuscripts of the Vulgate are not preserved, but many copies were in circulation by the Middle Ages and a need for standardization emerged as printed Bibles became the norm. The Vulgate was the text used for the early English translations of the Bible. The Council of Trent called for a critical edition of the Vulgate with moderate results, but the Pontifical Commission for the Establishment of the Text of the Vulgate in 1907 produced volumes that include Jerome's translations.

HELEN DOOHAN

See also JEROME, ST.; MANUSCRIPTS OF THE BIBLE.

W

WADDING, LUKE (1588–1657)

Born in Wexford, Ireland, Wadding grew up under English oppression of Catholics. He had to pursue his priestly vocation abroad, entering the Irish College in Lisbon in 1603. He took Franciscan vows in 1604, was ordained in 1613, studied theology at Salamanca, and then went to Rome in 1618. He represented the Spanish government in its efforts to get the doctrine of the Immaculate Conception defined. In 1625 he became head of the newly established Roman priory of St. Isidore, which he turned into a college for Irish Franciscans; in 1627 he helped to establish the Ludovician College for Irish secular priests. His star rose in the Vatican, and he became a consultor to the Holy Office, to the Index, and to the Congregation of Rites, as well as an advisor to the Congregation for the Propagation of the Faith in efforts to help Irish Catholics. Although nonresident in Ireland for decades, Wadding kept a strong interest in his native land and Church, advising Irish bishops and, in 1641, winning papal support to the cause of rebellious Irish Catholics. Wadding personally helped to secure weapons and ships for the Irish, and he was among those blamed for the rebellion's failure. A brilliant scholar, he produced the first edition of the works of John Duns Scotus (1639), combatted Jansenism (1652), and wrote *Annales Minorum,* an eight-volume history of the Franciscan Order (1625–1654), his greatest work, to which he added a bibliography, *Scriptores Ordinis Minorum* (1650). A personally humble man, Wadding worked for decades in Rome without ever accepting promotion to either the episcopate or the cardinalate. He combined the best of the priest, the patriot, and the scholar.

JOSEPH F. KELLY

See also CATHOLICISM, IRISH.

WAGES, JUST

See JUST WAGES.

WALSH, JAMES ANTHONY, M.M. (1867–1936)

James A. Walsh, a cofounder of Maryknoll was born in Boston, Massachusetts, in 1867. He completed studies at St. John's Seminary, Brighton, and was ordained a priest for the Boston Archdiocese in 1892. Following parish service, he was named Archdiocesan Director of the Society for the Propagation of the Faith in 1903. In 1907, with colleagues who included Mary Josephine Rogers (later a cofounder of Maryknoll) he began publishing *The Field Afar* to disseminate mission information. His work convinced him that the U.S. Church should assume responsibility to send personnel to the "foreign mission field." In 1911, together with Fr. Thomas F. Price, he organized the Catholic Foreign Mission Society of America. In 1933, he was consecrated a titular bishop in recognition of his tremendous contribution to the missionary dynamism of the U.S. Catholic Church. Walsh served as Superior Gen-

Bishop James Anthony Walsh, M.M.

eral of the Society from its founding until his death in 1936.

JANET CARROLL, M.M.

See also MARYKNOLL.

WALSINGHAM SHRINE

The English national shrine to Our Lady dates from the eleventh century, when it was claimed that a heavenly intervention directed the construction of a chapel modeled on the House of Nazareth. A religious order was instituted to tend the chapel and a statue was placed there. Pilgrims soon began to come, and their numbers grew during the medieval Marian age, the twelfth and thirteenth centuries, when England led Europe in teaching about Our Lady and her Immaculate Conception. Gradually, numbers of pilgrims from overseas came to Walsingham. Royalty enhanced the social status of the pilgrims: Henry III came in 1248; Edward I, in 1280, came barefoot in thanksgiving for his escape in a serious accident. The flow continued and many hostelries and chapels were constructed. The most famous of the latter was the Slipper Chapel, where pilgrims removed their shoes a mile away before walking to the shrine.

The sixteenth century was dramatic and damaging. In 1521 Henry VIII, following the example of his father, came to Walsingham with Queen Catherine. His father had given thanks for victory over a pretender to the throne, Lambert Simnel. Henry himself walked the last two miles barefoot, practically on ice. He sent gifts to the shrine until 1532. The great European humanist, Desiderius Erasmus, also came to Walsingham. He donated a *Carmen votivum* in Greek to Our Lady; and he wrote that the canons were richer in piety than in revenue.

The shrine was a victim of the Reformation. Henry's claim to supremacy over the Church tested the prior and priests of Walsingham. The prior temporized when tried with a number of others for high treason at Norwich. Five were martyred. In 1538 Thomas Cromwell's men arrived and ransacked the place. Catholic piety went into eclipse for over three hundred years. A poignant memory is the "Lament for Walsingham" written by Philip of Arundel, martyred under Elizabeth.

The revival came towards the end of the last century. The Slipper Chapel, which had been vandalized, was bought back and restored. Anglicans set up a church nearby. In 1934 Cardinal Bourne said the first Mass in the new Slipper Chapel. Pilgrimages and ecumenism benefit by the presence of Anglicans and Catholics praying to Our Lady at Walsingham.

MICHAEL O'CARROLL, C.S.Sp.

See also DEVOTIONS.

WAR, JUST

See JUST WAR.

WARD, BARBARA (1914–1981)

Born in 1914 in York, England, she distinguished herself at Sommerville College, Oxford, where she took an honors degree in economics, politics, and philosophy. After a brief stint at teaching, she joined *The Economist* in 1939, and was made foreign editor the following year. An indefatigable traveler and keen observer of human conditions, she enhanced her economic views with an acute sense of history, blended with her deep sense of Christian mission and compassion.

After World War II, she earned an international reputation for her mental acuity and her reformed analyses of the political and economic challenges of the poorer nations and continents. Governments and statesmen respected and sought her advice. Her first book, *The International Share-Out* (1938), dissected the colonial system and established her as a talented writer with the gift of presenting complex problems with unusual lucidity. Among her other writings are: *The West at Bay* (1948), *Faith and Freedom* (1954), *Five Ideas That Change the World* (1959), *India and the West* (1961), *The Rich Nations and the Poor Nations* (1962).

Barbara Ward

In 1960, she married Robert Jackson, an Australian who was later knighted. She was an ardent advocate of European union, and was farsighted in her political and economic forecasts on the emerging nations of Asia and Africa. Keenly conscious of the disparity between the rich and the poor, she viewed poverty as the enemy of peace; and world leaders, such as President Lyndon Johnson, valued the wisdom and counsel of this extraordinary woman who gave economics a human face. She died in 1981.

JOSEPH QUINN

See also LAITY, THEOLOGY OF THE; SOCIAL TEACHING OF THE CHURCH.

WARD, MAISIE (1889–1975)

Born in 1889, Maisie Ward was an English writer and lecturer, daughter of Wilfrid Ward, granddaughter of W. G. Ward and James Hope Scott (Oxford Movement converts). In 1926 she married Frank Sheed and they founded Sheed and Ward Publishers (U.S. branch opened 1933).

She wrote biographies of her parents, G. K. Chesterton, Caryll Houselander, Robert Browning, and a short study of his son Pen Browning, as well as *Young Mr. Newman* (covering Newman's early life—excluded from Wilfrid Ward's official biography) and an autobiography, *Unfinished Business.* Other works included *This Burning Heat, France Pagan?, Return to Chesterton, Be Not Solicitous, The Splendour of the Rosary, We Saw His Glory, Early Church Portrait Gallery,* and *To and Fro on the Earth.*

She lectured on literary and theological topics all over America and spoke outdoors for the Catholic Evidence Guild in London, Sydney, and New York until she was over eighty. She was also involved with social problems and movements: Dorothy Day and the Catholic Worker Movement in the 1930s; various cooperative and back-to-the-land movements in the U.S.A., Canada and Britain; Friendship House in the U.S.A.; the Taena Community in England; self-help groups of ex-mental patients in Australia and England; priest-workers in France; Vietnam draft resisters and their families. She cofounded the Catholic Housing Aid Society, the first housing aid group in Britain, which led to the creation of the national organization, Shelter. In her eighties she raised money to help a priest in India buy land where former "Untouchables" could live decently and grow their own food.

Eighty-three when her last book was published, she afterwards complained of feeling useless because she was not working. She died in 1975, and was survived by her husband, two children, and seven grandchildren.

ROSEMARY SHEED

See also BRITAIN, CHURCH IN; SHEED, F. J. (FRANK); SOCIAL RESPONSIBILITY, FINANCIAL; SOCIAL TEACHING OF THE CHURCH.

WAUGH, EVELYN (1903–1966)

Author; born in 1903 into a publishing and literary family, and educated at Oxford, where he was an undistinguished student. He was briefly and unhappily employed as an assistant schoolmaster, but that experience provided him with the material for his hugely successful *Decline and Fall* (1928). After his divorce from Evelyn Gardner in 1930, he became a Catholic. His literary career was greatly enhanced by the wide success of *Vile Bodies* (1930), *Black Mischief* (1932), *A Handful of Dust* (1934), and *Scoop* (1938).

His work was skillful, humorous, and satirical. He also made a name for himself as a journalist and as the author of perceptive travel books such as *Remote People* (1931), and *Waugh in Abyssinia* (1936). His wartime experiences in the Royal Marines and his service in Crete and Yugoslavia led him to write his great trilogy: *Men at Arms* (1952)—later retitled *Sword of Honor* (1965); *Officers and Gentlemen* (1955), and *Unconditional Surrender* (1961). In the interim, he wrote three of his best-known works: *Brideshead Revisited* (1945), *The Loved One* (1948), and *The Ordeal of Gilbert Pinfold* (1957).

In 1935, Waugh published an excellent biography of the Jesuit, Edmund Campion; years later, he also wrote an affectionate study of his friend, Ronald Knox. His autobiography, *A Little Learning* (1964), and his *Diaries* (1976, ed. M. Davie) and *Letters*

Evelyn Waugh

(1980, ed. M. Amory) give us a view of this sad, talented, and brilliant man, whose second marriage, to Laura Herbert in 1937, and a family of six children failed to bring him happiness. Unfortunately, his propensity for offensive snobbery often alienated those around him, but that did not veer critics from regarding him as one of the most talented writers of his age.

JOSEPH QUINN

See also BRITAIN, CHURCH IN.

WEIGEL, GUSTAVE (1906–1964)

Gustave Weigel was born in Buffalo, New York, on 15 January 1906. His parents had immigrated to the United States in 1902 from Alsace and Alsatian was spoken in their simple and frugal home. Gustave was the second of three children, the first of which died in infancy.

Weigel entered the Jesuit novitiate in 1922 at St. Andrew-on-Hudson near Poughkeepsie, New York. His philosophical and theological studies for the priesthood were made at Woodstock College, Maryland, between 1926 and 1934. He became particularly intrigued by the works of Immanuel Kant and Joseph Maréchal.

Weigel's impatience with traditional intellectual and spiritual paths was stated clearly in his 1934 tertianship diary: "I am making the Spiritual Exercises of St. Ignatius on the basis that they leave the soul in freedom. . . . I use my own ideas in these meditations. . . . I know that the ways taught me years ago are impossible. I shall trust the Spirit." Throughout his life he struggled with the problem of the surrender of his will to authority while preserving his treasured liberty intact.

Weigel did graduate studies in dogmatic theology at the Pontifical Gregorian University in Rome between 1935 and 1937, receiving his S.T.D. degree after completing his dissertation on the fifth-century theologian, Faustus of Riez. Due to the fact that his scholarship was not judged totally satisfactory, Gustave Weigel, who had initially been considered as a potential member of the faculty at the Gregorian University, was instead assigned to teach dogmatic theology at The Catholic University of Chile in Santiago where he served from 1937 to 1948.

With his impressive communicative abilities, his disarming frankness and simplicity, he charmed both Catholics and Protestants in the English and American communities in Santiago. Weigel's extensive popularity led to his removal from Chile in 1948. He simply did not fit the confining mold of the Chilean Jesuits.

Weigel returned to the United States in 1948, depressed, bitter, and lost for direction in his life. A new impetus was given, however, when John Courtney Murray invited him to become the specialist in Protestant theology for *Theological Studies.* With great energy and intelligence Weigel wrote extensive articles, analyzing the writings of Protestant theologians and Protestant ecclesial structures. He became a major pioneer in the promotion of ecumenism in the United States.

At Woodstock College, he became professor of ecclesiology in 1949, and of fundamental theology in 1951, and so served until his death. His theology of

Gustave Weigel, S.J.

the Church was quite traditional except for his emphasis on the Church as Mystery. He stressed that the Roman Catholic Church, as the Mystical Body of Christ, is a divinely instituted society and that the truth of that claim could best be demonstrated by the moral miracle of the Church's united and effective existence in the world.

From 1954 on, Weigel became a supreme activist in behalf of ecumenism. Speaking and writing extensively, his ecumenical style was based upon his remarkable memory and his magnetic personality. Ecumenism for him was, above all else, a conversation between differing brothers, leading to a type of unity which only God could give to the Church.

Frequently Weigel mentioned three suggested solutions to unity. Compromise: through give-and-take, a common basis is agreed upon and all melt into one Church. Comprehension: certain basic principles are accepted but interpreted differently by various Churches. Conversion: all Churches disband and join one remaining Church. All of these ways Weigel found wanting. He preferred the path of Convergence in which the Churches, gathered in conversation, would move closer and closer to one another. It was this coming together, not the achievement of unity, that was the true purpose of ecumenism.

His final contributions centered around the Second Vatican Council (1962–1965). Between 1960 and 1962 he served as a consultor to the Secretariat for Promoting Christian Unity during the preparatory period. He was not initially optimistic about the council's chances for Church renewal. However, he took new hope from the positive, pastoral, and ecumenical approach of Pope John XXIII. The third session in 1963, under the more curial-style leadership of Pope Paul VI, brought a return of pessimism to Weigel. He was exhausted by the divisive debates and their meager results which were "not good enough but far better than we deserved," he said.

Weigel was determined not to return for the council's fourth session. Although tired and disenchanted with conciliar processes, he had an abiding confidence that God's Spirit would straighten out any mess that human beings could make. He died suddenly in New York City on 3 January 1964 shortly after returning from the council, and he is buried at the Jesuit cemetery in Woodstock.

PATRICK W. COLLINS

See also AMERICAN CATHOLICISM; ECUMENISM; SOCIETY OF JESUS; VATICAN COUNCIL II.

WESLEY, JOHN (1703–1791)

John was the fifteenth child of an Anglican rector, Samuel Wesley, and a mother, Susannah, who believed that the best way to educate a child was to break the youngster's will and then guide the child in the direction (she believed) he ought to go. John inherited his father's fondness for ecclesiastical controversy and his Tory political views. He went to Christ Church, Oxford, soon to be joined there by his brother Charles (the Wesleys' eighteenth child), who founded the Holy Club, which met to read the Bible and to pray. Even in heavily clerical Oxford, they were ridiculed by the local high churchmen. Wesley also met with the spiritual writer, William Law, during his Oxford period. In 1735 the brothers went to the American colony of Georgia, but the rigorist Wesley, who preached against the slave trade and alcohol abuse, offended the colonists, and in 1737 he returned to England. In America he had met some Moravian Brethren, and early in 1738 he visited a Moravian at Herrnhut in Saxony. On 24 May 1738, back in England, listening to a Moravian read from Luther's *Preface to the Epistle to the Romans,* Wesley says "I felt my heart strangely warmed. I felt that I did trust in Christ, in Christ alone, for salvation. . . ." He plunged himself into popular preaching, only to find that the Anglican clergy did not want him in their churches. A friend from the Holy Club, George Whitefield, suggested that he then preach in public places, even in fields. Wesley did, and with remarkable results. The first crowds were small and sometimes hostile; on more than one occasion Wesley was the victim of rock-throwing and even beatings. This courageous man stayed his course, and soon huge crowds came at all hours, from 5:00 A.M. to the darkest night, and many experienced conversion. His followers were called Methodists, but it is uncertain how the name was first applied to them, although it was in use in the 1730s. Simple Christians responded to this messenger so patronized by the Hanoverian Church. Wesley firmly believed in free will, and this caused a split in 1752 with the Calvinist Whitefield. Wesley also wanted to remain in the Church of England, but his principles made that impossible. He never abandoned his rigorism, and he organized his communities along a simple method: classes of twelve for study and prayer (1742), a code of rules for doing good and avoiding evil (1743), a general consultation known as the Conference (1744), and the organization of neighboring groups into circuits (1746). Wesley stood by his program and, reflecting his mother's training, he had no mercy on those who put their own desires first, once excommunicating sixty-four people for a variety of reasons, including swearing, drunkenness, wife-beating, and idleness. But strict as he could be with those who defied him, he had charity toward everyone else, especially the marginalized. He organized a loan society for the needy, a school for poor children, and a home for widows. His principles of sobriety and industry guaranteed that sincere Methodists would prosper economically; Wesley approved of honestly earned money but he was personally fearful of wealth. He never benefitted financially from his work. Wesley's superb organization brought many lay people of the working classes into positions in the Church, yet another strain in his relations with the Anglican hierarchy. Wesley died before the Methodists broke with the Church of England. George Eliot's novel *Adam Bede* presents a good picture of the early Methodists in rural England.

JOSEPH F. KELLY

See also ANGLICANISM; METHODISTS, UNITED.

WITCHCRAFT

Seems to have had a place in all civilizations. It was generally described as an exercise of preternatural powers, usually by women who were thought to have some compact with evil spirits. In 1 Samuel 28:7-25 we have the story of the witch of Endor, and some point to Galatians 5:20 to illustrate the existence of witchcraft in NT times. In the Middle Ages superstition led to the persecution of witches even though such was officially forbidden. However, the Inquisition persecuted those connected with witchcraft when it was alleged that they had heretical leanings. Popular resentment led to the widespread condemnation and punishment of witches in the fourteenth century and thereafter. The frenzy was worsened by the exaggerated belief in the power of the devil by many followers of the early Protestant Reformers. The persecution of witches only ceased with the influence of the Enlightenment in the eighteenth century.

MICHAEL GLAZIER

See also DEMONOLOGY; MIDDLE AGES, THE; SATAN.

WOMEN IN THE CHURCH

The Church's opening to dialogue with contemporary cultures at the Second Vatican Council (1962–1965) helped set the stage for discussions about women in the Church. The council's renewal of the theology of the Church also contributed.

"Women" as an Issue in the Contemporary Church and Culture

Cultural Shifts. Just as the council opened, Pope John XXIII promulgated his 1963 social encyclical *Pacem in Terris.* In his discussion of justice in contemporary society he observed that one of the "signs of the times" was women's new consciousness of their human dignity and their growing refusal to be treated as objects or as less than full human persons (no. 41). He further observed that persons who become conscious of their rights in domestic and public life have the responsibility to claim them, while others have the obligation to honor such claims (no. 44). Echoing the spirit of the Pope's observations, the world's bishops at the council named the rising social aspirations of women as one of the global realities to which the message of the gospel needed to be addressed (*Gaudium et Spes,* Pastoral Constitution on the Church in the Modern World, 1965, no. 9). In both these Church documents from the 1960s, women everywhere are acknowledged as legitimately hoping for relief from the burdens of social and domestic inequality and for affirmation of their dignity as persons.

What the papal encyclical and the conciliar documents did not anticipate is that within a decade of the council's closing baptized Catholic women would begin questioning the Church itself about their dignity and their rights. How did that development occur? No simple explanation accounts for broad developments in human consciousness. But during these same decades of the 1960s and 1970s other observable events can be noted where the world's women publicly asserted their solidarity and began to claim their dignity and to declare their aspirations. In this new situation, women's voices began to counter the voices of Church authorities.

Casual observers often connect these developments to unrest promoted by the rise of the feminist movement in the United States and Western Europe. In retrospect, cultural historians are more likely to note, as Pope John XXIII did, that unrest among women was global; it was to find expression in multiple forms. First-world women identified aspects of male-dominated culture as the source of their experiences of injustice and oppression. Third-world women identified Western/European cultural dominance as the distorting force in their worlds, complicating further the inequity and injustice within their own cultures.

Women's widespread dissatisfaction with cultural constraints placed on them as women prompted regional and international initiatives to promote exchanges among women and men. The United Nations proclaimed a Decade of the Woman and sponsored an international assembly in Mexico City in 1975 to consider economic, educational, social, and political situations from women's perspectives. The World Council of Churches conducted a five-year study (1978–1982) of The Church as a Community of Women and Men, sponsoring local consultations, then six regional meetings in Ibadan, Nigeria; Bangalore, India; San Jose, Costa Rica; Beirut, Lebanon; Stony Point, New York; and Bad Sedeberg, West Germany; and finally an international conference in Sheffield, England. From within EATWOT (the Ecumenical Association of Third World Theologians) a Women's Commission formed in the 1980s, and theologically educated women in Africa, Asia, and Latin America—Catholic women among them—began to question traditions of Christian thought and practice. They wondered openly whether the Church of Jesus Christ is an ally or an opponent in women's quest for dignity and liberation from injustice. Unconvinced by official interpretations of the gospel tradition that have subordinated and marginalized women, Christian women began to offer alternative interpretations.

In the United States, the women's movement developed in two distinct but related forms. An outgrowth of the Presidential Commission established by John F. Kennedy and chaired by Eleanor Roosevelt, the *women's rights* movement generally affirmed the political, economic, educational, and social institutions of the country and then showed evidence that women had less access to and less opportunity within these than men. Since the 1960s the women's rights movement has sought, through the legislative and the judicial processes, to promote the cause of women and to correct institutional injustices and biases against women. The *women's liberation* movement emerged under other circumstances and focused its energy differently. The women's liberation movement took shape as it began to dawn on activist women in the civil rights movement of the 1960s that even in social movements for justice and equality activist men assumed the inferiority of women and took for granted their subordination to men. When the male-centeredness of all social dynamics became apparent among these women, women's consciousness-raising groups spread. From them rose the call for women's liberation through social transformation. The feminist critique of society's androcentrism (male-centeredness) and its patriarchal social order (male-dominance) finds its home in the women's liberation movement. Both the women's rights and the women's liberation movements were taking shape in the United States at the same time the proceedings of the Second Vatican Council were being disseminated.

Theology of the Church since Vatican II. While the Second Vatican Council only alluded to women in society and never directly addressed the question of women in the Church, the council considered at great length the question of relations within the community of the baptized. Pope John XXIII's goal of *aggiornamento* (updating) led the bishops and their theological consultants to conduct an in-depth reexamination of Church order and mission, even while Church office holders maintained institutional distinctiveness in the modern world by rejecting the culture's democratic impulses. The results of this conciliar reexamination can be found throughout the sixteen offical documents of the council; but the basic relations that are said to constitute the Church are presented most systematically in *Lumen Gentium* (Constitution on the Church).

The familiar perception that the hierarchy are the Church is rectified by the affirmation that the Church is the People of God, the community of the baptized, some of whom hold office through ordination (ch. 1). The theological recovery of the primacy of baptism for the constitution of the Church has been important for all subsequent theological discussions on women in the Church. Given this common ground for Christian life, why has gender been given such authority as the basis for restrictions on women's participation in the life of the Church?

Current Church Practice and Theological Discussion

Liturgy as Embodied Theology. How has the ordinary Catholic, who is neither a bishop nor a theologian, become aware of disputed questions about women in the Church? Again, the situation is complex; but the case can be made that discipline related to the liturgy is the concrete basis for Catholic people's being alerted to the question of women in the Church. The 1963 conciliar Constitution on the Liturgy (*Sacrosanctum Concilium*) stated that in the reform and renewal of the liturgy the "full and active participation by all the people is the aim to be considered above all else" (no. 14). To further this goal the lay liturgical ministries of reader (lector) and cantor were authorized. But the implementing legislation (1970, 1975) for these new liturgical ministries made distinctions about how women and men were to exercise these functions. For example, if bishops wished to authorize baptized women to read the Scriptures during the liturgy, they were also to designate a place outside the sanctuary from which the reading might be done. No comparable arrangement had to be made for lay men. The U.S. bishops petitioned Rome and received authorization (1971) for both women and men to read from the sanctuary. But the underlying question of the relative status of women and men in the exercise of liturgical ministries has continued to surface in other controversies about liturgical discipline: whether baptized girls as well as boys might assist the priest at the altar during Mass; whether women as well as men might have their feet washed in the Holy Thursday enactment of the Mandatum. Concrete liturgical experience tends to focus the Church's awareness of what might otherwise remain abstract theological issues.

Within this broader social and ecclesial questioning of what was and was not possible for baptized women, the possibility of women's ordination to the Catholic priesthood became a public issue at the first Women's Ordination Conference in Detroit in 1975. The ensuing theological discussions—on women's nature and role and the basis for the exclusion of women from priestly ordination—took place in unprecedented circumstances.

Women Doing Theological Reflection. For the first time in history, sizeable numbers of Catholic women had earned doctoral degrees in various theological disciplines and religious studies. With rare exceptions prior to the 1960s, Catholic women were denied access to advanced theological studies, except in separate theological institutes established especially for women. But by the 1970s a growing number of American Catholic lay women and women religious held faculty appointments in colleges and universities; their membership in professional societies put them in conversation with each other. They were well prepared to dialogue and debate with churchmen about what constituted authentic tradition. European women, too, had gained access to universities; but Church-state concordats requiring bishops to approve theological faculty appointments served (and still serves) to delay European women's professional development and growth in solidarity. Since the 1970s Third-world women theologians have been reflecting on the implications of the gospel for the transformation of their cultural situations, while First-world Catholic women's theological reflection has started to reshape magisterial and theological discussions of the Catholic tradition.

A single example of the latter development can be cited. In the mid-1970s the Catholic Biblical Association in the United States and the International Pontifical Biblical Commission were both considering whether the New Testament provided a definitive basis for excluding women from ordination. The Catholic Theological Society of America was reexamining theological traditions that asserted the subordination of women to men both in nature and in grace. The results of these investigations are reflected in *Inter Insigniores,* the 1977 declaration of the Roman Congregation for the Doctrine of the Faith on the question of the admission of women to the ministerial priesthood. In that document, the congregation concurs that the New Testament "on its own does not resolve in a clear fashion . . . the possibility of women acceding to the priesthood" (no. 19). It also "discards . . . explanations given by medieval theologians'' that women have a natural inferiority vis-à-vis men (no 37). The congregation then prepared a constructive argument, not dependent on the New Testament or medieval theories about women's nature, for maintaining nevertheless that only baptized men can be ordained to the ministerial priesthood. The 1977 declaration started new rounds of theological reflection and debate on what is authentic Catholic interpretation of the gospel tradition.

Commentators have noted the similarity of intent in the theological reflection being done by Catholic women and by other contemporary liberation theologians, whether the theological reflection is that done in base communities in Latin America or that being done by people of color in societies dominated by white Europeans. What these otherwise distinct theologies have in common is that each takes it as axiomatic that the God whose self-revelation comes to its fullness in Jesus Christ intends the relief of the oppressed. Theological reflection directed toward women's liberation is often called "feminist theology." In fact there are many feminist theologies: Jewish, Protestant, and Catholic being only the most publicly identifiable. "Feminist" refers at once to the theologians' commitments to put their reflection on their religious traditions at the service of the emancipation of women and also to their method of theological reflection. Catholic women and men doing feminist theology reflect on the Catholic tradition as insiders, using the conceptual tools of feminist theory (e.g., patriarchy and androcentrism, the hermeneutic of suspicion, and so on) to analyze and evaluate Church traditions of thought and practice that marginalize women and to offer alternative readings of Catholic tradition.

Documents from the Roman See have recently introduced the terms "Christian feminists" and "radical feminists," apparently as a way of distinguishing "authentic" reevaluation of the tradition from reevaluations that go "too far." However, since the terms have not been defined or their use examined, the terms do not serve to clarify. Other distinctions in terminology are more useful. Women "doubly marginalized" in Church and society, i.e., women who are poor or members of a racial minority as well as being women, have expressed criticism of much "feminist theology." They judge that First-world Catholic women who have been its principal practitioners are not sufficiently self-critical of their own identity as dominant and privileged white women; they do not advert to the fact that securing their rights in Western societies does little to benefit the majority of the world's women. Such criticism has given rise in the last decade to the "womanist theology" of African-Americans and the "*mujerista* theology" of Hispanic Catholic women. The distinct voices have heightened debate on authentic Catholic tradition. Nevertheless, the term "feminist theology" is often used to identify all these theological developments and their practical implications.

New Ministries for Women. While the theological reflection continues, the roles available to baptized women in Church ministry have grown significantly within the past twenty-five years. Some of these developments were officially authorized by the 1983 Code of Canon Law; others were the results of pastoral exigency, the responses of bishops locally and regionally to shortages of ordained priests. In traditional Catholic terminology, the Church's official ministry involves teaching, governance, and works of sanctification, including sacramental activity. In current practice at the end of the twentieth century, women not only participate but even provide creative pastoral and institutional leadership in regional, national, diocesan, and parish settings wherever official Church ministry is being done. Perhaps the most remarkable development is the emergence of the woman parish or mission administrator (often identified as "catechist" in Third-world countries), whose ministry corresponds to that of the ordained priest even in many sacramental matters.

This development of women exercising official ministry is not without its critics from many directions. Some see it positively as an achievement of women's rights in the Church. Some see it ambivalently or negatively as another instance of churchmen's readiness to use women to serve institutional purposes without "giving" them recognition as equal collaborators in the Church's mission. Others call it a modern breakdown of traditional discipline, Church authority's capitulation to the demands of secular culture.

In addition to their participation in official ministry, Catholic women have also emerged at the end of the twentieth century as lay leaders of the Church's mission to transform society in the spirit of the gospel. Public roles for the exercise of this ministry vary according to cultural circumstances. Christian women have served as organizers of labor cooperatives to improve women's economic circumstances, have banded in solidarity as community organizers against unjust social conditions, or, as with the Argentinian mothers of "the disappeared," have appeared publicly in silent witness against violent and corrupt political regimes. Where women have had access to cultural education, they have used this education to develop culturally appropriate strategies for the promotion of the gospel; Network, the Catholic social justice lobby for the United States Congress sponsored by American Catholic sisters, is a single case in point.

Prospects for the Future

Caution and Resistance. There are middle-class women in the Church who are wary of feminist theology because they are fundamentally wary of dialogue with modern secular culture and its agendas for women. They do not trust that the intellectually sophisticated Catholic feminist critique and reinterpretation of Catholic thought and practice will have positive results for women's lives or lead to greater evangelical authenticity. They suspect it will have the opposite effect, further weakening the Church and its presentation of the message of salvation. In this context, an anti-feminism movement, "Women for Faith and Family," has emerged in the U.S. Catholic Church, dedicated to defending the historical tradition of Catholic thought and practice concerning women and to challenging the judgments and even the authority of churchmen who are prepared to give feminist theology a hearing. This countermovement is part of the larger ongoing social process of the confrontation between tradition and modernity. It is also part of the larger process taking place in the postconciliar Church, namely, the Church in different cultures actively "receiving" the teachings of the Second Vatican Council and examining their implications.

In the practical order, the global movement for the emancipation of women from the constraints of traditional cultures is likely to continue as one of the "signs of the times" into the twenty-first century. It is just as likely that efforts to redefine women's roles will meet resistance from within those cultures. The Church will inevitably participate in that dynamic movement toward and resistance to women's social emancipation, since the Church is present in virtually every cultural situation, living with its roots in ancient civilizations.

Intelligent Development of the Tradition. The criterion for making judgments about institutional change and even transformation is not, however, what human cultures will tolerate or demand, but what the message and Holy Spirit of Jesus requires of the Church. Human intellect and spiritual discernment will both be in demand as the Church searches for wisdom about how it must order itself for the service of the gospel. Teresa of Avila's teaching may be apropos; this sixteenth-century mystic and reformer, named a Doctor of the Church by Pope Paul VI, wrote often about taking counsel on significant matters. On one occasion she noted that holiness and intelligence combined in one person were most likely to generate spiritual insight; but if the two could not be found in one person, intelligence should be preferred (*The Interior Castle* VI: 8, 8).

Women's intelligence, a resource underdeveloped and underutilized during the Church's first two millennia, is coming into its own at the opening of the twenty-first century. This intelligence has been evident in the practical order throughout Church history. Current interest in women's history has led to the recovery of well-documented but neglected records of women's competence and originality in organizing and administering a wide range of Church institutions, often but not always under the supervision of male authorities. But speculative intelligence and the development of theory are often considered to be men's prerogatives. So women's theological reflection and writings might well be the most unprecedented contribution of women to Church life in the next century. The interpretation of Scripture, the doctrines of Christ and the Trinity and grace, the nature of the Church, the foundations of moral judgment, and theological method itself have already been the subject of transformative reinterpretations by Catholic feminist theologians. No aspect of the tradition is likely to go unexamined by women only belatedly allowed to study the sources of Catholic faith and life.

Bishops, bishops' conferences, and the Roman See have been responding to these developments by reformulating aspects of the Church's teachings about women's identity and role. The failed efforts of the Catholic bishops of the United States during the decade of the 1980s to write a pastoral letter on the role of women demonstrated the difficulty of formulating a collaborative statement of authentic Catholic tradition concerning women. Individual bishops were often more successful in writing diocesan pastoral letters.

Pope John Paul II prepared an apostolic letter, *Mulieris Dignitatem,* on the dignity and vocation of women, in 1988. In it he acknowledged again the Church's desire to respond to the "signs of the times." He also cited his predecessor Pope Paul VI, who had observed that "it is evident that women are meant to form part of the living and working structure of Christianity in so prominent a manner that perhaps not all their potentialities have yet been made clear" (no. 1). The irenic treatment of particular topics indicates his conversance with contemporary feminist theological reflection on the traditional teaching about women. His teaching affirms the dignity and equality of women with men, while also maintaining distinctive and separate roles. He identifies motherhood and virginity as the two vocational paths of women, the teaching found in the New Testament in 1 Timothy 2, although he does not cite that passage. He grounds women's unsuitability for ordination in the biblical metaphor of divine-human espousal as it is found in Ephesians 5 and in the subsequent use of that metaphor in traditional teaching about the ministerial priesthood.

In each of these instances, Pope John Paul II set aside questions being posed to the tradition by Catholic feminist writers rather than responding to them. But questions posed as a result of cultural shifts in human consciousness do not quickly disappear. It is likely that restatement of traditional teaching and the continued questioning of traditional thought and practice by intelligent Catholic men and women have just begun. It is also likely that authentic developments in Catholic understanding of the role of women in the Church will come through consideration of living tradition, what women are actually doing in the service of the gospel at the end of the twentieth century.

MARY COLLINS, O.S.B.

See also LAITY, THEOLOGY OF THE; LITURGY; VOCATION.

WORD, LITURGY OF THE

See LITURGY OF THE WORD.

WORK

Work can be understood and experienced as drudgery—an experience imaged in the penalty God pronounced on Adam after the Fall: "By the sweat of your brow you will earn your bread." Insofar as this image controls our thinking and acting, work will be understood as something to be avoided; and work will be done only under close supervision and with the threat of dire consequences if one fails to work.

But there is another understanding and experience of work as well—one that sees work not as a divine penalty but as a way that a person "made in the image and likeness of God" participates in God's creative power. Work here is essential to our humanity—the means by which people reach out to bring fulfillment to the world, and, in so doing, bring fulfillment to themselves.

Without denying that work at times is indeed drudgery, the Roman Catholic tradition seeks to promote the vision of work as essential to human fulfillment and to delineate the factors necessary to make that vision a reality.

First, work is included among human rights. It is a human right because without it our dignity as a human being made in the image and likeness of the Creator God is threatened. It is a human right because it is a primary means by which we participate in and contribute to the good of society—which is also essential to our dignity as a human being.

(The right to work, as discussed here, must be distinguished from the "right to work" of anti-union legislation. On the right of employees to union representation, see "unions, labor.")

Second, recognizing that work can be drudgery, the conditions essential to developing a context within which work can bring fulfillment are set forth. Those conditions include the following: (1) The objective dimension of work (i.e., the product) is secondary to the subjective dimension (i.e., the worker). While the way in which the product is produced—e.g., the efficiency, the quality—are important, they must not be such as to diminish the dignity of the worker. (2) The work must be done in a way that builds up a sense of community among the workers. Each person must have a sense of making a contribution to the final product while at the same time sensing that the final product is the result of a joint effort of all involved. (3) The work must be done in a way that gives workers a voice in what they are doing. Workers must have a voice in factors affecting their work, not just negatively through a grievance procedure, but positively. This voice must not depend upon the willingness of superiors to listen but must be a structured means by which workers can make their voices heard.

THOMAS SCHINDLER

See also CREATION; LABOREM EXERCENS; UNIONS, LABOR.

"WORSHIP" (FORMERLY "ORATE FRATRES")

The first issue of *Orate Fratres* was published by the monks of St. John's Abbey, Collegeville, Minnesota, on the First Sunday of Advent, 1926. It was edited by Dom Virgil Michel with the help of other well-known pioneers of the liturgical movement, including Donald Attwater of England, William Busch, Gerald Ellard, S.J., Martin Hellriegel, Justine Ward, and James O'Mahony, O.F.M. Cap., of Ireland. Its aim was to develop a better understanding of the spiritual impact of the liturgy and to promote active participation in the worship of the Church. Since Michel's sudden death in 1938, the editorial policy has been primarily and successively under the direction of Godfrey Diekmann, Aelred Tegels, Michael Marx, and Kevin Seasoltz, all monks of St. John's Abbey. In 1951, twenty-five years after the founding of the journal, its name was changed to *Worship,* an indication of the growing interest in the use of the vernacular in liturgical celebrations.

"Orate Fratres," November 1926

Since the Second Vatican Council, the journal has tried to help Christian communities internalize the meaning of the extensive liturgical changes that have taken place in their churches, to evaluate critically the effectiveness of those reforms, and to search for new rituals that enable worshipers to praise and serve God and to minister to God's people in the midst of rapidly changing cultural patterns in the world. The journal has concentrated on a theoretical approach to liturgical issues; however, the editors have been convinced that the doctrinal study of liturgy is usually best situated at the level of concrete ritual structures and explicit pastoral problems. Before the council pastoral issues were most challengingly addressed by H. A. Reinhold in his column "Timely Tracts" (1938–1954); more recently they have been treated by Robert Hovda in "The Amen Corner" (1983–1992).

Although the journal is firmly rooted in both a Benedictine and a Roman Catholic tradition, its editorial policy has never been narrowly confessional, as the membership of the editorial board, the list of authors, and the subjects addressed in the journal indicate. The Benedictine tradition has regularly provided a hospitable context in which the human search for God in diverse traditions can both be discussed and experienced. Liturgy, much more effectively than theology, tends to emphasize the truths which unite Christians; hence it is important for ecumenical encounters. Since 1967 *Worship* has quite consciously sought to contribute to the ecumenical movement by the appointment of Protestant and Orthodox liturgical scholars to its editorial board.

The journal has also been distinguished for its covers and design. The first cover carried the work of Eric Gill. For over forty years now Frank Kacmarcik has designed both the covers and the layout of the journal.

R. KEVIN SEASOLTZ, O.S.B.

See also AMERICAN CATHOLICISM; BENEDICTINES; LITURGICAL MOVEMENT, THE.

WREATH, ADVENT

A circlet made of evergreen boughs and decorated with four candles, lit in succession to mark the beginning of each week of Advent. Traditionally, the colors of the candles match those of the Advent season—three purple and one rose. The wreath is suspended from the ceiling or placed on a stand in a house or church. The new *Book of Blessings* incorporates a formal blessing of the Advent wreath into the General Intercessions on the First Sunday (Mass) of Advent. *Catholic Household Blessings and Prayers* provides a blessing for the wreath at home, as well as prayers to be recited at the candle-lighting each evening.

JOSEPH QUINN

See also ADVENT.

Y

YOM KIPPUR

The Day of Atonement or *Yom Kippur* is the most solemn day on the Jewish calendar. Occurring on the tenth day of the month of Tishri, it follows close upon the New Year and remains the great autumnal observance as Passover is that of the spring. But its origin is remote, and provision for the day in the priestly tradition (Lev 16) represents generations of cultic practice. Predicated upon the holiness and mercy of God, the Day of Atonement answered Israel's deepening sense of sin. The Exile itself was regarded as a judgment. And as the Torah loomed ever larger in the nation's consciousness in the post-exilic period, anxiety at its infraction became the more acute.

Central to the Day of Atonement was the ritual performed by the high priest in the Temple. Amidst clouds of incense to shield him from the divine presence, the high priest entered the Holy of Holies. There in his confession he invoked the ineffable name once revealed to Moses (Exod 3:14). Then sprinkling the blood of a sacrificed bull on the mercy seat (*kapporeth*) he would expiate his own sins. To expiate the sins of the people and to purify the sanctuary he would sprinkle the blood of a sacrificed goat (Lev 16:15). Actually two goats had been presented: one for the Lord and one for Azazel who haunted the wilderness. The one for the Lord was sacrificed. The other, the scapegoat, was symbolically burdened with the guilt of the people and driven into the wilderness. Although the transfer of guilt to animals was known among primitive peoples, in Israel the scapegoat was first presented before the Lord because it is the Lord who brings about the expiation of sin and transfer of guilt.

With the fall of Jerusalem and the collapse of the Temple in A.D. 70 the ritual ceased. No longer would the high priest enter and then leave the divine presence "emerging like the morning star among the clouds" (Sir 50:6). Prayers and synagogue services replaced the Temple ritual. The rabbis taught that there was another atonement as effective as the Temple ritual, an atonement inherent in deeds of compassion and mercy. Emphasis would be placed on personal morality and increasingly on the spiritual aspect of religion rather than on the outward form. In keeping with acknowledgment of sin, fasting and penitence would characterize the Day of Atonement. On the eve of the observance the service begins with the plaintive and deeply moving *Kol Nidrē* to seek release from rash or unfilled promises to God.

In the New Testament reference to the Day of Atonement as the fast is found in Acts 27:9. In the seamless tunic which Jesus wore on his ascent of Calvary (John 19:23) there is possibly an allusion to the tunic worn by the high priest on the Day of Atonement (Exod 28:4; Lev 16:4). In Hebrews the Temple ritual is recalled by way of contrast to the superior advantage of Jesus' sacrifice on Good Friday (Heb 9–10:18). Similarly the sprinkling of blood on the mercy seat or *kapporeth* on the Day of Atonement points to Jesus Christ as the locus of what to the earliest Christians was an incomparably more effective expiation of sin (Rom 3:24, 25).

THOMAS BUCKLEY

YOUVILLE, MARGUERITE D' (1701–1771)

Saint, founder of the Congregation of the Sisters of Charity of the Hôpital Général of Montreal (Grey Nuns). She was the eldest daughter of a prominent aristocratic family of New France. Born at Varennes, Quebec on 15 October 1701, she was baptized Marie-Marguerite Dufrost de Lajemmerais. On 12 August 1722, she married François-Madeleine d'Youville at the church of Notre-Dame in Montreal; he died some eight years later on 4 July 1730.

Some key dates in Marguerite's life include 1727 through 1737: growing evidence of a burgeoning spiritual life was demonstrated in her embracing a simple lifestyle and devoting herself earnestly to prayer and good works, especially assisting the destitute; by year's end of 1737, she and three other companions vowed to dedicate their lives to the service of the poor. In 1747, the administration of the Hôpital Général and its restoration were entrusted to Mme d'Youville and her fledgling community. 1753 saw the regal recognition of the community and its management of the hospital. In 1755 there was ecclesiastical approbation of the rules of the new religious community.

A litany of trials and tribulations would accompany Mme d'Youville on her spiritual and human journey. Personal grief accompanied the loss of loved ones: her father, her husband, and four children who died in infancy. There were the repeated experiences of personal quasi-destitution and the economic misfortunes besetting the institutions she was asked to administer. Recurring health problems impeded the pursuit of her work. There were misunderstandings about her work within her own family and even malicious and slanderous gossip about the community in its early years. Political and ecclesiastical intrigues slowed down and even threatened to undermine the charting of a secure future for the Hôpital Général and that of her own religious community. To these one might add other ills of the time: epidemics, bad harvests and famine, and the ravages of fire and war.

Consolations were also evident during Marguerite d'Youville's lifetime. She could count on the sage advice of those Sulpician priests she chose as her spiritual directors. The priestly ordination of both her sons gave her great joy. The support of her companions gave her untold strength in pursuing the evangelical ideal of service to the poor. And the generosity of benefactors enabled her to make that dream a reality.

When Mme d'Youville died on 23 December 1771, the population of Montreal realized that they had lost a most compassionate and sensitive servant. They knew from experience that the service of the poor for her had no limitations of race or color nor those of nationality or gender. Civic and ecclesiastical leaders rejoiced that the Hôpital Général could look forward to a secure future because of the sound economic and management policies established by Marguerite d'Youville. The entire Church could look to her as a shining example of the Christian love command lived out heroically in the service of the needy. She had been a model wife and mother, a woman of integrity and character, a person of unflagging trust in Divine Providence, and a charismatic, deeply spiritual leader who had been able to instill in her companions and followers a deep respect and love for the radical demands of the gospel. It is these qualities of Marguerite d'Youville that Pope John Paul II proclaimed when he canonized her on 9 December 1990.

Saint Marguerite d'Youville's work is continued today by six autonomous branches of the Grey Nuns: Montreal (the original foundation), Quebec, Saint-Hyacinthe, Ottawa, Pembroke—all in Canada—and by the Grey Nuns of the Sacred Heart in the U.S.A. Mission posts of the Grey Nuns are also scattered throughout the world.

CAMILLE DOZOIS

See also CANADA, THE CATHOLIC CHURCH IN; RELIGIOUS LIFE; RELIGIOUS ORDERS.

Z

ZURBARÁN, FRANCISCO (1598–1664)

Born in 1598, Zurbarán was a Spanish painter flourishing in Seville. He concentrated in religious works suitable for churches and monasteries throughout Spain and its empire (saints and monks at prayer predominate). His style is marked by austerity and great spiritual power. Three periods of Zurbarán's art may be distinguished: After an apprenticeship painting devotionals in Seville, he established himself in Llerena in southern Spain. Building on the unidealized style of the region, his works of this period are characterized by straightforward realism, with clarity of color combined with dramatic shadow. They invariably make an effective religious statement. His second period begins with his return to Seville (1629). As early as 1634 he visited Madrid to receive a major commission from the king (*The Siege of Cadiz*); his style developed at this time due to his exposure to Baroque paintings, particularly the Italian, which he saw in the capital. *The Adoration of the Shepherds* (1638) reflects a greater magnificence and heroic style without the loss of his realism. Zurbarán's third period relates to the growing popularity of Murillo in the 1640s. Forced to compete in the softer style of his rival, Zurbarán's work suffered and, in the end, he was eclipsed by Murillo. He moved to Madrid in 1658, and died in 1664.

Portrait of Franciscan friar by Zurbarán, British Museum, London

DAVID BRYAN

See also ART, CHRISTIAN; MURILLO, BARTOLOMÉ ESTEBAN.

Contributors

MARY BARBARA AGNEW, C.PP.S., Villanova University, Pennsylvania
ANITA ALLSOPP, Edmonton, Alberta, Canada
ANTHONY D. ANDREASSI, St. Joseph's Seminary, Yonkers, New York
GERARD AUSTIN, O.P., The Catholic University of America, Washington, D.C.
GREGORY BAUM, McGill University, Montreal, Canada
JENNIFER BELISLE, The Catholic Worker, New York, New York
MICHAEL BLASTIC, O.F.M. CONV., Saint Bonaventure Friary, Washington, D.C.
VIVIAN BOLAND, O.P., Dominican House of Studies, Dublin, Ireland
JAMES BROCKMAN, S.J., Little Rock, Arkansas
DAVID BRYAN, Boston, Massachusetts
THOMAS BUCKLEY, St. John the Baptist Rectory, Essex, Massachusetts
R. EDMUND CAMPION, Manly, New South Wales, Australia
CLAUDIA CARLEN, I.H.M., Ann Arbor, Michigan
DENIS CARROLL, Dublin, Ireland
JANET CARROLL, M.M., United States Catholic China Bureau, Seton Hall University, South Orange, New Jersey
JULIANA M. CASEY, St. Louis, Missouri
JOHN L. CIANI, S.J., Georgetown University, Washington, D.C.
PAUL L. CIOFFI, S.J., Georgetown University, Washington, D.C.
TERESA CLEMENTS, D.M.J., Daughters of Mary and Joseph, Croydon, Surrey, England
MARY COLLINS, O.S.B., The Catholic University of America, Washington, D.C.
PATRICK W. COLLINS, Indianapolis, Indiana
COLMAN M. COOKE, St. Vincent de Paul Catholic Church, Holiday, Florida
JAMES A. CORIDEN, Silver Spring, Maryland
PATRICK J. CORISH, St. Patrick's College, Maynooth, Ireland
WILLIAM COSGRAVE, St. Peter's College, Wexford, Ireland
JOHN F. CRAGHAN, Appleton, Wisconsin
NICHOLAS M. CREARY, Office of Paulist History and Archives, Washington, D.C.

CHARLES E. CURRAN, Elizabeth Scurlock Professorship in Human Values, Southern Methodist University, Dallas, Texas
EUGENE W. DAVIS, Milton, Delaware
JOHN DEEDY, Rockport, Maine
PATRICIA DEFERRARI, Washington, D.C.
PATRICK M. DEVITT, Mater Dei Institute of Education, Dublin, Ireland
JOHN DILLON, Mother of God Community, Gaithersburg, Maryland
DANIEL DONOVAN, University of St. Michael's College, Toronto, Ontario, Canada
HELEN DOOHAN, Gonzaga University, Spokane, Washington
LEONARD DOOHAN, Dean of the Graduate School, Gonzaga University, Spokane, Washington
CATHERINE DOOLEY, O.P., The Catholic University of America, Washington, D.C.
MICHAEL DOWNEY, Bellarmine College, Louisville, Kentucky
CAMILLE DOZOIS, Newman Theological College, Edmonton, Alberta, Canada
ELIZABETH DREYER, Washington Theological Union, Silver Spring, Maryland
ANGELYN DRIES, O.S.B., Cardinal Stritch College, Milwaukee, Wisconsin
STEPHEN J. DUFFY, Loyola University, New Orleans, Louisiana
WILLIAM V. DYCH, S.J., Fordham University, Bronx, New York
DENIS EDWARDS, Catholic Church Office, Adelaide, South Australia
SEÁN FAGAN, S.M., Padri Maristi, Rome, Italy
E. R. FALARDEAU, S.S.S., Director, Office of Ecumenical and Interreligious Affairs, Albuquerque, New Mexico
JOHN D. FARIS, Chancellor, Diocese of Saint Maron, Brooklyn, New York
EDWARD FARRELL, Sacred Heart Seminary, Detroit, Michigan
M. JOHN FARRELLY, O.S.B., St. Anselm's Abbey, Washington, D.C.
MARY ANN FATULA, O.P., St. James the Less Convent, Columbus, Ohio
JAMES A. FISCHER, C.M., Saint Thomas Theological Seminary, Denver, Colorado
AUSTIN FLANNERY, O.P., Dominican Publications, Dublin, Ireland
EDWARD FOLEY, O.F.M. CAP., Catholic Theological Union, Chicago, Illinois
JOHN FORD, Associate Dean, School of Religious Studies, The Catholic University of America, Washington, D.C.
JOSEPH GALLAGHER, Baltimore, Maryland
THOMAS GALLAGHER, Albany, New York
ALICE GALLIN, O.S.U., St. Bonaventure University, Saint Bonaventure, New York
MARY GARVIN, S.N.J.M., Gonzaga University, Spokane, Washington
LINA GAUDETTE, S.P., Edmonton, Alberta, Canada
ROBERT C. GIBBONS, St. Vincent de Paul Seminary, Boynton Beach, Florida
JOAN GLAZIER, Clearwater, Florida
MICHAEL GLAZIER, Clearwater, Florida
PHILIP GLEESON, O.P., St. Mary's Priory, Dublin, Ireland
DONALD GRABNER, O.S.B., Conception Seminary College, Conception, Missouri
THOMAS H. GROOME, Boston College, Chestnut Hill, Massachusetts
RICHARD M. GULA, S.S., St. Patrick's Seminary, Menlo Park, California
JAMES HALEY, Wilmington, Delaware
JEREMY HALL, O.S.B., Convent of St. Benedict, St. Joseph, Minnesota
JOAN HALMO, Saskatoon, Canada
DENNIS HAMM, S.J., Creighton University, Omaha, Nebraska
JAMES P. HANIGAN, Duquesne University, Pittsburgh, Pennsylvania

Patrick Hannon, St. Patrick's College, Maynooth, Ireland
J. Hanrahan, c.s.b., St. Mark's College, Vancouver, British Columbia
Daniel J. Harrington, s.j., Weston School of Theology, Cambridge, Massachusetts
Wilfrid J. Harrington, o.p., St. Mary's Priory, Dublin, Ireland
Joanna Hastings, o.p., Dominican Sisters of the Perpetual Rosary, Milwaukee, Wisconsin
John Haught, Georgetown University, Washington, D.C.
Diana L. Hayes, Georgetown University, Washington, D.C.
Zachary Hayes, o.f.m., Catholic Theological Union, Chicago, Illinois
Charles C. Hefling, Boston College, Chestnut Hill, Massachusetts
Monika K. Hellwig, Georgetown University, Washington, D.C.
James Hennesey, s.j., Canisius College Jesuit Community, Buffalo, New York
Leslie J. Hoppe, o.f.m., Catholic Theological Union, Chicago, Illinois
John Hosie, s.m., St. Patrick's Presbytery, Grosvenor Place, New South Wales, Australia
Raymond Huel, The University of Lethbridge, Alberta, Canada
Robert P. Imbelli, Church of St. Theresa, Bronx, New York
Elizabeth A. Johnson, Fordham University, Bronx, New York
Frederick Jones, c.ss.r., Marianella, Dublin, Ireland
Teresita Kambeitz, o.s.u., Newman Theological College, Edmonton, Alberta, Canada
Christopher J. Kauffman, The Catholic University of America, Washington, D.C.
Carl R. Kazmierski, University of Ottawa, Ontario, Canada
Sean P. Kealy, c.s.sp., Blackrock College, Dublin, Ireland
Joseph F. Kelly, John Carroll University, Cleveland, Ohio
Thomas M. King, s.j., Georgetown University, Washington, D.C.
J. Leo Klein, s.j., Xavier University, Cincinnati, Ohio
Josephine Koeppel, o.c.d., Carmelite Monastery, Elysburg, Pennsylvania
Joseph A. Komonchak, The Catholic University of America, Washington, D.C.
Frances Krumpelman, s.c.n., Our Lady of Nazareth Convent, Wakefield, Massachusetts
Alice L. Laffey, College of the Holy Cross, Worchester, Massachusetts
Dermot A. Lane, Dublin, Ireland
James R. Langford, University of Notre Dame Press, Notre Dame, Indiana
Michael Lawler, Creighton University, Omaha, Nebraska
Richard Liddy, Seton Hall University, South Orange, New Jersey
Bríd Long, s.s.l., The Catholic University of America, Washington, D.C.
Mary Luti, Andover Newton Theological School, Newton Centre, Massachusetts
Vincent MacNamara, St. Patrick's Missionary Society, Dublin, Ireland
Sean MacReamoinn, Dominican Publications, Dublin, Ireland
Celine Mangan, o.p., Dublin, Ireland
Joseph Martos, Spalding University, Louisville, Kentucky
Marchita B. Mauck, Louisiana State University, Baton Rouge, Louisiana
Brian O. McDermott, s.j., Dean, Weston School of Theology, Cambridge, Massachusetts
Elizabeth McDonough, o.p., Archdiocesan Pastoral Center, Washington, D.C.
William C. McFadden, s.j., Georgetown University, Washington, D.C.
Mark G. McGowan, University of St. Michael's College, Toronto, Ontario, Canada

James McGrath, Bradenton, Florida
John McHale, Christian Classics, Inc., Westminster, Maryland
Robert McKeon, St. Joseph's College, University of Alberta, Edmonton, Canada
Louis McRedmond, Dublin, Ireland
Alan C. Mitchell, s.j., Georgetown University, Washington, D.C.
Paul Moglia, St. Joseph's Medical Center, Yonkers, New York
Jacques Monet, s.j., President, University of Sudbury, Ontario, Canada
Marcel Mongeau, o.m.i., Les Missionnaires Oblats de M.I., Sainte-Agathe-des-Monts, Quebec, Canada
David Motiuk, Edmonton, Alberta, Canada
Irene Moynihan, House of the Holy Innocents, Mt. Sinai, New York
J. J. Mueller, s.j., Bellarmine House, St. Louis, Missouri
Peter Douglas Murphy, Halifax, Nova Scotia, Canada
Suzanne Noffke, o.p., Middleton, Wisconsin
Michael O'Carroll, c.s.sp., Blackrock College, Dublin, Ireland
Patricia O'Connor, Springfield, Ohio
John F. O'Grady, Barry University, Port St. Lucie, Florida
Magdalen O'Hara, o.s.u., Wilmington, Delaware
Vincent O'Keefe, s.j., Kohlmann Hall, Bronx, New York
Kenneth O'Malley, c.p., Catholic Theological Union, Chicago, Illinois
Bernadette O'Neill, c.n.d., Red Deer, Alberta, Canada
William O'Neill, s.j., The Jesuit School of Theology at Berkeley, California
Kevin O'Rourke, o.p., St. Louis University School of Medicine, St. Louis, Missouri
Carolyn Osiek, r.s.c.j., Catholic Theological Union, Chicago, Illinois
John T. Pawlikowski, o.s.m., Assumption Church, Chicago, Illinois
Gérald Pelletier, Aylmer, Quebec, Canada
M. Basil Pennington, o.c.s.o., Trappist Monastery, Hong Kong, China
Peter C. Phan, The Catholic University of America, Washington, D.C.
John J. Pilch, Georgetown University, Washington, D.C.
Thomas R. Potvin, o.p., Provincial, Dominicans or Friars Preachers of Canada, Montreal, Quebec, Canada
David N. Power, o.m.i., The Catholic University of America, Washington, D.C.
Michael Prendergast, London, England
Tricia T. Pyne, Office of Paulist History and Archives, Washington, D.C.
Joseph Quinn, Wilmington, Delaware
Thomas P. Rausch, s.j., Loyola Marymount University, Los Angeles, California
John Renken, Catholic Pastoral Center, Springfield, Illinois
Nancy Ring, Le Moyne College, Syracuse, New York
Paul Robichaud, c.s.p., Office of Paulist History and Archives, Washington, D.C.
Denise Robillard, Montreal, Canada
Arturo Pérez Rodriguez, Tepeyac Institute, El Paso, Texas
Marie-Eloise Rosenblatt, Santa Clara University, Santa Clara, California
Theresa Sanders, Georgetown University, Washington, D.C.
Michael J. Scanlon, o.s.a., Villanova University, Pennsylvania
Thomas Schindler, Mercy Health Services, Farmington Hills, Michigan
R. Kevin Seasoltz, o.s.b., St. John's University, Collegeville, Minnesota
Albert C. Shannon, o.s.a., St. Thomas Monastery, Villanova, Pennsylvania
Rosemary Sheed, London, England

THOMAS J. SHELLEY, Saint Joseph's Seminary, Dunwoodie, Yonkers, New York
WILLIAM J. SHORT, O.F.M., Franciscan School of Theology, Berkeley, California
EDWARD S. SKILLEN, *Commonweal,* New York, New York
CHARLES D. SKOK, Gonzaga University, Spokane, Washington
LUKE STEINER, O.S.B., St. John's University, Collegeville, Minnesota
RAYMOND STUDZINSKI, O.S.B., The Catholic University of America, Washington, D.C.
DENNIS SWEETLAND, Saint Anselm College, Manchester, New Hampshire
CHARLES H. TALBERT, Wake Forest University, Winston-Salem, North Carolina
ANTHONY J. TAMBASCO, Georgetown University, Washington, D.C.
GEORGE H. TAVARD, Marquette University, Milwaukee, Wisconsin
DAVID D. THAYER, S.S., St. Mary's Seminary and University, Baltimore, Maryland
JEROME THEISEN, O.S.B., Abbot Primate, Collegio S. Anselmo, Rome, Italy
JAMES W. THOMASSON, Georgetown University, Washington, D.C.
MAUREEN A. TILLEY, Florida State University, Tallahassee, Florida
T. W. TILLEY, Florida State University, Tallahassee, Florida
THOMAS TOBIN, S.J., Loyola University, Chicago, Illinois
FAY TROMBLEY, S.C.I.C., Edmonton, Alberta, Canada
JULIA UPTON, R.S.M., St. John's University, Jamaica, New York
RICHARD VILADESAU, Fordham University, Bronx, New York
BENEDICT T. VIVIANO, O.P., Ecole Biblique, Jerusalem, Israel
PAUL WADELL, Catholic Theological Union, Chicago, Illinois
J.P.M. WALSH, S.J., Georgetown University, Washington, D.C.
MICHAEL J. WALSH, Heythrop College, London, England
LEONARD J. WEBER, Ethics Institute, University of Detroit Mercy, Detroit, Michigan
CHARLES K. WILBER, University of Notre Dame, Indiana
ROBERT WILD, Madonna House, Combermere, Ontario, Canada
R. B. WILLIAMS, O.P., Dominican Community, San Antonio, Texas
RONALD D. WITHERUP, S.S., Saint Patrick's Seminary, Menlo Park, California
RICHARD WOODS, O.P., Loyola University, Chicago, Illinois
IRA ZEPP, Western Maryland College, Westminster, Maryland

List of Illustrations

COLOR ART

PLATE 20
Dali, Salvador
The Sacrament of the Last Supper
© 1963, National Gallery of Art, Washington
Chester Dale Collection
1963.10.115

PLATE 21
Manet, Edouard, 1832–1883
The Mocking of Christ, 1865
190.3x148.3 cm
Gift of James Deering, 1925.703
© 1994, The Art Institute of Chicago
All Rights Reserved

PLATE 22
Chagall, Marc, 1887–1985
White Crucifixion, oil on canvas, 1938
154.3x139.7 cm
Gift of Alfred S. Alschuler, 1946.925
© 1994 The Art Institute of Chicago
All Rights Reserved

PLATE 23
Master of the Saint Lucy Legend
Pietà with Saints John the Baptist and Catherine of Alexandria
The Minneapolis Institute of Arts
Bequest of John R. Van Derlip
35.7.87

PLATE 24
Solimena, Francesco, Italian, 1657–1747
The Risen Christ Appearing to the Virgin
oil, ca. 1710, 222.5x169.x cm.
© The Cleveland Museum of Art
Mr. and Mrs. William H. Marlatt Fund
71.63

PLATE 25
Velazquez, Diego
The Supper at Emmaus
© 1983, The Metropolitan Museum of Art
Bequest of Benjamin Altman
14.40.631

PLATE 26
Book of Hours, ca. 15th century
Pentecost
MS7(BeanMS2) f298
Hill Monastic Microfilm Library
St. John's Abbey, Collegeville

PLATE 27
Frischauf, Clement, O.S.B.
Christ the Pantocrator
St. John's Abbey, Collegeville